INSIDE Oscar®

"A veritable encyclopedia of Oscariana . . . *Inside Oscar* is the one with the goods . . . You get most of the history . . . and the juicy scandal . . . without the screams and heavy breathing. Plus, this treasure actually contains a description of every Oscar ceremony, including preliminaries and postmortems: who arrived on whose arm, who presented which awards, who wore what, what they said (more or less), who didn't show up, who cried the hardest, who made what slips of the tongue. If that weren't enough, an appendix lists by year every nonimation, every rule change, even films that *weren't* nominated and should have been . . . *Inside Oscar* is as addictive as a bag of Fritos. Open it anywhere and you will sink into a sitting position and remain there reading until someone wrests the book away from you. This is the ultimate Oscar reference book—the book you want at your side on Oscar night to settle arguments, answer questions, etc."

The Village Voice

"The best book to date about the Academy Awards . . . Wiley and Bona superbly describe in detail the campaigns and behind-the-scenes politicking of the first . . . Oscar contests, then take you to the ceremonies for all the melodramatic and often comical goings-on backstage and onstage. Neither dry nor even somewhat dull, their book reads like a story populated by all the most esteemed performers in Hollywood."

The Pittsburgh Press

"For everyone who considered Oscar's night an annual holiday comes the boffo *Inside Oscar,* the fulsome compendium of everything you ever wanted to know about the Night of the Lemmings, er, oops, Golden Boy . . . each chapter contains an overview of the film year: the hits, flops and personalities that have made Hollywood the biggest Greased Hog Chase in six decades."

The Columbus Dispatch

[redacted]

INSIDE Oscar®

The Unofficial History of the Academy Awards®

By Mason Wiley & Damien Bona

Edited by Gail MacColl

[redacted]

BALLANTINE BOOKS • NEW YORK

Dedication

To Margaret and Bob —MW

To my parents, who let me stay up late on Oscar night —DB

 Published in the United States by Ballantine Books, a division of Random House, Inc., New York, and simultaneously in Canada by Random House of Canada Limited, Toronto.

Except where otherwise credited, all photographs courtesy of UPI/Bettmann Newsphotos.

Library of Congress Catalog Card Number: 88-91945
ISBN: 0-345-38177-7

Edited by Gail MacColl
Cover and text design by Charles Kreloff

Manufactured in the United States of America

First Edition: March 1986
Updated Edition: March 1987
Trade Paperback (Updated) Edition: November 1988
Fourth Updated Edition: February 1993

10 9 8 7 6 5 4 3 2

We are deeply indebted to our editor and friend Gail MacColl, who helped us pull this book together. We would have been in big trouble without her.

Cover: *Best Actor Marlon Brando and emcee Bob Hope at the 1954 Academy Awards ceremony.*

About the Authors page: *Best Supporting Actress Patty Duke and Bambi at the Governors' Ball after the 1962 Awards.*

Acknowledgments

Our agent, Lynn Seligman, and Bob Wyatt of Ballantine Books have stood by us from the beginning and we would like to thank them for their patience, which allowed us to research and write this book. We are also particularly grateful to our friend Charles Kreloff, whose design brought forth a better-looking book than we dared imagine. We thank Linda Rosenberg, Beth Pearson, Melissa Browne, and Anet Sirna-Bruder for their expert handling of a formidable production task.

Susan Bowling, Marc Eberhardt, Michael "Kitty" Johnson, D. J. Ziegler and Dan Woodruff deserve praise for being wonderful human beings, and we congratulate the Academy for hiring them. We are also very fond of the staff at the Academy's Margaret Herrick Library: Patrick Stockstill, Carol Cullen, Carol Epstein, Lisa Mosher, Susan Oka, Sam Gill and the late Terry Roach. We were familiar faces at the New York Public Library at Lincoln Center, too, and we salute the staff there: Richard Lynch, Christine Karatnytsky, David Bartholomew, Heidi Stock, Donald Fowle, Daniel Patri, and Roderick Bladel.

Also playing various roles in the saga of this book were Amy Bona, Neil Cohen, Emily Bona-Cohen, Margo Wiley, Helen Wiley, Rob and Shelley Ryan, Ellen Meltzer, Joe Smith, Bill Condon, Annie Waldrop, Judy Voelker, Bob Montgomery, Marion Romanick, Ezra Palmer and Jane Hamerslough, Sue Halpern, Linda Shreve, Doug Armato, George Robinson, Ira Hozinsky, Andy Dickos, Ed Sikov, Howard Karren, Stuart Byron, Vito Russo, Lee Beaupre, Robert Lord, Bill Rosenfield, Justin Ross, Dean Pitchford, Greer Garson, Stella Stevens, Olivia de Havilland, Evelyn Rudie, Margaret and Ted Perry, Rhoda Penmark, Ernest Gold, Stanley Kramer, Frederic Brisson, Sharon Williams, Genie Leftwich, Rosanna Arce, Jane Croes, Chris Ferrone, Timmie Battle, Kellam de Forrest, Cole Harrop, David Fincham, Les Cripe, Paul Dinas, Richard McCoy, Dorothy Perry, Angie De Vito and the Ce Bon Motel, Jonathan Roberts, Ron Fried, Mr. and Mrs. George Fisher, Lesa Logan, George Roberson, Tom Phillips, Helen Reynolds, Charles Champlin, Tony Walton, and Jack Thomas.

Additional Acknowledgments for Fourth Edition

We'd like to offer special thanks to Patrick Stockstill, Tom Phillips, Roy Leonard, Nina Newhouser, Duncan Murphy, Ryan Murphy, Jason Pomerance, Sandra Archer, Josh Karpf, Gilbert Cole, and Ralph Peña for their invaluable assistance in the preparation of this new edition.

Contents

Rob Lowe and Eileen Bowman at the 1988 Awards show.
Photo courtesy of AP Wide World

Introduction

A restaurant in Sausalito, California, has a sign on its door that reads CLOSED THE FOLLOWING NIGHTS: CHRISTMAS, EASTER, FOURTH OF JULY, HALLOWEEN AND ACADEMY AWARD NIGHT. This book is for the proprietors of that restaurant, and for everyone else who considers Oscar night an annual holiday.

We've tried to tell the Oscar tale the way Oscar fans talk about it, by treating each Awards year as a suspense story. Since it all comes down to who wins, we devote the first part of a chapter to the movies and stars who will be (or, in some unexpected cases, will not be) contestants in the Oscar race. The Nominations section reports on who made it to the first heat, with all the omens the Oscar pundits were looking at—critics' awards, box-office grosses, illnesses and personal conduct—when they made their predictions. The Big Night covers the ceremony itself, from the entrances when stars showed off their clothes, hairdos and escorts, to the memorable speeches, gaffes and backstage controversies that are a part of every Oscar show. The Aftermath section reports on what happened after the ceremonies: the celebrations, the wakes, and any twists of fate befalling Oscar winners and losers. The emcees, the presenters, the people who sang the Best Song nominees and the date, time and place of the ceremony are listed in The Big Night section. The nominations and information on rule changes and other points of interest marking noteworthy or amusing achievements form an appendix.

In documenting the Oscar race, we looked beyond the screen to such behind-the-scenes people as the studio moguls and gossip columnists who wielded a powerful influence in the Oscar campaigns. We also scoured the major Hollywood trade papers to see who was doing the most advertising and who was in the news.

This book is also about the history of Hollywood, as reflected in the Academy Awards. Everything from the coming of sound to the rise of the various screen guilds to the impact of television to the dissolution of the old studio system has had an effect on how the Oscars are distributed. History often repeats itself, and there are many stories about overnight successes, comebacks, pariahs and rivals in Oscar's annals. Every year someone is complaining that movies are too violent or sexy and every year there are box-office returns to prove that violence and sex sell tickets. Almost annually there is a producer with an expensive, high-minded movie that nobody wants to see and a veteran star whose vehicle is touted as his or her "Oscar movie." Many names that first appear as Supporting Acting candidates go on to become durable screen draws, while some top acting winners have one night of glory and are virtually never heard from again.

To many artists, the Academy Awards ritual is silly, meaningless and humiliating, but no one denies that there is an aura of fantasy about the secret envelope. As Federico Fellini remarked when he won his fourth Academy Award, "In the mythology of the cinema, Oscar is the supreme prize."

1927-28

"As you danced, you saw the most important people in Hollywood whirling past you."
—Janet Gaynor

In the beginning, there was Louis B. Mayer. And he looked over the kingdom of Hollywood and its glory and said, "This is good." And then he saw stirrings of unionism among studio craftsmen and he said, "This stinks."

Hollywood was a thriving factory town in 1926 and Louis B. Mayer, the head of Metro-Goldwyn-Mayer, was the big boss. When his family decided they wanted to live at the beach, Mayer assigned studio art director Cedric Gibbons to design the residence and a studio production manager to see that Gibbons' vision was built in six weeks. But Mayer couldn't get unionized studio laborers to construct his home—they cost too much. Thanks to an agreement signed by the nine Hollywood studios and five labor unions in November of 1926, it looked as if labor negotiations were going to be a constant headache to studio bosses, so before actors, writers and directors got in on the action Mayer decided to do something about it.

With the Studio Agreement barely a month old, Mayer invited three studio acolytes—leading man Conrad Nagel, director Fred Niblo (who had helmed MGM's biggest grosser, *Ben-Hur*) and Fred Beetson, head of the Association of Motion Picture Producers—to Sunday dinner at his now-completed Santa Monica beach house. At that meal, the four men concocted an industry organization that would mediate labor disputes. The more they talked, the more ambitious the organization became. In addition to labor settlements, the new association would improve the industry's image by helping the Hays Office to clean up screen content and by promoting technical advances. Mayer liked the idea of an elite club that would hold annual banquets. Membership would be open only to leading lights of the industry's five branches—actors, directors, writers, technicians, and producers. Mayer would be in charge of picking the members. Awards were never mentioned.

Overleaf: *Joseph Farnham proudly displays the only Award ever given in the short-lived Title Writing category; Farnham was also short-lived, two years later becoming the first Oscar winner to pass away.*

The First Supper

Mayer was so tickled with the idea that the very next week, he invited thirty-six industry bigwigs to a formal banquet at the Ambassador Hotel. On January 11, 1927, the guests listened as Mayer expanded on something called the International Academy of Motion Picture Arts and Sciences. Mayer said that membership was open to those who "had contributed in a distinguished way to the arts and sciences of motion picture production." Although Mayer stressed the democratic makeup of the organization, the guests looked around and saw that there were twice as many producers in the room as anybody else.

The giveaway to Mayer's intention were the two nonindustry people he wanted as Academy members—his lawyers. Edwin Loeb and George W. Cohen—the latter known around town as "the father of motion-picture contracts"—were appointed "special members" and were commissioned to draw up the Academy's Constitution and By-Laws. The remaining thirty-three guests signed up to become Academy Founders, too. The organization elected a chairman of the Committee on Plan and Scope—Louis B. Mayer.

See My Lawyer

Mayer's lawyers went right to work on the Academy's charter—dropping "International" from the name—and when they presented it, the Academy suffered its first snafu—a proofreader at the law firm had given the organization a further title change, "The Academy of Motion Picture Arts and/or Sciences." A new charter with the correct title was produced and submitted to the state of California. While the Academy waited for the state to grant it status as a nonprofit organization, it elected its first president—Douglas

Fairbanks, Sr. When the Academy became a legal corporation on May 4, 1927, it invited three hundred people to buy into the new corporation at a lavish banquet at the Biltmore Hotel, paid for by Louis B. Mayer.

Douglas Fairbanks was as successful selling $100 Academy memberships at that dinner as he had been hustling war bonds during World War I—231 guests became Academy members that night. Director Frank Woods, the Academy's secretary, wrote that Fairbanks reminded the gathering that "the screen and all its people were under a great and alarming cloud of public censure and contempt. Some constructive action seemed imperative to halt the attacks and establish the industry in the public mind as a respectable legitimate institution, and its people as reputable individuals."

An Award Is Born

Among the other activities of this new organization, President Fairbanks added, was the bestowing of "awards of merit for distinctive achievement." No one had thought beyond the concept of the award, though, so a Committee for the Awards of Merit was formed soon after the May 11, 1927, banquet. A year later, in July of 1928, the Awards committee finally had something to show for itself—a voting system. Each Academy member would cast one nominating vote in his branch. Period. Then a Board of Judges from each branch would count the votes and determine the nominations, turning them over to a Central Board of Judges. This Central Board was comprised of one representative from each branch and these five people would pick the Academy Award winners.

Attempting to obscure the insignificance of the members' votes, the Academy's rulebook emphasized the importance of being able to vote at all. "All members of the Academy are urged as a special duty and privilege to fill in their nominations for the Academy Awards of Merit with full recognition of the importance and responsibility of the act. Academy Awards of Merit should be considered the highest distinction attainable in the motion picture profession and only by the impartial justice and wisdom displayed by the membership in making their nominations will this desired result be possible."

Anything Goes

Coming up with categories for the Awards was tough, especially since Warner Brothers had introduced talking pictures with *The Jazz Singer* in late 1927. Because the talkie had caused such a sensation, the Awards Committee decided it was unfair to make silent pictures compete with it, and *The Jazz Singer* was ruled ineligible for either of the two Best Picture awards. The "Best Production" Award would go to "the most outstanding motion picture considering all elements that contribute to a picture's greatness." On the other hand, the "Artistic Quality of Production" Award would honor "the Producing Company, or Producer, who produced the most artistic, unique and/or original motion picture without reference to cost or magnitude."

Silent comedies were so popular and profitable that a few studios subsisted on nothing but slapstick features and shorts, so the Academy decided to give two directorial awards—one for "Comedy Direction" and one for "Directing." The Technical Branch was really at a loss on how to categorize work in its field, and lumped everything into an all-purpose "Engineering Effects" Award, to be given to the person who "rendered the best achievement in producing effects of whatever character obtained by engineering or mechanical means." Not included under this umbrella were cinematographers and interior decorators, who got their own categories. The writers' branch had dreamed up two awards—"Best Adaptation" and "Best Original Story"—but then decided at the last minute to add a third trophy for Title Writing, requiring the Academy to staple makeshift inserts into the printed ballot books.

"Miss Gaynor is not a member of the Academy. Why? God knows."
—William C. DeMille

It Was Good Then, It's Good Now

The Academy also sent out a reminder list of all the films that had opened in Los Angeles between August 1, 1927, and July 31, 1928, but then realized that it included films that had bowed before the August 1 date. As the votes began to pour in to the various boards of judges, the Academy discovered that members weren't paying attention to the reminder list anyway and were nominating films that were several years old, including *Stella Dallas* (1925), *The Gold Rush* (1925), and *The General* (1926) and the voting had to be done all over again.

The Competition

The most respected artist in Hollywood was Charles Chaplin, and the Little Tramp was eligible for the Awards with *The Circus*, his first film since his triumph with *The Gold Rush* three years earlier. The United Artists production was a big moneymaker, as was Gloria Swanson's UA release, *Sadie Thompson*. Swanson had produced the adaptation of Somerset Maugham's "Rain" with her mentor, Joseph P. Kennedy, who then decided the finished film was unreleasable. Kennedy sold the distribution rights to Joseph Schenck, chairman of the board of United Artists, who cleaned up at the box office when the film became a hit. Kennedy did not make a dime.

Challenging Swanson at the box office was a twenty-one-year-old newcomer named Janet Gaynor. Unlike the glamorous Gloria Swanson, a clotheshorse who had been married three times by the time she was thirty, Gaynor wore low heels and no makeup offscreen and lived with her mother. Onscreen, Gaynor had been a virginal heroine in three of the Fox Studios' biggest productions. The most ambitious and expensive was *Sunrise*, made in Hollywood by German director F.W Murnau. Subtitled "The Story of Two Humans," *Sunrise* was a dreamlike parable about a poor farmer tempted by an evil city woman to kill his loving wife, Gaynor.

Love Team

Sunrise was a succès d'estime for Fox, but the money came pouring in for another Gaynor vehicle, *Seventh Heaven*, a romantic melodrama set in Paris, directed by Frank Borzage and costarring Charles Farrell. When gossip columnist Louella Parsons of the Hearst papers learned that Gaynor had been cast in the film, she wrote that the actress was "too young and inexperienced to trust for such a fine property. Blanche Sweet is a more logical choice." Louella published an apology to Janet when *Seventh Heaven* was released and confessed her performance had moved her to tears. The public loved the combination of Gaynor and Farrell so much that Fox rushed them into another tearjerker directed by Borzage, *Street Angel*.

Causing almost as much a stir as Gaynor was Richard Barthelmess, a ten-year screen veteran at age thirty-two. Barthelmess had become a star as the leading man in D.W. Griffith's *Broken Blossoms* (1919) and *Way Down East* (1920). His costar, Lillian Gish, sighed, "He has the most beautiful face of any man who ever went before a camera." By 1927, Barthelmess had signed a deal with First National Pictures and went on to supply the company with two big hits: *The Patent Leather Kid* and *The Noose*. Both of these were melodramas, and the *New York Times* said that *The Patent Leather Kid* "carries a combination of crises and sentimental pathos best calculated to bring out Barthelmess' histrionic abilities." The ads for *The Noose* revealed that Barthelmess' abilities got a workout in this one, too: "Every known emotion will be stirred as this story of a gangster kid who would rather die than betray his mother's great secret is unfolded." In addition to these film credits, Barthelmess was one of the original founders of the Academy.

Just Passing Through

Paramount was blowing its horn over the man considered the greatest actor in the world. The studio had imported Emil Jannings, who had gained an international reputation as a tragedian in German silent films, and given him two strong roles as men who fall from grace to dereliction. In *The Last Command*, directed by compatriot Joseph von Sternberg, Jannings portrayed a former general of the czar's army who flees Russia only to wind up as a $7.50-a-day extra in Hollywood. In *The Way of All Flesh*, directed by Hollywood's Victor Fleming, the actor played a respectable member of the community who yields to temptation and is ruined. Although both of these films did very well at the box office, Jannings knew the end of his Hollywood career was near when *The Jazz Singer* opened and Al Jolson said, "You ain't heard nothing yet." Jannings had heard plenty. Rather than work on his English, he told Paramount he was going home to the Fatherland when his contract was up in 1929.

Paramount had lots of other stars, such as Clara Bow, Charles "Buddy" Rogers and Richard Arlen, the principals of *Wings*, the studio's extravaganza about World War I air battles. Directed by William Wellman, *Wings* represented the state of the visual art of filmmaking, with aerial photography, primitive color for certain battle scenes, and an early attempt at wide screen called Magnascope. In first-run engagements in major cities, there were even offstage machines to supply airplane noises. The story evoked tears—one of the two hero-buddies dies at the end—and the cast included twenty-six-year-old Gary Cooper and thirty-eight-year-old supporting actress Hedda Hopper, as one of the leading men's mothers. *Wings* was a smash hit.

The King of MGM

While Greta Garbo, Joan Crawford, and Norma Shearer brought cash into the studio, MGM's biggest critical success was a film without a major star—King Vidor's *The Crowd*. Filmed on location in New York, often with hidden cameras to capture a realistic glimpse of city life, *The Crowd* starred a former extra named James Murray in the role of an average man oppressed by the impersonality of urban life. Louis B. Mayer forecast nothing but doom for the bleak-visioned film, and exhibitors were offered their choice of either a realistic or happy ending to the movie. The public was intrigued, especially after the critics had gone on and on about the film's powerful subject matter, and *The Crowd* turned a tidy profit for MGM.

A Naked Man with a Sword

As the Academy members filled out their nomination ballots, the founders of the Academy deliberated over what kind of trophy, plaque or scroll the ultimate winners would receive. Mayer left the design of the award in the capable hands of Cedric Gibbons. While Gibbons was at an Academy meeting listening to Board members talk about the five branches and the need for a strong image for the film industry, he sketched away and then revealed his design: a naked man plunging a sword into a reel of film. The five holes on the reel, Gibbons explained, represented the Academy branches.

For the production of the statuette, the Academy gave $500 to an unemployed art school graduate named George Stanley, who sculpted Gibbons' design in clay. Alex Smith then cast the $13^1/_2$-inch, $6^3/_4$-pound statuette in tin and copper and gold-plated the whole thing. The Award was ready; now it was time for the first winners.

And Mayer Makes Six

The Central Board of Judges met to decide the final winners on February 15, 1929, and who was there to supervise the voting but Louis B. Mayer. At 6 A.M. on February 16, King Vidor's telephone rang. The caller was Sid Grauman, the

"Life without service isn't worthy living."
—Louis B. Mayer

man who had built the Chinese Theatre, and the representative of the producers' branch on the Central Board of Judges. He had the results. The Central Board had decided early on to give the Artistic Quality of Production Award to Vidor's *The Crowd*, but Mayer kept them up all night arguing against it. The Academy founder had reiterated one of the stated aims of the organization—"It will encourage the improvement and advancement of the arts and sciences of the profession by the interchange of constructive ideas and by awards of merit for distinctive achievements." What kind of constructive idea did a nonglamorous picture like *The Crowd* promote, the mogul asked, noting that the movie implied an average man could work hard and still not amount to anything. Mayer thought the best choice for the Artistic Award was Fox's *Sunrise*. To Mayer's way of thinking, F.W. Murnau was a world-respected artist who would bring honor to the organization, and a Fox victory would prove there was no collusion between Mayer, the Academy and MGM. By 5 A.M. the Central Board was sleepy and gave in.

The Winners

The results of the voting were printed on the back page of the *Academy Bulletin* on February 18. Winners were announced outright, with the other nominees given Honorable Mention. The winners would receive the golden statuettes; to lure the runnersup, the Academy promised scrolls. In the case of the two production awards, Artistic Quality of Production and Best Production, the stars of the winning films would get scrolls just for being in them. The Awards banquet was another three months off— it would take place in May at the Hollywood Roosevelt Hotel, of which Academy member Joe Schenck was president.

Gloria Swanson felt that her Honorable Mention for *Sadie Thompson* would only make Joe Kennedy feel worse, so she declined the Academy's invitation. The Best Actress winner, Janet Gaynor, would certainly be there, Fox told the Academy. So would the other Honorable Mention for Best Actress, RKO's Louise Dresser. The forty-seven-year-old actress was married to the general booking director of Fox and lived in Beverly Hills. Dresser's nomination—for her portrayal of a Polish immigrant named Mamma Pleznick in *A Ship Comes In*—was something of a surprise since the film, according to *Picture Play* magazine, was "a little, pictorial gem that seldom made the first-run theaters."

Academy Take-out

The Best Actor winner was Emil Jannings for both *The Way of All Flesh* and *The Last Command*. The recipient was grateful, but in a hurry. Since he was returning to Germany in a matter of weeks, Jannings sent the Academy a wire: "I therefore ask you to kindly hand me now already the statuette award to me. I want to take this opportunity to extend to you my heartfelt thanks for the honor bestowed upon me, which fills me with pride and joy which I shall cherish all my life as a kind of remembrance in recognition of my artistic activities in U.S.A." The Academy sent Jannings his statuette and he posed with it for the Paramount publicity department before heading back home.

The runners-up to Jannings were Richard Barthelmess for both *The Patent Leather Kid* and *The Noose* and Charles Chaplin for *The Circus*. Chaplin didn't make the grade with the Central Board of Judges and Louis B. Mayer; he was not mentioned for the Writing Award and he lost the Comedy Direction Award to Lewis Milestone for *Two Arabian Nights*, a farce about feuding buddies during World War I. As a consolation prize, the Academy announced that it was giving Le Charlot a Special Award "for versatility and genius in writing, acting, directing and producing *The Circus*."

The Academy also rubbed balm on Warners by giving a Special Award to *The Jazz Singer*, which it described as "the pioneer outstanding talking picture, which has revolutionized the industry." Although *The Jazz Singer* had been ineligible for the top awards, it did win Honorable Mention for Engineering Effects and Adaptation Screenplay. The winner for Best Original Story was Ben Hecht, who had publicly complained that director Josef von Sternberg had ruined his screenplay for *Underworld*. Hecht was suspicious of the new Academy, and was in New York the night he was supposed to receive his statuette.

The Big Night

"It was more like a private party than a big public ceremony," Janet Gaynor recalled. "It wasn't open to anyone but Academy members and as you danced, you saw the most important people in Hollywood whirling past you." After Louis B. Mayer had his fill of dancing, the program began with the premier demonstration of Western Electric's portable talking projection system, starring Academy President Douglas Fairbanks, handing the Best Production Award for *Wings* to studio head Adolph Zukor at Paramount's Astoria Studios in New York.

After the exhibition, guests dined on Jumbo Squab Perigeaux, Lobster Eugénie, Los Angeles Salad, Terrapin and Fruit Supreme. "The Blossom Room was a gorgeous sight, with its soft lantern lights shedding rays and shadows on the brilliant gowns and gay blooms. Thirty-six tables with their scintillating glassware and long tapers, each table bearing a replica in waxed candy of the gold statuette award, filled the entire floor space of the room," said the hotel's press release.

When the dessert plates were taken away, Chairman of the Evening William C. DeMille, Cecil B.'s brother, welcomed everyone and introduced Douglas Fairbanks. Then President Fairbanks struggled through an explanation of the voting rules and asked for brevity in acceptance speeches. As he called the winners' names, they marched up to his table to get their booty.

Frank Borzage walked off with his Directing Award for *Seventh Heaven* and King Vidor picked up his runner-up scroll for *The Crowd*. Gerald Duffy, a runner-up for the Title Writing Award, had died a few months earlier, so his mother came down from her home in Berkeley to accept his scroll. The Title Writing Award winner, Joseph Farnham, was present to receive his statuette, but he would soon be joining Duffy.

None of the three actors was there. "Mr. Chaplin is not here tonight, due to cold feet," William C. DeMille said. Richard Barthelmess was in New York, and winner Emil Jannings was in Germany, so Fairbanks read aloud Jannings' "Hand me now already the statuette award" telegram. Gloria Swanson, the throng was told, "is out of the city," but Best Actress runner-up Louise Dresser and Best Actress winner Janet Gaynor were present to get what was coming to them.

The only winner to pause and make a speech was Darryl F. Zanuck, production head at Warner Brothers, who picked up a Special Award for *The Jazz Singer*. "This award is dedicated to the late Sam Warner, the man responsible for the successful usage of the medium," Zanuck said. Warner had died the day before the film opened. As for special winner Charles Chaplin, William C. DeMille stood up again and informed the assembled that the absentee "has wired his high appreciation of the honor." After reading the wire, DeMille expanded, "I think he is the only one to whom the Academy has or ever will give a first award to one man for writing, directing, acting and producing a picture. It takes us back to the old days."

The Honorable Mention scroll to *The Crowd* for Artistic Quality of Production was accepted by none other than Louis B. Mayer. The final presentation was to *Wings* again, and this time Clara Bow, Buddy Rogers and Richard Arlen filed up to get their scrolls. Douglas Fairbanks had completed his duties swiftly—the awards were handed out in five minutes. When all the gold had been

Awards Ceremony

MAY 16, 1929, 8:00 P.M.
A BANQUET AT THE BLOSSOM ROOM OF THE HOLLYWOOD ROOSEVELT HOTEL

Your Hosts:
ACADEMY PRESIDENT DOUGLAS FAIRBANKS,
CHAIRMAN WILLIAM C. DEMILLE

Presenters

All Awards Presented by Douglas Fairbanks

given away, Fairbanks asked the statuette's sculptor, George Stanley, to stand up and take a bow.

Although the Awards presentation was concluded, the evening was far from over. According to columnist Jimmy Starr, "President Fairbanks, who asked for brevity in speeches, was not granted the favor by Chairman William C. DeMille, who lapsed into long adjectives describing the Academy and its activities in the last two years of operation." DeMille also lauded the Academy for its objectivity in selecting its winners. "Take Mr. Jannings, for instance," DeMille said. "He is not a member of the Academy—he is not even a citizen of our country—but it did not prevent the Academy from giving him the award. Miss Gaynor is not a member of the Academy. Why? God knows. I think she has been invited, in fact, I know she had had an invitation."

In an effort to meet civic and academic responsibility, the Academy invited just about every lecturer in the state of California: Mary Pickford revealed that the Motion Picture Relief Fund had officially withdrawn from the Community Chest; a professor from Stanford University reminisced about a recent visit to the school by a few Academy members; the Dean of the University of Southern California talked about the school's new course "Introduction to the Photoplay"; and Mrs. Edwin Jacobs of the Federated Women's Club thanked the Academy for allowing her group to preview films to determine if they were fit for family viewing.

William C. DeMille followed the academics to introduce the Academy's guests of honor, stage actor Sir Gilbert Parker and Fannie Hurst, the author of *Humoresque* and *Back Street*. Both Parker and Hurst rose and praised the Academy. Then DeMille introduced his brother Cecil, who spoke for a few minutes, as did Academy "founding fathers" Fred Niblo and Conrad Nagel. The main concern of Nagel was the spate of wisecracks that some industry members had been making at the expense of the Academy, and the founder stressed the organization's dedication to "promote harmony and solidarity among the different branches."

For the pièce de résistance, DeMille called upon "one of the Academy's oldest and staunchest supporters, and above all, one of the members of the Academy who has seen most truly its ideals and has hewn most closely to the line with the Academy in trying to achieve that ideal for which the Academy stands, Mr. Louis B. Mayer."

When the applause subsided, Mayer began, "When the Academy was first started, it was my thought that there must be a closer understanding between the artistic and business side of making pictures." About those wisecracks that Conrad Nagel talked about, Mayer said, "Personally, I have not heard much of it." The mogul then expressed the purpose of the Awards: "Life without service isn't worth living; give flowers to the living, don't wait until they are dead." He concluded by singling out President Herbert Hoover as the epitome of a life dedicated to service.

The ceremony lurched to a conclusion as Al Jolson rose and began to deflate the proceedings. "I noticed they gave *The Jazz Singer* a statuette," the entertainer said. "But they didn't give me one. I could use one; they look heavy and I need another paperweight. For the life of me, I can't see what Jack Warner can do with one of them. It can't say yes." The three hundred guests laughed and applauded, and the ceremony ended after Jolson finished singing.

Aftermath

When Best Actress winner Janet Gaynor was asked what the most exciting part of the ceremony was, the twenty-one-year-old exclaimed, "Meeting Douglas Fairbanks!" Jimmy Starr wrote in his column that some industry members felt that Gaynor's costar Charles Farrell had been slighted: "Many voiced their disappointment of this, but not openly to the Academy."

The first ceremony came and went without too much discussion, since no one in Hollywood had any idea how long Mayer's brainchild would last. But one aspect of the Academy had become a tangible reality: the award itself. "The little gold-washed statuette was thought, by skeptics and art lovers, a bit on the amatuerish side," wrote MGM screenwriter Frances Marion. "Still, I saw it as a perfect symbol of the picture business: a powerful athletic body clutching a gleaming sword with half of his head, that part which held his brains, completely sliced off."

1928-29

"Russian is a polite word for Yiddish."
—Mrs. Paul Muni

In only its second year, the Academy Awards were rocked by scandal.

The Warner Brothers followed the historic, partially-talking, *The Jazz Singer* with its first all-talking picture, *The Lights of New York,* in July of 1928. Critics realized that *The Lights of New York* was a standard melodrama, but there was nothing ordinary about the film's gross—it pulled in $2 million. Louis B. Mayer, who had stubbornly resisted sound by calling it a passing fad, went where the money was and ordered MGM to start producing talkies.

Any film would do, even one that had been filmed as a silent. Documentarian Robert Flaherty and MGM contract director W.S. "Woody" Van Dyke had traveled to the Marquesas Islands in the South Pacific to film *White Shadows in the South Seas,* a love story about an alcoholic doctor and a native woman. Mayer decided this silent would be Metro's first sound movie. Douglas Shearer, brother of MGM star Norma Shearer, took the reels of film to a New Jersey recording studio and dubbed sound effects and music—but no dialogue—onto the footage. The picture bowed in the summer of 1928 and the sound of ringing box-office cash registers told Mayer he had made the right decision.

History as Sex Comedy

Over at Paramount, the studio heads decided that the drawing power of Academy Award winner Emil Jannings and director Ernst Lubitsch weren't enough to guarantee good returns for the silent historical drama *The Patriot,* so some sound effects were synchronized to this film, too, before its August 1928 opening. The *New York Herald Tribune* loved the movie, about the murder of Czar Paul II by his good friend Count Pahlen, and commented, "Though the picture is essentially tragedy, Ernst Lubitsch, who directed, has made at least half of it that sort of sly, brilliant sex comedy that has turned his name into an adjective for a definite type of cinema farce." Emil Jannings, who had returned to Germany by the time of the film's release, won his usual great notices as the lusty czar, as did his costar, Hollywood character actor Lewis Stone. "There were those in the audience last night," wrote the *Herald Tribune,* "who thought Stone's triumph was more notable than the star's." As for the new sound track, the paper concluded, "The sound accompaniment isn't particularly helpful."

Overleaf: *Irving Thalberg poses with the Best Production Award for* Broadway Melody *with Academy President William C. DeMille. Eight years later, Thalberg's head would be an Award, too.*

All-Singing

Sound also meant that people could sing in movies for the first time, and all the major studios rushed the production of all-star revues that did not have plots but did have contract players singing and dancing, regardless of their abilities. There were *Fox Movie Tone Follies, Paramount on Parade,* and, the most financially successful of all, MGM's *Hollywood Revue*. The latter was the studio's amateur night—literally. Filmed during the "graveyard shift," 7 P.M. to 7 A.M., *Hollywood Revue* consisted of every star on the MGM lot doing a turn after he or she finished the day's shooting on a starring vehicle. Hosted by Jack Benny and Academy founder Conrad Nagel, the revue featured Marie Dressler and Bessie Love warbling "Singin' in the Rain" and Joan Crawford dancing. Mark Hellinger raved in the *New York Daily News,* "If this film doesn't catch on like wildfire, I am Calvin Coolidge's old electric horse."

Rat-a-Tat-Tat

Sound also increased the excitement of gangster movies, what with all those guns going off, and crime movies were among the biggest moneymakers in the early sound years. Paramount followed up the Academy Award–winning *Underworld* by reteaming director Josef von Sternberg with villain-star George Bancroft in *Thunderbolt,* a prison melodrama with dialogue by former *New Yorker* magazine theater critic Herman J. Mankiewicz. Bancroft played the title character, a convict who keeps a dog in his death-row cell but can't keep girlfriend Fay Wray from finding another man outside the big house. "There is a queer idea of humor in this film," wrote the *New York Times*. "While there may be, once in a while, a gangster who grins at death, this particular prison has all the inmates in the condemned cells as happy and hearty as if they were about to take a dip in the surf." There was no doubt, however, about Bancroft's performance. "When words roll from his tongue, one expects them to be punctuated by lightning," the *Times* noted.

The *Times* was more impressed with *Alibi,* which it called "by far the best of the gangster films, and the fact that it is equipped with dialogue makes it all the more stirring." The reviewer also lauded the film's sound recording. "When a taxicab engine is running, the noise is really like the real thing, and the same applies to other sounds." United Artists was glad to hear this, since the studio had ordered the film to be reshot with sound after production was completed. The result made a star out of Broadway actor Chester Morris, playing the lead, who was described by the *Times* as a "dyed-in-the-wool gunman."

Muni the Monkey

Another Broadway name lured to Hollywood was Muni Weisenfreund, an Austrian-born graduate of New York's Yiddish theater. The thirty-two-year-old actor moved to California with a seven-year contract at Fox, and the first thing the studio did was go to work on the new acquisition's name. "I like Muni for a last name, it's catchy and short," said one executive. "So's Rin-Tin-Tin," retorted the actor just dubbed Paul Muni. When he first read the studio's publicity release on him—"Mr. William Fox has personally discovered the celebrated Russian actor, Paul Muni"—he exclaimed, "I not only have a new name, I have a new nationality!" His wife Bella explained things to him: "Russian is a polite word for Yiddish."

The actor waited for the studio to come up with a vehicle for him and passed the time by joining the Academy at Louis B. Mayer's second membership drive banquet in 1928. Finally, Fox offered Muni the title role in *The Valiant,* a melodrama about a murderer who refuses to divulge his motive or his identity but looks forward to meeting his Maker. When Mr. William Fox looked at the rushes of the talkie, he screamed, "This Muni guy is terrible. How did we ever sign this monkey?" *Variety* gave the newcomer excellent notices—"His voice is rich and pleasant, his personality is strong and virile, and if he is not pretty, neither is Lon Chaney or Emil Jannings." But Fox still didn't have any confidence in the film, opening it cold in New York. "It wasn't a sneak preview," said Mrs. Muni, "it was a sneak release."

Fortunately, Fox opened the film on Broadway at the glamorous Roxy Theatre and owner S.L. Rothafel adored the movie, going so far as to run his own ads in the newspapers: "So great is my faith in this picture, confirmed by the opinions of the critics and the thousands who have sat spellbound and enthralled by its stark drama and human emotion, that I have persuaded Mr. William Fox to permit me to hold it over another week." *The Valiant* went on to make a pile of money.

A Lucky Rabbit's Foot

William Fox also had trouble with the leading man of *In Old Arizona,* the first talkie western. Raoul Walsh was supposed to play the outlaw hero and direct the film, but on the way back from a location in Utah, a jackrabbit jumped through the windshield of Walsh's car. The accident left the director-actor permanently blinded in the right eye, and unavailable to finish the film. Fox action director Irving Cummings was rushed in to take over behind the camera and Warner Baxter, an actor with undistinguished credits in silent films, was tapped to essay the lead.

Western fans had to do without the usual genre conventions for *In Old Arizona*. Because sound recording equipment had to be kept in stationary soundproof booths, such western standbys as chase scenes were dropped—a third of the movie took place indoors. Despite these setbacks, *In Old Arizona*, based on a story by O. Henry, had a gunfight, a cattle roundup, a twist ending, and Warner Baxter, whose good looks and deep voice brought lots of box-office dollars and fan mail to the studio.

That Gal Has Guts

As inspirational as Warner Baxter's emergence was, it paled next to the story of Betty Compson. Compson's father died when she was fifteen, leaving her and her mother broke. Compson earned money by playing the violin in a movie house in Salt Lake City and later toured with a vaudeville troupe. She and her mother moved to San Francisco and worked as domestics when Compson wasn't touring with her fiddle. While passing through Hollywood, Compson was noticed by Al Christie, who hired her to be a comedienne in his low-budget slapstick comedies. Compson worked her way up and was lured by Mack Sennett to appear in his comedies. Her career really took off when director George L. Tucker cast her opposite Lon Chaney in *The Miracle Man* in 1919. The film made her a star, but after three years, her popularity waned and Paramount decided not to renew her contract. Unable to find work in Hollywood, Compson accepted film offers in England, where she worked with such budding talent as art director Alfred Hitchcock on *Woman to Woman* in 1923. When her British films reestablished her, Hollywood beckoned Compson to come home. She returned to Paramount, but when her films failed to do well at the box office, the studio dropped her once again. This time, Compson stayed in Hollywood, working on "Poverty Row," a collection of penny-ante studios that paid poorly and required twenty hours of work a day. Compson often made two pictures at once.

Then, in a traffic jam on Wilshire Boulevard, Compson was recognized by the driver of a shiny roadster, director George Fitzmaurice, who yelled over to her, "Betty, how'd you like to play a marvelous part for me over at First National?"

"If you didn't see *The Barker,*" stated columnist Adela Rogers St. Johns in an article entitled "The Girl Who Came Back," "you missed a great moment in screen history. The first-night audience in Los Angeles greeted that comeback of Compson's with cheers that must have been very dear to her." Back in demand, the actress was rushed into *The Docks of New York*, with George (*Thunderbolt*) Bancroft, and *Weary River* with heartthrob Richard Barthelmess. According to *Liberty*, Compson was now a figure of awe to her coworkers. "If you mention Betty Compson's name to the legions of Hollywood, the reply invariably will be in the vernacular: 'that gal has guts.' "

A Boom for Sound

Ruth Chatterton had credits—impressive ones. The Broadway star of *Daddy Long Legs* was first called to Hollywood by Paramount, which used her perfect diction in verbose dramas about long-suffering heroines. MGM managed to convince the actress to come over to Culver City and remake the old war-horse *Madame X*, a tearjerker about a lady who has to give up her infant son and is ultimately defended in a murder trial by him. Directing the renowned stage actress was Lionel Barrymore, whom the studio selected because he was familiar with dialogue. Although this was Barrymore's first directing job, he proved to be innovative, becoming the first director to utilize the

"I want to wear smart clothes."
—Mary Pickford

mike boom—a microphone on a pole over the actors' heads, allowing them to move around the set without wandering out of range of the new-fangled sound recorders.

While Chatterton was emoting at MGM, Paramount had another stage legend before its cameras—Jeanne Eagels. The actress had a tour de force in an adaptation of Somerset Maugham's *The Letter,* but any hopes the studio had about building up the star for a long career were dashed when Eagels died of a heroin overdose on October 3, 1929.

No More Curls, Girls

"I am sick of Cinderella parts, of wearing rags and tatters," declared America's Sweetheart, Mary Pickford, as she looked for her first speaking part. "I want to wear smart clothes and play the lover." Hearing this, Lillian Gish urged the actress and cofounder of United Artists to buy the movie rights to a Helen Hayes vehicle then on Broadway, *Coquette,* about a flirtatious Southern woman who ruins the lives of several men. Pickford grabbed the play and then made headlines by cutting off her long blond curls and sending them to museums in Los Angeles and San Diego. Sporting a marcel wave, Pickford announced, "I am determined to give the performance of my career, and to give it my own way." The public turned out to see the new Mary Pickford in *Coquette,* but she soon got letters advising her to grow her hair back.

100% All Hit

Bessie Love, a screen name since 1916, when she costarred with Douglas Fairbanks and William S. Hart, was luckier than Pickford when she crossed over to sound films. Her big movie was MGM's first all-talking picture, and the studio pulled out all the stops. Mayer and company spared no expense on *The Broadway Melody,* a musical extravaganza that differed from anything seen on the screen before.

For one thing, the musical had a plot, albeit an old one about two sisters who find success and heartbreak on the Great White Way. For another thing, the film had a Nacio Herb Brown–Arthur Freed score filled with songs that would become standards, including "You Were Meant for Me" and the title tune. Then there was a sequence in Technicolor: a lavish, Ziegfeld-like production number entitled "Wedding of the Painted Doll." When MGM's young production chief, Irving Thalberg, saw this number he was underwhelmed and said "too static." Director Harry Beaumont had to shoot it all over again to satisfy the Boy Wonder. Douglas Shearer, by now really getting the hang of the sound equipment, suggested they just reuse the original recording of the music, thus inaugurating the technique of prerecording music for musical numbers.

MGM promoted the musical when it opened in February 1929 by decorating the exteriors of theaters with signs reading "100% All Talking! 100% All Singing! 100% All Dancing!" The critics called the film a step forward for the screen. *Film Daily* was amazed at how "the microphone and its twin camera poke themselves into backstage corners, into dressing rooms, into rich parties and hotel bedrooms." Best of all, the picture made an unheard-of $4 million. Louis B. Mayer was delighted; he had beaten the Warner Brothers, and everybody else, at the sound game.

Academy Housecleaning

Sound movies were so profitable that Hollywood was temporarily reprieved from the devastation of the stock-market crash. WALL ST. LAYS AN EGG was the way *Variety* headlined the news on October 30, 1929. The very next day, the trade paper announced the nominations for the second Academy Awards. The Academy had done some housecleaning and got rid of some unnecessary awards. The Engineering Effects Award was too vaguely worded to have any meaning, it was decided, and the desire to have a top award in each

"I must have someone—I want a grand love affair before I die."
—Betty Compson

category led the Academy to declare that the Comedy Direction and Artistic Quality of Production Awards were redundancies. And, in the space of one year, the Title Writing Award had become obsolete.

"The Academy wishes this year's bestowals to cover the new medium of talking pictures," stated the nomination ballot, which provided guidelines for judging talkies. The producers were asked to "name the best production, silent or talking, drama, comedy or musical production, with special reference to quality, public appeal, general excellence, and all elements that contribute to a motion picture's greatness." The actors were advised to keep an ear out for "speech and diction, if employed." Unlike the previous year, when the winners were announced months before the ceremonies, the Academy declared that it was withholding the names of the victors until the big night. There would be no scrolls for the runners-up this year, either; if you lost, you'd go home empty-handed.

The Nominations

The Academy didn't get all of the kinks out of the nominating process. The technicians had managed to nominate for Best Cinematography one of the movies for which Janet Gaynor had won Best Actress last year—*Street Angel*. The producers took the Academy's advice to consider musicals and nominated *The Broadway Melody* and MGM's other musical hit, *Hollywood Revue*. Fox's talkie western, *In Old Arizona*, and Paramount's virtually silent Ernst Lubitsch movie, *The Patriot*, had the most nominations—five each. *The Patriot*'s acting nominee was not last year's winner Emil Jannings, but Lewis Stone. Lionel Barrymore was nominated, too, for Best Director for *Madame X*.

Madame X herself, Ruth Chatterton, was up for Best Actress, as was the deceased Jeanne Eagels for *The Letter*. Betty Compson in *The Barker* and Bessie Love in *The Broadway Melody* capped their comebacks with nominations. Mary Pickford got credit for trying and was nominated for *Coquette*. The actors also gave a nomination to *Thunderbolt*'s George Bancroft, and to two of the ex-Broadway boys, Chester Morris in *Alibi* and Paul Muni in *The Valiant*.

Bye-Bye Monkey

Paul Muni's second job at Fox was the title role of *Seven Faces*. When the Lon Chaney bit failed to do the business of *The Valiant*, the studio decided that maybe Muni wasn't such a big draw after all and told him his third assignment was to play the villain in a Janet Gaynor–Charles Farrell love melodrama. When Muni balked at being demoted, Fox gave him his walking papers. Mr. and Mrs. Muni packed their bags for Broadway, not planning to wait around for the Awards ceremony.

It would have been a long wait anyway. Academy secretary Frank Woods said, "The development of talking pictures has made individual achievement of artists more difficult to judge. Sound has brought in a new element of screen art and a host of new people." The Central Board of Judges—comprised of one representative from each branch with Louis B. Mayer hanging around for good measure—took six months to deliberate.

The Betty Compson Saga Continues

In the meantime, an article about Betty Compson entitled "Too Many Guests" appeared in *Motion Picture* magazine. "What an odd and tragic freak of fate—that Betty Compson's brilliant comeback should be an indirect cause of the break-up of her home!" the writer sobbed. Compson was splitting up with her husband of two years, James Cruze, the rough-and-tumble director of *The Covered Wagon* and *The Pony Express*. "The Compson-Cruze estate, with its comparatively small house, was the most popular nightclub in town," the article continued. "The talkies presented new requirements. She had to study lines. Where was she to concentrate?"

Compson moved into her own apartment and

told a columnist: "Jim's a brutal man in some ways. Still, I don't know where I shall find anyone else who can measure up after Jim. I must have someone—I want a grand love affair before I die."

Tea for Five

Mary Pickford wanted an Academy Award, but she was worried about her chances. Her career in talkies was not going well. If *Coquette*'s box-office showing was disappointing, her subsequent teaming with husband Douglas Fairbanks in *The Taming of the Shrew* was an outright fiasco. Critics said the only notable aspect of the production was the screenplay credit "Written by William Shakespeare, Additional Dialogue by Sam Taylor." To overcome these setbacks, Pickford launched the first campaign to win an Academy Award, inviting all five members of the Central Board of Judges to tea at her mansion, Pickfair.

On the eve of the Awards, the *Los Angeles Times* observed, "Despite the alleged sophistication of these film folks, pulses will race as exceptionally as they did back in the days when they sat on the stage of the high school auditorium, awaiting the principal's final speech, and the subsequent thrilling trip to the center table from which the gold-sealed, blue-ribboned diplomas were dished out."

The Big Night

After dinner, the presentation began at 10:30 when a local radio station began an hour broadcast for the benefit of the uninvited. Speakers that evening included an actor who thought the legitimate stage needed an organization like the Academy, an electrical expert who mentioned recent developments in film technology, and another actor who praised the Academy for the positive influence it had on film actors, both on the screen and in labor negotiations, citing the 1927 contract between free-lance actors and the studios.

Then chairman of the evening William C. DeMille stood up and explained how the Central Board of Judges arrived at their decisions. "The achievements were judged with special reference to its value to the motion-picture industry and to the arts and sciences on which that industry rests. Each achievement was judged from all its aspects combined rather than on any single point of excellence."

DeMille began announcing winners, and the crowd noticed that many of them were among the thirty-six charter members of the Academy. The first Award, for Interior Decoration, went to the man who had designed the statuette, Cedric Gibbons, for *The Bridge of San Luis Rey*, a film set in Peru. The Cinematography Award went to another MGM film, its first sound picture, *White Shadows in the South Seas*, photographed on location. Ernst Lubitsch's *The Patriot* won the Screenplay Award. The Directing trophy went to Academy charter member Frank Lloyd for the silent costume spectacle, *The Divine Lady*. The Best Picture citation went to MGM's *The Broadway Melody*, and Louis B. Mayer, founder of the Academy, accepted the honor. The Best Actress was Academy charter member Mary Pickford for *Coquette*. The winner dabbed her wet eyes with her handkerchief and said, "I've forgotten my prepared speech." The Best Actor was Warner Baxter for *In Old Arizona*, who also forgot his lines and apologized for being overwhelmed.

Aftermath

For the first and only time in the history of the Awards, no movie won more than one trophy. MGM had the highest total with three victories. Despite Academy Secretary Frank Woods' talk about how the Central Board of Judges were evaluating "a host of new people," each recipient was a Hollywood veteran.

But discussion centered on how the Academy could possibly have given Best Actress to Mary Pickford in a movie nobody liked. Her defenders said that it was a nice gesture to give her credit for changing her image, but others pointed out knowingly that since Pickford was a charter member of the Academy, things weren't exactly on the up-and-up. One columnist wrote that the Mary Pickford victory proved "that the Academy is handing out its cups on a political or social basis," and on merit alone, the Award should have gone to Ruth Chatterton or the late Jeanne Eagels.

Accusations of favoritism grew to the point that the Academy announced that starting the following year it was introducing a more "democratic" method of selection in which every Academy member was eligible to vote on the final ballot. The Central Board of Judges would be discontinued and Louis B. Mayer would be just one of nearly three hundred voters.

Awards Ceremony

April 30, 1930, 8:00 p.m.
A Banquet at the Coconut Grove of the Ambassador Hotel, Los Angeles

Your Host:
Academy President William C. DeMille

Presenters

All Awards Presented by William C. DeMille

1929-30

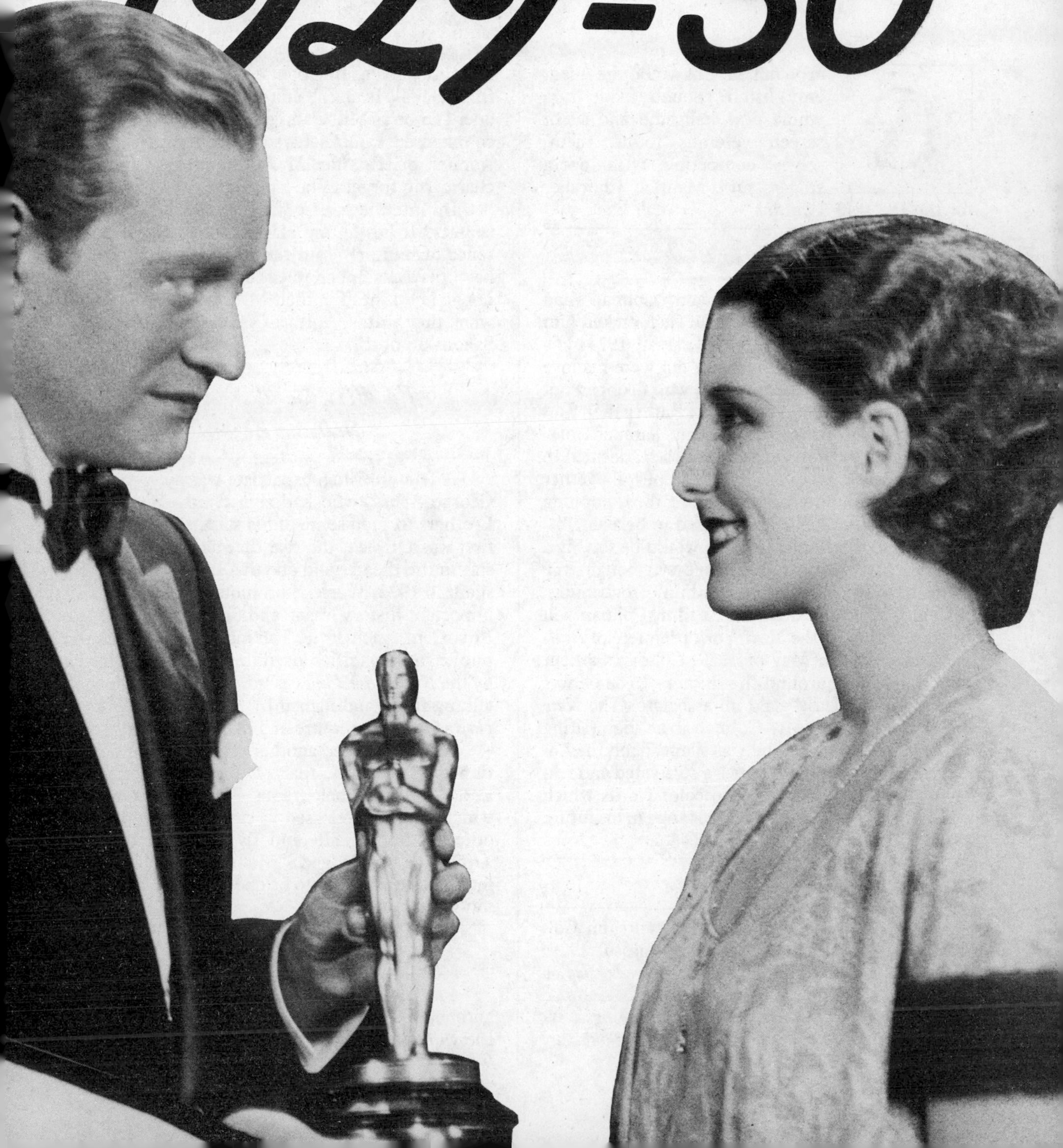

"Ronald Colman is as ingratiating when he talks as when he was silent."
—New York Times

Garbo talked, but would the Academy listen? Sound made it a whole new ballgame and silent screen veterans found themselves competing with opera singers and Maurice Chevalier for the 1929–30 Awards.

From Lover to Bulldog

Thirty-nine-year-old Ronald Colman had been a matinee idol since Lillian Gish picked him as her leading man in *White Sister* in 1924. His most popular films of the silent era were his love melodramas with Vilma Banky, who dropped out of pictures when sound came in. Rather than find him a new screen lover, producer Samuel Goldwyn, who had Colman under contract, decided to keep the actor away from love scenes altogether "until the sound tracks stop making those popping noises when the scene is supposed to be silent."

Instead of kissing, Colman would be solving a mystery in his first talkie. Goldwyn bought the rights to *Bulldog Drummond* for him, proclaiming: "What Chaplin is to the silent film, Colman will be to sound." At the New York premiere of *Bulldog Drummond* in May of 1929, Colman's ardent fans chased him around the theater. "Ronnie was shaking like a leaf," said an associate. The *New York Times* said, "Mr. Colman is as ingratiating when he talks as when he was silent," and the *Los Angeles Times* wrote, "He has a cultivated and resonant voice and an ability to color words which will probably permit him a large range in his future career."

The Gay Prisoner

Sam Goldwyn was already at work on Colman's future career, and by Christmas of 1929, there was another Colman talkie—*Condemned*, a romantic adventure about a prisoner who escapes from Devil's Island. "You may wonder how a prisoner can be as blithe and gay as Ronald Colman," commented Louella Parsons. "But you can only wonder briefly, for Mr. Colman has so much charm you forget to be logical."

In interviews, Colman was definitely pro-sound. "It has let me play a character who has a sense of humor!" said the British-born actor. "I have played somber roles for so long. People do not go about beating their breasts and being tragic when they suffer. At least I am certain that Anglo-Saxons do not!"

The First Gentlemen of the Talking Screen

A fellow British expatriate was sixty-year-old George Arliss, who had signed up with Warner Brothers to redo some of his stage successes. The first was *Disraeli,* the role that had made Arliss a star in the theater and one that he had filmed as a silent in 1923. Warners promoted the movie as an important history lesson and billed Arliss as "The First Gentlemen of the Talking Screen." Both the public and the critics loved the biography, praised by the *New York Times* as "the most distinguished talking film" and named by the readers of *Photoplay* as the best picture of 1929.

Arliss recreated another stage role that he had filmed as a silent, that of an evil Far Eastern leader, in the melodrama *The Green Goddess,* which Warners released in early 1930. It was another box-office hit, and the *New York Herald Tribune* acknowledged, "Mr. Arliss, a bit surprisingly, has turned out to be one of the most popular motion picture stars."

C'est Chevalier

Paramount went fishing across the Atlantic and hooked France's Maurice Chevalier, bringing the world-famous music-hall performer to Hollywood in 1929. Director Ernst Lubitsch cast the

Overleaf: *Norma Shearer, with Conrad Nagel, expresses the thrill of winning Best Actress in a publicity photo taken two days before the ceremony.*

"The long-awaited successor to Rudolph Valentino has arrived."
—Louella Parsons on Lawrence Tibbett

import in his first sound film, *The Love Parade*, a Ruritanian operetta with Jeanette MacDonald as a queen who marries a playboy count. American women loved the rougish persona of the Frenchman and the radio waves were filled with either Chevalier's singing or comics doing imitations of his singing. The *New York Times* called *The Love Parade* "a brilliantly directed film. Mr. Chevalier once again shows himself to be an artist in his particular line." His follow-up musical, *The Big Pond*, was equally profitable.

Vamoose, Valentino

MGM was looking beyond the city limits for new talent, too. "To bring you the new, vital figure for the further glory of your talking screen, MGM has reached into the highest realm—the Metropolitan Opera," bragged a studio release. "From this renowned company of immortal voices has been picked the greatest, your new star—Lawrence Tibbett!"

For his debut, MGM took a Franz Lehár operetta entitled *Gypsy Love* and turned it into *The Rogue's Song*, allowing the tall, athletic Tibbett to play a high-spirited ladies' man in MGM's first all-Technicolor feature. *The Rogue's Song* had a gala premiere at Grauman's Chinese, with Tibbett standing onstage after the ovation to sing a poem written by his wife, who was in the audience. Then he threw her a kiss, and she rose from her seat and threw a kiss back. Meanwhile, Louella Parsons was busy typing, "The long-awaited successor to Rudolph Valentino has arrived. He has the charm of a Ronald Colman, the rough appeal of a combined Victor McLaglen and George Bancroft, the insouciance of a John Gilbert, to say nothing of the finest male voice yet heard in the talkies."

Gloria Swanson—The Human Battering Ram

It was time, Gloria Swanson and mentor Joe Kennedy decided, for her to make her talkie debut. So Swanson and company cooked up a vehicle entitled *The Trespasser*, in which she got to wear beautiful gowns, suffer nobly and sing two songs. *The Trespasser* premiered in London first, to great reviews, and then went on to conquer New York. "No wonder London was bowled over by her sensitive interpretation," said the *New York Times*. "Although nineteen months have passed since this actress' previous production, *Sadie Thompson*, it was quite evident from the crowd that surged around the theatre that time has not dimmed Miss Swanson's popularity. In fact, one might say that she was almost killed with kindness, for the eager populace pressed her to the curb when she arrived and she had difficulty, with the aid of policemen, in entering the theatre." Swanson herself recalled in her autobiography, "As I felt my feet leave the ground, I could tell that someone behind me was standing on my train, so I screamed for one of the horsemen to pick it up. I was now completely horizontal, headfirst, face down, like a battering ram and that is the way they carried me through the crowd and into the theater lobby."

Swanson received more publicity when flacks created a "controversy" over whether she had used her own singing voice in the film. SWANSON STUDIOS SEND PROOF THAT ACTRESS CAN SING—AFFIDAVITS, TESTIMONY, ASSERTION SENT TO 'NEWS' REPORTER screamed the headline of the Dallas *News*. All this attention brought patrons to the box office, but Joe Kennedy was still unhappy. Unlike *Sadie Thompson*, which he produced and then sold the distribution rights to, *The Trespasser* earned Kennedy plenty of money but no credit. "He didn't think it was important enough to put his name on it," Swanson said, "until it opened and it was too late."

Garbo Talks

Exciting as the Swanson premiere was, it was rivaled five months later, according to the *New York Herald Tribune*. "The most eagerly and fearfully awaited cinema event since the talking pictures got their stride took place at the Capitol

"Good taste is good business."
—Will Hays

Theatre yesterday when the voice of that fascinating, inscrutable, almost legendary personage, Miss Greta Garbo, was heard upon the screen for the first time." Garbo's first sound film was Eugene O'Neill's *Anna Christie,* adapted by Frances Marion and directed by Clarence Brown. All MGM had to do was advertise "Garbo Talks!" to send legions of fans to check out her voice. They could relax, according to the *Herald Tribune*. "Her voice is revealed as a deep, husky, throaty contralto that posssesses every bit of that fabulous, poetic glamour that has made this distant Swedish lady the outstanding performer of the motion picture." *Anna Christie* was one of MGM's top moneymakers.

Garbo returned to her ill-fated-love plots and Adrian gowns in her second talkie, *Romance,* also directed by Clarence Brown. Her ability with dialogue now taken for granted, MGM thought nothing of casting the Swede as an Italian soprano in this story of a love-tormented diva. Carped one critic, "She even undertakes to exchange a few words in Italian with a passing organ grinder and they are moderately well spoken, but seldom during the length of this current offering does she convey the impression of being anything but Scandinavian."

The First Lady of the Screen

Garbo may have been MGM's most celebrated actress, but it was Norma Shearer who was billed by the studio as "The First Lady of the Screen." The man behind the moniker was Shearer's husband, Irving Thalberg, the head of production at the studio. Thalberg was determined to make his wife a star, and he carefully tailored vehicles for her. She had already made three talkies by the time *Their Own Desire* bowed at the end of 1929. The plot was farfetched—Shearer and leading man Robert Montgomery have an affair at the same time her father has one with his mother—but Mrs. Thalberg looked great in her chic Adrian wardrobe and bobbed hair. The *New York Times* wrote, "Miss Shearer's spontaneity and pleasing diction are worthy of a more plausible chronicle than that of this current film."

Nor was there much plausibility in Shearer's next film, *The Divorcée*. Based on a novel called *Ex-Wife*—the Hays Office ordered a title change—Shearer played a married woman who discovers that her husband has been fooling around. They divorce, she has affairs with his best friend and several other men, then they run into each other again in Paris and decide they are really in love after all. Critics scoffed but the public flocked to see risqué situations featuring three attractive leading men—Chester Morris as the husband, Robert Montgomery as the best friend and Conrad Nagel as another man—and, of course, gowns by Adrian.

Another Opera Singer

Paramount First Lady Ruth Chatterton, who had lost the Best Actress Award the previous year to Mary Pickford, was still suffering in films and making a lot of money for the studio as a result. In her biggest 1930 vehicle, *Sarah and Son,* she played a Viennese immigrant whose n'er-do-well husband sells their infant son to a wealthy family and then dies. Chatterton spends the rest of the film looking for the kid, while studying voice and becoming a Metropolitan Opera star in her spare time. The *New York Times'* critic wrote: "Miss Chatterton sustains the broken English for some of the scenes and in the later passages she cleverly contrives to make Sarah's English improve. This is quite a remarkable feat, especially before the microphone with constantly changing scenes spread over a period of six weeks or two months."

Death Is My Casting Agent

When Jeanne Eagels' unexpected death the previous year left Paramount without a tragedienne for *The Devil's Holiday,* the studio simply promoted Nancy Carroll—the star of musical pictures like *Sweetie* and *Honey*—to play the role of a golddigging manicurist. *The Devil's Holiday* somewhat resembled Gloria Swanson's *The Trespasser* in that Carroll also played a young bride paid off by her wealthy father-in-law, but Carroll's heroine was all too happy to take the money and run. By the end of the picture, however, she is asked by a Viennese psychiatrist to return to her husband, now mentally unbalanced after a fistfight with his brother, and she discovers she really loves him—just like Norma Shearer at the end of *The Divorcée*. The *New York Times* wrote, "Nancy Carroll, who has hitherto confined her screen efforts to light parts, undertakes a serious role and the excellence of her portrayal is surprising." Paramount reported that Carroll received more fan mail than anybody else on the lot.

Beery Behind Bars

The death of Lon Chaney in 1930 meant that MGM had to find someone else to play Butch, the hard-boiled murderer in Frances Marion's prison drama, *The Big House*. The studio picked as a replacement Gloria Swanson's ex-husband, 225-pound Wallace Beery. Beery had played either comic or villainous roles for the past fourteen years, often in support of big-name stars like Rudolph Valentino and Douglas Fairbanks. But in *The Big House* he had a role that required him to be both tough and sympathetic, moving one critic to rave, "Beery, as Butch, a murderer, does not make a false move or expression throughout this production." *The Big House*, which climaxes with an attempted jailbreak, was a box-office blockbuster. MGM took notice of the critical and popular reaction to Beery and cast him as the romantic interest of one of the studio's biggest stars, Marie Dressler, in the upcoming *Min and Bill*.

War Is Profitable as Hell

Carl Laemmle, the head of Universal, a studio that had yet to receive a single Academy Award nomination, went all out in 1930. He spent $1.2 million to film Erich Maria Remarque's antiwar novel, *All Quiet on the Western Front*. Lewis Milestone was the director, Laemmle's son, Carl, Jr., the producer, Broadway names Maxwell Anderson and George Abbott worked on the screenplay, and a thirty-one-year-old Broadway director named George Cukor was the dialogue director. The story of a group of German schoolboys who enlist in the army at the outbreak of World War I and become steadily disillusioned as they face the reality of combat, *All Quiet on the Western Front* was unusually strong screen fare—the American Legion threatened to picket because the film treated Germans sympathetically—but it was a critical success and a box-office champion. "The League of Nations could make no better investment than to buy the master print, reproduce it in every nation to show every year until the word 'war' is taken out of the dictionary," prescribed a Hollywood reviewer. *All Quiet* made Laemmle, known around town as Uncle Carl, the front-runner for the Best Picture Award.

The Nominations

Uncle Carl made it into the select circle when *All Quiet on the Western Front* was nominated for four Awards. Completely shut out was the Fox Company. This hadn't been William Fox's year. He had been wiped out by the stock-market crash, the government brought antitrust claims against him, and he had a wreck in his car that left him laid up for two months. Finally, he had to sell his film company to bankers for $18 million.

This was the first year that all Academy members got to nominate their peers directly, without boards of judges screening their votes. Academy members were also able to vote on the final ballot for the first time. MGM led the pack with fifteen nominations, followed by Paramount with eleven, United Artists with six, and Warners, four. Nominated for Best Director were three from MGM's stable: Clarence Brown for both *Anna Christie* and *Romance*, Robert Z. Leonard for *The Divorcée*, and King Vidor for *Hallelujah!* a God-vs.-the-Devil parable filmed in Tennessee with an all-black cast. Lewis Milestone was nominated for *All*

Quiet on The Western Front, and Ernst Lubitsch for *The Love Parade*.

Rating the Race

Goldwyn's Ronald Colman, Paramount's Maurice Chevalier, and Warners' George Arliss were each nominated for Best Actor in two films. MGM had placed two entries in the category—Lawrence Tibbett for *The Rogue's Song* and Wallace Beery for *The Big House*. The ex-Mrs. Beery was up for Best Actress for *The Trespasser*, along with fellow screen sufferers Nancy Carroll in *The Devil's Holiday* and Ruth Chatterton in *Sarah and Son*. Greta Garbo and Norma Shearer were nominated for two films each. The Awards ceremony was being held a mere seven months after the last one, to make up for lost time and to get the annual ritual on a regular schedule. The banquet sold out as soon as tickets went on sale.

The Big Night

Greta Garbo didn't come. Neither did George Arliss, who was on a trip to France. The mood was festive for those who did attend the crowded affair. After Louis B. Mayer got off the dance floor, dinner was served. Then the program began with Will Hays, the head of the industry's self-censorship board, giving a lecture on the connection between morality and business. "Good taste is good business, and to offend good taste is to fortify sales resistance," Hays expounded. "Nothing unclean can maintain growth and vitality. When a tree begins to collect blights, it begins to wither. So does reputation. So does business." Frances Marion, a nominee for the Writing Award, wrote later, "Hays rose and for fifty minutes extolled the virtues of the picture business since his Censor Board had eliminated its vices."

Academy founder Conrad Nagel acted as master of ceremonies and read a telegram from the Academy's previous emcee, William C. DeMille, who was off on a vacation. Nagel saluted Milton Sills, a recently deceased charter member of the Academy who was also a founder of Actors' Equity in 1913, calling him "one of the most faithful of workers for the good of the industry." Then the Academy treasurer stood up and gave a financial report.

Director John Cromwell started the Awards-giving by announcing that Lewis Milestone was Best Director for *All Quiet on the Western Front.* Colonel Nugent Slaughter announced that there was a new category for Sound Recording and the first winner was Norma Shearer's brother, Douglas, for *The Big House*. Universal's second Award was for Interior Decoration for Bing Crosby's first feature film, *King of Jazz*. Charles Rosher gave the Cinematography Award to Paramount's *With Byrd at the South Pole,* filmed on location. The Writing Award went to Frances Marion, author of *The Big House,* and just about everything else at MGM.

Louis B. Mayer declared the winner of the Best Picture Award—Universal's Carl Laemmle for bringing forth *All Quiet on the Western Front.* "I hear there's talk that the motion picture we honor tonight may win a Nobel Peace Prize," Mayer said. Laemmle picked up the statuette and commented, "Next to the thrill of becoming a grandfather, this is the proudest moment of my life."

British character actor Lawrence Grant, who supported Best Actor nominee Ronald Colman in *Bulldog Drummond,* revealed that Colman had lost Best Actor to George Arliss, who was cited for his impersonation of Benjamin Disraeli. The head of production at Warners, Darryl F. Zanuck, accepted the statuette for the vacationer. Grant then announced that the Best Actress winner was Norma Shearer, for *The Divorcée.* Mrs. Thalberg was present, and was reported to be "flustered" when she accepted. The Awards presentation over, Louis B. Mayer congratulated Carl Laemmle for his remarkable feat— Universal had tied with MGM by winning three Academy Awards.

Awards Ceremony

NOVEMBER 5, 1930, 8:00 P.M.
A BANQUET AT THE FIESTA ROOM OF THE AMBASSADOR HOTEL, LOS ANGELES

Your Host:
CONRAD NAGEL

Presenters

Director	John Cromwell
Sound Recording	Colonel Nugent Slaughter
Art Direction	William Cameron Menzies
Cinematography	Charles Rosher
Writing Achievement	Jack Cunningham
Production	Louis B. Mayer
Actor	Lawrence Grant
Actress	Lawrence Grant

Aftermath

Both George Arliss and Norma Shearer knew they were winners, because the Academy had asked them to pose with their statuettes two days before the banquet. A rumor persisted after the ceremony that MGM employees had been sent a memo asking them to vote for Norma Shearer. The rumor was never confirmed, but it was no secret that Mrs. Irving Thalberg got the red-carpet treatment at the studio. "What do you expect?" Joan Crawford was quoted as saying. "She sleeps with the boss."

1930-31

"American women talk always of their jewelry. They go to parties and drink cocktails, but it is such hollow enjoyment."
—Marlene Dietrich

Marlene Dietrich, James Cagney, Edward G. Robinson—Hollywood attracted new faces, but the Academy would hold out for old favorites at the 1930–31 Awards.

The biggest social event of the season was the marriage of Louis B. Mayer's daughter Irene to rising Paramount producer David O. Selznick. Their wedding was enough of a hometown event that Paramount threw a party for the pair at the Beverly Wilshire. As the bride remembered in her memoirs:

> *It was a brief social merger of Paramount and MGM, a command appearance. Midway in the evening there was a sudden hush, as though a cue had been given. Paramount's answer to MGM's Garbo, Marlene Dietrich, fresh from her triumph in* The Blue Angel, *made a spectacular entrance, followed by Josef von Sternberg. She strode across the full length of the enormous dance floor. The silence was broken by applause. She had arrived in Hollywood that day, and her debut caused such a flurry she practically seemed the guest of honor.*

After her European success in *The Blue Angel*, director Josef von Sternberg implored Dietrich to come to Hollywood with him. Dietrich, wary about leaving Germany, demanded that Paramount promise to release her from her contract with them after one movie if she didn't like the United States. "Otherwise, I wouldn't have come," she said. "I want nothing to do with a seven-year contract or anything like that. I have to look at the country first and know if it's good enough to bring my child over before I stay."

Von Sternberg gave Dietrich a deluxe American film debut—*Morocco*, an atmospheric romance about an entertainer who must choose between wealthy artist Adolphe Menjou and Foreign Legionnaire Gary Cooper. The director put every effort into making Dietrich appear mysterious and unattainable; the sound man complained that von Sternberg was making Dietrich whisper so much that he couldn't get a decent recording of her voice. Costar Gary Cooper was also perplexed. "It's bad enough that I don't understand a thing he's talking about," he said of von Sternberg, "but I don't even know what's going on in this movie."

Before either *Morocco* or *The Blue Angel* was released in the United States, Dietrich was causing a sensation in America simply by the way she dressed. She showed up at a posh Hollywood party in a yachting cap, a blazer, and white bell bottoms—every other woman there was in an evening gown. When a Paramount photographer snapped the star lounging at home in slacks, the impact on American fashion was immediate. "All over the country, the stores were raided for their small supplies of women's slacks," said Paramount's Adolph Zukor. "The rage was on."

The rage continued as *Morocco* and *The Blue Angel* opened and the public flocked to see the pants-wearer on film. In *Morocco*, von Sternberg had his protégée sing a song in a white tuxedo and end the number by kissing a woman. With the Depression causing movie attendance to drop, Adolph Zukor claimed that the box-office returns earned by Dietrich "saved" Paramount. Dietrich was happy, too, and brought her child over, but the star was still a little uncertain about Hollywood. "American women talk always of their jewelry," she said. "They go to parties and drink cocktails, but it is such hollow enjoyment. It makes me miserable."

The King Goes Forth

MGM decided to recognize the Depression and use it for a plot twist in Joan Crawford's latest vehicle, *Dance, Fools, Dance*. Crawford portrayed a rich girl whose fortune is wiped out by the Crash, so she turns to crime reporting. The Hays Office thought the film committed the crime of showing

Overleaf: *After referring to her as an "old firehorse," Best Actress loser Norma Shearer* (right) *hugs the winner, Marie Dressler.*

unchaperoned young adults going for a midnight swim in their underwear, but MGM managed to sneak the scene through by arguing that it was a convincing depiction of decadence. Audiences were more interested in the thirty-year-old unknown who played a gangster—Clark Gable. When the actor began receiving fan mail, the studio tagged him to play another gangster in *The Secret Six*, the follow-up melodrama to the previous year's successful *The Big House* by writer Frances Marion, director George Hill, and star Wallace Beery. *The Secret Six*—sporting one of Howard Hughes's contractees, Jean Harlow, in a supporting role—was a smash hit.

Gable portrayed a gangster again in *A Free Soul,* another adult drama for Norma Shearer in the mold of her Academy Award picture from the previous year, *The Divorcée,* although Thalberg seemed to be getting careless with his wife's reputation. *Film Daily* advised exhibitors: "Good audience picture although below the usual Shearer standard handicapped by weak story." The *New York Times* told readers: "Talking pictures are by no means elevated by the presentation of *A Free Soul.*"

Destiny by Heredity

Despite the mediocre reviews, *A Free Soul* was one of Norma Shearer's biggest moneymakers. The studio put its Academy Award push behind Lionel Barrymore, who played her alcoholic lawyer father. They publicized the fact that the actor had filmed the climactic trial scene, at the conclusion of which he drops dead, in just one take. The program for *A Free Soul* given out at first-run theaters read, "Lionel Barrymore, like his brother John and sister Ethel, was destined by heredity and training for a brilliant career in the theatre."

Triumph of an Ugly Duckling

By 1931, the most popular actress at MGM, or in Hollywood for that matter, was 62-year-old Marie Dressler, voted the number-one box-office star by *Motion Picture Herald*. Four years earlier, the former vaudeville star had been unable to find work, although she lied to her old friend, screenwriter Frances Marion, by telling her she had found bit parts here and there. Then one day Marion received a letter from another friend: "Don't believe Marie's bluff that she's got a good part in a picture. She's looking at the want ads. Says she would make a good housekeeper for some family. Can't you do something for her in Hollywood?" Marion did—she persuaded Irving Thalberg to cast Dressler in a silent comedy called *The Callahans and the Murphys* in 1927. From there, Dressler worked her way up at the studio, winning wide acclaim in a supporting role in Greta Garbo's *Anna Christie* in 1930. Then, Marion talked Thalberg into letting the actress have a starring role in *Min and Bill*, a screenplay that she had created with Dressler and Wallace Beery in mind.

"It is regrettable that Miss Dressler and Mr. Beery should have been cast for the first time together in this far from pleasant film," sniffed the *New York Times*. The picaresque movie followed the trials of Dressler, the owner of a waterfront dive, who battles with Beery, her boyfriend, and adopts a foundling, later killing the kid's mother when she wants her offspring back. Audiences loved the slapstick-and-sentimentality mix, and *Min and Bill* was MGM's top moneymaker for 1930. Although she played a guttersnipe in the film, Dressler was referred to by the studio as "The Grand Lady of Hollywood." Almost every article on her mentioned her autobiography, entitled *The Life Story of an Ugly Duckling,* and the actress' sixty-third birthday was celebrated by the studio with great ceremony. "I'm nothing special," Dressler said, wiping away tears at her party, "I've been having birthdays for many years now."

Youth and Beauty

Marie Dressler's Academy competition included Ann Harding, a twenty-eight-year-old blond beauty who had begun her acting career

"She's bound to have one of the most enviable careers in Hollywoood—if she gets a good agent."
—Wesley Ruggles on Irene Dunne

with the Provincetown Players in Greenwich Village before moving uptown to Broadway and finally to Hollywood. Harding made seven pictures during her first two years in films, getting her best notices for the adaptation of the Philip Barry comedy, *Holiday*. Fox then featured her in its expensive adaptation of *East Lynne*, a theatrical chestnut with the usual long-suffering heroine. "When Miss Harding appears, always attractively gowned, she captures one's full attention," wrote the *New York Times*. As for *East Lynne*, the *New York World* said, "The dean of modern tear-jerkers is not—could not possibly be—a great movie. But it has an individual splendor in its old-world, last-century manner." The movie was very popular, but it still couldn't pull the struggling Fox out of the red.

Nicely Dunne

RKO Radio was having a hard time balancing its books, too, and took a gamble by adapting Edna Ferber's western novel *Cimarron*, an epic about the settling of Oklahoma. The film company didn't stint on the production, which featured a recreation of the Oklahoma land rush of 1888 and enormous sets depicting the growth of a city over a forty-year period. Critics applauded *Cimarron* for being one of the few talkies to approach the visual sweep of the silents and the film made stars of the couple who played the leads: Richard Dix, a handsome hero from the silents, and Irene Dunne, an actress just starting out in films after her success on Broadway in *Show Boat*. Director Wesley Ruggles raved of his leading lady, "She can sing, play comedy or drama. She's bound to have one of the most enviable careers in Hollywood—if she gets a good agent." Although *Cimarron* was a prestigious box-office hit, RKO still managed to lose $5.5 million by the end of 1931.

Come Blow Your Horn

MGM had troubles with its epic, *Trader Horn*, filmed on location in Africa over a seven-month period by W.S. Van Dyke. Leading lady Edwina Booth, playing an abducted missionary's daughter who becomes the ruling white goddess of an African tribe, contracted African sleeping sickness and a fever from the tsetse fly and sued MGM for a million bucks. She won a settlement. Meanwhile, Irving Thalberg was ordering more footage to be shot in Hollywood and Mexico. The film finally opened after a year of production and earned $2 million. Unfortunately, it had cost MGM $3 million.

You Dirty Rat

Warner Brothers was doing things more economically. The studio that had brought forth sound was so successful that it had already absorbed First National Pictures. Almost as important as sound for the brothers Warner was the gangster film, a genre in which they had no rivals. The studio's first underworld smash was *Little Caesar*, starring a New York actor named Edward G. Robinson as an Italian immigrant who climbs to the top of gangsterdom. "*Little Caesar* becomes at Mr. Robinson's hands a figure out of Greek epic tragedy," said one reviewer.

Warners followed this hit with a picture made in twenty-six days for $150,000—*The Public Enemy*. James Cagney, as a gangster-on-the-rise, smashed a grapefruit in his moll's face, and the *New York Times* called his performance "remarkably lifelike." Jean Harlow popped up in this one, too, and MGM soon bought out her contract from Howard Hughes. *The Public Enemy* made over a million for Warners, but the studio began getting bad press from organizations that claimed gangster films were endangering society. The New York Patrolman's Benefit Association passed a resolution that called for a ban on films that "glorify the lives of gangsters, gunmen and racketeers." The Better Films Committee of Montclair, New Jersey, went further and said that the death of a twelve-year-old boy occurred because his murderer had recently seen a gangster movie. After the press raised the issue of violence, even James Cag-

"I'm sick of carrying guns and beating up women."
—James Cagney

ney commented, "I'm sick of carrying guns and beating up women. Movies should be entertaining, not bloodbaths."

Good Clean Wholesome Sadism

The violence was happening offscreen at Paramount, where director Norman Taurog was terrorizing his nephew, ten-year-old Jackie Cooper, by telling him that if he didn't cry for a scene, the director would be forced to shoot Jackie's dog. When Cooper began to bawl, the cameras started rolling and Taurog had another heartwarming scene for *Skippy,* a film based on a comic strip about a little boy. Cooper, a veteran of "Our Gang" comedy shorts, won great reviews but the *Herald Tribune* noted, "The film is pretty idealistic about the loyalty and inherent fitness of the children on your block and if it were not so admirably directed, it might have seemed just an elongated 'Our Gang' comedy without the gags." *Skippy* became so popular that a brand of peanut butter was named after it.

Broadway Babies

Paramount also did well with a more sophisticated comedy, *The Royal Family of Broadway,* adapted by Herman Mankiewicz and Gertrude Powell from Edna Ferber and George S. Kaufman's Broadway parody of the Barrymores. Fredric March, imitating flamboyant John Barrymore, walked off with the lion's share of the reviews. The film marked a step up for George Cukor, who codirected the picture at Paramount's studio in Astoria, Queens. Cukor had been the dialogue director on the previous year's *All Quiet on the Western Front. All Quiet*'s Academy Award–winning director, Lewis Milestone, also hit paydirt this year by adapting a Broadway comedy—Ben Hecht and Charles MacArthur's rowdy newspaper comedy *The Front Page,* with Adolphe Menjou as editor Walter Burns and screen newcomer Pat O'Brien as reporter Hildy Johnson.

The Nominations

Lightning struck twice for Lewis Milestone; for the second year in a row, he and his picture were nominated for Academy Awards. Not as fortunate were James Cagney and Edward G. Robinson—both *The Public Enemy* and *Little Caesar* were nominated only for Writing Awards. The Best Picture race was between the costly epics—RKO's *Cimarron,* with seven nominations, and MGM's *Trader Horn,* which was only nominated for Best Picture. The other nominees were Fox's *East Lynne,* and Paramount's *Skippy. Min and Bill*'s Marie Dressler was up against glamour girls Marlene Dietrich in *Morocco,* Ann Harding for *Holiday,* Irene Dunne (enough of a newcomer to have her name spelled wrong on the ballot) for *Cimarron* and Norma Shearer for *A Free Soul.* Shearer's screen lover, Clark Gable, was bypassed for her screen father, Lionel Barrymore, whose main competition was ten-year-old Jackie Cooper. Cooper's uncle and tormentor Norman Taurog was in the running for Best Director. The other Best Actor nominees were Adolphe Menjou for *The Front Page,* Richard Dix for *Cimarron,* and Fredric March for impersonating conominee Lionel Barrymore's brother in *The Royal Family of Broadway.*

Louis B. Mayer was in charge of the guest list for the Awards banquet, and he invited everybody he could think of: the governor of California, a former assistant U.S. attorney general, an admiral, a lieutenant commander, Will Hays, and 200 members of the American Newspaper Publishers Association, which just happened to be holding a convention in Los Angeles. But the mogul's most celebrated guest was Herbert Hoover's Vice President, Charles Curtis. Accompanying Curtis on his trip to the West Coast was the centerpiece of Washington society, his sister, Mrs. Dolly Gann, causing a furor among vying Hollywood hostesses. Mrs. Gann and the Vice President had already accepted one social invitation—they would be the houseguests of Mr. and Mrs. Louis B. Mayer.

The Big Night

The Academy had thought ahead by moving from the Ambassador Hotel to a more spacious room in the Biltmore to accommodate the swelling guest list, but nobody had thought about sending the table assignments out to the guests in advance. It took an hour for Academy officials to straighten things out and dinner, scheduled for 8, wasn't served until 9.

At 10:30, emcee Lawrence Grant introduced the guests of honor but forgot Mrs. Dolly Gann's name. When he remembered, he praised her warmth and affection. Conrad Nagel, a Founder of the Academy and nominee Ann Harding's co-star in *East Lynne*, asked the Academy to pay tribute to Thomas Edison, the previous year's Lifetime Academy Membership recipient, who had just passed away. The lights were dimmed and a shadow image of the late inventor flashed on a wall, the silence violated only by the thumps and clangs of the hotel elevators.

Outgoing Academy President William C. DeMille stood up and introduced the new president, M.C. Levee, who rose and praised Will Hays and Louis B. Mayer. Levee added that the evening also marked his seventeenth wedding anniversary, and "naturally, the happiest night of my life." Then everybody toasted Mrs. Levee.

The president of the American Newspaper Publishers Association was next, and the editor of Little Rock's *Arkansas Gazette* was not about to let Herbert Hoover's cohort get away unscathed. J.N. Heiskell began by commenting that since he was from Arkansas, there was no question that he was a Democrat. "Of course," Heiskell said of his home state, "there are some Republicans there and also other varmints." When the laughter died down, Heiskell launched into a spiel against Prohibition that was soundly applauded by the Hollywood crowd, many of whom had brought flasks with them. Vice President Curtis squirmed and stared down at his coffee cup. Heiskell also had the answer to the country's widespread unemployment problem; it would go away, he said, if the government would employ the unemployed to collect statistics on unemployment.

Vice President Curtis relaxed when Louis B. Mayer stepped up to the podium. The mogul praised his houseguests and talked a little bit about the Academy. One of Mayer's other banquet guests, the admiral, stood up and paid tribute to democracy. Will Hays read a tribute to the Hays Office, although a few reporters noted that some of the guests grew bored and began talking during Hays' address. The governor of California saluted Vice President Curtis, the movie industry, and Louis B. Mayer, who was also lauded by the ex-assistant attorney general as "beloved in the halls of Congress."

By the time Vice President Curtis walked up to make his remarks, Best Actor nominee Jackie Cooper had fallen asleep on Marie Dressler's arm. The Vice President didn't notice that he dropped a number of pages from his prepared speech on the way to the podium and they weren't missed. While Curtis rambled on about the picture industry's "glorious opportunity to render a great and steadying influence to your fellow Americans," comedian Roscoe Ates led a parade of guests to the hotel

Awards Ceremony

NOVEMBER 10, 1931, 8:00 P.M.
A BANQUET AT THE SALA D'ORO OF THE BILTMORE HOTEL, LOS ANGELES

Your Host:
LAWRENCE GRANT

Presenters

Scientific or Technical Awards	J. Theodore Reed
Cinematography	Karl Struss
Art Direction	Van Nest Polglase
Sound Recording	Colonel Nugent Slaughter
Writing Awards	Waldemar Young
Director	William K. Howard
Actress	Norma Shearer
Actor	George Arliss
Picture	B.P. Schulberg

"Like an old Model T Ford, I had to be cranked up."
—Marie Dressler

lobby, where he entertained them with his stuttering routine. Academy officials, seeing the exodus to the lobby, pleaded with Ates and his audience to return to the banquet hall in time to applaud the Vice President when he finished speaking.

It was midnight before the first awards were presented and these were the new Scientific and Technical Awards that went to machinery rather than to specific movies. For the third year in a row, the Cinematography Award went to a film shot outside of the United States. The winner was Floyd Crosby for *Tabu*, a silent shot in the South Seas with sound added later. The Interior Decoration Award went to the man who designed the growing city of *Cimarron*. The Sound Recording Award was won by the Paramount Sound Department for, among other things, capturing Marlene Dietrich's whispers in *Morocco*.

Five gangster movies were up for the two Writing Awards, but none of them won. *Cimarron*, grabbing its second Award, picked up the best Adapted Screenplay statuette, and the Best Original Screenplay Award went to a man who was in the midst of a lawsuit. "This is indeed a crazy business where I am being sued for plagiarism on one hand and given the statuette for originality on the other," said John Monk Saunders, author of *The Dawn Patrol*, before rejoining wife Fay Wray at their table.

Director William K. Howard presented the Direction Award by reading telegrams from the four losers urging the Academy to give the award to Norman Taurog for *Skippy*. Winner Taurog, a victim of a recent accident, hobbled to the dais on crutches and said he had sent a telegram rooting for Wesley Ruggles for *Cimarron*. The director also thanked his star, who was still slumbering on Marie Dressler's arm. No one bothered to wake Cooper up minutes later when George Arliss announced "the best performance of the year by a male actor—Lionel Barrymore in *A Free Soul*." The winner praised his fellow nominees, concluding with a tribute to the still sleeping Jackie Cooper.

Although she was a nominee herself, Norma Shearer made the Best Actress presentation. She revealed that the winner had been ill recently, "but when she came on the lot and heard the call 'Ready on the set, Miss Dressler,' she would charge across that lot like an old firehorse that hears the gong." When she learned that she had won for *Min and Bill*, Marie Dressler sat in stunned silence for a moment. "Like an old Model T Ford, I had to be cranked up," she confessed later. "I was scared stiff." Dressler eased Jackie Cooper into his mother's arms, headed for the podium, and noticed that, "Across the table, Frances Marion was smiling a triumphant I-told-you-so smile." The winner ended her speech by saying, "I have always believed that our lives should be governed by simplicity. But tonight, I feel very important. In fact, I think Dolly Gann should get up and give me her seat." Mrs. Gann laughed loudly, stood up, and offered her chair to the Best Actress.

Paramount head B.P. Schulberg named the Best Picture—RKO's *Cimarron*, which, with three Awards, making it the night's biggest winner. The guests then mingled and congratulated each other, with the exception of youngest Best Actor loser, who went straight home to bed.

Aftermath

Even though his film won a three Awards, the director of *Cimarron* complained that he had been shut out. "I wonder where I was when the picture was made as it was given the award for sets, production and adaptation, which possibly I had something to do with," said Wesley Ruggles.

Ruggles' was a lonely voice compared to the collective cry from the cinematographers who felt it wasn't fair for Hollywood studio movies to compete for the Award with silent films shot in exotic locations. The branch quickly rewrote the requirements for the Cinematography Award to read: "The best achievement in cinematography of a black-and-white picture photographed in America under normal production conditions." *Tabu*'s winner, Floyd Crosby, couldn't have cared less about the controversy. The cinematographer photographed documentaries for the next two decades, moving to commercial features with *High Noon* in 1952 and later to such drive-in favorites as *Attack of the Crab Monsters* (1957) and *How to Stuff a Wild Bikini* (1965). He also raised a son, rock musician David Crosby.

No matter how important the names on Louis B. Mayer's guest list, the trade journals wrote the entire evening off as a bore. *Daily Variety* called the affair "a long winded, verbose, political and dull evening of a nature which will repel many a Hollywoodian next year (unless memories dim and time makes 'em forget)." And the guest of honor, Vice President Charles Curtis, received the worst reviews of all. "That dull Republican oratory started dishes to rattling, silver to clinking and conversation to humming," recalled the *Hollywood Herald*, while columnist Homer Croy wrote, "Even if I live to be as old as redwood, I'll never forget that speech which to me is the nadir of all banquet speeches. George S. Kaufman could have written a play around it."

There was no dissent over the selection of Marie Dressler for Best Actress; yet, for the winner, the victory proved to be bittersweet. As Dressler recalled in a second autobiography, she lay in bed the morning after the Awards, reading the paper when she came across a small obituary for an obscure actress who had committed suicide and was to be buried in a pauper's grave. The actress had been one of Dressler's friends when she was just starting her career. "I looked back along the highway of the years," Dressler wrote. "Dark, pretty little Jane and big, homely Marie Dressler, dancing together in the pony ballet of a third-rate musical comedy in Kansas City, forty-odd years ago. Jane on Broadway, while Marie was still stalking the provinces. . . . And now Jane was dead at sixty, a self-confessed failure. And I, Marie Dressler, was alive, with the Academy Award of last night standing within reach of my hand. I slip the golden figure into a bureau drawer. I cannot bear to look at it just now."

1931-32

"When picture makers vote their own preferences, they are not for the sensational, the tawdry, the cheap, the sexy."
—Los Angeles Herald

Mickey Mouse wanted in on the action when the Academy rewarded Hollywood's success stories at the 1931–32 Awards.

Walt Disney, a 22-year-old commercial animator from Kansas City, came to Hollywood in 1923 with his brother Roy with the idea of making cartoons. By 1927, their partnership launched its first cartoon series, *Oswald the Rabbit*. Their company struck gold the following year when Walt introduced Mickey Mouse. The cartoon rodent started in silents and made the transition to sound quickly with Disney himself supplying the high-pitched voice. By 1932, Disney was turning out cartoons in lush colors with classical sound tracks—*Flowers and Trees* had music by Mendelssohn and Schubert. And Mickey Mouse had prospered, too. Many theaters were able to attract finicky Depression audiences by advertising that Mickey was on the bill.

As the Disney brothers became a force to be reckoned with, the Academy opened its doors to the animators by creating a category for short subjects. Not only would cartoons be given awards, but slapstick comedies and documentaries—which usually preceded feature films on theater programs—would be honored as well. To make the nominations in the new category, the Academy elected a committee of experts in the field that included Laurel and Hardy, Walt and Roy Disney, Mack Sennett, and Leon Schlesinger, the producer of the *Looney Tunes* series.

Tears and Tickets

Unlike the Disney boys, almost every other studio in Hollywood was on wobbly financial legs—Fox, Warner Brothers and Paramount each listed losses over $10 million. MGM, on the other hand, flourished. The studio with "More Stars Than There Are In Heaven" pulled in a profit of $8 million by putting their stars through familiar paces. Screenwriter Frances Marion designed *Emma,* another comedy tearjerker in the *Min and Bill* vein, for Marie Dressler. In this one, Dressler played a housekeeper who marries her employer only to be snubbed by his children. The film was as profitable as its predecessor.

Writer Marion had even bigger things in mind for Wallace Beery, creating for him the role of a broken-down boxer rejuvenated by his adoring son. Beery's costar was the box-office titan who had broken hearts in *Skippy* the year before, eleven-year-old Jackie Cooper. *The Champ* was MGM's highest-grossing film of the year and, while Cooper received most of the critical praise for his crying scenes, Beery established himself in the eyes of the studio as one of its top-drawing stars.

I Want to Be Alone

MGM's Irving Thalberg had a brainstorm: Why not take a star like Wallace Beery, who could carry a movie all by himself, and put him in a film with other big MGM stars? The result was *Grand Hotel,* Hollywood's first all-star melodrama. In order of billing, the stars in this glossy soap opera set in a Berlin hotel were Greta Garbo, John Barrymore, Joan Crawford, Wallace Beery, and Lionel Barrymore. Garbo said, "I want to be alone" to millions of moviegoers, who made the film both a box-office hit and another feather in the cap of MGM's Boy Wonder, Irving Thalberg.

With stars bringing in such large profits, Thalberg was eager to find more luminaries, so he imported names from Broadway. The team of Alfred Lunt and Lynn Fontanne was about as illustrious as any the American theater had to offer, so Thalberg hired them to recreate one of their stage hits, Ferenc Molnar's *The Guardsman,* at Culver City. "It is a pity that there are not more Fontannes, Lunts and Molnars to help out the screen," wrote the *New York Times'* reviewer, "for

Overleaf: *Helen Hayes is puzzled that she could win a Best Actress Award for a tearjerker like* The Sin of Madelon Claudet.

"Little Helen was going back to New York—a failure."
—Helen Hayes

then the medium of entertainment would be on a far higher level." Even with laudatory notices, the Lunts didn't have the drawing power of, say, Joan Crawford. But, based on the moderate success of *The Guardsman,* Louis B. Mayer was nonetheless optimistic enough to offer the acting couple a long-term contract. The Lunts decided to pass, and returned to the boards.

The Bride Who Didn't Want To

MGM had more luck with the debut of another Broadway light, Helen Hayes. The actress had followed her husband, writer Charles MacArthur, to Hollywood when he signed a contract with MGM, and Irving Thalberg began pestering Mrs. MacArthur about making a talkie as soon as she arrived. Hayes finally gave in, but began to rue ever listening to the Boy Wonder when her vehicle, a weeper about a sacrificial mother entitled *The Sin of Madelon Claudet,* proved so ridiculous that she was afraid Louis B. Mayer was going to stop filming on it. MacArthur stepped in for some rewriting, but the sneak preview of the finished product was still a disaster. "The studio was about to shelve it," Hayes said, "and that meant little Helen was going back to New York—a failure. But Mr. Thalberg took a look at it, told us all to cheer up, and to get to work on retakes. We did—and I know Charlie never worked harder."

Louis B. Mayer was originally in favor of shelving the movie, but when the mogul saw the second version he wept like a baby. After the film premiered, the *New York Times* said, "It is no wonder that the producer heads of MGM are enthusiastic over Helen Hayes' acting in her first picture, *The Sin of Madelon Claudet*. For this actress' superb portrayal in a difficult role leaves only the regret that the powers that be did not see fit to have her make her screen debut in a more cheerful study."

Samuel Goldwyn immediately hired Hayes to play Ronald Colman's wife in *Arrowsmith,* an adaptation of Sinclair Lewis' novel, directed by John Ford. Colman, Ford and Hayes were all praised for their work, and the sentimental drama made plenty of money. Helen Hayes, the reluctant movie actress, was now sought after by all the studios.

Give Me a Primitive Man

Heartened by the success of *Dracula* and *Frankenstein* over at Universal, Paramount's B.P. Schulberg thought it would be a good idea to drag out *Dr. Jekyll and Mr. Hyde*. Schulberg wanted character actor Irving Pichel in the title roles, but director Rouben Mamoulian disagreed, saying, "I want someone who can play Jekyll, and Pichel can only play Hyde!" The director preferred Fredric March, who had won a Best Actor nomination for his John Barrymore parody in *The Royal Family of Broadway*. "You're crazy," Schulberg responded, "Fredric March is a comedian." But Mamoulian's mind was made up. "He's a natural Jekyll," the director argued. "He's young, he's handsome, his speech is fine, and I'm sure he can play Hyde."

Schulberg gave March a chance and Mamoulian expanded on the reason behind his casting: "I don't want Hyde to be a monster. Hyde is not evil, he is the primitive, the animal in us, whereas Jekyll is a cultured man, representing the intellect. Hyde is the Neanderthal man, and March's makeup was designed as such." It took Wally Westmore three hours to apply March's makeup, but everyone said it was worth it. The critics saluted Fredric March's performance and the public took his Hyde as much to heart as it had Boris Karloff's Frankenstein and Bela Lugosi's Dracula.

The Good Bad Girl

Paramount's two most famous directors also helped bring in some desperately needed cash to the studio. Josef von Sternberg concocted another exotic picture for Marlene Dietrich, *Shanghai Express,* in which she played a vamp known as Shanghai Lili on board a train rushing through a Chinese civil war. Audiences still jumped at the chance to see Dietrich, as they did Maurice Chevalier, who starred in two operettas, *Smiling Lieutenant,* with Claudette Colbert, and *One Hour with You,* with Jeanette MacDonald.

The surprise hit of the year was Fox's romance about ordinary people, *Bad Girl,* which had no major stars. James Dunn and Sally Eilers, who usually starred in B-movies, played a lower-income couple struggling by in director Frank Borzage's love story that became an international success. The *New York Times* said the movie was "blessed with truth and simplicity" and the *Times of London* commented, "It is the measure of Mr. Borzage's achievement that the experience of this unsophisticated pair is momentous to us." The only problem with the picture was the title—there was no bad girl in *Bad Girl.*

The Shame of the Nation

One of Fox's ex-employees, Paul Muni, had returned to Broadway and covered himself with glory in *Counsellor-at-Law.* Hollywood became interested in him again, and Muni accepted Howard Hughes' offer to star in Howard Hawks' gangster film *Scarface: The Shame of the Nation.* Audiences were fascinated by Hawks' tragic vision of the immigrant kingpin, but some critics complained—as they had with *Little Caesar* and *The Public Enemy*—that the film glamorized violence and the criminal life. Others called it a masterpiece, including Samuel Weiss, a theater-chain owner, who wrote the *Hollywood Reporter* requesting that the Academy nominate the film for Best Picture. "Nothing like it has been done in the past year upon the stage or screen or in literature," Weiss claimed.

The Nominations

Scarface was completely shut out of the nominations. "I'm not disappointed for myself," said Paul Muni, "but I think it's the shame of the nation that Howard Hawks wasn't nominated."

Hawks wasn't alone in obscurity; the Academy allowed eight Best Picture nominations but only three Best Director nominees. Among the five directors who didn't get nominated along with their films were *Arrowsmith*'s John Ford and *Smiling Lieutenant*'s Ernst Lubitsch. Of the directors who were recognized, Hollywood columnist Sidney Skolsky said the race was a "toss-up" between Josef von Sternberg for *Shanghai Express* and Frank Borzage, "the favorite," for *Bad Girl.*

Some Hollywoodites thought the Academy had too many favorites and that former winners Borzage; Marie Dressler, nominated for *Emma*; and writer Frances Marion, nominated for *The Champ,* should not be able to win again. But the Academy voted down a petition for an exclusionary rule prohibiting repeat winners. According to columnist Jimmy Starr, Wallace Beery of *The Champ* held the lead in the Best Actor race over nominees Fredric March in *Dr. Jekyll and Mr. Hyde* and Alfred Lunt for *The Guardsman.* Starr maintained that Helen Hayes would be the Best Actress victor for *The Sin of Madelon Claudet* over Mrs. Lunt in *The Guardsman* and Marie Dressler, and that MGM's *Grand Hotel* would be the Best Picture winner.

No Sex Allowed

The *Hollywood Herald* applauded the Academy's choices, noting that *Red-Headed Woman,* a Jean Harlow gold-digging saga; *Shopworn,* a Barbara Stanwyck soap opera; *Possessed* and *Letty Lynton,* two Joan Crawford vehicles; "and their type" of film were not nominated. "Box office or not," the article concluded, "when picture makers vote their own preferences, they are not for the sensational, the tawdry, the cheap, the sexy. They wish to reward substantial effort." In the view of Elizabeth Yeaman of the *Hollywood Citizen-News,* the nominations of the Lunts showed how fair the Academy was: "*The Guardsman,* a classic bit of subtlety, was not a very great financial success. Add to these factors the knowledge that Lunt and Fontanne declined a film contract which would have netted them $1,000,000 cash, and you need nothing further to prove the nominations were not guided by prejudice."

They were not guided by an outpouring of popular approval, either. As the *Los Angeles Times'* Edwin Schallert said of the nominated Lunts, "The discriminating audiences, I will grant, like the industry itself, blessed the stars with its approval. But the favorites of the mass public would probably be found elsewhere." The *Los Angeles Record* took issue with a Best Original Story nomination for *What Price Hollywood*, which depicted the fall from grace of a drunken movie director. "*What Price Hollywood* wasn't an original story except in the technical sense," the journal insisted. "The authors only called to mind a few bits of common Hollywood history and stitched 'em up into a story." Just who did the stitching became a question the Academy had to answer when columnist Adela Rogers St. John said the Original Story was her idea and not that of the two rewrite men who received screen credit. The Academy investigated and agreed with her, telling RKO to give screen credit to St. John and then nominating her alone for the Award.

Mickey Mouse was a part of a mutual admiration society in the Short Films branch—judges Laurel and Hardy, Disney, Sennett and Leon (*Looney Tunes*) Schlesinger were all nominated for Awards. But Mack Sennett's brotherhood extended only so far. When he learned in advance that his nominated novelty short, *Wrestling Swordfish*, had lost to Pete Smith's *Swing High* by only three votes on the final ballot, Sennett called the Academy's attention to the rule book, which stated that a three-point difference was considered a tie vote. After the Academy's Executive Secretary declined the honor, the tie-breaking vote was turned over to the entire Academy membership—everybody was called to decide the superior novelty short.

Where Dietrich Goes, Zombies Follow

David O. Selznick thought that all voters should see all the nominees before they marked their final ballots and he persuaded the Academy to hold special screenings of the nominated films for Academy members at the Fox Criterion Theatre. "The revivals have not drawn heavily," observed the *Los Angeles Times*, which then reported that Marlene Dietrich had come to five screenings. The biggest draws at the Academy's film festival were Best Picture nominee *Arrowsmith* and Marie Dressler's Best Actress vehicle, *Emma*. A week later, the *Times* reported that the Criterion's business had picked up when the theater showed Bela Lugosi in *White Zombie*.

Attendance would be higher at the Awards ceremony. An extra row of tables accommodating sixty-five people had to be added to the Fiesta Room of the Ambassador Hotel. For the first time, there were reports of ticket scalping. Wishing to avoid last year's human traffic jam, the Academy mailed out seating assignments and floor diagrams a week in advance.

The Academy also thought about the promotional benefits of the ceremony and arranged a national radio broadcast of the Awards "as a goodwill medium for industry." To make sure there were no windbags on the bill this year, the Academy adopted a "no speechmaking" policy and invited no guests of honor. Will Hays, Hollywood's censor, tried to block the broadcast because it would keep listeners from going to the movies that evening; he was overruled. And *Film Daily* reminded the guests, "with a national hookup, those attending will have to get caught up with their sleep beforehand and not doze through proceedings as formerly."

The Big Night

Eleanor Barnes of the *Los Angeles Daily News* observed, "The Depression had brought about the unusual spectacle of two or three beauties appearing in gowns they wore at the recent Mayfair party. A preponderance of wine-colored velvet and brown velvet was evidenced." Another Academy first was a musical piece written expressly for the Awards banquet by Nat Finston, head of the Paramount music department. Louis B. Mayer danced with Helen Hayes, the only Best Actress nominee to show up. Marie Dressler was in New York, Lynn Fontanne on tour with her husband in St. Louis. Both Fredric March and Wallace Beery were present.

Academy President Conrad Nagel started the presentation after dinner by suggesting that all the men toast their wives. The first bit of business was the swearing in of newly elected Academy officers, and then various committee members were asked to stand and identify themselves. Nagel read a telegram from Douglas Fairbanks, who was at sea on the Indian Ocean. Fairbanks said that since he was on the other side of the international date line, he would know the winners a day before anybody else. Then Nagel informed the audience that Academy officials were just now tabulating the votes.

Despite the "no speechmaking" rule, Nagel embarked upon the reading of a lengthy cable from Will Hays. Then the guests were asked to pay silent tribute to three deceased men: director F.W. Murnau, film manufacturer George Eastman, and inventor Thomas Edison, receiving his second posthumous tribute at an Academy banquet.

Things were livelier when Walt Disney received the second Special Award in the Academy's five-year history, "for the creation of Mickey Mouse." For the occasion, Disney had created a special cartoon, *Mickey's Parade of Nominees,* in which all the acting nominees were caricatured in their nominated roles. The cartoon ended with Mickey apologizing, "I'm sorry. I can't come any further so I'll have to ask Mr. Disney to accept my prize for me." The previous Special Award recipient, Charlie Chaplin, was supposed to present Disney's statuette but once again he elected at the last minute to stay at home.

Mickey's happiness was short-lived when *Mickey's Orphans* lost the Best Cartoon Award to Disney's *Flowers and Trees,* the one with music by Mendelssohn and Schubert. A nattily attired Stan Laurel and Oliver Hardy marched up to receive their Best Comedy Short Award for *The Music Box* with producer Hal Roach. The winner of the contested Novelty Short Award was squeaky wheel Mack Sennett for *Wrestling Swordfish.*

Norma Shearer presented the Best Actor Award, but she did not read the name of the winner. The Academy had devised a more elaborate way to divulge his identity—his photograph was flashed on a wall while his voice was heard from the sound track. Fredric March was the victor for *Dr. Jekyll and Mr. Hyde.* "I must thank Wally

Awards Ceremony

NOVEMBER 18, 1932, 8:00 P.M.
A BANQUET AT THE FIESTA ROOM OF THE AMBASSADOR HOTEL, LOS ANGELES

Your Host:
ACADEMY PRESIDENT CONRAD NAGEL

Presenters

Scientific or Technical Awards	John M. Nickolaus
Sound Recording	John M. Nickolaus
Interior Decoration	Max Ree
Cinematography	Karl Struss
Special Award to Walt Disney	Conrad Nagel
Short Subjects	Conrad Nagel
Writing Awards	Howard Estabrook
Director	Norman Taurog
Actor	Norma Shearer
Actress	Lionel Barrymore
Picture	William LeBaron

"The Depression has brought about the unusual spectacle of two or three beauties appearing in gowns they wore at the recent Mayfair party."
—Los Angeles Daily News

Westmore, who made my task an easy one," March said. "Wally, who I consider a great artist, is responsible for the greater measure of my success." Louella Parsons turned to those at her table, whispering, "He's just being modest."

Before Lionel Barrymore gave out the Best Actress Award, he went on a harangue about the integrity of the Awards. "There is no power, however great, in any branch of motion pictures that can exert an atom of influence beyond the marking of that secret ballot, and no smash of commercial significance can dilute the fairness of the awards when so many and such varied opinions are responsible," Barrymore stressed, before proceeding to the duty at hand. Helen Hayes' face popped up on the wall and the crowd heard a snippet from the sound track of *The Sin of Madelon Claudet*. Hayes said the thrill of winning equaled her excitement when she gave birth to her daughter: "The only other time in my life when I really felt great or superb, all I could think to say was 'Gosh, isn't she red!' I hope I do better the second time, but I doubt it."

As Louis B. Mayer walked up to the podium to accept the Best Picture Award for MGM's *Grand Hotel*, Paramount's B.P. Schulberg was overseeing the Voting Committee as they reviewed the tabulations for the Awards. Suddenly, a vote-checker discovered that Wallace Beery was only one vote shy of Fredric March in the Best Actor race. Under the rules, this meant that Beery had tied with March. Schulberg sent an official to go find another statuette quick and had another messenger summon President Nagel. After Mayer was through with his gratitudes, Nagel called Wallace Beery to the dais. "Mr. Beery, it is my pleasure to announce that you have tied with Mr. March for the best male performance of the year for your splendid portrayal in *The Champ*." The crowd broke into the loudest applause since Laurel and Hardy's win. The *Los Angeles Times* reported, "This time lapse made the second award seem more like a consolation prize, but Beery nevertheless accomplished a very graceful acceptance."

The finale of the evening was a broadcast from New York. David O. Selznick was first on the wireless, followed by Best Actress loser Marie Dressler, who said, "It is honor enough for me to be mentioned for an award in company with Helen Hayes and Lynn Fontanne. Dear Helen, you will know that my hand clasps yours under the hand that hands you the gold prize which you have won so brilliantly." The Hollywood assemblage applauded Dressler, but there were gasps when she continued, "I am under strict doctor's orders to remain in New York for several weeks." No one in Hollywood had known that she was ill. Dressler would die of cancer two years later.

Aftermath

Just as the Academy had promised, the ceremony was over by 11 o'clock. Winners Helen Hayes and Frank Borzage congratulated each other; they were currently working together on *A Farewell to Arms*. As the guests resumed dancing, B.P. Schulberg revealed more information on the tabulations. Helen Hayes had received more votes than Marie Dressler and Lynn Fontanne put together; as for the Beery-March tie, the Paramount head said that Hedda Hopper may have been responsible. "On the final day of voting, Hedda showed up two minutes before the deadline," Schulberg said of the then-actress, "If she voted for Beery, she won the award for him."

Fredric March laughed over the whole outcome, as well as over the coincidence that he and Beery had also just adopted children. "It seems a little odd that Wally and I were given awards for best male performance of the year," he quipped. Columnist Homer Croy later wrote that the only reason March won was because Academy voters were fooled by his makeup. The *Los Angeles Times* took an equally dim view of the Academy's Best Picture choice, sneering, "*Grand Hotel* filled, it appeared, the requirements of bigness."

When Hayes appeared on the *Farewell to Arms* set the next day, costar Gary Cooper asked to see her statuette. "My God, I have no idea where it is!" Hayes screamed. She called her husband and he couldn't remember, either. A frantic search began, and the trophy was finally found locked in the trunk of MacArthur's car.

One person who learned his lesson from Hayes' success was Irving G. Thalberg. When he was debating whether or not to produce another hackneyed screenplay some time later, Thalberg decided to give it a shot. "Let's face it," he said. "We win Academy Awards with crap like *The Sin of Madelon Claudet*."

1932-33

"I want to make Art."
—Frank Capra

The Award got its nickname the year that the Academy's name was mud.

Despite a Best Picture Award for *Cimarron,* RKO Pictures was having trouble making money. After David O. Selznick became the studio's vice president in charge of production in 1931, things began looking up. Under the Selznick aegis, RKO released two giant hits—*King Kong* and *Flying Down to Rio,* the latter introducing the dance duo of Fred Astaire and Ginger Rogers. But Selznick's savvy was best displayed by his handling of a young, difficult actress from Broadway just signed by the studio—Katharine Hepburn.

A Beauty from Bryn Mawr

The twenty-three-year-old Bryn Mawr graduate got the deluxe treatment for her 1932 film debut. George Cukor was her director and John Barrymore her male lead in *A Bill of Divorcement,* the story of a man released from a mental institute who is reconciled with his headstrong daughter. Hepburn was rather headstrong herself during filming. When the last scene was completed, Hepburn said to Barrymore, "Thank goodness I don't have to act with you anymore." The Great Profile retorted, "I didn't know you ever had, darling."

Barrymore's opinion notwithstanding, Hepburn caused a sensation before she said a word; for her screen entrance Cukor had directed her simply to walk down a staircase and sigh. Her angular beauty was so different from the round kewpie-doll faces of most of her contemporaries that Connecticut-born Hepburn seemed almost as exotic as Dietrich or Garbo. RKO rushed her into three films for 1933: *Christopher Strong, Morning Glory,* and *Little Women,* an adaptation of Louisa May Alcott's Victorian novel, directed by George Cukor. *Christopher Strong* was a box-office flop, but Hepburn's performances in *Morning Glory,* in which she played a naïve actress, and *Little Women,* made her a household name.

But Hepburn was still viewed skeptically by Hollywood. A profile of the actress by the *Hollywood Citizen-News* read: "She delights in eccentric poses. Off the screen she wears blue denim overalls and hob-nailed boots. She carries a pet monkey and refuses to attend parties. One moment she admits and the next moment she denies a marriage to Ludlow O. Smith, a New York insurance man. She is one of six children. Her father is a reputable surgeon and her mother campaigns for birth control."

The Son-in-Law also Rises

Hepburn's mentor David O. Selznick, on the other hand, was becoming a Hollywood favorite thought to possess the Midas touch. When MGM's head of production, Irving Thalberg, collapsed from a heart ailment in December of 1933 and set sail for a European recuperation soon after, Louis B. Mayer asked Selznick, his daughter's husband, to assume the Thalberg reins. "The son-in-law also rises," cracked cynics, but Selznick showed them. Bringing over director George Cukor from RKO, Selznick out-Thalberged Thalberg with his first production, *Dinner at Eight,* an all-star adaptation of the Edna Ferber–George S. Kaufman play with Marie Dressler, John Barrymore, Wallace Beery, Jean Harlow, and Lionel Barrymore. The film's success at the box office led Mayer to offer Selznick a full-time job at Culver City.

The Lady from Poverty Row

"I want to make Art," Frank Capra declared. He also wanted to win an Academy Award. The problem for the Sicilian-born director was that he was not employed at a major studio but at Columbia Pictures, a small company located along Poverty Row. Determined nonetheless, Capra filmed a sentimental Damon Runyon story called "Mad-

Overleaf: *Emcee Will Rogers* (right) *and Best Director winner Frank Lloyd laugh as loser Frank Capra crawls back to his seat.*

"Thank goodness I don't have to act with you anymore."
—Katharine Hepburn to John Barrymore

ame La Gimp," about a poor street vendor who, through the aid of her gangster friends, passes herself off as a socialite for her visiting daughter. To portray the leading character, "Apple Annie," Capra chose seventy-five-year-old May Robson, an Australian-born stage actress who had most recently been seen in supporting roles at MGM.

Capra's efforts paid off—handsomely. *Lady for a Day* was both a commercial and critical bull's-eye. The *New York Herald Tribune* wrote: "The Lady in whose honor celluloid toasts are now being drunk in broken glass is May Robson, whose extraordinary performance has had more than anything else to do with the success of *Lady for a Day*. The picture itself has been justly celebrated as a vivaciously efficient example of first-chop hokum, manufactured with a skill that is almost savage in its ability to call its shots."

Now Tapping—Ruby and Dick

Warner Brothers also had a miracle worker over at Burbank, thirty-eight-year-old choreographer Busby Berkeley. In the space of a year, Berkeley revolutionized the movie musical with his geometric chorus lines and outrageous sense of humor: Mahatma Gandhi popping up at the end of the "Shuffle Off to Buffalo" number in *Forty-Second Street*, Ginger Rogers singing "We're in the Money" in pig latin while tap-dancing on a giant stack of coins in *Gold-Diggers of 1933*. By the time Berkeley was knocking a hole in the ceiling of a Warners sound stage for a trademark overhead shot for the swimming scenes in *Footlight Parade*'s "By a Waterfall" number, a Warners executive exclaimed, "Jesus, now Berkeley's going through the roof!" But so were his movies. The musicals, all three starring Ruby Keeler and Dick Powell as the ingenue couple, were the studio's most profitable films.

I Am a Star from Warner Brothers

When they weren't cranking out musicals, the brothers Warner were producing social-protest dramas. The most lucrative was *I Am a Fugitive From a Chain Gang*, starring Scarface himself, Paul Muni. The critics called it "raw" and "gritty" and the film had a powerful effect on Depression audiences. Muni had shown Fox, which had dropped him three years earlier—he was now a full-fledged box-office draw.

Shell-Shock Therapy

Fox was currently making a mint off the thirty-nine-year-old British-born matinee idol Leslie Howard. Of all the reasons given for actors going into show business, Howard's ranks with the strangest—his doctor had recommended it as therapy for shell shock suffered during World War I. He wasn't in the States long before Norma Shearer had used him twice and Mary Pickford had elected him to escort her through her last film venture, *Secrets*. Fox hired him to portray a time traveler who has the rotten luck to fall in love with a woman from a previous century in the romantic fantasy *Berkeley Square*. A critic wrote, "Mr. Howard is quite dashing, in both his 18th and 20th Century clothing."

Lloyd of London

Berkeley Square director Frank Lloyd was no stranger to period British clothes; the Scottish-born Hollywood veteran had won the 1928–29 Director Award for *The Divine Lady*, about the Lord Nelson–Lady Hamilton affair. Lloyd got another chance to vent his Anglophilia with *Cavalcade*, Fox's expensive adaptation of Noel Coward's historical pageant which had run for 405 performances on the London stage. The high-class soap opera impressed the critics but not the public, which flocked instead to Fox's slice of Americana, *State Fair*. This one starred Will Rogers as a farmer entering his pig in the Kansas State Fair, with Janet Gaynor as a daughter who finds romance with Lew Ayres.

A Face Like an Elephant's Behind

Not every Englishman in movies looked like Leslie Howard. Charles Laughton described himself as having "a face that looks like an elephant's behind. It would stop a sun dial." Nevertheless, the thirty-three-year-old became the movies' most celebrated new actor after his performance in the title role of *The Private Life of Henry VIII*. Because British producer Alexander Korda wasn't encumbered by the Hollywood Production Code, Laughton's Henry was far lustier than the British couple in Fox's *Cavalcade*, and American audiences loved watching His Royal Highness eat like a slob and bed women for fun and politics. Irving Thalberg was particularly impressed and cast Laughton in the latest Norma Shearer vehicle, *The Barretts of Wimpole Street*.

Is That a Pistol in Your Pocket?

Paramount also needed a new face. Desperately. The studio was declaring bankruptcy when in strutted Mae West, recruited to repeat her stage successes on film, even though one play, entitled *Sex*, had gotten her thrown in jail for ten days. Writing her own dialogue, West came up with outlandish lines like "Is that a pistol in your pocket or are you just glad to see me?" in order to throw off the censor, who would then permit her to retain a tamer line like "You can be had." In quick succession, West filmed *Night After Night*, *She Done Him Wrong*, and *I'm No Angel*—each making more money than the one before.

While West pulled Paramount out of the hole, she was being sent to hell from pulpits across the country. In New York, Monsignor Amleto Giovanni Cicognani boomed, "How shall the crimes that have their direct source in immoral motion pictures be measured? Catholics are called by God, the pope, the bishops, and the priests to a united and vigorous campaign for the purification of the cinema, which has become a deadly menace to morals." The Catholics formed the Legion of Decency to rate Hollywood movies on their moral content, and Joseph Breen of the Production Code Office told the studios that, from now on, the Production Code would be strictly administered. A film would not receive the all-important stamp of approval if it contained "obscenity in word, gesture, reference, song, joke or by suggestion (even when likely to be understood only by part of the audience)." But it would take more than a code to stop Mae West from getting her message across. As observed in the *New York Herald Tribune*, ". . . By her gift of rowdiness she writes into the work all of the qualities of hard-boiled hilarity that the producers have, in their sly way, pretended to cut out of it."

Tightening the Money Belt

President Franklin D. Roosevelt's bank holiday on March 5, 1933, dealt a severe blow to Hollywood, since most studios were operating on credit alone. The labor-negotiating wing of the Academy formed an Emergency Committee which recommended a 50 percent pay cut for all studio employees for two months. The trade unions quickly responded that, while Louis B. Mayer might be able to struggle by on half of his $8,000-a-week salary, $50-a-week technicians would have a harder time of it. The Academy revised its recommendation so that a sliding percentage of cuts would spare the lower-income employees, but this deal still wasn't good enough for the writers. In retaliation, the scribes formed the Screen Writers Guild on April 6, 1933, and the members of the new organization all resigned in writing from the Academy. The rest of Hollywood decided to give the Academy's pay cut a try.

When Sam Goldwyn and Jack Warner refused to restore full salaries at the end of the two-month period—the Academy had audited their books and documented their solvency—there were more resignations. Darryl F. Zanuck left his position as vice president in charge of production at Warners,

"How shall the crimes that have their direct source in immoral motion pictures be measured?"
—Msgr. Amleto Giovanni Cicognani

and Conrad Nagel stepped down as Academy president. Nagel was replaced by J. Theodore Reed, an assistant director at Paramount, who immediately issued a statement: "The Academy as a whole will be free from politics, and any taint of self-preservation in office."

A Star-Studded Exodus

Reed's claim proved to be bogus by October, when the Motion Picture Committee, of which the Academy president was a member, announced its new regulatory code, already approved by the National Recovery Administration. The producer-created code put a ceiling on the salaries of writers, actors and directors (but not on those of studio executives); demanded that talent agents had to be licensed by the same producers they would be doing business with; and declared that artists could not accept bids from other studios when their contracts were up for renewal until the original studio had definitely decided not to re-hire them. Now it was time for the actors to get organized.

Many of Hollywood's top stars—among them James Cagney, Jeanette MacDonald, Gary Cooper, Paul Muni—met at the house of character actor Frank Morgan, later known as the Wizard of Oz, and formed the Screen Actors Guild. Like the writers, the actors resigned from the Academy. The previous year's Best Actor, Fredric March, was elected second vice president of the guild, and two former acting nominees were also selected for duty—Vice President Adolphe Menjou and Third Vice President Ann Harding. The newly elected treasurer, Groucho Marx, claimed he went to a bordello after being sworn in, explaining, "It was the only safe place to go." But guild President Eddie Cantor spent Thanksgiving with United States President Franklin Roosevelt and persuaded the Chief Executive to remove many of the anti-labor provisions from the producers' code via executive order. Although Cantor's efforts calmed down the creative community, many members continued to regard the producer-dominated Academy with suspicion.

The Nominations

Two guild members were nominated despite their Academy resignations: Frances Marion was tapped for the Original Story Award for *The Prizefighter and the Lady,* and Paul Muni was named a Best Actor nominee for *I Am a Fugitive From a Chain Gang*. Muni's competition was all British—Leslie Howard for *Berkeley Square* and Charles Laughton for *The Private Life of Henry VIII*.

Director Frank Capra got his wish. *Lady for a Day* was nominated for four Academy Awards, becoming the first picture from Columbia to be recognized by the Academy. Capra was running neck-and-neck with Frank Lloyd for Fox's succés d'estime *Cavalcade,* also with four nominations. Paramount's *A Farewell to Arms* earned four nominations, and RKO's *Little Women* garnered three nods, including a directing nomination for George Cukor. Cukor and Selznick's collaboration at MGM—*Dinner at Eight*—was completely shut out. Warners managed two Best Picture nominations—*Forty-Second Street* and *I Am a Fugitive From a Chain Gang*. Other Best Picture nominees were United Artists' *The Private Life of Henry VIII* and Fox's *State Fair*. Paramount's *She Done Him Wrong* made the Best Picture lineup, but *auteur* Mae West wasn't nominated for anything. MGM's sole Best Picture nomination was *Smilin' Through,* a weepie starring Norma Shearer and Leslie Howard.

The Best Actress race pitted *Lady for A Day*'s May Robson against *Cavalcade*'s Diana Wynyard. The third nominee was Katharine Hepburn for *Morning Glory*. After her Hollywood triumph, Hepburn had returned to Broadway in a play entitled *The Lake,* but neither she nor the play were received well. In her famous review, Dorothy Parker quipped, "Miss Hepburn ran the gamut of emotions, from A to B." The play closed quickly, and Hepburn informed RKO she would be sailing

"The Academy as a whole will be free from politics, and any taint of self-preservation in office."
—J. Theodore Reed

off to a vacation in Europe on the night of the Awards ceremony.

In Hollywood, the press ignored the Academy's labor squabbles and played up the excitement of the Awards. "You'd be surprised how the greatest of stars who have won the coveted little bronze statues have them sitting in places of prominence in their homes," Louella Parsons wrote. "As eagerly as youngsters the world over anticipate St. Nick's Day, the grown-up boys and girls of the film colony look forward to the dinner." It had been a long wait since the last banquet; the Academy had decided to give the Awards on a calendar year basis, delaying this year's ceremony until 1934 in order to include all of 1933's movies.

Even guild members Frances Marion and Paul Muni were talked into going to the ceremonies by their studios, but Muni had no delusions. "Why go?" he argued. "I won't win. Americans don't like American actors." But he bought his first tuxedo for the occasion, just in case.

The Big Night

"Despite the wars and resignations which have shaken the Academy during the past eight months," wrote Elizabeth Yeaman of the *Hollywood Citizen-News*, "nearly everyone of importance in the motion picture industry was present." The only nominees who didn't make it were Charles Laughton, in England, and Katharine Hepburn, *en voyage*.

Leery of any more criticism from the film colony, the Academy took great pains to ensure that the ceremony would be a festive affair. The thankless responsibility of seating arrangements had been turned over to the studios in advance. To avoid an embarrassment like the previous year's eleventh-hour Best Actor tie, the Academy planned to announce the exact orders of finish in each race at the end of the evening. The party got off to a good start, according to the *Hollywood Reporter:* "Instead of massing the tables about a long speaker's table, the tables this year were arranged around the dance floor, and Duke Ellington's band dispensed 'hot' music for dancing. While the place was jammed with picture notables and executives, there was a noticeable increase of the younger element and a spirit of fun and gaiety prevailed."

Louis B. Mayer got in more dancing than usual because the presentation was delayed by the tardiness of Academy President J. Theodore Reed, who had car trouble. Once Reed got through with his opening remarks, emcee Will Rogers, star of the Best Picture nominee *State Fair*, began ribbing the audience. "This looks like the last roundup of the ermine," he began. "I got my courage to come here and talk to the highbrows and brains of the industry after I read that Sam Goldwyn had lectured at Harvard—and in person, too. Yeah, and the voice wasn't dubbed, either. I understand now that Harvard's writing back, 'Will you send us the English version?' " Rogers then turned nostalgic, reminiscing about "the old days of Republican rugged individualism, when Louis B. Mayer was photographed on the steps of the White House and when actors signing a contract at MGM had an Academy Award thrown in for good measure."

Following a demonstration of a new sound-recording machine, Rogers commenced the awards-giving with Best Cartoon. There was little suspense in this category, since Walt Disney's *Three Little Pigs* had made "Who's Afraid of the Big, Bad Wolf?" one of the most popular ditties in America. The audience roared when Rogers called Disney to the podium and the winner's head was covered in bandages. Disney had been injured in a polo match in which Will Rogers was also a participant. "Don't feel bad, I got whacked over the head with a mallet," the emcee said.

According to Frances Marion, Disney's speech had a long-range effect on Academy nomenclature. Ever since Academy librarian Margaret Herrick had exclaimed upon seeing the statuette, "It looks like Uncle Oscar!" the nickname had been used informally around the Academy and Hollywood. "Those who had never won the gold-plated honor referred to it disparagingly as the 'Oscar,' " Marion wrote. "But when Walt referred to the 'Oscar' in his speech, that name took on a different meaning, now that we had heard it spoken with sincere appreciation."

Will Rogers' technique for announcing the winners was to go directly to the opening of the envelope and reveal the victor. After the winner made his or her speech, Rogers called attention to

Awards Ceremony

MARCH 16, 1934, 8:00 P.M.
A BANQUET AT THE FIESTA ROOM AT THE AMBASSADOR HOTEL, LOS ANGELES

Your Host:
WILL ROGERS

Presenters

All awards presented by Will Rogers.

"Americans don't like American actors."
—Paul Muni

the other nominees and asked for a round of applause for them. Rogers' personal touch backfired with the Best Director Award. Rogers ripped open the envelope and said, "Well, well, well, what do you know. I've watched this young man for a long time. Saw him come up from the bottom, and I mean the bottom. It couldn't have happened to a nicer guy. Come up and get it, Frank!" An ebullient Frank Capra—his dream come true—jumped up from his table and made his way across the crowded room. As the spotlight searched for the winner, Capra waved his arms and shouted, "Over here!" The spotlight did land on Frank—Frank Lloyd, that is. The director of *Cavalcade* walked proudly to the dais where Rogers embraced him. A crestfallen Capra stood on the dance floor until a party behind him yelled, "Down in front!" Capra wrote in his autobiography that he then took "the longest, saddest, most shattering walk in my life. All my friends at my table were crying."

The crowd's approval of Frank Lloyd's triumph was not carried over to the Acting Awards. There was only polite applause when Rogers revealed that neither Leslie Howard nor Paul Muni had won but that the absent Charles Laughton was the champion for *The Private Life of Henry VIII*. The Best Actress Award went over even worse. "The ladies were not too happy when Katharine Hepburn won for *Morning Glory*," wrote Frances Marion in her autobiography. "Only those who had worked with her could testify to her friendliness. To others, she seemed 'high-hat.' " Rogers softened the blow by calling the losers—*Lady for a Day*'s May Robson and *Cavalcade*'s Diana Wynyard—to the dais, praising their performances, and handing each a rose.

The Awards returned to approval when Rogers declared that *Cavalcade* was the Best Picture. After producer Winfield Sheehan poured out his thanks, Rogers disclosed the results of the contests. *Cavalcade* had received 50 percent more votes than first runner-up, *A Farewell to Arms*, with *Little Women* in third place. Frank Capra had placed second in the director's race, with two votes more than *Little Women*'s George Cukor. Walt Disney's *Three Little Pigs* had trounced the competition with 80 percent of the votes. The acting races had tighter finishes, with May Robson a close second to Hepburn and Paul Muni right behind Charles Laughton.

As the guests rose for more dancing to Ellington's band, Bella Muni told her husband, "Well, at least you got a tuxedo out of it."

Aftermath

The *Hollywood Reporter* enjoyed the ceremony, raving, "The banquet was one of the most brilliant affairs that the Academy has ever held." The *Reporter* also congratulated the Academy on its business acumen: "The sell-out banquet kept the annual deficit low; two of the most expensive details were Duke Ellington's band and the statuettes—an even 1000 dollars."

The *Los Angeles Times* was also impressed by the party. "Proceedings at the Academy dinner, especially with reference to the losers, were handled with more grace than ordinarily," the paper said. "And Will Rogers was largely responsible . . . in imbuing the whole affair with a cheerful spirit." The *Times* commented on the outcome of the voting by noting that the "awards evidenced one thing—namely that sentiment was ruled out. Katharine Hepburn isn't a particularly popular choice around the film colony, yet she was chosen for first place regardless. This is also, in a degree, true of Charles Laughton. Sentiment would have favored May Robson and Leslie Howard."

Louella Parsons was upset at what she considered Hepburn's indifference to the honor. "Katy was not very gracious," Louella wrote in her column. "She didn't send a telegram of appreciation when unable to attend. Someone at RKO realized this and sent one." There was mail waiting for Best Director loser Frank Capra when he returned home—his relatives from Sicily had sent letters of congratulation, mistaking his nomination for a victory.

The *Hollywood Citizen-News* looked back over the six years of the Awards and made two observations. The first was that the Award now had a name, Oscar. The second had to do with the Academy's founder, Louis B. Mayer: "The fact that the Democrats are now in power had nothing whatever to do with the Academy Awards. But it was strange indeed to see MGM and its Republican chief executive claiming not a single award."

1934

"Bette Davis has all the sex appeal of Slim Summerville."
—Carl Laemmle

One actress brought the Academy to its knees in 1934, but it was a director from Poverty Row who took home all the Oscars.

When twenty-two-year-old Bette Davis stepped off the train in Los Angeles in 1930, she couldn't find the Universal Pictures representative who was supposed to meet her. He had returned to the studio and told the boss, "I didn't see anybody there who looked like an actress." Davis' future didn't look much brighter when studio head Carl Laemmle watched the rushes of one of her films and commented, "She has all the sex appeal of Slim Summerville." After Universal dropped her, Davis finagled a long-term contract at Warner Brothers. There, she had regular work but few good roles. Movies like *Parachute Jumper* and *Fashions of 1934* convinced Davis that she had to take matters into her own hands.

She pleaded with Jack Warner to offer her more challenging roles and, when that didn't work, begged him to loan her out to RKO, where director John Cromwell was preparing an adaptation of W. Somerset Maugham's *Of Human Bondage* for Leslie Howard. Warner couldn't understand why his contract actress would want to play Mildred, a slatternly Cockney waitress who torments a crippled intellectual, but he finally let Davis go just to get her off his back. "Mildred was her chance, once and for all, to make the big time," Cromwell said. She did make it; the critics called her an exciting new dramatic actress and even Somerset Maugham went public in his admiration of her performance. The only clouds around Davis' triumph were the low box-office grosses. A sneak previewer had written on his questionnaire, "This is a sordid and dirty picture" and most moviegoers agreed. But *Life* magazine said that Davis gave "probably the best performance ever recorded on the screen by a U.S. actress."

Claudette Colbert drops by the Biltmore on her way to New York to pick up a Best Actress Oscar from Shirley Temple, who was just about to accept her own Award.

White Tie, Top Hat and Tails

RKO had better luck with another Broadway graduate who hadn't fared much better than Davis in his screen test. "Can't act. Slightly bald. Can dance a little," was one executive's estimation of Fred Astaire, who made his film debut as the dancing partner of Joan Crawford when MGM tried her out in a musical. But RKO saw enthusiastic reaction to Astaire and partner Ginger Rogers in *Flying Down to Rio* and acquired Astaire's 1932 Broadway hit, Cole Porter's *The Gay Divorce*, to see if the two could carry a movie themselves. They could. Retitled by the studio to calm the Legion of Decency, *The Gay Divorcée* sent the team of Rogers and Astaire whirling to fourth position on the list of top box-office stars.

Another musical couple packing in audiences was Jeanette MacDonald and Maurice Chevalier, who made love behind closed doors in Ernst Lubitsch's operetta, *The Merry Widow*, at MGM. Harry Cohn, the president of tiny Columbia Pictures, wanted to get in on the operetta racket, so he began shopping around for available talent. He found a Metropolitan Opera star from Slabtown, Tennessee, named Grace Moore, who had made two films at MGM and was then fired for being overweight. Cohn went through five writers to concoct a story about a romance between a budding opera singer and her demanding teacher, and then he lured from Paramount director Victor Schertzinger, a former concert violinist and composer. Columbia's stockholders argued that this cultural package would not sell in the sticks, but Cohn retorted, "You jerks! Not everybody outside New York City lives in shanties beside the railroad tracks." The musical, entitled *One Night of Love*, became one of the year's top moneymakers and ushered in a vogue for movies about opera singers.

"That French broad likes money."
—Harry Cohn on Claudette Colbert

Gable Gets Spanked

Meanwhile, Cohn's star director, Frank Capra, was still determined to win an Oscar, especially after his humiliation at the previous year's banquet. Capra had another sentimental comedy ready for the next Awards, a romance between a runaway heiress and a reporter, called *Night Bus*. The director thought that MGM's Robert Montgomery would be perfect for the male lead, so Harry Cohn got on the phone to Louis B. Mayer. "Montgomery says there are too many bus pictures," Mayer responded. "And, Herschel, no offense, stars don't like changing their address from Culver City to Gower Street. But Herschel, you caught me in a good mood. I got an actor here who's being a bad boy. Wants more money. And I'd like to spank him. You can have Clark Gable." "Gable!" Cohn answered. "Would he do it?" "Herschel, you're talking to Louis B. Mayer."

Gable showed up drunk for his first appointment with Capra, but he did show up. The director couldn't seem to persuade any actress to play the heroine, even though he had been responsible for a Best Actress nomination for May Robson just the year before. Miriam Hopkins, Margaret Sullavan and Myrna Loy turned him down; Bette Davis was busy on *Of Human Bondage*. Capra approached Claudette Colbert, whose 1927 film debut he had directed—a flop that kept her off the screen for another two years. Colbert said no. Capra was getting nervous but Harry Cohn had an idea. "I hear that French broad likes money," he said. "Why don't you go see her personal?" When Capra offered Colbert $50,000 for a month's work, he had his leading lady.

No T-Shirts

Columbia took Robert Montgomery's observation to heart and changed the title from *Night Bus* to *It Happened One Night*. The comedy did not make enough money to be held over a second week at Radio City Music Hall, but word of mouth on the movie started to grow. Critics praised the fast-paced farce while underwear manufacturers complained that sales plummeted when Clark Gable took off his shirt on screen and was not wearing a T-shirt underneath. The popular demand for the film was so great that Radio City Music Hall brought it back for a return engagement. For the second year in a row, Frank Capra had hit a critical and commercial home run.

For Claudette Colbert, *It Happened One Night* was the first of a string of successes in 1934. Colbert didn't have Bette Davis' problem of undemanding roles—she played the lead in Cecil B. DeMille's epic *Cleopatra* at Paramount and then the pancake entrepreneur of *Imitation of Life* at Universal. By the end of the year, Colbert had joined her *It Happened One Night* costar Clark Gable on the list of top box-office names.

Baby, Take a Bow

The most spectacular success story of the year, however, belonged to a six-year-old girl. Show business was Shirley Temple's life. At age three, she was taking dance lessons and breaking into films, headlining a series of shorts called "Baby Burlesks" with her Marlene Dietrich imitation. Fox signed her for features, and was impressed when she stopped the show with the number "Baby Take a Bow" in *Stand Up and Cheer* in 1934. Loaned out to Paramount for the title role in its adaptation of the Damon Runyon short story "Little Miss Marker," the youngster came back to Fox a star—movie exhibitors ranked Temple a top box-office attraction. Fox put the tot in three starring vehicles that same year, and the six-year-old—like Mae West of Paramount—single-handedly kept the studio from going under.

Love and Laughs

Next to the Shirley Temple cult, the biggest news in movies was a new genre—the screwball comedy. *It Happened One Night* started the ball rolling in February and Howard Hawks followed

"The Academy is dwindling in importance, especially in Hollywood."
—Hollywood Citizen-News

up expertly with *Twentieth Century,* also released by Columbia, in May. The screenplay by Ben Hecht and Charles MacArthur allowed John Barrymore, as a flamboyant producer, to parody himself and gave Carole Lombard the chance to prove herself as a comedienne. On the heels of this box-office hit was MGM's *The Thin Man,* starring Lombard's ex-husband, William Powell. Director W.S. Van Dyke knocked this one off in sixteen days and made Myrna Loy a star by casting her as Powell's wisecracking socialite wife—she had been typecast as Oriental vamps for nearly a decade. Powell and Loy were so convincing a couple that fans wrote letters to them addressed "Mr. and Mrs. William Powell."

Actors on the Warpath

Neither the Screen Actors nor Screen Writers Guild had forgiven the Academy for taking sides with the producers over the NRA controversy the previous year, and the Actors Guild bulletin, *The Screen Player,* denounced the Academy on a regular basis throughout 1934. "The Academy, as everyone knows, was to hold banquets, confer statues and other forms of *ordres pour le merite* and incidentally police the industry," read one editorial. "The hitch, however, as it took quite a while for the talent classes to discover, lay in the fact that the policing was to be done by an oligarchy." Membership in the Screen Actors Guild—which required a resignation from the Academy—had swelled to such proportions that only ninety-five actors were left in the Academy to make 1934's nominations.

The Nominations

Those ninety-five nominated Claudette Colbert for Best Actress, for *It Happened One Night,* but cited neither of her screwball sisters, Myrna Loy and Carole Lombard. However, the omission that sent a jolt through Hollywood was Bette Davis'. A nomination for her breakthrough in *Of Human Bondage* seemed such a sure thing that no one could believe that she had not received a plurality of votes. The *Hollywood Reporter* demanded to see the tabulations but the Academy said nothing doing. Instead of Davis, the ninety-five judges had nominated Grace Moore in Columbia's *One Night of Love* and the perennial Norma Shearer for MGM's *The Barretts of Wimpole Street.*

Hollywood refused to let the Davis omission go down without a fight. The *Hollywood Citizen-News* declared, "The Academy is dwindling in importance, especially in Hollywood, and its current nominations have done much to harm it. Everyone in the profession is expressing amazement that Bette Davis is not even mentioned." The Academy was besieged with telegrams from Hollywood notables demanding a write-in final ballot to give Davis the chance she deserved. When nominee Norma Shearer joined the campaign for Bette, the Academy knew it had to do something.

Opinion or Propaganda

Nine days after the announcement of the nominations, the Academy's new president, writer Howard Estabrook, issued a statement:

> *Criticisms of the nominations for the 1934 Academy Awards have appeared with such uniform content that they raise the question as to whether these criticisms are based on genuine opinion or propaganda. With so many achievements of unquestioned merit each year, however, it is inevitable that certain differences of opinion should arise.*
>
> *Despite the fact that the criticism fails to take into consideration that the nominations have been made by the unrestricted votes of each branch, the awards committee has decided upon a change in the rules to permit unrestricted selection of any voter, who may write on the ballot his or her personal choice for the winners.*

In other words, Bette Davis was back in the running.

"The Academy Award is the Nobel Prize of motion pictures!"
—Leroy Johnston

No Drunks

The nominations were, nevertheless, a clear indication of Academy voters' favorites. *One Night of Love* had the highest total with six nominations. In addition to nods for Best Picture, Best Actress, Best Director and Best Sound, the movie was up for two new Awards, Best Film Editing and Best Score. The major Best Picture competition was Frank Capra's *It Happened One Night* with five nominations—including an unpredicted one for Clark Gable—and *The Thin Man,* with four nods, including one for William Powell. The third Best Actor nominee was Frank Morgan for a supporting role as the Duke of Florence in United Artists' lavish biography, *The Affairs of Cellini.* Non-nominee John Barrymore was not happy over his being overlooked for *Twentieth Century.* "This town is filled with hypocritical old biddies who are afraid that if I win, I'll show up drunk to accept it," Barrymore said, then added, "And I just might."

The remaining Best Picture nominees included Claudette Colbert's other hits, *Cleopatra* and *Imitation of Life,* and Norma Shearer's *The Barretts of Wimpole Street,* which also starred two other Oscar winners, Fredric March and Charles Laughton. None of Shirley Temple's movies were nominated, leaving Loretta Young's tribute to nursing, *The White Parade,* as Fox's only Best Picture nominee. An Academy favorite, Frank Borzage, made the lineup with a Ruby Keeler–Dick Powell musical, *Flirtation Walk,* and Warner Brothers sneaked in a James Cagney–Pat O'Brien adventure, *Here Comes the Navy.* Warners' ex-production head, Darryl F. Zanuck, had formed his own production company, Twentieth Century Pictures, and produced *The House of Rothschild,* a biography so opulent that George Arliss played two roles in it; Loretta Young was also in this Best Picture nominee. RKO scored a nomination with *The Gay Divorcée,* and the studio's former production head, David O. Selznick, produced the twelfth nominee, MGM's *Viva Villa,* with Wallace Beery in the title role.

Bette Packs the Wallop

Daily Variety yawned, "With a production year notable for its few sensational pictures and performances, Academy nominations lack the competitive wallop of previous years." The excitement that did exist surrounded Bette Davis. When the actress said she would attend the ceremony, the three official nominees for Best Actress declined the Academy's invitation. Still, Bette was nervous about the whole thing, as she later wrote in her memoirs: "The air was thick with rumors. It seemed inevitable that I would receive the coveted award. The press, the public and the members of the Academy who did the voting were sure I would win! Surer than I!"

The Big Night

On the day of the Awards, the *Hollywood Reporter* couldn't resist revealing that there was going to be the presentation of a Special Award at the ceremonies. Fox would not go unrewarded—Shirley Temple was receiving a miniature Oscar. Columnist Sidney Skolsky kept an eye on the child during dinner. "The Shirley Temple award is supposed to be a surprise and yet Shirley sits at her table from 8 o'clock on waiting to be surprised," he wrote. "Shirley had her dinner at home and she sits at the table breaking rolls and stuffing them with olives."

The emcee was humorist Irvin S. Cobb who began the proceedings by commenting, "I find myself between actors and producers, but I always thought the only thing between them was mutual distrust." The crowd laughed and applauded. Cobb was also handing out the Oscars, and he started by giving Walt Disney his third Best Cartoon Award in a row, for *The Tortoise and the Hare*. The Music category was christened when *One Night of Love* won the first Score Award. The new Best Song Award pitted Astaire–Rogers' "Carioca" from *Flying Down to Rio* against their "The Continental" from *The Gay Divorcée;* the latter won.

By the time of the Writing Awards, it was obvious that Academy voters were sticking with the original nominations and not taking advantage of the write-in ballot. *It Happened One Night* won the Adaptation Award, but it was reported that winner Robert Riskin was out on a date that night with non-nominee Carole Lombard.

As Cobb opened the envelope for Best Director, Frank Capra prepared himself for the defeat that had befallen him the previous year. "And the winner is . . . " Cobb began. "C'mon up and get it, Frank!" The room erupted with applause. Capra had invited the same guests from last year to his table and they assured him it was all right to go to the podium this time.

The *It Happened One Night* momentum continued when Cobb announced that the Best Actor was Clark Gable. The winner couldn't believe that Louis B. Mayer's "punishment" of loaning him out to Columbia had turned out so well. "I honestly never expected to win one of these," said the leading man. "There are too many good actors in this business. But I feel as happy as a kid and a little foolish they picked me." According to MGM publicists, Gable stepped down muttering to himself, "I'm still going to wear the same size hat."

The merriment quickly quieted down to a nervous silence when Cobb picked up the envelope with the name of the Best Actress. Bette Davis sat up straight. "And the winner is Claudette Colbert in *It Happened One Night,*" Cobb said. Davis did not change her smiling expression as Colbert's Oscar was accepted in absentia. Meanwhile, a member of the Academy's press committee, Leroy Johnston, was frantically searching the Los Angeles train station for Claudette Colbert, about to board the 20th Century for New York. When he found her, she shocked him by saying she didn't want to collect her Oscar. "I'll miss my train," she insisted, "and I'm not dressed." She was wearing a traveling suit and fur. "But it's the Nobel Prize of motion pictures!" Johnston yelled. That did it—she'd come. Johnston persuaded officials to hold the train for the Academy Award winner, and he and Colbert hopped in a car and headed for the Biltmore Hotel.

Back at the Bowl, the audience was giddy over little Columbia's Oscar sweep. Cobb held up the

Awards Ceremony

FEBRUARY 27, 1935 8:00 P.M.
A BANQUET AT THE BILTMORE BOWL OF THE BILTMORE HOTEL, LOS ANGELES

Your Host:
IRVIN S. COBB

Presenters

All Awards Presented by Irvin S. Cobb (Shirley Temple joined Cobb for the Best Actress Award)

Best Picture envelope, ripped it open, and exclaimed, "The winner is . . . you guessed it, it is something that . . ." The audience finished it for him, "Happened One Night!" Harry Cohn received the applause in the manner of his political idol, Benito Mussolini, but turned humble in his speech, thanking everyone who worked on the film. As for his part in the production, the mogul explained, "I was just an innocent bystander."

Shirley Temple's mother was preparing her for the Special Award just as Johnston's car pulled up with Claudette Colbert. Temple was pressed into service and asked to hand Colbert her statuette, which she dutifully did, standing on a chair. Colbert said, breathlessly, "I am afraid I am just going to be very foolish and cry. I was busy with retakes until the last minute and I wanted to get off for this vacation. And to take it, I have to catch the train tonight in order to reach New York by Sunday. But before I go, I want to tell you how grateful I am to Frank Capra. If it hadn't been for him, I wouldn't be here." As Bette Davis and everyone else applauded, Colbert posed for pictures with Temple and then departed. She was at the ceremony a full six minutes.

After Colbert hurried off, Cobb boomed, "There was one great towering figure in the cinema game, one artiste among artistes, one giant among the troupers, whose monumental, stupendous and elephantine work deserved special mention . . . Is Shirley Temple in the house?" The six-and-a-half-year-old marched out again and Cobb cooed, "Listen, you-all ain't old enough to know what this is all about. But, honey, I want to tell you that when Santa Claus wrapped you-all up in a package and dropped you down creation's chimney, he brought the loveliest Christmas present that was ever given to the world." Evidently, Temple did know what it was all about, and she tried to snatch the small Oscar out of Cobb's hand before he finished speaking.

Before the dancing resumed, Cobb revealed the order of the voting results. Clark Gable had narrowly defeated Frank Morgan, but his costar Colbert had won "in a walk." In second place was Norma Shearer, followed by Grace Moore—all original nominees.

Aftermath

"They threw a party for Harry Cohn," wrote *Daily Variety* the next day, but the biggest party had occurred after the ceremonies at Frank Capra's house, where the director celebrated the first clean sweep of the Awards—Best Screenplay, Best Director, Best Actor, Best Actress and Best Picture. Two of Capra's guests became embroiled in a drunken fistfight, one fellow fell in the goldfish pond, and the host polished off a magnum of champagne before passing out on his front lawn clutching his Oscar.

"I might be able to understand the hysterical enthusiasm for *It Happened One Night* if Hollywood had produced no picture of impressive artistry in the past year," complained Elizabeth Yeaman in the *Hollywood Citizen-News,* who thought that if the Academy had wanted to toast Columbia, it should have awarded *One Night of Love,* "a brilliant picture which marked a new milestone in the musical field. And, in the years to come, I hardly think that critics or the public will regard *It Happened One Night* as a great picture."

Bette Davis claimed in her autobiography that Jack Warner had sent instructions to his personnel to vote for anybody but her. She couldn't prove this charge, of course, but there was one bit of tangible evidence that Davis had made an impact on the Academy. "Not since that decision in 1934 was so cavalier a verdict allowed to take place," Davis wrote. "Price, Waterhouse was asked to step in the next year to count the votes, which they have done ever since."

1935

"Franchot and I are very deep friends. Until things are adjusted, we will remain as we are."
—Joan Crawford

Hollywood declared war on the 1935 Awards and the Academy had to pull out a secret weapon to get anyone to come to the Awards ceremony.

Tone Poem

MGM was always in the market for a playboy type to play the other man in romantic vehicles. In 1932, the studio had latched onto a twenty-seven-year-old stage actor named Franchot Tone. In no time, the former president of the Cornell Dramatic Club was making screen love to Jean Harlow and Joan Crawford and obviously enjoying himself—he proposed marriage to Joan Crawford in real life. But Crawford was worried about their competing careers; she was still unsettled from her divorce from Douglas Fairbanks, Jr. in 1933. That marriage had ended the moment Joan made it onto the list of top box-office stars, and Crawford didn't want the same thing to happen again. "Franchot and I are very deep friends," she told an interviewer. "Until things are adjusted, we will remain as we are."

Tone's career was taking off in 1935 when MGM loaned him out to Paramount for the Gary Cooper adventure *Lives of a Bengal Lancer,* directed by Henry Hathaway. Tone was able to shed his man-about-town image by playing a robust British soldier in nineteenth-century India in what became a runaway hit. Then Tone returned to MGM, for another romantic vehicle—his third Joan Crawford movie. On the set one day, Robert Montgomery, who was playing Crawford's main love interest, let Tone know that Irving Thalberg was coming by to offer him the role Montgomery had turned down in Thalberg's upcoming *Mutiny on the Bounty.* Sure enough, Thalberg appeared at lunchtime and told Tone, "You're going to get your big chance."

Overleaf: *D. W. Griffith performing the only job he could get in Hollywood—handing out Oscars to Victor McLaglen and fashion rebel Bette Davis.*

Thalberg's Ship Comes In

Big was, indeed, the word for *Mutiny on the Bounty*. Thanks to location shooting in Tahiti and numerous production setbacks—a technician drowned, a prop boat floated out to sea—Thalberg's adventure cost $2 million, becoming the most expensive movie since MGM's *Ben-Hur* in 1926. Louis B. Mayer was skeptical of the whole project, arguing that it didn't have any roles for female stars. Thalberg insisted, "People are fascinated by cruelty, and that's why *Mutiny* will have appeal." Although Clark Gable as Fletcher Christian and Charles Laughton as Captain Bligh had the leading roles, Franchot Tone had a showy monologue in the film's climactic court trial and garnered terrific personal notices when the picture opened to rave reviews. *Mutiny on the Bounty* went on to make almost as much money as *Ben-Hur*. Joan Crawford married Franchot Tone on October 11, 1935.

Ten Men = Bette Davis

Tone's star rose so quickly that Warners asked MGM for him to play opposite its dawning light, Bette Davis. The studio was planning to cash in on Davis's *Of Human Bondage* reputation with a drama called *Dangerous,* about a self-destructive actress who cripples her husband in a car wreck on her opening night. "I read the script carefully and sighed," Davis wrote in her autobiography. "It was maudlin and mawkish with a pretense at quality which in scripts, as in home furnishings, is often worse than junk. But it had just enough material in it to build into something if I approached it properly. It was lovely to play with Franchot Tone and I worked like ten men on that film . . ." The work was rewarded with critical praise and hefty box office. Jack Warner was delighted that Davis' brand of powerhouse performing was profitable and he demanded the full publicity treatment for his new dramatic star. Davis was the frequent subject of fan-magazine stories and the

"Dangerous had a pretense at quality which in scripts, as in home furnishings, is often worse than junk."
—Bette Davis

studio regularly shipped out pictures of Davis at nightclubs—many of which were shot on studio sets.

Tolstoi, Dickens, Selznick

Davis' rival in the tragedienne department was MGM's Greta Garbo, who decided that she wanted to play *Anna Karenina* again, having starred in a silent version, entitled *Love,* in 1927. For the first time in years, Irving Thalberg did not produce a Garbo picture—David O. Selznick did. Unlike the previous one, this version did not have a happy ending. The million-dollar production boasted Fredric March as Count Vronsky and gowns by Adrian. *Anna Karenina,* earning Garbo her best reviews and her highest grosses in years, was another triumph for David O. Selznick.

The producer had struck gold earlier in the year with another million-dollar adaptation of a literary classic, *David Copperfield,* directed by George Cukor. Charles Laughton had begun filming the role of Micawber, but Selznick agreed with the assistant who commented during the rushes, "Laughton looks as if he's going to molest the child." With Laughton out, Selznick came up with the offbeat casting of W. C. Fields. The film was very successful—Selznick was especially pleased when it was well received in London, where a critic called the movie "the most gracious work of film art that America has yet sent us." Inspired by his luck at MGM, Selznick informed the studio he was leaving to set up his own movie company.

Katharine Hepburn Meets Hedda Hopper

At Selznick's former haunt, RKO, Katharine Hepburn was doing well for herself in *Alice Adams,* an adaptation of Booth Tarkington's comedy of manners about a status-seeker in a small town. Fred MacMurray was the leading man and Hedda Hopper had a small part as a local snob, but Hepburn walked off with the picture and the reviews. Bette Davis herself said that Hepburn gave the best performance by an actress that year.

With Hepburn, as well as Fred Astaire and Ginger Rogers, on its team, RKO could afford to take a gamble on scenarist Dudley Nichols and director John Ford's adaptation of *The Informer,* Liam O'Flaherty's novel about a stool pigeon during the Irish rebellion of 1922. But since the property didn't sound very commercial, the studio allotted Ford only $218,000 and eighteen days to make the picture. The brooding title character was played by forty-nine-year-old Victor McLaglen, better known for happy-go-lucky leading parts in adventure movies. The film won sensational reviews—the *Baltimore Sun* placed it "among the five best pictures produced since the coming of sound"—but audiences, perceiving it as either arty or depressing or both, stayed away and *The Informer* managed to lose money.

Big Noise from New York

Awards-giving fever was contagious and the New York Film Critics, perhaps feeling they could be more objective than Hollywood, inaugurated their own annual awards on January 2, 1936. The scribes selected *The Informer* and John Ford as Best Picture and Best Director. They gave their Best Actress Award to Greta Garbo for *Anna Karenina* and Best Actor to Charles Laughton for *Mutiny on the Bounty* and *Ruggles of Red Gap,* a comedy in which he played an English valet making it in the Wild West.

The First Oscar Ad

For the first time in Oscar history, a studio campaigned in the trade journals for Academy consideration. The guilty party was MGM, promoting its adaptation of Eugene O'Neill's *Ah, Wilderness* with Wallace Beery and Lionel Barrymore. The ad was a cartoon depicting a statuette with the label AH, WILDERNESS around its neck while MGM's trademark, Leo the Lion, stood by with

"Looking to the Academy for representation was like trying to get laid in your mother's house. Somebody was always in the parlor watching."
—Dorothy Parker

arms outstretched. The copy read, "Leo, you've given so much . . . get ready to receive!"

The Nominations

Leo got ready to put his tail between his legs—*Ah, Wilderness* failed to receive a single nomination. The Academy mimicked the Gotham critics, nominating all of the film critics' winners, with one exception. Greta Garbo was not nominated for Best Actress, although her two main rivals, Katharine Hepburn in *Alice Adams* and Bette Davis in *Dangerous,* were. "Although nearly everyone in Hollywood secretly or openly admires Garbo, she has never won an award," wrote Elizabeth Yeaman in the *Hollywood Citizen-News*. "Perhaps she did not get the votes because everyone knows that she would not appear at a public banquet to accept it and that would pique them." Also considered less likely to pique were Merle Oberon for *The Dark Angel,* Miriam Hopkins for *Becky Sharp,* Elisabeth Bergner for the British drama *Escape Me Never,* and Claudette Colbert for *Private Worlds.*

There were six nominees for Best Actress because of tie votes; the Best Actor race, in contrast, was a battle between *The Informer*'s Victor McLaglen and the three stars of *Mutiny on the Bounty,* Clark Gable, Charles Laughton and Franchot Tone. *The Informer* and *Mutiny on the Bounty* were also dueling for the Best Picture Award, as were John Ford and two-time winner Frank Lloyd for the Best Director Oscar. The third directorial nominee was Henry Hathaway for *Lives of a Bengal Lancer*, also a Best Picture nominee.

Among the other Best Picture nominations were *Ruggles of Red Gap* and *Alice Adams*. There were plenty of expensive prestige items nominated, too, including Selznick's *David Copperfield*, Warner Brothers' million-dollar version of *A Midsummer Night's Dream* (with Mickey Rooney as Puck), and Darryl F. Zanuck's independently made *Les Miserables* with Charles Laughton and Fredric March. Musicals were popular and there were nominations for RKO's *Top Hat* with Rogers and Astaire, MGM's *Naughty Marietta,* the first teaming of Jeanette MacDonald and Nelson Eddy, and MGM's *Broadway Melody of 1936* with Eleanor Powell and Jack Benny. Jack Warner was disappointed that *Captain Blood,* the studio's million-dollar pirate movie which had made stars out of Errol Flynn and Olivia de Havilland, was nominated for Best Picture without winning a Director nomination for Michael Curtiz. But there was nothing Warner could do about it—at least not yet.

Another Guild, Another Nemesis

Hollywood's directors had decided they needed a guild, too, and on January 15, 1936, the Screen Directors Guild had been formed at King Vidor's house, with two-time Oscar winners Frank Borzage and Lewis Milestone in attendance. Like the actors and the writers, the directors had given up on the Academy as a forum for labor negotiations. "No one can respect an organization with the high-sounding title of the Academy of Motion Picture Arts and Sciences which has failed in every single function it has assumed," cried a guild newsletter. "The sooner it is destroyed and forgotten, the better for the industry." One member of the Writers Guild, Dorothy Parker, put it this way, "Looking to the Academy for representation was like trying to get laid in your mother's house. Somebody was always in the parlor watching."

On March 2, 1936, the guilds set their sights on the Academy banquet by sending their members telegrams. "You have probably been asked by your producer to go to the dinner," the message read. "We find that this is a concerted move to make people think that Guild members are supporting the Academy. The Board feels that since the Academy is definitely inimical to the best interests of the Guilds, you should not attend."

Upon learning of the telegram, Donald Gledhill, the executive secretary of the Academy, replied, "We are very much surprised by this sudden attack, but are holding our course without paying attention to it. The Awards are entirely

"It's the greatest business in the world."
—D. W. Griffith

nonpolitical and have nothing to do with the labor problems. They are entirely based on achievement." The guilds continued their criticism after Gledhill's statement. Ernest Pascal, president of the Writers Guild, told the *Los Angeles Times*, "We consider the Academy a company union with nothing in common with the Guild. We believe our members should have nothing to do with it under any circumstances."

Enter Price, Waterhouse

The Academy's newly elected president, Frank Capra, knew he had to act fast. Not only had the guilds abandoned the Academy, so had the studio bosses. "Short-sighted company heads couldn't care less," Capra wrote in his autobiography. "The Academy had failed them as an instrument of salary cuts during the bank-closing crisis. They withdrew their memberships and financial support, leaving the derelict organization in the care of a few staunch Academy-oriented visionaries dedicated to the continuance of the awards." Among the visionaries were David O. Selznick, Darryl F. Zanuck, Cecil B. DeMille and *Mutiny on the Bounty* nominees Frank Lloyd and Clark Gable.

With no studio funding, the Academy board of directors paid for the banquet and statuettes out of their own pockets. To assure the honesty of the tabulations—especially after the Fredric March–Wallace Beery tie of 1931–32 and Bette Davis' shutout in 1934—Capra hired the accounting firm of Price, Waterhouse to count the votes. Bending over backwards, the Academy once again allowed write-in votes, permitting the 640 Academy voters to ignore the nominations if they so chose. Jack Warner saw his big chance to win an Oscar for director Michael Curtiz and sent out a memo to all the Academy members at his studio "suggesting" they write in votes for Warners' movies all the way down the ballot.

With all of those concessions, Capra was still worried about the guild boycott. The Academy president decided the banquet needed a further lure to convince the nominees to attend. Then, it hit him—why not give a Special Award to the father of American cinema himself, D. W. Griffith, and turn the party into a testimonial dinner? Although the film pioneer had not been able to obtain financing for a movie since 1931, his achievements were still revered in Hollywood. Capra called the director in Kentucky and Griffith said he'd be honored to attend. The fifty-six-year-old honoree added that he would be on his honeymoon with his fourth wife, a twenty-six-year-old actress, and thought a visit to Hollywood would be a fine wedding trip. Capra broadcast the news of the Griffith tribute and kept his fingers crossed.

The Big Night

Daily Variety reported that the boycott did have an effect on the banquet: "There was not the galaxy of stars and celebs in director and writer groups which distinguished awards banquets of recent years. Banquet tickets were liberally sprinkled to secretaries and others on the various lots as a result." A few stars did attend. Best Actress nominee Merle Oberon was a member of Sam Goldwyn's party. While *The Informer*'s John Ford and Dudley Nichols stayed home, Best Actor nominee Victor McLaglen was resplendent in white tie and tails. And Clark Gable was present, chatting and laughing with directors Frank Capra and Frank Lloyd.

When guest of honor D. W. Griffith arrived with his wife, he was applauded by the other guests. Bette Davis' appearance also caused a commotion. The actress showed up for the formal affair in a simple checked dress.

The Awards presentation began around midnight. Pete Smith, presenting the Short Subject Awards, got a big laugh when he began, "Ladies and gentlemen, members of the Screen Actors Guild—I mean, the Academy of Motion Picture Arts and Sciences." Later, there were loud exclamations of surprise when—in the only instance in Academy history—a write-in candidate won. The Cinematography Award went to Hal Mohr for Warners' *A Midsummer Night's Dream*. The winner was lounging at home, but when the Academy called him to tell him he'd won, he and his wife dressed up and drove down to join the party. Meanwhile, Irving Thalberg grew nervous: *Mutiny on the Bounty* wasn't winning anything while John Ford's *The Informer* had claimed the awards for Best Score and for Best Adapted Screenplay.

Columbia's Harry Cohn mounted the podium to give the Best Picture Award and said, "Last year we won an armful of statuettes over at Columbia, so this year, we started out not to make any good pictures and we believe we succeeded." Columbia's sole nomination that year was for Best Sound Recording, a category in which each studio automatically received a nomination. It lost. After Cohn opened the Best Picture envelope, Thalberg could relax. The winner was *Mutiny on the Bounty*.

The star of *Birth of a Nation*, Henry B. Walthall, presented the Special Award to Griffith. The inscription on the statuette read: "For his distinguished creative achievements as director and producer and his invaluable initiative and lasting contributions to the progress of the motion picture arts." As Griffith walked to the rostrum, the crowd gave him the first standing ovation in Oscar history. The director said, "We had many worries in those days, small worries. Now you people have your worries and they are big ones. They have grown with the business—and no matter what its problems, it's the greatest business in the world." According to the *Hollywood Reporter*, the speech "brought tears to the eyes of the throng."

Griffith was also in charge of handing out some awards. The Best Director was the absent

Awards Ceremony

MARCH 5, 1936, 8:00 P.M.
A BANQUET AT THE BILTMORE BOWL OF THE BILTMORE HOTEL, LOS ANGELES

Your Host:
ACADEMY PRESIDENT FRANK CAPRA

Presenters

Dance Direction	Frank Capra
Music	Frank Capra
Song	Frank Capra
Short Subjects	Pete Smith
Film Editing	Rouben Mamoulian
Art Direction	Rouben Mamoulian
Cinematography	Rouben Mamoulian
Assistant Director	Rouben Mamoulian
Technical Awards	Nathan Levinson
Writing Awards	Robert Riskin
Picture	Harry Cohn
Special Award to D. W. Griffith	Henry B. Walthall
Director	D. W. Griffith
Actor	D. W. Griffith
Actress	D. W. Griffith

"The Oscar is the most valuable, but least expensive, item of world-wide public relations ever invented by any industry."
— Frank Capra

John Ford for *The Informer*. The Best Actor was the jubilant Victor McLaglen for *The Informer*. The last award was Best Actress; the winner was Bette Davis for *Dangerous*. "There was a shout from my table and everybody was kissing me," Davis recalled. But the actress was not altogether pleased. "It's a consolation prize. This nagged at me. It was true that even if the honor had been earned, it had been earned last year." Despite these thoughts, the winner put on a happy face at the podium and asked her director, Alfred E. Green, to take a bow. He wasn't there. So she asked Jack Warner to take a bow, which he did. Handing her the statuette, D. W. Griffith said, "You don't know how lucky you are, young lady." "I do," insisted Davis. "At your age, to be where you are," continued Griffith, "making all that money, fame, and everything."

After all the awards were given, Capra revealed the results of the voting. *Mutiny on the Bounty* had won by a wide margin, followed by *The Informer* and *Captain Blood*. Katharine Hepburn was behind Bette Davis, with Elisabeth Bergner in third place. Victor McLaglen's closest competitor for Best Actor wasn't one of the *Bounty* nominees but write-in candidate Paul Muni for Warners' *Black Fury*, a drama about coal miners. *Captain Blood*'s Michael Curtiz placed third in the Directors' race, behind Henry Hathaway for *Lives of a Bengal Lancer*. The party broke up sometime after 1 A.M.

Aftermath

The guilds called their boycott a success and bragged that only twenty members of the Actors Guild and thirteen of the Writers Guild were present. But Frank Capra stated that the Academy had emerged victorious: "The boycott fizzled—most of the winners were there."

The *New York Times* criticized the Academy's choices, claiming that *Mutiny on the Bounty* defeated *The Informer* because it was "from the more influential Metro lot." As for the Oscars that *The Informer* did win, the *Times* credited East Coast critics: "It was conceded in the industry that the picture had little chance of winning, but with all the disturbance caused by the Broadway lads, the picture could not be ignored."

Jack Warner, who had masterminded the Cinematography win for *A Midsummer Night's Dream*, did not consider Bette Davis' triumph sacrosanct. The mogul leased her face to Quaker Puffed Rice for advertisements that said, "Breakfast fit for a queen of the screen—Academy Award Winner Bette Davis." She wasn't treated like royalty at the studio, however, and she wrote:

> *Now that I had received the Academy Award, I had high hopes the studio would find me a great script. My hopes were soon shattered. I was cast in an absurd adaptation of Michael Arlen's* Golden Arrow *in which George Brent and I were alternately seen with a black eye. The whole affair was a black eye as far as I was concerned. . . . After 31 pictures, two Academy Award nominations and one Oscar, it was obvious I would have to do something drastic to change the situation.*

Davis walked out on the studio.

Meanwhile, Frank Capra and Dudley Nichols were playing tug-of-war with Nichols' Best Adapted Screenplay Oscar for *The Informer*. Capra sent the statuette to the winner, who sent it right back with a note, "To accept it would be to turn my back on nearly a thousand members who ventured everything in the long-drawn-out fight for a genuine writers' organization." Capra put the Oscar back in the mail with another note: "The balloting does not in any way take into account the personal or economic views of the nominees nor the graciousness with which they may be expected to receive the recognition." But Nichols was adamant and sent the Oscar back a second time. Capra gave up and the statuette remained at the Academy.

Nichols' behavior made the press wonder if director John Ford, treasurer of the Screen Directors Guild, was also refusing the Oscar. "I am proud to have received the honor," Ford said. "If I had planned to refuse it, I would not have allowed my name to go in nomination." Asked why he didn't attend the banquet, Ford responded, "I'm not a member of the Academy." When Ford accepted the statuette from the Academy a week after the ceremonies, the Directors Guild voted him out of office.

Boosted by the attention from the Academy, *The Informer* was re-released by RKO and finally made a profit. Frank Capra savored the irony; it proved what he had maintained all along, that the Oscar is "the most valuable, but least expensive, item of world-wide public relations ever invented by any industry."

1936

"Sound is only a baby."
—Leopold Stokowski

Now that the Academy was out of the studios' control, the moguls wanted Oscar more than ever.

Next to Fred Astaire and Ginger Rogers, America's favorite screen couple was William Powell and Myrna Loy, who were paired three times by MGM in 1936. They were reunited with *Thin Man* director W. S. Van Dyke and Asta the dog in *After the Thin Man,* which equaled the box-office success of the original, and they were joined by Jean Harlow and Spencer Tracy in *Libeled Lady,* a comedy about a newspaper-suing heiress. When Carole Lombard, Powell's real-life ex-wife, saw what he was doing for Loy and Harlow at MGM, she wanted him over at Universal. She got him and *My Man Godfrey* was Powell's third box-office smash that year.

Powell was back at MGM in no time; producer Hunt Stromberg needed the box-office draw of Powell and Loy for the studio's most expensive movie since *Mutiny on the Bounty*—a musical biography of Broadway showman Florenz Ziegfeld entitled *The Great Ziegfeld*. MGM spared no expense in the $2 million-plus extravaganza. Ziegfeld's original scenarist, set designer and dance director were called in to reproduce their former boss's stage triumphs—although traces of Busby Berkeley's style could be found in the musical numbers—and Ziegfeld star Fannie Brice was recruited to sing "My Man."

The finished film was three hours long, but proved to be a sound investment, more than doubling its production cost in box-office receipts. Powell, as Ziegfeld, and Loy, as his second wife Billie Burke, earned excellent notices, but reviewers spent most of their laudatory adjectives on newcomer Luise Rainer, who played Ziegfeld's first wife, Anna Held. The twenty-six-year-old Austrian actress had come to Hollywood the year before to replace Myrna Loy in a William Powell movie called *Escapade* when Loy felt that MGM wasn't offering her enough money. In *The Great Ziegfeld,* Rainer had a long telephone scene in which Held, having been dumped by Ziegfeld, congratulates him on his second marriage. By the time she hung up the phone, audiences were in tears.

Overleaf: *Louis B. Mayer allows Hunt Stromberg* (left), *the actual producer of Best Picture winner* The Great Ziegfeld, *to touch the statuette while toastmaster George Jessel stands ready with a spare.*

Shake, Rattle and Roll

Beating *The Great Ziegfeld* in the box-office race was another MGM epic, *San Francisco,* a movie so successful that *Motion Picture Story* wrote: "Now comes *San Francisco* with its fabulous dollar record to confound the trade, the critics and its own producers." Director W. S. Van Dyke's film had Clark Gable, Jeanette MacDonald (singing what would become the city's real-life anthem), rising MGM star Spencer Tracy and a ten-minute earthquake for a climax. After playing tough guys at Fox for a number of years, Tracy leapt to stardom when his contract was picked up by MGM. In addition to second leads in *Libeled Lady* and *San Francisco,* in 1936 the actor carried his own vehicle, *Fury,* a melodrama about an innocent fugitive directed by Germany's Fritz Lang. Spencer Tracy was on a roll.

David O. Selznick wasn't doing badly, either. His latest Dickens adaptation, *A Tale of Two Cities,* was a million-dollar epic starring Ronald Colman and 17,000 extras. The producer knew the picture had turned out well when he previewed it in a theater by the Pacific filled with "rowdy sailors and their dates. It was way overlength, but they loved it." The movie was Selznick's going-away gift to the studio before leaving to start Selznick International Pictures—*A Tale of Two Cities* netted MGM millions.

The Biopic Man

Warner Brothers was shelling out a million to adapt a book, too, but played it safe by going with Hervey Allen's 1,224-page bestseller, *Anthony Ad-*

"I never expected Romeo and Juliet to make money."
—Irving Thalberg

verse. Director Mervyn LeRoy told the art department to pull out the whole studio inventory for this costume romance about a swashbuckling adventurer, played by Fredric March, traveling the globe during the Napoleonic Wars. The two-hour-twenty-minute epic also starred Olivia de Havilland as the opera-singing heroine and screen newcomer Gale Sondergaard as the villainess.

Anthony Adverse was the studio's biggest hit that year, followed by *The Story of Louis Pasteur*, starring Paul Muni, who had implored Jack Warner to stop casting him in gangster movies. Playing the French scientist, Muni was proclaimed by critics as successor to George Arliss' "King of the Biopics" title. *Screen Story* magazine advised its readers, "You may not think that microbes, germs, toxins and rabies make very exciting screen fare but that's where you are mistaken," and labeled it "the most important picture of the year."

The sovereign of the small-scale hit was still Frank Capra, who once again provided Harry Cohn with a fortune in *Mr. Deeds Goes to Town*. Gary Cooper played the country rube in the big city in Capra's whimsical comedy, which added the words "pixilated" and "doodle" to the vernacular. Louella Parsons raved, "Great entertainment. And so original!"

Exit Irving Thalberg

Irving Thalberg wanted his wife, who had been absent from the screen since the birth of their second child, to come back in style, so he announced that thirty-six-year-old Norma Shearer would be playing Juliet to the Romeo of forty-four-year-old Leslie Howard. The producer hired a Shakespeare professor from Cornell, Dr. William Strunk, Jr., and told him: "Your job is to protect Shakespeare from us." George Cukor directed the $2 million production, which inspired the *New York Times* to comment that the studio had given the Bard "a jeweled setting in which the deep beauty of this romance glows and sparkles and gleams with breathless radiance." *Romeo and Juliet* did not earn back all of its cost, but Thalberg said, "I never expected it to make money."

The Boy Wonder was busy molding his upcoming projects—Greta Garbo in *Camille* and Luise Rainer and Paul Muni, the latter on loanout from Warners, in *The Good Earth*—when he died suddenly from pneumonia at age thirty-seven on September 14, 1936. All the studios in town closed down for the funeral, where the rabbi eulogized, "The love of Norma Shearer and Irving Thalberg was a love greater than that in the greatest motion picture I have ever seen—*Romeo and Juliet*." After the funeral, Norma Shearer went into seclusion, not to be seen in public for months.

Critics' Choice

The New York Film Critics passed over the widow Thalberg for their Best Actress Award and chose Luise Rainer for her performance as the jilted wife in *The Great Ziegfeld*. The New Yorkers voted Frank Capra's *Mr. Deeds Goes to Town* the Best Picture, but then ignored Capra by giving the Best Director award to Rouben Mamoulian for the musical *The Gay Desperado*. The Best Actor Award went to Walter Huston, recreating his Broadway role in Samuel Goldwyn's production of Sinclair Lewis' *Dodsworth*.

A Committee of Absentees

"Responding to criticism of the allegedly political method of choice," wrote the *New York Times* a few weeks after the film critics' selections, "the Academy changed its procedure. Instead of entire membership nomination, a committee of fifty, representing the five branches, will make the preliminaries." Academy President Frank Capra elaborated, "We feel that this committee of fifty will be able to give the various achievements of the year more individual discussion and consideration than could be done by the old method."

The fifty judges included Lionel Barrymore, Ronald Colman, Harold Lloyd and a new twosome around town—Clark Gable and Carole Lombard.

"You may not think that microbes, germs, toxins and rabies make very exciting screen fare but that's where you are mistaken."
—Screen Story

Many committee members had been associated with the year's biggest films: *A Tale of Two Cities'* producers, Charles R. Rogers and David O. Selznick; *Anthony Adverse*'s director, Mervyn LeRoy; *The Great Ziegfeld*'s producer, Hunt Stromberg, and its director, Robert Z. Leonard; and *San Francisco*'s director, W. S. Van Dyke. But, according to *Daily Variety,* by the time the fifty got around to voting on Best Song, Best Score and Best Sound, only thirty-three members showed up, Gable and Lombard not among them.

Capra made other changes. He got rid of the xenophobic qualifications in the Cinematography and Interior Decoration categories that all nominated films had to be made in America. To assuage the Screen Actors Guild, Capra augmented the number of acting nominees from three to five and added two new acting categories—Best Supporting Actor and Best Supporting Actress. Just as Capra had hoped, the actors began to get a little more interested in the Awards. The actors' organization announced, "The Guild this year intends to offer no objections to its members attending the dinner. It reserves the right, however, to change its attitudes in future years as the situation warrants."

The Nominations

There were a few bugs to be worked out in the division between the Acting Awards; somehow Stuart Erwin, the star of Fox's football comedy *Pigskin Parade,* was nominated for Best Supporting Actor while the second lead of *San Francisco,* Spencer Tracy, was in the running for Best Actor in a Leading Role. Rounding out the list of Best Actor nominees were William Powell for *My Man Godfrey,* Paul Muni for *The Story of Louis Pasteur,* Gary Cooper for *Mr. Deeds Goes to Town,* and Walter Huston, New York Film Critics winner, for *Dodsworth*.

Three of the five nominated directors were committee members—Robert Z. Leonard for *The Great Ziegfeld,* W. S. Van Dyke for *San Francisco,* and Academy President Frank Capra for *Mr. Deeds Goes to Town*—and their films were all in the running for Best Picture. So were Selznick's *A Tale of Two Cities,* Warners' *Anthony Adverse* and *The Story of Louis Pasteur,* Goldwyn's *Dodsworth,* and MGM's *Libeled Lady*. They were joined by Universal's *Three Smart Girls,* starring a fifteen-year-old singing newcomer named Deanna Durbin, whose popularity saved the studio from having to file for bankruptcy.

Norma Shearer was nominated for Best Actress for *Romeo and Juliet* which also got a Best Picture nomination. Shearer's competition was committee member Carole Lombard in *My Man Godfrey,* Luise Rainer in *The Great Ziegfeld,* Irene Dunne in the screwball comedy *Theodora Goes Wild,* and Gladys George, who made her talkie debut in Paramount's tearjerker, *Valiant Is the Word for Carrie* (later parodied by the Three Stooges as *Violent Is the Word for Curly*).

Sizing Up the Race

Daily Variety said that Walter Brennan was a "a cinch" for the Best Supporting Actor Award for *Come and Get It,* an adaptation of Edna Ferber's lumber-dynasty saga, with the "closest candidate" being Akim Tamiroff for playing a villainous Chinese general in *The General Died at Dawn*. The trade journal also wrote that veteran character actress Maria Ouspenskaya as a Viennese baroness in *Dodsworth* was "about even" with film neophyte Gale Sondergaard in *Anthony Adverse*.

Although *Daily Variety* claimed, "With the so-called inner circle antipathy of the extinct Screen Writers Guild and Screen Actors Guild members towards the Academy, there has not been any exuberance or enthusiasm with respect to the voting," the paper then proceeded to record the industry gossip on the contests. MGM's employees made up the bulk of the voting membership, it was rumored, and they would vote for Norma Shearer "unless the studio group has a last-minute change of heart and tosses its ballots toward Luise Rainer." *Daily Variety* added that Warners had the second highest total of Academy

"It is pretty easy to fool an audience with a little crêpe hair and a dialect."
—W. C. Fields

members on the payroll and alleged that vote-swapping and back-scratching was going on. Since Warners' Paul Muni was appearing in MGM's just-released *The Good Earth*, *Variety* reasoned that Warners would help MGM push the expensive *The Great Ziegfeld* for Best Picture if MGM assisted the Warner star in the Best Actor tournament. "It is more than likely that Warners would help Metro's entry along in return for getting support for Muni," the paper said.

The *Hollywood Reporter* thought that New York Film Critics Award winner Luise Rainer would bring home the bacon, but it wasn't sure what to make of the new star. "Something of a recluse, Miss Rainer surprised Hollywood two months ago by marrying, without preliminary fanfare or ballyhoo, the brilliant young playwright, Clifford Odets." Louis B. Mayer was sorry that the wedding had occurred, referring to the groom as "that rotten Communist." Nevertheless, the *Reporter* commented, there was no denying Rainer's versatility in hopping from the glamorous Anna Held in *The Great Ziegfeld* to the humble Chinese peasant in *The Good Earth*.

The Hottest Ticket in Town

Because the Academy's coffers were low, banquet tickets went for $5 for members and $10 for guests. The Academy, sensing a good racket, charged $25 for ringside seats. *Daily Variety* reported, "Many performers and technical workers feel that this is too steep and that ringside seats will probably be gobbled up by agents and others seeking to gain prominence by their presence at the banquet."

In spite of the carping over the ticket costs, the Academy sold all 1,150 seats to the dinner. The public's appetite for the Awards continued to grow, and *Daily Variety* wrote, "Traffic on the Academy's switchboard had become congested with incoming calls from fans expressing their views on the actors and actresses who should receive the year's awards."

The Big Night

There were only twenty-five actors left in the Academy, but being nominated was still considered an honor—all the nominees showed up, with the exception of Luise Rainer. Carole Lombard and Clark Gable double-dated with William Powell and his fiancée, Jean Harlow. Paul Muni appeared with his wife, and told reporters, "I hope something good comes out of it." Clearly enjoying himself was last year's Best Actor winner, Victor McLaglen, who, according to the *Hollywood Reporter,* "spent the evening shouting to his friends." Bette Davis was also back, this year formally gowned, to present the Best Actress Award. The last guest to arrive was Norma Shearer—her first appearance since her husband's funeral. Louis B. Mayer escorted the widow, who waved off photographers and went directly to her seat.

The voting had stopped at 5 P.M. that day and the Academy was planning to inform the press of the results at 8 P.M., while making the banquet guests wait for the ceremonial opening of the envelopes after 11. Some guests couldn't wait and sneaked down to the press room to get the news. When Carole Lombard and Jean Harlow visited the ladies' room during dinner, they found Best Actress nominee Gladys George in her cups. "I already heard," George confessed. "I thought I might be a dark horse but Luise Rainer won. She's going to win next year, too, look at the reviews. Mayer's trying to build her up and thought an Oscar would help, and he's trying to get rid of Shearer." Lombard said she didn't believe her and reminded her competitor that Mayer didn't have that kind of influence in the voting anymore.

MGM's flacks had heard the same story, though, and they rushed to call Rainer at home. But she wasn't interested. "I've just driven down from San Francisco," she protested, "and my face is all red from the sun and the wind." "Put on some makeup and get over here," the publicists demanded. The contractee did as she was told, and Mr. and Mrs. Odets arrived at 10:30, just before the Awards presentation began.

At 11, Academy President Frank Capra called the meeting to order and introduced the evening's toastmaster, George Jessel, who requested brevity in speeches by alluding to the recent abdication of King Edward VIII: "Two or three minutes is enough for anything. Remember, a fellow gave up the British Empire in two minutes." Walt Disney was then called upon to make the Short Subject Awards and became the first person in Oscar history to present himself an Award. This was Disney's fifth Cartoon Oscar in a row, but he still hadn't gotten the hang of acceptance speeches. "I tried to memorize it," he apologized, "but it didn't work." He then read his prepared speech.

Leopold Stokowski began the presentation of the Music Awards with a dissertation. "Sound is only a baby. It is eight years old. If sound goes as

Awards Ceremony

MARCH 4, 1937, 8:00 P.M.
A BANQUET AT THE BILTMORE BOWL OF THE BILTMORE HOTEL, LOS ANGELES

Your Host:
GEORGE JESSEL

Presenters

Short Subjects	Walt Disney
Scientific or Technical Awards	Lee De Forest
Music Awards	Leopold Stokowski
Dance Direction	Leopold Stokowski
Assistant Director	Frank Lloyd
Film Editing	Frank Lloyd
Sound Recording	Frank Lloyd
Art Direction	Frank Lloyd
Film Editing	Frank Lloyd
Cinematography	Frank Lloyd
Writing Awards	George Jessel
Special Award to March of Time	George Jessel
Director	George Jessel
Picture	George Jessel
Supporting Actor	George Jessel
Supporting Actress	George Jessel
Actor	Victor McLaglen
Actress	George Jessel

"*San Francisco confounds the trade, the critics and its own producers.*"
—*Motion Picture Daily*

far in the next eight years as it has in the past, it is interesting to see what will happen." Sidney Skolsky wrote, "Stokie made a dull speech." More entertaining was the mother of Seymour Felix; when her son won the Dance Direction Award for *The Great Ziegfeld,* the seventy-six-year-old woman gave the winner a one-person standing ovation.

George Jessel later read the names of the Best Director nominees and then called Frank Capra up to pick a winner. "I don't see how anybody could look over these nominees and pick one out," Capra responded. "Well, they all may be president of the Academy someday and they can select whom they please," Jessel said, handing Capra his second Oscar, for *Mr. Deeds Goes to Town.*

Jessel revealed the Best Picture winner—*The Great Ziegfeld.* Louis B. Mayer walked to the podium and asked Best Director loser Robert Z. Leonard to take a bow. "We have an arrangement in our studio where I make all the speeches," Mayer said, but he broke policy by bringing the film's actual producer, Hunt Stromberg, to the dais. "One thing I like about working with Louis B. Mayer," Stromberg commented, "I went to him and told him that the melody numbers of *The Great Ziegfeld* would cost $250,000 and he just said 'Shoot.' "

The new Supporting Awards were christened when Walter Brennan won for *Come and Get It* and Gale Sondergaard was honored for *Anthony Adverse.* Jessel talked about the vital importance of supporting players to movies, but the winners got plaques, not statuettes.

Victor McLaglen announced that the Best Actor was Paul Muni for *The Story of Louis Pasteur,* and then wouldn't stop talking. As Muni waited at the podium, McLaglen continued, "This Award goes to Muni for the second time [it was Muni's first Oscar]. My statuette I placed beside my bedside and while I am asleep it looks at me. Only recently, it told me it was lonely and wanted a pal. Paul, I give you this statuette. I will strive to get another one and hope you do the same." When he could get a word in edgewise, Muni said, "I have the greatest thrill of my life getting this. I will try to continue to work to make myself worthy of the Academy's high and meaningful honor." "Me, too," McLaglen piped up. When Muni spoke to Sidney Skolsky later, he confided, "Victor talked so long, for a minute there, I thought I was presenting the Award to him."

Bette Davis was supposed to give the Best Actress Award, but George Jessel never called her to the dais, plunging into the presentation himself. "Miss Rainer, I want to present you with the token of the finest acting in the 1936 season among Hollywood women stars," Jessel said. "Thank you very much," Rainer replied, "I am very glad to get it. I thank everybody who made me capable of getting it." Then she sat down.

Jessel revealed the order of finish. Rainer had been followed by Carole Lombard, with Norma Shearer in third place. Paul Muni was way ahead of second-place Gary Cooper in *Mr. Deeds Goes to Town,* but director Frank Capra had just squeaked by W. S. Van Dyke for *San Francisco* and Gregory La Cava for *My Man Godfrey.* MGM's *The Great Ziegfeld* had won out over Warners' *The Story of Louis Pasteur* by only a few votes. The film with the highest number of wins was Warners' *Anthony Adverse* with four Oscars.

The final ceremonial gesture of the evening was Capra's announcement of the inception of the Irving G. Thalberg Award, which would be given to the producer with the most distinguished body of work in a given year. "It is to encourage the pride, the fortitude, the good taste and tolerance that Thalberg put into pictures," Capra said. "It is to keep permanent his message: The stars brighten the night, the laughter of children is a message to the ear. Irving would have liked that." Apparently, the gathering liked it, too; there was a respectful ovation as everyone watched Norma Shearer hold back the tears.

Aftermath

The winners were hustled into the press room where they all posed with an all-purpose prop Oscar before a prop banquet table—even the Sup-

"My face is all red."
—Luise Rainer

porting winners got to hold the statuette, if only for a moment. Newsreel photographers made Luise Rainer repeat her acceptance speech eight times before she turned to Capra and asked, "Why don't you direct this?"

Bette Davis stormed in, wanting to know why she had been ignored. George Jessel apologized profusely and said he made a nervous oversight after Victor McLaglen took so long with the Best Actor Award. Jessel suggested that Davis pose with Muni for publicity pictures so that the public could see her evening gown; Davis took him up on it. As for Muni, he was sporting a Van Dyke beard for his role in the film he was currently making, *The Woman I Love*. *Daily Variety* wrote that Mrs. Muni wore her hair "parted Wally Simpson style," but that she wasn't happy with her husband's appearance: "Paul should have been clean-shaven for such a big occasion."

Meanwhile, the ballroom upstairs was a human traffic jam as lower-echelon studio workers crowded the dance floor to get a look at celebrities at ringside tables. When Mr. and Mrs. Harold Lloyd tried to dance, they realized that any serious movement was impossible. Fighting their way back to their table, they passed Tyrone Power and his date, Sonja Henie, heading out. "Not unless you're very brave," Lloyd warned them.

The *Hollywood Citizen-News* wrote: "Critics were generally of the opinion that Spencer Tracy would have won if he had been nominated for Supporting Actor for *San Francisco*." While most in Hollywood conceded that Paul Muni was deserving of the Best Actor Oscar, W. C. Fields had his reservations. "Any actor knows that comedy is more difficult, requires more artistry," Fields said. "It is pretty easy to fool an audience with a little crêpe hair and a dialect. It seems to me that a comedian who really makes people laugh should be as eligible for an award as a tragedian who makes people cry. This isn't a case of sour grapes with me because I didn't grow any grapes last year. I didn't even sow a wild oat."

"*The Great Ziegfeld* was the most controversial choice," the *Hollywood Citizen-News* continued, adding that Thalberg's friends were "upset over the skirting of *Romeo and Juliet*." Going further, the paper called *The Great Ziegfeld* "an atrocious production . . . a picture false in biography, a glittering avalanche of legs and tinsel," and concluded that "a truer demonstration of the stupidity and rank barbarism of these times had never been more ably given."

Louis B. Mayer was oblivious to the criticism. A few weeks later, he threw a *Great Ziegfeld* party at the French Room of the Ambassador Hotel. After four women dressed as Ziegfeld chorines wheeled out a giant cake, Mayer presented producer Hunt Stromberg with the Oscar. Billie Burke, Ziegfeld's widow, got a brooch from the mogul and all the other guests received miniature Oscar replicas. These mini-statuettes were clearly an infringement of the Academy's copyright, but Mayer wasn't worried about any lawsuits. After all, the Academy had been his idea in the first place.

1937

"Whores can make good wives; that has been proven."
—Irving Thalberg

Impostors, invalids and dummies walked off with the 1937 Awards.

The sudden and unexpected death of Irving Thalberg in 1936 made his final, yet-to-be-released films more keenly anticipated than any in his lifetime. One of these movies was *Camille* with Greta Garbo. Thalberg had instructed his three screenwriters—James Hilton, Frances Marion and Zoe Atkins—to update Dumas' antique plot. "The problem of a girl's past ruining her marriage doesn't exist anymore," Thalberg told them. "Whores can make good wives; that has been proven."

So the writers and director George Cukor made Robert Taylor's Armand merely very jealous of Marguerite's ex-suitor and concentrated on Garbo's performance. When the million-dollar production opened, Garbo dropped her reclusive act and showed up at the Hollywood premiere with Louis B. Mayer. The *New York Times* raved, "She is as incomparable in the role as legend tells us that Bernhardt was." The *Los Angeles Herald-Express* was equally enthusiastic: "If Greta Garbo is not Hollywood's greatest dramatic actress in her greatest dramatic role then I have been bewitched." *Camille* made more money than any Garbo film. Thalberg had done it again. Garbo followed *Camille* with *Conquest,* which did not earn back its cost in the United States although the European audience ultimately pulled the costume romance into the black. *The New Yorker* observed that, with co-star Charles Boyer playing Napoleon, for the first time "Garbo has a leading man who contributes more to the interest and vitality of the film than she does." After *Conquest,* Garbo told the studio she was taking a vacation.

Overleaf: *Best Actor winner Spencer Tracy, who managed to duck the ceremony by undergoing an appendectomy, finds he can't escape MGM's publicity flacks when his wife presents him with his Oscar.*

Day of the Locusts

The other posthumous Thalberg film exceeded the cost of *Ben-Hur*—a $2.8 million version of Pearl S. Buck's *The Good Earth* with Paul Muni and Luise Rainer that had opened just before they won their 1936 Oscars. "Irving, the public won't buy pictures about American farmers and you want to give them Chinese farmers?" Louis B. Mayer had argued, but Thalberg knew what he was doing. The epic included a sacrificial mother, the Chinese Revolution, and a climactic plague of locusts.

"The greatest photographic miracles in the history of motion pictures," extolled the *Los Angeles Evening Herald*. "The swarming of the locusts, I think, surpasses the earthquake in *San Francisco*." Although *The Good Earth* did not surpass *San Francisco* at the box office, it came close. *Silver Screen* magazine said that a lot of the credit went to Luise Rainer: "She was known to the public as a Viennese glamour gal. But it is a measure of Miss Rainer's artistic integrity that she became a Chinese peasant, mother of a starving brood, bowed down with the cares of Oriental womanhood and graying into old age. Can you imagine your Garbos and Dietrichs and Crawfords playing O-lan?"

"Any credit you give yourself isn't worth having," was Thalberg's explanation for why his name never appeared on his pictures, but Mayer decided he would get credit for *The Good Earth* and hired John Lee Mahin to write the testimony: "To the memory of Irving Grant Thalberg we dedicate this picture, his last great achievement."

Go Fish

When he wasn't writing tributes, Mahin was working on the screenplay of Rudyard Kipling's *Captains Courageous,* a million-dollar vehicle for child star Freddie Bartholomew. MGM assigned Spencer Tracy to play a Portuguese fisherman, but

"The public won't buy pictures about American farmers and you want to give them Chinese farmers?"
—Louis B. Mayer

he was uncomfortable with the accent. He didn't like his curled hairdo either, especially after Joan Crawford ran into him on the Metro lot and roared, "Oh my God, it's Harpo Marx!" Tracy felt better when *Captains Courageous* went on to become the studio's top moneymaker of the year and the winner of *Photoplay*'s readers' poll for the year's most popular film. The magazine said of Tracy, "In this difficult role, Tracy does masterful work. He realizes not only the outward character but the role's spiritual implications." Joan Crawford stopped laughing and costarred with Tracy in *Mannequin*, her first moneymaker in ages.

Weeping Buckets

Samuel Goldwyn, who had produced a silent version of the tearjerker *Stella Dallas* in 1925, dusted off the property for Barbara Stanwyck in 1937. Director King Vidor pulled out all the melodramatic stops and Stanwyck threw herself into the role of the working-class mother who sacrifices her child to high society. "Miss Stanwyck's portrayal is as courageous as it is fine," opined the *New York Times*.

Janet Gaynor had her share of suffering, too, in *A Star Is Born*, which Selznick International advertised as "The First Modern Dress Story in Technicolor." Producer David O. Selznick and director William Wellman adapted Robert Carson's story about a fading Hollywood matinee idol, played by Fredric March, who marries rising star Gaynor. Dorothy Parker and husband Alan Campbell were called in to add polish to the script. The filmmakers strove for such accuracy that Gaynor used her own Oscar in the Academy Awards scene. *Variety* said of the finished product, "Hollywood has taken it on the chin for a long time as the butt of many a stage farce. *A Star Is Born* is a compelling and moving reply in which the people of the studios are portrayed as human beings." The *New York Herald Tribune* said that Janet Gaynor gave "a beautifully rounded and appealing performance as the girl," and the *Los Angeles Herald-Express* commented, "Fredric March gives the most real performance I have ever seen."

Pitching Screwballs

Selznick, March and Wellman teamed again for another movie when Mrs. Selznick—Irene Mayer—mentioned over breakfast that Carole Lombard would be an interesting study in Technicolor. Selznick called up Ben Hecht and told him to write a Lombard comedy fast. The result was *Nothing Sacred*, a satire about a woman who pretends to be dying from radium poisoning as a publicity stunt. The picture packed them in at Radio City Music Hall at Thanksgiving and Lombard, one of the highest-paid performers in Hollywood, was dubbed "the Daffy Duse of Screen Comedy."

Her rival for the title was Irene Dunne, who scored in another screwball comedy, Leo McCarey's *The Awful Truth*. Earlier in the year, McCarey had worked for less than his usual salary to direct *Make Way for Tomorrow*, a drama about an elderly couple and their uncaring children. The movie opened on Mother's Day and the *Los Angeles Daily News* wrote, "*Make Way For Tomorrow* is so human it hurts." Paramount was certainly wounded when nobody came to see the movie. The studio's advertising department tried every angle: "Is Your Old Man a Crab?—See *Make Way For Tomorrow*" "Are You Chained to Your Inlaws?—See . . ." "Going to Get Married? See . . ." The film did so poorly that Adolph Zukor bought out the rest of McCarey's Paramount contract. The unemployed director had to think of something to sell, so he went to Harry Cohn at Columbia with the idea of a comedy about divorce.

Eluded Censors

Cohn had just alienated his star director, Frank Capra, by putting Capra's name on someone else's picture and distributing it in England as a Capra film. With hitmaker Capra gone, the mogul gave McCarey a chance, and almost anything he wanted: Irene Dunne as the wife, Cary Grant as the husband, Ralph Bellamy as Dunne's would-be second husband, and Asta the dog, on loan-out from MGM, as the pet. The actors learned that McCarey hadn't written a final script and that his working method was to sit and play the piano on the set before telling them what they were going to do in a scene. Cohn got wind of this, stormed onto the set, and boomed, "I hired you to make a great comedy so I could show up Frank Capra. The only one who's going to laugh at this is Capra."

"A rollicking comedy that should delight anyone," was the verdict of the *New York Sun*. "Mr. McCarey's direction has skillfully eluded all problems of censorship, concocting a comedy that is sometimes naughty but always nice. *The Awful Truth* is as merry as sleighbells." Cohn was so happy over the box-office returns that he offered to give McCarey a quarter of the profits if he would sign a three-year contract with Columbia. McCarey's response was a raspberry.

Ladykillers and Gentlemen

Ed Sullivan wrote, "Robert Montgomery, cocktail-shaking smarty of films, rebelled and asked to be assigned to *Night Must Fall*," based on the hit Broadway thriller. Louis B. Mayer thought that Montgomery was crazy for wanting to play a psychopathic murderer roaming the English countryside, but the actor was the president of the Screen Actors Guild, so the mogul let him have his way. The critics reacted the way that Montgomery had hoped they would; the *New York Daily News* said the film "lifts the MGM actor out of the lower brackets, where he has slipped because of shoddy material, into an eminent position among the top-notchers of Hollywood players." But *Variety* reported the bad news: "The appearance of Montgomery in a part which is the antithesis of his pattern may be art but it's not box office." The movie flopped.

Jack Warner was used to giving Paul Muni what he wanted, and the studio head didn't balk when the Oscar winner said he wanted to impersonate Emile Zola next. William Dieterle, who directed Muni as Louis Pasteur, was given a similar chore on *The Life of Emile Zola*, costarring Oscar-winner Gale Sondergaard as Mrs. Alfred Dreyfuss and Broadway name Joseph Schildkraut as her unlucky husband. Warners billed the star as "Mr. Paul Muni" and *Time* magazine declared it "the outstanding prestige picture of the season." The New York Film Critics bestowed their Best Picture and Best Actor awards on the movie and its star. *The Life of Emile Zola* was also Warners' top moneymaker of 1937.

Popularity Contest

Greta Garbo won her second New York Film Critics Award for *Camille*. The Best Director was Gregory La Cava for the immensely popular *Stage Door*, RKO's adaptation of the Edna Ferber–George S. Kaufman play about struggling actresses, starring every female name at the studio: Katharine Hepburn, Ginger Rogers, Lucille Ball, Eve Arden, Andrea Leeds and Ann Miller.

The New York critical body was microscopic compared to the Academy after president Frank Capra swelled the ranks of voters. With a new charter, the Academy made it official—no more involvement in labor-management business. And, in a final effort to win over members of the actors', directors', and writers' organizations, Capra got rid of the Academy's fifty-man nominating committee and invited all guild members to vote, whether they were members of the Academy or not. Even extras got to vote on the final ballot for Best Picture, Best Acting and Best Song awards. This meant a jump from the previous year's 800-odd voters to 15,000—with the extras representing 12,000 of those votes. Capra still had to plead with the guild leaders for permission to mail the ballots to their members, but they finally said okay.

"Lionel Barrymore already has one of those crummy little statues and now he wants you to have one."
—Louis Lighton to Spencer Tracy

The Nominations

Carole Lombard may have wished that Capra had kept the fifty-man nominating committee; she was not nominated for *Nothing Sacred*. "They don't give awards to comedy performances," she told reporters, overlooking the fact that Irene Dunne was nominated for *The Awful Truth*. Dunne's costar, Cary Grant, probably agreed with Lombard; he was about the only person connected with *The Awful Truth* who was not nominated—even Ralph Bellamy was in the running for Best Supporting Actor.

Tears, rather than laughs, dominated the Best Actress race, with Janet Gaynor nominated for *A Star Is Born,* Barbara Stanwyck for *Stella Dallas,* Luise Rainer for *The Good Earth* and Greta Garbo for *Camille*. Although Garbo was the expected winner, she shrugged off her nomination and said she wasn't changing her plans to visit Italy. Her traveling companion was reported to be conductor Leopold Stokowski, Deanna Durbin's costar in Universal's Best Picture nominee, *100 Men and a Girl*.

The picture with the highest number of nominations was Warners' *The Life of Emile Zola* with ten. Its Best Picture competition came from McCarey's *The Awful Truth* with six nominations, Selznick's *A Star Is Born* with seven, La Cava's *Stage Door* with four and the late Irving Thalberg's *The Good Earth* with five. Also in the Best Picture race was Samuel Goldwyn's *Dead End,* based on Sidney Kingsley's play; Frank Capra's *Lost Horizon,* based on James Hilton's best-selling fantasy; and Darryl F. Zanuck's disaster epic *In Old Chicago,* based on the desire to imitate the success of MGM's *San Francisco*. The tenth nominee was the *Photoplay* favorite, *Captains Courageous*.

Spencer Tracy's Portuguese accent got him on the Best Actor ballot. Joining him were "Mr." Paul Muni for *The Life of Emile Zola,* Fredric March for *A Star Is Born,* Charles Boyer in *Conquest,* and Screen Actors Guild President Robert Montgomery for *Night Must Fall*. When *Captains Courageous* producer Louis Lighton asked Tracy if he was going to attend the banquet, Tracy said he hadn't liked losing the previous year and that he thought Lionel Barrymore gave a better performance in *Captains Courageous* than he did. "Lionel doesn't care," Lighton snapped, "he already has one of those crummy little statues and now he wants you to have one. And you're going to get it. Everyone in town is going to vote for you."

Stormy Weather

John Lee Mahin was not happy when he was nominated for his screenplay for *Captains Courageous*. The nominee was the president of the Screen Playwrights, Inc., a splinter group from the Screen Writers Guild, which Mahin believed evinced Communist leanings. Mahin wasn't fond of the Academy, either, and wrote a letter to the trade papers complaining that Academy President Frank Capra had refused to allow the Screen Playwrights in on the Academy balloting because of their political views.

When Mahin announced that he was refusing his Best Screenplay nomination, Capra wrote him back: "In regard to the charge of unfair discrimination which your organization is belly-aching about, you know very well that you were given the same opportunity to participate in the Awards Committee as any other organization in Hollywood." Capra added that Mahin's nomination stood as a matter of record. "We don't care whether you accept it or throw it away or deposit it in that well-known place where everything is consigned in Hollywood."

Capra had taken care of Mahin, but Mother Nature proved too much for him to handle. A rainstorm begat a flood that stranded the Academy president in his Malibu home and sent a giant rubber whale from Warners floating down the Los Angeles River. The banquet was postponed a week and $750 worth of flowers was donated to hospitals. There were a number of Oscar nominees at those hospitals. Best Supporting Actress nominee Alice Brady, the odds-on favorite for her portrayal of Mrs. O'Leary in *In Old Chicago,* was laid up with a broken ankle. Best Actor nominee Spencer Tracy had appendicitis. And emcee George Jessel fell ill by the time the floodwaters subsided, and was replaced at the last minute by hillbilly comedian Bob "Bazooka" Burns.

Many of the healthier nominees weren't planning to attend the banquet because they didn't want to lose. Best Supporting Actor nominee Joseph Schildkraut of *The Life of Emile Zola* was told by his agent to stay home because the race was between Ralph Bellamy in *The Awful Truth* and veteran character actor H. B. Warner in *Lost Horizon.* Irene Dunne told reporters she "couldn't wait to be off to New York," and Paul Muni had plans for a trip, too. "It'll be less embarrassing for everybody if I'm in Palestine or Greece," the actor told Jack Warner. "Nobody wins two years in a row."

The Big Night

The extras stood out in the cold, watching the entrances of the stars they voted on, because they couldn't afford the $15-a-couple tab. None of the onlookers recognized the first arrival, Mrs. Spencer Tracy. Joan Blondell was more visible; she fell down as she stepped out of her limousine. When nominee Robert Montgomery arrived, he had a sinking feeling. "There was a line of MGM cameramen waiting with cameras poised," he recalled, "and they all looked self-conscious and turned aside. I knew immediately I wasn't going to get it or else they would have been dimpling and snapping my picture."

The guilds were officially represented at the banquet by their presidents, Montgomery for the actors, King Vidor for the directors and Dudley Nichols for the writers. In a further show of rec onciliation, Nichols had just recently accepted the Oscar for *The Informer* that he had turned down two years earlier. Along with the air of cooperation, the banquet was marked by an increase of showmanship. "For the first time," the *Hollywood Reporter* said, "the list of winners has been kept completely secret, even from the Academy. The Academy officials will learn the news simultaneously with the press just prior to the dinner."

The Awards portion of the evening began at 10:30 when President Capra greeted everyone and introduced Cecil B. DeMille, who declared that the Academy "is now free of all labor struggles." DeMille continued at length, prompting the *Hollywood Reporter* to remark, "DeMille broke his own speech record—35 minutes." One of DeMille's duties was to present a special plaque to the Museum of Modern Art for its film library. The honor was accepted by an honorary vice president of the museum—Louella Parsons.

Emcee Bob Burns followed DeMille and began by commenting, "I've been selected because I probably know less about motion pictures than anyone present and if anything goes wrong it can be blamed on my ignorance." The blame for the Best Song selection fell on the extras. When Irving Berlin revealed that the Gershwins' "They Can't Take That Away From Me," from an Astaire-Rogers musical, lost the Best Song Oscar to "Sweet Leilani," from a Bing Crosby musical, the buzz at the banquet was that the Gershwins were too sophisticated for the new voters. Everyone was happier when William Wellman accepted his Oscar for the Best Original Story for *A Star Is Born* by holding up the statuette and telling Selznick, "Here, David, you take it; you wrote more of it than I did."

The most celebrated winner of the evening was made of wood. Although ventriloquist Edgar

Awards Ceremony

March 10, 1938, 8:15 p.m.
A Banquet at the Biltmore Bowl of the Biltmore Hotel, Los Angeles

Your Host:
Bob "Bazooka" Burns

Presenters

Special Award to the Museum of Modern Art Film Library	Cecil B. DeMille
Film Editing	Cecil B. DeMille
Sound Recording	Cecil B. DeMille
Cinematography	Cecil B. DeMille
Art Direction	Cecil B. DeMille
Scientific and Technical Awards	Nathan Levinson
Short Subjects	Bob Burns
Dance Direction	Bob Burns
Song	Irving Berlin
Music Score	Dr. Arnold Schoenberg
Original Story	Howard Estabrook
Screenplay	Robert Riskin
Special Award to Edgar Bergen	Bob Burns
Assistant Director	Frank Capra
Special Award to Mack Sennett	W. C. Fields
Director	Frank Capra
Picture	Frank Capra
Supporting Actor	Bob Burns
Supporting Actress	Bob Burns
Actor	C. Aubrey Smith
Actress	C. Aubrey Smith
Thalberg Award	Douglas Fairbanks

"Thanks, but you gave it to me for the wrong picture."
—Leo McCarey

Bergen created Charlie McCarthy when he was in high school, the Academy decided to honor the dummy as he graduated from starring roles in comedy shorts to feature films—McCarthy was a star of *The Goldwyn Follies*. A tuxedoed Bergen carried a tuxedoed McCarthy to the podium where Burns presented them with a special Oscar—a minute wooden one with a movable mouth. "It's really remarkable that anyone could carve a statue so small . . . Why, it doesn't even shine," complained the dummy. "Carved out of wood! A bit of sarcasm, I suppose." Bergen rebuked Charlie's bad manners, and McCarthy apologized, "Well, thanks, even if it isn't gold . . . But if you have a gold one left over I'd like to have it."

In presenting the Best Director Award, Frank Capra said first that more than "just make pictures," directors must "strive always to make great pictures and think of something besides their salaries." The winner was *The Awful Truth*'s Leo McCarey, who had not forgotten *Make Way for Tomorrow*. "Thanks, but you gave it to me for the wrong picture," McCarey said. Jack Warner was not so particular when he won his first Best Picture Award for *The Life of Emile Zola*. "I want to express my special appreciation to Hal Wallis, to Henry Blanke, to William Dieterle, to Paul Muni and to every artist; to the writers and the entire *Zola* staff for having made possible a production that marks still another milestone in the history of the screen," the mogul stated. "They, and they alone, are entitled to the glory of having created the masterpiece this industry has so highly honored." Warner was so taken with his speech, he had it reprinted in trade-paper ads the next day.

W. C. Fields presented a Special Oscar to Mack Sennett, Hollywood's "King of Comedy," now retired and nearly penniless. The inscription read: "To Mack Sennett, for his lasting contributions to the comedy technique of the screen, the basic principles of which are as important today as when they were first put into practice, the Academy presents a Special Award to that master of fun, discoverer of stars, sympathetic, kindly, understanding comedy genius." The *Hollywood Reporter* called this bestowal, "another hilarious round."

Bob Burns reappeared to give the Supporting Actor and Actress Awards. First he named Joseph Schildkraut for *The Life of Emile Zola*. The winner had taken his agent's advice and was already asleep when Academy officials called him to tell him he'd won. Schildkraut was dressed and present when his name was called. Alice Brady, the Best Supporting Actress winner for *In Old Chicago*, was not there. She stayed home with her broken ankle. An unidentified gentleman accepted for her and left with her Oscar. He was never heard from again. Brady said she didn't send any representative and she had not received her Oscar. When the Academy couldn't find the impostor, they gave Brady another Oscar at an informal ceremony twelve days after the Awards.

Best Actor nominee Robert Montgomery's suspicions were confirmed when C. Aubrey Smith proclaimed Spencer Tracy the Best Actor winner for *Captains Courageous*. "It is privilege to be the stand-in for Spencer Tracy," said Louis B. Mayer at the podium. "Tracy is a fine actor, but he is most important because he understands why it is necessary to take orders from the front office." (When he heard Mayer's tribute later, Tracy asked, "Was that a compliment or a threat?") After Mayer finished, he brought up Mrs. Tracy, who merely said, "I accept this award on behalf of Spencer, Susie, Johnny and myself."

There was a loud gasp when C. Aubrey Smith announced the Best Actress winner. Screenwriter Frances Marion remembers, "The crowd at the dinner was amazed that Garbo lost to Rainer." Luise Rainer had won for *The Good Earth*. For the first time in Oscar history, an acting nominee won two years in a row. Academy officials had called the actress at home, and once again she rushed to the ceremony with husband Clifford Odets. The press forgave Rainer for not wearing makeup, but they thought Odets was carrying his proletarian attitudes too far by appearing in a business suit at a black-tie affair. Her speech was humble and brief.

The climactic bit of business was the bestow-

"Spencer Tracy is a fine actor, but he is most important because he understands why it is necessary to take orders from the front office."
—Louis B. Mayer

ing of the first Irving G. Thalberg Memorial Award to the producer with "the most consistent high quality of production." The Award, determined by a committee of fourteen drawn from the various branches, was given to 20th Century–Fox's Darryl F. Zanuck, one of the Academy's best friends during the labor troubles. Zanuck's productions that year were *In Old Chicago*, a remake of *Seventh Heaven*, and the John Ford–Shirley Temple collaboration, *Wee Willie Winkie*.

Aftermath

The banquet broke up around 2 A.M. One of the guests was a reporter from *Time* magazine, who commented that the statuette "strongly resembled radiator-cap sculpture." The magazine didn't think much of the Thalberg trophy, either, describing it as "an effeminate-looking bust of the late young MGM producer." *Time* also said that the Best Actor victory was most appreciated. "Last year's Oscar to Paul Muni disappointed many who thought Tracy deserved it for a row of consistently fine jobs. When this year's balloting named his difficult, pidgin-English part in *Captains Courageous*, many thought the score was about even."

The convalescing winner was deluged with phone calls at Good Samaritan Hospital. He finally instructed the nurse to unplug the phone, forcing MGM publicists to come up with a response for reporters. Their version: "Spencer Tracy cried when he heard the news and said, 'It's the nicest thing that's ever happened to me in my life. Now I've got to get well and get out of here as soon as possible.' "

The *New York Times* went after the choice of Darryl Zanuck for the Thalberg Award. "Mr. Zanuck's box-office score would be a potent argument in his behalf," wrote Frank S. Nugent. "His musical-comedy formulas have quite outdistanced Warners' early lead in that field, his romantic comedies with Tyrone Power and Loretta Young are models of juvenilia, his big shows, *In Old Chicago* and the like, manifest an uncanny marksmanship where superficial mass appeal is the target. But these and 'high quality' by the Thalberg standards are not even distant cousins. We hate to rub it in, but where was Mr. Zanuck when the ten-best lists went out?"

Louis B. Mayer placed ads in the trade papers thanking the Academy for the Oscars to Tracy and Luise Rainer, but he didn't bother giving Rainer any more good scripts. "The industry seemed to feel that having an Academy Award winner on their hands was sufficient to overcome bad story material, which was often handed out afterwards to stars under long-term contract," Rainer recalled. When she complained about her projects, the actress found herself being labeled "temperamental" by columnists. She believed that Oscar had brought "a change of one's image felt by others but not by oneself. One was acclaimed now; therefore one's doings, one's motives, one's every utterance seemed to have greater dimension and therefore suddenly became suspect. It seemed harder to continue one's work quietly."

On top of her problems at MGM, Rainer had problems at home. Clifford Odets' graphologist told him that sleeping with his wife drained his creative energy—the playwright insisted on separate bedrooms. After a year, Rainer had had it. "I couldn't face the 'star' career and the devastation of a broken marriage because I was simply too young and unsophisticated to handle it," she said. So the twenty-nine-year-old woman fled Hollywood and later married a publisher in London.

Rainer's immediate career decline after her Oscar victories led to the myth of the Oscar jinx, used to describe any performer whose subsequent work never lived up to the Academy's expectations. Rainer dismisses the Oscar jinx as "nonsense" and still has high regard for her two statuettes. When she visited Hollywood in 1983, she had the Academy replace one that had broken. "Actually it wasn't broken at all," she told the *Hollywood Reporter*. "I think it just got so tired standing there, holding that sword all those years, it just collapsed."

1938

"Boys Town does need your money, so keep it coming, Americans."
—Louis B. Mayer

Where Snow White led, Bob Hope followed.

Profits dipped at every film factory with one exception—Walt Disney Studios. The man who had won five Best Cartoon Oscars in a row jumped into the big leagues with the feature-length *Snow White and the Seven Dwarfs*. The animated film opened for Christmas 1937, but the only category the Academy could fit it into at the 1937 Awards was Best Score. By Christmas of 1938, *Snow White* had grossed more than $4 million, making it the number-one film of the year. The Academy didn't want to give a cartoon the Best Picture Award, but everyone agreed $4 million deserved some sort of recognition.

MGM still led the pack of live-action studios when it came to box-office pull. Leo the Lion scored highest with *Boys Town,* starring Spencer Tracy as a priest and Mickey Rooney as a juvenile delinquent. Originally planned as a B-movie about the real-life Father Flanagan who founded a correctional home in Nebraska, *Boys Town* became a million-dollar production when the MGM brass realized they had another *Captains Courageous*–style tearjerker on their hands. Norman Taurog, Oscar winner for directing little Jackie Cooper in *Skippy,* had a hundred youngsters to break hearts with in this one and he was very good at his job. Too good, according to the real Father Flanagan, who complained that MGM made Boys Town look so well managed that nobody remembered it was really a charity. Donations dropped dramatically enough for Louis B. Mayer to have to go on the radio saying, "Boys Town does need your money, so keep it coming, Americans."

T.B. or Not T.B.

Tuberculosis went up a notch in charitable donations after Americans saw Margaret Sullavan die of it in MGM's *Three Comrades*. Erich Maria Remarque, the author of *All Quiet on the Western Front,* had a knack for sad novels, and adapting his *Comrades* into a screenplay was F. Scott Fitzgerald—the movie was tragedy from the word go. "Miss Sullavan enters a very small company of movie actresses who can really act," remarked the *New York Post,* and Sullavan's fans came out to see her suffer in two more MGM handkerchief dramas that year—*Shopworn Angel* and *The Shining Hour*.

The citizenry of Boys Town, Nebraska, inspects the Oscar donated, grudgingly, by Best Actor winner Spencer Tracy.

Warner Brothers and Sisters

Over at Warners, Bette Davis was still having problems. An Oscar wasn't enough to convince Jack Warner to treat his contract actress like a star; he wouldn't give Davis good scripts or loan her out to RKO again to play Queen Elizabeth to Katharine Hepburn's Mary Queen of Scots. The moment Davis walked out on Warner in 1936, a British producer popped up with two film offers. Davis accepted and flew off to London, prompting Warner to file a breach-of-contract suit against her. Warner won the case, but Davis won the battle—she got better material. Her big 1938 vehicle was *Jezebel,* the drama of a Southern belle, played by Miriam Hopkins on Broadway. Davis got the best Warner could buy: gowns by Orry-Kelly, Henry Fonda as her leading man, John Huston as scriptwriter and William Wyler as director.

"That handsomely homely dynamo Wyler could make your life hell," Davis recalls in her autobiography. "It was he who screamed at me, 'Do you want me to put a chain around your neck? Stop moving your head!' " Davis found the role physically draining and her frequent illnesses delayed the expensive production. Henry Fonda had to leave before filming was over to attend the birth of his daughter, Jane. When the film finally wrapped, Davis' physician warned Warner, "She is not actually medically ill, but her general physical and emotional makeup is such that if we rush her into another picture, she will be in danger of a collapse." Davis recovered when *Jezebel*'s reviews

"Do you want me to put a chain around your neck?"
—William Wyler to Bette Davis

were sterling, the box office boffo and *Time* put her picture on the cover.

R-e-s-p-e-c-t

Davis wasn't the only Warners star who had to go to extreme lengths to get some respect from Jack Warner. James Cagney had been a consistent moneymaker for the studio, but he and the mogul had a lengthy contract squabble. The Academy, in its labor-negotiating days, had worked out a settlement between the actor and his employer, only to have Cagney name the Academy as a co-defendant in a lawsuit against Warners two years later. By 1938, Cagney and Warner had worked things out and the actor received one of his most popular roles since *Public Enemy* in *Angels with Dirty Faces*. Once again he was a gangster. "For Cagney, the picture is likely to bring added prestige for the bantam rooster of a racketeer is just the kind of part he plays best," proclaimed *Variety*.

Cagney soon had a tough-guy rival on the lot—John Garfield. The actor from the Lower East Side had been an extra standing behind Cagney in the 1933 Busby Berkeley musical *Footlight Parade* before moving back to New York and finding stardom on Broadway. Hollywood beckoned and the twenty-five-year-old actor came back to Warner Brothers to play a likable heel in *Four Daughters*, based on a Fannie Hurst story. "I believe *Four Daughters* is the best picture of my career," boasted Jack Warner in the trade-paper ads, and he was certainly proud of the fortune the movie earned him, as well as of his new star. *Newsweek* marveled, "John Garfield, a graduate of New York's Group Theatre, has never appeared on the screen before and is undoubtedly the outstanding film find of the year."

The director of both *Angels with Dirty Faces* and *Four Daughters* was Michael Curtiz, the Hungarian who was rapidly becoming Warners' all-purpose in-house director. Jack Warner was still grateful to him for making a star out of former bit player Errol Flynn in *Captain Blood* after Robert Donat bowed out of the title role. Now Warner was spending $2 million on *The Adventures of Robin Hood* for Flynn and Olivia de Havilland, but was worried that director William Keighley was treating the legend a little too solemnly. Out went Keighley, in came Curtiz, and Warners soon had what the *New York Herald Tribune* called "a swell entertainment." Curtiz had gone three for three in 1938.

From Britain

Robert Donat, the would-be Captain Blood, made his American film comeback by waiting for Hollywood to come to him in England. After co-starring with Charles Laughton in *The Private Life of Henry VIII* in 1932, Donat had come to Hollywood to star in *The Count of Monte Cristo*. The film was a hit, but Donat hadn't thought much of Los Angeles and went back to London. Director King Vidor wanted Donat to play the leading role in MGM's adaptation of A. J. Cronin's bestseller, *The Citadel*, so he convinced Louis B. Mayer to let him film it on location in England. Rosalind Russell was the love interest, and the supporting roles were played by stars of the London stage, including Ralph Richardson and Rex Harrison.

The Citadel was very popular, but MGM fared even better when it distributed another British-made film, *Pygmalion*, produced from George Bernard Shaw's own screenplay. "Not the least regard will be paid to American ideas except to avoid them as much as possible," Shaw announced, but producer Gabriel Pascal persuaded him to let Professor Higgins get the girl in the end. Wendy Hiller, the unknown who played Eliza Doolittle, was proclaimed "a radiant newcomer" by *Life*. *The New Yorker* said, "Leslie Howard, with that somewhat arid academic style of his, has a perfect comedy part; not for a long time have we seen him so at ease." And *Newsweek* favored Shaw's revisions: "The film surpasses the play."

"Not the least regard will be paid to American ideas except to avoid them as much as possible."
—George Bernard Shaw

Royal Bad Girl

MGM was still making movies in Culver City, too, the most expensive being Norma Shearer's post-Irving comeback, the $1.8 million two-hour-and-forty-five-minute *Marie Antoinette*. Everything was on a grand scale; Adrian designed costumes for everyone down to the Queen's poodles. Tyrone Power, Fox's leading box-office attraction, was borrowed to play opposite Shearer, but Charles Laughton was unavailable to portray Louis XVI, so a fat English character actor named Robert Morley, fresh from playing Oscar Wilde on Broadway, made his film debut in the role. Just as Thalberg predicted way back in 1933, *Marie Antoinette*, advertised as "The Life, The Sins of a Royal Bad Girl!," was a tremendous success for Norma Shearer. *Variety* said, "Miss Shearer shows progress as an actress and reveals certain capabilities heretofore kept from view."

Foreign Quotas

Political messages went over big in two 1938 films. "A French film challenges Hollywood," reported *Life* of Jean Renoir's World War I drama, *Grand Illusion,* with Erich von Stroheim and Jean Gabin. The American ads read, "One of the greatest films in any language," and the film, with dialogue in French, English and German, inspired the *New York Times* to utter, "Its virtues cannot be reduced to words."

For a foreign-language film, *Grand Illusion* did spectacularly well in the U.S., but it couldn't compare to the box-office grosses of the latest Frank Capra paean to individualism, *You Can't Take It With You*. Columbia's Harry Cohn paid $200,000 to acquire the rights to George S. Kaufman and Moss Hart's Pulitzer Prize–winning play, which was still running on Broadway when Capra's movie version opened. Jean Arthur and James Stewart were Capra's romantic leads, Lionel Barrymore Capra's mouthpiece, and Edward Arnold the capitalist who learns his lesson. Capra's name went right on the marquee with his stars, and he proved to be as big a magnet as they were. "You'll leave the movie house thinking it's pretty nice they have such things as movies," raved the Associated Press, "because movies have made you feel so very good."

London on the Hudson

Jack Warner was delighted that newcomer John Garfield placed third in the New York Film Critics Best Actor contest, behind second-place Spencer Tracy for *Boys Town* and *Test Pilot,* and first-place Warners star James Cagney for *Angels with Dirty Faces*. So that the two Warners actors would not compete with each other in the Oscar race, Warner demoted Garfield to the Best Supporting Actor race. Broadway name Margaret Sullavan won the New York Critics' Best Actress Award for *Three Comrades,* but neither Hollywood's Bette Davis nor Norma Shearer was runner-up. Second place had gone to British Wendy Hiller for *Pygmalion*. Britain claimed two other New York awards—*The Citadel* was Best Picture and Alfred Hitchcock Best Director for *The Lady Vanishes*.

The scribes inaugurated a Foreign Film Award and gave it to *Grand Illusion*. The *Hollywood Reporter* commented on "how burned the boys were in California over the Critics' votes going to foreign pictures. Asked how his new motion picture was reviewed in New York, a producer snapped, 'Considering it was made in America, it did very well in the notices.' " But the New Yorkers had not completely overlooked Hollywood—there was a special award to the year's most remarkable achievement, Walt Disney's *Snow White and the Seven Dwarfs*.

The Nominations

Grand Illusion was nominated by the Academy for Best Picture, as were *Pygmalion* and *The Citadel*. Both Leslie Howard and Robert Donat were competing for Best Actor with Yankees James

"You'll leave the movie house thinking it's pretty nice they have such things as movies, because movies have made you feel so very good."
—Associated Press

Cagney and Spencer Tracy, and Frenchman Charles Boyer in *Algiers*, his "Come-with-me-to-the-Casbah" role. *Pygmalion*'s Wendy Hiller was in the Best Actress race, along with Bette Davis, Norma Shearer and Margaret Sullavan. The fifth Best Actress nominee, Fay Bainter, pulled an unprecedented feat—she was nominated for both Best Actress and for Best Supporting Actress. Bainter supported Bette Davis in *Jezebel*, and was vying with her for the Best Actress Oscar for *White Banners*. *Screenland* magazine described her role in the latter: "Miss Bainter plays a strange woman who wanders out of a snowstorm to put new life and hope into the household of an absentminded schoolmaster and his disorganized family."

Director Michael Curtiz was nominated twice for Best Director—for *Angels with Dirty Faces* and *Four Daughters*. John Garfield held the lead in the Best Supporting Actor contest for *Four Daughters*. With Garfield, Fay Bainter, James Cagney and Bette Davis the expected winners in the four acting categories, all Jack Warner had to worry about was whether *The Adventures of Robin Hood* would defeat 20th Century–Fox's *Alexander's Ragtime Band*, an Irving Berlin musical, for Best Picture. The extras still voted for Best Picture and the acting Awards on the final ballot, but the Academy excluded them from the Best Song selection after the "Sweet Leilani" choice the previous year.

The Awards got dragged into the Hollywood labor wars one more time thanks to, of all people, Frank Capra. The Directors Guild saw what a great job Capra had done keeping the Academy afloat and elected him its president, too. He had his work cut out for him. Joseph Schenck of 20th Century–Fox was the head of the Association of Motion Picture Producers, and he refused to recognize the Directors Guild as the sole negotiating agent for directors. Capra called on the guild members to strike and then threatened to resign as president of the Academy and instigate a boycott of the Awards ceremony—which was only a week away—if the producers did not relent. The moguls had come to depend on the Awards for their publicity value and couldn't afford a strike, so Schenck told Capra that the AMPP was willing to meet the guild's demands. The banquet proceeded as if nothing had happened.

The Big Night

The gang from Warner Brothers was all there. Bette Davis swept in with an eight-man entourage that included current boyfriend William Wyler, ex-husband of fellow Best Actress nominee Margaret Sullavan. Spencer Tracy, hoping to pull off a Luise Rainer–style double win, came to the banquet, as did 1,250 other guests. A giant Oscar over the hotel entrance greeted them, and lead Oscar paperweights decorated place settings.

The Awards presentation began when Miliza Korjus, a former coloratura soprano from the Berlin Opera and a Best Supporting Actress nominee for MGM's biography of Richard Strauss, *The Great Waltz*, belted out "The Star-Spangled Banner." While Jerome Kern commenced the Music Awards by noting, "Of all the noises I think music is the least annoying," the Academy received a phone call from NBC Radio wanting to know why it had been double-crossed. The Academy had forbidden any radio coverage but, for several minutes, George Fisher had been broadcasting on local radio station KNX. Fisher, who had helped set up the hotel's public address system for the program, had also surreptitiously hung an extra microphone in the broadcast booth at the back of the room. Academy officials and Biltmore security guards began smashing through the door of the booth with axes, and Fisher decided it was time to sign off.

Had Fisher remained on the air a little longer, listeners would have heard the familiar voice of radio star Bob Hope, who was tapped for Oscar duty the year he arrived in Hollywood to make movies. Hope's theme song, "Thanks for the Memory," had been presented with a Best Song Oscar by Jerome Kern, and the orchestra reprised it as the comedian made his entrance. His assignment was to give the Short Subject Awards, but Hope took advantage of his captive audience. Eyeing the table holding the Oscars, Hope quipped, "Looks like Bette Davis' garage. I don't envy some of you. You make a good picture like *Marie Antoinette* once a year and then you sit down the other nine months and worry if it'll get an Academy Award." After a string of jokes, Hope gave Fred Zinnemann, who hadn't yet graduated to features, an Oscar for Best Two-Reel Short, and Walt Disney his sixth Cartoon Oscar.

Following Hope was novelist Lloyd C. Douglas, the author of *Magnificent Obsession*, who couldn't resist making a wisecrack when he announced George Bernard Shaw had won the Oscar for the screenplay of *Pygmalion*. "Mr. Shaw's story now is as original as it was three thousand years ago," Douglas observed. Shaw was not there to accept, or retort.

Edgar Bergen was back, this year to present a Special Award to the industry's two most profitable juveniles—Universal's Deanna Durbin and MGM's Mickey Rooney. Durbin was ready for the honor. "Two and a half years ago when I came into this business, I had one desire," the seventeen-year-old told the throng. "That was to be as good as I could be. Tonight you have made me very,

Awards Ceremony

FEBRUARY 23, 1939, 8:30 P.M.
A BANQUET AT THE BILTMORE BOWL OF THE BILTMORE HOTEL, LOS ANGELES

Your Host:
ACADEMY PRESIDENT FRANK CAPRA

Presenters

Music Awards	Jerome Kern
Cinematography	Frank Lloyd
Sound Recording	Frank Lloyd
Art Direction	Frank Lloyd
Short Subjects	Bob Hope
Writing Awards	Lloyd C. Douglas
Director	Fred Niblo
Picture	James Roosevelt
Special Awards	James Roosevelt
Thalberg Award	Joseph Schenck
Supporting Actor	Tyrone Power
Supporting Actress	Tyrone Power
Actor	Cedric Hardwicke
Actress	Cedric Hardwicke

"Isn't it beautiful and shiny, Mr. Disney?"
—Shirley Temple

very happy. My aspirations had not reached such a peak. I am extremely gratified." Mickey Rooney, eighteen, was on vacation, explained presenter Charlie McCarthy, who did a double take when he espied Frank Capra's bald spot at a nearby table. "Mickey, you're working too hard!" the dummy said. Bergen announced that Rooney's substitute acceptor was waiting in the audience. It was Mortimer Snerd.

There was a roar of approval when Fred Niblo revealed that the winner of the Best Director Award was Frank Capra for *You Can't Take It with You*. Capra was hardly over the surprise of winning his third Oscar when James Roosevelt, FDR's son and a Hollywood producer, announced that the Best Picture was *You Can't Take It with You*. Jack Warner applauded nervously—what was happening to the Warners sweep?

Capra admitted later that his triumph couldn't compare to the excitement of the next Award—a Special Oscar to Walt Disney for *Snow White and the Seven Dwarfs*. When the Academy said, "special," they weren't kidding. Instead of one lousy statuette, Disney received a specially designed trophy consisting of one Oscar, representing Snow White, flanked by seven dwarf Oscars descending in a row. The momentous task of making this presentation fell into the hands of Shirley Temple, now ten, who stood on a chair for the occasion. "Isn't it beautiful and shiny, Mr. Disney?" Temple asked. "Yes, I'm so proud of it, I'm going to burst," the winner said. "Oh, don't do that, Mr. Disney!" Temple exclaimed. Capra swore that this exchange "brought down the house."

As an inside joke, Capra asked Joseph Schenck, the head of the AMPP, to give the Thalberg Award, which was voted on by all Academy members that year. The winner was Hal Wallis, vice president in charge of production at Warner Brothers. Jack Warner began to relax a bit, but his comfort was cut short by Tyrone Power's announcement that the winner of the Best Supporting Actor Award was not John Garfield but, for the second time, Walter Brennan. Brennan had played an old coot in a Loretta Young vehicle called *Kentucky*. "The extras, again," Warner grumbled. But all was not lost for the mogul; Fay Bainter, as expected, won the Best Supporting Actress Oscar for *Jezebel*.

Sir Cedric Hardwicke stepped up to give the final acting Awards. The Best Actor was, for the second year in a row, Spencer Tracy for *Boys Town*. Tracy mainly praised Father Flanagan in his speech, saying, "If you have seen him through me, then I thank you." The double streak continued when Hardwicke called Bette Davis to the podium to claim Oscar number two for *Jezebel*. Davis gave all the credit to William Wyler and demanded that he take a bow. And then everybody danced.

Aftermath

"During this evening at the Academy, it was reported that a whisper of pique had been heard among the competitors," recalls screenwriter Frances Marion. "With only one Oscar a year for the best performer, was it cricket to let an individual actor or actress start a collection?"

For Davis, her Oscar win held a sense of déjà vu. No sooner had she won a second Oscar than she was feuding with Jack Warner over bad material again. She refused the next two scripts he offered her, and she was again put on suspension.

Tracy also found that winning an Oscar could spell trouble. For starters, the Academy made a mistake inscribing his trophy and sent it to him marked *Dick Tracy*. He sent it back to have the name fixed, and a MGM publicist announced that the actor was having the Oscar inscribed to Father Flanagan with plans to donate it to Boys Town. "Hold on a minute," Tracy protested, "I won it. I want to keep it." "But you have another one," the desperate publicist argued, afraid that Tracy was going to blow this humanitarian deed. "Not unless the Academy gives me another one to keep myself," Tracy insisted. The Academy obliged; Tracy had two, Boys Town one.

George Bernard Shaw also put up a fuss—he

was furious that the Academy was sending him anything at all. "It's an insult for them to offer me any honor, as if they had never heard of me before—and it's very likely they never have. They might as well send some honor to George for being King of England," the playwright declared. The Academy sent Shaw the Oscar anyway and Mary Pickford reported that when she visited him she saw the statuette proudly displayed on the mantel.

1939

"To me, Mr. Smith Goes to Washington is as great as Lincoln's Gettysburg speech."
—Hedda Hopper

Hollywood's giants played king of the mountain at the 1939 Awards and David O. Selznick won.

Frank Capra's fame was such that when he finished *Mr. Smith Goes to Washington,* the National Press Club insisted on throwing the premiere party in the nation's capital. The event was monumental enough for the club to open its doors to women for the first time in its history. There was a lot of indigestion at the dinner, however, when the gentlemen of the press saw themselves portrayed as heavy-drinking cynics in Capra's comedy about political corruption. The film was denounced in the U.S. Senate for "belittling the American system of government," and Joseph P. Kennedy, U.S. ambassador to England, wired President Roosevelt, the State Department, Will Hays and Harry Cohn to stop showing the movie overseas because it "will cause our allies to view us in an unfavorable light."

The Hollywood home team went on the defensive. Columnist Sheilah Graham called *Mr. Smith Goes to Washington* the "best talking picture ever made." Hedda Hopper swore, "To me, it is as great as Lincoln's Gettysburg speech." As the greenhorn scout leader who ends up in the Senate, James Stewart inspired *The Nation* to rave, "Now he is mature and gives a difficult part, with many nuances, moments of tragicomic impact. And he is able to do more than play isolated scenes effectively. He shows the growth of a character through experience." The review hoped that "after this success, Mr. Stewart in Hollywood will remain as uncorrupted as Mr. Smith in Washington." Harry Cohn wasn't above electioneering, though, and the mogul ran ads in the trade papers celebrating *Mr. Smith*'s unanimously favorable reviews. Prominently featured was *Screen Book*'s prediction: "Should win every Academy Award."

Best Supporting Actress winner Hattie McDaniel of Gone With the Wind *re-creates her moment of triumph for a newsreel filmed the day after the ceremony.*

Seven Strange Men

John Ford shared the laurels with Frank Capra as Hollywood's most critically acclaimed director, and he dazzled again in 1939 with, of all things, a western starring John Wayne, hero of countless low-budget cowboy movies from Republic and Monogram. *Variety* hailed "the beauty of *Stagecoach,*" which lay "not in its action nor its story, but in the powerful contrasts of personalities, the maturing of characters and the astounding suspense that director Ford achieves." The ads promised "2 Women on a Desperate Journey with 7 Strange Men," while *Life* called it "a sort of *Grand Hotel* on wheels." In the *New York Post,* Archer Winsten concluded that *Stagecoach* is "the best western since talking pictures began. It is so beautiful and exciting that maybe it ought not to be called a 'western.' "

Third Time Lucky

Just as *Stagecoach* served to introduce John Wayne to millions of moviegoers he hadn't reached before, *Wuthering Heights* presented them with a matinee idol from England, Laurence Olivier. This was Olivier's third shot at Hollywood stardom. In 1931 he had made three movies for RKO, but nobody paid attention and Olivier returned home. Two years later, he was back for the prestigious assignment of Greta Garbo's leading man in *Queen Christina* at MGM. No sooner had he started filming than Garbo, wanting to help out her ex-lover, John Gilbert, whose career had been done in by the talkies, decided she had to have him as her costar. Back to England Olivier went, where he emerged as one of the leading actors of the British stage. In 1939, Samuel Goldwyn asked him to try going Hollywood one more time.

The team of Olivier and Merle Oberon set audiences panting in Goldwyn's version of Emily Brontë's *Wuthering Heights*, directed by William Wyler. Viewers couldn't decide what impressed them more; Olivier's swarthy good looks or his in-

"Who wants to see some dame go blind and die?"
—Jack Warner

tense performance as Heathcliff. People also loved the atmosphere of the Yorkshire moors, even though the exterior shots were filmed in the San Fernando Valley. Hospitals reported that in the months following the release of *Wuthering Heights,* as many as a third of newborn girls were named Cathy after the film's heroine.

Cashing in Mr. Chips

MGM had already procured its own British matinee idol, Robert Donat, a year earlier for *The Citadel.* This year the studio sent him James Hilton's novel, *Goodbye, Mr. Chips,* about a lovable schoolteacher who ages from twenty-five to eighty-three. Sam Wood directed the sentimental tale in England, and Donat's costar was a young woman Louis B. Mayer had seen on the English stage in 1937 and signed immediately—Greer Garson. Both the critics and the public were moved to tears, and *Goodbye, Mr. Chips* made MGM a mint. Mayer considered Greer Garson his new protégée and rushed her into a starring vehicle, *Remember?*, a romantic comedy costarring Robert Taylor. The ads identified Garson as "Mrs. Chips," but moviegoers had short memories—*Remember?* didn't earn a nickel.

Lights Out

One actress who could do nothing but make money was Bette Davis, who had four hits in 1939: *Dark Victory, Juarez, The Old Maid* and *The Private Lives of Elizabeth and Essex. Dark Victory* had been an unsuccessful Broadway play with Tallulah Bankhead, and when Davis approached Jack Warner about buying the property he scoffed, "Who wants to see some dame go blind and die?" But Davis persevered and, figuring he owed her one, Warner gave in and let her play the socialite with a brain tumor. When *Dark Victory* opened early in the year, most of Hollywood conceded that the Best Actress Oscar was now spoken for and in the year-end poll of film exhibitors, Bette Davis was voted the second most popular actress in America, right behind Shirley Temple.

Garbo Laughs!

Ticket-buyers loved going to see Bette Davis suffer but they were no longer interested in spending time at a Greta Garbo tragedy. When theatre owner Harry Brandt called Garbo "box-office poison," MGM decided it was time to put her in a light comedy. There was still an attitude of nothing but the best for Garbo, and the studio assigned Ernst Lubitsch to direct *Ninotchka,* a romance about a coldhearted Russian spy who warms up under the influence of Paris nightlife. MGM's publicity genius Howard Dietz came up with the advertising slogan "Garbo Laughs!" After *Ninotchka* premiered, critics and audiences were laughing, too. And so were the executives at MGM, at that silly "box-office poison" label.

Dietrich Rides Again

Marlene Dietrich had also landed on the exhibitors' list of has-beens. She had been off the screen for two years, Hollywood having decided that the elaborate, European-flavored romances with which she was identified were out of vogue. The locale of her new movie was far from Morocco and Shanghai—*Destry Rides Again* took place in the American West. Dietrich played Frenchy, a saloon gal, to James Stewart's reluctant sheriff and she sang "The Boys in the Back Room" on a bar and wrestled with a jealous Una Merkel on the floor. The film opened in New York in November and the critics were ecstatic about the actress' flair for rowdy comedy. The *New York Daily News* wrote that "1939 will go down in cinema history as the year that turned Greta Garbo from the screen's greatest dramatic actress into one of its first comediennes and that brought that great sleeping beauty of the screen, Marlene Dietrich, back to life."

"The second coming of a great prophet couldn't match the first coming of Gable."
—Hollywood Reporter

Waiting for the Wind

The main topic of conversation in Hollywood throughout the year, however, was whether David O. Selznick would be able to pull off his mammoth undertaking of turning Margaret Mitchell's massive Civil War epic, *Gone With the Wind*, into a movie. For three years, gossip columns were filled with every conceivable detail about the production, and Selznick's search for an actress to play Scarlett O'Hara was one of the most successful publicity ploys in the history of Hollywood. Everyone in town knew that there had been problems during production, since director George Cukor had been replaced by Clark Gable's hunting buddy, Victor Fleming. Then Fleming had a nervous breakdown and was replaced by Sam Wood, the director of *Goodbye, Mr. Chips*. When the news came out that the picture had the unheard-of running time of three hours and forty minutes, rumors persisted that sheer logistics were turning this $4 million movie into "Selznick's Folly."

"It" Arrives

Despite the doomsayers, *Gone With the Wind* was undoubtedly the most eagerly awaited motion picture ever; a Gallup poll indicated that 56.5 million people were looking forward to it. When the film had its world premiere at Atlanta's Fox Theatre on December 15, the mayor gave all civic employees and school kids the day off and 300,000 people showed up to greet Selznick and company at the theater. A few days later the film opened in New York in an unprecedented dual premiere in two Times Square houses. The *New York Times*' Frank S. Nugent wrote, "Anyway, 'it' has arrived at last, and we cannot get over the shock of not being disappointed; we had almost been looking forward to that." By the time of the Hollywood premiere some two weeks later, no one thought that the *Hollywood Reporter* was overdoing it with the headline, "*Gone With the Wind*—Magnificent and Supreme Triumph of Film History." And when the box-office receipts were as unparalleled as the reviews, Harry Cohn and the others who had thought this was their year for the Oscars were running scared.

Revolution in New York

At the New York Film Critics meeting, proponents of *Mr. Smith Goes to Washington* refused to knuckle under; for thirteen long ballots, *Mr. Smith* and *Gone With the Wind* were tied, with neither side willing to budge. Finally, in order to go home, the critics reached a compromise and tossed the award to *Wuthering Heights*. The *Mr. Smith* contingent had to content itself with James Stewart's Best Actor win, the *Wind* contingent with a Best Actress award for Vivien Leigh's Scarlett O'Hara. Spreading the wealth, the newspaper crowd gave the Best Director award to John Ford for *Stagecoach*.

The *Hollywood Reporter* dubbed the results of the New York awards "a revolution." In addition to *Gone With the Wind*'s going one for four, the paper found it especially startling that "Bette Davis, who, up to this minute has won every critical voice as the best actress, had to take a back seat for Vivien Leigh." On the other hand, "we don't believe there will be much of a surprise on the selection of John Ford for the award for the best directing job of the year, because if ever direction stood out like a sore thumb, his work on *Stagecoach* was the greatest evidence of what fine direction could do for just an ordinary story."

The Nominations

If the New York Film Critics Awards had caused anyone to doubt that Selznick's magnum opus was the one to beat for the Academy Awards, *Gone With the Wind*'s record thirteen nominations put the issue to rest. In another year, such nominees as *Mr. Smith; Goodbye, Mr. Chips; Stagecoach; Ninotchka* and *Wuthering Heights* might well

"Laurence Olivier and Vivien Leigh are, for the moment, just about the most sacred of all Hollywood's sacred cows."
—Hollywood Reporter

have been front-runners, but this year their partisans could only hope for a major upset. Other Best Picture nominees just along for the ride were *Dark Victory,* Hal Roach's version of John Steinbeck's *Of Mice and Men,* Leo McCarey's *Love Affair* and MGM's musical-fantasy *The Wizard of Oz,* which had lost a million dollars for the studio.

The Best Director race provided a good opportunity for the competition to stem the *Gone With the Wind* tide since its nominee, Victor Fleming, was only one of at least three directors who worked on what was generally considered Selznick's achievement. Frank Capra was enormously popular and John Ford had the New York Film Critics Award going for him.

Still, Victor Fleming made it well known that he felt Selznick was taking too much credit for *Wind*'s success and that his own contributions were callously disregarded by the producer. Support for the martyred Fleming began to grow, and it seemed that perhaps the director of the biggest blockbuster in history might squeak by on a sympathy vote.

Move Over, Lindy

Chief among Fleming's supporters was Best Actor nominee Clark Gable, who claimed that Selznick's nit-picking had taken a year off the director's life. Gable had grown to dislike Selznick so much that he had threatened to skip the Atlanta premiere of the film. Mrs. Gable, a.k.a. Carole Lombard, finally persuaded her husband that Rhett Butler had to attend. Gable's reception in Atlanta had been so overwhelming that even Hollywood was amazed. "The second coming of a great prophet couldn't match the first coming of Gable," wrote an astonished *Hollywood Reporter.* "Lindbergh's arrival after his flight is the nearest thing to it."

Sacred Cows

Gable's nickname "The King" never seemed more appropriate, but his popularity by no means guaranteed him an Oscar. Both *Mr. Smith*'s James Stewart and *Mr. Chips'* Robert Donat had legions of admirers. The most popular Best Actor nominee of all was number-one box-office attraction Mickey Rooney, last year's winner of the Outstanding Juvenile Performance Award. The nineteen-year-old sensation was nominated for putting on a show in *Babes in Arms,* a Busby Berkeley musical. Louis B. Mayer publicly announced that he would use the Mick in a minimum of ten movies a year, while privately he asked the star of the Andy Hardy series to stop posing for publicity pictures at racetracks.

Wuthering Heights' Best Actor nominee Laurence Olivier loomed as a possible dark horse for the Oscar because of his romantic affiliation—he was engaged to Best Actress nominee Vivien Leigh. The wooing of Scarlett O'Hara by Heathcliff so captured the public's imagination that the *Hollywood Reporter* wrote that the two "are, for the moment, just about the most sacred of all Hollywood's sacred cows."

Garbo à-Go-Go

The hero worship didn't stop at the Los Angeles County line. *Time* treated Vivien Leigh like visiting royalty, running her picture on the cover of its Christmas-week issue. Having been sanctioned by the New York Film Critics, Leigh was favored for Best Actress, but one columnist thought that "Hollywood will stick by its favorite home-town girl, Bette Davis." Irene Dunne in *Love Affair,* Greer Garson in *Goodbye, Mr. Chips* and Greta Garbo in *Ninotchka* were also nominated, but they didn't stand a chance. MGM publicists nevertheless campaigned for Garbo by keeping gossip columnists informed of the recluse's activities. Typical items were "Garbo is examining naturalization laws and, it is believed, will file her first citizenship papers next week," and "Garbo, who's always wanted to be alone, is on a complete change of social diet on her numerous nightclub dates in New York." As for non-nominee Marlene Dietrich, she could shrug off her defeat to bad timing—Universal released *Destry Rides Again* in Los Angeles on January 12, 1940, a few hours after the Academy's extended eligibility deadline.

While the Academy had stated that "there should be no 'electioneering' or 'lobbying' as has been the case in the past," *Daily Variety* reported, "Paramount, for the first time, is really going after those Academy Oscars this year and is stimulating the studio voting urge with inciting posters stuck about the lot to get out and put the push behind the candidates." Paramount needed all the help it could get: the entire studio had five fewer nominations than *Gone With the Wind* alone.

The Big Night

Frank Capra had his hands full on Oscar night; in addition to being a nominee, he was a working director. In the last days of his presidential term he managed to make the Academy a fast $30,000 by selling Warners the right to film the banquet for a short subject. With Oscar-winning cinematographer Charles Rosher shooting away under Capra's direction, the Academy's 1,200 guests prepared for the roving cameras by dressing to the nines; *Daily Variety* estimated that "the ermine and mink and silks and satins that constituted the femme finery for the occasion represented an investment of better than half a million dollars."

The fans gave their loudest ovation to Vivien Leigh, who arrived on the arm of David O. Selznick. *Variety* took inventory of her outfit: "full-skirted flowered dress, covered with long ermine robe, heavy antique bracelet and huge precious stone pendant around the neck." Right behind Leigh was her fiancé, Laurence Olivier, with *his* arm around Olivia de Havilland, herself a Best Supporting Actress nominee for *Gone With the Wind*. De Havilland was wearing a "voluminous black evening dress with lace inserts and white ermine jacket." According to the *Hollywood Reporter,* "Every name of note in the industry in Hollywood was either a guest or a host." Three major names who were missing were nominees Robert Donat, Irene Dunne and Greta Garbo—apparently the MGM flacks hadn't convinced the Swede that she was really a party girl at heart.

One nominee who was very much visible was Hattie McDaniel, *Gone With the Wind*'s Mammy, and Olivia de Havilland's closest competitor for the Best Supporting Actress Oscar. The actress was covered in gardenias from head to collar and she received an ovation from the banquet guests as she and her date made their way to their table for two at the rear of the Coconut Grove.

Late arrivals were let in on some secrets. The *Los Angeles Times* had broken its vow with the Academy not to publish the names of winners until after the banquet. The 8:45 edition spilled the beans and Clark Gable and Bette Davis were among those who knew whether or not they were winners by the time they entered the Ambassador.

At 11, after dinner was finished, retiring Academy President Frank Capra opened the proceedings by reminding the guilds he was still on their side. "I believe the guilds should more or less conduct the operations and functions of the institution." He then introduced the new president, producer Walter Wanger, whom he described as "a fearless liberal." Wanger said that as president he would strive to create "an Academy that will see that our public relations are maintained on the same level as the great steel, iron and motor in-

Awards Ceremony

FEBRUARY 29, 1940, 8:30 P.M.
A BANQUET AT THE COCONUT GROVE AT THE AMBASSADOR HOTEL, LOS ANGELES

Your Host:
BOB HOPE

Presenters

Scientific and Technical Awards	Darryl F. Zanuck
Film Editing	Darryl F. Zanuck
Sound Recording	Darryl F. Zanuck
Cinematography	Darryl F. Zanuck
Art Direction	Darryl F. Zanuck
Special Effects	Darryl F. Zanuck
Music Awards	Gene Buck
Short Subjects	Bob Hope
Special Award to Judy Garland	Mickey Rooney
Director	Mervyn LeRoy
Writing Awards	Sinclair Lewis
Picture	Y. Frank Freeman
Special Award to Jean Hersholt, Ralph Morgan, Ralph Block and Conrad Nagel	Basil O'Connor
Thalberg Award	Dr. Ernest Martin Hopkins
Commemorative Award to Douglas Fairbanks	Walter Wanger
Supporting Actor	Fay Bainter
Supporting Actress	Fay Bainter
Actor	Spencer Tracy
Actress	Spencer Tracy

"I feel like I'm in Bette Davis' living room."
—Bob Hope

dustries." The audience heartily applauded and the only hitch to Wanger's speech was emigré director Alfred Hitchcock, seated at Wanger's guests of honor table, and fast asleep during the oration.

Darryl F. Zanuck gave out a slew of Awards and then Wanger introduced the "Rhett Butler of the air waves," Bob Hope, making his debut as master of ceremonies. "What a wonderful thing, this benefit for David Selznick," began Hope. There was loud, nervous laughter. Looking at the table of Oscars, the comedian echoed a joke from last year, "I feel like I'm in Bette Davis' living room."

Hope brought out Mickey Rooney by alluding to Fox's recent spate of historical biographies. "MGM plans to star Mickey Rooney in a super epic, portraying Don Ameche as a boy." The Mick presented his *Babes in Arms* leading lady, Judy Garland, with this year's miniature Oscar for the Outstanding Juvenile Performance for *The Wizard of Oz*. The seventeen-year-old returned the favor by singing "Over the Rainbow," which had earlier won Best Song. The costars moved to the press room, where photographers made Garland kiss Rooney so many times he spent the rest of the evening trying to get lipstick off his face.

Mervyn LeRoy settled the tight Best Director contest: the winner was Victor Fleming for *Gone With the Wind*. The audience sighed when David O. Selznick walked to the rostrum and explained that Fleming was "ill." Showing that there were no hard feelings, Selznick went on at length about the director's fine work.

Sinclair Lewis gave the writing Awards and had to wing it when neither of the winners showed up. *Gone With the Wind*'s Screenplay winner, Sidney Howard, had been run over by his tractor on his Massachusetts farm, thus becoming the first posthumous Oscar winner. Lewis Foster, the Original Story winner for *Mr. Smith Goes to Washington*, had a happier excuse for his absence: he was busily pacing the corridors of the L.A. hospital where his wife was giving birth.

Paramount executive Y. Frank Freeman was called upon to bestow the Best Picture Award. Since there was no longer any question as to what was going to win, Freeman kidded, "The only reason I was called upon to give this honor is because I have a Southern accent." When the producer of *Gone With the Wind* was called to the podium for the second time that night, Bob Hope quipped, "David, you should have brought roller skates." Handing Selznick the Award, Freeman drawled, "I present this trophy to you, David Selznick. But David, I never saw so many soldiers as were used in *Gone With the Wind*. Believe me, if the Confederate Army had had that many, we would have licked you damn Yankees." Selznick thanked the multitudes, but dwelled on Best Supporting Actress nominee Olivia de Havilland; clearly, he had read the *Los Angeles Times*. The crowd's reaction was recorded by *Movie and Radio Guide*: "There's a gasp at such outspoken praise, at the hint of disappointment he feels in her loss, then applause."

The Thalberg Award was given by Dr. Ernest Martin Hopkins, president of Dartmouth College, of which Academy President Wanger was an alumnus. Surveying his audience and its glitter, the academic observed, "It is the first time in my life that I have addressed such a gathering." After paying heed to the importance of the motion picture to "the eyes of the world," Dr. Hopkins gave the Thalberg bust to David O. Selznick, making his third visit to the microphone.

Fay Bainter announced the winners of the Supporting Awards. A timid and somewhat bewildered Thomas Mitchell nervously walked to the rostrum when he won Best Supporting Actor for *Stagecoach*. "I didn't think I was that good," confessed Mitchell, who had also played Scarlett O'Hara's father in *Gone With the Wind* and a newspaperman in *Mr. Smith*. "I don't have a speech, I'm too incoherent."

Bainter revealed the result of the Best Supporting Actress contest with a pomp usually reserved for coronations. "This is more than an occasion," Bainter proclaimed, her bosom swelling with such pride that it almost dislodged the fox stole clinging to her shoulders. "It is a tribute to a

"Hallelujah!" —Hattie McDaniel

country where people are free to honor noteworthy achievements regardless of creed, race or color." Since Bainter had felt no need to go on about equality when she gave the Award to Thomas Mitchell, it was obvious that the winner was Hattie McDaniel for *Gone With the Wind*. A "Hallelujah!" rang out from the back of the room and the audience gave McDaniel the biggest hand of the evening. McDaniel, beginning her studio-prepared speech with "This is the happiest moment of my life," pledged to be a credit to her race and to the motion-picture industry and thanked Selznick and her agent for helping her career. Then she choked, sobbed a barely audible "Thank you," and rushed back to her table, crying with her face buried in her hands. Loser Olivia de Havilland hurried from the Selznick table and ducked into the kitchen, where she burst into tears. Irene Mayer Selznick followed her, told her to grow up, that she'd have plenty of other chances for an Oscar and go to congratulate Hattie for her career pinnacle. "It was a learning experience for me," said Olivia, who promptly marched over to her costar's table to felicitate.

After this drama had settled down, Bob Hope introduced Spencer Tracy, presenter of the remaining acting Awards, by commending him for coming even though he was suffering from a strep throat. The Best Actor winner was the one absentee, Robert Donat for *Goodbye, Mr. Chips*. Although Tracy was a good friend of loser Clark Gable, he said he was "joyful" over Donat's victory and that he was sure his joy was "sincerely seconded by every past Award winner and the entire motion-picture industry."

Too nervous to eat earlier in the evening, Vivien Leigh could now relax. Tracy confirmed that she had won Best Actress for *Gone With the Wind*. She spoke briefly and ended by expressing gratitude to Tracy "for coming here tonight to give me the trophy after two days in the hospital." Observers noted that Bette Davis was waiting to congratulate Leigh when the winner got back to her table.

Aftermath

With the Awards over, the dissection of the choices began. The word was that Davis had lost to Leigh by a very small margin and that James Stewart had been neck-and-neck with Donat. Academy officials, steamed over the *Los Angeles Times'* breach of faith, were already discussing ways to protect the secrecy of the winners at next year's ceremony.

The *Hollywood Reporter* declared: "All that is Hollywood and all that ever hopes to be Hollywood turned out last night in a blaze of glory, with a fanfare and a pomp and circumstance that only the Academy Awards banquet can command." *Daily Variety* gave Spencer Tracy a headline all his own: TRACY QUITS HOSPITAL TO GIVE OSCARS. Tracy would never attend another Oscar ceremony.

Hattie McDaniel's victory was a top story. *Daily Variety* boasted: "Not only was she the first of her race to receive an Award, but she was also the first Negro ever to sit at an Academy banquet." An Oscar didn't mean total respect, however. A week later the paper noted, "In addition to her ability as an actress, Hattie McDaniel could pose as an ad for Aunt Jemima."

With a combination of eight Awards in competition and two Special Awards—production designer William Cameron Menzies' "mood enhancement" Award and Selznick's Thalberg—*Gone With the Wind* was now the all-time Oscar champ. Even so, the night turned out to be less than carefree for David O. Selznick. He regretted that Victor Fleming's illness had prevented a reconciliation and that Rhett Butler was sent home without an Oscar. In his biography of the producer, Bob Thomas recounts:

> *As he drove with [publicist] Russell Birdwell to the celebration party, David was strangely silent. Then he blurted, "I don't know why we didn't get the Best Actor Award for Gable. Somewhere you failed. You didn't put on the proper campaign; oth-*

erwise Clark Gable would have been sure to get it."

Later, after Birdwell didn't report to work for two days, Selznick called to apologize and said, "I was a pig. I worked so hard and waited so long, I got piggish and wanted everything."

Clark Gable was also upset with the way things had gone. Mrs. Gable tried to cheer up her husband on the way home: "Aw, don't be blue, Pappy. I just know we'll bring one home next year." "No, we won't," Gable responded. "This was it. This was my last chance. I'm never gonna go to one of these things again." "Not you, you self-centered bastard," Carole Lombard answered. "I mean me!"

1940

"All Ginger Rogers was interested in was the dough-re-mi on the dotted line."
—Louella Parsons

In 1940, the Academy decided the Awards ceremony should be a surprise party.

David O. Selznick was a busy man. In March 1940, less than a month after *Gone With the Wind* made its unprecedented sweep of the Oscars, the producer was back with his entry for the 1940 Awards. *Rebecca* was based on Daphne du Maurier's bestselling gothic love story and, after seeing what all that hype had done for *Gone With the Wind,* Selznick began whetting the public's appetite for the film version by having his flacks spread rumors about casting months before production. After Ronald Colman hemmed and hawed about playing the brooding leading man, Max de Winter, and William Powell was unavailable, Selznick cast Laurence Olivier, the heartthrob from *Wuthering Heights*. The producer then proceeded to tantalize the public over who would play the timid young Mrs. de Winter, a role that he felt was "second only to Scarlett O'Hara."

Scarlett O'Hara herself had been in the running, but Selznick felt Vivien Leigh's screen test was "terrible," so Laurence Olivier would not be acting opposite his fiancée. Others under consideration included Loretta Young, Margaret Sullavan, Olivia de Havilland and an unknown named Anne Baxter. But in the end, the producer decided that Olivia's sister, Joan Fontaine, had the vulnerability he was looking for. One columnist noted that if Fontaine, who had yet to achieve the popularity of her sister, "did not have an inferiority complex she would not be starring in *Rebecca*."

Selznick's big casting coup, however, was in signing Alfred Hitchcock, England's most successful director and the winner of the New York Film Critics Award in 1938 for *The Lady Vanishes*. Hitchcock's final British film was an adaptation of Daphne du Maurier's *Jamaica Inn,* but the fact that it died at the box office didn't shake Selznick's determination to have Hitchcock direct his du Maurier property. And Selznick never let Hitchcock forget whose property it was. The director, who was used to having free rein over his movies, was totally unprepared for Selznick's notorious memos, which came to him incessantly. More than two decades later Hitchcock commented, "When I came to America to direct *Rebecca,* David Selznick sent me a memo . . . I've just finished reading it . . . I think I may turn it into a motion picture . . . I plan to call it *The Longest Story Ever Told*."

But Hitch pulled it off—reviewers and audiences were bowled over by *Rebecca*. The *Los Angeles Times* called it a "worthy successor to *Gone With the Wind*." Olivier's status as a dashing romantic lead was solidified, Joan Fontaine was declared a star, and it was clear that Hitchcock's rotund figure was going to be part of Hollywood for a long time.

Real People

Rebecca opened in March, but it already had strong competition for the year-end Awards. *The Grapes of Wrath* had opened in January, and from the reviews it seemed likely that John Ford and Darryl F. Zanuck would be seeing Oscar's glory. Walter Winchell declared that the adaptation of John Steinbeck's novel about a nomadic Dust Bowl family was "better than the book." *New York Times* film critic Frank S. Nugent, who would later become John Ford's son-in-law and favorite screenwriter, wrote, "*The Grapes of Wrath* is just about as good as any picture has a right to be; if it was any better we just wouldn't believe our eyes." This type of talk led to record grosses in Times Square and the *Hollywood Reporter* predicted, "The effect that *Grapes* has had on New York audiences, we feel certain, will be more than duplicated in the other showings throughout the country, particularly in the hinterlands, which are

Best Actress hopeful Ginger Rogers arrives at the banquet with her most frequent companion—her mother.

"As for me, prizes are nothing. My prize is my work."
—Katharine Hepburn

certain to have a greater appreciation of the subject than a Gotham crowd."

Laugh, Clown, Laugh

The Grapes of Wrath was sobering stuff for 1940 audiences; those who preferred their social messages in a lighter vein had *The Great Dictator,* Charlie Chaplin's first film in four years. Not only did *The Great Dictator* give moviegoers their first chance to hear Chaplin speak on screen, it also presented the comedian in a dual role. Chaplin played both a Jewish barber one step removed from the Little Tramp, as well as Adolf Hitler, renamed Hynkel, Dictator of Tomania. Most critics called the film things like "important" and "urgent" and the finale in which Chaplin delivers a long, passionate plea for human decency was likened to Tom Joad's famous "they can't keep us down" speech in *The Grapes of Wrath.* President Roosevelt was so affected by the movie that Chaplin was invited to recite the speech at the Chief Executive's gala birthday party. The *Hollywood Reporter* noted that this marked "Chaplin's first official appearance in the District of Columbia since 1917 when he helped sell Liberty Bonds."

He's Okay

A number of reviewers felt that Hitler was hardly a laughing matter, but no one could help but crack up at Jack Oakie's Mussolini takeoff, Napaloni, dictator of Bacteria. Oakie was a cheerful comic from the Midwest who had starred in such programmers as *College Humor, College Rhythm* and *Collegiate*, and in this character part, critics finally took notice. *Daily Variety* marveled, "In *The Great Dictator* he throws his chest farther than Mussolini himself." Oakie had always been popular with the public. When, as a lark, he stopped by a theater in the San Fernando Valley showing *The Great Dictator* and signed autographs, the owner told him, "If you'd only let me advertise when you're coming, I wouldn't have to give away dishes."

Has-Been Hepburn

According to exhibitor Harry Brandt, to get people into a Katharine Hepburn movie in 1938, theater owners would have had to give away not only dishes, but also silverware, pots and pans, and maybe an automobile. Brandt put Hepburn, along with Joan Crawford, Marlene Dietrich, Greta Garbo, Edward Arnold and Mae West on his list of stars who were "box-office poison." Playwright Philip Barry came to Hepburn's rescue, tailoring the arrogant heroine of his new comedy *The Philadelelphia Story* to her personality. Agreeing to do the play on Broadway, the actress got not only a good role but a good deal—instead of a straight salary, she opted for a percentage of the profits and the film rights to the play. After becoming the toast of the Great White Way, Hepburn peddled the project in Hollywood, selling it to the highest bidder—MGM—and picking best friend George Cukor to direct.

Hepburn aided the film's box-office performance by taking the play on the road simultaneously with the movie's release. After the final performance in Philadelphia, she came on stage and told the audience that the comedy had saved her career because "most people considered me a has-been." She then asked the stage manager to keep the curtain up because "I don't ever want to see the curtain come down on 'our play.' " Telling the audience she wanted some souvenirs, Hepburn picked up a vase and a pair of andirons from the set, turned and walked off.

The movie version of *The Philadelphia Story* was a smash, and Hollywood welcomed Hepburn back with open arms. The *Hollywood Reporter* exhorted, "This lady is now the toast of the picture world, is the rave of every customer who has had an opportunity to see the picture and the performance." *Daily Variety* wisecracked that *The Philadelphia Story* was "a winner, in contrast to Philadelphia baseball" and "Katharine (Poison-at-the boxoffice) Hepburn seems to have discovered an antidote." Now that she was popular again, the

"If you'd only let me advertise when you're coming, I wouldn't have to give away dishes."

—Theater owner to Jack Oakie

town referred to her as "the new Katharine Hepburn." George Cukor wrote an essay with that title for the *Hollywood Reporter*'s year-end issue, in which he insisted,"It goes without saying that she has improved as an actress and that she is a more delightful and intelligent person than she was eight years ago."

No More Tap Shoes

Throughout the 1930s, it was Hepburn who got the plum dramatic parts at RKO while the studio kept Ginger Rogers doing what they felt she did best—musicals and light comedies. Now that Hepburn was at MGM, Rogers ruled the roost, insisting that her career be put on a no-dance diet. In December, the same month that her old rival opened in *The Philadelphia Story*, Ginger showed up as "Christopher Morley's White-Collar Girl" in the love story *Kitty Foyle*. The *New York Daily Mirror* raved, "Thrilling is the amazing development of the one-time Interstate Circuit hoofer and Broadway musical-comedy dancer who gives a spirited top-flight dramatic performance here, the equal of anything seen on the screen in years."

Since, as one columnist put it, RKO had been "sort of down in the mouth" for quite a while, it realized it had a good thing and decided that Ginger and *Kitty* should be pushed for Oscars. The studio gathered all of Rogers' good reviews and placed them in an ad in the trade papers under the heading "It's Unanimous!" The actress loved being in the spotlight, and in January she went to New York to be the guest of honor at the annual Stenographer's Ball. Emblematic of Ginger's popularity in Hollywood was that Louella Parsons was one of her biggest boosters even though Rogers had refused to appear gratis on the columnist's radio show. "All she was interested in, she explained, was the dough-re-mi on the dotted line, and apparently she meant what she said."

Great Scott

Kitty Foyle's director, Sam Wood, had also tackled Thornton Wilder in 1940, adapting *Our Town*, the drama set in a New Hampshire hamlet. He struck box-office gold with this one too, and again helped an ailing studio. United Artists was eager to field an entry in the Best Actress race, as well, placing its bets on newcomer Martha Scott, who was recreating her stage role as Emily Webb. Scott showed that she could make the Hollywood grade. *Daily Variety:* "Best Dressed Gal of the Week—Martha Scott at the Hollywood Brown Derby in a navy and white striped tailored suit designed by Irene Saltern featuring the new rounded shoulders."

Pistol Packin' Mama

Bette Davis made her annual bid for an Academy Award nomination with *The Letter*, William Wyler's remake of the Somerset Maugham tale for which Jeanne Eagels had been nominated in 1928–29. In the movie, Davis murders her lover, but in real life she married her lover, one Arthur Farnsworth, on New Year's Day, 1941. Neither Davis nor Warner Brothers did much Oscar campaigning, but Bette was up there with Martha Scott as a "Best Dressed Gal of the Week" for her "clever, self-designed slacks suit with a new kind of military aspect."

Scandal in New York

The New York Film Critics had good memories this year; eleven months after opening, *The Grapes of Wrath* won their awards for Best Picture and Best Director. For the acting awards, the critics chose Charlie Chaplin in *The Great Dictator* and Katharine Hepburn in *The Philadelphia Story*. But before Chaplin and Hepburn could savor their awards, scandal broke out. Critic Lee Mortimer of the *Daily Mirror* turned stoolie and revealed that Bosley Crowther had induced the scribes to vote

"If Joan Fontaine did not have an inferiority complex she would not be starring in Rebecca."
—New York Journal-American

for Chaplin with the argument "He'll be a swell free attraction for us" on the radio broadcast of the awards presentation. The disgruntled Mortimer also indicated that most of the critics had not favored Hepburn, switching their votes only after a filibuster by the fellow from the *World-Telegram.* Hedda Hopper reported that these revelations had severely damaged the Oscar chances of Hepburn and Chaplin and not even Chaplin's refusal of the New York award seemed to put him into Hollywood's good graces.

The Nominations

For the second year in a row, a David O. Selznick movie had the most Academy Award nominations; *Rebecca* led the pack with eleven, including nods for Laurence Olivier, Joan Fontaine, Alfred Hitchcock and Judith Anderson, the classical stage actress who shivered movie audiences as the creepy housekeeper Mrs. Danvers. Other films popular with Academy voters were *The Grapes of Wrath* and *The Letter* with seven nominations each, and *The Philadelphia Story, Our Town,* John Ford's *The Long Voyage Home* and Alfred Hitchcock's *Foreign Correspondent,* six apiece. In addition to Fontaine, Best Actress contenders were Ginger Rogers, Martha Scott, Bette Davis and the controversial New York winner, Katharine Hepburn.

Like Hepburn, Charlie Chaplin managed to sneak in. Besides Olivier, the other Best Actor candidates were Raymond Massey as *Abe Lincoln in Illinois,* Henry Fonda as Tom Joad in *The Grapes of Wrath* and James Stewart in *The Philadelphia Story.* Stewart had a steady stream of hits this year with *Destry Rides Again* in January and continuing with *The Shop Around the Corner, The Mortal Storm* and *The Philadelphia Story.* His role as a reporter in *The Philadelphia Story* was secondary to Katharine Hepburn's and even costar Cary Grant's, but since *The Philadelphia Story* opened in December, it was the Stewart film freshest in the voters' minds. The race seemed to be between ex-roommates Stewart and Fonda. Stewart had all those successes—and the fact that he hadn't won the previous year for *Mr. Smith Goes to Washington*—going for him and Fonda was riding on the affection for *The Grapes of Wrath.* At a New York nightclub, Fonda was urged by an emcee to come on stage—in his tuxedo—and recite his climactic speech from the movie. As an indication of his versatility, Fonda proved himself an adroit comedian in Preston Sturges' *The Lady Eve,* which opened around the time the nominations were released.

No Man o' War

Taking a gander at the nominations, *Daily Variety* stated, "This is what old-fashioned bookies would call an open race. Meaning that there is no Man o' War on the track . . . There is more betting on the current Oscar Derby than there was last year when *GWTW* galloped home by 40 lengths." *Daily Variety* was well-versed in such racing terms; bowing to the demand of its readers, it published the odds from Santa Anita every day. With its readership in mind, the paper gave the lowdown: "Odds of 8 to 5 are being offered that the winner of this year's Best Production Award will be decided between *Rebecca, Grapes of Wrath* and *Our Town.*"

Let's Do It Again

Although *Rebecca* had come in first in the *Film Daily* poll of the nation's movie reviewers, it had been shut out by the New York crowd and was only tenth with the National Board of Review, which selected *The Grapes of Wrath* as the year's best. Selznick knew he had to get on the stick if he was going to be a two-in-a-row Oscar winner. *Rebecca* had been out of circulation for several months, so the day after the nominations were announced, Selznick held a second gala "premiere" for *Rebecca* at the Hawaii Theatre, a B-movie showcase on Hollywood Boulevard. At this second premiere, Selznick read a joint resolution he had managed to wangle from the governor of California and the mayor of Los Angeles, temporarily changing the name of Hollywood Boulevard to "Rebecca Lane." He also unveiled an extremely large seat that had been installed in the Hawaii with the inscription RESERVED FOR ALFRED HITCHCOCK.

The Envelope, Please

In addition to the lack of a clear-cut favorite in any category, Hollywood was buzzing over the Academy's latest innovation—the sealed envelope. Having gotten burned by the *Los Angeles Times* the previous year when the paper published the voting results before it was supposed to, the Academy decided to have the identities of the winners remain absolutely secret until they were announced at the banquet. The suspense heightened the town's enthusiasm for the Awards so much that the Academy, swamped with requests for tickets, had to send back what the *Reporter* said was "$500 in reservations sent in by persons not identified with the business." Columnist George Phair poeticized, "No more the flu germs hang around to peril and affright us/Instead, the town is ailing with a wave of Oscaritis."

The Big Night

With the fanfare of a gaudy Hollywood premiere, the Academy installed a fifteen-foot neon Oscar over the doorway of the Biltmore Bowl. James Stewart was the only Best Actor nominee to come, but three Best Actress finalists were there: Bette Davis, Joan Fontaine and Ginger Rogers. Although not nominated for her American debut in *Down Argentine Way,* Fox's newest sensation, Carmen Miranda, entered like a winner—her silver turban really got the fans worked up. Unfortunately, the spectators were denied the pleasure of seeing the evening's most dramatic entrance: Carole Landis descending the grand stairway into the Biltmore Bowl only to have her slip drop from beneath her gown and land at her ankles.

Less conspicuous was party-crasher Helen Boardly, a reporter for the Manual Arts High School paper, who cornered Bette Davis in the lobby for an interview. Jane Plowman and Trudy Marshall, two winners of *Look* magazine's "Hollywood Visit Contest," were photographed for the magazine and covered by columnists. Some doubted that the contest was exactly on the up-and-up—Trudy had already appeared in a movie for Fox, *Secret Agent from Japan*.

The ceremony began at 8:45 with a radio address from President Roosevelt, broadcast nationally and through speakers outside the Biltmore for the benefit of the fans there. Roosevelt had been invited by his Academy counterpart Walter Wanger to attend the banquet, but the President said that the international situation being what it was, he had better stay put in Washington. For six minutes, Roosevelt lauded Hollywood for its defense fund-raising efforts, pushed his Lend-Lease bill and praised filmmakers for promoting "the American way of life."

Many of the Academy's guests couldn't hear the President. An Academy official was loudly telling them how they should look while listening because they were being photographed by a newsreel film crew. Feeling like an extra as the cameras filmed him applauding at the end of the speech, one wag remarked, "Surely we'll get a $7.50 check for this."

When Roosevelt finished, he was thanked by Walter Wanger and Bette Davis, who said, "Mr. President, I have followed your leadership for years with pleasure, but to follow you on tonight's program is not an easy task. I never dreamed I would be on the same bill as the President of the United States." Judy Garland sang "America" to the Chief Executive while her boyfriend, composer David Rose, listened at the MGM table where Louis B. Mayer writhed in Republican anguish. Dinner was then served.

At 10 o'clock a special birthday cake was brought out for Joan Bennett, a.k.a Mrs. Walter Wanger. After his wife was taken care of, Wanger gave a short speech in which he paid tribute to the

Awards Ceremony

FEBRUARY 27, 1941, 8:45 P.M.
A BANQUET AT THE BILTMORE BOWL OF THE
BILTMORE HOTEL, LOS ANGELES

Your Host:
ACADEMY PRESIDENT WALTER WANGER

Presenters

Film Editing	Darryl F. Zanuck
Sound Recording	Darryl F. Zanuck
Special Effects	Darryl F. Zanuck
Art Direction	Darryl F. Zanuck
Scientific and Technical Awards	Darryl F. Zanuck
Cinematography	Rosalind Russell
Special Award to Nathan Levinson	Col. J. O. Mauborgne
Short Subjects	Bob Hope
Special Award to Bob Hope	Walter Wanger
Music Awards	B. G. DeSylva
Writing Awards	Quentin Reynolds
Director	Frank Capra
Picture	Mervyn LeRoy
Supporting Actress	Lynn Fontanne
Actress	Lynn Fontanne
Supporting Actor	Alfred Lunt
Actor	Alfred Lunt

"Bette Davis drops in at these affairs every year for a cup of coffee and another Oscar."
—Bob Hope

industry, predicting that films would be greater than ever in 1941. Wanger also praised the Academy's founding fathers for conceiving the Academy fifteen years earlier: "It just shows what a Hollywood idea can do when it's right."

Darryl F. Zanuck, now using the appellation "Lieutenant Colonel," opened his presentation of the Technical Awards with a "little people" speech: "Technicians are very often editorially neglected. They are the people who work miracles and wonders behind the scenes." In presenting the Cinematography Awards, Rosalind Russell was more specific about what behind-the-scenes wonder-workers cameramen were: "It is miraculous how these unsung heroes make us actresses look—like we don't."

Wanger then introduced "Private" Bob Hope as emcee for the rest of the evening. Looking at the Oscars, Hope cracked, "What's the matter, did Selznick bring them back?" Spotting Bette Davis in the crowd, he said, "Bette drops in at these affairs every year for a cup of coffee and another Oscar . . . And how 'bout these secret ballots? Columnists have exerted every trick to discover the winners beforehand and when the last envelope was sealed, Price, Waterhouse had to open it again to let Sidney Skolsky out."

After Hope issued the Short Subjects Awards, Walter Wanger reappeared and said, as Hope stood by uncertainly, "It gives me a real pleasure to give a humanitarian award to Bob Hope, in recognition of his unselfish services for the motion-picture industry, a special plaque honoring him as the man who did the most for charity in 1940." Hope was speechless, finally saying,"I don't feel a bit funny. It's a kick—it's a beautiful thing." He kissed the plaque and then introduced the head of Paramount, B. G. DeSylva, to present the Music Awards: "He's just loaned me to Sam Goldwyn for one picture. Sort of a lend-louse bill."

The Academy had congratulated itself for getting the highly regarded British war correspondent Quentin Reynolds to give out the writing Awards, but the Board of Governors was soon ruing his presence. Reynolds had produced one of the one-reel Short Subject nominees, *London Can Take It,* about war conditions in Britain, but he had lost to *Quicker 'n a Wink*, a demonstration of stop-action photography made by MGM's Pete Smith, who had run campaign ads in *Daily Variety*. Now that he was at the dais, Reynolds went ahead and gave an acceptance speech anyway. He said he understood "why Hollywood and the Academy had engaged Mr. Price and Mr. Waterhouse to count the ballots. No one in the movie colony could count up to 12,000. Yes, there are a couple of producers who could count that high—but not in English." A columnist wrote that Reynolds "arrived with fanfare in Hollywood, but did not return with it."

Reynolds was quickly upstaged by the three writing winners. In an instance of life imitating art, Benjamin Glazer, accepting the Best Original Story Award for *Arise My Love,* an anti-isolationist comedy set in contemporary Europe, said that the name of his collaborator, John S. Toldy, was a pseudonym. Glazer added that "Toldy" was currently in Nazi Germany and he could not risk jeopardizing his partner's life by divulging his true identity to the guests at the Biltmore.

The tone lightened when Preston Sturges, who, the *Hollywood Reporter* said, "burst over Hollywood like a comet" in 1940, won the Original Screenplay Award for his political satire, *The Great McGinty*. The meteoric success told the audience, "Mr. Sturges isn't here this evening but I will be happy to accept the Award for him." The jocularity continued when Best Screenplay winner Donald Ogden Stewart stammered, "I envy the boys who get the Technical Awards. They don't have to get nervously drunk before. There has been so much niceness here tonight, that I am happy to say that I am entirely—and solely—responsible for the success of *The Philadelphia Story*."

Presenting the Best Director Award, Frank Capra called all the nominees to the podium and suggested they shake each other's hands for jobs well done. Warily, George Cukor, Alfred Hitchcock, Sam Wood and William Wyler followed or-

"Awards are nice, but I'd much rather have a job."
—Jane Darwell

ders. Then, recalling his own humiliation seven years earlier, Capra opened the envelope and discovered that the winner was John Ford for *The Grapes of Wrath,* who had told reporters that he and Henry Fonda would be in a boat off the coast of Mexico "for as long as the fish are biting." While the losing directors crawled back to their tables, Darryl Zanuck stepped forward and accepted for Ford, thanking John Steinbeck "for writing one of the great American novels."

President Wanger rematerialized to deliver another broadside. To the disappointment of the producers who had been longingly eyeing the Irving G. Thalberg Award all evening, Wanger declared that there would be no presentation of the Award because "the Academy did not think any individual in the industry deserved it." *Daily Variety* called this "the biggest surprise of the dinner."

Mervyn LeRoy came to the podium to present the Best Picture Award. At this point none of the nominees had received more than one Award, so last-minute bets were being made up to the opening of the envelope. David O. Selznick's ballyhooing had accomplished its aim: the winner was *Rebecca*. Although Selznick's achievement of consecutive Best Picture Oscars was a first, he apparently didn't have much to say about it—none of the accounts of the ceremony quoted him.

The final Awards, for acting, were given by the theater's Alfred Lunt and Lynn Fontanne. Appearing in Los Angeles on a road tour of *There Shall Be No Night,* the 1931–32 acting losers regally distributed the remaining trophies. The crowd warmly applauded the selection of Jane Darwell as Best Supporting Actress for *The Grapes of Wrath*. Darwell told reporters that she hadn't worked in seven months and that "awards are nice, but I'd much rather have a job."

The Best Supporting Actor Award did not go over as well with the audience. When Lunt called out the name of Walter Brennan—his third, and totally unexpected, win—for his role as Judge Roy Bean in *The Westerner,* the gathering gasped. Everyone had figured the winner would be either Jack Oakie or James Stephenson, who played Bette Davis' attorney in *The Letter*. Mrs. Jack Oakie burst into tears. Brennan meekly expressed his thanks, and during the applause, Oakie told friends that Brennan won because the extras always voted for him out of loyalty since he had come from their ranks.

The whistling and cheering resumed when Fontanne revealed that the Best Actress was Ginger Rogers in *Kitty Foyle*. According to the *Hollywood Reporter,* "There was a thunderous outburst of spontaneous approval as the little Rogers gal, overcome with emotion, was handed her Oscar." Ginger said as the tears washed down her cheeks, "This is the greatest moment of my life. I want to thank the one who has stood by me faithfully—my mother. " In fact, Ginger's mother *was* standing by her—Mrs. Lela Rogers had escorted her daughter to the rostrum. When the mama's girl had returned to her seat, loser Joan Fontaine, who also toiled at RKO, rushed over with congratulations.

The decibel level was raised even higher as James Stewart won Best Actor for *The Philadelphia Story*. Plate-rattling augmented the shrieks and clapping that carried the winner to the stage. True to his screen image, Stewart gulped loudly at the microphone before speaking slowly and carefully. "I want to assure you that this is a very, very important moment in my life," he began. "As I look around the room a warm feeling comes over me—a feeling of satisfaction, pride, and most of all, gratefulness for the encouragement, instruction and advantage of your experience that have been offered to me since I came to Hollywood and with all my heart I thank you." The *Los Angeles Examiner* observed, "As he has done in many a wild motion-picture scene, he stumbled dazedly back to his table amid shouts and applause."

Aftermath

After a night of revelry, James Stewart made his way home early in the morning. His current roommate, Burgess "Buzz" Meredith, was wait-

"There has been so much niceness here tonight, that I am happy to say that I am entirely—and solely—responsible for the success of The Philadelphia Story."
—Donald Ogden Stewart

ing up and, seeing the Oscar, cracked, "Where'd you get that thing—Ocean Park Pier?" Stewart called his father in Indiana, Pennsylvania, and Dad, who ran a hardware store, instructed his son to send him the statuette. There Jimmy Stewart's Oscar sat in a glass case that had formerly displayed kitchen knives.

When reporters located no-show Katharine Hepburn to get her reaction to the Awards, the actress insisted, "I was offered *Kitty Foyle* and I didn't want to play a soap opera about a shopgirl." Hepburn added, "Ginger was wonderful, she's enormously talented and she deserved the Oscar. As for me, prizes are nothing. My prize is my work."

As for Ginger, she took a day off to recuperate from celebrating. When she returned to the set of *Tom, Dick and Harry,* the entire cast and crew—including Burgess Meredith—greeted her in top hat and tails. Ginger was in such good spirits she gave a fake Oscar to Dorothy Panter for being the "Best Stand-In of 1940."

When Dudley Nichols, who had turned down the 1935 Screenplay Oscar for John Ford's *The Informer,* wired his felicitations to this year's winning director, Ford wrote back, "Awards are a trivial thing to be concerned with at times like these." Ford was being a little harsh; the Academy *had* contributed in its own way to British morale—British producer Alexander Korda's lavish *The Thief of Bagdad* had captured three technical Awards, more Oscars than any other film.

Twentieth Century–Fox took its contractee Jane Darwell to task for mouthing off about not getting work. Studio flacks told the press that over the past seven months she had worked at the studio for twenty-one weeks and an additional month at Warners on loanout. Furthermore, Zanuck called her personally the day after the Oscars to offer her a co-starring role in *Private Nurse,* starring Sheldon Leonard. Zanuck himself was criticized when the Fox Movie Tone News coverage of the Oscar ceremony included footage of only Fox's employees—Darwell, composer Alfred Newman and Zanuck accepting for Ford—receiving their Oscars.

The *Los Angeles Mirror* criticized the Academy for the sealed envelope, claiming it prevented the newspapers from meeting their deadlines and allowed the press to be scooped by radio. The Academy Awards, argued the *Mirror,* owed everything to press coverage and was showing a shocking lack of gratitude. But the secrecy element had captured the public's imagination and, by next year, the *Mirror* would be playing up the suspense aspect of the Awards just like everybody else.

1941

"Of course we fight. What two sisters don't battle?"
—Olivia de Havilland

Nineteen forty-one saw the outbreak of war—Joan Fontaine took on her sister Olivia de Havilland while Hollywood battled a young hotshot named Orson Welles.

Local Boy Makes Bad

RKO was hurting for money and it couldn't attract the top names in Hollywood because it couldn't afford them. So the studio began to hunt for new talent. It didn't take long for the company to find twenty-five-year-old Orson Welles; in fact, it would have been hard to overlook him. The young man had already made history with the Mercury Theatre broadcast of H.G. Wells' *The War of the Worlds* on Halloween night, 1938. Luckily for RKO, the Mercury Theatre was short on funds when the studio came a-courting, and Welles consented to come to Hollywood to make a movie.

After he got a tour of the studio facilities, Welles said, "This is the biggest toy-train set any boy ever had." For his film debut, Welles settled on a script by Herman J. Mankiewicz about an eccentric publishing tycoon, and recruited actors from the Mercury Theatre to interpret it. RKO gave him total artistic control because, after all, how much trouble could the tyro get into on such a small budget?

In her autobiography, *Tell It to Louella*, Louella Parsons boasts, "I believe I have carried only one grudge for any length of time and that was against Orson Welles. I feel justified." Parsons, who was employed by publisher William Randolph Hearst, explained:

> *When Orson, characterized as the "boy genius," came to Hollywood, I was one of his biggest boosters. He was born in Grande Tour, Illinois, just six miles from Dixon, and I had known his family. I was delighted to give a boost to a local boy who had made good.*
>
> *Then when I heard that the film he was making,* Citizen Kane, *was about Mr. Hearst, I called him to ask if this was so.*
>
> *"Take my word for it," he said, "it isn't. It's about a completely fictional publisher."*
>
> *I took his word, and so informed the Hearst editors who kept insisting that it did concern Mr. Hearst.*
>
> *Then Orson pulled one of the classic double crosses of Hollywood. He arranged for Hedda Hopper to see parts of the picture.*

Hedda couldn't wait to get on the phone to tell Hearst that Louella hadn't told him the truth—*Citizen Kane* was indeed about William Randolph Hearst. Some twenty years later, Louella wrote, "I am still horrified by the picture . . . The boy genius certainly used all his talents just to do a hatchet job."

T.K.O. RKO

Hearst's attorneys told the boss he had a good case for libel against RKO, so in late 1940 the publisher dangled the threat of a lawsuit before the studio's executives. RKO held up *Kane*'s release for two months until its lawyers convinced the studio that such a suit was groundless. In December 1940, Hearst retaliated by ordering his publications to omit all references to RKO and its films. The immediate effect of this executive order was the pulling of a laudatory review of *Kitty Foyle*, which RKO had just opened to qualify for the 1940 Oscars. And the publisher also let it be known that he would not look too favorably upon any theater chains that saw fit to book *Citizen Kane*. Afraid of losing the all-important newspaper advertisements, the major theater chains told RKO they wanted nothing to do with the movie.

Many of Hearst's friends came to his defense, and Hearst traveled in all the best circles: RCA

Best Actor winner Gary Cooper watches Best Actress winner Joan Fontaine gloat. Not pictured: Fontaine's sister, Best Actress loser Olivia de Havilland.

"I have carried only one grudge for any length of time and that was against Orson Welles. I feel justified."
—Louella Parsons

head David Sarnoff, Fox's Nicholas Schenck, MGM's Joseph Schenck, Sam Goldwyn, Louis B. Mayer, and various Rockefellers pleaded with RKO to take the publisher up on his offer to pay for the production cost himself if the studio would burn the negative of the film. Even when Hearst threw a bonus of several thousand dollars into his offer, RKO still said no.

Teaching 'Em a Lesson

Meanwhile, Orson Welles was busy alienating collaborator Herman J. Mankiewicz. During production, Mankiewicz, a Hollywood veteran, had been amused by the boy wonder's bravado, quipping, "There but for the grace of God goes God." But when the director said he wanted sole writing credit on the finished film, claiming that he had rewritten most of it, Mankiewicz took the matter down to the Screen Writers Guild, and got to keep his co-credit. Welles angered the Hollywood community further by calling film producers "stupid" in a lecture at New York's New School, and then committed blasphemy by scoffing that "David Selznick thinks *Gone With the Wind* is art and will go to his grave thinking so."

RKO had sought the advice of so many industryites on what to do with *Kane* that it seemed as if *tout le Hollywood* had seen the film before it opened and the studio scratched plans for a $5.50-a-ticket gala Los Angeles premiere. When *Citizen Kane* finally premiered in New York at the independently owned Palace Theatre on Broadway, Bosley Crowther of the *New York Times* wrote that *Kane* had come "within the withering spotlight as no other film has ever been before." The *New York Post* raved, "The interlocking jigsaw puzzle of human personalities and their relationships to each other simply doesn't appear in other American motion pictures. *Citizen Kane* has the field to itself." In Hollywood, Sidney Skolsky wrote, "I still remember what William Wyler, Leo McCarey and other great directors said after seeing *Citizen Kane.* They claimed that Welles, in his first effort, had given them all lessons." But Welles' biggest Hollywood booster was Louella's rival, Hedda Hopper, who, despite entreaties from Louis B. Mayer and Sam Goldwyn, went right ahead with her six-part radio program glorifying Welles' life and accomplishments. Though a cause célèbre, *Citizen Kane* was a failure to Hollywood's way of thinking—it didn't make money.

Sgt. Cooper and Lady Stanwyck

What was making money was *Sergeant York,* a patriotic tribute to a hillbilly World War I war hero, played by Gary Cooper, a perennial top ten box-office star. *Sergeant York* was the year's top-grossing film, and the Veterans of Foreign Wars were so moved that they gave Cooper their "Distinguished Citizenship Medal" at a ceremony attended by the real-life Sergeant Alvin York, who had insisted on Cooper when he sold the film rights to his life.

When he wasn't shooting Germans onscreen, Cooper was romping with Barbara Stanwyck in two other hits, Frank Capra's *Meet John Doe* and Howard Hawks' *Ball of Fire.* Stanwyck also scored with Henry Fonda in Preston Sturges' sex farce *The Lady Eve. Daily Variety* commented in March, "The Hollywood contingent is already nominating Barbara Stanwyck for a 1941 Oscar. By the time the next annual Awards banquet rolls around she will have been in three top roles, any one of which might qualify her for a statuette."

Stars on Parade

As the year unfolded, Stanwyck's Oscar competition appeared to be a lineup of some of Hollywood's most glamorous stars: Joan Crawford as an ugly crook who reforms after having her face remodeled in *A Woman's Face,* Greer Garson as a woman who opens an orphanage in *Blossoms in the Dust,* Bette Davis as Regina Giddens in *The Little Foxes,* and Olivia de Havilland as a plain-jane spinster who winds up with Charles Boyer in *Hold Back the Dawn.*

Hey, Wait for Me

At literally the last minute, Olivia's sister, Joan Fontaine, also found herself a Best Actress fa-

"You'll never work in this town again."
—Darryl F. Zanuck to Bette Davis

vorite for *Suspicion,* in which she played her second shy Hitchcock heroine. The movie was not scheduled to play Los Angeles until late January, but after Fontaine won the New York Film Critics prize, RKO wised up and got *Suspicion* into the Pantages for one day—January 11, the last day of eligibility for the '41 Awards. Then, in a rare show of camaraderie, Universal agreed to postpone the opening of its latest Deanna Durbin vehicle, *It Started with Eve,* so that RKO could have two theaters in which to display *Suspicion* for Academy voters.

Putting Orson in His Place

The New York Film Critics threw another curve ball in the Oscar game. The scribes chose *Citizen Kane* as their Best Picture, but passed over Orson Welles for Best Director. The critics chose their old favorite, John Ford, who won his fourth Critics Award for Fox's expensive family drama set in a Welsh mining town, *How Green Was My Valley,* which Darryl Zanuck had intentionally opened on the last day of Oscar eligibility in order to keep it fresh in Academy members' minds. The New Yorkers agreed with the Veterans of Foreign Wars and gave their Best Actor Award to *Sergeant York*'s Gary Cooper.

Despite the Critics Award, Gene Autry's Pittsburgh fan club was determined to turn the tide of a Cooper victory at the Academy banquet. The club obtained 27,398 signatures from thirty states on its petition, "An Oscar for Autry," and requested that the Academy nominate the top-ten cowboy star for one of his 1941 vehicles: *Sunset in Wyoming, Back in the Saddle* or *Sierra Sue.*

Doing It for Defense

The Academy's grandiose plans for the 1941 banquet were cut short with the news that the Japanese had bombed Pearl Harbor. Nightly blackouts prohibited the usual glitter and pomp, so traditional Hollywood glamour was suddenly out of the question. Bette Davis, the recently elected Academy president, proposed that the ceremony take place in a theater and be open to the public. She suggested that Rosalind Russell, a whiz at arranging charity events, be in charge of the proceedings, with the money earned from the $25 tickets going to the British War Relief. The Board of Governors sat in stunned silence. Finally, former Academy President Walter Wanger asked, "What have you got against the Academy, Bette?" Last year's Awards banquet chairman, Mervyn LeRoy, piped up that his feelings were hurt that Davis wanted Rosalind Russell for his job.

No Banquet

On December 17, the board announced that there would be no Academy banquet but that the Awards would be given in a different, yet to be determined format. In the words of the *Hollywood Reporter,* "Bejeweled stars with trailing ermine, and all the hothouse trappings that are traditional for that internationally renowned night is being sloughed in view of existing war conditions."

W.R. Wilkerson, *Reporter's* editor, took the news badly: "The Academy offers a poor example to all our people and makes a pretty hefty thrust at national morale by calling off an event that has been a good diversion for the movie bugs of our country—which means a big slice of the U.S. population."

The criticism came from as far away as Britain and Australia, where the press insisted that the excitement and the glamour of the ceremony would take their people's minds off of the fighting.

Bette Beats It

"I told you so," Bette Davis said. Still, the Academy wouldn't go along with her idea to invite the public to the party. Rumors began to circulate that Davis was about to resign the presidency in protest and Darryl F. Zanuck, the head of 20th Century–Fox, told the actress, who was under contract to Warner Brothers, "If you resign, you'll never work in this town again." Nevertheless, the

"There but for the grace of God goes God."
—Herman J. Mankiewicz

thirty-three-year-old Davis stepped down, citing time constraints and health reasons. Her predecessor, Walter Wanger, filled in as acting Academy president.

On January 30, the Academy announced that it was reinstating the banquet "to boost civil morale." The board had made some changes, though. The banquet was to be referred to as a "dinner," there would be music but no dancing, formal dress was eschewed, and women were not to wear orchids but donate the money they would have spent for them to the Red Cross. The board had considered serving food "similar to that served soldiers and other servicemen," but the idea was voted down.

The Nominations

Ex-Academy President Bette Davis was nominated for the fifth time for Best Actress, for *The Little Foxes*. Barbara Stanwyck was tapped for playing the nightclub entertainer who thaws out professor Gary Cooper in *Ball of Fire*, and Greer Garson was along for the ride as the noble heroine of *Blossoms in the Dust*. The press was most interested in the nominated sisters: Olivia de Havilland, for *Hold Back the Dawn*, and Joan Fontaine, for *Suspicion*. Fontaine kept her distance from reporters, but de Havilland told Louella Parsons, "I voted for her in *Rebecca* and I will probably vote for her again this year." When Louella asked her if she and her sister ever had disagreements, Olivia responded, "Of course we fight. What two sisters don't battle?"

Same Size Hat

Louella was also busy asking last year's Best Actress winner Ginger Rogers to name her choice for this year's Award. Rogers, who had turned down *Ball of Fire*, was enthusiastic about Barbara Stanwyck's interpretation of the role, causing another Hollywood columnist to write, "A lot of Hollywood's so-called first ladies of the screen are whopping mad at Rogers." Stanwyck also had a fan in Hedda Hopper, who called her "The most popular woman in Hollywood, because Barbara wears the same size hat she did when she arrived here."

Hopper had some definite ideas about the other Award categories, too. *Sergeant York* got her vote for Best Picture. Hedda said an Oscar for producer Jesse Lasky, who made the very first Hollywood feature in 1914, would be "the most popular Award the Academy could dish out. Jesse's had more ups and downs than any producer here, yet there's no more respected man in Hollywood and no one deserves the Award more." As for the four nominations—for Actor, Director, Producer and Coauthor—given Orson Welles for *Citizen Kane*, Hopper commented, "Orson Welles is still the most brilliant man of 1941."

Needless to say, Louella Parsons didn't share the sentiment. Rumors abounded that Louella was programming her minions to boo if *Kane* won a single Award at the dinner. *Kane*, with nine nominations, had been bested by *Sergeant York*, with eleven, and *How Green Was My Valley*, with ten. There seemed to be no doubt that Gary Cooper would grab the Best Actor Oscar from his competition, including Orson Welles, Robert Montgomery for *Here Comes Mr. Jordan*, and Walter Huston for *All that Money Can Buy*. Cary Grant, acknowledged as Hollywood's foremost light comedian, was at last nominated—for *Penny Serenade*, a tearjerker.

There He Goes Again

The appearance of *Sergeant York*'s Walter Brennan in the Supporting Actor race dismayed the other nominees, what with Brennan having gone three for three in the five-year existence of the Supporting Award. The *Los Angeles Times* commented, "If he is champion again . . . they ought to tender him a plaque as big as a signboard and put it out on some boulevard."

As the dinner approached, Hedda Hopper threatened to defy the Academy's ban on formal wear. "Would it break down anyone's morale to see our girls beautifully dressed?" she asked.

Academy President Walter Wanger was less concerned about what Hedda would show up in than he was over whether Joan Fontaine would show up at all. "Surely, you're attending the banquet?" he asked the nominee over the phone the morning of the dinner. "It isn't possible," she responded. "I don't want to stay up late and then rise at 6:30 A.M. to drive from Beverly Hills to the studio in Burbank." Moments later, Fontaine received another call, from her sister. "You have to attend," Olivia demanded. "Your absence will look odd." "But I haven't anything to wear," Fontaine protested. According to Fontaine's autobiography, "Within an hour, Olivia arrived with our usual saleslady from I. Magnin."

The Big Night

The featured speaker of the "dinner" was Wendell Willkie, the Republican presidential candidate who had run unsuccessfully against Roosevelt in 1940. Darryl Zanuck had invited him because he was toying with the idea of turning *One World*, Willkie's book of personal philosophy, into a movie. When Willkie was leaving New York to attend the "dinner," he told reporters he was on his way to Hollywood, where he was going to "speak at the movie banquet where they award those—you know, those little Okies." A newsman asked if he meant "Oscars." "That's it," Willkie said. "I wasn't sure what they called them."

On the eve of the ceremony, the Academy worried that everyone in Hollywood might be too scared to show up because of a recent bogus "air raid" over L.A. The secretary of war had claimed enemy agents were flying over filmdom, until the secretary of the navy shrugged it off as a false alarm. The Academy need not have worried. Sixteen hundred people attended—a record high, and extra tables were placed behind the orchestra to accommodate everyone.

Despite the Academy's dictate against formal wear, a number of women wore evening gowns, among them Linda Darnell, Ginger Rogers and, of course, Hedda Hopper. Loretta Young found a way to adhere to the Academy's request and still cause a fashion stir: she wore a pillbox hat made entirely of pearls.

The biggest excitement was over the competing siblings. Olivia de Havilland arrived first, on the arm of Burgess Meredith, who was being inducted into the army as a buck private the next day. Joan Fontaine made her entrance in her black dress shortly after, escorted by husband Brian Aherne. Columnist Harold Heffernan noted: "From 8 P.M. until close to 1 A.M., the two girls faced each other, chatting and smiling with forced gaiety and nonchalance. Meanwhile 1,600 sets of eyes shifted curiously from the entertainment above to the sisterly drama below."

Convinced that one of the sisters would win, Barbara Stanwyck stayed home. David O. Selznick called her from the dinner and talked her into coming. The remaining Best Actress nominees were also absent: Greer Garson was in Canada participating in a victory drive and Bette Davis was in Sugar Hill, New Hampshire. Other nominated no-shows included Best Actor nominees Robert Montgomery and Walter Huston.

In keeping with the downplay of glamour, there were no floral decorations. American flags dominated the entrance and the ballroom was bedecked with flags of the Allies. A gold American eagle kept watch over the podium, but this was not protection enough for Wendell Willkie—he sat between his bodyguard and Mrs. Walter Wanger.

After the guests finished eating, CBS Radio began a broadcast at 10:30 when Willkie stood up and saluted the film industry for being "among the

Awards Ceremony

FEBRUARY 26, 1942, 7:45 P.M.
A DINNER AT THE BILTMORE BOWL OF THE BILTMORE HOTEL, LOS ANGELES

Your Host:
BOB HOPE

Presenters

Film Editing	Darryl F. Zanuck
Sound Recording	Darryl F. Zanuck
Special Effects	Darryl F. Zanuck
Art Direction	William L. Pereira
Scientific or Technical Awards	Darryl F. Zanuck
Cinematography	George Barnes
Short Subjects	Bob Hope
Music Awards	B.G. DeSylva
Writing Awards	Preston Sturges
Special Awards	Mervyn LeRoy
Director	Cecil B. DeMille
Picture	David O. Selznick
Thalberg Award	David O. Selznick
Supporting Actor	James Stewart
Actor	James Stewart
Supporting Actress	Ginger Rogers
Actress	Ginger Rogers

"To the extras, a genius is someone who can't be a good guy."
—Daily Variety

first to appreciate fully true American sentiment" and for "disclosing the vicious character of Nazi plotting and violence."

The next speaker was Chinese Ambassador Dr. Hu Shih, who lightened things up by commenting, "I have never seen so many beautiful ladies in my life. I think I have seen more stars tonight than I have ever seen with my nearsighted eyes in the sky . . . The moving picture is one of the greatest inventions of mankind. It makes mankind happy."

Out came Bob Hope, who opened with a salute to Willkie. "To show how I feel about you," he began, turning his lapel to reveal a WILLKIE FOR PRESIDENT button, "I haven't given up yet, and there's one for Hoover under it." Noticing with whom Willkie was sitting, Bob kidded, "Politics does funny things. You lose and end up with Joan Bennett . . . And how 'bout that air raid Wednesday? That was no air raid, that was John Barrymore coming home from W.C. Fields' house."

Hope then decided to give out an Oscar of his own—a joke award to Jack Benny who had appeared in drag throughout most of 1941's *Charley's Aunt*. Hope announced that the award was "for being the best cigar-smoking sweater girl, and the outstanding example of lavender and old lacing" and then produced Benny's trophy—a bewigged Oscar in a skirt with a cigar in its mouth. The emcee commented, "Benny will no longer play any of these female roles because the government's taking his rubber girdle away from him." A surprised Benny responded, "I'm caught with my gags down . . . I've been waiting so long for an Oscar that I'm ready to accept anything from anybody."

Walt Disney won the Cartoon Award—for the tenth time—and his feature-length *Dumbo* won the Award for Scoring of a Musical. There were more Oscars to come for Disney; the Board of Governors voted *Fantasia* two Special Awards. Disney and RCA received one for "the advancement of the use of sound" and conductor Leopold Stokowski picked up one for "the creation of a new form of visualized music."

Academy voters had their choice of the blues or swing for the Best Song Award. The race was considered a dead heat between "Blues in the Night" and "Chattanooga Choo Choo," but the winner turned out to be the sentimental ballad "The Last Time I Saw Paris." The winning composer, Jerome Kern, was caught off guard—he was at home listening on the radio.

Louella Parsons' group applauded vigorously when the Cinematography Award went to *How Green Was My Valley* because Gregg Toland's celebrated deep-focus photography for *Citizen Kane* had been the predicted winner. Parsons' cheerleaders were booing the next minute when Preston Sturges revealed that the Best Original Screenplay Award went to the absent Orson Welles and Herman Mankiewicz for *Citizen Kane*. Others were screaming, "Mank! Mank! Where's Mank!" But the Hollywood veteran had stayed home because, as his wife explained, "He did not want to be humiliated. He thought he'd get mad and do something drastic when he didn't win." The absentees' Oscars were accepted by RKO president George Schaefer. According to Louella's biographer George Eells, "Privately, many of the same people who booed conceded that it was a superb film but the popular stance was to pretend disapproval."

Cecil B. DeMille embarked on a lengthy discourse as he presented the Best Director Award and made a shambles of it. "Some of the people who spoke before me have stolen the thunder, like Mr. Willkie and the Jap—I mean, Chinese—ambassador," DeMille said. The winner was John Ford for *How Green Was My Valley*. A still-flustered DeMille referred to the lieutenant commander as "Major Ford." The Oscar was accepted by Lieutenant Colonel Darryl F. Zanuck, who was back at the rostrum a few minutes later claiming the Best Picture Oscar for *How Green Was My Valley*.

David O. Selznick stepped up to the podium with the bust of Irving Thalberg, and announced that it was going to Walt Disney. Selznick praised the cartoonist for employing Bach, Beethoven and Tchaikovsky in *Fantasia*, "in which established music was used as the complete basis for the cre-

"Barbara Stanwyck wears the same size hat she did when she arrived here."
—Hedda Hopper

ation of the picture." He added that the cartoon "contributed to the musical education of the public." All the praise in the world could not obscure the fact that *Fantasia* was Disney's first box-office bomb, and Disney began weeping during his acceptance speech. "Thank you so much for this," the recipient said. "Maybe I should have a medal for bravery. We all make mistakes. *Fantasia* was one but it was an honest one. I shall now rededicate myself to my old ideals." There was a respectful ovation as the crybaby returned to his seat. Norma Shearer, still playing the widow Thalberg, walked over to Disney and kissed him.

Rosalind Russell took over as emcee and addressed the guest of honor as "Your Excellency, Mr. Willkie." She introduced James Stewart, on a one-day furlough from Camp Moffet, by saying that after Stewart won his Oscar "he didn't use it to go out and exploit himself for a larger salary—he went into the army at twenty-one bucks." Stewart presented the Best Supporting Actor Award, and somebody finally beat Walter Brennan—the winner was Donald Crisp for *How Green Was My Valley*. Crisp was also in uniform—he was a captain in Lewis Stone's station-wagon brigade for evacuating civilians in case of an air raid. Crisp, whose film career had begun with D.W. Griffith in 1908, told the audience, "Other old-timers should be given a chance and they, too, could win Awards." When Crisp returned to his seat, Walter Brennan came by and kissed him on the top of his head.

Stewart next announced that Gary Cooper was the Best Actor winner for *Sergeant York*. When Stewart handed Cooper the Oscar they fumbled and almost dropped it. They both laughed, then Stewart stepped away and Cooper smiled sheepishly at the microphone, lifting one foot off the floor. "It was Sergeant Alvin York who won this Award," he began, then added, "Shucks, I've been in the business sixteen years and sometimes dreamed I might get one of these things. That's all I can say . . . Funny, when I was dreaming I always made a good speech." And he and Stewart walked off, forgetting the Oscar on the podium.

Ginger Rogers came out to present the Best Supporting Actress Award to Mary Astor for *The Great Lie*. The winner reminded the assemblage that it had been twenty-two years since she first faced a movie camera and she thanked the two people she said had most helped her in the role of a vicious classical pianist: costar Bette Davis and Pyotr Ilyich Tchaikovsky.

Finally, it was time for the night's climax—the battle of the sisters would be settled. Nominee Barbara Stanwyck had arrived minutes earlier with husband Robert Taylor. Ginger Rogers ripped open the envelope and announced that the winner was the younger sister, twenty-four-year-old Joan Fontaine for *Suspicion*. Joan froze for a moment, then heard her sister whisper, "Get up there." Fontaine later recalled her thoughts at the moment of triumph: "All the animus we'd felt toward each other as children, the hair-pullings, the savage wrestling matches, the time Olivia fractured my collarbone, all came rushing back in kaleidoscopic imagery." By the time Fontaine got to the dais, she was in tears. Ginger Rogers started crying, too, as she handed her the Oscar. Columnist Jimmy Starr wrote that after Fontaine finished her thank-you's, she "returned to the table where Olivia shook her hand. Olivia smiled faintly."

Aftermath

Even though the dinner was a sellout, the 1941 affair lost $3,000—$500 more than the previous year's banquet had lost. Board member Darryl Zanuck didn't care at all—he was overjoyed over winning his first Best Picture Award. He was also rather surprised and said, "When I think of what I got away with . . . and won the Academy Award with the picture, it is really astonishing. Not only did we drop five or six characters, we eliminated the most controversial element in the book, which was the labor-and-capital battle in connection with the strike."

Less happy was Mrs. Cecil B. DeMille. Embarrassed by her husband's faux pas about the

"Well, Cecil, at last you have done something that Hollywood will remember."
—Mrs. Cecil B. DeMille

Chinese ambassador, she turned to him on the way home and said, "Well, Cecil, at last you have done something that Hollywood will remember."

Another sour note came from some of the losing songwriters who complained that "The Last Time I Saw Paris" should not have been eligible for an Oscar since it wasn't written expressly for a movie; the song had been published in 1940. Even its composer, Jerome Kern, had questioned its qualifying for an Academy Award and said he had voted for "Blues in the Night." *Time* wrote, "Hollywood has its nerve in claiming that nostalgic hit, since it was published without movie sponsorship before it was borrowed for *Lady Be Good*." *Daily Variety* theorized that the extras, who could once again vote for Best Song, had been responsible for electing the popular ballad.

Most of the postmortem discussion centered on the virtual shutting out of Orson Welles, who was off in South America scouting locations for a movie that would never materialize. RKO President George Schaefer sent Herman J. Mankiewicz his statuette with the message: "Congratulations and best wishes from a high-priced office boy." Mank made up for lost time and celebrated his Oscar victory with his friends for days afterward. One well-wisher gave him a blue tie with an Oscar painted on it that Mankiewicz wore everywhere.

Daily Variety speculated that the late release of *How Green Was My Valley* worked in its favor, "the public memory being as short as it is." The trade paper pontificated further on the Oscar results:

> *Now as to what happened to miracle of youth, Welles. Across the length and breadth of Hollywood there are none to quarrel with the prevailing opinion that the extras took care of him, to vent their wrath or their distaste of him. To them a genius is someone who can't be a good guy.*

The popular press was more interested in Fontaine's win over de Havilland. Olivia told reporters that she was delighted with her sister's good fortune, but *Life* heard the loser whisper to her friends, "If *Suspicion* had been delayed just a little, it wouldn't have gotten under the wire for this year's Award and I might have won. . . ."

1942

"Mrs. Miniver is propaganda worth a hundred battleships."
—Winston Churchill

Patriotism was the vogue in 1942, and the Academy Awards became a good-citizen contest.

Throughout 1942, Hollywood was helping to fight World War II—and was winning. The *Hollywood Reporter* headlined: ALL THE MAJOR COS. IN THE CHIPS and gloated that in combining war pictures and escapism, the studios were in "the best financial position they have occupied since the peak days of 1929."

Hollywood treated military leaders like royalty and dropping the names of commanding officers was the order of the day. One columnist reported that director Sam Wood was busting his buttons over "a letter received yesterday from one of Gen. 'Ike' Eisenhower's staff officers" informing him that Eisenhower had taken along a print of *Kings Row,* Wood's turn-of-the-century small-town soap opera, to entertain troops during their North African expedition. Winston Churchill was so impressed with Paramount's *Wake Island,* about one of the U.S.'s first skirmishes in the war, that he gave director John Farrow special permission "personally to get his brand-new Austin out of Canada and back to Beverly Hills." And Louis B. Mayer spread the word that Churchill had written to him to say that *Mrs. Miniver* is "propaganda worth a hundred battleships."

There'll Always Be an England

What *Mrs. Miniver* was worth to MGM was millions of dollars. Not only Americans, but people around the world were stirred by Greer Garson and Walter Pidgeon's struggle to maintain their middle-class existence amid the blitz. MGM's foreign office delighted in giving out reports that the British-homefront drama was breaking *Gone With the Wind*'s box-office records everywhere from Cairo to Trinidad to Buenos Aires. *Liberty* magazine typified critical reaction, saying that Garson's performance was "luminous," and *Mrs. Miniver* established Louis B. Mayer's protégée as the new first lady of the Metro lot.

Six months after *Mrs. Miniver* opened, Garson was back and Ronald Colman had her. The film was *Random Harvest,* based on a novel by James Hilton—one of the *Mrs. Miniver* screenwriters—about an amnesiac who becomes re-enamored of his wife. Metro was now bragging that this romantic drama was knocking down *Mrs. Miniver*'s records and *Daily Variety* marveled that so many people were seeing *Random Harvest* at Radio City Music Hall that the theater "frequently opens at 7:45 A.M., a precedent for this swank spot."

For the fifty-one-year-old Ronald Colman, 1942 brought him a comeback after a career slump. Earlier in the year he had starred in George Stevens' popular comedy *Talk of the Town,* and *Random Harvest* sealed his triumph, inspiring *Liberty* to write: "Devoted followers of Ronald Colman will cheer his finest performance." Colman was a devoted public servant, too—he volunteered his sonorous voice for government radio broadcasts when war broke out. He also economized at home, according to the *Hollywood Reporter:* "The Ronald Colmans are giving up their Beverly Hills house and going to live on their ranch. Last straw came when their pet (and last) butler was drafted the other day."

Yankee Doodle Jimmy

Louis B. Mayer's flag-waving for MGM was low-key compared to Jack Warner's fireworks for *Yankee Doodle Dandy.* Warner premiered the James Cagney musical in May with all the showmanship he could muster, charging $25,000 for the best seats at New York's Hollywood Theatre. From this one showing, he made $5,750,000 for the U.S. Treasury. He didn't do poorly for himself either; the biography of George M. Cohan became the studio's all-time top grosser.

Best Actress winner Greer Garson and Best Actor winner James Cagney pose with the Academy's wartime model—the plaster Oscar.

"Seventy percent of our American audiences are between the ages of sixteen and twenty-four. Do we want to scandalize them?"
—A member of the Hays Office

Warner congratulated himself in a trade-paper ad that read, "All of us who are Warner Brothers—actors, writers, directors, technicians—have one purpose and one only; to give you the kind of entertainment that raises your spirits, lifts your chin, and helps brighten things for any day ahead . . . We're glad that people feel that way about *Yankee Doodle Dandy,* because if they feel that way they feel good, and that's what we Americans are shooting for."

Yankee Doodle Dandy was James Cagney's last movie as a contract actor at Warners. Freed from his studio servitude, he made trade-paper headlines by forming his own production group with his brother—who had produced *Yankee Doodle Dandy*—and President Roosevelt personally requested that Cagney perform some numbers from the movie at his birthday party. Cagney was elected president of the Screen Actors Guild, and his first bit of business was to press charges against Chicago mobsters trying to stir up trouble in Hollywood. But, according to *Life,* the best was yet to come: "Cagney's performance as George M. Cohan may win him a 1942 Academy Award."

Rule Britannia

The Allied cause was forcefully set forth in Noel Coward's salute to the Royal Navy, *In Which We Serve*. The *Hollywood Reporter* noted that at an advance screening attended by Mary Pickford and Basil Rathbone, viewers "were so moved, they couldn't move." *In Which We Serve* was acclaimed as the last word in realism and everyone said what a genius writer-director-star Noel Coward was. "Obviously, Noel Coward is the guy Orson Welles thinks he is," Humphrey Bogart was quoted as saying.

But it wasn't all smooth sailing for Coward. The Hays Office didn't care for the way some of the British sailors talked and got out its scissors. Whereupon the British minister of information stood up in the House of Commons and attacked the Hays Office for being "too maiden-auntlike." The British producers cabled United Artists to stop distributing the movie in America, but the head of United Artists fired back a letter that defended the Hays Office for its "openmindedness" in allowing such words as "bloody," "hell" and "damn" to remain in the movie.

The Hays Office drew the line, though, at the appellation "bloody bastards" used to describe the German sailors. A Hays official explained, "Morally, we are obligated to protect the youngsters who attend our pictures. Seventy percent of our American audiences are between the ages of sixteen and twenty-four. Do we want to scandalize them?" Back east, *The New Yorker* observed, "Regarding Noel Coward's difficulties with the Hays Office over several earthy words in the sound track of his new war film, we can only say that we sympathize with the poor bastard."

Coward's ship was finally sunk when, on December 7, the Academy decided to move the eligibility deadline from the traditional January 12 to December 31 "to allow eight weeks, rather than six, to consider nominations and for gas rationing." MGM was able to rush Greer Garson's *Random Harvest* into one of its Los Angeles theaters with no trouble, but *In Which We Serve,* with no big-studio backing, was stuck with its early-January Hollywood premiere. The Oscar race could once again be All-American.

Orson Welles Meets Lupe Velez

There appeared little chance that the Academy would have any more trouble with wunderkind Orson Welles. His latest effort was a two-and-a-half-hour movie about a decaying American family called *The Magnificent Ambersons*. RKO executives thought they knew a dog when they saw one, so the family saga was cut down to eighty-eight minutes and released on a double bill with the Lupe Velez vehicle *Mexican Spitfire Sees a Ghost*. Just as RKO predicted, the movie flopped, although a few critics tracked it down and gave it favorable reviews.

"I shall pat each of the little darlings on the head until they drop dead."
—Monty Woolley

Wright on Both Counts

Next to *Yankee Doodle Dandy*, the most All-American film of the year was Samuel Goldwyn's baseball movie, *Pride of the Yankees*, the biography of Lou Gehrig, as played by Gary Cooper. Goldwyn enticed non-sports-fans by explaining, "It's not a baseball picture, it's a human drama." Mrs. Gehrig was played by twenty-four-year-old Teresa Wright, whom Goldwyn had signed to a longterm contract after seeing her on Broadway in *Life with Father*. His investment paid off immediately when Wright was nominated for Best Supporting Actress for her first film, 1941's *The Little Foxes*, with Bette Davis. By 1942, Teresa Wright was one of Hollywood's most sought-after actresses. Prior to *Pride of the Yankees*, she played an ingenue in *Mrs. Miniver* and upcoming was Alfred Hitchcock's *Shadow of a Doubt*, shortchanged out of the 1942 Oscar race by the same timetable switch that had knocked out *In Which We Serve*. *Photoplay* analyzed Wright's success: "The glamor-gorged public has snapped at sweet, unspoiled Teresa like a shipwrecked sailor at a T-bone steak."

A Doughnut and a Dance

Teresa Wright was going to have stiff Oscar competition not only from her costar in *Mrs. Miniver* but from former costar Bette Davis. The perennial nominee had one of her most popular films with *Now, Voyager*, a romance costarring Paul Henreid in which she went from frumpy spinster to fashion plate. Archer Winsten of the *New York Post* wrote: "Miss Davis handles her role with her usual but always exciting intensity." The film was based on a novel by the author of *Stella Dallas*, and Jack Warner was so impressed by its box-office performance that he gave Davis a raise.

Davis also went to work for the boys in the military. With fellow Warners star John Garfield, she organized a nonprofit coffee-and-doughnuts nightclub for servicemen in Southern California. The two of them talked dozens of personalities into participating in the Hollywood Canteen—the soldiers loved being served refreshments by Marlene Dietrich, dancing with Joan Crawford and gawking at Humphrey Bogart doing the dishes.

Do-Gooding with Roz

Rosalind Russell was working overtime, too. After scoring in the hit comedy *My Sister Eileen* and leading the *New York Herald Tribune* to exclaim, "It is her wry and persuasive portrayal of the pretty Eileen's older sister which stamps the film with most of its comic authority . . . the show owes a lot to her acute instinct for clowning," Russell held her own Christmas dinner for soldiers stationed in the California desert. The *Hollywood Reporter*'s "Rambling Reporter" made it clear that the party was no picnic: "Roz Russell and Freddie Brisson were on their feet from 1 in the afternoon until 3 A.M. Sunday—dishing out coffee, presents, etc. For 'dessert,' Roz grabbed a microphone and sang her version of 'River, Stay Away From My Door.' " And to top it off, Mrs. Brisson was pregnant, causing the *Reporter* to gasp, "All we can say is Praise the Lord and Pass the Obstetrician!"

My Country 'Tis of Thee

Greer Garson was no slouch in the line of duty, either. Although she hailed from Ireland, Garson was now 100 percent American. One columnist wrote, "Garson, grateful for everything this land has brought her, says she doesn't want to do anything but stay here and make movies, and sell war bonds between pictures." She did do at least one other thing— she fell in love with Richard Ney, the actor who had played her son in *Mrs. Miniver*. At twenty-four, Ney was nine years younger than Garson, but the image of *Mrs. Miniver* in a passionate embrace with her offspring was too tempting for journalists. The *Hollywood Reporter* noted, "The wire service boys were going currazy all day yesterday trying

"I do not, however, feel Katharine Hepburn should win."
—Joan Fontaine

to find out whether Greer Garson was really en route to a tryst with Richard Ney up at Tacoma, Wash."

Only Geniuses Need Apply

Neither Garson nor any of her fellow glamorous do-gooders impressed the New York Film Critics, who gave their Best Actress citation to Agnes Moorehead for her portrayal of the spinster aunt in Orson Welles' *The Magnificent Ambersons*. Moorehead was a radio actress and *Ambersons* was only her second film, the first being *Citizen Kane*. The New York crowd also thumbed their noses at Hollywood when they selected as Best Picture *In Which We Serve*. But for Best Actor, they went pure Hollywood—James Cagney in *Yankee Doodle Dandy*.

The Nominations

Not only was Agnes Moorehead nominated by the Academy—albeit in the Supporting Actress category—but to the surprise of all, *The Magnificent Ambersons* was nominated for Best Picture—maybe Lupe Velez had done Orson Welles some good after all. *Mrs. Miniver* entered the Oscar race with twelve nominations, followed by *The Pride of the Yankees* with eleven; *Yankee Doodle Dandy,* eight; and *Random Harvest,* seven. Both of the Yankees—James Cagney and Gary Cooper—were in the Best Actor contest with Ronald Colman and Mr. Miniver, Walter Pidgeon. The fifth slot had gone to Monty Woolley for *The Pied Piper,* a drama about a misanthrope who ends up rescuing kids from the Nazis. Woolley liked to live up to his curmudgeon image and when his director asked him to be patient with his young costars, he responded, "I shall pat each of the little darlings on their heads until they drop dead."

Columnist Edith Gwynn was bitter that her favorite was excluded, and she praised a cowboy star who had campaigned for him: "Nice gesture of Don Barry's. He's busy rounding up 'write-in' votes for Ronald Reagan, whose performance in *Kings Row* deserved an Oscar nomination in the first place." Reagan was not completely left out of the Academy Awards race, however; he was the star of a short nominated for Best Documentary, *Mr. Gardenia Jones*.

As expected, the Best Actress lineup was Greer Garson, Bette Davis, Rosalind Russell and Teresa Wright, who was also nominated for Best Supporting Actress for *Mrs. Miniver*. The fifth nominated actress was Katharine Hepburn for the comedy *Woman of the Year;* she had also acted as the agent of budding screenwriters Michael Kanin and Ring Lardner, Jr., pitching the property to Louis B. Mayer herself for $120,000. *Woman of the Year* was also Hepburn's first movie with Spencer Tracy, who got top billing.

Joan Jumps In

Taking a cue from predecessor Ginger Rogers, the reigning Best Actress Joan Fontaine figured she was supposed to select a preference in the current race. She told the press, "I believe Greer Garson should and will win. I do not, however, feel Katharine Hepburn should win. She belongs to the stage. Awarding the honor is an industry matter. Bette Davis' work in *Now, Voyager* is a triumph, but then there couldn't be the thrill for Bette as there is for an actress who has never won the Award."

Bette Davis did experience the thrill of upstaging the competition at least once. When *Redbook* magazine gave its Best Picture award to *Mrs. Miniver,* Davis offered to hold the award ceremony at the Hollywood Canteen. She then attracted most of the attention and became *Daily Variety*'s "Best Dressed Gal of the Week—a picture of utter simplicity in an all-black ensemble."

Willie's Smile

Daily Variety speculated on how the voting would go and reported, "Those on the inside were touting Metro to have the inside rail for a bevy of

Oscars with its productions *Mrs. Miniver* and *Random Harvest*. Extras, however, have been campaigning for James Cagney, president of SAG." Hedda Hopper was also campaigning and in her column she printed a letter to *Mrs. Miniver*'s director, who was off filming war documentaries. "To Maj. Willie Wyler, somewhere in North Africa," Hopper began. "Eight times I've seen you at the Academy dinner and watched the smile on your face when another director was presented with the little Oscar . . . So, wherever you are, I'm hoping, and so are all of your friends (and in spite of the many arguments you've had with many of them, they're still your friends, Willie) that in this year of grace 1943, you'll get the Award . . ." Even if he won, Wyler couldn't count on receiving a gold statuette. Due to the wartime metal shortage, the Academy announced that for the duration of the war, the Oscars would be made of plaster.

The Big Night

Once again, the Academy slapped a ban on formal wear, but *Daily Variety* still espied "a sprinkling of fancy dress among the femme guests." Greer Garson came with her mother and sat with costars Ronald Colman and Walter Pidgeon at Metro's table, headed by Louis B. Mayer with two publicity men kneeling in attendance behind him. Dinner began at 8:15 and the orchestra played the nominated songs, giving guests the pleasure of eating to the strains of *Hellzapoppin*'s "Pig Foot Pete."

The official ceremony started at 9:30, when Jeanette MacDonald launched into the national anthem. There were special guests ranging from armed forces representatives to consuls from Latin America; the place was so crowded, many guests had difficulty standing for the anthem. To the chagrin of those who had managed to stand, MacDonald launched into the second verse. As she sang, Private Tyrone Power of the marines and Private Alan Ladd of the army brought out the flag. Louella Parsons felt that "the most thrilling event of the Academy dinner was the unveiling of the American flag with 27,677 names of Hollywood who have answered Uncle Sam's call." Adding to the thrill was the tense moment when the flag refused to unfurl, but Privates Power and Ladd prevailed.

The military motif continued when Walter Wanger, who had decided to stay on as Academy president, introduced an army colonel who spoke for a while about the army. Paramount executive Y. Frank Freeman got the focus back to Hollywood as he started to give out Technical Awards. He hadn't gotten far when he was told to get off because the national radio broadcast was about to commence.

The radio program began with Chet Huntley introducing 1941's Best Supporting Actor, Donald Crisp, who read a telegram from President Roosevelt. The President apologized for not phoning in and congratulated Hollywood for "turning the tremendous power of the motion picture into an effective war instrument without the slightest resort to the totalitarian methods of our enemies."

Walter Wanger introduced California Governor Earl Warren, who talked about the mail he had received from servicemen telling him that American movies were second only to letters from home in their affections. After Warren's speech, CBS turned off its microphones and Y. Frank Freeman got back to the Awards.

When Freeman was finished, Bob Hope walked out and asked, "Y. Frank Freeman?" The emcee also made light of the war's effect on Hollywood. "The leading-man shortage is so great," the comedian said, "pretty soon we'll see Hedy Lamarr waiting to be kissed while they put a heating pad on Lewis Stone."

Awards Ceremony

MARCH 4, 1943, 8:30 P.M.
A BANQUET AT THE COCONUT GROVE OF THE AMBASSADOR HOTEL, LOS ANGELES

Your Host:
BOB HOPE

Presenters

Film Editing	Y. Frank Freeman
Sound Recording	Y. Frank Freeman
Special Effects	Y. Frank Freeman
Art Direction	William Cameron Menzies
Scientific and Technical Awards	Y. Frank Freeman
Cinematography	James Wong Howe
Short Subjects	Bob Hope
Music Awards	Irving Berlin
Director	Frank Capra
Special Awards	Mervyn LeRoy
Writing Awards	Mary C. McCall, Jr.
Documentary Awards	David O. Selznick
Picture	William Goetz
Thalberg Award	Walt Disney
Supporting Actor	Gary Cooper
Actor	Gary Cooper
Supporting Actress	Joan Fontaine
Actress	Joan Fontaine

"Now you've seen everything—MGM and 20th Century–Fox with their arms around each other."
—Bob Hope

Best Song nominee Irving Berlin found the courage to present the Best Song Award and his valor was rewarded—he won. "It's someone I've known for a good many years," the presenter said. "He's a nice kid and I think deserves it."

Colonel Frank Capra gave the Best Director Award in his army uniform, and the winner was *Mrs. Miniver*'s Lieutenant Colonel William Wyler. Mrs. Wyler accepted and boasted that her husband was busy filming a bombing raid over Germany. Hedda Hopper had sent her letter to Wyler to the wrong continent.

Bob Hope introduced the next presenter, *Random Harvest*'s Best Director loser Mervyn LeRoy, with a recollection: "He's the first producer who tested me for films. He advised me to return to New York." LeRoy gave out the surprise Special Awards. To compensate for the deadline switcheroo, the Board of Governors voted a certificate to Noel Coward for *In Which We Serve*, commemorating his "outstanding production achievement." The winner wasn't present. Charles Boyer got a certificate for "establishing the French Research Foundation in Los Angeles." Boyer received a nice hand, although later one killjoy reported, "Comparatively few people in Hollywood have even heard of this organization." The third Special Award went to MGM—and Louis B. Mayer—for making the highly successful *Andy Hardy* series. The certificate honored the films for their "achievement in representing the American way of life."

Before she got to the writing Awards, Writers Guild President Mary C. McCall, Jr., read a number of telegrams from government bigwigs who echoed each other with their references to, "our allies, the British." The British had some allies in the Academy—England's *The Invaders* was the surprise winner of Best Original Story, beating such all-American entries as *Yankee Doodle Dandy* and *The Pride of the Yankees*. MGM had a lock on the other writing Awards. Katharine Hepburn's chums won Original Screenplay for *Woman of the Year* and *Mrs. Miniver* took Best Screenplay.

Introduced by Hope as the "Wizard of Oscars," David O. Selznick read a telegram from Madame Chiang Kai-shek thanking Hollywood for "interpreting China to the world." Selznick then had the sizable task of announcing all the nominees for Best Documentary. In its second year of existence, this category had swelled from the original nine nominees to twenty-five in order to acknowledge every foreign country, every military branch, and every studio that had produced a war documentary. The Academy even suspended its winner-take-all rule and gave out four Oscars in this category: one to our allies the Australians, one to our allies the Russians, one to Frank Capra and the U.S. Army, and one to John Ford and the U.S. Navy.

William Goetz, Lieutenant Colonel Darryl Zanuck's stand-in as head of Fox during the war, gave the Best Picture Award to his father-in-law, Louis B. Mayer, who picked up the statuette for *Mrs. Miniver*. In accepting, Mayer put his hand on his daughter Edie's husband's shoulder and said, "You will be greater than I ever was." Bob Hope quipped, "Now you've seen everything—MGM and 20th Century–Fox with their arms around each other."

Mayer admitted that *Mrs. Miniver*'s producer, Sidney Franklin, really deserved the honor, but he was sick in bed. When Franklin, who also had produced *Random Harvest*, was declared the winner of the Thalberg Award by Walt Disney, it was Mrs. Franklin's turn to go to the podium. The widow Thalberg was not present—Norma Shearer had quit movies and married a ski instructor half her age.

At this point, *Mrs. Miniver* had notched four wins and, with the acting Awards coming up, Bob Hope joked, "If *Mrs. Miniver* keeps up like this, the government will put a ceiling on statuettes." Gary Cooper prefaced the acting Awards with the reminder, "It's possible to have this banquet only because men in uniform are being shot and killed on foreign battlegrounds." One man in uniform far away from the battlegrounds was Van Heflin,

"It's possible to have this banquet only because men in uniform are being shot and killed on foreign battlegrounds."
—Gary Cooper

winner of the Best Supporting Actor Award for MGM's *Johnny Eager*. The air force lieutenant was described by the *Hollywood Reporter* as "a little speechless," but he did manage to thank director Mervyn LeRoy, Louis B. Mayer, his pregnant wife, and also the air force, for giving him the night off.

Even though he was a nominee himself, Gary Cooper showed no remorse in announcing James Cagney as the Best Actor winner for *Yankee Doodle Dandy*. As Cagney bounded to the dais amid whistling and cheering, one person commented, "You don't have to be from MGM to win." When Cooper took a few steps back to allow Cagney the spotlight, the screen's quintessential tough guy threw his arms around the presenter and cried, "Please don't leave me!"

Finding the courage to let go, Cagney said, "I've always maintained that in this business you're only as good as the other fellow thinks you are. It's nice to know that you people thought I had done a good job. And don't forget it was a pretty good part, too." Cagney exited with George M. Cohan's famous line, "My mother thanks you, my father thanks you, my sister thanks you, and I thank you."

Joan Fontaine was in charge of announcing the Best Actress awards. The Best Supporting Actress winner was Teresa Wright for *Mrs. Miniver*. As Fontaine rattled off the names of the Best Actress nominees, the photographers swarmed around the MGM table where Garson was sitting. With Teresa Wright already taken care of, the Award went to Fontaine's favorite, Greer Garson in *Mrs. Miniver*. The photographers got a shot of her open-mouthed reaction to the news.

"I am practically unprepared," the winner began. "This is the most wonderful thing. I feel just like Alice in Wonderland." The Irish-born actress then praised the Academy for honoring industry members who weren't originally from America. "I may never win another statuette," she accurately prophesied, "but tonight is a memorable one; one that officially places the welcome mat for me. I shall cherish this evening and the kindness of my many friends forever." Garson then confessed that she did not consider acting a "competition," and added, "A nomination means that an actress had one of the five best roles and opportunities of the year and the actress had met the challenge."

Members of the audience, many of whom had gotten up for work at 6 A.M., began looking at their watches as Garson continued to stress the arbitrary nature of awards for another five minutes. It was after 1 A.M. by the time the winner had finished and somebody snickered, "Her acceptance speech was longer than her part."

The ceremony finally closed with an air of mystery as President Walter Wanger reminded the crowd, as he had at least three times earlier in the evening, that next year's presentation would be in a different format. Bob Hope added, "Don't forget to tip your waiters. You never know who is on your draft board."

Aftermath

In its coverage of the Awards, the *Hollywood Reporter* griped:

> *Never in the history of Academy dinners was there such a compression of tables and people. It was almost impossible to get through the aisles and, with tables stacked up as far as the bandstand, there wasn't a foot of space on the dance floor.*

The *Reporter*'s editor, W. R. Wilkerson, was so agitated about the whole thing that he ran three separate editorials condemning the affair. Day 1: "Probably no big event ever attracted more tiresome speakers voicing greater dullness and long-winded speeches, consuming, with the Awards, the better part of three hours." Day 2: "In short, the Motion Picture Academy of Arts and Sciences is a misnomer for a group that should call itself the Motion Picture Political Party of Pull and Palaver, with this annual dinner party its soapbox." Day 3: "Why load the platform with politicians and

"No one person could arrange anything so boring."
—Mary Pickford

professional jerks of every calibre?" *Daily Variety,* meanwhile, was miffed that the "usual ornate place cards with gilded replicas of the Oscars were missing."

Mary Pickford, Best Actress winner of 1928–29, also made her disapproval of the ceremony well known. After she and her husband, naval Lieutenant Buddy Rogers, managed to extricate themselves from the mob of onlookers outside the Ambassador, they discovered that the Academy had stuck the Academy founder at a table way in the back of the room, or, as Pickford told reporters, "in Arizona." She promptly resigned from the Academy because "the big studios buy up blocks of reservations and squeeze everybody else out." Pickford didn't like the speeches either, but she was hesitant to blame any individual: "No one person could arrange anything so boring."

The Academy's choices were also met with some disapproval. When a reporter asked one independent producer who won the Awards, the mini-mogul replied, "The Giants." The *New York World-Telegram* felt that the 4,500 extras who got to vote on Best Picture, Best Song and the Acting Awards held an imbalance of power. The paper scoffed, "That means the actors' taste prevails. *Mrs. Miniver* had the showy quality and nobility dear to any actor's heart."

Hedda Hopper, who had earlier voiced her support for William Wyler, now wanted to know why the Academy saw fit to honor a movie which wasn't even about Americans. The *Hollywood Citizen-News* further degraded the Academy's choice by pointing out, "And the cruelest blow of all is the report in England—among the 'common people' with whom it was supposed to deal—*Mrs. Miniver* has been a failure."

Mrs. Miniver herself, Greer Gerson, also came under attack. While the political speakers were the ones responsible for making the ceremony interminable, it was Greer Garson with her five-and-a-half minute speech who got the reputation for being a windbag. A few days after the Awards, Danny Kaye and wife Sylvia Fine threw a party where, as a parlor game, they presented their guests with mock Oscars. When Laird Cregar, who usually played hulking villains over at Fox, was given an award for "Best Female Impersonation of the Year," he mimicked Garson's polite English and said, "I am practically unprepared." Cregar then went on to parody Garson's entire acceptance speech by dragging it out to a ludicrous length. In no time, Hollywoodites started "remembering" that Garson bored everyone for over an hour and her speech became a Hollywood legend.

When interviewed for this book, Greer Garson said, "Please clear up this myth. It was funny for two weeks, but now I'm quite tired of it."

1943

"Jennifer Jones is a strange, restrained, shy girl."
—Louella Parsons

The private party was over—in 1943 the Academy Awards went public.

Jack Warner had the golden touch in 1943. In fact, Warner Brothers didn't even wait for the new year to begin its hit parade of '43. *Casablanca* premiered in New York in November 1942, just after Eisenhower led Allied troops in an invasion of . . . Casablanca, making the Moroccan city a household word. The critics were generally genial; *Newsweek* called the film "absorbing escapist entertainment," although the *New York World-Telegram* decided that *Casablanca* "is not the best of the recent Bogarts."

But columnist Irving Hoffman exulted, "New Yorkers like its timeliness, Bogart and Bergman and various bits of business in the picture, and Warners likes the big business it's doing, so everybody's happy." None happier than the Warners executives who had decided to stick with the title *Casablanca;* some thought it sounded like a Mexican beer and had argued that *Everybody Goes to Rick's* was catchier. When the movie opened in Los Angeles in January, the government again provided free publicity. Roosevelt and Churchill pledged to fight the Axis powers to the end at a meeting held in . . . Casablanca.

Jack Warner had another hit when he adapted Lillian Hellman's Broadway success *Watch on the Rhine*. Bette Davis, in a secondary role, received top billing in order to lure patrons, and the leading role was played by the star of the Broadway production, Paul Lukas, whose fifteen-year film career had been rather mediocre. In the *New York Times*, Bosley Crowther raved, "It is the first Hollywood film to go deeply into the fundamental nature of fascism." *Life* said that Lukas' "portrait of an anti-Nazi German is magnificent" and *Time* predicted an Oscar for the actor. Columnist Harriet Parsons declared that Lukas was now "back on top of the Hollywood heap."

Best Actress loser Ingrid Bergman, twenty-eight, congratulates birthday girl and best friend Jennifer Jones, twenty-five, who holds her present from the Academy.

Beast of Burden

Warners was also crowing that *This Is the Army,* Irving Berlin's rabble-rousing salute to both the army and show business, was the second highest-grossing movie of all time. To top it off, Jack Warner had the pleasure of seeing his patriotism saluted in the *Hollywood Reporter*. Editor W.R. Wilkerson cited such films as *Casablanca, Watch on the Rhine* and a reissue of 1939's *Confessions of a Nazi Spy* (with Paul Lukas as a Nazi) and wrote, "So long as some studio—any studio—is turning out product like the above, it would be an unjust criticism to say that Hollywood is not carrying its war burden."

Turning on the Heat

Ever since David O. Selznick brought her to America to star in *Intermezzo* in 1939, the Swedish-born, five-foot-ten Ingrid Bergman had been a well-regarded, straight-laced actress. In 1943, the public discovered that she could also be sexy and Bergman became a full-fledged star. She and Humphrey Bogart embraced to the strains of "As Time Goes By" in *Casablanca* and one reviewer proclaimed that the two of them "really turn on the heat."

It's in the Bag

Bergman followed *Casablanca* with the film version of Ernest Hemingway's Spanish Civil War novel, *For Whom the Bell Tolls*. Paramount sold the movie as their prestige item for the year, playing it only on a reserved-seat basis. After these initial engagements had ended, the studio bragged that it was withdrawing the film until sometime in 1945, when it would deign to release *For Whom the Bell Tolls* to the masses. Much of the large audience that paid the upscale prices didn't know from Hemingway; they rushed to *For Whom the Bell*

"Casablanca is not the best of the recent Bogarts." —*New York World-Telegram*

Tolls because of a much-publicized scene in which Bergman and Gary Cooper spend the night together in the same sleeping bag. The pair was so convincing in the scene that people began to speculate. Sometime later, when asked about a romance between Cooper and herself, Bergman responded, "Oh, I think Gary Cooper falls in love with all his leading ladies."

Reviewing *For Whom the Bell Tolls,* James Agee wrote that Bergman "really knows how to act, in a blend of poetic grace with quiet realism that almost never appears in American pictures." Giving Bergman a run for her raves was Katina Paxinou, the forty-two-year-old actress from the Greek stage who played the guerrilla fighter Pilar. She had impressed Paramount executives by telling them, "I come from generations of guerrillas. My grandmother learned her ABC's from a guerrilla chieftain in a cave. I know that Pilar. I know her well."

Mrs. Miniver Goes to France

Over at MGM, Greer Garson and Walter Pidgeon were showing quiet dignity again, this time in France in the biography *Madame Curie*. The Christmas release received mixed reviews—one critic noted, "We have a two-hour picture reaching a highpoint when two people stand together looking into a saucer"—but it did big business. The MGM publicity department broadcast that *Madame Curie* outgrossed both *Mrs. Miniver* and *Random Harvest* at Radio City Music Hall.

For the first time since the 1935 Awards, Metro ran an Oscar ad in the trade papers, an eight-page extravaganza printed on heavy stock. "MGM presents the immortal love story of Madame Curie," began the promo, which included pictures from the movie, the prediction that Louis B. Mayer would get another Oscar, and a series of laudatory quotations. The *Los Angeles Examiner,* for example, stated that *Madame Curie* "raises motion pictures to the realm of Shakespearean drama."

Ain't No Mountain High Enough

Opening on Christmas Day in L.A. was Fox's two-hour-and-forty-minute paean to religious visions, *The Song of Bernadette*. W.R. Wilkerson, editor of the *Hollywood Reporter,* was so taken with the film that he wrote on the front page of his publication:

> *Now that this industry has reached a perfection that affords a* Song of Bernadette, *ANYTHING is possible for it to accomplish. No concern is too deep, no sky is too high for it to reach out and select great thoughts to contribute to the thinking—and betterment—of this world.*

Darryl Zanuck wanted *Bernadette* to contribute some Oscars to his studio and Fox rigged up an elaborate advertisement. Like the *Madame Curie* job, this three-page ad was printed on heavy paper and began with the words, "The Story of a Masterpiece." On the next page was a full-color copy of a Norman Rockwell painting of actress Jennifer Jones, with the text indicating that the painting and the movie were "masterpieces."

Fox got some free hucksterism, as the *Hollywood Reporter* related: "The Catholic churches throughout the nation over the weekend appealed to their congregations to go see *The Song of Bernadette.*" Indeed, a reviewer in Toronto surmised that the appeal of this movie about Saint Bernadette of Lourdes seeing the Virgin Mary "is directed almost exclusively to members of the Roman Catholic faith." If so, there were a whole lot of Catholics out there and *The Song of Bernadette* racked up huge grosses. Those in the industry had a good laugh over a piece of casting for *Bernadette*: Zanuck's current paramour, Linda Darnell, played the Virgin Mary.

A Strange Girl

Movie fans wanted to know more about this newcomer Jennifer Jones. Press agents at Fox revealed that she had been discovered by David O. Selznick and that *Bernadette* was her first movie. It didn't take long, however, for reporters to uncover that Jones was really one Phyllis Isley, who had made a B-western with John Wayne and the serial *Dick Tracy's G-Men* over at Republic in 1939.

Thinking that it didn't jibe with her image as a saint, the studio told Jones to downplay the fact that she was married to actor Robert Walker and had two kids. And whatever she did, she was not to mention that the marriage was in trouble. Louella Parsons fell for the deception and printed that Jones was an available young miss. But when Jones' true marital status leaked out, Louella got back at the actress for making her a laughingstock, writing, "Jennifer Jones is a strange, restrained, shy girl, with little of the small talk and frivolous comments on life that characterize the average young woman of her years."

An Academy by Any Other Name. . .

Content in the knowledge that Warner Brothers had swept the New York Film Critics Awards, Jack Warner sat back and stood apart from the Oscar campaigning. The New York crew had selected *Watch on the Rhine* as Best Picture and its star Paul Lukas as Best Actor. Their Best Actress choice was Ida Lupino, playing an impoverished woman scheming to get her kid sister into showbiz in the Warners drama, *The Hard Way*. The jockeying for Academy Awards by the other studios, however, caused columnist Edith Gwynn to ask: "Why not give a statuette for the best 'we-want-an-Oscar' publicity campaign?" The winner would have been RKO for *Tender Comrade*. The studio had sneak previews of the movie at two theaters named the "Academy," one in Pasadena, the other in Inglewood. After the screenings, full-page ads told the results: "Academy reaction: It's the finest picture of the year" and "The Academy awarded Ginger praise such as we (or you) have not heard—or read—in a long, long time."

The Nominations

The Academy had quite a scare in mid-January when it got word that phony nominating ballots were circulating on college campuses in New York, Los Angeles, San Francisco and Pittsburgh. A vigilant Price, Waterhouse came through, tossing away any ballots received with the label "Public Voting Ballot for Academy Award Candidates" and the nominating proceeded without a hitch.

It continued to be Warner Brothers' year. With twenty-seven nominations, the studio led all others for the first time ever. *Casablanca* and *Watch on the Rhine* were both Best Picture nominees and Humphrey Bogart and Paul Lukas were up for Best Actor. If the studio was disappointed that New York winner Ida Lupino failed to make it, at least it had Joan Fontaine competing as a tragic teenage heroine in the period romance *The Constant Nymph*.

The film with the most nominations, though, belonged to Fox, which was rewarded for spending all that money on advertising. *The Song of Bernadette* had twelve and was the one to beat for Best Picture. Paramount also had a lot to show for its campaigning, because *For Whom the Bell Tolls* was second with nine nominations and MGM also had a Best Picture contender in *Madame Curie*. RKO's chicanery was for naught—*Tender Comrade* was completely ignored (although, years later, Ginger Rogers' mother would recite a line of Dalton Trumbo's dialogue—"Share and share alike, that's democracy"—to the House Un-American Activities Committee as an example of "Communist infiltration" of Hollywood). The passing of a year did not shake the loyalty of Noel Coward's fans and *In Which We Serve* was a Best Picture nominee, although it received only one other nomination, for Coward's original screenplay.

For Whom the Bell Tolls and *The Song of Bernadette* provided the two top candidates for Best Actress, Ingrid Bergman—who also had *Casablanca* to her credit—and Jennifer Jones. Rumors

"My grandmother learned her ABC's from a guerrilla chieftain in a cave."
—Katina Paxinou

of the burgeoning relationship between Jones, still married to Robert Walker, and her Svengali, David O. Selznick, married to Louis B. Mayer's daughter Irene, provided a tantalizing contrast to the actress' innocence as Saint Bernadette. Jones also received the first Golden Globe Award from the Hollywood Foreign Press Association. For the first time in six years, Bette Davis was not a Best Actress nominee, but Greer Garson got her fourth nod in five years for *Madame Curie*.

Jean Arthur received her first nomination for *The More the Merrier*. Although very popular with the public—her press agents said she had never been in a movie that lost money—the actress had the reputation of being uncooperative with the press and aloof from her fellow actors. Hedda Hopper called Arthur the "most criticized star in Hollywood." John Wayne, Arthur's costar in 1943's *The Lady Takes a Chance*, proved to be a gentleman and tried to set the record straight in *Screenland* magazine: "Unlike some stars I know, servicemen are always welcome on her set regardless of how tough a scene may be. . . . When they were there, Jean didn't go into her dressing room. She went over and talked to the boys for a long time."

The two guys from Warners were battling it out for Best Actor. Paul Lukas had the year's classiest reviews, but he really wasn't a marquee name. On the other hand, the *Hollywood Reporter* noticed, "This fellow Bogart is about the hottest thing on the screen today." Gary Cooper's performance in *For Whom the Bell Tolls* brought him his third nomination in a row; as M. Curie, Walter Pidgeon got his second.

The fifth contender for Best Actor was box-office giant Mickey Rooney in MGM's *The Human Comedy*. The studio had commissioned writer William Saroyan to do a script about a small town and he came up with one that required four-and-a-half hours of screen time. While someone else at the studio completely rewrote the script, Saroyan took his material and published it as a novel. His book came out the same week as the movie, became a bestseller, and Saroyan was nominated for Best Original Story. The rewriter wasn't nominated for anything.

Warner Realism

In a trade-paper ad, Jack Warner wrote an "Open Letter to the Warner Brothers nominees":

> *My brothers and I know that this magnificent record could not have been achieved without you and our fellow workers, all of whom understand the studio's realistic policy.*

No one was quite sure whether the realistic policy Jack was referring to was the studio's oft-stated intention to combine entertainment with social commitment or a veiled reference to his reputation as the toughest employer in town. The industry got a clue when, a few days later, MGM congratulated *its* nominees in a multipage ad, billing itself as "THE BEST COMPANY . . . and the MOST FRIENDLY."

Just 30 Seconds

As a further acknowledgment that there was a war on, Academy President Walter "What-have-you-got-against-the-Academy-Bette?" Wanger announced that this year there would be no Academy dinner. Instead, the Awards would be held in a public movie theater, just as Bette Davis had suggested two years earlier. By giving passes to two hundred members of the armed forces, the Academy was implementing another Davis idea—inviting non-industryites to come. As to Davis' suggestion of donating the proceeds to the war relief—well, two out of three's not bad.

The theater chosen was Grauman's Chinese on Hollywood Boulevard, and the Academy emphasized that this year's ceremony would be "streamlined." Recalling the endless stream of speeches at the 1942 Awards, the Board of Governors declared: "No outside speeches" and specifically requested brevity from the winners. "IF YOU WIN AN OSCAR YOU MAY SPEAK JUST 30 SECONDS" blared a *Daily Variety* headline.

Instead of speakers, the Academy promised a "variety show" featuring entertainers who had performed on USO tours to let Hollywood "see for the first time how its personalities entertained the boys abroad."

The Big Night

The Academy had forgotten that in previous years parking services had been provided by the hotel hosting the ceremony. But parking attendants did not come with Grauman's Chinese, so arriving guests were forced to fend for themselves and a steady stream of people entered the theater throughout the first half of the show. Fans complained that the cops had sectioned them off so far away from the theater's courtyard that they couldn't see the stars, who in turn griped that they couldn't greet their public. Photographers, however, were given free rein, and they increased the confusion by blocking the entrances of the celebrities.

The Academy dedicated the show to "the fighting men of the United Nations." The ceremony opened with Susanna Foster's rendition of "The Star-Spangled Banner." The *Los Angeles Times* reported that then "the curtain went up on the biggest Oscar you ever saw—12 feet if it was an inch. It gave everybody an awful start." Emcee Jack Benny came out and told the audience, "I'm here through the courtesy of Bob Hope's having a bad cold." Benny also noted that "It seems to me that to get a nomination a picture must have no laughs . . . and they tell me I've come pretty close to that a few times already."

The Technical Awards were given in the early portion of the program; all of the winners adhered to the Academy's request for brevity, saying "Thank you" and getting off. As Kay Kyser's band opened the variety show, ten tiers of seats holding the invited soldiers and sailors rose up at the rear of the stage. Their arrival got the most sustained applause of the night but they spent the rest of the evening watching participants' backs.

The Writing Awards followed the variety show, and William Saroyan ended up not only with a bestselling book but also an Oscar for his script of *The Human Comedy*. Noel Coward's *In Which We Serve* lost Original Screenplay to Norman Krasna's romantic comedy *Princess O'Rourke*, the climax of which has President Roosevelt bringing together lovers Olivia de Havilland and Robert Cummings. *The Song of Bernadette* lost Best Screenplay to *Casablanca*, a film that was rewritten daily on the set during filming. Best Director went to Michael Curtiz for *Casablanca*, who said that he had written acceptance speeches in 1938 and 1942 only to lose, so this year he had prepared nothing.

The radio broadcast of the show began with Donald Crisp announcing that the Best Supporting Actor was Charles Coburn for *The More the Merrier*. After Coburn got to the stage, presenter Crisp went on about how the winning performance was "one of the greatest ever seen on the screen." Coburn cut him off, "Yes, I'll accept the prize. You don't have to urge me." The winner then broke up the audience with "I hope that at the end of another fifty years of service in the theater, your

Awards Ceremony

MARCH 2, 1944, 8:00 P.M.
GRAUMAN'S CHINESE THEATRE, HOLLYWOOD

Your Host:
JACK BENNY

Presenters

Short Subjects	Walter Wanger
Special Award to George Pal	Walter Wanger
Music Awards	Dinah Shore
Film Editing	Y. Frank Freeman
Sound Recording	Y. Frank Freeman
Special Effects	Y. Frank Freeman
Scientific or Technical Awards	Y. Frank Freeman
Art Direction	Carole Landis
Cinematography	Rosalind Russell
Writing Awards	James Hilton
Director	Mark Sandrich
Documentary Awards	Howard Estabrook
Picture	Sidney Franklin
Thalberg Award	Darryl F. Zanuck
Supporting Actor	Donald Crisp
Supporting Actress	Teresa Wright
Actor	George Murphy
Actress	Greer Garson

"If you win an Oscar you may speak just thirty seconds."
—Daily Variety

children and your children's children will have enough courage to vote for me again."

Teresa Wright, dry-eyed this year, presented the Best Supporting Actress Award to Katina Paxinou, for *For Whom the Bell Tolls,* who expressed her admiration of the "boys" of the Allied powers "fighting for liberty and human dignity." The Greek actress continued, "I will share this Award in spirit with my friends at the Royal Theatre of Athens. I hope they are still alive, but I doubt it."

Song-and-dance man George Murphy bestowed the Best Actor Award on Paul Lukas for *Watch on the Rhine*. One columnist noted that the winner "handled his statue like a hot potato and nearly dropped it a couple of times while he stuttered thanks." When Lukas returned to his seat, loser Humphrey Bogart came over with congratulations.

Best Actress nominee Greer Garson didn't find her own name in the envelope when she presented the Award. The winner was Jennifer Jones for *The Song of Bernadette,* who trembled as she spoke and held on to the microphone for support. After making her thank-you's, Jones burst into tears and rested her head on Jack Benny's shoulder.

Producer Sidney Franklin announced that the winner of the Best Picture Award was *Casablanca*. The *Los Angeles Herald-Express* reported that the audience "gasped in amazement, then quickly regained its composure and heartily applauded the unexpected results." The UPI concurred: "*Casablanca* was a dark horse. Jack Warner seemed as surprised as everyone else when the plaster Oscar was thrust in his hand."

Aftermath

Losers Jean Arthur and Joan Fontaine and their husbands immediately took off for a bar on Rodeo Drive. Loser Ingrid Bergman, who had had a lock on Best Actress until *The Song of Bernadette* came along, ran backstage to congratulate friend Jennifer Jones, who was receiving felicitations not only for her Oscar but for her twenty-fifth birthday. The winner told Bergman, "I apologize, Ingrid. You should have won." "No, Jennifer, your Bernadette was better than my Maria."

A few days after the ceremony, the Screen Directors Guild announced that its members were seriously considering quitting the Academy. The guild's president, Mark Sandrich, fumed: "Our complaint is based on the fact that the directorial Award was relegated to the first part of the evening's program and was not carried on the broadcast." With time, however, bruised egos healed—Mark Sandrich agreed to produce next year's show.

Also feeling slighted was *Casablanca*'s producer Hal Wallis, who felt that he, not Jack Warner, should have received the Best Picture Oscar. Mollifying him somewhat was the fact that he had won his second Thalberg Award and the knowledge that each of the five movies he produced in 1943—*Casablanca, Watch on the Rhine, Air Force, Princess O'Rourke* and *This Is the Army*—had won at least one Academy Award. Still, when Wallis left to go to Paramount later in the year after two decades at Warners, insiders pointed to Jack Warner's Oscar night usurpation as a major cause.

Daily Variety pointed out how Fox's "prestige" campaign for *Bernadette* blew up in its face: at Oscar time, *Bernadette* was still in limited release at advanced ticket prices, which meant that those with the bulk of the voting power—the extras—had not yet been able to afford to go to the movie. A poll of voting extras showed that only 25 percent had seen *Bernadette,* whereas nearly all of them had seen—and voted for—*Casablanca*. Still, with four Oscars, *The Song of Bernadette* did better than *Madame Curie,* which was shut out.

Photoplay told its readers: "That the picture *Casablanca* won over several more elaborate productions proves Hollywood joins the world in its belief that entertainment is the aim and goal of every picture." But entertainment was no longer the aim of the ceremony. Bon vivants discovered that with the Awards having gone public they could no longer drink through the whole thing as in olden days. The *Hollywood Reporter* felt that

1943's presentations had a simple dignity that had been missing in the past: "All in all, it was a swell affair, finely handled and one that will now set a precedent that will most certainly eliminate the junk usually attendant at such affairs in the past."

But *Daily Variety* expressed another view: "All of the colorfulness of previous Academy Awards that took place in hotels was gone and the 16th annual Awards was just one of those things, so far as color, warmth and glamour are concerned."

1944

"It is the movie to prevent World War III."
—P.M.

Academy voters had a choice between a priest and a president, and when they made their selection they left one mogul mighty sore.

Going Paramount's Way

Director Leo McCarey wasn't a stranger to critical praise and Academy recognition—he had won Best Director in 1937 for *The Awful Truth*—but *Going My Way* was no screwball comedy. To make the success of this series of vignettes about a Catholic parish church even more unlikely, McCarey chose crooner Bing Crosby for the leading role of a young priest. But McCarey's mixture worked, with most critics echoing the *New York Post*'s Archer Winsten, who wrote, "The beauty and joy of *Going My Way* spring from the treatment of human relationships."

For the first time, critics called Bing Crosby an actor rather than a singer, and exhibitors named him the number-one box-office star of the year. His costar, Barry Fitzgerald, as an aging priest, was declared the discovery of 1944 even though the alumnus of the Abbey Theatre in Dublin had been in Hollywood since 1937, appearing in such hits as *Marie Antoinette* and *How Green Was My Valley*. *Life* told its readers to look out for "a wonderful Irishman named Barry Fitzgerald. His performance is one of the half-dozen finer things seen in motion pictures as they complete their first fifty years."

At the end of August, Paramount proclaimed that *Going My Way* had broken 2,420 house records. With business at such high levels, the trade papers were moved to rave about the film all over again. W.R. Wilkerson of the *Hollywood Reporter* enthused:

> *There's not much doubt that when the negative of* Going My Way *has been worn out through the printing of thousands of release prints, in years to come, this picture will accumulate the largest gross take of any picture of its day with the possible exception of* Gone With the Wind *and it's a good bet that the McCarey-Paramount clicker may even top the Selznick-MGM big grosser.*

Gone With the Wind's producer, David O. Selznick, meanwhile was overseeing the release of *Since You Went Away,* his latest attempt to duplicate *GWTW*'s success. He described it as an "epic of the American homefront." Costing a staggering $4.5 million dollars, *Since You Went Away* received mostly favorable reviews and did outstanding business. Louella Parsons called it "another great picture like *Gone With the Wind,*" but everyone else realized that Selznick did not have another *GWTW*. *The New Yorker* observed, "Mr. Selznick does not say that *Since You Went Away* is better than *Gone With the Wind*. He merely asks his performers to state in writing that *Since You Went Away* is the finest motion picture in which they have appeared. So they do this little thing, through the advertising department, and how they will reconcile it with their consciences is strictly up to them." Selznick did come up with an advertising circular containing everything nice anyone ever said about the film—it was forty pages long.

Darryl's Dream

But Selznick couldn't touch Darryl F. Zanuck in the self-aggrandizement department in 1944. The head of 20th Century–Fox let the industry know he would not be content with entertaining audiences—*his* movies would be instructive, too. Zanuck's big deal for '44, and his dream project, was *Wilson*, a two-and-a-half-hour, $5.2-million biography of the twenty-sixth president, Woodrow Wilson.

The Fox advertising department knew that *Wilson* was going to be a tough sell, so the ads promised, "A warm intimate human story . . . The color of a glamorous era . . . Roaring football

Overleaf: *Best Supporting Actor winner Barry Fitzgerald mourns the plaster Oscar he decapitated while practicing golf in his living room.*

"The people who vote in that free-for-all don't know on which side their crêpes Suzette are buttered."
—Tallulah Bankhead

games." But the critics responded just as Zanuck had hoped. The *New York Morning Telegraph* solemnized, "*Wilson* is one of the most important movies, not of the year, but of the era in which we all now find ourselves living," while *P.M.* pronounced it "the movie to prevent World War III."

After the film opened in August, "open letter" ads praising both *Wilson* and Zanuck began popping up in the trade papers. These were bought by Hollywood notables ranging from Samuel Goldwyn to the Hot Shots, house dancers at the Trocadero nightclub, who opined, "To our way of thinking, *Wilson* will go down in cinematic history as the film that actually made a vital contribution towards making the world a better one in which to live." Fox used eight pages of red, white and blue advertising to hype "WILSON—The most important event in fifty years of motion picture entertainment." From August through the close of the year, the studio also ran ads reprinting not only favorable reviews, but editorials and sections of the *Congressional Record*.

Wilson wasn't doing badly at the box office, either. During its eight-week premiere engagement at New York's Roxy, *Wilson* grossed $1,027,000, the highest take of a movie at any one theater up to that time.

Woodrow Wilson vs. God

By year's end, the "Rambling Reporter" sighed, "Boy! Would we have to tear our hair out if we had to choose a 'best' between *Going My Way* and *Wilson*." The makers of such highly touted films as *Double Indemnity, Lifeboat, Hail the Conquering Hero, Miracle of Morgan's Creek, Laura, Gaslight, Meet Me in St. Louis, None But the Lonely Heart, Thirty Seconds Over Tokyo* and—sorry, David—*Since You Went Away* were tearing their hair because they knew that they'd be stuck as also-rans to the big two. Zanuck scored another coup when he was invited to address the American Nobel Committee anniversary dinner in New York after the committee had honored *Wilson* as "a vital contribution to the cause of world peace."

But then it was Zanuck's turn to start the hair-tearing. The New York Film Critics made *Going My Way* their runaway Best Picture winner, with *Wilson* coming in third, behind Preston Sturges' home-front comedy, *Hail the Conquering Hero*. The critics also went for Leo McCarey for Best Director and Barry Fitzgerald for Best Actor. Much to Zanuck's chagrin, *Going My Way* was winning awards all over the place, including the *Film Daily* poll, the *Screen Guild* magazine poll, the *Photoplay* Gold Medal, and the Best Picture prize from *Leatherneck*, the official magazine of the United States Marine Corps. Zanuck did get one award from *Look* magazine "for his courage in producing *Wilson*."

David O. Selznick figured that if he was out of the running for Best Picture, he could still get an Oscar for one of his actors. It was a rare day during January 1945 that readers of trade papers were not greeted by a full-page photograph of a Selznick contractee on the back page. Selznick went especially heavily for Joseph Cotten in the wartime romance *I'll Be Seeing You*, but he also sprang for space for Claudette Colbert, Jennifer Jones and Shirley Temple in *Since You Went Away* and Ingrid Bergman in *Gaslight*. A Victorian suspense movie abut a husband who tries to drive his wife nuts, *Gaslight* was an MGM film with which Selznick had nothing to do, but he was a realist; Bergman had the best chance of anybody in his stable of stars. She had placed second to Tallulah Bankhead in *Lifeboat* with the New York Film Critics, and was well-liked in the industry for her talent, her cooperation and her steadily increasing box-office pull.

The Nominations

As expected, the nominations were dominated by *Going My Way* and *Wilson*, each of which was up for ten Oscars. Selznick received a Best Picture nomination for *Since You Went Away*. The other two nominees were *Gaslight* and Paramount's *Double Indemnity*, the James M. Cain story of murderous adulterers directed by Billy Wilder.

"You'll go to the Academy Awards or you'll never hear the end of it from me."
—Bing Crosby's mother

Tallulah Bankhead was unable to parlay her New York Film Critics Award into an Oscar nomination. Speculation was that the strong-willed Tallulah was too much of an industry outsider to appeal to Academy voters, having kissed off Hollywood a dozen years earlier. In her autobiography, Bankhead scoffed, "Did I get an Academy Oscar? No! The people who vote in that free-for-all don't know on which side their crêpes Suzette are buttered." Advertising paid off for David Selznick: Bergman and Colbert were up for Best Actress. So were Bette Davis, for the seventh time, for *Mr. Skeffington;* Greer Garson, for the fourth year in a row, for *Mrs. Parkington;* and Barbara Stanwyck for *Double Indemnity*. Originally, Stanwyck did not want to do *Double Indemnity*. After reading the script she went to Billy Wilder and said, "I love the script and I love you, but I'm a little afraid after all these years of playing heroines to go into an out-and-out cold-blooded killer." Wilder said simply, "Well, are you a mouse or an actress?" Stanwyck decided to make the film.

Both of the priests in *Going My Way,* Bing Crosby and Barry Fitzgerald, were competing for Best Actor, as were Alexander Knox, a.k.a. Woodrow Wilson, and two fellows who played not very nice people: Cary Grant, a Cockney ne'er-do-well in *None But the Lonely Heart,* and Charles Boyer, for doing dreadful things to Ingrid Bergman in *Gaslight*. When Crosby was asked if he thought he would win, he responded, "I don't think so. This guy—what's his name—Knox ought to make it."

Double Whammy

Everyone cried "Huh?" when Barry Fitzgerald got a Supporting Actor nomination to go with his Best Actor nod for the same performance. It had been assumed that he would place in the Supporting category—he didn't have a whole lot of screen time in *Going My Way*—leaving Best Actor open for leading man Crosby. It was all strictly legal, however; the Academy's official rules at the time stated: "Performances by an actor or actress in any supporting role may be nominated for either the Best Acting Award or the Award for Supporting Player." *Photoplay* argued that "no one can, in the same picture, be both—any more than a man in uniform can simultaneously be a lieutenant and a corporal—but the Academy achieved the impossible."

The prestige of the double nomination capped recent good news for Fitzgerald. A month before the nominations were disclosed, he had been found not guilty in the manslaughter death of an elderly woman whom he had hit with his car on Hollywood Boulevard. Not only was the actor acquitted of the charges, but the presiding judge sharply reprimanded the district attorney's office for issuing the complaint and the Los Angeles Municipal Court for ordering him to stand trial in the first place. Personal sympathy made his popularity increase even more and one columnist wrote, "Barry Fitzgerald has suddenly snuck up and become everybody's dream man."

Selznick the Incorrigible

Once the nominations were announced, David O. Selznick went back to fattening the bank accounts of *Daily Variety* and the *Hollywood Reporter* by buying ad space for his nominees: Claudette Colbert, Ingrid Bergman, Jennifer Jones and Monty Woolley, a Supporting Actor nominee for *Since You Went Away*. Selznick seemed convinced that the way to win Oscars was to point out other awards won by his players so that voters would feel in good company. Unfortunately for Selznick, none of these actors had won much of anything, but he did the best he could. CLAUDETTE COLBERT—THE WINNER. BEST ACTRESS*, blazed one. The asterisk drew attention to a footnote indicating that Colbert had received no prize; this was merely the opinion of the *Toronto Star*. Bergman's ad had the appearance of a news wire-service flash, datelined Iceland: THE AMERICAN TROOPS STATIONED HERE HAVE VOTED INGRID BERGMAN THE NUMBER ONE ACTRESS OF 1944. Selznick made sure he got his money's worth: the ad also noted that Jennifer Jones came in second in the voting. The mogul also tried the "Isn't it about time?" approach with Bergman in ads labeled BERGMAN THE INCOMPARABLE that showed the actress in 1939's *Intermezzo,* 1941's *Dr. Jekyll and Mr. Hyde* and Selznick's forthcoming *Spellbound.*

To ensure that no Award would seem of secondary importance, ceremony producer Mark Sandrich announced that the show would contain a "cinemontage"—film clips of every nominee in each category to be shown as the appropriate nominations were read. Another novelty: the Awards would be broadcast in their entirety—by the fledgling ABC network—so that even the winning director would be heard coast-to-coast.

The Big Night

Mark Sandrich never got to see if his innovations worked; a few days before the ceremony, the forty-four-year-old director died of a heart attack while playing gin rummy with his wife. It also didn't help matters that Hollywood was in the midst of a strike by set designers, illustrators and decorators, with other unions refusing to cross the picket lines.

Despite these troubles, the Los Angeles police reported that the Awards drew the biggest turnout of fans for a film event since the beginning of the war. Ingrid Bergman and Jennifer Jones arrived together for the second year in a row; Bergman even wore last year's dress. Once again a ban on formal wear was flouted by Hedda Hopper, who, in the courtyard of Grauman's Chinese, opened her coat to flash her evening gown to the crowd.

Bing Crosby decided to attend the ceremony only at the last minute. Paramount had discovered that their number-one star was not planning to go to the Awards and, at 6 o'clock that evening, sent publicity people on a manhunt. Der Bingle was found at the twelfth hole at the Lakeside Golf Course in casual clothes and no toupee. Bing told the flacks to call his parents and they'd go in his place. The publicity people did phone his mother, who insisted on speaking to her boy. She told him, "You'll go or you'll never hear the end of it from me." So Crosby dutifully put on a suit—but not his hairpiece—and went to the Chinese Theatre.

John Cromwell, director of *Since You Went Away,* was the host of the first portion of the show and, after dedicating the program to Mark Sandrich, saying "It's Mark's show and Mark would want us to get on," handed out the Technical Awards.

After the Awards-giving took a break for a variety show, the orchestra launched into "Thanks for the Memory." Explaining his appearance on the stage, Bob Hope said, "Anything to avoid paying the $12 ticket fee." Looking around the Chinese Theatre auditorium, he commented, "This is the first time I knew this was a theater. I've always thought it was a place where Darryl Zanuck sent his laundry." Hope was startled when President Walter Wanger stepped out and presented him with his second Special Award, a life membership in the Academy. This time Hope was not speechless: "Now I know how President Roosevelt feels," he said.

A Special Oscar went to eight-year-old Margaret O'Brien for her performances that year in *Meet Me in St. Louis, Jane Eyre, The Canterville Ghost* and *Lost Angel.* Hope held the child up so she could be heard over the radio microphone, saying, "Will you hurry up and grow up, please?"

Mervyn LeRoy handed the Best Director trophy to Leo McCarey, who was all set to recite his acceptance speech: "I want to thank Paramount for the picture, the actors for the wonderful per-

Awards Ceremony

March 15, 1945, 8:00 p.m.
Grauman's Chinese Theatre, Hollywood

Your Hosts:
John Cromwell and Bob Hope

Presenters

Documentary Awards	John Cromwell
Short Subjects	John Cromwell
Scientific or Technical Awards	John Cromwell
Film Editing	John Cromwell
Sound Recording	John Cromwell
Special Effects	John Cromwell
Scoring Awards	John Cromwell
Art Direction	John Cromwell
Song	Bob Hope
Cinematography	Bob Hope
Writing Awards	Hugo Butler
Director	Mervyn LeRoy
Life Membership to Bob Hope	Walter Wanger
Supporting Actor	Charles Coburn
Supporting Actress	Teresa Wright
Actor	Gary Cooper
Actress	Jennifer Jones
Thalberg Award	Norma Shearer
Picture	Hal Wallis

"I always thought Grauman's Chinese was a place where Darryl Zanuck sent his laundry."
—Bob Hope

formances and I want to thank God for the subject." But someone told him they were running overtime for the radio broadcast so all he got to say was "Thanks."

The winner of Best Supporting Actress was Ethel Barrymore for *None But the Lonely Heart*. The "cinemontage" clip of Barrymore was all the audience got to see of the absent winner as RKO's Charles Koerner accepted her Oscar from Teresa Wright. Barry Fitzgerald was there to pick up his Best Supporting Actor Oscar. *Daily Variety* noted that Fitzgerald "drew a round of applause such as greeted no other victor. And when it came to making his speech, he was just the kindly bashful priest he portrayed in *Going My Way*."

Gary Cooper was pressed into service to present the Best Actor Award because last year's winner, Paul Lukas, was sick with food poisoning after a trip to Mexico. The winner was Bing Crosby for *Going My Way*. Cooper called him to the stage, saying, "It is the greatest pleasure I've ever had to present to you the Best Acting Award for 1944 for your wonderful, superb performance."

"Superb?" asked Crosby. "Superb," Cooper insisted. "Oh, my heavens . . .," Crosby responded. "That is the best word I can think of at the moment for *Going My Way*," Cooper added. "Thank you very much, Gary. I couldn't be more surprised if I won the Kentucky Derby. Can you imagine the jokes Hope's going to write about this in his radio show? This will give him twelve straight weeks of material for his radio program, talking about me."

Hope couldn't wait for his radio show—the comedian sneaked out on stage and began making faces behind Crosby's back. Crosby didn't know why the audience was laughing, but he started chuckling himself and, pipe in hand, continued, "This is a real land of opportunity when Leo can take a broken-down old crooner and make an Academy Award winner out of him."

After Crosby and Cooper exited, Hope cracked that Crosby's winning an Oscar was like hearing that Sam Goldwyn was lecturing at Oxford. Jennifer Jones showed up to announce Best Actress. The winner was her friend Ingrid Bergman for *Gaslight*. Before handing Bergman the Oscar, Jones said, "Your artistry has won our vote and your graciousness has won our hearts." Bergman responded, "Tomorrow I go to work in a picture with Bing and Mr. McCarey [*The Bells of St. Mary's*]. And I'm afraid if I didn't have an Oscar, too, they wouldn't speak to me."

In the opinion of *Daily Variety*, the "most dramatic happening" of the ceremony came when Norma Shearer was introduced to present, for the first time, the Thalberg Award. The remarried Shearer handed the head of her former husband to Darryl Zanuck—his second Thalberg.

Zanuck's Award would have to serve as a consolation prize because *Going My Way* was named Best Picture. As in previous years, the studio head rather than the film's producer picked up the Oscar. Bob Hope, standing at the side of the stage when Hal Wallis announced the Paramount film the winner, made the most of the opportunity. The comedian was temporarily on suspension at the studio and when his boss, Buddy DeSylva, reached the stage, Hope got on his knees in a mock plea for forgiveness. He then took out a handkerchief and, to the audience's cheers, started shining DeSylva's shoes.

Aftermath

When Ethel Barrymore learned that she had won the Academy Award, she told friends she was "not particularly impressed." In her autobiography, she was downright blasé: "And of course it was very pleasant later to get the Oscar."

Barry Fitzgerald's win proved more dramatic. After celebrating with his roommate—his stand-in—and friends at Barney's Beanery, the actor practiced his golf swing at home, accidentally hitting his plaster statuette and decapitating it. Paramount was forced to shell out ten bucks for a spare. So Fitzgerald did, in a way, end up with two Oscars that year.

Losing Best Actress nominee Barbara Stanwyck told the press she was a member of the Ingrid Bergman Fan Club: "I don't feel at all bad about the Award because my favorite actress won it and has earned it by all her performances."

Darryl Zanuck was not such a good sport. Not content with another bust of the MGM Boy Wonder, he told friends and underlings that the Academy was obviously a corps of philistines if they could pass over *Wilson* as Best Picture. And until he died, he bitterly complained that his dream project did not receive the rewards he felt it so justly deserved.

1945

"People in Hollywood don't like me, and they've never regarded me as a good actress."
—Joan Crawford

A glamour gal and a reigning director were looking to get even at the 1945 Academy Awards.

Writer-director Billy Wilder was supposed to be on vacation when he bought four novels to read on the long train trip from Hollywood to New York—one of them a bestseller about a New York alcoholic, entitled *The Lost Weekend*. After Wilder read it, he started it all over again, taking notes on how he was going to adapt it as his next movie. By the time the train pulled in to Grand Central Station, Wilder had an outline and he called his erstwhile collaborator, Charles Brackett, in Los Angeles—it was 6 A.M. there—and asked him if he'd like to write with him again. Brackett consented immediately and was particularly drawn to the material—Mrs. Brackett was an alcoholic who rarely left the house.

On Location at Bellevue

Paramount was wary of the project, but let Wilder have his way, except for the casting. The director wanted a new Broadway actor named José Ferrer for the lead, but the studio felt "an attractive-looking hero" would make the film more commercial, so Paramount leading man Ray Milland was assigned to the role. Wilder shot much of the film on location in New York, around Third Avenue bars and Bellevue Hospital, and at times the movie had an almost documentary look. *The Lost Weekend* was so far from the usual studio movie that a preview audience in Santa Barbara didn't know how to take it—there was laughter and a steady stream of people walking out. Paramount executives were ready to shelve Wilder's mistake, but studio president Barney Balaban said, "Once we make a picture, we don't just flush it down the toilet!"

The studio opened the movie out of town—in London, where it was a hit. "London is on a praise binge for *The Lost Weekend*," remarked the *Hollywood Reporter*. "Even with the paper shortage it's gotten more comment than any picture since *Gone With the Wind*." Paramount announced plans to release the movie in the United States in November, in New York first, then Hollywood. "The most daring film that ever came out of Hollywood," raved the *New York Daily News*. All Gotham toasted Billy Wilder, who told the *New York Times*, "If *To Have and Have Not* has established Lauren Bacall as The Look, then *The Lost Weekend* should certainly bring Mr. Milland renown as The Kidney."

A week before the movie premiered in Hollywood, ads in the trade papers proclaimed, "*The Lost Weekend*. The Talk Has Started." One of the talkers was Hedda Hopper, who said, "*The Lost Weekend* tops them all. Ray Milland's portrayal is an engraved invitation for an Academy Award." The movie's reviews were so consistently favorable, Paramount advertised it as "The Most Widely Acclaimed Motion Picture in the History of the Industry." Even with the great notices and box office, a few studio executives wondered if the film would impress Academy members and there were discussions about hustling Ray Milland's follow-up vehicle—a lavish historical period romance called *Kitty*—as the company's major Oscar contender. "Paramount can't decide whether *Lost Weekend* or *Kitty* will be their entry for picture of the year," wrote Edith Gwynn. "Are they kidding?" *Kitty* was held back until 1946.

No More Shoulder Pads

Joan Crawford was going to show them. She walked out on MGM after eighteen years because Louis B. Mayer, believing she didn't have it in her to become a box-office draw again, was consigning her to routine projects. Crawford went over to Burbank and signed a three-picture deal with Jack Warner—at a reduced salary. Crawford was still a star, in her own mind at least, and she refused Warner's scripts for a year and a half, ultimately

Overleaf: *Unlike little Kay in* Mildred Pierce, *an "ill" Joan Crawford makes a miraculous recovery when her Oscar is personally delivered to her bedroom.*

"Once we make a picture, we don't just flush it down the toilet."
—The president of Paramount

taking herself off salary until he delivered the goods.

Bette Davis had turned down the title role in James M. Cain's *Mildred Pierce,* so producer Jerry Wald offered it to Crawford. "I love it! I love it!" Joan exclaimed over the phone to Wald. "It's exactly what I've been waiting for." There was still one obstacle; Warner's star director Michael Curtiz didn't want to work with Crawford. "She comes over here with her high-hat airs and her goddamn shoulder pads," the director complained. "Why should I waste my time directing a has-been?"

Crawford got rid of the shoulder pads and condescended to make a screen test for Curtiz. She got the part. At the party commemorating the end of filming, Curtiz silenced the revelers and said, "When I agreed to direct Miss Crawford, I felt she was going to be stubborn as a mule and I made up my mind to be plenty hard on her. Now that I have learned how sweet she is and how professional and talented she is, I take back even thinking those things about her." After the applause, Crawford gave Curtiz a gift—a specially designed pair of Adrian shoulder pads.

Seeing Is Believing

One of Crawford's first moves after leaving MGM had been to hire her own publicist, Henry Rogers. While she was still filming *Mildred Pierce,* Rogers received a phone call from producer Jerry Wald: "Call Hedda Hopper and tell her you were talking to me and I was raving to you about the great performance Joan Crawford is giving and that I'm certain she will be a strong contender for an Academy Award. Hedda will pay attention." Rogers did as instructed, and, sure enough, Hopper itemed, "Insiders at Warner Brothers Studios are saying that Joan Crawford is giving such a great performance in the early stages of *Mildred Pierce* that she'll be a strong contender for next year's Academy Award."

Then Rogers got a call from his client. "My telephone has been ringing since early this morning with people congratulating me on my performance," Joan said. "What's going on?" Rogers explained Wald's word-of-mouth Oscar strategy, but Crawford was skeptical. "People in Hollywood don't like me, and they've never regarded me as a good actress. But go ahead. We'll see what happens."

Things started happening right away. Producer Hal Wallis pulled Jerry Wald aside at a party and said that he had heard that Crawford was giving a sensational performance. "I'm curious where you heard about it," Wald asked. "I don't know," Wallis responded, "I guess I must have read it somewhere." Warners heard the industry grapevine too, and cooked up an ambitious advertising campaign for the movie. "Don't tell what Mildred Pierce did!" was the film's advertising slogan, and the line was parodied everywhere. A diner in downtown Los Angeles, for instance, displayed a sign that read: FOR 65 CENTS WE'LL NOT ONLY SERVE YOU A SWELL BLUE PLATE—WE'LL TELL YOU WHAT MILDRED PIERCE DID. Joan's comeback had become an anticipated event.

Minus the Glamour

"It gives me pleasure to report that Joan has come back for a second try at the screen minus the old glamour and with added poise and greater flexibility as an actress," commented the *New York Daily News.* "She gives the best performance of her career." The film was a runaway hit, and even James Agee confessed in *The Nation* that he loved every minute of it. When the public's attention swung back to Crawford, she was ready. The star was always available for interviews, and she talked about her new maturity. "When I was at Metro, I had to live up to a mold. Now I am a free spirit," she said. "Do you know, I never had a sense of humor, but I think I am beginning to develop one."

Henry Rogers was also busy, giving information to the gossips Crawford had not gotten around to talking to, and the trade papers were filled with items along the lines of, "Joan Crawford had a New York shoe store send 50 pairs of shoes out

"We could not keep the audience quiet from the time his name came on the screen."
—David O. Selznick

here—but those 846,573 hats she toted herself." Then there was the circulating industry wisecrack, "Crawford's Back and MGM Doesn't Have Her." The only dark spot on the actress' comeback was her divorce from her third husband, Phillip Terry, who was enjoying the best role of his career as Ray Milland's brother in *The Lost Weekend*. Crawford told columnists, "I want the kind of marriage I haven't had," but she told friends, "I owed Phillip an apology from the beginning."

The Ubiquitous Bergman

As well oiled as Crawford's campaign machine was, she faced considerable competition for the Oscar. The number-one female star in America was Greer Garson, and her latest, *The Valley of Decision*, in which she played a servant who marries into a wealthy family, was voted the favorite movie in a Gallup poll of fifty-five million for *Photoplay*. Another popular Oscar winner was Jennifer Jones, who played an amnesia victim in *Love Letters*. But Crawford's biggest threat was last year's winner—Ingrid Bergman.

"Nineteen forty-five is a Bergman year," declared David O. Selznick's publicists when three Bergman movies opened in New York. Ingrid played an oversexed Creole in Warner Brothers' *Saratoga Trunk*, a warm-hearted nun in Leo McCarey's sequel to *Going My Way* called *The Bells of St. Mary's*, and a psychiatrist with more than a passing interest in her male patient in Selznick's latest collaboration with Alfred Hitchcock, *Spellbound*. "Hollywood, it seems, decided to dispense with all actresses but Miss Bergman," observed the *New York Mirror*. "That is okay by me." But *Esquire* became worried: "Should Ingrid suddenly become unpopular or get herself involved in a scandal, the corporate life of the U.S. would dissolve like a pair of pasteboard shoes in a snowstorm."

Although Selznick was pushing his contract actress in his own *Spellbound*, it looked as if it would be *The Bells of St. Mary's* that would carry Bergman into the Oscar derby. Of Bergman's performance, *Hollywood Review* wrote, "It is probably the single greatest performance that any actress in motion pictures has ever given and, as magnificent as she also is in *Saratoga Trunk*, this is the jewel that crowns her illustrious career."

The Bells of St. Mary's, an anecdotal film about a parochial grammar school, was 1945's highest-grossing film, and it made more money than its predecessor, putting it third on the list of all-time moneymakers, behind *Gone With the Wind* and *This Is the Army*. Bing Crosby was back as Father Chuck "Dial O For" O'Malley, and columnists speculated that last year's Oscar winner could win again for playing the same character.

A New Face

Selznick's *Spellbound* boasted a dream sequence designed and executed by surrealist Salvador Dali, but the producer discovered that audiences were reacting mostly to the film's leading man, a twenty-nine-year-old newcomer named Gregory Peck. "We could not keep the audience quiet from the time his name came on the screen until we had shushed them through three or four sequences and stopped all the dames from 'oohing' and 'ahing' and gurgling," Selznick reported after the first preview. Peck hit Hollywood like a meteor that year because the war had drained the film industry of its leading men. The good-looking actor made a splash as a missionary priest in *The Keys of the Kingdom* and then went on to costar opposite Greer Garson in *The Valley of Decision* and Ingrid Bergman in *Spellbound*. Like Bergman, Peck seemed to be everywhere; also like Bergman he was under contract to David O. Selznick—an Oscar nomination appeared imminent.

Naming the Favorites

The New York Film Critics chose *The Lost Weekend* as their Best Picture, and they saluted Billy Wilder and Ray Milland with their Director and Actor Awards. Ingrid Bergman kayoed them with the one-two punch of *Spellbound* and *The*

Bells of St. Mary's and won the Best Actress Award. Bergman's victory did not bode well for Joan Crawford, but there was still a glimmer of hope: the National Board of Review made what *Daily Variety* referred to as "the eye-opening selection of Joan Crawford as best actress of the year."

The Nominations

It was so far, so good, for Joan Crawford's campaign—she was nominated for Best Actress along with Ingrid Bergman, Greer Garson, Jennifer Jones and Gene Tierney, who starred in the melodrama *Leave Her to Heaven,* the second highest-grossing film of the year after *The Bells of St. Mary's. Mildred Pierce* did well too, garnering six nominations, including Best Picture. Two of Joan's costars were competing in the Best Supporting Actress race—Eve Arden, who played her best friend, and seventeen-year-old Ann Blyth, who played her spoiled daughter, Veda Pierce. Another vicious seventeen-year-old was Joan Lorring, nominated for giving Bette Davis trouble in *The Corn Is Green.* Next to Blyth and Lorring, twenty-year-old Angela Lansbury was practically a veteran, earning her second Supporting Actress nomination for MGM's *The Picture of Dorian Gray.* The old lady of the category was forty-two-year-old Anne Revere, tapped for being Elizabeth Taylor's mother in Liz's first starring vehicle, *National Velvet.*

The Best Picture race was between *The Bells of St. Mary's,* with eight nominations, and *The Lost Weekend,* with seven. The same held for the Best Actor contest, with Bing Crosby vying with Ray Milland. Gregory Peck placed, along with another new heartthrob, Cornel Wilde, a star of B-movies who suddenly got the big buildup from Columbia when he was cast as Frédéric Chopin in *A Song to Remember.* Wilde's star rose so quickly that lyricist Johnny Mercer said a group of coeds from Cornell University had petitioned him to write a song called "I'm Just Wilde About Cornell."

The biggest surprise in the Academy's first round was the strong showing for the Gene Kelly musical *Anchors Aweigh*—the film was up for Best Picture and Kelly was nominated as an Actor. "Gene Kelly's innovation in film dancing did more than anything else in the last several years to yank movie musicals out of their accustomed rut," explained comedy director Norman Z. McLeod.

A Blessing from the House

For the second year in a row, the two major contenders for Best Picture were directed by Billy Wilder and Leo McCarey and Wilder had not forgotten that McCarey had taken home the Oscars last year. *The Lost Weekend* campaign continued at full speed; there was a plug from the House of Seagrams, a liquor company, which read, "Paramount has succeeded in burning into the hearts and minds of all who see this vivid screen story our own long-held and oft-published belief that . . . *some men should not drink!*, which might well have been the name of this great picture instead of *The Lost Weekend.*" Billy Wilder was telling his friends that in his acceptance speech he was going to thank W.C. Fields for providing him with such an outstanding research subject.

Humorist Fred Allen wrote to Best Director nominee Alfred Hitchcock that he thought Academy Award winners should be given statuettes in their own likenesses, adding, "Should you win, think how much more distinctive it would be for you to receive a balloon-shaped statuette rather than the skinny model."

The Big Night

Now that the war was over, the Oscars were made of gold again and the ceremony was a formal affair for everyone, not just Hedda Hopper.

Conspicuously absent was Best Actress nominee Joan Crawford. She had called Henry Rogers that morning and cried, "Henry, I can't do it, I'm so frightened. I know I'm going to lose." Despite entreaties from Rogers and Jerry Wald, she wouldn't budge and ran up a temperature of 104. She had her physician examine her and he pronounced her too ill to attend. Henry Rogers refused to say die and sent photographers to wait at Crawford's home, just in case. Also standing by were Joan's hairdresser and makeup man. Meanwhile at the Chinese Theatre, costar Ann Blyth showed up in a body cast; she had recently broken her spine. The other *Mildred Pierce* nominee, Eve Arden, managed to make it unscathed.

The show began at 8 o'clock with Johnny Green conducting the orchestra in the "Academy Hit Parade," a medley of previous Best Song winners. The new Academy president, actor Jean Hersholt, read telegrams from General Dwight Eisenhower and Admiral Chester Nimitz praising the motion-picture industry for its part in winning World War II. The audience listened respectfully, and no doubt gratefully, with the knowledge that this was probably the last year they would have to hear dissertations on "the war effort."

James Stewart, recently returned from the air force, was introduced as master of ceremonies. In contrast to Bob Hope and Jack Benny, the reticent actor skipped the jokes and the patter, offering only, "Let's get this show on the road." Among the prizes given out in this early portion of the program were Special Awards to Walter Wanger, for "his six years' service as president of the Academy," spent mostly in belatedly effecting ex-president Bette Davis' suggestions, and to Republic Studios for building itself a musical auditorium.

Best Scoring winner Miklos Rosza had, per-

Awards Ceremony

MARCH 7, 1946, 8:00 P.M.
GRAUMAN'S CHINESE THEATRE, HOLLYWOOD

Your Hosts:
BOB HOPE AND JAMES STEWART

Presenters

Short Subjects . . . . Y. Frank Freeman
Film Editing . . . . Frank Capra
Sound Recording . . . . Frank Capra
Special Effects . . . . Frank Capra
Special Award to Walter Wanger . . . . . Donald Nelson
Art Direction . . . . Ginger Rogers
Cinematography . . . . D.W. Griffith
Picture . . . . Eric Johnston
Writing Awards . . . . Bette Davis
Director . . . . William Wyler
Special Award to
The House I Live In . . . . George Murphy
Special Award to
Peggy Ann Garner . . . . George Murphy
Supporting Performances . . . . Van Heflin
Actor . . . . Ingrid Bergman
Actress . . . . Charles Boyer

Performers of Nominated Songs

(This was the first time that the nominated songs were performed on the show.)

"Accentuate the Positive" . . . . *
"Anywhere" . . . . Frank Sinatra
"Aren't You Glad You're You" . . . . *
"The Cat and the Canary" . . . . Dick Haymes
"Endlessly" . . . . Kathryn Grayson
"I Fall in Love Too Easily" . . . . Frank Sinatra
"I'll Buy That Dream" . . . . Kathryn Grayson
"It Might As Well Be Spring" . . . . Dick Haymes
"Linda" . . . . Kathryn Grayson
"Love Letters" . . . . Dinah Shore
"More and More" . . . . Kathryn Grayson
"Sleighride in July" . . . . Dinah Shore
"So in Love" . . . . Frank Sinatra
"Some Sunday Morning" . . . . Dinah Shore

*Bing Crosby was scheduled to sing these two songs but bowed out at the last minute. No record of who sang in his place exists.

"It's Four Roses against Old Granddad."
—Bob Hope

haps, an unfair publicity advantage over his competitors—he had introduced his score for *Spellbound* at a Hollywood Bowl concert the previous summer. His Award was presented by Ginger Rogers, who, according to one account, "was the sensation of the evening in a metallic gown featuring an almost frontless effect."

Ginger's dress was soon upstaged by a 10-by-20-foot flag on which there was a huge gold star with the number "118" and a blue star with "7926." The figures referred, respectively, to the number of film-industry personages who had died in the war and to the number of Hollywood men and women who had served and made it back. Those with good memories wondered about the Academy's arithmetic, which seemed off by 19,633 people. The 1942 banquet had featured a flag with a "27,677" figure—supposedly representing this same Hollywood corps.

The orchestra softly began playing service songs and onto the stage marched Hollywood war veterans Cesar "Butch" Romero (with the war over, "one of Hollywood's most popular escorts" was back in business); writers Robert Riskin, Sy Bartlett and Peter Viertel; writer-director John Huston; producer Gene Markey; grip Don Duffield, and June Carpenter, a secretary at Warners who had given up the glamour of Hollywood for the excitement of navy life. The seven of them exchanged war stories and then a hush fell over the audience. A spotlight centered on the gold star as a slide was projected with the words, "Who will speak for these?" It was then time for intermission.

Having decided that broadcasting the entire program was not an audience-grabber, ABC reverted to covering only the "major" Awards. The broadcast began with a second emcee, whom Jean Hersholt introduced as "Bob 'Academy' Hope." Since Hope often used his inability to win an Oscar as the basis of jokes, the Academy decided to make a joke of its own and President Hersholt presented the comedian with a tiny statuette. Hope responded in kind: "I've heard of the *Look* Award, but this is the first time I ever knew the *Reader's Digest* was in this racket . . . Sidney Skolsky must have posed for this one."

Summing up the Best Actor contest between Ray Milland and Bing Crosby, Hope said, "It's Four Roses against Old Granddad." Looking at the row of Oscars behind him, he scoffed, "They don't worry me—they're nothing but bookends with a sneer." After Hope's quips, the orchestra broke into "Auld Lang Syne" to herald the appearance of the Cinematography Awards presenter, D.W. Griffith, who, ten years after receiving his Special Oscar, still couldn't get a job in Hollywood. Hope introduced Griffith with, "He was out here before Crosby was, and the slogan then was 'Lionel Barrymore's back and Lillian Gish has got him.' "

For the first time, the nominated songs—or, at least parts of them—were performed by singers at the ceremony. The choruses of the fourteen numbers were individually sung by Kathryn Grayson, Dick Haymes, Dinah Shore and Frank Sinatra. Bing Crosby was supposed to sing the two nominees he had warbled in movies that year, "Accentuate the Positive" and "Aren't You Glad You're You," but at the last minute pulled a Houdini. Bob Hope got back at his buddy by snorting, "Crosby's been playing so many priest roles that when his friends come to visit him, he automatically passes around the plate."

William Wyler, back from filming bombing raids, gave Best Director to the homophonic Billy Wilder for *The Lost Weekend*. "Thank you, Mrs. Miniver," said Wilder to the presenter. Hope then introduced the recently installed successor to Will Hays as the official censor of the Motion Picture Association of America, cracking, "Eric Johnston is the man who tells Hollywood what's cooking and how far they can turn up the flame." Announcing Best Picture, Johnston exclaimed the winner with little-boy enthusiasm: "Oooooooh! It's *The Lost Weekend*."

This year's juvenile Award went to fifteen-year-old Peggy Ann Garner of *A Tree Grows in*

"I'm so glad! I'm so glad!"
—Ingrid Bergman

Brooklyn and *Junior Miss,* who beat out *National Velvet*'s fourteen-year-old Elizabeth Taylor for the miniature Oscar. George Murphy gave Special Awards to everyone connected with a "tolerance short subject," *The House I Live In,* which featured Frank Sinatra singing two songs and lecturing a cross section of young bullies about brotherhood and religious intolerance. Sinatra, director Mervyn LeRoy, producer Frank Ross (husband of Jean Arthur), writer Albert Maltz and the others involved with the film worked on it for free and RKO donated facilities for shooting. The movie was even given to theaters free of charge. Because of all this selflessness, the Board of Governors decided the fellows deserved *something* and gave them this Special Award.

Aping his *Going My Way* costar, Barry Fitzgerald decided at the last minute that he didn't want to be bothered with showing up to give the Supporting Awards as planned. Van Heflin took his place. There was a loud round of applause for the Best Supporting Actor winner, James Dunn, a Hollywood veteran who played the alcoholic father in *A Tree Grows in Brooklyn.* Academy voters may have figured that the younger Supporting Actress nominees would have ample opportunities for future awards—they chose the oldest contender, Anne Revere in *National Velvet.*

Ingrid Bergman, soon to find out whether she'd be a two-in-a-row winner, opened the envelope containing the name of the Best Actor. "Mr. Milland, are you nervous?" she asked. "It's yours!" Mr. Milland was nervous—his wife had to elbow him in the ribs to get him out of his seat. Once onstage, he continued to be speechless and merely grinned and bowed. Hope commented, "I'm surprised they just handed it to him. I thought they'd hide it in the chandelier."

Charles Boyer walked out to announce Best Actress. Nominees Greer Garson, Jennifer Jones and Gene Tierney were in the audience. Ingrid Bergman was backstage with Ray Milland. Joan Crawford was listening on the radio in her bedroom. When Boyer read the winner's name—Joan Crawford in *Mildred Pierce*—*Daily Variety* reported, "There was an explosion of applause in the house." According to Crawford's daughter Christina, Joan's "health seemed to improve dramatically," and she got out of bed and prettied herself for the expected onslaught of well-wishers. While Crawford was collecting herself at home, her director, Michael Curtiz, accepted her Award at the Chinese. "Miss Crawford is very, very ill," he explained. As Curtiz walked backstage, Ingrid Bergman ran to him, saying, "Oh, I'm so glad! I'm so glad!"

The winners all came back onstage and sang "The Star-Spangled Banner" to close the show. Then *The Lost Weekend* crowd sped to Romanoff's, the *Mildred Pierce* contingent to Joan Crawford's house.

Aftermath

Joan Crawford was now ready to receive guests in a coffee-colored negligee. Costar Ann Blyth and Van Johnson, president of the Joan Crawford Fan Club, were among the celebratory onlookers as Curtiz handed Crawford the statuette and photographers snapped away. "Usually I'm ready with the wisecracks," Crawford said, "but I can't say anything. My tears speak for me. I just don't see how anyone could stand this more than once. This is the greatest moment of my life." Joan added, "I voted for Ingrid Bergman myself."

"Joan may have been afraid to attend the Oscar ceremonies that night but she was also a great showwoman," wrote Henry Rogers in his memoirs. "The photo of her in bed clutching the Oscar pushed all the other winners off the front page. She was there all by herself." *Daily Variety* praised Crawford in its editorial the following day: "It was a notable moment for her. Hollywood, recognizing her grim determination and a driving force possessed by few actresses, rallied to her cause. Last night was Hollywood's way of paying homage to a great personality and a lovely woman."

Upon arriving at the Writers' Building on the Paramount lot the following day, *The Lost Weekend*'s Billy Wilder and Charles Brackett found that the other occupants of the building had prepared a congratulatory greeting—dozens of liquor bottles were hanging from every window.

For Best Actor Ray Milland, winning an Oscar was a fleeting moment to be savored. Riding with his wife in a limousine en route to the post-ceremony celebration, Milland directed the chauffeur to drive to the bridle path on Sunset Boulevard overlooking Hollywood. An MGM talent scout had brought the actor to this spot when he first arrived in Hollywood in 1930 and told him, "It all belongs to Ramon Novarro. He is the reigning romantic star at the moment, so tonight it belongs to him." Milland stood there with his Oscar, taking in the view of twinkling lights, and finally said, "Mr. Novarro, tonight they belong to me!"

1946

"Times have changed but Hollywood hasn't."
—Samuel Goldwyn

Hollywood went to war in 1946—the enemy was an invading force of foreign films.

The moguls had gotten campaigning for Oscars down to a science, having learned to save their biggest contenders until the end of the year. But while the Hollywood blockbusters were being primped and preened, several foreign films sneaked in and stole some of their thunder. In 1946, guys who wanted to impress their dates took them to European movies.

From Italy came Roberto Rossellini's *Open City,* featuring Anna Magnani and filmed on the streets of Rome in 1944 and '45 after the Allies had captured the city. *Life* wrote that *Open City,* a tribute to the anti-Nazi underground, "has an earthy verisimilitude which will make many American audiences think of it as a documentary film rather than as a plain melodrama. Its violence and plain sexiness steadily project a feeling of desperate and dangerous struggle which Hollywood seldom approaches." Walter Winchell was more to the point: "A slam bang-up job!"

France's *Children of Paradise,* in the words of the *New York Post*'s Archer Winsten, "challenges Hollywood on its own ground of grandeur." A romantic epic set in the theatrical districts of nineteenth-century Paris, *Children of Paradise* was secretly filmed by Marcel Carné during the German Occupation and reels of film were hidden throughout the city until the three-hour movie was completed. The film cost $1,250,000, part of that money going to replenish food for banquet scenes stolen by starving extras, and the *New York Times* heralded it as the "French reply to *Gone With the Wind.*"

Strictly Average

The majority of foreign hits in America, however, came from England. Noel Coward was back with *Brief Encounter,* about a love affair between two middle-aged people, based on one of his plays, and directed by David Lean, codirector of *In Which We Serve.* The *Saturday Review* wrote that "what is most exceptional about it is that it dares to allow its average characters to remain average" and praised the unglamorous stars Trevor Howard and Celia Johnson. The magazine raved that Johnson's face "is touched by life rather than retouched by an ever-hovering make-up man." The *New York Herald Tribune* felt that "*Brief Encounter* is so far removed from the ordinary run of screen romances that it speaks, as it were, in another cinematic language." With Rachmaninoff on the sound track, audiences cried and cried over the fatalistic lovers and *Brief Encounter* became one of the most successful foreign films yet.

Another British romance with classical music prominently featured, *The Seventh Veil,* was also a big hit in the States. As the stern guardian of a maladjusted girl, James Mason became an international star; *Look* reported that "several Hollywood studios are angling for Mason, whose American appeal is indicated by the violent reaction of a New York bobby soxer: 'He's so handsome, and so mean! Gee!'"

Do-It-Yourself Shakespeare

But the most successful foreign film of all was made by Laurence Olivier, known to American audiences as Heathcliff and Max de Winter. During the war, Olivier dreamed of starring in a film of Shakespeare's *Henry V,* feeling that the heroism of the title character paralleled the courage of the British people. Olivier asked William Wyler to direct. Wyler said, "Do it yourself," and Olivier did, filming in Ireland in 1944. *Time* was beside itself: "At last there has been brought to the screen, with such sweetness, vigor, insight and beauty that it seemed to have been written yesterday, a play by the greatest dramatic poet who ever lived." The *New York Daily News* said Olivier "has shown Hollywood the way to put Shakespeare on the screen."

World War II veteran Harold Russell wins two Oscars for the same performance, then decides to quit show business while he's ahead.

"Nobody else would have the nerve to do it! But it doesn't faze Sam Goldwyn. He never bats an eye."
—Darryl F. Zanuck

Bosley Crowther wrote that "Mr. Olivier's own performance of Henry sets a standard for excellence" and several critics found the climactic Battle of Agincourt the most exciting screen spectacle since *Birth of a Nation.* Instead of being put off by Shakespeare, audiences lined up to see Olivier in Technicolor; *Henry V* ran for forty-six weeks in New York.

Sam and Walter—Hollywood Sociologists

Hollywood took notice of what was happening. Samuel Goldwyn countered the European invasion with *The Best Years of Our Lives,* a drama about the adjustment problems of returning war veterans. He had been inspired to make the film after reading a *Time* magazine article in 1944 indicating that things were not all hunky-dory for soldiers when they left the service. Goldwyn decided the subject matter deserved the best he could get, so he hired famed war correspondent MacKinlay Kantor to write a story and Pulitzer Prize–winning playwright Robert Sherwood to adapt the story into a script. Then he assigned the film to his pet director, William Wyler, and put together a top-drawer cast headed by Fredric March, Myrna Loy, Dana Andrews and Teresa Wright.

With all this going for *Best Years,* Goldwyn still figured a little extra publicity couldn't hurt. The producer called a press conference and harumphed:

> *Times have changed but Hollywood hasn't . . . In film after film, we have the same old boy-meets-girl, the same old chase, the same tough guy stories, the same psychological melodramas . . .*

Goldwyn then sounded a clarion call:

> *Hollywood is facing a challenge. Today it is by the British, tomorrow it may be the French or the Italians or the Russians. To maintain its place, Hollywood must set aside the old formulas. It must find honest stories, stories with something important to say, stories that reflect these disturbing times in which we live.*

On the very same day that Goldwyn made these pronouncements, producer Walter Wanger made a similar analysis of the state of Hollywood. Just back from a trip to the Continent, the former Academy president said that the industry was in trouble with the foreign market because European audiences were clamoring for true-to-life movies. Said Wanger, it was high time to come up with a fresh, more mature viewpoint.

The World According to Zanuck

Darryl F. Zanuck was incensed when he heard his fellow producers mouthing off and decided that somebody had to stand up for Hollywood. Starting off with the assertion that "there is nothing wrong with Hollywood that cannot be cured by the liquidation of self-appointed oracles," Zanuck then personalized his defense, which was reprinted in the trades. Of Goldwyn he said,

> *The man's a genius when it comes to getting attention for his product. If he doesn't have any significant pictures to release, if he's putting out some little musical comedy or other, he will issue a statement that it is Hollywood's job to brighten the lives of the people and not worry them about serious issues. And then, when he has a significant picture to release and he knows it is going to be praised for its significance—something like* The Best Years of Our Lives*—he will wait until just a day before it comes out and issue a statement that Hollywood isn't producing enough significant pictures.*
>
> *My God! It's so obvious! Nobody else would have the nerve to do it! But it doesn't faze Sam. He never bats an eye.*

And Walter Wanger, opined Zanuck, was "a humdinger when it comes to popular oratory. He,

"Catholics may not, with a free conscience, attend Duel in the Sun, which appears to be morally offensive and spiritually depressing."
—Archbishop of Los Angeles

too, can do a lot to lift Hollywood from this mystical mire by solemnly promising not to produce any more films like *Salome, When She Danced* as long as he lives."

Zanuck's Second Coming

To combat the likes of *Henry V*, Darryl Zanuck would have the rest of Hollywood strive to make films like *The Razor's Edge*, an adaptation of Somerset Maugham's 1944 bestseller. Zanuck told everyone that he considered *The Razor's Edge*—Tyrone Power's around-the-world search for spiritual fulfillment—his finest achievement ever. The producer made sure that, as columnist Cecelia Ager put it, the movie was "heralded like the second coming."

The mixed reviews—good acting, murky story—didn't deter Zanuck, who found enough quotations extolling the movie and the performances of Tyrone Power, in his first postwar film, Gene Tierney, John Payne, Herbert Marshall and, especially, Anne Baxter and Clifton Webb, to keep the trade papers saturated with Oscar ads. He also had two gimmicks. Recollecting the success he had had with the portrait of Jennifer Jones in *The Song of Bernadette*, Zanuck again commissioned Norman Rockwell to transfer his impressions of *The Razor's Edge* to easel. In an advertisement, Zanuck reprinted the painting, a likeness of Tyrone Power with the torsoless heads of his costars hovering behind him. The ad informed the Hollywood community that "More than 250,000 copies of this famous NORMAN ROCKWELL painting have been requested by patrons of the Roxy Theatre where *The Razor's Edge* is still breaking box-office records."

Zanuck also tried snob appeal to sway Academy members—he reprinted a telegram from Somerset Maugham himself. "I have just seen *The Razor's Edge* and I am enthusiastic," Maugham wired. "I think the acting is superb and the production beyond all praise. I can only thank you for all you have done for me."

Real Life

Like Zanuck, Sam Goldwyn considered his film the year's Important Social Statement, and he advertised *The Best Years of Our Lives* as a major event. He readied Hollywood for the William Wyler film by premiering it in New York and then impressing the film colony by reprinting remarks from the East Coast critics. He had plenty of raves from which to choose and a two-page ad in the trades blazed: "It's Unanimous!" (Not quite; *The New Yorker* was unimpressed.) "Never before such cheers from the New York press." The *Daily News* called *Best Years* "the best picture from Hollywood since the end of the war" and *P.M.* felt "it must merit the gratitude of the whole country, indeed every country which war has maimed." To prove he wasn't bluffing about the seriousness of the movie, Goldwyn reprinted editorials from *Look* and the *New York Times*, which called it "a poignant drama of real life." The Los Angeles critics echoed their cross-country brethren when *Best Years* hit the West Coast on Christmas Day.

Dorothy Kilgallen wrote: "William Wyler means more to filmgoers than they know. He is full of unexpected magic." He was also full of unexpected trouble, as far as Sam Goldwyn was concerned. Wyler claimed that the producer had reneged on a promise to bill *The Best Years of Our Lives* as "A William Wyler Production." He then left Goldwyn's employ to form a production company, Liberty Pictures, with Frank Capra and George Stevens, a move that Goldwyn took as a personal affront. After a working relationship that had begun in 1936, Goldwyn and Wyler were no longer on speaking terms, the raves for *Best Years* notwithstanding.

Forget Gone With the Wind

Publicity-wise, no one could compare with what David O. Selznick was up to on *Duel in the*

"*It's a Wonderful Life* momentarily restored this reporter's faith in human nature."
—*New York Daily News*

Sun, the latest of his continuing attempts to outdo *Gone With the Wind*. Selznick set aside a then-astronomical advertising budget of over $1 million for his $7 million epic western. Teaser ads appeared as early as June 1945, a full year and a half before the movie was released. By January of 1946, *Duel in the Sun* ads were a daily fixture in the trade papers, so Selznick began distributing over five million *Duel in the Sun* matchbook covers as a change of pace.

As the film's December premiere drew near, Selznick's ads quoted various Hollywood notables, including Alfred Hitchcock, who was under contract to Selznick at the time, on the merits of *Duel in the Sun*. Two people gave Selznick exactly what he was looking for. Frank Capra felt that "*Duel in the Sun* is thrilling. It is as good or better than *Gone With the Wind*" and Mervyn LeRoy told Selznick, "All I can say is that the heat of *Duel in the Sun* will burn up all memories of *Gone With the Wind*."

But, suddenly, all those grandiose preparations were being undermined by a group of mere laborers. While the *Duel in the Sun* print was being processed, employees called a strike against Technicolor and it was touch-and-go whether the movie could open in time to qualify for the Oscars. The strike was settled in mid-December, Selznick got to work and finished a marathon reediting session just in time to get *Duel* into a Hollywood theater on December 30. The scope and production values of the movie were praised, but *Daily Variety* summed up critical reaction when it commented: "Actually, *Duel in the Sun* is a glorified Western." Although the public rushed in droves to see the film, Selznick did not have another *Gone With the Wind*.

Motif of Sex

In addition to the mixed reviews and inordinate production cost, Selznick was having trouble fending off a groundswell of criticism against the so-called immorality of movies. *Duel in the Sun*, also referred to as "Lust in the Dust," came in for the most heat. *Daily Variety* admitted that the film, which chronicled the passionate love affair between Jennifer Jones and Gregory Peck that ends with their shooting each other and dying in an orgasmic embrace, had "a motif of sex such as seldom has been pictured for the screen." The Catholic Church thought it was not a pretty picture.

After *Duel in the Sun* opened, the archbishop of Los Angeles directed priests to warn their parishioners that "pending classification by the Legion of Decency, they may not, with a free conscience, attend the motion picture *Duel in the Sun*, which appears to be morally offensive and spiritually depressing." Then *Tidings*, the official magazine of the archdiocese, spelled out the trouble spots: "It tends to throw audience sympathy on the side of sin"; "Jennifer Jones is unduly, if not indecently, exposed"; and "a character, acting as a minister of religion, parodies prayer and thus becomes a comical figure." Columnist Jimmy Fidler went so far as to pay for a full-page mea culpa in all the trade papers explaining that the rave he accorded the Selznick film was actually written by a member of his staff while he, Fidler, was in bed with the flu.

Vicious Crackpots

A torrent of complaints caused the management of the Egyptian Theatre on Hollywood Boulevard to replace the posters advertising *Duel in the Sun* to protect the public from Jennifer Jones' cleavage. Could this really be the actress who won an Oscar for playing Saint Bernadette? The *Hollywood Reporter* wrote that the Los Angeles D.A. was investigating "those 'poison pen' letters that some vicious crackpot has been sending to most of the columnists and reviewers here who have said anything good about Jennifer Jones and her performance in *Duel in the Sun*." Sheilah Graham reported that David O. Selznick had "hired a former FBI man in Washington to find out who's making the scurrilous attacks."

"Critics slap Hollywood by picking foreign pix."
—Daily Variety

The Best for Last

Two other movies expected to capture the enthusiasm of the Academy, *The Yearling* and *It's a Wonderful Life,* opened in Los Angeles on Christmas Day following earlier New York premieres. Getting wind of what the studios were up to, Hollywood columnists complained that the five films most highly touted for Oscars—*The Razor's Edge, Best Years, The Yearling, It's a Wonderful Life* and *Duel In the Sun*—were jammed into a five-week, year-end period.

The Finest Movie Ever Made

The Yearling, based upon Marjorie Kinnan Rawlings' Pulitzer Prize–winning novel about a boy and his fawn, had been kicking around at MGM for years. Originally bought with Spencer Tracy in mind, it was finally made with Gregory Peck and Jane Wyman as the kid's parents. MGM's publicity campaign included what *Daily Variety* called the "most ambitious policy in publicizing a motion picture locally via radio." The studio turned such stars as Greer Garson, Van Johnson and Robert Taylor into a cheering section for *The Yearling* and bought dozens of radio ads in which the celebrities fawned over the movie.

For print ads, there were the usual collection of raves; the UPI asserted, "*The Yearling* is what the Academy had in mind when it first dreamed up this Oscar business." Show business celebrities also stepped in, including playwright Moss Hart who said, "I wouldn't be sure, but *The Yearling* may be the finest movie ever made." Ads proudly displayed Marjorie Kinnan Rawlings' "wish for all authors as sensitive and satisfying a translation of their work to the screen."

It's a Wonderful Campaign

Frank Capra was back with his first movie since he had left Hollywood to make documentaries during the war. For *It's a Wonderful Life,* a fantasy in which a would-be suicide is shown what the world would be like had he not been born, the Capra-Wyler-Stevens production company Liberty Pictures ran ads for ten successive days prior to the premiere. Each ad featured a picture of one of the film's actors, starting with James Stewart and finishing with H.B. Warner, and included catchy comments from reviewers who had already seen the movie. Columnist Jimmy Starr allowed, "If I were an Oscar I'd elope with *It's a Wonderful Life* lock, stock and barrel on the night of the Academy Awards."

Long Drink of Water

The *New York Daily News* was so impressed with *It's a Wonderful Life* that it ran an editorial on the movie. The paper praised the heart-tugger because "it momentarlly restored this reporter's faith in human nature—quite some achievement after you've spent some time in the newspaper game." The editorial also praised James Stewart in that "he'd outdone all his previous performances." This was also Stewart's first movie since coming back from the war as an air force hero and *Modern Screen* told its readers, "The drought's over, girls. Your long drink of water's back. We can talk about Jimmy Stewart again."

Jack Warner's Pride and Joy

Jack Warner kept a low profile during the pre-Oscar season. Warners had planned to push *Deception*—a melodrama about a love triangle involving three neurotics, a composer, his mistress and a cellist—and its star, Bette Davis, as its major Oscar contender. When that film opened to less-than-enthusiastic response, however, the studio threw its weight behind Joan Crawford's post-Oscar vehicle, *Humoresque,* a remake of the Fannie Hurst novel that shifted the original's emphasis from maternal sacrifice to a love affair between two neurotics: a society dame and a violinist. À la Darryl Zanuck, Jack Warner announced to the industry in a two-page ad, "Now we are about to launch

"Larry Parks gives me the creeps."
—Al Jolson

Humoresque. Our studio has never, in all our years, been more proud of an achievement than we are of this one. /s/ Jack L. Warner." It was clear that Crawford was winning the battle to become queen of the Warners lot. But once *Humoresque* was released and no one got too worked up about it, the studio lost enthusiasm for the Oscars and Jack Warner watched from the sidelines.

Orchids for Olivia

Paramount and Universal-International were having it out over Olivia de Havilland's two Oscar-potential vehicles for the year, *To Each His Own* and *The Dark Mirror*. De Havilland was worried that a split in the voting might deprive her of a nomination. She decided that aging thirty years and suffering nobly in Paramount's well-mounted soap opera would get more votes than playing good-and-evil twins in Universal's psychological mystery melodrama—after all, even Maria Montez had done that bit for the studio in *Cobra Woman*—and she asked Universal to quit campaigning for her. Paramount thought that a floral motif would be a nice way to promote de Havilland. Each of her ads had pictures of flowers and the caption, "To Olivia de Havilland . . . A Great Actress" along with the standard laudatory quotations.

Rah, Rah, Roz

The most heavily advertised actress, however, was Rosalind Russell for her portrayal of the Australian nurse who worked against infantile paralysis in *Sister Kenny*. Her rather plebeian ads consisted of no artwork, just a simple green background and a single line a day urging an Oscar for the actress.

Year-End Wrap-Up

When the year-end East Coast film awards began rolling in, Hollywood really started getting antsy. The National Board of Review selected Laurence Olivier's *Henry V* as Best Picture, Olivier as Best Actor and *Open City*'s Anna Magnani as Best Actress. The New York Film Critics kept it domestic with *The Best Years of Our Lives* and William Wyler, but then went British in its acting choices, Olivier again and Celia Johnson for *Brief Encounter*. *Daily Variety* headlined: CRITICS SLAP HOLLYWOOD BY PICKING FOREIGN PIX IN THEIR 10 BEST OF YEAR, and Bosley Crowther of the *New York Times* explained the strong showing of European movies among critics by parroting Sam Goldwyn. Hollywood, he said, had "run dry of ideas."

Membership Drive

The Academy felt it no longer needed to court the Screen Actors, Writers and Directors guilds. So it let the guild members know that they could still take part in the nominating, but if they weren't also Academy members, they could forget about the final balloting. *Variety* explained the problem: "In past seasons thousands of ballots, like the seeds in the Biblical parable, were sown on barren ground. The result proved the Academy's contention that widespread mailing of election blanks was a waste of time and postage."

Following these voting changes, studio heads, who previously couldn't have cared less if their employees were Academy members, were suddenly clamoring for them to join up so they could do their bit for the in-house product. Membership doubled overnight, but with the exclusion of the guilds the number of people determining the Oscar winners was cut by over 80 percent, from 9,000 to 1,610.

The Nominations

David O. Selznick got a jolt—there was no Best Picture nomination for *Duel in the Sun*. The movie got only a crummy two nominations: the "unduly exposed" Jennifer Jones for Best Actress and Lillian Gish for Supporting Actress. Darryl

"In past seasons thousands of ballots, like the seeds in the Biblical parable, were sown on barren ground."
—Variety

Zanuck, Sam Goldwyn, Louis B. Mayer and Frank Capra got their Best Picture nominations, but *Henry V*, which had only one campaign ad, sneaked up and joined them. What Hollywood had feared would happen did happen and *Daily Variety* moaned: BIG THREAT FOR OSCARS BY BRITISH. *Henry V* also snared an Actor nomination for Laurence Olivier as well as Art Direction and Scoring nods. *Brief Encounter* was represented by Best Actress, Director and Screenplay nominations. In all, British movies received eleven nominations and there were writing nominations for France's *Children of Paradise* and Italy's *Open City*, cowritten by one F. Fellini.

Competing with Jennifer Jones and Celia Johnson were Olivia de Havilland for *To Each His Own*, Rosalind Russell for *Sister Kenny* and Jane Wyman for *The Yearling*. In addition to Olivier, the Best Actor contenders were Fredric March, a middle-aged war veteran in *The Best Years of Our Lives;* Gregory Peck, who continued to appear in nothing but hits, for *The Yearling;* and James Stewart for *It's a Wonderful Life*. Larry Parks snagged a Best Actor nomination for his performance as Al Jolson in *The Jolson Story,* a film produced by gossip columnist Sidney Skolsky. Parks was so authentic in his role that the real-life Al Jolson said, "The guy gives me the creeps watching him." Like Cornel Wilde last year, Parks went from negligible B-actor to overnight star by appearing in a popular musical biography for Columbia; in addition to his Oscar nomination, Parks was selected as "Man of the Year" by the Bobby Soxers of America.

Golden Globe Award winner Rosalind Russell was the only one of the ten Actress and Actor nominees to continue advertising after the nominations. She also had the advantage of a year-end release, while chief rival Olivia de Havilland's *To Each His Own* had opened the previous spring. De Havilland's performance did stay in people's minds through Eddy Howard's recording of "To Each His Own"; written to help exploit the film after it opened, the song remained on the charts through late autumn. Paramount still wasn't about to take any chances and rereleased *To Each His Own* in four Los Angeles theaters in January.

Oscar's Shrine

The Academy moved the Awards from the Chinese Theatre to the huge Shrine Auditorium in downtown Los Angeles. The place had 6,700 seats, and to fill them, the Academy sold tickets to the general public. The Academy Awards was no longer just an industry celebration.

Shortly before Oscar night, the *Los Angeles Times* predicted: "*The Yearling* should be the strongest contender for the Academy Awards because it is known to represent the surmounting of enormous obstacles and because its appeal is the most comprehensive of any picture released during 1946." On the other hand, columnist Ed Sullivan thought *The Best Years of Our Lives* was the "best bet of your life for an Academy Award." *Daily Variety* had these two entries neck-and-neck for Best Picture, but the *Hollywood Citizen-News* advised readers to watch out for a victory by *It's a Wonderful Life*, "a definite Academy Award dark horse." If Darryl Zanuck's picture seemed to be out of the running, at least *The Razor's Edge* had been named the year's best by the National Association of Barbers.

The Big Night

Time reported that Awards night involved "35 Oscars, 16 searching lights (crisscrossing shades of white, blue, red and orange), a 66-piece orchestra, 250 policemen, 90 ushers, 50 stagehands, 6 parking lots and 125 parking lot attendants." In the bleachers outside, 5,000 fans kept watch, giving their biggest round of cheers to Sonny Tufts, whose appearance, noted *Daily Variety*, "set the bobby-soxers to yipping and wiggling in their seats." The paper also wrote:

> *The yells hit a crescendo when one dazzlingly dressed gal and her tail-coated escort got out and headed for the doors. They faded down somewhat when someone in the bleachers shouted, "That isn't an actress, that's just somebody's wife!"*

The show wasn't even close to being a sellout and scores of leftover tickets were given to servicemen who were milling around outside. Although the Academy had expressly requested black tie, less than half of those attending came formally dressed. Sneered a Hollywood veteran, "That's what happens when you let in John Q. Public."

Onstage was a neoclassical setting consisting of a pylon backed by six Greek columns and topped by a five-foot gilt plastic replica of Oscar. The set was designed by MGM's Cedric Gibbons, an Art Direction nominee, and Jack Martin Smith.

The program opened with the "Parade of Stars," a silent compilation of Oscar-winning films with Ronald Reagan, Screen Actors Guild president and husband of Best Actress nominee Jane Wyman, standing onstage to provide the narration. Unfortunately, because of a snafu in the projection booth, the film was shown upside down and backwards and was projected on the ceiling instead of the screen. Reagan, oblivious to what was going on, continued to read from his "memory book": "This picture embodies the glories of our past, the memories of our present and the inspiration of our future."

Academy President Jean Hersholt told the audience that the previous evening the Board of Governors had voted to present four Special Awards. Three of them related to Best Picture nominees. In one fell swoop, the Academy took care of *Henry V* by giving absent Laurence Olivier an Oscar for

Awards Ceremony

MARCH 13, 1947, 8:45 P.M.
THE SHRINE AUDITORIUM, LOS ANGELES

Your Host:
JACK BENNY

Presenters

Short Subjects	Douglas Fairbanks, Jr.
Documentary Awards	Douglas Fairbanks, Jr.
Scientific or Technical Awards	Douglas Fairbanks, Jr.
Film Editing	Rex Harrison
Sound Recording	Rex Harrison
Special Effects	Rex Harrison
Scoring Awards	Lana Turner
Art Direction	Greer Garson
Cinematography	Ann Sheridan
Song	Van Johnson
Writing Awards	Robert Montgomery
Special Awards	Shirley Temple
Director	Billy Wilder
Picture	Eric Johnston
Thalberg Award	Donald Nelson
Supporting Actor	Anne Revere
Supporting Actress	Lionel Barrymore
Actor	Joan Fontaine
Actress	Ray Milland

Performers of Nominated Songs

"All Through the Day"	Dinah Shore
"I Can't Begin To Tell You"	Dick Haymes
"Ole Buttermilk Sky"	Hoagy Carmichael
"On the Atchison, Topeka and Santa Fe"	Dinah Shore
"You Keep Coming Back Like a Song"	Andy Russell

"Lana Turner is to an evening gown what Frank Lloyd Wright is to a pile of lumber."
—Rex Harrison

"his outstanding achievement." Hersholt must have heard Sam Goldwyn's pronouncements, because he said, "1946 gave us our first sight of many fine pictures made abroad during the war. To the commercial side of the industry, these pictures may have presented the rude visage of competition; to the creative branches, and that's what the Academy represents, they come as a refreshing wind."

A veteran who had lost his hands during the war, Harold Russell had been nominated as Best Supporting Actor for his performance in *The Best Years of Our Lives*. Since Russell was not a professional actor and his competition included four veteran character actors, the Board of Governors knew he was a long shot and they voted the one-shot actor an Award for "bringing hope and courage" to other veterans. Dean Stockwell, the eleven-year-old star of MGM's *The Green Years* lost out to Claude Jarman, Jr., the twelve-year-old star of MGM's *The Yearling*, in the board's selection of the outstanding child actor. The original juvenile Award winner, Shirley Temple, now the eighteen-year-old Mrs. John Agar, gave Jarman, Jr., his junior statuette.

With the fourth of the Special Awards, the Academy began the Life Achievement Award tradition, whereby somebody reckoned to be on the brink of death is handed an Oscar before it's too late. The recipient was director Ernst Lubitsch, who was ill and who, it turned out, would be dead in a matter of months. Presenter Mervyn LeRoy praised Lubitsch's subtlety: "The housebroken camera learned to stop at the closed door instead of peeking gawkily through the keyhole. A master of innuendo had arrived."

After handing out the Special Effects, Editing and Sound Awards, Rex Harrison introduced the presenter of the Music Awards by saying, "Lana Turner is to an evening gown what Frank Lloyd Wright is to a pile of lumber."

The program's producer Mervyn LeRoy had more than his share of headaches with the Best Song Awards. Bing Crosby, who had caused trouble for the Academy in this area the year before, had been asked to sing the nominated song "I Can't Begin to Tell You." He declined, claiming that it had been so long since he had performed before an audience that he would not feel comfortable. Dick Haymes was tapped for the honor. Then, a couple of days before the Awards, Frank Sinatra, who had agreed to do "You Keep Coming Back Like a Song," got wind of Crosby's refusal. Sinatra informed the Academy that he wasn't going to appear on the show after all. He explained that he had a good reason for bowing out—he was merely "following Crosby's footsteps." Singing heartthrob Andy Russell took over.

The night before the Awards, with everyone having rehearsed and everything set to roll, Judy Garland decided that she had stage fright and would have to cancel, leaving LeRoy with no one to warble "On the Atchison, Topeka and Santa Fe." But Dinah Shore came through; she was going to be singing "All Through the Day" and volunteered to do Garland's number, too.

For the Best Director Award, Billy Wilder and William Wyler reversed their positions of the previous year; Wilder handed Wyler the Oscar for *The Best Years of Our Lives,* calling it "the best-directed film I've ever seen in my life." The film maintained its momentum when Sam Goldwyn won the Thalberg Award as the year's outstanding producer; his other picture in 1946 was *The Kid from Brooklyn* with Danny Kaye.

It had been winning Awards right and left, so it was no surprise when motion picture censor Eric Johnston announced the Best Picture winner, "Ooooooh, it's *The Best Years of Our Lives*." If the revelation of Best Picture was less than startling, Johnston, at least, provided his own inadvertent entertainment. *Time* wrote, "Film czar Eric Johnston, who always provides a fragrant oratorical nosegay, was in top form." Johnston told the assembled, "Movies are immortal art—the first new art, in fact, since Greek drama." In accepting his first Best Picture Award, Sam Goldwyn concluded with a nod to songwriter-actor Hoagy Carmichael: "And last, but not least, I'd like to thank Hugo Carmichael."

"I don't know why she does that when she knows how I feel."
—Olivia de Havilland

The voters agreed with the Board of Governors that Harold Russell of *Best Years* should have an Award, and he was the winner of Best Supporting Actor. When the veteran made his way to the microphone to get his second Oscar, he was so overcome by the audience's response—the heartiest of the night—that he was reduced to tears. He then went backstage and told the press he had no plans to act again. Following Russell, the crippled Lionel Barrymore rolled out in his wheelchair to give the Best Supporting Actress Award to Anne Baxter for *The Razor's Edge*.

Ray Milland revealed the winner of the Best Actress Oscar by calling out the name of *To Each His Own*'s Olivia de Havilland. Described by *Time* as appearing "as gauzy and misty-eyed as a Walt Disney angel," de Havilland gushed, "I feel humble, too, as well as proud. I accept this Oscar in the name of my team as well as my own." She then proceeded to list her teammates—twenty-seven of them—from *To Each His Own*. This was actually the actress' second "Oscar" for *To Each His Own*. On the last day of production, director Mitchell Leisen and producer-writer Charles Brackett presented de Havilland with a live Oscar—a bald man in a gold body stocking.

One might have thought that publicity-conscious Joan Crawford would have jumped at the opportunity to bask in the spotlight as the outgoing Best Actress crowning the new Best Actor. The Academy assumed so, too, and invited her to present. Crawford accepted the offer, but stage fright was running rampant and on the eve of the Awards the actress reneged, remarking that live audiences gave her the willies. Louella Parsons reported that Olivia de Havilland's sister, 1941's Best Actress Joan Fontaine, "graciously consented to present the Academy Award after Joan Crawford left town." Fontaine settled the hotly contested Best Actor race: the winner was Fredric March for *The Best Years of Our Lives*. March was in New York and his Oscar was accepted by Cathy O'Donnell, who played Harold Russell's girlfriend in the movie. And that was the show.

Aftermath

Having given out the Best Actor Award, Joan Fontaine rushed backstage to congratulate her Best Actress sister. She approached Olivia de Havilland, who, in the darkness, seemed not to recognize her sibling. Olivia reached out her hand, suddenly realized who was coming toward her and abruptly turned away. "I don't know why she does that when she knows how I feel," Olivia said to her press agent, Henry Rogers. According to *Daily Variety*, "Joan stood there looking after her with a bewildered expression and then shrugged her shoulders and walked off." Fontaine ran into a photographer from the *Los Angeles Examiner* who asked her to pose congratulating her sister. "Really, I can't," she answered. "I haven't time."

Another photographer had had his camera poised at the right moment, and he captured Olivia snubbing Joan; the next day the picture was plastered all over the newspapers. News of the feud spread like a brushfire, and the two actresses seemed to pour gasoline on the flames. Both vehemently denied a radio report that they had hugged backstage. "Our relations have been strained for some time," maintained de Havilland. Henry Rogers explained, "The girls haven't spoken to each other for four months. This goes back for years and years, ever since they were children. They just don't have a great deal in common."

A second dark spot on Olivia's big night occurred when she dined after the ceremony with her producer, Charles Brackett, and he spilled gravy on her hand-painted dress.

Although two of the three writing Awards went to British films and Olivier had his Special Award, that didn't stop *Time*, *Newsweek* and others from howling that the Academy purposely ignored foreign entries. Also complaining about the Academy's choices was the Women's Christian Temperance Union. *Daily Variety* gave the low-

"Her classmates saw her dad in his pajamas."
—Florence Eldridge

down, writing that the ladies in the Union wished that

> *Academy voters weren't so partial to film characters who bend the elbow and dip the beak. Male stars who portrayed souses romped home with top honors. Ray Milland and Jimmie Dunn last year and Fredric March this year. Women tosspots get under the wire such as Anne Baxter. The Down-With-King-Alcoholers are worried that this may start a trend.*

Penny March, daughter of Fredric, had her own worries. Her mother, actress Florence Eldridge, told Broadway columnist Radie Harris, "The fact that Freddie won an Academy Award for his performance meant nothing to Penny. What was far more important to her was the embarrassing fact that her classmates saw her dad in his pajamas—and that he drank too much in the picture."

One of those actors vanquished by March also had to deal with a disgruntled fan. The morning after the Awards, James Stewart was awakened by a phone call from the owner of a local movie theater in Johnstown, Pennsylvania, the actor's home state. Said the exhibitor, "Mr. Stewart, I went to a lot of expense making lobby displays and things on your winning the Award and you didn't win it." He then asked Stewart if he could borrow his *Philadelphia Story* Oscar, which was in Stewart's father's hardware store. The theater operator added, "Then I'd put it up in the lobby with a little sign saying 'This is what it would have looked like if he had won!' "

Samuel Goldwyn had won, but one thing was clear: his next film would be made without the services of William Wyler. The seven Academy Awards for *The Best Years of Our Lives* did not lead the two feuders to call a truce. The press noted that at the mammoth post-Oscar party given by RKO executive Peter Revson, Goldwyn and Wyler studiously avoided each other, not even saying hello.

Eleven years later, the two were still going at it. In 1958, Wyler sued Goldwyn, charging that the producer had bilked him out of $400,000 of his share of the profits of *Best Years*. The suit was settled out of court but, needless to say, the two never worked together again after *The Best Years of Our Lives*.

A joke went around Hollywood after the Oscars that MGM was changing the title of *The Yearling* to *The Yearning,* but the triumphant Sam Goldwyn kept a straight face. The producer who had wept when he won the Thalberg Award dried his eyes and told *Life,* "It's not good enough to win an Oscar. Suppose next time I make a stinker. I'm worrying about that now."

1947

"I am naturally suspicious of deep thinkers in relation to motion pictures."
—Darryl F. Zanuck

Oscar night turned into Veteran's Day at the 1947 Academy Awards.

Darryl Zanuck was determined to improve the world and win an Oscar for it if it was the last thing he did. Having already missed out on Academy recognition for *Wilson* in 1944 and *The Razor's Edge* in 1946, the 20th Century–Fox head picked anti-Semitism as his important subject for 1947 and dared the Academy not to honor him.

His project was *Gentleman's Agreement*, based on Laura Z. Hobson's bestseller about a Gentile who passes for Jewish to write a series of articles on religious discrimination. To adapt the book, Zanuck lured Moss Hart from New York, despite the playwright's protest that "Hollywood is too comfortable, too luxurious for mental stimulus."

Hart managed to come up with a screenplay anyway, and Zanuck assigned director Elia Kazan to film it. Zanuck had been skeptical of the Broadway director when he first hired him in 1945, telling a producer, "I am naturally suspicious of deep thinkers in relation to motion pictures. They sometimes think so deep, that they miss the point . . . " The success of 1945's *A Tree Grows in Brooklyn* showed that Kazan could get the point and make a profit.

Why, Darryl, Why

With such a tony collection of talent, Zanuck wasn't about to let *Gentleman's Agreement*'s controversial subject matter stand in his way. Kazan recalls, "When Zanuck announced the picture, there was a terrific uproar from the rich Jews of the Hollywood community. And there was a meeting at Warner Brothers called, I think, by Harry Warner. At that meeting, as reported to me by Zanuck, all these wealthy Jews said: 'For Chrissake, why make that picture? We are getting along all right. Why raise the whole subject?' And Zanuck, in a polite way, told them to mind their own business."

Zanuck withstood recriminations from another religious group, too. Kazan remembered: "To the Catholics who got after him—they told him the leading lady couldn't be a divorced woman—Zanuck said, in effect, go f—— yourself."

The film starring Gregory Peck and Dorothy McGuire opened in New York in November and a *Hollywood Reporter* headline declared: GOTHAM RINGS WITH WILD APPLAUSE FOR "AGREEMENT." Social butterfly Elsa Maxwell exclaimed to gossip columnists, "It's the most unequivocally honest action picture ever shown. The Motion Picture Academy should devise a special Oscar for courage and present it to Darryl F. Zanuck. No one deserves it more."

Soon Zanuck was getting such awards, like the Thomas Jefferson Award for the Advancement of Democracy in the field of the arts from the Council Against Intolerance in America. *Look* magazine gave him a medal for producing the most important film of the year, calling it a "powerful indictment of a social wrong which a less courageous producer would have avoided."

Gentleman's Agreement didn't open in Hollywood until Christmas, but that didn't stop Zanuck from taking advantage of the advance publicity by running ads on the back cover of the trade papers in mid-November. "Tomorrow this page will carry the first in a series of reviews of the MOST WIDELY ACCLAIMED PICTURE in the history of Screen Achievement," the first ad promised. The series contained the assertion of the *New York Daily Mirror*'s Lee Mortimer: "I confidently expect this masterpiece to win the Academy Oscar." Zanuck kept this gimmick up for four months, and when he ran out of New York and Los Angeles critics to quote, he found ones in Boston, San Francisco, and even Pittsburgh. Fox's own ad line for the movie about intolerance: "The Picture That Calls a Spade a Spade!"

Presenter Anne Baxter gives Best Supporting Actor winner Edmund Gwenn her warmest regards.

"Hollywood is too comfortable, too luxurious for mental stimulus."
—Moss Hart

Other Victims

Gentleman's Agreement was not the only movie about anti-Semitism that year. Over at RKO, director Edward Dmytryk and producer Adrian Scott adapted a book by future director Richard Brooks about the murder of a homosexual by a bigot, making the victim Jewish in the movie. *Crossfire* was an immediate hit, thanks to its film-noirish suspense, but, on November 24, before Dmytryk and Scott could think about their Oscar acceptance speeches, they were cited for contempt of Congress for not testifying before the House Un-American Activities Committee. Being one-fifth of the "Hollywood Ten" did not help their Oscar chances, especially since their studio, which normally would have underwritten their Academy campaigns, fired them on November 28.

Schary's Babies

RKO's new head of production, Dore Schary, was ready to challenge Zanuck for a rack of Oscars with productions from his first year at the studio. RKO's potential Oscar winners were considerably lighter than *Gentleman's Agreement*: *The Bachelor and the Bobby Soxer,* a situation comedy with Cary Grant and Shirley Temple in the title roles; *The Farmer's Daughter,* another situation comedy with Loretta Young playing a housekeeper running for Congress; and *The Bishop's Wife,* a whimsical comedy about a do-gooding angel starring Cary Grant and Loretta Young.

RKO thought *The Bishop's Wife* had the best chance against Zanuck's movie, and, since it was produced by Samuel Goldwyn, the studio emphasized in ads that the film was a quality production, quoting *Newsweek:* "Insiders are betting that Sam Goldwyn will follow his prize-winning *The Best Years of Our Lives* by capturing 1947 Oscar recognition for *The Bishop's Wife.*" Just to make sure the film fantasy wasn't perceived as a trivial piece of fluff, the Associated Press was quoted as observing that "*The Bishop's Wife* is definitely an indication of a new trend in the movies toward an awareness of social responsibility." By the time of the film's premiere party on Christmas night in Hollywood, the columnists were already being quoted in the ads. Hedda Hopper saw "an Academy Award contender" and Ed Sullivan maintained that "Cary Grant gives an Academy Award performance."

It Was Murder

RKO had another movie opening Christmas night, but it was hardly lightweight fun—Eugene O'Neill's *Mourning Becomes Electra*. Dudley Nichols had done enough favors at the studio to be given free rein in adapting and directing O'Neill's lengthy tragedy with his dream cast—Katina Paxinou, Michael Redgrave and Rosalind Russell, who described the experience of filming in her autobiography: "It was murder. Katina Paxinou screaming and yelling all over the set; Michael Redgrave, a hell of a good actor, but nervous, taking pills to calm himself. . . ." Russell also worried whether movie audiences would care about Nichols' slavish devotion to the text— "O'Neill was his idol"—since his fidelity was resulting in a picture almost three hours long.

The *Hollywood Reporter*'s movie reviewer tried to help out the ambitious film: "It will be called a photographed stage play, but this it is not. Rather, *Mourning Becomes Electra* is a blend of many theatrical elements, funneled into a particular direction." But then the reviewer got down to the brass tacks of how hard a film this one would be to promote and noted that it "is being carefully handled in the same shrewd manner which made *Henry V* a resounding success in this country." This method was simply to let the Theatre Guild take it off the studio's hands and publicize it as a theatrical event playing exclusively at deluxe houses.

"*What an asset to Hollywood that Crawford gal is!*"
—*Columnist Florabel Muir*

Christmas Glut

With the studios putting their weight behind heavy dramas, *Daily Variety* editor Arthur Unger blasted, "It's time for Hollywood to start making pictures for the public, not the Academy." Unger warned that television was starting to drain the weekly moviegoing audience and that Hollywood better lighten up its fare if it wanted to continue to attract patrons. The editor didn't like the Christmas batch at all. "Everybody, with an exception or two, tried for the arty."

One film was so arty it quoted Shakespeare—*A Double Life*, directed by George Cukor and starring Ronald Colman. Since Colman had the juicy role of an actor playing Othello who goes mad offstage as well as on, Universal-International didn't beat around the bush with its ads: "The screen will welcome one of the year's greatest performances . . . starting Christmas day to qualify for Academy Award nomination." By early January, Colman's trade ads were asking, "Why is it so expert an actor as Ronald Colman has never won an Academy Award?" Columnist Louella Parsons printed an "open letter" that read like a mash note to the fifty-seven-year-old actor: "Dear Ronnie, I've seen *Othello* many times, but I prefer your performance as the jealous Moor against any of them." Even nightclub owner Mike Romanoff got into the act by placing a plug for Colman in the club's menus.

Darryl Zanuck read the writing on the menus and stepped up the campaigning for *Gentleman's Agreement*'s leading man. The "Rambling Reporter" gave an example of his wit: "Gregory Peck thinks all N.Y. directors should come to Hollywood; besides earning several thousand a week, they can make a few extras on the side." The handsome thirty-one-year-old was the cover boy of *Life* in December and then of *Time* in January, the latter headlining him as "The Average Man on the Flying Trapeze." Evidently, Peck thought his own Oscar chances were below average, confiding to columnist Radie Harris on the eve of a vacation, "I'll be back in time to see Ronnie Colman walk away with it."

Peck's *Gentleman's Agreement* costar John Garfield loomed as a dark horse. Garfield could afford to play a small role in *Gentleman's Agreement* because he was the star of another hit—*Body and Soul*. This prototypical boxing drama gave Garfield even better notices than his earlier triumphs, *The Postman Always Rings Twice* and *Four Daughters*. The *New York World-Telegram* opined that "he has developed into Hollywood's most vigorous talent." While the actor toiled in New York in an Experimental Theatre Production staged by Lee Strasberg, an ad ran in the *Hollywood Reporter:* "We have received many calls from members of the Academy who wanted to withhold their nominations for the best picture of 1947 until they had seen *Body and Soul*." Garfield's production company, Enterprise, used the ad to announce special screenings for Academy voters, a practice that was increasingly becoming an Academy tradition.

The Wizard of Roz

Publicist Henry Rogers had masterminded Joan Crawford and Olivia de Havilland's Oscar victories the previous two years and he was hoping to pick a winner for the third year in a row. Scouring the potential winners, Rogers decided that Rosalind Russell had the showiest role, so the publicist made an offer of his services to Russell's husband, producer Freddie Brisson, who took him up on it. To plan the campaign strategy, Rogers and an associate watched *Mourning Becomes Electra;* Rogers wrote later, "Neither of us remarked that we had dozed a couple of times during the film's screening."

Rogers' first tactic was persuading a casino in Las Vegas to post the betting odds on the Academy Awards race. The Vegas "experts" listed Rosalind Russell as the favorite in the Best Actress category, with 6-5 odds. The closest competitor was rising star Susan Hayward as an alcoholic in *Smash-Up: The Story of a Woman*, with 6-1. The Vegas blessing was followed by similar paeans from Los An-

"The Motion Picture Academy should devise a special Oscar for courage and present it to Darryl F. Zanuck."
—Elsa Maxwell

geles organizations. A local PTA chapter declared Russell "Actress of the Year"; a few weeks later, a sorority at UCLA named her "Hollywood's Best"; and a fraternity at USC called her "The Outstanding Actress of the Twentieth Century."

"Then we received unexpected help from legitimate sources," Rogers said, referring to Russell's victory at the Golden Globe Awards. Rogers also made sure that the actress was portrayed as a workhorse in the gossip columns: "Rosalind Russell is doing it the hard way in *The Velvet Touch.* She works 58 days straight—being in every scene." And then there were the Oscar ads in the trades, quoting critics like the one from the *New York World-Telegram,* who advised the actress to "clear a place on the mantelpiece for the Oscar."

Young at Heart

Even with Rogers' tireless efforts, Russell had to contend with RKO head Dore Schary's indifference to *Mourning Becomes Electra*—it wasn't one of his productions. If Schary had his druthers, the Oscar would go to Loretta Young for one of the movies he had produced for the studio, *The Farmer's Daughter.* Schary had brought the script with him to RKO when he left Selznick-International because Selznick was no longer interested in it—Ingrid Bergman had turned it down. Schary turned it into a moneymaker, thanks to the enduring popularity of Loretta Young, a twenty-year Hollywood veteran, who gallantly worked on a Swedish accent to play the heroine—a naive Minnesota farm girl.

When Oscar time approached, Schary didn't have to worry about Loretta's making the gossip columns—she was an old pro at the sport. Young's trip to England in January 1948 for the Royal Command Performance of *The Bishop's Wife* was duly covered in the society pages. In New York, Radie Harris wrote that at a cocktail party celebrating her return, "Loretta was full of the sobering effect of visiting England for the first time in ten years. 'Everything you read about conditions over there is an understatement until you see them for yourself. The well-to-do are suffering as well as the poor, because there is no such thing as a black market.' "

What a Gal!

Young's rival in the society pages was Joan Crawford, who threw a big party for Noel Coward around Oscar time. Columnist Florabel Muir was a guest and reported: "What an asset to Hollywood that Crawford gal is! She is everything the world wants a screen actress to be and who but she could entertain two ex-husbands with such eclat, Franchot Tone and Douglas Fairbanks, all the while on the arm of Greg Bautzer?" Crawford was also prepared for a second Oscar. Although Warners had Irene Dunne in *Life with Father* as a possible nominee, Dunne was a free-lance actress, so the studio pushed contractee Joan for *Possessed,* a film in which she played a schizophrenic so realistically that a woman sued, claiming that Crawford had observed her mental treatments at a local hospital and then copied her on the screen.

The Nominations

The *Los Angeles Daily News* wrote that Susan Hayward's nomination for Best Actress for *Smash-Up: The Story of a Woman* was "the most spontaneous nomination of the lot and people are talking about it everywhere in movietown."

People were giving a lot of the credit to former Academy President Walter Wanger, who had signed the struggling twenty-nine-year-old actress to a personal contract the previous year and produced *Smash-Up* himself to showcase her dramatic abilities. But Hayward's nomination by no means guaranteed her an Oscar; she was competing with four popular personalities: Joan Crawford, Dorothy McGuire, Loretta Young and Rosalind Russell. People were also talking about the nominations of Edward Dmytryk and Adrian Scott for *Crossfire,* and the film's Best Picture nomination, a vote of support for the blacklistees.

"Why is it so expert an actor as Ronald Colman has never won an Academy Award?"
—A trade paper ad

Another eyebrow-raiser was Charlie Chaplin's nomination for a Writing Award for *Monsieur Verdoux,* his black comedy that had failed at the box office, because many Hollywood conservatives had been badmouthing Le Charlot. For example, the *Hollywood Reporter*'s W. R. Wilkerson asked, "What's with this fellow Charlie Chaplin? What's with this fellow who, over a long period of years, has lived in this country, accepted its bounty, amassed millions of dollars, but who has constantly refused to become a citizen and who, on any and every occasion, has criticized our form of government, sought its repeal and fomented causes objectionable to our Democracy?"

The writers also nominated Vittorio DeSica's *Shoe-Shine,* the Italian art-house hit. Director Delmer Daves, the producer of the Awards show, tried to explain the omission of the Italian film in the other categories: "The wide spread of nominators did not have an opportunity to see it perhaps . . . It was nominated for the script because that special group, the writers, make it a point to see more foreign pictures than the rank and file of moviemakers."

The Academy's ongoing Anglophilia was represented by eight nominations for British films. David Lean's version of Dickens' *Great Expectations* even claimed Best Picture and Best Director nominations. Two fantasy films, *The Bishop's Wife* and *Miracle on 34th Street,* were also Best Picture nominees, as was Darryl Zanuck's *Gentleman's Agreement,* which led the pack with seven nominations. A confident Zanuck rented ad space on the last page of the trade papers to list the Academy screening schedules of the nominated films and to plead, "Academy members are urged to attend these showings so they may have complete knowledge of the industry's outstanding motion pictures of 1947."

Silver Anniversary

Best Actor nominee Ronald Colman tried to direct attention to one outstanding achievement—his performance—with a series of ads in which former Academy Award winners said they felt that Colman should join the winner's circle. His supporters were Greer Garson, Joan Crawford, Frank Capra, Ginger Rogers, Van Heflin, Charles Coburn, Jane Darwell, Walter Brennan, Donald Crisp and Ethel Barrymore, herself a Supporting Actress nominee for Alfred Hitchcock's *The Paradine Case*. Colman's sentimental edge—he was celebrating his twenty-fifth year in Hollywood—placed him way ahead of the other nominees: Gregory Peck, John Garfield, Michael Redgrave and one of Colman's best friends, William Powell, the New York Film Critics' winner for *Life with Father*. The critics had also picked *Gentleman's Agreement* for Best Picture, but they went British for Best Actress, choosing Deborah Kerr for *Black Narcissus* and *The Adventuress*.

It appeared that Fox had staked out the Supporting Awards. The ads for Edmund Gwenn, who played Santa Claus in *Miracle on 34th Street,* showcased Hedda Hopper's mandate: "Must get the Oscar for a supporting role." Celeste Holm, in only her second year in films, enjoyed the momentum of *Gentleman's Agreement* and the attention of admiring columnists who kept abreast of her social outings, such as the time she was "getting laughs" for showing up at the opening of a play by the ubiquitous Noel Coward "with her leg in a cast."

Just a few days before the Awards, *Daily Variety* printed the results of a poll it had taken of over two hundred Academy members. Their winners were: *Gentleman's Agreement,* Ronald Colman, Rosalind Russell, Edmund Gwenn, Celeste Holm and Elia Kazan. The newspaper said that 13 percent of the Academy's voters were represented in this tally and that "national political polls which reach 5 percent of the electorate have always proven deadly accurate." An indication of *Daily Variety*'s accuracy: listed in fourth place was Loretta Young for *The Bishop's Wife*—her nomination was for *The Farmer's Daughter*.

The Big Night

The suspense-killing results of *Variety*'s poll did not dampen excitement over the Awards, and the *Hollywood Reporter* wrote, "Some of the dyed-in-the-wool fans had been hanging tenaciously to their selected observation posts since before noon, and stayed there until the last limousine drove away." The stargazers withstood 30-degree weather and high winds to watch actresses display their bare-shouldered gowns. Although *Daily Variety* reported that, of the men entering the Shrine Auditorium, "only a scant handful heeded the warning that the event was to be formal," the *Hollywood Reporter* remarked, "The distaff side of the thespian profession really went to town in displaying the latest in frills, bustles and petticoats."

Florabel Muir commented that nominee Joan Crawford, who was in fifth place on *Daily Variety*'s poll, "made one of her rare appearances at the Academy's doin's . . . decked out in white crêpe covered all over with silver bugle beads." Once again, Crawford was found on "the arm of Greg Bautzer." Susan Hayward's husband, actor Jess Barker, was seen, "busy keeping fans and cameramen from stepping on the back of her skirt which trailed." Loretta Young appeared in a full-flowing emerald green silk taffeta dress, accompanied by her husband. As she brushed past the bleachers, one fan was heard sighing, "There goes her chances. Green is an unlucky color."

Young mingled with her friend Rosalind Russell, *Daily Variety*'s choice for Best Actress, who was dressed for victory in a white soufflé gown with highlights of shocking pink designed by studio costume designer Travis Banton, who stood nearby basking in the attention his creation was drawing.

Upstaging the actresses was someone in a gorilla suit advertising a varsity show at the University of Southern California. Quick-thinking flacks at RKO got plenty of pictures of the simian and claimed it was a stunt for its upcoming feature, *Mighty Joe Young*. Years later the story went around that inside the costume was political columnist Art Buchwald, then a college student.

The show began with a seventy-five-piece orchestra playing "The Star-Spangled Banner" as

Awards Ceremony

MARCH 20, 1948, 8:15 P.M.
THE SHRINE AUDITORIUM, LOS ANGELES

Your Hosts:
DICK POWELL AND AGNES MOOREHEAD

Presenters

Motion Picture Story and Original Screenplay	George Murphy
Scientific and Technical Awards	Robert Montgomery
Short Subjects and Documentary Awards	Shirley Temple
Special Effects	Larry Parks
Musical Scoring	Larry Parks
Sound Recording	Larry Parks
Supporting Actress	Donald Crisp
Director	Donald Crisp
Actor	Olivia de Havilland
Song	Dinah Shore
Art Direction	Dick Powell
Special Awards to Bill and Coo, Shoe-Shine, *William N. Selig, Albert E. Smith, Thomas Armat and George K. Spoor*	Jean Hersholt
Special Award to James Baskette	Ingrid Bergman
Cinematography	Agnes Moorehead
Supporting Actor	Anne Baxter
Screenplay	Anne Baxter
Film Editing	Anne Baxter
Picture	Fredric March
Actress	Fredric March

Performers of Nominated Songs

"A Gal in Calico"	Gordon MacRae
"I Wish I Didn't Love You So"	Dennis Day
"Pass That Peace Pipe"	Dinah Shore
"You Do"	Frances Langford
"Zip-a-Dee-Doo-Dah"	Johnny Mercer and the Pied Pipers

"I worked hard on my dress all week because I had a feeling that I ought to make some sacrifice if I were to win the Award."
—Celeste Holm

ABC began its fourth annual broadcast to an estimated 45 million radio listeners, and the five thousand fans outside the Shrine listened through speakers. A medley of Oscar-winning songs was followed by the revelation of the stage setting celebrating Oscar's twentieth anniversary—a giant birthday cake with statuettes instead of candles.

Academy President Jean Hersholt came onstage to announce that the theme of the evening was "Oscar's Family Album." The programs had been printed to resemble a photo album and home movies were shown of famous Hollywood stars when they were unknowns—among them, nominees Ronald Colman, William Powell, and John Garfield. The montage went on to a silent tribute to members of the movie colony who had died in 1947, including actor Harry Carey and director Ernst Lubitsch, and concluded with a clip of Grace Moore singing in her 1934 Oscar-nominated role in *One Night of Love*.

One of the innovations of the show was the jumbling of the usual order of presentation that had always begun with Technical Awards first and ended with the major Awards. The Academy claimed the jumbling made each Award equally important, but *Daily Variety* added, "This was arranged so that there won't be a rush for the exits when the big awards are made." The giving started when Valentine Davies won the Original Screen Story for *Miracle on 34th Street* and confessed the idea came to him when he was waiting in line at a department store.

Shirley Temple later announced that Tom and Jerry's choke hold on the Best Cartoon Award had been broken after four years by Tweety and Sylvester, who had made their debuts in Warners' winning *Tweetie Pie*. In contrast to the evening's previous winners, who had modestly said "Thank you" and left, cartoon producer Edward Selzer got a big laugh when he paused and said, "I'll take a minute because cartoons have saved many a show before."

Donald Crisp stepped out to give two more big ones away a few minutes later. The Best Supporting Actress was, just as the poll said she would be, *Gentleman's Agreement*'s Celeste Holm, who was in her seat, knitting. "I dropped the ball of yarn and it rolled underneath the seats," she revealed later. At the podium, she exclaimed, "Thank you for letting this happen. I'm happy to be part of an industry that can create so much understanding in a world that needs it so much."

Backstage, the new Oscar winner said she had made her blue-gray bouffant gown with tight bodice and shocking pink organza petticoat herself, finishing just hours before the show. "I worked hard on my dress all week because I had a feeling that I ought to make some sacrifice if I were to win the Award." Meanwhile, her director, Elia Kazan, was receiving the Best Director Award from Donald Crisp, but Kazan made no sartorial sacrifices himself—he wore a regular business suit. His speech was humble, too: "I guess, being a comparative newcomer to the industry, I'm more grateful than most for the help that I needed and received."

Samuel Goldwyn was scheduled to give the Thalberg Award this year, but the Board of Governors didn't think anybody deserved it, causing *Daily Variety* to snicker later, "An Oscar Derby without the Thalberg Award is a confession." Olivia de Havilland appeared to announce the Best Actor—Ronald Colman in *A Double Life*. "It looked for an instant as if the house would give Colman a standing ovation," the *Hollywood Reporter* observed. When Colman got a chance to speak, he said, "I am very happy and very proud and very lucky—lucky because I wouldn't be standing on this stage tongiht without the help of such people as Bill Goetz, Ruth Gordon, and Garson and Michael Kanin," and then exited with de Havilland and wept backstage.

The Awards distribution was interrupted after the Best Actor Award for a program of old footage called, "Twenty Years of Academy Awards." Afterward, the nominated songs were performed and Dinah Shore announced that the winner was "Zip-a-Dee-Doo-Dah," a novelty song from Walt Disney's *Song of the South* that was so popular that Carmen Miranda had included a

"When Zanuck announced the picture, there was a terrific uproar from the rich Jews of the Hollywood community."
—Elia Kazan

backwards version of it in her nightclub act entitled "Eedapiz Ooh Dad."

Dick Powell was assigned the Art Direction Awards and revealed the Black-and-White winner to be the British picture *Great Expectations*. Eighteen-year-old Jean Simmons, a British actress who had appeared in the film, accepted the Award for the absent winners. Before anyone knew it, the British were on a roll, as J. Arthur Rank's productions of *Great Expectations* and *Black Narcissus* swept the Art Direction and Cinematography Awards.

Since Jean Simmons had been asked to accept for any absent Britisher, she was a busy woman. "It mounted like a running gag," the *Reporter* said, "when she was called back for three more successive Awards." *Daily Variety* inferred, "The crowd voiced its approval of the proceedings, but it was readily apparent that the approval was more for Miss Simmons than for the fortunate winners." Miss Simmons did, indeed, win many admirers. Florabel Muir said she "was the only one I saw there whose nails were not tinted," and Cecil B. DeMille approached her, offering her a part in his upcoming epic, *Samson and Delilah*. She turned him down.

President Jean Hersholt returned to announce the Special Awards voted on by the Board of Governors the night before. The first one was a plaque to *Bill and Coo,* a novelty live-action film about lovebirds with human voices dubbed in, and the Award specifically honored the filmmaker's "artistry and patience." Republic Pictures had actively campaigned for the recognition with the help of Louella Parsons, who called *Bill and Coo* "the greatest picture of its kind."

The Academy's board apparently felt a lot of heat over *Shoe-Shine*'s poor showing in the nominations because Hersholt produced a statuette for Vittorio DeSica and company for proving "to the world that the creative spirit can triumph over adversity." Hersholt said the statuette would be on its way to Rome the next day and then proposed, "An international Award, if properly planned and carefully administered, would promote a closer relationship between American film craftsmen and those of other countries."

There was also a Special Oscar for James Baskette, who played "Uncle Remus" in Disney's *Song of the South* and sang "Zip-a-Dee-Doo-Dah" to a lot of cartoon animals. Hedda Hopper took full credit for this Award, writing in her autobiography that she had suggested it as a great humanitarian move on the Academy's part. Some members of the board opposed the Award because Baskette played a slave, and, in Hedda's words, "the feeling was that Negroes should play only doctors, lawyers and scientists." Hedda said Jean Hersholt had argued in Baskette's favor until four in the morning, at which point he gave his ultimatum: "If he doesn't receive an Oscar, I shall stand up tomorrow night and tell the world the whole disgraceful story." The board gave in, and Ingrid Bergman gave Baskette his Oscar.

Anne Baxter brought the show back to the competitive Awards when she named Edmund Gwenn the Best Supporting Actor for playing Santa Claus in *Miracle on 34th Street*. What else could the winner say but "Now I know there's a Santa Claus." Santa Claus must have liked the picture, because Baxter gave it a second writing Award, this one for Best Screenplay.

Fredric March stepped out and said that Oscar was a character with a heart. He invited the audience to listen to one statuette's heartbeat and the throng heard someone beat a kettledrum. He then announced that *Gentleman's Agreement* had been voted Best Picture, and Darryl Zanuck went to the stage to collect what was due him.

Zanuck started off with the usual humility: "This picture started as a gamble. We knew we were pioneering in an off-the-beaten-path film, but we weighed every sequence in the light of entertainment values . . . I would like to emphasize that *Gentleman's Agreement* was primarily planned for entertainment rather than for any social message. I believe this is the chief reason for the success of the film." Instead of ending with his personal gratitudes, though, he added, "This makes up for a sharp disappointment I suffered

"It's time for Hollywood to start making pictures for the public, not the Academy."
—Daily Variety

some years ago. I'm sure I will be forgiven for mentioning the name of the picture, *Wilson,* of which I am still proud."

After Zanuck's grievances were aired, March proceeded to the Best Actress Award. Since the *Daily Variety* poll had been batting 1.000, members of the audience were already leaving, "not too quietly" as the paper reported, when March opened the envelope, started to say "Rosalind . . ." then did a double take. The winner was Loretta Young for *The Farmer's Daughter*. *Daily Variety* said, "It was a right blustery windy night outside, but the gasp that arose from the audience when Miss Young's name was read by Fredric March just about matched the heaviest gust whipping around the Shrine Auditorium."

A story this good couldn't pass by Louella Parsons, who recounted, "I was seated directly behind Rosalind . . . never as long as I live will I forget that almost involuntary motion she made of leaning forward, almost rising from her seat. Then Roz got to her feet—leading the applause." According to Russell's husband, the loser said, "We're going to the party afterward anyway. I won't be bitter."

Loretta Young was in a state of shock. She made Fredric March show her the name in the envelope when she got to the stage and, convinced that she really did win, said, "Up to now, this occasion has been for me a spectator sport. But I dressed, just in case." The winner lapsed into profuse praise for her fellow nominees, and concluded by looking at Oscar and swooning, "And as for you . . . at long last!" She kissed the statuette and exited. Eyewitness Florabel Muir wrote: "The blood was racing so wildly when she walked off the stage with the unexpected Oscar in her hands, the diamond necklace around her throat was moving up and down in a trinkling sort of rhythm."

Aftermath

As Darryl Zanuck, Ronald Colman and Loretta Young stood backstage congratulating each other for the benefit of photographers, one reporter cracked, "So much for new talent—this trio's been around since silent pictures." For Young, recognition had come earlier than she anticipated: "I had never expected this in my lifetime," she confessed.

Meanwhile, the audience was filing out of the Shrine while the orchestra played "Auld Lang Syne." Rosalind Russell walked over to console designer Travis Banton, who had burst into tears when his model lost. "Poor Travis," Russell said, "I feel so sorry for him." Just then, Russell's publicist, a contrite Henry Rogers, approached her with an early issue of the *Los Angeles Times* with the headline: ROZ RUSSELL WINS OSCAR.

Another Best Actress loser, Susan Hayward, kept her chin up for the press. "I'll be nominated for an Oscar again," she swore. "Maybe not next year. Maybe I'll have to wait until the fifties. But I intend to win someday. That's my goal." She also admitted that her gown was the most expensive article of clothing she had ever bought. "But I can always wear the dress again," she said. Alas, it just wasn't Hayward's night, because minutes later she stormed into the ladies' room and complained to Sheilah Graham, "My husband stepped on my dress! All that money, down the drain!"

The big party afterward was Darryl Zanuck's wingding for one hundred at the Mocambo, where the band played until 4 A.M. Zanuck could afford the expense; he had opened *Gentleman's Agreement* in a wide, regular-priced engagement the week of the Awards. Good loser Rosalind Russell did show up and showed the world there were no hard feelings by embracing Loretta Young for photographers.

The next day, *Daily Variety* graded its own poll and deduced, "It wasn't as pure as Ivory soap," but gave itself credit for getting "$83\frac{1}{3}$ percent" correct. Columnists were struck by how the musical chairs of casting had led so many second- and fourth-choice players to Oscar victory. The "Rambling Reporter" claimed that Ingrid Bergman, Olivia de Havilland, and even Rosalind Russell had turned down *The Farmer's Daughter* before Loretta Young got it. The "Reporter" later al-

"Neither of us remarked that we had dozed a couple of times during the film's screening."
—Rosalind Russell's publicist

leged that Cary Grant, the non-nominee for *The Bishop's Wife,* had vetoed *A Double Life* because "Cary was leery of playing Shakespeare."

Critics found the show's "Family Album" theme as dull as a family reunion and wanted to know where Bob Hope and Jack Benny were when the Academy needed them. The *Hollywood Citizen-News* went further and suggested the Academy go all out with a variety show. "Why not have some big production numbers, too, a few hundred dancing Oscars, say. Or a couple of bird acts, maybe."

If the show wasn't so hot, the responses of the winners were irresistible to the press. Celeste Holm entertained columnists with her tale of how her husband was so excited, he locked her Oscar in their car for safekeeping and then lost the key. Grateful Ronald Colman invited director George Cukor to his home, where the Oscar stood proudly on the mantel. "I hope you've noticed how inconspicuously I've placed it!" the winner laughed.

But since she had saved the show with her surprise finale, Loretta Young was the queen of the post-ceremony publicity. Newsmen gathered at her home at 9 A.M. the next day, where they were informed that the Oscar winner, who had been out celebrating until 7 A.M., was not to be disturbed until 11 A.M., when she would rise and prepare for 12 o'clock mass. When she could finally fit the press into her Sunday schedule, Loretta told them, "My only regret about the whole thing is Roz Russell. And don't say 'poor Roz' because she will go on to win an Academy Award and then some. But it was cruel for the polls to come out and say that she was going to win. I hope that will discourage them from taking polls next year."

Daily Variety's poll continued for another decade, since it only added to the excitement and suspense. As for "poor Roz," she didn't even mention the 1947 Oscar race in her memoirs, but said that the "one grace note in the discord" of *Mourning Becomes Electra* was that she received "a rare, handwritten note from Eugene O'Neill telling me how much he loved my performance as Lavinia."

Another loser who looked on the bright side was William Powell. The fifty-five-year-old Powell sent a congratulatory telegram to fifty-seven-year-old Ronald Colman: "After all, it's a good thing you won instead of me, because you haven't many years left and I have so many ahead of me."

1948

"With all the heated rivalry going on, it wouldn't be a bad idea to hold the Oscar ceremonies in the boxing ring at the Hollywood Legion Stadium."
—A joke around town

Hollywood tried to shortchange the Academy at the 1948 Awards, and ended up forfeiting the Oscar.

Since Ingrid Bergman had been elevated to virtual sainthood by her fans since *The Bells of St. Mary's*, producer Walter Wanger decided to take the next step and cast her in the title role of his $8.7 million epic, *Joan of Arc*. Bergman had packed them in when she played the part in Maxwell Anderson's *Joan of Lorraine* on Broadway in 1946, and Wanger recruited the Academy Award–winning director of *Gone With the Wind*, Victor Fleming, to direct her in the movie version. When the two-hour-and-twenty-seven-minute movie bowed, critics and audiences found it long-winded and overproduced. "*Joan of Arc* is massive, eyefilling and pretentiously disappointing," opined the *New York Herald Tribune*, while the *New York Times* said of Bergman, "Her strength seems to lie in her physique rather than in her burning faith." The best reviews went to film newcomer José Ferrer, recreating his Broadway role as the Dauphin. Bergman knew it was time to change direction, so she sent a fan letter to Italian director Roberto Rossellini, telling him how much she had enjoyed *Open City* and *Paisan*, and that she would love to work for him "for the sheer pleasure of the experience."

Wanger, meanwhile, had an $8.7 million turkey on his hands. The independent producer plumbed all publications looking for good reviews—the *Reader's Digest* was his biggest supporter—and he had exhibitors writing the trade journals to put a stop to the rumors that no one was going to see the movie. "It not only renews the public's faith in Hollywood's ability to produce wholesome, worthwhile motion pictures," scribbled a theater owner from Pennsylvania, "but it also confirms my belief that our support of independent productions of this caliber is vital for the survival of our industry."

The Huston Dynasty

Maxwell Anderson came off better in the movie version of *Key Largo*, if only because director John Huston and writer Richard Brooks threw out most of his play and let Humphrey Bogart, Edward G. Robinson, Lauren Bacall, Claire Trevor and Lionel Barrymore do their stuff in the melodrama set in the Florida Keys. Jack Warner was impressed enough by the film to allow Huston to adapt a novel about three prospectors digging for gold in Mexico who destroy themselves through greed and betrayal. Expecting another hit vehicle for Humphrey Bogart, Warner was dismayed when the on-location shooting dragged on and the budget rose with no end in sight. The mogul screamed, "I know whose gold they're going after—mine!"

Treasure of Sierra Madre, costarring Huston's father, Walter, opened to unanimous raves. The *New York Times* headlined, GREAT DAY FOR THE HUSTONS, and in *The Nation* James Agee called it "one of the most visually alive and beautiful films I have ever seen." Unfortunately, American audiences thought they were going to see a movie in which their hero Bogart struck it rich, and they were disappointed to find he was playing an immoral louse. Huston's acclaimed film was no treasure at the box office.

Silence Is Golden

Jack Warner was also worried about *Johnny Belinda*, a melodrama designed to showcase rising name Jane Wyman. The actress had been playing second leads at the studio for years, commenting, "I'm either the star's confidante, adviser, chum, sister or severest critic." Wyman always fared better when she was loaned out, as she was to Paramount for the romantic interest in *The Lost Weekend*, and then to MGM for her Oscar-nominated role in *The Yearling*. Warner decided he had

Overleaf: *First-time father-and-son winners Walter Huston and John Huston appraise their treasure.*

"Who is going to like this?" —Jack Warner on Johnny Belinda

an exploitable star on his payroll and cast her in a drama about a deaf mute who has to fight for the custody of her illegitimate child.

When the studio head viewed the rushes, he saw that director Jean Negulesco was avoiding the traditional tearjerking approach of most sacrificial-mother sagas. "Who is going to like this?" Warner shouted. Negulesco was canned before filming was completed and another director finished things up. *Variety* said of the resulting film, "*Johnny Belinda* is a fine presentation of a tragedy with a happy ending." The movie became Warner's highest grosser of the year.

Invalids on Parade

Jane Wyman was not the year's only disabled heroine. Director Anatole Litvak was hopping around town directing Hollywood's foremost actresses in dramas about trapped, helpless women. At Paramount, he guided Barbara Stanwyck through an adaptation of *Sorry, Wrong Number,* a popular radio play about a bedridden heiress who discovers, over the telephone, that someone is planning to kill her. For Stanwyck, the movie offered her a chance at a tour de force—she got to be tough and tremulous—and critics called it her best role since her Oscar-nominated one in *Double Indemnity*.

Litvak then reported to 20th Century–Fox, where he toured Olivia de Havilland through a mental asylum in *The Snake Pit.* This was Darryl Zanuck's big one for the year, and the film's ad campaign reminded everyone that the production was "from the company which gave you *Gentleman's Agreement* last year." Louella Parsons said, "It is the most courageous subject ever attempted on the screen," and Walter Winchell swore, "Its seething reality gets inside of you." Zanuck also tried to pass the movie off as a catalyst for social reform and at one point *Daily Variety* gossip columnist Herb Stein interrupted his discussion of the film colony's social comings-and-goings to note: "Wisconsin is the seventh state to institute reforms in its mental hospitals as a result of *Snake Pit.*" Moviegoers were curious about what goes on inside asylums, and the picture was more profitable than *Gentleman's Agreement.*

Another Sister Slugfest

Olivia de Havilland's bid for a second Oscar was challenged by her old nemesis—kid sister Joan Fontaine. Although Fontaine's self-produced film, *Letter from an Unknown Woman,* had not created much of a stir at the box office, Max Ophuls' direction and Joan's performance as a love-struck-teenager-turned-tragic-middle-aged-woman had inspired compliments from the critics. After mailing invitations to the "Demand Re-Issue" of the movie at the end of the year, Fontaine ran trade-paper ads that quoted her Hollywood friends on how much they admired her. The Fontaine Fan Club included Joan Crawford, Charles Boyer, Zoe Atkins, Ronald Colman and Preston Sturges, who commented, "Joan Fontaine is as dazzling and disturbing in this as in everything else she does."

Hail Sir Larry

Olivia de Havilland won the first round when the New York Film Critics selected her as their Best Actress. The scribes followed through on their good reviews for *Treasure of Sierra Madre* by giving their Best Picture Award to the film and the Best Director citation to John Huston. Hollywood could handle these choices, but was rankled when the critics picked as Best Actor Laurence Olivier for *Hamlet,* giving him momentum in the Oscar race.

The international success of *Henry V* had inspired Olivier to tackle the tragedy of the melancholy Dane on film, and British producer J. Arthur Rank was happy to give him the money to try. King George VI was proud of Olivier, too, and knighted him while the film was in production. Still, Olivier had not forgotten what he had learned in Hollywood, and he told Alan Dent, who was helping him on the screenplay, that this *Ham-*

"As long as we turn out pictures like I Remember Mama we don't have to worry about the future of Hollywood."
—Hedda Hopper

let had to sell tickets. "One has to choose between making the meaning clear to twenty million cinemagoers and making two thousand Shakespearean experts wince, or not changing a word," Dent explained. "We decided to make the minority wince." The play was trimmed down from four hours to two hours and thirty minutes, Ophelia was played by Jean Simmons, the actress who had picked up four Oscars at the previous Awards show, and Olivier went blond for the title role.

Hamlet was a hot ticket, and Hollywood watched in amazement as the public turned out to see Shakespeare. *Motion Picture Herald* marveled, "The promoters have held the product so far from the accepted cinema patterns that they have given it distribution through the Theatre Guild and stage-type promotions addressed at a non-cinematic audience. Eschewing weekend engagements when film-minded persons dominate audiences, *Hamlet* had been held for the mid-week 'carriage trade.' " *Daily Variety* conceded that "Olivier appears to be tops among the candidates for best actor," but Universal, which distributed *Hamlet* in the U.S., ran no Oscar ads for the tragedy with an unhappy ending. One Hollywood company did publish an ad that bragged, "*Hamlet* comes to life on a Western Electric sound track."

Dance Fever

Commercial tie-ins were also the name of the game for the year's other major British import, *The Red Shoes*. Eagle-Lion, the small American releasing company that presented the ballet melodrama in the States, knew what it was doing when it held what *Daily Variety* termed "the largest number of advanced showings in its history." The previews were for the benefit of ballet-school instructors and merchandising heads of Los Angeles department stores who saw a gold mine in the romantic story about a possessed ballerina. Soon there was a thriving triangle trade: little girls who saw the movie bought slippers from stores to wear in dance classes.

The Nominations

The popularity of the British films was painfully brought home to Hollywood in the nominations: *The Red Shoes* was up for five Oscars, *Hamlet* for six, and both were nominated for Best Picture. Not to worry, said *Daily Variety,* the Best Picture race was between *The Snake Pit* with six nominations and *Johnny Belinda* with twelve. Jack Warner sent a telegram to Jean Negulesco, the director he had fired from *Johnny Belinda:* "Well, kid, we did it again!" Negulesco was a friend of fellow Director nominees John Huston and Anatole Litvak, and a columnist wrote, "Have you noticed that the three top directors for Academy Award honors are the closest of buddies and their buddies are having the damnedest time making a choice?"

One choice no Academy voter would have to make was whether or not to vote for *Joan of Arc* for Best Picture. Walter Wanger was livid when the Academy turned its back on his epic and nominated it for a measly seven Oscars. The nominations of Ingrid Bergman and José Ferrer did not assuage the producer, who felt personally insulted that neither the movie nor director Victor Fleming were tapped for honors. It was all the former Academy president could talk about.

Bogart Ostracized

The rest of Hollywood was agog at the Best Actor nominations. Laurence Olivier, as expected, was named, as were Lew Ayres for *Johnny Belinda,* Clifton Webb for the comedy hit *Sitting Pretty,* and screen newcomer Montgomery Clift for *The Search*. But where was Humphrey Bogart from *Treasure of Sierra Madre*? In Bogart's place was the left-field nomination of Dan Dailey for a Betty Grable musical, *When My Baby Smiles at Me*. Nobody had an explanation.

Because Olivier had the Best Actor trophy sewn up, *Daily Variety* opined, "Interest this year

"It looks to us as if the Academy Awards is going to fold."
—An executive at Columbia

will rest primarily in the best actress award." Ingrid Bergman's Joan of Arc would just be watching from the sidelines, as would nominee Irene Dunne's matriarch in *I Remember Mama*. Paramount gave dark horse Barbara Stanwyck a big push by breaking the ice and advertising the reissue of *Sorry, Wrong Number* on television; the studio was unsure if the TV promos would help Stanwyck's chances, but it reported that they were responsible for booming business.

Crazy and Dumb

Olivia de Havilland didn't have to worry about her sister this year—Joan Fontaine hadn't even made it to the nominations—but Jane Wyman was a different matter. When the news came that Wyman had won the London Film Critics Award, de Havilland's publicists sent cables to columnists pointing out that *The Snake Pit* had not opened in England yet. Both actresses campaigned on the basis of the painstaking research that went into their performances. After columnist Florabel Muir wondered if "they allowed contact dances among violent inmates of mental institutions" as depicted in *The Snake Pit,* she got a phone call from de Havilland verifying that she had attended several such dances herself. The actress' ads quoted the *Saturday Review,* which said, "Miss de Havilland gives one of those wonderfully unglamorized and true performances generally associated with only the more distinguished foreign films."

De Havilland had the luxury of dialogue in her role; Jane Wyman didn't have that much. "She has long been known as a fast-talking, wisecracking comedienne," *Liberty* magazine said, "but as the deaf mute she speaks not a word." *Life* detailed Wyman's efforts to study sign language and lipreading, noting, "To get the feeling of deafness she had her ears plugged while acting." Director Negulesco elaborated, "You could have shot a gun off behind her and even in close-up it wouldn't have registered on her face." In addition to stuffed ears, Wyman also had this year's sympathy vote. Before filming began, she had lost her premature baby, and, by the time the production was over, she and husband Ronald Reagan were divorcing. "I think I'll name *Johnny Belinda* co-respondent," Reagan quipped.

Behind the Scenes Drama

While the press raised its annual hoopla over the Oscar race, the Academy wondered whether the show would go on. The studios that had always funded the ceremony were looking for ways to tighten their belts in 1948, particularly the Big Five—MGM, Warners, Fox, Paramount and RKO. In May of 1948, the Supreme Court had told the Big Five they couldn't own both their movie theater chains and their studios without violating antitrust laws, so the theaters would have to go. Since the profits from the movie houses represented as much as half a studio's income, the moguls were devastated by this blow, which meant the film factories would have to live on their movies alone. Making matters worse, this was the year that television began beaming the World Series, Milton Berle and Ed Sullivan into American homes. Suddenly, theaters that had been filled to capacity during the war years were as empty as Monument Valley.

In December 1948, the Big Five got the message from their New York offices to cut expenses. The Academy Awards show was a good place to start. The quintet issued a statement to the Academy saying that they would no longer be subsidizing the ceremonies. Their official reason was that "the companies, as companies, were never members of the Academy . . . The companies should not be in the position where they can be accused of subsidizing an artistic and cultural force." *Time* magazine, when it found out about it, scoffed that this was "a pious explanation."

"I sure hate to vote for a Britisher, but what can you do?"
—An Academy voter

Jumping Mad

Academy President Jean Hersholt was so mad he threatened to resign, but the Board of Governors pleaded with him not to become another deserter. The president acquiesced on the condition that the board find a new president to begin office immediately after this year's ceremonies—if there were ceremonies this year. Hersholt decided to keep mum about the studio pullout, and the public was not aware of any problem. After negotiations with Hersholt, Jack Warner was willing to let the Academy hold a banquet on the still-standing castle set from the Errol Flynn costume epic, *The Adventures of Don Juan,* but the Academy's accountants figured the expenses of transforming the sound stage into a dining room would put them $15,000 in the red. Finally, Hersholt said to hell with the studios and announced that the show would be held in the Academy's 950-seat screening theater—a far cry from last year's ceremonies at the 6,700-seat Shrine Auditorium.

"Indignant Academy members kept the switchboard humming over the weekend as they registered protest over announcement," *Daily Variety* reported. "Goodly percentage of members, who pay $36 a year dues, beefed that they could see no reason for continuing to shell out that amount if they couldn't attend the show."

Playing Poverty

The *Hollywood Reporter*'s W.R. Wilkerson was also dismayed and wrote an editorial warning that the public has:

> *gotten the feeling that the bottom has just about fallen out of the motion picture industry generally and Hollywood particularly. Accordingly, any sign that will counteract this feeling, a move that will tell our customers that we are still alive and kicking, would be a most progressive accomplishment. For this reason, we feel that "playing poverty" with the conduct of this year's Awards is a particularly bad thing . . .*

The Academy was deluged with offers and suggestions. The Ambassador Hotel, host of five Academy banquets in the 1930s, argued that the Academy should return to the Coconut Grove and utilize the hotel's other ballrooms too, because "Academy members would prefer to wander from room to room, thus giving actresses a chance to show off their gowns and jewels." Hersholt was not convinced, and he vetoed another suggestion, put forth by a group of Academy members, to turn the show into a national event by staging it in New York's Madison Square Garden this year, in Chicago Stadium next, and then back to Hollywood after that. As for the offer from local TV stations to televise the show from the Academy Theatre as a news event, Hersholt said no on principle. *Daily Variety* quoted one wag on the controversy: "With all the heated rivalry going on, it wouldn't be a bad idea to hold the Oscar ceremonies in the boxing ring at the Hollywood Legion Stadium."

Despite the moguls' refusal to pay for the ceremony, many of them were planning their post-Awards celebratory bashes when *Daily Variety* published its annual Oscar poll. The trade paper predicted *Johnny Belinda* as Best Picture; Jane Wyman as Best Actress; John Huston as Best Director and his father, Walter, Best Supporting Actor for *Treasure of Sierra Madre;* and Claire Trevor Best Supporting Actress for playing Edward G. Robinson's alcoholic mistress in Huston's *Key Largo*. For the Best Actor result, the trade journal went into more detail:

> *. . . there were many expressions of distaste for British films. These were not strictly nationalistic in character, but appeared to stem from the general belief that English film tycoons have hurt the foreign market for American pictures. Olivier, who practically walked in, received most of his votes with the preface, "I sure hate to vote for a Britisher, but what can you do? He deserves it."*

The Big Night

The ceremonies were held during the first week in spring; it snowed. The nearest parking lot was several blocks away, so Hollywood's elite parked their cars and then rode in Academy-provided limousines to the theater. Though there was no room in the small auditorium for many Academy members, seating was found for the likes of Governor Earl Warren, Los Angeles Mayor Fletcher Bowron, Beverly Hills Mayor Otto Gerth and the police chiefs of both cities.

Academy President Jean Hersholt didn't mince words in his opening remarks. "There have been voices in the industry raised against the Academy," he lectured. "These voices always say the same thing: 'We don't want the Academy's standards foisted upon us—we want to make commercial pictures unhampered by considerations of artistic excellence.' " As a further slap in the face to the Big Five's New York offices, Hersholt said that without the Academy, Hollywood would not "be producing pictures with the variety, the distinction and the courage of the nominees." The president then announced that his successor in office would be screenwriter/ producer Charles Brackett.

Emcee Robert Montgomery, wearing a line of war medals on his tuxedo, brightened the proceedings with his request to the evening's winners: "If you want to acknowledge your indebtedness, please do it by letter or phone tomorrow." The Academy had played up to the studios somewhat by asking their contract starlets to distribute the Awards throughout the ceremony. Montgomery acted like the host of a bachelor party as he drooled over every actress presenter. "When you speak of Ava Gardner," his first introduction began, "you must admit that Mother Nature lingered over the job." Gardner, who had played Venus for Universal that year, read the name of the Documentary nominees and asked for "the magic envelope, if you please." The magic name inside was "O.O. Dull." Mr. Dull accepted his award and walked off in one direction while a confused Gardner went off in the other.

Sensing the Anglophobic sentiments of the audience, Montgomery prefaced the Writing Awards with the reminder that "William Shakespeare wasn't nominated." Out came MGM's new contractee, British Deborah Kerr, to announce that John Huston had won the Screenplay Oscar for *Treasure of Sierra Madre*. Huston simply held up the statuette and smiled. MGM's *The Search* won the Motion Picture Story Award, although

Awards Ceremony

MARCH 24, 1949, 8:00 P.M.
THE ACADEMY THEATRE, HOLLYWOOD

Your Host:
ROBERT MONTGOMERY

Presenters

Scientific and Technical Awards	George Murphy
Documentary Awards	Ava Gardner
Foreign Film	Louis Jourdan
Writing Awards	Deborah Kerr
Special Effects	Glenn Ford
Sound Recording	Ann Blyth
Short Subjects	Jeanne Crain
Film Editing	Wendell Corey
Art Direction	Arlene Dahl
Costume Design	Elizabeth Taylor
Cinematography	Robert Ryan
Music Awards	Kathryn Grayson
Supporting Actor	Celeste Holm
Supporting Actress	Edmund Gwenn
Special Awards	Jean Hersholt
Director	Frank Borzage
Actor	Loretta Young
Actress	Ronald Colman
Picture	Ethel Barrymore

Performers of Nominated Songs

"Buttons and Bows"	Jane Russell
"For Every Man There's a Woman"	Gordon MacRae
"It's Magic"	Doris Day
"This Is the Moment"	Jo Stafford
"The Woody Woodpecker Song"	Gloria Wood and Harry Babbitt

"William Shakespeare wasn't nominated."
—Robert Montgomery

the orchestra struck up the movie's theme before Kerr could get the authors' names out.

Of MGM's red-haired Arlene Dahl, Montgomery said, "She is responsible for men refusing to dream in black-and-white." Dahl entered to the strains of "A Pretty Girl Is Like a Melody" and revealed that the Black-and-White Art Direction Award was won by *Hamlet*. There was polite applause. The Color Award went to *The Red Shoes* which received a heartier ovation, if only because Hollywood's own Susan Hayward accepted.

Montgomery introduced the Academy's newest Award, for Costume Design, with the observation, "It is fitting that an actress would present this award." The presenter was MGM's seventeen-year-old Elizabeth Taylor, who made her entrance in a white taffeta gown to the tune of "Did You Ever See a Dream Walking?" One of the nominees was Edith Head for the lavish color musical *The Emperor Waltz*. As Head recounted in her memoirs:

> *There was no doubt in my mind that I would win that Oscar. I deserved it—for longevity if nothing else. I had been doing motion pictures before the Oscar even existed. And besides, my picture had the best costumes of any nominated picture. The serious competition was* Joan of Arc, *designed by Madame Karinska and Dorothy Jeakins. To my mind there was no way Ingrid Bergman's sackcloths and suits of armor could win over my Viennese finery.*

Academy voters were of a different mind, and Taylor announced that *Joan of Arc* was the winner. An excited Karinska charged up to the stage like a horse. As for Head, "Since I am not very emotional," she remembered, "no one knew that I was in shock. My husband squeezed my hand and we watched the remaining presentations, but I do not remember the rest of the evening." While Head sat there stupefied, the rest of Hollywood got nervous when Taylor gave the Black-and-White Costume trophy to *Hamlet*, the British entry's second victory.

Jane Russell was brought on by Montgomery with, "The nominated song 'Buttons and Bows' will now emanate from the lovely and talented throat of Miss Jane Russell." She was followed by Celeste Holm, "who literally burst across the Hollywood sky last year," but was in one piece when she entered to give the Best Supporting Actor Award. The winner was John Huston's father for *Treasure of Sierra Madre*. In contrast to the film's grizzled, unshaven prospector, a dapper, bespectacled Walter Huston mounted the stage and said, "Many years ago . . . many, many years ago [laughter] I raised a son and I said to him, 'If you ever become a writer or a director, please find a good part for your old man.' "

Edmund Gwenn, last year's Best Supporting Actor for *Miracle on 34th Street,* appeared and gave a personal progress report: "I'm just about able to venture down the street without being mobbed by small children." He then revealed that the Best Supporting Actress was Claire Trevor in *Key Largo*. The winner curtsied before the Price, Waterhouse representative and exclaimed, "From the bottom of my heart, this is one of the happiest moments of my life." Going Huston two better, she added, "I have three boys and I hope they grow up to be directors or writers so they can give their old lady a job."

Jean Hersholt rematerialized to give the Special Awards. The board had voted to give a juvenile trophy to nine-year-old Ivan Jandl for playing the orphan Montgomery Clift befriends in *The Search*. The Czechoslovakian child did not speak English and had learned the film's dialogue by rote. Nobody bothered to teach him an acceptance speech and his Award was picked up by director Fred Zinnemann. Sid Grauman, an Academy founder, received an Award for having "raised the standard of exhibition of motion pictures," presumably by building such famous rococo movie palaces as Grauman's Chinese and Egyptian theaters. Grauman, sixty-nine, said, "When I have my

"The first thing that came to my mind was 'Did I or didn't I put on my girdle tonight?'"
—Jane Wyman

thirty-fifth birthday, I'll look back and say they didn't forget me." He returned to his seat with the Oscar and, having gotten what he came for, fell asleep.

Hersholt dished out another unofficial lifetime achievement Oscar to Adolph Zukor, the chairman of the board of Paramount, for "services over forty years to the industry." Zukor's son picked up the Oscar. Then came the pièce de résistance. The Board of Governors had decided to make it up to ex-Academy President Walter Wanger for the Academy's not nominating his expensive movie for Best Picture with a Special Oscar for his "distinguished service to the industry in adding to its moral stature in the world community by his production of *Joan of Arc*." Hersholt added, "I have no doubt that the citation on this award you have just received expresses the sentiment of the vast picture-going audience who have already seen *Joan of Arc* and those who will in time see it."

This attention still wasn't enough for Wanger, who responded, "Notwithstanding the citation, I cannot accept this award except in the name of my partners Ingrid Bergman and Victor Fleming, who made this great picture possible." His partners couldn't have cared less since Bergman was off with Roberto Rossellini in Italy and Fleming had died two months earlier.

Jean Hersholt settled the question of the Thalberg Award, which *Daily Variety* had headlined as a "hot race" because the "producing of pictures based on themes hitherto untried requires plenty of confidence, especially in an uncertain market." The Board of Governors decided that Jerry Wald had the most guts for producing *Johnny Belinda* and *Key Largo*. Wald proved that the acrobatics were best left to Errol Flynn when he stumbled on the steps to the stage. At the podium he gushed, "I hope I can put back into the picture business half of what it's giving to me tonight."

Robert Montgomery returned to admire the Best Director presenter, two-time winner Frank Borzage. "So well preserved, too," the emcee mused. Borzage opened the envelope and said, "Again, John Huston." The winner was in a mood to celebrate: he lifted the statuette in the direction of his producer, saying, "If this were hollow and had a drink in it, I'd toast Henry Blanke."

Loretta Young entered to the sound of "The Most Beautiful Girl in the World," and stated, "I know what a memorable evening this will be for the winner." The Best Actor winner turned out to be the absent Laurence Olivier for *Hamlet*. After muted applause, Douglas Fairbanks, Jr., accepted for his friend.

Last year's Best Actor, Ronald Colman, had won newfound fame as a frequent guest star on Jack Benny's radio show and was introduced by Montgomery as "Jack Benny's neighbor" while a violin played out of tune. Colman declared that Jane Wyman had won Best Actress for *Johnny Belinda*. The winner's date was costar Lew Ayres, who remembered, "When Jane heard her name called, she stood up as though she were sleepwalking, dropped her bag and everything rolled out of it to the floor. She had a million coins and charms in her bag. Some of them are probably still under the seat at the Academy Theatre."

Wyman had a different version of her trip to the stage. "I heard my name called," she remembered, "and the first thing that came to my mind was 'Did I or didn't I put on my girdle tonight?' Then I thought 'So what? Let it bounce.' " Her acceptance speech was brief: "I accept this very gratefully for keeping my mouth shut for once. I think I'll do it again."

Montgomery didn't remark on the physical attributes of the next female presenter, Ethel Barrymore. He labeled her "the great lady of film," and she returned the compliment by saying she was "deeply honored" to give the Best Picture Oscar. Her honor quickly turned to disappointment when she saw that the winner inside the envelope was *Hamlet*, a film that she had publicly criticized for not being on par with her brother John's stage production. Douglas Fairbanks, Jr., was on stage again, and he tried to downplay the British-invasion angle by reminding the audience that Olivier

"At midnight, merchants hereabouts reported a strong run on aspirin."
—Hollywood Reporter

was hardly a stranger to Hollywood. "I'm sure that Larry, who lived and worked amongst us for so many years—no awards can be more touching than this. We should congratulate ourselves for having honored him twice," Fairbanks said, as half the audience began to head for the exits. Montgomery rushed out to say his final line before everybody disappeared: "Miss Ethel Barrymore, in a manner which gives us at the Academy a real sense of our responsibility to the honest creators of the motion-picture industry, you have closed our program."

Aftermath

"Is it any wonder the Warner boys (Harry and Jack) tossed a big party in the Mocambo Champagne Room?" queried columnist Florabel Muir as she surveyed Warners' bevy of winners: Jane Wyman, Walter and John Huston, Jerry Wald and Claire Trevor. Governor Warren and Mayor Bowron also managed to get invited to this shindig, and Elsa Maxwell was glimpsed reveling with the Hustons. Jack Warner presented Wyman with an "Old Methuselah," which, as Muir defined it, is "a bottle big enough to hold a case of champagne." Wyman said she was placing her Oscar on top of her TV set at home, while Claire Trevor confessed that her husband had already given her a miniature Oscar that day. Barbara Stanwyck, now a four-time loser, said, "If I get nominated next year, they'll have to give me the door prize, won't they? At least the bride should throw me the bouquet."

Despite his lack of enthusiasm for his Special Award, Walter Wanger began advertising *Joan of Arc* as the "Academy Special Award Picture" until the Board of Governors told him to cut it out because it was he, not his movie, that had been honored. Wanger's losses on *Joan of Arc* eventually forced him into bankruptcy and, even worse, into signing a three-picture deal with Monogram. Two years later Wanger became embroiled in a Hollywood scandal when, convinced that wife Joan Bennett was cheating on him, he shot her agent and supposed paramour in a Beverly Hills parking lot. Hollywood was stunned but sympathetic, and one observer told a reporter, "Walter was in a turbulent state of mind. He didn't shoot Jennings Lang—he shot the millions of people who didn't see *Joan of Arc*."

Laurence Olivier's Hollywood secretary got hold of him at 9 A.M., London time. The double Oscar winner told the press, "It is incredibly generous of Hollywood to confer their highest honor upon the British film industry. I personally have not deserved this honor but my associates have and I am happy, proud and most grateful for their sakes and for my own." Appearing on stage with his wife, Vivien Leigh, in *The School for Scandal*, Olivier was asked how he planned to celebrate. "Oh," he enthused, "perhaps an extra drink after tonight's show."

Most of Hollywood was not in a celebratory mood. The *Hollywood Reporter* wrote: "*Hamlet*'s ghost stalked Hollywood last night and in the most ghoulish seventy-five minutes the picture business ever experienced waltzed off with a flock of golden Oscars. At midnight, merchants hereabouts reported a strong run on aspirin." A guest was heard saying, "Although the orchestra had opened the proceedings with 'The Star-Spangled Banner,' in retrospect, maybe it was really 'God Save the King.' "

Academy President Hersholt waited until after the ceremony to reveal publicly that the Big Five had withdrawn their support for the Academy. As a result, the majors were made to look as if they were taking it out on the Academy because *Hamlet* had won. The brouhaha led three of the smaller studios—Universal-International, Republic and Columbia—to announce that they, too, were pulling out. One Columbia executive told the press, "Columbia, for the past few years, never thought the Academy officials handled the Awards presentations in the right manner. It looks to us as if the Academy Awards is going to fold."

But cooler heads prevailed. The *Hollywood Citizen-News* was one of several newspapers that shamed the studios back into funding the Awards. One editorial read: "The studios never miss a chance to exploit the Oscar symbol of the Academy in newspaper and magazine ads when a player or a picture is so honored. Yet, they won't support the Awards—the very persons who profit most from them!"

But one paper was still angry at the Academy. From his pulpit at the *Hollywood Reporter,* W.R. Wilkerson charged, "From ANYWAY you look at it, *Hamlet* was NOT the best picture of the year," and then asked rhetorically, "Have we a bunch of goofs among our Academy voters who, like many of the New York critics, kid themselves into believing that Britain is capable of making better pictures than Hollywood?"

Academy Governor Emmet Lavery put Wilkerson in his place by writing in *Saturday Review* that "a word of condemnation from him is, by a kind of inverted yet wonderfully appropriate logic, a guarantee of good conduct to the thoughtful citizens of the community." The governor concluded that Oscar had finally become his own man: "At the ripe old age of twenty-one, he has shown that he is free to vote as he pleases."

1949

"Olivia de Havilland was a star long before she became a great actress."
—Elsa Maxwell

War and politics, adultery and lonely spinsters—these were what the 1949 Academy Awards were made of.

After his anti-Semitism drama *Gentleman's Agreement* won Best Picture at the 1947 Academy Awards, Darryl F. Zanuck reportedly turned to an associate and cried, "Let's do it with a Negro!" The result was *Pinky*, about a light-skinned black woman who falls for a white doctor, and Zanuck figured its seriousness made it a natural for the Oscars. But critics complained that *Pinky* was too glossy, especially in comparison to several low-budget movies about the "Negro problem" that had opened earlier in the year. That Zanuck cast the pristine white actress Jeanne Crain as the black heroine didn't help matters; *Daily Variety* found that Crain "brings proper dignity and sincerity to her role, although she's not always convincing." *The New Yorker* shrugged off the whole enterprise: "The message of *Pinky* seems to be that colored girls, however fair, will find more happiness conducting themselves as Negroes in the warm-hearted South than they could passing as whites in Boston. I'm not sure I'm willing to take Mr. Zanuck's word for that."

May the Force Be With You

If the critical response to *Pinky* was a disappointment, Zanuck wasn't overly concerned. Shortly after the film opened, columnist Herb Stein leaked: "Those in the know say that Darryl Zanuck has another ace up his sleeve which he won't pull out until the eve of the Academy Award nominations with *12 O'Clock High*." In 1949, Hollywood reasoning held that one way to get audiences into theaters was letting all those World War II GI's relive their glory days. *12 O'Clock High* dealt with the psychological pressures felt by an air force division and Zanuck, who had been in that service branch, made the film because "there is no doubt in my mind that unquestionably it can serve as tremendous propaganda to stimulate interest in the air force."

Olivia de Havilland turns her two Best Actress Oscars into four—it's all done with mirrors.

Photoplay lamented that, despite the presence of Gregory Peck, "completely devoid of love interest, this is a man's picture." Nevertheless, Hedda Hopper called *12 O'Clock High* "the best picture I've seen this year" and Louella Parsons said, "when Academy voting time comes, it will be the picture to beat." *Time* praised the film because "it avoids such cinemilitary booby traps as self-conscious battle scenes and the women left behind or picked up along the way."

Hello, Sucker

Over at MGM, new chief of production Dore Schary wanted to make a war movie as his initial production because "it was imperative to do a film that would say the war was worth fighting despite the terrible losses . . . The men who fought this war were not suckers." But Dore Schary *was* a sucker, or so thought Louis B. Mayer, still the head of the studio. Mayer felt the last thing Americans wanted as an evening's entertainment was a film about an army battalion in the Battle of the Bulge, but he approved Schary's *Battleground* anyway. "It's a war picture, but let him make it," Mayer confidently told Nick Schenck, president of MGM's parent company, Loew's, Inc. "It will teach him a lesson."

The critics were lavish in their praise of *Battleground*. *Daily Variety* wrote: "The cutting humor of *What Price Glory?*, the eloquence of *Journey's End*, the pathos of *All Quiet on the Western Front*, the adventure of *Hell's Angels*, the sentiment of *The Big Parade* have all been combined in this extraordinary celluloid achievement." MGM promoted *Battleground* as "The Intimate Story of a Bunch of Fellows from Anybody's Home Town." So many people went to see these hometown boys that the film became MGM's highest grosser of this, its twenty-fifth year of existence. Industry veterans recalled that in 1925,

"The men who fought this war were not suckers."
—Dore Schary

Mayer had pooh-poohed production chief Irving Thalberg's wish to make a war movie but like *Battleground, The Big Parade* had been a huge hit.

Written in Blood

Republic's war movie, *Sands of Iwo Jima,* was its most expensive production ever, and the studio managed to get it into "prestige" first-run houses that normally wouldn't have touched its product. Walter Winchell went crazy over the movie: "The original story was written in blood by the glorious United States Marines! John Wayne must be everybody's idea of a good actor! He's immense in *Iwo Jima,* the best of the war pictures." The Christmas release also turned out to be the most successful movie in Republic's history and the studio felt that Oscars were in order. Although Republic was new to the Oscar game, it handled itself like an old pro; in addition to advertisements extolling the patriotism of *Sands of Iwo Jima,* the studio made direct-mail pleas to Academy voters on behalf of the film.

John Wayne had already received sterling reviews earlier in the year for John Ford's *She Wore a Yellow Ribbon,* and after *Sands of Iwo Jima,* the forty-two-year-old actor was voted America's number-one box-office star in the annual exhibitors' poll. To most people, *Sands of Iwo Jima* was a rousing action film. To John Wayne it was "a beautiful personal story." Because it dealt with a sergeant who whips young recruits into shape, Wayne later called *Sands of Iwo Jima,* "the story of Mr. Chips put in the military."

Harry Cohn—Role Model

Despite these war films, *Life* cited *All the King's Men* as "the most exciting film to come out of Hollywood this year." The political drama based on the Pulitzer Prize–winning roman à clef about Huey Long was made by writer-director Robert Rossen's own production company and distributed by Columbia. Studio head Harry Cohn didn't count the film among his favorites; even after *All the King's Men* opened to terrific reviews in New York, Rossen had to plead with the mogul to release it in Los Angeles in time to qualify for the Oscars. "Okay," Cohn finally agreed, "but don't expect me to put on a campaign." The *Los Angeles Daily News* declared that *King's Men* "rates all Oscars for the year" and Rossen went ahead and shelled out his own money for trade-paper ads, stressing the social importance of the movie. Epitomizing this approach was the grandiose, full-page announcement that *All the King's Men* received a "citation" from the New York University Center for Research as "one of the decade's 10 most distinguished films in the field of human relations."

For character actor Broderick Crawford, tyrannical politician Willie Stark was the role of a lifetime. After a decade of films like *Tight Shoes, South of Tahiti* and *North to the Klondike,* Crawford, thirty-seven, was hearing rave reviews. *Daily Variety* said: "Crawford delivers one of the most dynamic character studies the screen has ever glimpsed" and *Newsweek* wrote: "Crawford gives a performance that matches the story's crude eloquence and force." Crawford himself was incredulous. "This can't really be happening after all those westerns," he exclaimed. The word around Hollywood was that director Rossen had drawn such a forceful performance from Crawford by suggesting a role model for his crude character—Harry Cohn.

Now I'm Sexy

Like Crawford, Kirk Douglas was a journeyman actor receiving newfound critical acclaim. Douglas played a ruthless boxer in the low-budget sleeper *Champion* and found himself elevated to the big time. He told Hedda Hopper, "My agent had a costarring deal at a major studio. But I was tired of costarring. I decided it was now or never. I had to find out whether I could carry a picture. If I couldn't, I might as well get into some other

"Everybody thinks now I'm sexy and tough all of a sudden."
—Kirk Douglas

business." As a result of *Champion,* Douglas got a high-price long-term contract from Warner Brothers and was voted one of the year's top five male stars in the *Photoplay* poll. And, as he said, "Everybody thinks now I'm sexy and tough all of a sudden . . . Even my agent's nicer to me."

Mail Call

Douglas had one final fling as a supporting performer in 1949, playing a mild-mannered schoolteacher in *A Letter to Three Wives.* Writer-director Joseph L. Mankiewicz poked fun at the mores of married life in suburbia and wowed the critics with his wit in this tale of three friends who learn that one of their husbands has run off with another woman. *Time* called it "a bright, unusual comedy that sets itself some hurdles and clears them all—mostly with room to spare." But even with the great notices and a titillating ad line—"It's a Peek Into The Other Woman's Male!"—*Letter* proved too sophisticated to be more than a moderate financial success.

On the Square

William Wyler had not made a motion picture since his Oscar-winning *The Best Years of Our Lives,* but now, three years later, he was back with *The Heiress,* based on Henry James' *Washington Square.* When asked why it had taken so long, the director said, "Well, if I don't make any picture at least I'm not making a bad one. Anything is better than making a bad picture." Wyler could rest assured; the critics loved his study of a spinster who decides to marry over the objections of her father. Exhibitor Harry Brandt of "box-office poison" fame said, "I've seen every picture made in 1949 and this should not only win the Academy Award but get second and third place, too." *Variety,* however, predicted: "The majority of ticket buyers will find the nearly two hours soporific." The analysis proved accurate. *The Heiress* went as unwanted as its title character.

Lovely Livvy

That title character was played by Olivia de Havilland, and Elsa Maxwell wrote in *Photoplay* that "Olivia has become the girl to whom Hollywood producers turn when they have a movie that demands an actress who will discard her personality and her beauty to become, utterly, the character described by the author." She added, "Olivia, of course, was a star long before she became a great actress." Reviewers couldn't contain their enthusiasm over de Havilland, although many conceded, as one critic put it, "lovely Livvy has difficulty preventing her great personal beauty showing through the supposedly homely girl she plays."

Sam's Sham

Although Olivia's reviews seemed to leave all other actresses behind, Samuel Goldwyn, the former employer and current nemesis of her director, William Wyler, wasn't going to let her waltz home with the Oscar without a fight. In December, he proclaimed his latest release with an "open letter" advertisement:

> *It has been my good fortune to have produced many motion pictures which the public has established among its all-time favorites—such as* Wuthering Heights, The Secret Life of Walter Mitty, The Bishop's Wife, Pride of the Yankees *and, of course,* The Best Years of Our Lives.
>
> *Now I have made* My Foolish Heart. *I am genuinely convinced that the public will add* My Foolish Heart *to the roster of the finest of Goldwyn productions.*

The J.D. Salinger–based romantic drama didn't quite go over with either the press or the public except for one thing—*My Foolish Heart* provided a dramatic showcase for Susan Hayward as an unhappily married suburban wife and was certain to snag her another Oscar nomination.

"Anything is better than making a bad picture."
—William Wyler

Photoplay exulted, "Susan Hayward packs plenty of emotion in her portrayal of impetuous youth."

In the Apple

Great personal beauty notwithstanding, Olivia de Havilland won the New York Film Critics Award for the second year in a row. The Critics went with *All the King's Men* for Best Picture and Broderick Crawford for Best Actor. But, continuing to give at least one prize to a foreign film for the fourth consecutive year, the group named Britisher Carol Reed as Best Director for the Graham Greene suspense film *The Fallen Idol*.

The Nominations

Unexpected among the Best Actress nominees was Loretta Young, this year as a nun in *Come to the Stable.* Britain's Deborah Kerr, in her third year in Hollywood, received her first nomination for *Edward, My Son,* in which she played the distraught mother of a suicide. They were joined on the list by Susan Hayward, Jeanne Crain and, of course, Olivia de Havilland in the Best Picture nominee, *The Heiress*.

Of the triumvirate of year-end war movies, the most successful was *Battleground,* with six nominations; thanks to Dore Schary, MGM had a contender in major Oscar categories for the first time in three years. All the money spent promoting *Sands of Iwo Jima* got John Wayne a nomination, but none for Best Picture. *12 O'Clock High,* represented in the Best Picture and Best Actor (Gregory Peck) categories, failed to win a directing or writing nomination. Darryl Zanuck had run daily trade-paper ads for *12 O'Clock High,* but not a single one for *A Letter to Three Wives,* which was up for Best Picture, Director, and Screenplay. Similarly, Harry Cohn's laissez-faire attitude did not keep *All the King's Men* from getting seven nominations. The *Hollywood Reporter* gloated: "A highlight was the sharp drop in nominations among feature film product from foreign countries." British films received four nominations—two writing, one Art Direction, and a Director nod for Carol Reed—and the Italians managed to get away with two writing nominations.

Money Matters

With the film companies having another dismal year financially, the Academy again busied itself trying to figure out how to put on a halfway decent Awards ceremony without the studios' financial assistance. The entire Board of Governors was bereft of ideas. Suddenly, the studios' New York offices gave the okay for the companies to once more ante up for the show. The Hollywood moguls had convinced the New York bosses that money given to the Academy was an investment that paid off handsomely in publicity and increased business and that they would be idiots to let this worldwide public-relations opportunity slip by. With its bank account nicely padded, the Academy decided to rent the Pantages Theatre, a rococo movie palace on Hollywood Boulevard near Vine. After the plebeian Shrine Auditorium and the tiny Academy Theatre, the industry was thrilled that the Awards would be back in a glamorous setting.

Spilling the Beans

According to the annual *Daily Variety* poll, Best Picture would be *All the King's Men,* and Best Actor, Broderick Crawford, although *A Letter to Three Wives* and Kirk Douglas for *Champion* were possible upset winners. Olivia de Havilland had Best Actress sewn up and it was expected that Mercedes McCambridge, a radio actress making her screen debut with the small but showy role of Willie Stark's secretary in *All the King's Men,* would defeat her more seasoned Supporting Actress competition. Favored for Supporting Actor was Dean Jagger, who in making the switch from marginal leading man to character actor in *12 O'Clock High,* revealed that he was bald. *Time* wrote, "Jagger without his toupee seems to have launched a new career."

The Big Night

Although the results of many races seemed inevitable, most of the nominees showed up, evidently hoping for a Loretta Young–style come-from-behind victory; after all, Loretta was a nominee herself. Non-nominee Linda Darnell of *A Letter to Three Wives* was a good sport who not only came to the show but mingled with fans in the bleachers when most of the stars simply ignored them. *Daily Variety* noted: "Early arrivals pulling up in Cadillac convertibles disappointed most of the sightseers. As one of the wags put it, 'Up comes a Cadillac and out comes a secretary.' " Entering the Pantages, Jane Wyman, the previous year's Best Actress, told friends, "It ain't gonna be as good as last year."

The program opened with Academy President Charles Brackett speaking about the "solemnity of film" and stating that "newsreels have prevented us from whitewashing history." He then introduced the show's emcee, Paul Douglas, who, at forty-one, had become a movie star with his first film, *A Letter to Three Wives*. Douglas, complete with carnation, told the audience that in planning the show everyone demanded, "Get Douglas!" adding, "Well, you know how busy Kirk is." He then advised against long speeches: "I'll thank in advance all the writers, grips, hairdressers, cameramen, front offices and producers," he said. "And we'll also assume that without your mother the whole thing might not have been possible. Just thank your lucky stars, the voters and no one else."

He introduced Anne Baxter ("Aha, now there's a dish") and her husband, John Hodiak ("A pair of people who have put together a really handsome marriage"). The couple, who would divorce in 1953, presented the Cartoon Award to Warners' *For Scent-Imental Reasons,* starring screen newcomer Pepe Le Pew. Radio listeners got a treat when commentator Eve Arden gushed over the victory: "A wonderful cartoon. You probably remember it, about the little skunk. And the winner seems very happy, and I'm very happy for him. A wonderful cartoon, I remember it with great pleasure."

Paul Douglas said of presenter George Murphy, "He's so loved, you'd think he was dead." The future United States senator, wearing tails, responded, "I may not be dead, but I certainly feel

Awards Ceremony

MARCH 23, 1950, 8:00 P.M.
THE RKO PANTAGES THEATRE, HOLLYWOOD

Your Host:
PAUL DOUGLAS

Presenters

Special Effects . . . . Patricia Neal
Film Editing . . . . Mark Robson
Short Subjects . . . . Anne Baxter and John Hodiak
Sound Recording . . . . John Lund
Art Direction . . . . Barbara Hale and Ruth Roman
Documentary Awards . . . . George Murphy
Costume Design . . . . Peggy Dow and Joanne Dru
Cinematography . . . . . . June Allyson and Dick Powell
Scientific and Technical Awards . . . . José Ferrer
Foreign Film . . . . Micheline Presle
Special Award to Jean Hersholt . . . . . Ronald Reagan
Special Award to Bobby Driscoll . . . Donald O'Connor
Special Award to Fred Astaire . . . . Ginger Rogers
Special Award to Cecil B. DeMille . . Charles Brackett
Music Awards . . . . Cole Porter
Writing Awards . . . . James Hilton
Director . . . . Ida Lupino
Supporting Actor . . . . Claire Trevor
Supporting Actress . . . . Ray Milland
Actor . . . . Jane Wyman
Actress . . . . James Stewart
Picture . . . . James Cagney

Performers of Nominated Songs

"Baby, It's Cold Outside" . . . . Arlene Dahl, Ricardo Montalban, Betty Garrett and Red Skelton
"It's a Great Feeling" . . . . Jack Smith
"Lavender Blue" . . . . Gene Autry and the Cass County Boys
"My Foolish Heart" . . . . Ann Blyth
"Through a Long and Sleepless Night" . . . Dean Martin

"It ain't gonna be as good as last year."
—Jane Wyman

dressed for it." Murphy opened the envelope for Best Documentary Short Subject and rather nonchalantly commented, "Our first tie of the evening."

On the radio, Eve Arden really went to town over the Costume Awards. When Edith Head captured the Black-and-White prize, Arden told listeners, "The Award is long overdue her. As a matter of fact, we had our hair done at the same place this afternoon and I told her I was rooting strongly for her. Here she comes in a very interesting gown." Head wore her familiar dark glasses and black-and-white ensemble, but was too nervous to make a speech. Marjorie Best was among the Color winners, and Arden was beside herself: "This is really my department. She's designing for the new picture I'm in."

A highlight of the evening was the performance of Best Song nominee "Baby, It's Cold Outside," which Paul Douglas referred to as "the bachelor's anthem." Red Skelton elicited raucous laughter when he flubbed a line and said, "None of this I remember," even though he had sung it in the movie *Neptune's Daughter*. Then President Brackett returned and, in his Brahmin monotone, read a letter of greeting from President Truman.

Eve Arden's co-commentator, Ronald Reagan, climbed out of the radio booth and on to the stage, to the tune of "Take Me Out to the Ballgame," in honor of his earlier career as a baseball announcer. Wearing glasses to mark the seriousness of his task, Reagan gave a Special Award to "an actor of Academy Award stature," the never-nominated Jean Hersholt. Hersholt's Oscar was officially for "distinguished service to the motion picture industry," which really meant that as Academy president he had stood up to the heads of the industry when they tried to cut off funds.

Donald O'Connor good-naturedly alluded to the state of his film career at the time by apologizing, "Sorry, Francis couldn't be with me," as the orchestra played "Mule Train." O'Connor dropped on his knees to give a Special Oscar to Bobby Driscoll, twelve and a half years old, for his performances in *The Window* and *So Dear to My Heart*. Driscoll angelically said, "I want to thank God for giving me such a wonderful mother and father." Driscoll would be plagued by severe acne as an adolescent and his career would be over in a few years.

Ginger Rogers bounced out to bestow a Special Award on Fred Astaire, who spoke over a cable hookup from New York. "I'm so excited, I could do handsprings down Hollywood Boulevard," Astaire said. "As for you, Ginger, you've been much too gracious. Remember, I had a partner." "That's not what it says on the citation," quipped Lela Rogers' little girl.

Writer James Hilton got a cheap laugh when he gave the Story and Screenplay Award. One of the nominees for *Paisan* was Roberto Rossellini, much in the news for his affair with Ingrid Bergman. Hilton read Rossellini's name with an affected pronunciation that drew snickers from the same people who had given Bergman an Oscar five years earlier.

Paul Douglas joked that the Director Award would be presented by "the best-looking director in town." Ida Lupino strolled out and was soon handing Joseph L. Mankiewicz, who had just won Best Screenplay, his second Oscar of the evening. "Thank you, brother Lupino," the winner joshed. "She's listed in the membership list of the Directors Guild as Irving Lupino."

Claire Trevor, in a gown heavy on the flowers, announced that Dean Jagger in *12 O'Clock High* was Best Supporting Actor. "I feel as emotional as the dickens," the winner said. Best Supporting Actress was Mercedes McCambridge in *All the King's Men,* who enthused, "I just want to say to all beginning actresses, never get discouraged. Hold on. Just look—look what can happen!" Presenter Ray Milland told her, "Congratulations and thanks for a very distinguished speech."

Broderick Crawford was overcome when Jane Wyman awarded him his Oscar. Pausing before speaking, he finally began, "If my heart was to stop beating for a moment . . ." Olivia de Havil-

"We'll assume that without your mother the whole thing might not have been possible."
—Paul Douglas

land was more prepared when James Stewart gave her her second Best Actress trophy: "Your Award for *To Each His Own* I took as an incentive to venture forward. Thank you for this very generous assurance that I have not failed to do so."

For the last Award of the night, James Cagney announced that Best Picture was *All the King's Men*. A diplomatic Harry Cohn had stayed home that evening, telling producer-director-writer Robert Rossen to represent the film because, "It's your show." Having lost Best Director and Best Screenplay to Joseph Mankiewicz, a relieved Rossen admitted, "It's been a long evening. I just can't talk."

Aftermath

Backstage, Broderick Crawford's heartbeat had slowed down enough for him to laugh, saying, "My wife's in the car already. She's taking no chances on a recount." Like Ginger Rogers, Crawford was the apple of his mother's eye, and he said that he had obtained a ticket for Mom, actress Helen Broderick, but she was too nervous to come. As important to Crawford as his Oscar was his mother's comment, "I could find nothing wrong with your performance."

Meanwhile, Crawford's costar, Mercedes McCambridge, was telling reporters about her "lucky" dress. "It's thirteen years old. I wore it because I wore it when I won my first dramatic scholarship award and when I met my husband." One reporter asked her to pose for a picture "washing" Oscar in a nearby sink. "Oh, no," McCambridge shuddered, "I couldn't make fun of it."

Equally sober was Best Actress Olivia de Havilland, who told reporters, "When I won the first Award in 1946, I was terribly thrilled. But this time I felt solemn, very serious and . . . shocked. Yes, shocked! It's a great responsibility to win the Award twice."

The lack of surprise in any of the results didn't dim Hollywood's enthusiasm over the Oscar show. The *Hollywood Reporter* happily stated:

> *Hollywood last night returned to fundamental showmanship—staging a revitalized 22nd Annual Awards presentation for the first time at the very crossroads of the motion picture world—Hollywood and Vine—and forcefully served notice to the "prophets of gloom" of its resurgence as the undisputed entertainment medium for the great masses of the world.*

The *Reporter* was honest enough to mention, however, that there was "chagrin and disappointment" within the industry that no Thalberg Award was given. Shortly before the Awards, Darryl Zanuck had argued to the Board of Governors that the Thalberg was so important and prestigious it should only be given to a producer who receives a two-thirds majority from the voting board members, rather than the simple plurality required under the existing rules. The Academy adopted his suggestion but the producer may have rued ever bringing it up—a board member revealed that Zanuck was one vote shy of the requisite two-thirds.

Some songwriters groused that the winning "Baby, It's Cold Outside" shouldn't have qualified as a movie song. They protested that writer Frank Loesser and his wife had been performing the number at Hollywood parties for a good five years before he sold it to MGM. The Academy countered by saying that "Baby, It's Cold Outside" had not been performed *professionally* before the movie, so the supporters of the other nominees could forget any hopes that the Award would be disqualified.

A second Oscar brought prima donna behavior not from winner Olivia de Havilland, but from her husband, Marcus Goodrich. Two days after the Awards, de Havilland removed herself from the client list at the Kurt Frings Agency, a move that shocked Hollywood because of its timing and because of the high quality of films that the agency had rounded up for the actress. It was soon revealed that the reason behind her withdrawal was that the agency wanted to run a trade paper ad congratulating its client on her Oscar victory. Goodrich, who had written his wife's acceptance speech, insisted on approval of the ad's copy and demanded that it refer to the actress not as "Olivia de Havilland," but as "Miss" de Havilland. The agency demurred, no ad was placed and de Havilland went shopping for new representation. Thereafter, she made only occasional film appearances and, unfortunately, none of her post-Frings films—including *My Cousin Rachel* (1952), *That Lady* (1955) and *The Ambassador's Daughter* (1956)—approached the impact of her work of the late 1940s. The Goodriches divorced in 1952.

1950

"What'd you get that for, bowling?"
—José Ferrer to Gloria Swanson

The 1950 Academy Awards were all about comedies, commies and comebacks.

Oscar winners Billy Wilder and Charles Brackett held such exalted positions at Paramount that they were able to begin production on a film without giving the studio a copy of the script. All the Paramount executives knew about the project was the working title, *A Can of Beans,* and the terrific-sounding plots Billy Wilder spun at the story conferences. Little did the studio honchos know that Wilder's stories had absolutely nothing to do with the movie he was actually shooting. Wilder went to such lengths to protect his privacy, he locked the script up every night before leaving the studio.

The project was *Sunset Boulevard,* the story of a middle-aged silent-movie actress who pins her hopes for a comeback on a young, down-on-his-luck screenwriter. When Wilder approached his friend Mae West to play the faded star, she informed him that she was too young—only fifty-five. Mary Pickford was intrigued but wanted the movie to center on her and not the screenwriter, and Pola Negri threw a tantrum at the very suggestion of playing a has-been. Finally, Wilder asked the advice of fellow director George Cukor, who said he knew the perfect actress for the part: Gloria Swanson.

The fifty-one-year-old Swanson had made only one film in the past fifteen years and was now hosting a TV show in New York. She was interested, but was offended when Paramount insisted on a screen test. "My old studio," she screamed, "the one you might say I built, wants me to test for a part in a picture!" George Cukor phoned her and pleaded, "Gloria, it's the part you'll be remembered for," so she swallowed her pride, and took the test. Paramount liked her.

A week before filming was to begin, Montgomery Clift reneged on his contract and said he wouldn't play the part of the screenwriter-turned-gigolo. Apparently Clift was already playing the part; he was the companion of torch singer Libby Holman, thirty years his senior, who threatened to commit suicide if he made the movie. When Wilder couldn't persuade Fred MacMurray to take the role, he had Paramount order minor leading man William Holden, who had been kicking around Hollywood for a decade, to fill in.

Sic Transit Gloria

Paramount invited the biggest names in Hollywood to an industry preview of *Sunset Boulevard* in the summer of 1950. The reaction was mixed, to say the least. A weeping Barbara Stanwyck knelt before Gloria Swanson and kissed the hem of her silver lamé dress. Louis B. Mayer wasn't as laudatory. "You bastard!" he boomed to Wilder. "You have disgraced the industry that made and fed you. You should be tarred and feathered and run out of Hollywood."

Critics were kinder. *Time* raved: "It is a story of Hollywood at its worst told by Hollywood at its best" and *Newsweek* rewarded the movie with a cover story. William Holden was proclaimed an accomplished actor, and it was a special triumph for Swanson, who made the kind of comeback that Norma Desmond dreamed of. "A brilliant, haunting performance," praised *Look*. "It will make one more generation of moviegoers aware of her as a vivid screen personality."

Bette Davis Rises from the Dead

Over at 20th Century–Fox, Darryl Zanuck was most impressed that Joseph L. Mankiewicz had managed to win both the 1949 Director and Screenplay Oscars for *A Letter to Three Wives* over Columbia's highly respected *All the King's Men.*

Overleaf: *Best actor winner José Ferrer collects victory kisses from nominees Judy Holliday* (right) *and Gloria Swanson* (left)*—the Best Actress envelope has yet to be opened.*

"You should be tarred and feathered and run out of Hollywood."
—Louis B. Mayer to Billy Wilder

The mogul decided to produce Mankiewicz's next picture himself, and gave the writer-director carte blanche. Mankiewicz's new film was to be *All About Eve,* a caustic look at Broadway and backstage life, starring Claudette Colbert as a temperamental actress and featuring Fox's recent Oscar winners Anne Baxter and Celeste Holm. Just before production started, Colbert cracked a vertebra while skiing and Mankiewicz had to come up with another actress fast. Enter Bette Davis, finally out of her Warner Brothers contract. Davis had no trouble fitting into the role, going so far as to fall in love with leading man Gary Merrill, whom she married as soon as filming was completed.

In October, Zanuck opened the movie with great fanfare at New York's Roxy Theatre by initiating a policy of admitting no one after the movie had started. "The Men and Women of 20th Century–Fox" alleged in the New York newspaper ads: "When we first saw *All About Eve,* we became aware that its utter fascination and charm were immeasurably due to the fact that we were seeing it the only way it should be seen—from the beginning." But moviegoers didn't cotton to waiting outside in the cold when there were empty seats inside and by the time the film premiered in Los Angeles a few weeks later, Zanuck had dropped his "unprecedented policy."

In Hollywood, Zanuck heralded the film by reprinting all of the glowing New York newspaper reviews in their entirety in a nine-page trade ad. The reviewers toasted Mankiewicz and his cast—Celeste Holm, George Sanders, Thelma Ritter and newcomer Marilyn Monroe—but the highest praise was saved for Anne Baxter and Bette Davis. "Bette and Anne vie for acting honors, each in her own way being superb," opined the *New York Daily News.* Most critics were so delighted that Davis once again had a good part that they acted as if she had been away as long as Gloria Swanson; Rose Pelswick of the *New York Journal-American* declared, "Chalk up a terrific comeback for Bette Davis—comeback in the sense that here for the first time in years she's been given a role she really can—and does—sink her teeth into." Davis relished the acclaim—especially her first New York Film Critics Award—and she told Mankiewicz, "You resurrected me from the dead."

That Fat Jewish Broad

Meanwhile, Harry Cohn made headlines with the first million-dollar sale of a play when he bought a Garson Kanin Broadway comedy as a vehicle for Rita Hayworth. The Columbia head was stuck with an expensive property when Hayworth informed him that she was quitting movies to marry playboy Sheik Aly Khan. Judy Holliday, the understudy who had taken over the starring role on Broadway only three days before opening night and made the play a hit, was now breaking into movies as the second lead in the Spencer Tracy–Katharine Hepburn comedy *Adam's Rib.* But to Cohn, Holliday was "that fat Jewish broad"—and he continued to think she wasn't a big enough name to earn back his considerable investment.

Katharine Hepburn thought differently. Having made up her mind that her costar deserved a chance to recreate her role as *Born Yesterday's* dumb blonde, Hepburn began leaking items to gossip columns that "Judy Holliday is stealing *Adam's Rib* right under the noses of Spencer Tracy and Katharine Hepburn." Cohn believed what he read and began to get interested. *Adam's Rib* director George Cukor was assigned to direct *Born Yesterday* and he finally persuaded Cohn that Holliday should have the part after *Adam's Rib* opened in January of 1950 and she received wonderful reviews.

Frankly Speaking

To add marquee weight, Cohn cast the previous year's Best Actor winner Broderick Crawford as Holliday's vulgar tycoon boyfriend. Cukor suggested that Holliday's romantic interest be

"You resurrected me from the dead."
—Bette Davis to Joseph L. Mankiewicz

played by the fellow Billy Wilder was using in *Sunset Boulevard,* William Holden. Before filming began, Cukor had his cast perform the play in a theater on the Columbia lot and members of the film colony competed for his personal invitations to come watch.

In December, an ad entitled "Why *Born Yesterday* Opens Christmas Day" appeared in the trades and explained:

> *Let's be frank about it.*
>
> *It is being released early in Los Angeles because we think it is good enough to win an Academy Award and, under the rules, it must open before January 1 to become eligible.*
>
> *We know that only two comedies have won the Academy Award since 1934 . . .*
>
> You Can't Take It With You *and* It Happened One Night. *We know because we produced both of them.*
>
> *We think* Born Yesterday *will be the third. We know you will enjoy it.*
>
> *Columbia Pictures Corp.*

Born Yesterday won terrific reviews, earned a pile of money, and made Judy Holliday a movie star.

José Ferrer by a Nose

Another Broadway baby who was making a name for himself in movies was José Ferrer. After his Best Supporting Actor nomination two years earlier for his film debut in *Joan of Arc*, Ferrer returned to the screen in three roles in 1950. He played a South American dictator holding Cary Grant hostage in *Crisis* and an evil hypnotist terrorizing Gene Tierney in *Whirlpool*. So audiences wouldn't think of him completely as a villain, Ferrer re-created his Broadway success in Edmond Rostand's *Cyrano de Bergerac,* which, like Laurence Olivier's *Henry V* and *Hamlet,* was distributed via the Theatre Guild in reserved-seat engagements. *Cyrano de Bergerac* became the first Hollywood movie to be endorsed by the New York City Board of Education, causing *Daily Variety* to crack, "New York moppets can be excused officially from classes to attend weekday screenings."

Ferrer got competition for the Best Actor Oscar on Christmas Day when Universal-International released *Harvey,* the film version of a Pulitzer Prize–winning play about an eccentric whose best friend is an invisible six-foot rabbit. Reviewers were captivated by James Stewart as the kook and Josephine Hull, re-creating her Broadway role, as the protagonist's exasperated sister. The studio's Oscar ads employed the tag "Yes, everybody loves *Harvey.*" One of the film's most passionate admirers was Louella Parsons, who said, "I'm going to see it again—that's how much I loved it. You'll love James Stewart. I want to be the first to prophesy he'll be up for an Academy Award."

Here Comes Trouble

Before *Born Yesterday* premiered, Judy Holliday was one of 151 members of the entertainment industry listed in a book called *Red Channels* as having "alleged" Communist leanings. Harry Cohn breathed easier when J. Edgar Hoover assured him that he had sent his G-men to investigate Holliday and they hadn't come up with anything. Still, when *Born Yesterday* opened, the Catholic newspaper *Tidings* called the film "Communistic" because it suggested that political scandals were possible in America, and the Catholic War Veterans picketed some theaters with placards impugning the patriotism of Judy Holliday and Garson Kanin. Louella Parsons, for one, defended the film. "If there are any pink ideas in *Born Yesterday,*" the columnist claimed, "they are way over my head."

The Nominations

Finger-pointing was also going on in the Directors Guild, and Cecil B. DeMille was bitter that

"If there are any pink ideas in Born Yesterday, they are way over my head."
—Louella Parsons

Guild President Joseph L. Mankiewicz did not support his idea of an anti-Communist loyalty oath. DeMille tried to have President Mankiewicz impeached, but ended up resigning himself when his movement failed. Mankiewicz was equally popular with the Academy—*All About Eve* received a record fourteen nominations, while DeMille's *Samson and Delilah* was relegated to a few mentions in the Technical categories. Journalists acccused Anne Baxter of pulling an Eve Harrington herself when she was nominated for Best Actress along with Bette Davis, but the manipulating had been done by Darryl Zanuck, who had listed both Baxter and Davis as the film's stars.

Both Davis and Baxter would be competing with Eleanor Parker for *Caged,* the ultimate women's prison movie, and Judy Holliday, who survived the *Red Channels* scare. The Academy also had good tidings for Harry Cohn—*Born Yesterday* was nominated for five Awards, including Best Picture and Best Director for George Cukor. MGM managed two Best Picture nominations for two box-office hits: the lavish adventure film *King Solomon's Mines,* filmed on location in Africa, and the domestic comedy *Father of the Bride,* which brought Spencer Tracy his fourth Best Actor nomination. Instead of being tarred and feathered, Billy Wilder did very well with eleven nominations for *Sunset Boulevard,* including a surprise Supporting Actress nomination for the film's ingenue Nancy Olson, then Mrs. Alan Jay Lerner. Erich von Stroheim, who played Gloria Swanson's butler, did not take the news of his nomination for Supporting Actor at all well. He said he was too big a name for that category and threatened to sue Paramount over the indignity.

Ancient Enemies

José Ferrer had averaged an Oscar ad every two days in the trade papers, but he became the victim of bad timing when he was subpoenaed by HUAC a few weeks after winning a Best Actor nomination for *Cyrano de Bergerac*. Rather than letting all that campaign money go down the drain, Ferrer began ballyhooing his patriotism. In one ad, he pledged that he would swear under oath that he was neither Communist nor sympathizer. *Daily Variety* applauded his move: "Not only is he taking much of the steam out of the irresponsible accusations filed against him with the House Committee, he also will greatly lessen any box-office shock and financial loss."

Darryl Zanuck ran to Academy President Charles Brackett with the word that Hedda Hopper was planning to stand up, unfurl an American flag and storm out of the theater if Ferrer won Best Actor. This turned out to be just a rumor, but when Hopper heard about it after the show, she lamented not having thought of it.

Last-Minute Campaigning

Since Best Actress nominees Bette Davis and Gloria Swanson had sentiment going for them, Harry Cohn sought to endear newcomer Judy Holliday to Academy voters with abundant ads containing laudatory quotations from critics who had similarly praised now-famous performers in their career-establishing roles. The ads likened Holliday to Jean Harlow in *Hell's Angels,* Vivien Leigh in *Gone With the Wind,* and, yes, Bette Davis in *Of Human Bondage*.

Producer Charles Brackett helped his *Sunset Boulevard* star by telling the *New York Times* that Swanson "worked slavishly without complaint, often to two and three o'clock in the morning. It's the kind of trouping we don't have too much of in Hollywood nowadays." Swanson was now trouping on Broadway in a revival of *Twentieth Century* with José Ferrer. One of the play's gags had Swanson producing a prop Oscar and Ferrer quipping, "What'd you get that for, bowling?"

Since Ferrer and Swanson couldn't leave their show to go to Hollywood on Oscar night, Ferrer announced that he was hosting a birthday party for his costar at the La Zambra restaurant in New York on Awards night. New York residents Judy Holliday, Celeste Holm and Sam Jaffe, a Best Supporting Actor nominee for *The Asphalt Jungle*, decided to go to Ferrer's party rather than the Academy's, and Hollywood resident George Cukor said he would join them. The Academy quickly arranged to have a radio hookup in New York since so many of the potential winners would be there, and Gloria Swanson's birthday party became the Oscar Show East.

Bette Davis would be at neither show. She was somewhere on the Yorkshire moors filming a British movie called *Another Man's Poison* with Gary Merrill.

The *Daily Variety* poll predicted that *All About Eve* would win Best Picture, Best Director, Best Screenplay and Best Supporting Actor for George Sanders. Josephine Hull was expected to win Best Supporting Actress for *Harvey*. Hull's nominated costar, James Stewart, was not so lucky; José Ferrer topped the poll for Best Actor, although the paper warned that *Sunset Boulevard*'s William Holden and *The Magnificent Yankee*'s Louis Calhern, a thirty-year veteran, were hot on his heels. And for Best Actress, the poll picked Judy Holliday, although columnist Bob Thomas insisted on the eve of the Awards, "It's still a wide-open race, particularly among the fillies, and it's continuing right down to the wire."

The Big Night

The star who caused the biggest stir in the bleachers outside the Pantages Theatre was Elizabeth Taylor, fresh from her divorce from Nicky Hilton. Her escort was director Stanley Donen, whom columnists were calling her new romantic interest. Another twosome causing talk were Spring Byington, fifty-seven, and Charles Coburn, seventy-three. Cowboy star William "Hopalong Cassidy" Boyd—no longer making movies but bigger than ever, thanks to television reruns—arrived in a tuxedo and threw silver dollars to his fans.

The show began with a medley of the nominated songs that climaxed with the opening of the curtains and the revelation of the set designed by Paramount's Mitchell Leisen. The setting was classical columns flanked by obelisks with an oversized Oscar in the middle. Academy President and *Sunset Boulevard* producer Charles Brackett came out and reminded the audience that 1950 was "the year of Korea, Russian land grabs, household bomb shelters, violent shock treatment."

This year's master of ceremonies was last year's Special Oscar winner Fred Astaire, who described himself as a "hoofer with a spare set of tails." Requesting that acceptance speeches be held to a minimum, he reminisced about "one year at Grauman's when a girl took the Beverly Hills phone book up with her."

Astaire was shocked when he read what the Academy's writers had come up with as an introduction for Costume Design Award presenter Jan Sterling: "She is the sort of girl who makes a man want to go home and saw off his wife's head below the ankles." After Astaire looked back at his program to make sure he said that one correctly, Sterling presented the Black-and-White Award to *All About Eve*. Fox's chief designer Charles LeMaire and Edith Head, whom Bette Davis had personally requested, accepted their trophies. When Sterling revealed that Head had also won the Color Award for being part of the team that worked on DeMille's *Samson and Delilah*, the designer didn't return to the stage to claim her second Oscar. "I never thought I did good work for DeMille," she said later. "I always had to do what that conceited old goat wanted, whether it was correct or not."

Fred Astaire promised "two of the greatest entertainers in show business" and out came Dean Martin and Jerry Lewis to perform the nominated song from Walt Disney's *Cinderella*, "Bibbidi-Bobbidi-Boo." Dino sang the body of the lyrics while Jerry provided the "Boo" at the end of each

Awards Ceremony

MARCH 29, 1951, 8:00 P.M.
THE RKO PANTAGES THEATRE, HOLLYWOOD

Your Host:
FRED ASTAIRE

Presenters

Special Effects	Jane Greer
Film Editing	Debra Paget
Documentary Awards	Coleen Gray
Costume Design	Jan Sterling
Scientific and Technical Awards	David Wayne
Art Direction	Lex Barker and Arlene Dahl
Short Subjects	Phyllis Kirk
Sound Recording	Marilyn Monroe
Cinematography	Debbie Reynolds
Foreign Film	Marlene Dietrich
Honorary Awards	Charles Brackett
Music Awards	Gene Kelly
Writing Awards	Ruth Chatterton
Director	Leo McCarey
Supporting Actor	Mercedes McCambridge
Supporting Actress	Dean Jagger
Actor	Helen Hayes
Actress	Broderick Crawford
Picture	Ralph Bunche

Performers of Nominated Songs

"Be My Love"	Lucille Norman
"Bibbidi-Bobbidi-Boo"	Dean Martin and Jerry Lewis
"Mona Lisa"	Robert Merrill
"Mule Train"	Frankie Laine
"Wilhelmina"	Gloria DeHaven and Alan Young

"It was a tasteless exercise, even for the press."
—Gloria Swanson

chorus. As Martin sang, Lewis pantomimed that his partner had had a nose job.

Meanwhile, backstage, Marilyn Monroe, who had small but attention-getting parts in *The Asphalt Jungle* and *All About Eve,* was preparing herself for her debut on the Awards show. When she noticed that her dress was torn, Monroe burst into tears and said she couldn't go on. Fellow starlets Debra Paget, Jane Greer and Gloria DeHaven rushed over and consoled her while a fashion attendant did some quick mending. Monroe pulled herself together when it was time to present the Sound Award, but—in what would be her only appearance at the Academy Awards—she barely looked up from the podium when she was onstage.

Another Best Song nominee was "Mule Train," from a Republic western called *Singing Guns.* Frankie Laine stepped out with a whip to perform the number and chastised the orchestra for starting before he had cracked his whip. He tried to achieve the proper cracking sound, but murmured, "Whoops, that's not so good." When Laine instructed conductor Alfred Newman, "If I miss, cover up for me," Newman did just that, and Laine protested, "Wait a minute, kid, you didn't even give me a chance." When Laine finally was pleased with the whip's performance, he continued with the song.

Charles Brackett returned to herald the Honorary Awards, regretting that there was "no medal for glamour" because certainly the presenter of the Foreign Language Film Award would have earned it. Marlene Dietrich then glided onstage in a dress that was cut so high the audience audibly sighed over her legs. "Miss Dietrich is wearing a black Dior evening gown described as her 'battle gown,'" said radio commentator John Lund, her costar in *A Foreign Affair.* The Oscar, by the way, went to *The Walls of Malapaga,* a Franco-Italian production.

Charles Brackett was back to give an Honorary Award to George Murphy for "interpreting the film industry to the country at large." In the backstage pressroom later, Brackett clarified what that meant: "Murphy went through most of the forty-eight states talking about Hollywood." Then Brackett announced an Honorary Award to Louis B. Mayer for "distinguished service to the motion-picture industry." Brackett called the Academy Founder "one of our most distinguished citizens in Hollywood." Uncle Louis accepted the statuette and said that of all the moments in his life, "this stands out." Within months, Mayer himself was out of MGM and replaced by former chief of production Dore Schary after an acrimonious battle with Metro's parent company, Loews, Inc. Rumors were already circulating on Oscar night that Mayer's departure was imminent, so the audience at the Pantages made the most of this chance to give him a curtain call.

In contrast, things couldn't have been going better for fellow-nabob Darryl F. Zanuck. Not only had he been on the cover of *Time* earlier in the year as "Hollywood's most innovative mogul," but the Academy was giving him his third Thalberg Award. "As for myself," Zanuck said upon accepting, "I've been very lucky for winning a third time."

Ruth Chatterton, 1929–30 Best Actress nominee, was asked to present the writing Awards in honor of her new career as a novelist. Regally holding her spectacles before her, Chatterton noted that a husband-and-wife team had been nominated in each of the three writing categories. Edna and Edward Anhalt won the Award for Motion Picture Story for *Panic in the Streets,* but the other couples didn't make out as well. Frances Goodrich and Albert Hackett of *Father of the Bride* lost the Screenplay Award to Joseph L. Mankiewicz for *All About Eve,* and Ruth Gordon and Garson Kanin of *Adam's Rib* lost the Story and Screenplay Award to *Sunset Boulevard.* For the latter film, Oscars went to longtime collaborators Charles Brackett and Billy Wilder, and to their bridge partner, D.M. Marshman, who had suggested they give the old dame a lover.

Two-time Best Director winner Leo McCarey announced the winner of the Best Director

"I'm just a hoofer with a spare set of tails."
—Fred Astaire

Award—Joseph L. Mankiewicz, who became a two-time winning director himself. Mankiewicz also made the record books for being the only person to win both the Director and Screenplay Awards for two consecutive years. The winner was modest and made no speech.

Fred Astaire segued to the acting Awards by alluding to the East Coast party: "Whether they're having a lark or a wake we'll know in a few minutes." Mercedes McCambridge gave the Best Supporting Actor trophy to George Sanders for his portrait of a cynical theater critic named Addison DeWitt in *All About Eve*. Sanders accepted the Oscar, bowed to the audience, walked backstage and started crying. "I can't help it," wept Zsa Zsa Gabor's third husband. "This has unnerved me."

Cut to New York, where someone ran up to Sam Jaffe's table to tell him he had just lost to George Sanders. The press asked the remaining nominees to sit together at a table in the middle of the restaurant. Judy Holliday and Gloria Swanson met at the table and shook hands. José Ferrer sat between them. George Cukor took the seat next to Gloria Swanson, and Celeste Holm sat on his other side.

Back in Hollywood, Astaire introduced "last year's popular choice for Best Supporting Actor" Dean Jagger to present Best Supporting Actress. The winner was Josephine Hull for *Harvey*. Hull trotted up the aisle with her fur stole and pocketbook, stumbled at the top step and was assisted onto the stage. The winner applauded her studio, crediting Universal-International as "the gateway to the world."

Helen Hayes followed to give the Best Actor Award. The victor was José Ferrer in *Cyrano de Bergerac*. Gloria and Judy threw their arms around their host and gave him a dual bear hug. Ferrer made his way to the microphone while the Hollywood audience listened over the wire to screams and party noises. "Hello, three thousand miles away," greeted Hayes. "You must know that this means more to me than the honor accorded an actor," Ferrer's voice suddenly boomed over the air, "I consider it a vote of confidence and an act of faith and, believe me, I'll not let you down." According to *Life* magazine, when Ferrer gave his speech, "Gloria smiled and waved her snakelike arms about. Judy sat deathly still and repeated under her breath, 'I'm sick, sick, sick.'"

Ferrer returned to the table of nominees. A reporter plopped down the prop Oscar from *Twentieth Century* and asked Ferrer to pose with it. Then a photographer asked Holliday and Swanson to kiss him, one on each cheek, while he held the dummy Oscar. Yet another photographer wanted the two actresses to grapple for the trophy in the final moments before the Best Actress presentation. "It was a tasteless exercise, even for the press," Swanson wrote in her autobiography, "and Judy and I were both acutely embarrassed to go along with the galumphing horseplay, which, thank heaven, couldn't go on for long because the next fraught moment had come."

Broderick Crawford came onstage in Hollywood to settle the question of the year's Best Actress. In England, Bette Davis and the crew of *Another Man's Poison* were gathered around a radio, and Davis stood up expectantly when the Best Actress presentation began with the reading of the nominees. In New York, Gloria Swanson leaned over to Judy Holliday and whispered, "One of us is about to be very happy."

Crawford opened the envelope and said, "And the winner is Judy Holliday for *Born Yesterday*." Amid the screams at La Zambra, Gloria hugged Judy and said, "Darling, why couldn't you have waited till next year?" In England, Bette said to the assembled, "Good. A newcomer got it. I couldn't be more pleased." Back in New York, Holliday squeezed through the crowd of admirers to the microphones and began thanking everyone. Unfortunately, the radio connection had been knocked out since Ferrer's win, and Judy's speech didn't go any farther than the walls of the restaurant.

In Hollywood, Ethel Barrymore, who had been asked to be the proxy for the missing Best Ac-

"I'm sick, sick, sick."
—Judy Holliday

tress, walked uncertainly to the podium while technicians tried to figure out what had happened to the radio. "I am very happy to accept this award for her radiant performance, but I don't know what she wants me to say," Barrymore confessed.

Barrymore wandered off and Dr. Ralph Bunche of the United Nations came out from a different direction to give the Best Picture Award. "The motion-picture industry should be kept free," Dr. Bunche lectured, "and the Academy should act democratically." Then he revealed that the winner was *All About Eve*. Darryl F. Zanuck made his second trip to the stage to pick up the prize, and *Time*'s cover picture of him as a king wearing a celluloid crown now seemed dead on target.

Aftermath

In New York, the photographers were falling all over themselves in an attempt to get pictures of Gloria Swanson sportingly congratulating José Ferrer and Judy Holliday. *Life* noted, "Judy was too overcome to do more than stand around and sob and smile by turns. Gloria murmured, 'Judy, sweet, Judy, bless your heart' and maintained the old trouper tradition by saying airily it was just as well she hadn't won: it would have meant she had nothing left to look forward to in life." But Gloria put it differently in her memoirs: "Judy Holliday, when she dared to look at me at all, seemed to be pleading forgiveness."

Trapped by press and well-wishers, Holliday crawled under the winner's table and came up on the other side, where her husband and mother were. They left soon afterward and Judy was still crying because she felt so guilty about Gloria Swanson.

Gloria wasn't having such a great time, either. The attitude of the press bothered her. "It slowly dawned on me that they were unconsciously asking for a larger-than-life scene, or better still, a mad scene," she wrote. "More accurately, they were trying to flush out Norma Desmond." In England, Bette Davis didn't have that problem. When she left the cast party, she returned to her hotel and informed the desk she was not to be disturbed under any circumstances.

José Ferrer thoroughly enjoyed his party, and when a reporter asked if his speech was "political," the winner snapped, "You're goddamned right!" Ferrer also shouted to columnist Earl Wilson above the din of the revelers: "This is a direct rebuke to the people who tried maliciously to affect the voting by things that are (a) beside the point and (b) untrue."

But columnist Florabel Muir said not so fast, José: "I didn't cast my vote to vindicate you on the charges that you may have failed to be a good American citizen. As far as I'm concerned, the jury is still out on you on that category."

In Hollywood, the big postmortem party was at Ciro's, where the entertainment was provided by Sammy Davis, Jr., singing and doing his imitations. With the Best Actress and Actor absent from Hollywood, the press concentrated on a presenter. GRANDMA DIETRICH STEALS SHOW proclaimed *Daily Variety*'s headline. The paper went on to explain, "Marlene Dietrich was bestowing the foreign film award but she gave every woman there a lift by her startling denial of the fifties. She sauntered out with her sheath skirt slit to one knee and held 2,800 people in her instep."

Best Supporting Actress winner Josephine Hull was also given a glamour buildup. Flacks at Universal-International decreed that the actress had won her Oscar, coincidentally, on the same day she was celebrating her fiftieth year in show business. The day after the Awards, newsmen were invited to the studio to photograph the sixty-eight-year-old film star holding her Oscar before a giant anniversary cake as well-wishers Tony Curtis, Chill Wills, Tom Ewell and a man dressed in a rabbit suit looked on. The publicity didn't turn Hull's head; she completed one more movie—*The Lady from Texas*—and then retired. Fifty years was long enough.

1951

"I wish I were Kim Hunter tonight."
—Bette Davis

Price, Waterhouse put TNT in the envelopes at the 1951 Oscar ceremonies.

Gene Kelly had finally persuaded MGM to let him do it his way. The studio, in the midst of shifting from Louis B. Mayer to successor Dore Schary, gave the okay to a Kelly musical called *An American in Paris*. Although Kelly had cast an unknown nineteen-year-old ballerina from Paris for the lead and added a ballet number to the movie, MGM thought the hoofer couldn't get too carried away if producer Arthur Freed kept watch on the set.

An American in Paris opened with a bang in July and the critics raved about its Gershwin music, its ground-breaking choreography, its charming new star Leslie Caron and, most of all, about Gene Kelly. The musical made millions. But with all of this, Kelly wasn't happy. One goal eluded him. "There is a strange sort of reasoning in Hollywood that musicals are less worthy of Academy consideration than dramas," he said. "It's a form of snobbism, the same sort that perpetuates the idea that drama is more deserving of Awards than comedy."

Queen of the Prom

Drama was definitely heading for Awards in 1951, especially if it involved sex. Director George Stevens didn't clown around when he cast *A Place in the Sun*, his adaptation of Theodore Dreiser's *An American Tragedy*. If the audience was to sympathize with Montgomery Clift for knocking up and then knocking off sweet Shelley Winters, the girl he was doing it all for had better be worth it. She was. Twenty-year-old Elizabeth Taylor starred as the alluring debutante. "The real surprise of *A Place in the Sun* is the lyrical performance of Elizabeth Taylor," wrote *Look* magazine. "Always beautiful, Miss Taylor here reveals an understanding of passion and suffering that is electrifying." *A Place in the Sun* was hailed as a masterly literary adaptation by the critics, but the moguls ascribed its box-office success to teenagers—thousands of American girls showed up at their senior proms in facsimiles of the Edith Head–designed white debutante gown worn in the film by Elizabeth Taylor.

Your T-Shirt Is Ripped

The sex was so ripe in *A Streetcar Named Desire* that movie censors had to pluck some of the fruit from Tennessee Williams' Broadway smash. Director Elia Kazan imported the New York cast, save Jessica Tandy, who was replaced by Vivien Leigh, and then worked with the playwright himself to make the movie version of his tragedy as sweltering as its New Orleans setting. When the movie opened in the fall, Hollywood got word that many people were walking out on it, complaining that if this kind of filth was so big on Broadway, then it was no wonder Broadway was dying.

But the tide changed, and crowds began to form to see for themselves what had made others walk out in disgust. A main attraction was Marlon Brando, whose two assets were displayed on the film's posters: his good reviews and his physique. Critics referred to Brando's mixture of histrionics and carnal appeal as "the torn T-shirt school of acting."

The *Hollywood Reporter* marveled that either of the dramas had done so well. "We thought both of them would land on their nose when they got out in general release," the editor wrote, "because of the downbeat type of stories and because those stories were made so realistic." One of them did land with a thud in Gotham when the New York Film Critics ignored *A Place in the Sun* in their awards-giving. Their Best Picture winner was *A Streetcar Named Desire*, which also took Best Di-

Overleaf: *Listening to the Oscar broadcast in the privacy of her Greenwich Village apartment is Best Supporting Actress winner Kim Hunter with her husband, Bob.*

"There won't be anybody out here but those who know how to make B-pictures."
—Tennessee Williams

rector and Best Actress. Brando was passed over for Best Actor for Arthur Kennedy, playing a blind war veteran in *Bright Victory*.

Bogart's Cliffhanger

Humphrey Bogart took heart when Kennedy topped Brando in New York—maybe he could outrun Brando in Hollywood, where sentiment would be on his side. Bogart had just completed *The African Queen* with Katharine Hepburn, and just as soon as director John Huston had made his final cuts in London, producer Sam Spiegel defied acts of God to rush a print to Los Angeles to qualify for the Oscars. Spiegel himself carried the cans of film through a storm over the Atlantic, during a two-day customs holdup in Boston, and on the cross-country flight to Hollywood. The film opened to unanimously favorable reviews on the very last day of eligibility.

For the first time in his career, Bogart hired a press agent, who conducted a phone campaign aimed at making Academy members realize that Bogie had been making movies for over two decades. Publicly, Bogart was his usual cynical self, telling reporters, "The only honest way to find the best actor would be to let everybody play Hamlet and let the best man win. Of course, you'd get some pretty funny Hamlets that way."

Marlon Brando did not have a press agent. He didn't like to talk to columnists, either. "Marlon Brando flew out for the *Viva Zapata!* preem," the *Hollywood Reporter* remarked, "but went salooning around town with a friend instead, and in dungarees." Kirk Douglas, touted as a probable nominee for William Wyler's *Detective Story*, wasn't so casual; he actively campaigned with trade-paper ads.

More Laughs with Shelley

Shelley Winters didn't need to hire a press agent; the columnists gave her plenty of coverage as it was. "Shelley Winters dented her derrière when Ted Richmond pulled a chair out from under her in Universal's Sun Room. More laughs!" chortled Mike Connolly in the *Hollywood Reporter*. Paramount's Oscar ads reminded Academy members that Winters had brought tears to their eyes when her pathetic character talked on the phone to Montgomery Clift. Although hopeful, Winters expressed doubt about her chances to Sidney Skolsky, who had an idea. "Why don't you get your legion of boyfriends to join the Academy and vote for you?" he suggested. "Then you'd be a cinch."

Jane Wyman's Kidney

Shelley Winters wasn't the only one with friends in the fourth estate. Jane Wyman scored as a sacrificial nursemaid in *The Blue Veil* and Mike Connolly drummed up support for the actress by making Hollywood worry about her health. "Jane Wyman, who's been putting off that kidney operation," he projected, "may find herself in the hospital along about Oscar time."

Eleanor Parker, ballyhooing her performance as Kirk Douglas' distraught wife in *Detective Story*, was also no slouch at using the trade papers at Oscar time. In both the *Hollywood Reporter* and *Daily Variety*, she ran a facsimile of their front pages, with all the cover stories devoted to her. OHIO TO HONOR ELEANOR PARKER, announced the headline, followed by "Cedarville Citizens Back Favorite Daughter to Win Academy Award Oscar Race."

Poetry from Jack Warner

The success of *A Streetcar Named Desire* inspired Jack Warner to write public love letters to those responsible. First, the mogul serenaded the author with "Words have been the tools of mankind through the ages." Then Elia Kazan was regaled: "The director is the artist who paints the picture, he's the musician who tunes the intruments and he's the mason who builds the house." Warner blew a kiss to the cast: "You are the face

"The only honest way to find the best actor would be to let everybody play Hamlet and let the best man win."
—Humphrey Bogart

of the screen itself," and he embraced all the technicians, down to the last hairdresser, even though, "Your names never decorate marquees." To prove that his love wasn't blind, Warner's other ads proclaimed, "North, East, West, South—There has never been greater praise!" Among the many critical quotations was one from the *New York Times:* "Comments cannot do justice to the substance and artistry of this film."

The Screen Directors Guild gave their award to *A Place in the Sun*'s George Stevens and Paramount campaigned on the basis that it was time for the thirty-year veteran to get Academy recognition. After all, Elia Kazan had already won in 1947 for *Gentleman's Agreement.* Mike Connolly found something else that bothered him about Kazan: he had confessed membership in the Communist Party to HUAC but had refused to supply any evidence on his friends from the Group Theatre. When the columnist went on about this, Tennessee Williams wrote him, complaining, "Why pick on Kazan just because he made a mistake sixteen years ago and joined the Communist Party when he didn't know what it was all about? If you keep it up, there won't be anybody out here but those who know how to make B-pictures."

Allusions of Grandeur

Dore Schary, now the head of MGM, thought it would look good if he started out by winning the Best Picture Oscar, so the $7 million Biblical epic *Quo Vadis* was portrayed as the company's most important film since that David O. Selznick movie about the Civil War. In a three-page ad, MGM printed a "Supplement to the Sales Plan of *Quo Vadis,* The Greatest Motion Picture of All Time," which explained to potential exhibitors, "The quickest way to understand *Quo Vadis'* business is to compare it with *Gone With the Wind.*" And the *Hollywood Reporter* kept up the analogy: "If *Quo Vadis* wins the best picture Oscar, it'll be the second Technicolor item to do so, first being *GWTW.*"

Over at 20th Century–Fox, Darryl Zanuck had spent a bundle on a World War II drama, *Decision Before Dawn,* and he celebrated its December premiere by publishing a glossy, twelve-page insert in the trades praising himself for making the movie. "The screen gains in stature through films like *Decision Before Dawn,*" argued the promo. "Such pictures are made because men have courage and vision. And such a man is Darryl F. Zanuck."

The Nominations

In the Best Picture race, money spent on advertising was spent well. Both *Quo Vadis* and *Decision Before Dawn* made the lineup, knocking out more expected hopefuls *The African Queen* and *Detective Story,* although the latter did manage an Acting nomination for Eleanor Parker and a Supporting nod for Lee Grant. *Quo Vadis* crossed the line with eight nominations, but *Decision Before Dawn* squeaked by with only two, meaning that a Zanuck sweep was out of the question. The race was still between *A Place in the Sun* and *A Streetcar Named Desire,* with the fifth picture nominee, *An American in Paris,* along for the ride.

Kirk Douglas discovered that despite his best efforts, he had been left off the Best Actor list. Brando was there, with Humphrey Bogart, Arthur Kennedy, *Death of a Salesman*'s Fredric March and Montgomery Clift, who got swept along with *A Place in the Sun.*

A Streetcar Named Desire had hit for the cycle, with Marlon Brando and Vivien Leigh nominated in the leading categories and screen newcomers Karl Malden and Kim Hunter vying for Supporting Awards. The *Daily Variety* poll predicted that all four of them would be victorious, but that the Best Picture and Best Director Awards would go to *A Place in the Sun.*

Jack Warner would not have a picture of *Streetcar*'s cast holding their Oscars: only Karl Malden was planning to attend the show. Kim Hunter was rehearsing a play in New York. Vivien Leigh was appearing on Broadway with Laurence Olivier in a revolving presentation of Shakespeare's *Antony and Cleopatra* and Shaw's *Caesar and Cleopatra,* called by columnists "the most distinguished event of the season." Leigh said she thought Katharine Hepburn would win for *The African Queen.* As for Marlon Brando, he had no intention of being at the Awards, just on general principles.

Once again, the Academy voted down a move to broadcast the Awards on television, although this time the idea was spearheaded by the theater owners who, theoretically, had the most to lose the night of the ceremonies. Radio was still welcome, though, and the ABC network was scheduled to broadcast the show for the eighth consecutive year.

The Big Night

The fans began lining up outside the Pantages at 11:30 A.M. and the first celebrity they saw arrived at 7:00 P.M.—*An American in Paris'* Leslie Caron, who had the flu. The first nominee to appear was Humphrey Bogart with his pregnant wife, Lauren Bacall. Later, Best Actress nominee Shelley Winters rode up and exclaimed, "I'm running a fever of 101 but I had to come tonight!" For the occasion, Winters had commissioned Orry-Kelly to design an off-the-shoulder gown in her lucky color—mauve. Fans greeted Shelley's escort as "Mr. Granger," thinking he was Winter's ex-fiancé, Farley, when, in fact, he was Vittorio Gassman, whom she married later that year.

"The sleekly gowned gals were more numerous last year but the bouffant kids still outnumbered them," the *Hollywood Reporter* said of the forecourt parade. Nancy Davis walked in on the arm of her fiancé, Ronald Reagan, ex-husband of Best Actress nominee Jane Wyman. Nineteen-year-old Debbie Reynolds brought a pocketbook "crammed with Girl Scout cookies." Sheilah Graham observed, "Montgomery Clift, sitting with pal Kevin McCarthy, found everything too, too funny—rolling in the aisle at simple things like an usherette showing Brod Crawford to his seat." Outside, Best Director nominee Elia Kazan had a hard time getting in, explaining to security guards that someone in his party had walked in with his ticket.

Mitchell Leisen's stage setting with columns was similar to the previous year's, except that he had added a row of flowerpots. Academy President Charles Brackett's "state of the industry" speech assessed how movies had met the challenge of television. "Suddenly the movie industry was wide awake. *A Place in the Sun* revealed truth deeper than facts. The deeply perceived realities of *A Streetcar Named Desire* could stand up against Sid Caesar and Imogene Coca."

Brackett than began extolling the emcee, who stood behind him making faces. "We have settled for a genius. The man who went from Loew's Palace to Buckingham Palace, the same unspoiled kid from Brooklyn—Danny Kaye." The comedian's wife, Sylvia Fine, had a hand in writing his material, and Kaye's irreverent plea for short acceptance speeches had the audience laughing. "In the past, various subtleties have been used," Kaye

Awards Ceremony

March 20, 1952, 8:00 P.M.
The RKO Pantages Theatre, Hollywood

Your Host:
Danny Kaye

Presenters

Special Effects . . . . Sally Forrest
Documentary Awards . . . . Janice Rule
Film Editing . . . . Constance Smith
Costume Design . . . . Zsa Zsa Gabor
Scientific and Technical Awards . . . . . George Murphy
Art Direction . . . . Marge and Gower Champion
Short Subjects . . . . Lucille Ball
Sound Recording . . . . Cyd Charisse
Cinematography . . . . Vera-Ellen
Foreign Film . . . . Leslie Caron
Honorary Award to Gene Kelly . . . . . Charles Brackett
Thalberg Award . . . . Darryl F. Zanuck
Music Awards . . . . Donald O'Connor
Writing Awards . . . . Claire Booth Luce
Director . . . . Joseph L. Mankiewicz
Supporting Actor . . . . Claire Trevor
Supporting Actress . . . . George Sanders
Actor . . . . Greer Garson
Actress . . . . Ronald Colman
Picture . . . . Jesse Lasky

Performers of Nominated Songs

"In the Cool, Cool, Cool of the Evening" . . . . Danny Kaye and Jane Wyman
"A Kiss To Build a Dream On" . . . . Kay Brown
"Never" . . . . Dick Haymes
"Too Late Now" . . . . Jane Powell
"Wonder Why" . . . . Howard Keel

"The Academy asks that your speech be no longer than the movie itself."
—Danny Kaye

said, "trapdoors, disappearing microphones and an ex-blocker from Penn State. To no avail. This year, there is no attempt to muzzle anyone. The Academy asks that your speech be no longer than the movie itself."

The Costume Design Award presenter was an actress just breaking into films that year—Zsa Zsa Gabor. To make the presentation, Zsa Zsa borrowed her Adrian costume from her forthcoming debut picture, causing Louella Parsons to write, "Zsa Zsa's dress was daring, to put it mildly. She took it right out of *Lovely to Look At* and it showed more of her gams than did Marlene Dietrich's gown last year, but it didn't get the whistles." Gabor announced the "vinner" of the "Black-and-Vhite" Award, Edith Head, for "the Liz Taylor gown" in *A Place in the Sun*. Head daintily held her skirt as she hopped to the stage, silently picked up her trophy and hurried off. As a reporter was asking Head how many Oscars she possessed, the Color Award winners from *An American in Paris* came dashing in and Walter Plunkett answered, "Don't let her kid you. She owns a fifty-acre estate surrounded by a picket fence made of nothing but Oscars!"

"We could say about the girl that's presenting the Cartoon and Short Subject Awards," Danny Kaye began, "I wouldn't be surprised if she showed up in Levi's." Instead, Lucille Ball made her entrance in a pink evening gown designed by Mitchell Leisen. Lucy's TV show had premiered five months earlier and the audience gave the movie alumna a big hand. When the comedienne stumbled over the name of a French nominee, she said of the cue-card writers, "They loused up on their French."

Leslie Caron, still feeling the effects of her illness, stepped out to present an Honorary Award. Sheilah Graham wrote that the actress-dancer did a "duck walk" onstage. The Award was for the foreign-language film *Rashomon*, and was accepted by the Japanese consul in Los Angeles, who profusely praised the film's producer without once mentioning the director, Akira Kurosawa. *Daily Variety*'s George E. Phair was amused that the Academy was giving Oscars to the Japanese film industry and commented, "What a difference ten years make."

Charles Brackett returned to announce that on the previous evening, the Academy Board of Governors had voted Gene Kelly an Honorary Oscar for his "versatility" and "his brilliant achievements in the art of choreography on film." Alas, Kelly was out of town—in Germany. Stanley Donen, codirector of his upcoming musical, *Singin' in the Rain*, accepted for him.

Three-time winner Darryl Zanuck then revealed the recipient of the Thalberg Award—not, as anticipated, *Death of a Salesman*'s Stanley Kramer, not Dore Schary, but the producer of *An American in Paris*, Arthur Freed, who was also the producer of the Oscar show. Everyone gulped in astonishment but applauded warmly as Freed appeared onstage. "Twice the name Irving G. Thalberg has been the most important name in my professional life," the winner said. "First when I came to Metro to work for him—and tonight."

Donald O'Connor danced onstage with Danny Kaye and once again took a ribbing for playing in the "Francis" series when the orchestra played "Mule Train." O'Connor picked up the podium and cracked, "Thanks, this is the nicest award I've ever had." He presented the Music Awards and, after each one, threw the envelope over his shoulder. The Best Song Award went to "In the Cool, Cool, Cool of the Evening," and composer Hoagy Carmichael said, "They made a mistake. As I remember in former presentations, the name is Hugo," referring to Sam Goldwyn's famous 1946 Oscar gaffe.

"One of America's most distinguished women," Claire Booth Luce, had problems with the writing Awards. She called *Seven Days to Noon*, the winner of the Best Motion Picture Story, "Seven Days to the Moon," mispronounced James Agee's name and asked for help on pronouncing "John Huston." Alan Jay Lerner wasn't there to accept his Story and Screenplay

"Montgomery Clift, sitting with pal Kevin McCarthy, found everything too, too funny—rolling in the aisle at simple things like an usherette showing Brod Crawford to his seat."
—Sheilah Graham

Oscar for *An American in Paris,* but his third wife, Nancy Olson, picked it up for him, sighing into the microphone, "Congratulations, darling."

Joseph L. Mankiewicz prefaced the awarding of Best Director with the cryptic remark, "And in all cases, these men directed the picture." As expected, George Stevens won for *A Place in the Sun*—the *Daily Variety* poll had not made a mistake yet.

The poll's winning streak continued when Claire Trevor divulged the Best Supporting Actor and editorialized, "Oh, good, it's Karl Malden for *A Streetcar Named Desire*." The winner, a recently transplanted New Yorker, seemed confused about what he was supposed to do and walked to the wrong microphone. A stagehand directed him to the correct podium and Malden said, "I haven't been out here very long, but I can tell you how I feel—great!"

George Sanders revealed the Best Supporting Actress to be Kim Hunter in *A Streetcar Named Desire.* The winner heard her name over the radio in her Greenwich Village apartment, where she was failing to learn the rules of pinochle: "It was an effort to get my mind off the whole thing. It didn't work. I never did learn and I don't play it today." In Hollywood, proxy Bette Davis walked onstage, held her *All About Eve* costar's hand, and said, "I wish I were Kim Hunter tonight." Noticing that she had not been handed the statuette, Davis demanded, "Where is her Award?"

Greer Garson came out and asked, "This is hardly the time to be wordy, but if anyone would still like to hear it, I think I still have twenty minutes left over from a highly emotional speech I made a few years ago." Proceeding with the Best Actor Award, Garson opened the envelope and read the name—Humphrey Bogart for *The African Queen.* The audience gasped. "My wife let out a scream when my name was called," Bogart recalled. "She jumped four feet and almost had a miscarriage." Bogart scurried to the stage and, once there, stood in a daze. Garson tapped him on the shoulder, he turned around, and she handed him his Oscar. Bogart had earlier told his friend Nathaniel Benchley, "I'm not going to thank anyone; I'm just going to say I damn well deserve it." But when the big moment came, he said, "It's a long way from the heart of the Belgian Congo to the stage of the Pantages Theatre and I'm glad to say I'd rather be here," and then thanked John Huston, Katharine Hepburn, and Sam Spiegel.

Danny Kaye introduced Ronald Colman and commented at length about not delaying the presentation of the Best Actress Award because of the nervousness of the nominees. Colman finally got a chance to broadcast the winner—Vivien Leigh for *A Streetcar Named Desire,* who heard her name over the radio backstage in New York. Leigh's name was not what Shelley Winters heard. In her autobiography, the actress wrote, "When he opened the envelope, I'll swear to this day he said 'Shelley Winters.' I was almost to the steps leading up the stage when Vittorio tackled me." As Shelley crept back to her seat, Greer Garson came back onstage and scooped up Leigh's award.

The Best Picture Award was the responsibility of seventy-one-year-old producer Jesse Lasky, whom Kaye described as "a young sprout." Lasky opened the envelope and exclaimed, "Oh, my!" The audience held its breath as Lasky blurted out, "The winner is *An American in Paris*!" The roars of approval that had greeted the announcement of Arthur Freed's Thalberg Award were not repeated when he returned for his second Award that night but winner Freed was smiling nonetheless. "I'd like to thank MGM, a great studio with real courage and leadership." Then Lasky and Freed walked offstage, with Freed heading for the pressroom, where he gleefully declared, "It's a doubleheader!" Lasky jumped into a limousine and received a police escort to the airport. Changing from his tux to his business suit in the car, the film pioneer discovered that the pants to the suit were missing.

Aftermath

"The lineup for the photogs looked like it happened a long time ago with Davis, Greer Garson and Ronald Colman waving Oscars they hadn't won," Sheilah Graham observed. Bette

"I'll never let myself in for another emotional experience like that. Ye gods, I almost had a heart attack."
—Shelley Winters

Davis had been an unwilling photographer's model and Graham stated: "They practically had to carry her to the lensers." Once there, Davis kept insisting, "It isn't mine. I won mine a long time ago." To which Humphrey Bogart retorted, "Yeah, about twenty-five years ago."

Bogart was having a grand time talking to journalists. "I didn't prepare a winner speech, but I had a loser's speech ready," he claimed. When a reporter asked if he had changed his mind about all the nominees playing Hamlet, the winner quipped, "I could have beaten all of those bums, but I wouldn't have proposed that if Larry Olivier had been up. Any guy who calls himself 'Olivier' changed it from 'Oliver.'"

Shelley Winters admitted to reporters, "I'll never let myself in for another emotional experience like that. Ye gods, I almost had a heart attack in the theater." Best Supporting Actor loser Peter Ustinov, the villainous Nero of *Quo Vadis,* was bemused by the turn of events: "Someone called me in Europe in the middle of the night to tell me I hadn't won." Neither had his film, which lost all eight of its nominations, prompting Mike Connolly to inquire, "Quo Vadis, *Quo Vadis*?"

The real hard-luck story of the night was Mrs. Pauline Paulson's. After watching her film favorites depart the Pantages, the eighty-year-old grandmother fell in between the rows of bleachers and was rushed to Hollywood Receiving Hospital. Not to worry, for as *Daily Variety* noted, "Full insurance is carried to cover any accidents in the temporary bleachers erected for the fans."

Radie Harris believed that the Best Actress winner had an equally hard time that night. "Vivien's ordeal of waiting for the results was tougher, perhaps, than any of the other contestants. While she was playing in *Antony and Cleopatra* that night, twenty cameramen were waiting in the wings, alerted for her possible victory." Olivier had tried to prepare his wife for any disappointment by suggesting, "Maybe one kind gentleman will wait and take your picture anyway." But when they got the news from the Pantages, all the journalists demanded a shot of Olivier kissing the winner in her dressing room. Afterward, the Oliviers "celebrated quietly" in their West Fifty-fourth Street apartment. Meanwhile, in Hollywood, Jack Warner was frantic because *Streetcar* had to leave its Los Angeles theater in a week to make way for Abbott and Costello in *Jack and the Beanstalk.*

Radie Harris checked Bogart's New York "home"—the 21 Club—and saw a "scene of much gaiety, with all of Bogie's pals congregated to celebrate his Oscar victory in a beeg way." Back in Hollywood, the winner received a telegram from director John Huston: "Dear Bogie, Guess it was worth taking the old Queen down the Ulgana River." Army Archerd reported that once Bogart's backstage photo sessions were completed, he "anchored at Romanoff's for a week."

Mrs. Bogart gave her husband a present for winning—a full-sized replica of the *African Queen*'s tiller engraved with a line from the script: "Nature, Mr. Allnut, is what we're put in this world to rise above." Lauren Bacall later wrote, "He had really wanted to win for all his bravado—when push came to shove, he did care and was stunned that it was such a popular victory. He had never felt people in the town liked him much and hadn't expected such universal joy when his name was called."

Joy was not what everybody felt about *An American in Paris* as Best Picture. Sidney Skolsky said it was a "shocker" and suggested a recount. The *New York Times*'s Bosley Crowther, who had put the musical on his Ten Best list, fumed that it was unbelievable that the Academy had "so many people so insensitive to the excellencies of motion-picture art that they would vote for a frivolous musical picture over a powerful and pregnant tragedy."

The trade papers reported that Thalberg Award winner Arthur Freed had won "by unanimous vote" and the *Hollywood Reporter* went further in defense of the winner: "The dissenters have had plenty to say. They're saying 'It was a frame. A studio the size of MGM has too many votes and they can swing an award.' That's a lot of hogwash. The best picture ALWAYS wins and it's madc no difference whether that best was from the largest or the smallest studio."

MGM toasted its unexpected success with an ad that depicted Leo, the studio's mascot, looking at the Oscar and apologizing, "Honestly, I was just standing *In the Sun* waiting for *A Streetcar.*" The fact that the company won a Best Picture Award as soon as Louis B. Mayer left would have seemed to indicate that the new management knew what it was doing. But a few people knew better. Alan Jay Lerner recalled in his autobiography that one of the toughest obstacles in making *An American in Paris* was convincing MGM's New York office to fork over the $400,000 to film the climactic ballet number that became the musical's most celebrated scene. "Later Dore Schary intentionally or unintentionally took credit for that," Lerner wrote, "but Louis B. Mayer did it."

1952

"I don't want to compete with glamour queens and beauty gals."
—Shirley Booth

In 1952, the Academy Awards sold out to the enemy and found salvation.

Cecil B. DeMille's two-and-a-half hour circus extravaganza *The Greatest Show on Earth* premiered at Radio City Music Hall on January 10 and started pulling in millions instantly. The critics could enjoy being nasty to DeMille because his high grosses made him indestructible. The *New York Herald Tribune* chuckled, "The train wreck looks as luridly contrived as rubber octopuses, falling temples, and all the other divertissements of past epics." DeMille's box-office miracle was the high-water mark all year long—the closest anyone came to his totals was MGM with *Ivanhoe*, featuring twenty-year-old Elizabeth Taylor, but at year's end DeMille was still ahead by five million or so.

The film that won over the critics was *High Noon*. Stanley Kramer was able to produce the western independently when he got backing from a lettuce grower who made one demand: instead of Kramer's original choices for the lead—Marlon Brando or Montgomery Clift—the produce magnate insisted on Gary Cooper to play the sheriff. Bosley Crowther of the *New York Times* approved of the casting: "Mr. Cooper is at the top of his form in a type of role that has trickled like water off his back for years." Crowther also praised the western's anti-McCarthy statement: "It bears a close relation to things that are happening in the world today, where people are being terrorized by bullies and surrendering their freedoms out of senselessness and fear."

High Noon quickly climbed up the list of the year's top moneymakers, but life soon imitated art for one of the film's creators—writer Carl Foreman. While the western was in production, the author was subpoenaed by HUAC and he pleaded the Fifth. In no time, Hedda Hopper and her cohorts in the Motion Picture Alliance for the Preservation of American Ideals condemned Foreman and led a campaign to make him unemployable in Hollywood. By the time that *High Noon* won the New York Film Critics Award for Best Picture, the blacklisted Carl Foreman had moved to England.

Overleaf: *Her poodle safely home watching the show on TV, Best Actress favorite Shirley Booth arrives at the ceremony.*

The Duke in Ireland

Meanwhile, John Wayne, one of Hedda's colleagues in the preservation society, was heading to Ireland to make *The Quiet Man* for John Ford. Despite his three Best Director Oscars, Ford couldn't convince the major studios to bankroll his "first love story," a boisterous romance between an American boxer, Wayne, and a headstrong Irishwoman, Maureen O'Hara. The director finally made a deal with Republic Pictures—the home of cowboy and pulp adventure movies—and proved all the moguls wrong: the movie was both a commercial and a critical success. The *New York Herald Tribune* said the romp was filled with "the wild glee of the Irish when the mood of joy is upon them." Although the New York Film Critics gave their Director Award to *High Noon*'s Fred Zinnemann, Ford's friends in the Directors Guild awarded him their trophy for the Most Outstanding Directorial Achievement of 1952.

Bring on the Girls

Hollywood's female stars had custom-made Oscar vehicles tuning up for the Best Actress race. Joan Crawford, liberated from her Warner Brothers contract, picked *Sudden Fear* as her first freelance flight. In this RKO thriller, she played a mystery playwright who figures out that her young husband, Jack Palance, is plotting with his old girlfriend, Gloria Grahame, to kill her. "The scenario is designed to allow Miss Crawford a wide range of quivering reactions to vicious events," a critic observed. "With her wide eyes and forceful bearing, she is the woman for the job."

Reigning as the number-one actress at 20th

"If José Ferrer gets an Oscar for the best acting of the year, the Academy has my resignation."
—Hedda Hopper

Century–Fox, Susan Hayward landed a plum role as a crippled torch singer in *With a Song in My Heart* when vocalist Jane Froman told the studio that she wanted to be portrayed by Hayward in the biographical tearjerker. "She looks and acts like a singer, like myself," Froman argued, "but she has some tricks of her own." *Look* magazine agreed and noted, "From now on, the two women may be one in the public's mind." The movie was one of the year's top moneymakers.

C'mon Oscar, Let's Get Drunk

Bette Davis was also at Fox, making a low-budget film that she claimed was shot all in first takes. The vehicle was *The Star,* in which Davis played a down-on-her-luck Academy Award–winning actress who grabs her statuette, exclaims, "C'mon Oscar, let's go get drunk," and joyrides through Beverly Hills. Davis used one of her own Oscars for the scene. The ads promised "The Magnificent Bette Davis Giving Her Greatest Performance." Davis' fans were not disappointed.

Bette's old friend from her Warner Brothers days, Olivia de Havilland, was getting the glamour treatment from Fox with *My Cousin Rachel,* a Daphne du Maurier adaptation with a young British actor named Richard Burton as her leading man. The ads for this one said, "20th Century–Fox brings to the screen the most important book of the year." Almost as soon as the movie opened in December, there were Oscar ads for de Havilland in the trades ballyhooing this as her first movie since her last Oscar-winner, *The Heiress.* "Great acting by a great actress," these ads said. "Olivia de Havilland adds another brilliant performance to her gallery of distinguished portrayals."

The Kitchen Sink

The campaigns of these Hollywood stars were shot down by Shirley Booth, a forty-five-year-old Broadway character actress making her film debut. Hal Wallis bought the rights to Booth's stage success, William Inge's *Come Back, Little Sheba,* and provided the actress with a cast that included screen names Burt Lancaster and twenty-three-year-old Terry Moore, who, Hedda Hopper wrote, "is the envy of teen-agers, she's been flitting from Nicky Hilton to Bob Taylor to Bing Crosby!" Paramount released the drama at the end of the year with the tag line, "The picture marked for every box-office honor."

The *New York Herald Tribune* said, "Miss Booth is utterly realistic and at the same time most appealing, in an acting style like the best modern French and Italian motion pictures." Booth won the New York Film Critics Award and every other pre-Oscar trophy. An actress moviegoers had never heard of was suddenly the front-runner for the Oscar.

John Huston's Petticoats

John Huston hadn't learned his lesson the previous year with *The African Queen,* and this time he was rushing to meet the eligibility deadline with his biography of Toulouse-Lautrec, *Moulin Rouge.* Sheilah Graham reported, "John Huston arrives at the crack of dawn Thursday with the print and rushes it to the Johnston Office to learn if the can-can can pass the censor. He's keeping his petticoats crossed." *Daily Variety* took the film-maker to task for his Oscarmania and said, "The apparent rush to open the film here in time for Academy Award qualification has left it without the polish and finish it should have to make the most of its undeniable quality."

José Ferrer starred as the tiny Lautrec and his Oscar ads stressed that the actor had to play the whole movie on his knees. Sidney Skolsky scoffed, "Ferrer has been the only actor to campaign but José doesn't stand a chance of repeating."

Bad But Busy

MGM's Christmas present was the Hollywood exposé *The Bad and the Beautiful,* which it advertised as its "Boldest Drama of the Year." Kirk

"Ferrer has been the only actor to campaign but José doesn't stand a chance of repeating."
—Sidney Skolsky

Douglas played a tyrannical movie producer and the movie became a Hollywood guessing game as everyone tried to figure out which member of the film colony he was imitating.

MGM realized that another of *The Bad and the Beautiful*'s stars was attracting attention—Gloria Grahame, who played Dick Powell's Southern belle wife. Grahame seemed to have appeared in just about every hit movie that year. She menaced Joan Crawford in *Sudden Fear*, and played Angel, the Elephant Girl, in *The Greatest Show on Earth*. But it was MGM that campaigned for a Supporting Actress nomination for her.

Brando's Pile

Darryl F. Zanuck had high hopes for *Viva Zapata!*, a biography of Mexican revolutionary-turned-president Emiliano Zapata written by John Steinbeck, directed by Elia Kazan, and starring Marlon Brando, who, at age thirty, was talking about retirement. "One more film and I will have my pile," Marlon told the *Los Angeles Herald*. "My mother and father are taken care of. I have eight hundred head of cattle on my ranch in Nebraska. This should soon bring me an income of $80,000 a year. That will be enough. Any acting I do will be on the stage."

Zanuck had better luck with *My Cousin Rachel*'s Richard Burton, if only because he hadn't been making movies as long as Brando. "He is astonished by the salary he now commands," wrote Sidney Skolsky. "He carries a copy of his movie contract around in his pocket. He still can't believe the figures are true after his years of poverty." Zanuck listed his new "exciting star discovery" as a Supporting Actor to keep him out of the way of *High Noon*'s Gary Cooper and *Viva Zapata!*'s Marlon Brando.

Harry Cohn did not want to play the Oscar game with *The Member of the Wedding*, a film version of the Carson McCullers play. Directed by *High Noon*'s Fred Zinnemann, it did not fare well at the box office and Cohn laid the blame on the play's depressing plot and on screen newcomer Julie Harris. "She scares small children," the mogul claimed. His associates implored him to at least promote the film's other star, Ethel Waters, but all Cohn would do was list her as a Supporting Actress—he wasn't about to spend another dime on *The Member of the Wedding*.

The Nominations

Ethel Waters did not get nominated for Supporting Actress, but Julie Harris was tapped for Best Actress. When reporters asked her about her unexpected good fortune, Harris sounded like Harry Cohn. "Pictures make me look like a twelve-year-old boy who flunked his body-building course," she said. The ugly duckling was competing with Joan Crawford, Susan Hayward, Bette Davis and Shirley Booth.

Ignoring the New York Film Critics, who had picked Ralph Richardson for Best Actor for the British drama *Breaking the Sound Barrier*, the Academy chose to nominate instead Alec Guinness for the British comedy *The Lavender Hill Mob*. José Ferrer's campaigning was not in vain; he was named for *Moulin Rouge*, as were Gary Cooper for *High Noon*, Kirk Douglas for *The Bad and the Beautiful*, and, for the second year in a row, Marlon Brando, for *Viva Zapata!*

For the first time in its seventeen-year history, Republic boasted a Best Picture nominee. *The Quiet Man* was definitely in the running, with seven nominations, a total matched by two other Best Picture nominees, *High Noon* and *Moulin Rouge*. The remaining nominations went to the two films at the top of the box-office charts: *Ivanhoe* and *The Greatest Show on Earth*.

"Once again the pictures and the players which were most exploited dominated the nominations," the *Hollywood Citizen-News* complained. "A victim of this system is Ethel Waters." The big surprise in the Supporting Actress lineup was *Come Back, Little Sheba*'s Terry Moore. Most columnists preferred to think of the nominee as a

"She scares small children."
—Harry Cohn on Julie Harris

sex kitten—Mike Connolly joked, "The Award for Best Supporting Role should go to Terry Moore's bra."

High Noon's Katy Jurado had a corps of loyalists who were upset that the actress had not been nominated for Supporting Actress because producer Stanley Kramer had accidentally listed the entire cast as leading players. "Katy Jurado, who should have been nominated, is out campaigning for Gloria Grahame," reported Sidney Skolsky.

At Home with Joan Crawford

Oddsmakers indicated that Shirley Booth was the can't-miss favorite in the Best Actress race, but Joan Crawford wasn't about to let a nomination go by without getting every last drop of publicity out of it, starting at the very moment she got the news. "At the Photoplay Awards at the Beverly Hills Hotel," the *Hollywood Reporter* noted, "Joan Crawford, who wore real diamonds in her hair, got word from her director David Miller that she was up for an Academy Award and went to the powder room to cry her heart out." When producer Jerry Adler scoffed, "Oh, Joan, you must have expected it." The nominee replied, "Yes, but don't forget it took me twenty-five years to be able to expect it."

Crawford's family life was dutifully reported on in the post-nominations period. Sheilah Graham wrote: "Joan Crawford keeps her kids' baby teeth in velvet jewel boxes in the lower-right-hand drawer of her dressing table." And: "Christina Crawford and Butch Jenkins have called the whole thing off." Mike Connolly scooped everyone with: "Joan Crawford got rid of her son's collie puppy and Cliquot couldn't be happier." Cliquot, as everybody in Hollywood knew, was Crawford's poodle.

Body Blows

Two blacklisted writers turned up in the nominations for Best Screenplay—*High Noon*'s Carl Foreman and *Five Fingers*' Michael Wilson, an Oscar winner last year for *A Place in the Sun*. Mike Connolly was still angry at Wilson for taking the Fifth two years earlier, and he warned Academy voters, "If you give unfriendly witness Michael Wilson another Oscar this year, you'll be giving the Academy a body blow from which it may never recover."

Hey, Ma, I'm a News Event

Michael Wilson couldn't possibly have hit the Academy as hard as the studios did a week before the nominations were announced. With television eroding their audiences and profits, the studios were trimming all possible expenses and almost every company was laying off scores of employees. But on top of this, Universal-International, Columbia, Republic and Warner Brothers made a joint statement that they were no longer funding the Awards show. It was 1948 all over again. "It is ridiculous that we should have to face this uncertainty regarding support within this industry year after year," fumed Academy President Charles Brackett, now understanding why his predecessor Jean Hersholt had quit. No sooner had Brackett spoken than RCA contacted him, offering to buy the broadcast rights to the Awards and telecast them on its network, NBC. This took care of the uncertainty and an eager Brackett signed the deal for $100,000. For nominees who couldn't make it to the West Coast on the big night, NBC planned a New York Oscar ceremony, to be telecast from the Century Theatre in Columbus Circle. When the television plans were announced in Hollywood, MGM alone refused to allow any of its personalities to appear before the network camera. But head of production Dore Schary later changed his mind, explaining "the studio's players would be merely participating in a news event and not performing as actors." More likely, the *Hollywood Reporter* suggested, Schary was influenced by the strong reaction at the box office when Robert Taylor went on Ed Sullivan's TV show in January to plug the MGM movie *Above and Beyond*. If a sin-

"The Award for Best Supporting Role should go to Terry Moore's bra."
—Mike Connolly

gle actor's appearance could do so much, imagine the impact of a parade of stars advertising their new movies.

Missing Person

The climax of the telecast was to be a lineup of twenty-five Oscar winners, each proudly fondling his or her statuette, filmed the Sunday before the ceremony. During a break in the filming, Paul Muni chatted with Janet Gaynor, then turned to a reporter and asked, "Tell me—what was the name of the young lady I was talking to?"

The group was one shy of the scheduled twenty-five. Hedda Hopper reported, "Twenty-four stars gave up three hours last Sunday to be photographed except Vivien Leigh, who claimed Sunday was for social contacts, not work." If Hedda had checked her sources, she would have discovered that social contacts were the last thing preoccupying Leigh. The previous year's Best Actress winner was in Hollywood filming *Elephant Walk* and said she was "looking forward to giving the Award to Cooper," and had even picked out a dress in Paris for the occasion. But shortly before the Sunday filming of the past winners, Leigh suffered a violent nervous breakdown and was rushed to a sanatorium in England. Her bad fortune did not end there. As soon as she was settled into the sanatorium, thieves broke into her Chelsea home and stole clothing, silverware and her Oscar for *A Streetcar Named Desire*. Doctors thought it best that the convalescing actress not be told. Back in Hollywood, Elizabeth Taylor took over for Leigh in *Elephant Walk*.

Beware of Vultures

While the former winners were delighted to participate in the TV show, many of the nominees weren't so excited about going on television. Darryl Zanuck was in a tizzy because none of Fox's six acting nominees were planning to attend the ceremony. The mogul pleaded with Susan Hayward, the actress most likely to pull an upset over Shirley Booth, to postpone her trip to Europe. "I attended twice and I lost twice," Hayward retorted, "and I had to explain to some of those vultures who had been dying for me to lose how 'there'll always be a next day.' Well, I'm not going to make a TV spectacle of myself in front of a few million viewers and that's that!" Zanuck managed to find two representatives of Fox willing to attend: *With a Song in My Heart*'s Thelma Ritter, with her third consecutive Supporting Actress nomination, and Katherine DeMille—Mrs. Anthony Quinn—who would substitute for her husband, a Best Supporting Actor nominee for *Viva Zapata!* Quinn was filming a western in Mexico, along with Best Actor nominee Gary Cooper.

To the Academy's despair, it looked as if the lineup of twenty-four Oscar winners would just about be the only stars viewers would see. Kirk Douglas was filming in France and Alec Guinness didn't want to cross the Atlantic for an award he wouldn't win. Julie Harris was appearing in *I Am a Camera* in Baltimore and Marlon Brando was "on location in California." And Bette Davis was stuck in the hospital in New York after a jaw operation. "NBC wanted a photographer for 'The Star Awaits Her Third Oscar,'" reported Radie Harris, "but Bette, still bandaged and in terrible pain, was hardly in the mood to await anything but relief from her suffering."

Last-Minute Pitches

The *Daily Variety* poll decreed that *High Noon*, Gary Cooper, Shirley Booth, Gloria Grahame and Richard Burton would be the Oscar victors. Booth would be there in New York, although she assured the West Coast, "I found Hollywood most kind and generous." Hedda Hopper was busy with last-minute campaigning against her least favorite nominees. Still smoldering over Carl Foreman, the columnist reminded everyone of *High Noon*'s political overtones and plugged the entertainment value of *The Greatest Show on Earth*. Hedda also had it in for José Ferrer, writing, "I have talked with no one yet who was moved by his performance. If he gets an Oscar for the best acting of the year, the Academy has my resignation."

Dress for Success

Hopper's threat went unnoticed as Hollywood prepared itself for the new fashion demands that television made. NBC informed the gentlemen that harsh television lights made white shirts photograph too glaringly, so they were requested to send their tuxedo shirts to the network for a complimentary blue tint job. Women were told to wear pale colors like blue or gray. In case anyone had any questions, he or she could consult the official fashion adviser, Edith Head. According to the *Hollywood Reporter,* Best Supporting Actress nominee Terry Moore showed Head her "sexy black gown" and the fashion consultant promptly told her, "It won't photograph well." Claire Trevor, on the other hand, was way ahead of the game—she painted her hair gold. "It was too dark for TV," the Oscar winner explained, "and I wouldn't bleach it for one night."

The Big Night

It rained in both New York and Hollywood. Gloria Grahame was the first nominee to arrive at the Pantages, where celebrities found the going hazardous on the rain-slick forecourt. As *Life*'s photographer snapped away, a starlet named Sandra White slipped and fell down. When she discovered that her crinoline slip had come off during the tumble, the young actress threw the undergarment into her limo as the fans cheered. To prevent a similar occurrence, Pantages attendants sprinkled sawdust on the pavement.

Former winner Jane Wyman wore what one reporter called "garish TV makeup." Elizabeth Taylor showed up with her new husband, Michael Wilding, and glared at a newsman who asked, "Who are you with tonight, Liz?"

The only Best Actress nominee to appear in Hollywood was Joan Crawford, on the arm of her *Sudden Fear* director, David Miller. It was noted that she "graciously signed autographs as the crowd applauded." But Joan insisted, "I bet on Shirley Booth to win." As for Booth, she prepared for her expected night of triumph by turning on the TV set before she left her New York apartment. "I did it for my poodle, Pretty Prego," Booth explained to reporters. "She's very intelligent, and I wanted her to see it, just in case."

The television broadcast began with a scene from the original Oscar-winning Best Picture, *Wings*, followed by pictures of a modern jet. "Since then there have been many, many changes," intoned announcer Ronald Reagan. "Motion pictures stand today on the threshold of even wider horizons. Like this jet plane, the Awards themselves have been streamlined." Cut to Ronald Reagan standing outside in the rain. "We're having a little unusual California weather," he explained.

Inside the Pantages, the orchestra played the first Academy Award–winning song, "The Continental," as the camera roamed the auditorium looking for famous faces. Announcer Reagan was of little help—he was able to recognize only Merle Oberon. The stage curtains opened to reveal a set of ersatz marble columns, pots of shocking pink azaleas and a giant blue birthday cakc decorated with neon-lighted replicas of the Oscar. Every

Awards Ceremony

MARCH 19, 1953, 7:30 P.M.
THE RKO PANTAGES THEATRE, HOLLYWOOD
AND THE NBC CENTURY THEATRE, NEW YORK

Your Hosts:
BOB HOPE IN HOLLYWOOD,
CONRAD NAGEL IN NEW YORK
TELEVISED OVER NBC

Presenters

Costume Design . . . . Ginger Rogers
Documentaries . . . . Jean Hersholt
Film Editing . . . . Frank Capra
Art Direction . . . . . Joan Fontaine and James Stewart
Sound Recording . . . . Claire Trevor
Short Subjects . . . . Ray Milland and Jane Wyman
Cinematography . . . . Teresa Wright
Music Awards . . . . Walt Disney
Director . . . . Olivia de Havilland
Writing Awards . . . . Dore Schary
Supporting Actor . . . . Greer Garson
Supporting Actress . . . . Edmund Gwenn
Actor . . . . Janet Gaynor
Actress . . . . Ronald Colman
Picture . . . . Mary Pickford
Special Effects . . . . Loretta Young
Foreign Film . . . . Luise Rainer
Honorary Award to
Joseph M. Schenck . . . . Charles Brackett
Honorary Award to Harold Lloyd . . . Charles Brackett
Scientific and Technical Awards . . . . Anne Baxter
Honorary Award to Bob Hope . . . . . . Charles Brackett
Thalberg Award . . . . Charles Brackett

Performers of Nominated Songs

"Am I in Love?" . . . . Bob Hope and Marilyn Maxwell
"Because You're Mine" . . . . Billy Daniels
"High Noon (Do Not Forsake Me,
Oh My Darlin')" . . . . Tex Ritter
"Thumbelina" . . . . Celeste Holm
"Zing a Little Zong" . . Peggy Lee and Johnny Mercer

"Now my kids won't think I'm just another bum—they'll know what I do for a living."
—Anthony Quinn

time an Award was given in the course of the evening, the Oscars on the cake would light up with a celestial harp accompaniment from the orchestra pit. The giant Oscar on top of the cake, however, would not be lit until the climax of the show.

Academy President Charles Brackett, in his blue tuxedo shirt and a blue carnation, walked out to welcome viewers; since the Academy now had to entertain the public, Brackett decided to bypass his customary state-of-the-industry address and went straight to his introduction of the night's emcee—Bob Hope. Considered a Benedict Arnold for defecting to television, Hope hadn't been asked to host the Oscar show since 1946, but now that the Academy, too, had sold out, Bob was back.

"All over America, housewives are saying, 'Honey, put on your shirt, Joan Crawford's coming over,'" Hope began. "Television—that's where movies go when they die. How 'bout that Jack Warner, he still refers to television as that furniture that stares back." Commenting on the well-dressed audience, Hope said, "It looks like a PTA meeting in Texas." The host observed, "Look at all those Oscars, looks like Bette Davis' garage." Setting his sights on the birthday cake, Hope admitted, "I haven't seen anything so pretty since Hedda Hopper wore it."

The TV show jumped to New York, where former Academy President Conrad Nagel said, "We're having California weather, too." The cameras revealed a sparsely populated auditorium, and Nagel's excuse was: "The empty seats are for nominees in Broadway shows."

Back in Hollywood, Celeste Holm sang the nominated song "Thumbelina" to a face painted on her thumb. Then Ginger Rogers materialized to give the Costume Awards. Helen Rose, the Black-and-White winner for *The Bad and the Beautiful,* didn't make a speech and, being the first recipient of the night, wasn't sure how she was supposed to exit. Rogers took control of the situation and yelled, "Miss Rose wants to know which way she goes out." Rose was directed to the pressroom, where she later left her Oscar by mistake. Rogers then revealed that the Color Costume winner was Marcel Vertes for *Moulin Rouge*. Two people, however, walked to the stage to claim Oscars, and Ginger sputtered, "Oh, there are two of you—wouldn't you know?"

Presenting the Music Awards, Walt Disney made mincemeat of the nominees' names. Miklos Rosza became "Miklos Rosca." Conductor Adolph Deutsch hissed the correct pronunciation from the orchestra pit, but it didn't help. By the time he got to the Best Song Awards, Disney was changing "Am I in Love?" to "I Am in Love!" and couldn't make it all the way through Dimitri Tiomkin's name. Another faux pas evoked screams in the audience: Best Scoring of a Musical Picture winner Alfred Newman walked away, leaving his Oscar on the podium.

Non-nominee Olivia de Havilland presented the Best Director Award, which went to John Ford for *The Quiet Man*. The film's star, John Wayne, accepted for the director and paid a tribute to Ford by listing some of his earlier films, adding that the winner "will place this Oscar on his mantel with his five other Academy Awards."

Greer Garson walked out to present the Best Supporting Actor Award and the *Daily Variety* poll came a cropper when Richard Burton lost to Anthony Quinn for *Viva Zapata!* Katherine DeMille Quinn, accepting for her husband, was as surprised as everyone else and gasped at the podium, "I can hardly believe I'm here!"

The task of naming the Supporting Actress winner was given to Edmund Gwenn, who, five years after winning Supporting Actor for *Miracle on 34th Street,* was serenaded by Christmas music as he strolled onstage. He opened the envelope and announced, "Gloria Grahame for *The Bad and the Beautiful* . . . She's the Beautiful." A stunned-looking Grahame held on to her skirt as she walked to the stage. Gwenn handed her the Oscar and whispered, "Smile, you're on television." She smiled, gave brief thanks and got off fast.

There was clamorous applause when Janet Gaynor revealed that the Best Actor was Gary Cooper for *High Noon*. John Wayne was again the proxy and said, "I'm glad to see they're giving this

"Is this as big as Crosby's?"
—Bob Hope

to a man who has conducted himself throughout his years in this business in a manner that we can all be proud of him. And now, I'm going to go back and find my business manager, agent, producer, and three-name writers and find out why I didn't get *High Noon* instead of Cooper. Since I can't fire any of these very expensive fellas, I can at least run my 1930 Chevrolet into one of their big black new Cadillacs." Bob Hope lamented, "He gets pretty big laughs for a leading man."

Ronald Colman began reciting the names of the Best Actress nominees and the TV cameras ignored Joan Crawford in Hollywood and concentrated on Shirley Booth in New York, who was, indeed, the winner for *Come Back, Little Sheba*. Booth took off her fur coat, ran up the stairs and fell down to one knee, picked herself up and ran to the podium. "I am a very lucky girl," the stage veteran said. "I never could have done it alone. It has been a long, long climb. I guess this is the peak. I want to thank my old friends for their faith, my new friends for their hope, and everyone for their charity." When the winner returned to her seat, Danny Thomas gave her a solitary standing ovation.

Joan Crawford wasn't completely forgotten; the Best Actress presentation was followed by the chorus line of Oscar winners and there was Crawford cradling her *Mildred Pierce* statuette along with Loretta Young, Bobby Driscoll and Charlie McCarthy. "These twenty-five years have cast some long shadows," said the announcer as the former winners posed, "but shadows are never seen unless the sun is shining. Our film memories would mean far less were Hollywood not so brightly aglow tonight."

The Academy's big casting coup was the television debut of "Miss Mary Pickford" to present Best Picture. She opened the envelope and—to everyone's astonishment, including Pickford's—the winner was *The Greatest Show on Earth*. Back in New York, the audience at the Century could not even applaud and a voice asked, "Who decides these things, anyway?" The NBC cameramen were caught unprepared and had difficulty finding where Cecil B. DeMille was sitting—the producer was almost onstage before the cameras spotted him. Pickford reminded the winner, as she handed him the Oscar, "You and I were juveniles in Belasco's *Warrens of Virginia*." At his big moment, DeMille got humble and said, "I am only one little link in a chain that produced this film."

The Academy's equivalent of a gold watch went to Joseph M. Schenck, who had recently resigned from 20th Century–Fox to join Broadway producer Mike Todd in exploiting a new widescreen process called Todd-AO. Although Schenck had been sent up the river for tax evasion linked to his involvement with racketeers in 1941, he had been paroled after four months and returned to Fox as an "executive producer." The Academy saluted him with an Honorary Oscar "for long and distinguished service to the motion-picture industry." Brackett extolled, "All along the line he was generous—the Barney Baruch of the industry." The pillar of the community was "en route to New York," so his statuette was picked up by the 1927–28 Best Actress nominee from one of Schenck's films—Gloria Swanson. The proxy came onstage in glitter harlequin glasses, a mink stole and a pocketbook. She thanked everyone for Schenck, laughed and walked off.

Brackett then divulged that the Board of Governors had voted a third Honorary Oscar to Bob Hope. This one rewarded him for "his contribution to the laughter of the world, his service to the motion-picture industry, and his devotion to the American premise." An unprepared Hope said, "I don't believe it. Is this the same size as Crosby's? I hope he's still up—I've got to run over there." Making sure the trophy was genuine, Hope bit the Oscar's head.

The final tribute was the Thalberg Award. For this announcement, the big Oscar on top of the birthday cake lit up. The winner, again, was Cecil B. DeMille, who said, "I understand millions are watching on TV." They weren't—the networks had switched off after the Best Picture Award.

"Since I can't fire any of these expensive fellas, I can at least run my 1930 Chevrolet into one of their big black new Cadillacs."
—John Wayne

Aftermath

"I thought *High Noon* or *The Quiet Man* would get it," Cecil B. DeMille said backstage. His fellow juvenile, Mary Pickford, was asking reporters, "How do you like this blue dress? I rushed out and bought it at the last minute when they told me I better wear a blue or gray dress. All I have are black or white evening gowns." As Janet Gaynor and her husband, Adrian, walked through the backstage area reserved for journalists, Gaynor exclaimed: "Look dear, this is the way the press-room is in the movies—noisy with all the type-writers clicking."

Another star from the '20s was already enjoying herself at one of the after-parties. At Romanoff's, Joan Crawford reprised the Charleston number that made her famous in *Our Dancing Daughters* in 1928. Nearby, Jack Palance, the man who tried to kill her in *Sudden Fear*, did the rumba with Celeste Holm. At Chasen's, Stanley Kramer held a party for the *High Noon* crowd, although the movie ended up only winning three Awards: Best Actor for Gary Cooper, Best Score for Dimitri Tiomkin, and Best Song for "High Noon (Do Not Forsake Me, Oh My Darlin')". Lyricist Ned Washington exclaimed, "I feel like the mother of twins, only prouder." It was a good thing Washington didn't go to Ciro's, where Pearl Bailey entertained the crowd with her parody of the *High Noon* theme song. Meanwhile at the Mocambo, Piper Laurie—who for no particular reason had accepted T.E.B. Clarke's Story and Screenplay Award for *The Lavender Hill Mob*—took his Oscar and hid it under the table. "Got tired of explaining it wasn't mine," she said. "Sure wish it was."

Susan Hayward and her husband, Jess Barker, checked into the Grand Hotel in Rome, where there was a message from Hollywood at the desk. Hayward read it and sighed, "Thank God I didn't listen to Zanuck."

In New York, the Best Actress winner was apologetic. "I don't think it's fair I win," Shirley Booth said. "There is all the difference in the world between playing a character more than a thousand times, as I did, and getting your lines on the set in the morning and having to face the camera with them in the afternoon." Earl Wilson reported that Booth held the minority opinion: "Everybody around Broadway likes the selection and, above all, likes her. We would like to give the Academy an award for a perfect choice." Booth denied that the Oscar was pointing her in a new direction as a Hollywood star. "I don't want to compete with glamour queens and beauty gals," she shrugged. "As far as that goes, I might have stayed in bed." When the press was finished with her, Booth put on her fur coat, picked up her bouquet of four dozen red roses, and told her four male escorts they were heading for Sardi's. Back in Hollywood, Jerry Lewis was proposing a follow-up to Booth's vehicle: *Go Away, Little Shiksa*.

Hedda Hopper noted that it was a religious holiday in Cuernavaca, Mexico, where winners Gary Cooper and Anthony Quinn were shooting their western, and that "thousands of celebrants crowded the hotel." Their costar, Barbara Stanwyck, had thought ahead and bought a head—a four-thousand-year-old bust she dubbed "an Aztec Oscar." She gave it to Cooper; Quinn would just have to settle for the incredible news. "Frankly, I'm terribly surprised," Quinn said. "I didn't think I had a chance." Quinn was also overcome by the coincidence of his winning the same year as Cooper and DeMille: his first movie part was in *The Plainsman*, directed by Cecil B. DeMille and starring Gary Cooper. When asked why he seemed so thrilled about being recognized by the Academy, Quinn replied "because my kids won't think I'm just another bum. Now they'll know what I do for a living."

Gloria Grahame brought her Oscar to work with her the next day and then couldn't find it when it was time to go home. She spent two hours looking for it—a crewman had thought it was a prop and locked it up in the storage warehouse.

The Oscar show was a television event—it had

outdrawn every other show in television history. The newspaper critics gave the Academy good reviews. The *New York Journal-American* said, "The razzle-dazzle and triumphs of the Academy Awards presentations came into our living room last night and it was the greatest show to sizzle the coaxial yet." And the Academy got the official Hollywood seal of approval when *Variety*'s headline proclaimed 1ST MAJOR PIX-TV WEDDING BIG CLICK.

1953

"This is too much."
—Audrey Hepburn

Sex and Cinemascope battled it out for the 1953 Academy Awards.

Otto Preminger loosened Hollywood's corset with his adaptation of the Broadway bedroom comedy *The Moon Is Blue* by refusing to edit the words "virgin" and "pregnant" from the screenplay. The Breen Office, enforcer of the Motion Picture Production Code, told Preminger the words would have to be snipped out or he could forget the seal of approval. Preminger told them what they could do with their seal and arranged to distribute the movie without it. There were lines opening day to see the movie that the Catholic Church had given a "Condemned" rating, although one Catholic magazine caused an uproar when its reviewer, unaware of the "C" rating, raved, "It is hard to imagine a more irresistible piece!" Denounced as a smutmonger, Preminger cleaned up at the box office.

S.O.B.

When the news broke that Harry Cohn was going to make James Jones' tough-talking World War II novel *From Here to Eternity* into a movie, a joke went around town that he had bought the property "because he thinks everybody talks that way." The Columbia mogul was not as bold as Otto Preminger, however, and invited the Breen Office to tidy up the language in the film about army men, adulterous wives, and hookers in Hawaii on the eve of Pearl Harbor. Cohn wanted two big stars to play the film's daring love scene in the surf and he liked the idea of Burt Lancaster writhing with Joan Crawford. But after discussions with director Fred Zinnemann, Crawford announced that she was declining the role—she didn't like the costumes.

Deborah Kerr's agent called Cohn to suggest his client, who usually played regal ladies at MGM. "Why, you stupid son of a bitch," Cohn responded. "Get outta here!" He slammed down the phone. When Zinnemann and screenwriter Daniel Taradash dropped by for a casting conference, Cohn said, "You know who this stupid son of a bitch suggested? Deborah Kerr!" Zinnemann and Taradash turned and looked at each other and exclaimed, "What a great idea!" The British-born actress was signed and went to work on her American accent.

Cohn couldn't believe it either when Zinnemann decided to cast Montgomery Clift as a boxer who shacks up with a prostitute. Then Cohn insisted that one of Columbia's contract actresses play the prostitute role and the director picked Donna Reed, the goody-goody who had played James Stewart's wife in *It's a Wonderful Life*. What next, Cohn wondered.

Sinatra's Deal

Next, Eli Wallach said he was dropping out of his role as a private because he had a previous commitment to do Tennessee Williams' latest, *Camino Real*, on Broadway. Frank Sinatra jumped into action and began begging Cohn to give him the role. Frankie Boy had suffered a precipitous drop in popularity in record sales, concert attendance, and movie grosses, and even that last resort—television—had failed to restore him to his former celebrity. Confident that the part of Maggio would return him to the limelight, Sinatra went as far as offering to pay Cohn for the honor of being in the movie, but it wasn't until the mogul got a phone call from Mrs. Sinatra, Ava Gardner, that he decided to let the bobby-soxer's idol play the part for a salary of $8,000.

Sinatra got the last laugh on television when *From Here to Eternity* did so much business that Sid Caesar parodied it on his show. When the drama became Columbia's highest grossing film, Cohn wrote a letter to the trade papers, expressing his delight: "It is heartening to us—and to the industry—to know that the payoff in our business

Overleaf: *Best Actress winner Audrey Hepburn celebrates by littering her suite with congratulatory telegrams.*

"You know who this stupid son of a bitch suggested? Deborah Kerr."
—Harry Cohn

still exists for fine entertainment. Give them the kind of pictures they want and the American public—bless 'em—will still beat down your doors."

The Frank and Ava Show

Although Maggio was a secondary role in *From Here to Eternity,* Frank Sinatra walked away from the movie with the public spotlight planted firmly on him. Every result of his comeback was reported, from his scheduled film roles, to his switching record labels from Columbia to Capitol, to his IRS okay to invest in the Sands Hotel in Las Vegas. With all of this attention, Sinatra was, nonetheless, chosen as the least cooperative male star by the Hollywood Women's Press Club.

The problem started when word got out that Mr. and Mrs. Sinatra were splitting up. Army Archerd was one of many columnists who kept tabs on the couple's separate moves:

> *Frank Sinatra left for Las Vegas yesterday while Ava was busy getting her luggage out of L.A. Customs. (Oct. 8)*
>
> *Up to yesterday, Frank and Ava hadn't spoken and when asked about her arrival in Las Vegas, Frank replied: "I'd really like to know . . ." (Oct. 19)*
>
> *It must be final between Ava and Frankie. When asked if she were going to Las Vegas she countered with, "Why should I go to Vegas?" (Oct. 22)*

After a while, Sinatra got tired of the constant attention and didn't talk to journalists quite as often as he had before *Eternity*'s release.

Grace Period

Ava Gardner had done very well for herself in movies that year with *Mogambo,* a remake of Clark Gable's *Red Dust* with Gardner as Jean Harlow, Grace Kelly as Mary Astor, and Gable as Gable. Critics now called Gardner an actress instead of a pinup, and the public considered her the only sex symbol who rivaled Marilyn Monroe. Gardner's *Mogambo* costar, Grace Kelly, was also much in demand. Alfred Hitchcock had hired her for *Dial M for Murder* and *Rear Window* and Paramount picked her for *The Country Girl* with Bing Crosby and William Holden.

Kelly was also popular with gossip columnists. Mike Connolly claimed that "Grace Kelly resolved to date only single men in '54," while according to Army Archerd, "Bing Crosby and Grace Kelly are chatting in French between takes, 'Darling, *je vous aime beaucoup.*'"

Horse Opera

The American public still had to take kids to the movies, and that's where George Stevens came in. In contrast to the smoldering adults in *Eternity* and *Mogambo* was ten-year-old Brandon de Wilde, who broke hearts as the hero-worshipper in Stevens' *Shane*. This Technicolor western, filmed in the mountains of Utah with a big-name cast—Alan Ladd, Jean Arthur, Van Heflin, Jack Palance—garnered the same kind of reverential praise accorded the director's *A Place in the Sun* two years earlier. The *New York Times* said the film had "the quality of a fine album of paintings of the frontier," and the *New York Post* made it clear that "it's only a western in the sense that *Romeo and Juliet* is only a love story." The western was 1953's third highest grosser, coming right behind second-place *From Here to Eternity*.

Bigger than Life

Darryl Zanuck had his own approach to luring the TV audience back to movie theaters—he thought big. Television screens were small, therefore, the 20th Century–Fox head reckoned, movie screens should be at least one hundred times bigger. And thus, CinemaScope was born. Unlike 3-D, another gimmick that had debuted recently, Fox's innovation did not involve special glasses, just a wider screen and a new lens on the projector.

To showcase CinemaScope, Zanuck dusted

"It's only a western in the sense that Romeo and Juliet *is only a love story."*
*—*New York Post *on* Shane

off an old bestseller about a Roman tribune who refuses to crucify Jesus after trying on the Savior's garment. Richard Burton and Jean Simmons were cast in the leads to give *The Robe* a patina of respectability. The ads for the epic promised, "The supreme novel of our time as it was meant to be seen, heard, lived! The Miracle Story 'reaching out' to encompass you in its awe-inspiring and breathtaking grandeur." The ad copy went on so much about "The Anamorphic Process for the Miracle Mirror Screen with Stereophonic Sound," that one columnist suggested the police use the name of the new process for a sobriety test—"If he can say it he's sober, and probably works for 20th Century–Fox."

Daily Variety was astonished that in the *New York Daily News* "a review of *The Robe* was printed up front in general news section, on page five, not back in theatrical news pages. The review consumed almost the whole page." And what a review! Kate Cameron, using the paper's four-star rating system, gave *The Robe* eight stars—four for the movie, four more for CinemaScope.

The Robe rolled into Hollywood in glory. For the hometown premiere, Grauman's Chinese was given "a spic-and-span refurbishing," which, according to *Daily Variety,* translated into "all new seats, drapes, carpets and a majestic sign sweeping across its forecourt heralding CinemaScope and *The Robe.*" CinemaScope's inventor, Henri Chretien, was flown in from France and Army Archerd reminded his readers, "It's his first Coast visit since 1910."

Although the ads proclaimed, "It's Here! The Most Important Event in 59 Years of Hollywood History!" there were those who wondered what all the shouting was about. A professor of Latin at Columbia University wrote an essay for *Harper's* deriding the film's historical accuracy. Howling over the spectacular's resurrection of a Biblical character who would have been dead for twenty years by the time of the story, Dr. Gilbert Highet Anthon commented, "After this, it was no surprise to see a unit of the Regular Roman army marching to the drum and using bows and arrows, which is about as ridiculous as showing the U.S. Marines marching to the ukulele and using blowguns." Most moviegoers didn't seem to mind, and *The Robe* became the year's top-grossing film. CinemaScope was here to stay.

Brando's Torn Toga

Joseph L. Mankiewicz's four Oscars enabled him to take a stab at Shakespeare, and he assembled a dream cast for *Julius Caesar*—James Mason, John Gielgud, Louis Calhern, Greer Garson and Deborah Kerr. MGM handled the film carefully, opening it at the end of the year in a legitimate theater on Broadway—the Booth—so audiences could pretend they were at a play. The *New York Post* opined, "Every cultured person will want to see it." There were no prestigious legitimate theaters in Los Angeles in which to try this stunt, but MGM was able to prohibit the Four Star movie theater from selling popcorn during the engagement.

Mankiewicz realized that even the Bard sells more tickets if a little sex appeal is added, so his Marc Antony was played by Marlon Brando. A columnist joked that if MGM was really smart, it would have advertised the tragedy with a picture of Brando in a torn toga. Hollywood was impressed by the news of Brando's cooperation on the set and his willingness to have John Gielgud coach him on some line readings. The *New York Times'* Bosley Crowther wrote: "Happily, Mr. Brando's diction, which has been guttural and slurred in previous films, is clear and precise in this instance. In him, a major talent has emerged."

Hero-Heel Holden

At Paramount, Billy Wilder again cast a reluctant William Holden in a part nobody wanted—a double-dealing American in a Nazi POW camp in *Stalag 17*. When Holden urged Wilder to make his character more sympathetic, the director responded, "I was right with *Sunset Boulevard,* wasn't I?" *Life* verified that Wilder was

"Happily, Mr. Brando's diction, which has been guttural and slurred in previous films, is clear and precise in this instance."
—New York Times

correct again. "As acted by William Holden, *Stalag 17*'s hero-heel emerges as the most memorable character to come out in Hollywood this year." *Stalag 17* made a substantial amount of money and opened within a week of *The Moon Is Blue,* also starring Holden. The actor was now a bona fide box-office name.

Audacious Audrey

Paramount's important newcomer this year was twenty-four-year-old Audrey Hepburn, whose trip to stardom had been both swift and first class. At the age of twenty-one, while doing a bit part in a movie in Monte Carlo, Hepburn caught the eye of French writer Colette, who urged that the Belgian-born unknown be cast as the heroine of a stage version of her *Gigi*. After Hepburn triumphed on Broadway, Paramount cast her in the lead of William Wyler's *Roman Holiday,* a modern fairy tale about a princess who skips her royal duties to cavort in Rome with two Americans. Ads for the film said, "The man of every girl's dreams, Gregory Peck, meets the screen's most audacious new star, Audrey Hepburn." The public liked what they saw: the film became an international hit and Hepburn an international star.

After *Roman Holiday* opened, Hepburn was officially welcomed to Hollywood with a giant party thrown by Jules Stein, the head of MCA, the biggest talent agency in town. She was immediately signed by Billy Wilder for his new film, *Sabrina*. Columnists loved writing items about her, whether it was listing the number of celebrities who dropped by the set to meet her or commenting on what a dedicated actress she was. Army Archerd wrote, "Audrey Hepburn underwent minor surgery Tuesday and reported back to *Sabrina* yesterday without telling anyone."

Campaigning Time

When the New York Film Critics gave awards to *From Here to Eternity,* Burt Lancaster and Fred Zinnemann, Harry Cohn began lining up theaters for the film's national re-release. Paramount was happy that the Gotham tribe crowned Audrey Hepburn their Best Actress, because it indicated that *Sabrina* might have an Oscar-winning leading lady. If the studio could only get an Oscar for William Holden, it could advertise an All-Academy-Award cast.

But Holden's competition had marquees in his eyes, too. Interviewed on the set of his new western costarring Gary Cooper, Burt Lancaster said, "Well, I wouldn't ask for it myself, but now that I am making this picture with Coop, think of the marquee: 'Last Two Academy Award Winners in *Vera Cruz*,' Think of the box office!" The other contenders let the columnists do the talking. Army Archerd said: "Monty Clift's getting social—hired a private secretary in Gotham." And Mike Connolly reported: "Marlon Brando lunched at 20th with five gals, showed off his manners by personally seating each."

Darryl Zanuck thought a Best Actor nomination for Richard Burton would be good for *The Robe* and, though Burton himself was off playing Hamlet in Edinburgh with the Old Vic, the studio head made sure everyone knew the actor was still part of the home team. Publicity flacks issued denials from Burton that he had spoken snidely of the studios. "If I were going to blast Hollywood," he was quoted as saying, "I'd at least try to be witty about it." Alan Ladd did not have press agents working for his campaign; Paramount released *Shane* but did not promote Ladd, now a free-lance actor with no ties to his old studio.

The Nominations

Audrey Hepburn, Deborah Kerr and Ava Gardner cracked the list of Best Actress nominees, along with Leslie Caron for the box-office hit *Lili*. The fifth spot belonged to Maggie MacNamara for her film debut in *The Moon Is Blue;* she had just signed a contract with Darryl F. Zanuck at Fox. "What if Maggie MacNamara

"If he can say it he's sober, and probably works for 20th Century-Fox."
—Hollywood Reporter

wins?" warned *Daily Variety*. "It will mean that the Production Code carries no weight in the Oscar Derby."

Grace Kelly was nominated for Best Supporting Actress for *Mogambo*. Her major competition was *Eternity*'s Donna Reed, who was trying to get out of her contract with Harry Cohn because all the post-*Eternity* films he offered her were duds. "It's a matter of life and death!" was how she described the situation.

God and Glenn Ford on My Side

Shane did well and won six nominations, including Best Picture and two Best Supporting Actor candidates: Jack Palance as the villain and ten-year-old Brandon de Wilde. The honor did not turn Master de Wilde's head because his parents didn't tell him he was nominated; in fact, he wouldn't find out for another four years. Forty-year-old Burt Lancaster was the elder statesman of the Best Actor nominees: William Holden, thirty-five; Montgomery Clift, thirty-three; Marlon Brando, twenty-nine; and Richard Burton, twenty-eight.

Frank Sinatra was the only Best Supporting Actor nominee not in a movie from Paramount. The other nominees were the duo from *Shane*, Eddie Albert from *Roman Holiday*, and Robert Strauss, who was so delighted by his unexpected nomination for *Stalag 17* that he printed his acceptance speech in the trade papers in advance. Strauss' costar, Best Actor nominee William Holden, had a better shot at winning an Oscar because his friends were helping him out: Glenn Ford told publicists that he had turned down the Academy's offer to accept the Best Actor Award in the absence of Monty Clift and Burt Lancaster because he "makes no bones" about his pulling for William Holden. MGM, which had borrowed Holden from Paramount for *Executive Suite*, decided that an Academy Award plug would help sell the film, so—a week before the Awards were handed out—they introduced the nominee in the trailer as "the winner of the Best Male Acting Oscar."

No Pharaohs

Marlon Brando lost all the goodwill earned by his good manners when he suddenly broke his contract with Darryl Zanuck and bowed out of the newest CinemaScope bible spectacular, *The Egyptian*. Zanuck announced that he was suing the actor for $2 million. The *Hollywood Reporter* said, "Such conduct is nothing new with Brando, but nothing has been as drastic as this last stunt. So—why do any business with him?" Zanuck was having difficulty persuading other stars to appear in *The Egyptian*—Montgomery Clift turned down the part of a pharaoh.

Hondo and Dodo

One of the nominees for Best Motion Picture Story, western author Louis L'Amour, politely thanked the Academy for nominating his work but informed them that it wasn't really original. He had first published the idea for *Hondo*—a John Wayne 3-D western—as a short story in *Collier's* magazine entitled "The Gift of Cochise," and was thus ineligible by the rules. The Academy thanked him, gave him free tickets to the show and invited him to become a member of the Writers Branch.

Awards show producer Johnny Green was hoping that Doris Day, who had courteously agreed to sing "It's Magic" at the 1948 Awards, would reprise her radio hit "Secret Love" from the 1953 movie *Calamity Jane* on the show. But the former band singer let him in on a terrible secret. "I'm terrified of appearing before people!" Dodo confessed. Enter Ann Blyth, who was just beginning her operatic period at MGM and would be honored to perform the song. As Blyth began rehearsals, someone noticed that she was pregnant, stirring discussion about whether she should be seen belting the lyric "And my secret love's no secret anymore." High-level meetings were held, and it was decided that since Blyth was married, no impressionable young viewers would be corrupted.

Broadway Shows and No-Shows

The Academy declared war on the thunder-stealing *Daily Variety* poll and begged members not to respond to poll-takers' inquiries. The trade paper admitted that the Academy's attack had wounded its survey, but announced the winners as it saw them: *From Here to Eternity,* William Holden, Audrey Hepburn, Frank Sinatra, Donna Reed and director Fred Zinnemann. "Burt Lancaster was creeping up on William Holden as the polling ended," the paper added.

Both Audrey Hepburn and Deborah Kerr indicated they would attend the sister show in New York after their performances in their current Broadway plays, but the other Actress nominees said they weren't going at all. William Holden was the only Best Actor nominee planning to be in Hollywood for the Big Night. Even Bob Hope would be passing up the ceremony—Chrysler, sponsor of the comedian's television series, informed him he wasn't going to be telling any jokes on a show underwritten by Oldsmobile.

The Big Night

Since Hepburn and Kerr would both be latecomers, reporters outside New York's Century Theatre had to content themselves with the arrivals of Best Supporting Actress nominees Geraldine Page of *Hondo* and Thelma Ritter, up for the fourth consecutive year, for *Pickup on South Street*. Said Ritter on entering, "Now I know what it feels like to be the bridesmaid and never the bride."

The scene was livelier in Hollywood. Best Supporting Actress nominee Grace Kelly showed up on the arm of *Mogambo* costar Clark Gable. Fashion observers noted that "Miss Kelly wore a champagne tulle gown, embroidered with grape designs in gold paillettes," while "Mr. Gable was the only gentleman to wear an overcoat." *Daily Variety* surveyed what everybody else was wearing. "Full-skirted and strapless designs were most favored but several stars selected the sheath effect." Such a star was Mercedes McCambridge, the Supporting Actor Award presenter, who wore a net and satin gown with white inserts "like the fuzz on top of a strawberry soda," said she.

Best Supporting Actor hopeful Frank Sinatra showed up not with wife Ava but with two of his kids from his first marriage— Nancy, Jr., and Frank, Jr. His producer, Buddy Adler, stood nervously in the lobby and pleaded with photographers, "Don't ask me anything because I'm not responsible for what I say. I don't know what I'm doing." Harry Cohn's new protégé attracted attention nearby: "Kim Novak posed à la Marilyn Monroe for a good ten minutes," Mike Connolly observed, "striking every pose in Marilyn's book."

The television program began with the image of an Oldsmobile billboard on Hollywood Boulevard. An announcer said, "Ladies and gentlemen, tomorrow's headlines will be made here tonight. This is news. This is movietown's election night." Inside the Pantages, André Previn conducted the overture while the camera panned the audience looking for stars. "There's Rory Calhoun!" the announcer exclaimed. Members of the audience pointed to themselves on the monitors with the enthusiasm of an audience at a TV game show.

Academy President Charles Brackett began the proceedings with a speech about "how people thought movies were on the way out" until the

Awards Ceremony

MARCH 25, 1954, 8:00 P.M.
THE RKO PANTAGES THEATRE, HOLLYWOOD
AND THE NBC CENTURY THEATRE, NEW YORK

Your Hosts:
DONALD O'CONNOR IN HOLLYWOOD
FREDRIC MARCH IN NEW YORK
Televised over NBC

Presenters

Documentaries . . . . Elizabeth Taylor and Michael Wilding
Sound Recording . . . . Jack Webb
Short Subjects . . . Keefe Brasselle and Marilyn Erskine
Film Editing . . . . Esther Williams
Costume Design . . . . Gene Tierney
Art Direction . . . . Marge and Gower Champion
Cinematography . . . . Lex Barker and Lana Turner
Writing Awards . . . . Kirk Douglas
Director . . . . Irene Dunne
Supporting Actress . . . . Walter Brennan
Supporting Actor . . . . Mercedes McCambridge
Music Awards . . . . Arthur Freed
Actress . . . . Gary Cooper (on film)
Actor . . . . Shirley Booth (on film)
Picture . . . . Cecil B. DeMille
Special Effects . . . . Merle Oberon
Honorary Awards . . . . Charles Brackett
Scientific and Technical Awards . . . . . . Tyrone Power
Thalberg Award . . . . David O. Selznick

Performers of Nominated Songs

"The Moon Is Blue" . . . . Donald O'Connor and Mitzi Gaynor
"My Flaming Heart" . . . . Margaret Whiting
"Sadie Thompson's Song (Blue Pacific Blues)" . . . . Connie Russell
"Secret Love" . . . . Ann Blyth
"That's Amore" . . . . Dean Martin

"It's wonderful, but I think it's my year to retire."
—Walt Disney

technical and artistic revitalization of Hollywood in 1953 steered them straight. Then Brackett introduced the emcee, Donald O'Connor, who entered with a large notebook and explained, "I thought I was going to be the star of *This Is Your Life*." Echoing Brackett on the innovations in films, O'Connor said, "1953 was a big year for Hollywood—or, at least it was a wide year." When no one laughed, O'Connor continued, "On with the reading of the will," and introduced his cohost, Fredric March, in New York. "Hi, Dad," O'Connor greeted. There was a split-screen effect showing both men that brought ooohs from the Pantages audience.

After a bit of repartee between O'Connor and March, the audience was subjected to the first Oldsmobile commercial starring Paul Douglas, who in the space of a few years had gone from hosting the Oscar show to serving as radio commentator to his present turn as car pitchman. Clad in white tie and tails, Douglas introduced his cohost, "a new NBC star" named Betty White. The couple extolled the Oldsmobile in front of them and then scampered out of the way as a group of dancers gyrated around it.

Elizabeth Taylor wore a tomboy haircut as she and husband Michael Wilding gave both Documentary Oscars to Walt Disney, who was back onstage later to monopolize the Short Subject Awards, too. With his total of four statuettes, Disney told the audience, "Just gotta say one more word. It's wonderful, but I think it's my year to retire."

From Here to Eternity started its Awards conquest by winning the Sound and Editing Awards right away, but was slowed at the Costume Design Award presentation. Although Columbia's own Kim Novak did some more posing in one of Deborah Kerr's *Eternity* outfits that Joan Crawford had rejected, the Black-and-White Award went to Edith Head for Audrey Hepburn's royal gowns in *Roman Holiday*. Head didn't give a speech, but backstage she told reporters what she was going to do with her fifth Oscar: "I'm going to take it home and design a dress for it." After *The Robe* won the Color Costume Award, Donald O'Connor got in a dig at Darryl F. Zanuck: "If Mr. Douglas isn't ready for another commercial, Mr. Zanuck asked me to say something about *Wilson*." The audience laughed but television viewers were abruptly switched to Betty White, leaning on a car and asking, "How could any woman resist a design like this?"

"One of Hollywood's most distinguished citizens," Irene Dunne, made the Best Director presentation. It was clearly *From Here to Eternity*'s night and winning director Fred Zinnemann thanked the U.S. Pacific commander for letting him use Hawaii as a backdrop.

The "lovable" Walter Brennan named the Best Supporting Actress—Donna Reed for *From Here to Eternity*. The actress sprinted down the aisle with her arms moving pistonlike in front of her. "It was a long walk, I didn't think I would make it," she said at the podium. "As wonderful as *From Here to Eternity* was, what's even more wonderful is *Eternity* to here." She walked backstage, started crying, and was surprised when someone told her she had run to the stage. "I ran? I don't believe it."

Mercedes McCambridge was so moved by Reed's victory that she put in a personal observation: "I'm so glad about Donny!" McCambridge went down the list of Best Supporting Actor nominees and Frank Sinatra's name earned a round of anticipatory applause. McCambridge opened the envelope, jumped up and screamed, "Frank Sinatra!" The winner jubilantly trotted toward the stage and a fellow on the aisle playfully popped him on the butt with a program. Sinatra hugged O'Connor and kissed McCambridge. "Uh . . . that's a clever opening," the winner said, getting laughs. "If I start thanking everybody, I'll do a one-reeler [more laughter] . . . They're doing a lot of songs up here tonight but nobody asked me [laughter mixed with applause] . . . I love you, though." He walked off arm in arm with McCambridge and no one mentioned that in 1946 the Academy had asked him to sing and he had refused.

"I get a kick out of just being nominated."
—Thelma Ritter

Audrey Hepburn's show, *Ondine,* was letting out in New York and photographers stalked the nominee as she rode in her limousine with a police escort to the Century Theatre, taking her blond stage wig off during the trip. The first thing she did at the Century was beeline to an anteroom where she removed her stage makeup. The impatient cameramen gave her five minutes and then began banging on the door, yelling, "Hey, Skinny, come on out!" Hepburn had invited *Life*'s photographer into the dressing room and after the magazine was through with her, she made her entrance and joined her mother, a Dutch baroness, in the theater.

When Deborah Kerr entered with her husband a few minutes later, the photographers insisted that she kiss both her spouse and a nearby security guard before leaving her alone.

Hepburn and Kerr arrived just as Gary Cooper, on film from Mexico, was leading into the Best Actress Award. "Folks down here in Mexico are just as excited," Cooper said, then he ripped open an envelope and pulled out a blank piece of paper. "Shall I read it?" Donald O'Connor asked in Hollywood. The winner was Audrey Hepburn for *Roman Holiday*. In New York, a very confused young lady mounted the steps to the stage, turned suddenly, and began to wander off toward the wings. Fredric March guided the winner back to the podium. "This is too much," Audrey Hepburn sighed.

Shirley Booth appeared on the TV screen from her dressing room backstage in Philadelphia, where she was starring in a musical called *By the Beautiful Sea*. Booth chatted with her maid, put on her glasses, turned to the camera, said "Hello" and skipped down the names of nominees for Best Actor. To reveal the winner, Booth spoke on the phone to a Price, Waterhouse representative and responded, "Yes, I'll tell everyone." She faced the camera and said, "William Holden." In Hollywood, the *Stalag 17* star raced to the stage, where Donald O'Connor whispered to him that the show was running into overtime. Holden told the audience, "Thank you, thank you," and got off.

The Best Picture Award was given by "a man responsible for great films every year since this industry was born—Mr. Cecil B. DeMille." DeMille announced what everybody already knew—the winner was *From Here to Eternity*, which, with eight awards, tied *Gone With the Wind*'s record total.

The telecast ended, but the Academy had a few more scores to settle. Charles Brackett announced an Honorary Oscar to Otto Preminger's nemesis, Joseph I. Breen, head of the office bearing his name, "for his conscientious, open-minded and dignified management of the Motion Picture Production Code." Breen strode onstage as the orchestra played "Don't Fence Me In." Brackett handed him the trophy and congratulated Breen for preventing "wildcatting, self-appointed censorship boards from interfering with screen content."

Brackett then saluted Darryl F. Zanuck for "a process that is a shot in the arm to the whole industry." *The Robe* won only two of its five nominations, but CinemaScope got an Honorary Oscar for its debut. In accepting, Zanuck said that the new screen had been "accepted by millions of theatergoers." There were still a few holdouts in Hollywood, though; George Stevens, for one, told friends he thought the wide-screen format was appropriate only for photographing high school classes and snakes. After Zanuck exited, a white-haired David O. Selznick presented the Thalberg Award to none other than George Stevens, whose *Shane* had won only one of its six nominations. "Certainly it is a double-barreled honor to receive the Thalberg from the hands of David Selznick," the recipient said.

Aftermath

People were already departing the Century Theatre in New York as the events at the Pantages came to a close. Thelma Ritter commented, "I get a kick out of just being nominated," and Geraldine Page said she left her glasses at home and couldn't see anything anyway. Columnist Helen Gould couldn't find Deborah Kerr when everything was over: "Deborah left so quietly after the verdict

"It's a matter of life and death!"
—Donna Reed

that nobody got a chance to ask her how she felt about losing." Winner Audrey Hepburn wasn't so lucky. The photographers asked her to peck emcee Fredric March on the cheek. The actor responded, "I'll take a dozen of those!" When asked how she expected to celebrate, the twenty-four-year-old winner replied, "At home with Mother." Jean Hersholt said, "I am glad Audrey won or there wouldn't have been anyone here to give an Oscar to."

According to one columnist, Hepburn only gave her mother an hour, and then she and her fiancé, Mel Ferrer, joined Deborah Kerr and husband for post-Awards drinks at the Persian Room. Three evenings later, Audrey did it to Deborah again when she won the Tony Award as Broadway's Best Actress.

In Hollywood, the site of the biggest after-party was Romanoff's, where William Holden toasted Billy Wilder and said, "Of course, I knew it all the time." Loser Burt Lancaster also claimed clairvoyance and sent Holden a telegram that read: "Never had a doubt about the outcome for a moment." Holden evidently enjoyed himself because he woke up the next morning in his tuxedo in his easy chair surrounded by the neighborhood kids. His children had brought them in to look at the Oscar, which was resting in Daddy's lap.

The *From Here to Eternity* crowd was also making ribald toasts at Romanoff's, but one member of their party was missing. Frank Sinatra took his kids home and then, flushed with victory, took a solitary walk around Beverly Hills, until the police stopped him and asked him where he got that statuette. Back at his pad was a cable from Ava Gardner: "Congratulations, darling."

Hedda Hopper adored the sentimental aspects of Sinatra's victory, and went on about them at length:

> *Unpredictable as always, Frank went with his family to the Academy Awards show.*
>
> *"The minute my name was read, I turned around and looked at the kids. Little Nancy had tears in her eyes. For a second I didn't know whether to go onstage and get it or stay there and comfort her . . . I got Nancy a little miniature thing for her charm bracelet, a small Oscar medallion. The kids gave me a St. Genesius medal before the Awards, engraved with 'Dad, we will love you from here to eternity.' Little Nancy gave me a medal and said, 'This is from me and Saint Anthony.' That's her dear friend. She seems to get a lot done with St. Anthony, I guess she has a direct wire to him."*

Nancy and her father later reprised this night at the Academy Awards in the climax of the 1966 film, *The Oscar*. But, for the time being, Mike Connolly warned, "We hope Sinatra realizes the enormous responsibility that comes with this kind of success."

Connolly had sterner words for the winner of the Motion Picture Story Oscar. Ian McLellan Hunter was, according to the columnist, "in Mexico avoiding a House subpoena" the night he won for *Roman Holiday*. Connolly was upset that a proxy was allowed to accept the Oscar for the absent blacklistee, but the joke was ultimately on Connolly. Winner Hunter had merely served as a front for the man who had conceived the story of *Roman Holiday*—Dalton Trumbo, one of the Hollywood Ten.

Two conflicts ended happily. Best Supporting Actress winner Donna Reed was freed from her Columbia contract and, after a few more movies, moved on to her own, long-running TV series, *The Donna Reed Show*. And Best Actor loser Marlon Brando agreed to play Napoleon in an upcoming Fox movie, so Darryl F. Zanuck withdrew his $2 million lawsuit against the actor on April Fool's Day, 1954.

1954

"You bet I'll be there, but Brando will win it."
—Bing Crosby

The 1954 Oscar drama centered on babies, comebacks and Awards for good behavior.

The excitement started in the summer with the release of *On the Waterfront,* directed by Elia Kazan and starring Marlon Brando. Every studio in town had turned down the film about corruption in the longshoremen's union—Darryl Zanuck had screamed to Kazan, "Who the hell gives a shit about labor unions!"—but maverick independent producer Sam Spiegel said why not and raised the $820,000 necessary to shoot the thing in Hoboken, New Jersey.

When the critics got a look at the black-and-white movie with an Actors Studio cast and a Leonard Bernstein score they wrote paeans to it. *The New Yorker*'s John McCarten called it "the sort of galvanic movie we used to get when the Warner Brothers were riding herd on Al Capone and his associates." The *Hollywood Reporter* agreed: "After so many costume dramas, it may be just what the box office needs, for *On the Waterfront* is so stark and gripping that it can only be compared with *Little Caesar* and *The Public Enemy.*" The box office did need it, and the union melodrama jumped onto the list of the year's box-office champions.

One Glorious Meathead

The role of Terry Malloy gave Marlon Brando the best opportunity to strut his stuff since Stanley Kowalski, and he got even better reviews. *Time* said: "Brando in this show is one glorious meathead. The gone look, the reet vocabulary and the sexual arrogance are still the Brando brand of behavior. But for once the mannerisms converge, like symptoms to point out the nature of the man who has them. The audience may never forget that Brando is acting, but it will know that he is doing a powerful acting job." *Life* got more specific about Brando's popular appeal: "*On the Waterfront* is the most brutal movie of the year but it also contains the year's tenderest love scenes. Responsible for both is Marlon Brando."

A nattily attired Marlon Brando poses at home with his Best Actor Oscar.

The object of Brando's affection in these tender scenes was blond Eva Marie Saint, a young actress who had done mostly TV work. She made the cover of *Life* with the headline FROM TV TO STARDOM IN MOVIE 'WATERFRONT,' and in its review of the film, the *Hollywood Reporter* said that Saint's "haggard loveliness seems to have sprung from between the actual cobblestones of the docks. It makes the prettiness of the average starlet seem trivial."

Bing on a Binge

Despite the success of *On the Waterfront,* Paramount did not shrink from launching an Oscar blitz in December for its adaptation of Clifford Odets' *The Country Girl.* Before the film debuted in Hollywood, trade-paper ads reproduced glowing reviews from the New York critics, including the *World-Telegram*'s prediction that *The Country Girl* is "likely to become the favored picture of the year-end awards."

Paramount was counting on acting nominations for the film's two stars, Bing Crosby and Grace Kelly. Prior to the movie's release, Edward R. Murrow had interviewed Crosby on his *Person-to-Person* TV show and congratulated the actor on his change-of-pace role as drunken has-been entertainer:

> *You were an actor playing with great delicacy, restraint and understanding, a very difficult part, and my friends who are really experts in the business tell me that it may win an Academy Award, and I wouldn't be surprised if they're right!*

Watch That Baby Troupe

In the role of Crosby's unhappy wife, Grace Kelly wore glasses and drab housedresses and re-

"Grace Kelly's walkouts are unfortunately timed. Academy voters seem to be veering toward Judy."
—Mike Connolly

ceived the best reviews of her busy career—she had had no fewer than four movies released in 1954, including Alfred Hitchcock's *Dial M for Murder* and *Rear Window*. The *Hollywood Reporter* couldn't wait for *The Country Girl*'s December release and was already singing Kelly's praises in July:

> *Grace Kelly is going to be one of the great, great stars of this picture business NOT because of the romantic items—Kelly's lovers—but because she's a top actress, and any of you who have any doubts about this, grab a view of Paramount's* Country Girl *and watch that baby troupe.*

Most critics agreed with the *New York Post*'s Archer Winsten: "Kelly extends her range down to the bottoms of un-glamor, dead-faced discouragement . . . And she gives it everything a great actress could, one who was not handicapped by her own beauty."

The Heart Flutters and Bleeds

If Bing Crosby had his work cut out for him opposing Marlon Brando, Kelly had the equally formidable task of competing with Judy Garland. Garland had returned to movies in George Cukor's *A Star Is Born,* her first film since being unceremoniously fired from MGM in 1950, when she had proven too unreliable during the shooting of *Annie Get Your Gun*. Produced by her husband, Sid Luft, *A Star Is Born* seemed custom-made to showcase Garland's singing and dramatic abilities, but the production of the film seemed to take forever—the town was rife with rumors that Judy was up to her old tricks.

Warner Brothers ballyhooed the film's September 29 world premiere at the Pantages Theatre as the "Biggest Date in Entertainment History!" and the *Hollywood Reporter* joined in by declaring that this was "Hollywood's most eagerly anticipated film premiere in many years." The *Reporter*'s Mike Connolly couldn't believe his eyes at the sneak preview of the film:

> *Never have we seen people fight for seats as they did at this one . . . Were they rewarded? Yea verily.* Star *is an all-time great . . .*

Star's was the first premiere to be televised coast to coast; the interviews with arriving celebrities went over so well that the show was rebroadcast the very next night. And when Jack Warner boasted, "It's the greatest night in the history of the movies," Mike Connolly admitted, "We agreed with him."

Judy Garland and her costar James Mason—playing a washed-up-actor part not too far removed from Bing Crosby's—were covered with critical glory. The *New York Times'* Bosley Crowther wrote that director Cukor "gets performances from Miss Garland and Mr. Mason that make the heart flutter and bleed." But the film was too long, according to exhibitors, so Jack Warner cut a half hour out of the three-hour movie a week after the premiere. Despite the trimming, the word of mouth was not what the studio had hoped for and *A Star Is Born* was considered a box-office disappointment. At Oscar time, Warner did not place a single ad for his biggest release of the year.

Bogart's Silver Balls

If Harry Cohn was less than enthused about *On the Waterfront,* he still had a genuine in-house movie to crow about. He hoped that *The Caine Mutiny*, a project he had nurtured, would be Columbia's major Oscar contender. The film opened to mixed reviews—*The New Yorker* ho-hummed, "As pictures about the United States Navy go, *The Caine Mutiny* isn't bad"—but audiences enjoyed the courtroom histrionics and Humphrey Bogart's performance as the paranoid Captain Queeg with the scene-stealing habit of playing with silver balls. *The Caine Mutiny* became the second highest-grossing film of 1954, just behind *White Christmas,* starring Bing Crosby.

Another Bogart film venture in 1954 was Joseph L. Mankiewicz' *The Barefoot Contessa*. Al-

"It's as if they're trying to impose their psychiatric difficulties on the audience."
—Joan Crawford on Method actors

though this stinging portrait of Hollywood didn't gather the acclaim awarded *All About Eve,* Edmond O'Brien won kudos for his turn as a sweaty press agent. O'Brien was also respected for swallowing his pride when he learned that he would not be billed over the title as usual because Bogart's contract prevented it. "Bogie put his arm around me, bought me a drink and advised me to take below-the-line billing," O'Brien told interviewers. "After a few drinks, I agreed."

Ike Casts a Vote

MGM wasn't above using patriotism in promoting its most successful movie of the year, the musical *Seven Brides for Seven Brothers*. President Eisenhower was quoted in the ads, telling his fellow Americans, "If you haven't seen it, you should see it."

A Custom Is Born

Other innovative campaign tactics this year included Sam Spiegel's sending *free* tickets to Academy members for the reissue of *On the Waterfront*. Universal went one step further when it brought back its two top moneymakers, *Magnificent Obsession* and *The Glenn Miller Story,* in a "Special pre-Academy Award Nominations Engagement" at a cinema the studio called the "Hollywood Academy Theatre." This forced the Academy to take out its own trade-paper ad declaring, "There is only one theatre owned and operated by the Academy of Motion Picture Arts and Sciences. It is the Academy Theatre, 9038 Melrose Avenue."

The Nominations Show

Impressed with the high ratings of the first two televised Awards ceremonies, the Academy tried airing the announcement of the nominations on February 12, 1955. Jack Webb, the star of TV's *Dragnet,* was the show's major-domo, who explained that potential nominees were awaiting the news at various Hollywood nightclubs. Viewers saw a mink-clad Joan Crawford being led into Romanoff's by Mike Romanoff himself. Humphrey Bogart and Ann Higgenbothen, the editor of *Photoplay,* greeted everyone from a central table. Donna Reed and Sheilah Graham held court at Ciro's, and Greer Garson was the hostess at "Club NBC"—a TV studio decorated as a nightclub. The funniest participant was Louella Parsons, sharing duties with Irene Dunne at the Coconut Grove; the columnist read the nominations by looking through her jewel-encrusted opera glasses at the TV monitor a full foot and a half away.

Not very many nominees were there. Supporting Actress nominees Nina Foch, Jan Sterling and Katy Jurado (in an evening gown) were at Romanoff's; Lee J. Cobb, Edmond O'Brien and Tom Tully were the Supporting Actor nominees at Ciro's; Best Actor contender Dan O'Herlihy was at the Coconut Grove and Bogart at Romanoff's; and a pregnant Judy Garland hugged Jane Wyman at "Club NBC." Since there was not much for the nominees to do but stand and smile, the show won universally negative reviews; the *New York Times* commented, "The video and film industries can stop worrying about competition. The only thing they have to fear is co-operation." But NBC was happy; the show trounced the competition in the ratings.

The Nominations

Sam Spiegel proved he knew how to play the Oscar game. *On the Waterfront* joined former Best Picture winners *Mrs. Miniver, All About Eve* and *From Here to Eternity* as the only films to rake in five acting nominations, and it also became the first movie to have three people competing in the same category. But Best Supporting Actor contenders Rod Steiger, Lee J. Cobb and Karl Malden found three an unlucky number when the *Daily Variety* poll predicted that Edmond O'Brien would be rewarded for his lowly billing.

Marlon Brando's nomination was no surprise,

"Marlon Brando and I have a lot in common. He, too, has made many enemies."
—Bette Davis

but Sam Spiegel pulled a fast one with Eva Marie Saint—he listed his leading lady as a supporting actress, thus getting her away from the Garland vs. Kelly bout in the main arena. Saint's instant lead in the Supporting Actress category was confirmed by the *Daily Variety* poll, but some of her competitors trudged on nevertheless. Katy Jurado, nominated for *Broken Lance,* found a champion in columnist Army Archerd, who felt that the Academy had done her wrong once before by failing to nominate her for *High Noon* in 1952. Archerd kept his readers posted of Jurado's activities and thoughts during Oscar season. The Mexican-born actress, "happy for my country" because of the nomination, was also "saving her money to bring her children north of the border for their high school education." The agents of Jan Sterling, nominated for *The High and the Mighty,* celebrated themselves with an ad "marking 15 years to the day that we have been honored to represent Jan Sterling in her growth from schoolgirl actress to one of our finer dramatic talents."

Words and Music

The Best Song category was turning into a real battlefront as songwriters began to realize that an Oscar made sales of sheet music and records skyrocket. Four of the Best Song nominees had numerous ads; only "The Man That Got Away" was left to stand on its merits. Coral Records, not content to rely on trade-paper advertisements alone, mailed records to all Academy members so that they could hear "Hold My Hand" from *Susan Slept Here* as often as they liked.

Composer Dimitri Tiomkin was distressed because his popular theme song from *The High and the Mighty* would not be eligible for Best Song. Someone at the studio had arbitrarily removed the lyrics from the picture after its first preview. Tiomkin convinced Warner Brothers to reinstate the lyrics in a single print of the film shown in Los Angeles and suddenly the song was eligible. Tiomkin then advertised the fact by an elaborate means of Oscar campaigning—skywriting.

Psychiatric Difficulties

Having won the New York Film Critics, National Board of Review and Golden Globe Awards, *On the Waterfront* was the one to beat for Best Picture. The two main acting contests, on the other hand, were anything but an open-and-shut case, as the two leading contenders in each race had already won awards. Grace Kelly and Bing Crosby had grabbed the National Board of Review Awards, Kelly and Marlon Brando had taken home the New York Film Critics citations, while Crosby and Judy Garland snatched up the *Look* magazine awards. And all four of them won Golden Globes.

Marlon Brando may have become tired of losing Oscars, having been defeated for Best Actor three years in a row. There would be no more shots of him in a T-shirt this year; the Hollywood rebel now wore a sports jacket around town, inspiring one columnist to quip, "If Marlon Brando keeps it up, he'll win this year's Golden Apple Award as the most cooperative actor from the Hollywood Women's Press Club."

Bing Crosby, who had to be dragged to the ceremonies the year he won for *Going My Way,* told Army Archerd, "You bet I'll be there, but Brando will win it." Now a widower, Crosby kept the identity of his date for the show a secret, leaving gossips guessing.

Grace Kelly did *Life* magazine the favor of posing for its cover in her ice-blue satin backless Oscar-night evening gown, but in Hollywood she started receiving the kind of unwanted publicity that usually plagued Brando. Mike Connolly wrote that the actress was showing signs of temperament on the set, noting that her "walkouts are unfortunately timed. Academy voters seem to be veering toward Judy." The columnist also quoted Joan Crawford "on the torn T-shirt school of acting—'I don't like it. It's as if they're trying to impose their psychiatric difficulties on the audience.'"

By Oscar time, Judy Garland was eight

months pregnant. Jean Negulesco, the director of the Awards show as well as of Best Picture nominee *Three Coins in the Fountain,* regretted that her condition made it "inappropriate" for her to reprise Best Song nominee "The Man That Got Away." Garland had ordered a maternity gown by designer Michael Woulfe and was ready to attend the ceremonies but, two days before the show, prematurely gave birth to son Joey Luft. Jean Negulesco cursed Joey's arrival, wishing that the infant had waited until during the Awards: "That would have been the most fantastic *Medic* show of all time." Negulesco settled for what he could get and told NBC to put cameramen outside of Garland's third-story hospital room so that Bob Hope could talk to her on TV if she won.

Judy Garland would be otherwise engaged, but Negulesco decided the other acting nominees should do more than just sit and sweat out the show. He decided to give them all a chance to get onstage, inviting them to serve as presenters. Even Marlon Brando consented to the invitation.

The Big Night

The first nominee to arrive at the Pantages was Edmond O'Brien with his wife, Olga San Juan, at 6:30 P.M. The first Best Actor nominee to appear was Marlon Brando, in a tuxedo, with an entourage that included his agent, his secretary, his aunt and his father. One columnist described Brando as "looking somewhat bewildered," especially when he lost his father in the crowd.

Best Supporting Actor nominee Rod Steiger dated Best Supporting Actress nominee Katy Jurado, who created what the *Los Angeles Mirror-News* called a "minor sensation" in her "flame-colored gown which had at least four enormous red roses blooming across her shoulder." When the forecourt emcee complimented Jurado on the outfit, she elaborated, "It's a Dior and the bra and panties that came with it are flame-colored, too." When asked to describe her gown, Best Supporting Actress nominee Jan Sterling replied, "It's tight." Lauren Bacall, on the arm of Best Actor nominee Humphrey Bogart, flashed a diamond necklace and laughed, "You can see where my money goes."

Even the diamond-draped Bacall was overshadowed by Grace Kelly in her blue satin evening gown with full-length matching evening coat. *Daily Variety* reported that she "drew perhaps the biggest swarming of photogs of the evening," when she arrived, à la Brando, with her own crowd of admirers, among them Paramount boss Don Hartman and Edith Head. Kelly's costar was equally dapper. Bing Crosby, the last nominee to show up, was dressed in white tie, tails and top hat. He came with his steady date, twenty-one-year-old Kathryn Grant, thirty years his junior. Another forecourt surprise came when Walter Brennan was caught unawares by the *This Is Your Life* show, and the three-time Oscar winner was led away from the Pantages to a TV studio.

Judy Garland was not the only nominee experiencing motherhood. In New York, Best Supporting Actress nominee Eva Marie Saint told reporters she was expecting any day. Also in the

Awards Ceremony

MARCH 30, 1955, 7:30 P.M.
THE RKO PANTAGES THEATRE, HOLLYWOOD AND THE NBC CENTURY THEATRE, NEW YORK

Your Hosts:
BOB HOPE IN HOLLYWOOD,
THELMA RITTER IN NEW YORK
Televised over NBC

Presenters

Documentaries . . . . Grace Kelly
Sound Recording . . . . Tom Tully
Short Subjects . . . . Eva Marie Saint, Edmond O'Brien and Rod Steiger
Special Effects. . . . . Lee J. Cobb
Film Editing. . . . . Dorothy Dandridge
Costume Design . . . . Nina Foch and Jane Wyman
Art Direction. . . . . . . Jan Sterling and Dan O'Herlihy
Black and White Cinematography . . . . Humphrey Bogart
Color Cinematography. . . . . Katy Jurado
Director . . . . Marlon Brando
Motion Picture Story. . . . . Claire Trevor
Screenplay . . . . Karl Malden
Story and Screenplay. . . . . Audrey Hepburn
Music Awards . . . . Bing Crosby
Supporting Actress . . . . Frank Sinatra
Supporting Actor . . . . Donna Reed
Actress. . . . . William Holden
Actor. . . . . Bette Davis
Picture. . . . . Buddy Adler
Scientific and Technical. . . . . Lauren Bacall
Foreign Film. . . . . Jeanmaire
Honorary Award to Bausch & Lomb Optical Company . . . . Charles Brackett
Honorary Award to Kemp R. Niver . . . . Charles Brackett
Honorary Awards to Jon Whiteley and Vincent Winter . . . . Merle Oberon
Honorary Award to Greta Garbo . . . . Charles Brackett
Honorary Award to Danny Kaye . . . . Charles Brackett

Performers of Nominated Songs

"Count Your Blessings Instead of Sheep". . .Peggy King
"The High and the Mighty" . . . . Johnny Desmond and Muzzy Marcellino
"Hold My Hand" . . . . Tony Martin
"The Man That Got Away". . . . . . Rosemary Clooney
"Three Coins in the Fountain" . . . . Dean Martin

"The Oscar show is always a little better if things go wrong, so I had no need to feel guilty about letting them down."
—James Mason

New York audience were nominees Dorothy Dandridge, Karl Malden and Nina Foch. Audrey Hepburn, nominated for Best Actress for *Sabrina,* had already informed the Academy that she would be in London that evening, but Best Actor nominee James Mason agreed to give an Award in Hollywood and then didn't show. The Academy called his house, and the maid responded, "Mr. and Mrs. Mason went to San Francisco for the weekend. They expect to return home tomorrow." Mason admitted, several years later, that he "had no intention" of attending because "the Oscar show is always a little better if things go wrong, so I had no need to feel guilty about letting them down."

To accelerate the television show, Jean Negulesco dispensed with the reading of the nominations before each Award. Instead, he superimposed the lists of names over the image of the audience at the Pantages as it listened to the overture conducted by David Rose, Judy Garland's first husband. The idea backfired because the names were impossible to read and, as the night wore on, it became obvious that the pomp of reading the nominees was an integral part of the process that ends with the opening of the envelope.

The Hollywood set was a Daliesque, three-dimensional painted horizon. Onto it walked Academy President Charles Brackett to perform his function: he introduced Bob Hope. "Welcome to *You Bet Your Career,*" said Hope. "Cecil B. DeMille is about to make *The Eight Commandments*. He couldn't get two of them past the Breen Office. I just wanna say they should give a special award for bravery to the producer who produced a movie without Grace Kelly." Hope then introduced the hostess of the New York show, "lovely Thelma Ritter."

"Did Truman Capote get out of his hammock?" Hope asked.

"Yes," Ritter said.

"Is Marilyn Monroe there?" Hope queried.

"Yes, she just walked in with the Brothers Karamazov," Ritter responded, ridiculing Monroe's recent announcement that she wanted to play Grushenka. This banter was followed by a lengthy Oldsmobile commercial starring Lee Bowman. When the program switched back to Bob Hope, the emcee said, "Remember me? My clothes went out of style."

Grace Kelly appeared onstage with her pocketbook and presented the Documentary Feature Award to the Disney Studios' *The Vanishing Prairie.* Humphrey Bogart gave the Black-and-White Cinematography Award and then kidded around with Hope, lending the show the air of a friendly get-together. The two men caressed each other's faces and Bogie asked Hope, "Who does your makeup, Abbey Rents?" Then the comedian asked, "How do I get nominated?" "Go in for more serious roles," the three-time nominee answered. Hope then produced three silver balls from his pocket and began turning them with his fingers.

The Black-and-White Costume Award winner was the perennial Edith Head for *Sabrina*. The designer minced to the stage, grabbed her sixth Oscar and hurried off, defeating nominee Christian Dior for *Indiscretion of an American Wife*. Army Archerd wrote that Kim Novak was slated to accept for the French designer, had he won: "That would have been something, Novak accepting for Dior, the creator of the flat look! Wow!"

Marlon Brando strode onstage to announce that Best Director was his own director, Elia Kazan. The Turkish-born filmmaker accepted his second Oscar in New York and put the statuette face down on the podium while making his speech. After Kazan walked off, Brando and Hope cavorted with each other back in Hollywood. Hope brought up a conversation the two supposedly had as to how the comedian could get nominated for an Oscar. Brando reminded him that the first step was to hire a writer like Tennessee Williams. "Tennessee Williams?" questioned Hope. "I hired Tennessee Ernie." After he was finished clowning with Hope, Brando went backstage, where he was stopped by Officer Ben Kowski of the Warner Brothers police force, who demanded

"This is the one night I wish I smoked and drank."
—Grace Kelly

to see his identification card. An onlooker cleared up the problem and Kowski said, "Gee, I didn't know him from Adam."

When Karl Malden revealed *On the Waterfront* to be the winner of the Original Screenplay Award, writer Budd Schulberg toasted his father, B.P. Schulberg, head of Paramount when the studio won the first Best Picture Award for *Wings:* "Because of my old man . . . this little fellow gives me an added kick tonight."

Bob Hope got a chance at his favorite pastime—kidding Bing Crosby—by bringing out "old leather tonsils himself" to make the Music Awards presentation. Dimitri Tiomkin's efforts proved in vain in the Best Song category and the winner was "Three Coins in the Fountain." Lyricist Sammy Cahn said, "It took us fourteen years to get here." Tiomkin did win the Dramatic Score Award for *The High and the Mighty,* and when he walked onstage, Hope and Crosby bowed before him like palace guards. Tiomkin got in the best-remembered speech of the night: "I would like to thank my colleagues," he began, "Brahms, Bach, Beethoven, Richard Strauss—" The audience erupted into laughter and applause. "Unfortunately, I didn't intend to be funny," Tiomkin wrote later in his autobiography, *Please Don't Hate Me*. "I was misunderstood. What I wanted to say was something entirely serious, even solemn . . . What I wanted to express was a musician's homage to the heroes of the musical past."

Frank Sinatra declared that the winner of the Best Supporting Actress Award was Eva Marie Saint for *On the Waterfront*. The expectant mother cautiously made her way to the podium in New York and then dissolved into laughter. "I think I may have the baby right here," she said, earning more applause. Donna Reed stepped out in Hollywood to divulge that the Best Supporting Actor was Edmond O'Brien in *The Barefoot Contessa*. The Irishman quipped, "It can't be March 30, it must be March 17."

William Holden, who had not been permitted to make an acceptance speech when he won Best Actor the previous year, followed and said, "As I was going to say last year . . ." Just then Bob Hope ran up to Holden, whispered in his ear and pointed to his watch. The gag over, Holden revealed that the Best Actress winner was his costar Grace Kelly for *The Country Girl*. There were cries of "Bravo!" as Grace Kelly, pocketbook still in hand, shivered onstage and said, "The thrill of this moment prevents me from saying exactly what I feel."

The disappointment of the moment didn't prevent Judy Garland's husband from telling her exactly what he felt. According to Garland's biographer, Gerold Frank, as the TV technicians began dismantling their equipment, "Sid put his arms around Judy. 'Baby, f—— the Academy Awards, you've got yours in the incubator.'"

Back at the Pantages, Bette Davis, in Hollywood for the first time in three years, caused a sartorial commotion when she stepped onstage to present Best Actor. With her head shaven for her role as Queen Elizabeth in *The Virgin Queen,* Davis had commissioned a special getup for the Oscars. The *New York World-Telegram*'s Harriet van Horne described her: "She wore a sort of jeweled space helmet with shoes to match, and a black, off-the-shoulder dress that came to menacing points, front and back. Miss Davis may have borrowed the whole outfit from the *Captain Video* show, but I liked her for dressing dramatically and making an entrance."

Sidney Skolsky was ignoring Davis and keeping his eye on the two leading Actor nominees. Crosby was sitting directly in front of Brando. "They hadn't spoken a word to each other," Skolsky claimed, adding that Brando had chewed gum throughout the program, but stopped when Davis appeared. As soon as Davis announced the winner's name, "Marlon Brando for *On the Waterfront,*" the actor removed the gum and stood up. Crosby turned around, offered his hand and said, "Congratulations." Brando shook his hand, said "Thanks," and accepted his Award from the helmeted Davis. The Mumbler articulated, "I can't

"I would like to thank my colleagues: Brahms, Bach, Beethoven, Richard Strauss . . ."
—Dimitri Tiomkin

remember what I was going to say for the life of me. I don't think ever in my life that so many people were so directly responsible for my being so very, very happy." As the couple walked offstage, Davis turned to the Oscar winner and said, "It's nice to meet you."

There was little anticipation by the time Best Picture rolled around. *On the Waterfront* had already won seven Awards and its eighth win for Best Picture tied it with *Gone With the Wind* and last year's *From Here to Eternity*. After *Waterfront*'s producer, Sam Spiegel, had his moment in the sun, a member of the audience whispered, "And the picture didn't even have a title theme song."

Bob Hope summed up the program's message: "Get an Oldsmobile and drive to the movies. Good night from Oldsmobile." What Hope meant was that this was the end of the Oldsmobile-sponsored portion of the TV show, but there were still the Special Awards. Ninety percent of the NBC affiliates nevertheless misinterpreted Hope's line and signed off. Pandemonium also reigned at the Pantages; few people had paid attention to an earlier announcement about the final Awards and most of the audience began filing out of the theater. Academy officials had to head people off at the doors and steer them back to their seats.

After several technicians and juveniles were taken care of, Charles Brackett announced an Award for Greta Garbo, who hadn't made a movie since 1941, but had been the subject of a *Life* profile earlier in the year. The Swede did not show up and her Oscar was accepted in New York by the ex-wife of Supporting Actor winner Edmond O'Brien, Nancy Kelly, a recent Tony Award winner, who said, "In this year of awards, there's more than one Kelly, but there's only one Garbo." Unlike Garbo, Honorary Award winner Danny Kaye took advantage of his moment in the spotlight by making a plea for charity: "We can make the world understand the problems of our children." Then President Brackett made the announcement everybody was waiting for—the show was over.

Aftermath

A reporter asked Edmond O'Brien if he minded winning a mere Supporting Award. "No, you get the same Oscar," the winner replied. Best Actor Marlon Brando, meanwhile, was posing with an adulatory Bette Davis. "I have nothing but admiration for your work," she said. "My niece will be so jealous when she finds out I kissed her favorite actor." She then told reporters: "I was thrilled Marlon Brando was the winner. He and I have a lot in common. He, too, is a perfectionist. He, too, has made many enemies." So had Dimitri Tiomkin, who said that when his fellow composers caught up with him, they "berated me angrily for having cast accusation and ridicule on our profession."

When Davis was finished with Brando, he was hustled next to Grace Kelly, whose façade finally crumbled, "I can't believe they were saying my name," she sobbed. Brando fumbled for a cigarette, lit it, and then crushed it out when a cameraman asked him to put his arm around Kelly. A photographer instructed the actress to kiss the actor, but Kelly insisted, "I think he should kiss me." And so he did, twenty times, until all the photographers were satisfied. Brando was so euphoric that he started to kiss Hedda Hopper, until he suddenly recognized her and shook her hand instead.

Sidney Skolsky had cornered Brando's father, who said, "When I saw Marlon run up the steps to the stage, I said to myself, 'He's a good boy.'" Good enough to be respectful of his mother: "You see, it was just a year ago tonight that my Maw died and I don't feel too much like celebrating," Brando remarked. Nevertheless, at a post-Oscar party at his agent's house, Brando sat on a couch drinking champagne out of a coffee mug until he fell asleep.

Grace Kelly did her rejoicing at Romanoff's

with Bing Crosby, Kathryn Grant, Sarah Churchill, Charles Brackett, Merle Oberon and Edith Head. When Crosby arrived at the restaurant, co-loser Humphrey Bogart waved to him, "C'mon over and join the bad losers' table." Amid the reveling, Grace gushed, "This is the one night I wish I smoked and drank." Dean Martin and Jerry Lewis amused the crowd at Chasen's with their imitations of Brando (Jerry) and Crosby (Dean).

Judy Garland took the loss gracefully and told reporters that she was not disappointed. "After all, I was presented with my own special Oscar," said the proud mother. Hollywoodites reckoned that Grace, with vehicles in the wings at both Paramount and MGM, had had more studio support than the unemployed Judy, who, as it turned out, wouldn't make another film for six years. Garland did receive over a thousand telegrams of condolence. Groucho Marx wired: "Dear Judy, this is the biggest robbery since Brink's." And fellow loser Bing Crosby, remembering an award the two of them had managed to win, wrote, "I don't know about you, but I'm renewing my subscription to *Look*."

1955

"When I came out here, I was a green bumpkin. I put all my faith in the people I knew."
—Ernest Borgnine

The 1955 Academy Awards were a real-life fairy tale complete with a genuine princess and a frog prince.

Ernest Borgnine had a reputation as one of the meanest villains in movies (he beat Frank Sinatra to a pulp in *From Here to Eternity*) when he landed the lead in *Marty*, a low-budget, black-and-white expansion of a Paddy Chayefsky television drama about a Bronx butcher who falls in love with a plain Jane. Rumors circulated that producers Harold Hecht and Burt Lancaster made the movie expecting it to lose money so that they could claim it as a tax write-off, but then discovered that preview audiences were walking out smiling. *Variety* wrote: "If *Marty* is an example of the type of material that can be gleaned, then studio story editors better spend more time at home looking at television." The *New York Times* reported that Hecht and Lancaster used a policy of "screening the film intensively for community opinion-makers—such as ministers, shopkeepers and physicians—for two weeks previous to the opening."

The movie opened in art houses in April where it played for months—United Artists was in no hurry to release it in regular theaters, lest it be confused with run-of-the-mill Hollywood product. "Apart from the fact that *Marty* is one of the few recent films of American origin to offer dialogue that has some sort of verisimilitude," opined *The New Yorker*, "it has the virtues of being set forth in physical dimensions as modest as the story. It is neither high, wide, nor handsome, and it has been photographed with a camera designed to present films of the type we used to know and love before CinemaScope opened new and lunatic vistas for enjoyment."

Marty was the first American movie to win the Best Picture prize at the Cannes Film Festival. Betsy Blair (a.k.a. Mrs. Gene Kelly) won the Best Actress trophy while Ernest Borgnine, as Marty, shared the Best Actor honor with Spencer Tracy, whom Borgnine had supported as a villain in the suspense film *Bad Day at Black Rock*. *Time* raved, "Ernest Borgnine lives up to all the promise he showed as the sadist in *From Here to Eternity*, and at the same time brilliantly shatters the typecast he molded for himself in that picture. His Marty is fully what the author intended him to be—a Hamlet of Butchers." Comics loved him, too, and his most famous line in the film, "Whaddya feel like doing tonight?" became standard fodder in nightclub routines. Army Archerd laughed in *Daily Variety:* "Ernie Borgnine now rates $100,000 a picture, thanks to *Marty;* in '53 you could have gotten him for scale!"

Overleaf: *Best Actor winner Ernest Borgnine discovers that it wasn't a dream when wife Rhoda serves him Oscar in bed.*

Come Back, Jimmy Dean

As miraculous as Borgnine's sudden stardom was, it couldn't compare to the immediate cult-hood of James Dean. When the twenty-four-year-old actor bowed in Elia Kazan's adaptation of John Steinbeck's *East of Eden*, Bosley Crowther wrote in the *New York Times*, "He scuffs his feet, he whirls, he pouts, he sputters, he leans against walls, he rolls his eyes, he swallows his words, he ambles slack-kneed—all like Marlon Brando used to do. Never have we seen a performer so clearly follow another's style. Mr. Kazan should be spanked for permitting him to do such a sophomoric thing." Audiences didn't share Crowther's view—*East of Eden* raked in $5 million in the U.S. alone and Warner Brothers was swamped with requests for publicity photos of the new teen idol.

The James Dean fan club got serious when the actor fatally crashed his Porsche on September 30, 1955, just days after finishing George Stevens' *Giant*. When his second movie, *Rebel Without a Cause*, opened a month after the accident, teenagers eagerly lined up to see their martyred hero. *Daily Variety* wrote, "Under Nicholas Ray's socko direction, the Marlon Brando mannerisms displayed in the initialier are gone and the role here carries much greater audience sympathy and re-

"I've been a star for a good many years and I don't intend to change to a supporting actress now simply in hopes of winning an Oscar."
—Rosalind Russell

sponse as a result." The result was another hit for Warner Brothers. Army Archerd reported that when the late actor won a posthumous prize from an exhibitors' poll, "Hedda Hopper was the first to stand in tribute to Jimmy Dean when Grace Kelly called his name as Best Actor." Hopper was but one of Dean's fans; *Daily Variety* revealed that "James Dean topped the fan mail list at Warner Brothers, with 4,038 in January. Tab Hunter followed with 3,900." Other fans wrote Dean's screen father in *Rebel*, Jim Backus, for personal recollections, and Dean's real-life grandparents said they averaged thirty teary-eyed visitors a week at their home in Fairmount, Indiana.

Leader of the Rat Pack

Unlike the late Mr. Dean, Frank Sinatra was very much alive—and kicking. Sinatra had not let his 1953 Supporting Actor Oscar go to waste and the actor, who a couple of years earlier couldn't get a job, had made six films in two years. In number six, Otto Preminger's *The Man With the Golden Arm*, Sinatra portrayed a heroin addict with such realism that once again the Production Code seal was withheld from a Preminger film. This time the exhibitors didn't care about the censor and *Variety* headlined: ALL BIG CIRCUITS, FOR FIRST TIME, WILLING TO BOOK CODE-NIXED FILM. Sinatra pulled them into theaters like James Dean, and the critics were also adulatory. Arthur Knight in the *Saturday Review* called the singer "an actor of rare ability." He was popular in Hollywood, too. "Frank Sinatra had tears in his eyes when we walked up to him at the post–*Golden Arm* party to tell him his is one of Hollywood's all-time great performances," noted columnist Mike Conolly. "Any number of singers and musicians were at Otto Preminger's glittering preem party—Sinatra himself, Judy Garland, Rosemary Clooney, Noel Coward, Eddie and Debbie Fisher, Celeste Holm, Jerry Lewis, violinist Jack Benny."

Sinatra's Oscar ads called him "the hottest thing in show business," and, as proof, quoted *Time*'s evaluation that he was "currently in more demand than any other performer. A rating that stands second to none in pull or payoff." With this kind of status, Sinatra ruled what one columnist called "the Holmby Hills Rat Pack, as Humphrey Bogart so quaintly describes his little group." Columnist Connolly was the Boswell of the Rat Pack, regularly printing items about their activities, such as this Christmas 1955 tidbit: "Sinatra and Jimmy Van Heusen spent the entire Christmas Eve night wrapping young Nancy's gift—a Chevrolet. They gift-bound it in strips of cellophane."

A Royal Dressing Down

Last year's Best Actress, Grace Kelly, didn't have anyone talking about a second statuette for her performances in her two 1955 releases, but she continued to be the best-dressed woman on the screen, modeling Edith Head costumes as William Holden's wife in *The Bridges at Toko-Ri* and as Cary Grant's elegant girlfriend in Alfred Hitchcock's *To Catch a Thief*. "I think I am prouder of the clothes in that film than those in any other picture on which I have worked," said Head of *Thief*. "Grace played a wealthy heiress, giving me the opportunity to provide her with a luxurious wardrobe. She was breathtaking." Even without a critically acclaimed role, Kelly managed to upstage the year's potential Best Actress nominees when she announced that she was marrying Prince Rainier III of Monaco on April 6, 1956—just two weeks after the Oscar ceremonies. Many Hollywoodites cherished an invitation to the royal wedding as much as an Academy Award nomination; especially nervous were the costume designers, who coveted the prestige of creating the princess' wedding gown. When Kelly selected MGM's Helen Rose for the honor, Edith Head promptly informed the bride that she was designing a honeymoon travel outfit as a gift from Paramount. The Academy wasn't about to let Kelly get away unsaluted, so the actress was asked to present the Best Actor Award. It would be her final public appearance before flying off to Monaco.

"Magnani wants to be judged only on her performance, not her handshaking ability."
—Anna Magnani

The Oriental Look

Rivaling Grace Kelly's screen fashion show was Jennifer Jones—now married to mentor David O. Selznick—in 20th Century–Fox's CinemaScope romance *Love Is a Many-Splendored Thing*. Jones portrayed a Eurasian doctor involved with an Occidental war correspondent, William Holden, and led *Film Daily* to declare, "It's hard to believe that her measured steps, practiced speech and other Oriental characteristics are not her real personality." *Variety* was impressed with her Charles LeMaire costumes: "Miss Jones' Chinese gowns (and she wears a multitude of them) are the smartest thing any dress designer ever dreamed up." The *Hollywood Reporter* proclaimed the film "one of the best woman's pictures made in some years," and a lot of women went to see it; in addition to racking up a high box-office gross, the film dominated the radio airwaves with the Four Aces' recording of the title tune. *Photoplay*'s readers voted Mrs. Selznick the most popular actress of the year and boutiques reported a boom in Chinese cheong sam dresses.

Wounded Warblers

If an actress wanted to star in one of MGM's musical biographies, she had better be prepared to suffer. Eleanor Parker had to go the polio route as opera singer Marjorie Lawrence in *Interrupted Melody*. Eileen Farrell sang the arias on the sound track for Parker, but the actress did her own stumbling with such conviction that Otto Preminger cast her as Sinatra's crippled wife in *The Man With the Golden Arm*.

Doris Day did her own singing as blues singer Ruth Etting in *Love Me or Leave Me*, but while the picture made a bundle and her versions of Etting's songs climbed to the top of the charts, many of Day's fans did not cotton to her new image as a saloon singer. "I was deluged with mail attacking me for drinking, for playing a lewd woman, for the scant costumes I wore in the nightclub scenes," the actress recalled in her autobiography. "I answered every piece of mail . . . for I feel a performer has the same responsibility to his public that a politician has to the electorate."

James Cagney, as Etting's gangster husband Martin "The Gimp" Snyder, had no such identification problems. William K. Zinsser in the *New York Herald Tribune* wrote, "It's a high tribute to Cagney that he makes this twisted man steadily interesting for two hours." *New York Daily News* critic Kate Cameron did some checking and noted, "When I inquired if Snyder was touchy about the Cagney impersonation, which is supposed to be realistic, I was told he was so pleased with it that he offered to go to Chicago when the picture opens there, to help MGM's exploitation campaign."

Another torch singer, Lillian Roth, turned down Paramount's lucrative offer to film her best-selling autobiography, *I'll Cry Tomorrow*, coauthored by Mike Connolly, when MGM promised her less money but Susan Hayward in the starring role. "Millions wept unashamedly when Lillian Roth's extraordinary biography was sketched on Ralph Edwards' *This Is Your Life* TV program," heralded the studio's trade-paper ads, which boasted the slogan, "Filmed on Location . . . Inside a Woman's Soul!" MGM saved the release of the film until Christmas so that Hayward's battle with the bottle would be fresh in the minds of Academy voters. The *Hollywood Reporter* declared the actress gave "an intensely varied and expertly coordinated performance that comes to a heart-rending climax when she becomes a wretched, abandoned bum, accepting the embraces of any passing wino on skid row." And *Daily Variety* predicted hers was "a performance that can't miss being a major contender in the forthcoming Academy balloting for Best Actress."

Most Exciting Woman of All Time

Before helming Hayward in her Oscar bid, director Daniel Mann helped her Oscar competition—Anna Magnani. The Italian actress had been an international star since appearing in *Open City* in 1946 and one of her biggest fans was Tennessee Williams. "I never saw a more beautiful woman," the playwright exclaimed after meeting her in Rome in 1950, "enormous eyes, skin the color of Devonshire cream." He wrote a play, *The Rose Tattoo,* for her, but Magnani was afraid her English wasn't good enough and Maureen Stapleton played the part on Broadway. Williams insisted Magnani star in the movie version, going so far as having the script printed in both English and Italian. The actress was given the same team that had made Shirley Booth comfortable before the camera in *Come Back, Little Sheba*—director Daniel Mann and costar Burt Lancaster—and Williams supplied both the screenplay and the dressing room—his home in Key West, where part of the film was made.

"It's a tour de force of quality rarely seen on the screen," remarked *Daily Variety,* which projected big returns at the box office. "The play's reputation and smash performance by Anna Magnani, another name for animal magnetism, tee off the film as a natural for the carriage trade in selected showcases." The ads for the film called Magnani "One of the Most Exciting Women of All Time!" and *Time* joined in by dubbing her "the most explosive actress of her generation." Producer Hal Wallis begged her to return to Hollywood for the film's December premiere, arguing that her presence would aid her Oscar chances, but the actress replied, "No, thanks. Magnani wants to be judged only on her performance, not her handshaking ability."

More Wedding Bells

Hal Wallis could relax about the visibility of *The Rose Tattoo*'s other Oscar candidate, twenty-three-year-old Marisa Pavan, who played Magnani's love-struck daughter—she was in real-life love in full view of the gossip columnists. Finally, the *Hollywood Reporter* had the scoop on March 15: "Jean-Pierre Aumont asked Marisa Pavan to marry him and she said yes." There were still some things that had to be ironed out: "Marisa Pavan wants to wait until after Lent but Jean-Pierre Aumont wants the wedding right away, before Grace Kelly's."

Peggy Sings the Blues

Marisa Pavan had something to look forward to regardless of the whims of the Academy, but the idea of a Supporting Actress Oscar really gave Peggy Lee fever. The singer won plaudits for her dramatic turn as a Jazz Age baby who cracks up in a Jack Webb movie called *Pete Kelly's Blues* and, in her eagerness to attract the Academy's attention, she jumped the gun while appearing in Las Vegas in January. "How about those radio spot announcements for the Sands: 'Presenting Academy Award nominee Peggy Lee'?" asked Army Archerd. "They know something we don't?" From the Sands, Lee moved to the Coconut Grove in Hollywood, where Archerd interviewed her between shows and reported, "Peggy Lee hopes her current date is her last nitery stint. Sez she's been singing in saloons since she was 14 and she's had it." Understandably so, according to Mike Connolly's review of her Grove opening: "Peg almost fell flat on her face taking a bow . . . we were told she had dyed her shoes red to match her dress and that they stretched in the process and almost tripped her."

Nightclubbing with Natalie

Mike Connolly saw one of Peggy Lee's potential Supporting Actress rivals at her opening: "Natalie Wood, who was with Raymond Burr, ate a plate of mashed potatoes and nothing else for dinner. Said she's putting on poundage because wide screens make her look thin." Playing James Dean's love interest in *Rebel Without a Cause,* the seventeen-year-old Wood had shown audiences that she had matured considerably since learning to believe in Santa Claus in *Miracle on 34th Street.* Noting the popular response to his young contractee, Jack Warner told the press that he was

"Being an actress is such a humiliating business anyway, and as you get older it becomes more humiliating because you've got less to sell."
—Katharine Hepburn

pushing her for a nomination. Warner himself "chaperoned" Wood and Tab Hunter to a Hollywood party and she was seen around town with another young actor from *Rebel*, Nick Adams.

No Support for Roz

Harry Cohn was pushing Joshua Logan's adaptation of William Inge's *Picnic* as Columbia's big Oscar entry through elaborate ads that quoted practically everyone who worked on the film. For instance, film editor William A. Lyon explained that "when individual frames of film can catch your eye and impress you even before the scenes are spliced together, you know you've got a winner." When *Picnic* bowed in December, the *Hollywood Reporter* verified the claim: "Space does not permit a cataloguing of all Logan has accomplished, but it could form the basis for a notable lecture on what constitutes 'The Art of the Screen.'" When the *Reporter* went on to praise Rosalind Russell's performance as the old-maid schoolteacher—"Roz is hilariously funny, touchingly pathetic and, in her drunk scene, as horrifyingly menacing as a Greek Harpy, in her portrayal of this desperate woman who fears that life is passing her by"—Cohn began cranking up for a Supporting Actress campaign for Russell. "Now, hold on a minute, Harry," the actress told the mogul, "I've been a star for a good many years and I don't intend to change to a supporting actress now simply in hopes of winning an Oscar."

Cohn didn't have to take such flak from Columbia contractee Jack Lemmon, demoted to supporting for his role as Ensign Pulver in the immensely popular screen adaptation of *Mister Roberts*. Although *Mister Roberts* was a Warners movie, Cohn didn't think it would hurt to have an Oscar winner under contract. Henry Fonda, in the title role, graced the cover of *Life*, which proclaimed, "*Mister Roberts* is finally a movie." Hedda Hopper rejoiced, "*Mister Roberts* brings joy and laughter back to motion picture theaters." The comedy, costarring James Cagney, certainly brought patrons to theaters—it was the second highest-grossing film of the year, right behind *Cinerama Holiday*.

The Great Throbbing Thing

The New York Film Critics were not swayed by the box-office totals of *Cinerama Holiday* and stuck with their favorite, *Marty*, which won Best Picture and Best Actor. *Marty*'s first-time director, Delbert Mann, was passed over by the scribes for England's David Lean, for his adaptation of Arthur Laurents' play *The Time of the Cuckoo*, entitled *Summertime*. The star of this portrait of a spinster, Katharine Hepburn, came in second in the Best Actress voting, behind *The Rose Tattoo*'s Anna Magnani. Producer Hal Wallis was thrilled by Magnani's victory, which gave her the lead in the Oscar race, but was dismayed when he learned the actress still wasn't planning a return trip to Hollywood to attend the ceremonies. His publicists got to work trying to explain that Magnani was not snubbing the Academy. On January 17, according to Mike Connolly, the excuse was that "Magnani's son comes first. If he recovers from his recent operation satisfactorily, she'll come." By February 9, that had changed to "Anna Magnani is playing a nun in a movie shooting in Rome. It will prevent her presence here at Oscar time."

With *Marty*'s success in Cannes and New York, producers Harold Hecht and Burt Lancaster took aim at Hollywood. The producers allocated $400,000 for an Oscar campaign budget for the $343,000 movie, inspiring W. R. Wilkerson, editor of the *Hollywood Reporter*, to inquire, "Has there ever before in this business been a picture where the producer or the distributor spent more than the picture's cost in advertising?" Army Archerd explained why this precedent-breaking move was made: "Hecht-Lancaster hope the black-and-white narrow-screen luck of the past two Oscar winners, *On the Waterfront* and *From Here to Eternity*, holds up for *Marty*."

No stunt in the effort to attract Academy voters' attention was left untried. Borgnine acted as a guest butcher at the opening of a supermarket in Santa Monica, where he received a gold urn trophy from the Santa Monica Bay District Meatcutters Union. The union saluted him for portraying "the meatcutters of America as friendly, humble, sincere and accredited members of the human race." The dignity of the occasion was marked by nearby starlets in bathing suits holding placards that read, "I love Marty." The editor of *Box Office Digest* was so moved by the producers' promotional hoopla that he wrote: "It is the rare occurrence such as this that makes the motion picture business the great throbbing thing it is."

The Nominations

For the second year in a row, the Academy broadcast the reading of the nominations. This television show's format was simpler than the previous year's; instead of hopping around to Hollywood nightclubs, the program took place entirely in one TV studio, with Fredric March as the host. There were even fewer acting nominees in attendance this time, only six: Marisa Pavan, Natalie Wood (in a mink stole), Jack Lemmon, Arthur O'Connell, Susan Hayward and Ernest Borgnine. When their names were read, they all signed their names on a blackboard, just like on *What's My Line?* After June Haver announced James Dean's posthumous nomination for *East of Eden*, she said, "May God rest his soul. I would love to have the honor of writing his name on the board." Prefacing the Costume Design nominees, Sheree North worried about television censorship: "Last year's Award went to *Gate of Hell*—oops, can I say that?" Once again, the nominations show earned great ratings and terrible reviews. Academy members cried enough and the Board of Governors decided it was time to put the nominations show to rest.

The *Marty* campaign began to pay off when the film won eight nominations, a total tied by both *Love Is a Many-Splendored Thing* and *The Rose Tattoo*. These other two films didn't pose much of a threat to *Marty*'s Best Picture chances because they weren't nominated for either Best Director or any of the Screenplay Awards. Despite the looming sweep of *Marty*, nominee Frank Sinatra let it be known that he would be there if Ernest Borgnine failed to take home the prize; as Army Archerd put it, "Frank Sinatra, à la Grace Kelly, delayed his departure for Europe and will attend the Academy Awards." Sinatra's competition, Spencer Tracy, didn't give a second thought to his fifth nomination, for *Bad Day at Black Rock*, but told reporters, "It was a blatant omission on the part of the Academy to leave Henry Fonda out of the running. He was great in *Mister Roberts*."

The posthumous nomination of James Dean for *East of Eden*—the first since Jeanne Eagels' in 1928–29 for *The Letter*—was not enough for Hedda Hopper, who led the call for an Honorary Award. Academy President George Seaton had to remind the columnist that current Academy rules prevented nominees from winning Honorary Awards. "We're sentimental, too," Seaton said, "but that's the rule." The fifth Best Actor nominee was James Cagney of *Love Me or Leave Me*, who said he'd be a participant on the Oscar show.

Cagney's costar, Doris Day, wasn't as fortunate—she didn't make the lineup of Best Actress nominees. *Interrupted Melody*'s Eleanor Parker, *Love Is a Many-Splendored Thing*'s Jennifer Jones, *The Rose Tattoo*'s Anna Magnani and *I'll Cry Tomorrow*'s Susan Hayward were there, as was *Summertime*'s Katharine Hepburn, who seemed about as excited as her friend Spencer Tracy. When the *Hollywood Reporter* caught up with her in London on the set for her latest movie, a remake of *Ninotchka* entitled *The Iron Petticoat*, co-starring Bob Hope, Hepburn lashed out, "Why am I mean to reporters? Because they ask me things they have no business asking, like why do I wear pants? Being an actress is such a humiliating business anyway, and as you get older it becomes more humiliating because you've got less to sell."

"I'm known a little bit for being a nut."
—Jerry Lewis

Friendly Plugs

When there was no sign of Rosalind Russell on the nominations list, Army Archerd reported, "Roz Russell sez she didn't expect a nomination and doesn't know what all the fuss is about." The non-nominee then talked with Mike Connolly, who told readers, "Roz Russell's dough is on Susan Hayward." When her fourth nomination was official, Hayward used trade-paper ads to show off letters from colleagues applauding her performance. Producer Lawrence Weingarten was among her admirers and wrote: "Dear Susan: As one of those closest to you during the filming of *I'll Cry Tomorrow*—I feel I cannot withhold my expression of admiration and respect . . . I wish you every success in the Oscar race." Hayward also got a congratulatory plug from "Duke" Wayne and Dick Powell, costar and director, respectively, of her latest release, *The Conqueror,* in which Wayne played Genghis Khan and Hayward a Tatar princess.

Rosalind Russell was also plugging her *Picnic* costar Arthur O'Connell, who did get nominated in a supporting role. O'Connell received this letter in the trade papers:

> *Good morning Arthur:*
> *With everyone in the country acclaiming you, I want to make it known that I became your fan the day we started working together on* Picnic.
> *Your Oscar nomination is so richly deserved, and come Academy Award night the leader of the cheering section for you will be*
> *Your friend,*
> *Rosalind Russell*

Teenage Tuxedo

The surprise nominee in the Supporting Actor category was seventeen-year-old Sal Mineo as James Dean's fellow outcast in *Rebel Without a Cause*. Although Louella Parsons had deemed him "the teenage acting sensation of the year," nobody had figured that the Academy would act like his swooning fan club. Mike Connolly wrote that when the actor heard the news of his nomination over his television, "he got so excited he knocked over the dining-room table." Mineo immediately hung banners outside his home that read "Congratulations Sal" and sent a "Memo from Mineo" to the trade journals thanking the Academy for the recognition. Columnists paid more attention to him and Army Archerd revealed, ". . . Young Sal Mineo sez he has two ambitions. One, of course, is to win an Oscar, the other, to reach 18 so he won't require a welfare worker on stage." Mike Connolly announced that the nominee was ready to achieve the first ambition: "Sal Mineo got a butch haircut and tux for Oscar night."

Despite Mineo's grooming, the *Daily Variety* poll predicted that Academy voters would cast their ballots for Jack Lemmon in *Mister Roberts* in the Supporting Actor race. There was still lingering resentment over the appearance of stars in the supporting categories, as typified by the letter to the *Hollywood Reporter* by one industryite who wondered "what will become of the many wonderful supporting players who can hope only to qualify in the one category? Like many lovable old spinsters, their chances could surely become fewer as the years go by for that highly coveted Academy Award nomination."

Poll Predictions

The *Variety* poll decreed that a bona fide supporting player would win Best Supporting Actress—Jo Van Fleet as James Dean's mother in *East of Eden*. Van Fleet had left a successful Broadway career and cleaned up in Hollywood in her first year. In addition to her role in *East of Eden,* she supported Anna Magnani in *The Rose Tattoo* and, at age thirty-five, played the mother of Susan Hayward, thirty-seven, in *I'll Cry Tomorrow*.

Anna Magnani was the poll's choice for Best Actress, and the other categories were *Marty* all the way. Tyro Delbert Mann had already collected the Directors Guild Award and Paddy Chayefsky the Writers Guild trophy, so it appeared only a matter of time before Hecht-Lancaster would be claiming the Oscar gold. Mike Connolly reported on the eve of the ceremonies that at least one member of the *Marty* team was planning to enjoy himself: "Win or lose, Oscar nominee Ernest Borgnine is having a catered affair . . . His Saturday soiree, incidentally, is for Borgnine's in-laws, here on their first trip from the East to see him win (they hope!)."

The Big Night

Columnist Radie Harris lamented that at the Century in New York "there was none of the electric excitement of last year" even though several members of the *Marty* contingent were there. The Academy had requested former winner Shirley Booth to add celebrity to the New York end but she sent her regrets, explaining that "a past winner is like a horse brought back from pasture."

Things were livelier in Hollywood. One woman fainted outside the Pantages when there was a mad rush for seats in the bleachers. As two policemen carried the woman into the theater on a stretcher to administer first aid, a gawker remarked, "That's one way of getting in."

Ernest Borgnine and his wife, Rhoda, began the celebrity parade when they arrived at 6:45. A few minutes later Sal Mineo showed up with his mother and the *Hollywood Reporter* found that he "was strictly teenage heartthrob stuff for the bleacherites." Mike Connolly swore that "under the bright lobby lights, the difference in age between Marisa Pavan and her fiancé, Jean-Pierre Aumont, hardly showed. He kissed the bride-to-be before the fans." The columnist was then baffled because "Natalie Wood, Tab Hunter's date, looked like Marisa Pavan what with the Italian haircut and all." Army Archerd explained that "Natalie's crazy new coiffure was done by Tab Hunter." Connolly had no trouble recognizing another Supporting Actress nominee: "Peggy Lee, with Dewey Martin, looked like a strawberry ice cream soda in red dress, pink mink."

Ignoring the *Daily Variety* poll's cloudy outlook, Susan Hayward showed up escorted by the twin sons over whom she was fighting with ex-husband Jess Barker in an ongoing, headline-making custody case. Hayward confessed that her chances didn't look good, especially since she had broken a mirror just the day before. According to Hayward, her maid, Cleo, tried to offset the spell by burying the mirror in the backyard. Feeling sorry for her, one reporter gave Hayward a medal of the Infant of Prague as she entered the theater. Meanwhile, *Marty*'s moneyman Burt Lancaster told reporters, "We're gonna take 'em all."

As expected, the biggest ovation from the fans

Awards Ceremony

MARCH 21, 1956, 7:30 P.M.
THE RKO PANTAGES THEATRE, HOLLYWOOD AND THE NBC CENTURY THEATRE, NEW YORK

Your Hosts:
JERRY LEWIS IN HOLLYWOOD, CLAUDETTE COLBERT AND JOSEPH L. MANKIEWICZ IN NEW YORK
Televised over NBC

Presenters

Documentary Awards . . . . Eleanor Parker
Sound Recording . . . . Sal Mineo
Scientific and Technical Awards . . . . . Mel Ferrer and Claire Trevor
Short Subjects . . . . . Arthur O'Connell, Marisa Pavan and Jo Van Fleet
Art Direction . . . . Peggy Lee and Jack Lemmon
Costume Design . . . . Susan Hayward
Cinematography . . . . Cantinflas (on film)
Special Effects . . . . James Cagney
Foreign Film . . . . Claudette Colbert
Film Editing . . . . Jerry Lewis and Mr. Magoo (on film)
Original Story . . . . Joe Mantell
Screenplay . . . . Anna Magnani (on film)
Story and Screenplay . . . . Ernest Borgnine
Scoring Awards . . . . Frank Sinatra
Director . . . . Jennifer Jones (on film)
Song . . . . Maurice Chevalier
Supporting Actor . . . . Eva Marie Saint
Supporting Actress . . . . Edmond O'Brien
Actor . . . . Grace Kelly
Actress . . . . Marlon Brando (on film)
Picture . . . . Audrey Hepburn (on film)

Performers of Nominated Songs

"I'll Never Stop Loving You" . . . . Jane Powell
"Love Is a Many-Splendored Thing" . . . . Eddie Fisher
"Something's Gotta Give" . . . . Maurice Chevalier
"(Love Is) the Tender Trap" . . . . Dean Martin
"Unchained Melody" . . . . Harry Belafonte and Millard Thomas

"I had done an outstanding job and, in my estimation, the competition was very slim."
—Edith Head

was for Grace Kelly. On the morning of the Awards, the *Hollywood Reporter* remarked, "Grace Kelly, no nominee she, is nonetheless The Star of tonight's big do and don't doubt it for a second. There isn't a correspondent who hasn't begged, pleaded and/or demanded an interview, a photo, even a lock of her golden hair!"

Although Kelly got most of the attention, the bride-to-be didn't get the last laugh. As *Daily Variety* reported, "Just before 7:30 deadline time, Kim Novak proved to be the last of the star arrivals. An overhead light in the outer foyer exploded, shattering glass on the people below. Some wondered aloud if the explosion was tied to Miss Novak's arrival."

The television program began with a shot of Tony Curtis and wife Janet Leigh climbing out of an Oldsmobile outside the Pantages. As the camera gazed at guests making their entrances, Mel Ferrer announced, "You may be wondering what you're looking at—this is working Hollywood."

Academy President George Seaton walked out onstage to give a brief valedictory. He observed that "screens have become wider and wider" and "each nominated picture was shot in the actual locale." He then introduced "a young comedian I have always enjoyed. In the last twenty-four hours, I've learned to respect him."

Jerry Lewis was said comedian and he welcomed the audience to "our live television performance of *I'll Cry Tomorrow*." He explained that although he was not with his usual performing partner Dean Martin at the moment, "last night at the roulette wheel, he arranged it so we'll be in Las Vegas for another five years." Lewis said he had been given the emcee duties because the Academy couldn't locate Bob Hope—"he was at home."

Lewis then directed attention to the New York wing, and said hello to East Coast emcees Claudette Colbert and Joseph L. Mankiewicz, who told him, "We're amazed at the dignity with which you have conducted yourself so far." Jerry feigned hurt feelings and responded, "Amazed, Mr. Mankiewicz? The character with which I have been identified, that of a raucous buffoon, is merely a studied portrayal. In natural life, I am quite the antithesis. For your edification, when it comes to dignity, deportment and composure, I'll make a slob out of Ronald Colman." When Colbert laughed uproariously, Jerry rolled his eyes and cracked, "Keep laughing like that, honey."

After *Interrupted Melody* Best Actress nominee Eleanor Parker handed Documentary Oscars to one of Walt Disney's wildlife teams, she exited holding a surplus statuette. "Stop Eleanor!" screamed Lewis. "She has a hot award on her hands!" Jerry got more laughs at the conclusion of a two-minute-and-forty-five-second Oldsmobile commercial when he quipped, "And now, a brief word from the Academy."

Susan Hayward gave the Black-and-White Costume Design Award to her own movie. From the audience, Edith Head had to watch the woman chosen over her to design Grace Kelly's wedding gown claim another victory. Winner Helen Rose brought her pocketbook with her to the stage, just as Grace Kelly had the previous year, and thanked Hayward "for being so beautiful, which helps a lot."

Rose and Head were up for the Color Costume Award as well, Rose for *Interrupted Melody* and Head for designing Kelly's threads in *To Catch a Thief*. Head wrote in her memoirs, "I had done an outstanding job and, in my estimation, the competition was very slim." The Color Costume winner was Charles LeMaire for *Love Is a Many-Splendored Thing*. Head's reaction: "Charles LeMaire is a good friend of mine and I would tell him to his face that his designs were blah compared to my gowns. All the costumes Jennifer Jones wore were Chinese cheong sams, the traditional Chinese dress, which could have been purchased in Chinatown if Charles had wanted to. That loss was the single greatest disappointment of my costume-design career."

After *Love Me or Leave Me* Best Actor nominee James Cagney gave the Special Effects Award to Grace Kelly's *The Bridges at Toko-Ri,* he and Jerry engaged in a bit of repartee. Commenting on Cagney's nominated role as a wife-beater, Lewis

"They're dull, dreary, deadly, draggy, and they make us look like bums."
—Mike Connolly

asked in a plaintive, little-boy voice, "Why were you so mean to Doris Day? Joan Crawford, yeah, Doris Day, no." Jerry followed this with a you-dirty-rat Cagney imitation. Cagney provided the climax: he exited screaming, "I like it! I like it!"—in perfect imitation of Jerry Lewis.

Marty Supporting Actor nominee Joe Mantell was introduced by Lewis as "an actor's actor" before he gave the Motion Picture Story Award to *Love Me or Leave Me*. On film from Rome to read the nominees for the Screenplay Oscar was Anna Magnani, standing on a sound stage filled with statuary. Claudette Colbert revealed that the winner, in New York, was Paddy Chayefsky for *Marty*. After a long ovation, winner Chayefsky said, "I'm just really proud, thanks very much."

Marty's star, Ernest Borgnine, was up next, in Hollywood, revealing that *Interrupted Melody* had won Story and Screenplay—which didn't sit well with Army Archerd. The columnist wanted to know how the screenplay qualified as an original story when it was based on someone's autobiography. When MGM said the winning screenplay was not based on the book, Archerd exclaimed, "Aw, c'mon already!" Borgnine loitered onstage as the controversial winners walked away. Lewis returned to join him and they stood about idly. Finally, Jerry said to Ernie, "Well, whaddya feel like doing tonight?" Ernie said, "I don't know. Whaddya feel like doing?"

Frank Sinatra gave the Scoring Awards. When he mentioned his friend Alfred Newman as a nominee, Sinatra casually remarked, "There's old Pappy." Sinatra let out a brief cheer when Pappy won for *Love Is a Many-Splendored Thing*. The film's star, Jennifer Jones, was seen on film a few minutes later, sitting in a director's chair in London as a prelude to Best Director. The winner, in New York, was *Marty*'s Delbert Mann.

Eva Marie Saint, who went unnoticed by the bleacher crowds this year, announced that Jack Lemmon was the Best Supporting Actor for *Mister Roberts*. Lemmon had accidentally put his hand in a bucket of paint while posing for photographers outside the Pantages, but he was all cleaned up by the time he raced to the stage to gather his award. Edmond O'Brien appeared to name Jo Van Fleet Best Supporting Actress for *East of Eden*. The actress made her acceptance speech, walked backstage and sighed, "I could never go through this again." As soon as she realized she had lost, Peggy Lee left for her show at the Coconut Grove.

Grace Kelly, carrying a smaller pocketbook than she had the year before, made her big entrance to announce Best Actor. The winner was Ernest Borgnine for *Marty*. Borgnine kissed his wife, and, on his way to the stage, handed something to Jerry Lewis. At the podium he said, "At the risk of sounding repetitious, I just want to thank my mother for giving me the idea of going in and doing this . . . my pop for being steadfast and my lovely wife for helping me." Borgnine's mother was deceased, reporters revealed the next day.

The winner walked off and presenter Kelly remained onstage. Lewis first explained that Borgnine had handed him "$1.41 in a sock. We had a bet and he lost." Then Jerry got serious and turned to Grace. "I'm known a little bit for being a nut," he began. "It's the wish of the entire industry that you always have good health, good luck and a good life." After taking in the warm applause, Kelly peppily ran offstage. Jerry turned to the audience and said wistfully, "Now, if she'd only start chasing me."

After footage of Marlon Brando reading the Best Actress nominations from Manila, Jerry Lewis revealed the winner—Anna Magnani. An awed Marisa Pavan walked to the stage to accept for her *Rose Tattoo* costar, but when she got to the microphones, she laughed, "I prepared a speech, but I can't remember a word." Jerry reassured the youngster, "Don't worry, Dean has the same problem."

Audrey Hepburn, on film from London, heralded the Best Picture Award and told Lewis, "The Board of Governors asked me to give you this." She blew a kiss into the camera and Jerry remarked, "I can't wait to get home and see if it fits on the mantel." The winner was, of course,

"We're going to take 'em all!"
—Burt Lancaster

Marty, and producer Harold Hecht sounded as if he were running for political office: "It's very fortunate to live in a country where any man, no matter how humble his origins, can become president, and to be part of an industry where any picture, no matter how low its budget, can win an Oscar."

The show ended with Jerry Lewis reiterating the industry's slogan, "movies are better than ever." In New York, Claudette Colbert said goodbye and then added, "And congratulations to you, Jerry, you're the cutest."

Aftermath

Hecht-Lancaster spent another fortune on their post-Awards party and again received rave reviews. Army Archerd said the producers "coulda won another award Wednesday night for the best party of the season." Among the party highlights was Kim Novak, who according to Mike Connolly, "had a workout trying to keep her backless and almost-frontless dress up." Ernest Borgnine did the rumba with his mother-in-law while Harold Hecht was busy leading the orchestra and singing the *Marty* theme song until three in the morning.

In New York, *Marty* author Paddy Chayefsky wasn't as carefree. At the post-ceremony supper party, Chayefsky told reporters, "I would have been disappointed if I hadn't won. I believe *Marty* was the year's best." Then the Oscar winner refused to pose with Jayne Mansfield, Tina Louise or Monique Van Vooren, commenting, "That's not my kind of publicity." *Marty*'s director Delbert Mann had no such qualms and smiled along with Mansfield, who was currently appearing on Broadway in *Will Success Spoil Rock Hunter?*

Mike Connolly said that loser Susan Hayward "busted loose with a bang-up brawl, too, at her home in Van Nuys." Hedda Hopper was one of Hayward's guests, and she wrote: "Susan Hayward would never give a better performance in her life than she did when the Oscar went to Anna Magnani. Susan sang song after song and was the gayest of the few friends who gathered at her home." Telling reporters "I'll have to try harder next year," Hayward shrugged off any suggestion of ill will toward the winner. "It's not hard losing to a champ like Magnani," she said.

With the Best Actress out of town, many columnists concentrated on the final hours of Grace Kelly in Hollywood. The *Hollywood Reporter* had her post-ceremonies agenda: "Grace Kelly got home from George Seaton's Oscar party at 1 A.M., packed, got to bed at 3:30, got up at 5:30 after only two hours' sleep, packed some more, left the house at 8—looking gorgeous!—planed to New York at 9."

Before she left, Kelly did find time to fire off a thank-you note to Jerry Lewis for his kind words. The comedian was nearly as mobile as the bride-to-be that evening. According to the *Hollywood Reporter*, he flew back to Las Vegas at 2 A.M., stayed up all night waiting for the newspaper reviews of the telecast, and then at 10 A.M. "put in person-to-person 'thank-you' calls to every critic in Hollywood."

The critics adored Lewis. *Daily Variety* said, "It was a triumphant evening for Hollywood's emcee, who gagged and quipped with presenters and made it an evening of high carnival. It was a romp and gave the New York end a funereal air by comparison." One of Lewis' most celebrated bits was not seen by the television audience: during one of the Oldsmobile commercials, Jerry walked offstage, returned with a chair, and sat and yawned until the promo was over. The television reviewers saved all their unkind remarks for Oldsmobile and took the company to task for their unimaginative ads. "They're dull, dreary, deadly, draggy, and they make us look like bums," Mike Connolly growled.

The Oscar gave the Ernest Borgnine career a giant boost—he became one of the most sought-after character actors in town—but Borgnine learned that even fairy tales have to come to an end. He later sued Hecht-Lancaster to get out of what he considered an unfair contract, telling the press, "When I came out here, I was a green bumpkin. I put all my faith in the people I knew.

I expected them to do the same thing in return. But I was disappointed." He also grew disappointed with the "lovely wife" of his acceptance speech—he and the former Rhoda Kemins were divorced in 1958. Borgnine later told his third wife of thirty-eight days, Ethel Merman, what happened to his first marriage. "I won the Oscar, but Rhoda started wearing the dark glasses."

Jack Lemmon's story ended differently. Despite the "supporting" status of his Award, he was well on his way to a durable career as a leading man. A week after the ceremonies, the *Hollywood Reporter* spotted the thirty-one-year-old actor driving down Sunset Boulevard in a red Thunderbird with the Oscar in the front seat.

1956

"The kid's great."
—Mike Todd on Elizabeth Taylor

A huckster took the top honors at the 1956 Academy Awards, but a fallen woman stole the show.

Hollywood thought it had seen everything in terms of publicity—until Mike Todd came along. Todd, the Broadway impresario described by drama critic John Chapman as having "the soul of a pitchman and the ambition of a Napoleon," got his first taste of motion pictures as one of the original backers of Cinerama and the developer of his own wide-screen process called Todd-AO. His appetite sufficiently whetted, he announced that his first film would be an all-star, multimillion-dollar version of Jules Verne's *Around the World in 80 Days*.

Few thought Todd could succeed with his grandiose project, into which he sank mostly his own dough. "He fast-talked the men, sweet-talked the women, and conned them all into believing that only a top name could afford to take alphabetical billing," explained a production assistant when asked how Todd had lured the likes of Frank Sinatra, Marlene Dietrich and Noel Coward to take bit parts that Todd dubbed "cameos." Soon, being asked to participate in the movie became a Hollywood status symbol. During the on-location shooting, Todd kept himself in Hollywood's eye through trade-paper ads telling what was happening on the set, such as "cameo star" Peter Lorre's birthday party.

From the publicity it may have seemed like a lark, but Todd was a hard taskmaster. Gregory Peck got his walking papers for not taking his cameo as a cavalry officer seriously enough and director John Farrow was fired the very first day of shooting because Todd thought he took too long to set up the cameras. The producer also balked at giving Farrow and James Poe credit for the screenplay. Todd decided it would be more impressive for the script to be credited solely to humorist S. J. Perelman, and Todd had to be hauled down to a Writers Guild arbitration meeting before the other names were put in the credits.

When the three-hour movie, with a prologue narrated by Edward R. Murrow, was ready for release, Todd warned theater owners: "Do not refer to *Around the World in 80 Days* as a movie. It's not a movie. Movies are something you can see in your neighborhood theater and eat popcorn while you're watching them." Instead, exhibitors were to show the film "almost exactly as you would present a Broadway show in your theater."

If they were at a loss as how to do this, not to worry—Todd sent a manual to each theater, detailing how to organize reserved seating, raise ticket prices and schedule showings on a two-a-day basis. Taking no chances, Todd ordered managers to remove illuminated clocks near the screen, rip out undesirable seats and ban all refreshments, especially the dreaded popcorn. To complete the experience, moviegoers received programs, similar to the playbills at legitimate theaters, which listed the show's credits and "accomplishments," e.g., "Most species of animals photographed in their natural habitat."

Is It Art?

Reviewing the film in the *Saturday Review*, Hollis Alpert wrote:

> *Is it a movie? Is it art? Good Lord, these questions will have to wait until there is time for sober reflection. What it does seem to be without question is a good show—replete with high and low comedy, circus attractions, spectacles of various sorts, a great deal of attractive scenery and scores of familiar personalities.*

The *New York World-Telegram* was more direct: "There is only one proper summary of *Around the World in 80 Days:* Just one long loud Wheee-ee-ee!"

The movie racked up record grosses and, at the conclusion of its sixteen-month run at New

Overleaf: *Tyro producer Mike Todd holds the spoils of success: an Oscar and wife Elizabeth Taylor.*

"Cecil B. DeMille is to motion pictures what Winston Churchill is to statesmanship."
—Boston Herald

York's Rivoli Theatre, the management claimed that not once during the entire engagement was there an empty seat in the house. Todd had clearly shown Hollywood a thing or two about showmanship, and to make every red-blooded producer even more green with envy, he married twenty-five-year-old Elizabeth Taylor, half his age, a few months after the film's premiere.

Small Potatoes

Elizabeth Taylor, too, had an epic in 1956—George Stevens' *Giant,* based on Edna Ferber's three-decade saga about a Texas oil dynasty. Whereas Mike Todd reveled in the vastness of his project, Stevens was almost apologetic about his three-hour-eighteen-minute film. "The title embarrassed us when shooting," he told the press. "It's not a big film. It is interested in small things, smaller than usual because the background is so vast." But the critics agreed with the *New York Times'* Bosley Crowther, who called *Giant* "a heap of a film." One reviewer found it so big that it was "numbing at times."

Giant stood tall at the box office, too, and helped to establish Rock Hudson, playing Taylor's screen husband, as the number-one box-office attraction. After years of playing leading men in Universal's "women's pictures," Hudson finally earned notices as an actor; *Cue* magazine's reviewer found "new and unsuspected talent" in him. *Giant* also contained the last performance by James Dean, who had clashed with director Stevens. "I'll never work with him again," Stevens had said to a colleague during filming. But, by the time Dean had been killed in a car accident shortly after the film was completed, Stevens was telling reporters, "Dean is extraordinary. The film will be a real credit to him." Hedda Hopper was at it again and demanded that the Academy bequeath a special posthumous Oscar to Dean. This time she tried to convince the Academy by pointing out that Warner Brothers could mount the Oscar on a granite shaft over Dean's grave.

King Wants a Crack

The success of *Giant* fazed director King Vidor, who had adapted an even bigger novel, Leo Tolstoi's *War and Peace,* starring Audrey Hepburn and Henry Fonda. The advertising for the film promised: "It all flashes by in all too short three hours and 28 minutes . . . you'll wish there were more." This leviathan made some money, too, but Vidor said wistfully, "I wish Stevens would hold *Giant* back a year so I can have a crack at an Oscar."

Shall We Dance

Twentieth Century–Fox entered the advanced-price arena with its lavish adaptation of the Broadway musical *The King and I,* which, running a little over two hours, was practically a short subject next to the other releases. The studio imported Yul Brynner from Broadway to recreate his role as the king, and the bald-headed, bare-chested actor became an immediate sex symbol. Deborah Kerr, her singing dubbed by Marni Nixon, received high marks for her musical-comedy turn, which contrasted nicely with her dramatic performance in *Tea and Sympathy,* also released in 1956.

God's High Purpose

The biggest blockbuster of them all, however, was Cecil B. DeMille's *The Ten Commandments,* his first movie since the Oscar-winning *The Greatest Show on Earth.* Clocking in at three hours and forty minutes, it not only superseded all other films at the box office that year, it settled comfortably right behind *Gone With the Wind* on the list of all-time box-office champs. It also had the endorsement of the Los Angeles City Council, which unanimously passed a resolution that "*The Ten Commandments* will bring happiness to millions for years to come and everlasting inspiration for the whole family."

"American audiences have never forgiven Miss Bergman and she will not be received at the box office."
—Spyros Skouras, president of 20th Century–Fox

Paramount jumped into its Oscar campaign for the biblical spectacular with religious fervor. The studio's most elaborate ad in the trades was a ten-page booklet, bound like a Bible, which listed the glowing reactions of people from all walks of life. Hollywood was represented by Sheilah Graham's admission, "My daughter and I wept." The press was typified by the *Boston Herald*'s editorial proclaiming "Cecil B. DeMille is to motion pictures what Winston Churchill is to statesmanship." A housewife named Mrs. George E. Peters stated flatly, "Loving the Bible, the viewing of your ultimate production convinced me more than ever of the high purpose of mankind's Creator."

Thumb Sucker

Another of *The Ten Commandments*' supporters was New York's Cardinal Spellman, who held Cecil B. DeMille in much higher esteem than he did Tennessee Williams. Williams' latest affront to conventional mores was *Baby Doll,* a comedy about the attempted deflowering of a child bride by her husband's business rival. The cardinal didn't get the joke, and attacked the film from his pulpit at St. Patrick's Cathedral by drawing a parallel to the recent Russian invasion of Hungary.

Warners might as well have put Cardinal Spellman on the payroll for all of the publicity he generated. *Baby Doll* and its poster featuring twenty-five-year-old Carroll Baker seductively sucking her thumb inspired so much talk that even the reclusive Norma Shearer was glimpsed among the six-hundred Academy members turned away from the film's first Hollywood preview. As the movie's star, Karl Malden, told friends, "We've got to do something to get people away from TV." Warners had already hit paydirt in 1956 by slapping a "Recommended for Adults Only!" caveat on its adaptation of the Broadway play *The Bad Seed*, a thriller about a little girl who kills people because of her bad genes.

The Priceless Plum

The most heated discussions in Hollywood, however, centered not on big budgets, long movies or sex on the screen, but on a movie star of the 1940s—Ingrid Bergman.

Since leaving Hollywood in 1949, Bergman had been considered anathema by Hollywood producers because of her headline-making affair with Italian director Roberto Rossellini. By conceiving a child out of wedlock, Bergman had invoked the wrath of church groups and even had her name read into the *Congressional Record* as "a powerful influence for evil."

When director Anatole Litvak told Fox that he wanted Bergman to star in *Anastasia*—an "Is she or isn't she?" drama about a woman claiming to be the long-lost daughter of Russian Czar Nicholas II—the studio's New York head, Spyros Skouras, said absolutely not because "American audiences have never forgiven Miss Bergman and she will not be received at the box office." But the West Coast boys felt differently—Darryl Zanuck, now an independent producer at Fox, snapped to Skouras, "The Bergman case was inflated and publicized out of all proportion," and Bergman, eager to return to American films, signed to make *Anastasia,* despite Rossellini's view that the script was "junk."

The suspense over Litvak's gamble mounted when Ed Sullivan announced on his television show that he had visited the *Anastasia* set in England, had taken movies of "that great Swedish star" and was considering inviting her on his show. Noting that she was a "controversial figure," Sullivan asked his viewers to write in their opinion on whether "seven and a half years for penance" was enough. The response was 2,500 letters of approval against 1,500 of disapproval, but the harshest votes were cast against Sullivan himself. The *Hollywood Reporter* fumed, "We think Ed Sullivan went off the deep end" and criticized the host for not having the good taste to realize that if the public's response had been negative, it

"We've got to do something to get people away from TV."
—Karl Malden

would have been "quite disastrous to Fox's $3 million investment."

The December premiere of *Anastasia* was the hottest ticket of the year and the Hollywood audience burst into applause when "Starring Ingrid Bergman" flashed on the screen. Archer Winsten, writing in the *New York Post,* was similarly adulatory: "*Anastasia* is a royal pudding of grand quality and Ingrid Bergman is the priceless plum in it." The New York Film Critics named her Best Actress of the year and Bergman flew into New York for thirty-six hours to pick up the citation at the critics' annual dinner, where she was mobbed by the press and the public. *Anastasia* turned out to be one of the year's biggest moneymakers, and Ingrid Bergman had the inside track on the Best Actress Oscar.

The Nominations

Deborah Kerr won her third Best Actress nomination, for *The King and I,* and Katharine Hepburn her seventh, for *The Rainmaker*. The heroines of Warner Brothers' two "adults only" dramas also scored with the voters—Best Actress nominees Nancy Kelly of *The Bad Seed* and Carroll Baker of *Baby Doll*. But the biggest news was Ingrid Bergman's fifth nomination, leading Hedda Hopper, who had written reams on the Rossellini scandal, to declare that she hoped "that *Anastasia* will end the campaign of vilification against her."

There wasn't a chance for a small picture like *Marty* or *On the Waterfront* or a medium-sized one like *From Here to Eternity* to romp off with the Best Picture Oscar this year, because every Best Picture nominee was a long-running epic: *Around the World in 80 Days, The Ten Commandments, Giant, The King and I,* and *Friendly Persuasion,* William Wyler's popular two-hour-twenty-minute film about a Quaker family during the Civil War. One of *Friendly Persuasion*'s six nominations was for Adapted Screenplay, but there was no author listed with the nomination. The writer was Michael Wilson, who had been blacklisted ever since pleading the Fifth before the House Un-American Activities Committee in 1952. A week before the nominations were released, the Academy's Board of Governors passed a new rule that anybody who refused to talk to a Congressional committee couldn't get an Oscar. So, instead of Wilson's name, the nomination read "Writer ineligible for nomination under Academy bylaws."

The Academy had not bothered to tell anybody about this new rule until the nominations came out and the Writers Guild was not pleased. When the Academy wouldn't change the rule upon the Guild's protest, the Guild turned around and gave Wilson its award for Best Written American Drama. Speaking at the guild's award dinner, Groucho Marx mocked Hollywood's commiephobia, "Take, for example, *The Ten Commandments,* Original Story by Moses. The producers were forced to keep Moses' name off the writing credits because they found out he had once crossed the Red Sea."

The Big Boo-Boo

A second screenplay nomination brouhaha was dubbed by *Variety* as the "biggest boo-boo in Academy nomination history." Among the nominees for Best Motion Picture Story was *High Society,* although the MGM musical was an adaptation of *The Philadelphia Story* and, thus, wasn't an original story at all. Adding to the confusion was the fact that the nominated writers—Elwood Ullman and Edward Bernds—weren't the guys who had written the musical, either. Investigation revealed that Ullman and Bernds *had* written a film called *High Society* in 1956—only it was a Bowery Boys movie.

The laughter was loud and hard when Steve Broidy, president of Allied Artists, told the press, "This just proves what we've known all along—that the Bowery Boys series couldn't have lasted this long if not for the fine writers." At first, the Academy maintained that the Writers Branch had intended to nominate the Bowery Boys movie, but then Ullman and Bernds sent a telegram to the Board of Governors stating, "Since our nomina-

"I think he'd do well to spend a summer on a ranch."
—Gary Cooper on Anthony Perkins

tion is apparently a case of mistaken identity, we wish to withdraw our names from consideration." The governors breathed a sigh of relief, and one confessed that the board had been worried that "pranksters" might have voted for the Bowery Boys opus as a joke, which would have caused "no end of embarrassment to the Academy." Among the nominees that the Bowery Boys would have been competing against was Jean-Paul Sartre, nominated for the French film, *The Proud and the Beautiful*.

Starry Night

Since the Best Actress race had become a final referendum on welcoming Ingrid Bergman back, the Best Actor contest held more suspense. The New York Film Critics had selected Kirk Douglas for his portrayal of Vincent Van Gogh in *Lust for Life* as their Best Actor and the two-time Oscar loser tried harder this time at bat. Army Archerd reported that, after three years of marriage, "Anne and Kirk Douglas tossed their first Hollywood party—and it was a beaut—on the eve of their departure for Europe and *The Vikings*. Motif to match the Nordic epic decked the tent in the garden."

Yul Brynner was Douglas' biggest threat. In addition to *The King and I,* Brynner played a pharaoh in *The Ten Commandments* and the con man who sets up Ingrid Bergman in *Anastasia*. He followed this hat trick by winning the role of Dimitri in MGM's upcoming film of *The Brothers Karamazov*. In the space of a year, the newcomer had zoomed to the list of top ten box-office stars. "The most exciting male on the screen since Rudolph Valentino," raved *Redbook* and the news services reported that fourteen boys were suspended from a Des Moines, Iowa, high school for shaving their heads to achieve the "Yul Brynner Look." Columnist Art Buchwald asked the new movie star why he had created such a sensation, and Brynner replied, "I'm not of the can-kicking, shovel-carrying, ear-scratching, torn T-shirt school of acting. There are very few real men in the movies these days. Yet being a real man is the most important quality an actor can offer on the screen."

As for the other Best Actor nominees, Laurence Olivier's citation for *Richard III* was a surprise in itself and was ascribed to the fact that the film premiered on TV before it opened in theaters, thereby allowing the members of the Acting Branch to vote for him without having to leave the house to see the movie. James Dean's liability was the same as last year—he was dead. Rock Hudson's problem was that he was Rock Hudson and not taken seriously as an actor.

Scramble in Supporting

Jack Lemmon's success in the Supporting Actor category the previous year did not go unnoticed, and there was a mad scramble among leading players for a position in the lower acting ranks. Charlton Heston was offended and cried, "That's not the purpose of that Academy Award category," but the Screen Actors Guild turned a deaf ear to his proposal to ban stars from the Supporting Awards. Mickey Rooney in *The Bold and the Brave;* Don Murray, as Marilyn Monroe's leading man in *Bus Stop;* and Robert Stack, one of Lauren Bacall's leading men in *Written on the Wind,* denigrated their status on the ballot and were rewarded with nominations.

At the other extreme, Anthony Quinn, onscreen for all of nine minutes as Paul Gauguin in *Lust for Life,* snagged a nod, too. Only twenty-four-year-old Anthony Perkins, playing Gary Cooper's son in *Friendly Persuasion,* had what could be called a conventional supporting part. Perkins had received a studio buildup, including a *Life* cover story that quoted Gary Cooper on the budding star: "I think he'd do well to spend a summer on a ranch. It would toughen him up and he'd learn a lot from another kind of people."

The Supporting Actress heat was led by Dorothy Malone—another supporting nominee who had been billed above the title—for her role as Robert Stack's sister, who pines for Rock Hudson throughout *Written on the Wind*. One trade ad for the actress appeared with the disclaimer: "Miss Malone, who probably won't campaign for herself, is overdue for recognition as an actress who *creates characterizations in depth*. (This ad bought and paid for by friends of Dorothy Malone without her knowledge)."

Thanks for the Groceries

Mike Todd didn't rest when *Around the World in 80 Days* pulled in eight nominations, but continued his exorbitant promotion by running daily ads in the trade journals thanking everybody who worked on the film, from David Niven down to the caterer. Jules Verne was saluted for "giving me absolutely no trouble on billing or credits." Hedda Hopper reported that Todd was willing to pay for the Academy Awards telecast in order to spare everyone from the Oldsmobile commercials, but, as luck would have it, Todd didn't make his offer until the Academy was already contractually obligated to the car company. Just as well, Hedda pointed out, because personal sponsorship would have meant a disqualification of Todd's film from the Awards.

On the eve of the ceremony, the *Daily Variety* poll predicted *Written on the Wind*'s Robert Stack and Dorothy Malone for the Supporting Awards, Ingrid Bergman for Best Actress, Yul Brynner for Best Actor, George Stevens for Best Director for *Giant* and *Around the World in 80 Days* for Best Picture.

The Big Night

First to arrive at the Hollywood ceremony was Robert Stack and his new wife, Rosemarie. Stack told Mike Connolly that he was wearing the "St. Christopher–Mezuzah medal" that he last wore when he proposed to Rosemarie. Shelley Winters, accompanied by fiancé Anthony Franciosa, bumped her head as she tumbled out of her limousine and moaned, "Everything's gotta happen to me!" Maureen O'Hara was the victim of another of Ralph Edwards' *This Is Your Life* stunts as she approached the Pantages. Mike Connolly recorded, "Last we saw of her they were rushing her down the street and she was weeping."

Both the Pantages and Century theaters in New York had a set boasting a globe on top of a reel of film (as might have been expected, the Hollywood set was one up on New York—the Hollywood globe turned). Academy President George Seaton declared that the set implied that film is "a truly global medium." He added that the makers of this year's nominated Best Pictures roamed the world "not only for new effects but for content as well."

Seaton then introduced the "debonair Mr. Jerry Lewis." The brunt of Lewis' opening monologue was the cost and length of current films: "I didn't see all of *War and Peace,* because the kid in front of me grew up. *War and Peace* cost nine million dollars—that's more than the real war cost. *Giant* cost me three hundred dollars. Three dollars to get in and $297 to pay the baby-sitter." Lewis then introduced Celeste Holm in New York as "a credit to our profession" and the two hosts kissed each other via a split screen.

Once again, the acting nominees dispensed the Awards. First up was *Giant*'s Mercedes McCambridge, who gave a Technical Award to a fog machine and commented, "I bet it's hard to do one of those."

Eleven-year-old Patty McCormack, a Best Supporting Actress nominee for her performance as the murderess in *The Bad Seed,* strolled onstage

Awards Ceremony

MARCH 27, 1957, 7:30 P.M.
THE RKO PANTAGES THEATRE, HOLLYWOOD
AND THE NBC CENTURY THEATRE, NEW YORK

Your Hosts:
JERRY LEWIS IN HOLLYWOOD,
CELESTE HOLM IN NEW YORK
Televised over NBC

Presenters

Scientific and Technical Awards . . . . Mercedes McCambridge and Robert Stack
Documentary Awards . . . Mercedes McCambridge and Robert Stack
One- and Two-Reel Short Subjects . . . . Mickey Rooney
Cartoon . . . . Patty McCormack
Supporting Actor . . . . Nancy Kelly
Sound Recording . . . . Dorothy Malone
Costume Design . . . . Elizabeth Taylor
Special Effects. . . . . Dorothy Dandridge
Film Editing . . . . Kirk Douglas (on film)
Supporting Actress . . . . Jack Lemmon
Art Direction . . . . Marge and Gower Champion
Scoring—Dramatic or Comedy Picture . . . . Eva Marie Saint
Scoring—Musical Picture. . . . . Rock Hudson (on film)
Cinematography . . . . Claire Trevor
Honorary Award to Eddie Cantor . . . . . George Seaton
Jean Hersholt Humanitarian Award . . . . George Seaton
Thalberg Award. . . . . George Seaton
Foreign Film. . . . . George Seaton
Director . . . . Ingrid Bergman (on film)
Writing Awards . . . . Deborah Kerr
Song . . . . Carroll Baker
Actor. . . . . Anna Magnani
Actress. . . . . Ernest Borgnine
Picture. . . . . .Janet Gaynor

Performers of Nominated Songs

"Friendly Persuasion (Thee I Love)" . . . Tommy Sands
"Julie" . . . . Dorothy Dandridge
"True Love" . . . . Bing Crosby (on film)
"Whatever Will Be, Will Be (Que Sera, Sera)" . . . . Gogi Grant
"Written on the Wind" . . . . The Four Aces

"Everything's gotta happen to me!"
—Shelley Winters

with a tiny pocketbook to give the Cartoon Award and to provide Jerry Lewis with a lot of material. "She killed the critics—and most of the cast," the emcee said. "She's got a date with Peter Lorre, this child."

Jo Van Fleet presented the first Acting Award and revealed a major upset for Supporting Actor. Anthony Quinn won for his cameo in *Lust for Life*. Mickey Rooney turned to Robert Stack in the row behind him and said, "We wuz robbed." Quinn told the audience that this, his second Oscar, meant that he had won a fight over himself. He didn't elaborate.

Jerry Lewis said the Costume Design presenter was "the prettiest thing Mike Todd left out of *Around the World in 80 Days*"—Elizabeth Taylor, wearing a $25,000 diamond tiara given her by her husband. The audience laughed along with Liz when she read *Around the World*'s nomination and then watched her behave professionally when the winner turned out to be *The King and I*.

Jack Lemmon named the Best Supporting Actress: *Written on the Wind*'s Dorothy Malone, the night's most loquacious winner. By the time Malone began to thank the "Screen Actors and Screen Extras guilds because we've had a lot of ups and downs together," Jack Lemmon stuck his arm out in front of her and pointed to his watch. Malone and the audience chuckled and then she went right on thanking, "all the crews I've worked with."

Academy President George Seaton returned to give an Honorary Award to Eddie Cantor, who had almost been prevented from accepting it. Unbeknownst to most of the audience, Cantor had passed out in the lobby on the way into the theater. Academy officials were terrified that he had suffered a heart attack, but a quick thinker administered a shot of whiskey and Cantor was back on his feet as if nothing had happened.

Seaton gave the Thalberg Award to 20th Century–Fox's head of production, Buddy Adler, who had produced *Bus Stop* and *The Revolt of Mamie Stover* this year, but above all, he was the producer of *Anastasia* and, therefore, responsible for bringing back Ingrid Bergman. He expressed thanks to his predecessor Darryl Zanuck, a three-time Thalberg Award recipient.

For the first time, the Foreign Language Film Award was a competitive rather than an Honorary Award. Federico Fellini's *La Strada*, which starred Hollywood's own Anthony Quinn and Richard Basehart, was the winner. The Award was accepted by the film's producer, Italian mogul Dino DeLaurentiis, who had also produced King Vidor's *War and Peace*, while director Fellini smiled from the audience.

Ingrid Bergman appeared on film on a rooftop in Paris to introduce the Best Director Award. When she miscalled the Pantages "the Pantage Theatre," Jerry Lewis couldn't resist saying, "May I have the envelope plea?" Winner George Stevens for *Giant* stumbled on the stairs to the stage and then said, "The director's chair is a wonderful place to see the film."

Deborah Kerr, wearing what a columnist described as "two-hundred yards of nude chiffon," floated out to present the writing Awards. Kerr didn't mention the Bowery Boys' *High Society* when she read the nominations for Best Motion Picture Story. The winner was Robert Rich for *The Brave One* and Jesse Lasky, Jr., the vice president of the Writers Guild, accepted for him.

In the other troublesome writing category, Kerr's announcement showed that a rumored drive to honor the blacklisted Michael Wilson's work on *Friendly Persuasion* had fizzled—*Around the World in 80 Days* won the Best Adapted Screenplay Award. Given the credit squabble over the movie, it was appropriate that James Poe accepted for John Farrow and himself in Hollywood—making no acknowledgment of S. J. Perelman—while Perelman's representative accepted in New York.

Perelman's proxy, Hermione Gingold, emerged as the hit of the show. "I'm very proud to accept this objet d'art on behalf of Mr. Perelman," Gingold began imperiously, "who writes: he cannot be here for a variety of reasons, all of them spicy. He is dumbfounded, absolutely flum-

"It just goes to show, give the public what it wants and they'll show up."
—Billy Wilder

moxed. He never expected recognition for writing *Around the World in 80 Days* and in fact did so on the expressed understanding that the film would never be shown. He hopes he will be able to live up to it, or rather, to live it up. And he says, bless you all."

Last year's Best Actress Anna Magnani entered in a chinchilla stole and dark glasses; she evoked a loud ovation. She gave her belated thanks for last year's honor and then named this year's Best Actor—Yul Brynner for *The King and I*. The winner darted to the stage, shook Magnani's hand and then bowed to her. One observer said, "When Yul won, his whole bald head flushed a deep red." "I hope this isn't a mistake," Brynner said, "because I won't give it back for anything in the world." After he and Magnani exited, Jerry Lewis felt his hair uncertainly.

Ernest Borgnine wandered out to present Best Actress and announced, "Ingrid Bergman for *Anastasia*." There were shouts of approval mixed in with the thunderous applause. Cary Grant walked to the stage buttoning his tuxedo and accepted for his former costar. "Dear Ingrid," he said, "if you can hear me or see this, I want you to know we all send you our love and admiration." Bergman did in fact hear Grant—over the radio as she soaked in a bathtub in Paris. Backstage at the Pantages, Yul Brynner "shouted himself hoarse" over the outcome, although he had a conflict of interest since his *King and I* costar Deborah Kerr was among the losers.

Janet Gaynor, introduced by Jerry Lewis as "Jeanette," presented the Best Picture Award. The global motif of the stage setting was an accurate omen and *Around the World in 80 Days* was the victor. Mike Todd jumped out of his seat, started down the aisle, returned to embrace Elizabeth Taylor—nearly choking her—and then sprinted to the stage. At the steps, he stopped short and ascended in a dignified manner, only to break into a mad dash across the stage to the podium. Literally snatching the Oscar from Gaynor, Todd exclaimed, "I'm especially thrilled, this is my first time at bat. I'd like to thank you on behalf of the sixty-odd thousand people who worked on this show." Then the triumphant neophyte held his Oscar aloft as he walked off with a laughing Janet Gaynor.

Aftermath

Posing with the winners afterward, Anna Magnani was asked what kind of fur her chinchilla was. "Italian cat," she replied and then refused to honor a photographer's request that she kiss Yul Brynner's head. Buddy Adler held up his Thalberg Award and discovered it was made of plaster—the Academy hadn't found a bronze one in time for the show. Anthony Quinn said he didn't know if his second Oscar would help his career. "I'm going to be a director," he shouted. Quinn's sole directorial effort would be 1958's *The Buccaneer,* starring Yul Brynner. When he received bad reviews for that film, Brynner said, "In Hollywood, they like you until you're standing on a pedestal and they hand you an Oscar. Then they say, 'How did he get up there—let's knock him down.' "

Mike Todd couldn't get over his good fortune and muttered, "Imagine this—and being married to Liz, too." When Hedda Hopper inquired about Mrs. Todd's tiara, Todd looked the columnist in the eye and said, "Doesn't every girl have one?" The Todds, joined by friends Eddie Fisher and Debbie Reynolds, repaired to Romanoff's, where the producer interrupted his celebrating to complain that Liz had been cheated out of a nomination for *Giant*. "But it won't happen next year," he predicted, "she'll get it for *Raintree County*. The kid's great."

The trade journals overflowed with items about Todd's extravagant gifts and bets with his friends and employees; for example, he had wagered film editor Gene Ruggiero a thousand dollars against a box of cigars that Ruggiero would win the Editing Award—he did. The producer also placed a four-page ad thanking, alphabetically, the entire voting membership of the Academy, with the postscript, "If there are one or two of you who did

"They have a strange code of morals and ethics in Hollywood . . . they deserve all of the criticism they receive."
—Las Vegas Review Journal

not vote for us—thanks anyway—we're very mellow today."

This was the last Academy Awards ceremony that Louis B. Mayer attended, and the man who had dreamed up the organization in the first place had to make several phone calls before he could locate a pair of tickets. When the deposed head of MGM died later in 1957, his funeral was SRO, inspiring Billy Wilder to crack, "It just goes to show, give the public what it wants and they'll show up."

The television critics were growing more and more impatient with the lengthy commercials—which the Oldsmobile people referred to as "intermissions"—but according to Louella Parsons, the general feeling was "the obvious relief, including mine, that *Baby Doll* didn't win anything." Most reviewers raved about the warmth that Ingrid Bergman's victory radiated and MGM, deciding that the scandal was officially over, announced its plans to re-release *Gaslight,* its own Bergman Oscar winner, the week after the show. Nevertheless, Bergman hadn't won over everybody, especially not the *Las Vegas Review Journal,* which editorialized:

> *She is still Ingrid Bergman, the woman who so forgot her moral obligation to her family and her public to leave it all behind for a love tryst with Roberto Rossellini in Italy.*
>
> *The very fact that the Academy even considered Ingrid Bergman for an Oscar indicates the thinking of the so-called "better people" of Hollywood. They have a strange code of morals and ethics in Hollywood and their vision is so narrow that they deserve all of the criticism they receive.*

Any lingering indignation over Ingrid Bergman was nothing, however, compared to the confusion, controversy and antagonism that erupted as Hollywood began to realize that Robert Rich, the winner of the Best Motion Picture Story Award for *The Brave One,* didn't really exist. The Academy had been tricked. After all that effort to keep the blacklisted Michael Wilson out of the running, who should win an Oscar under a pseudonym but Dalton Trumbo, one of the original Hollywood Ten.

The Academy was also reminded of another embarrassment when Allied Artists screened the rushes of *Spook Chasers,* the newest Bowery Boys movie. One of the movie's stars, Huntz "Sach" Hall, quipped, "I think we've got another Academy Award nominee in this one."

1957

"Everyone knows the luster of the Academy Awards has been dimmed over the years, but until Joanne Woodward, no one in the movie colony ever made a public announcement about it."

—Joe Hyams

Death stalked the 1957 Academy Awards.

The Oscar race began in December when the studios released their major Academy candidates in a cinematic season that had Hollywoodites hopping from premiere to premiere. Louella Parsons was out of breath by January and sighed, "I have seen so many fine pictures these least few weeks that when voting comes around for the Academy Awards, it will be difficult to make decisions."

After the hoopla over the premieres subsided, Oscar pundits sorted out the Christmas releases and established the prime contenders. Twentieth Century–Fox was in the running with its two-hour-and-thirty-seven-minute adaptation of *Peyton Place,* the bestseller that had been thought too trashy to be filmed tastefully. Producer Jerry Wald licked that problem by casting Lana Turner and a crew of young, clean-scrubbed newcomers—including David Nelson of TV's *Ozzie and Harriet*—and filling the film with widescreen vistas of the New England countryside. Jack Moffitt, in his "Talking Shop" column in the *Hollywood Reporter* commented, "I think the whole industry can profit from a certain skill which Jerry Wald has exhibited . . . smut is still smut and Jerry is vigilant to avoid it. There was plenty of sophomoric sex in the scene where Lana Turner walked in on a necking party, but its shock value lay in the fact that it was a normal thing parents never get used to." Shock value translated into a box-office bonanza; when a Beverly Hills theater reported it had to turn away 900 people one rainy Saturday night, the *Hollywood Reporter* asked, "Who says the picture business is dead? Only some pictures are."

Newlyweds Paul Newman and Best Actress winner Joanne Woodward respond to the congratulatory orchid from Best Actress loser and new widow Elizabeth Taylor.

Still Pygmies

Interracial sex was the theme of Warners' *Sayonara,* a two-and-a-half-hour adaptation of James Michener's novel about the romance between an American soldier (Marlon Brando) and a Japanese entertainer (Miiko Taka). Going all out for the premiere, Warner Brothers turned its studio into a Japanese village complete with lanterns and Southern California natives of Japanese ancestry as hostesses. "Only stars and press are invited," informed the trades, and the stellar guests saw the movie in various screening rooms instead of in one auditorium. Evidently they liked what they saw because soon the producers were receiving congratulatory letters—via the trade journals—from Hollywood stalwarts Jack Benny, Cecil B. DeMille, Fred Astaire and Frank Capra, who wrote that it is "the kind of motion picture that proves to us what all secretly know—that the medium is terrific but that those of us who use it are still pygmies."

Another December contestant was Billy Wilder's adaptation of Agatha Christie's courtroom mystery *Witness for the Prosecution,* starring Charles Laughton, Tyrone Power, Marlene Dietrich and Elsa Lanchester. Since Warners had already used up the Hollywood social directory in ads plugging *Sayonara,* United Artists began quoting New York celebrities like Bennett Cerf, Oscar Hammerstein II, Moss Hart and Billy Rose, who said, "If there were more movies like it, I'd see more movies." *Witness* got publicity even farther east when it was chosen for a command performance in London and producer Arthur Hornblow, Jr., made the Royal Family sign pledges that they would not divulge the film's surprise ending to the Commonwealth.

"I'll Kwai Tomorrow"

Independent producer Sam Spiegel was back in action after his Academy triumph in 1954 with

"I never understood the part until I saw Guinness play it."
—Charles Laughton

On the Waterfront, and this time Columbia's Harry Cohn was all too happy to distribute his latest—the two-hour-forty-minute *The Bridge on the River Kwai.* Supreme Court Chief Justice Earl Warren attended the premiere, and afterward Spiegel threw a dinner party on a Manhattan rooftop for a thousand of his friends who, according to columnist Radie Harris, "all seemed to know each other." A highlight of the party was reading the film's good notices from the New York critics. "There will be no 'I'll Kwai Tomorrow' with these reviews," Harris predicted, and she was right. The *New York Post*'s Archer Winsten wrote: "*The Bridge on the River Kwai* is a long picture that moves with such intensity of feeling and reality on its Japanese prison camp adventure that it seems to have been short."

When *The Bridge on the River Kwai* began winning film critics awards right and left, the producers of *Twelve Angry Men,* a courtroom drama that had drawn critical acclaim earlier in the year, had to resort to also-ran tactics in their campaign ads. "Second Best Film of the Year—New York Film Critics," bragged their promos, which also saluted the film's debuting director, Sidney Lumet, for being the Critics' "Runner-up for Best Director."

The Long Arm of Coincidence

Alec Guinness, as the stiff-upper-lipped British commander in *Bridge,* seemed to win the Best Actor award from every critical group, and the actor, previously best known in the U.S. only to art-house audiences, became an American cover boy. *Life* called him "Alec the Great," *Time* ran him on the cover the week of the Oscar ceremonies, and the *Saturday Evening Post* alerted readers to a forthcoming profile with the teaser, "Learn about the psychological problem he had as a boy that may be responsible for making him an actor!"

Hollywood insiders laughed over the fact that *Witness for the Prosecution*'s Charles Laughton had originally been signed for Guinness' role in *Bridge* but bowed out due to illness. "This 'illness' later turned out to be a disguise for Laughton's desire to direct and star in a Broadway revival of *Major Barbara,*" Radie Harris reported. "So, now, by the long arm of coincidence, which is always working overtime in Hollywood, it's very conceivable that Alec may well be Laughton's No. 1 opponent in the Oscar sweepstakes." Laughton, typically indifferent to the Academy, campaigned for his opponent by telling people, "I never understood the part until I saw Guinness play it."

Guinness nevertheless had to contend with home-grown competition for the Academy's Best Actor trophy. Marlon Brando, for one, was looking more and more respectable—*Sayonara* had returned him to the list of top box-office stars, and the screen rebel was now a married man. By Oscar campaigning time, though, the Brandos were regulars in the gossip columns. Mike Connolly related, "Anna Kashfi Brando is discovering Marlon meant it when he said he wanted to be a bachelor on weekends. Except the weekends are stretching into weeks! Brando's visits to his bride have dropped to once every week or ten days and then only for a few hours. Anna, accordingly, is looking for a smaller place to roll around in until the baby arrives."

Brando's costar from 1952's *Viva Zapata!,* two-time Supporting Actor Oscar winner Anthony Quinn, had progresssed to a starring role opposite Anna Magnani in *Wild Is the Wind,* which opened in December. Quinn mounted a campaign that revolved around how cooperative his directors thought he was. *Wind*'s George Cukor verified that "he is a truly creative actor whose performance enriches any script he plays," and Federico Fellini, who had helmed Quinn in *La Strada* said, "He is the kind of actor who enables a director to make a great picture."

Tony's Titanic Snub

Quinn's romantic rival in *Wild Is the Wind* was Anthony Franciosa, who made a splash his first year in films with four hits: he recreated his Broadway success as a drug addict's put-upon brother in

"The medium is terrific but those of us who use it are still pygmies."
—Frank Capra

A Hatful of Rain, played a wolf in the romantic comedy *This Could Be the Night*, and a ruthless agent in Elia Kazan's political drama *A Face in the Crowd*. Like Brando, Franciosa was a gossip columnist's dream because of his marital situation—he was Shelley Winters' third husband. The *Hollywood Reporter* had this: "Oversea Spy-Eye-tem: Shelley's ex, Vittorio Gassman, and Shelley's present, Tony Franciosa, giving each other a titanic snub at the bar in Rome's Titanus Studio."

Franciosa started off 1958 with another hit, *The Long, Hot Summer*, Jerry (*Peyton Place*) Wald's adaptation of three William Faulkner stories costarring another couple making nuptial news—Paul Newman and Joanne Woodward, who wed in Las Vegas on January 29, 1958. Mrs. Newman had become an overnight success in *The Three Faces of Eve* after languishing under contract at Fox for two years. In the showy role of a schizophrenic, Woodward was praised as "the talk of the industry" by the *Hollywood Reporter*, which congratulated producer Nunnally Johnson for going "out on a limb" by casting her and predicted that "she'll probably win an Academy Award as a result."

No Respect

Woodward turned out to be more outspoken than most Oscar hopefuls and, when asked what she thought about winning the Best Actress Award, responded, "If I had an infinite amount of respect for the people who think I gave the greatest performance, then it would matter." Columnist Joe Hyams was impressed and wrote, "Everyone knows the luster of the Academy Awards has been dimmed over the years by commercialism, but until Joanne Woodward came along no one in the movie colony ever made a public announcement about it." Twentieth Century–Fox felt that the luster of the Academy Awards did matter and had its potential nominee do a trade-paper shampoo ad: "Joanne Woodward, beautiful Lustre-Creme girl, says: 'With *my* casual hair style, my hair just *has* to be shining clean and easy to manage.' "

Deborah Kerr, the star of Fox's *Heaven Knows, Mr. Allison*, was easier to manage than Woodward, but if the studio could count on the actress to be respectful toward Oscar, it couldn't rely on her for any self-promotion. With the New York Film Critics Award in her pocket, Kerr set off for Austria to make a movie, asking David Niven to accept the Oscar for her. Paramount got the same message from Anna Magnani, who had been enticed back to the U.S. for *Wild Is the Wind*. Magnani may have declined to campaign, but the theater showing her film seemed intent on sabotaging her chances, too. Producer Hal Wallis had to tell the manager of the Four Star in Los Angeles to stop flashing a subliminal popcorn ad during Magnani's climactic soliloquy.

Crossed Fingers and Machiavellian Mitts

Two other entrants in the Oscar Derby were glamour girls Lana Turner and Elizabeth Taylor. For the first time in their careers, they were considered actresses instead of decorative objects. Turner had been good material for gossip columnists from her "discovery" by the editor of the *Hollywood Reporter* in Schwab's Pharmacy in the '30s through four rocky marriages, and they were rooting for her at Oscar time. A recurring image in the trades was a sketch of a rose, accompanied by a glowing tribute, such as one columnist's comment, "An Oscar would look as good on her as a sweater." She also got "an unsolicited love letter" from *Peyton Place*'s young supporting cast, who wrote: "We were all frankly awed at the prospect of working with a star of your stature but your help and understanding was an incentive and challenge to all of us. Our fingers are crossed."

When Mike Todd wanted to capitalize on wife Elizabeth Taylor's good reviews as a demented Southern belle in *Raintree County*, she told him, as he put it, "to keep my Machiaevellian mitts off her Oscar campaign because she's out to run on merit alone." Despite Todd's alleged restraint, Mike

"Am I wearing too much the clothes?"
—Miyoshi Umeki

Connolly ran an item about a form letter going around town soliciting votes for Elizabeth Taylor.

Out Like Flynn

Like Turner and Taylor, Errol Flynn finally began receiving credit as an actor in 1957. His performance as an alcoholic in *The Sun Also Rises* was the turning point. "Why all the fuss?" the actor said, "After all, I was only playing myself." To prove his point, the bon vivant spent one weekend in January in a Chicago slammer after participating in a barroom brawl. Although prognosticators suggested him as a possibility for a Supporting Actor nomination, 20th Century–Fox listed him as a star, thus making him eligible only in the Best Actor category.

The favorite in the Supporting Actor race was Red Buttons, a former TV comic who couldn't get a job anywhere in show business until José Ferrer recommended the has-been to Joshua Logan for the part of an American sergeant who marries a Japanese woman in *Sayonara*. W. R. Wilkerson was so moved by Buttons' performance as a star-crossed lover that he commented in a front-page *Hollywood Reporter* editorial: "Red might stage such a comeback as did Frankie Boy after his Acad Award performance in *From Here to Eternity*." *Sayonara* made Buttons a hot commodity, and he was portraying a comic sergeant in *Imitation General* by the time Academy members were filling out their nomination ballots.

Japanese Import

As Red Buttons' ill-fated wife, twenty-eight-year-old Miyoshi Umeki became almost a household name. The Japanese-bred singer was discovered performing in San Fernando Valley nightclubs when she landed some television assignments that led to her film debut in *Sayonara*. The success of the movie allowed her to cross the Hollywood Hills and perform her act at the Mocambo. Columnists loved her broken English. At the *Sayonara* premiere, Umeki said to Hugh O'Brian, TV's Waytt Earp, "I think you shoot the gun admirably." And at the Editors Guild Awards, the kimono-clad actress asked a scantily dressed starlet, "Am I wearing too much the clothes?"

Umeki was not under contract to Warners, but Diane Varsi, who played Lana Turner's daughter in *Peyton Place*, had signed with 20th Century–Fox. After sneak-preview audiences indicated that Varsi was their favorite among *Peyton Place*'s group of newcomers, the studio gave the twenty-year-old actress the big buildup. She was a cover girl on *Modern Screen* and a frequent item in the columns whenever she went on a studio-arranged date—"Chummy Chewsome at Chasen's: Diane Varsi and director Curtis Harrington."

A Nympho by Any Other Name

Twenty-seven-year-old Carolyn Jones was gaining a reputation for playing beatniks, and she won acclaim for her five-minute role in Paddy Chayefsky's *The Bachelor Party*. Though her character was billed as "The Existentialist," Jones' trade-paper ads included this rave from Army Archerd: "Carolyn Jones is a stand-out as the nympho." Married to screenwriter Aaron Spelling, Jones oscillated from turns on TV's *Playhouse 90* to supporting roles in movies. Louella Parsons, lauding the actress' performance as Natalie Wood's "dizzy girlfriend" in 1958's *Marjorie Morningstar*, told readers, "Hollywood is talking about the repeated applause that interrupted Carolyn Jones' scenes at the first preview."

The Nominations

The Academy kicked the various Hollywood guilds out of the nominating process and, for the first time since the 1936 Awards, all the electing was done by Academy members alone. Instead of the usual 15,000 people voting, decisions were now being made by a select 1,780. One result of the change was that the Best Picture and Best Di-

"I was happy enough to know the Academy had finally decided to look beyond the glamorous shell."
—Lana Turner

rector nominations corresponded precisely for the first time. The 250 actors nominating this year, down from the 12,639 of yesteryear, obviously adored *Peyton Place,* which received five acting nominations: Lana Turner for Actress, Russ Tamblyn and Arthur Kennedy for Supporting Actor, and Diane Varsi and Hope Lange for Supporting Actress. Turner later wrote in her autobiography, "I didn't expect to win. I was happy enough to know the Academy had finally decided to look beyond the glamorous shell."

The husband-and-wife nominees from *Witness for the Prosecution,* Charles Laughton and Elsa Lanchester, hadn't done the first thing to campaign. And director Billy Wilder laughed at his nomination and later told an interviewer, "To give an Academy Award to a man who directs a play is like giving the removalists who took Michelangelo's *Pietà* from the Vatican to the New York World's Fair a first award in sculpture." The only one not laughing was non-nominee Marlene Dietrich. She had been so sure of a nomination that she began a recording of her current floor show in Las Vegas with the announcement "Ladies and gentlemen, we are proud to present the Academy Award nominee for *Witness for the Prosecution,* Miss Marlene Dietrich!" The introduction was rerecorded.

Cohn with the Wind

With eight nominations, *The Bridge on the River Kwai* loomed as a likely sweep, but its momentum was cut short when the credited author of the screenplay, Pierre Boulle, who had written the novel on which the film was based, accepted the British Academy Award and told the audience that he hadn't written all of the screenplay. Hollywood scuttlebutt had it that the real authors were blacklistees Carl Foreman and Michael Wilson. Producer Sam Spiegel was suddenly everywhere telling people that what Boulle had meant was that director David Lean and Spiegel himself had helped him by doing rewriting on the set. Carl Foreman even sent a cable from England to the trade papers to deny having had anything to do with the movie.

The controversy quieted down with the sudden death of Columbia's Harry Cohn, at age sixty-six. He died of a heart attack while on vacation in late February. His obituary in the *Hollywood Reporter* noted, "At the time of his death, in Cohn's office were lined up forty-five Oscars—mute testimony to the impact of the man on Hollywood's history." *Bridge* was now the sentimental choice and bookies bet that, come March 26, there would be a forty-sixth Oscar for Harry Cohn.

Diamonds Stay Home

Barbara Stanwyck told reporters, "If ever an actress deserved this highest honor, it is Deborah Kerr. And while there are certainly plenty of voters who feel the same way, I am going out and try to do something about it—real, active, door-to-door campaigning, I mean." Elizabeth Taylor, meanwhile, was the subject of daily ads in the trades chronicling her growth as an actress. Starting with her first MGM film appearance at age eleven in *Lassie Come Home,* the series of ads catalogued her entire career, ending with a photograph from 1956's *Giant.* In each ad was a picture of the mature Taylor from *Raintree County.*

Then, four days before the ceremony, Mike Todd took off for New York in his private plan, christened *The Lucky Liz,* to accept the Showman of the Year Award from the Friars Club. He never got there; the plane crashed in New Mexico. The widow Todd was all over the news. Army Archerd wrote, "The Todd-Taylor love story will take its place with the most dramatic and tragic amours of all time . . . Yesterday, Elizabeth Taylor had partially regained her composure, but still could only keep repeating the fact Todd didn't want her to take a chance by flying with a cold!" Taylor canceled her plans to attend the ceremony, and the $6,000 diamond tiara Todd bought for the occasion remained in its box.

The day after Todd's death, producer Don Hartman, the former head of Paramount who had escorted Grace Kelly to the Awards the year she won, dropped dead from a heart attack at age fifty-eight. A definite pall settled over Hollywood.

When columnists weren't eulogizing the recently deceased, they tried to drum up enthusiasm for the Awards by talking about what the women would be wearing. *Peyton Place*'s Jerry Wald was producing this year's Oscar show, and he declared a ban on the latest fashion rage from Paris—sack dresses. Barbara Stanwyck also spoke her mind on this issue: "The woman who spends a fortune on diets, reducing machines and massages and then lets some sad sack slip a shapeless sack over her slim shape should spend it on a psychiatrist instead!" And Mike Connolly advised, "Leave your diamonds home, girls—they glare too much for the telecasts."

For the final time, *Daily Variety* conducted its Oscar poll. The winners were *The Bridge on the River Kwai*, Alec Guinness, Joanne Woodward, and Red Buttons. The paper revealed that the "closest race is in Best Supporting Actress." Elsa Lanchester of *Witness for the Prosecution* won, but by "a very narrow margin." Both *Peyton Place*'s Diane Varsi and *The Bachelor Party*'s Carolyn Jones were close behind.

The Big Night

The first limousine to arrive in front of the Pantages carried Ernest and Rhoda Borgnine, but Clark Gable's cut in, so the King was the first celebrity the fans saw. Miyoshi Umeki appeared in a kimono on the arm of Wyatt Earp himself, Hugh O'Brian. When a reporter asked her onscreen lover, Red Buttons, for a quote, he replied, "Give you a quote? Give me a stomach!" Marlon Brando's plane from New York landed at 6:30 and he put on his tuxedo in his limousine. He did not take his wife to the show. His publicists were worried because Brando was considering—even back then—turning down the Oscar to protest Hollywood's treatment of minorities. The publicists told Brando they'd quit if he did.

Joanne Woodward explained that she had made her green evening gown all by herself and that she had spent seven hours at Fox's makeup department changing her hair from blond to strawberry. Paul Newman confessed he didn't "dig" her new look. Woodward was skeptical of the *Daily Variety* results and said, "Deborah Kerr will win." *Life* felt otherwise and assigned a photographer to cover Mrs. Newman.

The last nominee to arrive was Lana Turner, just back from a vacation in Acapulco with her boyfriend, underworld figure Johnny Stompanato, who, according to Turner's autobiography, had amused himself on the holiday by holding a revolver and warning her "just to remind you I have it and that it's aimed at you." Turner did not invite Mr. Stompanato to the Awards. Instead, her entourage included her mother, her teenage daughter Cheryl Crane, and publicity agent Glenn Rose. "My dress evoked the image of a mermaid, and I almost felt like one," Turner recalled, especially after she lost one of her high heels in the lobby and limped to her seat. Mr. Rose retrieved the slipper.

Academy President George Seaton opened the show with: "The message from the Board of Governors is brief but enchanting," and announced that there would be no commercial interruptions—the industry itself was sponsoring the show. The audience, remembering the Oldsmobile commercials of earlier years, applauded loudly. Seaton added that a pavilion adjacent to

Awards Ceremony

March 26, 1958, 7:30 p.m.
The RKO Pantages Theatre, Hollywood

Your Hosts:
James Stewart, Bob Hope, Rosalind Russell,
David Niven and Jack Lemmon
Televised over NBC

Presenters

Supporting Actor . . . . Lana Turner
Scientific and Technical Awards . . . . Hope Lange and Ronald Reagan
Documentary Awards . . . . Cyd Charisse and Ernest Borgnine
Supporting Actress . . . . Anthony Quinn
Short Subjects . . . . . Jennifer Jones and Rock Hudson
Sound Recording . . . . Dorothy Malone and Van Johnson
Special Effects . . . . June Allyson
Art Direction . . . . . Eva Marie Saint and Gregory Peck
Film Editing . . . Joanne Woodward and Paul Newman
Music Scoring . . . . . Anita Ekberg and Vincent Price
Cinematography . . . . Joan Collins
Foreign Film . . . . . . Dana Wynter and Fred Astaire
Writing Awards . . . . Doris Day and Clark Gable
Costume Design . . . . Wendell Corey and Robert Ryan
Director . . . . Sophia Loren
Actor . . . . Cary Grant
Song . . . . Maurice Chevalier
Actress . . . . John Wayne
Picture . . . . Gary Cooper
Honorary Awards . . . . Bette Davis

Performers of Nominated Songs

"An Affair To Remember" . . . . Vic Damone
"All the Way" . . . . Dean Martin
"April Love" . . . . Ann Blyth, Shirley Jones, Anna Maria Alberghetti, Jimmie Rodgers, Tommy Sands and Tab Hunter
"Tammy" . . . . Debbie Reynolds
"Wild Is the Wind" . . . . Johnny Mathis

"It was rather daring of me, I admit, but after all, there is just so much you can do with women's clothes at an affair like the Academy Awards."
—Rosalind Russell

the theater had been set up for newsmen and the TV audience saw a shot of a journalist drinking a cocktail in the tent. The Academy president also pointed out that, in an effort to streamline the proceedings, presenters would tote their envelopes with them, thus eliminating the time-wasting question, "May I have the envelope, please."

A medley of Oscar-winning songs followed, climaxed by the appearance of Mae West and Rock Hudson in a lascivious rendition of "Baby, It's Cold Outside." The audience got a rise out of Rock's offering Mae a cigarette and saying,"King-sized." Mae's retort: "Ummmmmm, it's not the men in your life, it's the life in your men!" Their duet ended with a long and realistic kiss as the audience clapped and howled like the Saturday night crowd at Minsky's. When the sixty-five-year-old West wiggled out afterward to the press pavilion, she was asked how she kept her figure. "Dumbbells, dear," she said, "and a daily one-mile walk on the sands of Santa Monica."

The first of the evening's five emcees was James Stewart, who announced that Don Murray and Janet Leigh had "drawn the assignment as Oscar sitters," meaning they got to hand the statuettes to the winners. The first award was Best Supporting Actor, presented by Lana Turner. The winner was *Sayonara*'s Red Buttons, whose run to the stage was described by the *Hollywood Reporter* as resembling "Puck on a pogo stick." On stage, Buttons wept softly and the audience laughed at his inability to speak. He thanked his agent, Marty Baum, and said, "I'm a very happy guy." When he got to the press backstage, he elaborated on winning: "It's like a bullet in the gut."

Ronald Reagan and Hope Lange gave out the Technical Awards, and while there was little emotionalism shown over their announcement at the Pantages, Army Archerd reported that Elizabeth Taylor, watching the awards at home on TV, "broke up when the Todd-AO award was made, could only watch the Awards intermittently afterwards."

Jack Lemmon replaced James Stewart as emcee and seemed somewhat pressured by show producer Jerry Wald's demand for expediency. "I haven't opened my mouth but I've already gotten a speed-up signal," were his first words. Following orders, Lemmon brought on Anthony Quinn to give the Best Supporting Actress Award. The winner was . . . not Lanchester, Jones, or Varsi, but Miyoshi Umeki for *Sayonara*. Umeki waddled up to the stage in her socks and sandals and was clearly as surprised as everyone else. "I really don't know what to say. I wish someone would help me now. I have nothing in my mind. Thank all American people."

Rock Hudson, perhaps still reeling from his antics with Mae West, illustrated the hazards of allowing someone other than the Price, Waterhouse representative to distribute the envelopes when he presented the Cartoon and Live Action Short Awards and opened the wrong envelopes. A little later, Zsa Zsa Gabor, in a black Edith Head creation, tripped out and said, "For me to break a little station should be easy, so c'mon, children, let us play." Translation: station break.

When the show returned, David Niven had become the emcee, and he announced that Don Murray and Janet Leigh had relinquished their position as Oscar sitters to "these charming newlyweds," Robert Wagner and Natalie Wood. As Mr. and Mrs. Wagner gazed adoringly at each other, Niven called for a close-up "to beautify living rooms all over America."

More newlyweds were on hand when Niven introduced "an exciting new star," Joanne Woodward, and her husband. "Will you read the nominations, Mr. Newman?" she asked. "A pleasure, Mrs. Newman," Paul said. Joanne begged off revealing the Film Editing winner: "You read it, I'm too nervous." The victor was *The Bridge on the River Kwai,* and the "Colonel Boogie March" theme filled the Pantages for the first time that evening.

The evening's fourth emcee was Rosalind Russell, who wore a beaded pajama costume from the movie she was currently filming, *Auntie Mame*. The audience gasped over Russell's getup, and she told a reporter afterward, "It was rather daring of

"Our fingers are crossed."
—The cast of Peyton Place

me, I admit, but after all, there is just so much you can do with women's clothes at an affair like the Academy Awards. You can either try to outdo the others in the plunging neckline or you can try to go all out in the bouffant gown. I decided to try a complete departure."

Cinematography Award presenter Joan Collins decided to try a pink silk gown with "the new balloon effect" that she designed herself. Collins couldn't wait to see who the winner was, so she broke Oscar decorum by tearing open the envelope, reading the contents to herself, and then getting on with the announcement of the nominees and the winner. Once again, the "Colonel Boogie March" filled the theater.

Because the industry was paying for the ceremony, Bob Hope didn't have a sponsor conflict this year and he was the last emcee. "I've just returned from Moscow," he began. "They didn't recognize me there, either. At least here they let the losers stay in town. They had a TV in every room, only it watches you." Commenting on the number of non-Hollywood films that were winning this evening, Hope said, "I think we're carrying this foreign aid too far."

Clark Gable and Doris Day walked out to the tune of "Teacher's Pet," to announce the writing winners. The Adapted Screenplay Award went to the mysterious author of *The Bridge on the River Kwai*. Pierre Boulle, the credited writer, wasn't there, but then again neither were rumored authors Carl Foreman and Michael Wilson. Instead, Kim Novak walked up, adjusting her tight gown as she moved, and breathlessly intoned, "My boss, the late Mr. Harry Cohn, was very proud of *The Bridge on the River Kwai*, as all of us at Columbia are." Novak then hurried off and said to reporters backstage, "This is the closest I'll ever come to one of these."

Meanwhile, onstage, Gable and Day were starting the cherished Oscar tradition of making fun of the names of the foreign nominees in the Original Screenplay category. The King and Dodo were particularly wary of the writers of Federico Fellini's *I Vitelloni* and, as Gable opened the envelope, Day quipped, "I hope you get Ennio Fliano." The winner was the easy-to-say George Wells for *Designing Woman*, who divulged, "The suggestion for the screenplay came from one of our industry's most designing women—Helen Rose."

Sophia Loren strolled onstage to name the Best Director and, as the strap of her gown slid down her arm, she said, "I'd like to thank the Academy for the recognition they've given Italian artists." Loren was supposed to engage in banter with Bob Hope, but when she flubbed the lead-in to his punch line and got a laugh, Hope cracked, "You catch on fast, honey." Loren rattled off the names of the nominees, asked for the envelope, realized that she was holding it, and laughed at herself. The winner, for *The Bridge on the River Kwai*, was David Lean, who, as he marched to the stage, was thinking: "Remember what you tell your actors: walk slowly!" At the podium, Lean said, "When we were sweating in the jungle for so long, I never dreamed that the bridge would bring us to Hollywood." Lean had spent so much time filming the movie in Ceylon that his wife, actress Ann Todd, had divorced him—on grounds of desertion.

The tension over the Best Actor Award was tightened when the Awards-giving stopped so that Burt Lancaster and Kirk Douglas could sing "It's Great Not to Be Nominated," a specialty number written by Sammy Cahn and Jimmy Van Heusen. Lancaster and Douglas playfully humiliated the nominees in the audience. "There's Marlon Brando, Hi y'all/That corny Southern drawl." Brando laughed and waved back. "Anthony Franciosa, you've got our vote/If he wins I'll cut my throat." Franciosa nervously smiled and chewed a fingernail while Mrs. Franciosa, Shelley Winters, roared with laughter. "Charles Laughton, he's great/Yeah, if you're voting for weight." Laughton didn't attend these things. "Anthony Quinn, isn't he uncanny/Your father would look great in a scene with Magnani." Quinn chuckled. "Alec flew all the way from Britain/Bully, Burt, that's why my teeth are grittin'." Guinness hadn't left Britain at all.

"It's like a bullet in the gut."
—Red Buttons

Lancaster and Douglas ended with a spectacular stunt—Douglas did a handstand over Lancaster, who then held him aloft while dancing offstage. Cary Grant entered from another direction to present the Award. The winner was Alec Guinness for *The Bridge on the River Kwai*, and the Academy's favorite British proxy, Jean Simmons, accepted for him.

John Wayne ambled out and, after Bob Hope helped him plug his latest picture, *The Barbarian and the Geisha*, he revealed the Best Actress—Joanne Woodward for *The Three Faces of Eve*. Woodward ran to the stage, holding up the front of her homemade dress. "I can only say I've been daydreaming about this since I was nine years old," she said. "I'd like to thank my parents for having more faith in me than anyone could."

Bob Hope called out Gary Cooper to name the Best Picture. To illustrate the fact that four of the five were in wide screen, the Academy lowered a CinemaScope screen to project film clips that totally dwarfed Cooper and Hope. The winner was *The Bridge on the River Kwai*. Producer Sam Spiegel claimed his Oscar, then went backstage and said he had played gin rummy with Mike Todd the night before he died.

The televised portion of the program ended here, but at the Pantages, Bette Davis was onstage handing out the Honorary Awards to, among others, former Academy President Charles Brackett and silent cowboy star Broncho Billy Anderson. These Awards were supposed to have been televised, too, but the show was running late by six minutes and the powers-that-be decided that Davis' portion had to go. As soon as she was finished, Davis walked off and fumed to the press that, earlier in the show, the Academy had found time for Donald Duck to narrate a history of film. "My segment was six minutes in length. Unfortunately, that was also the length of Mr. Duck's bit of film, and they chose Donald Duck. You always have to settle for less on TV."

Aftermath

The Academy's first post-ceremony Governor's Ball was held at the Bali Room of the Beverly Hilton Hotel, although the room was still undergoing refurbishing and Academy President George Seaton warned the revelers, "Don't put your heels down too heavily or we'll have more footprints here than at Grauman's." Pearl Bailey performed for the guests, and there was ice cream decked with miniature Oscars. Marlon Brando took one look and fled to his agent's house, where he ate fried chicken until 4:30 A.M.

Elizabeth Taylor did not make it to the ball, but Greta Garbo dropped by the Todd home that evening to pay her condolences. Taylor did send a bouquet of white orchids to Joanne Woodward at the party with the message "I'm so happy and pleased for you. Love, Elizabeth Todd—and Mike, too."

The evening wasn't much fun for Lana Turner, either. Turner and company waited and waited for their limousine to take them from the Pantages to the Beverly Hilton, but the driver had fallen asleep and never appeared. After taking a cab to the Governor's Ball, Turner and daughter Cheryl returned to their two-bedroom suite at the Bel-Air Hotel. Waiting for Lana in her bedroom was Johnny Stompanato, who beat the actress—still wearing her diamonds—for not taking him to the show.

"The incredible contrast of the evening," recalled Turner in her autobiography, "the exhilaration of the Awards ceremony . . . to this degradation, this vicious beating at the hands of a madman." Ten nights later, in Turner's new Beverly Hills home, Cheryl interrupted another fight between the couple by stabbing Stompanato to death with a knife from the cutlery set he had bought for the new house. The murder made headlines, but young Cheryl was acquitted.

Alec Guinness got the news of his Hollywood triumph the next day in England from his chauffeur as he was being driven to the set of *The Horse's*

Mouth. "Heard it on the wireless, sir," the driver mentioned. "You've won what they call an Oscar." When the press caught up with the winner, he told them, "No doorstop shenanigans for me. I'll put the Oscar on my mantel, which I realize makes for very dull copy, except that I'll put a mirror on the mantel so that I'll get a view of Oscar's back, too."

Life headlined: TENSION AND TRIUMPH FOR A YOUNG ACTRESS, and had a photo of Joanne Woodward the second before her name was called with the caption: "A 28-year-old girl, a year ago all but unknown, sits tensely in a theater seat waiting to see how her peers, the 2,000 leading figures in the movie industry, have judged her." The Associated Press went *Life* one better, with a picture of Woodward's mother, now living in Aiken, South Carolina, congratulating her daughter on the telephone while looking at a glamour photo of her Oscar-winning daughter.

Not all of Woodward's publicity was laudatory. Sidney Skolsky reprimanded the winner for her pre-victory, anti-Oscar comment and added, "She wasn't so flip after winning and Liz Taylor, loser and recent widow, gave her a bouquet." Skolsky also printed the telegram from four-time loser Deborah Kerr: "Congratulations Joanne and here I go again—always the bridesmaid, never the bride." Even husband Paul Newman made her feel like mud when he rhetorically asked Mike Connolly, "Isn't it too bad there have to be four unhappy ones for every happy one?"

Then there was the matter of Woodward's dress. A museum in Georgia wanted its first native Oscar winner to donate the gown to its collection and raised a stink when Joanne refused. "I spent $100 on the material, designed the dress and worked on it for two weeks," the winner argued. "I'm almost as proud of that dress as I am of my Oscar." Joanne couldn't win—back in California, Joan Crawford issued a statement: "Joanne Woodward is setting the cause of Hollywood glamour back twenty years by making her own clothes." Woodward eventually learned her lesson. When she appeared at the 1965 Academy Awards in a dress by Travilla, the 1957 Best Actress said, "I hope that it makes Joan Crawford happy."

Another controversy that took years to settle was the authorship of *The Bridge on the River Kwai* screenplay. It turned out that blacklistees Carl Foreman and Michael Wilson had indeed written the movie, and moreover, that Oscar winner Pierre Boulle had never written anything in English in his life. When Michael Wilson was anointed by the Screen Writers Guild with its life achievement award in 1976, presenter Carl Foreman jokingly suggested they write a letter to Boulle and ask, "'Say, by the way, do you think you might send us our Oscar, COD, and we will work out the custody for same between us?' " It took the Academy twenty-seven years to realize its mistake. On March 16, 1985, the authors finally got their Oscars when their widows picked up their statuettes at a special ceremony.

Although *Peyton Place* went 0 for 9 in the Awards tally, producer Jerry Wald didn't mind because his Oscar telecast received the most laudatory reviews of any in years. Louella Parsons was overwhelmed, and sighed, "What a night! The biggest and best Academy Awards in all its 30 years." Wald exclaimed, "We wanted to recapture some of the lost glamour of Hollywood and, from the reaction we've received, we succeeded completely." One official reaction came from Advertest Research Inc. of New Brunswick, New Jersey, which found that 63 percent of 600 adult viewers polled in New York had agreed that "seeing the old actors and actresses made me homesick to see a movie." But perhaps the highest praise was the report that, in Italy, the hottest ticket of the year was a bootleg tape of the Rock Hudson–Mae West duet of "Baby, It's Cold Outside."

1958

"Unless someone happens to be looking over my shoulder, I'll be voting for myself."
—David Niven

Homewreckers, tramps, adulterers and B-girls so dominated the 1958 Academy Awards—both on and offscreen—that Ingrid Bergman could return to Hollywood on Oscar night as a paragon of virtue.

One of the most eagerly anticipated films of 1958 was director Richard Brooks' version of Tennessee Williams' *Cat on a Hot Tin Roof* with its top-notch cast—Paul Newman as Brick, Judith Anderson as Big Mama and Burl Ives re-creating his Broadway role as Big Daddy. *Cat* was also the picture Elizabeth Taylor had just started filming when husband Mike Todd was killed in a plane crash earlier in the year. MGM's publicity flacks let it be known that Liz was acting with an unprecedented intensity as Maggie the Cat, a character who spends the whole movie begging her husband to go to bed with her. But Taylor proved that she didn't need a studio's publicity department to attract attention—she created Hollywood's biggest scandal since the Ingrid Bergman–Roberto Rossellini affair.

The press was still portraying Liz as the grieving widow when she stopped in New York in September before heading on to Europe. Her constant companion there was singer Eddie Fisher, best man at the Todds' wedding and star of a Gotham-based TV show. In February, Fisher and his wife, Debbie Reynolds, had named their son Todd, after Liz's husband. According to the gossips, Eddie and Debbie had a storybook marriage, and as late as July, Army Archerd reported, "Debbie Reynolds, now on a campaign to do straight dramas, had to turn down a *Devil's Disciple* offer because it would separate her from Eddie Fisher."

After *Cat on a Hot Tin Roof* opened to great reviews for all involved—the *New York Times*' headline was "The Fur Flies in *Cat*"—the paparazzi devoted even more attention to Taylor and began to notice that she was spending a great deal of time with Fisher. On September 9, when a Hollywood columnist asked Mrs. Fisher if something smelled fishy in New York, Debbie replied, "Eddie and Liz are very good friends. What's wrong with a friend taking a friend out in the evening?" Two days later, Reynolds announced her separation from Eddie Fisher and Liz canceled her European trip.

Best Actress winner Susan Hayward administers first aid to Best Actor winner David Niven.

Don't Blame Eddie

"I am still in love with my husband," Debbie told the press. "Do not blame him for what has happened. We were never happier than we have been in the last year."

Eddie begged to differ, and said, "The breakup is inevitable. We've been having problems for a long time and it has nothing to do with Liz Taylor." But as far as the press and the public were concerned, it had everything to do with Liz.

Hedda Hopper summed up her view of the arrangement: "Too bad Eddie Fisher isn't free so he and Liz could marry immediately; would serve them both right. We'd give that union just about six months—you can't build a marriage on sex alone."

Elizabeth Taylor was no longer the widow Todd to journalists but the woman-you-love-to-hate. Mike Connolly reported that Taylor threw a private soirée for Fisher and herself in October that she dubbed her "You-Can-All-Go-to-Hell Party." The National Association of Theatre Owners had planned to name Taylor their Star of the Year, but changed their minds, explaining, "The movie industry is at the mercy of public opinion and to award Miss Taylor the honor at a time like this is out of the question."

Sinning Spinster

The theater owners decided to give that Star of the Year citation to Deborah Kerr, even though she, too, was involved in scandal. "Hollywood was rocked back on its feet early this year," Louella Parsons reported, "when Deborah's husband of

"I want to be a full-time wife."
—Susan Hayward

many years, Tony Bartley, accused writer-charmer Peter Viertel of 'enticing the affections' of his beautiful actress-wife." When Mr. and Mrs. Bartley separated, an English court awarded the father custody of the couple's two daughters. Louella noted that on the set of *Separate Tables*, the heartbroken Kerr turned to costar David Niven and confessed: "It's a good thing I'm playing a drab spinster role in this picture. I feel like one." Hedda didn't want to miss out on this story either, and wrote, "Deborah spent her evening hours writing long letters to the dashing man of the world who had won her heart and to the children who owned it."

Moll Flanders, Move Over

In *Some Came Running* MGM had another movie starring gossip-column favorites. It was a romantic melodrama enacted by members of the town's ranking social club, the Rat Pack. Frank Sinatra and Dean Martin got top billing, but the club's lone female member, Shirley MacLaine, got the notices. Before the film's December opening, Army Archerd leaked that "word was all over town on Shirley MacLaine," and the reviewers verified the report. The *New York Herald Tribune* opined: "Miss MacLaine's part is that of a docile and affectionate tramp and she plays it with wonderful abandon." And the *Hollywood Reporter*'s Jack Moffitt felt that she "comes through with what is probably the most penetrating analysis of a good-hearted, hard-luck broad since Daniel Defoe gave us *Moll Flanders*." *Life* devoted a cover to lovable kook Shirley MacLaine and her tiny, look-alike daughter.

"Rozzamatazz"

Warners' big Christmas release featured another good-hearted broad. She was higher up the social scale but no less uninhibited—Rosalind Russell as *Auntie Mame*. *Time* raved about "Rozzamatazz" and the *New York Herald Tribune* admitted, "Nothing can really daunt the flamboyant Miss Russell, and when she sails onto the screen in a pair of her extraordinary pajamas and a Martini-tinted cape, flourishing a cigarette holder as long as a cane, the effect is electric and awesome." Warners advertised the fact that *Auntie Mame* was on its way to becoming the highest-grossing film of the year with a cartoon in the trades. It showed a long line in front of a theater box office headed by Frankenstein and the Wolf Man and was captioned, "*Everybody*'s going to see *Auntie Mame!*" Since Russell had discovered the property, played it on Broadway and made the movie deal with Jack Warner, the three-time Oscar loser was sure to get some sort of Academy recognition, but she refused to campaign. "I think Academy members vote only for what they see on the screen," she asserted.

I Want to Win!

Four-time loser Susan Hayward had no qualms at all about campaigning for Oscar and she went along with producer Walter Wanger's ballyhoo for her performance as a murderess in *I Want to Live!* The film graphically depicted the gas-chamber execution of a convicted killer—although the filmmakers maintained her innocence—and condemned capital punishment. Existentialist Albert Camus got in on the publicity action with his plug from Paris: "The story had to be told to the whole world; the world should see it and hear it. The day will come when such documents will seem to us to refer to prehistoric times and we shall consider them as unbelievable as we now find it unbelievable that in earlier centuries witches were burned or thieves had their right hands cut off."

In Hollywood, Clifton Webb claimed to have been so shaken up by Hayward's performance as a woman who walks bravely to the gas chamber that he sent producer Wanger the bill for a fifth of Scotch. The *New York Times'* Bosley Crowther cried: "She has never done anything so vivid or shattering," and his fellow critics agreed; Hay-

"Less folksongs, more gams."
—Mike Connolly

ward won Best Actress Award from the New York Film Critics.

Humble Hometown Boy

The New York Film Critics gave their Best Actor Award to David Niven for playing a pompous windbag who turns out to be a molester of women in *Separate Tables*. Winner Niven turned this award into a Hollywood cause by telling the community "I'm glad I struck a blow for Hollywood because New York always looks down its newspaper nose at 'Hollywood movie stars' and this time they gave an acting award to someone who learned what little he knows right here in Hollywood, starting as an extra." Niven spent $1,500 on trade ads that consisted simply of a picture of himself in character with the legend "New York Film Critics winner: Best Actor."

The producers of *Separate Tables*, Harold Hecht and Burt Lancaster of *Marty* fame, also thought that pictures spoke louder than words and one of their ads for Best Picture featured a still from the movie, framed and hanging on a wall alongside such works of art as the *Mona Lisa* and *Blue Boy*.

The Touchiest Problem

Challenging Hecht-Lancaster for flashiest Oscar campaign was producer-director Stanley Kramer, hustling *The Defiant Ones*, a plea for racial tolerance using the plot device of two escaped convicts—one black (Sidney Poitier), the other a white bigot (Tony Curtis)—handcuffed together. Most critics had been as sober as Arthur Knight of the *Saturday Review* in their praise:

> *At a time when most producers are turning out pictures that firmly shun the realities of the contemporary scene, either star-laden blockbusters or rock 'n' roll horror films, Mr. Kramer has boldly and eloquently dramatized what is unquestionably the touchiest problem of our day, the strained relations between Negro and white.* The Defiant Ones *is a film that he, the motion picture industry, and every American can be proud of.*

But Kramer also reprinted the reactions of the Hollywood folk who found it good, old-fashioned entertainment, like Mike Connolly, who wrote: "If we must have message pictures, let 'em be like *The Defiant Ones*, in which Kramer and Co. reach ecstasies of high-flown dramatics, wild arias of hell-for-leather action and arpeggios of thunderous suspense such as we've seldom seen."

Just as the *Separate Table* crowd had eschewed print in their trade paper ads, Kramer ran a full-page photo of just Poitier and Curtis' hands, cuffed together, rising out of a river. This shot became so familiar that Susan Hayward and her *I Want to Live!* director, Robert Wise, ran a gag ad showing the two of them handcuffed together while standing in a river. Kramer could laugh, secure in the knowledge that his film had cleaned up at the New York Film Critics Award, winning Picture, Director and Screenplay. But it was this last award that made the Academy uncomfortable.

Breaking the Rule

The winning authors of *The Defiant Ones* were Harold Jacob Smith and Nathan E. Douglas, the latter a pseudonym for a blacklisted writer named Ned Young. According to the Academy's anti-Communist rule, the "Douglas" name could not be on the ballot, although his "clean" collaborator's could. "A lot of people on the Board are unhappy about it," whispered an unnamed Academy governor to *Daily Variety*. "The climate has changed a little. People realize how absurd this rule is." On January 12, 1959, six weeks before the nominations were released, the Academy announced it was revoking the law because "experience has proven the bylaw to be unworkable and impractical to administer and enforce." Hedda Hopper was upset at this turn of events and wrote,

"You can't build a marriage on sex alone."
—Hedda Hopper

"Since our Academy now makes it legal for Commie writers to receive Oscars, some past winners, who are as bitter about this as I, tell me they'll return theirs." Nobody did.

Oui, Oui, Gigi

Defying *The Defiant Ones'* claim on Oscar was Arthur Freed's musical production of *Gigi*, boasting the best credits that MGM's money could buy: written by Frederick Loewe and Alan Jay Lerner, designed by Cecil Beaton (all three fresh from their 1956 Broadway triumph, *My Fair Lady*), directed by Vincente Minnelli, and starring Leslie Caron, Louis Jourdan and Maurice Chevalier. The *New York Post*'s Archer Winsten predicted, "It is going to be a hit, and it will run for a long, long time and it will please so many people on so many levels that one hesitates to estimate exactly what the proportion of the success will be." MGM treated the movie like a Broadway show and opened it in a legitimate theater on the Great White Way—the Royale—where it ran for six months and then moved on to a regular movie theater for close to a year.

The Nominations

Leo's kid-glove handling of *Gigi* paid off and the movie won nine nominations; for some reason none of them were for the actors, although MGM had virtually promised Maurice Chevalier that his Golden Globe Award for Best Actor assured him a similar nod from the Academy. *C'est la vie*. David Niven's money proved to be well spent, as was Stanley Kramer's—both Sidney Poitier and Tony Curtis were up for Best Actor for *The Defiant Ones*. The *Los Angeles Mirror-News* wrote that Curtis' nomination meant "his pretty-boy days of maudlin, meaningless films are over." Niven cabled Curtis: "Congratulations, chum, but I want to make one thing crystal clear. Unless someone happens to be looking over my shoulder, I'll be voting for myself." To which Curtis telegramed back: "Heartiest congratulations. I couldn't be happier if it was happening to me—and it is."

Paul Newman, nominated for the first time for *Cat on a Hot Tin Roof*, said he didn't plan to leave his Broadway show, *Sweet Bird of Youth*, and was going to send his mother to the ceremonies. Sidney Poitier was also on Broadway, in *A Raisin in the Sun*, and he, too, would stay east. Spencer Tracy, a two-time winner receiving his sixth nomination, for *The Old Man and the Sea*, had no intention of going or sending a proxy. Bob Hope said, "Tracy needs another Oscar like Zsa Zsa Gabor needs Ann Landers' lovelorn advice."

Liz Weeps, Shirley Dances

The Best Actress race was the most exciting event, and Louella Parsons recorded the nominees' reaction to the good news. Eddie Fisher informed Elizabeth Taylor, who promptly broke down crying and thanked Hollywood for not being vindictive. Susan Hayward got the word over her car radio as she and her husband returned from a day at the races, while Deborah Kerr learned of her good fortune in "far-off Klosters, Switzerland, with her new love, Peter Viertel." As for Shirley MacLaine, "that red-headed imp of emotion, was in the makeup department at Paramount having her hair lightened for her new picture. When word broke out that she had made it for *Some Came Running*, she let out a yip of joy, went into a war dance and splashed peroxide and ammonia all over the booth."

Each of the Actress nominees had a real shot at the Award, and ads proliferated in the trades. Warners even began tub-thumping Rosalind Russell despite her no-campaign policy. Columnists felt free to flaunt their favorites. Erskine Johnson reminded everyone that Mike Todd's alleged last words before boarding his ill-fated plane were "She doesn't have to worry about the Oscar. If Liz doesn't win it this year she will next year for *Cat*," while Mike Connolly informed everyone that producer "Hal Wallis paid for Shirley's Oscarobes by Edith Head."

"It's very likely the girls won't come face to face."
—Jerry Wald

The Supporting Races

Martha Hyer, playing the "good girl" who competes with MacLaine for Frank Sinatra in *Some Came Running,* had been one of the year's most visible campaigners with a series of pre-nomination ads for Best Supporting Actress. Although she was out of town when the nominations were released, the gossips had her reaction. "I was trying to dismount from my camel in front of the Sphinx when the hotel runner brought me the cable with the news," she explained, adding, "I'm sure of one vote—mine."

Auntie Mame's Peggy Cass, who repeated her stage role as Agnes Gooch, told *Daily Variety:* "I'm not wearing any sandwich boards, but I'm smiling a lot." Warners assigned flacks to help her out, and the *Hollywood Reporter* later broke this news: "Peggy Cass lost her contact lenses in her bean sprouts and egg foo yong at Don the Beachcomber's." *The Defiant Ones'* Cara Williams made news because of her impending divorce from John Drew Barrymore and her explanation of what went wrong: "We'll never reconcile because the three of us would never be happy together—John, myself and his psychiatrist." There was no news on screen newcomer Maureen Stapleton of *Lonelyhearts,* but reportedly *Separate Tables* nominee Wendy Hiller was toasted by her husband with a new car—a Triumph.

Human Drama and Pretty Girls

Two of the Supporting Actor nominees weren't above playing to the voters' sentimental streaks. *The Brothers Karamazov*'s Lee J. Cobb had a dramatic story about how Frank Sinatra lent him his Palm Springs home for a month. "My whole life seemed to change with that call from Frank," Cobb exclaimed. "It is as though a curtain had raised on an entirely new act of my life. I not only regained my health—I found love, happiness and peace of mind." Folksinger Theodore Bikel, who had played a Southern sheriff in *The Defiant Ones,* used the "land of opportunity" routine. The Academy's first Israeli nominee effused, "I think it amazing that a man from another land, who stepped into Hollywood two years ago and landed in America just four years ago, should be in the running for such a great honor!" But Sidney Skolsky didn't think he should get his hopes up: "Bikel would win in a cinch if beatniks voted."

The lead in the Best Supporting Actor contest was given to Burl Ives, who was not nominated for *Cat on a Hot Tin Roof* because MGM listed him in the Best Actor category. Ives was in the race for playing a corrupt land baron in *The Big Country,* which *Hollywood Reporter* referred to as "Big Daddy Goes West." The newspaper's Mike Connolly also had inside information on Ives' upcoming Las Vegas act: "Ives swings out with a 'Sing Out, Sweet Land' musical-type format for his Flamingo opening and will utilize the line girls—less folksongs, more gams."

Cover That Cleavage

Remembering the swell reviews it got last year, the Academy drafted Jerry Wald to produce the show and the industry was again willing to shell out to keep Oldsmobile at bay. Wald asked Rosalind Russell to present the Honorary Award the Academy had decided to give Maurice Chevalier and rumors abounded at rehearsals that this was a tipoff that she'd won Best Actress. Roz didn't have to worry about a faulty *Daily Variety* poll this year—the Academy had finally persuaded the paper to discontinue the survey. Wald also sent out letters to female guests warning, "There will be no cleavage on this year's Oscar Awards show. This was one of the major criticisms we received last year, that the necklines were too low. Most of the complaints came from the Middle West. If you need any help, a wardrobe mistress backstage is equipped with enough lace to make a mummy."

Wald was also prepared when reporters asked if he wasn't pushing his luck by inviting Debbie Reynolds and Elizabeth Taylor to the show. "The girls are big stars and they belong on the program," he argued. "They both wanted to be a part of it. We're not out to embarrass anybody, nor are we trying to put on a Coney Island sideshow. It's very likely the girls won't come face to face." Reynolds decided she didn't want to be a part of it and declined, excusing herself by saying that she had just returned from Spain.

Also returning from abroad was Ingrid Bergman, who came sweeping into town like Joan of Arc. Two nights before the Oscar ceremonies, Anita Louise and Buddy Adler hosted a welcome-back party for Bergman at the Crystal Room of the Beverly Hills Hotel and many film-colony members who had turned down offers to appear at the Awards show were there. David Niven was there, too, as he remembered in his autobiography:

> *Everyone at the party seemed to have voted for me; they didn't say so in so many words; they were content to signal the fact across the room by making a cross in the air and pointing to their own chests and winking knowingly.*
>
> *I was greatly encouraged until I caught the eye of Rosalind Russell, a nominee for Best Actress, for whom I had not voted . . . I found myself winking and pointing and drawing crosses in the empty air.*

The Big Night

All of the Best Actress nominees showed up with the exception of Deborah Kerr, who Louella Parsons said was in Europe to be close to her kids. The columnists verified that the two celebrities who created the greatest furor in the bleachers were Ingrid Bergman and Elizabeth Taylor. David Niven, one of the show's emcees, appeared calm, but his wife confessed, "I haven't slept in three days." The gown that caused the most talk was Vera-Ellen's; she wore a form-fitting gold lamé sheath and asked, "Why not? It's the way Oscar himself dresses!"

The telecast opened with William Holden and John Wayne greeting the television audience from the press tent outside the Pantages. The ceremony began with a filmed musical number in which Kirk Douglas and Burt Lancaster reprised their "It's Great Not to Be Nominated" number from the previous year's show. This duet ended with acrobatics; Kirk stood on Burt's shoulders and then they both executed somersaults. Producer Jerry Wald got a taste of impending doom when the screen rose prematurely at the Pantages, so that the live audience saw only the first part of the act.

Bob Hope strolled out and said, "We have a great show tonight. To give you some idea, Ed Sullivan is in *our* audience. Pictures were grim this year . . . I'm surprised Susan Hayward made it here. I'll be followed by David Niven—if the balloon arrives on time."

The first Award was for Best Supporting Actor and producer Wald, remembering the Bette Davis–Donald Duck controversy last year, had said, "We're not taking any chances this year. We put Bette on the first part of the show." Davis appeared on the arm of Anthony Quinn and named Burl Ives the winner for *The Big Country*. On the way to the stage, Ives patted *Teacher's Pet*'s Supporting Actor loser Gig Young on the shoulder. When the winner, sporting a western ribbon tie with his tuxedo, got to the podium, Bette Davis thrust the statuette toward him and proclaimed, "For you."

Awards Ceremony

APRIL 6, 1959, 7:30 P.M.
THE RKO PANTAGES THEATRE, HOLLYWOOD

Your Hosts:
BOB HOPE, DAVID NIVEN, TONY RANDALL, MORT SAHL, LAURENCE OLIVIER AND JERRY LEWIS
Televised over NBC

Presenters

Supporting Actor . . . . Bette Davis and Anthony Quinn
Scientific and Technical Awards . . . . Barbara Rush and Jacques Tati
Short Subjects . . . . Janet Leigh and Tony Curtis
Supporting Actress . . . . Shelley Winters and Red Buttons
Scoring of a Musical Picture . . . . June Allyson and Dick Powell
Sound . . . . Jane Wyman and Charlton Heston
Costume Design . . . . Wendell Corey and Ernie Kovacs
Film Editing . . . . Jean Simmons and Louis Jourdan
Documentary Awards . . . . Natalie Wood and Robert Wagner
Song . . . . Sophia Loren and Dean Martin
Special Effects . . . . Shirley MacLaine and Peter Ustinov
Scoring of a Dramatic or Comedy Picture . . . . Eva Marie Saint and Anthony Franciosa
Foreign Film . . . . Cyd Charisse and Robert Stack
Cinematography . . . . Doris Day and Rock Hudson
Honorary Award to Maurice Chevalier . . . . Rosalind Russell
Art Direction . . . . Vincent Price and Eddie Albert
Irving Thalberg Award . . . . Buddy Adler
Director . . . . Millie Perkins and Gary Cooper
Writing Awards . . . . . . Elizabeth Taylor, Dirk Bogarde and Van Heflin
Actress . . . . Kim Novak and James Cagney
Actor . . . . Irene Dunne and John Wayne
Picture . . . . Ingrid Bergman

Performers of Nominated Songs

"Almost in Your Arms" . . . . Anna Maria Alberghetti, Tuesday Weld, Connie Stevens, Nick Adams, Dean Jones and James Darren
"A Certain Smile" . . . . John Raitt, danced by Marge and Gower Champion
"Gigi" . . . . Tony Martin, danced by Taina Elg
"To Love and Be Loved" . . . . Eddie Fisher
"A Very Precious Love" . . . . Howard Keel and Rhonda Fleming

"You read the nominations and I'll describe the girls."
—Wendell Corey

Best Actor nominee Tony Curtis and his wife, Janet Leigh, announced that the Cartoon Award went to Bugs Bunny. The winner's producer, John W. Burton, said, "Bugs Bunny has finally made the grade. He's tried for eighteen years, rabbit's feet and all."

Emcee-nominee David Niven assumed the hosting duties and said he had been told to be informal. Accordingly, he took off his tails and draped them on the podium. Niven introduced the presenters of the Best Supporting Actress Award, Shelley Winters and Red Buttons, who revealed, "Miss Wendy Hiller for *Separate Tables*." The Award was accepted by her producer, Harold Hecht, who proved to have a limited vocabulary: "It's a great honor to accept this great honor for a great actress."

Ernie Kovacs, three cigars sticking out of his handkerchief pocket, and Wendell Corey presented the Costume Awards, which began with Corey's suggestion: "You read the nominations and I'll describe the girls." Among the costume models were Inger Stevens, wearing an Edith Head gown from *The Buccaneer*, and Jayne Mansfield, filling out one of Cecil Beaton's creations for *Gigi*. When Beaton was declared the winner, Mansfield left the other models and stood by the podium while producer Arthur Freed accepted the Oscar. Mansfield told reporters backstage that for this event she had bleached her eyebrows platinum to match her hair.

The third emcee was one of Mansfield's former costars, Tony Randall, who had been told by Jerry Wald to drop his monologue to keep the show moving briskly. Randall simply asked, "Who could follow David Niven?" Answer: "Nobody." Dean Martin and Sophia Loren appeared to introduce the team of singers who performed the nominated songs in one big medley. Eddie Fisher was a member of this team and some snickered at the fact that he was chosen to sing "To Love and Be Loved." When it came time to reveal the winning tune, Dino ad-libbed to Loren, "You open it, honey. I don't do sight bits." "What?" Sophia responded. The winner was "Gigi" and composer Frederick Loewe alluded to his recent cardiac surgery: "I want to thank you from the bottom of my somewhat battered heart."

Tony Randall introduced the next host, comedian Mort Sahl, who warned that his presence on the show would have an adverse effect. "We've just lost the college crowd," Sahl despaired. "All across the country they're saying 'Sell-out!'" More laughter followed when Shirley MacLaine and Peter Ustinov used the Special Effects Award presentation to show off their abilities to make funny noises with their mouths.

Joan Fontaine appeared onstage to welcome the fifth emcee, Laurence Olivier, who returned the compliment by commenting that Fontaine's performance in *Rebecca* "knocked me so far off the screen a few years ago." Olivier, too, felt the need to point out why he was chosen for the job. "I'm a change of pace from the previous hosts. The Academy wanted someone completely devoid of humor."

Cyd Charisse and Robert Stack presented the Foreign Film Award to *Mon Oncle* and director-star Jacques Tati accepted in French-flavored English. "I want to say a few words with my very bad English," he began. "I find people with the worst English talk more than the others." The winner went on to criticize the Academy for not having fully appreciated America's own film comedians in their heyday. "If Hollywood had not done so many funny pictures, I would not be here tonight. For all those great comedians, I am not the uncle, but the nephew. I respect Hollywood."

The introductory music to "Thank Heaven for Little Girls" filled the Pantages and the stage was filled with young Hollywood actresses in turn-of-the-century costumes specially designed by Cecil Beaton, who, according to Sheilah Graham, had refused to let Jayne Mansfield be one of the models because "Jayne's figure was too much for the gowns."

Olivier explained the purpose of this fashion show: "Among this bevy, you'll notice a Parisian landmark, but, unlike the Eiffel Tower, he belongs to the world." There was Maurice Chevalier,

"What?"
—Sophia Loren

wearing his costume from his unnominated role in *Gigi*, wandering among the "little girls." Rosalind Russell, in a shiny silk suit and a tall hat, walked out with an Oscar and handed it to Chevalier. "Can I kiss you, Auntie Mamie?" Chevalier asked, but, before he could say anything else, he was cut off by the "little girls" who sang "We're glad you're not young anymore." At this point, Anthony Franciosa, Robert Wagner and Rock Hudson were supposed to come out and sing a response, but Jerry Wald started worrying about taking too much time and axed the number at the last minute.

When the Chevalier tribute more or less ended, Laurence Olivier stepped aside for Jerry Lewis, the sixth and final emcee. "I'm proud to be a part of show business and MCA, the owners," Lewis began, only to stop and say, "This woman is drunk in the front row and I can't concentrate."

The Board of Governors took care of some more unfinished business when Buddy Adler, the head of production at Fox, presented the Thalberg Award to Jack Warner, who had recently given the industry quite a scare. On a pleasure trip through Europe, Warner had fallen asleep at the wheel of his Alfa-Romeo, crossed into the wrong lane, and was thrown through the windshield when a ten-ton truck hit the car. Mike Connolly detailed that "medicos packed him in ice for two days because of those second-degree burns and skull fracture." Warner was sufficiently pulled together by Awards night, and he humbly thanked the assembled for their good wishes.

Millie Perkins, a newcomer whose film debut *The Diary of Anne Frank* had just been released, and Gary Cooper presented the Best Director Award, which went to Vincente Minnelli for *Gigi*. The winner called it "just about the proudest moment of my life," a sentiment slightly undercut by the fact that he was simultaneously scratching his eye with his middle finger. Minnelli was followed by Miss "You-Can-All-Go-to-Hell" herself, Elizabeth Taylor, who helped out with the writing Awards. When the Original Screenplay went to "Nathan Douglas" and Harold Jacob Smith, for *The Defiant Ones*, Best Director loser Stanley Kramer shrugged to his companions, "At least we beat the blacklist."

Jerry Wald thought that since the Best Actress contest had garnered the most interest this year, it would be fun to have a distaff version of the Kirk Douglas–Burt Lancaster number "It's Great Not to Be Nominated." Explaining that "the Ritz Brothers are out of work," Jerry Lewis brought out Angela Lansbury, Dana Wynter and Joan Collins to sing "It's Bully Not to Be Nominated." Of Susan Hayward, the trio warbled, "She didn't let Walter Wanger down/I didn't know she was back in town." A reaction shot showed Hayward smiling faintly but appearing on the verge of tears. Of Shirley MacLaine, "There's a talent that's rare/If you like juvenile delinquent hair." MacLaine laughed and crinkled up her face. Of Elizabeth Taylor, "Tell me, darling, what's she got/Are you kidding, what do you think made the roof so hot?" Taylor forced a laugh. "Roz Russell, what a marvelous dame/Your mother could have scored as Auntie Mame." Russell seemed still to be waiting for the punch line. "We've done with every star/But darling, we forgot Deb-or-rah/Debra Paget?/No, Deborah Kerr." The applause for the trio was no more than respectable.

Kim Novak and James Cagney entered to end the suspense and they divulged the Best Actress winner—Susan Hayward for *I Want to Live!* There was sustained applause and cheers and a shaken Susan thanked her producer. "My special thanks to Walter Wanger, who made this possible." When Hayward walked backstage, Jerry Lewis turned to ask, "Will you hold the lady?" and asked Hayward to come back out and take another bow. She did, and Walter Wanger said to a friend, "Thank heavens, now we can all relax. Susie got what she's been chasing for twenty years."

John Wayne and Irene Dunne presented the Best Actor Award to David Niven for *Separate Tables*. "I'm so loaded down with good-luck charms I could hardly make it up the stairs," the winner said. "People have been saying thank you for Oscars for thirty years. All I can add is thank you."

"My God, have we fallen to this?"
—Spencer Tracy

Cary Grant was onstage next to introduce "a great actress and a great lady. Welcome back, Ingrid Bergman." This was Bergman's first public appearance in Hollywood since 1949 and the audience's response was suitably momentous. When the ovation finally died down, Bergman said, "Thank you for this most heartening welcome." She related how she had been sitting in the bathtub as she heard her name called over the radio when she won Best Actress two years earlier. Then she got on to naming the Best Picture winner: "The winner is *Gigi*."

To close the show, Mitzi Gaynor strolled out and burst into "There's No Business Like Show Business." As Gaynor charged into the second chorus, a part of the stage behind her rose from below with all the winners and presenters standing side by side and singing along. After two more choruses, Jerry Wald signaled to Jerry Lewis. There were twenty minutes of air time left! Keep on singing!

Lewis yelled, "Another twenty times!" Shirley MacLaine turned around to look at him as if he were crazy, but most of the stellar chorus just stood there as Lionel Newman's orchestra kept playing. A few people decided that they might as well start dancing, and soon the two lines of celebrities dissolved into dancing couples, among them: Cary Grant and Ingrid Bergman, Dimitri Tiomkin and Angela Lansbury, Natalie Wood and Robert Wagner, Tony Randall and Eva Marie Saint, Maurice Chevalier and Rosalind Russell, and Bob Hope and Zsa Zsa Gabor. While dancing with Sophia Loren, Dean Martin waltzed past the podium and grabbed himself an Oscar. Loren, as usual, looked bewildered. Jerry Lewis ad-libbed, "And they said that Dean and I wouldn't be on the same stage again!" Dean retorted, "He needs me." Watching the spectacle on TV at home, absentee Spencer Tracy said, "My God, have we fallen to this?"

The minutes crawled by. Jerry took a microphone and extemporized. "We are very sorry about Danny Thomas, whose show must have a three rating tonight . . . We would like to sing three hundred choruses . . . We're showing Three Stooges shorts to cheer up the losers . . . We'll have a test pattern for the next hour and twenty minutes." He turned to conductor Newman and asked, "May I have a baton?" Jerry then began conducting the orchestra, leaning over to Newman and adding, "We may get a bar mitzvah out of this." Some of the dancing celebrities thought it best to disappear from the stage and many members of the audience were well on their way out by this time. As Jerry picked up a trumpet and began hitting flat notes, NBC turned its cameras off and filled the rest of the time slot with a short film about pistols.

Aftermath

Time jeered that the ending of the Awards show was "an unplanned twenty-minute melee that had the somewhat sweaty aroma of a combination Arthur Murray, Lawrence Welk, Dick Clark, free-for-all." The winners couldn't have cared less. "This came as a big surprise," Burl Ives marveled. "I didn't think I'd get it. I thought Lee J. Cobb would get it." When asked what he'd do with his statuette, Big Daddy replied, "I don't know. Maybe use it as a figurehead on my schooner." David Niven's reaction to winning was honest: "Damn it, I must say I wanted to win and I'm happy I did." So was Best Picture winner MGM. The next day, telephone operators at the studio were instructed to answer, "M-Gigi-M."

Reporters requested the two winning actors to buss the winning actress, but Susan Hayward refused to kiss either of them or her Oscar. "I don't kiss anyone but my husband," she insisted. As Niven had done after he won the New York Film Critics Award, Hayward played up her victory as a triumph for Hollywood. "I guess this proves you don't have to be a Method actor," she observed. "Me, I'm strictly a product of the motion-picture industry." It was only at the ball at the Beverly Hilton that the actress realized that, in all of the excitement, she had left her purse and her coat at the Pantages. "Oh well, there was nothing impor-

"I find people with the worst English talk more than the others."
—Jacques Tati

tant in the coat," she shrugged, "except my sunglasses."

While Lowell E. Reddelings of the *Hollywood Citizen-News* liked the finale with the dancing participants and called it "a fitting climax to a memorable night," most people considered it an embarrassment. The vice president of United Artists found the show "inexcusable and amateurish" and put the blame on Jerry Wald. "The fact that the guy is a good motion-picture producer—and Wald has done many fine things—does not make him a good TV producer. We ought to hire a pro."

Jerry Wald took offense at the criticism and asked, rhetorically, "If it had been a championship bout and not the Oscarcast, and if one of the contenders was knocked out in the first round, would the viewers have squawked because they didn't see the additional fourteen rounds?" Jerry Lewis bore the brunt of the bad reviews for his handling of the final minutes, leading the show's television director, Alan Handley, to write to Lewis' critics personally to exonerate the comedian. Dorothy Kilgallen was Jerry's harshest judge; she didn't like anything about him, from his "ghastly evening shirt," to "his grisly accent," to "his cheap give-the-little-girl-another-hand treatment of Susan Hayward, who scarcely needed an assist from an egg-laying comedian in her hour of triumph." Hollywood was kinder and more sympathetic, even grateful because the show provided great material for jokes. "They timed this thing with a sundial" was Bob Hope's reaction.

Other negative comments came from those who still weren't ready to forgive Ingrid Bergman. The *Atlanta Chronicle* editorialized, "The honor accorded Ingrid Bergman at the Academy Awards ceremony and the thunderous ovation she received from spectators at the Pantages proved at least one point, insofar as we are concerned. Our ideas of moral values and those of the folks in Hollywood are widely separated."

But the criticism that the Academy found the hardest to accept came from one of the winners. When Best Supporting Actress Wendy Hiller was interviewed by the *London News Chronicle,* she said she thought the Academy was crazy for giving her an Award. "All you could see of me in the picture was the back of my head," she argued. "Unless they give some award for acting with one's back to the camera, I don't see how I could have won. They cut my two best scenes and they gave one to Rita Hayworth." When the interviewer said never mind all that, what do you think of the tribute, the winner scoffed, "Never mind the honor, though I'm sure it's very nice of them. I hope this award means cash—hard cash. I want lots of lovely offers to go filming in Hollywood, preferably in the winter so I can avoid all the horrid cold over here." Honorary winner Maurice Chevalier, meanwhile, instructed his agent, "Now we must get an Academy Award for the best dramatic performance."

A satisfied winner was Susan Hayward, who was interviewed at the Beverly Hills Hotel by columnist James Bacon the day after her victory. "I came here when I was nineteen and I've been here twenty years. I've had it, " she claimed, adding that now that she had an Oscar, "I want to be a full-time wife." Mr. and Mrs. Floyd Chalkley returned to their home in Carrollton, Georgia, where the citizenry threw Mrs. Chalkley a ticker-tape parade. Hayward's Oscar also closed a chapter in the life of producer Walter Wanger, an ex-president of the Academy and an ex-con for shooting Jennings Lang. "I made *I Want to Live!* Susan wins the Oscar, and so I was a bloody hero again."

Rosalind Russell refused to be upset over her fourth defeat and told reporters, "Well, I have to admit that nobody deserved it more than Hayward. If it had to be somebody else, I'm glad it was Susie." On the other hand, Russell's costar, Best Supporting Actress loser Peggy Cass, had had enough of Hollywood. "I'm going back to New York tonight," she told Earl Wilson after the ceremony. "These westerners—what do they know?"

1959

"I would not walk out of a picture for anything as trivial as a costume."
—Lana Turner

The 1959 Academy Awards was a chariot race between sex and religion—the only two things profitable on screen that year.

Although Otto Preminger had made loads of money defying the Hollywood Production Code throughout the '50s, the major studios had played by the Code's rules. At the end of the decade, however, the companies, realizing that sex sells, were no longer so intimidated by the Code. They still played it safe and looked for Code approval, but the censors were having to swallow stronger stuff.

The strongest stuff this year came from Otto Preminger himself. *Anatomy of a Murder* was his latest, and it first made headlines in March when Lana Turner left the production. LANA GIVES UP JUICY ROLE IN FILM RHUBARB, flashed the *New York Daily News*, which gave both sides of the story. Preminger claimed Turner didn't like her costumes, but the actress said, "I would not walk out of a picture for anything as trivial as a costume. It was simply impossible to deal with Mr. Preminger's unpredictable temper."

"I'll get an unknown and make her a new Lana Turner," vowed Preminger, and he cast Lee Remick as the wife who claims to have been raped by the man her husband is accused of murdering. When the film, starring James Stewart as the murderer's attorney and film newcomer George C. Scott as a prosecutor, opened in July, *Time* called it "a courtroom melodrama less concerned with murder than with anatomy." Its reviewer warned: "In scene after scene the customers are bombarded with such no-nonsense words as 'intercourse . . . contraceptive . . . spermatogenesis . . . sexual climax.' And even the least barkbound of spectators may find himself startled to hear, in his neighborhood movie house, extended discussion of what constitutes rape." One neighborhood that didn't want to hear it was Chicago. Preminger's personal plea couldn't sway Mayor Richard Daley from banning the film in the Second City. A Federal District Court order was more persuasive, stating that Preminger's movie "does not tend to excite sexual passion or undermine morals." The Production Code people felt the same way, happily giving him their seal.

"I couldn't decide whether to be dignified or sexy," admitted Best Supporting Actress winner Shelley Winters.

Room for Two

Daily Variety was impressed when *Anatomy of a Murder* made over $2 million in a mere six weeks, and the *Hollywood Reporter* predicted Lee Remick would cop a Best Actress nomination. The trades were also talking about a movie that did not earn the seal of approval from the censors, an independently distributed British film called *Room at the Top*. In the *Saturday Review*, Arthur Knight commented, "Its characters swear, curse, connive, commit adultery like recognizable (and not altogether unlikable) human beings. And the effect is startling."

As the young protagonist from the slums determined to improve his status, Laurence Harvey caught the eye of Hollywood. Army Archerd raved that he "throws himself into the bitterness of this role with an intenstity that strikes out from the screen at you." The British actor was immediately signed to such diverse upcoming projects as MGM's Elizabeth Taylor sex vehicle *Butterfield 8* and John Wayne's patriotic epic *The Alamo*. In the role of the middle-aged woman Harvey dumps, Simone Signoret interested American audiences almost as much as Brigitte Bardot had, and she became a popular figure around town when she accompanied husband Yves Montand to Hollywood later in the year so he could make a Marilyn Monroe movie. The news that *Room at the Top* had been banned in Atlanta only added to the film's publicity and box office.

Kissing Hitler

The state of Kansas was keeping up with Atlanta by deciding that Billy Wilder's transsexual

"I think Liz would have dragged Sebastian home by his ears and so saved them from considerable embarrassment."
—Tennessee Williams

farce *Some Like It Hot* contained material "regarded as too disturbing for Kansasans." The censors didn't mind Jack Lemmon and Tony Curtis' cross-dressing, but they said some of the intimate scenes between Curtis and Marilyn Monroe had to go. But in New York, the *Times'* Bosley Crowther pronounced the box-office smash "one of the most uninhibited and enjoyable antics to come out of Hollywood in years." Crowther was also hot for Marilyn. "Miss Monroe is not only superb as a comedienne but is also the answer to any red-blooded American boy's dream."

Monroe was a nightmare, though, to anyone who had to work with her. *Life* featured her on its cover, and then dissected her inside. "Directing Marilyn Monroe is not the unalloyed delight a man might think," the magazine informed. "She often reports late to work. Sometimes she does not come in at all." Her leading man certainly wasn't fond of her offscreen, and Tony Curtis said that kissing her "was like kissing Hitler." Her reputation grew more tarnished when the gossips itemed that 20th Century–Fox had to pull strings with the State Department to extend Yves Montand's special six-month visa because Marilyn's behavior kept delaying their movie, *Let's Make Love*.

Hip Doll

Next to Monroe, last year's bad girl—Elizabeth Taylor—was a pillar of professionalism. In *Suddenly, Last Summer,* the adaptation of Tennessee Williams' stage melodrama about homosexuality and cannibalism, the new Mrs. Eddie Fisher inspired the *Los Angeles Examiner* to exclaim, "Elizabeth Taylor plays with a beauty and passion which make her the commanding young actress of the screen." Her director, Joseph L. Mankiewicz, asserted, "You'll rarely come across a more honestly realized performance by an actress," and, within two months after the film's December release, Taylor had won a Golden Globe for the movie. Tennessee Williams thought folks were praising the actress because of her celebrity; as far as he could see, she was all wrong for the part. "It stretched credulity to believe that such a hip doll as our Liz wouldn't know she was being used for something evil," the playwright contended. "I think Liz would have dragged Sebastian home by his ears and so saved them from considerable embarrassment." John Wayne didn't buy the picture, either, announcing, "I don't intend to see it. The subject matter is too distasteful to be put on a screen designed to entertain a family—or any member of a decent family."

Certainly the set of *Suddenly, Last Summer* was no big happy family. Director Mankiewicz did not get along well with the actress playing Taylor's loony aunt—Katharine Hepburn. "We will resume shooting, Miss Hepburn," Mankiewicz reputedly screamed on the set one day, "when the Directors Guild card which I ordered for you arrives from Hollywood." Another report had Hepburn celebrating the conclusion of shooting by spitting in the director's face. But she, too, got great reviews, and the *Hollywood Reporter* cooed, "Hepburn lashes her part into thunder, no less." Mike Connolly said that "*Summer* seems a cinch to Oscarate Kate Hepburn opposite that other Hepburn."

Nun But the Best

That other Hepburn was Audrey, who played a troubled sister in *The Nun's Story*. Fred Zinnemann's film opened for a long run at Radio City Music Hall in June and became one of the year's five top grossing films. Zinnemann was praised for his "unfailing judgment and exquisite taste" and Audrey Hepburn was described as "brilliant," "luminous," and looking "like an Annunciation angel from any angle." After Zinnemann and Hepburn were awarded by the New York Film Critics, a trade ad reproduced a letter to producer Jack Warner from Jack Benny, who wrote, "My heartiest congratulations on *The Nun's Story* winning so many film critics awards. It is one of the most beautiful pictures I have ever seen."

"The subject matter is too distasteful to be put on a screen designed to entertain a family—or any member of a decent family."
—John Wayne

A Masterpiece of Interpretation

Catholicism wasn't the only faith on view. George Stevens got reverential reviews for *The Diary of Anne Frank,* based on the best-selling book. The *New York Herald Tribune* called the drama of a young Jewish girl hiding from the Nazis with her family and various neighbors "a masterpiece of interpretation" and "a tribute to American moviemaking." Standouts in the cast were Ed Wynn, the comedian who had been making a comeback in dramatic parts at the end of the decade, and Shelley Winters, who, one critic stated, fulfilled "all the early prophecies of her potential prowess." Another reviewer said, "Shelley Winters as Mrs. Van Daan is still Miss Winters but much less so than one would have expected and for me proves herself a very fine actress." Winters realized this role was her best since her last outing with George Stevens, *A Place in the Sun,* and she drummed up support for Supporting Actress honors by talking about how she had given the part her all; she confessed to Sidney Skolsky that she had had to gain 35 pounds for the movie.

Gross High, Sweet Chariot

The film that really put the fear of God in moviegoers was *Ben-Hur,* MGM's $15 million, three-hour-thirty-two-minute remake of its 1925 silent epic. MGM was struggling to stay solvent when the unholy success that Paramount had in 1956 with the late Cecil B. DeMille's *The Ten Commandments* inspired it to redo its most profitable Biblical spectacle. As the *Hollywood Reporter* put it, Leo "decided to shoot the works on *Ben-Hur* with the hope its successful production would give inspiration to the company and the whole picture business, aside from coining money." MGM assigned producer Sam Zimbalist, who had made *Quo Vadis,* to the project and picked DeMille's Moses, Charlton Heston, for the lead. When the crew headed for Rome for ten months of filming, Mike Connolly bade them farewell with the grim reminder, "MGM's future rides on the success or failure of *Ben-Hur.*"

Hollywood received regular dispatches from the set, and excitement began to rise when the editor of the *Hollywood Reporter* returned from his Roman holiday raving about the rushes of the chariot-race sequence that had taken two months to film. Then came word that producer Zimbalist had collapsed and died from the pressure of keeping the superproduction under control. At least five writers were said to have worked on the screenplay—Karl Tunberg, Christopher Fry, Maxwell Anderson, S. N. Behrman and Gore Vidal. The last-mentioned told friends that when he added a homosexual motivation to Heston's hero, director William Wyler responded, "Don't ever tell Chuck what it's all about or he'll fall apart."

Back in Hollywood, MGM's publicity department was as busy as the filmmakers, spending another $3 million on promotion, including commercial tie-ins that ranged from a hundred kinds of toys to a line of towels marked "Ben-His" and "Ben-Hers." The owner of Hollywood's Four Star Theatre was willing to spend $200,000 on redecoration to show the film, but the studio thought the Egyptian Theatre on Hollywood Boulevard was more appropriate. When the epic premiered there on November 24, the *Hollywood Reporter*'s headline was BEN-HUR EXTRAORDINARY, OF GREATER DIMENSION THAN ANY FILM OF OUR TIME.

The critics seconded director Wyler's description of the film as "Hollywood's first intimate spectacle," one going so far as to point out that only forty five minutes of the three-hour-plus movie were devoted to special effects. The New York Film Critics went and named it their Best Picture. But it was obvious from all the jokes about chariot races comedians were making on TV that *Ben-Hur*'s action scenes were what pulled audiences into theaters. The pageant yanked MGM out of the hole, grossing $80 million worldwide and

"Don't ever tell Chuck Heston what it's all about or he'll fall apart."
—William Wyler

breaking box office records everywhere except the United Arab Republic, which banned the movie because it was about Jews.

An Upper-Class Peyton Place

One of the biggest Oscar campaigns was launched by twenty-seven-year-old Robert Vaughn, who was trying to upgrade his stock. In 1958, he played the lead in *Teenage Caveman*. In 1959, when he won the part of a ne'er-do-well socialite framed on a murder charge in a Paul Newman movie called *The Young Philadelphians*—which *Daily Variety* described as "a kind of urban upper-class *Peyton Place*"—Vaughn saturated the trades with ads quoting his good notices and depicting his big drunk scene. He was nothing like that in real life, and Mike Connolly wrote that the young actor appeared at George Gobel's opening night at the Coconut Grove wearing "a black Chesterfield to help bring glamour back to Hollywood."

Another industrious youngster was twenty-one-year-old Susan Kohner, who had played a black girl passing for white in the movie Lana Turner did make this year, the box-office hit *Imitation of Life*. Kohner told Hedda Hopper, "When I went on a tour of the South, I was surprised when newspapermen asked me if I'd minded playing a Negro girl. The thought never entered my mind." Hopper concluded, "Susan's got her head screwed on right and takes no guff from anybody, to which I say hurrah for her." Joe Hyams asked her what she thought about her likely Best Supporting Actress nomination and Kohner responded, "Objectively speaking, I was very good because the role was so unlike my own character."

Gentleman's Agreement

Before the nominating began, two of the leading Best Picture probabilities were involved in political controversies. In the case of *Ben-Hur*, it was the politics of billing. The Screen Writers Guild determined that only one writer—Karl Tunberg—was entitled to screen credit for *Ben-Hur* and director William Wyler let out such a howl, particularly over the omission of Christopher Fry, that the guild placed an ad that read: "Mr. William Wyler is engaged in a systematic attack against the writing credits." The ad explained that Christopher Fry himself had not protested the guild's decision, so what was Wyler crying about?

The cries were even louder when *Anatomy of a Murder* director Otto Preminger announced that the writer of his next movie would be none other than Dalton Trumbo, the blacklistee who had finally confessed that he was the "Robert Rich" credited on the 1956 Oscar-winning *The Bold and the Brave* screenplay. The *New York Daily News* editorialized that in ignoring the blacklist, Preminger was violating a "gentleman's agreement" and concluded, "No law, of course, compels Mr. Preminger to go along with the Hollywood blacklist. But neither does any law require patriotic Americans to go and see the Preminger-Trumbo movie when it hits the screen." The "Trade Views" column of the *Hollywood Reporter* expressed its view of Mr. Preminger: "He's out for the fast buck—and he'll skirt all American tradition and all long-range industry protective measures to get that fast buck."

The Nominations

Ben-Hur won twelve Academy Award nominations, including Best Adapted Screenplay for Karl Tunberg. Best Picture nominee *Anatomy of a Murder* won six other nominations, none of them for Otto Preminger. Nor was *Murder*'s Lee Remick on the Best Actress list with Elizabeth Taylor, Simone Signoret and the two Hepburns. Instead, there was the woman named by theater owners as the top female draw—Doris Day—in *Pillow Talk*, a sex comedy costarring Rock Hudson and produced by Ross Hunter, who also did *Imitation of Life*. "I was surprised at being nominated . . . and even more surprised to find that

"We will resume shooting, Miss Hepburn, when the Directors Guild card which I ordered for you arrives from Hollywood."
—Joseph L. Mankiewicz

. . . I had shot up to number one at the box office," Day wrote later, adding that the sudden acclaim made her realize she had "to face the depressing fact that if you are number one, the only place you can go is down."

A Break You Dream Of

Producer Hunter did very well in the Supporting Actress category too, with three entries. *Imitation of Life* snagged two slots—for Susan Kohner and for Juanita Moore, the black actress who played Kohner's mother. Hunter hadn't even campaigned for Moore and he rushed to distribute the studio's biography of her to newsmen. According to the release, the actress had exclaimed upon getting the part, "This is the break every actress dreams of." *Pillow Talk*'s Thelma Ritter received her fifth nomination, but the four-time loser had no illusions and invited guests to her home on the night of the ceremonies for a "Come and Watch Me Lose Again" party. Shelley Winters of *The Diary of Anne Frank* said she'd definitely be at the Pantages on Oscar night even though her husband, Anthony Franciosa, wouldn't be able to make it.

Robert Vaughn found room on the list for Best Supporting Actor nominees. *Ben-Hur* had placed British actor Hugh Griffith, who played an Arab sheik; *The Diary of Anne Frank* put Ed Wynn over. *Anatomy of a Murder* reeled in two nods, for George C. Scott and for Arthur O'Connell. Nominee O'Connell leaped into the campaigning furor with the energy he had shown in the 1955 Oscar race, going as far as to appear on Pat Boone's TV show to do a number with Brigitte Bardot.

Laurence Harvey was an active campaigner once the nominations were announced and *Room at the Top* managed to nab six nominations: Best Picture, Best Actor, Best Actress, Best Screenplay, Best Director (it was Jack Clayton's first feature), and Best Supporting Actress for fifty-three-year-old Britisher Hermione Baddeley in an eleventh-billed part. Joe Hyams dubbed Laurence Harvey the "dark horse" of the Best Actor race. Jack Lemmon was nominated for his drag act in *Some Like It Hot* and Hedda Hopper insisted he "has got to get an Oscar." Lemmon's competition came from the New York Film Critics' Best Actor choice—James Stewart for *Anatomy of a Murder*. Gossips reasoned that Paul Muni's nomination for his role as an elderly doctor in his first film in thirteen years, *The Last Angry Man*, was helped immeasurably by his old movies playing on TV.

When *Ben-Hur*'s Charlton Heston showed up on the Best Actor lineup, many Hollywoodites did double takes, but columnists predicted that he would ride in on the epic's expected sweep of the Awards. One of the few categories *Ben-Hur* didn't have a claim on was Best Actress, which was a wide open race between Elizabeth Taylor, Audrey Hepburn, and Simone Signoret.

Shouldn't Happen to a Dog

A month before the ceremonies, the Screen Actors Guild went on strike over the issue of actors receiving residuals on post-1948 movies being shown on TV. Mike Connolly squelched a rumor that the end of the strike would be announced on the Oscar show by calling it "an idle dream from which 'clean-cut all-American' SAG prexy Ronald Reagan was supposed to emerge smelling like American Family Soap." Meanwhile, the ceremony was being prepared by Arthur Freed, the producer of last year's Best Picture winner, *Gigi*. Freed called in stage director John Houseman for help, and hired *Gigi*'s director Vincente Minnelli to wrestle with basic aesthetic questions, like whether Sammy Davis, Jr., should sing "High Hopes" in casual wear or a tux.

A different network, ABC, carried the ceremonies, and tried to make a whole evening of it by airing "Oscar Night in Hollywood" before the actual Academy show. The program consisted of Tony Randall and Betsy Palmer interviewing Laurence Harvey, Jack Lemmon, Arthur O'Connell, Susan Kohner, Fabian, Frankie Avalon, and

Nancy Sinatra, Jr., at the Brown Derby. The *Hollywood Reporter* scowled, "The preceding telecast might better not have happened to a dog," and only Buster Keaton, later in the evening the recipient of an Honorary Academy Award from the Board of Governors, got good reviews for his clowning as a waiter. Nevertheless, the show swamped the opposition, *Hennessey* and *Adventures in Paradise*, in the ratings.

The Big Night

Life put its money on Simone Signoret and, on the evening of the Awards, a photographer snapped her in her bungalow at the Beverly Hills Hotel waiting for Yves Montand as he practiced the number the Academy had invited him to perform on the show. The fans in the bleachers were rooting for Elizabeth Taylor, who arrived with her singer-husband. There was no sign of Best Supporting Actor nominee George C. Scott at the Pantages, but Robert Vaughn was there with Stella Stevens. "They're not butterflies in my stomach," Vaughn said, "they're eagles."

The show began when new Academy President B. B. Kahane stepped out and said, "The Academy is graceful . . . uh, grateful to present the Awards as a public service"—in other words, the industry was paying for the show to escape commercials. Unlike the multiple-host format of the past two years, there was only one emcee tonight—Bob Hope.

"Welcome to Hollywood's most glamorous strike meeting," Hope said. "I never thought I'd live to see the day when Ronald Reagan was the only actor working. What a country. Only here could you wait in your swimming pool for the boss to improve working conditions.

"How about the pictures this year?" the comedian asked. "Sex, persecution, adultery, cannibalism—we'll get those kids away from those TV sets yet. The Russians loved *On the Beach*—they thought it was a newsreel. Oh, by the way, William Wyler, your chariot's double-parked outside. Enough of bitterness, let's get on with the open hatred."

After Mitzi Gaynor handed the Documentary Short Subject Award to Ann Blyth, standing in for the absent winner, a bald gentleman in a white dinner jacket walked onstage and lingered uncertainly. Bob Hope walked out and informed him, "There's nothing left over." The confused wanderer returned to his seat while Hope got a laugh by shaking his head in mock exasperation.

Fernando Lamas "and his lovely Arlene Dahl" read the names of the Costume nominees as such models as Yvette Mimieux, Diane McBain and Robert Vaughn's date Stella Stevens displayed the outfits. Orry-Kelly won the Black-and-White Costume Award for *Some Like It Hot* and thanked Jack Lemmon and Tony Curtis, "who, as Louella would say, never looked lovelier." The Color Costume Award went to *Ben-Hur*—one nomination down, eleven to go.

Next, *Ben-Hur*'s romantic interest, Haya Har-

Awards Ceremony

APRIL 4, 1960, 7:30 P.M.
THE RKO PANTAGES THEATRE, HOLLYWOOD

Your Host:
BOB HOPE
Televised over ABC

Presenters

Documentary Awards . . . . Mitzi Gaynor
Costume Design . . . Arlene Dahl and Fernando Lamas
Special Effects. . . . . .Haya Harareet
Supporting Actor . . . . Olivia de Havilland
Sound . . . . Natalie Wood and Robert Wagner
Short Subjects . . . . Hope Lange and Carl Reiner
Supporting Actress . . . . Edmond O'Brien
Foreign Film. . . . . Eric Johnston
Film Editing . . . . Barbara Rush
Art Direction . . . . Angie Dickinson and Richard Conte
Cinematography. . . . . .Edward Curtis
Song . . . . Doris Day
Scoring of a Musical Picture . . . . Gene Kelly
Writing Awards . . . . . . Janet Leigh and Tony Curtis
Jean Hersholt Humanitarian Awards . . . B. B. Kahane
Director . . . . John Wayne
Actor. . . . . Susan Hayward
Actress. . . . . Rock Hudson
Picture. . . . . Gary Cooper

Performers of Nominated Songs

"The Best of Everything". . . . . Frankie Vaughan
"The Five Pennies" . . . . Joni James
"The Hanging Tree". . . . . Frankie Laine
"High Hopes". . . . . Sammy Davis, Jr.
"Strange Are the Ways of Love" . . . . Gogi Grant

"I'm trapped downstairs in the gentlemen's lounge."
—Stanley Shapiro

areet, described by Hope as "Ben's Her," gave the Special Effects Award to *Ben-Hur*. The three winners proclaimed it "the proudest moment of our lives," and Hope cracked, "Thank you, the three Ritz Brothers."

Hope later introduced Olivia de Havilland by informing the audience that the Best Supporting Actor presenter had traveled "all the way from Paris, France" for the honor. De Havilland was rewarded with a long ovation and, after reading the nominees, she asked, "May we reveal the winner please?" It was Hugh Griffith for his Arab sheik in *Ben-Hur*, and his Award was accepted by director William Wyler.

Hope brought on "the world's greatest nuclear physicist," non-nominee Fred Astaire of *On the Beach,* to introduce Simone Signoret's husband. Yves Montand sang a French song about a "failed dancer and waiter" and then performed a dance routine to "The Continental." He received polite applause.

Best Supporting Actress presenter Edmond O'Brien announced that the Academy had selected Shelley Winters for *The Diary of Anne Frank*. Winters sobbed, "It takes a lot of people to put this in your hand. You have to be nominated and voted." Shelley continued by thanking a number of those people and ended with, "And I'd like to thank the memory of that wonderful little girl, Miss Anne Frank, who wrote with such depth and perception about human beings."

Making his first Oscar appearance in thirteen years was the Motion Picture Association of America president, Eric Johnston, who brought his unique style to the naming of Best Foreign Film. "Oooooooh, it's *Black Orpheus*!" he marveled. The accepter of the Award made his speech in French, requiring Bob Hope to translate, "What he said was 'I did it all myself,' " after which Barbara Rush entered with a pocketbook to give *Ben-Hur* its fifth consecutive Award—for Film Editing.

Bob Hope prefaced the Art Direction Awards by explaining an art director's job: "He picks out furniture for the producer's house." *Ben-Hur* won its sixth Award. The vice president of Eastman Kodak appeared to give the Cinematography Awards and told the audience: "Film is a necessary element in the making of motion pictures." But there was a catch: "Without imagination, a camera is about as useful as a hip pocket in the Garden of Eden." *Ben-Hur* grabbed number seven.

After Gogi Grant warbled the last of the Best Song nominations, "Strange Are the Ways of Love"—which Bob Hope said got its "inspiration at a drive-in theater"—Best Actress nominee Doris Day walked out in petite white gloves to give the Award. The winner was "High Hopes" and lyricist Sammy Cahn said, "Thank," followed by composer Jimmy Van Heusen's "You." Day piped in, "Ha!"

Gene Kelly came out to give the music Awards and joked that because of the strike, "Marilyn Monroe showed up on the set and said: 'Where is everybody?' " Dramatic Score went to *Ben-Hur*—eight for eight.

Janet Leigh and her husband, Tony Curtis, announced the writing Awards after Leigh told a joke that ended, "That was no lady, that was my husband." *Ben-Hur*'s sweep got sidetracked when the Adapted Screenplay Award was voted to *Room at the Top*. The Best Story and Screenplay winners were the two writing teams who had worked on *Pillow Talk* without having met. One of the winners, Stanley Shapiro, still didn't get to meet his coauthors, and his partner, Maurice Richlin, read a note from him that explained, "I am trapped downstairs in the gentlemen's lounge. It seems I rented a faulty tuxedo. I'd like to thank you upstairs for this great honor."

Academy President B. B. Kahane returned to announce that the Jean Hersholt Humanitarian Award winner was Bob Hope. This was Hope's fourth honor from the Academy, but the comedian was unprepared and told Kahane, "I'll get you for this. I don't know what to say. I don't have writers for this type of work. This will hold the highest spot in my trophy room."

Hope then explained that John Wayne was

"This guy Charlton Heston is a nice fellow, but what a hamola."
—Aldo Ray

giving the Director Award because "he's just directed his first picture." Wayne described the job: "On the set, the director is the captain of the ship." After getting through the nominees, Wayne inquired, "May I tear open the envelope?" Permission granted, the Duke announced that the winner was William Wyler, and *Ben-Hur* was back on track.

The streak continued when Susan Hayward divulged the Best Actor—Charlton Heston. The winner kissed his wife and then stumbled on the way to the stage. "I feel like thanking the first secretary who let me sneak into a Broadway casting call," Heston said, going on to thank, among others, *Ben-Hur*'s uncredited writer, Christopher Fry.

Doris Day's costar, Rock Hudson, announced the Best Actress nominees and added, "Congratulations to those five talented ladies." As he opened the envelope, *Life* got a shot of Simone Signoret clutching her bosom in expectation. The winner was Simone Signoret, for *Room at the Top*. She kissed Rock twice and said, "I can't say anything. I wanted to be dignified and all that, but I can't." Nor could she keep her dress straps from sliding off her shoulders and down her arms. "You can't imagine what it means to me, being French," the actress added.

Gary Cooper, introduced as "the gentleman who invented the horse," gave the Best Picture Award to *Ben-Hur,* which ended up winning a record eleven Oscars. Producer Sam Zimbalist's widow accepted and said, "I believe my husband would tell you that *Ben-Hur* was the sum of his career. I think you know what it would have meant to him."

The television show was supposed to end with Robert Ryan and Wendell Corey interviewing the winners in the press tent outside the Pantages. But so many people had trampled the television cables in the tent over the course of the evening that the audio was kaput, and the segment consisted solely of Corey and Ryan saying "Good night."

Aftermath

When a reporter asked Charlton Heston backstage which scene in *Ben-Hur* he enjoyed filming the most, the winner responded, "I didn't enjoy any of it. It was hard work." Heston did like winning, and said to his director, a three-time winner, "I guess this is old hat to you." "Chuck," William Wyler retorted, "it never gets old hat." When the press hustled Humanitarian Award winner Bob Hope into the lineup, Wyler turned and asked him, "What did you do in *Ben-Hur*?" Hope replied, "I feel out of place with these other winners, like Zsa Zsa Gabor at a PTA meeting or Governor Faubus in Harlem." Best Song winners Sammy Cahn and Jimmy Van Heusen were similarly awed and confessed, "We're glad *Ben-Hur* didn't have a title song."

Simone Signoret said she had no idea *Room at the Top* would be so popular. "When we made it, we just thought it would be a picture we would like and some of our friends would like. Its success came as a great surprise." When asked what she thought of the Oscar ceremonies, the film actress commented, "It looks like something I've seen in the movies."

Shelley Winters was still crying backstage, but she perked up when the questions turned to fashion. "Simone and I are going to change the styles of the women of the world," she announced. "No more size eights!" Winters also saw an omen in her statuette. She would later say, "I brought my Oscar home and Tony took one look at it and I knew the marriage was over." The Franciosas were divorced later that year.

Buster Keaton was handed his Honorary Oscar at the Governors Ball, where he received a "spontaneous standing ovation." Bob Hope was still carried away by his special Award and said, "I now have two Oscars—I'll have my ears pierced tomorrow." Best Supporting Actress loser Susan Kohner said that she was glad she came out empty-handed. "It's better this way," said the twenty-one-year-old. "It was all too much too soon."

The Writers Guild was angry that Charlton Heston had mentioned writer Christopher Fry after all that trouble over the screenplay credit, but the actor insisted that Fry had been on the set regularly, helping him with his characterization. As far as actor Aldo Ray was concerned, Fry didn't help Heston enough, saying to Louella Parsons, "I think the Academy Awards are ridiculous. This guy Charlton Heston is a nice fellow, but what a hamola."

Hedda Hopper was fuming that the Academy honored an actress with leftist political views. "I never minded when the Democrats won," Hopper wrote, "but I drew the line when Simone Signoret hit the jackpot. I'm as broadminded as anyone, but that was ridiculous. Let her decorate her mantel with Picasso doves and the like. I got so mad, I upped and resigned from the Academy." Again.

1960

"Here, let me carry the Oscar."
—Eddie Fisher

From start to finish the 1960 Academy Awards were a pain in the neck.

"When I saw Noel Coward's *Brief Encounter,* my God it hit me hard," confessed Billy Wilder to Garson Kanin. "I couldn't get over it. And I thought about that picture endlessly, the way you do about a picture that has an emotional impact on you. Then I began to brood about one of the undeveloped characters, the guy who owns the apartment."

Wilder and coscreenwriter I.A.L. Diamond expanded on his brooding and the result was *The Apartment,* the story of corporate employee Jack Lemmon, who, in return for job promotions, lends his New York apartment to his bosses for extramarital trysts. While the director was working on the film, Columbia was promoting *Suddenly, Last Summer* with the provocative ad line "She knew she was being used for something evil"; Wilder decided to take advantage of the situation and heralded his movie with trade ads depicting Lemmon sitting in Central Park and the line "Suddenly, Last Winter—He knew his Apartment was being used for something evil."

"The funniest movie made in Hollywood since *Some Like It Hot,*" laughed *Time,* "*The Apartment* is a comedy of men's-room humor and water-cooler politics that now and then among the belly laughs says something serious and sad about the struggle for success, about the horribly small world of big business." The *New York Times* declared, "Mr. Lemmon, whose stock went zooming last year with *Some Like It Hot,* takes precedence as our top comedian by virtue of his work in this film." And *Variety* raved about leading lady Shirley MacLaine as the boss' mistress who falls for Lemmon: "Miss MacLaine, again in pixie hairdo, is a prize that's consistent with the fight being waged for her affections . . . Rather than a single human being, Miss MacLaine symbolizes the universal prey of convincing, conniving married men within the glass walls of commerce." Sidney Skolsky noted that a number of editorials chided the comedy for "the deplorable theme of immorality and promiscuousness," but they didn't stop *The Apartment* from more than doubling its $3-million cost at U.S. box offices alone.

A Blow to Mother Love

"To me, it's a fun picture," explained Alfred Hitchcock. "The processes through which we take the audience, you see, it's rather like taking them through the haunted house at the fairground or the roller coaster, you know." The source of all this fun was *Psycho,* a thriller the director shot with his *Alfred Hitchcock Presents* television crew on a budget of $800,000 and in black-and-white to resemble the exploitation quickies that were so profitable at drive-ins. Hitchcock came up with his own exploitational gimmicks to sell the movie: the ads depicted star Janet Leigh, in a bra, screaming, while the poster stated flatly, "No one will be admitted after the picture has started." Paramount was also taken aback by Hitchcock's daring—he had photographed Hollywood's first flushing toilet.

"You had better have a pretty strong stomach and be prepared for a couple of grisly shocks when you go to see Alfred Hitchcock's *Psycho,*" warned Bosley Crowther in the *New York Times.* "There is not an abundance of subtlety or the lately familiar Hitchcock bent toward significant and colorful scenery in this obviously low-budget job." *Time* worried that "a blow is dealt to mother love from which that sentiment may not recover," but audiences weren't concerned; latecomers waited patiently outside the theaters to see what all the screaming was about. *Psycho* was Paramount's biggest grosser since *The Ten Commandments* and had Hedda Hopper crying, "Oscar overdue for

Overleaf: *The day after, Eddie Fisher and Elizabeth Taylor show off her tracheotomy scar and the Oscar it won her.*

"Elmer really wasn't acting, that was me."
—Burt Lancaster.

Hitchcock—there's no justice if he doesn't get one for *Psycho*."

Sixty-four Teeth

Even children who arrived punctually couldn't get in to see *Elmer Gantry*, which was advertised with the ultimate promotional gimmick—an "Adults Only" label. Sinclair Lewis' novel had been condemned in 1927 for ridiculing religious leaders, and writer-director Richard Brooks told *Variety* that he had already heard from certain Protestant groups while the film was in production. "They attacked the project without ever reading the screenplay," he said. Brooks was nonetheless committed; after all, the late Sinclair Lewis had defended him in 1946 when the United States Marine Corps tried to sue Brooks over his first novel, *The Brick Foxhole*, which dealt with the murder of a homosexual. "*Elmer Gantry* is the story of a man who wants what everyone is supposed to want—money, sex and religion," interpreted Brooks. "He's the all-American Boy." So was Burt Lancaster, the star of Brooks' 1947 screenplay *Brute Force;* thirteen years later, Brooks persuaded Lancaster not only to play Gantry, but to co-produce the movie. The actor was happy to do it. "Some parts you fall into like an old glove. Elmer really wasn't acting, that was me."

Brooks' other casting ideas included Shirley Jones—the virginal heroine of Rodgers and Hammerstein musicals—as a prostitute; pop singer Patti Page, in her film debut, as a gospel singer; and Jean Simmons, who would fall in love with the director during shooting and later marry him, in the role of an evangelist based on Aimee Semple McPherson. The film got through only the first half of the book—and that half took up two hours and twenty-four minutes of screen time—but the critics didn't miss the second half. *Cue* magazine called it "a powerful and gripping motion picture, in many ways a far better movie than the book was a book." *Time* raved, "Hollywood's Gantry is Burt Lancaster, whose sixty-four teeth flash brighter than ever with a sort of brushed-in goodness," and the *New York Herald Tribune* observed, "Shirley Jones plays her part with as much energy as Lancaster does his, which is about as much as anyone can expect." They were too energetic for Ontario; *Variety* reported the province's censor began cutting the dialogue when Jones told her fellow hookers, "He rammed the fear of God into me."

The Sweet Smell of Success

Producer Jerry Wald, having hit the box-office bull's-eye with *Peyton Place,* turned to another racy author for his next film—D.H. Lawrence. Wald made *Sons and Lovers* near the writer's home in England's industrial Midlands for $535,000 and signed Wendy Hiller and Trevor Howard as his stars. To attract the teenagers again, Wald cut out the first half of the novel and concentrated the movie's ads on the son and his lovers. "The innocence of a girl like Miriam and the experience of a woman like Clara are part of a young man's growing up," teased one poster.

Newsweek informed readers that D.H. Lawrence had not been turned into Grace Metalious: "The Anglo-American collaborators who have dramatized *Sons and Lovers* have done a find job of bringing a genuine classic to the screen; it is treated with affection and respect in a performance that is first rate." Twentieth Century–Fox was relieved when the teenagers showed up after the film's original art-house runs were expanded. "Ironically," thought Bosley Crowther in The *New York Times,* "the most dynamic and emotional character in the film is the discarded miner-father, played brilliantly by Trevor Howard." Also praised was director Jack Cardiff, a former cinematographer, whose earlier film that year, *Scent of Mystery,* the first movie in Smell-O-Vision, wasn't as successful. Mike Connolly reported that at the premiere the "too-strong, smell-blowing gimmick sent many in the celebstudded premiere pews scurrying to the washrooms, handkerchiefs to their kissers, sick to their stomach."

Prometheus with Polio

Two movies based on historical dramas bowed in the fall. Stanley Kramer adapted *Inherit the Wind,* a play inspired by the 1925 Scopes "monkey trial" about the teaching of Darwin's theory of evolution in a Tennessee public school. Kramer cast Spencer Tracy and Fredric March as the battling lawyers and to make sure Hollywood understood the play's political parallels to recent history, hired the formerly blacklisted writer Nathan E. Douglas to pen the screenplay. Adolphe Menjou and his cohorts in the American Legion were critical, but Moss Hart, the president of the Authors League of America, sent Kramer a cable congratulating him. The movie got respectable reviews and so-so grosses, but *Time* carped, "There is Spencer Tracy, the Hollywooden archetype of the wise old man, who as the years and pictures go by acts less and less and looks more and more as though he had been carved out of Mount Rushmore."

Time also didn't think much of Dore Schary's adaptation of his Broadway tribute to FDR—*Sunrise at Campobello*. "Playing to posterity, Schary presents Roosevelt as a sort of Prometheus with Polio," the magazine said. Ralph Bellamy recreated his Broadway turn as the world's most famous infantile paralysis victim, and Mrs. Roosevelt was played by Greer Garson, who mimicked the former First Lady's speech and buck teeth. Hollis Alpert, in the *Saturday Review,* thought she did a great impression: "It's the kind of personal triumph that sometimes leads to Academy Awards, when the collective judgment involved in Hollywood's honor system operates with reasonableness and sound taste."

Move Over, DeMille

Stanley Kramer wasn't the only one to look for talent on the blacklist; executive producer Kirk Douglas hired Dalton Trumbo, one of the Hollywood Ten, to adapt Howard Fast's novel *Spartacus,* about a Roman slave rebellion, into a $12-million, three-hour-sixteen-minute epic. When director Anthony Mann had to drop out of the superproduction, Douglas replaced him with Stanley Kubrick, who had not been able to get a job for two years after the critical success and box-office failure of *Paths of Glory*. "At 32, with only four pix behind him," remarked *Variety,* "Kubrick has out-DeMilled the old master in spectacle, without ever permitting the story or the people who are the core of the drama to become lost in the shuffle . . . While the question of Trumbo's political position may again become an issue, there is no ignoring the man is a helluva craftsman." Hedda Hopper begged to differ, telling readers, "I happen to think *Spartacus* was one of the worst pictures I've ever seen and the script was written by Dalton Trumbo."

Moral Idiots

For 1960 audiences, there were a lot of familiar faces in *Spartacus;* Janet Leigh's real-life husband, Tony Curtis, was a slave, and her boyfriend from *Psycho,* John Gavin, was Julius Caesar. Mrs. Richard Brooks—Jean Simmons—was in this one, too, and during the film's reserved-seat engagement in Times Square, the usherettes wore gowns "just like the ones worn by Jean Simmons in the film." The *New York Herald Tribune*'s Paul V. Beckley singled out his favorite in the all-star cast: "But it is Peter Ustinov who comes near to making up entirely for everything sticky or generalized in the picture. He takes gleeful advantage of every chance the script or situation offers. He is at all times a delight. . . ."

Time was taken with the epic's villain—Laurence Olivier. "As might be expected," the magazine said, "Olivier makes a memorable Crassus, emerging as a voluptuary of power; a moral idiot whose only feelings are in his skin." Much of the same could be said of Archie Rice, the character Olivier played in the film version of John Os-

"It used to be that everyone tried to play the game on a level of elegance, but no more."
—Sammy Cahn

borne's *The Entertainer,* which, like *Spartacus,* appeared in October. Unlike the immensely popular *Spartacus, The Entertainer* never ventured out of the art house, but it earned great reviews.

The Greeks Had a Word for Her

The art-house smash of the year was made in Greece by a blacklisted American director—Jules Dassin's *Never on Sunday.* The ex-Hollywood director, who had directed *Brute Force* with Burt Lancaster, fled the United States in 1951 during the witch-hunts and worked in Europe. "I had time to think and feel," he recalled. "I began those years as a technician. I came out of them an artist." With $151,000, Dassin wrote, directed, and costarred in a comedy about an American in Greece who tries to reform a golden-hearted prostitute, played by Dassin's real-life fiancée, Melina Mercouri. "A big, laughing girl with a big sweet mouth has the most contagious personality of any foreign movie star to hit America in years," exclaimed *Life,* which explained that the name Melina was the Greek word for honey. Mercouri picked up the Best Actress award at Cannes, composer Manos Hadjidakis had an international hit record with the movie's theme song, and Dassin saw his low-budget film pull in $8 million worldwide. "The fact seems to be that when an art pic catches on, it no longer really is an 'art' pic," deduced *Variety.* "*Sunday,* though condemned by the Legion of Decency and lacking a Production Code seal, is playing theaters that otherwise would eschew an imported film."

Not everyone was captivated. Brendan Gill wrote in *The New Yorker*: "This is the fantasy that turns prostitutes into the epitome of all that is hearty, warm, and generous," and concluded, "What a bore!" Another critic was Mrs. Christine Gilliam, the censor of Atlanta, Georgia, who didn't want the film to play within the city limits. In a decision that made headlines, Judge Luther Alverson overruled Mrs. Gilliam, telling her that by her standards, the city could "deny a permit for the showing of such an innocuous film as *Bambi* if they so choose." Dassin said Mrs. Gilliam reminded him of his character in the film, "the generous, selfless, good-hearted American Boy Scout who is always trying to make everybody over in his image. In doing so, he louses everything up."

Hero Worship

Dassin's analogy did not reach the ears of John Wayne, who told the *Hollywood Reporter,* "I think we've all been going soft, taking freedom for granted." To do something about it, the Duke produced, directed, and starred as Davy Crockett in *The Alamo,* a three-hour-eighteen-minute roadshow western. Wayne spent fourteen years putting the project together, raising the $12-million budget by convincing two oilmen and the Yale Foundation, among others, to invest in what the *Reporter* called, "the most expensive picture made entirely on U.S. soil."

Wayne spent $1.5 million reproducing the Alamo itself and assembled a cast that appealed to everybody: *Room at the Top*'s Laurence Harvey for the art-house crowd and Frankie Avalon for the teen market. Wayne's son Patrick played a soldier, his four-year-old daughter Aissa appeared in a birthday-party scene and Chill Wills was around for comedy relief. Wayne told reporters, "I think it will be a timely reminder to Americans and the world that freedom does not come cheap and easy."

Neither does publicity—the Duke spent $1 million ballyhooing the film's opening, telling his backers, "One smart-alec remark from a newspaperman on opening day could cost us plenty." In addition to frequent promos in the Hollywood trade papers, a large color ad in the July 4 issue of *Life* heralded the epic with the slogan, "The Mission That Became a Fortress—the Fortress That Became a Shrine." The ad also included an essay—"There Were No Ghost Writers at the Alamo"—by Russell Birdwell, Wayne's publicist, who received a rumored $100,000 for his services. On the eve of the October premiere, ABC aired a special, "The Spirit of the Alamo," in which the

Duke read a letter by Davy Crockett and told viewers, "Nobody should come to see this movie unless he believes in heroes."

"It is too bad that one's enthusiasm tends to wilt somewhat during the several hours of incidental exposition that precedes the climax," said Paul V. Beckley in the *New York Herald Tribune,* while Bosley Crowther at the *Times* was grateful for the comic moments: "Chill Wills is the best man in the cast." Wayne decided to trim the history lesson down to two hours and forty-two minutes—his daughter's birthday party hit the cutting-room floor—but the western could not earn back its cost at the box office.

Slut of All Time

John Wayne's *Alamo* costar, Laurence Harvey, went directly from the western to make an example of what Wayne called the "trend in certain quarters of Hollywood to glorify all that is degrading in a small percentage of disreputable human beings" when he signed to play the wandering husband in MGM's *Butterfield 8. Variety* reported, "Alterations made of John O'Hara's 1935 novel by scenarists Charles Schnee and John Michael Hayes (among other things, they have updated it from the Prohibition era, spectacularized the ending, and refined some of the dialogue) have given it the form and pace it needs for best results on a modern screen." The dialogue was not refined enough for the actress the studio wanted for the leading role, Elizabeth Taylor. In one scene on a yacht, the script called for Taylor to purr to Harvey, "You can drop anchor anytime," and later she was to confess to him, "I was the slut of all time—till you came."

"This is the most pornographic script I have ever read," the actress told Sol Siegel, MGM's head of production. "I've been here for seventeen years and I was never asked to play such a horrible role as Gloria Wandrous. She's a sick nymphomaniac. I won't do it for anything." Siegel then informed her that she was obligated to make one more picture for MGM and she had no choice. "It's a terribly mean thing they've done to me," the contractee told UPI. "They have the power to keep me off the screen for the next two years unless I agree to do *Butterfield* and it looks as if that's what they're going to do." Since Fox was offering the actress a cool million to make *Cleopatra,* Taylor consented to make the MGM picture on three conditions: it would be filmed in New York instead of Hollywood; Helen Rose would design her costumes and Sydney Guilaroff her hairdos; and husband Eddie Fisher would play the one male character she doesn't sleep with.

"With Elizabeth Taylor to give it the box-office oomph it needs," predicted *Variety,* "*Butterfield 8,* for all its major shortcomings, seems certain to be huge Metro gold-winner." Hollis Alpert wrote, "Miss Taylor obviously tries hard to get a tragic quality—Lord, how she tries—but not even acting can help this script." *The New Yorker* advised readers to "pretend that it has nothing to do with Mr. O'Hara's novel; just call it 'Yukon 6' in your mind and judge it on its own sumptuously sordid terms." Most audiences did just that, prompting *Variety* to validate its prediction, "Metro sees Elizabeth Taylor's *Butterfield 8* equaling the blockbuster record of *Cat on a Hot Tin Roof.*" Taylor's reaction to the film's success: "I still say it stinks."

Matzo Opera

Elizabeth Taylor's *Cat on a Hot Tin Roof* costar Paul Newman was fighting the Palestinian War in Otto Preminger's *Exodus,* based on the Leon Uris novel that sold four million copies and remained on the bestseller list for eighty weeks. Although the epic was, at three hours and thirty-three minutes, the third longest movie, after *Gone With the Wind* and *The Ten Commandments,* United Artists reported a record advance sale of $1.6 million before the film's December premiere. *Time* wrote, "Greeted by Hollywood wise guys with vulgar hoots ('Preminger's matzo opera . . . the first Jewish Western'), *Exodus* nevertheless turns out—despite its duration . . . and an irritating

"I still say it stinks."
—Elizabeth Taylor

tendency to Zionist tirade—to be a serious, expert, frightening, and inspiring political thriller." Of a large cast that featured Ralph Richardson and Lee J. Cobb, most reviewers singled out twenty-two-year-old Sal Mineo as an Israeli freedom fighter. Bosley Crowther said he was "absolutely overwhelming" and Hedda Hopper predicted a Supporting Actor nomination for the "former young beatnik-type." Hedda admitted that she hadn't actually seen *Exodus* and wasn't going to—it was written by Dalton Trumbo.

Lassie Goes Aussie

Hopper much preferred the Christmas attraction at the Radio City Music Hall. "I don't know how many Oscars Fred Zinnemann's *The Sundowners* will get," she wrote, "but to me, it's the most distinguished film of the year, about real people, acted by real people." The stars of this saga about sheepherders in the Australian outback were Deborah Kerr and Robert Mitchum and the supporting cast included sheep, kangaroos, emus, platypuses, dingoes, and Peter Ustinov, who provided the comedy relief by carrying on with Glynis Johns as a flirtatious innkeeper. The *New York Times* described *The Sundowners* as "a slow, expansive, good-natured film, with many of those small, quiet virtues which somehow never quite seem to justify a running time of over two hours" and Roger Angell complained in *The New Yorker*, "The only suspense hangs on the question of whether Pop can restrain his taste for gambling, barroom brawling, and the loose foot long enough to make a down payment on a little gray home in the west—a dilemma perhaps more suitable for a half-hour *Lassie* episode."

Hedda Takes Manhattan

Deborah Kerr did hold the attention of the New York Film Critics long enough to win their Best Actress Award. Her former costar from *From Here to Eternity*, Burt Lancaster, was the critics' choice for Best Actor for *Elmer Gantry*. The scribes couldn't make up their minds over *The Apartment* and *Sons and Lovers* and—in an unprecedented move—gave their Best Picture and Best Director scrolls to both films. *The Apartment* did get to keep the Best Screenplay Award all to itself.

Hedda Hopper was upset over the New Yorkers' choices, moaning, "Love on the screen today is treated as satire, nearly always cynically or sadistically. Yet when a good love story comes along, it always pays off." Hedda was also bitter when she learned that the Academy was postponing the ceremonies to the third week in April. "Setting the Academy Awards back to mid-April is just plain silly," she protested. "It puts Hollywood's biggest and brightest honors on the caboose—coming in months after lesser groups have named their bests." But what drove Hopper really crazy was that the ceremony would no longer take place in Hollywood; the Academy was moving it to the Santa Monica Civic Auditorium. "I'm so mad, I'd like to broadcast from the highest mountain," the columnist shrieked. "We have so little glamour anymore, let's cling to what's left." Wanting to know what was wrong with the dependable Pantages Theatre on Hollywood Boulevard, Hopper discovered that it had lost too many seats when it was "modernized" for the wide-screen engagement of *Spartacus*. Seeing red, Hedda threatened, "If Dalton Trumbo gets an Oscar for either *Exodus* or *Spartacus*, the roof may blow off the Santa Monica Auditorium from boos and hisses."

Vote American

John Wayne's $75,000 Oscar campaign produced forty-three ads for *The Alamo* in the trade papers, quoting the likes of John Ford and Roy Rogers and Dale Evans on the magnificence of the film. "Oscar voters are being appealed to on a patriotic basis," argued columnist Dick Williams in the *Los Angeles Mirror*. "The impression is left that one's proud sense of Americanism may be suspected if one does not vote for *The Alamo*. This is grossly unfair. Obviously, one can be the most ardent of American patriots and still think *The Al-*

"We have so little glamour anymore, let's cling to what's left."
—Hedda Hopper

amo was a mediocre movie." When one of Wayne's ads documented the number of paychecks that went to American citizens during the making of the movie, Darryl Zanuck accused the Duke of a "vulgar solicitation of votes." Wayne retorted by calling Zanuck an "expatriate producer" for making films outside of the U.S.; Wayne made this charge while filming Howard Hawks' *Hatari!* in Africa.

Virus in Music Branch

The race for Best Song had turned into a personal arena for those two musical gladiators, Sammy Cahn and Dimitri Tiomkin. *Los Angeles Times* columnist Joe Hyams observed that "all the composers have taken out ads and all seem to have publicity agents and all are available for interviews." Hyams chose to interview Cahn, who was pushing "The Second Time Around" from Bing Crosby's *High Time*. Cahn had a mouthful to say:

> *The reason I've become so avidly competitive this year is that Tiomkin has made it a fight for life. Have you noticed what he's been doing with the ads and interviews and cocktail parties? The feud between Tiomkin and me began the year he wrote the theme music for* The High and the Mighty. *It would have been better if he had just gracefully accepted the fact that my song for the year, "Three Coins in the Fountain," was better, and let it go at that. Tiomkin has stimulated a virus that has infected every branch of the music industry.*

Dimi, hustling "The Green Leaves of Summer" from *The Alamo,* couldn't take this without saying a few words himself. Upon Tiomkin's invitation, Dick Williams interviewed the composer in "the trophy office of his big, old home in Hancock Park":

> *What is the duty of the Academy? I will tell you. I am interested in the Awards as a businessman. They increase my royalties.* High Noon *did more for me than all of my symphonic work combined. It doubled my royalties . . . I suffer for recognition here and the Academy Awards show to me is recognition . . . Composers have nothing to say about the product now . . . Four weeks was all I was allowed to write* The Alamo *score. For* Guns of Navarone, *it is five weeks. It is ruining my health and my heart.*

As if Cahn and Tiomkin didn't have enough to worry about, they had to compete with Manos Hadjidakis' "Never on Sunday." *Daily Variety* reported that Paul Francis Webster and Henry Mancini "were very worried at the Racquet Club (in Palm Springs) over dark-horse last-minute entry 'Never on Sunday.' Webster insists 'Sunday' will have to be sung in GREEK if performed on the Academy program."

A Little Ad Will Do Ya

Producer Ross Hunter was worried about *Never on Sunday*'s Melina Mercouri claiming a Best Actress nomination when Sidney Skolsky commented, "It's interesting to note that most of the actresses who are front-runners for an Oscar nomination portrayed 'bad girls'—as the Johnston Office calls them." Hunter tried to stem the tide by promoting Doris Day, who starred in his thriller *Midnight Lace*. Louella Parsons joined in by stressing Day's versatility while Hunter attempted to re-create the film's suspenseful moments in trade-paper ads. Readers saw a picture of Day with the headline: "Reel 6B, Scene 62, CLOSE-UP, Kit on a girder, paralyzed with fear . . . This is the point of no return. Behind her, a murderer. Ahead, a suicidal plunge!"

Two supporting hopefuls spared no expense in their pursuit of Oscar. Shirley Jones put the $5,000 she was saving to add a wing to her house into a campaign promoting her prostitute turn in *Elmer Gantry*. And an unknown named Peter Falk

"It appears more people voted for The Alamo than have seen it."
—Sidney Skolsky

advertised his performance in the gangster programmer, *Murder, Inc.*, with innumerable ads and appearances on TV talk shows. Sidney Skolsky was impressed and said, "If it happens, it'll be one of the rare times an actor in a 'B' picture got a nomination in the Oscar derby." Falk's success would not be as rare as Milton Berle's if the comic achieved his goal—getting nominated for *Let's Make Love*, a film in which he played himself.

The Nominations

Sidney Skolsky declared that "the biggest surprise" in the nominations was the Best Picture nod for *The Alamo*. "It appears more people voted for *The Alamo* than have seen it," he quipped. Hedda Hopper was thrilled, particularly because Dalton Trumbo wasn't nominated for anything. She wrote, "*The Alamo*, frowned on by liberals, got nominated and I believe has a good chance of winning." Her fellow columnists weren't so sure. Skolsky said, "This year there's no chariot race to make the race a runaway," and Louella Parsons admitted, "The Award race has never been as wide open."

The Apartment, Sons and Lovers and *The Sundowners* were the only Best Picture nominations with nominated directors. For *Elmer Gantry's* Richard Brooks, it was only the beginning of the bad news—a few hours after he learned he was not nominated for Best Director, Brooks saw a truck run into his sports car. Brooks was nominated for Best Adapted Screenplay, Burt Lancaster for Best Actor, and Shirley Jones got her money's worth with a Best Supporting Actress nod. Her biggest competition came from *Psycho*'s Janet Leigh, who told reporters, "I think I have just as good a chance as any of the other girls." Hitchcock received his fifth Best Director nomination and Paramount ran ads showing Leigh shaking hands with him as he sat in a director's chair marked "Mrs. Bates."

Burt Lancaster's rivals were Jack Lemmon for *The Apartment*, Trevor Howard for *Sons and Lovers*, Laurence Olivier for *The Entertainer*, and Spencer Tracy, winning his seventh nomination, for *Inherit the Wind*. Said Tracy, "I need another award like I need ten pounds." Milton Berle wasn't convincing enough to Academy voters, but Peter Falk won a Best Supporting Actor nomination—and made it pay off almost immediately. Hank Grant wrote in the *Hollywood Reporter*, "Unknown and unsung in Hollywood as recently as last Thanksgiving, Peter Falk is now about the most sought-after guest star by TV producers, not to mention a current flock of participation bids to star his own series."

The Mule That Roared

Falk's efforts at self-promotion paled next to Chill Wills'. When the supporting actor of *The Alamo* was nominated, he was not content to leave his fate in the hands of John Wayne's publicist Russell Birdwell, but hired his own press agent—one W.S. "Bow-Wow" Wojciechowicz—to help him pull ahead of the front-runners in the Supporting Actor race: *Exodus*' Sal Mineo and *Spartacus*' Peter Ustinov. Wojciechowicz kicked off the campaign by mailing out letters to Academy voters repeating a Hedda Hopper plug for Wills. When Hedda got wind of this tactic, she wrote, "On March 2, I wrote in my column that I hoped Chill Wills would get the Oscar. Now I learn that Chill has sent out letters using my name to influence Academy voters to vote for him and because of this he's just lost my vote." Despite the fact that Hopper claimed to have resigned from the Academy after Simone Signoret won the previous year, Wills apologized publicly to the columnist, adding, "Although my representative may have gone too far, it is possible that Miss Hopper has also."

His representative was just getting started. A series of ads listing every member of the Academy alphabetically appeared in the trades with a picture of Chill and the comment, "Win, lose or

"I'm sure his intentions were not as bad as his taste."
John Wayne

draw, you're all my cousins and I love you all."

After the ad with the *M*'s ran, Groucho Marx placed his own ad:

> *Dear Mr. Chill Wills, I am delighted to be your cousin, but I voted for Sal Mineo. Groucho Marx.*

Mort Sahl was so tickled by Groucho's antics that at the Screen Writers Guild Awards dinner, he suggested an Oscar be given to Marx for "Best Ad."

Then Bow-Wow sprang his pièce de résistance. On the Friday that Groucho's ad was printed in the *Hollywood Reporter*, the facing page featured a photo of the *Alamo* cast, a picture of Chill in his buckskin costume superimposed over them, and the copy line, "We of the *Alamo* cast are praying harder—than the real Texans prayed for their lives in the Alamo—for Chill Wills to win the Oscar as the Best Supporting Actor—Cousin Chill's acting was great. Your Alamo Cousins." *Daily Variety* had refused to run the ad.

By Monday, John Wayne had an open letter in *Daily Variety*. According to the Duke, "the Chill Wills ad published in the *Hollywood Reporter*, of which we had no advance knowledge, [contained] an untrue and reprehensible claim. No one in the Batjac organization [Wayne's production company] or in the Russell Birdwell office has been a party to his trade paper advertising. I refrain from using stronger language because I am sure his intentions were not as bad as his taste."

The *Los Angeles Times*' Joe Hyams had a good laugh over Wayne's letter. "There are those in Hollywood, including this writer, who think that for John Wayne to impugn Chill Wills' taste is tantamount to Jayne Mansfield criticizing a stripper for too much exposure." After picking up the Screen Directors Guild Award for *The Apartment*, Billy Wilder told the audience, "Keep praying, cousins! We hope Oscar will say the right thing this year."

Even Bow-Wow realized he'd gone too far this time and publicly apologized with his own ad. At $250 a page, the trades were making a mint off of all the *Alamo* cousins apologizing to one another. Bow-Wow confessed that "Wills did not know anything whatsoever about this ad and when he saw it he was madder than Wayne and Birdwell put together. I informed Wayne and Birdwell after the ad appeared that I was fully responsible." Chill was not satisfied. The actor, best known as the voice of Francis the Talking Mule, told Sheilah Graham, "I always had a very reputable name in this town. One day I'll get even with that so-and-so if it's the last thing I do."

Never in a Month of Sundays

Even with all of Chill Wills' fireworks, the most dramatic race was Best Actress. *Never on Sunday* racked up four nominations: Best Song, Best Original Screenplay, Best Director and Best Actress. When Melina Mercouri made the list with Elizabeth Taylor, Deborah Kerr, Greer Garson, and Shirley MacLaine, that meant there was no room for Doris Day. "Of course I'm disappointed," Day said to Sidney Skolsky, "but it's not the end of the world." Melina, on the other hand, didn't know quite what to think. She told Art Buchwald:

> *At the beginning I am very happy to have the honor, but what kind of honor is it? First Louella Parsons writes they shouldn't give it to a foreign actress but to a nice American girl like Doris Day who makes pictures in Hollywood and not overseas . . .*
>
> *The UA people say I can't win unless I go back to Hollywood and make a campaign for the Oscar. What kind of campaign should I make? I told them I'm not Kennedy. I'm an actress, not a politician. What do they want me to do—ring doorbells in Beverly Hills and say, "Good day. My name is Melina Mercouri and I would like you to vote for me as the best actress of the year."*
>
> *We have a saying in Greece that if you don't vote for yourself, the roof will fall down and the house will catch on fire. Why*

"One day I'll get even with that so-and-so if it's the last thing I do."
—Chill Wills

should I go back there and suffer? Before I was nominated, I was very happy and relaxed. Everybody loved me and the picture. Now I am not happy and I am not relaxed.

Mercouri decided to wait out the finish in Paris with Dassin, which was just as well, according to Sheilah Graham, who wrote on March 11, "There is no question about it now—Elizabeth Taylor will win the Oscar this year . . . popular sentiment was against her because of her tie-up to the Eddie Fisher–Debbie Reynolds marital smash. Now, everything is forgotten in the hope that this beautiful woman will regain her health and find a way of life that will bring her happiness."

Prescription: Oscar

Elizabeth Taylor had been in a London hospital for a month, and her condition took a turn for the worse a few weeks before the ceremony. *Newsweek* attempted to unscramble the various diagnoses: "The twenty-nine-year-old Taylor suffered first from a puzzling ailment—ascribed in turn to Malta Fever, an abscessed tooth (which was removed), a virus and meningism. Next, a brief attack of the flu. Last week, Miss Taylor came down with a severe case of pneumonia. Doctors called her condition 'grave' after performing a tracheotomy." But Taylor recovered and indicated she'd be there in Santa Monica on Oscar night.

All the other nominees abandoned hope. Louella Parsons heard from six-time nominee Deborah Kerr "from her home in Switzerland" that she thought Taylor should win not because she was ill, but because her performance was "superb." Melina Mercouri toyed with the idea of asking the other nominees to drop out of the race with her and let Liz win unanimously, but she dropped the idea. "I was afraid to suggest it because then everyone would think I was just trying to make publications," she told an interviewer. Shirley MacLaine, filming *My Geisha* in Japan, heard the news of the tracheotomy and canceled her plans to attend the ceremonies. MacLaine then called Taylor and asked Liz to accept for her if she won for *The Apartment*. Liz said she'd be delighted to, but nobody could imagine Taylor staggering to the podium for someone else's benefit.

The Big Night

The promise of Elizabeth Taylor's first public appearance since her operation lured 2,500 fans to the bleachers surrounding the Santa Monica Civic Auditorium. The first nominee they saw was Chill Wills, who told friends in the lobby, "Phone me in Forest Lawn tomorrow!" The fans didn't recognize Shirley Temple or Hedy Lamarr, but they went wild for TV star Gardner McKay as well as for Bobby Darin and Sandra Dee, who pulled up in a car that Hedda Hopper said cost $97,500. Darin's chief competitor for fan adulation was Sal Mineo, who arrived with Tuesday Weld. Mineo's father had promised to build him a special stand for his Oscar. "Pop's a casket maker," Army Archerd gleefully related. Mineo confessed to forecourt emcee Johnny Grant that "I've been unable to sleep for days," and that he had spent the previous afternoon pumping iron in the gym to forget the suspense.

But the crowd wanted Liz. Johnny Grant had to reassure the mob continually that she was going to arrive. The *Los Angeles Herald-Express* recorded that "a young man in Bermuda shorts, beachwalkers, and a suntan, but no shirt, got all the way to outdoor emcee Johnny Grant's podium and his voice over the loudspeaker asked, 'Is Liz here? She's well, isn't she?' " Then starlet Mara Massey arrived and was mistaken for Taylor—pandemonium broke loose. Just as the crowd had collected itself, the real Liz finally arrived. So did Burt Lancaster, but nobody paid any attention to him. The star of the forthcoming *Cleopatra* rolled up in a limousine purchased for her by Fox. The fans descended the bleachers and formed a human net, thirty persons deep, around the Eddie Fishers. One woman torpedoed herself through the throng and told the nominee, "I came from Riverside just to see you, honey. We all love you there—not a fan club, but just everybody!" After the police subdued the Riverside resident, Liz limped at a snail's pace into the theater. Husband Eddie remarked on her improving health: "She's in great shape—the blood clot in her leg is all healed."

Despite Eddie's opinion, the first thing Liz did after making it through the sea of newsmen and photographers was head for the ladies' room. She stayed there for fifteen minutes while her doctor, in a tux rented for him by the ever-thoughtful

Awards Ceremony

APRIL 17, 1961, 7:30 P.M.
SANTA MONICA CIVIC AUDITORIUM, SANTA MONICA

Your Host:
BOB HOPE
Televised over ABC

Presenters

Scientific and Technical Awards	Given during the commercials
Documentary Awards	Janet Leigh and Tony Curtis
Special Effects	Polly Bergen and Richard Widmark
Costume Design	Barbara Rush and Robert Stack
Supporting Actor	Eva Marie Saint
Jean Hersholt Humanitarian Award	Bob Hope
Sound	Paula Prentiss and Jim Hutton
Honorary Award to Stan Laurel	Danny Kaye
Short Subjects	Susan Strasberg and Wendell Corey
Foreign Film	Eric Johnston
Editing	Betty Comden and Adolph Green
Honorary Award to Hayley Mills	Shirley Temple
Supporting Actress	Hugh Griffith
Art Direction	Tina Louise and Tony Randall
Cinematography	Cyd Charisse and Tony Martin
Scoring Awards	Sandra Dee and Bobby Darin
Song	Jayne Meadows and Steve Allen
Director	Gina Lollobrigida
Writing Awards	Kitty Carlisle and Moss Hart
Honorary Award to Gary Cooper	William Wyler
Actor	Greer Garson
Actress	Yul Brynner
Picture	Audrey Hepburn

Performers of Nominated Songs

"The Facts of Life"	The Hi-Los
"Faraway Part of Town"	Sarah Vaughan
"The Green Leaves of Summer"	The Brothers Four
"Never on Sunday"	Connie Francis
"The Second Time Around"	Jane Morgan

"I didn't know there was any campaigning until I saw my maid wearing a Chill Wills button."
—Bob Hope

Eddie, stood guard outside. After the cops cleared the lobby, Liz made it to her auditorium seat and the show began. The only other Best Actress nominee who bothered to show up was Greer Garson, and she was scheduled to be a presenter.

The program started with André Previn conducting the orchestra in a medley of Arthur Freed and Nacio Herb Brown tunes as cameras panned seats empty due to a traffic snarl that had limousines clustered a quarter of a mile around the Civic Auditorium. Among those who did manage to arrive in time was a bewildered Jack Lemmon, shown on TV looking for his seat.

Academy President Valentine Davies introduced the master of ceremonies, Bob Hope, who opened with some wisecracks about all the campaigning. "The members of the Academy will decide which actor and actress has the best press agent. I didn't know there was any campaigning until I saw my maid wearing a Chill Wills button." Noting that Jack Lemmon was receiving his second nomination in a row, Hope worried, "My kids think their mother married the wrong lemon. And how 'bout those movies this year? *Exodus,* the story of the Republican Party; *Sons and Lovers,* the Bing Crosby family; *The Apartment,* the story of Frank Sinatra; *Never on Sunday,* about a Greek coffee break . . . ."

Hope then introduced "one of Hollywood's happiest couples," Janet Leigh and Tony Curtis—who would divorce the following year—to give the Documentary Awards. Almost two years after *Some Like It Hot,* the Curtis transvestism jokes continued and when Leigh was handed the envelope, she said, "Darling, do open this, you have the longest nails." A Costume Design Award went to *The Facts of Life* starring Bob Hope, who earlier in the year had told friends that he had a good chance to get nominated with this one. Edith Head was luckier and picked up her seventh Oscar for the film. She commented backstage, "There's nothing like a row of Oscars on a dress designer's desk for putting the fear of God into an actress who thinks she knows everything about dress designing."

Before bringing on Eva Marie Saint to present Best Supporting Actor, Bob took one last swipe at Chill Wills: "There are five actors being held down by their psychiatrists and their cousins." The winner was Peter Ustinov for *Spartacus,* and Mike Connolly confided that loser Chill brushed away a tear. Ustinov said, "Having been educated in English schools, we were taught for at least fifteen years of our lives how to lose gracefully and I've been preparing myself for that all afternoon . . . Now I don't know quite what to say." Hope returned to give the Jean Hersholt Award to producer Sol Lesser, who said a few words of gratitude and then went backstage and told reporters, "I wrote my own speech and rehearsed it for two days and then I had to read what they had on the TelePrompTer. It's just too mechanized." Meanwhile, onstage, Jane Morgan, introduced as "Dimitri Tiomkin's cousin," sang Sammy Cahn's "The Second Time Around," which Hope "dedicated to Joe DiMaggio and Marilyn Monroe."

Danny Kaye appeared to accept an Honorary Award for Stan Laurel, whose partner, Oliver Hardy, had died four years earlier. Since Laurel was ill and unable to attend, he wanted his friend Jerry Lewis to accept for him, but the Academy, for some reason, insisted on Kaye.

Viewers perked up when Eric Johnston, president of the Motion Picture Association of America, walked out to give, for the second consecutive year, the Best Foreign Film Award. Johnston joked, "Often these films require less translation than our own." The result was revealed in the inimitable Johnston style—"The winner is, Ooooooooooh, it's *The Virgin Spring*!" Ingmar Bergman was not present to pick up the trophy from the ebullient Johnston.

The dreaded "Never on Sunday" was the next nominated song. Bob Hope commented, "It was written by an out-of-town boy." It was performed by the star of MGM's *Where the Boys Are,* Connie Francis.

Hope then introduced the man who won Best Supporting Actor for "last year's sleeper," *Ben-Hur*'s Hugh Griffith. The British actor was in

"Thanks for the award to Billy Wilder. I'll be getting lots of compliments."
—William Wyler

town filming MGM's latest remake, *Mutiny on the Bounty,* and he said, "May I apologize for my unshaven appearance." He made his acceptance speech a year late, read the list of Best Supporting Actress nominees, and then declared, "And the chosen of these is Shirley Jones for *Elmer Gantry*." The *Los Angeles Herald-Express* said the winner looked "like Cinderella in a gold and white full-length bouffant gown with beaded bodice, beaded jacket and matching gold beads in her hair." Jones started at the beginning and thanked Rodgers and Hammerstein for giving her the big break. The winner walked offstage and smack into loser Janet Leigh, waiting to go on to perform a song. The two women laughed and embraced.

Meanwhile, the audience was laughing at one of the winning art directors from *Spartacus,* who was dumbfounded when Tina Louise handed him an Oscar. "This . . . art . . . uh," he began, groping for the words, "this award represents the culmination of a man's life and . . . and . . . his career in the movie industry . . . I can think of no . . . uh . . . greater . . . uh . . . achievement for a man . . ." Finally he froze altogether, until one of his co-winners pulled him away as the audience tittered. Bob Hope returned and quipped, "That fella has my diction coach."

The emcee brought on Sarah Vaughan to sing the nominated "Faraway Part of Town," which he "dedicated to the location of the Academy Awards tonight." After Vaughan finished singing, Steve Allen and Jayne Meadows came out to settle the heated Best Song contest. Hope introduced the couple as "the Adlai Stevenson of show business with his favorite bookmark." Dimitri Tiomkin and Sammy Cahn both lost—to "Never on Sunday." The Allens waited and waited for someone to pick up the statuette. While they waited, Steve ad-libbed, "In case you're tuning in late, welcome to *I've Got a Secret*"—the television show which featured Mrs. Allen as a panelist. Meadows, determined to find a recipient, looked out over the auditorium and asked, "Is there a Mr. Hadjidakis in the house?" Allen continued, "I guess he won't be here until Sunday. I'll stand here and write a song myself." Bob Hope rushed in and announced, "This is the moment I've been waiting for," and made a grab for the Oscar. Meadows snatched it out of the comedian's reach and walked offstage with the statuette herself.

Academy President Valentine Davies revealed the following day that French producer Raoul J. Levy had been asked to accept for the song. "He knew he was to accept any Awards given *Never on Sunday* and we have no idea why he didn't," the president stated. M. Levy protested, "Nobody told me I was supposed to accept." Director Dassin, in Paris, thought Hadjidakis had been in Hollywood all along. While others tried to sort it out, Jayne Meadows put the Oscar in a duffel bag and took it to New York, where, before she sent it to Hadjidakis, she displayed it on *I've Got a Secret*.

Best Director presenter Gina Lollobrigida said, in her Italian accent, "The winner is Billy Wilder for *The Apartment*." Then Wilder, after kissing Gina's hand, said in his German accent, "Thank you so much, you lovely, discerning people." Wilder was back onstage a few minutes later when Moss Hart and his wife, Kitty Carlisle, announced that he and I.A.L. Diamond had won Best Original Screenplay. "I couldn't be happier!" Kitty exclaimed when the duo approached the podium. Hart leaned over and whispered to Wilder as he handed him his second statuette, "This is the moment to stop, Billy." Wilder's speech was simply, "Thank you, I.A.L. Diamond"; Diamond's was, "Thank you, Billy Wilder." The Harts then revealed that Richard Brooks had won the Best Adapted Screenplay Oscar for *Elmer Gantry*. "The Bible says that first came the word," said the winner. "There are so many people to thank that I don't have time, so let's do this again."

William Wyler entered and thanked the audience for the two awards to Billy Wilder. "I'll be getting a lot of compliments for it," he explained. Wyler was there to give an Honorary Oscar to "the kind of American who's loved in the four corners of the earth." The recipient was Gary Cooper, who had already won two Oscars. He was not on hand to pick up his third and Wyler introduced "a close

"She's in great shape. The blood clot in her leg is all healed."
—Eddie Fisher

friend and worthy stand-in—James Stewart." Accepter Stewart began weeping during his speech and the audience buzzed—just how sick was Coop? Stewart didn't give any facts, but exited tearfully.

Bob Hope introduced Greer Garson by noting, "She played the part of Eleanor Roosevelt so convincingly that Westbrook Pegler now hates her." Garson skipped down the names of the Best Actor nominees and the camera found Burt Lancaster, in glasses; Jack Lemmon; and Trevor Howard, who was in town playing Captain Bligh in the *Mutiny on the Bounty* remake. The winner was Burt Lancaster, who took off his glasses. "When Miss Garson handed me this," he began, "she graciously said, 'So well earned,' a lovely thing to say. I want to thank all who expressed this kind of confidence by voting for me and right now I'm so happy I want to thank all the members who didn't vote for me."

There was absolute silence as Yul Brynner opened the envelope for the Best Actress Award. "And the winner is . . . Elizabeth Taylor." Liz threw her hands to her mouth and gasped, "I don't believe it!" The audience roared. Sal Mineo turned around and smiled as Eddie Fisher helped his wife out of her seat and escorted her to the top of the stairs, where she rewarded him with a kiss. Liz made it by herself to the podium, where she faced her audience in a Dior gown that did not conceal her scar. "I don't really know how to express my gratitude for this and for everything," she said. "All I can say is thank you, thank you with all my heart." She walked off to tumultuous applause, proceeded to a backstage bathroom, and fainted.

Audrey Hepburn had the final responsibility—the Best Picture Oscar. Billy Wilder collected his third statuette of the evening, but dedicated it to those less fortunate: "It would only be proper to cut it in half and give it to the two most valuable players—Jack Lemmon and Shirley MacLaine."

The TV cameras switched the home audience to the pressroom backstage, where Mitzi Gaynor and Wendell Corey promised viewers that they would be interviewing Elizabeth Taylor and Burt Lancaster. "How many of these shows have you seen?" asked Gaynor, adding, "I'm so glad Shirley Jones won, she looked so lovely." "I'm glad they all won," responded Corey, looking around for someone to interview. "Do you see any winners?" Gaynor inquired. "I don't see any." Neither did TV viewers—the show ended then and there.

Aftermath

Eddie Fisher found his wife in the backstage bathroom and offered assistance. "Here, let me carry the Oscar," he said. "It must be heavy for you." "It isn't," Liz assured him, "I'll carry it until it's too much. I waited a long time."

Taylor pulled herself together and headed for the pressroom, where Burt Lancaster was jumping up and down and hugging Billy Wilder. "*The Apartment* is one picture I'm happy to applaud!" the Best Actor declared, before catching Liz as she started to faint again. Shirley Jones said that she would not be instructing her agent to raise her price and that she didn't think that *Elmer Gantry* would type-cast her in prostitute roles. When a reporter noticed that her hem had torn, she sighed, "Oh, I expected that to happen." Richard Brooks posed with his Oscar, located his wife, and went out to wait for their limousine."Miss Jean Simmons' car," announced the valet.

At the Governors' Ball, the Eddie Fishers received a standing ovation. Mike Connolly reported, "*Life* and *Paris Match* had $20,000 of push-button camera gear on Liz." Taylor earned a cover photo on both magazines just by smoking a cigarette and looking at her Oscar. *Life* dubbed her "Hollywood's favorite convalescent" and Bob Hope remembered, "Everybody wondered whether she'd be able to make it up the aisle. But . . . she was still at the party, dancing and drinking champagne. That Oscar must have gotten the old adrenaline flowing." Liz told loser Greer Garson, "Your role as Mrs. Roosevelt was so much more demanding than mine was," and kidded, "The walk to the stage was the most exercise I've

"Hell, I even voted for her."
—Debbie Reynolds

gotten since leaving the London clinic." When a reporter asked if she was planning to raise her current million-dollar price tag, Liz shook her head and said, "After all, I don't want to be greedy."

Liz and Eddie finally left the ball at 12:15, and returned to the Beverly Hills Hotel for a nightcap with Audrey Hepburn, Mel Ferrer and Yul Brynner. Peter Ustinov remained at the ball and danced what the *Hollywood Citizen-News* described as "a mean cha-cha." The Best Supporting Actor spent the following day applying for a California driver's license. Mike Connolly observed that "Cary Grant, Deborah Kerr's stand-in, signed for every other dance on Gina Lollobrigida's program." John Wayne overcame any disappointment about *The Alamo* winning only the Best Sound Award—he was one of the last to leave the ball at 2:20 A.M.

Burt Lancaster lumbered to his Bel Air home in the early morning and turned to look at the hillside opposite his home. Earlier, his neighbors had erected a sign that read: GOOD LUCK, BURT. Now it said: CONGRATS, BURT. Inside was a telegram from David Niven: "Congratulations and welcome to the most exclusive club in the world." There was a more plebeian telegram waiting for Shirley Jones—one signed by every citizen of her hometown, Smithton, Pennsylvania, population 800.

Louella Parsons rejoiced in her column the next day: "Thank goodness our Oscars came back to America." Hedda Hopper was less jubilant: "Liz should have had the award for *Cat on a Hot Tin Roof*. And whoever thought that song 'Never on Sunday' was music?" Philip K. Scheuer of the *Los Angeles Times* did. "Why are so many commentators 'surprised' that 'Never on Sunday' won Best Song?" he asked. "It is the first fresh sound in a movie since 'The Third Man Theme.'"

Most press attention focused on the shocking news about Gary Cooper. *Life*, after poking fun at Liz's various ailments, wrote: "Then the word spread, and everyone knew what Gary Cooper has known and bravely accepted for weeks past—that he has cancer and is far down the road Humphrey Bogart once walked. The frolic and glitter dimmed. A few days later a Hollywood correspondent wired his New York office, 'I have never known this town to be so depressed.'" Cooper died less than a month later.

While the other also-rans paid off their expensive publicists, a cheerful Greer Garson saluted her publicists, Rogers and Cowan: "Well, boys, we didn't win, but we sure have a great scrapbook!" That's about all Greer had because the day after the Awards, somebody swiped her purse off a counter at a Beverly Hills emporium while she was discussing the ceremonies with salesgirls. Garson offered a reward and implored the thief, "Keep the valuables but please return my diary with my mother's photographs and her letters."

As the culprit made off with Garson's purse, Elizabeth Taylor held a press conference at her bungalow at the Beverly Hills Hotel. She wore a low-cut white blouse, with pink-and-white slacks. Surrounded by her children and her husband, Liz explained that after Eddie wound up his gig at the Desert Inn in Vegas, they would be embarking on a second honeymoon. After that, they would head for Rome and *Cleopatra*.

In Japan, Shirley MacLaine told reporters, "It couldn't have happened to a nicer person." Billy Wilder sent the loser a telegram that read, "Dear Shirley, You may not have a hole in your windpipe but we love you anyway."

Many years later, a reporter asked the first Mrs. Eddie Fisher about the second Mrs. Fisher's winning an Oscar because of a tracheotomy.

"Hell, I even voted for her," confessed Debbie Reynolds.

1961

"I am not a sexy pot."
—Sophia Loren

Hollywood lost its grip on the Academy Awards in 1961 and out-of-towners took home the Oscars.

Just about the only producer making money on a regular basis was Walt Disney, but Hollywood didn't think of *The Absent-Minded Professor* or *The Parent Trap* as Oscar material. The movie that had caused the most excitement during the summer and fall was *The Guns of Navarone,* a fanciful World War II adventure movie with a cast of Hollywood leading men—David Niven, Gregory Peck, Anthony Quinn. Even the critics had been amused by it. *The New Yorker* called it "one of those great big bow-wow, or maybe I should say bang-bang, movies that are no less thrilling because they are so preposterous," and *Time* recommended it as "the most enjoyable consignment of baloney in months."

Producer Joseph E. Levine was serving up more substantial fare. Having bought the foreign rights to an Italian neorealist film called *Two Women* for peanuts, he exploited the hell out of it in the United States. Capitalizing on the name of star Sophia Loren, Levine booked the subtitled film in theaters that usually showed Doris Day movies. His stratagem worked: general audiences accepted the subtitles and the film made almost as much money as a regular Hollywood movie.

For Sophia Loren, the film represented another kind of triumph. She had left Hollywood and returned to Italy because the studios couldn't find any roles that challenged her—her last Hollywood movie had been *A Breath of Scandal* with John Gavin. "I said before I am not a sexy pot," Loren said. "Now I can prove it." Playing a young mother who flees World War II Rome with her teenaged daughter and encounters attacking airplanes and Moroccan rapists, the former pinup girl led the *New York Herald Tribune* to say, "By virtue of her recent performance in *Two Women,* Miss Loren has won the critics to her cause. Before that, the Loren loyalists had no tangible evidence that their lady could act."

On the Shabby Side

Robert Rossen, of *All the King's Men* fame, had made a study of the lower depths called *The Hustler,* which its star, Paul Newman, thought was the perfect American arthouse movie. Twentieth Century–Fox thought otherwise, and, to Newman's horror, dumped the film in wide release in the fall with an ad campaign that the actor charged was "limited and unimaginative"—a poster of Newman in a torn T-shirt. The *New York Times* explained that the studio believed *The Hustler*'s appeal "might be limited because it deals with an almost unknown and rather shabby aspect of Americana—the poolroom hustle." But when *The Hustler* racked up high grosses, a Fox executive said, "We came to the conclusion that this picture had much wider appeal than we originally thought." And Spyros Skouras, the studio president, allowed, "For the first time in two years, I am smiling."

The critics smiled on *The Hustler*'s cast. *Life* said of comedian Jackie Gleason, who impersonated pool shark Minnesota Fats, "Gleason, who fled Hollywood because he could not get good parts, covers himself with glory." *Time* lauded George C. Scott for looking "as though he could sell hot air to the devil." And Piper Laurie returned to the screen after a four-year absence in the role of Newman's lover—a crippled, alcoholic short-story writer. "Laurie gets her first chance at a serious movie part after a series of syrupy roles as a flower-nibbling enchantress," commented *Life*. "She proves herself a fine, perceptive actress." But Paul Newman got the lion's share of the critical attention and the *New York Herald*

Overleaf: *Best Actress nominee Natalie Wood escorted by what Hedda Hopper dubbed her "consolation prize"—screen newcomer Warren Beatty.*

"I take the position that actors shouldn't be forced to out-advertise and out-stab each other."
—George C. Scott

Tribune said, "His standard is high but he has surpassed it this time."

Introducing Warren Beatty

Newman got some competition on teenaged girls' bulletin boards when Warren Beatty made his film debut as a young man who drives Natalie Wood crazy. The film was *Splendor in the Grass,* directed by Elia Kazan, billed as "the first play especially written for the screen by William Inge." Jack Warner went all out ballyhooing *Splendor,* because he saw it marking the emergence of Natalie Wood as an adult actress and a true box-office name—Beatty was along for the promotional ride. *Life* proclaimed him "the most exciting American male in movies," and Natalie Wood agreed. By the time of their movie's release, she and Warren were an item.

Beatty and Wood attracted so much attention that the *National Geographic* sent a photographer out to record them for a study of Southern California culture when the pair attended the premiere of Natalie's other movie that year. She had stretched her acting range by playing a Puerto Rican Juliet in *West Side Story.* Wood lip-synched the Stephen Sondheim lyrics while Marni Nixon, the voice of Deborah Kerr in *The King and I,* interpreted them. Archer Winsten of the *New York Post* said, "Natalie Wood, reaching heights she had never before remotely approached until her triumph in *Splendor in the Grass,* is heartbreaking in her exquisite projection of the role." Sidney Skolsky came right out with: "She is definitely the actress the others will have to beat for the Best Actress Oscar this year."

Ethnic Blurs

The Mirisch Brothers, executive producers of *West Side Story,* had toyed with the idea of casting Elvis Presley as the leader of the American street gang, with his followers played by Fabian, Frankie Avalon and Paul Anka. That was before director Jerome Robbins, who had "conceived, choreographed and directed" the musical on Broadway, convinced them otherwise. The Mirisches enlisted the aid of Robert Wise as producer and codirector to keep the film—and Robbins—moored to reality. Natalie Wood wasn't the only performer in the cast switching ethnicity: George Chakiris, the leader of the American gang in the London production, played Bernardo, the head of the Puerto Ricans, and his screen girlfriend was Rita Moreno, who had played a Siamese princess the last time she worked with Robbins, in *The King and I.*

"Working with Robbins was the greatest experience I've ever had," Chakiris said, "because it was Jerry who first showed me how a dancer could express himself in dancing rhythms and how an actor could intensify his dramatic performance with the graceful, expressive body movements of a dancer." But, in the codirector's opinion, the choreographer took too long showing his dancers how to express themselves and Wise told Robbins to jeté off the set after two and a half months of filming. Robbins' assistants helped Wise wrap up the film.

"Nothing short of a cinema masterpiece," sang the *New York Times,* and the *Herald Tribune* claimed that the film's "genius" was "at least five years ahead of its time." Louella Parsons wrote, "Tiny Rita Moreno, with the big flashing eyes, comes into her own in *West Side Story,*" and Hedda Hopper said, "A great dancer who can act is a rare thing. George Chakiris combines both talents sensationally in *West Side Story.*" The musical outgrossed *The Guns of Navarone* and the soundtrack was the most profitable in Hollywood history.

Oscar at Nuremberg

Moreno and Chakiris had high-class competition for Supporting Oscars. "So many stars have been squeezed into *Judgment at Nuremberg,*" explained *The New Yorker,* "that it occasionally

"I am America's number-one fan. I like your food—especially cornflakes."
—Maximilian Schell

threatens to turn into a judicial *Grand Hotel*." Stanley Kramer transformed a television drama about the Nuremberg war trials into a three-hour movie, sprinkling major names throughout and allowing some leading players to try on character roles. Montgomery Clift played a fellow who had been sterilized by the Nazis and Judy Garland portrayed a Gentile who had been imprisoned for befriending a Jew. But the actor who profited the most from *Nuremberg* was the one repeating his TV role—Maximilian Schell. "He is the least well-known performer in the giant all-star cast," Sidney Skolsky said, "until the movie is over." As the lawyer defending the Nazis, Schell declaimed with such "persuasive skill," said the *Washington Post*, "that the emotional temptation will be to root for his side."

A teaser ad appeared before the film opened and promised, "Once in a generation . . . a motion picture explodes into greatness." Kramer spent $150,000 on a promotional junket to get everyone to his premiere in West Berlin, where he had persuaded Mayor Willy Brandt to give a speech. "If the film serves justice," Mayor Brandt said, "we will welcome it and will still welcome it, even if we have to feel ashamed at many of its aspects." In America, it was welcomed by movie critics who felt, as *Cue* magazine did, that "Stanley Kramer is one of the few men in Hollywood with the courage to face, to discuss and risk his time and money on pictures that have something to say." Historian Arthur Schlesinger, Jr., wasn't quite sure what the picture was trying to say, and found it "without clear direction or logical conclusion." But with a cast including Richard Widmark, Burt Lancaster, Spencer Tracy and Marlene Dietrich and a controversial subject, the film did well in its reserved-seat engagements.

Schell made sure the American people got to know him as he hit the interviewing circuit. He presented himself as a dedicated artist: "I once went hungry for seven months waiting for a worthwhile part." His favorite place? "I am America's number-one fan. I like your food—especially cornflakes."

'Tis the Season to Campaign

The New York Film Critics anted up with their choices: *West Side Story* for Best Picture, Maximilian Schell for Best Actor, Robert Rossen for Best Director for *The Hustler*, and Sophia Loren for Best Actress for *Two Women*. If this last award made Natalie Wood nervous about her Oscar chances, there was more—Loren was back in the public eye when her Hollywood spectacle *El Cid* with Charlton Heston premiered in December to good reviews and excellent business.

But at least Wood knew she'd be nominated for best performance in a leading role; Warren Beatty wasn't so fortunate. He had also played Vivien Leigh's Italian gigolo in *The Roman Spring of Mrs. Stone*, but two leading-man roles weren't enough to convince Warner Brothers that the newcomer belonged in the Best Actor category and they listed him as a Supporting Actor. Beatty went to the Academy and asked them to strike his name from the ballot. Informed that his request had come too late, Beatty then told them that if nominated, he'd refuse the honor.

Maurice Chevalier, by contrast, was actively courting Oscar honors. His role as Leslie Caron's wealthy suitor in *Fanny* was his first nonsinging role in American films, and his agent put an ad in the trades that read "Introducing a new young dramatic star—Maurice Chevalier." Oscar pundits in the trade papers agreed on four thespians as likely Best Actor nominees: Paul Newman, Maximilian Schell, Maurice Chevalier and Burt Lancaster as a Nazi in *Judgment in Nuremberg*.

The Nominations

Newman and Schell made the final five, but the Actors' Branch passed over Lancaster for one of his *Nuremberg* costars, Spencer Tracy, receiving his eighth nomination. "Those actors," Tracy sighed, "they always vote for me." The actors also said *non* to M. Chevalier, giving their *oui* to his *Fanny* costar, Charles Boyer, who played Leslie

"I have to be genuinely in love with a girl to make a pass."
—George Chakiris

Caron's father. The fifth spot went to Stuart Whitman, an action-picture actor who had gone to England to play a reformed sex pervert in *The Mark*. *Daily Variety* reported that once nominated, Whitman nixed TV roles because he felt they would hurt his Oscar chances.

Piper Laurie, Sophia Loren and Natalie Wood were nominated for Best Actress, along with Geraldine Page as Tennessee Williams' martyred spinster in *Summer and Smoke* and Audrey Hepburn as Truman Capote's high-fashion bohemian in *Breakfast at Tiffany's*. Loren announced that she would fly in from Italy to attend the ceremonies out of gratitude for the honor, but the more she thought about it, the less she thought of it. "I decided that I could not bear the ordeal of sitting in plain view of millions of viewers while my fate was being judged," she wrote in her autobiography. "If I lost, I might faint for disappointment; if I won, I would also very likely faint with joy. I decided it would be better to faint at home." So Academy members wouldn't forget what she looked like, Loren appeared on the cover of *Time*, which commented, "A short time ago, all the serious attention toward Sophia Loren would have seemed as preposterous as the suggestion that Jimmy Hoffa might someday win a Nobel Prize." Back in Hollywood, Natalie Wood was a regular in the gossip columns thanks to her comings and goings with Beatty. There were also some tidbits that had nothing to do with him, such as Army Archerd's noting that San Quentin inmates voted Natalie "the girl I'd most like to be paroled with."

A Weird Beauty Contest

The Academy didn't have to concern itself about Warren Beatty making noise—Natalie's beau was not nominated for Best Supporting Actor. But the Academy did have to worry about George C. Scott. A week after being tapped for Best Supporting Actor for *The Hustler*, he asked the Academy to withdraw his name. The actor told the press that the Oscars were "like a weird beauty or personality contest. I take the position that actors shouldn't be forced to out-advertise and out-stab each other."

Burt Lancaster was baffled, saying, "His attitude really doesn't make any sense. He's under no pressure to take any ads. All he has to do is *not* take any ads." The Academy sent Scott a telegram saying that they weren't nominating him, they were nominating his performance. Scott explained to the press, "I did not send the telegram out of petulance or impudence. I meant it to be a constructive rather than a destructive move." Sidney Skolsky thought the whole affair was a publicity stunt and commented, "In fact, the biggest noise to date has been George C. Scott's declaring he didn't want to be a candidate."

No More Pepper Pot

In 1957, a publication named *Exposed* had run a story headlined RITA MORENO: COP-FIGHTING WILDCAT and listed her pinup titles: "The Cheetah," "The Chile Pepper" and "The Puerto Rico Pepper Pot." Now that she was a Best Supporting Actress nominee, Moreno was talking to the town's leading columnists, trying to change her image. The actress visited Louella Parsons, who wrote, "She is a very patriotic girl. She's been on two overseas tours to entertain the troops."

Moreno and Best Supporting Actor nominee George Chakiris were a duo in public, but the actor told Sidney Skolsky not to get the wrong idea, claiming, "I have to be genuinely in love with a girl to make a pass." Louella also talked to Chakiris and recorded her impression: "George is very soft-spoken and quiet, and his skin isn't nearly as dark in real life as it looks on the motion-picture screen."

A Coffee Break

Both Judy Garland and Montgomery Clift were nominated for supporting Oscars for their character bits in *Judgment at Nuremberg*. Louella Parsons thought it was ridiculous the stars were in the supporting races and likened the situation to "a bank president reducing himself to title of bookkeeper in order to get a coffee break." Sheilah Graham thought a new category should be instituted for "Best Star Cameo." Clift announced that he would not attend the ceremonies, but Garland, who was in the process of divorcing Sid Luft, indicated that she'd come.

Romantic Antics

Three days before the Academy's balloting closed, the Board of Governors announced that they were giving the Thalberg Award to Stanley Kramer, a Best Director nominee for *Judgment at Nuremberg*. *Daily Variety* editorialized that the governors' action "raises a basic question of ethics and, perhaps, even a suspicion that the Board of Governors is unwittingly misusing their influence."

No controversy raged, however—another scandal was more interesting. Word was getting back from the Rome location of *Cleopatra* that Elizabeth Taylor and Richard Burton were making like Ingrid Bergman and Roberto Rossellini a dozen years earlier. The Academy promptly asked Liz to give the Best Actor Award, but she declined. On the eve of the ceremonies, the *Los Angeles Herald-Examiner* ran a cartoon of the Oscar statuette stamped with the labels, "Emphasis on Sex and Adult Themes," "Rising Overseas Production," and "Liz's Romantic Antics." The caption read, "Somewhat Tarnished."

The Big Night

Warren Beatty and Natalie Wood created a stampede among photographers when they arrived at the Santa Monica Civic Auditorium forecourt. Gardner McKay, star of TV's *Adventures in Paradise*, pulled up with his date and his dog, Pussycat, and the bleacher crowds screamed and hollered. The Academy told the actor his pet would have to remain locked in his car during the show. Another TV star, Ty Hardin of *Bronco* fame, escorted Shelley Winters, holding her mink around her shoulders as she posed for photographers.

The paparazzi didn't have a lot of nominees to photograph that evening. Audrey Hepburn of *Breakfast at Tiffany's* flew in from Switzerland to attend, but on Oscar night she was sick in bed with a sore throat at the Beverly Hills Hotel. "I could kick myself," she moaned. "It was a long way to come to watch a television show in a hotel room. And I brought a pretty dress." Down the hall was Best Supporting Actress nominee Judy Garland. She said her son, Joey Luft, whose entrance into the world had precluded his mother's attendance at the 1954 Awards, was down with an earache and she thought she should be with him.

Garland's chief competition, Rita Moreno, appeared with date George Chakiris. Paul Newman came with Joanne Woodward. But, according to Mike Connolly, it was presenter Joan Crawford "who made the Star Entrance of the evening on Cesar Romero's arm, her smile outglittering the $250,000 worth of rocks she wore." Crawford was a big hit backstage, as well, where she had a champagne party in her dressing room for the stagehands, wardrobe women and make-up men.

Two firsts marked this evening's ceremony. For the first time, pickets used the media spotlight on the Oscars to trumpet their causes. A group calling itself the Hollywood Race Relations Bureau marched outside the Auditorium with placards reading "Film Equality for Negroes" and "All Negroes Want a Break." Twelve protesters were taken into custody for disturbing the peace, in-

Awards Ceremony

APRIL 9, 1962, 7:30 P.M.
THE SANTA MONICA CIVIC AUDITORIUM,
SANTA MONICA

Your Host:
BOB HOPE
Televised over ABC

Presenters

Documentary Awards . . . . George Chakiris and Carolyn Jones
Costume Design . . . . . . Eddie Albert and Dina Merrill
Supporting Actor . . . . Shirley Jones
Short Subject. . . George Hamilton and Glynis Johns
Film Editing . . . . . Angie Dickinson and Rod Taylor
Honorary Award to William L. Hendricks . . . . Greer Garson
Scoring Awards . . . . . Cyd Charisse and Tony Martin
Sound Recording . . . . Anthony Franciosa and Joanne Woodward
Special Effects. . . . . MacDonald Carey and Shirley Knight
Honorary Award to Jerome Robbins . . . . . . Gene Kelly
Supporting Actress . . . . Rock Hudson
Jean Hersholt Humanitarian Award. . . . . Charles Brackett
Cinematography. . . . . Vincent Edwards and Shelley Winters
Honorary Award to Fred L. Metzler. . . Wendell Corey
Art Direction . . . . Carroll Baker and Richard Chamberlain
Foreign Film. Eric Johnston
Thalberg Award. . . . . Arthur Freed
Song . . . . Debbie Reynolds
Writing Awards . . . . . Jack Lemmon and Lee Remick
Director . . . . Rosalind Russell
Actor. . . . . Joan Crawford
Actress. . . . . Burt Lancaster
Picture. . . . . Fred Astaire

Performers of Nominated Songs

"Bachelor in Paradise" . . . . Ann-Margret
"Love Theme From El Cid". . . . . Johnny Mathis
"Moon River" . . . . Andy Williams
"Pocketful of Miracles" . . . . Gogi Grant
"Town Without Pity" . . . . Gene Pitney

"Martinis for everybody!"
—Johnny Mercer

cluding one who had harassed Johnny Mathis as he entered the theater. The other Oscar first was the absence of Louella Parsons, who had come every year since the first party at the Roosevelt Hotel—this year she was laid up in the hospital with shingles.

The telecast began with Mary Costa singing "The Star-Spangled Banner" followed by an overture entitled "Oscar Fantasy Overture #1." During the musical interlude, the camera glided over the audience. There were many empty seats, but Gregory Peck, Stuart Whitman, Paul Newman and Joanne Woodward, Rita Moreno and George Chakiris were spotted by the camera, as was a young blond woman who had to get up off her seat because she was sitting on another woman's fur coat. The cameras did not find Sophia Loren. "On Academy Awards night, our house held the atmosphere of the waiting room in a maternity ward," Loren said. "I was smoking cigarette after cigarette and drinking cup after cup of coffee." Finally she asked her husband, producer Carlo Ponti, what he recommended for a tranquilizer. "Chloroform," he replied.

Back in Hollywood, Academy President Wendell Corey told the audience, "While we hope you'll be entertained, this is essentially a news event." The anchorman to this news special was "the nicest guy in town—Bob Hope." "Welcome to Judgment at Santa Monica," the comedian said. "I'm something new—a Method loser. How 'bout that George C. Scott?—he's sitting at home with his back to the set." The cameras caught Paul Newman laughing and clapping. "Jackie Gleason can't be here," Hope continued. "He's afraid of planes, and vice versa. *The Hustler*—that's about Bing's obstetrician."

Shirley Jones wiggled out in a skintight gown to reveal the winner of the Best Supporting Actor Award after Bob Hope reviewed the nominees: "Those in contention are fellas who played a juvenile delinquent, a Nazi, a gangster, a gambler and a poolroom hustler. Now you know why I turned down the title role in *The Albert Schweitzer Story*." For the first time, the TV cameras zoomed in on the acting nominees as their names were read, but there were only two Supporting Actor nominees present: Peter Falk, who had played a comic gangster in Frank Capra's last film, *Pocketful of Miracles*, and George Chakiris. The winner was a stunned-looking Chakiris for *West Side Story*. After being furiously hugged and kissed by Rita Moreno, he got to the stage, where he whispered to Shirley Jones, "Wow, I don't believe it." Speaking into the microphones, he said, "I don't think I'll talk too much. I'll just say thank you, thank you very much." In Rome, Sophia Loren was giving herself a manicure.

After a commercial in which Eve Arden showed how her maid poured fabric softener into her rinse water, Gene Kelly danced out to the music of "An American in Paris" and gave an Honorary Oscar to Jerome Robbins "for his brilliant achievements in the art of choreography on film." The smiling recipient thanked everyone except Robert Wise.

Then came another commercial, this one for Crest toothpaste, starring Kathryn Grant Crosby and baby daughter Mary Frances. When the scene returned to the Santa Monica Civic, Bob Hope interrupted the proceedings to ask, "Isn't Bing beautiful? He's fishing in Mexico and has his wife and year-old child hustling toothpaste. You can tell this is the off-season for 'White Christmas.' "

Rock Hudson marched out to announce the winner of Best Supporting Actress—Rita Moreno for *West Side Story*. She bounded to the podium with her pocketbook and shrieked, "I can't believe it! Good Lord! I leave you with that!"

Ex-Academy President Charles Brackett gave the Jean Hersholt Humanitarian Award—named in honor of the late ex-Academy president—to George Seaton, an ex-Academy president. Shelley Winters came on with TV's *Ben Casey*, Vince Edwards, to announce the Cinematography Awards. The Black-and-White winner was Eugene Shufton for *The Hustler*; the Award was accepted by Howard Keel, who said of the victor, "I don't know where he is." As Keel walked off, a man suddenly appeared at the podium. "Ladies and gentlemen,

"I just came here to present Bob Hope with his 1938 trophy."
—Gate-crasher Stan Berman

I'm the world's greatest gatecrasher and I just came here to present Bob Hope with his 1938 trophy," he announced, identifying himself as "Stan Berman." Berman gave the presenters a little trophy and said, "This is for Bob." Shelley Winters laughed through his whole spiel and assured him, "We'll give it to him." When Hope returned after the Color Award was given to *West Side Story*, he quipped, "Who needs Price, Waterhouse? All we need is a doorman." Sophia Loren changed from her lounging dress to her street clothes.

Hope announced that the nominated song "Bachelor in Paradise" would be sung by film newcomer Ann-Margret. A finger-snapping hand emerged from behind a screen. Then a purring sound heralded an emerging female figure in a tight gown. The red-headed singer posed coquettishly throughout the song and was rewarded with a long ovation. The applause was cut short when Eric Johnston, the head of the Motion Picture Association of America, stepped out to give a lecture on the universality of film before handing out the Foreign Film Award. In true Eric Johnston fashion, he opened the envelope and announced the winner, "Ooooooooooh! *Through a Dark Glass—Through a Glass Darkly*!" The star of this Ingmar Bergman film, Harriet Andersson, accepted and Eric said as he gave her the statuette, "And you told me you wouldn't win it!" "I'm sorry Ingmar is not here—I mean, Mr. Bergman; but he's just starting to write his new picture and he never leaves the country." Sophia Loren decided to switch back to her lounging outfit.

Arthur Freed gave Stanley Kramer his controversial Thalberg Award and the recipient said, "Unfortunately, I didn't know Irving Thalberg, but my grandmother and his mother were bridge partners." Then "Moon River" won Best Song and lyricist Johnny Mercer exclaimed, "Martinis for everybody!"

Mercer was followed by Jack Lemmon and Lee Remick, the stars of a then-filming drama about alcoholism, *Days of Wine and Roses*. They gave the Adapted Screenplay Award to Abby Mann for *Judgment at Nuremberg*. "A few years ago I retired to a room on Fifty-eighth Street in New York and I retired with some legal records of the Third Reich," the winner recalled. "And I went there because I believe a writer worth his salt at all has an obligation not only to entertain, but to comment on the world in which he lives, not only to comment, but maybe have a shot at reshaping that world." Mann walked backstage and told the press, "I'm afraid I came across too pompous out there." Meanwhile, Lemmon and Remick were making fun of the Russian and Italian names nominated for Original Screenplay. The winner was William Inge for *Splendor in the Grass*.

Rosalind Russell strode out in a sequined '20s headband to hand over the Best Director trophy—or trophies, as it turned out. Robert Wise and Jerome Robbins became the first dual winners for *West Side Story*. "Jerome, I told you!" Russell said when she presented Robbins with his Oscar. Neither winner mentioned or thanked the other.

Bob Hope said the presenter of the Best Actor Award was chosen specifically "for those who think young—Joan Crawford!" As Crawford made her entrance to the tune of "Sophisticated Lady," the cameras cut to Paul Newman, whose tuxedo pants had hiked up, exposing his calves. The winner was Maximilian Schell for *Judgment at Nuremberg*. The news was greeted enthusiastically in the hall, and the winner kissed Joan on the hand and then on the mouth. "This honors not only me, but the cast and that great old man who has been nominated for the eighth time now, Spencer Tracy," said Schell, who recalled entering the United States for the first time and telling the Customs official that he was an actor. "Good luck, boy" was the officer's reaction. "I can tell him now, I had it," Schell concluded.

Sophia Loren couldn't stand it anymore. It was after 6:00 A.M. Rome time and she hadn't heard a word. "Someone else got it and no one has the courage to call me!" she screamed. Her husband persuaded her to forget it and go to bed. She took off her makeup and her dress and hit the sack.

In Hollywood, Burt Lancaster strolled out to

"I'll be at a special table with Sid Luft and Eddie Fisher."
—Bob Hope

announce the Best Actress Award. As he read the names of the nominees, there was a big hand for Natalie Wood, sitting with a bespectacled Warren Beatty. Lancaster forgot to mention Loren and the audience cried out when he went for the envelope. "I was saving it," Lancaster apologized. "And Sophia Loren for *Two Women*. And the winner is . . . Sophia Loren for *Two Women*." Greer Garson came onstage to accept for "this wildly beautiful and talented girl. We do so wish you good health and happiness along with this award." Garson and Lancaster exited and Bob Hope said, "It must be wonderful to have enough talent just to send for one."

Fred Astaire, "who did to top hat and tails what Marlon Brando did to mumbling," presented the Best Picture Award. Fred looked pleased because the winner was a musical—*West Side Story*. Producer Robert Wise observed, "It's been a wonderfully exciting evening for *West Side Story*."

Bob Hope closed the show: "There'll be a victory celebration at the International Ballroom at the Hilton Hotel. I'll be there at a special table with Sid Luft and Eddie Fisher."

Aftermath

The telephone rang at Sophia Loren's house at 6:45 A.M. Rome time. It was Cary Grant calling.

"Darling, do you know?" he asked.

"*Know what?!?*" Loren screamed.

"Oh, darling, I'm so glad I'm the first to tell you. You won."

Loren began jumping and screaming. Her husband picked up the receiver and asked Grant, "Sophia win? Sophia win? True? True?" By the time the press found her, she was worn out and sighing, "*Mamma mia!* What a day!"

Though fatigued, Loren showed gratitude for her victory the next day by donating a pint of blood. She told Hollywood, "I started as a sex symbol, but it was as a symbol of mother love that I won an Oscar. And that gives me extra satisfaction."

In Hollywood, Maximilian Schell said he was glad he had won an Oscar because "no one in this country knows me yet." Later, Schell and winning screenwriter Abby Mann delivered the Oscar to Sophia Loren, who would be starring in their latest collaboration, *The Condemned of Altona*. Rita Moreno, after painting the town red with George Chakiris, refused to hand over her statuette for engraving. She packed it unmarked and headed to a film location in the Philippines.

"Natalie Wood was robbed," Hedda Hopper screamed, "but at least she got the nicest consolation prize—Warren Beatty." Hopper had her eye on another young actress that evening, too. "It sure was a big night for Ann-Margret," the columnist wrote. "She'd been watching Oscars handed out since she was in grade school and couldn't believe she was so close to all those big stars." The press agreed that Ann-Margret was the star of the show. The *Los Angeles Times* raved over "the sexy, exciting personality of a little cupcake, new to me, named Ann-Margret." Someone ran to the Oscar show's producer, Arthur Freed, and suggested that next year he hire Ann-Margret to sing all the nominated songs.

Another star born that evening was gatecrasher Stan Berman, who had already gained notoriety by invading parties for astronaut John Glenn and President John F. Kennedy. When he was not a party-crasher, the thirty-five-year-old Berman was a cabdriver from Brooklyn. He told reporters how he maintained his expensive hobby: "I just spend thirty-five dollars a week on myself and save the rest for gate-crashing expenses."

"On the whole it was a listless evening," *Daily Variety* complained of the ceremony. Reviewers bemoaned the lack of stars and the Academy began to worry that private Beverly Hills Oscar-watching parties were starting to drain the big party of its stars. Even Harold Mirisch, one of the executive producers of the Best Picture–winning *West Side Story*, had skipped the Academy's function to enjoy himself at Mrs. Charles Vidor's party.

Sidney Skolsky felt the fact that Oscars had gone to natives of Italy, Austria and Broadway indicated that Hollywood was in trouble: "Oscar today stands ironically as a symbol of Hollywood's lost supremacy rather than of its present glory." Skolsky wasn't even turned on by Ann-Margret. "She performed as if she were auditioning for the role of a stripper in *Gypsy*," the columnist scowled. "There's a time and there's a place . . ."

Whereas Ann-Margret was just getting started, Joan Crawford was cruising into decade number five as a professional movie star. "Joan was the kissingest girl at the party," Hedda Hopper said. "She bussed everybody except her partner, Butch Romero." While Crawford socialized, Hedda asked Romero if he enjoyed playing court jester to the Queen. "Sure do," the actor replied. "I've been doing it for years."

1962

"I didn't know if I had any talent anymore."
—Anne Bancroft

The 1962 Academy Awards were a tug-of-war between new discoveries and old favorites, with Joan Crawford acting as referee.

Anne Bancroft's Hollywood credits hadn't been so hot. In 1952, she had come to California from New York and got work in B-movies like *Gorilla at Large* and *The Kid from Left Field*. "Every picture I did was worse than the last one," she said. "I didn't know if I had any talent anymore." Bancroft went back to Broadway to find out. Two successive hit plays—*Two for the Seesaw* and *The Miracle Worker*—convinced her that she had gone into the right line of work.

Hollywood still wasn't so sure. When it came time to make the movie version of *Two for the Seesaw*, the producers played it safe and cast Shirley MacLaine in Bancroft's role. When the creative team behind *The Miracle Worker*—writer William Gibson, director Arthur Penn and producer Fred Coe—was approached by United Artists for a film version, they heard this offer: "We'll give you $5 million if you do it with Liz Taylor, $500,000 if you make it with Bancroft." The trio put their money on Bancroft and she played Annie Sullivan to stage costar Patty Duke's Helen Keller. *Variety* cheered, "Anne Bancroft and Patty Duke tackle the juicy but enormously exhausting roles with great artistry and conviction. It is very likely that re-enacting these roles on film posed the greatest challenge of all to their thespic resources." The movie was so widely applauded that fifteen-year-old Patty Duke was offered her own TV show. And columnists began touting Anne Bancroft as a contender for Best Actress—along with Shirley MacLaine.

Katharine Hepburn's Journey

Back in New York, a TV producer who liked to bring classical drama to the masses decided to branch out into movies with a film version of Eugene O'Neill's *Long Day's Journey Into Night*. Ely Landau was able to raise enough money to make the movie when Katharine Hepburn said she'd play the mother. The movie premiered at the Cannes Film Festival and the entire cast—Hepburn, Ralph Richardson, Jason Robards, Jr., and Dean Stockwell—won acting awards. The three-hour film christened a brand-new theater on New York's East Side with its exclusive, reserved-seat engagement. Theater parties were welcomed. Most critics saluted the movie for its aspirations, but *Time* carped about the star: "Hepburn is too vivid a presence for a woman who is largely an absence."

Best Actress winner Anne Bancroft in costume as Mother Courage (left), receives her Oscar from triumphant non-nominee Joan Crawford.

Grande Dame Guignol

While Hepburn got the royal treatment, Bette Davis and Joan Crawford were unloaded on the neighborhood theater circuit. Their vehicle was *What Ever Happened to Baby Jane*, a shocker about two reclusive ex-stars living in a crumbling Hollywood mansion. "Don't tell me about using two old broads in it," was the reaction of most studio heads when director Robert Aldrich peddled the property around Hollywood. "I won't give you a dime." So Aldrich made the low-budget movie independently, and Warner Brothers finally agreed to distribute it after the press began to get excited about the casting. The *New York Times* had headlined: TNT POTENTIAL EXPLOSION SEEN IN PAIRING OF BETTE DAVIS AND JOAN CRAWFORD.

The film was shot in twenty-one days, and Aldrich made sure that interviewers covered every single one of them. Hedda Hopper asked Joan how she had swallowed her pride and accepted second billing. "Naturally Bette gets top billing," Crawford smiled. "She plays the title role. There was no problem about it." Hopper went over to Bette to get the dirt, and the costar said, "In the area of being a worker and having drive, Joan and I are incredibly alike. But the exterior, well, nothing could be further apart." Aldrich reassured journalists that his two stars "didn't fight at all." The

"I feel like an altar boy invited to the Ecumenical Council in Rome."
—Victor Buono

only tense moment came when Crawford realized that someone had put Coca-Cola into the Pepsi machines she had installed on the set—the Pepsi board member stormed over to Aldrich and demanded, "Will you get that other soft drink out of there right now?"

For publicity's sake, Davis ran an ad in *Daily Variety* a month before *Baby Jane* bowed:

SITUATION WANTED,
WOMAN ARTIST

Mother of three—10, 11, & 15—divorcee. American. Thirty years experience as an actress in motion pictures. Mobile and more affable than rumor would have it. Wants steady employment in Hollywood (has had Broadway). Bette Davis, c/o Martin Baum, G.A.C. References upon request.

The gag was the talk of Hollywood—until *Baby Jane* opened. Studio heads kicked themselves when the has-beens turned out to be the most potent marquee duo since Martin and Lewis. The movie made a fortune overnight and *Time* raved, "Two aging screen queens—both of them going on 55—give a vigorous and talented answer to a question often asked: What Ever Happened to Joan Crawford and Bette Davis." If Warners was caught unprepared for the film's success, Bette and Joan were not—they both had their autobiographies in the bookstores: Davis' *The Lonely Life* and Crawford's *A Portrait of Joan*.

Altar Boy to the Stars

Peter Lawford had turned down the role of the mama's boy Bette Davis hires as her musical director in *Baby Jane*, commenting, "It's a spot I wouldn't have given to my dry cleaner." So Robert Aldrich instead cast a twenty-five-year-old, three-hundred-pound screen newcomer named Victor Buono, whom he had seen playing a beatnik on TV's *77 Sunset Strip*. "I feel like an altar boy invited to the Ecumenical Council in Rome," Buono rejoiced when he won the part. "I can't believe it's me emoting with two such stars." *Baby Jane* made Buono something of a star himself, and Frank Sinatra tapped the young actor to play comic parts in two of his rat-pack movies—*Four for Texas* and *Robin and the Seven Hoods*.

Walk Like a Movie Star

It was a big year for faded movie stars. In addition to Davis and Crawford, Geraldine Page played one in the screen version of Tennessee Williams' *Sweet Bird of Youth*. When director Richard Brooks asked her to walk down a staircase "like a movie star," Page made several attempts at being grandiose that Brooks rejected. "Well, then, how in the hell does a movie star walk down a staircase?" the actress asked. Brooks showed her a film clip of Bette Davis from *A Stolen Life* and the actress got the idea. "Don't say another word," Page told the director, "I know just how to do it." When the movie was released, the *New York Herald Tribune* called Page's "one of the most acute and unnerving performances put on film in a long, long time."

The king of the art-house circuit these days was Marcello Mastroianni, the star of *La Dolce Vita* and other Italian hits. When the comedy *Divorce, Italian Style* premiered in September, *The New Yorker* said Mastroianni "seems to appear in nearly every Italian picture that reaches these shores." The subtitled comedy made an unheard of $2.5 million in the American market, and *Parade* magazine made clear why: "Mastroianni has a dedicated following, particularly among women moviegoers who describe him as a Roman dreamboat and the sexiest male since Rudolph Valentino." *Time* profiled the actor and revealed that his playboy image was just an image. "He scorns the cafés of the Via Veneto," the newsmagazine said. "He is, in fact, a thoroughgoing family man, married for twelve years to his first and only wife."

"Mutiny on the Bounty has become famous for its trouble before it could become famous for anything else."
—The New Yorker

No Cannibalism, No Nothing

With all the noise about art-house movies, the editorial board of the *New York Daily News* felt it was its duty to alert readers to more wholesome fare. "If you're of a mind to take in a movie one of these days or evenings," the paper suggested, "a movie that's just sheer entertainment, involving positively no grim social problems, no dope or alcoholic agonies, no cannibalism, no nothing but Hollywood's show magic at its best—we can and do recommend *The Music Man*." Since Broadway director Morton DaCosta did such a successful job transferring *Auntie Mame* from stage to screen, Warners had allowed him to do it again with the Meredith Willson musical. With Robert Preston leading seventy-six trombones, the exuberant piece of Americana became Warners' biggest moneymaker of the year.

Darryl's Day

At two hours and thirty-one minutes, *The Music Man* was long, but it was shorter than Darryl F. Zanuck's recreation of D-Day, which took two hours and forty-nine minutes. For *The Longest Day*, Zanuck spent $10 million, hired 167 actors, and used 472 U.S. Army troops as extras. He also employed three directors but then claimed to have shot "65 percent" of the epic himself. "This was the greatest challenge any producer has faced at any time in the history of making motion pictures," the independent producer told *Life*.

But it was worth it, according to the *Washington Post*. "Zanuck's audacity," the paper said, "has created a spectacle as awesome, in its own way, as the real thing." "Stupendous," the *New York Times* proclaimed. "There are no more worlds to conquer." But *The New Yorker* complained that the members of Zanuck's all-star cast—including teen-throbs Fabian, Paul Anka and Tommy Sands—"make such fugitive appearances that the audience finds itself engaged in a distracting game of instant identification."

Twentieth Century–Fox was nevertheless impressed with *The Longest Day* and its producer. The Fox board was not so happy with the current studio head, Spyros Skouras, who was spending so much money on that Liz Taylor movie *Cleopatra*—$20 million and climbing—that the company was at its lowest financial ebb since the Depression. Pinning their hopes on *The Longest Day*, Fox kicked Skouras upstairs to the ceremonial post of chairman of the board and asked Zanuck to head production once again. Zanuck accepted the offer and promptly fired everybody on the Fox lot except the group working on the *Dobie Gillis* TV show. The board congratulated itself on its decision when the millions from *The Longest Day* pulled the corporation out of the red.

Brando Overboard

MGM was not as lucky as Fox this year. The *Christian Science Monitor* heralded Leo's latest epic remake, *Mutiny on the Bounty:* "MGM is grooming it carefully as the successor to its big 1959 success, *Ben-Hur*. *Mutiny* is following the *Ben-Hur* pattern—filmed in a grand manner on a wide screen, no lid on expenses, and no effort spared to recruit top talent at all levels." Soon MGM wished it had spared some of that effort. The studio had started shooting on location in Tahiti during the rainy season, and the six-month production schedule expanded to thirteen months and a bloated budget of $20 million.

Life sent a reporter to investigate. He blamed the film's problems on star Marlon Brando as much as Mother Nature. "Worst rebel of all was Brando," the magazine said, "who repeatedly delayed production by defying the director and impulsively revising his portrayal of Fletcher Christian, which turned the other stars against him." Brando defied three directors in all; Carol Reed was replaced by the sixty-six-year-old Lewis Milestone, with George Seaton stepping in for final retakes. When the three-hour movie finally lumbered into movie theaters in November, about the nicest thing anybody said about it was *The New*

"The first impression we had of him is that no man had the right to be so handsome."
—Boston Herald on Omar Sharif

Yorker's observation that "*Mutiny on the Bounty* has suffered the currently modish Hollywood misfortune of becoming famous for its trouble before it could become famous for anything else."

$300,000 for a Gulp of Water

Life held more admiration for the production crew on *Lawrence of Arabia*, which it called "one of the most difficult and expensive movies ever filmed." The duo responsible for *The Bridge on the River Kwai*—producer Sam Spiegel and director David Lean—was now spending three years and $15 million in the deserts of Saudi Arabia to tell the life story of British adventurer T.E. Lawrence. "Water had to be fetched 150 miles at $3 a gallon," *Life* explained. "When Lean recruited 5,000 camels for a scene, the price of water soared because camels can consume 20 gallons at a gulp—roughly $300,000 every time the herd tanked up."

Lean and company persevered and when the epic had its gala premiere at Christmastime, *Newsweek* exclaimed, "This is the first extravaganza that is not a circus." The *New York Daily News* blessed the movie with its highest rating of four stars and added, "If there were more stars in my Christmas pack, I would gladly give them to *Lawrence of Arabia*." The adventure introduced twenty-nine-year-old Egyptian matinee idol Omar Sharif, whom Louella Parsons dubbed "a new Valentino." Elinor Hughes of the *Boston Herald* interviewed the newcomer and wrote, "The first impression we had of him was that no man had the right to be so handsome."

The New Gal-Grabber

Omar Sharif was not the only actor causing hearts to flutter throughout *Lawrence*'s three hours and forty-two minutes. When Spiegel couldn't get Brando to play the title role because he was busy on the *Bounty*, the producer settled on a twenty-nine-year-old, blond, blue-eyed Irishman named Peter O'Toole. "On this day after Christmas, whatta showbiz pleasure to see a new star on the horizon—Peter O'Toole," declared Army Archerd. "And no question he's to be one. All the majors are trying to make deals with him after his *Lawrence* bow."

O'Toole's fans did not have to be disappointed with the knowledge that the dashing actor was, in reality, a family man like Marcello Mastroianni. The columnists played up the married Mr. O'Toole as a real-life ladies' man. Mike Connolly referred to him as "the sensational new gal-grabber" and Army Archerd despaired, "Too bad O'Toole won't be spending a lotta time in Hollywood—his personality is reminiscent of Errol Flynn." But Archerd reported that the new star was enjoying himself in Gotham. "In N.Y., he buddy-buddied with Jason Robards, Jr., but their late-nights-out finally got O'Toole 'barred' from the house by Mrs. Robards—Betty Bacall."

Good-bye, Hairbreadth Harry

Universal's Christmas gift was in black-and-white, a mere 129 minutes long, and was shot completely on the studio back lot. For *To Kill a Mockingbird*, its film version of Harper Lee's novel about growing up in Depression Alabama, the company's ad campaign was: "The Pulitzer Prize novel that has become a legend in its own time is now a memorable motion picture." *McCall's* magazine concurred, raving, "What a sheer delight to see a movie that informs, amuses, enchants and makes you think all at the same time." Although the movie didn't make as much money as Universal's Doris Day comedies, it became a box-office champ and led *Life* to squeal, "*Mockingbird* fairly sings out for this year's Oscar."

Critics were also singing the praises of Gregory Peck. Playing a widowed lawyer who defends a black man accused of rape, Peck stated, "I can honestly say that in twenty years of making movies, I never had a part that came close to being the real me until Atticus Finch." Peck had felt so strongly about the part that he had originally tried to buy the film rights to Lee's book himself. Studio flacks reported that after Peck played a nine-

"People have actually condoled with her real-life husband for having such a wicked wife."
—Sheilah Graham on Angela Lansbury

minute courtroom scene in one take, the actors playing jurors broke into applause. *Show* magazine said, "Gregory Peck, who for years has been almost indistinguishable from Hairbreadth Harry, drops the phony heroics long enough to give an intelligent performance."

Mr. Mid-Century

Jack Warner hadn't been taking notes during the *Baby Jane* success story. He wasn't excited about releasing Blake Edwards' alcoholism drama, *Days of Wine and Roses,* either, even though it starred Jack Lemmon. The mogul opened the black-and-white movie in a second-run house in Hollywood at the end of the year. "At least they did renovate the place first," Lemmon commented, "because the building looked as if it were condemned."

The public found the theater and the United Theater Owners named Jack Lemmon their Star of the Year. As the drunk, Lemmon inspired *Life* to say: "He writhes with the worst case of the screaming D.T.s ever shown on the screen." The *Hollywood Reporter* commented, "Lemmon, with his special quality of wry pathos, as genuine a man of the mid-century as any actor in films, does a magnificent job. There is very little he can't play." The *Reporter* liked his costar, Lee Remick, too: "She maintains a core of integrity at the base of her being, even in scenes of poignant despair and degradation."

Status Quo

Since the Best Actor and Actress races were filled with strong contenders, two studios panicked and tried to place their stars in the Supporting Acting categories. Allied Artists, née Monogram Pictures, told Peter Ustinov he could adapt Herman Melville's *Billy Budd* if he cast Warren Beatty, Dean Stockwell or Tony Perkins in the title role. Ustinov convinced them to let him use a twenty-three-year-old tyro from London named Terence Stamp. The *New York Times* celebrated Ustinov's choice, describing Stamp as "a new English actor with a sinewy, boyish frame and the face of a Botticelli angel." Steve Broidy, the president of Allied Artists, persuaded the Academy to give the kid a break and let him qualify in the Best Supporting Actor category even if he did play the hero. But Shelley Winters was upset when MGM listed her in the Supporting Actress category for playing the mother in *Lolita*. "I was the star of that picture!" Winters cried. "I want to go for broke!"

Commie Mommy

Shelley's competition was another memorable mother—Angela Lansbury as a Communist who sacrifices her son to the party in *The Manchurian Candidate*. Although Lansbury had received two successive Best Supporting Actress nominations when she first set foot in Hollywood in the mid-40s, her movie assignments began to go downhill, so she, like Anne Bancroft, hied herself to Broadway for character parts. The Great White Way revitalized her career as well, and Lansbury returned to films in her middle thirties to play the mothers of Warren Beatty, twenty-five; Elvis Presley, twenty-six; and ultimately Laurence Harvey, thirty-four, in *The Manchurian Candidate*. Sheilah Graham wrote, "She is so good in the vicious role of Mr. Harvey's mother that people have actually condoled with her real-life husband for having such a wicked wife."

The Nominations

Anne Bancroft was nominated for Best Actress for *The Miracle Worker,* but Shirley MacLaine of *Two for the Seesaw* was not. Geraldine Page was nominated for re-creating her stage role in *Sweet Bird of Youth,* Lee Remick for her alcoholic in *Days of Wine and Roses,* and Katharine Hepburn for her morphine addict in *Long Day's Journey Into Night*. That left one spot open for the *Baby Jane* stars. No columnist had the guts to ask Joan Crawford what she thought about her omis-

"I feel like a male Susan Hayward."
—Gregory Peck

sion. Bosley Crowther scoffed in the *New York Times* that Bette Davis' nomination "must have been meant as a joke," and the *Los Angeles Times* said, "Bette Davis' Baby Jane is galaxies away in outer space." But columnist Vernon Scott insisted that the nomination "has triggered one of the most astonishing comeback stories in movietown's scrapbook. Until the picture was released, Bette was as much in demand as high button shoes."

Bette Davis' friend Olivia de Havilland announced that she was flying in from Paris on Academy Awards night to watch Davis become the first actress to win three Oscars. "She's the greatest and the industry owes her this," de Havilland declared. "I don't think any other actress in the world would have chosen the style she used in *Baby Jane* or could have brought it off so magnificently." Davis had another fan, a young comedienne named Carol Burnett, who was rooting for her "because you just know that Bette's acceptance speech would be the wildest!"

Zsa Zsa Hepburn

The Academy did not have its annual guide in the New York Film Critics this year; a newspaper strike had led the critics to take vacations rather than vote. With open season on the Oscar race, nominees campaigned in earnest. Katharine Hepburn figured if she could get Judy Holliday an Oscar-winning role in 1950, then she could get herself an Oscar in 1962. The actress contacted all the columnists, including Sheilah Graham, who was amazed: "Hepburn, almost as much of a recluse as Garbo, is actually almost as accessible as Zsa Zsa Gabor. She'd love to win."

Nominee Anne Bancroft played it smart and didn't tell Hollywood I-told-you-so. "Even in my own eyes I was a failure," she confessed. "When I arrived in town, the movie industry was looking for sexpot glamour girls. I didn't qualify. Nor was I ever offered a top-flight movie. But there isn't any bitterness on my part. I wasn't as good an actress then as I am now." She was also a do-gooder now, co-chairing a UNICEF benefit with the real Helen Keller.

The Friendly Tune of $500,000

"I have nothing against Hollywood," said surprise Best Actor nominee Marcello Mastroianni for *Divorce, Italian Style*. "But today's best films are being made in Italy and the world's finest directors are working in Italy. So why should I leave Rome?" He wasn't even planning to leave to come to the Oscar ceremonies, so the pundits said *arrivederci* to Mastroianni's chances.

Fellow nominee Jack Lemmon was on a roll—this was his third Best Actor nomination in four years. *Life* published a profile that asked, "Does Everybody Here Like Jack?" The answer was yes, producers, directors, and "even his fellow actors like him." The nominee claimed he worried less about the Award than the new home he was building, saying, "If I devoted about ten percent as much thought to the Oscar as I do about the kitchen, I'd go crazy."

Still, Lemmon already had one Oscar from 1955. Gregory Peck, with nothing at home on the shelf, laughed over his fifth Best Actor nomination: "I feel like a male Susan Hayward." Peck and competitor Peter O'Toole were riding on the popularity of the only two Best Picture nominees that managed to win Best Director nominations—*To Kill a Mockingbird* and *Lawrence of Arabia*. Since *Birdman of Alcatraz* wasn't nominated in either category, competitor Burt Lancaster was going to stay home.

When Murray Schumach of the *New York Times* saw that *The Music Man*, *The Longest Day* and *Mutiny on the Bounty* were nominated for Best Picture, but had been completely shut out of the Director, Writing, and Acting categories, he charged, "Vote-swapping of outrageous proportions is indicated by this year's Oscar nominations for Best Picture. Undercover politics of Oscar campaigning combined with lavish advertising and publicity may make it almost impossible for

"Patty Duke is the kind of little girl every family would like to have."
—United Press International

any movie to be nominated for best film in the future unless it is distributed by the major companies."

Darryl F. Zanuck's feelings were hurt that someone thought that his World War II epic had not won its Best Picture nomination fairly and he replied, "I don't know who in the hell we could swap with. We only have twenty people working here who belong to the Academy." Nevertheless, *Daily Variety* couldn't resist pointing out that the nominations for *The Longest Day* and *Mutiny* were terrific "morale builders" for both Fox and MGM, and that *Bounty*'s producer Aaron Rosenberg was "frank to admit pleasant surprise at the Best Picture nomination."

Saint Omar

Telly Savalas was delighted over his Best Supporting Actor nomination for playing the villain in *Birdman of Alcatraz*. "It's great to have people all over the country recognize me and even ask me for my autograph," he said. Allied Artists got their angelic Supporting nominee, Terence Stamp from *Billy Budd,* to visit Hollywood and charm the columnists. Stamp told Sheilah Graham that when he had to bleach his hair for the movie, "My mother burst into tears." The other glamour boy in the category, Omar Sharif, said of his nomination, "It would be impossible for me to return to films in Egypt. I would like to make it in Hollywood." From every indication, he was doing just that, signing up for major films like *The Fall of the Roman Empire* with Sophia Loren and *The Yellow Rolls-Royce* with Ingrid Bergman. And Army Archerd cleared up one further matter about Sharif: "The affable (and red hot!) actor is Catholic, not Moslem." Betting was heavy that Sharif would triumph on Oscar night.

The columnists also declared Angela Lansbury the runaway favorite for *The Manchurian Candidate,* but the *Hollywood Reporter* estimated that "youngster Patty Duke's nod should help the sale of her TV series." Vernon Scott interviewed the nominee, now sixteen years old, and concluded, "Patty is best described as the kind of little girl every family would like to have."

Arlene of Arabia

Producer Sam Spiegel saw two good omens for *Lawrence of Arabia* on the eve of the ceremonies. The first was director David Lean's award from the Screen Directors Guild. The second was Arlene Dahl's prophecy in a column on Hollywood fashion: "In the past, one outstanding motion picture has been the fashion inspiration at the Academy Awards, for example *Ben-Hur* and *Gigi*. So it is this year. Columbia's *Lawrence of Arabia* sets the fashion pace." According to Dahl's preview, Rita Moreno was coming with a Cleopatra haircut and Harry Cohn's widow was wearing a dress modeled on Omar Sharif's Arabian costume. "Finally, my own gown and cape of flowing white chiffon," Arlene announced, "was directly inspired by the dramatic white Arabian costume Peter O'Toole wore as Lawrence."

Stage Door

The real Peter O'Toole was performing in the West End on Oscar night. Producer Spiegel tried to buy out the house so O'Toole could fly to Hollywood, but the management said it was impossible to reach all the patrons for refunds. Anne Bancroft was appearing on Broadway and she asked if Patty Duke could accept for her. The Academy turned down her request because Duke "was also a nominee and it would cause confusion and complicate press coverage." Bancroft thought the Academy's response was peculiar until she learned that a Hollywood star had volunteered to accept for any absent Best Actress nominee. Her name was Joan Crawford.

The Big Night

Best Supporting Actress nominee Angela Lansbury arrived with her hair piled into a cream-puff topknot. For luck, fellow nominee Patty Duke brought her pet chihuahua, Bambi, in a bowling bag which she checked during the ceremony. Ty Hardin brought his new wife, Marlene, who was flustered because her eye makeup had smeared on her homemade gown. Hardin's date from last year, non-nominee Shelley Winters, was also having problems with her dress—she couldn't find it. Winters had to be sewn into a last-minute replacement.

Bette Davis was there, in a gown similar to the Edith Head cocktail dress she had worn a decade earlier in *All About Eve*. Olivia de Havilland's Christian Dior gown arrived off an Air France jet just minutes before the ceremony began.

Joan Crawford did not allow sartorial matters to be left to such chance. She had contacted Edith Head weeks in advance for her Oscar dress and the designer asked, "I'm making you a silver gown, Joan—do you have the diamonds to go with it?"

"If I don't, I'll get them," Crawford said.

"That's what I love about you, doll!" Head exclaimed. And Joan was as good as her word; she topped off the beaded silver sheath dress with rocks on her fingers, wrists, neck and earlobes.

When Crawford walked down the forecourt with her adopted daughter Cindy and her escort, Cesar "Butch" Romero, the bleacher fans screamed and lunged forward with their autograph pads. Crawford made a beeline to the waving notebooks and began signing away, getting down on her knees to reach some of the blocked-off fans. Mike Connolly was dazzled by her backstage authority:

> *Joan reigned like a queen back there. She brought two Pepsi coolers stocked with bourbon, Scotch, vodka, gin, champagne and Pepsi, plus four kinds of cheese and all the fixin's. Watching the lobby goings-on via the monitor, Joan said, "Look at Eddie Fisher giving Ann-Margret all the camera play. That boy has great manners with his ladies."*

The telecast began with the voice of announcer Hank Sims: "These people, like most of us, are movie fans. You at home will join these stars. You will have a front-row seat." "These people" were the audience at the Santa Monica Civic, including the only Best Actor nominee to show, Gregory Peck.

The opening address was made by the master of ceremonies, Frank Sinatra, who alluded to the *Mona Lisa*, which was then on exhibition in Wash-

Awards Ceremony

April 8, 1963, 7:00 p.m.
The Santa Monica Civic Auditorium,
Santa Monica

Your Host:
Frank Sinatra
Televised over ABC

Presenters

Sound	Shelley Winters
Special Effects	Shelley Winters
Film Editing	Karl Malden
Documentary Awards	Miyoshi Umeki
Scoring Awards	Ginger Rogers
Supporting Actor	Rita Moreno
Short Subjects	Van Heflin
Costume Design	Eva Marie Saint
Supporting Actress	George Chakiris
Jean Hersholt Humanitarian Award	Frank Sinatra
Foreign Film	Wendell Corey
Art Direction	Gene Kelly
Cinematography	Donna Reed
Song	Frank Sinatra
Director	Joan Crawford
Writing Awards	Bette Davis
Actor	Sophia Loren
Actress	Maximilian Schell
Picture	Olivia de Havilland

Performers of Nominated Songs

All songs sung in a medley by Robert Goulet.

"I'm not Ed Begley."
—Ed Begley

ington, D.C. "The chick just sits there and smiles," Sinatra said. "Maybe that picture represents one man's personal vision. A picture he had to make so bad his brushes hurt."

The Awards-giving commenced when Shelley Winters walked out onstage, put on her glasses and began reading the nominees for the Sound Award. When Shelley accidentally referred to *The Music Man* as "Meredith Willson's *The Sound of Music,*" she caught her mistake, gasped, giggled, shuddered, stuttered and continued on uncertainly. She relaxed when she announced that *Lawrence of Arabia* was the winner. After revealing that *The Longest Day* had won Best Special Effects, the non-nominated Winters seemed loath to hand over the statuette. "This is very hard for an actress to let go of," she explained.

Rita Moreno came out in her Vidal Sassoon Egyptian cut and announced the nominees for Best Supporting Actor. The TV cameras showed Omar Sharif, Victor Buono and Ed Begley, who was wiping his nose. Telly Savalas' big close-up was lost because of a technical foul-up and his name was flashed over Patty Duke. The winner was Ed Begley for *Sweet Bird of Youth*. The surprise win was met with whistles and cheers, and Begley was so overwhelmed that his first words at the podium were, "I'm not Ed Begley." Among those the winner thanked "from my heart," was "my agent, George Morris." Morris may not have heard these kind words; it was reported that burglars had robbed his home that morning and stolen his TV set.

Audrey Hepburn was on film from Paris introducing the Costume Design Award. "This award is not only of great interest to every actress," Audrey said, "it is also important to women throughout the world." The Black-and-White winner was *What Ever Happened to Baby Jane?* Designer Norma Koch expressed "deepest appreciation to all the Baby Janes, wherever you are."

George Chakiris began the presentation of the Best Supporting Actress Award. When the cameras tried to cut to a close-up of *To Kill a Mockingbird*'s nine-year-old Mary Badham, she was completely blocked out by Victor Buono, sitting in the row in front of her. Chakiris drew a loud gasp when he declared: "The winner is Patty Duke for *The Miracle Worker*." The sixteen-year-old winner was awed by her good fortune, and all she could do was say "Thank you" while stroking the statuette. Chakiris placed a protective arm around her as they exited to enthusiastic applause.

Leading into Laurence Olivier's filmed introduction of the Best Director Award, Sinatra said, "There you go, Ollie." "A good director helps actors," Olivier declared. Then the orchestra struck up "Some Enchanted Evening" and Joan Crawford made her entrance in her silver gown to announce the Best Director, who turned out to be David Lean for *Lawrence of Arabia*. "This limey is deeply touched and greatly honored," he said.

Crawford walked off and Bette Davis entered to give the Writing Awards, telling the audience the screenwriters she knew "were among the surliest in Hollywood." Davis had trouble pronouncing the names of the three authors of *Divorce, Italian Style,* and when the film won the Original Screenplay Award, she announced the winners as "those three difficult Italian names for *Divorce, Italian Style*."

In a similar vein, Sinatra welcomed "the greatest pizza maker in the world—Miss Sophia Loren." The Best Actor presenter thanked Hollywood for her Oscar from last year and then read the name of the winner, "Gregory Peck for *To Kill a Mockingbird*." The winner took off his glasses and walked to the stage as various audience members shouted bravo. Peck came prepared and read aloud a list of names from the podium. When he walked off with Loren, she asked him, "Now when are we going to do a movie together?" In 1966—when they costarred in *Arabesque*.

Maximilian Schell came onstage and it was time for the most anticipated Award—Best Actress. Bette Davis and Olivia de Havilland sat in Frank Sinatra's dressing room holding hands as Davis chain-smoked. Joan Crawford was in the neighboring dressing room, pacing and puffing on

"Hollywood—that's where they give Academy Awards to Charlton Heston for acting."
—Shirley Knight

a cigarette. The TV director Richard Dunlap debated about showing the home viewers the scene backstage. "I couldn't," he remembered for *TV Guide*, "it would have been cruel." Schell opened the envelope and said, "And the winner is Anne Bancroft for *The Miracle Worker*." Dunlap adds:

> *Joan instantly stood erect—shoulders back, neck straight, head up. She stamped out her cigarette butt, grabbed the hand of the stage manager, who blurted afterward that she "practically broke all my fingers with her strength." Then she soared calmly on-stage with that incomparable Crawford composure. Backstage, Bette bit her cigarette and seemed to stop breathing. Joan was out there; suddenly it was her night.*

Crawford read a note from Anne Bancroft. "Quote. Here's my little speech. Dear Joan, there are three reasons why I won this award—Fred Coe, Arthur Penn and William Gibson. Thank you. Anne Bancroft. End quote." Crawford then walked off, holding hands with Maximilian Schell.

Olivia de Havilland left Bette Davis to go give the Best Picture Award. Frank introduced her as "a girl who's a French housewife born in Tokyo." De Havilland declared the winner to be *Lawrence of Arabia* and Sam Spiegel accepted by noting, "There's no magic formula for making pictures."

Aftermath

Anne Bancroft was jumping up and down for photographers in her apartment on West Eleventh Street. "Do you think you deserved to win?" a reporter asked. "Well, if that means I was better than anyone else," Bancroft said, turning and smiling at her fiancé, Mel Brooks, "the answer is yes!" Brooks laughed with her and at himself—he had warned his bride-to-be earlier, "You can't overcome the sentiment for Davis or Hepburn, they have thirty years over you." A reporter for the *New York Journal American* was equally fallible and wrote, "Anne Bancroft celebrated at home and her boyfriend, Mel Blanc, was with her."

Posing for photographers backstage in Hollywood, Gregory Peck said that the gold pocket watch and chain he was wearing used to belong to Harper Lee's father. Nearby, Ed Begley confessed, "Since *Lawrence of Arabia* was winning in droves, I just naturally assumed that Omar Sharif would get it." As for Sharif, he said, "It was best I didn't win for this wonderful role in such a great film—now I must prove myself. If I had won, I might not have the opportunity to pass this way again." But Shirley Knight, who had just lost Best Supporting Actress for the second year in a row, wasn't interested in coming back. "Hollywood," she told a reporter later in New York, "that's where they give Academy Awards to Charlton Heston for acting."

At the Governors' Ball, Best Supporting Actress winner Patty Duke released her chihuahua from the bowling bag and introduced it to the Oscar. Duke had clung to Joan Crawford during all the post-Awards picture-taking, but at the ball, Bette Davis came over to congratulate her. ABC was sufficiently impressed by her win—*The Patty Duke Show* premiered on TV in September.

Olivia de Havilland told the *Los Angeles Times:* "I'm crushed that Bette didn't win. Her victory would have been perfect continuity, tying yesterday, today and tomorrow." Hedda Hopper reported, "Joan was all over the ballroom at the party later, but Bette Davis sat quietly, surrounded entirely by family and friends."

Time dubbed Crawford "The Triumph of the Evening." Joan didn't want the evening to end, so she insisted on hand-delivering the statuette to Bancroft in New York. Bancroft's Broadway show, Bertolt Brecht's *Mother Courage,* advertised, "Annie Won It, And We've Got Her!"

The broadcast got good reviews, mainly because of the several surprise wins. The *Los Angeles Times* called it "one of the most unpredictable Academy Award runoffs in years" and the *Los Angeles Herald-Examiner* said the show was "highlighted by the biggest surprise upsets in its history."

When the *Los Angeles Times'* Joyce Haber asked Bette Davis years later what her feelings really were that evening in 1963, the actress said:

> *I was positive I would get it. So was everybody in town. I almost dropped dead when I didn't win. I wanted to be the first actress to win three times, but now it's been done, so I may as well give up. And, of course, the fact that Miss Crawford got permission to accept for any of the other nominees was hysterical. I was nominated but she was receiving the acclaim. It would have meant a million more dollars to our film if I had won. Joan was thrilled I hadn't.*

1963

"What if eight million Negroes decide to kick in their TV screens at the moment someone else's name is called."
—Sidney Poitier

Sex reared its ugly head in Hollywood and morality became the issue at the 1963 Academy Awards.

The film event of the year, according to the headlines, was the June 12 premiere of *Cleopatra*. Bosley Crowther of the *New York Times* called it "one of the great epic films of our day," but Judith Crist of the *New York Herald Tribune* labeled the four-hour-and-five-minute movie, "a monumental mouse." "Something's gotta give on the overlong *Cleopatra*," wrote Hollywood's Mike Connolly, "so they're slicing Rex Harrison's footage because Fox refuses to deprive the panting public of a single passionate frame of Lady L and her knight-at-arms." Fox trimmed the movie down to three and a half hours, then down to a mere three. Liz was vociferous in her complaint, telling reporters, "They had cut out the heart, the essence, the motivations, the very core, and tacked on all those battle scenes."

Taylor was involved in some battles herself. Liz sued Fox for failing to pay her a percentage of the gross—in addition to her $2,140,500 in salary and overtime pay. The studio retaliated by suing Burton and Taylor for $50 million for "depreciating" the film's commercial value by their "scandalous conduct and deportment," although studio executives admitted that the Taylor-Burton romance was what had made the movie such an eagerly awaited event. Taylor also sued husband Eddie Fisher for divorce, on the grounds of abandonment.

Cleopatra was the highest-grossing film of the year, but it still didn't make back enough money to recoup its $44 million price tag. Rex Harrison's lawyers had to remind the studio that he was supposed to receive equal billing with Liz and Dick—the poster had left out his picture completely—but, publicly, Harrison refused to call the movie a fiasco. "*Cleopatra* is an underrated motion picture," he asserted. "Unfortunately, its brilliance has been obscured by two years of gossip and scandal." Harrison was not obscured, and columnist Vernon Scott wrote, "Out of the scandal-blighted and costly wreckage of *Cleopatra*, actor Rex Harrison emerged unscathed with a performance that will almost surely win him an Oscar nomination."

Best Actor winner Sidney Poitier compares his first Oscar to Federico Fellini's third.

Another Matinee Idol

If Taylor and Burton titillated the public offscreen, *Tom Jones* excited it onscreen. British director Tony Richardson and playwright John Osborne, best known for "angry young man" dramas like *The Entertainer* and *Look Back in Anger*, decided to have some fun, so they adapted an eighteenth-century novel by Henry Fielding into a rollicking bedroom farce. David Picker, an executive at United Artists, persuaded the powers-that-be to pick up the English picture for peanuts and advertise it with sexy posters for its U.S. release. The ploy worked and the studio found itself with the highest-grossing foreign-made film ever distributed in America. It was so popular that a *New Yorker* cartoon depicted a patient wailing to his psychiatrist: "Doctor, what's my problem? *Tom Jones* depressed me."

The New York Film Critics gave the film its Best Picture and Best Director Awards, and their Best Actor citation went to the film's twenty-seven-year-old star, Albert Finney. The trio of Richardson, Osborne, and Finney conquered Broadway next, with an acclaimed dramatic production—*Luther*. "Albert Finney is sure to be a U.S. matinee idol before the year is out," proclaimed *Life*, and *Show* magazine claimed he was the "heir apparent to the throne held by Laurence Olivier."

Leslie Caron Puts Out

Another "adult" film from England starred Leslie Caron, who had fled Hollywood because "I had always played adolescents of one sort or another, and I expect they thought that was all I

"Out of the scandal-blighted and costly wreckage of Cleopatra, Rex Harrison emerged unscathed."
—Vernon Scott

could do." Caron convinced Bryan Forbes, the director of *The L-Shaped Room,* to cast her as the film's unwed pregnant heroine by arguing, "Everyone thinks French girls are easier to get into bed anyway." The director had to agree, and when the film opened in New York in May, the *Times* headlined: LESLIE CARON GROWS UP IN HARSH STORY. The *New York Post*'s Archer Winsten toasted Caron's change of pace: "British neorealism digs its grimy teeth into a luscious morsel in *The L-Shaped Room,* which presents a different Leslie Caron to the public that adored her as Lili, Gigi and Fanny."

Caron insisted on being referred to as an actress because her dancing days were finished, too; she told reporters that only once in the past six years had she broken her pledge never to dance again—she had shown the Queen of England how to do the twist.

Paul Newman's Special Province

Around the same time that *The L-Shaped Room* bowed, an ad appeared in *Daily Variety* heralding Paul Newman's latest work of American neorealism:

> *A picture comes along that grabs you by the throat. You sit there, spellbound. You say, 'This is the way it really is.' You don't merely see the picture, you live it. And when it's over, you've changed. You see life in a new way.* Hud *is such a motion picture.*

The *New York Times* said *Hud* was "a drama of moral corruption—of the debilitating disease of avaricious self-seeking—that is creeping across the land and infecting the minds of young people in this complex, materialistic age."

While Bosley Crowther praised it as "a profound contemplation of the human condition," audiences loved seeing Paul Newman play an amoral Texan who slept around a lot. "*Hud* is the sort of non-hero who has become Paul Newman's special province," said *Life* and *The New Yorker* remarked, "The Academy may as well give him an Oscar right now and get it over with."

The entire cast of *Hud* earned good reviews. Melvyn Douglas' virtuous patriarch and Brandon de Wilde's innocent nephew were touted as Best Supporting Actor nominees. But the cast member who really got the notices was Patricia Neal, as the housekeeper Paul Newman tries to rape. The *Washington Post* commented, "So fully did Miss Neal realize the part's potential that after seeing her play it one could not imagine any other actress in the role and it is heartening to find Miss Neal decisively recognized. The final salute should be a springtime Oscar."

Pat Neal was ready for recognition. She had first come to Hollywood in the '40s after some success on Broadway, but she became better known as the woman Gary Cooper was seeing than for any movie role. When the affair ended, Neal suffered a nervous breakdown. She recovered, married writer Roald Dahl and returned to New York, where she began to work on Broadway again—she costarred with fellow Hollywood exile Anne Bancroft in *The Miracle Worker*. Better offers came from Hollywood, and Neal made *Breakfast at Tiffany's* in 1961 and then *Hud*. But just as her career improved, Neal's personal life fell to pieces. In 1960, her four-month-old son was severely injured when a cab hit his baby carriage. The Dahls moved to England, where their seven-year-old daughter died of measles in 1962. The bad luck rubbed off on Neal's career, and she discovered that her character had been completely cut from Fox's *The Third Secret* because, as the studio explained, "It's simply a case of running time, of eradicating one plot tangent, and Miss Neal happened to be on that tangent." *Hud* put Neal back in the spotlight.

Bad Girls Finish First

Hedda Hopper did not like what she saw as the Academy's Best Actress hopefuls. "Ever since Judy Holliday lived in a sinful state with Paul Douglas [sic] in *Born Yesterday,* our heroines have been sliding downhill to fame. Bad girls finish

"Doctor, what's my problem? Tom Jones depressed me."
—New Yorker cartoon

first. Natalie Wood and Leslie Caron, portraying girls who have children out of wedlock, will doubtless be nominated," she predicted, referring to Natalie's 1963 vehicle with Steve McQueen, *Love With the Proper Stranger*.

Columnist Hazel Flynn, of the *Hollywood Citizen-News*, was also upset at how the Oscar season was shaping up. "Incidentally," she wrote on January 9, 1964, "The N.Y. critics should be slashed for choosing *Tom Jones*, the bawdy British film, as best picture of the year. As for the National Board of Review which chose *Tom Jones*, for shame! And I'm not through with them yet. I'm going to find out who appoints them and how come they had the nerve to recommend a bawdy film when their duty is to protect the American public from filth without and within."

A Great Service to Civilization

Hollywood columnists began looking around for American movies that could stop *Tom Jones* in its tracks. Elia Kazan had taped his father's recollections of emigrating from Greece and then filmed them in New York as a three-hour, black-and-white movie entitled *America, America*. The *Christian Science Monitor* said, "The American's feeling for his country can be solid as fact, yet hopelessly beyond words. Such a document as Lincoln's Gettysburg Address surmounts the difficulties with rare eloquence. Such a film as Elia Kazan's manages through cinema techniques to give a similar impression of heartfelt patriotism." When the film premiered in Hollywood just in time to qualify for Oscars, Jack Warner stated, "Through this picture, Elia Kazan has done a great service to civilization."

But Hollywood didn't go for it. The *Los Angeles Times* sniffed, "If Elia Kazan had made his Greek hero less scheming and ruthless, the kid's arrival on our soil could have been a much more moving thing than it is." Others noticed that the film was made by New York talent—cinematographer Haskell Wexler, editor Dede Allen—and the one Oscar winner among them was—of all people—Manos Hadjidakis, the Greek composer who had written "Never on Sunday." Kazan didn't help his campaign much by saying, "Producers are unnecessary, any good director is quite capable of producing his own pictures." And when the director visited Hollywood, he told Army Archerd, "I'm shocked—it's nothing but TV here, now."

A Constructive Image

Then the anti-*Tom Jones* columnists agreed upon it—they had the film that could fend off the amoral British onslaught. A TV director named Ralph Nelson had received $247,000 from United Artists to adapt a novella about a group of German nuns in the Arizona desert who con a vagabond into building a chapel for them. Nelson's casting coup was getting thirty-eight-year-old black actor Sidney Poitier to play the itinerant hero.

United Artists first sent the film to the Berlin Film Festival, where it won the Best Actor Award. Then the studio advertised the prize and sneaked the film to individual critics, who wrote advance reviews. By the time *Lilies of the Field* opened in October, everybody had already heard about it and the film became a sleeper. The *New York Times* liked *Lilies* but wisecracked, "It's *Going My Way* with a Negro." Not all reviewers were able to stomach the saccharine story; *Newsweek* frowned, "The screen overflows with enough brotherhood, piety, and honest labor to make even the kindest spectator retch."

Hazel Flynn rushed the news to Hollywood that at least one critical group had given its best picture award to *Lilies of the Field*. "The National Audience Board's West Coast Opinion Leader Survey gave *Lilies of the Field* the highest rating EVER GIVEN A MOTION PICTURE," she exclaimed, adding, "This is a film which will bring great credit on Hollywood if it gets the Oscar and it will also bring us great credit abroad for it builds a constructive image of our country, not a destructive one."

"I got myself into a sticky mess which couldn't work, didn't work and never should have worked."
—Patricia Neal

An Apology to Roddy McDowall

One of Liz Taylor's close friends was Roddy McDowall, who got great reviews for playing her nemesis Octavius in *Cleopatra,* but any hopes he had for a Best Supporting Actor Oscar hit a snag. By accident, Fox had listed the entire cast of thousands in *Cleopatra* as Leading Players on the Academy's ballot. When the mistake was discovered, the Academy said too late, everything's at the printers already. Fox pleaded, but all it could get out of the Academy was a pledge to change the rule next year so that Academy voters could determine for themselves what category to place a performer in.

The studio made it up to McDowall by printing a public apology in the trade papers:

> *We feel it is important that the industry realize that your electrifying performance as Octavius in* Cleopatra, *which was unanimously singled out by the critics as one of the best supporting actor performances by an actor this year, is not eligible for an Academy Award nomination in that category . . . due to a regrettable error on the part of 20th Century–Fox.*

Upset Stomach to Ex-Lax

With a wide-open competition in the race for Best Supporting Actor nominations, Nick Adams began furiously campaigning for the honor for his role as a man falsely accused of murder in *Twilight of Honor,* which Sidney Skolsky described as "a little picture MGM made to cash in on the popularity of Richard Chamberlain from TV." Most reviewers didn't mention Adams at all, but the actor found two notices, one from the *Los Angeles Herald-Examiner* and the other from columnist Vernon Scott, that said he "warrants" and "will be a cinch to win" the Best Supporting Oscar. These two quotations appeared over and over again as ads popped up regularly in the trade papers. Meanwhile, Adams, a member of the board of the Screen Actors Guild, gave a lot of interviews. "A nomination for me means that *Twilight of Honor* will bring in another million dollars and supply funds for more Hollywood pictures," he said. "Next, it means I, as a Hollywood star, can make more films in Hollywood and stop this runaway production which is killing Hollywood. I will never make a picture abroad."

Hedda Hopper liked this kind of talk and she dubbed Adams "a top contender for Best Supporting Actor." Another columnist was amused at Adams' campaign and laughed that pictures of the actor in his ads "ranged in every expression from Upset Stomach to Godzilla to Stopped Up Sinuses to Attila the Hun to Ex-Lax." Undaunted, Adams told Hazel Flynn, "I spent $8,000 on my ads and I would spend $88,000 to bring my performance to the attention of the voters." But Brandon de Wilde, twenty-one, refused to campaign at all for his role in *Hud,* arguing, "The people of my profession know whether or not I'm good enough to make the race. I don't need to prod them with reminders."

The Nominations

Brandon de Wilde was the only lead from *Hud* not to be nominated for an Oscar. His costar, Melvyn Douglas, was in the race for Best Supporting Actor with Bobby Darin—who had played a drugged hospital patient in *Captain Newman, M.D.*—and Nick Adams, who had gotten his money's worth. "Nick Adams called Bobby Darin to bury the hatchet—dates back to *Hell Is for Heroes* on the Redding, California, location," reported Army Archerd. "They haven't seen or spoken to each other since."

Darin was speaking to reporters. OSCAR NOMINATION HUMBLES A COCKY ACTOR headlined Sheilah Graham, noting that the young singer who had once claimed, "I want to be a legend by the

"The N.Y. critics should be slashed for choosing Tom Jones."
—Hazel Flynn

time I'm twenty-five," was now, at twenty-seven, "a new person. He feels more secure. Besides his nomination, another reason could be his now happy marriage with Sandra Dee. Or maybe he is just growing up."

The surprise Supporting Actor nominee was director John Huston as a cardinal in Otto Preminger's *The Cardinal*. Huston assured Hollywood that he was not planning a new career. "There was one great actor in my family and that's enough," Walter's son said. "I could never top him and I don't want to try." A good thing, according to the *Los Angeles Times,* which told readers to "put Huston's nomination down as a private Hollywood joke—'Well, at least he can act.' "

The lead in the Best Supporting Actor race was held by Huston and Hugh Griffith—who already had an Oscar from *Ben-Hur*—as a lusty squire in *Tom Jones,* which led the nominated pictures with ten nods in all. The runner-up was *Cleopatra*, a Best Picture nominee, with nine. Another Best Picture nominee was MGM's all-star Cinerama epic *How the West Was Won,* which, like *Cleopatra,* had no corresponding nomination for Best Direction. The *New York Times* again charged vote-swapping and concluded, "If either Metro or Fox spends a great deal of money on a movie, the members of the Academy may feel an obligation to reward those studios."

Beneath Contempt with Hedda

Now that the nominations were out, Hollywood columnists declared a full-scale war on *Tom Jones*. "The British have their Oscar race," cried Hazel Flynn. "Why are they trying to run away with ours? It took them until after World War II to even make a few good pictures." Hedda Hopper went to work on discrediting *Tom Jones'* Best Director nominee Tony Richardson, reminding readers that he was "a director Hollywood shrugged off some years ago after he did *Sanctuary*." Despite their criticism, *Tom Jones* was the definite front-runner, if only because Kazan's *America, America* was the only Best Picture nominee with a nominated director. *Hud* had a nominated director, Martin Ritt, but was not on the list for Best Picture.

To Hopper, the biggest crime was that *Lilies of the Field* was one of the Best Picture nominees without an anointed director. "Ralph Nelson stepped aside for Italian Federico Fellini," Hedda wrote, "whose *8½* in my opinion was beneath contempt." Fellini, whose films had already won two Foreign Film Awards, eagerly made plans to come to Los Angeles because he wanted to entice two Hollywood stars, Mae West and Groucho Marx, to appear in his next movie, *Juliet of the Spirits*. The Italian director attended all the Academy's preceremony cocktail parties and took his third trip to Disneyland, which he called, "*La Dolce Vita* for kids."

Best Hard Luck Story

Three actresses from *Tom Jones* placed on the Best Supporting Actress list. A fourth British Supporting Actress nominee was Margaret Rutherford, who had supplied the comic relief to *The V.I.P.'s*, Liz and Dick's other 1963 release, rushed out by MGM to capitalize on the scandal. MGM had just signed Rutherford to a long-term contract to play Agatha Christie's Miss Marple in a series of mystery movies, moving Hedda Hopper to write, "I'm happy Margaret Rutherford is up, even if she is English."

Hopper was happiest over the nomination of *Lilies of the Field*'s Lilia Skala, a hard-luck story if ever Hedda saw one. Skala had been a stage star in Vienna in the '30s, before fleeing Hitler and coming to America. Although she did work occasionally on the stage and television and had a small part in the film *Call Me Madam*, Skala's American work was mostly in a zipper factory and a hat factory—until she worked her way up to busboy in a restaurant. Even her good notices in *Lilies* failed to bring her steady theatrical employment. "When she received her nomination," Louella Parsons

"I spent $8,000 on my ads and I would spend $88,000."
—Nick Adams

wrote, "Lilia Skala was working for $1.50 an hour at the lost-and-found department of New York's City Center."

"I am deeply grateful to God for every step as it unfolds," Skala said. "Of course I am thrilled. I did not expect it. I have known too many disappointments in my life to count on anything." Complimentary Oscar travel expenses from United Artists didn't come until the actress told reporters, "I couldn't afford the trip to Los Angeles myself."

That Tight Little Isle

Hedda Hopper inspected the Best Actor list, saw the number of British nominees on it, and commented, "Wonder why we hate ourselves?" The columnist announced that she was voting for Sidney Poitier in *Lilies of the Field*. Then she aimed her pen at the Brits. "I'm not going to be narrow enough to claim these fellows can't act," she wrote. "They've had plenty of practice. The weather's so foul on that tight little isle that, to get in out of the rain, they all gather in theatres and practice Hamlet on each other."

Nevertheless, Albert Finney was the favorite because of *Tom Jones'* popularity. But the nominee declined the studio's offer to campaign in Los Angeles. He then dropped out of *Luther* on Broadway and went on vacation in the South Seas. Rex Harrison, nominated for giving his all to *Cleopatra,* had been in Hollywood for months filming *My Fair Lady* at Warners. Mrs. Harrison was popular around town, too, and she was nominated for Best Actress for her work in a British kitchen-sink drama called *This Sporting Life*. Rachel Roberts insisted that her husband's role was much harder than hers: "It's much more difficult to act in a spectacle, especially *that* spectacle." Nor did Roberts expect a new Hollywood career. "I haven't got the equipment," she said, laughing.

Mr. Harrison's competition included Mrs. Harrison's costar, twenty-nine-old Richard Harris, described by Hollywood as "Ireland's answer to Marlon Brando." Harris had worked—and feuded—with Brando on *Mutiny on the Bounty* and told columnists, "There are too many prima donnas in this business and not enough action." Harris was shooting *Major Dundee,* a Sam Peckinpah western, in Mexico when the nominations were released. "I've struck a blow for the Irish rebellion," he yelled.

Telegraph to the Globe

When the *Los Angeles Times* reviewed *This Sporting Life*, it observed that "Richard Harris makes Hud look like a Mama's Boy." The Mama's Boy, Best Actor nominee Paul Newman, was in New York, keeping his distance from the Academy. The two-time loser said he wanted Sidney Poitier to win and was not going to attend the ceremonies. He would be on Broadway performing in *Baby, Want a Kiss* with wife Joanne Woodward.

Newman's absence meant that Sidney Poitier would be the only American nominee at the Awards show. Although the actor himself made jokes about being the "dark horse," a campaign grew to select Poitier in an effort to stop the *Tom Jones* sweep. Since members of the Hollywood community—George Jessel, Judy Garland, Gregory Peck, *Hud* director Martin Ritt, Blake Edwards—had followed leader Charlton Heston on the August Civil Rights March on Washington, Sidney Skolsky was overwhelmed by the appropriateness of a Poitier victory:

> *If ever there was a year when the Negro should be honored it is this year for obvious reasons. It would pour soothing oil on the troubled racial waters and, besides, IT IS DESERVED. It would also telegraph to the globe that WE do not discriminate and thus give the lie to our so-called Communist friends who themselves really DO discriminate.*

There were plenty of ads for Poitier in the trade papers, but the actor was nervous about the political pressure his nomination was creating. "What if eight million Negroes decide to kick in their TV screens at the moment someone else's name is called," he asked. "Besides, I want to win because they think I'm a good actor." Sidney Skolsky himself had doubts about the Poitier campaign and predicted, on the eve of the ceremonies, an Albert Finney victory.

The Sympathy Vote

In the Best Actress contest, Natalie Wood was nominated for *Love with the Proper Stranger;* Leslie Caron for *The L-Shaped Room;* Shirley MacLaine for *Irma La Douce;* and Rachel Roberts for *This Sporting Life*. But all the pundits agreed that the Best Actress favorite was the New York Film Critics winner, Pat Neal for *Hud*, who took inventory of her career in interviews. "I didn't drop Hollywood, they dropped me," she said. "Hollywood has a way of indicating to contract artists that they are fed up with them—they feed them all the bad parts. I couldn't relax on camera, anyway, and I was trying too hard." When one reporter asked about Gary Cooper, Neal responded, "Oh, yes. That. Even more than my career, that did me in. I got myself into a sticky mess which couldn't work, didn't work, and never should have worked." The nominee would not be able to fly from England to attend the ceremonies because she was pregnant again and knew better than to push her luck. But then, Neal didn't have to rely on a personal appearance to get votes; as one press agent told Hazel Flynn, "I will vote for Pat Neal to win because she has had so much personal tragedy in her life."

The Big Night

The first nominee to arrive was Best Supporting Actor hopeful Nick Adams, a full hour and a half before the show began. "An usher said Nick Adams and wife arrived at 5:30," reported Sidney Skolsky, "went into the empty auditorium and practiced walking, skipping, trotting down the aisle to the stage." Most of the Academy's other guests weren't so punctual, thanks to highway construction that kept the limousines bumper to bumper all the way from Beverly Hills to Santa Monica. Many nominees didn't come at all; fifty-seven were missing. Harold Mirisch, one of the producers of the Oscar-winning *West Side Story*, had taken over from Mrs. Charles Vidor the role of host of the unofficial Oscar party for the non-nominated. His Beverly Hills Oscar-watching party was held in honor of newlyweds Peter Sellers and Britt Ekland, and a hundred guests chose to watch the show on the TV sets around the Mirisch home rather than see it live.

When the limousines finally started arriving, out popped Bobby Darin with his wife, Sandra Dee. Best Supporting Actor nominee John Huston brought Stella Stevens. *Hud*'s Melvyn Douglas was in Israel, so he had the non-nominated Brandon de Wilde substitute for him. Lilia Skala appeared in a new dress with a new pocketbook, courtesy of United Artists. Her only competitor in Hollywood was *Tom Jones*' Edith Evans, who wore a black and white gown with black gloves.

Wearing a Dior, Leslie Caron arrived with boyfriend Warren Beatty. His sister, Shirley MacLaine, came with her husband, Steve Parker, and told reporters, "I hope I don't win. I don't think it was my best performance." Then her husband stepped on the train of her gown and she headed straight backstage to have it ironed.

The last-minute arrivals of most guests created a stampede for the bars in the lobby. Walter Wanger, the ex-Academy president and current producer of *Cleopatra*, fought his way through the crowd and sighed, "There, the preliminary bone-breaking's over—when do they operate on me?"

Among the throng was Eddie Fisher and his date, identified as Jacqueline Kennedy's secretary, who wore her hair in the bouffant style made fashionable by her boss. Another guest was eighteen-year-old Pat Klay, of Woodland Hills, the winner of the Trini Lopez Dream Date Contest conducted by KRLA Radio. And Jody McCrea, featured in *Beach Party*, added to the crowd by picking a fan

Awards Ceremony

APRIL 13, 1964, 7:00 P.M.
THE SANTA MONICA CIVIC AUDITORIUM,
SANTA MONICA

Your Host:
JACK LEMMON
Televised over ABC

Presenters

Sound Recording	Steve McQueen
Sound Effects	Tuesday Weld
Special Visual Effects	Angie Dickinson
Short Subjects	Shirley MacLaine
Supporting Actor	Patty Duke
Film Editing	Sidney Poitier
Supporting Actress	Ed Begley
Documentary Awards	Debbie Reynolds
Costume Design	Donna Reed
Foreign Film	Julie Andrews
Song	Shirley Jones
Cinematography	James Stewart
Art Direction	Anne Baxter and Fred MacMurray
Scoring Awards	Sammy Davis, Jr.
Writing Awards	Edward G. Robinson
Director	Rita Hayworth
Actor	Anne Bancroft
Actress	Gregory Peck
Picture	Frank Sinatra

Performers of Nominated Songs

"Call Me Irresponsible"	Andy Williams
"Charade"	Andy Williams
"It's a Mad, Mad, Mad, Mad World"	James Darren
"More"	Katina Ranieri
"So Little Time"	Harve Presnell

"I'm never going to put myself through this shit no more."
—Sidney Poitier

out of the bleachers and inviting her to be his date. "I thought it would give the kid a thrill," McCrea shrugged.

The telecast began with Rock Hudson standing in the lobby—which was still filled with noisy people at the bar—inviting viewers to "take the family helicopter to Hollywood."

The audience applauded the set—a dramatic recreation of the nighttime view of Los Angeles from the Hollywood Hills. Emcee Jack Lemmon strolled out and exclaimed, "It's magic time." Many of Lemmon's jabs took aim at the effect of *Tom Jones* on screen content. "Our British cousins found out that just plain eating can be very sexy," he said. "We've revised the Production Code and now you can't show a couple eating unless they're married." Academy President Arthur Freed appeared and seemed happy about how the nominations had turned out. "Our Awards have now become international," he bragged.

Tuesday Weld had also been inspired by Jacqueline Kennedy, and exhibited a bouffant hairstyle as she presented the Sound Effects Award. Her hairdresser had not finished the job, however, and her hair collapsed and fell in her face as she read the nominations. Angie Dickinson followed in another bouffant to give the Special Effects Oscar. The winner was Emil Kosa, Jr., for *Cleopatra;* the middle-aged gentleman looked at Angie and said, "I wish I could take the lady home with me rather than this little Oscar."

Patty Duke stepped out in a dress with a daisy pattern and presented the Best Supporting Actor Award. The winner was Melvyn Douglas for *Hud*. Brandon de Wilde hopped to the stage to accept for his costar but Sidney Skolsky kept his eye on one of the losers. "I was fascinated by the face of Nick Adams," he wrote. "Nick looked like Instant Murder. I never believed I'd want to give Nick a prize, but really, he should be given an Oscar for his Portrait of a Loser. I'll say this for him: his face and emotions were honest."

Lemmon announced that the presenter of the Film Editing Award was "the actor I would most like to work with"—Sidney Poitier. The winning editor for *How the West Was Won* received the Oscar from Poitier and commented, "To take this from such a fine, fine actor is a great privilege and a great honor." Even with all this testimony, Poitier remained unconvinced that it was his night, and when he returned to his seat he sulked. "I can understand that this is an important moment and I have to be here for what it means to us as a people," the actor wrote in his autobiography, "but I'm never going to put myself through this shit no more—never again under no circumstances am I going to come here again and put myself through this."

Ed Begley presented the Best Supporting Actress Award as the five nominees paraded on film—even though nominees Lilia Skala and Edith Evans were in the audience. The winner wasn't. Peter Ustinov accepted for Margaret Rutherford of *The V.I.P.'s*.

Jack Lemmon introduced Best Foreign Film presenter Julie Andrews as "My Fair Lady," although Audrey Hepburn had by now completed filming the movie version of Andrews' Broadway success. The winner was *8½* and a jubilant Federico Fellini said, "I am particularly happy to receive this fabulous award because it comes to me on the eve of my next picture. I don't think a director about to start a job could wish for anything more stimulating and auspicious as this. *Arrivederci*." The director waved to the audience as he walked off with Julie Andrews and the Oscar.

Personal drama marked the Best Song category. A bouffanted Shirley Jones revealed that the winner was "Call Me Irresponsible," but mounting the stage was Jimmy Van Heusen with his collaborator's daughter. Laura Cahn said of her father, Sammy: "I'd like to express my thanks along with the thanks of my father." Cahn had been divorced that same day, and backstage Van Heusen said, "Sammy just didn't feel like showing up."

James Stewart, introduced as "a responsible American," gave the Black-and-White Cinematography Award to James Wong Howe, the four-foot-eleven-inch cinematographer of *Hud,* who

"Wait'll the NAACP hears about this!"
—Sammy Davis, Jr.

was almost completely obscured by the podium. Moving on to the Color Cinematography Award, Stewart read: "*The Cardinal*—Leon Shamroy; *Cleopatra*—Leon Shamroy. Gee, that's five years out of a man's life right there." The winner was Leon Shamroy for *Cleopatra*. The cinematographer was so excited, the first thing he did at the podium was whisper to Stewart, "Which one did I win for?"

Sammy Davis, Jr., this year wearing two rings, came out to present the Scoring Awards, but before he got to the nominations, he did a few impressions. His Jimmy Stewart followed Edward G. Robinson, and then Sammy did Jerry Lewis, whose TV show had just been an expensive flop. Jack Lemmon ran onstage and interrupted the Lewis mimicry. "Not on this network!" he yelled, getting a big laugh. But Davis topped him. As he was about to tear open the envelope for Best Adapted Score, the representative of Price, Waterhouse darted out to whisper an urgent message. Sammy reacted over the microphone, "They gave me the wrong envelope?" He turned to the audience: "Wait'll the NAACP hears about this!" Everyone laughed, including Sidney Poitier. "And about then the thought hits me," Poitier wrote, "what if some miracle's about to take place? I was not going to get up there and look dumb. The first thing they were going to say was, 'Here comes the first black actor to win the Academy Award and he can't even say nothing—dumb-dumb!' Think, Sidney, think, time is of the essence!"

Poitier had plenty of time to think as Sammy Davis continued. When he got the proper envelope, he put on his glasses and said, "I ain't gonna make no mistake about this!" The audience roared. After handing out the Awards, Davis launched into a medley of Best Song losers and was really cooking by the time he got to "Blues in the Night." "Let's do it one more time!" Davis exclaimed as the orchestra wound down. Davis received a long ovation when he stopped and Jack Lemmon declared upon returning to the stage, "He's a genius, that boy!"

Lemmon called out "one of the greats of the cinema," the never-nominated Edward G. Robinson, to present the Writing Awards. After announcing that *Tom Jones* won the Adapted Screenplay Oscar, Robinson peered at the nominees for Original Screenplay and despaired, "This looks a little formidable." So Jack Lemmon walked over to read the Italian names for *Four Days of Naples* and Fellini's *8 1/2*. Robinson had no problem reading the winner—James Webb for *How the West Was Won*. The writer, who began his career penning westerns at Republic in the '30s, said, "It took me as long to win this as it took to win the West."

The Best Director presenter, a bouffanted Rita Hayworth, was also nervous about reading names aloud in public. She had requested an envelope with extremely large type to counter her myopia, but when Hayworth got to the podium, the envelope was missing. She tried to read from the TelePrompTer, but *Tom Jones'* Tony Richardson came out as "Tony Richards." A breathless Jack Lemmon rushed up with the large-type envelope. Hayworth got even more nervous, opened the envelope and proclaimed the winner, "Tony Richards for *Tom Jones*." Dame Edith Evans rose up and accepted the trophy in black-gloved hands. "I'm so happy to take this back to Tony. It was very richly deserved."

"We're in the adrenaline section," Jack Lemmon announced, and a sleekly garbed Anne Bancroft stepped out to name Best Actor. According to Poitier, Lemmon's quip was correct: "I remember distinctly that my smile froze after a while and I could neither unsmile nor widen it. I was just stuck there with a lot of teeth exposed—just stuck." There was applause for the nominations of Rex Harrison and Paul Newman, cheers for Sidney Poitier's. Then Bancroft opened the envelope. The winner was Poitier for *Lilies of the Field*.

The orchestra surged into the hymn "Amen" and the audience screamed. Anne Bancroft jumped up and down. The winner walked to the stage in a daze. When he got there, Bancroft threw her arms around him and kissed him. "I looked

"She nearly lost her bird."
—Frank Sinatra

out at those thousands of faces," Poitier wrote, "and suddenly forgot my speech. Fortunately for me, they were still applauding." By the time they stopped, Poitier remembered what he was going to say: "It has been a long journey to this moment." Anne Bancroft was still jumping around when the couple walked off and Jack Lemmon noted, "A very special man." As they exited, Bancroft whispered to Poitier, "Live it up, chum, it doesn't last long."

The special man was followed by a "man who grants great dignity to this occasion," Gregory Peck. Reading the names of the Best Actress nominees, Peck paused for the ovation that erupted when Patricia Neal's picture was flashed on screen. The winner was Patricia Neal for *Hud*. Annabella, Tyrone Power's ex-wife, accepted and informed all, "Pat is expecting her fourth child in London. She wishes you a very special thank you."

Frank Sinatra materialized to give the Best Picture Oscar, which, he reminded, "is still, after thirty-six years, the highest honor given a motion picture." For *Tom Jones,* the film clip showed Albert Finney retrieving Susannah York's pet canary. "She nearly lost her bird," Sinatra quipped. The winner was *Tom Jones* and David Picker of United Artists accepted. *Tom Jones* and *Cleopatra* had tied with four Awards each.

Jack Lemmon came out to close the show: "When in Hollywood, do as the British and Romans do."

Aftermath

Backstage, Sammy Davis, Jr., ran up to Poitier and said, "Hey, I wanted to be the first one to win one of those, but that's okay, I'm not mad. And neither are my kids or the NAACP." When Sidney Skolsky offered his congratulations, Poitier ribbed him, "Man, how come you didn't pick me to win? Me, your pal from Schwab's yet?"

David Niven, who would have accepted for Albert Finney, told the winner, "I'm delighted you got it. Outside of the rather ignominious moment when I once voted for myself, it was the first time I picked a winner." Meanwhile, United Press International instructed its reporters to find Albert Finney, pronto. One did find him—on a boat off Waikiki. "When Albert Finney heard the news," the report went, "he raised his glass in a toast, 'To Sidney, well deserved.' Then he grabbed a newfound friend, Renette Wright, and said, 'Let's dance.' They joined the tourists in a wild twist on the after deck."

While the winners accepted congratulations, Rita Hayworth was morose over her bungling of Tony Richardson's name. "Is it the Taoists who practice disintegration?" she asked. "I think I'll try that and just disappear into the fog."

Betsy Drake managed to get through to Patricia Neal at 6 A.M. London time. Neal didn't mind having her sleep interrupted. "If we woke without hearing it," she explained, "then I'd lost. Naturally, I was thrilled to hear that phone ringing."

Back in Hollywood, a Best Actress loser garnered most of the attention. "As usual, the life of the party at the Beverly Hilton after the awards was Shirley MacLaine," said the *Los Angeles Herald-Examiner*. "She danced so vigorously that her gown came unbuttoned in the back and husband Steve Parker had to hastily prevent de-frocking."

The next day, Best Supporting Actress winner Margaret Rutherford made a statement from the set of her latest movie, *Murder, Ahoy*. "This Oscar is the climax of my career after twenty-eight years of filming. This may sound presumptuous at my age—I'm seventy-two next month—but I like to feel that this will be the starting point of a new little phase in films. I certainly hope it will be."

But the biggest news story was Sidney Poitier. Sidney Skolsky made it up to his pal from Schwab's by headlining his column, "Oscar—Civil Rights Leader." Poitier told the *New York Times,* "I'd like to think it will help someone, but I don't believe my Oscar will be a sort of magic wand that will wipe away the restrictions on job opportunities for Negro actors." His victory was magic enough for New York Mayor Robert Wagner to announce that New York was throwing a ticker-tape parade for Poitier and awarding him the Medal of the City at a ceremony at City Hall.

"Probably little noticed in the drama of the awards was Mr. Poitier's human response to his moment of happiness," pointed out the *New York Times'* television reviewer, Jack Gould. "He received his Oscar from Anne Bancroft, and, as anyone would in the circumstances, gave her an impulsive hug. In fictional television such a touchingly sincere and realistic scene would have been written out lest Southern sensibilities be disturbed."

Federico Fellini did not persuade Groucho Marx and Mae West to be in *Juliet of the Spirits*, but he felt his trip to the Academy Awards ceremony was definitely worth it. "That colored fellow is wonderful," the director said to Hollywood writer Melville Shavelson after the show. "You mean Poitier?" Shavelson asked. "No, the one who sang," Fellini replied. "Sammy Davis, Jr. He is a diamond. If only he could speak Italian!"

1964

"No Communist could dream of a more effective anti-American film to spread abroad than this one."
—Washington Post

The 1964 Academy Awards contest was a championship bout between two heavyweights—Audrey Hepburn and Julie Andrews.

In 1962, Stanley Kubrick sprang *Lolita* on Hollywood. Now, he had *Dr. Strangelove: Or How I Learned to Stop Worrying and Love the Bomb,* "the best American movie in years," according to *The New Yorker*. "A true satire with the whole human race as the ultimate target," wrote the *Saturday Review*. "I'm inclined to say that this mordant young director Kubrick has carried American comedy to a new high ground."

Others thought Kubrick was carrying things too far. "I am troubled," wrote Bosley Crowther of the *New York Times,* "by the feeling which runs all through the film, of discredit and even contempt for our whole military establishment." The *Washington Post* was more than troubled and editorialized, "No Communist could dream of a more effective anti-American film to spread abroad than this one." The air force quickly issued a statement that expressed its "belief" that safeguards would prevent such a mistaken dropping of the A-bomb from happening in real life.

"Never before has a political satire been an unqualified box-office bonanza," noted the *New York Herald Tribune*. "That theme for movies has been considered strictly taboo." But then, *Dr. Strangelove* was a news event. NBC called it "a true echo of our time!" In its "1964 Year End Review," *Time* included a picture of Peter Sellers in the title role on a cover montage under the headline THE NUCLEAR ISSUE.

Sellers was also a familiar sight on movie screens. He followed *Dr. Strangelove* with another hit, *The World of Henry Orient,* and then replaced Peter Ustinov in the role of a bumbling detective in Blake Edwards' comedy *The Pink Panther*. The bubble finally burst when Sellers collapsed from a heart attack while filming Billy Wilder's *Kiss Me, Stupid* and *he* was replaced by Ray Walston. When he recovered from surgery, Sellers returned to London and complained publicly that Wilder's set had always been bustling with visitors. "He was running a bloody Cook's Tour!" Sellers said.

Fun with Dick and Peter

Richard Burton and Elizabeth Taylor were used to crowds; they were the most photographed couple in the world. Forget that old news about trouble on the set of *Cleopatra*—Liz and Dick sold tickets. MGM was fluffing up *The Sandpiper* for them and producer Marty Ransohoff was telling gossips he wanted the beautiful couple to play *Macbeth*. But Burton didn't spend all his screen time with Taylor. In 1964, he costarred with Ava Gardner, Deborah Kerr, and the actress who had been Kubrick's Lolita, Sue Lyon, in *The Night of the Iguana,* and with Peter O'Toole in *Becket*.

Iguana's reviews were mixed, but *Becket,* a lavish historical spectacle, received high praise. The *Los Angeles Times* declared it "the stuff that awards are made of, both as picture and for acting" and the *New York Daily News* announced, "Other productions this year with pretensions towards Academy Awards will have to contend with *Becket,* which is [producer] Hal Wallis' masterpiece." Like Burton, O'Toole did not need a publicist—he was capable of attracting attention on his own. Mike Connolly reported: "Peter O'Toole and Jason Robards were the ruckus-raisers in the strictly-members-only Daisy Club, as though all you crazy Daisy cardholders didn't know, and Happy Lent to you too. . . ."

Beatlemania

O'Toole and Burton looked as old as Bob Hope next to the Beatles, who burst on the screen in *A Hard Day's Night*. When United Artists hired an American TV commercial director named

Overleaf: *Audrey Hepburn* (left) *and Best Actress winner Julie Andrews show, once and for all, that there are* no *hard feelings.*

"I can't wait to see My Fair Lady. I know I'll cry so hard I'll blot my eye out."
—Julie Andrews

Richard Lester to make a feature with the Fab Four the studio was hoping for something along the lines of an Elvis Presley vehicle. "This is going to surprise you—it may knock you right out of your chair," warned Bosley Crowther of the *New York Times,* "but the new film with those incredible chaps, the Beatles, is a whale of a comedy." The *New York Post* called it "the surprise of the century." The sound-track album was the biggest seller in the history of the recording industry. Grown-ups went to see the teen musical too, and they could bring their youngest kids because the *New York Daily News* swore, "It's clean wholesome entertainment."

A Very Square Person

As clean as *A Hard Day's Night* was, it wasn't nearly as wholesome, or as profitable, as *The Unsinkable Molly Brown,* and that was the way its star, Debbie Reynolds, liked it. "In European things, they can take a deeper look into characterization and do more things with sex," Reynolds asserted,"but I really think American films are much better. I'm a very square person." As Molly Brown, *Time* said Reynolds was "all charm, all bounce, all spirit and all fun, and it is impossible not to admire her." Louella Parsons exclaimed, "Debbie Reynolds is a revelation and is certain to earn herself an Oscar nomination . . . and perhaps an Oscar, too!" Reynolds had fans at NASA, as well. When astronauts Virgil "Gus" Grissom and John Young named their Gemini space capsule "Molly" in honor of the movie, Debbie sent them the lace handkerchief she used in the film and told them, "This is the greatest thing that's ever happened in my life."

Who's the Fairest of Them All

Debbie's Oscar chances were blasted into outer space, however, when Julie Andrews' *Mary Poppins* landed at Radio City Music Hall in September. Andrews had been deprived of re-creating her Broadway role as Eliza Doolittle in Jack Warner's $17 million movie version of *My Fair Lady* because the producer said nobody in the sticks had ever heard of her. "The criticism heaped upon Jack Warner for bypassing Julie," wrote Sheilah Graham, "has been like nothing I can remember in my years of reporting." *Time* opined, "Someone, somewhere, made the decision to include Andrews out of the movie version of *My Fair Lady.* There is an evil and rampantly lunatic force at loose in the world and it must be destroyed."

Jack Warner's choice for Eliza Doolittle was Audrey Hepburn. Hepburn couldn't sing, so reliable Marni Nixon, who had dubbed Deborah Kerr in *The King and I* and Natalie Wood in *West Side Story,* trilled in her place. Meanwhile, Julie Andrews decided to take Walt Disney's offer to star as a magical nanny because he was also offering a job to her husband, designer Tony Walton. Although Hepburn and Andrews were in town at the same time making the musicals, they never met.

"I feel very close to Julie," Audrey Hepburn said, "because we're both being asked the same thing—about getting or not getting the role. I feel as if we're going through the same thing." Andrews insisted that she was looking forward to the movie version of *My Fair Lady.* "I can't wait to see it," she said. "I know I'll cry so hard I'll blot my eye out."

Andrews didn't cry nearly as much as author P. L. Travers, who didn't like what Disney had done to *Mary Poppins.* But she was alone in her dismay. The *Saturday Review* predicted that the film would become a perennial classic like *The Wizard of Oz,* which was now a television fixture. *Mary Poppins* rose straight to the top of the year's moneymaking films and sold nearly as many sound-track albums as *A Hard Day's Night. Time* was once again one of Andrews' loudest cheerleaders: "If she did nothing but stand there smiling for a few hours, she would cast her radiance. It would be enough." *Newsweek* concurred and reported: "At the age of 29, Julie Andrews suddenly finds

"They said, 'Who cares about an old man making love to a broken-down old broad?' "
—Anthony Quinn

herself transformed into a full-fledged movie star." Julie had passed the test with flying colors; a month later, it was Audrey Hepburn's turn.

By George, She's Done Half of It

When *My Fair Lady* had its world premiere in New York in October, the *New York Times* stated, "The happiest thing about it is that Audrey Hepburn superbly justifies the decision of Jack Warner to get her to play the title role." But Hedda Hopper had her reservations: "With Marni Nixon doing the singing, Audrey Hepburn gives only half a performance." When other critics harped on the dubbing issue, Jack Warner was perplexed. "We've been doing this for years," he said. "We even dubbed Rin-Tin-Tin."

Rex in Wax

Audrey Hepburn's nonsinging was just about the only problem any of the critics had with *My Fair Lady*. Judith Crist called it "the best movie-musical news of the year." Army Archerd said that Rex Harrison's performance as Henry Higgins "is even better in the Warner film. He's a cinch to be in the Oscarace again this year." Twentieth Century–Fox quickly signed Harrison to make another musical, *Doctor Dolittle*, and the Movieland Wax Museum immortalized him in wax. The musical was very popular at Academy screenings; when the Academy turned away crowds at one showing, so many people came back for the hastily scheduled 11 P.M. showing of the three-hour movie that there was another mad scramble for seats. *My Fair Lady* became Warner Brothers' highest-grossing film, and one columnist remarked, "Jack Warner has turned gold into gold."

Bosoms, Blood and Sand

Another film with the Midas touch was the third installment of the James Bond series. Opening at Christmas, *Goldfinger* pulled in the highest gross of any single film that year. Coproducer Harry Saltzman explained the secret of his success: "We've gone back to the bedrock of Hollywood—bosoms, blood and sand!"

Zorba the Greek also premiered in December and *Time* called it "a grand uproarious bacchanalian bash." Of Anthony Quinn as the title character, the *New York Times* wrote, "He is Adam in the Garden of Eden, Odysseus on the windy plains of Troy." The two-time Oscar winner played a free-spirited vagabond who woos an old courtesan. Simone Signoret was his original costar, but she dropped out suddenly and was replaced by French actress Lila Kedrova, who had to learn English while making the film. "Nobody wanted to do this role," Quinn said after the good reviews came in. "Burl Ives and Burt Lancaster turned it down. They said, 'Who cares about an old man making love to a broken-down old broad?' "

Quinn Admits Love Child

The public cared a lot, though, about a middle-aged man making love to a twenty-three-year-old Italian woman, especially when he had a wife and kids waiting for him in the States. ACTOR QUINN ADMITS LOVE CHILD, screamed a *New York Daily News* headline on June 15, 1963, when the story came out that Quinn had fallen for a blond wardrobe mistress while working on *Barabbas* in Rome in 1961. The couple had two sons. The *New York Times* said, "The situation created something of an international outrage when it became public."

Psychics and Evil Geniuses

Jack Warner started writing his Oscar acceptance speech when the New York Film Critics named *My Fair Lady* the Best Picture and Rex Harrison the Best Actor. Audrey Hepburn did not win Best Actress; but then neither did Julie Andrews. The critics picked Kim Stanley for

"I'm sick about it."
—George Cukor

playing a devious medium in the British thriller *Seance on a Wet Afternoon*. The film opened in Hollywood on December 18 to qualify for the Awards and, although it was British-made, Hedda Hopper wrote of Stanley: "Hers is by far the best acting performance of the year." Sheilah Graham agreed: "Miss Stanley could walk away with the Oscar."

The New York Film Critics skipped over *My Fair Lady*'s George Cukor and elected *Dr. Strangelove*'s Stanley Kubrick as their Best Director. The Best Screenplay Award went to British playwright Harold Pinter for *The Servant*. Bosley Crowther wrote that he wished Rex Harrison had not won Best Actor because he preferred *The Servant*'s Dirk Bogarde "for his performance of the horrifying role of the evil genius. And he almost got it. He was beaten by one vote." Ads appeared in the Hollywood trade papers calling Academy nominators' attention to "Dirk Bogarde's controversial portrayal" in the movie that ran for seven months in one art house in New York.

Two Art-House Women

Harold Pinter had written another screenplay in 1964, *The Pumpkin Eater*, which starred Anne Bancroft as a woman who had a lot of babies. Bancroft won a lot of awards for the role—a Golden Globe, the London Film Critics citation and a trophy from the Cannes Film Festival. Another former Oscar winner with an art-house hit was Sophia Loren, who costarred with Marcello Mastroianni in the sexy, subtitled comedy *Marriage, Italian Style*. "Smashing Records Coast-to-Coast in Blockbuster Joseph E. Levine Style," boomed ads in the Hollywood trade papers with box-office figures confirming that the producer of *Two Women* had done it again. But Loren was still considered a Hollywood outsider, at least according to the ladies' room attendant at Chasen's in Beverly Hills. Columnist Shirley Eder interviewed the employee, who repeated what she had heard on the job: "All the people are sick of those foreign broads walking off with the Academy Award, so as far as I'm concerned, that eliminates Sophia Loren," the attendant said. "I can't name the winners, but I can tell you it won't be one of those foreign broads."

Young, Lovely and Slovenly

Fox's Christmas present was Robert Aldrich's latest grisly shocker, *Hush . . . Hush, Sweet Charlotte*. Bette Davis and Joan Crawford were originally costarring à la *What Ever Happened to Baby Jane?*, but after three days on the set, Joan entered a hospital, claiming "a respiratory ailment." When it looked as if Crawford might never come out, Davis suggested that Aldrich hire her old friend Olivia de Havilland to take over Joan's villainess role. The film provided Davis and Aldrich with another hit, putting Bette back to work on Oscar number three. "Bette Davis takes a running start for her 11th Oscar nomination," wrote Army Archerd, "guests on Johnny Carson's show January 28, the day ballots go out."

Another Hollywood institution who profited by the success of *Charlotte* was supporting actress Agnes Moorehead. "One of the best-groomed ladies of the screen, Miss Moorehead is a joy in the comic relief part of Velma, Charlotte's slovenly, sarcastic housekeeper," said the *New York Daily News*. Louella Parsons told Hollywood, "Aggie should be odds-on for Oscar in this."

Universal's Christmas release was a Cary Grant comedy called *Father Goose*. "This one could easily win Cary Grant an (overdue) Oscar nomination," thought Army Archerd. The preview of the film was something of a social event—Grant invited Joan Crawford to repay her for sending bottles of Pepsi to the movie's Jamaican location. Meanwhile, Columbia was trying to get Peter Sellers nominated for *Dr. Strangelove* in any category possible, advertising for him as Best Actor, then running ads for each of his three characters as separate Supporting Actor candidates.

"I've had this recurring nightmare that Rex loses to Anthony Quinn by one vote and I kill myself."
—Rachel Roberts

The Nominations

The *Los Angeles Times* headlined on its front page:

Academy Nominations Upset
JULIE ANDREWS CHOSEN,
AUDREY HEPBURN OMITTED

Mary Poppins had received thirteen nominations; *My Fair Lady,* twelve. "I think Audrey should have been nominated," said Julie Andrews. "I'm very sorry she wasn't." Not as sorry as George Cukor: "I'm sick about it," he confessed. Jack Warner wired his condolences to Audrey Hepburn in Rome, who was unavailable for comment, although she had said earlier that she had seen an hour and a half of *Mary Poppins* at Radio City Music Hall and thought Andrews was marvelous. In Hollywood, producer Mervyn LeRoy commented, "I'm very disappointed. I find it very mean of Hollywood not at least to have nominated this great actress."

Put the Blame on Marni

"She did the acting," *Daily Variety* conjectured, "but Marni Nixon subbed for her in the singing dept. and this is what undoubtedly led to her erasure." Warner executive Max Bercutt was infuriated by this explanation, and said, "If that's true, next time we have some star-dubbing to do out here we'll hire Maria Callas!"

Patricia Neal, last year's Best Actress winner, was all set to present the Best Actor Award this year, but then suffered three strokes the week before the nominations were revealed. So the Academy asked the non-nominated Audrey Hepburn to give the Award—which was expected to go to Rex Harrison.

Hepburn accepted the invitation and the *Hollywood Reporter* headlined on the front page: HEPBURN TO OSCARCAST. Mike Connolly wrote that Hepburn's sportsmanship "has captured this town's imagination like nothing since Mary Pickford said yes to Doug Fairbanks." Audrey wouldn't be handing the Award to her *Charade* costar, Cary Grant, because he wasn't nominated for *Father Goose*. Neither was Dirk Bogarde for *The Servant*. Nominee Rex Harrison said he'd be there to present an Award, too, but Mrs. Harrison was worried. "My ballot was sent to Portofino and arrived too late for me to vote," moaned Rachel Roberts. "I've had this recurring nightmare ever since that Rex loses to Anthony Quinn by one vote and I kill myself."

Quinn laughed when *Daily Variety* reviewed the Best Actor nominations with the comment, "Entire lineup are foreign, although Quinn is regarded as an American actor." "The Americans regard me as one of themselves at last," rejoiced the Mexican-born nominee, who said he'd be at the ceremony, with his European wife. His costar would be there, too. "I wonder how many Academy voters for the Best Supporting Actress Award realize that Lila Kedrova, who gives such a superb characterization of a fading beauty in *Zorba the Greek,* is only forty-five years old?" asked Mike Connolly.

Peter O'Toole was working in Paris with his Best Actor competition, Peter Sellers, on *What's New, Pussycat?* Sellers had no comment on his nomination for *Dr. Strangelove,* but O'Toole said that he didn't think he or his costar Richard Burton had a chance of winning for *Becket,* which copped a total of twelve Oscar nods, including Best Picture. "I think we'll probably knock each other off in the voting," he predicted, adding, "Perhaps they could cut an Oscar in half for us?"

Becket's John Gielgud placed in the Supporting Actor category, but the race was between *My Fair Lady*'s Stanley Holloway, who played Eliza Doolittle's father, and *Seven Days in May*'s Edmond O'Brien, who was campaigning on a nostalgia ticket. "Nominee Eddie O'Brien just wrapped up his twenty-fifth year in pix," informed *Daily Variety*. "RKO originally brought him west from his longhair legit'ing for *The Hunchback of Notre Dame*." O'Brien already had one Oscar, as did one

"I'm going to fall right outta bed."
—Agnes Moorehead

of his fellow nominees, Peter Ustinov, who was nominated this year for *Topkapi,* the picture he made after leaving the *The Pink Panther* to Peter Sellers.

Bewitched, Bothered and Nominated

"I'm going to fall right outta bed," Agnes Moorehead told Louella Parsons when she was called for her reaction to her fourth Supporting Actress nomination. Her victory was certain to Radie Harris, who covered Moorehead's appearance at a TV awards show: "Aggie, who accepted the *Bewitched* award for Elizabeth Montgomery, was just warming up for her *Hush, Hush* Oscar (what's 'hush, hush' about it, when everyone is predicting it out loud?)." Moorehead said she was "mad" to make another movie with Bette Davis and was sorry that neither Bette nor Olivia were nominated for Best Actress. The supporting actress was also delighted with Debbie Reynolds' Best Actress nod for *Molly Brown* because she was her costar in the upcoming *The Singing Nun.*

Debbie, trouping in Las Vegas, was prevented by laryngitis from commenting when the nominations were released. "Can you imagine, my daughter not being able to say a few thousand words?" her mother asked reporters. Debbie wrote down her sentiments on a pad for her mother to read to the press over the phone: "This has always been my dream. My heart is filled with gratitude and I'm thrilled beyond words to be honored by my own industry."

Nominee Kim Stanley was not coming to the ceremony because she was appearing in *The Three Sisters* in London; fellow nominees Sophia Loren and Anne Bancroft also indicated they would be absent. That left Debbie Reynolds and Julie Andrews. Despite Mike Connolly's item that "the Oscar voters we've met at the Academy screenings seem mostly agreed on Julie Andrews for next year's Best Actress nod for *The Sound of Music* and the doll they just adore this year is Debbie Reynolds," the 1964 Best Actress winner was an open secret the moment *The Sound of Music* premiered in March and Andrews smiled from the cover of *Life.* The Fox musical took off like the Gemini rocket and was headed for the biggest box-office gross since *Gone With the Wind.* Both Disney and Fox ran full-page ads congratulating Andrews on her nomination, and it was reported that Princess Grace requested a print of *Mary Poppins* for Caroline's birthday party.

With everyone being so friendly, the annual Golden Globe Awards was like a company picnic. After Jack Warner accepted *My Fair Lady*'s Best Picture award, emcee Andy Williams joked, "Mr. Warner's voice was dubbed by Marni Nixon." Best Actress winner Julie Andrews also got a laugh when she concluded her acceptance speech, "And finally, my thanks to the man who made all this possible, Jack Warner."

The Big Night

The teenagers in the bleachers gave a bigger hand to young Dick Chamberlain than they did to Max von Sydow," observed the *Hollywood Reporter*. Gregory Peck, a member of the Board of Governors, had personally called a number of older Hollywood stars and invited them to attend; showing up were Buster Keaton, Fay Wray, Ramon Novarro, and Francis X. Bushman.

Double-dating were a quartet from *My Fair Lady*. Best Supporting Actress nominee Gladys Cooper came with Jack Warner, while Audrey Hepburn was on the arm of Best Director hopeful George Cukor. "One of the last to enter the auditorium, almost unnoticed," said Army Archerd, "was Eddie Fisher."

Backstage, Joan Crawford stood waiting with two wardrobe assistants. She was scheduled to give the Best Director Award—which everyone assumed would go to the Screen Directors Guild winner, George Cukor—and she wanted to pay homage to her former director by wearing white or black as a tribute to *My Fair Lady*'s Ascot races scene. But there was one catch, as Edith Head recalled: "We had found out that the actress who was to present the Oscar just ahead of Joan had sampled both black and white fabrics, but she refused to tell us what color she was going to wear. Joan's solution was simple—do the dress in both colors. 'If she comes out in white, I'll wear black, and vice versa.' "

After the announcement that *Ben Casey* would not be seen that night, the telecast began with the overture to *My Fair Lady* as the camera looked around the audience for celebrities, finding Julie Andrews and husband Tony Walton—nominated for Best Costume Design for *Mary Poppins*—sitting in the row in front of Rex Harrison and Rachel Roberts, and, farther back, Audrey Hepburn and George Cukor in front of Jack Warner and Gladys Cooper. Another couple was Jane Fonda with her new husband, French director Roger Vadim. When the music stopped, Academy President Arthur Freed walked onto the candelabra-filled set, and said, "I think it's safe to say we live in troubled times." He then lauded movies for offering escape from these times.

The emcee was Bob Hope, who began, "Wel-

Awards Ceremony

APRIL 5, 1965, 7:00 P.M.
THE SANTA MONICA CIVIC AUDITORIUM,
SANTA MONICA

Your Host:
BOB HOPE
Televised over ABC

Presenters

Sound . . . . Claudia Cardinale and Steve McQueen
Sound Effects . . . . Angie Dickinson
Special Visual Effects . . . . Alain Delon
Supporting Actor . . . . Angela Lansbury
Documentary Awards . . . . Jimmy Durante and Martha Raye
Costume Design . . . Greer Garson and Dick Van Dyke
Short Subjects . . . . Merle Oberon
Honorary Award to William Tuttle. . . Rosalind Russell
Scoring Awards . . . . Debbie Reynolds
Scientific or Technical Awards . . . .Anthony Franciosa
Supporting Actress . . . . Karl Malden
Film Editing. . . . . Richard Chamberlain and Vincent Edwards
Cinematography. . . . Rock Hudson and Jean Simmons
Art Direction. . . . . Elizabeth Ashley and MacDonald Carey
Song . . . . Fred Astaire
Foreign Film. . . . . Rex Harrison
Writing Awards . . . . Deborah Kerr
Director . . . . .Joan Crawford
Actor. . . . . .Audrey Hepburn
Actress. . . . . Sidney Poitier
Picture. . . . . Gregory Peck

Performers of Nominated Songs

"Chim Chim Cher-ee". . . . The New Christy Minstrels
"Dear Heart" . . . . Andy Williams
"Hush . . . Hush, Sweet Charlotte" . . . . . . .Patti Page
"My Kind of Town". . . . . Nancy Wilson
"Where Love Has Gone". . . . . Jack Jones

"I think it's safe to say we live in troubled times."
—Arthur Freed

come to Santa Monica on the Thames. Tonight Hollywood is handing out the foreign aid. Before you can pick up your Oscar, you have to show your passport. Peter Sellers plays three roles and was nominated for Best Performance by a Showoff. Richard Burton doesn't know he's nominated yet. The phone is still off the hook." Then Hope turned and saw Mrs. Tony Walton. "Julie Andrews is up for *Mary Poppins,* Or How I Learned to Stop Worrying and Love Jack Warner." The television cameras showed both Warner and Andrews laughing. Then *My Fair Lady* won the first award—for Sound—and there was a shot of Rex Harrison applauding.

The orchestra played "I Enjoy Being a Girl" and out walked Angie Dickinson, who gave the Sound Effects Award to *Goldfinger*. Visiting America for the first time with his family, the winning British technician gushed, "This trip will be the most wonderful one of our lives." Then Alain Delon gave the Visual Effects Award to *Mary Poppins* and Julie Andrews was seen smiling and clapping.

Angela Lansbury read the names of the Best Supporting Actor nominees as Edmond O'Brien and Stanley Holloway squirmed in their seats. The winner was Peter Ustinov for *Topkapi*, who was off in London directing Sophia Loren as *Lady L*. Jonathan Winters accepted for him in Hollywood. "I don't know whether Peter expected this. I certainly didn't," Winters confessed. "Or I would have been sure to wear black socks."

As the orchestra began "Hello, Young Lovers," Jimmy Durante and Martha Raye marched out to demolish the titles of the Documentary nominees. Durante told Raye to act "scholarly and dignified," to which Raye responded, "It comes naturally to us Vassar girls." When the man who picked up the Feature Award sported long, flowing locks, Durante rubbed his own cranium and said, "Look at the hair on that guy!" The winning Documentary Short was made by the U.S. Information Agency and a handful of men ascended the stage. "Not a good-looking guy here," Durante commented.

Greer Garson and Dick Van Dyke appeared to present the Best Costume Design Award. Julie Andrews' husband lost to Cecil Beaton for *My Fair Lady*. Beaton's stand-in, Gladys Cooper, forgot her duties and sat clapping along with everyone else in the audience. Suddenly, she remembered what she was supposed to be doing there. The seventy-two-year-old actress sprinted down the aisle and ran to the table filled with statuettes. "Which one, does it matter?" Cooper asked a stagehand before picking up an Oscar. "Oh, it's been such a night!" she sighed.

Debbie Reynolds walked out to give the Music Awards, and made her new husband, shoe tycoon Harry Karl, the butt of repartee with Bob Hope. "That's a lovely full-length gown," the emcee complimented. "Don't tell Harry, but I'm barefoot," Reynolds responded. "So is Dolores," said Hope, referring to Mrs. Hope. The Original Score Award went to the Sherman brothers for *Mary Poppins* and, in the audience, Tony Walton took their picture with a pocket camera. Reynolds named André Previn the winner of the Best Adapted Score Award for *My Fair Lady* over *A Hard Day's Night, Mary Poppins* and *The Unsinkable Molly Brown*.

"I know how your hearts are fluttering, so I'll get on with it," said Best Supporting Actress presenter Karl Malden. Agnes Moorehead sat upright, but the winner was Lila Kedrova for *Zorba the Greek*. The recipient didn't believe she heard correctly, so she turned to her costar and asked, "Has it really happened?" "It has," confirmed Anthony Quinn. Kedrova held Quinn's face in her hands, and then hurried to the stage. She thanked her director, "Michael Cacoyannis, it is your fault, not mine. I will never, never forget it." When the couple walked offstage, Kedrova said, "I need a drink." Malden escorted her to Joan Crawford's dressing room.

The Academy's casting coup this year was arranging for TV's two most famous doctors—"Ben Casey" and "Dr. Kildare"—to present the Film Editing Awards. Bob Hope introduced Vince Edwards and Richard Chamberlain as "Method doc-

"I need a drink."
—Lila Kedrova

tors." "You open it, you're the surgeon," Chamberlain said. "That's a cutting remark," was Edwards' retort. *Mary Poppins* won the Oscar and Julie Andrews continued to smile.

Jean Simmons and Rock Hudson announced that the Black-and-White Cinematography winner was *Zorba the Greek,* but it was Hollywood's Arlene Dahl who walked to the stage and claimed the statuette. "Isn't he beautiful," said Dahl, admiring Oscar. She praised cinematographer Walter Lassally and added, "His brilliant camera work contributed enormously to *Zorba the Greek.*" The Color Cinematography Award went to *My Fair Lady*'s Harry Stradling, Sr., who was sitting with his wife's coat in his lap. Stradling thanked "Audrey Hepburn for her appreciation," and the cameras caught George Cukor whispering to Hepburn as Stradling walked off. A sense of déjà vu colored the Art Direction Awards. The Black-and-White winner was *Zorba the Greek,* and Vassilis Fotopoulos said, "It's a great honor for me and my country. It's very nice and sweet." There was a shot of Anthony Quinn laughing as the winner walked off. Then *My Fair Lady*'s Gene Allen received the Color trophy and commented, "Miss Audrey Hepburn really lights up those sets so that we can win these awards."

Fred Astaire announced that the Best Song winner was "Chim Chim Cher-ee" from *Mary Poppins*. The Sherman brothers made their second trip to the stage and said, "There are no words. All we can say is supercalifragelisticexpialidocious." Rex Harrison stepped forward to give the Foreign Film Award and Bob Hope congratulated him on his performance as Caesar in *Cleopatra*. "Oh, you noticed me in that, thank you," Harrison quipped, before giving the Oscar to producer Joseph E. Levine for Italy's *Yesterday, Today and Tomorrow*. Gene Kelly then introduced Judy Garland, who sang a Cole Porter medley. Garland was followed by her *Meet Me in St. Louis* costar, June Lockhart, who hawked toothpaste in a commercial.

It was time for the Writing Awards and for Joan Crawford's fashion riddle to be answered. Deborah Kerr made her entrance in white. Joan Crawford hightailed it to her dressing room with the black gown. Kerr gave the Adapted Screenplay Award to Edward Anhalt for *Becket,* who said,"I hope the TV audience appreciates the excitement of winning." The winners for the Original Screenplay Award had never met before; Peter Stone had rewritten Frank Tarloff's script for Cary Grant's movie *Father Goose*. "Our thanks to Cary Grant, who keeps winning these things for other people," Stone said. "He just stole my speech," followed Tarloff.

Bob Hope brought out "the best-looking tycoon you'll ever see—Joan Crawford." Crawford walked out, stopped, and bowed to the ovation. Then Hope reminded her, "Stop by my house afterwards and pick up a load of empties." Crawford read the nominations, opened the envelope and, with all the grandeur she could muster, announced, "And the winner is Mr. George Cukor for *My Fair Lady*." The applause was thunderous as Cukor walked to the stage and kissed Crawford's hand. "I'm very grateful, very happy and very lucky," the winner said.

Bob Hope introduced Audrey Hepburn, "who flew in all the way from Europe." Hepburn got the longest ovation yet, accompanied by a shot of Julie Andrews clapping for her. "Thank you very much," she whispered. She opened the envelope, smiled and proclaimed, "And the winner is Rex Harrison for *My Fair Lady*!" As Harrison walked to the stage, TV viewers saw Julie Andrews applauding nervously while, behind her, Rachel Roberts was clapping with all her might. Onstage, Andrews' Broadway costar Harrison hugged his movie costar five times, kissed her thrice and kept his arm around her throughout his acceptance. "I feel in a way I should split it in half between us," Harrison said, putting the Oscar on the podium. "Hold it up!" Audrey instructed him. "Deep love," Rex concluded, "to—uh—well, two fair ladies." "Yes!" Audrey agreed. They walked off arm in arm.

Bob Hope introduced Best Actress presenter Sidney Poitier by explaining how he had won his

"This is some delicatessen Joan's running, but I can't stand Pepsi in my vodka."
—Bob Hope

Oscar last year: "How could he have missed, he had all those nuns praying for him." Poitier revealed the winner—Julie Andrews for *Mary Poppins*. Andrews drew a breath when she heard her name and, as she walked to the stage, the cameras saw her costar, Dick Van Dyke, looking very satisfied. Andrews shook hands with Poitier and said, "I know you Americans are famous for your hospitality, but this is really ridiculous. I know where to start—Mr. Walt Disney gets the biggest thank you." Andrews ended by thanking everybody "for making me feel truly welcome in this country."

Before the final Award was made, Bob Hope read a telegram from Patricia Neal, now convalescing in England, that expressed her regrets at not being able to give the Best Actor Award. Then Gregory Peck popped out to bestow the Best Picture Oscar. Like Joan Crawford, Peck rose to his most stately to name the winner: "The Best Picture of the Year is *My Fair Lady*." Jack Warner did not receive the clamorous applause of Cukor, Harrison and Andrews—the clapping ended before he got all the way onstage. "I am indeed gratified to be here tonight," said the man who had been a studio head when the talkies were born. "It is something we'll always be proud of, and I speak of those in the back lot, the front lot, upstairs, and downstairs and everywhere."

Bob Hope walked on to make the closing remarks, but the orchestra swung into "That's Entertainment" so loudly that the master of ceremonies was temporarily drowned out. "That's the loudest background music I ever heard," Hope cracked. When the volume was lowered, Bob continued with his message. "Hollywood has become the celluloid United Nations," he began, ultimately ending with a joke: "The losers will now join hands and march on the British Embassy."

Aftermath

Julie Andrews stood backstage muttering, "I don't believe it. I don't believe it." Audrey Hepburn told reporters, "I'm thrilled for her, of course." When asked his interpretation of the Best Actress result, Rex Harrison responded, "I wouldn't consider it poetic justice. Julie was marvelous onstage but Audrey was wonderful, too." Mrs. Rex Harrison admitted, "I haven't seen *My Fair Lady* yet but I would really like to." Julie Andrews replied, "No, I wouldn't say revenge was sweet. There's no ill will." And even Jack Warner confessed, "I voted for Julie Andrews."

Those who weren't being grilled by the press were hovering in Joan Crawford's dressing room. Martha Raye burst in, exclaiming, "Quick, kids, something on the rocks!" Bob Hope stuck his head in and quipped, "This is some delicatessen Joan's running, but I can't stand Pepsi in my vodka." Crawford was having a terrific time, and she told Mike Connolly, "It always knocks me out to be backstage with big talents at the Oscarcast—I don't think I'll ever get over the sheer magic of people like Patti Page sitting around in dressing gowns or in tweeds one second and then the next switching to something bouffant and beautiful and glamorous and then going out there and knocking everybody cold."

At the Governors' Ball, Jonathan Winters swiped the miniature Oscar adorning his table's dessert and figured, "It's probably the only Oscar I'll ever get." The Rex Harrisons and the Vince Edwardses left the ball and went to Peter O'Toole's favorite nightclub, the Daisy, where comedian Dick Martin was performing. When the elegantly attired Oscar-goers entered, Martin did a double take and said, "One of us is dressed funny."

Audrey Hepburn skipped the after-parties and went to bed. The *Hollywood Reporter* stated that Hepburn spent the next morning shopping and then flew off to Spain that afternoon with one hundred pounds of excess luggage. Before she left, Hepburn sent Julie Andrews a large bouquet of paper flowers. When Andrews returned home from celebrating, her Oscar went into a box in the attic "until I find a suitable place to put it."

Columnist Marilyn Beck speculated that

"many flicker-folk believe Anthony Quinn lost to Rex Harrison because of his personal life. They think Tony's public admission of siring two families simultaneously outraged the industry's moral code and this negated his brilliant acting job in *Zorba*." Peter O'Toole had a simpler explanation for the turn of events and cabled his costar, "Burton, old buddy, you can't win 'em all."

Hedda Hopper was displeased that Lila Kedrova had stolen the Oscar from Hollywood's Agnes Moorehead. "I guess I'll remain a bridesmaid for the rest of my life," the loser told Hedda. The columnist had a few more thoughts about the outcome:

> *No American actor won. Either the rules will have to be changed or our actors will have to try harder. And did you notice that Oscar went home with those who acted, produced and directed good, clean family-type pictures? Proving that not only the rest of the country but Hollywood itself doesn't go for all that overabundance of sex and stripping.*

When Audrey Hepburn arrived home, there was a telegram waiting for her from Katharine Hepburn. "Don't worry about not being nominated," advised the wire. "Someday you'll get it for a part that doesn't rate it."

1965

"I like seeing my picture in the papers."
—Julie Christie

Julie Andrews was back for round two, defending her Oscar title against this year's discovery, Julie Christie.

Just as Julie Andrews received word in February 1965 that she had been nominated for Best Actress for *Mary Poppins*, her latest musical was opening. 'SOUND OF MUSIC' RESTORES FAITH IN THE ART OF MOTION PICTURES, headlined the *Hollywood Reporter*, which advised viewers, "If you sit quietly and let it take, it may also restore your faith in humanity." Then the reviewer talked about Andrews: "Once there was Mary Pickford, then there was Garbo, now there is Julie. She is very likely going to be the object of one of the most intense and sustained love affairs between moviegoers and a star in the history of motion pictures."

The $8 million adaptation of the Rodgers and Hammerstein Broadway musical earned back its cost after nine months of limited release, single-handedly pulling 20th Century–Fox out of the hole it had dug for itself making *Cleopatra*. *Time* called *The Sound of Music* "the most surprising financial success in decades. In city after city, house managers are proudly rounding up the names of fans who claim that they have seen the movie as many as 30 times." The *New York Times* investigated these infamous repeat viewers and uncovered a typist from Los Angeles who had seen the movie three hundred times, a little old lady in Wales who went to see it every day, and a fellow in Oregon who had seen the film so many times that he sent Fox a copy of the script that he had written from memory.

The critics loved making fun of the film that threatened to knock *Gone With the Wind* off the top of the box-office champs list. The *New York Herald Tribune*'s Judith Crist wrote, "All that was a sugar lump on stage has, courtesy of the super-spectacular screen, become an Alp." Writing in *Esquire*, Dwight MacDonald admitted, "There is something interesting about any man-made product that approaches perfection of its kind, also about any exercise of supreme professional skill, and this was both: pure, unadulterated kitsch, not a false note, not a whiff of reality." Even leading man Christopher Plummer was slightly embarrassed by the film's sentimentality, calling the movie "The Sound of Mucus."

Director Robert Wise said that things could have been worse. "We didn't go in for too-cute costumes or turreted castles," he said, "and we were careful not to overdo colors." But Richard Haydn, who played the impresario in the movie, placed most of the credit for the film's success on its star. "Julie's incredibly wholesome, she's everybody's wife, mother, daughter. It wouldn't have been the same picture with, say, Susan Hayward."

Bare-Breasted Women

Andrews' happy *Sound of Music* world contrasted sharply with Rod Steiger's in *The Pawnbroker*, which opened in April. Director Sidney Lumet went all out for realism in telling this story of a Jewish concentration-camp survivor who runs a Harlem pawnshop: when one of Steiger's black customers bared her breasts to get a good deal, stirring up memories of the pawnbroker's wife, Lumet showed the wife's breasts, too. The Production Code people said the breast shots would have to go or no seal of approval. Lumet and company appealed the decision and won. The *New York Times* reported that the nudity in *The Pawnbroker* was merely an exception to the association's still-existent ban and thus the censors' action was "an unprecedented move that will not, however, set a precedent." The Catholic Church condemned *The Pawnbroker*, apparently unswayed by Bosley Crowther's argument in the *Times* that "the few shots of bare-breasted women contribute forcibly to a comprehension of the emotional confusions."

American International Pictures—best known

Overleaf: *Best Actress winner Julie Christie expresses her appreciation.*

"William Wyler made me believe he actually hated me."
—Samantha Eggar

for Vincent Price horror flicks and Frankie and Annette beach movies—sold *The Pawnbroker* as the last word in contemporary film-making by advertising the movie with an Op Art poster. One columnist predicted that *The Pawnbroker* "will take its place with such films as *Marty* and *Dr. Strangelove* as classics of U.S. independent filmmaking." The filmmakers had run the movie by the 1964 Berlin Film Festival and picked up a Best Actor prize for Rod Steiger, before opening it in New York in 1965. "Steiger gives one of the great performances in movies," claimed *Newsweek*.

Samantha Eggar Unleashed

Winning the acting awards at the 1965 Cannes Film Festival was William Wyler's adaptation of John Fowles' novel *The Collector*. Both Terence Stamp, in the title role, and Samantha Eggar, as his captive, won honors, and Eggar accompanied the film when it opened in the United States in May. Columnist Vernon Scott interviewed the twenty-six-year-old British newcomer and wrote, "Miss Eggar shows a charming honesty. She visited Las Vegas and declares she 'hated' it." Eggar was also a little wary of her director, who had denied her lunch breaks and made her rehearse on the weekends. "I believe now that he kept me unnerved and high-strung," the actress said of William Wyler. "He made me believe he actually hated me, to get the performance out of me that he wanted." As far as the critics were concerned, Wyler's technique worked: the *New York Daily News* awarded the drama four stars, calling it "an electrifying experience," and *Time* described the leading lady as "a rare combination of acting talent and physical beauty." Hollywood beckoned, and Eggar signed to make a movie called *Walk Don't Run* with Cary Grant.

Suddenly, Minis Everywhere

Samantha Eggar's new stardom couldn't hold a candle, however, to the meteoric flash of her twenty-four-year-old compatriot, Julie Christie. The blond beauty became an international star thanks to *Darling*, a British-made morality tale about how empty the jet-set life is, written by Frederic Raphael and directed by John Schlesinger. "If the message in *Darling* is no great shakes," opined the *Saturday Review*, "the filmmaking itself is decidedly clever, representative of the new subtle look in British filmmaking."

Darling also ushered in a new look in fashion. "I remember when Mary Quant first introduced the miniskirt," said costume designer Anthony Powell. "It got a lot of press but it wasn't really accepted much beyond the mods in London. Then *Darling* came out and the public saw beautiful Julie Christie walking around in miniskirts. Suddenly, we saw minis everywhere." Sidney Skolsky wasted no time in interviewing Christie. "She looks a bit like Brigitte Bardot, like Joanne Woodward, like Juliet Prowse," wrote the columnist, "yet she retains her own individual look and personality." Skolsky asked Christie what she thought about her overnight success and she responded, "Success is a trap. I don't know if I am prepared for it." She then added with a sigh, "I like seeing my picture in the papers."

Lee Marvin Joins the In Crowd

When movie columnists weren't writing about Julie Christie that summer, they were profiling a character actor who had played villains in American films for fifteen years. "As soon as people see my face on a movie screen," Lee Marvin told *Life*, "they know two things: first, I'm not going to get the girl, and second, I'll get a cheap funeral before the picture is over." Two films changed all that. In June, Marvin appeared in the dual role of a drunken gunfighter and his evil twin brother in *Cat Ballou*, a cowboy parody that had Hedda Hopper swearing, "It's the kookiest Western I ever saw." Marvin, who won the 1965 Berlin Film Festival Best Actor Award, described the film in terms of a dating experience. "I'll tell you what it's really like. Ever go

"Ever go out with a silly girl who turned out to be really amusing?"
—Lee Marvin

out with a silly girl who turned out to be really amusing?"

Hot on the heels of *Cat Ballou* came a dramatic change of pace for Marvin, the role of a baseball player in the allegorical drama *Ship of Fools,* released in July. When the *New York Times* asked Marvin if he had read Katherine Anne Porter's Pulitzer Prize– and National Book Award–winning novel before making movie, he retorted, "Hell, no. A book by a seventy-two-year-old broad? Not me." Some movie critics echoed Marvin's estimation of the book; the *New York Daily News* gave *Ship of Fools* four stars because it "skillfully condensed Miss Porter's long, sometimes dull novel." There were no complaints about Marvin's performance, with many columnists remarking on the actor's double whammy. "*Cat Ballou,* a comedy Western that has started Oscar talk, and *Ship of Fools,* make Marvin an Oscar contender," wrote *Newsday.* "Now he may be able to call the shots, as to roles, and he may be able to carry a film."

New Male Charmer

Lee Marvin wasn't the only actor benefiting from *Ship of Fools.* Broadway actor Michael Dunn made his film debut as the ship's Greek chorus and inspired the *New York Daily News* to rave: "Michael Dunn, the fine dwarf actor, plays a German with a small body but a giant brain." In a more traditional movie-star vein was Oskar Werner, as the ship's doctor who has an affair with passenger Simone Signoret. *Time* called their love scenes "a duet of eye-to-eye messages that make dialogue seem beside the point, show-stoppers of stunning subtlety." Director Stanley Kramer said Werner was, "the new male charmer of the screen." The *New York Times* headlined its interview with the German-born actor, OSKAR WERNER—THEY'RE PRONOUNCING IT 'OSCAR WINNER'.

Critics weren't as optimistic for the filmmakers; "Their vessel is almost swamped by symbolism before it leaves port," snarled *Newsweek,* "and neither director Kramer nor screenwriter Abby Mann knows quite how to navigate it." But Simone Signoret came to the film's defense, telling the magazine, "Parts of the film are intentionally unsubtle as life was unsubtle then, rough, tough, incredible, unbelievable, but true. I have a European attitude toward this picture, I suppose. I think it says more than most, a picture that will be seen twice."

Free Thinkers

Audiences were more interested in seeing the Burtons' latest *roman à cinema, The Sandpiper.* In this MGM production shot in California's Big Sur area by director Vincente Minnelli, Richard Burton played a straying minister involved with Liz, a bohemian artist frequently referred to as a "freethinker" by reviewers. The *New York Times'* Bosley Crowther didn't think much of the picture and carped, "Doubtless as an exploitation gimmick, Elizabeth Taylor is frequently overexposed via low-cut sweaters and tops, and there is one scene where she is completely nude to the waist except for her hands barely covering focal points." The film's theme song, "The Shadow of Your Smile," became a radio and nightclub hit and the movie pulled in huge grosses. Burton was able to redeem himself in the critics' eyes later in the year with the espionage drama based on John le Carré's novel *The Spy Who Came in From the Cold,* which costarred Oskar Werner and Claire Bloom. *Spy* didn't make anywhere near the money that *The Sandpiper* did, yet Bosley Crowther liked it because it wasn't filled with James Bond gimmickry but was "realistic, and believable, too."

Latecomers

At Christmastime, David Picker, the United Artists executive who had shrewdly promoted *Tom Jones* to a Best Picture Oscar in 1963, was touting *A Thousand Clowns,* an adaptation of Herb Gardner's play starring Jason Robards as a nonconfor-

"When does Laurence Olivier sing 'Mammy'?"
—Inez Robb

mist and Martin Balsam as his stuffy brother. "Sooner or later . . . you'll fall in love with *A Thousand Clowns*," promised the ads, and *Newsweek* seconded it: "*A Thousand Clowns* tells its audience what it craves to hear—that every man, woman and child is a treasure-trove awaiting discovery." The picture opened in New York and Los Angeles to qualify for Oscars, but Picker had trouble persuading skeptical theater chains in other cities to book the comedy.

Having better luck at the box office was a film whose ads declared: "A motion picture that will make you laugh, break your heart and thrill you all within seconds!" The movie was *A Patch of Blue*, a fable about racial tolerance with Sidney Poitier as the hero and Shelley Winters as the villainess. "Can you imagine me using words like 'nigger' and 'wop'?" Winters asked a columnist, adding, "I've always found something to like in the characters I've played, but not this time. I really hate this woman. She blinds her daughter by accident when she was trying to blind her husband. And when the girl grows up, she beats her. How's that for a role?"

MGM tested 150 unknowns to find the actress to play Winters' luckless daughter, and chose one Elizabeth Hartman, twenty-two, of Youngstown, Ohio. "I believe I was lacking the things they wanted an actress to lack," reckoned Hartman to Sidney Skolsky, who made her the subject of one of his "Tintypes" profiles after she won glowing notices. Skolsky made the following observations about the actress: "She is shy, timid. She sleeps in a normal-size bed in sleeveless nightgowns. She always takes her Raggedy-Ann doll to bed with her."

Catch My Soul, Man

Another Christmas offering was a filmed record of the National Theatre of Great Britain's production of *Othello*. The title role was played by a black-faced Laurence Olivier, who inspired *Women's Wear Daily* to write, "If there was ever any doubt that Laurence Olivier was the finest actor in the English-speaking theater there can be none at all after seeing his Othello." But in Hollywood, columnist Inez Robb still had her doubts and said, "Olivier's performance was high camp. I was certainly in tune with the gentleman next to me who kept asking, 'When does he sing "Mammy"?'"

Boris Pasternak Meets Julie Christie

After David Lean won two Best Picture Awards for Columbia with *The Bridge on the River Kwai* and *Lawrence of Arabia*, MGM snapped him up for his next epic—an adaptation of Boris Pasternak's *Doctor Zhivago*. Lean didn't argue with success when it came to casting, and Egyptian Omar Sharif, who had become an international star in *Lawrence of Arabia*, played the title character, a Russian poet. And who better to portray the woman who bears his love child than British Julie Christie? Army Archerd heralded MGM's big one in early December: "*Zhivago* timetable: David Lean and his round-the-clock crew are due to complete editing today, turn the film over for scoring and dubbing of the 195 minute epic. The preem is only two weeks off."

"A masterpiece comparable to *Gone With the Wind*," claimed the *Los Angeles Herald-Examiner*, when *Zhivago* did open. The *Hollywood Reporter* went further: "*Doctor Zhivago* is more than a masterful motion picture; it is a life experience." But in New York, many critics felt that the film's three-hour-plus running time gave the impression they had spent their whole lives watching it. Judith Crist called it an "ultimately tedious epic-type soap opera," and *The New Yorker* complained that the "able actors have been given almost nothing to do except wear costumes and engage in banal small talk."

Running on a reserved-seat basis, *Doctor Zhivago* drew great word-of-mouth and became MGM's second most profitable film, right behind *Gone With the Wind*. Maurice Jarre's musical score, including "Lara's Theme," conquered the

"The bare-breasted women contribute forcibly to a comprehension of the emotional confusions."
—Bosley Crowther

record charts and Hallmark cards published a small book, "The Love Poems of Doctor Zhivago." But MGM's hopes of challenging *The Sound of Music* at the Oscars dimmed when the Directors Guild nominations were announced and David Lean wasn't even mentioned.

Julie vs. Julie

"Voom! Voom! It's Julie Christie," headlined *Newsweek* in its cover story of the actress for its Christmas issue, and now that Hollywood had gotten a second look at Julie Christie, Army Archerd wrote that she "is the year's British 'Julie' being touted for stardom. Ironically, she and boyfriend Don Bessant Christmas-dined here with Julie Andrews and Tony Walton. Miss C. is much like France's B. B., physically and vociferously—judging by the razorlike replies she tosses in an interview. A lotta copy will be penned on this talented lass."

Much of that copy centered on Christie's arrangement with her boyfriend. "People keep asking me why Don and I are not engaged," she said. "Well, because I don't want to get married. Some people can be married and some people cannot—it's as simple as that."

The Best Actress race was not so simple—would Julie Andrews win for being wholesome in *The Sound of Music* or would it be Julie Christie for being mod in *Darling*? Then there were other considerations, according to Sidney Skolsky: "Elizabeth Hartman for *A Patch of Blue* is the sleeper, the long-shot filly who could sneak in and win the Oscar Derby if the race between the Julies is so close they divide the votes." MGM sent reporters to Youngstown, Ohio, where Hartman still resided with her mother. "I'm just waiting for someone to offer me a part in a picture or a play," the actress told the press. "I'm climbing the walls, as a matter of fact." MGM did not use pictures of Hartman in her Oscar ads in the trade papers, but relied on a sight gag—a pair of sunglasses in a Price, Warehouse envelope—to remind Academy members that she had played a blind girl.

The Nominations

A Thousand Clowns received three nominations: Best Adapted Screenplay for Herb Gardner, Best Supporting Actor for Martin Balsam, and Best Picture. "On the basis of the Academy nomination, we finally got a theater in London to play it," David Picker rejoiced. But the film's competition included two formidable, hard-ticket epics—*The Sound of Music* and *Doctor Zhivago* with ten nominations each. When the Academy nominated David Lean for *Zhivago*, the nominee wondered, "But how could I have been when the Directors Guild didn't give us a nomination?" *Darling* was nominated for the same awards that it had won at the New York Film Critics—Best Picture, Best Director and Best Actress—and the Academy also nominated it for Best Original Screenplay and Best Costume Design. *Ship of Fools* was the fifth nominee for Best Picture, but Stanley Kramer was not nominated for Best Director. According to Army Archerd, Best Actress nominee Simone Signoret wept when she learned that Kramer had been bumped for Japanese director Hiroshi Teshigahara for *Woman in the Dunes*, a film that had won a special prize at the Cannes Film Festival the year before and was renowned for its sensual love scenes. But it didn't seem that Teshigahara's luck would continue in Hollywood if the Directors Guild Award was any indication—they picked Robert Wise for *The Sound of Music*, which Fox executives were now calling "The Mint."

Let's Stay Together

Best Actress nominees Simone Signoret, Elizabeth Hartman and Samantha Eggar looked on as the press clamored around the two Julies, who refused to suggest there was any rivalry between them. They even talked alike. Andrews said, "I'd like to win the Oscar, but being nominated for it is glory enough." Christie elaborated, "Of course, I'd love to win the Oscar, but, believe me, being

"For the first time, you can actually see the losers turn green."
—Bob Hope

nominated is praise enough." Andrews invited Christie to stay at her home for the Awards, but Christie's publicists persuaded her to stay at the Beverly Hills Hotel to make their job easier. "Our schedules were both so hectic," was how Christie explained her choice of accommodations.

Best Actor in a Documentary

The Best Actor nominations for Lee Marvin in *Cat Ballou,* Rod Steiger in *The Pawnbroker,* Richard Burton in *The Spy Who Came in From the Cold* and Oskar Werner for *Ship of Fools* didn't surprise anyone, but the nomination of Laurence Olivier in *Othello* did. In addition, practically half of the National Theatre company was nominated in supporting roles—Frank Finlay as Iago, Maggie Smith as Desdemona and Joyce Redman as Bianca. "The amazing thing is that the Academy has completely overlooked the fact that they are acting in a film which simply cannot be classified and analyzed as an achievement in genuine cinema," commented Bosley Crowther. "It is almost as though nominations for best acting were given to people in documentary films."

Rod Steiger campaigned in earnest for Best Actor for *The Pawnbroker,* hoping that Hollywood would not follow the lead of the New York Film Critics and give the Oscar to Oskar Werner. Steiger's small role in *Doctor Zhivago* was seen by more people than his starring turn in *The Pawnbroker,* but his trade-paper ads assured Academy voters that he had done a good job in that one, too.

It Feels Good

Lee Marvin did a lot of talking to columnists after he was nominated for *Cat Ballou.* "You're damn well right I like what's happening to the old career right now. I wasn't sure I was ever going to really make it. I waited a long time for this to happen—boy, it feels good."

Louella Parsons interviewed Marvin and reported, "He was wounded seriously during World War II and came back from the South Pacific with a rebellious attitude and in acting, he found an outlet for it." At the time of his nomination, Marvin was in the process of getting divorced after thirteen years of marriage. The *New York Daily News* gave an update on his situation: "Marvin shares financial success with family but now enjoys bachelor life in company of pretty starlet Michelle Triola."

Lynda Bird of Paradise

Another young woman dating a celebrity was the daughter of the President of the United States. Lynda Bird Johnson was going out with actor George Hamilton, and she called him one day and asked if he would take her to the Academy Awards, and please get his Hollywood home comfortable for her Secret Service men. According to one earwitness, Lynda Bird was excited enough to interrupt a professor in a class at the University of Texas when he announced that he was giving a test the following Monday; "I won't be here. I'm going to the Academy Awards that night with George Hamilton," she shouted.

For the first time, the Awards show was to be telecast in color, and to broadcast this news ABC showed trailers in movie theaters for weeks before the ceremony. Bob Hope, the show's emcee, was also the announcer for these trailers, and he enticed the audience with this thought: "Just think, for the first time, you can actually see the losers turn green."

The Big Night

It was the coldest night in Oscar history," commented the *Hollywood Reporter*. "Those weren't balmy ocean breezes that caught the ladies' silks and satins as they arrived, those were chilly strong winds." Julie Christie arrived with Don Bessant, who had designed her gold pajamas. *The Sound of Music*'s costume designer, Dorothy Jeakins, created Julie Andrews' kimono-style gown. Andrews, recently separated from Tony Walton, appeared on the arm of *Music*'s associate producer, Saul Chaplin. Samantha Eggar and Elizabeth Hartman came to the show, too.

"This is my first Oscar show," said Irene Ryan, of TV's *The Beverly Hillbillies*. "I hate getting dressed up. Granny Clampett's clothes are much more comfortable." *Daily Variety* said that "probably the most striking attire of the evening was Phyllis Diller's spectacular full-length, tricolored mink cape." Diller was upstaged, though, by Lynda Bird Johnson, in an orange dress with mink trim. The fans in the bleachers shrieked wildly as George Hamilton escorted Johnson into the auditorium, and Milton Berle quipped, "When I took out Woodrow Wilson's daughter they didn't make such a fuss." A fuss was made by an elderly lady dressed in fur and diamonds claiming to be George Hamilton's mother.

Lee Marvin and Michelle Triola were seated two rows ahead of Rod Steiger. Marvin turned around and said to Steiger before the show began, "You know why they put me ahead of you? Because when they call your name I am going to stick my big foot out and you are going to fall on your ass!" Steiger was Marvin's only target—none of the other Best Actor nominees showed up.

The television program began with the announcement that *The Avengers* would not be seen that evening. Then film clips from previous Awards shows were unspooled as announcer Hank Sims said, "This is Mr. Oscar's album." Pictures of the nominees flashed by, as an offscreen chorus sang, "Which new face, which new name, will rush down the aisle, to claim that golden statuette."

Awards Ceremony

April 18, 1966, 7:00 p.m.
The Santa Monica Civic Auditorium,
Santa Monica

Your Host:
Bob Hope
Televised over ABC

Presenters

Sound Recording . . . Patty Duke and George Hamilton
Special Visual Effects . . . . Dorothy Malone
Supporting Actor . . . . Lila Kedrova
Sound Effects . . . . Yvette Mimieux
Costume Design . . . . . James Garner and Lana Turner
Documentary Awards . . . . Milton Berle and Phyllis Diller
Short Subjects . . . . Don Knotts and Elke Sommer
Supporting Actress . . . . Peter Ustinov
Film Editing . . . . Jason Robards
Art Direction . . . Warren Beatty and Debbie Reynolds
Jean Hersholt Humanitarian Award . . . . Angie Dickinson
Cinematography . . . . Richard Johnson and Kim Novak
Scoring Awards . . . . James Coburn and Virna Lisi
Foreign Film . . . . Gregory Peck
Song . . . . Natalie Wood
Thalberg Award . . . . Arthur Freed
Director . . . . Shirley MacLaine
Writing Awards . . . . George Peppard and Joanne Woodward
Actor . . . . Julie Andrews
Actress . . . . Rex Harrison
Picture . . . . Jack Lemmon
Gold Medal to Bob Hope . . . . Arthur Freed

Performers of Nominated Songs

"The Ballad of Cat Ballou" . . . . The Smothers Brothers
"I Will Wait for You" . . . . Michel Legrand and Jane Morgan
"The Shadow of Your Smile" . . . . . . Barbara McNair
"The Sweetheart Tree" . . . . Robert Goulet
"What's New, Pussycat?" . . . . Liza Minnelli

"I hate getting dressed up. Granny Clampett's clothes are much more comfortable."
—Irene Ryan

The orchestra struck up the overture, "Richard Rodgers in Hollywood." The camera panned the audience and found Celeste Holm singing along to "It's a Grand Night for Singing," as well as Louella Parsons, now in a wheelchair but secure in the knowledge that she had outlasted Hedda Hopper, who had died two months earlier.

The audience ooohed and aaahed over this year's set—forty-two splashing water fountains. Unfortunately, the fountains made too much noise and had to be turned off anytime anyone spoke onstage. The first person to do so was Academy President Arthur Freed, who said, "Today, the motion picture is an international medium." Then he brought out Bob Hope.

"How 'bout this set?" Hope asked. "Looks like Lloyd Bridges' rumpus room. Sitting out there are the stars of today and the senators of tomorrow." The comedian contrasted himself with the Best Actor nominees: "I can't drink like Marvin, grunt like Steiger, enunciate like Olivier, and when it comes to Burton, I'm really in trouble." Hope welcomed Lynda Bird and said of her escort, "If he plays his cards right, he may be the second Hamilton in the White House," cheerfully forgetting that Alexander Hamilton was never President.

George Hamilton was the first presenter and he gave the Sound Award with Patty Duke. They made a few jokes about who they had been dating recently and then handed the Award to the team that recorded *The Sound of Music*. A few minutes later, twenty-year-old Liza Minnelli stepped out to sing the Best Song nominee "What's New, Pussycat?" Minnelli was followed by filmed interviews with former Oscar winners. Among the interviewees was this year's nominee Simone Signoret, who, asked what advice she would give to nominees, responded, "I don't give advice to anyone."

Lila Kedrova appeared to name the Best Supporting Actor. Michael Dunn and Martin Balsam were the only nominees present. "I am delighted to announce that the winner is Martin Balsam for *A Thousand Clowns*," Kedrova said. The cameras cut to the winner, who was being vigorously hugged and kissed by Shelley Winters.

James Garner and a bouffanted Lana Turner strolled out to give the Costume Design Award. When they announced that the Black-and-White winner was *Darling*, two more bouffanted blondes—Elke Sommer and Connie Stevens—rushed out to accept for the absent winner. Elke got there first and began reading a prepared speech. She heard giggling and asked, "What's going on behind me?" Seeing that Connie was there for the same reason, Elke said, "Both of us," and the two read the speech in unison. Winner Julie Harris had written, "Not only is the Oscar the highest honor in the motion-picture world, it is one of the highest in the world of fashion since much of the most exciting thinking in design is done by film people." As the two blondes walked off with the statuette, there was a shot of Julie Christie smiling and clapping. Her other release, *Doctor Zhivago*, won the Color Costume Design Oscar. Kathryn Grayson accepted the Award, and the cameras once again showed a smiling Julie Christie.

Christie was laughing out loud when Bob Hope segued into Cyd Charisse's dance number with this introduction: "Today's ballroom dances like the swim, the frug, the chicken and the monkey are really nervous disorders set to music." Charisse was different, according to Hope, who called her "a liquid poem."

Announcing that Peter Ustinov would be presenting the Best Supporting Actress Award, Hope reminded everyone that "his monogram is P.U." As Ustinov rattled off the nominees' names, *The Sound of Music*'s Peggy Wood and a bespectacled Shelley Winters were glimpsed sitting in the audience. The winner was Shelley Winters for *A Patch of Blue*, and the moment her name was announced, her calm facade crumbled. She took off her glasses, jogged to the stage, and sobbed throughout her acceptance speech:

> *Thank you very much, members of the Academy, for giving this to me the second time in*

"I am going to stick my big foot out and you are going to fall on your ass!"
—Lee Marvin to Rod Steiger

> *my life. I wish to thank very much my director, Mr. Guy Green, who truly understood the role I played better than I did and I would like to especially thank Mr. Pandro Berman for not only making such a sensitive, beautiful picture about a subject of integration, such as* A Patch of Blue *is, but for making the picture a box-office success which is very important for subjects like these.*

Winters was equally flustered when she stepped backstage to the pressroom and discovered that she had lost her diamond necklace. "Hey, I rented—I mean, I borrowed—it. Somebody please go find it." Orson Welles and Rita Hayworth's daughter Rebecca located the necklace and returned it to the two-time Oscar winner.

Meanwhile, Julie Andrews almost lost her white mink when Jason Robards announced that William Reynolds had won the Film Editing Oscar for *The Sound of Music*. "Oh, boy!" Julie exclaimed, applauding so quickly that the mink fell out of her lap and onto the floor. "There's a secret for winning the Oscar," Reynolds explained. "When in doubt, cut to Julie Andrews."

After Debbie Reynolds and Warren Beatty revealed that the winner of the Color Art Direction Award was *Doctor Zhivago*, there was another shot of Julie Christie smiling. She was one of the few people clapping for the British winners. There was louder applause when a bouffanted Angie Dickinson, wearing a long coat with fur collar and cuffs, gave the Jean Hersholt Humanitarian Award to Warner Brothers executive Edmond L. DePatie. The winner's speech was suspiciously similar to the one that Jack Warner used last year to accept the Best Picture Oscar for *My Fair Lady*—"Thanks from everyone from the back lot to the front office."

The Smothers Brothers had fun with the nominated song "The Ballad of Cat Ballou." Tom interrupted the singing a number of times to observe that "Cat Ballou practiced bad dental hygiene," and that "I'd like to take this opportunity for my brother and myself to accept this wonderful award." When the Smothers finished, Maurice Jarre won the Original Score Award for *Doctor Zhivago* and, after the orchestra quit playing "Lara's Theme," the French-born composer said, "It's the second time I get this big thing." The Adaptation Score Oscar went to *The Sound of Music* and composer Irwin Kostal paid tribute to "the great sound of Julie Andrews' voice."

Bob Hope introduced the nominated song "The Shadow of Your Smile" by commenting that it was from *The Sandpiper,* which he called, "Liz and Dick's Beach Blanket Party." When "The Shadow of Your Smile" won the Best Song Oscar, composer Johnny Mandel said, "This probably is the proudest moment I can remember." Then Arthur Freed returned to give the Thalberg Award to Best Director nominee William Wyler, who had produced *The Collector*. "I was an office boy and he was the assistant manager of a studio," Freed recalled of their early Hollywood days. There was no reaction shot of Samantha Eggar as her director-tormentor snatched up his prize.

Shirley MacLaine came out to give the Best Director Award to Robert Wise for *The Sound of Music*. Wise was shooting *The Sand Pebbles* in Taiwan, so the kimono-clad Julie Andrews made her way to the stage. "I love your dress," MacLaine whispered to Andrews as she handed her the statuette. "I know he's heart-broken not to be here," Andrews said of Wise, "but he's filming in Hong Kong."

Best Director loser David Lean was the next proxy, accepting the Adapted Screenplay Oscar for *Doctor Zhivago*'s Robert Bolt. Frederic Raphael wasn't there to pick up his Award for Best Original Screenplay either, so Connie Stevens—all by herself, this time—did the honors and shared a thought with the audience: "Original screenplay writers are still, I think, the foundation of the motion-picture industry."

Julie Andrews was back at the podium to announce the Best Actor winner. He was Lee Marvin for *Cat Ballou*. One eyewitness claimed that Rod

"It's the second time I get this big thing."
—Maurice Jarre

Steiger momentarily choked. Marvin bounded to the stage and said, "There are too many people for me to thank for my career." He concluded by alluding to his equine costar, "I think one-half of this belongs to some horse somewhere in the Valley." Walking offstage with Andrews, Marvin whispered to her, "It's kind of wonderful when it happens to you."

Rex Harrison appeared to settle the Best Actress contest. The cameras showed Julie Christie, Samantha Eggar and Elizabeth Hartman in the audience, and Julie Andrews waiting backstage. The winner was Julie Christie for *Darling*. The excited champion ran to the stage and plowed into Harrison, embracing him. Rex seemed the slightest bit nonplussed. Christie shed as many tears as Shelley Winters had as she choked, "I don't think I can say anything except thank everyone concerned, especially my darling John Schlesinger, for this great honor." As Harrison and Christie exited, the camera cut to Rod Steiger clapping for the winner.

Jack Lemmon began the presentation of the Best Picture Award, but was interrupted by Arthur Freed, who announced that Bob Hope was getting his fifth special Award from the Academy. This one was a gold medal for "distinguished service to our industry and the Academy." Freed told Hope, "You occupy a special place in the hearts of free men everywhere." Bob admitted, "I'm caught with my idiot cards down. Anybody who wants to look at this can come by my place—it'll be in the shrine." After Hope was taken care of, Lemmon finished the Best Picture announcement—*The Sound of Music*. The musical had tied with *Doctor Zhivago* with five Oscars each. Julie Andrews' date, associate producer Saul Chaplin, accepted for Robert Wise.

"The final decision is made by you at the box office," Bob Hope said to close the show. "Movies, the instant dream. And so, until next time, this meeting of the Great Society is adjourned." Most members of the audience were already walking up the aisles as the emcee made his concluding remarks.

Aftermath

Backstage, Julie Christie inspected her Oscar and asked Rex Harrison, "Why isn't my name on it?"

"They didn't know you were going to win, dear," Rex told her. "They'll take it from you and put your name on it and then you may put it on your mantel."

"But I haven't got a mantel!" Christie cried, dissolving into tears once again.

Meanwhile, Julie Andrews was busy being a good sport, rejoicing, "We did it! Best Picture! Isn't that great?" When reporters asked her about losing Best Actress, Andrews confessed, "You know, it's almost a relief not to win again. It's a little difficult to live up to that kind of image." A journalist cheered her up: "Now you don't have to worry about the Luise Rainer jinx."

Rod Steiger was also looking on the bright side. "Winning the nomination is an enormous help in getting directors to listen to me when I feel a scene isn't going right," he said. As for losing this year, he wrote it off to bad timing for an independent feature like *The Pawnbroker*. "When *The Sound of Music* gets an Academy Award, you know it's Hollywood's year."

As the winners posed with their statuettes, Martin Balsam told Shelley Winters, "I won because I didn't get it for *Breakfast at Tiffany's* in 1961." Lee Marvin told reporters that he had to beg director Robert Aldrich to let him leave the English location of his new film, *The Dirty Dozen*, to attend the ceremonies. When Marvin caught up with Michelle Triola, she sighed, "Well, that's over."

Edith Head, the show's fashion consultant, was livid that so many of the female presenters had worn white dresses in order to look tanned on color television. "I looked at all those white dresses and I thought we were doing a reprise of 'White Christmas,'" she complained. When asked about Julie Christie's gold pajamas, the seven-time Oscar-winning designer answered, "How did I know she was going to get dressed up as an Oscar until she got up onstage? Some people are just so independent that you expect them to dress differently. If she had come out in some proper little black dress and a string of pearls, we would all have been disappointed."

The press was definitely not disappointed, and a corps of photographers began stalking Christie and Don Bessant the moment they left the Santa Monica Civic Auditorium and headed for the Governors' Ball. "I can't say I'm sorry that Julie Andrews lost," the winner said. "She won it last year, after all." Tiring of the constant press attention, Christie and Bessant hopped in a limousine and headed for Palm Springs two days later to be the guests of Mr. Blackwell, compiler of the list of the world's worst-dressed women. Christie wasn't completely fed up with Hollywood's adulation, however—following behind her limo was a car holding all the flowers she had received from industry well-wishers, including a paper rose from Julie Andrews.

1966

"I've never heard those words on a screen before, but I've heard them at Coney Island."
—Head of the Catholic Office for Motion Pictures

The 1966 Academy Awards ceremony was a showdown between sisters, saints and sinners.

As it had with Harry Cohn and *From Here to Eternity,* Hollywood shook its collective head in disbelief when Jack Warner paid $500,000 for the film rights to *Who's Afraid of Virginia Woolf?* It was one thing for him to make a movie of *My Fair Lady,* quite another to film Edward Albee's controversial drama about one night in the lives of a bitter and abusive middle-aged couple. Its plethora of profanity, after all, had shocked even New York theater audiences.

Realizing that this was the part that would win her a third Oscar, Bette Davis tried to convince her old boss to follow Edward Albee's suggestion that she and Henry Fonda be cast as Martha and George. But writer-producer Ernest Lehman—whose most recent film was *The Sound of Music*—hit upon a brainstorm. To play the most celebrated fictional couple of the 1960s, he reasoned, why not get the decade's most celebrated real-life couple?

Hump the Hostess

At thirty-two, Elizabeth Taylor was a good fifteen years younger than her character, and her physical appearance was hardly appropriate for a disillusioned hag. Richard Burton admitted, "I know she has the stridency, but she's too young." And Burton was far from anyone's picture of the burnt-out professor he would be enacting. But, as *Newsweek* explained, the vehicle's "endless verbal karate provides a glittering metaphor for the life that a gossip-gulping public likes to think such people as Elizabeth Taylor and Richard Burton live off-screen." The film would mark the directorial debut of Mike Nichols, the former stand-up comedian who had become successful as a director of Neil Simon comedies on Broadway.

Throughout production, newspaper and magazine coverage kept *Virginia Woolf* in the public eye. Then the Motion Picture Association of America told Warner that he couldn't have actors talking like that and still expect a Production Code seal. When the film was screened for Warner Brothers executives, *Life* reported their reaction as: "My God, we've got a $7.5 million dirty movie on our hands." Nevertheless, Warner, Lehman and Nichols persevered and, on appeal, the Code Review Board bought the argument that the profanity was artistic. *Who's Afraid of Virginia Woolf?*—with its eleven "goddam's," seven "bastards's," five "son of a bitch's," and "screw you," "hump the hostess," "up yours" and "monkey nipples"—could proudly display the seal of approval. Similarly, the Catholic Office for Motion Pictures (né the Legion of Decency) did not condemn the film; its head admitted, "I've never heard those words on a screen before, but I've heard them at Coney Island."

When *Virginia Woolf* opened in June, the critics agreed that the risks had paid off. The *Hollywood Reporter* raved: "The screen has never held a more shattering and ravaging and indelible drama," and *Newsweek* found that "Burton's performance is a marvel of disciplined compassion." As for Liz, who had put on two dozen pounds for the role, *Variety* remarked that she "earned every penny of her reported $1,000,000 salary . . . Her characterization is at once sensual, cynical, pitiable, loathsome and tender." The combination of publicity, controversy and critical enthusiasm couldn't fail. *Virginia Woolf* was on its way to becoming 1966's number-one box-office hit.

What's It All About?

At the end of July, the *New York Daily News* announced, "People are going to stop talking about *Virginia Woolf* and start talking about *Alfie.*" A British film about a fellow who has sex every chance he gets had a parallel to the Burtons'

Overleaf: *No sibling rivalry here—Best Actress nominees Lynn* (left) *and Vanessa Redgrave* (right) *dash hopes for a de Havilland/Fontaine update.*

"I don't want to be the new anybody."
—Alan Arkin

film—it, too, was initially denied a Production Code seal. *Alfie*'s offense was not dirty words, but its inclusion of an abortion scene. Paramount couldn't believe it. After all, they argued, the abortion was used to expose the sordid results of promiscuity and, therefore, this was a very upstanding film. Star Michael Caine agreed, saying that the movie's point was that "the bloke realizes the damage he has done, becomes aware of the fact that his 'birds' leave him." The seal was granted.

Audiences lined up to be titillated by what *Newsday* called Alfie's "bawdy odyssey." And they also flocked to see Michael Caine, the actor who had made wearing glasses not only respectable but downright sexy in last year's espionage hit *The Ipcress File*. The *New York Daily News* positively drooled over him. An article entitled "Cockney Charmboy" began, "Well, girls, first it was the Beatles and then it was miniskirts, and now see what the British have sent us in the flicks—a cockney lad who's sure to be just our cup of tea."

The Most Beautiful Jailbird in the World

The British also sent over that summer an actress whom *Life* declared "a late-blooming sensation at the age of twenty-nine." In *Morgan*, an "anti-Establishment" black comedy, Vanessa Redgrave played the wife of an artist who thinks he's King Kong. *The New Yorker* called Michael Redgrave's daughter "a charming creature" and when the film became an unexpected hit, Hollywood took notice. Jack Warner signed her to play Guinevere in the film version of *Camelot*—another role Julie Andrews originated onstage—and at a press conference presenting Redgrave to Hollywood reporters, director Joshua Logan introduced her as "the most beautiful girl in the world." Redgrave herself was as interested in politics as in acting, having been arrested several times in London peace demonstrations. She told Sheilah Graham, "I'm about as far left-wing as it's possible to go."

French Kiss

French filmmaker Claude Lelouch spent $125,000 to make a love story with his friends and they called it simply *A Man and a Woman*. Allied Artists, né Monogram, picked up the subtitled romance for American release, despite *Variety*'s observation that "it has practically no story." It didn't need one. The film's heroine, thirty-four-year-old Anouk Aimée, entertained American audiences simply by rolling around in bed and putting on her makeup. George Cukor said he'd like to work with her. Americans were also humming Francis Lai's pop musical score; the sound track became an American bestseller. Pauline Kael called it "the most efficacious make-out movie of the swinging '60s."

I've Got to Be Me

Not every new face was from overseas. "A star is born," announced the *New York Daily News* of hometown son, Alan Arkin, a graduate of Chicago's Second City comedy troupe, making his first film appearance as the commander of the Russian sub in the Cold War comedy *The Russians Are Coming, the Russians Are Coming*. The *News* continued that "his changing facial expressions . . . are so fascinating I could hardly see what anybody else was doing when he was on the screen." *Life* noted that Arkin had been heralded as "the new Peter Sellers, the new Buster Keaton, the new Marx Brothers." The thirty-two-year-old actor said, "I don't want to be the new anybody."

Lemmon-Aid

Walter Matthau was no new face. Originally a stage actor, he had been in movies for a decade, usually playing villains. He went back to Broadway in the early 1960s, and won two Tony Awards for comedy—one for playing Oscar Madison, the slob half of *The Odd Couple*.

"I should think I'm the least educated in all my family."
—Lynn Redgrave

When he come back to Hollywood, Billy Wilder cast Matthau as an ambulance-chasing lawyer named "Whiplash Willie" Gingrich in *The Fortune Cookie*. The *San Diego Union* found that "seldom has an evil character been so funny" while *Life* deemed Matthau to be "the W.C. Fields of the '60s." *The Fortune Cookie* also marked the beginning of a long association between Matthau and Jack Lemmon. Matthau asked Lemmon why he took the costarring role when all he'd be doing was feeding him straight lines, and Lemmon said, "It was about time somebody fed you some decent lines."

Little Sister

In the fall, another performer in a comedy challenged Vanessa Redgrave as the most popular new film actress from England—her younger sister, twenty-three-year-old Lynn, playing an ugly duckling in *Georgy Girl*. The younger Redgrave, à la Liz Taylor, gained eighteen pounds to play Georgy, and the *New York Times* found her "funny as Judy Holliday in *Born Yesterday*, touching as Julie Harris in *Member of the Wedding*, haunting as Giulietta Masina in *La Strada*." *The New Yorker* allowed that "it is a measure of her success in the role that James Mason, in a stunning portrayal, fails to steal the picture from her."

Columnists couldn't wait to start comparing and contrasting the sisters, and their father, Sir Michael, gave the scoop: "It's awful hard not to love Vanessa," he said. "It's equally hard in a different way not to love Lynn. In the past, you know, Lynn has been overshadowed by her sister's dramatic talent so she nearly didn't become an actress." Lynn pretty much concurred, saying of her parents, her sister and her brother Corin, "They were all so brilliant and so beautiful. So naturally I was shy. I should think I'm the least educated in all my family." Vanessa, meanwhile, was rhapsodizing over her siblings: "We are the sprigs of a great and beautiful tree."

The Code Blows Up

Vanessa was back in the spotlight in December. After *Virginia Woolf* and *Alfie* had belatedly been given Production Code approval despite content that was prohibited by the Code, it was apparent that it was time for an overhaul. Under the guidance of its new head, Jack Valenti, a former special adviser to President Johnson, the MPAA came up with its 1966 model Code. The new Code did not ban sex and nudity outright; it merely asked for restraint when these subjects were broached.

The MPAA figured it could rest, but then came along Michelangelo Antonioni's *Blow-Up*. For the life of him, Valenti couldn't understand how a scene of sexual intercourse or glimpses of two teenage girls rolling around in the nude could possibly evidence "restraint." Even more annoying was that this movie was financed by an American company, good old MGM. No seal. MGM released the film anyway, although it copped out by taking its company name off the advertising.

People who had grown tired of talking about *Virginia Woolf* and *Alfie* had a new topic of conversation. *Look* praised *Blow-Up* because "it generates pure excitement with the use of film," but asked "But *what* does it mean? . . . Your guess is as good as mine." This continued to be the question at cocktail parties throughout the Christmas season and well into 1967 as *Blow-Up* became *the* movie to see. And the nude scenes didn't hurt business, either. Of star Vanessa Redgrave—who went topless—the *London Citizen* wondered, "What next for the greatest Redgrave of them all—yes, even including Sir Michael?"

More, More, More

"What next?" was also the question for many who thought that the movies were beginning to lose all sense of decency. It seemed as if to make money a movie had to either center on sex or else

"I'm about as left-wing as it's possible to go."
—Vanessa Redgrave

be a James Bond spoof. With no new 007 film released this year, millions of fans found consolation in the hugely successful *Our Man Flint* with James Coburn and *The Silencers,* the first of Dean Martin's Matt Helm movies.

But then, at the end of the year, Judith Crist could write, "At last we have the film for all seasons." The film was *A Man for All Seasons,* based on the Robert Bolt play about Sir Thomas More, the English chancellor who lost his head for refusing to sanction Henry VIII's first divorce. *Life* felt that it "could hardly have happened at a better time." Lest someone think that his movie was a trifle old-fashioned, director Fred Zinnemann said, "To me, the story of Thomas More is contemporary. What interests me are the feelings that man today and man 450 years ago had in common." *A Man for All Seasons* was at least contemporary enough to have Vanessa Redgrave in it—the actress had a cameo as Anne Boleyn.

Carpetbagging

A Man for All Seasons all but swept the New York Film Critics Awards and suddenly Paul Scofield, who played Thomas More, was challenging Richard Burton for the attention of Academy voters. *Virginia Woolf* had to make do with a tie Award for Best Actress, Elizabeth Taylor sharing with *Georgy Girl*'s Lynn Redgrave. Bosley Crowther, a *Virginia Woolf* partisan, was incensed enough to excoriate his fellow critics in print, claiming that they "have simply flipped their lids," and "voted like wild evangelists."

Virginia Woolf did even worse at the Golden Globes—it didn't win a single award. After a publicist asked Lynn Redgrave if she'd like to place trade-paper ads thanking the Hollywood Foreign Press for her Best Actress–Comedy award, she replied. "Think of that! They want me to spend $275 to thank them for giving me a couple of globes that probably cost a few guineas." Her co-star, James Mason, allowed the producers of *Georgy Girl* to promote him for Best Supporting Actor even though he had put his foot down when the same idea was suggested for his small role in 1964's *The Pumpkin Eater*. Back then he had fumed to Louella Parsons, "It's just plain dishonest for a star to be billed in the Supporting Actor category merely to be in the Oscar race! It's nothing short of carpetbagging and I'll have no part of it."

Since she didn't win any Golden Globes, Stella Stevens ran two suggestive centerfold photos in the trade papers to promote her performance as a sexpot in *The Silencers.* Milton Berle campaigned with more traditional ads for Best Supporting Actor; the most prominent quotation was "Milton Berle took on the demanding role of the agent in *The Oscar* like a Burton or Olivier."

The Nominations

Neither Uncle Miltie nor Stella Stevens was nominated, although Stevens didn't regret her campaign at all. "I did it for the work," she explained, "and I got a picture offer, too." The *Hollywood Reporter* analyzed the nominations and announced: "One thing can be said for Hollywood in its voting for nominations: it is not provincial. As many foreign artists got top nominations as Americans." Michelangelo Antonioni and Claude Lelouch were both up for Director and Writing Awards, and the Best Actress race included Anouk Aimée and sixty-five-year-old Ida Kaminska, for last year's Foreign Film winner from Poland, *The Shop on Main Street.* But what captured the public's fancy were two family affairs: the team of Dick and Liz was in the running, as were both Vanessa and Lynn Redgrave.

"Before the Oscar night is done, a gap could be put in the Redgrave girls' lives that they'll never be able to bridge," warned an anonymous Hollywoodite in *New York* magazine, but the sisters seemed to be enjoying themselves. Lynn said, "I'd be thrilled if Vanessa won it and I know Vanessa would feel the same way if I got the big prize." Vanessa's view was: "All this talk about the Oscar coming between Lynn and me . . . well, only

"She missed by the wink of an eye never being able to walk again."
—Anouk Aimée's doctor

those who don't know us could think that. None of it's very adult, really." She added, "But what's the use of kidding anyway? We shall probably just sit there, giggle—and watch Elizabeth Taylor walk away with it." The sisters did provide social notes: Vanessa divorced 1963 Best Director winner Tony Richardson shortly after the nominations were announced and Lynn married actor John Clark a week before the Awards.

When asked about her Oscar chances, Lynn replied, "Sure, Liz has something going for her after that marvelous performance. But I wouldn't be surprised if I were given the Academy Award. Liz isn't unbeatable." But Lynn also had to contend with an unforeseen circumstance—Anouk Aimée was trying the invalid angle that had been so successful for Elizabeth Taylor in 1960. In Los Angeles to acquaint herself with Hollywood and to attend the Golden Globes—she won Best Actress in a Drama—Aimée was injured when her husband accidentally pinned her against a garage with his car. "She missed by the wink of an eye never being able to walk again," said her doctor, who, coincidentally, was also Liz's physician. Aimée recovered in time for the ceremony.

With thirteen nominations, *Who's Afraid of Virginia Woolf?* led the pack. Second, with eight apiece, were *A Man for all Seasons* and *The Sand Pebbles*. The latter was Robert Wise's first film since *The Sound of Music*—a three-hour-thirteen-minute movie about an American gunboat in 1920s China starring Steve McQueen, on his way to the Top Ten Box Office list. McQueen was competing for Best Actor with Richard Burton, Paul Scofield, Alan Arkin and Michael Caine.

The Awards were obviously not an obsession for Paul Scofield. When Army Archerd asked his opinion about the preponderance of British actors nominated for Oscars over the past several years, Scofield asked, "Have there been?"

Being demoted paid off for James Mason, and he was up for Best Supporting Actor with Walter Matthau. The big three Best Picture nominees each swept in a contender in this category: *Virginia Woolf*'s George Segal, *All Seasons*' Robert Shaw, and *Sand Pebbles*' Mako. The latter was an unknown Japanese-born actor making his film debut; he deemed it "a great thrill to be nominated with such fine actors."

Next to the favorite Sandy Dennis—when *Who's Afraid of Virginia Woolf* was reviewed in *The New Yorker*, Edith Oliver said, "When a performance is as triumphant as Miss Dennis', any description seems irrelevant"—the Supporting Actress nominee causing the most excitement was Jocelyn LaGarde in *Hawaii*. Not only had she never acted before, she didn't speak English and learned her role as the Island queen phonetically. United Artists gave the nominee's vital statistics: six feet tall, 418 pounds, 52-48-54.

The Oscar show's producer, Joe Pasternak, decided that since sisters were running against each other for the first time since 1941, it would be fun to have Olivia de Havilland and Joan Fontaine hand out an award. Olivia was willing to fly in from Paris to participate but Joan said that flying to and from New York in a twenty-four-hour period would be too wearying.

Pasternak's big worry, though, was whether there would be any show at all. Thirteen days before the ceremony, the American Federation of Television and Radio Artists (AFTRA) went on strike against ABC. The Academy panicked—no strike settlement meant no TV show, which meant no $700,000 from ABC. Initially, the Academy talked about canceling the Awards but, bowing to industry pressure, decided to proceed as normal and ABC agreed to reimburse the Academy for any out-of-pocket expenses incurred in putting on the show. On the morning of the Awards it didn't look good and actresses went to their hairdressers doubting that their coiffures would get coast-to-coast coverage.

The Big Night

The strike was settled three hours before showtime; ABC's cameras were present—most stars were not. The Burtons were in France instead of Santa Monica so photographers concentrated on the Redgraves, all five of them—Lynn, Vanessa, Corin, Sir Michael and Lady Redgrave. Elke Sommer told reporters that her hair had been shaped by Gus LePre into the form of a reel of film. Ronald Reagan was making his first Academy appearance since being elected governor of California the previous November. Avoiding any appearance of a conflict of interest, Reagan resigned from the Academy the day he was sworn in.

The first thing home viewers saw were the entrances of Andy Devine, Ida Kaminska, Joan Blondell, the Redgraves, the Reagans, and Ginger Rogers to the accompaniment of "Another Opening, Another Show." Academy President Arthur Freed introduced "America's comic consciousness" and Bob Hope walked out. "What tension, what drama," he began, "and that was just waiting to see if the show would go on. Oscar, or as he's known around my house, the Fugitive. Pretty soon we're gonna have another category, Best Peformance by a Governor." There was a shot of Reagan laughing. "How 'bout Liz and Richard? They're a most unusual couple—they're both expecting." He ended with, "Let's get on with this farcical charade of vulgar egotism and pomposity."

The Sound Award was given by Raquel Welch, making her initial appearance on the Oscars. Welch had risen to overnight international sex stardom by appearing in a fur bikini in *One Million Years B.C.* and her copresenter Dean Jones told her, "You open the envelope, my eyes are busy." After they gave the Award, the camera witnessed Anouk Aimée checking her makeup in her compact.

Shelley Winters walked out to the strains of "Winter Wonderland" to name the Best Supporting Actor. She had chartered an airplane from Durango, New Mexico, where she was filming *The*

Awards Ceremony

April 10, 1967, 7:00 p.m.
the Santa Monica Civic Auditorium,
Santa Monica

Your Host:
Bob Hope
Televised over ABC

Presenters

Sound . . . . Dean Jones and Raquel Welch
Supporting Actor . . . . Shelley Winters
Cinematography . . . . . . Ann-Margret and Omar Sharif
Jean Hersholt Humanitarian Award . . . . Irene Dunne
Short Subjects . . . . Olivia de Havilland
Sound Effects . . . . Diahann Carroll
Documentary Awards . . . . Richard Harris and Barbara Rush
Special Visual Effects . . . . Fred MacMurray
Costume Design . . . . Candice Bergen and Robert Mitchum
Supporting Actress . . . . Sidney Poitier
Honorary Award to Y. Frank Freeman . . . Jack Valenti
Film Editing . . . . Lee Remick and James Stewart
Honorary Award to Yakima Canutt . . . . Charlton Heston
Foreign Film . . . . Patricia Neal
Art Direction . . . Rock Hudson and Vanessa Redgrave
Writing Awards . . . . . Fred Astaire and Ginger Rogers
Thalberg Award . . . . Arthur Freed
Scoring Awards . . . . Mary Tyler Moore and Dick Van Dyke
Song . . . . Dean Martin
Director . . . . Rosalind Russell
Actor . . . . Julie Christie
Actress . . . . Lee Marvin
Picture . . . . Audrey Hepburn

Performers of Nominated Songs

"Alfie" . . . . Dionne Warwick
"Born Free" . . . . Roger Williams and the Young Americans
"Georgy Girl" . . . . Mitzi Gaynor and the Ernie Flatt Dancers
"My Wishing Doll . . . . Jackie DeShannon
"A Time for Love" . . . . John Davidson

"Raquel, you open the envelope, my eyes are busy."
—Dean Jones

Scalphunters, after telling producer Jules Levy, "I'll be absolutely impossible to work with if you don't let me get to Santa Monica!" "Last year I was beside myself because I was a nominee," she informed the audience. "This year I still am because I'm not nominated." The only nominees present were Mako and Walter Matthau. The winner was Matthau for *The Fortune Cookie*. He removed his glasses, kissed his wife and climbed to the stage with his arm in a cast and his face bruised. "You had a hard time getting here," said Shelley. Matthau began his speech, "The other day, as I was falling off my bicycle . . ."

Handing out the Cinematography Awards, Omar Sharif suggested, "All right, Ann-Margret, let's begin." The Black-and-White winner was *Virginia Woolf*'s Haskell Wexler, who said in his speech: "I hope we can use our art for peace and love." Veteran cinematographer Hal Mohr accepted for *All Seasons'* Ted Moore and said, "I'm terribly sorry to be the wrong Mohr."

The Academy experimented this year with distributing clips from the Best Picture nominees throughout the show rather than lumping them together at the end. Bob Hope explained that this procedure was adopted "so you'll know how they'll look on TV."

The intensity of the applause greeting Short Subject presenter Olivia de Havilland showed that the audience appreciated her effort in coming from Paris. Olivia addressed the Redgrave sisters: "May I recommend what my sister Joan reminded me? There are three other nominees, too." Lynn and Vanessa looked at each other and giggled.

Bob Hope introduced the clip from *A Man for All Seasons* by saying, "It's no *Boy, Did I Get a Wrong Number* but it managed to sneak in." Mitzi Gaynor and the Ernie Flatt Dancers gyrated through a well-received version of the nominated song "Georgy Girl" and Robert Mitchum and Candice Bergen gave the Costume Awards to the winners of the Cinematography Awards—*Virginia Woolf* and *A Man for All Seasons*.

Sidney Poitier announced Best Supporting Actress. Only *All Seasons'* Wendy Hiller and *Hawaii*'s Jocelyn LaGarde were present. The winner was Sandy Dennis and her director, nominee Mike Nichols, accepted. "Sandy thanks you very much," he said. "I thank Sandy very much. It was nice to be up here."

Patricia Neal, two years after her stroke, walked out to present the Best Foreign Film Award and received a standing ovation. She told the crowd, "I'm sorry I've been away so long." Not unexpectedly, the winner was *A Man and a Woman*. Director Claude Lelouch apologized, "I'm sorry, I don't speak English," and then lapsed into French.

Rock Hudson and Vanessa Redgrave announced the Art Direction Awards. Even then, Vanessa had little patience with traditional Hollywood glamour. She put on her specs and matter-of-factly stated, "We are here to present the Black-and-White and then the Color Art Direction Awards." Knowing that the Directors Guild Award had gone to *All Seasons'* Fred Zinnemann, Black-and-White winner Richard Sylbert made sure that *Virginia Woolf*'s Mike Nichols would get some recognition that night. He thanked "a young director who directed his first picture."

A brief montage of Oscar-winning songs provided a musical introduction to the presenters of the Writing Awards—Fred Astaire and Ginger Rogers. As they descended the stairs, Fred impishly grabbed Ginger around the waist and executed a breathless impromptu spin. The audience cheered. Rogers and Astaire were so flushed with joy from the applause, they temporarily forgot themselves and held hands while reading the nominations. *Virginia Woolf* lost the Adapted Screenplay Oscar to *A Man for All Seasons*, and winner Robert Bolt said, "You really are incredibly generous to aliens." To make up for *A Man for All Seasons'* not having been nominated for Art Direction, Bolt thanked "John Box for working on a small budget." The Academy continued being generous to aliens when Claude Lelouch won his second statuette, for Original Screenplay for *A Man and a Woman*, and made another speech in French. Candice Bergen, thinking she was sup-

"If he'd won, he'd have been impossible to live with."
—Mrs. Steve McQueen

posed to accept for Lelouch, darted down the aisle, stopped short when she saw the Frenchman descending the other aisle, crouched down and tried to sneak back to her seat, as sixty million people watched.

Dean Martin, doing a drunken act, nearly tumbled down the stairs when he came on to give Best Song. "I waited so long I sobered up twice," he said, taking a drag from his cigarette. Dino laughed as he made a mess of the nominees' names. "Georgy Girl" became "Gregory Girl." "Four guys wrote this last one," he said of "A Time for Love," penned by Johnny Mandel and Paul Francis Webster. He then turned to the man from Price, Waterhouse and asked, "Now, you got a letter for me or something?" The winner was "Born Free," and lyricist Don Black thanked record producer Don Kirschner, soon to be the man behind the Archies and "Sugar, Sugar."

Rosalind Russell waltzed out to "Sophisticated Lady" and gave the Director Award to Fred Zinnemann for *A Man for All Seasons*. Zinnemann kissed the presenter's hand and said "I must thank the Columbia executives, especially Mike Frankovich, for their courage and enthusiasm with this project." The final Best Picture clip was *Virginia Woolf*, but by now everybody knew it didn't stand a chance.

Julie Christie came flying out in a polka-dot miniskirt to reveal the Best Actor winner. She read the nominations—Arkin, Caine and McQueen were in the audience—added, "Congratulations all," and proclaimed Paul Scofield the winner for *A Man for All Seasons*. Scofield's costar, Wendy "Never-mind-the-honor-I-hope-this-means-cash" Hiller, mounted the stage with her gloves and pocketbook to pick up the Oscar. She didn't give a financial estimation this time but turned philosophical: "There is something very special in being recognized in a country other than one's own."

Lee Marvin, presenting Best Actress, went down the list of "talented young ladies" and concluded, "Now how do you make a selection out of those five girls?" The Redgrave sisters didn't have to start worrying about a feud; the winner was Elizabeth Taylor for *Who's Afraid of Virginia Woolf?* Anne Bancroft accepted for the absentee.

Audrey Hepburn, in a short haircut, made the final presentation—Best Picture. She opened the envelope, dramatically declared, "The winner is . . . *A Man For All Seasons*!" and then handed the Oscar to Fred Zinnemann, who had directed her in *The Nun's Story*.

Aftermath

Producer Joe Pasternak was furious that so many nominees chose not to attend the ceremony. "It's an obligation the nominees owe the Awards. After all, people can make it from Europe or anywhere in the U.S. in one day." He lauded Shelley Winters for chartering a plane just to be a presenter. Dorothy Manners, Louella Parsons' successor at the Hearst papers, urged that any winner not attending the Awards be given a lousy certificate instead of an Oscar.

Elizabeth Taylor, singled out as the most glaring no-show, came up with the excuse that Dick was afraid of flying and wouldn't allow her to fly alone. No one bought this and Warner Brothers refused to send their Best Actress a congratulatory telegram. But Bob Hope condoled with Liz because "leaving Richard alone in Paris is like leaving Jackie Gleason locked in a delicatessen."

If Hollywood was ticked off at Liz, she was just as angry at them. She was so furious that Burton had lost for the fifth time that she refused to thank the Academy for her own Award. Reporters hoping to get her reaction were met by a publicist who snapped, "There will be no statement and no press conference." Liz did agree to pick up her Oscar later that year when Lord Mountbatten gave it to her at the British Academy Awards, where she won Best Foreign Actress for *Virginia Woolf*.

Sandy Dennis also took a lot of heat for not being present to receive the Academy's proclamation of her as a new star. "Enough already!" she finally cried and promised that if she was ever nominated again, she'd be sure to be there. On the other hand, no one much minded that Paul Scofield hadn't made it. The actor's reaction in England: "No doubt my wife and I will find time to share a bottle of champagne with someone."

Steve McQueen's wife was happy that her husband had lost. "If he'd won, he'd have been impossible to live with," she said, "not because of a big head but because he'd be worrying how to top himself next. I prayed he wouldn't win." Lynn Redgrave echoed the sentiment, telling Sheilah Graham, "At my age, while it was an honor to be nominated, the burden of winning would have been too much. It really was an enormous relief to hear them call Elizabeth Taylor's name."

Courtesy of Pictorial Parade, Inc.

1967

"Sock it to me, baby!"
—Sammy Davis, Jr.

The times, they were a-changin'.

My Fair Lady and *The Sound of Music* had left a big impression on their studios, and both Warners and Fox attempted to duplicate their successes in 1967. Jack Warner took another Lerner and Loewe musical from Broadway, and once again cast another actress in the Julie Andrews' role. Vanessa Redgrave was Jack Warner's Guinevere in *Camelot,* a $15 million road-show musical that opened in November to dreadful reviews. "Unfortunately, there is nothing royal about *Camelot*'s curious screen version," reported *Time.* "It has been brought crunchingly down to earth by the churlish touch of director Joshua Logan." Not even the presence of such popular young British actors as Redgrave and Richard Harris could revive the dinosaur production at the box office—*Camelot* failed to earn back its cost.

Fox shelled out $16 million to turn Hugh Lofting's children's book character Doctor Dolittle into another *Mary Poppins,* but the critics weren't charmed this time around. "Children-shmildren," said Archer Winsten of the *New York Post,* "let them go by themselves if they like it so much. I'm not going to pretend I wasn't bored silly." To Fox's chagrin, the kids weren't going either, and *Doctor Dolittle* garnered only a third of its cost at the box office. The experience reminded the actor in the title role, Rex Harrison, of one of his previous movies, and it wasn't *My Fair Lady.* "Excepting only that the hero did not fall in love with his leading lady, Chi-Chi the chimp," wrote Harrison in his autobiography, "*Doctor Dolittle* had all the hallmarks of *Cleopatra.* In one respect, *Dolittle* outdid Cleopatra; it administered a near-fatal body-blow to 20th century–Fox's finances."

Overleaf: *Sammy Davis, Jr., accepting somebody else's Oscar, sports love beads over his newest Nehru jacket; Barbra Streisand is presenting her "Bob Dylan" hairdo.*

Hello, Dolly and Barbra and Carol

Fox had already lined up two more multimillion-dollar musicals for the next two years—*Star!* with Julie Andrews, and *Hello, Dolly!* The studio decided against allowing Carol Channing to re-create her Broadway role in the latter, and chose twenty-seven-year-old Barbra Streisand instead, even though Streisand's debut movie, *Funny Girl,* had not yet been released. Deprived of their Broadway roles, Carol Channing and Julie Andrews appeared in Universal's *Thoroughly Modern Millie,* a modestly budgeted musical spoof of the '20s that producer Ross Hunter concocted when he couldn't obtain the screen rights to Andrews' first Broadway success, *The Boy Friend.* Opening in March, Andrews' third movie musical was yet another hit, with Carol Channing sharing the spotlight. *Newsweek* wrote of her performance: "Carol Channing is . . . well . . . Carol Channing."

Trini Lopez—Psychopath

The film that made the most money during 1967 was Robert Aldrich's *The Dirty Dozen,* a summer hit about a World War II army officer, played by Lee Marvin, who leads a special platoon of convicts—Charles Bronson, John Cassavetes and Trini Lopez—in a mission against the Nazis. The *New York Daily News* gave the action movie its highest rating and commented, "Possibly the most unique war drama ever filmed opened last night at the Capitol Theatre to the loudest blast of applause ever heard on old Broadway." But at the *New York Times,* Bosley Crowther was horrified. "A raw and preposterous glorification of criminal soldiers," the critic wrote, "a spirit of hooliganism that is brazenly antisocial, to say the least; a studied indulgence of sadism that is morbid and disgusting beyond words."

"A cheap piece of bald-faced slapstick."
—Bosley Crowther on Bonnie and Clyde

The Moron Trade

By August another film bowed which made *The Dirty Dozen* look like *Doctor Dolittle—Bonnie and Clyde*. Producer-star Warren Beatty had reportedly got down on his knees to beg Jack Warner to finance the film about the notorious Depression-era gangsters after two other studios had turned him down.

Bosley Crowther wished Warner had turned Beatty down when he saw the result of Beatty and Penn's efforts. "It is a cheap piece of bald-faced slapstick that treats the hideous depredations of that sleazy, moronic pair as though they were as full of fun and frolic as the jazz-age cut-ups in *Thoroughly Modern Millie*." *Newsweek*'s Joseph Morgenstern wasn't much kinder, calling the film a "squalid shoot-'em-up for the moron trade." The crowds that filed in to the movie didn't like being referred to as morons and both the *Times* and *Newsweek* were inundated with angry letters from *Bonnie and Clyde*'s fans. At *Newsweek*, Morgenstern gave the public the benefit of the doubt, saw the movie again, and retracted his original review. "*Bonnie and Clyde* knows perfectly well what to make of its violence," he said the second time around.

But Crowther refused to say die. "Evidently, there are people, including some critics, who feel that the deliberately buffoonized picture achieves some sort of meaningful statement for the time in which we live." Crowther then went on to quote from newspaper crime reports from the '30s to prove that the film distorted the "truth." The criticism didn't bother Warren Beatty. On the contrary, he told Sheilah Graham, "Bosley Crowther has been very helpful to us. His misguided moralizing about the film has made the other critics determined to be heard." One of the latter, Penelope Gilliatt of *The New Yorker*, wrote, "*Bonnie and Clyde* could look like a celebration of gangster glamour only to a man with a head full of wood shavings."

By November, things had gotten to the point that Bonnie Parker's sister was suing Warren Beatty and Warner Brothers for blackening Bonnie's memory and exposing her to hatred and ridicule. *Time* adjudged the film "not only the sleeper of the decade, but also, to a growing consensus of audiences and critics, the best movie of the year." The cast of little-knowns were suddenly household names. Gene Hackman, thirty-six, playing Clyde's brother, confessed, "I worry about my double chin. I know I'm not a leading man, but I still worry." Estelle Parsons, thirty-nine, who played Clyde's sister-in-law, gushed, "This is my first movie and I like movies more than plays because I don't have to be the same someone else every night." Most popular was Michael J. Pollard, twenty-eight, who balked when interviewer Nora Ephron asked if he were a hippie. "Hippies. They make them out to be bad. I'm not bad. I love everybody. Well, I like everybody."

A Faye Dunaway Sweep

Everybody seemed to love Faye Dunaway. Sheilah Graham wrote that at *Bonnie and Clyde*'s Paris premiere, the French public went "wild about Bonnie, pronounced here Bonnee—Faye Dunaway—who has single-handedly revolutionized the maxi-length of the 1930's." Dunaway was a hit in Italy, too, where director Vittorio De Sica told her, "I like you when you laugh because I feel your laughter is not going to be for long."

Dunaway certainly had a lot to laugh about for the time being. After two flop films earlier in the year, *The Happening* and Otto Preminger's *Hurry Sundown*, the actress had a winner and emerged a celebrity, thanks in part to her foresight: she returned $25,000 of her $60,000 salary for above-the-title billing. Now a sought-after leading lady—Steve McQueen wanted her next—Dunaway also become a fashion plate, modeling the "Bonnie Look" for *Life*. The *New York Daily News* reported, "Faye Dunaway's Poor Look wardrobe is sweeping the fashion world and is sweeping the

"I worry about my double chin. I know I'm not a leading man but I still worry."
—Gene Hackman

film's costume designer Theadora Van Runkle, heretofore an obscure fashion illustrator, right into the limelight and the heady world of celebrities."

They Call Me Mr. Poitier

In addition to violent movies like *Bonnie and Clyde,* Bosley Crowther was upset over the spate of inflammatory films about racial problems in America. "In a year that has dismally brought us a couple of bad, really bad, dramatic films intended to be about Negroes—including Otto Preminger's awful glop of neo-Uncle Tomism, *Hurry Sundown*—it is exciting and encouraging to have *In the Heat of the Night."* The Negro in question in *Heat* was Sidney Poitier, who had already had one hit film that year with *To Sir, with Love,* the story of a black teacher in a London slum school. In *Heat,* Poitier played a Philadelphia detective who grudgingly aids a Southern bigot sheriff, played by Rod Steiger, in solving a murder in a small Mississippi Town. "It's a crime melodrama which also makes a statement about our time," said director Norman Jewison, and *Life* agreed, calling the film "not merely a good whodunit or a fine demonstration that races can work together but first and foremost a drama of two deeply etched characters in conflict."

Newsweek stated that Poitier "could be ruling the American roost if parts were handed out on the basis of talent instead of pigment," but the lion's share of the reviews for *Heat* went to his costar. *Life,* for example, said that Rod Steiger "could so easily have been turned into a clownish caricature of the rube lawman. It is a wonderful piece of acting—humorous, shrewd and strong without being domineering or self-admiring."

Sidney's Supper

Poitier was also upstaged in his third hit of the year, Stanley Kramer's *Guess Who's Coming to Dinner,* the story of an interracial marriage that opened at Christmastime. Archer Winsten of the *New York Post* called it "a thought-provoking film that leads to a lot of healthy self-examination," pointing out that Secretary of State Dean Rusk's daughter had married a black man that same year. "You can't say it couldn't happen here," Winsten argued. But *Harper's* thought the filmmakers had been less than honest. "The Negro, it turns out, is a world-famous expert on international hygiene problems and in terms of character, he is a near-perfect mixture of Albert Schweitzer, Louis Pasteur and Ralph Bunche, while looking like Sidney Poitier, who plays the role. Who could resist that?"

Even the critics who scoffed couldn't resist the fact the *Guess Who's Coming to Dinner* marked the ninth and final teaming of Spencer Tracy and Katharine Hepburn, portraying the parents of the bride. Tracy was so physically incapacitated from a long illness that Hepburn and Kramer put their salaries in escrow so that Columbia could remake the film with another actor if Tracy became unable to finish filming. The filmmakers did not let the studio know that they only shot half-days with Tracy in order to preserve his strength, a precaution that was proved necessary when Tracy died just ten days after filming was completed. "It is a sentimental film and sentimental occasion," wrote *Time.* "Tracy and Hepburn were appearing before the cameras together for the last time and they knew it."

Hepburn on Her Head

Like Faye Dunaway, Hepburn became a *Life* cover girl, but instead of high fashion, she wore her usual casual slacks and white socks. The headline declared THE COMEBACK OF KATE, and inside, the magazine said the fifty-eight-year-old actress was "busier and more sought-after than ever." Hepburn was already working on her next picture, *The Lion in Winter,* and was about to begin her first Broadway musical, *Coco,* based on the life of Coco Chanel. She stood on her head for *Life*'s photographer and answered its reporter's questions about her continuing popularity. "I think they're beginning to think I'm not going to be around much

"He looked about three feet tall, so dead serious, so humorless, so unkempt."
—Katharine Ross on Dustin Hoffman

longer," she said. "And what do you know: they'll miss me like an old monument—like the Flatiron Building."

Plastics

Guess Who's Coming to Dinner became the second highest-grossing film in 1968, just behind another 1967 Christmas release—Mike Nichols' *The Graduate*. Fresh from his box-office triumph with *Who's Afraid of Virginia Woolf?*, Nichols signed a deal with independent producer Joseph E. Levine that allowed him to adapt a satiric novel by Charles Webb about a college graduate who has an affair with a friend of his parents'. Nichols said one of his ambitions behind the movie was "to stop the Los Angelesization of America," and the director took innumerable swipes at California consumerism, typified by the one-word career advice—"plastics"—given the title character. The *Saturday Review* raved, "Mike Nichols has made the freshest, funniest and most touching film of the year. He has filled it with delightful surprises, cheekiness, sex, satire, irreverence toward some of the most sacred of American cows, and, in addition, gives us the distinct feeling that the American film may never be quite the same again."

Among the innovations that Nichols wrought was a pop-score sound track performed by Simon and Garfunkel—the album quickly became number one on the charts and the paean to the film's temptress, "Mrs. Robinson," was a hit single. Anne Bancroft, as the immoral Mrs. Robinson—a role that Doris Day turned down because "it offended my sense of values"—had her most popular part since *The Miracle Worker*, and twenty-five-year-old Katharine Ross, as her pretty daughter, was proclaimed by Liz Smith in *Cosmopolitan* as "surely this year's Julie Christie." Ross had not had high hopes when she first saw the film's leading man, a thirty-year-old unknown named Dustin Hoffman. "He looked about three feet tall, so dead serious, so humorless, so unkempt" that the actress thought, "this is going to be a disaster." "An amazing new youngster," marveled the *New York Times*, which said Hoffman "makes you feel a little tearful and choked up while making you laugh yourself raw." The *New York Daily News* proclaimed him a new star, although "he is rather plain-looking, resembling both Sonny and Cher. In addition, he'll never threaten Rock Hudson's image."

The Graduate put Embassy Pictures, the company Joseph E. Levine had formed with the millions he made distributing Italian-made *Hercules* movies, on the list of important Hollywood studios. "We thought we had a commercial picture, but we didn't know what we had," the Boston-born mogul effused to *The New Yorker*. "It's absolutely incredible. There's no way to describe it. It's like an explosion, a dam bursting. The business just grows and grows."

Adios, Bosley

In his Sunday piece on *The Graduate,* Bosley Crowther said the satire was on a par with the Preston Sturges comedies of the '40s. Then at the end of the review, Crowther announced that he would be retiring from his position as film critic of the *New York Times*. The editorial board had persuaded the veteran that, after thirty-odd years, it was time for him to step down, especially if he couldn't relate to *Bonnie and Clyde*. Before he left for good, though, there was still the New York Film Critics Awards, and Crowther spearheaded the selection of *In the Heat of the Night* for Best Picture and Rod Steiger for Best Actor. Crowther went along with the choice of Mike Nichols for Best Director, but he couldn't stop his fellow critics from giving the Best Screenplay Award to Robert Benton and David Newman for *Bonnie and Clyde*.

The Senile Leading the Blind

The Critics' Best Actress was eighty-year-old Dame Edith Evans for playing a senile woman in a British industrial town in *The Whisperers*, a well-received art-house hit. *Time* had said, "She has

"They'll miss me like an old monument—like the Flatiron Building."
—Katharine Hepburn

created new proof that for great artists there is still no age limit." The Critics Award gave Evans the lead for the Oscar, but in Hollywood, Sheilah Graham was pulling for her favorite—Faye Dunaway. "I'd like to see her win the Oscar, as she's one of the new breed of stars, and a good actress—intelligent and beautiful."

For Academy voters who thought Faye Dunaway was too young and Dame Edith Evans too old, there was thirty-eight-year-old Audrey Hepburn. In the spring, Hepburn had traded quips with Albert Finney and worn miniskirts in the Frederic Raphael comedy *Two for the Road*. In the fall, she switched gears and played a blind woman tormented by heroin dealers in the thriller *Wait Until Dark*. When *Wait Until Dark* proved to be more profitable than *Camelot*, Warner Brothers decided a few Oscar ads weren't a bad idea.

A Failure to Communicate

Making nearly as much money for Warners as *Wait Until Dark* was *Cool Hand Luke*, a Paul Newman vehicle from Jack Lemmon's production company. Even at forty-two, Newman had no trouble maintaining his rebellious image as a cocky convict who defied authority and took off his shirt a lot. The film's ads capitalized on the comment Strother Martin's prison guard uttered every time Newman misbehaved—"What we have here is a failure to communicate"—and the line became a rallying cry for both sides of the generation gap.

While Newman, receiving his best reviews since *Hud*, was assured of a nomination, his costar, George Kennedy, playing a fellow inmate, was nervous about his chances in the Supporting Actor race. "With Warners pushing *Camelot* and *Bonnie and Clyde*, I'm afraid that not enough people will see *Cool Hand Luke*," Kennedy said, so he spent $5,000 on trade-paper ads to goad Academy members to see his performance. His ads depicted him carrying a wounded Paul Newman and were headlined "George Kennedy—Supporting."

Bye Bye, Black-and-White

A sign of the times was that few Hollywood movies were filmed in black-and-white anymore—only one in five. The reason: TV networks had made it clear they preferred to broadcast color movies, and the studios had gotten into the habit of selling all of their movies to television. The Academy decided to get rid of the Black-and-White and Color divisions of the visual Awards—Best Cinematography, Best Art Direction, and Best Costume Design—and give just one Oscar for each of the categories. By eliminating half of the nominations in these categories, the Academy made the competition tougher than ever.

Operation *Dolittle*

A memo from a publicist at Fox circulated around the studio. "The following has been decided regarding our Academy Award campaign for *Doctor Dolittle*," the message read. "Each screening will be preceded by champagne or cocktails and a buffet dinner in the studio commissary. *Doctor Dolittle* is the studio's prime target for Academy Award consideration." Their prime rib au jus dinner parties were very well-attended and non-Fox candidates began to get a little nervous.

The Nominations

For the first time in the nineteen-year history of the Costume Design Award, Edith Head was not nominated. The designer's work this year included *Barefoot in the Park; Hotel; Easy Come, Easy Go*, an Elvis Presley movie; and *Chuka*, an Ernest Borgnine western. The films nominated for Best Costume Design were *Thoroughly Modern Millie, Camelot, The Taming of the Shrew, The Happiest Millionaire* and *Bonnie and Clyde*. Head took her omission in stride and continued as volunteer fashion consultant to the Awards show.

The Oscar race was led by *Bonnie and Clyde* and *Guess Who's Coming to Dinner* with ten nomi-

"I hope to God I don't win an Oscar. It would really depress me if I did."
—Dustin Hoffman

nations each. *The Graduate* and *In the Heat of the Night* had seven each. All were nominated for Best Picture. The real surprise was the nominations won by the 20th Century–Fox production *Doctor Dolittle*. "It's outrageous!" Truman Capote screamed. "It simply proves that the Academy Awards is all politics and sentiment and nothing to do with merit." The novelist was particularly peeved that Richard Brooks' adaptation of his *In Cold Blood* had received four nominations—including Best Director—but was not up for Best Picture. *Doctor Dolittle,* however, was. "Anything allowing a *Dolittle* to happen is so rooked up it doesn't mean anything," Capote said.

Sayonara, Sidney

The Actors Branch nominated the late Spencer Tracy for the ninth year but not Sidney Poitier, the star of two of the Best Picture nominations. Nor was the theme song to *To Sir, with Love*—the number-one bestselling record of 1967 as sung by Lulu—nominated for Best Song. "It's the biggest mystery of all time," said Elmer Bernstein, a member of the Music Branch and of the Board of Governors. "Lyricist Don Black had just won the Oscar last year for 'Born Free' and the song was beautifully used in the picture."

Poitier's other male costar, Rod Steiger, was also nominated for Best Actor, for *In the Heat of the Night*. Having won his third nomination, Steiger hired a publicist who suggested a "Rod Steiger Film Festival" on a local television station. "The object was a simple and valid one," the flack argued. "If Steiger isn't one of the best actors in America, he's certainly the most versatile." Steiger himself told Army Archerd, "I've learned one thing about this business—and that's not to stake one's life on awards."

Rod Steiger had fellow nominee Dustin Hoffman's vote; too bad the newcomer wasn't a member of the Academy. "Steiger gave a performance that had many colors and facets to it," Hoffman said. "That's what acting is all about." When asked what he thought of the posthumous nomination for Tracy, Hoffman confessed, "I tried not to cry when I watched him, but it was impossible." Dustin made it clear he didn't want anything for himself. "I hope to God I don't win an Oscar tomorrow night. It would really depress me if I did. I really don't deserve it. It wasn't that important a part anyhow."

Your Presence Is Requested

Despite his misgivings, when personally contacted by new Academy President Gregory Peck, Hoffman said he would attend the ceremonies. President Peck called on all the nominees and invited Mrs. Spencer Tracy to accept for her husband. Katharine Hepburn was the lone holdout of the surviving nominees, but she agreed to film a segment for the show on the set of *The Lion in Winter* in France. Peck also made an effort to invite younger talent on the show as presenters; in addition to Dustin Hoffman, Supporting Actress nominee Katharine Ross and Barbra Streisand would be seen on the show.

Dress Code

The Academy wasn't completely joining the newer generation; glamour was too valuable a Hollywood asset to surrender to the latest fashion trends. Once again, a dress code was sent out to ceremony participants. Women were asked to forget what a sensation Julie Christie had created last year in a miniskirt and dress in long gowns. Men were reminded that this was a white-tie affair and that turtleneck sweaters, beads, beards, and unkempt hair were frowned upon. *Variety* reported that "the rule was taken amiss in certain N.Y. circles as evidence of Hollywood's unwillingness to move with the times and its own loss of style leadership."

Reality Intrudes

Columnists called it the most exciting Oscar race in years because almost all of the acting categories had room for surprises. But conjecture was cut short with the news four days before the ceremony that Dr. Martin Luther King, Jr., had been assassinated at a Memphis motel. The funeral service was planned for April 9 and five people slated to appear on the Awards show on April 8—Louis Armstrong, Diahann Carroll, Sidney Poitier, Sammy Davis, Jr., and Rod Steiger—notified the Academy that they would not participate if the show was held on the scheduled date. "I asked President Peck to postpone the Awards to show that someone cares," Sammy Davis, Jr., said on the *Tonight* show the day after the murder. "I certainly think any black man should not appear. I find it morally incongruous to sing 'Talk to the Animals' while the man who could make a better world for my children is lying in state."

Peck called a meeting of the Board of Governors, and they voted to postpone the Awards to the day after the funeral and to cancel the annual Governors' Ball completely. There were other adjustments to be made, Peck told the press. "This will principally concern Bob Hope's opening remarks," the president announced. "The writers will rewrite the script to conform with the dignity of the occasion." Bob Hope happily went along with the changes, and noted that he had once flown on the same plane with the late Dr. King, who had complimented him. "You know, Bob, you're so wonderful on the Academy Awards show," the civil rights leader had said. "We enjoy watching it every year."

The Big Night

In spite of the somber atmosphere, mogul Joseph E. Levine was in a festive mood—Mike Nichols had won the Directors Guild Award for *The Graduate*. A Best Picture Oscar would certainly put Embassy Pictures on the map. Katharine Ross came with a fellow wearing a cowboy hat and Dustin Hoffman, in white tie and tails, escorted Senator Eugene McCarthy's daughter, Ellen.

The *Bonnie and Clyde* gang took most of the bleacher fans' attention. Double threat Warren Beatty—he was nominated as a producer as well as an actor—escorted Julie Christie, who wore a floor-length skirt. Best Actress nominee Faye Dunaway arrived with director Jerry Schatzberg, Supporting nominee Gene Hackman came with his wife, and his co-nominee Michael Pollard arrived in a ruffled Beau Brummel tuxedo without the tie. Academy President Gregory Peck had to promise to appear on the Tony Awards in order to persuade theater producer David Merrick to permit Best Supporting Actress nominee Estelle Parsons to have the night off from her Broadway play, *The Seven Descents of Myrtle*. "When I got to the Coast, I was still hopeful of winning," Parsons said, "and then I saw the whole Hollywood crowd, which I don't feel a part of. So I just went in and smiled for the TV camera."

Forecourt emcee Army Archerd asked Mrs. Gregory Peck who had designed her gown. When she replied that it was an Yves St. Laurent, Archerd said, "Yes sir, he's really great, that Yves." Other interviewees included Sonny and Cher, who wore a cossack suit and Egyptian makeup, respectively. Phyllis Diller arrived in a 1930 Excalibur phaeton with her husband driving and her chauffeur in the back seat with her. Diller's gown was designed, she said, by Omar of Omaha, and she described her silver lamé dress with chinchilla stole and ostrich feathers as "a Brillo pad, stretched." Diller received a hearty hand from the fans, but was forgotten the moment Paul Newman showed up with his teenage daughter, Susan.

Awards Ceremony

APRIL 10, 1968, 7:00 P.M.
THE SANTA MONICA CIVIC AUDITORIUM,
SANTA MONICA

Your Host:
BOB HOPE
Televised over ABC

Presenters

Sound . . . . Carol Channing
Supporting Actor . . . . Patty Duke
Cinematography . . . . Dustin Hoffman and Katharine Ross
Short Subjects . . . . MacDonald Carey and Diahann Carroll
Documentary Awards . . . . Robert Morse and Barbara Rush
Costume Design . . . . Eva Marie Saint
Honorary Award to Arthur Freed . . . . Bob Hope
Special Visual Effects . . . . Natalie Wood
Sound Effects . . . . Richard Crenna and Elke Sommer
Supporting Actress . . . . Walter Matthau
Film Editing . . . . Dame Edith Evans
Jean Hersholt Humanitarian Award . . . . Rosalind Russell
Foreign Film . . . . Danny Kaye
Art Direction . . . . Rock Hudson and Shirley Jones
Scoring Awards . . . . Angie Dickinson and Gene Kelly
Song . . . . Barbra Streisand
Thalberg Award . . . . Robert Wise
Director . . . . Leslie Caron
Writing Awards . . . . . . Claire Bloom and Rod Steiger
Actor . . . . Audrey Hepburn
Actress . . . . Sidney Poitier
Picture . . . . Julie Andrews

Performers of Nominated Songs

"The Bare Necessities" . . . . Louis Armstrong
"The Eyes of Love" . . . . Lainie Kazan
"The Look of Love" . . . . Sergio Mendes and Brazil '66
"Talk to the Animals" . . . . Sammy Davis, Jr.
"Thoroughly Modern Millie" . . . Angela Lansbury and the Ronald Field Dancers

"Anything allowing a Dolittle to happen is so rooked up it doesn't mean anything."
—Truman Capote

The television show began with the orchestra playing an overture based on the film scores of Max Steiner. Then Academy President Gregory Peck said, "Last Monday was the fortieth anniversay of the Academy Awards. This has been a fateful week in the history of our nation and the two-day delay of this ceremony is the Academy's way of paying our profound respect to the memory of Dr. Martin Luther King, Jr. Of the five films nominated for Best Picture, two dealt with the subjects between the races. We must unite in compassion if we are to survive."

With his address out of the way, Peck introduced the emcee, Bob Hope, "who pricks the balloons of pomposity." Hope's writers had altered the script, all right:

> *Welcome to the Academy Awards, or, as it's known at my house, Passover. About the delay of two days, it didn't affect me, but it's been tough on the nominees. How would you like to spend two days in a crouch? We also voted a special Oscar to the ABC programming department. They just committed harakiri. The delay also hurt Kodak, the sponsor's image. This show took three days to develop.*

Among the other topics that Hope made light of was President Lyndon Johnson's recent announcement that he would not be running for reelection and the current Paris Peace talks on the Vietnam War. "I will not seek nor will I accept an Oscar," the comedian said. "Actually, I have a deal with the Academy—they'll negotiate if I stop bombing." Then Hope went after the nominees: "The women are all beautiful but Dame Edith Evans in a micro-miniskirt is too much [there was a shot of Dame Edith laughing]. How 'bout *The Graduate*? It proves that a girl's best friend is not necessarily her mother. And they nominated a kid like Dustin Hoffman—he made a picture he can't get in to see. Warren Beatty arrived in a truck with Faye Dunaway behind in a getaway car [there was a shot of Beatty, Dunaway, and Julie Christie laughing]. I don't know what the writers have been smoking this year."

Best Supporting Actress nominee Carol Channing, of *Thoroughly Modern Millie,* presented the Sound Award and exclaimed, "What a thrill for me to fondle an envelope even in transit." She handed the Oscar to the team who worked on *In the Heat of the Night*.

Patty Duke, a non-nominee this year for her performance in *Valley of the Dolls,* commented before naming the Best Supporting Actor, "It's unusual because an English actor isn't on the list." The winner was George Kennedy for *Cool Hand Luke*. Delighted that his homemade ads had paid off, the winner hustled to the stage and hugged Patty Duke. There was a reaction shot of a smiling Paul Newman. "I could cry," the forty-three-year-old recipient said. "I have to thank [director] Stuart Rosenberg for even being here. And I have to thank the Academy for the greatest moment of my life."

Katharine Hepburn appeared, on film, in her Eleanor of Aquitaine costume from *The Lion in Winter* to ruminate on Oscar's first decade. "It was a hell of a long time ago, but we weren't bad," she said, adding that "the most honored film of the period was an unpretentious film in a whole new style—*It Happened One Night*."

"Hi, kids," Bob Hope said, introducing *Graduate* stars Dustin Hoffman and Katharine Ross to present the Cinematography Award. The presenters were nervous and solemn, especially when their film lost to *Bonnie and Clyde*.

Diahann Carroll and MacDonald Carey stepped out to bestow the Short Subject Awards and encountered nothing but trouble. The podium holding the microphones didn't rise from the floor, an overhead boom didn't extend far enough to be used as a substitute, and when Bob Hope came to the rescue with a hand mike, that went dead, too. Finally, Carroll and Carey bent over to speak in the microphones on the floor. Evidently, the Academy did not send its dress code guidelines to the nominees in this category, because Live Action winner Christopher Chapman wore a turtle-

"I fall down when I stand up."
—Carol Channing

neck, while Cartoon winner Fred Wolf went all the way with a turtleneck, beads, a necklace and sideburns.

Martha Raye faked a pratfall and then read a letter from General William Westmoreland commending Hollywood for its work with the USO in boosting the morale of U.S. troops in Southeast Asia. Minutes later, a Documentary Feature Oscar went to French filmmaker Pierre Schoendoerffer for his antiwar film, *The Anderson Platoon*.

The Academy's second decade was saluted by Olivia de Havilland, filmed in the Louis XVI room in Versailles. She remarked on the introduction of the secret envelope and the most honored film of that era—*Gone With the Wind*. Then it was back to Hollywood and more flouting of the dress code with Best Costume Design winner John Truscott of *Camelot*, who wore a Nehru jacket and bell-bottom pants. "I don't know what to say," admitted the winner whose medieval costumes had won over the trend-setting clothing from *Bonnie and Clyde*, "so I'll just say thank you."

Walter Matthau, in sideburns, announced the winner of Best Supporting Actress—Estelle Parsons for *Bonnie and Clyde*. The winner ran laughing and crying to the stage, putting her hands to her face in awe. As soon as she held the Oscar, Parsons responded, "Boy, it's heavy!" There was a shot of her *Bonnie and Clyde* cohorts laughing and clapping. "I have to thank David Merrick, who let me out of my Broadway play—*The Seven Descents of Myrtle*—so I could be here this evening," the actress said. "Little did he know what he would mean to me, really. Thank you, it's really a great moment."

Disregarding her royal status, Bob Hope introduced "Miss Grace Kelly," who was on film from the Louis XV room of her palace in Monaco. The princess called the Academy's third, "a decade of firsts," and alluded to the addition of the Foreign Language Film Award. "The highest honored film was based on a book that people thought couldn't be turned into a movie," she recalled, "*From Here to Eternity*."

Edith Evans strode onstage in Hollywood to the tune of "There Is Nothing Like a Dame" to give the Film Editing Award. When Bob Hope asked her where she would like to go on a date, Evans replied, "How does the Pink Pussycat grab you?" The winning editor was Hal Ashby for *In the Heat of the Night*, who sported a beard and a turtleneck and said, "To repeat the words of a very dear friend of mine last year when he picked up his Oscar, I only hope we can use all of our talents and creativity towards peace and love." Ashby was quoting Haskell Wexler, winner of the last Black-and-White Cinematography Award, for *Who's Afraid of Virginia Woolf?*

Rosalind Russell stepped out to give the Jean Hersholt Humanitarian Award to a surprised Academy president, Gregory Peck, who didn't even have to wait to be an ex-president to get an Award. The Board of Governors had lied and told him somebody else was going to get it. "What a humbling experience to hear oneself described as a humanitarian," said Peck, before turning fund-raiser by suggesting that viewers donate to Dr. King's Southern Christian Leadership Conference.

The next film clip featured Best Actress nominee Anne Bancroft lounging in a toga by a pool while talking about the "forty years of the talking magic lantern" and "the most honored film in this decade—winner of eleven Academy Awards—*Ben-Hur*."

It was time for Sammy Davis, Jr., to sing "Talk to the Animals." Dressed in a Nehru jacket, beads and high-heeled shoes, Davis tore into the song, punctuating it with the ad libs "Sock it to me, baby!" and "Here come de judge, here come de judge!" When Davis was finished, Barbra Streisand walked out with her hair in a "Bob Dylan cut" to name the winner of the Best Song Oscar. Before she did, Bob Hope mentioned her upcoming movie, *Funny Girl*, adding, "You get a couple more quickies like that under your belt and you'll be ready to star with me." According to Rex Reed, when Streisand announced that the winner was "Talk to the Animals," "you could hear the 'Oh, nos' loudly in the theater." Standing in for

"Tell them who I am."
—George Cukor

the English composer-lyricist Leslie Bricusse was Sammy Davis, Jr., who accepted with a British accent: "It's absolutely marvelous. It's super!"

Bob Hope introduced Robert Wise, the director of *The Sound of Music,* as "the genius," and the director announced that the Thalberg Award was going to "the familiar figure of Alfred Hitchcock." The strains of "Funeral March of a Marionette" filled the auditorium and Hitchcock walked out to receive the only Oscar he'd ever get. "Thank you . . . very much," was his speech. "He ad-libs a lot, doesn't he?" Hope quipped.

Leslie Caron presented the Best Director Award and appeared thrilled that the winner was not the director of *Bonnie and Clyde* but the director of *The Graduate,* Mike Nichols. The French actress kissed him on both cheeks. "Until this moment, my greatest pleasure was making it," the winner said, and then thanked his cast and crew. "This Award belongs as much to them as to me. I'd like to wish my mother a happy birthday."

Rod Steiger and his pony-tailed wife, Claire Bloom, gave the writing Awards. The first one went to Stirling Silliphant for *In the Heat of the Night.* "I really have no speech," Silliphant said. "The Writers Guild doesn't allow us to do any speculative writing." William Rose, the author of the original screenplay for *Guess Who's Coming to Dinner* wasn't there to accept his Oscar, so director Stanley Kramer did it for him.

Best Actor presenter Audrey Hepburn wandered out and kissed Bob Hope. "Thank you, darling," the emcee said. Then Audrey got down to business. "If I may, I should like to congratulate all five gentlemen for their outstanding performances," she boldly stated before ripping open the envelope and announcing, "Rod Steiger for *In the Heat of the Night*!" There were bravos from the audience as Steiger walked to the stage and kissed Hepburn's hand. "I find it unbelievable. I find it overwhelming," Steiger said, before going on to thank "the Maharishi" and "the public for being so kind to me." He concluded with gratitude for "Mr. Sidney Poitier for the pleasure of his friendship which gave me the knowledge and understanding of prejudice to enhance my performance. Thank you—and we *shall* overcome."

When Poitier walked out to present the Best Actress Award, the audience gave him a prolonged ovation. "That's not bad for a man who started out chained to Tony Curtis," said the star of *The Defiant Ones.* "I hate to see these lovely ladies kept in any more suspense," Poitier said, as he began to name the nominees. He opened the envelope and an incredulous grin crossed his lips. "The winner is Katharine Hepburn for *Guess Who's Coming to Dinner*!" he exclaimed. There was a gasp from the audience and then, after a beat, sustained applause. Director George Cukor mounted the stage to accept for his friend and instructed Poitier, "Tell them who I am." "Ladies and gentleman, Mr. George Cukor," the presenter proclaimed. "It was a very hard decision for you to make," Cukor acknowledged after expressing Hepburn's thanks.

Joseph E. Levine straightened up in his seat as Julie Andrews walked out to give the Best Picture Award. The only problem was that Andrews did not announce Embassy's *The Graduate* as the victor. The winner was *In the Heat of the Night.* The cameras cut backstage to where Sidney Poitier, Claire Bloom and Rod Steiger were admiring Steiger's Oscar; the trio ran to the edge of the stage to hear producer Walter Mirisch's speech. The producer thanked director Norman Jewison "who brought it so vividly to life. We are grateful for your recognition of our efforts and your recognition of the lesson of *In the Heat of the Night.*" Then the winner walked off to receive his colleagues' congratulations.

"I've never seen six hours fly by so fast," commented Bob Hope, who turned serious for his final remarks. "Clichés have been replaced. Films reflect the human condition. The moguls shared something with the man in Atlanta—they had a dream," he said, summing up with the observation that "rioting and indifference are equal sins." The sermon over, the audience left for the afterparties around town.

"What a humbling experience to hear oneself described as a humanitarian."
—Gregory Peck

Aftermath

"I wanted to win it. It's important," Rod Steiger said in the pressroom. "It gives you greater latitude in the business and that means bigger and better parts. And I need that. I'm only forty-two. Paul Newman is forty-three, Brando is forty-three, but I look like their father." Was he going out to celebrate tonight? he was asked. "Not too late," the Oscar winner said, "I've got to be on a set tomorrow." Meanwhile, a reporter from the Tulsa *Tribune* stepped into the winner's circle, put his arm around Best Supporting Actor winner George Kennedy and asked to have their pictures taken. "Kennedy's wife is from Oklahoma," he explained to his colleagues.

Reporters asked Best Supporting Actress winner Estelle Parsons who designed her victory gown. "I bought it four years ago in a store," she confessed. One columnist asked if she was disappointed that *Bonnie and Clyde* won only two Awards out of ten nominations. "I felt surely we'd get Best Picture," Parsons responded, "but then nobody likes Warren Beatty. I like Warren very much, but he is not the kind of guy people say, 'Gee, he's a great guy.'" Nevertheless the paparazzi outside the Santa Monica Civic Auditorium hovered around Beatty and Christie as they exited empty-handed. *Newsweek* wrote that Beatty muttered, "We wuz robbed."

Back in the pressroom, Academy President Gregory Peck insisted that his Hersholt Award was on the level and that he didn't know anything about it. "The Board of Governors sent me out of the room when they voted," he maintained. "I told them, 'Don't do anything rash,' and when I came back, they told me I came in third." Nearby, Barbra Streisand and reporters were discussing her visible lack of enthusiasm over the Best Song Oscar going to "Talk to the Animals." "Quite honestly," Streisand said, "I don't think any of the nominated songs were worthy of an Oscar, so I couldn't pretend any excitement I couldn't feel."

Sammy Davis, Jr., was busy posing with the Best Song Oscar and detailing the specifics of his Nehru jacket: a Sy Devore formal made of black velvet with white satin lining. The singer said he had nineteen other Nehru jackets at home and he estimated the worth of his collection at $6,000. Davis didn't leave Leslie Bricusse's Oscar with the Academy to be engraved, but took it with him to the after-party at the Factory, which Best Supporting Actress loser Carol Channing was hosting.

Guest Rex Reed wrote that while Raquel Welch, Peter Lawford and Elke Sommer mingled, the hostess sat and "ate organic peaches from a Mason jar and grinned widely." Channing informed him that her beaded rhinestone evening gown weighed thirty-six pounds "and I fall down when I stand up." When Angela Lansbury made an entrance at the Factory in a slinky satin gown the crowd gave her a standing ovation. One of Channing's other guests entered and exited simultaneously—Dame Edith Evans. She told the press as she walked out of the discotheque, "It's too noisy and I can't get any cornflakes."

The hard-luck story of the night was Bosley Crowther's. The ex-film critic for the *New York Times* had secured an advisory position at Columbia and the studio was supposed to have given him the deluxe treatment on Awards night. Only there was no limousine waiting for him at the airport and no reservations or room for him at the Beverly Hills Hotel. According to the ubiquitous Rex Reed, Crowther "ended up on top of his luggage at three o'clock in the morning looking for a place to stay."

The *New York Times'* review of the Oscar show labeled Bob Hope's opening jokes about the delay "tasteless." The *Hollywood Reporter* called it "the year Oscar came home, albeit to the seaside suburbs, the year of the ruffled turtleneck, the 'Bonnie' and the Bob Dylan electric hairstyle." Columnist Inez Robb was not fond of Julie Andrews' short hairdo: "Miss Andrews might have gotten away with the extravaganza if only she had worn her hair on this occasion in anything but a butch cut. Even Yale crews have abandoned this coif."

Best Supporting Actor winner George Kennedy later bragged to columnist James Bacon that the Oscar increased his income ten times. "And socially, you can't imagine what happens," said Kennedy, a resident of the San Fernando Valley. "Soon my wife and I were receiving invitations to parties in Bel-Air and the homes of people who didn't know we existed before the Oscar. It's a status thing, no doubt about it."

When George Cukor got through to Best Actress winner Katharine Hepburn in Nice, she responded, "I'm very touched. I'm not sure if it was a tribute to my dramatic ability or rather a showing of friendship to Spence and me. But I'm glad I won it for Spence." One reporter scoffed, "She's the first person to win because her costar died." For an official response, Hepburn sent a telegram to the Academy: "It was delightful, a total surprise. I feel I have received a big, affectionate hug from my fellow workers. They don't usually give these things to the old girls, you know."

968

"Only nuts are interesting people."
—Roman Polanski

The impossible happened at the 1968 Academy Awards.

MGM was looking for another road-show hit along the lines of *Doctor Zhivago* when Stanley Kubrick, of all people, came along with an idea for a Cinerama movie set in outer space. The studio gave him $11 million and Kubrick made the film in complete secrecy at MGM's British sound stages, designing the special effects himself. Written for the screen by Kubrick and science-fiction novelist Arthur C. Clarke, *2001: A Space Odyssey* bowed on a reserved-seat basis in the spring and the *Los Angeles Times'* Charles Champlin announced, "Some of next year's Academy Awards are already bespoken. I spent the first half of the film nudging my wife black and blue and saying again and again 'I don't believe it.'"

In New York, they couldn't understand it. "A small sphere of intellectuals will feel that Kubrick has said something because one expects him to say something," concluded the *New York Daily News*. After Andrew Sarris of the *Village Voice* panned *2001*, a colleague persuaded him to see it again "under the influence of a smoked substance . . . somewhat stronger and more authentic than oregano." Sarris reversed his opinion in print the next week. The *New York Times'* William Kloman enjoyed himself, too, writing, "*Space Odyssey* is poetry. It asks for groovin', not understanding." The epic and its classical soundtrack were so popular, noted critic Frank Rich, that "you could not walk through a college quad without hearing Strauss' 'Thus Spoke Zarathustra' blaring from a stereo."

The Slick and the Sick

At Paramount Robert Evans, thirty-seven, was making a name for himself. The studio vice president had engineered two highly successful Neil Simon adaptations: *Barefoot in the Park* with Jane Fonda and Robert Redford in 1967, and *The Odd Couple* with Jack Lemmon and Walter Matthau. But comedy wasn't Evans' only interest, and he surprised Hollywood when he began to consider filming Ira Levin's gothic bestseller *Rosemary's Baby,* the story of a Manhattan housewife who bears Satan's child. The film rights belonged to William Castle, known as "the King of the B-Picture" for drumming up business for his horror films with such stunts as wiring theater seats or offering insurance policies in the lobby. Because Paramount wasn't about to fork over a lot of dough for a thriller, Evans and Castle decided to put a Polish art-house director named Roman Polanski, thirty-four, at the helm. As Castle explained, "I think Polanski's *Knife in the Water* is a classic and he made it on a shoestring." Evans offered the leading role to Jane Fonda, who turned it down.

Enter Mrs. Frank Sinatra. Twenty-three-year-old Mia Farrow, the daughter of Maureen O'Sullivan and director John Farrow, was a pro at making headlines. She won them when she married her fifty-year-old husband in 1966; when she joined the cast of TV's *Peyton Place;* and when she replaced her waist-length hair with a crewcut, but she had never received a good movie offer from Hollywood. Polanski hired her and said, "She has a neurotic quality good for Rosemary. Only nuts are interesting people."

One day Sinatra dispatched his lawyer to the set to inform his wife that he was filing for divorce. More headlines followed, and Sheilah Graham heralded the movie as the one "Mia Farrow gambled and lost on her marriage to make." *Time* wrote, "Even those who read the book are in for a shock: the very real acting talent of Mia Farrow." Although the Catholic Church condemned the film, the public lined up to see what the baby would look like. *Rosemary's Baby* produced another overnight sensation—seventy-one-year-old Ruth Gordon, receiving the best reviews of her acting career as Farrow's next-door-neighbor witch. While Farrow recovered from the breakup of her marriage in India with the Maharishi Yogi,

Overleaf: *Best Actress winner Barbra Streisand checks out her Oscar while presenter Ingrid Bergman checks out Barbra.*

columnist Dorothy Manners wrote in Hollywood, "With the Oscar Awards almost a year away, I've already awarded Best Actress honors to Mia Farrow."

John Cassavetes' Home Movie

Playing Farrow's husband was John Cassavetes, who took his salary and sank it into *Faces,* his $140,000 *cinema vérité* chronicle of a middle-aged L.A. couple's disintegrating marriage. Character actor John Marley played the husband and Lynn Carlin, formerly Robert Altman's secretary, portrayed the wife. Mrs. Cassavetes, Gena Rowlands, was a prostitute in the film, and another character actor, Seymour Cassel, was a pickup. Directed in an improvisational style, *Faces* premiered at the New York Film Festival. "It has the unevenness of a home movie, visually and audibly," observed the *New York Post,* and *Variety* sneered, "All technical aspects of *Faces* are poor." But Renata Adler, Bosley Crowther's replacement at the *New York Times,* called it "a movie so good that one can hardly believe it" and the *New York Daily News* awarded it four stars. When John Marley heard that he had won the Best Actor citation at the Venice Film Festival, the Hollywood veteran said, "I thought they meant some film group in Venice, California."

My Director, My Love

Another filmmaking couple was Paul Newman and Joanne Woodward, who raised $780,000 to film a story about a spinster schoolteacher in their home state of Connecticut. Newman made his directorial debut, and both Mr. and Mrs. waived salaries. "It was not at all like working in Hollywood, where the grips play poker and have no idea what the movie is about," Woodward explained. "Everyone from the little boy who helped the grips was involved."

If *Rachel, Rachel*'s production was small-scale, its exploitation campaign was handled with the care lavished on an epic. Publicist Warren Cowan, detailed his strategy: "First, we set up a great many trade screenings for eight people, usually in the cinema room of the Beverly Hills Hotel. Often, Paul Newman would join us afterwards for coffee. We had a big premiere in New York and we put Newman and Woodward on all of the TV talk shows. Then, the Newmans spent all of Labor Day posing for the cover of *Life.*"

Life praised the novice director for his "sensitive, slightly melancholy eye for something most American movies miss—the texture of ordinary life." The *Saturday Review* lauded Mrs. Newman and commented, "Suddenly we realize how much has been lost in the name of underplaying or 'cool.'" The public found Joanne and Paul almost as intriguing as Liz and Dick and *Rachel, Rachel* emerged a moneymaker.

Image Problem

A third do-it-yourselfer was Cliff Robertson, who told Sidney Skolsky, "I'm trying to become a definite image on the screen because this has been my career hang-up." Robertson definitely had an image problem—producers didn't seem to know he existed. Two of the television dramas that Robertson had starred in, "Days of Wine and Roses" and "The Hustler," went on to become movie vehicles for Jack Lemmon and Paul Newman, respectively, so Robertson bought the rights to a third one entitled "The Two Worlds of Charlie Gordon," based on a novel called *Flowers for Algernon.* "I wasn't going to be beaten out by some movie star," the actor said. Since the plot—a mentally retarded man undergoes a scientific experiment and becomes a genius, only to regress to his earlier state—didn't sound commercial, it took Robertson seven years to sell the property. Finally, a budding company named ABC Pictures gave it a chance, shortening the title to *Charly,* and Robertson got the recognition he craved. The *New York Daily News* declared, "I suspect no one could have replaced him in *Charly.* At long last, he has a film that shows his depth and range as an actor."

Tony Curtis was also searching for a change of

"I wasn't going to be beaten out by some movie star."
—Cliff Robertson

image. After four sex comedies in a row, he decided on something different—playing the title role in *The Boston Strangler*. The *New York Daily News* applauded this change of pace, too: "It's true what we've heard about Tony Curtis. Tony, his face changed by makeup, his body seemingly heavier, gives an extraordinary performance." Joyce Haber predicted in Hollywood, "Every columnist in the country will surely nominate him for an Oscar and deservedly so."

Pat's Back

The biggest comeback story of 1968, however, belonged to Patricia Neal. The actress felt she hadn't recovered enough from the stroke she suffered in 1965—which had left her semi-paralyzed and with a loss of memory and a severe speech impairment—to accept Mike Nichols' offer to play Mrs. Robinson in *The Graduate*. But when that film became one of the most profitable in Hollywood history, Neal was determined not to let another good part get away. In 1968, she landed the role of the mother of a returning war veteran in the adaptation of Frank D. Gilroy's Pulitzer Prize–winning play, *The Subject Was Roses*. Charles Champlin decreed, "Patricia Neal's return is triumphant," and *Time* said, "Patricia Neal's performance would be worth waiting a decade for."

Teen Romance by Bill Shakespeare

Teenagers who weren't interested in Patricia Neal's comeback went to see Franco Zeffirelli's sexy version of *Romeo and Juliet*, complete with nude scene. The director cast Leonard Whiting, seventeen, and Olivia Hussey, fifteen, as the lovers and clarified that his movie was "not created for people familiar with Shakespeare." Columnist Florabel Muir reported "Paramount will stage special teen premieres in key spots all over the country for its *Romeo and Juliet* . . . rock music stations and local discotheques will play an important role in getting youngsters into the theaters." The strategy worked. Weeping teenagers were so common a sight that the *New York Times* could not resist running a photograph of "Sad-eyed schoolgirls leaving the Paris Theatre." The "Love Theme" from the film sailed to the Top Ten and *Romeo and Juliet* became the most profitable Shakespearean film ever. *Life* attributed its success to the "convincing portrait of adolescents bursting with sexual hunger."

The Sound of Flop

There were a lot of tears being shed over at 20th Century–Fox, too. After *The Sound of Music*, the Fox executives were sure the public wanted musicals. And then *Doctor Dolittle* bombed. The executives kept their fingers crossed over *Star!*, a biography of Gertrude Lawrence by the duo who had been responsible for *The Sound of Music*—Julie Andrews and director Robert Wise. *Newsweek* brought the bad news: "The sets are tacky, the color abysmal, the length—three hours and ten minutes—unconscionable." *The Sound of Music* had not garnered good reviews either, the executives remembered, but it did have paying customers; once the first batch of old ladies saw *Star!*, the movie played to empty houses. The studio yanked *Star!* out of circulation, reedited it, retitled it *Those Were the Happy Days*, and tried again—it flopped again. Julie Andrews' box-office reign had come to an end and Richard Zanuck, Darryl's son and Fox's vice president in charge of production, started referring to *Star!* as "My Edsel."

Hello, Gorgeous

Zanuck couldn't console himself with the notion that musicals had gone out of style, because Columbia was doing fine with them. In the fall, the studio released *Funny Girl*, the film debut of Barbra Streisand, who had received a ton of publicity while the movie was in production. Joyce Haber had called her "a full-fledged monster" for treating veteran director William Wyler as if he were "a butler." Screenwriter Isobel Lennart said that working with Streisand was "a deflating, ego-crushing experience," and Sheilah Graham wrote, "Barbra Streisand's search for perfection in everything reminds me of how Shelley Winters had everyone walking up the wall when she first came to Hollywood."

Still, Columbia had enough confidence in Streisand's drawing power to charge a six-dollar top—an all-time high—for *Funny Girl*'s New York and Los Angeles engagements. *Newsday* wrote, "The script is just a vehicle for showing off one of the most exciting musical-comedy stars in a decade" and *Cosmopolitan*'s Liz Smith called Streisand "the greatest talent anywhere." The *Saturday Review* dissented: "She has a voice, of course. I've never liked it much . . . Sorry to say, I'm not much of a fan of her comic abilities, either." Streisand herself was disappointed with the way she looked onscreen, telling *Look*, "I thought they'd make me gorgeous. I always wanted to be pretty." But, as Isobel Lennart said, "Streisand has made life a lot better for a helluva lot of homely little girls." *Funny Girl* was the highest-grossing musical since *The Sound of Music* and played in one Times Square theater for over a year.

Consider Yourself Profitable

In December, Columbia released *Oliver!*, the song-and-dance version of *Oliver Twist*. "This is the first time we English have tried to compete with Hollywood in the musical department," said producer John Woolf, who asked Carol Reed, the director of *The Third Man* and *The Fallen Idol*, to helm the movie. Renata Adler of the *New York Times* dismissed the movie as "a cast-iron pastry," but her fellow reviewers adored it. *Time* pronounced it "a gleaming, steaming rum-plum pudding of a film" and Pauline Kael posited in *The New Yorker*, "It proves these multimillion-dollar productions can be beautifully made, if you know how." The *New York Daily News*' Wanda Hale threw all caution to the wind: "I'm going to stick my neck out and say it's the best musical I have ever seen."

Oliver!'s cast was not well known to Americans, but Hollywood knew talent when it saw it. The *Hollywood Citizen-News* declared that fifteen-year-old Jack Wild, as the Artful Dodger, "just has to be the most precocious film discovery of 1968." And columnist James Bacon reported that Hollywood was quite taken with Ron Moody's Fagin. "Hit of the Jim Backus party was Ron Moody," the columnist wrote. "He's returning home tomorrow. I told him to come back and meet people and he'll be able to take an Oscar home with him. He was of the opinion that Academy Awards are won solely on what's up on the screen."

The Great Kate

Last year's Best Actress, Katharine Hepburn, wasn't planning to go to any Hollywood parties—she wouldn't have to. When *The Lion in Winter* opened, columnists began referring to her as "the Great Kate." After the death of Spencer Tracy, Hepburn plunged into work, committing to a Broadway musical about Coco Chanel and signing to play Eleanor of Aquitaine to Peter O'Toole's Henry II in the film adaptation of James Goldman's short-lived Broadway play. *The Lion in Winter* premiered on a reserved-seat basis and audiences paid top prices to listen to Hepburn and O'Toole argue for two hours and fifteen minutes over which of their screen sons should be successor to the throne. The *Los Angeles Times*' Charles Champlin called it "the most literate movie of the year." The *Saturday Review* wrote of Hepburn, "There is a fusion, a merging of identities that makes this perhaps the finest characterization of her career." But Pauline Kael complained, "Hepburn plays Eleanor as a gallant great lady. She's about as tough as Helen Hayes." The *New York Daily News* said of O'Toole, "He'll be up for an Oscar and most likely take it home with him." But not every critic was swayed by the film; for example, *Time* carped, "Henry and Eleanor are reduced to a TV-sized version of the sovereigns next door, their epic struggle shrunk to sitcom squabbles."

"Everyone from the little boy who helped the grips was involved."
—Joanne Woodward

Trouble in Gotham

The critical division over *The Lion in Winter* reached a showdown at the New York Film Critics Awards. Everyone was polite when Joanne Woodward won Best Actress, and only slightly less so when Paul Newman won Best Director for *Rachel, Rachel* and Alan Arkin won Best Actor for playing a deaf-mute in *The Heart Is a Lonely Hunter*. But *Life*'s Richard Schickel hit the roof when John Cassavetes' *Faces* lost the Best Picture Award by one vote to *The Lion in Winter*. A witness told *Variety*'s Stuart Byron "some of those girls had tears in their eyes" when Schickel labeled the veteran critics "deadwood" for picking the historical drama. Schickel and three cohorts resigned in protest—they'd be back next year—and *Variety* predicted another victory for *The Lion in Winter*. "Never has a road-show film won the New York Film Critics Award and then gone on to lose the Oscar. So a defeat for *Lion* would be precedent-setting." This was good news to *Lion*'s producer, Joseph E. Levine, still smarting from *The Graduate*'s Oscar defeat last year.

How to Get Nominated

Alan Arkin's New York victory did not slow down Cliff Robertson's Best Actor campaign for *Charly*. As *Time* revealed, Robertson's efforts had been going on for months. "Starting in October, ads on his behalf were placed in the trade papers," the magazine reported. "The campaign culminated in a giant double-fold-out inserted in *Daily Variety*. Its contents: 83 favorable reviews of Robertson from a spectrum of journals."

That Redgrave Woman

Universal executives realized that the studio had nothing to show for itself this year, so they threw out their road-show entry, *Isadora,* a biography of dancer Isadora Duncan, a couple of months ahead of schedule. Charles Champlin scolded the studio: "The most conspicuous instance of self-defeat, Universal's *Isadora,* was rushed into release with its length and its pace seriously out of whack, with its intermission misplaced and its weaknesses given equal time with its strengths."

Isadora did have one asset—Vanessa Redgrave. Her performance knocked everyone out, but her antiwar activism—perceived as a mere eccentricity when she was nominated in 1966—preceded her. "Although the Academy officials keep denying it, the Oscar race is still basically a popularity contest and Vanessa Redgrave's violent political action has alienated some of the conservative Hollywood crowd," warned James Bacon. Redgrave antagonized that crowd even more by announcing that she was pregnant by her *Camelot* costar, Franco Nero: "I'm very happy, because having a baby is the most extraordinary thing that can happen to a woman." Universal didn't know how happy Hollywood would be about it, though, and ran ads in the trades reminding readers, "*The Academy Awards are not a popularity contest,*" adding. "Members should vote based on what they themselves have seen on the screen, not on what they've heard or read about a performance. We urge you not to vote until you have seen *Isadora*."

The Nominations

Isadora received a single nomination—for Best Actress. *Rosemary's Baby* received two nominations, but a Best Actress nod for Mia Farrow wasn't one of them. Dorothy Manners, who had predicted an Oscar for Farrow, was livid. "Obviously, Mia Farrow 'kooked' herself out of a nomination," the columnist deduced, continuing, "Vanessa Redgrave!!!?? I don't care what anybody says about her 'art.' This woman has led rallies in Hyde Park against the U.S.A. There's an element of irony here. Miss Redgrave is honored DESPITE her private-life activities. Mia is blocked out BECAUSE of hers."

Katharine Hepburn had done more than outdraw Mia Farrow in votes, she had topped Bette

Davis' record of ten nominations with her eleventh for *The Lion in Winter*. But her competition for Oscar number three was tough: Patricia Neal's comeback, Barbra Streisand's debut, and Joanne Woodward's reemergence. But a nomination was not enough for Woodward. When she saw that her husband wasn't nominated for Best Director, she saw red. "It's a total boycott!" Woodward screamed to Army Archerd. "I couldn't have been nominated for Best Actress or Estelle Parsons for Supporting Actress without his being the director. This negates the whole purpose of the Academy. I'm not going to go." Paul Newman told her, "You're being emotional," pointing out that *Rachel, Rachel* was a Best Picture nominee. A repentant Woodward said later, "My husband decided I should go and I do what he says."

More Surprises

James Bacon sided with Woodward when he saw that one of the Director nominees was Gillo Pontecorvo for *The Battle of Algiers*, an Italian film that had lost the Foreign Film Award two years earlier. "If I were Newman, I'd demand a recount," the columnist suggested. "This one smells." Maximilian Schell, who had beaten Newman as Best Actor in 1961 and who had turned director himself in 1968, said, "Only directors nominate directors and they're all jealous of Newman's brilliance with his first effort."

When *2001* failed to be nominated for Best Picture—*Funny Girl* was there instead—*Variety* observed, "Over-50 demographic age characteristics of Academy members was brought sharply home with lack of a best picture nomination for *2001*, this year's youth fave."

There were also surprises in the Best Actor race. Neither Tony Curtis in *The Boston Strangler* nor Walter Matthau in *The Odd Couple* was on the list, but standing tall with Peter O'Toole, New York Film Critics winner Alan Arkin and *Oliver!*'s Ron Moody was Alan Bates, as a persecuted Soviet Jew in *The Fixer*, Dalton Trumbo's adaptation of Bernard Malamud's novel that died at the box office. Sidney Skolsky wisecracked, "Alan Bates is only on the list because they needed a fifth nominee." Columnist Hank Grant congratulated a Best Actor nominee whose campaign had succeeded—Cliff Robertson. "Cliff's been burping with satisfaction," he wrote, "over the dozen cases of Pepsi sent him on *Too Late the Hero* location by Joan Crawford as her salute to his Oscar nomination for *Charly*."

Schlemiels and Godfathers

The *Hollywood Reporter*'s Hank Grant also had good things to say about Gene Wilder, nominated for Best Supporting Actor for his second film role, the schlemiel in Mel Brooks' *The Producers:* "Gene Wilder's Oscar nomination moves him into dueling contention with Dustin Hoffman for the title role in *Portnoy's Complaint*." Mel Brooks was nominated, too, for Original Screenplay. His competition included John Cassavetes for the screenplay of *Faces,* which also won supporting nods for Seymour Cassel and Lynn Carlin. Enough members of the Acting Branch went to see *Star!* to nominate Raymond Massey's son Daniel for portraying his real-life godfather, Noel Coward. According to the columnists, all this new talent would likely lose to the favorites in the Supporting contests—Ruth Gordon in *Rosemary's Baby* and Jack Albertson as Pat Neal's husband in *The Subject Was Roses*.

Joseph E. Levine said so far so good when Anthony Harvey won the Directors Guild Award for *The Lion in Winter* and both Bob Thomas and Sidney Skolsky predicted Oscars for the film, Harvey and Peter O'Toole. *The Lion in Winter* wouldn't make it a clean sweep, however, because, as Sheilah Graham reported, Barbra Streisand had not only Columbia behind her, but Fox and Paramount, which both had expensive Streisand musicals waiting in the wings. Still, there were those in the industry who resented the partial treatment the Academy had given Streisand by letting her become a voting member before she had even finished filming her first movie. Academy President

"The Santa Monica city fathers will be furious with me but I think their theater is a dreary barn."
—Gower Champion

Gregory Peck tried to explain: "When an actress has played a great role on the stage and is coming into films for what will obviously be an important career, it is ridiculous to make her wait two or three years for membership."

It's What's Happening

Peck also thought it ridiculous that the Academy Awards show should always be so listless and boring, so he asked Broadway director-choreographer Gower Champion to come in and spruce up the ceremonies. After thinking about it for five months, Champion accepted—reportedly without pay—on the condition that the show be moved from the Santa Monica Civic Auditorium to the Dorothy Chandler Pavilion at the Music Center in downtown L.A. "The Santa Monica city fathers will be furious with me, but I think their theater is a dreary barn," Champion said. Told that the Chandler didn't have a middle aisle, thus making it difficult for the winners to get to the stage, Champion got around the problem by adding a runway that would extend from the stage into the first two rows of the orchestra. For a stage setting, Champion selected a series of panels, mirrors and rear-projection effects because previous settings "always used to look like Tara." He also requested a looser dress code—black tie instead of white, and no tails, please.

The director wanted to eliminate all forecourt activity, including the fan-filled bleachers, because "It seems very Hollywood Boulevard to me." The Academy and the police informed him that two thousand fans were going to be there to ogle the stars and that bleachers were a necessary restraint. Champion had the temerity to state that the tradition of having Bob Hope as emcee was "a bore" and his alternative was to have ten "Friends of Oscar" who would serve as hosts and double as presenters. *TV Guide* reported that Hope sighed "Thank God" when Champion broke the news to him.

A Friend Indeed

Champion wanted Sophia Loren to be one of Oscar's friends, but she cabled him from Italy: "My little bambino will not let me travel to California." Warren Beatty had accepted the chore but he withdrew due to "illness." Radie Harris said in the *Hollywood Reporter* that "both Beatty and Julie Christie came down with mumps over the weekend," but *Women's Wear Daily* had a different prognosis: "The naked truth is Warren has a new friend (an English model, they say) and has been holed up in Palm Springs . . . nothing contagious." Beatty's rising temperature left the show minus one Friend and non-nominee Tony Curtis was called in as a replacement.

Cliff Hanger

President Peck made an attendance drive again this year and fifteen of the twenty acting nominees promised to come. Missing would be Alan Bates, Estelle Parsons, Peter O'Toole, Katharine Hepburn and Cliff Robertson. Having spent all that money on his campaign, Robertson was dying to attend, but director Robert Aldrich—who had let Lee Marvin leave the English set of *The Dirty Dozen* to pick up his Oscar for *Cat Ballou*—said that Robertson's departure from the Philippines set of *Too Late the Hero* would delay production and wreck the film's budget. Robertson offered to pay $75,000 to cover any losses and had arranged to fly to Los Angeles in President Ferdinand Marcos' personal jet, but Aldrich wouldn't budge. President Peck sent Aldrich a telegram pleading for Robertson's release. No way, the producer-director insisted.

Katharine Hepburn was a different story. She planned to watch the show on television in Los Angeles. Peck phoned and pleaded, but Hepburn informed him that she didn't want to be in the audience if she lost.

The Big Night

The first "big hand of the evening," said the *Hollywood Reporter*, went to the 5:42 arrival of Cesar "Butch" Romero, although this year the popular escort came stag. Cheers also greeted Loretta Young, Raquel Welch, Patricia Neal with Roald Dahl, and Romero's sometime date, Joan Crawford. Crawford's escort this year, George Frelinghuysen, told one columnist he had been taken aback when Joan piled into his Rolls with a bucket of ice and a bottle of vodka. Best Supporting Actress nominee Lynn Carlin wasn't recognized by the press or the fans. Vanessa Redgrave, arriving with Franco Nero, was welcomed with a placard in the bleachers reading: "A vote for Vanessa REDgrave is a vote for the Viet Cong."

After television viewers got the news that *The Big Valley* and the *Joey Bishop Show* would not be seen that night, there was a shot of the Dorothy Chandler Pavilion. Out popped nominees Ron Moody and Jack Wild, in character as Fagin and the Artful Dodger.

"Dodger, this here is the place where they're giving out all them golden Oscars tonight."

"What do you think the chance is of our winning one?"

"I don't rightly know, my dear, but if they don't give us one, we'll have to pinch it, won't we?"

The scene switched to the lobby of the pavilion, empty except for Gregory Peck. "It's kind of lonesome out here," Peck remarked as he headed for the auditorium doors. He mentioned than ten of Oscar's "best friends" were waiting inside—Warren Beatty was still listed as one of them on the program—and announced the first, Ingrid Bergman.

The next instant, Bergman was walking on to the stage to say, "It's nice to be back among old friends and some new ones, like Sidney Poitier." Poitier entered, walked to another part of the stage, and asked, "What could be nicer than an evening with friends like Ingrid Bergman and Jane Fonda?" Jane gushed, "What a spot to be in, be-

Awards Ceremony

APRIL 14, 1969, 7:00 P.M.
THE DOROTHY CHANDLER PAVILION, LOS ANGELES

Your Hosts:
THE FRIENDS OF OSCAR: INGRID BERGMAN, SIDNEY POITIER, JANE FONDA, FRANK SINATRA, NATALIE WOOD, WALTER MATTHAU, DIAHANN CARROLL, TONY CURTIS, ROSALIND RUSSELL AND BURT LANCASTER
Televised over ABC

Presenters

Supporting Actor	Frank Sinatra
Art Direction	Natalie Wood
Honorary Award to John Chambers	Walter Matthau
Documentary Awards	Diahann Carroll and Tony Curtis
Costume Design	Jane Fonda and the Soul Rascals
Sound	Rosalind Russell
Cinematography	Ingrid Bergman
Scientific or Technical Awards	Burt Lancaster and Natalie Wood
Supporting Actress	Tony Curtis
Foreign Film	Jane Fonda
Special Effects	Diahann Carroll and Burt Lancaster
Scoring of a Musical Picture	Marni Nixon and Henry Mancini
Writing Awards	Rosalind Russell and Frank Sinatra
Actor	Burt Lancaster
Short Subjects	Jane Fonda and Tony Curtis
Honorary Award to Onna White	Mark Lester and Diahann Carroll
Film Editing	Walter Matthau
Song	Frank Sinatra
Original Score	Rosalind Russell
Actress	Ingrid Bergman
Picture	Sidney Poitier

Performers of Nominated Songs

"Chitty Chitty Bang Bang"	Ingrid Bergman, Sidney Poitier, Paula Kelly and the UCLA Marching Band
"For Love of Ivy"	Abbey Lincoln
"Funny Girl"	Aretha Franklin
"Star!"	Frank Sinatra
"The Windmills of Your Mind"	José Feliciano

"A vote for Vanessa REDgrave is a vote for the Viet Cong."
—A protestor's poster

tween Sidney Poitier and Nancy Sinatra's dad." Frank responded with, "Thank you, Henry Fonda, Jr., and I think my spot's pretty groovy. I'm between Barbarella and that wonderful skier, Natalie Wood." Out came Wood with a broken leg and cast. Natalie allowed that "I love that man. Also this man—Walter Matthau." Matthau said, "I enjoy playing opposite Jack Lemmon, but it's a nice change of pace to be between Natalie Wood and Diahann Carroll," and Carroll asked, "Where else but in Hollywood could a girl from the Bronx come out on a night like this and introduce a boy from Brooklyn—Tony Curtis." "I'm from the Bronx, too," Tony corrected her, and then introduced "one of the great ladies of Hollywood, the original Auntie Mame, Rosalind Russell." Roz brought on the final Friend, "a man who's made forty-five pictures and, sad to say, none of them with me. What do you have to say for yourself—Burt Lancaster?" Lancaster came out as one of Champion's rear projectors went into action and flashed a photo of the embrace in the surf from *From Here to Eternity*. "You could have been in *From Here to Eternity,*" Lancaster told Russell, "but you don't body surf. Then there was another memorable scene." The projector flashed a photo of Sinatra after he had been beaten by Ernest Borgnine. "Poor baby," Burt sighed, giving Sinatra his cue to reappear and sing the nominated song "Star!"

After finishing the number, Sinatra looked at his picture from *From Here to Eternity* and quipped, "If I hadn't copped that Oscar, I'd still be working with Gene Kelly in sailor suits." As part of the new "informal" look, Champion had Sinatra sit on the edge of the runway while reading the nominees for Best Supporting Actor. The winner was the former vaudevillian Jack Albertson for *The Subject Was Roses*, who began to weep.

> *I didn't expect to be this moved. I'm glad I'm off the hook—the first one. It's not the first time I've been the opening act. I'd like to thank that wonderful, wonderful actress and a great woman, Patricia Neal.*

The television audience saw a thrilled Neal, clapping proudly as Albertson exited.

The Champion touch was felt during the presentation of the Costume Design Award. As Jane Fonda read the nominations, she was backed by an ersatz rock band, the Soul Rascals, and dancers wearing the nominated costumes. Romeo and Juliet did the jerk; *Lion in Winter*'s Henry II and Eleanor the frug; showgirls from *Star!* shimmied in their early '40s tassled outfits; Fagin, the Artful Dodger and Oliver bopped about; and, finally, one of the apes from *Planet of the Apes* was found sitting next to a surprised Jack Wild in the orchestra before bounding onstage to thrash among the other dancers. The winner, *Romeo and Juliet*'s Danilo Donati, was absent, so the barefoot Jane boogied out among the costumed dancers and handed the Oscar to Romeo, who held it aloft.

Tony Curtis crowned the Best Supporting Actress—Ruth Gordon, for *Rosemary's Baby*. "I can't tell you how encouraging a thing like this is," cracked the now seventy-two-year-old actress. "I remember the first film I was ever in, in 1915, and here we are in 1969 and I don't know why it took me so long, though I don't think I'm backward." She thanked her coworkers from *Rosemary's Baby* and concluded, "Thank all of you who voted for me and to all who didn't, please excuse me."

Jane Fonda confessed that her French husband made foreign-language films and pointed out that in France and Egypt, *Funny Girl* was a foreign-language film. Fonda then opened her mouth, only to be dubbed by Walter Matthau reading the Foreign Film nominees. The winner was *War and Peace,* a six-hour-thirteen-minute movie—and that was the edited American version—which the U.S.S.R. shelled out $100 million to make. The Award was accepted by Ludmila Savelyeva, who played Natasha in the film. Natalie Wood hobbled out to show off her fluency in Russian by translating Savelyeva's speech. Then Stanley Kubrick won an Oscar—for Special Effects.

The Lion in Winter claimed its first Oscar when James Goldman won the Adapted Screenplay

"The only female thing in 2001 is a computer with a noticeable lisp."
—Rosalind Russell

Award. "I've been told by people who've been through this experience that the smiles of joy that appear occasionally up here aren't smiles of joy but smiles of relief," the winner said. "It's absolutely true and I can't tell you how relieved I am."

Frank Sinatra wandered out again to give the Original Screenplay Award and asked, "What do I do here?" Out bolted Don Rickles with an idiot card. Champion thought that Rickles had "saved" the Emmy Awards show the previous year and brought the insult comedian on the Oscars to do his schtick.

"I've been watching Burt Lancaster's chest move," Rickles said. When Sinatra put his arm around him, Rickles snapped, "Get your arm off. You're big but I'm not your coolie. Later on, we're going to buy a Dick Haymes album and see what happened to your career." The two of them went down the list of nominees and when Rickles arrived at the two authors, one Italian and one Spanish, of *The Battle of Algiers,* he joked, "All these Italians. Let's have a linguini party." The winner was Mel Brooks for *The Producers,* who said, "I'll just say what's in my heart—ba-bump, ba-bump, ba-bump." He also thanked his film's distributor, "Joseph E. Levine and his wife Rosalie." Levine grinned broadly—little Avco Embassy had won both writing Oscars.

In an attempt to "juice up" the show, Champion moved the Best Actor Award to the middle of the proceedings with Burt Lancaster making the announcement. The winner was Cliff Robertson for *Charly*. Frank Sinatra walked onstage, hesitated, and walked off. "Frank will accept," Lancaster said, and Sinatra reappeared. "Cliff is filming in the Philippines. I wish him the joyous moment of his life." The camera cut to Joan Crawford clapping for the man who threw a typewriter at her in *Autumn Leaves*—a movie directed by the man responsible for Robertson's absence, Robert Aldrich.

The Cartoon Award was given by Tony Curtis and a former winner in this category, the Pink Panther. This year's victor was *Winnie the Pooh and the Blustery Day*. Cartoon director Wolfgang "Woolie" Reitherman accepted for Walt Disney—dead some two years now—whose last project was this Pooh short. Reitherman, wearing a Nehru jacket and over-sized medallion, was on the verge of tears as he spoke about "another memorable moment we've all shared with Walt."

When Sinatra introduced Aretha Franklin to sing "Funny Girl," he promised "a new old-fashioned soul shouter with a soul treatment." Aretha belted out the torch number in a gold dress with enormous tassle sleeves and a matching gold crown covered with foliage. When Franklin finished, Sinatra exclaimed, "She really tore it up, didn't she?" He then gave the Best Song Award to "The Windmills of Your Mind."

All the female "Friends of Oscar" lined up and Ingrid Bergman explained, "We are assembled, somewhat reluctantly, to give the Award for Best Director." The joke was that the nominated directors were trying "to make female stars obsolete." The presenters pointed out that only *Lion in Winter*'s Anthony Harvey had directed a major woman star. Franco Zeffirelli with *Romeo and Juliet* helmed "a teenaged newcomer"; *Oliver*'s Sir Carol Reed had a woman "who sang two songs and got choked for her trouble"; in *The Battle of Algiers,* Gillo Pontecorvo gave the audience "women extras with veils and army blankets"; as for Stanley Kubrick, "the only female thing in *2001* is a computer with a noticeable lisp." All the women opened envelopes but only Jane Fonda's contained the winner's name. For the first time ever, he turned out not to be the winner of the Directors Guild Award. *Lion in Winter*'s Anthony Harvey lost to *Oliver!*'s Sir Carol Reed. "Not having made a musical before," a surprised Sir Carol said modestly, "you can imagine what I owe to other people." Joseph E. Levine turned to Rosalie and shrugged; once again the Academy was standing up Avco Embassy Pictures.

The ghost of Oscar past was summoned up when the orchestra started playing "Thanks for the Memory" and Bob Hope arrived. Hope had decided to appear on the show when he heard that Martha Raye was being honored with the Jean

Hersholt Humanitarian Award for her Vietnam USO tours and the comedian was rarin' to go: "Pictures have been pretty wild this year, haven't they? Oscar has been more naked than usual . . . They're doing things on the screen today I wouldn't do in bed"—some applause—"even if I had the chance."

Hope then turned to praising Martha Raye for entertaining the troops: "She knows what they want—songs, laughs, as only she can do it. Such charge and excitement onstage that it would thrill even the spying Viet Cong. A great gal, a great lady, a great woman, our Colonel Maggie of the Boondocks, Miss Martha Raye! Ri' here!" Greeting the Academy, the audience and "our dear beautiful legend, Mr. Bob Hope," Raye started to speak, forgot her lines and giggled, "I'm so nervous." "Yes, but you're on," Hope reminded her. "This is the happiest day of my life—stateside," Raye confessed. The first woman to win the Hersholt, she was supposed to sing a song but she told Champion she "was too pent up." So Bob and Raye walked off, arm in arm.

Ingrid Bergman entered to give the Best Actress award. The presentation began with a montage of the nominees in their screen roles, courtesy of the projection machines. The audience applauded each actress as she appeared on the screen. Bergman went down the list of nominees, and the TV audience saw Patricia Neal, Vanessa Redgrave, Joanne Woodward and Barbra Streisand, who was holding Elliott Gould's hand. Bergman opened the envelope and said, "The winner is . . . it's a tie!" The audience cried out in shock. Bergman continued: "The winners are Katharine Hepburn for *The Lion in Winter* [applause] and Barbra Streisand for *Funny Girl* [applause and bravos]." Best Director loser Anthony Harvey, accepting for Hepburn, leaned forward in his seat and suggested to Streisand that they ascend together. They held hands as they walked to the stage and the audience got a second shock when it saw Streisand's see-through Scassi pajamas. Streisand added more drama when one of her bell-bottomed pants legs got caught on the stairs and ripped.

Harvey spoke first. "When I asked Miss Hepburn what she thought when she broke the record of nominations, she said, 'When you've lived as long as I have, anything is possible.' [Hepburn was fifty-nine.] I'm absolutely thrilled that it has." Then it was Streisand's turn. Looking at the Oscar, she said, "Hello, gorgeous," and, after the audience laughed, continued, "I'm very honored to be in such magnificent company as Katharine Hepburn . . . and, um, gee whiz, it's some kind of a wild feeling, um, sitting there tonight, I was thinking . . . um . . . the first script of *Funny Girl* was written when I was only eleven years old and, um, thank God it took so long to get it right, you know?"

Barbra and Anthony walked off. Although she had just addressed millions of people, Streisand stopped backstage before the pressroom and said, "I can't go out and face these people." She kept reporters waiting for fifteen minutes before she found the nerve to go in.

Sidney Poitier came out to announce the Best Picture, which, after Best Director, was anybody's guess. The winner was *Oliver!* and producer John Woolf thanked composer Lionel Bart, "without whom we'd have no film at all," but didn't mention Charles Dickens.

Gregory Peck closed the proceedings with, "On your way home, stop and see a movie. If you're already home, go out and see a movie."

Aftermath

Backstage, Ingrid Bergman was still trembling over the contents of the Best Actress envelope. She recounted that, when handing her the envelope, the Price, Waterhouse man, had told her to "read everything." "I thought he was referring to all the names of the nominees," she said.

Barbra Streisand told reporters, "Yeah, it was kind of unexpected, having two winners, huh? I know you won't believe it, but honestly, my work

"I think my spot's pretty groovy."
—Frank Sinatra

is my reward," which was exactly what Katharine Hepburn said when she lost to Ginger Rogers in 1940. Streisand added, "But the tension. I thought I was gonna faint."

Martha Raye sobbed softly and refused to pose kissing her Oscar. "If I do, I'll swallow it." Ruth Gordon, having lost two Screenwriting nominations and one try at Supporting Actress in the past, was a little calmer than Barbra and Martha. "My husband told me if I didn't win this time, he wouldn't bring me again," Mrs. Garson Kanin said. "But I figured even if I didn't win I got a new dress out of it. I feel absolutely groovy." Asked about costar Mia Farrow's failure to get a nomination, Gordon assured everyone, "She'll be back next year—she's going to win for *John and Mary*."

Jack Albertson was teary-eyed. "Frank Gilroy fought for a year to make sure I got this part in the movie and I shall never forget him for it," he said of the author of *The Subject Was Roses*. He added, "I've been kicking around this business about forty years and I'm not about to be knocked over by the red-carpet treatment." A year later he revealed the best part about winning the Oscar: "I get invited to a lot of pro-am tournaments now. Being an avid golfer, this has been the happiest year of my life."

Everyone lamented that Cliff Robertson wasn't around for the biggest event of his career, and Radie Harris wrote that the Academy was "fuming at Aldrich." Out in the Philippines, Michael Caine got the word about his costar over the AP wireless at 12:30 P.M. Philippines time. When Caine announced the news on the set, twenty Japanese actors, playing Robertson's enemies in the World War II film, suddenly broke character and tossed the winner in the air three times. They then produced fifteen bottles of sake they had brought from Tokyo just in case. Director Aldrich later threw a party at the Manila Sheraton Hilton that three thousand people tried to crash. "There hasn't been this much excitement since V-J day," marveled a Philippines government official.

Back in Hollywood, people wondered why Robertson's wife, Dina Merrill, didn't accept for her husband. The *Los Angeles Herald-Examiner* reported, "Cliff told Dina he didn't think he'd win so she watched with her mom—Mrs. Merriweather Post." But Radie Harris wrote, "Dina Merrill had agreed to accept for Cliff, but changed her mind."

Paul Newman and Joanne Woodward skipped the Governors' Ball and went to a friend's house. The next day Newman said, "There must be something wrong with a group that hands out awards and then has to send telegrams saying, 'Please come.' It should be fun to go to—not agony. There's something barbaric about it."

Columnist Joyce Haber did go to the ball at the Beverly Hilton and did nothing but complain: "The supper consisted of overdone filets carrying the discernible odor of Sterno. The room was overheated, the dance floor overcrowded, the seating arrangment the most inept of any party in a decade." Haber managed to put in a kind word for Joan Crawford: "The exotic boss of Pepsi-Cola was perfectly sober." Meanwhile, Joseph E. Levine was asking everybody why, for two years in a row, his Best Picture nominees failed to take Best Picture at the Oscars after having won the Directors Guild Award. Levine looked over sadly at the *Oliver!* table, where they couldn't get over their unexpected good fortune.

Gower Champion was greeted by a standing ovation when he entered the ball. Talk at the party, however, centered on the Best Actress tie as well as Barbra Streisand's see-through outfit. Don Rickles told *Women's Wear Daily* that he thought Streisand's pajamas were "smashing," but Edith Head pronounced them "shocking!"

As if her outfit wasn't enough, Barbra Streisand annoyed some Academy members when she left the ball early to host a party at her house. Prior to the Awards, Katharine Hepburn had told Sheilah Graham that she thought Streisand "has the most fantastic talent." And Streisand wired Hepburn: "It's marvelous being in such distinguished company, but do you have to sing, too?"

Skeptics doubted that the two actresses had drawn the exact same number of votes, but Price, Waterhouse's Frank Johnson declared, "I assure you it was a precise tie. We always do at least one recount, but you can imagine all the recounts we did on that one."

Three days after the ceremony, the following letter was printed in the *Hollywood Reporter:*

Barbra Streisand was recently admitted to Academy membership. There was, from among 2,000 eligible voters, a dead heat for Best Actress. It is logical to assume that Miss Streisand voted for herself. Therefore, had she not recently become eligible to vote, she would have lost by one vote.

Henry Randolph

1969

"You don't mind if I turn on?"
—Jane Fonda

Oscar served as peacemaker between the New Hollywood and the Old Guard at the 1969 Academy Awards.

Producers no longer had to worry about the Motion Picture Association of America withholding its seal of approval when the MPAA established a new rating system that classified movies in terms of content. A G rating meant anyone could see the movie, M meant it had mature subject matter but anyone could still get in, R meant the under-seventeen-year-olds would have to drag along their parents, and X meant they couldn't get in at all. No sooner had the new ratings system been established than United Artists released the first big-studio movie with an X tag, John Schlesinger's *Midnight Cowboy*.

The British director portrayed New York as seen from the gutter, and the *New York Daily News'* Wanda Hale exclaimed, "Whew! It's shocking—a horror film but extremely well done." Across town, at the *New York Times*, Vincent Canby commented, "It's not a movie for the ages, but having seen it, you won't ever again feel detached as you walk down West 42nd Street, avoiding the eyes of the drifters, stepping around the little islands of hustlers and closing your nostrils to the smell of rancid griddles."

Everybody's Talking

The lines waiting to get in to see *Midnight Cowboy* in its exclusive run at an East Side theater were far from the squalor of Forty-second Street, though, and United Artists executives relaxed when they discovered that an X rating did not mean box-office disaster, even if half of the film-going audience was prohibited from buying tickets. On the contrary, Dustin Hoffman's turn as a consumptive con man named Ratso Rizzo had the same perverse fascination for audiences as the Lon Chaney and Boris Karloff roles of two generations earlier. "By following up the glamorous *Graduate* with the dreggiest dropout imaginable," wrote Andrew Sarris, "Dustin Hoffman has achieved his aim of not becoming the Andy Hardy of the '60s and '70s." This was confirmed by the *Wall Street Journal*, which reported that the actor was "solidly proving that his phenomenal success on the screen is not to be short-lived."

Providing what glamour there was in the film was blond and blue-eyed Jon Voight, thirty-one, as the title character, a hick male hustler whose dreams are shattered in the big city. Michael Sarrazin had been John Schlesinger's first choice for the role, but when contractual obligations forced him out, the director reluctantly went along with the unknown Voight. "He just didn't seem to me to be the physical image of the cowboy," the British director said. The *Los Angeles Times'* Charles Champlin welcomed Voight as "a major addition to the family of important American actors," and Schlesinger was pleased with him, too. "Now, I can't imagine anyone else playing the role," he said. *Midnight Cowboy* not only boosted the career of Voight, but propelled singer Harry Nilsson into the top ten on the pop charts with the film's theme song, "Everybody's Talking."

Crowing Over Rooster

To most Americans, the word "cowboy" still meant John Wayne, who was having his biggest hit in years in the G-rated adaptation of Charles Portis' bestseller *True Grit*. Just the year before, Wayne had angered most critics with his pro–Vietnam War film, *The Green Berets;* as *True Grit*'s Rooster Cogburn, an overweight U.S. marshal with an eyepatch, Wayne had the same critics eating out of his hand. "The richest performance of his long career," crowed the *New York Times*, and Dan Wakefield wrote in the *Atlantic Monthly*, "Whether or not John Wayne ever joins the ACLU, he is a hell of a good actor who obviously took great relish in the opportunity to play a meaty role." The *Los Angeles Herald-Examiner* put forth

Overleaf: *Best Actress nominee Jane Fonda flashes a message to her fans in the bleachers.*

"Mama said, 'Go, baby, that's the kind of story I wish I could have done.'"
—Liza Minnelli

that an Oscar would be "a fitting tribute to his 40th anniversary in show business," and *Time* ran a cover story on him as an American institution. *Life,* on the other hand, was amused by the polar opposition of the year's most celebrated actors—Wayne and Hoffman—and contrasted them in a cover story entitled "Dusty and the Duke." Inside, the tops of the pages featured photos of Wayne in color, under which were pictures of Hoffman in black-and-white.

Blood and Guts

As *Time* glorified Wayne on the cover, its film reviewer Jay Cocks jumped the gun and wrote an advance review of another western—Sam Peckinpah's *The Wild Bunch.* Although this film starred such established Hollywood names as William Holden and Ernest Borgnine, Peckinpah presented an R-rated version of the Wild West with the most graphic, slow-motion gun battles since *Bonnie and Clyde*. Cocks maintained that the death scenes "have the agonizing effect of prolonging the moment of impact, giving each death its own individual horror." It was too much horror for Judith Crist, who called the film exploitative and "undoubtedly the worst movie of 1969." Peckinpah answered his critics: "Well, killing a man isn't clean and quick and simple—it's bloody and awful. And maybe if enough people come to realize that shooting somebody isn't just fun and games, maybe we'll get somewhere."

More Butch

For those who thought *True Grit* too square and *The Wild Bunch* too gory, there was the M-rated *Butch Cassidy and the Sundance Kid*. *Life*'s Richard Schickel, who had called *The Wild Bunch* "a film that someday may emerge as one of the most important records of the mood of our times," denigrated director George Roy Hill's facetious western: "It is *The Wild Bunch* for people who couldn't stand *The Wild Bunch*. That is to say, *Butch Cassidy and the Sundance Kid* is funny instead of grim, elegiac instead of horrifying." That was all right by the *New York Daily News,* which referred to it as "a laugh-in, a fun western." It was also the year's number-one money-maker. The reason: Paul Newman and Robert Redford, whose glamour poster began to outsell Newman's by the end of the year. The sound track by Burt Bacharach also went gold, and B.J. Thomas' single "Raindrops Keep Fallin' on My Head" became both a chartbuster and a permanent fixture in the Muzak library. Katharine Ross played the film's nominal love interest.

Looking for America

As outstanding as *Butch Cassidy*'s box office was, the western was still an expensive production to begin with, so its return on investment couldn't compare to Columbia's bonanza on a $340,000 outlay on another buddy picture. Columbia had hoped to emulate the success of American International's motorcycle genre by luring Peter Fonda, the star of AIP's *The Wild Angels* and *The Trip,* into making a bike epic under their aegis. Fonda, son of Henry, collaborated with producer William Hayward, son of Margaret Sullavan and agent Leland Hayward, and Terry Southern, the author of *Candy*. Dennis Hopper, who had just played a bad guy in *True Grit*, costarred with Fonda and directed the picture—*Easy Rider,* the odyssey of two drug pushers touring the modern West on motorcycles. Columbia's advertising slogan hit a responsive chord: "They went looking for America . . . and couldn't find it anywhere."

They found plenty of money, though—$19 million in the United States alone. The Georgia State Senate condemned the movie because "heroin-selling, pot-smoking LSD-taking motorcycle riders are portrayed as the good guys while those folks who comprise a portion of the 'silent majority' are made to look like creeps in the hayloft." Yet Hollywood executives adored it because as Pauline Kael observed in *The New Yorker,* "The movie attracts a new kind of 'inside' audience,

"I've won an Award. Richard never has, you know."
—Elizabeth Taylor

whose members enjoy tuning in together to a whole complex of shared signals and attitudes." The signals included a rock score with artists like Jimi Hendrix and Steppenwolf and an improvisational tone—Peter Fonda claimed "easily ninety percent of the film was ad-libbed."

The best ad-libber in it was Jack Nicholson, another AIP veteran who stepped into a supporting role at the last minute when Rip Torn dropped out. After delivering a long monologue about how America had gone to pot, while smoking a joint, Nicholson had Long Island's *Newsday* insisting, "If Nicholson doesn't get this year's Best Supporting Actor Oscar, there's no meaning to the Awards at all." Columnist Earl Wilson revealed, "This lad Nicholson's pro-pot and has used LSD."

So Long, BonBon

Time called *Easy Rider* "one of the ten most important motion picture events of the decade," but Peter Fonda still had to share the cover of the magazine with his sister and father. In an article entitled "The Flying Fondas," *Time* predicted, "In the '70s, the daughter will dominate the screen far more successfully than the father did in the '30s, '40s, '50s or '60s." This was high praise for an actress best known for playing a sex kitten in her husband's soft-core fantasies, but Mrs. Roger Vadim smashed her image in one fell swoop with her portrait of a disillusioned dance-marathon contestant in *They Shoot Horses, Don't They?* The *Hollywood Reporter* adjudged that "Jane Fonda gives a dramatic performance that turns her own previous career as a sex bonbon upside down" and the *San Francisco Chronicle* agreed, calling the movie "a turning point in the career of Henry Fonda's daughter. Maybe Henry will now be identified as Jane's father."

Baum-Shell

Jane wasn't the only one to benefit from the success of *They Shoot Horses, Don't They?*, the movie that Michael Sarrazin made instead of *Midnight Cowboy*. Director Sydney Pollack earned praise from the *New York Times* for pulling off "a spectacle of awesome despair." Perhaps the film's biggest success story belonged to Gig Young. His former agent, Marty Baum, did not forget him when he became the head of ABC-Cinerama Films, insisting that Young and another ex-client, Red Buttons, be cast in the film. Fonda and producers Robert Chartoff and Irwin Winkler were "shocked and furious" over the casting of Young, whose image as a light comedian did not jibe with his role—the cynical master of ceremonies. But after a few looks at the rushes, Fonda apologized to Young personally. "Puffy-eyed, unshaven, reeking of stale liquor, sweat and cigarettes, Young has never looked older or worse or acted better," raved the *Hollywood Reporter*. Baum predicted Young was in for a Red Buttons–style Oscar victory; *Life* declared, "If he doesn't get an Academy Award for his portrayal of human devastation, there is no justice."

Spouse Wars

In addition to Nicholson, Young faced Oscar competition from another man trying to change his image—Mr. Barbra Streisand. While his wife was trapped in gigantic screen versions of Broadway musicals, Elliott Gould made a splash in Paul Mazursky's *Bob & Carol & Ted & Alice*, which *Playboy* proclaimed "a funny, abrasive, bitingly accurate satire of American sex and marriage." Columbia came up with another enticing ad line—"Consider the possibilities"—and the comedy about wife-swapping intrigued a lot of customers. Critics dwelled not on Bob & Carol, played by Robert Culp and Natalie Wood, but on the reluctant swingers portrayed by Gould and the ex-Mrs. Cary Grant, Dyan Cannon. Vincent Canby said Gould was "very funny as the sort of man who'd wear his stretch socks to a group assignation," and Pauline Kael remarked, "Playing the bitch . . . Dyan Cannon—who looks a bit like Lauren Bacall and a bit like Jeanne Moreau, but the wrong bits—

"The Oscars are some sort of masturbatory fantasy."
—Elliott Gould

is most effective (really brilliant), I think, just because you don't like her."

Cuckoo for Oscar

When the daughter of Judy Garland and Vincente Minnelli heard about the part of a misfit college girl named Pookie Adams in *The Sterile Cuckoo,* "I went after the role; I mean I really campaigned for it, like camping on the producer's doorstep until he finally agreed." She got the part, which included what *Look* magazine described as "the longest telephone scene since Luise Rainer in *The Great Ziegfeld.*" "Liza Minnelli gives a performance which is so funny, so moving, so perfectly crafted and realized that it should win her an Academy Award," gushed Tommy Thompson in *Life,* while Sidney Skolsky reported, "She is excited by the thought of an Oscar nomination. She had an Oscar for a doll for a while." Minnelli's only regret was that her mother died four months before the film opened. "Mama would have been so proud, but she did read the script and she told me, 'Go, baby, that's the kind of story I wish I could have done.' "

Discordant Sounds

Minnelli didn't sing in *The Sterile Cuckoo* and it was probably just as well—the post–*Sound of Music* road-show musicals were heading their studios into bankruptcy. Universal imported Broadway's Bob Fosse to direct Shirley MacLaine in *Sweet Charity,* but the choreographer asked, "How do you make a G-rated musical about a prostitute?" Answer: You can't—it flopped. Paramount risked an M rating for the $20 million *Paint Your Wagon* starring Lee Marvin, Clint Eastwood and Jean Seberg, and *Saturday Review* questioned the studio's wisdom: "Paramount seems to have made a special search for stars who can't sing." MGM was optimistic when Peter O'Toole won great reviews in the musical version of *Goodbye, Mr. Chips,* but Molly Haskell of the *Village Voice* warned, "While the size of *Paint Your Wagon* simply emphasizes its pointlessness, the elephantineness of *Goodbye, Mr. Chips* is monstrous." The most successful of the 1969 musicals was Fox's $20 million version of *Hello, Dolly!* with Barbra Streisand—it only lost $3 million.

More Support From N.Y.

The New York Film Critics decided to have a bigger effect on the Oscar race and inaugurated its own Supporting Acting Awards. The initial winners were Jack Nicholson for *Easy Rider* and Dyan Cannon for *Bob & Carol & Ted & Alice*. Cannon told reporters, "I've suffered from the stigma of my marriage long enough. The award is really important to me. It indicates that some people think of me as an actress rather than as an ex-wife." The critics also thought of Jane Fonda as more than Henry's daughter and she picked up the Best Actress plaque. Jon Voight of *Midnight Cowboy* was the scribes' Best Actor.

After the critics picked the French-Algerian production *Z* for Best Picture and Costa-Gavras Best Director, publicist Max Bercutt leaped into action. When the political thriller based on an actual assassination in Greece opened in Hollywood at the end of the year, Bercutt conducted a $10,000 ad campaign in the trades flaunting the Critics' Awards and Charles Champlin's tribute in the *Los Angeles Times*, "Film-making at its best." Costa-Gavras was available for interviews and said, "I made *Z* first because I am Greek-born. Secondly, because I felt I would like to do something. Some people sign petitions, others go to the streets—I do something as a filmmaker." Meanwhile, Bercutt was doing something as a publicist. "I screened the film for twenty people or one person," he said. "I told them a nomination for *Z* would make the Academy look important worldwide."

Anne of the Thousand Filets

Bercutt's efforts were small potatoes compared to Universal's tub-thumping for its 11th-hour release. *Anne of the Thousand Days* was based

"I want to leave because I want to go on."
—Goldie Hawn

on Maxwell Anderson's twenty-year-old play about Henry VIII and Anne Boleyn and starred Richard Burton and Genevieve Bujold, a Canadian-born actress best known for the French art-house hits *King of Hearts* and *La Guerre est Finie*. The bad reviews—*Time* sneered, "*Anne of the Thousand Days* seems to have been made for one person: the Queen of England"—did not deter the studio from launching a $20,000 ad campaign in the trades. The British film played just one week in Los Angeles in December "for Academy Award consideration," but Academy members who missed it then could see it at Universal's special screenings highlighted by the world's best concession stand—filet mignon and champagne were served at each showing. The next day, the studio sent out thank-you letters to the Academy members who had come.

The Nominations

Anne of the Thousand Days led the field with 10 nominations; *Hello, Dolly!* had seven, *Z* five. *Z* even made the Best Picture lineup, but, as practically every Hollywood columnist pointed out, it was also nominated for Best Foreign Film, where it was sure to win. *They Shoot Horses, Don't They?* was in second place with nine nominations but Best Picture was not among them. Both *Anne* and *Dolly* were Best Picture nominees without corresponding Director nods, so the big prize was up for grabs between the M-rated *Butch Cassidy and the Sundance Kid* and the X-rated *Midnight Cowboy*, both with seven nominations. Undaunted, *Hello, Dolly!*'s producers reminded Academy voters in ads in the trade papers that *Hello, Dolly!* was "the only film nominated for a Best Picture Oscar with a G-rating for entire family entertainment and the only Best Picture nominee made in Hollywood by Hollywood craftsmen."

Barbra Streisand was not nominated for Best Actress for *Hello, Dolly!* but Elliott Gould, from whom she was now separated, was a Supporting Actor nominee for *Bob & Carol & Ted & Alice*. "The Oscars are some sort of masturbatory fantasy," Gould commented after receiving the good news. "People think, an Academy Award—now if I get a parking ticket I don't have to pay it. I don't put the Award down, but at my sanest, I would rather have a good three-man basketball game than sit there in my monkey suit." Nevertheless, the star of the just-released *M*A*S*H* was willing to be a presenter on the show, as was Barbra Streisand.

Gould's costar Dyan Cannon would also be running into her ex on the show; the Academy announced that it was giving an Honorary Oscar to Cary Grant, although Grant almost refused to accept it because a woman was naming him in a paternity suit and he wanted to avoid publicity.

Cannon's Supporting Actress competition included TV star Goldie Hawn, best known for dancing in a bikini with jokes painted on her body on *Rowan and Martin's Laugh-In*. During a break from the TV show, Hawn brought her dumb-blonde act to the movies as Walter Matthau's mistress in the film version of the Broadway comedy *Cactus Flower*. The Associated Press had reported, "Some observers predict, indeed, that Goldie will become as big a star as the late Marilyn," and *Time* gasped, "Goldie can really act." Hawn announced that she would appear in only four more *Laugh-In* episodes. "I want to leave because I want to go on."

Why Me?

Not all of the Supporting Actress nominees had Hawn's ambition. Twenty-four-year-old Catherine Burns played a bullied, overweight girl in her first film, Frank Perry's *Last Summer*. *Life* profiled the nominee and asked if she was a late bloomer. "I'm not even a late bloomer at all," Burns protested, "I'm a non-bloomer. I'm a walking out-group. I don't fit in anywhere."

Susannah York, nominated for her supporting part in *They Shoot Horses, Don't They?*, did not take the news well, wailing to Earl Wilson, "I felt a ghastly sickening thud when I got nominated and tried to get un-nominated. It angered me to be

"I felt a ghastly sickening thud when I got nominated."
—Susannah York

nominated without being asked. I was actually appalled. I don't think I have much of a chance and I didn't think that much of myself in it."

Jane Turns On

Henry Fonda didn't think much of himself when he learned that his son was nominated for Best Original Screenplay for the ad-libbing in *Easy Rider* and his daughter was in the running for Best Actress. "How in the hell would you like to have been in this business as long as I and then have one of your kids win an Oscar before you did?" he asked.

Jane, however, was looking forward to the big event. "You can't imagine what winning an Oscar does for your career," she enthused. "I'd love to get it." The actress' campaign was unorthodox, however; her way of getting publicity was being arrested in a pro-Indian demonstration. Jane's efforts at traditional Oscar publicity backfired, too. When Rex Reed interviewed her, she pulled out her stash and pipe and inquired, "You don't mind if I turn on, do you?" Sidney Skolsky's response was "I don't think the Academy will let her turn on."

Time interviewed twenty-seven-year-old Genevieve Bujold in an article entitled "A Kitten Purring Beethoven." "The odds are heavily against me," said the Best Actress nominee, who was determined to get something out of the experience. "I like moments of destiny. But even if I lose, the moment of loss will stay with me until I die." Also resigned to defeat was Jean Simmons, a surprise nominee as an unhappily married woman in *The Happy Ending,* directed by her husband, Richard Brooks. "I don't expect to win," said Simmons.

Maggie Smith's Best Actress nomination for *The Prime of Miss Jean Brodie* had also been unexpected because the film had opened in March and then disappeared. Although her reviews were excellent—Vincent Canby wrote, "There hasn't been such a display of controlled, funny, elegant theatricality in years"—columnist Nathan Cohen of the *Toronto Daily Star* attributed Smith's nomination to her appearance onstage in Los Angeles with the National Theatre Company in *The Beaux' Stratagem* in January when the nominations were voted. "She received that adoration that had been reserved for movie stars in the old days," Cohen noted. "Los Angeles was wild about her."

The Separated Cuckoo

When Smith followed the company back to England, the spotlight fell on nominee Liza Minnelli, who faced trauma after trauma. First, she suffered lacerations that required twenty-two stitches after a motorcycle accident with actor Tony Bill. "It was a cuckoo accident," Minnelli shrugged. "We were only going fifteen miles an hour." Henry Fonda quipped that if the mishap had happened before the voting ended, Liza would have won hands down. Then, on the day of the Awards, the news broke that Minnelli had separated from her husband, singer Peter Allen. "We're still friends, though," the nominee insisted. There was more heartache when Nancy Sinatra, Jr., backed out of singing the nominated song from Minnelli's movie, "Come Saturday Morning," because she discovered that the show would be directed by Jack Haley, Jr., her ex-fiancé (and future husband of Liza Minnelli). The *Chicago Tribune* explained, "The emotional strain of working with him through rehearsals might have been too much for her, since, supposedly, she's still torching for him."

Liz Sticks Neck Out

Sentimentality made John Wayne the heavy favorite in the Best Actor contest, but some columnists predicted surprise wins for one of the *Midnight Cowboy* stars—Dustin Hoffman or Jon Voight. Hoffman wasn't planning to attend, but Voight was, although he privately admitted he was rooting for John Wayne. Then there was Peter O'Toole, receiving his fourth nomination, for *Goodbye, Mr. Chips,* and Richard Burton, notching his sixth nomination with *Anne of the Thousand Days*. Burton laughed and said, "Oh, I suppose thirty years from now, Peter O'Toole and I will still be appearing on talk shows plugging for our first Oscar."

Not if Mrs. Burton had anything to do about it. "We want Richard to win an Oscar," said Elizabeth Taylor. "I've won an Award. Richard never has, you know." As opposed to the 1966 Awards, when the couple did not show for their dual nominations for *Virginia Woolf*, the Burtons made plans to attend the ceremony this year. CBS interviewed Liz and Dick a few weeks beforehand and Taylor again reminded everyone that Burton had not won for *Virginia Woolf*, "which I consider his greatest performance because the weak character is so much unlike him." Taylor also volunteered to present the Best Picture Award, her first Oscar appearance since her victory at the 1960 Awards. And, as if her presence wasn't enough, Liz promised to wear the $1.5 million diamond necklace that Burton had given her—the most publicized jewel since the Hope Diamond.

In spite of Taylor's politicking, director Howard Hawks threw a good-luck party for John Wayne the day he left the Tucson set of his latest western, *Rio Lobo*. "Don't you dare come back if you lose!" Hawks admonished his star. Wayne shot back, "I just may not come back if I win!"

The Big Night

The first star to show up was Mickey Rooney, who clocked in at 5:25. He was soon followed by nominee Gig Young, who came stag. Liza Minnelli came with her father and told Army Archerd, "My stitches were covered by the makeup man who gives me scars on the set of my new movie, *Tell Me That You Love Me, Junie Moon*." Jane Fonda arrived with Roger Vadim and, when she received a loud roar of approval from the bleacher fans, raised a fist and shouted, "Right on!"

Daily Variety noted that *Easy Rider*'s Dennis Hopper "was modishly resplendent in a velvet double-breasted tux and white ten-gallon hat. Presumably he removed the Stetson in the theater, but certainly not in the lobby. That would be you know—uncool." On Hopper's arm was his new wife, Michelle Phillips. John Wayne's *True Grit* costar, singer Glen Campbell, stood nearby in a chocolate-brown tuxedo and apache tie.

John Wayne caused the most commotion—he arrived with his wife and the fans wouldn't stop screaming, although one picket held a sign that read JOHN WAYNE IS A RACIST. A few demonstrators protested that only three black musicians were in the show's orchestra. Down the street, eighty pickets held placards criticizing the nominations of *The Wild Bunch* and *Butch Cassidy and the Sundance Kid* because they portrayed Latinos as "inferior, incompetent, worthless and ignorant." The *Hollywood Reporter* claimed that this last group became bored after a while, "perhaps taking interest in the arrival of Raquel Welch, the girl least likely to be mistaken for the Frito Bandito."

The TV show began with footage of an earlier generation of stars—Norma Shearer, Jean Harlow, Greta Garbo, Errol Flynn and Tony Martin—attending premieres, and then the focus switched to the nominees arriving that night. The cameras cut to the stage set, where the head of Genevieve Bujold as Anne Boleyn hung from above, along with pictures of the other nominees.

Awards Ceremony

APRIL 7, 1970, 7:00 P.M.
THE DOROTHY CHANDLER PAVILION, LOS ANGELES

Your Hosts:
THE FRIENDS OF OSCAR: CLAUDIA CARDINALE, ELLIOTT GOULD, MYRNA LOY, BARBARA MCNAIR, JON VOIGHT, FRED ASTAIRE, ELIZABETH TAYLOR, ALI MACGRAW, CLIFF ROBERTSON, KATHARINE ROSS, JAMES EARL JONES, CANDICE BERGEN, RAQUEL WELCH, CLINT EASTWOOD, JOHN WAYNE, BOB HOPE
Televised over ABC

Presenters

Sound .... Candice Bergen and Elliott Gould
Short Subjects ...... Myrna Loy and Cliff Robertson
Cinematography .... John Wayne
Film Editing .... Claudia Cardinale and James Earl Jones
Special Visual Effects .... Raquel Welch
Jean Hersholt Humanitarian Award .... Bob Hope
Scoring of a Musical Picture .... Elmer Bernstein and Shani Wallis
Original Score .... Barbara McNair and Cliff Robertson
Documentary Awards .... Fred Astaire and Bob Hope
Art Direction .... Myrna Loy and Jon Voight
Costume Design .... Candice Bergen
Honorary Award to Cary Grant .... Frank Sinatra
Foreign Film .... Claudia Cardinale and Clint Eastwood
Supporting Actor .... Katharine Ross
Supporting Actress .... Fred Astaire
Song .... Candice Bergen
Adapted Screenplay .... Katharine Ross and Jon Voight
Original Screenplay .... James Earl Jones and Ali MacGraw
Director .... Myrna Loy
Actor .... Barbra Streisand
Actress .... Cliff Robertson
Picture .... Elizabeth Taylor

Performers of Nominated Songs

"Come Saturday Morning" .... The Sandpipers
"Jean" .... Lou Rawls
"Raindrops Keep Fallin' on My Head ... B.J. Thomas
"True Grit" .... Glen Campbell
"What Are You Doing the Rest of Your Life? .... Michel Legrand

"How in the hell would you like to have been in this business as long as I and then have one of your kids win an Oscar before you do?"
—Henry Fonda

The ten heads pulled away as Academy President Gregory Peck walked onstage and announced, "I think you're about to see the most star-studded, surprise-packed Academy show of them all." The first surprise was that the FCC had a new rule requiring the Academy to explain the voting system on the air, just like any other contest. So Gregory Peck explained the rules, and the Price, Waterhouse representative took his traditional bow. "He holds the envelopes that will mean so much to so few," Peck said.

Instead of last year's ten "Friends of Oscar" there were sixteen this year. They all paraded out—John Wayne got the loudest applause—and the final one was described as "Everybody's Friend"—Bob Hope. The comedian didn't even have to open his mouth to get his first laugh: he was wearing a Rooster Cogburn eyepatch. "You remember me," Hope said, "Moshe." He took off the eyepatch and commented, "Welcome to the Academy Awards . . . or as it's known at my house, Mission Impossible . . . I know Liz Taylor's here, I saw a Brink's truck parked outside." The camera saw Richard Burton, wearing a gold vest, chuckling with the audience. "*The Sterile Cuckoo*—I thought that was the life of Tiny Tim," Hope cracked. "Don't tell Goldie Hawn, she thinks it's another taping of *Laugh-In*. This is not an Academy Awards, ladies and gentlemen, it's a freak-out."

Cliff Robertson appeared and gave the acceptance speech that Robert Aldrich prevented him from giving the previous year. "My apologies," Robertson said, "I respectfully dedicate my award to Charly." Then he brought on Glen Campbell to sing "True Grit." When Campbell was finished, out came John Wayne, who declared, "I'm an American movie actor. I work with my clothes on." There was some applause, then Wayne continued, "I have to. Horses are rough on your legs and your elsewheres." The Duke gave the Cinematography Award and commented, "It's a real, deep deep-down pleasure to read the list of men." The winning man was Conrad Hall for *Butch Cassidy and the Sundance Kid*, who saluted the film's leading lady. "I'd like to thank Katharine," her fiancé said. "She wanted me to have it."

Raquel Welch stepped out and informed, "I'm here for Special Visual Effects." The audience snickered. "There are two of them," Raquel went on, and the audience laughed. Then Welch gave the Oscar to *Marooned*, an outer-space thriller.

For the second year in a row, the Academy gave the Jean Hersholt Humanitarian Award to someone who had entertained troops in Vietnam. Bob Hope was back, toasting George Jessel: "The Award is for his consistent devotion to the cause of easing the pain and burdens of American servicemen in combat areas and hospitals throughout the world." Hope held Jessel's hand while he made the presentation, and Jessel responded, "For a minute, I thought I was dead. I've waited a long time, but it shows that God's delay is not God's denial."

When *Hello, Dolly!* won for Scoring of a Musical, Lionel Newman said of his cowinner, "Lennie Hayton couldn't make it tonight, but I'm sure he's just as gassed as I am. Thanks to Ernest Lehman for being so goddam beautifully difficult and the Fox Sound Department and the wonderful orchestra. I don't know what the hell I'm saying . . ."

Frank Sinatra presented the Honorary Oscar to Cary Grant, and Sammy Davis, Jr., led the standing ovation. "You're applauding my stamina," Grant replied. Then the actor who had retired in 1966 recited his speech:

> *You know, I may never look at this without remembering the quiet patience of the directors who were so kind to me, who were kind enough to put up with me more than once—some of them even three or four times. There were Howard Hawks, Alfred Hitchcock, the late Leo McCarey, George Stevens, George Cukor and Stanley Donen. And all the writers . . . Philip Barry, Dore Schary, Bob Sherwood, Ben Hecht, dear Clifford*

"This is not an Academy Awards, ladies and gentlemen, it's a freak-out."
—Bob Hope

> *Odets, Sidney Sheldon, and more recently Stanley Shapiro and Peter Stone. Well, I trust they and all the other directors, writers and producers, and leading women, have all forgiven me what I didn't know.*
>
> *I realize it's conventional and usual to praise one's fellow workers on these occasions . . . but why not? Ours is a collaborative medium; we all need each other!*

Grant concluded: "There's an even more glorious era right around the corner."

Best Foreign Film Award presenters Claudia Cardinale and Clint Eastwood proved that the columnists had been correct—*Z* won Best Foreign Film. The grateful producer said, "With this award, you help us."

Conrad Hall's fiancé, Katharine Ross, named the Best Supporting Actor—Gig Young for *They Shoot Horses, Don't They?* There was a shot of a happy Jane Fonda as Young ran to the stage. "I'm really quite speechless," the winner confessed. "In my heart, I have a special thanks—Mr. Martin Baum, who believed in me when no one else did." Then Fred Astaire revealed the Best Supporting Actress. Dyan Cannon, Cathy Burns, and *Midnight Cowboy*'s Sylvia Miles were in the audience, but the winner was not—Goldie Hawn for *Cactus Flower*. Raquel Welch returned to say, "Goldie's in England shooting a film," and grabbed the Oscar.

Candice Bergen, in a poncho, gave the Best Song Award to "Raindrops Keep Fallin' on My Head." Burt Bacharach, who had already won the Best Score Oscar, brought that statuette with him when he visited the podium for a second time. "It's so special," the double winner sighed. "Two of them . . . they'll be on our breakfast table tomorrow . . . our little girl—she's only four—she'll look at them and know they're special."

Katharine Ross and Jon Voight presented the Adapted Screenplay Award to the man who had written Voight's movie, Waldo Salt, whose daughter Voight was currently dating. Waldo hugged Jon and said, "I'd like to thank all the beautiful people who helped make it and, even more, all the beautiful people who will see it. May their numbers increase."

James Earl Jones, in Hollywood shooting *The Great White Hope*, and Ali MacGraw, wearing pants and fringe, revealed that the ad-libbing in *Easy Rider* had lost the Original Screenplay Award to William Goldman's script for *Butch Cassidy and the Sundance Kid*. Katharine Ross was the proxy and she accepted for "Bill." Myrna Loy came out to present Best Director, and again the winner was absent. Jon Voight accepted for *Midnight Cowboy*'s John Schlesinger. "John's shooting his next picture, *Sunday, Bloody Sunday*," Voight explained. "I think he's on the phone in the back."

The Best Actor Award was given by Barbra Streisand, wearing what *Women's Wear Daily*'s Chauncey Howell called "a nice pink bar-mitzvah-mother dress" with a matching pillbox hat. The first thing Streisand did was ask for the envelope, "Just in case I forget to ask for it later." She read the contents of the envelope, held it against her chest and laughed, "I'm not going to tell you." But she did—John Wayne for *True Grit*. The audience hollered like cowpokes at a roundup. The Duke whispered into Streisand's ear "Beginner's luck." Then Wayne looked at the audience and said, "Wow. If I had known that, I would have put that eyepatch on thirty-five years earlier!"

Cliff Robertson was in charge of the Best Actress Award. All the nominees were there expect for one. "The name is Maggie Smith for *The Prime of Miss Jean Brodie*." Smith was the absent one, and her award was accepted by an unidentified Alice Ghostley, who had costarred with Smith on Broadway in *New Faces of 1956*.

It was time for Elizabeth Taylor. Deeply tanned, Mrs. Burton wore an Edith Head dress with a décolletage that showcased the necklace. The rock was nevertheless upstaged by Liz herself as she unsuccessfully tried to mask her disappointment that Richard had lost again.

"Shut up, Bob Hope."
—Shirley MacLaine

Reading the Best Picture nominations, Taylor finally smiled when she handed the Oscar to Jerome Hellman, the producer of *Midnight Cowboy*.

Bob Hope returned to close the proceedings. "How 'bout this show. Wasn't it a goody, huh?" the comedian asked, consoling the losers. "There's a bright side to all of this. Remember, you can still run for governor." Hope then turned serious: "The troubled kooky characters that have peopled the screen are not examples to emulate but to learn from and try to understand and hopefully perhaps contrive help for . . . perhaps a time will come when all the fighting will be for a place in line outside the theater or a better seat inside."

Aftermath

"It's ironic that I got the Oscar for a role that was the easiest of my career," John Wayne said backstage. "I just hippity-hopped through it." Wayne was interviewed extensively by the reporter from the *Oklahoma City Oklahoman* because he was one of the few big winners the journalist felt free to cover. His paper had a policy of not publicizing X-rated movies. "I'm glad *Midnight Cowboy* won," the reporter said, "but, hell, I won't even be able to write about it."

Bob Hope stood around joking, "The show ran two hours, twenty minutes—which is the longest any show has run on ABC without being canceled." Gregory Peck was celebrating Maggie Smith's victory, which Sidney Skolsky described as the biggest upset since Loretta Young's win in 1947. "This is great," Peck rejoiced. "Now you can see it's not rigged." Meanwhile, in London, reporters swarmed the theater where Smith was opening in the London run of *The Beaux' Stratagem*. "I'm very surprised and very delighted," the winner said. "Does it make you nervous?" a reporter asked. "Who isn't nervous on opening night?" Smith retorted. In another part of town, Goldie Hawn also confessed surprise when she got the call, followed by flowers from her current costar, Peter Sellers.

When John Wayne left the Governors' Ball, a fan approached him for an autograph. "Any other night but tonight," the winner said. "This is my night to howl, and I couldn't see the paper anyway." Army Archerd reported that Wayne was feted until 4 A.M. by Mr. and Mrs. Richard Burton in their Beverly Hills Hotel bungalow. The Burtons also found time to send a basket of flowers to winner Gig Young with the note "Congratulations, baby. Elizabeth and Richard." Young responded, "Elizabeth and Richard? I don't know any Elizabeth and Richard. Why don't people sign their last names?"

Time magazine covered the ceremonies as seen at a Hollywood party thrown by Gwen Davis, the author of *The Pretenders*. Lee Marvin and Shirley MacLaine were among the guests. Goldie Hawn's victory was labeled "a joke," by the partygoers, but everyone was open-mouthed when Maggie Smith won. "Gee, they voted for talent," someone finally said. There were also derisive sounds when John Wayne was crowned, but Shirley MacLaine commented, "Tell 'em about America, John!" By the time Bob Hope was making his concluding lecture, Shirley yelled, "Shut up, Bob Hope," and the hostess turned off the TV set.

Henry Fonda was upset at Peter's collaborator, Dennis Hopper. "Any man who insists on wearing his cowboy hat to the Academy Awards and keeps it on at the dinner table afterwards ought to be spanked," Fonda said. And, according to columnist Shirley Eder, Edgar and Frances Bergen "were so furious at the way Candy was dressed they wouldn't speak to her!" Fashion critic Kitty Johnson likened Candy's Arnold Scassi poncho to "a particularly ugly tablecloth from a greasy spoon diner." Frances Bergen moaned, "She didn't have to be a presenter, but once she did, she should have conformed and worn something elegant." Army Archerd took *Hello, Dolly!*'s Lionel Newman to task: "Lionel Newman didn't disappoint his many pals in the industry who know his usual, salty language—but on Oscar night, Lionel?"

The only discouraging word that John Wayne heard came from the author of *True Grit,* Charles Portis. "He sent me a letter. Inside was a picture of some fat slob of a frontier sheriff with a big drooping mustache, and all he said in the letter was 'This is Rooster Cogburn,'" the Oscar winner said. "You know, it gave me a real letdown that I carry around to this day."

Wayne felt better when he received a telephone call from President Richard Nixon, who said, "The whole family watched the Awards and I just want to tell you I'm proud of you—on the screen and off." Wayne got another thrill when he returned to Tucson and the *Rio Lobo* set: the entire cast and crew, including his horse, greeted him wearing eyepatches.

1970

"I wouldn't like to think that I couldn't go to the launderette when I felt like it."
—Glenda Jackson

Just as the Academy Awards were being written off as obsolete, along came George C. Scott to make them front-page news again.

As the 1970s began, the only mogul still heading a studio was Fox's sixty-eight-year-old Darryl F. Zanuck—and he spent the year hanging on for dear life at the company he had founded thirty-five years earlier. Conglomerates were running movie companies now and they wanted cheap merchandise that turned a fast profit—*Easy Rider* was their idea of perfect product. As a result, Hollywood cranked out a rash of "anti-Establishment" movies aimed at the 18–30 market, leading Pauline Kael to comment, "Many of the best recent American movies leave you feeling there's nothing to do but get stoned and die . . ."

A lot of these youth movies starred Elliott Gould, who made the cover of *Time* as "A Star for an Uptight Age." He also made the list of 1970's top box-office stars, coming in at number five; Barbra Streisand was number nine. Gould's biggest success was Fox's *M*A*S*H*, a black comedy set in a surgical unit during the Korean War. Hollywood veteran and Oscar-winner Ring Lardner, Jr., wrote the screenplay and the directing reins fell into the hands of one Robert Altman, whose previous work was primarily in television. In addition to Gould, Altman rounded up a cast of little-known actors—Donald Sutherland, Sally Kellerman, Robert Duvall—and set them loose to improvise. Both the critics and audiences immediately took the irreverent, free-form film to their hearts. *Life* raved, "Its humor is not, as they say, in good taste. War is not in good taste either." The magazine added, "*M*A*S*H* is what the new freedom of the screen is all about." The *New York Times* marveled that it was "the first major American movie openly to ridicule belief in God."

In London, veteran Hollywood producer Hal Wallis hands the Oscar to Best Actress winner Glenda Jackson, who didn't dress for the occasion.

When inteviewers asked about his unheard-of use of overlapping dialogue, Altman shrugged. "I've been getting fired for doing it for the last fifteen years. Jack Warner fired me off a picture called *Countdown* because I had two actors talking at the same time."

Hawks and Doves

Darryl Zanuck always had a soft spot for war movies, and he called *M*A*S*H* "the funniest comedy ever made." Fox's *Patton*, however, released a few weeks after *M*A*S*H*, was more in keeping with the mogul's traditional view of the military. Producer Frank McCarthy, a retired brigadier general, had been hustling the biography of General George S. Patton for nearly two decades before Zanuck finally took him up on the idea. In 1965, McCarthy had commissioned a screenplay from twenty-six-year-old UCLA graduate Francis Ford Coppola, which the producer found "poetic, marvelous and rather shapeless." After a writer named Edmund H. North whipped the script into shape, it came time to cast the title role.

Burt Lancaster said no. So did Robert Mitchum. And Lee Marvin and Rod Steiger. Finally, McCarthy turned to forty-three-year-old George C. Scott, who said okay. Once filming started, McCarthy began to wonder if he had made the right choice. Scott constantly argued with him over the interpretation of Patton's character and the actor told the *London Sunday Times*, "It's an inadequate script and it's very difficult for me. Patton was misunderstood contemporaneously and he's misunderstood here—and I'm ashamed of being a part of it."

To attract the youth audience, Fox decided to label the movie *Patton: Salute to a Rebel,* and the film's poster read, "Patton was a rebel before it became fashionable. He rebelled against the Establishment—and its ideas of warfare." The subtitle and the campaign were scrapped the moment the studio realized the film didn't need them—even the kids were coming to see George C. Scott's critically acclaimed performance. "Superpatriots may

"Patton was misunderstood contemporaneously and he's misunderstood here—and I'm ashamed of being a part of it."
—George C. Scott

find their hero and antiwar viewers can point to the general as a vain glory seeker," was how *Cue* explained the film's widespread appeal. Richard Nixon made it clear which view he held: he screened *Patton* twice before ordering the invasion of Cambodia, leading *Life* to suggest that the President view *Snow White and the Seven Dwarfs* before making any other foreign-policy decisions.

Dean Martin Takes up Flying

Having turned down *Patton,* Burt Lancaster elected to be one of the stars in Ross Hunter's all-star *Airport,* a $10 million adaptation of an Arthur Hailey bestseller. Other stars on board included Dean Martin, Jean Seberg, Jacqueline Bisset, Van Heflin, and Helen Hayes, as a stowaway. In Hollywood, Joyce Haber declared, "The fabled Helen Hayes is more fabulous than ever," but in New York, Pauline Kael warned that "Helen Hayes does her lovable-old-trouper pixie act." As for the picture itself, one of the kindest things said about it was the *Washington Post*'s contention that "it may have an irresistible if dumbfounding, sort of popular appeal; even people who know it's lousy might be looking forward to it as a complacent evening of auld lang syne." *Airport* went on to become the highest-grossing Universal film yet.

The Intellectual's Raquel Welch

Airport did win the highest rating—four stars—from the *New York Daily News,* but the paper was equally generous with Ken Russell's sexually charged adaptation of D.H. Lawrence's *Women in Love,* calling it "a visual stunner and very likely the most sensuous film ever made." The advance word on the British film was that it contained a nude wrestling scene between 1968 Best Actor nominee Alan Bates and Oliver Reed, but when the movie was unveiled, talk centered on the unknown who played Gudrun, thirty-three-year-old Glenda Jackson. *Variety* said, "The girl's no stunner in the looks department, but she has punch and intelligence which give a sharp edge to all her scenes," and a publicist dubbed her "the intellectual's Raquel Welch."

When the *Christian Science Monitor* asked Jackson what she thought of her new fame, she responded, "It's ridiculous, when you think how hard I'm working right now, when for so many years nobody even knew I existed. But I don't want to wake up one morning and find myself stuck in the hermetically sealed, centrally heated, showbiz world, which can destroy you. I wouldn't like to think that I couldn't go to the launderette when I felt like it." On the other hand, Jackson confessed she drew her inspiration from Hollywood: "Bette Davis and Joan Crawford are my idols and I would love to meet them."

A Frog in Her Throat

Twenty-five-year-old Carrie Snodgress was also uncomfortable with overnight success. She made her debut in *Diary of a Mad Housewife,* playing a married Manhattanite who has an affair with Frank Langella. The critics proclaimed her a new talent—and voice. "Carrie Snodgress has charmingly bewildered or ironic gazes at her command, and a voice that harbors not just one frog but a whole family of batrachians to delicious effect," chortled John Simon, while *Newsweek* insisted she had "the husky gravel voice of a latter-day June Allyson." The Hollywood Foreign Press Association named her "Newcomer of the Year" and the *Hollywood Reporter* rumored that Ross Hunter was thinking of following *Airport* with a biography of Zelda Fitzgerald starring Carrie Snodgress.

But the dream was coming true a little fast for Snodgress, who didn't enjoy being one of the few contract actresses left at Universal. She told Rex Reed that the studio "warned me, don't talk about politics, don't talk about James Earl Jones—I used to go out with him but that was over five months ago and they're still uptight about it—don't criticize these creeps in the White House or support Jane Fonda or anything." The actress who had re-

"If George C. Scott wins, I'll resign from the Academy."
—Ross Hunter

fused to change her name was not about to change her life, either. "If being in this business depends on playing games, I'll get out of it," Snodgress maintained, adding that she shared one of Glenda Jackson's convictions: "I still go to the laundromat with my wash."

Black is Beautiful

Snodgress' ex-escort, James Earl Jones, was also doing well in movies. After springing to prominence on Broadway in *The Great White Hope,* Jones came to Hollywood for the movie version of the boxing drama. *Time* remarked, "In Jones' eight-ounce gloves, black is beautiful, black is ugly, black is violent, black is gentle, black is self-deceit, black is truth—in brief, black is a man, and a man is the world. It is the kind of pounding, feinting, bloody unbowing portrayal that insures an Academy Award nomination—and possibly the prize itself." Jones was invited to play *Othello* in Los Angeles around Academy Award time, and he accepted, but the actor had reservations about making the big time. "You might say I'm really the happiest in shoestring budgets somewhere off Broadway." His *The Great White Hope* costar, thirty-one-year-old Jane Alexander, felt the same way. After working in repertory in Washington, D.C., Alexander had tagged along with the play from off-off Broadway to Broadway to Hollywood. "The way my career has gone is all very exciting and a great surprise, but having had a go at being a film star really hasn't made any changes in me," she said, and she wasn't kidding. As soon as the filming was over, Alexander headed for a repertory theater in Connecticut.

The High and the Mighty

A new film star with no intention of leaving Hollywood was Jack Nicholson. After appearing in his first big-budget movie, the lavish Barbra Streisand musical *On a Clear Day You Can See Forever,* Nicholson got together with a group of friends to make a "relevant" picture about alienation, *Five Easy Pieces.* "Good vibrations are half the success of doing anything," said the film's director, Bob Rafelson, who had coproduced *Easy Rider.* "The physical ordeal of making a movie is enormous, so why not cut down on the hassle and hang out with pals?" Nicholson told *Time* about one of the ordeals of this particular movie: "We all took a vow to stay off pot. I'm the only person who stuck to it."

"A very modern film," mused Andrew Sarris when *Five Easy Pieces* premiered at the New York Film Festival, "elliptical, absurdist, harshly humorous, convulsively lyrical." The *New York Times* wrote that Nicholson's "wonderfully agile characterization of the bedeviled hero communicates at once a profound intimacy with psychic pain and a vivid appreciation for the absurd in life and in himself." *Variety* singled out Karen Black, last seen tripping with Peter Fonda in *Easy Rider,* as Nicholson's girlfriend, "one of those rare actresses who's not afraid to let herself look ugly if it suits the scene."

A Lean Investment

David Lean's $13.6 million *Ryan's Daughter* was MGM's last-ditch effort to have a reserved-seat-only hit on the order of Lean's *Doctor Zhivago.* Oscar-winner Robert Bolt wrote the title role for Mrs. Bolt, twenty-nine-year-old Sarah Miles. Unlike the earlier sweeping Lean epics, this one was primarily a love triangle, set against the Irish countryside, between Miles and Robert Mitchum, as her older husband, and Christopher Jones, as a young British officer. Mrs. Bolt garnered good reviews, as did John Mills in a supporting role as a mute village idiot, but Pauline Kael scoffed, "This is the kind of thing that gets people Academy Awards because the acting is so conspicuous." The crowds that had loved *Doctor Zhivago* didn't come to this one, but an investment is an investment and MGM placed twenty Oscar ads for *Ryan's Daughter* in the trade papers.

"Nothing would disgust me more morally than receiving an Oscar. I wouldn't have it in my home."
—Luis Buñuel

Love Means Big Box Office

When *Ryan's Daughter* failed to set the world on fire, industry analysts concluded that love stories were out of style. But then, at Christmas, came what *Time* declared "a phenomenon," adding, "There has been nothing like it in a generation." "It" was a movie starring the wife of the executive vice-president of Paramount. Mrs. Robert Evans was a top model who had just made a name for herself in movies by playing Philip Roth's Jewish princess Brenda Patinkin in *Goodbye, Columbus*. Looking for a second vehicle, Ali MacGraw came across a screenplay by a friend of hers from college. Every studio in town had already rejected the manuscript, but it made MacGraw cry. Evans went along with his wife and funded the project because "I thought it might be a good, small, profitable trend-bucker away from all those 'now' movies I hated." After three months, Evans found a willing director, and hired an actor from TV named Ryan O'Neal to play the leading man.

In the meantime, the screenwriter, a thirty-three-year-old associate professor at Yale named Erich Segal, turned the script into a book—an easy-to-read book. "I cut it to read in two hours," Segal explained, "because I wanted it to be a one-sitting experience like a movie." The book, entitled simply *Love Story,* zoomed to the top of the bestseller list and stayed there. Suddenly, Paramount had the most eagerly awaited picture of the year.

Love Story proved to be critic-proof. Although Judith Crist complained, "Its venality and infantilism make us reach for the barf bag instead of the Kleenex," the lines at the box office went all the way around city blocks. The moral of the story—"Love means never having to say you're sorry"—started a greeting-card avalanche and composer Francis Lai's "Theme from Love Story" became a hit record the moment Andy Williams was given lyrics to sing along. The movie made money so fast, it joined *Gone With the Wind* and *The Sound of Music* at the top of the all-time box-office champions list.

Preppies

As the film's tragic preppie, Oliver Barrett IV, Ryan O'Neal was crowned by the *New York Daily News* as "this year's Golden Boy." But the *New York Times* took a closer look: "You would think that this kid who played sweet Rodney Harrington in 519 of *Peyton Place*'s 540 TV episodes and is now reducing an entire nation to tears would at least come equipped with the right Ivy League credentials. You would be mistaken. Furthermore, not only isn't he from the East, he isn't even a kid. Ryan O'Neal has been married twice, has three children, and will be 30 years old on April 20. And he has a prison record." When interviewers came a-calling, O'Neal expanded on his acting technique: "I didn't worry a lot about whether I was preparing enough for the part. I'm not into study and research much. I just thought about it as a story about a man and a woman and I made sure I looked right. You know, the right scarf, the right sweater."

Golden Boy was a cipher next to his leading lady. Joyce Haber got so carried away she wrote, "She's the biggest female star since Marilyn Monroe." But Ali MacGraw, thirty, hadn't convinced everyone she was a Radcliffe student and many critics pointed out her acting limitations. Molly Haskell snickered, "Although she has mastered one effective expression—a smirking smile with eyes lowered—her shallowness subverts any speech longer than an expletive." But the Hollywood press defended the new star, and James Bacon said, "Ali is probably the movies' best instinctive actress since Elizabeth Taylor."

MacGraw certainly had the trappings of stardom—she started a fashion craze with her trademark knit hats and she put her prints in cement at Grauman's Chinese. *Time* couldn't resist making her its cover girl, and the headline read "The Return to Romance." Inside, the copy stated, "She

"I'm voting for myself."
—Jack Nicholson

is today's closest approximation of the old-style star, with the Beverly Hills mansion, the burgeoning career, the marriage to the industry, and the chance to become very, very rich." MacGraw's response to it all: "I think it's nice so many people are relating one to one and responding to *Love Story* because two people care about each other."

Chief Party Boy

Love Story didn't exist as far as the New York Film Critics Circle was concerned. The Gotham crowd was most impressed with *Five Easy Pieces,* which won Best Picture, Best Director for Bob Rafelson, and Best Supporting Actress for Karen Black. The critics' Best Supporting Actor Award winner was a seventy-one-year-old Native American named Chief Dan George, for *Little Big Man.* According to the *Los Angeles Times,* George "marched right into Sardi's in his celebration robes and had a ball." So did the Best Actress winner, Glenda Jackson, who received her citation from none other than Bette Davis. "Miss Davis should have this award in perpetuity," the recipient said. Best Actor victor George C. Scott was not present, but his wife, Colleen Dewhurst, accepted for him, commenting, "George thinks this is the only film award worth having."

Dewhurst's remark made producer Frank McCarthy nervous; he didn't want her husband to ruin *Patton*'s Oscar chances by refusing a nomination again—Scott had turned down a Supporting Actor nod in 1961. In contrast, the press eagerly awaited a refusal, if only to put some excitement in the Oscar race—Scott had won every film award there was. Five days before the nominations were to be announced, columnist Hank Grant flashed a bulletin: "According to a wire service report outta Spain yesterday morn, George C. Scott has done it again—announced he won't accept an Oscar if he wins (for *Patton*) because he doesn't like the way the Awards are handled. This will make Scott a big hero with provincial pals in the East whose prime pastime is putting down Hollywood. But here, he's admired only for his timing in making his blast after the Oscar nominations were closed Friday." Scott told reporters, "The ceremonies are a two-hour meat parade, a public display with contrived suspense for economic reasons."

The Nominations

George C. Scott *was* nominated for Best Actor, but the Academy did not send him a congratulatory telegram. *Five Easy Pieces* was nominated for four Oscars, including Best Picture, but not Best Director. *Patton* and *Airport* tied with ten nominations each. *Love Story* was nominated for seven Oscars, and *M*A*S*H* for five. The *Los Angeles Herald-Examiner* commented, "What is visible in the nominations is an industry in flux, and probably in confusion."

What really got the cynics going were those ten nominations for *Airport*. *Time* jeered, "Nominations included the usual number of mind-boggling mediocrities: *Airport,* for instance . . . To Hollywood, quality and high budgets are often synonymous." When a reporter rushed the good news to *Airport* star Burt Lancaster, he responded, "I don't know why it was nominated. It's the biggest piece of junk ever made."

Imitation of Life

Of the ten Oscars *Airport* was up for, producer Ross Hunter most wanted a Best Supporting Actress Award for Helen Hayes. The problem was that another one of *Airport*'s nominations was for Maureen Stapleton, also in the Best Supporting Actress category. "I called on Maureen before I left New York and expressed my feelings of guilt for throwing a luncheon at the Bistro for Helen Hayes," the producer assured the *Herald-Examiner,* "and she said I could go ahead and plug for a tie." Three days after the Bistro party, Hunter escorted Hayes to a tribute to Oscar Hammerstein II at USC; "Miss Hayes received deafening applause

"The Academy is only two or three years behind the critics."
—Gregory Peck

on her appearance," reported Hank Grant. The very next evening, Miss Hayes was at a party at the Beverly Hills Hotel thrown by the Actors' Fund, which gave her a citation for her "magnificent devotion to all causes which serve mankind." Miss Hayes returned the compliment by reading the "quality of mercy" speech from *The Merchant of Venice:* "It was one of the evening's most solemn moments and was received with mute respect," confirmed *Daily Variety*. For all this ballyhoo, Hayes wasn't even planning to go to the ceremonies—she had already promised Catholic University that she would perform *Long Day's Journey Into Night* on that date.

Hayes' Oscar competition included *M*A*S*H*'s "Hot Lips," Sally Kellerman, thirty-two, who was definitely going to be there on Oscar night. "All those years of watching it on TV," she exclaimed, "and now I actually get to go." Not only that, she was going to present an Oscar and sing a nominated song. While waiting for Oscar, Kellerman posed for five national magazine layouts, including one for Alfred Eisenstadt for *Life*. Lucille Ball went on the *Merv Griffin Show* and announced, "Sally is the closest thing to Garbo I've seen in years." Kellerman didn't let her newfound fame get completely out of hand, though—she turned down an offer by a cosmetic company to endorse "Hot Lips" lipstick.

Somebody's Baby

Best Actress nominee Sarah Miles was also looking forward to the big night. "My husband tells me it's worth going over just to see how well the show goes," said Mrs. Robert Bolt, who was also planning to give an Award. "I have no illusions about winning, but the American Oscar is the only award that carries any weight—ours is just a lot of shit. And getting nominated is quite important to me." Her compatriot Glenda Jackson wasn't going over because she claimed she couldn't afford to and United Artists hadn't made any overtures about paying. Although her starring role in the six-part *Masterpiece Theatre* TV series *Elizabeth R* gave her plenty of free advertising during the voting period, Glenda had her doubts about the whole experience: "It's like being pregnant with a child someone else may have for all your labor pains." That someone else might be Ali MacGraw, who announced her pregnancy during the voting period. But Mrs. Robert Evans bet her husband that someone else would win.

Up to Old Tricks

"If George C. wins," said Ross Hunter, echoing the late Hedda Hopper, "I'll resign from the Academy. He's ridiculing our Academy." David Niven took a lighter opinion: "It could be he just can't bear to hear someone else's name called out." Columnist James Bacon had an explanation for Scott's rejection: "It's an old trick inaugurated by Humphrey Bogart the year he won for *The African Queen*. After he was nominated, Bogie damned the Academy, the movie industry, starlets, stars and the studio bosses, and dared them to give it to him." Joyce Haber agreed that Scott was up to something: "He's usually reporter-shy, but has been talking to anyone and everyone ever since the Oscar nominations were announced."

The reluctant nominee landed on the cover of *Time* with the headline AN ACTOR'S ART: RAGE BENEATH THE SURFACE. Interviewer Mary Cronin cooed, "I liked him tremendously." And film critic Jay Cocks dwelled on Scott's devotion to his craft: "He even insisted on having moles on his face identical to Patton's and filled in part of his nose to make it more like the general's." The actor told the critic, "Film is not an actor's medium," and that his "real commitment is to the legitimate theater."

A Corrupting Influence

Scott wasn't the only nominee to reject the honor. Director Luis Buñuel was incensed that his film *Tristana* was up for Best Foreign Film. "Nothing would disgust me more morally than receiving an Oscar. Nothing in the world would

"Ali MacGraw is the biggest female star since Marilyn Monroe."
—Joyce Haber

make me go accept it. I wouldn't have it in my home," the director told *Variety*. "Even in refusing it, like this actor, one isn't free from its corrupting influence. Look at what happened to him when he said he wouldn't accept it. It was worth a *Time* cover."

Scott's fellow nominees didn't mind the extra attention when reporters asked them about the noisy actor. "Scott's position doesn't affront me," said Melvyn Douglas, sixty-nine, nominated as the patriarch in *I Never Sang for My Father*. "I'd accept the Oscar because there is gratification in getting any award." Ryan O'Neal confessed, "If I win, it will be because Scott backed out. I think Scott made an admirable stand, but for me, the nomination is a great honor." James Earl Jones concurred: "*Patton* was great and I think Scott deserves to win. I don't feel my life depends on winning the Award—but I love receiving trophies."

Jacko in Tennis Shoes

Best Actor nominee Jack Nicholson liked trophies, too. "I'm voting for myself," he told reporters, "though I don't expect to win it. Scott already has it sewn up, whether he likes it or not. But the Oscar is as valid as any award around." The Academy was delighted that a young Turk like Nicholson would be attending the show, but Hank Grant fretted over how he would dress: "Hope nominee Jack Nicholson will have the good taste not to wear patched Levi's and tennis shoes to the Oscar Awards tomorrow night. That's how he made the Golden Globes scene and he's telling pals he'll do it again. But this one, Jacko, is being telecast—to millions around the world."

Another worry was the latest fashion craze—hot pants. "If they're not on the right figure, we'll zoom into a close-up," television show director Richard Dunlap warned *Women's Wear Daily*. Dunlap had tonsorial concerns as well: "Lillian Gish says all male hairdressers are misogynists. They especially try to show off on these shows. Suddenly, you lose the face in all those wild hairstyles."

If I Were a Carpenter

The Oscar show was getting competition from Broadway's Tony Awards—which were also televised—and the *Hollywood Reporter* hinted: "Would that the Oscars could engender half of the enthusiasm and excitement projected by the Tonys, which were completely devoid of manufactured jokes for presenters, long-winded speeches by executives (not even brought onstage) and no awkward stage waits—particularly one of the boring and time-consuming may-I-have-the-envelope-please?" Oscar show producer Robert Wise insisted solely on "movie names" this year, which excluded General Omar Bradley, who wanted to accept for George C. Scott. Wise's strict enforcement of his screen-celebrity rule meant that the pop duo the Carpenters would not be able to sing their hit, the nominated song "For All We Know." The *Hollywood Reporter* noted that the sister-and-brother team then accepted an offer to speak on Wink Martindale's radio show and "trace their career, discuss music trends, but most of all, they will reveal their personal feelings and record industry bitterness when the Academy refused to let them sing on the Oscar show."

The Other Society

A couple of hours before the ceremony, Robert Wise got a call from Best Actress nominee Carrie Snodgress. "It's very hard for me not to come tonight and I'm not putting down the Academy, but I don't want to be a 'star' or 'Best Actress,'" the actress said. "I love my work and I'm praying this doesn't affect people's minds about my work or talent, but this is a whole other society I don't believe in." Wise asked, "But, Carrie, why did you go to the Golden Globes to get Newcomer of the Year?" Snodgress replied, "I went there because I thought I had to."

The Big Night

Goldie Hawn, last year's Best Supporting Actress winner, was the first celebrity to arrive, at 5:35 P.M., followed by Anne Francis. Jack Nicholson showed up wearing a dark suit with dark shirt and tie. His date was Michelle Phillips, who had just recently had her marriage to Dennis Hopper annulled. Mr. and Mrs. Robert Evans pulled up and the *Hollywood Reporter* commented, "Ali MacGraw wore what is becoming almost traditional for her public appearances, a knit skull cap and two-piece navy-blue dress with floor-length straight skirt." Erich Segal came with Jane Alexander, and Army Archerd explained, "They're old pals but haven't seen each other in twelve years."

According to *Variety*, "Most colorful arrival was Sessue Hayakawa and a contingent of Japanese-clad friends," but Chief Dan George left his celebration robes home and wore a dark suit with a necklace. His competition, John Mills of *Ryan's Daughter*, wore his arm in a sling—a London doorman had recently slammed a car door on his left hand. Producer Ross Hunter sported a $1,000 custom-made tuxedo and escorted his former protégée, Sandra Dee (née Alexandra Zuck). When Army Archerd asked after Hunter's usual date, Nancy Sinatra, Sr., the producer explained, "She's in Mexico because she's allergic to the pollen in the Los Angeles spring air." About his own Oscar chances, Hunter said, "I expect *Patton* to win."

Before the telecast began, writer Hal Kanter, serving as a "warm-up man," told the audience, "Keep it short, make your speeches shorter than George C. Scott's rejection." Then the cameras rolled, Quincy Jones struck up the orchestra, and a giant neon Oscar silhouette lit up around an oversized Oscar statue. Academy President Daniel Taradash asked, "What is the Academy?" and then delivered a lecture. The first Award went to *Patton* for Best Sound and one of the technicians thanked George C. Scott, "for his wonderful performance."

Maggie Smith, appearing in *Design for Living*

Awards Ceremony

APRIL 15, 1971, 7:00 P.M.
THE DOROTHY CHANDLER PAVILION, LOS ANGELES

Your Hosts:
BURT BACHARACH, HARRY BELAFONTE, RICHARD BENJAMIN, JOAN BLONDELL, JIM BROWN, GENEVIEVE BUJOLD, GLEN CAMPBELL, PETULA CLARK, ANGIE DICKINSON, MELVYN DOUGLAS, LOLA FALANA, JANET GAYNOR, GOLDIE HAWN, BOB HOPE, JOHN HUSTON, JAMES EARL JONES, SHIRLEY JONES, SALLY KELLERMAN, BURT LANCASTER, JOHN MARLEY, WALTER MATTHAU, STEVE MCQUEEN, SARAH MILES, RICARDO MONTALBAN, JEANNE MOREAU, MERLE OBERON, RYAN O'NEAL, GREGORY PECK, PAULA PRENTISS, EVA MARIE SAINT, GEORGE SEGAL, MAGGIE SMITH, GIG YOUNG; Televised over NBC

Presenters

Sound . . . . Shirley Jones and John Marley
Supporting Actor . . . . Maggie Smith
Cinematography . . . . Genevieve Bujold and James Earl Jones
Honorary Award to Orson Welles . . . . John Huston
Jean Hersholt Humanitarian Award . . . . Gregory Peck
Short Subjects . . . . Jim Brown and Sally Kellerman
Scoring Awards . . . . Joan Blondell and Glen Campbell
Special Visual Effects . . . . Lola Falana
Supporting Actress . . . . Gig Young
Documentary Awards . . . . Richard Benjamin and Paula Prentiss
Costume Design . . . . Merle Oberon
Art Direction . . . . Petula Clark and Bob Hope
Honorary Award to Lillian Gish . . . . Melvyn Douglas
Foreign Film . . . . Richardo Montalban and Jeanne Moreau
Film Editing . . . . Genevieve Bujold and Walter Matthau
Thalberg Award . . . . Burt Lancaster
Song . . . . Burt Bacharach and Angie Dickinson
Director . . . . Janet Gaynor and Ryan O'Neal
Adapted Screenplay . . . . Harry Belafonte and Eva Marie Saint
Original Screenplay . . . . Sarah Miles and George Segal
Actor . . . . Goldie Hawn
Actress . . . . Walter Matthau
Picture . . . . Steve McQueen

Performers of Nominated Songs

"For All We Know" . . . . Petula Clark
"Pieces of Dreams" . . . . Glen Campbell
"Thank You Very Much" . . . . Petula Clark, Sally Kellerman, Burt Lancaster and Ricardo Montalban
"Till Love Touches Your Life" . . . . Lola Falana
"Whistling Away the Dark" . . . . Shirley Jones

"All those years of watching it on TV and now I actually get to go."
—Sally Kellerman

in a neighboring theater, popped over to give the Best Supporting Actor Oscar. "Despite the proliferation of awards these days, Oscar remains the one symbol of achievement in the entertainment field that's recognized around the world," last year's Best Actress said, before ripping open the envelope. All of the nominees were present and the winner was John Mills for *Ryan's Daughter*. "I was not expecting to be standing here with Oscar," said the recipient, clutching the statuette with his good hand. "I was thrilled to be in the building. I was speechless for a year in Ireland and I'm utterly speechless this moment."

Smith was followed by James Earl Jones in his *Othello* robes—he, too, was giving a performance in a theater next door. Jones and Genevieve Bujold handed the Cinematography Award to Sarah Miles, accepting for *Ryan's Daughter*'s Freddie Young. "It's no surprise to me at all," Miles said. "He's won three before and this is his fourth. I hope he lives long enough to win five more."

A bearded John Huston stepped forth and said that Orson Welles had received only "half an Oscar" for the screenplay of *Citizen Kane* and that "tonight, the Academy wants to give him an Oscar all his own." Welles didn't attend the ceremonies to pick up this Oscar, either, and he accepted his Honorary Oscar on film. "For the public, I hope they understand it means more to me because it doesn't come from them, much less the critics," Welles said, smiling.

Gregory Peck came out to announce that Frank Sinatra was receiving the Jean Hersholt Humanitarian Award. "He has until now managed to keep quite well his humanitarianism out of the public view," Peck stated. Sinatra, who had announced his retirement from show business a few months earlier, appeared and said, "This is truly an all-consuming thrill for me. Why do you have to get famous to get an award for helping other people? . . . To Mr. and Mrs. John Doe, I want you to reach out and get your share." Sinatra held out his Oscar for the metaphorical couple to touch and there was a shot of a weeping Nancy Sinatra, Jr.

Gig Young came on to present the Best Supporting Actress Award. Television viewers saw Karen Black and Sally Kellerman, as well as *The Landlord*'s Lee Grant, who was adjusting her earrings. The winner was Helen Hayes for *Airport*. Hayes' second Oscar was accepted by Rosalind Russell, in a slit skirt, who said, "The first lady in theater is the first lady tonight in our hearts."

After handing the Costume Design Oscar to the British historical drama, *Cromwell*, Merle Oberon introduced "a special friend of Oscar with whom this show would not be official." The orchestra launched into a jazzed-up version of "Thanks for the Memory" and out walked Bob Hope. "Frank Sinatra announces he's quitting show business and they give him a humanitarian award. I saw a movie without Elliott Gould. I go back to the kind of movie when a girl says 'I love you,' and it's a declaration, not a demonstration." For the first time ever, the audience booed a Bob Hope joke. Shaken by the reaction, the comedian sped through his final gags, which included "Chief Dan George, he was all right; but why couldn't they give that part to an American?"

Hope hustled off and Melvyn Douglas appeared to give an Honorary Oscar to Lillian Gish. Army Archerd wrote, "The schmaltzy audience always digs seeing some of the greats get long overdue awards and the Lillian Gish Oscar brought a standing ovation, a pleasant chance to stand up." After everyone stretched, Gish reminisced, "Oh, all the charming ghosts I feel around me who should share this. It was our privilege for a little while to serve that beautiful thing, the film, and we never doubted for a moment that it was the most powerful thing, the mind and heartbeat of our technical century."

Goldie Hawn stepped out and recounted that, last year, she was in bed in London when the phone rang at 5 A.M. with the news that she had won an Oscar. Then she introduced a musical salute to the Beatles. "Their films had fantastic impact on film music," Hawn claimed—they had already won an Oscar that evening for Best Song Score for *Let It Be*. The Fab Four were not pres-

"The Oscar is the only award that carries any weight—ours is just a lot of shit."
—Sarah Miles

ent; in fact, they had disbanded the year before. Nor was the recipient of the Thalberg Award in the hall, so Liv Ullmann accepted for Ingmar Bergman. "This is my first visit to Los Angeles and I have enjoyed every moment of it," Ullmann said. "I have met many generous people. He has asked me to say to you that he is sitting on his little island in the Baltic writing a new script . . . and he believes that he shows his respect and gratefulness . . . by staying home finishing his script."

Ryan O'Neal and Janet Gaynor, introduced as the star of Fox, "the studio that is now Century City," named the Best Director—Franklin J. Schaffner for *Patton*. The winner was in Europe assembling *Nicholas and Alexandra* for Sam Spiegel, so *Patton*'s other star, Karl Malden, accepted. "Since he isn't here, let me say you couldn't have given it to a better fella. I know, I was there."

Eva Marie Saint and Harry Belafonte prefaced the Adapted Screenplay Award with: "Now the boy and girl are making love under the titles—where do we go now?" The winner was Ring Lardner, Jr., for *M*A*S*H,* who did not mention director Robert Altman but alluded to his previous Oscar for *Woman of the Year*. "At long last, a pattern has been established in my life," he said. "At the end of every twenty-eight years, I win one of these. So I will see you all again in 1999."

George Segal and Sarah Miles, wearing her Mary Queen of Scots costume from the London production of *Vivat! Vivat! Regina,* appeared to give the Original Screenplay Award, and Miles decided to have some fun with the scripted banter. When Segal asked her which films her husband had won Oscars for, Mrs. Bolt said, "He wrote—a little bit closer, it's me eyes," addressing the cue-card holder, "oh, yes, he wrote *Doctor Zhivago, A Man for All Seasons,* Rosie Ryan—oh, no." As the audience laughed, Segal began reading the nominees. Miles jumped in, "*Joe,* Norman Wexler, your turn," Segal suppressed laughter and continued, then it was Sarah's turn again. "*My Night at Maud's,* Eric Rohmer—oooh, I haven't seen that one." The winners were Francis Ford Coppola and Edmund H. North for *Patton*. The coauthors had never met, and they didn't get the opportunity here because Coppola was in New York directing *The Godfather*. North said, "I'd like to say one word if I may about the picture. I hope it's not just a war picture but a peace picture."

"Then, after about two hours and fifteen minutes," Army Archerd reported, "during which there were a great number of departures from the theater to respective rest rooms—it happened. The murmur before the announcement of George C. Scott told the tale why everyone was really there!" Presenter Goldie Hawn first noted that the term "Best Actor" was a misnomer and that "it is a specific achievement that is honored—a pertinent distinction." Then she dropped the formal posture and giggled, "Can't wait!" as she tore into the envelope. "Oh, my God!" she exclaimed. "The winner is George C. Scott!" The audience roared its approval. Producer Frank McCarthy accepted and praised the Academy for its choice.

Walter Matthau came out and quipped, "Next year, I'm going to try the George C. Scott routine . . . Did Goldie really say 'pertinent'?" Matthau then got around to the Best Actress Award—the winner was Glenda Jackson for *Women in Love*. Her Oscar was accepted by John Mills' daughter Juliet: "She's one-hundred-percent professional and this is a great night for professionals."

Steve McQueen made the final presentation, although there was no suspense as to what the Best Picture would be—*Patton*. Frank McCarthy returned to the podium and thanked both Darryl and Richard Zanuck, "who gave *Patton* firm support during the twenty years since I first proposed it." This was the last time Darryl Zanuck would be associated with the Oscars. The mogul had made one war movie too many. The $25 million retelling of the bombing of Pearl Harbor, *Tora! Tora! Tora!* was the latest movie to nearly do in 20th Century–Fox. Within a month of the Awards, Zanuck would be forced from office and given the title "Chairman Emeritus."

"Oh, all the charming ghosts I feel around me."
—Lillian Gish

Aftermath

With so few winners present, reporters interviewed any celebrity who happened to be milling about backstage. "Good, good, great!" was how Karl Malden reacted to George C. Scott's victory. "This adds some prestige to this organization." Gregory Peck concurred, saying, "The Academy is only two or three years behind the critics. I tried to get the young people involved in the Academy but it's impossible to reach them. People like Dennis Hopper and Peter Fonda belong to the Academy, but they wouldn't get involved." As Sarah Miles posed with her winning costar, John Mills, a reporter cracked, "It's appropriate she wore her Mary Queen of Scots outfit since she lost to the actress playing Queen Elizabeth on TV."

Miles enjoyed herself nevertheless and said her biggest thrill was meeting Lillian Gish at the ball, which Army Archerd described as "emphatically festive. All the losers showed up." There were so many of them that Hank Grant complained, "The tables were so crowded together, it was like trying to get out of East Berlin squeezing through to mingle with the mob. Once over the Berlin Wall, it was a joy to see John Mills reacting as an Oscar winner should. 'I'm still in a state of shock,' he said, with a smile broad enough to swallow a banana sideways. 'This has been such a thrill for me. I'm taking my Oscar to bed with me tonight. Otherwise, I'd awaken and feel it was only a beautiful dream!'"

As for the reveling losers, Robert Altman said, "I was happy enough with a nomination—I was sure they'd vote for another war." Columnist Radie Harris commented on "the crushing disappointment of Bob Evans . . . the marvelous sportsmanship of Ali MacGraw." Mrs. Evans didn't appear too upset, "I'm glad it's over," she said, adding that she had predicted that Glenda Jackson would win. As MacGraw chatted with Liza and Vincente Minnelli, *Love Story* author Erich Segal said his trip to Hollywood wasn't a total loss—he was scheduled to give a lecture on "The Future of Literature" at Beverly Hills High.

Although *Airport* won only one of its ten nominations—Hayes'—Ross Hunter rescinded his threat to resign after Scott's win. "But I still think he's ruined the Academy," the producer told James Bacon, while his date, Sandra Dee, confessed, "I voted for Scott." Hunter's main concern now was what to do with his expensive tuxedo: "I'll put the suit in wardrobe and try to use it in my next picture." Hunter was busy casting that next picture and he talked to Sally Kellerman and Liv Ullmann about his idea—a musical remake of *Lost Horizon*.

Helen Hayes had seen her victory on television, and when the press caught up with her, she cried, "I'm on the verge of tears. God bless those people in Hollywood!" Meanwhile, Vincent Canby wrote in the *New York Times*, "Helen Hayes' being absent spared her—and us—one of those worthy, embarrassing standing ovations for a performance that was, let's face it, just a teentsy-weentsy bit terrible."

Bette Davis called Glenda Jackson in England with the good news, and later the winner received a telegram from Joan Crawford. At a press conference, Jackson said, "I was amazed at how pleased I was." But she said that her success had mostly gone to her two-year-old son's head: "He's become so accustomed to photographers, he keeps asking for more flash."

George C. Scott claimed he had watched a hockey game on TV then gone to bed. He refused to talk to reporters, but Colleen Dewhurst told them, "George had to do what he did about the Oscar because that's the way he feels. But me? I want to win an award." Back in Hollywood, columnist Hank Grant was still insisting it was all a stunt, calling it "public relations at its best because his defiance was printed and aired all over the world, making him the most highly publicized nominee on the Oscar roster."

TRADITIONAL CHIC—FEW HOT PANTS was the *Hollywood Reporter*'s headline: only Darren

McGavin's wife sported the shorts. In the *Los Angeles Times,* Charles Champlin went after one particular participant: "Bob Hope's monologue, weary, bitter, and excruciatingly unfunny, was an embarrassment to everyone." And *Daily Variety* opined, "At forty-three, Oscar looked tired." But at least one person enjoyed herself; presenter Joan Blondell, who, after handing out a few statuettes, said she watched the rest of the show on a monitor in the Dorothy Chandler bar.

1971

"You can lead actresses to water and drink, but you can't make them wear what they don't want to."
—Edith Head

Hollywood's rebels took over the 1971 Academy Awards. As soon as Glenda Jackson won Best Actress from the New York Film Critics for Ken Russell's *Women in Love*, United Artists released Ken Russell's biography of Tchaikovsky that starred Glenda Jackson as the composer's insane wife—*The Music Lovers*. Rex Reed raved, "It's too bad Glenda won her award before people got a chance to see *The Music Lovers* because up to this shattering film everything has been an audition."

After *The Music Lovers*, Jackson balked when Russell asked her to play a sexually obsessed, hunchbacked, seventeenth-century nun in *The Devils*. "Please, Ken, don't ask me to go crazy and start tearing off my clothes again," she pleaded. Miffed, Russell offered the role to Vanessa Redgrave, who was being considered by director John Schlesinger and film-critic-turned-screenwriter Penelope Gilliatt for their movie about a love triangle. Vanessa decided to work with Russell, while Schlesinger and Gilliatt offered their movie to Glenda Jackson. Ken Russell's *The Devils* opened in the summer and was damned even by the critics who admired it; *Time* opined, "It is a movie so unsparingly vivid in its imagery, so totally successful in conveying an atmosphere of uncontrolled hysteria, that Russell himself seems like a man possessed." *Variety* wrote the whole thing off as a "relentlessly grotesque meller gone berserk."

Pipe Dream

Director Robert Altman was faring a little better than Russell with his follow-ups to *M*A*S*H*. Neither critics nor audiences knew what to make of *Brewster McCloud*, Altman's dark comedy about a loner who tries to fly like a bird in the Houston Astrodome. But *McCabe and Mrs. Miller*, his next film, had a number of passionate admirers, none more so than Pauline Kael, who wrote, "*McCabe and Mrs. Miller* is a beautiful pipe dream of a movie—a fleeting, almost diaphanous vision of what frontier life might have been." Gary Arnold of the *Washington Post* called it, "the best American movie since *Bonnie and Clyde*." The film starred Warren Beatty, as the naive entrepreneur McCabe, and Julie Christie as Mrs. Miller, a Cockney madam out west. Charles Champlin of the *Los Angeles Times* declared that Christie gave "the best performance of her career." Despite the praise, box office was spotty, and the western barely crawled into the black.

Overleaf: *After forty-four years, Charlie Chaplin finally shows up at an Awards ceremony—this time the Academy has guaranteed him an Oscar.*

The Soul of Neon

Jules Feiffer came to director Mike Nichols with an idea for a play about two men who never grow up emotionally. "I see it as a movie," Nichols responded. It turned into a Joseph E. Levine production with Jack Nicholson and Art Garfunkel as the two men, and Candice Bergen and Ann-Margret as two of their women. The critics were divided: *Saturday Review* said, "The most mature of all of those American films that have attempted to deal with the subject of sex in these ultra-liberated cinematic times." But Pauline Kael dismissed it as "a grimly purposeful satire about depersonalization and how we use each other sexually as objects, and, in Mike Nichols' cold, slick style, it is like a neon sign that spells out the soullessness of neon."

Ann-Margret, on the other hand, won good reviews for the first time in her film career. The actress, who had last appeared opposite Joe Namath in *C.C. and Company*, had *Time* raving: "It was like watching Minnie Mouse play Ophelia—brilliantly," while the *New York Times* proclaimed, "Ann-Margret acts!" *Life* put the actress on its cover, and she told the magazine's interviewer, "The critics had an image of me, and they wouldn't accept any other . . . I was a cartoon character. A joke."

Multimedia MacLaine

Another song-and-dance star switching images was Shirley MacLaine, who played a troubled upper-income New Yorker in Frank D. Gilroy's drama *Desperate Characters*. *Newsweek* said, "Miss MacLaine has done herself a favor, playing Sophie with a quiet, tasteful intelligence that effectively projects the confusion of a refugee wandering through a battle zone." MacLaine also forged new territory by writing a bestselling autobiography, *Don't Fall Off the Mountain*, and by appearing in a TV series, *Shirley's World*, which was canceled after a few episodes.

For a Good Time Call Jane

"If three years ago you would have said that the two leading actresses in the Oscar race were Ann-Margret and Jane Fonda, people would have thought you were crazy," commented Donia Mills in the *Washington Star-News*. But Jane Fonda had once again converted the critics to her cause, this time as a call girl stalked by a homicidal maniac in the thriller *Klute*. "It seems to me unquestionable that Jane Fonda here emerges as probably the finest screen actress of her generation with a mercurial, subtly shaded and altogether fascinating performance," commented Richard Schickel in *Life*.

But Warner Brothers began to sweat when Jane's antiwar activism persuaded a number of state legislatures to pass resolutions calling for a boycott of Jane Fonda movies. And in interviews, Fonda made the movie sound more like a political rally than a suspense film: "I took *Klute* because in it I expose a great deal of the oppression of women in this country—the system which makes women sell themselves for possessions." The Warners executives need not have worried; for whatever reasons, audiences turned out to see Jane Fonda and *Klute* turned a healthy profit.

Movie vs. Picture Show

Although *Daily Variety* had already reported, "The *Easy Rider* craze is over" and that low-budgeted anti-Establishment movies were as profitable as silent movies, Universal was hoping that the director who had started the craze—Dennis Hopper—could revitalize the genre with his next movie, about a film company in Peru, named *The Last Movie*. The title was prophetic. The *New York Times* referred to it as "an extravagant mess" and it lost money so quickly that Universal pulled it out of circulation within a matter of weeks.

Meanwhile, a thirty-two-year-old film critic named Peter Bogdanovich was making his first big-studio feature and telling interviewers, "My insight is to reject all those modern techniques. In too many movies, the camera is the star. My films are not about cameras, they're about people." The people in Bogdanovich's movie were from Larry McMurtry's novel about a small Texas town in the Eisenhower era, *The Last Picture Show*.

The author of books on John Ford, Fritz Lang and Allan Dwan, Bogdanovich purposefully aimed for an "old movie" look, going so far as to shoot the movie in black-and-white. His wife, Polly Platt, was the production designer and Ford, also the subject of a Bogdanovich documentary, served as casting director when the young director couldn't convince a member of Ford's stock company, Ben Johnson, to play a pivotal role. The problem arose when Johnson read the script and saw that the film contained profanity and nudity. "I don't like making movies you can't take the entire family to," Johnson said. Then the actor got a phone call from John Ford, asking him to play the part as a favor. "Yes sir, I will," Johnson responded.

When *The Last Picture Show* premiered at the New York Film Festival, the first thing the critics did was warn their readers not to confuse it with *The Last Movie*. *Newsweek* proclaimed it "the most impressive work by a young American direc-

"Please don't ask me to go crazy and start tearing off my clothes again."
—Glenda Jackson

tor since *Citizen Kane*." And Bogdanovich's old crony Andrew Sarris was amused by the turn of events: "Who would have thought a few years back that Bogdanovich would be traveling first-class on the express train of film history while Dennis Hopper was bumming a ride on a freight train headed for oblivion?" Bogdanovich himself worried, "I hope I'm not repeating what happened to Orson. You know, make a successful serious film like this early and then spend the rest of my life in decline." At least one aspect of Bogdanovich's life was pure Hollywood—he left his wife for his twenty-one-year-old star, Cybill Shepherd.

Slam-Bang

Bogdanovich had a competitor for the title of wunderkind in thirty-two-year-old William Friedkin. A former TV director, Friedkin had made movies that ranged from Sonny and Cher to Harold Pinter to Mart Crowley, but he had never had a box-office hit until he adapted a bestseller about a New York cop busting an international heroin ring—*The French Connection*. "It was really made in the editing room," the young director shrugged. "One of the easiest sequences to do was that chase scene." That scene involved a car pursuing an elevated train and it ranked with the chariot race in *Ben-Hur* in drawing power—audiences turned out to see what the critics were shouting about. "Pure dynamite," exclaimed Kathleen Carroll in the *New York Daily News*. "It's trigger-fast explosive scenes and high-tension sequences (the one in *Bullitt* pales in comparison) will have you literally gasping for breath." In Los Angeles, Joyce Haber gasped, "A movie that's fun—and I saw it twice."

Friedkin had tried everybody for the lead role of the cop—Steve McQueen, Jackie Gleason, columnist Jimmy Breslin—when he settled for his seventh choice, Gene Hackman, who jumped for it. "When I first read the part, it seemed like a chance to do all those things I watched Jimmy Cagney do as a kid," the actor said as he began his first starring film role. But once filming was under way, Hackman had second thoughts. "I found out very quickly that I'm not a violent person," Hackman said, "and these cops are surrounded by violence all the time. There were a couple of days when I wanted to get out of the picture." When filming was finished, Hackman returned to his usual character actor status as the villain in a melodrama with Lee Marvin, but after *The French Connection* opened in the fall to smash reviews and long lines, 20th Century–Fox was on the phone, asking him to be the leading man in its expensive new adventure movie, *The Poseidon Adventure*.

Critics' Choice

Glenda Jackson had made the right choice, as it turned out. When John Schlesinger and Penelope Gilliatt's *Sunday, Bloody Sunday*, premiered in the U.S. in the fall, *Variety* couldn't get over it: "The story's bisexual triangle differs in that it's not ménage à trois stuff." *Time* clarified, "*Sunday, Bloody Sunday* is an anomaly. It's text is sexual, but its theme is nothing less than the nature of affection." The film played well in urban areas, but suburbanites stayed home. Despite the film's limited box-office appeal, it provided a Hollywood boost to the career of Peter Finch, playing Jackson's rival for newcomer Murray Head. *Airport* producer Ross Hunter decided to "topline" Finch in his expensive musical remake of *Lost Horizon*.

If I Were a Rich Man

The road-show musical was now a dead genre, but Norman Jewison strove onward anyway with a $9 million adaptation of the Broadway hit, *Fiddler on the Roof*. For Tevye, Jewison passed over Zero Mostel, who had created the role, and went with a thirty-six-year-old Israeli named Chaim Topol, who had played the part for a year in London. United Artists thought his name was a mouthful for Americans, and the studio billed him simply as "Topol." When *Fiddler on the Roof* opened in November, it proved that families were still willing to troop to a downtown theater and pay inflated

"My films are not about cameras, they're about people."
—Peter Bogdanovich

prices to see a musical—the film ran over a year in Times Square. In the *Los Angeles Times,* Charles Champlin was impressed: "You have to be knocked out of your seat by the painstaking and inspired craftmanship you see and hear before you." *Life* profiled the new star and observed: "Topol is the kind of man who weeps without embarrassment when he is separated from his family . . . he is also a gung-ho type who has been politically active all his life, a sophisticate and connoisseur who collects Pissarros and Modiglianis and a millionaire impresario who is Israel's most successful show businessman."

Merry Christmas—Pow!

Time previewed three of the upcoming Christmas releases and commented, "Merry Christmas—Pow!" Ken Russell was back for the third time this year with an adaptation of Sandy Wilson's spoof of 1920s musicals, *The Boy Friend.* Reviewers expecting an escapist, paper-thin pastiche felt double-crossed when Russell portrayed the struggle of a Depression-era theatrical troupe putting on *The Boy Friend* in a show-within-a-movie framework. "An anti-musical" was how Pauline Kael labeled it, and the only performer to get unanimously good reviews was Glenda Jackson, in an unbilled cameo as the star who breaks her leg. Critics also had a difficult time with Sam Peckinpah's *Straw Dogs,* in which Dustin Hoffman, as a nebbish mathematician, proves his manhood by killing the hoodlums who attack his home—Kael called this one "a fascist work of art."

But Russell and Peckinpah looked like toddlers next to Stanley Kubrick, who unleashed his adaptation of Anthony Burgess' science-fiction novel *A Clockwork Orange* for the holidays. Like Russell's *The Devils, A Clockwork Orange* carried an X rating, and the film's violent depiction of the near future sparked such a controversy that it became the cover story of both *Time* and *Newsweek.* When Judith Crist of *New York* magazine praised it as a "masterpiece," an irate reader wrote the *New York Times*: "Would Judith Crist, one of the movie's more enthusiastic supporters, regard her own rape as being, possibly, a charitable act of self-assertion on the part of her attackers?"

Critical Support

Crist and her fellow critics stuck to their guns and named *A Clockwork Orange* the New York Film Critics' choice for Best Picture, with Kubrick their Best Director. Not forgetting their own, the critics let *Sunday, Bloody Sunday*'s Penelope Gilliatt share the Best Screenplay citation with Peter Bogdanovich and Larry McMurtry for *The Last Picture Show,* which swept the supporting acting awards: the winners were Ben Johnson and former-starlet-and-Lee-Strasberg graduate Ellen Burstyn. Jane Fonda walked off with the Best Actress Award with Shirley MacLaine in second place, but there was a dead heat between *The French Connection*'s Gene Hackman and *Sunday, Bloody Sunday*'s Peter Finch. On the last ballot, Hackman pulled ahead to garner the plaque.

The announcement of the Gotham decisions by no means meant the end of campaigning in Hollywood. Sam Spiegel had shelled out a bundle to film a bestselling biography of *Nicholas and Alexandra,* and, if the film did not go over as well as director Franklin J. Schaffner's previous epic, *Patton,* the producer was not about to allow a bunch of bad reviews stand in his way. Spiegel launched a massive trade-paper campaign, and his Alexandra, British stage actress Janet Suzman, gave plenty of interviews. Suzman was perhaps too candid with the press: "The film is entirely too long, what a gargantuan monster to condense into three hours. If I do more movies, I'd like to have some fun, look great in tacky things, meeting spy boats in the fog in a trench coat and smoking lots of cigarettes like Bette Davis. But nobody seems to make those movies anymore."

George C. Scott was back, in *The Hospital,* directed by *Love Story*'s Arthur Hiller and written by Paddy Chayefsky. Although the film critics overlooked Scott, United Artists placed a number of Oscar ads for him when the film bowed at the

"Just because I don't happen to resemble Tab Hunter or Ryan O'Neal doesn't mean I'm not virile."
—Gene Hackman

end of the year. Scott didn't raise a ruckus about the Oscar this year, and nobody asked him about it, either.

Hollywood veteran Hal Wallis didn't bother at all with the New Yorkers' opinions; the producer held up the release of his latest English historical epic, opening it in Los Angeles for just one week to qualify for the Oscars—just as he had done for *Anne of the Thousand Days* in 1969. His new effort moved to the next generation on the English throne—Queen Elizabeth vs. Mary Queen of Scots, the latter the subject of a bestselling biography by Lady Antonia Fraser. Wallis' Mary was Vanessa Redgrave, and his Elizabeth was Glenda Jackson, who had already played the queen on television earlier in the year. The Academy screenings of *Mary Queen of Scots* drew capacity crowds eager to see the two actresses go at one another, and Wallis didn't let them down—the film featured two encounters between the two queens, who historians argued had never met. Glenda Jackson answered the academics, "Just because no one recorded it doesn't mean they never saw each other."

The Nominations

When *Mary Queen of Scots* finally opened at Radio City Music Hall, *Time* laughed: "This is a *Love Story* with historical footnotes," but Hal Wallis had done it again—Vanessa Redgrave was nominated for Best Actress and the film was up for four other Oscars. Costar Glenda Jackson wasn't forgotten; she was cited for *Sunday, Bloody Sunday*, which was nominated for four Oscars in all, but not Best Picture. Producer Sam Spiegel had proven his mettle once again and *Nicholas and Alexandra* made off with a Best Picture nod and five other nominations, including Janet Suzman for Best Actress. Julie Christie was in the race as the single nomination for *McCabe and Mrs. Miller*. The only American in the Best Actress contest was Jane Fonda in *Klute*.

Best Picture nominees with nominated directors were *The French Connection* (eight nominations), *The Last Picture Show* (eight), *Fiddler on the Roof* (eight), and *A Clockwork Orange* (five). *The Boy Friend* and *Straw Dogs* were both nominated for their musical scores and nothing else.

Jeff Bridges' Bar Mitzvah

The Last Picture Show's ensemble cast dominated the supporting races. New York Film Critics winner Ben Johnson competed with his twenty-year-old costar, newcomer Jeff Bridges, son of Lloyd, who told his offspring after he saw the movie: "I understand now why you don't come to me anymore, you've got all the right makings for the job and I can't teach you anymore." "It was kind of like a bar mitzvah," Jeff told the *New York Post*. "'You are a man.'"

Life looked in on *The Last Picture Show*'s two Supporting Actress nominees: Film Critics winner Ellen Burstyn, thirty-nine, who played a sexy adulteress, and Cloris Leachman, forty-five, who played a frumpy one. The article was headlined TWO FRIENDS WHO HATE THE IDEA OF 'COMPETING,' and Burstyn confessed, "One part, the adult part, says that acting is not a sports contest. But the child part is saying, 'Ohhhh, a dream come true!'" Leachman said, "I think George C. Scott was so right. In a way giving the award is anti-everything actors are. Still, I really want to win." Leachman had been around Hollywood for years—she was the mother on *Lassie* for the 1957 season and was currently appearing in a supporting role on *The Mary Tyler Moore Show*—but had never been in the spotlight before: "I had decided a long time before I started that I wanted to have a husband and family. They came first. If I had wanted to be a star, I would have done things differently."

Ann-Margret Jumps In

"I get jumpy merely thinking about it and I'm thinking about it all the time," said Ann-Margret, a Best Supporting Actress nominee. "It would be

"I understand now why you don't come to me anymore, you've got all the right makings for the job and I can't teach you anymore."
—Lloyd Bridges to Jeff Bridges

incredible if I won, but just being nominated is a kind of vindication," she told reporters, adding that she had gained twenty pounds for the role. The *Portland Oregonian* sounded a good omen: "Ann-Margret's performance is to *Carnal Knowledge* what Frank Sinatra's was to *From Here to Eternity*." Her manager, Allan Carr, was approached at a party by non-nominee Shirley MacLaine, who was wearing a McGovern for President button. "What are you doing for the campaign?" Shirley asked. "Oh, we're taking a few ads in the trades," Carr replied.

Good Golly, Gene Hackman

Best Actor nominee Gene Hackman got the star treatment with trade ads and celebrity profiles. *Time* observed, "He has become one of the best-liked of Hollywood professionals, a shambling, shirt-sleeves type who actually uses words like 'golly' and 'gee' and is still married to his first wife after 14 years."

Hackman's main competition, Peter Finch, was lauded by Walter Matthau, who was nominated for playing an old codger in *Kotch*. "Finch probably had the most difficult role," Matthau said, "because it's difficult to play a fairy convincingly." *Fiddler on the Roof*'s Topol marched immediately to his superiors in the Israeli Army with the news of his nomination, and asked for liberty from his two-months active duty to attend the Oscar show. Permission was granted. As for the fifth nominee—George C. Scott for *The Hospital*—his producer Howard Gottfried and screenwriter Paddy Chayefsky promised the Academy that the nominee would show up this year "if we have to personally deliver him dead or alive."

Redgrave Passes, Fonda Accepts

Vanessa Redgrave would not be coming in any condition because the Nixon Administration would not let her. Grace Duncan, Isadora's daughter, told James Bacon, "Vanessa feels that the people of the United States don't like her and, besides, Attorney General John Mitchell has her visa on his desk." That was one radical out of the way, but Jane Fonda, who *was* planning to attend, spent the nomination period telling reporters, "I don't care about Oscar. I make movies to support my activist causes, certainly not for any honors." Jane also had a response when the Hollywood Women's Press Club voted her their annual "Sour Apple" Award: "It's odd that my exercise of freedom should be criticized by an organization whose freedom is so carefully insured by the Constitution. . . ."

The Gentleman Is a Tramp

Although the Academy could count on Jane Fonda to attend the ceremonies, nobody else wanted to get involved. Barbra Streisand refused an offer to present Best Picture, and a number of older stars declined because they didn't approve of the nomination of *A Clockwork Orange*. The show's producer, Howard W. Koch, wanted to avoid last year's scathing reviews and was desperate for a star attraction, like D. W. Griffith at the 1935 Awards. And then came the news that Charlie Chaplin was ending his twenty-year exile from the U.S. to accept an honor in New York from the Film Society of Lincoln Center. The Academy promptly invited the eighty-two-year-old to come west and receive something from it, too—his second Honorary Oscar. This time, he accepted. Chaplin's return to the States was front-page news and Candice Bergen took his picture in New York for the cover of *Life*.

The Academy announced that no other Honorary Awards would be given to make Chaplin's all the more special. Howard Koch said the show would be "nostalgic and glamorous" and that actresses were asked "to wear black, white or silver to comply with the theme, a salute to nostalgia, and to complement the noncolor background sets." When a number of actresses protested Koch's mandate, fashion consultant Edith Head commented, "You can lead actresses to water and drink, but you can't make them wear what they don't want to."

Modern Times

Some people, however, were less than delighted about Chaplin's homecoming. Columnist Nancy Anderson, of the Copley News Service, wrote, "I'm old enough to remember how he sat out WW II, helping neither his adopted country, this one, which had made him rich, nor his native one, England, which was fighting for its life. Too old, I suppose, to have enlisted, he didn't follow Joe E. Brown's example and do camp shows and benefits, nor did he do anything else, including pay his taxes." The *Los Angeles Herald-Examiner* got in on the criticism with a cartoon depicting an Oscar covered with banners that read "Chaplin's left-wing leanings" and "lives in Switzerland." The caption read: "Memories Are Short."

The Academy heard rumors that protesters were planning to demonstrate against Chaplin on Oscar night, so it was decided that the Honorary winner would make his entrance through the theater's underground garage. Academy President Daniel Taradash met Chaplin and his wife, Oona O'Neill, at Los Angeles International Airport and accompanied them on their limousine tour of Chaplin's old haunts. "It's all banks, banks, banks!" said Chaplin.

The Big Night

One of the first nominees to arrive was Jane Fonda, in a dark pants outfit, with Donald Sutherland. The only other Actress nominee to appear was Janet Suzman. The only Actor nominee missing was George C. Scott. All of the Supporting Actor nominees were present, but the only Supporting Actresses fans saw were Cloris Leachman and Ann-Margret, who told a reporter, "I know it's between Cloris Leachman and Ellen Burstyn but I'm still about to collapse." Her former costar, Joe Namath, entered with Raquel Welch on his arm.

The telecast began with the star of the just-released *Cabaret*, Joel Gray, dancing and singing in a production number entitled "Here's Hollywood." Then president Daniel Taradash stepped out to point out that there were only six more days to Charlie Chaplin's birthday. "We welcome him home," Taradash concluded, to loud applause.

Last year's Best Supporting Actress, Helen Hayes, was the first host, and she began with, "As George C. Scott didn't get around to saying last year, thank you." Hayes was stuck with the reading of the rules, and she had a difficult time reading the cue cards. "I hope to do it right," she fretted. "I'll be liable to get the Academy in trouble or investigated." Hayes was followed by Screen Actors Guild President John Gavin and Ann-Margret, who presented the Cinematography Award. Gavin picked Ann-Margret up and quipped, "I'd like to thank the Academy for this trophy." Ann-Margret laughed and gave the Oscar to *Fiddler on the Roof*. Director Norman Jewison accepted for the absent Oswald Morris and said, "It is true. He shot the whole picture through a lady's silk stocking."

Helen Hayes returned with index cards and glasses and began reading. "Presenting the Award for Visual Effects is the lovely Karen Black, whom we shall see in the film version of *Portnoy's Complaint*—" Hayes did a double-take and blushed. Black walked out and gave the Oscar to a trio from the Disney Studios, one of whom said, "A number of people have said in the Technical Awards

Awards Ceremony

April 10, 1972, 7:00 p.m.
The Dorothy Chandler Pavilion, Los Angeles

Your Hosts:
Helen Hayes, Alan King,
Sammy Davis, Jr., Jack Lemmon
Televised over NBC

Presenters

Cinematography . . . . . Ann-Margret and John Gavin
Special Visual Effects . . . . Karen Black and Richard Chamberlain
Short Subjects . . . . Cloris Leachman and Richard Roundtree
Supporting Actor . . . . Richard Harris and Sally Kellerman
Foreign Film . . . . Leslie Caron and Jack Valenti
Sound . . . . Sandy Duncan and Michael York
Supporting Actress . . . . Gene Hackman and Raquel Welch
Documentary Awards . . . . James Caan and Joey Heatherton
Costume Design . . . . Joe Namath and Cybill Shepherd
Art Direction . . . . Timothy Bottoms and Jennifer O'Neill
Scoring Awards . . . . . Betty Grable and Dick Haymes
Film Editing . . . . Red Buttons and Jill St. John
Song . . . . Joel Gray
Writing Awards . . . . Tennessee Williams
Director . . . . Frank Capra and Natalie Wood
Actress . . . . Walter Matthau
Actor . . . . Liza Minnelli
Picture . . . . Jack Nicholson
Honorary Award to Charlie Chaplin . . . . Jack Lemmon and Daniel Taradash

Performers of Nominated Songs

"The Age of Not Believing" . . . . Debbie Reynolds
"All His Children" . . . . Charley Pride and the Mitchell Singing Boys
"Bless the Beasts & Children" . . . . . . The Carpenters
"Life Is What You Make It" . . . . Johnny Mathis
"Theme From Shaft" . . . . Isaac Hayes

"This couldn't have happened to a nicer fella."
—Ben Johnson

there's not much excitement. I can assure you when you're up here the excitement is ecstatic."

Hayes turned over emcee duties to Alan King, who came out with a cigar and asked, "What is Alan King doing here? . . . I was turned down for a role because I was too Jewish—the role of Tevye." There was a shot of 1956 Supporting Actress winner Dorothy Malone laughing and clapping. King continued, "The reason you're so relaxed in L.A. is because you've got so many massage parlors out here." There was a shot of Jane Fonda and Donald Sutherland, who were not laughing.

Sally Kellerman and Richard Harris revealed that the Best Supporting Actor was Ben Johnson for *The Last Picture Show.* The veteran walked to the stage with his hands on his face, shaking his head in disbelief. A jubilant Richard Harris hugged him. "Boy, ain't that purty," the winner drawled. "I had a speech all rigged up for this, but the more I worked on it, the phonier it got. I'd like to thank Peter Bogdanovich and his lovely wife, Polly." Bogdanovich's date that night was Cybill Shepherd. "I'd also like to thank Mr. John Ford, who had a lot to do with my doing the show," Johnson said, taking a breath before adding, "What I'm about to say probably will stir up a lot of conversation around all over the country. It's something I'd like to leave in everyone's mind throughout the world." He paused dramatically. "This couldn't have happened to a nicer fella." The audience exploded with laughter and Richard Harris hugged him again.

Raquel Welch appeared onstage with Gene Hackman to give the Best Supporting Actress Award. The winner was Cloris Leachman for *The Last Picture Show.* Leachman hugged Raquel and kissed Gene and then laughed her way through a rambling speech, in which she thanked her piano and dancing teachers and "Dad, who paid the bills." After the winner walked off with the presenters, Alan King cracked, "Raquel Welch is my personal nominee for Best Living Action."

Sammy Davis, Jr., was the next emcee and he wore a peace symbol necklace and flashed a peace sign as he made his entrance. "Tonight, the Academy is honoring two films about my people," he said, "*Shaft* and *Fiddler on the Roof.*" Davis continued, "It's such a gas to be backstage and to follow on the podium my man, Alan King." Davis' first bit of business was introducing "my man, Isaac Hayes" to sing his nominated theme song from *Shaft.* As dancers gyrated amid flashing lights, Hayes, in a shirt made entirely of chains, rode out on an illuminated organ, singing, "I hear that cat Shaft's a bad mother—" "Shut your mouth!" interrupted the chorus. "But I'm talking about Shaft," protested Hayes. "And we can dig it," responded the singers. The audience thoroughly enjoyed this number, and their applause was augmented by Sammy Davis' reaction. "Isn't that something! Isn't that heavy!" he exclaimed, jumping up and down. "Isn't it nice to have the Lawrence Welk show back? By the way, Mr. Hayes' shirt was by Hillcrest Hardware."

When Jerry Greenberg picked up the Editing Oscar for *The French Connection,* he thanked "the New York subway system." The Carpenters settled an old score and sang another nominated song, and were followed by Joel Gray with the envelope for the Best Song Award. For the first time, a black man won in this category—Isaac Hayes for the "Theme from *Shaft.*" The singer had changed into a black velvet tuxedo with blue lapels that he rented especially for the occasion. "Three bodyguards—six feet, six inches and wearing guns—came in and spot-checked the store," recalled the Tuxedo Center's Roger Meunier in a later interview. "Then Isaac came in with three more bodyguards. He must have been wearing $200,000 in jewelry." At the podium, Hayes gave most of his thanks to his grandmother, "the lady who's here by me tonight, because years ago her prayers kept my feet on the path of righteousness. This is a thrill for me and in a few days, it'll be her eightieth birthday and this is her present."

Jack Lemmon was the final emcee and he brought out Tennessee Williams to give the Writing Awards. When the playwright got to the nominees for *The Garden of the Finzi-Continis,* he

"Isn't that something! Isn't that heavy!"
—Sammy Davis, Jr.

sighed, "Thank God I went to Italy!" The Original Screenplay winner was Paddy Chayefsky for *The Hospital,* who embraced Tennessee and then praised "the high caliber of the other nominees."

Natalie Wood and Frank Capra were responsible for the Director's Award, and Natalie gave the envelope to Capra and said, "I truly believe the winner would rather hear it from you." The winner was the same man who had won the Directors Guild Award— thirty-two-year-old William Friedkin, for *The French Connection*. He wore a ruffled tuxedo shirt and saluted someone in the audience.

Walter Matthau began the Best Actress presentation by noting, "The tradition has been for the previous year's Best Actor to present Best Actress, but for reasons beyond our control . . . " When the laughter was over, Matthau announced the Best Actress winner—Jane Fonda. Some journalists reported scattered boos mixed in with the applause, but the jeers weren't heard on television. Fonda mounted the stage, bowed, took the Oscar and said, "Thank all of you who applauded." Then, after what the *Hollywood Reporter* termed "a tense and meaningful pause," Jane continued, "There's a great deal to say, but I'm not going to say it tonight. I just want to thank you very much."

Best Actor presenter Liza Minnelli breezed out to the tune of "Cabaret" and dismissed the cue cards. "Can you flip them over? I'm not going to say any of that," she instructed the stagehand, after telling the audience, "You all look great." Ripping open the envelope, Minnelli quipped, "Are you guys as nervous as I am?" She jumped and screamed, "The winner is Gene Hackman in *The French Connection*!" The winner looked at the envelope before he spoke. "This is what it says," Hackman murmured when he saw it in writing. The winner thanked his acting teacher and "Billy Friedkin, who brought me through this one—I wanted to quit."

The Best Picture presenter was Jack Nicholson, wearing a print shirt and a McGovern button. After a film clip of the chase scene from *The French Connection*, Nicholson joked, "It sounded like I was on my way home." The winner was *The French Connection,* and producer Philip D'Antoni was awed. "To think that *The French Connection* will rank with all the other pictures that have come to this place," he said.

President Taradash returned for the finale, leading into a compilation of film clips by saying, "Time is Chaplin's dearest friend." The montage ended with the closing iris shot from *The Circus*. The movie screen went up, revealing Charlie Chaplin alone onstage. The standing ovation lasted for several minutes. The microphone at the podium echoed loudly when Chaplin first tried to speak, but when it quieted down, the silent star said, "Words are so futile, so feeble." Jack Lemmon appeared with the Little Tramp's hat and cane and Chaplin put the hat on—another ovation. Mrs. Chaplin made her way onstage, followed by all the winners, presenters, and the dancers from the *Shaft* number. Lemmon "invited" everyone to sing Chaplin's own composition, "Smile," but most of the celebrities simply crowded around Charlie as a recording of the song filled the auditorium. The Shell gasoline trademark was superimposed over Chaplin's face and the telecast ended.

Aftermath

"I put my trust in Peter Bogdanovich and he didn't let me down," said Ben Johnson backstage. "I'm glad to know I didn't let him down either." When a reporter asked him if he had let up on his opposition to R-rated movies, the winner said, "Well, I saw the picture once and I liked it, but I don't plan on seeing it again. And I still don't want my mother to see it, although she wants to."

Costar Cloris Leachman was insisting that Oscar would not come between her and loser Ellen Burstyn. "I kept hearing all this talk about Ellen and me and it's driving me crazy," she said. "Ellen and I became very close and permanent friends while we were making the movie and I certainly wouldn't want anyone to think a friendly award could come between us." Now that the friendly award was hers, Leachman expected some changes in life. "I'm at a point where I'm free to go out and have a little fun with my career. Some Oscar winners have dropped out of sight as if they were standing on a trapdoor. Others picked it up and ran with it. I'm going to run with it." Leachman soon had her own TV series, *Phyllis,* and she worked so often for Disney, Roger Corman and Mel Brooks that the *New York Times* ran a story on her headlined, "Oh, No, Not Cloris Leachman Again!"

"I know I'm not the conventional handsome star," apologized Gene Hackman, "but just because I don't happen to resemble Tab Hunter or Ryan O'Neal doesn't mean I'm not virile. There's a lot of romance in all of us." His director, William Friedkin, meanwhile, was scoffing when reporters asked him what it felt like to be the youngest director ever to win the Oscar. "I'm very much still in the learning process," Friedkin said. "Speaking personally, I think Stanley Kubrick is the best American filmmaker of the year. In fact, not just this year, but the best, period."

Jane Fonda made good her word not "to say it tonight." After posing for pictures, she left, and she and Sutherland dined at a Japanese restaurant in Los Angeles' Little Tokyo. Despite her snubbing the Governors' Ball, the *Hollywood Reporter* dubbed Jane "the little darling of the crowd" because of her surprisingly gracious speech. Her father had spoken to her before the Awards and said, "I implore you not to make a political statement." Fonda herself later revealed:

> *A woman who is much wiser than I am said to me, "You're a subjective individual, an elite individual. The Oscar is what the working class relates to when it thinks of people in the movies. It's important for those of us who speak out for social change to get that kind of acclaim."*

President Taradash didn't know if Chaplin would feel up to the Governors' Ball, but the Oscar winner beat a hasty path to the Beverly Hilton and stayed there until after 1:30 A.M. The Academy laid out an extravagantly Gallic menu in his honor: pâté, Chateaubriand, Moët et Chandon. After dinner, Chaplin was reunited for the first time in thirty years with his costar from *The Kid,* Jackie Coogan, now fifty-seven years old. When Groucho Marx offered his congratulations, Chaplin whispered, "Stay warm, Groucho, you're next." Army Archerd reported that Sammy Davis, Jr., whose last movie was *Salt and Pepper,* "reacted like a fan when Chaplin said he knew his work." Chaplin couldn't say the same for Raquel Welch, who had problems of her own, as Shirley Eder reported: "Raquel was plenty upset with Joe Namath, because he never asked her to dance at the ball afterwards."

The Chaplin protesters never materialized, although the Academy's extra security force did catch one wiseguy who tried to break into the Little Tramp's limousine during the show. When reporters asked Chaplin about his political leanings today, the eighty-two-year-old replied, "I've retired from all that political sort of thing. That's one thing about money and age; it makes you lazy."

1972

"All I really need is sunshine, love and growing things around me."
—Liza Minnelli

An American Indian stole the thunder at the 1972 Academy Awards.

When John Kander and Fred Ebb wrote the Broadway musical *Cabaret,* they designed it as a showcase for their friend Liza Minnelli. Producer-director Hal Prince thought Judy Garland's daughter too awkward and inexperienced for the show, and so, the musical version of Christopher Isherwood's *Berlin Stories* went on to become the biggest hit of the 1966–67 season starring Jill Haworth. By the time *Cabaret* was being made into a movie, Minnelli had turned into a star—with an Oscar nomination for *The Sterile Cuckoo* as a credential. The role of Sally Bowles was hers.

First-time producer Cy Feuer signed Broadway whiz Bob Fosse as director, ignoring the fact that Fosse's one prior film, *Sweet Charity,* was an expensive flop. The whole troupe took off to Germany for location shooting and Liza had high hopes: "We're trying to show the dirt and decadence and the perverse atmosphere of Berlin when the Nazis came to power. All the musical numbers take place inside the cabaret with real drag queens and cheap, tacky sets."

Cabaret opened in February and the *Los Angeles Times* called the film "an exquisitely sculpted milestone in the history of the film musical." Pauline Kael predicted "after *Cabaret,* it should be awhile before performers once again climb hills singing or a chorus breaks into song on a hayride." By year's end, Fosse was having his biggest Broadway hit ever in *Pippin* and conquering television with the musical special *Liza With a "Z."*

Sunshine, Love and Liza

If people loved Bob Fosse, they adored his star. Liza Minnelli "gives a performance so beautiful I can think of nothing to do but give thanks," said Roger Greenspun in the *New York Times.* In rapid succession, Liza made the covers of *Time, Newsweek* and *Life,* which proclaimed: "At 25, Liza Minnelli is still Judy's daughter, but now she is her own voice." Despite reaching this new level of stardom, Liza's philosophy remained simple: "All I really need," she told the *New York Times,* "is sunshine, love and growing things around me." The thing growing around her the most was her romance with nineteen-year-old Desi Arnaz, Jr. "Liza, wrought by anxieties, may be doing everything in her power to close the [age] gap," reported *Modern Screen.* "Her makeup is kookier, her clothes more far-out. Her energy is almost frenetic. With Desi she giggles, bubbles—like a teenager without a care in the world."

Cabaret also brought stardom to nightclub performer and Broadway actor Joel Grey, repeating his stage role as the master of ceremonies. *Saturday Review* effused, "Nothing like Mr. Grey has happened before, not on stage and not in films. He is totally outrageous, mocking, raucous, leering, a dreadfully delightful symbol of the overall decadence." Pauline Kael stated, "Joel Grey is every tantalizingly disgusting show-biz creep one has ever seen."

Brando's Back in Town

The unexpected excitement over *Cabaret* momentarily diverted attention from one of the most anticipated movies in years, *The Godfather,* premiering in March. Six years earlier, Paramount head Robert Evans had gotten his hands on a thirty-page treatment for a book called *Mafia* and liked it, so the studio paid unknown author Mario Puzo $35,000 for the rights. Evans sat back and watched the book, retitled *The Godfather,* become a phenomenally successful bestseller. The producer hired thirty-two-year-old Francis Ford Coppola to direct the film version, even though his last two movies had been bombs. Evans' reason: "He'll be easy to control." No sooner was Coppola signed than he began to argue with the Paramount brass about raising the budget and turning *The*

Overleaf: *Sacheen Littlefeather holds up the longest acceptance speech in Oscar history—all fifteen pages of Marlon Brando's rejection.*

"Joel Grey is every tantalizingly disgusting show-biz creep one has ever seen."
—Pauline Kael

Godfather into an epic instead of what the studio envisioned—a low-budget gangster thriller with an exploitable title.

Coppola's next issue was casting. Danny Thomas, Ernest Borgnine and lawyer Melvin Belli each made it known that he'd be perfect as patriarch Don Corleone. The studio mulled over such possibilities as Burt Lancaster, Orson Welles, George C. Scott and Edward G. Robinson, but Coppola was determined to have "one of the world's two greatest actors," Laurence Olivier or Marlon Brando, whom author Puzo claimed to have had in mind from the beginning. Olivier was unavailable, but as far as Paramount was concerned Brando wasn't even a contender—the troublemaker hadn't had a hit in a dozen years. But when the actor stuffed tissue paper in his mouth to make his own screen test, studio executives were impressed by his humility; when they *saw* the test, they signed Brando for $50,000 and a percentage of the profits.

Sons of a Gun

As one fan magazine put it, "The hunt for Corleone's sons was tantamount to finding *four* Scarlett O'Haras." It helped if you were a friend of Coppola's. One old buddy, John Cazale, got the minor role of Fredo and another, James Caan, tested for the three remaining sons. Coppola decided he would be most persuasive as Sonny, the one with the voracious sexual appetite. Robert Duvall, who had costarred with Caan in Coppola's *The Rain People,* signed for Tom Hagen, the adopted Irish son. Paramount wanted to see Warren Beatty, Jack Nicholson or Dustin Hoffman play Michael, the heir apparent. They scoffed at Coppola's suggestion of Al Pacino, a stage actor who hadn't made much of a splash playing a drug addict in *The Panic in Needle Park*. Pacino was pretty thin-skinned about the whole thing: "Francis knew I could do the part and so did I," he recalled, "but he kept asking me to test again and again. I didn't want to go . . . I don't go where I'm not wanted." Paramount finally relented, and Pacino celebrated his good fortune. "Once I got the role," he said, "I was waking up at four or five in the morning and going into the kitchen to brood over the role."

Class Clowns

Filming began in March 1971, and James Caan remembered, "Jesus, at first everybody was so uptight. Francis was a wreck and Pacino looked like he was going to die. But I gotta have fun, so Bobby Duvall and I started cutting up, and then Brando joined in. It got to the point where Brando and I couldn't look each other in the eye. We would just laugh." Paramount was laughing over Brando, too; not only did the actor refrain from tantrums, but he was having such a good time "mooning" people on the set that he worked an extra week without extra pay.

The Money Tree

"Promises to be the *Gone With the Wind* of gangster movies," heralded *Newsweek* when *The Godfather* opened and *Time* piped in that it has "the dynastic sweep of an Italian-American *Gone With the Wind*." "Hollywood has finally produced a money tree that won't stop growing," wrote Wayne Warga in the *Los Angeles Times,* and before long *The Godfather* passed *Gone With the Wind* for the number-one position on the all-time box-office list. The film also invaded the American vernacular—"Make him an offer he can't refuse" was soon in the repertoire of Madison Avenue copywriters and Borscht Belt comedians.

With his percentage of the profits, Marlon Brando got a whole lot of money, but on top of that he got back his respectability. *Newsweek* oozed, "There is no longer any need to talk tragically of Marlon Brando's career. His stormy two-decade odyssey through films good and bad, but rarely big enough to house his prodigious talents, has ended in triumph . . . At forty-seven, the king has returned to reclaim his throne."

Everyone connected with *The Godfather* made

"I'm an actor, not a star. Stars are people who live in Hollywood and have heart-shaped swimming pools."
—Al Pacino

out like gangbusters. Critics said Francis Ford Coppola had joined Peter Bogdanovich and William Friedkin as the future of American movies—the trio formed a production company. Robert Duvall, who was in several films released in 1972, was declared one of the foremost young character actors in movies and a *Newsweek* profile dubbed him "Man of Many Faces." James Caan had just starred in the football tearjerker *Brian's Song,* the highest-rated TV movie yet, and this one-two punch suddenly made him a star after nearly a decade of trying. He did have one complaint, however—"All the women I now meet expect me to perform like Sonny Corleone." And columnist Dorothy Manners sighed, "Though Marlon Brando is great in *The Godfather,* Al Pacino is the one who has the girls and women panting. He has enough animal magnetism to get himself locked up in a zoo!" Fame did not make Pacino giddy. The actor, who lived in a small apartment in Boston with his girlfriend, Jill Clayburgh, protested, "I'm an actor, not a star. Stars are people who live in Hollywood and have heart-shaped swimming pools."

Look Ma, No Clothes

Burt Reynolds had none of Pacino's compunctions. A veteran of a couple of television series and some B-movies, the thirty-six-year-old Reynolds *wanted* to be a star and worked to develop a following by making acerbic comments on the Johnny Carson show. When Reynolds took off his clothes for a centerfold in the April 1972 issue of *Cosmopolitan,* he became one of the biggest names in the business. Now that he had parlayed himself into a hot item, he wanted to be taken seriously as an actor. *Deliverance* helped him do it.

Based on poet James Dickey's bestseller and starring Jon Voight, *Deliverance* followed four suburbanites out to prove how macho they are by canoeing in the backwoods of Georgia. Reviewers praised the movie's visceral thrills—"A magnificent visual assault on the senses," raved *Time*—but hooted at its "intellectual pretensions." In the words of Vincent Canby, it was "an action melodrama that doesn't trust its action to speak louder than words on the order of 'Sometimes you gotta lose yourself to find something.' If anybody said that to me—seriously—in the course of a canoe trip, I think I'd get out and wade." *Deliverance* became the biggest moneymaker of the summer and, for once, people were mentioning Burt Reynolds not for the centerfold or his relationship with Dinah Shore, but for his acting abilities. The movie's popularity was helped by a bluegrass tune called "Dueling Banjos," which made its way into the top ten.

The Great Black Hope

Because *Superfly, Blacula* and lots of other "blaxploitation" movies were so popular, many reviewers sang hosannahs when they found *Sounder,* a film in the "humanistic" tradition of *Lilies of the Field. Sounder,* directed by Martin Ritt, was based on a children's book about a black sharecropping family during the Depression. *Variety* said the movie "transcends space, race, age and time" and *Black Stars* magazine hailed *Sounder* as "the film we've all waited for." Paul Winfield, playing the father sent to prison for stealing food for his wife and kids, told reporters: "The love and devotion the Lee family expresses in *Sounder* is what it is all about. This is the real black experience." He also groused that in other black films "those cats don't show any humor or emotions. They just get in and out of bed." And *Vogue* wrote of Cicely Tyson, who claimed she went without work for three years waiting for a decent role before playing the wife, "At long last a black woman as a human being with pride, dignity, strength and love . . . It's a complete change from those stereotypes as prostitute, drug addict, vacuous servant girl." Not everyone thought good intentions were enough. In the *New York Times,* Roger Greenspun complained that people were "treating *Sounder* not as a movie at all but rather as something unusually worthy, like the United Fund or a UNICEF Christmas card."

"The first time I heard a Billie Holiday record, I thought, 'What's so great about Billie Holiday?'"
—Diana Ross

Diana Takes a Holiday

The only time Diana Ross had ever acted was when she and fellow Supremes Mary and Cindy appeared as nuns on an episode of the *Tarzan* TV series in 1968. But now that Ross had been a successful solo act for a couple of years, her mentor, Motown head Berry Gordy, decided it was time for her to become a movie star. The vehicle he put together was *Lady Sings the Blues,* based on Billie Holiday's autobiography, but the singer of "Love Child" said, "The first time I heard a Billie Holiday record, I thought, 'What's so great about Billie Holiday?'"

Ross forged ahead, nevertheless, maintaining, "I tried to find the person that Billie Holiday was at home, that very few people knew about." *Rolling Stone* said of Ross' ultimate performance: "Every whisky breath she takes, each flutter of those heavy lids, all the unstudied nuance of her performance, each shrug of those exquisite shoulders, every ululation of the clavicles—it comes from a clairvoyant affinity for the period, the music, and most of all for the woman Billie Holiday might have been." White and black audiences alike swooned over the romantic clinches between Ross and Billy Dee Williams, whom one critic described as "sort of a black Clark Gable." Ross was now a film star with a smash movie and she was rewarded with a cover story in *Life,* "New Day for Diana," and a top-selling sound-track album. Even jazz purists who winced at Ross' rendition of "God Bless the Child" didn't mind too much; thanks to the movie, Lady Day's records were once again big sellers.

Liv in Hollywood

Diana Ross wasn't the only one getting that old movie-star treatment. Liv Ullmann had her face plastered on the front of *Time* with a caption heralding "Hollywood's New Nordic Star"—even though she had yet to be seen in a Hollywood movie. The thirty-three-year-old veteran of Ingmar Bergman films was currently on view in *The Emigrants,* a two-and-a-half hour movie from Sweden about immigrants settling in the American Midwest during the mid-nineteenth century. The *Christian Science Monitor* called this surprise hit "a Swedish *Gone With the Wind*" while the *Los Angeles Times* deemed it "the most beautiful and profoundly touching celebration of the American experience to come along in years." Soon after, Ingmar Bergman's latest, *Cries and Whispers,* opened in New York and won Ullmann the Best Actress Award from the New York Film Critics.

What really impressed the movie industry, however, was that instead of brooding for Bergman, Ullmann would now be making big-budget movies in Hollywood. *Time* exclaimed: "A new movie star is about to burst onto U.S. movie screens, starting with the release of *Lost Horizon* next spring." Excitement over Ullmann was so great that producer Mike Frankovich couldn't have cared less that Audrey Hepburn and Elizabeth Taylor were dying to be in his comedy about a chic, middle-aged divorcée, *40 Carats,* and revised the script so that the younger Ullmann could star. While in Hollywood, Ullmann made the gossip columns by being seen in the company of Warren Beatty, as well as Glenn Ford, but she admitted she was less than enthusiastic about the California life-style: "You never see anyone. Nobody in the streets. Nobody at the windows of houses."

The Two of Us

There was almost nobody in the movie *Sleuth,* either. The film version of the comedy-mystery stage success had a cast of exactly two actors, portraying romantic rivals trying to do each other in on an English country estate. Laurence Olivier, in his first starring role in six years, was the flamboyant cuckolded husband and, unable to sign Albert Finney or Alan Bates, director Joseph Mankiewicz went with Michael Caine as the younger man. Caine gave the assignment his all because, as he put it, "*Sleuth* was not only a game between people, but a game between two actors." His special preparation for this part? "To put it mildly," he said, "I do like to drink. But I didn't take a single one all during filming, in order to keep my mind absolutely sharp. I felt I needed that with Olivier."

His method worked. Although it was Olivier who won the New York Film Critics Award, on the West Coast the *Los Angeles Times* wrote, "The surprise and the pleasure of *Sleuth* is to discover Michael Caine as an actor of such range and ability giving as good as he gets from the pre-eminent actor of the English stage." What four-time Oscar winner Joe Mankiewicz got was his first hit since *Suddenly Last Summer* in 1959.

Topsy-Turvy

Producer Irwin Allen had won an Academy Award in 1952 for his documentary *The Sea Around Us* and then moved on to science-fiction movies such as *The Lost World* and TV shows such as *Lost in Space*. In 1972, he returned to cinema with *The Poseidon Adventure* starring Gene Hackman and four other Oscar winners, and in the process created a whole new genre—the all-star disaster epic. The premise was preposterous—passengers escaping from an ocean liner turned upside down by a tidal wave—but the public loved it. They especially loved Shelley Winters as an overweight Jewish grandmother. In the *New York Times,* Vincent Canby noted, "The audience clearly adores her, to such an extent that at one point, when it appeared the character might be having a heart attack, a lady in my row cried out with concern: 'Aw, come on, Shelley.'" *Newsweek* remarked that Winters "is plump enough these days to sink an ocean liner all by herself," but she hit all the talk shows demonstratively asserting that "I put on all this weight for the movie!" She also made sure everyone knew that this was only a temporary condition—under her contract the studio had to pay for her sessions at a fat farm.

Parents and Children

Another actress with a favorite line for interviewers was newcomer Jeannie Berlin, who got great reviews for playing an uncouth Jewish newlywed dumped by her husband in the Neil Simon comedy, *The Heartbreak Kid*. "Nobody believes me," she protested, "but, yes, I did have to test for the part just like anybody else"—even though the director was her mother, Elaine May. Berlin did pause from that line of thought to say, "I've been told I look like Anne Bancroft, Ingrid Bergman and, from some angles, Tiny Tim." *The Heartbreak Kid* also marked the return to movies of Eddie Albert, who had spent the previous six years on TV's *Green Acres* with Eva Gabor and Arnold the Pig. The critics were glad to have him back; the *New York Times* called him "superbly comic."

Albert had more to crow about this year than just his own good reviews. His son Edward Albert starred in the popular comedy *Butterflies Are Free,* as a blind musician trying to go it alone who becomes involved with Goldie Hawn, playing the "hippie" next door. In the annual exhibitors' Stars of Tomorrow poll, young Albert came in second, right behind Al Pacino. *Butterflies* also featured Eileen Heckart, re-creating her Broadway role as the domineering mother who, for the benefit of the film's targeted middle-aged audience, becomes the heroine of the piece. *Variety* reported, "Miss Heckart finally gets another role that enables her to display the versatility that has been evident for a long time in her stage roles."

East Side Kids

The New York Film Critics didn't give much guidance to Hollywood—*Cries and Whispers,* the Bergman picture which had not yet opened in Hollywood, dominated their awards. The critics couldn't decide whether to consider Marlon Brando and Al Pacino as leads or supporting players, so the two Corleones lost out to Laurence Oli-

"It's so much fun being nominated—everyone is a winner. And then—afterwards—there are four losers."
—Liv Ullmann

vier for Best Actor and Robert Duvall for Supporting Actor. Liv Ullmann in *Cries and Whispers* (but not *The Emigrants*) and Jeannie Berlin in *The Heartbreak Kid* won the feminine awards.

Back in Hollywood, the campaign was on. United Artists and Avco Embassy were fighting it out over Peter O'Toole, UA wanting him nominated for his Don Quixote in the disastrous but expensive *Man of La Mancha,* Avco pushing him as an Englishman who thinks he's Christ in its cult hit, *The Ruling Class*. Paramount instructed Academy voters that Brando was *the* lead in *The Godfather*—everyone else should be considered supporting. George C. Scott had directed a movie this year—something called *Rage*—and told the press he'd gladly accept an Oscar nomination.

The Nominations

As expected, *The Godfather* led the pack with eleven nominations, including Marlon Brando's first in fifteen years, and supporting nods for James Caan, Robert Duvall and Al Pacino. *Cabaret* was right behind with ten nominations, and since it had no double nominations in any category, its backers were bragging that it was competing in more categories than any other film. *The Emigrants,* a Foreign Film contender last year, was up for Best Picture—only the third foreign-language film so honored—while its sequel, *The New Land,* was nominated for Best Foreign Film. Best Picture nominee *Deliverance* had four nominations, although voters had not taken Burt Reynolds seriously enough to give him a nod. *Sounder* was the fifth Best Picture competitor, with four nominations, but director Martin Ritt was passed over for *Sleuth*'s Joseph L. Mankiewicz.

The Best Actress race attracted the most attention. With Liza Minnelli, Diana Ross, Cicely Tyson and Liv Ullmann in competition, the outcome was anybody's guess. Only Maggie Smith, playing Graham Greene's eccentric heroine for George Cukor in *Travels with My Aunt* was, by virtue of her previous win, out of the running. But then, during the voting period, a dark shadow fell on Ullmann's chances—*Lost Horizon* opened.

Cynics snorted that the two black nominees, Ross and Tyson, were bound to cancel each other out, but Motown decided to beef up Diana's chances by going all out with daily advertisements—full-page pictures of the actress in scenes from *Lady Sings the Blues*.

The anticipated sweep for *The Godfather* seemed a sure thing when Francis Ford Coppola won the Directors Guild Award. *Cabaret*'s Bob Fosse had some consolation when he won two Tony Awards for *Pippin* two days before the Oscar ceremonies. The Academy took away one of *The Godfather*'s nominations—a snoop discovered that composer Nino Rota had cribbed the film's popular "Love Theme" from his score from a 1958 Italian movie. Rota was out, John Addison's *Sleuth* score was in.

Marlon Brando had more than just *The Godfather* going for him. He had aped Burt Reynolds and taken his clothes off for the just-released and very controversial *Last Tango in Paris,* making him the most discussed man in America—Michael Caine, Laurence Olivier, Peter O'Toole and Paul Winfield didn't have a prayer. Winfield shrugged and said, "I'm just thrilled to be mentioned along with four of the world's greatest actors." Olivier told columnist Radie Harris that he wouldn't be at the ceremony: "It's an awfully long way to come and my face isn't going to look any prettier with all that egg on it."

Academy officials were a little nervous waiting for Brando to confirm whether he'd be attending the Awards. In January, he had refused his Golden Globe for *The Godfather* because there "is a singular lack of honor in this country today . . . and to accept an honor, however well-intended, is to subtract from the meager amount left." The headline of the *Hollywood Reporter* on the morning of the Academy Awards blared: BRANDO IS MYSTERY MAN AS OSCAR CURTAIN RISES. At the last minute Brando finally R.S.V.P.'d. He would be unable to attend the ceremony but he was sending a proxy.

The Big Night

Twenty pickets mingled across from the Dorothy Chandler Pavilion, hired by the producer of the X-rated science-fiction spoof *Flesh Gordon* because he was mad the Academy didn't nominate his movie for an Oscar for Visual Effects. Hank Grant reported, "One joker in the bleachers sporadically yelled, 'Here comes Marlon Brando,' which worked up the crowd considerably until they realized he was yelling 'Wolf' and almost tossed the rascal outta the stands." Another bleacher fan had as his date a life-sized cardboard cutout of Barbra Streisand. Among the real-life celebrities, the first to arrive were Eddie Albert and family. Burt Reynolds brought Dinah Shore, Liv Ullmann had her mother and her nominated director Jan Troell with her and said she felt sad the big night had arrived: "It's so much fun being nominated—everyone is a winner. And then—afterwards—there are four losers." Zsa Zsa Gabor's escort was World War II hero General Jimmy Doolittle. In contrast, Cesar "Butch" Romero was all alone.

Liza Minnelli had two escorts: her father Vincente and beau Desi Arnaz, Jr., with a crucifix outside his tuxedo. "If I don't win," laughed Liza, "I can think of it as just a nice party." "I know Shelley Winters or Susan Tyrrell is going to win," Supporting Actress nominee Eileen Heckart nervously said. "I just hope they pan the camera on me just once. I paid a lot of money for this dress"—a simple beige knit outfit with matching cloak—"and I want my mother in Columbus, Ohio, to be able to see it."

Meanwhile, Marlon Brando's stand-in, a woman wearing Apache garb, was introducing herself to the show's producer, Howard W. Koch. She also showed him the speech written by Brando she'd be reading if the actor won—all fifteen pages of it. "I'll give you forty-five seconds to make your statement," warned Koch. "If you go one second over I'll have you bodily removed from stage. I promise you I'm not afraid to do that."

The stage was made up to resemble an empty

Awards Ceremony

MARCH 27, 1973, 7:00 P.M.
THE DOROTHY CHANDLER PAVILION, LOS ANGELES

Your Hosts:
CAROL BURNETT, MICHAEL CAINE,
CHARLTON HESTON, ROCK HUDSON
Televised over NBC

Presenters

Sound .... Eddie Albert and Edward Albert
Special Achievement Award .... Merle Oberon
Short Subjects ...... Beatrice Arthur and Peter Boyle
Supporting Actress .... Robert Duvall and Cloris Leachman
Foreign Film........ Elke Sommer and Jack Valenti
Film Editing .... John Gavin and Katharine Ross
Supporting Actor ..... James Coburn and Diana Ross
Honorary Award to Charles S. Boren .... Richard Walsh
Documentary Awards .... Robert Wagner and Natalie Wood
Costume Design .... Marisa Berenson and Michael Caine
Art Direction .... Greer Garson and Laurence Harvey
Scoring Awards .... Dyan Cannon and Burt Reynolds
Cinematography .... Candice Bergen and Billy Dee Williams
Song .... Sonny and Cher
Honorary Award to Edward G. Robinson .... Charlton Heston
Jean Hersholt Humanitarian Award .... Frank Sinatra
Director .... Julie Andrews and George Stevens
Writing Awards .... Jack Lemmon
Actor .... Roger Moore and Liv Ullmann
Actress .... Gene Hackman and Raquel Welch
Picture .... Clint Eastwood

Performers of Nominated Songs

"Ben" .... Michael Jackson
"Come Follow, Follow Me" .... The Springfield Revival
"Marmalade, Molasses and Honey" ... Glen Campbell and the Mike Curb Congregation
"The Morning After" .... Connie Stevens
"Strange Are the Ways of Love" .... Diahann Carroll

"Marlon Brando very regretfully cannot accept this very generous Award."
—Sacheen Littlefeather

Hollywood sound stage and Angela Lansbury kicked off the show with a musical tribute to movies ranging from *Seventh Heaven* to *Cabaret*. Then Academy President Daniel Taradash made the invocation, noting that film criticism is "made by people who can't make movies." Then he added, "Tonight, the professionals are the reviewers."

The first of the evening's cohosts came onstage and the audience double-checked its programs—what was Clint Eastwood doing up there? Eastwood said that this "was supposed to be Charlton Heston's part of the show but for some reason he's not here . . . so who did they get? A guy who hasn't said three lines in twelve movies." He gamely went on, reading the cue card jokes about Moses and *The Ten Commandments*. Within minutes, Heston arrived, to the obvious relief of Eastwood, whom producer Koch had grabbed out of the audience and instructed, "You're going on!"—Ruby Keeler–style. Heston had gotten a flat tire on his way to the show, but didn't enlighten the audience or apologize for his tardiness, simply jumping in as if nothing had happened.

Supporting Actor nominee Eddie Albert presented the Sound Award with Edward Albert, whom he proudly referred to as "my son the movie star." Merle Oberon got a big hand for coming up from her home in Mexico to give a Special Oscar for Visual Effects to *The Poseidon Adventure*. She entered on a moving platform made to resemble the deck of a ship, but the mechanism malfunctioned and, for her efforts, Oberon nearly got knocked off.

Cloris Leachman, presenting Best Supporting Actress, announced that she had "a little gift of thanks for the Academy, it's something they've needed for a long time," and produced a letter opener. Copresenter Robert Duvall said, "I would like to thank you, too, but I didn't even watch the show last year," and then, spotting his pal from *The Godfather*, James Caan, added, "Hi, Jimmy, how are you?" Reading the list of nominees, Leachman pronounced "Susan Tyrrell in *Fat City*" and Duvall started saying "Shelley Winters . . ." and then laughed uproariously as he struggled to get through "in *The Poseidon Adventure*." The TV cameras cut to Winters wondering if it was her nomination or the juxtaposition of "*Fat City*" and her name that Duvall found so funny.

Shelley didn't get the opportunity to have it out with Duvall—the winner was Eileen Heckart in *Butterflies Are Free,* whose mother thus got a good long look at her dress. Among those the winner thanked was "the very first man who recommended me for this part, Howard Otway," best known for running Theatre 80 St. Marks, a revival house in New York where the projector is located behind the screen.

Carol Burnett took over as hostess and mentioned that she knew Joel Grey "when his name was Joel Katz. It's not easy for two kids named Minnelli and Katz to tap dance across Nazi Germany." Best Foreign Film was given by the inevitable Jack Valenti, head of the Motion Picture Association of America, and Elke Sommer, who, Burnett revealed, "is a beautiful lady who talks and acts in six languages." The winner was Luis Buñuel's *The Discreet Charm of the Bourgeoisie* and producer Serge Silberman accepted, telling everyone, "My English is only so-so."

Introducing Best Supporting Actor presenter Diana Ross—in a white silk tuxedo with rhinestone vest—Carol Burnett commented, "Why she left the Supremes, I'll never know." The winner was Joel Grey for *Cabaret,* and when his name was read, Liza Minnelli went haywire and kicked his chair furiously. "Don't let anybody tell you this isn't a terrific thrill," the winner effused. As Grey walked off, Burnett returned and, making no attempt to hide her delight, reminded the audience, "I knew him when he was Joel Katz." Francis Ford Coppola and the rest of *The Godfather* crowd was getting a little antsy; *Cabaret* had now won three Awards, their movie none.

The next host was Best Actor nominee Michael Caine, who said that "if it hadn't been for an American film called *The Caine Mutiny,* the bloke

"What Marlon Brando did this year could signal the death of Oscar as we know him."
—Rona Barrett

standing before you would still be called Maurice Micklewhite." He added that when he was growing up "the name didn't matter because what we would call each other would blow the tube out of your telly." Marisa Berenson then gave Best Costume Design to *Travels with My Aunt*. The television cameras caught director George Cukor sitting in his seat clapping happily. Suddenly, an arm reached from a few rows behind and pushed him, but it was still a while before Cukor realized *he* was supposed to be up there accepting for the absent winner.

The presentation of an Honorary Award to Edward G. Robinson, who had died two months earlier, began with the recorded voice of James Cagney praising his old friend from Warner Brothers, followed by a compilation of film clips. Robinson, who had never been nominated for an Oscar, had learned of the Award a week before his death and his widow read the acknowledgment he had written: "It couldn't have come at a better time in a man's life. Had it come earlier, it would have aroused deep feelings in me, still not so deep as now. I'm so very grateful to my rich, warm, creative, talented, intimate colleagues who have been my life's association. How much richer can you be?"

After people dressed up as Mickey Mouse, Donald Duck, and Goofy danced around onstage in tribute to the fiftieth anniversary of Walt Disney Studios, Frank Sinatra gave the Jean Hersholt Humanitarian Award to his friend Rosalind Russell. Sinatra referred to her acting nominations, telling the audience, "Knowing Roz as I do, she'd value this one more than the other four." And then Rock Hudson came out to be the final host of the show.

The Best Director Award was given by two-time winner George Stevens and Julie Andrews, the wife of director Blake Edwards. The winnner was not Directors Guild victor Francis Ford Coppola, but *Cabaret*'s Bob Fosse, who now had an Oscar to go with his Tony. Army Archerd wrote that the night's "biggest gasp from the Academy members—and guests—greeted the announcement." Fosse was as surprised as everyone else, saying, "I feel a little like Clint Eastwood—you're letting me stand up here because Coppola and Mankiewicz haven't shown up yet." He singled out his soon-to-be-ex-wife Gwen Verdon for thanks, calling her "a dear friend of mine." The score stood at *Cabaret*, seven Awards, *The Godfather*, none, and *The Godfather*'s producer Albert S. Ruddy later said, "When they announced Fosse for Director, I was ready to tear up my speech."

Ruddy could calm down a bit; Jack Lemmon gave the Adapted Screenplay Oscar to *The Godfather*. Mario Puzo's daughter accepted for him, and Francis Ford Coppola, in a red tuxedo jacket, admitted, "I was beginning to think I wasn't going to get up here at all." Jeremy Larner, writer of *The Candidate*, a film about a political campaign, punctuated his acceptance speech with a dig at President Richard Nixon. "I'd like to thank the political figures of our time, who have given me terrific inspiration," he said.

It was time for the Best Actor Award. Liv Ullmann and Roger Moore opened the envelope, and the winner was Marlon Brando. The young woman in Native American costume came to the podium, but she brushed away Roger Moore as he tried to hand her the Oscar. She turned to the audience and said:

> *Hello. My name is Sacheen Littlefeather. I'm Apache and I am president of the National Native American Affirmative Image Committee. I'm representing Marlon Brando this evening and he has asked me to tell you in a very long speech which I cannot share with you presently because of time but I will be glad to share with the press afterwards that he very regretfully cannot accept this very generous award. And the reasons for this being are the treatment of American Indians today by the film industry. [Some rumbling in the audience.] Excuse me*

"It's all a lot of crap."
—Robert Duvall

> *. . .[boos and claps] and on television in movie reruns and also with the recent happenings at Wounded Knee.*
>
> *I beg at this time that I have not intruded upon this evening and that we will, in the future, in our hearts and our understanding meet with love and generosity.*
>
> *Thank you on behalf of Marlon Brando.*

Nobody booed as Littlefeather went off to the pressroom to read Brando's statement to any members of the press who cared to listen. Those in the audience sat motionless, stunned by what had transpired.

Leading into Best Actress, Rock Hudson said, "Often to be eloquent is to be silent." Raquel Welch didn't wish to be eloquent; as she and Gene Hackman were about to name the Best Actress winner, she muttered, "I hope they haven't got a cause." The television cameras cut to the nominees, revealing that Diana Ross, not wanting to be seen in the same thing twice, had switched from her tuxedo into a black evening gown and fur. The winner was an ebullient Liza Minnelli. "Making the film of *Cabaret* was one of the happiest times of my entire life," she exclaimed. "Thank you for giving me this Award. You've made me very happy." The camera cut to Vincente Minnelli and Desi Arnaz, Jr., both looking very happy.

Clint Eastwood was back to give Best Picture, but first commented, "I don't know if I should present this Award on behalf of all the cowboys shot in John Ford westerns over the years." Even though by this point it had become something of a long shot, the winner was *The Godfather*. Producer Albert S. Ruddy said, "We were all getting nervous for a minute there," adding, "I want to make it quick because its past midnight in New York and I have some relatives who want to go to sleep."

Out lumbered John Wayne, who had a suggestion for ending the show: "Let's get all the winners and presenters out here to take a much-deserved bow. Whaddya say?" The gang joined the Duke, who said, "Now, why don't all of you out there on TV join with us in singing 'You Oughta Be in Pictures.' You better sing because I'll be watching and pow."

Wayne started singing—off-key—and a few people joined in, but nobody knew the lyrics past the first two lines. Hoping to avoid an embarrassing ending, director Marty Pasetta switched to highlights of the show as the credits rolled. When he ran out of highlights, the television audience was treated to the sight of John Wayne—still making a game try at the song—being dwarfed by Mickey Mouse standing behind him.

Aftermath

The television critic of the *Hollywood Reporter* wrote: "It was a very routine Oscar cast until a charming young woman by the name of Sashima [sic] Littlefeather blew the top off the TV set." And that was all anyone wanted to talk about. "My own reaction is that he has no guts," said Academy President Daniel Taradash. "If he had any class, he would have come down there and said it himself. That's my first reaction. My second is that I liked Jane Fonda's speech better." Best Actor loser Michael Caine concurred: "I think if the man wants to make a gesture, I agree entirely with what he did, but I think he should have stood up and done it himself instead of letting some poor little Indian girl take the boos." Caine had another thought: "And if you're going to make a humanitarian gesture, I think a man who makes $2 million playing that leader of the Mafia should at least give half of it to the Indians."

Charlton Heston said, "It was childish. The American Indian needs better friends than that." Paramount head Frank Yablans was perplexed, saying, "Personally, I think it's foolish. I always accept all my awards." Brando did have some supporters. Jane Fonda commented, "I thought what he did was wonderful." And producer Albert S. Ruddy defended his star: "Where is the time and

"Now, why don't all of you out there on TV join with us in singing 'You Oughta Be in Pictures.'"
—John Wayne

place for that kind of demonstration? It's whenever you have a moment that you would have the biggest audience . . . It's something I may not have said, but I certainly back him in his right to say it."

The *Hollywood Reporter* editorialized that "the tragedy of Mr. Brando's act is that while he sought to serve the welfare of the American Indian, nothing was gained but ill-will." Rona Barrett was so eager for everyone to know how she felt that she took out a full-page ad in the trade papers transcribing her remarks from a television broadcast. After stating that "the greatness of the United States lies in each man's right to expression without fear of being thrown in jail," she expressed her fear that "what Marlon Brando did this year could signal the death of Oscar as we know him . . ."

Barrett also turned investigative reporter and scooped that Sacheen Littlefeather was really a professional actress using the name Maria Cruz, that she had been selected "Miss American Vampire of 1970" and, in that capacity, had made personal appearances on behalf of MGM's *House of Dark Shadows*. Littlefeather told reporters later, "I thought if I came out alive, I'd be lucky." She also maintained, "I feel that I am doing the proper thing and I cannot help what people think," adding that "a very nice man and his son"—Eddie and Edward Albert—congratulated her and offered their support.

Despite all the brouhaha over Brando, reporters did find time to talk to the other winners. *The Godfather*'s Albert S. Ruddy said Best Picture presenter "Clint Eastwood is a friend of mine. I suggested that if some other movie won Best Picture, he announce *The Godfather* and eat the envelope." Francis Ford Coppola was still incredulous. Shaking his head, he acknowledged, "I was so sure I was going to win Best Director." His conqueror Bob Fosse would soon be winning the third jewel in entertainment's triple crown—an Emmy Award for directing TV's *Liza With a "Z"*. Joel Grey told the press he was hoping his next film role would be the title character in Bob Fosse's forthcoming *Lenny*. Fosse was noncommittal.

Best Supporting Actress Eileen Heckart lamented that, backstage, "they made me do something that was a bit tacky. I had to cuddle the Oscar and the worst thing was that I found myself doing it." Returning to her hotel after the Governors' Ball, Heckart found a note from her friend Marlene Dietrich instructing the winner to call her. When she did, Dietrich scolded her, "Eileen, your makeup was terrible." When she got back home to Connecticut, Heckart went to an unemployment office to apply for benefits. "They cheered me when I walked in," she said. "I'm very well known there."

One of the actresses Heckart defeated, Shelley Winters, was smarting that Robert Duvall had laughed at her in front of all those millions of people. Duvall tried to rectify things, giving the trade papers his explanation: "I respect Shelley as an actress and as an individual. How can I explain that my laugh had nothing to do with her?" Duvall had "spotted Jimmy Caan grinning wickedly at me" and "as anyone who worked with us can tell you, Caan always breaks me up." He concluded, "I apologize to Shelley for the unfortunate coincidence. At that moment I wouldn't have been able to stifle my laugh if I was announcing the arrival of the Pope."

Duvall added that he did not share his *Godfather* costar's disdain of Oscar: "I feel the people who give prizes in Hollywood are no more or less qualified than the New York Film Critics. I took a prize from them, so why not take one from Hollywood? It's all a lot of crap, but as long as it's there . . ."

Liza Minnelli said her only disappointment was the speech Rock Hudson delivered when introducing the Best Actress Award. "He said, 'In a horserace, bloodlines count and Liza's got the bloodlines,'" the Best Actress complained. "Well, I don't want to think I won because of my mother. That's why in my speech I said, 'Thank you for giving *me* this award.'"

At least Minnelli won an Award. In her autobiography, Best Actress loser Liv Ullmann recalled departing the theater, referring to herself in the third person: "Outside are hundreds of autograph-hunters and they hurl themselves at her, still remembering her from television. She has written her name a few times, when she hears a screech as from a thousand gulls. There comes the winner. The autograph books are torn from her, the name half written on a paper she is holding. She's almost trampled underfoot as they rush past her in their pursuit of the Successful One."

1973

"I never miss a Liv Ullmann musical."
—Bette Midler

Oscar wasn't the only naked man at the 1973 Academy Awards.

The year started off with the premiere of Ross Hunter's first movie since *Airport,* a $12 million musical remake of Frank Capra's 1937 film *Lost Horizon.* Hunter found room for everyone: *Butch Cassidy*'s Burt Bacharach and Hal David wrote the songs, and the cast included *Romeo and Juliet*'s Olivia Hussey, *M*A*S*H*'s Sally Kellerman, *Sunday, Bloody Sunday*'s Peter Finch, *Airport*'s George Kennedy, and *The Emigrants*' Liv Ullmann, who was found smiling on the cover of *Time.* The magazine said, "It was the biggest movie plum in years, the role of Katharine in the singing and dancing version of *Lost Horizon.*"

The plum turned out to be a prune; the critics hadn't had this much fun laughing at a movie since the days of Cecil B. DeMille. Vincent Canby chortled in the *New York Times,* "The High Lama's palace looks like Pickfair remodeled as a motel," and Pauline Kael reported, "The biggest laugh in the theater greeted the arrival of the young men of the village—Broadway style and mostly Caucasian men dancers, whose progeny in the film are Oriental." The studio, Columbia, promptly cut the dancers out of the movie, but they couldn't cut Bette Midler's remark to her concert audiences: "I call it Lost-Her Reason. I never miss a Liv Ullmann musical!"

The Non-Conformist

"I always wanted to know what Marlon Brando sounded like," said thirty-two-year-old Italian director Bernardo Bertolucci. "I've seen all his films, but in Italy he was always dubbed because audiences, even the critics, hate to read subtitles." So when Bertolucci had his first international hit, *The Conformist* in 1971, he took advantage of the acclaim and pitched an idea to his favorite American film actor, who accepted the offer immediately.

Last Tango in Paris had its premiere at the 1972 New York Film Festival, an evening described by the *New York Times* as "the night pent-up passions were unleashed on Philharmonic Hall—the night Bertolucci buffs went berserk bellowing 'Bravo,' the night open-mouthed matrons did their weak-kneed best to stagger out in a huff, and the night Pauline Kael stayed behind to confess for all to hear that Bertolucci's 'breakthrough' movie had impressed her as no other movie has in the last 20 years." At her typewriter for *The New Yorker,* Kael continued her raving, "This must be the most powerfully erotic movie ever made, and it may turn out to be the most liberating. Brando and Bertolucci have altered the face of an art form." She went on to compare its impact to that of Stravinsky's *Le Sacre du Printemps.*

Porno Brando

Newsweek compared it to Howard Hughes' *The Outlaw* when the film opened commercially in New York with a $5 ticket price—the going rate for porno theaters. That was fitting, thought William F. Buckley, who labeled the X-rated film "pornography disguised as art" without bothering to see it. *Playboy* featured nude pictures of forty-seven-year-old Brando with his twenty-year-old co-star Maria Schneider and United Artists predicted the highest gross in its history. *Time* declared that Brando with "his emotionally wrenching, coruscating performance fulfills all the promise he gave in *The Godfather* of regaining his old dominance, not only as an actor, but also as a star and a legend."

In Hollywood, director Robert Altman walked out of a screening in a daze, rhapsodizing, "Bertolucci has carried film honesty to its ultimate. How dare I make another movie?" Lucille Ball reacted differently: "I'd like to bash Brando in the nose and I have these three rings on!" When criticism mounted, Jack Lemmon defended the film. "*Last Tango in Paris* isn't a pornographic pic-

Ten-year-old Tatum O'Neal, the youngest Oscar winner ever, with her newest toy.

"How dare I make another movie?"
—Robert Altman

ture," the actor stated. "It's about a man leaning on sex because there's nothing for him at that terrible point in his life, that male menopause."

Middle-Aged Blues

Lemmon could identify with Brando, not only because he was the same age, but because he had just made his own male-menopause movie, *Save the Tiger*. Writer-producer Steve Shagan had schlepped his screenplay about a disillusioned Los Angeles garment-factory owner around for two years, but there were no takers. "Everyone was afraid to touch it," Lemmon said. "No one thought it had a chance even to make back its investment." When they finally found a backer, Lemmon worked for scale and the *Saturday Review* praised the result as "the first important film of 1973, and possibly the 1970s." But the executives had been correct; Paramount couldn't get anyone to see *Save the Tiger*. Lemmon's Hollywood friends admired him for trying—Joyce Haber wrote that "Jack Lemmon proves for all time he's one of the best living actors"—and the actor himself had no regrets: "I did *Save the Tiger* for nothing and I'm prouder of it than all those movies I made millions on all rolled into one."

A Period Piece in Mod Clothing

Glenda Jackson's 1973 challenge was *A Touch of Class,* a romantic comedy about adultery costarring George Segal and directed by Hollywood veteran Melvin Frank. "I always seem to be in controversial things and I wanted to do a big American comedy to see if I could do it," Jackson said when she took the assignment. *Newsweek* commented that the sixty-year-old director's sensibility "gives the movie the air of a period piece in mod clothing," but *Variety* sang, "The film conjures up the warmest memories of Leo McCarey and George Stevens at their best." *A Touch of Class* also brought back pleasant memories of box-office action—the film was an unexpected hit and ran for months. The *New Republic* said that "the delightful surprise is Glenda Jackson in a fast-and-funny light-comedy role and she is absolutely first-class."

Like Father, Like Daughter

Ryan O'Neal started to worry when his daughter Tatum developed an ulcer at age seven. Two years later, when director Peter Bogdanovich offered Tatum the chance to costar with her father in a comedy about a con man and his moppet sidekick during the Depression, her father urged her to take it. "This was her first opportunity to try to channel her energy and mind into something constructive," O'Neal explained. "And this movie would give her what she never had enough of—love."

Bogdanovich would not allow Tatum to look at the rushes but he assured reporters, "What makes her good is that she isn't professional. She's just being natural." But it took her a while to get natural. The *New York Daily News* reported, "Although Bogdanovich rarely does more than ten takes with an actor, the number went as high as 53 for Tatum. He admits it's a 'manipulated performance.' "

"A star is born!" cried Marilyn Beck when *Paper Moon* bowed in May. "Tatum O'Neal is the best kid actress I've ever seen since I was a kid," claimed Sidney Skolsky, sixty-eight. *Interview* magazine asked the new star if she'd pose for a nude layout, but her costar vetoed the idea, as well as any other career plans. "I want her to stop being a movie star and return to being a little girl," Ryan O'Neal said. "She can go back to all that when she's sixteen, if she's still interested."

He Earned It

A few months after *Paper Moon* came out, a movie called *The Paper Chase,* about struggling law students at Harvard, was released. Just before filming had begun on the picture, James Mason walked out of the part of a tyrannical professor. In desperation, director James Bridges called his ex-

"I always wanted to know what Marlon Brando sounded like."
—Bernardo Bertolucci

teacher from UCLA's Theatre Group, John Houseman, who had organized the Mercury Theatre with Orson Welles in 1937, and was currently heading the Juilliard School in New York. Houseman responded, "Get Edward G. Robinson." But Robinson was too ill, so Houseman, who had only acted once in a bit part in *Seven Days in May* in 1964, put his theories on acting into practice. *Time* graded the acting teacher: "It is a forbidding, superb performance, catching not only the coldness of such a man, but the patrician crustiness that conceals deep and raging contempt."

Whiz Kid

"This is in no shape to show an audience—it's unreleasable!" boomed Universal executive Ned Tanen after a sneak preview of a film by a twenty-nine-year-old director named George Lucas, a graduate of the USC film school. Lucas had been able to squeeze the film's $700,000 budget out of the studio only because his mentor, Francis Ford Coppola, said he'd personally oversee the production as executive producer. Lucas shot his film, a nostalgic comedy of teenage manners, in twenty-eight nights and spent $75,000 obtaining the rights to golden oldies of the late '50s and early '60s for the sound track. Despite the preview audience's spirited reaction to the movie, Ned Tanen thought it was awful. "You boys let me down," he screamed to Lucas and Coppola. "I went to bat for you and you let me down."

"You should get down on your knees and thank George for saving your job!" Coppola thundered back. "This kid has killed himself to make this movie for you. This movie's going to be a hit! The audience loves this movie—I saw it with my own eyes!" Tanen nevertheless made a few cuts in the picture and Universal finally released it in August.

"Few films have shown quite so well the eagerness, the sadness, the ambitions and small defeats of a generation of young Americans," praised *Time*, while the *Los Angeles Times*' Charles Champlin called *American Graffiti* "the warmest and most human comedy in a long time." It was also one of the most profitable—returning over $55 million in rentals and spinning out two bestselling sound-track albums. Vindicated at last, whiz kid George Lucas told the *New York Times*, "There's no message or speech, but you know that when the story ends, America underwent a drastic change. The early '60s was the end of an era. It hit us all very hard."

The Grand Tradition

Unlike George Lucas, producer Ray Stark was not hamstrung by a small budget, and he liked to make movies with big stars. The producer found a nostalgic love story for Barbra Streisand, but he couldn't persuade Warren Beatty to be her leading man. Enter Robert Redford, who was willing, able and available. *Variety* previewed this new Streisand vehicle and noted, "Her character does not sing in the story, but she sings the plaintive, and weak, title tune, much in the manner of Doris Day's title-tuning in her comedies of some years ago."

The Way We Were—the movie and the song—had audiences boo-hooing by the millions. Vincent Canby resented the way the film used the McCarthy trials as "a plot device of no more believability than an auto accident," but *Women's Wear Daily* told him to knock it off because the "film is so highly stylized it would be ludicrous to compare it with reality. In the grand tradition, everything is more gorgeous than it could possibly be in reality."

For female moviegoers, nothing was more gorgeous than Robert Redford, who emerged as the leading matinee idol of the day. And Barbra Streisand collected her best reviews since *Funny Girl*. The *New York Daily News* felt "Barbra Streisand does something quite remarkable in *The Way We Were*. She acts." And Molly Haskell confessed in the *Village Voice*, "I would trade many an art-film classic for the final exchange between Redford and Streisand in front of the Plaza." Streisand added to the film's publicity by giving gossip

"I'd like to bash Brando in the nose and I have three rings on!"
—Lucille Ball

columnists plenty to write about around the time of its release; one revealed, "Hollywood's inner circle is buzzing with the news of Barbra Streisand's passionate romance with a handsome hairstylist."

Joanne Woodward—Snow Queen

"Along with Barbra Streisand and Liza Minnelli," *Newsweek* commented, "Joanne Woodward is one of the few American actresses to consistently put the stamp of her personality on the films she makes." Having made an expensive, glossy star vehicle with Streisand, producer Ray Stark then made an inexpensive star vehicle with Woodward. The actress was reunited with her *Rachel, Rachel* screenwriter Stewart Stern, who came up with a domestic drama about a middle-aged Manhattan housewife, called *Death of a Snow Queen*. Columbia didn't like that title and released the film as *Summer Wishes, Winter Dreams*. *Variety* analyzed, "Although poky in the extreme, this could be a very touching, moving film for a certain age group. Unfortunately, not for the age group which frequents theaters." The movie did little business, but Sylvia Sidney was glad she had dropped out of a play to be in it because she considered her brief role as Woodward's mother—who dies of a heart attack on screen—to be "a wonderful part, in a beautiful film." Woodward, too, was proud of the picture. "I think it's a good film, but I can't stand that title. It's so meaningless."

No Rubber Stamp

Al Pacino followed his success in *The Godfather* by costarring with Gene Hackman in *Scarecrow,* a study of two drifters. Audiences preferred his year-end movie: *Serpico,* the true story of a New York cop who blew the whistle on corruption in the police force. Not only was *Serpico* a big Christmastime hit, but the poster of Pacino as the bearded cop adorned many an adolescent's wall. Kathleen Carroll announced in the *New York Daily News,* "Al Pacino gives a masterful performance as Serpico. He proves that, although there is a strong resemblance, he is no rubber-stamp Dustin Hoffman." Marilyn Beck wrote, "If Al Pacino doesn't walk away with an Academy Award, he should complain of robbery." But the actor was already complaining. "I couldn't exist just doing films," he said on the set of his latest movie. "I don't think you'll be seeing me in too many movies after *Godfather II*. I still want to play *Hamlet* and time is running out."

Mrs. Simon

One of Pacino's *Godfather* brothers, James Caan, found himself upstaged by his latest costar, a thirty-one-year-old film newcomer from daytime TV, Marsha Mason. After a supporting role in Paul Mazursky's *Blume in Love,* Mason portrayed a Seattle hooker with a black son in *Cinderella Liberty*. *Time* wrote, "This is the one about the sailor and the whore, and is there anyone out there who still cares?" *Women's Wear Daily* did, describing the leading lady as "an actress of amazing emotional power and resourcefulness." Few people saw *Cinderella Liberty* but everyone knew that, a few months earlier, Mason had tried out for a new Neil Simon play and that Simon, a widower of three months' standing, had fallen for her. After a whirlwind twenty-two-day courtship, the actress and the playwright were married. She got the part, too. "I have everything that anyone could possibly want," Mason told reporters. "I worked hard for it and I have the right to enjoy it."

The Second Time Around

Robert Redford was getting all the parts other people didn't want. *The Way We Were* was his because Warren Beatty had turned it down and the title role in the upcoming *The Great Gatsby*—the most wildly publicized movie since *The Godfather*—went to an eager Redford because Marlon Brando and Warren Beatty had said no. But before

"*Paper Moon* would give Tatum what she never had enough of—love."
—Ryan O'Neal

Gatsby was unleashed, the Golden Boy had one more 1973 release, *The Sting;* Redford got this one after Jack Nicholson turned it down.

Redford liked the script—a comedy about con men set in the 1930s, written by twenty-seven-year-old UCLA Film School graduate David S. Ward—and so did his *Butch Cassidy* cohorts, Paul Newman and director George Roy Hill. *The Sting* was made on the back lot at Universal Studios, with Edith Head designing the costumes and Scott Joplin's ragtime music used for the score. Hoping for another *Butch Cassidy*–style success, Universal scheduled *The Sting* as its major Christmas release.

Universal had given itself a Christmas present—all the theaters showing *The Sting* were filled with patrons. "This isn't a movie," *Time* jeered, "it's a recipe. The people who put *The Sting* together followed the instructions on the *Butch Cassidy* package." And *Newsweek* wisecracked, "*The Sting* reunites the screen's leading romantic couple—Paul Newman and Robert Redford." While the word of mouth kept box offices humming for months, a *New York Times* "Arts and Leisure" article despaired that the film's success meant that women were finished in films.

Risky Business

Even though Jack Nicholson didn't want to do *The Sting,* he had nothing but kind words for the script. "I like it," he said, "I like the period setting, the whole project, and I know it will be commercial. But I need to put my energies into a movie that really needs them. I need to take a risk." The movie Nicholson chose to pour his energies into was *The Last Detail,* which, like *Cinderella Liberty,* was based on a Darryl Ponicsan novel. Nicholson had read the book in galleys and had been instrumental in putting the project together. His friend Robert Towne wrote the expletive-filled screenplay about two veteran sailors escorting a teenaged recruit to a naval prison and Hal Ashby, director of the cult favorite *Harold and Maude,* was behind the camera. One of the actors Peter Bogdanovich had discovered in Texas for *The Last Picture Show,* twenty-two-year-old Randy Quaid, was playing the young sailor. "I know this might be the best part I will ever have," he admitted.

Columbia decided to keep the New York critics at bay and opened *The Last Detail* for a week in Los Angeles to qualify for the Oscars. *Boxoffice* magazine reported: "Hundreds of Academy members passed into the theater during the run, creating such a demand that extra switchboard operators were added after the first three days to handle the request for passes." "Jack Nicholson has never jumped out at us with quite such charm," raved the *Los Angeles Herald-Examiner.* "His raunchy sailor is something like James Cagney might have given us." And the *Los Angeles Times*' Charles Champlin wrote, "Randy Quaid's performance is one of the most likable, moving and skillful in a whole year's worth of memorable acting."

The Devil Made Her Do It

Warners had also put a lot of thought into its Christmas package and an executive told the *Hollywood Reporter* before the film opened, "It will reach its maximum potential this summer, right after it wins Academy Awards." The film, William Friedkin's first since winning an Oscar for *The French Connection,* was based on William Peter Blatty's bestselling thriller *The Exorcist,* about a little girl possessed by Satan.

When the production dragged on for months and the budget soared from $3 million to $10 million, the thirty-four-year-old Oscar winner said, "I'm not the most experienced director in the world and I don't feel there was any precedent for the picture in the way we decided to make it. I'm not a convert to the occult, but so much has gone cockeyed connected to this picture, it makes you wonder. Even my gaffer cut his toe off. The whole thing was a nightmare."

But for Warners, *The Exorcist* was a dream come true—it broke house records in every single

"Although there is a strong resemblance, Al Pacino is no rubber-stamp Dustin Hoffman."
—New York Daily News

theater where it played. The long, long lines of moviegoers waiting to be scared grew longer when TV reporters said that viewers were fainting and vomiting in disbelief. One theater usher told the *New York Times* that several people had suffered heart attacks and one woman a miscarriage. *The Exorcist* became Warner Brothers' most profitable film to date.

The Nightmare Continues

For William Friedkin, the nightmare still wasn't over. Pauline Kael hissed, "If *The Exorcist* had cost under a million or had been made abroad, it would almost certainly be an X film, but when a movie is an expensive as this one, the MPAA rating board doesn't dare to give it an X." In spite of the film's R rating, the District of Columbia banned children under seventeen from the film. Then 1949 Best Supporting Actress winner Mercedes McCambridge growled that Friedkin had promised her screen credit for supplying the voice of the devil emanating from the on-screen mouth of fourteen-year-old Linda Blair. "If people had heard her saying some of those obscenities, they would have fallen over laughing," McCambridge said. "Billy Friedkin promised me a special credit and then broke his promise. It's heartbreaking when a friend does that." Friedkin ultimately gave McCambridge screen recognition.

Brave New World

The New York Film Critics were not caught up in *The Exorcist* mania and they ignored the film in their awards. Joanne Woodward won Best Actress for *Summer Wishes, Winter Dreams* and Marlon Brando won Best Actor for *Last Tango in Paris*. Thirty-year-old Robert De Niro won the Best Supporting Actor citation for two low-budget movies, *Bang the Drum Slowly* and Martin Scorsese's *Mean Streets,* a hit at the New York Film Festival. The festival's biggest success was François Truffaut's *Day for Night*, which scored big with the critics, too. They named it Best Picture, Truffaut Best Director and Valentina Cortese Best Supporting Actress for playing an actress who couldn't remember her lines.

Day for Night was only eligible for Best Foreign Film in the Oscar race—according to the rules, it would be eligible for all the other categories the following year—but Ingmar Bergman's *Cries and Whispers* was definitely competing for this year's Oscars, as distributor Roger Corman reminded voters in trade-paper ads. "Here was one of the greatest directors in the world," said Corman, the producer-director of *The Masque of the Red Death,* "and he couldn't get a major release in the U.S.!" Having just set up his own distribution company, New World Pictures, Corman bought *Cries and Whispers* sight unseen in 1972 for $75,000. "Can you imagine being able to buy a Bergman picture for as little as that?" he gloated. "And after I saw it, I was even more excited." The *Hollywood Reporter* called the drama about four women, one of whom is dying of cancer, "a film of high seriousness and almost unrelieved agony," yet *Cries and Whispers* became the New York Film Critics Best Picture winner and the highest-grossing Bergman film ever released in the United States.

The Nominations

Cries and Whispers won five Oscar nominations, including Best Picture. *Last Tango in Paris* managed only two—for Marlon Brando and Bernardo Bertolucci. When an interviewer asked Best Director nominee Ingmar Bergman what he though of *Last Tango*, the Swede replied, "I don't think it's really about a middle-aged man and young girl, but about homosexuals. As it is now, it makes no sense as a film. But if you think about it in those terms, it becomes interesting." Bertolucci responded, "I accept all interpretations of my films. I'm not sure what my film says."

Brando's Best Actor competition came from Jack Lemmon, Jack Nicholson, Al Pacino and Robert Redford, nominated for *The Sting*. Redford's leading lady from *The Way We Were*, Barbra

"I've been told by sources in the Vatican that they have seen The Exorcist and liked it."
—William Friedkin

Streisand, was in the Best Actress race with Marsha Mason, Ellen Burstyn, Glenda Jackson and Joanne Woodward, who didn't like the course the Oscar race had taken. "The Oscar has become a political gesture, or a business gesture," complained Mrs. Newman. "People tell you it adds $5 million to a film's gross and I believe it, but that's not what the Oscar is for." Despite her opinion, Woodward made plans to attend the ceremony, hoping the Academy would imitate the New York Film Critics.

The Best Picture Oscar Race was between two American entries—*The Exorcist* and *The Sting,* both with ten nominations. *American Graffiti,* with five, was a dark horse, but surprise entry *A Touch of Class,* also with five but with no Director nomination, didn't have a chance. "The worst Best Picture nomination," scribbled *Chicago Today*'s Mary Knoblauch, "a nostalgic trip for the Hollywood crowd, made by a thirty-year veteran in the old studio star-system way."

When Robert De Niro didn't win a Best Supporting Actor nomination, a "NY trade vet" complained to *Variety,* "It's a New York picture and they hate us out there." Instead of De Niro, the Actors Branch nominated his *Bang the Drum Slowly* costar, Vincent Gardenia. The other nominees were Jack Gilford in *Save the Tiger,* Randy Quaid in *The Last Detail,* and two neophytes—playwright Jason Miller in *The Exorcist* and acting teacher John Houseman in *The Paper Chase.*

In Hollywood, everyone was talking about the Best Supporting Actress nominations. Both Linda Blair and Tatum O'Neal—whom Paramount had promoted for Best Actress—were in the contest. O'Neal was competing with her costar, Madeline Kahn, prompting Peter Bogdanovich to grouse, "I don't understand how Madeline Kahn, who's onscreen for maybe eighteen minutes, can be up against Tatum, who's in 100 of the 103 minutes of the film." Vincent Canby thought it was unfair for the moppets to be vying against his favorite, sixty-three-year-old Sylvia Sidney, for *Summer Wishes, Winter Dreams.* "How can Sylvia Sidney compete with the souped-up electronics and editing that went into Miss Blair's performance and with the preconditioned responses that were elicited by Miss O'Neal's?" One who was happy with the nominations was *American Graffiti*'s Candy Clark, who had borrowed $2,000 from her roommate Jeff Bridges to buy herself ads in *Daily Variety*—she was the only member of the movie's ensemble cast to be nominated.

No Laughing Allowed

An anonymous Woody Allen fan also ran an ad in *Daily Variety:* "Congratulations to the Academy for turning its back on talent and artistry once again by ignoring Woody Allen and his superb film *Sleeper* in the Academy Award nominations. Charlie Chaplin and the Marx Brothers never got any Oscars for their performances either. Doesn't anyone out there like to laugh?" As it turned out, Groucho Marx was getting an Honorary Oscar this year. Marx's live-in companion, Erin Fleming, was reputed to have approached various Academy members with the idea of the Award, and the Board of Governors eventually approved it. Presenting the Oscar would be Best Actor nominee Jack Lemmon, who was getting to be a familiar face at Academy functions—he handed out the Academy's student film awards, too.

Hepburn and Hayward—One Night Only

Show producer Jack Haley, Jr.'s big coup was luring the "Great Kate" to her first Oscar show. Katharine Hepburn consented to give the Thalberg Award to a man who had produced three of the movies she made with Spencer Tracy—on one condition: her appearance would be top secret. Rehearsals would be closed, she'd write her own speech, and Haley would get out of the dressing room she had used when *Coco* played the Dorothy Chandler Pavilion and let her stay there until it was time for her to go on.

The Hepburn surprise was camouflaged by

the news that Susan Hayward, who was terminally ill with cancer, was coming to town to give the Best Actress Oscar. The Oscar winner had recently suffered a brain tumor and subsequent cobalt treatments had reduced her to 85 pounds. Designer Nolan Miller created a green sequined gown with a high neck and long sleeves to conceal her emaciated figure. As for her cobalt-caused baldness, Miller exclaimed, "We're going out and getting you the goddamnedest red Susan Hayward wig that anyone has ever seen!" They also went out and borrowed a pile of jewelry from Van Cleef and Arpel's on Wilshire Boulevard; "Susan had been a very good customer there," Miller recalled. And her doctor gave her a large dose of Dilantin, a drug for the prevention of seizures, just in case.

In addition to Hayward's precarious condition, the Academy was afraid of the latest social craze—streaking. The idea of someone running across the stage stark raving naked sounded impossible, especially considering the Academy's tight security, but then who would have thought that Marlon Brando would be nominated the very year after his Indian demonstration? Hank Grant joked, "The Academy is well aware that Sacheen Littlefeather needs the work, even if it is only a one-nighter."

The Big Night

Variety described Oscar night as "an R-rated carnival in which publicity-hungry starlets bazoomed theatrically in the spotlight." Perennial starlet Edy Williams wore a fur coat and purred, "I didn't think it'd be so warm." She tore off the fur and revealed a leopard skin bikini. With Williams was a great Dane wearing a feathered collar. *Variety* reported that Williams made a big entrance, but not much else: "She attempted to shoehorn her way into the pressroom but was ousted." Williams had competition when Linda Lovelace, the star of *Deep Throat,* pulled up in a coach drawn by two white horses. She stepped down in a white lace dress and broad-rimmed hat to tell Army Archerd, "I'm here to meet a man I always wanted to know—Oscar."

Jack Nicholson came with Anjelica Huston and wore a red shirt with his tuxedo. Al Pacino flew in from *The Godfather Part II* location. Jack Lemmon came with his wife. Tatum O'Neal brought her grandparents and explained to Army Archerd that the tuxedo she was wearing was inspired by the clothing style of her good friend Bianca Jagger. Archerd added, "Tatum O'Neal's very short haircut was the work of Stanley Kubrick's daughter Vivien. Both lasses decided to trim each other's locks while their daddies were working on *Barry Lyndon.*"

Best Actor nominee Robert Redford didn't make it, but his non-nominated costar Paul Newman showed up with *his* nominated wife, Joanne Woodward. The Directors Guild Award winner, George Roy Hill of *The Sting,* entered smiling, but William Friedkin told Army Archerd he was still optimistic about *The Exorcist*'s chances. The director also reassured the forecourt emcee, "I've been told by sources in the Vatican that they have seen it and liked it."

The program began with Liza Minnelli belting out a Fred Ebb/John Kander song entitled "Oscar" and then Academy President Walter Mirisch walked out and asked, "What does the Academy do besides giving awards?" After his spiel,

Awards Ceremony

APRIL 2, 1974, 7:00 P.M.
THE DOROTHY CHANDLER PAVILION, LOS ANGELES

Your Hosts:
JOHN HUSTON, DIANA ROSS, BURT REYNOLDS, DAVID NIVEN
Televised over NBC

Presenters

Short Subjects . . . Linda Blair and Billy Dee Williams
Documentary Awards . . . . James Caan and Raquel Welch
Honorary Award to Henri Langlois . . . . . Jack Valenti
Sound . . . . Candice Bergen and Marcel Marceau
Film Editing . . . Richard Benjamin and Paula Prentiss
Jean Hersholt Humanitarian Award .Alfred Hitchcock
Art Direction . . . . . . .Sylvia Sidney and Paul Winfield
Costume Design . . . . Peter Falk and Twiggy
Cinematography . . . . Peter Lawford and Cicely Tyson
Foreign Film . . . . Yul Brynner
Song Score and/or Adaptation . . Donald O'Connor and Debbie Reynolds
Original Dramatic Score . . . Cher and Henry Mancini
Original Screenplay . . Marsha Mason and Neil Simon
Adapted Screenplay . . . . Angie Dickinson and Jason Miller
Song . . . . .Ann-Margret and Burt Bacharach
Supporting Actor . . . . Ernest Borgnine and Cybill Shepherd
Supporting Actress . . .Charles Bronson and Jill Ireland
Director . . . . Shirley MacLaine
Thalberg Award . . . . Katharine Hepburn
Honorary Award to Groucho Marx . . . . . Jack Lemmon
Actress . . . . Susan Hayward and Charlton Heston
Actor . . . . .Liza Minnelli and Gregory Peck
Picture . . . . Elizabeth Taylor

Performers of Nominated Songs

"All That Love Went to Waste" . . . . . . Dyan Cannon
"Live and Let Die" . . . . Connie Stevens
"Love" Jodie Foster and Johnny Whittaker
"The Way We Were" . . . . Peggy Lee
"You're So Nice to Be Around" . . . . . . .Telly Savalas

"I'm living proof that a person can wait forty-one years to be unselfish."
—Katharine Hepburn

Mirisch remarked that, for the first time, the show was dedicated to somebody—to the late Sam Goldwyn, who had recently passed away at age ninety-one.

The first emcee was Burt Reynolds, in a double-breasted tuxedo with ruffled shirt, who wrote his own material. "Right now in New York, Beverly Hills, Bel Air, all over the country, there are cocktail parties filled with people saying nasty, catty, snide remarks," Reynolds commented to laughter and applause. "It's true, they're putting us down about the way we're dressed, how unfunny we are, how unsophisticated we are—and you know where that comes from. They haven't been nominated, they haven't been invited, or they're just too chic to be here. So to all you people out there, from all of us in here—" and he gave the Bronx cheer.

After Reynolds introduced Documentary Award presenters James Caan and Raquel Welch, he commented, "Two biggies." When Caan flubbed a nomination credit, he confessed, "I was never real good at reading." "Then streak, honey, streak," retorted Raquel. The Documentary Feature Oscar went to a film about rodeo that Caan had personally campaigned for in the trade papers, and the Documentary Short Oscar went to a movie about Princeton University, which alumnus Joshua Logan had similarly promoted.

Candice Bergen read the nominations for the Sound Award while Marcel Marceau mimed them. After Marceau mock-vomited for *The Exorcist,* Bergen declared it the winner and handed a statuette to a gum-chewing technician. Then followed a clip from Best Picture nominee *Cries and Whispers,* featuring the line "I can't take it any longer. All that guilt," after which Burt Reynolds quipped, "On that happy note . . ."

Reynolds turned the emcee duties over to Diana Ross, who segued to the Costume Design Award, which would be the final battle between Dorothy Jeakins, the first winner in 1948, and Edith Head, who had never fully recovered from losing that year. Presenters Twiggy and Peter Falk, the latter introduced as "the man who set the raincoat back twenty years," read the nominees: "Dorothy Jeakins for *The Way We Were* . . . Edith Head for *The Sting*. And the winner is . . . Edith Head for *The Sting*." Head minced her way to the stage in a black-and-white dress, waving a white scarf. "Just imagine," she gushed at the podium, "dressing the two handsomest men in the world and then getting this."

Yul Brynner appeared and said, "The Best Foreign Language Film Award is an important award because this year's nominees are eligible for next year's Best Picture Award." This year's winner was *Day for Night* and the camera saw star Valentina Cortese kissing François Truffaut. "*Merci beaucoup*," the director said at the podium, "I am very happy. Why? Because *Day for Night* is about show people."

Diana Ross introduced her successor, John Huston, who departed from the script to criticize those who criticize Oscar "because they are afraid to appear unsophisticated, as if knocking it is the thing to do." He also debunked the myth that Oscars are bought. "These Awards have not been bought and paid for; Christ knows the ones you gave me weren't." Then Huston announced that the next nominated song would be performed by Telly Savalas.

Debbie Reynolds and Donald O'Connor divulged that the Song Score Oscar had gone to Marvin Hamlisch for *The Sting*. The twenty-nine-year-old winner ran to the stage with his hands above his head. "I'm very happy and I really wanted this," Marvin exclaimed. "I'm happy that my parents are here to see this." Mrs. and Mrs. Hamlisch were in for more when Henry Mancini and Cher, in a skirt and bikini top, named their son the winner of the Dramatic Score Oscar for *The Way We Were*. Marvin remarked, "What can I tell ya? I'd like to thank the makers of Maalox for making all this possible."

Huston introduced "the playwright of the Western world," Neil Simon, and Marsha Mason to give the Original Screenplay Award. When they

"Now I want a Tony, and an Emmy and a Grammy and I won't be satisfied until I get them."
—Marvin Hamlisch

were handed the envelope, Simon cracked, "Hey, we got mail." Marsha laughed. The young winner was David S. Ward for *The Sting*. Wearing a ruffled tuxedo shirt, he expressed his gratitude "to people for going to the movies, because if it wasn't for them, we wouldn't have this business to work in."

The Exorcist's Best Supporting Actor nominee, Jason Miller, assisted Angie Dickinson in giving the Adapted Screenplay Oscar to William Peter Blatty, who glumly hugged Miller and then thanked, "My parents, who came to this country on a cattle boat."

After Peggy Lee warbled "The Way We Were," Huston wandered out to introduce the Best Song Award and observed, "I think they were all superbly performed tonight." Burt Bacharach and Ann-Margret, in a sequined cap, announced that Marvin Hamlisch had won his third Oscar, for "The Way We Were." The camera found Hamlisch sitting with Liza Minnelli—he had been the rehearsal pianist on her first New York show in 1963. The lyricists of "The Way We Were," Alan and Marilyn Bergman, beat the composer to the stage, and Marilyn sighed, "Marvin, it's almost obscene how many of those you have." "I think we can talk as friends," said Marvin, now beside himself. "I feel as if I know you. You're terrific. I want to thank you, again, as it were. Thanks to Sam Spiegel—my first job. You've done it for this year."

Ernest Borgnine and Cybill Shepherd presented the Best Supporting Actor Award, but not before Cybill put in a few plugs for her paramour, Peter Bogdanovich. In Shepherd's words, John Houseman was nominated for "*Paper Moon*—oops, *Paper Chase*" and Randy Quaid was up for "*The Last Picture Show*—uh—*The Last Detail*." All the nominees were there and the winner was seventy-one-year-old John Houseman. "Almost for the first time in a long and tumultuous life, I'm almost speechless," he said, praising his director for "the unspeakable gall to select this aging and obscure schoolmarm for this perfectly glorious part" and singling out the perpetually non-nominated cinematographer Gordon Willis, "whose extremely dramatic camerawork did a great deal to create the character of Kingsworth."

David Niven was the final host and he called out Charles Bronson and Jill Ireland to crown the Best Supporting Actress. This category also drew perfect attendance, and the winner was ten-year-old Tatum O'Neal for *Paper Moon*. Her grandfather escorted her to the stage and she said simply, "All I really want to thank is my director Peter Bogdanovich and my father." Grandpa muttered something inaudible in the microphone and, since he wasn't identified, Andrew Sarris in the *Village Voice* wanted to know, "Who was that Humbert Humbert with her?"

Shirley MacLaine and Walter Matthau announced that the Best Director was George Roy Hill for *The Sting*—the film's sixth Oscar. Hill offered "a bit of advice for my fellow directors," which was hire the same people who worked on *The Sting*. "It helps, believe me," he said.

Niven returned and talked about the term "star" and concluded, "To me, this is a star—Katharine Hepburn." There were gasps as Hepburn trotted out in pantsuit and clogs. When the audience gave her a standing ovation, she gestured for them to sit down. "Thank you very, very much. I am naturally deeply moved. I'm also very happy that I didn't hear anyone call out, 'It's about time,'" she began. "I'm living proof that a person can wait forty-one years to be unselfish." She gave the Thalberg Award to Lawrence Weingarten, who admitted, "I feel completely incapable of responding to this outpouring of love. To have Katharine Hepburn and the Academy Award at the same time is an emotional package that I cannot cope with." He didn't have her for long; when they walked offstage, Hepburn stopped before the pressroom and whispered to Weingarten, "You don't need me anymore." And then she dashed off into the night in a limousine.

Jack Lemmon, in a tux with a red tie and matching handkerchief, was busy onstage pre-

"I'd like to thank Erin Fleming, who makes my life worth living."
—Groucho Marx

senting the Honorary Oscar to Groucho Marx. "The Marx Brothers were as revolutionary in their approach to humor as Karl Marx was to philosophy," Lemmon said, and out walked Groucho, looking unusually distinguished in white tie with a blue ribbon across his chest. "I wish Harpo and Chico were here to share this great honor," Groucho said, tearfully. "And I wish Margaret Dumont were here, too. She was a great straight woman even though she never got any of my jokes. I'd like to thank Erin Fleming, who makes my life worth living and who understands all my jokes."

David Niven led into the Best Actress presentation with, "Charlton Heston has created many miracles, just illusions on the screen, but in presenting our next award, he brings with him not an illusion, but the real thing—Miss Susan Hayward." Hayward took a step, paused for a moment, and Heston took her arm. "Easy, girl," he advised softly. When she made it to the podium, Hayward cut short a standing ovation and got down to business. Nominees Marsha Mason, Joanne Woodward and Ellen Burstyn were in the audience, Barbra Streisand was hiding backstage. The winner was the absentee—Glenda Jackson for *A Touch of Class*. Television viewers saw Joanne Woodward exclaim, "Oh, wow," while Ellen Burstyn wrinkled up her face and commented, "Hmm, what a surprise." Director Melvin Frank beat producer George Barrie to the stage, and, as the film's coauthor, he said, "She undoubtedly thanks her writers and I say you're welcome."

Liza Minnelli and Gregory Peck revealed the Best Actor—Jack Lemmon for *Save the Tiger*. The winner shook Jack Nicholson's hand, hugged his costar, Best Supporting Actor loser Jack Gilford, and made a victorious boxing gesture on his way to the stage. "I had a speech prepared in 1959—I've forgotten it," Lemmon said. "There has been some criticism of this Award, some of it justified, but I think it is one hell of an honor and I'm thrilled."

As Niven began to introduce Elizabeth Taylor as "a very important contributor to world entertainment and someone quite likely—" his speech was interrupted by screams and laughter. A naked man streaked by, flashing a peace sign. Henry Mancini struck up the orchestra with "Sunny Side Up" and TV director Marty Pasetta switched to another camera so viewers would be spared the sight of the gentleman's genitals. When the streaker ran offstage, the Academy security nabbed him, and dragged him to the pressroom for pictures—clothed. David Niven was amused, and prepared. "Ladies and gentlemen, that was bound to happen. Just think, the only laugh that man will probably ever get is for stripping and showing off his shortcomings." The camera cut to the audience, and even William Peter Blatty was laughing.

Niven returned to his introduction. "Someone quite likely to have breakfast, lunch and dinner at Tiffany's—Elizabeth Taylor." A tanned Taylor—in a Valentino gown and a hairdo by MGM's Sydney Guilaroff—sashayed out and laughed, "That's a pretty tough act to follow." Liz started in on the nominations, "*American Graffiti*, Universal-Lucasfilm, Ltd.—Limited? What does that mean? I'm really nervous, that upset me. I think I'm jealous." Taylor basked in the audience's laughter and then mispronounced William Peter Blatty's name. She opened the envelope and editorialized, "Oh, I'm so glad. It's *The Sting*." Producer Julia Phillips' long feather boa was caught on her chair, but after some tugging, she made it to the stage and babbled, "You can imagine what a trip this is for a Jewish girl from Great Neck—I get to win an Academy Award and meet Elizabeth Taylor at the same time." Liz laughed and introduced herself, and then Phillips and her two coproducers gave themselves a three-way hug.

Aftermath

"Liz was in a great mood that night," wrote one of the Academy's photographers on the contact sheet of the backstage pictures. Taylor hung around and posed with everyone. Nearby, Marvin Hamlisch said that the evening had changed his life. "Now I want a Tony, and an Emmy and a Grammy and I won't be satisfied until I get them,"

"Streak, honey, streak."
—Raquel Welch to James Caan

he insisted. Best Supporting Actor John Houseman said his part really wasn't so tough: "Since I now spend a great deal of time haranguing the young, the role was not all that alien or strange." Tatum O'Neal was calling long distance. "Daddy, Daddy!" the youngest Oscar winner ever cried into the receiver. "You did it?" Ryan asked in England. "Guess what I'm holding," Tatum demanded. "Is it gold?" her father asked. "No, I think it's bronze," Tatum answered.

Adapted Screenplay winner William Peter Blatty didn't know what to make of his Oscar, either. "The Academy should fold its tent and go back to baking apple strudel or whatever they can do well," the author complained. "*The Exorcist* is head and shoulders the finest film made this year or in several years. I sensed a backlash when the Writers, Directors and Editors Guild Awards fell through—and the writers gave the film a standing ovation at their screening." Blatty put the blame on one person in particular—seventy-four-year-old George Cukor. "Cukor spoke to key members of the Academy and persuaded them to eliminate the Special Effects Award, which our film certainly would have won. I think the film is touching a nerve and sometimes that nerve is very raw. Perhaps Mr. Cukor was disturbed, he has a narrow view of what constitutes outrage or obscenity." *Variety* remarked, "Cukor hasn't had such publicity since David O. Selznick replaced him as director of *Gone With the Wind*."

Jack Lemmon thoroughly enjoyed himself and told reporters that when he returned to the set of his new movie, a remake of *The Front Page*, "If Billy Wilder tries to give me any direction, I'll hit him right over the head with both my Oscars." Outside, Jack Nicholson confided to the *Chicago Tribune*, "I like the idea of winning at Cannes with *The Last Detail*, but not getting our own Academy Award hurt real bad. I did it in that movie, that was my best role. How often does one like that come along, one that fits you?"

Daily Variety was furious at the Academy for permitting a streaker to appear: "The incident was a most unfortunate lapse of judgment on the part of the Academy people responsible for the show, for they destroyed in a few seconds a forty-six-year history—often characterized by pomposity but nevertheless marked by propriety." Jack Haley, Jr., denied the streaking had been planned, arguing, "I would have used a pretty girl instead." The rest of the world wanted info on who the streaker was. He was thirty-three-year-old Robert Opal, who had managed to get backstage via a bogus press pass. Most critics praised Opal's performance, claiming he had enlivened a dull show that had little to offer other than a parade of Eddie Fisher's ex-wives—Debbie, Liz and Connie. Opal debuted as a stand-up comic in a Hollywood nightclub not long after the Oscar show; was a guest on the Mike Douglas show; and was hired to streak again by Allan Carr, for a party honoring Rudolf Nureyev and Marvin Hamlisch. Opal made headlines again in 1979 when he was found murdered in his sex paraphernalia shop in San Francisco.

Publicists said that Glenda Jackson was "surprised and delighted" when she learned of her unexpected second victory, but the actress told a different story to the *New York Times* a few years later. "I was working but I doubt that I would have been there even if I hadn't been," she said. "Watching it on television here in my hotel suite, I kept telling myself that I ought to turn it off and go to bed. I felt disgusted with myself—as though I were attending a public hanging . . . No one should have a chance to see so much desire, so much need for a prize, and so much pain when it was not given."

1974

"I do find Faye Dunaway tremendously temperamental. Off the stage, I find her impossible."
—Roman Polanski

Bob Hope returned to the Oscar show at the 1974 Awards—and all hell broke loose.

Francis Ford Coppola was king of the Paramount mountain. The *New York Times* profiled the thirty-five-year-old director and observed, "He lives in San Francisco, in the flamboyant style of a Hollywood rajah; he has his own office building, his own theater and his own Lear jet." "I don't want to be a director who just does one movie after another until you realize there's nobody behind the movies but a technician," Coppola declared. "I want to direct plays and a radio play and be involved in a lot of other projects."

It would be a while before Coppola would be branching out into other fields, though—four months after *The Godfather* won the Best Picture Award, Paramount announced a sequel, to be written and directed by Francis Ford Coppola. "Charlie Bludhorn talked me into doing it," the director explained, referring to the head of Gulf & Western, the conglomerate that had absorbed the studio. "He convinced me that it was a challenge to try and make a sequel to a very successful film and pull if off. I'm basically a gambler, so the challenge of it appealed to me."

But before Coppola could tackle the Corleone saga again, he had to take care of two other assignments. The first was the screenplay to Paramount's lavish version of *The Great Gatsby,* starring Robert Redford. Coppola knocked out a screenplay in three weeks and handed it over. Then he returned to a screenplay he wrote in 1969 about wiretapping—an activity recently popularized by the Nixon administration. Coppola directed *The Conversation* on a low budget at his own San Francisco studio, American Zoetrope. Starring Gene Hackman, the film featured many of Coppola's favorite actors—John Cazale, Cindy Williams, Frederic Forrest and Teri Garr.

While son Francis lives it up, Carmine Coppola uses both hands to hold on to a prop Oscar; he had already dropped and broken the real one.

Pots and Pans

"*The Great Gatsby,*" squawked *Vogue,* "has caused the greatest preproduction excitement since *Gone With the Wind.*" Paramount compared the search for an actress to play Daisy to Selznick's hunt for his Scarlett. According to the publicity, Mia Farrow finally won the role when she wrote Bob Evans, "Dear Bob, May I be your Daisy?" Farrow made the cover of the first issue of *People* and, inside, F. Scott Fitzgerald's daughter Scottie enthused, "Mia is the Daisy Father had in mind." Bob Evans asked Broadway's David Merrick to produce the picture, since he was a good friend of Scottie, who owned the rights to her father's novel. British director Jack Clayton was in charge of the production and *Women's Wear Daily* began talking about "the Gatsby look" in late 1972. Just before the film's premiere in the spring of 1974, *Time* ran a cover story on "The Great Gatsby Supersell." The magazine revealed that Paramount had arranged $6 million worth of product tie-ins, including one with Ballantine Scotch, although the film took place during Prohibition, and another with du Pont for their new "classic white" line of cookware. Scottie Fitzgerald complained, "You have turned *The Great Gatsby* into pots and pans."

Newsweek called the movie "an extraordinary white elephant" and some TV critics said it wasn't the filmmakers' fault, that "Fitzgerald's dialogue is unspeakable." *New York* magazine devoted a whole article detailing the historical inaccuracy of the costumes; "this hat could have been bought off the counter at Bloomingdale's," read one caption. The final straw came when *Esquire* featured Redford and Farrow on the cover of its year-end "Dubious Achievements" issue.

Nobody blamed Francis Ford Coppola for *The Great Gatsby* letdown, especially when *The Conversation* bowed soon afterward. "A film of triumphant style and overwhelming passion, white hot with American anguish," declared the *Hollywood Reporter*. *Newsweek* applauded: "*The Conversation* remains brilliantly original in its basic

"The Academy Awards are obscene, dirty and no better than a beauty contest."
—Dustin Hoffman

style and mood and prophetically American in its vision of a monitored society." The movie won the Best Film Award at the Cannes Film Festival, but it didn't earn back its cost at the box office. "It was not a film that I set out to earn a great fortune on," Coppola insisted. "I do think that a very awkward distribution made the difference between a picture that might have a profit and a picture that had a loss." In contrast, *The Great Gatsby* drew an unprecedented $18.6 million in advance booking fees from big-city, first-run theaters and was in the black before it was released. But irate exhibitors who were unable to recoup their advances forced Paramount to refund several million and by the end of its theatrical run in the United States, the film had collected a respectable but unspectacular $14.2 million.

Poe in L.A.

Robert Evans, who had stuck by Coppola during the making of *The Godfather,* was busy putting together his own surefire project. Divorced from Ali MacGraw—she had run off with Steve McQueen after costarring with him in a movie that Evans urged her to make for her career's sake—Evans was also separating himself from the business end of Paramount after working on the *Gatsby* project. He dropped out of his executive office and became an independent producer with a Paramount contract. His first picture under this new arrangement was a Robert Towne script called *Chinatown*.

Towne tailored the role of a private detective in '30s Los Angeles for the star of his *The Last Detail* screenplay, Jack Nicholson. Evans hired the reliable director of *Rosemary's Baby,* Roman Polanski, to make the movie, and Polanski said that when he read the femme fatale's part, "I kept picturing Faye Dunaway." The actress eagerly signed on to give her career a shot in the arm. "I sort of dropped the ball after *Bonnie and Clyde,*" she admitted to the *New York Times*.

"*Chinatown* is easier than anything I've ever done before," Polanski remarked to *Women's Wear Daily*. "We have a good crew, a great cameraman and great actors. I waste very little time with actors who aren't." When asked about rumors about Dunaway's temperament, the director replied, "I do find Faye tremendously temperamental. Off the stage, I find her impossible. It's hardly worth it, but it's worth it." Polanski also clashed with Towne over the film's ending; Towne's original was hopeful, but Polanski's final one was relentlessly bleak.

"*Chinatown* reminds you again—and thrillingly—that motion pictures are larger, not smaller, than life," wrote Charles Champlin in the *Los Angeles Times*. "They are not processed in drug stores and they are not television." *Newsweek* described it as "a brilliant cinematic poem in the style of Poe, circa 1974." *Saturday Review* said it was "superbly acted—especially by Jack Nicholson, who does everything so easily, casually, and appropriately that he hardly seems to be acting at all." Nicholson's face grinned on the cover of *Time* in a story entitled, "The Star with the Killer Smile," and his foot and handprints were put in cement in the forecourt of the Chinese Theatre. As for Faye Dunaway, Liz Smith agreed with Polanski that she was worth it: "Her insistence on perfection shines through. Ms. Dunaway is in the grand tradition of bizarre neurotic stars—like Bette Davis, Ida Lupino, Barbara Stanwyck. She's got it." She also got married that summer to twenty-eight-year-old singer Peter Wolf of the J. Geils Band, six years her junior. "It puts a definition on a relationship," the bride clarified. "A door has been closed."

Out of the Sewer

Over at Fox, writer-director Paul Mazursky was trying to cast the role of an old widower hitchhiking across country with his cat. Mazursky had written the role for James Cagney, who was not interested, and the studio wanted either Laurence Olivier or Frank Sinatra. Mazursky decided on fifty-five-year-old Art Carney, who happily put on old-age makeup. "I'm trying to change my im-

"Contrary to what Mr. Hoffman thinks, it is not an obscene evening."
—Frank Sinatra

age," said Ed Norton of TV's *The Honeymooners.* "You don't like going through life with your name synonymous with sewers." When *Harry & Tonto* premiered at the end of the summer, Pauline Kael declared, "Art Carney shows the great talent that he could never fully show on television." The actor told *Time* that he had recently conquered his alcoholism and that *Harry & Tonto* had produced another change in him. "Until the picture, I never liked cats," he said. "But Tonto is a helluva cat, never used a stand-in once."

Out of Control

Mr. and Mrs. Cassavetes were at it again, this time with *A Woman Under the Influence,* a movie about a marriage in which the wife suffers a nervous breakdown. "I knew many girls who had had breakdowns," said Gena Rowlands. "I drew little touches from each of them and a lot from myself. I don't mean I'm really going mad, but I'm a little crazy—we all are—and sometimes I let things go." Her husband was going crazy trying to secure control of the picture. "I just couldn't trust any studio to handle the picture correctly," the director confessed. "If anyone had interfered with my vision, I would probably have gone mad." Instead, he got his friend and leading man, Peter Falk, to help finance the film, which the star of the *Columbo* TV series was able to do. Cassavetes opened the film at the New York Film Festival and distributed it himself. *Newsweek* raved that Cassavetes "makes us confront our own deepest feelings, even as we cry 'Stop, enough!'" And Charles Champlin acclaimed Gena Rowlands' performance as "the most overpowering, gut-knotting, achingly believable and beautifully sympathetic portrayal I have watched in a very long time." Audiences came to watch her, too, and the low-budget independent feature raked in $6 million in domestic rentals.

Dirty Words

Bob Fosse didn't have John Cassavetes' problem. No sooner had the Oscar-winning director of *Cabaret* said he wanted to direct a biography of the late Lenny Bruce than United Artists gave him the go-ahead. What Fosse did have problems with was convincing Dustin Hoffman to play the title role. According to *The Films of Dustin Hoffman,* "Fosse desperately wanted Hoffman so much that at parties he would make a scene by half-jokingly falling to his knees, crawling to Dustin with his arms out, in the style of Jolson singing, begging the actor to take the part." Ultimately, Hoffman acquiesced and Fosse went to work. The New York Film Festival wanted to premiere *Lenny,* but the director said the editing wouldn't be finished in time. Part of the delay was due to the fact that Fosse was beginning work on a new Broadway musical, *Chicago.* By the time *Lenny* opened in November, Fosse had collapsed from exhaustion and undergone open-heart surgery.

"In the way that Fosse made *Cabaret* a landmark musical drama, he has now made *Lenny* a landmark contemporary biographical drama," cheered *Variety,* although Vincent Canby complained the film was "no more profound than those old movie biographies Jack Warner used to grind out about people like George Gershwin, Mark Twain and Dr. Ehrlich." Hoffman also aroused mixed responses. *Time* wrote, "Loving and loveless, adolescently joyful or darkly sadistic, paranoid and fearless, aggressive and pitiful, he gives a complex and mercurial performance." But Pauline Kael scoffed, "Hoffman makes a serious, honorable try, but his Lenny is a nice boy. Lenny Bruce was uncompromisingly not nice; the movie turns a teasing, seductive hipster into a putz."

There was little dissension, however, over the performance of Valerie Perrine as Bruce's stripper wife, Honey. "Valerie Perrine certainly landed one of the year's juiciest roles in *Lenny,* giving a performance that has Best Actress written all over it," announced Marilyn Beck. The *New York Times* profiled the thirty-one-year-old ex-Vegas showgirl in an article headlined VALERIE PERRINE OR THE RETURN OF THE HOLLYWOOD SEX KITTEN. "I've never had any acting lessons," Perrine indicated. "I don't know anything about Chavan-

"I really don't think about anything until I get on the set."
—Valerie Perrine

asky, or whatever you call him. I really don't think about anything until I get on the set."

All Aboard

Ingrid Bergman said of her first visit to the set of her new movie, "I felt absolutely awed when we first gathered together for a cast and crew party. I hadn't felt this excited since my first days in Hollywood." Sipping cocktails with Ingrid were her costars: Lauren Bacall, Vanessa Redgrave, Wendy Hiller, John Gielgud, Anthony Perkins and Sean Connery, among others. They were all playing murder suspects in Sidney Lumet's version of Agatha Christie's *Murder on the Orient Express* and Albert Finney, thirty-eight, was impersonating the far-older Hercule Poirot. Lumet, the director of *Serpico,* wasn't out for realism this time. "I want glamour, gaiety and humor," he said, bragging "not since the Marx Brothers in the stateroom has there been an assembly like this." When *Murder on the Orient Express* rolled off the line in late November, Judith Crist described it as "a feast—in any season." *Variety* raved "Finney is outstanding as Poirot, his makeup, wardrobe and performance a blend of topflight theater." *Newsweek* was a killjoy, however, carping that Lumet "simply has no feel for high-style," but audiences didn't seem to notice—the whodunit was so successful it launched a whole series of all-star Agatha Christie mystery movies.

Shake 'n' Bake

Stars who weren't slated for Agatha Christie movies found themselves cast in disaster movies, a genre spawned by the success of Irwin Allen's *The Poseidon Adventure*. Universal jumped on the bandwagon first by reviving Ross Hunter's *Airport* format in *Airport 1975,* starring Charlton Heston and George Kennedy, both of whom then punched into work on *Earthquake,* which the studio billed as "An Event." Ava Gardner and Genevieve Bujold were among the performers dodging the falling debris. *The New Yorker* rejoiced, "L.A. gets it," and called the film "an entertaining marathon of Grade-A destruction effects with B-picture stock characters spinning through it." The biggest effect was a loud noisemaker that Universal trademarked "Sensurround" and installed in theaters "to give moviegoers the sense of being in the epicenter of a major tremor." "There's no end to this if it hits," predicted producer Jennings Lang, "I can see eventual audience participation in a picture. They could sing, talk back at the screen, yell at it, anything."

Meanwhile, Fox and Warners had each bought the rights to books about burning skyscrapers and, rather than compete, they made Hollywood history by making a film together; thus, *The Tower* and *The Glass Inferno* begat Irwin Allen's production, *The Towering Inferno*. "Our aim is to entertain, but if while we're doing so we are able to alert the public to fire safety in high rises and the proper defenses to combat a fire emergency, that's just great!" the producer told interviewers.

Allen took the label "all-star" literally and his cast boasted Steve McQueen, Paul Newman, William Holden and Jennifer Jones. Fred Astaire played a con man and said, "It's a fun picture to make—it's all fire and water." And Faye Dunaway said to *People* that she was in it because "this is the kind of picture people want to see." When Paul Newman was asked if there was feuding over billing, the actor retorted, "Hell, we all know who the real star of this movie is—that damned fire."

Charles Champlin was reduced to press agentry in the *Los Angeles Times:* "More stars, more effects, more scale, more suspense, more crises, more impact, more of that feeling that you got your ticket's worth and then some!" The *New York Times'* Vincent Canby was keeping score, too, and said, "The special effects are smashing, better than those in *Earthquake* even without the brain-bending Sensurround." *The Towering Inferno* outgrossed *Earthquake* by almost $15 million, and *Variety* suggested the two films be combined on a double-bill called "Shake 'n' Bake."

"I can't carry a tune, but I was determined not to have Marni Nixon sing for me."
—Ellen Burstyn

The Quiet Chameleon

Christmas brought Francis Ford Coppola's *The Godfather Part II*. Brando wasn't in it, "because he was furious at Paramount's Frank Yablans who was furious at him for rejecting the Oscar," reported *Time*, which ran a story on the actor who was playing Don Corleone as a young man, thirty-year-old Robert De Niro. The magazine dubbed him "The Quiet Chameleon," explaining, "He researches a role like a counterintelligence agent cramming for a new identity." To research this role, De Niro spent six weeks in Sicily studying a local dialect—his only line of English in his subtitled performance was "I'll make him an offer he can't refuse." Although *Newsweek* said he gave "a tour de force," De Niro did not start packing for Hollywood. "He still lives in the same $75-a-month, two-room walk-up flat in which he grew up," said *Time*.

Coppola had fun casting the other roles in the sequel: Troy Donahue played one of the lovers of Connie Corleone, portrayed by Coppola's sister, Talia Shire. B-movie producer Roger Corman enacted a senator who interrogates an underworld figure played by playwright Michael V. Gazzo. And Actors Studio guru Lee Strasberg portrayed a Jewish gangster from Miami. Strasberg's prize pupil, Al Pacino, reprised his role as the don's youngest son, Michael, who becomes a bitter middle-aged man by the end of the film. Like De Niro, Pacino wasn't going to act like a star. "I'm the same now as I've always been—sort of a recluse," he swore. "People resent me for remaining myself when they think I should be acting like a superstar. I never wanted to be an actor and I don't particularly enjoy it. I have to act—there just isn't anything else for me."

Richard Schickel confirmed that Coppola's gamble had succeeded: "Francis Ford Coppola has made a richly detailed, intelligent film that uses overorganized crime as a metaphor to comment on the coldness and corruption of an overorganized modern world." Pauline Kael added: "The daring of *Part II* is that it enlarges the scope and deepens the meaning of the first film. Visually, *Part II* is far more complexly beautiful than the first, just as it's thematically richer, more shadowed, fuller." *Part II* cost twice as much to make as *Part I* and earned only about one-third as much at the box office, but since that translated into $30 million, Charles Bludhorn considered the sequel a good investment.

A Woman's Point of View

Warners was wary of investing $2.1 million in *Alice Doesn't Live Here Anymore,* a script that had made the rounds of all the studios. But Ellen Burstyn talked the company into it by arguing that it had been so long since a film presented a woman's point of view about women's real-life problems that any movie addressing the subject would be immediately embraced by an adult audience. Warners gave her the go-ahead and Burstyn began looking for a director. "I wanted someone who hadn't quite made it yet, who'd still be hungry," the actress said, so she asked Martin Scorsese, the director of *Mean Streets,* if he knew anything about women. "No," Scorsese replied, "this film will be a learning experience." "I thought that was a smashing answer," Burstyn responded. Scorsese was hired.

In *Alice,* Burstyn portrayed a widow in her mid-thirties who travels through the Southwest with her son, trying to get a job as a singer but winding up as a waitress. The film covered some of the same landscape as *Harry & Tonto,* in which Burstyn had played a supporting role as Art Carney's daughter, but *Alice* presented a new challenge for the actress—singing. "I have the worst voice," Burstyn despaired. "I can't carry a tune, but I was determined not to have Marni Nixon sing for me."

Warners opened *Alice* for one week in December in Hollywood to qualify for the Oscars, and the reviews were encouraging. Joyce Haber called Burstyn the "woman most deserving of an Oscar" and *Variety* praised Diane Ladd, as a fellow wait-

"You don't like going through life with your name synonymous with sewers."
—Art Carney

ress, for being "sort of a redneck Eve Arden." When the film bowed in New York in January, the critics were equally laudatory. Vincent Canby wrote that Burstyn was "one of the few actresses at work today (another is Glenda Jackson) who is able to seem appealing, tough, intelligent, funny and bereft, all at approximately the same moment." Burstyn added another feather to her cap by appearing on Broadway in the hit situation comedy, *Same Time, Next Year,* but she had it written into her contract that she could go to Hollywood on Oscar night.

Cable Enters the Picture

"Tonight, for the first time ever, you can enjoy an Academy screening right in your own home," announced a December 20 ad in *Daily Variety*. The screening was for Fox's *Claudine*, which was broadcast over Los Angeles' Z Channel, co-owned by Fox. Stanley Kauffmann described *Claudine* as "a Rock Hudson–Doris Day comedy-romance, updated and modified to be done by black people in New York," and Rex Reed welcomed it as "a refreshing change of pace from blaxploitation trash." *Claudine* had opened in the spring and bombed, but the studio was hoping that one of the leads, James Earl Jones or Diahann Carroll, could nab an Oscar nomination. Because of the dearth of women's roles, Carroll had the better chance, especially since her role as a welfare mother did not fit her image. "I have been searching desperately for a role in a film that was not a sophisticated, well-dressed, educated lady, which has been my image over the past seventeen years," the entertainer said. "I wanted to try another side of me." And so, when first choice Diana Sands died of cancer before production began, Carroll stepped into the title role.

Liv Her to Heaven

The New York Film Critics gave Jack Nicholson and Valerie Perrine a leg up in the Oscar race by voting them Best Actor and Best Supporting Actress, although United Artists continued to campaign for Perrine as Best Actress contender for *Lenny*. The Gotham crowd went Continental for the other awards: Federico Fellini's *Amarcord* won Best Picture and Best Director and Charles Boyer won Best Supporting Actor for Alain Resnais' *Stavisky*, which *Glamour* said "catches the chilly elegance that *The Great Gatsby* tries for but misses." Ingmar Bergman and Liv Ullmann wowed the critics again, this time winning Best Screenplay and Best Actress for *Scenes from a Marriage,* a movie that had been shown as a six-part series on Swedish television in 1973.

Bergman didn't have to worry about turning down another invitation to the Oscar ceremony this year; the Academy disqualified his movie because of a rule stating that a TV show had to play in theaters the same calendar year it was telecast. The film's American distributor, Don Rugoff, wrote the Academy, charging, "This is a technical rule which hampers the Academy's recognition of quality," and then asked why they hadn't been so picky in 1971 when they nominated *The Sorrow and the Pity* after it had been shown the year before on French TV. Another letter popped up in the *Los Angeles Times* demanding the Academy "make Liv Ullmann eligible." It was signed by a list of actresses, among them, Gena Rowlands, Diahann Carroll and Ellen Burstyn. A corp of directors, including Francis Ford Coppola, Martin Scorsese, Federico Fellini and Frank Capra, sent yet another letter, calling for Bergman's eligibility. And Vincent Canby protested in the *New York Times* that the rule was "the kind of technicality one usually encounters at obscure border stations in Central Asia."

The Academy would not budge, arguing that the request was too late; preliminary decisions had already been voted on in the technical branches. The *Hollywood Reporter* applauded its stand, advising critics, "Let's not make up new rules as we go along." Liv Ullmann told interviewers, "Perhaps all those actresses campaigning on my behalf is more gratifying than the award itself."

"I don't mean I'm really going mad, but I'm a little crazy."
—Gena Rowlands

Among the films in competition was one that Columbia was afraid to release. Although producer Bert Schneider was an Academy governor, his documentary *Hearts and Minds* was openly critical of U.S. involvement in Vietnam. One of President Lyndon Johnson's national security advisors claimed his interview in the film was "somewhat misleading" and asked that a temporary restraining order be placed on the movie. A Los Angeles Superior Court denied the request, but for Schneider the damage was done—Columbia wouldn't touch the movie. After six months of legal wrangling, Schneider arranged to have it distributed by Warner Brothers and entered it in the Academy's Documentary category. "It shouldn't be considered a documentary," Schneider said, "it should be considered a disaster epic, for that's what it surely is."

The Nominations

Hearts and Minds was nominated for Best Documentary, while Irwin Allen's disaster epic *The Towering Inferno* was up for Best Picture and seven other Oscars. *Earthquake* had to settle for four technical nominations. According to columnists, *The Towering Inferno* had a sure win in Best Supporting Actor nominee Fred Astaire. The hoofer's competition was a trio from *The Godfather Part II*—Michael V. Gazzo, Lee Strasberg and Robert De Niro. Kathleen Carroll of the *New York Daily News* said of the fifth nominee, "The steady barrage of ads promoting Jeff Bridges' performance in *Thunderbolt and Lightfoot* is the only possible explanation for his nomination."

Chinatown and *The Godfather Part II* led the race with ten nominations each; *The Godfather* won a slight lead when the Directors Guild crowned Coppola their best director, but Coppola still had memories of losing to Bob Fosse at the 1972 Oscars. These memories were rekindled by the presence of Fosse in the race; *Lenny* had seven nominations, including Best Picture and Best Director. Valerie Perrine was recognized as a Best Actress nominee, with her competition coming from Gena Rowlands, Faye Dunaway, Ellen Burstyn and Diahann Carroll, who had obviously profited from her exposure on cable TV. Coppola's *The Conversation* had been another cable offering and was another cable triumph—the film surprised everyone by being nominated for Best Picture, as well as for Best Original Screenplay.

Cold Feet and Personal Vanity

"The Academy Awards are obscene, dirty and no better than a beauty contest," said Best Actor nominee Dustin Hoffman on a Los Angeles talk show. Hoffman gave his tickets to the Oscar show to his parents. His fellow absentees would be nominees Albert Finney of *Murder on the Orient Express* and Al Pacino of *The Godfather Part II*. *Harry & Tonto*'s Art Carney said he'd be there, but the *New York Daily News* told him not to bother: "Not since Ray Milland guzzled his way to an Oscar in *The Lost Weekend* has an actor been such a sure bet as Jack Nicholson." The paper quoted "one well-known beauty" who said, "If only half the actresses with whom he's had affairs vote for him, he'll win by their ballots alone."

After all the campaigning, nominee Ellen Burstyn decided not to leave her Broadway show on Oscar night. "I won't win. I never do. I just get nominated," she said. When Marilyn Beck asked her about her third nomination, Burstyn shrugged, "There are so few decent roles for women these days, if you work, you get nominated." Gena Rowlands was a happier nominee, telling *Women's Wear Daily* she'd show up because "It adds greatly to the box office, especially since it's our picture. Plus there's a certain amount of personal vanity involved." Mrs. Cassavetes was also thrilled that her husband was finally recognized by the Academy with a Best Director nomination. "There are so many times you have the rug pulled out from under you, so it's very pleasing to have a little icing."

Gang of Four

The Academy went all out for a nostalgic hue to the telecast—all four emcees had been around since at least the '50s. Shirley MacLaine, forty, had just returned from a cultural exchange with mainland China and had written another autobiographical bestseller, *You Can Get There from Here*. MacLaine's *Sweet Charity* costar, Sammy Davis, Jr., forty-nine, had last been in the newspapers for hugging President Richard Nixon, who had just resigned. Shirley and Sammy were reunited with their former Rat Pack leader, Frank Sinatra, fifty-nine, who had returned to show business after retiring in 1971. Completing the picture of days gone by was Bob Hope, seventy-one, making his first Oscar show appearance since being booed in 1970.

The Academy had difficulty persuading a few other stars from the Golden Era to participate. The *Chicago Daily News* reported, "Cary Grant and Loretta Young are reluctant to appear as presenters for fear that *Lenny* . . . might win some awards. Friends say the two veteran screen stars don't want to be connected with what they term a 'dirty' movie." Shirley MacLaine's brother, Warren Beatty, thirty-seven, currently starring in *Shampoo,* was not offended by any of the Best Picture nominees and agreed to present the Award. With this group of friends and relatives in charge, the Academy promised "the show will have the comfortable feel of a family reunion."

The Big Night

Jack Nicholson, wearing a standard white tuxedo shirt this year, escorted Anjelica Huston through the torrential downpour that sent women scurrying with chinchilla coats held over their heads. Art Carney was the only other Best Actor nominee to show up. Ellen Burstyn was the only missing Best Actress nominee. The Best Supporting Actress category managed perfect attendance, meaning that Valentina Cortese made her second trip to Hollywood for last year's Best Foreign Film winner, *Day for Night*. François Truffaut, nominated for Best Director, stayed home this year, as did Roman Polanski. Bob Fosse was in Philadelphia working on *Chicago*. Francis Ford Coppola was very much in evidence, surrounded by his sister, Best Supporting Actress nominee Talia Shire, and his father, Best Score nominee Carmine Coppola. Two of Coppola's three Best Supporting Actor nominees were accounted for, but Robert De Niro was nowhere in sight. Fred Astaire had his daughter on his arm, and competitor Jeff Bridges brought his parents, as well as Susan George.

The telecast began with shots of arriving celebrities and when Lauren Bacall entered, the announcer called her "one of the greatest actresses never to win." Bacall was followed by two-time winner Peter Ustinov, plugging Gallo wines in a commercial. After announcer Hank Sims recalled the titles of the previous Best Picture winners—forty-six of them—Academy President Walter Mirisch made a brief appearance and then brought out Bob Hope, who began by commenting on the weather: "I didn't know Dustin Hoffman had that much power. If Dustin Hoffman wins, he's going to have a friend pick it up—George C. Scott. I think *The Godfather Part II* has an excellent chance of winning. Neither Mr. Price nor Mr. Waterhouse has been heard from in days. I'm wearing a tuxedo with a bulletproof cummerbund—who knows what will happen if Al Pacino doesn't win."

When Hope was finished, the curtain rose to reveal the set—an enormous bust of Oscar rising from the floor, flanked by large Oscar statues.

Awards Ceremony

APRIL 8, 1975, 7:00 P.M.
THE DOROTHY CHANDLER PAVILION,
LOS ANGELES

Your Hosts:
SAMMY DAVIS, JR., BOB HOPE, SHIRLEY MACLAINE,
FRANK SINATRA
Televised over NBC

Presenters

Supporting Actor . . . . Ryan and Tatum O'Neal
Short Films. . . Roddy McDowall and Brenda Vaccaro
Documentary Awards . . . . Lauren Hutton and Danny Thomas
Honorary Award to Jean Renoir . . . . . Ingrid Bergman
Special Achievement Award . . . . Bob Hope
Song . . . . Gene Kelly
Sound . . . . Joseph Bottoms and Deborah Raffin
Honorary Award to Howard Hawks . . . . . John Wayne
Scoring Awards . . . . Diahann Carroll and John (ny) Green
Costume Design . . . . Lauren Bacall
Supporting Actress . . . . Peter Falk and Katharine Ross
Art Direction . . . . Susan Blakely
Cinematography . . . . . . Jon Voight and Raquel Welch
Film Editing . . . . MacDonald Carey and Jennifer O'Neill
Foreign Film. . . . . Susan George and Jack Valenti
Jean Hersholt Humanitarian Award . . . . Frank Sinatra
Director . . . . Goldie Hawn and Robert Wise
Writing Awards . . . . James Michener
Actor . . . . Glenda Jackson
Actress . . . . Jack Lemmon
Picture . . . . Warren Beatty

Performers of Nominated Songs

"Benji's Theme (I Feel Love)" . Aretha Franklin, Jack Jones and Frankie Laine
"Blazing Saddles" . . . . Frankie Laine
"Little Prince" . . . . Jack Jones
"We May Never Love Like This Again" . . . . Aretha Franklin, Jack Jones and Frankie Laine
"Wherever Love Takes Me" . . . . Aretha Franklin

"Man, that's heavy. You know, as J.J. would say, 'Dyn-o-mite!'"
—Sammy Davis, Jr.

Ryan O'Neal and Tatum, in a low-cut dress, strolled out and Ryan explained the voting rules, with help from footage of Academy voters in action—Ricardo Montalban was seen attending an Academy screening. Then the two O'Neals announced the winner of the Best Supporting Actor Oscar—the sole absentee, Robert De Niro for *The Godfather Part II*. An ebullient Francis Ford Coppola rushed to the podium and exclaimed, "I'm happy that one of my boys made it. I think Robert De Niro is an extraordinary actor and he's going to enrich the films that will be made in the years to come."

Lauren Hutton and Danny Thomas declared the Best Documentary Feature to be *Hearts and Minds*. Coproducer Peter Davis, in a white suit, commented, "It's ironic to get a prize for a war movie while the suffering in Vietnam continues." He then thanked his sons, "who I hope will grow up in a country and atmosphere different from the one we had to portray in *Hearts and Minds* and who I hope will go to bed now." Bert Schneider, in a traditional tuxedo, stepped up to the microphone and said, "It is ironic that we're here at a time just before Vietnam is about to be liberated. I will now read a short wire that I have been asked to read by the Vietnamese people from the delegation for the Viet Cong at the Paris peace talks:

> *Please transmit to all our friends in America our recognition of all that they have done on behalf of peace and for the application of the Paris accords on Vietnam. These actions serve the legitimate interests of the American people and the Vietnamese people. Greetings of friendship to all American people.*

The producers walked off and then the Documentary Short winner Robin Lehman made an ecological pitch: "If the film says anything, it says let's save a little bit of nature for our children and ancestors to come."

Best Supporting Actress nominee Ingrid Bergman strode out to present and accept an Honorary Oscar for Jean Renoir, who had directed her in *Paris Does Strange Things* in 1957. The audience welcomed her with a standing ovation, but, in the pressroom, Bergman said, "I hope the ovation was for Renoir and not for me." Ingrid found out otherwise when the reporters refused to interrogate her about Renoir, but asked her if she thought she'd win tonight. After a few minutes, Bergman declared, "I thought you would ask questions about him but you didn't, so good-bye," and she walked out.

Meanwhile, Bob Hope was in a tizzy. Show producer Howard W. Koch reported that after Bert Schneider read the telegram, "Bob Hope pinned me up against the wall telling me I should do a disclaimer on the air, and Shirley MacLaine was screaming at me, 'Don't you dare!'" MacLaine didn't have much time to debate; after *Earthquake* grabbed two special Oscars—one for Visual Effects and one for Sensurround—it was time for her big entrance.

As the band struck up a fanfare, MacLaine came waltzing out with a train sailing behind her. "You're never going to believe this, but I'm Shirley MacLaine," she laughed. "It is so nice to be back home in show business. I've been a lot of places over the world the last few years, but I've never seen anything quite like this—this looks like Liberace's sauna bath." Shirley added, "It's like a class reunion backstage for me to sit once again with Frank Sinatra, Sammy Davis and Bob Hope. We laughed a lot and told each other lies about what we've been doing over the past few years. At least Sammy said he was sorry."

MacLaine introduced John Wayne, who gave an Honorary Oscar to director Howard Hawks. "Actors hate directors," Wayne explained, "and then the movie comes out, and they get great notices, and then they don't hate the director anymore." After reading a list of Hawks' movies, Wayne said, "He's made a lot of actors jump. I'm the director tonight. Hawks! Roll 'em. Get your skinny whatchamacallit out here!" The veteran got a standing ovation and Wayne handed him his Oscar, saying, "From movie fans everywhere." Hawks reminisced, "I remember visiting John Ford when he became sick and went out into the

"It is ironic that we're here at a time just before Vietnam is about to be liberated."
—Bert Schneider

desert to die. And he said, 'There's something I stole from you that tops the whole thing. I won the Oscar but you made a better picture. You're going to get one.'" Wayne pointed the way off when Hawks was finished. "This way," the Duke demanded. "No, this way," Hawks directed, leading Wayne off in the other direction. When they reached the pressroom, a journalist accused Wayne of being a racist. "You're mistaken," Wayne responded, and Hawks defended him. The reporter repeated his accusation and was then led off by Academy security guards.

On stage, Diahann Carroll and John Green revealed the winners of the Best Score Oscar—Nino Rota and Francis Ford Coppola's father, Carmine Coppola, for *The Godfather Part II*. The camera showed Francis' reaction: he was jumping up and down, whistling. Carmine Coppola climbed to the stage and apologized for his collaborator's absence, adding, "We worked very nicely together. I'd like to thank my son for my being up here." When Coppola senior returned to his seat, he dropped his Oscar—it broke. The Song Score Award went to Nelson Riddle for *The Great Gatsby,* who said, "I'd like to thank Jack Clayton, the English director, who had faith in me."

"An interesting thing happened in films last year," ruminated MacLaine. "Not many of us women were in any." This was a lead-in to the Costume Design Oscar, presented by Lauren Bacall. "Movies are influencing fashion again," Bacall proclaimed. "I like that because it means romance is back on the way. Are you ready for it? I am." For the first time ever, one studio produced all five nominees in a category—Paramount. The winner was *The Great Gatsby,* which won both of its two nominations. Designer Theoni V. Aldredge flew to the stage and said, "I love you, Jack, and I'm very, very proud to be a part of your film."

Peter Falk and Katharine Ross named the Best Supporting Actress—Ingrid Bergman for *Murder on the Orient Express,* her third Oscar. "It's always nice to win an Oscar," Bergman began, "but in the past he has shown he is very forgetful and has poor timing. Because last year when *Day for Night* opened, Valentina Cortese gave the most beautiful performance that all we actresses recognize. Here I am her rival and I don't like it all. There you are . . ." The camera found Cortese, with her arms out, blowing kisses to Bergman. "Please forgive me, Valentina," Ingrid pleaded, "I didn't mean to."

Shirley MacLaine introduced the next emcee by commenting that he has "more rings on his fingers than I can count. Ladies and gentlemen, the mad hugger himself, Sammy Davis, Jr.!" Davis wore his glasses and a small necklace with a star. Explaining that he and his wife were "real film freaks," Davis confessed, "I've never been as moved as I was tonight, I mean, standing over there, hearing that list of forty-six award-winning flicks. Man, that's heavy. You know, as J.J. would say, 'Dyn-o-mite!'" The audience applauded, but Davis cut them off. "May I just say something? I am so proud in one small way to be a part of this industry and like what *That's Entertainment* said, 'Boy, do we need it now!'" There was applause for this sentiment, and Davis said, "I just had to say it because I feel that way. Thank you for letting me be here."

Davis segued to the Art Direction Award, introducing presenter Susan Blakely as "Susan Berkerly." The actress laughed as she walked onstage with O.J. Simpson and gave the Oscar to *The Godfather Part II* without a word of protest. Sammy, on the other hand, was beside himself with guilt. "I would just like to take a moment out to apologize," Davis said when he returned. "Susan, I should have done it right." Davis' nervousness was due to the musical salute he was about to perform after *The Towering Inferno* picked up two more technical Oscars. "The Academy has graciously consented to let me pay tribute to The Man," Sammy said. "In silent films, The Man was Charlie Chaplin. In talking movies, it's Clark Gable. But when they talk about singing and dancing movies, this is The Man, man." Photos of Fred Astaire flashed on the screen and Shirley MacLaine returned with a hat and cane for Davis, who

"Sacheen Littlefeather accepted in good taste."
—Howard W. Koch

then went into his dance, ending up on his knees before Astaire in the orchestra. The audience gave its third standing ovation and Davis handed Astaire the hat and cane. "Thank you, Sammy," Astaire said.

A film clip of Frank Sinatra winning his 1953 Oscar was followed by the orchestra playing the singer's current theme song, "My Way." Sinatra entered and told the audience, "So many gifted people are making pictures like you do, with their clothes on. Contrary to what Mr. Hoffman thinks, it is not an obscene evening. It is not garish and it is not embarrassing." The emcee paused for applause. "I was also thinking that I'm glad I wasn't here with both the Coppolas and Frankie Laine, or there would have been an investigation. I also think Sammy looks better in an African caftan and I wish he'd go back to one. He looks like a headwaiter in a rib joint somewhere."

Sinatra was safely offstage when Goldie Hawn and Robert Wise revealed that Francis Ford Coppola was the winner of the Best Director Oscar for *The Godfather Part II*. "I almost won this a couple of years ago for the first half of the same picture, but that's not why we did *Part II*," Coppola said. He concluded by thanking his non-nominated cinematographer, "Gordo Willis," and added quickly, "Thanks for giving my dad an Oscar."

As Coppola spoke, Bob Hope was backstage waving a disclaimer he had written to Bert Schneider's speech at Frank Sinatra. "If you don't read it, I will," the comedian threatened. So Sinatra took the piece of paper and walked out to introduce the Writing Awards.

"Ladies and gentlemen, to deviate a second," Sinatra began, "I've been asked by the Academy to make the following statement regarding a statement made by a winner. The Academy is saying, 'We are not responsible for any political references made on the program and we are sorry they had to take place this evening.'" The announcement was met with both boos and applause. Sinatra continued, "And now to present the Writing Awards, the author of *Continental*—I mean, *Centennial*—James Michener." Sinatra scooted off and Michener gave the Adapted Screenplay Oscar to Francis Ford Coppola and Mario Puzo for *The Godfather Part II*. Only Puzo appeared and he asked, "Where's Francis?" All alone, the winner thanked "all the actors for bringing the book alive." The Original Screenplay winner was Robert Towne for *Chinatown* and he commented, "If you've ever been on a film that didn't quite work out, you know how much you owe to people if it did." The screenwriter did not mention Roman Polanski, but paid tribute to the leading man, "Jack, who was really magic."

Meanwhile, Frank Sinatra was getting heat offstage from Shirley MacLaine. "Why did you do that!?" she screamed. "You said you were speaking on behalf of the Academy. Well, I'm a member of the Academy and you didn't ask me. It was arrogant of you and Bob Hope not to submit it to the Board of Governors first." Sinatra dodged MacLaine and ran back onstage to announce, "Last year's winner of the Best Actress Award—Glenda Jackson." An unsmiling Jackson walked out and said, "Thank you, thank you twice in fact, and thank you for tonight." Jackson's task was to name the Best Actor. "The winner is Art Carney for *Harry & Tonto*," she said. Now Jack Nicholson wasn't smiling, but Art Carney impulsively kicked his foot in the air. The audience rewarded Carney further with a standing ovation—the fourth one—and Carney thanked Paul Mazursky for "a gem of a script" and his agent for his advice: "Do it. You are old."

Jack Lemmon appeared and said, "We are all incredibly fortunate tonight because I have lost my voice." The laryngitis victim croaked out the winner of the Best Actress Oscar—Ellen Burstyn for *Alice Doesn't Live Here Anymore*. Director Martin Scorsese came to the stage and reiterated the people Burstyn had asked him to thank, ending "and she asked me to thank myself."

Sinatra returned to introduce Shirley MacLaine's brother by alluding to his role as a hairdresser in *Shampoo:* "He wanted to touch mine,

"It's always nice to win an Oscar."
—Ingrid Bergman

but there's no possible way." Warren Beatty, in glasses, responded, "Thank you, Frank, you old Republican, you. I'll give you a wash and set anytime." Beatty gave the Best Picture Award to Francis Ford Coppola for *The Godfather Part II*, who said, "We tried to make a film that would be a really good film."

The four hosts were supposed to rush out and sing "That's Entertainment," but the *New York Post* reported that Sinatra refused to join in until Sammy Davis dragged him out onstage by his sleeve. "The world is a stage, the stage is a world of entertainment," the quartet sang as the winners and presenters filled the stage behind them. The camera recorded Danny Thomas kissing Glenda Jackson's hand and the show was over.

Aftermath

Backstage, Bob Hope called Schneider's speech "a cheap, cheap shot" and John Wayne bellowed that the producer "was a pain in the ass and outta line and against the rules of the Academy." A journalist asked Schneider why he didn't keep quiet like Jane Fonda, and he replied, "Jane deservedly won her Oscar for a fictional film, while we were talking to the issue of what our film was about. Frank Sinatra and Bob Hope are equally entitled to their point of view and I've no argument about their making a statement on their own, but it's wrong to drag the Academy into it."

"I never heard such controversy in my life!" wailed show producer Howard W. Koch. "The phones won't stop." When presenter Brenda Vaccaro stormed over to the producer and pointed out, "The Academy never interrupted its show to apologize for the streaker or Marlon Brando's Indian," Koch heard himself saying, "Sacheen Littlefeather accepted in good taste." Francis Ford Coppola came to Schneider's defense, arguing, "It's not a musical comedy, so the Academy in voting for that picture was sanctioning the message of that picture, which was in the spirit of Mr. Schneider's remarks." As for himself, Coppola promised to make good his claim to venture into other fields. A few months later, he launched a San Francisco–based magazine named *City*, which folded after one year.

Art Carney mugged for photographers and confessed, "On the way to the stage, I thought of saying in my speech, 'You're looking at an actor whose price has just doubled.'" Outside, four-time loser Jack Nicholson shrugged, "Maybe in 1976 I'll be the sentimental favorite."

At the Governors' Ball, Bob Hope ran around with telegrams from viewers angry at Schneider's speech, prompting Shirley MacLaine to laugh, "Bob Hope's so mad at me he's going to bomb Encino." Frank Sinatra said he was glad at least that Dustin Hoffman didn't win: "After those cracks he made, I'd have torn the place down." But *Lenny* producer Marvin Worth said, "I know Dustin wanted to win."

The following day, Art Carney received a phone call from his former TV costar. "Hey, Carney, what'd you do last night?" Jackie Gleason asked. "I went to see *Chinatown*," Carney retorted. Gleason had also worked with the Best Actress winner, back when she was a "Glee Girl" on his TV show, so he gave Ellen Burstyn a call, too. "I haven't heard from him in twenty years," Burstyn remarked to the *New York Post*'s Earl Wilson. She also said, "I wanted to win after I saw Art Carney win." Still, Burstyn didn't know what to make of the honor until two nights later, when Jack Lemmon and Walter Matthau appeared at the stage door with a liquor box. Burstyn's Oscar was inside. Over dinner, Burstyn turned to Matthau and asked, "What's really in that box, Walter? What does an Oscar mean?" "Let's put it this way, Ellen," Matthau said. "When you die, the newspapers will say, 'The Academy Award-winning actress Ellen Burstyn died today.'"

Best Supporting Actor Robert De Niro was also uncertain how he felt about winning when reporters finally caught up with him. "Well, lots of people who win the award don't deserve it, so it makes you a little cynical about how much it means," he told *Women's Wear Daily*. "Did it mean that much to me? Well, I don't know. It changes your life like anything that will change your life. People react to it. I mean, it's not bad winning it."

Best Supporting Actress Ingrid Bergman recalled in her autobiography, "Valentina was with me for the rest of the evening and we were photographed together. I was really sad that she hadn't gotten it, because she did deserve it. I realized later I had acted—as usual—too impulsively. Three other actresses had also been nominated, and they were also very good; they were kind of mad that I'd only mentioned Valentina. It would have been better if I'd kept my mouth shut altogether."

For Federico Fellini, winning his fourth Foreign Film Award with *Amarcord*, an Oscar posed no problem at all. "Of course it is a pleasure for me," the director said when he got the news in Italy. "In the mythology of the cinema, the Oscar is the supreme prize."

1975

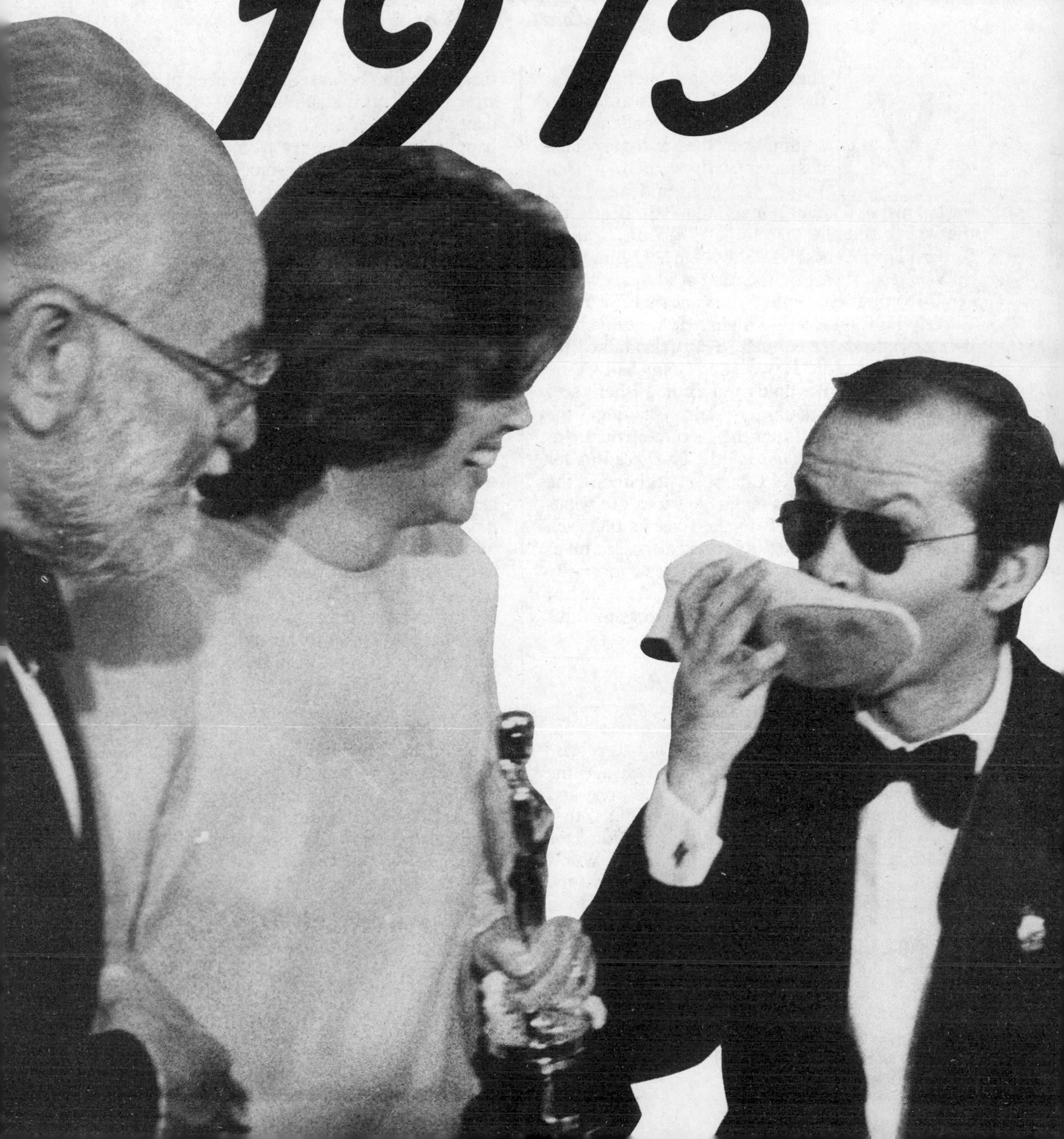

"Suddenly, I'm having to worry about my hair. I got hot rollers for the first time in my life."
—Louise Fletcher

Vengeance was Jack Nicholson's at the 1975 Academy Awards.

"I wanted to challenge the assumption that a hypersexual character with women, a Don Juan," said Warren Beatty, "is a misogynist or a latent homosexual." So Beatty got the writer and the director of *The Last Detail*—Robert Towne and Hal Ashby—to help him whip up *Shampoo*. It was an updating of Thomas Wycherly's Restoration comedy *The Country Wife,* set in Beverly Hills on election night, 1968, with a hairdresser instead of a eunuch. Beatty also talked Julie Christie, Goldie Hawn, Lee Grant and Carrie Fisher—Debbie Reynolds and Eddie Fisher's seventeen-year-old daughter—into playing the women in his life. When the picture opened, Judith Crist dubbed *Shampoo* "the *La Dolce Vita* for the 1970s" and Charles Champlin declared in the *Los Angeles Times,* "Its language wipes out whatever reticences were left in the screen's playback of life as spoken." The film's most discussed bit of dialogue regarded Julie Christie's wish to gratify Warren Beatty under a table at L.A.'s Bistro; *Shampoo* became one of the highest-grossing films in Columbia's history.

Ann-Margret Bounces Back

Columbia released two musicals in the spring. Ray Stark convinced Barbra Streisand to reprise *Funny Girl*'s Fanny Brice in *Funny Lady* and the sequel proved to be profitable. But the press and ticket-buyers responded more to the studio's other tuner—The Who's rock opera *Tommy*. Director Ken Russell went on record comparing The Who's work to Alban Berg's opera *Wozzeck* and cast the all-singing movie with everyone from Elton John to Jack Nicholson to Tina Turner. Ann-Margret played the mother of the title character, a deaf-dumb-and-blind pinball player, and said she identified with him because she had been incapacitated after falling off a stage in 1972. "Since the accident," the entertainer explained, "it makes me happier than ever to try to make people happy. They say 'see me, touch me, feel me' in *Tommy*. That's important. So often we go through life like zombies." Of her performance, Vincent Canby wrote in the *New York Times,* "Ann-Margret sings and dances as if the fate of Western civilization depends upon it."

Overleaf: *Best Actor winner Jack Nicholson shows producer Saul Zaentz and Best Actress Louise Fletcher what she can do with her shoe.*

Altman Goes Country

Before *Funny Lady* and *Tommy* could premiere, Pauline Kael was rushing to *The New Yorker* with an advance review of a musical by Robert Altman. United Artists had financed the director when he said he and Joan Tewkesbury were going to write a movie covering twenty-four characters in a five-day span in country music capital Nashville, Tennessee, but the studio neither understood nor liked the finished script. "Everybody else turned it down, too," Altman said. "I had to get independent financing." Once he got the cash, the director starting casting.

Susan Anspach had to bow out of a role of a singer who has a nervous breakdown, so Altman replaced her with the woman who had written some of the songs for the character, former backup singer Ronee Blakley. Louise Fletcher, who had been in Altman's previous film, *Thieves Like Us,* was working on a character based on her experience with her deaf parents, only to have Altman decide that TV comedienne Lily Tomlin would be perfect for the part. Tomlin admitted that she was skeptical: "When I got the part, I thought, 'I'm not her,' but as I looked at everybody else and saw how perfect they were, I thought Altman couldn't be wrong about me." Any fears the other twenty-three actors may have felt were allayed at Altman's daily conferences; *Newsweek* described them: "At the end of a typical day, the *Nashville* set would gather for drinks in the director's office with Altman himself—a stiff Scotch and soda in one hand, a joint in the other—leading the letting-go."

"So often we go through life like zombies."
—Ann-Margret

"At Robert Altman's new, almost three-hour film," wrote Pauline Kael, "you don't get drunk on images—you get elated." She predicted that UA's decision to withdraw the film "will probably rack up as a classic boner, because this picture is going to take off into the stratosphere." Altman cut the movie to two hours and forty minutes and Paramount picked it up, opening it in the summer at two small theaters across the street from Bloomingdale's. *Newsweek* devoted a cover story to the "Epic of Opryland" and the *Los Angeles Herald-Examiner* proclaimed, "The film is a landmark as significant to movie history as *The Birth of a Nation* and *Citizen Kane*."

But when *Nashville* premiered in the eponymous city, the residents didn't cotton to it. Brenda Lee denounced it as "a dialectic collage of unreality," and Webb Pierce, a singer famous for his guitar-shaped swimming pool, surmised "whoever put this out must have had a nightmare the night before." Loretta Lynn also had a beef: "I ain't seen the movie and I ain't going to; I'd rather see *Bambi*. Besides, if they wanted country music, they could have had the real thing. All they had to do was ask me." Despite Pauline Kael's stratospheric prediction, *Nashville* earned a mere $9 million in the U.S.

Bruce Makes a Splash

"*Jaws* was not a novel," argued actor Robert Shaw, "it was a story written by a committee, a piece of shit." But Darryl Zanuck's son Richard and partner David Brown had purchased Peter Benchley's bestseller about a rampaging great white shark and were determined to make it into a movie. Shaw came around when his wife, Mary Ure, said the script wasn't so bad and the actor signed on to the movie, to be directed by twenty-seven-year-old Steven Spielberg, who insisted on shooting on location—the Atlantic Ocean. "We could use a tank, but it just wouldn't look real," the director maintained, so the film crew spent the summer of 1974 at Martha's Vineyard waiting for the three mechanical sharks, nicknamed Bruce, to operate properly in salt water. Universal grew nervous when the sharks, costing $150,000 each, constantly malfunctioned, dragging out the shooting schedule and doubling the original budget. Zanuck and Brown managed to hold the studio executives off while the film's editor, Verna Fields, reported to work at the Vineyard. "If anybody in the audience laughs at the shark," she explained, "we're sunk."

Releasing the movie on June 30, 1975, was a major corporate undertaking, as *Newsweek* documented: "Like the novel, the movie was launched with an almost unprecedented promotional campaign, complete with cross-country tours by stars and $700,000 worth of prime-time TV time to trumpet its release in 450 theaters throughout the land." Pauline Kael went ga-ga over this one, too: "There are parts of *Jaws* that suggest what Eisenstein might have done if he hadn't intellectualized himself out of reach." But to the *New York Times* it was "nothing more than a creaky, old-fashioned monster picture reminiscent of *Creature from the Black Lagoon*."

Nobody paid any attention to the critics; there were lines at theaters even longer than the ones for *The Exorcist* and shark sightings rose at a hysterical rate. *Jaws* not only boosted the careers of stars Roy Scheider, Robert Shaw and Richard Dreyfuss, but made composer John Williams famous for his pounding shark theme music. The film's logo—a woman swimming above an open-mouthed shark—showed up in some form in political cartoons practically every day. Steven Spielberg was pronounced a genius and *Jaws* became the most profitable Hollywood movie to date—topping *The Godfather*, *Gone With the Wind* and *The Sound of Music*.

Nicholson Gets Around

Filmgoers who didn't want to wait in line for Bruce had their choice of two Jack Nicholson movies that summer. Director Michelangelo Antonioni told Nicholson he could only get backing for his latest art-house venture, *The Passenger*, if the

"It wasn't a bad year for movies, it was a terrible year."
—Charles Champlin

backers saw an American star's name above the title. Nicholson said count me in, telling journalists that playing the part of a man who switches identities with a corpse was "pure pleasure." Andrew Sarris wrote, "Nicholson comes through ultimately for Antonioni with a magnificent incarnation of alienated, doom-ridden modernity."

No matter how good the movie, the name Antonioni meant nothing outside of art houses, so Nicholson searched for a sure-fire commercial project and thought he had one in a caper movie called *The Fortune*. But the critics disagreed. "There is something hectic and ugly about watching a cad and a weasel trying to drown, however ineptly, an essentially defenseless innocent," *Newsweek* said, and audiences felt the same way—*The Fortune* didn't make a dime.

Pacino in Lavender

Variety announced that the latest Al Pacino–Sidney Lumet collaboration would be *The Boys in the Bank*, based on an actual 1972 Brooklyn bank robbery "by a bisexual man who was seeking money to finance a sex-change operation for his homosexual boyfriend." Lumet told the *New York Post* that he knew that his star could pull off this unusual role: "Al's very possibly a great actor. Maybe one for the ages, I don't know." Film newcomer Chris Sarandon, thirty-two, played the boyfriend and told the *New York Daily News:* "When I auditioned, I tried to capture the femininity of Blanche DuBois. Lumet said, 'Next time come back and think of Blanche as a hardhat.'" Pacino's real-life counterpart, John Wojtowicz, told *People* from his jail cell that the film was "only 30 percent true," adding, "I felt the movie in essence a piece of garbage." Retitled *Dog Day Afternoon*, the offbeat picture nonetheless found an audience and moved *Vogue* to comment, "Al Pacino moves through his movie with the epic nobility of a Greek tragedian and the sashay of a pitiful comedian."

Diana Has Designs

Motown and Paramount collaborated again to let Diana Ross suffer again, this time as a high-fashion designer in *Mahogany*. "In high school, I studied fashion design and costume illustration," Ross revealed, "but the only opportunity I ever had in this direction was in my own personal wear when I was with the Supremes. I used to talk to the guys who designed our clothes and tell them exactly what I thought we should wear." Diana didn't have to talk to anybody about the costumes in *Mahogany*—she designed all twenty-five of her gowns herself—but director Tony Richardson had to answer to Motown head Berry Gordy, who fired the British Oscar-winner because, according to *Variety,* he "didn't quite capture the feeling of blackness—the black point of view."

When Gordy himself took over the direction, *Time* observed, "Gordy took pen in hand and wrote the line that he says encapsulates *Mahogany*'s philosophical essence: 'Success is nothing without someone you love to share it with.' Such creativity sent *Mahogany* $1.25 million over its original $2.5 budget." *Mahogany*'s box-off success was minor, but its theme song, sung by Diana Ross and subtitled "Do You Know Where You're Going To?," went straight to the top of the charts.

Nicholson Cracks Up

Kirk Douglas threw in the towel. After trying for thirteen years to launch a movie version of his 1963 Broadway flop *One Flew Over the Cuckoo's Nest,* the actor turned over the film rights to Ken Kesey's cult novel to his son, Michael, best known for his role as a cop in TV's *The Streets of San Francisco*. Michael wasn't any more successful than Dad at hustling the property about a nonconformist in a mental hospital, until he took a cue from Michelangelo Antonioni and persuaded Jack Nicholson to star. Douglas was able to raise his $3 million budget independently—approximately a

"There are so few surefire Best Actress candidates this year that the list may be downright embarrassing."
—New York Times

third of it went to Nicholson—and hired director Milos Forman, who had left his native Czechoslovakia during the 1968 Soviet invasion and been looking for a Hollywood hit ever since. Finding an actress willing to play the villainous Nurse Ratched was more difficult—Anne Bancroft, Ellen Burstyn, Colleen Dewhurst, Angela Lansbury and Geraldine Page all said no. Then Forman looked at Altman's *Thieves Like Us* to see if Shelley Duvall would be right for the role of a prostitute in *Cuckoo's Nest* and found himself growing fascinated with the supporting performance of Louise Fletcher, whose husband produced the movie. A week before *Cuckoo's Nest* started filming, Mrs. Jerry Bick won the role of Nurse Ratched.

The film company retreated to the Oregon State Hospital where "each and every person associated with the production literally lived in the hospital for ten to twelve hours a day during the first three months of 1975," bragged the production notes. Many journalists also happened by the asylum. "Usually I don't have much trouble slipping out of a film role, but here I don't go home from a movie studio, I go home from a mental institution," Nicholson laughed to the *New York Daily News,* while telling *Time,* "It's a nice place to visit."

United Artists acquired the film after it was finished, and when *Cuckoo's Nest* premiered in November, Charles Champlin proclaimed it "the best American film of the year." Rona Barrett predicted "for Louise Fletcher, a sure Best Actress nomination as the bad, life-denying establishment boogiewoman, Big Nurse Ratched." Fletcher, who had only acted on TV before dropping out in 1962 to become a full-time mother, said of her new fame, "Suddenly, I'm having to worry about my hair. I got hot rollers for the first time in my life." Almost every reviewer brought up the Oscar when evaluating Jack Nicholson's performance, and the *New York Times Magazine* went out of its way to suggest the actor had all the trappings of a conventional movie star. An article entitled "The Conquering Anti-Hero" stated, "In earning power, he's right up there with Redford and Pacino and probably has surpassed Newman by now. Among producers, he's even more in demand than Gene Hackman for the classic anti-hero roles that went to Bogart and Tracy in the 1940s. He has the standard superstar's house in the chic mountains overlooking Beverly Hills—with Brando and Charlton Heston as neighbors."

The Secret Stanley

Warners was wondering about the drawing power of Ryan O'Neal, the star of the studio's expensive Christmas present—Stanley Kubrick's *Barry Lyndon*. The studio gave the filmmaker $2.5 million to adapt William Thackeray's novel, but Kubrick worked on the movie for two years, sending the budget to $11 million. "If a picture is flawed, that flaw is forever," Kubrick explained. "The ideal way to make a film would be to wrap up after every scene and go away for a month to think." The director experimented with all-natural light sources and thought nothing of taking four days to set up a scene with 1,000 burning candles. "Neither the press nor the bank-rolling Warner Bros. has an inkling of what to expect of *Barry Lyndon*," reported *New York* in September. "N.Y. executives who flew to London a few weeks ago to get a look at some footage in order to prepare the December opening advertising campaign could not even persuade Kubrick to show them the film." The director did tell them that when the movie won Oscars, "it'll go through the roof."

When the film premiered, *Time* devoted a cover story to "Kubrick's Greatest Gamble," with pictures showing how eighteenth-century England had been meticulously recreated by Kubrick's army of technicians. Judith Crist raved, "We are transported to another time and place, another Kubrick odyssey of extraordinary proportions, this one to engage the heart and mind and remain therein." But *Newsweek* said, "Kubrick has created an epic of esthetic self-indulgence, beautiful

"I ain't seen Nashville and I ain't going to; I'd rather see Bambi."
—Loretta Lynn

but empty." Andrew Sarris described it as "clearly the most expensive meditation on melancholy ever financed by a Hollywood studio." Many reviewers thought Ryan O'Neal was an odd choice to play the title character and were taken aback when Marisa Berenson, as his wife, remained silent for most of the picture. Warners hoped that Kubrick's Oscar predictions were correct—*Barry Lyndon* was going to need all the box-office help it could get.

Bonjour, Isabelle A.

Kubrick didn't have quite enough friends in the New York Film Critics Circle; *Barry Lyndon* ran second to *Nashville* for both the Best Picture and Best Director citations. Jack Nicholson beat out Al Pacino and Gene Hackman for Best Actor; *Nashville*'s Lily Tomlin won Best Supporting Actress over second-place Louise Fletcher for *Cuckoo's Nest;* and Alan Arkin grabbed the Best Supporting Actor honor for his role as a '30s movie director in the comedy *Hearts of the West*. The critics gave Best Actress to nineteen-year-old Isabelle Adjani, who played Victor Hugo's love-obsessed daughter in François Truffaut's *The Story of Adele H*. The press called her the hottest actress from France since Jeanne Moreau, and Truffaut told *People,* "France is too small for her. I think Isabelle is made for American cinema."

At the critics' awards ceremony, Lillian Gish glorified her, "The camera fell in love with that face, and what camera wouldn't. She's so beautiful—it's a face that has no angles." When Gish's tribute moved Adjani to tears, Lillian asked, "Don't you have a sister? You need a sister at times like this." Adjani was dry-eyed when reporters asked her if she thought the critics' award would help her Oscar chances. "I am not an American," she reminded them, "I didn't grow up with that will to win an award. I care about my work and I'm not interested in being part of a Hollywood package." But yes, she said, if nominated, she'd attend the Oscar show.

Just who would be nominated caused such concern that the *New York Times* ran an article in January entitled, "Do Any of These Actresses Rate an Academy Award?" "There are so few surefire candidates this year that the list may be downright embarrassing," feared Judy Klemesrud, who began the article by suggesting that the relatively unknown Marilyn Hassett might win for the inspirational drama *The Other Side of the Mountain*. A picture of Louise Fletcher was captioned, "In this weak year, a supporting role may win the Best Actress Oscar for Louise Fletcher." Klemesrud said of *Mahogany*'s Diana Ross, "Some observers say she has a good chance because of sentiment that it is time for a black woman to win."

Discordant Sounds in Music Branch

When Ross' song was not included in the preliminary nominations for the Best Song Award, the *Hollywood Reporter* editorialized, "The failure to even nominate 'Theme from Mahogany' once again points out the completely antiquated and biased structure of the music branch of the Academy, whose executive committee appears to be run like a restricted private club, with the primary objective being to exclude any 'undesirables' from its membership roster." Robert Altman was also furious that only one of *Nashville*'s songs made the list and accused the branch of a "terrible oversight and typical Academy cliquishness."

Two weeks after the preliminary nominations had been announced, the Music Branch decided to throw out the preliminaries voted by a seventeen-member committee and let all 207 branch members do the nominating. When the new ballots were counted, "Theme from Mahogany" had made the list. The song's composer, Michael Masser, immediately wrote an open letter to the trade papers stating, "I have tremendous admiration and respect for the Board of Governors who acted out of the highest principles in allowing the entire music branch to vote on eligibility this year." Rob-

"I'm ready to go back to work, yes I am."
—Mary Pickford

ert Altman didn't agree—only Keith Carradine's "I'm Easy," which was on the original preliminary list, appeared on the second.

It Was a Very Bad Year

Artistic merit was at a premium in 1975. "It wasn't a bad year for movies, it was a terrible year," commented Charles Champlin in his annual *Los Angeles Times* Oscar predictions article. His headline was "Picking the Best Film in a Nonvintage Year, " and Champlin foresaw the Best Picture nominees as *Cukoo's Nest, Nashville, Jaws, Dog Day Afternoon*, and *The Sunshine Boys*, an adaptation of a Neil Simon play starring Walter Matthau as an old comedian and George Burns, who replaced the late Jack Benny at the last minute, as his former partner. "The odds lengthen a bit on *Shampoo* and a bit further on *Barry Lyndon*," Champlin wrote. With open season in the Oscar game, film companies campaigned for almost every film released that year. *Cuckoo's Nest* had the biggest ad push—seventeen in *Daily Variety*—followed by *Barry Lyndon* with fifteen.

The Nominations

A documentary film crew recorded wunderkind Steven Spielberg's reaction as he watched the televised announcements of the nominations in his Los Angeles home. When the Best Director category rolled around, the nominees were: Robert Altman for *Nashville*, Milos Forman for *Cuckoo's Nest*, Stanley Kubrick for *Barry Lyndon*, Sydney Lumet for *Dog Day Afternoon*, and Federico Fellini for *Amarcord*, last year's Best Foreign Film winner. "I can't believe it? The went for Fellini instead of me!" Spielberg moaned, burying his face in his hands as the cameras rolled. *Jaws* was up for Best Picture, but its chances were pretty slim without a Best Director nomination. "It hurts because I feel it was a director's movie," Spielberg said. "But there was a *Jaws* backlash. The same people who had raved about it began to doubt its artistic value as soon as it began to bring in so much money."

"In the Best Actress competition, which had attracted special attention this year for what many saw as a dearth of Hollywood candidates," observed *Daily Variety*, "not one nominee appeared in a Hollywood studio production made in the U.S." The nominees were Louise Fletcher in the independently financed *Cuckoo's Nest;* Isabelle Adjani in the French *The Story of Adele H.*; Ann-Margret in the British *Tommy;* Glenda Jackson in *Hedda*, a film adaptation of the Royal Shakespeare Company's production of *Hedda Gabler;* and twenty-two-year-old Carol Kane in *Hester Street*, an independently made film completed in thirty-four days on a $400,000 budget.

Joan Micklin Silver had directed *Hester Street*, about Jewish immigrants in turn-of-the-century New York, and her husband Ray distributed the film himself, because, as he put it, "Unless a major is willing to put a lot of money in a film, it gets dropped." Rona Barrett asked the Best Actress nominee if she thought she had a chance to win and Kane laughed, and alluded to her parents, "Are you kidding? All I've got pulling for me are two Jews from Cleveland." As for Glenda Jackson, *People* chronicled that the nominee had forgotten to pay her $50 dues and that the Academy had revoked her ballot and her membership.

Burstyn vs. Fletcher

When last year's Best Actress winner, Ellen Burstyn, went on TV and asked Academy members not to vote for Best Actress this year to protest the lack of good roles for women, Louise Fletcher called her up and asked what she meant by it. "She hadn't meant anything personal, but it was personal and my feelings were hurt," Fletcher told the *New York Times*. "She hadn't even seen *Cuckoo's Nest* because she felt it would be too painful an experience. I told her that I thought it would have been nicer if she had said what she said in a year when she had been nominated." Fletcher was

"All I've got pulling for me are two Jews from New York."
—Carol Kane

also still sore at Robert Altman about being bumped from *Nashville*. "I must say that he took a part which I inspired and helped to write, and when he got angry with my husband over something else, he gave that part to someone else."

Ann-Margret, on the other hand, was nothing but grateful. "The nomination made me realize that the nomination for *Carnal Knowledge* was not a fluke," she said to the *Los Angeles Times*. "People around me told me they were responsible for my success and I believed them. Now I know I have something to give and that it is coming from inside me." Revenge was even sweeter when her mentor, George Burns, was also nominated, for Best Supporting Actor for *The Sunshine Boys*. Ann-Margret's first job was in Burns' Las Vegas show, although she left after eleven days to go to Hollywood. "You owe me six weeks pay at $1,100 a week," kidded the eighty-year-old Burns as he and the Best Actress nominee celebrated in front of reporters. Ann-Margret leaned over and bussed the comedian, who then replied, "The kisses cancel the debt."

Invaders From Z Channel

The Best Actor category proved the power of TV advertising. In addition to the expected Jack Nicholson for *Cuckoo's Nest*, Al Pacino for *Dog Day Afternoon*, and Walter Matthau for *The Sunshine Boys*, there were two actors in filmed stage plays that were broadcast on Los Angeles' Z Channel—members of the Acting Branch never had to leave their beds. James Whitmore imitated President Harry Truman in the "Theatrovision" production of *Give 'Em Hell, Harry!* and his Oscar campaign included trade-paper ads quoting President Gerald Ford, who waxed, "A superb performance." Maximilian Schell had performed in producer Ely Landau's "American Film Theatre" series production of Robert Shaw's *The Man in the Glass Booth*. The critics had not been as charitable to Schell as the Academy; the *Christian Science Monitor* wrote, "His performance is shrill and unmodulated, beginning at a feverish pitch and becoming wearisome as it continues." Robert Shaw was not a fan, either, and asked Landau to take his name off the credits.

People predicted, "*Cuckoo's Nest*, the trade figures, should bring Nicholson his long-overdue Oscar and public acceptance as the first American actor since Marlon Brando and James Dean with the elemental energy to wildcat new wells of awareness in the national unconscious." And the five-time nominee assured Rona Barrett he was coming to the show: "I get a kick out of movie stars," he said.

Supporting Sorority

Best Supporting Actress nominee Lily Tomlin said she enjoyed the Oscars because they are "classic American kitsch." Among her competition was her *Nashville* costar Ronee Blakley. Sylvia Miles, a supporting nominee in 1969 for *Midnight Cowboy*, got her second supporting nomination, for *Farewell, My Lovely*, but told *Variety*, "Anything I could say would be longer than my roles in both pictures." Brenda Vaccaro, nominated for *Jacqueline Susann's Once Is Not Enough*, told *Daily Variety* that she'd be attending with her ex-lover, *Cuckoo's Nest* producer Michael Douglas, and pointed out that she was also the godmother to Glenda Jackson's son. The fact that it is such a small world bothered the fifth nominee, *Shampoo*'s Lee Grant. "My big concern is would Brenda and Lily and I be talking once it's all over," Grant fretted. "We're very close friends, you know." The three-time nominee didn't want any more unpleasantness—her TV show, *Fay*, had just been canceled after a mere three weeks and she had gone on Johnny Carson's show to tell the world how unhappy she was about it.

Fashions a Must

"People from all over the world were writing in telling us to show more of the fashions," show producer Howard Koch remarked. "The marketing surveys showed us that people actually care more about the clothes than who wins. So we are paying strict attention this year to giving the public what it wants." The producer asked agent Irving "Swifty" Lazar to cancel his annual Oscar-watching party at the Bistro because it was drawing bigger stars than the Oscar ceremonies. Lazar refused, but Marisa Berenson pledged her allegiance to the Academy. "I, for one, love the tackiness of it all and I find some of the fashion things hysterical," she said, "but people want stars again and that's what the Oscars will attempt to do." Also lending moral support was fashion designer Halston, who was jetting in from New York to attend his first Oscar show and to watch presenters Elizabeth Taylor and Jacqueline Bisset model his designs.

One Oscar winner was going to be absent—eighty-three-year-old Mary Pickford, who would be receiving an Honorary Award. America's Sweetheart told *Newsweek*, "I could still be on the screen, you know. I'm ready to go back to work, yes I am." She would be onscreen again on Oscar night; a camera crew had already filmed Academy President Walter Mirisch as he handed the recluse her trophy at Pickfair. Pickford's husband, Charles "Buddy" Rogers, had ruled out a live appearance because "the sheer excitement of it would be too much for her."

The Big Night

Performed in broad daylight, the entrance ceremony has not much more glamour than a school fete—especially since most of the stars seemed to stay away this year, preferring to watch the rituals with coke spoon and TV set at home," sniffed *Time*. But a few stars managed to uphold Hollywood tradition, and at least some of them were sincere about it. *Daily Variety* wondered of one nominee, "Knowing her sense of satire, it's hard to say whether Lily Tomlin was having some fun with the night's fashion code, but she was elegant nonetheless, in white fur, silver metallic gown, all topped by a glittering silver tiara." Jack Nicholson sported dark glasses with his traditional tuxedo, and brought Anjelica Huston and his thirteen-year-old daughter with him. Competitor James Whitmore pulled up in a presidential-looking topcoat and said, "I have a cold."

Army Archerd revealed, "Michael Douglas escorted longtime g.f. and fellow nominee Brenda Vaccaro but their association is now in the 'friend' status as she's in the process of buying her own house." Douglas explained that his father was in Palm Springs because he said he didn't want to detract from his son's evening. *Cuckoo's Nest* director Milos Forman, the winner of the Directors Guild Award, arrived with his twelve-year-old identical twin sons, whom he had not seen since leaving Czechoslovakia in 1968. "The international publicity of the Academy Awards is important to the Communist leaders," Forman said, explaining how his kids were able to visit him. The boys didn't speak English, but they knew the name of their father's film—"Cuksunext!"

Best Supporting Actress nominee Sylvia Miles walked into the lobby and observed, "There was so much alcohol there that you either fought them or joined them, and you know I never fight." Equally peaceful were pickets from the United Farm Workers, who marched in an orderly fashion across the street, telling the *Hollywood Reporter*, "No axe to grind; we just need the publicity those cameras are giving us." Army Archerd

Awards Ceremony

MARCH 29, 1976, 7:00 P.M.
THE DOROTHY CHANDLER PAVILION, LOS ANGELES

Your Hosts:
WALTER MATTHAU, ROBERT SHAW, GEORGE SEGAL, GOLDIE HAWN, GENE KELLY
Televised over ABC

Presenters

Supporting Actress . . . . Joel Grey and Madeline Kahn
Special Achievement Awards . . . . Robert Blake
Short Films . . . . . Marisa Berenson and O.J. Simpson
Sound . . . . . Margaux Hemingway and Roy Scheider
Documentary Awards . . . . Beau Bridges and Marilyn Hassett
Jean Hersholt Humanitarian Award . . . . Charlton Heston
Art Direction . . . . Anthony Hopkins and Charlotte Rampling
Costume Design . . . . Telly Savalas
Supporting Actor . . . . . . Linda Blair and Ben Johnson
Scoring Awards . . . . Rod McKuen and Marlo Thomas
Cinematography . . . . Stockard Channing and Billy Dee Williams
Film Editing . . . . . . Isabelle Adjani and Elliott Gould
Foreign Film . . . . . Jacqueline Bisset and Jack Valenti
Song . . . . Burt Bacharach and Angie Dickinson
Thalberg Award . . . . William Friedkin
Director . . . . Diane Keaton and William Wyler
Writing Awards . . . . Gore Vidal
Honorary Award to Mary Pickford . . . . Walter Mirisch (on tape)
Actress . . . . Charles Bronson and Jill Ireland
Actor . . . . Art Carney
Best Picture . . . . Audrey Hepburn

Performers of Nominated Songs

"How Lucky Can You Get" . . . . Bernadette Peters
"I'm Easy" . . . . Keith Carradine
"Now That We're In Love" . . . . Steve Lawrence
"Richard's Window" . . . . Kelly Garrett
"Theme from Mahogany*"* . . . . Diana Ross (from Amsterdam)

"It's too bad we have no Thalbergs around today. There was a real creator—and so sweet and unassuming."
—Mervyn LeRoy

thought war was being declared when screenwriter Norman Wexler pulled out a toy rifle. When the security grabbed him, Wexler said he was only kidding.

There was more excitement in store for Archerd, as *Daily Variety* reported, "Timing of arrivals is a matter of luck and one had to feel sorry for John and Keith Carradine, who mounted Army Archerd's podium just as Liz burst from her car in bright red, diamonds flashing." Escorted by George Cukor and Halston, Elizabeth Taylor evoked the longest and loudest ovation from the bleachers, and she waved happily to the crowds.

The TV show began with footage of arriving stars; O.J. Simpson was described by the announcer as "actor and athlete *nonpareil.*" As the audience inside the auditorium waited, TV viewers saw Ray Bolger in a production number taped outside the theater the night before. The number ended with Bolger dancing in front of the live audience inside, which heartily applauded his finale. Academy President Walter Mirisch reminded everyone that the forty-eighth Oscar show "coincides with our nation's Bicentennial" and then introduced the first emcee, Walter Matthau.

The first Award was Best Supporting Actress and all the nominees were present, but when Ronee Blakley's name was listed, the TV audience was treated to a close-up of Best Supporting Actor nominee Chris Sarandon's wife, Susan. The winner was Lee Grant for *Shampoo*. Wearing an old wedding dress and a limp ribbon in her hair, Grant kissed her friend Lily Tomlin on the way to the stage. "I really must have won or why else would I wear an old wedding dress," she said, thanking "the artistic community for sustaining me through wins and losses." As she spoke, Grant saw someone offstage beckoning her to hurry up and finish. She walked off and said to him, "Hey, what is this?"

The live audience once again had to wait while TV viewers saw another musical number, this one the performance of the Best Song nominee "Theme from *Mahogany*," lip-synched live by Diana Ross via satellite from Amsterdam, where it was 4:30 A.M. A horse-drawn carriage bearing a fur-clad Ross rolled into view and the singer climbed down, crossed a bridge over a canal, waved to a passing boat, got back in the carriage and rode away waving to the camera—singing all the while.

Matthau turned the emcee job over to a giddy Robert Shaw, who had earlier stood on Army Archerd's podium and addressed the bleacher fans, saying, "Hello, girls." Shaw introduced the non-nominated stars of *The Other Side of the Mountain*, Marilyn Hassett and Beau Bridges, who gave the Documentary Short Oscar to a producer named Claire Wilbur. The next day, the *New York Post* ran a story announcing that Miss Wilbur had starred in a soft-core porno movie directed by Radley Metzger, but on Oscar night, she demurely skipped to the podium and exclaimed "Wow!" Then the presenters revealed that the Academy had skipped over Shirley MacLaine's foray into documentaries, *The Other Half of the Sky: A China Memoir*, for a skiing movie.

Shaw welcomed the "chic Greek," Telly Savalas, to handle the Costume Design Oscar, and Savalas responded, "Thank you, Bobby, baby." Savalas' copresenter, Jennifer O'Neill, said the winner was *Barry Lyndon* and designer Ulla-Britt Soderlund accepted in eighteenth-century costume: knickers, ruffled shirt, topcoat, three-cornered hat and a heart-shaped beauty mark.

Linda Blair and Ben Johnson stepped out to announce the Best Supporting Actor winner. Milos Forman's sons perked up when they heard the presenters mention "Brad Dourif for *One Flew Over the Cuckoo's Nest.*" When the winner turned out to be George Burns for *The Sunshine Boys*, the loud approval of the audience inspired the Forman *fils* to stand up and applaud their father. "Cut it out," Dad told them. "You are making fools of yourselves. We lost." The boys sat down, confused, while George Burns made his way to the podium. Recalling that his last picture was in 1939, the comedian commented, "This is all so exciting. I've decided to keep making one movie every thirty-six years. You get to be new again."

A little later, Marlo Thomas appeared with Rod McKuen, in sneakers, to give the Score Award. The winner was the show's conductor, John Williams, for *Jaws*. The orchestra broke into applause and McKuen quipped, "I think the orchestra likes him." When the composer thanked the non-nominated Steven Spielberg, loyalists applauded.

The show continued as George Segal asked his co-host, Goldie Hawn, if she knew how important a cinematographer was to a picture. "Yes," Goldie answered. "In *Shampoo,* if we could have found a way to get him under the table we could have made another $50 million." The camera cut to Goldie's former *Laugh-In* co-star, Lily Tomlin, who was not amused. The Cinematography Oscar went to *Barry Lyndon,* which was sweeping the visual Awards.

Isabelle Adjani came out with Elliott Gould. After reading the Editing nominees, Adjani said, "And the winners are . . ." "Indiana 86 to 68," piped in Gould, relaying the score of the NCAA basketball final. "Whaaa?" Adjani reacted. *Jaws* won the Award and Verna Fields again invoked the name of Spielberg, which again drew a smattering of applause.

Burt Bacharach and Angie Dickinson walked out smiling and gave the Best Song Oscar to Keith Carradine for "I'm Easy." The audience rewarded him with a long ovation. "Wow, it's heavy!" Carradine ejaculated when he first held the statuette. "I'd like to thank Robert Altman, he's done more for me than anyone." Carradine paid tribute to his father, "Thanks, Dad," and then went back to the pressroom and confessed, "Actually, I wrote the song three years ago."

William Friedkin gave the Thalberg Award to Mervyn LeRoy, who did not dwell on his famous credits, including *The Wizard of Oz* and *The Bad Seed,* but thanked the Academy: "I think they've done more for the world than ever by showing what Hollywood does and running all of these beautiful acts and beautiful scenes on Telstar, of which I am a stockholder." Backstage, LeRoy said of the man who inspired the Award, "It's too bad we have no Thalbergs around today. There was a real creator—and so sweet and unassuming."

By now, the Forman twins had lost interest in the show; one was playing with his bubble gum, the other was fast asleep. William Wyler and Diane Keaton, in a suit and tie, stepped out to present the Best Director Oscar. "Uhm, Mr. Wyler, you're more used to getting Oscars than giving them out," said Keaton, regarding the cue cards skeptically. "It's more fun," was Wyler's rejoinder. "All right now," gulped Keaton, pushing ahead with the nominations. The young Formans snapped to attention when they heard their father's name listed. Wyler announced, "And the winner is Milos Forman for *One Flew Over the Cuckoo's Nest.*" The boys jumped up and applauded, and Forman raced to the stage, where he explained the secret of his success: "I spent more time in mental institutions than the others."

Gore Vidal called the screenwriter "the unsung hero of the movies, the St. Sebastian of the LaBrea tar pits," and then distributed the writing Awards. Warren Beatty, coauthor of *Shampoo,* was just as unlucky as his sister Shirley—he also lost, to *Dog Day Afternoon,* for Best Original Screenplay. The winner, Frank Pierson, was absent because he was off directing Barbra Streisand in the second remake of *A Star Is Born.* Both of the authors of *Cuckoo's Nest* were there to claim their Adapted Screenplay Oscars, and Lawrence Hauben thanked "some of the most finest people I've ever known."

The live audience finally got to see a film sequence along with TV viewers—the trip to Pickfair. The camera roamed the mansion, still decorated in 1920s style, and found a portrait of Mary Pickford as a young woman. Pickford herself was propped up in a chair in a sitting room, and she wore a blond wig, a satin dress with a white fur collar, and pearls. President Mirisch handed her the Oscar—her second—and the ex-member of the Producers Branch said, "That's wonderful. You've made me very, very happy." She held the Oscar next to her face and a solitary tear descended from her eye.

"I get a kick out of movie stars."
—Jack Nicholson

Charles Bronson and his wife, Jill Ireland, announced the Best Actress Award. Glenda Jackson was the only missing nominee. The winner was Louise Fletcher, who said of her villainous role in *Cuckoo's Nest,* "It looks like you all hated me." Then she spoke to her deaf parents in Birmingham, Alabama, via sign language. "I want to thank you for teaching me to have a dream," she said, beginning to cry. "You are seeing my dream come true." For a moment there was total silence, and then thunderous applause.

Art Carney, in a blue tuxedo shirt, followed with the Best Actor envelope. Jack Nicholson still had on his dark glasses and James Whitmore wore regular glasses with a safety cord attached. The only other nominee present was Walter Matthau. The winner was Jack Nicholson, and the camera saw Matthau mutter to his wife, "It's about time." The audience yelled and whistled as Nicholson hopped to the stage, removing his glasses en route. Art Carney embraced him and Nicholson said, "I guess this proves there are as many nuts in the Academy as anywhere else." He went on to thank Mary Pickford for being "the first actor to get a percentage of her pictures"—applause—"and speaking of percentages, last but not least, my agent, who, about ten years ago, advised me that I had no business being an actor."

There was no suspense over the Best Picture outcome. Audrey Hepburn had the responsibility of proclaiming the winner—*One Flew Over the Cuckoo's Nest*. Michael Douglas was so excited about his film's sweep of the top five awards, he got his history wrong: "This is the first film to do so since *It Happened One Night* in 1937." When Douglas and coproducer Saul Zaentz walked off triumphantly, the camera saw a beaming Brenda Vaccaro applauding away.

Gene Kelly introduced "an international star, twice winner of an Academy Award," while backstage, an Academy official ran up to Elizabeth Taylor and said, "We're running out of time. Forget the cue cards and say anything." Taylor made her entrance in her deep red, strapless Halston gown and extemporized, "I have worked all over the world and found Hollywood in Rome, in France, in London. It came from here. I started here when I was ten years old, and it's always a thrill to come back." Taylor flung her arm out and whipped it back to her side. "Films have helped bring a sense of the American land, the American purpose, the American dream to people everywhere. Tonight, saluting the two-hundredth year of this land, the Bicentennial year, let us recall the original purpose and reaffirm that necessary dream."

She flung both her arms out, inviting the audience, "Please join us to sing 'America the Beautiful.'" The orchestra struck up the song and Gene Kelly returned to sing with Taylor. The audience reluctantly rose and the USC marching band, in full Trojan regalia, emerged from the orchestra pit and the side exits of the hall. All the presenters and winners were herded onstage, but Gene Kelly was the only one really singing—Taylor apparently didn't know the lyrics to "America the Beautiful." Jack Nicholson and the rest of the *Cuckoo's Nest* crowd were onstage, laughing hysterically.

Aftermath

"God, isn't it fantastic?" was Jack Nicholson's first utterance when he stepped into the pressroom. "When you were doing *Little Shop of Horrors* did you ever think it would lead to this?" a reporter asked. "Yes, I did," assured Nicholson, who put his dark glasses back on. "I have one more ambition," the Best Actor admitted, "that is to don gray chauffeur's livery and drive Milos Forman into Prague in a Rolls-Royce." A South American correspondent asked the winner what he had to say to his fans down there—"*Buenos días*." The same reporter asked Louise Fletcher what she thought about the complaints that hers was really a supporting role. "That's a terrible question and a terrible way to end the evening," she responded, but she confessed a few minutes later that she had not received any good film offers since *Cuckoo's Nest* had opened.

Producer Michael Douglas said, "The best

"This is glamour, the stars, the palm trees, the weather, the glitter."
—Halston

thing that could happen is that some studio heads go back and reread some of the scripts they've turned down." As for himself, Douglas predicted, "It's all downhill from here." Milos Forman commented, "I had been told by many people that the Academy is patriotic and chauvinistic and does not like to give this Award to foreigners. It is nice to know it is not so." When his sons caught up with him in the pressroom, Forman asked them, "Tell me anything in the world you want and I'll get it for you." His sons responded, "We want to meet that Columbo guy Peter Falk and then we want to see *Jaws*!"

One who was not so excited about *Cuckoo's Nest*'s sweep was the author of the original novel, Ken Kesey, who said, "I'd like to have subpoenas in some of those Award envelopes." Kesey was suing Michael Douglas for a bigger slice of the profits than he was receiving and was also hurt that no one mentioned him on the Awards show. "Oscar night should have been one of the great days of my life, like my wedding. I really love movies. When they can be turned around to break your heart like this, well, it's like something you never thought would happen."

George Burns did enjoy himself on Oscar night, telling reporters that the Oscar was pointing his career in a new direction, "I'm thinking of taking on Gentile roles and becoming the new Robert Redford." Asked how he planned to celebrate, the eighty-year-old replied, "I'm going home to have a bowl of soup—barley soup." Best Supporting Actor loser Burgess Meredith, nominated for *The Day of the Locust*, was outside commenting, "If the picture's not a hit, you might as well forget any possibility of an Academy Award, even if your performance is miraculous."

Lee Grant told reporters that a designer had offered to make her a new dress for free but that she had found the materials "sleazy," so she decided to hunt for an "old and beautiful dress" and found one in a secondhand store. "The first time I was married was in Hoboken and the second time was before a poker game. I never had a proper wedding until tonight." The bride was moved to tears when she arrived at the Governors' Ball and the fans waiting outside the Beverly Hilton gave her a round of applause. *Daily Variety* wrote, "Twice nominated before, Grant was a popular favorite, particularly because of sympathy over the cancellation of her *Fay* vidseries." After the ball, Michael Douglas threw a party at his house, attended by *Nashville*'s Robert Altman and Ronee Blakley.

Many of the Oscar show participants went directly to Swifty Lazar's party. Elizabeth Taylor breezed in and said of her improvising, "It was the closest I've come to doing a nightclub act." Gore Vidal showed up, too, observing, "Hollywood hasn't changed that much since I was under contract to MGM in the '50s." *Women's Wear Daily* was also at the party, and overheard agent Sue Mengers say of the Oscar show, "It's pathetic. Very unrepresentative of Hollywood. It needs total revamping." And Lazar added, "You can't help but cringe over the ineptitude of some of the presenters who mispronounce names and don't know what the hell is going on. Also, it is so old-fashioned to have a girl and a guy together when one person, like Gore Vidal or an Audrey Hepburn, can stand alone. It's unnecessary to always bring in some dumb-looking broad."

Columnist Dorothy Manners took issue with Swifty and his band of partygoers: "The people who presented the Academy Awards show . . . are far more representative of this industry than those who viewed it in a restaurant wielding their little stilettos. Lazar and Mengers have acquired personal fortunes from this industry. In the future, it would be far more becoming for them to bite their own tongues rather than bite the hands that feed them—at the Bistro." Producer Howard Koch jumped in, commenting, "It seems to me that someone who gets $3 million from a picture owes it to the industry that's making him rich to participate in the Academy Awards—especially if he's a nominee."

Best Actor nominee Al Pacino hadn't seen it that way, and Earl Wilson tracked him down "in jeans, without tie, in a Greenwich Village restaurant. He had no TV set." Pacino told the columnist that his performance in a workshop production of a play at the Public Theater was "a more important previous date" than the Oscars. When Wilson asked about the publicity value of the Awards, Pacino retorted, "Fame is a perversion of the natural human instinct for attention."

Halston held a different view. After announcing to the assembled at Swifty Lazar's party that henceforth the color of Liz's gown would be known as "Elizabeth Taylor red," the designer refused to echo the derogatory sentiments of the other guests. "This is glamour," he cooed, "the stars, the palm trees, the weather, the glitter. I came with a dream of what the Academy Awards were like and I'm going home with a full stomach."

1976

"Kids talk like sailors today—and adults just don't want to know."
—Jodie Foster

Death took home the Oscar at the 1976 Academy Awards.

"The hottest name in movies today," was what the *New York Daily News* called Lina Wertmuller, the forty-seven-year-old Italian director who was making art houses as profitable as commercial theaters with her pointedly Marxist satires starring Giancarlo Giannini. The director said of her leading man, "Those eyes are extraordinary; they seem to contain an independent life force—as if they could scream, curse, plead, argue, and make love." When the duo's latest collaboration, *Seven Beauties,* opened in early January, John Simon flew to Rome to interview Wertmuller for a *New York* magazine cover story entitled "The Most Important Film Director Since Bergman." "This is a milestone that future filmmakers will have to keep an eye on," Simon said of the film, "that future filmgoers will have to—will want to—keep in mind." In February, *Variety* reported that Lina Wertmuller had signed an exclusive four-picture deal with Warner Brothers, which outbid United Artists and Columbia for her services. A little later, she announced that her first Hollywood project would be a film starring Giancarlo Giannini and Candice Bergen, entitled *The End of the World in Our Usual Bed in a Night Full of Rain.*

Meaner Streets

Although he, too, had an Italian name, Martin Scorsese did not receive the red-carpet treatment that Wertmuller enjoyed. He had come across a Paul Schrader script called *Taxi Driver* about an urban vigilante, inspired by the Harry Chapin song "Taxi," but even the involvement of the producers of *The Sting* and the Oscar-winning star of *The Godfather Part II* failed to persuade a single studio to fund the picture. So Scorsese, producers Julia and Michael Phillips and star Robert De Niro agreed among themselves to accept small salaries and Scorsese offered the film again to Columbia with a budget of $2 million. David Begelman took them up on it, arguing he couldn't resist such a bargain.

Best Actress winner Faye Dunaway disproving Marty Feldman's claim that the bottom of the statuette is stamped "Made in Japan."

Scorsese still had another obstacle ahead of him—the California State Welfare Department, which did not want twelve-year-old Jodie Foster to play the film's child prostitute. "I was determined to win," fumed Mrs. Brandy Foster, Jodie's mother. "Here was some board trying to tell me what was too adult for my own daughter." Jodie submitted to four hours of psychological tests because, as she said, "They had to see if my morals would hold up during filming." The veteran actress was used to controversial parts; her first job, at age three, was getting her bathing suit bottom pulled down by a dog in a Coppertone ad. "Children today know about sex by the time they are ten," Jodie stated. "Kids talk like sailors today—and adults just don't want to know." The Welfare Department decided that Jodie could take care of herself.

The Grim Reaper also gave Scorsese a break, not claiming Bernard Herrmann—Hitchcock's favorite composer—until the day after he finished recording the film's score. The director described *Taxi Driver* as "a continuation of *Mean Streets*. It's a film dealing with religious anxiety, guilt and one man's attitudes toward women—attitudes that were arrested at age thirteen." Pauline Kael praised the film as "one of the few truly modern horror films" and Roger Ebert likened it to "a brilliant nightmare," but *Time* groused, "It is all too heavy with easy sociologizing to be truly moving." It was, however, profitable, earning $12 million in the U.S. alone and providing Robert De Niro with another scrapbook of glowing reviews. The *New York Post* said his acting "makes even the better movie performances of the past few years look artificial and bombastic by comparison."

"I worked hard at being a nerd."
—Sissy Spacek

Robert Redford vs. Richard Nixon

"Political films don't make money," studio executives told Robert Redford when he informed them he had optioned a book by *Washington Post* reporters Bob Woodward and Carl Bernstein about how they unraveled the Watergate scandal. "It's not a political film," Redford countered, "it's a detective story." The actor told the *New York Times* the film companies were "nervous about alienating their conservative constituency," but when Woodward and Bernstein's *All the President's Men* ruled the bestseller list for months, Warners forked over $9 million. Redford cast himself as Woodward and found his Bernstein in Dustin Hoffman. "What took you so long?" Hoffman asked when Redford finally popped the question.

Not arguing with success, Redford hired William Goldman, the author of *Butch Cassidy and the Sundance Kid,* to adapt the book into a screenplay, and Goldman commented, "Expectations are so high on this movie that if the film is only good, it won't be good enough." The *Washington Post*'s editor Ben Bradlee didn't think that Goldman's first draft was good enough, and told Redford, "Just remember, pal, that you go off and ride a horse or jump in the sack with some good-looking woman in your next film—but I am forever an asshole." According to the *Los Angeles Times,* Redford gave the screenplay to Woodward and Bernstein for suggestions: "Giving this invitation the broadest possible interpretation, Bernstein, together with his great and good friend Nora Ephron, rewrote the script, changing his character to a 'combination of Sherlock Holmes, Nero Wolfe and Casanova' while buddy Woodward emerged as 'a vapid, colorless Elmer Fudd worshipping at the shrine of Bernstein's brilliance.'" Redford rejected this version, telling Bernstein, "Errol Flynn is dead." Goldman did some more rewriting.

Newsweek documented the lengths Redford went to assure historical authenticity: "The sum of $200,000 alone is being spent re-creating at a Burbank studio the newsrooms of the *Washington Post,* aided by voluminous photographs taken by the film's art directors, the purchase of 200 desks identical to those at the newspaper and the shipment of 270 cartons of authentic litter gathered from newsroom desks and waste baskets." Ben Bradlee raved, "The set was just stunning."

"No picture since *Jaws,* a polar opposite, has attracted such advance participation," observed Roger Ebert when it became impossible to pass a newsstand without seeing Redford and Hoffman's faces—*Time, People, Parade, American Film* and *Rolling Stone* all ran cover stories on the movie. In the *Los Angeles Times,* Charles Champlin heralded the film as "an engrossing mystery movie, with atmosphere, suspense, surprise, conflict, danger, secret messages, clandestine meetings, heroes, villains and a cast of leading and supporting characters that might have emerged from an unlikely collaboration of, let us say, Gore Vidal and Raymond Chandler." The political film racked up $30 million in domestic rentals, prompting Dustin Hoffman to comment, "The real reason for the success of this picture is that Hoffman's back and Redford's got him. It's what the public always wanted: that beautiful WASP finally wound up with a nice Jewish boy."

L'Amour, L'Amour

Another couple audiences took to heart were the adulterous lovers in Jean-Charles Tacchella's French comedy *Cousin, Cousine*. "Like Chekhov, I don't judge or condemn or acquit my characters," Tacchella said. "I put a mirror before the audience and they laugh or smile or cry at their own images." Most Americans laughed, and *Cousin, Cousine,* broke the box-office records held by the former French champ, *A Man and a Woman*. The *New York Times* headlined U.S. LOVE AFFAIR WITH 'COUSINE' and asked star Marie-Christine Barrault, thirty-two, why the film was so popular. "I think they like it because it's the kind of film that makes people happy," the actress said. "It's a very positive movie, and in America, you don't have the habit of seeing this kind of movie here."

"It's what the public always wanted: that beautiful WASP finally wound up with a nice Jewish boy."
—Dustin Hoffman

De Palma's Period Piece

There certainly weren't any happy love birds in Brian De Palma's two 1976 movies. *Obsession* was the director's reworking of Hitchcock's *Vertigo,* with the same composer—Bernard Herrmann wrote this score before working on *Taxi Driver. Obsession* earned good notices, but De Palma didn't hit pay dirt until he adapted Steven King's novel *Carrie,* the story of an introverted high school student who ends up using her telekinetic powers to kill her abusive classmates at the senior prom. "She had to be a little bit of a nerd at times, to give the others girls motivation, so I worked hard at being a nerd," said Sissy Spacek, twenty six, whose third film this was. "I made a point of not fraternizing with the other actors." She spent her time instead with the art director, Jack Fisk, who was also her husband.

To play Spacek's religious-fanatic mother, De Palma lured Piper Laurie back to the screen after a fifteen-year absence—she had not worked since winning a Best Actress nomination for *The Hustler* in 1961. "I wouldn't say that I had a breakdown," Laurie explained, "I just had disgust. For a long time, I felt a real hostility about the things that happened to me in Hollywood, but now I look back on the person I was then with a kind of affection—I didn't know if I wanted to be a movie star or a really good actress." She enjoyed herself on *Carrie,* though: "It was so much fun," she enthused. "We all roared with laughter at the end of the day, especially the day I got it with all those knives."

"The best scary-funny movie since *Jaws,*" rejoiced Pauline Kael, "a teasing, terrifying, lyrical shocker, directed by Brian De Palma, who has the wickedest baroque sensibility at large in American movies." The shocker went on to bring United Artists $15 million from the U.S. alone and catapulted Sissy Spacek onto the cover of *Newsweek*—the magazine dubbed her "the most promising new actress in motion pictures." She also was the guest host on the hit TV show *Saturday Night Live,* playing Carrie "the day after the prom" and, in another skit, eight-year-old Amy Carter.

Gonna Fly Now

Thirty-year-old Sylvester Stallone didn't think his career was progressing fast enough, despite supporting roles in *Farewell, My Lovely* and *Death Race 2000*. With his wife pregnant and his rent overdue, the actor took the advice of his mother, an amateur astrologist, who predicted that his first success would be as a writer. Three and a half days later, Stallone had the first draft of a screenplay, inspired by the 1975 Muhammad Ali–Chuck Wepner title bout and set in Philadelphia, where Stallone had grown up in foster homes. Stallone said, "It's a film that I wanted to go to. It's an audience's inalienable right, when they go to a theater, to see something truly extraordinary, something that borders on day-dreamism."

He didn't feel there was anything particularly remarkable about the fact that it only took him half a week to knock out the script. He told the *New York Times,* "I'm astounded by people who take eighteen years to write something. That's how long it took that guy to write *Madame Bovary*. And was that ever on a bestseller list? No. It was a lousy book and it made a lousy movie."

The studios liked Stallone's script, called *Rocky,* and executives saw it as a possible vehicle for Burt Reynolds, James Caan or Ryan O'Neal. Then Stallone told them he would sell the script on one condition: he'd play the starring role. He only got one offer, from independent producers Robert Chartoff and Irwin Winkler. They hired John G. Avildsen, who had directed Jack Lemmon to an Oscar in *Save the Tiger,* for peanuts, and the producers told the press they mortgaged their houses to make sure the movie would be completed. United Artists agreed to distribute and the film's advertising line was "His life was a million-to-one shot."

"At the two screenings I have attended," wrote Charles Champlin, "*Rocky* got rousing sus-

"We don't just urinate in the streets." —William Holden

tained ovations the likes of which I can't remember hearing at a movie before." UA heard the applause as well, and gave Stallone the biggest publicity build-up since the old studio-system days. *New York* magazine, for example, described his rags-to-riches success story in a profile entitled "He Could Be a Contender." Stallone was so ubiquitous by the time of the film's premiere in November, the *New York Post* said he had "granted more interviews in recent months than any American short of Lillian Carter."

To Smell the Truth

Newsweek found the analogy apt, and commented, "Just as Jimmy Carter prevailed by harking back to the old values of love and trust, *Rocky* resembles nothing so much as a throwback—to the 1950s Cinderella hit *Marty* and to the 1930s brand of optimism known as 'Capra-corn.'" Frank Capra himself said, "I think it's the best picture in the last ten years. It's got my vote for the Oscars all the way down the line. When I saw it, I said, 'Boy, that's a picture I wish I had made.'" Most critics were equally captivated—even John Simon said, "*Rocky* is a pugnacious, charming, grimy, beautiful fairy tale"—but the *New York Times*' Vincent Canby was a holdout. "Not since *The Great Gatsby* two years ago," wrote the critic, "has any film come into town more absurdly oversold than *Rocky*."

Rocky became an overnight box-office champion, throwing the spotlight on Stallone and his costars. Talia Shire, best known as Francis Ford Coppola's sister, made it clear that she didn't win the role of Rocky's shy girlfriend—a thirty-year-old virgin—because of family connections. "I got it because I was called to audition and I went in and gave the best reading I had ever given in my life," she insisted. Character actor Burt Young, playing Shire's screen brother "Paulie," said, "You have to really respect the camera. It picks up the truth and it can smell a counterfeit performance." And Burgess Meredith, as Rocky's trainer, explained the film's appeal: "It's a refreshing change after things like *Taxi Driver* and *One Flew Over the Cuckoo's Nest*—brilliant pictures, perhaps, but not rooting pictures. It's the difference between watching a sunset and a snake." Stallone himself felt that it was the manliness of Rocky's character that had made the film a hit. "I don't think that even women's lib wants all men to become limp-wristed librarians," the actor told the *New York Times*. "There doesn't seem to be enough real men to go around."

Bound for Boredom

For United Artists, *Rocky* was a happy surprise, but the studio's prestige item was Hal Ashby's biography of Woody Guthrie, written by Robert Getchell of *Alice Doesn't Live Here Anymore* fame. The studio's first choices for the lead were Dustin Hoffman, Jack Nicholson, Robert De Niro and Bob Dylan, but none of them wanted it. UA settled for David Carradine, the star of *Death Race 2000* and the TV show *Kung Fu*. Marilyn Beck declared *Bound for Glory* "the film of the year, of the decade," and Molly Haskell wrote, "Ashby—working through a magnificent performance by Carradine—has converted technical virtuosity to his own ends, creating a richly ambiguous character study that sings and provokes and celebrates." But *Time* headlined its review, "Bound for Boredom," and Rex Reed complained, "Woody emerges in the script as stubborn, arrogant, selfish and stupid. And his songs stink." The *New York Daily News* asked Carradine if he'd attend the Oscar show if he were nominated. "Sure, I'd be flattered," he replied. "You know, I might even wear a tux." He added, "If I won the award, anyone could win it."

Mad as Hell

MGM's prestige effort was a Sidney Lumet production of a Paddy Chayefsky screenplay about television news—*Network*. "Television is democracy at its ugliest—give the people what they want," snapped the author of *Marty*, who clari-

"I don't think that even women's lib wants all men to become limp-wristed librarians."
—Sylvester Stallone

fied, "My rage isn't against television; it's against the dehumanization of people. People say to me, 'Jesus, you moved into some pretty surreal stuff' and I say: 'No, I still write realistic stuff. It's the world that's turned into a satire.' " Lumet wasn't sure how to cast the role of a newscaster who goes crazy on camera. "Walter Cronkite's a good friend of mine and John Chancellor is a good friend of Paddy's, but their news departments may not think a movie like this is 'dignified' enough." Neither anchor wanted the role, but Cronkite's daughter did get cast as a Patty Hearst–type terrorist. Henry Fonda turned down the role, too, but Peter Finch jumped at it. "I'm really excited about *Network*," Finch said when the part was his. "It's a delight to work in a movie where there are really significant lines to deliver. I love being a mouthpiece for Paddy Chayefsky."

Lumet also admitted that casting the female lead—a ruthless career woman—might be difficult. "With all the lack of good female roles, I can name you ten actresses who would have turned it down." The filmmakers narrowed their choices down to Jane Fonda or Faye Dunaway—the latter took it. William Holden portrayed her lover, but confessed that he was uncomfortable playing his first nude love scene: "I just feel there are certain things that require privacy. We don't just urinate in the streets." Dunaway reported how the love scene went: "All I know is that whenever we got into bed, Bill couldn't stop laughing." As the wife whom Holden's character cheats on, Lumet cast the cousin of his former wife, Gloria Vanderbilt. "It's a very short part," said auburn-haired stage actress Beatrice Straight, fifty-eight. "If you blink, you miss it, but it is a lucky break."

Many journalists didn't heed the movie's advertising slogan, "Prepare yourself for a perfectly outrageous motion picture," and came out of screenings livid. "There are valid things to say about TV news, but this movie didn't say them," charged NBC's Edwin Newman, while CBS's Walter Cronkite commented, "It's just a fantasy, a burlesque, amusing perhaps, but it doesn't bear any relationship to reality. And, besides that, they cut my daughter's part down to almost nothing."

"Like the Frank Capra films of the '30s and '40s (particulary *Meet John Doe*), it is half entertainment and half message, a populist plea for the individual against human institutions," wrote *Time*. The magazine went on to label *Network* "the most controversial movie of 1976" and reported that NBC retaliated by barring Sidney Lumet from a screening of a TV movie.

Gotham Goes Nuts for Ullmann

Chayefsky did not bark when the New York Film Critics gave him their Best Screenplay citation. Sylvester Stallone did not receive an award, but his costar, Talia Shire, won Best Supporting Actress. Liv Ullmann won her third Best Actress plaque from the critics, for Ingmar Bergman's *Face to Face*, a performance that John Simon described as "the most harrowing portrayal ever of a nervous breakdown." Robert De Niro won the Best Actor Award for *Taxi Driver* and the Best Picture winner was *All the President's Men*, which went on to win the top prizes from the National Board of Review and the National Society of Film Critics.

The Campaigns

Winning the critical triple crown didn't seem enough in the wake of all the hoopla over *Rocky* and *Network*, so Warners began reminding Academy voters in trade-paper ads that *All the President's Men* had once been a media event, too. "April 1976 . . . it BEGAN" read the ads, which featured collages of the magazine covers and newspaper articles that had been devoted to the movie way back when. The campaigners for *Rocky* and *Network* kept up with the *President's Men* advertisers in the papers, and UA also promoted *Bound for Glory*, which was not headed for any box-office glory without help from Oscar.

Network aimed for an acting sweep, and William Holden, Faye Dunaway, Peter Finch, Robert

"Television is democracy at its ugliest."
—Paddy Chayefsky

Duvall, Ned Beatty, and Beatrice Straight—with a quote from *Variety* calling her performance "one of the outstanding film memories of a lifetime"—all starred in their own ads. Since Paramount was exhibiting Liv Ullmann's prize-winning crack-up on Z Channel and UA was touting Talia Shire for Best Actress, Faye Dunaway was busy giving interviews. "My best work has been in the last two years," the actress told *Women's Wear Daily*. "I think it's largely because I don't go home to an empty house. Marriage has filled out my life in a way that it feeds my work and my work feeds my marriage."

Dunaway couldn't compare to her costar Peter Finch in the interview department. When MGM informed the actor that it was planning to promote him for Best Supporting Actor and William Holden for Best Actor, Finch screamed, "Absolutely not! Howard Beale was not a supporting role." Finch's publicist, Michael Maslansky, explained why the actor got so hot under the collar: "Peter wanted to win that Oscar. It was an obsession with him. Between August and January, Peter must have done three hundred interviews with foreign and domestic media." Publicly, Finch said of the Oscar race, "I hate the politics of the whole thing, but the nomination is a big help. I'm not even sure that winning is that important, but the nomination lets people know you're there." On January 14, Finch met Lumet at the Beverly Hills Hotel to appear on *Good Morning, America* and dropped dead of a heart attack in the lobby. It was front-page news.

The Nominations

Network won ten nominations, including a Best Actor nod for the late Peter Finch, who was nevertheless topped by the late Bernard Herrmann, who received two posthumous nominations for Best Score. *Rocky* also garnered ten nominations, including two for Sylvester Stallone. ODDITIES APLENTY IN OSCAR '76 NOMINEES, headlined *Variety*, which noted, "*Seven Beauties* and *Cousin, Cousine*, both nominated for Best Foreign Language pic, made surprising incursions into the acting categories as well." *Cousin, Cousine* placed Marie-Christine Barrault in the Best Actress race, and *Seven Beauties* put Giancarlo Giannini into the Best Actor contest. Lina Wertmuller became the first female nominee in the history of the Best Director category, and she was also taking on Paddy Chayefsky, Sylvester Stallone and *Cousin, Cousine*'s Jean-Charles Tacchella in the Original Screenplay tournament. Ingmar Bergman also found his way into the Best Director category, meaning that two of the Best Picture nominees did not have corresponding Best Director nominations—*Bound for Glory* and *Taxi Driver*. At least *Taxi Driver* saw two of its stars—Robert De Niro and Jodie Foster—in the acting divisions; *Bound for Glory* also failed to get David Carradine nominated.

To her relief, Talia Shire was nominated for Best Actress, and she told reporters, "It's thrilling to get a nomination because it means that things you were trying to do got across." Best Actor nominee William Holden felt the same way: "Of course it's exciting being nominated again after all these years. It's really an undeniable thrill—the only thrill for a film actor." *Rocky*'s director John G. Avildsen claimed the news of his nomination could not have come at a better time: he was in producer Robert Stigwood's office getting fired from a picture called *Saturday Night Fever*.

Rocky's Burgess Meredith thought he had a better shot for Best Supporting Actor this year than he did the previous year because "believe it or not, *Rocky* is my first smash hit out of 120 films. I had many successes artistically, but nothing like *Rocky*." The sixty-eight-year-old nominee told the *Hollywood Reporter* he liked the new Hollywood. "I'm glad the Louella Parsons days are over. In the old days, there were five men who ran the whole industry, who could make or break your career. Today it's a sane place, more fun and more private." Although Meredith was competing against Laurence Olivier as a vicious Nazi in *Marathon Man*—his ninth acting nomination—his biggest threat for the Oscar was first-

"Just remember, pal, that you go off and ride a horse or jump in the sack with some good-looking woman in your next film—but I am forever an asshole."
—Ben Bradlee to Robert Redford

time nominee Jason Robards as Ben Bradlee in *All the President's Men.*

Last year's Best Supporting Actress, Lee Grant, was in the running this year for *Voyage of the Damned,* an all-star melodrama in which she and Faye Dunaway played Jewish refugees fleeing Hitler. Grant said the movie was important to her because "it got a lot out of my system." She was also pleased with the nomination. "It never gets boring, even when you're just a contender. More than anything, it's a psychological boost, particularly when you've been nominated as often as I have," said the four-time nominee. *Carrie*'s Piper Laurie agreed. "I've never even won a turkey," the Supporting Actress nominee said. "It's all so much more than I ever expected when I took the part. Whatever happens, I'm really enjoying this. My friends and my daughter will see me on TV, at least for a flash." The youngest nominee, thirteen-year-old Jodie Foster, was asked by an eleven-year-old interviewer from *The Children's Express,* "Would the Academy Award change your personality?" "No, I don't think so," Jodie replied. "I think it would be just a really nice thing to have on my mantelpiece. Boy, I would love it. It would be so neat."

Streisand Wants In

Barbra Streisand was nominated for Best Song, having written her radio hit "Evergreen" for her remake of *A Star Is Born,* which was universally panned by the critics but made money anyway. Streisand's biggest competition came from Bill Conti's equally popular theme from *Rocky,* "Gonna Fly Now"—TV sports shows had already appropriated the anthem for their highlight spots—so Streisand overcame her fear of performing before live audiences and consented to sing on the Oscar show. Seventy-four-year-old Sammy Fain, the composer of a nominated song from a movie called *Half a House,* ran a trade ad that read: "It would be nice if we had a commercial record, but we don't. It would also be nice if we were in a widely seen motion picture, but we don't have that either." Fain then provided the telephone number to "Dial-a-Song," so Academy voters could call up and hear Fain's tape recording of the tune.

Director William Friedkin was in charge of the Oscar show and he was ruling out any depressing references to death. He vetoed a plan to have Loretta Young pay tribute to her recently deceased friend Rosalind Russell and he told Paddy Chayefsky to accept for the late Peter Finch—Friedkin didn't want a widow boo-hooing at the podium. The director invited Lillian Hellman, who had just published a McCarthy era memoir called *Scoundrel Time,* to give an award, hiring a private jet to pick her up in Martha's Vineyard. Friedkin's emcees were Richard Pryor, Ellen Burstyn, Jane Fonda and Warren Beatty. Gregg Kilday of the *Los Angeles Herald-Examiner* wrote of the four co-hosts, "Their very presence rings out like a gesture of defiance." Bob Hope would not be on the show; he would be preoccupied that night at a benefit at Baker University in Baldwin, Kansas.

The Big Night

Mrs. Peter Finch arrived in a mink stole and mingled with Paddy Chayefsky. Faye Dunaway, in black slacks, came with her husband, rock star Peter Wolf, and Talia Shire was on the arm of her husband, composer David Shire. It was Shire's costar, according to *Newsweek,* who caused the most commotion in the bleachers: "When Sylvester Stallone stepped out—his ruffled dress shirt open at the neck to display a Sicilian death's head pendant and a hint of white undershirt over his huge chest—the cheers crescendoed to a new level of primal enthusiasm." Stallone told his legion of fans upon entering, "My pumpkin is waiting. I'll see you later." Stallone was confident—*Rocky* had won him the Directors Guild Award.

As part of his modern new look, William Friedkin did away entirely with the traditional opening shots of arriving celebrities and began the telecast with Ann-Margret singing a specially written number entitled "It All Started in Someone's Head" against what *Daily Variety* described as an "all-purpose abstract set with light changes for mood." Ann-Margret was followed by Academy President Walter Mirisch, who spoke briefly and noted, "Like any other industry, motion pictures have had periods of great fertility as well as disturbing dry spells."

Richard Pryor, in white tie and tails, wandered out onstage and stood there with his mouth open. The camera saw Sylvester Stallone laughing. Finally, Pryor spoke: "I'm here to explain why black people will never be nominated for anything. This show is going out to seventy-five million people—none of them black. We don't even know how to vote. There's 3,349 people in the voting thing and only two black people—Sidney Poitier and Harry Belafonte. We're quitting. You'll have to listen to Lawrence Welk." Pryor then warned the nominees not to curse when they lost because of the omnipresent cameras. "We don't want to see you saying—" and the emcee's lips silently formed an obscenity.

A star from *Saturday Night Live,* Chevy Chase, executed one of his trademark stumbles as he made his entrance to explain the rules; Faye Dunaway and Jason Robards were glimpsed laughing at the pratfall. The comedian began speaking in Spanish, switched to English and made a mock acceptance speech, thanking "of course, my godmother, Aldo Ray." Suddenly,

Awards Ceremony

MARCH 29, 1977, 7:00 P.M.
THE DOROTHY CHANDLER PAVILION, LOS ANGELES

Your Hosts:
RICHARD PRYOR, JANE FONDA, ELLEN BURSTYN, WARREN BEATTY
Televised over ABC

Presenters

Supporting Actor	Tatum O'Neal
Costume Design	Tamara Dobson
Short Films	Marty Feldman
Special Visual Effects	Roy Scheider
Art Direction	Marthe Keller
Supporting Actress	Sylvester Stallone
Film Editing	William Holden
Sound	Red Skelton
Thalberg Award	Cicely Tyson
Cinematography	Donald Sutherland
Foreign Film	Pearl Bailey
Scoring Awards	Ann-Margret
Documentary Awards	Lillian Hellman
Song	Neil Diamond
Writing Awards	Norman Mailer
Director	Jeanne Moreau
Actor	Liv Ullmann
Actress	Louise Fletcher
Picture	Jack Nicholson

Performers of Nominated Songs

"Ave Satani"	Lee Vivante
"Come to Me"	Tom Jones
"Evergreen"	Barbra Streisand
"Gonna Fly Now"	Ben Vereen
"A World That Never Was"	Eddie Albert

"Thanks to you, darling, for sending the right vibes the right way."
—Mrs. Peter Finch

King Kong's hand swung out from stage left, holding an oversized envelope. "Ernest Borgnine, ladies and gentlemen," Chase said, then made a sexual innuendo about the hairy palm. Chase opened the envelope and went on, "This is an invitation to Tippi Hedren's party later. I can't make it."

While reading the rules, Chase laughed at the reference to the "secret ballot" and said of the specially selected Documentary, Short Subject and Foreign Language Film Awards, "I alone decide that." He declared that the results of the balloting are "only known to Price, Waterhouse and their wives and kids." The camera saw Liv Ullmann laughing as Chase concluded, "Should you be lucky enough to be picked by Mr. and Mrs. Price, Waterhouse, remember that handling and fondling of the Oscar itself must be limited to the upper torso."

The actress voted by exhibitors as the number-one female box-office attraction, thirteen-year-old Tatum O'Neal, walked out with her father to give the Best Supporting Actor Oscar. The only missing nominee was Laurence Olivier.The winner was Jason Robards for *All the President's Men*. Gingerly picking up the statuette, Robards said, "I think I'm following Chevy's instructions." The actor thanked Ben Bradlee "for being alive so I could come out and play with him."

Another comedian, bug-eyed Marty Feldman, appeared and quipped, "I would just like to point out that God made me in his own image." Feldman had his own jokes about Oscar. "It's not Jewish, you can tell," he said, turning the statuette upside down and reading, "It says 'Made in Hong Kong.'" When two producers came to claim the Live Action Short Oscar, Feldman threw it on the floor, broke it in two and handed each a half. Then Eddie Albert came out to sing Sammy Fain's Best Song nominee, which included the lyric "Sunburned girls in sleeveless jackets/Gaily swinging tennis rackets."

Ellen Burstyn, in a tuxedo with a blue ruffled shirt, took over as emcee and introduced the next nominated song—a Gregorian chant from the horror movie *The Omen*. Sylvester Stallone walked out afterward to loud applause, interrupted by the surprise appearance of Muhammad Ali. "I'm the real Apollo Creed!" Ali boomed. "You stole my script! Show me what you can really do!" Stallone and Ali sparred for a moment, and then they fell into a bear hug. "I just got to say one thing," Stallone interjected. "I may not win anything here in the form of an Oscar, but I really feel it's a privilege to be standing next to a living legend and it's something I'll always treasure for the rest of my life." Stallone was there to give the Best Supporting Actress Oscar. All of the nominees were present and the winner was *Network*'s Beatrice Straight. Lifting her statuette, Straight said, "It's very heavy and I'm the dark horse. It's a great, great thrill and totally unexpected." The actress thanked Paddy Chayefsky, "who writes what we all feel but cannot express."

Straight's screen husband, William Holden, presented the Editing Award, which went to *Rocky*. "It's a dream of a lifetime come true," gushed cowinner Scott Conrad. Red Skelton, introduced as "the king of the clowns," made a number of gags about public speakers and then gave the Sound Oscar to *All the President's Men*. Noting a safety net over the orchestra, Skelton joked, "Boy, it's the first time I ever worked with a net." Skelton was followed by Cicely Tyson, who gave the Thalberg Award to Pandro S. Berman, who had produced some of the Astaire-Rogers musicals of the '30s. "The marvelous thing about this medium," Berman said, "is that I could show my dreams as well as my feelings." Berman went backstage and said the old studio days weren't so bad. "When I wanted it badly enough, I got it on the screen."

"If a cameraman takes the day off, we all do," explained Donald Sutherland, handing the Cinematography Oscar to *Bound for Glory*'s Haskell Wexler, who was dressed like Ellen Burstyn. The winner said he was indebted to a "good crew, good people, good film." Tom Jones, dressed like

"This show is going out to 75 million people—none of them black."
—Richard Pryor

Sylvester Stallone with open shirt but crucifix instead of medallion, sang a nominated song and then Jane Fonda assumed the hosting duties. She wore an evening gown and a small flower behind her ear.

Fonda brought out a member of the United States delegation to the United Nations—Pearl Bailey. She explained to Red Skelton that the net over the orchestra was there to prevent a mishap like the one that had happened recently to Bing Crosby—Der Bingle fell off a stage while taping a TV special. "If I had fallen in, you would have seen the biggest bounce you've ever seen," Bailey said, moving on to the Foreign Film Award, which pitted *Seven Beauties* against *Cousin, Cousine*. The winner turned out to be *Black and White in Color,* from the Ivory Coast, and the flabbergasted producer, Arthur Cohn, exclaimed, "I feel a bit like Harry Truman when he was holding up the newspaper saying that Dewey had won the election."

Ann-Margret returned and announced that Leonard Rosenman, who had won the Song Adaptation Award for *Barry Lyndon* the previous year, had won again for adapting Woody Guthrie's songs for *Bound for Glory*. The winner reminded everyone that he composed original music, too, and thanked the non-nominated Hal Ashby, "a great director." Ashby's fans applauded. The late Bernard Herrmann struck out twice with the Best Score Oscar; Jerry Goldsmith won for *The Omen,* the first horror movie to win a Music Oscar.

Jane Fonda introduced "my friend," Lillian Hellman, whom she was portraying in her upcoming movie *Julia*. The audience rewarded Hellman with a standing ovation and the writer avowed her dedication to the category she was announcing, the Documentary Awards. But then Hellman continued, "I have a mischievous pleasure in being asked here tonight. I was once a respectable member of this community." She briefly recalled the blacklisting era, claiming the film industry confronted McCarthy "with the force and courage of a bowl of mashed potatoes." The camera watched former blacklist victim Lee Grant listening intently. Hellman wound things up by noting that she was here as a celebrity again and she "never thought it would happen." Both of the Documentary Oscars went to women, and both of them said, "I can't think of a greater honor than to receive this from Lillian Hellman."

Lillian's friend Jane Fonda returned and said, "This is the first time an executive producer has ever been asked to sing" and introduced the composer of "Evergreen" with "Right on, Barbra Streisand!" Streisand, in an Afro hairdo, sang her composition, while the lighting cast a faint halo around her head. When she was finished, her friend from her Brooklyn high school days, Neil Diamond, walked out to reveal that "Evergreen" had won the Best Song Oscar. "In my wildest dreams, I never thought I would win an Oscar for writing a song," Streisand said. Her collaborator, the diminutive Paul Williams, commented, "I was going to thank all the little people, then I remembered I am the little people."

Norman Mailer, also dressed like Ellen Burstyn, prefaced the writing Awards with a story about Voltaire at a male bordello: "Once a philosopher, twice a pervert" was the moral of the story. Mailer thought this held true for the screenwriter, too, because "he writes a line and gives it life, then the director comes along and gives it another life that's a perverted life." Best Original Screenplay winner Paddy Chayefsky accepted his Oscar for *Network* "in the name of all us perverts" and then said, "I don't, as a rule, in fact, I don't ever before remember making public acknowledgment of private and very personal feelings but I think it's time that I acknowledge two people who I could never really thank properly or enough." They turned out to be his wife and kid. Best Adapted Screenplay winner William Goldman, for *All the President's Men,* said, "I had all kinds of cute and humble things to say but I forgot them all." He did remember to acknowledge the once-again non-nominated cinematographer Gordon Willis.

Mrs. William Friedkin, Jeanne Moreau, presented the Best Director Award. Nominee Ingmar Bergman hadn't made it to L.A., but Lina Wertmuller was there with her hair in a pony tail. The

"The Oscar is not Jewish, you can tell."
—Marty Feldman

winner was John G. Avildsen for *Rocky,* who hugged Sylvester Stallone on his way to the stage. "I guess *Rocky* gave a lot of people hope," the winner said, adding, "Stallone gave his guts and his heart and his best shot."

Warren Beatty was the final emcee, and he observed, "And of course, there's always the temptation with an audience like this to say something political. But when I saw who was going to be on the show tonight—Lillian Hellman, Norman Mailer, Jane Fonda, Donald Sutherland—maybe the nicest thing I could do is say a few nice words about Reagan and Goldwater."

Because Liv Ullmann was just publishing her autobiography, *Changing,* Beatty introduced her as "actress and author." Her task was to read the name of the Best Actor; William Holden and Sylvester Stallone were the only nominees present. The winner was Peter Finch for *Network*. Paddy Chayefsky hustled to the stage and said, "For some obscure reason, I'm up here accepting an award for Peter Finch, or Finchie, as everybody who knew him called him. There's no reason for me to be here. There's only one person who should be up here, and that's the person Finch wanted to accept his award. Are you in the house, Eletha? C'mon up and get your Award." Mrs. Finch came to the stage, bearing flowers, her pocketbook and her mink coat. She leaned over the microphones and said:

> *I want to say thanks to the members of the Academy and my husband. I wish he were here tonight to be with us all. But since he isn't here, I'll always cherish this for him and before he died he said to me, "Darling, if I win I want to say thanks to my fellow actors who have given me encouragement over the years and thanks to Paddy Chayefsky who've given him the part and thanks to Barry [Finch's agent Barry Kross] who have tell us to come from Jamaica to come and do this part" and he said most of all, "Thanks to you, darling, for sending the right vibes the right way." And thanks to the members of the Academy Awards. Thank you all.*

As soon as Ullmann walked off with Chayefsky and Mrs. Finch, Louise Fletcher came out to determine her fate in the Best Actress category. All the nominees were in attendance, including Marie-Christine Barrault. The winner was Faye Dunaway for *Network*. "I didn't expect this to happen quite yet, but I thank you very much," Dunaway said. "I'm very grateful."

Beatty introduced the Best Director presenter, Jack Nicholson, who asked, "Who was that guy?" Nicholson also commented, "You will note that among films nominated this year, there isn't a single disaster movie, nor is there a nominated picture that even the most critical could consider a disaster." Nicholson opened the envelope and declared the winner—*Rocky*. Cheers emanated from the audience as the producers made their way down the row of seats. In all the excitement, Irwin Winkler accidentally hit Beatrice Straight in the head with his rear end. She did not look pleased, but appeared forgiving.

Winkler and Robert Chartoff grabbed Sylvester Stallone and pulled him up to the stage with them. Once at the podium, the trio raised their clasped hands triumphantly over their heads and Stallone instructed the producers to "Tell it like it is!" Chartoff said to Stallone, "I'd like to thank you for sharing your dreams with us and for giving a performance that has enriched all our lives. Thanks to the Academy for letting *Rocky,* a million-to-one underdog, go the distance." Winkler added, "Thanks for helping us to live out the dream of *Rocky*." The cameras showed Stallone's brother in the audience—his unbuttoned shirt was yellow. Stallone made the final remarks, "To all the Rocky's of the world, I love ya!"

Warren Beatty came back to say, "We want to thank all of you for watching us congratulate ourselves tonight." Then Ann-Margret returned to reprise the opening number, summoning up the ghost of Louis B. Mayer by concluding, "It all began in someone's head."

"My husband and I were left out in the freezing cold waiting for our rented limousine after all the beautiful people had already gone."
—Talia Shire

Aftermath

"I had no idea *Rocky* would be such a hit," Oscar-winner John G. Avildsen exclaimed backstage. "I thought it was going to be the second half of a double bill at a drive-in." When asked if he would direct a sequel, Avildsen said, "You bet! I'm looking forward to it and I think Sly has already written it."

"The greatest compliment I can have," Stallone was saying nearby, "and the greatest pleasure I'll have—is the fact that *Rocky* will be remembered, I think, much more than any other film ten to fifteen years from now." Stallone shrugged off not winning an Oscar himself: "We won the big one!" He did win the cover to *Newsweek*. The picture showed Stallone holding a giant-sized Oscar in the pressroom with the headline ROCKY KO'S HOLLYWOOD.

Mrs. Rocky, Talia Shire, did not remember the evening so fondly. The Best Actress loser told Shirley Eder that she and her husband "were left out in the freezing cold waiting for our rented limousine after all the beautiful people had already gone. Seems the chauffeur couldn't find his way from the underground garage up to the front door. And if anything ruined the evening for us, it was that and not the fact that I lost the Oscar to Faye."

Barbra Streisand did not have any transportation problems; she rented two limousines, one with a Barbra Streisand look-alike to fool the fans, and another to whisk her and boyfriend Jon Peters away. Streisand skipped the Governors' Ball, but Paul Williams went and enjoyed himself with Ann-Margret and Martin Scorsese, whose *Taxi Driver* came up empty-handed. Hank Grant wrote of the ball: "The hiring of Harry James and his band was an inspiration: all the good old standard sentimental ballads and toe-tapping swing tunes, such a welcome relief from all the raucous, ear-splitting rock bands which heretofore have emptied out black-tie affairs faster than a bomb threat."

William Friedkin ran up to Paddy Chayefsky and *Network* producer Howard Gottfried and ranted, "You guys lied to me. You didn't tell me what you had planned." Chayefsky said that Mrs. Finch "had no idea I was going to do it," but later revealed that he had written her speech himself and had rehearsed it with her. Chayefsky explained, "Friedkin said he didn't want any sentimentality and I didn't want to get in a fight, so I said I'd do it his way—but I figured if I got up there I'd call Eletha. I thought this is what movies are all about—'This is Mrs. Norman Maine' or like when Louise Fletcher spoke to her parents when she won." Howard Gottfried concurred, "We decided, between Paddy and me, we could not conceive of allowing this kind of injustice to take place. She was the proper recipient."

William Friedkin didn't win any friends in the industry, either. The *Hollywood Reporter* reviewed the show as "a crashing bore . . . that simply sophisticated us to tears." *Variety* mentioned the innuendos made by Chevy Chase, Marty Feldman and Norman Mailer and asked, "Has Hollywood taken leave of its public-image senses?" But the worst news came with the announcement of the TV ratings—it was the lowest-rated Oscar show ever.

The evening was far from dull for Faye Dunaway, who celebrated until morning, when a *Time* photographer snapped her in a bathrobe by a pool as she stared at her Oscar and piles of newspapers headlining her victory. Costar and Best Actor loser William Holden had been one of her well-wishers, but months later he winked at his business manager and said, "If the son of a bitch hadn't died, I could have had my second Oscar."

1977

"I'm an introvert. I don't want to be famous."
—George Lucas

Vanessa Redgrave turned Oscar's fiftieth birthday party into a political showdown.

Woody Allen wasn't talking. To the press and exhibitors, his new movie was simply the "New Woody Allen Film" and all that nervous UA executives knew was the working title, *Anhedonia*—i.e., the inability to enjoy oneself. When the movie, retitled *Annie Hall*, was ready for its spring release, Allen spilled enough beans to call it "a contemporary, loosely autobiographical, romantic comedy." After *Annie Hall* had its premiere at Filmex, the annual film festival held in Los Angeles—the city which, according to the film, had the sole cultural advantage of being able to turn right on a red light—Woody opened up some more: "I wanted it to be about . . . real people, real problems besetting some fairly neurotic characters trying to exist in male-female relationships in America in 1977. So it turns out to be more serious than anything I've ever tried before." The *New York Daily News* warned that "*Annie Hall* will likely be a trifle disconcerting for audiences who've been reduced to tears of laughter by Woody Allen; his new comedy is so tinged with sadness it tends to encourage actual weeping."

Annie Hall recounted the breakup of a relationship—Allen and Diane Keaton more or less playing themselves—and *Variety* raved, "In a decade largely devoted to male buddy-buddy films, brutal rape fantasies and impersonal special effects extravaganzas, Woody Allen has almost single-handedly kept alive the idea of heterosexual romance in American films." Those who turned to Allen for laughs didn't have to worry according to *Newsweek*'s Janet Maslin, who wrote that *Annie Hall* has "laughs as satisfying as those in any of Allen's other movies." John Simon was about the only dissenter; he carped that the film is "everything we never wanted to know about Woody's sex life and were afraid he'd tell us anyway."

Everyone except Simon was in love with Diane Keaton, who confirmed to Rex Reed, "Woody and I . . . we're beyond getting involved again with each other . . . He's my closest and dearest friend." "As Annie Hall," wrote Vincent Canby in the *New York Times*, "Miss Keaton emerges as Woody Allen's Liv Ullmann." She also emerged as a fashion trendsetter when women began aping the "Annie Hall" look—floppy hat, oversized man's shirt, vest, baggy chinos, tie, all with a wrinkled effect. One Seventh Avenue fashion coordinator surveyed the scene and concluded, "Not since *The Godfather* when clothes took on a gangster style has Hollywood had such an impact on fashion."

Spaced Out

"I loved the *Flash Gordon* comic books," effused George Lucas. "I loved the Universal serials with Buster Crabbe." But Universal didn't love Lucas' idea of making an outer-space adventure fantasy and told him to go peddle it somewhere else. Three weeks before his *American Graffiti* opened, 20th Century–Fox gave Lucas $15,000 to write the screenplay for *Star Wars*. Luckily for Lucas, he had his share of *Graffiti*'s profits to supplement his income because it took him three years to finish writing his screenplay and, believing a deal's a deal, he refused to ask for more money. When Lucas finally presented the script to Fox, the top brass had strong doubts about giving him $8.5 million for the science-fiction project, production chief Alan Ladd, Jr., convinced them to hand over the money.

Star Wars, which ended up costing around $10 million, opened in May and most reviewers were enthralled by the old-fashioned heroics and high-tech special effects highlighting the galactic battle between good and evil. Judith Crist wrote that "you exit with that satisfied Saturday-afternoon-at-the-movies-smile that feels so good." But Stanley Kauffmann detected a case of arrested devel-

Overleaf: *Best Supporting Actress winner Vanessa Redgrave, dining with her bodyguard at the Governors' Ball, keeps a lookout for Paddy Chayefsky.*

opment: "This picture was made for those (particularly males) who carry a portable shrine with them of their adolescence, a chalice of a self that was better then, before the world's affairs or—in any complex way—sex intruded." Lucas saw it differently. "Nobody except Disney makes movies for young people anymore," he lamented. "I want to open up the realm of space for them."

They, in turn, opened up their wallets for *Star Wars*—it became the most profitable film in history. *Newsweek* took a gander at the nation's movie theaters to report, "Not since the ominous jaws of a shark stirred the country's imagination two summers ago has a film generated such a cult following." The magazine talked to some of those cultists, like Lawrence Mitchell, a security guard from New York City, who had been back to see Luke Skywalker and his friends twenty-six times. His reason? "It's one of those straight movies that get away from sex, murder and rape." Bill Mason, a fourteen-year-old from Boston, had gone six times, mostly because he liked the film's comic-relief robots. "They're really wicked," he exclaimed. Hollywood's Chinese Theatre thought so, too—R2D2, C-3P0 and Darth Vader became the first nonhumans to have their footprints placed in the theater's courtyard since Roy Rogers' Trigger left his hoofmarks three decades earlier.

People noted, "Within three weeks, *Star Wars* posters were outselling Farrah Fawcett-Majors five to one." Everywhere consumers looked were *Star Wars* bubble-gum cards, watches, masks, towels, T-shirts, nightgowns, toys and lingerie, and a disco version of John Williams' theme music was making it to number one on the pop charts. All of which was disconcerting to George Lucas, who sighed, "I'm an introvert. I don't want to be famous."

Something for the Girls

Star Wars kept the kids and teenagers happy, but in the fall *Time* noticed that, for the first time in years, Hollywood was coming up with lots of good roles for actresses. The magazine noted "a determined trend-spotter can point to a handful of new films whose makers think that women can bear the dramatic weight of a production." *Newsweek* also picked up on this trend with a cover story called "Hollywood's New Heroines" and *People* decreed that 1977 "will be recorded as the year the holdout state of Hollywood finally ratified the Equal Rights Amendment."

Ladies on the Left

Newsweek's cover girl was Jane Fonda, who, earlier in the year, had proven that her politics didn't make her box-office poison when her caper comedy *Fun With Dick and Jane* became a sleeper hit. In October she was back with *Julia*, based on a portion of Lillian Hellman's memoirs about a childhood friend who had taught her political activism. Fonda had campaigned to play Hellman because, initially, director Fred Zinnemann didn't think she was right for the role. Zinnemann admitted that he and Fonda "had it out early. I told her this would not be a political-soapbox movie. Jane was disappointed, but the more you give in to her the more domineering she becomes."

Fonda pressed producer Richard Roth to sign her friend Vanessa Redgrave for the title role and Lillian Hellman loved the idea. Roth said, "Why not? It was perfect symmetry. The two most famous left-wing women of the '70s playing two left-wing women of the '30s. I liked it. Of course the fact that Jane and Vanessa were both terrific actresses didn't hurt, either. Not to mention they both agreed to work cheap." Zinnemann also had to speak to Redgrave about keeping politics off the set and, after the film was completed, he told an interviewer, "If Lillian Hellman had been along with Vanessa and Jane, I don't think I could have handled it." Meanwhile Fonda was telling *Women's Wear Daily*, "After playing endless characters who are neurotic or lost, I can't describe what it is like to play an intellectual woman and act out her deep commitment to a friend who is also a woman."

Time's Frank Rich decried that "for all the

"If Lillian Hellman had been along with Vanessa Redgrave and Jane Fonda, I don't think I could have handled it."
—Fred Zinnemann

taste, talent and money that have been lavished on the film, it is stubbornly lacking passion and life." But most reviewers were reverential toward *Julia*—Rex Reed called it "the quiet masterpiece we've all been waiting for." *Saturday Review*'s Arthur Schlesinger, Jr., marveled over the casting: "What an accomplished pair these two are! They play off each other wonderfully, Redgrave with her exquisite and steely passion, Fonda with her tremulous self-doubt and involuntary commitment. Each performance is a triumph of professional skill and personal spirit." Fonda and Redgrave weren't the only standouts in the cast; Charles Champlin praised Jason Robards' "brief but indelible portrait of Dash Hammett, irascible, powerful, wise, brutally honest."

For Those Who Think Young

Next up was Diane Keaton again, this time as a woman who frequents single bars and is killed when she brings home Mr. Wrong in the film version of bestseller *Looking for Mr. Goodbar*. Director Richard Brooks originally didn't want to do the movie, but then the sixty-seven-year-old filmmaker sensed a golden opportunity to scold the younger generation. "I became intrigued by the possibility of saying something about the lack of commitment young people seem to have today," he declared. "Their infatuation with the merely sensational; their desire for instant relief and gratification; their lack of sexual joy; and their disillusionment because everything didn't turn out the way TV commercials say it should."

Brooks didn't get through to those young people, however. Rumors drifted out of Hollywood that the under-forty crowd in the industry was doubled over with laughter during supposedly harrowing scenes at screenings of *Mr. Goodbar*, and *Time* snorted, "Not since Paddy Chayefsky in *Network* has a middle-aged filmmaker so cantankerously lashed out against the young." Andrew Sarris reported that the worried Brooks ordered screeningroom doors locked so that critics couldn't walk out on his film. Reviewers may have derided the film, but not its star, whose change-of-pace performance landed her on the covers of *Rolling Stone* and *Time*. Andrew Sarris was turned on by Keaton's "electrifying explicit sexuality," and concluded "with *Annie Hall* and *Looking for Mr. Goodbar* coming out of the same year, Diane Keaton is clearly the most dynamic woman star in pictures."

Dance, Ballerina, Dance

"For a long time, it was a movie nobody would touch," explained choreographer-turned-director Herbert Ross of *The Turning Point*, a project he conceived with his wife, ex-ballerina Nora Kaye, and writer Arthur Laurents. "Everybody kept asking, 'Who's interested in ballet?' And we kept saying we wanted to show what really goes into being a ballet dancer." Arthur Laurents told the *New York Daily News*, "The problem for Hollywood is that if a contemporary woman is allowed to be 'aggressive' in Hollywood terms she must either be what they consider unattractive physically, neurotic, or a neurotic bitch like Faye Dunaway in *Network*." So the filmmakers tried to counter this stereotype by sending their script, about the friendship between a working ballerina and one who dropped out of the business to raise a family, to two Hollywood "ladies"—Audrey Hepburn and Grace Kelly. "Grace loved the story and said she'd come out of retirement to play the ballet dancer who opts for marriage," Ross told the *New York Daily News*, "but then she showed the script to Prince Rainier and he told her he didn't want her to go back to work."

By the time Ross and company got a film commitment out of 20th Century–Fox, Hepburn was out of the project, too. Anne Bancroft stepped into the role of the ballerina, and Shirley MacLaine assumed the part of the mother, although she stressed to interviewers, "My compatibility with this part is nil . . . I would have had the baby and gone back to work; it wouldn't have been any problem in my mind at all."

For verisimilitude, the filmmakers cast Mik-

"The feud that's been talked about for years really exists. Olivia de Havilland and Joan Fontaine hate one another."
—Allan Carr

hail Baryshnikov as a sexy ballet star, but the dancer warned the press, "Acting is not my language at all. My part was small and I don't know if I could do real, serious acting." The Rosses cast their own godchild in the role of MacLaine's ambitious daughter, but Leslie Browne, a member of the corps de ballet of the New York City Ballet, had about as much confidence in her thespian abilities as Baryshnikov had in his. "Oh, I'd love to have both an acting career and a dancing career, but I don't think I could handle both," she told reporters. "I'm really just trying to succeed in ballet."

Time heralded *The Turning Point* with four stop-action photographs of Bancroft and MacLaine in the film's climactic catfight and the *Los Angeles Herald-Examiner* exclaimed, "It's great entertainment—bitchy, bold, awash with the theatrics of the heart." Vincent Canby thought he had seen it all before, "Although *The Turning Point* is set in the somewhat rare world of the ballet, it's essentially an old-fashioned backstage musical that contains every backstage cliché I can think of . . . ," but Judith Crist wasn't bothered by the familiarity. Calling the film "the movie-movie of the year," Crist advised readers, "You don't get this kind of movie too often anymore. When you do—wallow in it." Moviegoers did, to the tune of $17 million, and both Bancroft and MacLaine did fine by the reviewers. Bancroft won the National Board of Review Award for Best Actress and Molly Haskell wrote of MacLaine in *New York*, "The balance would be overwhelmingly in favor of the career woman were it not for Shirley MacLaine's magnificence in the role of the Oklahoma City housewife . . . She makes motherhood and family a living, breathing thing instead of a sitcom."

Horsefeathers

Richard Burton had not made a movie in three years and he hoped his double-whammy comeback in 1977 would put him back in the winner's circle. His first vehicle was as commercial as all get-out—*The Exorcist II, The Heretic,* a sequel to the 1973 smash hit. Part Two did not go over as well; in fact, the manager of a Hollywood Boulevard theater reported that the opening night audience grew so hostile they threw their refreshments at the screen. Warners quickly reedited the picture, cutting out the preposterous scenes that had elicited laughter, but the effort was in vain—*The Exorcist II* was one of the year's biggest fiascos.

Burton's second try was the film version of *Equus*, which Burton had played on Broadway to capacity audiences. Director Sidney Lumet, fresh from his triumph with *Network,* was in charge of the prestige project, and the cast was filled with admired British actors, including Peter Firth, who had originated the role of the troubled youth who pokes out horses' eyes in the Broadway production. *Time* brought the bad news when the film opened in exclusive engagements in the fall. "If ever there was a play that has no business being a movie, *Equus* is it," wrote Frank Rich. "Strip the stagecraft away, and all that remains is two-and-a-half hours of talky debate about shopworn ideas. The poor play stumbles and falls before it can break from the gate." *Equus* made even less money than *Exorcist II,* but Burton earned enough good notices personally—the *Los Angeles Times*' Kevin Thomas opined, "It represents the finest work of Richard Burton since *Who's Afraid of Virginia Woolf?*"—to give United Artists material for an Oscar campaign. The studio ran a number of Oscar ads in the trade papers, showed the movie on Z Channel, and kept their fingers crossed.

Quiet on the Set

Columbia executives, meanwhile, were tearing their hair out over Steven Spielberg's first movie since *Jaws,* a $22 million project the director called *Watch the Skies*. The *New York Times* reported that the feature "has been cloaked in almost as much secrecy as the Manhattan (atomic bomb) Project." *Time* tried to investigate and discovered, "Cast and crew have been forbidden to discuss the movie's content in interviews—security guards

"I love being regarded as a sex symbol, but I can't take it too seriously."
—John Travolta

have watched over its sets round the clock, at one point assiduously ejecting Spielberg when he showed up without his ID badge." Pestered by a reporter, Spielberg's leading man Richard Dreyfuss begged off with, "If I told you anything, Steven would kill me. All I can say is that in *Jaws,* the shark was the star of the film; in this film, the film is the star of the film." Spielberg himself told *American Film,* "I didn't clamp the lid down because of egocentric reasons . . . I wanted to surprise. And the only way in the world you're going to do that is by keeping quiet about what's in it."

Columbia executives feared the worst when someone from *New York* bribed his way into the film's initial sneak preview in Dallas, Texas, and reported, "I can understand all the apprehension. In my humble opinion, the picture will be a colossal flop." Although Columbia's stock dropped precipitously after this bleak forecast, the studio proceeded with its expensive press junket before the film's premiere. Journalists from around the country were flown in to meet the filmmakers and the cast, who spent the press conference showering praise on their director. "I want to thank you, Steven, for giving us this film," said producer Michael Phillips, while actress Melinda Dillon added,"I think of it as a religious film."

Columbia thought it was an act of God when the science-fiction film about UFO's, retitled *Close Encounters of the Third Kind*, opened to sensational reviews. "An incredible experience," waxed Rona Barrett, "Steven Spielberg proves himself to be a consummate movie-maker and an artist of rare insight." *Newsweek* blessed the movie with a cover story and inside Jack Kroll wrote, "*Close Encounters* is the friendliest, warmest science-fiction epic you've ever seen. It brings the heavens down to earth." Ray Bradbury told the *Los Angeles Times,* "*Close Encounters* is, in all probability, the most important film of our time." One of the few unconverted was Rex Reed, who called it "a wasteful depressing failure . . . Living in New York, I'm surrounded by enough intergalactic freaks already." But the film wasn't a failure at the box office—*Close Encounters* was an immediate box-office smash and became Columbia's most profitable film to date.

Simon Says

Robert De Niro wanted to try comedy, so he signed to play in a Neil Simon picture about a struggling actor entitled *Bogart Slept Here,* to be directed by Mike Nichols. After two weeks of filming, De Niro was out of the picture and Simon was explaining to reporters, "Robert De Niro is a very intense actor. He doesn't play joy very well."

Nichols went on to other projects and Simon rewrote the screenplay for Richard Dreyfuss, who, the playwright told *Time,* is "not the handsome type like Redford or a dramatic-actor type like Pacino or De Niro. Rick can do anything—and he is funnier than any of them." Simon also had definite ideas about the film's leading lady—he wanted his wife, Marsha Mason. "What I wanted from Marsha was the reality she could bring," he told the *New York Times.* "To cast a light comedienne would have made it artificial." Mrs. Simon assured the paper, "I think if I hadn't been married to Neil, I still would have been one of the actresses thought of for the role. I would never have done the film if I felt I wasn't qualified to do it, because I would lose all my self-respect." There was no hint of nepotism in the casting of Mason's young daughter; ten-year-old Quinn Cummings was a veteran of television commercials who had been pushed into the business by her neighbor, cinematographer James Wong Howe.

With Mike Nichols unavailable, Simon turned to Herbert Ross, who had directed *The Sunshine Boys* two years earlier and had just finished *The Turning Point.* Ross jumped at the chance, telling publicists that the comedy "is seriously about the need for human beings to trust one another and have faith no matter how many times they are disappointed or scared. This picture is really about believing in the ultimate good of people." There were no conflicts on the set this time around, and Dreyfuss told *Esquire,* "I could make that movie for the rest of my life."

"If I told you anything, Steven would kill me."
—Richard Dreyfuss

Vanilla-Flavored Escapism

The ads for the comedy, retitled *The Goodbye Girl,* said, "Thank you, Neil Simon for making us laugh about falling in love . . . again." Rex Reed was particularly grateful, writing, "It is just the kind of lump-in-the-throat comedy we need now. No nudity, violence, tragedy, killings or bloodshed. Just pure joy and happiness and vanilla-flavored escapism." The film opened moderately, but word-of-mouth turned it into the most successful Neil Simon movie yet. The *Los Angeles Times'* Charles Champlin differed with Simon's view of Marsha Mason and claimed, "She takes her place with the great screen comediennes."

But it was Dreyfuss, benefiting from the simultaneous release of *Close Encounters,* who amazed the critics. *Time* opined, "Dreyfuss is mature and sensitive at the same time—not to mention sexy and compassionate." The *New York Times Sunday Magazine* awarded the twenty-nine-year-old actor a cover story called, "Close Encounters with a Rising Star." "I always knew that I could be a star for this whole audience that didn't relate to John Wayne or Al Pacino," Dreyfuss said. "An urban, progressive, intellectually oriented audience, not too macho, people who read, people who listen to Paul Simon and Randy Newman. People like me."

Rock Cheapie

John Travolta's audience was younger than Dreyfuss'. "If I don't want to be considered a teen idol the rest of my life," he declared, "then it's my responsibility to give the serious film audience a product that's quality." Still, producer Robert Stigwood was thinking of all those teenage girls who bought *16* and *Tiger Beat* magazines just to look at the pictures of the twenty-three-year-old actor who starred as Vinnie Barbarino, the leader of the "Sweathogs" in the hit TV series *Welcome Back, Kotter,* when he signed Travolta to a million-dollar contract to make three movies. For the first movie, Travolta attempted to satisfy both audiences with a sociological musical based on a *New York* magazine article entitled "Tribal Rites of the New Saturday Night," about working-class youths in Brooklyn who spent their weekends dancing at the 2001 disco. Travolta trained three months for the acrobatic dancing scenes and, to ensure a dashing image, sewed his shirt into his pants so that his shirttails would not come flying out as he swaggered across 2001's illuminated dance floor. Previewing Paramount's Christmas release, titled *Saturday Night Fever, Variety* wrote it off as "nothing more than an updated '70s version of the Sam Katzman rock cheapies of the '50s."

The "cheapie" netted Paramount $74 million from the United States alone, and the film's sound track—which produced three number-one singles for the Bee Gees and two other top ten hits—became the biggest-selling movie sound track of all time. But that was just the beginning of *Saturday Night Fever*'s impact: discos suddenly began springing up in shopping malls and dance teachers across the country added "disco dancing" to their curricula. Steve Rubell, the owner of New York's Studio 54, tried to be above it all, insisting, "The dancing style in that movie is already passé in my club," but, by January, Studio's DJ's were spinning the Bee Gees' singles by popular demand. The 2001 disco itself became as picky as Studio 54 about its clientele, turning away hundreds who showed up to dance on the now-famous dance floor. Macy's got in on the craze by advertising facsimiles of Travolta's white suit with models imitating the actor's defiant pose and TV commercial parodies promoted everything from radio stations to stereo systems.

Travolta Fever

But the biggest promotion centered on John Travolta himself. From the film's opening scene, as the camera closed in on his shoes as he walked down a Brooklyn street to the strains of the Bee Gees' "Stayin' Alive," Travolta had reviewers rav-

"Acting is not my language at all."
—Mikhail Baryshnikov

ing like his *Tiger Beat* fans. "He's riveting, with a sexy message aimed directly at women that is not easily forgotten," responded Rona Barrett; "The man can boogie," observed *Newsweek*'s David Ansen; and Los Angeles TV critic David Sheehan stated,"Travolta has got to be the most exciting new screen presence to come along since Brando, Dean and Newman." *Time* featured him in a cover story entitled "Travolta Fever" and remarked, "Not even Sweathog freaks will be prepared for the new Travolta. His presence is electric, his dancing spectacular. In *Fever,* Travolta makes a rare leap for a stereotyped TV actor and lands as a real movie star."

But the magazine pointed out that Travolta's life was not a bed of roses; two weeks into filming, his lover, actress Diana Hyland, died of cancer. "The pain was on every inch of his body," recalled director John Badham. "Some of the best scenes in the picture were done in that advanced stage of grief." When the *New York Times* asked the heartthrob how it felt to be an overnight sensation, Travolta replied, "I love being regarded as a sex symbol, but I can't take it too seriously."

Retired Violinists

The film and record industries were both shocked when the Academy announced the preliminary selections in the technical categories. None of the top-ten hits from *Saturday Night Fever* were mentioned for Best Song, nor was the bestselling score itself among the semifinalists in the Song Score/Adaptation category.

Remembering that an appeal had worked for "Theme from *Mahogany,*" *Fever* producer Stigwood argued that "music critics and audiences have responded to the fresh sounds of the Bee Gees' compositions in unprecedented numbers" and asked for a revote. Howard W. Koch, in his first term as Academy president, said, "I feel badly. I hate this kind of controversy. But what are you going to do? The people voted. It's a democratic system." There was no revote, and an official of Stigwood's company complained to *People* that the Music Branch was made up of "retired violinists who probably still play 78s on their Victrolas."

Meanwhile, probable Supporting Actress nominee Vanessa Redgrave was having more than her share of troubles. One of the political activist's main concerns at this time was establishing a homeland for the Palestinian people, and to this end she had produced a propaganda film, *The Palestinians.* This, plus the fact that she had been seen in public with PLO leader Yasir Arafat, got the Jewish Defense League on her case. In late January, the JDL informed 20th Century–Fox that it would be picketing theaters showing *Julia* unless the studio vowed never to hire Redgrave again and to issue a statement denouncing her political activities. When Fox said nothing doing, the JDL reacted by letting white mice loose in theaters showing the picture. The rodents failed to stem attendance, so the JDL began threatening the Academy that they'd picket the Oscar show if Redgrave were nominated. "She transcends art by her politics," argued the Jewish newspaper *The Herald.* "Any Jewish person who goes to see that picture ought to have his head examined. You might just as well see Hitler's girlfriend and encourage her."

The Nominations

For all the anti-California sentiment in *Annie Hall,* the Academy still went ahead and welcomed Woody Allen into the record books—he was the first person to be nominated for Best Actor, Best Director and Best Screenplay since Orson Welles in 1941. His leading lady was also nominated for Best Actress—for *Annie Hall,* not *Mr. Goodbar.* The other hero to emerge from the nominations was Alan Ladd, Jr., the president of Fox, which garnered thirty-three nominations. Twenty-two of those nominations belonged to *Julia* and *The Turning Point,* which earned eleven each. *Julia* had four nominated performers—Jane Fonda, Maximilian Schell, Jason Robards and Vanessa Redgrave—and *The Turning Point* also had a quartet—Anne Bancroft, Shirley MacLaine, Mikhail Baryshni-

"Then Grace showed the script to Prince Rainier and he told her he didn't want her to go back to work."
—Herbert Ross

kov and Leslie Browne. Despite this vote of approval from the Actors' Branch, Baryshnikov said he'd be busy dancing on Oscar night. Because the Best Actress race had no front-runner, all the nominees planned to attend the show, with the exception of Anne Bancroft.

Leslie Browne's godfather, Herbert Ross, succeeded in having both of his 1977 movies nominated for Best Picture—*The Goodbye Girl* and *The Turning Point*. But Academy rules precluded Ross from competing against himself for Best Director and he was nominated for *The Turning Point*.

Closed Accounts

George Lucas and Steven Spielberg would be battling it out in the Best Director race, but Spielberg would just be watching from the sidelines for Best Picture—*Close Encounters* didn't make the top five, leading the *Christian Science Monitor* to ask, "What happened to *Close Encounters of the Third Kind*? Its blood brother, *Star Wars*, is lots of fun, but the picture that represents a whole year should have more heft—which is exactly what *Close Encounters* has to offer." The paper speculated that the Academy wasn't punishing Spielberg as much as it was Columbia Pictures, which had become embroiled in scandal when 1968 Best Actor winner Cliff Robertson discovered that company president David Begelman had forged his name on a few checks.

Best Actor nominee John Travolta was worried that his television background might hurt his chances, saying, "I hope aversions like that don't still influence the voting, because I really did try to go beyond Vinnie in *Saturday Night Fever*." *People* picked up on *Equus* nominee Richard Burton's "touching desire to win. He's been tirelessly making the talk-show circuit, apologizing profusely for his past overindulgence in good whiskey and bad movies." Meanwhile, Richard Dreyfuss tooted his own horn in the *New York Times:* "I was wonderful in *The Goodbye Girl*."

The Jewish Defense League R.S.V.P.'d Vanessa Redgrave's Supporting Actress nomination, pledging to be there demonstrating on the big night. The JDL whiled away the hours until showtime by calling in bomb threats to theaters exhibiting *The Palestinians*. *Julia*'s producer, Richard Roth, was getting fed up. "The Oscars are for merit as a performer and shouldn't have anything to do with politics," he argued. "I'm a Zionist, but I respect her right to have her views." The JDL then started picketing Roth's home, forcing him to move into the Beverly Hills Hotel for the duration.

Fifty Years Young

Since this was the fiftieth anniversary of the Academy Awards, the show's producer, Howard W. Koch, and "Executive Talent Consultant" Allan Carr claimed they would outdo all of the previous forty-nine ceremonies. "There will be an extended opening sequence of arrival," Koch told the press. "We will attempt to bring back the old Hollywood." They also wanted to use as many previous Oscar winners as they could and managed to corral nearly four dozen of them. Carr admitted to the *Los Angeles Herald-Examiner* that he had to promise presenters Joan Fontaine and Olivia de Havilland that their appearances would be spread far apart. "The feud that's been talked about for years really exists. They hate one another."

Carr couldn't persuade Elizabeth Taylor to appear because "she doesn't want to infringe on what should be Richard's big night." The *Herald-Examiner* revealed that Farrah Fawcett-Majors, one of *Charlie's Angels,* had become a genuine prima donna after agreeing to present an Award: "It took some doing to get a leading man whom Farrah Fawcett's advisors considered of great enough stature to serve as her Oscar copresenter. Their first suggestion was Laurence Olivier, then Cary Grant. And when neither of those gentlemen were willing, Farrah finally settled on sharing the stage with Marcello Mastroianni." The Italian actor wasn't coming to Los Angeles simply to escort Farrah to the podium; he was a Best Actor nominee for playing opposite Sophia Loren in the art-house hit *A Special Day*.

When Woody Allen won the Directors Guild Award, everyone wanted to know if the inveterate New Yorker would visit Hollywood to claim an Oscar. Allen, who had refused to allow his name to appear in UA's Oscar ads for *Annie Hall*, said he'd be at his usual place on Monday night—playing clarinet with the New Orleans Marching and Funeral Band at Michael's Pub on Manhattan's East Side. "I couldn't let down the guys," the Monday-night musician insisted. United Artists went ahead and ran *Annie Hall* on Los Angeles' Z Channel—it was the only Best Picture nominee to be broadcast—so Hollywoodites could listen to Allen make fun of them in their own homes.

The Big Night

Diane Keaton arrived wearing the "Annie Hall" look at its most extreme—high heels, rolled-up stockings, slacks, skirt, oversized sweater, jacket and scarf. Her escort was her sister. Jane Fonda, her hair red for her role in *The China Syndrome,* was in a pink sequined evening dress while her husband, Tom Hayden, wore a business suit. Hayden also economized on a baby-sitter—Fonda's two children came along. Best Actress nominee Marsha Mason was escorted by her husband, Neil Simon, a nominee for Best Original Screenplay. Richard Dreyfuss came with his current girlfriend and Richard Burton escorted his third wife, who wore gold lamé.

About seventy-five members of the Jewish Defense League shouted and waved anti-Redgrave signs while nearby some two hundred PLO members and sympathizers demonstrated in support of the nominee. Neither group saw Vanessa, who was deposited at the stage door by an ambulance. Redgrave's bodyguards were just about the only black people attending the show, a point made by another group of protestors, Blacks in Media Broadcasting Organization ("BIMBO"). A representative told *Daily Variety* that the Academy Awards show "adds to racism, segregation and a totally negative image of blacks" while honoring white "glory, success and superiority."

The telecast began with a montage of past winners receiving their Awards. There was footage of various freeways in Los Angeles, followed by shots of arriving celebrities. Debbie Reynolds danced out in a sequined tuxedo and sang "Look How Far We've Come." Then groups of past Oscar winners—including Ernest Borgnine, Louise Fletcher, Burl Ives and Dorothy Malone—walked out onstage without an introduction. Their names flashed on and off before anyone had a chance to read them and the army of winners milled about onstage as Academy President Howard W. Koch greeted the audience with "Being onstage with these Oscar winners, I'm really shook up." The winners continued standing aimlessly as former

Awards Ceremony

MARCH 29, 1978, 7:00 P.M.
THE DOROTHY CHANDLER PAVILION, LOS ANGELES

Your Host:
BOB HOPE
Televised over ABC

Presenters

Supporting Actress	John Travolta
Special Achievement Awards	Mark Hamill, R2D2 and C-3PO
Animated Short Film	Mickey Mouse, Jodie Foster and Paul Williams
Live Action Short Film	Jodie Foster and Paul Williams
Sound	William Holden and Barbara Stanwyck
Visual Effects	Joan Fontaine
Documentary Awards	Kirk Douglas and Raquel Welch
Scientific or Technical Awards	Billy Dee Williams
Art Direction	Greer Garson and Henry Winkler
Foreign Film	Eva Marie Saint and Jack Valenti
Supporting Actor	Michael Caine and Maggie Smith
Costume Design	Natalie Wood
Scoring Awards	John Green, Henry Mancini and Olivia Newton-John
Cinematography	Goldie Hawn and Jon Voight
Jean Hersholt Humanitarian Award	Bette Davis
Honorary Award to Margaret Booth	Olivia de Havilland
Film Editing	Farrah Fawcett-Majors and Marcello Mastroianni
Song	Fred Astaire
Thalberg Award	Stanley Kramer
Director	Cicely Tyson and King Vidor
Writing Awards	Paddy Chayefsky
Actress	Janet Gaynor and Walter Matthau
Actor	Sylvester Stallone
Picture	Jack Nicholson

Performers of Nominated Songs

"Candle on the Water"	Gloria Loring
"Nobody Does It Better"	Aretha Franklin
"The Slipper and the Rose Waltz"	Jane Powell
"Someone's Waiting for You"	Gloria Loring
"You Light Up My Life"	Debby Boone

Academy Presidents Bette Davis and Gregory Peck explained the voting procedures. The winners were still there when the camera cut to TV director Marty Pasetta in the control truck and Nelson Riddle in the orchestra pit. Finally, the cavalcade of winners received an offstage signal to exit and they marched off silently, never to be seen or heard from for the rest of the show. The *Hollywood Reporter* wrote, "High hopes for an extraordinary, solid-gold evening reflecting years of film excellence were dashed within the first few minutes."

The orchestra played "Thanks for the Memory" and out came Bob Hope, making his first Oscar appearance since the flap over *Hearts and Minds* three years earlier. The seventy-four-year-old comedian referred to the departing former winners as "the road company of the Hollywood Wax Museum" and then launched into his monologue:

> *They all have their Oscars—but are they happy? . . . I'm the only one that had to show my American Express card to get onstage . . . Liz Taylor's back on her farm in Virginia—still trying to milk a chicken [a shot of Richard Burton laughing] . . . And I just want to say, what a night—the furs, the jewels, the glamour. Looks like the opening of the Beverly Hills Taco Bell . . . I haven't seen so much expensive jewelry go by since I watched Sammy Davis, Jr.'s house sliding down Coldwater Canyon . . .*

John Travolta, with a white silk scarf flapping around his neck, came out to present the Best Supporting Actress Award. The winner was Vanessa Redgrave for *Julia*. Redgrave wore a simple black dress with a cloak, and glowed as she addressed the audience:

> *My dear colleagues, I thank you very much for this tribute to my work. I think that Jane Fonda and I have done the best work of our lives and I think this is in part due to our director, Fred Zinnemann [a cascade of applause].*
>
> *And I also think it's in part because we believed and we believe in what we were expressing—two out of millions who gave their lives and were prepared to sacrifice everything in the fight against fascist and racist Nazi Germany.*
>
> *And I salute you and I pay tribute to you and I think you should be very proud that in the last few weeks you've stood firm and you have refused to be intimidated by the threats of a small bunch of Zionist hoodlums [gasps followed by boos and a smattering of applause] whose behavior is an insult to the stature of Jews all over the world and their great and heroic record of struggle against fascism and oppression.*
>
> *And I salute that record and I salute all of you for having stood firm and dealt a final blow against that period when Nixon and McCarthy launched a worldwide witch-hunt against those who tried to express in their lives and their work the truth that they believed in [small sprinkling of boos and hisses]. I salute you and I thank you and I pledge to you [swelling of applause] that I will continue to fight against anti-Semitism and fascism.*

Redgrave and Travolta embraced and walked offstage together to rousing applause. Outside, protesters burned an effigy of the actress marked "Vanessa Is a Murderer."

After Redgrave's dramatic oratory, frivolity prevailed. *Star Wars'* R2D2, wearing a black bow tie, and C-3PO gave two Special Achievement Awards, including one for the fellow who had made the robot noises for *Star Wars*. On their way out, the robots passed Mickey Mouse as he came onstage to give the Animated Short Award with Jodie Foster and Paul Williams. It was also Mickey's fiftieth birthday and when the orchestra played the theme from *The Mickey Mouse Club*, the audience spontaneously clapped along. "Happy Birthday, Mickey," added Jodie. "You look good for fifty." And Williams joined in, "You

"You should be very proud that you've stood firm and have refused to be intimidated by the threats of a small bunch of Zionist hoodlums."
—Vanessa Redgrave

look great. Know what we're gonna get you for your birthday? . . . Two more fingers."

Debby Boone was present to sing the nominated song "You Light Up My Life," the bestselling record of the decade. Boone, who told reporters she dedicated the ballad to God every time she sang it, was joined on this rendition by "eleven young ladies affiliated with the John Tracy Clinic for the Deaf," who interpreted the lyrics through sign language. (Newspapers revealed later that these little girls were actually students from Torrance, California, and their signing mere mumbo-jumbo.) As Debby sang there was a shot of her father, Pat Boone, smiling in the audience. Backstage, Bob Hope said to no one in particular, "That Debby Boone sure is something."

Barbara Stanwyck and William Holden were on hand to give the Sound Award. When they got to the podium, Holden announced, "Before Barbara and I present this next Award, I'd like to say something." He told the audience that "thirty-nine years ago this month, we were working in a film together called *Golden Boy*. It wasn't going well, and I was going to be replaced . . . But due to this lovely human being and her interest and understanding and her professional integrity and encouragement and, above all, her generosity, I'm here tonight." Stanwyck was so shaken she could only sigh, "Oh, Bill," and the two friends embraced.

The first de Havilland sister out onstage was Joan Fontaine, who presented the Visual Effects Awards to *Star Wars*. Then Jane Powell's rendition of "The Slipper and the Rose Waltz" was interrupted by a sudden loud noise—a satin drop had fallen on a dancer who gamely continued through his paces despite being fully enveloped by the material. At the end of the number, Hope quipped, "For a minute there, I thought my girdle snapped."

The Supporting Actor Award was given by Maggie Smith and Michael Caine, who were currently filming roles as an Oscar nominee and her husband in *California Suite*. In the pursuit of realism, director Herbert Ross had, earlier in the evening, filmed the pair entering the Dorothy Chandler. Peter Firth was the only nominee present, but, for the second year, the winner was Jason Robards. The *Julia* costar was appearing on Broadway in O'Neill's *A Touch of the Poet* but Hope said, "I think he's playing bridge with Marlon Brando and George C. Scott." Robards was surprised about the crack. "See, they send you a thing in the mail: will you attend or will you not," he told the *New York Post*. "I sent it back weeks ago, saying sorry, I can't be there. They might not have told Michael and Maggie, but certainly Bob Hope knew it." He added under his breath, "Tasteless shit, anyway."

Bette Davis presented the Jean Hersholt Humanitarian Award to Charlton Heston. After stating emphatically that "Chuck wants no part of politics," Davis went down a list of the actor's charitable endeavors, concluding that he is a "man of conscience and, to boot, a darn good tennis player."

Marvin Hamlisch was joined by a subdued—only one ring, a bracelet and a lapel pin—Sammy Davis, Jr., who sang "Come Light the Candles," in which movie stars who had died during the past year were likened to the absent guests of a birthday party. While Sammy crooned, pictures of Peter Finch, Bing Crosby, Zero Mostel, Elvis Presley, Groucho Marx, Charlie Chaplin and Joan Crawford were flashed above him. When Sammy was finished, Best Actress nominee Shirley MacLaine yelled, "Bravo!"

Joan Fontaine must have been safely out of the way because Olivia de Havilland came out to give an Honorary Award to Margaret Booth, for thirty years the supervising film editor at MGM. De Havilland noted that Booth has "run a lot of celluloid through her Moviola." Marcello Mastroianni entered with Farrah Fawcett-Majors to hand out Best Film Editing. The Oscar went to *Star Wars* and Mrs. George Lucas was one of the recipients. Then Aretha Franklin sang "Nobody Does It Better" from a James Bond movie while some dancers fiddled around with hula hoops.

The Academy's custom of dusting off an

"I am that Zionist hoodlum she was talking about. It's just a pity I wasn't on the platform tonight. I would have gone for the jugular."
—Alan King

Award for its former presidents continued—Stanley Kramer gave the Thalberg Award to Walter Mirisch, who had held office from 1973 to 1977, and had kicked off his producing career with such films as *Bomba the Jungle Boy* and *Flight to Mars*. The Best Director Award was given by veteran director King Vidor and actress Cicely Tyson. When Steven Spielberg's nomination was read, he mouthed into the camera, "I love you, Amy," a Valentine to girlfriend Amy Irving. All of the nominees except one were present, and the winner was the absent Woody Allen for *Annie Hall*. No one stepped out to accept the statuette, so Tyson and Vidor congratulated Allen and then walked away.

Paddy Chayefsky was next. "Before I get on to the writing Awards," he began, "there's a little matter I'd like to tidy up . . . at least if I expect to live with myself tomorrow morning." He continued: "I would like to say, personal opinion, of course, that I'm sick and tired of people exploiting the Academy Awards [loud applause and bravos] for the propagation of their own personal propaganda. [more applause] I would like to suggest to Miss Redgrave that her winning an Academy Award is not a pivotal moment in history, does not require a proclamation and a simple 'Thank you' would have sufficed."

His own proclamation finished, Chayefsky said, "And now on to much more important matters," whereupon he started to tear open an envelope, stopping when the screams of the audience alerted him he hadn't read the nominees for Original Screenplay. *Annie Hall* won again; Woody Allen's cowriter, Marshall Brickman, had made the trip from New York. "I still have guilt when I make a right turn on a red light," he joked. When *Julia*'s Alvin Sargent accepted his Adapted Screenplay Oscar, he praised the real-life "Julia" and "all the things she stands for," adding, "I like to think this Oscar represents those things, and the free expression of all our good thoughts and feelings, no matter who we are or what we have to say."

Walter Matthau and Janet Gaynor, the first Best Actress winner, were called upon to settle the toss-up race of Best Actress. The winner was Diane Keaton for *Annie Hall*. Keaton giggled her way through her acceptance, "It's simply terrific . . . This is something . . ." After praising her fellow nominees, the winner laughingly concluded, "I just would like to say thanks to Woody and thank you, thank you very much."

Last year's Best Actress, Faye Dunaway, had been in a car wreck shortly before the show and so Sylvester Stallone took her place to present Best Actor. The orchestra heralded him with "Gonna Fly Now." "Catchy tune," he remarked. After reading the nominees, Stallone announced, "The new heavyweight champ is . . . Richard Dreyfuss." One observer swore that Richard Burton jumped out of his seat, but it was Dreyfuss who was punching the air as he bounded onto the stage. The stubble-chinned winner announced, "I didn't prepare anything." He paused and said, "Wait a minute . . . am I here?" and laughed, "I don't wanna leave." There was a shot of his girlfriend crying as he walked off.

Jack Nicholson showed up to award Best Picture. He made it official; for the first time since *Tom Jones* won in 1963, the Academy gave its top prize to a comedy—*Annie Hall* won its fourth Award of the night. All that remained was for Bob Hope to tie things up. He addressed John Wayne, who had undergone open-heart surgery earlier in the day. "Duke," he said, "we miss you tonight. We expect to see you amble out here in person next year, because nobody else can walk in John Wayne's boots." Hope also said, "The essence of our arts and sciences are dreams and hopes and faith in the future. That's why a half century is only the beginning." He concluded, "Just want you to know, if the Academy wants me back here in another half century, I'm available."

Aftermath

Backstage, Vanessa Redgrave told the press that Jewish extremist groups "do not represent the Jewish people and their behavior is an insult to

"I haven't seen so much expensive jewelry go by since I watched Sammy Davis, Jr.'s house sliding down Coldwater Canyon."
—Bob Hope

Jewish people all over the world." She also said, "Of course, I'm on the side of the Jews who have struggled in a most glorious struggle against fascism." When a reporter questioned the propriety of making a political statement on the Academy Awards, she responded that hers was not a political speech at all.

Asked his opinion of Redgrave's remarks, Jack Nicholson put on a blank face and said, "I guess it's fine. But I'm not a well-read person, you can see that. What are these Zionists? Are they reds? There've been threats? I've been skiing." Nicholson was the only person in town without an opinion. Comedian Alan King screamed, "I am that Zionist hoodlum she was talking about. It's just a pity I wasn't on the platform tonight. I would have gone for the jugular." Lester Persky, producer of Redgrave's upcoming movie *Yanks,* said, "I thought about firing her when I heard what she said. But that would have been suppression of free speech. Tomorrow I am telling her, 'Cut out the politics and learn your lines.'" Aaron Spelling, producer of *Charlie's Angels* and *The Love Boat,* moaned, "After Miss Redgrave's stupid remarks, had I been at home I would have turned off the set. But since I was in the audience all I could do was close my eyes a lot." As for Paddy Chayefsky, he was proud of the fact that "she tried to speak to me afterward and I cut her dead." Chayefsky later confessed producer Daniel Melnick had gotten hold of him in the men's room and convinced him to speak out.

Lynn Redgrave had been at an Oscar-watching party, and when Paddy Chayefsky started to criticize her sister, she gulped and said, "Oh, oh, trouble." Defending Vanessa were Karen Black and her husband, Kit Carson: "She's a very brave lady, and we mean that in a positive way." Actress Joan Hackett said, "I like her and one has to do what one has to do." And although he found some of her words ill-chosen, Moshe Mizrahi, the Israeli director of Foreign Film winner *Madame Rosa,* volunteered that "basically, she's right."

Los Angeles Herald-Examiner columnist Denis Hamill opined: "Paddy Chayefsky is a hypocrite when he stood up to criticize Vanessa Redgrave for using her speaking time after winning the Oscar for Best Supporting Actress to make a political statement. Anyone who castigates another person for exercising her right to free speech is making a political statement. Maybe you agree with him. But get it straight. He was pontificating. He was didactic. He was politicking."

Some people had gotten so worked up over Vanessa Redgrave they scarcely noticed the elaborate menu at the Governors' Ball in honor of the Awards' fiftieth anniversary: caviar, salmon and crab appetizer, lobster tail, "anniversary cake" and, to drink, Pouilly Fuissé, Moët et Chandon champagne, and Stolichnaya vodka. Academy President Howard W. Koch turned out to be an old softie, admitting, "I felt sorry for Vanessa because at the party afterwards she was sitting all alone with just her two bodyguards. No one else would sit with her and here it was her big night." Paddy Chayefsky perceived things differently. Seeing Vanessa make the rounds from table to table at the ball, chatting with other guests and kissing friends, Paddy steamed, "This is disgusting. Vanessa thinks she can get away with anything. How can she have the nerve to come here?"

Two of the actresses who lost to Vanessa had troubles of their own. While she was at the ceremony, Leslie Browne's room at the Beverly Hills Hotel was broken into; she lost a watch and a fur coat that was a gift from her godparents. Ten-year-old Quinn Cummings of *The Goodbye Girl* dropped a pierced earring in the ladies' room at the Beverly Hilton. Lauren Hutton, Mackenzie Phillips and disco singer Gloria Gaynor joined Quinn on their hands and knees and found the missing piece of jewelry in time to get back to the ball, where everyone was asked to light a match and sing "Happy Birthday" to Oscar. Immediately after the ball, Best Actor Richard Dreyfuss hopped into a chartered jet that whisked him back to New York, where, the next night, he had to appear in *Julius Ceasar* at the Public Theater. Best

"In my humble opinion, Close Encounters of the Third Kind will be a colossal flop."
—New York magazine

Actress loser Marsha Mason also left town—she was off to India to meditate with Swami Muktanada.

Because of the furor over Vanessa Redgrave, Hollywood overlooked the snub it got from Woody Allen. He left Michael's Pub at midnight and went straight home to bed without bothering to find out how *Annie Hall* was doing. The next day, after learning the Academy had chosen his film as the year's best, he still made no statement. A year later, Woody finally had something to say on the subject. "I know it sounds horrible," he admitted, "but winning that Oscar for *Annie Hall* didn't mean anything to me. I have no regard for that kind of ceremony. I just don't think they know what they're doing. When you see who wins those things—or doesn't win them—you can see how meaningless this Oscar thing is."

That wasn't how he felt fourteen years earlier. In 1964, the young comedian mused to the *Decatur* (Ill.) *Herald*, "I've done a lot of TV shows like the *Tonight Show, Hootenanny, Candid Camera* and the like. But I still haven't done the really big shows. I'd like ten minutes on a major show like Judy Garland's. Maybe if she doesn't want me I can be the host on the Academy Awards."

1978

"Warren, just think what you could have accomplished if you tried celibacy."
—Shirley MacLaine

Allan Carr fiddled while Jane Fonda burned at the 1978 Academy Awards.

By 1978, Jane Fonda was fully in business as a professional movie star—she had her own production company, a partnership with a fellow radical named Bruce Gilbert. Their first project was about the Vietnam War, but it took five years to get it off the ground. Fonda had commissioned a screenplay from Nancy Dowd in 1973, and the writer portrayed the consciousness-raising of two women involved with fighting men in a script called *Buffalo Ghost*. Fonda decided she needed a love story and turned the screenplay over to Waldo Salt, much to Dowd's chagrin. "The original was the best writing I've ever done," she protested, adding that the changes weren't too hot. "I'm ashamed. It is a male supremacist film; men choose between ideas and women choose between men."

Fonda chose Briton John Schlesinger to direct, but, as the shooting date approached, he felt less and less at home with the American-ness of the subject and dropped out. Hal Ashby enlisted, and offered the romantic lead, a disillusioned paraplegic, to Jack Nicholson, but he was busy. Fonda tried to interest Al Pacino, then Sylvester Stallone, but had no luck. Fonda's producer, Jerome Hellman, who made *Midnight Cowboy,* said that Fonda's choice for the second lead, Jon Voight, really wanted to play the part of the wheelchair veteran. When Fonda presented this idea to United Artists executive Mike Medavoy, he pleaded, "We'll pay you another million dollars to get a star." Fonda passed up the offer and hired Voight as her leading man, praising his devotion to his craft. "Voight's been living in a wheelchair for two months. When a foot falls off it, he reaches down with his hands to put it back up again." Bruce Dern stepped in as the jilted husband, but confessed to reporters, "I've been so many tortured vets. I would love to have played the Jon Voight role but no one asked me."

Overleaf: *Best Actress winner Jane Fonda is embraced by presenter Shirley MacLaine, who appears to be having second thoughts about those Warren Beatty wisecracks.*

Just before filming began, Waldo Salt fell ill, so Ashby asked his favorite film editor, Robert C. Jones, to do rewrites on the set. By the time filming was finished, there had been so many revisions to Nancy Dowd's original script that the Screen Writers Guild had to decide what the screen credits would be. The guild ruled that Dowd deserved "story" credit while Salt and Jones could keep "screenplay" credit. Dowd still went around disowning the movie, now called *Coming Home,* and *Ms.* magazine agreed with her analysis of the final script: "It's message seemed to be that doves are better than hawks in bed, and it was pious as well as sentimental."

Charles Champlin had nicer things to say in the *Los Angeles Times* when *Coming Home* opened in February: "Despite an overexplicit songtrack and some moments when the story in fact became a sermon, the movie effectively translated a changed national consciousness into credible and touching personal terms." The *Toronto Sun* called the film "*The Best Years of Our Lives* circa '78, with the same high standards and the same lofty morals of an earlier era." Mike Medavoy apologized when he saw Jon Voight's performance, while Liz Smith wrote that "Fonda has never been more beautiful. She epitomizes the glamorous movie star from beginning to end, as she changes from frigid tailor-made officer's wife to a jeans and T-shirted curly-top with a frizz of newfound freedom and sensuality."

The New Freedom

Writer-director Paul Mazursky was also exploring what he called "the new freedom that has come with the women's movement." He called his movie *An Unmarried Woman,* but told the *New York Times,* "What it is really all about is that it's

"I plan to wear the same James Riva dress I wore to the Awards last year."
—Jane Fonda

okay not to be married." Mazursky's heroine, a well-heeled Manhattan housewife, was played by thirty-three-year-old Jill Clayburgh, who had been hanging around Hollywood since 1973, playing wisecracking blondes. "Erica is the role this gifted actress has deserved for years and now that she has it, she doesn't fool around," said *Time,* and Andrew Sarris predicted, "She will be hard to beat as actress of the year." Clayburgh claimed her first Best Actress honor in May at the Cannes Film Festival, where the competition included Jane Fonda in *Coming Home.* Clayburgh said she wanted her newfound acclaim to lead "to more and more important parts in films. When I first moved to Hollywood, I didn't know if I'd ever have another part. I don't want to feel that way again."

Here Comes Mr. Beatty

By the summer, audiences weren't interested in the new freedom or Vietnam, and the box-office hits were *Grease* with John Travolta, *Foul Play* with Goldie Hawn and Chevy Chase, and *National Lampoon's Animal House* with John Belushi. Joining in on the lightweight fare was Warren Beatty, who said, "I kept returning to the idea of a romantic fantasy because that's what I wanted to see. Maybe I was even a little depressed because a couple of my friends had died." Beatty elected to modernize the 1941 comedy *Here Comes Mr. Jordan* because "it dealt with death and reincarnation. That made me want to see it particularly."

Beatty called his new version *Heaven Can Wait* and called on his friends to help out. Elaine May worked with him on the screenplay and Julie Christie agreed to be his leading lady after Kate Jackson turned him down. Beatty couldn't persuade Cary Grant to be an angel, so he settled for James Mason. And Dyan Cannon was signed to play the comic villainess. Buck Henry doubled as an actor—he played another angel—and as Beatty's codirector. "I was not upset by having two directors, but it was different," said James Mason. "When Warren was in front of the camera, he decided it would be a nice idea to have somebody with whom he was on good terms behind it; he didn't have to bother with keeping an eye on the other actors."

Paramount kept its publicity campaign firmly on Beatty, and, in March, bought full-page ads in both the *New York* and *Los Angeles Times* depicting him standing on a cloud in a sweat suit with angel wings. There was no film title mentioned, just an offer from Paramount giving away free posters. "The only thing we sell in the movie business is magic," explained Paramount's Gordon Weaver. "We took this poster and thought it was magic because looking at it makes you feel good, so we decided to give it away to people." They gave away over 100,000 posters. The Beatty collectors also bought *Time* when Warren smiled off the cover with the headline "Mister Hollywood." Critic Frank Rich wrote the fan letter inside:

> *He is a millionaire many times over but lives in two small, slovenly kept hotel rooms. He travels with the fastest crowd in the country but rarely drinks and never snorts or smokes. He is offered the best jobs in the profession but turns most of them down. His idea of sin is to eat ice cream. His idea of a great time is to talk on the phone. His idea of heaven is to spend hours debating the pros and cons of Proposition 13. He wears dirty jeans three days in a row, chews vitamin pills and remembers everything. He makes coast-to-coast plane reservations for six consecutive flights, then misses all of them. Almost the only appurtenance consonant with his celebrity is an address book Don Juan would envy.*

Of the movie itself, Stephen Farber wrote, "One of the most appealing genres of the '40s was the supernatural comedy and Warren Beatty's new movie, *Heaven Can Wait,* revives that lost art. Beatty has challenged himself throughout his career; now he deserves credit for bringing fantasy

"When I first moved to Hollywood, I didn't know if I'd ever have another part. I don't want to feel that way again."
—Jill Clayburgh

back to the screen." He also brought in over $50 million at U.S. box offices.

Chekhov on Long Island

When Woody Allen challenged himself with *Interiors*, a drama about a WASP household rocked by divorce, *The New Yorker*'s Penelope Gilliatt wrote, "The theme its characters express is very Chekhovian. It is pinned to the idea that the simplest, hardest, and most admirable thing to do is to act properly through a whole life." Geraldine Page played the wife who falls apart when her husband abandons her for Maureen Stapleton, portraying a Jewish woman who wears red. Liz Smith said, "If you have always wanted to see a Bergman movie undubbed and performed in English, *Interiors* seems to be that film (one wouldn't want to call it a mere 'movie')." Woody denied aping Ingmar, although he did tell a British TV talk show host, "It's a film about women, which has been a very big theme of his."

So Long, Ingrid

Allen had competition from the real thing that fall when Ingmar Bergman unveiled *Autumn Sonata*, about the stormy relationship between a mother and daughter. "It goes without saying that I look forward to turning the camera on two such women as Ingrid Bergman and Liv Ullmann," the director said when he announced the casting, but Ingrid, who had been trying to get together to make a film with Ingmar for thirteen years, had reservations when she finally got a screenplay from him. "Look, this script is terribly depressing," she said to him. "In life, I have three daughters and we do have our little discussions from time to time—but this! Can't we have a little joke here and there?" "No jokes," Ingmar insisted. "We're not doing your story." Still, Ingrid told interviewers, "There's a lot of me in *Autumn Sonata*. I was terribly nervous when my daughter said she was going to see the film."

Bergman relaxed when she read the reviews. Roger Ebert paeanized, "Now working with one of the supreme film directors, Ingrid Bergman is able to use not only her star qualities but also every last measure of her artistry and her humanity." When the consensus on the film's success was in, the sixty-five-year-old Bergman announced that she was leaving movies forever. "My first film in America was *Intermezzo* and I played a concert pianist. Now I'm playing a concert pianist in *Autumn Sonata*. My career has come full circle."

St. Holly

Gary Busey's film career was just getting started. The actor had already gained rock 'n' roll fame as a drummer with the pseudonym Teddy Jack Eddy when he won the title role in *The Buddy Holly Story*. Although his musical experience touring with Leon Russell and Kris Kristofferson was an asset, Busey claimed he won the role of the late singer because "they finally realized I have the same-sized teeth." Vincent Canby said the actor had more than that: "Mr. Busey's performance is tremendous, full of drive, eccentric life and the sort of idiosyncrasy that creates a screen personality that the public will remember. *The Buddy Holly Story* should be Mr. Busey's breakthrough movie." Busey said there were two critics in particular that he wanted to impress: "I'm glad Mr. and Mrs. Holly got to see this movie and see their son portrayed in an innocent way."

Got to Go Disco

While Gary Busey was singing "Peggy Sue," composer Giorgio Moroder was bringing a disco beat to movie sound tracks. Moroder had a dance-club hit with his chase music from *Midnight Express*, a thriller directed by Britain's Alan Parker, a celebrated creator of TV commercials. *Midnight Express*, based on a book by a young American imprisoned in Turkey for possession of hashish, allowed Parker to depict horrifying scenes of violence. Those scenes led the Turkish embassy to complain, "The film does not recount 'brutal ex-

"It's okay not to be married."
—Paul Mazursky

perience based on fact' but rather based on misinterpretation and outright fabrications of the hashish smuggler." Producer Peter Guber couldn't understand why the Turks were so upset. "A film like this offers an experience," the producer exclaimed. "It's like a roller-coaster ride—scary when you're on it, but it comes out okay at the end."

"It is impossible to imagine a more exciting movie," Rona Barrett said, predicting that *Midnight Express* "stands a good chance of rivaling the cult status of *Cuckoo's Nest* because in its way it again deals with the fundamental battle of men against mindless authority." The *Los Angeles Herald-Examiner* gave a lot of the credit to Giorgio Moroder: "Not since the terrifying sound track in *Psycho* has music meant so much to a film." The movie netted Columbia over $15 million in the United States, but Pauline Kael complained: "*Midnight Express* is single-minded in its brutal manipulation of the audience; this is a clear-cut case of the use of film technique split off from any artistic impulse."

Beauty Pageant

Director Terence Malick's artistic impulse, along with Nestor Almendros' cinematography, were the stars of *Days of Heaven*. Richard Gere, Brooke Adams and playwright Sam Shepard portrayed the film's love triangle, but the critics only talked about the film's idyllic depiction of the wheat fields of Texas before World War I. *Time* said, "There is enough beauty here for a dozen movies," and Charles Champlin wrote, "Its summoning up of the resources of sight and sound is without parallel in this or many recent years." Despite the critical ballyhoo, *Days of Heaven* did not lure ticket-buyers, no matter how hard Paramount tried to push it.

Fonda Checks In, Smith Cleans Up

Jane Fonda returned in the fall in a western named *Comes a Horseman*. Jason Robards played the villain, a land baron, and James Caan played the hero, a drifter who hooks up with Fonda's oppressed cattle rancher. The one who rode off with the reviews was a fifty-eight-year-old stuntman who had once doubled for Montgomery Clift in *Red River*. *Variety* said, "The only really good part in the film is Richard Farnsworth's Dodge, Fonda's aging hand." *Comes a Horseman* didn't cause a stampede at the box office, but for Fonda, it was only a temporary setback. By Christmas, she was exchanging wisecracks with Alan Alda in the latest Neil Simon–Herbert Ross collaboration, *California Suite,* which made $30 million in the United States.

Producer Ray Stark hired an all-star cast for the film version of Simon's Broadway success, a quartet of one-act plays set in the Beverly Hills Hotel, and the critics' favorites were Maggie Smith and Michael Caine as an Academy Award nominee and her bisexual husband. "Smith and Caine trade barbs, bites and solace with a classic stylishness that recalls the matrimonial jousting of William Powell and Myrna Loy's Nick and Nora Charles," praised *Newsweek*. "Fussing over her awful party dress, voraciously scrounging the halls for leftovers after her defeat, or merely uttering the word 'bizarre,' Smith finds laughs in corners few actresses would think to explore."

A Vietnam Cocktail

"I really don't want to do anything until *Raging Bull,*" Robert De Niro admitted when Michael Cimino, whose only previous directorial credit was a Clint Eastwood movie, approached him with a screenplay about steelworkers in a Slovak community in Pennsylvania whose lives are changed when they fight in Vietnam. But De Niro read the script and changed his mind. "I liked the story and the dialogue," he said. "It was so simple and it seemed so real to me." With De Niro intersted, the thirty-seven-year-old Cimino worked out a deal with a production company called EMI, which immediately ran an ad in *Variety* showing De Niro wearing sunglasses as he

"I knew I wouldn't like The Deer Hunter. It's about two things I didn't care about: Vietnam and poor people."
—Allan Carr

sat on a truck with a gun. The film's title was *The Deer Hunter*.

De Niro headed for the steel mills of Mingo Junction and Steubenville, Ohio. "I talked with the millworkers, drank and ate with them, played pool," the actor said. "I tried to become as close to being a steelworker as possible and I would have worked a shift at the mill, but they wouldn't let me." Meanwhile, Cimino was lining up a cast of young New York actors: Christopher Walken, John Savage, and John Cazale, who was going out with a twenty-seven-year-old blonde he had played opposite in *Measure for Measure* in Central Park—Meryl Streep. Cimino cast the young actress in the biggest female role, but Streep said of her character, "Linda is essentially a man's view of a woman. Someone who's beaten down a lot by everybody, but who never gets angry about that." The actress was willing to make concessions in order to be near Cazale, who confessed to Cimino that he was terminally ill with cancer. The director refused to let EMI replace the ailing actor and Cazale completed the film. He died five months later, before the film was released.

Just when to release *The Deer Hunter* was a thorny question for Universal. "The picture will die if we open it cold," despaired Universal's Buddy Young. "It must have awards to give it the stature it needs to be successful." For advice, the studio turned to Ann-Margret's manager. "I was sitting in my cabana drinking champagne," recalled Allan Carr to the *Los Angeles Times*. "I knew I wouldn't like it. It's about two things I didn't care about: Vietnam and poor people, directed by this guy Cimino who I remember directing Ann-Margret in Canada Dry ads five years ago. Three hours of Pittsburgh steelworkers. After lunch at my hangout, Ma Maison, I went to see the film for friendship reasons. By the middle of the movie, I was crying so hard I had to go to the men's room to put cold water on my face." When Carr recovered, he instructed Universal to scrap its scheduled fall release date and open *The Deer Hunter* for one week only in December in Los Angeles and New York. "I know it will be the cocktail-party movie at Christmastime," Carr insisted.

"To my mind, *The Deer Hunter* is a major achievement in American movies," opined Arthur Knight in the *Hollywood Reporter*. "It is the great American film of 1978." David Denby of *New York* magazine wrote, "Just when it seemed time to announce that the American cinema had died as an art form, *The Deer Hunter* arrives to restore a little hope." "Of course, every performance in New York and L.A. was sold out that week," Carr gloated, but he arranged special screenings for Hollywoodites who couldn't get in. "Robert De Niro reclaims his title as our finest young dramatic male star," proclaimed *Life*, while Rona Barrett said, "Christopher Walken is a particular revelation. His early charm and later disintegration make for a devastating performance—one deserving of an Oscar nomination."

Manhattan Is Kind

Carr and Cimino won over the New York Film Critics Circle, which named *The Deer Hunter* the Best Picture of the year. Terrence Malick took the Director honor for *Days of Heaven;* Jon Voight claimed the Best Actor citation for *Coming Home;* Ingrid Bergman nabbed the Best Actress plaque for *Autumn Sonata;* and Maureen Stapleton won the Best Supporting Actress Award for *Interiors*. The critics agreed with Rona Barrett and selected Christopher Walken Best Supporting Actor for *The Deer Hunter*. "I know what I'm doing on stage," Walken said, "but in films, I have to depend on the kindness of strangers."

The Campaigns

Walken also had the backing of a studio, and Universal mailed out promos for *The Deer Hunter* and *Same Time, Next Year,* starring Ellen Burstyn and Alan Alda, directly to Academy voters' homes. Columbia led the trade-paper advertising with over fifteen ads each for *Midnight Express* and *California Suite*, both of which played on Z Chan-

"I still haven't seen The Deer Hunter, but ours is the best picture."
—Jane Fonda

nel, along with *Coming Home, Heaven Can Wait, Interiors,* and *An Unmarried Woman.*

Producer Norman Twain wasn't about to count solely on TV exposure for Jill Clayburgh, and publicized the fact that she was appearing at the Long Beach Theater Festival in David Rabe's *In the Boom, Boom Room.* "I'm trying to say that here's a lady who is out here working in a play for very little money, as a labor of love," Twain said to the *Los Angeles Times.* "That has got to influence people, the fact that she is in town and she's working as an actress who is serious about her craft."

Gary Busey didn't think he had much of a chance at winning an Oscar after Jon Voight won the New York Film Critics Award, but his press agent, Bob Levinson, ordered, "Shut up and listen. You're entitled to the award." Busey did as told and held a press conference with the Hollywood Foreign Press, which later rewarded him with a nomination for Best Actor in a Musical or Comedy at their annual Golden Globe Awards. Busey lost to Warren Beatty, but Levinson was not deterred. His client grinned from the cover of *Rolling Stone* and accepted an award from *US* magazine on *The Merv Griffin Show.* Busey told *US* that he didn't think Oscar night was such a big deal: "It's just another excuse to get drunk or something."

Busey's potential competition included Sir Laurence Olivier, this time a Nazi-chaser in *The Boys From Brazil.* Twentieth Century–Fox's trade-paper campaign for Olivier disturbed novelist Harold Robbins. "I thought Larry was much better in *The Betsy* than in *The Boys From Brazil,*" said Robbins, the author of *The Betsy.* "I was willing to spend $100,000 of my own money to push him for an Oscar, but it was useless my spending my money for advertisements if there was no ground support for the idea. And there wasn't."

The Nominations

When the Academy announced that Laurence Olivier was nominated for Best Actor for *The Boys From Brazil,* the *Miami Herald* retorted, "Nobody connected with the trashy *Boys From Brazil* should earn as much as a free ticket to Academy Award night." Olivier was getting more than a free invitation; the Academy guaranteed him an Oscar by giving him an Honorary Award "for the full body of his work, for the unique achievements of his entire career and his lifetime of contribution to the art of film." Since he was passing through town anyway so that his seventeen-year-old son could interview at UCLA, Olivier said he'd come to the ceremony—it would be the first time he attended as a nominee since he was nominated for *Wuthering Heights* in 1939.

Pay-TV conquered the nominations list: the only Best Picture nominee which had not been broadcast was *The Deer Hunter. Days of Heaven,* which Paramount held away from TV, was only nominated for technical Oscars, while *Midnight Express, An Unmarried Woman* and *Interiors* were in the major races. Universal's comedy blockbuster, *National Lampoon's Animal House,* didn't win a single nomination, not even a Best Supporting Actor nod for John Belushi, who had made the cover of *Newsweek* when the film made $74 million domestically. Gary Busey, who did get nominated, was the guest host of *Saturday Night Live* and Jane Curtin kidded him on the air that "practically nobody" saw *The Buddy Holly Story* and "practically everybody saw John Belushi in *Animal House.*" Belushi didn't think his omission was so funny, and declined the Academy's invitation to be a presenter on the show.

Predictions and R.S.V.P.

Best Actress nominee Ingrid Bergman wasn't coming either, because she was ill and decided to stay home, despite columnist Ruth Batchelor's prediction of a Bergman victory: "Hollywood is still guilty for tossing her out so many years ago and she has been ill." In the Actor race, columnists pointed out that the last person to be nominated for the same four Oscars that Warren Beatty was up for had been Orson

"Oscar night is just another excuse to get drunk."
—Gary Busey

Welles in 1941 for *Citizen Kane;* then the same columnists forecast a Jon Voight win for Best Actor. "In 1969, I was really kind of rooting for John Wayne," Voight confessed. "I thought Dusty and I would cancel each other out, anyway. John Wayne won and I was happy. I didn't want it because I didn't really want the responsibility that year. Maybe this year, I'll be able to handle the responsibility."

John Wayne was coming this year, too. Like Ingrid Bergman, Wayne was ill; he had undergone open-heart surgery in January. Wayne couldn't confirm that he'd make it to the ceremonies, but he said he was going to try. Show producer Jack Haley, Jr., asked both Gregory Peck and Audrey Hepburn to stand by in case of a Wayne absence, and he invited Johnny Carson to be the emcee.

When Haley okayed a specialty number written by Fred Ebb and Larry Grossman that paid tribute to eligible songs that were not nominated for Oscars, the Music Branch let out a collective howl. Marilyn Bergman snapped, "What that piece of material doesn't consider is that perhaps the Academy was correct in overlooking the songs. Perhaps they didn't make distinguished contribution to the dramatic structure of the movie." Haley responded, "This branch has been embroiled in controversy for the last ten years and they're very thin-skinned. I threatened to walk off the show and then Johnny Carson said if I walked, they could get a new emcee." The Academy relented and Steve Lawrence and Sammy Davis, Jr., were permitted to sing the medley, entitled "Oscar's Only Human." Haley was not as successful at persuading last year's Best Actress to give an Award. Diane Keaton said no and she meant it.

The Oscar show's costume consultant, Ron Talsky, called the feminine nominees and told them how to dress: "Not comfort, not what's in style, but glamour with a capital G." Best Supporting Actress nominee Maureen Stapleton said to Talsky that she'd be wearing a five-year-old Stavropoulos "If I can get into it—I have to wear a tight girdle." Stapleton's rival, Meryl Streep, said she went shopping at Bonwit Teller. "I was looking for something very simple that didn't look like a nightgown," the nominee explained. "I wanted something my mother would not be ashamed of." Talsky tracked down Ellen Burstyn, a Best Actress nominee for *Same Time, Next Year*, on location in Texas. "It's pretty hard to shop in El Paso," Burstyn informed the designer. And Jane Fonda's answer was direct: "I plan to wear the same James Riva dress I wore to the Awards last year."

Fonda on the Warpath

Fonda was also busy campaigning for the Oscar, telling reporters, "The movie means more to me than any movie I've done so far and if *Coming Home* wins Awards, it means that it's going to be rereleased and the audience I know is there for it will be able to see it in larger numbers. The letters I've gotten from veterans—all the way to the guy who was wounded in World War II and hasn't made love to his wife in thirty years. The movie changed their relationship." The *San Fernando Valley News* predicted a Fonda victory because "Hollywood wants to forgive her for being right about Nixon."

Then Fonda received a phone call at one in the morning: "It was Julie Christie. She was hysterical," Jane reported. "They had shown *The Deer Hunter* at the Berlin Film Festival and people were screaming." Christie said herself to *Variety*, "The film presents the Vietcong as subhuman and sadistic, though they effectively resisted both France and the United States, which possessed enormous means of warfare." In Hollywood, Fonda began campaigning against *The Deer Hunter*. "I hope it doesn't win," she told the *Los Angeles Herald-Examiner*. "I haven't seen it—I'm afraid to. My friends told me about it, though, and I just think it's amazing that good people can see the movie and not even consider the racism."

Jane's father, Henry, shared his daughter's cavalier attitude about seeing all the nominees before marking his Oscar ballot. Mrs. Fonda told *Chicago Tribune* critic Gene Siskel that she and another actor's wife had filled out their husbands' ballots a number of times. Academy President Howard W. Koch quickly issued a statement after Mrs. Fonda's remarks: "I'm sure this sort of thing happens on the rare occasion. Anyone who talks about it, however, is very foolish."

The Big Night

John Wayne's trailer pulled up at 4:30 P.M. and his daughter accompanied him backstage, where he received an ovation. "Hell, I'd have gotten sick before if I knew I'd get this kind of treatment," the Duke laughed, before heading for the bed where he would lie until he was due onstage hours later. Producer Jack Haley, Jr., whose divorce from Liza Minnelli had become final that very day, stopped by his dressing room and discovered a sign on the door: UNMARRIED MAN.

When the stars began to arrive, Donna Summer earned a loud reception from the bleacher fans as she danced down the walkway. But the loudest screams greeted Warren Beatty, who arrived with Diane Keaton, in blue slacks. Honorary winner Laurence Olivier and his son walked in unnoticed, but Army Archerd recognized Maureen Stapleton and called her up to his podium. "You're no stranger to the Academy Awards," the forecourt emcee said. "That's right," Stapleton retorted, "I'm a two-time loser."

Gwen Jones surveyed the fashions for the *Los Angeles Herald-Examiner* and reported, "With the exception of Gary Busey, who wore an orange calico print shirt, striped ribbon tie and black velvet suit, almost everyone showed up tastefully dressed." Jon Voight showed up with the Vietnam veteran who had been his technical adviser on the film, and the nominee made a point of shaking his fellow nominees' hands. He didn't shake Robert De Niro's hand because he wasn't there. Lauren Bacall was present, and producer Lester Persky walked over to her at the bar in the lobby to discuss her recently published autobiography, *By Myself*. "I've just read your book," Persky said. "You know it would make a good movie." "Lester, it's not for sale," the author replied.

This year's protesters included Blacks in Media Broadcasting Oranization (BIMBO), who came last year, and two groups demonstrating against *The Deer Hunter,* which had won the Directors Guild Award. The Hell No, We Won't Go Committee waved placards that read NO OSCARS

Awards Ceremony

APRIL 9, 1979, 7:00 P.M.
THE DOROTHY CHANDLER PAVILION, LOS ANGELES

Your Host:
JOHNNY CARSON
Televised over ABC

Presenters

Honorary Award to Walter Lantz . . . . Robin Williams
Supporting Actor . . . . Dyan Cannon and Telly Savalas
Scientific or Technical Awards . . . . Maggie Smith and Maureen Stapleton
Short Films. . . . . . . Robby Benson and Carol Lynley
Documentary Awards . . . . Mia Farrow and David L. Wolper
Art Direction. . . . . . Shirley Jones and Ricky Schroder
Costume Design . . . . Ray Bolger and Jack Haley
Film Editing. . . . . Dom De Luise and Valerie Perrine
Visual Effects . . . . Steve Martin
Sound . . . . . . Margot Kidder and Christopher Reeve
Cinematography. . . . . James Coburn and Kim Novak
Song . . . . Ruby Keeler and Kris Kristofferson
Scoring Awards . . . . . Dean Martin and Raquel Welch
Honorary Award to the Museum of Modern Art. Gregory Peck
Honorary Award to King Vidor . . . . . Audrey Hepburn
Foreign Film. . . . . . . Yul Brynner and Natalie Wood
Jean Hersholt Humanitarian Award. . . . . Jack Valenti
Supporting Actress . . . . George Burns and Brooke Shields
Writing Awards . . . . . . Lauren Bacall and Jon Voight
Director . . . . Francis Ford Coppola and Ali MacGraw
Honorary Award to Laurence Olivier . . . . . Cary Grant
Actress. . . . . Richard Dreyfuss and Shirley MacLaine
Actor. . . . . Ginger Rogers and Diana Ross
Picture. . . . . John Wayne

Performers of Nominated Songs

"Hopelessly Devoted to You" . . . . Olivia Newton-John
"Last Dance" . . . . Donna Summer
"The Last Time I Felt Like This" . . . . Johnny Mathis and Jane Olivor
"Ready to Take a Chance Again" . . . . Barry Manilow
"When You're Loved". . . . . Debby Boone

"Hollywood wants to forgive Jane Fonda for being right about Nixon."
—San Fernando Valley News

FOR RACISM and the Vietnam Veterans Against the War distributed statements that said: "Many of us were part of the antiwar movement ten years ago. Tonight we are opposing another war, one that never happened, except in the mind of Michael Cimino." A number of protesters clashed with police and thirteen people were arrested for "inciting to riot." The police also had to deal with a man dressed in a full-sized duck outfit—they made sure he wasn't part of the show before escorting him away.

The telecast began with disco music as the camera zoomed in close on the theater, neatly avoiding the protesters. Academy President Howard W. Koch introduced "a national treasure," Johnny Carson, who began with a monologue: "Welcome to the fifty-first Academy Awards, two hours of sparkling entertainment spread over a four-hour show . . . I see a lot of new faces, especially on the old faces . . . *Heaven Can Wait*—a real fantasy about Warren Beatty not being able to find a body he could use."

Carson brought out "America's newest comedy sensation," Robin Williams, who alluded to "those of you with a buzz on." Williams and Woody Woodpecker gave an Honorary Oscar to Woody's creator, animator Walter Lantz. "Thanks for drawing me and a nice paycheck for thirty-eight years," the cartoon bird said. Backstage, Lantz said Woody's inspiration came on his honeymoon: "This bird outside our room drove us crazy."

Carson introduced Danny Thomas to read the voting rules, advising, "For you people watching at home, this might be a good time to make some dip." When Thomas was through, the emcee said, "What Danny was trying to say was who gets the most votes wins."

Heaven Can Wait's Best Supporting Actress nominee Dyan Cannon sighed, "It's really an honor just to be nominated," and then revealed that the Best Supporting Actor was Christopher Walken for *The Deer Hunter*. The winner sprinted to the stage, a lock of hair falling over his forehead as he made his speech. After his thanks, Walken asked, "Which way do I go?" As Cannon exited with Walken, her fellow nominees Maureen Stapleton of *Interiors* and Maggie Smith of *California Suite* marched out to present the Scientific or Technical Awards, and when they were finished, Carson cracked, "I'm glad the suspense is over in that category."

Donna Summer sang "Last Dance" amid mirrors and flashing lights as discophiles in the audience yelped at various crescendos. *The Deer Hunter* won the Editing Award and winner Peter Zinner said, "Growing up in Austria, I used to indulge in this fantasy that I would win an Oscar." *The Deer Hunter* won another Oscar, for Sound, and then Debby Boone, wearing a tiny crucifix, sang a song from *The Magic of Lassie*.

James Coburn and Kim Novak, in a sleek black gown, gave the Cinematography Oscar to the Spanish-born Nestor Almendros for *Days of Heaven*. The winner began in Spanish, "Hello to all Spanish-speaking people in the United States," and then converted to English to say, "Thanks to Terrence Malick. These images belong entirely to him. This Oscar, it should be for him."

The Best Song Oscar was handled by Rhodes scholar Kris Kristofferson and Ruby Keeler, who had recently suffered a stroke. The trouper walked out with a cane topped with a carved dog's head and won a standing ovation. Keeler divulged that the winner was "Last Dance" and songwriter Paul Jabara hopped to the stage in a tux with a string tie. "Thanks for coming to my bar mitzvah," he said. Backstage, Jabara elaborated on how he won Donna Summer's affection for his song. "I wanted to play the song for her, but she was so busy, I finally put a cassette of the song in her bathroom and locked the door," he revealed. "After she heard it ten times, she said she loved it."

Meanwhile, the controversial "Oscar's Only Human" number was being introduced by Paul Williams, who explained why the songs weren't honored by the Academy: "Tall people don't nominate short people." He called out "two giants of the music industry" and Steve Lawrence and Sammy Davis, Jr., strutted their way through

"Somebody told Dean Martin he was going to a Ruth Buzzi roast."
—Johnny Carson

thirty songs—only three of which were from the last two decades: "Stayin' Alive," "New York, New York," and Sammy's personal hit, "The Candy Man." In spite of the Music Branch's bickering, the audience gave the performers sustained applause.

Raquel Welch and Dean Martin were in charge of the Scoring Awards, and Carson said Martin was lured because "somebody told him he was going to a Ruth Buzzi roast." Welch walked out in a tight, low-cut, blue-sequined jump suit and Martin winked at the audience: "I'll lay eight to five that only two of you were looking at me." Disco triumphed once again, and Giorgio Moroder, in red glasses, claimed his Oscar for *Midnight Express*. Backstage, the composer confessed, "I wanted to get the sound of a heartbeat and we tried a real heartbeat but it wasn't authentic enough. I don't know whether I should tell you this but in the end we had to use a drum."

George Burns, eighty-three, and his current leading lady, Brooke Shields, thirteen, presented the Best Supporting Actress Oscar. All the nominees were there and the winner was Maggie Smith—her second Oscar—for *California Suite*. "I would very much like for Michael Caine to be here with me," Smith said. "It should be split down the middle."

The writing Awards were assigned to Lauren Bacall and Jon Voight, who handed the Original Screenplay Oscars to the trio responsible for *Coming Home*. Nancy Dowd, Waldo Salt and Robert C. Jones were all smiles, but Dowd reminded everyone, "I wrote my screenplay in 1973." The Adapted Screenplay winner Oliver Stone said that he hoped his winning for *Midnight Express* would lead to "some consideration for all the men and women who are still in prison tonight."

King Vidor finally got the recognition Louis B. Mayer denied him the first year of the Oscars when he received an Honorary Oscar from Audrey Hepburn, the star of his 1956 adaptation of *War and Peace*. "I hope this can be an inspiration to all those who didn't make it the first twenty-five years," said the eighty-three-year-old director.

Just before giving the Best Director Oscar, Ali MacGraw heard the news that her eight-year-old son by Robert Evans was in Malibu Emergency Hospital receiving stitches after a freak accident with a baseball bat. Any hope MacGraw had of rushing through the presentation was dashed when copresenter Francis Ford Coppola launched into a spiel about "digital electronics." Scratching continuously at his beard, Coppola predicted a "communications revolution just around the corner that will make the Industrial Revolution seem like a small-town tryout." When Coppola concluded, MacGraw rushed in, "And, in the spirit of this wonderful new cinema of the future, we're very, very honored to announce the nominees." "And the winner is," Coppola announced, "my colleague and *paisan*, Michael Cimino." MacGraw kissed Cimino and then wiped the lipstick off his cheek. "At a time like this," Cimino said, "it is difficult to leaven pride with humility, but I'm proud to be here and proud of our work." The director thanked his cast and crew, "and most especially I embrace Robert De Niro for his dedication and for his great dignity of heart." Then Cimino and Coppola headed for the pressroom; MacGraw, for Malibu.

With no introduction, Cary Grant was onstage, going on about Honorary winner Laurence Olivier. "Those of us who have had the joy of knowing him since he came to Hollywood, warmly and fondly, and yet respectfully call him Larry," Cary said. "He represents the ultimate in acting." Olivier, bearded for his role as Zeus in a MGM's *Clash of the Titans*, stepped out to a standing ovation. Then he spoke:

> *Oh dear friends, am I suppose to speak after that? Cary, my dear old friend for many a year, from the earliest years of either of us working in this country. Thank you for that beautiful citation and the trouble you have taken to make it and all the warm generosities in it. Mr. President and governors of the Academy, committee members, fellows, my very noble and approved good masters, my*

"Oscar doesn't mean anything in England. They don't know quite what they are."
—Maggie Smith

colleagues, my friends, my fellow students. In the great wealth, the great firmament of your nation's generosities this particular choice may perhaps be found by future generations as a trifle eccentric, but the mere fact of it—the prodigal, pure, human kindness of it—must be seen as a beautiful star in that firmament which shines upon me at this moment dazzling me a little, but filling me with the warmth of the extraordinary elation, the euphoria that happens to so many of us at the first breath of the majestic glow of a new tomorrow. From the top of this moment, in the solace, in the kindly emotion that is charging my soul and my heart at this moment, I thank you for this great gift which lends me such a very splendid part in this, your glorious occasion. Thank you.

The camera saw Jon Voight half rising out of his seat, throwing his hands in the air and exclaiming, "Oh, wow!" Over at the *New York Times*, John O'Connor was less impressed, writing, "Olivier lapsed into a curiously rambling, slightly sticky, extended metaphor about stars and firmaments."

Richard Dreyfuss presented the Best Actress Oscar with Shirley MacLaine, who editorialized, "I want to take this opportunity to say how proud I am of my little brother, my dear, sweet, talented brother." The audience laughed, but MacLaine continued, "Just imagine what you could accomplish if you tried celibacy." The camera caught Beatty and Diane Keaton sitting with frozen smiles as the audience tittered uncertainly. "Not me, Jack," quipped Dreyfuss, who proceeded with the nominations. The winner was Jane Fonda for *Coming Home*. Fonda ran into the open arms of Shirley MacLaine. There were a few astonished chuckles when Fonda began her speech in sign language. At a Hollywood Oscar-watching party, Louise Fletcher thought for a minute that Fonda was parodying her speech. "I'm signing part of what I'm saying tonight because while we were making the movie, we all became more aware of the problems of the handicapped," Fonda explained. "Over fourteen million people are deaf. They are the invisible handicapped and can't share this evening, so this is my way of acknowledging them." Fonda stopped signing to thank her two children, sitting in the audience, "for forgiving me my absences." The winner thanked a number of other people connected with the movie, but Nancy Dowd wasn't one of them.

Ginger Rogers waited for Diana Ross to descend a staircase and then the pair gave the Best Actor Award. Rogers made a slip of the tongue and announced the nomination of "Warren Beatty in *Love—Heaven Can Wait*." Then Ross revealed that the winner was Jon Voight for *Coming Home*. Voight hugged costar Bruce Dern on the way on the stage. "I don't think there's an actor here or watching this proceeding tonight who doesn't acknowledge a great debt to the continuing legacy of Laurence Olivier," Voight said, thanking Bruce Dern, producer Jerome Hellman, director Hal Ashby, and "Jane, whose great dignity as a human being—it's a good thing she's not here to see this—is very moving to me." By the time Voight got to "the people in the chairs and the veterans," he was sobbing.

"Last year, an American institution stood right here and said some heartfelt words about another American institution," Johnny Carson said, leading into a clip of Bob Hope telling John Wayne, "Duke, we miss you tonight. We expect to see you amble out here in person next year, because nobody else can walk in John Wayne's boots." Carson said, "Ladies and gentlemen, Mr. John Wayne," and a gaunt Wayne walked out. There was another standing ovation, and the TV audience saw Laurence Olivier standing up for John Wayne.

"That's just about the only medicine a fella'd ever really need," the Duke drawled. "Believe me when I tell you that I'm mighty pleased that I can amble down here tonight. Well, Oscar and I have something in common. Oscar first came to the Hollywood scene in 1928—so did I. We're both a little weather-beaten but we're still here, and plan to be around a whole lot longer. My job here to-

"Am I supposed to speak after that?"
—Laurence Olivier

night is to identify your five choices for the outstanding picture of the year and announce the winner, so let's move 'em out!" Wayne did more than that, he shot 'em full of mispronunciations. Michael Cimino became "Michael Chipino," Warren Beatty was "Warner Beatty" and Paul Mazursky turned out to be "Paul Mazurki," as in character actor Mike Mazurki. The winner was *The Deer Hunter* and Michael Cimino returned and said, "I love you madly. Thank you."

When *The Deer Hunter*'s producers departed, Carson detained Wayne and told him "a few friends want to say hello." All the presenters and winners, including Jane Fonda, returned to greet the Duke. Sammy Davis, Jr., gave him one of his patented hugs and the show was over.

Aftermath

A publicist tried to arrange a shouting match backstage by instructing Jane Fonda to enter the pressroom while Michael Cimino was in there defending his movie. "I am puzzled by the pickets," Cimino was saying as Fonda walked in. "I didn't know there were pickets outside the theater until I got inside and somebody told me about them." Jane realized that she had been set up, so she smiled and left the room.

Cimino was stuck there, dodging questions about the scene in which the Vietcong make Robert De Niro and company play Russian Roulette. "It was a dramatic device," the director leveled with them. "It symbolized nothing; it moved the story along." When a reporter asked if he had distorted history, Cimino answered, "We're not trying to rewrite history, nor should we. We're moviemakers. We're not doing newsreels; that's what movies are about."

Oliver Stone, the winning author of *Midnight Express,* was given the same going-over about historical accuracy, and he echoed Cimino: "We weren't making a documentary." When asked why the events in the autobiography didn't correspond to those of the film, Stone stated: "We felt the book didn't have the dramatic cohesion the film needed. For instance, the lunatic asylum was originally in the early part of the story. I moved it to the end because I felt things should keep getting worse and that a lunatic asylum was the bottom line."

Maggie Smith didn't have Oliver Stone's assurance, admitting, "I've won two Oscars and I still don't begin to understand film acting." The double winner emphasized that she appreciated Oscars, though, "unlike in the movie, I won't go back to London until next week—I want to enjoy the feeling of being a winner." A journalist inquired if London would celebrate her victory, too, but Smith shrugged, "Oh, no, Oscar doesn't mean anything in England. They don't know quite what they are."

Christopher Walken said he didn't think winning an Oscar would be enough to make him want to move to Los Angeles. "However," the New Yorker responded, "I guess I will start thinking of myself as a movie actor rather than a stage actor after this." Walken added that his winning over John Hurt for *Midnight Express* meant that he was entitled to higher billing on the new picture they were making together, Michael Cimino's *Heaven's Gate*. The star of *Heaven's Gate,* Kris Kristofferson, was backstage, too, urging support for Cesar Chavez' boycott of Chiquita bananas.

Jon Voight wasn't talking politics. "I think there is a lot to talk about, but tonight I'm just very happy to be up here," he said. But he was ready to give credit where credit was due: "I have to thank Jane Fonda's husband Tom Hayden for getting me this role and the Oscar. I was originally offered the part of Jane's husband, but I wanted this one and Tom worked as my drama coach and backed me up to win this part instead."

When the press had had enough of Michael Cimino, he was ushered out to the left as Jane Fonda was brought back in from the right. Asked which of her two Oscars meant more to her, the double winner responded, "This is better because *Coming Home* means so much to me. We've been living with it for eight years." Someone brought up *The Deer Hunter*. "I still haven't

"Oh, wow!"
—Jon Voight

seen it," Fonda replied, "but ours is the best picture."

The Deer Hunter pickets were still outside. The Academy, afraid of more violence, asked its guests to forego the custom of waiting for their limousines outside and to walk to them in the underground garage. This new route proved perilous for Honorary winner Walter Lantz; when he got to his car, he discovered that he had been pickpocketed.

Columnists called Warren Beatty a good sport for showing up at the Governors' Ball after losing all four of his nominations, but Liz Smith wrote, "The big surprise to me about Hollywood's morning after is the general joy that Warren's *Heaven Can Wait* flunked out in the winning. Warren is enviously admired and grudgingly respected in the business, but many feel that his ego is too big and they don't like him personally." Jack Haley, Jr., didn't like seeing Beatty's date, Diane Keaton, walking about at the Governors' Ball after refusing to be a presenter on the show. Haley's date, Kim Novak, mixed business with pleasure by looking for job offers. "I'm kind of itchy to come back," Novak said. "I sense a mood in Hollywood of getting back to pictures that I really want to do. *An Unmarried Woman* is the kind of film I mean—something without sex and violence but with something to say." John Wayne skipped the ball; after the show, he got back in his trailer and went home. The Duke died two months later.

Lord Olivier, on the other hand, attended the Governors' Ball and then moved on to Swifty Lazar's party, where he had a late dinner with two of his former costars, Natalie Wood and Robert Wagner. Maggie Smith ended up there, too, where she celebrated with costar Michael Caine. Warren Beatty and Diane Keaton entered and commiserated with Warren's codirector, nominee Buck Henry, who didn't go to the ceremonies but watched them on TV at the Bistro with Lauren Hutton. *The Deer Hunter* brigade also showed up and toasted Allan Carr, who proclaimed Michael Cimino "the next David Lean." A grateful Christopher Walken told Carr, "You can keep my Oscar six months of the year because you were so instrumental in getting the picture recognized."

Market analyst Stuart Byron wrote of Carr's campaign, "The company brought out of mothballs a variation of the reserved-seat playoff pattern by which '60s blockbusters were sold, and the movie took on an aura of uniqueness which led to key awards by the New York Film Critics and the Academy." The *New York Times* claimed that Carr's success was all a matter of timing. Aljean Harmetz wrote, "According to one Los Angeles journalist sensitive to industry nuances, there was almost a rustle of embarrassment when the award was announced. 'Early on, we all thought the film was powerful but flawed,' he says. 'Now I think there have been a lot of second thoughts that emphasized the flawed. When the picture's name was read, it was as if you had proposed to a girl and were horrified she had accepted. I had the peculiar feeling that, if the ballots had gone out one week later, *The Deer Hunter* wouldn't have won.'"

1979

"The people who don't think All That Jazz is a flaming goddamned masterpiece are apt to tell you it's the worst piece of self-indulgent claptrap they ever sat through."
—Playboy

Dustin Hoffman returned as the prodigal son at the 1979 Academy Awards.

"I had a terrible image," said Sally Field, thirty-two. "Because I had appeared in the TV series *Gidget* and *The Flying Nun,* nobody every suggested me for a movie. Who in America would have wanted to pay to see anything like me in the movies? I was a continual put-down, a national joke, a running gag. Bob Hope, every comedian, had jokes about *The Flying Nun* that went straight to my heart; I couldn't separate myself from the role and I thought they were laughing at me."

Natural Bounce

Field finally separated from the *Flying Nun* persona when she split into sixteen different personalities in the 1977 TV-movie, *Sybil.* After winning an Emmy for her performance as a schizophrenic, Field had credibility as an actress, but she still wasn't offered much in the way of movie roles outside of her costarring appearances in Burt Reynolds' movies—they were an item offscreen. Enter director Martin Ritt, fifty-nine, who was trying to cast the title role of *Norma Rae,* the story of a poor Southern textile worker who becomes active in the unionization of her company. Jane Fonda didn't want the part, and neither did Jill Clayburgh or Faye Dunaway. Finally, Sally Field received a copy of the script. Burt Reynolds read it and said, "May I have the envelope, please? And the winner is Sally Field for *Norma Rae.*" She took the part, and Ritt told interviewers, "In my opinion, she's going to be one of Hollywood's biggest stars; she's sexy, funny, photogenic, zany, bouncy and tough—possibly another Carole Lombard."

When *Norma Rae* opened in March, the *Hollywood Reporter* wrote, "Martin Ritt has always demonstrated his deep concern for the poor and inarticulate. So far as the movies are concerned, he has become their voice—and in *Norma Rae,* it is an eloquent voice indeed." But *Newsweek* complained, "What *Norma Rae* really tells us is that Hollywood is still capable of making condescending paeans to the 'little people' with all the phoniness of yesteryear." *People* profiled "the real Norma Rae," Crystal Lee Sutton, and observed, "So far she hasn't a dime to show for the filmed version of her life or from the magazine article and book from which it was drawn." When Sutton was critical of Ritt's interpretation of her story, the director replied, "She's obviously no longer the free spirit of my movie. She's turned into a middle-class bourgeois woman who doesn't want anyone to know about her life."

The critics did give Ritt credit for hiring the right actress for the part. "With her sassy charm and her natural bounce, Sally Field transforms Norma Rae into one of the most zesty, beguiling heroines in screen history," remarked the *New York Daily News,* and Vincent Canby declared in the *New York Times* that: "Her triumph in *Norma Rae* is to have shucked off at long last all need to associate her with her TV beginnings, not because they are vulgar but because the performance she gives is as big as the screen that presents it."

Fonda's Nuclear Fondue

Jane Fonda, meanwhile, was doing her radicalization act again in a movie about the dangers of nuclear energy. Actor-producer Michael Douglas had a story called *Power,* about a TV news team that accidentally witnesses an emergency at a nuclear plant, and Richard Dreyfuss was supposed to play Douglas' fellow journalist, but when he dropped out, the role switched genders. Fonda had been trying to film the life of Karen Silkwood, the late nuclear energy safety activist, but the project was tied up with too many legal complications, so Fonda signed on with Douglas, and arranged to have her own production company coproduce. For her role as a TV reporter who is pressured by her

Best Actor winner Dustin Hoffman, a vigorous campaigner, sizes up Alec Guinness, who won his second Oscar without even making a movie.

bosses to look beautiful, Fonda decided to change her hair color, and turned to her husband, Tom Hayden, for advice. "I've never had a relationship with a redhead," he said.

The role of a conscience-stricken nuclear plant employee was rejected by both Jack Nicholson and Robert Redford, so Douglas turned to someone involved in films against nuclear proliferation—Jack Lemmon, who had narrated two documentaries. "When Michael Douglas gave me the script, I flipped," Lemmon said. "A whole year went by and I literally did not work because I was afraid that if I did something else and this finally did jell I might lose it on a physical conflict."

Retitled *The China Syndrome,* the movie opened in March to praise from the critics and pans from the energy companies. An executive at Westinghouse called it "an overall character assassination of an entire industry" and the Edison Electric Institute said the film required "a suspension of disbelief by the audience in order to provide its thrills." But two weeks after the premiere, life imitated art at a nuclear power plant on Three Mile Island, Pennsylvania, where a leak sent radioactive steam escaping into the atmosphere. When reporters rushed to ask Michael Douglas about this bonanza of free publicity, the producer exclaimed, "I've never had an experience like this. It goes beyond the realm of coincidence; it's enough to make you religious." It made *The China Syndrome* a hit, with domestic rentals of over $26 million.

Woody's Girls

Woody Allen returned to *Annie Hall* terrain in *Manhattan,* a modern-day *La Ronde* photographed in black-and-white by Gordon Willis. The women whirling past Allen in this roundelay were Diane Keaton, as a neurotic editor; Meryl Streep, as his lesbian first wife; and seventeen-year-old Mariel Hemingway, as his faithful lover. In the *Saturday Review* Arthur Schlesinger, Jr., rhapsodized,"Mariel Hemingway acts with the ecstatic gravity of one for whom love is close and death unimaginably distant." Andrew Sarris raved, "Woody Allen's *Manhattan* has materialized out of the void as the one truly great American film of the '70s. It tops *Annie Hall* in brilliance, wit, feeling and articulation." *Variety* put it simply: "Woody Allen never seems to tire of topping himself."

Peter Yates Stretches

"Concentrating exclusively on big-budget films can lead to creative suicide," stated British director Peter Yates, fifty. "After *The Deep,* I had to do something different. I felt it was time to get back to characters and human relationships. And I wanted to make a film about class distinction in America. Coming from England, I was always told that it doesn't exist here. But of course, it does." Yates found what he was looking for in two scripts written by thirty-five-year-old Steve (né Stoyan) Tesich, a Yugoslavian immigrant who had attended Indiana University on a wrestling scholarship. "The script I wrote eight years ago was about the annual Little 500 bicycle race between the school's fraternities and the townies," said Tesich, "and the other, about the fathers of the townies who worked in the limestone quarries around Bloomington, I wrote six years ago. It was Peter's idea to combine them." The new script was called *Breaking Away* and Yates persuaded Fox to put up the $2.4 million to make the film on location in Bloomington. Persuading actress Barbara Barrie to play the hero's mother took a lot of effort on Yates' part. "I don't think I'm quite right," the New Yorker told the director. "She's such a plain, down-home kind of woman, and I—well, I feel I'm more sophisticated." But a job is a job and Barrie packed her bags for Bloomington.

"The kids in *Breaking Away* are not heroin addicts, muggers, vampires, duck-tailed cretins from *Grease,* pelvis-churning disco dummies or freaks from outer space," rejoiced Rex Reed when the film opened in August. "They are neither

"I'm such a long shot I think anyone who bets on me should get a toaster, like they give out in banks, for having made the investment."
—Bob Fosse

trendy nor retarded, but real people with real emotions and needs and gently embroidered senses of humor." *Time* said, "This is the kind of small, starless film that big studios sometimes do not know what to do with." This claim was substantiated by *Film Comment,* which referred to *Breaking Away* as the year's "worst-marketed film," explaining "the summer playoff permitted no time for the low-key film to build word of mouth." Fox was preoccupied with the summer performance of *Alien,* an outer space horror movie that the studio opened on the anniversary of the *Star Wars* premiere. *Alien* scared up $45 million; Fox dubbed *Breaking Away*'s mere $9 million "disappointing."

They Came from TV

The star of Fox's TV show *M*A*S*H,* Alan Alda, had his primary residence in New Jersey, and, to have someting to do on his frequent five-hour flights to the Coast, the actor wrote a screenplay for himself about a senator who has an affair. But when *The Seduction of Joe Tynan* bowed in August, it was Alda's costars who got the attention. Janet Maslin wrote that Meryl Streep, as Alda's mistress, was "more stunning with each new appearance on the screen." And the *Saturday Review* opined, "The best thing about the film, however, is the superb rendition by that splendid actor Melvyn Douglas of an aging Southern senator."

Writer James L. Brooks, a creator of TV's *The Mary Tyler Moore Show* and *Taxi,* was also branching out into films, with a romantic comedy entitled *Starting Over,* starring Burt Reynolds, Jill Clayburgh and Candice Bergen. Reynolds counted on the urban comedy to do to his good-ole-boy image what *Norma Rae* did to Sally Field's flying-nun identity. *Variety* assured the actor that he had attained his goal: "It's a performance that should get the critics off his back once and for all." The critics left him alone, but Hollywood didn't seem to notice. "I hoped that the critical success of *Starting Over* would mean I would be offered similar roles. I wasn't." Reynolds said. "I can't see over the top of the scripts on my desk, but they're all the same as *Smokey and the Bandit.*"

He's Out

The critics were all over director Franco Zeffirelli for updating *The Champ* for Jon Voight. "If it was shameless when Wallace Beery and Jackie Cooper first played it," declared *Newsweek,* "it's downright decadent in the hands of the operatic Zeffirelli." Faye Dunaway, having rejected *Norma Rae,* played the kid's high-fashion mother and led *Time* to comment that her "repertoire of neurotic mannerisms brings back unwanted memories of her performance in *Chinatown,* even to the point of imbuing *The Champ* with bizarre incestuous undercurrents."

Foreign Sex

The sex symbol of the art house was Hanna Schygulla, the star of Rainer Werner Fassbinder's satire about Germany's postwar economic miracle, *The Marriage of Maria Braun.* The film premiered at the New York Film Festival and then settled down for a year's run at one theater in New York. "With her bee-stung lips, poodle-cut blond hair and blood-raising sensual fullness, Schygulla is one of the ripest and funniest screen images in years—an improbable cross between Dietrich and Harlow," drooled David Denby in *New York* magazine. "She raises screen acting to a new level of sexual knowingness." New Yorker Films knew it had a hot commodity in Schygulla and, according to industry observer Stuart Byron, the company "hired the gilt-edged publicity firm of Maslansky-Koenigsberg to thump the tubs for the German actress. The 'Academy campaign' will cost $35,000. It'll probably work, too."

Byron called *Maria Braun*'s $1 million gross "blockbuster status for an import," but the Germany entry paled next to the French sex farce picked up by United Artists—*La Cage aux Folles.* The studio thought the comedy about two homo-

"If Justin Henry loses again, we'll have to give him a lifetime achievement award."
—Dustin Hoffman

sexuals, directed by Edouard Molinaro, would draw a few bucks in urban markets and the reviews were mixed: *Newsweek* said, "In any language, the film is laugh-out-loud funny," and *Time* called it "a giddy, unpretentious and entirely lovable film." But Vincent Canby at the *New York Times* wasn't laughing so hard. "*La Cage aux Folles* is naughty in the way of comedies that pretend to be sophisticated but actually serve to reinforce the most popular conventions and most witless stereotypes." To United Artists' amazement, *La Cage aux Folles* was a runaway hit all over America. Andrew Sarris documented, "Everywhere I went, and particularly out on sybaritic Long Island, the only topic of film conversation was *La Cage aux Folles*. I couldn't get on a tennis court or sit at a dinner table without being regaled about the glories of this hot-weather sleeper." The comedy became one of the highest grossing foreign-language films ever, pulling in over $7 million—it grossed $2 million alone at a tiny Manhattan theater where it ran for nineteen months.

A Divine Debut

Although the success of *La Cage aux Folles* threw Hollywood for a loop, the studios had been trying for years to lure a singer who first made her mark parodying Carmen Miranda in a gay bathhouse in New York. From the Continental Baths, Bette Midler went on to conquer Broadway with two record-breaking concerts, while her hit recording of the 1941 Best Song nominee, "Boogie Woogie Bugle Boy of Company C," inspired the surviving Andrews Sisters to make their own Broadway comeback. The Divine Miss M was terribly picky about screenplays, though; she turned down *Nashville, The Fortune, Foul Play* and *Rocky*. "We're looking for something to make Bette a legend," explained her personal manager, Aaron Russo. Finally, they came across a script called *The Pearl*, based on the life of the late Janis Joplin. "I chose it because it was a big film, with music, sound and lights, not an everyday picture," Midler said. "I don't know if I'll ever get a part like that again. I hope I do." Fox produced the picture, renamed *The Rose*, and Midler said of filmmaking, "Well, I loved my trailer."

"The word's out that Bette Midler's going to be Oscar-nominated for her first movie, *The Rose*, and it's a little premature since she's only been filming two weeks," said Earl Wilson. "But her director, Mark Rydell, says she was brilliant in some emotional street scenes, chasing her man, Frederic Forrest, yelling, crying, with the mascara running." Pauline Kael confirmed the advance word when *The Rose* opened in November: "The picture is shaped to tear you up, and, as one of the Dionysian stars (such as Janis Joplin) who ascended to fame in the '60s and OD'd, all within a few years, Midler gives a paroxysm of a performance—it's scabrous yet delicate, and altogether amazing." Midler returned to Broadway in a show called *Divine Madness* after the film's premiere, and she instructed her audience to see her movie. "It's great and I get to die at the end," the actress said. Enough of her fans followed orders and *The Rose* was another success for Bette Midler.

Heart of Coppola

Frederic Forrest was almost unavailable for Bette Midler to chase in *The Rose* because he was involved in the latest Francis Coppola epic (the director had dropped the "Ford" from his name, except for the "Francis Ford Coppola Presents" credit above the title of any film made by his studio, Omni Zoetrope). Zoetrope's most ambitious effort was to be *Apocalypse Now*, an updating of Conrad's *Heart of Darkness* set during the Vietnam War. John Milius had approached Coppola with the idea in 1967, and George Lucas was supposed to have directed it after *American Graffiti*, but he became busy with *Star Wars*, so Francis thought he'd take it on, and the trouble started.

Although the director coaxed Marlon Brando to play the film's villain, an insane army officer, Coppola couldn't convince another star to portray the hero, whose mission is to find and rub out Brando. Robert Redford and Jack Nicholson said

"If I want to be up for an Academy Award, I'm either going to have to play a tour de force of some kind or have a tracheotomy just before the nominations."
—Burt Reynolds

no thanks, as did three former Coppola stars, Gene Hackman, Al Pacino and James Caan. Finally, Steve McQueen consented, but a month before filming started, Coppola told *Women's Wear Daily,* "I've got a $17 million picture uncast. I had Steve McQueen and all that group, but they all backed out at the last minute because they didn't want to spend six months in the jungle." Coppola replaced McQueen with Harvey Keitel and started shooting on location in the Philippines. There he fired Keitel and replaced him with Martin Sheen, thirty-seven, who had a heart attack. Brando did not cause Coppola any trouble, although the director was caught off-guard when the actor reported to work ninety pounds overweight.

By the spring of 1979, the director had a 150-minute version of the movie that he entered in the Cannes Film Festival, which he called "an out-of-town tryout." The jury made *Apocalypse Now* share the Best Picture palm with Volker Schlöndorff's adaptation of Gunter Grass' *The Tin Drum,* but Coppola made the most of it by walking onstage holding Schlöndorff's hand triumphantly over their heads. "It's taken a long, long time, but I feel I've staged a real piece of work about an important American era," Coppola said. "I think it's a monument."

"*Apocalypse Now* was worth the wait," *Variety* declared when the movie opened in exclusive engagements, complete with free programs. "Alternately a brilliant and bizarre film, Francis Coppola's four-year 'work-in-progress' offers the definitive validation of the old saw, 'War is hell.'" But *New West* magazine argued, "Coppola has come up with a movie that unwittingly mirrors the spirit of the Vietnam war: a heartless exercise in logistics, a monumentally oversized catastrophe." The *New York Daily News* wrote, "Only Robert Duvall seems to have realized that for an actor to be noticed in this psychedelic horror show, he must play it big, and his performance as the rabid militarist, who is so supremely cocky he never so much as flinches when standing in the line of fire, is so full of manic energy he all but leaps off the screen."

A Horse Is a Horse

Omni Zoetrope's other production wasn't such a headache to make; director Carroll Ballard filmed the children's book *The Black Stallion* without a hitch and the film premiered at the New York Film Festival. *Time* said Caleb Deschanel's photography "consists of one stunning view after another: coral seas, scarlet sunsets, moonlight landscapes, stormy skies. Almost every shot is suitable for framing." The acting honors went to Mickey Rooney, described by *New York* magazine as "a figure out of a semi-mystical past." *Variety* was more direct: "Mickey Rooney gives his best screen performance in years." For Rooney, *The Black Stallion* was one half of his double-whammy comeback; he and Ann Miller had just opened to critical acclaim and capacity audiences on Broadway in a burlesque revue called *Sugar Babies*.

All That Ego

Coppola's old Oscar adversary, Bob Fosse, was also having problems with his latest project—an autobiographical probe called *All That Jazz*. Richard Dreyfuss left this picture, too, so Fosse hired Roy Scheider to play the hero, a sexually compulsive choreographer-director juggling a Broadway musical and a motion picture who has a heart attack. Fosse was such a stickler for realism, he enlisted the cardiac surgical team of a New York hospital for the film's graphic open-heart surgery scene and gave them screen credit. Scheider told *Playboy* about another method Fosse used to bring the element of truth to the movie: "Of course, many women in the cast were women whom Bob had gone with at one time, which I found very interesting, though, of course, all were hired strictly on the basis of talent." Scheider added, "This is Bob Fosse's *8 1/2*. We never discussed the Fellini film, yet Fosse has the same wonderful confusion about women in his movie." Fosse also had Fellini's cinematographer, Giuseppe Rotunno, to blend the fantasy scenes seam-

"Most actors want to play Othello, but all I've really wanted to play is Chance the Gardener."
—Peter Sellers

lessly within his portrait of the New York theater world.

When *All That Jazz* opened in December, *Playboy*'s Bruce Williamson prophesied, "The people who don't think Bob Fosse's *All That Jazz* is a flaming goddamned masterpiece are apt to tell you it's the worst piece of self-indulgent claptrap they ever sat through." Vincent Canby called it an "uproarious display of brilliance, nerve, dance, maudlin confessions, inside jokes, and especially ego"; Liz Smith said it was "a dazzling, overlong, and flawed ego trip"; and *Variety* opined it was "all that jazz and plenty of ego." Fosse protested, "I'm afraid of saying, yes, there is a lot of me in Joe Gideon because people have used the word 'self-indulgent' about the film, but critics are constantly saying that an artist should draw more from himself and less from others. This is what I've done. So why do I get this reaction? It frightens me."

Roy Scheider, however, was delighted at the attention he received when *All That Jazz* premiered just days before he opened on Broadway in Harold Pinter's *Betrayal*. "This is a different plateau; it's the place I've always wanted to get to," the actor said. "It's the place where people say, 'Hey, this guy is an actor. He can do this and he can do that—he can surprise us.'"

Peter Sellers Takes a Chance

Jerzy Kosinski was surprised when he published his novel *Being There*, about a simpleton named Chance the Gardener, and received a telegram from the fictional character. "Available in my garden or outside of it. C. Gardener," read the telegram, which included a telephone number. Kosinski called up and Peter Sellers answered. "This character was created for me to play on the screen," the actor asserted. "Since my heart attack in 1964, my life has been dictated by chance." Sellers took no chances with the screen adaptation, and sent the book to Hal Ashby in 1973, when the director was editing *The Last Detail*. "Neither of us had the power then to raise the money for it," Ashby said, but after he directed *Shampoo* and *Coming Home* and Sellers resurrected the *Pink Panther* series, a production company called Lorimar decided they were good investments and came through with the cash.

Kosinski wrote the screenplay and marveled at Sellers' skill at portraying the imbecile who, through luck, becomes President of the United States. "Nobody thought Chance was even a character, yet Peter knew that man," the author said. "Most actors want to play Othello, but all I've really wanted to play is Chance the Gardener," Sellers told interviewers. "I feel what the character, the story is all about is not merely the triumph of a simple man, an illiterate; it's God's message again that the meek shall inherit the earth."

Costar Shirley MacLaine thought Laurence Olivier would be perfect as the billionaire who launches the simpleton's political career, but he turned the role down. "I called Larry about it the other day," MacLaine said. "He didn't like the idea of being in a film with me masturbating." Melvyn Douglas, seventy-eight, had no such qualms, and took the part.

The critics agreed that Sellers was born to play Chance when *Being There* bowed in December. The *Wall Street Journal* wrote, "Mr. Sellers makes Chance not simply amusing but also the sweetest of simpletons as well." So popular was Sellers that buttons bearing one of Chance's lines in the film—"I like to watch"—became big sellers for sidewalk vendors. *Variety* felt that "Melvyn Douglas almost steals the film with his spectacular performance as the dying financial titan. Avoiding all clichés, the veteran actor movingly creates a crusty old character of full human dimensions."

Dustin Hoffman Finds Motherhood

Unlike Peter Sellers, Dustin Hoffman did not feel fated to make the film version of Avery Corman's bestselling novel about a child-custody battle, *Kramer vs. Kramer*. Nevertheless, producer Stanley Jaffe envisioned a Dustin Hoffman vehicle, written by Robert Benton and directed by François Truffaut. Benton didn't see it that way—

"I always thought the actors were hired to ruin the writer's lines."
—Robert Benton

he wanted to direct, too. Jaffe consented and then the two of them tried to entice Hoffman, who rejected Benton's first draft. Several drafts later, Hoffman said he would do the film if he could improvise, demand extra takes, and oversee the editing. "I've never let an actor in on the writing or the editing before," responded Benton. "I always thought the actors were hired to ruin the writer's lines." Benton swallowed his pride and Hoffman was in.

To play the wife who walks out on Hoffman, the trio wanted Kate Jackson, one of *Charlie's Angels*, but Columbia executive Sherry Lansing opposed the choice, suggesting Meryl Streep instead. Streep had met Hoffman earlier at an audition, as she reminisced to *Time:* "He came up to me and said, 'I'm Dustin—burp—Hoffman' and he put his hand on my breast. What an obnoxious pig, I thought."

The filmmakers had difficulty with the actor playing Hoffman and Streep's son—six-year-old Justin Henry. "The first few days his concentration was terrible," Hoffman reported. "He kept looking at the camera. He was like a young colt or, more accurately, he was a normal six-year-old. By the third week, he was becoming an actor." Someone asked the burgeoning actor what his favorite film was. "*Jaws 2!*" Justin exclaimed. "What about *Jaws?*" was the next question. "Oh," Justin shrugged, "that was before my time."

Hoffman with Strings

When *Kramer vs. Kramer* opened as Columbia's big Christmas release, Charles Champlin gave it his blessing in the *Los Angeles Times:* "*Kramer vs. Kramer* is as nearly perfect a film as can be." When Michael Douglas exited the Los Angeles premiere, he told *Women's Wear Daily:* "Dustin's is the first performance I've seen that will give Jack Lemmon something to worry about when the Academy Awards roll around." Lemmon had more worries when *Time* devoted a cover story to the movie and said of Hoffman, "Like Diane Keaton in *Annie Hall*, he has turned the screen into a mirror, a magical looking glass into his own head and heart." Hoffman revealed that the role had made him long to give birth to a child himself and the magazine noted, "When he was preparing to play Ted Kramer, he kept staring at young mothers and pregnant women, especially the pregnant woman wheeling children in carriages. 'They have an aura that you don't see in a man with his kids,' he said. 'I hear music when I see them—definitely strings.'"

Hollywood took notice of another change in Hoffman—he was actually cooperating with the publicity department. "The normally press-shy actor has been promoting the film as he's never promoted one of his pictures before," reported Liz Smith. "And recently, at one of the *Kramer* New York unveilings, it reached the point of extreme. Hoffman endeared himself to a group of about 30 photographers by posing—by himself, with his parents, with juvenile costar Justin Henry, and then with Justin and Justin's parents—for 20 minutes."

Costar Justin also earned great reviews: the *New York Daily News* said he was "an astonishingly natural actor with none of the affectations that plague most child stars" and Rex Reed called him "a saffron-haired dumpling." Justin didn't fall for the hoopla. "People think I'm a big-shot movie star," the now eight-year-old told *Time*. "This hasn't changed me at all." Meryl Streep also declined to see herself in grandiose terms. "I don't care about being a star," the actress informed *New York* magazine. "I feel horribly embarrassed in a limousine. I'd rather that they humanize the subways. I don't want a mink coat." Still, Meryl was celebrated by the press as the great blond hope for having appeared in *Manhattan, The Seduction of Joe Tynan,* and *Kramer vs. Kramer*. The *Ladies' Home Journal* dubbed her "a throwback to what used to be called 'a classy dame.' "

Marsha Mason Muscles In

For all the excitement over Streep, she had not played a leading role yet in a film and there

"I have no idea why they don't nominate me. Maybe if I bought a house in Hollywood I'd have a better chance."
—Gordon Willis

were still a few vacancies in the Best Actress contest. When producer Ray Stark read Vincent Canby's paean to Hanna Schygulla in the *New York Times*—promoting her as a possible Best Actress winner—the Hollywood veteran thought it ridiculous that the Oscar would be wasted on a German actress in an art-house movie, especially when he had a tour de force by Marsha Mason, a two-time loser, waiting in the wings. So Stark rushed the release of *Chapter Two* from spring 1980 to December 1979 to qualify. *Chapter Two* represented a unique challenge for Mason—she was portraying a character based on herself. Neil Simon's play was about his whirlwind marriage to Mason and their subsequent problems when he discovered he was still hung up over his late first wife. Mason was not in the original Broadway production because, as she explained to the *New York Times,* "It would have been weird to do the role at that time." She did feel ready to tackle the movie version, though—"I feel much more separated from it now." "Mason is as fetching as ever," raved Stanley Kauffmann, "the ideal magazinestory heroine, with suggestions of Nanette Fabray and Rosalynn Carter blended into a funny, sexy, appealingly snuffy persona."

The Awards Season

There was only one first-ballot winner at the New York Film Critics—Dustin Hoffman for Best Actor for *Kramer vs. Kramer,* which also won Best Picture. Woody Allen made off with the Best Director citation for *Manhattan* and Steve Tesich took the Best Screenplay plaque for *Breaking Away.* Sally Field in *Norma Rae* edged out Bette Midler in *The Rose* and won Best Actress. Melvyn Douglas earned sixteen votes for *The Seduction of Joe Tynan* but won Best Supporting Actor with forty-six points for *Being There*. Meryl Streep garnered thirty-two points for *The Seduction of Joe Tynan* and then thirty-three points for *Kramer vs. Kramer;* the critics decided to give her the Best Supporting Actress Award for both movies, but Streep wasn't at the party to accept it. Married to sculptor Donald Gummer, Streep became a mother in real life just two months before the critics' bash, and a representative announced that she couldn't make it because her infant was sick. "Oh, little baby," Sally Field was overheard saying to herself.

Field and Hoffman became a virtual traveling team as they won almost all of the pre-Oscar awards—Hoffman even accepted his Los Angeles Film Critics Award on *The Merv Griffin Show*. Hoffman's award enthusiasm dimmed a bit at the Golden Globes ceremony when Justin Henry lost two awards—including Most Promising Male Newcomer to *The Champ*'s ten-year-old Ricky Schroder—and burst into tears. When Dustin inevitably won, he said in his speech: "I think awards are silly. They put very talented people against one another and they hurt a lot when you don't win." Hoffman told reporters he sympathized with his costar: "What Justin was feeling was what I had been feeling when I lost awards in the past." Everyone cheered up, though, when Bette Midler, winning two awards—Best Actress in a Musical and Most Promising Female Newcomer—shimmied to the podium and joked, "As Joan Crawford once said, 'I'll show ya a pair of Golden Globes!'"

The Nominations

Kramer vs. Kramer won nine nominations, tied by *All That Jazz*. Bob Fosse couldn't believe it, but he told Marilyn Beck that his movie "doesn't have a chance. It's going to be mostly *Kramer vs. Kramer*. I'm such a long shot I think anyone who bets on me should get a toaster, like they give out in banks, for having made the investment." Fosse was also skeptical because, for the third time, he was competing with Francis Coppola, whose *Apocalypse Now* had eight nominations.

Michael Douglas could not expect another *One Flew Over the Cuckoo's Nest*–style sweep for *The China Syndrome;* the film won only four nominations, failing to be nominated for either Best Picture or Best Director. Columnist James Bacon

"As Joan Crawford once said, 'I'll show ya a pair of Golden Globes!'"
—Bette Midler

contended that nominee Jack Lemmon still had a shot at Oscar number three: "There are a lot of Academy voters who will tell you that Lemmon's performance was the best of a career that has already produced two Oscars." The likelihood of nominee Jane Fonda earning her third statuette appeared slimmer, as journalists began to suggest that her roles were becoming awfully similar. In reporting the nominations for the *New York Times,* Aljean Harmetz wrote, "Jane Fonda, who won last year as the gradually radicalized army wife in *Coming Home* is back for her gradually radicalized television reporter in *The China Syndrome.*"

"Perhaps the biggest surprise in any major category," Harmetz continued, "was the fifth directorial nomination—Edouard Molinaro for the sunny French farce about a pair of middle-aged homosexuals, *La Cage aux Folles.*" Molinaro was also nominated for Adapted Screenplay, and the movie about transvestites won a third nomination—for Costume Design. Molinaro's directorial nomination bumped New York Film Critics winner Woody Allen from the list. *Manhattan* earned only two nominations—Original Screenplay and Best Supporting Actress for Mariel Hemingway—meaning that Gordon Willis' photography went unrecognized again. *Daily Variety* termed the omission of Willis and Caleb Deschanel for *The Black Stallion* "the talk of the town." Willis said, "I have no idea why they don't nominate me. Maybe if I bought a house in Hollywood I'd have a better chance." Conrad Hall told *Variety* it wasn't Willis' New York residence that bothered the Cinematography Branch. "The veterans want to see the eyes, always the eyes," he said, referring to Willis' characteristically dark photography. "They said they would have been fired if they'd shot that way." Caleb Deschanel confessed, "I'm disappointed. The fact that so many people told me I was sure to get the nomination has made it harder to take. On the other hand, who am I? I'm just a young punk making his name in this business. But to ignore Gordon Willis is a crime."

Deschanel could go commiserate with Burt Reynolds. Not only was Sally Field a nominee, but so were both of his costars from *Starting Over*—Jill Clayburgh and Candice Bergen—while he was overlooked. The fifth Best Actor nominee turned out to be Al Pacino—his fifth nod—for . . . *And Justice for All,* a picture largely dismissed by the critics. As for Reynolds, he was the guest host of *Saturday Night Live* the week the nominations were announced, and the first joke on the show centered on his being excluded from the Oscar race. One by one, the cast members consoled him until finally he exploded and banged Gilda Radner's head inside a locker. Offstage, Reynolds told reporters, "If I want to be up for an Academy Award, I'm either going to have to play a tour de force of some kind or have a tracheotomy just before the nominations."

Sally Field was also sounding off about the Academy. "I think it's exploitative, overcommercialized, frequently offensive and shouldn't be televised," she told reporters, even though industry pundits ascribed *Norma Rae*'s surprise Best Picture nomination to Fox's massive trade-paper campaign. "Sure, I'll be there," the nominee said. "If I said I wasn't coming, they'd still go on with the show."

Show producer Howard W. Koch said this year's theme would be "The Elegant '80s" and explained, "It will be a feeling of dressing up—back to the '40s and '50s. We will have style in the sets and costumes. We will be as elegant as we can." To ensure elegance, costume designer Bob Mackie was the show's fashion consultant. "Thank God we're past the era when it was fashionable not to be fashionable and to show up wearing jeans or Indian buckskins," Mackie exclaimed to the *Hollywood Reporter.* When the designer called Sally Field, she told him, "I know nothing about clothes. You can design for me anything you want." She then told reporters, "I'm leaving it all up to Bob and have no idea what he'll put me in, though it probably will be pinafores to suit my personality."

The Big Night

The first celebrity to arrive was TV's Kristy McNichol. Cesar "Butch" Romero rolled up and told Army Archerd he hadn't missed an Oscar ceremony since *It Happened One Night* won in 1934. Bo Derek, who became the country's top pinup after playing the title role in *10*, came alone and explained why her husband wasn't with her: "It's not his thing. He took Shirley Temple when he was sixteen. That was his first and last time." *Daily Variety* reported that there were no protesters this year, just three Jesus freaks across the street, but there was the annual appearance of "sometime-actress Edy Williams, in an abbreviated bikini bottom, glitter on her body and an almost-sheer shirt, pulling a sheep dog on a leash."

Sally Field wore her Bob Mackie outfit: a white suit with a beaded Hawaiian shirt underneath the jacket. Her escort was not Burt Reynolds, but comedian David Steinberg. Jill Clayburgh came with playwright David Rabe, Bette Midler with actor Peter Riegert, Marsha Mason with Neil Simon, and Jane Fonda brought her family again—daughter Vanessa Vadim wore a tuxedo while husband Tom Hayden wore his standard suit. Dustin Hoffman also brought his family—his parents and his new wife. The only other Actor nominee present was Jack Lemmon. Roy Scheider was watching the show from Joe Allen's restaurant in New York, and Al Pacino and Peter Sellers weren't paying attention at all. "I never go to those things," Sellers had said earlier. "I'm very antisocial."

Mickey Rooney and Ann Miller got the night off from *Sugar Babies* to be presenters. Miller had asked Halston to design her gown and the designer consented on one condition: "You won't wear one of those tacky wigs." When Army Archerd asked *Black Stallion* Supporting Actor nominee Rooney if he felt this was his year, the born-again Christian said, "I'm just so pleased, my cup runneth over." Rooney's competition, Frederic Forrest of *The Rose*, entered with white hair—he was currently filming the latest Omni Zoetrope production,

Awards Ceremony

APRIL 14, 1980, 6:00 P.M.
THE DOROTHY CHANDLER PAVILION, LOS ANGELES

Your Host:
JOHNNY CARSON
Televised over ABC

Presenters

Supporting Actress	Cloris Leachman and Jack Lemmon
Art Direction	Ann Miller and Mickey Rooney
Scoring Awards	Dolly Parton and Ben Vereen
Jean Hersholt Humanitarian Award	Douglas Fairbanks, Jr.
Costume Design	Robert Hays and Kristy McNichol
Visual Effects	Farrah Fawcett and Harold Russell
Documentary Awards	Persis Khambatta and William Shatner
Short Films	Lauren Hutton and Telly Savalas
Special Award for the Moviola	Richard Gere
Honorary Award to Hal Elias	Walter Mirisch
Foreign Film	Ann-Margret and Jack Valenti
Special Achievement Award	Johnny Carson
Thalberg Award	Kirk Douglas
Cinematography	Jamie Lee Curtis and George Hamilton
Song	Gene Kelly and Olivia Newton-John
Film Editing	Bo Derek and Christopher Reeve
Supporting Actor	Walter Matthau and Liza Minnelli
Honorary Award to Alec Guinness	Dustin Hoffman
Director	Goldie Hawn and Steven Spielberg
Writing Awards	Neil Simon
Actor	Jane Fonda
Actress	Richard Dreyfuss
Picture	Charlton Heston

Performers of Nominated Songs

"I'll Never Say Goodbye"	Melissa Manchester
"It Goes Like It Goes"	Dionne Warwick
"It's Easy to Say"	Dudley Moore and Helen Reddy
"The Rainbow Connection"	Kermit the Frog
"Through the Eyes of Love"	Melissa Manchester

"Thank God we're past the era when it was fashionable not to be fashionable and to show up wearing jeans or Indian buckskins."
—Bob Mackie

Hammett. Justin Henry looked like a miniature Tom Hayden in his dark suit. Accompanied by his parents, Justin told Army Archerd that he had already written his speech. The oldest nominee, Melvyn Douglas, didn't bother to come. "The whole thing is absurd, my competing with an eight-year-old," he told reporters.

The telecast began with helicopter shots of the Griffith Observatory and the Hollywood sign, followed by the arriving celebrities. Henry Mancini led the orchestra in a overture of themes from the Best Score nominees, including his own *10,* from which he played *Bolero*. Hank Sims then announced the Academy's new president, "the distinguished writer, Mr. Fay Kanin." Ms. Kanin walked out laughing and said, "Movies have become a national treasure."

Master of ceremonies Johnny Carson entered to the tune of "You Ought to Be in Pictures" and commented, "It says something about our times that the only lasting relationship is in *La Cage aux Folles*. Who says they don't write good feminine parts anymore?" Justin Henry, Carson said, "has the distinction of being the only Hollywood actor not in Britt Ekland's memoirs." The cameras saw a bewildered Justin wondering why everyone was laughing. On the subject of Bo Derek, Carson said, "Forty years ago Butterfly McQueen wore the same hairdo and nobody cared." Bob Fosse, with date Julie Hagerty, had to endure more criticism when the emcee cracked, "In *All That Jazz* with Roy Scheider, they opened up his chest and his ego had already spread all over his body."

Cloris Leachman and Jack Lemmon gave the first Award—Best Supporting Actress. All the nominees were there and the winner was Meryl Streep for *Kramer vs. Kramer*. Streep had obviously forgiven Hoffman for their first meeting and she bussed him on the way to the stage. "Holy mackerel!" she exclaimed at the podium. "I'd like to thank Dustin Hoffman and Robert Benton, to whom I owe this. To Justin . . ." and she blew him a kiss. When she returned to her seat, Justin walked over to inspect the Oscar.

Mickey Rooney, in a ruffled tuxedo shirt, and Ann Miller, in her blue Halston and her hair pulled into a pony tail, danced out to give the Art Direction Oscar—Ann spun around so the audience could see the back of her dress. Rooney put his glasses on upside down, and then they got down to business. *All That Jazz* won. After the winners gave thanks, they exited backstage with the presenters. "All right, guys," Rooney instructed them, "this is your big night, so live it up." "Good luck to you, later on," they told the Best Supporting Actor nominee. "Ahhh," laughed the Mick, "I don't take this award crap seriously."

Dolly Parton and Ben Vereen announced the Scoring Awards and Vereen could not restrain his excitement when his movie, *All That Jazz,* won the Original Song Score Award. "Yesssss!" he yelled, jumping up and down. There was a reaction shot of Fosse and Hagerty, who were smiling but still incredulous. "I'm in that movie!" Vereen continued, while Parton, with a noticeable edge in her voice, said, "Oh, that's terrific," and progressed to the next category. After they gave the Score Award, Vereen and Parton walked off while Carson quipped, "They make a lovely pair, don't they?" Minutes later, *All That Jazz* claimed the Costume Design Oscar—Fosse's movie had gone three for three.

Farrah Fawcett and Harold Russell, the amputee who had won Best Supporting Actor in 1946 and was now making a comeback in a film called *Inside Moves,* presented the Visual Effects Oscar, which went to Fox's *Alien*. Carlo Rambaldi climbed to the stage and said, "Three years ago when I was up here for *King Kong,* I didn't know English and I said 'Thank you.' Now I learn very well English and I say thank you very much."

William Shatner and Persis Khambatta, the stars of *Star Trek—The Motion Picture,* gave the Documentary Feature Oscar to Ira Wohl for his film about his retarded cousin, entitled *Best Boy*. "So what's a nice Jewish boy from Queens doing in a nice place like this?" Wohl said. "With documentaries, it's not always easy to get people to come and see it." When Wohl began to thank "my

"Three years ago, I wasn't even in the ball game—and now I'm in the Super Bowl."
—Mickey Rooney

cousins Frances and Norman," there were giggles from the audience, but the recipient continued, "my aunt and uncle who are no longer alive, my aunt Pearl, my uncle Max, and cousin Philly . . ." Wohl left after speaking for three minutes and 58 seconds and Shatner said, "I'm glad he didn't have a larger family." The winner of the Documentary Short Oscar was briefer, saying, "All my life I've wanted one of these."

Donald O'Connor led a musical salute to choreography in films and was rewarded with a standing ovation, led by Mickey Rooney, who had taken over for O'Connor in the final Francis the Talking Mule movie. Then Carson returned to introduce the Foreign Film Award presenter, Motion Picture Association of America head Jack Valenti: "He's not the most electric personality, but he's filled the charisma void left by the passing of Conrad Nagel." After his traditional "film is the universal language" spiel, Valenti revealed that Volker Schlöndorff had won for *The Tin Drum*. "You know, it's the first Award ever given to a film of my country. There's been lots of reasons for that, we know!" Schlöndorff shouted, then calmed down and continued, "But I take it as a tribute to my fellow directors over there and for all those whose traditions we want to pick up and follow, and who worked and lived here, I mean, Fritz Lang, Billy Wilder, Ernst Lubitsch, F. W. Murnau and G. W. Pabst. You all know them. You welcomed them. Thank you very much."

Johnny Carson was in charge of the Special Achievement Award to Alan Splet for his Sound Effects Editing work on *The Black Stallion*, but when Splet failed to materialize, the comedian commented, "It always happens. First George C. Scott doesn't show, then Marlon Brando, and now Alan Splet." Ray Stark was present to accept his Irving G. Thalberg Award from Kirk Douglas, who told the audience, "Ray does what Irving used to do." "Thank you, Kirk, I couldn't have said it better myself," said the producer whose maneuvering of *Chapter Two* showed that he was, indeed, as crafty as Thalberg.

Carson rushed out and announced, "We just heard from Alan Splet. He missed the off-ramp at the Music Center and he's somewhere in Ensenada—but he's on his way here." The *All That Jazz* momentum was cut short when *Apocalypse Now* won the Cinematography Oscar. "Francis, thank you for the freedom to express myself in *Apocalypse Now*," said Vittorio Storaro. More sentiment was expressed by composer David Shire, who accepted the Best Song Oscar for the theme song to *Norma Rae* by remarking, "I'd like to thank my young son and his mother, Talia Shire, who taught my heart something it needed to know before I could find out what my music could really be about." The Shires divorced a few months later.

"Here's an Alan Splet update," Carson reported. "He's had trouble with his carburetor outside of Barstow." Bo Derek and Christopher Reeve gave the Editing Oscar to *All That Jazz*'s Alan Heim, who thanked "my wife and family and friends for putting up with a year of obsessive behavior." Then Walter Matthau and Liza Minnelli stepped out to reveal the Best Supporting Actor. The winner was the sole absentee—Melvyn Douglas for *Being There*. The camera saw Justin Henry roll his head back as if to say, "Not again." Carson was back and quipped, "It's not Melvyn Douglas' fault he's not here. He's in a car pool with Alan Splet." Even Justin laughed.

Dustin Hoffman was onstage to give an Honorary Oscar to the 1957 Best Actor winner Alec Guinness. Hoffman said that he spent the last few weeks taking in Guinness' films and "to watch his work is to be a student of him." Guinness walked out to a standing ovation and said, "Thank you, Mr. Hoffman, for your overgenerous words and all that deep research work you did." The actor confessed, "I feel very fraudulent taking this but, letting no expression cross my face," he broke into a smile, "I'm grabbing this while the going's good." He took the Oscar and walked offstage.

Bob Fosse sat nervously as Steven Spielberg opened the Best Director envelope. The winner was Robert Benton for *Kramer vs. Kramer*. Benton kissed his wife and son, tripped slightly on the way to the stage, and thanked "all the people at Colum-

"I sat home alone like a wounded Citizen Kane, visualizing Sally dancing with Dustin Hoffman at the Academy ball."
—Burt Reynolds

bia, past and present." He also saluted his agent, Sam Cohn.

Neil Simon, who had failed to get an Oscar nomination for *Chapter Two* even after Ray Stark sent out one hundred fifty copies of the script to journalists, was compensated by being put in charge of the writing Awards. The Best Original Screenplay winner was *Breaking Away*'s Steve Tesich, who, like Robert Benton, had Sam Cohn as his agent. "Where's Sam, I need Sam up here," the writer fretted. "I was going to do original stuff." Tesich thanked "the present Fox people," and reminisced about "seeing *Stagecoach* in Yugoslavia. I'm grateful to send back a film that's just like the one I saw originally. The good and bad still fight it out and the good wins." The Adapted Screenplay winner was Robert Benton for *Kramer vs. Kramer*, who once again tripped en route to the podium. "This really is one of the five best days of my whole life," Benton declared.

Jane Fonda strolled out to name the Best Actor. "I'm very pleased to tell you the nominees," Fonda said, "and to remind you that each has given a remarkable body of work in their careers." This was a prelude to a brief tribute to each nominee. Fonda said of Al Pacino, "He's virtually a specialist in showing the darker side of life." Academy members were in a lighter mood, though, and the winner was Dustin Hoffman in *Kramer vs. Kramer*. The audience erupted with whistles and cheers as Hoffman kissed his wife, his mother, Justin Henry, Meryl Streep and Jack Lemmon. He only shook Mickey Rooney's hand. Onstage, Hoffman glanced at his Oscar and remarked, "He has no genitalia and he's holding a sword. I'd like to thank my mother and father for not practicing birth control. We are laughed at when we are up here sometimes for thanking, but when you work on a film you discover that there are people who are giving that artistic part of themselves that goes beyond a paycheck and they are never up here."

Hoffman began thanking some of these people, and mentioned Justin Henry: "If he loses again, we'll have to give him a lifetime achievement award." The camera saw Justin beaming. "I'm up here with mixed feelings," Hoffman said. "I've criticized the Academy before, with reason. I refuse to believe that I beat Jack Lemmon, that I beat Al Pacino, that I beat Peter Sellers . . . We are part of an artistic family. There are sixty thousand actors in the Screen Actors Guild who don't work. You have to practice accents while you're driving a taxicab 'cause when you're a broke actor, you can't write and you can't paint. Most actors don't work and a few of us are so lucky to have a chance. And to that artistic family that strives for excellence, none of you have ever lost and I am proud to share this with you and I thank you." Dustin's mother was in tears as he walked off. Carson editorialized, "I think we can all agree that was beautifully said."

Richard Dreyfuss hopped out to crown the Best Actress. Opening the envelope, Dreyfuss laughed, "I'm not going to tell you." But he did—the winner was Sally Field for *Norma Rae*. Shaking her fist triumphantly as she walked to the podium, Field announced, "I'm going to be the one to cry tonight, I'll tell you that right now. They said this couldn't be done." The actress thanked her cinematographer, then added, "Marty Ritt is Norma Rae; he's fought all his life to put on films that have something to say." She concluded by thanking her two sons: "No matter how many awards I win, if it weren't for them, I wouldn't be worth a damn." As Field walked off with Dreyfuss to loud applause, she held the Oscar over her head.

It was anticlimactic when Charlton Heston revealed that the Best Picture was *Kramer vs. Kramer*, but producer Stanley Jaffe was definitely escstatic. "Oh, boy!" he exclaimed at the podium. Everyone came out to sing "That's Entertainment" shortly thereafter, as the winners and presenters stood uncertainly onstage until the telecast ended.

Aftermath

"Hey!" a voice cried out from the ladies' room. "Somebody left an Oscar in here!" "Oh, my

"I do feel like the Academy is slacking off in the class quotient—after all, I won."
—Sally Field

God!" screamed Meryl Streep. "How could I have done that? It shows how nervous I really am." While Streep retrieved her trophy, Foreign Film winner Volker Schlöndorff was being grilled by the press on exactly what he meant by that crack that "we all know why" Germany had never won an Oscar. "I did not intend to say that the country was being penalized by the Academy for its Nazi past," the director explained. "I meant that all our great directors came over here and took their talent with them. We had no fathers to copy."

With no Melvyn Douglas around to interview, reporters focused on Best Supporting Actor loser Mickey Rooney, who didn't appear very upset. "Believe me, win, lose, or draw or otherwise, I'm just so proud to be an infinitesimal part of a great evening," the trouper said. "Remember, three years ago, I wasn't even in the ball game—and now I'm in the Super Bowl."

Sally Field did not take such a grand view. "I do feel like the Academy is slacking off in the class quotient—after all, I won," she stated. "It's like the Groucho Marx line about I wouldn't want to be in a club that would have me as a member." Someone asked if the Best Actress Award at the Cannes Film Festival meant more to her, but Field said, "No, the Oscar means more. This is my state and my home. I've wanted to be an actress since I was two and growing up in Encino."

No one asked Field the whereabouts of Burt Reynolds, but he told a reporter later, "I sat home alone like a wounded Citizen Kane, visualizing her dancing with Dustin Hoffman at the Academy ball. After that, nothing was the same. I had become obsessed with the notion that two stars could not coexist."

Hoffman made the most of his evening, instructing his waiter at the Governors' Ball, "Don't stop with the champagne! Keep it coming!" The Best Actor celebrated with his *Kramer* collaborators, and toasted his *Lenny* director, Bob Fosse. In New York, Fosse's latest leading man, Roy Scheider, was consoling his fifteen-year-old daughter, who began weeping at Joe Allen's when her father lost. Newspaper photographers snapped Scheider as he comforted his child, but the Best Actor loser maintained that he was happy for his *Marathon Man* costar. "This was Dustin Hoffman's year," he said, "just as it was Jack Nicholson's year, just as it was John Wayne's year."

The Soviet newspaper *Tass* was critical of the Academy's choices, arguing, "*The China Syndrome* was the best U.S. movie of the year and should have won an Academy Award." The paper charged that its favorite movie lost because it was "too close to the truth, which is unacceptable under Hollywood's canon." What show producer Howard W. Koch found unacceptable was Documentary winner Ira Wohl's long acceptance speech. On a local Los Angeles radio show, Koch said, "There's a lot of controversy about putting those Documentary Awards on the air. I don't know whether we should continue that, whether we should give Oscars to the people who come from nowhere." Wohl happened to be on the freeway listening on his car radio, and he pulled over and called the station. "It's true that maybe I did talk a little long," the Oscar winner said, "but what really infuriates me is the attitude somebody like Howard Koch takes. My movie is every bit as legitimate as any film he's ever made and I would like to think it's going to be remembered much longer than most of his. I happen to come from New York and I'm sure he came from somewhere else originally." As it turned out, Koch was also from New York, and Dustin Hoffman's paean to the Screen Actors Guild was a minute longer than Wohl's speech.

The day after the ceremony, Justin Henry returned to his home in Rye, New York, where he finally won an award—his Bobcat badge from Cub Scout Pack 5.

1980

"I think me and Sissy were probably twin sisters in a past life."
—Loretta Lynn

Life—and death—imitated art at the 1980 Academy Awards.

"After my book came out," said Loretta Lynn of her autobiography, "they wanted to make a TV thing about me, but I said no. Why do something like that when a real movie will end up on TV someday anyway?" So the country singer who was named after Loretta Young held out until Universal made a movie offer. She told the movie company it could explore any aspect of her life "good or bad, as long as it's the truth. I didn't worry about what they'd do to me. But I didn't want my husband to be offended in any way—or any of his people. Like his drinking—I'm not ashamed, but I didn't want them to make him a drunk because that would have been wrong."

To cast herself, Lynn looked through a pile of photographs of actresses and stopped when she got to one of red-haired, freckle-faced Sissy Spacek. "That's her," the singer said, "there's the coal miner's daughter." But Spacek, a native of Texas, wasn't so sure. "I was leery of the part, skeptical of playing a contemporary figure who appears on television all the time," the actress said, but she agreed to meet Loretta. "I just loved her," Spacek raved afterward. "She and I are the same size—five feet two and one-half inches and there is something so familiar about her. It was like meeting a long-lost friend." Spacek went brunette and did her own singing for the part, as did blond Beverly D'Angelo as the ill-fated Patsy Cline. Tommy Lee Jones bleached his hair blond to play Loretta's husband, Doolittle Lynn, and the actor also recommended the performer who was to play Loretta's father—Levon Helm, drummer for The Band. "It was fun," the thirty-nine-year-old-musician told *People*, "nothing strenuous like memorizing the Gettysburg address."

"You don't have to know anything much about Loretta Lynn in order to have a good time at *Coal Miner's Daughter*," said *The New Yorker*, while Stanley Kauffmann wrote in the *New Republic*, "Some of us keep asking for American movies that speak of the variedness of America. Much of the time this picture does part of that job. It means a lot more to me than the bloated *Nashville*, with its strain to be an All-American metaphor." *Newsweek* said that as Loretta, Spacek "demonstrates anew that she is one of the most gifted chameleons on the screen." To Universal's delight, *Coal Miner's Daughter* made $40 million in the United States. When Marilyn Beck asked the actress if she thought she'd win an Oscar nomination, Spacek blushingly replied, "Oh heavens, oh gosh. I don't really think I deserve that. I feel that my award was getting to play the role—and getting to know Loretta Lynn." As for Loretta, she cried all the way through the picture and said, "I think me and Sissy were probably twin sisters in a past life."

Overleaf: *Coal miner's daughter strikes gold—Loretta Lynn and Sissy Spacek with their Best Actress Oscar.*

Ace in the Hole

Producer Charles A. Pratt was interested in adapting Pat Conroy's autobiographical novel *The Great Santini*, about a youth's clash with his martinet military father, and he knew the perfect actor for one of the roles. "Bob Duvall wanted to do it very badly," Pratt said. "He's the son of a navy officer and the story sort of paralleled his own life." Robert Duvall's screen son was played by twenty-five-year-old Michael O'Keefe, who called his role "the first I've ever played with any depth of character." Although filmed in Conroy's hometown of Beaufort, South Carolina, the movie bombed in both North and South Carolina when Orion released it in November 1979. The studio tried a variety of new titles—*The Ace; Son of Heroes;* and *Reaching Out*—but the movie flopped wherever the studio opened it: Fort Wayne, Cincinnati, San Diego, Sacramento and Peoria. "We had nothing to sell but quality," said writer-director Lewis John Carlino. "There were no big stars. Orion tested it, but based on the response, they feared the

"The liberal notion seems to be that you're not making anything worthwhile unless it's about the poor."
—Robert Redford

poor reviews in New York would kill the chances to sell the ancillary rights."

Orion decided to make what money it could and sold the film to cable TV and to the airlines as an in-flight movie, but refused to sponsor the movie in New York. Producer Pratt managed to raise the funds to open the movie in one Manhattan theater and the critics finally got a look at it. Vincent Canby was moved to write in the *New York Times*, "Now it's about time to recognize Robert Duvall as one of the most resourceful, most technically proficient, most remarkable actors in America today . . . I think he may well be the best we have, the American Olivier." And Rex Reed found Michael O'Keefe very much to his liking. "Michael O'Keefe is just about the best young actor to emerge on the screen from obscurity since Montgomery Clift." *The Great Santini* broke house records in New York, and Pratt told the press, "Let's face it, they made a monumental blunder. The trouble is that filmmakers aren't running the industry anymore. They don't know and they don't care how your soul and guts are involved in a picture. Movies are just canned goods to them." But Pratt's success story extended only as far as the Hudson River; cable TV premiered *The Ace* two weeks after *The Great Santini* opened in Gotham and the picture never made a cent in any other city.

Ellen Burstyn Never Says Die

It just wasn't Lewis John Carlino's year at the box office. He had also tailored a screenplay for Ellen Burstyn about faith healing, a subject the actress had been interested ever since a healer had cured her son of an injury in a mere ten days after doctors had said it would take months. Burstyn recruited many of her friends—Eva Le Gallienne, Lois Smith, Sam Shepard—to play the film's Midwestern characters and hired a professional faith healer from California as a technical supervisor and occasional medic.

"Because *Resurrection* is about a contemporary faith healer, Universal had the bright idea that the film would appeal to the Midwest and the Bible Belt, so they decided to test-market it in rural areas before exposing it to the cynical New York critics," Burstyn said. "They designed an ad campaign that made it look like a horror film, so they got the horror-film buffs instead of the people who would like to have a beautiful spiritual experience." After flopping in the South, *Resurrection* rose again in New York, where Liz Smith asked, "Is Universal nuts? Ellen Burstyn is at the very least a national treasure. Her performance in this one is simply luminous. The miracles in *Resurrection* are wonderfully believable, certainly no more freaky than some of the experiments that take place at Duke University."

But these glowing critical notices weren't enough to make Ellen Burstyn happy. "Now Universal has gotten discouraged over the low grosses and given up. I am so discouraged that I really feel devastated. Everyone who sees the film seems to love it—I've had people tell me it changed their life—so I simply will not give up on a film I believe so strongly in and I'm going to fight for the success of *Resurrection* if it kills me." The actress inspired her cohorts from the Actors Studio to help out, and Rex Reed warned readers, "Don't be surprised if you run into June Havoc or Eli Wallach outside the Citicorp Building passing out leaflets urging people to see *Resurrection* because it's good for their souls." This method didn't work, either, and a Universal executive said, "We've tried everything, but let's face it— God isn't commercial." But Burstyn begged to differ. "It's that commercial Hollywood mentality that's not working when they'd rather drag a good film down with them than be proven wrong. I get so frustrated and sick, I wonder why I got into this business in the first place."

No Bucks for Howard Hughes

Universal was also having problems with *Melvin and Howard*, a $7.5 million film about Melvin Dummar, the Utah gas station owner who claimed to be a beneficiary of Howard Hughes' will. "It's

"I get so frustrated and sick, I wonder why I got into this business in the first place."
—Ellen Burstyn

nice to make a movie that is a reminder that human relations have beneficial outcomes," said director Jonathan Demme. "Films don't zero in on this much, unless it's in an exaggerated sense, like people teaming up to hurt a killer or catch a shark." Demme discovered after an exhibitors' screening that theater owners thought *Melvin and Howard* could use a shark. "They did not clamber all over one another trying to book this film," the director admitted. "I read some of their reactions and one wrote, 'It's funny, but it's not really a comedy' and another wrote, 'It's a nice movie, but I don't understand why it was made.' " Universal wondered why, too, and the film sat on the shelf for seventeen months.

With nothing to lose, the studio allowed *Melvin and Howard* to play the New York Film Festival as the opening night attraction. *Newsweek* wrote, "*Melvin and Howard* takes on the deeply satisfying glow of a classic folk tale, lovingly told," and Andrew Sarris said that Jason Robards, as Howard Hughes toward the end of his life, "does a haunting cameo." "But the picture belongs to Mary Steenburgen, who is the new Jean Arthur, and about time, too," proclaimed *Time*. The *New York Daily News* agreed, stating that Steenburgen as Melvin's first wife "is as adorably giddy as the late Judy Holliday." The actress had been discovered by Jack Nicholson when he was casting *Goin' South* in 1978 and she married the leading man of her next movie—Malcolm McDowell in 1979's *Time After Time*. Steenburgen seemed to have everything an actress could want except a hit movie. Universal's Ned Tanen told Marilyn Beck that, outside of New York, nobody cared about the folk tale. "We couldn't drag 'em in if we gave dishes away," he said.

Robert Redford Finds the Dark Side

"I wouldn't mind moving away from the role of, uh, a glamour figure of cartoon proportions," said Robert Redford. "I've felt tremendously reduced by that. I've been grateful for a lot of it—no complaints—but I have felt reduced." To expand himself, the actor turned producer again and optioned a novel he had read in galley form, *Ordinary People*, that went on to become a bestseller. "The liberal notion seems to be that you're not making anything worthwhile unless it's about the poor," Redford said, explaining why he was adapting a story about upper-middle-class WASPs in Chicago. "It's about the status quo and whether it's worth the trouble it takes to maintain it.

"You can only do so much as an actor," Redford went on, and he cast himself as the film's director while casting the rest of the picture against type. Donald Sutherland, described by Redford as "about as off-center as you can get," was assigned the role of a straitlaced businessman. For the role of his unyielding wife, "We considered Lee Remick, a wonderful actress," Redford said, "but I became interested in the dark side of Mary Tyler Moore." The forty-two-year-old TV star, having terminated her hit situation comedy, insisted she was the woman for the role. "There is a dark side," Moore confessed. "I tend not to be as optimistic as Mary Richards. I have an anger in me that I carry from my childhood experiences—I expect a lot of myself and I'm not too kind to myself." Redford also looked to TV when Gene Hackman backed out of the role of a psychiatrist—*Taxi*'s Judd Hirsch stepped in between episodes to film his part in ten days. To play Hirsch's patient, a teenager who blames himself for his brother's death, Redford selected nineteen-year-old Timothy Hutton, the son of actor Jim Hutton, who had died of cancer four months before filming began. Paramount didn't think a heavy family drama would pack audiences in, so the studio focused the film's publicity on the film's glamorous director. "I don't care if people go to see it just because I directed it," Redford said, "just as long as I get them into the theaters."

No More Sunshine Girl

"Never a very expressive actor, he has turned to directing to reveal a depth of feeling he couldn't seem to manage in front of the camera," wrote

"You're a crazy man. You're hired." —Mel Brooks to David Lynch

Kenneth Turan in *New West* when *Ordinary People* premiered in September. The *New York Daily News* decorated the film with four stars and called it "a soul-searching, penetratingly honest movie, one that recognizes the limitations of us all, while urging us to scale the barriers that prevent us from reaching out to one another." Pauline Kael in *The New Yorker,* didn't feel that way, and said the movie "is essentially a simple-minded, old-fashioned tearjerker, in a conventional style."

Timothy Hutton inspired conventional fan worship in audiences and reviewers. "Jumpy, nervous, intense, hostile to an adult world that doesn't understand him, Hutton's Conrad is one of the truest portrayals of an adolescent in torment we have had since the long-lost days of James Dean," wrote Turan. Like Dean, Hutton saw himself as a Hollywood outsider and told interviewers, "I don't like the whole Hollywood scene. If I went to a party—and I wouldn't—but if I went there looking to talk to somebody about Faulkner's *Light in August,* someone would say, 'Hey, who has the option on that? Let's have lunch.'" Despite his distaste for the social life, the actor was a favorite of the gossip columnists. "Tim Hutton and Patti Reagan Davis let their romance simmer down to just friendship," Hank Grant wrote in his column in the *Hollywood Reporter*. "He won't be accompanying her to papa Ronald's inauguration, after all."

"Mary Tyler Moore deserves some kind of award for her courage in exploring the coldness that can sometimes be found at the heart of those all-American girls she often plays," applauded *Time,* and the *New York Times* headlined, SUNSHINE GIRL BECOMES GIRL YOU'LL LOVE TO HATE. The actress told the paper that she drew on memories of raising her own son, now twenty-three and working in the mailroom of a TV network in Los Angeles. "I was kind of a perfectionist mother and I demanded a lot of him," she confessed. "I think I was responsible for a lot of alienation, although we've since become very close. So I brought some of that to the part, and enlarged and magnified it." A month after the film's release, Moore's son committed suicide. President Carter called with his condolences, while Marilyn Beck reported, "Some sources believe that the role Mary Tyler Moore plays—as a mother whose eldest son has died—has taken on too heavy a sense of reality since the tragic death of her own son last month." A film executive said, 'It's just too downbeat a story to appeal to the masses in these trying times. It's not going to lose money, but it's certainly not going to be the blockbuster that was predicted.'"

I Am Not an Animal

Paramount's other major fall release wasn't a bundle of laughs, either, although it was produced by Mel Brooks. The comic angered the producers of a Broadway play called *The Elephant Man* when he announced that he was making a movie with the same title about the same subject—John Merrick, a hideously deformed man who became a celebrity in turn-of-the century London. Brooks got away with it because Merrick's story was in the public domain, but the movie producer did make a settlement out of court with the Broadway producers who claimed that Brooks had ruined the film sale of their play.

Brooks lined up a cast of English names—Wendy Hiller, John Gielgud, Anthony Hopkins and John Hurt as Merrick—and found a role for Mrs. Brooks, Anne Bancroft, playing a regal actress who reads from *Romeo and Juliet* with the title character and exclaims, "Why, you're not an Elephant Man at all! You're Romeo!" This prestige property was placed at the feet of David Lynch, whose only claim to fame was an extremely low-budget midnight movie called *Eraserhead,* about a weirdo couple and their gelatinous offspring. "You're a crazy man," Brooks told Lynch. "You're hired."

"*The Elephant Man* is a moving glimpse into the dark alleys of human existence," exhorted *Variety*. "Those seeking shock and sensationalism will be disappointed and, hopefully, chastised by the experience." The *New York Times* overheard a

"Being sober for so many years is getting interesting."
—Peter O'Toole

patron in a lobby say after he saw the movie, "He was ugly, but he was a nice guy. I would've liked to know a guy like that." Director Lynch wasn't surprised by the film's commercial appeal, noting, "Hollywood will probably consider *Elephant Man* a 'different' movie, but, for me, it is very mainstream." So mainstream, in fact, that J. Hoberman, the avant-garde film critic of the *Village Voice*, accused the former underground filmmaker of going totally Hollywood. "The film congratulates itself at every turn, not forgetting to congratulate its audience as well, most spectacularly when Merrick is taken to the theater and awarded a standing ovation by his fellow spectators. Like them, you're encouraged to feel good about yourself just for having seen it."

The critics congratulated John Hurt for his performance and echoed the *Times*' Vincent Canby, who wrote, "It can't be easy to act under such a heavy mask." Hurt didn't have to worry about anonymity, after all; when *The Elephant Man* came out, he was starring on TV in *Masterpiece Theatre*'s adaptation of *Crime and Punishment*.

Peter O'Toole Plays God

Hurt's compatriot, Peter O'Toole, also went two for two that season. He was starring as *Macbeth* at the Old Vic when he appeared onscreen as the flamboyant director in *The Stunt Man*. Richard Rush had been trying to film Paul Brodeur's novel, about a fugitive who gets involved with a film crew, for nine years, but every single studio rejected the script even though O'Toole had promised to star. Finally, Rush found the money from an independent producer and former shopping center magnate named Mel Simon. Simon couldn't persuade the studios to distribute the finished picture, so, after two years of waiting, Rush arranged to have a theater in Seattle exhibit the movie. When *The Stunt Man* became the highest-grossing film in Seattle, Fox took another look and decided to release it.

"So startling and breathtakingly new it literally defies description," declared Rona Barrett, describing *The Stunt Man* as "a triumph conjured by an alchemist." The *Los Angeles Herald-Examiner* named it "a popular work of modernist art" and said "O'Toole is an acting sorcerer. An ethereal figure with strength, which is how most imagine God." O'Toole maintained he wasn't playing the Lord but imitating director David Lean, and the actor joined in the praise of his current director. "I think Rush himself is presenting a new syntax to cinema," O'Toole said. "It's such a brilliant film and a work I cherish. But for some reason, many studio executives— those watchdogs, those guardians of sense and sensibility—they just nodded off."

Meanwhile, the English critics crucified O'Toole's *Macbeth;* one critic called it "the silliest thing I have ever seen," and another opined, "the worst Shakespearean disaster since the burning of the Globe." But the executive board of the Globe adored O'Toole; he sold out every performance and wiped out the theater's $300,000 debt. "It's nice to be popular again with the executive suite, or with the sweet executives," replied O'Toole. "Nineteen eighty was a funny old year—ups and downs, swings and roundabouts—I adored it. Also, being sober now for so many years is getting interesting."

The Giggly Executive

"I wasn't happy with just being an actress and knowing my lines, sitting back and waiting for someone to create something for me," Goldie Hawn said. "Also, there aren't many scripts around. Period. I found myself turning down everything. Finally, I asked myself, 'What's stopping me from doing it myself?'" Three of Hawn's friends approached her with an idea for a comedy about a pampered woman who joins the army. "I loved it so much that I walked into Warner Brothers and said this is going to be my next picture," the actress recalled. "If I don't make it here, I'll make it somewhere else." She made it at Warner Brothers, serving as its executive producer.

"It didn't interfere with my sex life."
—Robert De Niro

"Goldie Hawn has such frothy charm that she manages to get laughs out of ancient routines about a tenderfoot going through the rigors of basic training," wrote Pauline Kael when *Private Benjamin* became the box-office champ of the fall. Stuart Byron observed, "*Private Benjamin* is far and away the biggest-grossing movie with a female as its sole main player, which is certainly a challenge to conventional Hollywood assumptions (men can star alone, while women need a costar of either sex)." Hawn was back at Christmas with her *Foul Play* costar Chevy Chase in a Neil Simon comedy entitled *Seems Like Old Times;* this one wasn't as successful as *Private Benjamin*—it only made $22 million domestically. *Newsweek* was impressed by Hawn's business acumen and featured her on the cover with the headline SOLID GOLDIE. "When Goldie Hawn walks into a room," the magazine said, "what people invariably expect is the giggly dimwit who made her name flubbing her lines on *Laugh-In* thirteen years ago. Well, Goldie does giggle. She can look like a Barbie doll. But if Goldie Hawn is a dumb blonde, Henry Kissinger is a dopey brunet. At thirty-five, this former go-go girl's back-to-back successes have made her the most popular actress in the country."

The Robert De Niro Diet

"I just can't fake acting," Robert De Niro insisted. "I know movies are an illusion, and maybe the first rule is to fake it, but not for me, I'm too curious. I want to deal with all the facts of the character, thin or fat." De Niro had his work cut out for him in *Raging Bull,* in which he played prizefighter Jake LaMotta at both his professional peak and middle-aged decline. LaMotta trained De Niro himself, and told the *New York Daily News,* "Bobby's a main-event fighter. I'm not kidding. He's thirty-five, but he moves and hits like a nineteen-year-old. Anytime he wants to quit acting, I could easily make him into a champion, he's that good." But De Niro made it clear to *Newsweek* he wasn't switching jobs. "Fighting really turns me off," the actor said. "There's got to be some kind of guilt in deliberately taking punches."

The film production shut down for four months so that De Niro could gain fifty-six pounds for the later scenes. Among those waiting for De Niro to reach obesity was a thirty-seven-year-old manager of an Italian restaurant named Joe Pesci, who had given up acting eight years earlier. He then received a message at his restaurant that Robert De Niro called; De Niro had remembered him from the one film he had made—a gangster movie called *The Death Collectors.* "I don't want to go back to acting unless I get a part that proves I'm good," Pesci told De Niro and director Martin Scorsese over dinner. The two filmmakers described the role of LaMotta's brother Joey, and De Niro said, "It's a good role, not a great role." Pesci took it anyway and worked out with Joey La Motta, who, like his brother, was interested in seeing himself in a movie.

The restaurant manager also discovered the film's leading lady, Cathy Moriarty, when her picture flashed on the wall of a disco in Mount Vernon, New York. The seventeen-year-old had never heard of Robert De Niro, but she liked the idea of being in a movie. Moriarty didn't find acting the role of LaMotta's wife Vickie too tough. "We talked about a scene until we got the feeling down," she told the *New York Post.* "If the feeling was there, then the scene just came."

A Meaty Roll

When De Niro tipped the scales at 225 pounds, *Life* came round with cameras clicking. "It didn't interfere with my sex life," the star assured the magazine. "I mean, some women never give a look unless they find out who I am, but believe it or not, some liked me fat—thought I was a big teddy bear." One girl who dissented was his five-year-old daughter. "My daughter got so she was terribly embarrassed for her friends to see me," he said. "After all, I looked like an animal."

"One of the most repugnant and unlikable screen protagonists in some time," remarked *Va-*

"I did scenes of violence and sex because the general hypocrisy didn't allow it."
—Roman Polanski

riety, and CBS's Pat Collins said *Raging Bull* "surely ranks as one of the most significant movies ever made. De Niro is a contender for sure for the Oscar." Jake LaMotta had mixed feelings: "When I saw the film, I was upset. I kind of look bad in it. Now I realized it was true. I was a no-good bastard. It's not the way I am now, but the way it was then." The *New York Daily News* reported that Joe Pesci's comeback was "praised by all but the real Joseph La Motta who, it turns out, is filing a $2.5 million suit against the moviemakers for a portrait he considers unflattering." Pesci's discovery didn't have that problem. "Tall and strong-looking, Cathy Moriarty has a beautiful glassy presence, like Kim Novak in her *Man with the Golden Arm* days, and the same mute sexuality," applauded Pauline Kael.

The *Hollywood Reporter* quoted one critic of De Niro's acting style—Marcello Mastroianni. "By nature the actor is a kind of wonder who can allow himself to change personalities," the Italian said. "If you don't know how to do this, it's better to change professions. I think it's ridiculous to imagine that to play a taxi driver or a boxer you have to spend months and months 'studying' the life of cabdrivers and the weight of fighters." Fortunately for De Niro, Mastroianni was not a member of the Academy.

A Valentine from Roman Polanski

"A decade ago, I was promoting realism. I did scenes of violence and sex because the general hypocrisy didn't allow that," said Roman Polanski. "Now violence has been exploited to such an extent that I am tired of it and nostalgic for romance." Polanski was also on the lam, from the Los Angeles Police Department. On the eighth anniversary of the Sharon Tate murder, the director had been thrown in jail for forty-two days for psychiatric evaluation after having sex with a thirteen-year-old girl. The day before he was scheduled to be sentenced by a judge who had already told the press he wanted further tests, Polanski informed producer Dino De Laurentiis he was skipping town and couldn't make a movie for him. De Laurentiis responded by giving Polanski $1,000 in pocket money.

Polanski fled to France, where he began to think of his late wife, Sharon, and their plans long ago to adapt Thomas Hardy's *Tess of the D'Urbervilles*. French producer Claude Berri helped him make the movie by raising the money independently, and Polanski cast in the title role his ex-girlfriend, Nastassia Kinski, seventeen. "It's a modern story, but very unlike Polanski's other films," Kinski told interviewers. "It corresponds to what he really is, but rarely shows." To capture all the seasons of the story, Polanski and crew spent nine months filming.

The three-hour *Tess* opened in 1979 in Germany, where it was panned. No American company would touch it; one studio executive told Marilyn Beck, "We're not in a gambling mood today, not when you're talking about having to release a movie in a minimum of 600 theaters at $1,500 a print. We just don't have the money to throw around anymore." The *Los Angeles Times'* critic Charles Champlin saw the movie at the Cannes Film Festival and scolded the American film industry in print a year later when *Tess* had still not been distributed in the United States. Finally, Frank Price of Columbia said, "Even though I thought it was a wonderful movie, I had reservations about it commercially. Then I found that the picture stayed with me and, ultimately, I decided we could release it."

"They thought it could win awards," Polanski said, explaining why the movie was scheduled for only one week in December in New York and Los Angeles. Charles Champlin called it "the best film of the year," and *Newsweek* said it was "a rigorously classical, beautiful film, faithful to the novel's reticence, outrage and deep conviction." Columbia abandoned its one-week policy when the company realized it had a hit—every performance sold out. The *Hollywood Reporter* stated, "One of the most unexpected box-office success stories of the year is that of *Tess*." The film was dedicated "To Sharon" and Polanski said his only disap-

"I was driving to the studio when the radio announced the nominations. I almost ran into a wall."
—Paramount head Barry Diller

pointment over the film's success was that "she can't enjoy it."

The New York View

The only award *Tess* won from the New York Film Critics was the cinematography plaque. The New Yorkers decided the restaurant manager from the Bronx did the best job in the Supporting Actor category, and Joe Pesci said, "It may not last, but if I get an Oscar nomination, I'm going to the Awards and taking my mother and daughter." Robert De Niro was the critics' Best Actor, Sissy Spacek the Best Actress for *Coal Miner's Daughter* and *Ordinary People* was their Best Picture. *Melvin and Howard* won many of the Gotham awards: Best Director for Jonathan Demme, Best Screenplay for Bo Goldman and Best Supporting Actress for Mary Steenburgen, who couldn't make it to the awards dinner at Sardi's because she had given birth to a baby girl three days earlier.

Steenburgen got another chance to pick up an award when she won Best Supporting Actress from the National Society of Film Critics. Bo Goldman received another trophy and *Melvin and Howard* won the Best Picture award. Peter O'Toole was this critics group's Best Actor for *The Stunt Man,* and when *Variety* asked him about his Oscar chances, O'Toole replied, "I'd adore to win. Wouldn't you? The fact I've lost five times intrigues one even more."

The Nominations

"In something of a surprise," wrote Aljean Harmetz in the *New York Times,* "two movies about different sorts of grotesque human beings tied with the most nominations"—*The Elephant Man* and *Raging Bull* both had eight. *Coal Miner's Daughter* followed with seven, including a Best Picture nomination, but Sissy Spacek was the only cast member to win a nomination. *Ordinary People* managed six nominations, although Paramount was expecting more. "I was driving to the studio when the radio announced that *Elephant Man, Raging Bull* and *Coal Miner's Daughter* were the big winners," said studio head Barry Diller. "I almost ran into a wall." All the principals of *Ordinary People* were nominated except Donald Sutherland, who told the *Today* show the next day, "I'm not surprised. I know that community and I didn't expect a nomination."

Ellen Burstyn was vindicated by the Actors Branch, which nominated her for Best Actress and Eva Le Gallienne for Best Supporting Actress for *Resurrection.* Executive producer Goldie Hawn was rewarded with a Best Actress nomination for *Private Benjamin,* which also won a Best Supporting Actress nomination for the film's comic villainess, Eileen Brennan. And Gena Rowlands, in *Gloria,* got a second Best Actress nomination for a film directed by husband John Cassavetes.

The Academy, unlike the public, did not shun *Melvin and Howard,* and the film won three nominations: Best Original Screenplay, Best Supporting Actress for Mary Steenburgen and Best Supporting Actor for two-time winner Jason Robards. *Ordinary People* managed two Best Supporting Actor nominations, for Timothy Hutton and Judd Hirsch, while *Raging Bull* placed nominees Joe Pesci and Cathy Moriarty, in each Supporting category. *The Great Santini*'s Michael O'Keefe was a Supporting contender, and his screen father, Robert Duvall, was taking on *Raging Bull*'s Robert De Niro in the Best Actor contest. Peter O'Toole earned his sixth Best Actor nomination for *The Stunt Man* and Jack Lemmon garnered nomination number seven for *Tribute,* the movie version of his Broadway play about a dying press agent. The fifth Best Actor nominee was the man under all the makeup, *The Elephant Man*'s John Hurt.

Even with *The Elephant Man*'s eight nominations, there was one Hollywood crowd that felt the film had been slighted—the makeup artists. They had recommended an Honorary Oscar, but the Board of Governors nixed the idea. The makeup people let out such a protest that the board promised to look into setting up a regular Award for Best Makeup the following year, but it wouldn't relent on its refusal to give a statuette to *The Elephant Man*. Also unrelenting was Los Angeles District Attorney John Van de Kamp when he saw that *Tess*'s six nominations included one for Best Director. "If Roman Polanski returns to Los Angeles or anywhere in the country, we would have him arrested to go before a judge to face sentencing," he announced.

Return of *Taxi Driver*

The day of the Awards, as caterers prepared for the post-Oscar parties and hair-dressers went to work on the nominees, a young man named John Hinckley, Jr., was busy shooting President Ronald Reagan in the chest in Washington. Hinckley apparently was trying to impress actress Jodie Foster à la Robert De Niro in *Taxi Driver*. In Hollywood, reports on whether the Oscar show had been postponed were as frequent as updates on the President's condition. At 2 P.M. Pacific time, the Academy made if official—the show would not go on as scheduled but would be held the following evening. Doctors reported that Reagan was out of danger and recovering by late afternoon, so many of the celebrity-watchers already in the bleachers wanted to know why the Academy was making them come back tomorrow. "It isn't fair," said one spectator. "He didn't die." Another fan was puzzled, saying, "The thing I don't understand is how can they have all those stars' telephone numbers to call them up and tell them to come back later."

The Big Night

Protesters showed up waving placards that read WHO WILL WIN BEST WHITE ACTRESS AND BEST WHITE ACTOR? Other demonstrators held signs that ranged from ROMAN POLANSKI IS A PERVERT to WE LOVE YOU RONALD REAGAN to JESUS SAVES. An ABC page named Thomas Rogers wore a green ribbon on his lapel—the national symbol of solidarity for citizens concerned over a series of unsolved murders of black Atlanta children—as he escorted arriving celebrities from their limousines to the theater. When Robert De Niro—making his first appearance at the Oscars—pulled up with his wife and the rest of the *Raging Bull* crowd, he asked Thomas what the ribbon stood for. Thomas told him and De Niro asked if he had another one that he could wear; the page took his off and pinned it on the Best Actor nominee's tuxedo.

The bleacher fans gave a loud chorus of boos when Best Actress nominee Ellen Burstyn ignored them, the press and forecourt emcee Army Archerd and walked directly into the theater. Half an hour later, Ellen Burstyn showed up again and surprised Army Archerd when she happily ascended his podium; the emcee did a double take and realized the earlier arrival had just been a look-alike. Then Erik Estrada appeared in his highway patrol outfit from his TV show *CHiPs* and threw his leather gloves into the bleachers. It turned out that this was another look-alike and the police escorted him away. There was no mistaking Edy Williams; this year the eternal starlet wore what *Daily Variety* described as "a layer of amber Saran Wrap sprinkled lightly with gold glitter."

Timothy Hutton came with his mother and Diane Lane, and told Archerd he spent the day riding his bike by the beach and playing video games to overcome the tension. Joe Pesci brought his mother and daughter, and the real Jake LaMotta came to see how his biography would fare. Loretta Lynn and her husband came, too, as did Sissy Spacek and her husband. Diana Ross appeared on the arm of Michael Jackson, and Billy Dee Williams entered with his wife, flashing a peace sign to the bleachers.

The show began when the announcer heralded "John Carson" and the emcee said, "Because of the incredible events of yesterday, that old adage that the show must go on seemed relatively unimportant." Reporting that the President's

Awards Ceremony

MARCH 31, 1981, 7:00 P.M.
THE DOROTHY CHANDLER PAVILION, LOS ANGELES

Your Host:
JOHNNY CARSON
Televised over ABC

Presenters

Supporting Actor . . . . Jack Lemmon and Mary Tyler Moore
Award of Merit for the Optical Printer . . . Lily Tomlin
Short Films. . . . . Alan Arkin and Margot Kidder
Art Direction . . . . Peter O'Toole and Sissy Spacek
Costume Design . . . . Nastassia Kinski and Sigourney Weaver
Visual Effects . . . . Jack Valenti
Sound . . . . Bernadette Peters and Billy Dee Williams
Foreign Film. . . . Brooke Shields and Franco Zeffirelli
Original Score . . . . The Nichols Brothers
Film Editing . . . . . Richard Pryor and Jane Seymour
Supporting Actress . . . . Diana Ross and Donald Sutherland
Song . . . . . . Angie Dickinson and Luciano Pavarotti
Writing Awards . . . . Peter Ustinov
Honorary Award to Henry Fonda . . . . Robert Redford
Cinematography. . . . Blythe Danner and Steve Martin
Director . . . . George Cukor and King Vidor
Actor. . . . . Sally Field
Actress. . . . . Dustin Hoffman
Picture. . . . . Lillian Gish

Performers of Nominated Songs

"Fame". . . . . Irene Cara
"9 to 5". . . . . Dolly Parton
"On the Road Again". . . . . Willie Nelson
"Out Here on My Own" . . . . Irene Cara
"People Alone". . . . . Dionne Warwick

"It's Reagan's strongest attack on the arts since he signed with Warner Brothers."
—Johnny Carson

prognosis was good, Carson said it was the Chief Executive's "express wishes" that the Academy unspool the welcoming address he had made a week earlier. A screen was lowered and the audience saw a happy Reagan sitting in the White House saying, "It's surely no state secret that Nancy and I share your interest in the results of this year's balloting." The President led into this year's ceremonial theme, "Film Is Forever," by commenting, "I've been trapped in some film forever myself." Ronald Reagan was followed by Lucie Arnaz, who led a production number that paid tribute to film personalities who had died in the past year—Steve McQueen, Peter Sellers, Alfred Hitchcock and Mae West. The number ended with a tap-dancing finale, although an Academy spokesman later revealed the taps had been prerecorded.

Academy President Fay Kanin stepped out in harem pants and thanked everybody for waiting an extra day for the ceremonies and then elaborated on the nominations. "They detail the struggle of human beings to stay human," she said, adding, "Movies will help preserve our most essential marvel—our humanity." Johnny Carson returned with his monologue, and Reagan didn't get off as easy this time. "The President has asked for severe cuts in aid to the arts and humanities. It's Reagan's strongest attack on the arts since he signed with Warner Brothers." The audience roared with applause, and Carson laughed, "I'll bet he's up and around now."

The first Award was Supporting Actor, and presenters Jack Lemmon and Mary Tyler Moore forgot to mention the nominee from *Melvin and Howard*. "How could we overlook Jason Robards?" Moore asked as she caught herself in time. ABC's camera also goofed, showing director Martin Scorsese when *The Great Santini*'s Michael O'Keefe was mentioned. The winner was Timothy Hutton for *Ordinary People*. The twenty-year-old sat stunned until his mother gave him a push. Hutton turned to shake director Robert Redford's hand and tripped. "He caught me and kept me from falling completely on my face," Hutton recalled later. At the podium, the winner made his thanks and concluded, "I'd like to thank my father. I wish he were here." Hutton revealed that when he returned to his seat, "I had this feeling that somebody was looking at me. I turned and it was Peter O'Toole, who was in the row across from me. He turned and said, quietly, 'I wish Daddy were here, too.' Wow, it was so incredible."

O'Toole soon had the whole audience agog as he began to ramble when presenting the Art Direction Oscar. "One forgives him precipitous staircases for his true work bench, the fabled . . ." he paused, then remembered "drawing board which he uses hundreds and hundreds of times . . ." Copresenter Sissy Spacek stood by amused and waited for O'Toole to finish. The winner was *Tess,* and when Pierre Guffroy began speaking in French, the orchestra jumped in with music so he'd get the hint to get off. Backstage, O'Toole confessed, "It's very nerve-racking being a presenter, especially with Japanese names to pronounce." Spacek told the press, "See y'all later."

Tess was on a winning streak when Nastassia Kinski and Sigourney Weaver walked down opposing staircases, kissed and then declared Nastassia's movie the winner of the Costume Oscar. Carson got in his annual licks at MPAA head Jack Valenti, introducing him as "not the world's most thrilling speaker. I suggest while you're listening to him you do not drive or operate heavy machinery."

Johnny Carson described Foreign Film Award presenter Brooke Shields, fifteen, as "star of stage, screen and pants." Shields and her *Endless Love* director Franco Zeffirelli revealed that the popular nominees—François Truffaut's *The Last Metro* and Akira Kurosawa's *Kagemusha*—were bested by the Russian love story *Moscow Does Not Believe in Tears,* which nobody in the United States except the voters in this category had seen.

Alluding to Richard Pryor's near-fatal acci-

"I'm not going to let you pass."
—Dolly Parton

dent the previous summer while free-basing cocaine, Carson said, "He makes the world a much happier place to be and I am glad he is living in it." Pryor escorted Jane Seymour—who Carson noted was missing three performances of *Amadeus* on Broadway—to the stage to give the Editing Oscar. "Most film editors are grouches," Pryor explained, gulping, "there go all my future close-ups." *Raging Bull*'s winner, Thelma Schoonmaker, was all smiles, as was Jake La Motta, who won a TV close-up.

Neil Diamond was supposed to give the Best Supporting Actress Award with Diana Ross but the postponement meant he had to bow out. Filling in for him was good sport and non-nominee Donald Sutherland, who won a hearty round of applause. Eva Le Gallienne of *Resurrection* was the only nominee who stayed home and the winner was Mary Steenburgen. "Well, I'm gonna have to figure out something new to dream about, that's for sure," she said, going on to thank "my folks in Arkansas for always believing against all odds that something like this was going to happen. If anybody had a patron saint, it was me. In 1977 when he insisted on casting me as his leading lady in a film called *Goin' South,* everybody told him he was crazy, but thank goodness for me he was and is, Jack Nicholson." The *Melvin and Howard* team were thanked "for the plain, old-fashioned fun it was to work with you," and Steenburgen concluded with a tribute to her husband, "I must thank you, Malcolm, for making life so nice that I feel like tap-dancing."

The Best Song race was between two Top 40 hits—Dolly Parton's "9 to 5" and Irene Cara's "Fame." The latter won, but songwriters Dean Pitchford and Michael Gore found making their way to the stage difficult when songwriter Parton jumped up at the end of the row, threw her arms out and laughed, "I'm not going to let you pass." "Can you imagine trying to get around Dolly Parton?" Pitchford said later. Finally, the loser embraced the winners and let them go. "MGM's had a history of bringing musicals to the screen and so I'm very grateful to be part of such an exciting musical that feels like the '80s," Pitchford said. Backstage, reporters asked Pitchford, thirty, if he was the youngest person to win the Best Song Oscar, but Rona Barrett answered for him, "Marvin Hamlisch was younger."

Peter Ustinov was in charge of the writing Oscars, and the Adapted Screenplay Award went to *Ordinary People*. The camera loitered on Goldie Hawn as winner Alvin Sargent walked to the podium, where he said, "It's a film about all of us trying to understand all of us." Bo Goldman received yet another Award for his Original Screenplay for *Melvin and Howard*. "Tonight I am here for *Melvin and Howard* but there are years in between when there are no Awards, so tonight I'd like to mention some men who have taught me a lot." After mentioning directors he had worked with, Goldman thanked Universal's Ned Tanen "for his deep pockets" and Melvin Dummar, whom Goldman misnamed "Melvin Howard, for sharing his life with me."

Robert Redford was onstage next, saying, "I have a lot of pride to be here." He hadn't won anything, but was presenting an Honorary Oscar to Henry Fonda. After a series of film clips—that concluded with a scene from the upcoming *On Golden Pond*—the seventy-five-year-old recipient hobbled out with a cane to a standing ovation. "It's been a very rewarding forty-six years for me and this has got to be the climax," Fonda declared. When he exited, Carson said, "Those are the special moments that make this show." It wasn't special enough to Fonda's son Peter, who told reporters, "I was only disappointed that I didn't get to give him the Award."

George Cukor received some direction from King Vidor when presenting the Director Oscar—Vidor had to point out where the cue cards were. The winner was first-time director Robert Redford, who humbly thanked his colleagues and hurried offstage.

Carson introduced "one of the most vital actresses in film," and out came Sally Field to pres-

"I hate to see Mary Tyler Moore lose because she's always been one of my real favorites, but there she was, pitted against Sissy."
—Sissy Spacek's father

ent Best Actor. All the nominees were in the auditorium but the one who got to go up onstage was Robert De Niro. Still wearing the green ribbon on his lapel, De Niro said at the podium, "I'm a little nervous, I'm sorry. I forgot my lines so the director wrote them down." The cameras saw Martin Scorsese laughing. The actor went on to thank Jake LaMotta, "Vickie LaMotta and all the other wives, Joey LaMotta, even though he's suing us. I want to thank my mother and father for having me and my grandmothers and grandfathers for having them." De Niro covered all bases by concluding with gratitude for "everyone else involved in the film and I hope that I can share this with anyone that it means anything to and the rest of the world and especially with all the terrible things that are happening . . . I love everyone." De Niro headed back toward his seat, but Sally Field grabbed him and dragged him to the pressroom.

All the Best Actress nominees were present when Dustin Hoffman read their names, prefacing each with "Miss." Miss Goldie Hawn waved to the camera when her nomination was mentioned but it was Miss Sissy Spacek's name that was in the envelope. The winner thanked Loretta Lynn, "the lady who gave me all that hair," and her husband "Dooley." The camera saw Mr. and Mrs. Doolittle Lynn smiling in the audience—Mr. Lynn was not wearing a tie with his tuxedo. Spacek continued by thanking "my own Dooley, Tommy Lee Jones," and ended with a tribute to her "mama and daddy."

The Best Picture presenter was eighty-four-year-old Lillian Gish, who earned the evening's third standing ovation. Gish described each of the five nominees and called *The Elephant Man*, "the story of one of history's most unfortunate men." *The Elephant Man*'s misfortune at the Oscars—the film had lost seven of its eight nominations—became total when Gish revealed that the winner was *Ordinary People*. Producer Ronald L. Schwary pulled a hesitant Robert Redford back onstage. All that Redford said was, "Thank you very much." With that, he hustled off and the show was over.

Aftermath

Robert De Niro did not stay in the pressroom long. One reporter asked him about the connection between *Taxi Driver* and the assassination attempt. "I don't know about the story," De Niro insisted, "I don't want to discuss the matter now." When the reporter pressed the question, De Niro retorted, "Look, I said what I wanted to say out there. You're all very nice, but that's it." He stormed out and joined his *Raging Bull* cohorts at a private party at Ma Maison.

Sissy Spacek did not have such weighty matters on her mind. "Just to be nominated makes me feel like a real actress. I used to watch the Oscars growing up, so all of this is like a dream come true, like living out a fantasy." Her parents were watching at home in Quitman, Texas, where her father told the *Dallas Times Herald*, "I hate to see Mary Tyler Moore lose because she's always been one of my real favorites, but there she was, pitted against Sissy. We were a little worried there." Her high school biology teacher told the paper, "When they announced that Sissy'd won the award, we all jumped up and started hollering. I'm real fond of Sissy. She was a real go-getter. Always out in front."

"I'm really fortunate and surprised. I didn't think enough people had seen the film," admitted Best Supporting Actress Mary Steenburgen. When asked her immediate plans, Steenburgen got specific, "Well, tonight I have to go home first and feed my baby, but then Malcolm and I are going to the ball and I plan to dance my feet off."

There wasn't a lot of room at the ball this year; because of the postponement, the Academy had to share the ballroom at the Beverly Hilton with the conventioneers at the American Film market. There was even less space when Richard Pryor showed up with his three-hundred-pound bodyguard. One guest who lingered and enjoyed himself was Best Director Robert Redford, who said, "It's ironic I won for directing, but no less acceptable." Other guests stayed at the ball longer than they'd planned because the car valets were swamped. "I'll be lucky if I get my car by Thursday," griped one Hollywoodite.

Best Supporting Actress loser Diana Scarwid told Marilyn Beck that she wasn't surprised that she'd lost. "I didn't have a studio behind me," she said. "What really disappointed me was that, in this year of gloom and violence on screen, our movie was pulled from release so fast it didn't have a chance." *The Elephant Man*'s John Hurt also aired his grievances with the columnist, saying, "De Niro is already 'bankable.' With me, the Oscar would have helped in terms of setting up films, actually getting a film off the ground, getting it financed."

Thomas Rogers, the page who had given Robert De Niro his green ribbon, later told *California* magazine of one other celebrity who was upset at the evening's turn of events. "I was escorting Brooke Shields to her limousine, and she was complaining to her mother that Robert Redford didn't stop and talk to her," he said. "She's a beautiful, talented lady, but you could see the little girl in her when she saw her idol. She was as starstruck as any other girl. I told her Robert Redford was probably in a hurry. Maybe next year."

1981

"On Golden Pond gave all of us the chance to say out loud something you could admit to yourself only at night."
—Jane Fonda

Old favorites took the gold at the 1981 Academy Awards.

When he turned sixty in 1973, Burt Lancaster said he'd play no more romantic leads because "at my age, I'd look ridiculous." He added that he would make an exception for the part of an older man who becomes obsessed with a young girl. Eight years later, playwright John Guare gave the 1960 Best Actor such a part in *Atlantic City*. Appearing onscreen for the first time ever without makeup, Lancaster played an overaged penny-ante hood who falls for a young woman stalked by the mob. *Atlantic City* was the second American film for French art-house director Louis Malle, who said, "I left France because I was losing my curiosity. In every new situation, I'd have the impression that I'd lived it before."

Independently made, *Atlantic City* was picked up for distribution by Paramount and opened in April with little publicity; the critics did the drumbeating for it. "When you leave the theater," predicted Pauline Kael, "you may feel light-headed, as if there were no problems in the world that couldn't be solved." Burt Lancaster made off with some of the best reviews of his career. Vincent Canby heralded his performance as "one of Mr. Lancaster's most remarkable creations, a complex mixture of the mangy and magnificent," and Pauline Kael thought "if this was a stage performance, the audience would probably give him a standing ovation." *Newsweek* liked leading lady Susan Sarandon, calling her "touching and funny—a truly fresh performance." Despite the good reviews, the public stayed away and *Atlantic City* was exhibited only in a handful of cities.

Summer Fantasies

Paramount didn't weep long over *Atlantic City*'s disappointing box office; the studio had the first-time collaboration of the two most profitable names in movies—George Lucas and Steven Spielberg. Spielberg reminisced about a vacation that he had spent with Lucas in Hawaii the week *Star Wars* opened four years earlier: "We were sitting on the beach one day building a sand castle and we were fantasizing about movies we'd always wanted to make. Lucas told me the *Raiders of the Lost Ark* story and I just said, 'I'd love to do that' and he said, 'Well, I've retired. I'm not directing anymore, so it's yours.'"

Two-time winner Jane Fonda makes good her promise to get an Oscar for her dad.

The story was about a heroic archeologist named Indiana Jones, who overcomes all obstacles to locate the Ark of the Covenant before the Nazis can claim it for the glory of Hitler. Lucas served as executive producer and wrote the script with Lawrence Kasdan. "The story was based on the serial matinees I loved when I was kid," confessed Lucas. "I wondered why they didn't make movies like that anymore. I still wanted to see them." Director Spielberg pointed out an important difference in the two men's sensibilities: "I think George was inspired by the serials when he wrote the script with Larry Kasdan. I was more inspired by comic books, like *The Green Lantern, Blackhawk*, and *Sgt. Rock*."

To play Indiana Jones, the filmmakers wanted the star of Chaz cologne commercials, Tom Selleck, but the actor said he had a better offer to be the star of a TV detective series called *Magnum P. I.* So Lucas enlisted one of his *Star Wars* players, Harrison Ford, to portray the fedora-wearing hero. Because Spielberg's previous movie *1941* had been an expensive flop—*People* had said "the prodigy became a prodigal"—the previously profligate director finished this one twelve days ahead of schedule and spent no more than his $20 million budget.

Once again, the major newsmagazines did the work of Paramount's publicists—*Time, People* and *Newsweek* all had cover stories when *Raiders of the Lost Ark* bowed in the summer. *Newsweek*'s David Ansen wrote, "If *Raiders* proves to be the summer movie everyone wants to see, it's not because these movie-mad maniacs studied their demographics

"Everybody thinks Sir John Gielgud reads Chaucer all day, and, in fact, he loves reading Harold Robbins."
—Dudley Moore

charts, but because they made the movie *they* wanted to see. It's a boy's adventure made by the genre's greatest fans, fans who happen to have a touch of genius." But some critics refused to return to their childhoods. Archer Winsten, in his fifth decade of reviewing at the *New York Post*, opined "this picture represents an enormous expenditure of productive opulence and imaginative cinematic creativity for the delight of an empty head. It says nothing of consequence," and Pauline Kael lamented that if Lucas "weren't hooked on the crap of his childhood—if he brought his resources to bear on some projects with human beings in them—there is no imagining the result."

For the time being, Lucas could imagine just how much money he and Spielberg were raking in off *Raiders*. Eclipsed by *Superman II* early in the summer, *Raiders* soon overtook all comers, and by the end of the year was number four on the all-time box-office champ list, behind *Star Wars*, *Jaws* and *The Empire Strikes Back*—all of which happened to be Lucas or Spielberg enterprises.

Drunken Dudley

Writer-director Steve Gordon, a former Madison Avenue director, swore that his movie, *Arthur*, was also inspired by films of the 1930s, likening it to *My Man Godfrey*, *It Happened One Night* and other screwball comedies of the Depression era. When Dudley Moore read the script about a spoiled drunken millionaire and the girl from Queens he falls in love with even though it means disinheritance, he raved, "Ten laughs a page. Instead of one laugh every ten pages." The reviewers laughed a lot, too. "The combination of wit, taste, charm, timing, both elegant and lowdown humor, and this miraculous cast is irresistible," exclaimed Sheila Benson in the *Los Angeles Times*, and *Variety* was happy that "Dudley Moore is back in top-*10* form."

But even with Moore and Liza Minnelli in the leads, the lion's share of the attention went to Sir John Gielgud, as a no-nonsense butler. Rex Reed called Sir John's "a character of the most curmudgeonly charm since Clifton Webb dumped oatmeal on that spoiled brat in *Sitting Pretty*." Even his costars got in on the adulation. "You want to hug him until you cry," declared Liza, while Dudley revealed, "He was always coming out with these sweet, corny theatrical anecdotes, and he's got a sort of mucky sense of humor. I mean everybody thinks he reads Chaucer all day, and in fact, he loves reading Harold Robbins." Although the *SoHo Weekly News* complained "no amount of laughter could mask the movie's crude, greedy heart," audiences enjoyed the antics of the inebriated super-rich and *Arthur* was the year's biggest comedy hit, making $42 million domestically. The movie's theme song, sung by Christopher Cross, also went gold.

No Names, Please

Neil Simon had written a comedy about an alcoholic, too, but he didn't want to play it strictly for laughs. He had rewritten his 1970 Broadway comedy-drama *The Gingerbread Lady*, about a dipsomaniacal actress and retitled it *Only When I Laugh*. "And to avoid any of the confrontations I've had with producers in the past over casting," the playwright told the *New York Post*, "I decided to do this one myself. I didn't want anyone telling me we had to have superstar names."

One name Simon was determined to have in the credits was Mrs. Simon's—Marsha Mason. "Now that Marsha's matured so much as an actress," her husband stated, "I decided this was an ideal vehicle for her." *Newsweek*'s David Ansen agreed, commenting that Mason "has grown enormously as an actress since her cloying performance in *The Goodbye Girl*." Producer Simon also cast Kristy McNichol as Mason's understanding daughter, James Coco as an overweight actor and Joan Hackett as an aging socialite. "I rarely leave a film wanting to take the people I've just seen home to Mother," Rex Reed confessed, "but I'd be proud to know everyone in this one." According to the *Hollywood Reporter*'s "The Great Life" column, Hollywood partygoers were proud to

"Of all the actresses today, only Faye Dunaway has the talent and class and the courage it takes to make a real star."
—Joan Crawford

know one cast member: "Producer Lester Persky told Joan Hackett, a knockout in a black derby slanted over her forehead and a $1,500 handwoven coat of many colors by London's Kate Kelly ('I couldn't resist it at Bendel's'), that she has to rev up a publicity campaign to win a Best Supporting Actress Academy Award for her superb performance in *Only When I Laugh.*"

Possessed

Joan Crawford once said, "Of all the actresses today, to me, only Faye Dunaway has the talent and the class and the courage it takes to make a real star." Crawford didn't live to see Dunaway tackle her most challenging role—Joan Crawford. Christina Crawford had fascinated four million readers with *Mommie Dearest,* her own *I Remember Mama,* and gossip columnists followed the production of the film version closely. "You think Christina Crawford was tough on her mother Joan in the book *Mommie Dearest?*" asked Liz Smith. "It wouldn't be a patch on anything written by anyone involved in the making of the movie of the same name with Faye Dunaway. They say her Fayeness is ruling the roost in a manner unheard of since Crawford's heyday."

When the movie was ready to be unveiled, director Frank Perry spilled it all to Rex Reed: "Let's face it. Faye went bananas. She *became* Joan Crawford . . . She was possessed, she was obsessed, and she didn't make life easy for anybody." But he added, "Now that it's over, crazy or not, she was sensational and I'd work with her again tomorrow." Dunaway concurred that indeed she had been taken over by Joan Crawford, and said, "It took me two months before I was able to regain my own personality."

Most critics thought Dunaway worked wonders with her schizophrenic school of acting. In the *New York Times,* Janet Maslin wrote, "Miss Dunaway's work here amounts to a small miracle, as one movie queen transforms herself passionately and wholeheartedly into another," and Pauline Kael applauded a "startling ferocious performance." On the other hand, columnist Marilyn Beck sneered, "If you want to see the most flagrant case of overacting in decades, see what Faye Dunaway does to Joan Crawford in this picture."

Paramount noticed that a lot of people were treating *Mommie Dearest* as high camp, so the advertising department came up with a one-time-only ad that referred to the scene where Crawford beats Christina with a wire hanger. The ad showed a hanger, a line from the script, "No wire hangers . . . ever!" and the tag line, "The biggest mother of them all." Producer Frank Yablans was upset enough to sue Paramount, calling the ad "obscene, vulgar, offensive, salacious and embodies a racial slur of the poorest taste." But, as far as Christina Crawford was concerned, the ad was nothing compared to what Paramount had done to her book. "They turned it into a Joan Crawford movie!" wailed the authoress.

If at First You Don't Succeed . . .

Premiering the same day as *Mommie Dearest, The French Lieutenant's Woman* also offered a bravura challenge for an actress. John Fowles' 1968 bestseller about a "free-spirited" young woman and her passion for a betrothed army man had been eluding filmmakers for a decade. Fred Zinnemann, Franklin J. Schaffner, Richard Lester, Michael Cacoyannis, Lindsay Anderson and Mike Nichols worked with various screenwriters to devise a viable concept for a movie and all gave up. The difficulty was that, although the book's story takes place in 1867, the narrator is firmly planted in the late 1960s, making modern-day observations and references to the likes of Freud, Marx and Marshall McLuhan.

Director Karel Reisz and screenwriter Harold Pinter decided to give it a try, and Reisz admitted that they could have just told the Victorian story but, "what with the two points of view, it would have been cowardly not to have tried something." What they tried was a parallel, contemporary love story between two actors who are portraying the

"Let's face it. Faye went bananas."
—Frank Perry

Victorian lovers in a movie. *Ms.* thought the motif worked nicely: "The film has its own integrity the way, to use a flattering example, Verdi's *Otello* does in relation to Shakespeare's," but Vincent Canby argued that the device "illuminates nothing more about the differences between the manners and mores of 1867 and 1981 than any reasonably alert 1981 adult might be expected to bring into the movie theater uninstructed."

Dime-Store Baby

Back in 1968, John Fowles thought Vanessa Redgrave would make the ideal French Lieutenant's woman. A dozen years later, he put his money on Meryl Streep. Even so, he said that "she was very shy about me. When I appeared on the set, she'd hide. She had some extraordinary notion that I didn't want an American actress. But there's no English actress of her age group who could have done it." The coveted role landed Streep on the cover of *Time,* and now that Sidney Skolsky had retired, the magazine took it upon itself to give the actress a "Tintype" profile: "Streep is now and forever a New Yorker without a trace of a tan or of West Coast showbiz gloss. She bounces into a magazine photo session, wearing a dime-store sun dress and dark glasses held together by a safety pin. She is . . . a resolute rider of the subways . . . Streep is a liberal who is outraged by the Reaganauts in Washington and a feminist who supports the ERA and who gets angry at the way films exploit women in sex scenes." The *Los Angeles Herald-Examiner* raved, "We can believe this woman is all things—crazy, visionary, pure, despoiled—because Streep has incorporated all the possibilities into her performance." But the *New York Daily News* thought the actress "seems somewhat constrained for a woman who . . . is supposed to represent the untamed forces of nature."

Running for England

A second British period piece opened in the United States during the fall. Producer David Puttnam, best known for *Midnight Express,* said, "I wanted to make a film like *A Man for All Seasons* about someone who didn't behave in an expedient manner." He had to go back to the 1924 Olympics to find his story—a tale of two British runners who go for the gold for reasons other than the glory of England; one is a theological student who runs to express his love of God, the other a Jew who wants to show up anti-Semites at Oxford. When *Chariots of Fire* opened at the 1981 Cannes Film Festival, *Variety* reported: "Seldom perhaps has any British film gone to bat with as much emotional commitment riding on it . . . Many in the British industry have come to regard it as a test of whether indigenous British films can successfully compete nowadays in the marketplace with sex and violence, sans a big budget and uppercase marquee talent . . . Its launch, handling and promotion is becoming little short of a crusade."

In the United States, the New York Film Festival helped out by giving *Chariots of Fire* their prestigious opening night slot. Although *Film Comment*'s Richard Corliss snickered that the film was "a hymn to the human spirit as if scored by Barry Manilow," *Variety* contended the film was ready-made for American audiences, "As between the slapstick comedy and scary contrived schlockers that predominate in the current marketplace, *Chariots* offers jaded fans an uncommon chance to relate to believable people in a drama of affecting emotion and tension plus more than a little social and psychological complexity."

Variety's claim was verified by Harry Francis, the manager of the Bruin Theatre in Westwood, who declared in an ad in the trade papers, "In my fifty years as a theatre manager, I have never witnessed such a thrilling reaction to a film as *Chariots of Fire*. The words 'wonderful, heartwarming,' 'I love it,' 'beautiful film' are told to me by countless patrons. Once the show starts, no one leaves their seats." Vangelis' score, with its anachronistic synthesizer, became a favorite of both television sport shows and American record buyers. The film's opening scene of athletes running on the beach in slow motion was immediately usurped by parod-

"Warren Beatty has an interesting psychology. He has always fallen in love with girls who have just won or been nominated for an Academy Award."
—Leslie Caron

ists and TV commercials. In short, *Chariots of Fire* was a hit and became the highest-grossing imported film in the United States to date.

News Hounds

Kurt Luedtke quit his job as executive editor of the *Detroit Free Press* and wrote a screenplay about a newspaper reporter who ruins lives through her shoddy journalism and then hides behind the First Amendment. Whereas five years earlier members of the press were cinematic supermen in *All the President's Men, Absence of Malice,* starring Paul Newman and Sally Field, portrayed them as villains.

Predictably, the press questioned the accuracy of the drama. The *Columbia Journalism Review* argued the "film is grotesquely distorted" and a *New York Daily News* reporter maintained that the reporting techniques depicted "seem to be impossible on a major daily." Liz Smith also had her beef: "If Jane Fonda had done *Absence of Malice* instead of Sally Field, would Jane have allowed her character to sleep with Paul Newman in the movie?" But Smith was willing to be fair to the film, adding, "In spite of reservations that this movie is probably an insult to women journalists, it is extremely enjoyable, thought-provoking and certainly Paul Newman's best work in ages." Critics also praised Melinda Dillon as a woman driven to suicide because of a newspaper article; Pauline Kael classified her as "that rarest of critters—an actress who thinks out completely new characters."

Running Ragged

When E.L. Doctorow published his historical novel *Ragtime* in 1975, Dino de Laurentiis announced with great fanfare that he had purchased the movie rights to the critically acclaimed best-seller for Robert Altman, whose *Nashville* was called the cinematic equivalent to Doctorow's sweeping, multi-character work. When Altman and de Laurentiis had a falling out later, the mogul took the film rights to Milos Forman, whose *One Flew Over the Cuckoo's Nest* had beaten *Nashville* for Best Picture, and made more money, anyway. Forman proved himself to be a master at publicity when he coaxed his Martha's Vineyard neighbor, eighty-one-year-old James Cagney, out of a twenty-year retirement to play the New York City police commissioner, and then got Norman Mailer to play the assassinated Stanford White.

Although Paramount found the $32 million period piece impossible to sell to the public, two screen newcomers nevertheless profited from their appearances in the epic. Twenty-year-old Elizabeth McGovern, whose only previous film role was that of Timothy Hutton's girlfriend in *Ordinary People,* played Evelyn Nesbitt as a ding-a-ling and earned a *Newsweek* cover as "A New Breed of Actor." *People* told readers, "Critics already have cheered Elizabeth's gloriously daffy portrayal, credited her with the year's most memorable nude scene, and reached all the way back to Carole Lombard to discover an ingenue of comparable comedic talent."

Thirty-year old Howard E. Rollins, Jr., as a fictional black character who seizes J.P. Morgan's library to protest racial injustice, had *Variety* heralding his "intense screen magnetism that bodes instant star status" and had *Playboy* calling him "a sure bet to become a star overnight." But Rollins didn't fall for the hype, telling *US* magazine, "Everybody tells me to look for big things after *Ragtime,* but there are very few decent roles for black actors today. Unless the film industry really believes in my talent, I just don't see it happening." It didn't happen, so the actor signed on to a TV soap opera, *Another World.*

Commie Dearest

Paramount wasn't as concerned over *Ragtime*'s box-office fizzle—after all, that was de Laurentiis' money—as it was over the millions it had poured into Warren Beatty's latest concoction. In contrast to the romantic fantasy *Heaven Can Wait,* Beatty was now working on an expensive epic

"Jane Fonda has begun to look like the Ladies' Home Journal cover girl."
—Gregg Kilday

about Communism. Back in the '60s, Beatty accompanied his then-girlfriend Natalie Wood to her ancestral homeland—Russia—where he met a woman who claimed to have been a lover of John Reed, the American journalist who witnessed the Russian Revolution and was a fervent leader of the American Communist Party. For years, Beatty nurtured the idea of a film biography of Reed, and, after his success with *Heaven Can Wait,* he convinced Paramount to put up the dough for *Reds.*

Production began in August 1979 with Maureen Stapleton as Emma Goldman, Jack Nicholson as Eugene O'Neill and Beatty's current girlfriend, Diane Keaton, as Reed's wife, Louise Bryant. "Warren has an interesting psychology," noted ex-girlfriend Leslie Caron. "He has always fallen in love with girls who have just won or been nominated for an Academy Award." After filming in the United States, Beatty and company moved to Finland, which stood in for Russia, since the U.S.S.R. said *nyet* to Beatty's idea of shooting on location.

It took nine months to edit *Reds* and two days before the December premiere, Marilyn Beck reported that "Beatty is at the point of exhaustion . . . I'm told his doctors warned him months ago to take it easier, but as one of his aides reports, 'He just cared too much about the picture to let it out of his hands.'" Beatty's fatigue forced him to drop out of promoting the picture—which Paul Morrissey had dubbed "Commie Dearest"—prompting the *New York Times'* Aljean Harmetz to comment, "*Reds* also lost immense amounts of publicity, including cover stories in *Newsweek* and the *New York Times Magazine,* because Mr. Beatty threw a news blackout over the movie." The *New York Daily news* quoted a "marketing insider" who opined that Beatty "may have committed the biggest faux pas in the last fifty years of filmmaking by opting to play the prima donna, making himself unavailable for publicity."

"I would like to state here, now, and without equivocation," declared Arthur Knight in the *Hollywood Reporter,* "that I regard Warren Beatty's *Reds* as the single most important, creative and original American production since Orson Welles' *Citizen Kane,*" and the *Los Angeles Herald-Examiner* averred, "If *Dr. Zhivago* and *Citizen Kane* mated, the result might be *Reds.*" *Newsweek* said, "Diane Keaton's Louise Bryant is the film's greatest triumph—a rich, complex portrait of a woman one comes to love, but only after struggling through a maze of ambiguous responses." *Variety* claimed, "Nicholson's O'Neill, played as a romanticist in cynic's clothing, is a major delight," and Vincent Canby said Maureen Stapleton was "marvelous and earthy, as Emma Goldman." Stanley Kauffmann insisted, "Beatty gives here the best self-directed film performance since Olivier's *Henry V.*" But even with all this hoopla, *Reds* did middling business when it opened at Christmas and Paramount realized that if it was going to recoup its investment, *Reds* would have to be a big winner at the Academy Awards.

Something for Dad

Like Warren Beatty, Jane Fonda had a dream project. She wanted to appear in a movie with her father Henry, especially now that his failing health meant his working days were limited. As he entered his late seventies, she found a vehicle—*On Golden Pond,* a semisuccessful Broadway play about a man learning to accept old age. Jane's company would produce the picture and she would play the daughter with whom he had never had a close relationship. Katharine Hepburn signed on as the understanding wife.

Hepburn and Fonda *père,* who had never met, formed a mutual admiration society. She: "Working with Henry brings tears to my eyes. He's so sensitive, so giving an actor." He: "What a joy to be acting with Katharine. She can play all the levels of a scene, and always is able to do something so fresh with a slight gesture or a look." Jane Fonda was busy saying things like, "I've always thought of *On Golden Pond* as a present to my father . . . *On Golden Pond* gave all of us the chance to say out loud something you could admit to yourself only at night." There seemed to be so much niceness around that a reporter asked Hepburn if it was true the cast and crew sensed an aura of magic. "Magic on the set?" the Great Kate scoffed. "Who told you all that stuff? . . . They're all romantic." Magic certainly wasn't what Jane felt when she had her big, somewhat autobiographical, scene with her father. She confessed that "I was sick, I had a headache, I couldn't eat. Things were coming from way deep down that I couldn't handle."

Newsweek heralded "that resonant once-in-a-lifetime cast—Fonda, Hepburn, Fonda —which automatically turns *On Golden Pond* into an event in movie-star mythology." The two septuagenarians were featured on the front of *Time* under the heading "Golden Oldies." Vincent Canby proclaimed, "Mr. Fonda gives one of the great performances of his long, truly distinguished career," while *New York* called Katharine Hepburn "goosey and likable." To the public, *On Golden Pond* became an irresistible Auld Lang Syne event. Even Jane Fonda professed amazement when it turned into the year's sleeper hit, earning over $60 million in domestic rentals.

Year-End Wrap-Up

Reds got a boost in its Oscar quest when both the National Board of Review and the New York Film Critics named it Best Film, but the epic also found a surprisingly strong challenger in *Atlantic City,* which won the top prize from the Los Angeles Film Critics and National Society of Film Critics Awards. A Hollywood veteran swept the Best Actor citations, only it wasn't Henry Fonda—Burt Lancaster seemed to be winning everything in sight. The New York Film Critics' choice for Best Actress was Glenda Jackson as poet Stevie Smith in *Stevie* but she was already out of the running for the Academy Award. *Stevie* was three years old and its distributor had already released the film in Los Angeles for Oscar consideration back in 1978. The supporting awards from the critics' groups were dominated by John Gielgud in *Arthur* and Maureen Stapleton in *Reds.*

Don't Vote for Me

Carol Burnett asked Universal to discontinue the trade-paper ads promoting her for Best Actress in Alan Alda's ode to middle-aged friendships, *The Four Seasons.* She deemed her performance, "Okay, no gem. Certainly not Academy Award caliber," and argued, "The whole Oscar thing can get so silly with everyone and their uncle taking out ads. I don't want to be a part of it—unless I deserve it."

Similarly, the Polish government didn't want Academy members to vote for the country's official Best Foreign Language Film entry. In late November, Poland had yanked its original submission in the Oscar race, a pro-government drama called *The Shivers,* and substituted Andrzej Wajda's celebration of the Solidarity trade union, *Man of Iron.* Two days later, martial law was declared. "*Man of Iron* is the best piece of propaganda Solidarity could ask for," said an executive from United Artists, which released the film in America. "It was obviously slipped in as the official nominee by somebody who knew what was coming. We think the government has been too busy to notice." When the government finally did notice, it requested that the Academy remove *Man of Iron* from consideration and replace it with a film the government approved of. The Academy declared its own martial law, and *Man of Iron* remained the official Polish entry.

The Nominations

Carol Burnett was not nominated, but *Man of Iron* was, and with all the political brouhaha, it was an odds-on favorite to win. For the second time, Warren Beatty received four nominations and *Reds* was up for twelve Oscars, the highest total since *Who's Afraid of Virginia Woolf?*'s thirteen in 1966. In second place with ten nominations was *On Golden Pond.* Army Archerd reported that Henry Fonda, "who was not having one of his better weeks, was cheered enormously when wife

"John Belushi was something of a special effect himself."
—Dan Aykroyd

Shirlee told him of *On Golden Pond*'s nominations. And when she said he was among them, Fonda yelled, 'Holy Mackeloney.'" In the *Los Angeles Herald-Examiner,* Gregg Kilday looked at the two top contenders and noted "if the 54th annual Academy Award nominations prove anything, it's that the brash talents of the New Hollywood of the '70s are now thoroughly ensconced as the New Establishment of the '80s . . . For if Beatty has taken on the mantle of David Lean . . . then Jane Fonda has begun to look like the *Ladies' Home Journal* cover girl."

Paramount easily outdistanced all other studios with thirty-three nominations, including three Best Picture contenders—*Reds, Raiders of the Lost Ark* and *Atlantic City*. The Paramount trio was facing *On Golden Pond* and *Chariots of Fire*. Missing from the Best Actress lineup was *Mommie Dearest*'s Faye Dunaway, a strong second in the New York critics' voting. Gregg Kilday surmised, "Apparently Hollywood hasn't forgiven Faye Dunaway for her audacious performance as Joan Crawford . . . for Dunaway was ignored and the movie's makeup and costumes which contributed to her impersonation, were given the cold shoulder, too." According to Aljean Harmetz, the biggest surprise was Susan Sarandon's nomination as Best Actress for *Atlantic City*—Paramount had been running ads listing her as a Supporting Actress. Harmetz wrote that "a flabbergasted Miss Sarandon said today that even she had voted for herself in the Supporting Actress category." Sarandon was up against Katharine Hepburn, making her twelfth go at the Oscars; Diane Keaton in *Reds*; Meryl Streep in *The French Lieutenant's Woman*; and Marsha Mason in *Only When I Laugh*, who was meditating in India when she got the news.

Paul Newman had his first nomination in fourteen years to go along with his reemergence as a moneymaker, but Burt Lancaster, last nominated in 1962, was disappointed his own choice for Best Actor hadn't been nominated—Harrison Ford in *Raiders of the Lost Ark*. "He's a remarkably good actor," said the star of *Crimson Pirate*. "In that role you have to bring something special to it, to be funny as well as a good actor." The fifth actor nominee was Dudley Moore for *Arthur* who admitted to *Entertainment Tonight* that Henry Fonda was the sentimental favorite. "I think I know how it will turn out," Moore said.

Maureen Stapleton, a three-time Supporting Actress loser, realized she had a good chance of walking off with the Award this year for her Emma Goldman in *Reds,* so she prepared for the occasion by going on a diet and treating herself to a new dress. "But," she warned Radie Harris, "I'm not expecting to compete with Jane Fonda's fabulous figure or her wardrobe." Another *Reds* nominee, Jack Nicholson, told Army Archerd, "I'm pretty sure Sir John Gielgud will win—and that's jake with me. I like a nice, relaxed evening. I'm hoping for a win for Warren." So was columnist James Bacon: "If my idol Warren Beatty doesn't win at least one Oscar this year, he should yell robbery." Vincent Canby felt *Reds* was the one to beat, arguing, "After all, Warren Beatty has paid his dues, has taken a huge gamble and won, and has, to boot, made a remarkable film." And besides, Beatty had already won the Directors Guild Award so everything was in order for a *Reds* triumph. One of the few prognosticators with a different view was the *Village Voice*'s Andrew Sarris, who predicted, "*Chariots of Fire* will get the votes of all the joggers."

On With the Show

When John Belushi, scheduled to present the Visual Effects Award with Dan Aykroyd, died from a drug overdose a few weeks before the ceremony, show producer Howard W. Koch made Aykroyd pledge that he wouldn't mention his deceased friend on the show. "I wouldn't be part of a tribute to Belushi," Koch assured Marilyn Beck. "I couldn't face myself if I were."

Supporting Actor nominee John Gielgud told the Academy he wouldn't be at the ceremony, but asked that Michael York be allowed to accept for him. Koch, perhaps fearful of another Sacheen Littlefeather, said absolutely not, the Academy now had a rule against proxy acceptances. Then the Academy turned around and made an exception for two members of the *On Golden Pond* crowd. Nominated editor Robert L. Wolfe had died, so his wife was welcomed to come onstage if he won. Henry Fonda was too ill to come, so the Academy became sentimental and said that Jane, a Best Supporting Actress nominee, could accept for her father. There was talk about setting up cameras at Fonda's Bel Air home, just as cameramen had been poised at Judy Garland's hospital window for the 1954 Awards, but Koch vetoed the idea. "All else aside," he said to Marilyn Beck, "it would take away credibility from the Awards. If he wins, it would look like we knew about it in advance."

Alice Faye came to the rehearsal for a musical tribute to composer Harry Warren, but then found out that on her big number she'd be joined by Gregory Hines and Debbie Allen. "I was supposed to sing three bars of 'You'll Never Know' but I didn't know anyone else was going to sing it," she explained to Army Archerd. "If anyone was going to sing that song, I thought it was going to be me. It was one of those things that hit me and my husband [Phil Harris] the wrong way. And he absolutely forbade me to go on." So Faye, who introduced the 1943 Oscar winner in *Hello, Frisco, Hello,* and Harris left the rehearsal and headed home to Palm Springs.

The Big Night

First to arrive on the rainy, windy night was singer and Best Song nominee Peter Allen, wearing tails and a gold lamé cummerbund. Diane Keaton, on the arm of Warren Beatty, showed up in a black leather top, black slacks and black kid gloves that had the *Los Angeles Herald-Examiner* commenting that while the outfit "might not have been the most stylish at the Academy Awards, it certainly was the most practical." Supporting Actress nominee Joan Hackett said the hell with the weather and happily modeled her own design—a white, sequined strapless gown and matching cape, topped off with earrings that were actually Christmas tree ornaments she had bought for $1.95. Jane Fonda, the one-time fashion militant who had defiantly worn the same gown to the 1977 and '78 Awards, was dressed in a gold Valentino, inspiring Janet Maslin of the *New York Times* to remark, "As Jane Fonda . . . develops more and more of a radiant movie-queen air, she makes it all too clear how rare that quality is today." Fonda's husband Tom Hayden stuck to his usual conservative three-piece suit. Ernest Thompson, the writer of *On Golden Pond,* wore a white scarf and matching white-framed sunglasses; having just separated from ex-child star Patty McCormack of *The Bad Seed* fame, he brought Diana Ross as his date. *Atlantic City*'s Burt Lancaster brought his teenage granddaughter, and Susan Sarandon came with Richard Gere.

The television show began with announcer Hank Sims intoning, "Around the world, people are gathering—London, New York, Chicago—to watch filmmakers in a rainy Los Angeles twilight, already dressed for evening, come together to make tomorrow's headlines and another chapter of Hollywood history." Viewers saw a number of stars arriving, including Roger Moore, whom Sims called "maybe the handsomest man alive," and John Schneider from TV's *The Dukes of Hazzard*.

Academy President Fay Kanin proudly told the audience, "I don't think we've ever honored an array of films with more diversity or power." She then introduced emcee Johnny Carson, who started off by commenting on the weather: "Sad to think that $40,000 worth of hairdos are floating

Awards Ceremony

MARCH 29, 1982, 6:00 P.M.
THE DOROTHY CHANDLER PAVILION, LOS ANGELES

Your Host:
JOHNNY CARSON
Televised over ABC

Presenters

Supporting Actress	Timothy Hutton
Art Direction	Karen Allen and Howard E. Rollins, Jr.
Makeup	Kim Hunter and Vincent Price
Thalberg Award	Roger Moore
Original Score	Liberace, William Hurt and Kathleen Turner
Costume Design	Morgan Fairchild and Robert Hays
Visual Effects	Dan Aykroyd
Short Films	Paul Williams and Debra Winger
Cinematography	Chevy Chase and Rachel Ward
Honorary Award to Barbara Stanwyck	John Travolta
Sound	Christopher Atkins and Kristy McNichol
Foreign Film	Ornella Muti and Jack Valenti
Film Editing	Ursula Andress and Harry Hamlin
Song	Bette Midler
Jean Hersholt Humanitarian Award	Gregory Peck
Supporting Actor	Carol Burnett and Joel Grey
Director	Jack Lemmon and Walter Matthau
Writing Awards	Jerzy Kosinski
Actress	Jon Voight
Actor	Sissy Spacek
Picture	Loretta Young

Performers of Nominated Songs

"Arthur's Theme"	Christopher Cross
"Endless Love"	Lionel Richie and Diana Ross
"The First Time It Happens"	Kermit the Frog and Miss Piggy
"For Your Eyes Only"	Sheena Easton
"One More Hour"	John Schneider

"And so tonight, my golden boy, you've got your wish."
—Barbara Stanwyck

down the street," and then mentioned Nancy Reagan's attempt to donate her clothes as tax write-offs, "I have never seen such lovely designer gowns. Did you ladies borrow them from the Smithsonian? . . ."

The men from Price, Waterhouse brought out the envelopes and Johnny assured everyone that they "really know how to keep a secret—they also handled the distribution of *Atlantic City*." Timothy Hutton went down the roster of Best Supporting Actress nominees and then announced the winner—Maureen Stapleton in *Reds*. The actress started up, stopped, looked back to make sure she was indeed the winner, blew kisses to Warren Beatty and made it up to the podium, saying, "I'm thrilled, happy, delighted—sober! It is an evening for thanks, I'm sorry . . . I want to thank Troy, New York, my children, my family, my friends, and everybody I ever met in my entire life, and my inspiration, Joel McCrea." As Hutton and Stapleton, waving the Oscar over her head, trotted off, there was one of the evening's many shots of Warren Beatty, Diane Keaton and Jack Nicholson, who smiled and said, "Ooh, Joel McCrea."

This year, the Board of Governors had acquiesced and given its blessing for a Makeup Award. Voters chose the werewolves of *An American Werewolf in London* over the robots of *Heartbeeps* and winner Rick Baker said, "I'd like to thank the Academy for creating this new category and I'm honored to be the first winner." Next, Sheena Easton sang the nominated song "For Your Eyes Only" from the James Bond movie, while various Bond villains—Dr. No, Odd Job, Blowfeld (holding a toy cat) and Richard Kiel as Jaws—prowled around the set. The number ended with Easton and a dancer posing as 007 blasting off in a rocket. This served as the preface to the Thalberg Award for the series' producer Albert "Cubby" Broccoli, given by Roger Moore, who was currently having a salary dispute with his boss.

The Music Awards began with the credits to the 1955 film, *Sincerely Yours*, starring Liberace. Then a screen rose up and there was Liberace in person, wearing sequined tails with embroidered green roses, seated at a mirrored piano adorned by candelabra. "I've done my part for motion pictures," Mr. Showmanship joked, "I've stopped making them." After playing the themes from the five nominated Original Scores, Liberace asked, "Who better to give the Scoring Awards than the stars of *Body Heat*—Kathleen Turner and William Hurt?" The pair announced Vangelis' score for *Chariots of Fire* as the winner.

After dancers modeling creations by the Costume Design nominees paraded onstage, Robert Hays and Morgan Fairchild proclaimed that the winner was, again, *Chariots of Fire*, which Bloomingdale's had recently been featuring in a promotional fashion tie-in. Winner Milena Canonero paid tribute to her fellow nominees by name, adding, "I think we're all marvelous . . . but I've got it." *Chariots'* producer David Puttnam later recounted that when his film won Best Costume Design, "I knew that was the end for *Reds*. I looked at Warren Beatty, and I think he knew also." Next, Dan Aykroyd gave the Visual Effects Oscar to *Raiders of the Lost Ark*, but only after he broke his promise to Howard W. Koch and said, "My partner would have loved presenting this Award with me. He was something of a special effect himself."

John Travolta brought out Barbara Stanwyck, receiving an Honorary Oscar for her career's work, and the audience gave her the only standing ovation of the night. "I tried many times to get it, but I didn't make it," the four-time nominee recalled. She thanked "the remarkable crews we had the privilege to work with . . . *my* wonderful group, the stunt men and women who taught me so well." She ended with a tribute to an actor who had died several months earlier: "A few years ago, I stood on this stage with William Holden as a presenter. I loved him very much and I miss him. He always wished that I would get an Oscar." Raising the statuette as her eyes filled with tears, Stanwyck concluded, "And so tonight, my golden boy, you've got your wish."

After the Harry Warren tribute without Alice

"I bear no grudges. My heart is as big as the sky and I have a mind that retains absolutely nothing."
—Bette Midler

Faye, Johnny Carson cracked, "Having turned down an opportunity to go into the jean business with his brother Sergio, Jack Valenti and Ornella Muti will present the Foreign Language Film Award." The expected political statement didn't take place—*Man of Iron* lost out to Hungary's *Faust* update, *Mephisto*. Director István Szábo came onstage and called out to his leading man, Klaus Maria Brandauer, "Klaus, come with me, I'm so alone up here." Klaus shot up to the stage, and the two men embraced and danced a jig. After they walked off, Carson couldn't resist, "Later at the Governors' Ball, they plan to announce their engagement."

Bette Midler arrived to award Best Song, and stole the show by making a shambles of the pomp and circumstance. "So this is what it actually feels like to be up here, this is fantastic. I've been waiting for two years for the Academy to call me up and tell me they made a mistake. But do I bear a grudge—no, no. I bear no grudges. My heart is as big as the sky and I have a mind that retains absolutely nothing. This is the Oscars. We have to be dignified, as dignified as humanly possible. That is why I have decided to rise to the occasion," whereupon she lifted her breasts with her hands. The audience howled, and Midler went in for the kill:

> *The Best Original Song is a song that was actually written for the picture and not just some piece of junk the producer found in the piano bench, you dig? . . . "Arthur's Theme," also known as "The Best That You Can Do," also known as that song about the moon and New York City also known as Four on a Song . . . a nice piece of music. "Endless Love" from the endless movie [shot of Joan Hackett laughing]* Endless Love. *How do you like it so far, kids? Music and lyrics were written by the extremely rich Lionel Richie. . . . From* The Great Muppet Caper, *"The First Time It Happens," music and lyrics by Joe "It's Not Easy Being Green" Repozo . . . "For Your Eyes Only," from* For Your Eyes Only, *and they weren't kidding, I couldn't watch a single frame, music by Bill Conti [the show's musical director. Bette turned to the orchestra and asked] How are you taking this, guys? And my personal fave rave, "One More Hour" . . . Okay, that was fun, I enjoyed it.*

The winners were the four songwriters it took to assemble "Arthur's Theme," and cowriter Carole Bayer Sager told Midler, "I love getting this from you." "I know you do," snapped back Bette.

Carol Burnett and Joel Grey announced that the Best Supporting Actor was the absent John Gielgud in *Arthur*. Michael York was nowhere in sight. Jack Nicholson had not even bothered to take off his sunglasses.

Jack Lemmon and Walter Matthau stepped out to the *Odd Couple* theme to give Best Director. The victor was a bespectacled Warren Beatty. "Miss Keaton," the winner said cautiously, "I know that public expressions like this can be embarrassing sometimes and that my chances of speaking with you privately are at the moment excellent, but I do want to tell you that you do make every director you work with look good and I think what they're trying to tell me here tonight—thank God—is that I'm no exception." The cameras found a smiling Miss Keaton. "Mr. Nicholson," Beatty continued, "I know that you're enjoying my being up here almost as much as I am in being here." Mr. Nicholson grinned behind his glasses. Beatty then expressed his gratitude to Paramount president Barry Diller and Gulf & Western head Charles Bludhorn for bankrolling an expensive movie about American communism, saying, "I think it reflects more particular credit on the freedom of expression we have in our American society and the lack of censorship from the government or the people who put up the money."

Beatty was also up for the next Award, Best Original Screenplay. The winner, however, was *Chariots of Fire*. Writer Colin Welland exclaimed, "What you've done for the British film industry!"

"I've done my part for motion pictures. I've stopped making them."
—Liberace

and then warned the American industry, "You may have started something: The British are coming!" For Adapted Screenplay, the Academy chose *On Golden Pond*. Ernest Thompson, his white scarf draped over his shoulders, dashed to the stage, jumped up, gave a little one-two punch in the air and bear-hugged embarrassed presenter Jerzy Kosinski. After bussing his Oscar on its head, Thompson gave his speech: "I wrote *On Golden Pond* as a play four years ago for two reasons. First, I was out of work as an actor and, second, because I believe I had something to say and a burning need to say it. I'd like to thank a few people who believed in me as a writer before it was popular to do so." Among those thanked were "an incredible company of actors for making my words sound so intelligent and funny." To close, he told the audience, "I'm so proud and if you would all see me later, I would love to suck face with you all." Janet Maslin wrote in the *New York Times* that Thompson "exemplified everything that can be wrong with the Oscars and its winners."

Another white scarf appeared, this one wrapped around the neck of Jon Voight, who decided to make do without a tie. All of the Best Actress nominees were present save Katharine Hepburn. And the winner was—for the fourth time—Katharine Hepburn in *On Golden Pond*. There was a roar of surprise and the television cameras caught a close-up of an overwhelmed Jane Fonda. Voight didn't bother with the cue cards, extemporizing, "I don't think there's anyone here or watching who doesn't appreciate the amount of love and gratitude represented by this Oscar selection tonight and we all send our love to Katharine."

Sissy Spacek entered and recalled, "when I was growing up in Texas, Academy Awards night was the big night of the year . . . It's still that way for me and it's an honor to be here tonight." Spacek confirmed what everyone expected—the Best Actor winner was Henry Fonda. Jane came onstage, hugged Sissy and, for a good four minutes, accepted her father's Award. She began by breathlessly saying, "Oh, Dad, I'm so happy and proud for you," and then proceeded to go down a list of all the things she imagined he must be thinking: how much he respected the other nominees, how uncomfortable he is about competition and how he'd want to thank "the wonderful cast—Dougie McKeon, Dabney Coleman, me—he's a proud father." Jane also did her bit for tourism, saying, "He also feels very lucky to have been able to spend a summer in such a beautiful part of our country, northern New Hampshire." Turning folksy, Jane addressed her father again: "Dad, me and the grandkids will be right over."

Johnny Carson glowingly described Loretta Young as a Hollywood legend and then the actress appeared, posing casually at the top of a staircase. She blew a kiss to someone in the audience and flowed down the stairs as if she were about to enter through the doors on her old television show. After admitting that "reality" is an integral part of movies, Young lectured, "Fortunately, reality, contrary to some beliefs, is not restricted to sordid or shocking themes, nor gritty, gutter language, nor gratuitous violence, et cetera. Reality is also healthy, wholesome love and romance. It's courage, adventure, inspiration and heroism. This year, some tasteful filmmakers have rediscovered that fact and I am delighted for one and we are all enriched because of it." Andrew Sarris chuckled, "Loretta Young's reincarnation as a censorious schoolmarm was close to being a campy debacle." One reason was that the first clip, from *Atlantic City*, had to be bleeped twice because of Burt Lancaster's language.

The news in the envelope caused an avalanche of obscenities to be uttered throughout Hollywood. *Chariots of Fire* was the out-of-left-field winner. Producer David Puttnam joked, "Just for thirty seconds, I wish I were Bette Midler," and then said, "You are the most extraordinary, generous people on God's earth, not just the Academy, to whom we are thankful, but as a country to have taken what is an absolutely Cinderella picture and awarded it this and come to it in droves." Puttnam brought up Best Director loser Hugh Hudson, who looked as if he felt underappre-

"Hell, if I hadn't won, I wouldn't have been able to walk with my head up anymore."
—Henry Fonda

ciated. The *Hollywood Reporter* looked at its watch and noted, "At three hours and thirty-two minutes, the Oscar telecast came in 12 minutes longer than Beatty's *Reds*."

Aftermath

Backstage, Barbara Stanwyck answered questions about her health. "I feel fine. Thank God I'm breathing," the seventy-four-year-old actress said. "Of course I was disappointed those times I was nominated before and lost. Anyone who says they're not is lying. I never thought I had anything in the bag . . . I'd like to do more as an actress, and better. It might be in a wheelchair but what the hell."

To the inevitable, "Did you expect to win?" Maureen Stapleton—at fifty-six, the youngest among this year's winning actors— said, "Yes, because I'm old and tired and I deserved it and I lost three times before." How did Joel McCrea inspire her? "Just looking at him . . . and because he's always been a good actor and because I'm madly in love with him." When one reporter asked, "How does it feel to be recognized as one of the greatest actresses in the world?" Stapleton retorted, "Not nearly as exciting as if I were acknowledged as one of the greatest lays in the world." As for her director, one reporter said that backstage Warren Beatty gave "one of the best performances of his career." Asked if he felt gyped that the anticipated sweep for *Reds* turned into a mere three wins, Beatty responded, "I think we were treated very nicely."

Less diplomatic was *Chariots*' David Puttnam, who blasted Warren Beatty in print. Marilyn Beck claimed that Puttnam was "bitter" that Hugh Hudson had lost Best Director to Warren Beatty and quoted the British producer as saying, "Hugh is without a doubt a better director than Warren is, or ever will be. And so are Steven Spielberg and Louis Malle." He also asserted that Beatty's Oscar win was "proof the Academy was acknowledging he could raise $50 million to make a picture."

Most of the industry had equally strong objections to the Best Picture victory by Puttnam's movie. The *New York Post* headlined: HOLLYWOOD FUMING OVER WIN BY 'CHARIOTS OF FIRE' and quoted an unidentified "top official at the Academy": "I'm afraid this could be the beginning of a trend we saw in the 1960s. Twenty years ago, we started a love affair with the English that lasted about ten years. Their actors and actresses could do no wrong. We have extremely talented people here in America and I don't want them to get short shrift."

The *London Daily Star* was bursting with pride as it gloated to its readership that "our actors, writers and producers collected FIVE glittering Oscars—and ended up stealing the show from the fabulous Fondas and Warren Beatty's blockbuster *Reds*." The British actor who had won, seventy-seven-year-old Sir John Gielgud, said he'd be putting his Oscar on a shelf in his bathroom and professed to be amused by the whole thing. "It's extraordinary to have that Oscar after wonderful things like a knighthood," the Shakespearean actor chortled. "To think that people who've never heard of me before now think of me as a kind of name."

Even if the British had taken the top prize, Hollywood was nonetheless buoyed by the sentimental turn the two top acting Awards had taken. Janet Maslin of the *New York Times* argued, however, that "certainly Katharine Hepburn was not named Best Actress because of any groundswell among Academy members who felt she needed a fourth Oscar; she won because the voters lacked enthusiasm for Diane Keaton or Meryl Streep, the true leading contenders in that category." Hepburn told the press, "I was so dumbfounded. I'm so touched that my fellow actors cared to vote for me, a dear old thing."

After the Awards show, the press hightailed it to Henry Fonda's home. The bedridden actor had slipped into a bathrobe and was made up by Shotgun Britton, a makeup artist who had first worked with Fonda on *Let Us Live* in 1938. Fonda had grown a beard that he pledged not to shave off until he regained his health. After receiving Jane, Tom, the grandkids, and a few well-wishers—including Ernest Thompson and Diana Ross—Fonda retired for the night. Wife Shirlee reminded everyone, "He's still a very sick man." The Best Actor died five months later, on August 12, 1982.

After the ceremony, Mrs. Fonda said to *Time*, "I told him that he was going to win, and wouldn't that be wonderful after so long a time waiting for it? Talking about the Oscar was another way of not letting him fade away. When he won, I flew into his arms. He held me tight and I saw the tears in his eyes and they told me he was overwhelmed with a profound sense of happiness. 'Hell, if I hadn't won,' he said, 'I wouldn't have been able to walk with my head up anymore.' "

1982

"I was really hell to be around."
—Jessica Lange

Two pacifists battled it out at the 1982 Academy Awards.

"The worst part about being me," said Jack Lemmon, "is when people want me to make them laugh." Nobody was laughing at his latest movie, *Missing,* least of all the U.S. State Department. Political filmmaker Costa-Gavras based the film on *The Execution of Charles Horman,* a nonfiction book that alleged the United States had a hand in covering up the death of American citizens during the CIA-led overthrow of Chilean President Salvador Allende's democratic government. Lemmon played a conservative businessman and Sissy Spacek his daughter-in-law searching for his missing son in an unnamed South American country. Universal didn't have to worry about the film missing out on publicity; two days before *Missing* opened in February, the State Department released a three-page statement denying any "possibility that U.S. Government officials might have initiated, condoned or failed to act effectively" in Horman's disappearance and murder.

In the *New York Times,* Vincent Canby called *Missing* "Mr. Costa-Gavras' most beautifully achieved political melodrama to date, a suspense thriller of real cinematic style." But *Time* seemed to be harkening back to Sam Goldwyn's "Want-to-send-a-message-call-Western Union" attitude: "A story that could have made for a brisk jeremiad on *60 Minutes* is stretched to 122 minutes of heroes fuming and villains purring their oleaginous apologies." *Newsweek* found that "the odd pairing of Lemmon and Spacek is inspired. The clash of their acting styles is their clash of characters, and they work brilliantly together as they make their prickly progress from foes to allies." But to the public, *Missing* sounded too much like the evening news and, outside of urban areas and college towns, the film was a bust at the box office.

Competing Best Actresses Jessica Lange and Meryl Streep relax together, secure in the knowledge that neither is going home empty-handed.

His and Hers

Julie Andrews, the musical sweetheart of the 1960s, had a rough time of it in the '70s, starring in a mere three movies, all directed by her husband, Blake Edwards. Only one of the three was a hit, and everyone was so busy looking at Bo Derek in *10* that Julie went unnoticed. In 1981, she exposed her breasts in her husband's *cinema à clef, S.O.B.*, and the following year further demolished her sugar-and-spice persona by playing a woman who poses as a female impersonator in *Victor/Victoria.* This musical farce, set in a storybook Paris of the 1930s, took a look at sexual role-playing, and Vincent Canby instructed readers of the *New York Times,* "Get ready, set and go—immediately to the Ziegfeld Theater, where Blake Edwards today opens his *chef d'oeuvre,* his cockeyed crowning achievement." Columnist Bob Thomas called *Victor/Victoria* "a marvelous mixture of genders, a blatant attack on sexual attitudes that is both challenging and hilarious."

Julie Andrews basked in the kind of glowing reviews she had gotten when she first started making movies. Liz Smith called her "divine," *Newsweek,* "a delight," and Judith Crist cheered, "Julie Andrews is simply brilliant. All the gifts that sparkled in her Broadway and film musicals glitter in her maturity; she is pure enchantment as performer and as actress." Playing a gay cabaret performer, longtime musical-comedy star Robert Preston also won huzzahs, with Canby effusing, "It's a rich wonderful characterization, topping—I think—his memorable performances in *The Music Man* on the stage and the screen." Lesley Ann Warren, a former Disney ingenue who of late had been playing tramps in TV movies, put on a platinum wig and spoke through her nose to portray an archetypal dumb blonde; Stanley Kauffmann of the *New Republic* was awed that the actress "plays her as if the character had just been in-

"What I really need is a friend I can talk to—somebody who can give me all the answers."
—Steven Spielberg

vented." Not everyone joined in the fun, though. Rex Reed claimed that Julie Andrews looked like David Bowie and groused, "It's all very trashy and offensive, not to mention sophomoric."

A Boy and His Alien

At the end of June, the cover of *People* proclaimed: WOW! A MOVIE TO STEAL AMERICA'S HEART. Steven Spielberg was back, and once again he told the press about the gestation of his new movie. In 1980, he was in Tunisia making *Raiders of the Lost Ark* and "I was kind of lonely at the time. My girlfriend was back in Los Angeles. I remember saying to myself, 'What I really need is a friend I can talk to—somebody who can give me *all* the answers." Harrison Ford's girlfriend, screenwriter Melissa Matheson, was also hanging out in Tunisia, and she and Spielberg decided that in those lonely times, a gentle creature from outer space might fit the bill. And thus was *E.T.: The Extra-Terrestrial* born.

As usual, Spielberg ordered secrecy on the set and during filming went on record to state that no matter what anyone may have heard, "E.T. did *not* stand for "Extra-Terrestrial." The jig was up when *E.T.* premiered on closing night at the Cannes Film Festival. Rex Reed covered the scene, announcing that Spielberg "showed the Godards and the Antonionis and the Fassbinders who had bored everyone into a state of catatonia for the previous two weeks how real movies are made." Some critics pointed out that the fantasy about a cute little boy and his cute little alien friend was essentially a souped-up version of *Lassie, Come Home,* but Pauline Kael dubbed *E.T.* "a dream of a movie—a bliss-out," and on the West Coast, Sheila Benson of the *Los Angeles Times* suggested, "It may be the film of the decade and possibly the double decade."

E.T. was everywhere, from political cartoons to bumper stickers that pleaded E.T. PHONE HOME. Neil Diamond was so moved that he recorded an inspirational song, "Turn On Your Heart Light," which was popular both on the radio and at wedding receptions. When Spielberg approved more than fifty spinoff licenses to entrepreneurs, business analysts predicted over a billion dollars in sales. From day one, *E.T.* set box-office records, and in January 1983, Spielberg toppled his pal George Lucas on the all-time champ list. *E.T.* was now the top moneymaker in history.

Apple Pie and Sex

Bearing the Spielberg imprimatur, *E.T.* could hardly be called a surprise hit, but another of the summer's most popular items came from out of nowhere. Richard Gere was a star who had never had a big hit, Debra Winger was no household name, director Taylor Hackford's one previous feature, *The Idolmaker,* caused no stir at all, and the story was the old saw about the ragged recruit made a man by the military. Nevertheless, *An Officer and a Gentleman* earned a whopping $55 million at U.S. box offices by combining patriotism with enough steamy love scenes to become the make-out movie of the year. Charles Champlin of the *Los Angeles Times* called it "tropically sexy, unabashed, uninhibited and unashamed of calling forth big emotional responses in several flavors."

In addition to Winger and Gere, the film boosted the career of Louis Gossett, Jr., a black actor who was cast in a role that had been originally offered to white performers. But Gossett still had to put up with segregation; director Hackford told the actor playing the tough drill instructor that it might be a good idea not to socialize with the other cast members. "Lou is such a charming, lovely guy," said Hackford, "that I didn't want him going out to dinner and drinking with the other actors. I thought if he got to know them too well, they might start to giggle if he showed up on the set the next morning and started yelling at them." Being quarantined paid off. "Gossett's whiplike edge manages to make a hackneyed character almost fresh," wrote *Newsweek*, and *Variety* raved, "Gossett does more with his eyes and a facial reaction than others accomplish with pages of dialogue."

"It was such a relief to let it all hang out."
—Paul Newman

Drinking Again

On the wagon for several years now, Peter O'Toole said "I don't miss booze. I still cause mayhem. I'll always love to frolic, but now I can remember what I've done." The actor had to summon up those dear dead days and remember what it was like to be soused when he made the comedy *My Favorite Year*. O'Toole played a perpetually drunk matinee idol appearing on a live television variety show in 1954, and first-time director Richard Benjamin fretted, "My greatest fear in this thing was to be given this national treasure and somehow mess it up for him." He didn't. *California* magazine wrote, "Peter O'Toole's performance as a star playing a star is superlative. He doesn't hold the screen, he owns it." *Time* meanwhile was delighted that the one-time staple of historical epics "has turned into an utterly unique comic actor, a man who seems to have dedicated himself to the cause of giving decadence a good name."

Paul Newman's Blemishes

All year long, employees of 20th Century–Fox referred to *The Verdict* as "Paul Newman's Academy Award movie." Newman had a showy role as a dissipated, alcoholic lawyer and Hollywood quickly realized that the five-time nominee was hungry for the Award. His baby blues sparkled on the cover of *Time* under the heading "The Verdict on Newman: QUITE A GUY." Inside, Newman reviewed all of his movies, climaxing with his opinion of his performance in *The Verdict:* "It was such a relief to let it all hang out in the movie—blemishes and all." *Time* reminded, "He is also a fine director, a hard-charging sports-car racer, a campaigner for nuclear freeze and a big man in salad dressing," an allusion to his much-publicized foray into food marketing with his own concoction that had his picture plastered on the bottle.

Newman's Oscar front-runner status was solidified when the critics got a look at *The Verdict.* Janet Maslin said in the *New York Times,* "A solidly old-fashioned courtroom drama such as *The Verdict* could have gotten by with a serious, measured performance from its leading man, or it could have worked well with a dazzling movie-star turn. The fact that Paul Newman delivers both makes a clever, suspenseful, entertaining movie even better." Newman's courtroom adversary was seventy-three-year-old James Mason, and *California* declared that "Mason has not given such an effective, delicately modulated, powerhouse performance in at least a decade." Audiences lined up in large numbers for *The Verdict,* and Newman also kept in the public eye with public-service announcements promoting the use of seat belts and political commercials advocating nuclear disarmament.

Speaking in Tongues

Meryl Streep followed *The French Lieutenant's Woman* with another coveted role from a bestselling novel. Goldie Hawn and Marthe Keller had made public statements that they could do wonders as the Polish concentration-camp survivor in the movie version of William Styron's *Sophie's Choice,* but Streep did them one better. She approached director Alan J. Pakula, fell to her knees and said, "I have to play this role." Pakula said okay and Streep went to work mastering the two other languages spoken by her character. A dumbstruck Marilyn Beck advised her readers, "When you see *Sophie's Choice,* you'll find it hard to believe German and Polish aren't Meryl's native languages."

Critics faulted *Sophie's Choice* for being too reverential toward its source—"a handsome, doggedly faithful and astoundingly tedious adaptation," yawned *Variety*—but they were equally reverential toward Streep. Comparisons to Garbo were prevalent, and Charles Champlin called Streep's "the most moving performance by an actress, intellectually and emotionally, that I've seen in a very long time indeed." But *New York Daily News* had yet to become a believer: "It is a re-

"I feel cheated never being able to know what it's like to get pregnant, carry a child and breast-feed."
—Dustin Hoffman

markable display of acting ability, but it is also, like the movie itself, a little too studied and calculating."

Hell to Be Around

Like *Sophie's Choice, Frances* was a downbeat Christmas release with an extravagant role for an actress. But while Meryl Streep already had top credentials, the star of *Frances,* Jessica Lange, had to live down her past. To most people, she was still the innocuous ingenue of the *King Kong* remake. "I just didn't get another part for two years after *King Kong,*" Lange recalled. "I decided to go back to New York and pick up acting classes where Hollywood interrupted me. I had a contract with Dino de Laurentiis, and he paid me a salary, so I didn't have to support myself as a waitress anymore." After a small role as the Angel of Death for Bob Fosse in *All That Jazz* and a negligible comedy, Lange attracted some critical enthusiasm—but no audience—in the remake of *The Postman Always Rings Twice.* She impressed that movie's editor, Graeme Clifford, enough for him to cast her in a movie he was directing about the doomed movie actress Frances Farmer, whose fierce independence got her thrown out of Hollywood and into mental institutions. Lange identified with the part and told writer Vito Russo there was a "cosmic connection" between herself and Farmer.

The *Los Angeles Times'* Sheila Benson praised "a soaring performance . . . a combination of forcefulness, intelligence and a haunting sensuality." Vincent Canby pondered and decided, "The only comparable triumph I can remember is Sophia Loren's in 1961 when, after decorating a number of less-than-terrific films, she suddenly burst into our consciousnesses in *Two Women* as an actress of bravura talents." As pleasant as the result was, making *Frances* was no lark. Lange said, "All through life I've harbored anger rather than expressed it at the moment. Once I started on *Frances,* I discovered it was literally a bottomless well. It devastated me to maintain that for eighteen weeks, to be immersed in this state of rage for twelve to eighteen hours a day. It spilled all over into other areas of my life. I was really hell to be around." Kim Stanley, who played her loony mother in the film, told Lange, "Make a comedy as fast as you can. Get your mind off this."

Gender Gap

A couple of weeks later, Lange did just that, taking on leading-lady duties in *Tootsie.* When Dustin Hoffman had finished *Kramer vs. Kramer,* he was, he recalled, "very excited about a new feeling—what makes a man, what makes a woman, what is gender?" He and his friend, playwright Murray Schisgal, had numerous bull sessions about these issues. "Suddenly," said Hoffman, "he asked me this question: 'What kind of woman would you be if you were a woman?' And I said 'What a great question.'" To have that question answered, Hoffman took a script he had come across about an actor who pretends to be a woman in order to land a part, and gave it to Schisgal—and eventually five other writers—to fashion as a vehicle for him." Four years later, after two directors had dropped out, *Tootsie* was ready to roll.

Director Sydney Pollack was about to start filming and, he said, "I didn't know anything about *Victor/Victoria* until it opened and I read this poem by Vincent Canby in the *New York Times* and my heart sank. So I ran over to the Ziegfeld to see it, and I loved it. But I knew that my film was going to be very different. I was *not* making a farce. I wanted a realistic comedy about actors. I was still a little depressed, though." Hoffman wanted *Tootsie* to be realistic, too, so much so that he went around New York City in his woman's clothing to make sure he was convincing. Hoffman accosted his *Midnight Cowboy* costar Jon Voight at the Russian Tea Room. Reported *Newsweek,* "José Ferrer, trapped in an elevator by a strange lady in glasses, turned red at the woman's indecent proposal."

Tootsie had no grandiose special effects, large-scale action scenes or elaborate sets, but still ended up costing $22 million. "One of the best movie

"I'm truly looking forward to the Academy Awards. I've reached the point where I enjoy such weird do's."
—James Mason

farces in years," raved the *Los Angeles Herald-Examiner*. "It's a real wing-ding." As for the leading man, *Variety* felt that "Hoffman triumphs in what must stand as one of his most brilliant performances. Although hardly blessed with what one could consider feminine or even adrogynous features, his Dorothy is entirely plausible and, physically, reasonably appealing." The actor was busy on the interview circuit, reporting that, "I feel cheated never being able to know what it's like to get pregnant, carry a child and breast-feed." *Ms.* magazine applauded Hoffman's newfound feminist sensitivity, and writer Susan Dworkin rhapsodized that during filming Hoffman so well conveyed the sexist humiliation suffered by women that a weeping wardrobe worker came up to him on the set and said, "Oh, Dusty, that's it, that's just what we go through, that's just how we feel."

For all that, the hero in *Tootsie* still dumps his plain Jane girlfriend for the blonde beauty played by Jessica Lange. Although she didn't get the guy, Teri Garr did get praise from Pauline Kael, who said she was "becoming the funniest neurotic dizzy dame on the screen." Lange amazed the critics even more. Andrew Sarris swooned, "Let it be recorded for the year 2022 that in the year 1982 a bedazzled reviewer for the *Village Voice* suddenly discovered that Jessica Lange was more of a knockout than Frances Farmer ever was, that she was everything Marilyn Monroe was supposed to be in *Some Like It Hot,* and a great deal more besides." Aljean Harmetz reported that "directors and producers who ridiculed Jessica Lange four years ago are 'developing projects' for her now," and her ex-director Bob Fosse declared, "I've never seen anybody go from so cold to so hot." While *Frances* made next to no money for Universal, *Tootsie* went on to become the highest grossing picture in Columbia's history.

Little Brown Man

Sir Richard Attenborough, the British actor-turned-director, never tired of telling reporters, "The filming of Gandhi's life possessed me for the past twenty years. Nothing was more important to me. It took me over completely. It became an obsession." As Attenborough put it, the studios "felt a film about a little brown man in a sheet carrying a beanpole wasn't exactly going to pack them in," and Hollywood told him to go chase his windmills somewhere else. Finally, he got together the $20-odd million from independent investors, including the government of India, which kicked in $7 million, and off he went to follow that dream. Filming completed, Attenborough was back in Hollywood looking for a distributor and, he claimed, "Every single company that had turned it down over the last twenty years bid for it." Frank Price, chairman of the board of Columbia, said, "When I saw two hours of footage, I knew I had to have it. I haven't seen a film the likes of it since David Lean's epics. But it's much bigger than *Lawrence of Arabia*."

Having gotten it, Columbia had to figure out how to sell it. Somebody came up with a catchy slogan and a full year before its Christmas '82 opening, four-page trade-paper ads on heavy stock were already proclaiming *Gandhi* "a world event." A billboard on Sunset Boulevard told drivers the same thing all through 1982. Arthur Knight of the *Hollywood Reporter* must have thought this a marvelous slogan because he wrote, "*Gandhi* is more than a superb movie; it's a cinematic event . . . It is probably the most important film made in the last decade." Rex Reed stated that the three-hour-and-eight-minute movie "is the kind of massive accomplishment for which ordinary adjectives like 'brilliant' or 'sweeping' or 'magnificent' seem anemic and inadequate."

But some critics felt that their fellows were reviewing the man and not the movie. In the *Village Voice*, Elliot Stein carped that "anything which might have puzzled or offended Western audiences about this great, tough and often ambiguous world figure had been bowdlerized. The skimpy, sanitized residue had been wrapped in a salable package of sentiment." An obscure, half-Indian member of the Royal Shakespeare Company named Ben Kingsley (né Krishna Bhanji) had the

"Everyone is understandably sick of the sight of those repulsive-looking, rubberized E.T. dolls."

—Kathleen Carroll

title role, and he prepared for the part by meditating in his hotel room, surrounded by photographs of the Mahatma. The preparation worked fine. *Variety* marveled that Kingsley "has captured nuances in speech and movement which makes it seem as though he has stepped through black-and-white newsreel into the present Technicolor reincarnation."

Liz Smith praised Columbia's publicists for their bit in the huckstering of *Gandhi:* "These New Yorkers went for class and made tie-ins with the peace movement, Coretta King, Andrew Young, UNICEF and the National Council of Churches. They even influenced the Martin Luther King Peace Prize for Sir Richard Attenborough." The knight was the first show-business personality to be awarded this honor and he marched by Coretta Scott King's side from the Ebenezer Baptist Church to the Georgia State Capitol on the civil rights leader's birthday. Back in India, filmmakers were incensed that their own government had given a foreign enterprise $7 million that they could have used themselves and members of the country's Untouchables caste were so upset over the short shrift given their plight in the movie they took to unleashing snakes in theaters where it was playing.

A Time for Giving

The Los Angeles Film Critics decided that nothing before or since could approach the summer's big movie and they named *E.T.* the year's Best Picture and Steven Spielberg Best Director. The New York crew, however, went with the Christmas hits, choosing *Gandhi* and *Tootsie*'s Sydney Pollack. The awards season wasn't going well at all for Paul Newman; Ben Kingsley was taking home prize after prize, although the National Society of Film Critics shared the wealth by naming Dustin Hoffman Best Actor. Also on a winning streak was Meryl Streep for *Sophie's Choice*. Streep's dominance meant that the critics couldn't acknowledge Jessica Lange's Cinderella story, but then the New York Film Critics came up with a solution. After bestowing their Best Actress award on Streep, they declared that in *Tootsie,* Lange was actually a supporting actress, so they could have their Meryl and Jessica, too. The L.A. crew had given their Best Supporting Actress award to stage actress Glenn Close as the unemotional feminist mother in *The World According to Garp*. The film version of John Irving's bestseller won both groups' Supporting Actor awards—John Lithgow as the transsexual ex-football player, Roberta Muldoon. Lithgow said of his performance, "My first appearance is a sight gag. Then in the course of the film, you get very close to Roberta. The character is a controlled person with a happy equilibrium who helps other people through their lapses. She's admirable and I love the part."

Campaign Time

Since *Missing* had been out of circulation for a good six months, Universal decided to refresh Academy voters' memories by mailing out a twelve-page, eleven-by-fourteen-inch booklet about the movie. But once again the government came through with free advertising when a former ambassador to Chile and two fellow officials made headlines by suing the studio for libel. At the same time, the U.S. Department of Justice labeled as "propaganda" *If You Love This Planet,* a Canadian anti-arms-race short submitted for consideration as Best Documentary; the ruling required the film to carry a disclaimer whenever shown in the United States.

The *New York Daily News* ran an exposé charging that the studios had spent nearly $2 million trying to win nominations. Gordon Weaver, Paramount's vice president for worldwide marketing, protested that his company had a rational campaign policy: "We do it only for those who deserve the acclaim. Otherwise this whole thing becomes a joke and the Academy is no joke." Then the studio turned around and ran full-page ads extolling the artistry of *Friday the 13th—Part 3 in 3D*.

The Nominations

Film Comment's gag that the Academy consists of the last three thousand liberals in America may well have been true. Not only was *Missing* nominated for Best Picture, but that piece of "propaganda," *If You Love This Planet*, was one of the five finalists for Best Documentary Short Subject. With nine nominations, Best Picture nominee *E.T.* was only in the show position, *Gandhi* led with eleven nominations and *Tootsie* had ten. The fifth Best Picture contender was *The Verdict*. Jessica Lange was up for both Best Actress and Supporting Actress, the first person so honored since Teresa Wright in 1942.

Meryl Streep's competition was pretty much conceding the Best Actress race. "I've never reacted to a performance as I did to hers in *Sophie's Choice*," said *Missing*'s Sissy Spacek. "It left me so overcome with emotion I sobbed for a full ten minutes." And Debra Winger's parents told *People*, "The nomination thrilled us and was a wonderful tribute to Debra, but all three of us feel Meryl Streep deserves it." Nominated for the first time in seventeen years, *Victor/Victoria*'s Julie Andrews had to settle for being, as Andrew Sarris put it, "forgiven at long last for *The Sound of Music*." The only one who doubted Streep's victory was Meryl herself. On one TV interview, she opened her blouse to show that she was so nervous she had hives.

The year's biggest surprise was the six nominations for the West German film *Das Boot*, the highest total ever for a foreign-language movie. *Das Boot* was the most expensive film ever made in Germany and even though critics were divided on the World War II submarine drama, it found a ready audience. The film stayed at one Beverly Hills theater for most of 1982.

Screen newcomer Ben Kingsley was up for Best Actor, but the rest of the field consisted of veterans of the Oscar race: *Missing*'s Jack Lemmon had his eighth nomination; *My Favorite Year*'s Peter O'Toole his seventh; *The Verdict*'s Paul Newman his sixth; and *Tootsie*'s Dustin Hoffman his fifth. Three of the acting nominees this year were crossdressers—in addition to Julie Andrews and Dustin Hoffman, Supporting Actor Robert Preston had gone drag—and John Lithgow was a transsexual. After forty-five years in movies, first-time nominee Robert Preston chuckled to Army Archerd, "I figure all it takes is longevity." Of the Supporting Actor race, agreed to be the closest of the acting contests, Preston joked, "This is a year when almost everyone except Lou Gossett was in drag—and that's why Gossett will win."

If Gossett did seem to have a slight lead, it may have been because people began to realize it had been nineteen years since a black had won an acting Oscar and blacks in the Hollywood community held a reception for Gossett. At the tribute, 1963 Best Actor Sidney Poitier recalled how he felt when he was "within touching distance of an Academy Award" and said of the guest of honor, "It will be inconceivable if he doesn't win."

Also inconceivable, according to Supporting Actress nominee Teri Garr, was Jessica Lange's Supporting Actress nomination. Garr told Liz Smith, "I am thrilled by the nomination, but what really hurts is that I think Jessica Lange was the leading lady in *Tootsie*. I played the supporting part with the director telling me 'we can't make you look too good in this movie' and I was a real good sport about it and then I have to share the nomination. Well, I am a little bugged by that."

No one could have foreseen it, but the blockbuster *E.T.* had turned into an underdog. People simply seemed to have O.D.'d on the film; Kathleen Carroll wrote in the *New York Daily News*, "Everyone is understandably sick of the sight of those repulsive-looking rubberized *E.T.* dolls." Moreover, the death of actor Vic Morrow and two children in July during the making of *Twilight Zone—The Movie*, which Spielberg was coproducing, started a backlash. *Film Comment* wondered "whether Academy members will see the tragedy as an all-but-inevitable by-product of young directors who'll try anything for effect." In contrast, Richard Attenborough's twenty-year odyssey made for a good humaninterest story and as industry analyst Lee Beaupré observed, "By voting for *Gandhi,* an Academy member can feel noble. He can also figure he's helping to add the millions of dollars to the potential gross that winning Best Film could mean for the picture."

If Spielberg's chances looked slim, it looked as if Paul Newman wasn't even going to show up on Oscar night. His official explanation was that he couldn't get away from the Florida set of his new film, *Harry and Son,* but *People* quoted an unnamed "studio exec" who insisted that " 'Paul was pouting' because the prestigious acting awards in New York and L.A. had already gone to Kingsley and Hoffman." Then, at the last minute, Newman told Army Archerd, "They made me an offer I couldn't refuse," explaining that, without his knowledge, his film crew had voted to work an extra day so he could attend the Awards. Newman's costar from *The Verdict,* Supporting Actor nominee James Mason, who had been a no-show the two other times he was nominated, was definitely coming this year. He told Marilyn Beck, "I'm truly looking forward to it. I've reached the point where I enjoy such weird do's."

Apparently George C. Scott had reached the same point. In town to pitch his new project, *The Last Days of Patton,* the renegade of the 1970 Awards called the Academy to see if it could scrounge up tickets for wife Trish Van Devere and himself. The Academy found him two seats in the back of the orchestra.

The Big Night

When George C. Scott and his wife tried to enter the Dorothy Chandler Pavilion without speaking to forecourt announcer Army Archerd, Archerd yelled over the microphone, "Your Oscar is waiting for you at the Academy, Wilshire and Lapeer." Paul Newman and Joanne Woodward, as well as California Governor George Deukmejian, were hardly noticed when they arrived; the crowd saved its loudest cheers for TV star Tom Selleck and movie beefcakes Sylvester Stallone and Christopher Reeve. A pregnant Meryl Streep appeared in a gold maternity dress on the arm of her husband. Jessica Lange came with her brother and admitted she was nervous about the prospect of losing twice. Protesters wearing skull masks and army fatigues waved a sign that read: MISSING: 35,000 IN EL SALVADOR, FILMED ON LOCATION BY RONALD REAGAN PRODS. DIRECTED BY JEANE KIRKPATRICK. Concerned with conditions closer to home were employees of the Hungry Tiger Restaurant, the Academy's backstage caterer, who protested the restaurant's hiring practices.

The telecast began with a trip around the world in one hundred seconds, glimpsing movie theaters showing some of the nominated films in London, Rio de Janeiro, Tokyo, Sydney, Rome, Paris and Times Square. The cameras zoomed over the Hollywood sign and the four hosts—Walter Matthau, Liza Minnelli, Dudley Moore and Richard Pryor—ran onstage to sing the opening number, "It All Comes Down to This." Minnelli, perhaps self-conscious because her recent Los Angeles concert had been panned by *Daily Variety* as "Liza With a Zzzz," was the only member of the quartet to show any enthusiasm and she energetically tapped her foot.

Academy President Fay Kanin walked out in a beaded flapper dress and kept up the travelogue motif by sharing her trip to Amsterdam with the audience. Kanin had visited Anne Frank's house and related how touched she was that young Anne had pinned pictures of movie stars to the wall. Minnelli returned as the first emcee and cracked,

Awards Ceremony

April 11, 1983, 6:00 p.m.
The Dorothy Chandler Pavilion, Los Angeles

Your Hosts:
Walter Matthau, Liza Minnelli, Dudley Moore, Richard Pryor
Televised over ABC

Presenters

Foreign Film . . . . Luise Rainer and Jack Valenti
Supporting Actor . . . . Susan Sarandon and Christopher Reeve
Makeup . . . . Jane Russell and Cornel Wilde
Short Subjects . . . . Kristy McNichol and Matt Dillon
Scoring Awards . . . . Cher and Placido Domingo
Thalberg Award . . . . Charlton Heston
Costume Design . . . . Ann Reinking and Steve Guttenberg
Visual Effects . . . . .Elizabeth McGovern and Eddie Murphy
Sound Effects Editing . . . . Jamie Lee Curtis and Carl Weathers
Documentary Awards . . . . .Jobeth Williams and David Wolper
Art Direction . . . . Margot Kidder and William Shatner
Cinematography . . . . Nastassia Kinski and Michael Keaton
Honorary Award to Mickey Rooney . . . . Bob Hope
Sound . . . . Lisa Eilbacher and David Keith
Editing . . . . Raquel Welch and Tom Selleck
Song . . . . Olivia Newton-John
Supporting Actress . . . . Sigourney Weaver and Robert Mitchum
Screenplay . . . . Philip Dunne
Director . . . . Billy Wilder
Actress . . . . .Sylvester Stallone
Actor . . . . John Travolta
Picture . . . . Carol Burnett

Performers of Nominated Songs

"Eye of the Tiger" . . . . .Sandahl Bergman and The Temptations
"How Do You Keep the Music Playing?" . . . . Patti Austin and James Ingram
"If We Were in Love" . . . . Melissa Manchester
"It Might Be You" . . . . Stephen Bishop
"Up Where We Belong" . . . . Joe Cocker and Jennifer Warnes

"You really know how to show a foreign agent a good time."
—Terri Nash

"Richard, Dudley and Walter are still rehearsing our opening number." The reading of the rules was dispensed with in the most imaginative way yet: fast talker John Moschitta, the star of many TV commercials, zipped through the lengthy explanation in twenty-five seconds.

With Johnny Carson absent, annual Foreign Language Film presenter Jack Valenti was spared his annual insult. Accompanying him was the two-time Oscar winner described by Minnelli as "the legendary Luise Rainer," who was making her first Oscar appearance since the 1952 Awards. In interviews in the trade papers, Rainer debunked the "Oscar jinx" myth and claimed it was the pressures of her "monstrous" marriage to Clifford Odets that made her cut short her film career. Ironically, this year's twice-nominated *Frances* detailed Odets' affair with Frances Farmer while he was married to Rainer. Rainer declared the sentimental romance *To Begin Again* Best Foreign Language Film, the first Spanish film to win the Award.

Presenters Susan Sarandon and Christopher Reeve grimaced as they prefaced the Supporting Actor Award. She: "Funny, Chris, two of those performances could have been performed by women." He: "Yeah, I guess you're trying to say this Oscar derby is partly a drag race." The winner was Lou Gossett for *An Officer and a Gentleman,* and as the actor rose from his seat, viewers saw his young son Satie vehemently shaking his head no. Onstage, Gossett explained, "I tried to get my kid to come up here to share this with me." The winner went on to say, "I've got a spirit that guides me, starting from a great-grandmother who died at the age of 117," and concluded with a salute to the other nominees, "And all you other four guys, this is ours."

The hard-luck story of the night began to unfurl with the presentation of Best Animated Short Subject. Presenter Kristy McNichol found the name of the Polish nominee for *Tango* more than she could handle. "Zbigniew Rybcyznski—something," she said and then laughed. When he turned out to be the winner, Kristy changed his name to "Zbigniewski Sky." Through his interpreter, Rybcyznski commented, "I made a short film, so I will speak very short . . . I am dreaming that someday I will speak longer from this place." The audience laughed, the director and his female interpreter kissed and the orchestra, thinking the winner was finished, started up with a dignified version of the Warner Brothers "Looney Tunes" theme. The interpreter raised her hand like a schoolteacher and told the audience, "It's not over yet . . . He has important message." Copresenter Matt Dillon then felt the urge to play security guard and began pushing Rybcyznski away from the podium. The winner placated the impatient presenters by kissing McNichol and shaking Dillon's hand as the interpreter explained, "It's a Slavic custom; we are very warm people." The interpreter's garbled version of Rybcyznski's message was, "On the occasion of the film like *Gandhi,* which will portray Lech Walesa and Solidarity."

While Matt Dillon butchered the names of Michael Toshiyuki Uno and the film *Sredni Vashtar* in presenting the Live Action Short Award, Rybcyznski was backstage telling the press, "I chose to name my film *Tango* because everyday life has its rhythms, but basically life is grotesque." He found out just how grotesque when he stepped outside for a cigarette break, only to be barred from reentering by a guard. Rybcyznski repeated the only English he knew, "I have Oscar," but the guard was skeptical of this man in a tuxedo and tennis shoes. A fed-up Rybcyznski kicked the obstinate guard, a scuffle ensued and the director was thrown into the slammer. The Oscar winner asked for the only Hollywood lawyer he had heard of, Marvin Mitchelson, who, upon hearing the request, said, "First bring me an interpreter and then tell me how to pronounce his name." Charges were dropped, and Rybcyznski mused that the experience had taught him that "success and defeat are quite intertwined."

Foul-ups were occurring onstage, too. Introducing clips from an earlier Scientific Awards ceremonies, Liza Minnelli was unprepared when a giant screen came down, and she jumped in mid-

"The Oscar seemed to have been confused with the Nobel Peace Prize."
—Janet Maslin

sentence. This snafu was followed by the presentation of the Jean Hersholt Award by Charlton Heston, introduced as someone who "adds dignity and stature to any occasion." Heston was put to the test when he described the actor for whom the Humanitarian Award is named and promised clips of his performances, saying, "Here is Jean Hersholt." He turned around, looked at the blank screen for a few seconds and added, "I *think* here is Jean Hersholt." Still no clips. Heston faced the audience and said, "Never mind. Jean Hersholt was a wonderful man. Come up to the house, I'll show you the film later on." The Award went to former Academy President Walter Mirisch, who already had a Thalberg and a Best Picture Oscar.

Dudley Moore took over as host from his *Arthur* costar, and when the orchestra greeted him with "Arthur's Theme," he yelled, "Shut up!" Moore then told the audience, "My pants are killing me." It was time for the Costume Design Award and Aljean Harmetz wrote, "When *Gandhi* took the Award for Best Costumes, it was all over." Cowinner Bhanu Athaiya, wearing a sari and carrying her purse, started the tributes to Richard Attenborough, thanking him "for focusing world attention on India." Later, *E.T.* won the new Sound Effects Editing Award, and a technician thanked two individuals for "their sick breathing," as well as "various horses and otters" for their contributions.

The winner of the Documentary Short Subject Award was the controversial *If You Love This Planet*. Coproducer Terri Nash said, "Well, you really know how to show a foreign agent a good time," adding, "for their tremendous effort in promoting *If You Love This Planet*, I'd like to thank the U.S. Department of Justice." Her fellow winner Edward Le Lorrain said, "Oscar for peace." The filmmakers got more good news five months later when a federal judge ruled the Justice Department's "propaganda" label unconstitutional.

Richard Pryor assumed hosting chores after an exchange with Dudley Moore, who complimented him on his tuxedo: "A lovely suit. Is it expensive?" "A little bit," replied Pryor. "Fireproof." Bob Hope strode onstage and received a standing ovation. "It was time to stretch, huh?" the seventy-nine-year-old comedian asked, before showing film clips of Honorary Award winner Mickey Rooney. The footage completed, the screen rose to reveal the diminutive veteran, who walked over and kissed Bob Hope. After the ovation subsided, Bob handed Rooney his statuette and said, "To you, Mick, with love." Rooney said, "This is for sixty years of work, so they tell me. It's really for six minutes of fun, of love and joy." The Mick candidly reflected on his career: "When I was nineteen years old, I was the number-one star for two years. When I was forty, nobody wanted me. I couldn't get a job." He thanked the producers of his stage musical *Sugar Babies* for revitalizing his career and concluded that he was so overcome with emotion that "I'd love to kiss even Louis B. Mayer." There was a shot of George C. Scott roaring with laughter.

Next was a musical tribute to Irving Berlin, although Ethel Merman, the star of the Academy's 1962 tribute to Irving, had to bow out because of the flu, leaving the singing and dancing to Bernadette Peters and Peter Allen. Afterward, a stagehand tumbled off one of the number's moving staircases and the noise interrupted Richard Pryor's introduction of final host Walter Matthau.

After taking forever to get onstage, Sigourney Weaver and Robert Mitchum gave the Best Supporting Actress Oscar. All the nominees were present and the winner was Jessica Lange in *Tootsie*. At the podium, Lange held up the envelope and said breathlessly, "Says right there." She attempted to pour balm by commenting, "I feel real lucky to have been a part of *Tootsie* and to have worked with actors like . . . Teri Garr." Lange was also grateful "to have had Dustin Hoffman as my leading lady." The *New York Times'* Vincent Canby noted that this Award meant Best Actress "was going not to her but to Meryl Streep. Getting one award at the expense of another can't be much fun. It's like being patted on the head and kicked in the stomach."

"Is it still this year?"
—Dudley Moore

"I wrote a long movie and I'm going to make a long speech," threatened the Original Screenplay winner, *Gandhi*'s John Briley. He thanked "Dickie, for having the faith and courage to trust me with his dream" as well as "Gandhi himself." Donald Stewart, cowinner of the Adapted Screenplay Oscar for *Missing,* acknowledged "a lot of very brave people . . . but above all to Charles Edmund Horman," the deceased subject of the film.

Billy Wilder, who told reporters, "I'm doing this show so my relatives in Vienna will know I'm still alive," gave the Best Director Oscar. In announcing Sir Richard Attenborough the winner, Wilder mimicked the Indians in *Gandhi* by pressing his hands together. "I'm totally bowled over by this," Attenborough said as he fondled the Oscar throughout his speech. This time the valiant ones associated with *Gandhi* were "Frank Price and Columbia Pictures for their courage in agreeing to distribute it." He ended by toasting his fellow nominees by name.

Sylvester Stallone editorialized by announcing the Best Actress winner as "Marvelous Meryl Streep." At the podium, the winner noticed something on the floor, bent over to pick it up, and explained, "It's my speech," and collapsed with embarrassed laughter. After she had pulled herself together, Streep sighed, "Oh, boy. No matter how much you try to imagine what this is like, it's just so incredibly thrilling right down to your toes." She then read the names of almost everyone associated with *Sophie's Choice,* including her German and Polish coaches.

John Travolta settled the Best Actor contest. It was now Ben Kingsley's turn to pay homage to Attenborough and, after removing his glasses, he described his director as "another great man of vision and courage." Kingsley then added, "This is an Oscar for vision, for courage, for acting and for peace."

Gandhi had already won seven Oscars, so Best Picture presenter Carol Burnett tried to drum up interest by commenting, "It should be a five-way tie." No such excitement; the winner was *Gandhi* and Richard Attenborough's second speech resembled a political-science lecture: "Your great folk hero, Martin Luther King, Jr., was inspired by Gandhi. Lech Walesa, that noble Polish patriot, came out of prison the other day and said that what he had attempted to do was not going to work. The only way in which we could find human dignity and peace was through the philosophies and teachings of Gandhi." Attenborough concluded, "It's not me . . . you truly honor. You honor Mahatma Gandhi and his plea to all of us to live in peace." Janet Maslin moaned in *The New York Times,* "The Oscar seemed to have been confused with the Nobel Peace Prize."

"Is it still this year?" asked Dudley Moore after Attenborough left and the four hosts were reunited onstage. It was, but back East it was well into the next morning.

Aftermath

Backstage, Richard Attenborough was still sounding as if he were running for office: "That's what we should be saying around the world to Mr. Reagan, Mr. Andropov and Mrs. Thatcher. That we don't want confrontation." When the press steered him back to the fun stuff—the Oscar race itself—the double winner admitted to having been "scared stiff" since *Gandhi* had been the predicted winner. "I'd rather we were like *Chariots of Fire* to come in from left field," Attenborough said. Meryl Streep, due in two and a half months, told reporters that one day she would tell her child, "You were there, darling." Meanwhile, Lou Gossett was giving advice to his fellow black actors; they should follow his lead—"Don't just look for black roles. Just look for good roles."

Paul Newman maintained, "I flew to the Coast only to prove I'm a good loser." John Lithgow related to Cindy Adams, "When Lou Gossett won, my mother punched the set." Teri Garr told *Entertainment Tonight,* "I expected it 'cause I think Jessica won for *Frances* and well deserved." After she made her acceptance speech, Jessica's father told reporters at his Cloquet, Minnesota, home, "I

"I'd love to kiss even Louis B. Mayer."
—Mickey Rooney

told her to say 'hello' to all of us, but I guess she got too excited and forgot."

The show itself was panned even more than usual in the press. *Daily Variety* said, "Color the 1983 edition of the 1982 Awards program bland," and Andrew Sarris huffed and puffed, "Make no mistake about it, the Oscar ceremony is now intentionally designed to inflict as much pain and suffering as possible on both its participants and its viewers." The *Los Angeles Times'* Howard Rosenberg was a little more sympathetic: "But you know how it is, if you like picnics, you put up with the flies," he argued, and asked, "Perennial flaws and sillies? Of course. Yet who *cannot* like an Oscar telecast?"

The *Hollywood Reporter*'s Hank Grant opined, "The post-Oscars Governors' Ball at the Bev-Hilton certainly made up for a rather lacklustre Awards show," noting that the place was "filled to capacity, where in previous balls, you could sometimes shoot an arrow across the room and not hit anyone." Part of the reason was that Swifty Lazar was in New York putting on a production of *Porgy and Bess* at Radio City Music Hall and could not throw his usual party. Most of the losing nominees were at the ball, including Debra Winger, who hadn't bothered to go to the actual ceremonies. James Mason switched from his tux to a more comfortable cashmere dinner jacket. After dinner, Fay Kanin announced, "It's Howard's birthday!" and the crowd sang "Happy Birthday" to Howard W. Koch, who had fallen through a trapdoor during rehearsals. Leaving the party at 2 A.M., Ben Kingsley had to wait a half-hour for his limousine. When hecklers chanted at him that "fame is fleeting," the Best Actor whispered to his wife, "A little fame is better than none." Robert Preston said, "I honestly hate to leave, but I have to go home and walk my dog." Hating it even more was Richard Attenborough, the last celebrant to go home.

The next day, Attenborough had to contend with unusually vociferous criticism of the Academy's choices. Even fans of *Gandhi* wondered about that Costume Design Award—Rex Reed steamed, "For what—wrinkled sheets, burlap sacks and loincloths?" Vincent Canby complained, "*E.T.* and *Tootsie* are films. *Gandhi* is a laboriously illustrated textbook." His colleague at the *New York Times* agreed; Janet Maslin predicted, "Someday, the sweep that brought *Gandhi* eight Academy Awards may be known as one of the great injustices in the annals of Oscardom." Loser Steven Spielberg was more philosophical. "Look, we tried our best," he joked. "We stuffed the ballot boxes, we just didn't stuff them enough." In an interview with the *Los Angeles Times* Spielberg said, "We were almost precluded from awards because people feel we've already been amply rewarded . . . The tendency is for important films to win over popcorn entertainment. History is more weighty than popcorn."

One member of the anti-*Gandhi* faction took action. A few days after the Awards, a tiny ad appeared in *Daily Variety:*

> *To the members of the Academy: I would surely like you to see* The Verdict *once more and tell me what Paul Newman has to do to win an Academy Award.*
>
> *Supervisor Ed Jones*
> *Ventura County*

1983

"The attitude in Hollywood is that what they do in England is somehow better than what we do here."
—Robert Duvall

The 1983 Academy Awards was a party rewarding years of service—and Barbra Streisand was not invited.

It was only October, and Aljean Harmetz was already forecasting the Oscar race in the *New York Times.* Harmetz polled a number of "Hollywood executives" and discovered, "They agree, first, that it has been a bad year for art and believe that no movie released so far will be nominated for best picture." Aljean's revelation was bad news for Universal, which, back in March, had released *Tender Mercies,* a drama about an alcoholic country singer who is rehabilitated through the love of a good woman. Horton Foote had written the screenplay for his friend Robert Duvall and the film was made for $5 million in thirty-five days. Although Duvall said of his Australian director, Bruce Beresford, "He never once said 'What do you think?' to the actors," the actor received the best reviews of any performer that year. "Robert Duvall's versatility knows no limit," exclaimed Janet Maslin in the *New York Times,* while the *Hollywood Reporter*'s Robert Osborne said Duvall gave "a performance that should win him the Oscar next April."

A Radical Departure

Another film Harmetz unceremoniously dismissed from the race was Columbia's *The Big Chill,* cowritten and directed by Lawrence Kasdan, best known for his work on George Lucas and Steven Spielberg movies. *The Big Chill,* however, was far removed from the escapism of *Return of the Jedi;* it was about, as coscreenwriter Barbara Benedek put it, "rationalization and choices and coming into the world." Kasdan wanted to make a movie detailing what campus radicals of the '60s were up to in the '80s and he asked Benedek, the wife of his lawyer, to collaborate. It was the former social worker's first screenplay, and she told the *Los Angeles Times,* "The issues came first, then the characters." The film's eventual characters were reunited at the funeral of a friend. "We finished the script on a Friday and on a Monday we got the rejection from the Ladd Company," Benedek recalled, "and began looking for another home."

The writers found one at Johnny Carson Productions, which arranged for Columbia to distribute. Kasdan cast the ensemble film with rising stars—Glenn Close, William Hurt, Jobeth Williams, Kevin Kline, Tom Berenger, Mary Kay Place, Jeff Goldblum, and Meg Tilly—and then filled the sound track, *American Graffiti*–style, with vintage pop records from the '60s. "The feel-good movie of 1983," grooved *Time.* "The eight star actors deserve one big Oscar." The *Los Angeles Herald-Examiner* praised Kasdan as "one of the few writer-directors around now with an old-fashioned sense of honor about narrative craftsmanship and functional, economic storytelling." Some critics pointed out that the film's plot was rather similar to John Sayles' low-budget *Return of the Secaucus Seven* of 1980, but there was no comparison at the box office. "I am happy to report that now this movie has garnered $30 million [in gross] after only two months," gloated Liz Smith. "It is a testament to the fact that some moviegoers actually want to hear dialogue onscreen and explore meaningful relationships, as they say, rather than just watching car crashes and other junk."

Days of Hype

Since *Tender Mercies* and *The Big Chill* weren't going to make the grade, Harmetz pressed her Hollywood sources as to what films would get nominated. "Without hesitation," she reported, "most executives rattle off the names of the following five unreleased movies which they believe will be the probable nominees." These films were *The Right Stuff, Terms of Endearment, Star 80, Silkwood* and *Yentl.*

The first one out was *The Right Stuff,* a $27-

Presenter Dolly Parton shows everyone whom she voted for as Best Actor winner Robert Duvall reaches for his Oscar.

"I didn't want to make a film about astronauts."
—Philip Kaufman

million, three-hour-and-ten-minute adaptation of Tom Wolfe's book about the early days of the space race. Producers Robert Chartoff and Irwin Winkler paid the author half a million for the film rights in 1978, outbidding Universal, which saw it as another vehicle for John Belushi and Dan Aykroyd. The producers asked William Goldman, who won an Oscar for adapting *All the President's Men,* to tackle the screenplay. Goldman proceeded, and cut out all the stuff about the test pilots that preceded the astronauts in the story.

"I didn't want to make a film about astronauts," director Philip Kaufman told the *Los Angeles Times,* "I wanted to do test pilots. They'd been sold as astronauts, but I saw them as representing something old, not something new. I was looking for some jeopardized qualities in the American experience, qualities that maybe we'd begun to lose in these days of hype." Out went William Goldman. Kaufman himself rewrote the script, reinstated the Chuck Yeager character—the first man to break the sound barrier—and hired playwright-actor Sam Shepard to portray him. *Film Comment* observed that the director "had cast Shepard a little in the way one puts a poster on one's wall," and *Newsweek* declared, "Sam Shepard's matinee-idol status should be established forever with this role . . ."

The John Glenn Story

The *Hollywood Reporter*'s Arthur Knight loved *The Right Stuff,* declaring it "the picture of the year, one that its producers can be proud of, the industry can be proud of and one which Americans can be proud of." *Newsweek* and *Time* were both worried what effect the epic might have on the Presidential campaign of former astronaut John Glenn. *Time* commented that, through flattering casting, the Democratic candidate was portrayed by Ed Harris, thirty-two, a "blond, bristle-topped actor who has blue laser eyes, a quick-fire smile, and more charisma than his real-life model." *Newsweek* apparently agreed, and ran a photo of Harris instead of Glenn for its cover story entitled CAN A MOVIE HELP MAKE A PRESIDENT?

"I think the public thinks it's 'The John Glenn Story,' " worried Pamela Reed, an actress who played an astronaut's wife in the picture, when asked why the picture fizzled at the box office from opening day. Producer Robert Chartoff said, "The puzzle to me about *The Right Stuff* is that everyone thinks it's the hoopla around the film that kept people away. But hoopla didn't keep people away from *Jaws.*" But Chartoff had learned his lesson when he confided to Aljean Harmetz, "We thought that any kind of publicity space was good space. Now we think certain segments of the public aren't going to the movie because they think it's a responsibility—not a fun movie." It took *The Right Stuff* four months to earn what most hit movies make in a couple of weekends. Sam Shepard did all right by himself, however: he was dubbed by *People* magazine one of "the 25 Most Intriguing People of 1983." According to the magazine, Shepard's achievements included "his affair with 1982 Oscar winner Jessica (*Tootsie*) Lange."

Old Boob Question

The Ladd Company had another one of Harmetz's golden five—Bob Fosse's *Star 80,* based on the murder of a *Playboy* playmate by her jealous husband. The director said he was intrigued by a Pulitzer Prize–winning essay by Teresa Carpenter in the *Village Voice* on the death of Dorothy Stratten. "It was the guy's story that interested me," Fosse said. "His milieu—sleazy nightclubs—I could deal with that portion of the story and it's also about Hollywood. I suppose there is a bit of anger in me about Hollywood that I have to get out."

Mariel Hemingway, now twenty-two years old, was interested in getting into the role of Stratten, but Fosse told her she had physical drawbacks. "The old boob question," he elaborated. "You can't cast a girl unless she has them." So Hemingway went out and got them—via plastic

"I decided I didn't want to go through life being looked on as just an athletic tomboy."
—Mariel Hemingway

surgery. Fosse gave her the part, maintaining, "She has a certain innocence." On the subject of her surgery, Mariel insisted to *People* magazine, "I didn't do it for the role. It was for me, truly . . . I decided I didn't want to go through life being looked on as just an athletic tomboy." *People* defended the actress by comparing her to Oscar winners who had made similar sacrifices of the flesh: emaciated Meryl Streep in *Sophie's Choice,* bloated Robert De Niro in *Raging Bull,* and tanned Ben Kingsley in *Gandhi.* "A real downer of a movie," complained Kathleen Carroll in the *New York Daily News.* "One is forced to spend two hours in uncomfortably close contact with someone who, at best, is an irritating creep." Eric Roberts, as Stratten's husband Paul Snider, had Marilyn Beck announcing, "He seems certain to be a front-runner in the Oscar race." But Andrew Sarris felt the way Kathleen Carroll did, writing, "The trouble is that Fosse and Roberts have made Snider too monotonously odious to warrant such attention." The critics who did like the movie found it difficult to praise in appealing terms; Rex Reed called it "one bruising blockbuster" and Gene Siskel compared it to "witnessing a fatal car wreck in slow motion a second time; you want to tell the passengers to get out of the car." The Ladd Company couldn't persuade audiences to go into theaters showing *Star 80,* even after Hemingway showed off her new look in a ten-page *Playboy* spread. "Nobody talks about the movie, everybody talks about her boobs," Fosse protested.

Coming to Terms

Paramount pinned its hopes on *Terms of Endearment,* a project initiated by Jennifer Jones when she optioned the film rights to Larry McMurtry's novel about a willful mother and headstrong daughter as a vehicle for herself. Shopping for a director, Jones made the mistake of approaching Jim Brooks, the creator of *The Mary Tyler Moore Show,* who began to envision a movie without Jennifer Jones in it. He asked Paramount to buy the film rights from her. "Once Jennifer Jones sold the film rights to Paramount," reported the *Los Angeles Times,* "there was not a single actress in auditioning distance who wasn't foaming to do *Terms.*" Oscar winners Anne Bancroft and Louise Fletcher were talked to, but the actress Brooks actually cast was four-time nominee Shirley MacLaine because "In all that time, she was the only one who ever saw it as a comedy." Sissy Spacek was originally scheduled to play MacLaine's daughter, but by the time production commenced, she had been replaced by Debra Winger, the star of *An Officer and a Gentleman.*

"For three months I walked around with pregnancy pads," said Winger, describing her preparation for the role. "Every two weeks I added weights. I slept with the pads. My back was killing me. I never gave in." Winger's demand for realism seemed a bit much to her costar. "Debra insisted that I, and her parents, call her by the character's name, Emma," recalled MacLaine. "I understood the torture she was going through, but I just don't work that way." MacLaine's methods were equally unorthodox, though; she communicated with the dead. "My real role model was Martha Mitchell," the actress told reporters. "She was in my mind all the time. I always felt like she was hovering while I was working."

Brooks was looking for help when it came time to cast the character he invented for the film—MacLaine's lecherous, potbellied, middle-aged neighbor who becomes her lover. "You needed a male star," Brooks said, "but you couldn't get a male star to do it because the part was short and because the actor had to give up his vanity." Burt Reynolds was all too happy to play the part, insisting, "It's the role I'm looking for—walking around holding your stomach in at forty-seven is hard work," but a prior commitment kept him away. So the role was played by Jack Nicholson, also forty-seven, who said, "I'm in my forties and if I'm going to continue to grow as a person and an artist, I can't keep playing thirty-five-year-old ideas of romance."

"I had busted my butt in L.A. for eight years to get work and no one wanted to know me."
—Cher

Mother's Day

Kathleen Carroll enjoyed *Terms of Endearment* far more than *Star 80;* the *New York Daily News* reviewer awarded Brooks' film four stars and raved, "Here, at long last, is a juicy, utterly captivating movie that not only features wonderfully human characters, but actually dares to deal with the joys and frustrations of maintaining a mother-and-daughter relationship at a time when the average Hollywood movie is concerned mostly with overwrought computers." *Daily Variety* declared, "Teaming off Shirley MacLaine and Jack Nicholson at their best makes *Terms of Endearment* an enormously enjoyable offering for Christmas" and said the two stars were "always reminiscent of Hepburn and Bogart." *Newsweek* described Debra Winger as "the girl with the most sensually husky voice since Bacall," and Janet Maslin wrote in the *New York Times,* "Miss Winger again shows herself to be an astonishingly vital screen actress, able to imbue even the relatively drab Emma with urgency and passion." *Terms of Endearment* made $25 million in two months, and Army Archerd reported, "Oscar nominations are a cinch for Nicholson, Shirley MacLaine, Debra Winger and Brooks in his first outing as a director." Winger confessed the Oscar prediction "makes me very nervous—I don't like to think about it," but MacLaine had no trouble telling Aljean Harmetz she'd "like to win the Oscar and if I did win it I would think I deserved it."

Meryl Meltdown

A probable opponent for MacLaine was Meryl Streep, this year with an Oklahoma accent as the nuclear-energy martyr Karen Silkwood. Mike Nichols directed and scenarist Nora Ephron called her friend Alice Arlen and asked her to collaborate, and the two New Yorkers went to work. "We had the best time writing this," Arlene effused to the *Los Angeles Times,* but Ephron added, "Like any reporter, you start feeling guilty at some point because you're thinking, this is a fabulous story and yet someone's dead."

Cher nearly dropped dead when Mike Nichols came backstage during her appearance on Broadway in *Come Back to the Five and Dime, Jimmy Dean, Jimmy Dean* and asked her to costar with Meryl Streep. "I think at that moment I lost my hearing first, then my vision. I had busted my butt in L.A. for eight years to get work and no one wanted to know me." Nichols wanted her to play Karen Silkwood's lesbian housemate and, like Elizabeth Taylor in *Virginia Woolf,* she would have to go ugly for the part. Cher was not enamored of her blue-collar wardrobe. "The first day I put on Dolly's clothes, I started to cry. I wanted to look a little bit better."

Twentieth Century-Fox wasn't going to make the same mistake that the Ladd Company did with *The Right Stuff* by selling *Silkwood* as a political film. "We were careful not to link *Silkwood* to the nuclear issue," said marketing executive Jack Brodsky to *Film Comment.* "If people read the stuff on the front page and see it on TV, they're going to stay away from the movie." Fox sold it as a thriller and the public bought it.

"Whether or not Cher is a great actress, I'm still not sure," wrote Vincent Canby in the *New York Times,* "but when you take away those wild wigs she wears on television, and substitute something a little less riveting for her crazy Bob Mackie gowns, there's an honest, complex screen presence underneath." Cher put the wig back on for her *People* magazine cover story, CHER FINDS A NEW LIFE, but made no bones about wanting an Oscar to erase her image as a Las Vegas showgirl. "If Michelangelo painted in Caesar's Palace, would that make it any less art?" she asked.

The Singing Yeshiva

Like Shirley MacLaine, Barbra Streisand drew on supernatural inspiration. "My brother in-

"It might mean I'd get more scripts without other actors' coffee stains on them."
—Michael Caine

vited a medium, a nice, ordinary-looking, Jewish lady with blond hair, to his house," the actress told *People*. "We sat around a table with all the lights on and put our hands on it. And then it began. The table started to spell out letters with its legs." According to Streisand, it was her late father who was sending the message. "It sounds crazy but I know it was my father who was telling me to be brave, to have the courage of my convictions, to sing proud!" The experience was enough to make Streisand plunge into *Yentl,* a musical version of an Isaac Bashevis Singer short story called "Yentl, the Yeshiva Boy" that Streisand had optioned in 1968. Singer protested Streisand's alterations in his story—"She's a young girl who dresses as a boy to study the Talmud, not to sing songs"—but Streisand was determined to do it her way, all of it—writing, producing, starring and directing. When Hollywoodites carped that she was becoming too ambitious, Bette Davis reminded Streisand, "It's only the best fruit the birds pick at."

Streisand took her crew to Czechoslovakia to shoot the $16 million production, and Amy Irving, playing the romantic rival, said the director could not have been more dedicated. "She'd fix my hair ribbons, brush an eyelash off my cheek, paint my lips to match the color of the fruit on the table," Irving remembered. "I was like her little doll that she could dress up."

The normally reclusive Streisand was everywhere when *Yentl* opened in November: the cover of *Life, Billboard, Harper's Bazaar, People*. The ABC news show *20/20* devoted an entire hour to Geraldo Rivera's interview, and Barbra was frequently mentioned in the gossip columns as she made the social rounds. When the film opened, Radie Harris declared in the *Hollywood Reporter,* "It was the year that Barbra Streisand as *Yentl* established herself as the most versatile single talent since Orson Welles," and Liz Smith rushed in with the news, "Audiences are reacting as if they were in the Broadway theater. They sometimes stand up and applaud Barbra, repeatedly, as if at a live performance."

Amy Irving saw that all Streisand's fussing had paid off for her, too. In *New York* Magazine, David Denby rhapsodized, "Amy Irving's witchlike beauty has never been more seductive." Said Irving herself, "It wouldn't matter if I was terrible in *Yentl*. It's making money and suddenly I'm hot." So was Streisand: the movie made $20 million, the album was a big seller and Gary Arnold wrote in the *Washington Post,* "It would constitute a Hollywood scandal if Barbra Streisand were denied an Oscar nomination for her direction of *Yentl*."

A Flat Tire and a Bomb

Bonnie Bedelia and Jane Alexander weren't quite as lucky as Streisand: they both had strong starring roles in flops. Bedelia played America's first female championship drag racer in *Heart Like a Wheel* and Alexander portrayed a mother surviving nuclear attack in *Testament*. The only problem was that nobody wanted to see a movie about drag racing or about nuclear holocaust. Despite the box-office doldrums, Marilyn Beck said that Bedelia was a "good bet" for an Oscar nomination, and Robert Osborne called Alexander "a cinch."

Carry On, Caine

One of the year's surprise hits was *Educating Rita*, an adaptation of a London comedy about a working-class college student who brightens the life of her alcoholic professor. Michael Caine gained thirty-five pounds to play the worn-out academic, but director Lewis Gilbert, who had introduced Caine to film audiences as *Alfie* nearly twenty years before, refused to go Hollywood for the female role. Columbia wanted Dolly Parton for the leading lady but Gilbert insisted on the actress who had created the part on stage, thirty-four-year-old Julie Walters. When the critics began talking about Oscar in their reviews, Columbia invited the Cockney actress to Hollywood, where she won raves from everyone. Robert Osborne pronounced her "one of the most refreshing visitors we've had in these surroundings for some

"I was like a doll she could dress up."
—Amy Irving

time" and the British-American Chamber of Commerce of Beverly Hills held a ceremony to dub her "Star of the Year." Walters enjoyed the visit, but didn't sign any contracts. "I don't like the future sewn up," she said. "I like an open book, the feeling that anything can happen."

The British Are Coming

One of the soirées that Walters attended was the Hollywood premiere of *The Dresser,* Peter Yates' adaptation of Ronald Harwood's play about an aging Shakespearean actor and his faithful valet. The film bowed in New York and Los Angeles in December in order to qualify the two starring performances for Oscars: Albert Finney's as the old actor—Finney was only forty-seven—and Tom Courtney's as the effeminate assistant. *Daily Variety* said the actors' work was good enough to lift the picture to "the realm of the commercially accessible." By opening the picture in tiny theaters, Columbia was able to brag in trade ads that the movie was a frequent sellout.

Another British actor to appear at Oscar's eleventh hour was Tom Conti, who popped up as a drunken Scottish poet on a lecture tour in New England in *Reuben, Reuben,* written by Julius Epstein, the seventy-four-year-old Hollywood veteran who had won an Oscar already for *Casablanca*. "Before anyone marks any ballot," reminded Robert Osborne, "they'd be doing themselves (and Oscar) a disservice if they don't see Tom Conti in *Reuben, Reuben.*" The movie debuted in late December, and Vincent Canby hailed it for having "the kind of appreciation for the oddness of words you seldom find in films."

A Bunch of Losers

In an article headlined PICKING WINNERS FROM A BATCH OF LOSERS, *USA Today* columnist Jack Mathews wrote, "The enthusiasm level at Saturday's year-end awards voting of the Los Angeles Film Critics Association was so low you would have thought they'd gathered to cite Joan Rivers for good taste." Both the Los Angeles and the New York critics picked *Terms of Endearment* as the Best Picture, Shirley MacLaine Best Actress and Robert Duvall Best Actor for *Tender Mercies*. In the most dramatic moment in New York, Cher lost the Best Supporting Actress Award by one vote to Linda Hunt, a four-foot-nine-inch actress who portrayed a half-Chinese male photographer in *The Year of Living Dangerously*. Cher also lost to Hunt in Los Angeles, where she tied for second place with Alfre Woodard, who had played a backwoods illiterate in Martin Ritt's box-office flop *Cross Creek*. Jack Nicholson won Best Supporting Actor in both cities, but only Los Angeles picked *Terms of Endearment*'s James L. Brooks for Best Director. The New Yorkers chose Ingmar Bergman, for what he promised was his last movie—the three-hour-and-forty-five-minute *Fanny and Alexander,* his biggest success in the United States.

Malibu Uprising

Fox led the trade-paper advertising with fifty pages' worth of ads for *Silkwood,* and twenty-six for the Bonnie Bedelia vehicle *Heart Like a Wheel*. Charles Durning was the most avid campaigner for Best Supporting Actor, this year for his comic Nazi in the remake of *To Be or Not to Be* with Mel Brooks and Anne Bancroft. Robert Radnitz, the producer of *Cross Creek,* could not talk Universal into screening his money-losing movie during the ballot-marking period, so he arranged to have his neighborhood theater—in Malibu—exhibit the movie. Because Universal wouldn't pay for ads in the traders, either, Radnitz made up his own handbills and had the neighborhood kids distribute them. In contrast, no one heard a peep out of Best Actor hopeful Robert Duvall because, as Marilyn Beck reported, "He doesn't want it to seem as though he's campaigning."

MGM/UA wondered if their campaigning for *Yentl* was in vain when the Directors Guild announced its nominations in January and Barbra Streisand was not on the list with Jim Brooks, Ingmar Bergman, *The Right Stuff*'s Philip Kaufman,

"It's mostly the women reviewers who are attacking me."
—Barbra Streisand

Tender Mercies' Bruce Beresford, and *The Big Chill's* Lawrence Kasdan. The California chapter of the National Organization for Women released a statement: "We view this as another attempt to keep women in their place by not recognizing the quality and quantity of women's input into American society, and in this case because the film *Yentl* has feminist overtones, it is apparent that Miss Streisand is, too, being discriminated against because of her conviction and for being a woman."

The Nominations

If the Directors Guild made Streisand feel unwelcome, the Academy made her feel like a pariah—Streisand wasn't nominated for anything. *Yentl* pulled in five nominations—Best Picture was not among them. Two other of Aljean Harmetz' October top prize predictions failed to be realized: *Silkwood* managed only five nominations, and *Star 80* was completely forgotten. *Terms of Endearment* was the big winner, with eleven nominations, followed by *The Right Stuff* with eight, although writer-director Philip Kaufman must have felt like Barbra Streisand—he, too, was totally bypassed in the writing and directing categories. "The day's biggest upset," wrote Harmetz in her *New York Times* report on the nominations, was the selection of Peter Yates as a Best Director nominee for *The Dresser,* a Best Picture contestant that garnered five nominations in all. Harmetz did not seem surprised that two of the movies she had not mentioned in October, *Tender Mercies* and *The Big Chill,* were competing in the Best Picture contest. She did note one breakthrough: cinematographer Gordon Willis was finally nominated, for Woody Allen's parody of documentaries, *Zelig*.

The Gandhi Treatment

After the nominations were announced, Johnny Carson quipped, "Now Barbra Streisand really knows the meaning of The Big Chill." Columnist Jack Mathews took her omission more seriously. "Streisand had no choice but to take this personally, since the film itself pulled five nominations," he argued. A group calling itself P.E.P. (Principles, Equality and Professionalism in Film) did take it personally—they announced they'd be picketing on Oscar night. "We are not avid Barbra Streisand fans by any means," Simmone Sheffield, one of the demonstrators, told the *Los Angeles Herald-Examiner,* "but the way the Academy treated her is really the spark that lit the flame. She worked fifteen years to make that movie—just like Richard Attenborough worked twenty years on *Gandhi*—but even though the movie represents a significant accomplishment, the Academy doesn't want to admit that a woman is responsible for it."

Yentl's sole acting nominee was Amy Irving, who told Marilyn Beck that she was "devastated" by what happened to Barbra. But the director called the nominee and instructed, "Go and enjoy yourself. Don't worry about me." So Irving felt free to exclaim, "It is one of the high points of my life." When Beck asked another question about Streisand, Irving reminded the columnist that an Oscar "would certainly help me more, businesswise, than it would her."

Good Sports

Irving was competing in what the *Los Angeles Times* labeled "the toughest category of the year, with no clear winner apparent." Nominee Glenn Close also had to deal with ostracized costars—she was the single acting nominee for *The Big Chill.* She dashed any reporters' hopes of jealousy among cast members by insisting, "I think it shows how close we all were that every one of them called me to congratulate me as soon as they found out." When she made plans to leave her starring role in Tom Stoppard's *The Real Thing* to celebrate her second nomination in a row, Close's Broadway producers advertised the canceled performance with the explanation, "Glenn Close has been called to the Academy Awards for her performance in *The Big Chill.*"

The director of *The Real Thing,* Mike Nichols, was up for Best Director for *Silkwood,* which

"I once passed a kidney stone during the opening night of a show."
—Rip Torn

garnered Meryl Streep her fifth nomination and Cher her first. Not heeding Vincent Canby, Cher ordered an Oscar gown from Bob Mackie and showed up to win a Golden Globe Award in a black leather mini-skirt. Giving both Close and Cher a run for the race was the critics' choice, *The Year of Living Dangerously*'s Linda Hunt, who confessed to Cindy Adams that she never dreamed her male role would bring her such recognition. "My sole interest was the director. I wanted to work with Peter Weir," the New York actress said, adding that she was still not sure if her performance was any good. "Until I see it alone in a regular theater, I can't honestly judge my work."

Go England

"I guess it's me against the limeys," Best Actor nominee Robert Duvall jested with the *New York Daily News* when he discovered that his fellow nominees were all British. "The attitude with a lot of people in Hollywood is that what they do in England is somehow better than what we do here," said Duvall, who dropped the incommunicado act as soon as he was nominated, giving plenty of interviews. His two rivals from *The Dresser* didn't try to compete with Duvall's campaign at all. Army Archerd reported that Albert Finney was too "busy legiting in London" to campaign and Tom Courtenay told the *Los Angeles Times*, "Yes, I expect to be there for the ceremonies, but not because I choose to, frankly. I'm coming for Peter Yates." The *Hollywood Reporter*'s social column, "The Great Life," snapped a picture of *Reuben, Reuben*'s Tom Conti attending a wrap party for his latest Hollywood-financed movie, a romantic spy adventure costarring *The Big Chill*'s non-nominated Jobeth Williams. "Isn't it a fact that Tom Conti's asking price since his Oscar nomination has rocketed from $100,000 per film to $1 million?" asked Robert Osborne in his column. "And you can use that as Example A in any future discussions when asked to name two or three reasons why people lust after Academy Awards." The fifth nominee, Michael Caine of *Educating Rita*, attended a party honoring a visiting compatriot, Prince Andrew, and told *Entertainment Tonight* his reason for lusting for an Oscar: "It might mean I'd get more scripts without other actors' coffee stains on them."

The Heaviest Prejudice in the World

"Eight Oscar nominations failed to add much fuel to the wide national launching of *The Right Stuff* Friday," reported *USA Today*, "and the astronaut film now seems certain to plunge into the record books as the most acclaimed box-office flop of the past year." Once again, Sam Shepard emerged unscathed—he was nominated for Best Supporting Actor. So was Rip Torn, who received his first nomination, thanks to those Malibu screenings of *Cross Creek*. The fifty-three-year-old actor gave a number of interviews and told Marilyn Beck that he hoped his nomination would get rid of his reputation as an unprofessional actor. "People are finally realizing I'm one of the few actors who has never missed a performance," Torn said. "I've worked with broken legs, arms, ankles. I once passed a kidney stone during the opening night of a show."

Repeat nominees John Lithgow, nominated this year for *Terms of Endearment*, and Charles Durning, tapped for *To Be Or Not to Be*, both admitted that the Oscar would probably go to the man who had swept the critics' supporting actor awards—Jack Nicholson for *Terms of Endearment*. *Rolling Stone* interviewed the shoo-in, who talked publicly for the first time about his illegitimate birth. Liz Smith quoted Nicholson as saying later, "Illegitimacy is still the heaviest prejudice in the world."

Mother vs. Daughter

Jane Alexander made the Best Actress lineup for *Testament*, but Bonnie Bedelia didn't—*Heart Like a Wheel* was only nominated for Costume Design. *Educating Rita*'s nominated Julie Walters made plans to visit Hollywood again on Oscar night, but most pundits predicted that the statuette would go to Shirley MacLaine for *Terms of Endearment*. Although *Esquire* pronounced nominee Debra Winger the "New American Woman" and the twenty-eight-year-old actress was in the news campaigning for Democratic hopeful Gary Hart and dating Nebraska governor Robert Kern, forty, she didn't stand a chance against her forty-nine-year-old costar.

"Barring an upset by Winger or Streep," advised the *Los Angeles Times*, "look for MacLaine to finally deliver the acceptance speech she's been rehearsing for twenty-six years." MacLaine practiced her public speaking before the ceremony by accepting Barnard College's Woman of the Year for Achievements in the Arts trophy and by promoting her third bestselling autobiography, *Out on a Limb*. In her latest tome, MacLaine speculated on her former lives; she claimed to have been a native of Atlantis, a monk in the Himalayas, and the former daughter of her current daughter, Sachi Parker, twenty-seven. MacLaine was planning her present life expertly—she was set to open her one-woman show on Broadway the week after the Oscar ceremonies. As Liz Smith reported on the day of the Awards ceremony, no detail was overlooked: "*Playbill* magazine has written two biographies of Shirley MacLaine for her current show . . . One of them has Shirley winning the Oscar . . . The other has Shirley merely nominated. The program goes to press tomorrow with whichever biography is correct and we'll know tonight!"

The Big Night

Posters of Barbra Streisand greeted the Academy's guests as thirty demonstrators waved placards that read: IF YENTL WAS ANSEL, SHE'D BE NOMINATED and SCORE—1927–PRESENT, BEST DIRECTOR NOMINATIONS: MEN—273; WOMEN—1. Amy Irving paid the posters no mind, as she appeared on the arm of Steven Spielberg. The Supporting Actress nominee wore a Ralph Lauren black velvet skirt and antique lace blouse that caused the *Los Angeles Times* to observe, "Irving looked delicate—much smaller than she appeared to be in the movie."

The antique look was very popular this year—both Mary Tyler Moore and Best Actress nominee Jane Alexander wore blue Edwardian-style gowns. Glenn Close sported a black antique lace dress by Anne Ross and told Army Archerd, "For some reason, I'm more nervous this year." Not as nervous as Cher, who self-consciously checked her lipstick with her tongue every time she felt a camera on her. The thirty-seven-year-old nominee wore a tastefully slinky Bob Mackie and was escorted by her boyfriend, actor Val Kilmer, twenty-four, and her son, Elijah Allman, seven, who wore a black tux, black shirt and white tie. Linda Hunt came with her parents and told reporters, "My fingers are crossed." Alfre Woodard, the surprise nominee from *Cross Creek*, said she didn't expect to win, but "getting to go to the Academy Awards is like being invited to the palace."

Woodard's nominated costar, Texan Rip Torn, brought four of his five children, his mother and his cousin—Sissy Spacek. When the actress mounted the forecourt podium, Army Archerd forgot which member of the family was being honored and asked Sissy, "This makes four for you, huh?" Mr. and Mrs. Robert Duvall were accompanied by Mr. and Mrs. Johnny Cash. A wary Tom Courtenay stayed near Peter Yates, and Michael Caine held his wife's hand tightly. Caine predicted a Duvall victory, but said he came anyway because "I live in this town and I support the Oscars."

Awards Ceremony

APRIL 9, 1984, 6:00 P.M.
THE DOROTHY CHANDLER PAVILION, LOS ANGELES

Your Host:
JOHNNY CARSON
Televised over ABC

Presenters

Supporting Actor . . . . Mary Tyler Moore and Timothy Hutton
Tribute to David Niven . . . . Cary Grant
Short Subjects . . . . . . Jane Alexander and Michael Caine
Sound Effects Editing . . . . Daryl Hannah and Kevin Bacon
Scientific and Technical Awards . . Joan Collins and Arnold Schwarzenegger
Editing . . . . Robert Wise
Sound . . . . Christie Brinkley and Michael Keaton
Cinematography . . . . Joanna Pacula and Anthony Franciosa
Foreign Film . . . . John Gavin and Jack Valenti
Documentary Awards . . . . Holly Palance and Jack Palance
Visual Effects . . . . Cheech and Chong
Costume Design . . . . Twiggy and Tommy Tune
Art Direction . . . . . . Jane Powell and Ricardo Montalban
Original Song . . . . Jennifer Beals and Matthew Broderick
Original Score . . . . Gene Kelly and Ray Bolger
Adaptation Score . . . . Neil Diamond
Supporting Actress . . . . Dyan Cannon and Gene Hackman
Writing Awards . . . . Sissy Spacek and Mel Gibson
Jean Hersholt Humanitarian Award . . . . . . Frank Sinatra
Director . . . . Richard Attenborough
Honorary Award to Hal Roach . . . . . . Jackie Cooper and Spanky McFarland
Actor . . . . Dolly Parton and Sylvester Stallone
Actress . . . . Liza Minnelli and Rock Hudson
Picture . . . . Frank Capra

Performers of Nominated Songs

"Flashdance . . . What a Feeling" . . Irene Cara and forty-four boys and girls from the National Dance Institute
"Papa, Can You Hear Me?" . . . . Donna Summer
"Over You" . . . . Mac Davis
"The Way He Makes Me Feel" . . . . . . Jennifer Holliday
"Maniac" . . . . Herb Alpert & the Tijuana Brass and Lani Hall

"Getting to go to the Academy Awards is like being invited to the palace."
—Alfre Woodard

Caine's costar, Julie Walters, was a photographer's delight in her black leather dress with matching leather jacket. The British actress happily posed and told everyone her outfit was made by the people who design the Princess of Wales' gowns. Walters felt confident about the night's outcome, explaining, "I called my bookmaker the night before I left London and he said it was twenty to one—against!" The Best Actress favorite, Shirley MacLaine, also appeared informed. "I feel so peaceful," she told reporters as she entered with her daughter; they were both wearing shiny peach-colored dresses by Fabrice. "We're all mothers and daughters tonight," MacLaine told Archerd as Sachi stood by, smiling.

Meryl Streep came with her husband and told *Entertainment Tonight,* "It's the most exciting part of the industry, the night it all comes together and you get to see the movie stars." Her nominated screenwriters, Nora Ephron and Alice Arlen, had flown in from New York and giggled to the *Los Angeles Times,* "We're like two little suburban ladies out on the town." A reluctant-looking Debra Winger was on the arm of Paramount head Barry Diller. Winger didn't speak to reporters, nor did the last arrival, Jack Nicholson, with Anjelica Huston, who nevertheless got the loudest ovation from the fans.

Show producer Jack Haley, Jr., had told *Daily Variety* earlier that he had a "mandate" to "streamline" the show, "to shorten it and make it more glamorous." But things got off to a bad start when the opening TV shot of arriving guests was upside down. Then Academy President Gene Allen walked out and stumbled over his speech in which he thanked the nominees for giving audiences movie memories. Johnny Carson rushed in to put the show back on balance. "As you can tell if you saw our opening shot tonight," the emcee began, "people are literally standing on their heads with excitement."

Haley's idea of a streamlined show began when Carson introduced "a gentleman for whom the 'versatile' might have been coined." Out walked Sammy Davis, Jr., wearing two rings, who reminded everyone, "In 1934, some important categories were added to the Awards." Davis then introduced Shirley Temple, who came out with her Special Oscar from 1934. After she talked about winning that, she reminisced over the Best Song race that year. Then she asked the star who performed the winning song to stand up in the audience and take a bow, which Ginger Rogers dutifully did.

The Awards-giving commenced a half hour into the show. The first Oscar was for Best Supporting Actor and the only missing nominee was Sam Shepard. Jack Nicholson received the loudest ovation of the nominees, and the viewers saw his eyebrows raised in amusement from behind his dark glasses. The glasses came off when Nicholson's name was called and the winner kissed presenter Mary Tyler Moore's hand. Nicholson saluted the other nominees, gave his thanks and said, "I was going to talk a lot about how Shirley and Debra inspired me, but I understand they're planning an interpretive dance later right after the Best Actress Award to explain everything about life." He concluded by encouraging, "All you rock people down at the Roxy and up in the Rockies, rock on." As Nicholson walked off, the camera saw a smiling and clapping Shirley MacLaine sitting next to an unsmiling Robert Duvall.

When the Technical Awards rolled around, many of *The Right Stuff* winners proved to be as loyal as Barbra Streisand's devotees. The Sound Effect Editing victor said, "I'd like to thank Phil Kaufman for having the vision to make *The Right Stuff* the way it is." One of the Sound winners went on about "a guy who was always there pushing from the outside of the envelope, giving us the time and the enthusiasm and strength to carry on to give a sound track to his great picture—Phil Kaufman!" And a film editor said, "We must thank our marvelous, beautiful—we love you, Phil Kaufman—director for his leadership, dedication and vision he gave us."

Ingmar Bergman was also a popular employer, as revealed when *Fanny and Alexander* collected four Oscars. Cinematographer Sven

"We're all mothers and daughters tonight."
—Shirley MacLaine

Nykvist accepted his second Oscar for a Bergman movie and said, "The time has come to thank and I would like to thank a man who I have had the good fortune to work with for about twenty-five years on twenty-two pictures—Ingmar Bergman." Art director Anna Asp was so flabbergasted that all she said was, "I didn't prepare anything to say, but I can say that I'm very happy to be here." Producer Jorn Bonner accepted the Foreign Film Award for the picture in a thick Swedish accent and said, "Thanks to the members of the Academy for having good taste."

The writing was on the wall when Jennifer Beals, the star of *Flashdance,* strutted out in a black gown to reveal the Best Song Award. Although two songs from *Yentl* were nominated, the winner was the title tune to *Flashdance*, a bestselling single from performer-composer Irene Cara.

Yentl did claim one Oscar when Neil Diamond, in a tux with sequined lapels, announced that the musical had won Best Score Adaptation. "I'm very grateful for this. I'm very grateful, too, for the privilege of the experience of having worked on *Yentl,*" said Marilyn Bergman, adding, "Life has a way of imitating art in very interesting ways."

Because the show stopped to ask the wife of the president of the International Olympic Committee to stand up and take a bow, and then toasted Donald Duck on his fiftieth birthday, the program was completing its third hour by the time the final Awards were given out. Cher licked her lips one last time as the TV camera turned on her during the reading of the Best Supporting Actress nominees. The winner was Linda Hunt, who kissed her father and walked to the stage as the crowd cheered. Presenter Dyan Cannon bent over to hug the short actress and looked for a second as if she were going to pick the winner up. At the podium, Hunt stood on a platform and said, "There was an Indonesian phrase in the film which translates into English as 'water from the moon' and it means that which is unattainable, the impossible, that which one can never have or know. Making *The Year of Living Dangerously* was, to me, water from the moon." Hunt dedicated her Oscar to her parents and director Peter Weir and concluded, "To everyone I love, this is the sign": she kissed her thumb and raised it triumphantly.

Rip Torn's cousin Sissy Spacek revealed that the Best Original Screenplay Oscar went to a fellow Texan, *Tender Mercies'* Horton Foote, who clapped his hands in joy as he ran to the stage. Foote expressed his gratitude "particularly to my old and dear friend Robert Duvall for his marvelous work which was the heart and soul of our film." Foote's emotionalism was restrained compared with that of the Best Adapted Screenplay winner—James Brooks for *Terms of Endearment*. The winner kissed both of his leading ladies on the way to the stage and then thanked Jennifer Jones in his speech. Brooks nervously wiped the podium with his hand as he thanked his cast, his family and "Paramount, first and last, the only ones who'd make the movie."

Frank Sinatra stepped out to present the Jean Hersholt Humanitarian Award without checking to see if he could read the cue cards—he couldn't. The audience finally let out a few chuckles when the Chairman of the Board called the recipient a "Godfather . . . of . . . of . . . Goodness." Mike Frankovich, a former studio head at Columbia, walked out and said, "To receive it from Frank Sinatra makes it a little more special." Sinatra did not accompany Frankovich to the pressroom after they walked offstage but headed directly for his limousine instead.

Meanwhile, Sir Richard Attenborough trotted out to name Best Director. Only Peter Yates and James L. Brooks were there, and Brooks won his second Oscar of the evening. "No!" Brooks exclaimed when he heard his name called, but the clapping of his wife and Amy Irving, who was sitting beside him, convinced him that it was true. "I feel like I've been beaten up—it's strange," he said, before expressing more thanks and wiping the podium some more. Then two members of Our Gang, Jackie Cooper and Spanky McFarland,

"I feel like I've been beaten up—it's strange."
—James L. Brooks

came out and gave an Honorary Oscar to producer Hal Roach, ninety-two, who proceeded to reminisce about 1912.

"Okay, folks, we're into our fourth hour now," cracked Carson. "Let's check the board and see how much we've raised." Dolly Parton and Sylvester Stallone strode out to present Best Actor and Michael Caine confessed later, "I figured if they had a country-and-western star to give out the Award, I wasn't going to win." Parton made Caine feel more doubtful when she loudly cheered Duvall's nomination. The winner was Robert Duvall, who wore a cowboy tux with western tie. There was a long ovation, a shot of Johnny Cash and June Carter clapping, and Dolly Parton threw her arms around the winner and said, laughing, "I think you're just the greatest, I really do." Duvall said, "I'm very excited, very happy, very moved, very everything tonight," and went on to brag that Johnny Cash, Willie Nelson and Waylon Jennings had also complimented him on his performance.

Rock Hudson did not make Frank Sinatra's mistake when he gave the Best Actress Award with Liza Minnelli. "There's nothing easy about awarding an Oscar—or reading these cue cards!" he began, stopping to pull his glasses out of his pocket. The audience rewarded him with a round of applause. Shirley MacLaine took hold of Sachi's hand as Minnelli described her role as a "colorful, witty, multi-dimensional widow and mother, whose stormy relationship with her daughter causes them both to grow." Debra Winger's bare shoulders heaved as the camera bore down on her when her nomination was read. "Oh, Rock," Liza said as she ripped open the envelope. "The winner is Shirley MacLaine!" A jubilant MacLaine hugged Sachi, kissed two gentlemen in her row, hugged and whispered to Debra Winger, ran to the stage, hugged Rock, hugged Liza and beheld her Oscar. "I'm going to cry because this show has been as long as my career," she said, adding, "I'm not going to thank everybody I ever met in my entire life, although, with the way my mind has been going lately, probably everybody I've ever met in my entire life and in the other life I might have had had something to do with this." MacLaine praised James L. Brooks, Jack Nicholson—"to have him in bed was such middle-aged joy," she said—and Debra Winger. When Shirley talked about Winger's "turbulent brilliance," the camera saw Debra shrugging and laughing. MacLaine concluded: "God bless that potential that we all have for making anything possible if we think we deserve it." She held up her Oscar, turned to depart, and said quickly, "I deserve this." The audience laughed and gave her another ovation.

Only Best Picture remained unannounced, but it would be a few minutes before it was divulged. First, Carson had to introduce Roger Moore, who introduced Frank Capra, eighty-six, who walked out to the tune of "High Hopes." Capra had difficulty reading the cue cards even though he was holding them in his hands; the Academy switched to a prerecorded announcement of the nominees when it became clear that Capra was going to take all night. He finally got to the part about opening the envelope and the winner was the producer of *Terms of Endearment*—James L. Brooks. Steven Spielberg and *The Big Chill* producer Michael Shamberg shook Brooks' hand as he made his way to the stage for the third time. "I want to tell you that Debra Winger worked on this picture in countless ways for about a year with about as much as a person can give to a picture," he said, ending, "This is an extraordinary evening for us, there's no way to express the gratitude."

"Ladies and gentlemen, before we say good night and good-bye until next year, which is coming up soon . . . ," Carson said as the show came to a close after a record three hours and forty-two minutes. There was a final film clip of the late Ethel Merman singing at the 1962 ceremonies, and then Liza Minnelli and Sammy Davis, Jr., danced out singing "There's No Business Like Show Business." They were joined by the presenters and winners as the TV credits and voting rules flashed

"It's only the best fruit the birds pick at."
—Bette Davis

by. The camera lingered on Shirley MacLaine, hugging Gene Hackman and Jack Nicholson, until the telecast ended.

Aftermath

"I had a physical weakening in the knees," Shirley MacLaine marveled backstage. "I don't know what I said. Was it all right?" A reporter asked the Best Actress if she thought she had won for her performance or her body of work. "Both," MacLaine replied, "and for my body, too." Nearby Jack Nicholson was holding his second Oscar and raving, "I feel happy with this. I'm going to go for a lot more, you know; I'm after three or four more and it feels great." When *USA Today* asked how he would celebrate this evening, the winner said, "I'm going down to the Roxy, get loaded, tell a lot of fake jokes." He was already kidding around; he asked balding Robert Duvall, "Where's your hair?" The Best Actor laughed and explained to reporters that Horton Foote had written his first movie, *To Kill a Mockingbird*. "So I've come full circle," Duvall said. Linda Hunt was also seeing her career in cosmic terms. "They said I would be limited as an actress," she declared. "No one ever discouraged me from doing it; they only said you must prepare yourself to be limited. And how I feel is that I'm not going to be limited—the sky's the limit."

"At the Acad's Board of Governors' Ball at the Bev-Hilton," noted Army Archerd, "we were surprised to find singer Michael Jackson cowering in a doorway off the ballroom's main entrance, with friend Steven Spielberg and bodyguards flanking his entrance/departure." While Jackson avoided the press, Rip Torn's mother chatted with *Entertainment Tonight*. "It was fabulous," she exclaimed. "So much more interesting than on TV." Torn's family enjoyed the ball, but Robert Duvall did not. The Best Actor tried to bring some of his friends with him, but the Academy said there wasn't enough food, so Duvall joined his companions for some hamburgers over at Johnny Cash's house.

"It looked like New Year's Eve in L.A. during/after the Oscars," Army Archerd reported, "with the celebrants/participants/observers driving around town from party-to-party during/after the awards." A lot of that traffic was in the direction of Swifty Lazar's party at the Bistro. Liza Minnelli entered with Michael Jackson, who wore a blue sequined band jacket, aviator sunglasses, and trademark glove. Jackson never ventured far from Minnelli's side, although he did consent to pose for a picture with Michael Caine. The actor said the picture was for his daughter.

The *New York Daily News'* Liz Smith broadcast that "by 12:15, most people had departed agent Swifty Lazar's big Beverly Hills bash. Debra Winger came by at 12 midnight with Paramount tycoon Barry Diller—she took one look at the dregs and split." One report had Winger catching up with her *Terms of Endearment* family—MacLaine, Nicholson and Brooks—at the private club called On the Rocks. Shirley's brother Warren Beatty was there to assist in the celebrating, and the winners posed for what they called their "graduation picture."

The Board of Governors was inundated with phone calls from friends informing them how lousy and long the show was. *TV Guide* pointed out that the TV ratings dropped this year and chastised the Academy, "Film is a lively art. It does not deserve a deadly awards show." The *New York Daily News* editorial page inquired "Did it strike you while watching the Oscars, how many of the movies were about drunks?" and went on to illustrate that all five of Best Actor nominees played some sort of lush.

Robert Duvall was profiled by *Newsweek* in a story entitled A CHAMELEON'S CRAFT: OSCAR-WINNER DUVALL IS NOT A MOVIE STAR; HE'S AN ACTOR. Shirley MacLaine fared even better—she got a *Time* cover with the headline GETTING HER KICKS AT 50. Her birthday was feted at a gala party in a Manhattan nightclub that had once been a church. Sachi accompanied her mother to this event, too, and again they wore complementary outfits. At the conclusion of her Broadway show, which earned favorable reviews and sensational box office, MacLaine would introduce "the man I've been sleeping with lately." She would then produce her Oscar and audiences never failed to cheer. "This has been the best year of my life," MacLaine told *Time*.

As for Barbra Streisand, she was hopping from *Yentl* premiere to *Yentl* premiere in Europe, where she got a lot of attention. Federico Fellini saluted her in Rome, and the French were so taken with the film they gave her their Officer of Arts and Letters Award. At the Jerusalem premiere in honor of a new study center at Hebrew University that Streisand had funded and dedicated to her father, a reporter asked why *Yentl* hadn't done better with the Academy. Streisand retorted, "In Hollywood, a woman can be an actress, a singer, a dancer—but don't let her be too much more."

1984

"If Sally hadn't been so good in Gidget or The Flying Nun, do you think anyone would remember her in those roles?"
—Robert Benton

Ugly ducklings turned into swans at the 1984 Academy Awards.

Robert Towne's passion was to write and direct the definitive screen version of Edgar Rice Burroughs' Tarzan story, and the Oscar-winning writer toiled eight years on his script. He never got a chance to direct the movie, however, because he was coerced into selling his rights to the property in order to complete *Personal Best,* his directorial debut, which had run way over budget. Warner Brothers assigned British director Hugh Hudson, fresh from his *Chariots of Fire* triumph, to Towne's project and Hudson brought in another writer for fine-tuning. Towne removed his name from the script and replaced it with "P. H. Vazak"—his sheep dog. Countered Hudson, "Towne should have left his name on the film. That would have been honest."

Going Ape

When the $30 million *Greystoke: The Legend of Tarzan, Lord of the Apes* opened in the spring to big business, Vincent Canby effused in the *New York Times,* "*Greystoke* is unlike any other Tarzan movie you've ever seen. It is a wonderful original." Upstaging newcomer Christopher Lambert as Tarzan was eighty-one-year-old Ralph Richardson as the ape man's dotty grandfather. *Newsweek*'s Jack Kroll exclaimed, "The great Sir Ralph Richardson makes the old earl a marvelously Dickensian character," but the knighted actor wasn't around to appreciate his good notices—he died on October 10, 1983, five months before the film was released.

Three days before *Greystoke* bowed, columnist Liz Smith revealed that the film's leading lady, Calvin Klein jeans model Andie McDowell, had not been able to overcome her thick Southern drawl and that all her dialogue had to be redubbed by Glenn Close. "Now don't bother to ask either Glenn or Warner's about this," Smith advised. "Everybody has dummied up in the best whatever-are-you-talking-about fashion. But I'm here to tell you it's Glenn whose voice will appear to emerge from Andie's luscious lips."

Close Encounters

Audiences who wanted to *see* Glenn Close only had to wait a week until *The Stone Boy,* a low-budget family drama costarring Robert Duvall, premiered, although next to nobody did. Close had also signed for another low-budget film, James Ivory's adaptation of Henry James' *The Bostonians,* but dropped out when Robert Redford wooed her to appear in his first starring vehicle in four years, an adaptation of Bernard Malamud's *The Natural.* Although the part wasn't exactly the dream role she had hoped for—"Finally I got to play opposite every woman's fantasy, Redford, and I never got to touch him!"—the actress found herself in a hit movie when *The Natural* opened in May. Close's good fortune continued when, a month later, she won a Tony Award for her starring role in Tom Stoppard's *The Real Thing.* Despite this winning streak, Close confessed to the *Los Angeles Times,* "I'm still very hungry for the best roles."

A Tri-Star Is Born

The Natural was produced by Tri-Star Pictures, a brand-new studio formed by another studio, a TV network, and a cable-TV company—Columbia, CBS and Home Box Office. *Film Comment* observed that *The Natural,* the studio's first big production, "pulled a respectable $25 million and served notice that Tri-Star could be a contender."

The fledgling studio waited until September to release its major Oscar contender, *Places in the Heart,* 1979 Oscar winner Robert Benton's recollection of his Depression-era childhood, filmed on location in his hometown of Waxahachie, Texas. "I wanted a simple, clear picture—almost like a snapshot album—of what that town was like,"

Sally Field finally gets some self-respect.

"Finally I got to play opposite every woman's fantasy, Redford, and I never got to touch him!"
—Glenn Close

said the writer-director, who hired up-and-coming actors Ed Harris, Amy Madigan and Lindsay Crouse to play the citizenry.

Benton reserved the film's central role, a widow struggling to hold on to her farm, for 1979 Best Actress winner Sally Field. Even an Academy Award hadn't convinced Field that she had shaken her TV bubblehead image and she fretted that *Norma Rae* was a fluke, since none of her subsequent films had done much for her career. But she trusted Robert Benton, who gentlemanly defended her earlier work, "If Sally hadn't been so good in *Gidget* or *The Flying Nun,* do you think anyone would remember her in those roles?"

The Dust Bowl Trilogy

Tri-Star got what it was looking for when CBS critic Pat Collins raved, "An American masterpiece, the movie to beat for the Academy Award." Collins' comment became a part of the film's advertising campaign, which featured a picture of Sally posing stoically with two children in a field—photographed on location in Malibu. But Tri-Star wasn't the only company with a rural epic that fall, and the press referred to *Places in the Heart* as one-third of "The Dust Bowl Trilogy."

Jessica Lange had been approached to star in *The River,* Universal's modern-day drama about a Tennessee farming couple besieged by mortgage foreclosures and flash floods, but the Oscar-winning actress chose instead to produce her own farm vehicle for Walt Disney. *Country,* the story of an Iowa couple besieged by mortgage foreclosures and a tornado, costarred Lange's real-life leading man, Sam Shepard, and opened the New York Film Festival in September, thereby getting the jump on *The River,* starring Oscar winner Sissy Spacek, which wouldn't bow until Christmas. When critic Gene Siskel asked her why *Country* and *The River* had so much in common, Lange responded, "I think these films have only a vague similarity to each other." But columnist Harry Haun snickered, "C'mon now, do you *really* think it's a coincidence that the cow in the new Sissy Spacek–Mel Gibson movie *The River* is named Jessica?"

When the returns were in, *Places in the Heart* made more at the box office than the other two farm movies combined. It also restored Sally Field's confidence: she proceeded to find a new husband, a new house (a $1.5 million Brentwood "manse," according to the *Hollywood Reporter*), and, finally, the nerve to produce a picture for her own production company. "It's survival," Sally explained, "just plain old survival—and it's tough."

Blind Ambition

Places also gave a boost to the career of John Malkovich, a Chicago-trained stage actor who played a character based on Benton's blind great-uncle. Benton boasted of the young actor, "He's some kind of bizarre genius and his instincts are so true that you don't need to change him," adding, "and one of his great ambitions is to work with Pia Zadora." Prior to his turn as a blind man, Malkovich made his film debut as a "hard-drinking, dope-smoking free-lance photographer," as the Warner Brothers publicity department described his role in *The Killing Fields,* the latest film from *Chariots of Fire* producer David Puttnam.

The basis of *The Killing Fields* was an article in the *New York Times Magazine* by Pulitzer Prize–winning journalist Sydney Schanberg about his search for his Cambodian interpreter Dith Pran, who had been imprisoned by the Khmer Rouge for four years before escaping to Thailand. When producers courted Schanberg for the film rights, they discovered that Puttnam was one step ahead of them—he had already had lunch with the reporter a month earlier, having read about his reunion with Pran in *Time.* "Because it was so heavily synopsized," said Puttnam of the news item, "it read like boy meets girl, boy loses girl, boy finds girl again, which is a terrific narrative spine for anything." Schanberg's agent, Sam Cohn, told his client, "You won't get the most money, but if I were you, I'd go with Puttnam."

"I am not a movie star."
—Dr. Haing S. Ngor

A Member of the Wedding

Having grabbed Schanberg's sanction, the producer chose Roland Joffé, whose previous work was with the BBC and the Old Vic, to direct the $14 million film. "Anyone talented will bust his guts on his first feature film," Puttnam explained. He didn't want big name stars either, and cast Sam Waterston, forty-four, as Schanberg. Finding someone to play Dith Pran was more difficult. Puttnam and Joffé interviewed over three hundred expatriate Cambodians in California before casting agent Pat Golden saw a photo of Dr. Haing S. Ngor enjoying himself at a wedding reception. Upon investigating, Golden learned that Ngor's Cambodian escape was a virtual rerun of Pran's but with a difference—whereas Pran's loved ones had fled and were waiting for him in the U.S., Dr. Ngor watched almost his entire family die of starvation.

The thirty-five-year-old gynecologist was eager to make the film "to show the world how the Communists really were, what they did to my country," but he doubted he would get the part. "I am not a movie star," he said. "The producer or director want to choose a handsome young guy." But Ngor's impassioned audition convinced the filmmakers he was the man for the role. "When he looked out the window," recalled director Joffé, "he did not see the Warners parking lot on a Sunday afternoon, which I did—he saw Phnom-Penh."

Vincent Canby approved the casting when *The Killing Fields* appeared in November, writing, "Dr. Ngor reveals an extraordinary screen presence." Columnist Bob Thomas announced that after a decade in films, "Sam Waterston comes into his own," while the *Los Angeles Times*' Sheila Benson said, "What Roland Joffé has done in recreating the blind panic of what would happen to you in that situation under those war conditions is extraordinary." One of the film's few critics was Dr. Ngor himself, who told reporters, "The film is real, but not real enough; the cruelty of the Khmer Rouge is not bad enough." But Dr. Ngor found that his new fame brought fringe benefits: a niece he had not seen in ten years read an article about the film in her home in France and recognized her uncle. When they met again, *Time* was there to synopsize this reunion, too. "I found all of my family that is left," he rejoiced. "I can't speak anymore. I am happy."

A New Leaf

In casting the coveted roles in Peter Shaffer's Tony-winning play *Amadeus*, director Milos Forman picked actors not much better known than Dr. Haing S. Ngor. "I felt very funny about seeing Mozart played by, let's say, Dustin Hoffman, because audiences will not believe this Mozart," said Forman. "It was the same with Salieri, which is really the major role. I didn't want someone familiar like Jack Nicholson or Donald Sutherland that audiences would recognize."

To play Antonio Salieri, Mozart's jealous rival, Forman went with F. Murray Abraham, a forty-four-year-old New York actor who usually played character roles, most notably a leaf in a Fruit of the Loom underwear commercial. "Forman saw or heard from every major actor in the English language to do this role—and we're talking very famous actors whose names alone are worth millions and millions to a movie—and he chose me," marveled Abraham. "I'm not worth very much to a movie except for my talent." The director selected Tom Hulce, one of the juveniles from *National Lampoon's Animal House*, for Mozart because "He can speak obscenely but also make you believe that he could write divine music."

The John McEnroe of Music

Forman eschewed Hollywood soundstages as well and filmed on location in Czechoslovakia. "Prague is a gem," he said, "because it's possible to pivot the camera a full three hundred and sixty degrees and never encounter a modern vision."

"I'm tired of words like 'prestige' and 'dedication.'"
—Howard E. Rollins, Jr.

The location also represented a homecoming for the director, who hadn't made a film in his native land since the Russian invasion of 1968. He hired many of his countrymen and gave them their first taste of Hollywood opulence—$500,000 was spent on wigs alone. "At first, it felt like a costume party," said Hulce. "It took all of half an hour just to put on my wig."

"A thrilling deployment of the highest arts of the medium," sang Charles Champlin in the *Los Angeles Times,* but Pauline Kael hooted in *The New Yorker,* "Forman trudges through the movie as if every step were a major contribution to art." F. Murray Abraham had *Los Angeles Magazine*'s Merrill Shindler sighing, "He gave himself heart and soul to the role of Salieri and when he was on screen—which was through most of the film—goose bumps would flow up and down my spine." On the other hand, *Variety* echoed the sentiments of many reviewers, who felt the title character had become overly Americanized: "As played by Tom Hulce, Mozart emerges as the John McEnroe of classical music, an immature brat with loads of talent, but with little human dimension." Nevertheless, *Amadeus* attracted a sizable adult audience, inspiring Orion Pictures to try to lure the youth market with a music video that mixed scenes from the film with footage of Michael Jackson, Billy Idol and Eddie Van Halen. Alas, the kids didn't fall for it, and MTV quit showing the video after a couple of weeks.

Bargain Basement Prestige

Director Norman Jewison also worried about attracting the youth audience because, he acknowledged, "I can't make pictures about spaceships, I'm not interested in them." Jewison was interested in exploring race relations, as he had in 1967's Best Picture, the murder mystery *In the Heat of the Night.* "I hitchhiked through the South in 1945 when I was eighteen and passed the Missouri town where the last lynching had taken place," the director reminisced. "They told me I rode in the pick-up truck that dragged the victim through the streets—that was said with a great deal of pride, which astounded me." These memories were rekindled when Jewison read Charles Fuller's Pulitzer Prize–winning *A Soldier's Play,* a murder mystery set in a segregated Southern army base during World War II. Jewison decided this would be his next project but it wasn't easy finding someone to finance the film version—even though he was willing to waive his usual $1.5 million salary. "I just went from studio to studio and got down on my knees and asked them for the money," he said. Columbia finally agreed to shell out a mere $6 million—half the budget of the average studio movie.

Anticipating critical praise for *A Soldier's Story,* Columbia gave the movie a slow prestige release. The studio's president for distribution and marketing, Ashley Boone, told the *New York Times*' Aljean Harmetz that his job was "to attach this movie to the idea of quality," but the film's star, Howard E. Rollins, Jr., had heard this spiel before. Making his first picture since his 1981 Best Supporting Actor nomination for Milos Forman's *Ragtime,* Rollins earned only $40,000 for starring in *A Soldier's Story.* "This project is being referred to as 'special,' 'unusual,' 'different,' but when you cut through the bullshit, it's because it's a black production," the actor complained to *Moviegoer* magazine. "I'm tired of words like 'prestige' and 'dedication.' Sure, we're dedicated, but for no money." But at least Rollins was in a success—Boone's "quality" campaign worked. Not only did Norman Jewison win a Bill of Rights Award from the American Civil Liberties Union for his "commitment to civil rights," but the *Hollywood Reporter* had this tidbit: "Jewison, who usually refuses all requests to lend prints of his films for the Bel Air circuit and/or living room screenings, has okayed a request from Michael Jackson."

A Terrible Thing to Waste

Jewison had recruited members of the off-Broadway Negro Ensemble Company to re-create their roles, and the critics singled out Adolph Cae-

"One studio said they would give us the money if we had an explicit rape scene in the cave."
—producer John Brabourne

sar, fifty-one, as the ill-fated martinet Sergeant Waters. Jack Kroll wrote in *Newsweek,* "His portrait of a tragically twisted spirit is exact, uncompromising and indelible." Previously, Caesar's biggest claim to fame had been that he was the voice in United Negro College Fund commercials intoning, "A mind is a terrible thing to waste," so when he heard the raves, he plunged into a campaign for Best Supporting Actor. "Sure, I'd like to win it," Caesar told *Entertainment Tonight.* "I'd like to make lots of money and good films."

A Horror Story

Fourteen years had passed since the last David Lean movie. "After *Ryan's Daughter,* I had such terrible notices that I really lost heart," he confessed. The worst came when Lean attended a party in his honor at the Algonquin Hotel thrown by the National Society of Film Critics and a few of the hosts began voicing their objections to the movie. "How could the man who made *Brief Encounter* make such garbage as *Ryan's Daughter* was the point of the attack," a witness told Aljean Harmetz. "He sat it out for an hour and a half. It hurt him very deeply."

Eleven years later, producers John Brabourne and Richard Goodwin called Lean with the news that they had obtained the film rights to the late E. M. Forster's novel *A Passage to India,* which Lean had tried to buy in 1958, when the author told him no sale. Procuring the film rights was one thing; getting the money for the production was another. Producer Brabourne characterized the hunt for investors as "a horror story. One studio said they would give us the money if we had an explicit rape scene in the cave. Another said it was a waste having an elderly woman as a central character because young people are bored by old people." Ultimately, the filmmakers were able to piece together the film's $14.5 million budget from tax shelters, individual investors, HBO, EMI, Columbia and David Lean, who put some of his own money in.

Judy Freaks Out

The director cast Australia's Judy Davis, thirty, as the naive Miss Quested after a two-hour interview. When Davis gave her interpretation of what happened in the caves—"She can't cope with her own sexuality, she just freaks out"—Lean told her the part was hers. Davis eagerly signed on, but Dame Peggy Ashcroft put up a fight when Lean asked her to be the enigmatic Mrs. Moore. "Mr. Lean, I'm seventy-five years old," she protested. "So am I," he retorted. Although Ashcroft had just worked in India on the TV miniseries *The Jewel in the Crown,* she admitted, "I thought, 'Oh dear, I really don't want to do it,' but it's very difficult to turn down a Lean film." Lean also had to overcome the restrictions of British Equity in order to employ the thirty-eight-year-old Indian actor Victor Banerjee as the hapless Dr. Aziz. When Lean got his way,the casting made headlines in India. "It was a matter of national pride that an Indian was cast instead of an Asian from England," observed Banerjee.

Lean didn't have to worry about the critics this time. Vincent Canby stated, "Mr. Lean's *A Passage to India* is by far his best work since *The Bridge on the River Kwai* and *Lawrence of Arabia* and perhaps his most humane and moving film since *Brief Encounter.*" *Time* profiled the director in a cover story entitled "An Old Master's New Triumph," in which Steven Spielberg declared, "I think he has a much broader movie vocabulary than a lot of directors, including myself." The Directors Guild feted him in Los Angeles with a weekend tribute, and the guest of honor confided to his colleagues, "You know what I'd really love to do, and you'll all roar with laughter—I'd love to do a musical."

Blue-Collar Tastes

Arriving in Hollywood simultaneously with *A Passage to India,* but with much less fanfare, was another literary adaptation—*The Bostonians.* After

"I'm still in shock over that one."
—Rex Reed

Glenn Close walked out on him, producer Ismail Merchant flew to London and lunched with Vanessa Redgrave, who had earlier turned down the role of the ardent feminist because she found her "unrelentingly morbid." Redgrave reconsidered and signed a contract that evening, but then the U.S. State Department wouldn't let her in the country. "Even Senator Moynihan couldn't help," recalled Merchant. "But a marvelous immigration officer called me to say he loved my film *The Europeans* and he would speed things up." "Vanessa Redgrave's performance is a wonder to behold," applauded *Newsweek*'s David Ansen when the film ran in art-house engagements. Spurred by the good reviews, Frank Moreno, the film's independent distributor, placed a few Oscar ads in the trade papers, but leveled with *Variety* that Henry James "probably doesn't appeal to blue-collar audiences."

Blue-collar and white-collar audiences alike flocked to *Beverly Hills Cop*, the one unqualified hit of the Christmas season, grossing more than $200 million. The original script was designed for Sylvester Stallone as an action vehicle, but when he left as a result of "creative differences," Paramount revamped the story for contractee Eddie Murphy, who ad-libbed all over the place and turned the police thriller into a raucous comedy. *Newsweek* dubbed him "Mr. Box Office" and *Daily Variety* referred to him as "Eddie the Engine." His costar Judge Rheinhold called him "a comedic Mozart," but the twenty-three-year-old Murphy insisted he had another idol: "I want to direct, write, score and produce—like Chaplin used to." *Daily Variety* reported that he could have just about anything he wanted: "Paramount Pictures, anxious to show that it is holding on to some of its most prized assets, has negated Eddie Murphy's old contract and given him a new agreement with more money, more perks and permanent production offices on the Paramount lot." The office Murphy got had belonged to Sylvester Stallone.

Critical Shock Waves

David Lean's comeback became official when the New York Film Critics and the New York–based National Board of Review named *A Passage to India* Best Picture and Lean Best Director. But in Los Angeles the fair-haired boy was Milos Forman, who won both the Los Angeles Film Critics and Golden Globe awards. There was no consensus at all regarding the Best Actor awards. The Los Angeles scribes couldn't make up their minds and voted a tie between *Amadeus*' F. Murray Abraham and Albert Finney as a drunk in *Under the Volcano*, John Huston's adaptation of Malcolm Lowry's cult classic, which was a box-office disaster. The National Board of Review chose *Passage*'s Victor Banerjee while the New York Film Critics, after several ballots, surprised everyone by picking Steve Martin in the comedy fantasy *All of Me*, in which he played a character possessed by Lily Tomlin. A week later, voter Rex Reed told his readers, "I'm still in shock over that one."

The critics weren't able to come up with a consensus on the best supporting actor, either. The Los Angeles group anointed *A Soldier's Story*'s Adolph Caesar, the National Board chose *Places in the Heart*'s John Malkovich, the Golden Globe went to *The Killing Fields*' Dr. Haing S. Ngor, and the New York Critics, pulling another surprise, selected Sir Ralph Richardson for *Greystoke*. The late actor's Academy campaign was already in full swing in Hollywood—Warner Brothers had invited Academy members to a three-week retrospective of Richardson's films that culminated with a seven-day showing of *Greystoke*. The Los Angeles critics declared *Passage*'s Dame Peggy Ashcroft the year's outstanding supporting actress, handing best actress to Kathleen Turner for two movies—the hit adventure comedy *Romancing the Stone* and Ken Russell's erotic extravaganza *Crimes of Passion*. Their New York counterparts gave Ashcroft their award as best lead actress, picking Christine Lahti as best supporting actress

"It's a fairy tale, a dream come true."
—F. Murray Abraham

for playing a tough dame in the Goldie Hawn vehicle *Swing Shift*.

Peggy Takes the Lead

Delighted by her acclaim in the box-office disappointment, Lahti told the Gotham critics at their annual party that she was glad they had not made her compete with Ashcroft, adding, "Of course, since the announcement of the awards, Peggy and I have both been asked to pose for *Playboy*." Ashcroft and the entire crowd roared, but the biggest laugh came when Steve Martin accepted by commenting, "It is a great honor to have been given this award by so many distinguished critics—and Rex Reed." Mr. Reed was not present.

Columbia, which had been hustling Ashcroft for a Supporting Actress nomination, suddenly switched tracks and began running trade ads promoting her as a Best Actress Oscar candidate. "With this placement decision," observed columnist Robert Osborne, "Dame Peggy becomes the one actress that the others will have to beat for Oscar's primary female prize, and it now leaves a virtual open field to those supporting fillies who didn't previously have a chance to win." Among the studios taking advantage of this development were MGM/UA, which tub-thumped six-time nominee Geraldine Page for her two scenes as a cop's mother in the little-seen *The Pope of Greenwich Village,* and Tri-Star, campaigning for a third-in-a-row nomination for *The Natural*'s Glenn Close. Close's ads were just a few of nearly one hundred that Tri-Star bought in each of the trade papers. Its biggest effort was the forty-five solicitations for *Places in the Heart,* but the nascant company huckstered just about every film it released in its first year, even *Supergirl*.

The Clint and Jeff Traveling Show

Although he didn't win any critics' awards, Clint Eastwood conducted the most visible personal campaign, with fourteen ads commemorating his superlative reviews for playing a kinky cop in *Tightrope*. The trade papers also had updates on Eastwood's European sojourn, during which he received tributes from film societies in Munich, London, and Paris, where he was decorated by the Ministry of Culture as a Chevalier des Arts et Lettres. Meanwhile, Jeff Bridges journeyed through America, visiting Boston, St. Louis, Denver, San Francisco, and, on three separate trips, New York, in order to remain in the public eye after starring as a sweet-natured extra-terrestrial in *Starman*. The head of publicity for the film noted, "He's wonderful to look at and friendly to talk to and the press likes him." So did Hollywood. "Within the movie industry," commented *New York* magazine, "Bridges is thought of as a hard-working, untemperamental actor."

Despite their self-ballyhooing, Eastwood and Bridges remained long shots, so columnist Marilyn Beck checked in on a sure thing: "Steve Martin, anxiously awaiting tomorrow's announcement of Academy Award nominees, reports, 'Three months ago I wasn't even thinking I'd be included, but now so many people are talking about it, they've got me all worked up.' "

The Nominations

"Steve Martin, where art thou?" asked Robert Osborne when the comedian's name was missing from the list of Best Actor nominees. The columnist pointed out that Martin was only the third actor ever to be honored by the New York Film Critics and then ostracized by the Academy, adding, "If it's any consolation, Steve, those other two actors were Sir Ralph Richardson and Sir John Gielgud." Richardson was luckier than Martin this year; he received a posthumous Supporting Actor nomination for *Greystoke*, which also won an Adapted Screenplay nomination for Robert Towne's dog. Rex Reed had the last laugh: "By ignoring Steve Martin, this may be the first time in history the Oscars make more sense than the New York Film Critics."

The Los Angeles Film critics saw both of their

"I thought it was a typo."
—Woody Allen

Best Actor choices, Albert Finney and F. Murray Abraham, make the grade. Finney was as excited by his fourth nomination as he had been by his other three—he was nowhere to be seen. For F. Murray Abraham, though, "It's a fairy tale, a dream come true." When the Brooklyn resident attended the Hollywood luncheon honoring the nominees, he realized, "The difference between these people and me is that I had to wear a name tag: 'Hi, I'm an Academy Award nominee. My name is . . .' " Another Best Actor nominee at the luncheon was Abraham's costar Tom Hulce, and the two screen rivals embraced for photographers. *The Killing Fields*' Best Actor candidate, Sam Waterston, was as blasé as Albert Finney. "This has never been part of my daydream," he admitted, but he did promise to be there Oscar night. The fifth nominee was *Starman*'s Jeff Bridges; Aljean Harmetz pronounced him "the biggest surprise in the acting categories." As for *Passage*'s non-nominated Victor Banerjee, he accepted his National Board of Review Award and told the audience he was looking "for a blunt instrument that I can use on the Academy when I get back to Los Angeles."

Go Milk a Cow

"It used to be an actress had to play a hooker to be guaranteed a nomination; now she's got to milk a cow," quipped Gregg Kilday in the *Los Angeles Herald-Examiner* when he saw that all three Dust Bowl heroines were nominated. Academy members decided that Dame Peggy Ashcroft was a supporting actress after all, but *A Passage to India* still received a Best Actress nomination for dark horse Judy Davis. The fifth nominee was Vanessa Redgrave for *The Bostonians*. The *Los Angeles Times*' Dale Pollack reminded voters that Redgrave was "one of the most controversial winners in Oscar history for her fiery anti-Zionist speech at the 1977 Awards," and another columnist scoffed, "Don't expect the Academy to give Redgrave another chance to hijack the Oscar show." Nevertheless, Redgrave was warmly received when she was the only Best Actress candidate to attend the nominees' luncheon and she refused to talk politics during a two-hour interview with the *Los Angeles Times*. She wasn't going to be at the Awards ceremony, anyway; five days before the ceremony, her father, Sir Michael Redgrave, died, and Vanessa and Peggy Ashcroft canceled their Oscar plans and returned to England for the funeral.

Who's Laughing Now

OSCAR GETS SERIOUS headlined the *New York Post*'s announcement of the nominations, and columnist Diana Maychick remarked, "In his usual elitist fashion, Oscar thumbed his nose at the most popular movies of 1984." The Best Picture nominees were all moderate box-office successes: *Amadeus* (11 nominations), *A Passage to India* (11), *The Killing Fields* (7), *Places in the Heart* (7) and *A Soldier's Story* (3). *People* magazine was upset that box-office blockbusters *Ghostbusters* and *Beverly Hills Cop* were overlooked and asked "Can Oscar laugh?" while the staff of *Film Comment* carped, "More than ever, the Academy's middle-aged, middle-brow membership seemed estranged from the films people were paying to see," a complete reversal from the days when the Academy was ridiculed for honoring box-office successes such as *The Greatest Show on Earth*.

It's Only a Game

"I thought it was a typo," said Woody Allen when he discovered he had received two nominations for his comedy *Broadway Danny Rose*. "Movie fans weren't the only ones surprised by Woody Allen's Best Director nomination," reported Bill Harris. "The Academy itself was caught unprepared. They didn't even have a biography or a photograph to hand out" to the press corps. Allen's nomination bumped *A Soldier's Story*'s Norman Jewison from the directors' line-up, but the fifty-eight-year-old non-nominee shrugged off the snub to the *Los Angeles Times*, saying, "Oh, years ago it would have bothered me a lot." The

"It's like a religious experience, old boy."
—Irving "Swifty" Lazar

Directors Guild gave the lead to *Amadeus'* Milos Forman by giving him its annual award, and the director told an interviewer, "If you take the Oscar too seriously, as some sort of final judgment, you're in trouble. But if you take it as a game, it's wonderful." Competitor David Lean wasn't playing the game very well, and at a party for the Foreign Film nominees, complained, "The people at the heads of studios can't or won't read. It makes you wonder if there shouldn't be a hell of a shake-up at the studios."

The Killing Fields had a sentimental favorite in Supporting Actor nominee Dr. Haing S. Ngor. Many pundits compared the non-professional to Harold Russell, the double amputee of *The Best Years of Our Lives* who claimed the Supporting Oscar in 1946. Noriyuki "Pat" Morita, a comic nominated for playing a Japanese karate master in the crowd-pleasing *The Karate Kid,* protested, "One thing that lets me feel as though I've got a real shot is that I felt mine was an acting job and I feel, to a large degree, Dr. Ngor was playing Dr. Ngor." But Dr. Ngor replied to such criticism, "I got my license from the Khmer Rouge school of acting." John Malkovich, nominated for *Places in the Heart*, joked that his chances weren't so hot: "I'm up against two Orientals, one of them being Haing, and a black guy and a dead actor." That "black guy," Adolph Caesar, was fully enjoying his moment in the limelight and invited *Entertainment Tonight* to spend Oscar day with him as he drank a good luck toast with friends—"Here's to peace in our times—a piece of Oscar"—and had a tiff with his wife over who should carry the tickets. Mrs. Caesar prevailed, snapping them up in her purse.

"Will Oscar get interesting?" asked Suzy, who wrote in her column that "*anything*" would be more entertaining than "the predictable boring, smug shows the Academy has dumped on us for years." Since last year's show had dragged on for three hours and forty-two minutes, the Academy assembled a brand-new creative team and told them their main concern was speed. Gregory Peck, the creative team's head, went on ABC's *Good Morning America* to tell the public, "I'm willing to make a bet that we'll hold the show down to three hours." Hoping for another ratings blockbuster like the 1984 Olympics, ABC advertised the show in *TV Guide* with the slogan "The Glamour. The Gold. The Glory!" The show's sleek new format precluded Johnny Carson; the Academy didn't have time for his annual monologue. Spurned by Oscar, Carson made plans to attend Irving "Swifty" Lazar's perennial party, which was undergoing some changes itself. The agent moved the soiree after twenty-five years from the Bistro to Spago on the Sunset Strip because "it's the in place, where all the movie stars go anyway." When a KABC reporter asked him why his guests would enjoy watching a TV show at a party, the host replied, "It's like a religious experience, old boy."

The Big Night

The first nominee to arrive was Noriyuki "Pat" Morita at 4:10 P.M. Diana Ross followed soon thereafter, shouting to the press and the bleacher fans, "This is America! America is about stars and music and motion pictures and it's all here!" Also present was a protester waving a placard that read BACK TO BLACKLISTING . . . NO NUDITY, NO CUSSING, NO HOMOS, NO LEFTISTS. Edy Williams made her annual appearance in a décolletage emblazoned with the legend ADOPT-A-PET DAY—MAR. 30. Non-nominee Steve Martin said, "I just drove up hoping to be on the pre-Oscar show. Everybody knows this is where the excitement really is."

The excitement reached a crescendo with the arrival of the expected winner of the Song Score Award—Prince, the rock star whose vanity musical, *Purple Rain*, pulled in $32 million for Warner Bros. Roger Ebert reported the nominee rolled up "with twenty uniformed escorts on motorcycles around his purple limousine that the paint was still wet on." Prince entered like a sheik in a purple sequined hooded cape with two women from his band in attendance. Victor Banerjee wore a black Nehru jacket and brought the acceptance speech his costar Peggy Ashcroft wanted him to read if she won, but the Academy promptly informed him its post–Sacheen Littlefeather no-proxy policy was still in effect. Director David Lean, nominated for Best Director, Best Adapted Screenplay and Best Film Editing, announced he was also celebrating his seventy-seventh birthday that evening.

The Bridges family—Jeff, father Lloyd, brother Beau, respective wives—arrived en masse, as did the Sally Field entourage—her mother, her new husband, and a son. Seven-time nominee Geraldine Page came with two sons and said, "I'm almost the champion of the losers. I'm always sure I'll lose and I'm right every time." First-time nominee Christine Lahti rhapsodized, "This is all so surreal." As Lahti spoke, Debbie Reynolds mounted forecourt emcee Army Archerd's podium, grabbed his microphone, and said to the crowd, "This is my new husband, Richard Ham-

Awards Ceremony

MARCH 25, 1985, 6:00 P.M.
THE DOROTHY CHANDLER PAVILION, LOS ANGELES

Your Host:
JACK LEMMON
Televised over ABC

Presenters

Supporting Actor . . . . Linda Hunt
Documentary Short Subject . . . . Michael Douglas
Documentary Feature . . . . Kathleen Turner
Makeup . . . . Lonette McKee and Kelly LeBrock
Sound . . . . Amy Irving and Gregory Hines
Cinematography . . . . Diana Ross and Tom Selleck
Supporting Actress . . . . Ryan O'Neal
Jean Hersholt Humanitarian Award . . . . . . Gene Kelly
Art Direction . . . . Steve Martin
Scientific or Technical . . . . Janet Leigh (on film)
Visual Effects . . . . Candice Bergen and William Hurt
Honorary Award to National Endowment for the Arts . . . . Glenn Close
Writing Awards . . . . Burt Lancaster and Kirk Douglas
Original Score . . . . . . Ann Reinking and Jeff Bridges
Original Song Score . . . . Kathleen Turner and Michael Douglas
Costume Design . . . . . Jennifer Beals and Glenn Close
Animated Short Subjects . . . . Ann Reinking and Jeff Bridges
Live Action Short Film . . . . Kathleen Turner and Tom Selleck
Actor . . . . Shirley MacLaine
Song . . . . Gregory Hines
Editing . . . . Genevieve Bujold and William Hurt
Honorary Award to James Stewart . . . . Cary Grant
Foreign Film . . . . Faye Dunaway and Placido Domingo
Director . . . . Steven Spielberg
Actress . . . . Robert Duvall
Picture . . . . Laurence Olivier

Performers of Nominated Songs

"Ghostbusters" . . . . Ray Parker, Jr., and Dom DeLuise
"Let's Hear It for the Boy" . . . . Deniece Williams
"Against All Odds (Take a Look at Me Now)" . . . . Ann Reinking
"Footloose" . . . . Debbie Allen
"I Just Called to Say I Love You" . . . . . . Diana Ross

"I just drove up hoping to be on the pre-Oscar show."
—Steve Martin

lin. Say hello, Richard." Last year's Best Actor, Robert Duvall, returned and gave a progress report: "As for the business end, the Award hasn't helped a bit."

Before the show commenced, Richard Crenna admonished winners that they'd better not speak longer than forty-five seconds or else a red light would go on and the orchestra would drown them out. Meanwhile, backstage, a few Academy officials were having second thoughts about permitting the visibly pregnant but unwed Amy Irving to appear as one of the celebrity cohosts. Scheduled presenter Steven Spielberg, the father of Irving's child, threatened to desert if Amy was not allowed on the show. The opposition relented.

The telecast began with the arrival of Motion Picture Association of America head Jack Valenti—the Academy had promised him this coverage if he'd forego his usual "film is the universal language" speech on the show. Emcee Jack Lemmon stepped on stage and said, "Brevity is the soul of wit; in that sense, we hope to have a very soulful evening for you." Academy President Gene Allen welcomed three countries that were tuning in for the first time: Poland, Denmark and the People's Republic of China. Then followed a parade of ten celebrity cohosts, including Best Actor nominee Jeff Bridges, Best Supporting Actress nominee Glenn Close, mother-to-be Amy Irving and non-nominee Kathleen Turner, who declared, "Bring on the envelopes."

Last year's Best Supporting Actress, Linda Hunt, strutted out to name the Best Supporting Actor. All four of the living nominees were present and Hunt added,"God's blessing be with Sir Ralph Richardson." The winner was Dr. Haing S. Ngor, who flew into the arms of Sam Waterston. Haing tried to pull Sam to the stage with him, but Sam begged off. On stage, Dr. Ngor triumphantly raised the Oscar over his head and said,"This is unbelievable, but so is my entire life." He thanked everyone down to "the casting lady who found me for this role," and concluded by expressing his gratitude to Warner Bros. and "God—Buddha—that I am even here tonight." Dr. Ngor headed backstage to meet the press, but he didn't give the reporters a chance to ask any questions, launching instead into a tirade about the film not being realistic enough and how his family and his "sweetheart" had died. According to *TV Guide,* he summed up by "describing in gruesome detail how he'd been tortured by the Khmer Rouge guerrillas. Reporters listened in stunned silence."

Kathleen Turner announced that the Documentary Feature Oscar went to *The Times of Harvey Milk,* the biography of the slain San Francisco politician that Turner defined as "a film about American values in conflict." Producer Richard Schmiechen was a bit more specific when he thanked the title character "for his courage, for his pride in being gay and for his hope that one day we will all live together in a world of mutual respect."

Amadeus picked up the first technical trophy, for Makeup, and veteran Dick Smith praised "Murray Abraham, whose genius brought my old Salieri makeup to such glorious life." Minutes later, the *Amadeus* sound team was thanking "all the people in Czechoslovakia" as well as "Wolfgang, for writing it all down." But the *Amadeus* momentum was slowed when *The Killing Fields* claimed the Cinematography Oscar.

Ryan O'Neal revealed that the winner of the Best Supporting Actress Oscar was the only absent nominee—Dame Peggy Ashcroft. To Victor Banerjee's amazement, Angela Lansbury left her seat and rushed to the stage. "I know it would have been her dearest wish to be here with you all on this incredibly happy, joyous occasion for her, but I also know that you understand the circumstances which prevented it," Lansbury said, without elaborating. Instead, she lauded her "dear friend" for "her consummate artistry, her delicacy and beauty."

Steve Martin earned a big hand when he appeared to give the Art Direction Award. "Hi, I'm Steve Martin. They asked me to say that. They said, 'Steve, we're in China tonight.' I said, 'They know me in China! Billions of 'em.' I can't walk down the street in China—'Steve, how's it going?

"I could never imagine this in my wildest dreams."
—Prince

What are you doing here?' " The camera showed Dr. Haing S. Ngor laughing with the audience. *Amadeus* won its third Oscar and the Czech set decorator thanked Milos Forman.

Eddie Murphy's witticisms in *Beverly Hills Cop* lost the Original Screenplay Award to *Places in the Heart*. A choked-up Robert Benton saluted "Miss Sally Field; without her genius and courage I would not be standing here tonight." The camera found a smiling Sally as Benton ended with thanks to "the people of Waxahachie." David Lean and Robert Towne's dog were bested for the Best Adapted Screenplay Award by *Amadeus*' Peter Shaffer, who said with the pride of an agent, "my great pleasure now is that Mozart has now reached millions and millions of people who had not heard him before." When *A Passage to India*'s Maurice Jarre won the Score Award a minute later, he sighed,"I was lucky Mozart wasn't eligible this year."

Kathleen Turner proclaimed Prince the winner of the Best Song Score Oscar for *Purple Rain* and he was escorted to the stage by two band members as Bill Conti's orchestra played a stately version of the film's title song. The musician's fans gave him a second chorus of cheers when he reached the podium. "Thank you very much," Prince said, and introduced the young ladies. "This is Lisa and this is Wendy." After the women were applauded, Prince admitted, "This is very unbelievable. I could never imagine this in my wildest dreams." At Lazar's Spago party, Beverly Sills yelled back to the screen, "I can't believe it either!" After thanking every member of his band "and, most of all, God," Prince and company exited the stage, bypassed the pressroom, returned to the purple limo, and went dancing at Tramp.

The next big ovation greeted an elephant that was led onstage to model a costume from *A Passage to India*. There was a close-up of David Lean laughing, but he quieted down when the Oscar went to the Czech who designed *Amadeus*. "This is the biggest and happiest day of my film career," said Theodor Pistek, "because it is my first American movie."

Albert Finney was the only nominee missing when Shirley MacLaine ripped open the Best Actor envelope. The winner was F. Murray Abraham for *Amadeus*. After being kissed by his wife, the New York actor rose, straightened his green tuxedo tie, and walked over and kissed Milos Forman. Abraham rushed up the stairs in his cowboy boots and confessed, "It would be a lie if I told you I didn't know what to say because I've been working on this speech for about twenty-five years, but you're not going to hear any of those speeches because none of them are under forty-five seconds. It's easy to gamble everything when you have nothing to lose and Milos Forman had everything to lose when he gave such brilliant roles to Tom Hulce and me. His courage became my inspiration. There's only one thing missing for me tonight, and that's to have Tom Hulce standing by my side." This sentiment provoked "bravos" from the audience, and home viewers were treated to a lengthy close-up of a moved Tom Hulce. Abraham was tempted to leave 'em applauding, but he rushed back to the podium screaming, "Wait a minute. I still have more time—half of this statue belongs to my beloved wife, Kate."

After Diana Ross unsuccessfully tried to entice the audience into clapping along with her rendition of the Best Song nominee "I Just Called to Say I Love You," Gregory Hines settled the question of which Top 10 hit would win the Oscar. "I Just Called To Say I Love You" 's Stevie Wonder was the winner and the blind songwriter wore a tieless tux with multicolored sequinned lapels. "I'd like to accept this Award in the name of Nelson Mandela," stated Wonder, referring to the South African civil rights leader who has been in prison since 1964. Dionne Warwick and Gene Wilder were also thanked. Then David Lean lost his second Award when *The Killing Fields*' Jim Clark, wearing a brown tie with his tux, accepted the Film Editing Oscar. Clark plugged Lean's upcoming competitor, "Roland Joffé, making his film debut as a veteran director!"

Cary Grant walked out and recalled making *The Philadelphia Story* with his Oscar-winning

"I hope I won't let the occasion down too badly."
—Laurence Olivier

costar James Stewart, and then gave Stewart a second Oscar—an Honorary one—for "his fifty years of memorable performances, for his high ideals, both on and off the screen, with the respect and affection of his colleagues." The recipient also won the first standing ovation of the evening. Stewart thanked "everybody who was there with me, helping me to get along so well between 'action' and 'cut,' " singling out Frank Capra and other directors "who so generously and brilliantly guided me through the no-man's land of my own good intentions." His final tribute was to "the audience—all you wonderful folks out there. Thank you for being so kind to me over the years. You've given me a wonderful life."

Father-to-be Steven Spielberg appeared with the Best Director envelope and said, "This seems a fitting moment for us to pay our respects to the French director François Truffaut." After the audience applauded the late star of *Close Encounters of the Third Kind,* Spielberg revealed that David Lean had completely struck out. "I'm very proud because this is an American movie on which a lot of Czechoslovakian artists and technicians collaborated," said *Amadeus*' Milos Forman, "and to get this kind of recognition from the members of the Academy for this kind of collaboration is very encouraging for more than artistic or box office reasons."

Best Actress presenter Robert Duvall prefaced by saying that all the nominees had played "roles which also served as role models." Judy Davis, dressed in what *Entertainment Tonight* called "punk suffragette," seemed amused by the notion of Miss Quested as a role model. Two of the farmers' wives, Jessica Lange and Sally Field, wore black strapless gowns, while Sissy Spacek sported a man's white suit. The winner, for the second time, was Sally Field, who shook her head in disbelief when she heard the verdict. En route to the stage, she turned and looked over to Robert Benton, raising her arms over her head in a "we did it" gesture. The director was in for more appreciation when the winner started speaking. "Oh, Benton, what you did for me, you changed my life, truly. This means so much more to me this time, I don't know why. I think the first time I hardly felt it because it was all too new." Field thanked her cast, "my players," and then her family,"for having patience with this obsession of me." In a throbbing voice, she concluded, "I haven't had an orthodox career and I wanted more than anything to have your respect. The first time I didn't feel it, but this time I feel it and I can't deny the fact you like me—right now, you *like* me!" The audience responded with a spontaneous burst of laughter and applause and viewers saw costars John Malkovich and Lindsay Crouse and Best Actress loser Sissy Spacek react to Field's emotionalism.

"Ladies and gentlemen, we have, as always, saved the very best of the best for last," promised Jack Lemmon, bringing on Lord Laurence Olivier to present the Best Picture Oscar. The actor, in a ruffled tuxedo shirt, enjoyed the evening's second standing ovation. Oscar-show writer Larry Gelbart had come up with a snappy one-liner for Olivier—portraying the producer as "a man of humility, pride, stamina, imagination, and, as we say in Parliament, a man with a lot of chutzpah!"—but it quickly became apparent to Gelbart and the rest of the Academy that Lord Larry had thrown away the script and was winging it. "Dear ladies and gentlemen, thank you," he said, "I hope I won't let the occasion down too badly." But he was off to a bad start when he opened the envelope without reading the nominees. The audience buzzed with apprehension as oblivious Olivier continued on, declaiming with theatrical flourish, "The winner is *Amadeus*!" Applause broke out, and producer Saul Zaentz shook hands with Faye Dunaway and loser David Puttnam on his way to the stage."Gregory Peck and Larry Gelbart asked me to speak for fifty-five minutes to make it a four-hour show, but I only have thirty-two minutes prepared," Zaentz commented, to the amusement of the hall. The producer corrected Olivier's oversight by naming the competition and observing, "The five pictures nominated all had a curious relationship in the fact

"I think on some level I must be monumentally unsophisticated."
—Sally Field

that the filmmakers who made them had to fight and overcome many obstacles to make their films."

Zaentz didn't meet his thirty-two minute prediction, but at three minutes and fifty-eight seconds, he gave the longest acceptance speech of the night. By the time the winners and the elephant were paraded on stage for the finale, Gregory Peck had lost his bet—the show ran over its three-hour goal by ten minutes and thirty seconds.

Aftermath

"When I won for *Norma Rae,*" Sally Field reminisced backstage, "all I could think about was that I was going to fall down, I'm going to humiliate myself . . . my emotional life was blocked by this ridiculous 'don't look like a jerk' feeling." When asked to comment on her appeal, the two-time winner replied, "I think on some level I must be monumentally unsophisticated. There must be something very ordinary about me. I look like a lot of people you might have grown up with." *USA Today*'s Monica Collins dismissed Field's "you like me" address as a "teary, 'I'm OK—you're OK' acceptance speech," but Gene Siskel praised it as "one of the most open, honest admissions of the nervousness that every performer has . . . a beautiful moment." TV commentator Steve Edwards told his viewers, "This is the night Gidget got respect."

Best Actor F. Murray Abraham was almost as self-effacing as Field. "I still ride the subway and no one recognizes me," he insisted. A reporter asked if his Oscar would transform him into a leading man. "C'mon, do I look like a leading man?" Abraham retorted. "Cary Grant, now that's a leading man." Another journalist asked if, at the very least, an Oscar meant he would never have to work in commercials again. "I may do them—Olivier does them," he said. Surely, the press demanded, the Oscar would have some good effect on him. "Well," Abraham said, smiling, "I don't believe my wife has ever made love to an Academy Award winner before."

The *Los Angeles Times* remarked that Abraham's producer and director looked "content but utterly calm, as if they were picking up a library book rather than a fistful of Oscars," but backstage Milos Forman cooed, "I love this show! I love the Oscars!" The émigré director was also happy because he had just learned that *Amadeus* had been cleared for distribution in Czechoslovakia, making it his first American movie to be shown there. A second Oscar didn't alter Forman's philosophy on the Awards. "It's a game," he maintained, "and we'll celebrate tonight and not to worry because tomorrow's another day. Another day, another game."

"I've covered the Night of the 100 Stars and I've just been to the British Film Academy Awards, but *this* is a party," exclaimed Dith Pran, as he celebrated with *The Killing Fields* platoon at the Governors' Ball. Jeff Bridges' mother made her way over to one of her son's former costars, Sam Waterston, to tell him, "We rooted for Jeff but we rooted for you, too." According to *Entertainment Tonight,* "Adolph Caesar and his wife were the smoothest celebrity dancers," and the loser paid one last visit to the TV program to quote *Hamlet:* "How all occasions do inform against me and spur my dull revenge."

Three-time loser David Lean was also at the ball, remarking, "It never gets easier. You worry and wonder and keep telling yourself you haven't got a chance of winning—but it still hurts when you lose." He did have one cause for celebrating—Peggy Ashcroft's victory. "I'm sure she's the most amazed person in the business," Lean said. "She didn't even think she was terribly good in the film." But the director couldn't congratulate the winner because she had taken her phone off the hook in London. After flying in from Los Angeles, Ashcroft came down with the flu, thereby missing both the Oscars and Sir Michael Redgrave's funeral. The London *Sunday Times* empathized with the invalid and her "shock of lying in bed and seeing, 8,000 miles away, someone other than her nominee pick up her first-ever Oscar." Gregory Peck got through later in the day and apologized

"I still ride the subway and no one recognizes me."
—F. Murray Abraham

for "the terrible, unintentional mix-up." Ashcroft told the *Times* that, through Victor Banerjee, she had wanted to thank India "for inspiring E. M. Forster and Lean, for making the literature and art possible." The winner, nevertheless, wrote a thank-you note to friend Angela Lansbury and picked up her statuette from Sir Richard Attenborough twelve days later.

"The best show in town *wasn't* the Oscars," headlined the *Los Angeles Herald-Examiner*, "The Lazars' party at Spago is their best yet." "This party is so private," mused Cynthia Allison, a television reporter standing outside the restaurant as Laurence Olivier, Sally Field and Steve Martin mingled inside, "maybe it's like the Oscars when they originally started, when it was just a big family party, no press was allowed inside, and everybody just had a bash." Liz Smith concurred and asked in her column, "Why doesn't the Academy get wise and try to employ Mary and Swifty to help plan the official show and the Academy's own largely ignored party?"

Columnist Smith also reprimanded the Academy for the backstage squabble over Amy Irving."The whole thing is to laugh," she wrote."Just imagine anybody in Hollywood these days taking a high moral 'attitude' over an unwed mother! These people are denizens of a business that gives us things like *Porky's Revenge*." And Stevie Wonder's support for Nelson Mandela drew a response from the South African government—they banned his music.

Time opined, "This year's ceremony was not one of the world's longest. But, except for the introduction of a beguiling elephant . . . it was still one of the most boring." And Shirley MacLaine told *Women's Wear Daily*, "It was so precision-like that a little bit of the heart went out of it. Everyone was so concerned about the clock and the blinking red light. They were afraid to feel because feeling takes time." But the worst news for the Academy came with *Daily Variety*'s headline OSCARCAST HITS BOTTOM IN RATINGS. The shortened show "plunged to the lowest rating ever," causing Academy President Gene Allen to conclude, "You can't win."

Army Archerd reported on the reception held for someone who did win, "Sally Field returned to the Florence, Ariz. (pop. 3,723), location of *Murphy's Romance*, to find this banner across Main St.: 'You Found a Place in Our Hearts.' " F. Murray Abraham was similarly greeted in the lobby of his Eastern Parkway apartment building, where his neighbors had festooned the room with signs proclaiming WELCOME HOME, SALIERI. The New York tabloids treated him like a conquering hero; the *Post* dubbed him the "Crown (Heights) Prince of H'Wood" and the *News* called him "the biggest winner in Brooklyn since the Dodgers." Reporters stopped by to photograph the winner eating breakfast the next morning and learned that he had already received film offers from Lina Wertmuller and Arnold Schwarzenegger. Meanwhile, down the street, hardware store owner Jerry Wald informed the *Post*, "Because of people like him, this neighborhood is coming back."

On the West Coast, news hounds followed career counselor Dr. Ngor as he showed off his Oscar to his coworkers at the Asian Refugee Center. "I had to come to work today. I scheduled two appointments," he said. The doctor added that the best part of winning was "now, I represent Cambodian people to the world." Hollywood columnist James Bacon groused, "For the life of me, I can never understand why they give Oscars to nonactors who, in all probability, will never work again." But Dr. Ngor had news for Bacon—he had just hired an agent from the same office that handled Milos Forman.

1985

"Cher doesn't trust men and I don't blame her."
—Peter Bogdanovich

Someone's name was left off Oscar's guest list, turning the 1985 Academy Awards into a free-for-all.

Love Has No Middle Ground

Australian director Peter Weir was in the Central American country of Belize, preparing his new film, *The Mosquito Coast*, when he was informed that the financing had fallen through. He called his agent and said, "I need work. Find me what they call a 'go' project." The agent found a project at Paramount set to go in three weeks—all it needed was a director. Weir took the job, read the script about a Philadelphia cop hiding out among the Amish, and said, "*Witness* is full of clichés, but melodrama is a valid form of entertainment." When the director tried to eliminate the cliché of a love scene, first-time screenwriters Earl W. Wallace and William Kelley complained to producer Edward S. Feldman that the late-comer was ruining their work. Said Wallace, "When you're talking a love story, either it happens or it doesn't happen, there's no middle ground. That's what we had to fight for." Paramount wanted the love story.

Paul Newman and Tom Selleck turned it down, so producer Feldman asked himself, "Who of the younger actors today would look good in the big Amish hat like Gary Cooper did as a Quaker? Who's Gary Cooper today?" His answer was the same actor who had replaced Tom Selleck when he turned down *Raiders of the Lost Ark*—Harrison Ford. Filming took place on location around Lancaster, Pennsylvania and the filmmakers rented a farmhouse from a non-Amish couple who first checked with their neighbors. "They said it wouldn't bother them and now they are even asking for souvenirs," said Paula Krantz to the *New York Times*. Five Amish boys got so carried away they paid a crew member to drive them to Southern California, a situation which sounded to Edward S. Feldman like "the plot of a teenage sex comedy."

Non-nominee Cher manages to upstage Best Supporting Actor winner Don Ameche.

Witness was no sex comedy but it was sexy. Andrew Sarris was thrilled that Ford and Kelly McGillis, as the Amish love interest, "have resurrected that marvelous Look that passed between men and women in films gone by and that I thought had gone forever in the so-called liberated age of instant gratification and nonrepression." Pauline Kael, on the other hand, agreed with Peter Weir that *Witness* was cliché-ridden, calling the film "a compendium of scenes I had hoped never to see again. There's the city person stranded in the sticks and learning to milk a cow and—oh, yes—having to get up at 4:30 a.m. to do it." Despite the efforts of the "National Committee for Amish Religious Freedom" to lead a boycott against the film "as a pocket-book reprimand to all who would exploit the Amish for gain," *Witness* was the first big hit of 1985.

Cher and Share Alike

Witness opened the Cannes Film Festival in May, but *Variety* reported "it did not win a standing ovation from the SRO glitterati in the Grand Auditorium." Opening night was topped off with a fireworks display, but another American entry in the Festival later provided even more excitement—a verbal shooting match. *Mask* was a movie about a dying teenager with a disease that has made him grotesquely deformed. Cher starred as the kid's mother, a dope-addict member of a bike gang. *Entertainment Tonight*'s Leonard Maltin said, "Cher gives a terrific performance. She's a likely contender for next year's Academy Award." The movie was Peter Bogdanovich's first box-office success in ages, but he was unhappy and sued Universal for going behind his back and changing the music on the soundtrack from Bruce Springsteen to Bob Seger. By the time of Cannes, the director and his star were going at one another,

"It's a comedy, Jack."
—John Huston

too. "Don't invite Cher and Peter Bogdanovich to the same festival," warned Roger Ebert. "At opposing press conferences an hour apart, they gladly shared their low opinion of each other." Cher on Bogdanovich: "I never listened to his direction because I never liked it." Bogdanovich on Cher: "She doesn't trust men and I don't blame her . . . I had to use every trick in the book to get that performance out of her, then Cher told the U.S. press I had nothing to do with her performance." Cher won Best Actress at Cannes; the only catch was she had to split the honor with co-winner Norma Aleandro, the star of the Argentine political drama, *The Official Story*. Director John Boorman, presenting the award at the closing ceremonies, told the actress, "Ma chère Cher—sorry you have to share."

The Gay Anarchist

William Hurt, the Best Actor winner at Cannes for *Kiss of the Spider Woman*, didn't have to share his award with anyone. Based on the novel by Argentinean writer Manuel Puig, *Kiss of the Spider Woman* detailed the relationship between two cell-mates in a South American prison—a Marxist political prisoner and a homosexual window dresser who passes the time by spinning out the plots of his favorite movies. Argentinean-born director Hector Babenco's first choices were Burt Lancaster as the gay character Molina and Raul Julia as the leftist. When Lancaster had a heart attack before funding was raised, Babenco turned to William Hurt. "Listen, my first impulse is to say no because I think you are too handsome, you are too well built," the director said, but he allowed Hurt to audition. He got the job. Turned down by all the Hollywood studios, Babenco eventually got his money from several independent—mostly Brazilian—sources, and about the only thing the two American stars got upfront were decent hotel rooms in Brazil. "To prepare for the part," wrote *Women's Wear Daily*, "Hurt explains he explored Molina's world—the gay bars and dance places of Sao Paolo, which he travelled in the company of a Brazilian dancer."

When Brazil entered the final product at Cannes, it still had no distributor; one executive snarled, "We don't like anarchist projects." After Hurt's victory, *Kiss* was finally picked up for U.S. release by a small independent company called Island Alive, but its troubles weren't over. "We couldn't get people to screenings," a public relations executive told the *New York Times*. "So we called them on an individual basis and tried to make them feel guilty. We must have had thirty to fifty screenings in New York before it opened." The critics liked what they saw. "If Busby Berkeley had ever made a movie about politics and illusion," analogized *Time*'s Richard Schickel, "it might have come out something like this infectious, sobering film." As for the acting, the *New York Times*' Janet Maslin wrote, "If Mr. Hurt has never been so daringly extroverted on the screen before, Mr. Julia has never been so restrained." *Kiss* was the art-house hit of the year, but Island Alive didn't last long; in November, the company halved itself into "Island" and "Alive."

The Hustons, Part Two

In a summer dominated by science-fiction, teen-oriented comedies and Sylvester Stallone going to Viet Nam, there was one movie other than *Kiss of the Spider Woman* aimed at adults—John Huston's *Prizzi's Honor*. The director sent Richard Condon's novel, a black comedy about a dimwitted Mafia hitman, to his old *Chinatown* costar, Jack Nicholson, who had been living with Huston's daughter Anjelica for years. "I saw it like a humorless person would," admitted Nicholson when he read the book. "I read it as a very straight sort of story, and didn't really get it." When the first draft of the script didn't make things clearer, Huston put his arm around the actor and whispered, "Jack, it's a comedy."

The studio heads didn't get it either, and producer John Foreman shopped the Nicholson-

"Now I'm going into the deep section of the pool."
—Steven Spielberg

Huston combo around until finally ABC's motion picture division agreed to bankroll the picture. Kathleen Turner signed as Nicholson's lover-rival, and the supporting cast included character actors Robert Loggia, John Randolph, and New York acting teacher William Hickey, 56, as the eighty-three-year-old Don of a Brooklyn crime family. In the showy role of Nicholson's vengeful ex-fiancée, Huston cast his daughter, who had acted for him once before, at the age of fifteen, in a disastrous flop called *A Walk with Love and Death*. Having studied acting in the meantime, Anjelica was ready this go-round. She told the press that she and her costar stayed in separate hotels during filming because "There were elements of the hit man in Jack at the time and I didn't want to be around him too much."

During production, the *New York Post* observed that "veteran director Huston, seventy-eight, looked frail during the shoot and needed to rest after walking half a block," but when the movie came out, Pauline Kael raved, "If John Huston's name was not on *Prizzi's Honor*, I'd have thought a fresh new talent had burst on the scene, and he'd certainly be the hottest new director in Hollywood," adding that the movie is "like *The Godfather* acted out by The Munsters." The entire cast received hosannahs, but it was Anjelica Huston, as the Brooklyn Mafia princess, who the *New York Times*'s Aljean Harmetz declared "ran off with the picture." Although a market executive at 20th Century–Fox stated that the ad campaign was designed "to let the public know it's okay to laugh with the film," another executive revealed that not all of the public was catching on: "The movie is weak in the South and young people don't like it." But audiences in metropolitan areas loved it; over half of the film's grosses came from a quintet of cities: New York, Los Angeles, Chicago, San Francisco and Boston.

Spielberg Goes Off Deep End

Steven Spielberg had the adolescent market cornered; in addition to his new, much-ballyhooed TV series *Amazing Stories*, he had produced two summer hits, *The Goonies* and *Back to the Future*, the latter the year's most profitable film. But Spielberg saved his biggest challenge for Christmas. As he put it: "It's as if I've been swimming in water up to my waist all my life—and I'm great at it—but now I'm going into the deep section of the pool." Translation: he was going to make a movie out of Alice Walker's *The Color Purple*, a Pulitzer–prize winning novel about an oppressed Southern black woman. One Hollywood wag referred to Spielberg's gamble as "Close Encounters With the Third World."

To play the story's protagonist, Spielberg cast Whoopi Goldberg (née Caryn Johnson), a thirty-five-year-old stand-up comedienne who had just hit the big time after Mike Nichols produced her one-woman show on Broadway. Spielberg had met her at a party where she mimicked E.T. landing in Oakland, getting strung out on drugs, and winding up in jail. "He loved it and he said, 'I think I might be directing *The Color Purple* and it's yours if you want it,' " Goldberg recalled. Although she had never been in a film before, the comedienne said she grew up watching old movies in a Manhattan housing project, thus giving her a rapport on the set with fellow movie buff Spielberg. "He would say, 'I want Ray Milland in *The Lost Weekend*' and I would know exactly what he meant," Goldberg said. "We didn't have to spend hours discussing it." The role of Goldberg's strong-willed step-daughter went to another first-time actress; Oprah Winfrey was a Chicago talk show host whom *Color*'s coproducer Quincy Jones noticed while flipping channels in his hotel room. When Winfrey heard about the film, she said, "I prayed at night, 'Dear God, find me a way to get into this movie.' I would have done anything: 'best boy' or 'water girl.' " Tina Turner was first choice for the role of a sultry blues singer, but she passed, so Spielberg went with Margaret Avery, whom he had directed in a commercial fifteen years earlier. Like Winfrey, Avery had relied on divine guidance. "When I learned what an incredible

"At first, I was very kind. Now I'm just ready to slap them."
—Oprah Winfrey

amount of talent they were seeing," she said, "I got down on my knees and prayed, 'Give me the confidence to go on.' "

Spielberg took another big step by marrying Amy Irving, who earlier in the year had given birth to their son, Max. But on the eve of the film's Christmastime premiere the director confessed to opening night jitters: "The biggest risk, for me, is doing a movie about *people* for the first time in my career—and failing . . . It's the risk of being judged—and accused of not having the sensibility to do character studies." The *Hollywood Reporter*'s Arthur Knight made no such accusations. "To those who think of Steven Spielberg solely as the creator of science-fiction adventure movies or high-tech horror tales, *The Color Purple* will come as an exhilarating surprise," he wrote. "For all its darker colorations, the film is an ode to the goodness of mankind." The *Today Show*'s Gene Shalit pulled out all the stops, exclaiming, "It should be against the law not to see *The Color Purple*."

But other critics didn't grade the director so highly. The *Philadelphia Inquirer* complained that Spielberg "has shaved off most of its scratchy edges and washed away a lot of the rude glimmers that ran through it . . . He has taken Walker's bitter colloquial anthem and turned it into a big Hollywood tear-jerker." *Time*'s Richard Corliss scoffed that the characters were drawn with "Norman Rockwell attitudes"; the *New York Daily News* thought "it might have been directed by the late Walt Disney"; and *Variety* called it a "fairy tale." Goldberg also got mixed notices. To *New York*'s David Denby, she was "coy and calculating . . . She uses her huge eyes like a cartoon pussycat," but *Newsweek*'s David Ansen wrote, "From the start you can sense Celie's hidden strength in Goldberg's rivetting presence. This is powerhouse acting, all the more so because the rage and exhilaration are held in reserve."

Spielberg had to deal with more than film critics. Dozens of people picketed the Hollywood premiere, arguing that the film reenforced racial stereotypes by portraying black men as sadistic brutes. Protests from both the NAACP and a group called the Coalition Against Black Exploitation continued through the movie's release. Oprah Winfrey said that when people accused her of playing an Aunt Jemima role, "At first, I was very kind. Now I'm just ready to slap them." Coproducer Quincy Jones responded, "it's impossible to put the whole story of the black race in America into one picture. That's too much of a burden for any picture to take." Yet, the controversy only fueled interest in the film, and *The Color Purple* soon joined the list of top-grossers along with the other Spielberg megahits.

Streep on Safari

Bowing the same day as Spielberg's opus was Universal's expensive shot at the Academy Awards, *Out of Africa*. For years, such directors as Orson Welles, David Lean and Nicholas Roeg wanted to make a film version of Danish writer Karen Blixen's memoirs of life in Africa from 1914 to 1931, but the ethereal quality of her writing stymied them. Sydney Pollack said, "I thought it was too delicate, that there was no way to do it as a movie," but he decided to film it anyway, with a screenplay by Kurt Luedtke that drew upon three books by Blixen and two about her. Looking for an actress to play the writer, the director "went to Europe to meet with all the wonderful actresses—German, Scandinavian, English. Then I met Meryl Streep in New York for twenty-five minutes and I fell in love with her." Pollack did not look far and wide for an actor to play Blixen's British lover; he chose Robert Redford, a personal friend and a box-office name who did not resemble the character he was playing—a totally bald, six-foot, six-inch Englishman.

Filming took place in Kenya, but not everyone was happy about it. An editorial in the *Kenya Times* griped, "To require independent Kenyans to play inferior to a white memsahib in a movie, just because Karen Blixen, in her book, saw

"Dear God, I knows dat I been blessed."
—Margaret Avery

Kenyans as inferior is taking it too far. The Ministry of Information should not allow foreign film firms to come here and insult us on our own soil just because some racist author wrote a racist book ages ago." There was also controversy when it was discovered that black extras culled from local tribes were paid only half as much as white extras. The filmmakers contended that it was simple supply-and-demand economics, but once the story broke, they equalized salaries.

Six weeks before the film's premiere, Marilyn Beck reported, "Universal is busy batting down reports that the drama lacks chemistry between its two stars. And right now director Sydney Pollack is still working to whittle down *Africa* from its first rough-cut length of more than four hours." The *Hollywood Reporter* gave the studio a Christmas gift by rhapsodizing, "*Out of Africa* is a splendid, beautifully composed love story in a resplendent holiday film and it should appeal to a world-wide audience." More glad tidings came from *Time*'s Richard Schickel, who called it "the free-spirited, fullhearted gesture that everyone has been waiting for the movies to make all decade long." Playing Scrooge, however, was Andrew Sarris, who felt the epic "plods along at an elephantine pace," and called it "a failed love story. A lumpy simulated travelogue." Some critics said Meryl Streep gave her best performance, while others were beginning to feel enough was enough with her movie accents. Liz Smith snickered that in Denmark, "Streep's accent has become something of a national joke. One TV station ran film snippets and asked viewers to call in. Most Danes agreed that Meryl sounds like she's from somewhere, but not from Denmark."

The cast member who received nothing but praise was Klaus Maria Brandauer, the Austrian actor who played Blixen's ne'er-do-well husband. Brandauer told the *Los Angeles Times* he had met the character's real-life nephew who had requested, "Please do everything to make him charming because he was a charming man." Gene Siskel was so charmed he said, "Brandauer, one of the great actors of the world today, is spectacular." Also hailed were Milena Canonero's costumes; *Newsweek* predicted "the impressive richness and beauty of the African colors and clothes promise to set off a far-ranging fashion trend," and the promise was kept when sales skyrocketed at Banana Republic, a chain of stores specializing in safari-wear. With so much box-office and critical success, Universal executives waited anxiously for the year-end critics' awards.

Island Girl

Universal did win Best Picture when the Los Angeles Critics began the awards season, but the winner wasn't *Out of Africa*. The award went to *Brazil*, a bleak, $15 million, two-and-a-half-hour comedy, directed by Monty Python's Terry Gilliam and set in an Orwellian society, which the studio had considered unreleasable. The only reason the critics saw it was because Gilliam sneaked them in to screenings that Universal was having to attract buyers who might take the albatross off its back. Cashing in on the surprise win, the studio rushed *Brazil* in theaters to qualify for the Oscar. The Los Angeles scribes did not completely forget *Out of Africa*—Meryl Streep was named Best Actress. William Hurt won Best Actor for *Kiss of the Spider Woman*, meaning little Island Pictures was making it in the big league. The small company was also ready with a challenger for the Best Actress Oscar, and Streep's costar was partially responsible.

Peter Masterson, a Texas-born stage director, was itching to direct a movie, so his friend Robert Redford advised, "You ought to pick something from your home you feel deeply about." Masterson picked *The Trip To Bountiful*, a 1953 television play written by his second cousin, Horton Foote, about an old Texas woman who wants to return to her childhood home before she dies. The film cost $3 million and starred Geraldine Page, sixty-one. The director said, "I just let Geraldine act. But she warned me to watch out for when she was up to her 'old tricks.' Whenever she started to screw up her face, I would tell her—in a nice way." Vincent

"I called every person in the Academy and said if they couldn't get out of the house I would show it to them there."
—Menahem Golan

Canby had nice things to say: "As Mrs. Watts, Geraldine Page has never been in better form. . . . It's a wonderful role, and the performance ranks with the best things Miss Page has done on screen." But Howard Kissel of *Women's Wear Daily* identified with the movie's supposedly shrewish daughter-in-law: "Carrie is played by Geraldine Page with her grating voice, peevish manner and her usual collection of nervous tics. Who would want such a thing in the house?"

Island's Oscar campaign suffered a setback when the New York Film Critics gave their Best Actress plaque to Cher's cowinner from Cannes, Norma Aleandro in *The Official Story*. *Village Voice* columnist Michael Musto quoted the Argentinean actress's acceptance speech: "I'm not sure if I'm drimming, but that's okay because it's a beautiful drim." The New Yorkers gave the bulk of their prizes to *Prizzi's Honor*—Best Picture, Best Director, Best Actor (Jack Nicholson's record-setting fifth win from this group) and Best Supporting Actress for Anjelica Huston. *Out of Africa*'s Klaus Maria Brandauer got the Best Supporting Actor plaque. Best Foreign Film went to *Ran*, directed by a man almost as old as John Huston, seventy-five-year-old Akira Kurosawa.

Japanese War Lords

Patience was chief among Kurosawa's virtues; finishing his screenplay in 1973, he waited eight years to get the money to film it. The man behind Luis Buñuel's last films, French producer Serge Silberman, finally stepped in and helped Kurosawa find the $12 million budget for *Ran*, the most expensive movie ever made in Japan. Kurosawa spun the story of a 16th Century war lord betrayed by his sons, and when he told Emi Wada he wanted period costumes, he wasn't kidding. The clothes were entirely hand-made and were woven and dyed to match colors of the sixteenth-century because Kurosawa felt modern hues weren't bright enough. Wada had her work cut out for her: 1500 costumes, including those for 250 horses. It took her three years. Kurosawa used 1400 extras and thought nothing of waiting for proper cloud formations—shooting went on for nine months. He told reporters on the set, "I am devoting myself to this. I may not be alive so long. I will spend all my remaining energy to complete it."

Ran had its world premiere at the Tokyo Film Festival, but Kurosawa didn't attend. When it opened the New York Film Festival in the fall, Kurosawa winged over to enjoy a standing ovation in the hall and a party afterwards at Tavern On The Green. The *New York Times* compared the movie to Griffith's *Birth of a Nation*, Abel Gance's *Napoleon*, and Eisenstein's *Ivan the Terrible*. Archer Winsten, in his swan song after fifty years at the *New York Post*, appreciated Emi Wada's costumes: "The war scenes are magnificently staged with what seems thousands of men and horses galloping into the fray, color-coded to indicate the different groups. This is necessary because otherwise you'd never be able to guess who's attacking whom." Meanwhile, back in Japan, the Movie Producers Association, steamed at Kurosawa for standing up the Tokyo Film Festival, retaliated by passing over *Ran* as Japan's Foreign Film entry in the Oscar race, picking a film about Alzheimer's disease instead. A representative of New York's Japan Society explained, "He snubbed them and now they're paying him back." But Kurosawa's Oscar chances weren't completely blown away: Sidney Lumet told the *Los Angeles Times* he was soliciting fellow Directors Branch members to nominate Kurosawa and he had at least one disciple in Arthur Penn, who scolded the Japanese film industry, "To overlook the work of a man who is at the very peak of his career seems gravely unjust."

Runaway Campaigns

Kurosawa was involved in another movie receiving a big Oscar push—sort of. Over twenty years earlier, he had written a screenplay about convicts who hijack a train as their escape vehicle. The script ultimately fell into the hands of producers Menahem Golan and Yorum Globus, who were eager to eradicate the less-than-prestigious

"The company is shocked and dismayed."
—Warner Brothers
trade paper ad

image of their company, The Cannon Group, best known for Charles Bronson and Chuck Norris exploitation films. The producers brought in a slew of writers to rewrite Kurosawa—but keeping his name prominent in the credits—and hired Andrei Konchalovsky, a Russian now living in Brentwood, to direct the film, called *Runaway Train*. Jon Voight consented to playing the hardened prisoner who masterminds the escape because, "I had this adolescent enthusiasm about playing a tough guy for a change." Although the *Hollywood Reporter* wrote off the philosophical action film as "Moby Diesel," Golan and Globus promoted the hell out of *Runaway Train*, celebrating its opening with a seven-page spread in the *Reporter* and continuing with two dozen trade paper ads during the nominating season. Golan bragged to the *Los Angeles Times* that Cannon had "spent $150,000 on the trade paper ad campaign and another $30,000 on a series of screenings for Academy members that included—in about thirty instances—private screenings in the homes of voters too feeble to get to a theatre." Golan elaborated, "I called every person in the Academy and said if they couldn't get out of the house I would show it to them there."

"It's worth noting that the two holiday releases getting the most Oscar talk," pontificated the *Hollywood Reporter*'s Martin Grove, "are from the two majors with the greatest management stability." Stable or not, neither Warner Bros. nor Universal were taking any chances on their costly investments. From Warners, Academy members received a forty-four page souvenir booklet of *The Color Purple* done up in a fake book binding. As a keepsake of *Out of Africa*, Universal sent out a portfolio of color photographs of the Dark Continent and Meryl Streep, which, wrote Aljean Harmetz, one voter dismissed as "the National Geographic ploy."

The one campaign ad that made everyone stand up and notice appeared on the very last day of the nominating period, long after most members had already submitted their ballots. "Dear God," the ad began, "My name is Margaret Avery. I knows dat I been blessed by Alice Walker, Steven Spielberg, and Quincy Jones." Among the other revelations Avery had for the Lord was that "Now I is up for one of the nominations fo' Best Supporting Actress alongst with some fine, talented ladies that I is proud to be in the company of." The epistle was signed, "Your little daughter Margaret Avery." The actress maintained that she had consulted Alice Walker before running the ad and that Walker had approved it, but one thing was certain, no campaign had raised as many eyebrows since 1960 when Chill Wills asked voters to remember the Alamo.

The Nominations

God smiled on his little daughter Margaret Avery, but not on her director. The *Los Angeles Herald-Examiner* headlined:

Africa, Purple 11, Spielberg 0

Out of Africa and *The Color Purple* tied with eleven nominations each, but Spielberg, who had already won a Directors Guild nomination, was not in the Academy's Director race. Sydney Pollack was there, as were the directors of the other three Best Picture nominees: *Prizzi's Honor*'s John Huston, *Witness*' Peter Weir, and *Kiss of the Spider Woman*'s Hector Babenco. The fifth nominee was Akira Kurosawa for *Ran*, which pulled in a total of four nominations. Japan's official entry for Best Foreign Film didn't get nominated for anything. As for the Los Angeles Critics' favorite, *Brazil*, it won two nominations, for Art Direction and Original Screenplay.

But it was the Spielberg snub, dubbed by the *New York Post* as "Omission Impossible," that everybody wanted to talk about. Columnist Kirk Honeycutt chortled, "What wouldn't you have given to be a fly on the wall over at Spielberg's headquarters on Wednesday?" But the director knew better than to repeat his humiliation of ten years earlier when cameras caught him getting the news the Academy had rejected him for *Jaws* in favor of Federico Fellini; this time the non-nominee was, as the *Los Angeles Herald-Examiner* put

"It means a lot to me, but next year it's going to be a Trivial Pursuit question."
—Meg Tilly

it, "vacationing on a yacht in some undisclosed waters."

Under a Cloud

With no Spielberg around for a response, Warner Bros. jumped into action with a trade paper ad that expressed "sincere appreciation" to the Academy for the eleven nominations and then concluded, "At the same time, the company is shocked and dismayed that the movie's primary creative force—Steven Spielberg—was not recognized." Aljean Harmetz reported that "a number of people . . . made the assumption that Spielberg had masterminded the statement," although Warners denied the accusation. Columnist Martin Grove warned, "It would be best for all concerned that the ballotting not take place under a cloud" and recommended that the Academy "appoint a blue-ribbon panel" to investigate "any organized effort to dissuade voters from nominating Spielberg." Academy President Robert Wise said forget it, maintaining that the members of the Directors Branch "voted their artistic and creative feelings." One member, Henry Jaglom, vented his feelings, telling the *Los Angeles Times*, "The nominations for Babenco and Kurosawa are great. The whole thing is a sign the Directors Branch is growing up." Of the non-nominee, Jaglom said, "He took this wonderful material and turned it into zip-a-dee *Song of the South*." The *Los Angeles Herald-Examiner*'s Gregg Kilday shot back, "*Out of Africa* isn't a model of documentary realism, either, a fact purists seem willing to overlook." The one unperturbed voice was John Huston's, who told Army Archerd that Spielberg "has had so much success, he can afford to miss a beat." Huston could afford to be so sanguine; with Spielberg out of the running, he now held the lead in the Best Director race.

Talk to the Animals

A Huston victory had the extra appeal of echoing the 1948 Oscars when he won two Awards and directed his father Walter to a Best Supporting Actor Award; this year daughter Anjelica had swept the film critics' awards and was the shoo-in for Best Supporting Actress. "I'm offered parts these days as opposed to sort of having to go along and try to squeeze into interviews," rejoiced the nominee. The one pre-Oscar trophy Anjelica had lost was the Golden Globe, which went to Meg Tilly for playing a nutty nun in *Agnes of God*. "It means a lot to me," said Tilly of her Academy nomination, "but next year it's going to be a Trivial Pursuit question." The press flocked around the competing nominees from *The Color Purple*. When TV cameras found Oprah Winfrey reacting to the news, she was jumping up and down on her desk. Calming down, she said her nomination was a vindication, "I always knew I'd be an actress since I was growing up on the farm in Mississippi and sitting in the pig pen talking to those pigs." The *New York Times* headlined its profile of the actress, "Troubled Girl's Evolution Into an Oscar Nominee." Margaret Avery also took advantage of the media attention and toured the country on the talk-show circuit. When *People* gave her a hard time about her "Dear God" letter, she snapped, "That ad cost me a kitchen stove. It's easy to give lip service to thanking God, but I wanted to do something that would force me to give up something. I had been wanting a stove for ten years."

Popularity Contests

Jack Nicholson won his eighth nomination; William Hurt, his first. Hurt's producer, David Weisman, gave all the credit to the Cannes Film Festival, "Often we, in America, look to Europeans, especially the French, to tell us things that are new and different are O.K." Another first-time nominee was Harrison Ford, whose nomination prompted the *Los Angeles Times*' Shiela Benson to complain that, after his turns in the *Star Wars* and *Indiana Jones* serials, "Ford had to become Serious before he got his nomination." *Witness* producer Edward S. Feldman had another explanation for the film's eight nominations,

"I think Don Ameche will win it and I think he should—95,000 years in the movies."
—William Hickey

"*Witness* got terrific help from the airlines. About 150 Academy members told me they saw it on a plane." The most surprising nomination, wrote most columnists, was James Garner's, as Sally Field's love interest in the May-December love story *Murphy's Romance*. Jack Mathews of the *Los Angeles Times* wrote that Garner "Would win if it were a popularity contest, and it often is." Even more surprising than Garner's nomination, thought the *New York Daily News*' Kathleen Carroll, was the Academy's fifth contestant: "The January mud slides made travel so difficult that the fact *Runaway Train* was reportedly the only movie available for viewing in rainswept Malibu may explain why its two leading actors, Jon Voight and Eric Roberts, received much-coveted nominations." Nominee Voight was as grateful as Margaret Avery, telling Army Archerd, "Whatever I find that God wants me to do, I'm available."

Age Before Beauty

Columnists didn't give Voight's co-star, Eric Roberts, a prayer for the Supporting Actor Award but expected the Oscar to go instead to New York Film Critics winner Klaus Maria Brandauer. The nominee was in Vienna playing *Hamlet* when the nominations were announced; when his gig was over, he flew to Los Angeles to enjoy the Oscar hoopla. Despite Brandauer's popularity, he was competing with a sentimental favorite—1930s leading man Don Ameche receiving his first nomination for the sci-fi hit, *Cocoon*. Wrote Kathleen Carroll, "Ameche is adorably impish as a dapper bon vivant and he brings the house down with his gloriously triumphant breakdancing." Army Archerd called up the nominee and reported, "Don Ameche, seventy-seven years young, said, 'We oldsters fall into it once in a while.'" After Ameche announced he was also celebrating his fiftieth year in show business, fellow nominee William Hickey of *Prizzi's Honor* told a reporter, "I think Don Ameche will win it and I think he should—95,000 years in the movies."

All Sorts of Tacky People

Hickey's friend Geraldine Page was making her eighth try for an Oscar for *The Trip To Bountiful*, vying with newcomer Whoopi Goldberg and two-time winner Meryl Streep, on her sixth nomination for *Out of Africa*. The remaining slots were filled by former winners Anne Bancroft as a no-nonsense Mother Superior in *Agnes of God* and Jessica Lange as country singer Patsy Cline in *Sweet Dreams*. Observed Sheila Benson of the most conspicuous non-nominee, "Her shared Golden Palm at Cannes this year may not have been distinction enough to soothe generally outraged feelings in the industry over director Peter Bogdanovich's ruckus with Universal and the loser may have been Cher." The only nomination *Mask* won was for Makeup. Cher and Bogdanovich had to settle for the honors they did win later in the month from the Academy of Family Films and Family Television. Undaunted, Cher agreed to be a presenter on the show, taking consolation in the fact that her cowinner at Cannes, Norma Aleandro, wasn't nominated either, although *The Official Story* was up for Best Foreign Film and Original Screenplay. Then the Academy asked Aleandro to give the Foreign Film Award on the telecast, indicating what everybody expected the winner would be.

Though she had sentiment on her side, Geraldine Page protested, "I'd love to be champion for the most nominations without ever winning. The loser doesn't have to get up there and make a fool of herself." Still, she confessed to *People*, "I love the Oscars. All sorts of tacky people win. And watching everyone run up and down those aisles is just adorable." When the magazine pressed her about what she'd wear to the ceremonies, the perennial nominee replied, "Oh, I'll probably wear what I wore last year: a skirt I bought at a Hutchinson, Kansas thrift shop, with a blouse I found in an Indian shop on Broadway." Competitor Meryl Streep could have recycled the maternity gown she wore when she won for *Sophie's Choice*—Mr. and

"If you are making a statement, thank God, and I love you for it."
—Steven Spielberg

Mrs. Donald Gummer were expecting their third child during Oscar time. "So good, she's starting to get on people's nerves," wrote Jack Mathews of Streep's annual acclaim, and even Geraldine Page kidded about her frequent film accents, "People are beginning to wonder if she can talk normal." Whoopi Goldberg was ready to concede the race to either actress, telling *People* that Page "really deserves it" while quipping to the *New York Post*, "If Meryl wins, her husband can sculpt me an Oscar. That'll do fine." Goldberg herself won a Grammy Award for a comedy album and told the press what she thought of the Academy's Directors Branch, "It's a small bunch of people with small minds who chose to ignore the obvious."

Steven's Wonderful Life

The Directors Guild agreed with Goldberg and the *Los Angeles Times* called their awards dinner, "Spielberg's Revenge—Hollywood Style." After Milos Forman handed him his prize, Spielberg told the crowd, "I am floored by this. This is the last thing I expected. If some of you are making a statement, thank God, and I love you for it . . . I never won anything before." When the press got a hold of him, Spielberg finally spilled his guts about his non-nomination, "Certainly anyone's feelings would have been hurt, but with all the support I've received from people the last few weeks, I started to feel like Jimmy Stewart in *It's A Wonderful Life*."

"Will Academy members get on the bandwagon," wondered Aljean Harmetz, "or will they feel the director has been adequately comforted?" Since *The Color Purple* couldn't win Best Director, John Huston still maintained the lead because, as Kirk Honeycutt explained, the director "is ill and might never get another chance at Oscar." Despite his age and health, Huston found it necessary to quash romantic rumors. Hank Grant scooped, "No surprise, John Huston is denying rampant reports (printed elsewhere) that he quietly tied the knot with his Puerto Vallarta housekeeper–nurse Maricela Fernandez."

Include Kurosawa In

At the Academy's fifth annual nominee luncheon, the producer of this year's telecast, Stanley Donen, announced that the Best Picture Award would be given by Billy Wilder, Federico Fellini and Akira Kurosawa. The Best Director nominee was coming to town for both the Oscars and a special Directors Guild party where he would be given an honorary membership. The only Director nominee who made the luncheon was Sydney Pollack, recently endorsed by Kirk Honeycutt, who predicted, "*Out of Africa* is the kind of film Academy voters love to honor—big, serious and long. . . . Look for Pollack to win at the wire." Whoopi Goldberg was the only Best Actress nominee to attend and she enthused, "It's like candyland." Her costars Oprah Winfrey and Margaret Avery came, too, but none of the four *Color Purple* producers, including Steven Spielberg, put in an appearance.

"Will Spielberg be there Oscar night?" inquired a *Los Angeles Herald-Examiner* headline, but the luncheon no-show assured, "I wouldn't miss the ceremonies for anything." He did decline an offer to present Best Actor because "I felt under the current circumstances that my presence as a presenter might diminish the importance of the actual award." Though he couldn't persuade Spielberg, producer Stanley Donen convinced a number of ex-MGM contractees to participate in a musical tribute to their Alma Mater and Mikhail Baryshnikov to dance a salute to Fred Astaire, Gene Kelly and James Cagney. Then Army Archerd had this item: "Baryshnikov's ailing knee has KO'd a spectacular Oscar number." And, just a few days later, *Variety* reported that Federico Fellini "fractured a leg last week while shopping with his wife Giulietta Masina on Via Marguetta in Rome." John Huston pulled a Ruby Keeler and said he'd go on in Fellini's place.

All the major nominees were planning to attend the Awards with the exception of *Witness'* Peter Weir and Harrison Ford—financing for *The*

"It's like candyland."
—Whoopi Goldberg

Mosquito Coast finally had materialized and they were filming in Belize, where they planned to watch the Oscar show via satellite dish. The Academy attempted to attract others by distributing a sixteen-page "Viewer's Guide" to the ceremonies in nineteen newspapers around the country. The ad in *TV Guide* invited viewers to "the biggest Hollywood party of the year," and highlighted one of the show's cohosts, Robin Williams, in an effort to improve the telecast's sagging ratings. Aljean Harmetz, describing the usual frenzy of preshow preparations, commented, "this week, however, the usual hype seems to be mixed with genuine excitement and a feeling that there will be more than the usual one big surprise."

The Big Night

Ronald Reagan chose Oscar day to bomb Libya but in Hollywood people were too busy preparing for the show to notice. A group of homeless people were among the first to arrive in the bleachers and one of them told the Associated Press, "We took advantage and slept here last night. Usually we are thrown out of the Music Center area." The homeless group later gave up their choice seats to some fans in exchange for egg salad sandwiches. Making her ninth appearance outside the Dorothy Chandler Pavilion was twenty-three-year-old Dee Dee Dube of Torrance who had nothing but praise for her fellow bleacher-ites: "They aren't so rude as last year. They are civilized, even in this heat."

The first celebrity that Dube and friends saw was William Hickey, who arrived at 4:30. The *Hollywood Reporter* noted that "receiving the biggest ovations and cheers from the fans were Tom Selleck, Michael J. Fox and Whoopi Goldberg, followed closely by Huey Lewis, Phil Collins, and Lionel Richie." Margaret Avery told Army Archerd, "I will always thank God that Tina Turner was not able to do *The Color Purple*." The opponents of Avery's movie, the Coalition Against Black Exploitation, picketed across the street but they chatted with Army Archerd, too. "A very positive experience," said a spokesperson for the group. "Ordinary people in the crowd come up to us and ask why we object to the film." Objecting to the Best Director nominations was someone with a poster paraphrasing a line from *The Color Purple*: "I think it pisses God off, if you walk by *The Color Purple* and don't notice Steven Spielberg." Spielberg himself walked by without being noticed by the crowd; he had earlier told Army Archerd he was too nervous to come up to his podium. The director nominated in lieu of Spielberg did go up to Archerd's platform but, reported *Daily Variety*, Akira Kurosawa "silently nodded to those in the bleachers, who just as politely appeared to nod back."

Covering the celebrity entrances for a local TV station, 1962 Best Supporting Actress Patty Duke

Awards Ceremony

MARCH 24, 1986, 6:00 P.M.
THE DOROTHY CHANDLER PAVILION, LOS ANGELES

Your Hosts:
JANE FONDA, ALAN ALDA, ROBIN WILLIAMS
Televised over ABC

Presenters

Supporting Actress . . . . Marsha Mason and Richard Dreyfuss
Visual Effects . . . . Molly Ringwald
Animated Short Films . . Kermit the Frog, Scooter and Jim Henson
Costume Design . . . . Audrey Hepburn
Documentrary Feature . . . . Louis Gossett, Jr.
Makeup . . . . Teri Garr
Sound . . . . Irene Cara
Supporting Actor . . . . Cher
Jean Hersholt Humantarian Award . . . . Bob Hope
Documentary Short Subject . . . . Ally Sheedy and Steve Guttenberg
Art Direction . . . . Rebecca DeMornay and Michael J. Fox
Honorary Award to Paul Newman . . . . Sally Field
Sound Effects Editing . . . . Michael Winslow
Honorary Award to Alex North . . . . Quincy Jones
Live Action Films . . . . Chuck McCann and Jim McGeorge (as Laurel and Hardy)
Actress . . . . F. Murray Abraham
Cinematography . . . . Jon Cryer
Foreign Film . . . . . Norma Aleandro and Jack Valenti
Editing . . . . Whoopi Goldberg
Music Awards . . . . Debbie Reynolds, Gene Kelly and Donald O' Connor
Writing Awards . . . . Larry Gelbart
Director . . . . Barbra Streisand
Actor . . . . Sally Field
Picture . . . . John Huston, Akira Kurosawa and Billy Wilder

Performers of Nominated Songs

"Miss Celie's Blues (Sister)" . . . . Tata Vega
"The Power of Love" . . . . Huey Lewis and The News
"Say You, Say Me" . . . . Lionel Richie
"Separate Lives" . . . . Stephen Bishop
"Surprise, Surprise" . . . . Gregg Burge

"I'm sorry, ladies and gentlemen. I'm afraid we have to do the show."
—Robin Williams

was a celebrity herself to the arriving stars who congratulated her on her recent marriage and election as president of the Screen Actors Guild. "Patty, my darling, how are you?" asked Best Actress nominee Anne Bancroft as she hugged her *Miracle Worker* costar. Duke began to fill her in on recent personal events but Bancroft interjected, "I know you got married! And you're president of things and all. You've got to run for President of the United States!" Politics weren't discussed when Bob Hope, eighty-two, stopped by to brag that he was making his twenty-fifth Oscar appearance. Asked if he was nominated this year, Hope joked, "No, and not only that, they sent my bribery check back." Cesar "Butch" Romero, seventy-nine, announced that he'd been coming to the ceremonies even longer than Bob Hope but Ginger Rogers, seventy-four, claimed this was only her "fourth or fifth" time at an Oscar show. As to whether she'd be participating, Rogers quipped, "No, I'm just a viewer tonight. Not a doer. A viewer."

The first thing viewers saw was Robin Williams standing between two smiling gentlemen in tuxedoes whom Williams introduced as the Price, Waterhouse representatives. "So you guys know who won, right? You have all the envelopes right in there?" he asked, pointing to the men's briefcases. "What do you say we open those suckers up right now? C'mon, we haven't read the rules yet, we can go away. We can read 'em all out now and—bang—we can go to the party." Despite further cajoling, the accountants wouldn't budge so Williams told the audience, "I'm sorry, ladies and gentlemen, I gave it my best shot. I'm afraid we have to do the show."

After the first cluster of commercials, Ginger Rogers appeared, in a clip from the 1934 musical, *Flying Down To Rio*. Scenes of the film's famous airplane number were interspersed with shots of Teri Garr piloting a modern-day plane over Los Angeles with women again dancing on the wings. Garr's plane then showed up on the stage of the Dorothy Chandler where she cavorted with dancers and sang an ode to Hollywood that called the place "a state of mind that everyone wants to get in, a private club that very few are ever let in." Columnist Liz Smith didn't get into the spirit of the number, calling Garr "a major klutz."

Emcees Alan Alda and Jane Fonda came on stage to announce, "There are so many people around the world watching that we're calling on the linguistic services of our cohost, Mr. Robin Williams." The couple sent greetings to the People's Republic of China, India, and France—which were receiving a live telecast for the first time—while Williams translated the salutations into the native languages. Fonda gave "a special hello and congratulations to the Philippines" where Ferdinand Marcos had just been given the boot. For his Filippino "translation," Williams alluded to Mrs. Marcos—"Come on down! Some of these shoes have never been worn! Check it out!"

Marsha Mason and her Oscar-winning costar from *The Goodbye Girl*, Richard Dreyfuss, appeared to announce Best Supporting Actress. Margaret Avery reached back to shake Oprah Winfrey's hand. The winner was Anjelica Huston in *Prizzi's Honor*, who wore a self-designed emerald green gown. "This means a lot to me," the winner began, "since it comes from a role in which I was directed by my father. And I know it means a lot to him." Because of a cast on his left elbow (the result of a skiing accident), Jack Nicholson could only approximate clapping by hitting his leg with his good arm. Before going backstage, Huston went back to the audience to embrace Nicholson again.

Irene Cara performed a song called "Here's To The Losers" while clips of also-ran Best Picture nominees were shown, including Stanley Donen's *Seven Brides For Seven Brothers*, John Huston's *Treasure of Sierra Madre*, Sydney Pollack's *Tootsie* and three Spielberg films, *Jaws*, *Raiders of the Lost Ark* and, receiving especially strong applause, *E.T.* Introduced by scenes from Stanley Donen's *Funny Face*, Audrey Hepburn came on stage in a sari-like pink gown which she later described as "the prettiest in Givenchy's collection. He loaned it to me." Army Archerd wrote,

"I did receive my Academy booklet on how to dress like a serious actress."
—Cher

"This year even the standing ovations came early, when thirty-eight minutes into the show all-time favorite Audrey Hepburn made her entrance. It's usually two hours before everyone gets to his feet." Hepburn wiped away a tear and said, "Thank you, thank you very much." Costume designer Emi Wada was rewarded for her three years of toiling on *Ran*. The kimono-clad winner was accompanied by a male translator who brought down the house when he expressed her thanks "also to my wife . . . oh, to my husband." Michael Westmore, a third-generation makeup artist, accepted the Makeup Award for *Mask* by reminding the audience "my family name has been in the business for years but it's kind of gotten lost over the years with all the new people coming in," and ended by exclaiming, "We got an Oscar in the family!"

Jane Fonda introduced the Best Supporting Actor presenter as "one of the most glamorous people of this or any business—and you'd better believe it, wait'll you see what's gonna come out here." Out came Cher in a Vampirella outfit designed by Bob Mackie, featuring black stretch pants, knee-high suede boots, bejeweled loin cloth, bare midriff, a black wool jersey with metal brass plate and, topping it off, a huge Mohawk head-piece. After letting the audience get a load of her costume, the non-nominee informed them, "As you can see I did receive my Academy booklet on how to dress like a serious actress." The winner was Don Ameche in *Cocoon*; before he could get to the podium, the audience had given its second standing ovation of the evening. The moment was enhanced by James Horner's wistful theme from *Cocoon*, played by Lionel Newman's orchestra which was piping the music in from another building several miles away. Cher gave the seventy-seven-year-old actor a kiss and he addressed the audience, "To all you members of the Academy, this esteemed gentleman here [pointing to his Oscar] says that you have given to me your recognition, you've given to me your love, you have given to me, and I hope I have earned, your respect. For all these, I am deeply grateful."

"Right now you're about to see a man break a world's record," promised Alan Alda, "it's his record and it's for appearing on the Oscar show more than anybody else—an incredible twenty-four times." Out came the man who, forty-six years earlier, was making Don Ameche jokes—Bob Hope. "I think they oughtta give me an Oscar just for attendance, don't you?" joked Hope. "But I'm happy to be here at this annual Hollywood lottery," he said, before adding a punchline he had used at the 1967 Awards, "known at my house as Passover." He continued, "I love seeing Don Ameche win, I think that's a beautiful thing [applause]. Isn't that great? And he did it with break-dancing. And all these years I tried to do it with great acting . . . First it was George Burns, now Don Ameche, I hope it's a trend." But then Hope got down to the real reason he was there—the Jean Hersholt Humanitarian Award. Reading from index cards, Hope narrated clips of Buddy Rogers' movies before pronouncing that "Buddy's biggest role was as a humanitarian." To prove his point, he mentioned some of the recipient's favorite charities, including the Boy Scouts of America and the Navy League, and acknowledged that Rogers was a regular fixture "on skid row" every Christmas Eve. Hope handed the statuette to Mary Pickford's eighty-one-year-old widower, who promised he'd go home and "proudly put it beside Mary's two Oscars."

Possibly because Hope was posing backstage with Rogers, there was no replay of the 1974 *Hearts and Minds* brouhaha when director Deborah Schaeffer accepted the Documentary Short Subject Award for *Witness To War*. She commented, "We would like to dedicate this Award to the memory of Archbishop Oscar Romero, who was murdered six years ago today in El Salvador, and to all of those who are keeping his spirits and dreams alive by working to prevent another Vietnam War in Central America."

After 1968 Best Actor Cliff Robertson extolled AT & T in a commercial, Sally Field walked out to explain that the Award to six-time loser Paul Newman differed from Honorary Oscars "given to individuals whose careers are behind them or who

"I think they oughta give me an Oscar just for attendance, don't you?"
—Bob Hope

are contemplating retirement. Well, tonight's recipient is hardly ready to retire. In fact, at this very moment, he's working on a film set in Chicago." Newman was making *The Color of Money*, a sequel to *The Hustler*, which had earned him a nomination in 1961. Even the Academy's guarantee that he wouldn't go home empty-handed could not persuade Newman to appear in person. "I certainly want to thank the members of the Academy," Newman told the audience via satellite from the Chicago set, "and I'm especially grateful that this does not come wrapped as a gift certificate to Forest Lawn." Leaning against a canvas chair in sweater and slacks, Newman looked on the bright side, "Tonight has provided a lot of nourishment and a kind of permission to risk and maybe surprise myself a little bit in the hope that my best work is down the pike in front of me and not in back of me." Joanne Woodward's husband later told Gene Siskel that while "I was relieved that I finally had evened the score with my wife," he found the timing of the Award "very strange."

When Fonda and Alda turned over the hosting duties to Robin Williams, the comedian stepped out dressed in a totally white tuxedo and proceeded to split into several personalities. He was Paul Lynde appraising Fonda's glittering décolletage. "Look at these sequins, everywhere, go crazy!"; an unctuous TV host: "Hello, I'm Robin Leach. Welcome to 'Lifestyles of the Rich and Nervous' "; and a TV viewer in China: "Quick, Chin Woh, Irving Thalberg Award, we can't miss this!" But Williams saved his best cracks for the man who was threatening Bob Hope's record of most Oscar appearances, "For those of you who are keeping track, there are only four more Awards to go to Jack Valenti, so get ready." As the camera watched long-time Oscar-goer Geraldine Page laughing, Williams continued, "Jack 'Boom-Boom' Valenti is waiting for you baby. He's hot and ready to go!"

Before Valenti appeared, Quincy Jones presented an Honorary Award to composer Alex North, who had an even worse track record than Paul Newman—fifteen unsuccessful nominations. The Academy finally took action when North failed to be nominated for the score to *Prizzi's Honor* because there was no Music Score—Adaptation category due to a lack of entries. "I think this is the nicest and most pleasant way of getting an Oscar," said the perennial bridesmaid. North made "a humble plea" that Hollywood quit making movies with "blatant, bloody violence."

"The live audience was . . . quite surprised by the early appearance of the Best Actress Award," wrote Army Archerd. Geraldine Page was the most unprepared of all; she had kicked off her shoes and stuck them under a seat. "From the accounting firm of F. Murray and Abraham," announced Robin Williams, "the chairman of the board, F. Murray Abraham." Playing the role of presenter to the hilt, Abraham dramatically darted his eyes back and forth as he named the nominees. Jessica Lange, wearing eyeglasses, sat calmly next to Sam Shepard, but Geraldine Page chewed her nails as the audience applauded her nomination. Abraham ripped the envelope and gasped, "Ohhh . . . I consider this woman the greatest actress in the English language!" Anne Bancroft rolled her eyes and said, "Oh, God," but Lange turned to Shepard and smiled, "It's Geraldine." When Abraham excitedly confirmed it, Meryl Streep and Whoopi Goldberg leapt to their feet, clapping. Soon the whole place was standing, except the winner, who was looking for her shoes. "My mind blew a fuse," she later explained. Once she found her pumps, Page kissed her husband Rip Torn, hugged her son, held John Huston's hand as she stepped around his oxygen tank, and got bussed by William Hickey as she walked down the aisle. With the orchestara playing the hymn "Faith of Our Fathers," Page was greeted on stage by Abraham who was now genuflecting before her. At the podium, Page giggled and basked in the standing ovation and then yelled "Murray, come here," but Abraham stood aside, signaling for her to speak. "I wanted to say to Murray while he's here, thank you for the Mirror Repertory Company which we're both members of—" she said, turning to see Abraham's response, which turned out to be a

"Let's see which one you like, you really, really like."
—Sally Field

stage direction: shut up about that and give a speech! "Thank Horton Foote for this," she began, garnering more applause. She thanked cast and crew and concluded "But mainly, it's Horton's fault." She cradled the statuette and walked over to Abraham's waiting arms.

Out of Africa picked up its third technical trophy when David Watkin claimed the Cinematography Award, saying "A while ago I was sitting in a theater watching one of my movies next to a friend of mine who is a film director . . . he touched me on the arm and said, 'That's beautiful; you're very clever,' so I explained it was a second-unit shot." After the laughter subsided, Watkin thanked *Out of Africa*'s two second-unit cinematographers who supplied the "flying material" and the "animal photography."

Robin Williams returned to bring out "a man you've never heard of but have to listen to anyway . . . here he is, ladies and gentlemen, you've been waiting for him, Mr. Jack 'Boom-Boom' Valenti!" The head of the Motion Picture Producers Association acted as if he hadn't heard the introductory remarks as he escorted Norma Aleandro onstage. Valenti's usual "universal language of film" speech was given a new twist as he expounded on how videocassettes would now make foreign films more accessible than ever. He raised his hands and smiled when Aleandro opened the envelope and exclaimed, "The winner is—bless you—*The Official Story*!" Aleandro gave Valenti an earthy hug and, finishing with him, hugged director Luis Puenzo, who ended his speech with a reminder that "on another March 24, ten years ago, we suffered the last military coup in my country. We will never forget this nightmare, but we are certain now to begin with our new dreams." According to *Variety*, they began that very minute: "The city of Buenos Aires seemed to explode, despite the fact that it was two o'clock in the morning, Argentine time. It was the first Best Foreign Film Oscar for Argentina and for Latin America."

The Award-giving stopped for the tribute to MGM musicals. Howard Keel sang a song called "Once A Star, Always A Star" honoring the Metro alumna who swirled around him: June Allyson, Leslie Caron, Cyd Charisse, Marge Champion, Kathryn Grayson, Jane Powell, Debbie Reynolds, Ann Miller and Esther Williams, who came out of the floor amid red smoke. Rachel Horovitz, one of the extras hired to occupy seats in the orchestra when celebrities got up to go elesewhere, told the *Los Angeles Daily News*, "They were concerned that the production number with the old stars wouldn't work, so they asked all the seat fillers to lead the standing ovation." Donen needn't have worried; the standing ovation was genuine and was the longest of the night. Radie Harris enthused in the *Hollywood Reporter* that Donen had taken the stars and "made them all look so great that it should have been dedicated to plastic surgery!" Next, Best Actress loser Whoopi Goldberg, wearing a simple black dress with pearls, gave the Editing Award. When the winner for *Witness* turned out to be in Belize with Peter Weir and Harrison Ford, Goldberg said, "I'm sure that if Thom Noble were here he'd like to thank his mother, as some of us might have thanked ours."

Larry Gelbart honored the "survivors of a system that would have made the Marquis de Sade cry uncle"—screenwriters. The three authors of *Witness*, winning Best Original Screenplay, identified with Gelbart's remarks; none of them thanked Peter Weir. Earl W. Wallace did allow, "I'd like to thank all the marvelous talent that converged on our screenplay," but William Kelley thanked only "Paramount and [producer] Ed Feldman for taking our script and making the vision we had." Backstage, the winners told the press that Peter Weir had wanted to change everything. *Out of Africa*'s Kurt Luedtke, winner for Best Screenplay Based on Material from Another Medium, didn't mention director Sydney Pollack, but did pay tribute to rewrite man David Rayfiel and to his leading lady, whom he referred to as "Mrs. Gummer."

"Two-time Oscar winner" Barbra Streisand walked out after a film montage of directors at work, synchronized to her singing Stephen Sondheim's "Putting It Together"; the film clips included Streisand in action directing *Yentl*, for

"Ba-boom, ba-boom, ba-boom."
—William Hurt

which she received no nominations. "A director is part artist, part politician, part father-confessor and part Jewish mother," Streisand explained. As she ripped open the envelope, Hector Babenco smoothed his hair and straightened his tie, just in case. "Memories . . . " Streisand sang. None of the directors moved. "Sydney Pollack!" the presenter screamed. John Huston turned to his companion to ask "Who?" Anne Bancroft, the star of the first movie Pollack ever directed, was sitting beside the victor, laughing and clapping, and her husband Mel Brooks slapped him on the back as he went down their row. En route to the stage, Pollack stopped before Steven Spielberg and shook his hand. At the podium, Pollack accepted a hug and a kiss from his leading lady in *The Way We Were*, before praising a studio executive, "Frank Price made this film possible; he had the courage when it mattered the most and it was easy to say no." After thanking a multitude, the director finished with, "I can't leave this podium without saying I could not have made this film without Meryl Streep." As the camera caught a blushing Streep holding a hand to her face amid applause, Pollack continued, "She is astounding, personally, professionally, in all ways. I can't thank her enough."

Sally Field made fun of her notorious acceptance speech by prefacing the Best Actor Award with "Let's see which one you like, you really, really like." The winner was William Hurt in *Kiss of the Spider Woman*, who grabbed the top of his head in shock. Hector Babenco was grabbing him next, engulfing him in a ferocious bear hug. Producer David Weisman sprinted over to get his hug, but had to wait until after Hurt embraced his current paramour, Marlee Matlin. The winner clapped as he headed towards the stage, where he hugged Sally Field and accepted the off-stage congratulations yelled out by Robin Williams. Hurt started his speech by saluting his non-nominated costar, "I share this with Raul." Imitating the sound of his heart, "Ba-boom, ba-boom, ba-boom," Hurt admitted, "I didn't expect to be here so I don't know what I'm going to say." He ultimately thanked "the courageous people of Brazil" and concluded, "I'm very proud to be an actor." Observed Rex Reed, "One of the night's major sighs of relief came when Hurt, who has committed verbal suicide on more than one occasion with long-winded, incoherent speeches about the metaphysics of acting, said a simple 'thank-you' and mercifully left the stage."

The fifth and final standing ovation marked the entrances of the Best Picture presenters as the titles of their films flashed on large screens. John Huston came first, followed by Billy Wilder and Akira Kurosawa. The camera got a look at Steven Spielberg as he applauded the trio of titans. "Kurosawa doesn't speak very good English," noted a representative of ABC, explaining why the Japanese director received subtitles when he read the nomination of *Out of Africa*. He stared cautiously for a moment before blurting out his version of the name "Pollack" and the delighted nominee roared with laughter. Both Kurosawa and Huston begged off from reading the winner, so Billy Wilder made the announcement. The *Los Angeles Herald-Examiner* reported, "Each of the four acting winners . . . drew cheers when announced . . . But the biggest Award—Best Picture for *Out of Africa*—was greeted with silence by the hundreds of reporters back stage." In the auditorium, however, Sydney Pollack was a conquering hero. Mel Brooks slapped him on the back again, and he chatted with the three presenters before facing the microphone. "This is a wonderful evening for all of us," Pollack began. "If I left out anybody before, I'll hope you'll understand it was just because of all the pressure." Then he chased after the three veterans, who had already ambled off. Alan Alda ran out to say "Goodnight!"; Jane Fonda said "Goodnight!"; Robin Williams said "Ciao!" As the telecast ended, one of the final images was Cesar Romero pointing to show his date the quickest way out of the theater.

Aftermath

Backstage, Buddy Rogers reminisced about the first Oscar Awards banquet, where he had sat

"I was legitimately stoned on pain pills."
—Jack Nicholson

next to Clara Bow. "A *Twilight Zone* chill crept over the crowd as everyone realized he was actually *there*," noted the *Village Voice*'s Michael Musto. Geraldine Page was dealing with more current events. "Now when it comes to actually getting the little monster," she said, pointing to her Oscar, "it has to do with a lot of things. This may be because it was eight times, it may be because it was Carrie Watts and not another role. We don't know what made it slide into my welcoming arms this way, but I know what got me nominated—I did a damned good job." The press corp cheered in agreement. Asked where she purchased her evening gown, Page explained it was a costume from her current New York play, a revival of Somerset Maugham's *The Circle*. One reporter wanted to know if she thought she had any more award-worthy performances in her. "I hope so," Page retorted, "I don't want to stop now. It's just getting interesting."

Don Ameche didn't want to stop yet, either, but he said, "I haven't had a job offer since we stopped filming the movie seventeen months ago. If they ask me, I'll do it." When someone pointed out he had had three offers for TV series since *Cocoon*, the veteran admitted he had turned them down because "I've laid off for so long, I'm not about to do something I don't believe in." The actor didn't believe in the Oscar as a personal goal. "I don't know that it had the same importance years ago that it has today," he said. "Acting was not my whole life, as it was with some others. Hank Fonda, he comes to mind, he lived to act. It's kind of sad he had to wait so long to get the recognition he so craved." Ameche got further recognition a few months later when *Playgirl* named him one of the ten sexiest men in America.

Anjelica Huston had to deal with the disappointment of a press that didn't get the photo opportunity it craved. "Why Can't the Oscars be as Dramatic as the Movies?" wondered the *Los Angeles Times*, which had a photographer ready backstage with a picture of Anjelica's father and grandfather holding their "set of family Oscars" in 1948. "What'll you say to your father?" a reporter asked. "I just think we'll hug for a long time, probably," she said. Having grown up around Oscars, Anjelica presumably knew the value of her statuette, so someone asked her to evaluate "having one." She responded, "It means I get to look at it a lot."

Reporters seeking more profound answers turned to William Hurt, named by *Variety* "the most philosophical winner of the night." "My honor is my work, there is none greater, but there are so many people who do good work, who are as good as I am who are not up here," the Best Actor said, adding, "But, yes, it is a fantasy." Somebody inquired why he hadn't turned down the Award if he feels actors shouldn't compete. "Because I'm not a politician," Hurt replied. "I won an honor. I'm glad to accept." He hadn't felt that way originally, he confessed to Jack Kroll when *Esquire* made him a cover boy under the title "The Leading Man, 1986." The winner almost didn't attend the ceremony but "It was Steven Spielberg who set me straight. He told me it was a big deal and I should go . . . If people are going to honor you, how dare you not accept that?"

With no one from *The Color Purple* around backstage, Sydney Pollack had to answer the big question of the night: what about the complete shut-out of all eleven nominations for the Spielberg movie? "It's a difficult spot you've put me in," responded Pollack, "and I can't win no matter how I answer that question. I don't want to put a damper on the evening by trying to speculate on an undiplomatic question with an undiplomatic answer." But the press did get out of him that "It was a strange night. I didn't know what to expect. I thought Mr. Huston would get it."

Dinner at the Governor's Ball consisted of Norwegian salmon, rack of lamb, and lemon-mousse dessert wrapped in a white chocolate envelope with a red seal. "Of recent Best Actors," observed Paul Rosenfield of the *Los Angeles Times*, "maybe only Hurt is elusive enough to go undisturbed at a back table." While Hurt celebrated with Raul Julia, Geraldine Page whooped it up with Rip Torn and F. Murray Abraham; Rosen-

"It was a strange night."
—Sydney Pollack

field said of the two acting winners, "neither works ballrooms." Supporting Actor loser Klaus Maria Brandauer showed up and said he was happy for Don Ameche, "a man who is so long around the business." The *Los Angeles Times* watched Elizabeth Taylor blow in on the arm of George Hamilton and was glad to see her: "The trim Taylor, who takes over the dance floor, keeps the paparazzi happy and brings authentic nostalgia: Thirty odd years ago Oscar show producer Stanley Donen was the steady beau of La Taylor." She also found time to console Brandauer; an eyewitness for the *New York Post* said the couple "talked forever." Few of the gang from *The Color Purple* showed up at the party, but Steven Spielberg was there. Observed Paul Rosenfield, "He seems never to miss the Governor's Ball."

"Khadafy Put in Turnaround for Swifty's Spago Party," headlined the *Los Angeles Herald-Examiner*, where reporter Jeannine Stein surveyed the agent's soirée amid news updates flashing on giant TV monitors: "Sam Donaldson was keeping the country apprised of the goings-on in Libya, but a scant few were paying attention." Even the President's son, Ron Reagan, Jr., was unfazed; he was busy covering the party for *Good Morning America*. Audrey Hepburn, meanwhile, was busy getting Tom Selleck's autograph for her son. When Elizabeth Taylor inevitably appeared, Hepburn asked if her necklace was from jewelry designer Kenny Lane. "No," replied Taylor, "Richard Burton." Hepburn pointed to Taylor's earrings and again inquired, "Kenny Lane?" "No," Taylor told her, "Mike Todd."

Sydney Pollack didn't make it to the Lazar party, leaving John Huston to be the center of attention. Jack Nicholson and Anjelica Huston got stuck in traffic on Sunset Boulevard, so Huston chatted with Sam Shepard while Jessica Lange pulled out their table to accomodate the pregnant Meryl Streep. "Later," *Women's Wear Daily* reported, "Lange and Shepard necked discreetly as celebrity guests craned their necks." By that time, Huston had returned to his hotel, where Anjelica and Jack joined him for champagne. Nicholson told Army Archerd there were no hard feelings over *Prizzi's Honor*'s having won just one Oscar, "We got what we wanted. It was extremely heartwarming, and thank God it came early in the evening—I was legitimately stoned on pain pills." There had been genuine tragedy for John Randolph, the actor who played Nicholson's father in *Prizzi's Honor*. During the ceremonies, Mrs. Randolph, actress Sarah Cunningham, said she wasn't feeling well, collapsed in the Dorothy Chandler lobby, and died.

Two nights later, John Huston handed Akira Kurosawa his honorary membership in the Directors Guild as Sydney Pollack looked on. Kurosawa was introduced to the director he'd most wanted to meet, Vincente Minnelli, who would die in four months. Asked his opinion of the Oscar show, Kurosawa said, "I wouldn't say I didn't like it, but it was a little long." Television reviewers, more familiar with past telecasts than Kurosawa, were much more enthusiastic. "Surprise! An Oscar Entertains!" headlined *Time*, and the *New York Times*' John J. O'Connor heralded it as "the best Oscar show in years, perhaps ever." O'Connor, like many critics, singled out Robin Williams who, he wrote, "brought the event's comic tone thumpingly into the 1980's. This was no longer the topical-gag world of Bob Hope or even Johnny Carson." Then came the bad news: once again the show earned the lowest ratings in Oscar history. "Unfortunately," philosophized Stanley Donen, "in television, people only know if it's good or bad after they see it."

All of the reviewers had something to say about Cher. Representing the negative camp, the *Orange County Register* snorted that she resembled "a drug-crazed Indian porcupine." But Andrew Sarris appreciated her appearance, writing in the *Village Voice*, "Cher is rapidly emerging as the Jean Harlow of our generation, a warm, honest, amiably sluttish straight-shooter with both men and women." Cher also snagged an invitation to pose for a Blackglama "What becomes a Legend most?" ad—for which she insisted upon wearing her Oscar outfit headpiece—as well as a

"My mind blew a fuse."
—Geraldine Page

role in the upcoming Jack Nicholson movie. Anjelica Huston had also auditioned for the film but didn't get the part. "I was more upset by it because I had won," the Best Supporting Actress told Aljean Harmetz. "It made me feel not having to prove myself any more was an illusion at best."

Also upset was Willis Edwards of the Beverly Hills/Hollywood chapter of the NAACP. Joe Morgenstern of the *Los Angeles Herald-Examiner* wrote that Edwards executed "one of the more breathtaking pirouettes in Hollywood history" by turning around and accusing the Academy of a "slap in the face" to blacks by not giving any Oscars to *The Color Purple* after having accused the film of racism. Edwards explained his contradictory positions by saying, "I still feel it is a stereotypical portrayal of blacks but the acting was fabulous." Meanwhile, the international press was buzzing around the Tel Aviv hotel where Spielberg was staying with his wife, who was making a movie for Cannon. Pressed for a statement, Spielberg told the gaggle of reporters, "When I'm sixty, Hollywood will forgive me—I don't know for what, but they'll forgive me."

"In the end, it really wasn't much of a contest after all," summed up columnist Gregg Kilday. "Pollack's detour to shake Spielberg's hand as he made his way to the stage played like a laying of hands, a welcoming gesture suggesting that Spielberg, for enduring the controversy gracefully, had finally earned membership in the club." As for Frank Price, the executive Sydney Pollack had thanked so profusely in his acceptance speech, the future wasn't so rosy. Six months later Aljean Harmetz was reporting, "Mr. Price's resignation was asked for Monday night by Sidney J. Sheinberg, president and chief operating officer of MCA, Inc., Universal's corporate parent." Universal had had a crummy summer at the box-office and Sheinberg and Price "were overheard screaming at each other over who should be blamed for the failure of George Lucas's $35 million film about a duck from another planet." So Price was out of Universal and the studio replaced him with George Lucas's long-time lawyer.

1986

"If you make a popular movie, you start to think where have I failed?"
—Woody Allen

Independents sneaked off with the Oscars at the 1986 Awards as the Academy tangled, once again, with Bette Davis.

In compiling their 1985 ten-best lists, many critics couldn't resist saying that none of the year's movies could equal the Woody Allen movie due to open in February. When the director heard the enthusiastic response he moaned, "If you make a popular movie, you start to think where have I failed? I must be doing something that's unchallenging, or reinforcing prejudices of the middle class, or being simplistic or sentimental." Orion, however, was thrilled and, for the first time, held a national press tour of stars for a Woody Allen film. Woody didn't participate, but costar Michael Caine did. "I've never been to the Mid-West," admitted Caine, "because they don't go see my pictures. But I think they'll be seeing this one."

Hannah and Her Sisters, a comedy-drama about a New York actress and the relationships among members of her family, was based, Allen explained, on his "romanticized perception" of Mia Farrow. "She's very stable . . . and I thought if she had two unstable sisters, it would be interesting." The film's central set was Farrow's actual apartment, which to Allen, was "perfect for me because I always go over there anyhow"; and he relied on her family for much of the cast. Her real-life mother, Maureen O'Sullivan, played the same role on screen and all seven of Farrow's children had small parts. "I have a tremendous attraction to movies or plays or books that explore the psyche of women, particularly intelligent ones," Allen said, while Farrow mentioned another of her boyfriend's concerns, "He could have been a fashion designer. He's interested in women's clothes."

When the film opened, Andrew Sarris proclaimed, "as *Manhattan* was the great American film of the '70s, *Hannah and Her Sisters* is the great American film of the '80s," but Pauline Kael thought the director was too infatuated with the Farrow clan, writing "It might be time for Woody Allen to make a film with a whole new set of friends." *Hannah* was Allen's highest-grossing movie since *Annie Hall,* though it wasn't Farrow but Dianne Wiest, as her more neurotic sister, who was singled out by reviewers. *New York*'s David Denby called hers "a sly, tough, dead-accurate performance that should cause a sensation."

Overleaf: *Paul Newman's proxy, Academy President Robert Wise, waits patiently while former Academy president Bette Davis, the Best Actor presenter, observes decorum.*

Carry on Caine

Michael Caine did all right for himself, too, as Farrow's adulterous husband. *Newsweek*'s David Ansen called him "both sympathetic and exasperating, equally a torturer and the one who is tortured." Because of his torturous work schedule—four films in 1986—Caine's press agent was billing him as "the busiest actor in Hollywood." He showed up at art houses a few months later in a supporting role as a polished pimp in the British *film noir, Mona Lisa*. Bob Hoskins played the lead, an ex-con hired by Caine to chauffeur an enigmatic prostitute, but Hoskins was quick to point out the difference between himself and his costar, "Now, Michael's a star; he has that kind of glamour. I actually couldn't live Michael's international kind of life-style." Even snagging the Best Actor award at the Cannes Film Festival didn't change Hoskins's self-estimation. "I don't think I'm the sort of material movie stars are made of—I'm five-foot-six-inches and cubic," he claimed. "My own mum wouldn't call me pretty." Nonetheless, Hoskins had the *New York Daily News*'s Kathleen Carroll under his spell, "He makes you believe this thick-skulled Frog Prince actually possesses an inner beauty."

A Pain in the Neck

"I can't do another period picture, another literary adaptation," sighed director James Ivory, after filming Henry James's *The Bostonians* with

"My own mum wouldn't call me pretty."
—Bob Hoskins

his collaborators of twenty years, producer Ismail Merchant and screenwriter Ruth Prawer Jhabvala. Still, time was running out on the trio's option on *A Room with a View* from E. M. Forster's estate and Jhabvala had already written the script, so she and Merchant told Ivory to "just get on with it." Merchant made the rounds in Hollywood where every studio rejected the comedy of mores about a repressed English girl who discovers passion on a trip to Italy in the days before the First World War. "They all said it's a wonderful script but will Americans be interested in it?" Merchant recalled.

The filmmakers finally managed to get $3 million from English sources and the small American distributor Cinecom; production took place on location in England and Florence, Italy, under austere circumstances. "Nobody travels first class," Ivory said, "no sybaritic life-style, no fancy hotels." Two-time Oscar winner Maggie Smith, fifty-one, concurred, saying "everybody has to muck in." Still, she was willing to put up with the Poverty Row conditions to play the heroine's prim spinster cousin—whom she described as "a pain in the neck"—because "frankly, at my age, I always feel lucky to get any film roles at all." Watching the movie, Roger Ebert also felt fortunate and opined that "the story moved slowly for the same reason you try to make ice cream last: because it's so good."

A Room with a View bowed in New York in March at the Paris Theatre and, by the end of June, there was a party at the neighboring Plaza Hotel to celebrate the film's passing the $1 million mark at that theatre alone. The film did extraordinarily well elsewhere, too, and the *New York Times's* Aljean Harmetz marveled that it was playing in places like Boise and Des Moines where no Merchant/Ivory picture had ever gone before. Responded Ivory, "Audiences are not stupid, they're crying out for better entertainment. It's up to television and movie companies to try and give them that and not be afraid they're talking over their heads." Producer Merchant had a slightly different take, saying *A Room with a View* was so popular because "it's the story of three good-looking, handsome young people."

In the Bush

Opening the same time as *A Room with a View* was another low-budget film by an American director with British financing, Oliver Stone's *Salvador*. The writer-director was planning to make an action movie about the adventures of contemporary war correspondent Richard Boyle, but when the journalist took Stone to El Salvador, the filmmaker had an epiphany: "I was so revolted and angered by what I saw that I knew just what kind of movie this was going to be."

Hollywood would have preferred the action movie, so Stone got the film's $4 million budget from England's Hemdale Company and took no salary himself. Although the role wouldn't pay much, James Woods, determined to get away from the second-lead psychotics he usually played, harangued the director over lunch, "I can give you 103 reasons why I should play the lead. I was *born* to play it." "And I fell for that line," Stone remembered later. When he suggested Woods take a field trip to El Salvador, the actor shot back, "I do not have to go visit a country to understand the abuse of human rights." Filming in Mexico did make Woods understand the amenities of Hollywood: "Talk about motor homes," he said, "we didn't even have bathrooms on the set, so we always tried to shoot near some shrubbery for the crew."

The *New York Post*'s Archer Winsten came out of retirement to review *Salvador* and found that "the picture is exciting and it does speak its own mouthful. It probably takes the decent side with the angels (peasants) against the force of slaughter and repression." Michael Sragow of the *San Francisco Examiner* exulted, "James Woods chews through *Salvador* like a chain saw." Alas, *Salvador* did not have the same fairy-tale ending at the box-office as *A Room with a View;* it played briefly in a handful of cities and then disappeared.

"Blue Velvet is not a normal picture."
—David Lynch

Join the Navy

In contrast, audiences couldn't stay away from a summer movie that held a cheerier view of battle, *Top Gun,* in which Tom Cruise played a modern-day navy pilot. Producers Jerry Bruckheimer and Don Simpson proclaimed that their movie celebrated "the emotion of triumph" and the U.S. Navy was happy to supply them with the necessary jets and aircraft carriers for the tale. Reflecting on the film's achievement as the highest-grosser of the year, Simpson told *Premiere* their secret was that they "pay a lot of attention to the traditional elements of story—especially beginning, middle and end." Bruckheimer added, "Don and I lead with our hearts, rather than our heads." Oliver Stone was not impressed, commenting, "the message of this movie is 'I get a girlfriend if I start World War III.' "

Scary Monsters

Another summer hit featured military action, albeit with a feminist, sci-fi slant. In *Aliens,* Sigourney Weaver reprised her role as Captain Ripley from 1979's *Alien* and once again did battle with monsters at a hapless space station. *Newsweek* noted that "Next to her wonderfully human macho, most recent *male* action heroes look like very thin cardboard," and *Time* decorated Weaver with a cover story. The actress said she returned to the part because "it gives you the opportunity to do something you'd only do in classical theater, which is to play a warrior." But Weaver insisted that her warrior was not a right-wing fantasy: "I give money to anti-gun legislation. For me, the biggest problem on this film is that I hate guns and I don't think Ripley is a gun person at all. I want to make sure that in those scenes, although I look like I'm handling it, I don't turn into a marine."

Lend an Ear

Even eerier than *Aliens* was David Lynch's surrealistic drama, *Blue Velvet,* a film that began with an extreme close-up of ants in the grass crawling on a detached human ear. Lynch told the unnerving story of a small-town teenaged boy trying to find out to whom the ear belongs. J. Hoberman of the *Village Voice* said the film "could be described as *Archie and Veronica in the Twilight Zone* or John Hughes meets Luis Buñuel or *The Hardy Boys on Mars.*" Director Lynch himself stated, "It's not a normal picture." When urban audiences lined up to check it out, David Denby of *New York* dubbed the film "the cult movie of the year and perhaps of the decade." *Time* called it "perhaps the first film since 1972's *Last Tango in Paris* to scandalize its audience." And some critics. Rex Reed confessed, "I haven't the vaguest idea what *Blue Velvet* is about, except the desecration of a pop tune I danced to the night of my senior prom. . . . It should score high with the kind of sickos who like to smell dirty socks and pull the wings off butterflies, but there's nothing here for sane audiences."

Hopper on the Wagon

Blue Velvet was hardly a mainstream motion picture, but it did offer one irresistible, pure Hollywood feature—a comeback. Playing what one critic called "maybe the vilest sadistic creep in movie history," Dennis Hopper hadn't managed to win so much acclaim for a movie since *Easy Rider,* and columnists loved him for kicking alcoholism and drug addiction. "Now he's an outstanding endorsement for sobriety," wrote Marilyn Beck, who named him one of 1986's Best Comebacks, along with Bette Midler and Gumby. Interviewed by the *Hollywood Reporter*'s "Celebrity Spotlight," Hopper explained that he called on emotional and sense memories à la Lee Strasberg for *Blue Velvet*'s drug scenes instead of resorting to his old methods, "Normally I would

"Normally I would have taken cocaine."
—Dennis Hopper

have taken cocaine to get that sort of frenzy or I would have used amyl nitrate in the mask."

The Silver Hustler

Unlike the "rediscovered" Hopper, Paul Newman had never been far from the spotlight. If the *New York Times* wasn't headlining "Paul Newman Gives $40,000 to the Neediest Cases Fund" then the *Los Angeles Times* was reporting that the actor "likes to eat cantaloupe while showering in his Westport, Conn., home. After his wife, Joanne Woodward, complained about the rinds, he tried unsuccessfully to have a garbage disposal installed in their tub." His film projects attracted attention, too, especially when the six-time Oscar loser announced he was recreating the role that had won him his second nomination—pool shark Fast Eddie Felson of *The Hustler*.

Newman read *The Color of Money,* the sequel novel by *The Hustler* author Walter Tevis and said, "It reminded me that Eddie wasn't completed at the end of the first film like some other people I had played, and I began wondering what he would be doing now." The actor called in Martin Scorsese for advice, and the director told him to keep the title but get rid of the story. They enlisted another novelist, Richard Price, as a screenwriter, and the three of them sat around Newman's Malibu home, concocting a new plot about Eddie's educating a young rookie.

The Disney Company was delighted with the project, particularly since *Top Gun*'s Tom Cruise wanted the costarring role. When the movie opened in the fall, Newman and Cruise posed for the cover of *Life*, Newman for the cover of the *New York Times Magazine,* and there were articles on the film in everything from *New Woman* to *Playboy*. *Variety* later confirmed the film's success: "Sales of pool tables and billiards-related supplies have leaped dramatically since the October release of Buena-Vista's pool-themed, *The Color of Money*, mirroring a phenomenon that occurred when *The Hustler* bowed in 1961 and set off national interest in pool." Newman's reviews were just as laudatory as in 1961, but his publicist, Warren Cowan, swore, "If I were to suggest to Paul some kind of an Oscar campaign, he'd hang up on me." In spite of Newman's misgivings, Disney publicist Christine Lamonte told the *Los Angeles Times,* "Friends were saying that this would be Paul Newman's film for an Oscar before I'd even seen the movie. I think this has a lot to do with the fact that we really want him to win an Oscar—don't we?"

Seen and Not Heard

When a reporter asked Newman's leading lady from the earlier film, Piper Laurie, for her opinion of the sequel, she responded, "It was very hard to connect with *The Hustler* except at one point when a character refers to something in the past. Then I felt a little pang." Laurie did feel the joy of being in a popular movie again that fall with a supporting role in *Children of a Lesser God*. The 1980 Tony-winning play about a defiant young deaf woman and her sensitive teacher had been in development for years—Al Pacino and Robert Redford had both considered it—until Paramount packaged it with William Hurt and director Randa Haines, who had never made a feature before but had won acclaim for a TV movie about incest. Haines thought playwright Mark Medoff's adaptation was overly sentimental and got another writer to fashion it into "a knock-down, drag-out love story, tougher and grittier." Meanwhile the producers gruelled through a six-month search throughout the United States, Canada, Sweden, and the United Kingdom for a deaf actress to play the leading role. Their hunt ended when they saw a video of a Chicago production and were captivated not by the star but by a nineteen-year-old in a small role. Attested associate producer Candy Koethe, "Marlee Matlin took to the camera like a fish to water."

Matlin also took to publicity like an old-style Hollywood starlet and provided plenty of good copy. Hearing impaired as a result of an illness at eighteen months, Matlin admitted to the *Los*

"I guess I have a Zorba spirit."
—Marlee Matlin

Angeles Herald-Examiner that in high school, "I was very outgoing, gregarious and wild," and told the *New York Daily News:* "I guess I have a Zorba spirit because I like being free and doing what I want. I used to be a very angry deaf person, like Sarah in *Children* . . . I even wrote a letter to President Ford asking why he didn't have closed captions for his TV speeches. He didn't answer." But best of all, according to gossip columnists, Matlin said it was "love at first sight" when she met her thirty-five-year-old costar and, as soon as filming was completed, she moved into William Hurt's Central Park West apartment.

The film won Matlin more admirers. The *Chicago Tribune*'s Dave Kehr rhapsodized that "The expressivity of her gestures recalls the time when the movies themselves could not hear and made the very best of it—the thirty years of silent film." Hurt received his share of praise, as did Piper Laurie as Matlin's mother, but *Children* itself received mixed grades. Vincent Canby felt that watching it "is like being on a cruise to nowhere aboard a ship with decent service and above-par fast-food. Everything has been carefully programmed so that there are no surprises, no discoveries, nothing to do except sit." And deaf audiences complained the movie was hard to follow. "Mr. Hurt is a pretty good signer," said Joy Ann Hershkowitz, a teacher at a school for the deaf in Brooklyn, to the *New York Times,* "but he often has his back to the camera."

At the Hop

"I never had a prom," said Kathleen Turner. "My father died the week before my prom took place." The loss of a parent at a young age made her "dream of hearing someone you love so desperately and haven't had contact with for so long say, 'honey.' " The thirty-one-year-old actress was able to enact this dream and have her prom, too, when she made *Peggy Sue Got Married,* a fantasy about a forty-two-year-old woman who attends her high school reunion and travels back in time to when she was seventeen. Debra Winger was set for the part, but when a back injury forced her out, director Francis Coppola—himself a replacement after Jonathan Demme and Penny Marshall—needed a star to obtain financial backing for the film. Enter Turner, who bragged to interviewers, "I'm bankable."

Best known for playing sultry *femmes fatales,* the actress fretted about Peggy Sue, "I just worry about her so much. I mean, the girl is so *nice,*" but noted one drawback to playing her: "It's one of the ugliest periods I've ever been costumed in—petticoats, those hideous socks, saddle shoes, and bras with points. Nothing's long or sleek and that's what I look good in." When the movie bowed at the New York Film Festival, *Vogue*'s Molly Haskell wrote of Turner, "In her richest performance yet, she blends the poignancy of a Capra heroine with the tough, sardonic insight of an eighties' woman." But Pauline Kael carped, "Turner gives her role a good try, but she's miscast, or, rather, it's an unwritten part—Peggy Sue doesn't exist except to worry about marrying the right man."

Sister, Sister

If *Peggy Sue* were to bag Turner her first nomination, her likely competition included the three Oscar winners starring in the film version of Beth Henley's Pulitzer Prize–winning play, *Crimes of the Heart.* Maverick mogul Dino de Laurentiis picked up the property after the major studios turned down the teaming of Diane Keaton, Jessica Lange, and Sissy Spacek as Henley's eccentric Southern sisters. Reporters appeared at the North Carolina location snooping out possible feuds and ego clashes. No such luck. The stars shared a house near the set for dressing rooms and Lange enthused, "It was like a girl's dormitory over there." Spacek insisted that "not only do we have an incredible amount of things in common, we genuinely like each other," and Keaton bubbled, "they are both spectacular women." Even Lange's daughter, Alexandra, five, and Spacek's daughter, Schuyler, four, became close. Kathleen Carroll of

"It was like a girl's dormitory over there."
—Jessica Lange

the *New York Daily News* kept up the good feelings when *Crimes* premiered in December, calling Keaton "a jittery comic delight," Lange "deliciously brassy," and Spacek "divinely dizzy." Audiences didn't share the press's fascination, though, and de Laurentiis's sisters failed to have the box-office pull of Woody Allen's triumvirate.

If at First You Don't Succeed . . .

A film de Laurentiis decided not to make also opened in December—Oliver Stone's *Platoon*. "I had a deal where I agreed to write *Year of the Dragon* at a reduced fee if he would back *Platoon* with me as director," Stone said. Only the deal fell through, with de Laurentiis getting his *Dragon* script but Stone not getting his movie. "I wasted a year of my life for that man, but I have to admit I liked working with Michael Cimino and I learned a lot from him," the director shrugged.

Waiting for *Platoon* to be produced was nothing new for Stone—he had written the script in 1976. *Platoon* was based on his combat experiences in Vietnam when the twenty-one-year-old stockbroker's son and Yale dropout eagerly joined up and served fourteen months with the 25th Infantry Division. Although written in a few months, the script was no rush job. "It took me eight years to get to that screenplay, because I couldn't deal with it before," said the disillusioned vet. "I finally sat and dealt with the war as I had known about it realistically." No studio wanted the result, however; remembered Stone, "They said it was too grim, too down, too realistic." Producer David Puttnam had liked it enough to hire Stone to adapt 1978's *Midnight Express,* which won him an Oscar as well as steady employment penning screenplays for the next decade. Once he got the rights to *Platoon* back from de Laurentiis, Stone hooked up with producer Arnold Kopelson, best known around Hollywood for *Porky's,* and they convinced Hemdale to come to the financial rescue again. "We felt we couldn't do any worse than we did with *Salvador,*" reasoned Hemdale's John Daly. The filmmakers were not as persuasive with the same military that had been so kind to *Top Gun;* Kopelson recalled, "The U.S. government would not give us any assistance after they read the script."

Philippine Holiday

Stone offered James Woods another job, but the actor declined when he learned of the jungle locations. "I couldn't take the mud," Woods confessed. Tom Berenger, usually a handsome leading man, consented to be an evil, scar-faced sergeant and Willem Dafoe, a member of a New York experimental theatre group who so far had portrayed only villains on screen, agreed to play a good and virtuous one. Emilio Estevez passed on the innocent hero, so his brother Charlie Sheen signed on. Other showbiz relatives in the cast were Matt Dillon's brother Kevin and Anthony Quinn's son Francesco. All of them were whisked off to the Philippines and thrown into boot camp for two weeks with an ex-marine hired by the director for verisimilitude and tactical advice. Stone himself played the role of drill sergeant on the set to perfection; at one point when Sheen refused to go topless and risk injury from flying debris, Stone taunted, "Are you a little pussy from Malibu? Played too much volleyball all your life?" As Sheen later related to *People,* "I got so pissed off I ripped the shirt off, did the scene and had scars on my back for weeks." Despite the hardships, all the actors remained loyal to Stone, who, in turn, was faithful to one of his directors: his finished film ended with a special thanks to Michael Cimino.

Orion agreed to distribute the movie and *Variety* headlined "Orion Poised for Its *Platoon* March." The studio was well prepared, the trade journal reported, because an "executive v.p. for ad/pub/promo . . . has carefully orchestrated a publicity buildup keyed to rave reviews and a unique marketing campaign centered on the director's personal experience." Orion pounced on Vincent Canby's rave and highlighted it in their ads: "A singular achievement . . . vivid, terse, exceptionally moving . . . the tension builds and never

"Are you a little pussy from Malibu?"
—Oliver Stone to Charlie Sheen

lets up . . . a major piece of work." And on the west coast, the *Los Angeles Times*'s Sheila Benson dubbed Oliver Stone, "a Goya with a camera."

Forward, March

Audiences responded in such large numbers that the media started doing the publicity work for Orion. A month after giving the film a mixed review, *Time* made it a cover story and declared "*Platoon* the picture is now *Platoon* the phenomenon." The *New York Post* ran into actor Tony Roberts on his way into a crowded theatre and asked him why he'd come. "It is something that anyone who wants to be fully informed should see," he replied, "a very important picture."

Platoon became too important to be ignored in political circles. On the campaign trail, Democratic frontrunner Gary Hart declared that "every teenager in America should see *Platoon* while they make out in the balcony." In the neoconservative magazine *Insight*, John Podhoretz squawked that "Stone's effort to use his sleazy little story as a metaphor for the American experience in Southeast Asia blackens the sacrifice of every man and woman who served the United States in the Vietnam war (including Stone)." In Hollywood, Elia Kazan told Robert Osborne, "I think *Platoon* is the best of the Year." But Chuck Norris, the star of *Missing in Action* and *Missing in Action 2—The Beginning*, complained to the *Los Angeles Times*, "There's so much damn negativity in the world . . . I don't want to have to face that when I go to the movies." Mickey Rooney was of two minds. "*Platoon* was magnificent but it's just so catastrophic," he said. "They should have had a sign outside that said, 'No Women Allowed.' "

Negative Campaigning

Most of the film critics societies voted before the *Platoon* groundswell and both the New Yorkers and the Angelenos were unwavering in their devotion to *Hannah and Her Sisters,* awarding it Best Picture and Best Supporting Actress for Dianne Wiest. Gotham annointed Woody Allen Best Director as well, but L.A. pulled a surprise by electing David Lynch for the infamous *Blue Velvet.* A few weeks later, the National Society of Film Critics not only honored Lynch, but named his movie the best of the year. Woody Allen, who skipped both the New York and Los Angeles critics award dinners, told Orion to keep his name off any Oscar ads for *Hannah* and worked further to avoid the Academy's ceremony by telling *Daily Variety*'s Army Archerd, "My favorite movie of the year is *Blue Velvet*." Columnist Harry Haun said that Allen's strategy was working: "The first most popular film on Beverly Hills's private screening circuit is *Blue Velvet*, which most of Hollywood's elite walked out on when it was in theatres, but now that it has collected all those year-end awards, they're having to crawl back and see the whole thing for Oscar consideration."

With Dennis Hopper getting so much publicity for *Blue Velvet,* Orion hustled out *its* Dennis Hopper picture in Los Angeles in time for Oscar eligibility. *Hoosiers* was a sentimental tale about an Indiana high school basketball team in the '50s with Hopper as the town drunk who becomes rehabilitated for the sake of his son. The L.A. Film Critics cited Hopper for both films; the National Society of Film Critics for *Blue Velvet* only. Orion got on the stick and provided lots of screenings and trade paper ads so Academy voters would know its little movie existed.

Disney worried whether Academy members would remember Paul Newman since the majority of the critics organizations hadn't; *Mona Lisa*'s Bob Hoskins cleaned up in the Best Actor races. The one critics' prize Newman did claim was the National Board of Review's. Accepting the honor at a party at the Whitney Museum, the perennial Oscar bridesmaid told *Entertainment Tonight*, "When you look down the pike and see that your work is finite, these awards mean more than when you're a kid." Taking no chances of a split vote, Disney demoted Newman's costar Tom Cruise to Supporting Actor in its Oscar trade paper ads.

"There's so much damn negativity in the world."
—Chuck Norris

A Global Affair

There was no consensus among the critics circles on the actress of the year; Kathleen Turner and Sissy Spacek each earned a citation but neither seemed to have a lock on the Oscar derby. Spacek clearly outperformed her *Crimes of the Heart* costars in the publicity game. Diane Keaton didn't participate in de Laurentiis's promotional tour at all, and Jessica Lange sabotaged her chances with the Hollywood Foreign Press Association by arriving for a press conference and then refusing to budge from her limo when she heard she was expected to pose for individual photos with every member of the Association. Spacek happily complied and smiled along with the journalists; she was the only one from the cast nominated by the group for its Golden Globe Award, which she ultimately won.

By the time the Globes were handed out at the end of January, the *Platoon* juggernaut was running roughshod, claiming Best Picture (Drama), Best Director, and Best Supporting Actor for Tom Berenger. Accepting his prize, Oliver Stone postulated that "through this award, you're acknowledging the Vietnam veteran." *Children of a Lesser God*'s Marlee Matlin also received her first trophy that night and charmed the audience during her acceptance by pointing to her interpretor and signing, "I'm not much of a speaker—he is."

The success of *Platoon* spilled over to Oliver Stone's previous film and *Salvador* became a hot item at Hollywood video stores. Hemdale went all out with trade paper ads for the box-office dud and ran the film on cable-TV in Hollywood. James Woods wasn't about to miss out on the publicity so he dropped in on the *Tonight Show* to trade jokes with Johnny Carson and say that he adlibbed some of *Salvador*'s best lines.

Men with a Mission

The fuss over *Platoon* didn't stop Oliver Stone's old boss, David Puttnam, from trying to hype his latest uplifting experience to an Oscar. Puttnam's entry this year was *The Mission*, a $23 million epic about eighteenth-century missionaries in South America, written by three-time Oscar winner Robert Bolt, and directed by *The Killing Fields*'s Roland Joffe. *The Mission* seemed blessed when it became the first British movie in thirteen years to win the Palme d'Or at the Cannes Film Festival, but in America, most reviewers weren't as reverential. *Time*'s Richard Schickel sneered, "it confuses the importance of the subject with its own smug self-importance," and others hooted at Robert De Niro's anachronistic Lower East Side accent. In spite of the critics, Warner Bros. set aside a small fortune to convert Academy voters. Murray Weissman, the film's public relations director, explained his philosophy to *Entertainment Tonight:* "No picture can be a serious contender in the race for under $100,000 . . . You have to keep that picture available for Academy members to see. You even want members of their families to see it so that when they talk about it at home—and everybody does—that your son, your daughter and your maid are all having an input to possibly influence you."

The Nominations

For the first time since the 1955 debacle, the Academy attempted a national telecast of the announcement of the nominations. Only this time, the point was to appear live on the network morning news shows, meaning that Hollywood would have to be ready for the East Coast at 5:30 in the morning. "The Academy tried to soften the inconvenience by serving coffee, juice, rolls and Bloody Marys," wrote Jack Mathews in the *Los Angeles Times*, "but there was much grumbling among the crowd gathered there, like so many extras, for the Academy's network toadying." After last year's supporting winners, Anjelica Huston and Don Ameche, read the nominations with Academy President Robert Wise, the *Herald-Examiner*'s Gregg Kilday surveyed the networks' handling of the event. ABC's *Good Morning, America* featured

"No picture can be a serious contender in the race for under $100,000."
—Murray Weissman

David Hartman and Joel Siegel "bouncing up and down in their club chairs with unrestrained excitement"; and Robert Osborne of the CBS *Morning Show* "held his peace until the reading of the nominations was completed, and then almost started to cry since his favorite, *Stand By Me,* had received just one mention. Back in the New York studio, Mariette Hartley offered soothing noises." As for NBC's *Today,* observed Kilday, it "didn't cut to the Academy until Wise and Co. had vanished from the stage."

USA Today called the nominations "A nod to non-Hollywood," noting that the leading Best Picture contenders, *Platoon* and *A Room with a View,* each with eight nominations, were "made largely outside the Hollywood system." *Top Gun* received four nominations, but they were in the technical and music categories. John Powers chuckled in the *L.A. Weekly* that "This year they didn't even *pretend* that the big-studio films were worth nominating. How could they?" *The Mission*'s expensive campaign did result in seven nominations, including Picture and Director, tying it with *Hannah and Her Sisters. Children of a Lesser God* was the fifth Best Picture nominee, although Randa Haines was not among the Director nominees. The press corps cheered the announcement of David Lynch for *Blue Velvet,* but critics Charles Champlin and Jeffrey Lyons went on the radio a few hours later condemning the choice as "an abomination" and "an outrage," speculating that Haines was denied a nomination because of "Academy sexism." Lynch's own reaction was more benign. "I'd like to thank Woody Allen," he said.

Blue Velvet's likeliest acting nominee, Dennis Hopper, invited Leeza Gibbons of *Entertainment Tonight* over to his house to watch him watch the nominations telecast. The actor couldn't believe his ears when his category came on: "*Hoosiers? Hoosiers?* I got it for *Hoosiers?* That's amazing." Gibbons was oblivious to Hopper's surprise, but she was really beside herself when the nominee immediately received a congratulatory phone call from Warren Beatty. Hopper looked on the bright side and commented, "I might have a possibility of winning, only because *Hoosiers* parallels my life a lot, as I'm a recovering alcoholic." His competition included *Platoon*'s sergeants, Tom Berenger and Willem Dafoe, and Denholm Elliott of *A Room with a View.* The fifth nominee was *Hannah*'s workaholic Michael Caine, who was en route to the Bahamas to film *Jaws: the Revenge.*

A year after receiving his Honorary Award, Paul Newman nabbed his seventh nomination, but to take home the gold he'd have to best the critics' darling, Bob Hoskins. Despite pundits calling Newman a shoo-in as the sentimental favorite, Aljean Harmetz warned that because the actor "lives in the East and has kept himself aloof from the industry, the sentiment is qualified." The *Platoon* trickle-down theory worked and enough actors rented *Salvador* or watched it on L.A.'s Z Channel to nominate James Woods, who was fast asleep when his name was called. "I couldn't stand the idea of getting up at 5:30 A.M. to be disappointed one more time," he said. Admitting that he had been "always kind of cynical about Hollywood and everything," the nominee suddenly sounded like a member of the Hollywood Chamber of Commerce: "This is the greatest town on earth today." When Woods celebrated with Oliver Stone, who received a writing nomination for *Salvador* in addition to his expected pair of nods for *Platoon,* the director brought up an old score, "You should have gone to Salvador; it would have made a difference." "This picture was released in two theatres for ten minutes and I get a nomination," Woods retorted. "Aren't you happy yet?"

All that Jazz

Another Actor nominee was saxophonist Dexter Gordon for his role as a dissolute, expatriate jazz saxophonist in *'Round Midnight.* While some columnists wondered how hard it could be for a musician to portray a musician, director Bertrand Tavernier defended his star: "He *is* acting. He's using a lot of himself, like Cooper and Wayne used a lot of themselves—their essence. But he is not just playing himself." Fellow actor William Shat-

"If I were to suggest to Paul some kind of Oscar campaign, he'd hang up on me."
—Paul Newman's publicist

ner said Gordon had his vote, "Whether it was art or being, it was illuminating." Most profiles of the nominee erroneously claimed that *'Round Midnight* was Gordon's film debut; while serving time for a drug rap, he had scored a bit part when 1955's *Unchained* was filmed on location at his prison.

Last year's Best Actor William Hurt had the chance to make it two in a row and his *Children* and real-life costar Marlee Matlin was also nominated. Paramount issued their official statements—Hurt: "I am truly pleased. I hope I can find the strength to bear it with the grace it deserves." Matlin: "I feel great . . . I'm gonna scream later."—then reported the couple would not be available for Oscar publicity. Plenty of publicity was being written about them anyway. Liz Smith scooped that Hurt was "fresh out of the Betty Ford Clinic" after "being treated for alcoholism." Rex Reed grumbled that Matlin, like Dexter Gordon, was undeserving because she wasn't really acting, but he figured she'd be victorious because the Academy "would like to see her give her acceptance speech in sign language the way Louise Fletcher did."

Matlin was in a three-way race with *Peggy Sue*'s Kathleen Turner and *Crimes of the Heart*'s sole Actress nominee Sissy Spacek. Sigourney Weaver of *Aliens* was, as columnist Bob Thomas noted, "the first actress to win an Oscar nomination in the kind of role usually reserved for such performers as Sylvester Stallone and Arnold Schwarzenegger." "I feel quite lucky," Weaver rejoiced. "I don't think I have any chance of getting it, actually, which makes me glad because I can go that night without biting my fingernails." The fifth slot went to Jane Fonda for playing an alcoholic, over-the-hill actress who wakes up next to a dead guy in the murder-mystery *The Morning After*. Director Sidney Lumet woke Fonda with the news and reported, "She really was not expecting it." Neither were some critics who agreed with Dave Kehr's wisecrack in the *Chicago Tribune* that the aerobics queen "has the best muscle tone of any alcoholic in history."

Jane Fonda wasn't as stunned as *Children of a Lesser God*'s Supporting Actress nominee Piper Laurie, who told *USA Today,* that "when I heard my name I slapped my forehead so hard I nearly knocked myself out!" Prognosticators felt Laurie was out of the race, too, which they maintained was between Maggie Smith for *A Room with a View* and Dianne Wiest for *Hannah and Her Sisters*. Unlike her director, Wiest had no compunction about attending the ceremony and arranged to have the evening off from her current off-Broadway show. "Dianne Wiest Makes Neurosis a Success Story" was the headline of the *New York Times* profile of the nominee, which remarked that the actress's professional fortune had come at a time of personal disappointment: "A three-year romance with Sam Cohn, her agent, has come to an end, although he will continue to manage her career." Maggie Smith did not make plans to leave London, informing reporters, "It's a long way to go for a weekend."

The Goldwyn Follies

Samuel Goldwyn, Jr., was in charge of the show and, in the never-ending attempt to get it in under three hours, recommended keeping the documentary and short film winners out of the Dorothy Chandler Pavilion. An ABC inner-office memo reported that when the Academy board voted down Goldwyn's suggestion it was "an extremely stormy session. . . . Sam is extremely upset by this result and is now bringing back the blinking red light which will begin at the end of thirty seconds to signal the acceptors to get off the stage." Goldwyn did convince the Academy to throw all the nominated songs together in one number despite another ABC memo that stated individual song performances were necessary "in order that we have *some* entertainment to break up the monotony of the many awards." But the mogul couldn't find any takers for his opening number based on Frank Loesser's "Fugue for Tinhorns" with new lyrics; Frank Sinatra, Dean Martin, Steve Martin, and Rodney Dangerfield all said thanks but no thanks. Sighed Goldwyn, "I was warned not to take on this ordeal—it's a human

"It's a human taffy-pull."
—Samuel Goldwyn, Jr.

taffy-pull." Marty Pasetta, directing his sixteenth Oscar telecast, was more hard-boiled; *Entertainment Tonight* reported that during rehearsals, he told Costume Design presenter Lauren Bacall "she was not the pope and to refrain from blessing the audience."

On the eve of the ceremony, Andrew Sarris mused, "What makes *Platoon* such an overwhelming winter-book favorite for the Oscar is its exquisite timing. . . . It has taken this long for the bitter, harrowing ambiguities of the Vietnam War to break the Teflon barrier of Ramboism and Reaganism to the mainstream audiences necessary to certify an Oscar winner." Johnny Carson thought it appropriate that *Platoon* was the frontrunner: "If you think Vietnam was long and painful, wait till you see the Oscar show." Among the cheerleaders for Stone's film was Mrs. Anthony Quinn, who boasted to Cindy Adams, "All my sons are excellent actors like my husband. Francesco is in the Academy-Award–nominated movie *Platoon*." At which point her husband butted in, "That's not like me—I haven't been in a nominated movie in twenty years."

The Academy and ABC were not glad about Paul Newman's hemming and hawing over whether he'd attend the ceremony. When he missed the annual nominees luncheon, *Entertainment Tonight* said he was "also a question mark for Oscar night." Three days before the show, Newman sent his regrets, blaming his busy schedule editing *The Glass Menagerie*. Marilyn Beck couldn't resist telling readers that his decision "comes as no surprise to this reporter," adding, "As I predicted in February, there would be no way Newman would subject himself to publicly playing the role of Good Loser again." The actor gave another reason to the Associated Press: "I'm superstitious. I've been there seven times and lost. Maybe if I stay away I'll win."

The Big Night

For the second year, a group of homeless people camped outside of the Dorothy Chandler. One of them, Mike Neely, explained to the *Herald-Examiner*, "Part of the lure of coming to Hollywood is making it in the movies. Well, guess what? Not everyone makes it. Some of us wind up on the streets." The paper reassured Hollywood that Neely's group "did not plan on making a spectacle in front of the TV cameras." "We just want the stars to see us," Neely said. Another contingent held a large sign asking the question "Heaven or Hell?," while, farther down the bleachers, sat "The Laguna Platooners," seven women from Orange County dressed in battle fatigues who rode up in a limousine belonging to their neighbor, John Wayne's widow, Pilar.

As usual, Cesar "Butch" Romero and date were among the first celebrities to arrive on the unusually warm evening. To keep up the glamour quotient, the Academy invited previous acting winners; most of those who showed up were from the Supporting categories: Red Buttons, George Kennedy, Haing S. Ngor, who was talking up a book or movie of his life story, and Rita Moreno who, according to the *Hollywood Reporter*, "showed off her backside to the delighted fans." Current Supporting candidate Dennis Hopper brought along a tiny TV to watch the Indiana vs. Syracuse NCAA basketball final. Dianne Wiest brought Sam Cohn as her date. Her costar in the movie Woody Allen was now shooting, Supporting Actor nominee Denholm Elliott, said he was particularly anxious because, "Unfortunately, I've lost my pink plastic turtle good luck charm."

Daily Variety and the *Hollywood Reporter* agreed that the greatest round of applause in the forecourt went to cohost Chevy Chase. Best Actor nominee Bob Hoskins, after spending the day giving interviews, escorted his wife and stated ebulliently, "I'm here for a party." James Woods arrived with his fiancée, Sarah Owen, and professed that, as a result of his nomination, "You sort of feel you're part of the business. Finally."

Awards Ceremony

MARCH 30, 1987, 6:00 P.M.
THE DOROTHY CHANDLER PAVILION, LOS ANGELES

Your Hosts:
PAUL HOGAN, CHEVY CHASE, GOLDIE HAWN
Televised over ABC

Presenters

Writing Awards . . . . Shirley MacLaine
Sound . . . . Marlee Matlin
Supporting Actress . . . . Anjelica Huston and Don Ameche
Sound Effects Editing . . . . Chevy Chase
Costume Design . . . . Lauren Bacall
Original Score . . . . Bette Midler
Art Direction . . . . Isabella Rossellini and Christopher Reeve
Cinematography . . . . Jennifer Jones
Documentary Short Subject . . . . Helena Bonham-Carter and Matthew Broderick
Thalberg Award . . . . Richard Dreyfuss
Visual Effects . . . . William Shatner and Leonard Nimoy
Documentary Feature . . . . Oprah Winfrey
Supporting Actor . . . . Sigourney Weaver and Jeff Bridges
Song . . . . Bernadette Peters
Makeup . . . . Rodney Dangerfield
Animated Short Subject . . Tom Hanks and Bugs Bunny
Live Action Short Film . . . . Sonia Braga and Michael Douglas
Actress . . . . William Hurt
Editing . . . . Molly Ringwald
Foreign Film . . . . Anthony Quinn
Honorary Award to Ralph Bellamy . . . . . Karl Malden
Director . . . . Elizabeth Taylor
Actor . . . . Bette Davis
Picture . . . . Dustin Hoffman

Performers of Nominated Songs

"Glory of Love" . . . . Peter Cetera
"Life in a Looking Glass" . . . . Tony Bennett
"Mean Green Mother from Outer Space" . . Levi Stubbs
"Somewhere Out There" . . . . Natalie Cole and James Ingram
"Take My Breath Away" . . . . . . Melba Moore and Lou Rawls

"I hope my earrings don't fall off."
—Sigourney Weaver

Academy veteran Sissy Spacek knew the ropes. "The first time I did this, my mouth tasted like cotton," the five-time nominee recalled. "Now I know and carry Tic-Tacs in my purse." First-timer Kathleen Turner modeled a backless midnight blue gown which one observer wrote was cut "to (at least) her twenty-third vertebrae" and told the fans, "I wouldn't miss this for the world!" Sigourney Weaver, in a strapless Geoffrey Beene, was all but conceding the race, commenting, "I hope my earrings don't fall off, that's the only thing I'm nervous about." Male fashion plates, according to the *Herald-Examiner,* included Best Actor nominee Dexter Gordon in "a Lord Byron look with satin bow, vest and tweed jacket" and Director nominee David Lynch "in a string tie that could have come from an old shoe." Marlee Matlin wore a lavender lace dress with baby's breath in her hair, completing the ensemble with black horn-rimmed glasses. She clung to William Hurt's arm as she ascended Army Archerd's podium, where the bleacherites, having been rehearsed by the forecourt emcee, welcomed her by signing "congratulations." Said Archerd, "I wanted to show her the courtesy to be able to greet her that way."

The telecast began with the three crooners Sam Goldwyn found to sing "Fugue for Tinhorns": Telly Savalas, Pat Morita, and Dom De Luise. "After the worst opening to an Oscar telecast in living memory," asked the *Los Angeles Herald-Examiner*'s David Gritten, "where could things go from here?" To Academy President Robert Wise, who advised the TV audience, "Don't be deceived by the glitz and glamour of this evening. This is not the way we look and sound while we ply our trades. We wear blue jeans and pants suits and T-shirts and hair shirts. . . . We don't talk nice like this." But viewers only saw the glitz and glamour when the camera cut to Best Actress nominee Jane Fonda, resplendent in a sleek black gown and white kid gloves. Her husband, state assemblyman Tom Hayden, wore his customary business suit, but their teenage son Troy made his own statement with a solid white tuxedo with ruffled shirt.

The first cohost was Paul Hogan, the Australian tourism pitchman who shocked Hollywood when his movie *Crocodile Dundee* became the second-highest grossing film of the year. Wearing a white jacket, Hogan, a nominee for Original Screenplay, allowed, "I realize I'm not exactly the odds-on favorite, but I traveled 38,000 miles for this . . . if they read out someone else's name instead of mine, it's not going to be pretty."

As "Thus Spake Zarathustra" filled the auditorium, a flying saucer landed on stage, and out popped Shirley MacLaine, kidding her mystic image: "To you that may seem like special effects; to me, that's basic transportation." After a montage of notable screen dialogue—beginning with Paul Newman and Robert Redford uttering an expletive in *Butch Cassidy and the Sundance Kid*—MacLaine announced that Adapted Screenplay Award had gone to *A Room with a View*. Director James Ivory accepted for the absent winner, saying, "There is an idea that Ruth Jhabvala is a very shy person, a sort of recluse, but I can tell you if she were here tonight and not absolutely one half way around the world, she'd be up here in a flash to get this award." Woody Allen defeated Oliver Stone for the Original Screenplay Oscar and MacLaine accepted twice for the no-show: "Once for his body, which is in Michael's Pub playing the clarinet, and once for his spirit which is here. I know."

Taking over as host, Chevy Chase alluded to a line from one of Paul Hogan's TV commercials, "In Hollywood, when we say 'Throw another shrimp on the barbie,' it means we're getting rid of our agents." The camera eyed a laughing Sam Cohn. Turning topical, Chase said "Golan and Globus of Cannon Films paid Sylvester Stallone 12 million for his last picture; they were under the impression the money for the contras was being diverted to them."

Marlee Matlin stepped out with her interpretor to present the Award Sam Goldwyn, Jr., swore she suggested giving—Best Sound. The winners were the crew from *Platoon,* and, as they walked up a side aisle, they passed Original Screenplay

"Now I carry Tic-Tacs in my purse."
—Sissy Spacek

loser Paul Hogan who made good his promise: his unsmiling countenance was not a pretty picture. After one of the Sound victors gave his gratitude, another started to speak, but Lionel Newman's orchestra began playing and the fellow's microphone was turned off. Chevy Chase finished for him, "He said, 'Thanks. A lot.' "

All of the Best Supporting Actress nominees were present save Maggie Smith, and the winner was Dianne Wiest, who exclaimed, "Gee, this isn't like what I imagined it would be in the bathtub." She ended her thanks with a tribute to "my dearest friend, Sam Cohn." Backstage, a reporter asked if Woody Allen looked down his nose at her for attending the Oscars, and Wiest responded, "Oh, no, he's thrilled that I came" and revealed that the director held up shooting because "Denhôlm and I are here."

Wiest's fellow nominee from *Hannah,* Michael Caine, was not there. Delays in the filming of *Jaws: The Revenge* had marooned him in the Bahamas and snafued plans to have him give the Award for Sound Effects Editing. In his hotel room, Caine drank with his makeup man and watched Chevy Chase make the presentation on TV. After a comedy montage of familiar scenes redubbed with inappropriate sound effects, e.g., a gladiator movie mixed to a Jane Fonda workout tape, *Aliens* won and the winner read off a list of names. Lauren Bacall's voice was heard next, over a clip from her film debut in *To Have and Have Not*, commenting "See that suit? It was my first outfit in films and I loved it. It never occurred to me that it was soon to become famous. Six months after the film came out, different versions of that little check suit started popping up all over the country." Bacall then emceed a fashion show of Oscar winner Theoni V. Aldridge's impressions of how this year's Best Costume nominees "might become the clothes of tomorrow," even though they were all period movies. Chorus boys looking like lounge lizards in shiny suits danced around female models in contemporary evening wear "inspired" by, among others, the Catholic bishops' cassocks in *The Mission*. *Variety* wrote of the fashion preview, "It wasn't hopeful." The winner was *A Room with a View,* which had a total costume budget of only $30,000.

Original Score presenter Bette Midler sashayed out flapping her long red shawl as if it were a pair of wings. "I know you're all on the edge of your seats wondering whom I'm going to trash this evening," she said, but then disappointed those who had laughed in anticipation. "I hate to tell you this, folks, there is no trashing to be done in this category. . . . We'll save the cheap shots for the People's Choice Awards." The victorious Herbie Hancock of *'Round Midnight* lauded the "unsung heroes" who "suffered and even died for this music," which he called "this greatest of all expressions of the creative spirit of humankind—jazz." Stating that "praise has long been overdue," Hancock listed a few jazz artists—Bud Powell, Lester Young, Thelonius Monk, Charlie Parker, and Billie Holiday—but the Academy thought the end of his speech was overdue and Newman struck up the orchestra again. Recognizing the cue, Hancock shut up and exited.

Isabella Rossellini, the star of *Blue Velvet* and the off-screen companion of director David Lynch, plugged her movie by wearing blue velvet to present the Art Direction Oscar. Her copresenter, Christopher Reeve, a Merchant-Ivory alumnus, threw objectivity to the wind by cheering when *A Room with a View* received its third Oscar. In contrast, Jennifer Jones was a jittery case of nerves as she stepped out to give the Cinematography Award to *The Mission*'s Chris Menges, who wouldn't settle for a handshake but won a kiss from the presenter.

While actor Pierce Brosnan hawked Diet Coke in a commercial, James Woods left his seat to have a drink in the lounge, where he ran into his competition, Bob Hoskins and Dexter Gordon. "We all bought each other drinks and we all sat around and toasted Paul Newman," he later told KABC-TV. When the commercial ended, Chevy Chase pretended to be caught picking his nose as the show resumed. He joshed, "We have it on good authority that this part of the show is being

"Hi, I'm Elizabeth Taylor."
—Elizabeth Taylor

taped by people who can't stay up late so let me just say, Good Morning, Mr. President. You, too, Nancy. Just kidding. Anyway, he'll forget I said it . . . But she won't." *A Room with a View*'s Helena Bonham-Carter then appeared in a dress she said backstage cost sixty dollars to award the Documentary Short Subject Oscar to Vivienne Verdon-Roe for her antinuke film, *Women—For America, for the World*. Verdon-Roe was interrupted with applause when she appealed, "Let's improve our efforts to care for each other."

Richard Dreyfuss narrated a short documentary on Irving G. Thalberg, describing the mogul as "a shy, sensitive young man" who "had the courage when it was necessary to fire director Eric von Stroheim." When the clips were over, television viewers saw a glum-looking group in the audience identified as "The Thalberg Family." Dreyfuss then claimed that "whatever color the movies are now is due in great part" to the recipient of this year's Thalberg Award, Steven Spielberg. The star of *Jaws* and *Close Encounters* quoted the director on the source of his cinematic inspiration, "I use my childhood and go back there to find ideas and stories, all those horrible traumatic years I spent as a kid became what I do today." Winning the evening's first standing ovation, Spielberg had trouble balancing Thalberg's bust on the podium; after it fell over twice, he kept one hand on it while telling the crowd, "I'm resisting like crazy to use Sally Field's line from two years ago." He effused that it was "a great honor following in the footsteps of some of my heroes" who had won Thalbergs, among them Cecil B. DeMille and Ingmar Bergman, and then said of his generation, "I think in our romance with technology and our excitement at exploring all the possibilities of film and video, I think we have partially lost something that we now have to claim." He further explained that "it's time to renew our romance with the word" and after offering an apologia, "I'm as culpable as anyone in exalting the image at the expense of the word," Spielberg theorized that "only a generation of readers will spawn a generation of writers."

"It is a tie," proclaimed Documentary Feature presenter Oprah Winfrey. Canadian winner Brigitte Berman brought her pocketbook with her and addressed the subject of her film, bandleader Artie Shaw, "Thank you, Artie, for trusting me with your life's story." The two American producers of the cowinner, *Down and Out in America*, about the homeless, brought up their director, who turned out to be 1975 Best Supporting Actress Lee Grant. Grabbing one of their Oscars, Grant held it aloft and announced, "This is for the people who are still down and out in America."

Her earrings firmly fastened, Sigourney Weaver strode onstage with Jeff Bridges to present the Supporting Actor Oscar. The winner was the one nominee who wasn't present, Michael Caine for *Hannah and Her Sisters*. "Having worked with him, I know how much he deserved it," Weaver said of her costar from *Half-Moon Street*, yet another of Caine's 1986 releases. Meanwhile, at the annual Irving Lazar party at Spago, where the actor was a regular, David Frost observed that his victory was "the most emotional moment of the night." Caine's wife and daughter basked in the party-goers' felicitations and then called the winner in Nassau. Mrs. Caine reported afterwards, "Natasha asked him if he was nervous and he said he was too drunk to be nervous."

Sam Goldwyn's touch was evident when all five nominated songs were performed together as one production number with Bernadette Peters serving as the musical bridge by warbling about being "lost in a movie" between the songs. Ever-worried about its image, the Academy deleted a few of the saltier lyrics from one nominee, "Mean Green Mother from Outer Space." The winning song was the number-one hit from *Top Gun*, "Take My Breath Away," the film's only Oscar. Composer Giorgio Moroder, accepting his third Oscar, said, "There were so many great songs this year and this I really like."

A blond Rodney Dangerfield made jokes about his wife's facelift—"Just my luck, there was another just like it underneath"—before handing the Makeup Oscar to the duo responsible for turn-

"Oh, reaaaallly."
—Bette Davis

ing Jeff Goldblum into the title character in *The Fly*. Tom Hanks introduced his Animated Short Film copresenter as "one of the most honored characters in the history of animated cartoons," and there was a silhouette of Mickey Mouse; "Mickey" turned out to be the outline of the back of a chair from which emerged Bugs Bunny, who was disappointed at not handing out Best Actress.

That job went to William Hurt, who had acted opposite four of the nominees. Kathleen Turner smiled grimly, Marlee Matlin nervously brushed her hair back, Sigourney Weaver looked content, and Sissy Spacek savored a last Tic-Tac. Jane Fonda, the one actress who hadn't played a love scene with him, held her daughter Vanessa Vadim's hand as he read her name. "The winner is Marlee Matlin," Hurt said and then signed. Matlin shook her head in disbelief and then climbed the stairs as a sign flashed on an onstage screen crediting her as the editor of *Top Gun*. At the podium, Matlin shook Hurt's hand, kissed him, and shook his hand again. During the prolonged ovation, viewers were treated to a close-up of loser Jane Fonda saying, "That's great." Through her interpreter, Matlin thanked the cast and crew of her film, "particularly William Hurt for his great support and love," and her family, who she said was with her that night. She concluded by signing, "I love you." Army Archerd wrote, "the audience at home could not see the warm and long embrace she received from William Hurt as she came offstage."

The music from *Zorba the Greek* provided the accompaniment for a film montage of Anthony Quinn, the Foreign Language Film Award presenter. Fons Rademakers, the Dutch director of the winning *The Assault*, said that his Oscar had a request for the audience, "Please don't let subtitles scare you off as much as they seem to do from time to time." He then asked his statuette, "Did I talk late or well?" Alex North's music from *A Streetcar Named Desire* heralded Karl Malden, who, in lieu of film clips, gave Honorary Oscar recipient Ralph Bellamy's résumé: President of Actors Equity for twelve years, founding member of the Screen Actors Guild, Academy Governor, and one hundred films, "always the friend but never getting the girl. Sounds familiar," observed Malden. "But he says now in his eighty-third year that he will keep making films until he does get the girl." After the night's second standing ovation, Bellamy prophesized, "I expect to be around for quite a while longer and I look forward to working with those of you with whom I haven't worked." His next set of costars were the Fat Boys.

Chevy Chase stepped out to note that the show was running late and speakers would have to speed up their speeches or else. Then he dropped through a trap door. The Best Director presenter got a laugh simply by stating the obvious: "Hi, I'm Elizabeth Taylor." Wearing a low-cut pink antebellum gown recalling *Raintree County*, Taylor thanked all the directors she had worked with and gushed, "My heart fills with admiration now as I contemplate the nominees for this year's Best Directorial Achievement. God bless them all." David Lynch clutched a piece of blue velvet for luck but the cameraman couldn't locate Oliver Stone until the envelope was being opened. Stone got plenty of air time, though, when Taylor called his name. "Thank you for this Cinderella ending," he began, going on to reprise his Golden Globe speech and lecturing the assemblage that "what you're saying is that for the first time you really understood what happened over there . . . and that it should never, ever in our lifetime happen again." After pausing for applause, Stone turned to show biz, paying tribute to his publicist, Marion Billings, and Hemdale's John Daly, "who gave me a shot when nobody else would." His final paean was personal, "to my wife, Elizabeth, whose deep abiding love got me through the despair."

Clips from *Jezebel, The Letter, The Little Foxes, What Ever Happened to Baby Jane?*, and *All About Eve* and Max Steiner's music from *Now, Voyager* proclaimed the arrival of Bette Davis, seventy-eight, making her first Oscar appearance since her 1983 stroke. Davis received the third standing ovation and won laughs the moment she opened her mouth, "Oh, reaaaallly, thank you."

"I don't believe John Wayne ever went to war."
—Oliver Stone

Wearing glasses and holding cue cards, Davis immediately got down to business. As scenes of the Best Actor nominees started to roll, she announced Bob Hoskins. A few seconds later, realizing she neglected to cite his film, Davis mentioned *Mona Lisa;* clips of Dexter Gordon were being shown at this point, however, so show director Marty Pasetta cut off Davis's microphone, meaning that the other nominees went unnamed. Pasetta did turn it back on in time to hear Davis proclaim the winner: the sole absentee, Paul Newman. Announcer Hank Sims intoned that Robert Wise, who had directed Newman in *Somebody Up There Likes Me,* would accept. Wise began, "Paul wanted everybody to know that after coming here for seven other occasions like this—" but Davis interrupted, "You must let me say something about you first." Wise cut in with, "Wait a minute, darling." "Just a minute," persisted Davis, "I would like to congratulate Paul. I'm sure he's listening. He's not here tonight. And this Award, Paul, is long overdue." Davis turned her attention to Newman's proxy, who stood by sheepishly as she introduced him as "the winner of two Oscars himself," gesturing theatrically and grandiloquently naming his credits, "*The Sound of Music! West Side Story!*" All finished, Davis instructed Wise, "Now you get on." "Thank you my dear," he replied and the audience applauded Davis's colorful performance. Pasetta decided there was no more time for Newman's speech and once again unplugged the mike, had the orchestra play a fanfare, and switched to a long shot of the stage from the rear of the auditorium as Wise vainly tried to read the winner's sentiments.

Pasetta's camera cut to Chevy Chase and Goldie Hawn standing at the other end of the stage. Hawn attempted to proceed, "To present the Award for Best Picture—" but was interrupted as the audience laughed over Wise and Davis's continued presence on stage. Hawn looked over to the other podium and asked, "Are you guys done yet?" She then cracked up and the laughter increased, followed by another hand for Davis and Wise; a confused Hawn and Chase stood there for another moment until he prodded her, "Go ahead." The audience roared with more laughter. Hawn still could not get a hold of herself so Chase began the segue to Best Picture presenter Dustin Hoffman.

Any time that Pasetta might have saved by eliminating Newman's acceptance was for naught because Hoffman extemporized for two minutes and forty seconds, quoting tennis star Jimmy Connors about putting out "115 percent," before he got around to the nominees. The *Los Angeles Times* quoted an Academy official that when Hoffman spoke, "I looked at the Teleprompter, but none of what he said was there." "Fortunately for the egocentric Hoffman," wrote the *Hollywood Reporter*'s Richard Hack, "we didn't control the trap door." After the audience politely applauded the conclusion of Hoffman's panegyric, the presenter accidentally opened the envelope before reading the nominees, grinning embarrassedly. When Hoffman made it official that *Platoon* was the picture of the year, producer Arnold Kopelson and his wife jumped to their feet in an embrace. Mrs. Kopelson kissed her husband on the cheek and then wiped off the lipstick with her hand. The producer hugged his director while Mr. and Mrs. Anthony Quinn clapped for their son's boss in the row directly behind them. At the podium, Kopelson expressed the humble hope that "if, perhaps, *Platoon* could influence people in this and other countries in the world to hesitate before they engage in war, to demand facts and ask questions before the bombs, then we, not just those of us that made *Platoon,* but the entire motion picture industry will have succeeded beyond our wildest imagination." Kopelson ended with something rather more realistic; lifting his Oscar, he shouted, "I will cherish this forever!" As he walked off, there was a shot of antiwar veteran Jane Fonda smiling and applauding while, in the row ahead, Dexter Gordon, looking bored, sat doing neither.

Presumably Hawn and Chase were not referring to the just-annointed Best Picture when they advised, "Wherever you live in this weary world, whatever your problems may be at this moment,

"Now that I've lost, I'm going to be a rebel again."
—James Woods

go to a movie tomorrow and you'll feel better." All of the show's participants came out to mill about onstage, including Robert Wise and Bette Davis, who were holding hands as, superimposed over them, the credits ran: "Directed by Marty Pasetta . . . Associate Director—Marty Pasetta, Jr. . . . Stage Managers—. . . Gregory Pasetta . . . ."

Aftermath

"Looking back on your life now," *Entertainment Tonight*'s Jeanne Woolfe queried Oliver Stone backstage, "does this Oscar in some way make the Vietnam experience worthwhile?" "I used the war rather than letting the war use me," the director answered, "and that's the best revenge I could get." Stone still held a grudge against a 1949 Best Actor nominee, though: "I love John Wayne but *Sands of Iwo Jima* sent me to Vietnam believing that it was exciting and I could make a man out of myself. I don't believe John Wayne ever went to war." Steven Spielberg was battling a barrage of questions about his Award being compensation for the snub over *The Color Purple*. "I don't look upon this Award as amends for anything that some people think I deserved a year ago, or three years ago, or five years ago," he said, pointing out that his prize was "obviously not a statuette, it's a bust of Irving Thalberg." The *L.A. Weekly* made the same distinction, snickering that his was "an award to Spielberg the producer, presumably for endowing the world with such seminal works as *The Money Pit* and *Young Sherlock Holmes*." Elaborating on his acceptance speech, Spielberg said, "I never read very much and I was full of movies and television when I was growing up; after a while it recycles and becomes like a big Xerox machine."

Despite the onstage confusion, Bette Davis "was as spunky and quick-witted as ever backstage," raved the *Hollywood Reporter*. Davis was disappointed that the Best Actor hadn't shown up. "I would have had great fun because Mr. Newman and I were about three blocks apart in Westport, Connecticut, for about eight years and we never met," she said, explaining that "we moved to Westport not to see any actors or anything to do about the industry." Reminiscing about early Oscar ceremonies, Davis sighed, "The Academy Awards have completely changed because we had them in beautiful hotel rooms and we had no time limit on our speeches. There is an impersonality to this now via television."

Marlee Matlin, on the other hand, pontificated on how TV allowed millions to share her victory. "I have to believe that a lot of deaf people are jumping up and down," she signed. "Not only a lot of deaf people, but a lot of other people as well, because of the changes that have taken place in society. It's not just for white Anglo-Saxon hearing people anymore." When a reporter mentioned Rex Reed's skepticism about her acting talent, Matlin said, "I felt very angry and I wouldn't mind meeting this person." But that introduction would have to wait, because Matlin headed off to make merry at the Governors' Ball and Irving Lazar's party with William Hurt in tow. KABC's Steve Edwards told his viewers that Matlin's victory "somehow or other makes us all feel good or a little bigger tonight."

The *Los Angeles Times* covered both the Ball and Swifty Lazar's do and was disappointed in both. The paper worried that the Governors' Ball might be a dying institution. "There was not even a real dance floor," the *Times* complained, adding, "in another clue to the ball's diminished stature, the *paparazzi* not only left early—they barely tried for entry to the ballroom." Photographers were able to get shots of Sigourney Weaver, who had removed her earrings, and James Woods, who said, "Now that I've lost, I'm going to be a rebel again." Dianne Wiest sounded more wistful: "You look forward to it, you get your party dress, you hope your shoes fit, and then it's gone. It's like a dream."

To many of Swifty Lazar's old friends, Spago was a nightmare. The *Times* noted that "Lazar, who has proclaimed long and loud in the past about 'his' guest list and 'his' friends and who will come and who will not, seemed to be letting any and everyone in—including an overwhelming number of camera crews, reporters, and bright,

"I never read very much."
—Steven Spielberg

obnoxious lights." One invitee groused, "I liked it better when we had it at the Bistro. These have just gotten too big." The verdict of the *Times:* "Unless Lazar somehow is able to pull in the reins on his annual A-List bash, it might be headed for 'B-dom.' " Guest Kathleen Turner wasn't worried about the Lazars' social rank; she was still numb from the telecast. "I thought if they took another ten minutes to get to Best Actress I was going to die," the loser gasped. "It's cruel and inhumane!"

Back at the Governors' Ball, "well before midnight," reported the *Times's* Paul Rosenfield, "this year's Cinderella, Oliver Stone, gave a thumbs-up sign to his party. Then quietly, under his breath almost, he said, 'We could just walk.' " Their destination was La Scala, six blocks away, where Hemdale was throwing its own party for the *Platoon* cast, crew, and boot-camp trainer, who came in his full marine dress. The revelers hailed Stone with hearty cries and backslapping and his statuette was passed around for all to examine. Arnold Kopelson joined in the celebration that went on into the early morning hours, but there were headaches later when the producer sued Hemdale for allegedly withholding his share of the profits.

Although Paul Newman wasn't at Spago, his publicist, Warren Cowan, was and he reported his client's quip over the phone, "I'm on a roll now, and maybe now I can get a job." Shirley MacLaine wasn't crazy about accepting substitutes and lamented his absence on his night of triumph, saying, "I would have loved to have seen his face when his name was announced." A month later, Newman attended a party honoring bestselling author Danielle Steele at Cowan's home and was surprised when Mrs. Cowan, Barbara Rush, suddenly handed him his Award. "He seemed embarrassed when presented the Oscar statuette (now engraved) by Rush," observed Army Archerd. Loretta Young walked over and asked, "Was it too little, too late?" Newman nodded affirmatively.

Entertainment Tonight's Leonard Maltin spoke for most reviewers by complaining that "three big winners didn't show up to pick up their statues—seeing a still photo of Paul Newman or Woody Allen or Michael Caine doesn't exactly pack an emotional wallop, does it?" *Daily Variety* was happy that, at least, the TV ratings rose this year—by 1 percent—and observed, "It's the first time in three years the program hasn't hit all-time-low status." Woody Allen fans had to content themselves with a news photo identical to the one shown when he won for *Annie Hall:* him playing jazz clarinet at Michael's Pub in Manhattan. Allen's star, Michael Caine, was flashier. The crew of *Jaws: The Revenge* greeted him the next day with a chorus of "Hail, Britannia," and as soon as the movie wrapped, the English actor made up for lost time. He hurried back to Beverly Hills where *Good Morning America*'s Chantal interviewed him on his back patio and asked him to recite what would have been his acceptance speech. "If any producers are watching," he said, "I promise not to price myself out of the market." In a *People* cover story, Caine vowed, "I feel a performance is in me that will get the leading Oscar."

Marlee Matlin discovered that her Oscar caused an unforeseen reaction in William Hurt. "It really shocked him when I won the Oscar," the twenty-two-year-old actress confided later to *Glamour*, "because it took him a long time to win. He had gone through a great deal; I had just started." By the fall, she was telling interviewers the romance was over. "I wouldn't say we are friends, but I am happy with myself."

The Music Branch was not happy with Herbie Hancock winning the Oscar for Original Score since his soundtrack was, as a member told the *Los Angeles Times*, "more memorable for its jazz standards than Hancock's original work." The disgruntled composers responded by adding a codicil to their eligibility requirements excluding future "scores diluted by the use of tracked or preexisting music."

While the Music Branch quietly made its changes, public attention focused on Bette Davis's presentation of the Best Actor Award. With everyone asking what happened, an Academy spokesman told the Associated Press a few days after the telecast that the snafu was all Davis's fault. "She

"It's cruel and inhumane."
—Kathleen Turner

got off track a bit, as Bette does from time to time," the unidentified authority said. "She's a wonderful lady, but she rambles on and got off cue. Marty Pasetta was faced with a time problem—the show was twenty minutes over its planned three hours—and needed to move things along." When Davis learned the Academy was using her as a scapegoat, she called *Entertainment Tonight* for a press conference to tell "what really happened."

Wearing the same evening gown from the broadcast and standing before her two Oscars, the actress recalled that after she named Bob Hoskins, "someone rushed onstage and said 'go to the winner.' . . . Although utterly perplexed, I did as I was told." Things got more perplexing because "to my amazement and without a chance to say Mr. Wise will accept for Mr. Newman, Mr. Wise was at my side making a speech of acceptance." It wasn't until Davis saw a tape of the show that she realized that after she introduced him, "Mr. Wise and I were no longer part of the Oscar show. We were completely done away with." Davis then went on the offensive. "It was not my fault that they were overtime," she bristled. "We had rehearsed the entire show the night before and I am tired of taking the blame from the press."

Davis got in more licks as a guest on Joan Rivers's show where she scoffed that "It seems that Mr. Pasetta feels I never recovered from my stroke." As for *Entertainment Tonight*'s report that the incident so incensed the actress that she would never again deign to appear on an Oscarcast, "That is not true," Davis clarified. "But," she added, "I would want to change the *director*, no doubt."

1987

"There is nothing Sally Kirkland won't talk about."
—San Francisco Chronicle

Joan Fontaine and Olivia de Havilland flirted with disaster at the sixtieth Academy Awards, where dutiful children and out-of-towners made off with the glory.

After making her notorious appearance at the 1985 Academy Awards, Cher returned to work, filming three movies in a row. First up was *The Witches of Eastwick,* starring Jack Nicholson and based on John Updike's bestseller. "I didn't like *Witches,*" she told *Film Comment,* "but I took it because of Jack." Cher joined Susan Sarandon and Michelle Pfeiffer as a trio of modern-day witches sparring with Nicholson's misogynist devil. According to Cher, there was plenty of sparring on the set with the producers. "We were always referred to as the girls," she recalled, "and I don't want anybody calling me 'the girls' in that way. We had lousy facilities, lousy trailers." Cher did have kind words for Nicholson, calling him "a man who feels that women are smarter and better than men," but even he was useless when the actresses didn't have costumes for certain scenes. Cher called her personal couturier, Bob Mackie, and instructed him to send some things over. The critics called *Witches* Nicholson's show; "No one really has a chance as long as Jack Nicholson, in a samurai hairdo and brocade lounging robe, is chewing up the scenery as Van Horn. He hams it up with a gleeful vengeance," chortled the *New York Daily News's* Kathleen Carroll. The comedy was a summer hit, but Cher dismissed it as "just an okay piece of fluff."

Lasse's Great Adventure

When *Rolling Stone* asked Nicholson his favorite movie of the year, he chose *My Life as a Dog,* director Lasse Hallstrom's Swedish film about a young boy who is sent to live with relatives while his mother dies from tuberculosis. The gentle comedy bowed during the spring without much hoopla; Jeff Lipsky, the president of the film's U.S. distributor, Skouras Pictures, said the company's coffers were so low, exhibitors had to come up with their own methods of advertising. In Minneapolis, a theatre-owner sent a ten-year-old boy around town in a sandwich board poster accompanied by a sheep dog. The combination of critical reaction—the *Boston Globe* opined that the movie "resonates with a charm and beauty that hasn't been seen since Fellini's *Amarcord*"—and word of mouth turned the film into such a long-running art-house hit that, by the fall, its Los Angeles ads were already informing Academy members they would be admitted free to any performance. President Lipsky elaborated on his Oscar campaign plans to the *Hollywood Reporter;* they included mailing posters "to everybody in the acting, writing, and directing branches. . . . We will send out those one-sheets prior to Christmas so they can even be used as Christmas gifts."

Savoring the fruits of a hard-fought campaign, Best Actress nominee Sally Kirkland turns cheerleader for the fans in the bleachers.

Connery by Armani

Skouras's box-office success was, nonetheless, peanuts compared to Paramount's summer jackpot, led by Eddie Murphy's *Beverly Hills Cop II*, the year's highest-grosser, and Brian DePalma's *The Untouchables*. Although the latter was based on an old TV series, it was a deluxe movie package, complete with a wardrobe by Giorgio Armani and a screenplay by Pulitzer Prize–winner David Mamet. The movie's reviews were mixed but the praise was unanimous for Sean Connery as the veteran Irish cop who takes Elliot Ness under his wing in Prohibition-era Chicago. *Time*'s Richard Schickel wrote that Connery's character "is a weary, steady man, very clearly seen by an actor whose every gesture is wryly informed by the humorous and uncynical knowledge of a lifetime."

Sex and Violence

Prior to *The Untouchables*, Paramount had announced that Brian De Palma would be directing

"It was like having two hours of foreplay and no orgasm."
—Adrian Lyne

Michael Douglas in "an Alfred Hitchcock–type thriller" called *Diversions,* but he decided not to because the plot was too similar to Clint Eastwood's *Play Misty for Me.* John Boorman and John Carpenter also nixed the project about a psychopathic one-night stand, so *Flashdance*'s Adrian Lyne got the call. Finding an actress to play the vengeful woman was as hard as getting a director; first-choices Isabel Adjani and Debra Winger were not interested, and Barbara Hershey was unavailable. Then Michael Douglas's brother Eric showed the script to his friend Glenn Close, who told her agent she was "willing to do anything" for the part. "I wanted to break out of the kind of roles I used to do because I was boring myself," explained the screen earth mother. Lyne was standoffish. "Glenn certainly wasn't an obvious choice because she's not obviously erotic." After Close submitted to a screen test, the director told her the part was hers—if she lost ten pounds. A slimmer Close reported to work and jumped into the explicit love scenes, but at first, she confessed later to the *New York Daily News,* "I had to have a margarita every ten minutes."

When Paramount tested the movie, now called *Fatal Attraction,* audiences were enthralled until the very end, when Close's temptress frames Douglas's paramour with her suicide. "People were unsatisfied with an off-camera solution," Lyne observed of the booing crowds. "It was like having two hours of foreplay and no orgasm." Two months before the opening, the director and his stars trooped back to the film's Bedford, New York, location at a cost of $1.3 million to make sure the thriller ended with a bang. *New York* asked Paramount what was going on and the official spokesperson replied, "They are just doing pick-up shots and backgrounds, nothing dramatic."

Variety reviewed the new version, which ended with Douglas drowning a knife-wielding Close and his wife shooting her to finish the job, and cheered, "The screws are tightened expertly in this suspenseful thriller about a flipped-out femme who makes life hell for the married man who scorns her." *Newsweek*'s David Ansen resented the sell-out and chided, "A smattering of psychological veracity gets cynically chucked out the window for the sake of cheap thrills."

Paramount knew the box-office value of cheap thrills and *Fatal Attraction* immediately began earning almost as much money for the studio as *Beverly Hills Cop II.* "The attraction to Adrian Lyne's flashy slasher seems unstoppable," remarked the *Hollywood Reporter* of the movie's worldwide grosses, and *Time* soon gave *Fatal Attraction* a cover story in which Richard Corliss attributed the movie's success to its being "like velcro: any theory can attach itself to the story and take hold." In the *L.A. Reader,* John Powers mentioned two leading theories: "Although some people argue that this film is about AIDS terror (see what happens when you screw around), *Fatal Attraction* is much more about men's fear and hatred of women." Marilyn Beck championed it as "the year's greatest deterrent to marital infidelity," but coproducer Sherry Lansing thought *Fatal Attraction* was simply a movie anyone could identify with. "All of us have made a call in the middle of the night when we shouldn't have," she observed. "I've never boiled a rabbit, but I've made phone calls." If further proof of the movie's position as what the *Los Angeles Times* called a "socioeconomic phenomenon" was needed, Oprah Winfrey, Phil Donohue, and Geraldo Rivera all dedicated shows to victims of "real life Fatal Attractions."

The Most Hated Woman in America

Glenn Close defended the Grand Guignol finale because "people get so disturbed about my character they want to get some sort of revenge." She didn't take it personally, telling the *New York Times,* "I'm following in a great tradition. Think of all the great villains Bette Davis and Joan Crawford played." *Vogue* appreciated that tradition, dubbing hers "The Most Talked-About Performance of the Year," and commenting "Close should be congratulated for making a great career swerve in a very dangerous vehicle." The supermarket tabloids labeled her "The Most Hated Woman in America," and grew even more fascinated when

"I've never boiled a rabbit, but I've made phone calls."
—Sherry Lansing

Radie Harris scooped in the *Hollywood Reporter* that "Glenn Close is discovering that life often imitates art. . . . Now, she is enceinte again, but in this *unreel* condition, the identity of the father is still a mystery." Not for long. He turned out to be John Starke, who had worked on the production of *The World According to Garp*, the movie that had typecast her as a nurturing mother in the first place. Starke was also Close's business associate in her booming new career as a screen siren. Producers began keeping her in mind for steamy roles for the first time because, as Allan Carr put it to Marilyn Beck, "who knew she was sexy before?"

A Boy's-Eye View

When Sherry Lansing reminded John Boorman he could have been the director profiting from *Fatal Attraction*'s box-office boom, he told her, "it wouldn't have made as much money if I'd taken the assignment. For one thing, I wouldn't have allowed you to use that ending." The helmer of tough action pictures like *Deliverance* and *Point Blank,* Boorman went on to make as radical a departure as Glenn Close by taking a fond look back at his childhood in World War II Britain in *Hope and Glory*. "It took me years before I was able to open my heart with this kind of honesty," Boorman said, but the desire to complete the film while his octogenarian mother was still alive to see it inspired him to finish his script, which he promptly showed to his family. "I wouldn't have made it had they disapproved," he reassured the *New York Times,* but admitted that his older sister "collapsed and took to her bed for three days. All the things she'd been up to as a teenager that she'd thought she'd got away with had actually been observed by a small boy."

No producer in Britain was interested in Boorman's memoirs so the director took his irreverent portrait of the homefront to the enemy and obtained his financing from Germany, as well as nineteen other countries. Compatriot David Puttnam, now in Hollywood as the newly installed chairman of Columbia Pictures, supplied the final funds for Boorman's $9.5 million budget and guaranteed U.S. distribution. Describing the project as "a foreign film shot on location in England," Boorman commenced filming at an abandoned airstrip where he recreated and then destroyed his old neighborhood. Determined to avoid the clichéd "spirit of the Blitz: stiff upper lip and all those ludicrous things," Boorman showed war as a young boy's playground, more reminiscent of *Our Gang* than *Mrs. Minivor*. "It's hard to believe that a great comedy could be made of the Blitz, but John Boorman has done it," exclaimed Pauline Kael when *Hope and Glory* premiered at the New York Film Festival.

Puttnam Packs Up

No sooner had the glowing reviews appeared then Coca-Cola, the owner of Columbia, ousted Puttnam from his post after a corporate coup. Columbia's new management released *Hope and Glory* in only fifty theatres with little advertising; Boorman's hopes for a wider release were dashed when the new studio heads had a falling out with the massive Cineplex Odeon theatre chain, which then refused to book the movie for Christmas. The director did get one wish, however; his mother saw the film and "was very moved by it," not even minding that her son revealed she had been in love with her husband's best friend. Boorman said that "with both men dead, she was glad to have it out in the open."

China, Italian Style

The Puttnam pickup that sparked the fight with Cineplex Odeon was Bernardo Bertolucci's $25 million saga about twentieth-century China, *The Last Emperor*. In 1984, after two years in Hollywood preparing an adaptation of Dashiell Hammett's *Red Harvest* to star Jack Nicholson, Bertolucci was distraught when the project fell apart. "I wanted to disappear, to go as far as possible from the West," the director of *Last Tango in Paris* said. "So, from the far West, I went to the Far East." His passport was the autobiography of

Pu Yi, who was made emperor of the Manchu dynasty in 1908 at age three only to be deposed three years later in a life of downward mobility—he wound up as a gardener in Peking in the 1960s. "I was fascinated by the character of a man who was kidnapped by history," recounted Bertolucci. "It's the story of a metamorphosis, of a dragon who is turned into a butterfly."

After Bertolucci and his brother-in-law, Mark Peploe, converted Pu Yi's life into a screenplay, the director and British producer Jeremy Thomas spent the next two years talking the Chinese government into allowing them to shoot on location. *Variety* reported the final deal: Thomas and Bertolucci "have secured unprecedented cooperation from the People's Republic of China," including permission to film in the previously verbotten Forbidden City, in exchange for distribution rights in China. Thomas was not as persuasive with either British or American studios, so he sweet-talked British merchant banks into bankrolling the epic by reminding them that it was "a project that would give them contacts and links into China." Bertolucci filmed for six months in China and Italy to cover sixty years of Chinese history, using 19,000 extras, 9,000 costumes, and four actors in the title role. David Puttnam saw a forty-minute excerpt of the two-hour-and-forty-five-minute spectacle and decided immediately that Columbia should release it in America; he was fired by the time *The Last Emperor* opened in November.

Sitting on the Emperor

"Turning Bernardo Bertolucci loose in the treasure chest of Imperial China is like locking a chocaholic inside a Godiva factory for the night," raved *Newsweek*'s David Ansen. "Bertolucci creates images other people just dream about; he may be the last emperor of the epic cinema." But the *New Republic*'s Stanley Kauffmann kvetched that "Pu Yi is simply an eccentricity of history, worth a paragraph in the *Reader's Digest*, not a nearly three-hour film." The *New York Daily News* shared the opinion of most reviewers, that the film was a "visually thrilling historical drama" but the catch was a "lack of emotional involvement."

The new regime at Columbia made its lack of interest in *The Last Emperor* clear when it reneged on a commitment to Cineplex Odeon to play the movie at 150 of the chain's theatres. The *Los Angeles Herald-Examiner*'s Richard Natale reported that all of Hollywood was wondering, "Is it conceivable that as astute an executive as Victor Kaufman, the studio's heir apparent, would deliberately put the kibosh on a potential major grosser (and certain Best Picture nominee) to further embarrass the dismissed David Puttnam? It was apparent after its first weekend that *The Last Emperor* had a high want-to-see—in much the same way as last year's *Platoon*. Whereas Orion Pictures immediately expanded the film's playdates, Columbia has largely sat on *Emperor*."

Shanghai Steve

While Columbia was acting as if *The Last Emperor* was an unwanted child, Warner Brothers was treating *its* Far East epic like a favorite son since it was directed by Steven Spielberg. The forty-year-old Thalberg Award winner told the *New York Times* he "had decided to do a movie with grown-up themes and values, although spoken through a voice that hadn't changed through puberty yet." He found what he was looking for in J. G. Ballard's autobiographical novel *Empire of the Sun*, about a ten-year-old British boy in Shanghai who spends World War II in a Japanese prison camp. When the $35 million, two-hour-thirty-one-minute adventure—photographed in China, Spain, and England—debuted as Warner's major Christmas release, Andrew Sarris, a longtime Spielberg detractor, became one of his biggest boosters. "What I did not anticipate was that Spielberg would so completely overwhelm my skepticism that I am almost prepared to vote his most recent production the best picture of the year," he wrote, adding that he "was stirred and moved on a scale I had forgotten still existed." Despite Sarris's conversion, other critics were less enthused. The *Chicago Tri-*

"I think I lept into his arms."
—James L. Brooks on William Hurt

bune's Dave Kehr opined that the movie wasn't "drawn from observation or introspection but from some vague impressions of what a masterpiece should be—impressions gathered in this case largely from the somber epics of David Lean, with a dose of René Clement's *Forbidden Games*." *Variety* accurately predicted that the "lack of a strong narrative might well keep ultimate b.o. at a lower level than is customary for the director." *Empire of the Sun* made even less money than *1941*.

Greed

Last year's Best Director, Oliver Stone, was prepared for disappointment, telling *Premiere*, "I would rather turn something out fast, get it over with, give the gold crown to somebody else . . . I'm not expecting the same critical praise or the same box office I got for *Platoon*." He spun the same type of morality tale, though, in *Wall Street*, with *Platoon* star Charlie Sheen playing another innocent, this time in New York's financial market instead of Vietnam. As Gordon Gekko, the film's corrupt corporate raider, Stone cast Michael Douglas, who had just filmed *Fatal Attraction*, despite the fact that "I was warned by everyone in Hollywood that Michael couldn't act." Calling the character "a bit of a prick," Douglas relished the part because "villains have always done a lot for actors' careers." When shooting started, Stone may have wondered if he should have heeded Hollywood about his star. "I was amazed, for an actor who has done so many movies, how nervous he was in the beginning," Stone recalled. "He couldn't believe it when on the first day I gave him three pages of monologue." Douglas hung in there, because, he said, his father, Kirk, had told him that he was finally about to become a real actor, who could play a heel as well as a hero.

Just as Douglas's *The China Syndrome* had benefited from the publicity surrounding the Three Mile Island nuclear accident, *Wall Street* profited from the October 19 stock market crash, two months before its release. Vincent Canby enjoyed the "tantalizing Sidney Sheldon–like peek into the boardrooms and bedrooms of the rich and powerful," and *Films and Filming*'s Brian Baxter claimed "no other mainstream director is even attempting such a devastating critique of American society as Stone has successfully done in three movies. Let's hope the CIA hasn't got a contract out on him." But the voice of the financial community was not impressed by *Wall Street*. "A silly, pretentious melodrama that panders to the current fascination with insider trading," wrote Julie Salamon in the *Wall Street Journal*.

Michael Douglas's reviews were strictly blue chip. *New York*'s David Denby noted, "He's never acted with this kind of gusto and power before," and in the *Los Angeles Times*, Lawrence Christon commented, "It appears he's tapped into a lifetime of personal observations of high-level power types in action—the movie looks as though it could easily have been transferred to studio executive suites in Hollywood." The acclaim made Douglas as familiar a face as Glenn Close on the covers of tabloids, which warned his ten-year marriage might be on its last legs.

Hits and Misses

Last year's fairy tale Oscar romance, William Hurt and Marlee Matlin, had long been pfffft by the time their follow-ups to *Children of a Lesser God* bowed in December. Matlin played a small role in the political satire *Walker*, which was shown in a few theatres for a few days and then forgotten, but Hurt continued on a roll by starring in James L. Brooks's first movie since his *Terms of Endearment* Oscar sweep. "The Oscar gives you the right to make whatever movie you want next," the writer-director-producer said, but it took him a couple of years to decide what he wanted: "We're all becoming so involved with our work, it's become work as family, work as home, work as sex. And I wanted to trace how those changes have come about, what they mean to our lives." The workplace Brooks chose was television news, an area he knew from toiling as a newswriter for CBS in the '60s and from his days as a producer of *The*

"Sometimes I feel like an old hooker."
—Cher

Mary Tyler Moore Show in the '70s. After two years of hanging out in newsrooms to see how things had changed, he sat down "to write a true triangle," he told the *New York Times*. "The minute one of the men seemed to be winning, I made an effort to shore up the relationship."

Brooks had Debra Winger in mind for the romantic object, a neurotically driven news producer, and wrote the part of a gifted-but-not-very-sexy reporter for an old friend, comedian-filmmaker Albert Brooks. Once Brooks hit upon the idea of casting William Hurt as the handsome and amiable dunce who becomes a network anchorman, he decided that no other actor could play the role and he might as well scrap the project if Hurt wasn't interested. When the actor said yes, Brooks "was like a cat. I think I leapt into his arms." And to top it off, Jack Nicholson volunteered to do a couple of scenes as a network anchor free of charge, according to Liz Smith. With everything going along so smoothly, Debra Winger announced she was pregnant, sending the director on a six-month search for a replacement. Two days before rehearsals and still with no leading lady, someone suggested Brooks have a look at a twenty-nine-year-old New York stage actress from Georgia named Holly Hunter. He signed her right away, avowing, "God was my casting director."

The critics tended to agree. "Holly Hunter gives one of the finest screen performances I've ever seen," claimed Mike Clark in *USA Today*, "a performance so natural, yet packed with so much discernible detail, that it somehow seems simultaneously off-the-cuff and crafted." Her costars also heard hosannahs; in the *Philadelphia Inquirer*, Carrie Rickey said, "Albert Brooks' is one of the indelible movie characters of the decade," and the *Hollywood Reporter*'s Duane Byrge thought "William Hurt is magnificent. . . . He fits what seem to be contradictory qualities, dumb ambition and decency, into the fabric of a completely drawn character." Janet Maslin cooed, "The real star is behind the camera, since the writer, director, and producer has given his film such uncompromising intelligence and such enormous appeal." The popularity of *Broadcast News* propelled it onto the covers of *Newsweek* and *People;* in the latter, Dan Rather called the film "an appropriate warning about the dangers of whom you put on the air," but Tom Brokaw protested, "It vastly exaggerates the conflict between the serious and the lightweight."

Moon Over Brooklyn

Opening the same day as *Broadcast News* was another, less heralded, romantic comedy, *Moonstruck,* Cher's third movie of the year. Her second, *Suspect,* a thriller in which she played an attorney, had come and gone in the fall with little excitement; Pauline Kael complained of the filmmakers, "Probably these fellows were just so proud of not having made the woman a bimbo that they didn't notice they'd made her a lummox." *Moonstruck* had been written by playwright John Patrick Shanley for Sally Field, who couldn't satisfy a studio that she'd be believable as the film's Italian-American heroine. When Norman Jewison bought the script, Cher was his first choice to play the plain, forty-ish widow who blossoms when she falls for her fiancé's brother. As the actress brushed up on her Brooklynese with cast member Julie Bovasso, the celebrated dialect coach for the cast of *Prizzi's Honor,* members of the New York theatrical community began scrambling to portray the rest of Cher's family. "Word came very fast that there was this great screenplay around," said Olympia Dukakis, fifty-six. "I and a couple of thousand actors knew about it." She won the part of Cher's philosophical mother, but her husband, Louis Zorich, lost the role of the philandering father to Vincent Gardenia. Although Shanley made director Jewison agree to no fiddling with his dialogue, Dukakis was permitted to insert one line, telling Cher, "Your life is going down the toilet!"

The *Los Angeles Times*'s Sheila Benson called *Moonstruck* "an incredibly *nourishing* comedy, filled as it is like rigatoni with warmth, cheer and terrific snappy dialogue." Chris Chase wrote in the *New York Daily News,* that "In a movie full of

"Jack turned fifty on this project, most of the time he looked seventy."
—Meryl Streep

good things, Olympia Dukakis may just be the best." The *New York Times* profiled author Shanley and praised him as "a playwright whose obsessive passions are expressed in richly melodic language." As for the leading lady, Pauline Kael was much happier this time: "Cher isn't afraid to be a little crazy here, and she's devastatingly funny and sinuous and beautiful." Bruce Kirkland seconded it in the *Toronto Sun:* "Cher, in a dizzying virtuoso act, makes all the right moves."

Cher, Cher, Everywhere

Cher knew the publicity game, too. In the months surrounding *Moonstruck*'s release, she was on every conceivable magazine cover, from *Newsweek* to *Health and Fitness.* In addition, the forty-one-year-old star kept the gossip sheets intrigued by living with twenty-three-year-old Robert Camilletti, made the top ten charts with her first new record in years, and appeared on the *David Letterman Show* for a reunion with Sonny Bono, himself pursuing new career opportunities by running for mayor of Palm Springs. The *Hollywood Reporter*'s Robert Osborne let it be known that "Cher was the eleventh-hour savior for the Academy Monday night when she stepped into the boots left vacant by Glenn Close (confined on location in Arizona . . .) at the Academy's salute in New York to the late Johnny Mercer." And she continued to play gym queen in her sixth year as celebrity spokesperson for Jack LaLanne health clubs, encouraging couch potatoes, "If you can make yourself look more interesting, you've got more of a choice of people being interested in you, I guess." Cher analyzed her popularity to the *New York Times Magazine:* "Sometimes I feel like an old hooker. You know, just because they've stayed alive and stayed around, people start to respect them." When asked about her desire to win an Oscar, Cher insisted she had learned a valuable lesson from a former costar, "Meryl Streep told me a long time ago you don't do movies to get Oscars or get awards, you just do them because you really love doing them."

A Couple of Drunks

Even Streep was not above posing for a glamour shot for the cover of *Life* under the legend "On Top—And Tough Enough to Stay There" when her latest costarring vehicle with Jack Nicholson rolled up just in time to qualify for the Oscars—*Ironweed.* "This movie is like nothing anyone's seen on screen in thirty years," producer Keith Barish promised Marilyn Beck, heralding his $27 million adaptation of William Kennedy's Pulitzer Prize–winning novel about alcoholic drifters in Depression Albany. "It's got humor, drama, pathos." His stars got in on the prerelease hype by paying tribute to each other: "Helen is one of Meryl's greatest transformations"; "Jack turned fifty on this project, most of the time he looked seventy . . . but what he's done is tremendous." *People* toasted them both, "They are two of the greatest actors on the planet," but Janet Maslin wondered "why audiences in the market for a big-budget Christmas film should be drawn to anything as downbeat and actionless as this one." They weren't, but Tri-Star filled the trade papers with Oscar ads anyway and hired a publicist whose job was described by one studio executive: "What he does is organize a lot of screenings for small groups of influential people and sells the movie to them. He's like a Mercedes salesman. He calls the next day and says, 'Well, how's it drive? Is that a car or what?' "

Radio Days

This Christmas's Vietnam movie was as big a smash as *Platoon,* only it happened to be a comedy. Although *Good Morning, Vietnam* was based on a real person, a popular and irreverent disc jockey for Armed Forces Radio in Saigon named Adrian Cronauer, its *raison d'être* was fitting Robin Williams's manic, free-form comic routines into the framework of a movie. "I tried to take advantage of Robin's amazing mind and give him absolute freedom," director Barry Levinson said and

"They're telling us that we live in a decent society and I don't believe that."
—Wallace Shawn

the critics assured him he had succeeded. Vincent Canby called *Good Morning, Vietnam* "a breakthrough for Mr. Williams, who for the first time in movies, gets a chance to exercise his restless, full-frontal comic intelligence" while Michael Wilmington of the *Los Angeles Times* averred, "Blazing away brilliantly, ad-libbing on camera, Williams is like a man possessed: a Crazy Eddie of showbiz dada." Unlike the comedian's six previous films, *Good Morning, Vietnam* was a box-office titan, holding the number-one position for two months. Williams was appreciative because "this is the first role that calls upon me to do what I do best—me." That was fine for the real Adrian Cronauer, who quipped "Robin was the me I would have liked to have been."

Duse and Don'ts

Robin Williams had the luxury of a smash hit, but Sally Kirkland had nothing but her own spunk going for her when she ballyhooed her performance in *Anna*, a little-seen independent film made for $700,000. Kirkland had gained notoriety two decades earlier by being the first actress to appear totally nude on stage in *Sweet Eros*, by throwing money on the floor of the New York Stock Exchange with Abbie Hoffman and Jerry Rubin, and by showing up on the cover of *Screw*, naked and riding a pig. Moving to the West Coast in the early '70s, Kirkland gave acting classes and became an ordained minister in the Church of the Movement of Spiritual Inner Awareness. She had only limited success in movies, however, including small roles in *The Sting* and *The Way We Were*, so after her performance as *Anna*'s expatriate Czech actress struggling in New York—Sheila Benson singled it out as a "Little Gem Amid All the Flashy Biggies"—Kirkland set out to buck the odds and win a nomination by doing her own tubthumping. The *San Francisco Chronicle* marveled, "There is nothing Kirkland won't talk about," and she startled the audience at the San Francisco Film Festival by reminiscing about a suicide attempt at age twenty-three while having an affair with Rip Torn when Geraldine Page was pregnant. Kirkland also hired two leading publicists, Dale Olson in Hollywood and John Springer in New York, and by early December the trades had full-page ads quoting everyone from Rex Reed to the *B'nai B'rth Messenger*. The actress mailed letters to every Academy member—even though only those in the Acting Branch were eligible to nominate her—and her friend Shelley Winters personally made 150 phone calls soliciting votes on her behalf. Kirkland's self-appraisal: "I don't want to sound like an egotist, but I think of myself as the Eleanora Duse of the twentieth century."

Space Gobblers

Kirkland's publicity budget was dwarfed by the massive campaign sums studios were shelling out for previous Oscar winners Richard Attenborough, Barbra Streisand, and Faye Dunaway, whose current movies weren't exactly packing them in. Surveying the first round of trade paper ads, Marc Cooper noted in *Premiere*, "The most voracious space gobblers early in the current campaign were *Cry Freedom, Nuts,* and *Barfly*." The last was Dunaway's own *Ironweed*, an alcoholic's tour of Los Angeles bars drawn from Charles Bukowski's personal experiences, that Cannon Films was touting as its likeliest Oscar contender. *Cry Freedom*, Attenborough's $23 million, two-hour-thirty-five-minute antiapartheid drama, had already laid an egg in its initial urban bow. Gambling on Oscar nominations, Universal held back on a major release until February, and, hoping to improve its odds, revamped the film's posters to resemble the one from *Out of Africa*, the studio's last big winner. *Cry Freedom*'s most probable nominee was Denzel Washington for portraying Steven Biko, so Universal pushed him for Best Actor even though his character is killed off halfway through the movie. *Nuts*, an adaptation of a Broadway flop about a prostitute trying to prove her sanity while on trial for murder, starred and was produced by Streisand, who also wrote the musical score. By year's end, "there was already wide spec-

"Shut up, you fool!"
—John Simon

ulation that Warner Brothers had pushed too hard too soon on *Nuts*," commented Cooper. "Barbra Streisand's look-at-me-Ma performance led industry wags to dub the film *Mentl*—a pointed reference to *Yentl*, which failed to win her an Oscar." But Murray Weissman, Warner Brothers's publicist, disagreed. "We're very, very careful not to overhype, overcampaign," he said emphatically on *Entertainment Tonight* as he sat between two giant ads for *Nuts* and *Empire of the Sun*.

Off and Running

Warner Brothers could feel justified in its hype when the National Board of Review, the first group to announce its year-end awards, gave best picture and director citations to the Spielberg opus. Sean Connery, who had also hired a public relations firm for Oscar purposes, was the unanimous choice for best supporting actor. *Us* disclosed that his campaign was now in full gear, "though Connery intensely dislikes doing interviews, he'll allow the agency to trot him out for 'select projects,' " such as the cover of a glossy edition of the *Hollywood Reporter* and a Barbara Walters special. His publicist couldn't count on any more awards from the critics; the rest of the supporting actor trophies went to Morgan Freeman for playing a vicious pimp in *Street Smart,* a Christopher Reeve movie from Cannon that lasted for two weeks in the spring. Vanessa Redgrave was New York's choice for supporting actress as Joe Orton's crafty agent in *Prick Up Your Ears*, but the National Board and the Los Angeles critics elected *Moonstruck*'s Olympia Dukakis, who suddenly took the lead in the Oscar race within days of her picture's release.

The National Board named Michael Douglas best actor for *Wall Street,* but made Holly Hunter of *Broadcast News* share best actress with Lillian Gish, eighty-seven, who starred in the low-budget *The Whales of August*. The public had been more interested in reading reports of off-screen antagonism between Gish and costar Bette Davis than in actually seeing the movie, but the Board's acknowledgment of Gish—they threw in a lifetime achievement award to her, too—prompted Oscar talk about D. W. Griffith's star. The *Hollywood Reporter*'s Martin Grove quoted one "insider": "Since Lillian Gish has never won an Oscar and this is probably her last film, she'll win if she's nominated."

Holly Hunter didn't have to worry about Gish as far as the other critics groups were concerned; the newcomer nabbed best actress honors from both the New York and Los Angeles circles, although on the West Coast she had to split the award with cowinner Sally Kirkland, whose campaign was going great guns. Robert Osborne itemed in the *Hollywood Reporter* that "Sally Kirkland not only pulled a Golden Globe nomination for her superb *Anna* performance but many of her pals, including . . . Dale Olson and several of Kirkland's thespian friends are planning an 'Actors and Others for Sally Kirkland'(!) cocktail-buffet din in her honor at Olson's home." Among the guests were Robert De Niro and Leonard Maltin, who brought along an *Entertainment Tonight* camera crew.

What Kind of Fool Am I?

Steve Martin, who had updated José Ferrer's Oscar-winner *Cyrano de Bergerac* in the comedy *Roxanne,* took joint possession of the L.A. critics award with Jack Nicholson, tapped for both *The Witches of Eastwick* and *Ironweed*. Martin also copped a scroll from the National Society of Film Critics and Nicholson a plaque from the New York Circle, who cited his unbilled *Broadcast News* cameo, too. The *Los Angeles Times* listed the two actors as "shoo-ins" for Oscar nominations in December, but Steve Martin, like Cher, had given up on awards. "I would have turned handsprings to have gotten nominated for *All of Me*," he told the *Times*. "It's not as important as it would have been several years ago."

The National Society of Film Critics gave best picture to the late John Huston's final film, *The Dead*, and the Los Angeles crowd stood firmly be-

"My position is that of a quiet fatalist."
—Marcello Mastroianni

hind John Boorman's *Hope and Glory*. The New York awards party was a testimonial to *Broadcast News*, with only one sour moment. When actor-playwright Wallace Shawn presented the screenplay plaque, he stated that he trusted James L. Brooks more than "the networks and the people who put out the *New York Times*, I don't respect them. They're telling us that we live in a decent society and I don't believe that." Then, in what *Variety* described as "an unusual heckling incident," John Simon screamed at Shawn, "Shut up, you fool!"

Waiting for Oscar

Michael Douglas and Sally Kirkland kept up their winning streaks by earning Golden Globes for drama. The comedy victors were Robin Williams and Cher, the latter taking the opportunity to thank her fans for standing by her through her career ups and downs. David Puttnam was history but the Hollywood Foreign Press remembered him well, granting their Best Drama globe to *The Last Emperor* and the Best Comedy one to *Hope and Glory*. Despite this encouragement, John Boorman was uneasy because he believed Columbia wasn't conducting much of a campaign for *Hope and Glory*. "The Puttnam label" was hurting his chances, so Boorman asked producer Jake Eberts to tell the Hollywood press, "Although David has been truly good to us, the project was committed before he got involved. . . . It just makes me sick to think the studio is holding back because people think it's a Puttnam film." Boorman wasn't the only one with a sinking feeling. Steven Spielberg had managed to win a Directors Guild Award nomination, but then so had *My Life as a Dog*'s Lasse Hallstrom. Showing up at the National Board of Review ceremony on the eve of the Oscar nominations, Spielberg presaged, "I have a strong feeling I won't be nominated this year, just a hunch."

The Nominations

Once again, the nominations were announced at 5:30 in the morning in order to make the East Coast morning news programs and, in doing the honors, Academy President Robert Wise and Shirley MacLaine proved Spielberg a psychic. Although *Empire of the Sun* got six Oscar nominations, they were all in the technical categories. "David Puttnam, who was deposed as head of Columbia Pictures last fall, came up the big winner in the sixtieth annual race for the Oscar," declared Aljean Harmetz as *The Last Emperor* led with nine nominations and *Hope and Glory* snared five. President Robert Wise remarked that Puttnam had the support of "most of the creative people in Hollywood. It was the executives in the suites who had problems with him." Competing for Best Picture against Columbia's two entries were *Broadcast News, Moonstruck,* and *Fatal Attraction,* which Sheila Benson dubbed "the one major outrage." *Fatal*'s producer Sherry Lansing was equally shocked. "It's amazing the police didn't come," she exclaimed to Army Archerd. "I screamed so loud I woke up the entire neighborhood." Lansing also confided to Cindy Adams that "I was sleeping alone, so I called Glenn Close, who was calling me at the same moment." Shirley MacLaine was a spoilsport; in a follow-up interview on CBS's *This Morning,* she said she hadn't seen *Fatal Attraction* because "I'm not interested in stabbing and stuff."

Since Steven Spielberg had bombed out in the Best Picture category as well, Roger Ebert called "the Academy's biggest snub" the bumping of James L. Brooks from the Best Director lineup even though *Broadcast News* had seven nods. Those posters that Skouras Pictures sent out did the trick because the Directors Branch nominated *My Life as a Dog*'s Lasse Halstrom in Brooks's stead. The Writers Branch nominated him, too. "It's a miracle!" cheered Skouras's Jeff Lipsky. "Eighteen months ago, the director didn't think he'd get distribution in the U.S." "Academy vot-

"Now I won't have to go and lose to Cher."
—Lillian Gish

ers showed unprecedented preference for directors from abroad," noted *USA Today*, "all five Best Director slots went to foreigners," even though two of them, British Adrian Lyne of *Fatal Attraction* and Canadian Norman Jewison of *Moonstruck*, were picked for purely Hollywood product. James Brooks refused to criticize the category's international flavor. "I don't think we want to start an America First movement," he said. "Let's not bring back Wendell Wilkie."

Being a foreigner didn't help Sir Richard Attenborough; all he had to show for himself was a humanitarian award from the Film Teachers Association of Los Angeles. Those expensive campaigns didn't pay off for Faye Dunaway or Barbra Streisand either. The *Hollywood Kids*, a cheerful "scandal sheet" given out gratis throughout Los Angeles, told Streisand and Spielberg, "Face it, they hate you!"

One campaign that did work was Sally Kirkland's. "I think I bit all my fingernails off," the nominee bubbled to *Show-Biz Today*'s Bill Tush. "I was crying for five minutes even before I heard my name for fear of rejection." Kirkland had her work cut out for her—the *Los Angeles Times* called Best Actress the year's "most competitive" race. Kirkland's rivals were Cher in *Moonstruck*, Glenn Close in *Fatal Attraction*, Holly Hunter in *Broadcast News*, and Meryl Streep, receiving her seventh nomination, for *Ironweed*.

Streep's costar Jack Nicholson was up for the ninth time and *Broadcast News*'s William Hurt received his third nomination in a row. Michael Douglas, a 1975 Oscar winner as a producer, now had a chance of having a matched set with an acting nomination for *Wall Street*, the film's sole mention. Marcello Mastroianni became an Oscar finalist for the third time for playing a romantic buffoon in the Italian *Dark Eyes*, which had already netted him a best actor award at Cannes. The film's American distributor, Island Pictures, had actively sought a nomination, but Mastroianni wasn't worked up over their machinations. "My position is that of a quiet fatalist," the sixty-three-year-old international star responded when HBO tracked him down in Europe. "If I win a prize, I am happy. If I don't win, it doesn't matter."

"One surprise," maintained *Newsday*, "was that Robin Williams was nominated for essentially doing his free-form stand-up act in *Good Morning, Vietnam*." With Williams rounding out the Actor list, Liz Smith carped, "I wasn't happy that Steve Martin's really creative performance in *Roxanne* was passed over. His work in that charming movie was vastly superior, for instance, to Robin Williams's." Another Martin supporter, the Westwood *Village View*, suggested "Maybe he should costar with Streisand in a film directed by Spielberg and the weight of having such a triple cabash will offset each other resulting in nominations for all. It couldn't hurt." Two weeks later, Martin received the Harvard Hasty Pudding Club Man of the Year award; asked if this honor made up for the Academy's slight, he said, "Yes, it does, because it's such a prestigious award and so few people have gotten one."

The Actors Branch ignored the ads hustling *Cry Freedom*'s Denzel Washington and *Broadcast News*'s Albert Brooks as Best Actor candidates and nominated them for Supporting Actor. A letter in the *Los Angeles Times* pondered why it was Brooks and not his screen rival William Hurt in the lower category, deducing, "Perhaps it is true: the good-looking guys *do* succeed over the smart and funny ones," but Brooks was grateful to be noticed at all. He admitted to *People*, "If the others had gotten nominated and I didn't, I would have killed myself." The critics' darling Morgan Freeman and *Moonstruck*'s Vincent Gardenia were also in the running, but Sean Connery was expected to wipe out the competition. A publicist informed the *Los Angeles Times*, "He would have to commit a felony not to win."

Columnist Jack Mathews was pleased that the voters "were able to ignore the hype of the Lillian Gish–Bette Davis pairing in *The Whales of August* and vote a Best Supporting Actress nomination for the one great performance in the film—Ann Sothern's." The Supporting Actress nominee called to console Gish, who told her she was actually re-

"I do deserve to win."
—Glenn Close

lieved because "Now I won't have to go and lose to Cher." *Whales* was Sothern's first film in thirteen years, and the one-time MGM star hoped the Oscar publicity, as well as the revival of her 1950s sitcom *Private Secretary* on cable television, would mean more job offers. Walking with a cane as a result of an accident a decade-and-a-half ago when a stage prop fell on her, the seventy-eight-year-old actress bristled at the tag Oscar prognosticators had given her. "I don't like being the sentimental favorite," she retorted. "I want to win if I win because I did a good job. That's all." Sothern had tough competition from *Moonstruck*'s Olympia Dukakis, whose family was on a roll—the day before the nominations, her cousin, Massachusetts governor Michael Dukakis, won the New Hampshire Democratic presidential primary; now they were both front-runners.

Sally Forth

Sally Kirkland was back on the campaign trail within hours of the nominations, appearing on talk shows and chumming it up again with the press. She made it clear that she was no mere flash in the pan because "three scripts were messengered to me today as a result of this morning, all starring roles." Kirkland also knew where to be seen, showing up at a tribute to Jimmy Stewart hosted by Nancy Reagan, and happily appearing as a presenter at the twenty-fifth annual Publicists Guild of America Awards. A special edition of the *Hollywood Reporter* spotlighted her with an article entitled "A 20th-Century Muse," and she starred in a three-page spread in *People*, telling the magazine she wanted to win because "I will be the happiest woman in the world and my belief in God will be reaffirmed." If the Lord failed her, Kirkland had other powers on her side. As she recounted to Cindy Adams, "Liza Minnelli brought me an antique, enamaled, gold-leaf butterfly pin which her family had passed from member to member for years. Liza wore it the night she won, and, she said, it brings luck. She told me to wear it That Night."

Broadcast Blues

James L. Brooks could have used a field of four-leaf clovers. The Directors Guild of America passed up the chance to compensate the non-nominee à la Steven Spielberg and *The Color Purple* by annointing Bernardo Bertolucci instead. With *The Last Emperor* enjoying the status of the movie to beat for the Oscar, Bertolucci found he was liking Hollywood more and more. He told *Movieline* magazine, "I think Los Angeles is really beautiful. It is like the Forbidden City in *The Last Emperor*—huge empty spaces, very fancy, lonely, desperate, narcissistic. It's fantastic." Even Mrs. Rupert Murdoch, wife of the co-owner of 20th Century–Fox, inadvertantly plugged the competition instead of *Broadcast News* in a chat with George Christy of "The Great Life." After a discussion of her remodeling plans, the subject switched to movies and Mrs. 20th Century–Fox raved, "And the family and I all loved *The Last Emperor*. Seeing it's like going to China."

The stars of *Broadcast News* weren't helping the studio's cause either. William Hurt kept his customary resistance to self-promotion and Holly Hunter called a moritorium on all publicity once the picture opened because she was otherwise engaged in the L.A. production of a Sam Shepard play. Cindy Adams was among the columnists who censured her for not behaving like a good nominee, "Holly Hunter, who I am told will be The Name for the next twenty years, but whom almost no one heard of an hour ago, is an uptight lady who told even friendly journalists: 'I will not be interviewed.' Okay by me, lady." Somebody was talking to Adams, though, because she dished that Hunter was now an item with one of her costars—Marlee Matlin's ex, William Hurt.

Robin Williams became grist for the gossip mills, too. *People* ran a sensational cover story about the comedian's "Public triumph, private anguish" that centered on his "love affair with his son's nanny that has left his wife embittered." The *Hollywood Reporter*'s Hank Grant confirmed it the

"All I can say is you'll see a lot of miniaturized real people."
—Marty Pasetta

week before the ceremonies: "No surprise that Robin Williams and wife Valerie have decided to make their eight-month stipulation final in divorce court." Conversely, the actor's agent was explaining to the *Los Angeles Times* that the Oscar nomination had lifted his professional life to an all-time high, "Robin Williams has become a bankable star. Not only are the studios willing to offer him movies, they're willing to tear apart movies they have to suit them to Robin's talent."

Most Oscar pundits predicted that Williams would not be able to overcome hometown success story Michael Douglas, who had said that earlier in his acting career he had been intimidated by the reputation of his father. Kirk proudly accompanied his son and daughter-in-law to the People's Choice Awards where, claiming the trophy for Favorite Movie Actor, Michael squelched rocky marriage rumors by giving all his gratitude to his wife and child. Kirk's smile waivered only at the following press conference when Michael said the award "makes me realize that maybe I've been around for a while." The seventy-one-year-old Douglas recoiled in mock horror.

Glenn Close was the recipient of the Favorite Movie Actress trophy and *Parade* magazine was another fan, predicting an Oscar victory because "She deserves it." Close concurred. "I do deserve to win," she said on the pretaped Oscar Night Barbara Walters TV show, after taking the interviewer on a tour of her basement to see her old movie costumes. Cher was on later in the same show, and Walters summed up her appeal in the introduction: "Is there a more fascinating personality in pictures today than Cher? Just three years ago, Cher wasn't sure that Hollywood would take her seriously as an actress and tonight she is nominated for an Academy Award. But success hasn't changed the outspoken, outrageous, funny, and touching, Cher." Coca-Cola, one of the Oscar show's sponsors, was worried that Cher's taste in revealing clothes hadn't changed either, and demanded to see her gown before the ceremonies; Cher demurred. The Best Actress contest had as many people guessing as her outfit—*USA Today* headlined Oscar day that "Cher is no shoo-in for the gold," cautioning that a "Cher backlash may rear its unfriendly head."

Big Stars and Miniaturized People

"It will be a terrific show because no one knows who is going to win," predicted Samuel Goldwyn, Jr., in his sophomore year as producer of the show, which was changing its venue. "We want our sixtieth Awards to be a special occasion even by the Academy's standards," said Robert Wise, discussing the Academy's defection from the Dorothy Chandler Pavilion after eighteen years to the 6,000-seat Shrine Auditorium. Wise expounded that the move would enable "our entire membership to have the chance to enjoy" the program and, in addition, the Shrine's management was able to give the Academy more rehearsal time to get the musical numbers right. And to top it off, the Shrine had an adjacent banquet hall for the Governor's Ball. "It will save everybody a wait for their cars," gloated Wise, although he conceded, "It's not as beautiful down there, but there's a character and tone to it." As for the somewhat run-down neighborhood, the Shrine's manager told the *Los Angeles Herald-Examiner* not to worry, he spent $160,000 to surround the parking lots with eight-foot-high iron fences.

To commemorate sixty years of Oscars, the Academy planned to kick off the telecast with actors from each of the fifty-nine Best Pictures making an entrance in the forecourt. Invitations were mailed out and thirty-nine thespians accepted, *Grand Hotel*'s Greta Garbo not among them. *Lawrence of Arabia*'s Omar Sharif and *Oliver!*'s Ron Moody traveled from Europe and *Rebecca*'s Joan Fontaine was coming in full knowledge that her sister would be there, not only representing *Gone With the Wind*, but presenting an Oscar as well. Since the Shrine was the site of the 1946 Awards where Olivia de Havilland had snubbed her backstage, Fontaine was asking for trouble—which she got as soon as she checked in at the Beverly Hills Hotel and discovered her room was just a few doors away from Olivia's. Fontaine moved to another floor.

The Academy had its own troubles when the Writers Guild called a strike five weeks before the Awards and refused to grant a waiver for the Oscar broadcast. "We feel management is really playing hardball this time," said Melville Shavelson, an Oscar show veteran who quit the program. With only half of the program written, producer Goldwyn said "the show must go on and will," optimistically telling Marilyn Beck that the lack of a script means "we end up with a lot of ad libs, and that could be good; the prepared speeches are what the public seems to like the least." To ensure the quality of the ad libs, Goldwyn recruited a number of comedians, including Best Actor nominee Robin Williams, to bestow the statuettes. Marty Pasetta, directing his seventeenth telecast, was also confident things would go smoothly. "I've got a lot of tricks, but I don't want to ruin the surprise," he teased the *Hollywood Reporter*. "All I can say is you'll see a lot of miniaturized real people."

The one fear the Academy did admit to was limousine gridlock, so, on Oscar morn, both trade papers printed road maps and driving directions and the *Hollywood Reporter* stressed "Traffic will be heavy at the time you will be arriving at the Shrine—allow extra travel time."

The Big Night

"It looks like D. W. Griffith's *Intolerance* with those giant Oscars holding up the Shrine," Samuel Goldwyn quipped to forecourt emcee Army Archerd, who was sweltering in a tuxedo in the ninety-degree afternoon sun, but soon the scene resembled the flight from Egypt in C. B. DeMille's *The Ten Commandments*. "The traffic jam was among the most horrendous in Los Angeles history," reported Liz Smith of the snarl that forced Oscargoers to abandon their limousines and dash the final mile to the mosque-like structure. The leading man from the first Picture winner, *Wings*'s Buddy Rogers, entered unscathed, but the star from the second, *The Broadway Melody*'s Anita Page, seventy-seven, collapsed from the scorching heat, causing even more delays as paramedics rushed her to the hospital. *Rebecca*'s Joan Fontaine managed to arrive on time without the help of the Academy's escort—who never materialized—but her sister wasn't so lucky. Olivia de Havilland had to hop out of her car and hike ten blocks in order to be there to hand out an award. Robert Osborne recounted that "she and others were all dressed to the nines, hurrying off to a gaga glamour event while rushing past taco stands, donut shops and gawking onlookers, the latter munching on hot dogs and cradling babies, surprised at the unexpected passerby."

Caught in the stampede were the nine-months-pregnant Glenn Close, Meryl Streep, and Ann Sothern, who trotted with her cane as quickly as she could. Sally Kirkland was punctual, and had plenty of time to parade around the forecourt in her black décolletage, waving her arms to the bleacherites. "This is the happiest day of my life!" she exclaimed. "I feel like a movie star!" *Hope and Glory*'s John Boorman surveyed the cheering throng and said, "It makes you feel the movies aren't dead after all." With bandages on their wrists and teased blonde hair, the women from Orange County who had come in *Platoon* fatigues last year were now rooting for *Fatal Attraction* by dressing like Glenn Close in white dresses splat-

Awards Ceremony

April 11, 1988, 6:00 P.M.
The Shrine Auditorium, Los Angeles

Your Host: Chevy Chase
Televised over ABC

Presenters

Visual Effects	Sean Connery
Supporting Actress	Glenn Close and Michael Douglas
Art Direction	Olivia de Havilland
Cinematography	Mel Gibson and Danny Glover
Animated Short Film	Tom Selleck and Mickey Mouse
Documentary Short Subject	Joan Chen and John Lone
Documentary Feature	Steve Guttenberg
Sound	Billy Crystal
Supporting Actor	Cher and Nicolas Cage
Editing	Sean Young and Rob Lowe
Thalberg Award	Jack Lemmon
Song	Liza Minnelli and Dudley Moore
Original Score	Jennifer Grey and Patrick Swayze
Actor	Marlee Matlin
Scientific and Technical Awards	Shirley Jones (on film)
Live Action Short Film	Pee-wee Herman
Costume Design	Darryl Hannah and Kevin Costner
Director	Robin Williams
Makeup	John Candy
Writing Awards	Audrey Hepburn and Gregory Peck
Foreign Film	Faye Dunaway and James Garner
Actress	Paul Newman
Picture	Eddie Murphy

Performers of Nominated Songs

"Storybook Love"	Willy DeVille
"Nothing's Gonna Stop Us Now"	Starship and Gloria Estefan
"(I've Had) The Time of My Life"	Bill Medley and Jennifer Warnes
"Cry Freedom"	George Fenton and Jonas Gwangwa
"Shakedown"	Little Richard

"Good evening, Hollywood phonies."
—Chevy Chase

tered with fake blood. Said one *Fatal Attraction* supporter, "All men should see that picture. I hope my ex-husband saw it. He got off easy." The group waved rubber knives when they saw Michael Douglas but he was the picture of marital stability arriving with wife, Diandra. The Best Actor front-runner said father Kirk got cold feet and stayed home at the last minute. Douglas's wife from *Wall Street*, Sean Young, was panned by the *Orange County Register*'s fashion critic who complained that she "carried a silly parasol that matched her dusty blue Bob Mackie gown; she came across as a wacky Southern belle." The Mackie outfit everyone was dying to see had not arrived as the show began; Cher and her entourage—boyfriend, mother, sister, daughter, and son—were still stuck in the sea of limousines.

"At the six P.M. starting gun, the row in front of us was almost entirely empty and our row was but half filled," observed Archerd, once inside, where "at six-thirty P.M. people were still fighting their way into the auditorium. . . . The latecomers didn't miss much." The show started with a Michael Kidd production number based on the opening song from *A Chorus Line* that only generated audience enthusiasm when two rows of Oscars came to life and revealed themselves to be dancers in gold costumes. Announcer Hank Sims introduced, "The President of the Academy of Motion Picture Arts and Sciences, Mr. Robert Wise," but home viewers saw instead Demi Moore starring in a commercial for Coca-Cola. After the break, Sims tried again, "In actuality . . . Mr. Robert Wise." "To make the occasion just a shade more festive," the President said, "I have a remarkable piece of news for everyone who in the world who cares deeply about the art of motion pictures." Everyone in Hollywood figured that the writers' strike must have been settled but the bulletin turned out to be that the Academy was getting a new library.

"Good evening, Hollywood phonies," host Chevy Chase greeted the audience. Marty Pasetta cut to Joan Fontaine, who was not laughing. Chase's monologue included a tirade against critics—whose job he claimed is "to tear apart the work of hundreds of artists over a two-year period in the space of two minutes"—and a word for two non-nominees, "If you're relatively young or too funny and your name begins with Steve or Steven, you are not eligible." When the comedian jested that "I have it on good authority that Cher will be, in fact, dressed; apparently, she has decided against the simple but elegant wardrobe of just the dress-shields and odor-eaters and is going for the full body covering," there was no reaction shot of Cher, who was only now arriving at the forecourt. "Cher, you almost missed it!" scolded *Entertainment Tonight*'s Leeza Gibbons as the nominee hurried by. "Yeah, I almost did, but I'm here now!" she retorted. Marilyn Beck was there, too, observing that "Cher was greeted with the loudest screams of the day, but even the unbridled enthusiasm (and a few fans wearing Cher masks) didn't convince her to take off the velvet cape covering her Bob Mackie creation."

Back inside, Chevy Chase promised "an exciting look" at eighty years of special visual effects, but the audience was only aroused at the end of the montage when a figure emerged from a blast of light and a cloud of green smoke and intoned, "The name's Connery, Sean Connery." The crowd was on its feet for the night's first standing ovation as Bill Conti's orchestra played the James Bond Theme. After the Visual Effects Oscar went to *Innerspace*, another Spielberg production that had bombed that year, Marty Pasetta unveiled his "miniaturized real people"—a shot of half-a-dozen men and women standing around a giant, revolving Oscar that would be superimposed on screen every time an Award was handed out.

Cher and company strode in and discovered that their chairs were occupied by seat-fillers. Waiting in the aisle for them to move, Cher was told by a production assistant to scram because her group was blocking the camera's view of her costar Olympia Dukakis, who was up for the next Award. As the Cher family retreated up the aisle, Glenn Close and Michael Douglas walked onstage. Douglas evoked laughter just by hesitating

"Why not?"
—Olivia de Havilland

and glancing warily at Close's impending motherhood. All of the nominees were present, but only Olympia Dukakis had *Entertainment Tonight* watching the telecast with her family back in New Jersey. Dukakis's mother, eighty-six, couldn't stand the suspense and buried her hands in her face as Close ripped open the envelope. When her daughter was declared Best Supporting Actress, Mama caught her breath and wept. "I have to get up there and say something; I'm going to make a fool of myself," Dukakis later admitted was her first thought. After thanking her colleagues and her family, she finished by promoting her most famous relative. Lifting the Oscar above her head, Dukakis shouted, "Okay, Michael, let's go!"

Cher slipped into her seat as "Tara's Theme" and a career highlight film welcomed Olivia de Havilland, who garnered the evening's second standing ovation. Television viewers could not see if Joan Fontaine remained seated. "As an actress, I've spanned eight centuries on the screen, from Robin Hood's England through the Civil War to the present day," the two-time Oscar winner began. "All of us who have traveled through history in the movies are especially indebted to the Art Director." Although *Daily Variety* believed that de Havilland "showcased graciousness with her intro," Vincent Canby wrote that she emoted "as if she were Portia talking about the quality of mercy." When the triumphant trio from *The Last Emperor* came onstage, de Havilland offered congratulations and shook their hands; one winner moved to kiss her, so de Havilland laughed and said, "Why not?," offering her cheek. *The Last Emperor*'s reign continued when Vittorio Storaro claimed the Cinematography Oscar and got unintended laughs by stating the film was "the result of twenty years of collaboration with Bernardo Bertolucci, a long, difficult, hard journey. . . . "

Marty Pasetta had difficulties with his special effects when the finale to the Animated Short Film presentation backfired because a seat-filler inadvertently sat down in a chair already "occupied" on TV by Minnie Mouse. Saccharinity followed with the Michigan-based winners of the Documentary Short Subject Oscar for a film called *Young at Heart*. Sue Marx gave "A special thanks to the stars of our little movie, my daddy, who's right over there, who just celebrated his eighty-seventh birthday last week [applause] and his new bride, eighty-five." Cowinner Pamela Conn kissed her Oscar and lifted it over her head four times, before parting with, "We did something right!"

Charlton Heston stepped out to wax nostalgic and introduce a six-and-a-half-minute montage of past Oscar ceremonies that somehow included Greta Garbo, who never attended an Academy function. The show went from its memorable past to the present when Steve Guttenberg of the *Police Academy* movies appeared to give the Documentary Feature Oscar to Aviva Slesin for her movie about the Algonquin Round Table. "I made a film about a family of friends in New York in the '20s," Slesin said. "It was a good family; they worked together, they supported each other, they hired each other." And what did they accomplish? "They all became famous." Billy Crystal broke up the audience with his imitation of Rin Tin Tin—he stuck his tongue through a photo of the dog and panted—and then awarded the Sound Oscar to *The Last Emperor*. From his seat next to his wife, Clare Peploe, Bertolucci laughed with and pointed at the two technicians as they exited the stage waving their statuettes.

After a clip from *Moonstruck*, Cher made her entrance with costar Nicolas Cage to give Best Supporting Actor. She concealed her costume by wearing her velvet cloak around her shoulders and torso, allowing only a waist-down peek at its sheer material. All the nominees were present and Albert Brooks's fans started cheering the second his film clip appeared on the screen. Sean Connery's name was in the envelope, though, and Burt Lancaster led the second standing ovation for the actor. "Ladies and gentlemen, friends, and a few enemies," Connery began, "this is the sixtieth anniversary of these Academy Awards and I realized just the other day that my first one and only

"I'll be eternally grateful to you, Dad."
—Michael Douglas

attendance was thirty years ago—Patience truly is a virtue." He concluded, "If such a thing as a wish accompanied this award, mine would be that we ended the writers' strike." Connery grabbed a glass of wine on his way to the press tent, where he said, "The first thing I'm going to do is have a few drinks—oops, I've started somewhat early."

Recycling a gag from last year, Chevy Chase was caught picking his nose after a commercial, and then *The Last Emperor* picked up its fourth Oscar. Film editor Gabriella Christiani thanked Bertolucci and finished by quoting another *auteur*, "As Godard says, now I'm going home to cry."

Jack Lemmon came out with the Thalberg Award, which he said was the "heaviest Award we give" before dropping it on a tray on the podium. He mentioned that only twenty-five people had been given this Award in its fifty-year history, "so mere mortals need not apply." Mentioning some of those twenty-five, Lemmon admitted that "the man that we are honoring tonight may be a little sardonic about this whole thing but, oh, will he fit right in with the crowd he is joining." The audience rose to acknowledge "a master of the art of the movie, unfailingly true to himself and his audience," Billy Wilder, whom Lemmon bussed on the cheek. The recipient handed the Award to the presenter because "I have a feeling it is going to break." Wilder began his five-minute speech by thanking the Academy and "all the millions of fans I have all over the world—the civilized world." He saved his most heartfelt gratitude, for "one specific gentleman, without whose help I would not be standing here tonight. I have forgotten his name but I have never forgotten his compassion." The fellow turned out to be the American consul in Mexicali, Mexico, who, in 1934, gave Wilder permanent entry into the United States even though the Jewish refugee from Nazi Germany did not have the proper papers. Hearing that Wilder wrote movies, the official admonished him, " 'Write some good ones.' I've tried ever since." *Daily Variety* felt that the story "was touching and, more importantly, had a point," but the *Los Angeles Times* wisecracked that Wilder's "anecdote about his career lasted almost as *long* as his career." The winner ended with "I hope you're watching, I.A.L. because part of this is your's. So get well, will you?" Wilder's longtime collaborater I.A.L. Diamond died of cancer ten days later.

The nominees for Best Original Song were performed in a cluster with Liza Minnelli and Dudley Moore singing whimsical introductions to the numbers. The winner was "(I've Had) The Time of My Life" from Vestron's *Dirty Dancing*, and, as the three songwriters made their way to the stage, Sally Kirkland, Vestron's lone acting nominee, flailed around wildly, jumping out of her seat and "giving five" to one of the winners, Donald Markowitz. His fellow tunesmith Franke Previte thanked "the man upstairs and my parents for the best duet of all." *The Last Emperor* went five-for-five by winning the Original Score trophy and the audience hooted like fans at a rock concert when one of the three composers, David Byrne of Talking Heads, stood before the microphone in a modish Nehru jacket. "This is a lot of fun," he admitted, "but it's more fun doing it."

Best Actor presenter Marlee Matlin didn't wear glasses this year, but her bow to fashion came at a price. "I have contact lenses on and they don't seem to be working very well," she told the gathering through her interpreter. For the occasion, Matlin had studied with a voice coach and announced the nominees herself. Her former flame, William Hurt, wasn't there to hear his name, nor was Marcello Mastroianni, but Robin Williams roared and applauded when Matlin mimicked his way of saying "*Good Mooooooorning, Vietnam!*" As usual, Jack Nicholson did not remove his dark glasses for his close-up, and he didn't have to later, either; the winner was Michael Douglas, who kissed his wife and shook Albert Brooks's hand on the way to the stage. "A large part of this belongs to Oliver Stone, not only as the director, but for having the courage to cast me in a part that not many people thought I could play," Douglas said, calling Gordon Gekko "the best part I've ever had in my career." Turning personal, he dedicated his award to his parents and stepparents, "particularly

"When I was little, my mother said, 'I want you to be something.'"
—Cher

to my father, who I don't think ever missed one of my college productions, for his continued support and for helping a son step out of a shadow. I'll be eternally grateful to you, Dad." This sentiment evoked raucous applause from the crowd; Jack Nicholson was seen whistling his approval. The *New York Times*'s Janet Maslin was more impressed with another member of the Douglas clan: "the evening's best performance by a spouse came from Diandra Douglas, who wept extravagantly." Douglas departed by addressing his son, "Good night, Cameron. I love you," then went backstage and confessed to Joel Siegel that "I have a nine-year-old son now and I already missed one of his third-grade plays."

Third-grade–level humor prevailed as Peewee Herman attempted to present the Live Action Short Film Award but was thwarted when a villainous robot crashed through a set, demanding the Sound Effects Editing Oscar that had been given at a previous ceremony to *RoboCop*. Peewee escaped by being lifted by a wire to the top of the Shrine proscenium, where he remained until rescued by an actor dressed as RoboCop walked down an aisle firing lasers at the belligerent android. The camera caught Olympia Dukakis walking in the line of fire as she attempted to return to her seat unnoticed. When the cyborg was vanquished, Herman was lowered back down to the podium, scoring a laugh by saying, "I'll be right back to present the Oscar as soon as I change my pants." Despite *The Last Emperor*'s sweep, the only one to thank David Puttnam was a winner in this category, Jonathan Sanger, whose comedy short, *Ray's Male Heterosexual Dance Hall*, had been sponsored under the auspices of Puttnam's Discovery Program for new talent. Covering all political bases, Sanger also expressed gratitude to the present Columbia heads "for finding a way to keep the program alive."

Costume Design presenter Darryl Hannah remembered another forgotten man, plugging her non-nominated *Roxanne* costar Steve Martin by putting on a fake nose before handing the statuette to *The Last Emperor*'s John Acheson, who was keeping score. "This is number six?" he asked. "My mother used to say that a little bit of encouragement goes a long way, so I'd like to thank the Academy sincerely for this huge piece of encouragement." He went on to thank 250 people in five countries.

With a bushy moustache and old-fashioned tuxedo, Robin Williams looked more like a backwoods preacher than a movie star and he greeted the audience with an imitation of the recently disgraced television evangelist Jimmy Swaggert: "Thank you fellow members of the Congregation of God. I have sinned!" He kidded that Swaggert "will atone for his sins by publishing a magazine called *Repenthouse*." Switching personalities, Williams announced, "In order not to violate the writers' strike, I will be channeling the spirit of George Jessel," and began droning in the tones of the 1969 Jean Hersholt Humanitarian Award recipient, "Director, from the Latin word, 'Director,' meaning he who cashes the first check." The comedian soon gave up on being possessed by the Toastmaster General, claiming, "I can't keep that up, it's too hard—Sorry, Shirley, I'm sorry baby." KABC's Cynthia Allison, at the Swifty Lazar party, reported that Shirley MacLaine "didn't even crack a smile" over Williams's reference. Back at the Shrine, Robin was wondering, "Does Woody Allen dream in black-and-white and, if so, does Ted Turner buy them and color them in? Ted, who didn't give you the crayons as a boy?" He then defined a writer-director-producer as "one of the few creatures on the planet who can blow smoke up his own ass"; the line got the biggest laugh of the show, but *Daily Variety* clucked that "it was the night's only fall from grace," and left a blank space when reprinting the joke. Williams finally got around to giving Best Director but threw in one more gag at the last minute: "And the winner is . . . And the Academy, along with the Oscar, this year is giving out a green card." Lasse Halstrom and Bernardo Bertolucci didn't seem to get it, but Bertolucci did get the Oscar and the night's fifth standing ovation. Williams shyly handed him the statuette and stepped away, but

"The Academy, along with the Oscar, this year is giving out a green card."
—Robin Williams

Bertolucci reached over and grabbed him by the neck, pulling him over and kissing his cheek. As Williams meekly withdrew, the winner said:

> *As an Italian, as a European, the Academy Awards has always seemed to me like a distant ceremony, something fascinating, very remote. Something I really didn't belong to. Then one day,* The Last Emperor *got nine nominations and everything changed, immediately. I became immediately a kind of Oscar victim. I started to learn the rules of the game and to check the odds, to start with the colitis.*

Bertolucci added, "I want to do a Chinese kow-tow to the Academy because this is one of the strongest emotions in my life and I can't hide it." After he thanked China and his cast and crew, it became obvious his romance with L.A. had reached the erotic stage by his closing remark, "I was just thinking that if New York is the Big Apple, to me, Hollywood tonight is the Big Nipple."

There were only a handful of Awards left, so Joan Fontaine turned to Roddy McDowell, the mascot for 1941's *How Green Was My Valley,* and asked, "When are we going on?" "Later, later," he assured *Rebecca*'s second Mrs. de Winter, as Audrey Hepburn and Gregory Peck appeared onstage and won standing ovation number six. They announced Oscar number eight for *The Last Emperor,* Adapted Screenplay, and Mark Peploe expressed gratitude to his sister's husband, saying "I want to thank Bernardo for taking me to China." The writer thanked another Italian filmmaker, Michelangelo Antonioni, "who first showed me a film of Bernardo's . . . he has made us both believe in movies for years." Bertolucci had been in the pressroom and almost didn't make it back to pick up his second statuette. "I've been walking all around," he explained, "and they didn't let me in and then I showed my statue and they let me in and I just came in time."

"Wow!" ejaculated the Original Screenplay winner, *Moonstruck*'s John Patrick Shanley. "I don't care, man. I don't care if we're supposed to be cool. This"—his voice rising to a crescendo—"is incredible!" The writer thanked "everybody who ever punched or kissed me in my life and everybody who I ever punched or kissed," as well as "the multimedia princess, Cher."

For some reason, the orchestra ended the next commercial break with a fanfare from *Jesus Christ Superstar* and then Chevy Chase brought out "two of the classiest performers around," Faye Dunaway and James Garner, to present Best Foreign Language Film. Garner got to utter the inevitable "universal language of film" slogan and there were clips of such Hollywood stars as Groucho Marx, Cary Grant, and Jack Nicholson dubbed in different languages. Director Louis Malle's autobiographical look at his World War II childhood, *Au Revoir, Les Enfants,* was the heavy favorite, and Malle and his wife, Candice Bergen, were sitting nervously in the Shrine, but the surprise winner was Denmark's *Babette's Feast,* a movie emphasizing the life-affirming qualities of Art, specifically the art of gourmet cooking. Orion had given the Danish movie an upscale publicity stunt by arranging to have New York's Petrossian and Los Angeles's L'Ermitage restaurants recreate the title dinner at a hundred bucks a pop; the *New York Post* tagged the ploy, "You've seen the movie, now eat the meal." *Babette*'s director, Gabriel Axel, indicated he knew he was supposed to speak "quickly, short, and in English, okay," but he had charming difficulty with all three. Nevertheless, his feelings were made clear when he said, "In this evening I have learned in the beautiful world of our, everything are possible."

The audience was on its feet a seventh time for last year's Best Actor no-show Paul Newman, who appeared to crown the Best Actress. Hearing their names announced, Meryl Streep laughed with excitement, Cher remained stone-faced despite deafening applause, Holly Hunter grinned as she looked around her, Glenn Close smiled serenely, and Sally Kirkland, shaking visibly, chewed on her lip. Newman declared Cher the champion and Kirkland's face dropped for a second, but then she joined in the applause. Meryl Streep leapt out of

"If New York is the Big Apple, to me, Hollywood tonight is the Big Nipple."
—Bernardo Bertolucci

her seat cheering and the rest of the auditorium quickly followed suit. Cher embraced Rob Camilletti, daughter Chastity, and son Elijah Blue. Her mother was not sitting with her, but her screen mother, Olympia Dukakis, was nearby and ran over to hug her. As she marched down the aisle, Cher's shawl slipped off, revealing a tiny tattoo on her right arm; at the stairs, she stumbled and lost her left earring. "Shit," she muttered, nonchalantly flinging her wrap over her shoulder and ascending as Paul Newman offered her his hand but not a kiss. Giving the audience their first unobstructed view of her get-up—an Erte-like, transparent silk net gown laced with antique black bugle beads—Cher burst out laughing at what Army Archerd dubbed "the biggest ovation of all." Trying to be serious, the Best Actress commenced, "Now I want to really, really, really say something," but the idea amused her and she cracked up again. She regained composure and tried again: "When I was little, my mother said, I want you to be something." She went on to thank "everyone I worked on with the movie," singling out her hairdresser and "my makeup man, who had a lot to work with"; when she mentioned "my children, who've been so wonderful," viewers saw Chastity hanging on to Rob Camilletti, who wiped away a tear. Cher continued by thanking "the women that I was nominated along with, because I feel really, really good because they were so great and I also would like to thank Mary Louise Streep, who . . . I feel . . . so unbelievable that I did my first movie with her and now I was nominated with her and I feel really thankful." Streep blew her friend a kiss, waved, and yelled "Bravo!," even though Cher had made three films before *Silkwood*. The winner finished by conjecturing, "I don't think that this means that I am somebody, but I guess I'm on my way."

Eddie Murphy informed everyone that he initially wanted to turn down the Academy's invitation to present Best Picture "because they haven't recognized black people in the motion picture industry," citing the fact that after sixty years only three black actors had won Oscars. "I'll probably never win an Oscar for saying this," predicted the star of *The Golden Child*. "Actually, I might not be in any trouble because the way it's been going, it's about every twenty years we get one, so we ain't due until about 2004." Like some other recent bestowers of Best Picture—Frank Capra, Laurence Olivier, and Dustin Hoffman—Murphy messed up, forgetting to mention one of the nominees until the cries of alarm from the audience tipped him off. *The Last Emperor* completed its nine-for-nine sweep and became the Academy's most honored movie since 1961's *West Side Story*. Producer Jeremy Thomas said, "This is a truly imperial evening for me," and that the Oscar "is a real affirmation for me that independent cinema can be epic and quite popular." Taking a mild swipe at Columbia's handling of the film, Thomas averred that "I hope this Oscar will mean that many, many more people can see this picture in America." Bernardo Bertolucci was given a final testimonial as his producer thanked him for "inviting me on this incredible voyage of discovery."

Chevy Chase closed the show with: "What a night. Goodnight, everybody. Thanks for coming." As the closing credits, including one for the people who made Pee-wee Herman fly, rolled by, Gregory Peck kissed Liza Minnelli and John Lone, the *Last Emperor*'s adult Pu Yi, embraced Bernardo Bertolucci.

Aftermath

Asked in the press tent where he would keep his two Oscars, Bernardo Bertolucci figured, "I live in Rome, but my wife's English, so I go often to London, so maybe one in Rome and one in London." As for the popularity of his movie, he reasoned, "*The Last Emperor* goes to fill up a need of the audiences everywhere in the world for a big movie. The audience is happy to go to a movie like in the past in a space in the darkness where they can have all together the same dream. Cinema is a great cathedral for collective hypnosis." The press was less interested in his theory about cinema than in what he meant by that "Big Nipple" comment.

"It would never occur to a filmmaker to go to Atlanta and tell them how to make a soft drink."
—Billy Wilder

"Nine nominations is a kind of overdose of the milk of gratification," Bertolucci explained. "It was just a joke."

Bertolucci's producer was getting miffed at the insistent questions about David Puttnam's role in the success of *The Last Emperor*. "He didn't produce the film," Jeremy Thomas finally reminded everyone. *Daily Variety* tracked Puttnam down in Toronto to hear his reaction to the Academy's choices. "I feel great," the former mogul maintained. "I was asked to join Columbia to give the studio some prestige, and I have to believe the Coke people are proud tonight." Puttnam added he wished that the Academy had not shut out *Hope and Glory*. "I bleed for John Boorman," he said, "I was so hoping he'd win something." When Bertolucci was queried about Puttnam, he contended, "I am very sad he couldn't go on with his job," but, a week later, Liz Smith spotted the director lunching with Puttnam's replacement Dawn Steele "in the Russian Tea Room's superbooth 1." They may not have had much appetite, because *Variety* was reporting on "the failure of Main Street U.S.A. to line up around the block for *The Last Emperor*." Despite ads exhorting audiences, "Don't miss the most honored film in twenty-five years," Columbia's puzzled head of distribution admitted that "in the smaller markets the urgency to see the picture is just not there—even with the panache and cachet of nine Academy Awards." *Variety* recognized a familiar show-biz syndrome, and pointed out "the stix are nixing" the pic.

Having no movie at Columbia's mercy, Billy Wilder didn't worry about offending the powers-that-be. "It would never occur to a filmmaker to go to Atlanta and tell them how to make a soft drink," the director of *One, Two, Three* riposted. "I worked at Paramount for eighteen years; they were making fifty pictures a year. Now they're making four or five, and they're always looking over your shoulder. In the old days, we had the moguls—at least you knew whose behind to kiss." A reporter asked how he'd most like to be remembered. "As a great lover," Wilder snapped, while Jack Lemmon helped usher him out of the tent with the announcement, "Mr. Wilder has to point his peter at the porcelain."

Sean Connery told the press there was no way he'd play James Bond again. "I'm too old for that now," acknowledged the Best Supporting Actor. But when CBS's David Dow wondered if his next role as Harrison Ford's father in the third Indiana Jones's installment made him feel old, Connery said, "No, not particularly. It's only a movie." Michael Douglas was asked how he thought his father would react to his victory. "He'll say, 'Son, I'm really tired of hearing about you,' " laughed the Best Actor, reiterating that he always doubted he could ever be as good an actor as Kirk Douglas, "My father carved a very strong image, and it took a long while for me to find mine." The *Los Angeles Times* caught up with Kirk, who "watched at home alone with my wife, which is a good thing because I would have hated to have people see me cry. . . . I've always thought Michael had the potential to be a great actor, and I'm delighted that other people think so, too."

Olympia Dukakis said she'd be keeping her Oscar in her kitchen because, just like her *Moonstruck* family, "that's where we all seem to hang out in the house." As happy as she was, Dukakis stressed that "It's a mistake to think I've been waiting for this all my life. I've been working, not waiting. This is the icing on the cake." She was amused by her newfound celebrity, though. "People see me on the street and yell, 'You're life's going down the toilet.' " Fielding questions about her cousin Michael, who had seen *Moonstruck* just the night before, the actress predicted 1988 would be "the year of the Dukaki; when the year began, the name was not too familiar." The presidential candidate watched her victory while at a fund-raiser in Staten Island and then he rushed off to the restaurant featured in the movie—the Grand Ticino in Greenwich Village—where he awaited her phone call. Television crews on both coasts filmed their conversation as Michael told her, "This is the first step. I hope this is an omen for next Tuesday"—the New York primary. The governor also did some acting of his own by

"I'm too old for that now."
—Sean Connery

watching a tape of Olympia's win and pretending it was live for the benefit of the TV journalists. When the cameras were finished with them, Olympia called her mother, who said, "Now the whole world knows what a wonderful actress you are."

Like the Dukakis matriarch, Cher's mother spent some time with *Entertainment Tonight* Oscar night, commenting on her daughter's acceptance speech. "She used to be upset because she didn't think she was as pretty as the other little girls," Georgia Holt recalled. "I would tell her, 'You're special and being special is better.' " The *Village Voice*'s Michael Musto confirmed that her daughter was a hit backstage: "Finally, the climax—Cher, the feel-good winner from the feel-good movie, entered the tent saying, 'I feel I've given my first born to get this dress' and added that Theda Bara would have been proud of her look." In New York, Bob Mackie was fretting to the *Post*, "I hope people don't think it's fashion. It isn't. It's like dressing a charactor in a movie." Back in Hollywood, Joel Siegal was asking her about her acting abilities. "It's unbelievable to me but I might really be a great actress," she mused. "When I'm dead, maybe people will say that." For the present, she was still "singer-entertainer Cher" in ABC News's Oscar report, which ended with a rear view of her outfit "for those viewers who didn't get a good look at Cher's dress."

The Best Actress stopped to sign autographs for fans partitioned off behind an iron fence as she headed next door to the Governors' Ball. The orchestra revolved on a stage under three twenty-four-foot Oscars in the center of the hall which, Army Archerd wrote, had been converted "into a wonderland, with the flaws of the old place cleverly camouflaged in gold and candlelight." The menu included mesquite-grilled baby rack of lamb, fresh salmon, California free-range chicken, and 12,000 edible flowers. Despite the convenient location, the *Los Angeles Daily News* reported, "most of the major stars avoided the Governors' Ball that followed the Oscar ceremonies in favor of Swifty's."

Irving and Mary Lazar, stung by the charges of overcrowding at last year's party, pared their guest list by forty people and clamped down on television cameras inside Spago. The Lazars were so adamant about security that a guard barred a woman from entering the restaurant until she identified herself as the wife of owner Wolfgang Puck. Walter Matthau entertained the waiters by doing magic tricks while Barry Diller, chairman of 20th Century–Fox, griped that *Broadcast News* "was swept away; we were annihilated, and that makes me angry." Accepting congratulations from television reporter Cynthia Allison on her fourth nomination out of seven movies, Glenn Close replied, "Maybe someday I might actually win." Two weeks later, the actress gave birth to a daughter.

USA Today noted that while "the older, establishment crowd" was at the Lazars', which was over by one o'clock, "much of the younger film crowd either party hopped or attended private parties elsewhere." According to the *Los Angeles Times*, the "hippest post-Oscar party" was the $500-a-ticket benefit for an organization aiding Central American refugees held at Le Mondrian Hotel, which was still going strong at three A.M.; one of the restaurants catering the affair was Spago. Helena's, a private club in the Silverlake district, was host to Jack Nicholson, Meryl Streep, Kathleen Turner, and Michael Douglas, who showed up with twenty people, including his mother.

"Sally Kirkland, trying to smile bravely after her exuberant campaign, made all the parties—the Ball, Spago, and Helena's with her mom, Sally Kirkland, Sr., winding at 4 ayem," revealed Archerd. "Then her mom was stuck in her hotel elevator until 5:30. Whatta night!" Disappointed but not discouraged by the results, Kirkland was already plotting future campaigns. The actress discussed her film offers with the *Hollywood Reporter*, describing one as "such a shocking plot, a tragedy, and it's definitely a potential award-winning part."

The *Herald-Examiner* complained that host Chevy Chase "just doesn't give the Oscar show the big-time sheen and elegance it gets from a Johnny

"If they'd stepped out of the Police Academy series they couldn't have been any less effective."
—Martin Grove on the L.A.P.D.

Carson," and an unnamed Academy official whispered to the *Los Angeles Times* that 80 percent of the host's material was on the Teleprompter but the improvised remainder showed "a lack of class and style." The *Times*'s TV critic, Howard Rosenberg, felt the same way about the whole show, calling it "the Michael Dukakis and George Bush of TV awards programs: parched, drab and leaden." The three-hour-and-thirty-three-minute ceremony nonetheless reversed the recent downward trend in the ratings and the Academy won its biggest viewing audience in four years.

Olympia Dukakis was on view again the next week when her Oscar proved indeed to be an omen for cousin Michael; she appeared on front pages all over the country as she stood next to him celebrating his victory in the New York primary. Cher also had political connections—the day after the Awards, her ex-husband was elected mayor of Palm Springs. Mayor Bono's celebrity still couldn't compare to the Best Actress's; Cher was publicly congratulated in newspapers on both coasts by the Sands Hotel, which placed ads showing her wearing black leather and chains to promote her upcoming Atlantic City gig. Criticized for mentioning her hairdresser but not her director in her acceptance speech—KABC's Gary Franklin huffed, "You don't make that kind of an oversight when you're a professional"—Cher took out ads of her own in the trade papers, a three-page bouquet thanking the Academy, the director, producer, author, and cast of *Moonstruck,* and a couple others, including Bob Mackie and *Silkwood*'s director "Mike 'I Picked You Up From The Gutter' Nichols."

"AMPAS Honks Horn Over Traffic; Shrine Return Hinges On Solving 'Mess,' " headlined *Daily Variety,* which noted that Los Angeles Mayor Tom Bradley himself had been imprisoned in the nonmoving mass of vehicles on his way to the show. "Hizzoner was so concerned that he called in top brass from the Dept. of Transportation the first thing yesterday morning," the journal reported. While Bradley interrogated the department, the *Hollywood Reporter*'s Martin Grove ridiculed "the police cadets directing traffic—if they'd stepped out of the *Police Academy* series they couldn't have been any less effective." The columnist also beefed that the cops ignored the "bright orange windshield stickers" intended to grant Oscargoers the right-of-way and even allowed "non-Oscar cars" to drive in lanes "supposedly reserved only for Oscar guests." Not only were the stickers useless, they were permanent. "Those who fought their way through the traffic were left with two nasty strips of orange paper securely glued to the inside of their windshields," Grove fumed about the "orange battle scars."

While the Academy debated a return engagement at the Shrine, Joan Fontaine said count her out. Relating her troubles on Oscar night, the 1941 winner explained to the *Herald-Examiner*'s Mitchell Fink that her limo never returned to pick her up after the ball. "After an hour of standing in the cold, two ladies I never met gave us a lift back to the hotel." Since she paid for her whole trip to Los Angeles herself, "except for the missing limousine," Fontaine vowed that this was her last Oscar show, stating, "From now on, they can muck it up by themselves."

1988

"It will be the antithesis of tacky."
—Allan Carr

Allan Carr realized his childhood dream of producing the Oscar show and turned the Academy Awards into such a laughing stock that a studio sued.

Bunny Makes Money

Fifty years after her debut, Disney's Snow White made a comeback, appearing along with such other prominent screen names as Betty Boop, Daffy Duck, and Droopy Dog. For the second time in her career, she was in the year's highest grossing film. In *Who Framed Roger Rabbit,* a coproduction between producer Steven Spielberg and the Walt Disney studio, director Robert Zemeckis mixed cartoon stars with flesh-and-blood actors in a send-up of '40s hard-boiled detective movies. Charles Champlin of the *Los Angeles Times* rejoiced that the concoction "reminds you thrillingly that even after a century, the movies have not exhausted their magic," but Stanley Kauffmann opined in the New Republic, "The plot, the gags, the action are so stupid and strained, so unfunnily parodic, that the film's only interest is in wondering how they did it." Disney confidently flooded the toy market with merchandise, but the reviewer from *Variety* wasn't going to be buying any Roger products—he found the title character to be "an obnoxious, irritating rabbit with no discernible charm."

Triple Play

"Could it be—a summer movie that's actually for grown-ups?" marveled *Newsweek*'s David Ansen when Ron Shelton's adult comedy *Bull Durham* opened amid the kiddie shows. *"Bull Durham* is just that: a funny, sexy, literate love story about minor-league baseball, sex, love, and prayers answered and unanswered." A former minor-league second baseman, screenwriter Shelton decided to direct his script about a love triangle between a catcher, a pitcher, and a baseball groupie in North Carolina because "I felt the dialogue I write needs to be handled fairly carefully; it's odd, it's not very linear." Kevin Costner, having established himself as a sex symbol in *The Untouchables* and *No Way Out,* slid easily into the role of the seasoned catcher who declares his passion for "the small of a woman's back, the hanging curve ball, good Scotch, and long, slow, deep, soft, wet kisses that last for three days." Cashing in on Costner's appeal, Orion promoted the movie by giving away posters of the actor, but costar Susan Sarandon was more attracted to his screen rival, Tim Robbins. The couple moved in together after filming and started a family. The film's success startled Hollywood but, as Roger Angell explained later to *Premiere,* "This is the baseball movie real fans had waited for."

For Crichton Out Loud

Another R-rated comedy hit starred two Costner costars from the ill-fated 1985 western, *Silverado:* John Cleese and Kevin Kline. *A Fish Called Wanda,* a farce about a London jewelry heist by a quartet of double-dealing oddballs, was written by ex-Monty Python member Cleese in the spirit of the 1951 classic from England's Ealing Studios, *The Lavender Hill Mob.* Executive producer Cleese even selected the *auteur* of that comedy to direct *Wanda*, but it wasn't the first time that he had employed seventy-seven-year-old Charles Crichton; when, a few years earlier, the veteran director couldn't get a job in features, Cleese hired him to make management training films for his video company. Joked Cleese, "He's the only director I've ever worked with who's still trying to get over the impact of the talkies."

When he first saw the screenplay, Kline was confused; the slapstick role of a moronic sociopath was his, while Cleese himself "was relegated

Overleaf: *Allan Carr demonstrates how he will bring the Academy to its knees.*

"He's the only director I've ever worked with who's still trying to get over the impact of the talkies."
—John Cleese on Charles Crichton

to the romantic lead. I told him you've written the John Cleese part for me." Cleese instructed Kline, "I want this performance to make Dennis Hopper's acting in *Blue Velvet* look restrained." Rounding out the gang of thieves were Jamie Lee Curtis as a curvy femme fatale, and one of Cleese's Monty Python comrades, Michael Palin, as an animal lover with the worst cinematic stutter since Porky Pig.

Wanda bowed to mixed reviews; *Time*'s Richard Schickel deemed it "the next best thing to a Looney Tunes–Merrie Melodies summerfest" while *The New Yorker*'s Terrence Rafferty complained that "Crichton's direction is too drab and poky for the material." Kevin Kline also divided critical reaction. Kathleen Carroll of the *New York Daily News* chortled that "Kline has a high old time spewing out four-letter words and just generally chewing the scenery," but, in the *New York Post,* V. A. Musetto carped that the actor "gets on your nerves with his incessant barrage of stupidity and insults. You want to drown him about halfway through the movie."

Wanda producer Michael Shamberg also had to deal with criticism from unexpected sources when the A.S.P.C.A. argued that the deaths of small dogs and a fish were not proper fodder for comic effects. The producer rejoined that "nobody's upset that an old lady dies, or a man is run over by a steamroller." Shamberg calmed a group called the National Stuttering Project by signing a letter they had prepared, assuring moviegoers that "it was never our intention" that Palin's hit man "be taken as a portrayal of all people who stutter."

Good Lord!

Wanda's controversy was nothing compared to the storm Martin Scorsese created at summer's end. Having grown up wanting to be a priest—only to have his ambition kayoed when he flunked the entrance exam at the Jesuit-run Fordham College—the Catholic director still harbored religious fantasies. A self-confessed fan of Biblical epics like *Quo Vadis* and *The Robe*, Scorsese had visions of adapting the story of Christ into a movie, remarking, "This has been in my head since I was a child—how I would do scenes about Jesus."

In 1972, Barbara Hershey, the star of Scorsese's first Hollywood movie, a Roger Corman–produced cheapie entitled *Boxcar Bertha,* gave the director a copy of Nikos Kazantzakis' 1950s novel *The Last Temptation of Christ* because she was impressed by how "deeply religious" he was. The book rekindled Scorsese's hopes of putting the life of Christ on screen but it wasn't until 1983 that the bio was ready to roll, with Aidan Quinn in the title role for Paramount. A ballooning budget and 5,000 letters of protest from Christian groups objecting to the book's all-too-human portrait of Christ made the studio pull the plug at the last minute. Scorsese then persuaded France's Minister of Culture, Jack Lang, to ante up $5 million of his government's money, until the Archbishop of Paris put up a stink and the offer was withdrawn. The defeated director went on to make two other features before Universal came in as a saviour and funded the project. By then, Quinn was out and Willem Dafoe in, but Barbara Hershey was still available to play Mary Magdalene. The cast trouped to Morocco and worked for scale because, as Hershey put it, "It was like going on a Crusade."

Scorsese Gets Nailed

Fundamentalist Christians also had a mission—to stop the completed film from being shown. Something called the Campus Crusade for Christ offered to throw $10 million Universal's way if the company would hand over all prints of the movie. Seventy-five hundred people demonstrated at the studio with posters saying "The Greatest Story Ever Distorted" and "Universal Is Anti-Christian"; because the pickets had to park their cars in the studio lot, Universal made $4,500 off the protest. MCA head Lew Wasserman got a double dose of demonstrations, with

"Jesus never did that!"
—Bobbie Bible

groups showing up in Beverly Hills both at his temple and his home. A new version of the passion play was presented outside chez Wasserman: a protester dressed in a business suit as a movie mogul flogged a dress-extra Jesus at the foot of a cross.

Roy Rogers and Dale Evans were among the Tinseltown signatories of a petition protesting a film none of them had seen, and another nonviewer, Mother Theresa, pinned her hopes on American Catholics: "If they will implore the power of God through increased recitation of the Holy Rosary . . . then our Blessed Mother will see that this movie is removed from your land." Taking advantage of all this free publicity, Universal moved the picture's release up a month ahead of schedule. The Christians retaliated by threatening to bomb theaters or, at least, slash movie screens.

On opening day, the media staked out those theaters brazen enough to show *Last Temptation* after the fundamentalists' threats and weren't disappointed when hundreds of pickets brandished posters warning the hundreds waiting to go in to "Get Off That Line Before It's Too Late." Scanning the ticket buyers in Manhattan, the *New York Native*'s Ed Sikov spotted "Tiny Tim, who was wearing a lot of rouge," and in the heartland, the *Chicago Sun-Times* recorded that "a topless woman twice drove by and waved to some 150 people picketing." The first person to buy a ticket in Los Angeles, identifying himself as Bobbie Bible, was thrown out for yelling a number of times during the film, "Jesus never did that!" Meanwhile, across town at the Directors Guild, Warren Beatty and other members held a press conference in support of Scorsese, reading a short statement from the absent Clint Eastwood: "Freedom of expression is the American way."

If he had his fellow filmmakers' support, Scorsese couldn't convert all the reviewers. While David Ehrenstein of the *Los Angeles Herald-Examiner* called *Last Temptation* "One of the most serious, literate, complex and deeply felt religious films ever made," the *New York Times'* Vincent Canby felt that "for all of its sincerity," the two-hour-forty-four-minute epic "seems to be the longest movie ever made." Rex Reed called it "a 10-ton turkey" and complained "They spent millions of dollars on this film just to prove how terrible everyone looks in sandals." Despite sell-out crowds early in its run, *The Last Temptation of Christ* ultimately earned Universal less money than the bribe offered by the Campus Crusade.

Jodie Grows Up

A veteran of an earlier Scorsese scandal, the thirteen-year-old Jodie Foster of *Taxi Driver* was now a twenty-five-year-old reactivating her Hollywood career with another risky role after her sojourn at Yale. *Variety* reported, "Last year it was *Fatal Attraction* and this fall's anti-sex story from Jaffe/Lansing is *The Accused.*" Inspired by a 1984 case in which four men were tried for raping a woman on a pool table in New Bedford, Massachusetts, the film indicted not only the rapists but also the bystanders who encouraged them. Producer Sherry Lansing elaborated on the film's heroine: "We purposely chose a woman who might be perceived—and I hate this word, but I don't know what other word to use—as a slut. She's not a debutante, do you know what I mean?"

"I can't stop playing a victim just because of John Hinckley," the actress said when reporters asked her about the man responsible for the postponement of the 1980 Oscar show. "Being a victim is unfortunately a big part of women's lives." *Vanity Fair* detailed the rigors of portraying this particular victim: "The gang rape took five days to film . . . Foster had broken blood vessels over her eyes from crying on cue. Her body was bruised." Relief came with the glowing reviews: "It is the sort of role Jodie Foster has been training for and she invests Sarah with nuances of character that might have escaped a lesser actress," raved the *London Evening Standard.* Producer Lansing hoped "that no one seeing *The Accused* will ever believe that rape is sexy." It was a lesson lost, however, on television critic Michael Medved who, giving his Oscar predictions on CNN,

"She suffers. She emotes. She gets raped on screen in a very sexy scene."
—Michael Medved

picked Foster because "She suffers. She emotes. She gets raped on screen in a very sexy scene."

Hoover's Heroes

Another real-life crime, the 1964 murder of three civil rights workers in Philadelphia, Mississippi, was the basis of Alan Parker's *Mississippi Burning,* which provoked as fiery a reaction as *The Last Temptation of Christ.* The British director dealt not with the civil rights workers themselves—whom he bumps off in the opening moments—but with a pair of fictitious white FBI agents, portrayed by Gene Hackman and Jesus himself, Willem Dafoe. During production Parker boasted that his film "won't be just another tacky detective story. I have the final cut, and I will do justice to the people who died." His star wasn't so sure. "I was worried about the liberties the script takes," fretted Hackman after filming yet another cop-movie action scene, "but the picture couldn't have been made otherwise."

Sheila Benson of the *Los Angeles Times* was aghast at the movie's focus: *"Mississippi Burning* is missing a lot more than three civil rights workers. Parker seems to have left out black activism altogether . . . To judge from this film, neither the Student Non-Violent Coordinating Committee nor the Congress of Racial Equality existed." The *New York Post*'s David Edelstein lambasted the film for suggesting that the goals of the civil rights movement were only achieved through violence: "Parker is like a highbrow, left-wing Sylvester Stallone . . . he functions on the same Neanderthal level." Among the film's passionate defenders were the *Wall Street Journal*'s Julie Salomon, who wrote "I feel it is safe to say this film moved me more powerfully than any other this year," and *Time*'s Richard Schickel, who concurred that "narrow historical criticism somehow seems irrelevant to a movie that so powerfully reanimates the past for the best of reasons: to inform the spirit of today and possibly tomorrow."

As a result of the controversy, the sheepish Hackman found himself in the uncomfortable position of defending the movie against activist Julian Bond on *Nightline.* Other skeptics included journalist David Halberstam, who sneered in a *Time* cover story, "Parker has taken a terribly moving and haunting story and he has betrayed it, turned it into a Martin-and-Lewis slapstick between the two cops," and *Essence*'s film historian Donald Bogle who carped, "At heart, *Mississippi Burning* is a white-man's burden movie that trashes its black subjects while it celebrates the courage of its white heroes." One moviegoer so disliked the picture he filed an $8 million libel action against Orion; Lawrence Rainey, the notorious local sheriff at the time of the murders, charged that the movie made him seem like "a terrible person."

An Ovitz Blitz

About the only aspect of *Mississippi Burning* critics could agree on was Gene Hackman's performance—"awesome," raved *Sight and Sound*—and the actor, who appeared in four other 1988 releases, enjoyed a glamour buildup in a *New York Times Magazine* cover story entitled "Hollywood's Uncommon Everyman." His chief Oscar competition came from a classmate from his student days at the Pasadena Playhouse, Dustin Hoffman. "He wore a suede vest with no shirt and sandals," Hackman remembered. "He was considered outlandish. I was older than everybody and Dusty was the oddball. We kind of hit it off as soon as we knew each other."

Now that "Dusty" was a superstar, CAA head Michael Ovitz wanted to package him in a script called *Rain Man,* about two middle-aged brothers, one a con man, the other mentally retarded, who become involved with the Mafia on a cross-country trip. The agent thought Hoffman would be perfect as the sleazy sibling but the actor desired instead the showier role of the disabled man. Ovitz then got the bright idea of pairing Hoffman with another client, box-office king Tom Cruise. When Barry Morrow, the script's original author, pointed out that the heartthrob

"This is the worst work of my life."
—Dustin Hoffman

was a good twenty years too young for the role, he was given his walking papers.

In the following months, three different writers took turns trying to get the bugs out of the project. Somewhere along the line Hoffman's character made a switch from being mentally retarded to being an autistic savant, and the Mafia angle was deep-sixed. After director Martin Brest, also represented by Ovitz, took a hike during development, the agent sought other members of the CAA stable: Steven Spielberg and then Sydney Pollack, who had said that directing Hoffman in *Tootsie* had been the worst experience of his life; Pollack brought in two more writers before he, too, skedaddled. Ovitz's fourth and final recruit was Barry Levinson, who reinstated writer number three, Ronald Bass, to do another rewrite. Hoffman passed the time waiting for the production to begin by hanging out with three dozen autistic people and the doctors who treated them. He and Cruise got additional pointers by going bowling on a double date with an autistic man and his brother.

After sticking with *Rain Man* for two years, Hoffman decided, three weeks into shooting, that he wanted out. "Get Richard Dreyfuss," he told his director. "Get somebody, Barry, because this is the worst work of my life." The actor was persuaded to stay and was allowed to reshoot his first five days. Hoffman said the key to his monochromatic performance was to "find those autistic parts of myself. Because I'm convinced that we're all a little bit autistic, just like we're all a little bit crazy."

The biggest box-office hit of the Christmas season, *Rain Man* was labeled by Bob Thomas of U.P.I. as "the most original and compelling American drama since *One Flew Over the Cuckoo's Nest."* More typical of the reviews, however, was Dave Kehr's contention in the *Chicago Tribune* that the film "slips irreversibly into the so-what category. Even the superstar presence of Dustin Hoffman and Tom Cruise can't save the picture from its creeping familiarity and heart-sinking predictability." Although his part wasn't as flashy as his costar's, Cruise nevertheless heard a welcome change from the critical rancor that had greeted his summer smash, *Cocktail;* the saga of a lady-killer bartender was voted 1988's worst movie by a *Los Angeles Times* nationwide poll of print reviewers. Hoffman's autistic turn was generally hailed as "impressive" and "impeccable," but Pauline Kael, denigrating the movie as "kitsch," declared *"Rain Man* is Dustin Hoffman humping one note on a piano for two hours and eleven minutes."

Nymphet No More

The director who first put Hoffman in a blockbuster, Mike Nichols, came across a comedy screenplay that had been languishing for a couple of years at 20th Century-Fox and felt it would sum up the Reagan Era just as *The Graduate* had embodied the '60s. *Working Girl* was a fable about a secretary from Staten Island who schemes her way to success on Wall Street, a plot that *New York*'s David Denby defined as *"All About Eve* in reverse. This time, it's the young hustler who is moral and true." Fox was delighted with Nichols' choice of Harrison Ford for the love interest, but the studio got edgy when the director passed on Cher, Goldie Hawn, and Shelley Long for the female lead and selected Melanie Griffith. The actress, determined to change her party-girl image, confided to *Newsweek* that she related to her character's determination: "Tess correlated a lot with me and my career. Like finally saying 'OK, I'm going to do this part because I know I can.' That's what Tess did, and that's what I feel I've done—against everybody saying, 'Oh, you're just a sexpot or a nymphet.' Or 'You're a problem, you drink too much, you do drugs,' or 'You're wild.' " The magazine went on to document, "While filming *Working Girl,* she was still drinking (in some scenes she is visibly puffy)."

"At last—and it's long deserved—Melanie Griffith emerges as a full-blown star," rhapsodized Kirk Honeycutt in the *Hollywood Reporter,* "Combining intuitive comic timing, a savvy instinct for the subtext and a sex quotient big

"They all go back to Mama, don't they?"
—Suzy

enough to fuel a major city, Griffith totally captivates." When the press focused on the new star, she was ready with an inspiring tale of redemption—since making the movie, she had dried out at the Hazelden Center in Minnesota, reunited with her ex-husband, Don Johnson of TV's *Miami Vice,* and was expecting her second child. "I feel my life's become a fairy tale," Tippi Hedren's daughter stated in her cover story in *Vanity Fair,* "with true love at the end and the two of us the most fortunate people around."

Working Girl had a second strong role for an actress, a villainous yuppie financier played with gusto by Sigourney Weaver. "I've always wanted to play a Rosalind Russell–type role. I hadn't been in this kind of broad comedy for a while," remarked Weaver. Plus "after spending all that time in Africa, it was nice to just roll out of bed in the morning and go to work." The actress was referring to the three months she had spent in the near-freezing mountains of Rwanda impersonating slaughtered zoologist Diane Fossey for *Gorillas in the Mist,* a job that included carrying camera equipment up the hills and mingling with the eponymous simians. A male gorilla initially charged at her, but later, according to the studio's publicity, it became "habituated to Weaver and played an active role in the film."

French Kisses

When the members of the Royal Shakespeare Company headed home after completing their Broadway run of *Les Liaisons Dangereuses,* Christopher Hampton's adaptation of a 200-year-old French novel about kinky aristocrats, the producers shelved their plans to keep the show running with Glenn Close in the cast, doubting that she'd sell tickets. Two weeks later, *Fatal Attraction* opened. After shelling out $400,000 for rights to Hampton's play, the film producers protected their investment by signing a big movie star for the leading female role—Glenn Close.

Upon learning that director Milos Forman was also planning to make a film from the public domain novel, Lorimar executives offered him their vehicle but he nixed them. Eventually the company followed author Hampton's suggestion of his fellow countryman, Stephen Frears, who had gained a reputation with his caustic examinations of Margaret Thatcher's Britain in the art-house favorites *My Beautiful Laundrette* and *Sammy and Rosie Get Laid.* In addition to Close, the film's French aristocrats included such Yankees as John Malkovich, Michelle Pfeiffer, and Keanu Reeves. Frears was delighted with his star-spangled cast, paenizing, "Americans deal with such big feelings. They act with such intensity. I love to hear the American accents. My heart soars." The cast wasn't the only thing Americanized—for easier audience consumption, the film's title was changed to *Dangerous Liaisons.*

The novel took place in 1782, but the movie's time period was moved back two decades for purely practical reasons: The huge wigs that were fashionable in the later era "would make it very hard to shoot two heads in close-up," explained costume designer James Acheson. "Instead, the harder silhouette of 1760 and the smaller-headed look that goes with it seemed to serve our purposes better." Frears and company easily won the race to have an adaptation of *Les Liaisons Dangereuses* on screen. Milos Forman didn't get around to starting what would be his $30 million flop until after Frears had finished shooting his $15 million film.

Gossips heralded the production with rumors that Pfeiffer and Malkovich had continued their romantic clinches off-screen. Columnist Suzy dished that "John Malkovich, actor of many parts—and probably a man of just as many—is back with his actress wife Glenne Headley, and it's all over with beautiful actress Michelle Pfeiffer. (They all go back to Mama, don't they?)" Malkovich remained mum but did say that, far from being a stuffy costume drama, *Dangerous Liaisons* was "like something right out of *Dynasty.*" Peter Travers of *People* agreed, advising, "Don't expect *Masterpiece Theater* gentility. This baby bites!" Glenn Close further demolished her goody two-shoes image to great acclaim. "Close is chilling, a formidable, cunning puppeteer," wrote *Newsweek*'s David Ansen. "Here, in a performance of controlled venom and deeply hidden pathos, she's superb." Michelle Pfeiffer was also lauded and had Pauline Kael proclaiming her "paradisiacally beautiful." *Variety* noted that even though *Dangerous Liaisons* had snob appeal, "It also smolders with a timeless boudoir bawdiness, seasoned with eye-catching, R-rated nudity," and praised the Warner Brothers advertising department, which sold the highbrow movie by featuring cleavage in the print ads. Ted Arno, a vice-president of Loew's theaters, raved that "Campaign-wise, they did a helluva job with the beautiful women."

Gloomy and Goofy

John Malkovich was involved in another Christmas release, this time as the executive producer of the film version of Anne Tyler's quirky, best-selling novel *The Accidental Tourist,* about a gloomy gus who separates from his wife but is revitalized by the love of a daffy dog trainer. Mary Steenburgen, Laura Dern, Amy Madigan, and JoBeth Williams came to read for the female parts with star William Hurt and writer-director Lawrence Kasdan and were all in for a surprise; *Premiere* printed, "Each sailed in, blithely expecting to be the only actress present, and instead found a pack of competitors in front of Kasdan's tightly closed office door." For all of that, Kasdan chose none of them and opted for Hurt's *Body Heat* costar Kathleen Turner as the wife and the spouse of another *Silverado* actor, Mrs. Jeff Goldblum, Geena Davis, as the kook. Once cast, Davis told *Entertainment Tonight* how seriously she took her assignment. "From now on, I'll be Muriel when somebody reads the book after seeing the movie. They'll only be able to think of me."

A few days before the movie opened, the New York Film Critics gave their Best Picture award to "the sleepwalkish *Accidental Tourist,* a choice that provoked loud 'huhs???' from coast to coast," penned Peter Rainer of the *Los Angeles Times.* Some critics took their fellow voters to task in their reviews. "Everything about this glum and self-important adaptation of Anne Tyler's upper-cute novel is dim," snarled Richard Schickel. "Dim too is the judgment of the New York Film Critics Circle." The editors of *Movieline* gave Hurt a special award for "Best Autistic Performance," but *Playboy*'s Bruce Williamson defended the film, calling it "romantic, real and endearing." Mike Clark of *USA Today* thought "Geena Davis almost steals the film," although Janet Maslin found her adorableness "quite insufferable." "Libby Gelman-Waxner," *Premiere*'s singular columnist, wrote "seeing the film put me into a coma—I'm not kidding you. All I remember is watching William Hurt sitting in an armchair, blinking his little pink eyes, and the next thing I knew the usher was shaking me awake."

The Dingo Did It

The New York Critics overlooked the actors from Kasdan's film, honoring instead the stars of 1981's *The French Lieutenant's Woman* in two of 1988's least sympathetic roles. Meryl Streep wore a black Moe Howard wig and spoke with a Paul Hogan accent in *A Cry in the Dark,* a true story about an Australian woman who claims a dingo was the real culprit when she is accused of offing her kid. Best Actor Jeremy Irons won for playing crazy twin brother gynecologists in David Cronenberg's intense psychological drama, *Dead Ringers.* Praise notwithstanding, audiences stayed away in droves from both of these star vehicles; J. Hoberman of the *Village Voice* was not surprised about the commercial fate of Irons' picture, because "how do you promote a movie in which a deformed uterus becomes a subject for dinner conversation?"

Awards Smorgasbord

At year's end, no film or performer dominated the choices of the various critics groups.

Only Supporting Actor Dean Stockwell as a hapless Mafia don in *Married to the Mob* and Ron Shelton's screenplay for *Bull Durham* were cited more than once. Claiming various Best Picture and/or Director awards were *Mississippi Burning, Dead Ringers, The Unbearable Lightness of Being, A World Apart,* and *Little Dorrit,* a six-hour British version of the Charles Dickens novel.

As if Oscar prognosticators weren't confounded enough by the unruly melange of award winners, the Hollywood Foreign Press Association managed to add to the confusion. The only choices from a critics' group to receive a Golden Globe were Los Angeles winner Tom Hanks, for the popular body-switching fantasy *Big,* and National Board of Review champion Jodie Foster, who had to settle for a three-way tie for Best Actress (Drama) with Sigourney Weaver for *Gorillas in the Mist* and Shirley MacLaine, winning her fourth Globe, this time for playing an elderly, autocratic music teacher in *Madame Sousatzka.* With four awards, *Working Girl* was the Foreign Press' big winner; Sigourney Weaver won a second time as Best Supporting Actress and Melanie Griffith charmed everyone by using an epithet in her excited acceptance speech. *Rain Man* was named Best Picture (Drama), and Dustin Hoffman found the approval from the Foreign Press that had been denied him from the critics' circles. In contrast to Griffith's bubbly gratitudes, the actor's screed did not win him any new fans. Fumed Michael Musto in *The Village Voice,* "Monotonously thanking everyone from his failed fellow nominees to his hairdresser . . . Dustin still seemed to be doing *Rain Man.* Such a perverse mix of mock-humility and unctuous self-satisfaction hasn't been seen since Maria Montez pleaded for the cobra jewels."

The Nominations

"Warner sweeps to Oscar lead" headlined the *Hollywood Reporter,* but despite their two Best Picture nominees, Warner Brothers executives didn't have all that much to get excited about—neither *Dangerous Liaisons* nor *The Accidental Tourist* received Best Director nominations, thereby making them highly unlikely winners. In fact, although the inconsistencies of the pre-Oscar awards had made it seem that Best Picture would be a free-for-all, the suspense was killed once the nominations were announced. *Rain Man* was the only film nominated for both Best Director and Best Screenplay so, as Jack Mathews wrote in the *Los Angeles Times,* "The Oscar race this year is going to resemble a friendly game of bingo. The center spot—Best Picture—is free. Just write down *Rain Man* and move on."

Despite all the furor, *Mississippi Burning* managed to inspire seven nominations including Best Picture, and *Working Girl,* the fifth Picture nominee, finessed a total of six nods, but neither was up for Original Screenplay. Because all five contenders had been released in December, fans of such summer non-nominees as *Who Framed Roger Rabbit* (which received six technical nominations) and *Bull Durham* (a single mention for Original Screenplay) accused the Academy of amnesia. Of the latter film, the *L.A. Herald-Examiner*'s David Ehrenstein shrugged, "the Academy apparently wasn't as turned on as the rest of us." The Directors Branch did remember two July movies, annointing Charles Crichton's comeback with *A Fish Called Wanda* and thumbing its collective nose at the religious right by nominating *bête noire* Martin Scorsese.

Human Beings at Their Worst

The Best Actor race had been forecast as a contest among "the 4-H Club" but William Hurt failed to join Gene Hackman, Tom Hanks, and Dustin Hoffman. Jeremy Irons was also left out in the cold. "I got a big response from people in Los Angeles when I wasn't nominated," Irons said. "People I hardly knew wrote to me to say they thought it was a disgrace I was passed over. But it's not a life-enhancing movie, and the Oscars being the sort of birthday party of the movies, I think they like movies that show human beings at their best, not at their worst, which is what *Dead Ringers* was, so I sort of understood it."

The two contenders who did make the Actor lineup were Edward James Olmos as a math teacher at an East L.A. high school in the low-budget but inspirational *Stand and Deliver* and Ingmar Bergman alumnus Max von Sydow as a Swedish emigrant in the life-enhancing Danish Foreign Film nominee *Pelle The Conqueror*. Aljean Harmetz commented in the *New York Times* that "Mr. Olmos had been considered a long shot; Mr. von Sydow received little mention as a possible nominee." These dark horses hadn't been idle, though. Von Sydow's campaign had kicked off in early December when the *Hollywood Reporter*'s Robert Osborne reminded everyone, "Unbelievable, but Max has never been an Academy Award nominee before, despite the portfolio of consistently great work," and the Swedish actor was feted by the Women in Film Institute at the Zanuck Theater on the 20th Century-Fox lot. The *Los Angeles Times* reported that "Olmos' backers, including his agent and the film's investors, launched their marketing campaign for the actor several weeks ago after concluding that the studio wasn't doing enough." Their strategy paid off when Olmos appeared on *Good Morning America* as the nominations were announced and got to relish the news on camera.

The biggest surprise to soothsayers was the omission of Shirley MacLaine among the Best Actress finalists: Glenn Close, Melanie Griffith, Meryl Streep, Sigourney Weaver, and Jodie Foster. The last got news of her nomination as she waited for her plane to take off from Rome. "A man from Alitalia came right out on the tarmac and brought me a telex," she told *USA Today*. "And the people on the plane clapped for me. It was nice." The prepared nominee had purchased a short, strapless aqua body-hugging dress with a big bow in back that she had seen in a boutique window while "walking down the street in Italy." Foster also sent congratulatory telegrams to her fellow nominees that read, according to Sigourney Weaver's paraphrasing, "the nomination is the glory and the rest of it is one great party." The race was a toss-up but it was generally conceded that Streep and Weaver were out of the running. Noting in *TV Guide* that Glenn Close "has been nominated five times, most spectacularly last year in *Fatal Attraction*," Kenneth Turan predicted her victory because "that is the kind of morning-after grievance the Academy most enjoys redressing." Roger Ebert expected Foster to triumph "not only because of the strong social message in *The Accused*, but also because she has been respected by the movie community since her days as an uncommonly intelligent child actress." An anonymous Academy member told the *New York Daily News* why he was voting for Melanie Griffith: "I'm a softie. Anyone who can come back from a bout with alcohol, and whose mother is one of my favorite actresses, is the person for me."

Sigourney Weaver at least had the consolation of also being nominated for Best Supporting Actress in *Working Girl*, secure in the knowledge that all four performers who had previously accomplished this feat had taken home the secondary award. Nevertheless, her *Gorillas in the Mist* studio wasn't giving up; the studio sent four-color mailers to Academy members, inviting them to screenings followed by a dinner of carrot linguine carbonara. At the Directors Guild Awards ceremony, Carl Reiner wisecracked, "I have in my house more color reproductions of Sigourney Weaver and a beautiful gorilla than I need."

Despite the Academy's attached note on the nominating ballot, "don't put leading actors in supporting roles," the majority of the Supporting Actress nominees were above-the-title stars: Weaver, Michelle Pfeiffer, and Geena Davis. The press corp applauded the unexpected nomination of *Working Girl*'s true supporting player, Joan Cusak, while *Mississippi Burning*'s Frances McDormand was, as predicted, the fifth nominee.

A Fish Called Wanda's Kevin Kline was the only Supporting Actor nominee not to have received at least one pre-Oscar award. Dean Stockwell of *Married to the Mob* accepted *Entertainment Tonight*'s invitation to follow him around on

"No one has ever seen anything like this!"
—Allan Carr

Oscar day. Eighteen-year-old River Phoenix, winner of the National Board of Review scroll for his portrayal of the sensitive son of '60s radicals in *Running on Empty*, attended the Academy's nominees luncheon and confessed, "I never dreamed I'd be up here today, but I guess my agent thought I would be." Martin Landau, the former TV spy who won a Golden Globe as a shady but kind-hearted financier in Francis Ford Coppola's *Tucker*, exclaimed, "As a kid in Brooklyn, I dreamed of this. I think everyone does." In contrast, *Little Dorrit*'s Alec Guinness, who already had two Oscars, was dubbed by the *Hollywood Reporter* as "the coolest of all those who did get a nomination this session. Guinness sent word through his representatives that he may be available to discuss the nomination . . . in a week or so."

Making a last-ditch effort to win the hearts and minds of the Academy's liberal membership, Orion tried a new ad campaign in which prominent blacks and the families of the three slain men attested to the veracity of *Mississippi Burning*. At least Orion had something to push; Columbia, which had garnered nine Oscars the past year with *The Last Emperor*, did not receive a single 1988 nomination. The Feature Documentary race received as much press attention as any category when Errol Morris' award-winning *The Thin Blue Line*, an art-house triumph so successful it led to the overturning of the murder conviction of a Texas man, hadn't sufficiently impressed the Academy's documentary judges to be nominated. The *Los Angeles Times* dug deeper and discovered that "at the committee screening, enough members raised their hands to have the film stopped before it was completed."

Can't Stop the Carr

The Academy turned the task of producing the telecast over to Allan Carr, the flashy progenitor of *Can't Stop the Music* and *Where the Boys Are '84*, but in the news more recently because of his medical problems. The *Hollywood Reporter*'s Robert Osborne itemed, "In early September he goes into the hospital for a hip operation, à la Bette Davis and Sammy Davis," and Army Archerd revealed that, once tapped by the Academy, "Allan Carr, recuping after hip surgery at Cedars-Sinai, held his first Oscar '89 meeting in his hospital room with Academy prez Dick Kahn." Promoting himself as much as the awards, Carr later held a press conference a full four months before the ceremony at his Beverly Hills home, where a six-foot Oscar statue stood guard in the front yard. "There are just things in your life you always dream about doing," cooed the self-described "child of the movies." "It's the highest honor you can get from the Academy, other than winning one." The impresario insisted there was no personal gain involved: "You don't get paid to do the Academy Awards. People don't realize that"; he also pledged a patriotic devotion to his assignment, "America wants the Academy Awards; America loves the Academy Awards and this year we're definitely giving them something to read about."

Promising a high glamour quotient, Carr gurgled, "I just want as many great people as we can possibly get. We're casting the presenters as if we were casting a movie. We want famous costars who are known for making pictures together, or are married, or couples, or what I call 'compadres,' like Michael Caine and Sean Connery." The *Los Angeles Times*' Paul Rosenfield overheard the producer on the phone with the hustling publicist of a certain actress: "I like her. We were at the fat farm in England together three years ago—she's terrific, but I've got biggies on the waiting list."

In actuality, Carr was having problems wrangling luminaries. Two MGM glamour girls, Ava Gardner and Lana Turner, declined the showman's offer because they wanted people to remember them as they were on screen. Florida resident Sophia Loren preferred to rest up for a benefit she was doing for the University of Miami a few nights later. Pointing out that Melanie Griffith would be doing both the Oscars *and* the Florida gig, Carr testily commented, "It would

"Being asked to perform at the Academy Awards is like being asked to the White House."
—Rob Lowe

have been very easy for Miss Loren to do if she wanted to." An insulted Loretta Young said she wanted no part of the event unless she could be the sole Best Picture presenter as she had been at the 1981 Awards; the seventy-five-year-old Oscar winner's attitude shocked Carr because, "I was offering her Rudolf Nureyev as a copresenter!" The producer's brainstorm to have Roger and Jessica Rabbit present the Honorary Animation Award to their creator, Richard Williams, fizzled when he "found that it was so complicated to do it right that it would take nine months and be prohibitively expensive." Roseanne Barr turned down her invitation, arguing, "No, it's not fair to the Academy Awards. I'm still a TV star."

Bardot, Dodo, and No-Shows

Bona-fide movie names who also refused were Barbra Streisand, Elizabeth Taylor, Paul Newman, Joanne Woodward, Rex Harrison, Maureen O'Hara, and Mia Farrow. Even Carr's former client, Ann-Margret, would be missing—she had a previous engagement on Oscar night in Las Vegas. Brigitte Bardot was willing to fly from Europe to do the show but only if she were allowed to talk about her favorite cause. "We are not planning on Sacheen Littlefeather—or a speech on animal rights," Carr retorted. "We're on her side and I promise there are no furs on the show." Another animal fanatic did agree to appear, explained the producer. "Doris Day is doing it because a dog sitter was found and she felt comfortable leaving Carmel."

The Carr touch extended to decorating the exterior of the auditorium—"Six million tulips are being flown in from Holland. The Shrine's going to look like an Easter basket"—and providing an "exclusive, stars-only" green room called "Club Oscar" for V.I.P.s waiting in the wings to go on. *Vanity Fair* mentioned that not only were there celebrities at the rehearsals but that "Carr's acupuncturist was a fixture backstage, where Carr . . . sometimes took meetings with needles sticking out of him, clad only in a towel."

Promises, Promises

For entertainment value, Carr commissioned a song entitled "I Want to Be an Oscar Winner" to be warbled by a group of "Hollywood's brightest young stars" including Connie Stevens and Eddie Fisher's daughter Joely, Carol Burnett's daughter Carrie Hamilton, and Tyrone Power, Jr. "I think it's going to be a show-stopper," the producer predicted. "The audience is going to be on their feet, screaming in the theater. No one has ever seen anything like this!"

Even more grandiose was the hooplameister's plans for the opening number. "You don't want to miss the beginning," he teased *Daily Variety*. "When the curtain goes up, you want to be in your seat." The producer called a second press conference, this one to show off the sets for the extravaganza, depicting his version of the Cocoanut Grove nightclub, circa 1937, to feature such stars of the 1930s and '40s as Dorothy Lamour who, Carr boasted to Cindy Adams, "lost thirty pounds for this." His biggest casting coup was convincing Oscar night party-giver Irving "Swifty" Lazar to play himself "going from table to table trying to make a book deal." For younger audiences, he drafted Rob Lowe to make his singing debut. "Being asked to perform at the Academy Awards is like being asked to the White House," the young innocent explained to the *New York Daily News*. "You don't ask questions."

On Oscar day, the *Hollywood Reporter* remarked, "Producer Allan Carr, who has been banging the drum loudly for this year's gala and generated tons of press coverage, has little left to say that hasn't already been said." Despite Carr's vow that, "If nothing else, this will be the most beautiful Academy Awards of all time. It will be the antithesis of tacky," *Los Angeles Magazine* confided that the promoter "has some of the Academy's conservatives edgy about what the flamboyant producer may come up with."

The Big Night

The first celebrities to arrive were those *Last Temptation* critics, Roy Rogers and Dale Evans, decked out in cowboy duds for their roles in Carr's opening number. Reported Marilyn Beck, "Three times as many fans were able to pay homage to their favorite stars thanks to the expanded bleachers Carr had built this year. Carr even had several Porta-Johns built for the fans' convenience." One of these idolators, Tim Allen from Houston, told the *Long Beach Press-Telegram*, "I don't care for these new stars. I'm just hoping for a shot of Doris Day." He was destined for disappointment. The evening's first bad omen had earlier occurred some 300 miles north in Carmel, when Day was strolling the grounds of an inn she owned. Dodo tripped on a water sprinkler, had to have stitches, and canceled her Oscar appearance.

The group of women from Orange County who annually play dress-up to acknowledge their favorite nominee imitated Sigourney Weaver by wearing jungle khakis and clutching stuffed gorillas. Going for the Glenn Close look, however, was a trio from San Francisco's gay theater company, the Sisters of Perpetual Indulgence; the three men, in wigs and powdered faces, were outfitted in mid-18th-century gowns and held signs beckoning "Come out, Hollywood." Jodie Foster arrived with actor Julian Sands and various family members, but the *Los Angeles Herald-Examiner* said the loudest cheers greeted Melanie Griffith, who came with *her* mother and Don Johnson. Double-nominee Sigourney Weaver was escorted by her husband and her parents from New York. Recently separated from Tom Hayden, Jane Fonda was also part of a family group, coming with her children Vanessa Vadim and Troy Hayden.

Unlikely to end up on stage tonight, Meryl Streep jovially admitted that she picked up her blouse-and-pants ensemble at a store in Mystic, Connecticut, for a measly sixty bucks. River Phoenix's date was costar Martha Plimpton, while

Awards Ceremony

MARCH 29, 1989, 6:00 P.M.
THE SHRINE AUDITORIUM, LOS ANGELES

Televised over ABC

Presenters

Supporting Actress .... Melanie Griffith and Don Johnson
Sound .... Kim Novak and James Stewart
Sound Effects Editing .... Kim Novak and James Stewart
Makeup ... Cybill Shepherd and Robert Downey, Jr.
Original Score .... Patrick Swayze
Honorary Award to the National Film Board of Canada .... Donald Sutherland and Kiefer Sutherland
Art Direction .... Willem Dafoe and Gene Hackman
Costume Design .... Bo Derek and Dudley Moore
Original Song .... Sammy Davis, Jr. and Gregory Hines
Foreign Film ..... Candice Bergen, Jacqueline Bisset, and Jack Valenti
Supporting Actor ..... Michael Caine, Sean Connery, and Roger Moore
Visual Effects .... Beau Bridges, Jeff Bridges, and Lloyd Bridges
Documentary Short Subject .... Geena Davis and Jeff Goldblum
Documentary Feature ..... Edward James Olmos and Max von Sydow
Special Achievement Award to Richard Williams .... Charles Fleischer and Robin Williams
Cinematography ..... Demi Moore and Bruce Willis
Short Films .... Carrie Fisher and Martin Short
Actor .... Michael Douglas
Editing .... Farrah Fawcett and Ryan O'Neal
Scientific and Technical Awards ..... Angie Dickinson
Original Screenplay .... Amy Irving and Richard Dreyfuss
Adapted Screenplay .... Michelle Pfeiffer and Dennis Quaid
Director .... Goldie Hawn and Kurt Russell
Actress .... Tom Cruise and Dustin Hoffman
Picture .... Cher

Best Song nominees were not performed this year

"I've got a lovely bunch of cocoanuts."
—Merv Griffin

former child star Dean Stockwell arrived with an *Entertainment Tonight* camera crew in his limo. "You look like a storybook princess!" correspondent Leeza Gibbons ejaculated as Geena Davis breezed by in Bill Hargate's ice-blue satin gown with bustle and train, capped off by a diamond necklace. "It's one of those potentially once-in-a-lifetime things," replied Mrs. Goldblum. Adding to the fairy tale quality was the limo sent over from Disney bearing a duo wearing Roger Rabbit and Mickey Mouse costumes.

One hour before showtime, Allan Carr had yet to slip into his sequined tuxedo; wearing a windbreaker and boating shoes, he was preoccupied with ogling the arriving stars and telling reporters, "If it goes as well as it did in dress rehearsal three hours ago, I'll be in show business heaven." As he spoke, 1987 nominee Sally Kirkland busily worked the crowd, regaling anyone who would listen with the news that *Anna* was now available on video. Kirkland's vanquisher from the previous year, Cher, returned in a black, fringed go-go dress and made a beeline to shake the outreaching arms from the bleachers. Asked on TV if he was having a good time, Dustin Hoffman responded, "It's hard to enjoy it without a Valium." Cindy Adams recounted that "Max von Sydow showed me what he had done for luck. He turned his wife around and kicked her in the butt. 'In my country that's how we wish each other good fortune.' "

The broadcast began with a crane shot through the trees in front of the Shrine. Commercial sponsors were given top billing, followed by the forecourt entrances of nominees Jodie Foster, Sigourney Weaver, Glenn Close, Tom Hanks, and Edward James Olmos, who was with the person he portrayed, teacher Jamie Escalante. Presenters caught by the TV cameras as they showed up included "comedy legend" Lucille Ball and Allan Carr's friend, "beautiful and elegant" Jacqueline Bisset.

Army Archerd served double duty this year, interviewing arrivals and then participating in the opening of the show himself. Standing in the Shrine lobby, the columnist announced, "And now ladies and gentlemen, here's one of the great legends of Hollywood. She's back with us tonight—Miss Snow White." Portrayed by actress Eileen Bowman, this sparklingly dressed Snow White possessed a breathlessly screechy voice as she engaged in repartee with Archerd. "I'm a little late, though. Can you tell me how to get into the theater?" she asked. Archerd: "That's easy, Snow. Just follow the Hollywood stars." Echoed a munchkin-sounding chorus, "Follow the Hollywood stars." Indeed, two fantasy movies from the 1930s were being amalgamated; when the camera revealed Snow White's feet, she was wearing Dorothy's ruby red slippers from *The Wizard of Oz*.

Singing "I Only Have Eyes for You," Snow White then went to the front row of the orchestra, where she forced a reluctant Michelle Pfeiffer to hold her hand. Martin Landau, Tom Hanks, and Sigourney Weaver were in for the same treatment from the squeaking Snow. *Vanity Fair* observed, "The looks of horror on their faces were unforgettable." Snow's next stop was the Cocoanut Grove stage set where the featured attraction was talk-show host/game-show producer/casino owner Merv Griffin, who enacted an even earlier incarnation of himself by singing a hit from his days as Freddie Martin's boy singer, "I've Got a Lovely Bunch of Cocoanuts." At Carr's night club that evening were 1985's Jean Hersholt Humanitarian winner Buddy Rogers, Roy Rogers and Dale Evans, Dorothy Lamour, Vincent Price and wife Coral Browne, Alice Faye, her ex-husband Tony Martin, and his current "beautiful wife," Cyd Charisse; each of them had approximately three seconds of air time before being unceremoniously whisked away from the camera. The impresario's supposed big coup never materialized; Swifty Lazar, on the counsel of George Stevens, Jr., who had warned an appearance would be undignified, had come to his senses and stayed with his guests at Spago.

And the opening continued. Griffin addressed the fairy tale character, "Isn't it exciting, Snow? Isn't it thrilling? It gets better. Meet your

"I have supported one or two actresses in the past."
—Don Johnson

blind date—Rob Lowe." Looking as if he already realized this was a mistake, Lowe gamely joined his date in a duet of the Creedence Clearwater song "Proud Mary," with the new lyrics "Rolling, rolling, keep the cameras rolling." Meanwhile, heads popped out of the tables at the Cocoanut Grove as the furniture started dancing, joined by heavy-set waitresses wearing oversized Carmen Miranda headpieces. The *Los Angeles Herald-Examiner*'s television reviewer Andy Klein said the dancers were "dressed like tropical mixed drinks," adding that "The whole production number resembled the sort of nightmare you might have after imbibing too many such drinks."

And the opening continued. The Cocoanut Grove was replaced by a replica of the Chinese Theater while an off-stage chorus trilled, "Dreams come true, dreams come true, in the Grauman's Chinese Theater!" Lowe kissed Snow on the hand and a chorus line of ushers made like the Rockettes, doing their kicks while singing "Hooray for Hollywood." Johnny Mercer's original lyrics were replaced with the likes of "When you're down in the dumps/Try on Judy Garland's pumps."

Finally the opening concluded by going from Snow White to Cinderella: Lily Tomlin "accidentally" lost one of her shoes as she marched down a staircase to make a welcoming address. She seemed as agog by what had just transpired as the audience, noting that "More than a billion and a half people watched that. And at this very moment they're trying to make sense of it." Behind her, a stagehand could be seen retrieving her shoe. To the relief of all, the show cut to the first batch of commercials. One of the promos was the first of a series for Revlon directed by *Big*-helmer Penny Marshall.

Academy President Richard Kahn, a member of the Public Relations branch, delivered another welcoming address. After the antics of Snow White and Rob Lowe, Kahn's remarks had an unintentional irony when, remembering the Academy's Founding Fathers, he commented, "I don't see how any of them could have envisioned this." Tom Selleck made a third opening statement to explain that the show would have no master of ceremonies. He mentioned that the first Academy Awards were handed out in five minutes and that as for tonight's show, "I hope it'll seem like five minutes and that you'll end up asking for more."

As the orchestra played "The Second Time Around," an announcer hailed Supporting Actress presenters Melanie Griffith and "her best friend, Don Johnson." The enceinte Griffith wore a white Southern belle maternity dress and nervously allowed that "we don't want to sound stupid." Johnson advised, "Why don't you take a couple of deep breaths and relax and pretend you're in Lamaze class." There was tittering in the audience and then the former Hollywood ladies' man claimed that it was appropriate that he was giving this award because, "Let's face it, I have supported one or two actresses in the past." His laughs were topped by Griffith's retort: "Yeah, and one or two have supported you." When they got around to the awards, clips of the nominees, all of whom were present, aired, giving the home audience the chance to witness Michelle Pfeiffer contemplating her screen love scene with John Malkovich. Griffith and Johnson inaugurated another Carr innovation during the presentation, changing the famous "And the winner is" to "And the Oscar goes to." The *Los Angeles Times* thought the switch was merely semantics. "Call the winners whatever you will, the losers are going to know they've lost."

In an upset, the victor was not Sigourney Weaver but *The Accidental Tourist*'s Geena Davis. The radiant Davis quickly bussed her husband and glided to the stage. Allan Carr's pal Jacqueline Bisset received a close-up as she applauded. Davis started by thanking Anne Tyler "for writing such a wonderful book," and then listed: "My dear friend Larry Kasdan, Bill Hurt, Ruth Meyers, our wonderful costume designer . . . my wonderful acting coach Roy London, and my other wonderful acting coach and darling husband, Jeff Goldblum." The camera cut to a grinning Goldblum (with L.A. mayor Tom Bradley beaming behind him), but the *Village Voice*'s Cynthia Heimel quoted a guest at her Oscar-watching party: "I predict Geena's win will put a rift in her and Jeff's relationship."

Jane Fonda, in a revealing black, sequinned bolero jacket, introduced the first Best Picture film clip by exhorting everyone to see the nominees in their entirety. "I mean, see them, in a theater," the exercise queen demanded. "You wanna watch videotapes, I know some terrific videotapes you can watch." After the bathtub scene in *Rain Man* unspooled, Fonda brought on "my father's best friend and one of the screen's great beauties," James Stewart and Kim Novak. After joking about fear of heights, transvestism, and Stewart's trademark protracted line readings, the costars of *Vertigo* and *Bell, Book and Candle* gave the Sound Award to a Clint Eastwood box-office flop, his biography of Charlie Parker, *Bird.* They also bestowed the Sound Effects Editing statuette to *Who Framed Roger Rabbit,* and cowinner Louis L. Edemann advised his wife and kids to "clear the mantle." Memories of the opening number were then evoked, via a car commercial in which Disney cartoon characters—the Seven Dwarfs, Mickey and Minnie Mouse, et al.—spilled out of a Lumina in front of the Chinese theater.

The Makeup Award to Geena Davis' other 1988 release, *Beetlejuice,* was given by Cybill Shepherd and Robert Downey, Jr. whose connection was as costars in the current comedy, *Chances Are.* Because of Doris Day's injury, Patrick Swayze came on stage without a partner and recalled that when he was a child, "musical comedies were my pacifier." He introduced a series of clips from the movies on which Allan Carr cut his teeth—musicals of the 1950s. Said Swayze, "These magicians definitely had a hand in seducing me." The montage ranged from Judy Garland performing "Get Happy" in *Summer Stock* to June Haver and Gene Nelson in *The Daughter of Rosie O'Grady.* The segment was well received, but Kay Gardella of the *New York Daily News* harrumphed, "I'd like to have a dollar for every time I've seen Gene Kelly do 'Singin' in the Rain.' " Swayze returned to announce that the Original Score Award went to *The Milagro Beanfield War*'s Dave Grusin. The composer was home in Santa Fe, because, his friends Alan and Marilyn Bergman explained, he figured he didn't stand a chance since Robert Redford's first movie since winning an Oscar eight years ago had come and gone without causing a ripple.

Olivia Newton-John, whose cinematic claim to fame was the Allan Carr production of *Grease* ten years earlier, came out to do nothing more than introduce Donald and Kiefer Sutherland. The father and son awarded an Honorary Oscar to their compatriots at the National Film Board of Canada, which was celebrating its fiftieth anniversary. Next, Anjelica Huston set up the clip from *Mississippi Burning,* after which the film's stars, Gene Hackman and Willem Dafoe, appeared to give the Art Direction Oscar. The screen Jesus explained why his head was now shaved: "I came here from Auschwitz," where he was making *Triumph of the Spirit* with Best Actor nominee Edward James Olmos. The audience's response struck Janet Maslin as odd. "Only in the peculiar atmosphere of Oscar night could the mention of Auschwitz get a hand." The winner for Art Direction was *Dangerous Liaisons.*

To the strains of Ravel's "Bolero"—also known over the past decade as "Theme from *10*"—Bo Derek and Dudley Moore arrived for the Costume Design presentation. "Your hair looks different," Moore quipped to his former costar, who had long ago given up her cornrows. He also joked that "It's ironic that we should be here tonight presenting Best Costume Design, when as I recall. . . ." The audience laughed before the actual punchline so Moore murmured, "It's hardly worth reading the rest of the paragraph." The winner was James Acheson for what Moore labeled "his line of seductive French sportswear" in *Dangerous Liaisons.* Acheson, who had also won this award last year, thanked "the wonderful group of actresses that withstood the rigors of 18th-century corsetting with such pa-

"Knock yourself out, Boom-Boom."
—Candice Bergen to Jack Valenti

tience and good humor." A commercial for a Disney theme park then refreshed everyone's memory of the Snow White curtain-raiser.

Billy Crystal did assorted bits of business such as imagining Yul Brynner in *The Babe Ruth Story* (reaction shot of Robin Williams roaring), and George Bush and Dan Quayle in *Of Mice and Men* ("Tell me about the Contras, George") (shot of John Cleese laughing). After popping a cough drop in his mouth to illustrate how easy it is to feign tap dancing noise (shot of Jack Nicholson beside himself), Crystal introduced clips of movie tap scenes; receiving the biggest hand were the Nicholas Brothers who had been dumped from Carr's opening number the day before because it was running long. The footage culminated with the soon-to-be-released musical *Tap,* and out came the film's two stars, Gregory Hines and Sammy Davis, Jr. In what was to be his final Oscar appearance, Davis said "Get your VCRs ready," and a montage of past Oscar-show performances of nominated songs rolled, beginning with the 1957 Mae West–Rock Hudson duet of "Baby, It's Cold Outside" misidentified as taking place in 1949. Among the other clips were a pre-plastic surgery Michael Jackson doing "Ben" from 1972 and Best Actress nominee Jodie Foster dueting with Johnnie Whitaker on "Love" when she was ten. Afterward, Hines inquired, "Was that you singing 'Talk to the Animals'?" "No," deadpanned Davis, "I was the one singing 'Ben.' " None of this year's nominees would be seen in any future such montages because Carr had decided the song finalists wouldn't be performed, even though the category was down to just three nominations. The Award went to Carly Simon for "Let the River Run," from *Working Girl.* "Come on up here, Carly," instructed Sammy, and the winner, in a jumper that resembled one of Michael Keaton's costumes in *Beetlejuice,* thanked her husband in the audience and told her kids over the airwaves, "If you found a television set on that island where you are, your Mama's really proud."

The two stars of George Cukor's final film, *Rich and Famous,* Jacqueline Bisset and Candice Bergen, prefaced the Foreign Language Award by conversing in French while humorous subtitles ran on the screen: "Don't wait up for me, Louis," Bergen supposedly informed her husband, director Louis Malle. "There's chicken in the refrigerator." The women were accompanied by the inevitable Jack Valenti, and Bergen told the M.P.A.A. head, "Knock yourself out, Boom-Boom." For the second year in a row, the winner was from Denmark. Bille August, the director of *Pelle the Conqueror,* allowed as to how "I made a film about very poor immigrants coming to Denmark and here I'm standing in my tuxedo with this shiny thing." Posing backstage with August, Bergen was still sore that *Babette's Feast* had bested her husband's *Au Revoir, Les Enfant* at the last ceremony. "It was robbery," Mme. Malle maintained.

After a rerun of the car commercial with all the Disney critters, Barbara Hershey showed the *Accidental Tourist* clip, preceding Michael Caine and Sean Connery, who presented the Award they had claimed the last two years—Best Supporting Actor. Caine proceeded to read the acceptance speech he wasn't around to give two years ago; he praised his wife and daughter, Woody Allen and Swifty Lazar, while Connery pointed to himself, encouraging Caine to thank him. In the midst of these high jinks, a third "compadre," the bearded Roger Moore, entered unannounced and grabbed the speech out of Caine's hands. "I'm not on this list," the actor groused as the other two asked the interloper to identify himself. "Bond," responded Moore but Caine disagreed: "It's David Puttnam. I thought they sent you back to England," alluding to the short-tenured ex-head of Columbia.

Alec Guinness was the only candidate not in the Shrine and the Oscar went to Kevin Kline, to the surprise of most predictors, the other nominees, and Kline himself. He chastely kissed his bride of three weeks, Phoebe Cates, and shook Screenplay nominee John Cleese's hand on his way to the stage, where he said, "There's a lot of

Brits here tonight. Scary. But I have to thank a few of them myself." He concluded by praising Best Director nominee "Charlie Crichton, who, at seventy-seven, proves that, even with twenty-five years off, there's no such thing as growing old when you've got a dream," and, as the orchestra began playing get-off music, he hurriedly said, "And I'd like to thank my wife, Phoebe." Backstage, the winner admitted to Joel Siegel that his tribute to Crichton was "inane . . . cornball stuff—it's from watching the Oscar show."

Onstage, Lloyd, Beau, and Jeff Bridges were giving the Visual Effects prize to *Who Framed Roger Rabbit* and one of the technicians thanked the late cartoonist Tex Avery, who had helped to create Bugs Bunny and Chilly Willy. Walter Matthau materialized to say that Bob Hope and Lucille Ball would be appearing next. "Some of these people won't be around much longer," producer Carr had predicted, a sentiment shared by the audience, which gave the duo the night's first standing ovation. Curiously, the camera focused on a bored Michelle Pfeiffer clapping and standing along with everyone else. For the occasion, Ball wore a black, sequinned Bob Mackie with a daring slit. ("It has a slit that goes right up her behind," her husband Gary Morton filled in Cindy Adams.) Upon hearing the warm reception, the eighty-five-year-old Hope was off and running: "I haven't seen so many gorgeous girls since I spent Father's Day with Steve Garvey." Lucy cackled at the one-liner. Hope: "But I've got the most gorgeous girl right by my side, Lucille Ball, right there." He elicited more applause when he pointed out that he had been on the Oscars twenty-six times, to which Lucy pointed out that he had never won. "I may take a Chilean grape," riposted Hope, making sport of a current poisoning scare. His other jibes included a dig at both Salman Rushdie and one of Dustin Hoffman's less successful films. "The Ayatollah Khomeni called me. He wanted to know who wrote *Ishtar*" and, of course, one at Washington, "Dan Quayle's visit to the White House—*The Accidental Tourist.*" Ball got a laugh in edgewise when she remarked of her four screen teamings with Hope, "Talk about your dangerous liaisons."

The two comics had the task of introducing "nineteen of the hottest young people in pictures"—in other words, the "I Wanna Be an Oscar Winner" number. The participants were dressed in everything from tuxedos to T-shirts and included Rob Lowe's brother Chad, as well as twenty-three-year-old Corey Parker and Patrick Dempsey, also twenty-three, who happened to be Parker's stepfather, having married Corey's forty-eight-year-old mother. Olivia Newton-John's husband Matt Latanzi was included as a "young person," even though he had costarred with Jacqueline Bisset and Candice Bergen in *Rich and Famous* eight years ago. Corey Feldman moonwalked, Christian Slater and Tyrone Power, Jr. played pirates and fought over Ricki Lake's hand, Broadway's Savion Glover tapped and everybody did some steps, regardless of ability. Janet Maslin fretted that the number "inspired no confidence in Hollywood's future."

The announcer introduced Jeff Goldblum and "Academy Award Winner Geena Davis" and the stars of *The Fly* stepped out to the strains of "Flight of the Bumblebee." The couple awarded the Documentary Short Oscar to *You Don't Have to Die,* about children with cancer. Probable also-rans Max von Sydow and Edward James Olmos—also with an Aushwitz hairdo—entered the stage arm-in-arm and, after Olmos kissed von Sydow on the hand, gave the Documentary Feature trophy to *Hotel Terminus,* Marcel Ophuls' four-and-a-half-hour account of Nazi Klaus Barbie. The winner said "There are a lot of people to thank because it's a very long film. There are whole countries to thank." Backstage, the recipient said his documentary would have been even lengthier had Claude Lannsman not already covered some of the same material in the eight-hour *Shoah.*

Anne Archer was greeted by the sounds of "The Most Beautiful Girl in the World," when she served as a preamble for the *Dangerous Liaisons* clip. Robin Williams contributed to the evening's Disney motif by wearing Mickey Mouse

"You never see Robert De Niro's face on a watch."
—Robin Williams

ears and gloves. He introduced himself: "Good evening. I'm Dan Quayle. And welcome to a kinder, gentler Oscar." Folding back one ear, he said, "Look. Vincent van Mouse." He pointed out that "You never see Robert De Niro's face on a watch," and observed, "Behind every great man, they say there's a great behind." Charles Fleischer, the voice of Roger Rabbit, joined Williams in a rap song done in the voices of cartoon characters and in presenting an Honorary Award to *Roger Rabbit*'s animation director, Richard Williams. As the recipient entered holding an Oscar, there was a reaction shot of the wife of the show's musical director, Mrs. Marvin Hamlisch. Animator Williams credited "Steven Spielberg for having the enormous prestige to midwife the whole thing," and promised in summation, "The best is yet to come!"

"Thank God, no designer is to blame," huffed the front page of *Women's Wear Daily* when Demi Moore, with husband Bruce Willis, marched out in a self-created ensemble of bustier, half skirt and bicycling shorts. "Head to toe, Demi was clearly the Worst Dressed actress at the Oscars." Presenting Cinematography, the couple gave the audience a look at the wretched home movies Willis took of Moore feeding their infant. The Oscar winner was *Mississippi Burning*'s sole victor, Peter Bizou, who stated the obvious, "It's a great honor to be here, and a great thrill." Then another Disney theme park commercial helped to prevent memories of Rob Lowe and Snow White from dimming.

Short Film presenters Carrie Fisher and Martin Short arrived on stage—wearing the same dress. When Fisher complained that Short had shown poor judgment in choosing an identical outfit, he shot back, "Carrie, you have hundreds of dresses. I have four." Muttered Fisher, "Men. You can't live with them and you can't kill them." Animated Short Film recipient John Lassiter bragged that his *Tin Toy* was the first computer-generated film to win the Award. Minimalist comedian Steven Wright, coproducer and star of the Live Short winner *The Appointments of Dennis Johnson,* said, "This was for the Short Film category. We're really glad we cut out the other sixty minutes."

In a change from the usual protocol of gender-switching, last year's Best Actor, Michael Douglas, gave the male award. All the nominees were there to hear him declare Dustin Hoffman, in *Rain Man,* the victor. Hoffman kissed his wife and two other women in his party, as well as Gene Hackman who was sitting across the aisle. On the way to the podium, he shook Edward James Olmos' hand. Sporting what the *Philadelphia Daily News* dubbed "a Yasser Arafat–style stubble," Hoffman took time before speaking to gaze upon the second standing ovation of the evening. This show of respect afforded a fourth close-up of Jacqueline Bisset. Saluting his fellow nominees "even if you didn't vote for me," Hoffman smiled and said, "I didn't vote for you guys, either." He went on for almost as long as his record-setting speech of 1979, hemming and hawing his way through paeans to his hospitalized father who had recently had a stroke and to autistic people everywhere. In his two-and-a-half minutes at the microphone, Hoffman never got around to thanking costar Tom Cruise or director Barry Levinson. Liz Smith later snarled in her column about "his general egotism in thinking he never has to be prepared and the fact that he always puts on an act, tugging our heartstrings with fake-mannered awkwardness."

Ali McGraw set up the clips from the final Best Picture nominee, *Working Girl,* and welcomed "a man to die for, at least I did the only time I worked with him," her *Love Story* costar, Ryan O'Neal. Out strutted the second unmarried cohabitating couple of the night, appearing because producer Carr believed the audience ached for them. "The public hasn't seen Farrah and Ryan together in a long, long time!" he had proclaimed, so Ryan O'Neal and Farrah Fawcett presented the fourth Oscar to *Roger Rabbit,* for Film Editing.

"Oscar's special friend," Angie Dickinson, in a white, feathery gown *Woman's Wear Daily* described as her "duck costume," narrated the flashbacks to an earlier evening when the Scientific and Technical Awards were distributed to Dolby Sound, the zoom lens, and Eastman-Kodak, which was celebrating its 100th anniversary. "It was a beautiful evening," Dickinson rejoiced. "I'm in awe of all this technical and scientific expertise."

The costars of a largely forgotton love story, Richard Dreyfuss and Amy Irving from 1980's *The Competition,* announced that *Rain Man* had won Best Original Screenplay. Of the many writers who worked on it, only Barry Morrow and Ron Bass received screen credit and Oscars. As they walked up, the orchestra played Leroy Anderson's "Typewriter Song," a tune most closely associated with Jerry Lewis. Although Carr had promised the writers that they'd both be able to make speeches, the orchestra started up after Bass finished, so Morrow remained speechless. Dennis Quaid and Michelle Pfeiffer, who were neither costars, compadres, companions, nor a couple, handed the Adapted Screenplay Oscar to Christopher Hampton for *Dangerous Liaisons.* The writer said, "This is great, but anyone would fly across the Atlantic to get a kiss from Michelle Pfeiffer." He also thanked author Choderlos de Laclos "who's having about as good a year as it's possible to have if you're a dead writer."

Best Director presenters Goldie Hawn and her longtime companion Kurt Russell heard the orchestra play "Isn't It Romantic" for their entrance. Russell addressed Tom Cruise and Barry Levinson: "Your buddy Dustin Hoffman is going crazy backstage because he didn't have time to thank you." Then Hawn began the banter she later told *Vanity Fair* she and Russell conceived "while they were taking a shower together." She commented that they fit into the theme of the show as costars, campadres, companions, and as a couple. "There's only one thing we're not—married," added Russell. "Is that a proposal?" asked a giggly Hawn, prompting the audience to whoop and clap. "Well," Russell hesitated for a pregnant moment, before acceding to a supposed offstage signal to go on with the award. Goldie got laughs by feigning disappointment. Every nominee was present except Charles Crichton, who had already crossed the big pond once for the Directors Guild awards, which he had lost. The DGA's winner was the Academy's, too—Barry Levinson for *Rain Man.* Knowing how his bread was buttered, Levinson said, "I have to thank Michael Ovitz who worked to keep this movie alive."

Levinson's stars came on to announce Best Actress. Having already indulged himself nearly three minutes while on stage and then a few more seconds with Kurt Russell's proxy statement, Dustin Hoffman took up more time by saying "In my nervousness, I left out the director's name [as he was still doing] and I left out Tom's name. Tom, thank you very much. I love you very much." Cruise, the third presenter with a shaved head—his for *Born on the Fourth of July*—put his arm around Hoffman and then offered that the five Best Actress contenders "have proven to be as resilient as they are talented."

All of the nominees were present and the winner was Jodie Foster for *The Accused.* Army Archerd wrote she earned "the biggest scream of surprise and approval from the audience." She kissed Julian Sands, her brother, and her mother, and tugged up her blue decolletage before she walked down the aisle, giving a second tug at the top of the stairs just to make sure nothing peeked out. As Foster made her way to the podium, Jacqueline Bisset was accorded her fifth close-up. Cruise and Hoffman kissed her and Jodie said, "This is such a big deal and my life is so simple. There are very few things—there's love and work and family. And this movie is so special to us because it was all three of those things." Her final felicitations were to "most importantly, my mother, Brandy, who taught me all of my finger paintings were Picassos and that I didn't have to be afraid. And mostly that cruelty might be very human and it might be very cultural, but it's not acceptable." Before she visited the press room, a voice on the public address system requested,

"I have Oscar diarrhea."
—Allan Carr

"Please, no questions regarding Mr. Hinckley. This is Oscar night."

Ever the rebel, Best Picture bestower Cher was the only presenter to break Carr's edict as she revived "And the winner is . . . *Rain Man.*" Producer Mark Johnson also disobeyed Carr. "The producer says we're not allowed to thank our family, we're supposed to wait until we go backstage and use the pay phones, but he doesn't know my family," he said, going on to salute his wife, his two foster children, and his mother. He also paid obeisance to Ovitz and cited United Artists, "a wonderful studio that really doesn't exist anymore."

Because the show clocked in at three hours and fifteen minutes, Cher was given the signal to end it as soon as possible. "We hope you had a good time," said the gracious hostess, signing off with "Good night, everybody, God bless ya," and then hightailing it off the stage.

Aftermath

In the press room, Allan Carr might have gotten an inkling that maybe things hadn't gone over as well as he had hoped. The *Hollywood Reporter* heard a member of the fourth estate ask, " 'But Allan—why Snow White? What's the connection between her and, well, the whole Cocoanut Grove theme of the show?' With a laser glare from Carr: 'It's called theatrical.' " Alice Faye lamented that she and her fellow veterans were relegated to no more than "dress extras." Roger Ebert was also bellyaching. When Carr asked reporters how they were enjoying the backstage spread, the critic snapped, "The food isn't so good." The *Reporter* was amazed that of the dozens of stars present, the only one to whom Carr had provided an individual dressing room was . . . Merv Griffin.

Jodie Foster was chuckling backstage. Holding up her Oscar, the Best Actress answered where it was going to go. "For the moment, he's going to stay in these hands, he's not going anywhere, prisoner of Jodie . . . I rented three videos last night at the video place and they said if I brought this in I would get them free. So you can bet this is going back to the store tomorrow." For the next week, Foster carried the trophy around in her car trunk to show it off to people. Bette Davis, who wouldn't live to see another Oscar ceremony, sent her approval through Cindy Adams' column. "Someone told me years ago to keep my eye on Jodie Foster. And I have. And look what happened. She's damn good. She's a young Bette Davis."

Asked if winning the Oscar meant that she was a serious actress, Geena Davis nodded, saying "That's why I wore a serious dress." Of the impending Governors' Ball, the Oscar winner said, "I can't wait . . . how often do you get to go to an actual ball?" Dustin Hoffman, the star of Davis' first movie, *Tootsie,* couldn't believe how lucky *Rain Man* was since "the picture was literally cancelled three or four different times." Because he had the flu, there would be no celebratory revelry for Hoffman, although he hung around long enough to be interviewed on *Nightline.* Forrest Sawyer wanted to know what he thought his father's reaction was. "I doubt he was watching because he's still in a coma" was the cheery response.

Everyone else headed to the Governors' Ball, which, like last year, was located right next door. On her way in, an unbowed Sigourney Weaver smiled and said, "I figure I made history. I'm the only nominee who's lost twice in one night." Later, she told Ryan Murphy of the *New York Daily News,* "It was horrible, everybody was so embarrassed for me that nobody wanted to talk to me. They should have an anteroom for the losers. And I made my parents fly all the way out for it and they were disappointed for me."

According to Army Archerd, there wasn't such a good time to be had by anyone. The columnist vented his spleen in *Daily Variety:* "Now let's talk about the Board of Governors' Ball. Better we don't talk about it. Who were all those people there? And where did they get tickets? No one from the industry was at our table.

"One of the most grotesque television broadcasts in recent memory."
—David Ehrenstein

And at the so-called star tables, the principals were being hounded by amateur photographers and autograph seekers—guests at what is supposed to be an industry event." As compensation, guests took home 1,600 bottles of cologne and 9,600 truffles.

Three hundred invitees crowded into Spago, where one member of the graying "A-List," Jackie Collins, raved to TV journalists, "It's *the* hot party." Other hot partygoers included Don Rickles, Bob Newhart, and George Hamilton, who came with one of his ex-wives. *Women's Wear Daily* observed that "Tom Cruise must have liked the roar of the crowd outside, because he made not one but two entrances." Five-time loser Glenn Close arrived in her earth-mother mode, telling the press corp, "When it's all over with, I'm going home to my little girl." Her consolation prize was singing the National Anthem a few days later for the New York Mets on Opening Day. *Entertainment Tonight* bid adieu to a rather glum Dean Stockwell, who gamely asserted that "We just had such a great time." A giddier Robin Williams quipped of Allan Carr, "I hear he's doing the Nobel Prizes next."

Party-regular Michael Caine waited ten minutes for a *Nightline* interview while a technical snafu was worked on before getting fed up and going into the soiree. Kathleen Turner had more patience and did chat on the show. Her reward was being given a citation by *Premiere* for the year's "Worst TV Appearance" for her eye-rolling and pseudo-Spanish accent. A bigger hit was Lucille Ball, making her swan song appearance three weeks before her death. The comedienne was seen in public for the last time waiting outside Spago with her husband for their car. As a crowd of celebrity-watchers cheered her on, the seventy-seven-year-old former Goldwyn Girl gave them chorine-like kicks through the sexy slit in her gown.

Women's Wear Daily wrote that "Hollywood's younger, hip set" eschewed Spago to attend the El Rescate benefit at Vertigo. The *Los Angeles Times* made this party sound about as appealing as Army Archerd's version of the Governors' Ball because "the doormen, who insisted that the club wasn't ready to receive partygoers, acted as if they were shepherding a standard Friday-night club crowd instead of prepaid ticket holders"; many guests, who had spent $100, missed the Oscar telecast. In addition, "dessert arrived without silverware. Waiters simply told guests to take pieces of cake off of trays. Hungry guests who complied discovered, to their dismay, that they were holding cold, wet hunks of ice cream cake." *Movieline* concurred, saying that "Tongues were wagging all over town the next day about the way supposed guests were treated, including being cursed at by the staff, and at least one woman was manhandled by a guard." Making matters worse, fire marshals decided the place was overcrowded and they joined in blocking people from entering. Harrison Ford waited outside for a while, then decided to go home. Among those who managed to get in to hear Bonnie Raitt, Steven Stills, and Holly Near perform after the Awards were Jane Fonda, Robert Downey, Jr., Senator Alan Cranston, and Rob Lowe, who, according to *Movieline*, "ran from the press."

Robert Mitchum and Milton Berle hosted a fund-raiser at Mondrian for The Better World Society—an organization founded by Ted Turner which, in the words of *TV Guide*, "tries to improve the world through television"—but those busy fire marshals decreed that this party, too, was overbooked and they prevented Clint Eastwood from going in. Army Archerd later spotted the star "down the street at Dan Tana's . . . in T-shirt and leather jacket, dining as the Oscar show ended." Mike Nichols and wife Diane Sawyer threw a post-awards dinner at the Ivy for his colleagues Sigourney Weaver, Meryl Streep, Carly Simon, and Kurt Russell.

Gene Siskel was peeved about the selection of two of the performers: "Both supporting actors, I don't think, were playing supporting roles," but rival Roger Ebert termed Davis' win "historic because it announced her arrival, I think, as a major star." She got high marks from fashion critics,

"It was the best television show I've ever seen."
—Ronald Reagan

too. But all was not rosy for the surprise winner; after appearing with her husband on the cover of *GQ* as "Hollywood's Most Adorable Couple," Mr. and Mrs. Jeff Goldblum separated in 1990 and divorced in 1991.

Allan Carr didn't want the evening to end, resting his head on Leeza Gibbons' shoulder on *Entertainment Tonight* and effusing to Bill Tush on *Showbiz Today*, "I could babble on; I have Oscar diarrhea." Tush sent him off with, "Go enjoy everything that's coming to you out there." Co-reporter Mark Haefeli gave Carr a taste of what to expect by guessing that if the producer had read the reviews, "he must have a very sour stomach. . . . It was mutual bicoastal criticism," citing one reviewer's evaluation of the show as "a flaming wreck."

David Ehrenstein of the *Herald-Examiner* led the assault by christening Carr's baby, "one of the most grotesque television broadcasts in recent memory." CBS's Dennis Cunningham rated the show against its predecessors: "61 out of 61," adding, "We know whom to blame, don't we, Allan Carr?" As far as *Variety* was concerned, "Tech credits were dismal . . . Presenters were confused . . . Most humor was flat or pointless." Most observers zeroed in on the two production numbers. The *Hollywood Reporter*'s Miles Belle called the Stars of Tomorrow tunefest "a bad rerun of *Fame*," and the *New York Times*' Janet Maslin wrote that the opening segment "deserves a permanent place in the annals of Oscar embarrassments." The *Philadelphia Inquirer*'s Desmond Ryan wondered, "Can anyone who lived through it forget such gruesome low points?" And George Christy of the *Hollywood Reporter*'s "The Great Life" column despaired that, "insiders agreed that the many Oscar-cast distaffers were gowned in fashion disasters; a pity that the Russians, who viewed the show for the first time, may aspire to emulating these fashion victims, believing that this is the 'good taste' of America."

A couple of participants emerged unscathed. The *Herald-Examiner* felt "the brief appearances by Billy Crystal and Robin Williams raised the energy level of the proceedings so substantially that we can only hope that next year the Academy will just turn the whole show over to them." The over-the-years montage of the Best Song performances received good notices, too.

"Snow White" herself, Eileen Bowman, won a *Los Angeles Times* profile in which the twenty-two-year-old San Diego native revealed that she had never even watched an Oscar show before but did have experience impersonating the fairy tale heroine. She was playing her in "Beach Blanket Babylon," a risqué musical revue at the Sands Hotel in Las Vegas. "I've always loved Snow White because she's nice," Bowman said, admitting, "To tell you the truth, I've never seen the movie." Her sister added, "Her goal was to be Snow White at Disneyland . . . I don't think it will happen now."

Bowman had been Carr's fifth choice for the role, after rejections from Lucie Arnaz, Ellen Greene, Pia Zadora, and Lorna Luft, who told her former boss, "That's great for an unknown, but I've worked too hard to be somebody." Michael Musto termed Luft's decision "the best career move ever made." Rob Lowe was less fortunate. The catcalls over his singing were soon drowned out by the clamor over a scandalous videotape that surfaced a few months later, documenting his encounter with two women in an Atlanta hotel room during the 1988 Democratic National Convention. "Overnight, after the Atlanta tape, he became comedy fodder in talk-show monologues. He was tabloid-television bait," recorded the *New York Times*. "To avoid prosecution, since one of his partners in the episode was sixteen years old, Mr. Lowe agreed to perform twenty hours of community service over two years." But he couldn't dispel the joke: "If Snow White married Rob Lowe, she'd be Snow Lowe."

No sooner were the scathing reviews out then another dose of bad news came in. The normally litigious Academy found itself on the receiving end for a change. The Walt Disney Co. filed a lawsuit for copyright infringement, unfair competition, and violation of the California antidilution

"*Because the Academy did something kinda Dopey, Disney sure is Grumpy.*"
—*Variety*

laws because of the "unauthorized and unflattering" use of Disney's Snow White character. Or, as *Variety* put it, "Because the Academy did something kinda Dopey, Disney sure is Grumpy." Before taking legal action, Disney had offered the Academy an opportunity to apologize publicly and the matter would have been forgotten but, according to the studio's president Frank Wells, "For its own reasons, however, the Academy did not accede to our requests." Robin Williams's Mickey Mouse ears were not a part of the suit, a Disney spokesperson explained, because "we think Robin's use was fair parody," letting the star of the studio's soon-to-be-released *Dead Poets Society* off the hook. Allan Carr turned Perry Mason and worked on his jurisprudence, informing *New York Daily News* columnist William Norwich that he was planning to "base his case around the fact that Snow White was a character from fairy tale literature long before she went to work for Walt Disney."

A week after the brouhaha began, the Academy decided it had a loser and President Richard Kahn issued an apology for the infringement "and for unintentionally creating the impression that Disney had participated in or sanctioned the opening production number." Disney pulled back its lawyers and sicked them on a day-care center in Florida that was illegally decorating its walls with images of Mickey Mouse.

The Academy's Board of Governors had been more shocked and appalled at Carr's show than anyone else. "The phone rang off the hook yesterday, much of it on the subject of the squeaky 'Snow White,'" reported Robert Osborne. What really rankled the Academy nabobs was the fact that the public humiliation wouldn't go away. Steve Martin poked fun of the show on the Tony Awards telecast later in the spring and hallowed theater critic Walter Kerr suggested that "a limit might be placed on the number of couples permitted to hang around the microphone jesting about their unmarried, but probably fertile, state. After two or three instances, this gets to be bragging." Snow White even popped up in "Doonesbury," telling Rick that after the Oscars, "Mr. Eisner was livid! He called me a tramp, and accused me of doing it just to meet Rob Lowe!"

While the lawsuit played itself out, a flustered Allan Carr went on the defensive, letting everyone know that he had a fan in former president Ronald Reagan, who, he claimed, had called him at six in the morning after the ceremonies to say, "I used to go to the Cocoanut Grove to watch the Oscars. It was the best television show I've ever seen." The producer invited Charles Champlin, critic emeritus of the *Los Angeles Times,* over to his house to plead his case. During the interview, "Carr was padding about in bare feet, sipping a vodka and grapefruit juice" and "said defiantly, the flowers, the mail, and the calls all indicated that the industry had loved his handiwork." The producer indicated that even Ovitz had cabled, "You brought show business back to the movie business," and that a message from Jennifer Jones raved, "You delivered." Interestingly, when Army Archerd had reported on the same Jones missive the day before, it had read "In my opinion you produced the *Gone with the Wind* of the Oscar shows."

Seventeen of Hollywood's most distinguished citizens, including Oscar-winners Gregory Peck, Billy Wilder, Fred Zinnemann, Paul Newman, Joseph L. Mankiewicz, and Julie Andrews, begged to differ with Jones. They made their feelings known in a letter to the Academy in which they called Carr's presentation "an embarrassment to both the Academy and the entire motion picture industry . . . It is neither fitting nor acceptable that the best work in motion pictures be acknowledged in such a demeaning fashion." As a result of the epistle, the Academy set up an Awards Presentation Review Committee to try to figure out why the show received such unprecedented criticism "and what we should do in the future." Former Directors Guild president Gilbert Cates headed the committee, which recommended that the telecast's producer receive a salary for his efforts. As it happened, Cates himself was given the job for the subsequent broadcast, so he pocketed the $150,000 honorarium.

"Jodie Foster is a young Bette Davis."
—Bette Davis

A year later, a *Vanity Fair* article started off with, "You've got to give him this, at least. Allan Carr promised everyone an Academy Awards show they would never forget. No one can say he didn't deliver. That's why Gil Cates is producing the Oscars this time around." "Beach Blanket Babylon" creator Steven Silver laughingly tried to excuse the opening fiasco to the magazine: "It was supposed to be just a send-up of Hollywood, using elements people were familiar with, but there were a lot of different people throwing in a lot of different ideas . . . It turned out to be the worst number in the history of television." The article went on, "Friends say that Carr was devastated by the uproar, and that he seems to have spent most of the last year holed up in Hawaii and Palm Springs."

Two-and-a-half years after the infamous ceremony, *Variety* spotlighted the producer in its "Missing Persons Corner" feature, observing "Last Seen: Oscars Debacle." This article began, "The phrase goes: 'It ain't over till the fat lady sings.' For the career of Allan Carr, the fat lady was replaced by Rob Lowe, whose 'Proud Mary' duet with Snow White kicked off a disastrous 1989 Oscar cast that brought the producer's career to a screeching halt. Carr has been stalled ever since." Discussing several projects that had fallen by the wayside, *Variety* concluded that the deal maker "seems to have lost his touch since the Oscars," and noted that "Carr didn't return calls" for the profile.

The impresario did find himself in the public eye in one completed post-Oscar endeavor, even if it wasn't his project. Jane and Michael Stern gave him an entire chapter of his own in their 1990 best seller, *The Encyclopedia of Bad Taste.* There he was, permanently ensconced alongside Leisure Suits, Lava Lamps, and Twinkies.

1989

"If anyone figures that out, call me."
—George Bush

The term "Oscar Race" took on new meaning at the 1989 Academy Awards.

Farm Team

Kevin Costner continued to rise. Having scored with a baseball picture last year, he took a swing at another, but whereas *Bull Durham* had been praised for its realistic, earthy view of the sport, *Field of Dreams* had its head in the clouds. The sentimental fantasy featured Costner as an Iowa farmer who hears voices and decides it would be a good idea to tear up his cornfield and turn it into a baseball diamond so that the ghosts of Shoeless Joe Jackson and his teammates from the banished 1919 Chicago "Black Sox" could play ball. On top of this, the hero's dead father wants to see what all the fuss is about so he drops in from the graveyard, too, and father and son have a last game of catch at the end. Adapting the 1982 book *Shoeless Joe,* director Phil Alden Robinson, a former industrial filmmaker, had to make one major revision. In the novel, author J. D. Salinger had somehow ended up in the mix, but the recluse's lawyers informed Robinson that if he attempted to include the writer as a character in the movie he'd be sorry; Salinger's role was refashioned as a fictional '60s radical played by James Earl Jones, who waxed poetic over a time when baseball was segregated.

Sneak Previews' Jeffrey Lyons called *Field of Dreams* the best movie of the 1980s, and Roger Ebert said the film is "so perfect, it's like a miracle," but warned that it "will not appeal to grinches and grouches and realists." Of which there were many. In *Time,* Richard Corliss sneered that the movie "is the male weepie at its wussiest" and *Film Comment*'s editor Harlan Jacobson decried the film as a paean to "non-ethnic, vanilla ice cream America." President George Bush was another critic, shaking his head after a White House screening and commenting, "If anybody figures that out, call me." Meanwhile, Libby Gelman-Waxner mused in *Premiere,* "God forbid Kevin should bring back Einstein or Gandhi, or even Cary Grant. Maybe I should bring back Aunt Bertha by building a K-Mart in my backyard so she can return to buy makeup and girdles." To console himself after the wise-guy reviews, Robinson found solace in the hundreds of letters from estranged sons who said they had rapprochements with their fathers after seeing Kevin do it on screen.

The popular success of *Field of Dreams* cemented Costner's star status and provided an ancillary attraction. In the film the mysterious voice tells Costner, "If you build it, they will come." The message could also have been directed to Dan Lansing, the owner of the Dyersville, Iowa, farm where the movie was shot. Lansing kept the baseball field intact and come they did, as thousands of pilgrims, inspired by the film's uplift, headed to Iowa from as far away as France, gratefully leaving donations in a coffee can. The head of the local Chamber of Commerce, Connie Trenkamp, told the *Los Angeles Times* that "It could be the next Mount Rushmore. Seriously." Under the auspices of Lansing's neighbors Al and Rita Ameskamp, left field, which had been on their side of the property line, reverted to farm land. Commented Al, "I really don't see what they see over there. And I got no regrets. A lot of the neighbors say 'I'm glad you plowed it up.'"

Joking for Dollars

Costner couldn't hold a candle, though, to Jack Nicholson's star power, which ignited the year's biggest money-maker. By the time it opened, *Batman* had been so ballyhooed that the *Los Angeles Times* reported, "Studio marketing executives claim their audience research reveals awareness and want-to-see factors that are 'off

After playing Daniel Day-Lewis's selfless mother in My Left Foot, *Brenda Fricker steps out of character.*

"Usually, you're losing your virginity."
—Ethan Hawk

the charts' (literally, according to one effusive publicist, who put the awareness factor at '100% or more.')." *Batman* earned a record $42.7 million its opening weekend, and a month later its merchandising had pulled in six times that amount. Oscar-winning art director Paul Sylbert told the *Los Angeles Times* the credit belonged to the production designer who constructed the highly stylized, foreboding rendition of Gotham City. "Anton Furst was the triumph of the movie . . . In fact, he triumphed over the movie. The picture was so bad that all you looked at was the design." Three children analyzing the movie for the "Kidsday" section of *Newsday* "found it better than any film we've seen" and Liz Smith joined in with, "Personally, I adored every second of *Batman.*" Au contraire, crabbed *Boxoffice*, which said the movie "has a lumbering, claustrophobic feel to it which is lethal." The film's director Tim Burton summed it up for *Details* later. "There were parts I liked, but overall it was boring."

For playing the comic villain Joker (and receiving top billing over the title caped-player, Michael Keaton), Nicholson wheeled and dealed for fifteen percent of the box office and all the spinoffs. By year's end, magazines were trumpeting his take to be $60 million. Around the same time, tabloids documented his breakup after seventeen years with Anjelica Huston when it became known that another woman was giving birth to a second child by him.

Cool School

Another two-time Oscar winner, Dustin Hoffman, was going to mark his debut as a director/actor in a story about a charismatic English teacher who instills a love of poetry in his prep school students back in 1959. Hoffman dropped out and Peter Weir and Robin Williams then took charge of *Dead Poets Society;* although the latter had relatively little screen time, Touchstone sold the drama as another Robin Williams laughfest. When he had originally looked at Tom Schulman's melodramatic script—which featured a student committing suicide because his mean father won't let him take part in amateur theatrical productions and the teacher himself dying of leukemia—the comic said nothing doing. The illness angle was eliminated and Williams' anachronistic monologues were in.

Michael Wilmington of the *Los Angeles Times* called *Dead Poets Society* "a moving elegy for every inspired teacher who suddenly opened up a world before their wondering students" and to Marilyn Beck it was "a magnificent, haunting, thinking person's picture." Or at least a thinking adolescent's picture, felt David Edelstein of the *New York Post*, who ridiculed the movie as *"Animal House* for the *Masterpiece Theater* set," but acknowledged that it "will mean a lot to some people, though, especially if they're twelve years old." In *New York* magazine, David Denby had a good laugh at the plot of the film: "The teachers and administrators tear their hair out over the boys' going off to recite poetry—my God, what a scandal." *Dead Poets Society* struck enough of a chord with teenagers to earn nearly a hundred million dollars at ticket windows and it also meant a lot to the young actors appearing in it. Ethan Hawk, who played a pathologically shy student, explained: "It's not often an eighteen-year-old gets to do a film so special. Usually, you're losing your virginity." The film was so popular that the wife of one of the producers tried to claim responsibility for its success in *People*, suggesting that she had helped conceive the picture's design by taking Peter Weir on shopping trips to Ralph Lauren boutiques. Months after the film's premiere, the real-life teacher who was the model for screenwriter Schulman still hadn't gotten around to seeing the film. "To tell you the truth, I didn't know who Robin Williams was," admitted University of Connecticut professor Samuel F. Pickering. "I finally saw him on TV the other day. He's a nut."

"*They are always looking for a golden white boy.*"
—Spike Lee

Shootout at the Cannes Corral

While moviegoers spent their money on summer escapist fare like *Indiana Jones and the Last Crusade* and *Honey, I Shrunk the Kids,* journalists were expending news ink on a $6 million film, Spike Lee's *Do the Right Thing.* The portrait of the Bedford-Stuyvesant neighborhood that erupts into racial violence after a young black man is killed by cops first created debate at its premiere at the Cannes Film Festival. Jane Fonda, the glittery presenter of the top award, the Palme d'Or, announced that the winner was not Lee but twenty-six-year-old writer-director Steven Soderbergh for his film debut, *sex, lies and videotape.* Lee complained that "they are always looking for a golden white boy." The buzz around the festival was that the jury's president, German director Wim Wenders, lobbied against honoring *Do the Right Thing* because its protagonist, played by Lee himself, "wasn't heroic." Hearing this, Lee pointed to the lead character in Soderbergh's film and bellowed, "What's heroic about a fucking pervert who interviews women about their sex lives on TV?" When a reporter from *USA Today* asked why there was no depiction of drug use in his film, Lee retorted, "You don't ask that question about *Rain Man* and *Working Girl.*" On a plane from Nice to Paris, a member of the Cannes jury, Sally Field, leaned over a row of seats, took the director's hand and said: "I'm so sorry. I fought for your movie till the end, and I'd do it again."

Dyn-O-Mite!

Awaiting Lee in the USA was a neoconservative columnist for *New York* magazine, Joe Klein, who took it upon himself to fan the fires of racial fears by writing "Spike Lee's reckless new movie . . . opens on June 30 (in not too many theaters near you, one hopes.)" While he expected white filmgoers to have civilized discussions on the "irresponsible" film's message, Klein prophesized that "black teenagers won't find it so hard . . . *white people are your enemy,*" and, as a result, he predicted, race riots would break out at every venue. He foresaw that the movie might very well help defeat black New York City mayoral candidate David Dinkins. Lee maintained that his urban drama's ambiguous attitude toward mob violence showed that there are no easy answers to racism and *Do the Right Thing* simply mirrored society: "It's an examination of race relations between different ethnic groups in the city, how in the last eight years, the whole thing had been polarized by 'Hizzoner,' Mayor Ed Koch." And contrary to Klein's assessment, Lee believed that New Yorkers who saw his film would throw Koch out.

Nightline and *Oprah* devoted shows to *Do the Right Thing* and, emblematic of the controversy, *Newsweek* printed two reviews. David Ansen panegyrized, "You leave this movie stunned, challenged and drained . . . it's the funkiest and most informed view of racism an American filmmaker has given us," but his colleague Jack Kroll was of a Klein-ian bent, cautioning, "this movie is dynamite under every seat." Other critics were lukewarm. Terrence Rafferty wrote in the *New Yorker* that the "movie isn't likely to cause riots (as some freaked-out commentators have suggested)," but lamented that it "winds up bullying the audience—shouting to us rather than speaking to us." Andrew Sarris was disappointed when he saw it after all the hubbub as "the most overrated movie of the year." But looking at the movie on purely aesthetic terms, the *Village Voice*'s Georgia Brown wrote of *Do the Right Thing:* "The most beautiful American film of the year looks like Godard crossed with Minnelli." Roger Ebert was another booster, picking it as the best of the year in his annual tally.

In a role Lee offered first to Robert De Niro—an Italian-American pizzeria owner in the African-American neighborhood—Danny Aiello received the best reviews of the film's many actors

"I'm so sorry."
—Sally Field

in a multiracial cast. Amused that the actor and the director had such acclaim together when they were poles apart politically, the *Village Voice* reported that "Aiello's views are enough to make most Hollywood liberals shudder."

Joe the Jerk

When political columnist Bill Reel went to investigate Joe Klein's ominous premonition on opening day, he wrote, "I sat in the aisle seat in my Bermuda shorts with pale legs prominent and I thought, 'I sure hope he's wrong.'" Instead, when the movie was over, the audience, which Reel estimated to be ninety percent black, "walked out quietly. The mood leaving the theater was pensive and sober." Joe Klein proved to be an inept prognosticator; not a single disturbance broke out anywhere. Brent Staples of the *New York Times* zeroed in on the inherent racism of the doomsayers whose "fear suggests a view of black America: an enraged, conspiratorial mass out beyond the perimeter, waiting for the drumbeat that will cue their rampage." The only thing even approaching an incident occurred outside New York's Ziegfeld theater where last summer Christian groups had picketed *The Last Temptation of Christ.* This time it was the Jewish Defense League, protesting Lee's use of the song "Fight the Power" by the group Public Enemy, whom the J.D.L. branded anti-Semitic. As for Joe Klein's other prediction, David Dinkins handily defeated "Hizzoner" in the Democratic primary and went on to become mayor. Klein himself turned up on *Oprah* and got panned. The *Amsterdam News*'s Abiola Sinclair snickered that Klein was "trying to defend his position, amid guffaws and poo-poos from the largely white audience. He looked like the jerk he is."

What's My Motivation?

Woody Allen also became involved in the New York mayoralty contest at a pre-election press conference for Dinkins in which the Oscar winner defended Jackie Mason, who had joked that "Jews vote for blacks out of guilt" while campaigning for Dinkins' Republican rival Rudolph Giuliani. "I think, you know, that he's a comedian and he's always kidding around, there's no malice or racism in his position at all," said Allen. "I do think that people make decisions, you know, out of guilt as a motivation." Certainly the lead character in Allen's new movie, *Crimes and Misdemeanors,* did. In the film, a wealthy doctor, played by Martin Landau, has his demanding mistress, Anjelica Huston, murdered and then learns to ignore his conscience. In a parallel plot, a schlemiel film buff, played by guess who, loses the woman of his dreams, Mia Farrow, to an oily television producer, portrayed in an uproarious caricature by Alan Alda. Vincent Canby opined in the *New York Times* that the narrative "has the richness and breadth of a novel told with the concision of a densely packed short story." *Variety* felt that "Landau's thesping is another career milestone," while Jack Kroll deemed Alda's sleazoid "repellently funny." Casting a nay vote was one Leon Wieseltier, literary editor of *The New Republic,* who stated "It is a matter of honor to hate this film. There is not a frame of it that fails to degrade, to debase and to demean something precious. It is the work of a consumer, a voyeur, a coward, a philistine, a creep. It is a stain on the culture that produced it." Martin Landau said poppycock and rhapsodized his director, saying that doing a Woody Allen movie "is like working with Shakespeare."

Olivier II

Twenty-eight-year-old Kenneth Branagh went Landau one better—for his directing debut he actually did work with the Bard. When *Henry V* bowed in the fall, reviewers marveled at the sheer nerve it took to remake a film that Laurence Olivier had done so indelibly forty-four years earlier. The *New York Times* ran an editorial on the subject, concluding that the new movie "soars with invention" and was the better of the two.

Unlike Olivier's stylized, pageant-like piece of propaganda that had been designed to whip up the morale of the British public during World War II, Branagh's gritty rendition was, in the words of the *London Observer,* "made for a generation that has the Indo-China war and the Falklands campaign just behind it and is wary of calls to arms." Or as the *Los Angeles Times*' Michael Wilmington put it, "If Olivier gave us the glint of sunlight on armor and the wind roaring through the pennants and flags, Branagh gives us the rot, the mold, the wounds and the crusted blood underneath."

The Belfast-born Branagh was unknown in America, but he was a household name in Britain through television appearances and his touring Renaissance Theater Company. With the financial aid of Prince Charles, the actor/director founded the troupe at age twenty-six after spending two years with the Royal Shakespeare Company, which he denounced as overly bureaucratic. By the time he was twenty-seven, he had already written his autobiography—a best seller in England—and a profile of Branagh in the British edition of *GQ* declared "He is vehement, impassioned, massively impatient and meeting a fool drives him into paroxysms of despair." Branagh shot his $7 million film in seven weeks (Olivier had taken nearly that long just on the Battle at Agincourt) and said he wanted "to make a popular film that will both satisfy the Shakespearean scholar and the punter who likes *Crocodile Dundee.*" He also claimed he had "done a crash course in film history . . . I have watched endless war films, from *Chimes at Midnight* to *Platoon* and *Oh, What a Lovely War* to *The Longest Day.*" When quizzed why he was adapting this particular work, Branagh responded, "I'm not making this film to see if I can score a draw with Olivier, but because I passionately believe that all of Shakespeare's plays need to be constantly re-interpreted."

Reviewers loved Branagh the actor as much as Branagh the director. Pauline Kael praised, "This actor's earthy, doughy presence is the wrapping for his beautiful, expressive voice. Emotion pours out of it with surprising ease; he's conversational without sacrificing the poetry. His readings are a source of true pleasure. Listening to him, you think, with an instrument like that, he can play anything." His leading lady was crazy for him, too; after the film wrapped, Branagh married Emma Thompson, his Princess Katherine. The only drawback to the success of *Henry V* was exposed in *People*: "Kenneth Branagh wants it known that he is tired of being called the new Laurence Olivier." He confided to the magazine, "the comparison is ludicrous to me—so much puff. I find it extraordinary that people can compare a man who produced a lifetime's work with someone still under thirty." *People* translated: "In other words, we haven't seen anything yet."

Michelle, Ma Belle

A second first-time director, Steve Kloves, twenty-nine, told the story of two brothers with a third-rate lounge lizard piano act and the alluring singer who joins them. The director admitted, "This is not a movie that has an extraordinary plot." The casting gimmick of *The Fabulous Baker Boys* was Beau and Jeff Bridges, appearing onscreen together for the first time, but Michelle Pfeiffer stole the picture by undulating on a piano while warbling a make-out version of the Eddie Cantor song, "Makin' Whoopee." Janet Maslin cheered that Pfeiffer was "setting some new standard for cinematic slinkiness," and dubbed her "devastatingly gorgeous." Pfeiffer, however, insisted she was getting sick of reviewers babbling about her looks. "I think there's this misnomer about beautiful people that basically life is not tough on them, that bad things don't happen to beautiful people," the actress told the USA network's *Hollywood Insider*. "It's another form of prejudice." Nonetheless, her beauty graced the cover of *Newsweek* which averred, "The prospect of spending the '90s watching this gifted, funny, versatile beauty is one of those sweet anticipations that will make it a little easier getting through the rain to the local cinema."

Get on the Good Foot

Irishman Jim Sheridan was yet another debuting director who wowed the critics. *My Left Foot,* his biography about Christy Brown, the writer and artist who had cerebral palsy, unspooled at the New York Film Festival and moved Pauline Kael to declare it a "great, exhilarating movie"; she also claimed that the moment in which Brown learns his beloved is engaged to another man "may be the most emotionally wrenching scene I've ever experienced at the movies." A more measured response came from the *Chicago Tribune*'s Dave Kehr who wrote, "Stylistically, it must be said that *My Left Foot* is an adequate but ordinary film" which he compared to "a typical Movie of the Week," the only difference being "the relative openness with which it treats questions of sex and romance."

To prepare for his role, Daniel Day-Lewis spent two months at a Dublin clinic for children with cerebral palsy and learned to paint as Brown had—with a brush between his toes—and even began signing autographs with his foot. When a reporter from *Rolling Stone* asked if this was a difficult accomplishment, the actor shot back, "What do you think? You're an intelligent woman, don't demean yourself by asking those kinds of questions." On the set, he never once got out of his wheelchair and for the six weeks of filming he spoke only in the grunts of his character and depended upon the crew to feed him. The reviewers were grateful for all he went through. Sheila Benson of the *Los Angeles Times* raved, "He is sly, funny, as swift as he can be with those squash-shaped syllables, wicked, mordant and openly romantic," while down in the Valley, Bob Strauss of the *Los Angeles Daily News* praised the performance but seemed a little put off by it: "Daniel Day-Lewis displays so many unpleasant characteristics of cerebral palsy that you're thoroughly convinced the actor has the disease." Playing Brown's mum, Brenda Fricker, known in England as the star of a medical soap opera, "Casualty," also won plaudits in the United States; David Ansen noted that she "shows us a strong, good woman without a trace of stickiness."

Cruising for a Bruising

Daniel Day-Lewis wasn't the only heartthrob to spend time in a wheelchair. Ron Kovic, a Long Islander who enlisted to fight in Vietnam, was shot and became paralyzed, later chronicled his conversion from a rah-rah patriot to a leading opponent of the War in the 1976 National Book Award winner, *Born on the Fourth of July.* Kovic wrote a screen adaptation in 1977 which producer Martin Bregman was on the verge of filming for Universal, but interest dried up after the similarly themed *Coming Home*—on which Kovic had served as consultant—bowed and stole the thunder. Oliver Stone joined the crusade as a cowriter and Bregman arranged financing from a German consortium, with Al Pacino as Kovic, Daniel Petrie directing, and Orion distributing the film. Kovic began hanging out at Studio 54 with Pacino, until the funding fell through four days before shooting. Stone recalled, "Al got cold feet. It was a heartbreak. I just wanted to hide. I became semicomatose, and Ron became a complete basket case." On top of all that, Kovic was suddenly persona non grata at Studio 54 where owner Steve Rubell barked at him, "Who are you?" "When he did that, I left New York," said Kovic, who headed for L.A.

Years later, the success of Stone's *Platoon* led Universal President Tom Pollock—formerly Stone's lawyer—to take the *Born on the Fourth of July* script out of mothballs. He greenlighted the picture on the condition that Stone make the epic on the cheap and cast a major name in the lead. The director hired the country's biggest star, Tom Cruise, who instead of his $9 million asking price, worked for scale and a percentage of the profits. Universal's Pollock thought the casting was perfect and not only because of Cruise's box-office clout: "Tom Cruise is America's all-American boy. The film's journey is more powerful

"If I were George Bush, I'd shoot myself."
—Oliver Stone

when it is made by the maverick from *Top Gun*. It's not only Ron who goes through this wrenching story, it is Tom Cruise—our perception of Tom Cruise." Ron Kovic admitted that he had his doubts about the poster boy from that cinematic paean to the military ("I wondered if he had the depth to play me") until they met, and Cruise immediately hugged him. "I felt an instant rapport with him that I never experienced with Pacino," said Kovic. "We talked for hours in the kitchen and I began to cry . . . I felt like a burden was lifted, that I was passing all this on to Tom."

Like Daniel Day-Lewis, Cruise spent time in hospitals getting to know paraplegics, and he tooled around Westwood with Kovic in matching wheelchairs. He also did two stints in boot camp and, according to Stone, "At one point I talked him into injecting himself with a solution that would have totally paralyzed him for two days. Then the insurance company—the killer of all experience—said no because there was a slight chance that Tom would have ended up permanently paralyzed." Cruise acknowledged that he had only a vague recollection of the Vietnam war: "I remember bits and pieces on the news, but for a seven-year-old, Walter Cronkite was just the lead-in to *Batman*." Stone hypothesized that as a result of the film, "a part of Tom has passed from youth to middle age."

The director publicized the movie's December opening by saying things like "We have a fascist security state running this country . . . Orwell did happen. But it's so subtle that no one noticed. If I were George Bush, I'd shoot myself. Existentially, there's no hope. His soul is dead." His star stuck to more conventional forms of tub-thumping like appearing on Arsenio Hall, who referred to him as "Home Boy" and got him to talk about how, when he was seven, his eleven-year-old sister and her friends used him for kissing practice. Of the bust-up of his marriage to Mimi Rogers, Cruise confided, "She wishes me the best, I wish her the best, and we're just looking forward to moving on with our lives."

Cruise wound up as cover boy for *Premiere, Rolling Stone,* and *Time,* which proclaimed "He carries the film heroically, like a soldier bearing a wounded comrade across a battlefield." David Denby concurred, "*Born on the Fourth of July* is a relentless but often powerful piece of work, dominated by Tom Cruise's impassioned performance." Some right-wingers jumped on what they alleged to be Stone's anti-Americanism and were particularly peeved at a fictional scene in which Kovic is attacked by Nixon delegates at the 1972 Republican convention. Columnist Pat Buchanan, a vigorous jogger who got out of duty in Vietnam because of a "bad knee," ranted that, unlike Kovic and Stone, most Vietnam vets "emerged as stronger, better men, the best of their generation, still aware that there are things in this life, and this country, worth fighting for, dying for, and living for."

The leading man's reviews were not all approbations—Pauline Kael wrote, "Cruise gets through Stone's noisy Stations of the Cross without disgracing himself, but he's negligible"—but he got a rave from the critic he most cared about. "I'm extremely proud of his performance," said Ron Kovic. "On the last day of shooting, I gave Tom my Bronze Star, the medal I won in Vietnam. I told him it was for his heroic performance."

History Lesson

A second Christmas release dealt with another bitterly divisive American war. Strolling through the Boston Common one day, producer Freddie Fields noticed a statue honoring the 54th Regiment of the Massachusetts Volunteer Infantry, a Civil War fighting group made up of black men. "I'm always intrigued by things I never knew anything about," said Fields. "I knew a lot about the Civil War but not this . . . When I realized that nobody else knew about the incident, I realized that this was a movie that had to be made." Director Edward Zwick, best known as a perpetrator of the yuppie television show, *thir-*

"*Morgan Freeman wouldn't consider playing an Uncle Tom.*"
—*Alfred Uhry*

tysomething, used to see that same statue while an undergrad at Harvard; he agreed that "no one—white or black—knows the story, which is scandalous. The black actors in the film didn't know, except Morgan Freeman, who is a very studied man."

Cast as an angry runaway slave who joins the regiment, Denzel Washington insisted that he didn't want the film to be another *Mississippi Burning* or *Cry Freedom,* the white-focused anti-apartheid film for which he received a Supporting Actor nomination. "I did express my concern to Ed and Freddie that the movie not be about whites, and I think the film reflects this," said the actor. He later told *Essence* that making the film "has made me feel stronger about being an American—an African-American, yeah—but every bit an American. We've sweated and bled and died for this land. It is ours. We have a right to it."

"*Glory* has the sweep and magnificence of a Tolstoy battle tale or a John Ford saga of American history," saluted *Variety* but, while lauding the film as "an eloquent, heart-tugging Civil War epic," Kevin Thomas of the *Los Angeles Times* conceded that "without its fresh focus on the role of the black soldiers in the Civil War, *Glory* would seem old-fashioned in its unabashedly sentimental conflict between good and evil." Denzel Washington received the most attention of the cast; labeling him "charismatic," David Ansen raved, "Washington, oozing angry defiance, is extraordinary." Pauline Kael, though, felt that "when he's about to be whipped, he pulls open his shirt and flips his hands in the air in a gesture that spells out 'Method Actor.'" James McPherson, author of *Battle Cry of Freedom,* the Pulitzer Prize–winning history of the Civil War, weighed in with expert testimony in *The New Republic:* "Celebrating their fiftieth anniversary on the screen, Scarlett O'Hara and Rhett Butler are still teaching false and stereotyped lessons about slavery and the Civil War to millions of viewers. *Glory* will throw a cold dash of realism over the moonlight-and-magnolia portrayal of the confederacy."

Lena Horne wrote a fan letter to Freddie Fields through Liz Smith's column, congratulating him "because he and his colleagues have created something of immense value that should be seen by everyone—especially the children." But when defeated mayoral candidate Ed Koch tried to see it at an Upper East Side theater, fellow patrons noticed him and chanted "Koch has cops kill blacks." Reported the *Post,* "Koch's bodyguards quickly ushered the mayor out of the theater at the movie's end."

More Morgan

Morgan Freeman had another, bigger part in a film that opened the same week as *Glory.* In the film version of the Pulitzer Prize–winning off-Broadway long-runner, *Driving Miss Daisy,* the actor recreated his role of a black chauffeur who spends a quarter of a century working for an old Jewish woman in Georgia. Before the three-character play opened in New York in 1985, the screen rights had been snapped up by David Brown, Richard D. Zanuck, and Zanuck's third wife, Lili Fini Zanuck. Soon afterward, longtime partners Brown and Zanuck dissolved their union and Mr. and Mrs. Zanuck had a new entity, The Zanuck Company. They tapped playwright Alfred Uhry, Jr. to do his own adaptation and even though they didn't have a deal with any studio, proceeded to cast the film. That done, they shopped the project around town to uninterested studios, although one executive thought it had possibilities if they dropped Freeman and turned it into an Eddie Murphy/Bette Midler vehicle. "This is getting embarrassing," despaired the old-guard Mr. Zanuck. "We're being turned down by people I've never heard of." The plucky Zanucks managed to trim the budget by about $5 million and Warner Brothers agreed to ante up the same amount. The producers pulled together the remaining $2 million from the two British companies that had bankrolled Best Picture winners *Chariots of Fire* and *Gandhi.*

The Kindness of Zanucks

Just about every actress of a certain age—including Bette Davis, Katharine Hepburn, Angela Lansbury, and Lucille Ball—had checked out the play and expressed interest in playing the titular dowager. The producers, however, had their eyes on a woman from their earlier films *Cocoon* and *Cocoon: The Return*. "Relax, ladies," itemed the *Hollywood Reporter*'s Robert Osborne. "Unless something unforeseen happens, that juicy role-of-roles in Zanuck/Brown's film version of *Driving Miss Daisy* will be played onscreen by (drumroll here) Jessica Tandy." The columnist hoped "maybe this will also make up to the actress the fact she didn't get within miles of being asked to do the film version of a great Broadway role she once created, namely Tennessee Williams' *A Streetcar Named Desire*. In fact, the first film role Tandy was offered after doing *Streetcar* and winning all sorts of Broadway awards and kudos was, gulp!, as Lana Turner's maid in a remake of *The Merry Widow*." The grateful Tandy said, "You take a risk if you get an old lady of eighty like me to play a part like this. You don't know whether I'm going to fade by the wayside or just have to go by 4 o'clock." A nervous Warner Bros. had enough doubts that the studio made her pay her own $130,000 insurance premium.

The fifty-two-year-old Freeman was delighted with his new costar: "It's an incredible kick to be acting with her. She's just turned eighty and her stamina—wow! I'm having one of those times in a young actor's life—I'm working with a legend." Appearing in four 1989 releases, Freeman confessed he had gone through a dry period in the early 1980s and that he once ended up working at a hot dog stand. Asked why an actor of his stature would be so unemployable, he acknowledged that it was probably "because I was lipping off about how I felt about the scripts. I was a bit angry. I've grown up a bit. I don't demand white writers write black anymore."

The third character, Miss Daisy's son who hires the driver, was played by *Saturday Night Live* alum Dan Aykroyd, so eager to escape the juvenilia in which he had been trapped that he offered his services for a nominal fee. To helm the movie, the Zanuck's hired Bruce Beresford, even though his first adaptation of a Southern-based Pulitzer Prize–winning play, *Crimes of the Heart*, had bombed in 1986. More recently, his earlier 1989 release, the Tom Selleck comedy-mystery fiasco *Her Alibi*, had caused Vincent Canby to proclaim, "The makers of *The January Man* can rest easy because their's is no longer the worst picture of the year."

While the play was still running in New York, *Driving Miss Daisy* opened at a gala premiere in Washington, D.C., then moved to a handful of small art theaters to appreciative reviews. Jay Carr of the *Boston Globe* marveled, "While Freeman stakes his claim as an American actor second to none, Tandy, at the age of eighty, seems to have passed beyond technique into something like pure essence." And NBC's Pia Lindstrom preferred the film version of *Driving Miss Daisy* to the play "because instead of the characters sitting in chairs onstage, it's actually better to see Miss Daisy, the proud, penny-pinching old woman, actually being driven to the Piggly Wiggly." Surveying its Oscar chances, the *L.A. Weekly*'s Anne Thompson made no bones about it, "Like last year's front-runner *Rain Man*, it's an entertaining, unthreatening movie with just the right patina of seriousness to make people feel enobled after seeing it," and *The Bergen Record*'s Diana Maychick agreed that "its theme of aging could hit home for at least half the voters."

Word of mouth turned the film into a major sleeper and a relieved studio reimbursed Tandy for the insurance and threw in a $500,000 advance share of the profits, doing the same for Freeman, Aykroyd, Beresford, and Uhry. The Zanucks were featured in profile after profile lionizing them for having the vision to produce this improbable windfall. A *USA Today* article, which

"I'm not some Reno waitress who married a rich man and likes to act like she's Perle Mesta."
—Lili Fini Zanuck

quoted Richard as saying "You'd have to be smoking opium to think this movie would be a big hit," repeated the couple's claim that in twelve years of marriage they had never spent a night apart. *Vanity Fair* showcased their brand-new Sun Valley chalet in a photo spread in which the thirty-five-year-old Mrs. Zanuck stressed, "I'm not some Reno waitress who married a rich man and likes to act like she's Perle Mesta."

Do the Right Campaign

A month before *Driving Miss Daisy* had even opened, Universal was commencing the annual Oscar frenzy with the first trade paper ad—for *Do the Right Thing.* Not forgetting its other hopefuls, Universal also plugged *Born on the Fourth of July* and *Field of Dreams,* the latter with promos encouraging members to "Remember the feeling." Kevin Costner remembered the feeling he had had as an Award presenter two years earlier and told CBS' Steve Kmetko, "The Oscars made my pits wet, so I don't figure to go back there unless I'm nominated."

The National Board of Review was the first critics' group to weigh in, singling out *Driving Miss Daisy,* Morgan Freeman, and *The Fabulous Baker Boys*' Michelle Pfeiffer. The Board didn't reward *Daisy*'s director Bruce Beresford, honoring instead tyro Kenneth Branagh. The New York Critics Circle created a new directing category for Branagh to win—Best First Feature; they handed veteran Paul Mazursky the regular director award for his adaptation of Isaac Bashevis Singer's *Enemies, a Love Story,* which additionally earned Lena Olin the supporting actress scroll for playing one of the bigamist hero's three wives. Anjelica Huston portrayed another of the wives and, when promoting the movie on the *Today Show,* Gene Shalit asked her, "Do you think it's possible for a guy to love three women at the same time?" "Yes, unfortunately, it is," responded Anjelica. "Men are more prone to, how shall I say, spreading themselves around." The National Society of Film Critics later spread the wealth by giving Huston their supporting actress citation.

The big winner in Gotham was *My Left Foot,* claiming best picture and actor for Daniel Day-Lewis, after a reportedly fractious session. Georgia Brown wrote an article in the *Village Voice* implicitly accusing her colleagues of being anti-black for virtually ignoring *Do the Right Thing,* which that very same day was winning three Los Angeles Film Critics' Awards. Brown was not only irked by her colleagues' treatment of Spike Lee but when Denzel Washington of *Glory* and Alan Alda of *Crimes and Misdemeanors* were tied for Supporting Actor, "and Alda won on the next ballot, excuse me, fellow members, but I felt a chill." Director Lee and his movie had led on the New Yorkers' first ballot but both were in fifth place on their final ones. Richard Corliss of *Time* had a less sinister explanation for *Do the Right Thing*'s poor showing. Writing in *Premiere,* he noted that, as the voting goes on, "The question shifts from 'What film do I think is the best?' to 'What film is the least deplorable of the finalists?' . . . Some NYFCC members passionately liked *Do the Right Thing,* and some dispassionately disliked it. So *My Left Foot,* a mild, minor film that nobody could hate, was chosen. Apathy ruled the day."

The New York and Los Angeles groups were in sync with their screenplay winner, *Drugstore Cowboy,* Gus van Sant's low budget, deadpan account of a group of small-time, thieving junkies featuring former teen rave Matt Dillon and beat novelist William S. Burroughs. The National Society did even better by *Drugstore Cowboy,* citing it for Best Picture, Best Director, and Screenplay. Avenue, the independent company distributing the picture, got cracking, hogging the back covers of the trade papers with ads bragging about their critical booty.

Daniel Day-Lewis won three of the four critics' trophies while Michelle Pfeiffer topped him with a clean sweep. The *Boston Herald*'s James Verniere had an explanation for the actress's streak: "I think we can write off the enthusiasm for her as the Testosterone Vote." Pfeiffer had to

"The Oscars made my pits wet."
—Kevin Costner

share her L.A. award with *sex, lies and videotape*'s Andie MacDowell, who laughed and told *Entertainment Tonight*, "I was just really excited to be able to get some work that I thought would be able to show I could act." Spike Lee was there in the Big Orange basking in glory as the winner of the Picture, Director, and Screenplay awards and theorizing, "It's going to help us definitely with the Oscar nominations. This carries a lot more weight than the New York Film Critics, and that's not just sour grapes because we didn't win anything there. Eighty-five percent of the Academy voting members live here in the L.A. area." Lee was wrong about one thing: the New York critics did give one prize to *Do the Right Thing,* for cinematography—curiously one of the few awards it didn't win from the Angelenos, who elected *The Fabulous Baker Boys* instead.

Global Dreams

The Golden Globes ceremony happened to fall on the twenty-second anniversary of Ron Kovic's paralyzing injury and it turned out to be a celebration of *Born on the Fourth of July*. Winning Best Screenplay with Oliver Stone, Kovic proudly held his Globe above his head as the audience gave him a standing ovation. At the microphone, Kovic extolled, "No matter how difficult it may get, believe in your dreams. Because life is worth living and your dreams do come true. They came true for Ron Kovic tonight." His life story also won Best Picture (Drama), Director, and Actor (Drama) for Tom Cruise. Notwithstanding that this was Cruise's first award, the *New York Daily News* had already stated that, Oscar-wise "the Best Actor race is already over, in the eyes of many critics and insiders." Among those that Cruise defeated at the Globes was the original would-be cinematic Ron Kovic, Al Pacino, in *Sea of Love*.

The Foreign Press gave Jessica Tandy her first award. Although Tandy's vanquisher in the critical arena, Michelle Pfeiffer, sang several songs in *The Fabulous Baker Boys,* she was assigned to, and won in, the Globes' Drama category, thus paving the way for the *Miss Daisy* star to triumph in the Comedy/Musical competition. Tandy's costar Morgan Freeman and *Driving Miss Daisy* itself also won in their categories, even though director Bruce Beresford wasn't nominated. *Glory*'s Best Supporting Actor winner Denzel Washington said, "Mom, I didn't wear a tie, I'm sorry," while *Steel Magnolias*' Supporting Actress champion Julia Roberts did wear a tie, and an oversized man's suit, and intrigued everyone by thanking, "Most of all, my best friend, my beautiful blue-eyed, green-eyed friend, who gives me everything." The night was a washout for Spike Lee—*Do the Right Thing* didn't win any of the four Golden Globes for which it was nominated. Lee also bombed out later in the Directors Guild nominations, which didn't include *Daisy*'s Bruce Beresford either.

Personal Appearances

Kenneth Branagh wasn't nominated for Golden Globes as either an actor or a director but he was making time in Hollywood nonetheless. His Renaissance Theater Company had fortuitously been booked to make its American debut during Oscar campaign season at the Mark Taper Forum—right next door to the Dorothy Chandler Pavilion. The company's repertory of *King Lear* and *A Midsummer's Night Dream* became a hot ticket in L.A., and lest this be lost on those Academy voters living on the east coast, a large ad appeared in the Arts and Leisure section of the *New York Times* on opening day, heralding "Sold Out Before We Open!" Branagh also appeared on the *Tonight* show and Johnny Carson liked him so much he invited him back a few weeks later.

That other Britisher, Daniel Day-Lewis, also had a live appearance scheduled. In December, it was announced that, along with his director Jim Sheridan and members of Christy Brown's family, Day-Lewis would appear at a Capitol Hill showing of *My Left Foot*. The screening would be part of "Call for Action"—a day of lobbying support for Senator Tom Harkin's proposed American Disabilities Act, legislation which would outlaw discrimination against the disabled. The film's composer, Hollywood's own Elmer Bernstein, chatted with Robert Osborne about the movie's poor business in England "because it was incredibly manhandled there, sold as if it were a clinical film which was off-putting. It's been handled very well here in the States."

Isabelle vs. Isabelle

Another out-of-towner making the rounds was Isabelle Huppert. A presenter at the Golden Globes Awards dinner, Huppert was on the make for an Oscar nomination for the French film, *Story of Women*, about a WWII abortionist, which had been named Best Foreign Film by both the National Board and the New York critics. Hollywood columnist Martin Kasindorf mentioned that the actress "was the guest of honor at a glitzy hotel reception here a few days ago . . . A publicist whispered to Huppert that much of *la presse Americaine* was represented. She charmed the room with her good command of English." Huppert's picture was not France's entry in the Academy's Foreign Film category, that being *Camille Claudel,* a biography of the sculptor financed by its star, Isabelle Adjani. Winning the Cesar—the "French Oscar" for the part—the outspoken Adjani read from Salman Rushdie's *Satanic Verses* in her acceptance speech. Orion mailed videos of her film to Academy voters, finding a taker in Arlene Dahl, who told *People* she nominated its star as Best Actress. When the magazine inquired if she had viewed the *Do the Right Thing* tape that Universal had sent to all Academy members, Dahl replied she hadn't gotten it until a few days before the deadline and "By then, I had already mailed my ballot."

The Nominations

"It's Valentine's Day," announced the new Academy President Karl Malden, standing next to Geena Davis at 5:30 A.M. "The Academy has a few valentines to hand out this morning." Even though *Driving Miss Daisy*'s ten valentines led the pack, the film didn't seem to have the best shot for Best Picture because it failed a tried and true litmus test—its director was not nominated, and no film since 1931–1932's *Grand Hotel* had grabbed the top prize under these circumstances. Charles Champlin of the *Los Angeles Times* dubbed Bruce Beresford's omission "the single largest astonishment" among the nominations. Marilyn Beck reported, "Producers Richard and Lili Zanuck, in London on the way to the Berlin Film Festival . . . said they were waiting by the phone for the results of Wednesday's Academy Award nominations 'like people awaiting a call from the governor.' " Author Alfred Uhry was even more wracked with suspense when he attempted to watch the nominations on CNN and the network "cut away when they got to the writers." Uhry was filled in on his nomination by the Zanucks when they called to congratulate, but no one knew how to send condolences to the left-out Beresford who was filming in Nigeria. As a way of explanation, Richard said, "The only thing that I can think of is that the Academy might think with such great actors all the director has to do is shout 'action.' " *Daisy*'s three lead actors did place, and when Dan Aykroyd's publicist phoned him with the news, he responded, "We'll have to celebrate; now, I'm going back to sleep."

Beresford couldn't shrug off his snub on anti-Australian discrimination because his compatriot Peter Weir was in the Directors' race for *Dead Poets Society,* which had four nominations, including Picture and Actor for Robin Williams. The actor said that when he heard the news, "I danced around the house in the nude." Marilyn Beck was a party pooper. "C'mon now," scoffed the columnist. "He pretty much played Robin Williams and it was pretty much a supporting role." When Roger Ebert, livid that *Do the Right Thing* was not up for either Picture or Director, labeled *Dead Poets*' nod the single worst nomination of the year, he received boos from the studio audience at Disney World. Disney honchos were thrilled the company had earned only its second Best Picture nomination in its sixty-year history and immediately decided to move up the film's video release date to March 28. The studio had been less successful with its other major Oscar push. The campaign to make *The Little Mermaid* the first cartoon nominated for Best Picture was for naught; this result undoubtedly pleased children's author Maurice Sendak who had criticized Disney's film for "a total contradiction of the original" Hans Christian Andersen fairy tale: "This movie is about getting married, having cupcakes for bras and going to live in White Plains somewhere."

Born on the Fourth of July was second to *Miss Daisy* in nominations, and one of its eight nods *was* for Best Director. Still, the movie had its own Achilles heel—as the *Boston Herald* pointed out, it "has been running out of steam at the box office, and it doesn't leave viewers happy." Oliver Stone's platoon of nominees included Ron Kovic, who rejoiced to the AP, "This is truly one of the happiest and most triumphant moments of my life." The director, with four nominations and two Oscars already, was more blasé, telling the *Miami Herald*'s Ryan Murphy, "I'm working hard. Work is all there is, man."

In *Daily Variety*'s view, "Perhaps the biggest surprise in the competition," was that *"My Left Foot,* the first Irish production ever to score a best picture nomination," turned out "to be such a major contender in the Oscar sweepstakes." Tyro Jim Sheridan was nominated twice for his direction and for his coauthorship of the screenplay. The *Hollywood Reporter* tried to speak with "exhilarated" Actor nominee Daniel Day-Lewis in London, but "he ran out in the street when he heard the news and couldn't be corralled for an interview." Supporting Actress candidate Brenda Fricker stayed in one place and told *Entertainment Tonight,* "Of course it's an accolade for an actress to be nominated for an Oscar because Oscar is a thing I've watched on television while eating fish and chips from a newspaper . . . and suddenly, you're a part of that machine." *Variety* compiled the film's weekly box-office tally after the nominations and reported the happy news: *"My Left Foot* did toe-tapping biz as it danced from 98 to 279 pubs."

The fifth Best Picture nominee was *Field of Dreams,* whose director shared Bruce Beresford's fate; no one was too upset by Phil Alden Robinson's omission, however, since his script was nominated. Even though the movie ended up with only a trio of nominations (James Horner's score was the third), producer Lawrence Gordon was still happy to speak to the press about the commonality he perceived among the five Best Picture finalists: "They're all personal stories about people."

Hollywood Blackout

Do the Right Thing's partisans—including Spike Lee—were the most vocal critics of the Academy's selections after the film ended up with just two nominations: Supporting Actor for Danny Aiello and Original Screenplay. Going up against Lee in the latter race was his Cannes rival, Steven Soderberg, the only mention *sex, lies and videotape* received from the Academy. Lee told the *New York Post,* "We wuz robbed." He did have a theory: "Historically, the Academy goes for a different kind of film—*On Golden Pond, Driving Miss Daisy,* that sort of thing. Morgan is a great actor, but their comfort level is higher with him driving around Miss Daisy than with Mookie throwing a garbage can through Sal's pizzeria . . . I'm not going to slit my wrist. I know this is a film that people will be talking about for twenty years." Savoring the one nomination he did have, the author said "Hey, I'm just going to put it all behind me and show up and have a good time." The *Post*'s David Edelstein wouldn't say die, though, complaining that Freeman's character in *Daisy* was "that kind of Uncle Tom black you don't see represented anymore." Retorted Alfred Uhry, "I think anybody who says that Hoke is Uncle Tom is too young to know what they're

"That's part of the sickness of America, that you have to think in terms of who wins, who loses."
—Marlon Brando

talking about, basically. Morgan Freeman wouldn't consider playing an Uncle Tom."

The Hollywood community was less surprised about Lee than about the failure of Freddie Fields's epic to place in the top race. Angie Dickinson told *Premiere* that she was "appalled that *Glory* was left off the list—it's a superb film" and Andrew Sarris speculated that it "may have opened too late in the year to penetrate the nursing-home precincts of the Academy." When *Premiere* queried Dickinson what she thought of Lee's brush-off, the actress responded, *"Do the Right Thing* was a very nice picture, but I didn't think it deserved to be one of the five nominees." The *Los Angeles Times* was so vexed over the poor showings of *Do the Right Thing* and *Glory* in the major categories that it ran an editorial accusing Academy members of racism. An incensed Academy President Karl Malden sent a letter to the *Times* boasting that "The members of the Academy have done more to combat racial hatred and racial misunderstanding than all the editorial writers in all the newspapers in the world."

Of its five nominations, *Glory* stood the best chance of winning with Best Supporting Actor contender Denzel Washington, who happened to be filming a movie with Spike Lee. Washington wouldn't have to worry about Alan Alda again; the *Crimes and Misdemeanors* star was not nominated, although his costar Martin Landau was, for the second year in a row. Marveled Army Archerd, "Woody Allen even sent him an Oscar congrats wire!" *Variety* observed that Marlon Brando's unexpected supporting nod for the anti-apartheid drama *A Dry White Season* "is sure to provoke extraordinary attention since Brando publicly blasted the cutting of what he considered his most important scene from the pic." The press gasped when his name was announced and Joel Siegel joshingly wondered, "What Indian chief is he going to find this time?" The actor hadn't revised his opinion of the Academy Awards from the Sacheen Littlefeather days. In a CBS interview with Connie Chung, during which he made funny faces and spoke lovingly of Laurel and Hardy, Brando blasted the competitive aspects of the Oscars: "That's part of the sickness of America, that you have to think in terms of who wins, who loses . . . We always think in extreme terms. What's the point?"

Who's That Girl?

Brando's former *Streetcar* costar Jessica Tandy had a much better chance of winning; *Newsweek* flat-out asked, "Could you vote against Jessica Tandy?" In interviews, critics' favorite Michelle Pfeiffer conceded the Actress race to Tandy and the other nominees resigned themselves to watching from the sidelines. Jessica Lange grabbed her fifth nomination as a lawyer who defends her father against charges of Nazi war crimes in the box-office disappointment *Music Box*. Laughed Lange, "I always hear or read that if I don't do another hit soon it's going to be too bad for me. But I can't approach things from that direction."

Even less commercially successful was nominee Pauline Collins' picture *Shirley Valentine*, which nonetheless had a fan in high places. Queen Elizabeth II had been reported to be "tickled pink" with the movie and to have shown it to palace visitors. Although Collins had already won an Olivier in London and a Tony in New York for playing the eponymous neglected British housewife and had been a regular on the PBS series *Upstairs, Downstairs,* she was still fairly obscure among the general public; on the morning of the nominations, the *CBS Morning News*' cohost Kathleen Sullivan referred to the forty-eight-year-old actress as a "girl I've never heard of." One of the two Isabelles made the list. "I didn't think I had a chance," said the amazed Adjani, who made plans to come stateside and was one of only six acting nominees to attend the Academy's annual luncheon. The other Isabelle, Mlle. Huppert, was a good sport about not being nominated and agreed to go to Switzerland to present the Gordon Sawyer Technical Award to the inventor of the zoom lens.

"All I got was free champagne at restaurants for two weeks and then that stopped."
—Dianne Wiest

Handicapping the Races

If Tandy had Best Actress sewn up, the Best Actor competition was nip-and-tuck. To become the youngest actor ever to triumph in his category, twenty-seven-year-old Tom Cruise would have to knock off Morgan Freeman and Daniel Day-Lewis, as well as *Henry V*'s Kenneth Branagh. Branagh had a double dose of good news; he joined screen icons Orson Welles, Warren Beatty, and Woody Allen as the only people to be nominated for both Best Actor and Director in the same year; Allen himself was among his Best Director competition. The bad news for Branagh was that neither he nor Robin Williams were talked about optimistically. The three-way race was so tight that Oscar analysts put forth convoluted theories in making a guess as to who would win. David Edelstein of the *New York Post* came up with, "An interesting scenario: Cruise and Day-Lewis split the wheelchair vote, leaving the prize for Freeman." *Newsweek* thought Tom Cruise, the People's Choice Award winner, would beat its own preference, Daniel Day-Lewis, because the "Academy likes *American* handicapped people better," while *ShowBiz Today*'s Martin Grove warned, "Most Academy voters don't earn $9 million for a film like Cruise; they may express their jealousy." *Entertainment Weekly*'s Owen Gleiberman believed Day-Lewis' work was "simply too fine to ignore." But noting that Morgan Freeman had been well reviewed in four films, Jack Mathews of the *Los Angeles Times* said that "the Academy has a tendency to reward actors for the recent body of their work; on that score, Freeman is ahead on points."

Good Morning, America's Joan Lunden was flabbergasted at the Supporting Actress nomination for Julia Roberts in *Steel Magnolias* since all her fellow cast members—Shirley MacLaine, Sally Field, and Olympia Dukakis—were passed over. "So many stars in that movie and *she* gets it," clucked the morning host. After the final Oscar voting had closed, Martin Grove cursed the timing of Roberts' smash follow-up vehicle for bowing too late to help her, speculating that she "would have won had her new hit *Pretty Woman* opened during the ballotting." At least she had *USA Today* in suspense: "Hot newcomer nominee Julia Roberts' date is a mystery." Pundits predicted the race would be between *My Left Foot*'s Brenda Fricker and the *Enemies* wives, Lena Olin and Anjelica Huston, with *Variety* dubbing Olin "the narrow favorite." The fifth nominee, *Parenthood*'s Dianne Wiest, had seen it all before. After netting the 1986 Best Supporting Actress Oscar, recalled Wiest, "I thought I'll never be able to read all those scripts. I sat there patiently waiting and all I got was free champagne at restaurants for two weeks and then that stopped."

Block Voting

For the second year in a row, the Academy's Documentary Committee took heat for ignoring the critics' darling. *Roger and Me* recorded director Michael Moore's two-and-a-half-year attempt to meet General Motors chairman Roger Smith and threw a sarcastic glance at the economic devastation caused by the company's cavalier closing of factories in Flint, Michigan. Pre-Oscar, Moore had enjoyed the kind of success most documentarians only dream of. After acclaim at the New York Film Festival, Warner Brothers shelled out $3 million for distribution rights to the $250,000 movie, which then landed on more ten-best lists than any other movie and actually had people lining up to see it. The tide turned when a *Film Comment* exposé revealed that Moore had played fast and loose with real-life chronology and that he bent facts to fit into his populist agenda. Other dissenting voices joined in saying that because of its distortions the film should not even be considered a documentary and Moore himself seemed to agree. "I guess I'd describe *Roger and Me* as a dark comedy," the filmmaker told *People*, "A cross between *Grapes of Wrath* and *Pee-wee's Big Adventure*."

Moore's unorthodox techniques didn't sit

"A Snow White piñata would be a good idea."
—Billy Crystal

well with the strait-laced Academy Documentary Committee, and the panel's chairman Mitchell Block called the movie "unethical." When *Roger and Me* failed to be nominated after winning four critics' prizes, forty-five documentary filmmakers signed a letter of protest, urging a write-in vote for the movie. And on the subject of ethics, some protestors pointed out that Chairman Block was the president of Direct Cinema, a documentary distribution company which, per chance, had three of the year's five nominations. Informed of this coincidence, the Academy's executive director, Bruce Davis, responded, "Well, I'll be darned. I thought it was only two. That is very interesting."

The No-Snow Show

"The one word I can give you is dignity, a dignified show," promised Academy President Karl Malden of the first show of his tenure. The 1951 Best Supporting Actor winner admitted of the previous broadcast, "Some of the people in the Academy felt the show got a little out of control." This year, Malden persuaded Gilbert Cates, who had turned down earlier Academy offers, to do producing honors, because, as *Daily Variety* stated, "Cates, a veteran film and TV director known for his tasteful work in both media, will attempt to rectify the damage the last Oscar show did to the Academy's reputation." He had his work cut out for him, as *Entertainment Weekly*'s Jess Cagle reminded everyone, "Let's face it: Last year's Oscar telecast was the worst in history. That's not opinion; it's a fact."

Cates happened to have been the head of the committee analyzing what made Allan Carr's production such a fiasco but now that he had the job he skirted around, openly criticizing his predecessor. "Every producer brings his own personality to it," he said. "His was a great Allan Carr show." As for his concept of Oscar, Cates continued, "Most people knew about the Academy Awards when they were three, four, and five years old, and they've been kind of watching every year. It's almost like a national holiday in a way." Hoping to keep up the holiday spirit, Cates recruited former Laker Girl and current pop star Paula Abdul to choreograph, and Billy Crystal, one of last year's few bright spots, to emcee. Cracked Crystal at the Academy press conference, "I think a Snow White piñata would be a good idea."

Calling it "a party thrown around the world," Cates expanded, "The world is changing, and hopefully the awards show is changing, matching the changes in the world." For starters, the Oscar show would now be broadcast in Poland. Honoring the end of the Cold War, Cates announced that several Oscars would be presented live at sister ceremonies in London, Moscow, Sydney, and Buenos Aires via satellite hook-up. Price, Waterhouse was sending bonded couriers with locked metal boxes to each capital. "There are certainly possibilities for things to go awry," said the accounting firm's Dan Lyle, adding defensively, "but they won't." Ilmar Taska, the segment producer from Moscow, explained to CNN, "It is symbolic in many ways. You can really see how the borders are losing their importance." There was a single Academy member who resided in the Soviet Union, but director Elem Klimov lamented to the *Boston Herald*, "I pay dues annually as all other members but the ballot arrives two months after it is posted in the U.S.A., so I am deprived of the opportunity to vote in any of the categories." Comedian Crystal had his concerns about a worldwide audience. "Jokes are harder when it's global," he said. "There's the possibility of offending people without meaning to offend them, just because our sensibilities and our points of view about comedy are different."

Academy Lock-Out

Although the whole world was invited, many Hollywoodites found it impossible to get in when the Academy decided to move the ceremony back to the Dorothy Chandler Pavilion after two years at the Shrine Auditorium. With the seating capacity reduced from nearly 7,000 to 3,000, a lottery was held to determine which Academy members would get the remaining tickets after the nominees, dignitaries, and Cesar "Butch" Romero were served. Losing members were incensed that dutifully paying their membership dues was no longer a guarantee to be where the action was. Cates and Malden were so bombarded with requests that they took out full-page ads in the trade papers addressed to "Our Friends in the Industry" and saying they'd be "extremely grateful" if people would stop pestering them. The pair reminded that "There are lots of great Awards-night parties around town, many of which benefit worthy charities. Please consider enjoying the show at one of those this time around." A churlish Cates even suggested that "If they want to attend badly enough, fly down to Buenos Aires." With all this in-fighting, CNN's Sandy Kenyon scooped that the Academy, counting on Woody Allen's absence, gave away his tickets, but still reserved a seat for "Marlon Brando, in the unlikely event that he'll attend."

One member the Academy didn't have to worry about accommodating was last year's producer. When *Vanity Fair* inquired of Allan Carr where he planned to spend this Oscar night, he replied, China, because "I've never been and I wanted to see it."

The Big Night

Brando was the only acting nominee not to show. Daniel Day-Lewis arrived early, wearing a black frock coat and clutching an ivory rosary. Danny Aiello had his own charm, a coin that "my friend Carmine had blessed by the Pope." His director, Spike Lee, carted a camera and wore a Sabato Russo black suit with vest but no tie, topped off with an orange, red, and green Kente scarf from Kenya and a flattop hat that the *Santa Monica Outlook* said "made him look like a traveling priest in a western." Cartoonist R. Crumb, recording his impressions for *Premiere*, wrote that Lee "seemed to be wandering around by himself looking lost." Non-nominee Michael Moore showed up in black tie, white sneakers, and an Illinois State Film Commission cap as he accepted a "People's Award" for *Roger and Me* in a sidewalk bestowal across the street by a crowd that *Variety* described as "45 homeless people and homeless organizations' reps." "This is a nicer award," responded the recipient. While fans dressed as either baseball players, Miss Daisy, or Batman cheered in the bleachers, the *Long Beach Press-Telegram* interviewed a man it found "scavenging for cans under the stands." "I used to follow who got nominated," he said, "but when you live on the streets, you don't get to catch a lot of movies."

Fashion was on the mind of *Women's Wear Daily*, which proclaimed, "It was more like the Armani Awards Monday night as most of the big-time stars—male and female—dumped the glitz and opted for Giorgio's greatest hits." The Italian designer had outfitted Denzel Washington, Steve Martin, Tom Hanks, Jeff Goldblum, Dennis Hopper, emcee Billy Crystal, last year's Best Actress Jodie Foster, and the two top contenders in this year's race, Jessica Tandy and Michelle Pfeiffer. *WWD* called Pfeiffer's "sleek navy column" with pearls "sheer Ecstasy," while the *New York Post*'s Cindy Adams wrote, "Forget the 17-year-old tawny-haired twinkies. Last night the Big Star was Jessica Tandy" in her beaded jacket with

Awards Ceremony

MARCH 26, 1990, 6:00 P.M.
THE DOROTHY CHANDLER PAVILION, LOS ANGELES

Your Host:
BILLY CRYSTAL
Televised over ABC

Presenters

Supporting Actor . . . . Geena Davis
Art Direction . . . . Glenn Close and Mel Gibson (in London)
Original Score . . . . Steve Martin
Makeup . . . . Elizabeth McGovern and Kenneth Branagh
Foreign Film . . . . Natalia Negoda and Jack Lemmon (in Moscow)
Supporting Actress . . . . Kevin Kline
Live Action Short Film . . . . John Candy and Rick Moranis
Animated Short Film . . . . Bugs Bunny
Jean Hersholt Humanitarian Award . . . . Walter Matthau
Editing . . . . Jessica Tandy and Morgan Freeman
Gordon E. Sawyer Award Isabelle Huppert (on tape)
Sound . . . . Rachel Ward and Bryan Brown (in Sydney)
Sound Effects Editing . . . . Rachel Ward and Bryan Brown (in Sydney)
Cinematography . . . Melanie Griffith and Tom Hanks
Actress . . . . Gregory Peck
Costume Design . . . . Candice Bergen
Visual Effects . . . . . . Dan Aykroyd and Chevy Chase
Honorary Award to Akira Kurosawa . . . George Lucas and Steven Spielberg
Original Song . . . . . . Paula Abdul and Dudley Moore
Documentary Awards . . . . Norma Aleandro and Charlton Heston (in Buenos Aires)
Writing Awards . . . . Jane Fonda
Director . . . . . Robert De Niro and Martin Scorsese
Actor . . . . Jodie Foster
Picture . . . . Warren Beatty and Jack Nicholson

Performers of Nominated Songs

"After All" . . . . James Ingram and Melissa Manchester
"The Girl Who Used to Be Me" . . . . Patti Austin
"I Love to See You Smile" . . . . Randy Newman
"Kiss the Girl" . . . . Geoffrey Holder
"Under the Sea" . . . . Geoffrey Holder

"If this had happened early in our marriage, we'd be divorced now."
—Hume Cronyn

navy skirt. The shoo-in told the columnist, "I bet my agent a hundred dollars it was Michelle Pfeiffer," and the nominee's husband whispered, "If this had happened early in our marriage, we'd be divorced by now." Checking out Pfeiffer's date, Adams deduced, "Fisher Stevens of suburban Illinois flashed more jewelry than she. Three-stud earrings. Diamonds and emeralds. All on the left ear. They say he's an actor. Me, I figure he's a jeweler." Despite her glamorous facade, Pfeiffer confessed, "The Oscars just terrify me. I'd rather stay home and watch it on TV."

Another nominee in Armani, Julia Roberts, felt the same way. "I'm nervous and excited. I want to sit down," she said when the press swarmed around her and her mystery date, who turned out to be the Armani-clad Kiefer Sutherland, the "green-eyed, blue-eyed friend" of her Golden Globe speech. Her competition, Brenda Fricker, in a beaded blue tunic with pants, was also getting the glamour treatment. *Entertainment Tonight* had tagged along ever since she "arrived from London on Saturday night to an instant whirlwind of Oscar parties that had the Irish actress a bit overwhelmed." The TV show had followed her Oscar day "for a round of talk shows," and had gone to the beauty parlor with her.

The "official Oscar fashion coordinator," Fred Hayman of Beverly Hills, fretted about the Armani onslaught. "I'm not sure that they were glamorous enough," but he could comfortably point to a few nominees in dresses that his boutique had provided gratis. Pauline Collins, just off the plane, had stopped by the store, as did Jessica Lange who, in a gold metallic-spangled bustier with clinging ivory chiffon long skirt, arrived on the arm of her brother. Anjelica Huston was rankled that Hayman had already revealed her choice, a black strapless, on an Oscar preview program so she pulled a fast one and showed up in a red strapless instead. Her date was ex-Governor Jerry Brown.

A non-movie star proved "a crowd favorite," according to *USA Today*, when Adapted Screenplay nominee Ron Kovic came with his parents, whom he had portrayed so brutally onscreen, after having scored tickets for them at the last minute. "My dad didn't even have time to get a tux, so he's wearing the gray suit he always wears," said Kovic. Though she wasn't nominated for playing a fifty-one-year-old virgin in *The Old Gringo*, Jane Fonda emerged as the most talked-about star of the night when she popped up smiling and holding hands with cable television magnate Ted Turner. *Newsweek* praised "her newly fashioned body swathed in a blue Valkyrie-in-love dress with glittery abstract breast plate," from Gianni Versace. Fonda dismissed a possible romance, saying "We're just friends. He makes me laugh," but Turner intimated more. "We're dating, that's obvious, and we're having a good time." Gossips had more to gape over when Tom Cruise rolled up holding his mother's hand while his newest leading lady, Australia's Nicole Kidman, held on to his other arm. "Tom Cruise must have figured he had it made because he was the dead-last star to arrive at the theater," concluded Cindy Adams.

The obligatory opening shots of the forecourt featured Arnold Schwarzenegger entering with wife Maria Shriver and mother-in-law Eunice Shriver and 1963 Best Actress Patricia Neal, in a white movie-star turban, walking in unannounced behind Robin Williams. Then Karl Malden was on stage giving the kind of speech that usually prefaces the Foreign Language Film Award. "This is one of those nights when one world is more than a philosophical dream, but a reality," the Academy President intoned. "Films have leaped across national boundaries, overcome disparate languages . . . it's time to celebrate and party tonight." Injecting a touch of sadism into the celebration, Malden added, "And for you nominees, I dare you to be relaxed tonight." The party started with a Chuck Workman montage "100 Years of the Movies," that had the temerity to feature Disney's Snow White, as well as Brando in *Last Tango in Paris* and President Malden in *A Streetcar Named Desire*, who won another round of applause from the audience. In five minutes of

"Is that for me or are you just glad I'm not Snow White?"
—Billy Crystal

clips, Workman managed to include two different shots each of Sylvester Stallone and Eddie Murphy and highlights from *Bill and Ted's Excellent Adventure* and *Look Who's Talking.* Jack Nicholson, who was seen in a couple of clips, laughingly complained backstage that Workman chose Michael Keaton's Batman rather than his Joker.

To the strains of "It Had to Be You," Billy Crystal materialized on stage and responding to the applause, asked "Is that for me or are you just glad I'm not Snow White?" Alluding to the Workman montage and a recent plagiarism suit against Eddie Murphy, the comic said, "There are 330 pieces of film in that five-minute montage and what's amazing is that, according to Paramount, not one has yet to go into profits." The audience loved the joke and Crystal was on a roll. "Jack Nicholson's so rich, Jon Peters still cuts his hair," brought howls, and calling *Driving Miss Daisy* "the movie that apparently directed itself" received cheers. Of Jessica Tandy, he remarked, "At eighty years of age, tonight she would become the second oldest Oscar recipient ever. The first is Shirley MacLaine who is 915, I believe."

In New York, the *Post*'s David Edelstein wrote, "Crystal got off a few good ones (and some bad racist ones, too)." One of the latter occurred when he paid tribute to Spike Lee for his screenplay nomination—accompanied by a close-up of the chapeau-wearing nominee—and then zapped him by adding, "based on an idea by Art Buchwald," linking Lee to Eddie Murphy because they're both black. The audience actually booed when the stand-up said, "MGM is being bought by an Italian who's promised only one small change: from now on the lion's not going to roar, he's going to be taking the Fifth." Crystal recovered quickly, kidding, "All right, I'll bring out Jack Valenti now," but he waded back into racial waters by joking that executives at Columbia, now owned by "the great Japanese Sony Corporation," kept turning every one of his story pitches into Godzilla movies. Crystal wound it up by asking, "Where is that big, terrible number that usually opens the Oscars?" He told the grateful audience, "You won't be seeing that tonight," and then launched into his own Best Picture medley, combining "Me and My Shadow" with *My Left Foot* and, to the tune of "Walking My Baby Back Home," singing "Gee it's great / in a segregated state / Driving Miss Daisy back home."

The 1988 Best Supporting Actress was described by *USA Today:* "Even more stunning than last year, Geena Davis stuck with designer Bill Hargate, who created a sleek, shirred off-the-shoulder RED dress with long sleeves, highlighted with Harry Winston diamonds." The jewels came with their own bodyguards. Davis allowed, "This first award of the evening may have been the most difficult to decide" and then announced that Best Supporting Actor went to Denzel Washington in *Glory.* The winner kissed his wife and his mother and garnered applause when he referred to *Glory* as "what I consider to be at least one of the five best films of the year." There were teary reaction shots when he went on, "God bless you, my mother, I love you, my beautiful wife Pauletta . . . My son said he was going to make one of these out of clay for me, now I've got the model for him." Washington ended by paying homage "to the 54th, the black soldiers who helped to make this country free."

A Diet Coke commercial featuring the show's choreographer Paula Abdul followed and then the program cut to its first international hook-up. At the Ritz Hotel in London at 3:30 A.M., Glenn Close and Mel Gibson, about to star in Franco Zeffirelli's version of *Hamlet*, were on hand to present Best Art Direction and each made an erroneous statement: Close saying that *Henry V* was up for Best Picture and Gibson stating that this would be the first Oscar given outside of Southern California, forgetting the sister shows held in New York in the mid-1950s. *Batman* won the sole Award for which it was nominated and, back at the Dorothy Chandler, Anton Furst was amused. "Me, instead of Jack Nicholson?" he wondered. "I love it. It's great. He made my sets look so small." Thanking "the Bat Gang, the A-1 team I

"Prince didn't help me on this one."
—Kim Basinger

work with, but this is mine anyway," Furst tried to find his set decorator Peter Young in the audience, unaware that he was standing right behind him. "I came up here with you," said Young, his only comment before the orchestra drowned him out and he and his cowinner were hustled offstage. A year-and-a-half later, Furst leapt to his death from an L.A. parking garage.

Billy Crystal introduced "a man who's chest is bigger than Madonna's"—Arnold Schwarzenegger. The muscle man's function on the show was to introduce Kim Basinger, who floated out in a cuckoo antebellum gown that had the Russian word for love patched on its single sleeve. "Demi Moore proved it last year," pontificated *WWD*. "Actresses shouldn't design their own dresses. This year, Kim Basinger whipped up an agonizing half-jacket, half-strapless self-creation." David Ehrenstein wrote she "looked like Glenda the Good Witch after six or seven Scotches." As if her appearance wasn't enough, Basinger departed from the script to scold the voters over the nominations: "We have five great films here and they are great for one reason: They tell the truth. But there is one film missing from the list that deserves to be honored because, ironically, it might tell the biggest truth of all. And that's *Do the Right Thing*." ABC's microphones caught the applause in the orchestra but missed out on the hissing in the balconies. "OK, so on to business," Basinger continued, preluding the clip of *Dead Poets Society* by confiding, "when I saw this movie I fell in love with it at a very special time in my life . . . I really like this ad that I saw in the paper, it says, 'It makes you cry, it makes you laugh, and it makes you care.' What more could there be?" *WWD* had more ammunition. "The dress was as stupid as Kim's speech." Basinger wouldn't talk with the press, except to deny that her current flame had a hand in her dress. "Prince didn't help me on this one," she insisted. "It's a Kim Basinger original." She later said that, after her presentation, she "stripped off that gown, because it was taking up four seats in the audience." After she returned to her seat, Spike Lee, whom she had never met, passed her a thank-you note.

There was more sartorial drama according to *Newsweek* when Julia Roberts "appeared in a mud-colored Armani tank top without benefit of supporting undergarments." Roberts' job was to introduce the first song nominee, Randy Newman's "I Love to See You Smile," illustrated by a montage of grinning movie stars, monsters, and cartoon characters. Then Steve Martin joked, "Before the show could be broadcast from Russia this year there had to be an international agreement that there'd be no opening production number," and then lampooned one country's tough drug laws by quipping, "We were going to go live from Malaysia but the TV crew was hanged at the airport." After the inevitable double entendre about the Scoring award, the comedian presented the Oscar to *The Little Mermaid*'s Alan Menken, who said, "First of all, I'd like to thank my collaborator, Howard Ashman, who encouraged me to take the opportunity to compose my first film score." Kenneth Branagh and Elizabeth McGovern then gave the Makeup Oscar to *Driving Miss Daisy*. Lynn Barber thanked "Bruce Beresford for an incredible job . . . and my little girl, Mica, at home, yes, honey, you may take this to show-and-tell on Friday."

For the second remote, the telecast jumped to Moscow at the Russian Concert Hall next to Red Square where Jack Lemmon and the star of *Little Vera*, Natalia Negoda, said it was "Five minutes to 7:00 A.M. Tuesday morning." Citing a technical audio glitch, Lemmon joked, "Isn't that a beautiful echo?" Best Foreign Film went to *Cinema Paradiso* but producer Franco Cristaldi took so long talking about the significance of the date March 28 in his life that director Giuseppe Tornatore didn't get a chance to speak. Even worse, noted *Screen International*, "In an unfortunate twist of fate, the Italian audience watching the live transmission . . . was denied the chance of seeing its favorite film-maker . . . Just as Giuseppe Tornatore walked up to the podium . . . the transmission was interrupted by those unwelcome

"Anybody who gives birth twenty-two times deserves one of these."
—Brenda Fricker

commercial breaks." Tornatore was able to speak backstage, and said he found Hollywood "more amusing than I thought."

The husband of Phoebe Cates, last year's Best Supporting Actor Kevin Kline, prefaced the Supporting Actress presentation by thanking "Uncle Gil" and mentioning that "From 1937 up until this very moment there have been 107 Oscar recipients for Supporting roles. I am very proud to be here to help add another name to that most distinguished list, if I do say so myself." Brenda Fricker was the name he added and viewers saw her mutter, "I don't believe it." The actress thanked "Christy Brown just for being alive. I'd like to thank Mrs. Brown, his mother. Anybody who gives birth twenty-two times deserves one of these."

The Best Song nominees from *The Little Mermaid* followed, in a production number that *Variety* panned, saying troubadour Geoffrey Holder "lip-synched so poorly that it was painful." After Spike Lee starred in a Nike commercial he directed, Bugs Bunny presented the Animated Short Oscar to twenty-seven-year-old West German twins Christoph and Wolfgang Laurenstein, whose mother had sewed the costumes for the miniature figures featured in their seven-minute film *Balance,* which they had shot in their basement. Christoph held his statuette and commented, "So, what could I say?, It's very exciting to be here in L.A. on this stage with this great guy." His brother retorted, "That's what I wanted to say, too."

Walter Matthau showed up to give the Jean Hersholt Humanitarian Award to former Academy President Howard Koch, who also earned a standing ovation. The band played "The More I See You" and the audience was going to see a lot of Koch. When he produced the 1979 Oscar broadcast, Koch griped that Documentary Feature winner Ira Wohl had wasted time thanking members of his family. Now Koch himself was going down the list of his kin but unlike Wohl, he couldn't remember everyone's name and he called to his wife in the audience to help him out with the grandchildren's identities.

Jessica Lange strutted onstage to set up the *Driving Miss Daisy* clip with the thought, "Isn't it a wonderful surprise when, against all odds, a small, off-Broadway two-character play can not only get made in this town but become one of the most successful, most acclaimed films of the year?" Jessica Tandy and Morgan Freeman, in his mauve moiré muffler, cumberbund, and bow tie, followed and proved to be uncomfortable with the silly banter they were given. Freeman appeared in two of the Best Editing nominees but the award went not to *Daisy* or *Glory* but to *Born on the Fourth of July*. Cowinner David Brenner thanked Oliver Stone for "one of the greatest experiences of my life . . . Thank you for letting us help you to realize your vision" and there was a close-up of Tom Cruise. Tom Selleck then indulged in an old-fashioned welcome to "one of France's most beautiful technical achievements, the winner of Best Actress at the Venice Film Festival for her role in *The Story of Women,* Miss Isabelle Huppert." A tape showed her giving the Gordon E. Sawyer award to Pierre Angenieux in Geneva.

From Europe, the show cut to Australia where Rachel Ward, Bryan Brown, and a jovial crowd were in a restaurant at the Sydney Opera House. Brown told Hollywood that Australia is "18 hours ahead of you. This place is filled with people out to lunch." Ward told her husband that "no one can understand a word you're saying." The winner for Best Sound was *Glory* and back at the Dorothy Chandler, when a third sound person tried to get in his thanks, the orchestra cut him off. The camera caught Denzel Washington laughing at his dilemma. *Glory* won Oscar number three when seventy-two-year-old Freddie Francis nabbed Best Cinematography and thanked "All you lovely people over here at the Academy for always making us so welcome when we come over here. We love you all and we're available for September." Backstage, Francis was more critical: "*Glory* is a great picture. It's the one that I am most proud to be associated with. I was shocked that it was not nominated for Best Picture or that

"I don't feel that I understand cinema yet."
—Akira Kurosawa

Ed Zwick was not nominated for Best Director." At Lazar's Spago party, producer Freddie Fields was compensated for any disappointment when Sherry Lansing rejoiced over his movie's Oscar wins by jumping onto his lap.

Billy Crystal paused "to say hello to a dear friend of all of ours who's at home watching us tonight. Why don't we give a nice round of applause and send our love to Mr. Sammy Davis, Jr." The ailing entertainer, whom Crystal used to imitate on *Saturday Night Live,* passed away six weeks later.

Gregory Peck announced that the Best Actress Oscar went to Jessica Tandy. Morgan Freeman ran out of his seat to steady the octogenarian down the aisle and an instantaneous standing ovation greeted her. "I never expected in a million years that I would be in this position, it's a miracle," the winner exclaimed, "and I thank my lucky stars and Richard and Lili Zanuck who had the faith to give me this wonderful chance, and, also, most especially, to that forgotten man, my director, Bruce Beresford." Beresford's second mention of the evening drew applause. The actress finished by thanking agent "Sam Cohn, who takes such good care of me," and lifting the statuette over her head and declaring, "I am on Cloud 9!" She headed backstage and fretted, "I forgot to thank Morgan and my husband!"

Paula Abdul's dances for the Costume Oscar presentation were unanimously criticized for their inappropriateness, particularly when "Hoke" breakdanced and a jitterbugging "Miss Daisy" was lifted in the air and opened her legs to the audience. Opined Janet Maslin, "This alone was enough to bring back a flood of awful Oscar memories." Before presenter Candice Bergen could finish reading the Costume Design winner's name—*Henry V*'s Phyllis Dalton—Kenneth Branagh was heard yelling his delight. As Dalton made her way to the stage, the camera saw the jubilant Branagh accepting the congratulations of those sitting around him.

Chevy Chase rubbed it in to losing Supporting Actor nominee Dan Aykroyd, saying that he had voted for Martin Landau and that "Danny Aiello was probably a little better than you." The pair presented the Special Effects Oscar to *The Abyss,* an award for which 20th Century-Fox had campaigned by mailing out a half-hour cassette with all the effects so that Academy voters wouldn't have to spend two hours and twenty minutes watching the whole movie. All four technicians managed to get in brief words of gratitude before Bill Conti's orchestra started up.

Jack Valenti introduced George Lucas and Steven Spielberg as the progenitors of eight of the ten all-time top-grossing films, which he dubbed "an incredible creative achievement." The *New York Post*'s David Bianculli reprimanded Valenti: "Great equation for Hollywood to send out to the international community: creativity equals box-office receipts." Spielberg explained that an Honorary Oscar was going "to a man who many of us believe is our greatest living filmmaker and all of us know as one of the few true visionaries ever to work in our medium." Akira Kurosawa was said visionary and his work was summarized through a montage assembled by *Time* film critic Richard Schickel, ending with a quote by Kurosawa setting forth that hoariest of cliches, "In a mad world, only the mad are sane." The audience made its third standing ovation as the camera saw Kurosawa rise from his seat in front of Mr. and Mrs. Marvin Hamlisch. Onstage, the recipient was greeted by a remote from Tokyo, where his film crew spoke to him in Japanese; because television director Jeff Margolis chose to cover the scene in a long shot, the home audience couldn't begin to make out the subtitles on the monitor and was left in the dark about what was being said. Back in Tokyo, a crew member rolled out a giant birthday cake and exhorted, "Everyone at the Music Center, please join us" in singing "Happy Birthday." Most of the Hollywood crowd did as requested, but the camera caught Martin Scorsese with his mouth closed. Through his translator, Kurosawa said he didn't buy the hype. "I have to ask if I really deserve it. I'm a little worried because I don't feel that I understand cinema yet."

"I am really bored by those questions."
—Steven Spielberg

At the end of his humble speech, he said in English, "Thank you." Army Archerd reported, "Kurosawa received a second ovation from the film-centered audience after the TV cameras had already left him." Backstage, a reporter asked Spielberg about his being snubbed by Academy voters and the former Irving G. Thalberg winner reddened and shot back, "Not to mean any disrespect to you personally, but I am really bored by those questions."

An "Academy Award winner this evening, Mr. Denzel Washington" reappeared to say that the Best Song nominee from *Chances Are* would now be performed. Paula Abdul and Dudley Moore then annointed "Under the Sea" as this year's winner. Vowed lyricist Howard Ashman, "I won't do fish jokes, just say a couple of thank-yous." Later, amid the celebration at the Governors' Ball, his collaborator Alan Menken, remembered, "At the party, Howard told me he was really happy and then he said that when we got back to New York we would have to talk. That was unlike him. Usually if he had something to say he would say it. I went to his house the following Thursday, and he told me he had AIDS. I was devastated." Ashman would die a year later.

About an hour before the ceremony began, Gilbert Cates had learned that saboteurs in Buenos Aires were threatening to cut the cable if the Argentinian television technicians didn't get more money, but they were apprehended and, to the strains of "Don't Cry for Me, Argentina," the show proceeded to Buenos Aires as if nothing happened. Charlton Heston and Norma Alejandro were onstage at the Theatre Colon with the president of Argentina and his wife sitting in the same box Juan and Eva Peron used to frequent. Heston misstated history by saying that his copresenter had won an Oscar for *Gaby—A True Story*. The pair announced that the Documentary Short had gone to a movie about the Johnstown Flood produced by veteran documentarian Charles Guggenheim, who had received his first Oscar in this category in 1964 and his first nomination in 1956. "Thank God Noah didn't make films," joshed Guggenheim. Billy Crystal then joked that Heston and Alejandro "are going to do a full-contact Lambada"—referring to an erotic dance then on the last legs of its short-lived vogue. Heston riposted, "C'mon, Billy. You know I can't dance the LaMam . . . LaMamba. Hell, I can't even pronounce it." The Documentary Feature statuette went to *Common Threads: Stories from the Quilt*, or, as Alejandro pronounced it, "the kilt." Director Robert Epstein thanked "Elizabeth Taylor for her support and her heroic efforts in fighting AIDS and to all those fighting AIDS, especially the gay and lesbian community, thank you for leading the nation with courage and dignity and urgency. May our government soon follow." Epstein's comments marked the first time AIDS had been mentioned at the Oscars, but this wasn't Epstein's first trophy, having won in this category five years earlier for *The Times of Harvey Milk*. In an interview with *Outweek*, Epstein later jested, "We know the first Oscar is gay. We're not sure about the new one. He's really cute. We hope they get along."

As at Cannes, Screenplay presenter Jane Fonda was in the position to settle the battle between Spike Lee and Steven Soderbergh, but this one was a draw. To *Newsday*'s Linda Winer, the outcome was "the final outrage . . . to pass over Lee's screenplay in favor of *Dead Poets Society*—a sappy plea for repressed rich white boys to free themselves through literature." Spike Lee could be seen getting up so that the winner could pass by and, at the podium, Schulman earned unexpected laughs by thanking "my wife Miriam who supported me during the terrible years when I couldn't get a job in this town." One of Schulman's next scripts, *Medicine Man*, sold for $1.5 million. Ron Kovic, in his wheelchair in the aisle at the end of the row containing the Adapted Screenplay nominees, had to make way for *Driving Miss Daisy*'s Alfred Uhrey. "I guess I'm lucky that my grandmother was such a terrible driver," said Uhry, who singled out "the great and unheralded Bruce Beresford." This author also won laughs when he thanked each of his six children by name "for keeping things in perspective, and Mama and Will, if you're watching, this is for you."

Anjelica Huston was onstage saying "Since I was raised in Ireland, I'm proud to be introducing the first Irish film ever to be nominated for Best Picture—*My Left Foot*." Then it was time for Billy Crystal to reminisce, "When I was a film major at New York University in 1968, one of my professors was a struggling young director and he told me that my work was intense but always out of focus and his never was." After a montage of a "series of what has become a perfect blend of actor and director," Crystal brought out Robert De Niro and Martin Scorsese. De Niro had spent much of the show in the satellite truck outside the theater, fascinated by the technology, but when he came onstage, critics made fun of his "sheepdog" look. The Oscar went to the Directors Guild winner Oliver Stone, who kissed Ron Kovic on his way up. "My deepest thanks for your acknowledgment that Vietnam is not over, although some people say it is," Stone started. "Vietnam is a state of mind that continues all over the world, for as long as man, in his quest for power, interferes in the affairs of other men." Turning to his colleagues, the director saluted "Ron Kovic for his largeness of heart" and "Tom Cruise for making Ron's dream come true." Backstage, Stone decided to wait for the result of the Best Picture category before going into the pressroom.

Jodie Foster told the five Best Actor nominees, "You have moved me, moved the Academy, moved the people." She then ripped open the envelope with her black leather gloves with white stitching and read "Daniel Day-Lewis." The night's "loudest cheer went up" at Spago, reported *People*, and the audience at the Dorothy Chandler awarded him with the night's fourth standing ovation. One wag muttered, "Oh, he was just playing himself." "You've just provided me with the makings of one helluva weekend in Dublin," he began, to gales of laughter. Citing the youngster who had played his character as a child, Day-Lewis said, "I shared Christy's life for a while with a remarkable young actor called Hugh O'Connor . . . I'm truly grateful to you that, in honoring me with this award, you're encouraging Christy to carry on making his mark." As Day-Lewis started back to his seat, Foster redirected him backstage. A *New York Times* editorial approvingly observed that with his morning suit, "looking at Daniel Day-Lewis was like seeing Shelley plain," but hairdresser James Spadaro sniffed to columnist William Norwich about the state of the winner's locks: "Long hair like Daniel Day-Lewis' can work, but it has to be clean."

Michelle Pfeiffer introduced a clip of Judy Garland singing "Over the Rainbow" but, as the *New Yorker*'s Hal Rubenstein rejoined, the mood "was shattered by the reedy, sharp whisper-singing of another, lesser voice and before you could say 'What the hell are you doing here—you haven't made a movie in twelve years' three times fast, Diana Ross's hair, nails, and requisite white beaded gown were imploring us to sing along with her lazy self." Ross, who like Kurosawa was celebrating a birthday, came out in a different dress than the one she was wearing when she entered the Pavilion hours earlier. Liza Minnelli had nixed Cates' offer to perform the 1939 Best Song winner because "Nobody could sing it better than my mother." So it was Ross who ordered, "Sing with me, Los Angeles. Everyone." On the stage, a giant bank of video monitors attempted to show participants from the other Oscar cities joining in, but the clashing images provided such a hodgepodge of pictures that it was nearly impossible to make anything out. Amid the confusion, however, Mel Gibson could be glimpsed wolfing food into his mouth instead of warbling. As usual, Ross ended by striking a diva pose. In the pressroom, a reporter pondered aloud, "Didn't she marry a rich man? She doesn't have to do this."

Jack Nicholson, with a $7,500 Batman pin on his lapel, and Warren Beatty stepped out to give Best Picture. One critic thought the couple looked "as if they wandered in from a stag party." The jocular duo named *Driving Miss Daisy*, but an attempt by a few bodies to start a standing ovation

"I think they gave it to me because I'm the oldest."
—Jessica Tandy

fizzled. Producer Richard Zanuck carried on the family tradition of complaining during a Best Picture acceptance speech by grousing, "We're up here for one very simple reason and that's the fact that Bruce Beresford is a brilliant director, it's as simple as that." Lili Fini Zanuck, only the second woman to earn this top prize, said, "I hope I'm as religious all the rest of the year as I've been the last two months . . . I would very much like to thank the Academy for honoring us and making my mama so proud."

Billy Crystal said goodnight in different languages, but, in *TV Guide*'s estimation, he was too late: "By the time *Driving Miss Daisy* drove away with the Best Picture Oscar, more than a quarter of the viewers who had been tuned to the telecast two hours earlier had tuned out."

Aftermath

Oliver Stone ambled into the pressroom after losing the final award. "He was depressed and he had an Oscar in his hand!" observed Jack Mathews of the *Los Angeles Times*. "I thought my film was honest in the spirit of its time, but it still drew an ugly attack by the right-wing in our country," the director alleged. "It's a tough film, a relentless movie. It's political, and I know it made a lot of people angry."

Denzel Washington was more pleased. "It's good to be part of the club," he said. "So many people expected me to win, it put a lot of pressure on me." "Denzel will be back for Best Actor next year," predicted Spike Lee about their upcoming collaboration, *Mo' Better Blues*. He wasn't. The writer-director hung around backstage to be interviewed on *Nightline* where he told Forrest Sawyer, "Universal tried as much as they could to get people to see the film. They can't put a gun to the Academy members' heads and make them see the film." Gene Siskel was on the same show and revealed that Jessica Tandy had confessed she hadn't seen Lee's movie. The stone-faced Lee rarely smiled, except when his fellow guest, Dennis Hopper, steamed over the omission of *Drugstore Cowboy,* argued, "I thought it was the best drug movie that I've ever seen."

Last year's Best Actress winner, Jodie Foster, was asked what winning meant. "Everything," said the actress, sporting a new red bob for her role in *The Silence of the Lambs*. "Best year I ever had." Things were not so rosy for this year's champion. "I'm out of work and there's nothing on the horizon," said Jessica Tandy, and *Variety* worried, "There aren't a lot of parts for senior citizens. If people complain that there are no parts for women in their forties, what about women in their eighties?" Tandy had not enjoyed her status as a shoo-in, saying, "It worried me a great deal that everyone seemed to think that I was going to win because I would think that would put a jinx on it . . . I think maybe they gave it to me because I'm the oldest." It was established that she was six months older than the previous age record-holder, George Burns, also eighty. "Well, good for me," she reacted. "I'm lucky they trusted me with such a part; they could have given it to someone with more experience."

A victor who had not been a sure thing, Daniel Day-Lewis, described his feelings when his name was called. "I suppose it's the sort of reaction that you have when you're involved in a major road accident except that the benefit was somewhat more pleasurable," he philosophized. "But you've won every award in the book for this part," squealed *Entertainment Tonight*'s Leeza Gibbons. "Well, this isn't just any award." When somebody suggested that his role should have been played by an actual disabled actor, Day-Lewis replied, "I can't disagree with that, but the film wouldn't have been made with a disabled actor mainly because of the hypocrisy of the industry." Of his post-Oscar plans, Day-Lewis said, "I'm going to spend a few months just sitting and looking at it."

After playfully grabbing Day-Lewis' crotch for photographers, Brenda Fricker admitted she had aped Shelley Winters by gaining weight for the role. Remarking that she had bet $50 that Lena Olin would triumph, Fricker said, "I'm still

"*We know the first Oscar is gay. We're not sure about the new one.*"
—*Robert Epstein*

suffering from shock and disbelief. I don't even have a mantel to put this on. I'll have to buy a new home." Several weeks later she chatted with Joan Lunden when *Good Morning, America* did a show from Bath, England. "It's weird," was Fricker's evaluation of being an Academy Award winner. "I come down and the Oscar's still sitting on the table and I think, 'What's that doing in my house still?' "

The Governors' Ball was held under a tent in the Music Center's plaza, where guests dined on grilled veal chops with lemon soy sauce, served with wild rice pancakes and sesame seeds filled with shiitake mushrooms. There was one extra portion because, recounted the show's rabble-rouser, Kim Basinger, "A lot of people wouldn't get near me after the Oscars. I walked across to this Governors' Ball and walked out and went home back to the hotel. No parties, no Spago." Anjelica Huston and Jerry Brown moved on to a fund-raiser for the AIDS Hospice Foundation at the Directors Guild. A spokesperson told the *Los Angeles Times* that the organization hadn't done too much publicity for the fete because "since it was our first one, we didn't want to oversell." It still managed to net $85,000. Huston and Brown also popped up at El Rescate's third Oscar night benefit for Central American refugees, hosted by Esai Morales and last year's Actor nominee Edward James Olmos at the Mondrian Hotel. Jackson Browne and Dr. John performed and guests were also entertained by video images of families carrying child-size coffins in El Salvador on panels of monitors. This party made $90,000 and drew Jodie Foster, Oliver Stone, Billy Crystal, Jane Fonda and Ted Turner, and last year's Oscar show participant, Rob Lowe. In a replay from last year, fire marshals doused some party plans, preventing sixty-five would-be revelers in a line outside from entering. Inside the Mondrian someone joked to the *L.A. Weekly* that with Irving Lazar's guests including the likes of Gene Kelly, James Stewart, and Raquel Welch, the "A-List" at Spago stood for "Ancient."

Perhaps it was the promise of chocolate Oscar-shaped lollipops that brought an overflowing mob to Spago, where *People* testified, "Warren Beatty (sans Madonna) sneaked in through the back door with Jack Nicholson and flirted with Richard Gere's heartthrob, model Cindy Crawford (she appeared flattered but maintained her distance)." Paparazzi got the shot they were looking for when Anjelica Huston, making the rounds with Brown, showed up and chatted with Nicholson. "We were talking about the Oscars." Nicholson reassured *WWD,* "I didn't tell her she should have won, because the losers make all the money. Remember that!" The fashion paper noted "The party got better and better as big winners like producers Lili and Richard Zanuck . . . Denzel Washington and Oliver Stone arrived." A few hours later, Stone hopped a helicopter before dawn to shoot an acid sequence for his new movie *The Doors* in an Arizona desert.

Party regular Michael Caine described the Spago crowd to *Good Morning, America*'s Chantal: "They are nice people who all know each other. All the nasty people we leave behind tonight. Only the good people come." If that was the case, members of the disabled community might have wondered what Joan Collins was doing there. Collins had gushed to an interviewer from KABC-TV, "I'm thrilled about Daniel Day-Lewis . . . for somebody that is as good-looking as he is to make himself look as ugly as he is in every way is . . . a total work of art." Organizations for the disabled thought Collins was a piece of work herself and Marta Russell of the Media Access Office wrote her, "We hope you understand that a human being with cerebral palsy would take offense being characterized as 'ugly.' " A letter to the *Hollywood Reporter* indicated that disabled persons "protest Joan Collins' insidious remark and challenge her to a higher level of consciousness."

The Academy was given a similar challenge over two of the show's jokes. Steve Martin's wisecrack about Malaysia led to that country's canceling its planned rebroadcast of the ceremony. Even worse, Billy Crystal's joke about the MGM's Leo

"I'm lucky that my grandmother was such a terrible driver."
—Alfred Uhry

the Lion taking the Fifth brought angry wires from three Italian-American groups. Limousine mogul and George Steinbrenner–confidante William Fugazy of the Coalition of Italo-American Foundation charged that the line was "insensitive and inane . . . the audience clearly rebelled against Crystal's prejudicial remarks"; the National Italian-American Foundation called it "a cheap-shot joke against Italian-Americans"; and Vincent Romano of the Commission for Social Justice, a wing of the Order of Sons of Italy, seethed, "Italian-Americans are constantly portrayed as bums, bigots, or buffoons." Two days later, fifty-two Congressmen wrote Karl Malden to say Crystal "soiled the reputations of the thirty-eight members of the United States Congress who are descended from Italian parents and grandparents as well as twenty-six million citizens of Italian heritage who live throughout this free and loving land." The Congressional leaders demanded an apology "to those who were defamed and affronted by this racist, meanly offered sick joke. If that apology is not forthcoming, we pledge you that millions of Americans will neither forget nor forgive this painful breach."

Billy Crystal ducked reporters by going on vacation. President Malden didn't get off so easily. At first he refused to placate the furious voices, calling the protestors "awfully thin-skinned." A week later, he changed his tune and went on TV to say halfheartedly, "If they want an apology, I will apologize if that's what they want. But I don't think there's anything to apologize for."

Most reviewers gave show producer Cates and company high marks. "The movie industry breathed a huge collective sigh of relief Monday night," reported *Variety* on its front page, ". . . there were off-beat winners and off-color humor." Kay Gardella in the *New York Daily News* called the show "a distinct improvement over last year's." As to the three-hour-thirty-seven-minute running time, Gilbert Cates shrugged, "Well, there were four or five standing ovations for starters and at about forty-five seconds each, that's four minutes right there." *The Hollywood Reporter* let it be known that the show could have been even longer had a computer not warned the Academy the show was running late, prompting them to cut Meg Ryan's fake orgasm scene in *When Harry Met Sally* . . . redubbed into four languages. No one cared much for the around-the-world bit; the *Los Angeles Daily News* felt "The remote segments were about as special as Minicam reports on the local news." Paula Abdul's dances were also roundly criticized—*USA Today* said that the *Little Mermaid* number "made you wish for a clip from the cartoon"—but she still ended up winning an Emmy for Best Choreography. Other than the Italian groups, the majority of observers lauded the emcee. "Thank God for Billy Crystal—and that's all I'm going to say about that," penned columnist Suzy. When she interviewed him months later on one of her shows, Barbara Walters began with, "Billy Crystal, oh, he's probably had the best year of his life."

The off-Broadway production of *Driving Miss Daisy* began advertising, "It all started here," but others wanted to know what hath *Daisy* wrought. While *Jet* was upset that Morgan Freeman lost, labeling the snub "a tradition of passing over black actors for the coveted 'Best Actor' Oscar," David Denby in *New York* magazine argued the Best Picture winner was "a dream whose innocence and charm cannot conceal that the white character has all the power . . . This movie provides an image of a black man . . . that a white audience can feel comfortable with. For many whites, it may be the only kind of relationship with blacks that they can feel at ease with." Fresh from the *Do the Right Thing* soundtrack, rap group Public Enemy's new album included a song "Burn, Hollywood, Burn" containing a sarcastic reference to "Miss Daisy." *Do the Right Thing*'s losing Supporting Actor nominee did at last receive one honor—two days after the Awards, Le Dufy Hotel in West Hollywood served as their "Celebrity Recipe of the Day" Lentils à la Danny Aiello.

"Miss Daisy" herself, Jessica Tandy, was

"We're dating, that's obvious, and we're having a good time."
—Ted Turner on Jane Fonda

treated with kid gloves. Janet Maslin decreed her "the evening's most beautiful presence," and, on the *Tonight Show,* Jay Leno joked about her range in *Miss Daisy:* "Jessica Tandy ages from age sixty-seven to ninety. The last time an actress aged that quickly was when the judge made Zsa Zsa Gabor put her real age on her driver's license." Jessica was quickly added as a prize at a "Fantasy Auction" at Sotheby's in New York; the highest bidder would "drive with Miss Daisy" in a limo tour with the actress capped off by dinner at the Palm Court of the Plaza Hotel. When Dotson Rader caught up with the Cronyns that summer for a glowing portrait in *Parade* entitled "What's Their Secret?", he observed Jessica taking Hume's hand and saying to him, "I have been aware of the fact, wherever we are, of suddenly telling you that I am happy. Not for any specific reason . . . I love you and I'm happy to greet the day and be with you. When you're young, you don't think that, because you take it for granted. Oh, it's so wonderful to be able to feel that now!"

1990

"It's important for me to win . . . because it's not been done since 1939."
—Whoopi Goldberg

The 1990 Oscars ended up on the wrong side of the law.

Disney's Whore

Writer J. F. Lawton's script *3000* was a bleak tale of a wealthy man who hires a drug-addicted prostitute for a week and then tosses her back on the streets of Hollywood. The author described his theme as "The idea that men would rather buy women than respect them." That all changed when the people at Disney got their hands on the screenplay. Originally, the studio merely wanted an upbeat ending, with a reformed heroine opening up a day-care center, but then, following the dictates of the self-declared "romantic and sentimentalist" director Garry Marshall, a slew of writers refashioned the story into a variation of Cinderella; the streetwalker now has a proverbial heart of gold, is shown the finer things in life, and ends up with a filthy rich husband. Author Lawton shrugged about the enterprise, "When you sell a script, it's theirs. You've got to accept what happens to it."

Julia Roberts read *3000* and loved "this dark and dingy story." When she later saw it sweetened into a romantic comedy now called *Pretty Woman*, she admitted, "it was a real mind twist." Still, Roberts tried out for, and won, the role of the prostitute, and Richard Gere, who himself had played a hustler a decade earlier in *American Gigolo*, was cast as Prince Charming. Rewrites continued through shooting and Roberts recalled, "We had this writer on the set—his name was Marty—and Garry would always say, 'Marty, come up with something funny for this.' And this poor guy would be running around with eight different lines."

Pretty Woman opened a week before Roberts lost the Supporting Actress Oscar for *Steel Magnolias* and her reviews were rapturous. Janet Maslin of the *New York Times* wrote that the twenty-two-year-old actress with her wide-mouthed smile "is so enchantingly beautiful, so funny, so natural and such an absolute delight that it is hard to hold anything against the movie." "She's got 'It,' whatever 'It' is in 1990," Andrew Sarris rhapsodized in the *New York Observer,* and if that intangible wasn't enough, "she demonstrates a Chekovian flair for mingling farce and pathos with force and panache." The public was equally hooked on her hooker, and *Pretty Women* dominated box-office charts for months, giving Hollywood a chance to dream of new markets of revenue—female moviegoers. Roberts' triumph was cinched when the exhibitors' poll of the year's top ten box-office stars placed her as number two on the list, behind only Arnold Schwarzenegger; the last woman to finish so high was Barbra Streisand back in 1977.

Tricky Dick

Disney was also banking on Warren Beatty to have mass appeal. A new film adaptation of the *Dick Tracy* comic strip had been kicking around Hollywood since the mid-1970s, at one point being rumored as a directorial debut for Diane Keaton. In 1985, Paramount greenlighted the production to star Beatty with Martin Scorsese directing. When that fell through, Beatty, who had been a childhood fan of the cartoon dick, eventually struck a deal with Disney that gave him $9 million to produce, direct, write, act, and have final cut. As usual on a Beatty film, tabloids followed his offscreen romantic involvements with the leading lady, in this case, Madonna, who was hoping that playing a character named Breathless Mahoney would finally jump-start her moribund film career. When presented with the songs

Kathy Bates boldly shows Jeremy Irons her mini-Oscar good-luck charm, thus risking a suit by the Academy for copyright infringement.

"*What is this highbrow shit?*"
—*Madonna*

Stephen Sondheim had written for her, she had her doubts, recalling, "I totally rejected them at first. I said, 'What is this highbrow shit?' "

While *Dick Tracy* was still in production, *Batman* opened and Disney executives began salivating as they gazed upon the scads of money being pulled in by that cinematic comic book adaptation and its even more profitable merchandising items. Disney planned accordingly. Among the Dick Tracy products poised for purchase were two-way wrist radios, yellow fedoras, and $300 silk pajamas. *Variety* had ill tidings for the studio, however, quoting a toy executive whose market research convinced him not to buy licensing rights: "None of the kids knew who Dick Tracy was." The trade paper also noted that a year ago the ubiquitous Batman symbol "became so hip that kids shaved it into their heads and absorbed it into their psyches." Despite Disney's splattering a silhouette of Beatty all over the place, "there are no indications that the Tracy logo will follow Batman's lead of becoming a fashionable summer scalp design."

Beatty said he wanted to "recapture my point of view at the age of six or seven when I was really interested in the strip . . . I began to get interested in that childlike feeling about the thrill of bright, primary colors." To this end, production designer Richard Sylbert and costume designer Milena Canonero limited themselves to the seven bright colors used by cartoonist Chester Gould in the original strip. "I never shot on a back lot in my life—44 pictures," sighed Sylbert. "It's rat poison, but we had to do it." Eleanor Ringel of the *Atlanta Journal-Constitution* described the film's design as "Batman Lite . . . It's a rainbow-splashed underworld, situated somewhere between Bertolt Brecht and 'Toontown."

Although Howie Movshovitz of the *Denver Post* applauded that *Dick Tracy* was "coherent and joyful, and it takes you into a world that's a gas to visit," Stanley Kauffman surmised in *The New Republic,* "It must have been fun to make it . . . for the viewer, there's much less fun" and *People* declared that Beatty looked "jowly and wan." James Caan and Dustin Hoffman had cameos as heavies but the villain with the most screen time was Al Pacino as the hunchbacked Big Boy Caprice; Pacino was a replacement for Beatty's *Bonnie and Clyde* cohort, Gene Hackman, who had suffered a heart attack. "It's the first real comedic part I've ever had on screen," Pacino rejoiced to *Premiere*. *Entertainment Weekly*'s Owen Gleiberman noted that "Pacino's abrasive scenery chewing gives the picture a jolt of energy. Still there's not much charm to this ranting performance." Almost everyone was thrilled by the prosthetics that brought to life such bizarre-looking bad guys as "Flat Top" and "Little Face," but even this feeling was not unanimous. Carped Andrew Sarris, "The old comic strip concentrated on one glandularly disturbed villain for each episode. When you see them all in one room, you feel as if you are trapped in a hospital burn unit."

Disney may have felt burned, too. *Dick Tracy*'s opening weekend grosses were half of *Batman*'s and on Monday the company's stock tumbled $4.625 a share. The film did eventually lumber its way to the $100 million mark and turned a profit but, as *Premiere* put it, "the *Batman*-style marketing was a dismal flop. (Want to buy a Dick Tracy T-shirt, cheap?)."

Whoopi Cranks It Up

To the surprise of industry analysts, the summer's biggest blockbuster was not a sequel, an action film, or a Tom Cruise vehicle but an improbable love story about a murdered yuppie whose spirit comes back to earth to save his girlfriend from the killer. Screenwriter Bruce Joel Rubin began pitching the mystical love story *Ghost* in 1984, finally selling it to Paramount which, to Rubin's horror, assigned Jerry Zucker of *Airplane!* fame as director. To Rubin's delight, he and Zucker hit it off and they went to work on the casting. After a number of leading men turned down the title character, Rubin suggested Patrick Swayze because "he broke down and cried on a

"Ghost isn't awful enough to be a great trash movie, but it often comes close."
—Julie Salamon

Barbara Walters interview." Demi Moore played his common-law widow, a downtown Manhattan loft-dweller, but finding the psychic through whom the spirit returns was tougher. After six months of looking for an unknown, Zucker finally offered Whoopi Goldberg the job. She could use it, because after her Oscar nomination for *The Color Purple* in 1985, her career consisted of flop after flop. *Premiere* had so little faith in the movie that in making its predictions of the summer releases the magazine listed it as a likely also-ran, along with the likes of *Ducktales the Movie* and *The Exorcist III*.

Paramount publicists had been spending most of their energy promoting the Tom Cruise disappointment *Days of Thunder* but when they got around to *Ghost* they shelled out $75,000 to mount billboards with a picture of Swayze and Moore in a perfume ad–style embrace, embued with an otherworldly blue light and the simple tag line: "Believe." The studio also delivered little bottles of champagne to women's magazine editors after buying ad space from them. Most critics remained infidels. Terrence Rafferty of *The New Yorker* sneered that "there's not a trace of wit or irony in it," and the *Wall Street Journal*'s Julie Salamon scoffed "*Ghost* isn't awful enough to be a great trash movie, but it often comes close."

Labeling the supernatural tearjerker "modest," David Bartholomew of *Film Journal* nevertheless pinpointed its popularity by calling *Ghost* "an ideal date movie." The film's target audience of young women dragged their boyfriends to it and the movie made more money its second weekend than its first. The love story used the Righteous Brothers' rendition of 1955 Best Song nominee "Unchained Melody" as a theme song, and the record was back on the charts twenty-five years after they recorded it; due to a scene in which Swayze and Moore use clay as a sexual aid, enrollment for pottery classes zoomed. The three stars received career lifts, especially Whoopi Goldberg for providing comic relief amid the suds. Duane Byrge of the *Hollywood Reporter* wrote, "It's one of the best kook parts in recent years and Goldberg cranks it up. Chanting, chaffing, crabbing—she's a hoot." Amy Taubin of the *Village Voice* theorized that Paramount had Disney to thank for *Ghost*'s success because *Pretty Woman* "primed audiences to want more girls and boys gazing into each other's eyes and making emotional commitment." *Ghost* went on to beat out *Pretty Woman* as the top grossing movie of the year.

That Old Gang of Mine

The critics were more interested in *GoodFellas*, earning Martin Scorsese his best reviews since *Raging Bull* a decade earlier. Chronicling the life and times of the real-life and still-living Henry Hill, a Brooklyn kid who spent twenty-five years in the Mafia before turning government witness, *GoodFellas* was described by its director as "a mob home movie." Scorsese had known gangsters first hand from his Little Italy childhood but his memories were not fond. "It's like my mother says, 'They're bloodsuckers,'" he explained, reminiscing that "As a little boy I remember waiting a long time for a haircut, and then this flashy guy just walked in and sat down when it was my turn."

Although Scorsese felt that *GoodFellas* was "a morality play like most of my movies," Valley residents attending a sneak preview in Sherman Oaks didn't see it that way. "People got so angry that they stormed out of the theater," recalled Scorsese. "They thought it was an outrage that I made these people so attractive." The director maintained that "I wanted the audience to feel it was hanging out with these guys in a bar." He was also bracing himself for brickbats from his fellow Italian-Americans but hoped they'd "understand that it's time that we can really talk openly about this aspect of being Italian-American, not have it idealized or mythologized, or shown as comedy. I'm just trying to show it straight—with all its attraction and all its horror."

In the *New York Times*, Vincent Canby called *GoodFellas* "both the most politically serious and

"It's like my mother says, 'They're bloodsuckers.'"
—Martin Scorsese

most evilly entertaining movie yet made about organized crime," and Shelia Benson of the *Los Angeles Times* marveled, "To see an artist working at the peak of his power, everything extraneous stripped away, every element there for a purpose, is an extraordinary exhilaration." *GoodFellas* marked Robert De Niro's sixth appearance in a Scorsese picture, but critical attention centered on two names lower down in the credits. Joe Pesci reunited with his *Raging Bull* director to create a particularly psychotic gang member in what *New York*'s David Denby called "an astounding performance." Pesci allowed that it was sometimes hard for him to get under the skin of his demented character, especially when he shoots a teenager over a trivial slight. To justify the act, the actor explained, "I told myself that the kid would have grown up to be a rat anyway." The cokehead Mrs. Henry Hill was played by Lorraine Bracco, the wife of Scorsese regular Harvey Keitel, and she had Pauline Kael cheering, "She has a hot, bright vitality." Academy member Kaye Ballard told *Entertainment Weekly* she was nominating Scorsese's mother Catherine for her bit as psycho Pesci's adoring mother. Henry Hill himself, now with a different identity under the Federal Witness Protection Program, credited Scorsese's work, saying, "Had I the opportunity to direct the movie myself—if I knew anything about directing—I don't think I could have done a better job."

Scorsese and company did take a few critical hits. Tom Carson of the *L.A. Weekly* felt that Pesci "behaves as if moments before each scene was shot, some prankster whispered in his ear that this role could make him a star—and every second he's up there, he's acting the bejezus out of it." Andrew Sarris confessed that "I have encountered a few gangsters in my salad days . . . but I never felt the slightest twinge of involvement with the relentlessly mediocre hoods in *GoodFellas*." Bruce Cutler, mouthpiece for New York crime boss John Gotti, alleged that *GoodFellas* was "a government propaganda movie. It makes a hero out of paid government witnesses, pokes fun at everybody in the movie, trivializes terrible acts of violence." Asked if Gotti had seen the film, his lawyer asserted, "He is too intelligent to waste his time to see nonsensical movies like that."

Immaculate Marty

In addition to directing *GoodFellas*, Scorsese was trying his hand as a producer with an adaptation of *The Grifters*, a 1963 novel by the late, *roman noir* cult writer Jim Thompson. To film the downbeat tale of three small-time bunko artists—a young man, his new girlfriend, and the teenaged mother who had abandoned him at birth—Scorsese chose Englishman Stephen Frears of 1988's *Dangerous Liaisons*, who was thrilled to be filming in Los Angeles. Frears explained to the *Village Voice*, "I've kind of run out of steam about Britain. It's so narrow and the British establishment is so depressing." Elaborating on the contrast between his homeland and the States, Frears said, "In England, because everything is a secret, you are attracted to secrecy. Here it's so open I'll tell anyone anything." A pause. "But that can't be true because you still don't know who killed Kennedy."

Frears approached Anjelica Huston about playing the tough-as-nails mother, but while she was mulling it over, he called her back to say sorry, he was going with Melanie Griffith, a decision he later described as "foolish!" Because of the book's incestuous overtones—the two women are look-alikes—Frears and Scorsese chose Annette Bening (who had played the Glenn Close part in the Milos Forman version of *Les Liaisons Dangereuses*) to tangle with Griffith, with John Cusack rounding out the cast. Shortly thereafter, Griffith left the project and Frears sent the script to Huston, whom he described as "a very strong woman who can look at terrible things with strength and grace." She was amused when she took a gander at the director and producer at a meeting at West Hollywood's Chateau Marmont: "They were a very funny pair. Marty was immaculately dressed, the tie in the right place and speaking incredibly fast. And Stephen, on the other hand, his hair was sticking up; he was barefoot and he looked like he had just rolled out of bed." Huston signed on and there was some thought given to Cher taking over Bening's part, but Frears decided body types be damned. Producer Scorsese also did the voice-over narration at the beginning of the film.

Two other Jim Thompson adaptations had failed to cause a stir earlier in the year, so to make this one seem special, distributor Miramax opened *The Grifters* in Los Angeles and New York for one week only "For Academy Award Consideration." The majority of critics thought it merited such consideration. *Newsday*'s Gene Seymour wrote, "This is definitive, hard-bop storytelling; it's low-grade feverish tone is sustained throughout by the cool precision of its craftsmanship . . . You give a taut, complex and somewhat kinky script to director Stephen Frears and you get shrewd social history wrapped in melodrama." The *Hollywood Reporter* warned that "Frears uncovers the seamy underbelly of L.A. in a way that makes *Chinatown* look like Mayberry."

Pauline Kael wrote of the peroxided Anjelica Huston: "She's overpoweringly sexual; young men might find her frightening." In *Rolling Stone*, Peter Travers, citing her earlier 1990 performance as a horrible hag in Nicolas Roeg's children's film, *The Witches*, scribbled that Huston "confirms her position as the most exciting actress now working in movies. Meryl Streep gets the press, but it's Huston—in film after film, in large roles and small—who keeps astounding us." A drawback to the spotlight was that the actress once again had to field questions about Jack Nicholson. When one reporter asked if she and Nicholson were now friends, Huston thought for a while and said, "I think the word 'friendship' sort of implies a happy and concrete communication. And I wouldn't use 'friendship' as an appellation for the last year, certainly."

Annette Bening, too, came in for her share of appreciation. Jami Bernard of the *New York Post* declared, "Bening is shaping up as quite a tidbit" and Kathleen Carroll, scabbing at the *New York Daily News* while her fellow writers were out on strike, predicted that the actress is "such a saucy vamp, the role could be her ticket to stardom."

Shirley Does Debbie

Bening had also played a tiny part as an actress in Mike Nichols' latest, *Postcards from the Edge*, an adaptation of the novel by a child of Hollywood, Carrie Fisher, who wrote the script herself. Meryl Streep played the troubled daughter of a famous movie star, portrayed by Shirley MacLaine, and Nichols demanded such realism that interiors of MacLaine's home were shot in the Hollywood residence of Eddie Fisher's third wife, Connie Stevens. Looking forward to her first L.A. work experience, Streep said, "I've never made one before in Hollywood; I've only been out there for the Academy Awards and stuff like that." It was worth it, said the transplanted Connecticut resident, to have a chance with Fisher's dialogue, "a stylish, verbal thing, you know, it just really cackles." MacLaine was more hesitant, checking first with Carrie's mom, Debbie Reynolds, to make sure there would be no hard feelings for her portrait of a megalomaniac. Stanley Kauffmann raved, "Shirley MacLaine gives an even more vivid performance of the devoted-competitive mother than she did in *Terms of Endearment.*" *Time*'s Richard Corliss dipped back to the '30s for a comparison for Streep: "like the late Irene Dunne, she adds spin and sizzle to every *bon mot.*" Even *Premiere*'s "Libby Gelman-Waxner" enjoyed Streep doing comedy. "It's like watching Queen Elizabeth get tipsy on wine coolers at a royal picnic." Columnist Marilyn Beck didn't have much fun, though; she was too busy being incensed over "scenes of drug abuse that drew howls of laughter from the industry crowd with whom I screened the movie. A sad commentary on the business—and too many people in it."

"Is there a heaven or a hell?"
—Jeremy Irons

High Society

Like Scorsese, director Oliver Stone expanded his operations by linking up with frequent colleague Edward S. Pressman (*The Hand, Wall Street*) to produce *Reversal of Fortune*, based on lawyer Allan Dershowitz's book about overturning the attempted murder conviction of Claus van Bulow. Also like Scorsese, Stone and Pressman hired a non-American to direct: the Iranian-born, South American–raised, French resident with Swiss and German parents, Barbet Schroeder, whose offbeat portfolio ranged from taking a blistering look at the Ugandan dictator in the documentary *Idi Amin Dada* to letting Faye Dunaway loose on Skid Row in *Barfly*. Playing the blue-blooded-fashion-plate-turned-vegetable Sunny von Bulow was Glenn Close, who talked a former Broadway costar into taking second billing and playing opposite her as the inscrutable European twice accused of attempted murder. Jeremy Irons, who had proven adept at humanizing unsavory characters in *Dead Ringers*, refrained from meeting the real von Bulow, but he did consult with friends and acquaintances of the socialite and got additional pointers by watching his TV appearances with Phil Donahue and Barbara Walters. Actors' Equity President Ron Silver played his legal saviour, the Harvard-based Dershowitz.

Screenwriter Nicholas Kazan (son of Elia) described his adaptation as "a legal detective story. I was attempting to do for the appeals process what *All the President's Men* did for investigative journalism." Although the film did detail Dershowitz's painstaking work on the case, by the time Schroeder was through, the story had turned into what *New York*'s David Denby deemed "perhaps the most potent screen satire of the upper class since *Citizen Kane.*" Tom Carson of the *L.A. Weekly* called the film "an elegant, brazen, maliciously funny black comedy," and the director said he was "very flattered" that the critics got the joke because transforming a true-life tragedy into something droll was, contrary to expectations, "my ambition from the beginning. I thought it was some kind of very strange, weird comedy." William Norwich, the *Daily News'* Boswell of New York's upper crust, had a laugh at the production designer's expense. "I was amused," he tattled, during a scene in which Sunny's two children are watching television. "They sit on an ottoman, like little princely people in a Velasquez painting." Norwich had been to the Newport estate and "grand as Clarendon Court was, there were soft, comfortable chairs for watching TV, and the children slouched just like you and I."

As for Irons' version of von Bulow, the *L.A. Weekly*'s Carson chortled that he "suggests Boris Karloff playing Cary Grant." Calling it "a brilliant comic performance," Dave Kehr wrote in the *Chicago Tribune* that "Irons' von Bulow is easily the most attractive and entertaining movie heavy since James Mason's villain in *North by Northwest.*" Alan Dershowitz's verdict was "Irons is a better Claus von Bulow than Claus von Bulow." The actor was on record as saying he thought von Bulow was innocent, but when the Associated Press posed that question, he turned philosophical, responding, "Is there a heaven or a hell? The sad thing is we don't know." Rex Reed, however, was not afraid to give his opinion of von Bulow, adding as an aside to his review of *Reversal of Fortune:* "There's no question that Claus was a sick sister."

Costner's Revenge

A more traditional screen hero was Kevin Coster, who was also branching out as the mogul behind two productions. First up was *Revenge*, a melodrama in which he matched wits with drug kingpin/cuckolded husband Anthony Quinn. The movie received atrocious reviews ("lethally boring"—David Denby) and died at the box office, putting an end to the perception that Costner was infallible. The star had somehow convinced financially shaky Orion to distribute his next movie, about a U.S. Cavalry officer who deserts the Army to live with an Indian tribe. Not only was

"That's the way we used to make them."
—Ronald Reagan

Costner's project a western—a genre that had been *outré* for years—but he promised it would be lengthy, would feature no other stars, would concentrate on a realistic depiction of Native American culture and have the enigmatic title *Dances with Wolves*. Plus a good chunk of it wouldn't even be in English, but in Lakota Sioux with subtitles. And he wanted final cut. Costner was willing to bow to Hollywood convention in two respects: the film would include a love story involving a white woman who conveniently happened to be adopted by the tribe already and would have Costner's customary nude scene.

When filming started to go over schedule and Costner sank $2 million of his salary back into the project, Hollywood wags began referring to the project as "Kevin's Gate" and "Costner's Last Stand" and the rest of the industry shook their heads that he had turned down *The Hunt for Red October* and *Bonfire of the Vanities* for *this*. Whatever self-doubts Costner may have held about directing quickly dissipated. "I knew I had it the first day I saw dailies," he said. "I was really happy. I thought, "Yeah, I can do this." When studio executives finally got a look at the three-hour movie, they weren't so sure; according to *Entertainment Weekly*, their reaction was "an awkward silence." Things continued to go abysmally when *Dances with Wolves* had its glitzy premiere at a Washington, D.C., benefit for the Smithsonian Institute's Museum of the American Indian; first the projector broke down and then the projectionist put the reels on out of order.

Orion gamely went ahead and opened the movie in eight cities, taking artistic control over one aspect of the film. Although Costner appears onscreen with a mustache, studio publicists thought he was much more attractive clean-shaven, so the facial hair was shorn for print ads. "You make compromises," the coproducer-actor-director acknowledged grimly. "A wistful, poignant and entertaining movie, a loving look at a way of life and a people that have all but disappeared," praised the *San Francisco Chronicle* while Roger Ebert declared, "The movie is a simple story, magnificently told. It has the sweep and clarity of a western by John Ford." The *Hollywood Reporter*'s Duane Byrge also mentioned the director of *Fort Apache* and *She Wore a Yellow Ribbon:* "*Dances with Wolves* de-mythologies Ford and other western makers' blarney of the murderous nature of the Indians and the John Wayne round-'em-up mentality."

Others thought Costner had plenty of blarney of his own. "Goofy and even simpleminded," opined the *L.A. Reader*'s Henry Sheehan, while J. Hoberman of the *Village Voice* denigrated the film as a "grade school fantasy . . . like a multipart series from *The Wonderful World of Disney*." Critics also poked fun at the New Age consciousness of Costner's character who, snorted *Time*'s Richard Schickel, came across as a "1990s Yuppie who suddenly decides to take his Sierra Club membership seriously." Just starting out in his career as a film critic, ex-Gotham Mayor Ed Koch was also acerbic, dismissing the epic as "a fairy tale for children." The most devastating comments, though, came from Pauline Kael, who would soon retire after twenty-four years at *The New Yorker*. To wit: "Costner has feathers in his hair and feathers in his head" and "This epic was made by a bland megalomaniac (The Indians should have named him Plays with Camera)."

Orion executives could have been knocked over with a feather when *Dances with Wolves* started a stampede to cinemas, soon raking in over $100 million. Equally surprising was the way it appealed to all segments of the public: Costner was inducted into both the Sioux nation *and* the National Cowboy Hall of Fame. Previous Cowboy honoree Ronald Reagan, whom Costner treated to a birthday screening, was also a staunch fan. "That's the way we used to make them," approved the ex-President, forgetting that he usually shot and killed Indians onscreen.

Kansas City Confidential

It had taken four years for *Dances with Wolves* to go from a vision that writer Michael Blake got

"Don't write a script, it'll just end up in a pile."
—Kevin Costner

"while sitting around Kevin and Cindy's house" to a screenplay. There had been a novel in between because Costner had sagely advised, "Don't write a script, it'll just end up in a pile. Write a book first." Joanne Woodward had to wait much longer to realize her dream of a film version of *Mrs. Bridge*, Evan S. Connell's account of an upper-middle-class Kansas City WASP family in the 1930s and '40s—she had been ready to go ever since the book's publication in 1959. While having dinner with them, Woodward learned that Ismail Merchant and James Ivory were also admirers of the novel and its 1969 follow-up *Mr. Bridge*. The actress told the two partners that if they got film rights to the books she'd be willing to slash her salary to star. Woodward hadn't made a film in several years but her husband was also at dinner and said if he liked the script, they could count him in, too. Because the Newmans treated the picture as a charity case, Merchant and Ivory were able to lop off $5 million from the budget and pulled it off for $7.5 million.

Paul Newman seemed to expect some audiences to have difficulty with the movie. "You could describe the story as being about absolutely nothing," he admitted to the *New York Times*, "but it really is about absolutely everything . . . about life and love and the family." Jami Bernard of the *New York Post* was not alone in describing the leisurely, anecdotal family album as "a snooze." A more sympathetic voice could be heard across the sea. "What Hollywood likes nowadays is the perversely named 'high concept movie.' That is, a film that can be summed up in a single, simple sentence, in which the only difficult word permitted is Schwarzenegger," noted Philip French of the *London Observer*, saying of *Mr. and Mrs. Bridge*, "this funny and moving film is . . . at least the equal of Bergman's *Scenes from a Marriage*." Kathleen Carroll thought "It would be proper and fitting if both Mr. and Mrs. Newman won Oscars." That outcome would serve to reward the pair for having, like many others before them, acclimated themselves to Merchant-Ivory's penurious ways. "The film is very tough," Woodward told the *New York Times*, adding that at the end of one fourteen-hour day, rather than attending a production party, "I got into the tub with a glass of sherry and two Advils."

Daddy's Little Girl

Another family saga was the budgetary antithesis of the Newmans'. For years, talk of a third installment in *The Godfather* series had persisted despite director Francis Coppola's steady professions of disinterest. "I had deliberately left Michael for dead," the director had said. "I never thought to visit him again." Paramount chairman Frank Mancuso offered Coppola creative carte blanche to revisit the Corleones with a sort of Mafioso version of *King Lear*. That artistic freedom, combined with a $5 million base salary plus fifteen percent of the gross, eventually swayed the director, whose finances and reputation had both been in shambles. "I'm very embarrassed about my career over the last ten years," admitted the auteur of *One from the Heart* and *Rumble Fish*.

From the beginning, there were setbacks. Coppola wanted six months to work on the script with Mario Puzo; the studio gave them six weeks. Then Coppola lost a main character when Robert Duvall refused to reprise his role of family *consigliere* Tom Hagan, protesting, "I did not think it was fair that they offered the lead actor four-and-a-half times to five times as much as they offered me." Frantic rewrites followed. Emphasis was directed toward Pacino's screen daughter, a smart beauty to be played by Winona Ryder. Filming had not been going on for a month, when the studio, worried that the director was up to his old profligate ways, replaced his line producer with a company man to hold him in check. But worst of all, when Winona Ryder arrived in Rome straight from a grueling shoot on Cher's Oscar follow-up, *Mermaids*, she claimed she was suffering from exhaustion. A doctor took a look at her and agreed, sending her packing. Spending Christmas break on the set in Italy, Coppola's daughter Sofia, nineteen, was about to step into the shower

"I did not think it was fair that they offered the lead actor four-and-a-half times to five times as much as they offered me."
—Robert Duvall

at her hotel when a production assistant got ahold of her to say she was stepping into Winona's role. "Very weird day," recollected Sofia. It was strange over at Paramount, too, where executives were reportedly "shocked" by the sudden switch; even costars Al Pacino and Coppola's sister Talia Shire tried to talk Francis out of it. Coppola had his way and Aunt Talia maintained that the studio should be grateful to her niece: "Francis couldn't wait. And by Sofia being there, he was able to keep himself very centered. So her contribution was enormous, not because of her performance, but because she helped keep the film going, kept it together." Commented costar George Hamilton, "They brought in a coach, they worked on her hair. They asked what I thought, I didn't know." But it wasn't as if Sofia had never acted onscreen before—she was the infant who is baptized at the end of the first *Godfather*.

All of these carryings-on piqued the press during the four-and-a-half month production and *Time* gossiped that the $44 million budget had ballooned to $100 million, although the official price tag from the *Wall Street Journal* was $55 million. Another worry was the movie's release date. It was bad enough that *GoodFellas* had already stolen some of the gangland thunder but now the studio fretted that the movie might not be finished in time for Oscar eligibility. While Coppola and crew feverishly sat in the editing room, Paramount gloomily pushed back the autumn release date. Studio executives breathed a sigh of relief when they announced that *The Godfather III* would be Paramount's Christmas day present to the world.

Death on Christmas Day

While calling *The Godfather Part III*, "definitely one of the best American movies of the year," Michael Wilmington of the *Los Angeles Times* said, "it's still a disappointment. It fails on the highest level. It's not the capstone we might have wanted Coppola to make, not quite a fitting climax." The *Village Voice*'s J. Hoberman thought that "Although the movie is not altogether superfluous, it can't help but suggest Mark Twain's forgotten *Tom Sawyer* sequels." But then Hoberman felt that all those people who considered the original *Godfathers* the best Hollywood movies since *Citizen Kane* guilty of "sloppy judgment," naming several more worthy claimants, among them *Detour*, *Kiss Me Deadly*, and *The Naked Kiss*.

In his third rendition of Michael Corleone, Al Pacino's reviews were as good as ever. This go around had the character old, sick, and trying to go legit and *Variety* raved, "Pacino is magnificent . . . more animated than he was going onto his deep freeze in *Part II*." Playing Pacino's illegitimate nephew by *Part I*'s long-gone James Caan, thirty-one-year-old Andy Garcia received the kind of star-is-born response that had greeted Pacino in the first picture. Calling him "sure and sexy," Janet Maslin cooed that Garcia's "high-voltage performance . . . not only insures him a bright future but suggests that the series may have one as well." In sharp contrast, Sofia Coppola received some of the most vicious critical condemnations to which any individual was ever subjected; John Simon's lacerations are simply too cruel to bear repeating. Despite her Valley Girl speech patterns, Sofia did find a few sympathetic critics including Pauline Kael who wrote, "I came to like her." Gary Franklin of KABC-TV in Los Angeles was also an admirer, calling Sofia's role "magnificently played" and on a later broadcast he excitedly read a telegram of thanks from her papa.

A New York City television station sent out a crew to interview people attending the movie's first Christmas Day showing; one man complained about the film's showcasing the Catholic Church's involvement with the Mafia and concluded, "It can't light a candle to the other two." *The Godfather Part III* then showed up again on the 11 o'clock news that night. In a Long Island movie house, the violence on the screen was eclipsed by that in the auditorium as gunfights broke out, leaving one young man dead and sev-

"I'm very embarrassed about my career over the last ten years."
—Francis Ford Coppola

eral others injured. Eerily, during the shooting of his film's climatic assassination scene in an opera house, Coppola had observed, "There's a long tradition of people getting killed in theaters."

In and Out of Bed

Two veterans from earlier *Godfather* films were also on view during the Christmas season. James Caan was on the receiving end as he played a bedridden writer held captive by a crazed admirer in *Misery.* Screenwriter William Goldman had adapted Stephen King's novel with Kathy Bates in mind for the looney lady and she was familiar with Stephen King's thriller. "A friend of mine handed me the book to read in New York and said, 'Hey, when they do the movie of this, you have to play Annie Wilkes,'' she recalled. With her film work limited to supporting roles in a few movies, including *Dick Tracy*, director Rob Reiner looked for a bigger name to smash Caan's legs, even though he admitted thinking, "Wow, Bates was just perfect." But Bette Midler, Reiner discovered, "was frightened that if she created this character then that is how people would start thinking about her and that would ruin her image." So Bates got the part and she was prepared. "I was fortunate to see a program about nurses who kill on Geraldo one afternoon," the actress said. "He's a great source for this stuff."

Most reviewers found Bates all there was to like in a movie that the *Village Voice*'s Georgia Brown wrote off as "instantly disposable." In the *L.A. Weekly*, John Powers said that "Bates' terrifically entertaining turn as Annie is the best reason to see this movie-with-the-soul-of-a-gizmo." The praise served to assuage the actress's dismay over losing the chance to repeat her award-winning role in the film adaptation of *Frankie and Johnny in the Claire de Lune.* Prior to the release of *Misery*, *Pretty Woman*'s Garry Marshall decided the role of a plain-looking coffee shop waitress would be better served by siren Michelle Pfeiffer. A year later, *Frankie and Johnny* opened and did less than half the business of *Misery.*

Meanwhile, "Meathead" Reiner's ex-wife and Garry Marshall's sister, "Laverne," Penny Marshall, was directing an Oscar winner from *The Godfather II.* For *Awakenings*, Robert De Niro was offered his choice of parts: a victim of sleeping sickness who, after nodding off for forty years, gets a wake-up call through an experimental drug, or the nebbishy doctor who administers it to him. The actor chose the former because, "I hate to use the word challenging but in some ways, that's what it was" and Robin Williams took the other role. A memoir by best-selling neurologist Dr. Oliver Sacks served as the basis of the movie, which for authenticity's sake, was filmed in a genuine Brooklyn psychiatric hospital. "It was weird," Williams recalled of the location shooting. "There was a guy always yelling 'Hey, Mork!' 'Hey, Laverne!' "

Kathleen Carroll found De Niro's Rip van Winkle "simply astounding" but the *Boston Globe* bitched, "oddly heartless . . . His performance is little more than two-plus hours of rigorous isometrics." Word on Williams ranged from "extraordinary" *(Variety)* to "egregiously ego-stroking" (Dave Kehr, *Chicago Tribune*). *Good Morning America*'s Joel Siegel gushed that *Awakenings* is "One of those rare and precious films that make you realize how wonderful it is just to be alive." *Village Voice* columnist Michael Musto, however, had so little patience for the movie's would-be affirmation of life that his year-end round-up had a sardonic list of "Fave Lines from The Crappy *Awakenings*" including "The human spirit is more powerful than any drug, and *that* is what needs to be nourished."

Hordes of Awards

The National Board of Review kicked off the Awards season by splitting its Best Actor prize between *Awakenings'* doctor and patient. "You can't separate the two. One cannot possibly have worked without the other," a Board spokesperson said of Robin Williams and Robert De Niro. The Board's real man of the hour, though, was Kevin Costner as *Dances with Wolves* won Best Picture and Best Director. Mia Farrow was named Best Actress as a bored housewife given magical powers in *Alice,* her latest turn with Woody Allen. The Supporting Awards went to Joe Pesci for *GoodFellas* and Winona Ryder as the troubled teen in *Mermaids*, the enervating movie that had paved the way for Sofia Coppola's big break.

The National Board may have whetted Costner's appetite, but he went hungry through the rest of the critics' awards. *GoodFellas* and Martin Scorsese swept in New York, Los Angeles, and at the National Society voting. Joanne Woodward in *Mr. and Mrs. Bridge* and Robert De Niro in both *GoodFellas* and *Awakenings* won lead acting honors in New York, and Jeremy Irons in *Reversal of Fortune* and Anjelica Huston in *The Grifters* and *The Witches* triumphed in the other two contests. Joe Pesci picked up a Supporting nod in L.A., but the New Yorkers and the Nationals annointed Bruce Davison in American Playhouse's *Longtime Companion.* "Heartbreaking and absolutely convincing," the *New Yorker*'s Terrence Rafferty wrote of Davison's performance as a gay man dealing with the AIDS plague, "a beautiful piece of acting." Supporting Actress honors were divided among Lorraine Bracco in *GoodFellas* (L.A.), Annette Bening in *The Grifters* (National), and Jennifer Jason Leigh (NY) who enacted prostitutes in two little-seen films, *Last Exit to Brooklyn* and *Miami Blues*.

Too Much Kevin

It was up to the Hollywood Foreign Press to get *Dances with Wolves* back on track. Although Kevin Costner lost Best Actor (Drama) to Jeremy Irons, he did receive a Golden Globe as Best Director and was able to see *Dances with Wolves* win Best Picture and Best Screenplay. Addressing the price of fame when accepting the Picture prize, Costner despaired "You suddenly start to see yourself on every newsstand . . . and it's maybe too much Kevin."

As popular as Kevin was, he still had to compete in newspapers with Commander-in-Chief George Bush, whose occupying troops in the Persian Gulf had actually begun fighting three days before the Golden Globes show, making it a less giddy gala than usual. Best Actress (Drama) went to *Misery*'s Kathy Bates, who gazed upon the audience and announced, "I realize as I think back over the years, that these are the faces that reached into my heart years ago and made me want to become an actor." On the Comedy/Musical side, the winner was Julia Roberts in *Pretty Woman*, who wore a better-fitting suit than she did when she had won a Globe the year before. The actress saved her biggest thanks for her beau Kiefer Sutherland, "who supports me through everything and brings so much happiness to my life." French actor Gerard Depardieu was in the bathroom when he was named Best Actor (Comedy/Musical) for his first American film, *Green Card*, a Peter Weir comedy about a marriage of convenience that Disney sold as another *Pretty Woman* via look-alike ads. When he got to the podium, Depardieu, who had removed the tie from his tux, delivered what the *Los Angeles Times* characterized as a "rousingly incoherent acceptance speech." An encouraged Orion Classics mailed out to Academy voters cassettes of Depardieu's other 1990 release, a remake of José Ferrer's 1950 Oscar winner, *Cyrano de Bergerac*, that had already earned him the Cesar Award. He got good notices stateside, too; Vincent Canby rated Depardieu's, "The Cyrano that will make all other actors hesitate before they take on the role." Through the diligence of Disney, Depardieu's mug graced the cover of *Premiere*, which inside revealed one of his hobbies, "Between jobs, Depardieu slaughters his own cattle."

Warner's was worried when the Foreign Press completely shut out *GoodFellas*. Lorraine Bracco lost the Supporting Actress Globe to Whoopi Goldberg in *Ghost*, who admitted "I really did want this," and Joe Pesci was conquered by Bruce Davison. In his acceptance, Davison alluded to the Persian Gulf events, saying, "I have

"The time has come to get back to our roots."
—Jeffrey Katzenberg

a hope and a prayer that, as we evolve as a species, we can devote as much of our intelligence and our intuition and our courage and our will to the war against AIDS as we do in our war against each other." Davison's wish seemed to startle Patrick Swayze, a Best Actor loser from *Ghost*, who looked on disapprovingly, failing to clap along with the other guests.

The Bush/Katzenberg Follies of 1991

George Bush's Persian escapade took some of the spotlight away from the Oscar campaigns, as well. Although a small group of performers, including Susan Sarandon, Margot Kidder, and Woody Harrelson, expressed opposition to the military action, a whole gaggle of stars got together to record a song for U.S. troops in the Gulf. Among these crooners were Billy Crystal, Whoopi Goldberg, Meryl Streep, and Kevin Costner, who proclaimed, "The guys over there are fighting for me so I can at least half-way ruin this song for them."

A domestic issue was also riveting Hollywood's attention. Although Disney was delivering on its pledge to Beatty to mount an Oscar campaign to rival *Reds* for *Dick Tracy*, his picture was getting no respect from the studio. In mid-January, a splenetic twenty-eight page memo by Disney head Jeffrey Katzenberg using *Dick Tracy* as a scapegoat was leaked to *Daily Variety* and suddenly became *de rigeur* reading in Tinseltown. In an inner-office call to arms, Katzenberg railed, "Costs have escalated, profitability has slipped, and our level of risk has compounded. The time has come to get back to our roots." If the Beatty vehicle were offered today, Katzenberg theorized, Disney would "soberly conclude it's not a project we should choose to get involved in." An anonymous producer explained it all to the *New York Times*. "He wants Hollywood and Wall Street to know that Disney learned a lesson from *Dick Tracy* and won't make the same mistake again." The same day the document hit the news, the trades were also announcing that Walt Disney Co. chairman Michael Eisner earned $11 million in 1990.

Orion sent Academy members a 144-page book, $15.95 retail, about the making of *Dances with Wolves*, and Paramount mailed them an embossed "Family Album" of *The Godfather Part III*. Nearly every Oscar hopeful delivered cassettes, even the independents. In addition, Samuel Goldwyn, Jr. dispatched oversized postcards reminding voters of *Longtime Companion*. Jim Sheridan and Neal Pearson, the director and producer of last year's triumphant *My Left Foot*, were back with *The Field*, a murky Irish real-estate drama, starring 1963 Best Actor nominee Richard Harris. After a ten-year absence from films spent mostly touring in a reprise of his film role as *Camelot*'s King Arthur, Harris was now keeping a high profile on the party circuit. Those who didn't see Harris at a soiree were likely to see his face in the barrage of ads Avenue Pictures placed on the back pages of *Daily Variety*.

Dinner with Diane

The *Los Angeles Times* reported that the only Oscar wannabe from a non-major studio movie who didn't have a cassette to mass-mail to voters was Diane Ladd; in *Wild at Heart*, David Lynch's first feature since *Blue Velvet*, Ladd had impersonated a crazed mother chasing down her runaway daughter, played by her real-life offspring Laura Dern. Sam Goldwyn, Jr. didn't see any reason to ante up for a campaign for the critically and financially disappointing film even though Ladd had won a Golden Globe nomination for supporting actress, so Ladd did it herself. Wheedling twenty tapes out of the film's video distributor, Ladd wrote letters to members inviting them to borrow one; she estimated that 300 voters saw *Wild at Heart* this way. The actress went so far as to invite Academy members over for spaghetti dinner and a movie afterward; twenty took her up on it, including Esther Williams, Abe Vigoda, and longtime friend Shelley Winters, who later made phone calls for the cause.

"The picture got sixty percent poor reviews!"
—Howard W. Koch

The Nominations

"Last year 300 attended the sunrise services and today 450 were at the live 5:38 ayem announcements of the nominations," reported Army Archerd, who mused "Maybe audiences are looking for a break from the live drama in the Persian Gulf." CNN felt so, breaking from its war coverage to broadcast Academy President Karl Malden and Denzel Washington as they officially started the Oscar race. Almost every reporter recounted that there were audible gasps when Golden Globe winner Julia Roberts was tapped for a Best Actress nomination and again when *Ghost* scored with a Best Picture nod. Howard W. Koch, *Ghost*'s executive producer, was astounded—"The picture got sixty percent poor reviews!" he reminded Archerd—and producer Lisa Weinstein said, "I was completely shocked myself . . . but I totally understand the cynicism. It is a lightweight film." Peter Travers in *Rolling Stone* blasted it as the most striking of "the blatant idiocies among the year's Oscar nominations." The *Los Angeles Times'* Sheila Benson chalked it up to "the state of war . . . *Ghost* says that the dead are not forgotten," and even to the health epidemic, "It's not too far-fetched to suggest that in this age of AIDS, a ghostly lover is the safest kind to have."

As expected, *Dances with Wolves* dominated with twelve nominations, the most for a film since *Reds'* dozen in 1981. Three of those nods were for Kevin Costner, which may have provided a discouraging sense of déjà vu for Martin Scorsese, whose *GoodFellas* nabbed six mentions. Remembering his defeat at the hands of Robert Redford, another actor-turned director, Scorsese confessed to Janet Maslin, "I have to go back to that night ten years ago because that was when I understood that the kind of pictures I would be making would be outside the mainstream of Hollywood production . . . Still, Hollywood's highest honor is the Oscar and you can't just say it isn't given accurately—John Ford had six." His producer, Irwin Winkler, looked on the bright side. "I think the critics' response has been so strong that it dissuaded the Academy from not recognizing it. The Academy doesn't like violence that is too graphic. They like nice family films. *Dances* is unique and special in its time because nobody's done a western in years."

That other mobster movie, *The Godfather Part III,* bested *GoodFellas* by one nomination, including the first Academy recognition in eleven years for former wunderkind Francis Coppola. Cinematographer Gordon Willis received his first nomination for the series and Supporting Actor Andy Garcia received his first nomination ever. Al Pacino, however, was not among the Best Actor nominees; instead he found himself competing against Garcia in Supporting for his caricature in *Dick Tracy. Godfather III* producer Fred Roos remonstrated, "Al not getting nominated has almost spoiled everything else. I thought Al was the surest bet we had. Maybe his performance was taken for granted."

Warren Beatty could feel some vindication against Jeffrey Katzenberg because his film received a total of seven nominations, although none of them were for the producer-actor-director. His songwriter, Stephen Sondheim, was in the running to pick up an Oscar to go along with all of his Tonys, but he would have to overcome rock star Jon Bon Jovi, who had just defeated him for a Best Song Golden Globe.

A Penny Dropped

Awakenings drew mentions for Best Picture, Robert De Niro, and Adapted Screenplay but director Penny Marshall and costar Robin Williams went wanting. When *USA Today* asked her about it, Marshall took the long view. "*Big* got two nominations; this time I got three. I'll inch up gradually." Shirley MacLaine didn't make the cut either for *Postcards from the Edge*, but Meryl Streep earned her ninth nomination, and her third one during a pregnancy. "If I got one, Shirley certainly should have," responded Meryl. "She

"After that I had plenty of rapes, too many to count."
—Gerard Depardieu

was the right arm of the relationship." Streep's competition this go-round was Julia Roberts, Kathy Bates, Joanne Woodward, and Anjelica Huston for *The Grifters,* which was up for director and screenplay, but not for picture. Similarly, *Reversal of Fortune* was left out of the top race after garnering nominations for its director, screenwriter, and Jeremy Irons.

Richard Harris' efforts were rewarded and CNN's Sandy Kenyon called it a "rare instance that a campaign is responsible for the nomination." The press doted on the twenty-seven year gap between Harris' two nominations, from the angry young man of *A Sporting Life* to the cantankerous old geezer of *The Field.* The nominee told the *Los Angeles Times,* "I'm sixty years old. I know how to deal with it. I'm not expecting too much. Enjoying the ride, that's it." Riding with him on Oscar night would be *Entertainment Tonight,* which revealed that his designer, Versace, screamed when Harris showed him mismatched footwear for his tux.

Gerard Depardieu was remembered, not for *Green Card* but for *Cyrano de Bergerac,* which was also in the running for Best Foreign Film, Costumes, Art Direction, and Makeup. Gene Siskel called the last nomination the year's silliest, saying that all the nominees "did was find a nice-fitting big nose for an actor who already has one." "Even with a nomination, it's OK," Depardieu maintained, "it's already an award." It was a good thing that Depardieu was content with a nomination because whatever outside chance he had to win went kaput when *Time* reprinted statements that the Frenchman had made to *Film Comment* in 1978. "It was my friend Jackie . . . who took me along on my first rape. One thing led to another and, hup!! . . . that was that," he recollected. "It was normal. After that I had plenty of rapes, too many to count." Depardieu's appalling conclusion was "Violence isn't committed by those who do the act but by the victims, the ones who permit it to happen." After the outraged reaction in America, French Minister of Culture Jack Lang maintained that it was Depardieu who was the victim and he attacked *Time* for what he claimed was a "violent, mean and lowly" campaign against France's number one cinematic export.

Pundits decreed that the one sure thing outside of *Dances with Wolves* was Supporting Actress contender Whoopi Goldberg, who was facing *The Grifters'* Annette Bening, *Dances with Wolves'* white woman Mary McDonnell, *GoodFellas'* Lorraine Bracco, and pasta chef Diane Ladd; the unprepared Academy only had a black-and-white photo of Ladd to display during the nominations show. Supporting Actor was considered the year's toughest race. Joe Pesci joined fellow gangsters Garcia and Pacino, and partisans of *GoodFellas* thought that he was their best hope; not only had Pesci topped *Premiere*'s readers' poll, he was also showing versatility in his slapstick role as a bumbling burglar in the comedy gold mine, *Home Alone,* starring the hottest name in show business—ten-year-old Macauley Culkin. Pesci himself was rooting for his competition, saying "I'm honored to be mentioned in the same breath as Al Pacino." *Dances with Wolves* showed up in this category, too, with Graham Greene, a native American from Canada. But Pesci's biggest challenger was *Longtime Companion*'s Bruce Davison, who said, "I feel I'm carrying the torch for the people represented in this film." Joel Siegel prophesied he would win because, "Everyone in Hollywood knows someone who's died of AIDS."

Sophia and Myrna

Given the high number of beloved performers without Oscars, the news that the Board of Governors was bestowing an Honorary one on 1961 Best Actress Sophia Loren seemed crazy. The next day the Academy announced that Myrna Loy, who never once managed a nomination throughout 125 movies in her fifty-four-year career, would also be crowned with an Honorary Oscar. The Academy insisted that this was not an afterthought because of the flap over Loren, but claimed that the news about Sophia had been leaked, thus precluding the organization from an-

"I'd suggest that this is pretty snotty even for a magazine with a large number of critical bullies on its staff."
—Stephen King

nouncing the two winners in tandem as planned. The fifty-six-year-old Loren took advantage of the attention and invited *Entertainment Tonight* for a cruise on a ninety-foot yacht at the Williams Island, Florida, resort where she "spends much of her time." "I don't even know if I deserve it," Loren said modestly, but then boasted of another of her achievements: "I'm very good at Scrabble because I'm Italian and I learned Latin at school." Smiling with satisfaction, she reminisced, "I won Peter O'Toole and Richard Burton," who, coincidentally, are also the two biggest Oscar losers with seven unsuccessful nominations. Asked about this year's actresses, Loren favored "Julia Roberts, she's so nice, she's so fragile. I like her very, very much."

Just a Movie Star

Barbara Walters walked arm in arm with the twenty-three-year-old Roberts on her Oscar night special, in which the new star said of her relationship with Kiefer Sutherland, "Forever love, this is it." A wedding date was set soon after the Oscars, with the ceremony to take place on the 20th Century-Fox lot. Rex Reed opined, "For a pretty girl like Julia Roberts, an Oscar nomination is still a little too much, I don't think she's proved herself yet as an actress." The *Hollywood Reporter*'s Robert Osborne came to her defense, referring to hers as a "personality performance like Audrey Hepburn in *Roman Holiday*," and her director Garry Marshall piped in with, "She's not just a movie star, she's an extremely talented actress." The actress herself would not dwell on her Oscar chances with one interviewer, saying, "I don't expect it, I don't anticipate it, and I don't find it healthy even to consider it or talk about it."

Out on a Limb with Liz

The general feeling was that the Best Actress would be one of the two nominees from Miramax movies, Joanne Woodward or Anjelica Huston, even though contenders from independent studios historically had a poor Oscar track record. Going against the grain was Liz Smith who wrote, "Maybe it's 'out on a limb with a chain saw' time, but I have a feeling Ms. Bates will take home the Oscar. Hers is the kind of work Academy voters just love to honor—case in point, physically unprepossessing actress comes out of nowhere (by Hollywood terms) and gives a dazzling, perhaps once-in-a-lifetime performance . . . A good 80% of her onscreen time is in close-up." When *Entertainment Weekly* listed the stigma of the Stephen King horror genre as working against Bates' Oscar chances, the irate author wrote the magazine and snarled, "I'd suggest that this is pretty snotty even for a magazine with a large number of critical bullies on its staff." Meanwhile, Liz Smith warned fans that Joanne Woodward vowed she wasn't leaving the East Coast for Oscar night; in fact, the Hollywood premiere of *Mr. and Mrs. Bridge* had been the first time Woodward visited Los Angeles in six years.

The Home Stretch

Robert De Niro was saluted in early March at a Waldorf-Astoria bash thrown by the American Museum of the Moving Image. One of his well-wishers was Oscar foe Jeremy Irons, who told the *New York Times*, "He is America's greatest living actor." The week before the Oscars, Martin Scorsese was feted in Hollywood at the Moving Picture Ball of the American Cinematheque, where De Niro marveled, "seeing Marty standing around when we were kids—that we'd ever wind up this way. It's a classic movie story." But Kevin Costner's success story still outshined theirs, particularly after the Directors Guild granted him its blessing. The bespectacled greenhorn confided to the throng, "It's interesting to be in a room with directors because I feel almost kind of like going back to the seventh grade when you were in a locker room talking about sex for the first time, there were some questions you wanted to ask." Costner's keynote address at the Independent Feature-Project Spirit Awards did not go over

"Hollywood's highest honor is the Oscar and you can't say it isn't given accurately—John Ford had six."
—Martin Scorsese

well, according to the *L.A. Weekly*, which reported that he "unloaded a truly embarrassing speech, liberally sprinkled with fucks and shits (perhaps he thinks you have to talk ballsy to the independent crowd); rambled on about 'creativity' and 'individualism'; . . . and singled out as 'an inspiration to all independent filmmakers' no less than Creative Artists Agency's Michael Ovitz" who happened to be sitting at a prominent table.

The *E!* network reported that Kevin did miss a few parties: "Costner has canceled all industry social events, including this weekend's Hollywood tribute to Martin Scorsese, because he feels over-exposed." Nevertheless, he was seen sermonizing about the Academy ceremony on *Entertainment Tonight*. "People who watch them should be inspired by the speeches they hear enough to come and want to make movies. If somebody sitting somewhere in America goes, 'I want to go there and I want to to do that . . .' that's what Oscars should be about." *Showbiz Today* recorded the sacrifice Costner made for the integrity of his work. "I didn't sell my film to the airlines; I just blew about 2 million bucks there, because they wanted to cut it." But *Entertainment Tonight* told viewers not to worry about Costner's standing on any breadlines—the American star received a lucrative sum for hustling malt liquor on Japanese television.

Whoopi Goldberg discussed the historical significance of a victory by a black woman with Barbara Walters. "It's important for me to win . . . because it's not been done since 1939." The frontrunner called the other nominees and said let's have lunch, post-Oscars, the winner treats. They all accepted. But at the Academy's nominees luncheon, Army Archerd reported that responsibility of being the shoo-in had taken its toll on Whoopi. "She's been suffering from a severe case of hives that had almost completely closed her eyes—and also caused her to gain weight. She's feeling better, not 100%."

Happier celebrants at the Academy's feed were Diane Ladd and Annette Bening. None of the Actress nominees came and Richard Harris was the only Actor to attend, which was no surprise because Harris was ubiquitous during Oscar season. William Goldman wrote in *New York*, "He worked the town better than Reagan ever worked a room. There wasn't a voter's cheek he didn't kiss." Supporting Actors present at the luncheon were Bruce Davison, Graham Greene, and Andy Garcia, who, surprised by all the press, said, "I thought this was going to be a little lunch at the Beverly Hilton; I used to work here as a waiter so I knew they were kind of boring lunches."

Cates Pontificates

Show producer Gilbert Cates promised *Daily Variety*, "The tone and content will reflect the Persian Gulf situation. It won't be a frivolous show, or inappropriate to the times." Afraid that the ceremony might be an attractive target for an Iraqi terrorist, the Academy planned to beef up security measures extensively; for starters, the Shrine would be patrolled by bomb-sniffing dogs.

The cocky Cates was willing to take at least one risk, however. Flushed from the critical success of last year's show, the producer dared to revert to opening the show with a big splashy production number, just two years after Allan Carr's Snow White foozle. Emphasizing the show's theme of "100 Years of Movies," Debbie Allen's choreography would start off in Paris via Cates' ever-ready satellite and end up on the stage of the Shrine. Cates bragged that director Jeff Margolis' plan was "one of the most complicated and difficult numbers ever attempted on television. I almost stutter as I start to think about it."

Another concern was impromptu speech-makers, à la Kim Basinger last year. Said the Academy's press agent Bob Werden to *Variety*, "If they say something like, 'Let's bring the boys back safely,' that's not really a political statement anyway . . . We won't cut them off, except if they go into a 15-minute speech, and then we might go

"There's no shit list."
—Gilbert Cates

to a commercial." Gilbert Cates responded to *Interview*'s question about picking the presenters, "You mean is there a shit list? No, there's no shit list." Indeed, Cates had even welcomed Kim Basinger herself back, to give the Scoring Award with her new costar and beau, Alec Baldwin.

The Big Night

A cease-fire had been called in the Gulf a week before Oscar night, but the Academy still examined its guests' pocketbooks and made everyone pass through an airport-like security check—everyone, that is, except for Bob Hope, who was given special dispensation. Academy spokesperson Bob Werden argued, "He's like the American flag. Are you going to make him go through a metal detector?"

The fans in the stands were made to endure much greater hardships. Whereas in the past people were free to stake claims and camp out as soon as the bleachers went up, this year they were cordoned off from the area until 8 A.M. Adding to the degradation, the fans weren't allowed to bring food or drink or cameras or binoculars; some of them maintained a sense of humor, beseeching to reporters, "Water, water, water!" One gawker complained to the *San Diego Union* that guards had confiscated her Snickers bar because "they said we'd throw them at the stars." A security guard had little sympathy for her, telling the paper, "Candy bars can hold an explosive device." "I think there's paranoia in the air," Hermosa Beach resident Diane Echert scoffed to the *Los Angeles Daily News* but, rather than give up her food and camera, she forsook the bleachers and watched the proceedings from across the street.

Members of the press had it as bad as the bleacher fans thanks to the downpours inundating Los Angeles during the day. The *Hollywood Reporter* recounted that "Photographers, who were told they couldn't bring in umbrellas because it was a security risk, were soaked as security guards stood under a tent near the front arrivals area." Justice was served, though, when "Suddenly the entire tent drooped, spilling water on the security guards to the amusement of the lensmen." The rain had ended by the afternoon, but WNBC-TV's Pia Lindstrom noted that the special red carpet with a gold Oscar on it outside the Shrine was drenched and workers were still trying to vacuum it dry when people started arriving.

No Middle East terrorists were on hand, but

Awards Ceremony

MARCH 25, 1991, 6:00 P.M.
THE SHRINE AUDITORIUM, LOS ANGELES

Your Host:
BILLY CRYSTAL
Televised over ABC

Presenters

Supporting Actress	Denzel Washington
Sound	Dianne Wiest
Makeup	Anne Archer
Supporting Actor	Brenda Fricker
Live Action Short Film	Chevy Chase and Martin Short
Animated Short Film	Woody Woodpecker
Honorary Award to Myrna Loy	Anjelica Huston
Costume Design	Annette Bening
Scientific and Technical Awards	Geena Davis
Visual Effects	Jack Valenti
Thalberg Award	Michael Douglas
Original Score	Kim Basinger and Alec Baldwin
Editing	Danny Glover and Kevin Kline
Art Direction	Susan Sarandon and Richard Gere
Documentary Awards	Phoebe Cates and Ron Silver
Sound Effects Editing	Whoopi Goldberg and Andy Garcia
Cinematography	Glenn Close
Foreign Film	Dustin Hoffman
Writing Awards	Jodie Foster and Anthony Hopkins
Honorary Award to Sophia Loren	Gregory Peck
Original Song	Ann-Margret and Gregory Hines
Actress	Daniel Day-Lewis
Actor	Jessica Tandy
Director	Tom Cruise
Picture	Barbra Streisand

Performers of Nominated Songs

"Blaze of Glory"	Jon Bon Jovi
"I'm Checkin' Out"	Reba McEntire
"Promise Me You'll Remember"	Harry Connick, Jr.
"Somewhere in My Memory"	Children's Choir
"Sooner or Later (I Always Get My Man)"	Madonna

"To all you Sally Kirkland fans out there . . . I love you!"
—Sally Kirkland

waiting to greet guests were sixty AIDS activists from ACT-UP picketing with a banner decrying "102,000 Plus Deaths from AIDS—Two Films Not Enough." Other ACT-UP members held placards warning, "AIDSPHOBIA. Protect yourself from Hollywood." The organization had sent "SILENCE = DEATH" buttons to Academy members several weeks earlier and was again handing them out at the Shrine. The only attendees to wear the pins were presenter Susan Sarandon, Tim Robbins, and *Longtime Companion*'s Bruce Davison, who had to explain its significance to E!'s celebrity interviewer Dagne Hultgreen.

The first arrivals were Whoopi Goldberg with her daughter Alex, who had just made the Supporting Actress favorite a new grandmother. Outfitted in black sequins by Nolan Miller, of "Dynasty" legend, Goldberg told Cindy Adams that if the predictions were correct, "Boy, will I celebrate. But the first thing I'll do to celebrate is to take off these damn shoes." Annette Bening, with her parents and Ed Begley, Jr., showed up in a champagne-colored costume by Albert Wolsky from the movie she was making, Warren Beatty's *Bugsy*. Lorraine Bracco, in Valentino, brought her parents and husband Harvey Keitel, who gleefully told one reporter how he had assisted his wife's preparation that day. "I helped her take a shower."

"Here's the one you've been waiting for," heralded Army Archerd as Mr. and Mrs. Kevin Costner, both in shades, stepped through the metal detectors to the forecourt with his parents, drawing what *Daily Variety* described as a "predictably huge reaction" from the formerly disgruntled fans. Martin Scorsese brought his father and non-nominated mother, too. Francis Coppola, in a suit, carried a bottle of wine from his own vineyard which he was planning to give as his personal gift to whomever won Best Director. Daughter Sofia accompanied him and was having another weird day, telling KABC-TV interviewers Steve Edwards and Tawny Little, "It's strange because Sophia Loren was right next to me so I heard my name being screamed. Then I realized it was Sophia Loren. It's exciting, though."

Neither Robert De Niro nor Al Pacino posed for the papparazzi, but TV captured Pacino's embrace of cocontestant Andy Garcia. "If I win, I'll turn my Oscar over to Al; it was a great error that he wasn't nominated for this film," said Garcia. Joe Pesci continued to root for him, too. "I kind of hope Al gets it," said the nominee, who had, in the words of Cindy Adams, "a stunner wife attached to him like she was on life support." "I can enjoy it a lot more than ten years ago," Pesci told Edwards and Little, claiming he didn't have a speech. "I can assure you that all it's going to be is 'Thank You.' "

Jeremy Irons quipped, "It's like being in the circus," as nearby, "perennial starlet" Edy Williams paraded around and alluded to the Gulf War by holding a rabbit she named "Schwarzkopf." Song nominee Jon Bon Jovi was about to speak to forecourt king Army Archerd when 1987 nominee Sally Kirkland butted in and declared, "To all you Sally Kirkland fans out there . . . I love you!" And when it was Raul Julia's turn to chat with Archerd, a woman nearby repeatedly saluted while yelling "Spider Woman, Spider Woman!" Observed *Movies USA*, "She was obviously insane, but there was nothing to be done." Dustin Hoffman charmed reporters asking who had designed his tuxedo. "I don't know. I rented it," he replied. Both Kathy Bates and Julia Roberts came with their fiancés while *Entertainment Tonight*'s Leonard Maltin, attending his first Oscar show, enthused, "It's an adrenaline rush the likes of which I don't ever think I've felt before." *Women's Wear Daily* was wowed over the presence of two other movie buffs, "Both Gianni Versace and Giorgio Armani actually went to the show." Half of the ten male acting nominees were in Armani designs.

Recalling Kim Basinger's homemade horror from last year, the *Los Angeles Times'* Maureen Sajbel adjudged that she "redeemed herself—though just barely—with a pink ball gown that required an attendant to carry her train." Anjelica

"Anjelica just now looked at it, not too pleased."
—Michael Castner

Huston should have hired help, according to E!'s Michael Castner, who witnessed her arrival directly ahead of Tom Cruise and bride Nicole Kidman: "Anjelica Huston was right in front of them. Nicole accidentally stepped on part of Anjelica's costume and ripped the lining out of it, but they didn't say anything about it. Tom kind of grabbed his face like 'My God, I can't believe you did that!' Anjelica just now looked at it, not too pleased. She has no idea who is responsible."

Announcer Les Marchak began the telecast with "This celebration of the world's most compelling entertainment is proudly shared with you by the Academy . . . And Revlon, the Prudential. . . ." Playing prognosticator, Marchak named *The Silence of the Lambs'* Anthony Hopkins a "sure nominee for next year's Oscar" but flopped as an Oscar historian by referring to a never nominated actor as "Ron Silver, Academy Award winner." Bob Hope was described as "a legend not only at Oscar time but all year long," while the suddenly blond Julia Roberts, seen kissing Kiefer Sutherland was, of course, "the pretty woman herself."

"Hello, everybody, I'm back . . . Welcome to our party," greeted Academy President Karl Malden, who explained that the show's 100 years of film theme was based on Edison's 1891 patent application for his camera and his projector. Malden then sent the audience, via satellite, to Paris, where Michael Caine said, "It's 3:15 A.M. here . . . I am standing in the middle of history. In this very room in the Hotel Scribe, in 1895, for the first time anywhere, an audience gathered to witness a minor miracle. Pictures that moved." The cockney Caine was chosen after Shrine no-show Gerard Depardieu declined Cates' offer to star in the opener. The Lumiere Brothers' short films of a Paris street scene and a couple feeding their baby were shown, followed by a shot of an approaching train. Just as the story about the Lumieres' original viewers has it, this Paris audience leapt up in terror. Suddenly, back at the Shrine, television actress Jasmine Guy and the rest of Debbie Allen's dancers, dressed to look like the Paris audience, leapt through a screen onto the stage and went into their steps as film clips continued to play. Piped-in music led to an ersatz *West Side Story* gang rumble occurring as the Teenage Mutant Ninja Turtles frolicked on film and, at another point, an amalgam of gladiators and Civil War soldiers joined together for "The Battle Hymn of the Republic." As "His truth is marching on" was sung, the accompanying film clip featured Spike Lee about to throw a garbage can through Danny Aiello's window in *Do the Right Thing*. *Variety* sneered, "the dancers resembled little more than pesky flies buzzing around the screen," but Gene Kelly, watching at Spago, called it "sensational." At the end of the number, director Jeff Margolis cut to Susan Sarandon and Tim Robbins, who had removed their "SILENCE = DEATH" pins.

Hosting for the second year, Billy Crystal plugged his upcoming dude ranch comedy, *City Slickers*, by riding in on a horse; he handed the animal to a valet and then beeped a remote car lock. Crystal opened with "It doesn't matter who wins tonight because Sadaam Hussein will claim he did . . . I think all of us feel that we are very fortunate that there are no Americans fighting tonight anywhere [applause] . . . except at Paramount," a reference to the recent deposal of studio head and Coppola booster Frank Mancuso. "Madonna called me herself and said, 'Bill, who do I have to fax to get on this show?' " Crystal told Best Actress nominee Kathy Bates, "I'm your number one fan. I actually have the *Misery* home game, which is a home hobbling kit." Hearing the audience's tepid response to the joke, the comedian explained, "I'm referring to that great scene when Kathy took a sledgehammer and she crippled the legs of a writer so he couldn't leave and he had to finish his manuscript. Which is not an original idea in Hollywood—it's page eight of the Katzenberg memo." Reprising a bit from last year, Crystal performed another one-man production number kidding the Best Picture nominees. After descending into the audience to kiss the hand of Al Pacino on the front row, Crystal

"Madonna seems to be moving away from Marilyn and toward Jayne Mansfield."
—WWD

delivered his *Godfather III* parody to the tune of "Speak Softly Love": "This is the story about a man called Corleone/This man killed everyone, so now he's home alone." To grateful applause, he ended on his knee, crying, "You like me!"

Presenting Best Supporting Actress, Denzel Washington, in a white Armani dinner jacket, told the nominees, "it would be sadistic of me to prolong the agony." The winner was Whoopi Goldberg, who kissed Andy Garcia sitting in front of her and then bussed her daughter. When Washington presented her with her statuette, a disbelieving Goldberg hesitated before touching it. Goldberg said, "Ever since I was a little kid, I wanted this . . . My brother's sitting there and he's saying 'Thank God we don't have to listen to that anymore,' . . . my mom's home, everybody's watching." She acknowledged costar Patrick Swayze "who's a stand-up guy and who went to them and said 'I want to do it with her.' " She concluded, "I come from New York. As a little kid I lived in the projects and you're the people I watched, you're the people that made me want to be an actor. I am proud to be an actor. And I'm gonna keep on acting." The applause was deafening as she exited with Washington's arm around her. The *New York Post* dispatched a reporter to Goldberg's old project on West 25th Street where fifteen-year-old resident Yvette Marisol was inspired, "You can tell she came from here from her attitude—she's not one of those stuck-up people."

The Sound Award was prefaced by one of the earliest examples of sound on film—an unknown vaudevillian singing a version of "Ma, He's Making Eyes at Me," in which the duck he is holding quacks out the "Ma." "Very weird," commented Crystal. Dianne Wiest gave the award to a quartet from *Dances with Wolves.* One winner praised his wife "for convincing me I would love the prairie," a second said, "It's a great birthday present!" and a third one said "My wife—" and then was drowned out by the orchestra.

Jack Lemmon introduced a clip from *Ghost* and Anne Archer presented Best Makeup to *Dick Tracy.* John Caglione, Jr. thanked Warren Beatty "for taking a chance on two guys from Brooklyn" and Doug Dexler apologized to the stars "who suffered countless applications of glue and rubber." Then Billy Crystal prepared the audience for "the NC-17 portion of our really big show." Harkening back to her "Material Girl" period, a bleached Madonna rose out of the floor dripping in diamonds lent from Harry Winston. She warbled Sondheim's "Sooner or Later" in a white rhinestone and pearl encrusted decolletage, kid gloves, and ermine by Bob Mackie. "What kept up Madonna's gown?" asked Army Archerd. "$10,000!" answered Mackie's partner Ray Aghayan. *WWD* sniffed, "she seems to be moving away from Marilyn and towards Jayne Mansfield." The singer supplemented Sondheim's lyrics with an updated line of Monroe's: "Talk to me, General Schwarzkopf. Tell me all about it." For a finale, she turned and wiggled her rear for the audience but home viewers didn't see it—director Jeff Margolis was shooting her from the front.

Immediately after the commercial break, a number of people could be seen crouching and scurrying back to their seats. "Hurry up, hurry up," chided Crystal. He then introduced "a great actress," Best Supporting Actor presenter Brenda Fricker in a tuxedo-inspired outfit. "It's really nice to be back," said last year's Supporting Actress, who had co-starred with Richard Harris in *The Field.* Bruce Davison still had on his "Silence = Death" button and Graham Greene mouthed, "Hi, Mom." But the victor was Joe Pesci, who shook his head in wonder. Pesci's entire speech consisted of "It's my privilege. Thank you."

There was a commotion going on as Chevy Chase and Martin Short made their way out to present the Live Action Short Film Award. David Lacaillade, a member of ACT-UP, rose from his seat in the rear orchestra and screamed, "Hollywood is a bunch of hypocrites! AIDS Action Now! 102,000 Dead! People Are Dying!" Before he could get to "What are you doing?", as Lacaillade later told *Premiere*, "the security people grabbed me and walked me backward down the ramp, back through the doors, across the lobby and finally up with my nose against a wall." The activist's broadside went unheard and unseen by the television audience, although Martin Short briefly turned to look out at the hullabaloo. The comics bantered about the category they were presenting. Chase: "I was under the impression that a short film was a film made by Martin Short." Short: "Oh-ho. No, no, no. A film by Martin Short is called a classic." *Newsday*'s John Anderson figured the two presenters "may have had a bet to see who could kill his own career faster. They seemed to be on stage forever." The winner was Adam Davidson for *The Lunch Date*, who became the first non-documentary filmmaker to move up from an Academy Student Film Award to a real Oscar. The son of Gordon Davidson, the artistic director of L.A.'s Mark Taper Forum, the winner earned unexpected laughs when he confessed of his film, "It really is just a ten-minute student film I did for class" at Columbia University. Then the Animated Short award was presented to Nick Park's *Creature Comforts* by Woody Woodpecker, who was celebrating his fiftieth anniversary. Phil Rosenthal of the *Los Angeles Daily News* called Short and Chase's routine "horrendously unfunny" but the silver lining was that they made Woody Woodpecker "less annoying by comparison."

Anjelica Huston came onstage and declared that "Some actresses take us by storm. Some, like the lady we pay tribute to with an Honorary Oscar steal quietly into our hearts. Myrna Loy had a sweet way with a sharp line and she could communicate more with a delicately raised eyebrow than most performers can with a raised voice . . . Myrna Loy created an ideal of womanliness that is both an enduring achievement and an enduring inspiration." After a montage of clips ranging from Loy's early Asian roles to *The Best Years of Our Lives* with a lot of slapstick in between, the camera cut to Loy in her New York apartment. The actress rivaled Joe Pesci in terms of brevity, as she said merely, "You've made me very happy. Thank you very much." *Daily Variety* printed, "It was an effective moment," but Liz Smith huffed, "It saddened and angered many that nobody thought to give an Oscar to Myrna Loy, even five years ago. Now Miss Loy is painfully fragile. (And the idea to have her accept 'live'—from her New York apartment—wasn't a good one either.)"

Joe Pesci was back, clutching his Oscar. "I still can't talk," the Best Supporting Actor said, which he then proved by flubbing his lines and begging forgiveness. He was a replacement for absent co-star Macauley Culkin, introducing "Somewhere in My Memory," the nominated song from their *Home Alone*. The number resembled a leftover from the Radio City Christmas pageant, as children walked out of holiday packages while adults danced around in teddy bear and bunny costumes. Billy Crystal explained that Macauley "is watching the show this evening with his new girlfriend, Cher." Liz Smith didn't think other children would be watching by this point and complained "they put Madonna's sizzling and sexy 'Sooner or Later' number on early but saved the charming children's dance number 'Somewhere in My Memory' until after 9 P.M. (Eastern time). Many tots were already in bed."

Receiving the same "great actress" appellation from Billy Crystal as Brenda Fricker was Supporting Actress loser Annette Bening, who appeared to reveal the Costume Design winner in the *Bugsy* gown that would win the award the following year. Tonight, though, Warren Beatty's *Dick Tracy* lost to *Cyrano de Bergerac*. Winner Franca Squarciapino said "I am moved, thank you" and then launched into French. Backstage, when a reporter asked her a question in English, all the winner could do was respond, "No capisce."

A blond Geena Davis, who *WWD* said "looked the part of a movie star," came onstage and said, "Hi. Now through the miracle of science we can go back, back to a more innocent time, a time when we were young and naive. It was, well, three weeks ago." Highlights of the actress's presentation of the Scientific and Technical Awards were then shown after which Danny Aiello introduced the *GoodFellas* clip. "When movie critics, moviemakers and moviegoers all agree," said Aiello, "well you can bet your popcorn that movie is worth your time."

After a one-year absence, Motion Picture Association of America head Jack Valenti was back as a sitting target for the show's host. "If you thought Madonna was exciting, here is a showstopper," deadpanned Crystal and Valenti's entrance was accompanied by an angelic choir. Instead of his usual Foreign Film gig, Valenti presented Visual Effects and didn't even get to open an envelope since it had previously been determined that the effects in *Total Recall* were so far beyond the competition ("they created a universe that never before existed," in Valenti's words) as to render a vote pointless. Two of the technicians were able to speak but as winner number three said, "I'd like to thank—," Bill Conti's orchestra silenced him.

Another non-competitive award followed, the Irving G. Thalberg Memorial Award to Richard Zanuck and David Brown, the producing team that had split up a couple years earlier. Presenter Michael Douglas maintained that the recipients' "work is consistent both in theme and quality, for in almost every Zanuck and Brown film, gallant individuals struggle courageously against impossible odds to achieve improbable but inspiring success." A collection of film clips was intended to reinforce this hypothesis, but it remained unclear how such fluff as *The Sting* and *Cocoon* fit in; notably, the pair's '70s blaxploitation effort, *Willie Dynamite*, went unmentioned. The occasion turned into a testimonial to Darryl Zanuck as Richard bragged that his dad had been the first recipient of the Thalberg Award and David Brown thanked Papa Zanuck for bringing him out to Hollywood in the first place. Brown also praised "my non-voting beautiful wife" and the camera cut to the smiling editor of *Cosmopolitan*, Helen Gurley Brown.

Presenting Original Score with Alec Baldwin, Kim Basinger replaced her *Do the Right Thing* harangue from last year with the kind of smarmy joke that is standard for this category, sighing "It really is better when it's done to music." When nobody laughed, Baldwin raised his hands to his face in mock embarrassment. After Debbie Allen's dancers enacted snippets from the five nominated scores in universally panned interpretations, Basinger editorialized "Tough choice," and declared *Dances with Wolves* the Academy's selection, the western's second award. Five-time winner John Barry, who had nearly died three years earlier from a ruptured esophagus, praised his doctors, to whom he had already dedicated the soundtrack album.

Dances was on a roll when its editor Neil Travis won its third Oscar and said, "I grew up in a motion picture family so this little guy represents the fulfillment of a lifetime dream . . . It also belongs to Michael Blake, who gave us a closer look at the big, wounded hearts of the Native American people . . . Kevin, let's do it again." Backstage, he informed the press if he hadn't voted for himself, he would have picked *GoodFellas*. "That was a brilliantly edited film."

For the first time, Meryl Streep missed an Oscar show due to her obstetrician's orders, so she canceled her introduction to Reba McIntire's rendition of the nominated song Streep had sung in *Postcards from the Edge*. Cates had asked non-nominee Shirley MacLaine to substitute for Streep, but she was performing her Vegas act in Detroit that evening. So Crystal did the honors, calling her "the very best country singer in the country today." "The audience was visibly affected by Reba McIntire's performance," reported Army Archerd, "only a week after the tragedy of her troupe dying in a plane crash."

Set decorator Rick Simpson of *Dick Tracy* joined the list of winners cut down by conductor Conti before speaking even though cowinner Richard Sylbert had kept his word of thanks concise. Sylbert's gratitude had been to Warren Beatty. "This is the first opportunity I've had to

"Let's face it, Gone With the Wind was about me."
—Sally Field

thank him, not only for this picture but the past as well." There was a reaction shot of *Dick Tracy* star Madonna, sitting on the front row with her date, Michael Jackson, who wore two gloves for the occasion.

"Thanks for the Memories" drifted out of the orchestra pit next. *Newsday*'s John Anderson accused Bob Hope of having "shamelessly stalled his routine waiting for a standing ovation that never came." While the guests at the *Village Voice*'s Cynthia Heimel's Oscar-watching party "cringed at the hair plugs in his scalp," Hope plowed ahead. "I remember when they first handed out the Oscars in 1927—I was home alone, too." Television caught Al Pacino laughing and clapping as Hope continued, "I couldn't be here tonight in spirit, so I'm here in person." Naturally, the comedian poked fun of the Gulf War that had just claimed 148 American and over 100,000 Iraqi lives, "It was over like a big burst, it was like Rosanne Barr sitting on a whoopee cushion." He told kids to always pay for their movie tickets because "the Japanese need the money." Negative "oooohs" emanated from the audience but Hope had a rejoinder, "—to pay Michael," a reference to Madonna's thirty-two-year-old date who just five days before had signed what *People* called "the biggest deal in music history" with Sony.

Hope's purpose was to introduce Chuck Workman's montage of stars naming the first film they had seen. Observed the comedian, "Going to the movies is like sex—you always remember the first one"; Hope's co-star from *The Iron Petticoat*, Katharine Hepburn, kicked things off by waxing offscreen over Cecil B. DeMille's silent *Manslaughter*. Candice Bergen said "*Snow White* . . . It took me about thirty years to recover from that one," and Matt Dillon couldn't recall the title of his initial movie but said, "I think it must have had Charlton Heston in it because he was in every first movie that I ever saw." Ronald Reagan was also confused because instead of answering the question, went on about his preferences, "I always liked the westerns because it's the good against the evil with the good always winning out." A number of this year's nominees mentioned their initial film forays: Anjelica Huston—her father's *Moulin Rouge*, although she liked *Tammy Tell Me True* better; Richard Harris—*Snow White;* Joanne Woodward—*Dracula;* Andy Garcia—*Mr. Hulot's Holiday;* Gerard Depardieu—*Bird Man of Alcatraz;* and Kevin Costner, who reminisced, "I asked my mother what that said because there was something beautiful about the red letters and she said *Ben-Hur.*" Macauley Culkin couldn't recall any other movies he had seen besides *Home Alone* and Sally Field really liked *Gone With the Wind* because "Let's face it, it was about me!"

"Whoever gets this one right inevitably goes on to win the pool," Ron Silver hypothesized before giving the Documentary Feature award to previous winner Barbara Kopple, this time for *American Dream.* As producer Arthur Cohn went on about "today more than ever the free world owes the United States deep respect and gratitude," Kopple could be heard imploring him to hurry up before Conti's musicians attacked. She managed to get in, "I'd like to dedicate this film to the people of the Midwest and the families and the meatpackers in Austin, Minnesota, whose American dream is so precious and so vital. They went out on strike for their slice of the American dream and were permanently replaced. Lastly, for James Michael Carroll, whose life was so violently interrupted. He will be deeply missed."

Robert De Niro, who, Cynthia Heimel charged, wore "his hair in a flip like Marilyn Quayle," lackadaisically read the TelePrompter to prelude the *Dances with Wolves* clip. "Mr. De Niro gained seventy-five pounds to do that introduction," joked Billy Crystal. Then Whoopi Goldberg returned with Andy Garcia to give the Sound Effects Editing trophy to Alec Baldwin's movie, *The Hunt for Red October.* Glenn Close stepped out in a black-and-blue Geoffrey Beene with matching gloves and awarded *Dances with Wolves* its fourth trophy, for Cinematography. Dean Semler squinted at the audience and said, "It's a bit like facing 3,000 buffalo." He thanked

"I'd love to meet Claus von Bulow and tell him what he's all about."
—Jeremy Irons

his wife, "the blond bombshell from Down Under," and ended with, "I'm a very proud little Aussie up here tonight to accept this."

Dustin Hoffman, with stubble on his face and tennis shoes to go with his rented tux, revealed Best Foreign Film, which everyone thought would go to either France's *Cyrano de Bergerac* or the first nominee from China, the controversial *Ju Duo;* the Communist government had tried to withdraw the entry from the race, but failing that, barred director Zhang Yimou from coming to California, despite a petition signed by other nominees Martin Scorsese, Stephen Frears, and Joanne Woodward. "A major surprise," opined *Daily Variety*, when "the winner was the film that had received the least advance publicity," the Swiss film about Turkish emigrants, *Journey of Hope.*" Director Xavier Koller responded, "I can't believe it myself . . . My special thanks go, first of all, to the family down in Turkey . . . who lost their son in October '88 crossing the mountains into Switzerland." "Ironically," noted *Screen International*, "the Oscars were not broadcast in Switzerland this year due to the high TV license fee demanded for the awards." The *Hollywood Reporter* recorded that "The surmise among the foreign press members backstage . . . was that refusal for *Cyrano* had to do with anti-French sentiment among Academy members regarding that country's film quotas." Daniel Toscan du Plantier, the head of Unifrance, was prone to agree, condemning the Academy in *Le Figaro* for having "again chosen to honor an obscure low-budget movie from a country virtually without cinema over a powerful film acclaimed in its own country and around the world." The Academy's Bruce Davis responded, "It has the whiff of sour grapes."

Crystal welcomed *The Silence of the Lambs* stars Anthony Hopkins and Jodie Foster, the latter in a daring Armani suit that *Newsweek* said offered "twin peeks, she seemed to have lost her shirt. Maybe she'll find it by the next Oscar show, which is sure to be the Year of the Lamb." "Dorothy Parker once said the two most beautiful words in the English language are: 'Check enclosed,'" Foster said, ushering in the Original Screenplay Oscar. The prize went to *Ghost*'s Bruce Joel Rubin, the only one of the nominees who hadn't also directed his film. Rubin said, "I have to tell you I'm just honored to be associated with a film that not only acknowledges the spiritual nature of man but affirms it," thanking "everyone at Paramount, all the executives, past and present, who were involved in this film and who believed in it . . . and my wife Blanche who, six years ago, put our house on the market, quit her job, and said we were moving to Hollywood. Thanks, hon." Backstage, Rubin told skeptical journalists, "They decided to vote their hearts over their intellects, let's say, or over their aesthetics . . . Even though there are a lot of cynics out there who kind of laugh at what it is, a huge number of people didn't laugh."

Back onstage, Hopkins and Foster were giving *Dances with Wolves* its fifth Oscar, for Adapted Screenplay. Michael Blake brought up to the podium Doris Leader Charge, a teacher from Rosebud, South Dakota, who had been the film's language adviser, to translate his speech into Lakota. "I had intended if I was fortunate enough to win this magnificent award to direct my remarks to young people," Blake said. "My success began when I started to read books. Dreams come out of books and the dream that came to me was to do something beneficial for as many people as I could . . . Hold on to your dreams. Don't let anyone take them away. Never give up." Janet Maslin felt that Blake's sentiments "suggested the possibility of a Sioux greeting-card industry." Backstage, the writer said, "I get up glad to be alive another day. Just waking up in the morning is a big, exciting thing. I have Hodgkin's disease. I kind of live from blood test to blood test, like all cancer patients."

Onstage, Debra Winger promoted the clip to *Awakenings* with, "I defy anyone with a heartbeat to keep a dry eye." A clip of Sophia Loren handing Gregory Peck his 1962 Best Actor Oscar followed, as did the present-day Peck, who goofed when saying of the Honorary Winner, "millions

"Here you are, you clever man."
—Jessica Tandy to Jeremy Irons

who saw and loved her Oscar-winning performance in *The Women*," George Cukor's brittle all-female comedy, instead of Vittorio De Sica's neorealism, *Two Women*. Peck mused that "Critics have been trying for years to describe what makes Sophia so uniquely Sophia" and then a collection of film clips revealed that despite their thirty-year age difference, Loren and Myrna Loy each had had Clark Gable and Cary Grant as leading men. Sophia entered in a Valentino to the only standing ovation of the night and held back tears during the lengthy applause, during which there was a closeup of her favorite, Julia Roberts. "I remember my first Oscar," Loren said. "It was so overwhelming for me that the terror of having to face you all made me find so many excuses not be with you thirty years ago. Tonight, I'm still scared but I'm not alone and I will share this eventful evening with the three men in my life: my husband Carlo Ponti, without whom I wouldn't be the person I am today," which was all Ponti needed to hear to stand up in the orchestra and wave, "and my two sons, Carlo, Jr. and Edourdo, that taught me to conjugate the verb 'to love.' " The Scrabble champion concluded, "Words are very difficult to find for me to express it all in this wonderful moment in my life, so I will try to revert to my native language and say simply, 'Grazie, America.' "

Ann-Margret announced that Stephen Sondheim had beat out Jon Bon Jovi for Best Song. Since the winner was absent, another close-up of Madonna and Michael had to suffice. Then Crystal made a wisecrack about *My Left Foot*. "Daniel Day-Lewis, he wasn't the actual first choice for that role—it was Jerry Lewis." Realizing the audience found the joke in bad taste, Crystal alibied that "They told me to stretch . . . That's what I did." Out strode Day-Lewis, in a vicar's frock coat again, to name this year's Best Actress. The chosen one was Kathy Bates, who, stunned by the news and the attendant roar, closed her eyes for a second, then turned to kiss her fiancé, Tony Campisi, and to bearhug her director, Rob Reiner. On her way to the stage, she passed by Anjelica Huston and stuck out her hand. Anjelica rose and as she started to kiss the winner on the cheek, Jeff Margolis decided to cut to a close-up of Danny Glover. Grasping a good luck charm on a tassel, Bates began, "I'd like to thank the Academy—I've been waiting a long time to say that." She stated her appreciation of Rob Reiner "for giving me a chance," William Goldman, Stephen King, and her costar. "I would like to say that I really am your number one fan, Jimmy." She laughed when she greeted "my friends watching at the Sea Palace on 9th Avenue" but choked when she thanked "my mom at home and my dad (pause) who I hope is watching somewhere, I would like to say thank you."

"How nice it is to be back," said Jessica Tandy, who was attired in a gold-and-black beaded Pauline Trigere that the L.A. *Daily News* deemed "gorgeous." Tandy's head was almost bald due to chemotherapy treatments and the *New York Observer* loved the fact that "Instead of going the wig route, à la Tina Turner or Dolly Parton, she opted for reality . . . She looked great." As the actress read the names of the Best Actor nominees, Kevin Costner nervously wiped his face with his hands, while an unsmiling Robert De Niro didn't appear to be enjoying himself, either. The winner was Jeremy Irons, who leaned over to kiss costar Glenn Close in the row ahead of him. On the way to the stage, he took Madonna's hand and kissed her. "Here you are, you clever man," said Tandy, as he swept her up for a long embrace. Irons thanked his makeup artists, "the people who made me look like that," his screen wife, "Glenn, for finally persuading me to do it," Barbet Schroeder as well as his *Dead Ringers* director David Cronenberg, "some of you may understand why," and his offscreen wife, working actress Sinead Cusack. "Lastly, if I may cut the call of a telephone to London where my wife is trying to keep awake in a hotel room, 'I wish you were here to help me carry this because you helped me win it.' " Irons stood to revel in the audience's applause until the Academy's anonymous blond handler pulled him off backstage.

"Words, bad words, were forming in my mouth."
—Whoopi Goldberg

The clip from *The Godfather Part III* was prefaced by a ponytailed Jeff Bridges, wearing what Cindy Adams described as "a yellow and red and green and blue and black vest. He looked like a salad fell on him." Then Billy Crystal was back with "Some people say there are no real movie stars anymore. I say they're wrong. Ladies and gentlemen, Tom Cruise." The actor was there to reveal that Francis Ford Coppola's bottle of wine would be going to Kevin Costner, who kissed his wife and then sprinted up the stairs to the podium. Once there, he held his statuette aloft for the peanut gallery. Costner expressed his debt to his production company, "Majestic, the same people who came down to Mexico and watched my little slide show and tried to figure out through all of my boyish enthusiasm that I was deadly serious about making this movie," and, inevitably, "to Michael Ovitz, for his careful reconstruction that helped me finish *Dances* without making me compromise my dream. Finally, I'd like to share this with my wife and my parents, who I am so happy that we are alive to share this together."

That left one award, presented by "two-time Oscar winner" Barbra Streisand, who strutted out to the strains of "Evergreen" in a black gown slit to the thigh. There was a drumroll as she announced the final victor—*Dances with Wolves*, its seventh Oscar. Costner shook Richard Harris' hand, later explaining that Harris "is part of the first date I had with my wife . . . We saw *Camelot*"; he walked in a circle while waiting for coproducer Jim Wilson to extricate himself from Mary McDonnell's embrace. Jim grabbed Kevin's neck, and the two ascended the stage where Streisand kissed both presenters; waiting for the applause to die down, Costner walked over for another smooch. A dry-mouth Wilson said, "I didn't drink any water—it was smart." A more prepared Costner said, "It's very easy for people to trivialize what we do sometimes and they do it in ways of saying, well, if it's such a big deal, how come nobody remembers who last year won the Oscar? I've got a real flash for you: I will never forget what happened here tonight. My family will never forget what happened here tonight. My native American brothers and sisters across the country, especially the Lakota and Sioux will never forget. People I went to school with will never forget." At this last point, the audience started laughing. At her party in New York, the *Voice*'s Cynthia Heimel asked, "just wondering, do the Indians get any money?"

Billy Crystal climbed back on his horse and exhorted, "My new movie opens June 12. It's called *City Slickers*. There's a billion people watching, what am I, nuts?" The three-and-a-half hour ceremony terminated with closing credits, one for Giorgio Armani for Crystal's formal wear, though *WWD* thought "maybe he should have waived it—raisin is an icky color for a tux jacket."

Aftermath

Just as she had promised Cindy Adams, Whoopi Goldberg immediately took off her shoes backstage. She then told the press that as soon as she heard that she had won, "Words, bad words, were forming in my mouth—things beginning with 'f' and 's.' Then I remembered where I was." Now that she was away from the podium, she could say "I'm fucking thrilled." When asked if the picture had made her more spiritual, she howled and said, "No! If anything, it's taught me to get a piece of the 'backend,' meaning a piece of the action." Her winning screenwriter Bruce Rubin was also talking dollars and cents. His deal with Paramount called for four percent of his film's profits, but despite its $500 million worldwide gross, studio accountants claimed that *Ghost* had yet to go into the black. "I'm hoping Paramount will be good to me," he said optimistically. *People* revealed that Rubin was now a sought-after rewrite man earning $100,000 a week.

Screen tough guy Joe Pesci explained why he had given one of the shortest acceptance speeches on record: "There were so many people to thank, I was afraid that if I started I couldn't stop and would get booed." He was also sorry that Al Pacino lost, and he refused to have his head

"If you think you're a great actor 'cause you won an Oscar you're crazy."
—Joe Pesci

turned by the Academy recognition: "If you think you're a great actor 'cause you won an Oscar you're crazy . . . There are a lot of people who think this and they have a lot of problems. You have to be lucky."

Kevin Costner thought back on his adolescence. "I was never a big achiever in high school so I'm not used to this kind of thing," the double-winner admitted. *Newsday*'s Martin Kasindorf observed that "For a man who has had months to prepare his on-camera acceptance speech and backstage musings, Costner appeared surprisingly ill at ease and repeatedly untactful on the night of his greatest career triumph." He claimed that his Oscar success was "not the greatest thing in my life. My life is bigger than the movies and my ideas are bigger than the movies." Meanwhile, his editor Neil Travis was dispelling the rumor that Costner hadn't actually directed *Dances with Wolves* all by himself. He "was the sole director as far as I was concerned," said Travis, although he did say that Kevin Reynolds had shot some second-unit footage. Travis later took out a trade paper ad saying "The pressure on that stage was a bitch" and thanked "the supertalented" Costner "for trusting me with your firstborn."

Kathy Bates elaborated on her acceptance speech reference to her ninety-year-old father who had died two years earlier. He had originally given her the money to go to New York to pursue her acting career and "I just wish he could have been here tonight," she said, again fighting the urge to cry. "I think he really would have gotten a kick out of it." Bates cheered herself up by announcing the nuptials in her future. "Now that this is over we're going to plan our wedding." When somebody asked about her ensemble, she said it was a gift from her agent who picked it out, and her diamond ear clips were on loan from van Cleef and Arpel. The tassel she had carried with her to the podium held a teeny-tiny Oscar given her that day by a jeweler friend for luck. Back in New York, her friends at the Sea Palace put a glossy of the actress in the restaurant's window along with a sign of congratulations.

The first thing Best Actor Jeremy Irons did backstage was have a cigarette. Playing humble, the Briton told reporters that "As a whole, I think we're not as good as film actors as Americans." Asked whether he would now try to meet Claus von Bulow, Irons joked that "We may meet at dinner sometime. I'd love to meet him and tell him what he's all about. But the man's had enough invasion of his privacy without my calling him." A question about his footwear—deck shoes—led to this answer, "I feel the need to have my feet on the ground."

Unfortunately for Irons, for the first time ever, smoking was banned at the Governors' Ball, held next door to the Shrine. The *Los Angeles Times'* reporter found "miles of neon, mammoth lasers, black-and-white blowups of classic movie posters and waiters of both sexes clad in black unisex turtlenecks with Day-Glo cummerbunds." He also observed that Dustin Hoffman "was in a jovial mood, hugging everyone in sight, using the party-favor perfume for after-shave." Francis Ford Coppola's father Carmine, the Best Song loser among the film's seven Oscar losses, felt ill at the Ball and had to be taken away by ambulance; and although the diagnosis from Army Archerd was that he had suffered only a "very slight stroke," the Oscar-winning composer died a month later.

Kevin Costner's parents accompanied their son when the *Dances with Wolves* set slipped out of the Ball to attend a hush-hush private soiree at the Columbia Bar and Grill, where, the *Hollywood Reporter*'s Robert Osborne wrote, Costner did "a bit of an Indian dance with Graham Greene." The celebration continued until 4:00 A.M. and the guest list included former Costner costars and colleagues Andy Garcia, Susan Sarandon, Lawrence Kasdan, and, naturally, Michael Ovitz. Hangovers came the next day when *Daily Variety* headlined, "Dances No $ Savior for Orion," because the company's stocks just took a post-Oscar dip.

Farther west on Sunset, James Stewart and wife Gloria had been the first to arrive at the

"My life is bigger than the movies and my ideas are bigger than the movies."
—Kevin Costner

Irving Lazar affair at Spago and were the first to leave since Stewart had to hightail it to Stringfellows where he and Ginger Rogers were feted for the fiftieth anniversary of their Oscar wins. "I must have signed 200 autographs," Stewart told Army Archerd. At Swifty's during the opening number, noted the *Los Angeles Times:* "A waitress in one of the restaurant's upstairs offices decided she'd rather watch the Home Shopping Network than the Oscars. Unfortunately, her set controlled the fourteen monitors in the dining area. For twenty seconds, the Lazars' 140 guests were in the TV world of zirconium necklaces and discount microwave ovens." Among the elite were British former Oscar winners Maggie Smith and Ben Kingsley in town making movies, as well as American talent Ed MacMahon and his *Tonight Show* producer Fred De Cordova. When Governor Pete Wilson appeared, Lazar let him in but not his body guards—there wasn't enough room. Allan Carr also showed his face and played TV critic, grumbling "The show needs chemistry between the presenters. The audience is looking for a magical moment of two stars together. The Old Guard doesn't really think that's important. But it is, after all, a television show, and people want *Photoplay* magazine." According to *Women's Wear Daily*, Spago "was a snore until Madonna and Michael Jackson walked in at 11 P.M." Witnessed *People*, "After whispering and giggling in Michael's ear, the Material Girl abandoned her one-night Boy Toy and hopped over to Warren Beatty's table where heavy breathing and light necking ensued." The *London Times* observed that "judging by his expression, she talked dirty" to Beatty. *People* kept tabs on Jackson who "tit-for-tat, dandled Diana Ross on *his* lap before Madonna returned and joined him for a grand exit." When Whoopi Goldberg, Jeremy Irons, Kathy Bates, and their entourages entered to do more celebrating, the *Los Angeles Times* calculated, "The median age in the room dropped twenty years in twenty minutes."

As for other dos, El Rescate's $150-a-plate dinner-dance at Maple Drive had 250 attendees, almost a thousand less than last year thanks to limitations imposed by the city of Beverly Hills; the organization still managed to pull in $75,000. Susan Sarandon and Tim Robbins were at this party, too, and a reporter asked Robbins how he liked the Oscar show. "I never can get into those dance numbers," the actor admitted, adding that "I'd much rather see Brecht." A party of *Dances with Wolves* partisans in the Wilshire district was, according to *Hollywood Drama-Logue,* "the largest gathering of Native American actors ever gathered." The guest of honor was Sacheen Littlefeather, who took some of the credit for raising Hollywood's consciousness. "I knew many years ago that real Indian people in real Indian movies would be successful," said Marlon Brando's 1973 proxy. "My mother said I was ten years ahead of my time. Obviously, now people are ready."

The night's most eclectic guest list, no doubt, was at the Roxbury Supper Club, for a $1,000-a-plate dinner honoring 1961 Thalberg Award winner, Stanley Kramer. This benefit for the American Foundation of the Performing Arts attracted Eddie Fisher, Jerry Vale, Joni Mitchell, Morton Downey, Jr., Morey Amsterdam, Ron Silver, Cesar "Butch" Romero, the Pet Shop Boys, Bert Parks, Phyllis Diller, Mickey Dolenz, and ex-President and Mrs. Ford. The *Santa Monica Outlook* didn't think it was much of a bash because "Kramer huddled with his family in a red velvet corner booth of the 'V.I.P. Room' following dinner, then left midway through the affair." A "nervous press agent" explained, "Uh, Stanley's in a weird mood. He's just feeling kind of, uh, uh, quiet."

Lovebirds Julia Roberts and Kiefer Sutherland did not make the scene after the show, or later at the altar. A few days before the wedding, Roberts called the whole thing off.

Oscar show producer Gilbert Cates had to face the music the morning after in reviews that weren't as upbeat as last year's. "It was a long day's journey into night for Oscar, one of the most effective sleeping pills of the year," carped Rick du Brow of the *Los Angeles Times*, and the *Wash-*

"My mother said I was ten years ahead of my time."
—Sacheem Littlefeather

ington Post's Tom Shales complained that it was "more of a fizzle than usual." On the other hand, the *Hollywood Reporter*'s Miles Beller felt, "This year Oscar got it right," and David Bianculli wrote in the *New York Post*, "give last night's telecast credit, at least, for not getting everything wrong." Pauline Kael boasted she "laughed all the way through" the show because of the *Dances with Wolves* sweep. The host also drew mixed notices. *Entertainment Weekly*'s Jim Mullen called Crystal "the best thing about the Oscars," while *Variety* hated his "pimping his latest flick." Kay Gardella of the *New York Daily News* kvetched that "over such a long haul his nasal voice begins to grate on one's nerves like fingernails on a blackboard. He may have a sinus condition that needs attention. So does his material." Tom Carsin of the *L.A. Weekly* wrote, "It's a terrifying measure of the Academy's savvy that they think of Billy Crystal as a young, hip comedian. As an emcee, Crystal may actually beat Bob Hope for intolerability." One hundred eighty degrees away was Leonard Maltin who fretted that Crystal "was a little too hip for the room at times"; he generally loved the show because "Emotions ran high and they gave us all a chance to feel vicariously what it might be like to win this kind of award . . . good guys finishing first and the part of Hollywood we all like best, a happy ending." The ending was even happier when the Academy's broadcast cleaned up at the Emmys later in the year, winning trophies for Crystal, the writing, and the show itself.

A week after the ceremony, *Daily Variety*'s top story was that Martin Scorsese "has entered into a rare, exclusive, six-year motion picture producing and directing deal with Universal Pictures," whose chairman, Tom Pollock, raved that the director "is a unique animal who doesn't want to play Hollywood games and go to lunch everywhere; he wants to make movies." This turn of fortune was not enough for *GoodFellas'* supporters, still angry over Scorsese's going home empty-handed on Oscar night. Janet Maslin denigrated the Academy as "an organization capable of deeming Kevin Costner a better director than Martin Scorsese (the evening's single biggest outrage)." Gene Seymour of *Newsday* demanded to know "What is it going to take? What wheels does Martin Scorsese have to grease? Who does he have to buy off? Or knock off?" *Premiere* characterized Scorsese as being "angry and disappointed" over his loss and he told the magazine, "I wish I could be like some of the other guys and say, 'No, I don't care about it.' But for me, a kid growing up on the Lower East Side watching from the first telecast of the Oscars, there's a certain magic out there." Two Scorsese veterans expressed their opinions. Harvey Keitel reasoned that "Maybe he got what he deserves—exclusion from the mediocre." *Taxi Driver*'s Jodie Foster said "When you look at the ten old ladies who put down *Dances with Wolves* instead of *GoodFellas*—I don't know. The Oscars are like bingo. Who cares?" And as for the "rare" deal with Universal, the studio decided not to make the director's next project, deeming the $30 million budget for an adaptation of Edith Wharton's *The Age of Innocence* too dear a price for the prestige of having that "unique animal" in its employ.

1991

"Billy Crystal?—I crap bigger than him."
—Jack Palance

The 1991 Oscars went psycho.

Eat and Run

When Jodie Foster and Anthony Hopkins showed up at the previous Academy Awards to present the Writing Awards, *USA Today* reported "They drew louder applause than most of this year's crop." The duo was currently in theaters starring in *The Silence of the Lambs* and as Hopkins approached the Shrine auditorium, KABC-TV interviewer Steve Edwards greeted him with, "This is your rehearsal for next year." Responded Hopkins, "If you say so."

Based on a best-selling novel by Thomas Harris, *The Silence of the Lambs* told the story of a female FBI agent tracking down the serial killer of young women. At a prison for the criminally insane she seeks the counsel of an expert who knows the workings of the psychotic mind since he, too, is a homicidal maniac, known as "Hannibal the Cannibal," for not only killing his victims but eating them, too. The film had been intended to serve as Gene Hackman's directorial debut but he backed out; Liz Smith reported " 'He always gets cold feet,' says one who knows him well." Orion then approached Jonathan Demme, who said, "The idea of a film about a serial killer repels me"; after reading the book, however, he signed on because he was enamored of the feisty heroine. Citing his first movies—a pair of Roger Corman cheapies—a women's prison flick, *Caged Heat*, and *Crazy Mama*, in which Cloris Leachman led a group of desperadoes—Demme laughed, "I obviously still love doing movies about strong women in difficult circumstances."

Demme's *Married to the Mob* star Michelle Pfeiffer tentatively agreed to play the G-Woman but changed her mind because, said Demme, "she was really frightened of the material"; according to the *Los Angeles Herald-Examiner*, the only thing the actress was afraid of was a small paycheck—Orion wouldn't give her the $2 million she wanted. Pfeiffer was replaced by Jodie Foster, who had learned of the book from *Vanity Fair* interviewer Jesse Kornbluth. "She isn't a version of Rambo. It's all about her brain," said the 1988 Oscar winner, looking for a follow-up. "And it's not about some sort of squealy thing running around in her underwear either." Louis Gossett, Jr. claimed that he was on the verge of getting the part of Dr. Hannibal Lecter but ultimately the filmmakers "didn't want to cast a black man as a cannibal." Instead they chose a Welshman, Anthony Hopkins, an Emmy winner for playing Hitler, who shrugged, "I just seem to get cast in these sorts of parts." He wasn't complaining, though, because playing Hannibal the Cannibal "was great fun . . . a great chance to play a game, to flirt with something that's so diabolical, knowing it's only a fiction." The actor said that the voice he worked out to express his character's controlled madness was a "combination of Truman Capote and Katharine Hepburn," the actress with whom he made his film debut in *The Lion in Winter*.

Opening on Valentine's Day, *The Silence of the Lambs* was deemed by Janet Maslin of the *New York Times* to be a "phenomenally skillful adaptation." The movie thoroughly spooked Rex Reed who called it "hair-frying, a masterwork of unbearable maximum anxiety and tension that will leave you limp as a dead butterfly's wing." *Variety* praised Hopkins as "the personification of brilliant, hypnotic evil, and the screen jolts with electricity whenever he is on"; Duane Byrge of the *Hollywood Reporter* deemed his performance "spectacularly unnerving." Philip Wuntch of the *Dallas Morning News* wrote that "Foster has the less showy role. But she plays it with quiet authority, sly humor, and a stalwart grace under pressure . . . she must share the screen with assorted kooks and two outright maniacs. She

Overleaf: *Seventy-two-year-old Best Supporting Actor Jack Palance gets down.*

"He's endowed with all the fag clichés homophobes have doted on for decades."
—Stephen Harvey

does so without sliding into the background."

Not everyone liked *Silence.* Gene Siskel sneered that its heroine-vs.-psycho conclusion "is nothing more than a grisly version of every mad-slasher picture you've ever missed." It's much worse than that, thought Ron Rosenbaum of *Mademoiselle* who lambasted *The Silence of the Lambs* as a "snuff film . . . a sick pornography of butchery." The now retired Pauline Kael got her licks in, too, telling *Newsday,* "the film has no soul. It's pulp material treated as art, and I think that's a bit of a fraud. I like my pulp treated more like pulp, as in *The Grifters.*" Greg Rutkowski, an executive with the AMC theater chain that did very well with this attraction, came to its defense: "Demme is a bizarre guy and there's no question that he presses some different buttons, but he's not appealing to prurient interests."

Precious Poodle

The most vociferous critics were gay activists horrified by the characterization of the film's serial killer. As Stephen Harvey, associate curator in the Department of Film of the Museum of Modern Art, put it, "he's endowed with all the fag clichés homophobes have doted on for decades: bleached locks, whiny voice, frilly glad rags and, choicest of all, the love of a teensy white poodle named Precious." Richard Jennings of the Gay and Lesbian Alliance Against Defamation (GLAAD) lamented that "This film is a continuation of Hollywood's appalling track record of portraying gays in negative ways" and warned that it "could potentially encourage gay bashing." Jonathan Demme told the *Village Voice* that "homophobia is one of the cowardly manifestations of the sickness of American males," and so was mortified at being accused of it. The director pleaded with David Ehrenstein of *The Advocate:* "Listen, you've got to believe me. I didn't want this picture to send out the wrong signals. I am *not* a homophobe." He insisted that "I don't understand how anyone could think he's gay." When Ehrenstein pointed out that the murderer keeps the severed head of a male lover in his garage, Demme argued that the dead guy was just an experimental one-night stand from years ago. A few gay people sided with the director. "I was not offended by the film," said Stephen Bennett, head of the AIDS Project L.A. "The villain was a psychopathic mess, not representative of the gay community." Nevertheless, activist organizations picketed the film and passed out flyers asking moviegoers to pass up *The Silence of the Lambs.*

A boycott was the last thing Orion needed; despite the success of *Dances with Wolves*—for which the studio still reportedly owed Kevin Costner's company $3 million—it remained on the precipice of bankruptcy. *Silence* helped with a theatrical gross of over $100 million and a healthy profit when it was released on video on October 24 in time for the Halloween horror market. *People* declared that, "Not since 1960, when Janet Leigh turned on the shower in *Psycho,* has a film quite touched off the seismic tremors of terror which have accompanied *The Silence of the Lambs.* Hannibal Lecter has become the Norman Bates of the '90s, and moviegoers are flocking to see him."

Having a Wild Weekend

Gay characters weren't the only ones stuck in Hollywood stereotyping. Callie Khouri sighed, "So many times you go to the movies, and what woman up there would you want to be? None of them." The thirty-three-year-old music video producer wanted things to change but "I figured maybe the only way that's going to happen is if I wrote it myself." She came up with a world-weary waitress and a naive housewife whose weekend in the country turns riotous when they shoot a would-be rapist and take it on the lam through the American southwest in their Thunderbird convertible. Britisher Ridley Scott, best known for directing such brooding action films as *Alien* and *Blade Runner,* decided to produce the script, titled *Thelma & Louise,* because he was attracted to the lead characters. "I like strong women," he said. "In fact, I don't like polite women at all. Because

"I didn't realize that everyone would be so touchy."
—Susan Sarandon

then I'm forced to be polite, which I don't like." Meryl Streep and Goldie Hawn were the first choices for the fugitives, but Streep was unavailable and Hawn's agent at C.A.A. insisted the film would be a bad career move. Producer Scott was so taken with second choices Geena Davis as wide-eyed Thelma and Susan Sarandon as jaded Louise that "when I began interviewing other directors about the project, I became so jealous that someone else would be spending time with these fantastic women, I hired myself."

Amy Dawes of *Variety* called *Thelma & Louise* "a thumpingly adventurous road pic" and raved that "Despite some delectably funny scenes between the sexes, Scott's latest pic isn't about women vs. men. It's about freedom, like any good road picture. In that sense, and in many others, it's a classic." Terrence Rafferty of *The New Yorker* found the story "preposterous," but conceded that "Davis and Sarandon are so vivid and likable that they carry us past the plot's most obvious contrivances; a little disbelief seems a small price to pay for being allowed to remain in their company." *Thelma & Louise* was released by MGM, which was in almost as bad financial shape as Orion, and the studio had to postpone the film's premiere for two months until enough lucre was gathered to mount a decent publicity campaign. Fortunately, the film's two take-charge female characters captivated moviegoers and made a profit.

Sensitive Guys

Most of the movie's males tended to be mean or dumb but during production Scott said "I am hoping that the film is done with such humor that men will be able to laugh at themselves rather than take it too seriously." Fat chance. Richard Johnson, gossip columnist of the *New York Daily News*, went ballistic. The leads "give terrific performances," he admitted, "but this female buddy movie is ridiculous. It justifies armed robbery, manslaughter, and chronic drunken-driving as exercises in consciousness-raising. It glorifies suicide. And it is so degrading to men, with pathetic stereotypes of testosterone-crazed behavior that Loew's Theaters should ban it immediately," since the chain had blackballed a misogynistic Andrew Dice Clay concert movie. Janet Maslin fired back that "The aspects of this film that have raised the greatest furor are features that would be virtually routine in a comparable movie about men. So it requires the use of a double standard to feel that *Thelma & Louise* fails to depict exemplary behavior when the masculine road movie has never pretended to do anything of the sort." Andrew Sarris noted in *New York Observer* that the movie "touches a nerve in both sexes that seems to give as much pain to males as it does pleasure to females . . . Yes, Virginia, there is a difference between men and women. *Thelma & Louise* exacerbates it at every opportunity." Such was the case *chez* Sarris, for while he called the heroines' climactic plunge "tragic," his wife, critic Molly Haskell, found it "triumphant." Sides weren't drawn strictly according to gender lines. Sheila Benson of the *Los Angeles Times* was a traitor, harrumphing that feminism "has to do with responsibility, equality, sensitivity, understanding—not revenge, retributive sadistic behavior." *Variety*'s Anne Thompson observed that the film was getting "the kind of media attention that turns a movie into a cultural phenomenon," and the furor landed *Thelma & Louise* on the cover of *Time*. It was also a topic on *Oprah* where, after labeling it "a female buddy movie," Roger Ebert was chastised—to the audience's cheers—by a woman who insisted, "No, it isn't. It's about sisterhood."

The three women connected with *Thelma & Louise* all spoke out on the controversy. Geena Davis said, "It's not just wrong to raise our little girls to be nice and polite and sweet all the time and always say yes, it's life-threatening." Asked if the film was hostile toward men, writer Callie Khouri responded, "I don't think it is. I think it is hostile toward idiots." And Susan Sarandon told *Redbook*, "I didn't realize that everyone would be so touchy. I mean, did people think *Pretty Woman*

"I wasn't going to let some fool from Idaho or Encino direct a movie about living in my neighborhood."
—John Singleton

was such a great role model? Did they think it's better to get your way by giving blow jobs?"

Singleton Sensation

A cluster of movies made by young black directors unspooled in the summer of 1991, including nineteen-year-old Matty Rich's *Straight Out of Brooklyn*, twenty-nine-year-old Joseph B. Vasquez's *Hangin' with the Homeboys*, and Spike Lee's interracial love story, *Jungle Fever*, which made the cover of *Newsweek*; at age thirty-five, Lee was now the grand old man of the Black Renaissance. The most popular entry with both critics and audiences, though, was twenty-three-year-old John Singleton's *Boyz N the Hood*, a slice of life drama about three boyhood friends in South Central Los Angeles that served as a cautionary tale against drugs and gang warfare. Singleton was a graduate of the U.S.C. film school, where he concentrated in script writing because "if it ain't on the page, it ain't on the stage." He twice won the school's Jack Nicholson screenwriting award—the second time for *Boyz N the Hood*—and two weeks after graduation signed with C.A.A. When Columbia made a bid on the script, Singleton insisted that he also get to direct the movie—even though his previous filmmaking experience consisted of two silent 8 mm. shorts. "I wasn't going to let some fool from Idaho or Encino direct a movie about living in my neighborhood," he boasted. Studio head Frank Price could see his logic and decided to give Singleton a shot because "he has enormous self-confidence and assurance. In fact, the last time I'd met someone that young with so much self-assurance was Steven Spielberg." Singleton cast one established actor, Larry Fishburne, along with a group of new marquee names: Cuba Gooding, Jr., Morris Chestnut, Desi Arnaz Hines II, and the rap musician about whom Singleton said, "What Toshiro Mifune is to Akira Kurosawa, Ice Cube is to me." The young director retreated to his old stomping grounds to shoot the film and told studio honchos "horror stories" about the South Central area because he figured "it keeps them out of the way."

Roger Ebert was on hand at the Cannes Film Festival where "In the kind of spontaneous display of enthusiasm granted only rarely by festival audiences, *Boyz N the Hood* received a tumultuous ovation." Ebert described the film as "not simply a brilliant directorial debut, but an American film of enormous relevance." Preparing for the American premiere, Singleton proved to be as provocative an interviewee as Oliver Stone, telling *Downtown* magazine several months after the L.A.P.D. beating of Rodney King that "Where I come from, cops are nothing more than donut eatin', gun totin' Nazis." And when he started to recount to another reporter how his eighth-grade class cheered when Ronald Reagan got shot, his mother scolded, "Don't say anything political, because this might be a Republican magazine. You don't know who owns these magazines."

Jami Bernard of the *New York Post* deemed Singleton's "a remarkable writing-directing debut" although she was disturbed that "The fear and loathing of women hangs like a glop over the entire production." Also hanging over Singleton's triumph was the violence that broke out on opening day in several theaters from Jersey City to Universal City, resulting in two deaths and over thirty injuries. The director, who concluded his film with the plea "Increase the Peace," was saddened but he saw no reason to shoulder the blame for the disturbances. "I didn't create the conditions under which people shoot each other," averred Singleton. "This happens because there's a whole generation of people who feel disenfranchised." *Variety* talked to an unnamed theater exhibitor about the violence. "Across the country, when you play a film like this in a gang-related area, you have to be prepared," he philosophized. "But it's worth it. You'll make five times per screen what you would have if you played the same film in the suburbs instead." Columbia's investment was well worthwhile, too. The $6 million *Boys N the Hood* earned $57 domestically, making it the most profitable movie of the year.

"I wanted a woman of the '90s, someone who wanted to do more than wait for her prince to come."
—Linda Woolverton

Robin Williams Nude

Robin Williams returned in an update of the myth of Parsifal entitled *The Fisher King*, about an abrasive New York radio talk-show host who incites a caller into going on a murder spree. The guilt-ridden deejay becomes a dissipated wreck until he's redeemed by a gentle homeless person, Parry—get it?—who enlists his help in rescuing the Holy Grail from a millionaire's house. Paired with Jeff Bridges as the shock-jock, Robin Williams played the eccentric street person, but if he thought he could just do his Robin Williams riffs, director Terry Gilliam had news for him. "One of the first things I said to Robin was whatever funniness is here is going to be based on pain," said the director. "Robin works himself up. Tears are flowing. He is playing it frighteningly naked." Literally. Viewers got to see Williams frolicking in the nude in Central Park.

Pia Linstrom of WNBC-TV raved that the *The Fisher King* is "wild, wonderful and crazy." David Denby, who felt that director Gilliam had "made some of the most spectacular messes in the history of movies," chalked it up as another one, saying the film "has a glazed, forced, megalomanically jumbled quality that is, at times, exceptionally unpleasant." David Ansen of *Newsweek* felt that Williams "puts all his mercurial comic brilliance in the service of his character (well, almost all)" but that it was Jeff Bridges as the reformed creep "who holds the whole thing together. His subtle corrosive performance encompasses the movie's extravagant range of tones." Former Jonathan Demme star Mercedes Ruehl played Bridges' lover, a hard-edged video store owner, and Janet Maslin declared that she "again proves herself to be a fiery comedian graced with superb timing." But then there was Andrew Sarris rolling his eyes that "Ms. Ruehl adds new dimensions to nasal ethnicity with the pushiest performance since Marie Dressler's Tugboat Annie. I mean this undoubtedly talented actress *indicates* every second she is on the screen. She will not be denied." *The Fisher King* was the third of the year's movies about a smug yuppie undergoing terrible hardships to find his "inner child," but it proved much more popular with audiences than either *The Doctor* or Mike Nichols' *Regarding Henry*, the latter memorable only for its later parody by an X-rated video entitled *Regarding Heinie*.

It's an Art Film, Stupid

Disney also dusted off an old myth, following up its smash *The Little Mermaid* with *Beauty and the Beast*, again with a score by the Oscar-winning duo of Alan Menken and Howard Ashman. A Disney executive said that the production team had screened Jean Cocteau's sumptuous 1946 version of the story but that "it seemed to be about two people who had dinner a lot and it had psychosexual overtones, so we went with our own story." Scripter Linda Woolverton, a veteran of Saturday morning cartoons like *My Little Pony*, was the first woman to write an animated feature for Disney and, in adapting the fairy tale, was sounding almost like Callie Khouri. "Belle is a feminist," the author said of her heroine. "I'm not critical of Snow White or Cinderella . . . they reflected the values of their time. But it just wasn't in me to write a throwback. I wanted a woman of the '90s, someone who wanted to do more than wait for her prince to come." Which meant that the character sat around and read books.

The studio devised an elaborate plan to ensure that *Beauty and the Beast* wouldn't be considered just another kiddie cartoon. Eight months before the film was scheduled to be released, composer Menken, studio head Jeffrey Katzenberg, the film's two directors, and Walt's nephew Roy Disney greeted the press in New York and Los Angeles with snippets of the movie and a spiel that portrayed *Beauty and the Beast* as the natural heir to such Disney classics as *Snow White* and *Bambi*, lest the reporters think it was akin to the newer stuff like *Oliver and Company*. As "an industry observer" explained to the *Los Angeles Times*,

"If Watts went up in flames tomorrow and everyone died, I don't think they'd care."
—Bette Midler

"Katzenberg is feeling pressure these days and this is his baby. He'd like to finish this year in a blaze of glory."

The studio managed to get the unfinished cartoon accepted into the New York Film Festival that fall as a "work in progress." *Vogue* reported that a lot of work was left to be done because "*the Beast* was at times no more than a few angry pencil lines whirling on a white background." Nevertheless, the Lincoln Center highbrows gave the cartoon a ten-minute standing ovation and, setting the groundwork for Hollywood word of mouth, Disney then showed it at the Los Angeles County Museum of Art. Attempting to sell the finished film to baby-boomers and not just their kids, the Disney ballyhoo department came up with a separate advertising campaign the grown-ups could call their own. In lieu of cute cartoon animated kitchen utensils for the children's market, this ad featured the title characters silhouetted with a light glowing between them as they danced in front of the Beast's castle and the tag line, "The most beautiful love story ever told." And Jeffrey Katzenberg promised, "When you see the movie, you'll think you're watching Richard Gere and Julia Roberts."

The studio's release pattern also befitted a prestige item. Prior to its national distribution, *Beauty and the Beast* opened in New York at a single theater across from Bloomingdale's, while in Los Angeles, it was the premiere attraction at El Capitan, a newly refurbished Hollywood Boulevard palace from the 1920s, with the theater's elaborate ornamentation uncovered for the first time in fifty years; as a sort of minor-league Radio City Music Hall, El Capitan also featured a ten-minute show in which the ushers sang onstage before picking up discarded popcorn boxes around the auditorium with large plastic bags.

Beauty and the Beast left the *Hollywood Reporter*'s Duane Byrge starry-eyed: "Steeping with magical moments and bursting with vitality, this scrumptuously grand movie will be one of the year's great performers, and every seventh year hence it will continue to cast its wondrous spells over as-yet-unborn viewers." David Ansen raved, "Sophisticated and funny, romantic and scary, *Beauty and the Beast* is an instant classic." Caryn James of the *New York Times* admitted to a crush on the cartoon Beast, whom she dubbed the year's "Most Romantic Leading Man," and who "has a certain sex appeal—let's not say animal magnetism—that very little girls may not appreciate till they're older." Frank Rich, the *Times'* drama critic, answered his own question of "What is the best Broadway musical comedy score of 1991?" with: "Make no mistake about it, it is the score that Alan Menken and Howard Ashman wrote for *Beauty and the Beast*." Rich felt that the songs "have a spark that is missing from most contemporary Broadway musicals" and noted the passing of forty-year-old lyricist Ashman, who was also the executive producer. Ashman had died of AIDS while the film was in production and never saw the final product.

A Losing Bette

Bette Midler had had a home at Disney since her 1986 comeback *Down and Out in Beverly Hills* but now *Beauty and the Beast*'s Belle had supplanted her as Queen of the Lot. The studio said no thanks to Midler's dream project, a saga about a brassy USO entertainer spanning three wars and fifty years, but 20th Century-Fox welcomed her with open arms. "I'm a big Bette Midler fan," gushed studio chairman Joe Roth, "and this was our only opportunity to be in the Bette Midler business." *For the Boys* had been in development at Midler's production company for a half-dozen years but Mark Rydell, the director of her Oscar-nominated *The Rose*, felt that still wasn't long enough. He agreed to do the film only if Woody Allen's ex-partner Marshall Brickman was brought in for more rewrites; by the time *For the Boys* went into production, there had been forty-one drafts of the script. Rydell said "Disney has made her a star by putting her in light mindless comedies, but for the most part the material is not worthy of her talent. This was the first script since

"I don't know what issues he has unresolved with his own mother."
—Barbra Streisand on Mike Wallace

The Rose that I think is on the same level." Midler agreed. "It takes advantage of all my abilities," she enthused to the *London Times*. "This character is probably the most exciting I've ever had a chance to play. She ages, she sings, she dances, she chews the scenery." So that no one would think that the film's other major character, an entertainer played by James Caan, was based on Bob Hope, he was made Jewish. And director Rydell warned that even though *For the Boys* was a musical, it "will be quite disturbing and realistic . . . You'll see singing and dancing next to scenes of death." His wish for the movie? "At the end of this film, I want the audience to stagger out supporting each other."

An optimistic Fox spared no expense in prerelease advertising and Midler did scores of interviews, sometimes focusing on her happy private life ("I love my house and my garden. I love to sew and I bake," quoted *Entertainment Weekly*), other times grieving for the friends she lost to AIDS and speaking of social inequalities ("And I really do blame the White House. As the saying goes, the fish stinks from the head," she told *Newsday*, adding "If Watts went up in flames tomorrow and everyone died, I don't think they'd care."). She also got some unsolicited publicity when Geraldo Rivera published his memoirs of sexual conquests and described Midler as sexually "insatiable." Her response: "He's such a toad!" Midler prefaced a special invitational screening of her $45 million, two-and-a-half-hour vehicle at the Motion Picture Academy by singing several songs with an eighteen-piece orchestra—her first live performance in years—and then waited for the reviews.

Rex Reed was beside himself: "For the boys, for the girls, and the whole human race. There is only one word to describe this movie and the word is fabulous." The *Hollywood Reporter* cheered that Midler "struts her considerable stuff to the staccato-steppin' max," and in *Newsday*, Frank DeCaro presumed to speak for the gay male audience: "For us boys—Bette fans from way back—*For the Boys* is not just a Midler showcase, but a date with the woman of our dreams, a reacquaintance with our heroine in open-toed shoes, the forever Divine Miss M." As for her costar, Andrew Sarris wrote "The burned-out James Caan serves in much the same capacity here as he did opposite Kathy Bates in *Misery*, as the George Brent of the '90s, setting up his ferocious leading ladies for Oscars."

Bernard Weinraub, Hollywood reporter for the *New York Times,* delivered the bad news: audiences were shunning Midler's vehicle. Weinraub wrote "because of the high budget and the high expectations stirred by its stars and director, few films this year have prompted such post-mortems and anguish in Hollywood." *Lear*'s reported that *"For the Boys*, though by and large favorably reviewed, was the most high-profile flop of the holiday season. The pain of this failure sent Midler into seclusion."

If things weren't bad enough, one Mark Harris was considering suing Midler. The forty-two-year-old hairdresser had recently married seventy-five-year-old invalid Martha Raye and claimed that Midler's movie was a rip-off of the Big Mouth's life. Despite the failure of *For the Boys*, Harris had his own dream project, a retelling of his courtship of Raye, who ideally would be played by Estelle Parsons. And who should play Harris? "I see either Alec Baldwin or Sylvester Stallone," he told *Entertainment Tonight.*

Down Memory Lane

Another diva in a year-end release was Barbra Streisand, but she refrained from singing in *The Prince of Tides*, not even a song over the final credit crawl. She did, however, direct and coproduce the film. Streisand said she has a favorite saying: "The journey into the past is the only way forward." It was only natural, then, that she'd be attracted to Pat Conroy's best-selling 1986 novel in which a female psychiatrist helps an aging good ol' boy and his suicidal sister confront the demons of their screwed-up childhood. At one time, it was thought the story would make a swell reunion for Streisand, Robert Redford, and director Sydney Pollack but those other two parts of the *Way We Were* triumvirate went on to do *Havana* instead. Nick Nolte signed up to be analyzed by and make love to Streisand's Dr. Lowenstein. The director tattled that Nolte "wasn't comfortable playing a romantic leading man. He calls himself a character actor. I kept saying 'Yeah, yeah, sure, sure, but let me cut your hair.' "

To play the story's fierce matriarch, Streisand considered hiring Irene Worth to play the character's later scenes, but, in the end, she let Kate Nelligan do the whole role, even though she was ten years younger than Nolte. The director picked her own son Jason Gould to play her screen son after he passed his audition. Gould maintained that making the film with his mom "was like working for any director, except I would eat lunch with her." Author Pat Conroy was hired to touch up another writer's earlier incarnation of the script. Of Streisand, Conroy said, "I enjoyed working with her. I'd heard through the press she was a monster. She turned out to be a total delight. I was stunned." Kate Nelligan agreed that the director was "very real, very kind" and she enjoyed Nolte as well. "Whenever Nick's around, there goes the neighborhood. He's just so terribly low-rent it's comical."

Streisand Schmoozes

Variety's editor-in-chief Peter Bart was impressed by all the tub-thumping Streisand was doing for her movie, noting that she "has been both persuasive and ubiquitous, smiling from practically every magazine cover and chatting earnestly about her traumatic childhood on virtually every TV show." Her old acquaintance Mike Wallace, who had first put her on the air when she was nineteen, welcomed her to *60 Minutes* and then gave her a hard time about her relationship with her mother, whom he also interviewed. When asked "Are you proud of your daughter?" Diana Kind retorted, "Who wouldn't be?" "I was shocked to be attacked," Barbra confessed afterward on Larry King's show, putting the blame on Mike. "I don't know what issues he has unresolved with his own mother." After all, Streisand said later to King, she credited her mom with her career direction. "One time my mother got mad at me, I did something bad . . . she kind of hit me a little bit, so I pretended I was deaf. And it got her. And I did it for hours and hours and I did it well. I thought, 'Hey, I can act!' "

Columbia was so high on *The Prince of Tides* that it moved the release date back to Christmas so that the film would be fresher in the minds of Oscar voters. David Elliott of the *San Diego Union* praised the film as a "great tidal wave of feeling" and David Denby wrote that "Middlebrow seriousness of this sort—soul-searching examination of family and love and destiny—has just about gone out of our movies, and while watching *Prince,* which is extremely absorbing, I realized how much I missed it."

Scornful Shrinks

In contrast, an indignant psychiatrist wrote to *New York* complaining that the movie "misrepresented the role of a female psychiatrist as a seductive and manipulative character who takes advantage of an emotionally crippled man. What occurred on the screen could be grounds for malpractice." Gene Siskel ridiculed *The Prince of Tides* as "an overwrought drama," in which "Streisand takes an important subject—child abuse—with a script less sophisticated than the average TV talk show. The simple solution to life's problems: Talk about them in one cathartic scene with a shrink and they disappear."

Variety raved that in giving the "performance of a lifetime . . . Nolte courageously leaves himself naked on screen" while the *Philadelphia Inquirer*'s Carrie Rickey called the actor "extraordinary" and opined that "the director and her male lead are astonishingly matched, working off each other like seasoned dance partners." Columbia chairman Mark Canton bragged to the *Hollywood Reporter*'s Martin Grove that Nolte's "always been a fine actor, but rarely have you seen any actor get this many great reviews." Kathleen Carroll of the *New York Daily News* thought Nolte should thank his director who "is generous to a fault when it comes to letting her co-star upstage her." But Streisand didn't neglect herself completely. *Variety* giggled that "the director unabashedly shows off her shapely legs in repeated close-ups" and others singled out her long fingernails which the *Village Voice*'s Georgia Brown called "these grotesque little finger-extensions like Freddy Krueger or Ming the Merciless."

Scorsese Scores

After making *The Prince of Tides*, Nick Nolte became part of another dysfunctional screen family. Steven Spielberg planned to remake J. Lee Thompson's thriller *Cape Fear*, in which Robert Mitchum personified evil and terrorized Gregory Peck's brood. Then Spielberg decided that "I wasn't in the mood, it's as simple as that. I just couldn't find it inside me to make a scary movie about a family being preyed on by a maniac." He decided instead to make a movie with Robin Williams and Julia Roberts about Peter Pan growing up, yet his company Amblin still owned the remake rights to the thriller. Robert De Niro was hot to do the Robert Mitchum role, so he and Spielberg descended upon Martin Scorsese, who read the script three times. "And three times I hated it," he recalled. "And it's like *Cape Fear*? A remake? Who wants to be bothered. This is insane." Scorsese couldn't relate to the script's all-American family—"they were like Martians to me"—and was actually rooting for the psycho to off them. Spielberg came up with a solution: Scorsese should rewrite it.

In Scorsese's version the goody two-shoes bunch has become racked with adultery and frustration, with Nolte a detached husband and Jessica Lange his depressed wife saddled with a moody, sexually curious teenage daughter. Scorsese had his biggest budget ever ($34 million), shot in widescreen for the first time, and had the pleasure of recycling Bernard Herrmann's score from the 1962 original. The director said that "I just want to challenge myself. I've made so many films about Italians!" but he also readily admitted that "I set out to make a picture that was more mainstream and more 'commercial,' whatever that was. I just hope it makes money," he sighed to *Premiere*.

Which was exactly the problem, thought David Sterritt of the *Christian Science Monitor*: "the fierce resonance of *Taxi Driver* gives way here to shock effects and horror-movie twists geared to making audiences shriek rather than think." Kathleen Carroll agreed, complaining that "The movie is eventually reduced to the absurd extremes of a blood and gore horror flick" and that by the time it was all over she felt "as worked over as a punch-drunk fighter." But Owen Gleiberman of *Entertainment Weekly* didn't think Scorsese was slumming at all, maintaining that the director "has taken the original film and teased out a richly satisfying layer of moral complexity." Arousing considerable attention was an intense nine-minute scene in which De Niro's stalker corners the daughter, played by Juliette Lewis, in a school auditorium and leads her through a discussion of her carnal interests before getting her to suck his thumb. David Ansen singled out De Niro's "lip-smacking, blackly comic portrayal of psychopathic self-righteousness" while the *New York Post*'s Jami Bernard was most impressed at how the eighteen-year-old "Lewis is completely in tune with the sexual schizophrenia that marks early womanhood."

When Universal first screened the movie for Academy members in November, the audience hissed when the closing credits came up. Nevertheless the horror film did have a happy ending for Scorsese because *Entertainment Weekly* was able to report that with *Cape Fear* "Scorsese has attained something that has always stayed just out of his grasp: a mass audience."

"I was looking for someone to make me good. When I met her, I felt relief."
—Warren Beatty on Annette Bening

Warren in Love

Warren Beatty also crossed over to the other side of the law. Just as he had claimed that his film version of *Dick Tracy* had its gestation in his childhood perusals of comic strips, Beatty was now saying that the life of gangster Bugsy Siegel "was a helluva story and I've been interested in it since I was a kid." Back in 1984, Beatty had commissioned a script from writer-director James Toback, whom *Spy* had immortalized as a relentless New York pick-up artist with lousy come-on lines, e.g., "I'm a member of the Harvard Club." After twenty-five drafts, Toback had fine-tuned the story of the debonair but crazy mobster Ben Siegel, who hung out with movie stars and invented Vegas by building a casino in the Nevada desert. *Movieline* observed that by the time Beatty was satisfied with the script he was "already a decade too old to portray the bad boy who died at age forty-one." Even though the only movie in the last fifteen years that Beatty had starred in without directing himself was *Ishtar*, he entrusted the project to another—*Rain Man*'s Oscar-winning Barry Levinson.

For the role of Bugsy's love interest, Beatty and Levinson considered the up-and-coming actress Annette Bening. Just before *The Grifters* opened, Beatty had met her at a shopping mall pizza joint and said, "I was looking for someone to make me good. When I met her, I felt relief." When Bening attended the Academy luncheon after being nominated for the Stephen Frears' film, *USA Today* reported, "Now sporting brown hair, she laughed off questions about a Madonna-like on-set romance as 'ridiculous.' " Rumors persisted and soon gossip-maven Suzy was buzzing that "The love scenes between Warren, who plays the handsome gangster Ben "Bugsy" Siegel—he was catnip to women—and his costar Annette Bening, who portrays sexy starlet Virginia Hill, will make you forget Breathless Mahoney ever met Dick Tracy (Warren did a long time ago)." Come July, they couldn't contain it any longer. Their publicists broke the news that Warren and Annette were expecting a baby. Barry Levinson swore that nobody on the set had a clue. "I was totally naive," the director said. "They didn't exactly go strolling arm in arm." That Hollywood's most famous modern-day Lothario was entering the ranks of fatherhood made worldwide headlines, with one paper blaring "From Cad to Dad!" "I wish I had thought of that," Bette Midler told *Vanity Fair*, when she heard of the impending birth. "It's like this big P.R. deal. It's shocking it's so cynical." It was also priceless publicity for the $40 million movie, especially since Tri-Star was trying to convince a public that had tired of underworld films that *Bugsy* was actually a romance and not a gangster film at all; the cryptic tag line for the movie's advertising was "Glamor was the Disguise." Beatty himself described the film as "a hell of a tug of war between a man and a woman who were passionately in love. It's a slugfest." As for his significant other, Beatty called her "the Michael Jordan of actresses."

Stephen Schiff of *Vanity Fair* felt that "*Bugsy* makes you believe in movies again. It is the sort of sprawling energetic American movie you remember from the golden age." Bob Strauss of the *L.A. Daily News* wrote "Just when you thought that Hollywood had abandoned the art of glamorous adult entertainment along comes *Bugsy*." Andrew Sarris thought about the good old days and groused that, "This was the kind of gangster yarn that Jimmy Cagney and Joan Blondell could rattle off in seventy minutes three times a year for Warner Brothers in the '30s, and with considerably more flair and energy." William Arnold of the *Seattle Post-Intelligencer* raved over "a volcanic, tour-de-force performance" by Beatty and *Rolling Stone*'s Peter Travers said that Bening "makes a knockout impression." But *Variety* thought that "Virginia Hill remains a one-dimensional and annoying stick figure," and Eric Menken of the *L.A. Reader* joshed that Beatty "manages a little more life than he did as Dick Tracy. He showed that at least some of his facial muscles function."

"Let's face it, the public can only take this good-guy story about me for so long."
—Kevin Costner

And Beatty Makes Three

The Bening-Beatty baby girl made her appearance—thirteen days behind schedule—a couple of weeks after *Bugsy* premiered. Kathlyn Beatty weighed in at 8 lbs., 11 ozs. A staffer at Cedars-Sinai hospital told the *New York Daily News* after Bening's difficult Cesarean section, "Warren looked quite disturbed when he came out of the delivery room." Bening's mother said that once Beatty calmed down, he was "like a silly schoolboy, he can't keep his eyes off the child." Beatty was also sounding pretty silly when he went on the *Today* show to trade baby stories with Katie Couric, who got it out of him that his child's nickname was "Grumpee Munchkee. It's been shortened to Munch and to Burble-Gurble." Mother Couric bragged that her infant's pseudonym was "Pea Pie." "I shudder to think," recoiled Beatty. When spoilsport Couric brought up that *Bugsy*'s $40 million gross was considered disappointing, the producer replied, "It did better than I ever thought it would . . . it's not an escapist delight."

Costner's Clout

Another matinee idol, Kevin Costner was already an established father figure with three children. Thanks to the recent addition of two Oscars to the family, he was the big man in Hollywood. "He understands the clout he has and he's going to use it," stated his producing partner Jim Wilson in a worshipful *Vanity Fair* cover story entitled "Costner in Control." "He intends to make one or two movies a year, peppering the commercial ones with the controversial ones. He knows he's the biggest star in the world right now because he appeals to every common denominator." Filling his popcorn quota, Costner played a laid-back Sherwood Forest hero who has a Bryan Adams rock song for theme music and tells Moorish sidekick Morgan Freeman "I hear ya" in *Robin Hood: Prince of Thieves.* The movie was a big hit with kids and earned over $100 million. "Let's face it, the public can only take this good-guy story about me for so long," the star exclaimed after a mocking interview in print by the *New York Times*' Maureen Dowd and an onscreen put-down by Madonna in her vanity documentary, *Truth or Dare.*

While filming *Robin Hood,* Costner received the new Oliver Stone script that Harrison Ford and Mel Gibson had already rejected. "I let my wife, Cindy, read it," the actor remembered, "and I told her that I just didn't feel so strongly about this movie that I'd upset our big plans to go away together camping in the mountains with our kids." Cindy believed differently. "She's never been so outspoken about something in my career," Kevin said. "I know she felt it was important." The screenplay was based on former New Orleans district attorney Jim Garrison's 1988 book *On the Trail of the Assassins,* about his failed conspiracy case on the murder of President Kennedy. "It read like a Dashiell Hammett whodunit," enthused Oliver Stone to *Esquire* when he read Garrison's tome. "It starts out as a bit of a seedy crime with small traces, and then the gumshoe district attorney follows the trail, and the trail widens and widens, and before you know it, it's no longer a small-town affair. That seemed to me to be the kernel of a very powerful movie." He adapted the book with Garrison's New York editor, Zachary Sklar, combining it with Texas historian Jim Marrs' assassination theory guide *Crossfire.* Stone envisioned the D.A. as "somewhat like a Jimmy Stewart character in an old Capra movie," and Costner fit the bill because of "his moral simplicity, and a quiet understatement . . . he's comfortable with himself. He serves my function perfectly, because he anchors the movie in conventional morality." Costner approved of Stone, too, telling *Time,* "Oliver's a patriot and I believe with him that the impact of this movie will be liberating," so he signed on for $7 million, plus a percentage.

"I'm looking for work, as an actor or actress."
—Walter Matthau

Stone was out for more stars, explaining to the *Los Angeles Times*, "The supporting cast provides a map of the American psyche; familiar, comfortable faces that walk you through a winding path in the dark woods. Warner's thought it was too costly to have them, but these actors all waived their nominal fees to help the picture." "The movie I most wanted to be in in my life," said Donald Sutherland, who played a Washington sage, and Sissy Spacek, as Costner's long-suffering wife, said "I was raised not to talk about religion or sex or politics and I think it's good to talk about all those flammable subjects." A Hollywood liberal of long standing, Jack Lemmon didn't have any scenes with his *Odd Couple* costar, Walter Matthau, who was just happy for the job, quipping to "The Great Life"'s George Christy, "I'm looking for work, as an actor or an actress." Tommy Lee Jones and last year's Oscar winner Joe Pesci may not have been sure to which category they belonged as Stone cast them as gay conspirators who frolic in drag at orgies.

When the company trouped to the New Orleans location, Rosemary James, a reporter who had covered the Garrison trial, wrote a letter to the *Times-Picayune* warning, "Now comes a gullible from La La Land with a $40 million budget who wants to regurgitate all of that garbage. Many of us who call New Orleans home are offended by the fact that, once again, our city is about to be propelled into the limelight as a subject of national ridicule." The reception was no better in Dallas, where it took repeated requests and $50,000 for permission to film on the Book Depository's sixth floor opposite Dealy Plaza. Stone wasn't as persuasive with Arlington Cemetery, which nixed renting out Kennedy's grave as a set, so Stone recreated the tomb in Dallas. The last of the seventy-nine days of principal photography was in D.C. on the Capitol Mall, and Costner, who had played golf with the current president the day before, brought a Bush daughter-in-law to the set to sightsee.

Character Assassination

Assassination buffs whom Stone had consulted began criticizing him, one carping to *Esquire*, "He's so sure of himself, so arrogant and cocky, but that happens, I guess, after you win a few Oscars." Seventy-eight-year-old researcher Harold Weisberg was so unhappy that the movie was centering on Garrison, whom he maintained "could not find a pubic hair in a whorehouse at rush hour," that he leaked an early draft of the script to the *Washington Post*, which in turn headlined: "Dallas in Wonderland: Oliver Stone's Version of the Kennedy Assassination Exploits the Edge of Paranoia." The article, written by the paper's national security reporter, George Lardner, huffed that "there isn't space to list all the errors large and small" in the script. *Time* also saw this draft and in *its* preemptive strike, mocked Stone for buying into Garrison who, it said, was on the "far-out fringe" of conspiracy theorists, and the *Chicago Tribune* joined in by arguing that Garrison was not an appropriate cinematic hero. In what would prove to be one of the paper's few sympathetic articles on *JFK*, Richard Bernstein of the *New York Times* pointed out that "rarely, if ever, has a movie attracted such assault before anybody has seen it, even before most of it had been filmed." Stone, who noted that the script had undergone substantial changes since Harold Weisberg had gotten ahold of it, found these prerelease volleys "immoral" and Costner agreed, telling *GQ*, "To grab his script and leak it borders on being a kind of criminal act."

The director worked around the clock to pull the countless bits into a coherent three-hour movie for the scheduled December opening. Stone felt he would continue to be a target for "a thousand and one vultures out there, crouched on their rocks," so Warner Bros. hired Bobby Kennedy's old campaign manager, Frank Makiewicz, son of *Citizen Kane* cowriter Herman Mankiewicz, to ballyhoo the property in the Capi-

"Call me a guerilla historian."
—Oliver Stone

tal by setting up meetings with Washington insiders and counter "some of the sensational and hostile stuff about him." Stone got into a furious argument with the *Washington Post*'s executive editor Ben Bradlee, who demanded to know, "Who the hell does this punk think he is, anyway?" To which the director responded, "Jason Robards played that guy? It should have been Rod Steiger!" As usual, Stone hit the stump and gave colorful quotes to the press. "Call me a guerilla historian," he told the *Los Angeles Times*, depicting his film as "a battle over the meaning of my generation with the likes of Dan Quayle, a battle between official mythology and disturbing truth."

When the epic was ready for Christmas, Stone might well have thought there was conspiracy going on against him at the *New York Times*. Political columnist emeritus Tom Wicker kicked off the diatribe in a "How Dare He!" Sunday piece just before *JFK*'s release, blasting Stone for using his filming prowess to celebrate "a travesty of legal process." Next, Vincent Canby ripped into it on opening day and Janet Maslin put in a follow-up pan in a later Sunday article. With just about every columnist at the paper having a go at Stone's film, *Entertainment Weekly* started keeping count, reporting that in the first few weeks of release, the *Times* "has found room for at least twenty articles on the picture"—including an Op-Ed piece by Stone himself.

Among other publications, the *Newark Star-Ledger*'s Bob Campbell laughed that "*JFK* is even nuttier than advanced reports suggested" and the *Hollywood Reporter*'s Duane Byrge ended his notice with, "While Oliver Stone has certainly stirred up the waters, with good conscience and, in J.F.K.'s own parlance, 'with vigah,' most people are likely to regard *JFK* as B.S." The *New Yorker*'s Terrence Rafferty pronounced "For all its apparent meticulousness, *JFK* finally seems as muddled and as hastily thrown together as the Warren Commission Report." Despite the prerelease denigrations by their editors, both *Time* and the *Washington Post*'s Hal Hinson put *JFK* on their 10 Best List. Even though the cover of *Newsweek* blared "The Twisted Truth of *JFK:* Why Oliver Stone's New Movie Can't Be Trusted," inside David Ansen proposed, "Two cheers for Mr. Stone, a troublemaker for our times." Roger Ebert named it the best picture of the year and Warner's went into gear with new TV commercials starring average moviegoers who talked about how much they enjoyed the film, as well as copy in the print ads that read, "The movie Americans must see . . . The story that won't go away."

Critics wouldn't go away either, as Stone's history lesson became a media phenomenon. John Connally, who as governor of Texas, was wounded in the car in the Kennedy slaying, told *CBS This Morning*, "It's a propaganda film. I think it reflects the hangup that Oliver Stone has about the military and Vietnam . . . At one time or another in the film, he involves the CIA, the FBI, the Secret Service, the military, the Warren Commission, President Johnson, and the Mafia. You know, this is ludicrous." Senator Arlen Spector, whose "magic bullet" theory Stone ridicules in the film's climax, told reporters, "I'm going to find some time during the holiday season to see this movie because I like fiction." Humorist Mark O'Donnell drew a cartoon featuring a car with the bumper sticker, "Honk If You Shot JFK." Stone's cowriter Zachary Sklar argued that "Since nobody agrees on anything, nobody is distorting history. The only official history is the Warren Commission Report and that nobody believes." And *Newsday*'s Jack Mathews observed that another Christmas release "is as much a blend of fact and supposition as *JFK* . . . yet, no one has freaked out over the authenticity of *Bugsy*."

A Sailor in Every Port

New Orleans newspaperwoman Rosemary James was back to challenge Tommy Lee Jones' impersonation of Clay Shaw, "Not the least bit the raging queen as was portrayed by Oliver Stone." Gay activists weren't pleased either, as a

"They shafted me."
—Ted Tally on the New York Film Critics Circle

newsletter from the Gay & Lesbian Alliance Against Defamation read, "*JFK* equates gay men with moral degeneracy . . . contrasting [Costner's] family life to the orgiastic decadence of the film's gay villains . . . while ignoring the sex lives of his heterosexual villains." Stone attempted to assuage his gay audience by talking with *The Advocate* and saying that he wouldn't deny ever having a homosexual experience. When the reporter pressed for details, Stone retorted, "You mean which sailors, which ports? Forget it."

Returning to Washington, Stone had meetings with key members of Congress about opening secret files on the Kennedy assassination which were not scheduled to be released until 2029. While in town, he spoke to the National Press Club where he attacked Dan Rather, Tom Wicker, Anthony Lewis, George Lardner, and George Will, saying of his detractors, "When confronted with the crime of the century, they stand mute." *The Nation* likened *JFK*'s impact to that of *Uncle Tom's Cabin* and soon the movie, too, was affecting change in Washington. Both ex-President Ford, a member of the Warren Commission who called the film "a desecration to the memory of President Kennedy," and the deceased's brother, Senator Edward Kennedy, who said he had no plans to see the picture, called for releasing the files to answer the public's questions. With that, *ShowBiz Today*'s Martin Grove predicted "*JFK* will be nominated because it proves what Academy members want to believe about their art form, that it can actually change the real world."

And They're Off

Back in fantasyland, the L.A. Critics' Circle started the campaign rolling by celebrating Warren Beatty's *Bugsy*, which won Best Picture, Director, and Screenplay. Beatty himself had to settle for a second-place finish in the Best Actor race behind Nick Nolte for *The Prince of Tides*. Mercedes Ruehl was named Best Actress for *The Fisher King*, which had been a close runner-up for every award that *Bugsy* had won. Beatty the actor could take solace from his award from the National Board of Review which, just as it had last year allowed Robert De Niro and Robin Williams to share a prize for *Awakenings*, also split Best Actress between *Thelma & Louise*'s Susan Sarandon and Geena Davis. The Board named *The Silence of the Lambs* Best Picture, with Jonathan Demme copping the Director prize and Anthony Hopkins relegated to the Supporting Actor category. Kate Nelligan won Supporting Actress, not for *The Prince of Tides*, but for the flop romantic comedy *Frankie and Johnny* in which she cracked wise as a waitress.

Ignored in L.A., *The Silence of the Lambs* was not simply the favorite of the New York Film Critics, it was the first film ever to sweep all four of the group's top awards: Picture, Director, Actor (Anthony Hopkins), and Actress (Jodie Foster). But when Ted Tally's screenplay lost to David Cronenberg's adaptation of *Naked Lunch*, the *Silence* author groused to the *Washington Post*, "They shafted me; they acted like this movie was born in a Federal Express envelope on the way to Jodie Foster's house." Tally fought back by hiring a publicist for the Oscar race, saying "I feel like an idiot doing it, but I might have felt even worse if I hadn't." Overcoming the vehement protestations of John Simon, the New Yorkers decided to count the two stars of *Thelma & Louise* as a single entity; the Sarandon/Davis tag team lost to Foster by a 30 to 25 vote. *Boyz N the Hood*'s John Singleton won the New Director Award.

A year after *The Silence of the Lambs* had premiered, gay activists were not in a forgive-and-forget mood. Several tuxedo-clad members of ACT-UP crashed the New York Critics' awards ceremony at Rockefeller Center's Pegasus Room and handed out leaflets linking the group's Best Picture with horrendous gay-bashing statistics. Jonathan Demme expressed solidarity with the protestors but once again asserted that he had clearly made his film's prissy serial killer a heterosexual. Though in Chapter 11 and still owing Demme $364,000, Orion spent $325,000 on an

> *"Even if I thought your movie was the best picture, I wouldn't vote for it."*
> *—an Academy member to Disney*

Oscar campaign for its critics' favorite, distinguished by the mailing of video and audiocassettes of the film packaged in a sleek black gift box.

Stone Soul Picnic

Oliver Stone had to rely on his friends from the Hollywood Foreign Press for the chance to make a speech as he won his fifth Golden Globe for directing *JFK*. As was his wont, Stone proceeded to lecture the Foreign Press about their mind-set. "I think what you're really recognizing here tonight is that a terrible lie was told to us twenty-eight years ago," he explained. "I hope this film can be the first step in, maybe, trying to right it again." He didn't get the chance to return to the podium and elaborate because the voters spread the gold this year, with each of the five contenders for Best Picture (Drama) winning a single award. *Bugsy* ended up with only Best Picture. *The Prince of Tides* was represented by Nick Nolte's Best Actor award, *Silence of the Lambs* by Jodie Foster, and Callie Khouri won Best Screenplay for *Thelma & Louise*. Supporting honors went to Jack Palance for kidding his "one tough hombre" persona in the Billy Crystal vehicle *City Slickers*, and Mercedes Ruehl in *The Fisher King*. Backstage, Ruehl vowed to reporters, "I shall never waitress again and you are my witnesses!"

Beauty and the Bette

The Foreign Press decided that a cartoon was the Best Comedy or Musical film of the year; *Beauty and the Beast* also won for its score and title song. Lyricist Howard Ashman's sister accepted his award and remarked that "Howard was forty years old. When I think of what he could have contributed, it breaks my heart." Robin Williams received the Best Actor (Comedy/Musical) Globe for *The Fisher King* and his female counterpart was *For the Boys*' Bette Midler who said, "I'm very touched." Tears welled up as she acknowledged, "It makes me very, very happy that the Hollywood Foreign Press recognized our work when the American public dismissed us." The *Hollywood Reporter* observed that, meeting the press backstage, the usually ebullient "Midler roamed from rage to resignation" as she vented much of the frustration she felt over the failure of *For the Boys*, which was "a big, big shock. I doubt everything now. The reviews were all right. The performance at the box office was pathetic." Asked how she had gotten through this difficult two-month period, she responded. "What makes you think I'm through it?" Changing the subject, a reporter asked if she would like to be reunited on screen with her costar from *Down and Out in Beverly Hills*, fellow Golden Globe winner Nick Nolte. "Not especially," replied Midler, adding with a laugh that "I don't have a 'thing' for Nick. I'm not developing one and I'm sure he's not developing one for me either."

Ad Wars

Disney executives quivered with joy that *Beauty and the Beast* earned more Globes than any other film because, as David Fox of the *Los Angeles Times* observed, "The Globes have begun to take on a role in the Oscar race akin to New Hampshire's role in presidential politics. In other words, like New Hampshire, the Globe voters may not be a big group, but they have influence." Steadfast in their determination that their cartoon be seen as a serious work of art, the studio placed trade paper ads quoting every critic who had accepted its contention that *Beauty and the Beast* was legitimate Best Picture material. Disney also got into a spat with Tri-Star over who had bragging rights regarding critical favor. When the latter advertised *Bugsy* as "The Most Critically Acclaimed Film of the Year," Disney retaliated with *Beauty and the Beast* ads that claimed "Only one film can truly be called the best reviewed film of the year." The animated feature lost some goodwill among Academy members who were sent videos of the film. As Marilyn Beck reported, "those who settle down to see *Beauty and the Beast*

"Not only would I go, but every girl in the world wants to have a party dress."
—Laura Dern

in the privacy of their homes have been in for a surprise." "Here I got the whole family together and we were all excited," one voter told the *Los Angeles Times*, "only to find that the tape was a ten-minute promo." Disney did not have much trust in Academy voters and feared video piracy. Beck said that getting an advertising tape "made one writer/producer so mad he phoned the studio and declared, 'Even if I thought your movie was the best picture, I wouldn't vote for it.' "

Although the Academy instructed voters "to be on guard against inappropriate attempts to influence you and to register your displeasure with anyone who might make such an attempt," *Entertainment Weekly* reported that Tri-Star spent a million bucks to extol the virtues of *Bugsy, The Fisher King,* and *Terminator 2: Judgment Day*. Columbia mailed videos of last summer's *Boyz N the Hood* to voters and trumpeted the film's home video release in January with the news that the cassette contained a two-minute public service announcement written and directed by John Singleton for the United Negro College Fund. Academy members could also count on receiving a glossy photo book for *The Prince of Tides*, as well as a personal letter from Columbia head Mark Canton asking them to remember Barbra on their ballots. The *Reporter* quoted one studio marketing executive who had said that, due to the recession, campaigning was "an area that can be cut back. In fact, the filmmakers themselves are also saying, 'Hey, it's okay because we realize it's not Oscar potential.' " But Paramount had made so much money from *The Addams Family* that it could afford a joke ad for "Thing," the movie's torsoless hand.

Home Remedies

Laura Dern and her mother, Diane Ladd, who both received Golden Globe nominations for their 1930s' period piece, *Rambling Rose*, would have loved some of that cash Paramount was throwing around for laughs. Unfortunately, their studio, Carolco, was the latest Hollywood company to be on the brink, even though it was behind Arnold Schwarzenegger's *Terminator 2*, the year's number one blockbuster. Edgar J. Scherick, the executive producer of *Rambling Rose*, shelled out his own money to pay for a joint trade paper ad for Dern, who played a guileless, free-spirited young woman, and Ladd, the matriarch of the well-to-do family she turns upside down. Not only were the two actresses without a studio-backed campaign, but Carolco could only afford to make 200 prints of their acclaimed film and none of them were playing anywhere; the ad did, however, give a phone number for voters to call if they'd like to borrow a videotape of the film. Director Martha Coolidge told the *Hollywood Reporter* she had chipped in "a few grand" to make the videos because "I love this movie and I think these two women deserve to have their performances seen and considered."

Dern took the campaign to television by chatting with Arsenio Hall about her acting genes: she had been conceived while Bruce Dern and Diane Ladd were costarring in Roger Corman's *The Wild Angels*. "My family portrait is my father dead with a joint in his mouth and my mother laying her head on his shoulder. He's wearing some bizarre biker helmet." Mother and daughter were interviewed by *Entertainment Tonight*, and when Dern acknowledged that some of her friends, "wanting to be cool, young actors, say 'If I ever got nominated, I wouldn't go, man,' " Ladd cried out in disgust. Laura continued, "Not only would I go, but every girl in the world wants to have a party dress."

Michael Lerner was another Oscar hopeful who took matters into his own hands. *USA Today* called the character actor a "scene-stealer found guilty of armed robbery" for his three scenes as a boorish 1930s' studio mogul in *Barton Fink*. The Coen Brothers' movie was an arty apocalyptic Hollywood story seen by few people and liked by even fewer. "What the hell was that movie about?!! Does anybody know?" pleaded comedian Rosie O'Donnell. "They should have given

Cliffs Notes on the way into that movie." Still, Lerner knew Oscar caliber personal reviews when he heard them so he hired a publicist to make sure other people heard them, too. The flack got the heavy-set actor seen at premieres and Hollywood parties, and Lerner ran three different black-and-white, homemade trade paper ads in which he was able to brag that the Los Angeles Film Critics had picked him as Best Supporting Actor; unlike the single ad that 20th Century-Fox had taken out for him, Lerner's gave Academy members the dates and times for *Barton Fink* screenings as well as information about free on-site parking. Helping Lerner's chances was Anthony Hopkins, who won *Premiere*'s readers' poll in both the lead and supporting categories. "It means somebody out there likes you," responded the double-winner. Despite having only forty-five minutes of screen time, Hopkins defied pundits who considered him a shoo-in for Supporting and told Orion to push him for Best Actor, rationalizing to *USA Today* that to do otherwise would have been "like begging for it: 'Please give me an Oscar.' "

Unified and Divided

This year's most passionate campaign centered on a movie made far away from Hollywood. The New York Film Critics, National Board of Review, and the Hollywood Foreign Press all selected the German *Europa, Europa* as Best Foreign Film. Oscar voters, though, would not have the opportunity to reward this true story of a Jewish youth who passes as an Aryan during World War II and must go to great lengths to make sure nobody sees his circumcised penis. Voting for the first time since the German reunification, the German Expert Union—the committee in charge of selecting a movie for Oscar Foreign Film consideration—gave *Europa, Europa* thumbs down. Citing the fact that the film's director, Angnieska Holland, was not of German blood but hailed from Poland and that there were as many francs in the budget as deutschemarks, the Export Union's head, Manfred Steinkuhler, declared "*Europa, Europa* is certainly not a German film," despite its German producer, cast, and crew. He also mouthed off to *Der Spiegal* that the film was "an embarrassment," while another committee member labeled it "junk"; the panelists couldn't come up with anything else to send in its place, so Germany would be sitting out this year's Foreign Film race.

Director Holland mentioned that, in spite of her Polish heritage, West Germany had been happy to be represented by her *Angry Harvest* at the 1985 Oscars. She declared that it was the Holocaust theme of *Europa, Europa* coupled with her own Jewishness that led the Union to reject the film. "I was really shocked at how the minds of the people changed after the unification. The arrogance and xenophobia which was hidden is now official," she railed. "They felt guilty many, many years after the war, but it was official guilt. This time is over." The director contended that "*Europa, Europa* is the victim of the same xenophobia and stupidity it depicted." The film's producer Artur Brauner blasted the selection committee and, as *Variety* observed, "The fact that Brauner is Jewish is seldom missing from debates on the subject." Indeed, when a member of the Export Union criticized Brauner he did so by accusing him of "*chutzpah*."

Back in the States, this contretemps was covered not only by Tinseltown trade papers, but in the national press as well; *Newsweek* used the committee's rebuff as the starting point for an essay considering reunified Germany's hesitancy about "coming to terms with the past." In the trades, thirty members of the German film community, including directors Wim Wenders, 1983 Oscar nominee Wolfgang Petersen, and Volker Schlondorff (whose 1979 *The Tin Drum* was the last German film to win the Foreign Oscar), the twice-nominated cinematographer Michael Ballhaus, and actors Hannah Schygulla and Senta Berger, placed an open letter to director Holland, congratulating her on the film's success in America and regretting the committee's decision. The signatories also acknowledged that "As German

"It's hard because I don't want to be bitter."
—Barbra Streisand

filmmakers we are well aware of the special responsibility the past imposes upon us." The Academy wouldn't budge, though; Foreign Language Committee head Fay Kanin, a former Academy president, issued a statement through *Entertainment Weekly*: "I regret that it fell between the cracks but that's Germany's business, not ours."

Looking to the future, the film's American distributor, Orion Classics, was thinking that Germany's snub of *Europa, Europa* might work out to its advantage. Tom Bernard, an Orion Classics vice-president, understated, "I think the reason behind *Europa, Europa* is rather obvious"; exploiting voter resentment and sympathy, the company sent letters to Academy members urging them to see the film and reminded them that it was eligible in all other categories, including Best Picture. The 281 members of the Directors Branch got more than a letter; Orion Classics presented each of them with a *Europa, Europa* videocassette. Oscar prognosticators began to wonder. With passions running high over *Europa, Europa* and with Barbra Streisand's *The Prince of Tides* a popular success and a Directors Guild nominee, could there possibly be *two* women nominated for Best Director?

The Nominations

There was a full moon when Karl Malden and Kathleen Turner made the early morning announcements. "Welcome to another of Oscar's greatest moments," piped up Malden, plugging the Academy's just-released historical video. *Europa, Europa*'s Angnieska Holland was nominated—for Best Adapted Screenplay, not Director. *The Prince of Tides* took in an impressive seven nominations including Best Picture, but Barbra Streisand's name was not among the Best Director finalists; the category remained a "No Women Allowed" club. Columbia's Mark Canton denounced the omission as "truly shocking." Army Archerd reported that "Barbra watched the Oscar announcements 'live' via CNN at her London hotel. You can imagine how she felt." There to attend her film's Royal premiere with Princess Diana, Streisand said that while "disappointed" about the director's race, she was "thrilled" that her film was appreciated by the other branches, and that she could still take home an Oscar as coproducer. The non-nominee elaborated to *Variety* that "I'm trying not to take it too personally. It's hard because I don't want to be bitter. I don't take it as a personal affront. I look at it as a larger problem." Alluding to the admiration (and Best Director Oscar) that Warren Beatty received for producing, directing, and starring in *Reds*, Streisand pondered that "It's as if a man is allowed to feel passionate commitment about his work, and a woman is allowed to feel passionate commitment only about a man."

Warren Beatty's sister, Shirley MacLaine, phoned in to Streisand with condolences, as did Goldie Hawn and Meryl Streep. Streisand calmed them down by saying her "Directors Guild nomination means more—getting it from my peers." She got mileage out of her Academy exclusion though, appearing in a surprise spot with Madonna and Roseanne Arnold on *Saturday Night Live* and accepting a Grammy Legend Award and informing the throng in Radio City Music Hall, "I can't tell you how gratifying it is to be appreciated for what you do by your peers."

Warren Beatty was still sitting pretty with the Academy. *Bugsy* led all comers with ten nominations. Only twice in the last twenty-five years had Best Picture not been won by the film that led or tied for the most nominations, but the sobering reality was that those two exceptions were the Warren Beatty productions *Reds* and *Bonnie and Clyde*.

Cartoon Mania

Disney's hard campaign work paid off and *Beauty and the Beast* made the Best Picture race, a result that drew cheers from the early risers on hand for the announcement. Peter Jennings ran a story about the historic first on *ABC World News*

"You have to see this princess."
—Warren Beatty

Tonight but cartoon buff Leonard Maltin admitted that only "in a year as mediocre as 1991" could "this terrific film" be a finalist. The nomination "enables the Academy to congratulate itself for recognizing animation as a legitimate movie form, after only 50 or 75 years," wrote David Hinckley of the *New York Daily News*. "It's too bad it can't now give retroactive Oscars to the hundreds of Warner Bros. cartoons that are better than *Beauty*, an okay Disney film propelled by full-barrel Disney hype." *Beauty* had a total of six nominations, including three of the Best Song nominees, one of which was sure to win over the nominated Bryan Adams hit from *Robin Hood*, although Music Branch member Herschel Burke Gilbert warned the *Los Angeles Daily News*, "Those groups that don't understand music vote on the tunes they hear most on the radio." Disney began advertising, "For the first time in Motion Picture history, an animated feature has been nominated for Best Picture," with an exhortation, "Be a part of history!" A contented Roy Disney said, "I have no problem taking credit for it. I won't apologize for beating my own drum. Look at Oliver Stone. Electioneering clearly helps."

JFK received eight nominations, Kevin Costner not among them. Kenneth Turan of the *Los Angeles Times* noted that while "controversy is something the staid Academy has always studiously avoided . . . Stone's blood-red passion has become a badge of honor rather than a scarlet letter." Reacted Stone, now a ten-time nominee, "Considering what this film has been through, it's really nice to hear from your peers that they recognize the values in your film."

The fifth nominee, garnering seven nominations, was *The Silence of the Lambs*. Anthony Hopkins learned of his Best Actor nomination in Switzerland where he was working on Richard Attenborough's biography of Charlie Chaplin; his director approached him with the news but because of Attenborough's *faux* sober expression, "I thought he was going to tell us we were delayed again because of the weather."

Hopkins was part of a three-way race with four-time nominee Beatty and *The Prince of Tides*' Nick Nolte. When Liz Smith called Beatty to talk about *Bugsy*'s strong showing, he was more interested in his daughter: "She's amazing; just fantastic. You have to see this princess." Nick Nolte maintained that "I've been working twenty years to tell stories, not necessarily to gather awards. If this is recognition for good work, and I'm one of the actors doing good work—that's the way I accept it." Also in the race—but not in Best Picture nominees—were *The Fisher King*'s Robin Williams (nomination number three) and *Cape Fear*'s Robert De Niro (his sixth).

Women Together

Kathlyn Beatty's mom Annette Bening was left out among the Best Actress nominees, a development that disappointed her dad, who told Army Archerd, "I think the picture kinda works because of her." Both stars of what *Today*'s Bryant Gumbel damned as "the man-hating movie," *Thelma & Louise*, were nominated for Best Actress, as were director Ridley Scott and writer Callie Khouri. Referring to Geena Davis and Susan Sarandon as "this year's Siamese twins," *Us* worried that they would cancel each other out. The two stars didn't mind. "I'm so pleased that Geena and I have been honored together," said Sarandon of her second nomination. "I never would have gotten in the car without her." The 1988 Supporting Actress winner, Davis agreed that "the most fun thing is that we both got nominated."

Nineteen-eighty-eight's Best Actress Jodie Foster was also vying for a second statuette, having already been beatified by *Entertainment Weekly* as "Entertainer of the Year," not just because of her performance in *The Silence of the Lambs* but also for making her directorial debut with the story of a child genius, *Little Man Tate*; the magazine wrote of the former child star, "Overachievement becomes her." The *London Times* maintained, "Insecurity is rampant in Hollywood. The Oscars are the ultimate test of popu-

"Our world is still falling apart."
—Juliette Lewis

larity, which is why Jodie Foster should win Best Actress again." Bette Midler had friends in the Actors Branch who provided balm for her hurt feelings by annointing her performance as one of the year's best; it was the only nomination for *For the Boys*. And enough people had seen *Rambling Rose* to give not only Laura Dern a Best Actress nomination but also her mom, Diane Ladd, a Supporting citation; the mother-daughter nominations were an Academy first.

Diane Ladd had been up all night before the nominations expending nervous energy by cleaning her apartment. She didn't have the nerve to watch the telecast but got her good news first from Shelley Winters and then from Laura. Ladd's competition ranged from eighteen to eighty-two. Nineteen-eighty-nine's Best Actress Jessica Tandy became the oldest-acting nominee ever as a spinner of tales in the sleeper hit *Fried Green Tomatoes*, and Kate Nelligan was among the *Prince of Tides* contenders. Golden Globe winner Mercedes Ruehl was also in the running while *Cape Fear*'s teenager, Juliette Lewis, had a singular reaction to her recognition: the nomination, she said, "doesn't change anything. It doesn't change the condition of the world. Our world is still falling apart."

Gandhi Goes Gangster

Like Laura Dern and Diane Ladd, Michael Lerner's do-it-yourself campaign paid off big. The rotund *Barton Fink* actor went to a pal's house to watch the nominations and he told Ryan Murphy of the *New York Daily News* that once Kathleen Turner said his name, "I didn't hear anything after that. I was jumping up and down so hard I broke my friend's chair. I swear to you! Then I started to cry." Tommy Lee Jones was the only cast member from *JFK* to be nominated, and two actors from *Bugsy* made the cut: Harvey Keitel, who was also prominent in *Thelma & Louise*, and Ben Kingsley, whose Meyer Lansky was a far cry from his 1982 Best Actor role as Gandhi. "The future now for me is playing villains—bad guys, not nice people," Kingsley told *E!*, ending with an Edgar Allen Poe-like simile, "That's just the way the pendulum swings sometimes." Everyone agreed that the sentimental favorite in this category was *City Slickers*' Jack Palance, whose thirty-eight-year gap since his last nomination (for *Shane*) tied Helen Hayes' record waiting period. *ShowBiz Today* tracked him down at a Cowboy Hall of Fame affair gala in Oklahoma City, where the actor pulled an aw-shucks-it-was-just-the-role routine, "I think bunches of actors would have done that and done it well."

Boyz N the Oscar Race

Another record was set in the Best Director category where, at age twenty-four, John Singleton of *Boyz N the Hood* shattered Orson Welles' record as the youngest directorial nominee by two years. On top of that, no other black person had ever been up for Best Director. "It's really cool, so cool. I'm the first person in my neighborhood to get an Oscar nomination," laughed Singleton. He was also nominated for Original Screenplay and was chosen "Person of the Week" by ABC's *World News Tonight* which revealed that he had grown up next door to a drive-in movie theater watching movies silently. While directing the new, ultrahyped Michael Jackson music video, Singleton paid tribute to one of his fellow nominees: "Jonathan Demme gave me a little pep talk before I started filming. The things he talked about helped me to get nominated."

Spike Lee, whose *Jungle Fever* received no nominations—not even for Stevie Wonder's songs which the Music Branch had ruled ineligible "because the lyric and melody of each song was not clearly audible and intelligible"—slammed the Academy Awards as "a popularity contest, voted on mostly by white males over fifty years old" at an address at Richard Nixon's alma mater, Whittier College. Academy President Malden, who fit the demographic of Lee's prototypical Academy voter, retorted, "I can only speak for the Actors Branch, of which I am a

"I don't think that drag queens can come anywhere near that in terms of importance."
—Sy Gomberg

member, and it's fifty percent made up of women" and noted that Lee himself was an Academy voter. The Academy's executive director, Bruce Davis, used Singleton's breakthrough as compensation for the Streisand snub: "I do not think the Directors Branch is a hotbed of discrimination." Describing the directors' group as "pretty liberal, both in the political sense and in the other sense . . . these are some of the people least tainted by this kind of thing, not only in the industry but in the world." One of the branch's most liberal members, Oliver Stone, told *Daily Variety,* "I'm sad for Barbra. It's the nature of the Academy—a lot of heartbreak and a lot of triumph."

No TVs

The Documentary Committee once again made the Academy look like a geriatric center by ignoring the year's most decorated entry. Jennie Livingston's *Paris Is Burning*, about the subculture of New York City transvestites, had been named Best Documentary by all three major critics' groups but didn't rate a nomination with the Academy's committee members despite a trade paper campaign by Miramax. The company mailed a letter to Bruce Davis and rejoined that "one might conclude that a successful theatrical release is grounds for disqualification," and Andy Klein of the *L.A. Reader* accused the Academy of rewarding "utterly conventional, well-meaning and not very inspired work." Robert Redford, the producer of another documentary the Academy passed up, signed what *Variety* termed "the official protest letter" calling for a revamping of the nominating process.

The whole issue might have remained a question of the nominating group's dubious taste, but then Sy Gomberg, the chairman of the Feature Documentary Committee, opened his trap. In an interview with the *L.A. Daily News*, Gomberg compared *Paris Is Burning* to the films his group did nominate and asked, "Is this as important a subject as death on the job, or the conscience of the German officers? I don't think that drag queens can come anywhere near that in terms of importance."

Having fended questions about sexism, Bruce Davis now had to deal with questions of homophobia, especially after the organization Out in Film demanded that the Academy "publicly censure Mr. Gomberg for his bigoted remarks." The executive director insisted that what Gomberg meant was "that some subjects have more intrinsic weight than others," and "it takes a fair amount of willful misreading to turn it into something anti-gay." Director Jenny Livingston said, "As a Jew of German descent, I can say that the point of studying history is to see how history repeats itself . . . the homophobia and racism of today is as significant as the anti-Semitism and homophobia of forty years ago."

A Gay Old Time

The outcry expanded three weeks before the ceremony when the *New York Daily News* headlined, "Gays set to crash Oscars: Protest promised on telecast." Reporter Ryan Murphy broke the story that activist groups Queer Nation and Out in Film had been planning all year for a "peaceful yet powerful" interruption "during the presentation of a major award or shortly beforehand" to protest gay stereotyping in movies and to call for more money for AIDS research. According to Murphy, the Academy could also look forward to the distribution of "a Hollywood map of gay stars' homes." Bob Werden, the Academy's publicity coordinator, responded, "Look, if a dancer leaves the kick-line and begins to protest, we have no time to stop them. This is live TV. People who work for us who plan on protesting, however, should be aware that if they do disrupt the ceremony, they are in danger of losing their jobs." Richard Roeper of the *Chicago Sun-Times* thought an interruption might not be such a bad idea: "Let's at least hope they have the good sense to do it during one of those horrifying musical numbers." CNN interviewed the organizers and

"It's never been my concern whether I'm appreciated or not."
—Nick Nolte

learned, "they plan to out some of Hollywood's gay community, including a Best Actress nominee."

Lunch with the Stars

"I'm even shocked to be here," averred Jodie Foster at the Academy's eleventh annual nominees' luncheon, "because it's not one of those Oscar performances. My character is very spare and very subtle and not flashy at all." Michael Lerner's publicist encouraged him to continue being seen in all the right places so he, of course, attended. The *Hollywood Reporter*'s Robert Osborne was impressed by the "snap-crackle-pop level of the star power" at the event when Barbra Streisand, Nick Nolte, Anthony Hopkins, Warren Beatty and Annette Bening, Juliette Lewis, Geena Davis, and Bette Midler were there chomping on the poached salmon. Laura Dern was with her mother, who espoused an acrobatic devotion to her offspring. "People say to me, do you and Laura compete? No, we shouldn't compete with our kids, good God Almighty," said Diane Ladd. "We should take our children and let them stand on our shoulders and hopefully, maybe, they will be able to see further than we did." Three William Morris agents threw Ladd another luncheon which Army Archerd attended, raving "we were putting away the corn fritters, catfish, and fried chicken." Attendee Roseanne Arnold wasn't as pleased, complaining, "It wasn't very good food, it was Southern."

Active Actors

The three leading Actor candidates battled it out for postnomination attention. Beatty went to Washington to appear before Congress to promote legislation requiring labels on videos of films that had been altered. "It will give an honest description to the consumer," advocated citizen Beatty. He also journeyed to Paris to become a Commander of Arts & Letters in the French Culture Ministry and then crossed the Channel to lecture at Oxford about the impact of AIDS. But the Beatty topper came two weeks before the Oscars when Lauren Sydney of CNN's *ShowBiz Today* announced, "I never thought I'd read this one. Warren Beatty, for years one of the world's most talked-about bachelors, is now a married man." The only guest at the nuptials was the maid of honor—baby Kathlyn.

Beatty couldn't steal all the attention away from Nick Nolte who, at age fifty-two, was *People*'s choice this year as "The Sexiest Man Alive!" described as "Strong, sensitive, and squared away at last, he's a man's man that women can't resist." The sex symbol told *E!*, "It's never been my concern whether I'm appreciated or not." Meanwhile, Anthony Hopkins had the new art-house hit *Howard's End* to keep him in the public eye. He also appeared on Barbara Walters' Oscar night special, where he did his impersonations of Brando, Olivier, and Gielgud. Quoting Sir John, mimic Hopkins said, "I saw that awful, disgusting film of yours, *The Silence of the Lambs*. It terrified me, I couldn't see it again."

Hello La-La-Land

Like Gielgud, *Newsweek* questioned "The slice-and-dice factor" that could hurt *Silence*'s chances in a Best Picture race the *Los Angeles Times* deemed "wide open. The early handicapping of Hollywood's big night has been all over the lot—no movie has emerged as the runaway favorite." The *Wall Street Journal* reminded readers that "The Academy has often nominated extremely violent films, such as last year's *GoodFellas*, for Best Picture, but far less frequently handed them the actual award."

The Directors Guild dual ceremonies were packed on both coasts, but the Los Angeles contenders, Stone, Streisand, Scott, and Levinson, had to look at the monitors to see the winner, Jonathan Demme for *The Silence of the Lambs*. "This will show them out there in La-La Land," the jubilant recipient said over the hook-up to Hollywood. "I'm the 44th white male to receive

"I'm afraid, doggone it, it's another Oscar for Oliver Stone."
—Michael Medved

this award, which I have confused feelings about." Martin Grove was not confused, declaring on *ShowBiz Today* that, "After much thought, I think Jonathan Demme did ruin his Oscar chances by calling Los Angeles 'La-La Land.'" Grove then predicted Picture and Director victories for *Bugsy*. Bernard Weinraub reported that "Realizing his mistake, Demme issued a three-page apology, calling his words 'stupid' and 'borne of the hometown euphoric frenzy when a New Yorker actually gets the nod.'"

TV critic Michael Medved wrote Demme off anyway, and whined, "I'm afraid, doggone it, it's another Oscar for Oliver Stone." "Family values" proponent Medved did see a silver lining, though, prophesizing that *Beauty and the Beast* would become the first G-rated Best Picture winner since 1968's *Oliver!*, because "the sleaze vote, the feel-bad vote, will be divided by the other four movies." *Entertainment Weekly*'s Oscar prediction tote board called for a close victory by *The Silence of the Lambs*. Army Archerd heralded the latest boost for *JFK:* "Today, Sen. David Boren (D-Okla.) introduces the Senate Joint Resolution entitled Assassination Disclosure Act of 1992." Oliver Stone rejoiced, "They deserve an Oscar for their courage and vision as leaders in the battle to make the American government open and fully accountable." Meanwhile, *Newsday*'s Jack Mathews argued for *The Prince of Tides*, saying "An old-fashioned love story set against family tragedy, it has more of the soaring humanistic elements most voters like than any other nominee." A cheeky Roger Ebert predicted an Oscar for Stone but otherwise a sweep for *Silence*—Picture, Actor, Actress—based on "the hundreds of people who have mentioned the film to me since it opened in February 1991. They won't stop talking about it."

It's Terry, I'm in L.A.

When *Newsday* asked Gilbert Cates about his third go-around as producer of the Oscar show, he said, "Three years is enough. It's better for the show if the same person doesn't do it year after year. I think you need a certain amateur enthusiasm to have it sing out." Cates was certainly giddy when he considered having the Honorary Oscar to Indian director Satyajit Ray presented by none other than Mother Teresa. "The notion of Mother Teresa mixing and mingling with Madonna and Barbra and Nick and Warren and all the other stars—and maybe even showing up at Irving (Swifty) Lazar's famous post-Oscar party," laughed Bernard Weinraub, "was finally deemed inappropriate, even by Hollywood standards." Reasoned Cates, "People would accuse us of not having the right tone." The *Times* also noted that "Recession chic is dictating a modest approach to this year's awards festivities," except at Spago. "Do you think for one minute that someone like Mrs. Brooke Astor or the Rockefellers cut down on their food or caviar?" Lazar queried the paper. "The answer is no, no, no. Everything we've done in the past will remain the same."

Emcee Billy Crystal's plans for a big opening by bungee jumping from the top of the stage was kayoed by an insurance company. He thought of alternatives as he nursed the flu and missed some rehearsals. Susan Sarandon's baby wasn't due for three weeks but her obstetrician in California was given an orchestra seat directly behind her just in case—her doctor just happened to be the wife of Gilbert Cates. That took care of her, but with the show moving back to the smaller Dorothy Chandler Pavilion after being at the giant Shrine Auditorium, Cates and President Malden would be hearing the same grumblings from ticketless members they had to deal with two years ago. Once again they printed a letter in the trade papers "To Our Friends in the Industry," reminding their *amis* that "the laws of physics can't be suspended on Oscar night," then informing them that a lottery would be held to determine who would be able to attend; they requested that the losers "bear your bad luck with good grace." Army Archerd snickered, "Do you mean if Lew

Wasserman sends in his response, and isn't picked, he can't go to the Oscars?" CNN's Bill Tush confirmed that the invitations were a racket: "One ticket source claims his agency receives their tickets from older actors who no longer work and would rather have the money."

Waiting in the Wings

The Friday before the show, Queer Nation conducted a civil-disobedience training seminar in West Hollywood's Plummer Park in preparation for the Big Night. "Some of this town's biggest names are having major anxiety attacks over the gay threats," itemed Richard Johnson, but the Academy itself seems resigned toward them. Cates remarked, "In the final analysis, it's part of what makes the Academy Awards special, people don't know what to expect" and Bruce Davis considered the attempt to upstage the show "a kind of interesting little contest." The controversy whetted the news media's appetite as well. On Oscar day, the *CBS Evening News* warned, "This year a few actors who aren't in the script are waiting in the wings," while ABC's *World News Tonight* mentioned that the gay pickets had already failed in their call for a boycott of homophobic films, including the current Michael Douglas starrer, *Basic Instinct*, with its man-loathing psycho lesbian villain: "Protests over these movies certainly have not kept the audiences away and what audiences like has a lot to do with who wins tonight."

The Big Night

Positioned outside the Dorothy Chandler, *Good Morning, America*'s Chantal surveyed the scene and reported that in addition to the usual forecourt hoopla, there was "another show, this one on the street. It was called Gay Protestors vs. the Police. More than 100 police, many of them with riot gear and on horseback, pushed protestors off the street." *NYQ* was on the scene and reported that "Over a hundred demonstrators turned out on Oscar night for 'Night of the Livid Queers.' " The pickets carried signs demanding "Hollywood, Stop Censoring Our True Queer Lives!," protesting that *Paris Is Burning*'s "Jenny Livingston Was Robbed!" and revealing the identity of the murderer in *Basic Instinct*. *USA Today* observed that "Two men briefly lay down on the carpet and kissed, while others climbed the large gold Oscar statue outside the Pavilion and stuck suggestive stickers on its behind and groin." The stickers read "Fag."

One activist, Lynda Montgomery, explained to *Good Morning America* that "All of the big revolts, Stonewall . . . everything that's ever gone on in history has been the result of some people who were really angry" and some demonstrators expressed their ire by smashing plastic statuettes. Ten protestors were arrested and television cameras caught members of Darryl Gates' police force wearing rubber gloves and using their billy clubs against the crowd. Homophobia wasn't confined to the movie studios and *NYQ* took stock of "a small group of fundamentalists, wearing bandanas and tattoos. Some provoked activists with taunts like 'It's your own fault you're going to die of AIDS and go to Hell.' " These bastions of Christian charity carried signs bearing the legends "Homo Sex Is a Sin" and "Down with Dirty Movies."

Army Archerd dispatched news from the front: "Price, Waterhouse reps . . . who have been delivering the secret vote results for years, were given security escorts for the first time." Best Director hopeful Oliver Stone arrived to cries of

Awards Ceremony

MARCH 30, 1992, 6:00 P.M.
THE DOROTHY CHANDLER PAVILION, LOS ANGELES

Your Host:
BILLY CRYSTAL
Televised over ABC

Presenters

Supporting Actor . . . . Whoopi Goldberg
Makeup . . . . Rebecca De Mornay and Christopher Lloyd
Supporting Actress . . . . Joe Pesci
Art Direction . . . . Annette Bening
Thalberg Award . . . . Steven Spielberg
Sound Effects Editing . . . . Sharon Stone and Antonio Banderas
Editing . . . . Geena Davis and Susan Sarandon
Live Action Short Film . . . . Dana Carvey and Mike Myers
Animated Short Film . . . . Belle and The Beast
Costume Design . . . . Demi Moore
Foreign Film . . . . Sylvester Stallone
Sound . . . . Daryl Hannah and Edward James Olmos
Scientific and Technical Awards . . . . Tom Hanks
Gordon E. Sawyer Award . . . . Ray Bradbury
Documentary Awards . . Spike Lee and John Singleton
Cinematography . . . . Richard Gere
Visual Effects . . . . Laura Dern and Diane Ladd
Original Score . . . . Patrick Swayze
Honorary Award to Satyajit Ray . . . Audrey Hepburn
Writing Awards . . . . Anjelica Huston and Robert Duvall
Actor . . . . Kathy Bates
Original Song . . . . Shirley MacLaine and Liza Minnelli
Actress . . . . Michael Douglas
Director . . . . Kevin Costner
Picture . . . . Elizabeth Taylor and Paul Newman

Performers of Nominated Songs

"Beauty and the Beast" . . . . Angela Lansbury, Celine Dion, and Peabo Bryson
"Belle" . . . . Paige O'Hara, Jerry Orbach, and Richard White
"Be Our Guest" . . . . Paige O'Hara, Jerry Orbach, and Richard White
"(Everything I Do) I Do It for You" . . . Bryan Adams
"When You're Alone" . . . . Amber Scott

"It's your own fault you're going to die of AIDS and go to Hell."
—a counterprotestor

"Shame! Shame!" According to Archerd, Stone "was frankly concerned for his own safety." The nervous nominee told the forecourt emcee, "It would be something if I was assassinated by some CIA man disguised as a homosexual. Then they'd have to do my life story." Stone looked on the bright side: "It's not easy to make a movie that offends everyone. I'm proud of that. I feel the opposite of Sally Field."

Field herself, on hand to introduce the *Beauty and the Beast* clip, didn't like the demonstrators, telling *Entertainment Tonight*, "I believe disrupting the ceremony and being strident like they are doesn't do anybody any good." A broader-minded Audrey Hepburn defended them: "It's a free country and they should protest if they feel like it." Nick Nolte, in a black-shirted tux with a red AIDS awareness ribbon on the lapel, also expressed solidarity: "It's all right, I've been protesting since the '60s."

A demonstrator's placard, "For Worst Picture—*The Silence of the Lambs*," greeted a red-ribboned Jodie Foster, who made a fashion statement in her beige Armani jacket with beaded blouse and trousers. She told *Women's Wear Daily*, "Beauty is part of what I do. I don't know why, but I think there is this strange tradition where people think that people who are smart can't look good." *WWD* looked around and pouted that "the lack of bad taste cast a bland pallor over the parade of surprisingly subdued gowns grazing the red carpet." *Vanity Fair* liked Annette Bening "in a simple, long, navy-blue Armani dress, with her hair swept up in an aristocratic do." Cindy Adams noted that Bening "wore a very chunky diamond bracelet but a very small diamond ring. The ring was real." "Sure. We're married," confirmed Mrs. Beatty to Archerd, proving it by "the sparkler on her left hand." The forecourt emcee led the bleacher fans in serenading Mr. Beatty with "Happy Birthday."

At Spago, Beatty's former co-star Madonna arrived for dinner and discovered she was seated at Walter Cronkite's table. "I didn't expect to meet her," admitted the surprised newsman, "but then, she didn't expect to meet me." Roseanne and Tom Arnold came to the Lazar fete for the first time; given their place cards, Roseanne loudly asked, "What are these for?" Then she saw where their table was. "We love sitting next to the john at Spago," she commented. "Yeah, it's the best seat in the house." *Newsday*'s spy phoned in that "Church of Scientology member Tom Cruise and wife Nicole Kidman were there in body and soul. They reportedly 'all but had sex' during dinner."

Back at the Dorothy Chandler, *E!* asked John Singleton for his reaction to the proceedings, which he felt were "like the Rose Parade, but instead of floats you have long gowns and people." He also insisted that he had no intention of resting on his laurels: "I don't want to be sitting up in front of a Seven-Eleven asking for quarters and talking about *Boyz N the Hood.*" Wearing a Valentino gown was Bette Midler, who, gossipped Claudia Cohen, "lost ten pounds to fit into this dress on an all-liquid, all-juice diet." Midler told journalists, "I'm so glad this night is here. I'll be so happy when it's over, no matter what happens."

Barbra Streisand, on the arm of Jason Gould, wore a pinkish beige pleated gown with matching jacket by Welsh designer Patricia Lester and what one fashion critic called "crimped broomstick hair." Hairdo of the night belonged to the first arrival, nineteen-year-old Supporting Actress nominee Juliette Lewis who had twisted her locks into severe cornrows. *USA Today*'s fashion observer Elizabeth Snead penned that she looked "as if she had been attacked by a lawn mower." "I really liked the way it looked and I wanted my face out there," Lewis confided to *Entertainment Tonight*, adding that she didn't know who had designed her '20s-style gown because she had bought it for $150 at a thrift shop. Her date was actor Brad Pitt, who had made love to Geena Davis in *Thelma & Louise*, but now only had eyes for the sci-fi coiffed Lewis: "She's so smooth, you know. Like from another planet, but a nice planet." Lewis' competitor Jessica Tandy was also

"We love sitting by the john at Spago. Yeah, it's the best seat in the house."
—Roseanne Arnold

tonsorially noteworthy, with a full head of blond hair after last year's chemotherapy look. The 1989 Best Actress told Cindy Adams that fame had not gone to her head: "I still take the subway. The riders sometimes shake my hand."

Michael Lerner showed up after spending the day with *Entertainment Tonight*, which had accompanied him to the bank, to lunch with his brothers, through the phone call to Mom in Miami, and on a final trip to take out the trash, which the actor did in his formal wear. From the ankles down, Lerner preferred a preppy look—green boating shoes without socks. "These are my good luck shoes," he explained to reporters. His date was Diane Baker, who had returned to films with a small role in *The Silence of the Lambs*. Laura Dern was with Vincent Spano and allowed, "Mom is nervous so I'm relaxed." Diane Ladd came with an entourage: her agent, *Fatal Attraction* writer James Dearden, her screen son Lukas Haas, and her mother from Alabama. Ladd said of Oscar, "His name may not be Bill Bailey, but I'd like to see him come on home." When last year's Supporting Actress victor Whoopi Goldberg materialized with Timothy Dalton, *E!*'s Dagne Hultgreen inquired, "Last year you had hives, how are you doing this year?" Replied Whoopi, "I've got my period."

The broadcast began with a street scene outside the Dorothy Chandler with no protestors visible. The corn was ripe as announcer Les Marchak narrated the clips of arrivals: "Young, beautiful and talented—a winning combination in any league—Darryl Hannah," "one of Hollywood's bright new stars—Rebecca De Mornay" (who had made *Risky Business* with Tom Cruise back in 1983). Then onstage was the Academy president. Like the vast majority of the show's participants and winners, Karl Malden wore a red ribbon and, still pushing the Academy's video, began with "Tonight, we expect more golden moments from Oscar." After inviting everyone to visit the Academy's new library, a "spanking new center for motion picture study," Malden got things going with, "First we have some joyful business to take care of here." A Chuck Workman montage of screen comedy then unspooled. Along with Chaplin, Keaton, and Laurel & Hardy clips, the montage included this year's nominees Warren Beatty, Bette Midler, Nick Nolte, Laura Dern, and Jack Palance. As a sop to the protestors, the late comic actor Divine was shown licking his lips, but Workman scored a snicker from the audience at Paul Rubens' expense with his line, "There's a lot of things you don't know about me, Dotty," from *Pee-wee's Big Adventure*. The montage's biggest laughs came from Woody Allen theorizing about a conspiracy in the Kennedy assassination in *Annie Hall* and Kevin Costner's statement to Susan Sarandon in *Bull Durham*, "I believe Lee Harvey Oswald acted alone."

When the clips were finished, viewers could check out the seating arrangements. Bette Midler was behind Anthony Hopkins and in front of Ben Kingsley, while on the other side of the aisle, the Warren Beattys were next to the Hume Cronyns, who had the Nick Noltes on their other side. The camera caught Nolte suddenly laughing at what turned out to be Billy Crystal's replacement gag for his bungee jump. The comedian was rolled out on a stretcher wearing Hannibal Lecter's mask. Janet Maslin called this "a wicked, show-stopping entrance." Anthony Hopkins put his glasses on to get a better look and laughed delightedly. Unstrapped from his stretcher, Crystal repeated last year's joke with a remote car lock and then aped Snow White by accosting an audience member. Anthony Hopkins rose as the comedian approached him and Crystal, in an Anthony Hopkins voice, said, "I'm having some of the Academy over for dinner. Care to join me?" "Anytime," replied Hopkins.

Crystal returned to the stage and flung off the mask with, "I look like the goalie from the SAG hockey team." Plunging into his monologue, the host continued, "Welcome to the Oscars, or as it's known tonight, *Cape Fear* . . . A quadraplex is where you see one movie but hear four . . . Tonight we have the first cartoon ever nominated,

"Welcome to the Oscars, or as it's known tonight, Cape Fear."
—Billy Crystal

not counting Dan Quayle." This last crack earned cheers and whoops. John Singleton was flattered with a close-up when Crystal praised "the youngest writer-director ever nominated . . . *Boyz N the Hood*—the David Duke story." Ben Kingsley also got camera time when the emcee discussed his two nominated roles: "Gandhi and Lasky, two men with a vision and neither ate pork." Of Warren Beatty, Crystal said, "First he did press. Then he became a father. Then he got married and today is his birthday. I remember when people just used to take out trade ads."

The announcement that there would be no opening production number brought deafening applause and then Crystal launched into his customary medley of Best Picture nominees. *Beauty and the Beast* was parodied to the melody of the *Patty Duke Show* theme song, ending with "Actors/Are out of a job." *The Silence of the Lambs* became the Oscar-winning "The Shadow of Your Smile" ("A bouillabaisse of cheeks and necks and arms") and "Toot-Toot-Tootsie" became "Bug-Bug-Bugsy." The biggest response came when Crystal sent up "Three Coins in the Fountain" for *JFK*—"Three shots in the Plaza/Whodunnit, Mr. Stone?/The CIA or Homer Simpson/The FBI or Vic Damone?"—and "Don't Rain on My Parade" with "Seven nominations on the shelf/did this film direct itself?" This *Prince of Tides* reference afforded the first of what would be many shots of Barbra Streisand in the front row, sitting in front of Kevin Costner. She smiled. *WWD* carped about Crystal's Armani tux, "Last year, it was a brown monstrosity, and this year, it was made of . . . velvet, perfect for an opening night in the Catskills."

At the end of the first commercial break, several audience members could be seen scurrying back to their seats; "Hurry up, we were so worried about you," chided Crystal. The host brought out "a good friend of mine," Whoopi Goldberg, to name the Best Supporting Actor. All the nominees were present and the winner was Jack Palance, sporting the same gray silk dinner suit he had worn to the Cowboy Hall of Fame but no red AIDS ribbon. "I had no idea I would be the first award," Palance later said of the moment when he sat stunned while daughter Holly kissed his cheek and then wiped off the lipstick. Onstage, he shook Goldberg's hand and then kissed her cheek. Liz Smith wrote of what transpired next: "Considered a 'sentimental' favorite, Palance, in accepting, sure didn't wallow in *that* emotion." "Billy Crystal?" he began, referring to his *City Slickers* co-star, "I crap bigger than him." The audience reacted with startled amusement to his unexpected off-color wit. "You know," the winner continued, "there's a time when you reach a certain age plateau where the producers say, 'Well, what do you think? Can we risk it?' " To demonstrate his virility, Palance suddenly moved away from the podium, got down on the floor, and started doing push-ups; by the time he was doing them one-handed, the crowd was applauding and roaring its approval. Returning to the microphone, Palance kept up the blue humor: "As far as the two-handed push-ups are concerned, you can do that all night. Doesn't make any difference if she's there or not. Besides, it's a hell of a lot less expensive." The closest he came to standard acceptance speech sentiment was his conclusion that on his first film set in 1949, the producer told him, " 'you're gonna win the Academy Award.' Can you believe it, forty-two years later, he was right. How'd this sonofabitch know?" Backstage, Palance asked the press if, when he was on the floor, "Did you think I was dead out there?"

Crystal knew his costar had provided him with ample fodder, and he got laughs by saying Palance "is backstage on the Stairmaster." As for his own poor Academy showing for the same film, the comedian said, "I know why I wasn't nominated. It's because I'm a woman." A real woman, Rebecca De Mornay, who *WWD* said "looked just like Marilyn" in a low-cut satin Nolan Miller gown that the actress called "the real reason I went to the Academy Awards," strutted out to give the Makeup Oscar with *The Addams Family*'s Uncle Fester, Christopher Lloyd. Kenneth Turan of the *Los Angeles Times* took note of "the Academy's desire, in a time of declining box office, to be audience-friendly with a reliance on crowd-pleasing gimmicks," beginning with the arrival of the mechanical "Thing" from Lloyd's movie dashing across the stage with the envelope. And so began the technical sweep of *Terminator 2*, with one of the makeup artists thanking "the guy who sat in that chair everyday and made all this work—Arnold Schwarzenegger!"

Angela Lansbury was next, introducing two songs from *Beauty and the Beast*, performed onstage by the singers who had sung them, unseen, in the film, including Jerry Orbach, who delivered a rousing, Broadway-style version of "Be Our Guest." Last year's Supporting Actor winner, Joe Pesci, came out to read the names of the Best Supporting Actress nominees, who, he said, "range in age from None of Your Business to How Dare You Ask." All five women were there, Diane Ladd clutching a rose. The winner was Mercedes Ruehl for *The Fisher King*, the second victor not wearing a red ribbon; instead, she sported a black Valentino about which she had said on the forecourt, "The final fitting was at one o'clock today." For her big speech, Ruehl proclaimed, "At this moment, dreadful memories have suddenly transformed themselves into nothing more than the sort of charming and amusing anecdotes for my memoirs." She remembered playwright Albert Innuarto "and the late Joe Papp, who gave me my first shot on the New York stage." She went backstage and asked reporters, "Did it sound too prepared? Only thirty years of preparation, but hey." Then she called Bethesda, Maryland, to speak with "Mommy and Daddy."

Up front, Crystal was scoring with, "Jack Palance just bungee jumped off the Hollywood sign . . . a little decaf, Jack." Suddenly serious, Crystal explained "for our global audience" what the red ribbons meant: "a symbol of AIDS awareness to show our solidarity with the people suffering from this epidemic and the people who are fighting every day to wipe it off the face of the earth." Then this year's symbol of motherhood, Annette Bening, laughed as she disclosed that the Art Direction winner was *Bugsy*.

Steven Spielberg walked out carrying a bust, which he gave to "my valued colleague and great and loyal friend," this year's Irving G. Thalberg Award recipient, George Lucas. The producer thanked "the thousands of talented men and women, robots and aliens and others with whom I've been lucky enough to share the creative experience . . . my teachers from kindergarten through college, their struggle—and it was a struggle—to help me learn to grow . . . All of us who make motion pictures are teachers, teachers with loud voices, but we'll never match the power of a teacher who is able to whisper into a student's ear. Thank you, Francis [Coppola] for being my mentor . . . and my two daughters, they have taught me more and enriched my life beyond anything imaginable." When Lucas was done, Spielberg smirked that "There's someone else who wants to say congratulations to you," directing Lucas to a video screen satellite hook-up to the Atlantis Space Shuttle in orbit. Commander Charles Bolden, surrounded by his crew, said "We are carrying a special celebrity aboard our spaceship." The guest was an Oscar that floated in the ship's zero-gravity atmosphere. Army Archerd snitched that although Spielberg pretended it was live, the spot "was pretaped for safety."

"The shuttle just rendezvoused with Jack Palance, who somehow launched himself into orbit," joked Billy Crystal. *Terminator 2* claimed Oscar two when the Sound Effects Editing award was presented by Pedro Almodóvar fixture Antonio Banderas and Sharon Stone, star of the notorious *Basic Instinct*. Because of a death threat, the actress thought it prudent to hire a bodyguard for the evening. Marilyn Beck reported that backstage, Stone "posed for pictures in the photo area but was whisked by her publicist past the area where print journalists were waiting, no doubt with pointed questions."

Denzel Washington slyly alluded to his upcoming biography of Malcolm X directed by Spike Lee when he introduced the clip of *JFK* with, "Arguably the most controversial movie of the decade—so far." Stars of this year's other controversial movie came from opposite sides of the stage, met, and put their arms around each other's waists. *Newsweek* said that the Valentino-clad Susan Sarandon "wore the world's sexiest maternity gown" while Geena Davis, who towered over her, was "looking like Big Bird in dust ruffles" with her Bill Hargate-Ruth Myers can-can dancer ensemble. They presented the Editing Oscar not to their movie but to *JFK*. "It's rare that a man has the courage to consistently seek out the higher truth," attested Joe Hustings. "John F. Kennedy was such a man, Oliver Stone is such a man." Expanded cowinner Pietro Scalia, "Making a movie with Oliver Stone is like going into battle . . . in the language of cinema, we have opened an historical debate." Then a commercial followed touting Thalberg winner George Lucas' new TV show, *The Young Indiana Jones Chronicles*.

The stars of the TV-to-cinema crossover hit *Wayne's World*, Mike Meyers and Dana Carvey, gave the Live Action Short Film Award to *Session Man*. Coproducer Seth Winston addressed his children, watching in England "where it's 5 o'clock in the morning. You might as well stay up all night." For the third year in a row, cartoon characters presented the Animated Short Oscar. Beauty and the Beast showed up to award *Manipulation* which, from the clip, looked like a cartoon about bondage. Demi Moore bestowed the Costume Design Award to *Bugsy*'s Albert Wolsky, who wore no red ribbon and toasted his producer-star for having "created an elegant and impeccable taste and climate for us." Backstage, *WWD* asked Wolsky whose dress he liked best tonight and he replied that he liked Susan Sarandon and Geena Davis because, "They were funny together." "A great star," Sylvester Stallone, presented the somewhat tarnished Foreign Language Film Award to Italy's sunny anti-war fable, *Mediterraneo*. Director Carlo Ono said, "I'm sorry. I don't speak English," but did manage to get across the film's main theme: "Please stop the wars—life is better."

Terminator 2 marched on, winning Best Sound. Four technicians mounted the stage, but when the second one began to speak, the orchestra rudely drowned him out and the camera swung to the other side of the stage, where "an actor of charm and depth" entered, John Candy. *NYQ*'s Robin Podolsky reported that "Queer Nation . . . said forty-five demonstrators who had bought tickets and had been seated in the auditorium, stood up during John Candy's presentation speech and began to yell, 'Out of the closets and onto the screen.' Private security forces hustled them out of the auditorium and they were not arrested." Nor were they heard by the at-home audience. Onstage, Candy introduced a production number for the Best Song nominee "When You're Alone" from Steven Spielberg's Peter Pan movie. The stage was filled with kids flying on wires and when it was over, Billy Crystal commented that "Jack Palance is the father of all those children."

Tom Hanks, in white tie and tails, playfully described the Scientific and Technical Awards, saying that "Jim Doyle's dense, low-hanging fog machine has already revolutionized low-hanging fog" and "drag modules . . . and tripod heads make much better use of the compound silicone than is on display here this evening." The Gordon E. Sawyer Award went to special effects master Ray Harryhausen, whose wonderful movie monsters paraded by in a montage, followed by footage of him receiving the Award at an earlier function from his boyhood friend, science-fiction author Ray Bradbury.

John Singleton, wearing a checkered tie, and Spike Lee, with white tie, came out to present the Documentary Awards. Seeing the duo leaning casually on the podium, the *New York Times*'s Woody Hochswender wrote that "they delivered their speeches as if they were ordering coffee and a buttered roll at Nedick's." Jami Bernard of the *New York Post* chastised Lee for mispronouncing " 'Thailand' as if it contained a body part off of Hannibal Lecter's dinner plate." In lieu of Jenny Livingston's drag queens, the Award went to a

"*Thank you and boycott G.E.!*"
—*Debra Chasnoff*

much more urgent movie about singers in the chorus of the San Francisco Opera company. Backstage, one of the winning producers harrumphed that "Some of the films that were not nominated didn't deserve to be nominated."

There was real excitement as Debra Chasnoff stepped up to receive the Documentary Short Oscar for *Deadly Deception: G.E., Nuclear Weapons, and Our Environment.* Chasnoff inveighed against "the company that falsely claims it brings good things to life." She praised "Kim, my life partner, who always had faith in me, and our son Noah, who reminds us on a daily basis why it's so important not to give up." Her finale was, "Thank you and boycott G.E.!" Army Archerd confirmed that, "She electrified the audience with her condemnation of G.E." One hold-out was Kevin Costner, who did not join in with the thunderous applause. Reuters reassured stockholders the next day that "Chasnoff's comments had no immediate effect on G.E. shares, which initially rose before closing down 25 cents a share to $75.75 on the New York Stock Exchange." The corporation promptly informed the *Wall Street Journal* that the incident had "no impact at all," regardless of the footage of nuclear contamination seen by an audience of one billion people, and a public relations expert concurred: "The old rule of thumb is that you have to repeat it three to four times to the average person on the street before even a powerful point really sinks in." But Infact, the cooperative that Chasnoff named in her speech, told the paper it received seventy requests for the film by mid-afternoon the next day, particularly from newspapers and residents near G.E.'s nuclear facilities. Chasnoff had more immediate concerns when a backstage reporter asked if "Kim" was a man or a woman. "A woman," she clarified "and I'm really sorry I didn't say it."

More activism followed when Cinematography presenter Richard Gere deviated from the script to remind everyone about the significance of the red ribbons. "I think an appropriate thing to think about is what you can do about it," Gere declared. "In this day and age when defense budgets are shrinking, we can take some of that defense money and put it in AIDS research." This suggestion met with loud approval. Gere dedicated the Award to Nestor Almendros, the cinematographer who had died of AIDS-related lymphoma a few weeks earlier: "He won an Oscar for that first film, which was also my first film, *Days of Heaven*, en francais, *Moisson du Ciel.*" (Gere's film debut was actually 1975's *Report to the Commissioner.*) This year's Cinematography prize went to the absent Robert Richardson for *JFK.*

"We have a true pioneer in our audience tonight," was Crystal's Ed Sullivan-esque lead-in to the recognition of 100-year-old Hal Roach. After a montage of the producer's work—Laurel & Hardy and Our Gang (including a shot of Spanky McFarlane's butt)—the 1983 Honorary Award winner slowly rose from his seat as the audience did the same, leading into a lengthy standing ovation. When everybody sat down, Crystal attempted to go on with his schtick, but Roach was still standing in the aisle, addressing the audience. The show had just communicated with the shuttle in outer space but it couldn't relay Roach's words in the orchestra. Viewers saw the mute figure of Roach talking, then heard rising applause, and ultimately saw a technician rushing over with a microphone. By then it was too late; Roach had said what he had to say and returned to his seat, unaware of the man's presence or, indeed, of any problem at all. When the camera returned to Crystal, he was ready: "I think that's fitting because Mr. Roach started in silent films." The grateful audience howled. Crystal proceeded with his gag, in which he was superimposed onto a clip of Laurel & Hardy's dancing in *Way Out West*; Andrew Sarris denigrated the stunt as an "insensitive intrusion . . . into . . . one of the screen's most magical manifestations of male camaraderie." This would prove to be Mr. Roach's last public appearance; he passed away six months later.

Laura Dern said, "Hi, Mommy"; Diane Ladd said "Hi, Laura," and they honored *Terminator 2* with its fourth Oscar, for Best Sound. This quartet of winning technicians had learned from their colleagues' earlier ignominious fate at the microphone, and each one rushed through an acceptance before Bill Conti's band could do its damage. Director James Cameron, in the audience with leading lady Linda Hamilton, heard testimonials to his "genius" and his "vision," as well as an exhortation that "he's got to get one of these soon."

Patrick Swayze introduced "dance impressions" of the Best Score nominations by choreographer Debbie Allen "who did such a wonderful job on last year's Oscars, and no wonder, she was my mom's student." Allen's dancers went into their steps, Swayze said, "Yeah, way to go, Debbie," and then gave the statuette to Alan Menken for *Beauty and the Beast.* "On behalf of all the composers, I want to thank Debbie Allen for that, that was just great," Menken started. "Most of all, I want to thank my late partner and friend Howard Ashman. Howard, I wish you could have seen the finished product, I wish you could have heard the completed score. I know you would have been proud."

Jack Valenti, showing off his White House ties, commented, "There was one of the wittier occupants of the Oval Office, President John F. Kennedy, who once said that a committee was twelve people doing the work of one." Then the Motion Picture Association head flubbed his introduction of UNICEF-activist Audrey Hepburn with, "It's my good fortune to know one person who does the work of twelve, uhh, of one." Hepburn was Mother Teresa's replacement as the presenter of Satyajit Ray's Oscar and she glided out in an appropriately Indian-style, one-shouldered Givenchy and bussed Valenti French-style, on both cheeks. "Unfortunately, Mr. Ray is not well and cannot be with us tonight," said Hepburn, "but he is able to speak with us from his hospital room in Calcutta." The Academy had permitted the director to accept in bed—à la Joan Crawford—which was in keeping with the movie maven's speech: "This is a sobering experience for me to be here tonight to receive this magnificent Award, certainly the best achievement of my movie-making career. As a small schoolboy, I was terribly interested in cinema, became a film buff, wrote to Deanna Durbin, got a reply, was delighted. Wrote to Ginger Rogers, didn't get a reply. Then I wrote a twelve-page letter to Billy Wilder after seeing *Double Indemnity.* He didn't reply either (laughs). Well, there you are." Ray died a month later.

Billy Crystal had a news flash: "Jack Palance has just won the New York primary." Then Robert Duvall, in a western-style tux without a red ribbon, and Anjelica Huston in a black minidress, came out to give the Writing Awards, both of which went to the winners of the Writers Guild Awards. Ladies' man James Toback of *Bugsy* lost Original Screenplay to *Thelma & Louise*'s Callie Khouri. The winner hugged her husband and son and said, "For everybody that wanted to see a happy ending for Thelma and Louise, to me, this is it . . . Geena and Susan, I think you've made the world a better place." The camera saw Sarandon blow her a kiss as, behind her, Gilbert Cates' flashing timer was telling Khouri she only had thirty more seconds. Khouri assured everyone that her husband "wasn't the model for any of the characters. In fact, my brother was (laughter). I'm just kidding." Backstage, she said, "I don't think criticism of *Thelma & Louise* as a male-bashing movie was warranted. I'm kind of glad for the controversy, though, because more people saw the movie." Ted Talley's publicist had earned his money when the author claimed the first Oscar for *The Silence of the Lambs.* Jonathan Demme jumped up to embrace Talley on the way to the stage and the feeling was mutual, for the writer paeanized him as "a director of awesome talent and generosity and one of the finest men I've ever known." Jodie Foster could be seen in the audience shaking her fist triumphantly.

Kathy Bates strolled out to give Best Actor. Robert De Niro was nowhere to be seen, Anthony Hopkins had on his glasses, and Nick Nolte nervously chewed gum. Columnist Richard Johnson noted that "in the pressroom, a huge roar of approval went up when Hopkins was announced." In the auditorium, the actor—who wasn't wearing

"So, Liza, why don't you and I and some other real-life human beings next year get together and make a musical of our own?"
—Shirley MacLaine

a red ribbon—garnered the night's second standing ovation. He removed his specs on the way to the podium, where he hugged and kissed Bates, who, too, had won an Oscar for playing a sicko. Holding his statuette above him, Hopkins acknowledged the audience's cheers and after paying tribute to his fellow nominees, said "First of all, I want to say hello to my mother. She's in Wales watching this on television . . . My father died eleven years ago tonight, so maybe he had something to do with this . . . I have many people to thank here in Los Angeles who, over the years, have given me tremendous support and without whose help I wouldn't be here, I know." As Hopkins headed off, the *Los Angeles Times*' Kenneth Turan witnessed Warren Beatty leave his seat to "walk over to offer condolences" to fellow loser Nick Nolte.

Seguing to the Best Song Award, Crystal had trouble with a long-winded introduction to Liza Minnelli and Kathlyn Beatty's aunt, Shirley MacLaine. He saved himself by mocking Democratic presidential hopeful Bill Clinton's admission that, although he once tried marijuana, he "didn't inhale." The audience applauded the put-down. "So, Liza," Shirley said, "why don't you and I and some other real-life human beings next year get together and make a musical of our own?" Minnelli responded, "We should get that other buddy of ours, you know, the singer, the actress, that girl over there, that funny girl." "The director," MacLaine corrected. "The director we would most like to work with." The crowd applauded and Barbra Streisand blew kisses and mouthed, "You are so sweet, I love you." Then Shirley wisecracked, "Some other life." The Oscar went to the title song from *Beauty and the Beast*. Composer Alan Menken gave his thanks and then said of his late lyricist, "Accepting for Howard will be Bill Launch." Launch, an architect, said,

> *Howard and I shared a home and a life together and I'm very happy and very proud to accept this for him. But it is bittersweet. This is the first Academy Award given to someone we've lost to AIDS. In working on* Beauty and the Beast, *Howard faced incredible personal challenges but always gave his best. What made that possible was an atmosphere of understanding, love, and support, something everyone facing AIDS not only needs but deserves. There's an inscription at Howard's grave in Baltimore. It reads, "Oh, that he had one more song to sing." We'll never hear that song, but I'm deeply grateful for this tribute to what he's left behind. For Howard, I thank you.*

Janet Maslin was moved by Lauch's "tremendous sad dignity," and Leonard Maltin remarked, "No symbolic show of support could really approach the depth of feeling that came when the late Howard Ashman was celebrated."

Ironically, this memorial was followed by Michael Douglas, star of the dreaded *Basic Instinct*, who revealed that the Best Actress winner was Jodie Foster, the star of the dreaded *The Silence of the Lambs*. Foster accepted the statuette from the actor with whom she costarred in her first film, Disney's *Napoleon and Samantha*, and said, "This has been such an incredible year and I would like to direct this to all the women who came before me who never had the chances that I've had and the survivors and the outcasts, my blood, my tradition." She continued that "I'd like to thank all the people in this industry who have respected my choices and who have not been afraid of the power and the dignity that entitles me to." The actress thanked Jesse Kornbluth, Anthony Hopkins ("the reason I'm here . . . quid pro quo, doctor"), and "my guru, Jonathan Demme, not just for his talent but for his goodness." As she did in her acceptance speech three years earlier, Foster signed off by paying tribute to "most of all, my mother Brandy. . . ."

Coming out to preface a film clip, Jessica Tandy made like MacLaine and Minnelli with her own salute to Streisand. "When Gil Cates asked me to introduce one, I chose the one directed by

"Ummmmm."
—Jonathan Demme

a very talented lady and why she wasn't nominated, oh, well, never mind." Another close-up of Streisand waving and blowing kisses preceded the *Prince of Tides* clip, followed by a shot of Nick Nolte, unsmiling but still enjoying his gum.

Kevin Costner, whom *WWD* criticized for looking "puffy and faintly ridiculous with his new Caesar haircut," strode out to crown Best Director. The winner was Jonathan Demme for *The Silence of the Lambs.* Seeing his victory on the pressroom monitor, Jodie Foster exclaimed, "No way!" Demme kissed his wife, then turned tongue-tied, "Uh, well, in the context of my movie-loving life, this is unanticipated," he began, going on for a rambling three-minute-thirty-five second acceptance speech which contained, according to *Entertainment Weekly*'s count, ninety-four "uhs." "I wanted very much to salute John Singleton, Matty Rich, Jodie Foster, Ernest Dickerson, and a bunch of new people," Demme said, to applause. "I'm thrilled to be able to invoke the recent memory of two great men, two great filmmakers, Hal Ashby and Martin Ritt . . . Finally I've obviously got to say Hi, Mom and thanks for transferring your love of movies to me and thanks Dad for making me think I could actually be a part of this industry and, uh—thank you." Sniped Liz Smith, "He must never, ever, under any circumstances, speak in public again. Not unless he can get 'Ummmmmm' out of his vocabulary (And here we all thought 'you know' was bad!)."

A clip from *Cat on a Hot Tin Roof* led to Elizabeth Taylor and Paul Newman regally coming onstage. "We were looking pretty good back then," said Newman. "Hey, I think we're still looking pretty good," responded Taylor, who had recently celebrated her 60th birthday at a Disneyland bash attended by 1,000 guests including Michael Lerner and Diane Ladd. Taylor smiled at her costar from *The Only Game in Town* when Newman read *Bugsy*'s nomination, but the title in the envelope was *The Silence of the Lambs* and the film's three producers each spoke. Edward Saxon thanked "Orion Pictures for their support and unwavering commitment to artistic freedom throughout the years . . . and Jonathan Demme, my mentor and dear friend." Kenneth Utt addressed the telecast's producer, "Gil, I need a Teleprompter. I feel like John Wayne, I'm ten feet tall." Utt thanked Mrs. Utt, Angie, "who's been the star of our family for fifty years." Ron Bozman finished things off by praising "my brother in Texas" and "the family of filmmakers Jonathan has assembled." Meanwhile, Anthony Hopkins was on the phone to Wales, saying "Mom, we just won Best Picture."

"And I would like to thank my wife Janis, without whose soup tonight would not have been possible," said Billy Crystal, who had a bulletin: "I've just been informed that Jack Palance will be hosting the TV show next year, so good night." He walked off-stage and the names of the sponsors appeared on the screen, beginning with "Ultra Slim-Fast: The Delicious, Nutritious Way to Lose Weight."

Aftermath

"Everyone I ever went to school with all the way down to the 7th grade called me with the odds," Mercedes Ruehl said backstage in response to a question about how her nomination had changed her life. "Even my supermarket treats me differently. I used to throw on a trench coat, my hair in pins, dark glasses. Now at the Grand Union they stop squeezing the bananas to see how I'm dressed."

Jack Palance was asked how he would celebrate. "I don't drink, what in the hell can I do?" he quipped. Palance hadn't voted in this year's Oscars and "the only film I saw this year was *Beauty and the Beast*, which I adored . . . because of my granddaughter," whom he was sorry he had forgotten to mention in his speech. Someone asked where he'd put his Oscar. "On my head," replied Palance.

"Backstage, Palance had some competition from Anthony Hopkins," commented CNN, as Dr. Lecter kidded the press, "If I hadn't won, you'd all be in trouble." *Good Morning America*'s

"We only meet on award nights."
—Susan Sarandon on Geena Davis

Joel Siegel marveled to viewers that "In real life, he's so unassuming, nothing at all like the character he played." When asked how the folks in Wales were doing, Hopkins said "They're all crying. They're getting smashed on champagne for the moment." As to why his macabre film was so popular, Hopkins mused, "It's really about Beauty and the Beast again . . . a man trapped in a monstrous brain . . . like Quasimodo . . . Strange enough, I believe it was a potential for love, because he loves Clarice . . . he loves her courage."

Nobody demanded to know why the Best Actor wasn't wearing a red ribbon, while the Best Actress, who was sporting one, was asked for her opinion of the gay demonstration. "Protest is American," Foster stated. "It's not against the law. Criticism is also good. Anything other than that falls into the category of undignified." When the *Santa Cruz Sentinal* wanted to know who she had expected to win, Foster said, "I didn't know. Anybody else but me." Her director also had to answer to the protestors. "My life is full of positive gay characters and, yet, my movies aren't. I wish to see them become more and more that way," Demme declaimed. "I don't accept *Silence* being targeted for negative portrayals of gay people 'cause we didn't have any in it." Wary of offending anyone, Demme added, "I endorse the protest."

Entering the Governors' Ball, Spike Lee said he "was surprised because usually they don't give awards to so-called genre movies, slasher films." Winners usually reveled at the Governors' Ball but the *Silence* crowd had their own dinner party at Rex in downtown L.A. Foster told the press waiting outside, "I don't know what to do with myself. I just keep smiling, my face hurts." Inside, reported *USA Today*'s Jeannie Williams, Foster "swung from hug to hug, kiss to kiss, clutching a tall champagne glass in her little gloved hands, her Armani blouse slipping further open all the time." Jodie sat with her family, next to Anthony Hopkins' table, a group that included critic Roger Ebert—who had been rooting for *JFK*—and his fiancée Chaz Hammel-Smith. Dinner consisted of lamb chops and chianti. The winners watched their speeches again, and Hopkins murmured, "They really did stand . . . it was the greatest moment of my life." When a journalist asked Orion's Christine LaMonte if the studio had the cash to pay for this spread, she snapped, "How dare people question it. Don't we deserve to celebrate? We knew in February that we had a winner and there were monies allocated for the Academy campaign and the party." Hopkins told the SAG magazine, "After I got home and got to bed, later I woke up at four in the morning and went down to the parlor to take a look at it—just to make sure it was real." Two hours later, Jonathan Demme had a similar problem with reality, admitting to Joseph Gelmis of *Newsday* that he "awoke in his Los Angeles hotel room at six yesterday morning bathed in a cold sweat and feeling delayed shock at the hubbub that had engulfed him from the moment he won." Remarked Demme, "I don't feel it's going to be a part of my identity or change my life. But, man, it sure puts the spotlight on you." Janet Maslin confirmed it when she spotted Demme a few weeks later at Cannes: "This year, as an Oscar winner, he attracted such a crowd of onlookers on the Carlton terrace while trying to conduct a private conversation that he was forced to go somewhere else."

There were other Governors' Ball truants. "We were bad and skipped the Ball," Susan Sarandon and Tim Robbins whispered to *USA Today* at the annual El Rescate Oscar night fundraiser. "I went home to my hotel and took off all my jewels that were borrowed and then I came here," informed Sarandon, who said that despite their affection for each other, she and costar Geena Davis didn't see each other much: "We only meet on award nights." Oliver Stone also made the younger El Rescate scene, while Sally Field told CNN she had showed up at Spago for "schmoozing, eating, and being in the 'in' crowd." Supporting Actress also-ran Kate Nelligan went to the Lazar bash where "I was just

"A one-arm push-up is hard for me to do."
—Mr. Olympia

looking at everybody's jewelry. There was a lot of great jewelry in there." Gossip Claudia Cohen scooped that "Everyone said Liza's in love. She was here at Spago nuzzling her constant companion Billy Stritch." Paul Newman told Cohen, "I do the Oscar show every five years to remind people out here I'm still alive."

Newsday's Linda Stasi observed, "What a difference a year makes. Last year's glamorous material girl (in a Bob Mackie dress and $4 million worth of Harry Winston jewelry) was this year's totally immaterial girl. Wearing a polka-dotted blouse and French beret, Madonna quickly left the party before her ex-beau/Oscar loser Warren Beatty arrived with wife Annette Bening." Mrs. Beatty said of *Bugsy*'s disappointing 2-out-of-10 Oscar showing, "C'est la vie," but a *Los Angeles Times* article entitled "Why Did *Bugsy* Roll Snake Eyes?" quoted a studio executive who attested, "people in the Academy felt *Bugsy* was being jammed down their throats, what with the overwhelming ads and brochures."

Roseanne Arnold raved to CNN about the "Pizza crust with cream cheese and smoked salmon on top with some caviar—that made the night and made up for all the really boring conversations." Among the other guests that the Arnolds might have conversed with were Audrey Hepburn, Shirley MacLaine, Bette Midler, Harvey Keitel, Whoopi Goldberg, Kathy Bates, Walter Matthau, Mercedes Ruehl, Gene Siskel, and John Waters. Despite still having the flu, Billy Crystal dropped by at Spago to hear good notices and kid around with Jack Palance, who exclaimed, "I've had so much coffee and so many sweet drinks, I'm flying." Another Lazar guest, Ben Kingsley, said he was glad he lost to Palance because "Otherwise, we wouldn't have had all those jokes."

The reviewers liked Crystal's performance, too. Janet Maslin praised "his opening monologue which set the evening's clever and iconoclastic tone" and Anna Quindlen, an Op/Ed page columnist at the *New York Times*, declared the comic "has made the Oscar telecast worth staying awake for." At the *New York Daily News*, Kay Gardella chimed in with, "His performance was flawless. His ad libs were as funny as his scripted material . . . Hollywood did itself proud."

Kenneth Turan of the *Los Angeles Times* felt that "Like any good Hollywood movie, the Oscars kept their satisfying secrets until nearly the very end. But once Anthony Hopkins' lip-smacking Hannibal Lecter upset Nick Nolte for Best Actor at the nearly three-hour mark, it was clear this particular evening was going to belong with a vengeance to *The Silence of the Lambs* . . . giving a Best Picture Award to as bloody and non-inspirational film as this has to be some kind of first in the Academy's long and curious history." *Variety*'s "Buzz" column mused, "Anyone notice that, unlike most recent Oscar winners, no one thanked Mike Ovitz this year?"

USA Today chatted with Lee Haney, winner of the Mr. Olympia title "eight years running," about Palance's performance and he raved, "A one-arm push-up is hard for me to do. It's extremely impressive for a man of his age—of any age." In no time, the Supporting Actor winner was starring in an after-shave commercial in which he bragged, "I don't need an after-shave to make me feel like a man." The seventy-two-year-old met with publishers about a physical fitness book with an introduction by Billy Crystal and he also testified before the Congress' Select Council on Aging, where he did more push-ups.

Liz Smith chirped of Barbra Streisand that she "went home empty-handed, but she sat in the audience like a trouper, looking great, and behaving adorably. A great class act, a great star, and a great director, Streisand has really grown up!" A few weeks later, the star turned fifty, which was duly noted by many newscasts. "Barbra celebrated her milestone during three days of festivities which culminated at the home of producer Jon Peters, her former beau," reported *Hello!*, which observed party-goers Jason Gould, Elliott Gould, Elliott's other son, Sam, Barbra's mother Diana, and "butlers dressed in period costume."

"I do the Oscar show every five years to remind people out here I'm still alive."
—Paul Newman

Turns out that the party's motif was inspired by the other Best Picture nominee without a Director nomination, as the magazine documented: "As her many friends arrived at Jon's twelve-acre estate in Beverly Park in the Los Angeles area, they entered through a pink and purple cardboard gate cut in the shape of the fairy tale castle in *Beauty and the Beast*." Streisand also got around to lashing out at the critics of her onscreen fingernails, scoffing in a *Newsweek*'s "My Turn" column, "as if women can't get medical degrees *and* manicures, be professional *and* glamorous."

As for the promised gay disruption of the Oscar show, Liz Smith reported that "mere seconds after the show finally left the airwaves, many were breathing sighs of relief that nothing untoward had occurred inside the Dorothy Chandler Pavilion." Marilyn Beck was crying rip-off about "The much-touted map supposedly 'outing' gay celebrities—distributed only on the north side of the boulevard, and then only on request . . . It was a reproduction of a Beverly Hills map with the names of some supposed gay and lesbian celebrities on the back—some misspelled, some widely known in Hollywood circles to be gay, others unquestioned straight public figures."

Vanessa Pace of Queer Nation was happy with the event. "I rate the action as a success because we got our point across," she pronounced to *NYQ*. "Last year there was an attempt at an AIDS protest inside, and this year, the celebrities were falling all over themselves to demonstrate AIDS awareness." A *New York Daily News* editorial entitled "Queer night at the Oscars" congratulated gay role models Debra Chasnoff and Bill Lauch: "Here were two examples of the kinds of homosexual lives that rarely make it onto the silver screen." Liz Smith wondered, "Maybe the activists finally realized (and was this the plan all along?) that the mere threat of disruption had heightened awareness of their complaint." *Advocate* columnist Lance Loud validated Smith's parenthetical, chuckling over the "hilarious rumors" that were "an act of guerrilla terrorism." *Newsweek* declared, "And an Oscar should have gone to . . . those gay activists who had everybody convinced they would disrupt the Academy Awards to protest Hollywood homophobia."

The *New York Post* reported that "Hollywood had also been wondering if an Oscar-nominated actress would bow to pressure from protest groups and reveal her homosexuality during the ceremony . . . She did not." The *Advocate* gave Jodie Foster another honor to go with her Oscar, its sarcastic "Sissy" award, presented to her as the "Silence is Golden award—Need We Say More?" A nicer sentiment was expressed by Jesse Kornbluth, who told the *New York Post* of Foster's remembering him in her speech, "It was so out-of-the-blue and incredibly nice and unnecessary, but this is not a person who forgets anything." Gregg Kilday summed it up in the *Los Angeles Times*: "The industry sees her as one of their own, delivering on all her early promise."

Two days after the ceremony, Motion Picture Association head Jack Valenti issued a seven-page statement in which he called *JFK* "a monstrous charade," filled with "hallucinatory bleatings" and "accusatory lunacy." The former aide to President Johnson even referred to the Third Reich: "In much the same way, young German boys and girls in 1941 were mesmerized by Leni Reifenstahl's *Triumph of the Will*, in which Adolf Hitler was depicted as a newborn God . . . No wonder that many young people, gripped by the movie, leave the theater convinced they have been witness to the truth." Valenti told the *New York Times* that he had given Oliver Stone a break: "Indeed, I waited to speak out because I didn't want to do anything which might affect this picture's theatrical release or the Oscar balloting," but "I owe where I am today to Lyndon Johnson. I could not live with myself if I stood by mutely and let some filmmaker soil his memory." Stone, of course, wasn't going to let Valenti have the last word. "While I respect Jack Valenti's enduring loyalty to President Johnson," the director said, "I find his emotional diatribe off the mark . . . The overwhelming majority of Americans—and not

"I'd like to thank all the people in this industry who have respected my choices and who have not been afraid of the power and the dignity that entitles me to."

—Jodie Foster

just the young, whom Mr. Valenti puts down as too impressionable—agree with the central thesis of my film: that President Kennedy was killed by a conspiracy, which included people in the government."

Another Best Director also-ran made the news again soon after Oscar night. As John Singleton penned later for *Premiere*, "On Wednesday, April 29, at 3:15, I was driving north on the 405 freeway toward predominately white Simi Valley, the city that served as one of the locations of my second film, *Poetic Justice*. In between coolin' to CDs of A Tribe Called Quest and Black Sheep, I decided to turn on my portable, state-of-the-art Sony Watchman, a gift from a studio executive. What I saw pissed me off. Four white policemen had been found not guilty on charges of beating an African-American brother nearly to death . . . The shock of this verdict sent me into such a fury that I decided to make a detour." Singleton went to the Simi Valley courthouse, where "My assistant, Shorty, who happens to stand over six foot seven and weigh 360 pounds, easily carved a path for me through the crowd of onlookers and media vermin." News cameras caught Singleton telling the assembled: "The jury has lit the fuse to the bomb from which many innocent people will feel the shrapnel." Three hours later, the rioting began in Singleton's South Central L.A. neighborhood, continuing for days and resulting in the deaths of fifty-seven people. After his TV appearance, *Premiere* asked Singleton for his views, and he blamed "President George Herbert Walker Bush—whose response to the verdict was 'The court system has worked' " and warned, "The fuse is waiting to be lit by the next gross, inconsiderate action by the powers that be. No justice, no peace."

Nominations

This appendix lists every Award the Academy has ever bestowed, from the Best Picture statuette all the way down to the certificate given the technician who built a machine that makes artificial snow. Bob Hope's various medals and trophies are here, too. If nominations were announced with an Award, they are also included. In addition to the Academy's official data, we have added our own statistics. Under "Rule Changes," we chart all the times that the Academy has added or dropped an Award, changed the title of an Award, prohibited anyone from voting for an Award, or prohibited anyone from being eligible for an Award. Under "Points of Interest," we record the noteworthy achievements of nominees and winners: who the youngest and the oldest were, who was related to one another, who was making a film debut, and who had the highest total of nominations and Oscars. To shed further light on the Academy's nominees, we have also listed a few eligible films, songs, and foreign films that the Academy, for whatsoever reason, chose to ignore. **Winners are indicated by a ★ next to their names or titles.**

Founding Fathers

The original members of the Academy were: Actors Branch—leading men Richard Barthelmess (First National), Jack Holt (Columbia), Conrad Nagel (MGM), and Milton Sills (First National), swashbuckler Douglas Fairbanks (United Artists) and comedian Harold Lloyd (Pathé); Directors Branch—Cecil B. DeMille (Pathé), Frank Lloyd (First National), Henry King (independent), Fred Niblo (MGM), John M. Stahl (MGM) and Raoul Walsh (independent); Writers Branch—Joseph Farnham (MGM), Benjamin F. Glazer (Pathé), Jeanie MacPherson (worked for DeMille), Bess Meredyth (independent), Carey Wilson (MGM) and Frank Woods (Famous Players-Lasky); Technicians Branch—J. Arthur Ball (cinematographer and color engineer), Cedric Gibbons (head of the MGM art department) and Roy J. Pomeroy (head of Paramount's special effects department); and Producers Branch—Fred Beetson, Charles H. Christie (low-budget Christie slapstick comedies), Sid Grauman (theater owner of Chinese Theatre fame), Milton E. Hoffman (Paramount), Jesse L. Lasky (Famous Players–Lasky), M.C. Levee (First National), Louis B. Mayer (MGM), Joseph M. Schenck (United Artists), Irving Thalberg (MGM), Harry and Jack Warner (Warner Brothers) and Mary Pickford.

1927–28

Production

The Last Command, Paramount. Produced by J.G. Bachmann, with B.P. Schulberg.
The Racket, Caddo, UA. Produced by Howard Hughes.
Seventh Heaven, Fox. Produced by William Fox.
The Way of All Flesh, Paramount. Produced by Adolph Zukor and Jesse L. Lasky.
★ *Wings*, Paramount. Produced by Lucien Hubbard.

Artistic Quality of Production

Chang, Paramount.
The Crowd, MGM.
★ *Sunrise*, Fox.

Actor

Richard Barthelmess in *The Noose* (First National) and *The Patent Leather Kid* (First National).
Charles Chaplin in *The Circus* (Chaplin, UA).
★ Emil Jannings in *The Last Command* (Paramount) and *The Way of All Flesh* (Paramount).

Actress

Louise Dresser in *A Ship Comes In* (Pathé–RKO Radio).
★ Janet Gaynor in *Seventh Heaven* (Fox), *Street Angel* (Fox) and *Sunrise* (Fox).
Gloria Swanson in *Sadie Thompson* (United Artists).

Director

★ Frank Borzage for *Seventh Heaven* (Fox).
Herbert Brenon for *Sorrell and Son* (United Artists).
King Vidor for *The Crowd* (MGM).

Comedy Direction

Charles Chaplin for *The Circus* (Chaplin, UA).
★ Lewis Milestone for *Two Arabian Knights* (United Artists).
Ted Wilde for *Speedy* (Paramount).

Writing

(ADAPTATION)

Glorious Betsy, Warner Bros. Anthony Coldeway.
The Jazz Singer, Warner Bros. Alfred Cohn.
★ *Seventh Heaven*, Fox. Benjamin Glazer.

(ORIGINAL STORY)

The Last Command, Paramount. Lajos Biro.
The Patent Leather Kid, First National. Rupert Hughes.
★ *Underworld*, Paramount. Ben Hecht.

(TITLE WRITING)

The Private Life of Helen of Troy, First National. Gerald Duffy.
The Fair Co-ed, MGM. Joseph Farnham.
Laugh, Clown, Laugh, MGM. Joseph Farnham.
★ *Telling the World*, MGM. Joseph Farnham.
Oh Kay!, First National. George Marion, Jr.

Cinematography

Devil Dancer, United Artists. George Barnes.
Drums of Love, United Artists. Karl Struss.
Magic Flame, United Artists. George Barnes.
My Best Girl, Pickford, UA. Charles Rosher.
Sadie Thompson, United Artists. George Barnes.
★ *Sunrise*, Fox. Charles Rosher and Karl Struss.
The Tempest, United Artists. Charles Rosher.

Interior Decoration

★ *The Dove*, United Artists. William Cameron Menzies.
Seventh Heaven, Fox. Harry Oliver.
Sunrise, Fox. Rochus Gliese.
★ *The Tempest*, United Artists. William Cameron Menzies.

Engineering Effects

The Jazz Singer, Warner Bros. Nugent Slaughter.
The Private Life of Helen of Troy, First National. Ralph Hammeras.
★ *Wings*, Paramount. Roy Pomeroy.

Special Awards

Warner Bros. for producing *The Jazz Singer*, the outstanding pioneer talking picture, which has revolutionized the industry (statuette).

Charles Chaplin for versatility and genius in writing, acting, directing and producing *The Circus* (statuette).

Points of Interest

Lonely at the top: Best Picture nominee *The Racket* received no other nominations.

Eligible Films That Failed to Be Nominated for Best Picture

Metropolis, A Girl in Every Port, Love, Beau Geste, London After Midnight.

1928–29

Production

Alibi, Feature Productions, UA. Produced by Roland West.
★ *Broadway Melody*, MGM. Produced by Harry Rapt.
Hollywood Revue, MGM. Produced by Harry Rapt.
In Old Arizona, Fox. Winfield Sheehan, studio head.
The Patriot, Paramount. Produced by Ernst Lubitsch.

Actor

George Bancroft in *Thunderbolt* (Paramount).
★ Warner Baxter in *In Old Arizona* (Fox).
Chester Morris in *Alibi* (Feature Productions, UA).
Paul Muni in *The Valiant* (Fox).
Lewis Stone in *The Patriot* (Paramount).

Actress

Ruth Chatterton in *Madam X* (MGM).
Betty Compson in *The Barker* (First National).
Jeanne Eagels in *The Letter* (Paramount).
Bessie Love in *Broadway Melody* (MGM).
★ Mary Pickford in *Coquette* (Pickford, UA).

Director

Lionel Barrymore for *Madame X* (MGM).
Harry Beaumont for *Broadway Melody* (MGM).
Irving Cummings for *In Old Arizona* (Fox).
★ Frank Lloyd for *The Divine Lady* (First National), *Weary River* (First National) and *Drag* (First National).
Ernst Lubitsch for *The Patriot* (Paramount).

Writing

(ACHIEVEMENT)

In Old Arizona, Fox. Tom Barry.
The Leatherneck, Pathé. Elliott Clawson.
Our Dancing Daughters, MGM. Josephine Lovett.
★ *The Patriot*, Paramount. Hans Kraly.
The Valiant, Fox. Tom Barry.
Wonder of Women, MGM. Bess Meredyth.

Cinematography

The Divine Lady, First National. John Seitz.
Four Devils, Fox. Ernest Palmer.
In Old Arizona, Fox. Arthur Edeson.
Our Dancing Daughters, MGM. George Barnes.
Street Angel, Fox. Ernest Palmer.
★ *White Shadows in the South Seas*, MGM. Clyde DeVinna.

Interior Decoration

★ *The Bridge of San Luis Rey,* MGM. Cedric Gibbons.
Dynamite, Pathé. Mitchell Leisen.
Hollywood Revue, MGM. Cedric Gibbons.
The Iron Mask, United Artists. William Cameron Menzies.
The Patriot, Paramount. Hans Dreier.
Street Angel, Fox. Harry Oliver.

Special Awards

None given this year.

Points of Interest

1. Gone but not forgotten: Jeanne Eagles becomes first posthumous acting nominee.
2. Share the wealth: For first and only time, no film wins more than one Award.
3. My one and only: Mitchell Leisen, later one of Hollywood's top directors of light comedies, receives his only Academy Award nomination—for Interior Decoration.
4. Time is not of the essence: *Street Angel,* a winner for Actress last year, nominated for Cinematography and Interior Decoration.

Rule Changes

1. The fewer the merrier: Artistic Quality of Production, Comedy Direction, Title Writing and Engineering Effects no longer given.

Eligible Films That Failed to Be Nominated for Best Picture

Steamboat Bill, Jr.; The Wedding March; West of Zanzibar; Our Dancing Daughters.

1929–30

Production

★ *All Quiet on the Western Front,* Universal. Produced by Carl Laemmle, Jr.
The Big House, MGM. Produced by Irving G. Thalberg.
Disraeli, Warner Bros. Produced by Jack L. Warner, with Darryl F. Zanuck.
The Divorcée, MGM. Produced by Robert Z. Leonard.
The Love Parade, Paramount. Produced by Ernst Lubitsch.

Actor

★ George Arliss in *Disraeli* (Warner Bros.).
George Arliss in *The Green Goddess* (Warner Bros.).
Wallace Beery in *The Big House* (MGM).
Maurice Chevalier in *The Love Parade* (Paramount).
Maurice Chevalier in *The Big Pond* (Paramount).
Ronald Colman in *Bulldog Drummond* (Goldwyn, UA).
Ronald Colman in *Condemned* (Goldwyn, UA).
Lawrence Tibbett in *The Rogue Song* (MGM).

Actress

Nancy Carroll in *The Devil's Holiday* (Paramount).
Ruth Chatterton in *Sarah and Son* (Paramount).
Greta Garbo in *Anna Christie* (MGM).
Greta Garbo in *Romance* (MGM).
★ Norma Shearer in *The Divorcée* (MGM).
Norma Shearer in *Their Own Desire* (MGM).
Gloria Swanson in *The Trespasser* (Kennedy, UA).

Director

Clarence Brown for *Anna Christie* (MGM).
Clarence Brown for *Romance* (MGM).
Robert Z. Leonard for *The Divorcée* (MGM).
Ernst Lubitsch for *The Love Parade* (Paramount).
★ Lewis Milestone for *All Quiet on the Western Front* (Universal).
King Vidor for *Hallelujah* (MGM).

Writing

(ACHIEVEMENT)

All Quiet on the Western Front, Universal. George Abbott, Maxwell Anderson and Dell Andrews.
★ *The Big House,* MGM. Frances Marion.
Disraeli, Warner Bros. Julian Josephson.
The Divorcée, MGM. John Meehan.
Street of Chance, Paramount. Howard Estabrook.

Cinematography

All Quiet on the Western Front, Universal. Authur Edeson.
Anna Christie, MGM. William Daniels.
Hell's Angels, United Artists. Gaetano Gaudio and Harry Perry.
The Love Parade, Paramount. Victor Milner.
★ *With Byrd at the South Pole,* Paramount. Joseph T. Rucker and Willard Van Der Veer.

Interior Decoration

Bulldog Drummond, Goldwyn, UA. William Cameron Menzies.
★ *King of Jazz,* Universal Herman Rosse.
The Love Parade, Paramount. Hans Dreier.
Sally, First National. Jack Okey.
The Vagabond King, Paramount. Hans Dreier.

Sound Recording

★ *The Big House,* MGM. Douglas Shearer.
The Case of Sergeant Grischa, RKO Radio. John Tribby.
The Love Parade, Paramount. Franklin Hansen.
Raffles, Goldwyn, UA. Oscar Lagerstrom.
Song of the Flame, First National. George Groves.

Special Awards
None given this year.

Points of Interest

1. Nothing to it: Lawrence Tibbett nominated for film debut.
2. They're always good: Greta Garbo, Norma Shearer, George Arliss, Ronald Colman and Maurice Chevalier each have double nominations.

Rule Changes

1. New addition: "Sound Recording."
2. About time: Nominations voted by all members of each branch. Entire membership votes on final ballot.

Eligible Films That Failed to Be Nominated For Best Picture

The Cocoanuts, Hell's Angels, Hallelujah!, Applause.

1930–31

Picture
★ *Cimarron*, RKO Radio, Produced by William LeBaron.
East Lynne, Fox. Winfield Sheehan, studio head.
The Front Page, Caddo, UA. Produced by Howard Hughes.
Skippy, Paramount. Adolph Zukor, studio head.
Trader Horn, MGM. Produced by Irving G. Thalberg.

Actor
★ Lionel Barrymore in *A Free Soul* (MGM).
Jackie Cooper in *Skippy* (Paramount).
Richard Dix in *Cimarron* (RKO Radio).
Fredric March in *The Royal Family of Broadway* (Paramount).
Adolphe Menjou in *The Front Page* (Caddo, UA).

Actress
Marlene Dietrich in *Morocco* (Paramount).
★ Marie Dressler in *Min and Bill* (MGM).
Irene Dunne in *Cimarron* (RKO Radio).
Ann Harding in *Holiday* (RKO Pathé).
Norma Shearer in *A Free Soul* (MGM).

Director
Clarence Brown for *A Free Soul* (MGM).
Lewis Milestone for *The Front Page* (Caddo, UA).
Wesley Ruggles for *Cimarron* (RKO Radio).
★ Norman Taurog for *Skippy* (Paramount).
Josef Von Sternberg for *Morocco* (Paramount).

Writing
(adaptation)
★ *Cimarron*, RKO Radio. Howard Estabrook.
The Criminal Code, Columbia. Seton Miller and Fred Niblo, Jr.
Holiday, RKO Pathé. Horace Jackson.
Little Ceasar, Warner Bros. Francis Faragoh and Robert N. Lee
Skippy, Paramount. Joseph L. Mankiewicz and Sam Mintz.

(ORIGNAL STORY)
★ *The Dawn Patrol*, Warner Bros.-First National. John Monk Saunders.
Doorway to Hell, Warner Bros.-First National. Rowland Brown.
Laughter, Paramount. Harry D'Abbadie D'Arrast, Douglas Doty and Donald Ogden Stewart.
The Public Enemy, Warner Bros.-First National. John Bright and Kubec Glasmon.
Smart Money, Warner Bros.-First National. Lucien Hubbard and Joseph Jackson.

Cinematography
Cimarron, RKO Radio. Edward Cronjager.
Morocco, Paramount. Lee Garmes.
The Right to Love, Paramount. Charles Lang.
Svengali, Warner Bros.-First National. Barney "Chick" McGill.
★ *Tabu*, Paramount. Floyd Crosby.

Interior Decoration
★ *Cimarron*, RKO Radio. Max Ree.
Just Imagine, Fox. Stephen Goosson and Ralph Hammeras.
Morocco, Paramount. Hans Dreier.
Svengali, Warner Bros.-First National. Anton Grot.
Whoopee, Goldwyn, UA. Richard Day.

Sound Recording
MGM Studio Sound Department.
★ Paramount Studio Sound Department.
RKO Radio Studio Sound Department.
Samuel Goldwyn Sound Department.

Special Awards
None given this year.

Scientific or Technical
CLASS I (STATUETTE)
Electrical Research Products, Inc., RCA-Photophone, Inc., and RKO Radio Pictures, Inc., for noise reduction recording equipment.
DuPont Film Manufacturing Corp. and Eastman Kodak Co. for supersensitive panchromatic film.

CLASS II (PLAQUE)
Fox Film Corp. for effective use of synchro-projection composite photography.

CLASS III (CITATION)

Electrical Research Products, Inc., for moving coil microphone transmitters.

RKO Radio Pictures, Inc., for reflex type microphone concentrators.

RCA-Photophone, Inc., for ribbon microphone transmitters.

Points of Interest

1. Lonely at the top: Best Picture nominees *East Lynne* and *Trader Horn* received no other nominations.
2. Nothing to it: Irene Dunne nominated her first year in movies.

Rule Changes

1. New addition: "Scientific or Technical Awards."
2. The name of the game: "Production" becomes "Picture" so that voters won't judge films solely on the basis of size and logistics.
3. On second thought. . . . :Division of Writing Award into "Adaptation" and "Original Story" reinstated.
4. It's less bother this way: Sound Recording Award given to studio sound department without reference to individual films. Up to five examples of sound recording submitted by each company to the Sound Committee which made four nominations. Academy members "in good standing" vote on final ballot.

Eligible Films That Failed to Be Nominated for Best Picture

City Lights, Little Caesar, The Public Enemy, Holdiay, The Blue Angel, The Dawn Patrol, Dracula, Tabu.

1931–32

Picture

Arrowsmith, Goldwyn, UA. Produced by Samuel Goldwyn.
Bad Girl, Fox. Winfield Sheehan, studio head.
The Champ, MGM. Produced by King Vidor.
Five Star Final, First National. Produced by Hal B. Wallis.
★ *Grand Hotel*, MGM. Produced by Irving Thalberg.
One Hour with You, Paramount. Produced by Ernst Lubitsch.
Shanghai Express, Paramount. Adolph Zukor, studio head.
Smiling Lieutenant, Paramount. Produced by Ernst Lubitsch.

Actor

(Note: Two winners this year.)
★ Wallace Beery in *The Champ* (MGM).
Alfred Lunt in *The Guardsman* (MGM).
★ Fredric March in *Dr. Jekyll and Mr. Hyde* (Paramount).

Actress

Marie Dressler in *Emma* (MGM).
Lynn Fontanne in *The Guardsman* (MGM).
★ Helen Hayes in *The Sin of Madelon Claudet* (MGM).

Director

★ Frank Borzage for *Bad Girl* (Fox).
King Vidor for *The Champ* (MGM).
Josef von Sternberg for *Shanghai Express* (Paramount).

Writing

(ADAPTATION)
Arrowsmith, Goldwyn, UA. Sidney Howard.
★ *Bad Girl*, Fox. Edwin Burke.
Dr. Jekyll and Mr. Hyde, Paramount. Karl Struss.
★ *Shanghai Express,* Paramount. Lee Garmes.

(ORIGNAL STORY)
★ *The Champ*, MGM. Frances Marion.
Lady and Gent, Paramount. Grover Jones and William Slavens McNutt.
Star Witness, Warner Bros. Lucien Hubbard.
What Price Hollywood, RKO Radio. Adela Rogers St. John.

Cinematography

Arrowsmith, Goldwyn, UA. Ray June.
Dr. Jekyll and Mr. Hyde, Paramount. Karl Struss.
Shanghai Express, Paramount. Lee Garmes.

Interior Decoration

A Nous la Liberté (French). Lazare Meerson.
Arrowsmith, Goldwyn, UA. Richard Day.
★ *Transatlantic,* Fox. Gordon Wiles.

Sound Recording

★ Paramount Studio Sound Department.

Short Subjects

(CARTOONS)
★ *Flowers and Trees,* Walt Disney, UA.
Mickey's Orphans, Walt Disney, Columbia.
It's Got Me Again, Leon Schlesinger, Warner Bros.

(COMEDY)
The Loud Mouth, Mack Sennett.
★ *The Music Box,* Hal Roach, MGM (Laurel & Hardy).
Stout Hearts and Willing Hands, RKO Radio (Masquers Comedies).

(NOVELTY)
Screen Souvenirs, Paramount.
Swing High, MGM (Sport Champions).

★ *Wrestling Swordfish*, Mack Sennett, Educational (Cannibals of the Deep).

Special Award

Walt Disney for the creation of Mickey Mouse (statuette).

Scientific or Technical

CLASS I (STATUETTE)

None.

CLASS II (PLAQUE)

Technicolor Motion Picture Corp. for their color cartoon process.

CLASS III (CITATION)

Eastman Kodak Co. for the Type II-B Sensitometer.

Points of Interest

1. Lonely at the top: Best Picture nominees *Five Star Final*, *One Hour with You*, *Smiling Lieutenant* and winner *Grand Hotel* received no other nominations.
2. Not a peep was heard from the others: No nominees other than winning Paramount in Sound Recording category.

Rule Changes

1. New addition: "Short Subjects" Awards (Cartoon, Comedy and Novelty).
2. Foreigners need not apply: Only films shot in America eligible for Cinematography.
3. Include us out: Tired of arbitrating arguments over credits, Academy leaves it up to studios to decide if a work constitutes an "Original Story" or "Adapted Screenplay."

Eligible Films That Failed to Be Nominated for Best Picture

Scarface, What Price Hollywood, Frankenstein, Freaks, Tarzan The Ape Man, Red Dust.

1932–33

Picture

★ *Cavalcade*, Fox. Winfield Sheehan, studio head.
A Farewell to Arms, Paramount. Adolph Zukor, studio head.
42nd Street, Warner Bros. Produced by Darryl F. Zanuck.
I Am a Fugitive from a Chain Gang. Warner Bros. Produced by Hal B. Wallis.
Lady for a Day, Columbia. Produced by Frank Capra.
Little Women, RKO Radio. Produced by Merian C. Cooper, with Kenneth MacGowan.
The Private Life of Henry VIII, London Films, UA (British). Produced by Alexander Korda.
She Done Him Wrong, Paramount. Produced by William Le Baron.
Smilin' Thru, MGM. Produced by Irving Thalberg.
State Fair, Fox. Winfield Sheehan, studio head.

Actor

Leslie Howard in *Berkeley Square* (Fox).
★ Charles Laughton in *The Private Life of Henry VIII* (London Films, UA-British).
Paul Muni in *I Am a Fugitive from a Chain Gang* (Warner Bros.).

Actress

★ Katharine Hepburn in *Morning Glory* (RKO Radio).
May Robson in *Lady for a Day* (Columbia).
Diana Wynyard in *Cavalcade* (Fox).

Director

Frank Capra for *Lady for a Day* (Columbia).
George Cukor for *Little Women* (RKO Radio).
★ Frank Lloyd for *Cavalcade* (Fox).

Writing

(ADAPTATION)

Lady for a Day, Columbia. Robert Riskin.
★ *Little Women*, RKO Radio. Victor Heerman and Sarah Y. Mason.
State Fair, Fox. Paul Green and Sonya Levien.

(ORIGINAL STORY)

★ *One Way Passage*, Warner Bros. Robert Lord.
The Prizefighter and the Lady, MGM. Frances Marion.
Rasputin and the Empress, MGM. Charles MacArthur.

Cinematography

★ *A Farewell to Arms*, Paramount. Charles Bryant Lang, Jr.
Reunion in Vienna, MGM. George J. Folsey, Jr.
Sign of the Cross, Paramount. Karl Struss.

Interior Decoration

★ *Cavalcade*, Fox. William S. Darling.
A Farewell to Arms, Paramount. Hans Dreier and Roland Anderson.
When Ladies Meet, MGM. Cedric Gibbons.

Sound Recording

★ *A Farewell to Arms*, Paramount. Harold C. Lewis.
Forty-second Street, Warner Bros. Nathan Levinson.
Golddiggers of 1933, Warner Bros. Nathan Levinson.
I Am a Fugitive from a Chain Gang, Warner Bros. Nathan Levinson.

Assistant Director

★ Charles Barton, Paramount.
★ Scott Beal, Universal.

★ Charles Dorian, MGM.
★ Fred Fox, United Artists.
★ Gordon Hollingshead, Warner Bros.
★ Dewey Starkey, RKO Radio.
★ William Tummel, Fox.

Short Subjects

(CARTOONS)

Building a Building, Walt Disney, UA.
The Merry Old Soul, Walter Lantz, Universal.
★ *The Three Little Pigs,* Walt Disney, UA.

(COMEDY)

Mister Mugg, Universal (Comedies).
Preferred List, RKO Radio (Headliner Series #5).
★ *So This Is Harris,* RKO Radio (Special).

(NOVELTY)

★ *Krakatoa,* Educational (Three-reel Special).
Menu, Pete Smith, MGM (Oddities).
The Sea, Educational (Battle for Life).

Special Awards

None given this year.

Scientific or Technical

CLASS I (STATUETTE)

None.

CLASS II (PLAQUE)

Electrical Research Products, Inc., for their wide-range recording and reproducing system.

RCA-Victor Co., Inc., for their high-fidelity recording and reproducing system.

CLASS III (CITATION)

Fox Film Corp., Fred Jackman and Warner Bros. Pictures, Inc., and Sidney Sanders of RKO Studios, Inc., for their development and effective use of the translucent cellulose screen in composite photography.

Points of Interest

1. Lonely at the top: Best Picture nominees *She Done Him Wrong* and *Smilin' Thru* received no other nominations.
2. Nothing to it: Diana Wynyard nominated for film debut.

Rule Changes

1. New addition: "Assistant Director."
2. Foreigners need not apply: Only films shot in America eligible for Interior Decoration Award.

Eligible Films That Failed to Be Nominated for Best Picture

King Kong, Trouble in Paradise, Design for Living, Back Street, Babes in Toyland, Tugboat Annie, Duck Soup, Dinner at Eight, The Invisible Man, The Mummy.

1934

Picture

The Barretts of Wimpole Street, MGM. Produced by Irving Thalberg.
Cleopatra, Paramount. Produced by Cecil B. DeMille.
Flirtation Walk, First National. Produced by Jack L. Warner and Hal Wallis, with Robert Lord.
The Gay Divorcée, RKO Radio. Produced by Pandro S. Berman.
Here Comes the Navy, Warner Bros. Produced by Lou Edelman.
The House of Rothschild, 20th Century, UA. Produced by Darryl F. Zanuck, with William Goetz and Raymond Griffith.
Imitation of Life, Universal. Produced by John M. Stahl.
★ *It Happened One Night,* Columbia. Produced by Harry Cohn.
One Night of Love, Columbia. Produced by Harry Cohn, with Everett Riskin.
The Thin Man, MGM. Produced by Hunt Stromberg.
Viva Villa, MGM. Produced by David O. Selznick.
The White Parade, Fox. Produced by Jesse L. Lasky.

Actor

★ Clark Gable in *It Happened One Night* (Columbia).
Frank Morgan in *Affairs of Cellini* (20th Century, UA).
William Powell in *The Thin Man* (MGM).

Actress

★ Claudette Colbert in *It Happened One Night* (Columbia).
Grace Moore in *One Night of Love* (Columbia).
Norma Shearer in *The Barretts of Wimpole Street* (MGM).

Director

★ Frank Capra for *It Happened One Night* (Columbia).
Victor Schertzinger for *One Night of Love* (Columbia).
W. S. Van Dyke for *The Thin Man* (MGM).

Writing

(ADAPTATION)

★ *It Happened One Night,* Columbia. Robert Riskin.
The Thin Man, MGM. Frances Goodrich and Albert Hackett.
Viva Villa, MGM. Ben Hecht.

(ORIGINAL STORY)

Hide-Out, MGM. Mauri Grashin.
★ *Manhattan Melodrama*, MGM. Arthur Caesar.
The Richest Girl in the World, RKO Radio. Norman Krasna.

Cinematography

Affairs of Cellini, 20th Century, UA. Charles Rosher.
★ *Cleopatra*, Paramount. Victor Milner.
Operator 13, MGM. George Folsey.

Interior Decoration

Affairs of Cellini, 20th Century, UA. Richard Day.
The Gay Divorcée, RKO Radio. Van Nest Polglase and Carroll Clark.
★ *The Merry Widow*, MGM. Cedric Gibbons and Frederic Hope.

Sound Recording

Affairs of Cellini, 20th Century, UA. Thomas T. Moulton.
Cleopatra, Paramount. Franklin Hansen.
Flirtation Walk, First National. Nathan Levinson.
The Gay Divorcée, RKO Radio. Carl Dreher.
Imitation of Life, Universal. Gilbert Kurland.
★ *One Night of Love*, Columbia. Paul Neal.
Viva Villa, MGM. Douglas Shearer.

Assistant Director

Scott Beal for *Imitation of Life*, Universal.
Cullen Tate for *Cleopatra*, Paramount.
★ John Waters for *Viva Villa*, MGM.

Music

(SONG)

"Carioca" (*Flying Down to Rio*, RKO Radio); Music by Vincent Youmans. Lyrics by Edward Eliscu and Gus Kahn.
★ "The Continental" (*The Gay Divorcée*, RKO Radio); Music by Con Conrad. Lyrics by Herb Magidson.
"Love in Bloom" (*She Loves Me Not*, Paramount); Music by Ralph Rainger. Lyrics by Leo Robin.

(SCORE)

The Gay Divorcée, RKO Radio. RKO Radio Studio Music Dept.; Max Steiner, head. Score by Kenneth Webb and Samuel Hoffenstein.
The Lost Patrol, RKO Radio. RKO Radio Studio Music Dept.; Max Steiner, head. Score by Max Steiner.
★ *One Night of Love*, Columbia. Columbia Studio Music Dept.; Louis Silvers, head. Thematic music by Victor Schertzinger and Gus Kahn.

Film Editing

Cleopatra, Paramount. Anne Bauchens.
★ *Eskimo*, MGM. Conrad Nervig.
One Night of Love, Columbia. Gene Milford.

Short Subjects

(CARTOONS)

Holiday Land, Mintz, Columbia.
Jolly Little Elves, Universal.
★ *The Tortoise and the Hare*, Disney, UA.

(COMEDY)

★ *La Cucaracha*, RKO Radio (Special).
Men in Black, Columbia (Broadway Comedies).
What, No Men!, Warner Bros. (Broadway Brevities).

(NOVELTY)

Bosom Friends, Educational (Treasure Chest).
★ *City of Wax*, Educational (Battle for Life).
Strikes and Spares, MGM (Oddities).

Special Award

Shirley Temple, in grateful recognition of her outstanding contribution to screen entertainment during the year 1934 (miniature statuette).

Scientific or Technical

CLASS I (STATUETTE)

None.

CLASS II (PLAQUE)

Electrical Research Products, Inc., for their development of the vertical cut disc method of recording sound for motion pictures ("hill and dale recording").

CLASS III (CITATION)

Columbia Pictures Corp. for their application of the vertical cut disc method ("hill and dale recording") to actual studio production, with their recording of the sound on the picture *One Night of Love*.

Bell and Howell Co. for their development of the Bell and Howell fully automatic sound and picture printer.

Points of Interest

1. Lonely at the top: Best Picture nominees *Here Comes the Navy*, *The House of Rothschild* and *The White Parade* received no other nominations.
2. Moe, Larry, Curly and Oscar: The Three Stooges' film *Men in Black* nominated for Best Comedy Short Subject, but loses to first Technicolor movie, *La Cucaracha*.
3. What about me?: In Best Score category, Award went to studio music department head, not to persons who actually wrote the score. Original music of winning *One Night of Love* cowritten by Best Director loser Victor Schertzinger.

Rule Changes

1. New additions: "Film Editing," "Song" and "Score" Awards.

2. Just because you rewrote it doesn't mean you're going to get an Oscar for it: Directors declared ineligible for Writing Awards.
3. No false modesty: For nominations in Interior Decoration, Film Editing, Song and Score categories, members of respective branches vote for one of their own works and at least one of somebody else's. For Sound Recording, each studio's sound department head submits what he decides is studio's best work.
4. Back to the drawing board: Assistant Directors in Academy vote to determine three nominees for Assistant Director Award. Entire membership votes for final winner.
5. Do whatever you want: Write-ins allowed in all categories.

Eligible Films That Failed to Be Nominated for Best Picture

The Scarlet Empress, The Merry Widow, It's a Gift, Sons of the Desert, Twentieth Century.

Eligible Songs That Failed to Be Nominated

"Cocktails for Two" (Arthur Johnston and Sam Coslow)—*Murder at The Vanities;* "Did You Ever See a Dream Walking?" (Harry Revel and Mack Gordon)— *Sitting Pretty;* "I Only Have Eyes for You" (Harry Warren and Al Dubin)—*Dames;* "I'm in the Mood for Love" (Jimmy McHugh and Dorothy Fields)—*Every Night at Eight;* "Let's Fall in Love" (Harold Arlen and Ted Koehler)—*Let's Fall In Love;* "My Old Flame" (Arthur Johnston and Sam Coslow)—*Belle of the Nineties;* "The Object of My Affection" (Pinky Tomlin, Coy Poe and Jimmy Grier)—*Times Square Lady;* "On the Good Ship Lollipop" (Richard Whiting and Sidney Clare)—*Bright Eyes;* "Love Is Just Around the Corner" (Lewis E. Gensler and Leo Robin)—*Here Is My Heart.*

1935

Picture

Alice Adams, RKO Radio. Produced by Pandro S. Berman.
Broadway Melody of 1936, MGM. Produced by John W. Considine, Jr.
Captain Blood, Warner Bros.–Cosmopolitan. Produced by Hal Wallis, with Harry Joe Brown and Gordon Hollingshead.
David Copperfield, MGM. Produced by David O. Selznick.
The Informer, RKO Radio. Produced by Cliff Reid.
Les Miserables, 20th Century, UA. Produced by Darryl F. Zanuck.
Lives of a Bengal Lancer, Paramount. Produced by Louis D. Lighton.
A Midsummer Night's Dream, Warner Bros. Produced by Henry Blanke.
★ *Mutiny on the Bounty*, MGM. Produced by Irving Thalberg, with Albert Lewin.
Naughty Marietta, MGM. Produced by Hunt Stromberg.
Ruggles of Red Gap, Paramount. Produced by Arthur Hornblow, Jr.
Top Hat, RKO Radio. Produced by Pandro S. Berman.

Actor

Clark Gable in *Mutiny on the Bounty* (MGM).
Charles Laughton in *Mutiny on the Bounty* (MGM).
★ Victor McLaglen in *The Informer* (RKO Radio).
Franchot Tone in *Mutiny on the Bounty* (MGM).

Actress

Elisabeth Bergner in *Escape Me Never* (Wilcox, UA) British).
Claudette Colbert in *Private Worlds* (Paramount).
★ Bette Davis in *Dangerous* (Warner Bros.).
Katharine Hepburn in *Alice Adams* (RKO Radio).
Miriam Hopkins in *Becky Sharp* (Pioneer, RKO Radio).
Merle Oberon in *The Dark Angel* (Goldwyn, UA).

Director

★ John Ford for *The Informer* (RKO Radio).
Henry Hathaway for *Lives of a Bengal Lancer* (Paramount).
Frank Lloyd for *Mutiny on the Bounty* (MGM).

Writing

(ORIGINAL STORY)
Broadway Melody of 1936, MGM. Moss Hart.
The Gay Deception, Lasky, Fox. Don Hartman and Stephen Avery.
★ *The Scoundrel*, Paramount. Ben Hecht and Charles MacArthur.

(SCREENPLAY)
★ *The Informer*, RKO Radio. Dudley Nichols.
Lives of a Bengal Lancer, Paramount. Achmed Abdullah, John L. Balderston, Grover Jones, William Slavens McNutt and Waldemar Young.
Mutiny on the Bounty, MGM. Jules Furthman, Talbot Jennings and Carey Wilson.

Cinematography

Barbary Coast, Goldwyn, UA. Ray June.
The Crusades, Paramount. Victor Milner.
Les Miserables, 20th Century, UA. Gregg Toland.
★ *A Midsummer Night's Dream*, Warner Bros. Hal Mohr.

Interior Decoration

★ *The Dark Angel*, Goldwyn, UA. Richard Day.
Lives of a Bengal Lancer, Paramount. Hans Dreier and Roland Anderson.
Top Hat, RKO Radio. Carroll Clark and Van Nest Polglase.

Sound Recording

The Bride of Frankenstein, Universal. Gilbert Kurland.
Captain Blood, Warner Bros. Nathan Levinson.
The Dark Angel, Goldwyn, UA. Goldwyn Sound Dept. Thomas T. Moulton.
I Dream Too Much, RKO Radio. Carl Dreher.
Lives of a Bengal Lancer, Paramount. Franklin Hansen.
Love Me Forever, Columbia. John Livadary.
★ *Naughty Marietta,* MGM. Douglas Shearer.
1,000 Dollars a Minute, Republic. Republic Sound Dept.
Thanks a Million, 20th Century–Fox. E. H. Hansen.

Assistant Director

★ Clem Beauchamp for *Lives of a Bengal Lancer* (Paramount).
Eric Stacey for *Les Miserables* (20th Century, UA).
★ Paul Wing for *Lives of a Bengal Lancer* (Paramount).
Joseph Newman for *David Copperfield* (MGM).

Music

(SONG)

"Cheek to Cheek" (*Top Hat,* RKO Radio); Music and Lyrics by Irving Berlin.
"Lovely to Look At" (*Roberta,* RKO Radio); Music by Jerome Kern. Lyrics by Dorothy Fields and Jimmy McHugh.
★ "Lullaby of Broadway" (*Gold Diggers of 1935,* Warner Bros.); Music by Harry Warren. Lyrics by Al Dubin.

(SCORE)

★ *The Informer,* RKO Radio. RKO Radio Studio Music Dept.; Max Steiner, head. Score by Max Steiner.
Mutiny on the Bounty, MGM. MGM Studio Music Dept.; Nat W. Finston, head. Score by Herbert Stothart.
Peter Ibbetson, Paramount. Paramount Studio Music Dept.; Irvin Talbot, head. Score by Ernst Toch.

Film Editing

David Copperfield, MGM. Robert J. Kern.
The Informer, RKO Radio. George Hively.
Les Miserables, 20th Century, UA. Barbara McLean.
Lives of a Bengal Lancer, Paramount. Ellsworth Hoagland.
★ *A Midsummer Night's Dream,* Warner Bros. Ralph Dawson.
Mutiny on the Bounty, MGM. Margaret Booth.

Dance Direction

Busby Berkeley for "Lullaby of Broadway" number and "The Words Are in My Heart" number from *Gold Diggers of 1935* (Warner Bros.).
Bobby Connolly for "Latin from Manhattan" number from *Go Into Your Dance* (Warner Bros.) and "Playboy from Paree" number from *Broadway Hostess* (Warner Bros.).
★ David Gould for "I've Got a Feeling You're Fooling" number from *Broadway Melody of 1936* (MGM) and "Straw Hat" number from *Folies Bergere* (20th Century, UA).
Sammy Lee for "Lovely Lady" number and "Too Good to Be True" number from *King of Burlesque* (20th Century–Fox).
Hermes Pan for "Piccolino" number and "Top Hat" number from *Top Hat* (RKO Radio).
Leroy Prinz for "Elephant Number—It's the Animal in Me" from *Big Broadcast of 1936* (Paramount) and "Viennese Waltz" number from *All the King's Horses* (Paramount).
B. Zemach for "Hall of Kings" number from *She* (RKO Radio).

Short Subjects

(CARTOONS)

The Calico Dragon, Harman-Ising, MGM.
★ *Three Orphan Kittens,* Disney, UA.
Who Killed Cock Robin?, Disney, UA.

(COMEDY)

★ *How to Sleep,* MGM (Miniatures).
Oh, My Nerves, Columbia (Broadway Comedies).
Tit for Tat, Hal Roach, MGM (Laurel & Hardy).

(NOVELTY)

Audioscopiks, MGM.
Camera Thrills, Universal.
★ *Wings over Mt. Everest,* Educational.

Special Award

David Wark Griffith, for his distinguished creative achievements as director and producer and his invaluable initiative and lasting contributions to the progress of the motion picture arts (statuette).

Scientific or Technical

CLASS I (STATUETTE)

None.

CLASS II (PLAQUE)

Agfa Ansco Corp. for their development of the Agfa infrared film.
Eastman Kodak Co. for their development of the Eastman Pola-Screen.

CLASS III (CITATION)

Metro-Goldwyn-Mayer Studio for the development of anti-directional negative and positive development by means of jet turbulation, and the application of the method to all negative and print processing of the entire product of a major producing company.
William A. Mueller of Warner Bros.—First National Studio Sound Dept. for his method of dubbing, in which the level of the dialogue automatically controls the level of the accompanying music and sound effects.
Mole-Richardson Co. for their development of the "Solarspot" spot lamps.
Douglas Shearer and MGM Studio Sound Dept. for their automatic control system for cameras and sound recording machines and auxiliary stage equipment.

Electrical Research Products, Inc., for their study and development of equipment to analyze and measure flutter resulting from the travel of the film through the mechanisms used in the recording and reproduction of sound.

Paramount Productions, Inc., for the design and construction of the Paramount transparency air turbine developing machine.

Nathan Levinson, director of Sound Recording for Warner Bros.–First National Studio for the method of intercutting variable density and variable area sound tracks to secure an increase in the effective volume range of sound recorded for motion pictures.

Points of Interest

1. Lonely at the top: Best Picture nominee *Ruggles of Red Gap* received no other nominations.
2. Too close for comfort: Although rules called for only three nominations in acting categories, ties resulted in four actors and six actresses on final ballot.
3. Then what was so good about it?: *Mutiny on the Bounty* is last Best Picture winner to receive no other Award.
4. Out of left field: Cinematographer Hal Mohr becomes first and only write-in winner.

Rule Changes

1. New addition: "Dance Direction."
2. Do whatever you want again: Write-in votes allowed for second and final year.

Eligible Films That Failed to Be Nominated for Best Picture

The Thirty-Nine Steps, Steamboat 'Round the Bend, A Night at the Opera, The Bride of Frankenstein, The Devil Is a Woman.

Eligible Songs That Failed to Be Nominated

"About a Quarter to Nine" (Harry Warren and Al Dubin)—*Go Into Your Dance;* "Animal Crackers in My Soup" (Ted Koehler, Irving Ceasar and Ray Henderson)—*Curly Top;* "Broadway Rhythm" (Arthur Freed and Nacio Herb Brown)—*Broadway Melody of 1936;* "I Won't Dance" (Jimmy McHugh, Dorothy Fields and Oscar Hammerstein II)—*Roberta;* "The Lady in Red" (Allie Wrubel and Mort Dixon)—*In Caliente;* "Lulu's Back in Town"—(Harry Warren and Al Dubin)—*Broadway Gondolier;* "She's a Latin from Manhattan" (Harry Warren and Al Dubin)—*Go Into Your Dance;* "I Wished on the Moon" (Ralph Rainger and Dorothy Parker)—*The Big Broadcast of 1936;* "It's Easy to Remember" (Richard Rodgers and Lorenz Hart)—*Mississippi.*

1936

Picture

Anthony Adverse, Warner Bros. Produced by Henry Blanke.
Dodsworth, Goldwyn, UA. Produced by Samuel Goldwyn, with Merritt Hulbert.
★ *The Great Ziegfeld*, MGM. Produced by Hunt Stromberg.
Libeled Lady, MGM. Produced by Lawrence Weingarten.
Mr. Deeds Goes to Town, Columbia. Produced by Frank Capra.
Romeo and Juliet, MGM. Produced by Irving Thalberg.
San Francisco, MGM. Produced by John Emerson and Bernard H. Hyman.
The Story of Louis Pasteur, Warner Bros. Produced by Henry Blanke.
A Tale of Two Cities, MGM. Produced by David O. Selznick.
Three Smart Girls, Universal. Produced by Joseph Pasternak, with Charles Rogers.

Actor

Gary Cooper in *Mr. Deeds Goes to Town* (Columbia).
Walter Huston in *Dodsworth* (Goldwyn, UA).
★ Paul Muni in *The Story of Louis Pasteur* (Warner Bros.).
William Powell in *My Man Godfrey* (Universal).
Spencer Tracy in *San Francisco* (MGM).

Actress

Irene Dunne in *Theodora Goes Wild* (Columbia).
Gladys George in *Valiant Is the Word for Carrie* (Paramount).
Carole Lombard in *My Man Godfrey* (Universal).
★ Luise Rainer in *The Great Ziegfeld* (MGM).
Norma Shearer in *Romeo and Juliet* (MGM).

Supporting Actor

Mischa Auer in *My Man Godfrey* (Universal).
★ Walter Brennan in *Come and Get It* (Goldwyn, UA).
Stuart Erwin in *Pigskin Parade* (20th Century–Fox).
Basil Rathbone in *Romeo and Juliet* (MGM).
Akim Tamiroff in *The General Died at Dawn* (Paramount).

Supporting Actress

Beulah Bondi in *The Gorgeous Hussy* (MGM).
Alice Brady in *My Man Godfrey* (Universal).
Bonita Granville in *These Three* (Goldwyn, UA).
Maria Ouspenskaya in *Dodsworth (Goldwyn, UA).*
★ Gale Sondergaard in *Anthony Adverse* (Warner Bros.).

Director

★ Frank Capra for *Mr. Deeds Goes to Town* (Columbia).
Gregory La Cava for *My Man Godfrey* (Universal).
Robert Z. Leonard for *The Great Ziegfeld* (MGM).
W. S. Van Dyke for *San Francisco* (MGM).
William Wyler for *Dodsworth* (Goldwyn, UA).

Writing

(ORIGINAL STORY)

Fury, MGM. Norman Krasna.
The Great Ziegfeld, MGM. William Anthony McGuire.
San Francisco, MGM. Robert Hopkins.
★ *The Story of Louis Pasteur*, Warner Bros. Pierre Collings and Sheridan Gibney.
Three Smart Girls, Universal. Adele Commandini.

(SCREENPLAY)

After the Thin Man, MGM. Frances Goodrich and Albert Hackett.
Dodsworth, Goldwyn, UA. Sidney Howard.
Mr. Deeds Goes to Town, Columbia. Robert Riskin.
My Man Godfrey, Universal. Eric Hatch and Morris Ryskind.
★ *The Story of Louis Pasteur*, Warner Bros. Pierre Collings and Sheridan Gibney.

Cinematography

★ *Anthony Adverse*, Warner Bros. Gaetano Gaudio.
The General Died at Dawn, Paramount. Victor Milner.
The Gorgeous Hussy, MGM. George Folsey.

Interior Decoration

Anthony Adverse, Warner Bros. Anton Grot.
★ *Dodsworth*, Goldwyn, UA. Richard Day.
The Great Ziegfeld, MGM. Cedric Gibbons, Eddie Imazu and Edwin B. Willis.
Lloyds of London, 20th Century–Fox. William S. Darling.
The Magnificent Brute, Universal. Albert S. D'Agostino and Jack Otterson.
Romeo and Juliet, MGM. Cedric Gibbons, Frederic Hope and Edwin B. Willis.
Winterset, RKO Radio. Perry Ferguson.

Sound Recording

Banjo on My Knee, 20th Century–Fox. E. H. Hansen.
The Charge of the Light Brigade, Warner Bros. Nathan Levinson.
Dodsworth, Goldwyn, UA. Oscar Lagerstrom.
General Spanky, Roach, MGM. Elmer A. Raguse.
Mr. Deeds Goes to Town, Columbia. John Livadary.
★ *San Francisco*, MGM. Douglas Shearer.
The Texas Rangers, Paramount. Franklin Hansen.
That Girl from Paris, RKO Radio. J. O. Aalberg.
Three Smart Girls, Universal. Homer G. Tasker.

Assistant Director

Clem Beauchamp for *Last of the Mohicans* (Reliance, UA).
William Cannon for *Anthony Adverse* (Warner Bros.)
Joseph Newman for *San Francisco* (MGM).
Eric G. Stacey for *Garden of Allah* (Selznick, UA).
★ Jack Sullivan for *The Charge of the Light Brigade* (Warner Bros).

Music

(SONG)

"Did I Remember" (*Suzy*, MGM); Music by Walter Donaldson. Lyrics by Harold Adamson.
"I've Got You Under My Skin" (*Born to Dance*, MGM); Music and Lyrics by Cole Porter.
"A Melody from the Sky" (*Trail of the Lonesome Pine*, Paramount); Music by Louis Alter. Lyrics by Sidney Mitchell.
"Pennies from Heaven" (*Pennies from Heaven*, Columbia); Music by Arthur Johnston. Lyrics by Johnny Burke.
★ "The Way You Look Tonight" (*Swing Time*, RKO Radio); Music by Jerome Kern. Lyrics by Dorothy Fields.
"When Did You Leave Heaven" (*Sing Baby Sing*, 20th Century–Fox); Music by Richard A. Whiting. Lyrics by Walter Bullock.

(SCORE)

★ *Anthony Adverse*, Warner Bros. Studio Music Dept., Leo Forbstein, head. Score by Erich Wolfgang Korngold.
The Charge of the Light Brigade, Warner Bros. Studio Music Dept., Leo Forbstein, head. Score by Max Steiner.
The Garden of Allah, Selznick International Pictures Music Dept., Max Steiner, head. Score by Max Steiner.
The General Died at Dawn, Paramount Studio Music Dept., Boris Morros, head. Score by Werner Janssen.
Winterset, RKO Radio Studio Music Dept., Nathaniel Shilkret, head. Score by Nathaniel Shilkret.

Film Editing

★ *Anthony Adverse*, Warner Bros., Ralph Dawson.
Come and Get It, Goldwyn, UA. Edward Curtiss.
The Great Ziegfeld, MGM. William S. Gray.
Lloyds of London, 20th Century–Fox. Barbara McLean.
A Tale of Two Cities, MGM. Conrad A. Nervig.
Theodora Goes Wild, Columbia. Otto Meyer.

Dance Direction

Busby Berkeley for "Love and War" number from *Gold Diggers of 1937* (Warner Bros.).
Bobby Connolly for "1000 Love Songs" number from *Cain and Mabel* (Warner Bros.).
★ Seymour Felix for "A Pretty Girl Is Like a Melody" number from *The Great Ziegfeld* (MGM).
Dave Gould for "Swingin' the Jinx" number from *Born to Dance* (MGM).
Jack Haskell for "Skating Ensemble" number from *One in a Million* (20th Century–Fox).
Russell Lewis for "The Finale" number from *Dancing Pirate* (RKO Radio).
Hermes Pan for "Bojangles" number from *Swing Time* (RKO Radio).

Short Subjects

(CARTOONS)

★ *Country Cousin*, Walt Disney, UA.

Old Mill Pond, Harman-Ising, MGM.
Sinbad the Sailor, Paramount.

(ONE-REEL)
★ *Bored of Education*, Hal Roach, MGM (Our Gang).
Moscow Moods, Paramount (Headliners).
Wanted, A Master, Pete Smith, MGM (Pete Smith Specialties).

(TWO-REEL)
Double or Nothing, Warner Bros. (Broadway Brevities).
Dummy Ache, RKO Radio (Edgar Kennedy Comedies).
★ *The Public Pays*, MGM (Crime Doesn't Pay).

(COLOR)
★ *Give Me Liberty*, Warner Bros. (Broadway Brevities).
La Fiesta De Santa Barbara, MGM (Musical Revues).
Popular Science J-6-2, Paramount.

Special Awards

March of Time for its significance to motion pictures and for having revolutionized one of the most important branches of the industry—the newsreel (statuette).

W. Howard Greene and Harold Rosson for the color cinematography of the Selznick International Production, *The Garden of Allah* (plaques).

Scientific or Technical

CLASS I (STATUETTE)

Douglas Shearer and MGM Studio Sound Department for the development of a practical two-way horn system and a biased Class A push-pull recording system.

CLASS II (PLAQUE)

E. C. Wente and the Bell Telephone Laboratories for their multicellular high-frequency horn and receiver.

RCA Manufacturing Co., Inc., for their rotary stabilizer sound head.

CLASS III (CITATION)

RCA Manufacturing Co., Inc., for their development of a method of recording and printing sound records utilizing a restricted spectrum (known as ultra-violet light recording).

Electrical Research Products, Inc., for the ERPI "Type Q" portable recording channel.

RCA Manufacturing Co., Inc., for furnishing a practical design and specifications for a non-slip printer.

United Artists Studio Corp. for the development of a practical, efficient and quiet wind machine.

Points of Interest

1. Lonely at the top: Best Picture nominee *Libeled Lady* received no other nominations.
2. It was good, but it was no *Libeled Lady*: *My Man Godfrey* received six nominations—for Direction, Screenplay and all four Acting Awards—but was not nominated for Best Picture.
3. Nothing to it: Maria Ouspenskaya nominated for film debut. Gale Sondergaard becomes first winner for film debut.
4. Hum the title: "Pennies from Heaven" became the first title song to be nominated for Best Song.
5. Spanky and Alfalfa meet Oscar: Our Gang became Oscar winners in One-Reel Short Subject category for *Bored of Education*.

Rule Changes

1. New additions: "Supporting Actor" and "Supporting Actress" and "Color Short Subjects."
2. We'll be the judge of that: Committee of fifty makes all nominations except for Dance Direction and Assistant Direction Awards. Candidates for Interior Decoration, Cinematography, Film Editing, Sound and Music Awards submit what they consider their best work to the Committee as well as recommending at least one other work.
3. Back to the drawing board: A third method for the Assistant Director Award—committee of fifty makes list of potential nominees from which Directors Branch culls the five final nominees.
4. Open door policy: All English-language films, regardless of national origin, again eligible for nominations for Picture, Acting, Directing and Writing Awards.

Eligible Films That Failed to Be Nominated for Best Picture

My Man Godfrey, Fury, Magnificent Obsession, Modern Times, Show Boat, Swing Time, Desire.

Eligible Songs That Failed to Be Nominated

"Easy to Love" (Cole Porter)—*Born to Dance;* "A Fine Romance" (Jerome Kern and Dorothy Fields)—*Swing Time;* "I Love to Sing-a" (Harold Arlen and E. Y. Harburg)—*The Singing Kid;* "I'm an Old Cowhand" (Johnny Mercer)—*Rhythm on the Range;* "Let's Face the Music and Dance" (Irving Berlin)—*Follow the Fleet;* "Pick Yourself Up" (Jerome Kern and Dorothy Fields)—*Swing Time;* "San Francisco" (Gus Kahn, Bronislau Kaper and Walter Jurman)—*San Francisco.*

1937

Picture

The Awful Truth, Columbia. Produced by Leo McCarey, with Everett Riskin.
Captains Courageous, MGM. Produced by Louis D. Lighton.
Dead End, Goldwyn, UA. Produced by Samuel Goldwyn, with Merritt Hulbert.
The Good Earth, MGM. Produced by Irving Thalberg, with Albert Lewin.
In Old Chicago, 20th Century–Fox. Produced by Darryl F. Zanuck, with Kenneth MacGowan.
★ *The Life of Emile Zola*, Warner Bros. Produced by Henry Blanke.
Lost Horizon, Columbia. Produced by Frank Capra.
100 Men and a Girl, Universal. Produced by Charles R. Rogers, with Joe Pasternak.
Stage Door, RKO Radio. Produced by Pandro S. Berman.
A Star Is Born, Selznick International, UA. Produced by David O. Selznick.

Actor

Charles Boyer in *Conquest* (MGM).
Fredric March in *A Star Is Born* (Selznick, UA).
Robert Montgomery in *Night Must Fall* (MGM).
Paul Muni in *The Life of Emile Zola* (Warner Bros.).
★ Spencer Tracy in *Captains Courageous* (MGM).

Actress

Irene Dunne in *The Awful Truth* (Columbia).
Greta Garbo in *Camille* (MGM).
Janet Gaynor in *A Star Is Born* (Selznick, UA).
★ Luise Rainer in *The Good Earth* (MGM).
Barbara Stanwyck in *Stella Dallas* (Goldwyn, UA).

Supporting Actor

Ralph Bellamy in *The Awful Truth* (Columbia).
Thomas Mitchell in *The Hurricane* (Goldwyn, UA).
★ Joseph Schildkraut in *The Life of Emile Zola* (Warner Bros.).
H. B. Warner in *Lost Horizon* (Columbia).
Roland Young in *Topper* (Roach, MGM).

Supporting Actress

★ Alice Brady in *In Old Chicago* (20th Century–Fox).
Andrea Leeds in *Stage Door* (RKO Radio).
Anne Shirley in *Stella Dallas* (Goldwyn, UA).
Claire Trevor in *Dead End* (Goldwyn, UA).
Dame May Whitty in *Night Must Fall* (MGM).

Director

William Dieterle for *The Life of Emile Zola* (Warner Bros.).
Sidney Franklin for *The Good Earth* (MGM).
Gregory La Cava for *Stage Door* (RKO Radio).
★ Leo McCarey for *The Awful Truth* (Columbia).
William Wellman for *A Star Is Born* (Selznick, UA).

Writing

(ORIGINAL STORY)
Black Legion, Warner Bros. Robert Lord.
In Old Chicago, 20th Century–Fox. Niven Busch.
The Life of Emile Zola, Warner Bros. Heinz Herald and Geza Herczeg.
100 Men and a Girl, Universal. Hans Kraly.
★ *A Star Is Born*, Selznick, UA. William A. Wellman and Robert Carson.

(SCREENPLAY)
The Awful Truth, Columbia. Viña Delmar.
Captains Courageous, MGM. Marc Connolly, John Lee Mahin and Dale Van Every.
★ *The Life of Emile Zola*, Warner Bros. Heinz Herald, Geza Herczeg and Norman Reilly Raine.
Stage Door, RKO Radio. Morris Ryskind and Anthony Veiller.
A Star Is Born, Selznick, UA. Alan Campbell, Robert Carson and Dorothy Parker.

Cinematography

Dead End, Goldwyn, UA. Gregg Toland.
★ *The Good Earth*, MGM. Karl Freund.
Wings over Honolulu, Universal. Joseph Valentine.

Interior Decoration

Conquest, MGM. Cedric Gibbons and William Horning.
A Damsel in Distress, RKO Radio. Carroll Clark.
Dead End, Goldwyn, UA. Richard Day.
Every Day's a Holiday, Major Prods. Paramount. Wiard Ihnen.
The Life of Emile Zola, Warner Bros. Anton Grot.
★ *Lost Horizon*, Columbia. Stephen Goosson.
Manhattan Merry-Go-Round, Republic. John Victor MacKay.
The Prisoner of Zenda, Selznick, UA. Lyle Wheeler.
Souls at Sea, Paramount. Hans Dreier and Roland Anderson.
Vogues of 1938, Wanger, UA. Alexander Toluboff.
Wee Willie Winkie, 20th Century–Fox. William S. Darling and David Hall.
You're a Sweetheart, Universal. Jack Otterson.

Sound Recording

The Girl Said No, Grand National. A. E. Kaye.
Hitting a New High, RKO Radio. John Aalberg.
★ *The Hurricane*, Goldwyn, UA. Thomas Moulton.
In Old Chicago, 20th Century–Fox. E. H. Hansen.
The Life of Emile Zola, Warner Bros. Nathan Levinson.
Lost Horizon, Columbia. John Livadary.
Maytime, MGM. Douglas Shearer.
One Hundred Men and a Girl, Universal. Homer Tasker.

Topper, Roach, MGM. Elmer Raguse.
Wells Fargo, Paramount. L. L. Ryder.

Assistant Director

C. C. Coleman, Jr. for *Lost Horizon* (Columbia).
Russ Saunders for *The Life of Emile Zola* (Warner Bros.).
Eric Stacey for *A Star Is Born* (Selznick, UA).
Hal Walker for *Souls at Sea* (Paramount).
★ Robert Webb for *In Old Chicago* (20th Century–Fox).

Music

(SONG)

"Remember Me" (*Mr. Dodd Takes the Air*, Warner Bros.); Music by Harry Warren. Lyrics by Al Dubin.
★ "Sweet Leilani" (*Waikiki Wedding*, Paramount); Music and Lyrics by Harry Owens.
"That Old Feeling" (*Vogues of 1938*, Wanger, UA); Music by Sammy Fain. Lyrics by Lew Brown.
"They Can't Take That Away from Me" (*Shall We Dance*, RKO Radio); Music by George Gershwin. Lyrics by Ira Gershwin.
"Whispers in the Dark" (*Artists and Models*, Paramount); Music by Frederick Hollander. Lyrics by Leo Robin.

(SCORE)

The Hurricane, Samuel Goldwyn Studio Music Dept., Alfred Newman, head. Score by Alfred Newman.
In Old Chicago, 20th Century–Fox Studio Music Dept., Louis Silvers, head. Score: No composer credit.
The Life of Emile Zola, Warner Bros. Studio Music Dept., Leo Forbstein, head. Score by Max Steiner.
Lost Horizon, Columbia Studio Music Dept., Morris Stoloff, head. Score by Dimitri Tiomkin.
Make a Wish, Principal Productions: Lesser, RKO Radio. Dr. Hugo Riesenfeld, musical director. Score by Dr. Hugo Riesenfeld.
Maytime, MGM Studio Music Dept., Nat W. Finston, head. Score by Herbert Stothart.
★ *One Hundred Men and a Girl*, Universal Studio Music Dept., Charles Previn, head. Score: No composer credit.
Portia on Trial, Republic Studio Music Dept., Alberto Colombo, head. Score by Alberto Colombo.
The Prisoner of Zenda, Selznick International Pictures Music Dept., Alfred Newman, musical director. Score by Alfred Newman.
Quality Street, RKO Radio Studio Music Dept., Roy Webb, musical director. Score by Roy Webb.
Snow White and the Seven Dwarfs, Walt Disney Studio Music Dept., Leigh Harline, head. Score by Frank Churchill, Leigh Harline and Paul J. Smith.
Something to Sing About, Grand National Studio Music Dept., C. Bakaleinikoff, musical director. Score by Victor Schertzinger.
Souls at Sea, Paramount Studio Music Dept., Boris Morros, head. Score by W. Franke Harling and Milan Roder.
Way Out West, Hal Roach Studio Music Dept., Marvin Hatley, head. Score by Marvin Hatley.

Film Editing

The Awful Truth, Columbia. Al Clark.
Captains Courageous, MGM. Elmo Vernon.
The Good Earth, MGM. Basil Wrangell.
★ *Lost Horizon*, Columbia. Gene Havlick and Gene Milford.
100 Men and a Girl, Universal. Bernard W. Burton.

Dance Direction

Busby Berkeley for "The Finale" number from *Varsity Show* (Warner Bros.).
Bobby Connolly for "Too Marvelous for Words" number from *Ready, Willing and Able* (Warner Bros.).
Dave Gould for "All God's Children Got Rhythm" number from *A Day at the Races* (MGM).
Sammy Lee for "Swing Is Here to Stay" number from *Ali Baba Goes to Town* (20th Century–Fox).
Harry Losee for "Prince Igor Suite" number from *Thin Ice* (20th Century–Fox).
★ Hermes Pan for "Fun House" number from *Damsel in Distress* (RKO Radio).
Leroy Prinz for "Luau" number from *Waikiki Wedding* (Paramount).

Short Subjects

(CARTOONS)

Educated Fish, Paramount.
The Little Match Girl, Charles Mintz, Columbia.
★ *The Old Mill*, Walt Disney, RKO Radio.

(ONE-REEL)

A Night at the Movies, MGM (Robert Benchley).
★ *Private Life of the Gannetts*, Educational.
Romance of Radium, Pete Smith, MGM (Pete Smith Specialties).

(TWO REEL)

Deep South, RKO Radio (Radio Musical Comedies).
Should Wives Work, RKO Radio (Leon Errol Comedies).
★ *Torture Money*, MGM (Crime Doesn't Pay).

(COLOR)

The Man Without a Country, Warner Bros. (Broadway Brevities)
★ *Penny Wisdom*, Pete Smith, MGM (Pete Smith Specialties).
Popular Science J-7-1, Paramount.

Irving G. Thalberg Memorial Award

Darryl F. Zanuck.

Special Awards

Mack Sennett for his lasting contribution to the comedy technique of the screen, the basic principles of which are as important today as when they were first put into practice, the Academy presents a Special Award to that master of fun, discoverer of stars, sympathetic, kindly, understanding comedy genius—Mack Sennett (statuette).

Edgar Bergen for his outstanding comedy creation, Charlie McCarthy (wooden statuette).

The Museum of Modern Art Film Library for its significant work in collecting films dating from 1895 to the present and for the first time making available to the public the means of studying the historical and aesthetic development of the motion picture as one of the major arts (scroll certificate).

W. Howard Greene for the color photography of *A Star Is Born*. (This Award was recommended by a committee of leading cinematographers after viewing all the color pictures made during the year—plaque.)

Scientific or Technical

CLASS I (STATUETTE)

Agfa ANSCO Corp. for Agfa Supreme and Agfa Ultra Speed pan motion picture negatives.

CLASS II (PLAQUE)

Walt Disney Prods., Ltd., for the design and application to production of the Multi-Plane Camera.

Eastman Kokak Co. for two fine-grain duplicating film stocks.

Farciot Edouart and Paramount Pictures, Inc., for the development of the Paramount dual screen transparency camera setup.

Douglas Shearer and the MGM Studio Sound Department for a method of varying the scanning width of variable density sound tracks (squeeze tracks) for the purpose of obtaining an increased amount of noise reduction.

CLASS III (CITATION)

John Arnold and the MGM Studio Camera Department for their improvement of the semi-automatic follow focus device and its application to all of the cameras used by the MGM Studio.

John Livadary, Director of Sound Recording for Columbia Pictures Corp., for the application of the biplanar light valve to motion picture sound recording.

Thomas T. Moulton and the United Artists Studio Sound Department for the application to motion picture sound recording of volume indicators which have peak reading response and linear decibel scales.

RCA Manufacturing Co., Inc., for the introduction of the modulated high-frequency method of determining optimum photographic processing conditions for variable width sound tracks.

Joseph E. Robbins and Paramount Pictures, Inc., for an exceptional application of acoustic principles to the soundproofing of gasoline generators and water pumps.

Douglas Shearer and the MGM Studio Sound Department for the design of the film drive mechanism as incorporated in the ERPI 1010 reproducer.

Points of Interest

1. Finalists for the Thalberg Award (nominated and voted by a special committee): Pandro S. Berman, RKO, for *Stage Door, Damsel in Distress*. Samuel Goldwyn, Goldwyn, for *Dead End, The Hurricane, Stella Dallas,* and *Woman Chases Man*. David O. Selznick, Selznick International, for *Nothing Sacred, The Prisoner of Zenda,* and *A Star is Born*. Hunt Stromberg, MGM, for *Maytime, Night Must Fall,* and *The Firefly*. * Darryl F. Zanuck, Fox, for *In Old Chicago, Seventh Heaven,* and *Wee Willie Winkie*.

Rule Changes

1. You're all invited: All members of Actors, Directors and Writers Guilds nominate and vote. Extras vote on final ballot.
2. Not in my category, you don't: Only Academy branch members nominated and voted Awards for Interior Decoration, Cinematography, Sound Recording and Film Editing.
3. Yours for the asking: Every studio guaranteed a nomination for Interior Decoration, Sound Recording, and Score simply by submitting an entry.
4. Music appreciation: Final vote on Score Award restricted to select set of "directors, production executives, studio composers, conductors and a representative number of orchestra musicians who have been employed by various studios during the year."
5. On second thought . . . : Directors again eligible for Writing Awards.
6. New addition: "The Irving G. Thalberg Memorial Award."

Eligible Films That Failed to Be Nominated for Best Picture

Angel, Nothing Sacred, Make Way for Tomorrow, History Is Made at Night, You Only Live Once, The Hurricane, Stella Dallas, Easy Living, Shall We Dance, A Day at the Races, Way Out West.

Eligible Songs That Failed to Be Nominated

"A Foggy Day" (George and Ira Gershwin)—*A Damsel in Distress;* "The Folks Who Live on the Hill" (Jerome Kern and Oscar Hammerstein II)—*High, Wide and Handsome;* "Hooray for Hollywood" (Richard Whiting and Johnny Mercer)—*Hollywood Hotel;* "I've Got My Love to Keep Me Warm" (Irving Berlin)—*On the Avenue;* "In the Still of the Night" (Cole Porter)—*Rosalie;* "Let's Call the Whole Thing Off" (George and Ira Gershwin)— *Shall We Dance;* "Nice Work If You Can Get It" (George and Ira Gershwin)—*A Damsel in Distress;* "September in the Rain" (Harry Warren and Al Dubin)—*Melody for Two;* "Someday My Prince Will Come" (Frank Churchill and Larry Morey)—*Snow White and the Seven Dwarfs;* "Song of the Marines (We're Shovin' Right Off)" (Harry Warren and Al Dubin)—*The Singing Marine;* "They All Laughed" (George and Ira Gershwin)—*Shall We Dance;* "This Year's Kisses" (Irving Berlin)—*On the Avenue;* "Too Marvelous for Words" (Richard Whiting and Johnny Mercer)—*Ready, Willing and Able;* "Whistle While You Work" (Frank Churchill and Larry Morey)—*Snow White and the Seven Dwarfs;* "In the Still of the Night" (Cole Porter)—*Rosalie.*

1938

Picture

The Adventures of Robin Hood, Warner Bros. Produced by Hal B. Wallis, with Henry Blanke.
Alexander's Ragtime Band, 20th Century–Fox. Produced by Darryl F. Zanuck, with Harry Joe Brown.
Boys Town, MGM. Produced by John W. Considine, Jr.
The Citadel, MGM (British). Produced by Victor Saville.
Four Daughters, Warner Bros.–First National. Produced by Hal B. Wallis, with Henry Blanke.
Grand Illusion, R.A.O., World Pictures (French). Produced by Frank Rollmer and Albert Pinkovitch.
Jezebel, Warner Bros. Produced by Hal B. Wallis, with Henry Blanke.
Pygmalion, MGM (British). Produced by Gabriel Pascal.
Test Pilot, MGM. Produced by Louis D. Lighton.
★ *You Can't Take It with You,* Columbia. Produced by Frank Capra.

Actor

Charles Boyer in *Algiers* (Wanger, UA).
James Cagney in *Angels with Dirty Faces* (Warner Bros.).
Robert Donat in *The Citadel* (MGM) (British).
Leslie Howard in *Pygmalion* (MGM) (British).
★ Spencer Tracy in *Boys Town* (MGM).

Actress

Fay Bainter in *White Banners* (Warner Bros.).
★ Bette Davis in *Jezebel* (Warner Bros.).
Wendy Hiller in *Pygmalion* (MGM) (British).
Norma Shearer in *Marie Antoinette* (MGM).
Margaret Sullavan in *Three Comrades* (MGM).

Supporting Actor

★ Walter Brennan in *Kentucky* (20th Century–Fox).
John Garfield in *Four Daughters* (Warner Bros.).
Gene Lockhart in *Algiers* (Wanger, UA).
Robert Morley in *Marie Antoinette* (MGM).
Basil Rathbone in *If I Were King* (Paramount).

Supporting Actress

★ Fay Bainter in *Jezebel* (Warner Bros.).
Beulah Bondi in *Of Human Hearts* (MGM).
Billie Burke in *Merrily We Live* (Roach, MGM).
Spring Byington in *You Can't Take It with You* (Columbia).
Miliza Korjus in *The Great Waltz* (MGM).

Director

★ Frank Capra for *You Can't Take It with You* (Columbia).
Michael Curtiz for *Angels with Dirty Faces* (Warner Bros.).
Michael Curtiz for *Four Daughters* (Warner Bros.).
Norman Taurog for *Boys Town* (MGM).
King Vidor for *The Citadel* (MGM) (British).

Writing

(ORIGINAL STORY)

Alexander's Ragtime Band, 20th Century–Fox. Irving Berlin.
Angels with Dirty Faces, Warner Bros. Rowland Brown.
Blockade, Wanger, UA. John Howard Lawson.
★ *Boys Town,* MGM. Eleanore Griffin and Dore Schary.
Mad About Music, Universal. Marcella Burke and Frederick Kohner.
Test Pilot, MGM. Frank Wead.

(SCREENPLAY)

Boys Town, MGM. John Meehan and Dore Schary.
The Citadel, MGM (British). Ian Dalrymple, Elizabeth Hill and Frank Wead.
Four Daughters, Warner Bros. Lenore Coffee and Julius J. Epstein.
★ *Pygmalion,* MGM (British). George Bernard Shaw; adaptation by Ian Dalrymple, Cecil Lewis and W. P. Lipscomb.
You Can't Take It with You, Columbia. Robert Riskin.

Cinematography

Algiers, Wanger, UA. James Wong Howe.
Army Girl, Republic. Ernest Miller and Harry Wild.
The Buccaneer, Paramount. Victor Milner.
★ *The Great Waltz,* MGM. Joseph Ruttenberg.
Jezebel, Warner Bros. Ernest Haller.
Mad About Music, Universal. Joseph Valentine.
Merrily We Live, Roach, MGM. Norbert Brodine.
Suez, 20th Century–Fox. Peverell Marley.
Vivacious Lady, RKO Radio. Robert de Grasse.
You Can't Take It with You, Columbia. Joseph Walker.
The Young in Heart, Selznick, UA. Leon Shamroy.

Interior Decoration

★ *The Adventures of Robin Hood,* Warner Bros. Carl J. Weyl.
The Adventures of Tom Sawyer, Selznick, UA. Lyle Wheeler.
Alexander's Ragtime Band, 20th Century–Fox. Bernard Herzbrun and Boris Leven.
Algiers, Wanger, UA. Alexander Toluboff.
Carefree, RKO Radio. Van Nest Polglase.

Goldwyn Follies, Goldwyn, UA. Richard Day.
Holiday, Columbia. Stephen Goosson and Lionel Banks.
If I Were King, Paramount. Hans Dreier and John Goodman.
Mad About Music, Universal. Jack Otterson.
Marie Antoinette, MGM. Cedric Gibbons.
Merrily We Live, Roach, MGM. Charles D. Hall.

Sound Recording

Army Girl, Republic. Charles Lootens.
★ *The Cowboy and the Lady*, Goldwyn, UA. Thomas Moulton.
Four Daughters, Warner Bros. Nathan Levinson.
If I Were King, Paramount. L. L. Ryder.
Merrily We Live, Roach, MGM. Elmer Raguse.
Sweethearts, MGM. Douglas Shearer.
Suez, 20th Century–Fox. Edmund Hansen.
That Certain Age, Universal. Bernard B. Brown.
Vivacious Lady, RKO Radio. James Wilkinson.
You Can't Take It with You, Columbia. John Livadary.

Music

(SONG)

"Always and Always" (*Mannequin*, MGM); Music by Edward Ward. Lyrics by Chet Forrest and Bob Wright.
"Change Partners and Dance with Me" (*Carefree*, RKO Radio); Music and Lyrics by Irving Berlin.
"The Cowboy and the Lady" (*The Cowboy and the Lady*, Goldwyn, UA); Music by Lionel Newman. Lyrics by Arthur Quenzer.
"Dust" (*Under Western Stars*, Republic); Music and Lyrics by Johnny Marvin.
"Jeepers Creepers" (*Going Places*, Warner Bros.); Music by Harry Warren. Lyrics by Johnny Mercer.
"Merrily We Live" (*Merrily We Live*, Roach, MGM); Music by Phil Craig. Lyrics by Arthur Quenzer.
"A Mist Over the Moon" (*The Lady Objects*, Columbia); Music by Ben Oakland. Lyrics by Oscar Hammerstein II.
"My Own" (*That Certain Age*, Universal); Music by Jimmy McHugh. Lyrics by Harold Adamson.
"Now It Can Be Told" (*Alexander's Ragtime Band*, 20th Century–Fox); Music and Lyrics by Irving Berlin.
★ "Thanks for the Memory" (*Big Broadcast of 1938*, Paramount); Music by Ralph Rainger. Lyrics by Leo Robin.

(SCORE)

★ *Alexander's Ragtime Band*, 20th Century–Fox. Alfred Newman.
Carefree, RKO Radio. Victor Baravalle.
Girls School, Columbia. Morris Stoloff and Gregory Stone.
Goldwyn Follies, Goldwyn, UA. Alfred Newman.
Jezebel, Warner Bros. Max Steiner.
Mad About Music, Universal. Charles Previn and Frank Skinner.
Storm over Bengal, Republic. Cy Feuer.
Sweethearts, MGM. Herbert Stothart.
There Goes My Heart, Roach, UA. Marvin Hatley.
Tropic Holiday, Paramount. Boris Morros.
The Young in Heart, Selznick, UA. Franz Waxman.

(ORIGINAL SCORE)

★ *The Adventures of Robin Hood*, Warner Bros. Erich Wolfgang Korngold.
Army Girl, Republic. Victor Young.
Blockade, Wanger, UA. Werner Janssen.
Blockheads, Roach, UA. Marvin Hatley.
Breaking the Ice, RKO Radio. Victor Young.
The Cowboy and the Lady, Goldwyn, UA. Alfred Newman.
If I Were King, Paramount. Richard Hageman.
Marie Antoinette, MGM. Herbert Stothart.
Pacific Liner, RKO Radio. Russell Bennett.
Suez, 20th Century–Fox. Louis Silvers.
The Young in Heart, Selznick, UA. Franz Waxman.

Film Editing

★ *The Adventures of Robin Hood*, Warner Bros. Ralph Dawson.
Alexander's Ragtime Band, 20th Century–Fox. Barbara McLean.
The Great Waltz, MGM. Tom Held.
Test Pilot, MGM. Tom Held.
You Can't Take It with You, Columbia. Gene Havlick.

Short Subjects

(CARTOONS)

Brave Little Tailor, Disney, RKO Radio.
Mother Goose Goes Hollywood, Disney, RKO Radio.
★ *Ferdinand the Bull*, Disney, RKO Radio.
Good Scouts, Disney, RKO Radio.
Hunky and Spunky, Paramount.

(ONE-REEL)

The Great Heart, MGM (Miniatures).
★ *That Mothers Might Live*, MGM (Miniatures).
Timber Toppers, 20th Century–Fox (Ed Thorgensen-Sports).

(TWO-REEL)

★ *Declaration of Independence*, Warner Bros. (Historical Featurette).
Swingtime in the Movies, Warner Bros. (Broadway Brevities).
They're Always Caught, MGM (Crime Doesn't Pay).

Irving G. Thalberg Memorial Award

Hal B. Wallis.

Special Awards

Deanna Durbin and Mickey Rooney for their significant contribution in bringing to the screen the spirit and personification of youth, and as juvenile players setting a high standard of ability and achievement (miniature statuette trophies).

Harry M. Warner in recognition of patriotic service in the production of historical short subjects presenting signficant episodes in the early struggle of the American people for liberty (scroll).

Walt Disney for *Snow White and the Seven Dwarfs,* recognized as a significant screen innovation which has charmed millions and pioneered a great new entertainment field for the motion picture cartoon (one statuette—seven miniature statuettes).

Oliver Marsh and Allen Davey for the color cinematography of the MGM production *Sweethearts* (plaques).

For outstanding achievement in creating special photographic and sound effects in the Paramount production *Spawn of the North:* special effects by Gordon Jennings, assisted by Jan Domela, Dev Jennings, Irmin Roberts and Art Smith; transparencies by Farciot Edouart, assisted by Loyal Griggs; sound effects by Loren Ryder, assisted by Harry Mills, Louis H. Mesenkop and Walter Oberst (plaques).

J. Arthur Ball for his outstanding contributions to the advancement of color in motion picture photography (scroll).

Scientific or Technical

CLASS I (STATUETTE)

None.

CLASS II (PLAQUE)

None.

CLASS III (CITATION)

John Aalberg and the RKO Radio Studio Sound Dept. for the application of compression to variable area recording in motion picture production.

Byron Haskin and the Special Effects Dept. of Warner Bros. Studio for pioneering the development and for the first practical application to motion picture production of the triple head background projector.

Points of Interest

1. Nothing to it: John Garfield nominated for film debut.
2. On the way up: One-Reel Short Subject winner, *That Mothers Might Live,* directed by future Best Director winner Fred Zinnemann.
3. Up there with the big boys: Because each studio and production company could submit automatic nominations for Cinematography, Art Direction, Sound and the Scoring Awards, Hal Roach Studios ended up with seven nominations and Republic with four.
4. Finalists for the Thalberg Award: Samuel Goldwyn, for *Adventures of Marco Polo, Goldwyn Follies* and *The Cowboy and the Lady;* Joe Pasternak, Universal, for *Mad About Music* and *That Certain Age;* David O. Selznick, for *Adventures of Tom Sawyer* and *The Young in Heart;* Hunt Stromberg, MGM, for *Marie Antoinette* and *Sweethearts;* Hal B. Wallis, Warner Brothers, for *The Adventures of Robin Hood, Boy Meets Girl, Brother Rat, Four Daughters, Jezebel, The Sisters* and *A Slight Case of Murder;* Walter Wanger, for *Algiers, Blockade* and *Trade Winds.*
5. Two-timer: Fay Bainter nominated for both Best Actress and Best Supporting Actress.
6. Renaissance man: Irving Berlin nominated for both Original Story and Song.

Rule Changes

1. Okay, you don't have to compete with Tchaikovsky anymore: "Score" Award divided into "Score" (regardless of source) and "Original Score." Composers, rather than studio music department heads, now receive the Awards.
2. Tone deaf: Extras not allowed to vote for Best Song.
3. The fewer the merrier: Assistant Director and Dance Direction no longer given.

Eligible Films That Failed to Be Nominated for Best Picture

Bringing Up Baby, Holiday, Mayerling, Three Comrades, Algiers, Blockheads, Bluebeard's Eighth Wife.

Eligible Songs That Failed to Be Nominated

"Love Walked In" (George and Ira Gershwin)—*Goldwyn Follies;* "Our Love Is Here to Stay" (George and Ira Gershwin)—*Goldwyn Follies;* "Small Fry" (Hoagy Carmichael and Frank Loesser)—*Sing You Sinners;* "You Must Have Been a Beautiful Baby" (Harry Warren and Johnny Mercer)—*Hard to Get;* "Two Sleepy People" (Hoagy Carmichael and Frank Loesser)—*Thanks for the Memory.* (From 1938 through 1945, each studio's music department submitted a single song which would then automatically be nominated. Omissions during these years are therefore the responsibility of the studios and not the Academy.)

1939

Picture

Dark Victory, Warner Bros. Produced by David Lewis.

★ *Gone With the Wind,* Selznick, MGM. Produced by David O. Selznick.

Goodbye, Mr. Chips, MGM (British). Produced by Victor Saville.

Love Affair, RKO Radio. Produced by Leo McCarey.

Mr. Smith Goes to Washington, Columbia. Produced by Frank Capra.

Ninotchka, MGM. Produced by Sidney Franklin.

Of Mice and Men, Roach, UA. Produced by Lewis Milestone.

Stagecoach, Wanger, UA. Produced by Walter Wanger.
The Wizard of Oz, MGM. Produced by Mervyn LeRoy.
Wuthering Heights, Goldwyn, UA. Produced by Samuel Goldwyn.

Actor

★ Robert Donat in *Goodbye, Mr. Chips* (MGM) (British).
Clark Gable in *Gone With the Wind* (Selznick, MGM).
Laurence Olivier in *Wuthering Heights* (Goldwyn, UA).
Mickey Rooney in *Babes in Arms* (MGM).
James Stewart in *Mr. Smith Goes to Washington* (Columbia).

Actress

Bette Davis in *Dark Victory* (Warner Bros.).
Irene Dunne in *Love Affair* (RKO Radio).
Greta Garbo in *Ninotchka* (MGM).
Greer Garson in *Goodbye, Mr. Chips* (MGM) (British).
★ Vivien Leigh in *Gone With the Wind* (Selznick, MGM).

Supporting Actor

Brian Aherne in *Juarez* (Warner Bros.).
Harry Carey in *Mr. Smith Goes to Washington* (Columbia).
Brian Donlevy in *Beau Geste* (Paramount).
★ Thomas Mitchell in *Stagecoach* (Wanger, UA).
Claude Rains in *Mr. Smith Goes to Washington* (Columbia).

Supporting Actress

Olivia de Havilland in *Gone With the Wind* (Selznick, MGM).
Geraldine Fitzgerald in *Wuthering Heights* (Goldwyn, UA).
★ Hattie McDaniel in *Gone With the Wind* (Selznick, MGM).
Edna May Oliver in *Drums Along the Mohawk* (20th Century–Fox).
Maria Ouspenskaya in *Love Affair* (RKO Radio).

Director

Frank Capra for *Mr. Smith Goes to Washington* (Columbia).
★ Victor Fleming for *Gone With the Wind* (Selznick, MGM).
John Ford for *Stagecoach* (Wanger, UA).
Sam Wood for *Goodbye, Mr. Chips* (MGM) (British).
William Wyler for *Wuthering Heights* (Goldwyn, UA).

Writing

(ORIGINAL STORY)

Bachelor Mother, RKO Radio. Felix Jackson.
Love Affair, RKO Radio. Mildred Cram and Leo McCarey.
★ *Mr. Smith Goes to Washington*, Columbia. Lewis R. Foster.
Ninotchka, MGM. Melchior Lengyel.
Young Mr. Lincoln, 20th Century–Fox. Lamar Trotti.

(SCREENPLAY)

★ *Gone With the Wind*, Selznick, MGM. Sidney Howard.
Goodbye, Mr. Chips, MGM (British). Eric Maschwitz, R. C. Sherriff and Claudine West.
Mr. Smith Goes to Washington, Columbia. Sidney Buchman.
Ninotchka, MGM. Charles Brackett, Walter Reisch and Billy Wilder.
Wuthering Heights, Goldwyn, UA. Ben Hecht and Charles MacArthur.

Cinematography

(BLACK-AND-WHITE)

First Love, Universal. Joseph Valentine.
The Great Victor Herbert, Paramount. Victor Milner.
Gunga Din, RKO Radio. Joseph H. August.
Intermezzo: A Love Story, Selznick, UA. Gregg Toland.
Juarez, Warner Bros. Tony Gaudio.
Lady of the Tropics, MGM. Norbert Brodine.
Only Angels Have Wings, Columbia. Joseph Walker.
The Rains Came, 20th Century–Fox. Arthur Miller.
Stagecoach, Wanger, UA. Bert Glennon.
★ *Wuthering Heights*, Goldwyn, UA. Gregg Toland.

(COLOR)

Drums Along the Mohawk, 20th Century–Fox. Ray Rennahan and Bert Glennon.
Four Feathers, Denham, UA. Georges Perinal and Osmond Borradaile.
★ *Gone With the Wind*, Selznick, MGM. Ernest Haller and Ray Rennahan.
The Mikado, Universal. William V. Skall.
The Private Lives of Elizabeth and Essex, Warner Bros. Sol Polito and W. Howard Greene.
The Wizard of Oz, MGM. Hal Rosson.

Interior Decoration

Beau Geste, Paramount. Hans Dreier and Robert Odell.
Captain Fury, Roach, UA. Charles D. Hall.
First Love, Universal. Jack Otterson and Martin Obzina.
★ *Gone With the Wind*, Selznick, MGM. Lyle Wheeler.
Love Affair, RKO Radio. Van Nest Polglase and Al Herman.
Man of Conquest, Republic. John Victor Mackay.
Mr. Smith Goes to Washington, Columbia. Lionel Banks.
The Private Lives of Elizabeth and Essex, Warner Bros. Anton Grot.
The Rains Came, 20th Century–Fox. William Darling and George Dudley.
Stagecoach, Wanger, UA. Alexander Toluboff.
The Wizard of Oz, MGM. Cedric Gibbons and William A. Horning.
Wuthering Heights, Goldwyn, UA. James Basevi.

Sound Recording

Balalaika, MGM. Douglas Shearer.
Gone With the Wind, Selznick, MGM. Thomas T. Moulton.
Goodbye, Mr. Chips, MGM (British). A. W. Watkins.
The Great Victor Herbert, Paramount. Loren Ryder.
The Hunchback of Notre Dame, RKO Radio. John Aalberg.
Man of Conquest, Republic. C. L. Lootens.
Mr. Smith Goes to Washington, Columbia. John Livadary.
Of Mice and Men, Roach, MGM. Elmer Raguse.
The Private Lives of Elizabeth and Essex, Warner Bros. Nathan Levinson.

The Rains Came, 20th Century–Fox. E. H. Hansen.
★ *When Tomorrow Comes,* Universal. Bernard B. Brown.

Music

(SONG)

"Faithful Forever" (*Gulliver's Travels,* Paramount); Music by Ralph Rainger. Lyrics by Leo Robin.
"I Poured My Heart into a Song" (*Second Fiddle,* 20th Century–Fox); Music and Lyrics by Irving Berlin.
★ "Over the Rainbow" (*The Wizard of Oz,* MGM); Music by Harold Arlen. Lyrics by E. Y. Harburg.
"Wishing" (*Love Affair,* RKO Radio); Music and Lyrics by Buddy De Sylva.

(SCORE)

Babes in Arms, MGM. Roger Edens and George E. Stoll.
First Love, Universal. Charles Previn.
The Great Victor Herbert, Paramount. Phil Boutelje and Arthur Lange.
The Hunchback of Notre Dame, RKO Radio. Alfred Newman.
Intermezzo: A Love Story, Selznick, UA. Lou Forbes.
Mr. Smith Goes to Washington, Columbia. Dimitri Tiomkin.
Of Mice and Men, Roach, UA. Aaron Copland.
The Private Lives of Elizabeth and Essex, Warner Bros. Erich Wolfgang Korngold.
She Married a Cop, Republic. Cy Feuer.
★ *Stagecoach,* Walter Wanger, UA. Richard Hageman, Frank Harling, John Leipold and Leo Shuken.
Swanee River, 20th Century–Fox. Louis Silvers.
They Shall Have Music, Goldwyn, UA. Alfred Newman.
Way Down South, Lesser, RKO Radio. Victor Young.

(ORIGINAL SCORE)

Dark Victory, Warner Bros. Max Steiner.
Eternally Yours, Walter Wanger, UA. Werner Janssen.
Golden Boy, Columbia. Victor Young.
Gone With the Wind, Selznick, MGM. Max Steiner.
Gulliver's Travels, Paramount. Victor Young.
The Man in the Iron Mask, Small, UA. Lud Gluskin and Lucien Moraweck.
Man of Conquest, Republic. Victor Young.
Nurse Edith Cavell, RKO Radio. Anthony Collins.
Of Mice and Men, Roach, UA. Aaron Copland.
The Rains Came, 20th Century–Fox. Alfred Newman.
★ *The Wizard of Oz,* MGM. Herbert Stothart.
Wuthering Heights, Goldwyn, UA. Alfred Newman.

Film Editing

★ *Gone With the Wind,* Selznick, MGM. Hal C. Kern and James E. Newcom.
Goodbye, Mr. Chips, MGM (British). Charles Frend.
Mr. Smith Goes to Washington, Columbia. Gene Havlick and Al Clark.
The Rains Came, 20th Century–Fox. Barbara McLean.
Stagecoach, Wanger, UA. Otho Lovering and Dorothy Spencer.

Special Effects

Gone With the Wind, Selznick, MGM. Photographic: John R. Cosgrove. Sound: Fred Albin and Arthur Johns.
Only Angels Have Wings, Columbia. Photographic: Roy Davidson. Sound: Edwin C. Hahn.
The Private Lives of Elizabeth and Essex, Warner Bros. Photographic: Byron Haskin. Sound: Nathan Levinson.
★ *The Rains Came,* 20th Century–Fox. Photographic: E. H. Hansen. Sound: Fred Sersen.
Topper Takes a Trip, Roach, UA. Roy Seawright.
Union Pacific, Paramount. Photographic: Farciot Edouart and Gordon Jennings. Sound: Loren Ryder.
The Wizard of Oz, MGM. Photographic: A. Arnold Gillespie. Sound: Douglas Shearer.

Short Subjects

(CARTOONS)

Detouring America, Warner Bros.
Peace on Earth, MGM.
The Pointer, Walt Disney, RKO Radio.
★ *The Ugly Duckling,* Walt Disney, RKO Radio.

(ONE-REEL)

★ *Busy Little Bears,* Paramount (Paragraphics).
Information Please, RKO Radio.
Prophet Without Honor, MGM (Miniatures).
Sword Fishing, Warner Bros. (Vitaphone Varieties).

(TWO-REEL)

Drunk Driving, MGM (Crime Doesn't Pay).
Five Times Five, RKO Radio (Special).
★ *Sons of Liberty,* Warner Bros. (Historical Featurette).

Irving G. Thalberg Memorial Award

David O. Selznick.

Special Awards

Douglas Fairbanks (Commemorative Award)—recognizing the unique and outstanding contribution of Douglas Fairbanks, first president of the Academy, to the international development of the motion picture (statuette).
The Motion Picture Relief Fund—acknowledging the outstanding services to the industry during the past year of the Motion Picture Relief Fund and its progressive leadership. Presented to Jean Hersholt, President; Ralph Morgan, Chairman of the Executive Committee; Ralph Block, First Vice-President; Conrad Nagel (plaques).
Judy Garland for her outstanding performance as a screen juvenile during the past year (miniature statuette).
William Cameron Menzies for outstanding achievement in the use of color for the enhancement of dramatic mood in the production of *Gone With the Wind* (plaque).
The Technicolor Company for its contributions in success-

fully bringing three-color feature production to the screen (statuette).

Scientific or Technical

CLASS I (STATUETTE)

None.

CLASS II (PLAQUE)

None.

CLASS III (CITATION)

George Anderson of Warner Bros. Studio for an improved positive head for sun arcs.

John Arnold of MGM Studio for the MGM mobile camera crane.

Thomas T. Moulton, Fred Albin and the Sound Department of the Samuel Goldwyn Studio for the origination and application of the Delta db test to sound recording in motion pictures.

Farciot Edouart, Joseph E. Robbins, William Rudolph and Paramount Pictures, Inc., for the design and construction of a quiet portable treadmill.

Emery Huse and Ralph B. Atkinson of Eastman Kodak Co. for their specifications for chemical analysis of photographic developers and fixing baths.

Harold Nye of Warner Bros. Studio for a miniature incandescent spot lamp.

A. J. Tondreau of Warner Bros. Studio for the design and manufacture of an improved sound track printer.

Multiple Award for important contributions in cooperative development of new improved Process Projection Equipment:

F. R. Abbott, Haller Belt, Alan Cook and Bausch & Lomb Optical Co. for faster projection lenses.

Mitchell Camera Co. for a new type process projection head.

Mole-Richardson Co. for a new type automatically controlled projection arc lamp.

Charles Handley, David Joy and National Carbon Co. for improved and more stable high-intensity carbons.

Winton Hoch and Technicolor Motion Picture Corp. for an auxiliary optical system.

Don Musgrave and Selznick International Pictures, Inc., for pioneering in the use of coordinated equipment in the production *Gone With the Wind*.

Points of Interest

1. Nothing to it: Greer Garson nominated for film debut.
2. Thirteen and counting: *Gone With the Wind* sets new record with thirteen nominations.
3. King of the mountain: *Gone With the Wind* sets new record with eight wins.
4. Belly laughs: Among Cartoon Committee members selecting nominees was Alfred Hitchcock.
5. Slumming: Two-reel Short Subject winner *Sons of Liberty* starred Supporting nominee Claude Rains and former Best Supporting Actress Gale Sondergaard and was directed by 1938 double nominee Michael Curtiz.

Rule Changes

1. New addition: "Special Effects."
2. The more the merrier: Cinematography divided into separate Black-and-White and Color categories.
3. Open door policy: English-language films now eligible in all categories.
4. One less chance: No more than one nomination per person in Best Director category.

Eligible Films That Failed to Be Nominated for Best Picture

The Lady Vanishes, Only Angels Have Wings, Young Mr. Lincoln, The Women, Intermezzo: A Love Story, Four Feathers, Gunga Din, Alexander Nevsky, Midnight, The Old Maid, The Roaring Twenties.

Eligible Songs That Failed to Be Nominated

"Good Morning" (Arthur Freed and Nacio Herb Brown)—*Babes in Arms;* "Lydia, the Tattooed Lady" (Harold Arlen and E. Y. Harburg)—*At the Circus,* "The Lady's in Love with You" (Burton Lane and Frank Loesser)—*Some Like It Hot.*

1940

Picture

All This, and Heaven Too, Warner Bros. Produced by Jack L. Warner and Hal B. Wallis, with David Lewis.

Foreign Correspondent, Wanger, UA. Produced by Walter Wanger.

The Grapes of Wrath, 20th Century–Fox. Produced by Darryl F. Zanuck, with Nunnally Johnson.

The Great Dictator, Chaplin, UA. Produced by Charles Chaplin.

Kitty Foyle, RKO Radio. Produced by David Hempstead.

The Letter, Warner Bros. Produced by Hal B. Wallis.

The Long Voyage Home, Argosy-Wanger, UA. Produced by John Ford.

Our Town, Lesser, UA. Produced by Sol Lesser.

The Philadelphia Story, MGM. Produced by Joseph L. Mankiewicz.

★ *Rebecca,* Selznick, UA. Produced by David O. Selznick.

Actor

Charles Chaplin in *The Great Dictator* (Chaplin, UA).

Henry Fonda in *The Grapes of Wrath* (20th Century–Fox).

Raymond Massey in *Abe Lincoln in Illinois* (RKO Radio).
Laurence Olivier in *Rebecca* (Selznick, UA).
★ James Stewart in *The Philadelphia Story* (MGM).

Actress
Bette Davis in *The Letter* (Warner Bros.).
Joan Fontaine in *Rebecca* (Selznick, UA).
Katharine Hepburn in *The Philadelphia Story* (MGM).
★ Ginger Rogers in *Kitty Foyle* (RKO Radio).
Martha Scott in *Our Town* (Lesser, UA).

Supporting Actor
Albert Basserman in *Foreign Correspondent* (Wanger, UA).
★ Walter Brennan in *The Westerner* (Goldwyn, UA).
William Gargan in *They Knew What They Wanted* (RKO Radio).
Jack Oakie in *The Great Dictator* (Chaplin, UA).
James Stephenson in *The Letter* (Warner Bros.).

Supporting Actress
Judith Anderson in *Rebecca* (Selznick, UA).
★ Jane Darwell in *The Grapes of Wrath* (20th Century–Fox).
Ruth Hussey in *The Philadelphia Story* (MGM).
Barbara O'Neil in *All This, and Heaven Too* (Warner Bros.).
Marjorie Rambeau in *Primrose Path* (RKO Radio).

Director
George Cukor for *The Philadelphia Story* (MGM).
★ John Ford for *The Grapes of Wrath* (20th Century–Fox).
Alfred Hitchcock for *Rebecca* (Selznick, UA).
Sam Wood for *Kitty Foyle* (RKO Radio).
William Wyler for *The Letter* (Warner Bros.).

Writing
(ORIGINAL STORY)
★ *Arise, My Love*, Paramount. Benjamin Glazer and John S. Toldy.
Comrade X, MGM. Walter Reisch.
Edison the Man, MGM. Hugo Butler and Dore Schary.
My Favorite Wife, RKO Radio. Leo McCarey, Bella Spewack and Samuel Spewack.
The Westerner, Goldwyn, UA. Stuart N. Lake.

(ORIGINAL SCREENPLAY)
Angels Over Broadway, Columbia. Ben Hecht.
Dr. Ehrlich's Magic Bullet, Warner Bros. Norman Burnside, Heinz Herald and John Huston.
Foreign Correspondent, Wanger, UA. Charles Bennett and Joan Harrison.
The Great Dictator, Chaplin, UA. Charles Chaplin.
★ *The Great McGinty*, Paramount. Preston Sturges.

(SCREENPLAY)
The Grapes of Wrath, 20th Century–Fox. Nunnally Johnson.
Kitty Foyle, RKO Radio. Dalton Trumbo.
The Long Voyage Home, Argosy-Wanger, UA. Dudley Nichols.
★ *The Philadelphia Story*, MGM. Donald Ogden Stewart.
Rebecca, Selznick, UA. Robert E. Sherwood and Joan Harrison.

Cinematography
(BLACK-AND-WHITE)
Abe Lincoln in Illinois, RKO Radio. James Wong Howe.
All This, and Heaven Too, Warner Bros. Ernest Haller.
Arise, My Love, Paramount. Charles B. Lang, Jr.
Boom Town, MGM. Harold Rosson.
Foreign Correspondent, Wanger, UA. Rudolph Maté.
The Letter, Warner Bros. Gaetano Gaudio.
The Long Voyage Home, Argosy-Wanger, UA. Gregg Toland.
★ *Rebecca*, Selznick, UA. George Barnes.
Spring Parade, Universal. Joseph Valentine.
Waterloo Bridge, MGM. Joseph Ruttenberg.

(COLOR)
Bitter Sweet, MGM. Oliver T. Marsh and Allen Davey.
The Blue Bird, 20th Century–Fox. Arthur Miller and Ray Rennahan.
Down Argentine Way, 20th Century–Fox. Leon Shamroy and Ray Rennahan.
North West Mounted Police, DeMille, Paramount. Victor Milner and W. Howard Greene.
Northwest Passage, MGM. Sidney Wagner and William V. Skall.
★ *The Thief of Bagdad*, Korda, UA (British). George Perinal.

Interior Decoration
(BLACK-AND-WHITE)
Arise, My Love, Paramount. Hans Dreier and Robert Usher.
Arizona, Columbia. Lionel Banks and Robert Peterson.
The Boys from Syracuse, Universal. John Otterson.
Dark Command, Republic. John Victor Mackay.
Foreign Correspondent, Wanger, UA. Alexander Golitzen.
Lillian Russell, 20th Century–Fox. Richard Day and Joseph C. Wright.
My Favorite Wife, RKO Radio. Van Nest Polglase and Mark-Lee Kirk.
My Son, My Son, Small, UA. John DuCasse Schulze.
Our Town, Lesser, UA. Lewis J. Rachmil.
★ *Pride and Prejudice*, MGM. Cedric Gibbons and Paul Groesse.
Rebecca, Selznick, UA. Lyle Wheeler.
Sea Hawk, Warner Bros. Anton Grot.
The Westerner, Goldwyn, UA. James Basevi.

(COLOR)
Bitter Sweet, MGM. Cedric Gibbons and John S. Detlie.
Down Argentine Way, 20th Century–Fox. Richard Day and Joseph C. Wright.
North West Mounted Police, DeMille, Paramount. Hans Dreier and Roland Anderson.
★ *The Thief of Bagdad*, Korda, UA. Vincent Korda.

Sound Recording

Behind the News, Republic. Charles Lootens.
Captain Caution, Roach, UA. Elmer Raguse.
The Grapes of Wrath, 20th Century–Fox. E. H. Hansen.
The Howards of Virginia, Columbia. Jack Whitney, General Service.
Kitty Foyle, RKO Radio. John Aalberg.
North West Mounted Police, DeMille, Paramount. Loren Ryder.
Our Town, Lesser, UA. Thomas Moulton.
The Sea Hawk, Warner Bros. Nathan Levinson.
Spring Parade, Universal. Bernard B. Brown.
★ *Strike up the Band*, MGM. Douglas Shearer.
Too Many Husbands, Columbia. John Livadary.

Music

(SONG)

"Down Argentine Way" (*Down Argentine Way*, 20th Century–Fox); Music by Harry Warren. Lyrics by Mack Gordon.
"I'd Know You Anywhere" (*You'll Find Out*, RKO Radio); Music by Jimmy McHugh. Lyrics by Johnny Mercer.
"It's a Blue World" (*Music in My Heart*, Columbia); Music and Lyrics by Chet Forrest and Bob Wright.
"Love of My Life" (*Second Chorus*, Paramount); Music by Artie Shaw. Lyrics by Johnny Mercer.
"Only Forever" (*Rhythm on the River*, Paramount); Music by James Monaco. Lyrics by Johnny Burke.
"Our Love Affair" (*Strike Up the Band*, MGM); Music and Lyrics by Roger Edens and Georgie Stoll.
"Waltzing in the Clouds" (*Spring Parade*, Universal); Music by Robert Stolz. Lyrics by Gus Kahn.
★ "When You Wish Upon a Star" (*Pinocchio*, Disney, RKO Radio); Music by Leigh Harline. Lyrics by Ned Washington.
"Who Am I?" (*Hit Parade of 1941*, Republic); Music by Jule Styne. Lyrics by Walter Bullock.

(SCORE)

Arise, My Love, Paramount. Victor Young.
Hit Parade of 1941, Republic. Cy Feuer.
Irene, Imperadio, RKO Radio. Anthony Collins.
Our Town, Lesser, UA. Aaron Copland.
The Sea Hawk, Warner Bros. Erich Wolfgang Korngold.
Second Chorus, Paramount. Artie Shaw.
Spring Parade, Universal. Charles Previn.
Strike Up the Band, MGM. Georgie Stoll and Roger Edens.
★ *Tin Pan Alley*, 20th Century–Fox. Alfred Newman.

(ORIGINAL SCORE)

Arizona, Columbia. Victor Young.
Dark Command, Republic. Victor Young.
The Fight for Life, U.S. Government–Columbia. Louis Gruenberg.
The Great Dictator, Chaplin, UA. Meredith Willson.
The House of Seven Gables, Universal. Frank Skinner.
The Howards of Virginia, Columbia. Richard Hageman.
The Letter, Warner Bros. Max Steiner.
The Long Voyage Home, Argosy-Wanger, UA. Richard Hageman.
The Mark of Zorro, 20th Century–Fox. Alfred Newman.
My Favorite Wife, RKO Radio. Roy Webb.
North West Mounted Police, DeMille, Paramount. Victor Young.
One Million B.C., Roach, UA. Werner Heymann.
Our Town, Lesser, UA. Aaron Copland.
★ *Pinocchio*, Disney, RKO Radio. Leigh Harline, Paul J. Smith and Ned Washington.
Rebecca, Selznick, UA. Franz Waxman.
The Thief of Bagdad, Korda, UA. Miklos Rozsa.
Waterloo Bridge, MGM. Herbert Stothart.

Film Editing

The Grapes of Wrath, 20th Century–Fox. Robert E. Simpson.
The Letter, Warner Bros. Warren Low.
The Long Voyage Home, Argosy-Wanger, UA. Sherman Todd.
★ *North West Mounted Police*, DeMille, Paramount. Anne Bauchens.
Rebecca, Selznick, UA. Hal C. Kern.

Special Effects

The Blue Bird, 20th Century–Fox. Photographic: Fred Sersen. Sound: E. H. Hansen.
Boom Town, MGM. Photographic: A. Arnold Gillespie. Sound: Douglas Shearer.
The Boys from Syracuse, Universal. Photographic: John P. Fulton. Sound: Bernard B. Brown and Joseph Lapis.
Dr. Cyclops, Paramount. Photographic: Farciot Edouart and Gordon Jennings. Sound: No credit listed.
Foreign Correspondent, Wanger, UA. Photographic: Paul Eagler. Sound: Thomas T. Moulton.
The Invisible Man Returns, Universal. Photographic: John P. Fulton. Sound: Bernard B. Brown and William Hedgecock.
The Long Voyage Home, Argosy-Wanger, UA. Photographic: R. T. Layton and R. O. Binger. Sound: Thomas T. Moulton.
One Million B.C., Roach, UA. Photographic: Roy Seawright. Sound: Elmer Raguse.
Rebecca, Selznick, UA. Photographic: Jack Cosgrove. Sound: Arthur Johns.
The Sea Hawk, Warner Bros. Photographic: Byron Haskin. Sound: Nathan Levinson.
Swiss Family Robinson, RKO Radio. Photographic: Vernon L. Walker. Sound: John O. Aalberg.
★ *The Thief of Bagdad*, Korda, UA. Photographic: Lawrence Butler. Sound: Jack Whitney.
Typhoon, Paramount. Photographic: Farciot Edouart and Gordon Jennings. Sound: Loren Ryder.

Women in War, Republic. Photographic: Howard J. Lydecker, William Bradford and Ellis J. Thackery. Sound: Herbert Norsch.

Short Subjects

(CARTOONS)

★ *Milky Way,* MGM (Rudolph Ising Series).
Puss Gets the Boot, MGM (Cat and Mouse Series).
A Wild Hare, Schlesinger, Warner Bros.

(ONE-REEL)

London Can Take It, Warner Bros. (Vitaphone Varieties).
More about Nostradamus, MGM.
★ *Quicker 'N a Wink,* Pete Smith, MGM.
Siege, RKO Radio (Reelism).

(TWO-REEL)

Eyes of the Navy, MGM (Crime Doesn't Pay).
Service With the Colors, Warner Bros. (National Defense Series).
★ *Teddy, the Rough Rider,* Warner Bros. (Historical Featurette).

Irving G. Thalberg Memorial Award

Not given this year.

Special Awards

Bob Hope, in recognition of his unselfish services to the motion picture industry (special silver plaque).

Colonel Nathan Levinson for his outstanding service to the industry and the Army during the past nine years, which has made possible the present efficient mobilization of the motion picture industry facilities for the production of Army training films (statuette).

Scientific or Technical

CLASS I (STATUETTE)

20th Century–Fox Film Corp. for the design and construction of the 20th Century Silenced Camera developed by Daniel Clark, Grover Laube, Charles Miller and Robert W. Stevens.

CLASS II (PLAQUE)

None.

CLASS III (CITATION)

Warner Bros. Studio Art Department and Anton Grot for the design and perfection of the Warner Bros. water ripple and wave illusion machine.

Points of Interest

1. Nothing to it: Martha Scott nominated for film debut.
2. Double dose: Directors Sam Wood and Alfred Hitchcock each had two movies nominated for Best Picture.

Rule Changes

1. New addition: "Original Screenplay."
2. The more the merrier: Interior Decoration divided into separate Black-and-White and Color categories.

Eligible Films That Failed to Be Nominated for Best Picture

Waterloo Bridge, The Shop Around the Corner, The Mortal Storm, They Drive by Night, Christmas in July, His Girl Friday, My Favorite Wife, Destry Rides Again, Pride and Prejudice, The Bank Dick, All This and Heaven Too.

Eligible Songs That Failed to Be Nominated

"I Concentrate on You" (Cole Porter)—*Broadway Melody of 1940;* "I Hear Music" (Burton Lane and Frank Loesser)—*Dancing on a Dime;* "See What the Boys in the Back Room Will Have" (Frederick Hollander and Frank Loesser)—*Destry Rides Again.*

1941

Picture

Blossoms in the Dust, MGM. Produced by Irving Asher.
Citizen Kane, RKO Radio. Produced by Orson Welles.
Here Comes Mr. Jordan, Columbia. Produced by Everett Riskin.
Hold Back the Dawn, Paramount. Produced by Arthur Hornblow, Jr.
★ *How Green Was My Valley,* 20th Century–Fox. Produced by Darryl F. Zanuck.
The Little Foxes, Goldwyn, RKO Radio. Produced by Samuel Goldwyn.
The Maltese Falcon, Warner Bros. Produced by Hal B. Wallis.
One Foot in Heaven, Warner Bros. Produced by Hal B. Wallis.
Sergeant York, Warner Bros. Produced by Jesse L. Lasky and Hal B. Wallis.
Suspicion, RKO Radio. Produced by RKO Radio.

Actor

★ Gary Cooper in *Sergeant York* (Warner Bros.).
Cary Grant in *Penny Serenade* (Columbia).
Walter Huston in *All That Money Can Buy* (a.k.a. *The Devil and Daniel Webster*) (RKO Radio).
Robert Montgomery in *Here Comes Mr. Jordan* (Columbia).
Orson Welles in *Citizen Kane* (Mercury, RKO Radio).

Actress

Bette Davis in *The Little Foxes* (Goldwyn, RKO Radio).
★ Joan Fontaine in *Suspicion* (RKO Radio).
Greer Garson in *Blossoms in the Dust* (MGM).
Olivia de Havilland in *Hold Back the Dawn* (Paramount).
Barbara Stanwyck in *Ball of Fire* (Goldwyn, RKO Radio).

Supporting Actor

Walter Brennan in *Sergeant York* (Warner Bros.).
Charles Coburn in *The Devil and Miss Jones* (RKO Radio).
★ Donald Crisp in *How Green Was My Valley* (20th Century–Fox).
James Gleason in *Here Comes Mr. Jordan* (Columbia).
Sydney Greenstreet in *The Maltese Falcon* (Warner Bros.).

Supporting Actress

Sara Allgood in *How Green Was My Valley* (20th Century–Fox).
★ Mary Astor in *The Great Lie* (Warner Bros.).
Patricia Collinge in *The Little Foxes* (Goldwyn, RKO Radio).
Teresa Wright in *The Little Foxes* (Goldwyn, RKO Radio).
Margaret Wycherly in *Sergeant York* (Warner Bros.).

Director

★ John Ford for *How Green Was My Valley* (20th Century–Fox).
Alexander Hall for *Here Comes Mr. Jordan* (Columbia).
Howard Hawks for *Sergeant York* (Warner Bros.).
Orson Welles for *Citizen Kane* (Mercury, RKO Radio).
William Wyler for *The Little Foxes* (Goldwyn, RKO Radio).

Writing

(ORIGINAL STORY)

Ball of Fire, Goldwyn, RKO Radio. Thomas Monroe and Billy Wilder.
★ *Here Comes Mr. Jordan*, Columbia. Harry Segall.
The Lady Eve, Paramount. Monckton Hoffe.
Meet John Doe, Warner Bros. Richard Connell and Robert Presnell.
Night Train, 20th Century–Fox (British). Gordon Wellesley.

(ORIGINAL SCREENPLAY)

★ *Citizen Kane*, Mercury, RKO Radio. Herman J. Mankiewicz and Orson Welles.
The Devil and Miss Jones, RKO Radio. Norman Krasna.
Sergeant York, Warner Bros. Harry Chandlee, Abem Finkel, John Huston and Howard Koch.
Tall, Dark and Handsome, 20th Century–Fox. Karl Tunberg and Darrell Ware.
Tom, Dick and Harry, RKO Radio. Paul Jarrico.

(SCREENPLAY)

★ *Here Comes Mr. Jordan*, Columbia. Sidney Buchman and Seton I. Miller.
Hold Back the Dawn, Paramount. Charles Brackett and Billy Wilder.
How Green Was My Valley, 20th Century–Fox. Philip Dunne.
The Little Foxes, Goldwyn, RKO Radio. Lillian Hellman.
The Maltese Falcon, Warner Bros. John Huston.

Cinematography

(BLACK-AND-WHITE)

The Chocolate Soldier, MGM. Karl Freund.
Citizen Kane, Mercury, RKO Radio. Gregg Toland.
Dr. Jekyll and Mr. Hyde, MGM. Joseph Ruttenberg.
Here Comes Mr. Jordan, Columbia. Joseph Walker.
Hold Back the Dawn, Paramount. Leo Tover.
★ *How Green Was My Valley*, 20th Century–Fox. Arthur Miller.
Sergeant York, Warner Bros. Sol Polito.
Sun Valley Serenade, 20th Century–Fox. Edward Cronjager.
Sundown, Wanger, UA. Charles Lang.
That Hamilton Woman, Korda, UA. Rudolph Maté.

(COLOR)

Aloma of the South Seas, Paramount. Wilfred M. Cline, Karl Struss and William Snyder.
Billy the Kid, MGM. William V. Skall and Leonard Smith.
★ *Blood and Sand*, 20th Century–Fox. Ernest Palmer and Ray Rennahan.
Blossoms in the Dust, MGM. Karl Freund and W. Howard Greene.
Dive Bomber, Warner Bros. Bert Glennon.
Louisiana Purchase, Paramount. Harry Hallenberger and Ray Rennahan.

Interior Decoration

(BLACK-AND-WHITE)

Citizen Kane, Mercury, RKO Radio. Perry Ferguson and Van Nest Polglase; Al Fields and Darrell Silvera.
Flame of New Orleans, Universal. Martin Obzina and Jack Otterson; Russell A. Gausman.
Hold Back the Dawn, Paramount. Hans Dreier and Robert Usher; Sam Comer.
★ *How Green Was My Valley*, 20th Century–Fox. Richard Day and Nathan Juran; Thomas Little.
Ladies in Retirement, Columbia. Lionel Banks, George Montgomery.
The Little Foxes, Goldwyn, RKO Radio. Stephen Goosson; Howard Bristol.
Sergeant York, Warner Bros. John Hughes; Fred MacLean.
Son of Monte Cristo, Small, UA. John DuCasse Schulze; Edward G. Boyle.
Sundown, Wanger, UA. Alexander Golitzen; Richard Irvine.
That Hamilton Woman, Korda, UA. Vincent Korda; Julia Heron.
When Ladies Meet, MGM. Cedric Gibbons and Randall Duell; Edwin B. Willis.

(COLOR)

Blood and Sand, 20th Century–Fox. Richard Day and Joseph C. Wright; Thomas Little.

★ *Blossoms in the Dust*, MGM. Cedric Gibbons and Urie McCleary; Edwin B. Willis.

Louisiana Purchase, Paramount. Raoul Pene du Bois; Stephen A. Seymour.

Sound Recording

Appointment for Love, Universal. Bernard B. Brown.

Ball of Fire, Goldwyn, RKO Radio. Thomas Moulton.

The Chocolate Soldier, MGM. Douglas Shearer.

Citizen Kane, Mercury, RKO Radio. John Aalberg.

The Devil Pays Off, Republic. Charles Lootens.

How Green Was My Valley, 20th Century–Fox. E. H. Hansen.

The Men in Her Life, Columbia. John Livadary.

Sergeant York, Warner Bros. Nathan Levinson.

Skylark, Paramount. Loren Ryder.

★ *That Hamilton Woman*, Korda, UA. Jack Whitney, General Service.

Topper Returns, Roach, UA. Elmer Raguse.

Music

(SONG)

"Baby Mine" (*Dumbo*, Disney, RKO Radio); Music by Frank Churchill. Lyrics by Ned Washington.

"Be Honest With Me" (*Ridin' on a Rainbow*, Republic); Music and Lyrics by Gene Autry and Fred Rose.

"Blues in the Night" (*Blues in the Night*, Warner Bros.); Music by Harold Arlen. Lyrics by Johnny Mercer.

"Boogie Woogie Bugle Boy of Company B" (*Buck Privates*, Universal); Music by Hugh Prince. Lyrics by Don Raye.

"Chattanooga Choo Choo" (*Sun Valley Serenade*, 20th Century–Fox); Music by Harry Warren. Lyrics by Mack Gordon.

"Dolores" (*Las Vegas Nights*, Paramount); Music by Lou Alter. Lyrics by Frank Loesser.

★ "The Last Time I Saw Paris" (*Lady Be Good*, MGM); Music by Jerome Kern. Lyrics by Oscar Hammerstein II.

"Out of the Silence" (*All American Co-Ed*, Roach, UA); Music and Lyrics by Lloyd B. Norlind.

"Since I Kissed My Baby Goodbye" (*You'll Never Get Rich*, Columbia); Music and Lyrics by Cole Porter.

(SCORING OF A DRAMATIC PICTURE)

★ *All That Money Can Buy*, RKO Radio. Bernard Herrmann.

Back Street, Universal. Frank Skinner.

Ball of Fire, Goldwyn, RKO Radio. Alfred Newman.

Cheers for Miss Bishop, Rowland, UA. Edward Ward.

Citizen Kane, Mercury, RKO Radio. Bernard Herrmann.

Dr. Jekyll and Mr. Hyde, MGM. Franz Waxman.

Hold Back the Dawn, Paramount. Victor Young.

How Green Was My Valley, 20th Century–Fox. Alfred Newman.

King of the Zombies, Monogram. Edward Kay.

Ladies in Retirement, Columbia. Morris Stoloff and Ernst Toch.

The Little Foxes, Goldwyn, RKO Radio. Meredith Willson.

Lydia, Korda, UA. Miklos Rozsa.

Mercy Island, Republic. Cy Feuer and Walter Scharf.

Sergeant York, Warner Bros. Max Steiner.

So Ends Our Night, Loew-Lewin, UA. Louis Gruenberg.

Sundown, Wanger, UA. Miklos Rozsa.

Suspicion, RKO Radio. Franz Waxman.

Tanks a Million, Roach, UA. Edward Ward.

That Uncertain Feeling, Lubitsch, UA. Werner Heymann.

That Woman Is Mine, Universal. Richard Hageman.

(SCORING OF A MUSICAL PICTURE)

All American Co-ed, Roach, UA. Edward Ward.

Birth of the Blues, Paramount. Robert Emmett Dolan.

Buck Privates, Universal. Charles Previn.

The Chocolate Soldier, MGM. Herbert Stothart and Bronislau Kaper.

★ *Dumbo*, Disney, RKO Radio. Frank Churchill and Oliver Wallace.

Ice Capades, Republic. Cy Feuer.

The Strawberry Blonde, Warner Bros. Heinz Roemheld.

Sun Valley Serenade, 20th Century–Fox. Emil Newman.

Sunny, RKO Radio. Anthony Collins.

You'll Never Get Rich, Columbia. Morris Stoloff.

Film Editing

Citizen Kane, Mercury, RKO Radio. Robert Wise.

Dr. Jekyll and Mr. Hyde, MGM. Harold F. Kress.

How Green Was My Valley, 20th Century–Fox. James B. Clark.

The Little Foxes, Goldwyn, RKO Radio. Daniel Mandell.

★ *Sergeant York*, Warner Bros. William Holmes.

Special Effects

Aloma of the South Seas, Paramount. Photographic: Farciot Edouart and Gordon Jennings. Sound: Louis Mesenkop.

Flight Command, MGM. Photographic: A. Arnold Gillespie. Sound: Douglas Shearer.

★ *I Wanted Wings*, Paramount. Photographic: Farciot Edouart and Gordon Jennings. Sound: Louis Mesenkop.

The Invisible Woman, Universal. Photographic: John Fulton. Sound: John Hall.

The Sea Wolf, Warner. Photographic: Byron Haskin. Sound: Nathan Levinson.

That Hamilton Woman, Korda, UA. Photographic: Lawrence Butler. Sound: William H. Wilmarth.

Topper Returns, Roach, UA. Photographic: Roy Seawright. Sound: Elmer Raguse.

A Yank in the R.A.F., 20th Century–Fox. Photographic: Fred Sersen. Sound: E. H. Hansen.

Short Subjects

(CARTOONS)

Boogie Woogie Bugle Boy of Company B, Lantz, Universal.

Hiawatha's Rabbit Hunt, Schlesinger, Warner Bros.
How War Came, Columbia (Raymond Gram Swing Series).
★ *Lend a Paw,* Disney, RKO Radio.
The Night Before Christmas, MGM (Tom and Jerry Series).
Rhapsody in Rivets, Schlesinger, Warner Bros.
The Rookie Bear, MGM (Bear Series).
Rhythm in the Ranks, Paramount (George Pal Puppetoon Series).
Superman No. 1, Paramount.
Truant Officer Donald, Disney. RKO Radio (Donald Duck).

(ONE-REEL)
Army Champions, Pete Smith, MGM (Pete Smith Specialties).
Beauty and the Beach, Paramount (Headliner Series).
Down on the Farm, Paramount (Speaking of Animals).
Forty Boys and a Song, Warner Bros. (Melody Master Series).
Kings of the Turf, Warner Bros. (Color Parade Series).
★ *Of Pups and Puzzles,* MGM (Passing Parade Series).
Sagebrush and Silver, 20th Century–Fox (Magic Carpet Series).

(TWO-REEL)
Alive in the Deep, Woodard Productions, Inc.
Forbidden Passage, MGM (Crime Doesn't Pay).
The Gay Parisian, Warner Bros. (Miniature Featurette Series).
★ *Main Street on the March,* MGM (Special).
The Tanks Are Coming, Warner Bros. (National Defense Series).

Documentary

Adventures in the Bronx, Film Assocs.
Bomber, U.S. Office for Emergency Management Film Unit.
Christmas Under Fire, British Ministry of Information, Warner Bros.
★ *Churchill's Island,* Canadian Film Board, UA.
Letter from Home, British Ministry of Information.
Life of a Thoroughbred, 20th Century–Fox.
Norway in Revolt, March of Time. RKO Radio.
Soldiers of the Sky, 20th Century–Fox.
War Clouds in the Pacific, Canadian Film Board.

Irving G. Thalberg Memorial Award

Walt Disney.

Special Awards

Rey Scott for his extraordinary achievement in producing *Kukan,* the film record of China's struggle, including its photography with a 16mm camera under the most difficult and dangerous conditions (certificate).

The British Ministry of Information for its vivid and dramatic presentation of the heroism of the RAF in the documentary film *Target for Tonight* (certificate).

Leopold Stokowski and his associates for their unique achievement in the creation of a new form of visualized music in Walt Disney's production *Fantasia,* thereby widening the scope of the motion picture as entertainment and as an art form (certificate).

Walt Disney, William Garity, John N. A. Hawkins and the RCA Manufacturing Company, for their outstanding contribution to the advancement of the use of sound in motion pictures through the production of *Fantasia* (certificates).

Scientific or Technical

CLASS I (STATUETTE)
None.

CLASS II (PLAQUE)
Electrical Research Products Division of Western Electric Co., Inc., for the development of the precision integrating sphere densitometer.
RCA Manufacturing Co. for the design and development of the MI-3043 Uni-directional microphone.

CLASS III (CITATION)
Ray Wilkinson and the Paramount Studio Laboratory for pioneering in the use of and for the first practical application to release printing of fine grain positive stock.
Charles Lootens and the Republic Studio Sound Dept. for pioneering the use of and for the first practical application to motion picture production of Class B push-pull variable area recording.
Wilber Silvertooth and the Paramount Studio Engineering Dept. for the design and computation of a relay condenser system applicable to transparency process projection, delivering considerably more usable light.
Paramount Pictures, Inc., and 20th Century–Fox Film Corp. for the development and first practical application to motion picture production of an automatic scene slating device.
Douglas Shearer and the MGM Studio Sound Dept. and to Loren Ryder and the Paramount Studio Sound Department for pioneering the development of fine grain emulsions for variable density original sound recording in studio production.

Points of Interest

1. Nothing to it: Sydney Greenstreet, Patricia Collinge and Teresa Wright nominated for film debuts. Orson Welles received four nominations for his first film, *Citizen Kane.*

Rule Changes

1. New addition: "Documentary."
2. And I helped: For the Interior Decoration Awards, set dec-

orators receive a "certificate of merit." Art directors still receive Oscars.

3. The name game: "Score" and "Original Score" become "Scoring of a Dramatic Picture" and "Scoring of a Musical Picture."

Eligible Films That Failed to Be Nominated for Best Picture

Meet John Doe, High Sierra, Pepe Le Moko, Blood and Sand, Swamp Water, Major Barbara, The Strawberry Blonde, The Lady Eve, Never Give a Sucker an Even Break.

Eligible Song That Failed to Be Nominated

"This Time the Dream's on Me" (Harold Arlen and Johnny Mercer)—*Blues in the Night.*

1942

Picture

The Invaders, Ortus, Columbia (British). Produced by Michael Powell.
Kings Row, Warner Bros. Produced by Hal B. Wallis.
The Magnificent Ambersons, Mercury, RKO Radio. Produced by Orson Welles.
★ *Mrs. Miniver,* MGM. Produced by Sidney Franklin.
The Pied Piper, 20th Century–Fox. Produced by Nunnally Johnson.
The Pride of the Yankees, Goldwyn, RKO Radio. Produced by Samuel Goldwyn.
Random Harvest, MGM. Produced by Sidney Franklin.
The Talk of the Town, Columbia. Produced by George Stevens.
Wake Island, Paramount. Produced by Joseph Sistrom.
Yankee Doodle Dandy, Warner Bros. Produced by Jack Warner and Hal B. Wallis, with William Cagney.

Actor

★ James Cagney in *Yankee Doodle Dandy* (Warner Bros.).
Ronald Colman in *Random Harvest* (MGM).
Gary Cooper in *The Pride of the Yankees* (Goldwyn, RKO Radio).
Walter Pidgeon in *Mrs. Miniver* (MGM).
Monty Woolley in *The Pied Piper* (20th Century–Fox).

Actress

Bette Davis in *Now, Voyager* (Warner Bros.).
★ Greer Garson in *Mrs. Miniver* (MGM).
Katharine Hepburn in *Woman of the Year* (MGM).
Rosalind Russell in *My Sister Eileen* (Columbia).
Teresa Wright in *The Pride of the Yankees* (Goldwyn, RKO Radio).

Supporting Actor

William Bendix in *Wake Island* (Paramount).
★ Van Heflin in *Johnny Eager* (MGM).
Walter Huston in *Yankee Doodle Dandy* (Warner Bros.).
Frank Morgan in *Tortilla Flat* (MGM).
Henry Travers in *Mrs. Miniver* (MGM).

Supporting Actress

Gladys Cooper in *Now, Voyager* (Warner Bros.).
Agnes Moorehead in *The Magnificent Ambersons* (Mercury, RKO Radio).
Susan Peters in *Random Harvest* (MGM).
Dame May Whitty in *Mrs. Miniver (MGM).*
★ Teresa Wright in *Mrs. Miniver* (MGM).

Director

Michael Curtiz for *Yankee Doodle Dandy* (Warner Bros.).
John Farrow for *Wake Island* (Paramount).
Mervyn LeRoy for *Random Harvest* (MGM).
Sam Wood for *Kings Row* (Warner Bros.).
★ William Wyler for *Mrs. Miniver* (MGM).

Writing

(ORIGINAL STORY)

Holiday Inn, Paramount. Irving Berlin.
★ *The Invaders,* Ortus, Columbia (British). Emeric Pressburger.
The Pride of the Yankees, Goldwyn, RKO Radio. Paul Gallico.
The Talk of the Town, Columbia. Sidney Harmon.
Yankee Doodle Dandy, Warner Bros. Robert Buckner.

(ORIGINAL SCREENPLAY)

One of Our Aircraft Is Missing, Powell, UA (British). Michael Powell and Emeric Pressburger.
The Road to Morocco, Paramount. Frank Butler and Don Hartman.
Wake Island, Paramount. W. R. Burnett and Frank Butler.
The War Against Mrs. Hadley, MGM. George Oppenheimer.
★ *Woman of the Year,* MGM. Michael Kanin and Ring Lardner, Jr.

(SCREENPLAY)

The Invaders, Ortus, Columbia (British). Rodney Ackland and Emeric Pressburger.
★ *Mrs. Miniver,* MGM. George Froeschel, James Hilton, Claudine West and Arthur Wimperis.
The Pride of the Yankees, Goldwyn, RKO Radio. Herman J. Mankiewicz and Jo Swerling.
Random Harvest, MGM. George Froeschel, Claudine West and Arthur Wimperis.

The Talk of the Town, Columbia. Sidney Buchman and Irwin Shaw.

Cinematography

(BLACK-AND-WHITE)

Kings Row, Warner Bros. James Wong Howe.

The Magnificent Ambersons, Mercury, RKO Radio. Stanley Cortez.

★ *Mrs. Miniver,* MGM. Joseph Ruttenberg.

Moontide, 20th Century–Fox. Charles Clarke.

The Pied Piper, 20th Century–Fox. Edward Cronjager.

The Pride of the Yankees, Goldwyn, RKO Radio. Rudolph Maté.

Take a Letter, Darling, Paramount. John Mescall.

The Talk of the Town, Columbia. Ted Tetzlaff.

Ten Gentlemen from West Point, 20th Century–Fox. Leon Shamroy.

This Above All, 20th Century–Fox. Arthur Miller.

(COLOR)

Arabian Knights, Wanger, Universal. Milton Krasner, William V. Skall and W. Howard Greene.

★ *The Black Swan,* 20th Century–Fox. Leon Shamroy.

Captains of the Clouds, Warner Bros. Sol Polito.

Jungle Book, Korda, UA. W. Howard Greene.

Reap the Wild Wind, DeMille, Paramount. Victor Milner and William V. Skall.

To the Shores of Tripoli, 20th Century–Fox. Edward Cronjager and William V. Skall.

Interior Decoration

(BLACK-AND-WHITE)

George Washington Slept Here, Warner Bros. Max Parker and Mark-Lee Kirk; Casey Roberts.

The Magnificent Ambersons, Mercury, RKO Radio. Albert S. D'Agostino; Al Fields and Darrell Silvera.

The Pride of the Yankees, Goldwyn, RKO Radio. Perry Ferguson; Howard Bristol.

Random Harvest, MGM. Cedric Gibbons and Randall Duell; Edwin B. Willis and Jack Moore.

The Shanghai Gesture, Arnold, UA. Boris Leven.

Silver Queen, Sherman, UA. Ralph Berger; Emile Kuri.

The Spoilers, Universal. John B. Goodman and Jack Otterson; Russell A. Gausman and Edward R. Robinson.

Take a Letter, Darling, Paramount. Hans Dreier and Roland Anderson; Sam Comer.

The Talk of the Town, Columbia. Lionel Banks and Rudolph Sternad; Fay Babcock.

★ *This Above All,* 20th Century–Fox. Richard Day and Joseph Wright; Thomas Little.

(COLOR)

Arabian Nights, Wanger, Universal. Alexander Golitzen and Jack Otterson; Russell A. Gausman and Ira S. Webb.

Captains of the Clouds, Warner Bros. Ted Smith; Casey Roberts.

Jungle Book, Korda, UA. Vincent Korda; Julia Heron.

★ *My Gal Sal,* 20th Century–Fox. Richard Day and Joseph Wright; Thomas Little.

Reap the Wild Wind, DeMille, Paramount. Hans Dreier and Roland Anderson; George Sawley.

Sound Recording

Arabian Nights, Wanger, Universal. Bernard Brown.

Bambi, Disney, RKO Radio. Sam Slyfield.

Flying Tigers, Republic. Daniel Bloomberg.

Friendly Enemies, Small, UA. Jack Whitney, Sound Service, Inc.

The Gold Rush, Chaplin, UA. James Fields, RCA Sound.

Mrs. Miniver, MGM. Douglas Shearer.

Once Upon a Honeymoon, RKO Radio. Steve Dunn.

The Pride of the Yankees, Goldwyn, RKO Radio. Thomas Moulton.

Road to Morocco, Paramount. Loren Ryder.

This Above All, 20th Century–Fox. E. H. Hansen.

★ *Yankee Doodle Dandy,* Warner Bros. Nathan Levinson.

You Were Never Lovelier, Columbia. John Livadary.

Music

(SONG)

"Always in My Heart" (*Always in My Heart,* Warner Bros.); Music by Ernesto Lecuona. Lyrics by Kim Gannon.

"Dearly Beloved" (*You Were Never Lovelier,* Columbia); Music by Jerome Kern. Lyrics by Johnny Mercer.

"How About You?" (*Babes on Broadway,* MGM); Music by Burton Lane. Lyrics by Ralph Freed.

"It Seems I Heard that Song Before" (*Youth on Parade,* Republic); Music by Jule Styne. Lyrics by Sammy Cahn.

"I've Got a Gal in Kalamazoo" (*Orchestra Wives,* 20th Century–Fox); Music by Harry Warren. Lyrics by Mack Gordon.

"Love Is a Song" (*Bambi,* Disney, RKO Radio); Music by Frank Churchill. Lyrics by Larry Morey.

"Pennies for Peppino" (*Flying with Music,* Roach, UA); Music by Edward Ward. Lyrics by Chet Forrest and Bob Wright.

"Pig Foot Pete" (*Hellzapoppin',* Universal); Music by Gene de Paul. Lyrics by Don Raye.

"There's a Breeze on Lake Louise" (*The Mayor of 44th Street,* RKO Radio); Music by Harry Revel. Lyrics by Mort Greene.

★ "White Christmas" (*Holiday Inn,* Paramount); Music and Lyrics by Irving Berlin.

(SCORING OF A DRAMATIC OR COMEDY PICTURE)

Arabian Nights, Universal. Frank Skinner.

Bambi, Disney, RKO Radio. Frank Churchill and Edward Plumb.

The Black Swan, 20th Century–Fox. Alfred Newman.

The Corsican Brother, Small, UA. Dimitri Tiomkin.

Flying Tigers, Republic. Victor Young.

The Gold Rush, Chaplin, UA. Max Terr.

I Married a Witch, Cinema Guild, UA. Roy Webb.
Joan of Paris, RKO Radio. Roy Webb.
Jungle Book, Korda, UA. Miklos Rozsa.
Klondike Fury, Monogram. Edward Kay.
★ *Now, Voyager*, Warner Bros. Max Steiner.
The Pride of the Yankees, Goldwyn, RKO Radio. Leigh Harline.
Random Harvest, MGM. Herbert Stothart.
The Shanghai Gesture, Arnold, UA. Richard Hageman.
Silver Queen, Sherman, UA. Victor Young.
Take a Letter, Darling, Paramount. Victor Young.
The Talk of the Town, Columbia. Frederick Hollander and Morris Stoloff.
To Be or Not to Be, Lubitsch, UA. Werner Heymann.

(SCORING OF A MUSICAL PICTURE)
Flying with Music, Roach, UA. Edward Ward.
For Me and My Gal, MGM. Roger Edens and Georgie Stoll.
Holiday Inn, Paramount. Robert Emmett Dolan.
It Started with Eve, Universal. Charles Previn and Hans Salter.
Johnny Doughboy, Republic. Walter Scharf.
My Gal Sal, 20th Century–Fox. Alfred Newman.
★ *Yankee Doodle Dandy*, Warner Bros. Ray Heindorf and Heinz Roemheld.
You Were Never Lovelier, Columbia. Leigh Harline.

Film Editing
Mrs. Miniver, MGM. Harold F. Kress.
★ *The Pride of the Yankees*, Goldwyn, RKO Radio. Daniel Mandell.
The Talk of the Town, Columbia. Otto Meyer.
This Above All, 20th Century–Fox. Walter Thompson.
Yankee Doodle Dandy, Warner Bros. George Amy.

Special Effects
The Black Swan, 20th Century–Fox. Photographic: Fred Sersen. Sound: Roger Heman and George Leverett.
Desperate Journey, Warner Bros. Photographic: Byron Haskin. Sound: Nathan Levinson.
Flying Tigers, Republic. Photographic: Howard Lydecker. Sound: Daniel J. Bloomberg.
Invisible Agent, Universal. Photographic: John Fulton. Sound: Bernard B. Brown.
Jungle Book, Korda, UA. Photographic: Lawrence Butler. Sound: William H. Wilmarth.
Mrs. Miniver, MGM. Photographic: A. Arnold Gillespie and Warren Newcombe. Sound: Douglas Shearer.
The Navy Comes Through, RKO Radio. Photographic: Vernon L. Walker. Sound: James G. Stewart.
One of Our Aircraft Is Missing, Powell, UA (British). Photographic: Ronald Neame. Sound: C. C. Stevens.
Pride of the Yankees, Goldwyn, RKO Radio. Photographic: Jack Cosgrove and Ray Binger. Sound: Thomas T. Moulton.
★ *Reap the Wild Wind*, DeMille, Paramount. Photographic: Farciot Edouart, Gordon Jennings and William L. Pereira. Sound: Louis Mesenkop.

Short Subjects
(CARTOONS)
All Out For V, 20th Century–Fox.
The Blitz Wolf, MGM.
★ *Der Fuehrer's Face*, Disney, RKO Radio.
Juke Box Jamboree, Lantz, Universal.
Pigs in a Polka, Schlesinger, Warner Bros.
Tulips Shall Grow, Paramount (George Pal Puppetoon).

(ONE-REEL)
Desert Wonderland, 20th Century–Fox (Magic Carpet Series).
Marines in the Making, MGM (Pete Smith Specialties).
★ *Speaking of Animals and Their Families*, Paramount (Speaking of Animals).
United States Marine Band, Warner Bros. (Melody Master Bands).

(TWO-REEL)
★ *Beyond the Line of Duty*, Warner Bros. (Broadway Brevities).
Don't Talk, MGM (Two-reel Special).
Private Smith of the U.S.A., RKO Radio (This Is America Series).

Documentary
A Ship Is Born, U.S. Merchant Marines, Warner Bros.
Africa, Prelude to Victory, March of Time, 20th Century–Fox.
★ *Battle of Midway*, U.S. Navy, 20th Century–Fox.
Combat Report, U.S. Army Signal Corps.
Conquer by the Clock, Office of War Information, RKO Pathé. Frederic Ullman, Jr.
The Grain that Built a Hemisphere, Coordinator's Office, Motion Picture Society for the Americas. Walt Disney.
Henry Browne, Farmer, U.S. Department of Agriculture, Republic.
High Over the Borders, Canadian National Film Board.
High Stakes in the East, Netherlands Information Bureau.
Inside Fighting China, Canadian National Film Board.
It's Everybody's War, Office of War Information, 20th Century–Fox.
★ *Kokoda Front Line*, Australian News Information Bureau.
Listen to Britain, British Ministry of Information.
Little Belgium, Belgian Ministry of Information.
Little Isles of Freedom, Warner Bros. Victor Stoloff and Edgar Loew.
★ *Moscow Strikes Back*, Artkino (Russian).
Mr. Blabbermouth, Office of War Information, MGM.
Mr. Gardenia Jones, Office of War Information, MGM.
New Spirit, U.S. Treasury Department. Walt Disney.
★ *Prelude to War*, U.S. Army Special Services.
The Price of Victory, Office of War Information, Paramount. Pine-Thomas.

Twenty-one Miles, British Ministry of Information.
We Refuse to Die, Office of War Information, Paramount. William C. Thomas.
White Eagle, Cocanen Films.
Winning Your Wings, U.S. Army Air Force, Warner Bros.

Irving G. Thalberg Memorial Award
Sidney Franklin.

Special Awards
Charles Boyer for his progressive cultural achievement in establishing the French Research Foundation in Los Angeles as a source of reference for the Hollywood motion picture industry (certificate).
Noel Coward for his outstanding production achievement in *In Which We Serve* (certificate).
MGM Studio for its achievement in representing the American way of life in the production of the *Andy Hardy* series of films (certificate).

Scientific or Technical
CLASS I (STATUETTE)
None.

CLASS II (PLAQUE)
Carroll Clark, F. Thomas Thompson and the RKO Radio Studio Art and Miniature Departments for the design and construction of a moving cloud and horizon machine.
Daniel B. Clark and the 20th Century–Fox Film Corp. for the development of a lens calibration system and the application of this system to exposure control in cinematography.

CLASS III (CITATION)
Robert Henderson and the Paramount Studio Engineering and Transparency Departments for the design and construction of adjustable light bridges and screen frames for transparency process photography.
Daniel J. Bloomberg and the Republic Studio Sound Department for the design and application to motion picture production of a device for marking action negatives for pre-selection purposes.

Points of Interest

1. Nothing to it: William Bendix nominated his first year in movies.
2. Two-timer: Teresa Wright nominated for Best Actress and Best Supporting Actress.
3. Share the wealth: Documentary has four cowinners.
4. Renaissance man: Best Song winner Irving Berlin also nominated for Best Original Story.
5. The sound of silence: Charlie Chaplin's 1925 silent comedy *The Gold Rush,* reissued with narration, sound effects and music, nominated for Best Sound Recording.

Rule Changes

1. The name game: "Scoring of a Dramatic Picture" becomes "Scoring of a Dramatic or Comedy Picture."

Eligible Films That Failed to Be Nominated for Best Picture

To Be or Not to Be, The Palm Beach Story, Sullivan's Travels, Saboteur, Gentleman Jim, The Major and the Minor, Now, Voyager, Once Upon a Honeymoon.

Eligible Songs That Failed to Be Nominated

"Arthur Murray Taught Me Dancing in a Hurry" (Victor Schertzinger and Johnny Mercer)—*The Fleet's In;* "At Last" (Harry Warren and Mack Gordon)—*Orchestra Wives;* "Be Careful, It's My Heart" (Irving Berlin)—*Holiday Inn;* "I Don't Want to Walk Without You" (Jule Styne and Frank Loesser)—*Sweater Girl;* "I Remember You" (Victor Schertzinger and Johnny Mercer)—*The Fleet's In;* "I'll Remember April" (Don Raye, Gene De Paul and Pat Johnston)—*Ride 'Em Cowboy;* "I'm Old Fashioned" (Jerome Kern and Johnny Mercer)—*You Were Never Lovelier;* "Jingle Jangle Jingle" (Joseph J. Lilley and Frank Loesser)—*The Forest Rangers;* "Moonlight Becomes You" (Jimmy van Heusen and Johnny Burke)—*Road to Morocco;* "Serenade in Blue" (Harry Warren and Mack Gordon)—*Orchestra Wives;* "Tangerine" (Victor Schertzinger and Johnny Mercer)—*The Fleet's In;* "There Will Never Be Another You" (Harry Warren and Mack Gordon)—*Iceland;* "I Had the Craziest Dream" (Harry Warren and Mack Gordon)—*Springtime in the Rockies.*

1943

Picture
★ *Casablanca,* Warner Bros. Produced by Hal B. Wallis.
For Whom the Bell Tolls, Paramount. Produced by Sam Wood.
Heaven Can Wait, 20th Century–Fox. Produced by Ernst Lubitsch.
The Human Comedy, MGM. Produced by Clarence Brown.
In Which We Serve, Two Cities, UA (British). Produced by Noel Coward.
Madame Curie, MGM. Produced by Sidney Franklin.
The More the Merrier, Columbia. Produced by George Stevens.
The Ox-Bow Incident, 20th Century–Fox. Produced by Lamar Trotti.
The Song of Bernadette, 20th Century–Fox. Produced by William Perlberg.

Watch on the Rhine, Warner Bros. Produced by Hal B. Wallis.

Actor

Humphrey Bogart in *Casablanca* (Warner Bros.).
Gary Cooper in *For Whom the Bell Tolls* (Paramount).
★ Paul Lukas in *Watch on the Rhine* (Warner Bros.).
Walter Pidgeon in *Madame Curie* (MGM).
Mickey Rooney in *The Human Comedy* (MGM).

Actress

Jean Arthur in *The More the Merrier* (Columbia).
Ingrid Bergman in *For Whom the Bell Tolls* (Paramount).
Joan Fontaine in *The Constant Nymph* (Warner Bros.).
Greer Garson in *Madame Curie* (MGM).
★ Jennifer Jones in *The Song of Bernadette* (20th Century–Fox).

Supporting Actor

Charles Bickford in *The Song of Bernadette* (20th Century–Fox).
★ Charles Coburn in *The More the Merrier* (Columbia).
J. Carrol Naish in *Sahara* (Columbia).
Claude Rains in *Casablanca* (Warner Bros.).
Akim Tamiroff in *For Whom the Bell Tolls* (Paramount).

Supporting Actress

Gladys Cooper in *The Song of Bernadette* (20th Century–Fox).
Paulette Goddard in *So Proudly We Hail* (Paramount).
★ Katina Paxinou in *For Whom the Bell Tolls* (Paramount).
Anne Revere in *The Song of Bernadette* (20th Century–Fox).
Lucile Watson in *Watch on the Rhine* (Warner Bros.).

Director

Clarence Brown for *The Human Comedy* (MGM).
★ Michael Curtiz for *Casablanca* (Warner Bros.).
Henry King for *The Song of Bernadette* (20th Century–Fox).
Ernst Lubitsch for *Heaven Can Wait* (20th Century–Fox).
George Stevens for *The More the Merrier* (Columbia).

Writing

(ORIGINAL STORY)

Action in the North Atlantic, Warner Bros. Guy Gilpatric.
Destination Tokyo, Warner Bros. Steve Fisher.
★ *The Human Comedy*, MGM. William Saroyan.
The More the Merrier, Columbia. Frank Ross and Robert Russell.
Shadow of a Doubt, Universal. Gordon McDonell.

(ORIGINAL SCREENPLAY)

Air Force, Warner Bros. Dudley Nichols.
In Which We Serve, Two Cities-UA (British). Noel Coward.
The North Star, Goldwyn, RKO Radio. Lillian Hellman.
★ *Princess O'Rourke*, Warner Bros. Norman Krasna.
So Proudly We Hail, Paramount. Allan Scott.

(SCREENPLAY)

★ *Casablanca*, Warner Bros. Julius J. Epstein, Philip G. Epstein and Howard Koch.
Holy Matrimony, 20th Century–Fox. Nunnally Johnson.
The More the Merrier, Columbia. Richard Flournoy, Lewis R. Foster, Frank Ross and Robert Russell.
The Song of Bernadette, 20th Century–Fox. George Seaton.
Watch on the Rhine, Warner Bros. Lillian Hellman and Dashiell Hammett.

Cinematography

(BLACK-AND-WHITE)

Air Force, Warner Bros. James Wong Howe, Elmer Dyer and Charles Marshall.
Casablanca, Warner Bros. Arthur Edeson.
Corvette K-225, Universal. Tony Gaudio.
Five Graves to Cairo, Paramount. John Seitz.
The Human Comedy, MGM. Harry Stradling.
Madame Curie, MGM. Joseph Ruttenberg.
The North Star, Goldwyn, RKO Radio. James Wong Howe.
Sahara, Columbia. Rudolph Maté.
So Proudly We Hail, Paramount. Charles Lang.
★ *The Song of Bernadette*, 20th Century–Fox. Arthur Miller.

(COLOR)

For Whom the Bell Tolls, Paramount. Ray Rennahan.
Heaven Can Wait, 20th Century–Fox. Edward Cronjager.
Hello, Frisco, Hello, 20th Century–Fox. Charles G. Clarke and Allen Davey.
Lassie Come Home, MGM. Leonard Smith.
★ *The Phantom of the Opera*, Universal. Hal Mohr and W. Howard Greene.
Thousands Cheer, MGM. George Folsey.

Interior Decoration

(BLACK-AND-WHITE)

Five Graves to Cairo, Paramount. Hans Dreier and Ernst Fegte; Bertram Granger.
Flight for Freedom, RKO Radio. Albert S. D'Agostino and Carroll Clark; Darrell Silvera and Harley Miller.
Madame Curie, MGM. Cedric Gibbons and Paul Groesse; Edwin B. Willis and Hugh Hunt.
Mission to Moscow, Warner Bros. Carl Weyl; George J. Hopkins.
The North Star, Goldwyn, RKO Radio. Perry Ferguson; Howard Bristol.
★ *The Song of Bernadette*, 20th Century–Fox. James Basevi and William Darling; Thomas Little.

(COLOR)

For Whom the Bell Tolls, Paramount. Hans Dreier and Haldane Douglas; Bertram Granger.
The Gang's All Here, 20th Century–Fox. James Basevi and Joseph C. Wright; Thomas Little.
★ *The Phantom of the Opera*, Universal. Alexander Golitzen and John B. Goodman; Russell A. Gausman and Ira S. Webb.

This Is the Army, Warner Bros. John Hughes and Lt. John Koenig; George J. Hopkins.
Thousands Cheer, MGM. Cedric Gibbons and Daniel Cathcart; Edwin B. Willis and Jacques Mersereau.

Sound Recording

Hangmen Also Die, Arnold, UA. Jack Whitney, Sound Service, Inc.
In Old Oklahoma, Republic. Daniel J. Bloomberg.
Madame Curie, MGM. Douglas Shearer.
The North Star, Goldwyn, RKO Radio. Thomas Moulton.
The Phantom of the Opera, Universal. Bernard B. Brown.
Riding High, Paramount. Loren L. Ryder.
Sahara, Columbia. John Livadary.
Saludos Amigos, Disney, RKO Radio. C. O. Slyfield.
So This Is Washington, Votion, RKO Radio. J. L. Fields, RCA Sound.
The Song of Bernadette, 20th Century–Fox. E. H. Hansen.
This Is the Army, Warner Bros. Nathan Levinson.
★ *This Land Is Mine,* RKO Radio. Stephen Dunn.

Music

(SONG)

"Change of Heart" (*Hit Parade of 1943,* Republic); Music by Jule Styne. Lyrics by Harold Adamson.
"Happiness Is a Thing Called Joe" (*Cabin in the Sky,* MGM); Music by Harold Arlen. Lyrics by E. Y. Harburg.
"My Shining Hour" (*The Sky's the Limit,* RKO Radio); Music by Harold Arlen. Lyrics by Johnny Mercer.
"Saludos Amigos" (*Saludos Amigos,* Disney, RKO Radio); Music by Charles Wolcott. Lyrics by Ned Washington.
"Say a Prayer for the Boys Over There" (*Hers to Hold,* Universal); Music by Jimmy McHugh. Lyrics by Herb Magidson.
"That Old Black Magic" (*Star Spangled Rhythm,* Paramount); Music by Harold Arlen. Lyrics by Johnny Mercer.
"They're Either Too Young or Too Old" (*Thank Your Lucky Stars,* Warner Bros); Music by Arthur Schwartz. Lyrics by Frank Loesser.
"We Mustn't Say Good Bye" (*Stage Door Canteen,* Lesser, UA); Music by James Monaco. Lyrics by Al Dubin.
"You'd Be So Nice to Come Home To" (*Something to Shout About,* Columbia); Music and Lyrics by Cole Porter.
★ "You'll Never Know" (*Hello, Frisco, Hello,* 20th Century–Fox); Music by Harry Warren. Lyrics by Mack Gordon.

(SCORING OF A DRAMATIC OR COMEDY PICTURE)

The Amazing Mrs. Holliday, Universal. Hans J. Salter and Frank Skinner.
Casablanca, Warner Bros. Max Steiner.
The Commandos Strike at Dawn, Columbia. Louis Gruenberg and Morris Stoloff.
The Fallen Sparrow, RKO Radio. C. Bakaleinikoff and Roy Webb.
For Whom the Bell Tolls, Paramount. Victor Young.
Hangmen Also Die, Arnold, UA. Hanns Eisler.
Hi Diddle Diddle, Stone UA. Phil Boutelje.
In Old Oklahoma, Republic. Walter Scharf.
Johnny Come Lately, Cagney, UA. Leigh Harline.
The Kansan, Sherman, UA. Gerard Carbonara.
Lady of Burlesque, Stromberg, UA. Arthur Lange.
Madame Curie, MGM. Herbert Stothart.
The Moon and Sixpence, Loew-Lewin, UA. Dimitri Tiomkin.
The North Star, Goldwyn, RKO Radio. Aaron Copland.
★ *The Song of Bernadette,* 20th Century–Fox. Alfred Newman.
Victory Through Air Power, Disney, UA. Edward H. Plumb, Paul J. Smith and Oliver G. Wallace.

(SCORING OF A MUSICAL PICTURE)

Coney Island, 20th Century–Fox. Alfred Newman.
Hit Parade of 1943, Republic. Walter Scharf.
The Phantom of the Opera, Universal. Edward Ward.
Saludos Amigos, Disney, RKO Radio. Edward H. Plumb, Paul J. Smith and Charles Wolcott.
The Sky's the Limit, RKO Radio. Leigh Harline.
Something to Shout About, Columbia. Morris Stoloff.
Stage Door Canteen, Lesser, UA. Frederic E. Rich.
Star Spangled Rhythm, Paramount. Robert Emmett Dolan.
★ *This Is the Army,* Warner Bros. Ray Heindorf.
Thousands Cheer, MGM. Herbert Stothart.

Film Editing

★ *Air Force,* Warner Bros. George Amy.
Casablanca, Warner Bros. Owen Marks.
Five Graves to Cairo, Paramount. Doane Harrison.
For Whom the Bell Tolls, Paramount. Sherman Todd and John Link.
The Song of Bernadette, 20th Century–Fox. Barbara McLean.

Special Effects

Air Force, Warner Bros. Photographic: Hans Koenekamp and Rex Wimpy. Sound: Nathan Levinson.
Bombardier, RKO Radio. Photographic: Vernon L. Walker. Sound: James G. Stewart and Roy Granville.
★ *Crash Dive,* 20th Century–Fox. Photographic: Fred Sersen. Sound: Roger Heman.
The North Star, Goldwyn, RKO Radio. Photographic: Clarence Slifer and R. O. Binger. Sound: Thomas T. Moulton.
So Proudly We Hail, Paramount. Photographic: Farciot Edouart and Gordon Jennings. Sound: George Dutton.
Stand by for Action, MGM. Photographic: A. Arnold Gillespie and Donald Jahraus. Sound: Michael Steinore.

Short Subjects

(CARTOONS)

The Dizzy Acrobat, Universal. Walter Lantz, producer.
The Five Hundred Hats of Bartholomew Cubbins, Paramount (Puppetoon). George Pal, producer.

Greetings, Bait, Warner Bros. Leon Schlesinger, producer.
Imagination, Columbia. Dave Fleischer, producer.
Reason and Emotion, Disney, RKO Radio. Walt Disney, producer.
★ *Yankee Doodle Mouse,* MGM. Frederick Quimby, producer.

(ONE-REEL)
★ *Amphibious Fighters,* Paramount. Grantland Rice, producer.
Cavalcade of the Dance With Veloz and Yolanda, Warner Bros. (Melody Master Bands). Gordon Hollingshead, producer.
Champions Carry On, 20th Century–Fox (Sports Reviews). Edmund Reek, producer.
Hollywood in Uniform, Columbia (Screen Snapshots #1, Series 22). Ralph Staub, producer.
Seeing Hands, MGM (Pete Smith Specialty). Pete Smith, producer.

(TWO-REEL)
★ *Heavenly Music,* MGM. Jerry Bresler and Sam Coslow, producers.
Letter to a Hero, RKO Radio (This Is America). Fred Ullman, producer.
Mardi Gras, Paramount (Musical Parade). Walter MacEwen, producer.
Women at War, Warner Bros. (Technicolor Special). Gordon Hollingshead, producer.

Documentary
(SHORT SUBJECTS)
Children of Mars, This Is America Series, RKO Radio.
★ *December 7th,* U.S. Navy, Field Photographic Branch, Office of Strategic Services.
Plan for Destruction, MGM.
Swedes in America, Office of War Information, Overseas Motion Picture Bureau.
To the People of the United States, U.S. Public Health Service, Walter Wanger, Prods.
Tomorrow We Fly, U.S. Navy, Bureau of Aeronautics.
Youth in Crisis, March of Time, 20th Century–Fox.

(FEATURES)
Battle of Russia, Special Service Division of the War Department.
Baptism of Fire, U.S. Army, Fighting Men Series.
★ *Desert Victory,* British Ministry of Information.
Report from the Aleutians, U.S. Army Pictorial Service, Combat Film Series.
War Department Report, Field Photographic Branch, Office of Strategic Services.

Irving G. Thalberg Memorial Award
Hal B. Wallis.

Special Award
George Pal for the development of novel methods and techniques in the production of short subjects known as Puppetoons (plaque).

Scientific or Technical
CLASS I (STATUETTE)
None.

CLASS II (PLAQUE)
Farciot Edouart, Earle Morgan, Barton Thompson and the Paramount Studio Engineering and Transparency Departments for the development and practical application to motion picture production of a method of duplicating and enlarging natural color photographs, transferring the image emulsions to glass plates and projecting these slides by especially designed stereopticon equipment.
Photo Products Department, E.I. duPont de Nemours and Co., Inc. for the development of fine-grain motion picture films.

CLASS III (CITATION)
Daniel J. Bloomberg and the Republic Studio Sound Department for the design and development of an inexpensive method of converting Moviolas to Class B push-pull reproduction.
Charles Galloway Clarke and the 20th Century–Fox Studio Camera Department for the development and practical application of a device for composing artificial clouds into motion picture scenes during production photography.
Farciot Edouart and the Paramount Studio Transparency Department for an automatic electric transparency cueing timer.
Willard H. Turner and the RKO Radio Studio Sound Department for the design and construction of the phono-cue starter.

Points of Interest

1. The family way: Jean Arthur, nominated as Best Actress for *The More the Merrier,* was married to Frank Ross, the Original Story and Best Screenplay nominee for the film.
2. No blues in the night for Harold: Composer Harold Arlen receives three nominations in a single category—"Happiness Is a Thing Called Joe," "My Shining Hour" and "That Old Black Magic" all nominated as Best Song.
3. The real thing: Supporting Acting Award winners are now given statuettes instead of plaques.

Eligible Films That Failed to Be Nominated for Best Picture

Shadow of a Doubt, Old Acquaintance, Holy Matrimony, Hangmen Also Die, Five Graves to Cairo, Cabin in the Sky, The Cat People, I Walked with a Zombie.

Eligible Songs That Failed to Be Nominated

"Cow Cow Boogie" (Don Raye, Gene de Paul, Benny Carter)—*Revillee With Beverly;* "Hit the Road to Dreamland" (Harold Arlen and Johnny Mercer)—*Star Spangled Rhythm;* "One for My Baby" (Harold Arlen and Johnny Mercer)—*The Sky's the Limit.*

1944

Picture

Double Indemnity, Paramount. Produced by Joseph Sistrom.
Gaslight, MGM. Produced by Arthur Hornblow, Jr.
★ *Going My Way,* Paramount. Produced by Leo McCarey.
Since You Went Away, Selznick, UA. Produced by David O. Selznick.
Wilson, 20th Century–Fox. Produced by Darryl F. Zanuck.

Actor

Charles Boyer in *Gaslight* (MGM).
★ Bing Crosby in *Going My Way* (Paramount).
Barry Fitzgerald in *Going My Way* (Paramount).
Cary Grant in *None But the Lonely Heart* (RKO Radio).
Alexander Knox in *Wilson* (20th Century–Fox).

Actress

★ Ingrid Bergman in *Gaslight* (MGM).
Claudette Colbert in *Since You Went Away* (Selznick, UA).
Bette Davis in *Mr. Skeffington* (Warner Bros.).
Greer Garson in *Mrs. Parkington* (MGM).
Barbara Stanwyck in *Double Indemnity* (Paramount).

Supporting Actor

Hume Cronyn in *The Seventh Cross* (MGM)
★ Barry Fitzgerald in *Going My Way* (Paramount).
Claude Rains in *Mr. Skeffington* (Warner Bros.)
Clifton Webb in *Laura* (20th Century–Fox).
Monty Woolley in *Since You Went Away* (Selznick, UA).

Supporting Actress

★ Ethel Barrymore in *None But the Lonely Heart* (RKO Radio).
Jennifer Jones in *Since You Went Away* (Selznick, UA).
Angela Lansbury in *Gaslight* (MGM).
Aline MacMahon in *Dragon Seed* (MGM).
Agnes Moorehead in *Mrs. Parkington* (MGM).

Director

Alfred Hitchcock for *Lifeboat* (20th Century–Fox).
Henry King for *Wilson* (20th Century–Fox).
★ Leo McCarey for *Going My Way* (Paramount).
Otto Preminger for *Laura* (20th Century–Fox).
Billy Wilder for *Double Indemnity* (Paramount).

Writing

(ORIGINAL STORY)
★ *Going My Way,* Paramount. Leo McCarey.
A Guy Named Joe, MGM. David Boehm and Chandler Sprague.
Lifeboat, 20th Century–Fox. John Steinbeck.
None Shall Escape, Columbia. Alfred Neumann and Joseph Than.
The Sullivans, 20th Century–Fox. Edward Doherty and Jules Schermer.

(ORIGINAL SCREENPLAY)
Hail the Conquering Hero, Paramount. Preston Sturges.
The Miracle of Morgan's Creek, Paramount. Preston Sturges.
Two Girls and a Sailor, MGM. Richard Connell and Gladys Lehman.
★ *Wilson,* 20th Century–Fox. Lamar Trotti.
Wing and a Prayer, 20th Century–Fox. Jerome Cady.

(SCREENPLAY)
Double Indemnity, Paramount. Raymond Chandler and Billy Wilder.
Gaslight, MGM. John L. Balderston, Walter Reisch and John Van Druten.
★ *Going My Way,* Paramount. Frank Butler and Frank Cavett.
Laura, 20th Century–Fox. Jay Dratler, Samuel Hoffenstein and Betty Reinhardt.
Meet Me in St. Louis, MGM. Irving Brecher and Fred F. Finkelhoffe.

Cinematography

(BLACK-AND-WHITE)
Double Indemnity, Paramount. John Seitz.
Dragon Seed, MGM. Sidney Wagner.
Gaslight, MGM. Joseph Ruttenberg.
Going My Way, Paramount. Lionel Lindon.
★ *Laura,* 20th Century–Fox. Joseph LaShelle.
Lifeboat, 20th Century–Fox. Glen MacWilliams.
Since You Went Away, Selznick, UA. Stanley Cortez and Lee Garmes.
Thirty Seconds Over Tokyo, MGM. Robert Surtees and Harold Rosson.
The Uninvited, Paramount. Charles Lang.
The White Cliffs of Dover, MGM. George Folsey.

(COLOR)
Cover Girl, Columbia. Rudolph Maté and Allen M. Davey.
Home in Indiana, 20th Century–Fox. Edward Cronjager.
Kismet, MGM. Charles Rosher.
Lady in the Dark, Paramount. Ray Rennahan.
Meet Me in St. Louis, MGM. George Folsey.
★ *Wilson,* 20th Century–Fox. Leon Shamroy.

Interior Decoration

(BLACK-AND-WHITE)

Address Unknown, Columbia. Lionel Banks and Walter Holscher; Joseph Kish.

The Adventures of Mark Twain, Warner Bros. John J. Hughes; Fred MacLean.

Casanova Brown, International, RKO Radio. Perry Ferguson; Julia Heron.

★ *Gaslight,* MGM. Cedric Gibbons and William Ferrari; Edwin B. Willis and Paul Huldschinsky.

Laura, 20th Century–Fox. Lyle Wheeler and Leland Fuller; Thomas Little.

No Time for Love, Paramount. Hans Dreier and Robert Usher; Sam Comer.

Since You Went Away, Selznick, UA. Mark-Lee Kirk; Victor A. Gangelin.

Step Lively, RKO Radio. Albert S. D'Agostino and Carroll Clark; Darrell Silvera and Claude Carpenter.

(COLOR)

The Climax, Universal. John B. Goodman and Alexander Golitzen; Russell A. Gausman and Ira S. Webb.

Cover Girl, Columbia. Lionel Banks and Cary Odell; Fay Babcock.

The Desert Song, Warner Bros. Charles Novi; Jack McConaghy.

Kismet, MGM. Cedric Gibbons and Daniel B. Cathcart; Edwin B. Willis and Richard Pefferle.

Lady in the Dark, Paramount. Hans Dreier and Raoul Pene du Bois; Ray Moyer.

The Princess and the Pirate, Goldwyn, RKO Radio. Ernst Fegte; Howard Bristol.

★ *Wilson,* 20th Century–Fox. Wiard Ihnen; Thomas Little.

Sound Recording

Brazil, Republic. Daniel J. Bloomberg.

Casanova Brown, International, RKO Radio. Thomas T. Moulton, Goldwyn Sound Department.

Cover Girl, Columbia. John Livadary.

Double Indemnity, Paramount. Loren Ryder.

His Butler's Sister, Universal. Bernard B. Brown.

Hollywood Canteen, Warner Bros. Nathan Levinson.

It Happened Tomorrow, Arnold, UA. Jack Whitney, Sound Service Inc.

Kismet, MGM. Douglas Shearer.

Music in Manhattan, RKO Radio. Stephen Dunn.

Voice in the Wind, Ripley-Monter, UA. W. M. Dalgleish, RCA Sound.

★ *Wilson,* 20th Century–Fox. E. H. Hansen.

Music

(SONG)

"I Couldn't Sleep a Wink Last Night" (*Higher and Higher,* RKO Radio); Music by Jimmy McHugh. Lyrics by Harold Adamson.

"I'll Walk Alone" (*Follow the Boys,* Feldman, Universal); Music by Jule Styne. Lyrics by Sammy Cahn.

"I'm Making Believe" (*Sweet and Lowdown,* 20th Century–Fox); Music by James V. Monaco. Lyrics by Mack Gordon.

"Long Ago and Far Away" (*Cover Girl,* Columbia); Music by Jerome Kern. Lyrics by Ira Gershwin.

"Now I Know" (*Up in Arms,* Avalon, RKO Radio); Music by Harold Arlen. Lyrics by Ted Koehler.

"Remember Me to Carolina" (*Minstrel Man,* PRC); Music by Harry Revel. Lyrics by Paul Webster.

"Rio de Janeiro" (*Brazil,* Republic); Music by Ary Barroso. Lyrics by Ned Washington.

"Silver Shadows and Golden Dreams" (*Lady Let's Dance,* Monogram); Music by Lew Pollack. Lyrics by Charles Newman.

"Sweet Dreams Sweetheart" (*Hollywood Canteen,* Warner Bros.); Music by M. K. Jerome. Lyrics by Ted Koehler.

★ "Swinging on a Star" (*Going My Way,* Paramount); Music by James Van Heusen. Lyrics by Johnny Burke.

"Too Much in Love" (*Song of the Open Road,* Rogers, UA); Music by Walter Kent. Lyrics by Kim Gannon.

"The Trolley Song" (*Meet Me in St. Louis,* MGM); Music and Lyrics by Ralph Blane and Hugh Martin.

(SCORING OF A DRAMATIC OR COMEDY PICTURE)

Address Unknown, Columbia. Morris Stoloff and Ernst Toch.

The Adventures of Mark Twain, Warner Bros. Max Steiner.

The Bridge of San Luis Rey, Bogeaus, UA. Dimitri Tiomkin.

Casanova Brown, International, RKO Radio. Arthur Lange.

Christmas Holiday, Universal. H. J. Salter.

Double Indemnity, Paramount. Miklos Rozsa.

The Fighting Seabees, Republic. Walter Scharf and Roy Webb.

The Hairy Ape, Levey, UA. Michel Michelet and Edward Paul.

It Happened Tomorrow, Arnold, UA. Robert Stolz.

Jack London, Bronston, UA. Frederic E. Rich.

Kismet, MGM. Herbert Stothart.

None But the Lonely Heart, RKO Radio. C. Bakaleinikoff and Hanns Eisler.

The Princess and the Pirate, Goldwyn, RKO Radio. David Rose.

★ *Since You Went Away,* Selznick, UA. Max Steiner.

Summer Storm, Angelus, UA. Karl Hajos.

Three Russian Girls, R & F Prods., UA. Franke Harling.

Up in Mable's Room, Small, UA. Edward Paul.

Voice in the Wind, Ripley-Monter, UA. Michel Michelet.

Wilson, 20th Century–Fox. Alfred Newman.

Woman of the Town, Sherman, UA. Miklos Rozsa.

(SCORING OF A MUSICAL PICTURE)

Brazil, Republic. Walter Scharf.

★ *Cover Girl,* Columbia. Carmen Dragon and Morris Stoloff.

Higher and Higher, RKO Radio. C. Bakaleinikoff.

Hollywood Canteen, Warner Bros. Ray Heindorf.
Irish Eyes Are Smiling, 20th Century–Fox. Alfred Newman.
Knickerbocker Holiday, RCA, UA. Werner R. Heymann and Kurt Weill.
Lady in the Dark, Paramount. Robert Emmett Dolan.
Lady Let's Dance, Monogram. Edward Kay.
Meet Me in St. Louis, MGM. Georgie Stoll.
The Merry Monahans, Universal. H. J. Salter.
Minstrel Man, PRC. Leo Erdody and Ferde Grofé.
Sensations of 1945, Stone, UA. Mahlon Merrick.
Song of the Open Road, Rogers, UA. Charles Previn.
Up in Arms, Avalon, RKO Radio. Louis Forbes and Ray Heindorf.

Film Editing

Going My Way, Paramount. Leroy Stone.
Janie, Warner Bros. Owen Marks.
None But the Lonely Heart, RKO Radio. Roland Gross.
Since You Went Away, Selznick, UA. Hal C. Kern and James E. Newcom.
★ *Wilson,* 20th Century–Fox. Barbara McLean.

Special Effects

The Adventures of Mark Twain, Warner Bros. Photographic: Paul Detlefsen and John Crouse. Sound: Nathan Levinson.
Days of Glory, RKO Radio. Photographic: Vernon L. Walker. Sound: James G. Stewart and Roy Granville.
Secret Command, Columbia. Photographic: David Allen, Ray Cory and Robert Wright. Sound: Russell Malmgren and Harry Kusnick.
Since You Went Away, Selznick, UA. Photographic: John R. Cosgrove. Sound: Arthur Johns.
The Story of Dr. Wassell, Paramount. Photographic: Farciot Edouart and Gordon Jennings. Sound: George Dutton.
★ *Thirty Seconds Over Tokyo,* MGM. Photographic: A. Arnold Gillespie, Donald Jahraus and Warren Newcombe. Sound: Douglas Shearer.
Wilson, 20th Century–Fox. Photographic: Fred Sersen. Sound: Roger Heman.

Short Subjects

(CARTOONS)
And to Think I Saw It on Mulberry Street, Paramount (Puppetoon). George Pal, producer.
The Dog, Cat and Canary, Columbia (Screen Gems).
Fish Fry, Universal. Walter Lantz, producer.
How to Play Football, Disney, RKO Radio. Walt Disney, producer.
★ *Mouse Trouble,* MGM. Frederick C. Quimby, producer.
My Boy, Johnny, 20th Century–Fox. Paul Terry, producer.
Swooner Crooner, Warner Bros.

(ONE-REEL)
Blue Grass Gentlemen, 20th Century–Fox (Sports Review). Edmund Reek, producer.
Jammin' the Blues, Warner Bros. (Melody Master Bands). Gordon Hollingshead, producer.
Movie Pests, MGM (Pete Smith Specialty). Pete Smith, producer.
50th Anniversary of Motion Pictures, Columbia (Screen Snapshots #9, Series 23). Ralph Staub, producer.
★ *Who's Who in Animal Land,* Paramount (Speaking of Animals). Jerry Fairbanks, producer.

(TWO-REEL)
Bombalera, Paramount (Musical Parade). Louis Harris, producer.
★ *I Won't Play,* Warner Bros. (Featurette). Gordon Hollingshead, producer.
Main Street Today, MGM (Two-reel Special). Jerry Bresler, producer.

Documentary

(SHORT SUBJECTS)
Arturo Toscanini, Motion Picture Bureau, Overseas Branch, Office of War Information.
New Americans, This Is America Series, RKO Radio.
★ *With the Marines at Tarawa,* U.S. Marine Corps.

(FEATURES)
★ *The Fighting Lady,* 20th Century–Fox and U.S. Navy.
Resisting Enemy Interrogation, U.S. Army Air Force.

Irving G. Thalberg Memorial Award

Darryl F. Zanuck.

Special Awards

Margaret O'Brien, outstanding child actress of 1944 (miniature statuette).
Bob Hope for his many services to the Academy (a Life Membership in The Academy of Motion Picture Arts and Sciences).

Scientific or Technical

CLASS I (STATUETTE)
None.

CLASS II (PLAQUE)
Stephen Dunn and the RKO Radio Studio Sound Department and Radio Corporation of America for the design and development of the electronic compressor-limiter.

CLASS III (CITATION)
Linwood Dunn, Cecil Love and Acme Tool Manufacturing Co. for the design and construction of the Acme-Dunn Optical Printer.
Grover Laube and the 20th Century–Fox Studio Camera Department for the development of a continuous loop projection device.
Western Electric Co. for the design and construction of the 1126A Limiting Amplifier for variable density sound recording.
Russell Brown, Ray Hinsdale and Joseph E. Robbins for the

development and production use of the Paramount floating hydraulic boat rocker.

Gordon Jennings for the design and construction of the Paramount nodal point tripod.

Radio Corporation of America and the RKO Radio Studio Sound Department for the design and construction of the RKO reverberation chamber.

Daniel J. Bloomberg and the Republic Studio Sound Department for the design and development of a multi-interlock selector switch.

Bernard B. Brown and John P. Livadary for the design and engineering of a separate soloist and chorus recording room.

Paul Zeff, S.J. Twining and George Seid of the Columbia Studio Laboratory for the formula and application to production of a simplified variable area sound negative developer.

Paul Lerpae for the design and construction of the Paramount traveling matte projection and photographing device.

Points of Interest

1. Nothing to it: Angela Lansbury nominated for film debut.
2. Two-timer: Barry Fitzgerald nominated for Best Actor and Best Supporting Actor for same performance.
3. Attention auteurists: Leo McCarey becomes the first to win both a writing and a directing Oscar.
4. Kudos for Kurt: Composer Kurt Weill nominated for Scoring of a Musical Picture for *Knickerbocker Holiday,* competing with another score of his, *Lady in the Dark.* Both lose.

Rule Changes

1. The fewer the merrier: Henceforth, only five Best Picture nominees.
2. The silent majority: Extras no longer participate.

Eligible Films That Failed to Be Nominated for Best Picture

Laura, Phantom Lady, Ministry of Fear, Meet Me in St. Louis, Lifeboat, Hail the Conquering Hero, The Miracle of Morgan's Creek, Cover Girl, The Uninvited, Curse of the Cat People.

Eligible Songs That Failed to Be Nominated

"The Boy Next Door" (Ralph Blane and Hugh Martin)—*Meet Me in St. Louis;* "Don't Fence Me In" (Cole Porter)—*Hollywood Canteen;* "Have Yourself a Merry Little Christmas" (Ralph Blane and Hugh Martin)—*Meet Me in St. Louis;* "Is You Is or Is You Ain't (Ma' Baby)?" (Louis Jordan and Billy Austin)—*Follow the Boys;* "Spring Will Be a Little Late This Year" (Frank Loesser)—*Christmas Holiday.*

1945

Picture

Anchors Aweigh, MGM. Produced by Joe Pasternak.

The Bells of St. Mary's, Rainbow, RKO Radio. Produced by Leo McCarey.

★ *The Lost Weekend,* Paramount. Produced by Charles Brackett.

Mildred Pierce, Warner Bros. Produced by Jerry Wald.

Spellbound, Selznick, UA. Produced by David O. Selznick.

Actor

Bing Crosby in *The Bells of St. Mary's* (Rainbow, RKO Radio).

Gene Kelly in *Anchors Aweigh* (MGM).

★ Ray Milland in *The Lost Weekend* (Paramount).

Gregory Peck in *The Keys of the Kingdom* (20th Century–Fox).

Cornel Wilde in *A Song to Remember* (Columbia).

Actress

Ingrid Bergman in *The Bells of St. Mary's* (Rainbow, RKO Radio).

★ Joan Crawford in *Mildred Pierce* (Warner Bros.).

Greer Garson in *The Valley of Decision* (MGM).

Jennifer Jones in *Love Letters* (Wallis, Paramount).

Gene Tierney in *Leave Her to Heaven* (20th Century–Fox).

Supporting Actor

Michael Chekhov in *Spellbound* (Selznick, UA).

John Dall in *The Corn Is Green* (Warner Bros.).

★ James Dunn in *A Tree Grows in Brooklyn* (20th Century–Fox).

Robert Mitchum in *The Story of G.I. Joe* (Cowan, UA).

J. Carrol Naish in *A Medal for Benny* (Paramount).

Supporting Actress

Eve Arden in *Mildred Pierce* (Warner Bros.).

Ann Blyth in *Mildred Pierce* (Warner Bros.).

Angela Lansbury in *The Picture of Dorian Gray* (MGM).

Joan Lorring in *The Corn Is Green* (Warner Bros.).

★ Anne Revere in *National Velvet* (MGM).

Director

Clarence Brown for *National Velvet* (MGM).

Alfred Hitchcock for *Spellbound* (Selznick, UA).

Leo McCarey for *The Bells of St. Mary's* (Rainbow, RKO Radio).

Jean Renoir for *The Southerner* (Loew-Hakim, UA).

★ Billy Wilder for *The Lost Weekend* (Paramount).

Writing

(ORIGINAL STORY)

The Affairs of Susan, Wallis, Paramount. Laszlo Gorog and Thomas Monroe.

★ *The House on 92nd Street*, 20th Century–Fox. Charles G. Booth.
A Medal for Benny, Paramount. John Steinbeck and Jack Wagner.
Objective, Burma, Warner Bros. Alvah Bessie.
A Song to Remember, Columbia. Ernst Marischka.

(ORIGINAL SCREENPLAY)
Dillinger, Monogram. Philip Yordan.
★ *Marie-Louise*, Praesens Films (Swiss). Richard Schweizer.
Music for Millions, MGM. Myles Connolly.
Salty O'Rourke, Paramount. Milton Holmes.
What Next, Corporal Hargrove? MGM. Harry Kurnitz.

(SCREENPLAY)
★ *The Lost Weekend*, Paramount. Charles Brackett and Billy Wilder.
Mildred Pierce, Warner Bros. Ranald MacDougall.
Pride of the Marines, Warner Bros. Albert Maltz.
The Story of G.I. Joe, Cowan, UA. Leopold Atlas, Guy Endore and Philip Stevenson.
A Tree Grows in Brooklyn, 20th Century–Fox. Frank Davis and Tess Slesinger.

Cinematography
(BLACK-AND-WHITE)
The Keys of the Kingdom, 20th Century–Fox. Arthur Miller.
The Lost Weekend, Paramount. John F. Seitz.
Mildred Pierce, Warner Bros. Ernest Haller.
★ *The Picture of Dorian Gray*, MGM. Harry Stradling.
Spellbound, Selznick, UA. George Barnes.

(COLOR)
Anchors Aweigh, MGM. Robert Planck and Charles Boyle.
★ *Leave Her to Heaven*, 20th Century–Fox. Leon Shamroy.
National Velvet, MGM. Leonard Smith.
A Song to Remember, Columbia. Tony Gaudio and Allen M. Davey.
The Spanish Main, RKO Radio. George Barnes.

Interior Decoration
(BLACK-AND-WHITE)
★ *Blood on the Sun*, Cagney, UA. Wiard Ihnen; A. Roland Fields.
Experiment Perilous, RKO Radio. Albert S. D'Agostino and Jack Okey; Darrell Silvera and Claude Carpenter.
The Keys of the Kingdom, 20th Century–Fox. James Basevi and William Darling; Thomas Little and Frank E. Hughes.
Love Letters, Wallis, Paramount. Hans Dreier and Roland Anderson; Sam Comer and Ray Moyer.
The Picture of Dorian Gray, MGM. Cedric Gibbons and Hans Peters; Edwin B. Willis, John Bonar and Hugh Hunt.

(COLOR)
★ *Frenchman's Creek*, Paramount. Hans Dreier and Ernst Fegte; Sam Comer.
Leave Her to Heaven, 20th Century–Fox. Lyle Wheeler and Maurice Ransford; Thomas Little.
National Velvet, MGM. Cedric Gibbons and Urie McCleary; Edwin B. Willis and Mildred Griffiths.
San Antonio, Warner Bros. Ted Smith; Jack McConaghy.
A Thousand and One Nights, Columbia. Stephen Goosson and Rudolph Sternad; Frank Tuttle.

Sound Recording
★ *The Bells of St. Mary's*, Rainbow, RKO Radio. Stephen Dunn.
The Flame of the Barbary Coast, Republic. Daniel J. Bloomberg.
Lady on a Train, Universal. Bernard B. Brown.
Leave Her to Heaven, 20th Century–Fox. Thomas T. Moulton.
Rhapsody in Blue, Warner Bros. Nathan Levinson.
A Song to Remember, Columbia. John Livadary.
The Southerner, Loew-Hakim, UA. Jack Whitney, General Service.
They Were Expendable, MGM. Douglas Shearer.
The Three Caballeros, Disney, RKO Radio. C. O. Slyfield.
Three Is a Family, Master Productions, UA. W. V. Wolfe, RCA Sound.
The Unseen, Paramount. Loren L. Ryder.
Wonder Man, Goldwyn, RKO Radio. Gordon Sawyer.

Music
(SONG)
"Accentuate the Positive" (*Here Come the Waves*, Paramount); Music by Harold Arlen. Lyrics by Johnny Mercer.
"Anywhere" (*Tonight and Every Night*, Columbia); Music by Jule Styne. Lyrics by Sammy Cahn.
"Aren't You Glad You're You" (*The Bells of St. Mary's*, Rainbow, RKO Radio); Music by James Van Heusen. Lyrics by Johnny Burke.
"The Cat and the Canary" (*Why Girls Leave Home*, PRC); Music by Jay Livingston. Lyrics by Ray Evans.
"Endlessly" (*Earl Carroll Vanities*, Republic); Music by Walter Kent. Lyrics by Kim Gannon.
"I Fall in Love Too Easily" (*Anchors Aweigh*, MGM); Music by Jule Styne. Lyrics by Sammy Cahn.
"I'll Buy That Dream" (*Sing Your Way Home*, RKO Radio); Music by Allie Wrubel. Lyrics by Herb Magidson.
★ "It Might As Well Be Spring" (*State Fair*, 20th Century–Fox); Music by Richard Rodgers. Lyrics by Oscar Hammerstein II.
"Linda" (*The Story Of G.I. Joe*, Cowan, UA); Music and Lyrics by Ann Ronell.
"Love Letters" (*Love Letters*, Wallis, Paramount); Music by Victor Young. Lyrics by Edward Heyman.
"More and More" (*Can't Help Singing*, Universal); Music by Jerome Kern. Lyrics by E. Y. Harburg.
"Sleighride in July" (*Belle of the Yukon*, International, RKO

Radio); Music by James Van Heusen. Lyrics by Johnny Burke.

"So in Love" (*Wonder Man*, Goldwyn, RKO Radio); Music by David Rose. Lyrics by Leo Robin.

"Some Sunday Morning" (*San Antonio*, Warner Bros.); Music by Ray Heindorf and M. K. Jerome. Lyrics by Ted Koehler.

(SCORING OF A DRAMATIC OR COMEDY PICTURE)

The Bells of St. Mary's, Rainbow, RKO Radio. Robert Emmet Dolan.

Brewster's Millions, Small, UA. Lou Forbes.

Captain Kidd, Bogeaus, UA. Werner Janssen.

Enchanted Cottage, RKO Radio. Roy Webb.

Flame of the Barbary Coast, Republic. Dale Butts and Morton Scott.

G.I. Honeymoon, Monogram. Edward J. Kay.

Guest in the House, Guest in the House, Inc., UA. Werner Janssen.

Guest Wife, Green Tree, Prods., UA. Daniele Amfitheatrof.

The Keys of the Kingdom, 20th Century–Fox. Alfred Newman.

The Lost Weekend, Paramount. Miklos Rozsa.

Love Letters, Wallis, Paramount. Victor Young.

The Man Who Walked Alone, PRC. Karl Hajos.

Objective, Burma, Warner Bros. Franz Waxman.

Paris, Underground, Bennett, UA. Alexander Tansman.

A Song to Remember, Columbia. Miklos Rozsa and Morris Stoloff.

The Southerner, Loew-Hakim, UA. Werner Janssen.

★ *Spellbound*, Selznick, UA. Miklos Rozsa.

The Story of G.I. Joe, Cowan, UA. Louis Applebaum and Ann Ronell.

This Love of Ours, Universal. H. J. Salter.

The Valley of Decision, MGM. Herbert Stothart.

The Woman in the Window, International, RKO Radio. Hugo Friedhofer and Arthur Lange.

(SCORING OF A MUSICAL PICTURE)

★ *Anchors Aweigh*, MGM. Georgie Stoll.

Belle of the Yukon, International, RKO Radio. Arthur Lange.

Can't Help Singing, Universal. Jerome Kern and H. J. Salter.

Hitchhike to Happiness, Republic. Morton Scott.

Incendiary Blonde, Paramount. Robert Emmett Dolan.

Rhapsody in Blue, Warner Bros. Ray Heindorf and Max Steiner.

State Fair, 20th Century–Fox. Charles Henderson and Alfred Newman.

Sunbonnet Sue, Monogram. Edward J. Kay.

The Three Caballeros, Disney, RKO Radio. Edward Plumb, Paul J. Smith and Charles Wolcott.

Tonight and Every Night, Columbia. Marlin Skiles and Morris Stoloff.

Why Girls Leave Home, PRC. Walter Greene.

Wonder Man, Goldwyn, RKO Radio. Lou Forbes and Ray Heindorf.

Film Editing

The Bells of St. Mary's, Rainbow, RKO Radio. Harry Marker.

The Lost Weekend, Paramount. Doane Harrison.

★ *National Velvet*, MGM. Robert J. Kern.

Objective, Burma, Warner Bros. George Amy.

A Song to Remember, Columbia. Charles Nelson.

Special Effects

Captain Eddie, 20th Century–Fox. Photographic: Fred Sersen and Sol Halprin. Sound: Roger Heman and Harry Leonard.

Spellbound, Selznick, UA. Photographic: Jack Cosgrove. Sound: No credits listed.

They Were Expendable, MGM. Photographic: A. Arnold Gillespie, Donald Jahraus and R. A. MacDonald. Sound: Michael Steinore.

A Thousand and One Nights, Columbia. Photographic: L. W. Butler. Sound: Ray Bomba.

★ *Wonder Man*, Goldwyn, RKO Radio. Photographic: John Fulton. Sound: A. W. Johns.

Short Subjects

(CARTOONS)

Donald's Crime, Disney, RKO Radio (Donald Duck). Walt Disney, producer.

Jasper and the Beanstalk, Paramount (Jasper Puppetoon). George Pal, producer.

Life with Feathers, Warner Bros. (Merrie Melodies). Eddie Selzer, producer.

Mighty Mouse in Gypsy Life, 20th Century–Fox (Terrytoon). Paul Terry, producer.

Poet and Peasant, Universal (Lantz Technicolor Cartune). Walter Lantz, producer.

★ *Quiet Please*, MGM (Tom & Jerry Series). Frederick Quimby, producer.

Rippling Romance, Columbia (Color Rhapsodies).

(ONE-REEL)

Along the Rainbow Trail, 20th Century–Fox (Movietone Adventure). Edmund Reek, producer.

Screen Snapshots 25th Anniversary, Columbia (Screen Snapshots). Ralph Staub, producer.

★ *Stairway to Light*, MGM (John Nesbitt Passing Parade). Herbert Moulton, producer.

Story of a Dog, Warner Bros. (Vitaphone Varieties). Gordon Hollingshead, producer.

White Rhapsody, Paramount (Sportlights). Grantland Rice, producer.

Your National Gallery, Universal (Variety Views). Joseph O'Brien and Thomas Mead, producers.

(TWO-REEL)

A Gun in His Hand, MGM (Crime Does Not Pay). Chester Franklin, producer.

The Jury Goes Round 'N' Round, Columbia (All Star Comedies). Jules White, producer.

The Little Witch, Paramount (Musical Parade). George Templeton, producer.

★ *Star in the Night*, Warner Bros. (Broadway Brevities). Gordon Hollingshead, producer.

Documentary

(SHORT SUBJECTS)

★ *Hitler Lives?*, Warner Bros.

Library of Congress, Overseas Motion Picture Bureau, Office of War Information.

To the Shores of Iwo Jima, U.S. Marine Corps.

(FEATURES)

The Last Bomb, U.S. Army Air Force.

★ *The True Glory*, Governments of Great Britain and USA.

Irving G. Thalberg Memorial Award

Not given this year.

Special Awards

Walter Wanger for his six years service as President of the Academy of Motion Picture Arts and Sciences (special plaque).

Peggy Ann Garner, outstanding child actress of 1945 (miniature statuette).

The House I Live In, tolerance short subject; produced by Frank Ross and Mervyn LeRoy; directed by Mervyn LeRoy; screenplay by Albert Maltz; song "The House I Live In," music by Earl Robinson, lyrics by Lewis Allen; starring Frank Sinatra; released by RKO Radio (statuette).

Republic Studio, Daniel J. Bloomberg and the Republic Sound Department for the building of an outstanding musical scoring auditorium which provides optimum recording conditions and combines all elements of acoustic and engineering design (certificates).

Scientific or Technical

CLASS I (STATUETTE)

None.

CLASS II (PLAQUE)

None.

CLASS III (CITATION)

Loren L. Ryder, Charles R. Daily and the Paramount Studio Sound Department for the design, construction and use of the first dial-controlled step-by-step sound channel line-up and test circuit.

Michael S. Leshing, Benjamin C. Robinson, Arthur B. Chatelain and Robert C. Stevens of 20th Century–Fox Studio and John G. Capstaff of Eastman Kodak Co. for the 20th Century-Fox film processing machine.

Points of Interest

1. Two-timer: Don Siegel directed both the winning Documentary Short, *Hitler Lives?*, and the winning Two-Reel Short, *Star in the Night*.
2. Nothing to it: John Dall nominated for Best Supporting Actor for film debut.

Eligible Films That Failed to Be Nominated for Best Picture

A Tree Grows in Brooklyn, The Southerner, Leave Her to Heaven, To Have and Have Not, The Woman in the Window, The Clock, Murder, He Says, Scarlet Street, They Were Expendable, The Picture of Dorian Gray.

Eligible Songs That Failed to Be Nominated

"Baltimore Oriole" (Hoagy Carmichael and Paul Francis Webster)—*Johnny Angel;* "How Little We Know" (Hoagy Carmichael and Johnny Mercer)—*To Have and Have Not;* "It's a Grand Night for Singing" (Richard Rodgers and Oscar Hammerstein II)—*State Fair;* "Like Someone in Love" (Jimmy Van Heusen and Johnny Burke)—*Belle of the Yukon;* "The More I See You" (Harry Warren and Mack Gordon)—*Billy Rose's Diamond Horseshoe.*

1946

Picture

★ *The Best Years of Our Lives*, Goldwyn, RKO Radio. Produced by Samuel Goldwyn.

Henry V, Rank–Two Cities, UA (British). Produced by Laurence Olivier.

It's a Wonderful Life, Liberty, RKO Radio. Produced by Frank Capra.

The Razor's Edge, 20th Century–Fox. Produced by Darryl F. Zanuck.

The Yearling, MGM. Produced by Sidney Franklin.

Actor

★ Fredric March in *The Best Years of Our Lives* (Goldwyn, RKO Radio).

Laurence Olivier in *Henry V* (J. Arthur Rank–Two Cities, UA) (British).

Larry Parks in *The Jolson Story* (Columbia).

Gregory Peck in *The Yearling* (MGM).

James Stewart in *It's a Wonderful Life* (Liberty Films, RKO Radio).

Actress

★ Olivia de Havilland in *To Each His Own* (Paramount).
Celia Johnson in *Brief Encounter* (Rank, U-I) (British).
Jennifer Jones in *Duel in the Sun* (Selznick International).
Rosalind Russell in *Sister Kenny* (RKO Radio).
Jane Wyman in *The Yearling* (MGM).

Supporting Actor

Charles Coburn in *The Green Years* (MGM).
William Demarest in *The Jolson Story* (Columbia).
Claude Rains in *Notorious* (RKO Radio).
★ Harold Russell in *The Best Years of Our Lives* (Goldwyn, RKO Radio).
Clifton Webb in *The Razor's Edge* (20th Century–Fox).

Supporting Actress

Ethel Barrymore in *The Spiral Staircase* (RKO Radio).
★ Anne Baxter in *The Razor's Edge* (20th Century–Fox).
Lillian Gish in *Duel in the Sun* (Selznick International).
Flora Robson in *Saratoga Trunk* (Warner Bros.).
Gale Sondergaard in *Anna and the King of Siam* (20th Century–Fox).

Director

Clarence Brown for *The Yearling* (MGM).
Frank Capra for *It's a Wonderful Life* (Liberty, RKO Radio).
David Lean for *Brief Encounter* (Rank, U-I) (British).
Robert Siodmak for *The Killers* (Hellinger, Universal).
★ William Wyler for *The Best Years of Our Lives* (Goldwyn, RKO Radio).

Writing

(ORIGINAL STORY)
The Dark Mirror, U-I. Vladimir Pozner.
The Strange Love of Martha Ivers, Wallis, Paramount. Jack Patrick.
The Stranger, International, RKO Radio. Victor Trivas.
To Each His Own, Paramount. Charles Brackett.
★ *Vacation from Marriage*, London Films, MGM (British). Clemence Dane.

(ORIGINAL SCREENPLAY)
The Blue Dahlia, Paramount. Raymond Chandler.
Children of Paradise, Pathé-Cinema, Tricolore (French). Jacques Prévert.
Notorious, RKO Radio. Ben Hecht.
The Road to Utopia, Paramount. Norman Panama and Melvin Frank.
★ *The Seventh Veil*, Rank, Universal (British). Muriel Box and Sydney Box.

(SCREENPLAY)
Anna and the King of Siam, 20th Century–Fox. Sally Benson and Talbot Jennings.
★ *The Best Years of Our Lives*, Goldwyn, RKO Radio. Robert E. Sherwood.
Brief Encounter, Rank, U-I (British). Anthony Havelock-Allan, David Lean and Ronald Neame.
The Killers, Hellinger, U-I. Anthony Veiller.
Open City, Minerva Films (Italian). Sergio Amidei and Federico Fellini.

Cinematography

(BLACK-AND-WHITE)
★ *Anna and the King of Siam*, 20th Century–Fox. Arthur Miller.
The Green Years, MGM. George Folsey.

(COLOR)
The Jolson Story, Columbia. Joseph Walker.
★ *The Yearling*, MGM. Charles Rosher, Leonard Smith and Arthur Arling.

Interior Decoration

(BLACK-AND-WHITE)
★ *Anna and the King of Siam*, 20th Century–Fox. Lyle Wheeler and William Darling; Thomas Little and Frank E. Hughes.
Kitty, Paramount. Hans Dreier and Walter Tyler; Sam Comer and Ray Moyer.
The Razor's Edge, 20th Century–Fox. Richard Day and Nathan Juran; Thomas Little and Paul S. Fox.

(COLOR)
Caesar and Cleopatra, Rank, UA (British). John Bryan.
Henry V, Rank, UA (British). Paul Sheriff and Carmen Dillon.
★ *The Yearling*, MGM. Cedric Gibbons and Paul Groesse; Edwin B. Willis.

Sound Recording

The Best Years of Our Lives, Goldwyn, RKO Radio. Gordon Sawyer.
It's a Wonderful Life, Liberty, RKO Radio. John Aalberg.
★ *The Jolson Story*, Columbia. John Livadary.

Music

(SONG)
"All Through the Day" (*Centennial Summer*, 20th Century–Fox); Music by Jerome Kern. Lyrics by Oscar Hammerstein II.
"I Can't Begin to Tell You" (*The Dolly Sisters*, 20th Century–Fox); Music by James Monaco. Lyrics by Mack Gordon.
"Ole Buttermilk Sky" (*Canyon Passage*, Wanger, Universal); Music by Hoagy Carmichael. Lyrics by Jack Brooks.
★ "On The Atchison, Topeka and Santa Fe" (*The Harvey*

Girls, MGM); Music by Harry Warren. Lyrics by Johnny Mercer.

"You Keep Coming Back Like a Song" (*Blue Skies*, Paramount); Music and Lyrics by Irving Berlin.

(SCORING OF A DRAMATIC OR COMEDY PICTURE)

Anna and the King of Siam, 20th Century–Fox. Bernard Herrmann.

★ *The Best Years of Our Lives*, Goldwyn, RKO Radio. Hugo Friedhofer.

Henry V, Rank, UA (British). William Walton.

Humoresque, Warner Bros. Franz Waxman.

The Killers, Universal. Miklos Rozsa.

(SCORING OF A MUSICAL PICTURE)

Blue Skies, Paramount. Robert Emmett Dolan.

Centennial Summer, 20th Century–Fox. Alfred Newman.

The Harvey Girls, MGM. Lennie Hayton.

★ *The Jolson Story*, Columbia. Morris Stoloff.

Night and Day, Warner Bros. Ray Heindorf and Max Steiner.

Film Editing

★ *The Best Years of Our Lives*, Goldwyn, RKO Radio. Daniel Mandell.

It's a Wonderful Life, Liberty, RKO Radio. William Hornbeck.

The Jolson Story, Columbia. William Lyon.

The Killers, Hellinger, Universal. Arthur Hilton.

The Yearling, MGM. Harold Kress.

Special Effects

★ *Blithe Spirit*, Rank UA (British). Visual: Thomas Howard. Audible: No credit.

A Stolen Life, Warner Bros. Visual: William McGann. Audible: Nathan Levinson.

Short Subjects

(CARTOONS)

★ *The Cat Concerto*, MGM (Tom & Jerry). Frederick Quimby, producer.

Chopin's Musical Moments, Universal (Musical Miniatures). Walter Lantz, producer.

John Henry and the Inky Poo, Paramount (Puppetoon). George Pal, producer.

Squatter's Rights, Disney–RKO Radio (Mickey Mouse). Walt Disney, producer.

Walky Talky Hawky, Warner Bros. (Merrie Melodies). Edward Selzer, producer.

(ONE-REEL)

Dive-hi Champs, Paramount (Sportlights). Jack Eaton, producer.

★ *Facing Your Danger*, Warner Bros. (Sports Parade). Gordon Hollingshead, producer.

Golden Horses, 20th Century–Fox. (Movietone Sports Review). Edmund Reek, producer.

Smart as a Fox, Warner Bros. (Varieties). Gordon Hollingshead, producer.

Sure Cures, MGM (Pete Smith Specialty). Pete Smith, producer.

(TWO-REEL)

★ *A Boy and His Dog*, Warner Bros. (Featurettes). Gordon Hollingshead, producer.

College Queen, Paramount (Musical Parade). George Templeton, producer.

Hiss and Yell, Columbia (All Star Comedies). Jules White, producer.

The Luckiest Guy in the World, MGM (Two-reel Special). Jerry Bresler, producer.

Documentary

(SHORT SUBJECTS)

Atomic Power, 20th Century–Fox.

Life at the Zoo, Artkino.

Paramount News Issue #37, Paramount.

★ *Seeds of Destiny*, U.S. War Department.

Traffic with the Devil, MGM.

(No Features nominated this year.)

Irving G. Thalberg Memorial Award

Samuel Goldwyn.

Special Awards

Laurence Olivier for his outstanding achievement as actor, producer and director in bringing *Henry V* to the screen (statuette).

Harold Russell for bringing hope and courage to his fellow veterans through his appearance in *The Best Years of Our Lives* (statuette).

Ernst Lubitsch for his distinguished contributions to the art of the motion picture (scroll).

Claude Jarman, Jr., outstanding child actor of 1946 (miniature statuette).

Scientific or Technical

CLASS I (STATUETTE)

None.

CLASS II (PLAQUE)

None.

CLASS III (CITATION)

Harlan L. Baumbach and the Paramount West Coast Laboratory for an improved method for the quantitative determination of hydroquinone and metol in photographic developing baths.

Herbert E. Britt for the development and application of formulas and equipment for producing cloud and smoke effects.

Burton F. Miller and the Warner Bros. Studio Sound and Electrical Departments for the design and construction of a motion picture arc lighting generator filter.

Carl Faulkner of the 20th Century–Fox Studio Sound Department for the reversed bias method, including a double bias method for light valve and galvanometer density recording.

Mole Richardson Co. for the Type 450 super high intensity carbon arc lamp.

Arthur F. Blinn, Robert O. Cook, C. O. Slyfield and the Walt Disney Studio Sound Department for the design and development of an audio finder and track viewer for checking and locating noise in sound tracks.

Burton F. Miller and the Warner Bros. Studio Sound Department for the design and application of an equalizer to eliminate relative spectral energy distortion in electronic compressors.

Marty Martin and Hal Adkins of the RKO Radio Studio Miniature Department for the design and construction of equipment providing visual bullet effects.

Harold Nye and the Warner Bros. Studio Electrical Department for the development of the electronically controlled fire and gaslight effect.

Rule Changes

1. Y'all vote: Awards for Art Direction, Cinematography, Sound, Editing, Special Effects and Musical Scoring now voted upon by entire Academy membership, not special committees of respective branch members.
2. The silent majority: Although Guild members still take part in nominating process, only Academy members vote for final Awards.
3. I didn't see any I liked: No Feature Documentary nominations or Award this year.

Eligible Films That Failed to Be Nominated for Best Picture

Notorious, Children of Paradise, The Big Sleep, Gilda, The Postman Always Rings Twice, My Darling Clementine, Brief Encounter, Open City, Caesar and Cleopatra, Detour, Cluny Brown, The Stranger, Duel in the Sun.

Eligible Songs That Failed to Be Nominated

"The Anniversary Song" (Al Jolson)—*The Jolson Story;* "Give Me the Simple Life" (Harry Ruby and Rube Bloom)—*Wake Up and Dream;* "On the Boardwalk at Atlantic City" (Josef Myrow and Mack Gordon)—*Three Little Girls in Blue;* "Personality" (Jimmy Van Heusen and Johnny Burke)—*Road to Utopia;* "Put the Blame on Mame" (Allan Roberts and Doris Fisher)—*Gilda;* "You Make Me Feel So Young" (Josef Myrow and Mack Gordon)—*Three Little Girls in Blue;* "If I'm Lucky" (Josef Myrow and Eddie DeLange)—*If I'm Lucky;* "In Love in Vain" (Jerome Kern and Leo Robin)—*Centennial Summer.*

1947

Picture

The Bishop's Wife, Goldwyn, RKO Radio. Produced by Samuel Goldwyn.

Crossfire, RKO Radio. Produced by Adrian Scott.

★ *Gentleman's Agreement,* 20th Century–Fox. Produced by Darryl F. Zanuck.

Great Expectations, Rank-Cineguild, U-I (British). Produced by Ronald Neame.

Miracle on 34th Street, 20th Century–Fox. Produced by William Perlberg.

Actor

★ Ronald Colman in *A Double Life* (Kanin, U-I).

John Garfield in *Body and Soul* (Enterprise, UA).

Gregory Peck in *Gentleman's Agreement* (20th Century–Fox).

William Powell in *Life with Father* (Warner Bros.).

Michael Redgrave in *Mourning Becomes Electra* (RKO Radio).

Actress

Joan Crawford in *Possessed* (Warner Bros.).

Susan Hayward in *Smash Up—The Story of a Woman* (Wanger, U-I).

Dorothy McGuire in *Gentleman's Agreement* (20th Century–Fox).

Rosalind Russell in *Mourning Becomes Electra* (RKO Radio).

★ Loretta Young in *The Farmer's Daughter* (RKO Radio).

Supporting Actor

Charles Bickford in *The Farmer's Daughter* (RKO Radio).

Thomas Gomez in *Ride the Pink Horse* (U-I).

★ Edmund Gwenn in *Miracle on 34th Street* (20th Century–Fox).

Robert Ryan in *Crossfire* (RKO Radio).

Richard Widmark in *Kiss of Death* (20th Century–Fox).

Supporting Actress

Ethel Barrymore in *The Paradine Case* (Selznick).

Gloria Grahame in *Crossfire* (RKO Radio).

★ Celeste Holm in *Gentleman's Agreement* (20th Century–Fox).

Marjorie Main in *The Egg and I* (Universal-International).

Anne Revere in *Gentleman's Agreement* (20th Century–Fox).

Director

George Cukor for *A Double Life* (Kanin, U-I).

Edward Dmytryk for *Crossfire* (RKO Radio).

★ Elia Kazan for *Gentleman's Agreement* (20th Century–Fox).

Henry Koster for *The Bishop's Wife* (Goldwyn, RKO Radio).
David Lean for *Great Expectations* (Rank-Cineguild, (U-I) (British).

Writing

(ORIGINAL STORY)

A Cage of Nightingales, Gaumont, Lopert Films (French). Georges Chaperot and Rene Wheeler.
It Happened on Fifth Avenue, Roy Del Ruth, Allied Artists. Herbert Clyde Lewis and Frederick Stephani.
Kiss of Death, 20th Century–Fox. Eleazar Lipsky.
★ *Miracle on 34th Street*, 20th Century–Fox. Valentine Davies.
Smash Up—The Story of a Woman, Wanger, U-I. Dorothy Parker and Frank Cavett.

(ORIGINAL SCREENPLAY)

★ *The Bachelor and the Bobby-Soxer*, RKO Radio. Sidney Sheldon.
Body and Soul, Enterprise, UA. Abraham Polonsky.
A Double Life, Kanin Prod., U-I. Ruth Gordon and Garson Kanin.
Monsieur Verdoux, Chaplin, UA. Charles Chaplin.
Shoeshine, Lopert Films (Italian). Sergio Amidei, Adolofo Franci, C. G. Viola and Cesare Zavattini.

(SCREENPLAY)

Boomerang!, 20th Century–Fox. Richard Murphy.
Crossfire, RKO Radio. John Paxton.
Gentleman's Agreement, 20th Century–Fox. Moss Hart.
Great Expectations, Rank-Cineguild, U-I (British). David Lean, Ronald Neame and Anthony Havelock-Allan.
★ *Miracle on 34th Street*, 20th Century–Fox. George Seaton.

Cinematography

(BLACK-AND-WHITE)

The Ghost and Mrs. Muir, 20th Century–Fox. Charles Lang, Jr.
★ *Great Expectations*, Rank-Cineguild, U-I (British). Guy Green.
Green Dolphin Street, MGM. George Folsey.

(COLOR)

★ *Black Narcissus*, Rank-Archers, U-I (British). Jack Cardiff.
Life with Father, Warner Bros. Peverell Marley and William V. Skall.
Mother Wore Tights, 20th Century–Fox. Harry Jackson.

Art Direction—Set Decoration

(BLACK-AND-WHITE)

The Foxes of Harrow, 20th Century–Fox. Lyle Wheeler and Maurice Ransford; Thomas Little and Paul S. Fox.
★ *Great Expectations*, Rank-Cineguild, U-I (British). John Bryan; Wilfred Shingleton.

(COLOR)

★ *Black Narcissus*, Rank-Archers, U-I (British). Alfred Junge.
Life with Father, Warner Bros. Robert M. Haas; George James Hopkins.

Sound Recording

★ *The Bishop's Wife*, Goldwyn, RKO Radio. Goldwyn Sound Department.
Green Dolphin Street, MGM. MGM Sound Department.
T-Men, Reliance Pictures. Eagle-Lion, Sound Services, Inc.

Music

(SONG)

"A Gal in Calico" (*The Time, the Place and the Girl*, Warner Bros.); Music by Arthur Schwartz. Lyrics by Leo Robin.
"I Wish I Didn't Love You So" (*The Perils of Pauline*, Paramount); Music and Lyrics by Frank Loesser.
"Pass That Peace Pipe" (*Good News*, MGM); Music and Lyrics by Ralph Blane, Hugh Martin and Roger Edens.
"You Do" (*Mother Wore Tights*, 20th Century–Fox); Music by Josef Myrow. Lyrics by Mack Gordon.
★ "Zip-A-Dee-Doo-Dah" (*Song of the South*, Disney–RKO Radio); Music by Allie Wrubel. Lyrics by Ray Gilbert.

(SCORING OF A DRAMATIC OR COMEDY PICTURE)

The Bishop's Wife, Goldwyn, RKO Radio. Hugo Friedhofer.
Captain from Castile, 20th Century–Fox. Alfred Newman.
★ *A Double Life*, Kanin, U-I. Miklos Rozsa.
Forever Amber, 20th Century–Fox. David Raksin.
Life with Father, Warner Bros. Max Steiner.

(SCORING OF A MUSICAL PICTURE)

Fiesta, MGM. Johnny Green.
★ *Mother Wore Tights*, 20th Century–Fox. Alfred Newman.
My Wild Irish Rose, Warner Bros. Ray Heindorf and Max Steiner.
Road to Rio, Hope-Crosby, Paramount. Robert Emmett Dolan.
Song of the South, Disney–RKO Radio. Daniele Amfitheatrof, Paul J. Smith and Charles Wolcott.

Film Editing

The Bishop's Wife, Goldwyn, RKO Radio. Monica Collingwood.
★ *Body and Soul*, Enterprise, UA. Francis Lyon and Robert Parrish.
Gentleman's Agreement, 20th Century–Fox. Harmon Jones.
Green Dolphin Street, MGM. George White.
Odd Man Out, Rank–Two Cities, U-I (British). Fergus McDonnell.

Special Effects

★ *Green Dolphin Street*, MGM. Visual: A. Arnold Gillespie and Warren Newcombe. Audible: Douglas Shearer and Michael Steinore.
Unconquered, Paramount. Visual: Farciot Edouart, Dever-

eux Jennings, Gordon Jennings, Wallace Kelley and Paul Lerpae. Audible: George Dutton.

Short Subjects

(CARTOONS)

Chip an' Dale, Walt Disney, RKO Radio (Donald Duck). Walt Disney, producer.

Dr. Jekyll and Mr. Mouse, MGM (Tom & Jerry). Frederick Quimby, producer.

Pluto's Blue Note, Walt Disney, RKO Radio (Pluto). Walt Disney, producer.

Tubby the Tuba, Paramount (George Pal Puppetoon). George Pal, producer.

★ *Tweetie Pie,* Warner Bros. (Merrie Melodies). Edward Selzer, producer.

(ONE-REEL)

Brooklyn, U.S.A., U-I (Variety Series). Thomas Mead, producer.

★ *Goodbye Miss Turlock,* MGM (John Nesbitt Passing Parade). Herbert Moulton, producer.

Moon Rockets, Paramount (Popular Science). Jerry Fairbanks, producer.

Now You See It, MGM. Pete Smith, producer.

So You Want to Be in Pictures, Warner Bros. (Joe McDoakes). Gordon Hollingshead, producer.

(TWO-REEL)

Champagne for Two, Paramount (Musical Parade Featurette). Harry Grey, producer.

★ *Climbing the Matterhorn,* Monogram (Color). Irving Allen, producer.

Fight of the Wild Stallions, U-I (Special). Thomas Mead, producer.

Give Us the Earth, MGM (Special). Herbert Morgan, producer.

A Voice Is Born, Columbia (Musical Featurette). Ben Blake, producer.

Documentary

(SHORT SUBJECTS)

★ *First Steps,* United Nations Division of Films and Visual Education.

Passport to Nowhere, RKO Radio (This Is America Series). Frederic Ullman, Jr., producer.

School in the Mailbox, Australian News and Information Bureau.

(FEATURES)

★ *Design for Death,* RKO Radio. Sid Rogell, executive producer; Theron Warth and Richard O. Fleischer, producers.

Journey into Medicine, U.S. Department of State, Office of Information and Educational Exchange.

The World Is Rich, British Information Services. Paul Rotha, producer.

Irving G. Thalberg Memorial Award

Not given this year.

Special Awards

James Baskette for his able and heart-warming characterization of Uncle Remus, friend and storyteller to the children of the world (statuette).

Bill and Coo, in which artistry and patience blended in a novel and entertaining use of the medium of motion pictures (plaque).

Shoeshine—the high quality of this motion picture, brought to eloquent life in a country scarred by war, is proof to the world that the creative spirit can triumph over adversity (statuette).

Colonel William N. Selig, Albert E. Smith, Thomas Armat and George K. Spoor, the small group of pioneers whose belief in a new medium, and whose contributions to its development, blazed the trail along which the motion picture has progressed, in their lifetime, from obscurity to world-wide acclaim (statuettes).

Scientific or Technical

CLASS I (STATUETTE)

None.

CLASS II (PLAQUE)

C. C. Davis and Electrical Research Products, Division of Western Electric Co., for the development and application of an improved film drive filter mechanism.

C. R. Daily and the Paramount Studio Film Laboratory, Still and Engineering Departments for the development and first practical application to motion picture and still photography of a method of increasing film speed as first suggested to the industry by E.I. duPont de Nemours & Co.

CLASS III (CITATION)

Nathan Levinson and the Warner Bros. Studio Sound Department for the design and construction of a constant-speed sound editing machine.

Farciot Edouart, C. R. Daily, Hal Corl, H. G. Cartwright and the Paramount Studio Transparency and Engineering Departments for the first application of a special antisolarizing glass to high intensity background and spot arc projectors.

Fred Ponedel of Warner Bros. Studio for pioneering the fabrication and practical application to motion picture color photography of large translucent photographic backgrounds.

Kurt Singer and the RCA-Victor Division of the Radio Corporation of America for the design and development of a continuously variable band elimination filter.

James Gibbons of Warner Bros. Studio for the development and production of large dyed plastic filters for motion picture photography.

Points of Interest

1. We're on a roll now: Two-Reel Short Subject Award for *Climbing the Matterhorn* only Oscar ever for Monogram Studios.
2. Nothing to it: Richard Widmark nominated for his film debut. Tweety and Sylvester win Best Cartoon for film debut.

Rule Changes

1. The name game: Interior Decoration retitled "Art Direction—Set Decoration."

Eligible Films That Failed to Be Nominated for Best Picture

Body and Soul, Black Narcissus, Zero for Conduct, Odd Man Out, Nightmare Alley, Out of the Past, Monsieur Verdoux, Ivan the Terrible, Smash Up—The Story of a Woman.

Eligible Songs That Failed to Be Nominated

"Chiquita Banana" (Leonard McKenzie, Garth Montgomery and William Wirgers)—*This Time for Keeps;* "Golden Earrings" (Jay Livingston, Ray Evans and Victor Young)—*Golden Earrings;* "Time After Time" (Jule Styne and Sammy Cahn)—*It Happened in Brooklyn.*

1948

Picture

★ *Hamlet*, Rank–Two Cities, U-I (British). Produced by Laurence Olivier.
Johnny Belinda, Warner Bros. Produced by Jerry Wald.
The Red Shoes, Rank-Archers, Eagle-Lion (British). Produced by Michael Powell and Emeric Pressburger.
The Snake Pit, 20th Century–Fox. Produced by Anatole Litvak and Robert Bassler.
Treasure of Sierra Madre, Warner Bros. Produced by Henry Blanke.

Actor

Lew Ayres in *Johnny Belinda* (Warner Bros.).
Montgomery Clift in *The Search* (Praesens Films, MGM) (Swiss).
Dan Dailey in *When My Baby Smiles at Me* (20th Century–Fox).
★ Laurence Olivier in *Hamlet* (J. Arthur Rank–Two Cities, U-I) (British).
Clifton Webb in *Sitting Pretty* (20th Century–Fox).

Actress

Ingrid Bergman in *Joan of Arc* (Sierra Pictures, RKO Radio).
Olivia de Havilland in *The Snake Pit* (20th Century–Fox).
Irene Dunne in *I Remember Mama* (RKO Radio).
Barbara Stanwyck in *Sorry, Wrong Number* (Wallis, Paramount).
★ Jane Wyman in *Johnny Belinda* (Warner Bros.).

Supporting Actor

Charles Bickford in *Johnny Belinda* (Warner Bros.).
José Ferrer in *Joan of Arc* (Sierra Pictures, RKO Radio).
Oscar Homolka in *I Remember Mama* (RKO Radio).
★ Walter Huston in *Treasure of Sierra Madre* (Warner Bros.).
Cecil Kellaway in *The Luck of the Irish* (20th Century–Fox).

Supporting Actress

Barbara Bel Geddes in *I Remember Mama* (RKO Radio).
Ellen Corby in *I Remember Mama* (RKO Radio).
Agnes Moorehead in *Johnny Belinda* (Warner Bros.).
Jean Simmons in *Hamlet* (Rank–Two Cities, U-I) (British).
★ Claire Trevor in *Key Largo* (Warner Bros.).

Director

★ John Huston for *Treasure of Sierra Madre* (Warner Bros.).
Anatole Litvak for *The Snake Pit* (20th Century–Fox).
Jean Negulesco for *Johnny Belinda* (Warner Bros.).
Laurence Olivier for *Hamlet* (Rank–Two Cities, U-I) (British).
Fred Zinnemann for *The Search* (Praesens Films, MGM) (Swiss).

Writing

(MOTION PICTURE STORY)
The Louisiana Story, Robert Flaherty, Lopert. Frances Flaherty and Robert Flaherty.
The Naked City, Hellinger, U-I. Malvin Wald.
Red River, Monterey Productions, UA. Borden Chase.
The Red Shoes, Rank-Archers, Eagle-Lion (British). Emeric Pressburger.
★ *The Search*, Praesens Films (MGM) (Swiss). Richard Schweizer and David Wechsler.

(SCREENPLAY)
A Foreign Affair, Paramount. Charles Brackett, Billy Wilder and Richard L. Breen.
Johnny Belinda, Warner Bros. Irmgard Von Cube and Allen Vincent.
The Search, Praesens Films (MGM) (Swiss). Richard Schweizer and David Wechsler.

The Snake Pit, 20th Century–Fox. Frank Partos and Millen Brand.
★ *Treasure of Sierra Madre*, Warner Bros. John Huston.

Cinematography

(BLACK-AND-WHITE)

A Foreign Affair, Paramount. Charles B. Lang, Jr.
I Remember Mama, RKO Radio. Nicholas Musuraca.
Johnny Belinda, Warner Bros. Ted McCord.
★ *The Naked City*, Hellinger, U-I. William Daniels.
Portrait of Jennie, The Selznick Studio. Joseph August.

(COLOR)

Green Grass of Wyoming, 20th Century–Fox. Charles G. Clarke.
★ *Joan of Arc*, Sierra Pictures, RKO Radio. Joseph Valentine, William V. Skall and Winton Hoch.
The Loves of Carmen, Beckworth Corporation, Columbia. William Snyder.
The Three Musketeers, MGM. Robert Planck.

Art Direction—Set Decoration

(BLACK-AND-WHITE)

★ *Hamlet*, Rank–Two Cities, U-I (British). Roger K. Furse; Carmen Dillon.
Johnny Belinda, Warner Bros. Robert Haas; William Wallace.

(COLOR)

Joan of Arc, Sierra Pictures, RKO Radio. Richard Day; Edwin Casey Roberts and Joseph Kish.
★ *The Red Shoes*, Rank-Archers, Eagle-Lion (British). Hein Heckroth; Arthur Lawson.

Sound Recording

Johnny Belinda, Warner Bros. Warner Bros. Sound Department.
Moonrise, Marshall Grant Prods., Republic. Republic Sound Department.
★ *The Snake Pit*, 20th Century–Fox. 20th Century–Fox Sound Department.

Music

(SONG)

★ "Buttons and Bows" (*The Paleface*, Paramount); Music and Lyrics by Jay Livingston and Ray Evans.
"For Every Man There's a Woman" (*Casbah*, Marston, U-I); Music by Harold Arlen. Lyrics by Leo Robin.
"It's Magic" (*Romance on the High Seas*, Warner Bros.); Music by Jule Styne. Lyrics by Sammy Cahn.
"This is the Moment" (*That Lady in Ermine*, 20th Century–Fox); Music by Frederick Hollander. Lyrics by Leo Robin.
"The Woody Woodpecker Song" (*Wet Blanket Policy*, Lantz, UA Cartoon); Music and Lyrics by Ramey Idriss and George Tibbles.

(SCORING OF A DRAMATIC OR COMEDY PICTURE)

Hamlet, Rank–Two Cities, U-I (British). William Walton.
Joan of Arc, Sierra Pictures, RKO Radio. Hugo Friedhofer.
Johnny Belinda, Warner Bros. Max Steiner.
★ *The Red Shoes*, Rank-Archers, Eagle-Lion (British). Brian Easdale.
The Snake Pit, 20th Century–Fox. Alfred Newman.

(SCORING OF A MUSICAL PICTURE)

★ *Easter Parade*, MGM. Johnny Green and Roger Edens.
The Emperor Waltz, Paramount. Victor Young.
The Pirate, MGM. Lennie Hayton.
Romance on the High Seas, Warner Bros. Ray Heindorf.
When My Baby Smiles at Me, 20th Century–Fox. Alfred Newman.

Film Editing

Joan of Arc, Sierra Pictures, RKO Radio. Frank Sullivan.
Johnny Belinda, Warner Bros. David Weisbart.
★ *The Naked City*, Hellinger, U-I. Paul Weatherwax.
Red River, Monterey Productions, UA. Christian Nyby.
The Red Shoes, Rank-Archers, Eagle-Lion (British). Reginald Mills.

Costume Design

(BLACK-AND-WHITE)

B. F.'s Daughter, MGM. Irene.
★ *Hamlet*, Rank–Two Cities, U-I, British. Roger K. Furse.

(COLOR)

The Emperor Waltz, Paramount. Edith Head and Gile Steele.
★ *Joan of Arc*, Sierra, RKO Radio Pictures. Dorothy Jeakins and Karinska.

Special Effects

Deep Waters, 20th Century–Fox. Visual: Ralph Hammeras, Fred Sersen and Edward Snyder. Audible: Roger Heman.
★ *Portrait of Jennie*, The Selznick Studio. Visual: Paul Eagler, J. McMillan Johnson, Russell Shearman and Clarence Slifer. Audible: Charles Freeman and James G. Stewart.

Short Subjects

(CARTOONS)

★ *The Little Orphan*, MGM (Tom & Jerry). Fred Quimby, producer.
Mickey and the Seal, Walt Disney, RKO Radio (Pluto). Walt Disney, producer.
Mouse Wreckers, Warner Bros. (Looney Tunes). Edward Selzer, producer.
Robin Hoodlum, United Productions of America, Columbia (Fox & Crow). United Productions of America, producer.
Tea for Two Hundred, Walt Disney, RKO Radio (Donald Duck). Walt Disney, producer.

(ONE-REEL)

Annie Was a Wonder, MGM (John Nesbitt Passing Parade). Herbert Moulton, producer.

Cinderella Horse, Warner Bros. (Sports Parade). Gordon Hollingshead, producer.

So You Want to Be on the Radio, Warner Bros. (Joe McDoakes). Gordon Hollingshead, producer.

★ *Symphony of a City,* 20th Century–Fox (Movietone Specialty). Edmund H. Reek, producer.

You Can't Win, MGM (Pete Smith Specialty). Pete Smith, producer.

(TWO-REEL)

Calgary Stampede, Warner Bros. (Technicolor Special). Gordon Hollingshead, producer.

Going to Blazes, MGM (Special). Herbert Morgan, producer.

Samba-Mania, Paramount (Musical Parade). Harry Grey, producer.

★ *Seal Island,* Walt Disney, RKO Radio (True Life Adventure Series). Walt Disney, producer.

Snow Capers, Universal-International (Special Series). Thomas Mead, producer.

Documentary

(SHORT SUBJECTS)

Heart to Heart, Fact Film Organization. Herbert Morgan, producer.

Operation Vittles, U.S. Army Air Force.

★ *Toward Independence,* U.S. Army

(FEATURES)

The Quiet One, Mayer-Burstyn. Janice Loeb, producer.

★ *The Secret Land,* U.S. Navy, MGM. O. O. Dull, producer.

Irving G. Thalberg Memorial Award

Jerry Wald.

Special Awards

Monsieur Vincent (French)—voted by the Academy Board of Governors as the most outstanding foreign language film released in the United States during 1948 (statuette).

Ivan Jandl for the outstanding juvenile performance of 1948 in *The Search* (miniature statuette).

Sid Grauman, master showman, who raised the standard of exhibition of motion pictures (statuette).

Adolph Zukor, a man who has been called the father of the feature film in America, for his services to the industry over a period of forty years (statuette).

Walter Wanger for distinguished service to the industry in adding to its moral stature in the world community by his production of the picture *Joan of Arc* (statuette).

Scientific or Technical

CLASS I (STATUETTE)

None.

CLASS II (PLAQUE)

Victor Caccialanza, Maurice Ayers and the Paramount Studio Set Construction Department for the development and application of "Paralite," a new lightweight plaster process for set construction.

Nick Kalten, Louis J. Witti and the 20th Century–Fox Studio Mechanical Effects Department for a process of preserving and flame-proofing foliage.

CLASS III (CITATION)

Marty Martin, Jack Lannon, Russell Shearman and the RKO Radio Studio Special Effects Department for the development of a new method of simulating falling snow on motion picture sets.

A. J. Moran and the Warner Bros. Studio Electrical Department for a method of remote control for shutters on motion picture arc lighting equipment.

Points of Interest

1. Nothing to it: José Ferrer nominated for film debut.

Rule Changes

1. New addition: "Costume Design."
2. The fewer the merrier: Original Screenplay dropped.
3. The name game: "Original Story" becomes "Motion Picture Story."

Eligible Films That Failed to Be Nominated for Best Picture

Portrait of Jennie, Red River, Fort Apache, Letter from an Unknown Woman, A Foreign Affair, The Lady from Shanghai, The Pirate, Unfaithfully Yours, The Paleface.

Eligible Songs That Failed to Be Nominated

"A Couple of Swells" (Irving Berlin)—*Easter Parade;* "It's a Most Unusual Day" (Jimmy McHugh and Harold Adamson)—*A Date with Judy;* "Steppin' Out with My Baby" (Irving Berlin)—*Easter Parade.*

1949

Picture

★ *All the King's Men,* Rossen, Columbia. Produced by Robert Rossen.

Battleground, MGM. Produced by Dore Schary.

The Heiress, Paramount. Produced by William Wyler.

A Letter to Three Wives, 20th Century–Fox. Produced by Sol C. Siegel.

12 O'Clock High, 20th Century–Fox. Produced by Darryl F. Zanuck.

Actor

★ Broderick Crawford in *All the King's Men* (Rossen, Columbia).
Kirk Douglas in *Champion* (Kramer, UA).
Gregory Peck in *12 O'Clock High* (20th Century–Fox).
Richard Todd in *The Hasty Heart* (Warner Bros.).
John Wayne in *Sands of Iwo Jima* (Republic).

Actress

Jeanne Crain in *Pinky* (20th Century–Fox).
★ Olivia de Havilland in *The Heiress* (Paramount).
Susan Hayward in *My Foolish Heart* (Goldwyn, RKO Radio).
Deborah Kerr in *Edward My Son* (MGM).
Loretta Young in *Come to the Stable* (20th Century–Fox).

Supporting Actor

John Ireland in *All the King's Men* (Rossen, Columbia).
★ Dean Jagger in *12 O'Clock High* (20th Century–Fox).
Arthur Kennedy in *Champion* (Kramer, UA).
Ralph Richardson in *The Heiress* (Paramount).
James Whitmore in *Battleground* (MGM).

Supporting Actress

Ethel Barrymore in *Pinky* (20th Century–Fox).
Celeste Holm in *Come to the Stable* (20th Century–Fox).
Elsa Lanchester in *Come to the Stable* (20th Century–Fox).
★ Mercedes McCambridge in *All the King's Men* (Rossen, Columbia).
Ethel Waters in *Pinky* (20th Century–Fox).

Director

★ Joseph L. Mankiewicz for *A Letter to Three Wives* (20th Century–Fox).
Carol Reed for *The Fallen Idol* (London Films, SRO) (British).
Robert Rossen for *All the King's Men* (Rossen, Columbia).
William A. Wellman for *Battleground* (MGM).
William Wyler for *The Heiress* (Paramount).

Writing

(MOTION PICTURE STORY)
Come to the Stable, 20th Century–Fox. Clare Booth Luce.
It Happens Every Spring, 20th Century–Fox. Shirley W. Smith and Valentine Davies.
Sands of Iwo Jima, Republic. Harry Brown.
★ *The Stratton Story*, MGM. Douglas Morrow.
White Heat, Warner Bros. Virginia Kellogg.

(SCREENPLAY)
All the King's Men, Rossen, Columbia. Robert Rossen.
The Bicycle Thief, De Sica, Mayer-Burstyn (Italian). Cesare Zavattini.
Champion, Kramer, UA. Carl Foreman.
The Fallen Idol, London Films, SRO (British). Graham Greene.
★ *A Letter to Three Wives*, 20th Century–Fox. Joseph L. Mankiewicz.

(STORY AND SCREENPLAY)
★ *Battleground*, MGM. Robert Pirosh.
Jolson Sings Again, Columbia. Sidney Buchman.
Paisan, Rossellini, Mayer-Burstyn (Italian). Alfred Hayes, Federico Fellini, Sergio Amidei, Marcello Pagliero and Roberto Rossellini.
Passport to Pimlico, Rank-Ealing, Eagle-Lion (British). T.E.B. Clarke.
The Quiet One, Film Documents, Mayer-Burstyn. Helen Levitt, Janice Loeb and Sidney Meyers.

Cinematography

(BLACK-AND-WHITE)
★ *Battleground*, MGM. Paul C. Vogel.
Champion, Kramer, UA. Frank Planer.
Come to the Stable, 20th Century–Fox. Joseph LaShelle.
The Heiress, Paramount. Leo Tover.
Prince of Foxes, 20th Century–Fox. Leon Shamroy.

(COLOR)
The Barkleys of Broadway, MGM. Harry Stradling.
Jolson Sings Again, Columbia. William Snyder.
Little Women, MGM. Robert Planck and Charles Schoenbaum.
Sand, 20th Century–Fox. Charles G. Clarke.
★ *She Wore a Yellow Ribbon*, Argosy, RKO Radio. Winton Hoch.

Art Direction—Set Decoration

(BLACK-AND-WHITE)
Come to the Stable, 20th Century–Fox. Lyle Wheeler and Joseph C. Wright; Thomas Little and Paul S. Fox.
★ *The Heiress*, Paramount. John Meehan and Harry Horner; Emile Kuri.
Madame Bovary, MGM. Cedric Gibbons and Jack Martin Smith; Edwin B. Willis and Richard A. Pefferle.

(COLOR)
Adventures of Don Juan, Warner Bros. Edward Carrere; Lyle Reifsnider.
★ *Little Women*, MGM. Cedric Gibbons and Paul Groesse; Edwin B. Willis and Jack D. Moore.
Saraband, Rank-Ealing, Eagle-Lion (British). Jim Morahan, William Kellner and Michael Relph.

Sound Recording

Once More, My Darling, U-I, Universal-International Sound Department.
Sands of Iwo Jima, Republic. Republic Sound Department.
★ *12 O'Clock High*, 20th Century–Fox. 20th Century–Fox Sound Department.

Music

(SONG)

★ "Baby, It's Cold Outside" (*Neptune's Daughter*, MGM); Music and Lyrics by Frank Loesser.

"It's a Great Feeling" (*It's a Great Feeling*, Warner Bros.); Music by Jule Styne. Lyrics by Sammy Cahn.

"Lavender Blue" (*So Dear to My Heart*, Disney, RKO Radio); Music by Eliot Daniel. Lyrics by Larry Morey.

"My Foolish Heart" (*My Foolish Heart*, Goldwyn, RKO Radio); Music by Victor Young. Lyrics by Ned Washington.

"Through a Long and Sleepless Night" (*Come to the Stable*, 20th Century–Fox); Music by Alfred Newman. Lyrics by Mack Gordon.

(SCORING OF A DRAMATIC OR COMEDY PICTURE)

Beyond the Forest, Warner Bros. Max Steiner.

Champion, Kramer, UA. Dimitri Tiomkin.

★ *The Heiress*, Paramount. Aaron Copland.

(SCORING OF A MUSICAL PICTURE)

Jolson Sings Again, Columbia. Morris Stoloff and George Duning.

Look for the Silver Lining, Warner Bros. Ray Heindorf.

★ *On the Town*, MGM. Roger Edens and Lennie Hayton.

Film Editing

All the King's Men, Rossen, Columbia. Robert Parrish and Al Clark.

Battleground, MGM. John Dunning.

★ *Champion*, Kramer, UA. Harry Gerstad.

Sands of Iwo Jima, Republic. Richard L. Van Enger.

The Window, RKO Radio. Frederic Knudtson.

Costume Design

(BLACK-AND-WHITE)

★ *The Heiress*, Paramount. Edith Head and Gile Steele.

Prince of Foxes, 20th Century–Fox. Vittorio Nino Novarese.

(COLOR)

★ *Adventures of Don Juan*, Warner Bros. Leah Rhodes, Travilla and Marjorie Best.

Mother Is a Freshman, 20th Century–Fox. Kay Nelson.

Special Effects

★ *Mighty Joe Young*, Cooper, RKO Radio.

Tulsa, Wanger, Eagle-Lion.

Short Subjects

(CARTOONS)

★ *For Scent-imental Reasons*, Warner Bros. (Looney Tunes). Edward Selzer, producer.

Hatch Up Your Troubles, MGM (Tom & Jerry). Fred Quimby, producer.

Magic Fluke, UPA, Columbia (Fox & Crow). Stephen Bosustow, producer.

Toy Tinkers, Disney, RKO Radio. Walt Disney, producer.

(ONE-REEL)

★ *Aquatic House-Party*, Paramount (Grantland Rice Sportlights). Jack Eaton, producer.

Roller Derby Girl, Paramount (Pacemaker). Justin Herman, producer.

So You Think You're Not Guilty, Warner Bros. (Joe McDoakes). Gordon Hollingshead, producer.

Spills and Chills, Warner Bros. (Black-and-White Sports Review). Walton C. Ament, producer.

Water Trix, MGM (Pete Smith Specialty). Pete Smith, producer.

(TWO-REEL)

Boy and the Eagle, RKO Radio. William Lasky, producer.

Chase of Death, Irving Allen Productions. Irving Allen, producer.

The Grass Is Always Greener, Warner Bros. Gordon Hollingshead, producer.

Snow Carnival, Warner Bros. Gordon Hollingshead, producer.

★ *Van Gogh*, Canton-Weiner. Gaston Dichl and Robert Haessens, producers.

Documentary

(SHORT SUBJECTS)

(*Note: Two winners this year.*)

★ *A Chance to Live*, March of Time, 20th Century–Fox. Richard de Rochemont, producer.

1848, A. F. Films, Inc. French Cinema General Cooperative, producer.

The Rising Tide, National Film Board of Canada. St. Francis-Xavier University (Nova Scotia), producer.

★ *So Much for So Little*, Warner Bros. Cartoons, Inc. Edward Selzer, producer.

(FEATURES)

★ *Daybreak in Udi*, British Information Services. Crown Film Unit, producer.

Kenji Comes Home, A Protestant Film Commission Prod. Paul F. Heard, producer.

Irving G. Thalberg Memorial Award

Not given this year.

Special Awards

The Bicycle Thief (Italian)—voted by the Academy Board of Governors as the most outstanding foreign language film released in the United States during 1949 (statuette).

Bobby Driscoll, as the outstanding juvenile actor of 1949 (miniature statuette).

Fred Astaire for his unique artistry and his contributions to the technique of musical pictures (statuette).

Cecil B. DeMille, distinguished motion picture pioneer, for thirty-seven years of brilliant showmanship (statuette).

Jean Hersholt for distinguished service to the motion-picture industry (statuette).

Scientific or Technical

CLASS I (STATUETTE)

Eastman Kodak Co. for the development and introduction of an improved safety base motion picture film.

CLASS II (PLAQUE)

None.

CLASS III (CITATION)

Loren L. Ryder, Bruce H. Denney, Robert Carr and the Paramount Studio Sound Department for the development and application of the supersonic playback and public address system.

M. B. Paul for the first successful large-area seamless translucent backgrounds.

Herbert Britt for the development and application of formulas and equipment producing artificial snow and ice for dressing motion-picture sets.

André Coutant and Jacques Mathot for the design of the Eclair Camerette.

Charles R. Daily, Steve Csillag and the Paramount Studio Engineering, Editorial and Music Departments for a new precision method of computing variable tempo-click tracks.

International Projector Corp. for a simplified and self-adjusting take-up device for projection machines.

Alexander Velcoff for the application to production of the infrared photographic evaluator.

Rule Changes

1. Back to the drawing board: Former "Original Screenplay" category returns as "Story and Screenplay."

Eligible Films That Failed to Be Nominated for Best Picture

She Wore a Yellow Ribbon, On the Town, The Fallen Idol, White Heat, They Live by Night, Gun Crazy.

1950

Picture

★ *All About Eve*, 20th Century–Fox. Produced by Darryl F. Zanuck.

Born Yesterday, Columbia. Produced by S. Sylvan Simon.

Father of the Bride, MGM. Produced by Pandro S. Berman.

King Solomon's Mines, MGM. Produced by Sam Zimbalist.

Sunset Boulevard, Paramount. Produced by Charles Brackett.

Actor

Louis Calhern in *The Magnificent Yankee* (MGM).

★ José Ferrer in *Cyrano de Bergerac* (Kramer, UA).

William Holden in *Sunset Boulevard* (Paramount).

James Stewart in *Harvey* (U-I).

Spencer Tracy in *Father of the Bride* (MGM).

Actress

Anne Baxter in *All About Eve* (20th Century–Fox).

Bette Davis in *All About Eve* (20th Century–Fox).

★ Judy Holliday in *Born Yesterday* (Columbia).

Eleanor Parker in *Caged* (Warner Bros.).

Gloria Swanson in *Sunset Boulevard* (Paramount).

Supporting Actor

Jeff Chandler in *Broken Arrow* (20th Century–Fox).

Edmund Gwenn in *Mister 880* (20th Century–Fox).

Sam Jaffe in *The Asphalt Jungle* (MGM).

★ George Sanders in *All About Eve* (20th Century–Fox).

Erich von Stroheim in *Sunset Boulevard* (Paramount).

Supporting Actress

Hope Emerson in *Caged* (Warner Bros.).

Celeste Holm in *All About Eve* (20th Century–Fox).

★ Josephine Hull in *Harvey* (U-I).

Nancy Olson in *Sunset Boulevard* (Paramount).

Thelma Ritter in *All About Eve* (20th Century–Fox).

Director

George Cukor for *Born Yesterday* (Columbia).

John Huston for *The Asphalt Jungle* (MGM).

★ Joseph L. Mankiewicz for *All About Eve* (20th Century–Fox).

Carol Reed for *The Third Man* (Selznick–London Films, SRO) (British).

Billy Wilder for *Sunset Boulevard* (Paramount).

Writing

(MOTION PICTURE STORY)

Bitter Rice, Lux Films (Italian). Giuseppe De Santis and Carlo Lizzani.

The Gunfighter, 20th Century–Fox. William Bowers and Andre de Toth.

Mystery Street, MGM. Leonard Spigelgass.

★ *Panic in the Streets*, 20th Century–Fox. Edna Anhalt and Edward Anhalt.

When Willie Comes Marching Home, 20th Century–Fox. Sy Gomberg.

(SCREENPLAY)

★ *All About Eve*, 20th Century–Fox. Joseph L. Mankiewicz.

The Asphalt Jungle, MGM. Ben Maddow and John Huston.

Born Yesterday, Columbia. Albert Mannheimer.

Broken Arrow, 20th Century–Fox. Michael Blankfort.

Father of the Bride, MGM. Frances Goodrich and Albert Hackett.

(STORY AND SCREENPLAY)

Adam's Rib, MGM. Ruth Gordon and Garson Kanin.
Caged, Warner Bros. Virginia Kellogg and Bernard C. Schoenfeld.
The Men, Kramer, UA. Carl Foreman.
No Way Out, 20th Century–Fox. Joseph L. Mankiewicz and Lesser Samuels.
★ *Sunset Boulevard*, Paramount. Charles Brackett, Billy Wilder and D.M. Marshman, Jr.

Cinematography

(BLACK-AND-WHITE)

All About Eve, 20th Century–Fox. Milton Krasner.
The Asphalt Jungle, MGM. Harold Rosson.
The Furies, Wallis, Paramount. Victor Milner.
Sunset Boulevard, Paramount John F. Seitz.
★ *The Third Man*, Selznick–London Films, SRO (British). Robert Krasker.

(COLOR)

Annie Get Your Gun, MGM. Charles Rosher.
Broken Arrow, 20th Century–Fox. Ernest Palmer.
The Flame and the Arrow, Norma-F.R., Warner Bros. Ernest Haller.
★ *King Solomon's Mines*, MGM. Robert Surtees.
Samson and Delilah, DeMille, Paramount. George Barnes.

Art Direction—Set Decoration

(BLACK-AND-WHITE)

All About Eve, 20th Century–Fox. Lyle Wheeler and George Davis; Thomas Little and Walter M. Scott.
The Red Danube, MGM. Cedric Gibbons and Hans Peters; Edwin B. Willis and Hugh Hunt.
★ *Sunset Boulevard*, Paramount. Hans Dreier and John Meehan; Sam Comer and Ray Moyer.

(COLOR)

Annie Get Your Gun, MGM. Cedric Gibbons and Paul Groesse; Edwin B. Willis and Richard A. Pefferle.
Destination Moon, Pal, Eagle-Lion. Ernst Fegte; George Sawley.
★ *Samson and Delilah*, DeMille, Paramount. Hans Dreier and Walter Tyler; Sam Comer and Ray Moyer.

Sound Recording

★ *All About Eve*, 20th Century–Fox. 20th Century–Fox Sound Department.
Cinderella, Disney, RKO Radio. Disney Sound Department.
Louisa, U-I. Universal-International Sound Department.
Our Very Own, Goldwyn, RKO Radio. Goldwyn Sound Department.
Trio, Rank–Sydney Box, Paramount (British).

Music

(SONG)

"Be My Love" (*The Toast of New Orleans*, MGM); Music by Nicholas Brodszky. Lyrics by Sammy Cahn.
"Bibbidy-Bobbidi-Boo" (*Cinderella*, Disney, RKO Radio); Music and Lyrics by Mack David, Al Hoffman and Jerry Livingston.
★ "Mona Lisa" (*Captain Carey, USA*, Paramount); Music and Lyrics by Ray Evans and Jay Livingston.
"Mule Train" (*Singing Guns*, Republic); Music and Lyrics by Fred Glickman, Hy Heath and Johnny Lange.
"Wilhelmina" (*Wabash Avenue*, 20th Century–Fox); Music by Josef Myrow. Lyrics by Mack Gordon.

(SCORING OF A DRAMATIC OR COMEDY PICTURE)

All About Eve, 20th Century–Fox. Alfred Newman.
The Flame and the Arrow, Norma-F.R., Warner Bros. Max Steiner.
No Sad Songs for Me, Columbia. George Duning.
Samson and Delilah, DeMille, Paramount. Victor Young.
★ *Sunset Boulevard*, Paramount. Franz Waxman.

(SCORING OF A MUSICAL PICTURE)

★ *Annie Get Your Gun*, MGM. Adolph Deutsch and Roger Edens.
Cinderella, Disney, RKO Radio. Oliver Wallace and Paul J. Smith.
I'll Get By, 20th Century–Fox. Lionel Newman.
Three Little Words, MGM. André Previn.
The West Point Story, Warner Bros. Ray Heindorf.

Film Editing

All About Eve, 20th Century–Fox. Barbara McLean.
Annie Get Your Gun, MGM. James E. Newcom.
★ *King Solomon's Mines*, MGM. Ralph E. Winters and Conrad A. Nervig.
Sunset Boulevard, Paramount. Arthur Schmidt and Doane Harrison.
The Third Man, Selznick–London Films, SRO (British). Oswald Hafenrichter.

Costume Design

(BLACK-AND-WHITE)

★ *All About Eve*, 20th Century–Fox. Edith Head and Charles LeMaire.
Born Yesterday, Columbia. Jean Louis.
The Magnificent Yankee, MGM. Walter Plunkett.

(COLOR)

The Black Rose, 20th Century–Fox. Michael Whittaker.
★ *Samson and Delilah*, DeMille, Paramount. Edith Head, Dorothy Jeakins, Elois Jenssen, Gile Steele and Gwen Wakeling.
That Forsyte Woman, MGM. Walter Plunkett and Valles.

Special Effects

★ *Destination Moon,* Pal. Eagle-Lion.
Samson and Delilah, DeMille. Paramount.

Short Subjects

(CARTOONS)

★ *Gerald McBoing-Boing,* UPA, Columbia (Jolly Frolics Series). Stephen Bosustow, executive producer.
Jerry's Cousin, MGM (Tom & Jerry). Fred Quimby, producer.
Trouble Indemnity, UPA, Columbia (Mr. Magoo Series). Stephen Bosustow, executive producer.

(ONE-REEL)

Blaze Busters, Warner Bros. (Vitaphone Novelties). Robert Youngson, producer.
★ *Grandad of Races,* Warner Bros. (Sports Parade). Gordon Hollingshead, producer.
Wrong Way Butch, MGM (Pete Smith Specialty). Pete Smith, producer.

(TWO-REEL)

Grandma Moses, Falcon Films, Inc., A.F. Films. Falcon Films, Inc., producer.
★ *In Beaver Valley,* Disney, RKO Radio (True-Life Adventures). Walt Disney, producer.
My Country 'Tis of Thee, Warner Bros. (Featurette Series). Gordon Hollingshead, producer.

Documentary

(SHORT SUBJECTS)

The Fight: Science Against Cancer, National Film Board of Canada in cooperation with the Medical Film Institute of the Association of American Medical Colleges.
The Stairs, Film Documents, Inc.
★ *Why Korea?,* 20th Century–Fox Movietone. Edmund Reek, producer.

(FEATURES)

★ *The Titan: Story of Michelangelo,* Michelangelo Co., Classics Pictures, Inc. Robert Snyder, producer.
With These Hands, Promotional Films Co., Inc. Jack Arnold and Lee Goodman, producers.

Irving G. Thalberg Memorial Award

Darryl F. Zanuck.

Honorary Awards

George Murphy for his services in interpreting the film industry to the country at large (statuette).
Louis B. Mayer for distinguished service to the motion picture industry (statuette).
The Walls of Malapaga (Franco-Italian)—voted by the Board of Governors as the most outstanding foreign language film released in the United States in 1950 (statuette).

Scientific or Technical

CLASS I (STATUETTE)

None.

CLASS II (PLAQUE)

James B. Gordon and the 20th Century–Fox Studio Camera Department for the design and development of a multiple image film viewer.
John Paul Livadary, Floyd Campbell, L.W. Russell and the Columbia Studio Sound Department for the development of a multitrack magnetic re-recording system.
Loren L. Ryder and the Paramount Studio Sound Department for the first studio-wide application of magnetic sound recording to motion picture production.

CLASS III (CITATION)

None.

Points of Interest

1. The family way: Each writing category had a husband-and-wife team competing—Edna and Edward Anhalt, Frances Goodrich and Albert Hackett, Ruth Gordon and Garson Kanin.
2. Fourteen and counting: *All About Eve* sets new record with fourteen nominations, topping *Gone With the Wind*'s thirteen.

Rule Changes

1. The name game: "Special Awards" now called "Honorary Awards."

Eligible Films That Failed to Be Nominated for Best Picture

Rules of the Game, Winchester '73, The Third Man, The Asphalt Jungle, Adam's Rib, Kind Hearts and Coronets, In a Lonely Place, Caged, The Fuller Brush Girl.

1951

Picture

★ *An American in Paris,* MGM. Produced by Arthur Freed.
Decision Before Dawn, 20th Century–Fox. Produced by Anatole Litvak and Frank McCarthy.
A Place in the Sun, Paramount. Produced by George Stevens.
Quo Vadis, MGM. Produced by Sam Zimbalist.
A Streetcar Named Desire, Feldman, Warner Bros. Produced by Charles K. Feldman.

Actor

★ Humphrey Bogart in *The African Queen* (Horizon, UA).
Marlon Brando in *A Streetcar Named Desire* (Feldman, Warner Bros.).
Montgomery Clift in *A Place in the Sun* (Paramount).
Arthur Kennedy in *Bright Victory* (U-I).
Frederic March in *Death of a Salesman* (Stanley Kramer, Columbia).

Actress

Katharine Hepburn in *The African Queen* (Horizon, UA).
★ Vivien Leigh in *A Streetcar Named Desire* (Feldman, Warner Bros.).
Eleanor Parker in *Detective Story* (Paramount).
Shelley Winters in *A Place in the Sun* (Paramount).
Jane Wyman in *The Blue Veil* (Wald-Krasna, RKO Radio).

Supporting Actor

Leo Genn in *Quo Vadis* (MGM).
★ Karl Malden in *A Streetcar Named Desire* (Feldman, Warner Bros.).
Kevin McCarthy in *Death of a Salesman* (Kramer, Columbia).
Peter Ustinov in *Quo Vadis* (MGM).
Gig Young in *Come Fill the Cup* (Warner Bros.).

Supporting Actress

Joan Blondell in *The Blue Veil* (Wald-Krasna, RKO Radio).
Mildred Dunnock in *Death of a Salesman* (Kramer, Columbia).
Lee Grant in *Detective Story* (Paramount).
★ Kim Hunter in *A Streetcar Named Desire* (Feldman, Warner Bros.).
Thelma Ritter in *The Mating Season* (Paramount).

Director

John Huston for *The African Queen* (Horizon, UA).
Elia Kazan for *A Streetcar Named Desire* (Feldman, Warner Bros.).
Vincente Minnelli for *An American in Paris* (MGM).
★ George Stevens for *A Place in the Sun* (Paramount).
William Wyler for *Detective Story* (Paramount).

Writing

(MOTION PICTURE STORY)

The Bullfighter and the Lady, Republic. Budd Boetticher and Ray Nazarro.
The Frogmen, Warner Bros. Oscar Millard.
Here Comes the Groom, Paramount. Robert Riskin and Liam O'Brian.
★ *Seven Days to Noon*, Boulting Bros., Mayer-Kingsley–Distinguished Films (British). Paul Dehn and James Bernard.
Teresa, MGM. Alfred Hayes and Stewart Stern.

(SCREENPLAY)

The African Queen, Horizon, UA. James Agee and John Huston.
Detective Story, Paramount. Philip Yordan and Robert Wyler.
La Ronde, Commercial Pictures (French). Jacques Natanson and Max Ophuls.
★ *A Place in the Sun*, Paramount. Michael Wilson and Harry Brown.
A Streetcar Named Desire, Feldman, Warner Bros. Tennessee Williams.

(STORY AND SCREENPLAY)

★ *An American in Paris*, MGM. Alan Jay Lerner.
The Big Carnival, Paramount. Billy Wilder, Lesser Samuels and Walter Newman.
David and Bathsheba, 20th Century–Fox. Philip Dunne.
Go for Broke! MGM. Robert Pirosh.
The Well, Popkin, UA. Clarence Greene and Russell Rouse.

Cinematography

(BLACK-AND-WHITE)

Death of a Salesman, Kramer, Columbia. Frank Planer.
The Frogmen, 20th Century–Fox. Norbert Brodine.
★ *A Place in the Sun*, Paramount. William C. Mellor.
Strangers on a Train, Warner Bros. Robert Burks.
A Streetcar Named Desire, Feldman, Warner Bros. Harry Stradling.

(COLOR)

★ *An American in Paris*, MGM. Alfred Gilks and John Alton.
David and Bathsheba, 20th Century–Fox. Leon Shamroy.
Quo Vadis, MGM. Robert Surtees and William V. Skall.
Show Boat, MGM. Charles Rosher.
When Worlds Collide, Pal, Paramount. John F. Seitz and W. Howard Greene.

Art Direction—Set Decoration

(BLACK-AND-WHITE)

Fourteen Hours, 20th Century–Fox. Lyle Wheeler and Leland Fuller; Thomas Little and Fred J. Rode.
House on Telegraph Hill, 20th Century–Fox. Lyle Wheeler and John DeCuir; Thomas Little and Paul S. Fox.
La Ronde, Commercial Pictures (French). D'Eaubonne.
★ *A Streetcar Named Desire*, Feldman, Warner Bros. Richard Day; George James Hopkins.
Too Young to Kiss, MGM. Cedric Gibbons and Paul Groesse; Edwin B. Willis and Jack D. Moore.

(COLOR)

★ *An American in Paris*, MGM. Cedric Gibbons and Preston Ames; Edwin B. Willis and Keogh Gleason.
David and Bathsheba, 20th Century–Fox. Lyle Wheeler and George Davis; Thomas Little and Paul S. Fox.
On the Riviera, 20th Century–Fox. Lyle Wheeler and Leland Fuller; Joseph C. Wright, Thomas Little and Walter M. Scott.

Quo Vadis, MGM. William A. Horning, Cedric Gibbons and Edward Carfagno; Hugh Hunt.

Tales of Hoffmann, Powell-Pressburger, Lopert (British) Hein Heckroth.

Sound Recording

Bright Victory, U-I. Leslie I. Carey, sound director.

★ *The Great Caruso*, MGM. Douglas Shearer, sound director.

I Want You, Goldwyn, RKO Radio. Gordon Sawyer, sound director.

A Streetcar Named Desire, Feldman, Warner Bros. Col. Nathan Levinson, sound director.

Two Tickets to Broadway, RKO Radio. John O. Aalberg, sound director.

Music

(SONG)

★ "In the Cool, Cool, Cool of the Evening" (*Here Comes the Groom*, Paramount); Music by Hoagy Carmichael. Lyrics by Johnny Mercer.

"A Kiss to Build a Dream On" (*The Strip*, MGM); Music and Lyrics by Bert Kalmar, Harry Ruby and Oscar Hammerstein II.

"Never" (*Golden Girl*, 20th Century–Fox); Music by Lionel Newman. Lyrics by Eliot Daniel.

"Too Late Now" (*Royal Wedding*, MGM); Music by Burton Lane. Lyrics by Alan Jay Lerner.

"Wonder Why" (*Rich, Young and Pretty*, MGM); Music by Nicholas Brodszky. Lyrics by Sammy Cahn.

(SCORING OF A DRAMATIC OR COMEDY PICTURE)

David and Bathsheba, 20th Century–Fox. Alfred Newman.

Death of a Salesman, Kramer, Columbia. Alex North.

★ *A Place in the Sun*, Paramount. Franz Waxman.

Quo Vadis, MGM. Miklos Rozsa.

A Streetcar Named Desire, Feldman, Warner Bros. Alex North.

(SCORING OF A MUSICAL PICTURE)

Alice in Wonderland, Disney, RKO Radio. Oliver Wallace.

★ *An American in Paris*, MGM. Johnny Green and Saul Chaplin.

The Great Caruso, MGM. Peter Herman Adler and Johnny Green.

On the Riviera, 20th Century–Fox. Alfred Newman.

Show Boat, MGM. Adolph Deutsch and Conrad Salinger.

Film Editing

An American in Paris, MGM. Adrienne Fazan.

Decision Before Dawn, 20th Century–Fox. Dorothy Spencer.

★ *A Place in the Sun*, Paramount, William Hornbeck.

Quo Vadis, MGM. Ralph E. Winters.

The Well, Popkin, UA. Chester Schaeffer.

Costume Design

(BLACK-AND-WHITE)

Kind Lady, Walter Plunkett and Gile Steele.

The Model and the Marriage Broker, 20th Century–Fox. Charles LeMaire and Renie.

The Mudlark, 20th Century–Fox. Edward Stevenson and Margaret Furse.

★ *A Place in the Sun*, Paramount. Edith Head.

A Streetcar Named Desire, Feldman. Warner Bros. Lucinda Ballard.

(COLOR)

★ *An American in Paris*, MGM. Orry-Kelly, Walter Plunkett and Irene Sharaff.

David and Bathsheba, 20th Century–Fox. Charles LeMaire and Edward Stevenson.

The Great Caruso, MGM. Helen Rose and Gile Steele.

Quo Vadis, MGM. Herschel McCoy.

Tales of Hoffmann, Powell-Pressburger, Lopert (British). Hein Heckroth.

Special Effects

★ *When Worlds Collide*, Pal, Paramount.

Short Subjects

(CARTOONS)

Lambert, The Sheepish Lion, Disney, RKO Radio (Special). Walt Disney, producer.

Rooty Toot Toot, UPA, Columbia (Jolly Frolics). Stephen Bosustow, executive producer.

★ *Two Mouseketeers*, MGM (Tom & Jerry). Fred Quimby, producer.

(ONE-REEL)

Ridin' the Rails, Paramount (Sportlights). Jack Eaton, producer.

The Story of Time, A Signal Films Production by Robert G. Leffingwell, Cornell Film Company (British).

★ *World of Kids*, Warner Bros. (Vitaphone Novelties). Robert Youngson, producer.

(TWO-REEL)

Balzac, Les Films Du Compass, A.F. Films, Inc. (French); Les Films Du Compass, producer.

Danger Under the Sea, U-I. Tom Mead, producer.

★ *Nature's Half Acre*, Disney, RKO Radio (True-Life Adventure). Walt Disney, producer.

Documentary

(SHORT SUBJECTS)

★ *Benjy*. Made by Fred Zinnemann with the cooperation of Paramount Pictures Corp. for the Los Angeles Orthopaedic Hospital.

One Who Came Back, Owen Crump, producer. (Film sponsored by the Disabled American Veterans, in cooperation with the United States Department of Defense and the Association of Motion Picture Producers.)

The Seeing Eye, Warner Bros. Gordon Hollingshead, producer.

(FEATURES)

I Was a Communist for the F.B.I., Warner Bros. Bryan Foy, producer.

★ *Kon-Tiki*, Artfilm Prod., RKO Radio (Norwegian). Olle Nordemar, producer.

Irving G. Thalberg Memorial Award

Arthur Freed.

Honorary Awards

Gene Kelly in appreciation of his versatility as an actor, singer, director and dancer, and specifically for his brilliant achievements in the art of choreography on film (statuette).

Rashomon (Japanese)—voted by the Board of Governors as the most outstanding foreign language film released in the United States during 1951 (statuette).

Scientific or Technical

CLASS I (STATUETTE)

None.

CLASS II (PLAQUE)

Gordon Jennings, S. L. Stancliffe and the Paramount Studio Special Photographic and Engineering Departments for the design, construction and application of a servo-operated recording and repeating device.

Olin L. Dupy of MGM Studio for the design, construction and application of a motion picture reproducing system.

Radio Corporation of America, Victor Division, for pioneering direct positive recording with anticipatory noise reduction.

CLASS III (CITATION)

Richard M. Haff, Frank P. Herrnfeld, Garland C. Misener and the Ansco Film Division of General Aniline and Film Corp. for the development of the Ansco color scene tester.

Fred Ponedel, Ralph Ayres and George Brown of Warner Bros. Studio for an air-driven water motor to provide flow, wake and white water for marine sequences in motion pictures.

Glen Robinson and the MGM Studio Construction Department for the development of a new music wire and cable cutter.

Jack Gaylord and the MGM Studio Construction Department for the development of balsa falling snow.

Carlos Rivas of MGM Studios for the development of an automatic magnetic film splicer.

Points of Interest

1. Nothing to it: Lee Grant nominated for film debut.
2. Slumming: Director Fred Zinnemann won Documentary Short Subject Award.

Rule Changes

1. A sometimes thing: Special Effects made an "other" Award, not necessarily given every year.

Eligible Films That Failed to Be Nominated for Best Picture

The African Queen, Strangers on a Train, Orpheus, The River, La Ronde, The Day the Earth Stood Still, The Thing.

Eligible Songs That Failed to Be Nominated

"Happy Trails" (Dale Evans)—*Pals of the Golden West;* "Silver Bells" (Jay Livingston and Ray Evans)—*The Lemon Drop Kid.*

1952

Picture

★ *The Greatest Show on Earth*, DeMille, Paramount. Produced by Cecil B. DeMille.

High Noon, Kramer, UA. Produced by Stanley Kramer.

Ivanhoe, MGM. Produced by Pandro S. Berman.

Moulin Rouge, Romulus, UA. Produced by John Huston.

The Quiet Man, Argosy, Republic. Produced by John Ford and Merian C. Cooper.

Actor

Marlon Brando in *Viva Zapata!* (20th Century–Fox).

★ Gary Cooper in *High Noon* (Kramer, UA).

Kirk Douglas in *The Bad and the Beautiful* (MGM).

José Ferrer in *Moulin Rouge* (Romulus, UA).

Alec Guinness in *The Lavender Hill Mob* (Rank-Ealing, U-I) (British).

Actress

★ Shirley Booth in *Come Back, Little Sheba* (Wallis, Paramount).

Joan Crawford in *Sudden Fear* (Kaufman, RKO Radio).

Bette Davis in *The Star* (Friedlob, 20th Century–Fox).

Julie Harris in *The Member of the Wedding* (Kramer, Columbia).

Susan Hayward in *With a Song in My Heart* (20th Century–Fox).

Supporting Actor

Richard Burton in *My Cousin Rachel* (20th Century–Fox).

Arthur Hunnicutt in *The Big Sky* (Winchester, RKO Radio).

Victor McLaglen in *The Quiet Man* (Argosy, Republic).

Jack Palance in *Sudden Fear* (Kaufman, RKO Radio).
★ Anthony Quinn in *Viva Zapata!* (20th Century–Fox).

Supporting Actress

★ Gloria Grahame in *The Bad and the Beautiful* (MGM).
Jean Hagen in *Singin' in the Rain* (MGM).
Colette Marchand in *Moulin Rouge* (Romulus, UA).
Terry Moore in *Come Back, Little Sheba* (Wallis, Paramount).
Thelma Ritter in *With a Song in My Heart* (20th Century–Fox).

Director

Cecil B. DeMille for *The Greatest Show on Earth* (DeMille, Paramount).
★ John Ford for *The Quiet Man* (Argosy, Republic).
John Huston for *Moulin Rouge* (Romulus, UA).
Joseph L. Mankiewicz for *Five Fingers* (20th Century–Fox).
Fred Zinnemann for *High Noon* (Stanley Kramer, UA).

Writing

(MOTION PICTURE STORY)

★ *The Greatest Show on Earth*, DeMille, Paramount. Frederic M. Frank, Theodore St. John and Frank Cavett.
My Son John, Rainbow, Paramount. Leo McCarey.
The Narrow Margin, RKO Radio. Martin Goldsmith and Jack Leonard.
The Pride of St. Louis, 20th Century–Fox. Guy Trosper.
The Sniper, Kramer, Columbia. Edna Anhalt and Edward Anhalt.

(SCREENPLAY)

★ *The Bad and the Beautiful*, MGM. Charles Schnee.
Five Fingers, 20th Century–Fox. Michael Wilson.
High Noon, Kramer UA. Carl Foreman.
The Man in the White Suit, Rank-Ealing, U-I (British). Roger MacDougall, John Dighton and Alexander Mackendrick.
The Quiet Man, Argosy, Republic. Frank S. Nugent.

(STORY AND SCREENPLAY)

The Atomic City, Paramount. Sydney Boehm.
Breaking the Sound Barrier, London Films, UA (British). Terence Rattigan.
★ *The Lavender Hill Mob*, Rank-Ealing, U-I (British). T.E.B. Clarke.
Pat and Mike, MGM. Ruth Gordon and Garson Kanin.
Viva Zapata!, 20th Century–Fox. John Steinbeck.

Cinematography

(BLACK-AND-WHITE)

★ *The Bad and the Beautiful*, MGM. Robert Surtees.
The Big Sky, Winchester, RKO Radio. Russell Harlan.
My Cousin Rachel, 20th Century–Fox. Joseph LaShelle.
Navajo, Bartlett-Foster, Lippert. Virgil E. Miller.
Sudden Fear, Kaufman, RKO Radio. Charles B. Lang, Jr.

(COLOR)

Hans Christian Andersen, Goldwyn, RKO Radio. Harry Stradling.
Ivanhoe, MGM. F.A. Young.
Million Dollar Mermaid, MGM. George J. Folsey.
★ *The Quiet Man*, Argosy, Republic. Winton C. Hoch and Archie Stout.
The Snows of Kilimanjaro, 20th Century–Fox. Leon Shamroy.

Art Direction—Set Decoration

(BLACK-AND-WHITE)

★ *The Bad and the Beautiful*, MGM. Cedric Gibbons and Edward Carfagno; Edwin B. Willis and Keogh Gleason.
Carrie, Paramount. Hal Pereira and Roland Anderson; Emile Kuri.
My Cousin Rachel, 20th Century–Fox. Lyle Wheeler and John DeCuir; Walter M. Scott.
Rashomon, RKO Radio (Japanese). Matsuyama H. Motsumoto.
Viva Zapata!, 20th Century–Fox. Lyle Wheeler and Leland Fuller; Thomas Little and Claude Carpenter.

(COLOR)

Hans Christian Andersen, Goldwyn. RKO Radio, Richard Day and Clave; Howard Bristol.
The Merry Widow, MGM. Cedric Gibbons and Paul Groesse; Edwin B. Willis and Arthur Krams.
★ *Moulin Rouge*, Romulus, U.A. Paul Sheriff; Marcel Vertes.
The Quiet Man, Argosy, Republic Frank Hotaling; John McCarthy, Jr. and Charles Thompson.
The Snows of Kilimanjaro, 20th Century–Fox. Lyle Wheeler and John Decuir; Thomas Little and Paul S. Fox.

Sound Recording

★ *Breaking the Sound Barrier*, London Films. UA (British). London Film Sound Department.
Hans Christian Andersen, Goldwyn, RKO Radio. Goldwyn Sound Department; Gordon Sawyer, sound director.
The Promoter, Rank-Neame, U-I (British). Pinewood Studios Sound Department.
The Quiet Man, Argosy, Republic. Republic Sound Department; Daniel J. Bloomberg, sound director.
With a Song in My Heart, 20th Century–Fox. 20th Century–Fox Sound Department; Thomas T. Moulton, sound director.

Music

(SONG)

"Am I in Love" (*Son of Paleface*, Paramount); Music and Lyrics by Jack Brooks.
"Because You're Mine" (*Because You're Mine*, MGM); Music by Nicholas Brodszky. Lyrics by Sammy Cahn.
★ "High Noon (Do Not Forsake Me, Oh My Darlin')" (*High*

Noon, Kramer, UA); Music by Dimitri Tiomkin. Lyrics by Ned Washington.

"Thumbelina" (*Hans Christian Andersen*. Goldwyn, RKO Radio); Music and Lyrics by Frank Loesser.

"Zing a Little Zong" (*Just for You*, Paramount); Music by Harry Warren. Lyrics by Leo Robin.

(SCORING OF A DRAMATIC OR COMEDY PICTURE)

★ *High Noon*, Kramer, UA. Dimitri Tiomkin.
Ivanhoe, MGM. Miklos Rozsa.
The Miracle of Our Lady of Fatima, Foy, Warner Bros. Max Steiner.
The Thief, Popkin, UA. Herschel Burke Gilbert.
Viva Zapata!, 20th Century–Fox. Alex North.

(SCORING OF A MUSICAL PICTURE)

Hans Christian Andersen, Goldwyn, RKO Radio. Walter Scharf.
The Jazz Singer, Warner Bros. Ray Heindorf and Max Steiner.
The Medium, Transfilm-Lopert (Italian). Gian-Carlo Menotti.
Singin' in the Rain, MGM. Lennie Hayton.
★ *With a Song in My Heart*, 20th Century–Fox. Alfred Newman.

Film Editing

Come Back, Little Sheba, Wallis, Paramount. Warren Low.
Flat Top, Monogram. William Austin.
The Greatest Show on Earth, DeMille, Paramount. Anne Bauchens.
★ *High Noon*, Kramer, UA. Elmo Williams and Harry Gerstad.
Moulin Rouge, Romulus, UA. Ralph Kemplen.

Costume Design

(BLACK-AND-WHITE)

Affair in Trinidad, Beckworth, Columbia. Jean Louis.
★ *The Bad and the Beautiful*, MGM. Helen Rose.
Carrie, Paramount. Edith Head.
My Cousin Rachel, 20th Century–Fox. Charles LeMaire and Dorothy Jeakins.
Sudden Fear, Kaufman, RKO Radio. Sheila O'Brien.

(COLOR)

The Greatest Show on Earth, DeMille, Paramount. Edith Head, Dorothy Jeakins and Miles White.
Hans Christian Andersen, Goldwyn, RKO Radio. Clave, Mary Wills and Madame Karinska.
The Merry Widow, MGM. Helen Rose and Gile Steele.
★ *Moulin Rouge*, Romulus. UA. Marcel Vertes.
With a Song in My Heart, 20th Century–Fox. Charles LeMaire.

Special Effects

★ *Plymouth Adventure*, MGM.

Short Subjects

(CARTOONS)

★ *Johann Mouse*, MGM (Tom & Jerry). Fred Quimby, producer.
Little Johnny Jet, MGM (MGM Series). Fred Quimby, producer.
Madeline, UPA, Columbia (Jolly Frolics). Stephen Bosustow, executive producer.
Pink and Blue Blues, UPA, Columbia (Mister Magoo). Stephen Bosustow, executive producer.
Romance of Transportation, National Film Board of Canada (Canadian). Tom Daly, producer.

(ONE-REEL)

Athletes of the Saddle, Paramount (Sportlights Series). Jack Eaton, producer.
Desert Killer, Warner Bros. (Sports Parade). Gordon Hollingshead, producer.
★ *Light in the Window*, Art Films Prods., 20th Century–Fox (Art Series). Boris Vermont, producer.
Neighbours, National Film Board of Canada (Canadian). Norman McLaren, producer.
Royal Scotland, Crown Film Unit, British Information Services (British).

(TWO-REEL)

Bridge of Time, London Film Prod., British Information Services (British).
Devil Take Us, Theatre of Life Prod. (Theatre of Life Series). Herbert Morgan, producer.
Thar She Blows!, Warner Bros. (Technicolor Special). Gordon Hollingshead, producer.
★ *Water Birds*, Disney, RKO Radio (True-Life Adventure). Walt Disney, producer.

Documentary

(SHORT SUBJECTS)

Devil Take Us, Theatre of Life Prod. Herbert Morgan, producer.
The Garden Spider (Epeira Diadema), Cristallo Films, I.F.E. Releasing Corp. (Italian). Alberto Ancilotto, producer.
Man Alive!, UPA for the American Cancer Society. Stephen Bosustow, executive producer.
★ *Neighbours*, National Film Board of Canada, Mayer-Kingsley, Inc. (Canadian). Norman McLaren, producer.

(FEATURES)

The Hoaxters, MGM. Dore Schary, producer.
Navajo, Bartlett-Foster Prod., Lippert Pictures, Inc. Hall Bartlett, producer.
★ *The Sea Around Us*, RKO Radio. Irwin Allen, producer.

Irving G. Thalberg Memorial Award

Cecil B. DeMille.

Honorary Awards

George Alfred Mitchell for the design and development of the camera which bears his name and for his continued and dominant presence in the field of cinematography (statuette).

Joseph M. Schenck for long and distinguished service to the motion picture industry (statuette).

Merian C. Cooper for his many innovations and contributions to the art of motion pictures (statuette).

Harold Lloyd, master comedian and good citizen (statuette).

Bob Hope for his contribution to the laughter of the world, his service to the motion picture industry, and his devotion to the American premise (statuette).

Forbidden Games (French)—Best Foreign Language Film first released in the United States during 1952 (statuette).

Scientific or Technical

CLASS I (STATUETTE)

Eastman Kodak Co. for the introduction of Eastman color negative and Eastman color print film.

Ansco Division, General Aniline and Film Corp., for the introduction of Ansco color negative and Ansco color print film.

CLASS II (PLAQUE)

Technicolor Motion Picture Corp. for an improved method of color motion picture photography under incandescent light.

CLASS III (CITATION)

Projection, Still Photographic and Development Engineering Departments of MGM Studio for an improved method of projecting photographic backgrounds.

John G. Frayne and R.R. Scoville and Westrex Corp. for a method of measuring distortion in sound reproduction.

Photo Research Corp. for creating the Spectra color temperature meter.

Gustav Jirouch for the design of the Robot automatic film splicer.

Carlos Rivas of MGM Studio for the development of a sound reproducer for magnetic film.

Points of Interest

1. Nothing to it: Julie Harris nominated for film debut. Richard Burton and Colette Marchand nominated for first American films. Shirley Booth wins Best Actress for film debut.
2. The family way: Best Supporting Actor Anthony Quinn married to daughter of Best Picture and Thalberg Award winner Cecil B. DeMille.
3. Slumming: 1935 Best Actor winner Victor McLaglen nominated for Supporting Actor.

Eligible Films That Failed to Be Nominated for Best Picture

Singin' in the Rain, The Bad and the Beautiful, Rancho Notorious, The Man in the White Suit, The Lavender Hill Mob, Pat and Mike, Bend of the River.

Eligible Songs That Failed to Be Nominated

"Angel Eyes" (Matt Dennis)—*Jennifer;* "Make 'Em Laugh" (Arthur Freed and Nacio Herb Brown)—*Singin' in the Rain;* "No Two People" (Frank Loesser)—*Hans Christian Andersen.*

1953

Picture

★ *From Here to Eternity,* Columbia. Produced by Buddy Adler.
Julius Caesar, MGM. Produced by John Houseman.
The Robe, 20th Century–Fox. Produced by Frank Ross.
Roman Holiday, Paramount. Produced by William Wyler.
Shane, Paramount. Produced by George Stevens.

Actor

Marlon Brando in *Julius Caesar* (MGM).
Richard Burton in *The Robe* (20th Century–Fox).
Montgomery Clift in *From Here to Eternity* (Columbia).
★ William Holden in *Stalag 17* (Paramount).
Burt Lancaster in *From Here to Eternity* (Columbia).

Actress

Leslie Caron in *Lili* (MGM).
Ava Gardner in *Mogambo (MGM).*
★ Audrey Hepburn in *Roman Holiday* (Paramount).
Deborah Kerr in *From Here to Eternity* (Columbia).
Maggie McNamara in *The Moon Is Blue* (Preminger-Herbert, UA).

Supporting Actor

Eddie Albert in *Roman Holiday* (Paramount).
Brandon de Wilde in *Shane* (Paramount).
Jack Palance in *Shane* (Paramount).
★ Frank Sinatra in *From Here to Eternity* (Columbia).
Robert Strauss in *Stalag 17* (Paramount).

Supporting Actress

Grace Kelly in *Mogambo* (MGM).
Geraldine Page in *Hondo* (Wayne-Fellows, Warner Bros.).
Marjorie Rambeau in *Torch Song* (MGM).
★ Donna Reed in *From Here to Eternity* (Columbia).
Thelma Ritter in *Pickup on South Street* (20th Century–Fox).

Director

George Stevens for *Shane* (Paramount).
Charles Walters for *Lili* (MGM).
Billy Wilder for *Stalag 17* (Paramount).
William Wyler for *Roman Holiday* (Paramount).
★ Fred Zinnemann for *From Here to Eternity* (Columbia).

Writing

(MOTION PICTURE STORY)

Above and Beyond, MGM. Beirne Lay, Jr.
The Captain's Paradise, London Films, Lopert-UA (British). Alec Coppel.
Hondo, Wayne-Fellows, Warner Bros. (Writer Louis L'Amour ineligible for nomination under Academy by laws.)
Little Fugitive, Burstyn Releasing. Ray Ashley, Morris Engel and Ruth Orkin.
★ *Roman Holiday*, Paramount. Ian McLellan Hunter. (Later accredited to Dalton Trumbo.)

(SCREENPLAY)

The Cruel Sea, Rank-Ealing, U-I (British). Eric Ambler.
★ *From Here to Eternity*, Columbia. Daniel Taradash.
Lili, MGM. Helen Deutsch.
Roman Holiday, Paramount. Ian McLellan Hunter and John Dighton.
Shane, Paramount. A.B. Guthrie, Jr.

(STORY AND SCREENPLAY)

The Band Wagon, MGM. Betty Comden and Adolph Green.
The Desert Rats, 20th Century–Fox. Richard Murphy.
The Naked Spur, MGM. Sam Rolfe and Harold Jack Bloom.
Take the High Ground, MGM. Millard Kaufman.
★ *Titanic*, 20th Century–Fox. Charles Brackett, Walter Reisch and Richard Breen.

Cinematography

(BLACK-AND-WHITE)

The Four Poster, Kramer, Columbia. Hal Mohr.
★ *From Here to Eternity*, Columbia. Burnett Guffey.
Julius Caesar, MGM. Joseph Ruttenberg.
Martin Luther, Louis de Rochemont Assocs. Joseph C. Brun.
Roman Holiday, Paramount. Frank Planer and Henry Alekan.

(COLOR)

All the Brothers Were Valiant, MGM. George Folsey.
Beneath the 12 Mile Reef, 20th Century–Fox. Edward Cronjager.
Lili, MGM. Robert Planck.
The Robe, 20th Century–Fox. Leon Shamroy.
★ *Shane*, Paramount. Loyal Griggs.

Art Direction—Set Decoration

(BLACK-AND-WHITE)

★ *Julius Caesar*, MGM. Cedric Gibbons and Edward Carfagno; Edwin B. Willis and Hugh Hunt.
Martin Luther, Louis de Rochemont Assocs. Fritz Maurischat and Paul Markwitz.
The President's Lady, 20th Century–Fox. Lyle Wheeler and Leland Fuller; Paul S. Fox.
Roman Holiday, Paramount. Hal Pereira and Walter Tyler.
Titanic, 20th Century–Fox. Lyle Wheeler and Maurice Ransford; Stuart Reiss.

(COLOR)

Knights of the Round Table, MGM. Alfred Junge and Hans Peters; John Jarvis.
Lili, MGM. Cedric Gibbons and Paul Groesse; Edwin B. Willis and Arthur Krams.
★ *The Robe*, 20th Century–Fox. Lyle Wheeler and George W. Davis; Walter M. Scott and Paul S. Fox.
The Story of Three Loves, MGM. Cedric Gibbons, Preston Ames, Edward Carfagno and Gabriel Scognamillo; Edwin B. Willis, Keogh Gleason, Arthur Krams and Jack D. Moore.
Young Bess, MGM. Cedric Gibbons and Urie McCleary; Edwin B. Willis and Jack D. Moore.

Sound Recording

Calamity Jane, Warner Bros. Warner Bros. Sound Department; William A. Mueller, sound director.
★ *From Here to Eternity*, Columbia. Columbia Sound Department; John P. Livadary, sound director.
Knights of the Round Table, MGM. MGM Sound Department; A.W. Watkins, sound director.
Mississippi Gambler, U-I. Universal-International Sound Department; Leslie I. Carey, sound director.
War of the Worlds, Pal, Paramount. Paramount Sound Department; Loren L. Ryder, sound director.

Music

(SONG)

"The Moon Is Blue" (*The Moon Is Blue*, Preminger-Herbert, UA); Music by Herschel Burke Gilbert. Lyrics by Sylvia Fine.
"My Flaming Heart" (*Small Town Girl*, MGM); Music by Nicholas Brodszky. Lyrics by Leo Robin.
"Sadie Thompson's Song (Blue Pacific Blues)" (*Miss Sadie Thompson*, Beckworth, Columbia); Music by Lester Lee. Lyrics by Ned Washington.
★ "Secret Love" (*Calamity Jane*, Warner Bros.); Music by Sammy Fain. Lyrics by Paul Francis Webster.
"That's Amore" (*The Caddy*, Paramount); Music by Harry Warren. Lyrics by Jack Brooks.

(SCORING OF A DRAMATIC OR COMEDY PICTURE)

Above and Beyond, MGM. Hugo Friedhofer.
From Here to Eternity, Columbia. Morris Stoloff and George Duning.
Julius Caesar, MGM. Miklos Rozsa.
★ *Lili*, MGM. Bronislau Kaper.
This Is Cinerama, Cinerama Prods. Corp. Louis Forbes.

(SCORING OF A MUSICAL PICTURE)

The Band Wagon, MGM. Adolph Deutsch.
Calamity Jane, Warner Bros. Ray Heindorf.
★ *Call Me Madam*, 20th Century–Fox. Alfred Newman.

5,000 Fingers of Dr. T., Kramer, Columbia. Frederick Hollander and Morris Stoloff.
Kiss Me Kate, MGM. André Previn and Saul Chaplin.

Film Editing

Crazylegs, Bartlett, Republic. Irvine (Cotton) Warburton.
★ *From Here to Eternity*, Columbia. William Lyon.
The Moon Is Blue, Preminger-Herbert, UA. Otto Ludwig.
Roman Holiday, Paramount. Robert Swink.
War of the Worlds, Pal, Paramount. Everett Douglas.

Costume Design

(BLACK-AND-WHITE)
The Actress, MGM. Walter Plunkett.
Dream Wife, MGM. Helen Rose and Herschel McCoy.
From Here to Eternity, Columbia. Jean Louis.
The President's Lady, 20th Century–Fox. Charles LeMaire and Renie.
★ *Roman Holiday*, Paramount. Edith Head.

(COLOR)
The Band Wagon, MGM. Mary Ann Nyberg.
Call Me Madam, 20th Century–Fox. Irene Sharaff.
How to Marry a Millionaire, 20th Century–Fox. Charles LeMaire and Travilla.
★ *The Robe*, 20th Century–Fox. Charles LeMaire and Emile Santiago.
Young Bess, MGM. Walter Plunkett.

Special Effects

★ *War of the Worlds*, Pal, Paramount.

Short Subjects

(CARTOONS)
Christopher Crumpet, UPA, Columbia (Jolly Frolics). Stephen Bosustow, producer.
From A to Z-Z-Z-Z, Warner Bros. (Looney Tunes). Edward Selzer, producer.
Rugged Bear, Disney, RKO Radio (Donald Duck). Walt Disney, producer.
The Tell-Tale Heart, UPA, Columbia (UPA Cartoon Special). Stephen Bosustow, producer.
★ *Toot, Whistle, Plunk and Boom*, Disney, Buena Vista (Special Music Series). Walt Disney, producer.

(ONE-REEL)
Christ Among the Primitives, IFE Releasing Corp. (Italian). Vincenzo Lucci-Chiarissi, producer.
Herring Hunt, National Film Board of Canada, RKO Pathé, Inc. (Canadian). (Canada Carries On Series).
Joy of Living, Art Film Prods., 20th Century–Fox (Art Film Series). Boris Vermont, producer.
★ *The Merry Wives of Windsor Overture*, MGM (Overture Series). Johnny Green, producer.
Wee Water Wonders, Paramount (Grantland Rice Sportlights Series). Jack Eaton, producer.

(TWO-REEL)
★ *Bear Country*, Disney, RKO Radio (True-Life Adventure). Walt Disney, producer.
Ben and Me, Disney, Buena Vista (Cartoon Special Series). Walt Disney, producer.
Return to Glennascaul, Dublin Gate Theatre Prod., Mayer-Kingsley Inc.
Vesuvius Express, 20th Century–Fox (CinemaScope Shorts Series). Otto Lang, producer.
Winter Paradise, Warner Bros. (Technicolor Special). Cedric Francis, producer.

Documentary

(SHORT SUBJECTS)
★ *The Alaskan Eskimo*, Disney, RKO Radio. Walt Disney, producer.
The Living City, Encyclopaedia Britannica Films, Inc. John Barnes, producer.
Operation Blue Jay, U.S. Army Signal Corps.
They Planted a Stone, World Wide Pictures, British Information Services (British). James Carr, producer.
The Word, 20th Century–Fox. John Healy and John Adams, producers.

(FEATURES)
The Conquest of Everest, Countryman Films Ltd. and Group 3 Ltd., UA (British). John Taylor, Leon Clore and Grahame Tharp, producers.
★ *The Living Desert*, Disney, Buena Vista. Walt Disney, producer.
A Queen Is Crowned, J. Arthur Rank Organization, Ltd., U-I (British). Castleton Knight, producer.

Irving G. Thalberg Memorial Award

George Stevens.

Honorary Awards

Pete Smith for his witty and pungent observations on the American scene in his series of "Pete Smith Specialties" (statuette).

20th Century–Fox Film Corporation in recognition of their imagination, showmanship and foresight in introducing the revolutionary process known as CinemaScope (statuette).

Joseph I. Breen for his conscientious, open-minded and dignified management of the Motion Picture Production Code (statuette).

Bell and Howell Company for their pioneering and basic achievements in the advancement of the motion picture industry (statuette).

Scientific or Technical

CLASS I (STATUETTE)
Professor Henri Chretien and Earl Sponable, Sol Halprin, Lorin Grignon, Herbert Bragg and Carl Faulkner of 20th Century–Fox Studios for creating, developing and engi-

neering the equipment, processes and techniques known as CinemaScope.

Fred Waller for designing and developing the multiple photographic and projection systems which culminated in Cinerama.

CLASS II (PLAQUE)

Reeves Soundcraft Corp. for their development of a process of applying stripes of magnetic oxide to motion picture film for sound recording and reproduction.

CLASS III (CITATION)

Westrex Corp. for the design and construction of a new film editing machine.

Points of Interest

1. Nothing to it: Maggie McNamara nominated for film debut.
2. The family way: Ava Gardner and husband Frank Sinatra both nominated.
3. Slumming: Oscar-winning composer and music arranger Johnny Green wins One-reel Short Subject Award.
4. Another king of the mountain: *From Here to Eternity* ties *Gone With the Wind* for most Academy Awards—eight.

Eligible Films That Failed to Be Nominated for Best Picture

Gentlemen Prefer Blondes, The Band Wagon, Lili, The Big Heat, Stalag 17, Pickup on South Street, The Naked Spur.

Eligible Song That Failed to Be Nominated

"That's Entertainment" (Arthur Schwartz and Howard Dietz)—*The Band Wagon.*

1954

Picture

The Caine Mutiny, Kramer, Columbia. Produced by Stanley Kramer.

The Country Girl, Perlberg-Seaton, Paramount. Produced by William Perlberg.

★ *On the Waterfront,* Horizon-American, Columbia. Produced by Sam Spiegel.

Seven Brides for Seven Brothers, MGM. Produced by Jack Cummings.

Three Coins in the Fountain, 20th Century–Fox. Produced by Sol C. Siegel.

Actor

Humphrey Bogart in *The Caine Mutiny* (Kramer, Columbia).

★ Marlon Brando in *On the Waterfront* (Horizon-American, Columbia).

Bing Crosby in *The Country Girl* (Perlberg-Seaton, Paramount).

James Mason in *A Star Is Born* (Transcona, Warner Bros.).

Dan O'Herlihy in *Adventures of Robinson Crusoe* (Dancigers-Ehrlich, UA).

Actress

Dorothy Dandridge in *Carmen Jones* (Preminger, 20th Century–Fox).

Judy Garland in *A Star Is Born* (Transcona, Warner Bros.).

Audrey Hepburn in *Sabrina* (Paramount).

★ Grace Kelly in *The Country Girl* (Perlberg-Seaton, Paramount).

Jane Wyman in *Magnificent Obsession* (Universal-International).

Supporting Actor

Lee J. Cobb in *On the Waterfront* (Horizon-American, Columbia).

Karl Malden in *On the Waterfront* (Horizon-American, Columbia).

★ Edmond O'Brien in *The Barefoot Contessa* (Figaro, UA).

Rod Steiger in *On the Waterfront* (Horizon-American, Columbia).

Tom Tully in *The Caine Mutiny* (Kramer, Columbia).

Supporting Actress

Nina Foch in *Executive Suite* (MGM).

Katy Jurado in *Broken Lance* (20th Century–Fox).

★ Eva Maria Saint in *On the Waterfront* (Horizon-American, Columbia).

Jan Sterling in *The High and the Mighty* (Wayne-Fellows, Warner Bros.).

Claire Trevor in *The High and the Mighty* (Wayne-Fellows, Warner Bros.).

Director

Alfred Hitchcock for *Rear Window* (Patron, Inc., Paramount).

★ Elia Kazan for *On the Waterfront* (Horizon, Columbia).

George Seaton for *The Country Girl* (Perlberg-Seaton, Paramount).

William Wellman for *The High and the Mighty* (Wayne-Fellows, Warner Bros.).

Billy Wilder for *Sabrina* (Paramount).

Writing

(MOTION PICTURE STORY)

Bread, Love and Dreams, Titanus, I.F.E. Releasing Corp. (Italian). Ettore Margadonna.

★ *Broken Lance,* 20th Century–Fox. Philip Yordan.

Forbidden Games, Times Film Corp. (French). François Boyer.
Night People, 20th Century–Fox. Jed Harris and Tom Reed.
There's No Business Like Show Business, 20th Century–Fox. Lamar Trotti.

(SCREENPLAY)
The Caine Mutiny, Kramer, Columbia. Stanley Roberts.
★ *The Country Girl*, Perlberg-Seaton, Paramount. George Seaton.
Rear Window, Patron, Inc., Paramount. John Michael Hayes.
Sabrina, Paramount. Billy Wilder, Samuel Taylor and Ernest Lehman.
Seven Brides for Seven Brothers, MGM. Albert Hackett, Frances Goodrich and Dorothy Kingsley.

(STORY AND SCREENPLAY)
The Barefoot Contessa, Figaro, UA. Joseph Mankiewicz.
Genevieve, Rank-Sirius, U-I (British). William Rose.
The Glenn Miller Story, U-I. Valentine Davies and Oscar Brodney.
Knock on Wood, Dena Prods., Paramount. Norman Panama and Melvin Frank.
★ *On the Waterfront*, Horizon-American, Columbia. Budd Schulberg.

Cinematography
(BLACK-AND-WHITE)
The Country Girl, Perlberg-Seaton, Paramount. John F. Warren.
Executive Suite, MGM. George Folsey.
★ *On the Waterfront*, Horizon-American, Columbia. Boris Kaufman.
Rogue Cop, MGM. John Seitz.
Sabrina, Paramount. Charles Lang, Jr.

(COLOR)
The Egyptian, 20th Century–Fox. Leon Shamroy.
Rear Window, Patron, Inc., Paramount. Robert Burks.
Seven Brides for Seven Brothers, MGM. George Folsey.
The Silver Chalice, Saville, Warner Bros. William V. Skall.
★ *Three Coins in the Fountain*, 20th Century–Fox. Milton Krasner.

Art Direction—Set Decoration
(BLACK-AND-WHITE)
The Country Girl, Perlberg-Seaton, Paramount. Hal Pereira and Roland Anderson; Sam Comer and Grace Gregory.
Executive Suite, MGM. Cedric Gibbons and Edward Carfagno; Edwin B. Willis and Emile Kuri.
Le Plaisir, Meyer-Kingsley (French). Max Ophuls.
★ *On the Waterfront*, Horizon-American, Columbia. Richard Day.
Sabrina, Paramount. Hal Pereira and Walter Tyler; Sam Comer and Ray Moyer.

(COLOR)
Brigadoon, MGM. Cedric Gibbons and Preston Ames; Edwin B. Willis and Keogh Gleason.
Desirée, 20th Century–Fox. Lyle Wheeler and Leland Fuller; Walter M. Scott and Paul S. Fox.
Red Garters, Paramount. Hal Pereira and Roland Anderson; Sam Comer and Ray Moyer.
A Star Is Born, Trenscona, Warner Bros. Malcolm Bert, Gene Allen and Irene Sharaff; George James Hopkins.
★ *20,000 Leagues Under the Sea*, Disney, Buena Vista. John Meehan; Emile Kuri.

Sound Recording
Brigadoon, MGM. Wesley C. Miller, sound director.
The Caine Mutiny, Columbia. John P. Livadary, sound director.
★ *The Glenn Miller Story*, U-I. Leslie I. Carey, sound director.
Rear Window, Patron, Inc., Paramount. Loren L. Ryder, sound director.
Susan Slept Here, RKO Radio. John O. Aalberg, sound director.

Music
(SONG)
"Count Your Blessings Instead of Sheep" (*White Christmas*, Paramount); Music and Lyrics by Irving Berlin.
"The High and the Mighty" (*The High and the Mighty*, Wayne-Fellows, Warner Bros.); Music by Dimitri Tiomkin. Lyrics by Ned Washington.
"Hold My Hand" (*Susan Slept Here*, RKO Radio); Music and Lyrics by Jack Lawrence and Richard Myers.
"The Man That Got Away" (*A Star Is Born*, Transcona, Warner Bros.); Music by Harold Arlen. Lyrics by Ira Gershwin.
★ "Three Coins in the Fountain" (*Three Coins in the Fountain*, 20th Century–Fox); Music by Jule Styne. Lyrics by Sammy Cahn.

(SCORING OF A DRAMATIC OR COMEDY PICTURE)
The Caine Mutiny, Kramer, Columbia. Max Steiner.
Genevieve, Rank-Sirus, U-I (British). Muir Mathieson.
★ *The High and the Mighty*, Wayne-Fellows, Warner Bros. Dimitri Tiomkin.
On the Waterfront, Horizon-American, Columbia. Leonard Bernstein.
The Silver Chalice, Saville, Warner Bros. Franz Waxman.

(SCORING OF A MUSICAL PICTURE)
Carmen Jones, Preminger, 20th Century–Fox. Herschel Burke Gilbert.
The Glenn Miller Story, U-I. Joseph Gershenson and Henry Mancini.
★ *Seven Brides for Seven Brothers*, MGM. Adolph Deutsch and Saul Chaplin.
A Star Is Born, Transcona, Warner Bros. Ray Heindorf.

There's No Business Like Show Business, 20th Century–Fox. Alfred Newman and Lionel Newman.

Film Editing

The Caine Mutiny, Kramer, Columbia. William A. Lyon and Henry Batista.

The High and the Mighty, Wayne-Fellows, Warner Bros. Ralph Dawson.

★ *On the Waterfront*, Horizon-American, Columbia. Gene Milford.

Seven Brides for Seven Brothers, MGM. Ralph E. Winters.

20,000 Leagues Under the Sea, Disney, Buena Vista. Elmo Williams.

Costume Design

(BLACK-AND-WHITE)

The Earrings of Madame De . . . , Arlan Pictures (French). Georges Annenkov and Rosine Delamare.

Executive Suite, MGM. Helen Rose.

Indiscretion of an American Wife, DeSica, Columbia. Christian Dior.

It Should Happen to You, Columbia. Jean Louis.

★ *Sabrina*, Paramount. Edith Head.

(COLOR)

Brigadoon, MGM. Irene Sharaff.

Desirée, 20th Century–Fox. Charles LeMaire and Rene Hubert.

★ *Gate of Hell*, Daiel, Edward Harrison (Japanese). Sanzo Wada.

A Star Is Born, Transcona, Warner Bros. Jean Louis, Mary Ann Nyberg and Irene Sharaff.

There's No Business Like Show Business, 20th Century–Fox. Charles LeMaire, Travilla and Miles White.

Special Effects

Hell and High Water, 20th Century–Fox.

Them!, Warner Bros.

★ *20,000 Leagues Under the Sea*, Walt Disney Studios.

Short Subjects

(CARTOONS)

Crazy Mixed Up Pup, Lantz, U-I. Walter Lantz, producer.

Pigs Is Pigs, Disney, RKO Radio. Walt Disney, producer.

Sandy Claws, Warner Bros. Edward Selzer, producer.

Touché, Pussy Cat, MGM. Fred Quimby, producer.

★ *When Magoo Flew*, UPA, Columbia. Stephen Bosustow, producer.

(ONE-REEL)

The First Piano Quartette, 20th Century–Fox. Otto Lang, producer.

The Strauss Fantasy, MGM. Johnny Green, producer.

★ *This Mechanical Age*, Warner Bros. Robert Youngson, producer.

(TWO-REEL)

Beauty and the Bull, Warner Bros. Cedric Francis, producer.

Jet Carrier, 20th Century–Fox. Otto Lang, producer.

Siam, Disney, Buena Vista. Walt Disney, producer.

★ *A Time Out of War*, Carnival Prods., Denis and Terry Sanders, producers.

Documentary

(SHORT SUBJECTS)

Jet Carrier, 20th Century–Fox. Otto Lang, producer.

Rembrandt: A Self-Portrait, Distributors Corp. of America. Morrie Roizman, producer.

★ *Thursday's Children*, British Information Services (British). World Wide Pictures and Morse Films, producers.

(FEATURES)

The Stratford Adventure, National Film Board of Canada, Continental (Canadian). Guy Glover, producer.

★ *The Vanishing Prairie*, Disney, Buena Vista. Walt Disney, producer.

Irving G. Thalberg Memorial Award

Not given this year.

Honorary Awards

Bausch & Lomb Optical Company for their contributions to the advancement of the motion picture industry (statuette).

Kemp R. Niver for the development of the Renovare Process which has made possible the restoration of the Library of Congress Paper Film Collection (statuette).

Greta Garbo for her unforgettable screen performances (statuette).

Danny Kaye for his unique talents, his service to the Academy, the motion picture industry, and the American people (statuette).

Jon Whiteley for his outstanding juvenile performance in *The Little Kidnappers* (miniature statuette).

Vincent Winter for his outstanding performance in *The Little Kidnappers* (miniature statuette).

Gate of Hell (Japanese)—Best Foreign Language Film first released in the United States during 1954 (statuette).

Scientific or Technical

CLASS I (STATUETTE)

Paramount Pictures Inc., Loren L. Ryder, John R. Bishop and all the members of the technical and engineering staff for developing a method of producing and exhibiting motion pictures known as VistaVision.

CLASS II (PLAQUE)

None.

CLASS III (CITATION)

David S. Horsley and the Universal-International Studio Special Photographic Department for a portable remote control device for process projectors.

Karl Freund and Frank Crandell of Photo Research Corp. for the design and development of a direct reading brightness meter.

Wesley C. Miller, J.W. Stafford, K.M. Frierson and the MGM Studio Sound Department for an electronic sound printing comparison device.

John P. Livadary, Lloyd Russell and the Columbia Studio Sound Department for an improved limiting amplifier as applied to sound level comparison devices.

Roland Miller and Max Goeppinger of the Magnascope Corp. for the design and development of a cathode ray magnetic sound track viewer.

Carlos Rivas, G.M. Sprague and the MGM Studio Sound Department for the design of a magnetic sound editing machine.

Fred Wilson of the Samuel Goldwyn Studio Sound Department for the design of a variable multiple-band equalizer.

P.C. Young of the MGM Studio Projection Department for the practical application of a variable focal length attachment to motion picture projector lenses.

Fred Knoth and Orien Ernest of the Universal-International Studio Technical Department for the development of a hand portable, electric, dry oil-fog machine.

Points of Interest

1. Three on a match: Three actors from one film—Lee J. Cobb, Karl Malden and Rod Steiger of *On the Waterfront*—nominated in same category.
2. Yet another king: *On the Waterfront* ties *Gone With the Wind* and *From Here to Eternity* for most Academy Awards—eight.

Rule Changes

1. The more the merrier: After being an "other" Award for three years, "Special Effects" becomes a regular category.

Eligible Films That Failed to Be Nominated for Best Picture

Johnny Guitar, The Earrings of Madame De . . . , Magnificent Obsession, A Star Is Born, Sabrina, The Wild One, Beat the Devil, Rear Window, Carmen Jones.

1955

Picture

Love Is a Many-Splendored Thing, 20th Century–Fox. Produced by Buddy Adler.

★ *Marty*, Hecht-Lancaster, UA. Produced by Harold Hecht.

Mister Roberts, Orange, Warner Bros. Produced by Leland Hayward.

Picnic, Columbia. Produced by Fred Kohlmar.

The Rose Tattoo, Wallis, Paramount. Produced by Hal Wallis.

Actor

★ Ernest Borgnine in *Marty* (Hecht-Lancaster, UA).

James Cagney in *Love Me or Leave Me* (MGM).

James Dean in *East of Eden* (Warner Bros.).

Frank Sinatra in *The Man With the Golden Arm* (Preminger, UA).

Spencer Tracy in *Bad Day at Black Rock* (MGM).

Actress

Susan Hayward in *I'll Cry Tomorrow* (MGM).

Katharine Hepburn in *Summertime* (Lopert-Lean, UA) (Anglo-American).

Jennifer Jones in *Love Is a Many-Splendored Thing* (20th Century–Fox).

★ Anna Magnani in *The Rose Tattoo* (Wallis, Paramount).

Eleanor Parker in *Interrupted Melody* (MGM).

Supporting Actor

Arthur Kennedy in *Trial* (MGM).

★ Jack Lemmon in *Mister Roberts* (Orange, Warner Bros.).

Joe Mantell in *Marty* (Hecht-Lancaster, UA).

Sal Mineo in *Rebel Without a Cause* (Warner Bros.).

Arthur O'Connell in *Picnic* (Columbia).

Supporting Actress

Betsy Blair in *Marty* (Hecht-Lancaster, UA).

Peggy Lee in *Pete Kelly's Blues* (Mark VII, Warner Bros.).

Marisa Pavan in *The Rose Tattoo* (Wallis, Paramount).

★ Jo Van Fleet in *East of Eden* (Warner Bros.).

Natalie Wood in *Rebel Without a Cause* (Warner Bros.).

Director

Elia Kazan for *East of Eden* (Warner Bros.).

David Lean for *Summertime* (Lopert-Lean, UA) (Anglo-American).

Joshua Logan for *Picnic* (Columbia).

★ Delbert Mann for *Marty* (Hecht-Lancaster, UA).

John Sturges for *Bad Day at Black Rock* (MGM).

Writing

(MOTION PICTURE STORY)

★ *Love Me or Leave Me*, MGM. Daniel Fuchs.

The Private War of Major Benson, U-I. Joe Connelly and Bob Mosher.
Rebel Without a Cause, Warner Bros. Nicholas Ray.
The Sheep Has 5 Legs, U.M.P.O. (French). Jean Marsan, Henry Troyat, Jacques Perret, Henri Verneuil and Raoul Ploquin.
Strategic Air Command, Paramount. Beirne Lay, Jr.

(SCREENPLAY)
Bad Day at Black Rock, MGM. Millard Kaufman.
Blackboard Jungle, MGM. Richard Brooks.
East of Eden, Warner Bros. Paul Osborn.
Love Me or Leave Me, MGM. Daniel Fuchs and Isobel Lennart.
★ *Marty,* Hecht-Lancaster, UA. Paddy Chayefsky.

(STORY AND SCREENPLAY)
The Court-Martial of Billy Mitchell, United States Pictures, Warner Bros. Milton Sperling and Emmet Lavery.
★ *Interrupted Melody,* MGM. William Ludwig and Sonya Levien.
It's Always Fair Weather, MGM. Betty Comden and Adolph Green.
Mr. Hulot's Holiday, GBD International Releasing (French). Jacques Tati and Henri Marquet
The Seven Little Foys, Hope Enterprises, Inc., and Scribe Prods., Paramount. Melville Shavelson and Jack Rose.

Cinematography

(BLACK-AND-WHITE)
Blackboard Jungle, MGM. Russell Harlan.
I'll Cry Tomorrow, MGM. Arthur E. Arling.
Marty, Hecht-Lancaster, UA. Joseph LaShelle.
Queen Bee, Columbia. Charles Lang.
★ *The Rose Tattoo,* Wallis, Paramount. James Wong Howe.

(COLOR)
Guys and Dolls, Goldwyn, MGM. Harry Stradling.
Love Is a Many-Splendored Thing, 20th Century–Fox. Leon Shamroy.
A Man Called Peter, 20th Century–Fox. Harold Lipstein.
Oklahoma!, Hornblow, Magna Corp. Robert Surtees.
★ *To Catch a Thief,* Hitchcock, Paramount. Robert Burks.

Art Direction—Set Decoration

(BLACK-AND-WHITE)
Blackboard Jungle, MGM. Cedric Gibbons and Randall Duell; Edwin B. Willis and Henry Grace.
I'll Cry Tomorrow, MGM. Cedric Gibbons and Malcolm Brown; Edwin B. Willis and Hugh B. Hunt.
The Man With the Golden Arm, Preminger, UA. Joseph C. Wright; Darrell Silvera.
Marty, Hecht-Lancaster, UA. Edward S. Haworth and Walter Simonds; Robert Priestley.
★ *The Rose Tattoo,* Wallis, Paramount. Hal Pereira and Tambi Larsen; Sam Comer and Arthur Krams.

(COLOR)
Daddy Long Legs, 20th Century–Fox. Lyle Wheeler and John DeCuir; Walter M. Scott and Paul S. Fox.
Guys and Dolls, Goldwyn, MGM. Oliver Smith and Joseph C. Wright; Howard Bristol.
Love Is a Many-Splendored Thing, 20th Century–Fox. Lyle Wheeler and George W. Davis; Walter M. Scott and Jack Stubbs.
★ *Picnic,* Columbia. William Flannery and Jo Mielziner; Robert Priestley.
To Catch a Thief, Hitchcock, Paramount. Hal Pereira and Joseph McMillan Johnson; Sam Comer and Arthur Krams.

Sound Recording

Love Is a Many-Splendored Thing, 20th Century–Fox. Carl W. Faulkner, sound director.
Love Me or Leave Me, MGM. Wesley C. Miller, sound director.
Mister Roberts, Warner Bros. William A. Mueller, sound director.
Not As a Stranger, Kramer UA. RCA Sound Department; Watson Jones, sound director.
★ *Oklahoma!,* Hornblow, Magna. Todd-AO Sound Department; Fred Hynes, sound director.

Music

(SONG)
"I'll Never Stop Loving You" (*Love Me or Leave Me,* MGM); Music by Nicholas Brodszky. Lyrics by Sammy Cahn.
★ "Love Is a Many-Splendored Thing" (*Love Is a Many-Splendored Thing,* 20th Century–Fox); Music by Sammy Fain. Lyrics by Paul Francis Webster.
"Something's Gotta Give" (*Daddy Long Legs,* 20th Century–Fox); Music and Lyrics by Johnny Mercer.
"(Love Is) The Tender Trap" (*The Tender Trap,* MGM); Music by James Van Heusen. Lyrics by Sammy Cahn.
"Unchained Melody" (*Unchained,* Bartlett, Warner Bros.); Music by Alex North. Lyrics by Hy Zaret.

(SCORING OF A DRAMATIC OR COMEDY PICTURE)
Battle Cry, Warner Bros. Max Steiner.
★ *Love Is a Many-Splendored Thing,* 20th Century–Fox. Alfred Newman.
The Man With the Golden Arm, Preminger, UA. Elmer Bernstein.
Picnic, Columbia. George Duning.
The Rose Tattoo, Wallis, Paramount. Alex North.

(SCORING OF A MUSICAL PICTURE)
Daddy Long Legs, 20th Century–Fox. Alfred Newman.
Guys and Dolls, Goldwyn, MGM. Jay Blackton and Cyril J. Mockridge.
It's Always Fair Weather, MGM. André Previn.
Love Me or Leave Me, MGM. Percy Faith and George Stoll.

★ *Oklahoma!*, Hornblow, Magna Corp. Robert Russell Bennett, Jay Blackton and Adolph Deutsch.

Film Editing

Blackboard Jungle, MGM. Ferris Webster.

The Bridges at Toko-Ri, Perlberg-Seaton, Paramount. Alma Macrorie.

Oklahoma!, Hornblow, Magna Corp. Gene Ruggiero and George Boemler.

★ *Picnic*, Columbia. Charles Nelson and William A. Lyon.

The Rose Tattoo, Wallis, Paramount. Warren Low.

Costume Design

(BLACK-AND-WHITE)

★ *I'll Cry Tomorrow*, MGM. Helen Rose.

The Pickwick Papers, Renown, Kingsley International (British). Beatrice Dawson.

Queen Bee, Columbia. Jean Louis.

The Rose Tattoo, Wallis, Paramount. Edith Head.

Ugetsu, Datei, Edward Harrison Releasing (Japanese). Tadaoto Kainoscho.

(COLOR)

Guys and Dolls, Goldwyn, MGM. Irene Sharaff.

Interrupted Melody, MGM. Helen Rose.

★ *Love Is a Many-Splendored Thing*, 20th Century–Fox. Charles LeMaire.

To Catch a Thief, Hitchcock, Paramount. Edith Head.

The Virgin Queen, 20th Century–Fox. Charles LeMaire and Mary Wills.

Special Effects

★ *The Bridges at Toko-Ri*, Paramount.

The Dam Busters, Associated British Picture Corp., Ltd., Warner Bros. (British).

The Rains of Ranchipur, 20th Century–Fox.

Short Subjects

(CARTOONS)

Good Will to Men, MGM. Fred Quimby, William Hanna and Joseph Barbera, producers.

The Legend of Rock-A-Bye Point, Lantz, U-I. Walter Lantz, producer.

No Hunting, Disney, RKO Radio. Walt Disney, producer.

★ *Speedy Gonzales*, Warner Bros. Edward Selzer, producer.

(ONE-REEL)

Gadgets Galore, Warner Bros. Robert Youngson, producer.

★ *Survival City*, 20th Century–Fox. Edmund Reek, producer.

3rd Ave. El, Carson Davidson Prods., Ardee Films. Carson Davidson, producer.

Three Kisses, Paramount. Justin Herman, producer.

(TWO-REEL)

The Battle of Gettysburg, MGM. Dore Schary, producer.

★ *The Face of Lincoln*, University of Southern California, Cavalcade Pictures. Wilbur T. Blume, producer.

On the Twelfth Day . . ., Go Pictures, George Brest & Assocs. George K. Arthur, producer.

Switzerland, Disney, Buena Vista. Walt Disney, producer.

24 Hour Alert, Warner Bros. Cedric Francis, producer.

Documentary

(SHORT SUBJECTS)

The Battle of Gettysburg, MGM. Dore Schary, producer.

The Face of Lincoln, University of Southern California, Cavalcade Pictures. Wilbur T. Blume, producer.

★ *Men Against the Arctic*, Disney, Buena Vista. Walt Disney, producer.

(FEATURES)

Heartbreak Ridge, René Risacher Prod., Tudor Pictures (French). René Risacher, producer.

★ *Helen Keller in Her Story*, Nancy Hamilton Presentation. Nancy Hamilton, producer.

Irving G. Thalberg Memorial Award

Not given this year.

Honorary Award

Samurai, The Legend of Musashi (a.k.a. *The Seven Samurai*) (Japanese)—Best Foreign Language Film first released in the United States during 1955 (statuette).

Scientific or Technical

CLASS I (STATUETTE)

National Carbon Co. for the development and production of a high-efficiency yellow flame carbon for motion picture color photography.

CLASS II (PLAQUE)

Eastman Kodak Co. for Eastman Tri-X panchromatic negative film.

Farciot Edouart, Hal Corl and the Paramount Studio Transparency Dept. for the engineering and development of a double-frame, triple-head background projector.

CLASS III (CITATION)

20th Century–Fox Studio and Bausch & Lomb Co. for the new combination lenses for CinemaScope photography.

Walter Jolley, Maurice Larson and R.H. Spies of 20th Century–Fox Studio for a spraying process which creates simulated metallic surfaces.

Steve Krilanovich for an improved camera dolly incorporating multi-directional steering.

Dave Anderson of 20th Century–Fox Studio for an improved spotlight capable of maintaining a fixed circle of light at constant intensity over varied distances.

Loren L. Ryder, Charles West, Henry Fracker and Paramount Studio for a projection film index to establish proper framing for various aspect ratios.

Farciot Edouart, Hal Corl and the Paramount Studio Transparency Department for an improved dual stereopticon background projector.

Points of Interest

1. Nothing to it: Jo Van Fleet, Director Delbert Mann, Screenwriter Paddy Chayefsky, and Cartoon star Speedy Gonzales win for film debuts. Best Actress Anna Magnani wins for first English-language film.
2. Gone but not forgotten: James Dean becomes second posthumous acting nominee.
3. Getting the jump on Patty Duke: Helen Keller wins in Documentary Feature category as star of *Helen Keller in Her Story*.

Rule Changes

1. You, too, can win a statuette: Set Decorators now receive Oscars, not plaques.

Eligible Films That Failed to Be Nominated for Best Picture

Rebel Without a Cause; East of Eden; The Night of the Hunter; To Catch a Thief; It's Always Fair Weather; Kiss Me Deadly; Ugetsu; Bad Day at Black Rock; The Wages of Fear; The Seven Year Itch; The Phenix City Story; Blackboard Jungle; Female on the Beach.

Eligible Songs That Failed to Be Nominated

"Baby, You Knock Me Out" (André Previn, Betty Comden and Adolph Green)—*It's Always Fair Weather,* "Ballad of Davy Crockett" (George Bruns and Tom Blackburn)—*Davy Crockett, King of the Wild Frontier*—"I Like Myself" (André Previn, Betty Comden and Adolph Green)—*It's Always Fair Weather.*

1956

Picture

★ *Around the World in 80 Days,* Todd, UA. Produced by Michael Todd.
Friendly Persuasion, Allied Artists. Produced by William Wyler.
Giant, Warner Bros. Produced by George Stevens and Henry Ginsberg.
The King and I, 20th Century–Fox. Produced by Charles Brackett.
The Ten Commandments, DeMille, Paramount. Produced by Cecil B. DeMille.

Actor

★ Yul Brynner in *The King and I* (20th Century–Fox).
James Dean in *Giant* (Warner Bros.).
Kirk Douglas in *Lust for Life* (MGM).
Rock Hudson in *Giant* (Warner Bros.).
Sir Laurence Olivier in *Richard III* (Laurence Olivier Prod., Lopert Films) (British).

Actress

Carroll Baker in *Baby Doll* (Newtown, Warner Bros.).
★ Ingrid Bergman in *Anastasia* (20th Century–Fox).
Katharine Hepburn in *The Rainmaker* (Wallis, Paramount).
Nancy Kelly in *The Bad Seed* (Warner Bros.).
Deborah Kerr in *The King and I* (20th Century–Fox).

Supporting Actor

Don Murray in *Bus Stop* (20th Century–Fox).
Anthony Perkins in *Friendly Persuasion* (Allied Artists).
★ Anthony Quinn in *Lust for Life* (MGM).
Mickey Rooney in *The Bold and the Brave* (Filmakers Releasing Org., RKO Radio).
Robert Stack in *Written on the Wind* (U-I).

Supporting Actress

Mildred Dunnock in *Baby Doll* (Newtown, Warner Bros.).
Eileen Heckart in *The Bad Seed* (Warner Bros.).
Mercedes McCambridge in *Giant* (Warner Bros.).
Patty McCormack in *The Bad Seed* (Warner Bros.).
★ Dorothy Malone in *Written on the Wind* (U-I).

Director

Michael Anderson for *Around the World in 80 Days* (Todd, UA).
Walter Lang for *The King and I* (20th Century–Fox).
★ George Stevens for *Giant* (Warner Bros.).
King Vidor for *War and Peace* (Ponti-De Laurentiis, Paramount) (Italo-American).
William Wyler for *Friendly Persuasion* (Allied Artists).

Writing

(MOTION PICTURE STORY)

★ *The Brave One,* King Bros., RKO Radio. Robert Rich (a.k.a. Dalton Trumbo).
The Eddy Duchin Story, Columbia. Leo Katcher.
High Society, Allied Artists. Edward Bernds and Elwood Ullman (withdrawn from final ballot).
The Proud and the Beautiful, Kingsley International (French). Jean-Paul Sartre.
Umberto D., Harrison & Davidson Releasing (Italian). Cesare Zavattini.

(SCREENPLAY—ADAPTED)

★ *Around the World in 80 Days,* Todd, UA. James Poe, John Farrow and S.J. Perelman.
Baby Doll, Newtown, Warner Bros. Tennessee Williams.
Giant, Warner Bros. Fred Guiol and Ivan Moffat.

Lust for Life, MGM. Norman Corwin.

Friendly Persuasion, Allied Artists. (Writer Michael Wilson ineligible for nomination under Academy bylaws.)

(SCREENPLAY—ORIGINAL)

The Bold and the Brave, Filmakers Releasing Org., RKO Radio. Robert Lewin.

Julie, Arwin, MGM. Andrew L. Stone.

La Strada, Ponti-De Laurentiis, Trans-Lux Dist. Corp. (Italian). Federico Fellini and Tullio Pinelli.

The Lady Killers, Ealing, Continental Dist. (British). William Rose.

★ *The Red Balloon*, Lopert Films (French). Albert Lamorisse.

Cinematography

(BLACK-AND-WHITE)

Baby Doll, Newtown, Warner Bros. Boris Kaufman.

The Bad Seed, Warner Bros. Hal Rosson.

The Harder They Fall, Columbia. Burnett Guffey.

★ *Somebody Up There Likes Me*, MGM. Joseph Ruttenberg.

Stagecoach to Fury, Regal Films, 20th Century–Fox. Walter Strenge.

(COLOR)

★ *Around the World in 80 Days*, Todd, UA. Lionel Lindon.

The Eddy Duchin Story, Columbia. Harry Stradling.

The King and I, 20th Century–Fox. Leon Shamroy.

The Ten Commandments, DeMille. Paramount. Loyal Griggs.

War and Peace, Ponti-De Laurentiis, Paramount (Italo-American). Jack Cardiff.

Art Direction—Set Decoration

(BLACK-AND-WHITE)

The Magnificent Seven (a.k.a. *Samurai*), Toho. Kingsley International (Japanese). Takashi Matsuyama.

The Proud and the Profane, Perlberg-Seaton, Paramount. Hal Pereira and A. Earl Hedrick; Samuel M. Comer and Frank R. McKelvy.

The Solid Gold Cadillac, Columbia. Ross Bellah; William R. Kiernan and Louis Diage.

★ *Somebody Up There Likes Me*, MGM. Cedric Gibbons and Malcolm F. Brown; Edwin B. Willis and F. Keogh Gleason.

Teenage Rebel, 20th Century–Fox. Lyle R. Wheeler and Jack Martin Smith; Walter M. Scott and Stuart A. Reiss.

(COLOR)

Around the World in 80 Days, Todd, UA. James W. Sullivan and Ken Adam; Ross J. Dowd.

Giant, Warner Bros. Boris Leven; Ralph S. Hurst.

★ *The King and I*, 20th Century–Fox. Lyle R. Wheeler and John DeCuir; Walter M. Scott and Paul S. Fox.

Lust for Life, MGM. Cedric Gibbons, Hans Peters and Preston Ames. Edwin B. Willis and F. Keogh Gleason.

The Ten Commandments, DeMille, Paramount. Hal Pereira, Walter H. Tyler and Albert Nozaki; Sam M. Comer and Ray Moyer.

Sound Recording

The Brave One, King Bros., RKO Radio. John Myers, sound director.

The Eddy Duchin Story, Columbia. Columbia Studio Sound Department; John Livadary, sound director.

Friendly Persuasion, Allied Artists. Westrex Sound Services, Inc.; Gordon R. Glennan, sound director; and Samuel Goldwyn Studio Sound Department; Gordon Sawyer, sound director.

★ *The King and I*, 20th Century–Fox. 20th Century–Fox Studio Sound Department; Carl Faulkner, sound director.

The Ten Commandments, DeMille, Paramount. Paramount Studio Sound Department; Loren L. Ryder, sound director.

Music

(SONG)

"Friendly Persuasion (Thee I Love)" (*Friendly Persuasion*, Allied Artists); Music by Dimitri Tiomkin. Lyrics by Paul Francis Webster.

"Julie" (*Julie*, Arwin, MGM); Music by Leith Stevens. Lyrics by Tom Adair.

"True Love" (*High Society*; Siegel, MGM); Music and Lyrics by Cole Porter.

★ "Whatever Will Be, Will Be (Que Será, Será)" (*The Man Who Knew Too Much*, Filwite Prods., Paramount); Music and Lyrics by Jay Livingston and Ray Evans.

"Written on the Wind" (*Written on the Wind*, U-I); Music by Victor Young. Lyrics by Sammy Cahn.

(SCORING OF A DRAMATIC OR COMEDY PICTURE)

Anastasia, 20th Century–Fox. Alfred Newman.

★ *Around the World in 80 Days*, Todd, UA. Victor Young.

Between Heaven and Hell, 20th Century–Fox. Hugo Friedhofer.

Giant, Warner Bros. Dimitri Tiomkin.

The Rainmaker, Wallis, Paramount. Alex North.

(SCORING OF A MUSICAL PICTURE)

The Best Things in Life Are Free, 20th Century–Fox. Lionel Newman.

The Eddy Duchin Story, Columbia. Morris Stoloff and George Duning.

High Society, Siegel, MGM. Johnny Green and Saul Chaplin.

★ *The King and I*, 20th Century–Fox. Alfred Newman and Ken Darby.

Meet Me in Las Vegas, MGM. George Stoll and Johnny Green.

Film Editing

★ *Around the World in 80 Days*, Todd, UA. Gene Ruggiero and Paul Weatherwax.

The Brave One, King Bros., RKO Radio. Merrill G. White.

Giant, Warner Bros. William Hornbeck, Philip W. Anderson and Fred Bohanan.
Somebody Up There Likes Me, MGM. Albert Akst.
The Ten Commandments, DeMille, Paramount. Anne Bauchens.

Costume Design

(BLACK-AND-WHITE)

The Magnificent Seven (a.k.a. *Samurai*), Toho, Kingsley International (Japanese). Kohei Ezaki.
The Power and the Prize, MGM. Helen Rose.
The Proud and Profane, Perlberg-Seaton, Paramount. Edith Head.
★ *The Solid Gold Cadillac,* Columbia. Jean Louis.
Teenage Rebel, 20th Century–Fox. Charles LeMaire and Mary Wills.

(COLOR)

Around the World in 80 Days, Todd, UA. Miles White.
Giant, Warner Bros. Moss Mabry and Marjorie Best.
★ *The King and I,* 20th Century–Fox. Irene Sharaff.
The Ten Commandments, DeMille, Paramount. Edith Head, Ralph Jester, John Jensen, Dorothy Jeakins and Arnold Friberg.
War and Peace, Ponti-De Laurentiis, Paramount (Italo-American). Marie De Matteis.

Special Effects

Forbidden Planet, MGM. A. Arnold Gillespie, Irving Ries and Wesley C. Miller.
★ *The Ten Commandments,* DeMille, Paramount. John Fulton.

Short Subjects

(CARTOONS)

Gerald McBoing-Boing on Planet Moo, UPA, Columbia. Stephen Bosustow, producer.
The Jaywalker, UPA, Columbia. Stephen Bosustow, producer.
★ *Mister Magoo's Puddle Jumper,* UPA, Columbia. Stephen Bosustow, producer.

(ONE-REEL)

★ *Crashing the Water Barrier,* Warner Bros. Konstantin Kalser, producer.
I Never Forget a Face, Warner Bros. Robert Youngson, producer.
Time Stood Still, Warner Bros. Cedric Francis, producer.

(TWO-REEL)

★ *The Bespoke Overcoat,* Romulus Films, George K. Arthur, producer.
Cow Dog, Disney, Buena Vista. Larry Lansburgh, producer.
The Dark Wave, 20th Century–Fox. John Healy, producer.
Samoa, Disney, Buena Vista. Walt Disney, producer.

Documentary

(SHORT SUBJECTS)

A City Decides, Charles Guggenheim & Assocs.
The Dark Wave, 20th Century–Fox. John Healy, producer.
The House Without a Name, U-I. Valentine Davies, producer.
Man in Space, Disney, Buena Vista. Ward Kimball, producer.
★ *The True Story of the Civil War,* Camera Eye Pictures. Louis Clyde Stoumen, producer.

(FEATURES)

The Naked Eye, Camera Eye Pictures. Louis Clyde Stoumen, producer.
★ *The Silent World,* Filmad-F.S.J.Y.C., Columbia (French). Jacques-Yves Cousteau, producer.
Where Mountains Float, Brandon Films (Danish). The Government Film Committee of Denmark, producer.

Foreign Language Film

The Captain of Kopenick (Germany).
Gervaise (France).
Harp of Burma (Japan).
★ *La Strada* (Italy).
Qivitoq (Denmark).

Irving G. Thalberg Memorial Award

Buddy Adler.

Jean Hersholt Humanitarian Award

Y. Frank Freeman.

Honorary Award

Eddie Cantor for distinguished service to the film industry (statuette).

Scientific or Technical

CLASS I (STATUETTE)

None.

CLASS II (PLAQUE)

None.

CLASS III (CITATION)

Richard H. Ranger of Rangertone, Inc., for the development of a synchronous recording and reproducing system for quarter-inch magnetic tape.
Ted Hirsch, Carl Hauge and Edward Reichard of Consolidated Film Industries for an automatic scene counter for laboratory projection rooms.
The Technical Departments of Paramount Pictures Corp. for the engineering and development of the Paramount lightweight horizontal-movement Vista Vision camera.
Roy C. Stewart and Sons of Stewart-Trans Lux Corp. Dr. C.R. Daily and the Transparency Department of Paramount Pictures Corp. for the engineering and develop-

ment of the HiTrans and Para-HiTrans rear projection screens.

The Construction Department of MGM Studio for a new hand-portable fog machine.

Daniel J. Bloomberg, John Pond, William Wade and the Engineering and Camera Departments of Republic Studio for the Naturama adaptation to the Mitchell camera.

Points of Interest

1. Talk to me: Original Screenplay Award winner, *The Red Balloon,* has no dialogue.
2. Nothing to it: Don Murray nominated for film debut, Eileen Heckart in first year in movies.
3. Gone but still not forgotten: For the second year in a row, James Dean receives posthumous nomination.
4. Better late . . .: After twenty-two nominations, Victor Young, composer of *Around the World in 80 Days,* finally wins an Oscar—posthumously.
5. You're the top!: Highest rated Oscar broadcast ever.

Rule Changes

1. Better dead than red: No one may be nominated for an Oscar if he had admitted Communist Party membership and has not renounced that membership, if he has refused to testify before a Congressional Committee or if he has refused to respond to a subpoena from such committee.
2. New addition: "The Jean Hersholt Humanitarian Award" instituted to honor charitable endeavors.
3. The name game: "Story and Screenplay" now "Screenplay—Original"; "Screenplay" becomes "Screenplay—Adapted."
4. The more the merrier: Foreign Language Film becomes regular category.

Eligible Films That Failed to Be Nominated for Best Picture

The Searchers, Baby Doll, Written on the Wind, The Man Who Knew Too Much, Invasion of the Body Snatchers, The Girl Can't Help It, Mother 1905, The Killing, Bhowani Junction, All That Heaven Allows, Autumn Leaves, The Bad Seed.

Eligible Songs That Failed to Be Nominated

"The Girl Can't Help It" (Bobby Troup)—*The Girl Can't Help It;* "Love Me Tender" (Elvis Presley and Vera Matson)—*Love Me Tender.*

1957

Picture

★ *The Bridge on the River Kwai,* Horizon, Columbia. Produced by Sam Spiegel.

Peyton Place, Wald, 20th Century–Fox. Produced by Jerry Wald.

Sayonara, Goetz, Warner Bros. Produced by William Goetz.

12 Angry Men, Orion-Nova, UA. Produced by Henry Fonda and Reginald Rose.

Witness for the Prosecution, Small-Hornblow, UA. Produced by Arthur Hornblow, Jr.

Actor

Marlon Brando in *Sayonara* (Goetz, Warner Bros.).

Anthony Franciosa in *A Hatful of Rain* (20th Century–Fox).

★ Alec Guinness in *The Bridge on the River Kwai* (Horizon, Columbia).

Charles Laughton in *Witness for the Prosecution* (Small-Hornblow, UA).

Anthony Quinn in *Wild Is the Wind* (Wallis, Paramount).

Actress

Deborah Kerr in *Heaven Knows, Mr. Allison* (20th Century–Fox).

Anna Magnani in *Wild Is the Wind* (Wallis, Paramount).

Elizabeth Taylor in *Raintree County* (MGM).

Lana Turner in *Peyton Place* (Wald, 20th Century–Fox).

★ Joanne Woodward in *The Three Faces of Eve* (20th Century–Fox).

Supporting Actor

★ Red Buttons in *Sayonara* (Goetz, Warner Bros.).

Vittorio de Sica in *A Farewell to Arms* (Selznick, 20th Century–Fox).

Sessue Hayakawa in *The Bridge on the River Kwai* (Horizon, Columbia).

Arthur Kennedy in *Peyton Place* (Wald, 20th Century–Fox).

Russ Tamblyn in *Peyton Place* (Wald, 20th Century–Fox).

Supporting Actress

Carolyn Jones in *The Bachelor Party* (Norma, UA).

Elsa Lanchester in *Witness for the Prosecution* (Small-Hornblow, UA).

Hope Lange in *Peyton Place* (Wald, 20th Century–Fox).

★ Miyoshi Umeki in *Sayonara* (Goetz, Warner Bros.).

Diane Varsi in *Peyton Place* (Wald, 20th Century–Fox).

Director

★ David Lean for *The Bridge on the River Kwai* (Horizon, Columbia).

Joshua Logan for *Sayonara* (Goetz, Warner Bros.).

Sidney Lumet for *12 Angry Men* (Orion-Nova, UA).

Mark Robson for *Peyton Place* (Wald, 20th Century–Fox).

Billy Wilder for *Witness for the Prosecution* (Small-Hornblow, UA).

Writing

(SCREENPLAY—BASED ON MATERIAL FROM ANOTHER MEDIUM)

★ *The Bridge on the River Kwai*, Horizon, Columbia. Pierre Boulle. (Later accredited to Carl Foreman and Michael Wilson.)

Heaven Knows, Mr. Allison, 20th Century–Fox. John Lee Mahin and John Huston.

Peyton Place, Wald, 20th Century–Fox. John Michael Hayes.

Sayonara, Goetz, Warner Bros. Paul Osborn.

12 Angry Men, Orion-Nova, UA. Reginald Rose.

(STORY AND SCREENPLAY—WRITTEN DIRECTLY FOR THE SCREEN)

★ *Designing Woman*, MGM. George Wells.

Funny Face, Paramount. Leonard Gershe.

Man of a Thousand Faces, U-I. Ralph Wheelright; R. Wright Campbell, Ivan Goff and Ben Roberts.

The Tin Star, Perlberg-Seaton, Paramount. Barney Slater and Joel Kane; Dudley Nichols.

Vitelloni, API-Janus (Italian). Federico Fellini, Ennio Flaiano and Tullio Pinelli.

Cinematography

An Affair to Remember, Wald, 20th Century–Fox. Milton Krasner.

★ *The Bridge on the River Kwai*, Horizon, Columbia. Jack Hildyard.

Funny Face, Paramount. Ray June.

Peyton Place, Wald, 20th Century–Fox. William Mellor.

Sayonara, Goetz, Warner Bros. Ellsworth Fredericks.

Art Direction—Set Decoration

Funny Face, Paramount. Hal Pereira and George W. Davis; Sam Comer and Ray Moyer.

Les Girls, Siegel, MGM. William A. Horning and Gene Allen; Edwin B. Willis and Richard Pefferle.

Pal Joey, Essex-Sidney, Columbia. Walter Holscher; William Kiernan and Louis Diage.

Raintree County, MGM. William A. Horning and Urie McCleary; Edwin B. Willis and Hugh Hunt.

★ *Sayonara*, Goetz, Warner Bros. Ted Haworth; Robert Priestley.

Sound

Gunfight at the O.K. Corral, Wallis, Paramount. Paramount Studio Sound Department; George Dutton, sound director.

Les Girls, Siegel, MGM. MGM Studio Sound Department; Dr. Wesley C. Miller, sound director.

Pal Joey, Essex-Sidney, Columbia. Columbia Studio Sound Dept.; John P. Livadary, sound director.

★ *Sayonara*, Goetz, Warner Bros. Warner Bros. Studio Sound Dept.; George Groves, sound director.

Witness for the Prosecution, Small-Hornblow, UA. Samuel Goldwyn Studio Sound Department; Gordon Sawyer, sound director.

Music

(SONG)

"An Affair to Remember" (*An Affair to Remember*, Wald, 20th Century–Fox); Music by Harry Warren. Lyrics by Harold Adamson and Leo McCarey.

★ "All the Way" (*The Joker Is Wild*, Paramount); Music by James Van Heusen. Lyrics by Sammy Cahn.

"April Love" (*April Love*, 20th Century–Fox); Music by Sammy Fain. Lyrics by Paul Francis Webster.

"Tammy" (*Tammy and the Bachelor*, U-I); Music and Lyrics by Ray Evans and Jay Livingston.

"Wild Is the Wind" (*Wild Is the Wind*, Wallis, Paramount); Music by Dimitri Tiomkin. Lyrics by Ned Washington.

(SCORE)

An Affair to Remember, Wald. 20th Century–Fox. Hugo Friedhofer.

Boy on a Dolphin, 20th Century–Fox. Hugo Friedhofer.

★ *The Bridge on the River Kwai*, Horizon, Columbia. Malcolm Arnold.

Perri, Disney, Buena Vista. Paul Smith.

Raintree County, MGM. Johnny Green.

Film Editing

★ *The Bridge on the River Kwai*, Horizon, Columbia. Peter Taylor.

Gunfight at the O.K. Corral, Wallis, Paramount. Warren Low.

Pal Joey, Essex-Sidney, Columbia. Viola Lawrence and Jerome Thoms.

Sayonara, Goetz, Warner Bros. Arthur P. Schmidt and Philip W. Anderson.

Witness for the Prosecution, Small-Hornblow, UA. Daniel Mandell.

Costume Design

An Affair to Remember, Wald, 20th Century–Fox. Charles LeMaire.

Funny Face, Paramount. Edith Head and Hubert de Givenchy.

★ *Les Girls*, Siegel, MGM. Orry-Kelly.

Pal Joey, Essex-Sidney, Columbia. Jean Louis.

Raintree County, MGM. Walter Plunkett.

Special Effects

★ *The Enemy Below*, 20th Century–Fox. Walter Rossi.

The Spirit of St. Louis, Hayward-Wilder, Warner Bros. Louis Lichtenfield.

Short Subjects

(CARTOONS)

★ *Birds Anonymous,* Warner Bros. Edward Selzer, producer.

One Droopy Knight, MGM. William Hanna and Joseph Barbera, producers.

Tabasco Road, Warner Bros. Edward Selzer, producer.

Trees and Jamaica Daddy, UPA, Columbia. Stephen Bosustow, producer.

The Truth About Mother Goose, Disney, Buena Vista. Walt Disney, producer.

(LIVE ACTION SUBJECTS)

A Charity Tale, National Film Board of Canada. Kingsley International. Norman McLaren, producer.

City of Gold, National Film Board of Canada, Kingsley International. Tom Daly, producer.

Foothold on Antarctica, World Wide Pictures, Schoenfeld Films. James Carr, producer.

Portugal, Disney, Buena Vista. Ben Sharpsteen, producer.

★ *The Wetback Hound,* Disney, Buena Vista. Larry Lansburgh, producer.

Documentary

(SHORT SUBJECTS)

Not given this year.

(FEATURES)

★ *Albert Schweitzer,* Hill and Anderson Prod., Louis de Rochemont Assocs. Jerome Hill, producer.

On the Bowery, Rogosin, Film Representations, Inc. Lionel Rogosin, producer.

Torero!, Producciones Barbachano Ponce, Columbia (Mexican). Manuel Barbachano Ponce, producer.

Foreign Language Film

The Devil Came at Night (Germany).

Gates of Paris (France).

Mother India (India).

★ *The Nights of Cabiria* (Italy).

Nine Lives (Norway).

Irving G. Thalberg Memorial Award

Not given this year.

Jean Hersholt Humanitarian Award

Samuel Goldwyn.

Honorary Awards

Charles Brackett for outstanding service to the Academy (statuette).

B.B. Kahane for distinguished service to the motion picture industry (statuette).

Gilbert M. ("Broncho Billy") Anderson, motion picture pioneer, for his contributions to the development of motion pictures as entertainment (statuette).

The Society of Motion Picture and Television Engineers for their contributions to the advancement of the motion picture industry (statuette).

Scientific or Technical

CLASS I (STATUETTE)

Todd-AO Corp. and Westrex Corp. for developing a method of producing and exhibiting wide-film motion pictures known as the Todd-AO System.

Motion Picture Research Council for the design and development of a high efficiency projection screen for drive-in theaters.

CLASS II (PLAQUE)

Société D'Optique et de Mécanique de Haute Precision for the development of a high speed vari-focal photographic lens.

Harlan L. Baumbach, Lorand Wargo, Howard M. Little and the Unicorn Engineering Corp. for the development of an automatic printer light selector.

CLASS III (CITATION)

Charles E. Sutter, William B. Smith, Paramount Pictures Corp. and General Cable Corp. for the engineering and application to studio use of aluminum lightweight electrical cable and connectors.

Points of Interest

1. Nothing to it: Miyoshi Umeki wins for film debut; Diane Varsi and director Sidney Lumet nominated for theirs.
2. Renaissance man: Oscar-winning writer-director Leo McCarey nominated for Song.
3. I didn't see any I liked: No nominations for Documentary Short Subject.

Rule Changes

1. The fewer the merrier: In Cinematography, Art Direction and Costume Design categories, no distinction made between black-and-white and color films. For Music Scoring, no distinction made between musical and nonmusical films. Separate categories of One-Reel and Two-Reel Short Subjects combined into "Live Action Short Subjects." "Motion Picture Story" and "Screenplay—Original" joined as "Story and Screenplay."
2. The name game: "Sound Recording" becomes "Sound."

Eligible Films That Failed to Be Nominated for Best Picture

Paths of Glory, Sweet Smell of Success, A Face in the Crowd, Paris Does Strange Things, Funny Face, Les Girls, Run of the

Arrow, The Incredible Shrinking Man, Will Success Spoil Rock Hunter?, Jailhouse Rock.

Submitted Film Rejected by the Foreign Language Film Award Committee

The Seventh Seal (Sweden), directed by Ingmar Bergman.

Eligible Songs That Failed to Be Nominated

"It's Not for Me to Say" (Robert Allen and Al Stillman)—*Lizzie;* "Jailhouse Rock" (Jerry Leiber and Mike Stoller)—*Jailhouse Rock;* "Loving You" (Jerry Leiber and Mike Stoller)—*Loving You;* "Mean Woman Blues" (Claude De Metrius)—*Loving You;* "Teddy Bear" (Kal Mann and Bernie Lowe)—*Loving You;* "Think Pink" (Roger Edens and Leonard Gershe)—*Funny Face;* "Treat Me Nice" (Jerry Leiber and Mike Stoller)—*Jailhouse Rock.*

1958

Picture

Auntie Mame, Warner Bros. Jack L. Warner, studio head.
Cat on a Hot Tin Roof, Avon, MGM. Produced by Lawrence Weingarten.
The Defiant Ones, Kramer, UA. Produced by Stanley Kramer.
★ *Gigi,* Freed, MGM. Produced by Arthur Freed.
Separate Tables, Hecht-Hill-Lancaster, UA. Produced by Harold Hecht.

Actor

Tony Curtis in *The Defiant Ones* (Kramer, UA).
Paul Newman in *Cat on a Hot Tin Roof* (Avon, MGM).
★ David Niven in *Separate Tables* (Hecht-Hill-Lancaster, UA).
Sidney Poitier in *The Defiant Ones* (Kramer, UA).
Spencer Tracy in *The Old Man and the Sea* (Hayward, Warner Bros.).

Actress

★ Susan Hayward in *I Want to Live!* (Wanger-Figaro, UA).
Deborah Kerr in *Separate Tables* (Hecht-Hill-Lancaster, UA).
Shirley MacLaine in *Some Came Running* (Siegel, MGM).
Rosalind Russell in *Auntie Mame* (Warner Bros.).
Elizabeth Taylor in *Cat on a Hot Tin Roof* (Avon, MGM).

Supporting Actor

Theodore Bikel in *The Defiant Ones,* (Kramer, UA).
Lee J. Cobb in *The Brothers Karamazov* (Avon, MGM).
★ Burl Ives in *The Big Country* (Anthony-Worldwide, UA).
Arthur Kennedy in *Some Came Running* (Siegel, MGM).
Gig Young in *Teacher's Pet* (Perlberg-Seaton, Paramount).

Supporting Actress

Peggy Cass in *Auntie Mame* (Warner Bros.).
★ Wendy Hiller in *Separate Tables* (Hecht-Hill-Lancaster, UA).
Martha Hyer in *Some Came Running* (Siegel, MGM).
Maureen Stapleton in *Lonelyhearts* (Schary, UA).
Cara Williams in *The Defiant Ones* (Kramer, UA).

Director

Richard Brooks for *Cat on a Hot Tin Roof* (Avon, MGM).
Stanley Kramer for *The Defiant Ones* (Kramer, UA).
★ Vincente Minnelli for *Gigi* (Freed, MGM).
Mark Robson for *The Inn of the Sixth Happiness* (20th Century–Fox).
Robert Wise for *I Want to Live!* (Wanger-Figaro, UA).

Writing

(SCREENPLAY—BASED ON MATERIAL FROM ANOTHER MEDIUM)
Cat on a Hot Tin Roof, Avon, MGM. Richard Brooks and James Poe.
★ *Gigi,* Freed, MGM. Alan Jay Lerner.
The Horse's Mouth, Lopert-UA (British). Alec Guinness.
I Want to Live!, Wanger-Figaro, UA. Nelson Gidding and Don Mankiewicz.
Separate Tables, Hecht-Hill-Lancaster, UA. Terence Rattigan and John Gay.

(STORY AND SCREENPLAY—WRITTEN DIRECTLY FOR THE SCREEN)
★ *The Defiant Ones,* Kramer, UA. Nathan E. Douglas and Harold Jacob Smith.
The Goddess, Perlman, Columbia. Paddy Chayefsky.
Houseboat, Paramount. Melville Shavelson and Jack Rose.
The Sheepman, MGM. James Edward Grant and William Bowers.
Teacher's Pet, Perlberg-Seaton, Paramount. Fay and Michael Kanin.

Cinematography

(BLACK-AND-WHITE)
★ *The Defiant Ones,* Kramer, UA. Sam Leavitt.
Desire Under the Elms, Hartman, Paramount. Daniel L. Fapp.
I Want to Live!, Wanger-Figaro, Inc., UA. Lionel Lindon.
Separate Tables, Hecht-Hill-Lancaster, UA. Charles Lang, Jr.
The Young Lions, 20th Century–Fox. Joe MacDonald.

(COLOR)
Auntie Mame, Warner Bros. Harry Stradling, Sr.
Cat on a Hot Tin Roof, Avon, MGM. William Daniels.
★ *Gigi,* Freed, MGM. Joseph Ruttenberg.

The Old Man and the Sea, Hayward, Warner Bros. James Wong Howe.

South Pacific, Magna Corp., 20th Century–Fox. Leon Shamroy.

Art Direction—Set Decoration

(BLACK-AND-WHITE OR COLOR)

Auntie Mame, Warner Bros. Malcolm Bert; George James Hopkins.

Bell, Book and Candle, Phoenix, Columbia. Cary Odell; Louis Diage.

A Certain Smile, 20th Century–Fox. Lyle R. Wheeler and John DeCuir; Walter M. Scott and Paul S. Fox.

★ *Gigi,* Freed, MGM. William A. Horning and Preston Ames; Henry Grace and Keogh Gleason.

Vertigo, Hitchcock, Paramount. Hal Pereira and Henry Bumstead; Sam Comer and Frank McKelvy.

Sound

I Want to Live!, Wanger-Figaro, UA. Samuel Goldwyn Studio Sound Department; Gordon E. Sawyer, sound director.

★ *South Pacific,* Magna Corp., 20th Century–Fox. Todd-AO Sound Department; Fred Hynes, sound director.

A Time to Love and a Time to Die, U-I. Universal-International Studio Sound Department; Leslie I. Carey, sound director.

Vertigo, Hitchcock, Paramount. Paramount Studio Sound Department; George Dutton, sound director.

The Young Lions, 20th Century–Fox. 20th Century–Fox Studio Sound Department; Carl Faulkner, sound director.

Music

(SONG)

"Almost in Your Arms (Love Song from *Houseboat*)" (*Houseboat,* Paramount); Music and Lyrics by Jay Livingston and Ray Evans.

"A Certain Smile" (*A Certain Smile,* 20th Century–Fox); Music by Sammy Fain. Lyrics by Paul Francis Webster.

★ "Gigi" (*Gigi,* Freed, MGM); Music by Frederick Loewe. Lyrics by Alan Jay Lerner.

"To Love and Be Loved" (*Some Came Running,* Siegel, MGM); Music by James Van Heusen. Lyrics by Sammy Cahn.

"A Very Precious Love" (*Marjorie Morningstar,* Sperling, Warner Bros.); Music by Sammy Fain. Lyrics by Paul Francis Webster.

(SCORING OF A DRAMATIC OR COMEDY PICTURE)

The Big Country, Anthony-Worldwide, UA. Jerome Moross.

★ *The Old Man and the Sea,* Hayward, Warner Bros. Dimitri Tiomkin.

Separate Tables, Hecht-Hill-Lancaster, UA. David Raksin.

White Wilderness, Disney, Buena Vista. Oliver Wallace.

The Young Lions, 20th Century–Fox. Hugo Friedhofer.

(SCORING OF A MUSICAL PICTURE)

The Bolshoi Ballet, Czinner-Maxwell, Rank Releasing (British). Yuri Faier and G. Rozhdestvensky.

Damn Yankees, Warner Bros. Ray Heindorf.

★ *Gigi,* Freed, MGM. André Previn.

Mardi Gras, Wald, 20th Century–Fox. Lionel Newman.

South Pacific, Magna Corp., 20th Century–Fox. Alfred Newman and Ken Darby.

Film Editing

Auntie Mame, Warner Bros. William Ziegler.

Cowboy, Phoenix, Columbia. William A. Lyon and Al Clark.

The Defiant Ones, Kramer, UA. Frederick Knudtson.

★ *Gigi,* Freed, MGM. Adrienne Fazan.

I Want to Live!, Wanger-Figaro, UA. William Hornbeck.

Costume Design

(BLACK-AND-WHITE OR COLOR)

Bell, Book and Candle, Phoenix, Columbia. Jean Louis.

The Buccaneer, DeMille, Paramount. Ralph Jester, Edith Head and John Jensen.

A Certain Smile, 20th Century–Fox. Charles LeMaire and Mary Wills.

★ *Gigi,* Freed, MGM. Cecil Beaton.

Some Came Running, Siegel, MGM. Walter Plunkett.

Special Effects

★ *tom thumb,* Galaxy Pictures, MGM. Tom Howard.

Torpedo Run, MGM. A. Arnold Gillespie; Harold Humbrock.

Short Subjects

(CARTOONS)

★ *Knighty Knight Bugs,* Warner Bros. John W. Burton, producer.

Paul Bunyan, Walt Disney Prods., Buena Vista Film Distribution. Walt Disney, producer.

Sidney's Family Tree, Terrytoons, 20th Century–Fox. William M. Weiss, producer.

(LIVE ACTION SUBJECTS)

★ *Grand Canyon,* Walt Disney Prods., Buena Vista. Walt Disney, producer.

Journey into Spring, British Transport Films, Lester A. Schoenfeld Films. Ian Ferguson, producer.

The Kiss, Cohay Prods., Continental Distributing, Inc. John Patrick Hayes, producer.

Snows of Aorangi, New Zealand Screen Board. George Brest Assocs.

T Is for Tumbleweed, Continental Distributing, Inc. James A. Lebenthal, producer.

Documentary

(SHORT SUBJECTS)

★ *AMA Girls,* Disney Prods., Buena Vista. Ben Sharpsteen, producer.

Employees Only, Hughes Aircraft Co. Kenneth G. Brown, producer.

Journey into Spring, British Transport Films, Lester A. Schoenfeld Films. Ian Ferguson, producer.

The Living Stone, National Film Board of Canada. Tom Daly, producer.

Overture, United Nations Film Service. Thorold Dickinson, producer.

(FEATURES)

Antarctic Crossing, World Wide Pictures, Lester A. Schoenfeld Films. James Carr, producer.

The Hidden World, Small World Co. Robert Snyder, producer.

Psychiatric Nursing, Dynamic Films, Inc. Nathan Zucker, producer.

★ *White Wilderness,* Disney Prods., Buena Vista. Ben Sharpsteen, producer.

Foreign Language Film

Arms and the Man (Germany).

La Venganza (Spain).

★ *My Uncle* (France).

The Road a Year Long (Yugoslavia).

The Usual Unidentified Thieves (a.k.a. *Big Deal on Madonna Street*) (Italy).

Irving G. Thalberg Memorial Award

Jack L. Warner.

Jean Hersholt Humanitarian Award

Not given this year.

Honorary Award

Maurice Chevalier for his contributions to the world of entertainment for more than half a century (statuette).

Scientific or Technical

CLASS I (STATUETTE)

None.

CLASS II (PLAQUE)

Don W. Prideaux, Leroy G. Leighton and the Lamp Division of General Electric Co. for the development and production of an improved 10-kilowatt lamp for motion picture set lighting.

Panavision, Inc., for the design and development of the Auto Panatar anamorphic photographic lens for 35mm CinemaScope photography.

CLASS III (CITATION)

Willy Borberg of the General Precision Laboratory, Inc., for the development of a high speed intermittent movement for 35mm motion picture theater projection equipment.

Fred Ponedel, George Brown and Conrad Boye of the Warner Bros. Special Effects Dept. for the design and fabrication of a new rapid-fire marble gun.

Points of Interest

1. King of the mountain: *Gigi* sets new record for most Academy Awards—nine.
2. Renaissance man: Oscar-winning actor Alec Guinness nominated for Adapted Screenplay for *The Horse's Mouth*.
3. Nothing to it: Maureen Stapleton nominated for film debut.

Rule Changes

1. The more the merrier: Cinematography again divided into separate Color and Black-and-White Awards. For Musical Scoring, distinction again made between musicals and nonmusicals.
2. Better red than dead: Anti-Communist clause dropped.

Eligible Films That Failed to Be Nominated for Best Picture

Vertigo, Touch of Evil, Some Came Running, The Tarnished Angels, Man of the West, Indiscreet, The Last Hurrah.

Submitted Film Rejected by the Foreign Language Film Award Committee

The Magician (Sweden), directed by Ingmar Bergman.

Eligible Songs That Failed to Be Nominated

"Hard-Headed Woman" (Claude De Metrius)—*King Creole;* "I Remember It Well" (Alan Jay Lerner and Frederick Loewe)—*Gigi;* "Teacher's Pet (Joe Lubin)—*Teacher's Pet;* "Thank Heavens for Little Girls" (Alan Jay Lerner and Frederick Loewe)—*Gigi.*

1959

Picture

Anatomy of a Murder, Preminger, Columbia. Produced by Otto Preminger

★ *Ben-Hur,* MGM. Produced by Sam Zimbalist.

The Diary of Anne Frank, 20th Century–Fox. Produced by George Stevens.

The Nun's Story, Warner Bros. Produced by Henry Blanke.

Room at the Top, Romulus, Continental (British). Produced by John and James Woolf.

Actor

Laurence Harvey in *Room at the Top* (Romulus, Continental) (British).

★ Charlton Heston in *Ben-Hur* (MGM).

Jack Lemmon in *Some Like It Hot* (Ashton-Mirisch, UA).

Paul Muni in *The Last Angry Man* (Kohlmar, Columbia).

James Stewart in *Anatomy of a Murder* (Preminger, Columbia).

Actress

Doris Day in *Pillow Talk* (Arwin, U-I).

Audrey Hepburn in *The Nun's Story* (Warner Bros.).

Katharine Hepburn in *Suddenly, Last Summer* (Horizon, Columbia).

★ Simone Signoret in *Room at the Top* (Romulus, Continental) (British).

Elizabeth Taylor in *Suddenly, Last Summer* (Horizon, Columbia).

Supporting Actor

★ Hugh Griffith in *Ben-Hur* (MGM).

Arthur O'Connell in *Anatomy of a Murder* (Preminger, Columbia).

George C. Scott in *Anatomy of a Murder* (Preminger, Columbia).

Robert Vaughn in *The Young Philadelphians* (Warner Bros.).

Ed Wynn in *The Diary of Anne Frank* (20th Century–Fox).

Supporting Actress

Hermione Baddeley in *Room at the Top* (Romulus, Continental) (British).

Susan Kohner in *Imitation of Life* (U-I).

Juanita Moore in *Imitation of Life* (U-I).

Thelma Ritter in *Pillow Talk* (Arwin, U-I).

★ Shelley Winters in *The Diary of Anne Frank* (20th Century–Fox).

Director

Jack Clayton for *Room at the Top* (Romulus, Continental—British).

George Stevens for *The Diary of Anne Frank* (20th Century–Fox).

Billy Wilder for *Some Like It Hot* (Ashton-Mirisch, UA).

★ William Wyler for *Ben-Hur* (MGM).

Fred Zinnemann for *The Nun's Story* (Warner Bros.).

Writing

(SCREENPLAY—BASED ON MATERIAL FROM ANOTHER MEDIUM)

Anatomy of a Murder, Preminger, Columbia. Wendell Mayes.

Ben-Hur, MGM. Karl Tunberg.

The Nun's Story, Warner Bros. Robert Anderson.

★ *Room at the Top*, Romulus, Continental (British). Neil Paterson.

Some Like It Hot, Ashton-Mirisch, UA. Billy Wilder and I.A.L. Diamond.

(STORY AND SCREENPLAY—WRITTEN DIRECTLY FOR THE SCREEN)

The 400 Blows, Zenith International (French). François Truffaut and Marcel Moussy.

North by Northwest, Hitchcock, MGM. Ernest Lehman.

Operation Petticoat, Granart, U-I. Paul King and Joseph Stone; Stanley Shapiro and Maurice Richlin.

★ *Pillow Talk*, Arwin, U-I. Russell Rouse and Clarence Greene; Stanley Shapiro and Maurice Richlin.

Wild Strawberries, Janus Films (Swedish). Ingmar Bergman.

Cinematography

(BLACK-AND-WHITE)

Anatomy of a Murder, Preminger, Columbia. Sam Leavitt.

Career, Wallis, Paramount. Joseph LaShelle.

★ *The Diary of Anne Frank*, 20th Century–Fox. William C. Mellor.

Some Like It Hot, Ashton-Mirisch, UA. Charles Lang, Jr.

The Young Philadelphians, Warner Bros. Harry Stradling, Sr.

(COLOR)

★ *Ben-Hur*, MGM. Robert L. Surtees.

The Big Fisherman, Rowland V. Lee, Buena Vista. Lee Garmes.

The Five Pennies, Dena, Paramount. Daniel L. Fapp.

The Nun's Story, Warner Bros. Franz Planer.

Porgy and Bess, Goldwyn, Columbia. Leon Shamroy.

Art Direction—Set Decoration

(BLACK-AND-WHITE)

Career, Wallis, Paramount. Hal Pereira and Walter Tyler; Sam Comer and Arthur Krams.

★ *The Diary of Anne Frank*, 20th Century–Fox. Lyle R. Wheeler and George W. Davis; Walter M. Scott and Stuart A. Reiss.

The Last Angry Man, Kohlmar, Columbia. Carl Anderson; William Kiernan.

Some Like It Hot, Ashton-Mirisch, UA. Ted Haworth; Edward G. Boyle.

Suddenly, Last Summer, Horizon, Columbia. Oliver Messel and Wiliam Kellner; Scot Slimon.

(COLOR)

★ Ben-Hur, MGM. William A. Horning and Edward Carfagno; Hugh Hunt.

The Big Fisherman, Rowland V. Lee, Buena Vista. John DeCuir; Julia Heron.

Journey to the Center of the Earth, 20th Century–Fox. Lyle R. Wheeler, Franz Bachelin and Herman A. Blumenthal; Walter M. Scott and Joseph Kish.

North by Northwest, Hitchcock, MGM. William A. Horning, Robert Boyle and Merrill Pye; Henry Grace and Frank McKelvy.

Pillow Talk, Arwin, U-I. Richard H. Riedel; Russell A. Gausman and Ruby R. Levitt.

Sound

★ *Ben-Hur,* MGM. MGM Studio Sound Department; Franklin E. Milton, sound director.

Journey to the Center of the Earth, 20th Century–Fox. 20th Century–Fox Sound Dept.; Carl Faulkner, sound director.

Libel! MGM (British). MGM London Sound Dept.; A.W. Watkins, sound director.

The Nun's Story, Warner Bros. Warner Bros. Studio Sound Dept.; George R. Groves, sound director.

Porgy and Bess, Goldwyn, Columbia. Samuel Goldwyn Studio Sound Dept.; Gordon E. Sawyer, sound director; and Todd-AO Sound Dept.; Fred Hynes, sound director.

Music

(SONG)

"The Best of Everything" (*The Best of Everything,* Wald, 20th Century–Fox); Music by Alfred Newman. Lyrics by Sammy Cahn.

"The Five Pennies" (*The Five Pennies,* Dena, Paramount); Music and Lyrics by Sylvia Fine.

"The Hanging Tree" (*The Hanging Tree,* Baroda Warner Bros.); Music by Jerry Livingston. Lyrics by Mack David.

★ "High Hopes" (*A Hole in the Head,* Sincap, UA); Music by James Van Heusen. Lyrics by Sammy Cahn.

"Strange Are the Ways of Love" (*The Young Land,* C.V. Whitney, Columbia); Music by Dimitri Tiomkin. Lyrics by Ned Washington.

(SCORING OF A DRAMATIC OR COMEDY PICTURE)

★ *Ben-Hur,* MGM. Miklos Rozsa.

The Diary of Anne Frank, 20th Century–Fox. Alfred Newman.

The Nun's Story, Warner Bros. Franz Waxman.

On the Beach, Kramer, UA. Ernest Gold.

Pillow Talk, Arwin, U-I. Frank DeVol.

(SCORING OF A MUSICAL PICTURE)

The Five Pennies, Dena, Paramount. Leith Stevens.

Li'l Abner, Panama and Frank, Paramount. Nelson Riddle and Joseph J. Lilley.

★ *Porgy and Bess,* Goldwyn, Columbia. André Previn and Ken Darby.

Say One for Me, Crosby, 20th Century–Fox. Lionel Newman.

Sleeping Beauty, Disney, Buena Vista. George Bruns.

Film Editing

Anatomy of a Murder, Preminger, Columbia. Louis R. Loeffler.

★ *Ben-Hur,* MGM. Ralph E. Winters and John D. Dunning.

North by Northwest, Hitchcock, MGM. George Tomasini.

The Nun's Story, Warner Bros. Walter Thompson.

On the Beach, Kramer, UA. Frederic Knudtson.

Costume Design

(BLACK-AND-WHITE)

Career, Wallis, Paramount. Edith Head.

The Diary of Anne Frank, 20th Century–Fox. Charles LeMaire and Mary Wills.

The Gazebo, Avon, MGM. Helen Rose.

★ *Some Like It Hot,* Ashton-Mirisch, UA. Orry-Kelly.

The Young Philadelphians, Warner Bros. Howard Shoup.

(COLOR)

★ *Ben-Hur,* MGM. Elizabeth Haffenden.

The Best of Everything, Wald, 20th Century–Fox. Adele Palmer.

The Big Fisherman, Rowland V. Lee, Buena Vista. Renie.

The Five Pennies, Dena, Paramount. Edith Head.

Porgy and Bess, Goldwyn, Columbia. Irene Sharaff.

Special Effects

★ *Ben-Hur,* MGM. Visual: A. Arnold Gillespie and Robert MacDonald. Audible: Milo Lory.

Journey to the Center of the Earth, Joseph M. Schenck Enterprises, Inc. and Cooga Mooga Film Prods., Inc., 20th Century–Fox. Visual: L. B. Abbott and James B. Gordon. Audible: Carl Faulkner.

Short Subjects

(CARTOONS)

Mexicali Shmoes, Warner Bros. John W. Burton, producer.

★ *Moonbird,* Storyboard-Harrison. John Hubley, producer.

Noah's Ark, Disney, Buena Vista. Walt Disney, producer.

The Violinist, Pintoff Prods., Kingsley International. Ernest Pintoff, producer.

(LIVE ACTION SUBJECTS)

Between the Tides, British Transport Films, Schoenfeld Films (British). Ian Ferguson, producer.

★ *The Golden Fish,* Les Requins Associes, Columbia (French). Jacques-Yves Cousteau, producer.

Mysteries of the Deep, Disney, Buena Vista. Walt Disney, producer.

The Running, Jumping and Standing-Still Film, Lion International, Kingsley-Union Films (British). Peter Sellers, producer.

Skyscraper, Burstyn Film Enterprises. Shirley Clarke, Willard Van Dyke and Irving Jacoby, producers.

Documentary
(SHORT SUBJECTS)

Donald in Mathmagic Land, Disney, Buena Vista. Walt Disney, producer.

From Generation to Generation, Cullen Assocs., Maternity Center Assoc. Edward F. Cullen, producer.

★ *Glass,* Netherlands Government. George K. Arthur–Go Pictures (The Netherlands). Bert Haanstra, producer.

(FEATURES)

The Race for Space, Wolper, Inc. David L. Wolper, producer.

★ *Serengeti Shall Not Die,* Okapia-Film Prod., Transocean Film (German). Bernhard Grzimek, producer.

Foreign Language Film
★ *Black Orpheus* (France).
The Bridge (German).
The Great War (Italy).
Paw (Denmark).
The Village on the River (The Netherlands).

Irving G. Thalberg Memorial Award
Not given this year.

Jean Hersholt Humanitarian Award
Bob Hope.

Honorary Awards
Lee de Forest for his pioneering inventions which brought sound to the motion picture (statuette).

Buster Keaton for his unique talents which brought immortal comedies to the screen (statuette).

Scientific or Technical
CLASS I (STATUETTE)

None.

CLASS II (PLAQUE)

Douglas G. Shearer of MGM, Inc., and Robert E. Gottschalk and John R. Moore of Panavision, Inc., for the development of a system of producing and exhibiting wide-film motion pictures known as Camera 65.

Wadsworth E. Pohl, William Evans, Werner Hopf, S.E. Howse, Thomas P. Dixon, Stanford Research Institute and Technicolor Corp. for the design and development of the Technicolor electronic printing timer.

Wadsworth E. Pohl, Jack Alford, Henry Imus, Joseph Schmit, Paul Fassnacht, Al Lofquist and Technicolor Corp. for the development and practical application of equipment for wet printing.

Dr. Howard S. Coleman, Dr. A. Francis Turner, Harold H. Schroeder, James R. Benford and Harold E. Rosenberger of the Bausch & Lomb Optical Co. for the design and development of the Balcold projection mirror.

Robert P. Gutterman of General Kinetics, Inc., and the Lipsner Smith Corp. for the design and development of the CF-2 Ultra-sonic Film Cleaner.

CLASS III (CITATION)

Ub Iwerks of Walt Disney Prods. for the design of an improved optical printer for special effects and matte shots.

E.L. Stones, Glen Robinson, Winfield Hubbard and Luther Newman of the MGM Studio Construction Dept. for the design of a multiple-cable remote-controlled winch.

Points of Interest

1. King of the mountain: *Ben-Hur* sets new record for most Academy Awards—eleven.

Eligible Films That Failed to Be Nominated for Best Picture

Some Like It Hot; The 400 Blows; Wild Strawberries; Suddenly, Last Summer; Rio Bravo; The Horse Soldiers; North by Northwest; Operation Petticoat; Journey to the Center of the Earth; Imitation of Life.

Submitted Films Rejected by the Foreign Language Film Award Committee

The World of Apu (India), directed by Satyajit Ray; *Fires on the Plain* (Japan), directed by Kon Ichikawa; *Nazarin* (Mexico), directed by Luis Buñuel.

1960

Picture
The Alamo, Batjac, UA. Produced by John Wayne.

★ *The Apartment,* Mirisch, UA. Produced by Billy Wilder.

Elmer Gantry, Lancaster-Brooks, UA. Produced by Bernard Smith.

Sons and Lovers, Wald, 20th Century–Fox. Produced by Jerry Wald.

The Sundowners, Warner Bros. Produced by Fred Zinnemann.

Actor
Trevor Howard in *Sons and Lovers* (Wald, 20th Century–Fox).

★ Burt Lancaster in *Elmer Gantry* (Lancaster-Brooks, UA).

Jack Lemmon in *The Apartment* (Mirisch, UA).

Laurence Olivier in *The Entertainer* (Woodfall, Continental) (British).

Spencer Tracy in *Inherit the Wind* (Kramer, UA).

Actress

Greer Garson in *Sunrise at Campobello* (Schary, Warner Bros.).
Deborah Kerr in *The Sundowners* (Warner Bros.).
Shirley MacLaine in *The Apartment* (Mirisch, UA).
Melina Mercouri in *Never on Sunday* (Melinafilm, Lopert Pictures) (Greek).
★ Elizabeth Taylor in *Butterfield 8* (Afton-Linebrook, MGM).

Supporting Actor

Peter Falk in *Murder, Inc.* (20th Century–Fox).
Jack Kruschen in *The Apartment* (Mirisch, UA).
Sal Mineo in *Exodus* (Preminger, UA).
★ Peter Ustinov in *Spartacus* (Bryna, U-I).
Chill Wills in *The Alamo* (Batjac, UA).

Supporting Actress

Glynis Johns in *The Sundowners* (Warner Bros.).
★ Shirley Jones in *Elmer Gantry* (Lancaster-Brooks, UA).
Shirley Knight in *The Dark at the Top of the Stairs* (Warner Bros.).
Janet Leigh in *Psycho* (Hitchcock, Paramount).
Mary Ure in *Sons and Lovers* (Wald, 20th Century–Fox).

Director

Jack Cardiff for *Sons and Lovers* (Wald, 20th Century–Fox).
Jules Dassin for *Never on Sunday* (Melinafilm, Lopert Pictures) (Greek).
Alfred Hitchcock for *Psycho* (Hitchcock, Paramount).
★ Billy Wilder for *The Apartment* (Mirisch, UA).
Fred Zinnemann for *The Sundowners* (Warner Bros.).

Writing

(SCREENPLAY—BASED ON MATERIAL FROM ANOTHER MEDIUM)
★ *Elmer Gantry*, Lancaster-Brooks, UA. Richard Brooks.
Inherit the Wind, Kramer, UA. Nathan E. Douglas and Harold Jacob Smith.
Sons and Lovers, Wald, 20th Century–Fox. Gavin Lambert and T.E.B. Clarke.
The Sundowners, Warner Bros. Isobel Lannart.
Tunes of Glory, Lopert Pictures (British). James Kennaway.

(STORY AND SCREENPLAY—WRITTEN DIRECTLY FOR THE SCREEN)
The Angry Silence, Beaver Films, Lion International (British). Richard Gregson and Michael Craig; Bryan Forbes.
★ *The Apartment*, Mirisch, UA. Billy Wilder and I.A.L. Diamond.
The Facts of Life, Panama and Frank, UA. Norman Panama and Melvin Frank.
Hiroshima, Mon Amour, Zenith International (French-Japanese). Marguérite Duras.
Never on Sunday, Melinafilm, Lopert Pictures (Greek). Jules Dassin.

Cinematography

(BLACK-AND-WHITE)
The Apartment, Mirisch, UA. Joseph LaShelle.
The Facts of Life, Panama and Frank, UA. Charles B. Lang, Jr.
Inherit the Wind, Kramer, UA. Ernest Laszlo.
Psycho, Hitchcock, Paramount. John L. Russell.
★ *Sons and Lovers*, Wald, 20th Century–Fox. Freddie Francis.

(COLOR)
The Alamo, Batjac, UA. William H. Clothier.
Butterfield 8, Afton-Linebrook, MGM. Joseph Ruttenberg and Charles Harten.
Exodus, Preminger, UA. Sam Leavitt.
Pepe, Sidney, Columbia. Joe MacDonald.
★ *Spartacus*, Bryna, U-I. Russell Metty.

Art Direction—Set Direction

(BLACK-AND-WHITE)
★ *The Apartment*, Mirisch, UA. Alexander Trauner; Edward G. Boyle.
The Facts of Life, Panama and Frank, UA. Joseph McMillan Johnson and Kenneth A. Reid; Ross Dowd.
Psycho, Hitchcock, Paramount. Joseph Hurley and Robert Clatworthy; George Milo.
Sons and Lovers, Wald, 20th Century–Fox. Tom Morahan; Lionel Couch.
Visit to a Small Planet, Wallis, Paramount. Hal Pereira and Walter Tyler; Sam Comer and Arthur Krams.

(COLOR)
Cimarron, MGM. George W. Davis and Addison Hehr; Henry Grace, Hugh Hunt and Otto Siegel.
It Started in Naples, Paramount. Hal Pereira and Roland Anderson; Sam Comer and Arrigo Breschi.
Pepe, Sidney, Columbia. Ted Haworth; William Kiernan.
★ *Spartacus*, Bryna, U-I. Alexander Golitzen and Eric Orbom; Russell A. Gausman and Julia Heron.
Sunrise at Campobello, Schary, Warner Bros. Edward Carrere; George James Hopkins.

Sound

★ *The Alamo*, Batjac, UA. Samuel Goldwyn Studio Sound Dept.; Gordon E. Sawyer, sound director; and Todd-AO Sound Dept.; Fred Hynes, sound director.
The Apartment, Mirisch, UA. Samuel Goldwyn Studio Sound Dept.; Gordon E. Sawyer, sound director.
Cimarron, MGM. MGM Studio Sound Dept.; Franklin E. Milton, sound director.
Pepe, Sidney, Columbia. Columbia Studio Sound Dept.; Charles Rice, sound director.
Sunrise at Campobello, Schary, Warner Bros. Warner Bros. Studio Sound Dept.; George R. Groves, sound director.

Music

(SONG)

"The Facts of Life" (*The Facts of Life*, Panama and Frank, UA); Music and Lyrics by Johnny Mercer.

"Faraway Part of Town" (*Pepe*, Sidney, Columbia); Music by André Previn. Lyrics by Dory Langdon.

"The Green Leaves of Summer" (*The Alamo*, Batjac, UA); Music by Dimitri Tiomkin. Lyrics by Paul Francis Webster.

★ "Never on Sunday" (*Never on Sunday*, Melinafilm, Lopert Pictures) (Greek); Music and Lyrics by Manos Hadjidakis.

"The Second Time Around" (*High Time*, Crosby, 20th Century–Fox); Music by James Van Heusen. Lyrics by Sammy Cahn.

(SCORING OF A DRAMATIC OR COMEDY PICTURE)

The Alamo, Batjac, UA. Dimitri Tiomkin.

Elmer Gantry, Lancaster-Brooks, UA. André Previn.

★ *Exodus*, Preminger, UA. Ernest Gold.

The Magnificent Seven, Mirisch-Alpha, UA. Elmer Bernstein.

Spartacus, Bryna, U-I. Alex North.

(SCORING OF A MUSICAL PICTURE)

Bells Are Ringing, Freed, MGM. André Previn.

Can-Can, Suffolk-Cummings, 20th Century–Fox. Nelson Riddle.

Let's Make Love, Wald, 20th Century–Fox. Lionel Newman and Earle H. Hagen.

Pepe, Sidney, Columbia. Johnny Green.

★ *Song Without End*, Goetz, Columbia. Morris Stoloff and Harry Sukman.

Film Editing

The Alamo, Batjac, UA. Stuart Gilmore.

★ *The Apartment*, Mirisch, UA. Daniel Mandell.

Inherit the Wind, Kramer, UA. Frederic Knudtson.

Pepe, Sidney, Columbia. Viola Lawrence and Al Clark.

Spartacus, Bryna, U-I. Robert Lawrence.

Costume Design

(BLACK-AND-WHITE)

★ *The Facts of Life*, Panama and Frank, UA. Edith Head and Edward Stevenson.

Never on Sunday, Melinafilm, Lopert Pictures (Greek). Denny Vachlioti.

The Rise and Fall of Legs Diamond, United States Prod., Warner Bros. Howard Shoup.

Seven Thieves, 20th Century–Fox. Bill Thomas.

The Virgin Spring, Janus Films (Swedish). Marik Vos.

(COLOR)

Can-Can, Suffolk-Cummings, 20th Century–Fox. Irene Sharaff.

Midnight Lace, Hunter-Arwin, U-I. Irene.

Pepe, Sidney, Columbia. Edith Head.

★ *Spartacus*, Bryna, U-I. Valles and Bill Thomas.

Sunrise at Campobello, Schary, Warner Bros. Marjorie Best.

Special Effects

The Last Voyage, Stone, MGM. A.J. Lohman.

★ *The Time Machine*, Galaxy, MGM. Gene Warren and Tim Baar.

Short Subjects

(CARTOONS)

Goliath II, Disney, Buena Vista. Walt Disney, producer.

High Note, Warner Bros.

Mouse and Garden, Warner Bros.

★ *Munro*, Rembrandt Films, Film Representations. William L. Snyder, producer.

A Place in the Sun, George K. Arthur–Go Pictures (Czechoslovakian). Frantisek Vystrecil, producer.

(LIVE ACTION SUBJECTS)

The Creation of Woman, Trident Films, Sterling World Distributors (Indian). Charles F. Schwep and Ismail Merchant, producers.

★ *Day of the Painter*, Little Movies, Kingsley-Union Films. Ezra R. Baker, producer.

Islands of the Sea, Disney, Buena Vista. Walt Disney, producer.

A Sport Is Born, Paramount. Leslie Winik, producer.

Documentary

(SHORT SUBJECTS)

Beyond Silence, U.S. Information Agency.

A City Called Copenhagen, Statens Filmcentral, Danish Film Office (Danish).

George Grosz' Interregnum, Educational Communications Corp. Charles and Altina Carey, producers.

★ *Giuseppina*, Schoenfeld Films (British). James Hill, producer.

Universe, National Film Board of Canada, Schoenfeld Films (Canadian). Colin Low; producer.

(FEATURES)

★ *The Horse with the Flying Tail*, Disney, Buena Vista. Larry Lansburgh, producer.

Rebel in Paradise, Tiare Co. Robert D. Fraser, producer.

Foreign Language Film

Kapo (Italy).

La Verité (France).

Macario (Mexico).

The Ninth Circle (Yugoslavia).

★ *The Virgin Spring* (Sweden).

Irving G. Thalberg Memorial Award

Not given this year.

Jean Hersholt Humanitarian Award
Sol Lesser.

Honorary Awards
Gary Cooper for his many memorable screen performances and the international recognition he, as an individual, has gained for the motion picture industry (statuette).

Stan Laurel for his creative pioneering in the field of cinema comedy (statuette).

Hayley Mills for *Pollyana,* the most outstanding juvenile performance during 1960 (miniature statuette).

Scientific or Technical
CLASS I (STATUETTE)

None.

CLASS II (PLAQUE)

Ampex Professional Products Co. for the production of a well-engineered multi-purpose sound system combining high standards of quality with convenience of control, dependable operation and simplified emergency provisions.

CLASS III (CITATION)

Arthur Holcomb, Petro Vlahos and Columbia Studio Camera Dept. for a camera flicker indicating device.

Anthony Paglia and the 20th Century–Fox Studio Mechanical Effects Dept. for the design and construction of a miniature flak gun and ammunition.

Carl Hauge, Robert Grubel and Edward Reichard of Consolidated Film Industries for the development of an automatic developer replenisher system.

Points of Interest

1. The family way: Actress nominee Melina Mercouri engaged to Director and Original Screenplay nominee Jules Dassin.
2. Cartoonal knowledge: Political cartoonist Jules Feiffer is creator of Best Cartoon winner *Munro.*
3. Three-timer: Billy Wilder wins three Oscars for one film.

Eligible Films That Failed to Be Nominated for Best Picture

Psycho; Lola Montes; Hiroshima, Mon Amour; Bells Are Ringing; Home From the Hill; Spartacus.

Submitted Film Rejected by the Foreign Language Film Award Committee

Late Autumn (Japan), directed by Yasujiro Ozu.

Eligible Songs That Failed to Be Nominated

"G.I. Blues" (Sid Tepper and Roy C. Bennett)—*G.I. Blues;* "Lonely Boy" (Paul Anka)—*Girls Town;* "North to Alaska" (Mike Phillips)—*North to Alaska;* "Swingin' School" (Kal Mann, Bernie Lowe and Dave Appell)—*Because They're Young;* "Where the Boys Are" (Neil Sedaka and Howard Greenfield)—*Where the Boys Are.*

1961

Picture
Fanny, Mansfield, Warner Bros. Produced by Joshua Logan.

The Guns of Navarone, Foreman, Columbia. Produced by Carl Foreman.

The Hustler, Rossen, 20th Century–Fox. Produced by Robert Rossen.

Judgment at Nuremberg, Kramer, UA. Produced by Stanley Kramer.

★ *West Side Story,* Mirisch–B&P Enterprises, UA. Produced by Robert Wise.

Actor
Charles Boyer in *Fanny* (Mansfield, Warner Bros.).

Paul Newman in *The Hustler* (Rossen, 20th Century–Fox).

★ Maximilian Schell in *Judgment at Nuremberg* (Kramer, UA).

Spencer Tracy in *Judgment at Nuremberg* (Kramer, UA).

Stuart Whitman in *The Mark* (Stross-Buchman, Continental) (British).

Actress
Audrey Hepburn in *Breakfast at Tiffany's* (Jurow-Shepherd, Paramount).

Piper Laurie in *The Hustler* (Rossen, 20th Century–Fox).

★ Sophia Loren in *Two Women* (Ponti, Embassy—Italian).

Geraldine Page in *Summer and Smoke* (Wallis, Paramount).

Natalie Wood in *Splendor in the Grass* (Kazan, Warner Bros.).

Supporting Actor
★ George Chakiris in *West Side Story* (Mirisch–B&P Enterprises, UA).

Montgomery Clift in *Judgment at Nuremburg* (Kramer, UA).

Peter Falk in *Pocketful of Miracles* (Franton, UA).

Jackie Gleason in *The Hustler* (Rossen, 20th Century–Fox).

George C. Scott in *The Hustler* (Rossen, 20th Century–Fox).

Supporting Actress
Fay Bainter in *The Children's Hour* (Mirisch–Worldwide, UA).

Judy Garland in *Judgment at Nuremberg* (Kramer, UA).
Lotte Lenya in *The Roman Spring of Mrs. Stone* (Seven Arts, Warner Bros.).
Una Merkel in *Summer and Smoke* (Wallis, Paramount).
★ Rita Moreno in *West Side Story* (Mirisch–B&P Enterprises, UA).

Director

Federico Fellini for *La Dolce Vita* (Astor Pictures) (Italian).
Stanley Kramer for *Judgment at Nuremberg* (Kramer, UA).
Robert Rossen for *The Hustler* (Rossen, 20th Century–Fox).
J. Lee Thompson for *The Guns of Navarone* (Foreman, Columbia).
★ Robert Wise and Jerome Robbins for *West Side Story* (Mirisch–B&P Enterprises, UA).

Writing

(SCREENPLAY—BASED ON MATERIAL FROM ANOTHER MEDIUM)

Breakfast at Tiffany's, Jurow-Shepherd, Paramount. George Axelrod.
The Guns of Navarone, Foreman, Columbia. Carl Foreman.
The Hustler, Rossen, 20th Century–Fox. Sidney Carroll and Robert Rossen.
★ *Judgment at Nuremberg*, Kramer, UA. Abby Mann.
West Side Story, Mirisch–B&P Enterprises, UA. Ernest Lehman.

(STORY AND SCREENPLAY—WRITTEN DIRECTLY FOR THE SCREEN)

Ballad of a Soldier, Kingsley International-M.J.P. (Russian). Valentin Yoshov and Grigori Chukhrai.
General Della Rovere, Continental Distributing (Italian). Sergio Amidei, Diego Fabbri and Indro Montanelli.
La Dolce Vita, Astor Pictures (Italian). Federico Fellini, Tullio Pinelli, Ennio Flaiano and Brunello Rondi.
Lover Come Back, Shapiro-Arwin, U-I. Stanley Shapiro and Paul Henning.
★ *Splendor in the Grass*, Kazan, Warner Bros. William Inge.

Cinematography

(BLACK-AND-WHITE)

The Absent-Minded Professor, Disney, Buena Vista. Edward Colman.
The Children's Hour, Mirisch-Worldwide, UA. Franz F. Planer.
★ *The Hustler*, Rossen, 20th Century–Fox. Eugen Shuftan.
Judgment at Nuremberg, Kramer, UA. Ernest Laszlo.
One, Two, Three, Mirisch-Pyramid, UA. Daniel L. Fapp.

(COLOR)

Fanny, Mansfield, Warner Bros. Jack Cardiff.
Flower Drum Song, Hunter, U-I. Russell Metty.
A Majority of One, Warner Bros. Harry Stradling, Sr.
One-Eyed Jacks, Pennebaker, Paramount. Charles Lang, Jr.
★ *West Side Story*, Mirisch–B&P Enterprises, UA. Daniel L. Fapp.

Art Direction—Set Decoration

(BLACK-AND-WHITE)

The Absent-Minded Professor, Disney, Buena Vista. Carroll Clark; Emile Kuri and Hal Gausman.
The Children's Hour, Mirisch-Worldwide, UA. Fernando Carrere; Edward G. Boyle.
★ *The Hustler*, Rossen, 20th Century–Fox. Harry Horner; Gene Callahan.
Judgment at Nuremberg, Kramer, UA. Rudolph Sternad; George Milo.
La Dolce Vita, Astor Pictures (Italian); Piero Gherardi.

(COLOR)

Breakfast at Tiffany's, Jurow-Shepherd, Paramount. Hal Pereira and Roland Anderson; Sam Comer and Ray Moyer.
El Cid, Bronston, Allied Artists. Veniero Colasanti and John Moore.
Flower Drum Song, Hunter, U-I. Alexander Golitzen and Joseph Wright; Howard Bristol.
Summer and Smoke, Wallis, Paramount. Hal Pereira and Walter Tyler; Sam Comer and Arthur Krams.
★ *West Side Story*, Mirisch–B&P Enterprises, UA. Boris Leven; Victor A. Gangelin.

Sound

The Children's Hour, Mirisch-Worldwide, UA. Samuel Goldwyn Studio Sound Dept.; Gordon E. Sawyer, sound director.
Flower Drum Song, Hunter, U-I. Revue Studio Sound Dept.; Waldon O. Watson, sound director.
The Guns of Navarone, Foreman, Columbia. Shepperton Studio Sound Dept.; John Cox, sound director.
The Parent Trap, Disney, Buena Vista. Walt Disney Studio Sound Dept.; Robert O. Cook, sound director.
★ *West Side Story*, Mirisch–B&P Enterprises, UA. Todd-AO Sound Dept.; Fred Hynes, sound director; and Samuel Goldwyn Studio Sound Dept.; Gordon E. Sawyer, sound director.

Music

(SONG)

"Bachelor in Paradise" (*Bachelor in Paradise*, Richmond, MGM); Music by Henry Mancini. Lyrics by Mack David.
"Love Theme from *El Cid* (The Falcon and the Dove)" (*El Cid*, Bronston, Allied Artists); Music by Miklos Rozsa. Lyrics by Paul Francis Webster.
★ "Moon River" (*Breakfast at Tiffany's*, Jurow-Shepherd, Paramount); Music by Henry Mancini. Lyrics by Johnny Mercer.
"Pocketful of Miracles" (*Pocketful of Miracles*, Franton, UA); Music by James Van Heusen. Lyrics by Sammy Cahn.
"Town Without Pity" (*Town Without Pity*, Mirisch-Gloria,

UA); Music by Dimitri Tiomkin. Lyrics by Ned Washington.

(SCORING OF A DRAMATIC OR COMEDY PICTURE)
★ *Breakfast at Tiffany's*, Jurow-Shepherd, Paramount. Henry Mancini.
El Cid, Bronston, Allied Artists. Miklos Rozsa.
Fanny, Logan, Warner Bros. Morris Stoloff and Harry Sukman.
The Guns of Navarone, Foreman, Columbia. Dimitri Tiomkin.
Summer and Smoke, Wallis, Paramount. Elmer Bernstein.

(SCORING OF A MUSICAL PICTURE)
Babes in Toyland, Disney, Buena Vista. George Bruns.
Flower Drum Song, Hunter, U-I. Alfred Newman and Ken Darby.
Khovanshchina, Artkino (Russian). Dimitri Shostakovich.
Paris Blues, Pennebaker, UA. Duke Ellington.
★ *West Side Story*, Mirisch–B&P Enterprises, UA. Saul Chaplin, Johnny Green, Sid Ramin and Irwin Kostal.

Film Editing
Fanny, Mansfield, Warner Bros. William H. Reynolds.
The Guns of Navarone, Foreman, Columbia. Alan Osbiston.
Judgment at Nuremberg, Kramer, UA. Frederic Knudtson.
The Parent Trap, Disney, Buena Vista. Philip W. Anderson.
★ *West Side Story*, Mirisch–B&P Enterprises, UA. Thomas Stanford.

Costume Design
(BLACK-AND-WHITE)
The Children's Hour, Mirisch-Worldwide, UA. Dorothy Jeakins.
Claudelle Inglish, Warner Bros. Howard Shoup.
Judgment at Nuremberg, Kramer, UA. Jean Louis.
★ *La Dolce Vita*, Astor Pictures (Italian). Piero Gherardi.
Yojimbo, Toho Company (Japanese). Yoshiro Muraki.

(COLOR)
Babes in Toyland, Disney, Buena Vista. Bill Thomas.
Back Street, Hunter, U-I. Jean Louis.
Flower Drum Song, Hunter, U-I. Irene Sharaff.
Pocketful of Miracles, Franton, UA. Edith Head and Walter Plunkett.
★ *West Side Story*, Mirisch–B&P Enterprises, UA. Irene Sharaff.

Special Effects
The Absent Minded Professor, Disney, Buena Vista Dist. Co. Robert A. Mattey and Eustace Lycett.
★ *The Guns of Navarone*, Carl Foreman Prod., Columbia. Visual: Bill Warrington. Audible: Vivian C. Greenham.

Short Subjects
(CARTOONS)
Aquamania, Disney, Buena Vista. Walt Disney, producer.
Beep Prepared, Warner Bros. Chuck Jones, producer.
★ *Ersatz (The Substitute)*, Zagreb Film, Herts-Lion International Corp.
Nelly's Folly, Warner Bros. Chuck Jones, producer.
Pied Piper of Guadalupe, Warner Bros. Friz Freleng, producer.

(LIVE ACTION SUBJECTS)
Ballon Vole (Play Ball!), Ciné-Documents, Kingsley International.
The Face of Jesus, Jennings-Stern, Inc. Dr. John D. Jennings, producer.
Rooftops of New York, McCarty-Rush-Gaffney, Columbia.
★ *Seawards the Great Ships*, Templar Film Studios, Schoenfeld Films.
Very Nice, Very Nice, National Film Board of Canada, Kingsley International.

Documentary
(SHORT SUBJECTS)
Breaking the Language Barrier, U.S. Air Force.
Cradle of Genius, Plough Prods., Lesser Films (Irish). Jim O'Connor and Tom Hayes, producers.
Kahl, Dido-Film-GmbH., AEG-Filmdienst (German).
L'Uomo in Grigio (The Man in Gray) (Italian). Benedetto Benedetti, producer.
★ *Project Hope*, Klaeger Films. Frank P. Bibas, producer.

(FEATURES)
La Grande Olimipade (Olympic Games 1960), Cineriz (Italian).
★ *Le Ciel et la Boue (Sky Above and Mud Beneath)*, Rank Films (French). Arthur Cohn and René Lafuite, producers.

Foreign Language Film
Harry and the Butler (Denmark).
Immortal Love (Japan).
The Important Man (Mexico).
Placido (Spain).
★ *Through a Glass Darkly* (Sweden).

Irving G. Thalberg Memorial Award
Stanley Kramer.

Jean Hersholt Humanitarian Award
George Seaton.

Honorary Awards
William Hendricks for his outstanding patriotic service in the conception, writing and production of the Marine Corps film, *A Force in Readiness*, which has brought honor to the Academy and the motion picture industry (statuette).

Fred L. Metzler for his dedication and outstanding service to the Academy of Motion Picture Arts and Sciences (statuette).

Jerome Robbins for his brilliant achievements in the art of choreography on film (statuette).

Scientific or Technical

CLASS I (STATUETTE)

None.

CLASS II (PLAQUE)

Sylvania Electric Products, Inc., for the development of a hand held high-power photographic lighting unit known as the Sun Gun Professional.

James Dale, S. Wilson, H.E. Rice, John Rude, Laurie Atkin, Wadsworth E. Pohl, H. Peasgood and Technicolor Corp. for a process of automatic selective printing.

20th Century–Fox Research Dept., under the direction of E.I. Sponable and Herbert E. Bragg, and Deluxe Laboratories, Inc. with the assistance of F.D. Leslie, R.D. Whitmore, A.A. Alden, Endel Pool and James B. Gordon for a system of decompressing and recomposing CinemaScope pictures for conventional aspect ratios.

CLASS III (CITATION)

Hurletron, Inc., Electric Eye Equipment Division, for an automatic light changing system for motion picture printers.

Wadsworth E. Pohl and Technicolor Corp. for an integrated sound and picture transfer process.

Points of Interest

1. Two heads are better: For first time, two codirectors win Best Director Award.

Eligible Films That Failed to Be Nominated for Best Picture

Breakfast at Tiffany's; Breathless; L'Avventura; Yojimbo; The Misfits; One, Two, Three; Two Rode Together; The Absent-Minded Professor; Little Shop of Horrors.

Submitted Films Rejected by the Foreign Language Film Award Committee

Last Year at Marienbad (France), directed by Alain Resnais; *La Notte* (Italy), directed by Michelangelo Antonioni.

Eligible Songs That Failed to Be Nominated

"Can't Help Falling in Love" (George Weiss, Hugo Peretti and Luigi Creatore)—*Blue Hawaii;* "Let's Twist Again" (Kal Mann and Dave Appell)—*Twist Around the Clock.*

1962

Picture

★ *Lawrence of Arabia*, Horizon-Spiegel-Lean, Columbia. Produced by Sam Spiegel.

The Longest Day, Zanuck, 20th Century–Fox. Produced by Darryl F. Zanuck.

The Music Man, Warner Bros. Produced by Morton Da Costa.

Mutiny on the Bounty, Arcola, MGM. Produced by Aaron Rosenberg.

To Kill a Mockingbird, Pakula-Mulligan-Brentwood, U-I. Produced by Alan J. Pakula.

Actor

Burt Lancaster in *Bird Man of Alcatraz* (Hecht, UA).

Jack Lemmon in *Days of Wine and Roses* (Manulis-Jalem, Warner Bros.).

Marcello Mastroianni in *Divorce—Italian Style* (Embassy Pictures) (Italian).

Peter O'Toole in *Lawrence of Arabia* (Horizon-Spiegel-Lean, Columbia).

★ Gregory Peck in *To Kill a Mockingbird* (Pakula-Mulligan-Brentwood, U-I).

Actress

★ Anne Bancroft in *The Miracle Worker* (Playfilms, UA).

Bette Davis in *What Ever Happened to Baby Jane?* (Seven Arts–Associates & Aldrich Co., Warner Bros.).

Katharine Hepburn in *Long Day's Journey into Night* (Landau, Embassy).

Geraldine Page in *Sweet Bird of Youth* (Roxbury, MGM).

Lee Remick in *Days of Wine and Roses* (Manulis-Jalem, Warner Bros.).

Supporting Actor

★ Ed Begley in *Sweet Bird of Youth* (Roxbury, MGM).

Victor Buono in *What Ever Happened to Baby Jane?* (Seven Arts–Associates & Aldrich Co., Warner Bros.).

Telly Savalas in *Bird Man of Alcatraz* (Hecht, UA).

Omar Sharif in *Lawrence of Arabia* (Horizon-Spiegel-Lean, Columbia).

Terence Stamp in *Billy Budd* (Harvest, Allied Artists).

Supporting Actress

Mary Badham in *To Kill a Mockingbird* (Pakula-Mulligan-Brentwood, U-I).

★ Patty Duke in *The Miracle Worker* (Playfilms, UA).

Shirley Knight in *Sweet Bird of Youth* (Roxbury, MGM).

Angela Lansbury in *The Manchurian Candidate* (Axelrod-Frankenheimer, UA).

Thelma Ritter in *Bird Man of Alcatraz* (Hecht, UA).

Director

Pietro Germi for *Divorce—Italian Style* (Embassy Pictures) (Italian).

★ David Lean for *Lawrence of Arabia* (Horizon-Spiegel-Lean, Columbia).

Robert Mulligan for *To Kill a Mockingbird* (Pakula-Mulligan-Brentwood, U-I).

Arthur Penn for *The Miracle Worker* (Playfilms, UA).

Frank Perry for *David and Lisa* (Heller-Perry, Continental).

Writing

(SCREENPLAY—BASED ON MATERIAL FROM ANOTHER MEDIUM)

David and Lisa, Heller-Perry, Continental. Eleanor Perry.

Lawrence of Arabia, Horizon-Spiegel-Lean, Columbia. Robert Bolt.

Lolita, Seven Arts, MGM, Vladimir Nabokov.

The Miracle Worker, Playfilms, UA. William Gibson.

★ *To Kill a Mockingbird,* Pakula-Mulligan-Brentwood, U-I. Horton Foote.

(STORY AND SCREENPLAY—WRITTEN DIRECTLY FOR THE SCREEN)

★ *Divorce—Italian Style,* Embassy Pictures (Italian). Ennio de Concini, Alfredo Giannetti and Pietro Germi.

Freud, Huston, U-I. Charles Kaufman and Wolfgang Reinhardt.

Last Year at Marienbad, Astor Pictures (French). Alain Robbe-Grillet.

That Touch of Mink, Granley-Arwin-Shapiro, U-I. Stanley Shapiro and Nate Monaster.

Through a Glass Darkly, Janus Films (Swedish). Ingmar Bergman.

Cinematography

(BLACK-AND-WHITE)

Bird Man of Alcatraz, Hecht, UA. Burnett Guffey.

★ *The Longest Day,* Zanuck, 20th Century–Fox. Jean Bourgoin and Walter Wottitz.

To Kill a Mockingbird, Pakula-Mulligan-Brentwood, U-I. Russell Harlan.

Two for the Seesaw, Mirisch-Argyle-Talbot-Seven Arts. UA. Ted McCord.

What Ever Happened to Baby Jane?, Seven Arts–Associates & Aldrich Co., Warner Bros. Ernest Haller.

(COLOR)

Gypsy, Warner Bros. Harry Stradling, Sr.

Hatari!, Malabar, Paramount. Russell Harlan.

★ *Lawrence of Arabia,* Horizon-Spiegel-Lean, Columbia. Fred A. Young.

Mutiny on the Bounty, Arcola, MGM. Robert L. Surtees.

The Wonderful World of the Brothers Grimm, MGM and Cinerama. Paul C. Vogel.

Art Direction—Set Decoration

(BLACK-AND-WHITE)

Days of Wine and Roses, Manulis-Jalem, Warner Bros. Joseph Wright; George James Hopkins.

The Longest Day, Zanuck, 20th Century–Fox. Ted Haworth, Leon Barasa and Vincent Korda; Gabriel Bechir.

Period of Adjustment, Marten. MGM. George W. Davis and Edward Carfagno; Henry Grace and Dick Pefferle.

The Pigeon That Took Rome, Lienroe, Paramount, Hal Pereira and Roland Anderson; Sam Comer and Frank R. McKelvy.

★ *To Kill a Mockingbird,* Pakula-Mulligan-Brentwood, U-I. Alexander Golitzen and Henry Bumstead; Oliver Emert.

(COLOR)

★ *Lawrence of Arabia,* Horizon-Spiegel-Lean, Columbia. John Box and John Stoll; Dario Simoni.

The Music Man, Warner Bros. Paul Groesse; George James Hopkins.

Mutiny on the Bounty, Arcola, MGM. George W. Davis and J. McMillan Johnson; Henry Grace and Hugh Hunt.

That Touch of Mink, Granley-Arwin-Shapiro, U-I. Alexander Golitzen and Robert Clatworthy; George Milo.

The Wonderful World of the Brothers Grimm, MGM and Cinerama. George W. Davis and Edward Carfagno; Henry Grace and Dick Pefferle.

Sound

Bon Voyage, Disney, Buena Vista. Walt Disney Studio Sound Dept.; Robert O. Cook, sound director.

★ *Lawrence of Arabia,* Horizon-Spiegel-Lean, Columbia. Shepperton Studio Sound Dept.; John Cox, sound director.

The Music Man, Warner Bros. Warner Bros. Studio Sound Dept.; George R. Groves, sound director.

That Touch of Mink, Granley-Arwin-Shapiro, U-I. Universal City Studio Sound Dept.; Waldon O. Watson, sound director.

What Ever Happened to Baby Jane?, Seven Arts–Associates & Aldrich Co., Warner Bros. Glen Glenn Sound Dept.; Joseph Kelly, sound director.

Music

(SONG)

★ "Days of Wine and Roses" (*Days of Wine and Roses,* Manulis-Jalem, Warner Bros.); Music by Henry Mancini. Lyrics by Johnny Mercer.

"Love Song from *Mutiny on the Bounty* (Follow Me)" (*Mutiny on the Bounty,* Arcola, MGM); Music by Bronislau Kaper. Lyrics by Paul Francis Webster.

"Song from *Two for the Seesaw* (Second Chance)" (*Two for the Seesaw,* Mirisch-Argyle-Talbot-Seven Arts, UA); Music by André Previn. Lyrics by Dory Langdon.

"Tender Is the Night" (*Tender Is the Night,* 20th Century–

Fox); Music by Sammy Fain. Lyrics by Paul Francis Webster.

"Walk on the Wild Side" (*Walk on the Wild Side*, Feldman–Famous Artists, Columbia); Music by Elmer Bernstein. Lyrics by Mack David.

(MUSIC SCORE—SUBSTANTIALLY ORIGINAL)

Freud, Huston, U-I. Jerry Goldsmith.

★ *Lawrence of Arabia*, Horizon-Spiegel-Lean, Columbia. Maurice Jarre.

Mutiny on the Bounty, Arcola, MGM. Bronislau Kaper.

Taras Bulba, Hecht, UA. Franz Waxman.

To Kill a Mockingbird, Pakula-Mulligan-Brentwood, U-I. Elmer Bernstein.

(SCORING OF MUSIC—ADAPTATION OR TREATMENT)

Billy Rose's Jumbo, Euterpe-Arwin, MGM. George Stoll.

Gigot, Seven Arts, 20th Century–Fox. Michel Magne.

Gypsy, Warner Bros. Frank Perkins.

★ *The Music Man*, Warner Bros. Ray Heindorf.

The Wonderful World of the Brothers Grimm, MGM and Cinerama. Leigh Harline.

Film Editing

★ *Lawrence of Arabia*, Horizon-Spiegel-Lean, Columbia. Anne Coates.

The Longest Day, Zanuck, 20th Century–Fox. Samuel E. Beetley.

The Manchurian Candidate, Axelrod-Frankenheimer, UA. Ferris Webster.

The Music Man, Warner Bros. William Ziegler.

Mutiny on the Bounty, Arcola, MGM. John McSweeney, Jr.

Costume Design

(BLACK-AND-WHITE)

Days of Wine and Roses, Manulis-Jalem, Warner Bros. Don Feld.

The Man Who Shot Liberty Valance, Ford, Paramount. Edith Head.

The Miracle Worker, Playfilms, UA. Ruth Morley.

Phaedra, Dassin-Melinafilm, Lopert Pictures. Denny Vachlioti.

★ *What Ever Happened to Baby Jane?*, Seven Arts–Associates & Aldrich Co., Warner Bros. Norma Koch.

(COLOR)

Bon Voyage, Disney, Buena Vista. Bill Thomas.

Gypsy, Warner Bros. Orry-Kelly.

The Music Man, Warner Bros. Dorothy Jeakins.

My Geisha, Sachiko, Paramount. Edith Head.

★ *The Wonderful World of the Brothers Grimm*, MGM and Cinerama. Mary Wills.

Special Effects

★ *The Longest Day*, Darryl F. Zanuck Prods., 20th Century–Fox. Visual: Robert MacDonald; Audible: Jacques Maumont.

Mutiny on the Bounty, Arcola Prod., MGM. Visual: A. Arnold Gillespie; Audible: Milo Lory.

Short Subjects

(CARTOONS)

★ *The Hole*, Storyboard Inc., Brandon Films. John and Faith Hubley, producers.

Icarus Montgolfier Wright, Format Films, UA. Jules Engel, producer.

Now Hear This, Warner Bros.

Self-Defense—For Cowards, Rembrandt Films, Film Representations. William L. Snyder, producer.

Symposium on Popular Songs, Disney, Buena Vista. Walt Disney, producer.

(LIVE ACTION SUBJECTS)

Big City Blues, Mayfair Pictures. Martina and Charles Huguenot van der Linden, producers.

The Cadillac, United Producers Releasing. Robert Clouse, producer.

The Cliff Dwellers, (a.k.a. One Plus One). Group II Film Prods., Schoenfeld Films. Hayward Anderson, producer.

★ *Heureux Anniversaire* (Happy Anniversary), Atlantic Pictures Corp. (French). Pierre Etaix and J.C. Carrière, producers.

Pan, Mayfair Pictures. Herman van der Horst, producer.

Documentary

(SHORT SUBJECTS)

★ *Dylan Thomas*, TWW Ltd., Janus Films (Welsh). Jack Howells, producer.

The John Glenn Story, Department of the Navy, Warner Bros. William L. Hendricks, producer.

The Road to the Wall, CBS Films, Department of Defense. Robert Saudek, producer.

(FEATURES)

Alvorada (Brazil's Changing Face), MW Filmproduktion (German). Hugo Niebeling, producer.

★ *Black Fox*, Image Prods., Heritage Films. Louis Clyde Stoumen, producer.

Foreign Language Film

Electra (Greece).

The Four Days of Naples (Italy).

The Keeper of Promises (The Given Word) (Brazil).

★ *Sundays and Cybèle* (France).

Tlayucan (Mexico).

Irving G. Thalberg Memorial Award

Not given this year.

Jean Hersholt Humanitarian Award

Steve Broidy.

Honorary Awards

None given this year.

Scientific or Technical

CLASS I (STATUETTE)

None.

CLASS II (PLAQUE)

Ralph Chapman for the design and development of an advanced motion picture camera crane.

Albert S. Pratt, James L. Wassell and Hans C. Wohlrab of the Professional Division, Bell & Howell Co., for the design and development of a new and improved automatic motion picture additive color printer.

North American Philips Co., Inc., for the design and engineering of the Norelco Universal 70/35mm motion picture projector.

Charles E. Sutter, William Bryson Smith and Louis C. Kennell of Paramount Pictures Corp. for the engineering and application to motion picture production of a new system of electric power distribution.

CLASS III (CITATION)

Electro-Voice, Inc., for a highly directional dynamic line microphone.

Louis G. MacKenzie for a selective sound effects repeater.

Points of Interest

1. Nothing to it: Victor Buono nominated for film debut.

Rule Changes

1. The name game: The Music Scoring Awards now classified as "Music Score—Substantially Original" and "Scoring of Music—Adaptation or Treatment."

Eligible Films That Failed to Be Nominated for Best Picture

Jules and Jim, Lolita, The Man Who Shot Liberty Valance, Viridiana, Hatari!, Advise and Consent, The Manchurian Candidate, Peeping Tom, Days of Wine and Roses, What Ever Happened to Baby Jane?, Experiment in Terror, Sweet Bird of Youth.

Eligible Songs That Failed to Be Nominated

"I've Written a Letter to Daddy" (Frank DeVol and Lukas Heller)—*What Ever Happened to Baby Jane?*; "Peppermint Twist" (Joey Dee and Henry Glover)—*Hey, Let's Twist.*

1963

Picture

America, America, Athena, Warner Bros. Produced by Elia Kazan.

Cleopatra, Wanger, 20th Century–Fox. Produced by Walter Wanger.

How the West Was Won, MGM and Cinerama. Produced by Bernard Smith.

Lilies of the Field, Rainbow, UA. Produced by Ralph Nelson.

★ *Tom Jones,* Woodfall, UA-Lopert (British). Produced by Tony Richardson.

Actor

Albert Finney in *Tom Jones* (Woodfall, UA-Lopert) (British).

Richard Harris in *This Sporting Life* (Wintle-Parkyn, Reade-Sterling-Continental) (British).

Rex Harrison in *Cleopatra* (Wanger, 20th Century–Fox).

Paul Newman in *Hud* (Salem-Dover, Paramount).

★ Sidney Poitier in *Lilies of the Field* (Rainbow, UA).

Actress

Leslie Caron in *The L-Shaped Room* (Romulus, Columbia) (British).

Shirley MacLaine in *Irma La Douce* (Mirisch-Phalanx, UA).

★ Patricia Neal in *Hud* (Salem-Dover, Paramount).

Rachel Roberts in *This Sporting Life* (Wintle-Parkyn, Reade-Sterling-Continental) (British).

Natalie Wood in *Love with the Proper Stranger* (Boardwalk-Rona, Paramount).

Supporting Actor

Nick Adams in *Twilight of Honor* (Perlberg-Seaton, MGM).

Bobby Darin in *Captain Newman, M.D.* (Brentwood-Reynard, Universal).

★ Melvyn Douglas in *Hud* (Salem-Dover, Paramount).

Hugh Griffith in *Tom Jones* (Woodfall, UA-Lopert) (British).

John Huston in *The Cardinal* (Preminger, Columbia).

Supporting Actress

Diane Cilento in *Tom Jones* (Woodfall, UA-Lopert) (British).

Dame Edith Evans in *Tom Jones* (Woodfall, UA-Lopert) (British).

Joyce Redman in *Tom Jones* (Woodfall, UA-Lopert) (British).

★ Margaret Rutherford in *The V.I.P.'s* (MGM).

Lilia Skala in *Lilies of the Field* (Rainbow, UA).

Director

Federico Fellini for *Federico Fellini's 8½* (Embassy Pictures) (Italian).

Elia Kazan for *America, America* (Athena, Warner Bros.).
Otto Preminger for *The Cardinal* (Preminger, Columbia).
★ Tony Richardson for *Tom Jones* (Woodfall, UA-Lopert) (British).
Martin Ritt for *Hud* (Salem-Dover, Paramount).

Writing

(SCREENPLAY—BASED ON MATERIAL FROM ANOTHER MEDIUM)

Captain Newman, M.D., Brentwood-Reynard, Universal. Richard L. Breen, Phoebe and Henry Ephron.
Hud, Salem-Dover, Paramount. Irving Ravetch and Harriet Frank, Jr.
Lilies of the Field. Rainbow, UA. James Poe.
Sundays and Cybèle, Columbia (French). Serge Bourguigon and Antoine Tudal.
★ *Tom Jones*, Woodfall, UA-Lopert (British). John Osborne.

(STORY AND SCREENPLAY—WRITTEN DIRECTLY FOR THE SCREEN)

America, America, Athena, Warner Bros. Elia Kazan.
Federico Fellini's 8½, Embassy Pictures (Italian). Federico Fellini, Ennio Flaiano, Tullio Pinelli and Brunello Rondi.
The Four Days of Naples, Titanus, MGM (Italian). Pasquale Festa Campanile, Massino Franciosa, Nanni Loy, Vasco Pratolini and Carlo Bernari.
★ *How the West Was Won*, MGM and Cinerama. James R. Webb.
Love with the Proper Stranger, Boardwalk-Rona, Paramount. Arnold Schulman.

Cinematography

(BLACK-AND-WHITE)

The Balcony, Allen-Hodgdon, Reade-Sterling-Continental Dist. George Folsey.
The Caretakers, Bartlett, UA. Lucien Ballard.
★ *Hud*, Salem-Dover, Paramount. James Wong Howe.
Lilies of the Field, Rainbow, UA. Ernest Haller.
Love with the Proper Stranger, Boardwalk-Rona, Paramount. Milton Krasner.

(COLOR)

The Cardinal, Preminger, Columbia. Leon Shamroy.
★ *Cleopatra*, Wanger, 20th Century–Fox. Leon Shamroy.
How the West Was Won, MGM and Cinerama. William H. Daniels, Milton Krasner, Charles Lang, Jr. and Joseph LaShelle.
Irma La Douce, Mirisch-Phalanx, UA. Joseph LaShelle.
It's a Mad, Mad, Mad, Mad World, Kramer, UA. Ernest Laszlo.

Art Direction—Set Decoration

(BLACK-AND-WHITE)

★ *America America*, Athena, Warner Bros. Gene Callahan.
Federico Fellini's 8½, Embassy Pictures (Italian). Piero Gherardi.
Hud, Salem-Dover, Paramount. Hal Pereira and Tambi Larsen; Sam Comer and Robert Benton.
Love with the Proper Stranger, Boardwalk-Rona, Paramount. Hal Pereira and Roland Anderson; Sam Comer and Grace Gregory.
Twilight of Honor, Perlberg-Seaton, MGM. George W. Davis and Paul Groesse; Henry Grace and Hugh Hunt.

(COLOR)

The Cardinal, Preminger, Columbia. Lyle Wheeler; Gene Callahan.
★ *Cleopatra*, Wanger, 20th Century–Fox. John DeCuir, Jack Martin Smith, Hilyard Brown, Herman Blumenthal, Elven Webb, Maurice Pelling and Boris Juraga; Walter M. Scott, Paul S. Fox and Ray Moyer.
Come Blow Your Horn, Essex-Tandem, Paramount. Hal Pereira and Roland Anderson; Sam Comer and James Payne.
How the West Was Won, MGM and Cinerama. George W. Davis, William Ferrari and Addison Hehr; Henry Grace, Don Greenwood, Jr. and Jack Mills.
Tom Jones, Woodfall, UA-Lopert (British). Ralph Brinton, Ted Marshall and Jocelyn Herbert; Josie MacAvin.

Sound

Bye Bye Birdie, Kohlmar-Sidney, Columbia. Columbia Studio Sound Dept. Charles Rice, sound director.
Captain Newman, M.D., Brentwood-Reynard, Universal. Universal City Studio Sound Dept.; Waldon O. Watson, sound director.
Cleopatra, Wanger, 20th Century–Fox. 20th Century–Fox Studio Sound Dept.; James P. Corcoran, sound director; and Todd-AO Sound Dept., Fred Hynes, sound director.
★ *How the West Was Won*, MGM and Cinerama. MGM Studio Sound Dept.; Franklin E. Milton, sound director.
It's a Mad, Mad, Mad, Mad World, Kramer, UA. Samuel Goldwyn Studio Sound Dept.; Gordon E. Sawyer, sound director.

Music

(SONG)

★ "Call Me Irresponsible" (*Papa's Delicate Condition*, Amro, Paramount); Music by James Van Heusen. Lyrics by Sammy Cahn.
"Charade" (*Charade*, Donen, Universal); Music by Henry Mancini. Lyrics by Johnny Mercer.
"It's a Mad, Mad, Mad, Mad World" (*It's a Mad, Mad, Mad, Mad World*, Kramer, UA); Music by Ernest Gold. Lyrics by Mack David.
"More" (*Mondo Cane*, Cineriz Prod., Times Film); Music by Riz Ortolani and Nino Oliviero. Lyrics by Norman Newell.
"So Little Time" (*55 Days at Peking*, Bronston, Allied Artists); Music by Dimitri Tiomkin. Lyrics by Paul Francis Webster.

(MUSIC SCORE—SUBSTANTIALLY ORIGINAL)

Cleopatra, Wanger, 20th Century–Fox. Alex North.
55 Days at Peking, Bronston, Allied Artists. Dimitri Tiomkin.
How the West Was Won, MGM and Cinerama. Alfred Newman and Ken Darby.
It's a Mad, Mad, Mad, Mad World, Kramer, UA. Ernest Gold.
★ *Tom Jones*, Woodfall, UA-Lopert (British). John Addison.

(SCORING OF MUSIC—ADAPTATION OR TREATMENT)

Bye Bye Birdie, Kohlmar-Sidney, Columbia. John Green.
★ *Irma La Douce*, Mirisch-Phalanx, UA. André Previn.
A New Kind of Love, Llenroc, Paramount. Leith Stevens.
Sundays and Cybèle, Columbia (French) Maurice Jarre.
The Sword in the Stone, Disney, Buenta Vista. George Bruns.

Film Editing

The Cardinal, Preminger, Columbia. Louis R. Loeffler.
Cleopatra, Wanger, 20th Century–Fox. Dorothy Spencer.
The Great Escape, Mirisch-Alpha, UA. Ferris Webster.
★ *How the West Was Won*, MGM and Cinerama. Harold F. Kress.
It's a Mad, Mad, Mad, Mad World, Kramer, UA. Frederic Knudtson, Robert C. Jones and Gene Fowler, Jr.

Costume Design

(BLACK-AND-WHITE)

★ *Federico Fellini's 8½*, Embassy Pictures (Italian). Piero Gherardi.
Love with the Proper Stranger, Boardwalk-Rona, Paramount. Edith Head.
The Stripper, Wald, 20th Century–Fox. Travilla.
Toys in the Attic, Mirisch-Claude, UA. Bill Thomas.
Wives and Lovers, Wallis, Paramount. Edith Head.

(COLOR)

The Cardinal, Preminger, Columbia. Donald Brooks.
★ *Cleopatra*, Wanger, 20th Century–Fox. Irene Sharaff, Vittorio Nino Novarese and Renie.
How the West Was Won, MGM and Cinerema. Walter Plunkett.
The Leopard, Titanus, 20th Century–Fox. Piero Tosi.
A New Kind of Love, Llenroc, Paramount. Edith Head.

Special Visual Effects

The Birds, Hitchcock, Universal. Ub Iwerks.
★ *Cleopatra*, Wanger, 20th Century–Fox. Emil Kosa, Jr.

Sound Effects

A Gathering of Eagles, Universal. Robert L. Bratton.
★ *It's a Mad, Mad, Mad, Mad World*, Kramer, UA. Walter G. Elliott.

Short Subjects

(CARTOONS)

Automania 2000, Pathé Contemporary Films. John Halas, producer.
★ *The Critic*, Pintoff-Crossbow Prods., Columbia. Ernest Pintoff, producer.
The Game (Ingra), Rembrandt Films–Film Representations. Dusan Vukotic, producer.
My Financial Career, National Film Board of Canada. Walter Reade-Sterling-Continental Distributing. Colin Low and Tom Daly, producers.
Pianissimo, Cinema 16. Carmen D'Avino, producer.

(LIVE ACTION SUBJECTS)

The Concert, King Corp., George K. Arthur–Go Pictures. Ezra Baker, producer.
Home-Made Car, Schoenfeld Films. James Hill, producer.
★ *An Occurrence at Owl Creek Bridge*, Janus Films. Paul de Roubaix and Marcel Ichac, producers.
Six-Sided Triangle, Lion International. Christopher Miles, producer.
That's Me, Pathé Contemporary Films. Walker Stuart, producer.

Documentary

(SHORT SUBJECTS)

★ *Chagall*, Auerbach-Flag Films. Simon Schiffrin, producer.
The Five Cities of June, U.S. Information Agency. George Stevens, Jr., producer.
The Spirit of America, Spotlite News. Algernon G. Walker, producer.
Thirty Million Letters, British Transport Films. Edgar Anstey, producer.
To Live Again, Wilding Inc. Mel London, producer.

(FEATURES)

Le Maillon et la Chaine (The Link and the Chain). Films Du Centaure-Filmartic (French). Paul de Roubaix, producer.
★ *Robert Frost: A Lover's Quarrel With the World*, WGBH Educational Foundation. Robert Hughes, producer.
The Yanks Are Coming, David L. Wolper Prods. Marshall Flaum, producer.

Foreign Language Film

★ *Federico Fellini's 8½* (Italy).
Knife in the Water (Poland).
Los Tarantos (Spain).
The Red Lanterns (Greece).
Twin Sisters of Kyoto (Japan).

Irving G. Thalberg Memorial Award

Sam Spiegel.

Jean Hersholt Humanitarian Award

Not given this year.

Honorary Awards

None given this year.

Scientific or Technical Awards

CLASS I (STATUETTE)

None.

CLASS II (PLAQUE)

None.

CLASS III (CITATION)

Douglas G. Shearer and A. Arnold Gillespie of MGM Studio for the engineering of an improved Background Process Projection System.

Points of Interest

1. The family way: Rex Harrison and wife Rachel Roberts both nominated.
2. Renaissance man: Oscar-winning writer-director John Huston nominated for Supporting Actor.
3. Cartoon character: Mel Brooks is writer-director of cartoon winner, *The Critic.*

Rule Changes

1. The more the merrier: "Special Effects" divided into "Special Visual Effects" and "Sound Effects."

Eligible Films That Failed to Be Nominated for Best Picture

Hud, The Birds, The Great Escape, The Nutty Professor, The Leopard, Bye Bye Birdie.

Eligible Songs That Failed to Be Nominated

"Beach Party" (Gary Usher and Roger Christian)—*Beach Party;* "Bye Bye Birdie" (Charles Strouse and Lee Adams)—*Bye Bye Birdie.*

1964

Picture

Becket, Wallis, Paramount. Produced by Hal B. Wallis.

Dr. Strangelove or: How I Learned to Stop Worrying and Love the Bomb, Hawk Films, Columbia. Produced by Stanley Kubrick.

Mary Poppins, Disney, Buena Vista. Produced by Walt Disney and Bill Walsh.

★ *My Fair Lady,* Warner Bros. Produced by Jack L. Warner.

Zorba the Greek, Rochley, International Classics/20th Century–Fox. Produced by Michael Cacoyannis.

Actor

Richard Burton in *Becket* (Wallis, Paramount).

★ Rex Harrison in *My Fair Lady* (Warner Bros.).

Peter O'Toole in Becket (Wallis, Paramount).

Anthony Quinn in *Zorba the Greek* (Rochley, International Classics/20th Century–Fox).

Peter Sellers in *Dr. Strangelove or: How I Learned to Stop Worrying and Love the Bomb* (Hawk Films, Columbia).

Actress

★ Julie Andrews in *Mary Poppins* (Disney, Buena Vista).

Anne Bancroft in *The Pumpkin Eater* (Romulus, Royal Films International/Columbia) (British).

Sophia Loren in *Marriage Italian Style* (Champion-Concordia, Embassy) (Italian).

Debbie Reynolds in *The Unsinkable Molly Brown* (Marten, MGM).

Kim Stanley in *Seance on a Wet Afternoon* (Attenborough-Forbes, Artixo) (British).

Supporting Actor

John Gielgud in *Becket* (Wallis, Paramount).

Stanley Holloway in *My Fair Lady* (Warner Bros.).

Edmond O'Brien in *Seven Days in May* (Joel, Paramount).

Lee Tracy in *The Best Man* (Millar-Turman, UA).

★ Peter Ustinov in *Topkapi* (Filmways, UA).

Supporting Actress

Gladys Cooper in *My Fair Lady* (Warner Bros.).

Dame Edith Evans in *The Chalk Garden* (Hunter, Universal).

Grayson Hall in *The Night of the Iguana* (Seven Arts, MGM).

★ Lila Kedrova in *Zorba the Greek* (Rochley, International Classics/20th Century–Fox).

Agnes Moorehead in *Hush . . . Hush, Sweet Charlotte* (Associates & Aldrich Co., 20th Century–Fox).

Director

Michael Cacoyannis for *Zorba the Greek* (Rochley, International Classics/20th Century–Fox).

★ George Cukor for *My Fair Lady* (Warner Bros.).

Peter Glenville for *Becket* (Wallis, Paramount).

Stanley Kubrick for *Dr. Strangelove or: How I Learned to Stop Worrying and Love the Bomb* (Hawk Films, Columbia).

Robert Stevenson for *Mary Poppins* (Disney, Buena Vista).

Writing

(SCREENPLAY—BASED ON MATERIAL FROM ANOTHER MEDIUM)

★ *Becket,* Wallis, Paramount. Edward Anhalt.

Dr. Strangelove or: How I Learned to Stop Worrying and Love the Bomb, Hawk Films, Columbia. Stanley Kubrick, Peter George and Terry Southern.

Mary Poppins, Disney, Buena Vista. Bill Walsh and Don DaGradi.

My Fair Lady, Warner Bros. Alan Jay Lerner.

Zorba the Greek, Rochley, International Classics/20th Century–Fox. Michael Cacoyannis.

(STORY AND SCREENPLAY—WRITTEN DIRECTLY FOR THE SCREEN)

★ *Father Goose,* Granox, Universal. S.H. Barnett; Peter Stone and Frank Tarloff.

A Hard Day's Night, Shenson, UA (British). Alan Owen.

One Potato, Two Potato, Cinema V. Orville H. Hampton and Raphael Hayes.

The Organizer, Reade-Sterling-Continental (Italian). Age, Scarpelli and Mario Monicelli.

That Man from Rio, Lopert (French). Jean-Paul Rappeneau, Ariane Mnouchkine, Daniel Boulanger and Philippe De Broca.

Cinematography

(BLACK-AND-WHITE)

The Americanization of Emily, Ransohoff, MGM. Philip H. Lathrop.

Fate Is the Hunter, Arcola, 20th Century–Fox. Milton Krasner.

Hush . . . Hush, Sweet Charlotte, Associates & Aldrich Co., 20th Century–Fox. Joseph Biroc.

The Night of the Iguana, Seven Arts, MGM. Gabriel Figueroa.

★ *Zorba the Greek,* Rochley, International Classics/20th Century–Fox. Walter Lassally.

(COLOR)

Becket, Wallis, Paramount. Geoffrey Unsworth.

Cheyenne Autumn, Ford-Smith, Warner Bros. William H. Clothier.

Mary Poppins, Disney, Buena Vista. Edward Colman.

★ *My Fair Lady,* Warner Bros. Harry Stradling.

The Unsinkable Molly Brown, Marten, MGM. Daniel L. Fapp.

Art Direction—Set Decoration

(BLACK-AND-WHITE)

The Americanization of Emily, Ransohoff, MGM. George W. Davis, Hans Peters and Elliot Scott; Henry Grace and Robert R. Benton.

Hush . . . Hush, Sweet Charlotte, Associates & Aldrich Co., 20th Century–Fox. William Glasgow; Raphael Bretton.

The Night of the Iguana, Seven Arts, MGM. Stephen Grimes.

Seven Days in May, Joel, Paramount. Cary Odell; Edward G. Boyle.

★ *Zorba the Greek,* Rochley, International Classics/20th Century–Fox. Vassilis Fotopoulos.

(COLOR)

Becket, Wallis, Paramount. John Bryan and Maurice Carter; Patrick McLoughlin and Robert Cartwright.

Mary Poppins, Disney, Buena Vista. Carroll Clark and William H. Tuntke; Emile Kuri and Hal Gausman.

★ *My Fair Lady,* Warner Bros. Gene Allen and Cecil Beaton; George James Hopkins.

The Unsinkable Molly Brown, Marten, MGM. George W. Davis and Preston Ames; Henry Grace and Hugh Hunt.

What a Way to Go, Apjac-Orchard, 20th Century–Fox. Jack Martin Smith and Ted Haworth; Walter M. Scott and Stuart A. Reiss.

Sound

Becket, Wallis, Paramount. Shepperton Studio Sound Dept.; John Cox, sound director.

Father Goose, Granox, Universal. Universal City Studio Sound Dept.; Waldon O. Watson, sound director.

Mary Poppins, Disney, Buena Vista. Walt Disney Studio Sound Dept.; Robert O. Cook, sound director.

★ *My Fair Lady,* Warner Bros. Warner Bros. Studio Sound Dept.; George R. Groves, sound director.

The Unsinkable Molly Brown, Marten, MGM. MGM Studio Sound Dept.; Franklin E. Milton, sound director.

Music

(SONG)

★ "Chim Chim Cher-ee" (*Mary Poppins,* Disney, Buena Vista); Music and Lyrics by Richard M. Sherman and Robert B. Sherman.

"Dear Heart" (*Dear Heart,* Warner Bros.); Music by Henry Mancini. Lyrics by Jay Livingston and Ray Evans.

"Hush . . . Hush, Sweet Charlotte" (*Hush . . . Hush, Sweet Charlotte,* Associates & Aldrich Co., 20th Century–Fox); Music by Fank DeVol. Lyrics by Mack David.

"My Kind of Town" (*Robin and the 7 Hoods,* Warner Bros.); Music by James Van Heusen. Lyrics by Sammy Cahn.

"Where Love Has Gone" (*Where Love Has Gone,* Embassy, Paramount); Music by James Van Heusen. Lyrics by Sammy Cahn.

(MUSIC SCORE—SUBSTANTIALLY ORIGINAL)

Becket, Wallis, Paramount. Laurence Rosenthal.

The Fall of the Roman Empire, Bronston, Paramount. Dimitri Tiomkin.

Hush . . . Hush, Sweet Charlotte, Associates & Aldrich Co., 20th Century–Fox. Frank DeVol.

★ *Mary Poppins,* Disney, Buena Vista. Richard M. Sherman and Robert B. Sherman.

The Pink Panther, Mirisch, UA. Henry Mancini.

(SCORING OF MUSIC—ADAPTATION OR TREATMENT)

A Hard Day's Night, Shenson, UA (British). George Martin.

Mary Poppins, Disney, Buena Vista. Irwin Kostal.

★ *My Fair Lady,* Warner Bros. André Previn.

Robin and the 7 Hoods, Warner Bros. Nelson Riddle.

The Unsinkable Molly Brown, Marten, MGM. Robert Armbruster, Leo Arnaud, Jack Elliott, Jack Hayes, Calvin Jackson and Leo Shuken.

Film Editing

Becket, Wallis, Paramount. Anne Coates.
Father Goose, Granox, Universal. Ted J. Kent.
Hush . . . Hush, Sweet Charlotte, Associates & Aldrich Co., 20th Century–Fox. Michael Luciano.
★ *Mary Poppins*, Disney, Buena Vista. Cotton Warburton.
My Fair Lady, Warner Bros. William Ziegler.

Costume Design

(BLACK-AND-WHITE)

A House Is Not a Home, Greene-Rouse, Embassy Pictures. Edith Head.
Hush . . . Hush, Sweet Charlotte, Associates & Aldrich Co., 20th Century–Fox. Norma Koch.
Kisses for My President, Pearlayne, Warner Bros. Howard Shoup.
★ *The Night of the Iguana*, Seven Arts, MGM. Dorothy Jeakins.
The Visit, DeRode, 20th Century–Fox. Rene Hubert.

(COLOR)

Becket, Wallis, Paramount. Margaret Furse.
Mary Poppins, Disney, Buena Vista. Tony Walton.
★ *My Fair Lady*, Warner Bros. Cecil Beaton.
The Unsinkable Molly Brown, Marten, MGM. Morton Haack.
What a Way to Go, Apjac-Orchard, 20th Century–Fox. Edith Head and Moss Mabry.

Special Visual Effects

★ *Mary Poppins*, Disney, Buena Vista. Peter Ellenshaw, Hamilton Luske and Eustace Lycett.
7 Faces of Dr. Lao, Pal, MGM. Jim Danforth.

Sound Effects

★ *Goldfinger*, Broccoli-Saltzman-Eon, UA (British). Norman Wanstall.
The Lively Set, Universal. Robert L. Bratton.

Short Subjects

(CARTOONS)

Christmas Cracker, National Film Board of Canada, Favorite Films of California.
How to Avoid Friendship, Rembrandt Films, Film Representations. William L. Snyder, producer.
Nudnik #2, Rembrandt Films, Film Representations. William L. Snyder, producer.
★ *The Pink Phink*, Mirisch-Geoffrey, UA. David H. DePatie and Fritz Freleng, producers.

(LIVE ACTION SUBJECTS)

★ *Casals Conducts: 1964*, Thalia Films, Beckman Film Corp. Edward Schreiber, producer.
Help! My Snowman's Burning Down, Pathé Contemporary Films. Carson Davidson, producer.
The Legend of Jimmy Blue Eyes, Topaz Film Corp. Robert Clouse, producer.

Documentary

(SHORT SUBJECTS)

Breaking the Habit, American Cancer Society, Modern Talking Picture Service. Henry Jacobs and John Korty, producers.
Children Without, National Education Association, Guggenheim Productions.
Kenojuak, National Film Board of Canada.
★ *Nine from Little Rock*. U.S. Information Agency, Guggenheim Productions.
140 Days Under the World, New Zealand National Film Unit, Rank Film Distributors of New Zealand. Geoffrey Scott and Oxley Hughan, producers.

(FEATURES)

The Finest Hours, Le Vien Films, Columbia. Jack Le Vien, producer.
Four Days in November, David L. Wolper Prods., UA. Mel Stuart, producer.
The Human Dutch, Haanstra Filmproductie. Bert Haanstra, producer.
★ *Jacques-Yves Cousteau's World Without Sun*, Columbia. Jacques-Yves Cousteau, producer.
Over There, 1914–18, Zodiac Prods., Pathé Contemporary Films. Jean Aurel, producer.

Foreign Language Film

Raven's End (Sweden).
Sallah (Israel).
The Umbrellas of Cherbourg (France).
Woman in the Dunes (Japan).
★ *Yesterday, Today and Tomorrow* (Italy).

Irving G. Thalberg Memorial Award

Not given this year.

Jean Hersholt Humanitarian Award

Not given this year.

Honorary Award

William Tuttle for his outstanding makeup achievement for *7 Faces of Dr. Lao* (statuette).

Scientific or Technical

CLASS I (STATUETTE)

Petro Vlahos, Wadsworth E. Pohl and Ub Iwerks for the conception and perfection of techniques for Color Traveling Matte Composite Cinematography.

CLASS II (PLAQUE)

Sidney P. Solow, Edward H. Reichard, Carl W. Hauge and Job Sanderson of Consolidated Film Industries for the design and development of the versatile Automatic 35mm Composite Color Printer.

Pierre Angenieux for the development of a ten-to-one Zoom Lens for cinematography.

CLASS III (CITATION)

Milton Forman, Richard B. Glickman and Daniel J. Pearlman of ColorTran Industries for the advancements in the design and application to motion picture photography of lighting units using quartz iodine lamps.

Stewart Filmscreen Corporation for a seamless translucent Blue Screen for Traveling Matte Color Cinematography.

Anthony Paglia and the 20th Century–Fox Studio Mechanical Effects Dept. for an improved method of producing Explosion Flash Effects for motion pictures.

Edward H. Reichard and Carl W. Hauge of Consolidated Film Industries for the design of a Proximity Cue Detector and its application to motion picture printers.

Edward H. Reichard, Leonard L. Sokolow and Carl W. Hauge of Consolidated Film Industries for the design and application to motion picture laboratory practice of a Stroboscopic Scene Tester for color and black-and-white film.

Nelson Tyler for the design and construction of an improved Helicopter Camera System.

Points of Interest

1. The family way: Best Actress Julie Andrews married to Costume Design nominee Tony Walton.
2. Nothing to it: Lila Kedrova wins Supporting Actress for her first English-language film.

Eligible Films That Failed to Be Nominated for Best Picture

The Servant, The Night of the Iguana, The Pink Panther, The World of Henry Orient, Goldfinger, A Hard Day's Night, Hush . . . Hush, Sweet Charlotte.

Eligible Songs That Failed to Be Nominated

"And I Love Her" (John Lennon and Paul McCartney)—*A Hard Day's Night;* "Can't Buy Me Love" (John Lennon and Paul McCartney)—*A Hard Day's Night;* "Goldfinger" (Leslie Bricusse and Anthony Newley)—*Goldfinger;* "A Hard Day's Night" (John Lennon and Paul McCartney)—*A Hard Day's Night;* "I Should Have Known Better" (John Lennon and Paul McCartney)—*A Hard Day's Night;* "If I Fell" (John Lennon and Paul McCartney)—*A Hard Day's Night;* "I'm Happy Just to Dance with You" (John Lennon and Paul McCartney)—*A Hard Day's Night;* "Pass Me By" (Cy Coleman and Carolyn Leigh)—*Father Goose;* "Tell Me Why" (John Lennon and Paul McCartney)—*A Hard Day's Night;* "This Boy" (John Lennon and Paul McCartney)—*A Hard Day's Night.*

1965

Picture

Darling, Anglo-Amalgamated, Embassy (British). Produced by Joseph Janni.

Doctor Zhivago, Ponti, MGM. Produced by Carlo Ponti.

Ship of Fools, Kramer, Columbia. Produced by Stanley Kramer.

★ *The Sound of Music,* Argyle, 20th Century–Fox. Produced by Robert Wise.

A Thousand Clowns, Harrell, UA. Produced by Fred Coe.

Actor

Richard Burton in *The Spy Who Came in from the Cold* (Salem, Paramount).

★ Lee Marvin in *Cat Ballou* (Hecht, Columbia).

Laurence Olivier in *Othello* (B.H.E., Warner Bros.) (British).

Rod Steiger in *The Pawnbroker* (Ely Landau, American International).

Oskar Werner in *Ship of Fools* (Kramer, Columbia).

Actress

Julie Andrews in *The Sound of Music* (Argyle, 20th Century–Fox).

★ Julie Christie in *Darling* (Anglo-Amalgamated, Embassy) (British).

Samantha Eggar in *The Collector* (Columbia).

Elizabeth Hartman in *A Patch of Blue* (Berman-Green, MGM).

Simone Signoret in *Ship of Fools* (Kramer, Columbia).

Supporting Actor

★ Martin Balsam in *A Thousand Clowns* (Harrell, UA).

Ian Bannen in *The Flight of the Phoenix* (Associates & Aldrich Co., 20th Century–Fox).

Tom Courtenay in *Doctor Zhivago* (Ponti, MGM).

Michael Dunn in *Ship of Fools* (Kramer, Columbia).

Frank Finlay in *Othello* (B.H.E., Warner Bros.) (British).

Supporting Actress

Ruth Gordon in *Inside Daisy Clover* (Park Place, Warner Bros.).

Joyce Redman in *Othello* (B.H.E., Warner Bros.) (British).

Maggie Smith in *Othello* (B.H.E., Warner Bros.) (British).

★ Shelley Winters in *A Patch of Blue* (Berman-Green, MGM).

Peggy Wood in *The Sound of Music* (Argyle, 20th Century–Fox).

Director

David Lean for *Doctor Zhivago* (Ponti, MGM).

John Schlesinger for *Darling* (Embassy) (British).

Hiroshi Teshigahara for *Woman in the Dunes* (Pathé Contemporary Films) (Japanese).

★ Robert Wise for *The Sound of Music* (Argyle, 20th Century–Fox).
William Wyler for *The Collector* (Columbia).

Writing

(SCREENPLAY—BASED ON MATERIAL FROM ANOTHER MEDIUM)

Cat Ballou, Hecht, Columbia. Walter Newman and Frank R. Pierson.
The Collector, Columbia. Stanley Mann and John Kohn.
★ *Doctor Zhivago*, Ponti, MGM. Robert Bolt.
Ship of Fools, Kramer, Columbia. Abby Mann.
A Thousand Clowns, Harrell, UA. Herb Gardner.

(STORY AND SCREENPLAY—WRITTEN DIRECTLY FOR THE SCREEN)

Casanova '70, Embassy (Italian). Age, Scarpelli, Mario Monicelli, Tonino Guerra, Giorgio Salvioni and Suso Cecchi D'Amico.
★ *Darling*, Anglo-Amalgamated, Embassy (British). Frederic Raphael.
Those Magnificent Men in Their Flying Machines, 20th Century–Fox. Jack Davies and Ken Annakin.
The Train, Les Prods., UA. Franklin Coen and Frank Davis.
The Umbrellas of Cherbourg, Landau Releasing (French). Jacques Demy.

Cinematography

(BLACK-AND-WHITE)

In Harm's Way, Preminger, Paramount. Loyal Griggs.
King Rat, Coleytown, Columbia. Burnett Guffey.
Morituri, Arcola-Colony, 20th Century–Fox. Conrad Hall.
A Patch of Blue, Berman-Green, MGM. Robert Burks.
★ *Ship of Fools*, Kramer, Columbia. Ernest Laszlo.

(COLOR)

The Agony and the Ecstasy, International Classics, 20th Century–Fox. Leon Shamroy.
★ *Doctor Zhivago*, Ponti, MGM. Freddie Young.
The Great Race, Patricia-Jalem-Reynard, Warner Bros. Russell Harlan.
The Greatest Story Ever Told, Stevens, UA. William C. Mellor and Loyal Griggs.
The Sound of Music, Argyle, 20th Century–Fox. Ted McCord.

Art Direction—Set Decoration

(BLACK-AND-WHITE)

King Rat, Coleytown, Columbia. Robert Emmet Smith; Frank Tuttle.
A Patch of Blue, Berman-Green, MGM. George W. Davis and Urie McCleary; Henry Grace and Charles S. Thompson.
★ *Ship of Fools*, Kramer, Columbia. Robert Clatworthy; Joseph Kish.
The Slender Thread, Paramount. Hal Pereira and Jack Poplin; Robert Benton and Joseph Kish.
The Spy Who Came in from the Cold, Salem, Paramount. Hal Pereira, Tambi Larsen and Edward Marshall; Josie MacAvin.

(COLOR)

The Agony and the Ecstasy, International Classics, 20th Century–Fox. John DeCuir and Jack Martin Smith; Dario Simoni.
★ *Doctor Zhivago*, Ponti, MGM. John Box and Terry Marsh; Dario Simoni.
The Greatest Story Ever Told, Stevens, UA. Richard Day, William Creber and David Hall; Ray Moyer, Fred MacLean and Norman Rockett.
Inside Daisy Clover, Park Place, Warner Bros. Robert Clatworthy; George James Hopkins.
The Sound of Music, 20th Century–Fox. Boris Leven; Walter M. Scott and Ruby Levitt.

Sound

The Agony and the Ecstasy, International Classics, 20th Century–Fox. 20th Century–Fox Studio Sound Dept.; James P. Corcoran, sound director.
Doctor Zhivago, Ponti, MGM. MGM British Studio Sound Dept.; A.W. Watkins, sound director; and MGM Studio Sound Dept.; Franklin E. Milton, sound director.
The Great Race, Patricia-Jalem-Reynard, Warner Bros. Warner Bros. Studio Sound Dept.; George R. Groves, sound director.
Shenandoah, Universal. Universal City Sound Dept.; Waldon O. Watson, sound director.
★ *The Sound of Music*, 20th Century–Fox. 20th Century–Fox Studio Sound Dept.; James P. Corcoran, sound director; and Todd-AO Sound Dept.; Fred Hynes, sound director.

Music

(SONG)

"The Ballad of Cat Ballou" (*Cat Ballou*, Hecht, Columbia); Music by Jerry Livingston. Lyrics by Mack David.
"I Will Wait for You" (*The Umbrellas of Cherbourg*, Landau Releasing) (French); Music by Michel Legrand. Lyrics by Jacques Demy.
★ "The Shadow of Your Smile" (*The Sandpiper*, Filmways-Venice, MGM); Music by Johnny Mandel. Lyrics by Paul Francis Webster.
"The Sweetheart Tree" (*The Great Race*, Patricia-Jalem-Reynard, Warner Bros.); Music by Henry Mancini. Lyrics by Johnny Mercer.
"What's New Pussycat?" (*What's New Pussycat?*, Famous Artists-Famartists, UA); Music by Burt Bacharach. Lyrics by Hal David.

(MUSIC SCORE—SUBSTANTIALLY ORIGINAL)

The Agony and the Ecstasy, Internationsl Classics, 20th Century–Fox. Alex North.

★ *Doctor Zhivago*, Ponti, MGM. Maurice Jarre.
The Greatest Story Ever Told, Stevens, UA. Alfred Newman.
A Patch of Blue, Berman-Green Prod., MGM. Jerry Goldsmith.
The Umbrellas of Cherbourg, Landau Releasing (French). Michel Legrand and Jacques Demy.

(SCORING OF MUSIC—ADAPTATION OR TREATMENT)
Cat Ballou, Hecht, Columbia. DeVol.
The Pleasure Seekers, 20th Century–Fox. Lionel Newman and Alexander Courage.
★ *The Sound of Music*, Argyle, 20th Century–Fox. Irwin Kostal.
A Thousand Clowns, Harrell, UA. Don Walker.
The Umbrellas of Cherbourg, Landau Releasing (French). Michel Legrand.

Film Editing
Cat Ballou, Hecht, Columbia. Charles Nelson.
Doctor Zhivago, Ponti, MGM. Norman Savage.
The Flight of the Phoenix, Associates & Aldrich Co., 20th Century–Fox. Michael Luciano.
The Great Race, Patricia-Jalem-Reynard, Warner Bros. Ralph E. Winters.
★ *The Sound of Music*, Argyle, 20th Century–Fox. William Reynolds.

Costume Design
(BLACK-AND-WHITE)
★ *Darling*, Anglo-Amalgamated, Embassy (British). Julie Harris.
Morituri, Arcola-Colony, 20th Century–Fox. Moss Mabry.
A Rage to Live, Mirisch-Araho, UA. Howard Shoup.
Ship of Fools, Kramer, Columbia. Bill Thomas and Jean Louis.
The Slender Thread, Paramount. Edith Head.

(COLOR)
The Agony and the Ecstasy, International Classics, 20th Century–Fox. Vittorio Nino Novarese.
★ *Doctor Zhivago*, Ponti, MGM. Phyllis Dalton.
The Greatest Story Ever Told, Stevens, UA. Vittorio Nino Novarese and Marjorie Best.
Inside Daisy Clover, Park Place, Warner Bros. Edith Head and Bill Thomas.
The Sound of Music, Argyle, 20th Century–Fox. Dorothy Jeakins.

Special Visual Effects
The Greatest Story Ever Told, Stevens, UA. J. McMillan Johnson.
★ *Thunderball*, Broccoli-Saltzman-McClory, UA (British). John Stears.

Sound Effects
★ *The Great Race*, Patricia-Jalem-Reynard, Warner Bros. Tregoweth Brown.
Von Ryan's Express, 20th Century–Fox. Walter A. Rossi.

Short Subjects
(CARTOONS)
Clay or the Origin of Species, Harvard University, Pathé Contemporary Films. Eliot Noyes, Jr., producer.
★ *The Dot and the Line*, MGM. Chuck Jones and Les Goldman, producers.
The Thieving Magpie (La Gazza Ladra). Allied Artists. Emanuele Luzzati, producer.

(LIVE ACTION SUBJECTS)
★ *The Chicken* (Le Poulet), Pathé Contemporary Films (French). Claude Berri, producer.
Fortress of Peace, Farner-Looser Films, Cinerama. Lothar Wolff, producer.
Skaterdater, Byway Prods., UA. Marshall Backlar and Noel Black, producers.
Snow, Manson Distributing. Edgar Anstey, producer.
Time Piece, Muppets, Inc., Pathé Contemporary Films. Jim Henson, producer.

Documentary
(SHORT SUBJECTS)
Mural on Our Street, Henry Street Settlement, Pathé Contemporary Films. Kirk Smallman, producer.
Ouverture, Mafilm Prods., Hungarofilm-Pathé Contemporary Films.
Point of View, Vision Associates Prod., National Tuberculosis Assoc.
★ *To Be Alive!*, Johnson Wax. Francis Thompson, Inc., producer.
Yeats Country, Aengus Films for the Dept. of External Affairs of Ireland. Patrick Carey and Joe Mendoza, producers.

(FEATURES)
The Battle of the Bulge . . . The Brave Rifles, Mascott Prods. Laurence E. Mascott, producer.
★ *The Eleanor Roosevelt Story*, American International. Sidney Glazier, producer.
The Forth Road Bridge, Random Film Prods., Shell-Mex and B.P. Film Library. Peter Mills, producer.
Let My People Go, David L. Wolper Prods. Marshall Flaum, producer.
To Die in Madrid, Altura Films Inernational. Frederic Rossif, producer.

Foreign Language Film
Blood on the Land (Greece).
Dear John (Sweden).
Kwaidan (Japan).

Marriage Italian Style (Italy).
★ *The Shop on Main Street* (Czechoslovakia).

Irving G. Thalberg Memorial Award
William Wyler.

Jean Hersholt Humanitarian Award
Edmond L. DePatie.

Honorary Award
Bob Hope for unique and distinguished service to our industry and the Academy (gold medal).

Scientific or Technical
CLASS I (STATUETTE)
None.

CLASS II (PLAQUE)
Arthur J. Hatch of the Strong Electric Corporation, subsidiary of General Precision Equipment Corporation, for the design and development of an Air Blown Carbon Arc Projection Lamp.
Stefan Kudelski for the design and development of the Nagra portable 1/4″ tape recording system for motion picture sound recording.

CLASS III (CITATION)
None.

Points of Interest

1. Nothing to it: Elizabeth Hartman and Michael Dunn nominated for film debuts.

Eligible Films That Failed to Be Nominated for Best Picture

Help!, Cat Ballou, Repulsion, Contempt, Inside Daisy Clover, The Naked Kiss.

Submitted Film Rejected by the Foreign Language Film Award Committee

Gertrud (Denmark), directed by Carl Theodor Dreyer.

Eligible Songs That Failed to Be Nominated

"Another Girl" (John Lennon and Paul McCartney)—*Help!;* "Baby, the Rain Must Fall" (Elmer Bernstein and Ernest Sheldon)—*Baby, the Rain Must Fall*; "Catch Us If You Can" (Dave Clark and Lenny Davidson)—*Catch Us If You Can;* "Ferry Cross the Mersey" (Gerry Marsden)—*Ferry Cross the Mersey;* "Forget Domani" (Riz Ortolani and Norman Newell)—*The Yellow Rolls-Royce;* "Help!" (John Lennon and Paul McCartney)—*Help!;* "Listen, People" (Graham Gouldman)—*When the Boys Meet the Girls;* "The Night Before" (John Lennon and Paul McCartney)—*Help!;* "Sunshine, Lollipops and Rainbows" (Marvin Hamlisch and Howard Liebling)—*Ski Party;* "Ticket to Ride" (John Lennon and Paul McCartney)—*Help!;* "You're Gonna Hear From Me" (André and Dory Previn)—*Inside Daisy Clover;* "You're Gonna Lose That Girl" (John Lennon and Paul McCartney)—*Help!;* "You've Got to Hide Your Love Away" (John Lennon and Paul McCartney)—*Help!*.

1966

Picture
Alfie, Sheldrake, Paramount (British). Produced by Lewis Gilbert.
★ *A Man for All Seasons*, Highland, Columbia. Produced by Fred Zinnemann.
The Russians Are Coming, The Russians Are Coming, Mirisch, UA. Produced by Norman Jewison.
The Sand Pebbles, Argyle-Solar, 20th Century–Fox. Produced by Robert Wise.
Who's Afraid of Virginia Woolf? Chenault, Warner Bros. Produced by Ernest Lehman.

Actor
Alan Arkin in *The Russians Are Coming, The Russians Are Coming* (Mirisch, UA).
Richard Burton in *Who's Afraid of Virginia Woolf?* (Chenault, Warner Bros.).
Michael Caine in *Alfie* (Sheldrake, Paramount) (British).
Steve McQueen in *The Sand Pebbles* (Argyle-Solar, 20th Century–Fox).
★ Paul Scofield in *A Man for All Seasons* (Highland, Columbia).

Actress
Anouk Aimée in *A Man and a Woman* (Allied Artists) (French).
Ida Kaminska in *The Shop on Main Street* (Prominent Films) (Czechoslovakia).
Lynn Redgrave in *Georgy Girl* (Everglades, Columbia) (British).
Vanessa Redgrave in *Morgan!* (Quintra, Cinema V) (British).
★ Elizabeth Taylor in *Who's Afraid of Virginia Woolf?* (Chenault, Warner Bros.).

Supporting Actor
Mako in *The Sand Pebbles* (Argyle-Solar, 20th Century–Fox).
James Mason in *Georgy Girl* (Everglades, Columbia) (British).
★ Walter Matthau in *The Fortune Cookie* (Phalanx-Jalem-Mirisch, UA).

George Segal in *Who's Afraid of Virginia Woolf?* (Chenault, Warner Bros.).

Robert Shaw in *A Man for All Seasons* (Highland, Columbia).

Supporting Actress

★ Sandy Dennis in *Who's Afraid of Virginia Woolf?* (Chenault, Warner Bros.).

Wendy Hiller in *A Man for All Seasons* (Highland, Columbia).

Jocelyn Lagarde in *Hawaii* (Mirisch, UA).

Vivien Merchant in *Alfie* (Sheldrake, Paramount) (British).

Geraldine Page in *You're a Big Boy Now* (Seven Arts).

Director

Michelangelo Antonioni for *Blow-Up* (Ponti, Premier Productions) (British).

Richard Brooks for *The Professionals* (Brooks, Columbia).

Claude Lelouch for *A Man and a Woman* (Les Films 13, Allied Artists) (French).

Mike Nichols for *Who's Afraid of Virginia Woolf?* (Chenault, Warner Bros.).

★ Fred Zinnemann for *A Man for All Seasons* (Highland, Columbia).

Writing

(SCREENPLAY—BASED ON MATERIAL FROM ANOTHER MEDIUM)

Alfie, Sheldrake, Paramount (British). Bill Naughton.

★ *A Man for All Seasons*, Highland, Columbia. Robert Bolt.

The Professionals, Pax Enterprises, Columbia. Richard Brooks.

The Russians Are Coming The Russians Are Coming, Mirisch, UA. William Rose.

Who's Afraid of Virginia Woolf? Chenault, Warner Bros. Ernest Lehman.

(STORY AND SCREENPLAY—WRITTEN DIRECTLY FOR THE SCREEN)

Blow-Up, Ponti, Premier Productions (British). Michelangelo Antonioni, Tonino Guerra and Edward Bond.

The Fortune Cookie, Phalanx-Jalem-Mirisch, UA. Billy Wilder and I.A.L. Diamond.

Khartoum, Blaustein, UA. Robert Ardrey.

★ *A Man and a Woman*, Les Films 13, Allied Artists (French). Claude Lelouch and Pierre Uytterhoeven.

The Naked Prey, Theodora, Paramount. Clint Johnston and Don Peters.

Cinematography

(BLACK-AND-WHITE)

The Fortune Cookie, Phalanx-Jalem-Mirisch, UA. Joseph LaShelle.

Georgy Girl, Columbia (British). Ken Higgins.

Is Paris Burning? Transcontinental Films-Marianne, Paramount. Marcel Grignon.

Seconds, Paramount. James Wong Howe.

★ *Who's Afraid of Virginia Woolf?* Chenault, Warner Bros. Haskell Wexler.

(COLOR)

Fantastic Voyage, 20th Century–Fox. Ernest Laszlo.

Hawaii, Mirisch, UA. Russell Harlan.

★ *A Man for All Seasons*, Highland, Columbia. Ted Moore.

The Professionals, Pax Enterprises, Columbia. Conrad Hall.

The Sand Pebbles, Argyle-Solar, 20th Century–Fox. Joseph MacDonald.

Art Direction—Set Decoration

(BLACK-AND-WHITE)

The Fortune Cookie, Phalanx-Jalem-Mirisch, UA. Robert Luthardt and Edward G. Boyle.

The Gospel According to St. Matthew, Reade-Continental (Italian). Luigi Scaccianoce.

Is Paris Burning?. Transcontinental Films-Marianne, Paramount. Willy Holt; Marc Frederix and Pierre Guffroy.

Mister Buddwing, DDD-Cherokee, MGM. George W. Davis and Paul Groesse; Henry Grace and Hugh Hunt.

★ *Who's Afraid of Virginia Woolf?*, Chenault, Warner Bros. Richard Sylbert; George James Hopkins.

(COLOR)

★ *Fantastic Voyage*, 20th Century–Fox. Jack Martin Smith and Dale Hennesy; Walter M. Scott and Stuart A. Reiss.

Gambit, Universal. Alexander Golitzen and George C. Webb; John McCarthy and John Austin.

Juliet of the Spirits, Rizzoli Films (Italian). Piero Gherardi.

The Oscar, Greene-Rouse, Embassy. Hal Pereira and Arthur Lonergan; Robert Benton and James Payne.

The Sand Pebbles, Argyle-Solar, 20th Century–Fox. Boris Leven; Walter M. Scott, John Sturtevant and William Kiernan.

Sound

Gambit, Universal. Universal City Studio Sound Dept.; Waldon O. Watson, sound director.

★ *Grand Prix*, Douglas-Lewis-Frankenheimer-Cherokee, MGM. MGM Studio Sound Dept.; Franklin E. Milton, sound director.

Hawaii, Mirisch, UA. Samuel Goldwyn Studio Sound Dept.; Gordon E. Sawyer, sound director.

The Sand Pebbles, Argyle-Solar, 20th Century–Fox. 20th Century–Fox Studio Sound Dept.; James P. Corcoran, sound director.

Who's Afraid of Virginia Woolf?, Chenault, Warner Bros. Warner Bros. Studio Sound Dept.; George R. Groves, sound director.

Music

(SONG)

"Alfie" (*Alfie*, Sheldrake, Paramount) (British); Music by Burt Bacharach. Lyrics by Hal David.

★ "Born Free" (*Born Free*, Open Road–Atlas Films, Columbia) (British); Music by John Barry. Lyrics by Don Black.
"Georgy Girl" (*Georgy Girl*, Everglades, Columbia) (British); Music by Tom Springfield. Lyrics by Jim Dale.
"My Wishing Doll" (*Hawaii*, Mirisch, UA); Music by Elmer Bernstein. Lyrics by Mack David.
"A Time for Love" (*An American Dream*, Warner Bros.); Music by Johnny Mandel. Lyrics by Paul Francis Webster.

(ORIGINAL MUSIC SCORE)
The Bible, DeLaurentiis-Seven Arts, 20th Century–Fox. Toshiro Mayuzumi.
★ *Born Free*, Open Road-Atlas Films, Columbia (British). John Barry.
Hawaii, Mirisch, UA. Elmer Bernstein.
The Sand Pebbles, Argyle-Solar, 20th Century–Fox. Jerry Goldsmith.
Who's Afraid of Virginia Woolf?, Chenault, Warner Bros. Alex North.

(SCORING OF MUSIC—ADAPTATION OR TREATMENT)
★ *A Funny Thing Happened on the Way to the Forum*, Frank, UA. Ken Thorne.
The Gospel According to St. Matthew, Reade-Continental (Italian). Luis Enrique Bacalov.
Return of the Seven, Mirisch, UA. Elmer Bernstein.
The Singing Nun, MGM. Harry Sukman.
Stop the World—I Want to Get Off, Warner Bros. Al Ham.

Film Editing
Fantastic Voyage, 20th Century–Fox. William B. Murphy.
★ *Grand Prix*, Douglas-Lewis-Frankenheimer-Cherokee, MGM. Fredric Steinkamp, Henry Berman, Stewart Linder and Frank Santillo.
The Russians Are Coming, The Russians Are Coming, Mirisch, UA. Hal Ashby and J. Terry Williams.
The Sand Pebbles, Argyle-Solar, 20th Century–Fox. William Reynolds.
Who's Afraid of Virginia Woolf?, Chenault, Warner Bros. Sam O'Steen.

Costume Design
(BLACK-AND-WHITE)
The Gospel According to St. Matthew, Reade-Continental (Italian). Danilo Donati.
Mandragola, Europix-Consolidated (Italian). Danilo Donati.
Mister Buddwing, DDD-Cherokee, MGM. Helen Rose.
Morgan!, Quintra, Cinema V (British). Jocelyn Rickards.
★ *Who's Afraid of Virginia Woolf?*, Chenault, Warner Bros. Irene Sharaff.

(COLOR)
Gambit, Universal. Jean Louis.
Hawaii, Mirisch, UA. Dorothy Jeakins.
Juliet of the Spirits, Rizzoli Films (Italian). Piero Gherardi.
★ *A Man for All Seasons*, Highland, Columbia. Elizabeth Haffenden and Joan Bridge.
The Oscar, Green-Rouse, Embassy. Edith Head.

Special Visual Effects
★ *Fantastic Voyage*, 20th Century–Fox. Art Cruickshank.
Hawaii, Mirisch, UA. Linwood G. Dunn.

Sound Effects
Fantastic Voyage, 20th Century–Fox. Walter Rossi.
★ *Grand Prix*, Douglas-Lewis-Frankenheimer-Cherokee, MGM. Gordon Daniel.

Short Subjects
(CARTOONS)
The Drag, National Film Board of Canada, Favorite Films. Wolf Koenig and Robert Verall, producers.
★ *Herb Alpert and the Tijuana Brass Double Feature*, Paramount. John and Faith Hubley, producers.
The Pink Blueprint, Mirisch-Geoffrey-DePatie-Freleng, UA. David H. DePatie and Friz Freleng, producers.

(LIVE ACTION SUBJECTS)
Turkey the Bridge, Samaritan Prods., Schoenfeld Films. Derek Williams, producer.
★ *Wild Wings*, British Transport Films, Manson Distributing. Edgar Anstey, producer.
The Winning Strain, Winik Films, Paramount. Leslie Winik, producer.

Documentary
(SHORT SUBJECTS)
Adolescence, M.K. Prods. Marin Karmitz and Vladimir Forgency, producers.
Cowboy, U.S. Information Agency. Michael Ahnemann and Gary Schlosser, producers.
The Odds Against, Vision Associates Prod. for The American Foundation Institute of Corrections. Lee R. Bobker and Helen Kristt Radin, producers.
Saint Matthew Passion, Mafilm Studio, Hungarofilm.
★ *A Year Toward Tomorrow*, Sun Dial Films for Office of Economic Opportunity. Edmund A. Levy, producer.

(FEATURES)
The Face of Genius, WBZ-TV, Group W, Boston. Alfred R. Kelman, producer.
Helicopter Canada, Centennial Commission, National Film Board of Canada. Peter Jones and Tom Daly, producers.
Le Volcan Interdit (The Forbidden Volcano). Cine Documents Tazieff, Athos Films. Haroun Tazieff, producer.
The Really Big Family, David L. Wolper Prod. Alex Grasshoff, producer.
★ *The War Game*, BBC Prod. for the British Film Institute, Pathé Contemporary Films. Peter Watkins, producer.

Foreign Language Film

The Battle of Algiers (Italy).
Loves of a Blonde (Czechoslovakia).
★ *A Man and a Woman* (France).
Pharaoh (Poland).
Three (Yugoslavia).

Irving G. Thalberg Memorial Award

Robert Wise.

Jean Hersholt Humanitarian Award

George Bagnall.

Honorary Awards

Y. Frank Freeman for unusual and outstanding service to the Academy during his thirty years in Hollywood (statuette).

Yakima Canutt for achievements as a stunt man and for developing safety devices to protect stunt men everywhere (statuette).

Scientific or Technical

CLASS I (STATUETTE)

None.

CLASS II (PLAQUE)

Mitchell Camera Corporation for the design and development of the Mitchell Mark II 35mm Portable Motion Picture Reflex Camera.

Arnold & Richter KG for the design and development of the Arriflex 35mm Portable Motion Picture Reflex Camera.

CLASS III (CITATION)

Panavision Incorporated for the design of the Panatron Power Inverter and its application to motion picture camera operation.

Carroll Knudson for the production of a Composers Manual for Motion Picture Music Synchronization.

Ruby Raksin for the production of a Composers Manual for Motion Picture Music Synchronization.

Points of Interest

1. Nothing to it: Alan Arkin, Mako, Jocelyn Lagarde, Vivien Merchant and director Mike Nichols nominated for film debuts.
2. The family way: Nominees Richard Burton and Elizabeth Taylor were married at the time. Nominees Lynn and Vanessa Redgrave were—and still are—sisters.

Rule Changes

1. The name game: "Music Score—Substantially Original" becomes "Original Music Score."

Eligible Films That Failed to Be Nominated for Best Picture

Blow-Up, Georgy Girl, Masculine-Feminine, A Funny Thing Happened on the Way to the Forum, The Wild Angels.

Submitted Films Rejected by the Foreign Language Film Award Committee

Young Torless (Germany), directed by Volker Schlondorff; *Persona* (Sweden), directed by Ingmar Bergman.

Eligible Songs That Failed to Be Nominated

"Darlin' Be Home Soon" (John B. Sebastian)—*You're a Big Boy Now;* "A Must to Avoid" (P. F. Sloan)—*Hold On.*

1967

Picture

Bonnie and Clyde, Tatira-Hiller, Warner Bros.–Seven Arts. Produced by Warren Beatty.

Doctor Dolittle, Apjac, 20th Century–Fox. Produced by Arthur P. Jacobs.

The Graduate, Nichols-Turman, Embassy. Produced by Lawrence Turman.

Guess Who's Coming to Dinner?, Kramer, Columbia. Produced by Stanley Kramer.

★ *In the Heat of the Night,* Mirisch, UA. Produced by Walter Mirisch.

Actor

Warren Beatty in *Bonnie and Clyde* (Tatira-Hiller, Warner Bros.–Seven Arts).

Dustin Hoffman in *The Graduate* (Nichols-Turman, Embassy).

Paul Newman in *Cool Hand Luke* (Jalem, Warner Bros.–Seven Arts).

★ Rod Steiger in *In the Heat of the Night* (Mirisch, UA).

Spencer Tracy in *Guess Who's Coming to Dinner?* (Kramer, Columbia).

Actress

Anne Bancroft in *The Graduate* (Nichols-Turman, Embassy).

Faye Dunaway in *Bonnie and Clyde* (Tatira-Hiller, Warner Bros.–Seven Arts).

Dame Edith Evans in *The Whisperers* (Seven Pines, UA/Lopert) (British).

Audrey Hepburn in *Wait Until Dark* (Warner Bros.–Seven Arts).

★ Katharine Hepburn in *Guess Who's Coming to Dinner?* (Kramer, Columbia).

Supporting Actor

John Cassavetes in *The Dirty Dozen* (Aldrich, MGM).

Gene Hackman in *Bonnie and Clyde* (Tatira-Hiller, Warner Bros.–Seven Arts).

Cecil Kellaway in *Guess Who's Coming to Dinner?* (Kramer, Columbia).

★ George Kennedy in *Cool Hand Luke* (Jalem, Warner Bros.–Seven Arts).

Michael J. Pollard in *Bonnie and Clyde* (Tatira-Hiller, Warner Bros.–Seven Arts).

Supporting Actress

Carol Channing in *Thoroughly Modern Millie* (Hunter, Universal).

Mildred Natwick in *Barefoot in the Park* (Wallis, Paramount).

★ Estelle Parsons in *Bonnie and Clyde* (Tatira-Hiller, Warner Bros.–Seven Arts).

Beah Richards in *Guess Who's Coming to Dinner?* (Kramer, Columbia).

Katharine Ross in *The Graduate* (Nichols-Turman, Embassy).

Director

Richard Brooks for *In Cold Blood* (Pax Enterprises, Columbia).

Norman Jewison for *In the Heat of the Night* (Mirisch, UA).

Stanley Kramer for *Guess Who's Coming to Dinner?* (Kramer, Columbia).

★ Mike Nichols for *The Graduate* (Nichols-Turman, Embassy).

Arthur Penn for *Bonnie and Clyde* (Tatira-Hiller, Warner Bros.–Seven Arts).

Writing

(SCREENPLAY—BASED ON MATERIAL FROM ANOTHER MEDIUM)

Cool Hand Luke, Jalem, Warner Bros.–Seven Arts. Donn Pearce and Frank R. Pierson.

The Graduate, Nichols-Turman, Embassy. Calder Willingham and Buck Henry.

In Cold Blood, Pax Enterprises, Columbia. Richard Brooks.

★ *In the Heat of the Night,* Mirisch, UA. Stirling Silliphant.

Ulysses, Walter Reade–Continental Distributing. Joseph Strick and Fred Haines.

(STORY AND SCREENPLAY—WRITTEN DIRECTLY FOR THE SCREEN)

Bonnie and Clyde, Tatira-Hiller, Warner Bros.–Seven Arts. David Newman and Robert Benton.

Divorce American Style, Tandem-National General, Columbia. Robert Kaufman; Norman Lear.

★ *Guess Who's Coming to Dinner?,* Kramer, Columbia. William Rose.

La Guerre Est Finie, Sofracima-Europa, Brandon Films (French). Jorge Semprun.

Two for the Road, Donen, 20th Century–Fox. Frederic Raphael.

Cinematography

★ *Bonnie and Clyde,* Tatira-Hiller, Warner Bros.–Seven Arts. Burnett Guffey.

Camelot, Warner Bros.–Seven Arts. Richard H. Kline.

Doctor Dolittle, Apjac, 20th Century–Fox. Robert Surtees.

The Graduate, Nichols-Turman, Embassy. Robert Surtees.

In Cold Blood, Pax Enterprises, Columbia. Conrad Hall.

Art Decoration—Set Decoration

★ *Camelot,* Warner Bros.–Seven Arts. John Truscott and Edward Carrere; John W. Brown.

Doctor Dolittle, Apjac, 20th Century–Fox. Mario Chiari, Jack Martin Smith and Ed Graves; Walter M. Scott and Stuart A. Reiss.

Guess Who's Coming to Dinner?, Kramer, Columbia. Robert Clatworthy; Frank Tuttle.

The Taming of the Shrew, Royal Films International, Columbia. Renzo Mongiardino, John DeCuir, Elven Webb and Giuseppe Mariani; Dario Simoni and Luigi Gervasi.

Thoroughly Modern Millie, Hunter, Universal. Alexander Golitzen and George C. Webb; Howard Bristol.

Sound

Camelot, Warner Bros.–Seven Arts. Warner Bros.–Seven Arts Studio Sound Dept.

The Dirty Dozen, Aldrich, MGM. MGM Studio Sound Dept.

Doctor Dolittle, Apjac, 20th Century–Fox. 20th Century–Fox Studio Sound Dept.

★ *In the Heat of the Night,* Mirisch, UA. Samuel Goldwyn Studio Sound Dept.

Thoroughly Modern Millie, Hunter, Universal. Universal City Studio Sound Dept.

Music

(SONG)

"The Bare Necessities" (*The Jungle Book,* Disney, Buena Vista); Music and Lyrics by Terry Gilkyson.

"The Eyes of Love" (*Banning,* Universal); Music by Quincy Jones. Lyrics by Bob Russell.

"The Look of Love" (*Casino Royale,* Famous Artists, Columbia); Music by Burt Bacharach. Lyrics by Hal David.

★ "Talk to the Animals" (*Doctor Dolittle,* Apjac. 20th Century–Fox); Music and Lyrics by Leslie Bricusse.

"Thoroughly Modern Millie" (*Thoroughly Modern Millie,* Hunter, Universal); Music and Lyrics by James Van Heusen and Sammy Cahn.

(ORIGINAL MUSIC SCORE)

Cool Hand Luke, Jalem, Warner Bros.–Seven Arts. Lalo Schifrin.

Doctor Dolittle, Apjac, 20th Century–Fox. Leslie Bricusse.

Far from the Madding Crowd, Appia, MGM. Richard Rodney Bennett.
In Cold Blood, Pax Enterprises, Columbia. Quincy Jones.
★ *Thoroughly Modern Millie,* Hunter, Universal. Elmer Bernstein.

(SCORING OF MUSIC—ADAPTATION OR TREATMENT)
★ *Camelot,* Warner Bros.–Seven Arts. Alfred Newman and Ken Darby.
Doctor Dolittle, Apjac, 20th Century–Fox. Lionel Newman and Alexander Courage.
Guess Who's Coming to Dinner?, Kramer, Columbia. DeVol.
Thoroughly Modern Millie, Hunter, Universal. André Previn and Joseph Gershenson.
Valley of the Dolls, Red Lion, 20th Century–Fox. John Williams.

Film Editing
Beach Red, Theodora, UA. Frank P. Keller.
The Dirty Dozen, Aldrich, MGM. Michael Luciano.
Doctor Dolittle, Apjac, 20th Century–Fox. Samuel E. Beetley and Marjorie Fowler.
Guess Who's Coming to Dinner?, Kramer, Columbia. Robert C. Jones.
★ *In the Heat of the Night,* Mirisch, UA. Hal Ashby.

Costume Design
Bonnie and Clyde, Tatira-Hiller, Warner Bros.–Seven Arts. Theadora Van Runkle.
★ *Camelot,* Warner Bros.–Seven Arts. John Truscott.
The Happiest Millionaire, Disney, Buena Vista. Bill Thomas.
The Taming of the Shrew, Royal Films International, Columbia. Irene Sharaff and Danilo Donati.
Thoroughly Modern Millie, Hunter, Universal. Jean Louis.

Special Visual Effects
★ *Doctor Dolittle,* Apjac, 20th Century–Fox. L.B. Abbott.
Tobruk, Gibraltar-Corman, Universal. Howard A. Anderson, Jr. and Albert Whitlock.

Sound Effects
★ *The Dirty Dozen,* Aldrich, MGM. John Poyner.
In the Heat of the Night, Mirisch, UA. James A. Richard.

Short Subjects
(CARTOONS)
★ *The Box,* Brandon Films. Fred Wolf, producer.
Hypothese Beta, Films Orzeaux, Pathe Contemporary Films. Jean-Charles Meunier, producer.
What on Earth!, National Film Board of Canada, Columbia. Robert Verrall and Wolf Koenig, producers.

(LIVE ACTION SUBJECTS)
Paddle to the Sea, National Film Board of Canada, Favorite Films. Julian Biggs, producer.
★ *A Place to Stand,* T.D.F. Prod. for Ontario Dept. of Economics and Development, Columbia. Christopher Chapman, producer.
Sky Over Holland, Ferno Prod. for The Netherlands, Seneca International. John Ferno, producer.
Stop, Look and Listen, MGM. Len Janson and Chuck Menville, producers.

Documentary
(SHORT SUBJECTS)
Monument to the Dream, Guggenheim Prods. Charles E. Guggenheim, producer.
A Place to Stand, T.D.F. Prod. for The Ontario Department of Economics and Development. Christopher Chapman, producer.
★ *The Redwoods,* King Screen Prods. Mark Harris and Trevor Greenwood, producers.
See You at the Pillar, Associated British-Pathé Prod. Robert Fitchett, producer.
While I Run This Race, Sun Dial Films for VISTA. Carl V. Ragsdale, producer.

(FEATURES)
★ *The Anderson Platoon,* French Broadcasting System. Pierre Schoendoerffer, producer.
Festival, Patchke Prods. Murray Lerner, producer.
Harvest, U.S. Information Agency. Carroll Ballard, producer.
A King's Story, Jack Le Vien Prod. Jack Le Vien, producer.
A Time for Burning, Quest Prods. for Lutheran Film Associates. William C. Jersey, producer.

Foreign Language Film
★ *Closely Watched Trains* (Czechoslovakia).
El Amor Brujo (Spain).
I Even Met Happy Gypsies (Yugoslavia).
Live for Life (France).
Portrait of Chieko (Japan).

Irving G. Thalberg Memorial Award
Alfred Hitchcock.

Jean Hersholt Humanitarian Award
Gregory Peck.

Honorary Award
Arthur Freed for distinguished service to the Academy and the production of six top-rated Awards telecasts (statuette).

Scientific or Technical
CLASS I (STATUETTE)
None.

CLASS II (PLAQUE)
None.

CLASS III (CITATION)
Electro-Optical Division of the Kollmorgen Corporation for

the design and development of a series of Motion Picture Projection Lenses.

Panavision Incorporated for a Variable Speed Motor for Motion Picture Cameras.

Fred R. Wilson of the Samuel Goldwyn Studio Sound Dept. for an Audio Level Clamper.

Waldon O. Watson and the Universal City Studio Sound Dept. for new concepts in the design of a Music Scoring Stage.

Points of Interest

1. Nothing to it: Dustin Hoffman and Faye Dunaway nominated during first year in movies.
2. Without a stitch: For the first time since the creation of the Costume Design Award, Edith Head not nominated.

Rule Changes

1. The fewer the merrier: All divisions between Color and Black-and-White films eliminated.

Eligible Films That Failed to Be Nominated for Best Picture

In Cold Blood, Two for the Road, Accident, King of Hearts, La Guerre Est Finie, Point Blank, El Dorado, The Dirty Dozen, Up the Down Staircase, Reflections in a Golden Eye.

Submitted Films Rejected by the Foreign Language Film Award Committee

Father (Hungary), directed by Istvan Szabo; *China Is Near* (Italy), directed by Marco Bellocchio.

Eligible Songs That Failed to Be Nominated

"The Happening" (Eddie Holland, Brian Holland, Lamont Dozier and Frank DeVol)—*The Happening;* "This Is My Song" (Charlie Chaplin)—*A Countess from Hong Kong;* "To Sir, with Love" (Marc London and Don Black)—*To Sir, with Love;* "Valley of the Dolls" (André and Dory Previn)—*Valley of the Dolls.*

1968

Picture

Funny Girl, Rastar, Columbia. Produced by Ray Stark.

The Lion in Winter, Haworth, Avco Embassy. Produced by Martin Poll.

★ *Oliver!,* Romulus, Columbia. Produced by John Woolf.

Rachel, Rachel, Kayos, Warner Bros.–Seven Arts. Produced by Paul Newman.

Romeo and Juliet, B.H.E.-Verona-De Laurentiis, Paramount. Produced by Anthony Havelock-Allan and John Brabourne.

Actor

Alan Arkin in *The Heart Is a Lonely Hunter* (Warner Bros.–Seven Arts).

Alan Bates in *The Fixer* (Frankenheimer-Lewis, MGM).

Ron Moody in *Oliver!* (Romulus, Columbia).

Peter O'Toole in *The Lion in Winter* (Haworth, Avco Embassy).

★ Cliff Robertson in *Charly* (ABC–Selmur, Cinerama).

Actress

(Note: Two winners this year)

★ Katharine Hepburn in *The Lion in Winter* (Haworth, Avco Embassy).

Patricia Neal in *The Subject Was Roses* (MGM).

Vanessa Redgrave in *Isadora* (Hakim, Universal).

★ Barbra Streisand in *Funny Girl* (Rastar, Columbia).

Joanne Woodward in *Rachel, Rachel* (Kayos, Warner Bros.–Seven Arts).

Supporting Actor

★ Jack Albertson in *The Subject Was Roses* (MGM).

Seymour Cassel in *Faces* (Cassavetes, Reade–Continental).

Daniel Massey in *Star!* (Wise, 20th Century–Fox).

Jack Wild in *Oliver!* (Romulus, Columbia).

Gene Wilder in *The Producers* (Glazier, Avco Embassy).

Supporting Actress

Lynn Carlin in *Faces* (Cassavetes, Reade-Continental).

★ Ruth Gordon in *Rosemary's Baby* (Castle, Paramount).

Sondra Locke in *The Heart Is a Lonely Hunter* (Warner Bros.–Seven Arts).

Kay Medford in *Funny Girl* (Rastar, Columbia).

Estelle Parsons in *Rachel, Rachel* (Kayos, Warner Bros.–Seven Arts).

Director

Anthony Harvey for *The Lion in Winter* (Haworth, Avco Embassy).

Stanley Kubrick for *2001: A Space Odyssey* (Polaris, MGM).

Gillo Pontecorvo for *The Battle of Algiers* (Igor–Casbah, Allied Artists) (Italian).

★ Carol Reed for *Oliver!* (Romulus, Columbia).

Franco Zeffirelli for *Romeo and Juliet* (B.H.E.–Verona–De Laurentiis, Paramount).

Writing

(SCREENPLAY—BASED ON MATERIAL FROM ANOTHER MEDIUM)

★ *The Lion in Winter,* Haworth, Avco Embassy. James Goldman.

The Odd Couple, Koch, Paramount. Neil Simon.
Oliver!, Romulus, Columbia. Vernon Harris.
Rachel, Rachel, Kayos, Warner Bros.–Seven Arts. Stewart Stern.
Rosemary's Baby, Castle, Paramount. Roman Polanski.

(STORY AND SCREENPLAY—WRITTEN DIRECTLY FOR THE SCREEN)
The Battle of Algiers, Igor-Casbah, Allied Artists (Italian). Franco Solinas and Gillo Pontecorvo.
Faces, Cassavetes, Walter Reade-Continental. John Cassavetes.
Hot Millions, Albert, MGM. Ira Wallach and Peter Ustinov.
★ *The Producers,* Glazier, Avco Embassy. Mel Brooks.
2001: A Space Odyssey, Polaris, MGM. Stanley Kubrick and Arthur C. Clarke.

Cinematography
Funny Girl, Rastar, Columbia. Harry Stradling.
Ice Station Zebra, Filmways, MGM. Daniel L. Fapp.
Oliver!, Romulus, Columbia. Oswald Morris.
★ *Romeo and Juliet,* B.H.E.–Verona-DeLaurentiis, Paramount. Pasqualino De Santis.
Star!, Wise, 20th Century–Fox. Ernest Laszlo.

Art Direction—Set Direction
★ *Oliver!,* Romulus, Columbia. John Box and Terence Marsh; Vernon Dixon and Ken Muggleston.
The Shoes of the Fisherman, Englund, MGM. George W. Davis and Edward Carfagno.
Star!, Wise, 20th Century–Fox. Boris Leven; Walter M. Scott and Howard Bristol.
2001: A Space Odyssey, Polaris, MGM. Tony Masters, Harry Lange and Ernie Archer.
War and Peace, Mosfilm, Reade-Continental (Russian). Mikhail Bogdanov and Gennady Myasnikov; G. Koshelev and V. Uvarov.

Sound
Bullitt, Solar, Warner Bros.–Seven Arts. Warner Bros.–Seven Arts Studio Sound Dept.
Finian's Rainbow, Warner Bros.–Seven Arts. Warner Bros.–Seven Arts Studio Sound Dept.
Funny Girl, Rastar, Columbia. Columbia Studio Sound Dept.
★ *Oliver!,* Romulus, Columbia. Shepperton Studio Sound Dept.
Star!, Wise, 20th Century–Fox. 20th Century–Fox Studio Sound Dept.

Music
(SONG—ORIGINAL TO THE PICTURE)
"Chitty Chitty Bang Bang" (*Chitty Chitty Bang Bang,* Warfield, UA); Music and Lyrics by Richard M. Sherman and Robert B. Sherman.
"For Love of Ivy" (*For Love of Ivy,* ABC–Palomar, Cinerama); Music by Quincy Jones. Lyrics by Bob Russell.
"Funny Girl" (*Funny Girl,* Rastar, Columbia); Music by Jule Styne. Lyrics by Bob Merrill.
"Star!" (*Star!,* Wise, 20th Century–Fox); Music by Jimmy Van Heusen. Lyrics by Sammy Cahn.
★ "The Windmills of Your Mind" (*The Thomas Crown Affair,* Mirisch–Simkoe-Solar, UA); Music by Michel Legrand. Lyrics by Alan and Marilyn Bergman.

(ORIGINAL SCORE—FOR A MOTION PICTURE [NOT A MUSICAL])
The Fox, Stross, Claridge Pictures. Lalo Schifrin.
★ *The Lion in Winter,* Haworth, Avco Embassy. John Barry.
Planet of the Apes, Apjac, 20th Century–Fox. Jerry Goldsmith.
The Shoes of the Fisherman. Englund, MGM. Alex North.
The Thomas Crown Affair, Mirisch-Simkoe-Solar, UA. Michel Legrand.

(SCORE OF A MUSICAL PICTURE—[ORIGINAL OR ADAPTATION])
Finian's Rainbow, Warner Bros.–Seven Arts. Ray Heindorf.
Funny Girl, Rastar, Columbia. Walter Scharf.
★ *Oliver!,* Romulus, Columbia. John Green.
Star!, Wise, 20th Century–Fox. Lennie Hayton.
The Young Girls of Rochefort, Warner Bros.–Seven Arts (French). Michel Legrand and Jacques Demy.

Film Editing
★ *Bullitt,* Solar, Warner Bros.–Seven Arts. Frank P. Keller.
Funny Girl, Rastar, Columbia. Robert Swink, Maury Winetrobe and William Sands.
The Odd Couple, Koch, Paramount. Frank Bracht.
Oliver!, Romulus, Columbia. Ralph Kemplen.
Wild in the Streets, American International. Fred Feitshans and Eve Newman.

Costume Design
The Lion in Winter, Haworth, Avco Embassy. Margaret Furse.
Oliver!, Romulus, Columbia. Phyllis Dalton.
Planet of the Apes, Apjac, 20th Century–Fox. Morton Haack.
★ *Romeo and Juliet,* B.H.E.–Verona-DeLaurentiis, Paramount. Danilo Donati.
Star!, Wise, 20th Century–Fox. Donald Brooks.

Special Visual Effects
Ice Station Zebra, Filmways, MGM. Hal Millar and J. McMillan Johnson.
★ *2001: A Space Odyssey,* Polaris, MGM. Stanley Kubrick.

Short Subjects
(CARTOONS)
The House That Jack Built, National Film Board of Canada, Columbia. Wolf Koenig and Jim Mackay, producers.
The Magic Pear Tree, Bing Crosby Prods. Jimmy Murakami, producer.
Windy Day, Hubley Studios, Paramount. John and Faith Hubley, producers.

★ *Winnie the Pooh and the Blustery Day,* Disney, Buena Vista. Walt Disney, producer.

(LIVE ACTION SUBJECTS)

The Dove, Coe-Davis, Schoenfeld Films. George Coe, Sidney Davis and Anthony Lover, producers.

Duo, National Film Board of Canada, Columbia.

Prelude, Prelude Company, Excelsior Dist. John Astin, producer.

★ *Robert Kennedy Remembered,* Guggenheim Prods., National General. Charles Guggenheim, producer.

Documentary

(SHORT SUBJECTS)

The House that Ananda Built, Films Division, Government of India. Fali Bilimoria, producer.

The Revolving Door, Vision Associates for American Foundation Institute of Corrections. Lee R. Bobker, producer.

A Space to Grow, Office of Economic Opportunity for Project Upward Bound. Thomas P. Kelly, Jr. producer.

A Way Out of the Wilderness, John Sutherland Prods. Dan E. Weisburd, producer.

★ *Why Man Creates,* Saul Bass & Associates. Saul Bass, producer.

(FEATURES)

A Few Notes on Our Food Problem, U.S. Information Agency. James Blue, producer.

★ *Journey into Self,* Western Behavioral Sciences Institute. Bill McGaw, producer.

The Legendary Champions, Turn of the Century Fights. William Cayton, producer.

Other Voices, DHS Films. David H. Sawyer, producer.

Young Americans, The Young Americans Prod. Robert Cohn and Alex Grasshoff, producers. (Ineligible for nomination under Academy bylaws.)

Foreign Language Film

The Boys of Paul Street (Hungary).

The Fireman's Ball (Czechoslovakia).

The Girl with the Pistol (Italy).

Stolen Kisses (France).

★ *War and Peace* (Russia).

Irving G. Thalberg Memorial Award

Not given this year.

Jean Hersholt Humanitarian Award

Martha Raye.

Honorary Awards

John Chambers for his outstanding makeup achievement for *Planet of the Apes* (statuette).

Onna White for her outstanding choreography achievement for *Oliver!* (statuette).

Scientific or Technical

CLASS I (STATUETTE)

Philip V. Palmquist of Minnesota Mining and Manufacturing Co., to Dr. Herbert Meyer of the Motion Picture and Television Research Center, and to Charles D. Staffell of the Rank Organization for the development of a successful embodiment of the reflex background projection system for composite cinematography.

Eastman Kodak Company for the development and introduction of a color reversal intermediate film for motion pictures.

CLASS II (PLAQUE)

Donald W. Norwood for the design and development of the Norwood Photographic Exposure Meters.

Eastman Kodak Company and Producers Service Company for the development of a new high-speed step-optical reduction printer.

Edmund M. DiGiulio, Niels G. Petersen and Norman S. Hughes of the Cinema Product Development Company for the design and application of a conversion which makes available the reflex viewing system for motion picture cameras.

Optical Coating Laboratores, Inc., for the development of an improved anti-reflection coating for photographic and projection lens systems.

Eastman Kodak Company for the introduction of a new high speed motion picture color negative film.

Panavision Incorporated for the conception, design and introduction of a 65mm hand-held motion picture camera.

Todd-AO Company and the Mitchell Camera Company for the design and engineering of the Todd-AO hand-held motion picture camera.

CLASS III (CITATION)

Carl W. Hauge and Edward H. Reichard of Consolidated Film Industries and E. Michael Meahl and Roy J. Ridenour of Ramtronics for engineering an automatic exposure control for printing-machine lamps.

Eastman Kodak Company for a new direct positive film, and to Consolidated Film Industries for the application of this film to the making of post-production work prints.

Points of Interest

1. Nothing to it: Jack Wild, Lynn Carlin and Sondra Locke nominated for film debuts; Barbra Streisand wins for hers.
2. Renaissance man: Stanley Kubrick nominated for Director, Story and Screenplay, and Special Effects. Wins last Award.
3. Indian givers: When the Academy learns that Documentary Feature winner *Young Americans* played at a theater in North Carolina in 1967, it rescinds the Award, giving it to second-place finisher *Journey into Self*.
4. Didn't you used to be Gomez?: Live Action Short Subject nominee *Prelude* directed, produced and written by actor John Astin, who also starred.

Rule Changes

1. The fewer the merrier: Best Sound Effects no longer given.
2. The name game: "Song" becomes "Song—Original to the Picture"; "Original Music Score" becomes "Original Score—for a Motion Picture (Not a Musical)"; "Scoring of Music—Adaptation or Treatment" becomes "Score of a Musical Picture (Original or Adaptation)."

Eligible Films That Failed to Be Nominated for Best Picture

2001: A Space Odyssey; Petulia; Rosemary's Baby; Pretty Poison; Belle du Jour; The Good, the Bad, and the Ugly; Weekend; Bullitt; Planet of the Apes; The Killing of Sister George.

1969

Picture

Anne of the Thousand Days, Wallis, Universal. Produced by Hal B. Wallis.

Butch Cassidy and the Sundance Kid, Hill-Monash, 20th Century–Fox. Produced by John Foreman.

Hello, Dolly! Chenault, 20th Century–Fox. Produced by Ernest Lehman.

★ *Midnight Cowboy,* Hellman-Schlesinger, UA. Produced by Jerome Hellman.

Z, Reggane Films-O.N.C.I.C., Cinema V (Algerian). Produced by Jacques Perrin and Hamed Rachedi.

Actor

Richard Burton in *Anne of the Thousand Days* (Wallis, Universal).

Dustin Hoffman in *Midnight Cowboy* (Hellman-Schlesinger, UA).

Peter O'Toole in *Goodbye, Mr. Chips* (Apjac, MGM).

Jon Voight in *Midnight Cowboy* (Hellman-Schlesinger, UA).

★ John Wayne in *True Grit* (Wallis, Paramount).

Actress

Genevieve Bujold in *Anne of the Thousand Days* (Wallis, Universal).

Jane Fonda in *They Shoot Horses, Don't They?* (Chartoff-Winkler-Pollack, ABC Pictures, Cinerama).

Liza Minnelli in *The Sterile Cuckoo* (Boardwalk, Paramount).

Jean Simmons in *The Happy Ending* (Pax Films, UA).

★ Maggie Smith in *The Prime of Miss Jean Brodie* (20th Century–Fox).

Supporting Actor

Rupert Crosse in *The Reivers* (Ravetch-Kramer-Solar, Cinema Center, National General).

Elliott Gould in *Bob & Carol & Ted & Alice* (Frankovich, Columbia).

Jack Nicholson in *Easy Rider* (Pando-Raybert, Columbia).

Anthony Quayle in *Anne of the Thousand Days* (Wallis, Universal).

★ Gig Young in *They Shoot Horses, Don't They?* (Chartoff-Winkler-Pollack, ABC Pictures, Cinerama).

Supporting Actress

Catherine Burns in *Last Summer* (Perry-Alsid, Allied Artists).

Dyan Cannon in *Bob & Carol & Ted & Alice* (Frankovich, Columbia).

★ Goldie Hawn in *Cactus Flower* (Frankovich, Columbia).

Sylvia Miles in *Midnight Cowboy* (Hellman-Schlesinger, UA).

Susannah York in *They Shoot Horses, Don't They?* (Chartoff-Winkler-Pollack/ABC Pictures, Cinerama).

Director

Costa–Gavras for *Z* (Reggane Films-O.N.C.I.C., Cinema V) (Algerian).

George Roy Hill for *Butch Cassidy and the Sundance Kid* (Hill-Monash, 20th Century–Fox).

Arthur Penn for *Alice's Restaurant* (Florin Prod., UA).

Sydney Pollack for *They Shoot Horses, Don't They?* (Chartoff-Winkler-Pollack, ABC Pictures, Cinerama).

★ John Schlesinger for *Midnight Cowboy* (Hellman-Schlesinger, UA).

Writing

(SCREENPLAY—BASED ON MATERIAL FROM ANOTHER MEDIUM)

Anne of the Thousand Days, Wallis, Universal. John Hale, Bridget Boland and Richard Sokolove.

Goodbye, Columbus, Willow Tree, Paramount. Arnold Schulman.

★ *Midnight Cowboy,* Hellman-Schlesinger, UA. Waldo Salt.

They Shoot Horses, Don't They?, Chartoff-Winkler-Pollack, ABC Pictures, Cinerama. James Poe and Robert E. Thompson.

Z, Reggane Films-O.N.C.I.C., Cinema V (Algerian). Jorge Semprun and Costa-Gavras.

(STORY AND SCREENPLAY—BASED ON MATERIAL NOT PREVIOUSLY PUBLISHED OR PRODUCED)

Bob & Carol & Ted & Alice, Frankovich, Columbia. Paul Mazursky and Larry Tucker.

★ *Butch Cassidy and the Sundance Kid,* Hill-Monash, 20th Century–Fox. William Goldman.

The Damned, Pegaso-Praesidens, Warner Bros. Nicola Badalucco, Enrico Medioli and Luchino Visconti.

Easy Rider, Pando-Raybert, Columbia. Peter Fonda, Dennis Hopper and Terry Southern.

The Wild Bunch, Feldman, Warner Bros. Walon Green, Roy N. Sickner and Sam Peckinpah.

Cinematography

Anne of the Thousand Days, Wallis, Universal. Arthur Ibbetson.

Bob & Ted & Carol & Alice, Frankovich, Columbia. Charles B. Lang.

★ *Butch Cassidy and the Sundance Kid,* Hill-Monash, 20th Century–Fox. Conrad Hall.

Hello, Dolly! Chenault, 20th Century–Fox. Harry Stradling.

Marooned, Frankovich-Sturges, Columbia. Daniel Fapp.

Art Direction—Set Decoration

Anne of the Thousand Days, Wallis, Universal. Maurice Carter and Lionel Couch; Patrick McLoughlin.

Gaily, Gaily, Mirisch-Cartier, UA. Robert Boyle and George B. Chan; Edward Boyle and Carl Biddiscombe.

★ *Hello, Dolly!,* Chenault, 20th Century–Fox. John DeCuir, Jack Martin Smith and Herman Blumenthal; Walter M. Scott, George Hopkins and Raphael Bretton.

Sweet Charity, Universal. Alexander Golitzen and George C. Webb; Jack D. Moore.

They Shoot Horses, Don't They?, Chartoff-Winkler-Pollack, ABC Pictures, Cinerama. Harry Horner; Frank McKelvy.

Sound

Anne of the Thousand Days, Wallis, Universal. John Aldred.

Butch Cassidy and the Sundance Kid, Hill-Monash, 20th Century–Fox. William Edmundson and David Dockendorf.

Gaily, Gaily, Mirisch-Cartier, UA. Robert Martin and Clem Portman.

★ *Hello, Dolly!,* Chenault, 20th Century–Fox. Jack Solomon and Murray Spivack.

Marooned, Frankovich-Sturges, Columbia. Les Fresholtz and Arthur Piantadosi.

Music

(SONG—ORIGINAL TO THE PICTURE)

"Come Saturday Morning" (*The Sterile Cuckoo,* Boardwalk, Paramount); Music by Fred Karlin. Lyrics by Dory Previn.

"Jean" (*The Prime of Miss Jean Brodie,* 20th Century–Fox); Music and Lyrics by Rod McKuen.

★ "Raindrops Keep Fallin' on My Head" (*Butch Cassidy and the Sundance Kid,* Hill-Monash, 20th Century–Fox); Music by Burt Bacharach. Lyrics by Hal David.

"True Grit" (*True Grit,* Wallis, Paramount); Music by Elmer Bernstein, Lyrics by Don Black.

"What Are You Doing the Rest of Your Life?" (*The Happy Ending.* Pax Films, UA); Music by Michel Legrand. Lyrics by Alan and Marilyn Bergman.

(ORIGINAL SCORE—FOR A MOTION PICTURE [NOT A MUSICAL])

Anne of the Thousand Days, Wallis, Universal. Georges Delerue.

★ *Butch Cassidy and the Sundance Kid,* Hill-Monash, 20th Century–Fox. Burt Bacharach.

The Reivers, Ravetch-Kramer-Solar, Cinema Center, National General. John Williams.

The Secret of Santa Vittoria, Kramer, UA. Ernest Gold.

The Wild Bunch, Feldman, Warner Bros. Jerry Fielding.

(SCORE OF A MUSICAL PICTURE [ORIGINAL OR ADAPTATION])

Goodbye, Mr. Chips, Apjac, MGM. Leslie Bricusse and John Williams.

★ *Hello, Dolly!,* Chenault, 20th Century–Fox. Lennie Hayton and Lionel Newman.

Paint Your Wagon, Lerner, Paramount. Nelson Riddle.

Sweet Charity, Universal. Cy Coleman.

They Shoot Horses, Don't They?, Chartoff-Winkler-Pollack, ABC Pictures, Cinerama. John Green and Albert Woodbury.

Film Editing

Hello, Dolly!, Chenault, 20th Century–Fox. William Reynolds.

Midnight Cowboy, Hellman-Schlesinger, UA. Hugh A. Robertson.

The Secret of Santa Vittoria, Kramer, UA. William Lyon and Earle Herdan.

They Shoot Horses, Don't They?, Chartoff-Winkler-Pollack, ABC Pictures, Cinerama. Fredric Steinkamp.

★ *Z,* Reggane Films-O.N.C.I.C., Cinema V (Algerian). Françoise Bonnot.

Costume Design

★ *Anne of the Thousand Days,* Wallis, Universal. Margaret Furse.

Gaily, Gaily, Mirisch-Cartier, UA. Ray Aghayan.

Hello, Dolly!, Chenault, 20th Century–Fox. Irene Sharaff.

Sweet Charity, Universal. Edith Head.

They Shoot Horses, Don't They?, Chartoff-Winkler-Pollack, ABC Pictures, Cinerama. Donfeld.

Special Visual Effects

Krakatoa, East of Java, ABC Pictures, Cinerama. Eugene Lourie and Alex Weldon.

★ *Marooned,* Frankovich-Sturges, Columbia. Robbie Robertson.

Short Subjects

(CARTOONS)

★ *It's Tough to Be a Bird,* Disney, Buena Vista. Ward Kimball, producer.

Of Men and Demons, Hubley Studios, Paramount. John and Faith Hubley, producers.

Walking, National Film Board of Canada. Columbia. Ryan Larkin, producer.

(LIVE ACTION SUBJECTS)

Blake, National Film Board of Canada, Vaudeo Inc. Doug Jackson, producer.

★ *The Magic Machines,* Fly-By-Night Prods., Manson Distributing. Joan Keller Stern, producer.

People Soup, Pangloss Prods., Columbia. Marc Merson, producer.

Documentary

(SHORT SUBJECTS)

★ *Czechoslovakia 1968,* Sanders-Fresco Film Makers for U.S. Information Agency. Denis Sanders and Robert M. Fresco, producers.

An Impression of John Steinbeck: Writer, Donald Wrye Prods. for U.S. Information Agency. Donald Wrye, producer.

Jenny Is a Good Thing, A.C.I. Prod. for Project Head Start. Joan Horvath, producer.

Leo Beuerman, Centron Prod. Arthur H. Wolf and Russell A. Mosser, producers.

The Magic Machines, Fly-By-Night Prods., Manson Distributing. Joan Keller Stern, producer.

(FEATURES)

★ *Arthur Rubinstein—The Love of Life,* Midem Prod. Bernard Chevry, producer.

Before the Mountain Was Moved, Robert K. Sharpe Prods. for the Office of Economic Opportunity. Robert K. Sharpe, producer.

In the Year of the Pig, Emile de Antonio Prod. Emile de Antonio, producer.

The Olympics in Mexico, Film Section of the Organizing Committee for the XIX Olympic Games.

The Wolf Men, MGM. Irwin Rosten, producer.

Foreign Language Film

Adalen '31 (Sweden).

The Battle of Neretva (Yugoslavia).

The Brothers Karamazov (U.S.S.R.).

My Night with Maud (France).

★ *Z* (Algeria).

Irving G. Thalberg Memorial Award

Not given this year.

Jean Hersholt Humanitarian Award

George Jessel.

Honorary Award

Cary Grant for his unique mastery of the art of screen acting with the respect and affection of his colleagues (statuette).

Scientific or Technical

CLASS I (STATUETTE)

None.

CLASS II (PLAQUE)

Hazeltine Corporation for the design and development of the Hazeltine Color Film Analyzer.

Fouad Said for the design and introduction of the Cinemobile series of equipment trucks for location motion picture production.

Juan de la Cierva and Dynasciences Corporation for the design and development of the Dynalens optical image motion compensator.

CLASS III (CITATION)

Otto Popelka of Magna-Tech Electronics Co., Inc., for the development of an Electronically Controlled Looping System.

Fenton Hamilton of MGM Studio for the concept and engineering of a mobile battery power unit for location lighting.

Panavision Incorporated for the design and development of the Panaspeed Motion Picture Camera Motor.

Robert M. Flynn and Russell Hessy of Universal City Studios, Inc., for a machine-gun modification for motion picture photography.

Points of Interest

1. Nothing to it: Catherine Burns nominated for film debut.
2. Two-timer: *Z* first film nominated for both Best Foreign Film and Best Picture.
3. The family way: Jane Fonda and brother Peter both nominated.

Rule Changes

1. The name game: "Story and Screenplay—Written Directly for the Screen" becomes "Story and Screenplay—Based on Material Not Previously Published or Produced."

Eligible Films That Failed to Be Nominated for Best Picture

They Shoot Horses, Don't They?; Alice's Restaurant; The Wild Bunch; Easy Rider; Bob & Carol & Ted & Alice; Once Upon a Time in the West; Stolen Kisses; Take the Money and Run; If . . . ; Medium Cool; I Am Curious (Yellow); Boudu Saved From Drowning; Sweet Charity.

Submitted Film Rejected by the Foreign Language Film Award Committee

Fellini's Satyricon (Italy), directed by Federico Fellini.

Eligible Songs That Failed to Be Nominated

"Ballad of Easy Rider" (Roger McGuinn)—*Easy Rider;* "Mama Tried" (Merle Haggard)—*Killers Three;* "My Personal Property" (Cy Coleman and Dorothy Fields)—*Sweet Charity.*

1970

Picture

Airport, Hunter, Universal. Produced by Ross Hunter.
Five Easy Pieces, BBS Productions, Columbia. Produced by Bob Rafelson and Richard Wechsler.
Love Story, Paramount. Produced by Howard G. Minsky.
*M*A*S*H*, Aspen, 20th Century–Fox. Produced by Ingo Preminger.
★ *Patton*, 20th Century–Fox. Produced by Frank McCarthy.

Actor

Melvyn Douglas in *I Never Sang for My Father* (Jamel, Columbia).
James Earl Jones in *The Great White Hope* (Turman, 20th Century–Fox).
Jack Nicholson in *Five Easy Pieces* (BBS Productions, Columbia).
Ryan O'Neal in *Love Story* (Paramount).
★ George C. Scott in *Patton* (20th Century–Fox).

Actress

Jane Alexander in *The Great White Hope* (Turman, 20th Century–Fox).
★ Glenda Jackson in *Women in Love* (Kramer-Rosen, UA).
Ali MacGraw in *Love Story* (Paramount).
Sarah Miles in *Ryan's Daughter* (Faraway, MGM).
Carrie Snodgress in *Diary of a Mad Housewife* (Perry, Universal).

Supporting Actor

Richard Castellano in *Lovers and Other Strangers* (ABC Pictures, Cinerama).
Chief Dan George in *Little Big Man* (Hiller-Stockbridge, Cinema Center, National General).
Gene Hackman in *I Never Sang for My Father* (Jamel, Columbia).
John Marley in *Love Story* (Paramount).
★ John Mills in *Ryan's Daughter* (Faraway, MGM).

Supporting Actress

Karen Black in *Five Easy Pieces* (BBS Productions, Columbia).
Lee Grant in *The Landlord* (Mirisch-Cartier, UA).
★ Helen Hayes in *Airport* (Hunter, Universal).
Sally Kellerman in *M*A*S*H* (Aspen, 20th Century–Fox).
Maureen Stapleton in *Airport* (Hunter, Universal).

Director

Robert Altman for *M*A*S*H* (Aspen, 20th Century–Fox).
Federico Fellini for *Fellini Satyricon* (Grimaldi, UA) (Italian).
Arthur Hiller for *Love Story* (Paramount).
Ken Russell for *Women in Love* (Kramer-Rosen, UA).
★ Franklin J. Schaffner for *Patton* (20th Century–Fox).

Writing

(SCREENPLAY—BASED ON MATERIAL FROM ANOTHER MEDIUM)
Airport, Hunter, Universal. George Seaton.
I Never Sang for My Father, Jamel, Columbia. Robert Anderson.
Lovers and Other Strangers, ABC Pictures, Cinerama. Renee Taylor, Joseph Bologna and David Zelag Goodman.
★ *M*A*S*H*, Aspen, 20th Century–Fox. Ring Lardner, Jr.
Women in Love, Kramer-Rosen, UA. Larry Kramer.

(STORY AND SCREENPLAY—BASED ON FACTUAL MATERIAL OR MATERIAL NOT PREVIOUSLY PUBLISHED OR PRODUCED)
Five Easy Pieces, BBS Productions, Columbia. Bob Rafelson and Adrien Joyce.
Joe, Cannon Releasing. Norman Wexler.
Love Story, Paramount, Erich Segal.
My Night at Maud's, Pathé Contemporary (French). Eric Rohmer.
★ *Patton*, 20th Century–Fox. Francis Ford Coppola and Edmund H. North.

Cinematography

Airport, Hunter, Universal. Ernest Laszlo.
Patton, 20th Century–Fox. Fred Koenekamp.
★ *Ryan's Daughter*, Faraway Prods., MGM. Freddie Young.
Tora! Tora! Tora!, 20th Century–Fox. Charles F. Wheeler, Osami Furuya, Sinsaku Himeda and Masamichi Satoh.
Women in Love, Kramer-Rosen, UA. Billy Williams.

Art Direction—Set Decoration

Airport, Hunter, Universal. Alexander Golitzen and E. Preston Ames; Jack D. Moore and Mickey S. Michaels.
The Molly MaGuires, Tamm, Paramount. Tambi Larsen; Darrell Silvera.
★ *Patton*, 20th Century–Fox. Urie McCleary and Gil Parrondo; Antonio Mateos and Pierre-Louis Thevenet.
Scrooge, Waterbury, Cinema Center, National General. Terry Marsh and Bob Cartwright; Pamela Cornell.
Tora! Tora! Tora!, 20th Century–Fox. Jack Martin Smith, Yoshiro Muraki, Richard Day and Taizoh Kawashima; Walter M. Scott, Norman Rockett and Carl Biddiscombe.

Sound

Airport, Hunter, Universal. Ronald Pierce and David Moriarty.
★ *Patton*, 20th Century–Fox. Douglas Williams and Don Bassman.
Ryan's Daughter, Faraway, MGM. Gordon K. McCallum and John Bramall.
Tora! Tora! Tora!, 20th Century–Fox. Murray Spivack and Herman Lewis.

Woodstock, Wadleigh-Maurice, Warner Bros. Dan Wallin and Larry Johnson.

Music

(SONG—ORIGINAL TO THE PICTURE)

★ "For All We Know" (*Lovers and Other Strangers*, ABC Pictures, Cinerama); Music by Fred Karlin. Lyrics by Robb Royer and James Griffin (a.k.a. Robb Wilson and Arthur James).

"Pieces of Dreams" (*Pieces of Dreams*, RFB Enterprises, UA); Music by Michel Legrand. Lyrics by Alan and Marilyn Bergman.

"Thank You Very Much" (*Scrooge*, Waterbury, Cinema Center, National General); Music and Lyrics by Leslie Bricusse.

"Till Love Touches Your Life" (*Madron*, Four Star-Excelsior Releasing); Music by Riz Ortolani. Lyrics by Arthur Hamilton.

"Whistling Away the Dark" (*Darling Lili*, Geoffrey, Paramount); Music by Henry Mancini. Lyrics by Johnny Mercer.

(ORIGINAL SCORE)

Airport, Hunter, Universal. Alfred Newman.

Cromwell, Irving Allen, Columbia. Frank Cordell.

★ *Love Story*, Paramount. Francis Lai.

Patton, 20th Century–Fox. Jerry Goldsmith.

Sunflower, Sostar, Avco Embassy. Henry Mancini.

(ORIGINAL SONG SCORE)

The Baby Maker, Wise, National General. Fred Karlin and Tylwyth Kymry.

A Boy Named Charlie Brown, Mendelson-Melendez, Cinema Center, National General. Rod McKuen, John Scott Trotter, Bill Melendez, Al Shean and Vince Guaraldi.

Darling Lili, Geoffrey, Paramount. Henry Mancini and Johnny Mercer.

★ *Let It Be*, Beatles-Apple, UA. The Beatles.

Scrooge, Waterbury, Cinema Center Films, National General. Leslie Bricusse, Ian Fraser and Herbert W. Spencer.

Film Editing

Airport, Hunter, Universal. Stuart Gilmore.

*M*A*S*H*, Aspen, 20th Century–Fox. Danford B. Greene.

★ *Patton*, 20th Century–Fox. Hugh S. Fowler.

Tora! Tora! Tora!, 20th Century–Fox. James E. Newcom, Pembroke J. Herring and Inoue Chikaya.

Woodstock, Wadleigh-Maurice, Warner Bros. Thelma Schoonmaker.

Costume Design

Airport, Hunter, Universal. Edith Head.

★ *Cromwell*, Irving Allen, Columbia. Nino Novarese.

Darling Lili, Geoffrey, Paramount. Donald Brooks and Jack Bear.

The Hawaiians, Mirisch, UA. Bill Thomas.

Scrooge, Waterbury, Cinema Center, National General. Margaret Furse.

Special Visual Effects

Patton, 20th Century–Fox. Alex Weldon.

★ *Tora! Tora! Tora!*, 20th Century–Fox. A.D. Flowers and L.B. Abbott.

Short Subjects

(CARTOONS)

The Further Adventures of Uncle Sam: Part Two, Haboush Company, Goldstone Films. Robert Mitchell and Dale Case, producers.

★ *Is It Always Right to Be Right?*, Stephen Bosustow Prods., Schoenfeld Films. Nick Bosustow, producer.

The Shepherd, Cameron Guess and Associates, Brandon Films. Cameron Guess, producer.

(LIVE ACTION SUBJECTS)

★ *The Resurrection of Broncho Billy*, University of Southern California, Dept. of Cinema, Universal. John Longenecker, producer.

Shut Up . . . I'm Crying, Robert Siegler Prods., Schoenfeld Films. Robert Siegler, producer.

Sticky My Fingers . . . Fleet My Feet, American Film Institute, Schoenfeld Films. John Hancock, producer.

Documentary

(SHORT SUBJECTS)

The Gifts, Richter-McBride Prods. for the Water Quality Office of the Environmental Protection Agency. Robert McBride, producer.

★ *Interviews with My Lai Veterans*, Laser Film Corp. Joseph Strick, producer.

A Long Way from Nowhere, Robert Aller Prods. Bob Aller, producer.

Oisin, an Aengus Film. Vivien and Patrick Carey, producers.

Time Is Running Out, Gesellschaft für bildende Filme. Horst Dallmayr and Robert Menegoz, producers.

(FEATURES)

Chariots of the Gods, Terra-Filmkunst GmbH. Dr. Harald Reini, producer.

Jack Johnson, The Big Fights. Jim Jacobs, producer.

King: A Filmed Record . . . Montgomery to Memphis, Commonwealth United Prod. Ely Landau, producer.

Say Goodbye, a Wolper Prod. David H. Vowell, producer.

★ *Woodstock*, Wadleigh-Maurice. Warner Bros. Bob Maurice, producer.

Foreign Language Film

First Love (Switzerland).

Hoa-Binh (France).

★ *Investigation of a Citizen Above Suspicion* (Italy).

Paix Sur Les Champs (Belgium).
Tristana (Spain).

Irving G. Thalberg Memorial Award

Ingmar Bergman.

Jean Hersholt Humanitarian Award

Frank Sinatra.

Honorary Awards

Lillian Gish for superlative artistry and for distinguished contribution to the progress of motion pictures (statuette).

Orson Welles for superlative artistry and versatility in the creation of motion pictures (statuette).

Scientific or Technical

CLASS I (STATUETTE)

None.

CLASS II (PLAQUE)

Leonard Sokolow and Edward H. Reichard of Consolidated Film Industries for the concept and engineering of the Color Proofing Printer for motion pictures.

CLASS III (CITATION)

Sylvania Electric Products, Inc., for the development and introduction of a series of compact tungsten halogen lamps for motion picture production.

B.J. Losmandy for the concept, design and application of micro-miniature solid state amplifier modules used in motion picture recording equipment.

Eastman Kodak Company and Photo Electronics Corporation for the design and engineering of an improved video color analyzer for motion picture laboratories.

Electro Sound Incorporated for the design and introduction of the Series 8000 Sound System for motion picture theatres.

Points of Interest

1. Nothing to it: Jane Alexander and Carrie Snodgress nominated for film debuts.
2. Rock steady: Documentary Feature winner *Woodstock* first documentary nominated for Film Editing.

Rule Changes

The name game: "Score of a Musical Picture (Original or Adaptation)" becomes "Original Song Score"; "Original Score—for a Motion Picture (Not a Musical)" becomes "Original Score"; "Story and Screenplay—Based on Material Not Previously Published or Produced" becomes "Story and Screenplay—Based on Factual Material Not Previously Published or Produced."

Eligible Films That Failed to Be Nominated for Best Picture

Women in Love, Little Big Man, The Honeymoon Killers, Putney Swope, The Private Life of Sherlock Holmes, Darling Lili, On a Clear Day You Can See Forever, Beyond the Valley of the Dolls.

Eligible Songs That Failed to Be Nominated

"Let It Be" (John Lennon and Paul McCartney)—*Let It Be;* "The Long and Winding Road" (John Lennon and Paul McCartney)—*Let It Be;* "Suicide Is Painless" (Johnny Mandel and Michael Altman)—*M*A*S*H.*

1971

Picture

A Clockwork Orange, Hawk Films, Warner Bros. Produced by Stanley Kubrick.

Fiddler on the Roof, Mirisch-Cartier, UA. Produced by Norman Jewison.

★ *The French Connection,* D'Antoni-Schine-Moore, 20th Century–Fox. Produced by Philip D'Antoni.

The Last Picture Show, BBS productions, Columbia. Produced by Stephen J. Friedman.

Nicholas and Alexandra, Horizon, Columbia. Produced by Sam Spiegel.

Actor

Peter Finch in *Sunday, Bloody Sunday* (Janni, UA) (British).

★ Gene Hackman in *The French Connection* (D'Antoni-Schine-Moore, 20th Century–Fox).

Walter Matthau in *Kotch* (ABC Pictures, Cinerama).

George C. Scott in *The Hospital* (Gottfried-Chayefsky-Hiller, UA).

Topol in *Fiddler on the Roof* (Mirisch-Cartier, UA).

Actress

Julie Christie in *McCabe & Mrs. Miller* (Altman-Foster, Warner Bros.).

★ Jane Fonda in *Klute* (Gus, Warner Bros.).

Glenda Jackson in *Sunday, Bloody Sunday* (Janni, UA) (British).

Vanessa Redgrave in *Mary, Queen of Scots* (Wallis, Universal).

Janet Suzman in *Nicholas and Alexandra* (Horizon, Columbia).

Supporting Actor

Jeff Bridges in *The Last Picture Show* (BBS Productions, Columbia).

Leonard Frey in *Fiddler on the Roof* (Mirisch-Cartier, UA).

Richard Jaeckel in *Sometimes a Great Notion* (Newman-Foreman, Universal).

★ Ben Johnson in *The Last Picture Show* (BBS Productions, Columbia).

Roy Scheider in *The French Connection* (D'Antoni-Schine-Moore, 20th Century–Fox).

Supporting Actress

Ellen Burstyn in *The Last Picture Show* (BBS Productions, Columbia).

Barbara Harris in *Who Is Harry Kellerman, and Why Is He Saying Those Terrible Things About Me?* (Cinema Center, National General).

★ Cloris Leachman in *The Last Picture Show* (BBS Productions, Columbia).

Margaret Leighton in *The Go-Between* (World Film Services, Columbia).

Ann-Margret in *Carnal Knowledge* (Icarus, Avco Embassy).

Director

Peter Bogdanovich for *The Last Picture Show*, BBS Productions, Columbia.

★ William Friedkin for *The French Connection*, D'Antoni-Schine-Moore, 20th Century–Fox.

Norman Jewison for *Fiddler on the Roof*, Mirisch-Cartier, UA.

Stanley Kubrick for *A Clockwork Orange*, Hawks Films, Warner Bros.

John Schlesinger for *Sunday, Bloody Sunday*, Janni, UA (British).

Writing

(SCREENPLAY—BASED ON MATERIAL FROM ANOTHER MEDIUM)

A Clockwork Orange, Hawks Films, Warner Bros. Stanley Kubrick.

The Conformist, Paramount (Italian). Bernardo Bertolucci.

★ *The French Connection*, D'Antoni-Schine-Moore, 20th Century–Fox. Ernest Tidyman.

The Garden of the Finzi-Continis, Cinema V (Italian). Ugo Pirro and Vittorio Bonicelli.

The Last Picture Show, BBS Productions, Columbia. Larry McMurtry and Peter Bogdanovich.

(STORY AND SCREENPLAY—BASED ON FACTUAL MATERIAL OR MATERIAL NOT PREVIOUSLY PUBLISHED OR PRODUCED)

★ *The Hospital*, Gottfried-Chayefsky-Hiller, UA. Paddy Chayefsky.

Investigation of a Citizen Above Suspicion, Columbia (Italian). Elio Petri and Ugo Pirro.

Klute, Gus Prod., Warner Bros. Andy and Dave Lewis.

Summer of '42, Mulligan-Roth, Warner Bros. Herman Raucher.

Sunday, Bloody Sunday, Janni, UA (British). Penelope Gilliatt.

Cinematography

★ *Fiddler on the Roof*, Mirisch-Cartier, UA. Oswald Morris.

The French Connection, D'Antoni-Schine-Moore, 20th Century–Fox. Owen Roizman.

The Last Picture Show, BBS Productions, Columbia. Robert Surtees.

Nicholas and Alexandra, Horizon, Columbia. Freddie Young.

Summer of '42, Mulligan-Roth, Warner Bros. Robert Surtees.

Art Direction—Set Decoration

The Andromeda Strain, Wise, Universal. Boris Leven and William Tuntke; Ruby Levitt.

Bedknobs and Broomsticks, Disney, Buena Vista. John B. Mansbridge and Peter Ellenshaw; Emile Kuri and Hal Gausman.

Fiddler on the Roof, Mirisch-Cartier, UA. Robert Boyle and Michael Stringer; Peter Lamont.

Mary, Queen of Scots, Wallis, Universal. Terence Marsh and Robert Cartwright; Peter Howitt.

★ *Nicholas and Alexandra*, Horizon, Columbia. John Box, Ernest Archer, Jack Maxsted and Gil Parrondo; Vernon Dixon.

Sound

Diamonds Are Forever, Broccoli-Saltzman, UA. Gordon K. McCallum, John Mitchell and Alfred J. Overton.

★ *Fiddler on the Roof*, Mirisch-Cartier, UA. Gordon K. McCallum and David Hildyard.

The French Connection, D'Antoni-Schine-Moore, 20th Century–Fox. Theodore Soderberg and Christopher Newman.

Kotch, ABC Pictures, Cinerama. Richard Portman and Jack Solomon.

Mary, Queens of Scots, Wallis, Universal. Bob Jones and John Aldred.

Music

(SONG—ORIGINAL TO THE PICTURE)

"The Age of Not Believing" (*Bedknobs and Broomsticks*, Disney, Buena Vista); Music and Lyrics by Richard M. Sherman and Robert B. Sherman.

"All His Children" (*Sometimes a Great Notion*, Newman-Foreman, Universal); Music by Henry Mancini. Lyrics by Alan and Marilyn Bergman.

"Bless the Beasts and Children" (*Bless the Beasts and Children*, Columbia); Music and Lyrics by Barry DeVorzon and Perry Botkin, Jr.

"Life Is What You Make It" (*Kotch*, ABC Pictures, Cinerama); Music by Marvin Hamlisch. Lyrics by Johnny Mercer.

★ "Theme from *Shaft*" (*Shaft*, MGM); Music and Lyrics by Isaac Hayes.

(ORIGINAL DRAMATIC SCORE)

Mary, Queen of Scots, Wallis, Universal. John Barry.

Nicholas and Alexandra, Horizon, Columbia. Richard Rodney Bennett.

Shaft, MGM. Isaac Hayes.

Straw Dogs, ABC Pictures, Cinerama. Jerry Fielding.

★ *Summer of '42,* Mulligan-Roth, Warner Bros. Michel Legrand.

(SCORING: ADAPTATION AND ORIGINAL SONG SCORE)

Bedknobs and Broomsticks, Disney, Buena Vista. Richard M. Sherman, Robert B. Sherman and Irwin Kostal.

The Boy Friend, Russflix, MGM (British). Peter Maxwell Davies and Peter Greenwell.

★ *Fiddler on the Roof,* Mirisch-Cartier, UA. John Williams.

Tchaikovsky, Dimitri Tiomkin–Mosfilm Studios (U.S.S.R.). Dimitri Tiomkin.

Willie Wonka and the Chocolate Factory, Wolper, Paramount. Leslie Bricusse, Anthony Newley and Walter Scharf.

Film Editing

The Andromeda Strain, Wise, Universal. Stuart Gilmore and John W. Holmes.

A Clockwork Orange, Hawks Films, Warner Bros. Bill Butler.

★ *The French Connection,* 20th Century–Fox. Jerry Greenberg.

Kotch, ABC Pictures, Cinerama. Ralph E. Winters.

Summer of '42, Mulligan-Roth, Warner Bros. Folmar Blangsted.

Costume Design

Bedknobs and Broomsticks, Disney, Buena Vista. Bill Thomas.

Death in Venice, Alfa Cinematografica-P.E.C.F., Warner Bros. Piero Tosi.

Mary, Queen of Scots, Wallis, Universal. Margaret Furse.

★ *Nicholas and Alexandra,* Horizon, Columbia. Yvonne Blake and Antonio Castillo.

What's the Matter with Helen? Filmways-Raymax, UA. Morton Haack.

Special Visual Effects

★ *Bedknobs and Broomsticks,* Disney, Buena Vista. Alan Maley, Eustace Lycett and Danny Lee.

When Dinosaurs Ruled the Earth, Hammer, Warner Bros. Jim Danforth and Roger Dicken.

Short Subjects

(ANIMATED FILMS)

★ *The Crunch Bird,* Maxwell-Petok-Petrovich Prods., Regency Films. Ted Petok, producer.

Evolution, National Film Board of Canada. Columbia. Michael Mills, producer.

The Selfish Giant, Potterton Prods., Pyramid Films. Peter Sander and Murray Shostak, producers.

(LIVE ACTION FILMS)

Good Morning, E/G Films, Seymour Borde & Associates. Denny Evans and Ken Greenwald, producers.

The Rehearsal, Cinema Verona Prod., Schoenfeld Films. Stephen F. Verona, producer.

★ *Sentinels of Silence,* Producciones Concord, Paramount. Manuel Arango and Robert Amram, producers.

Documentary

(SHORT SUBJECTS)

Adventures in Perception, Han van Gelder Filmproduktie for Netherlands Information Service. Han van Gelder, producer.

Art Is . . . , Henry Strauss Associates for Sears, Roebuck Foundation. Julian Krainin and DeWitt L. Sage, Jr., producers.

The Numbers Start with the River, A WH Picture for U.S. Information Agency. Donald Wrye, producer.

★ *Sentinels of Silence,* Producciones Concord, Paramount. Manuel Arango and Robert Amram, producers.

Somebody Waiting, Snider Prods., for University of California Medical Film Library. Hal Riney, Dick Snider and Sherwood Omens, producers.

(FEATURES)

Alaska Wilderness Lake, Alan Landsburg Prods. Alan Landsburg, producer.

★ *The Hellstrom Chronicle,* David L. Wolper, Cinema V. Walon Green, producer.

On Any Sunday, Brown-Solar, Cinema V. Bruce Brown, producer.

The RA Expeditions, Swedish Broadcasting Company, Interwest Film Corp. Lennart Ehrenborg and Thor Heyerdahl, producers.

The Sorrow and the Pity, Cinema V (French). Marcel Ophuls, producer.

Foreign Language Film

Dodes'Ka-Den (Japan).

The Emigrants (Sweden).

★ *The Garden of the Finzi-Continis* (Italy).

The Policeman (Israel).

Tchaikovsky (U.S.S.R.).

Irving G. Thalberg Memorial Award

Not given this year.

Jean Hersholt Humanitarian Award

Not given this year.

Honorary Award

Charles Chaplin for the incalculable effect he has had in making motion pictures the art form of this century (statuette).

Scientific or Technical

CLASS I (STATUETTE)

None.

CLASS II (PLAQUE)

John N. Wilkinson of Optical Radiation Corporation for the development and engineering of a system of xenon arc lamphouses for motion picture projection.

CLASS III (CITATION)

Thomas Jefferson Hutchinson, James R. Rochester and Fenton Hamilton for the development and introduction of the Sunbrute system of xenon arc lamps for location lighting in motion picture production.

Photo Research, a Division of Kollmorgen Corporation, for the development and introduction of the film-lens balanced Three Color Meter.

Robert D. Auguste and Cinema Products Co. for the development and introduction of a new crystal controlled lightweight motor for the 35mm motion picture Arriflex camera.

Producers Service Corporation and Consolidated Film Industries, and to Cinema Research Corporation and Research Products, Inc., for the engineering and implementation of fully automated blow-up motion picture printing systems.

Cinema Products Co. for a control to actuate zoom lenses on motion picture cameras.

Points of Interest

1. Nothing to it: Janet Suzman nominated for film debut.

Rule Changes

1. The name game: "Cartoons" become "Animated Films"; "Original Score" becomes "Original Dramatic Score"; "Original Song Score" becomes "Scoring: Adaptation and Original Song Score."

Eligible Films That Failed to Be Nominated for Best Picture

Dirty Harry; McCabe and Mrs. Miller; Carnal Knowledge; Sunday, Bloody Sunday; The Go-Between; The Conformist; Straw Dogs; Play Misty for Me; Death in Venice; The Boy Friend; Bananas; Harold and Maude; The Wild Rovers.

Eligible Songs That Failed to Be Nominated

"Brown Sugar" (Mick Jagger and Keith Richard)—*Gimme Shelter;* "But I Might Die Tonight" (Cat Stevens)—*Deep End;* "Wild Horses" (Mick Jagger and Keith Richard)—*Gimme Shelter.*

1972

Picture

Cabaret, ABC Pictures, Allied Artists. Produced by Cy Feuer.

Deliverance, Warner Bros. Produced by John Boorman.

The Emigrants, Svensk Filmindustri, Warner Bros. (Swedish). Produced by Bengt Forslund.

★ *The Godfather,* Ruddy, Paramount. Produced by Albert S. Ruddy.

Sounder, Radnitz/Mattel, 20th Century–Fox. Produced by Robert B. Radnitz.

Actor

★ Marlon Brando in *The Godfather* (Ruddy, Paramount).

Michael Caine in *Sleuth* (Palomar, 20th Century–Fox).

Laurence Olivier in *Sleuth* (Palomar, 20th Century–Fox).

Peter O'Toole in *The Ruling Class* (Keep, Avco Embassy).

Paul Winfield in *Sounder* (Radnitz/Mattel, 20th Century–Fox).

Actress

★ Liza Minnelli in *Cabaret* (ABC Pictures, Allied Artists).

Diana Ross in *Lady Sings the Blues* (Motown-Weston-Furie, Paramount).

Maggie Smith in *Travels with My Aunt* (Fryer, MGM).

Cicely Tyson in *Sounder* (Radnitz/Mattel, 20th Century–Fox).

Liv Ullmann in *The Emigrants* (Svensk Filmindustri, Warner Bros.) (Swedish).

Supporting Actor

Eddie Albert in *The Heartbreak Kid* (Palomar, 20th Century–Fox).

James Caan in *The Godfather* (Ruddy, Paramount).

Robert Duvall in *The Godfather* (Ruddy, Paramount).

★ Joel Grey in *Cabaret* (ABC Pictures, Allied Artists).

Al Pacino in *The Godfather* (Ruddy, Paramount).

Supporting Actress

Jeannie Berlin in *The Heartbreak Kid* (Palomar, 20th Century–Fox).

★ Eileen Heckart in *Butterflies Are Free* (Frankovich, Columbia).

Geraldine Page in *Pete 'N' Tillie* (Ritt-Epstein, Universal).

Susan Tyrrell in *Fat City* (Rastar, Columbia).

Shelley Winters in *The Poseidon Adventure* (Irwin Allen, 20th Century–Fox).

Director

John Boorman for *Deliverance* (Warner Bros.).

Francis Ford Coppola for *The Godfather* (Ruddy, Paramount).

★ Bob Fosse for *Cabaret* (ABC Pictures, Allied Artists).

Joseph L. Mankiewicz for *Sleuth* (Palomar, 20th Century–Fox).

Jan Troell for *The Emigrants* (Svensk Filmindustri, Warner Bros.) (Swedish).

Writing

(SCREENPLAY—BASED ON MATERIAL FROM ANOTHER MEDIUM)

Cabaret, ABC Pictures, Allied Artists. Jay Allen.

The Emigrants, Svensk Filmindustri, Warner Bros. (Swedish). Jan Troell and Bengt Forslund.

★ *The Godfather*, Ruddy, Paramount. Mario Puzo and Francis Ford Coppola.

Pete 'N' Tillie, Ritt-Epstein, Universal. Julius J. Epstein.

Sounder, Radnitz/Mattel, 20th Century–Fox. Lonne Elder, III.

(STORY AND SCREENPLAY–BASED ON FACTUAL MATERIAL OR MATERIAL NOT PREVIOUSLY PUBLISHED OR PRODUCED)

★ *The Candidate*, Redford-Ritchie, Warner Bros. Jeremy Larner.

The Discreet Charm of the Bourgeoisie, Siberman, 20th Century–Fox (French). Luis Buñuel and Jean-Claude Carrière.

Lady Sings the Blues, Motown-Weston-Furie, Paramount. Terence McCloy, Chris Clark and Suzanne de Passe.

Murmur of the Heart, Continental Distributing (French). Louis Malle.

Young Winston, Open Road, Columbia. Carl Foreman.

Cinematography

Butterflies Are Free, Frankovich, Columbia. Charles B. Lang.

★ *Cabaret*, ABC Pictures, Allied Artists. Geoffrey Unsworth.

The Poseidon Adventure, Irwin Allen, 20th Century–Fox. Harold E. Stine.

"1776," Jack L. Warner, Columbia. Harry Stradling, Jr.

Travels with My Aunt, Fryer, MGM. Douglas Slocombe.

Art Direction—Set Decoration

★ *Cabaret*, ABC Pictures, Allied Artists. Rolf Zehetbauer and Jurgen Kiebach; Herbert Strabel.

Lady Sings the Blues, Motown-Weston-Furie, Paramount. Carl Anderson; Reg Allen.

The Poseidon Adventure, Irwin Allen, 20th Century–Fox. William Creber; Raphael Bretton.

Travels with My Aunt, Fryer, MGM. John Box, Gil Parrondo and Robert W. Laing.

Young Winston, Open Road, Columbia. Don Ashton, Geoffrey Drake, John Graysmark and William Hutchinson; Peter James.

Sound

Butterflies Are Free, Frankovich, Columbia. Arthur Piantadosi and Charles Knight.

★ *Cabaret*, ABC Pictures, Allied Artists. Robert Knudson and David Hildyard.

The Candidate, Redford-Ritchie, Warner Bros. Richard Portman and Gene Cantamessa.

The Godfather, Ruddy, Paramount. Bud Grenzbach, Richard Portman and Christopher Newman.

The Poseidon Adventure, Irwin Allen, 20th Century–Fox. Theodore Soderberg and Herman Lewis.

Music

(SONG—ORIGINAL TO THE PICTURE)

"Ben" (*Ben*, Bing Crosby Prods., Cinerama); Music by Walter Scharf. Lyrics by Don Black.

"Come Follow, Follow Me" (*The Little Ark*, Radnitz, Cinema Center, National General); Music by Fred Karlin. Lyrics by Marsha Karlin.

"Marmalade, Molasses & Honey" (*The Life and Times of Judge Roy Bean*, First Artists, National General); Music by Maurice Jarre. Lyrics by Marilyn and Alan Bergman.

★ "The Morning After" (*The Poseidon Adventure*, Irwin Allen, 20th Century–Fox); Music and Lyrics by Al Kasha and Joel Hirschhorn.

"Strange Are the Ways of Love" (*The Stepmother*, Crown International); Music by Sammy Fain. Lyrics by Paul Francis Webster.

(ORIGINAL DRAMATIC SCORE)

Images, Hemdale–Lion's Gate Films, Columbia. John Williams.

★ *Limelight*, Chaplin, Columbia. Charles Chaplin, Raymond Rasch and Larry Russell.

Napoleon and Samantha, Disney, Buena Vista. Buddy Baker.

The Poseidon Adventure, Irwin Allen, 20th Century–Fox. John Williams.

Sleuth, Palomar Pictures, 20th Century–Fox. John Addison.

(SCORING: ADAPTATION AND ORIGINAL SONG SCORE)

★ *Cabaret*, ABC Pictures, Allied Artists. Ralph Burns.

Lady Sings the Blues, Motown-Weston-Furie, Paramount. Gil Askey.

Man of La Mancha, PEA Produzioni Europee Associate Prod., UA. Laurence Rosenthal.

Film Editing

★ *Cabaret*, ABC Pictures, Allied Artists. David Bretherton.

Deliverance, Warner Bros. Tom Priestley.

The Godfather, Ruddy, Paramount. William Reynolds and Peter Zinner.

The Hot Rock, Landers-Roberts, 20th Century–Fox. Frank P. Keller and Fred W. Berger.

The Poseidon Adventure, Irwin Allen, 20th Century–Fox. Harold F. Kress.

Costume Design

The Godfather, Ruddy, Paramount. Anna Hill Johnstone.

Lady Sings the Blues, Motown-Weston-Furie, Paramount. Bob Mackie, Ray Aghayan and Norma Koch.

The Poseidon Adventure, Irwin Allen, 20th Century–Fox. Paul Zastupnevich.
★ *Travels with My Aunt*, Fryer, MGM. Anthony Powell.
Young Winston, Open Road, Columbia. Anthony Mendleson.

Short Subjects

(ANIMATED FILMS)
★ *A Christmas Carol*, American Broadcasting Company Film Services. Richard Williams, producer.
Kama Sutra Rides Again, Lion International Films. Bob Godfrey, producer.
Tup Tup, Zagreb Film-Corona Cinematografica, Manson Distributing. Nedeljko Dragic, producer.

(LIVE ACTION FILMS)
Frog Story, Gidron Productions, Schoenfeld Films. Ron Satlof and Ray Gideon, producers.
★ *Norman Rockwell's World . . . An American Dream*, Concepts Unlimited, Columbia. Richard Barclay, producer.
Solo, Pyramid Films, UA. David Adams, producer.

Documentary

(SHORT STORIES)
Hundertwasser's Rainy Day, Argos Films-Schamoni Film Prod. Peter Schamoni, producer.
K-Z, Nexus Films. Giorgio Treves, producer.
Selling Out, Unit Productions Films. Tadeusz Jaworski, producer.
★ *This Tiny World*, A Charles Huguenot van der Linden Production. Charles and Martina Huguenot van der Linden, producers.
The Tide of Traffic, BP-Greenpark. Humphrey Swingler, producer.

(FEATURES)
Ape and Super-Ape, Netherlands Ministry of Culture, Recreation and Social Welfare. Bert Haanstra, producer.
Malcolm X, Warner Bros. Marvin Worth and Arnold Perl, producers.
Manson, Merrick International. Robert Hendrickson and Laurence Merrick, producers.
★ *Marjoe*, Cinema X, Cinema V. Howard Smith and Sarah Kernochan, producers.
The Silent Revolution, Leonaris Films, Eckehard Munck, producer.

Foreign Language Film

The Dawns Here Are Quiet (U.S.S.R.).
★ *The Discreet Charm of the Bourgeoisie* (France).
I Love You Rosa (Israel).
My Dearest Señorita (Spain).
The New Land (Sweden).

Irving G. Thalberg Memorial Award

Not given this year.

Jean Hersholt Humanitarian Award

Rosalind Russell.

Honorary Awards

Charles S. Boren, leader for 38 years of the industry's enlightened labor relations and architect of its policy of nondiscrimination. With the respect and affection of all who work in films (statuette).
Edward G. Robinson, who achieved greatness as a player, a patron of the arts and a dedicated citizen . . . in sum, a Renaissance man. From his friends in the industry he loves (statuette).

Special Achievement Award

For Visual Effects: L.B. Abbott and A.D. Flowers for *The Poseidon Adventure*, Irwin Allen, 20th Century–Fox.

Scientific or Technical

CLASS I (STATUETTE)
None.

CLASS II (PLAQUE)
Joseph E. Bluth for research and development in the field of electronic photography and transfer of video tape to motion picture film.
Edward H. Reichard and Howard T. La Zare of Consolidated Film Industries and Edward Efron of IBM for the engineering of a computerized light valve monitoring system for motion picture printing.
Panavision Incorporated for the development and engineering of the Panaflex motion picture camera.

CLASS III (CITATION)
Photo Research, a Division of Kollmorgen Corporation, and PSC Technology, Inc., Acme Products Division, for the Spectra Film Gate Photometer for motion picture printers.
Carter Equipment Company, Inc., and Ramtronics for the Ramtronics light-valve photometer for motion picture printers.
David Degenkolb, Harry Larson, Manfred Michelson and Fred Scobey of DeLuxe General Incorporated for the development of a computerized motion picture printer and process control system.
Jiro Mukai and Ryusho Hirose of Canon, Inc., and Wilton R. Holm of the AMPTP Motion Picture and Television Research Center for development of the Canon Macro Zoom Lens for motion picture photography.
Philip V. Palmquist and Leonard L. Olson of the 3M Company, and Frank P. Clark of the AMPTP Motion Picture and Television Research Center for development of the Nextel simulated blood for motion picture color photography.
E. H. Geissler and G. M. Berggren of Wil-Kin, Inc., for engineering of the Ultra-Vision Motion Picture Theater Projection System.

Points of Interest

1. Nothing to it: Diana Ross nominated for film debut.
2. Eight is enough: *Cabaret* wins the most Academy Awards—eight—without being named Best Picture.
3. Those oldies but goodies: Even though it was made in 1952, Charlie Chaplin's *Limelight* wins Original Dramatic Score Award because it did not play in Los Angeles until 1972.
4. Two for one: Foreign Language Film nominee *The New Land* is a sequel to Best Picture nominee *The Emigrants*.

Rule Changes

1. A sometime thing again: "Special Visual Effects" becomes "Special Achievement Award" and is not necessarily given every year.

Eligible Films That Failed to Be Nominated for Best Picture

Frenzy; Lady Sings the Blues; The Heartbreak Kid; Play It Again, Sam; What's Up, Doc?; The Ruling Class; Images; Limelight.

Submitted Films Rejected by the Foreign Language Film Award Committee

Fellini's Roma (Italy), directed by Federico Fellini; *La Salamandre* (Switzerland), directed by Alain Tanner.

Eligible Songs That Failed to Be Nominated

"Money" (John Kander and Fred Ebb)—*Cabaret;* "Superfly" (Curtis Mayfield)—*Superfly*.

1973

Picture

American Graffiti, Lucasfilm/Coppola Company, Universal. Francis Ford Coppola, producer, Gary Kurtz, co-producer.

Cries and Whispers, Svenska Filminstitutet-Cinematograph AB Prod., New World Pictures (Swedish). Ingmar Bergman, producer.

The Exorcist, Hoya, Warner Bros. William Peter Blatty, producer.

★ *The Sting*, Bill/Phillips–Hill, Zanuck/Brown, Universal. Tony Bill, Michael and Julia Phillips, producers.

A Touch of Class, Brut Prods., Avco Embassy. Melvin Frank, producer.

Actor

Marlon Brando in *Last Tango in Paris* (UA).

★ Jack Lemmon in *Save the Tiger* (Filmways-Jalem-Cirandinha, Paramount).

Jack Nicholson in *The Last Detail* (Acrobat, Columbia).

Al Pacino in *Serpico* (De Laurentiis, Paramount).

Robert Redford in *The Sting* (Bill/Phillips–Hill, Zanuck/Brown, Universal).

Actress

Ellen Burstyn in *The Exorcist* (Hoya, Warner Bros.).

★ Glenda Jackson in *A Touch of Class* (Brut, Avco Embassy).

Marsha Mason in *Cinderella Liberty* (Sanford, 20th Century–Fox).

Barbra Streisand in *The Way We Were* (Rastar, Columbia).

Joanne Woodward in *Summer Wishes, Winter Dreams* (Rastar, Columbia).

Supporting Actor

Vincent Gardenia in *Bang the Drum Slowly* (Rosenfield, Paramount).

Jack Gilford in *Save the Tiger* (Filmways-Jalem-Cirandinha, Paramount).

★ John Houseman in *The Paper Chase* (Thompson-Paul, 20th Century–Fox).

Jason Miller in *The Exorcist* (Hoya, Warner Bros.).

Randy Quaid in *The Last Detail* (Acrobat, Columbia).

Supporting Actress

Linda Blair in *The Exorcist* (Hoya, Warner Bros.).

Candy Clark in *American Graffiti* (Lucasfilm-Coppola, Universal).

Madeline Kahn in *Paper Moon* (Directors Company, Paramount).

★ Tatum O'Neal in *Paper Moon* (Directors Company, Paramount).

Sylvia Sidney in *Summer Wishes, Winter Dreams* (Rastar, Columbia).

Director

Ingmar Bergman for *Cries and Whispers* (New World Pictures) (Swedish).

Bernardo Bertolucci for *Last Tango in Paris* (UA).

William Friedkin for *The Exorcist* (Hoya, Warner Bros.).

★ George Roy Hill for *The Sting* (Bill/Phillips-Hill-Zanuck/Brown, Universal).

George Lucas for *American Graffiti* (Lucasfilm/Coppola, Universal).

Writing

(SCREENPLAY—BASED ON MATERIAL FROM ANOTHER MEDIUM)

★ *The Exorcist*, Hoya, Warner Bros. William Peter Blatty.

The Last Detail, Acrobat, Columbia. Robert Towne.

The Paper Chase, Thompson-Paul, 20th Century–Fox. James Bridges.

Paper Moon, Directors Company, Paramount. Alvin Sargent.
Serpico, De Laurentiis, Paramount. Waldo Salt and Norman Wexler.

(STORY AND SCREENPLAY—BASED ON FACTUAL MATERIAL OR MATERIAL NOT PREVIOUSLY PUBLISHED OR PRODUCED)
American Graffiti, Lucasfilm/Coppola, Universal. George Lucas, Gloria Katz and Willard Huyck.
Cries and Whispers, New World Pictures (Swedish). Ingmar Bergman.
Save the Tiger, Filmways-Jalem-Cirandinha, Paramount. Steve Shagan.
★ *The Sting,* Bill/Phillips-Hill-Zanuck/Brown, Universal. David S. Ward.
A Touch of Class, Brut, Avco Embassy. Melvin Frank and Jack Rose.

Cinematography
★ *Cries and Whispers,* New World Pictures (Swedish). Sven Nykvist.
The Exorcist, Hoya, Warner Bros. Owen Roizman.
Jonathan Livingston Seagull, Bartlett, Paramount. Jack Couffer.
The Sting, Bill/Phillips-Hill-Zanuck/Brown, Universal. Robert Surtees.
The Way We Were, Rastar, Columbia. Harry Stradling, Jr.

Art Direction—Set Decoration
Brother Sun, Sister Moon, Euro International-Vic Film Ltd., Paramount. Lorenzo Mongiardino and Gianni Quaranta; Carmelo Patrono.
The Exorcist, Hoya, Warner Bros. Bill Malley; Jerry Wunderlich.
★ *The Sting,* Bill/Phillip-Hill-Zanuck/Brown, Universal. Henry Bumstead; James Payne.
Tom Sawyer, Jacobs, Reader's Digest, UA. Philip Jefferies; Robert de Vestel.
The Way We Were, Rastar, Columbia. Stephen Grimes; William Kiernan.

Sound
The Day of the Dolphin, Icarus, Avco Embassy. Richard Portman and Lawrence O. Jost.
★ *The Exorcist,* Hoya, Warner Bros. Robert Knudson and Chris Newman.
The Paper Chase, Thompson-Paul Prods., 20th Century–Fox. Donald O. Mitchell and Lawrence O. Jost.
Paper Moon, Directors Company, Paramount. Richard Portman and Les Fresholtz.
The Sting, Bill/Phillips-Hill-Zanuck/Brown, Universal. Ronald K. Pierce and Robert Bertrand.

Music
(SONG)
"All That Love Went to Waste" (*A Touch of Class,* Brut, Avco Embassy); Music by George Barrie. Lyrics by Sammy Cahn.
"Live and Let Die" (*Live and Let Die,* Eon, UA); Music and Lyrics by Paul and Linda McCartney.
"Love" (*Robin Hood,* Disney, Buena Vista); Music by George Bruns. Lyrics by Floyd Huddleston.
★ "The Way We Were" (*The Way We Were,* Rastar, Columbia); Music by Marvin Hamlisch. Lyrics by Alan and Marilyn Bergman.
"You're So Nice to Be Around" (*Cinderella Liberty,* Sanford Prod., 20th Century–Fox); Music by John Williams. Lyrics by Paul Williams.

(ORIGINAL DRAMATIC SCORE)
Cinderella Liberty, Sanford, 20th Century–Fox. John Williams.
The Day of the Dolphin, Icarus, Avco Embassy. Georges Delerue.
Papillon, Corona-General Productions, Allied Artists. Jerry Goldsmith.
A Touch of Class, Brut, Avco Embassy. John Cameron.
★ *The Way We Were,* Rastar, Columbia. Marvin Hamlisch.

(SCORING: ORIGINAL SONG SCORE AND/OR ADAPTATION)
Jesus Christ Superstar, Jewison-Stigwood, Universal. André Previn, Herbert Spencer and Andrew Lloyd Webber.
★ *The Sting,* Bill/Phillips-Hill-Zanuck/Brown, Universal. Marvin Hamlisch.
Tom Sawyer, Jacobs, Reader's Digest, UA. Richard M. Sherman, Robert B. Sherman and John Williams.

Film Editing
American Graffiti, Lucasfilm/Coppola, Universal. Verna Fields and Marcia Lucas.
The Day of the Jackal, Warwick Films, Universal. Ralph Kemplen.
The Exorcist, Hoya, Warner Bros. Jordan Leondopoulos, Bud Smith, Evan Lottman and Norman Gay.
Jonathan Livingston Seagull, Bartlett, Paramount. Frank P. Keller and James Galloway.
★ *The Sting,* Bill/Phillips-Hill-Zanuck/Brown, Universal. William Reynolds.

Costume Design
Cries and Whispers, New World Pictures (Swedish). Marik Vos.
Ludwig, Mega Film S.p.A. Prod., MGM. Piero Tosi.
★ *The Sting,* Bill/Phillips-Hill-Zanuck/Brown, Universal. Edith Head.
Tom Sawyer, Jacobs, Reader's Digest, UA. Donfeld.
The Way We Were, Rastar, Columbia. Dorothy Jeakins and Moss Mabry.

Short Subjects
(ANIMATED FILMS)
★ *Frank Film,* a Frank Mouris Prod. Frank Mouris, producer.

The Legend of John Henry, Bosustow-Pyramid Films. Nick Bosustow and David Adams, producers.

Pulcinella, Luzzati-Gianini Prod. Emanuele Luzzati and Guilo Gianini, producers.

(LIVE ACTION FILMS)

★ *The Bolero,* Allan Miller Production. Allan Miller and William Fertik, producers.

Clockmaker, James Street Prods. Richard Gayer, producer.

Life Times Nine, Insight Prods. Pen Densham and John Watson, producers.

Documentary

(SHORT STORIES)

Background, D'Avino and Fucci-Stone Prods. Carmen D'Avino, producer.

Children at Work (Paisti Ag Obair), Gael-Linn Films. Louis Marcus, producer.

Christo's Valley Curtain, Maysles Films. Albert and David Maysles, producers.

Four Stones for Kanemitsu, A Tamarind Prod. (producer credit not established).

★ *Princeton: A Search for Answers,* Krainin-Sage Prods. Julian Krainin and DeWitt L. Sage, Jr., producers.

(FEATURES)

Always a New Beginning, Goodell Motion Pictures. John D. Goodell, producer.

Battle of Berlin, Chronos Film. Bengt von zur Muehlen, producer.

★ *The Great American Cowboy,* Merrill-Rodeo Film Prods. Kieth Merrill, Producer.

Journey to the Outer Limits, National Geographic Society and Wolper Prods. Alex Grasshoff, producer.

Walls of Fire, Mentor Prods. Gertrude Ross Marks and Edmund F. Penney, producers.

Foreign Language Film

★ *Day for Night* (France).

The House of Chelouche Street (Israel).

L'Invitation (Switzerland).

The Pedestrian (Federal Republic of West Germany).

Turkish Delight (The Netherlands).

Irving G. Thalberg Memorial Award

Lawrence Weingarten.

Jean Hersholt Humanitarian Award

Lew Wasserman.

Honorary Awards

Henri Langlois for his devotion to the art of film, his massive contributions in preserving its past and his unswerving faith in its future (statuette).

Groucho Marx in recognition of his brilliant creativity and for the unequalled achievements of the Marx Brothers in the art of motion picture comedy (statuette).

Special Achievement Award

Not given this year.

Scientific or Technical

CLASS I (STATUETTE)

None.

CLASS II (PLAQUE)

Joachim Gerb and Erich Kastner of the Arnold and Richter Company for the development and engineering of the Arriflex 35BL motion-picture camera.

Magna-Tech Electronic Co., Inc., for the engineering and development of a high-speed re-recording system for motion-picture production.

William W. Valliant of PSC Technology, Inc., Howard F. Ott of Eastman Kodak Company, and Gerry Diebold of the Richmark Camera Service, Inc., for the development of a liquid-gate system for motion picture printers.

Harold A. Scheib, Clifford H. Ellis and Roger W. Banks of Research Products Incorporated for the concept and engineering of the Model 2101 optical printer for motion-picture optical effects.

CLASS III (CITATION)

Rosco Laboratories, Inc., for the technical advances and the development of a complete system of light-control materials for motion-picture photography.

Richard H. Vetter of the Todd-AO Corporation for the design of an improved anamorphic focusing system for motion-picture photography.

Points of Interest

1. Nothing to it: Tatum O'Neal wins Supporting Actress for film debut. Linda Blair and Jason Miller nominated for film debuts.
2. Three-timer: Marvin Hamlisch wins three Oscars, tying with Billy Wilder for most Academy Awards for feature films by an individual in one year.
3. Renaissance man: Foreign Language nominee *The Pedestrian* directed by 1961 Best Actor Maximilian Schell.
4. A little child shall lead them: At ten years old, Supporting Actress Tatum O'Neal is youngest person ever to win an Oscar.
5. The family way: Film Editor nominee Marcia Lucas is the wife of *American Graffiti*'s Director and Original Screenplay nominee, George Lucas.

Rule Changes

1. The name game: "Song—Original to the Picture" becomes "Song"; "Scoring: Adaptation and Original Song Score" becomes "Original Song Score and/or Adaptation."

Eligible Films That Failed to Be Nominated for Best Picture

Mean Streets, The Last Detail, Paper Moon, The Long Goodbye, Blume in Love, O Lucky Man!, The Harder They Come, Last Tango in Paris, Serpico, The Way We Were, Enter the Dragon.

Eligible Songs That Failed to Be Nominated

"Are You Man Enough?" (Dennis Lambert and Brian Potter)—*Shaft in Africa;* "The Harder They Come" (Jimmy Cliff)—*The Harder They Come;* "Knockin' on Heaven's Door" (Bob Dylan)—*Pat Garrett and Billy the Kid;* "You Can Get It If You Really Want It" (Jimmy Cliff)—*The Harder They Come.*

1974

Picture

Chinatown, Evans, Paramount. Produced by Robert Evans.
The Conversation, Directors Company, Paramount. Produced by Francis Ford Coppola.
★ *The Godfather Part II*, Coppola Company, Paramount. Produced by Francis Ford Coppola; Gray Frederickson and Fred Roos, co-producers.
Lenny, Worth, UA. Produced by Marvin Worth.
The Towering Inferno, Irwin Allen, 20th Century–Fox/Warner Bros. Produced by Irwin Allen.

Actor

★ Art Carney in *Harry and Tonto* (20th Century–Fox).
Albert Finney in *Murder on the Orient Express* (G.W. Films, Paramount).
Dustin Hoffman in *Lenny* (Worth, UA).
Jack Nicholson in *Chinatown* (Evans, Paramount).
Al Pacino in *The Godfather Part II* (Coppola, Paramount).

Actress

★ Ellen Burstyn in *Alice Doesn't Live Here Anymore* (Warner Bros.).
Diahann Carroll in *Claudine* (Third World Cinema-Selznick-Pine, 20th Century–Fox).
Faye Dunaway in *Chinatown* (Evans, Paramount).
Valerie Perrine in *Lenny* (Worth, UA).
Gena Rowlands in *A Woman Under the Influence* (Faces International).

Supporting Actor

Fred Astaire in *The Towering Inferno* (Irwin Allen, 20th Century–Fox/Warner Bros.).
Jeff Bridges in *Thunderbolt and Lightfoot* (Malpaso, UA).
★ Robert De Niro in *The Godfather Part II* (Coppola, Paramount).
Michael V. Gazzo in *The Godfather Part II* (Coppola, Paramount).
Lee Strasberg in *The Godfather Part II* (Coppola, Paramount).

Supporting Actress

★ Ingrid Bergman in *Murder on the Orient Express* (G.W. Films, Paramount).
Valentina Cortese in *Day for Night* (Warner Bros.) (French).
Madeline Kahn in *Blazing Saddles* (Warner Bros.).
Diane Ladd in *Alice Doesn't Live Here Anymore* (Warner Bros.).
Talia Shire in *The Godfather Part II* (Coppola, Paramount).

Director

John Cassavetes for *A Woman Under the Influence* (Faces International).
★ Francis Ford Coppola for *The Godfather Part II* (Coppola, Paramount).
Bob Fosse for *Lenny* (Marvin Worth, UA).
Roman Polanski for *Chinatown* (Evans, Paramount).
François Truffaut for *Day for Night* (Warner Bros.) (French).

Writing

(ORIGINAL SCREENPLAY)

Alice Doesn't Live Here Anymore, Warner Bros. Robert Getchell.
★ *Chinatown,* Evans, Paramount. Robert Towne.
The Conversation, Directors Company, Paramount. Francis Ford Coppola.
Day for Night, Warner Bros. (French). François Truffaut, Jean-Louis Richard and Suzanne Schiffman.
Harry and Tonto, 20th Century–Fox. Paul Mazursky and Josh Greenfeld.

(SCREENPLAY ADAPTED FROM OTHER MATERIAL)

The Apprenticeship of Duddy Kravitz, International Cinemedia Centre, Paramount. Mordecai Richler and Lionel Chetwynd.
★ *The Godfather Part II,* Coppola, Paramount. Francis Ford Coppola and Mario Puzo.
Lenny, Worth, UA. Julian Barry.
Murder on the Orient Express, G.W. Films, Paramount. Paul Dehn.
Young Frankenstein, Gruskoff/Venture Films-Crossbow-Jouer, 20th Century–Fox. Gene Wilder and Mel Brooks.

Cinematography

Chinatown, Evans, Paramount. John A. Alonzo.
Earthquake, Robson-Filmakers Group, Universal. Philip Lathrop.
Lenny, Worth. UA. Bruce Surtees.

Murder on the Orient Express, G.W. Films, Paramount. Geoffrey Unsworth.

★ *The Towering Inferno*, Irwin Allen, 20th Century–Fox/Warner Bros. Fred Koenekamp and Joseph Biroc.

Art Direction—Set Decoration

Chinatown, Evans, Paramount. Richard Sylbert and W. Stewart Campbell; Ruby Levitt.

Earthquake, Robson-Filmakers Group, Universal. Alexander Golitzen and E. Preston Ames; Frank McKelvy.

★ *The Godfather Part II*, Coppola, Paramount. Dean Tavoularis and Angelo Graham; George R. Nelson.

The Island at the Top of the World, Disney, Buena Vista. Peter Ellenshaw, John B. Mansbridge, Walter Tyler and Al Roelofs; Hal Gausman.

The Towering Inferno, Irwin Allen, 20th Century–Fox/Warner Bros. William Creber and Ward Preston; Raphael Bretton.

Sound

Chinatown, Evans, Paramount. Bud Grenzbach and Larry Jost.

The Conversation, Directors Company, Paramount. Walter Murch and Arthur Rochester.

★ *Earthquake*, Robson-Filmakers Group, Universal. Ronald Pierce and Melvin Metcalfe, Sr.

The Towering Inferno, Irwin Allen, 20th Century–Fox/Warner Bros. Theodore Soderberg and Herman Lewis.

Young Frankenstein, Gruskoff/Venture Films-Crossbow-Jouer, 20th Century–Fox. Richard Portman and Gene Cantamessa.

Music

(SONG)

"Benji's Theme (I Feel Love)" (*Benji*, Mulberry Square); Music by Euel Box. Lyrics by Betty Box.

"Blazing Saddles" (*Blazing Saddles*, Warner Bros.); Music by John Morris. Lyrics by Mel Brooks.

"Little Prince" (*The Little Prince*, Donen, Paramount); Music by Frederick Loewe. Lyrics by Alan Jay Lerner.

★ "We May Never Love Like This Again" (*The Towering Inferno*, Irwin Allen, 20th Century–Fox/Warner Bros.); Music and Lyrics by Al Kasha and Joel Hirschhorn.

"Wherever Love Takes Me" (*Gold*, Avton, Allied Artists); Music by Elmer Bernstein. Lyrics by Don Black.

(ORIGINAL DRAMATIC SCORE)

Chinatown, Robert Evans, Paramount. Jerry Goldsmith.

★ *The Godfather Part II*, Coppola, Paramount. Nino Rota and Carmine Coppola.

Murder on the Orient Express, G.W. Films, Paramount. Richard Rodney Bennett.

Shanks, Castle, Paramount. Alex North.

The Towering Inferno, Irwin Allen, 20th Century–Fox/Warner Bros. John Williams.

(SCORING: ORIGINAL SONG SCORE AND/OR ADAPTATION)

★ *The Great Gatsby*, Merrick, Paramount. Nelson Riddle.

The Little Prince, Stanley Donen, Paramount. Alan Jay Lerner, Frederick Loewe, Angela Morley and Douglas Gamley.

Phantom of the Paradise, Harbor Prods., 20th Century–Fox. Paul Williams and George Aliceson Tipton.

Film Editing

Blazing Saddles, Warner Bros. John C. Howard and Danford Greene.

Chinatown, Robert Evans, Paramount. Sam O'Steen.

Earthquake, Robson-Filmakers Group, Universal. Dorothy Spencer.

The Longest Yard, Ruddy, Paramount. Michael Luciano.

★ *The Towering Inferno*, Irwin Allen, 20th Century–Fox/Warner Bros. Harold F. Kress and Carl Kress.

Costume Design

Chinatown, Robert Evans, Paramount. Anthea Sylbert.

Daisy Miller, Directors Company, Paramount. John Furness.

The Godfather Part II, Coppola, Paramount. Theadora Van Runkle.

★ *The Great Gatsby*, Merrick, Paramount. Theoni V. Aldredge.

Murder on the Orient Express, G.W. Films, Paramount. Tony Walton.

Short Films

(ANIMATED FILMS)

★ *Closed Mondays*, Lighthouse Productions. Will Vinton and Bob Gardiner, producers.

The Family That Dwelt Apart, National Film Board of Canada. Yvon Mallette and Robert Verrall, producers.

Hunger, National Film Board of Canada. Peter Foldes and Rene Jodoin, producers.

Voyage to Next, Hubley Studio. Faith and John Hubley, producers.

Winnie the Pooh and Tigger Too, Disney, Buena Vista. Wolfgang Reitherman, producer.

(LIVE ACTION FILMS)

Climb, Dewitt Jones Productions. Dewitt Jones, producer.

The Concert, The Black and White Colour Film Company, Ltd. Julian and Claude Chagrin, producers.

★ *One-Eyed Men Are Kings*, C.A.P.A.C. Productions (Paris). Paul Claudon and Edmond Sechan, producers.

Planet Ocean, Graphic Films. George V. Casey, producer.

The Violin, Sincinkin, Ltd. Andrew Welsh and George Pastic, producers.

Documentary

(SHORT SUBJECTS)

City Out of Wilderness, Francis Thompson Inc. Francis Thompson, producer.

★ *Don't,* R.A. Films. Robin Lehman, producer.
Exploratorium, Jon Boorstin Prod. Jon Boorstin, producer.
John Muir's High Sierra, Dewitt Jones Prods. Dewitt Jones and Lesley Foster, producers.
Naked Yoga, Filmshop Prod. Ronald S. Kass and Mervyn Lloyd, producers.

(FEATURES)
Antonia: A Portrait of the Woman, Rocky Mountain Prods. Judy Collins and Jill Godmilow, producers.
The Challenge . . . A Tribute to Modern Art, World View. Herbert Kline, producer.
The 81st Blow, Ghetto Fighters House. Jacquot Ehrlich, David Bergman and Haim Gouri, producers.
★ *Hearts and Minds,* Touchstone-Audjeff-BBS Prod., Zuker/Jaglom-Rainbow Pictures, Warner Bros. Peter Davis and Bert Schneider, producers.
The Wild and the Brave, E.S.J.—Tomorrow Entertainment-Jones/Howard Ltd. Natalie R. Jones and Eugene S. Jones, producers.

Foreign Language Film
★ *Amarcord* (Italy).
Cats Play (Hungary)
The Deluge (Poland).
Lacombe, Lucien (France).
The Truce (Argentina).

Irving G. Thalberg Memorial Award
Not given this year.

Jean Hersholt Humanitarian Award
Arthur B. Krim.

Honorary Awards
Howard Hawks—A master American filmmaker whose creative efforts hold a distinguished place in world cinema (statuette).
Jean Renoir—a genius who, with grace, responsibility and enviable devotion through silent film, sound film, feature, documentary and television, has won the world's admiration (statuette).

Special Achievement Awards
For Visual Effects: Frank Brendel, Glen Robinson and Albert Whitlock for *Earthquake*, a Universal-Mark Robson-Filmakers Group Production, Universal.

Scientific or Technical
CLASS I (STATUETTE)
None.

CLASS II (PLAQUE)
Joseph D. Kelly of Glen Glenn Sound for the design of new audio control consoles which have advanced the state of the art of sound recording and rerecording for motion picture production.
The Burbank Studios Sound Department for the design of new audio control consoles engineered and constructed by the Quad-Eight Sound Corporation.
Samuel Goldwyn Studios Sound Department for the design of a new audio control console engineered and constructed by the Quad-Eight Sound Corporation.
Quad-Eight Sound Corporation for the engineering and construction of new audio control consoles designed by the Burbank Studios Sound Department and by the Samuel Goldwyn Studios Sound Department.
Waldon O. Watson, Richard J. Stumpf, Robert J. Leonard and the Universal City Studios Sound Department for the development and engineering of the Sensurround System for motion picture presentation.

CLASS III (CITATION)
Elemack Company of Rome, Italy, for the design and development of their Spyder camera dolly.
Louis Ami of the Universal City Studios for the design and construction of a reciprocating camera platform used when photographing special visual effects for motion pictures.

Points of Interest

1. Nothing to it: Michael V. Gazzo and Lee Strasberg nominated for their film debuts.
2. The family way: Francis Ford Coppola wins three Oscars, father Carmine wins Original Dramatic Score and sister Talia Shire nominated for Best Supporting Actress. Gena Rowlands nominated for Best Actress, husband John Cassavetes for Best Director.
3. Clothes make the studio: All Costume Design nominees are Paramount films—first time ever one studio gets all nominations in a category.

Rule Changes

1. The name game: "Story and Screenplay—Based on Factual Material or Material Not Previously Published or Produced" becomes "Original Screenplay"; "Screenplay—Based on Material from Another Medium" becomes "Screenplay Adapted from Other Material"; "Short Subjects" becomes "Short Films."

Eligible Films That Failed to Be Nominated for Best Picture

The Three Musketeers, Harry and Tonto, Alice Doesn't Live Here Anymore, Badlands, A Woman Under the Influence, Blazing Saddles, Young Frankenstein.

Submitted Film Rejected by the Foreign Language Film Award Committee

The Middle of the World (Switzerland), directed by Alain Tanner.

Eligible Song That Failed to Be Nominated

"On and On" (Curtis Mayfield)—*Claudine*.

1975

Picture

Barry Lyndon, Hawk Films, Warner Bros. Produced by Stanley Kubrick.

Dog Day Afternoon, Warner Bros. Produced by Martin Bregman and Martin Elfand.

Jaws, Zanuck/Brown, Universal. Produced by Richard D. Zanuck and David Brown.

Nashville, ABC Entertainment-Weintraub-Altman, Paramount. Produced by Robert Altman.

★ *One Flew over the Cuckoo's Nest,* Fantasy Films, UA. Produced by Saul Zaentz and Michael Douglas.

Actor

Walter Matthau in *The Sunshine Boys* (Stark, MGM).

★ Jack Nicholson in *One Flew over the Cuckoo's Nest* (Fantasy Films, UA).

Al Pacino in *Dog Day Afternoon* (Warner Bros.).

Maximilian Schell in *The Man in the Glass Booth* (Landau, AFT Distributing).

James Whitmore in *Give 'em Hell, Harry!* (Theatrovision, Avco Embassy).

Actress

Isabelle Adjani in *The Story of Adele H* (New World Pictures) (French).

Ann-Margret in *Tommy* (R.S.O., Columbia).

★ Louise Fletcher in *One Flew over the Cuckoo's Nest* (Fantasy Films, UA).

Glenda Jackson in *Hedda* (Royal Shakespeare-Barrie/Enders, Brut Productions).

Carol Kane in *Hester Street* (Midwest Films).

Supporting Actor

★ George Burns in *The Sunshine Boys* (Stark, MGM).

Brad Dourif in *One Flew over the Cuckoo's Nest* (Fantasy Films, UA).

Burgess Meredith in *The Day of the Locust* (Hellman, Paramount).

Chris Sarandon in *Dog Day Afternoon* (Warner Bros.).

Jack Warden in *Shampoo* (Rubeeker, Columbia).

Supporting Actress

Ronee Blakley in *Nashville* (ABC Entertainment-Weintraub-Altman, Paramount).

★ Lee Grant in *Shampoo* (Rubeeker, Columbia).

Sylvia Miles in *Farewell, My Lovely* (Kastner-ITC, Avco Embassy).

Lily Tomlin in *Nashville* (ABC Entertainment-Weintraub-Altman, Paramount).

Brenda Vaccaro in *Jacqueline Susann's Once Is Not Enough* (Koch, Paramount).

Director

Robert Altman for *Nashville* (ABC Entertainment-Weintraub-Altman, Paramount).

Federico Fellini for *Amarcord* (New World Pictures) (Italian).

★ Milos Forman for *One Flew over the Cuckoo's Nest* (Fantasy Films, UA).

Stanley Kubrick for *Barry Lyndon* (Hawk Films, Warner Bros.).

Sidney Lumet for *Dog Day Afternoon* (Warner Bros.).

Writing

(ORIGINAL SCREENPLAY)

Amarcord, New World Pictures (Italian). Federico Fellini and Tonino Guerra.

And Now My Love, Avco Embassy (French). Claude Lelouch and Pierre Uytterhoeven.

★ *Dog Day Afternoon,* Warner Bros. Frank Pierson.

Lies My Father Told Me, Pentimento-Pentacle VIII, Columbia. Ted Allan.

Shampoo, Rubeeker, Columbia. Robert Towne and Warren Beatty.

(SCREENPLAY ADAPTED FROM OTHER MATERIAL)

Barry Lyndon, Hawk Films, Warner Bros. Stanley Kubrick.

The Man Who Would Be King, Columbia/Allied Artists. John Huston and Gladys Hill.

★ *One Flew over the Cuckoo's Nest,* Fantasy Films, UA. Lawrence Hauben and Bo Goldman.

Scent of a Woman, Dean Films, 20th Century–Fox (Italian). Ruggero Maccari and Dino Risi.

The Sunshine Boys, Stark, MGM. Neil Simon.

Cinematography

★ *Barry Lyndon,* Hawk Films, Warner Bros. John Alcott.

The Day of the Locust, Jerome Hellman, Paramount. Conrad Hall.

Funny Lady, Rastar, Columbia. James Wong Howe.

The Hindenburg, Robert Wise-Filmakers Group, Universal. Robert Surtees.

One Flew over the Cuckoo's Nest, Fantasy Films, UA. Haskell Wexler and Bill Butler.

Art Direction—Set Decoration

★ *Barry Lyndon*, Hawk Films. Warner Bros. Ken Adam and Roy Walker; Vernon Dixon.

The Hindenburg, Robert Wise-Filmakers Group, Universal. Edward Carfagno; Frank McKelvy.

The Man Who Would Be King, Columbia/Allied Artists. Alexander Trauner and Tony Inglis; Peter James.

Shampoo, Rubeeker, Columbia. Richard Sylbert and W. Stewart Campbell; George Gaines.

The Sunshine Boys, Stark, MGM. Albert Brenner; Marvin March.

Sound

Bite the Bullet, Pax Enterprises, Columbia. Arthur Piantodosi, Les Fresholtz, Richard Tyler and Al Overton, Jr.

Funny Lady, Rastar, Columbia. Richard Portman, Don MacDougall, Curly Thirlwell and Jack Solomon.

The Hindenburg, Robert Wise-Filmakers Group, Universal. Leonard Peterson, John A. Bolger, Jr., John Mack and Don K. Sharpless.

★ *Jaws*, Zanuck/Brown, Universal. Robert L. Hoyt, Roger Heman, Earl Madery and John Carter.

The Wind and the Lion, Herb Jaffe, MGM. Harry W. Tetrick, Aaron Rochin, William McCaughey and Roy Charman.

Music

(ORIGINAL SONG)

"How Lucky Can You Get" (*Funny Lady*, Rastar, Columbia); Music and Lyrics by Fred Ebb and John Kander.

★ "I'm Easy" (*Nashville*, ABC-Weintraub-Altman, Paramount); Music and Lyrics by Keith Carradine.

"Now That We're in Love" (*Whiffs*, Brut, 20th Century–Fox); Music by George Barrie. Lyrics by Sammy Cahn.

"Richard's Window" (*The Other Side of the Mountain*, Filmways-Larry Peerce, Universal); Music by Charles Fox. Lyrics by Norman Gimbel.

"Theme from *Mahogany* (Do You Know Where You're Going To)" (*Mahogany*, Jobete, Paramount); Music by Michael Masser. Lyrics by Gerry Goffin.

(ORIGINAL SCORE)

Birds Do It, Bees Do It, Wolper, Columbia. Gerald Fried.

Bite the Bullet, Pax Enterprises, Columbia. Alex North.

★ *Jaws*, Zanuck/Brown, Universal. John Williams.

One Flew over the Cuckoo's Nest, Fantasy Films, UA. Jack Nitzsche.

The Wind and the Lion, Jaffe, MGM. Jerry Goldsmith.

(SCORING: ORIGINAL SONG SCORE AND/OR ADAPTATION)

★ *Barry Lyndon*, Hawk Films, Warner Bros. Leonard Rosenman.

Funny Lady, Rastar, Columbia. Peter Matz.

Tommy, R.S.O., Columbia. Peter Townshend.

Film Editing

Dog Day Afternoon, Warner Bros. Dede Allen.

★ *Jaws*, Zanuck/Brown, Universal. Verna Fields.

The Man Who Would Be King, Columbia/Allied Artists. Russell Lloyd.

One Flew over the Cuckoo's Nest, Fantasy Films, UA. Richard Chew, Lynzee Klingman and Sheldon Kahn.

Three Days of the Condor, De Laurentiis, Paramount. Frederic Steinkamp and Don Guidice.

Costume Design

★ *Barry Lyndon*, Hawk Films, Warner Bros. Ulla-Britt Soderlund and Milena Canonero.

The Four Musketeers, Salkind, 20th Century–Fox. Yvonne Blake and Ron Talsky.

Funny Lady, Rastar, Columbia. Ray Aghayan and Bob Mackie.

The Magic Flute, Surrogate Releasing (Swedish). Henny Noremark and Karin Erskine.

The Man Who Would Be King, Columbia/Allied Artists. Edith Head.

Short Films

(ANIMATED)

★ *Great*, Grantstern, British Lion Films Ltd. Bob Godfrey, producer.

Kick Me, Swarthe Productions. Robert Swarthe, producer.

Monsieur Pointu, National Film Board of Canada. René Jodoin, Bernard Longpré and André Leduc, producers.

Sisyphus, Hungarofilms. Marcell Jankovics, producer.

(LIVE ACTION)

★ *Angel and Big Joe*, Salzman Productions. Bert Salzman, producer.

Conquest of Light, Louis Marcus Films Ltd. Louis Marcus, producer.

Dawn Flight, Lansburgh Productions. Lawrence M. Lansburgh and Brian Lansburgh, producers.

A Day in the Life of Bonnie Consolo, Barr Films. Barry Spinello, producer.

Doubletalk, Beattie Productions. Alan Beattie, producer.

Documentary

(SHORT SUBJECTS)

Arthur and Lillie, Department of Communication, Stanford University. Jon Else, Steven Kovacs and Kristine Samuelson, producers.

★ *The End of the Game*, Opus Films Ltd. Claire Wilbur and Robin Lehman, producers.

Millions of Years Ahead of Man, BASF. Manfred Baier, producer.

Probes in Space, Graphic Films. George V. Casey, producer.

Whistling Smith, National Film Board of Canada. Barrie Howells and Michael Scott, producers.

(FEATURES)

The California Reich, Yasny Talking Pictures. Walter F. Parkes and Keith F. Critchlow, producers.

Fighting for Our Lives, A Farm Worker Film. Glen Pearcy, producer.

The Incredible Machine, The National Geographic Society, Wolper Prods. Irwin Rosten, producer.

★ *The Man Who Skied Down Everest,* Crawley Films. F.R. Crawley, James Hager and Dale Hartleben, producers.

The Other Half of the Sky: A China Memoir, MacLaine Productions. Shirley MacLaine, producer.

Foreign Language Film

★ *Dersu Uzala* (U.S.S.R.).

Land of Promise (Poland).

Letters from Marusia (Mexico).

Sandakan No. 8 (Japan).

Scent of a Woman (Italy).

Irving G. Thalberg Memorial Award

Mervyn LeRoy.

Jean Hersholt Humanitarian Award

Jules C. Stein.

Honorary Award

Mary Pickford, in recognition of her unique contributions to the film industry and the development of film as an artistic medium (statuette).

Special Achievement Awards

For Sound Effects: Peter Berkos for *The Hindenburg,* Robert Wise-Filmakers Group, Universal.

For Visual Effects: Albert Whitlock and Glen Robinson for *The Hindenburg,* Robert Wise-Filmakers Group, Universal.

Scientific or Technical

CLASS I (STATUETTE)

None.

CLASS II (PLAQUE)

Chadwell O'Connor of the O'Connor Engineering Laboratories for the concept and engineering of a fluid-damped camera-head for motion-picture photography.

William F. Miner of Universal City Studios, Inc. and the Westinghouse Electric Corporation for the development and engineering of a solid-state, 500 kilowatt, direct-current static rectifier for motion-picture lighting.

CLASS III (CITATION)

Lawrence W. Butler and Roger Banks for the concept of applying low inertia and stepping electric motors to film transport systems and optical printers for motion-picture production.

David J. Degenkolb and Fred Scobey of Deluxe General, Inc., and John C. Dolan and Richard Dubois of the Akwaklame Company for the development of a technique for silver recovery from photographic wash-waters by ion exchange.

Joseph Westheimer for the development of a device to obtain shadowed titles on motion-picture films.

Carter Equipment Co., Inc., and Ramtronics for the engineering and manufacture of a computerized tape punching system for programming laboratory printing machines.

The Hollywood Film Company for the engineering and manufacture of a computerized tape punching system for programming laboratory printing machines.

Bell & Howell for the engineering and manufacture of a computerized tape punching system for programming laboratory printing machines.

Fredrik Schlyter for the engineering and manufacture of a computerized tape punching system for programming laboratory printing machines.

Points of Interest

1. Nothing to it: Brad Dourif, Chris Sarandon, Ronee Blakley and Lily Tomlin nominated for film debuts.
2. The family way: Three-time Best Actress nominee Shirley MacLaine nominated for Documentary Feature, while her brother, Warren Beatty, one-time Best Actor nominee, is nominated for Original Screenplay.

Rule Change

1. The name game: "Original Dramatic Score" becomes "Original Score"; "Song" becomes "Original Song."

Eligible Films That Failed to Be Nominated for Best Picture

Shampoo, The Man Who Would Be King, Night Moves, The Romantic Englishwoman, Love and Death, The Rocky Horror Picture Show.

Submitted Films Rejected by the Foreign Language Film Award Committee

India Song (France), directed by Marguerite Duras; *Every Man for Himself and God Against All/The Mystery of Kasper Hauser* (West Germany), directed by Werner Herzog.

Eligible Song That Failed to Be Nominated

"Let's Do It Again" (Curtis Mayfield)—*Let's Do It Again.*

1976

Picture
All the President's Men, Wildwood, Warner Bros. Produced by Walter Coblenz.
Bound for Glory, UA. Produced by Robert F. Blumofe and Harold Leventhal.
Network, Gottfried/Chayefsky, MGM/UA. Produced by Howard Gottfried.
★ *Rocky,* Chartoff-Winkler, UA. Produced by Irwin Winkler and Robert Chartoff.
Taxi Driver, Bill/Phillips-Scorsese, Columbia. Produced by Michael Phillips and Julia Phillips.

Actor
Robert De Niro in *Taxi Driver* (Bill/Phillips-Scorsese, Columbia).
★ Peter Finch in *Network* (Gottfried/Chayefsky, MGM/UA).
Giancarlo Giannini in *Seven Beauties* (Medusa Distribuzione, Cinema 5) (Italian).
William Holden in *Network* (Gottfried/Chayefsky, MGM/UA).
Sylvester Stallone in *Rocky* (Chartoff-Winkler, UA).

Actress
Marie-Christine Barrault in *Cousin, Cousine* (Northal Films) (French).
★ Faye Dunaway in *Network* (Gottfried/Chayefsky, MGM/UA).
Talia Shire in *Rocky* (Chartoff-Winkler, UA).
Sissy Spacek in *Carrie* (Redbank Films, UA).
Liv Ullmann in *Face to Face* (Cinematograph, A.B., Paramount) (Swedish).

Supporting Actor
Ned Beatty in *Network* (Gottfried/Chayefsky, MGM/UA).
Burgess Meredith in *Rocky* (Chartoff-Winkler, UA).
Laurence Olivier in *Marathon Man* (Evans-Beckerman, Paramount).
★ Jason Robards in *All the President's Men* (Wildwood, Warner Bros.).
Burt Young in *Rocky* (Chartoff-Winkler, UA).

Supporting Actress
Jane Alexander in *All the President's Men* (Wildwood, Warner Bros.).
Jodie Foster in *Taxi Driver* (Bill/Phillips-Scorsese, Columbia).
Lee Grant in *Voyage of the Damned* (ITC, Avco Embassy).
Piper Laurie in *Carrie* (Redbank Films, UA).
★ Beatrice Straight in *Network* (Gottfried/Chayefsky, MGM/UA).

Director
★ John G. Avildsen for *Rocky* (Chartoff-Winkler, UA).
Ingmar Bergman for *Face to Face* (Cinematograph, A.B., Paramount) (Swedish).
Sidney Lumet for *Network* (Gottfried/Chayefsky, MGM/UA).
Alan J. Pakula for *All the President's Men* (Wildwood, Warner Bros.).
Lina Wertmuller for *Seven Beauties* (Medusa Distribuzione, Cinema 5) (Italian).

Writing
(SCREENPLAY WRITTEN DIRECTLY FOR THE SCREEN)
Cousin, Cousine, Northal Films (French). Jean-Charles Tacchella and Daniele Thompson.
The Front, Columbia. Walter Bernstein.
★ *Network,* Gottfried/Chayefsky, MGM/UA. Paddy Chayefsky.
Rocky, Chartoff-Winkler, UA. Sylvester Stallone.
Seven Beauties, Medusa Distribuzione, Cinema 5) (Italian). Lina Wertmuller.

(SCREENPLAY BASED ON MATERIAL FROM ANOTHER MEDIUM)
★ *All the President's Men,* Wildwood, Warner Bros. William Goldman.
Bound for Glory, UA. Robert Getchell.
Fellini's Casanova, Universal (Italian). Federico Fellini and Bernadino Zapponi.
The Seven-Per-Cent Solution, Herbert Ross/Winitsky-Sellers, Universal. Nicholas Meyer.
Voyage of the Damned, ITC, Avco Embassy. Steve Shagan and David Butler.

Cinematography
★ *Bound for Glory,* UA. Haskell Wexler.
King Kong, De Laurentiis, Paramount. Richard H. Kline.
Logan's Run, David, MGM. Ernest Laszlo.
Network, Gottfried/Chayefsky. MGM/UA. Owen Roizman.
A Star Is Born, Barwood/Peters-First Artists, Warner Bros. Robert Surtees.

Art Direction—Set Direction
★ *All the President's Men,* Wildwood. Warner Bros. George Jenkins; George Gaines.
The Incredible Sarah, Strauss–Reader's Digest, Seymour Borde & Associates. Elliot Scott and Norman Reynolds.
The Last Tycoon, Spiegel-Kazan, Paramount. Gene Callahan and Jack Collis; Jerry Wunderlich.
Logan's Run, David, MGM. Dale Hennesy; Robert de Vestel.
The Shootist, Frankovich/Self-De Laurentiis, Paramount. Robert F. Boyle; Arthur Jeph Parker.

Sound

★ *All the President's Men,* Wildwood, Warner Bros., Arthur Piantadosi, Les Fresholtz, Dick Alexander and Jim Webb.

King Kong, De Laurentiis, Paramount. Harry Warren Tetrick, William McCaughey, Aaron Rochin and Jack Solomon.

Rocky, Chartoff-Winkler, UA. Harry Warren Tetrick, William McCaughey, Lyle Burbridge and Bud Alper.

Silver Streak, Yablans, 20th Century–Fox. Donald Mitchell, Douglas Williams, Richard Tyler and Hal Etherington.

A Star Is Born, Barwood/Peters–First Artists, Warner Bros. Robert Knudson, Dan Wallin, Robert Glass and Tom Overton.

Music

(ORIGINAL SONG)

"Ave Satani" (*The Omen,* 20th Century–Fox); Music and Lyrics by Jerry Goldsmith.

"Come to Me" (*The Pink Panther Strikes Again,* Amjo, UA); Music by Henry Mancini. Lyrics by Don Black.

★ "Evergreen (Love Theme from *A Star Is Born*)" (*A Star Is Born,* Barwood/Peters-First Artists, Warner Bros.); Music by Barbra Streisand. Lyrics by Paul Williams.

"Gonna Fly Now" (*Rocky,* Chartoff-Winkler, UA); Music by Bill Conti. Lyrics by Carol Connors and Ayn Robbins.

"A World that Never Was" (*Half a House,* Lenro Productions, First American Films); Music by Sammy Fain. Lyrics by Paul Francis Webster.

(ORIGINAL SCORE)

Obsession, Litto, Columbia. Bernard Herrmann.

★ *The Omen,* 20th Century–Fox. Jerry Goldsmith.

The Outlaw Josey Wales, Malpaso, Warner Bros. Jerry Fielding.

Taxi Driver, Bill/Phillips-Scorsese, Columbia. Bernard Herrmann.

Voyage of the Damned, ITC Entertainment, Avco Embassy. Lalo Schifrin.

(ORIGINAL SONG SCORE AND ITS ADAPTATION OR ADAPTATION SCORE)

★ *Bound for Glory,* UA. Leonard Rosenman.

Bugsy Malone, Goodtimes Enterprises, Paramount. Paul Williams.

A Star Is Born, Barwood/Peters-First Artists, Warner Bros. Roger Kellaway.

Film Editing

All the President's Men, Wildwood, Warner Bros. Robert L. Wolfe.

Bound for Glory, UA. Robert Jones and Pembroke J. Herring.

Network, Gottfried/Chayefsky, MGM/UA. Alan Heim.

★ *Rocky,* Chartoff-Winkler, UA. Richard Halsey and Scott Conrad.

Two-Minute Warning, Filmways/Peerce-Feldman, Universal. Eve Newman and Walter Hannemann.

Costume Design

Bound for Glory, UA. William Theiss.

★ *Fellini's Casanova,* Universal (Italian). Danilo Donati.

The Incredible Sarah, Strauss–Reader's Digest, Seymour Borde & Associates. Anthony Mendleson.

The Passover Plot, Coast Industries-Golan-Globus, Atlas Films. Mary Wills.

The Seven-Per-Cent Solution, Herbert Ross/Winitsky-Sellers, Universal. Alan Barrett.

Short Films

(ANIMATED)

Dedalo, Cineteam Realizzazioni. Manfredo Manfredi, producer.

★ *Leisure,* Film Australia. Suzanne Baker, producer.

The Street, National Film Board of Canada. Caroline Leaf and Guy Glover, producers.

(LIVE ACTION)

★ *In the Region of Ice,* American Film Institute. Andre Guttfreund and Peter Werner, producers.

Kudzu, A Short Production. Marjorie Anne Short, producer.

The Morning Spider, The Black and White Colour Film Company. Julian Chagrin and Claude Chagrin, producers.

Nightlife, Opus Films, Ltd. Claire Wilbur and Robin Lehman, producers.

Number One, Number One Productions. Dyan Cannon and Vince Cannon, producers.

Documentary

(SHORT SUBJECTS)

American Shoeshine, Titan Films. Sparky Greene, producer.

Blackwood, National Film Board of Canada. Tony Ianzelo and Andy Thompson, producers.

The End of the Road, Pelican Films. John Armstrong, producer.

★ *Number Our Days,* Community Television of Southern California. Lynne Littman, producer.

Universe, Graphic Films Corp for NASA. Lester Novros, producer.

(FEATURES)

★ *Harlan County, U.S.A.,* Cabin Creek Films. Barbara Kopple, producer.

Hollywood on Trial, October Films/Cinema Associates. James Gutman and David Helpern, Jr., producers.

Off the Edge, Pentacle Films. Michael Firth, producer.

People of the Wind, Elizabeth E. Rogers Productions. Anthony Howarth and David Koff, producers.

Volcano: An Inquiry into the Life and Death of Malcolm Lowry,

National Film Board of Canada. Donald Brittain and Robert Duncan, producers.

Foreign Language Film

★ *Black and White in Color* (Ivory Coast).
Cousin, Cousine (France).
Jacob, the Liar (German Democratic Republic).
Nights and Days (Poland).
Seven Beauties (Italy).

Irving G. Thalberg Memorial Award

Pandro S. Berman.

Jean Hersholt Humanitarian Award

Not given this year.

Honorary Awards

None given this year.

Special Achievement Awards

For Visual Effects: Carlo Rambaldi, Glen Robinson and Frank Van Der Veer for *King Kong*. De Laurentiis, Paramount.

For Visual Effects: L.B. Abbott, Glen Robinson and Matthew Yuricich for *Logan's Run*, Saul David, MGM.

Scientific or Technical

CLASS I (STATUETTE)

None.

CLASS II (PLAQUE)

Consolidated Film Industries and the Barnebey-Cheney Company for the development of a system for the recovery of film-cleaning solvent vapors in a motion-picture laboratory.

William L. Graham, Manfred G. Michelson, Geoffrey F. Norman and Siegfried Seibert of Technicolor for the development and engineering of a continuous, high-speed, Color Motion Picture Printing System.

CLASS III (CITATION)

Fred Bartscher of the Kollmorgen Corporation and to Glenn Berggren of the Schneider Corporation for the design and development of a single-lens magnifier for motion-picture projection lenses.

Panavision Incorporated for the design and development of super-speed lenses for motion-picture photography.

Hiroshi Suzukawa of Canon and Wilton R. Holm of AMPTP Motion Picture and Television Research Center for the design and development of super-speed lenses for motion-picture photography.

Carl Zeiss Company for the design and development of super-speed lenses for motion-picture photography.

Photo Research Division of the Kollmorgen Corporation for the engineering and manufacture of the spectra TriColor Meter.

Points of Interest

1. Nothing to it: Burt Young nominated for film debut.
2. Gone but not forgotten: Peter Finch first actor to win Oscar posthumously.
3. Renaissance woman: 1969 Supporting Actress nominee Dyan Cannon nominated for Best Live Action Short Film, which she wrote, directed and coproduced.

Rule Changes

1. The name game: "Original Screenplay" becomes "Screenplay Written Directly for the Screen" and "Screenplay Adapted from Other Material" becomes "Screenplay Based on Material from Another Medium." "Original Song Score and/or Adaptation" becomes "Original Song Score and Its Adaptation or Adaptation Score."

Eligible Films That Failed to Be Nominated for Best Picture

Family Plot; Carrie; The Outlaw Josey Wales; Robin and Marian; Next Stop, Greenwich Village; The Tenant; The Last Tycoon; The Bad News Bears.

Submitted Films Rejected by the Foreign Language Film Award Committee

Xica (Brazil), directed by Carlos Diegues; *Cria* (Spain), directed by Carlos Saura; *Jonah Who Will Be 25 in the Year 2000* (Switzerland), directed by Alain Tanner.

Eligible Song That Failed to Be Nominated

"Car Wash" (Norman Whitfield)—*Car Wash*.

1977

Picture

★ *Annie Hall*, Rollins-Joffe, UA. Produced by Charles H. Joffe.
The Goodbye Girl, Stark, MGM/Warner Bros. Produced by Ray Stark.
Julia, 20th Century–Fox. Produced by Richard Roth.
Star Wars, 20th Century–Fox. Produced by Gary Kurtz.
The Turning Point, Hera Productions, 20th Century–Fox. Produced by Herbert Ross and Arthur Laurents.

Actor

Woody Allen in *Annie Hall* (Rollins-Joffe, UA).
Richard Burton in *Equus* (Winkast, UA).
★ Richard Dreyfuss in *The Goodbye Girl* (Stark, MGM/Warner Bros).
Marcello Mastroianni in *A Special Day* (Canafox Films, Cinema 5) (Italian).
John Travolta in *Saturday Night Fever* (R.S.O., Paramount).

Actress

Anne Bancroft in *The Turning Point* (Hera Productions, 20th Century–Fox).
Jane Fonda in *Julia* (20th Century–Fox).
★ Diane Keaton in *Annie Hall* (Rollins-Joffe, UA).
Shirley MacLaine in *The Turning Point* (Hera Productions, 20th Century–Fox).
Marsha Mason in *The Goodbye Girl* (Stark, MGM/Warner Bros.).

Supporting Actor

Mikhail Baryshnikov in *The Turning Point* (Hera Productions, 20th Century–Fox).
Peter Firth in *Equus* (Winkast, UA).
Alec Guinness in *Star Wars* (20th Century–Fox).
★ Jason Robards in *Julia* (20th Century–Fox).
Maximilian Schell in *Julia* (20th Century–Fox).

Supporting Actress

Leslie Browne in *The Turning Point* (Hera Productions, 20th Century–Fox).
Quinn Cummings in *The Goodbye Girl* (Stark, MGM/Warner Bros.).
Melinda Dillon in *Close Encounters of the Third Kind* (Columbia).
★ Vanessa Redgrave in *Julia* (20th Century–Fox).
Tuesday Weld in *Looking for Mr. Goodbar* (Fields, Paramount).

Director

★ Woody Allen for *Annie Hall* (Rollins-Joffe, UA).
George Lucas for *Star Wars* (20th Century–Fox).
Herbert Ross for *The Turning Point* (Hera Productions, 20th Century–Fox).
Steven Spielberg for *Close Encounters of the Third Kind* (Columbia).
Fred Zinnemann for *Julia* (20th Century–Fox).

Writing

(SCREENPLAY WRITTEN DIRECTLY FOR THE SCREEN)
★ *Annie Hall,* Rollins-Joffe, Woody Allen and Marshall Brickman.
The Goodbye Girl, Stark, MGM/Warner Bros. Neil Simon.
The Late Show, Lion's Gate, Warner Bros. Robert Benton.
Star Wars, 20th Century–Fox. George Lucas.
The Turning Point, Hera Productions, 20th Century–Fox. Arthur Laurents.

(SCREENPLAY BASED ON MATERIAL FROM ANOTHER MEDIUM)
Equus, Winkast Company, UA. Peter Shaffer.
I Never Promised You a Rose Garden, Scherick/Blatt, New World Pictures. Gavin Lambert and Lewis John Carlino.
★ *Julia,* 20th Century–Fox. Alvin Sargent.
Oh, God!, Warner Bros. Larry Gelbart.
That Obscure Object of Desire, First Artists (Spain). Luis Buñuel and Jean-Claude Carrière.

Cinematography

★ *Close Encounters of the Third Kind,* Columbia. Vilmos Zsigmond.
Islands in the Stream, Bart/Palevsky, Paramount. Fred J. Koenekamp.
Julia, 20th Century–Fox. Douglas Slocombe.
Looking for Mr. Goodbar, Freddie Fields, Paramount. William A. Fraker.
The Turning Point, Hera Productions, 20th Century–Fox. Robert Surtees.

Art Direction—Set Decoration

Airport '77, Lang, Universal. George C. Webb; Mickey S. Michaels.
Close Encounters of the Third Kind, Columbia. Joe Alves and Dan Lomino; Phil Abramson.
The Spy Who Loved Me, Eon, UA. Ken Adam and Peter Lamont; Hugh Scaife.
★ *Star Wars,* 20th Century–Fox. John Barry, Norman Reynolds and Leslie Dilley; Roger Christian.
The Turning Point, Hera Productions, 20th Century–Fox. Albert Brenner; Marvin March.

Sound

Close Encounters of the Third Kind, Columbia. Robert Knudson, Robert J. Glass, Don MacDougall and Gene S. Cantamessa.
The Deep, Casablanca Filmworks, Columbia. Walter Goss, Dick Alexander, Tom Beckert and Robin Gregory.
Sorcerer, Friedkin, Paramount/Universal. Robert Knudson, Robert J. Glass, Richard Tyler and Jean-Louis Ducarme.
★ *Star Wars,* 20th Century–Fox. Don MacDougall, Ray West, Bob Minkler and Derek Ball.
The Turning Point, Hera Productions, 20th Century–Fox. Theodore Soderberg, Paul Wells, Douglas O. Williams and Jerry Jost.

Music

(ORIGINAL SONG)
"Candle on The Water (*Pete's Dragon,* Disney, Buena Vista); Music and Lyrics by Al Kasha and Joel Hirschhorn.
"Nobody Does It Better" *(The Spy Who Loved Me,* Eon, UA); Music by Marvin Hamlisch. Lyrics by Carole Bayer Sager.
"The Slipper and the Rose Waltz (He Danced with Me/She Danced with Me)" *(The Slipper and the Rose—The Story*

of Cinderella, Paradine Co-Productions, Universal); Music and Lyrics by Richard M. Sherman and Robert B. Sherman.

"Someone's Waiting for You" *(The Rescuers,* Disney, Buena Vista); Music by Sammy Fain. Lyrics by Carol Connors and Ayn Robbins.

★ "You Light Up My Life" *(You Light Up My Life,* Session Company, Columbia); Music and Lyrics by Joseph Brooks.

(ORIGINAL SCORE)

Close Encounters of the Third Kind, Columbia. John Williams.

Julia, 20th Century–Fox. Georges Delerue.

Mohammad—Messenger of God, Filmco International, Yablans. Maurice Jarre.

The Spy Who Loved Me, Eon, UA. Marvin Hamlisch.

★ *Star Wars,* 20th Century–Fox. John Williams.

(ORIGINAL SONG SCORE AND ITS ADAPTATION OR ADAPTATION SCORE)

★ *A Little Night Music,* Sascha-Wien/Kastner, New World Pictures. Jonathan Tunick.

Pete's Dragon, Disney, Buena Vista. Al Kasha, Joel Hirschhorn and Irwin Kostal.

The Slipper and the Rose—The Story of Cinderella, Paradine Co-Productions, Universal. Richard M. Sherman, Robert B. Sherman and Angela Morley.

Film Editing

Close Encounters of the Third Kind, Columbia. Michael Kahn.

Julia, 20th Century–Fox. Walter Murch and Marcel Durham.

Smokey and the Bandit, Rastar, Universal, Walter Hannemann and Angelo Ross.

★ *Star Wars,* 20th Century–Fox. Paul Hirsch, Marcia Lucas and Richard Chew.

The Turning Point, Hera Productions, 20th Century–Fox. William Reynolds.

Costume Design

Airport '77, Lang, Universal. Edith Head and Burton Miller.

Julia, 20th Century–Fox. Anthea Sylbert.

A Little Night Music, Sascha-Wien/Kastner, New World Pictures. Florence Klotz.

The Other Side of Midnight, Yablans, 20th Century–Fox. Irene Sharaff.

★ *Star Wars,* 20th Century–Fox. John Mollo.

Visual Effects

Close Encounters of the Third Kind, Columbia. Roy Arbogast, Douglas Trumbull, Matthew Yuricich, Gregory Jein and Richard Yuricich.

★ *Star Wars,* 20th Century–Fox. John Stears, John Dykstra, Richard Edlund, Grant McCune and Robert Blalack.

Short Films

(ANIMATED FILMS)

The Bead Game, National Film Board of Canada. Ishu Patel, producer.

The Doonesbury Special, Hubley Studio. John and Faith Hubley and Garry Trudeau, producers.

Jimmy the C, Motionpicker Production. James Picker, Robert Grossman and Craig Whitaker, producers.

★ *Sand Castle,* National Film Board of Canada. Co Hoedeman, producer.

(LIVE ACTION)

The Absent-Minded Waiter, Aspen Film Society. William E. McEuen, producer.

Floating Free, Trans World International. Jerry Butts, producer.

★ *I'll Find a Way,* National Film Board of Canada. Beverly Shaffer and Yuki Yoshida, producers.

Notes on the Popular Arts, Saul Bass Films. Saul Bass, producer.

Spaceborne, Lawrence Hall of Science Production for the Regents of the University of California with the cooperation of NASA. Philip Dauber, producer.

Documentary

(SHORT SUBJECTS)

Agueda Martinez: Our People, Our Country, Esparza Production. Moctesuma Esparza, producer.

First Edition, Sage Productions. Helen Whitney and DeWitt L. Sage, Jr., producers.

★ *Gravity Is My Enemy,* a Joseph Production. John Joseph and Jan Stussy, producers.

Of Time, Tombs and Treasure, a Charlie/Papa Production. James R. Messenger and Paul N. Raimondi, producers.

The Shetland Experience, Balfour Films. Douglas Gordon, producer.

(FEATURES)

The Children of Theatre Street, Mack-Vaganova Company. Robert Dornhelm and Earle Mack, producers.

High Grass Circus, National Film Board of Canada. Bill Brind, Torben Schioler and Tony Ianzelo, producers.

Homage to Chagall—The Colours of Love, a CBC Production. Harry Rasky, producer.

Union Maids, a Klein, Reichert, Mogulescu Production. James Klein, Julia Reichert and Miles Mogulescu, producers.

★ *Who are the DeBolts? And Where Did They Get Nineteen Kids?* Korty Films/Charles M. Schulz, Sanrio Films. John Korty, Dan McCann and Warren L. Lockhart, producers.

Foreign Language Film

Iphigenia (Greece).

★ *Madame Rosa* (France).

Operation Thunderbolt (Israel).

A Special Day (Italy).
That Obscure Object of Desire (Spain).

Irving G. Thalberg Memorial Award
Walter Mirisch.

Jean Hersholt Humanitarian Award
Charlton Heston.

Honorary Awards
Margaret Booth for her exceptional contribution to the art of film editing in the motion picture industry (statuette).

Gordon E. Sawyer and Sidney P. Solow in appreciation for outstanding service and dedication in upholding the high standards of the Academy of Motion Picture Arts and Sciences (medal of commendation).

Special Achievement Awards
For Sound Effects Editing: Frank Warner for *Close Encounters of the Third Kind*, Columbia.

For Sound Effects: Benjamin Burtt, Jr., for the creation of the alien, creature and robot voices in *Star Wars*, 20th Century–Fox.

Scientific or Technical
CLASS I (STATUETTE)

Garrett Brown and the Cinema Products Corp. engineering staff under the supervision of John Jurgens for the invention and development of Steadicam.

CLASS II (PLAQUE)

Joseph D. Kelly, Emory M. Cohen, Barry K. Henley, Hammond H. Holt and John Agalsoff of Glen Glenn Sound for the concept and development of a post-production audio processing system for motion picture films.

Panavision, Incorporated for the concept and engineering of the improvements incorporated in the Panaflex Motion Picture Camera.

N. Paul Kenworthy, Jr. and William R. Latady for the invention and development of the Kenworthy Snorkel Camera System for motion picture photography.

John C. Dykstra for the development of the Dykstraflex Camera and Alvah J. Miller and Jerry Jeffress for the engineering of the Electronic Motion Control System used in concert for multiple exposure visual effects motion picture photography.

The Eastman Kodak Company for the development and introduction of a new duplicating film for motion pictures.

Stefan Kudelski of Nagra Magnetic Recorders, Incorporated, for the engineering of the improvements incorporated in the Nagra 4.2L sound recorder for motion picture production.

CLASS III (CITATION)

Ernst Nettmann of the Astrovision Division of Continental Camera Systems, Inc., for the engineering of its Snorkel Aerial Camera System.

EECO (Electronic Engineering Company of California) for developing a method for interlocking non-sprocketed film and tape media used in motion picture production.

Dr. Bernhard Kuhl and Werner Block of Osram, GmbH for the development of the HMI high-efficiency discharge lamp for motion picture lighting.

Panavision, Incorporated (2 citations), for the design of Panalite, a camera-mounted controllable light for motion picture photography and for the engineering of the Panahead gearhead for motion picture cameras.

Piclear, Inc., for originating and developing an attachment to motion picture projectors to improve screen image quality.

Points of Interest

1. Nothing to it: Mikhail Baryshnikov, Peter Firth, Leslie Browne and Quinn Cummings nominated for film debuts.
2. The family way: Marsha Mason and husband Neil Simon both nominated. Film Editor winner Marcia Lucas is married to Director and Original Screenplay nominee George Lucas.
3. Aping Orson: Woody Allen first person nominated for Actor, Director and Screenplay since Orson Welles for *Citizen Kane* in 1941.

Rule Changes

1. Here we go again: Visual Effects again made a regular, competitive Award although no longer called "Special" Visual Effects.

Eligible Films That Failed to Be Nominated for Best Picture

Close Encounters of the Third Kind; Saturday Night Fever; Handle with Care; The Late Show; Providence; Aguirre, the Wrath of God; New York, New York; 1900; The Gauntlet; Three Women; Outrageous!.

Submitted Films Rejected by the Foreign Language Film Award Committee

Soldier of Orange (The Netherlands), directed by Paul Verhoevan; *The American Friend* (German Federal Republic), directed by Wim Wenders.

Eligible Songs That Failed to Be Nominated

"The Greatest Love of All" (Michael Masser and Linda Creed)—*The Greatest;* "If I Can't Have You" (The Bee Gees)—*Saturday Night Fever;* "More Than a Woman" (The Bee Gees)—*Saturday Night Fever;* "New York, New York" (John Kander and Fred Ebb)—*New York, New York;* "Night Fever" (The Bee Gees)—*Saturday Night Fever;* "Staying Alive" (The Bee Gees)—*Saturday Night Fever.*

1978

Picture

Coming Home, Hellman, UA. Produced by Jerome Hellman.

★ *The Deer Hunter,* EMI Films/Cimino, Universal. Produced by Barry Spikings, Michael Deeley, Michael Cimino and John Peverall.

Heaven Can Wait, Dogwood, Paramount. Produced by Warren Beatty.

Midnight Express, Casablanca–Filmworks, Columbia. Produced by Alan Marshall and David Puttnam.

An Unmarried Woman, 20th Century–Fox. Produced by Paul Mazursky and Tony Ray.

Actor

Warren Beatty in *Heaven Can Wait* (Dogwood, Paramount).

Gary Busey in *The Buddy Holly Story* (Innovisions-ECA, Columbia).

Robert De Niro in *The Deer Hunter* (EMI Films/Cimino, Universal).

Laurence Olivier in *The Boys from Brazil* (ITC, 20th Century–Fox).

★ Jon Voight in *Coming Home* (Hellman, UA).

Actress

Ingrid Bergman in *Autumn Sonata* (Personafilm GmbH Production, Sir Lew Grade–Martin Starger–ITC, New World Pictures) (Swedish).

Ellen Burstyn in *Same Time, Next Year* (Mirisch-Mulligan, Universal).

Jill Clayburgh in *An Unmarried Woman* (20th Century–Fox).

★ Jane Fonda in *Coming Home* (Hellman, UA).

Geraldine Page in *Interiors* (Rollins-Joffe, UA).

Supporting Actor

Bruce Dern in *Coming Home* (Hellman, UA).

Richard Farnsworth in *Comes a Horseman* (Chartoff–Winkler, UA).

John Hurt in *Midnight Express* (Casablanca–Filmworks, Columbia).

★ Christopher Walken in *The Deer Hunter* (EMI Films/Cimino, Universal).

Jack Warden in *Heaven Can Wait* (Dogwood, Paramount).

Supporting Actress

Dyan Cannon in *Heaven Can Wait* (Dogwood, Paramount).

Penelope Milford in *Coming Home* (Hellman, UA).

★ Maggie Smith in *California Suite* (Stark, Columbia).

Maureen Stapleton in *Interiors* (Rollins-Joffe, UA).

Meryl Streep in *The Deer Hunter* (EMI Films/Cimino, Universal).

Director

Woody Allen for *Interiors* (Rollins-Joffe, UA).

Hal Ashby for *Coming Home* (Hellman, UA).

Warren Beatty and Buck Henry for *Heaven Can Wait* (Dogwood, Paramount).

★ Michael Cimino for *The Deer Hunter* (EMI Films/Cimino, Universal).

Alan Parker for *Midnight Express* (Casablanca–Filmworks, Columbia).

Writing

(SCREENPLAY WRITTEN DIRECTLY FOR THE SCREEN)

Autumn Sonata, Personafilm GmbH Production. Sir Lew Grade–Martin Starger–ITC. New World Pictures (Swedish). Ingmar Bergman.

★ *Coming Home,* Hellman, UA. Story by Nancy Dowd. Screenplay by Waldo Salt and Robert C. Jones.

The Deer Hunter, EMI Films/Cimino, Universal. Michael Cimino, Deric Washburn, Louis Garfinkle and Quinn K. Redeker.

Interiors, Rollins-Joffe, UA. Woody Allen.

An Unmarried Woman, 20th Century–Fox. Paul Mazursky.

(SCREENPLAY BASED ON MATERIAL FROM ANOTHER MEDIUM)

Bloodbrothers, Warner Bros. Walter Newman.

California Suite, Stark, Columbia. Neil Simon.

Heaven Can Wait, Dogwood, Paramount. Elaine May and Warren Beatty.

★ *Midnight Express,* Casablanca–Filmworks, Columbia. Oliver Stone.

Same Time, Next Year, Mirisch-Mulligan, Universal. Bernard Slade.

Cinematography

★ *Days of Heaven* OP, Paramount. Nestor Almendros.

The Deer Hunter, EMI Films/Cimino, Universal. Vilmos Zsigmond.

Heaven Can Wait, Dogwood, Paramount. William A. Fraker.

Same Time, Next Year, Mirisch-Mulligan Universal. Robert Surtees.

The Wiz, Motown/Universal. Oswald Morris.

Art Direction

The Brink's Job, De Laurentiis, Universal. Dean Tavoularis and Angelo Graham; George R. Nelson.

California Suite, Stark, Columbia. Albert Brenner; Marvin March.

★ *Heaven Can Wait*, Dogwood, Paramount. Paul Sylbert and Edwin O'Donovan; George Gaines.

Interiors, Rollins-Joffe, UA. Mel Bourne; Daniel Robert.

The Wiz, Motown/Universal. Tony Walton and Philip Rosenberg; Edward Stewart and Robert Drumheller.

Sound

The Buddy Holly Story, Innovisions–ECA, Columbia. Tex Rudloff, Joel Fein, Curly Thirlwell and Willie Burton.

Days of Heaven, OP, Paramount: John K. Wilkinson, Robert W. Glass, Jr., John T. Reitz and Barry Thomas.

★ *The Deer Hunter*, EMI Films/Cimino, Universal. Richard Portman, William McCaughey, Aaron Rochin and Darrin Knight.

Hooper, Warner Bros. Robert Knudson, Robert J. Glass, Don MacDougall and Jack Solomon.

Superman, Dovemead, Ltd.–Salkind, Warner Bros. Gordon K. McCallum, Graham Hartstone, Nicholas Le Messurier and Roy Charman.

Music

(ORIGINAL SONG)

"Hopelessly Devoted to You" (*Grease*, R.S.O/Allan Carr, Paramount); Music and Lyrics by John Farrar.

★ "Last Dance" (*Thank God It's Friday*, Casablanca–Motown, Columbia); Music and Lyrics by Paul Jabara.

"The Last Time I Felt Like This" (*Same Time, Next Year*, Mirisch-Mulligan, Universal); Music by Marvin Hamlisch. Lyrics by Alan and Marilyn Bergman.

"Ready to Take a Chance Again" (*Foul Play*, Miller–Milkis/Higgins, Paramount); Music by Charles Fox. Lyrics by Norman Gimbel.

"When You're Loved" (*The Magic of Lassie*, The International Picture Show Company); Music and Lyrics by Richard M. Sherman and Robert B. Sherman.

(ORIGINAL SCORE)

The Boys From Brazil, ITC, 20th Century–Fox. Jerry Goldsmith.

Days of Heaven, OP, Paramount. Ennio Morricone.

Heaven Can Wait, Dogwood, Paramount. Dave Grusin.

★ *Midnight Express*, Casablanca–Filmworks, Columbia. Giorgio Moroder.

Superman, Dovemead, Ltd.–Salkind, Warner Bros. John Williams.

(ORIGINAL SONG SCORE AND ITS ADAPTATION OR ADAPTATION SCORE)

★ *The Buddy Holly Story*, Innovisions–ECA, Columbia. Joe Renzetti.

Pretty Baby, Malle, Paramount. Jerry Wexler.

The Wiz, Motown/Universal. Quincy Jones.

Film Editing

The Boys from Brazil, ITC, 20th Century–Fox. Robert E. Swink.

Coming Home, Hellman, UA. Don Zimmerman.

★ *The Deer Hunter*, EMI Films/Michael Cimino, Universal. Peter Zinner.

Midnight Express, Casablanca Filmworks. Columbia. Gerry Hambling.

Superman, Dovemead, Ltd.–Salkind, Warner Bros. Stuart Baird.

Costume Design

Caravans, Ibex–F.I.D.C.I., Universal. Renie Conley.

Days of Heaven, OP, Paramount. Patricia Norris.

★ *Death on the Nile*, Brabourne-Goodwin, Paramount. Anthony Powell.

The Swarm, Warner Bros. Paul Zastupnevich.

The Wiz, Motown/Universal. Tony Walton.

Short Films

(ANIMATED)

Oh My Darling, Nico Crama Productions. Nico Crama, producer.

Rip Van Winkle, Will Vinton/Billy Budd. Will Vinton, producer.

★ *Special Delivery*, National Film Board of Canada. Eunice Macaulay and John Weldon, producers.

(LIVE ACTION)

A Different Approach, Jim Belcher/Brookfield. Jim Belcher and Fern Field, producers.

Mandy's Grandmother, Illumination Films. Andrew Sugerman, producer.

Strange Fruit, The American Film Institute. Seth Pinsker, producer.

★ *Teenage Father*, New Visions Inc. for the Children's Home Society of California. Taylor Hackford, producer.

Documentary

(SHORT SUBJECTS)

The Divided Trail, Jerry Aronson Productions: Jerry Aronson, producer.

An Encounter with Faces, Films Division, Government of India. K. Kapil, producer.

★ *The Flight of the Gossamer Condor*, Shedd. Jacqueline Phillips Shedd, producer.

Goodnight Miss Ann, August Cinquegrana Films. August Cinquegrana, producer.

Squires of San Quentin, J. Gary Mitchell Film Company: J. Gary Mitchell, producer.

(FEATURES)

The Lovers' Wind, Ministry of Culture & Arts of Iran. Albert Lamorisse, producer.

Mysterious Castles of Clay, Survival Anglia Ltd. Alan Root, producer.

Raoni, a Franco-Brazilian Production. Michel Gast, Barry Williams and Jean-Pierre Dutilleux, producers.

★ *Scared Straight!*, Golden West Television. Arnold Shapiro, producer.

With Babies and Banners: Story of the Women's Emergency Brigade, A Women's Labor History Film Project Production. Anne Bohlen, Lyn Goldfarb and Lorraine Gray, producers.

Foreign Language Film

★ *Get Out Your Handkerchiefs* (France).

The Glass Cell (German Federal Republic).

Hungarians (Hungary).

Viva Italia! (Italy).

White Bim Black Ear (U.S.S.R.).

Irving G. Thalberg Memorial Award

Not given this year.

Jean Hersholt Humanitarian Award

Leo Jaffe.

Honorary Awards

Walter Lantz for bringing joy and laughter to every part of the world through his unique animated motion pictures (statuette).

Laurence Olivier for the full body of his work, for the unique achievements of his entire career and his lifetime of contribution to the art of film (statuette).

King Vidor for his incomparable achievements as a cinematic creator and innovator (statuette).

The Museum of Modern Art Department of Film for the contribution it has made to the public's perception of movies as an art form (statuette).

Linwood G. Dunn, Loren L. Ryder, and Waldon O. Watson in appreciation for outstanding service and dedication in upholding the high standards of the Academy of Motion Picture Arts and Sciences (medals of commendation).

Special Achievement Awards

For Visual Effects: Les Bowie, Colin Chilvers, Denys Coop, Roy Field, Derek Meddings, and Zoran Perisic, for *Superman*, Dovemead Ltd., Salkind, Warner Bros.

Scientific or Technical

ACADEMY AWARD OF MERIT (STATUETTE)

Eastman Kodak Company for the research and development of a Duplicating Color Film for Motion Pictures.

Stefan Kudelski of Nagra Magnetic Recorders, Incorporated, for the continuing research, design and development of the Nagra Production Sound Recorder for Motion Pictures.

Panavision, Incorporated, and its engineering staff under the direction of Robert E. Gottschalk, for the concept, design and continuous development of the Panaflex Motion Picture Camera System.

SCIENTIFIC AND ENGINEERING (PLAQUE)

Ray M. Dolby, Ioan R. Allen, David P. Robinson, Stephen M. Katz and Philip S. J. Boole of Dolby Laboratories, Incorporated, for the development and implementation of an improved Sound Recording and Reproducing System for Motion Picture Production and Exhibition.

TECHNICAL ACHIEVEMENT AWARD (CITATION)

Karl Macher and Glenn M. Berggren of Isco Optische Werke for the development and introduction of the Cinelux-ULTRA lens for 35mm Motion Picture Projection.

David J. Degenkolb, Arthur L. Ford and Fred J. Scobey of Deluxe General, Incorporated, for the development of a Method to Recycle Motion Picture Laboratory Photographic Wash Waters by Ion Exchange.

Kiichi Sekiguchi of Cine-Fi International for the development of the Cine-Fi Auto Radio Sound System for Drive-in Theaters.

Leonard Chapman of Leonard Equipment for the design and manufacture of a small, mobile, motion picture camera platform known as the Chapman Hustler Dolly.

James L. Fisher of J.L. Fisher, Incorporated, for the design and manufacture of a small, mobile, motion picture camera platform known as the Fisher Model Ten Dolly.

Robert Stindt of Production Grip Equipment Company for the design and manufacture of a small, mobile, motion picture camera platform known as the Stindt Dolly.

Points of Interest

1. Tying Orson: Warren Beatty first person to be nominated for Actor, Director, Screenplay and as producer of a Picture nominee since Orson Welles for *Citizen Kane* in 1941.

Rule Changes

1. Here we go again: Visual Effects reclassified as a "Special Achievement Award."
2. The name game: The three classes of "Scientific or Technical Awards" reclassified as "Academy Award of Merit," "Scientific and Engineering" and "Technical Achievement Award."

Eligible Films That Failed to Be Nominated for Best Picture

Days of Heaven, Interiors, Stevie, Girl Friends, Blood Brothers, Halloween, National Lampoon's Animal House.

Submitted Film Rejected by the Foreign Language Film Award Committee

The Chess Players (India), directed by Satyajit Ray.

Eligible Songs That Failed to Be Nominated

"Grease" (Barry Gibb)—*Grease;* "You're the One That I Want" (John Farrar)—*Grease.*

1979

Picture

All That Jazz, Columbia/20th Century–Fox. Produced by Robert Alan Aurthur.

Apocalypse Now, Omni Zoetrope, UA. Francis Coppola, producer. Coproduced by Fred Roos, Gray Frederickson and Tom Sternberg.

Breaking Away, 20th Century–Fox. Produced by Peter Yates.

★ *Kramer vs. Kramer,* Jaffe, Columbia. Produced by Stanley R. Jaffe.

Norma Rae, 20th Century–Fox. Produced by Tamara Asseyev and Alex Rose.

Actor

★ Dustin Hoffman in *Kramer vs. Kramer* (Jaffe, Columbia).

Jack Lemmon in *The China Syndrome* (Douglas/IPC Films, Columbia).

Al Pacino in . . . *And Justice for All* (Malton Films Limited, Columbia).

Roy Scheider in *All That Jazz* (Columbia/20th Century–Fox).

Peter Sellers in *Being There* (Lorimar Film-Und Fernsehproduktion GmbH Production, UA).

Actress

Jill Clayburgh in *Starting Over* (Pakula/Brooks, Paramount).

★ Sally Field in *Norma Rae* (20th Century–Fox).

Jane Fonda in *The China Syndrome* (Douglas/IPC Films, Columbia).

Marsha Mason in *Chapter Two* (Stark, Columbia).

Bette Midler in *The Rose* (20th Century–Fox).

Supporting Actor

★ Melvyn Douglas in *Being There* (Lorimar Film–Und Fernsehproduktion GmbH Production, United Artists).

Robert Duvall in *Apocalypse Now* (Omni Zoetrope, UA).

Frederic Forrest in *The Rose* (20th Century–Fox).

Justin Henry in *Kramer vs. Kramer* (Jaffe, Columbia).

Mickey Rooney in *The Black Stallion* (Omni Zoetrope, UA).

Supporting Actress

Jane Alexander in *Kramer vs. Kramer* (Jaffe, Columbia).

Barbara Barrie in *Breaking Away* (20th Century–Fox).

Candice Bergen in *Starting Over* (Pakula/Brooks, Paramount).

Mariel Hemingway in *Manhattan* (Rollins-Joffe, UA).

★ Meryl Streep in *Kramer vs. Kramer* (Jaffe, Columbia).

Directing

★ Robert Benton for *Kramer vs. Kramer* (Jaffe, Columbia).

Francis Coppola for *Apocalypse Now* (Omni Zoetrope, UA).

Bob Fosse for *All That Jazz* (Columbia/20th Century–Fox).

Edouard Molinaro for *La Cage aux Folles* (Les Productions Artistes Associés Da Ma Produzione SPA, UA).

Peter Yates for *Breaking Away* (20th Century–Fox).

Writing

(SCREENPLAY WRITTEN DIRECTLY FOR THE SCREEN)

All That Jazz, Columbia/20th Century–Fox. Robert Alan Aurthur and Bob Fosse.

. . . *And Justice for All,* Malton Films Limited, Columbia. Valerie Curtin and Barry Levinson.

★ *Breaking Away,* 20th Century–Fox. Steve Tesich.

The China Syndrome, Douglas/IPC Films, Columbia. Mike Gray, T.S. Cook and James Bridges.

Manhattan, Rollins-Joffe, UA. Woody Allen and Marshall Brickman.

(SCREENPLAY BASED ON MATERIAL FROM ANOTHER MEDIUM)

Apocalypse Now, Omni Zoetrope, UA. John Milius and Francis Coppola.

★ *Kramer vs. Kramer,* Stanley Jaffe Productions, Columbia. Robert Benton.

La Cage Aux Folles, Les Productions Artistes Associés Da Ma Produzione SPA, UA. Francis Veber, Edouard Molinaro, Marcello Danon and Jean Poiret.

A Little Romance, Pan Arts, Orion. Allan Burns.

Norma Rae, 20th Century–Fox. Irving Ravetch and Harriet Frank, Jr.

Cinematography

All That Jazz, Columbia/20th Century–Fox. Giuseppe Rotunno.

★ *Apocalypse Now,* Omni Zoetrope, UA. Vittorio Storaro.

The Black Hole, Walt Disney, Buena Vista. Frank Phillips.

Kramer vs. Kramer, Jaffe, Columbia. Nestor Almendros.

1941, A-Team/Spielberg, Universal/Columbia. William A. Fraker.

Art Direction—Set Decoration

Alien, 20th Century–Fox. Michael Seymour, Les Dilley and Roger Christian; Ian Whittaker.

★ *All That Jazz,* Columbia/20th Century–Fox. Philip Rosenberg and Tony Walton; Edward Stewart and Gary Brink.

Apocalypse Now, Omni Zoetrope, UA. Dean Tavoularis and Angelo Graham; George R. Nelson.

The China Syndrome, Douglas/IPC Films, Columbia. George Jenkins; Arthur Jeph Parker.

Star Trek—The Motion Picture, Century, Paramount. Harold Michelson, Joe Jennings, Leon Harris and John Vallone; Linda Descenna.

Sound

★ *Apocalypse Now,* Omni Zoetrope, UA. Walter Murch, Mark Berger, Richard Beggs and Nat Boxer.

The Electric Horseman, Rastar /Wildwood/Pollack, Columbia. Arthur Piantadosi, Les Fresholtz, Michael Minkler and Al Overton.

Meteor, Meteor Productions, American International. William McCaughey, Aaron Rochin, Michael J. Kohut and Jack Solomon.

1941, A-Team/Spielberg, Universal/Columbia. Robert Knudson, Robert J. Glass, Don MacDougall and Gene S. Cantamessa.

The Rose, 20th Century–Fox. Theodore Soderberg, Douglas Williams, Paul Wells and Jim Webb.

(ORIGINAL SONG)

★ "It Goes Like It Goes" (*Norma Rae,* 20th Century–Fox); Music by David Shire. Lyrics by Norman Gimbel.

"The Rainbow Connection" (*The Muppet Movie,* Henson, Lord Grade/Starger, AFD); Music and Lyrics by Paul Williams and Kenny Ascher.

"Song from *10* (It's Easy to Say)" (*10,* Geoffrey, Orion); Music by Henry Mancini. Lyrics by Robert Wells.

"Theme from *Ice Castles* (Through the Eyes of Love)" (*Ice Castles,* International Cinemedia Center Columbia); Music by Marvin Hamlisch. Lyrics by Carole Bayer Sager.

"Theme from *The Promise* (I'll Never Say 'Goodbye')" (*The Promise,* Fred Weintraub–Paul Heller, Universal); Music by David Shire. Lyrics by Alan and Marilyn Bergman.

Music

(ORIGINAL SCORE)

The Amityville Horror, Professional, American International. Lalo Schifrin.

The Champ, MGM. Dave Grusin.

★ *A Little Romance,* Pan Arts, Orion. Georges Delerue.

Star Trek—The Motion Picture, Century, Paramount. Jerry Goldsmith.

10, Geoffrey, Orion. Henry Mancini.

(ORIGINAL SONG SCORE AND ITS ADAPTATION OR ADAPTATION SCORE)

★ *All That Jazz,* Columbia/20th Century–Fox. Ralph Burns.

Breaking Away, 20th Century–Fox. Patrick Williams.

The Muppet Movie, Henson, Lord Grade/Starger, AFD. Paul Williams and Kenny Ascher.

Film Editing

★ *All That Jazz,* Columbia/20th Century–Fox. Alan Heim.

Apocalypse Now, Omni Zoetrope, UA. Richard Marks, Walter Murch, Gerald B. Greenberg and Lisa Fruchtman.

The Black Stallion, Omni Zoetrope, UA. Robert Dalva.

Kramer vs. Kramer, Jaffe, Columbia. Jerry Greenberg.

The Rose, 20th Century–Fox. Robert L. Wolfe and C. Timothy O'Meara.

Costume Design

Agatha, Sweetwall-Casablanca, First Artists Presentation, Warner Bros. Shirley Russell.

★ *All That Jazz,* Columbia/20th Century–Fox. Albert Wolsky.

Butch and Sundance: The Early Days, 20th Century–Fox. William Theiss.

The Europeans, Merchant Ivory, Levitt-Pickman. Judy Moorcroft.

La Cage Aux Folles, Les Productions Artistes Associés Da Ma Produzione SPA Production, UA. Piero Tosi and Ambra.

Visual Effects

★ *Alien,* 20th Century–Fox. H. R. Giger, Carlo Rambaldi, Brian Johnson, Nick Allder and Denys Ayling.

The Black Hole, Walt Disney, Buena Vista. Peter Ellenshaw, Art Cruickshank, Eustace Lycett, Danny Lee, Harrison Ellenshaw and Joe Hale.

Moonraker, UA. Derek Meddings, Paul Wilson and John Evans.

1941, A-Team/Spielberg, Universal/Columbia. William A. Fraker, A. D. Flowers and Gregory Jein.

Star Trek—The Motion Picture, Century, Paramount. Douglas Trumbull, John Dykstra, Richard Yuricich, Robert Swarthe, Dave Stewart and Grant McCune.

Short Films

(ANIMATED)

Dream Doll, Godfrey Films/Zagreb Films/Halas and Batchelor, Film Wright. Bob Godfrey and Zlatko Grgic, producers.

★ *Every Child,* National Film Board of Canada. Derek Lamb, producer.

It's So Nice to Have a Wolf Around the House, AR&T Productions for Learning Corporation of America. Paul Fierlinger, producer.

(LIVE ACTION)

★ *Board and Care,* Ron Ellis Films. Sarah Pillsbury and Ron Ellis, producers.

Bravery in the Field, National Film Board of Canada. Roman Kroitor and Stefan Wodoslawsky, producers.
Oh Brother, My Brother, Ross Lowell Productions, Pyramid Films, Inc. Carol and Ross Lowell, producers.
The Solar Film, Woldwood Enterprises Inc. Saul Bass and Michael Britton, producers.
Solly's Diner, Mathias/Zukerman/Hankin Productions. Harry Mathias, Jay Zukerman and Larry Hankin, producers.

Documentary

(SHORT SUBJECTS)

Dae, Vardar Film/Skopje.
Koryo Celadon, Charlie/Papa Productions, Inc.
Nails, National Film Board of Canada.
★ *Paul Robeson: Tribute to an Artist,* Janus Films, Inc.
Remember Me, Dick Young Productions, Ltd. Dick Young, producer.

(FEATURES)

★ *Best Boy,* Only Child Motion Pictures, Inc.: Ira Wohl, producer.
Generation on the Wind, More Than One Medium. David A. Vassar, producer.
Going the Distance, National Film Board of Canada.
The Killing Ground, ABC News Closeup Unit. Steve Singer and Tom Priestley, producers.
The War at Home, Catalyst Films/Madison Film Production Co. Glenn Silber and Barry Alexander Brown, producers.

Foreign Language Film Award

The Maids of Wilko (Poland).
Mama Turns a Hundred (Spain).
A Simple Story (France).
★ *The Tin Drum* (Federal Republic of Germany).
To Forget Venice (Italy).

Irving G. Thalberg Memorial Award

Ray Stark.

Jean Hersholt Humanitarian Award

Robert Benjamin.

Honorary Awards

Hal Elias for his dedication and distinguished service to the Academy of Motion Picture Arts and Sciences (statuette).
Alec Guinness for advancing the art of screen acting through a host of memorable and distinguished performances (statuette).
John O. Aalberg, Charles G. Clarke and John G. Frayne in appreciation for outstanding service and dedication in upholding the high standards of the Academy of Motion Picture Arts and Sciences (medals of commendation).

Special Achievement Award

Sound Editing: Alan Splet, for *The Black Stallion,* Omni Zoetrope, UA.

Scientific or Technical

ACADEMY AWARD OF MERIT (STATUETTE)

Mark Serrurier for the progressive development of the Moviola from the 1924 invention of his father, Iwan Serrurier, to the present Series 20 sophisticated film editing equipment.

SCIENTIFIC AND ENGINEERING AWARD (PLAQUE)

Neiman-Tillar Associates for the creative development, and to Mini-Micro Systems, Incorporated, for the design and engineering of an Automated Computer Controlled Editing Sound System (ACCESS) for motion picture post-production.

TECHNICAL ACHIEVEMENT AWARD (CITATION)

Michael V. Chewey, Walter G. Eggers and Allen Hecht of MGM Laboratories for the development of a Computer-controlled Paper Tape Programmer System and its applications in the motion picture laboratory.
Irwin Young, Paul Kaufman and Fredrik Schlyter of Du Art Film Laboratories, Incorporated, for the development of a computer-controlled Paper Tape Programmer System and its applications in the motion picture laboratory.
James S. Stanfield and Paul W. Trester for the development and manufacture of a device for the repair or protection of sprocket holes in motion picture film.
Zoran Perisic of Courier Films, Limited, for the Zoptic Special Optical Effects Device for motion-picture photography.
A. D. Flowers and Logan R. Frazee for the development of a device to control flight patterns of miniature airplanes during motion-picture photography.
Photo Research Division of Kollmorgen Corporation for the development of the Spectra Series II Cine Special Exposure Meter for motion picture photography.
Bruce Lyon and John Lamb for the development of a Video Animation System for testing motion-picture animation sequences.
Ross Lowell of Lowel-Light Manufacturing, Incorporated, for the development of compact lighting equipment for motion-picture photography.

Points of Interest

1. A little child shall lead them: Supporting Actor nominee Justin Henry, nine, youngest performer nominated for an Oscar.
2. Nothing to it: Justin Henry nominated for film debut.

Rule Changes

1. Here we go again: Visual Effects again becomes a regular competitive Award.

Eligible Films That Failed to Be Nominated for Best Picture

Manhattan, 10, Fedora, Despair, The Marriage of Maria Braun, Picnic at Hanging Rock, The China Syndrome, Escape from Alcatraz, The Warriors.

1980

Picture

Coal Miner's Daughter, Schwartz, Universal. Produced by Bernard Schwartz.

The Elephant Man, Brooksfilms, Paramount. Produced by Jonathan Sanger.

★ *Ordinary People,* Wildwood, Paramount. Produced by Ronald L. Schwary.

Raging Bull, Chartoff–Winkler, United Artists. Produced by Irwin Winkler and Robert Chartoff.

Tess, a Renn-Burrill Société Française de Production (S.F.P.), Columbia. Produced by Claude Berri, Timothy Burrill, Co-producer.

Actor

★ Robert De Niro in *Raging Bull* (Chartoff–Winkler, United Artists).

Robert Duvall in *The Great Santini* (Bing Crosby Productions, Orion).

John Hurt in *The Elephant Man* (Brooksfilms, Paramount).

Jack Lemmon in *Tribute* (Turman-Foster/Michaels-Drabinsky, 20th Century–Fox).

Peter O'Toole in *The Stunt Man* (Melvin Simon, 20th Century–Fox).

Actress

Ellen Burstyn in *Resurrection* (Universal).

Goldie Hawn in *Private Benjamin* (Warner Bros.).

Mary Tyler Moore in *Ordinary People* (Wildwood, Paramount).

Gena Rowlands in *Gloria* (Columbia).

★ Sissy Spacek in *Coal Miner's Daughter* (Schwartz, Universal).

Supporting Actor

Judd Hirsch in *Ordinary People* (Wildwood, Paramount).

★ Timothy Hutton in *Ordinary People* (Wildwood, Paramount).

Michael O'Keefe in *The Great Santini* (Bing Crosby Prod., Orion).

Joe Pesci in *Raging Bull* (Chartoff–Winkler, United Artists).

Jason Robards in *Melvin and Howard* (Linson/Phillips/Demme, Universal).

Supporting Actress

Eileen Brennan in *Private Benjamin* (Warner Bros.).

Eva Le Gallienne in *Resurrection* (Universal).

Cathy Moriarty in *Raging Bull* (Chartoff–Winkler, United Artists).

Diana Scarwid in *Inside Moves* (Goodmark, Associated Film Distribution).

★ Mary Steenburgen in *Melvin and Howard* (Linson/Phillips/Demme, Universal).

Director

David Lynch for *The Elephant Man* (Brooksfilms, Paramount).

Roman Polanski for *Tess* (Renn-Burrill, Société Française de Production (S.F.P., Columbia).

★ Robert Redford for *Ordinary People* (Wildwood, Paramount).

Richard Rush for *The Stunt Man* (Melvin Simon Productions, 20th Century–Fox).

Martin Scorsese for *Raging Bull* (Chartoff–Winkler, UA).

Writing

(SCREENPLAY WRITTEN DIRECTLY FOR THE SCREEN)

Brubaker, 20th Century–Fox. W. D. Richter and Arthur Ross.

Fame, MGM, Christopher Gore.

★ *Melvin and Howard,* Linson/Phillips/Demme-Universal. Bo Goldman.

Mon Oncle D'Amerique, Philippe Dussart-Andrea Films T.F. 1, New World Pictures. Jean Gruault.

Private Benjamin, Warner Bros. Nancy Meyers, Charles Shyer and Harvey Miller.

(SCREENPLAY BASED ON MATERIAL FROM ANOTHER MEDIUM)

Breaker Morant, Australian Film Commission–South Australian Film Corporation Seven Network and Pact Productions, New World Pictures/Quartet/Films Incorporated. Jonathan Hardy, David Stevens and Bruce Beresford.

Coal Miner's Daughter, Schwartz, Universal. Tom Rickman.

The Elephant Man, Brooksfilms, Paramount. Christopher Devore, Eric Bergren and David Lynch.

★ *Ordinary People,* Wildwood, Paramount. Alvin Sargent.

The Stunt Man, Melvin Simon, 20th Century–Fox. Lawrence B. Marcus and Richard Rush.

Cinematography

The Blue Lagoon, Columbia. Nestor Almendros.

Coal Miner's Daughter, Schwartz, Universal. Ralf D. Bode.

The Formula, MGM. James Crabe.

Raging Bull, Chartoff–Winkler, UA. Michael Chapman.

★ *Tess,* Renn–Burrill, Société Française de Production (S.F.P.), Columbia. Geoffrey Unsworth and Ghislain Cloquet.

Art Direction—Set Decoration

Coal Miner's Daughter, Schwartz, Universal. John W. Corso; John M. Dwyer.

The Elephant Man, Brooksfilms, Paramount. Stuart Craig and Bob Cartwright; Hugh Scaife.

The Empire Strikes Back, Lucasfilm, 20th Century–Fox. Norman Reynolds, Leslie Dilley, Harry Lange and Alan Tomkins; Michael Ford.

Kagemusha (The Shadow Warrior), Toho Co., Ltd–Kurosawa Productions, Ltd. 20th Century–Fox. Art Direction: Yoshiro Muraki.

★ *Tess,* Renn–Burrill, Société Française de Production (S.F.P.), Columbia. Art Direction: Pierre Guffroy and Jack Stevens.

Sound

Altered States, Warner Bros. Arthur Piantadosi, Les Fresholtz, Michael Minkler and Willie D. Burton.

Coal Miner's Daughter, Schwartz, Universal. Richard Portman, Roger Heman and Jim Alexander.

★ *The Empire Strikes Back,* Lucasfilm, 20th Century–Fox. Bill Varney, Steve Maslow, Gregg Landaker and Peter Sutton.

Fame, MGM. Michael J. Kohut, Aaron Rochin, Jay M. Harding and Chris Newman.

Raging Bull, Chartoff–Winkler, United Artists. Donald O. Mitchell, Bill Nicholson, David J. Kimball and Les Lazarowitz.

(ORIGINAL SONG)

★ "Fame" (*Fame,* MGM); Music by Michael Gore. Lyrics by Dean Pitchford.

"Nine to Five" (*Nine to Five,* 20th Century–Fox); Music and Lyrics by Dolly Parton.

"On the Road Again" (*Honeysuckle Rose,* Warner Bros); Music and Lyrics by Willie Nelson.

"Out Here on My Own" (*Fame,* MGM); Music by Michael Gore. Lyrics by Lesley Gore.

"People Alone" (*The Competition.* Rastar, Columbia); Music by Lalo Schifrin. Lyrics by Wilbur Jennings.

Music

(ORIGINAL SCORE)

Altered States, Warner Bros. John Corigliano.

The Elephant Man, Brooksfilms, Paramount. John Morris.

The Empire Strikes Back, Lucasfilm, 20th Century–Fox. John Williams.

★ *Fame,* MGM. Michael Gore.

Tess, Renn–Burrill, Société Française de Production (S.F.P.), Columbia. Philippe Sarde.

Film Editing

Coal Miner's Daughter, Schwartz, Universal. Arthur Schmidt.

The Competition, Rastar, Columbia. David Blewitt.

The Elephant Man, Brooksfilms, Paramount. Anne V. Coates.

Fame, MGM. Gerry Hambling.

★ *Raging Bull,* Chartoff-Winkler, UA. Thelma Schoonmaker.

Costume Design

The Elephant Man, Brooksfilms, Paramount. Patricia Norris.

My Brilliant Career, Margaret Fink Films Pty., Ltd., Analysis Film Releasing. Anna Senior.

Somewhere in Time, Rastar–Stephen Deutsch–Universal. Jean-Pierre Dorleac.

★ *Tess,* Renn–Burrill, Société Française de Production (S.F.P.), Columbia. Anthony Powell.

When Time Ran Out, Warner Bros. Paul Zastupnevich.

Short Films

(ANIMATED)

All Nothing, Radio Canada. Frederic Back, producer.

★ *The Fly,* Pannonia Film, Budapest. Ferenc Rofusz, producer.

History of the World in Three Minutes Flat, Michael Mills Productions Ltd. Michael Mills, producer.

(LIVE ACTION)

★ *The Dollar Bottom,* Rocking Horse Films Limited, Paramount. Lloyd Phillips, producer.

Fall Line, Sports Imagery, Inc. Bob Carmichael and Greg Lowe, producers.

A Jury of Her Peers, Sally Heckel Productions. Sally Heckel, producer.

Documentary

(SHORT SUBJECTS)

Don't Miss with Bill, John Watson and Pen Densham's Insight Productions Inc. John Watson and Pen Densham, producers.

The Eruption of Mount St. Helens, Graphic Films Corporation. George Casey, producer.

It's the Same World, Dick Young Productions, Ltd. Dick Young, producer.

★ *Karl Hess: Toward Liberty,* Hallé/Ladue, Inc. Peter W. Ladue and Roland Hallé, producers.

Luther Metke at 94, U.C.L.A. Ethnographic Film Program. Richard Hawkins and Jorge Preloran, producers.

(FEATURES)

Agee, James Agee Film Project. Ross Spears, producer.

The Day After Trinity, Jon Else Productions. Jon Else, producer.

★ *From Mao to Mozart: Isaac Stern in China,* The Hopewell Foundation. Murray Lerner, producer.

Front Line, David Bradbury Productions. David Bradbury, producer.

The Yellow Star—The Persecution of European Jews, 1933–45, Chronos Films. Bengt von zur Muehlen, producer.

Foreign Language Film

Confidence (Hungary).
Kagemusha (*The Shadow Warrior*) (Japan).
The Last Metro (France).
★ *Moscow Does Not Believe in Tears* (U.S.S.R.).
The Nest (Spain).

Irving G. Thalberg Memorial Award

Not given this year.

Jean Hersholt Humanitarian Award

Not given this year.

Special Achievement Award

For Visual Effects: Brian Johnson, Richard Edlund, Dennis Muren, and Bruce Nicholson for *The Empire Strikes Back*, Lucasfilm, 20th Century–Fox.

Honorary Award

Henry Fonda, the consummate actor, in recognition of his brilliant accomplishments and enduring contribution to the art of motion pictures (statuette).

Fred Hynes in appreciation for outstanding service and dedication in upholding the high standards of the Academy of Motion Picture Arts and Sciences (medal of commendation).

Scientific or Technical

ACADEMY AWARD OF MERIT (STATUETTE)

Linwood G. Dunn, Cecil D. Love and Acme Tool and Manufacturing Company for the concept, engineering and development of the Acme-Dunn Optical Printer for motion picture special effects.

SCIENTIFIC AND ENGINEERING AWARD (PLAQUE)

Jean-Marie Lavalou, Alain Masseron and David Samuelson of Samuelson Alga Cinema S.A. and Samuelson Film Service, Limited, for the engineering and development of the Louma Camera Crane and remote control system for motion picture production.

Edward B. Krause of Filmline Corporation for the engineering and manufacture of the micro-demand drive for continuous motion picture film processors.

Ross Taylor for the concept and development of a system of air guns for propelling objects used in special-effects motion picture production.

Dr. Bernard Kühl and Dr. Werner Block of Osram GmbH for the progressive engineering and manufacture of the Osram HMI light source for motion-picture color photography.

David A. Grafton for the optical design and engineering of a telecentric anamorphic lens for motion-picture optical-effects printers.

TECHNICAL ACHIEVEMENT AWARD (CITATION)

Carter Equipment Company for the development of a continuous contact, total immersion, additive color motion picture printer.

Hollywood Film Company for the development of a continuous-contact, total-immersion, additive-color motion picture printer.

André DeBrie S.A. for the development of a continuous contact, total immersion, additive color motion picture printer.

Charles Vaughn and Eugene Nottingham of Cinetron Computer Systems, Incorporated, for the development of a versatile general purpose computer system for animation and optical effects motion picture photography.

John W. Lang, Walter Hrastnik and Charles J. Watson of Bell and Howell Company for the development and manufacture of a modular continuous contact motion picture film printer.

Worth Baird of LaVezzi Machine Works, Incorporated, for the advanced design and manufacture of a film sprocket for motion picture projectors.

Peter A. Regla and Dan Slater of Elicon for the development of a follow focus system for motion picture optical effects printers and animation stands.

Points of Interest

1. Nothing to it: Supporting Actor Timothy Hutton wins for film debut; Robert Redford wins for directing debut; Michael O'Keefe, Cathy Moriarty and Diana Scarwid nominated for film debuts.
2. Never too late: Supporting Actress nominee Eva Le Gallienne, eighty-two, oldest performer ever nominated for an Oscar.

Rule Changes

1. Here we go again: Visual Effects again considered a Special Achievement Award.
2. The fewer the merrier: "Original Song Score and Its Adaptation or Adaptation Score" category done away with.

Eligible Films That Failed to Be Nominated for Best Picture

Melvin and Howard, Stardust Memories, My Brilliant Career, Return of the Secaucus Seven, Dressed to Kill, American Gigolo.

Submitted Films Rejected by the Foreign Language Film Award Committee

Bye Bye Brazil (Brazil), directed by Carlos Diegues; *Every Man for Himself* (Switzerland), directed by Jean-Luc Godard.

Eligible Songs That Failed to Be Nominated

"Call Me" (Giorgio Moroder and Deborah Harry)—*American Gigolo*; "Ghosts of Cape Horn" (Gordon Lightfoot)—*Ghosts of Cape Horn*; "It's My Turn" (Michael Masser)—*It's My Turn*; "Late in the Evening" (Paul Simon)—*One Trick Pony*; "Look What You've Done for Me" (Boz Scaggs)—*Urban Cowboy*; "Lookin' for Love" (Bob Morrison, Wanda Mallette and Patti Ryan)—*Urban Cowboy*; "On the Radio" (Giorgio Moroder)—*Foxes*.

1981

Picture

Atlantic City, International Cinema Corporation, Paramount. Produced by Denis Heroux.

★ *Chariots of Fire*, Enigma, The Ladd Company/Warner Bros. Produced by David Puttnam.

On Golden Pond, ITC Films/IPC Films, Universal. Produced by Bruce Gilbert.

Raiders of the Lost Ark, Lucasfilm, Paramount. Produced by Frank Marshall.

Reds, J.R.S., Paramount. Produced by Warren Beatty.

Actor

Warren Beatty in *Reds* (J.R.S., Paramount).

★ Henry Fonda in *On Golden Pond* (ITC Films/IPC Films, Universal).

Burt Lancaster in *Atlantic City* (International Cinema Corporation, Paramount).

Dudley Moore in *Arthur* (Rollins, Joffe, Morra and Brezner, Orion).

Paul Newman in *Absence of Malice* (Mirage, Columbia).

Actress

★ Katharine Hepburn in *On Golden Pond* (ITC Films/IPC Films, Universal).

Diane Keaton in *Reds* (J.R.S., Paramount).

Marsha Mason in *Only When I Laugh* (Columbia).

Susan Sarandon in *Atlantic City* (International Cinema Corporation, Paramount).

Meryl Streep in *The French Lieutenant's Woman* (Parlon, UA).

Supporting Actor

James Coco in *Only When I Laugh* (Columbia).

★ John Gielgud in *Arthur* (Rollins, Joffe, Morra and Brezner, Orion).

Ian Holm in *Chariots of Fire* (Enigma, The Ladd Company/Warner Bros.).

Jack Nicholson in *Reds* (J.R.S., Paramount).

Howard E. Rollins, Jr., in *Ragtime* (Paramount).

Supporting Actress

Melinda Dillon in *Absence of Malice* (Mirage, Columbia).

Jane Fonda in *On Golden Pond* (ITC Films/IPC Films, Universal).

Joan Hackett in *Only When I Laugh* (Columbia).

Elizabeth McGovern in *Ragtime* (Paramount).

★ Maureen Stapleton in *Reds* (J.R.S., Paramount).

Director

★ Warren Beatty for *Reds* (J.R.S., Paramount).

Hugh Hudson for *Chariots of Fire* (Enigma, The Ladd Company/Warner Bros.).

Louis Malle for *Atlantic City* (International Cinema Corporation, Paramount).

Mark Rydell for *On Golden Pond* (ITC Films/IPC Films, Universal).

Steven Spielberg for *Raiders of the Lost Ark* (Lucasfilm, Paramount).

Writing

(SCREENPLAY WRITTEN DIRECTLY FOR THE SCREEN)

Absence of Malice, Mirage, Columbia. Kurt Luedtke.

Arthur, Rollins, Joffe, Morra and Brezner, Orion. Steve Gordon.

Atlantic City, International Cinema Corporation, Paramount. John Guare.

★ *Chariots of Fire*, Enigma, The Ladd Company/Warner Bros. Colin Welland.

Reds, J.R.S., Paramount. Warren Beatty and Trevor Griffiths.

(SCREENPLAY BASED ON MATERIAL FROM ANOTHER MEDIUM)

The French Lieutenant's Woman, Parlon, UA. Harold Pinter.

★ *On Golden Pond*, ITC Films/IPC Films, Universal. Ernest Thompson.

Pennies from Heaven, Hera, MGM. Dennis Potter.

Prince of the City, Orion/Warner Bros. Jay Presson Allen and Sidney Lumet.

Ragtime, Paramount. Michael Weller.

Cinematography

Excalibur, Orion. Alex Thomson.

On Golden Pond, ITC Films/IPC FIlms, Universal. Billy Williams.

Ragtime, Paramount. Miroslav Ondricek.

Raiders of the Lost Ark, Lucasfilm, Paramount. Douglas Slocombe.
★ *Reds,* J.R.S., Paramount. Vittorio Storaro.

Art Direction

The French Lieutenant's Woman, Parlon, United Artists. Assheton Gorton; Ann Mollo.
Heaven's Gate, UA. Tambi Larsen; Jim Berkey.
Ragtime, Paramount. John Graysmark, Patrizia Von Brandenstein and Anthony Reading; George De Titta, Sr., George De Titta, Jr. and Peter Howitt.
★ *Raiders of the Lost Ark,* Lucasfilm, Paramount. Norman Reynolds and Leslie Dilley; Michael Ford.
Reds, J.R.S., Paramount. Richard Sylbert; Michael Seirton.

Sound

On Golden Pond, ITC Films/IPC Films, Universal. Richard Portman and David Ronne.
Outland, The Ladd Company, Warner Bros. John K. Wilkinson, Robert W. Glass, Jr., Robert M. Thirlwell and Robin Gregory.
Pennies from Heaven, Hera, MGM. Michael J. Kohut, Jay M. Harding, Richard Tyler and Al Overton.
★ *Raiders of the Lost Ark,* Lucasfilm, Paramount. Bill Varney, Steve Maslow, Gregg Landaker and Roy Charman.
Reds, J.R.S., Paramount. Dick Vorisek, Tom Fleischman and Simon Kaye.

Music

(ORIGINAL SONG)

★ "Arthur's Theme (Best That You Can Do)" (*Arthur,* Rollins, Joffe, Morra and Brezner, Orion); Music and Lyrics by Burt Bacharach, Carole Bayer Sager, Christopher Cross and Peter Allen.
"Endless Love" (*Endless Love,* Polygram/Barish/Lovell, Universal); Music and Lyrics by Lionel Ritchie.
"The First Time It Happens" (*The Great Muppet Caper,* Henson/ITC Film, Universal); Music and Lyrics by Joe Raposo.
"For Your Eyes Only" (*For Your Eyes Only,* EON, United Artists); Music by Bill Conti. Lyrics by Mick Leeson.
"One More Hour" (*Ragtime,* Paramount); Music and Lyrics by Randy Newman.

(ORIGINAL SCORE)

★ *Chariots of Fire,* Enigma, The Ladd Company/Warner Bros. Vangelis.
Dragonslayer, Barwood/Robbins, Paramount. Alex North.
On Golden Pond, ITC Films/IPC Films, Universal. Dave Grusin.
Ragtime, Paramount. Randy Newman.
Raiders of the Lost Ark, Lucasfilm, Paramount. John Williams.

Film Editing

Chariots of Fire, Enigma, The Ladd Company/Warner Bros. Terry Rawlings.
The French Lieutenant's Woman, Parlon, UA. John Bloom.
On Golden Pond, ITC Films/IPC Films, Universal. Robert L. Wolfe.
★ *Raiders of the Lost Ark,* Lucasfilm, Paramount. Michael Kahn.
Reds, J.R.S., Paramount. Dede Allen and Craig McKay.

Costume Design

★ *Chariots of Fire,* Enigma, The Ladd Company/Warner Bros. Milena Canonero.
The French Lieutenant's Woman, Parlon, UA. Tom Rand.
Pennies from Heaven, Hera, MGM. Bob Mackie.
Ragtime, Paramount. Anna Hill Johnstone.
Reds, J.R.S., Paramount. Shirley Russell.

Make-Up

★ *An American Werewolf in London,* Lycanthrope/Polygram, Universal. Rick Baker.
Heartbeeps, Phillips/Universal. Stan Winston.

Visual Effects

Dragonslayer, Barwood/Robbins, Paramount. Dennis Muren, Phil Tippett, Ken Ralston and Brian Johnson.
★ *Raiders of the Lost Ark,* Lucasfilm, Paramount. Richard Edlund, Kit West, Bruce Nicholson and Joe Johnston.

Short Films

(ANIMATION)

★ *Crac,* Société Radio–Canada. Frederic Back, producer.
The Creation, Will Vinton Productions. Will Vinton, producer.
The Tender Tale of Cinderella Penguin, National Film Board of Canada. Janet Perlman, producer.

(LIVE ACTION)

Couples and Robbers, Flamingo Pictures Ltd. Christine Oestreicher, producer.
First Winter, National Film Board of Canada. John H. Smith, producer.
★ *Violet,* American Film Institute. Paul Kemp and Shelley Levinson, producers.

Documentary

(FEATURES)

Against Wind and Tide: A Cuban Odyssey, Seven League Productions, Inc. Susanne Bauman and Paul Neshamkin, producers.
Brooklyn Bridge, Florentine Films. Ken Burns, producer.
Eight Minutes to Midnight: A Portrait of Dr. Helen Caldicott, The Caldicott Project. Mary Benjamin, Susanne Simpson and Boyd Estus, producers.
El Salvador: Another Vietnam, Catalyst Media Productions. Glenn Silver and Tete Vasconcellos, producers.

★ *Genocide,* Arnold Schwartzman Productions, Inc. Arnold Schwartzman and Rabbi Marvin Hier, producers.

(SHORT SUBJECTS)

Americas in Transition, Americas in Transition, Inc. Obie Benz, producer.

★ *Close Harmony,* A Nobel Enterprise. Nigel Noble, producer.

Journey for Survival, Dick Young Productions, Inc. Dick Young, producer.

See What I Say, Michigan Women Filmmakers Productions. Linda Chapman, Pam Leblanc and Freddi Stevens, producers.

Urge to Build, Roland Hallé Productions, Inc. Roland Hallé and John Hoover, producers.

Foreign Language Film

The Boat Is Full (Switzerland).
Man of Iron (Poland).
★ *Mephisto* (Hungary).
Muddy River (Japan).
Three Brothers (Italy).

Irving G. Thalberg Award

Albert R. "Cubby" Broccoli.

Jean Hersholt Humanitarian Award

Danny Kaye.

Gordon E. Sawyer Award

Joseph B. Walker.

Honorary Award

Barbara Stanwyck, for superlative creativity and unique contribution to the art of screen acting (statuette).

Special Achievement Award

For Sound Effects Editing: Benjamin P. Burtt, Jr., and Richard L. Anderson for *Raiders of the Lost Ark*, Lucasfilm, Paramount.

Scientific or Technical

ACADEMY AWARD OF MERIT (STATUETTE)

Fuji Photo Film Company Ltd. for the research, development and introduction of a new ultra-high-speed color negative film for motion pictures.

SCIENTIFIC AND ENGINEERING AWARD (PLAQUE)

Leonard Sokolow for the concept and design and Howard Lazare for the development of the Consolidated Film Industries' Stroboscan motion picture film viewer.

Richard Edlund and Industrial Light and Magic, Incorporated, for the concept and engineering of a beam-splitter optical composite motion picture printer.

Richard Edlund and Industrial Light and Magic, Incorporated for the engineering of the Empire Motion Picture Camera System.

Edward J. Blasko and Dr. Roderick T. Ryan of the Eastman Kodak Company for the application of the Prostar Microfilm Processor for motion picture title and special optical effects production.

Nelson Tyler for the progressive development and improvement of the Tyler Helicopter motion picture camera platform.

TECHNICAL ACHIEVEMENT AWARD (CITATION)

Hal Landaker for the concept and Alan D. Landaker for the engineering of the Burbank Studios' Production Sound Department 24-frame color video system.

Bill Hogan of Ruxton, Ltd. and Richard J. Stumpf and Daniel R. Brewer of Universal City Studios' Production Sound Department for the engineering of a 24-frame color video system.

Ernst F. Nettman of Continental Camera Systems, Inc., for the development of a pitching lens for motion picture photography.

Bill Taylor of Universal Studios for the concept and specifications for a Two Format, Rotating Head, Aerial Image Optical Printer.

Peter D. Parks of Oxford Scientific Films for the development of the OSF microscopic photography.

Dr. Louis Stankiewicz and H. L. Blanchford for the development of Baryfol sound barrier materials.

Dennis Muren and Stuart Ziff of Industrial Light and Magic, Incorporated, for the development of a Motion Picture Figure Mover for animation photography.

Points of Interest

1. Nothing to it: Howard E. Rollins, Jr., and Hugh Hudson nominated for film debuts.
2. The Hepburn scorecard: Katharine Hepburn's twelfth nomination breaks her own record as most nominated performer. She is the only performer to win four times.
3. The family way: Henry Fonda and daughter Jane both nominated.
4. Never too late: Henry Fonda, seventy-six, and Katharine Hepburn, seventy-four, become oldest Best Actor and Actress winners.
5. Aping himself: Warren Beatty nominated for Best Actor, Director, Screenplay and as producer of a Best Picture nominee for the second time.

Rule Changes

1. New additions: "Make-Up"; Gordon E. Sawyer Award, honoring life-time achievements in scientific or technical fields.
2. Here we go again: Visual Effects again becomes a regular competitive category.

Eligible Films That Failed to Be Nominated for Best Picture

Pennies from Heaven, S.O.B., Cutter's Way, Body Heat, Strange Behavior, My Dinner with Andre, The Howling, Rich and Famous, Mommie Dearest.

Submitted Films Rejected by the Foreign Language Film Award Committee

Pixote (Brazil), directed by Hector Babenco (ruled ineligible); *Diva* (France), directed by Jean-Jacques Beineix; *Lili Marleen* (German Federal Republic), directed by Rainer Werner Fassbinder.

1982

Picture

E.T.—The Extra-Terrestrial, Universal. Produced by Steven Spielberg and Kathleen Kennedy.

★ *Gandhi,* Indo–British Films, Columbia. Produced by Richard Attenborough.

Missing, Universal/PolyGram, Universal. Produced by Edward and Mildred Lewis.

Tootsie, Mirage/Punch, Columbia. Produced by Sydney Pollack and Dick Richards.

The Verdict, Fox-Zanuck/Brown, 20th Century–Fox. Produced by Richard D. Zanuck and David Brown.

Actor

Dustin Hoffman in *Tootsie* (Mirage/Punch, Columbia).

★ Ben Kingsley in *Gandhi* (Indo–British Films, Columbia).

Jack Lemmon in *Missing* (Universal/Polygram, Universal).

Paul Newman in *The Verdict* (Fox–Zanuck/Brown, 20th Century–Fox).

Peter O'Toole in *My Favorite Year* (Gruskoff, MGM/UA).

Actress

Julie Andrews in *Victor/Victoria* (MGM, MGM/UA).

Jessica Lange in *Frances* (Brooksfilm/EMI, Universal/AFD).

Sissy Spacek in *Missing* (Universal/PolyGram, Universal).

★ Meryl Streep in *Sophie's Choice* (ITC/Pakula-Barrish, Universal/AFD).

Debra Winger in *An Officer and a Gentleman* (Lorimar/Elfand, Paramount).

Supporting Actor

Charles Durning in *The Best Little Whorehouse in Texas* (Universal/RKO/Miller–Milkis–Boyett, Universal).

★ Louis Gossett, Jr. in *An Officer and a Gentleman* (Lorimar/Elfand, Paramount).

John Lithgow in *The World According to Garp* (Warner Bros.).

James Mason in *The Verdict* (Fox–Zanuck/Brown, 20th Century–Fox).

Robert Preston in *Victor/Victoria* (MGM, MGM/UA).

Supporting Actress

Glenn Close in *The World According to Garp* (Warner Bros.).

Teri Garr in *Tootsie* (Mirage/Punch, Columbia).

★ Jessica Lange in *Tootsie* (Mirage/Punch, Columbia).

Kim Stanley in *Frances* (Brooksfilm/EMI, Universal/AFD).

Lesley Ann Warren in *Victor/Victoria* (MGM, MGM/UA).

Director

★ Richard Attenborough for *Gandhi* (Indo/British Films, Columbia).

Sidney Lumet for *The Verdict* (Fox–Zanuck/Brown, 20th Century–Fox).

Wolfgang Petersen for *Das Boot* (Bavaria Atelier GmbH Productions, Columbia) (German).

Sidney Pollack for *Tootsie* (Mirage/Punch, Columbia).

Steven Spielberg for *E.T.—The Extra-Terrestrial* (Universal).

Writing

(SCREENPLAY WRITTEN DIRECTLY FOR THE SCREEN)

Diner, Weintraub, MGM/UA. Barry Levinson.

E.T.—The Extra-Terrestrial, Universal. Melissa Matheson.

★ *Gandhi,* Indo/British Films, Columbia. John Briley.

An Officer and a Gentleman, Lorimar/Elfand, Paramount. Douglas Day Stewart.

Tootsie, Mirage/Punch, Columbia. Don McGuire, Larry Gelbart and Murray Schisgal.

(SCREENPLAY BASED ON MATERIAL FROM ANOTHER MEDIUM)

Das Boot, Bavaria Atelier GmbH, Columbia. Wolfgang Petersen (German).

★ *Missing,* Universal/PolyGram, Universal. Costa–Gavras and Donald Stewart.

Sophie's Choice, ITC/Pakula-Barrish, Universal/AFD. Alan J. Pakula.

The Verdict, Fox–Zanuck/Brown, 20th Century–Fox. David Mamet.

Victor/Victoria, MGM, MGM/UA. Blake Edwards.

Cinematography

Das Boot, Bavaria Atelier GmbH, Columbia. Jost Vacano (German).

E.T.—The Extra-Terrestrial, Universal. Allen Daviau.

★ *Gandhi,* Indo/British Films, Columbia. Billy Williams and Ronnie Taylor.

Sophie's Choice, ITC/Pakula–Barrish, Universal/AFD. Nestor Almendros.

Tootsie, Mirage-Punch, Columbia. Owen Roizman.

Art Direction—Set Decoration

Annie, Rastar, Columbia. Dale Hennesy; Marvin March.

Blade Runner, Michael Deeley–Ridley Scott, Ladd Company/Sir Run Run Shaw. Lawrence G. Paull and David Snyder; Linda DeScenna.

★ *Gandhi,* Indo/British Films, Columbia. Stuart Craig and Bob Laing; Michael Seirton.

La Traviata, Accent Films B.V./RAI–Radiotelevisione Italiana, PSO. Franco Zeffirelli; Gianni Quaranta.

Victor/Victoria, MGM, MGM/UA. Rodger Maus, Tim Hutchinson and William Craig Smith; Harry Cordwell.

Sound

Das Boot, Bavaria Atelier GmbH, Columbia. Milan Bor, Trevor Pyke and Mike Le-Mare (German).

★ *E.T.—The Extra-Terrestrial,* Universal. Buzz Knudson, Robert Glass, Don Digirolamo, and Gene Cantamessa.

Gandhi, Indo/British Films, Columbia. Gerry Humphreys, Robin O'Donoghue, Jonathan Bates, and Simon Kaye.

Tootsie, Mirage/Punch, Columbia. Arthur Piantadosi, Les Fresholtz, Dick Alexander, and Les Lazarowitz.

Tron, Disney, Buena Vista. Michael Minkler, Bob Minkler, Lee Minkler, Jim La Rue.

Music

(ORIGINAL SONG)

"Eye of the Tiger" (*Rocky III,* Chartoff/Winkler/UA, MGM/UA); Music and Lyrics by Jim Peterik and Frankie Sullivan III.

"How Do You Keep the Music Playing?" (*Best Friends,* Timberlane Films, Warner Bros.); Music by Michel Legrand. Lyrics by Alan and Marilyn Bergman.

"If We Were in Love" (*Yes, Giorgio,* MGM, MGM/UA); Music by John Williams. Lyrics by Alan and Marilyn Bergman.

"It Might Be You" (*Tootsie,* Mirage/Punch, Columbia); Music by Dave Grusin. Lyrics by Alan and Marilyn Bergman.

★ "Up Where We Belong" (*An Officer and a Gentleman,* Lorimar/Elfand, Paramount); Music by Jack Nitzsche and Buffy Sainte-Marie. Lyrics by Will Jennings.

(ORIGINAL SCORE)

★ *E.T.—The Extra-Terrestrial,* Universal. John Williams.

Gandhi, Indo/British Films, Columbia. Ravi Shankar and George Fenton.

An Officer and a Gentleman, Lorimar/Elfand, Paramount. Jack Nitzsche.

Poltergeist, MGM/Spielberg, MGM/UA. Jerry Goldsmith.

Sophie's Choice, ITC/Pakula–Barrish, Universal/AFD. Marvin Hamlisch.

(ORIGINAL SONG SCORE AND ITS ADAPTATION OR ADAPTATION SCORE)

Annie, Rastar, Columbia. Ralph Burns.

One from the Heart, Zoetrope Studios, Columbia. Tom Waits.

★ *Victor/Victoria,* MGM, MGM/UA. Leslie Bricusse and Henry Mancini.

Film Editing

Das Boot, Bavaria Atelier GmbH, Columbia. Hannes Nikel (German).

E.T.—The Extra-Terrestrial, Universal. Carol Littleton.

★ *Gandhi,* Indo/British Films, Columbia. John Bloom.

An Officer and a Gentleman, Lorimar/Elfand, Paramount. Peter Zinner.

Tootsie, Mirage/Punch, Columbia. Fredric Steinkamp and William Steinkamp.

Costume Design

★ *Gandhi,* Indo/British Films, Columbia. John Mollo and Bhanu Athaiya.

La Traviata, Accent Films B.V./RAI–Radiotelevisione Italiana, PSO. Piero Tosi.

Sophie's Choice, ITC/Pakula–Barrish, Universal/AFD. Albert Wolsky.

Tron, Disney, Buena Vista. Elois Jenssen and Rosanna Norton.

Victor/Victoria, MGM, MGM/UA. Patricia Norris.

Make-up

Gandhi, Indo/British Films, Columbia. Tom Smith.

★ *Quest for Fire,* International Cinema Corp., 20th Century–Fox (credits in controversy).

Visual Effects

Blade Runner, Michael Deeley–Ridley Scott, Ladd Company/Sir Run Run Shaw. Douglas Trumbull, Richard Yuricich, and David Dryer.

★ *E.T.—The Extra-Terrestrial,* Universal. Carlo Rambaldi, Dennis Murren, and Kenneth F. Smith.

Poltergeist, MGM/Steven Spielberg, MGM/UA. Richard Edlund, Michael Wood and Bruce Nicholson.

Sound Effects Editing

Das Boot, Bavaria Atelier GmbH, Columbia. Mile Le-Mare (German).

★ *E.T.—The Extra-Terrestrial,* Universal. Charles L. Campbell and Ben Burtt.

Poltergeist, MGM/Spielberg, MGM/UA. Stephen Hunter Flick and Richard L. Anderson.

Short Films

(ANIMATED)

The Great Cognito, Will Vinton Prods. Will Vinton, producer.

The Snowman, Snowman Enterprises Ltd. John Coates, producer.

★ *Tango*, Film Polski. Zbigniew Rybczynski, producer.

(LIVE ACTION)

Ballet Robotique, Bob Rogers and Company. Bob Rogers, producer.

★ *A Shocking Accident*, Flamingo Pictures, Ltd. Christine Oestreicher, producer.

The Silence, American Film Institute. Michael Toshiyuki Uno and Joseph Benson, producers.

Split Cherry Tree, Learning Corp. of America. Jan Saunders, producer.

Sredni Vashtar, Laurentic Film Prods. Ltd. Andrew Birkin, producer.

Documentary

(SHORT SUBJECTS)

Gods of Metal, Richter Prods. Robert Richter, producer.

★ *If You Love This Planet*, National Film Board of Canada. Edward Le Lorrain, producer.

The Klan: A Legacy of Hate in America, Guggenheim Prods., Inc. Charles Guggenheim and Werner Schumann, producers.

To Live or Let Die, American Film Foundation. Freida Lee Mock, producer.

Traveling Hopefully, Arnuthfonyus Films Inc. John G. Avildsen, producer.

(FEATURES)

After the Axe, National Film Board of Canada. Sturla Gunnarsson and Steve Lucas, producers.

Ben's Mill, Public Broadcasting Associates, Odyssey. John Karol and Michael Chalufour, producers.

In Our Water, Foresight Films. Meg Switzgable, producer.

★ *Just Another Missing Kid*, Canadian Broadcasting Corp. John Zaritsky, producer.

A Portrait of Giselle, Wishupon Prods. Joseph Wishy, producer.

Foreign Language Film

Alsino and the Condor (Nicaragua).

Coup de Torchon (Clean Slate) (France).

The Flight of the Eagle (Sweden).

Private Life (U.S.S.R.).

★ *Volver a Empezar (To Begin Again)* (Spain).

Irving G. Thalberg Memorial Award

Not given this year.

Jean Hersholt Humanitarian Award

Walter Mirisch.

Gordon E. Sawyer Award

John O. Aalberg for his technological contributions to the motion picture industry.

Honorary Award

Mickey Rooney for fifty years of versatility in a variety of memorable film performances (statuette).

Scientific or Technical

ACADEMY AWARD OF MERIT (STATUETTE)

August Arnold and Erich Kaestner for the concept and engineering of the first operational 35mm, hand-held, spinning-mirror reflex, motion picture camera.

SCIENTIFIC AND ENGINEERING AWARD (PLAQUE)

Colin F. Mossman and the Research & Development group of Rank Film Laboratories, London, for the engineering and implementation of a 4000-meter printing system for motion picture laboratories.

Santee Zelli and Salvatore Zelli of Elemack Italia S.R.L., Rome, Italy, for the continuing engineering, design and development that has resulted in the Elemack Camera Dolly Systems for motion picture production.

Leonard Chapman for the engineering design, development and manufacture of the PeeWee Camera Dolly for motion picture production.

Dr. Mohammad S. Nozari of Minnesota Mining & Manufacturing Company for the research and development of the 3M Photogard protective coating for motion picture film.

Brianne Murphy and Donald Schisler of Mitchell Insert Systems, Inc., for the concept, design and manufacture of the MSI Camera Insert Car and Process Trailer.

Jacobus L. Dimmers for the engineering and manufacture of the Teccon Enterprises' magnetic transducer for motion picture sound recording and playback.

TECHNICAL ACHIEVEMENT AWARD (CITATION)

Richard W. Deats for the design and manufacture of the "Little Big Crane" for motion picture production.

Constant Tresfon and Adriaan De Rooy of Egripment, and Ed Phillips and Carlos de Mattos of Matthews Studio Equipment, Inc., for the design and manufacture of the "Tulip Crane" for motion picture production.

Bran Ferren of Associates & Ferren for the design and development of a computerized lightning-effect system for motion picture photography.

Christie Electric Corp. and LaVezzi Machine Works, Inc., for the design and manufacture of the Ultramittent film transport for Christie motion picture projectors.

Points of Interest

1. Nothing to it: Glenn Close nominated for film debut.
2. The family way: Actress nominee Julie Andrews married to Blake Edwards, nominee for Screenplay Based on Material from Another Medium.
3. Triple play: Three of the five Best Song nominees by husband-and-wife team Alan and Marilyn Bergman.

4. Slumming: 1976 Director winner John G. Avildsen nominated for Documentary Short.
5. Two-timer: Jessica Lange nominated for Actress and Supporting Actress—first time since 1942.
6. Open door policy: West Germany's *Das Boot* sets foreign-language film record with six nominations.

Rule Changes

1. New addition: "Sound Effects Editing."
2. The more the merrier: "Song Score and Its Adaptation or Adaptation Score" is reinstated.
3. The name game: "Song" becomes "Original Song."

Eligible Films That Failed to Be Nominated for Best Picture

48 Hours, An Officer and a Gentleman, Victor/Victoria, Veronika Voss, Lola, Gregory's Girl, The Road Warrior, Poltergeist, Eating Raoul.

Submitted Films Rejected by the Foreign Language Film Award Committee

Fitzcarraldo (German Federal Republic), directed by Werner Herzog; *The Night of the Shooting Stars* (Italy), directed by Paolo and Vittorio Taviani.

Eligible Songs That Failed to Be Nominated

"Theme from *Cat People*" (Giorgio Moroder and David Bowie)—*Cat People;* "Making Love" (Burt Bacharach and Carole Bayer Seger)—*Making Love;* "Somebody's Baby" (Jackson Browne and Danny Kortchmear)—*Fast Times at Ridgemont High.*

1983

Picture

The Big Chill, Carson Productions Group, Columbia. Produced by Michael Shamberg.

The Dresser, Goldcrest/Television Limited/World Film Services, Columbia. Produced by Peter Yates.

The Right Stuff, Chartoff–Winkler, Ladd Company, Warner Bros. Produced by Irwin Winkler and Robert Chartoff.

Tender Mercies, EMI—Antron Media, Universal/AFD. Produced by Philip S. Hobel.

★ *Terms of Endearment,* Brooks, Paramount. Produced by James L. Brooks.

Actor

Michael Caine in *Educating Rita* (Acorn, Columbia).

Tom Conti in *Reuben, Reuben* (Saltair/Walter Shenson, Taft, 20th Century–Fox International Classics).

Tom Courtenay in *The Dresser* (Goldcrest/Television Limited/World Film Services, Columbia).

★ Robert Duvall in *Tender Mercies* (EMI—Antron Media, Universal/AFD).

Albert Finney in *The Dresser* (Goldcrest/Television Limited/World Film Services, Columbia).

Actress

Jane Alexander in *Testament* (Entertainment Events, American Playhouse, Paramount).

★ Shirley MacLaine in *Terms of Endearment* (Brooks, Paramount).

Meryl Streep in *Silkwood* (ABC Motion Pictures, 20th Century–Fox).

Julie Walters in *Educating Rita* (Acorn, Columbia).

Debra Winger in *Terms of Endearment* (Brooks, Paramount).

Supporting Actor

Charles Durning in *To Be or Not to Be* (Brooksfilms, 20th Century–Fox).

John Lithgow in *Terms of Endearment* (Brooks, Paramount).

★ Jack Nicholson in *Terms of Endearment* (Brooks, Paramount).

Sam Shepard in *The Right Stuff* (Chartoff–Winkler, Ladd Company, Warner Bros.).

Rip Torn in *Cross Creek* (Radnitz/Ritt/Thorn EMI Films, Universal).

Supporting Actress

Cher in *Silkwood* (ABC Motion Pictures, 20th Century–Fox).

Glenn Close in *The Big Chill* (Carson Productions Group, Columbia).

★ Linda Hunt in *The Year of Living Dangerously* (Fields, Metro-Goldwyn-Mayer Production, MGM/UA).

Amy Irving in *Yentl* (United Artists/Ladbroke Feature/Barwood, MGM/UA).

Alfre Woodard in *Cross Creek* (Radnitz/Ritt/Thorn EMI, Universal).

Director

Bruce Beresford for *Tender Mercies* (EMI—Antron Media, Universal/AFD).

Ingmar Bergman for *Fanny & Alexander* (Cinematograph AB for the Swedish Film Institute/the Swedish Television SVT 1, Sweden/Gaumont, France/Personafilm and Tobis Filmkunst BRD Production, Embassy).

★ James L. Brooks for *Terms of Endearment* (James L. Brooks, Paramount).

Mike Nichols for *Silkwood* (ABC Motion Pictures Production, 20th Century–Fox).

Peter Yates for *The Dresser* (Goldcrest Films/Television Limited/World Film Services Production, Columbia).

Writing

(SCREENPLAY WRITTEN DIRECTLY FOR THE SCREEN)

The Big Chill, Carson Productions Group, Columbia. Lawrence Kasdan and Barbara Benedek.

Fanny & Alexander, Cinematograph AB for the Swedish Film Institute/the Swedish Television SVT1, Sweden/Gaumont, France/Personafilm and Tobis Filmkunst, BRD, Embassy. Ingmar Bergman.

Silkwood, ABC Motion Pictures, 20th Century–Fox. Nora Ephron and Alice Arlen.

★ *Tender Mercies*, EMI—Antron Media, Universal/AFD. Horton Foote.

WarGames, Goldberg, MGM/UA. Lawrence Lasker and Walter F. Parkes.

(SCREENPLAY BASED ON MATERIAL FROM ANOTHER MEDIUM)

Betrayal, Horizon, 20th Century–Fox International Classics. Harold Pinter.

The Dresser, Goldcrest/Television Limited/World Film Services, Columbia. Ronald Harwood.

Educating Rita, Acorn, Columbia. Willy Russell.

Reuben, Reuben, Saltair/Walter Shenson, Taft, 20th Century–Fox International Classics. Julius J. Epstein.

★ *Terms of Endearment*, Brooks, Paramount. James L. Brooks.

Cinematography

★ *Fanny & Alexander*, Cinematograph AB for Swedish Film Institute/Swedish Television SVT1, Sweden/Gaumont, France/Personafilm and Tobis Filmkunst, BRD, Embassy. Sven Nykvist.

Flashdance, Polygram, Paramount. Don Peterman.

The Right Stuff, Chartoff–Winkler, Ladd Company, Warner Bros. Caleb Deschanel.

WarGames, Goldberg Production, MGM/UA. William A. Fraker.

Zelig, Rollins-Joffe Orion, Warner Bros. Gordon Willis.

Art Direction—Set Decoration

★ *Fanny & Alexander*, Cinematograph AB for the Swedish Film Institute/the Swedish Television SVT 1, Sweden/Gaumont, France/Personafilm and Tobis Filmkunst, BRD, Embassy. Anna Asp; Susanne Lingheim.

Return of the Jedi, Lucasfilm, 20th Century–Fox. Norman Reynolds, Fred Hole and James Schoppe; Michael Ford.

The Right Stuff, Chartoff–Winkler, Ladd Company, Warner Bros. Geoffrey Kirkland, Richard J. Lawrence, W. Stewart Campbell and Peter Romero; Pat Pending and George R. Nelson.

Terms of Endearment, James L. Brooks, Paramount. Polly Platt; Tom Pedigo.

Yentl, United Artists/Ladbroke Feature/Barwood Production, MGM/UA. Roy Walker and Leslie Tomkins; Tessa Davies.

Sound

Never Cry Wolf, Walt Disney, Buena Vista. Alan R. Splet, Todd Boekelheide, Randy Thom and David Parker.

Return of the Jedi, Lucasfilm, 20th Century–Fox. Ben Burtt, Gary Summers, Randy Thom and Tony Dawe.

★ *The Right Stuff*, Chartoff–Winkler, Ladd Company, Warner Bros. Mark Berger, Tom Scott, Randy Thom and David MacMillan.

Terms of Endearment, Brooks, Paramount. Donald O. Mitchell, Rick Kline, Kevin O'Connell and James Alexander.

WarGames, Goldberg, MGM/UA. Michael J. Kohut, Carlos de Larios, Aaron Rochin and Willie D. Burton.

Music

(SONG)

★ "Flashdance . . . What a Feeling" (*Flashdance*, Polygram, Paramount); Music by Giorgio Moroder. Lyrics by Keith Forsey and Irene Cara.

"Maniac" (*Flashdance*, Polygram, Paramount); Music and Lyrics by Michael Sembello and Dennis Matkosky.

"Over You" (*Tender Mercies*, EMI Presentation—Antron Media, Universal/AFD); Music and Lyrics by Austin Roberts and Bobby Hart.

"Papa, Can You Hear Me?" (*Yentl*, United Artists/Ladbroke Feature/Barwood, MGM/UA); Music by Michel Legrand. Lyrics by Alan and Marilyn Bergman.

"The Way He Makes Me Feel" (*Yentl*, United Artists/Ladbroke Feature/Barwood, MGM/UA); Music by Michel Legrand. Lyrics by Alan and Marilyn Bergman.

(ORIGINAL SCORE)

Cross Creek, Radnitz/Ritt/Thorn EMI, Universal. Leonard Rosenman.

Return of the Jedi, Lucasfilm, 20th Century–Fox. John Williams.

★ *The Right Stuff*, Chartoff–Winkler, Ladd Company, Warner Bros. Bill Conti.

Terms of Endearment, Brooks, Paramount. Michael Gore.

Under Fire, Lions Gate, Orion. Jerry Goldsmith.

(ORIGINAL SONG SCORE OR ADAPTATION SCORE)

The Sting II, Lang, Universal. Lalo Schifrin.

Trading Places, Aaron Russo, Paramount. Elmer Bernstein.

★ *Yentl*, United Artists/Ladbroke Feature/Barwood, MGM/UA. Michel Legrand, Alan and Marilyn Bergman.

Film Editing

Blue Thunder, Rastar, Columbia. Frank Morris and Edward Abroms.

Flashdance, Polygram, Paramount. Bud Smith and Walt Mulconery.

★ *The Right Stuff*, Chartoff–Winkler, Ladd Company, Warner

Bros. Glenn Farr, Lisa Fruchtman, Stephen A. Rotter, Douglas Steward and Tom Rolf.

Silkwood, ABC Motion Pictures, 20th Century–Fox. Sam O'Steen.

Terms of Endearment, Brooks, Paramount. Richard Marks.

Costume Design

Cross Creek, Radnitz/Ritt/Thorn EMI, Universal. Joe I. Tompkins.

★ *Fanny & Alexander,* Cinematography AB for the Swedish Film Institute/the Swedish Television SVT 1, Sweden/Gaumont, France/Personafilm and Tobis Filmkunst BRD, Embassy, Marik Vos.

Heart Like a Wheel, Aurora/20th Century–Fox. William Ware Theiss.

The Return of Martin Guerre, Société Française de Production Cinematographique/Société de Productions des Films Marcel Dassault—FR 3 Production, European International Distribution. Anne-Marie Marchand.

Zelig, Rollins-Joffe Orion, Warner Bros. Santo Loquasto.

Sound Effects Editing

Return of the Jedi, Lucasfilm, 20th Century–Fox. Ben Burtt.

★ *The Right Stuff,* Chartoff–Winkler, Ladd Company, Warner Bros. Jay Boekelheide.

Short Films

(ANIMATED)

Mickey's Christmas Carol, Walt Disney. Burny Mattinson, producer.

Sound of Sunshine—Sound of Rain, Hallinan Plus. Eda Hallinan, producer.

★ *Sundae in New York,* Motionpicker Productions. Jimmy Picker, producer.

(LIVE ACTION)

★ *Boys and Girls,* Atlantis Films Ltd. Janice L. Platt, producer.

Goodie-Two-Shoes, Timeless Films, Paramount. Ian Emes, producer.

Overnight Sensation, a Bloom Film Production. Jon N. Bloom, producer.

Documentary

(SHORT SUBJECTS)

★ *Flamenco at 5:15,* National Film Board of Canada. Cynthia Scott and Adam Symansky, producers.

In the Nuclear Shadow: What Can the Children Tell Us?, Impact Productions. Vivienne Verdon-Roe and Eric Thiermann, producers.

Sewing Woman, DeepFocus Productions. Arthur Dong, producer.

Spaces: The Architecture of Paul Rudolph, Eisenhardt Productions Inc. Robert Eisenhardt, producer.

You Are Free (Ihr Zent Frei), Brokman/Landis. Dea Brokman and Ilene Landis, producers.

(FEATURES)

Children of Darkness, Children of Darkness Productions. Richard Kotuk and Ara Chekmayan, producers.

First Contact, Arundel Productions. Bob Connolly and Robin Anderson, producers.

★ *He Makes Me Feel Like Dancin',* Edgar J. Scherick Associates. Emile Ardolino, producer.

The Profession of Arms (War Series Film #3), National Film Board of Canada. Michael Bryans and Tina Viljoen, producers.

Seeing Red, Heartland Productions. James Klein and Julia Reichert, producers.

Foreign Language Film

Carmen (Spain).

Entre Nous (France).

★ *Fanny & Alexander* (Sweden).

Job's Revolt (Hungary).

Le Bal (Algeria).

Irving G. Thalberg Memorial

Not given this year.

Jean Hersholt Humanitarian Award

M. J. "Mike" Frankovich.

Gordon E. Sawyer Award

Dr. John G. Frayne.

Honorary Award

Hal Roach, in recognition of his unparalleled record of distinguished contributions to the motion picture art form (statuette).

Special Achievement Awards

Visual Effects: Richard Edulund, Dennis Muren, Ken Ralston and Phil Tippett for *Return of the Jedi,* Lucasfilm, 20th Century–Fox.

Scientific or Technical

ACADEMY AWARD OF MERIT (STATUETTE)

Dr. Kurt Larche of OSRAM GmbH, for the research and development of xenon short-arc discharge lamps for motion picture projection.

SCIENTIFIC AND ENGINEERING AWARD (PLAQUE)

Jonathan Erland and Roger Dorney of Apogee, Inc., for the engineering and development of a reverse bluescreen traveling matte process for special-effects photography.

Gunnar P. Michelson for the engineering and development of an improved, electronic, high-speed, precision light valve for use in motion picture printing machines.

Gerald L. Turpin of Lightflex International Ltd. for the design, engineering and development of an on-camera device providing contrast control, sourceless fill light and special effects for motion picture photography.

TECHNICAL ACHIEVEMENT AWARD (CITATION)

William G. Krokaugger of Mole-Richardson Co. for the design and engineering of a portable, 12,000 watt, lighting-control dimmer for use in motion picture production.

Charles L. Watson, Larry L. Langrehr, and John H. Steiner for the development of the BHP electro-mechanical fader for use on continuous motion picture contact printers.

Elizabeth D. De La Mare of De La Mare Engineering, Inc., for the progressive development and continuous research of special effects pyrotechnics originally designed by Glenn W. De La Mare for motion picture production.

Douglas Fries, John Lacey, and Michael Sicrist for the design and engineering of a 35mm reflex conversion camera system for special effects photography.

Jack Cashin of Ultra-Stereo Labs, Inc., for the engineering and development of a 4-channel, stereophonic, decoding system for optical motion picture sound track reproduction.

David J. Degenkolb for the design and development of an automated device used in the silver recovery process in motion picture laboratories.

Points of Interest

1. Nothing to it: Julie Walters nominated for film debut; James L. Brooks wins for his directing debut.
2. Gender bender: Best Supporting Actress Linda Hunt first person to win for playing someone of the opposite sex.
3. Plain Janes: No films considered worthy of Make-Up Award.

Rule Changes

1. The name game: "Original Song Score and Its Adaptation or Adaptation Score" becomes "Original Song Score or Adaptation Score."

Eligible Films That Failed to Be Nominated for Best Picture

Yentl, Star 80, Risky Business, Flashdance, Betrayal, Zelig, Local Hero, King of Comedy, The Hunger, The Fourth Man.

Submitted Film Rejected by the Foreign Language Film Award Committee

And the Ship Sails On (Italy), directed by Federico Fellini.

1984

Picture

★ *Amadeus*, Zaentz, Orion. Produced by Saul Zaentz.
The Killing Fields, Goldcrest/International Film Investors, Warner Bros. Produced by David Puttnam.
A Passage to India, G. W. Films Ltd., Columbia. Produced by John Brabourne and Richard Goodwin.
Places in the Heart, Tri-Star. Produced by Arlene Donovan.
A Soldier's Story, Caldix, Columbia. Produced by Norman Jewison, Ronald L. Schwary and Patrick Palmer.

Actor

★ F. Murray Abraham in *Amedus* (Zaentz, Orion).
Jeff Bridges in *Starman* (Columbia).
Albert Finney in *Under the Volcano* (Ithaca, Universal).
Tom Hulce in *Amadeus* (Zaentz, Orion).
Sam Waterston in *The Killing Fields* (Goldcrest/International Film Investors, Warner Bros.).

Actress

Judy Davis in *A Passage to India* (G. W. Films Ltd., Columbia).
★ Sally Field in *Places in the Heart* (Tri-Star).
Jessica Lange in *Country* (Touchstone, Buena Vista).
Vanessa Redgrave in *The Bostonians* (Merchant Ivory, Almi).
Sissy Spacek in *The River* (Universal).

Supporting Actor

Adolph Caesar in *A Soldier's Story* (Caldix, Columbia).
John Malkovich in *Places in the Heart* (Tri-Star).
Noriyuki "Pat" Morita in *The Karate Kid* (Columbia).
★ Haing S. Ngor in *The Killing Fields* (Goldcrest/International Film Investors, Warner Bros.).
Ralph Richardson in *Greystoke: The Legend of Tarzan, Lord of the Apes* (Warner Bros.).

Supporting Actress

★ Peggy Ashcroft in *A Passage to India* (G. W. Films Ltd., Columbia).
Glenn Close in *The Natural* (Tri-Star).
Lindsay Crouse in *Places in the Heart* (Tri-Star).
Christine Lahti in *Swing Shift* (Warner Bros.).
Geraldine Page in *The Pope of Greenwich Villagbe* (UA Koch/Kirkwood, MGM/UA).

Director

Woody Allen for *Broadway Danny Rose* (Rollins-Joffe, Orion).
Robert Benton for *Places in the Heart* (Tri-Star).
★ Milos Forman for *Amadeus* (Zaentz, Orion).
Roland Joffé for *The Killing Fields* (Goldcrest/International Film Investors, Warner Bros.)
David Lean for *A Passage to India* (G. W. Films Ltd., Columbia).

Writing

(SCREENPLAY WRITTEN DIRECTLY FOR THE SCREEN)

Beverly Hills Cop, Simpson-Bruckheimer Murphy, Paramount. Daniel Petrie, Jr. Story by Danilo Bach and Daniel Petrie, Jr.

Broadway Danny Rose, Rollins-Joffe, Orion. Woody Allen.

El Norte, Island Alive/Cinecom International. Gregory Nava and Anna Thomas.

★ *Places in the Heart,* Tri-Star. Robert Benton.

Splash, Touchstone, Buena Vista. Lowell Ganz, Babaloo Mandel and Bruce Jay Friedman. Screen story by Bruce Jay Friedman. Story by Brian Grazer.

(SCREENPLAY BASED ON MATERIAL FROM ANOTHER MEDIUM)

★ *Amadeus,* Zaentz, Orion. Peter Shaffer.

Greystoke: The Legend of Tarzan, Lord of the Apes, Warner Bros. P. H. Vazak and Michael Austin.

The Killing Fields, Goldcrest/International Film Investors, Warner Bros. Bruce Robinson.

A Passage to India, G. W. Films Ltd., Columbia. David Lean.

A Soldier's Story, Caldix, Columbia. Charles Fuller.

Cinematography

Amadeus, Zaentz, Orion. Miroslav Ondricek.

★ *The Killing Fields,* Goldcrest/International Film Investors, Warner Bros. Chris Menges.

The Natural, Tri-Star. Caleb Deschanel.

A Passage to India, G. W. Films Ltd., Columbia. Ernest Day.

The River, Universal. Vilmos Zsigmond.

Art Direction—Set Decoration

★ *Amadeus,* Zaentz, Orion. Patrizia Von Brandenstein; Karel Cerny.

The Cotton Club, Totally Independent, Orion. Richard Sylbert; George Gaines.

The Natural, Tri-Star. Angelo Graham and Mel Bourne; Bruce Weintraub.

A Passage to India, G. W. Films Ltd., Columbia. John Box; Hugh Scaife.

2010, Hyams, MGM. Albert Brenner; Rick Simpson.

Sound

★ *Amadeus,* Zaentz, Orion. Mark Berger, Tom Scott, Todd Boekelheide and Chris Newman.

Dune, De Laurentiis, Universal. Bill Varney, Steve Maslow, Kevin O'Connell and Nelson Stoll.

A Passage to India, G. W. Films Ltd., Columbia. Graham Hartstone, Nicolas Le Messurier, Michael A. Carter and John Mitchell.

The River, Universal. Nick Alphin, Robert Thirwell, Richard Portman and David Ronne.

2010, Hyams, MGM. Michael J. Kohut, Aaron Rochin, Carlos De Larios and Gene S. Cantamessa.

Music

(ORIGINAL SONG)

"Against All Odds (Take a Look at Me Now)" (*Against All Odds,* New Visions, Columbia); Music and Lyrics by Phil Collins.

"Footloose" (*Footloose,* Melnick, Paramount); Music and Lyrics by Kenny Loggins and Dean Pitchford.

"Ghostbusters" (*Ghostbusters,* Columbia); Music and Lyrics by Ray Parker, Jr.

★ I Just Called to Say I Love You" (*The Woman in Red,* Orion); Music and Lyrics by Stevie Wonder.

"Let's Hear It for the Boy" (*Footloose,* Melnick, Paramount); Music and Lyrics by Dean Pitchford and Tom Snow.

(ORIGINAL SCORE)

Indiana Jones and the Temple of Doom, Lucasfilm, Paramount. John Williams.

The Natural, Tri-Star. Randy Newman.

★ *A Passage to India,* G. W. Films Ltd., Columbia. Maurice Jarre.

The River, Universal. John Williams.

Under the Volcano, Ithaca, Universal. Alex North.

(ORIGINAL SONG SCORE)

The Muppets Take Manhattan, Tri-Star. Jeffrey Moss.

★ *Purple Rain,* Purple Films, Warner Bros. Prince.

Songwriter, Tri-Star. Kris Kristofferson.

Film Editing

Amadeus, Zaentz, Orion. Nena Danevic and Michael Chandler.

The Cotton Club, Totally Independent, Orion. Barry Malkin and Robert O. Lovett.

★ *The Killing Fields,* Goldcrest/International Film Investors, Warner Bros. Jim Clark.

A Passage to India, G. W. Films Ltd., Columbia David Lean.

Romancing the Stone, El Corazon, 20th Century-Fox. Donn Cambern and Frank Morriss.

Costume Design

★ *Amadeus, Zaentz,* Orion. Theodor Pistek.

The Bostonians, Merchant Ivory, Almi. Jenny Beavan and John Bright.

A Passage to India, G. W. Films Ltd., Columbia. Judy Moorcroft.

Places in the Heart, Tri-Star. Ann Roth.

2010, Hyams, MGM. Patricia Norris.

Make-Up

★ Amadeus, Zaentz, Orion. Paul LeBlanc and Dick Smith.

Greystoke: The Legend of Tarzan, Lord of the Apes, Warner Bros. Rick Baker and Paul Engelen.

2010, Hyams, MGM. Michael Westmore.

Visual Effects

Ghostbusters, Columbia. Richard Edlund, John Bruno, Mark Vargo and Chuck Gasper.

★ *Indiana Jones and the Temple of Doom*, Lucasfilm, Paramount. Dennis Muren, Michael McAlister, Lorne Peterson and George Gibbs.

2010, Hyams, MGM. Richard Edlund, Neil Krepela, George Jensen and Mark Stetson.

Short Films

(ANIMATED)

★ *Charade*, Sheridan College. Jon Minnis, producer.

Doctor Desoto, Sporn Animation. Morton Schindel and Michael Sporn, producers.

Paradise, National Film Board of Canada. Ishu Patel, producer.

(LIVE ACTION)

The Painted Door, Atlantis Films Ltd., National Film Board of Canada. Michael MacMillan and Janice L. Platt, producers.

Tales of Meeting and Parting, American Film Institute—Directing Workshop for Women. Sharon Oreck and Lesli Linka Glatter, producers.

★ *Up*, Pyramid Films. Mike Hoover, producer.

Documentary

(SHORT SUBJECTS)

The Children of Soong Ching Ling, UNICEF and the Soong Ching Ling Foundation.

Code Gray: Ethical Dilemmas in Nursing, The Nursing Ethics Project/Fanlight Prods. Ben Achtenberg and Joan Sawyer, producers.

The Garden of Eden, Florentine Films, Lawrence R. Hott and Roger M. Sherman, producers.

Recollections of Pavlovsk, Leningrad Documentary Film Studio. Irina Kalinina, producer.

★ *The Stone Carvers*, Wagner Productions. Marjorie Hunt and Paul Wagner, producers.

(FEATURES)

High Schools, Guggenheim Productions. Charles Guggenheim and Nancy Sloss, producers.

In the Name of the People, Pan American Films. Alex W. Drehsler and Frank Christopher, producers.

Marlene, Braun Pictures/OKO Film Production. Karel Dirka and Zev Braun, producers.

Streetwise, Bear Creek Productions. Cheryl McCall, producer.

★ *The Times of Harvey Milk*, Black Sand Educational Productions, Inc. Robert Epstein and Richard Schmiechen, producers.

Foreign Language Film

Beyond the Walls (Israel).

Camila (Argentina).

★ *Dangerous Moves* (Switzerland).

Double Feature (Spain).

War-Time Romance (U.S.S.R.).

Irving G. Thalberg Memorial Award

Not given this year.

Jean Hersholt Humanitarian Award

David L. Wolper.

Gordon E. Sawyer Award

Linwood G. Dunn.

Honorary Awards

National Endowment for the Arts (statuette).

James Stewart for 50 years of meaningful performances, for his high ideals, both on and off the screen, with the respect and affection of his colleagues.

Special Achievement Award

Sound Effects Editing: Kay Rose for *The River*, Universal.

Scientific or Technical

ACADEMY AWARD OF MERIT (STATUETTE)

None.

SCIENTIFIC AND ENGINEERING AWARD (PLAQUE)

Donald A. Anderson and Diana Reiners of 3M Co. for the development of "Cinetrak" Magnetic Film #350/351 for motion picture sound recording.

Barry M. Stultz, Ruben Avila and Wes Kennedy of Film Processing Corp. for the development of FPC 200PB Fullcoat Magnetic Film for motion picture sound recording.

Barry M. Stultz, Ruben Avila and Wes Kennedy of Film Processing Corp. for the formulation and application of an improved soundtrack stripe to 70mm motion picture film, and John Mosely for the engineering research involved therein.

Kenneth Richter of Richter Cine Equipment for the design and engineering of the R-2 Auto-Collimator for examining image quality at the focal plane of motion picture camera lenses.

Gunther Schaidt and Rosco Laboratories, Inc., for the development of an improved, nontoxic fluid for creating fog and smoke for motion picture production.

John Whitney, Jr., and Gary Demos of Digital Prods., Inc., for the practical simulation of motion picture photography by means of computer-generated images.

TECHNICAL ACHIEVEMENT AWARD (CERTIFICATE)

Nat Tiffen of Tiffen Manufacturing Corp. for the production of high-quality, durable, laminated color filters for motion picture photography.

Donald Trumbull, Jonathan Erland, Stephen Fog and Paul Burk of Apogee, Inc., for the design and development of the "Blue Max" high-power blue-flux projector for traveling matte composite photography.

Jonathan Erland and Robert Bealmear of Apogee, Inc., for

an innovative design for front projection screens and an improved method for their construction.

Howard J. Preston of Preston Cinema Systems for the design and development of a variable speed control device with automatic exposure compensation for motion picture cameras.

Points of Interest

1. Nothing to it: John Malkovich nominated for first year in films, director Roland Joffé nominated for film debut. Dr. Haing S. Ngor first actor to win for first film.
2. The family way: Supporting Actress nominee Geraldine Page married to cousin of Actress nominee Sissy Spacek, Rip Torn.
3. See no evil: Stevie Wonder first blind Oscar winner.
4. Move over, Thelma: Seven-time loser Geraldine Page tops record of six losses by Thelma Ritter and Deborah Kerr and matches record of seven losses held by Richard Burton and Peter O'Toole.
5. Making it up to Mozart: *Amadeus* given special Oscar for music adaptation.
6. Renaissance men: David Lean nominated for Director, Adapted Screenplay and Editing; 1961 Actor winner Maximillian Schell directed Documentary Feature nominee *Marlene*.
7. New kid on the block: The Best Picture winner is distributed by a new studio—six-year-old Orion Pictures.

Rule Changes

1. The less the merrier: Sound Effects Editing not given as competitive award; the branch gives Award to *The River* without asking the rest of the Academy for its opinion.
2. The name game: "Origninal Song Score or Adaptation Score" becomes "Original Song Score."

Eligible Films That Failed To Be Nominated for Best Picture

Once Upon a Time in America, Ghostbusters, Splash, Beverly Hills Cop, Tightrope, Choose Me, Crimes of Passion, Stranger than Paradise, The Terminator.

Eligible Songs That Failed To Be Nominated

"Breakin' . . . There's No Stopping Us" (Gary Remal and Michael Boyd)—*Breakin';* "The Heat Is On" (Keith Forsey and Harold Faltermeyer)—*Beverly Hills Cop;* "I Can Dream About You" (Dan Hartman)—*Streets of Fire;* "Purple Rain" (Prince)—*Purple Rain.*

1985

Picture

The Color Purple, Warner Bros. Produced by Steven Spielberg, Kathleen Kennedy, Frank Marshall and Quincy Jones.

Kiss of the Spider Woman, H.B. Filmes/Sugarloaf Films, Island Alive. Produced by David Weisman.

★ *Out of Africa*, Universal. Produced by Sydney Pollack.

Prizzi's Honor, ABC Motion Pictures, 20th Century–Fox. Produced by John Foreman.

Witness, Feldman, Paramount. Produced by Edward S. Feldman.

Actor

Harrison Ford in *Witness* (Feldman, Paramount).

James Garner in *Murphy's Romance* (Fogwood Films, Columbia).

★ William Hurt in *Kiss of the Spider Woman* (H.B. Filmes/Sugarloaf Films, Island Alive).

Jack Nicholson in *Prizzi's Honor* (ABC Motion Pictures, 20th Century–Fox).

Jon Voight in *Runaway Train* (Cannon).

Actress

Anne Bancroft in *Agnes of God* (Columbia).

Whoopi Goldberg in *The Color Purple* (Warner Bros).

Jessica Lange in *Sweet Dreams* (HBO Pictures/Silver Screen Partners, Tri–Star).

★ Geraldine Page in *The Trip to Bountiful* (Bountiful, Island).

Meryl Streep in *Out of Africa* (Universal).

Supporting Actor

★ Don Ameche in *Cocoon* (Fox/Zanuck–Brown, 20th Century–Fox).

Klaus Maria Brandauer in *Out of Africa* (Universal).

William Hickey in *Prizzi's Honor* (ABC Motion Pictures, 20th Century–Fox).

Robert Loggia in *Jagged Edge* (Columbia).

Eric Roberts in *Runaway Train* (Cannon).

Supporting Actress

Margaret Avery in *The Color Purple* (Warner Bros.).

★ Anjelica Huston in *Prizzi's Honor* (ABC Motion Pictures, 20th Century–Fox).

Amy Madigan in *Twice in a Lifetime* (Bud Yorkin Productions).

Meg Tilly in *Agnes of God* (Columbia).

Oprah Winfrey in *The Color Purple* (Warner Bros.).

Director

Hector Babenco for *Kiss of the Spider Woman* (H.B. Filmes/Sugarloaf Films, Island Alive).

John Huston for *Prizzi's Honor* (ABC Motion Pictures, 20th Century–Fox).
Akira Kurosawa for *Ran* (Greenwich Film/Nippon Herald Films/Herald Ace, Orion Classics).
★ Sydney Pollack for *Out of Africa* (Universal).
Peter Weir for *Witness* (Feldman, Paramount).

Writing

(SCREENPLAY WRITTEN DIRECTLY FOR THE SCREEN)

Back to the Future, Amblin Entertainment, Universal. Robert Zemeckis and Bob Gale.
Brazil, Embassy International Pictures, Universal. Terry Gilliam, Tom Stoppard and Charles McKeown.
The Official Story, Historias Cinematograficas/Cinemania and Progress Communications, Almi (Argentine). Luis Puenzo and Aida Bortnik.
The Purple Rose of Cairo, Rollins–Joffe, Orion. Woody Allen.
★ *Witness*, Feldman, Paramount. Earl W. Wallace and William Kelley. Story by William Kelley, Pamela Wallace and Earl W. Wallace.

(SCREENPLAY BASED ON MATERIAL FROM ANOTHER MEDIUM)

The Color Purple, Warner Bros. Menno Meyjes.
Kiss of the Spider Woman, H.B. Filmes/Sugarloaf Films, Island Alive. Leonard Schrader.
★ *Out of Africa*, Universal. Kurt Luedtke.
Prizzi's Honor, ABC Motion Pictures, 20th Century–Fox. Richard Condon and Janet Roach.
The Trip to Bountiful, Bountiful, Island. Horton Foote.

Cinematography

The Color Purple, Warner Bros. Allen Daviau.
Murphy's Romance, Fogwood Films, Columbia. William A. Fraker.
★ *Out of Africa*, Universal. David Watkin.
Ran, Greenwich Film/Nippon Herald Films/Herald Ace, Orion Classics. Takao Saito, Masaharu Ueda and Asakazu Nakai.
Witness, Feldman, Paramount. John Seale.

Art Direction—Set Decoration

Brazil, Embassy International Pictures, Universal. Norman Garwood; Maggie Gray.
The Color Purple, Warner Bros. J. Michael Riva; Linda De Scenna.
★ *Out of Africa*, Universal. Stephen Grimes; Josie MacAvin.
Ran, Greenwich Film/Nippon Herald Films/Herald Ace, Orion Classics. Yoshiro Muraki and Shinobu Muraki.
Witness, Feldman, Paramount. Stan Jolley; John Anderson.

Sound

Back to the Future, Amblin Entertainment, Universal. Bill Varney, B. Tennyson Sebastian II, Robert Thirlwell and William B. Kaplan.
A Chorus Line, Embassy Films Associates/Polygram, Columbia. Donald O. Mitchell, Michael Minkler, Gerry Humphreys and Chris Newman.
Ladyhawke, Warner Bros./20th Century–Fox, Warner Bros. Les Fresholtz, Dick Alexander, Vern Poore and Bud Alper.
★ *Out Of Africa*, Universal. Chris Jenkins, Gary Alexander, Larry Stensvold and Peter Handford.
Silverado, Columbia. Donald O. Mitchell, Rick Kline, Kevin O' Connell and David Ronne.

Music

(ORIGINAL SONG)

"Miss Celie's Blues (Sister)" (*The Color Purple*, Warner Bros.); Music by Quincy Jones and Rod Temperton. Lyrics by Quincy Jones, Rod Temperton and Lionel Richie.
"Power of Love" (*Back to the Future*, Amblin Entertainment, Universal); Music by Chris Hayes and Johnny Colla. Lyrics by Huey Lewis.
★ "Say You, Say Me" (*White Knights*, New Visions, Columbia); Music and Lyrics by Lionel Richie.
"Separate Lives (Love Theme from *White Knights*)" (*White Knights*, New Visions, Columbia); Music and Lyrics by Stephen Bishop.
"Surprise, Surprise" (*A Chorus Line*, Embassy Films Associates/Polygram, Columbia). Music by Marvin Hamlisch. Lyrics by Edward Kleban.

(ORIGINAL SCORE)

Agnes of God, Columbia. George Delerue.
The Color Purple, Warner Bros. Quincy Jones, Jeremy Lubbock, Rod Temperton, Caiphus Semenya, Andrae Crouch, Chris Boardman, Jorge Calandrelli, Joel Rosenbaum, Fred Steiner, Jack Hayes, Jerry Hey and Randy Kerber.
★ *Out of Africa*, Universal. John Barry.
Silverado, Columbia. Bruce Broughton.
Witness, Feldman, Paramount. Maurice Jarre.

Film Editing

A Chorus Line, Embassy Films Associates/Polygram, Columbia. John Bloom.
Out of Africa, Universal. Fredric Steinkamp, William Steinkamp, Pembroke Herring and Sheldon Kahn.
Prizzi's Honor, ABC Motion Pictures, 20th Century–Fox. Rudi Fehr and Kaja Fehr.
Runaway Train, Cannon. Henry Richardson.
★ *Witness*, Feldman, Paramount. Thom Noble.

Costume Design

The Color Purple, Warner Bros. Aggie Guerard Rodgers.
The Journey of Natty Gann, Disney/Silver Screen Partners II, Buena Vista. Albert Wolksy.
Out of Africa, Universal. Milena Canonero.
Prizzi's Honor, ABC Motion Pictures, 20th Century–Fox. Donfeld.

★ *Ran*, Greenwich Film/Nippon Herald Films/Herald Ace, Orion Classics. Emi Wada.

Makeup

The Color Purple, Warner Bros. Ken Chase.

★ *Mask*, Universal. Michael Westmore and Zoltan Elek.

Remo Williams: The Adventure Begins, Clark/Spiegel/Bergman, Orion. Carl Fullerton.

Visual Effects

★ *Cocoon*, Fox/Zanuck-Brown, 20th Century–Fox. Ken Ralston, Ralph McQuarrie, Scott Farrar and David Berry.

Return to Oz, Disney/Silver Screen Partners II, Buena Vista. Will Vinton, Ian Wingrove, Zoran Perisic and Michael Lloyd.

Young Sherlock Holmes, Amblin Entertainment/Winkler/Birnbaum, Paramount. Dennis Muren, Kit West, John Ellis and David Allen.

Sound Effects Editing

★ *Back to the Future*, Amblin Entertainment, Universal. Charles L. Campbell and Robert Rutledge.

Ladyhawke, Warner Bros./20th Century–Fox, Warner Bros. Bob Henderson and Alan Murray.

Rambo: First Blood Part II, Anabasis Investments, Tri–Star. Frederick J. Brown.

Short Films

(ANIMATED)

★ *Anna & Bella*, The Netherlands. Cilia Van Dijk, producer.

The Big Snit, National Film Board of Canada. Richard Condie and Michael Scott, producers.

Second Class Mail, National Film & Television School. Alison Snowden, producer.

(LIVE ACTION)

Graffiti, The American Film Institute. Dianna Costello, producer.

★ *Molly's Pilgrim*, Phoenix Films. Jeff Brown, producer.

Rainbow War, Bob Rogers and Company. Bob Rogers, producer.

Documentary

(SHORT SUBJECTS)

The Courage to Care, United Way. Robert Gardner, producer.

Keats and His Nightingale: A Blind Date, Rhode Island Committee for the Humanities. Michael Crowley and James Wolpaw, producers.

Making Overtures—The Story of a Community Orchestra, Rhombus Media, Inc. Barbara Willis Sweete, producer.

★ *Witness to War: Dr. Charlie Clements*, Skylight Picture. David Goodman, producer.

The Wizard of the Strings, Seventh Hour. Alan Edelstein, producer.

(FEATURES)

★ *Broken Rainbow*, Earthworks Films. Maria Florio and Victoria Mudd, producers.

Las Madres—The Mothers of Plaza de Mayo, Film Arts Foundation. Susana Munoz and Lourdes Portillo, producers.

Soldiers in Hiding, Filmworks, Inc. Japhet Asher, producer.

The Statue of Liberty, Florentine Films. Ken Burns and Buddy Squires, producers.

Unfinished Business, Mouchette Films. Steven Okazaki, producer.

Foreign Language Film

Angry Harvest (Federal Republic of Germany).

Colonel Redl (Hungary).

★ *The Official Story* (Argentina).

3 Men and a Cradle (France).

When Father Was Away On Business (Yugoslavia).

Irving G. Thalberg Memorial Award

Not given this year.

Jean Hersholt Humanitarian Award

Charles "Buddy" Rogers.

Gordon E. Sawyer Award

Not given this year.

Honorary Awards

Paul Newman in recognition of his many memorable and compelling screen performances and for his personal integrity and dedication to his craft (statuette).

Alex North in recognition of his brilliant artistry in the creation of memorable music for a host of distinguished motion pictures (statuette).

John H. Whitney for cinematic pioneering (Medal of Commendation).

Scientific or Technical

ACADEMY AWARD OF MERIT (STATUETTE)

None.

SCIENTIFIC AND ENGINEERING AWARD (PLAQUE)

Imax Systems Corporation for a method of filming and exhibiting high-fidelity, large-format, wide-angle motion pictures.

Ernst Nettmann of E.F. Nettmann & Associates for the invention, and Edward Phillips and Carlos DeMattos of Matthews Studio Equipment, Inc., for the development, of the Cam-Remote for motion picture photography.

Myron Gordin, Joe P. Crookham, Jim Drost and David Crookham of Musco Mobile Lighting, Ltd., for the invention of a method of transporting adjustable, high-intensity luminaires and their application to the motion picture industry.

TECHNICAL ACHIEVEMENT AWARD (CERTIFICATE)

David W. Spencer for the development of an Animation Photo Transfer (APT) process.

Harrison & Harrison, Optical Engineers, for the invention and development of Harrison Diffusion Filters for motion picture photography.

Larry Barton of Cinematography Electronics, Inc., for a Precision Speed, Crystal-Controlled Device for motion picture photography.

Alan Landaker of The Burbank Studios for the Mark III Camera Drive for motion picture photography.

Points of Interest

1. Nothing to it: Whoopi Goldberg and Oprah Winfrey nominated for film debuts.
2. The family way: Best Supporting Actress Anjelica Huston is daughter of Director nominee John Huston, and is the first third-generation Oscar winner after her father and grandfather.
3. Never too late: John Huston, seventy-nine, oldest person nominated as Best Director.
4. The bilingual man: Best Supporting Actor nominee Klaus Maria Brandauer is also the star of the Hungarian Foreign Film nominee, *Colonel Redl*.
5. Cheaper by the dozen: twelve individuals nominated for Original Score for *The Color Purple* set record for most people sharing a single nomination.
6. Whoops: Claude Lanzmann's two-part, nine-hour-plus documentary *Shoah*—which was not submitted for Best Documentary—ruled ineligible for other categories because somebody forgot to show part two in Los Angeles in 1985.
7. Buy American: For the first time, all 10 nominees for Best Actor and Best Actress were born in the United States.

Rule Change

1. The fewer the merrier: Original Song Score not given this year.

Eligible Films That Failed to Be Nominated for Best Picture

Ran, Brazil, The Purple Rose of Cairo, Desperately Seeking Susan, After Hours, Lost in America, Heaven Help Us, Blood Simple, The Emerald Forest, Dreamchild, Wetherby, Pee-wee's Big Adventure.

Eligible Songs That Failed to Be Nominated

"Crazy for You" (Jon Lind and John Bettis)—*Vision Quest*; "Don't You (Forget About Me)" (Keith Forsey and Steve Schiff)—*The Breakfast Club*; "Into the Groove" (Madonna and Steve Bray)—*Desperately Seeking Susan*; "Rhythm of the Night" (Diane Warren)—*Berry Gordy's The Last Dragon*; "St. Elmo's Fire (Man in Motion)" (David Foster and John Parr)—*St. Elmo's Fire*; "A View to a Kill" (Duran Duran and John Barry)—*A View to a Kill*; "We Don't Need Another Hero (Thunderdome)" (Terry Britten and Graham Lyle)—*Mad Max Beyond Thunderdome*.

1986

Picture

Children of a Lesser God, Sugarman, Paramount. Produced by Burt Sugarman and Patrick Palmer.

Hannah and Her Sisters, Rollins-Joffe, Orion. Produced by Robert Greenhut.

The Mission, Warner Bros./Goldcrest/Kingsmere, Warner Bros. Produced by Fernando Ghia and David Puttnam.

★ *Platoon*, Hemdale, Orion. Produced by Arnold Kopelson.

A Room with a View, Merchant Ivory, Cinecom. Produced by Ismail Merchant.

Actor

Dexter Gordon in *'Round Midnight* (Warner Bros.).

Bob Hoskins in *Mona Lisa* (Palace/Handmade, Island).

William Hurt in *Children of a Lesser God* (Sugarman, Paramount).

★ Paul Newman in *The Color of Money* (Touchstone, Buena Vista).

James Woods in *Salvador* (Hemdale Releasing).

Actress

Jane Fonda in *The Morning After* (Lorimar, 20th Century–Fox).

★ Marlee Matlin in *Children of a Lesser God* (Sugarman, Paramount).

Sissy Spacek in *Crimes of the Heart* (De Laurentiis Entertainment Group).

Kathleen Turner in *Peggy Sue Got Married* (Rastar, Tri-Star).

Sigourney Weaver in *Aliens* (20th Century–Fox).

Supporting Actor

Tom Berenger in *Platoon* (Hemdale, Orion).

★ Michael Caine in *Hannah and Her Sisters* (Rollins-Joffe, Orion).

Willem Dafoe in *Platoon* (Hemdale, Orion).

Denholm Elliott in *A Room with a View* (Merchant Ivory, Cinecom).

Dennis Hopper in *Hoosiers* (De Haven, Orion).

Supporting Actress

Tess Harper in *Crimes of the Heart* (De Laurentiis Entertainment Group).

Piper Laurie in *Children of a Lesser God* (Sugarman, Paramount).

Mary Elizabeth Mastrantonio in *The Color of Money* (Touchstone, Buena Vista).

Maggie Smith in *A Room with a View* (Merchant Ivory, Cinecom).

★ Dianne Wiest in *Hannah and Her Sisters* (Rollins-Joffe, Orion).

Director

Woody Allen for *Hannah and Her Sisters* (Rollins-Joffe, Orion).

James Ivory for *A Room with a View* (Merchant Ivory, Cinecom).

Roland Joffe for *The Mission* (Warner Bros./Goldcrest/Kingsmere, Warner Bros.).

David Lynch for *Blue Velvet* (Blue Velvet S.A., De Laurentiis Entertainment Group).

★ Oliver Stone for *Platoon* (Hemdale, Orion).

Writing

(SCREENPLAY—WRITTEN DIRECTLY FOR THE SCREEN)

"Crocodile" Dundee, Rimfire, Paramount. Story by Paul Hogan. Screenplay by Paul Hogan, Ken Shadie, and John Cornell.

★ *Hannah and Her Sisters,* Rollins-Joffe, Orion. Woody Allen.

My Beautiful Laundrette, Working Title/SAF Production/Film Four Int'l, Orion Classics. Hanif Kureishi.

Platoon, Hemdale, Orion. Oliver Stone.

Salvador, Hemdale Releasing. Oliver Stone and Richard Boyle.

(SCREENPLAY—BASED ON MATERIAL FROM ANOTHER MEDIUM)

Children of a Lesser God, Sugarman, Paramount. Hesper Anderson and Mark Medoff.

The Color of Money, Touchstone, Buena Vista. Richard Price.

Crimes of the Heart, De Laurentiis Entertainment Group. Beth Henley.

★ *A Room with a View,* Merchant Ivory, Cinecom. Ruth Prawer Jhabvala.

Stand By Me, Act III, Columbia. Raynold Gideon and Bruce A. Evans.

Cinematography

★ *The Mission,* Warner Bros./Goldcrest/Kingsmere, Warner Bros. Chris Menges.

Peggy Sue Got Married, Rastar, Tri-Star. Jordan Cronenweth.

Platoon, Hemdale, Orion. Robert Richardson.

A Room with a View, Merchant Ivory, Cinecom. Tony Pierce-Roberts.

Star Trek IV: The Voyage Home, Bennett, Paramount. Don Peterman.

Art Direction—Set Decoration

Aliens, 20th Century–Fox. Peter Lamont; Crispian Sallis.

The Color of Money, Touchstone, Buena Vista. Boris Leven; Karen A. O'Hara.

Hannah and Her Sisters, Rollins-Joffe, Orion. Stuart Wurtzel; Carol Joffe.

The Mission, Warner Bros./Goldcrest/Kingsmere, Warner Bros. Stuart Craig; Jack Stephens.

★ *A Room with a View,* Merchant Ivory, Cinecom. Gianni Quaranta and Brian Ackland-Snow; Brian Savegar and Elio Altramura.

Sound

Aliens, 20th Century–Fox. Graham V. Hartstone, Nicolas Le Messurier, Michael A. Carter, and Roy Charman.

Heartbreak Ridge, Warner Bros. Les Fresholtz, Dick Alexander, Vern Poore, and William Nelson.

★ *Platoon,* Hemdale, Orion. John "Doc" Wilkinson, Richard Rogers, Charles "Bud" Grenzbach, and Simon Kaye.

Star Trek IV: The Voyage Home, Bennett, Paramount. Terry Porter, Dave Hudson, Mel Metcalfe, and Gene S. Cantamessa.

Top Gun, Simpson/Bruckheimer, Paramount. Donald O. Mitchell, Kevin O'Connell, Rick Kline, and William B. Kaplan.

Music

(ORIGINAL SONG)

"Glory of Love" (*The Karate Kid II,* Columbia); Music by Peter Cetera and David Foster. Lyrics by Peter Cetera and Diane Nini.

"Life in a Looking Glass" (*That's Life!,* Paradise Cove/Ubilam, Columbia); Music by Henry Mancini. Lyrics by Leslie Bricusse.

"Mean Green Mother from Outer Space" (*Little Shop of Horrors,* Geffen, Warner Bros.); Music by Alan Menken. Lyrics by Howard Ashman.

"Somewhere Out There" (*An American Tail,* Amblin, Universal); Music by James Horner and Barry Mann. Lyrics by Cynthia Weil.

★ "Take My Breath Away" (*Top Gun,* Simpson/Bruckheimer, Paramount); Music by Giorgio Moroder. Lyrics by Tom Whitlock.

(ORIGINAL SCORE)

Aliens, 20th Century–Fox. James Horner.

Hoosiers, De Haven, Orion. Jerry Goldsmith.

The Mission, Warner Bros./Goldcrest/Kingsmere, Warner Bros. Ennio Morricone.

★ *'Round Midnight,* Warner Bros. Herbie Hancock.

Star Trek IV: The Voyage Home, Bennett, Paramount. Leonard Rosenman.

Film Editing

Aliens, 20th Century–Fox. Ray Lovejoy.
Hannah and Her Sisters, Rollins-Joffe, Orion. Susan E. Morse.
The Mission, Warner Bros./Goldcrest/Kingsmere, Warner Bros. Jim Clark.
★ *Platoon*, Hemdale, Orion. Claire Simpson.
Top Gun, Simpson/Bruckheimer, Paramount. Billy Weber and Chris Lebenzon.

Costume Design

The Mission, Warner Bros./Goldcrest/Kingsmere, Warner Bros. Enrico Sabbatini.
Otello, Cannon. Anna Anni.
Peggy Sue Got Married, Rastar, Tri-Star. Theadora Van Runkle.
Pirates, Carthago Films/Accent Cominco, Cannon. Anthony Powell.
★ *A Room with a View*, Merchant Ivory, Cinecom. Jenny Beaven and John Bright.

Makeup

The Clan of the Cave Bear, Warner Bros./PSO, Warner Bros. Michael G. Westmore and Michele Burke.
★ *The Fly*, Brooksfilms Ltd., 20th Century–Fox. Chris Walas and Stephan Dupuis.
Legend, Legend Co., Universal. Rob Bottin and Peter Robb-King.

Visual Effects

★ *Aliens*, 20th Century–Fox. Robert Skotak, Stan Winston, John Richardson, and Suzanne Benson.
Little Shop of Horrors, Geffen, Warner Bros. Lyle Conway, Bran Ferren, and Martin Gutteridge.
Poltergeist II: The Other Side, Victor-Grais, MGM. Richard Edlund, John Bruno, Garry Waller, and William Neil.

Sound Effects Editing

★ *Aliens*, 20th Century–Fox. Don Sharpe.
Star Trek IV: The Voyage Home, Bennett, Paramount. Mark Mangini.
Top Gun, Simpson/Bruckheimer, Paramount. Cecelia Hall and George Watters II.

Short Films

(ANIMATED)

The Frog, The Dog and The Devil, New Zealand National Film Unit. Hugh MacDonald and Martin Townsend, producers.
★ *A Greek Tragedy*, CineTe pvba. Linda Van Tulden and Willem Thijssen, producers.
Luxo Jr., Pixar Productions. John Lasseter and William Reeves, producers.

(LIVE ACTION)

Exit, Rai Radiotelevisione Italiana/RAI-UNO. Stefano Reali and Pino Quartullo, producers.
Love Struck, Rainy Day Productions. Fredda Weiss, producer.
★ *Precious Images*, Calliope Films, Inc. Chuck Workman, producer.

Documentary

(SHORT FILMS)

Debonair Dancers, Alison Nigh-Strelich, producer.
The Masters of Disaster, Indiana Univ. Audio Visual Center. Sonya Friedman, producer.
Red Grooms: Sunflower in a Hothouse, Polaris Entertainment. Thomas L. Neff and Madeline Bell, producers.
Sam. Aaron D. Weisblatt, producer.
★ *Women—For America, for the World*, Educational Film & Video Project, Vivienne Verdon-Roe, producer.

(FEATURES)

(Note: Two winners this year)
★ *Artie Shaw: Time Is All You've Got*, Bridge Film. Brigitte Berman, producer.
Chile: Hasta Cuando?. David Bradbury, producer.
★ *Down and Out in America*, Feury. Joseph Feury and Milton Justice, producers.
Isaac In America: A Journey with Isaac Bashevis Singer, Amram Nowak Associates. Kirk Simon, producer.
Witness to Apartheid, Production of Developing News, Inc. Sharon I. Sopher, producer.

Foreign Language Film

★ *The Assault* (The Netherlands).
Betty Blue (France).
The Decline of the American Empire (Canada).
My Sweet Little Village (Czechoslavakia).
"38" (Austria).

Irving G. Thalberg Memorial Award

Steven Spielberg

Jean Hersholt Humanitarian Award

Not given this year.

Gordon E. Sawyer Award

Not given this year.

Honorary Award

Ralph Bellamy for his unique artistry and his distinguished service to the profession of acting (statuette).
E. M. "Al" Lewis in appreciation for outstanding service in upholding Academy standards (medal of commendation).

Scientific or Technical

ACADEMY AWARD OF MERIT (STATUETTE)

None.

SCIENTIFIC AND ENGINEERING AWARD (PLAQUE)

Bran Ferren, Charles Harrison, and Kenneth Wisner of Associates and Ferren for the concept and design of an advanced optical printer.

Richard Benjamin Grant and Ron Grant of Auricle Control Systems, Inc., for their invention of the Film Composer's Time Processor.

Metro-Goldwyn-Mayer Laboratories, Inc., and Technical Film Systems, Inc., for the design and engineering of a Continuous Feed Printer.

Robert Greenberg, Joel Hynek, and Eugene Mamut of R/Greenberg Associates Inc., and Dr. Alfred Thumin, Elan Lipschitz, and Darryl A. Armour of the Oxberry Division of Richmark Camera Service, Inc., for the design and development of the RGA/Oxberry Compu-Quad Special Effects Optical Printer.

Dr. Fritz Sennheiser of Sennheiser Electronics Corp., for the invention of an interference tube directional microphone.

Boss Film Corp., for the design and development of a zoom aerial (ZAP) 65m optical printer.

William L. Fredrick and Hal Needham for the design and development of the Shotmaker Elite camera car and crane.

TECHNICAL ACHIEVEMENT AWARD (CERTIFICATE)

Lee Electric (Lighting), Ltd., for the design and development of an electronic, flicker-free, discharge lamp control system.

Peter D. Parks of Oxford Scientific Films' Image Quest Division for the development of a live aerocompositor for special-effects photography.

Matt Sweeney and Lucinda Strub for the development of an automatic capsule gun for motion picture special effects.

Carl E. Holmes of Carl E. Holmes Co. and Alexander Bryce of The Burbank Studios for the development of a mobile D.C. power supply for motion pictures production photography.

Bran Ferren of Associates and Ferren for the invention of a laser synchro-cue system for applications in the motion picture industry.

John L. Baptista of Metro-Goldwyn-Mayer Laboratories, Inc., for the development and installation of a computerized silver recovery operation.

David W. Samuelson for the development of programs incorporated into a portable computer for motion picture cinematographers based on new algorithms developed in conjunction with W. B. Pollard.

Hal Landaker and Alan Landaker of The Burbank Studios for the development of the Beat System lo-frequency cue track for motion picture production and sound recording.

Points of Interest

1. Nothing to it: Marlee Matlin's win for film debut.
2. Renaissance woman: 1975 Best Supporting Actress winner Lee Grant is director of Documentary Feature cowinner, *Down and Out in America*.
3. Renaissance man: Director-stuntman Hal Needham wins a plaque for designing a "camera car and crane."

Eligible Films That Failed to Be Nominated for Best Picture

Blue Velvet, Salvador, Down and Out in Beverly Hills, That's Life, Stand By Me, Desert Bloom, Aliens, The Fly, My Beautiful Laundrette, Something Wild, Manhunter, She's Gotta Have It, Sid & Nancy, Parting Glances.

Submitted Films Rejected by the Foreign Language Film Award Committee

Men . . . (Federal Republic of Germany), directed by Doris Dorrie; *The Sacrifice* (Sweden), directed by Andrei Tarkovsky.

Eligible Songs That Failed to Be Nominated

"Coming Around Again" (Carly Simon)—*Heartburn;* "Danger Zone" (Giorgio Moroder and Tom Whitlock)—*Top Gun;* "If You Leave" (OMD)—*Pretty in Pink;* "Live to Tell" (Madonna and Patrick Leonard)—*At Close Range;* "Sweet Freedom" (Rod Temperton)—*Running Scared;* "Wild Wild Life" (David Byrne)—*True Stories.*

1987

Picture

Broadcast News, 20th Century–Fox. Produced by James L. Brooks.

Fatal Attraction, Jaffe/Lansing, Paramount. Produced by Stanley R. Jaffe and Sherry Lansing.

Hope and Glory, Davros Production Services Ltd., Columbia. Produced by John Boorman.

★ *The Last Emperor*, Hemdale, Columbia. Produced by Jeremy Thomas.

Moonstruck, Palmer & Jewison, MGM. Produced by Patrick Palmer and Norman Jewison.

Actor

★ Michael Douglas in *Wall Street* (Oxatal, 20th Century–Fox).

William Hurt in *Broadcast News* (20th Century–Fox).

Marcello Mastroianni in *Dark Eyes* (Excelsior TV & RAI Uno, Island).

Jack Nicholson in *Ironweed* (Taft Entertainment/Barish, Tri-Star).

Robin Williams in *Good Morning, Vietnam* (Touchstone, Buena Vista).

Actress

★ Cher in *Moonstruck* (Palmer & Jewison, MGM).

Glenn Close in *Fatal Attraction* (Jaffe/Lansing, Paramount).

Holly Hunter in *Broadcast News* (20th Century–Fox).

Sally Kirkland in *Anna* (Magnus, Vestron).

Meryl Streep in *Ironweed* (Taft Entertainment/Barish, Tri-Star).

Supporting Actor

Albert Brooks in *Broadcast News* (20th Century–Fox).

★ Sean Connery in *The Untouchables* (Linson, Paramount).

Morgan Freeman in *Street Smart* (Cannon).

Vincent Gardenia in *Moonstruck* (Palmer & Jewison, MGM).

Denzel Washington in *Cry Freedom* (Marble Arch, Universal).

Supporting Actress

Norma Aleandro in *Gaby—A True Story* (Brimmer, Tri-Star).

Anne Archer in *Fatal Attraction* (Jaffe/Lansing, Paramount).

★ Olympia Dukakis in *Moonstruck* (Palmer & Jewison, MGM).

Anne Ramsey in *Throw Momma from the Train* (Rollins, Morra & Brezner, Orion).

Ann Sothern in *The Whales of August* (Alive/Circle Associates, Alive).

Director

★ Bernardo Bertolucci for *The Last Emperor* (Hemdale, Columbia).

John Boorman for *Hope and Glory* (Davros Production Services Ltd., Columbia).

Lasse Hallstrom for *My Life as a Dog* (Svensk Filmindustri/Filmteknik, Skouras) (Swedish).

Norman Jewison for *Moonstruck* (Palmer & Jewison, MGM).

Adrian Lyne for *Fatal Attraction* (Jaffe/Lansing, Paramount).

Writing

(SCREENPLAY WRITTEN DIRECTLY FOR THE SCREEN)

Au Revoir, Les Enfants, NEF, Orion Classics (French). Louis Malle.

Broadcast News, 20th Century–Fox. James L. Brooks.

Hope and Glory, Davros Production Services Ltd., Columbia. John Boorman.

★ *Moonstruck*, Palmer & Jewison, MGM. John Patrick Shanley.

Radio Days, Rollins-Joffe, Orion. Woody Allen.

(SCREENPLAY BASED ON MATERIAL FROM ANOTHER MEDIUM)

The Dead, Liffey Films, Vestron. Tony Huston.

Fatal Attraction, Jaffe/Lansing, Paramount. James Dearden.

Full Metal Jacket, Natant, Warner Bros. Stanley Kubrick, Michael Herr, and Gustav Hasford.

★ *The Last Emperor*, Hemdale, Columbia. Mark Peploe and Bernardo Bertolucci.

My Life as a Dog, Svensk Filmindustri/Filmteknik, Skouras (Swedish). Lasse Hallstrom, Reidar Jonsson, Brasse Brannstrom, and Per Berglund.

Cinematography

Broadcast News, 20th Century–Fox. Michael Ballhaus.

Empire of the Sun, Warner Bros. Allen Daviau.

Hope and Glory, Davros Production Services Ltd., Columbia. Philippe Rousselot.

★ *The Last Emperor*, Hemdale, Columbia. Vittorio Storaro.

Matewan, Red Dog Films, Cinecom. Haskell Wexler.

Art Direction—Set Decoration

Empire of the Sun, Warner Bros. Norman Reynolds; Harry Cordwell.

Hope and Glory, Davros Production Services Ltd., Columbia. Anthony Pratt; Joan Woollard.

★ *The Last Emperor*, Hemdale, Columbia. Ferdinando Scarfiotti; Bruno Cesari.

Radio Days, Rollins-Joffe, Orion. Santo Loquasto; Carol Joffe, Les Bloom, and George DeTitta, Jr.

The Untouchables, Linson, Paramount. Patrizia Von Brandenstein; Hal Gausman.

Sound

Empire of the Sun, Warner Bros. Robert Knudson, Don Digirolamo, John Boyde, and Tony Dawe.

★ *The Last Emperor*, Hemdale, Columbia. Bill Rowe and Ivan Sharrock.

Lethal Weapon, Warner Bros. Les Fresholtz, Dick Alexander, Vern Poore, and Bill Nelson.

RoboCop, Tobor Pictures, Orion. Michael J. Kohut, Carlos DeLarios, Aaron Rochin, and Robert Wald.

The Witches of Eastwick, Warner Bros. Wayne Artman, Tom Beckert, Tom Dahl, and Art Rochester.

Music

(ORIGINAL SONG)

"Cry Freedom" (*Cry Freedom*, Marble Arch, Universal); Music and lyrics by George Fenton and Jonas Gwangwa.

★ "(I've Had) The Time of My Life" (*Dirty Dancing*, Vestron/Great American Films Ltd., Vestron); Music by Franke Previte, John DeNicola, and Donald Markowitz. Lyrics by Franke Previte.

"Nothing's Gonna Stop Us Now" (*Mannequin*, Gladden Entertainment, 20th Century–Fox); Music and lyrics by Albert Hammond and Diane Warren.

"Shakedown" (*Beverly Hills Cop II*, Simpson/Bruckheimer/Murphy, Paramount); Music by Harold Faltermeyer and Keith Forsey. Lyrics by Harold Faltermeyer, Keith Forsey, and Bob Seger.

"Storybook Love" (*The Princess Bride*, Act III Communications, 20th Century–Fox); Music and lyrics by Willy DeVille.

(ORIGINAL SCORE)

Cry Freedom, Marble Arch, Universal. George Fenton and Jonas Gwangwa.
Empire of the Sun, Warner Bros. John Williams.
★ *The Last Emperor*, Hemdale, Columbia. Ryuichi Sakamoto, David Byrne, and Cong Su.
The Untouchables, Linson, Paramount. Ennio Morricone.
The Witches of Eastwick, Warner Bros. John Williams.

Film Editing

Broadcast News, 20th Century–Fox. Richard Marks.
Empire of the Sun, Warner Bros. Michael Kahn.
Fatal Attraction, Jaffe-Lansing, Paramount. Michael Kahn and Peter E. Berger.
★ *The Last Emperor*, Hemdale, Columbia. Gabriella Cristiani.
RoboCop, Tobor Pictures, Orion. Frank J. Urioste.

Costume Design

The Dead, Liffey Films, Vestron. Dorothy Jeakins.
Empire of the Sun, Warner Bros. Bob Ringwood.
★ *The Last Emperor*, Hemdale, Columbia. James Acheson.
Maurice, Merchant Ivory, Cinecom. Jenny Beaven and John Bright.
The Untouchables, Linson, Paramount. Marilyn Vance-Straker.

Makeup

Happy New Year, Columbia. Bob Laden.
★ *Harry and the Hendersons*, Universal/Amblin, Universal. Rick Baker.

Visual Effects

★ *Innerspace*, Warner Bros. Dennis Muren, William George, Harley Jessup, and Kenneth Smith.
Predator, 20th Century–Fox. Joel Hynek, Robert M. Greenberg, Richard Greenberg, and Stan Winston.

Short Films

(ANIMATED)

George and Rosemary, National Film Board of Canada. Eunice Macaulay, producer.
★ *The Man Who Planted Trees*, Societe Radio-Canada/Canadian Broadcasting Corporation. Frederic Back, producer.
Your Face. Bill Plympton, producer.

(LIVE ACTION)

Making Waves, The Production Pool Ltd. Ann Wingate, producer.
★ *Ray's Male Heterosexual Dance Hall*, Chanticleer Films. Jonathan Sanger and Jana Sue Memel, producers.
Shoeshine, Tom Abrams Productions. Robert A. Katz, producer.

Documentary

(SHORT SUBJECT)

Frances Steloff: Memoirs of a Bookseller, Winterlude Films, Inc. Deborah Dickson, producer.
In the Wee Wee Hours. . . . Univ. of Southern California School of Cinema/TV, producer.
Language Says It All, Tripod. Megan Williams, producer.
Silver Into Gold, Department of Communications, Stanford Univ. Lynn Mueller, producer.
★ *Young at Heart*, Sue Marx Films, Inc. Sue Marx and Pamela Conn, producers.

(FEATURE)

Eyes on the Prize: America's Civil Rights Years/Bridge to Freedom 1965, Blackside, Inc. Callie Crossley and James A. DeVinney, producers.
Hellfire: A Journey from Hiroshima. John Junkerman and John W. Dower, producers.
Radio Bikini, Crossroads Film Project, Ltd. Robert Stone, producer.
A Stitch for Time, Peace Quilters Production Company, Inc. Barbara Herbich and Cyril Christo, producers.
★ *The Ten-Year Lunch: The Wit and Legend of the Algonquin Round Table*. Aviva Films. Aviva Slesin, producer.

Foreign Language Film

Au Revoir, Les Enfants (France).
★ *Babette's Feast* (Denmark).
Course Completed (Spain).
The Family (Italy).
Pathfinder (Norway).

Irving G. Thalberg Memorial Award

Billy Wilder.

Jean Hersholt Humanitarian Award

Not given this year.

Gordon E. Sawyer Award

Fred Hynes.

Honorary Awards

None given this year.

Special Achievement Award

For Sound Effects Editing: Stephen Flick and John Pospisil for *RoboCop*, Tobor Pictures, Orion.

Scientific or Technical

ACADEMY AWARD OF MERIT (STATUETTE)

Bernard Kuhl and Werner Block and to the OSRAM GmbH research and development department for the invention and continuing improvement of the OSRAM HMI light source for motion picture photography. (Recipients previously were awarded a certificate, then a plaque for the device.)

SCIENTIFIC AND ENGINEERING AWARD (PLAQUE)

Willi Burth and Kinotone Corp., for the invention and development of the non-rewind platter system for motion picture presentation.

Montage Group for the development, and Ronald C. Barker and Chester L. Schuler for the invention, of the Montage Picture Processor electronic film editing system.

Colin F. Mossman and Rank Film Laboratories' Development Group for a fully automated handling system for improving the productivity of high-speed film processing.

Eastman Kodak Co., for the development of Eastman Color High Speed Daylight Negative Film 5297/7297 and for the development of Eastman Color High Speed SA Negative Film 5295 for blue-screen traveling matte photography (two plaques).

Fritz Gabriel Bauer for the invention and development of the improved features of the Moviecam Camera System.

Zoran Perisic of Courier Films Ltd., for the Zoptic dual-zoom front projection system for visual effects photography. (Recipient was previously awarded a certificate for the device.)

Carly Zeiss Co., for the design and development of a series of superspeed lenses for motion picture photography. (Recipient was previously awarded a certificate for the device.)

TECHNICAL ACHIEVEMENT AWARD (CERTIFICATE)

Ioan Allen of Dolby Laboratories, Inc., for the Cat. 43 playback-only noise reduction unit and its practical application to motion picture sound recordings.

John Eppolito, Wally Gentleman, William Mesa, Les Robley, and Geoff Williamson for refinements to a dual-screen, front-projection image-compositing system.

Jan Jacobsen for the application of a dual-screen, front-projection system to motion picture special effects photography.

Thaine Morris and Davis Pier for the development of DSC Spark Devices for motion picture special effects.

Tadeuz Krzanowski of Industrial Light & Magic., Inc., for the development of a Wire Rig Model Support Mechanism used to control the movements of miniatures in special effects.

Dan C. Norris and Tim Cook of Norris Film Products for the development of a single-frame exposure system for motion picture photography.

Points of Interest

1. Ellis Island: No U.S.-born director nominated for Best Director.
2. Nothing Rotten: Denmark wins first Foreign Film Oscar.

Rule Changes

1. The Hancock Amendment: No musical score eligible for Best Original Score if "diluted by the use of tracked or pre-existing music."
2. Here we go again: Sound Effects Editing given as a non-competitive, Special Achievement Award.

Eligible Films That Failed to Be Nominated for Best Picture

Housekeeping, The Dead, Full Metal Jacket, House of Games, Radio Days, Jean de Florette, Manon of the Spring, My Life as a Dog, Law of Desire, Maurice, Sammy and Rosie Get Laid, Raising Arizona, Swimming to Cambodia, The Stepfather, River's Edge, The Witches of Eastwick, The Untouchables, RoboCop, Prick Up Your Ears.

Submitted Film Rejected by the Foreign Language Film Award Committee

Wings of Desire (Federal Republic of Germany), directed by Wim Wenders.

Eligible Songs That Failed to Be Nominated

"Hungry Eyes" (Franke Previte and John DeNicola)—*Dirty Dancing;* "She's Like the Wind" (Patrick Swayze and Stacy Widelitz)—*Dirty Dancing;* "Who's That Girl" (Madonna and Patrick Leonard)—*Who's That Girl.*

1988

Picture

The Accidental Tourist, Warner Bros. Produced by Lawrence Kasdan, Charles Okun, and Michael Grillo.

Dangerous Liaisons, Lorimar, Warner Bros. Produced by Norma Heymen and Hank Moonjean.

Mississippi Burning, Zollo, Orion. Produced by Frederick Zollo and Robert F. Colesberry.

★ *Rain Man*, Guber-Peters Co., United Artists. Produced by Mark Johnson.

Working Girl, 20th Century-Fox. Produced by Douglas Wick.

Actor

Gene Hackman in *Mississippi Burning* (Zollo, Orion).

Tom Hanks in *Big* (20th Century-Fox).

★ Dustin Hoffman in *Rain Man* (Guber-Peters Co., United Artists).
Edward James Olmos in *Stand and Deliver* (Menendez/Musca & Olmos, Warner Bros.).
Max von Sydow in *Pelle the Conqueror* (Per Holst/Kaerne Films, Miramax).

Actress
Glenn Close in *Dangerous Liaisons* (Lorimar, Warner Bros.).
★ Jodie Foster in *The Accused* (Jaffe-Lansing, Paramount).
Melanie Griffith in *Working Girl* (20th Century-Fox).
Meryl Streep in *A Cry in the Dark* (Cannon Entertainment/Golan-Globus, Warner Bros.).
Sigourney Weaver in *Gorillas in the Mist* (Warner Bros., Warner Bros./Universal).

Supporting Actor
Alec Guinness in *Little Dorrit* (Sands Films, Cannon).
★ Kevin Kline in *A Fish Called Wanda* (Shamberg-Prominent Features, MGM).
Martin Landau in *Tucker: The Man and His Dream* (Lucasfilm, Paramount).
River Phoenix in *Running on Empty* (Lorimar, Warner Bros.).
Dean Stockwell in *Married to the Mob* (Mysterious Arts-Demme, Orion).

Supporting Actress
Joan Cusack in *Working Girl* (20th Century-Fox).
★ Geena Davis in *The Accidental Tourist* (Warner Bros.).
Frances McDormand in *Mississippi Burning* (Zollo, Orion).
Michelle Pfeiffer in *Dangerous Liaisons* (Lorimar, Warner Bros.).
Sigourney Weaver in *Working Girl* (20th Century-Fox).

Director
Charles Crichton for *A Fish Called Wanda* (Shamberg-Prominent Features, MGM).
★ Barry Levinson for *Rain Man* (Guber-Peters Co., United Artists).
Mike Nichols for *Working Girl* (20th Century-Fox).
Alan Parker for *Mississippi Burning* (Zollo, Orion).
Martin Scorsese for *The Last Temptation of Christ* (Testament, Universal/Cineplex Odeon).

Writing
(SCREENPLAY WRITTEN DIRECTLY FOR THE SCREEN)
Big, 20th Century-Fox. Gary Ross and Anne Spielberg.
Bull Durham, Mount Co., Orion. Ron Shelton.
A Fish Called Wanda, Shamberg-Prominent Features, MGM). John Cleese. Story by John Cleese and Charles Crichton.
★ *Rain Man*, Guber-Peters Co., United Artists. Ronald Bass and Barry Morrow. Story by Barry Morrow.
Running on Empty, Lorimar, Warner Bros. Naomi Foner.

(SCREENPLAY BASED ON MATERIAL FROM ANOTHER MEDIUM)
The Accidental Tourist, Warner Bros. Frank Galati and Lawrence Kasdan.
★ *Dangerous Liaisons*, Lorimar, Warner Bros. Christopher Hampton.
Gorillas in the Mist, Warner Bros./Universal. Anna Hamilton Phelan. Story by Anna Hamilton Phelan and Tab Murphy.
Little Dorrit, Sands Films, Cannon. Christine Edzard.
The Unbearable Lightness of Being, Zaentz Co., Orion. Jean-Claude Carriere and Philip Kaufman.

Cinematography
★ *Mississippi Burning*, Zollo, Orion. Peter Biziou.
Rain Man, Guber-Peters Co., United Artists. John Seale.
Tequila Sunrise, Mount Co., Warner Bros. Conrad Hall.
The Unbearable Lightness of Being, Zaentz Co., Orion. Sven Nykvist.
Who Framed Roger Rabbit, Amblin Entertainment/Touchstone, Buena Vista. Dean Cundey.

Art Direction—Set Decoration
Beaches, Touchstone/Silver Screen Partners III, Buena Vista. Albert Brenner; Garrett Lewis.
★ *Dangerous Liaisons*, Lorimar, Warner Bros. Stuart Craig; Gerard James.
Rain Man, Guber-Peters Co., United Artists. Ida Random; Linda DeScenna.
Tucker: The Man and His Dream, Lucasfilm, Paramount. Dean Tavoularis; Armin Ganz.
Who Framed Roger Rabbit, Amblin Entertainment/Touchstone, Buena Vista. Elliot Scott; Peter Howitt.

Sound
★ *Bird*, Malpaso, Warner Bros. Les Fresholtz, Dick Alexander, Vern Poore, and Willie D. Burton.
Die Hard, 20th Century-Fox. Don Bassman, Kevin F. Cleary, Richard Overton, and Al Overton.
Gorillas in the Mist, Warner Bros., Warner Bros./Universal. Andy Nelson, Brian Saunders, and Peter Handford.
Mississippi Burning, Zollo, Orion. Robert Litt, Elliot Tyson, Rick Kline, and Danny Michael.
Who Framed Roger Rabbit, Amblin Entertainment/Touchstone, Buena Vista. Robert Knudson, John Boyd, Don Digirolamo, and Tony Dawe.

Music
(ORIGINAL SONG)
"Calling You" (*Bagdad Cafe*, Pelemele Film, Island); Music and lyrics by Bob Telson.
★ "Let the River Run" (*Working Girl*, 20th Century-Fox); Music and lyrics by Carly Simon.
"Two Hearts" (*Buster*, N.F.H., Hemdale); Music by Lamont Dozier. Lyrics by Phil Collins.

(ORIGINAL SCORE)

The Accidental Tourist, Warner Bros. John Williams.

Dangerous Liaisons, Lorimar, Warner Bros. George Fenton.

Gorillas in the Mist, Warner Bros., Warner Bros./Universal. Maurice Jarre.

★ *The Milagro Beanfield War*, Redford/Moctesuma Esparza, Universal. Dave Grusin.

Rain Man, Guber-Peters Co., United Artists. Hans Zimmer.

Film Editing

Die Hard, 20th Century-Fox. Frank J. Urioste and John F. Link.

Gorillas in the Mist, Warner Bros., Warner Bros./Universal. Stuart Baird.

Mississippi Burning, Zollo, Orion. Gerry Hambling.

Rain Man, Guber-Peters Co., United Artists. Stu Linder.

★ *Who Framed Roger Rabbit*, Amblin Entertainment/Touchstone, Buena Vista. Arthur Schmidt.

Costume Design

Coming to America, Murphy, Paramount. Deborah Nadoolman.

★ *Dangerous Liaisons*, Lorimar, Warner Bros. James Acheson.

A Handful of Dust, Stage Screen, New Line. Jane Robinson.

Sunset, Hudson Hawk, Tri-Star. Patricia Norris.

Tucker: The Man and His Dream, Lucasfilm, Paramount. Milena Canonero.

Makeup

★ *Beetlejuice*, Geffen Film Co., Geffen/Warner Bros. Ve Neill, Steve LaPorte, and Robert Short.

Coming to America, Murphy, Paramount. Rick Baker.

Scrooged, Linson, Paramount. Tom Burman and Bari Dreiband-Burman.

Visual Effects

Die Hard, 20th Century-Fox. Richard Edlund, Al DiSarro, Brent Boates, and Thaine Morris.

★ *Who Framed Roger Rabbit*, Amblin Entertainment/Touchstone, Buena Vista. Ken Ralston, Richard Williams, Edward Jones, and George Gibbs.

Willow, Lucasfilm/Imagine Entertainment, MGM. Dennis Muren, Michael McAlister, Phil Tippett, and Chris Evans.

Sound Effects Editing

Die Hard, 20th Century-Fox. Stephen H. Flick and Richard Shorr.

★ *Who Framed Roger Rabbit*, Amblin Entertainment/Touchstone, Buena Vista. Charles L. Campbell and Louis L. Edemann.

Willow, Lucasfilm/Imagine Entertainment, MGM. Ben Burtt and Richard Hymns.

Short Films

(ANIMATED)

The Cat Came Back, National Film Board of Canada. Cordell Barker, producer.

Technological Threat, Kroyer Films, Inc. Bill Kroyer and Brian Jennings, producers.

★ *Tin Toy*, Pixar. John Lasseter and William Reeves, producers.

(LIVE ACTION)

★ *The Appointments of Dennis Jennings*, Schooner Productions, Inc. Dean Parisot and Steven Wright, producers.

Cadillac Dreams, Cadillac Dreams. Matia Karrell and Abbee Goldstein, producers.

Gulah Tales, Georgia State University. George deGolian and Gary Moss, producers.

Documentary

(SHORT SUBJECTS)

The Children's Storefront, Simon and Goodman Picture Company, Karen Goodman, producer.

Family Gathering, Lise Yasui. Lise Yasui and Ann Tegnell, producers.

Gang Cops, Center for Visual Anthropology and the School of Cinema/Television, University of Southern California. Thomas B. Fleming and Daniel J. Marks, producers.

Portrait of Imogen, Pacific Pictures. Nancy Hale and Meg Partridge, producers.

★ *You Don't Have to Die*, Tiger Rose/Filmworks, Inc. William Guttentag and Malcolm Clarke, producers.

(FEATURE)

The Cry of Reason—Beyers Naude: An Afrikaner Speaks Out, Worldwide Documentaries, Inc. Robert Bilheimer and Ronald Mix, producers.

★ *Hotel Terminus: The Life and Times of Klaus Barbie*, The Memory Pictures Company. Marcel Ophuls, producer.

Let's Get Lost, Little Bear Films, Inc. Bruce Weber and Nan Bush, producers.

Promises to Keep, Durrin Productions, Inc. Ginny Durrin, producer.

Who Killed Vincent Chin?, Film News Now Foundation/ Detroit Educational Television Foundation. Renee Tajima and Christine Choy, producers.

Foreign Language Film

Hanussen (Hungary).

The Music Teacher (Belgium).

★ *Pelle the Conqueror* (Denmark).

Salaam Bombay! (India).

Women on the Verge of a Nervous Breakdown (Spain).

Irving G. Thalberg Memorial Award

Not given this year.

Jean Hersholt Humanitarian Award
Not given this year.

Gordon E. Sawyer Award
Gordon Henry Cook.

Honorary Awards
Eastman Kodak, an Academy Honorary Award in recognition of the company's fundamental contributions to the art of motion pictures during the first century of film history (statuette).

The National Film Board of Canada, an Academy Honorary Award in recognition of its 50th anniversary and its dedicated commitment to originate artistic, creative, and technological activity and excellence in every area of filmmaking (statuette).

Special Achievement Award
For Animation Direction: Richard Williams for *Who Framed Roger Rabbit*, Amblin Entertainment/Touchstone, Buena Vista.

Scientific or Technical
ACADEMY AWARD OF MERIT (STATUETTE)

Ray Dolby and Ioan Allen of Dolby Laboratories, Inc. for their continuous contributions to motion picture sound through the research and development programs of Dolby Laboratories.

SCIENTIFIC AND ENGINEERING AWARD (PLAQUE)

Roy W. Edwards and the engineering staff of Photo-Sonics, Inc. for the design and development of the Photo-Sonics 35mm-4ER high-speed motion picture camera with reflex viewing and video assist.

The Arnold & Richter engineering staff, Otto Blaschek, and Arriflex Corp. for the concept and engineering of the Arriflex 35-3 motion picture camera.

Bill Tondreau of Tondreau Systems/Alvah Miller and Paul Johnson of Lynx Robotics/Peter A. Regla of ELICON/Dan Slater/Bud Elam, Joe Parker and Bill Bryan of Interactive Motion Control/Jerry Jeffress, Ray Feeney, Bill Holland, and Kris Brown for their individual contributions and the collective advancements they have brought to the motion picture industry in the field of motion control technology.

TECHNICAL ACHIEVEMENT AWARD (CERTIFICATE)

Grant Loucks of Alan Gordon Enterprises, Inc. for the design concept, and Geoffrey H. Williamson of Wilcam for the mechanical and electrical engineering, of the Image 300 35mm high-speed motion picture camera.

Michael V. Chewey 3d for the development of the motion picture industry's first paper tape reader incorporating microprocessor technology.

BHP, Inc., successor to the Bell & Howell Professional Equipment Division, for the development of a high-speed reader incorporating microprocessor technology for motion picture laboratories.

Hollywood Film Co. for the development of a high-speed reader incorporating microprocessor technology for motion picture laboratories.

Bruce W. Keller and Manfred G. Michelson of Technical Film Systems for the design and development of a high-speed light valve controller and constant current power supply for motion picture laboratories.

Dr. Antal Lisziewicz and Glenn M. Berggren of ISCO-OPTIC GmbH for the design and development of the Ultra-Star series of motion picture lenses.

James K. Branch of Spectra Cine, Inc. and William L. Blowers and Nasir J. Zaidi for the design and development of the Spectra CineSpot one-degree spotmeter for measuring the brightness of motion picture screens.

Bob Badami, Dick Berntein, and Bill Berntein of Offbeat Systems for the design and development of the Streamline Scoring System, Mark IV, for motion picture music editing.

Gary Zeller of Zeller International Ltd. for the development of Zel-Jel fire protection barrier for motion picture stunt work.

Emanuel Trilling of Trilling Resources Ltd. for the development of Stunt-Gel fire protection barrier for motion picture stunt work.

Paul A. Roos for the invention of a method known as Video Assist, whereby a scene being photographed on motion picture film can be viewed on a monitor and/or recorded on videotape.

Points of Interest

1. No dice, twice: Sigourney Weaver first person nominated for lead and supporting awards in same year who doesn't win an Oscar.
2. Short laughs: Comedian Steven Wright is coproducer and star of Live Action Short Subject winner, *The Appointments of Dennis Jennings*.

Rule Changes

1. The fewer the merrier: Because only nineteen songs are eligible for consideration, Song category limited to three nominations.

Eligible Films That Failed to Be Nominated for Best Picture

Bull Durham, A Fish Called Wanda, Dead Ringers, The Last Temptation of Christ, The Unbearable Lightness of Being, The Thin Blue Line, The Accused, Little Dorrit, Beetlejuice, Married to the Mob, Crossing Delancey, White Mischief, High

Season, Matador, Boyfriends and Girlfriends, Another Woman, Bagdad Cafe, Hairspray.

Submitted Films Rejected by the Foreign Language Film Award Committee

Commissar (U.S.S.R.), directed by Alexander Askoldov; *La Lectrice* (France), directed by Michel Deville; *Red Sorghum* (People's Republic of China), directed by Zhang Yimou.

Eligible Songs That Failed to Be Nominated

"Da Butt" (Marcus Miller and Mark Stevens)—*School Daze;* "Kokomo" (Mike Love, Terry Melcher, John Phillips, and Scott MacKenzie)—*Cocktail.*

1989

Picture

Born on the Fourth of July, Ho & Ixtlan, Universal. Produced by A. Kitman Ho and Oliver Stone.

Dead Poets Society, Touchstone/Silver Screen Partners IV, Buena Vista. Produced by Steven Haft, Paul Junger Witt, and Tony Thomas.

★ *Driving Miss Daisy*, Zanuck Co., Warner Bros. Produced by Richard D. Zanuck and Lili Fini Zanuck.

Field of Dreams, Gordon Co., Universal. Produced by Lawrence Gordon and Charles Gordon.

My Left Foot, Ferndale/Granada, Miramax. Produced by Noel Pearson.

Actor

Kenneth Branagh in *Henry V* (Renaissance Films/BBC, Goldwyn).

Tom Cruise in *Born on the Fourth of July* (Ho & Ixtlan, Universal).

★ Daniel Day-Lewis in *My Left Foot* (Ferndale/Granada, Miramax).

Morgan Freeman in *Driving Miss Daisy* (Zanuck Co., Warner Bros.).

Robin Williams in *Dead Poets Society* (Touchstone/Silver Screen Partners IV, Buena Vista).

Actress

Isabelle Adjani in *Camille Claudel* (Films Christian Fechner-Lillith Films-Gaumont-A2 TV France-Films A2-DD, Orion Classics).

Pauline Collins in *Shirley Valentine* (Gilbert/Russell, Paramount).

Jessica Lange in *Music Box* (Carolco, Tri-Star).

Michelle Pfeiffer in *The Fabulous Baker Boys* (Gladden Entertainment/Mirage, 20th Century-Fox).

★ Jessica Tandy in *Driving Miss Daisy* (Zanuck Co., Warner Bros.).

Supporting Actor

Danny Aiello in *Do the Right Thing* (Forty Acres and a Mule Filmworks, Universal).

Dan Aykroyd in *Driving Miss Daisy* (Zanuck Co., Warner Bros.).

Marlon Brando in *A Dry White Season* (MGM/Weinstein, MGM).

Martin Landau in *Crimes and Misdemeanors* (Rollins-Joffe, Orion).

★ Denzel Washington in *Glory* (Tri-Star).

Supporting Actress

★ Brenda Fricker in *My Left Foot* (Ferndale/Granada, Miramax).

Anjelica Huston in *Enemies, A Love Story* (Morgan Creek, 20th Century-Fox).

Lena Olin in *Enemies, A Love Story* (Morgan Creek, 20th Century-Fox).

Julia Roberts in *Steel Magnolias* (Rastar, Tri-Star).

Dianne Wiest in *Parenthood* (Imagine Entertainment, Universal).

Director

Woody Allen for *Crimes and Misdemeanors* (Rollins-Joffe, Orion).

Kenneth Branagh for *Henry V* (Renaissance Films/BBC, Goldwyn).

Jim Sheridan for *My Left Foot* (Ferndale/Grenada, Miramax).

★ Oliver Stone for *Born on the Fourth of July* (Ho & Ixtlan, Universal).

Peter Weir for *Dead Poets Society* (Touchstone/Silver Screen Partners IV, Buena Vista).

Writing

(SCREENPLAY WRITTEN DIRECTLY FOR THE SCREEN)

Crimes and Misdemeanors, Rollins-Joffe, Orion. Woody Allen.

★ *Dead Poets Society*, Touchstone/Silver Screen Partners IV, Buena Vista. Tom Schulman.

Do the Right Thing, Forty Acres and a Mule Filmworks, Universal. Spike Lee.

sex, lies and videotape, Outlaw, Miramax. Steven Soderbergh.

When Harry Met Sally . . ., Castle Rock, Columbia. Nora Ephron.

(SCREENPLAY BASED ON MATERIAL FROM ANOTHER MEDIUM)

Born on the Fourth of July, Ho & Ixtlan, Universal. Oliver Stone and Ron Kovic.

★ *Driving Miss Daisy*, Zanuck Co., Warner Bros. Alfred Uhry.

Enemies, A Love Story, Morgan Creek, 20th Century-Fox. Roger L. Simon and Paul Mazursky.

Field of Dreams, Gordon Co., Universal. Phil Alden Robinson.

My Left Foot, Ferndale/Grenada, Miramax. Jim Sheridan and Shane Connaughton.

Cinematography

The Abyss, 20th Century-Fox. Mikael Salomon.

Blaze, Touchstone/Silver Screen Partners IV, Buena Vista. Haskell Wexler.

Born on the Fourth of July, Ho & Ixtlan, Universal. Robert Richardson.

The Fabulous Baker Boys, Gladden Entertainment/Mirage, 20th Century-Fox. Michael Ballhaus.

★ *Glory*, Tri-Star. Freddie Francis.

Art Direction—Set Decoration

The Abyss, 20th Century-Fox. Leslie Dilley; Anne Kuljian.

The Adventures of Baron Munchausen, Prominent Features & Laura Film, Columbia. Dante Ferretti; Francesca Lo Schiavo.

★ *Batman*, Warner Bros. Anton Furst; Peter Young.

Driving Miss Daisy, Zanuck Co., Warner Bros. Bruno Rubeo; Crispian Sallis.

Glory, Tri-Star. Norman Garwood; Garrett Lewis.

Sound

The Abyss, 20th Century-Fox. Don Bassman, Kevin F. Cleary, Richard Overton, and Lee Orloff.

Black Rain, Jaffe-Lansing/Douglas, Paramount. Donald O. Mitchell, Kevin O'Connell, Greg P. Russell, and Keith A. Wester.

Born on the Fourth of July, Ho & Ixtlan, Universal. Michael Minkler, Gregory H. Watkins, Wylie Stateman, and Tod A. Maitland.

★ *Glory*, Tri-Star. Donald O. Mitchell, Gregg C. Rudloff, Elliott Tyson, and Russell Williams II.

Indiana Jones and the Last Crusade, Lucasfilm Ltd., Paramount. Ben Burtt, Gary Summers, Shawn Murphy, and Tony Dawe.

Music

(ORIGINAL SONG)

"After All" (*Chances Are*, Tri-Star); Music by Tom Snow. Lyrics by Dean Pitchford.

"The Girl Who Used to Be Me" (*Shirley Valentine*, Gilbert/Russell, Paramount); Music by Marvin Hamlisch. Lyrics by Alan and Marilyn Bergman.

"I Love to See You Smile" (*Parenthood*, Imagine Entertainment, Universal); Music and lyrics by Randy Newman.

"Kiss the Girl" (*The Little Mermaid*, Disney/Silver Screen Partners IV, Buena Vista); Music by Alan Menken. Lyrics by Howard Ashman.

★ "Under the Sea" (*The Little Mermaid*, Disney/Silver Screen Partners IV, Buena Vista); Music by Alan Menken. Lyrics by Howard Ashman.

(ORIGINAL SCORE)

Born on the Fourth of July, Ho & Ixtlan, Universal. John Williams.

The Fabulous Baker Boys, Gladden Entertainment/Mirage, 20th Century-Fox. David Grusin.

Field of Dreams, Gordon Co., Universal. James Horner.

Indiana Jones and the Last Crusade, Lucasfilm Ltd., Paramount. John Williams.

★ *The Little Mermaid*, Disney/Silver Screen Partners IV, Buena Vista. Alan Menken.

Film Editing

The Bear, Renn, Tri-Star. Noelle Boisson.

★ *Born on the Fourth of July*, Ho & Ixtlan, Universal. David Brenner and Joe Hutshing.

Driving Miss Daisy, Zanuck Co., Warner Bros. Mark Warner.

The Fabulous Baker Boys, Gladden Entertainment/Mirage, 20th Century-Fox. William Steinkamp.

Glory, Tri-Star. Steven Rosenblum.

Costume Design

The Adventures of Baron Munchausen, Prominent Features & Laura Film, Columbia. Gabriella Pescucci.

Driving Miss Daisy, Zanuck Co., Warner Bros. Elizabeth McBride.

Harlem Nights, Murphy, Paramount. Joe I. Tompkins.

★ *Henry V*, Renaissance Films/BBC, Goldwyn. Phyllis Dalton.

Valmont, Berri/Renn, Orion. Theodor Pistek.

Makeup

The Adventures of Baron Munchausen, Prominent Features & Laura Film, Columbia. Maggie Weston and Fabrizio Sforza.

Dad, Universal/Amblin Entertainment. Dick Smith, Ken Diaz, and Greg Nelson.

★ *Driving Miss Daisy*, Zanuck Co., Warner Bros. Manlio Rocchetti, Lynn Barber, and Kevin Haney.

Visual Effects

★ *The Abyss*, 20th Century-Fox. John Bruno, Dennis Muren, Hoyt Yeatman, and Dennis Skotak.

The Adventures of Baron Munchausen, Prominent Features & Laura Film, Columbia. Richard Conway and Kent Houston.

Back to the Future, Part III, Universal/Amblin Entertainment, Universal. Ken Ralston, Michael Lantieri, John Bell, and Steve Gawley.

Sound Effects Editing

Black Rain, Jaffe-Lansing/Douglas, Paramount. Milton C. Burrow and William L. Manger.

★ *Indiana Jones and the Last Crusade*, Lucasfilm Ltd., Paramount. Ben Burtt and Richard Hymns.

Lethal Weapon 2, Warner Bros. Robert Henderson and Alan Robert Murray.

Short Films

(ANIMATED)

★ *Balance*, Lauenstein. Christoph Lauenstein and Wolfgang Lauenstein, producers.

Cow, "Pilot" Co-op Animated Film Studio/VPTO Videofilm. Alexander Petrov, producer.

The Hill Farm, National Film & Television School. Mark Baker, producer.

(LIVE ACTION)

Amazon Diary, Determined Prods. Robert Nixon, producer.

The Childeater, Stephen-Tammuz Productions Ltd. Jonathan Tammuz, producer.

★ *Work Experience*, North Inch Production Ltd. James Hendrie, producer.

Documentary

(SHORT SUBJECTS)

Fine Food, Fine Pastries, Open 6 to 9, David Petersen Prods. David Petersen, producer.

★ *The Johnstown Flood*, Guggenheim Prods., Inc. Charles Guggenheim, producer.

Yad Vashem: Preserving the Past to Ensure the Future. Ray Errol Fox, producer.

(FEATURES)

Adam Clayton Powell, RKB Prods. Richard Kilberg and Yvonne Smith, producers.

★ *Common Threads: Stories from the Quilt*, Telling Pictures and The Couturie Co. Robert Epstein and Bill Couturie, producers.

Crack USA: County Under Siege, Half-Court Prods. Ltd. Vince DiPersio and William Guttentag, producers.

For All Mankind, Apollo Associates/FAM Prods., Inc. Al Reinert and Betsy Broyles Breir, producers.

Super Chief: The Life and Legacy of Earl Warren, Quest. Judith Leonard and Bill Jersey, producers.

Foreign Language Film

Camille Claudel (France).

★ *Cinema Paradiso* (Italy).

Jesus of Montreal (Canada).

Waltzing Regitze (Denmark).

What Happened to Santiago (Puerto Rico).

Irving G. Thalberg Memorial Award

Not given this year.

Jean Hersholt Humanitarian Award

Howard W. Koch.

Gordon E. Sawyer Award

Pierre Angenieux.

Honorary Award

Akira Kurosawa, for accomplishments that have inspired, delighted, enriched, and entertained audiences and influenced filmmakers throughout the world (statuette).

Scientific or Technical

SCIENTIFIC AND ENGINEERING AWARD (PLAQUE)

J.L. Fisher of J.L. Fisher, Inc. for the design and manufacture of a small, mobile motion picture camera platform known as the Fisher Model Ten Dolly.

James Ketcham of JSK Engineering for excellence in engineering and the broad adaptability of the SDA521B Advance/Retard system for magnetic film sound dubbing.

J. Noxon Leavitt for the invention of and Istec, Inc. for the continuing development of the Wescam Stabilized Camera System.

Klaus Resch for the design and Eric Fitz and FGV Schmidle & Fitz for the development of the Super Panther MS-180 Camera Dolly.

Geoffrey H. Williamson of Wilcam Photo Research, Inc. for the design and development and Robert D. Auguste for the electronic design and development of the Wilcam W-7 200 frames-per-second Vista Vision Rotating Mirror Reflex Camera.

TECHNICAL ACHIEVEMENT AWARD (CERTIFICATE)

Dr. Leo Catozzo for the design and development of the CIR-Catozzo Self-Perforating Adhesive Tape Film Splicer.

Magna-Tech Electronic Co. for the introduction of the first remotely controlled Advance/Retard function for magnetic film sound dubbing.

SPECIAL COMMENDATION

To the members of the engineering committees of the Society of Motion Picture and Television Engineers (SMPTE). By establishing industry standards, they have greatly contributed to making film a primary form of international communication.

Points of Interest

1. Never too late: Jessica Tandy, eighty, oldest performer to win an Oscar.
2. Nothing to it: Kenneth Branagh and Jim Sheridan nominated for Director for film debuts.
3. Renaissance man: Kenneth Branagh nominated for Actor and Director.
4. Driving itself: *Driving Miss Daisy* first film to win Best Picture without a Director nominee since *Grand Hotel* in 1931–32.

Eligible Films That Failed to Be Nominated for Best Picture

Crimes and Misdemeanors, Do the Right Thing, sex, lies and videotape, Casualties of War, Drugstore Cowboy, Heathers, True Love, Henry V, Scenes from the Class Struggle in Beverly Hills, Roger and Me, Under the Sun of Satan, Scandal, High Hopes, The Adventures of Baron Munchausen, Mystery Train, Story of Women, Jacknife, Glory, Enemies: A Love Story, New York Stories, Skin Deep.

Submitted Films Rejected by the Foreign Language Film Award Committee

My 20th Century (Hungary), directed by Ildiko Enyedi; *Time of the Gypsies* (Yugoslavia), directed by Emir Kusturica.

1990

Picture

Awakenings, Columbia. Produced by Walter F. Parks and Lawrence Lasker.
★ *Dances with Wolves*, Tig, Orion. Produced by Jim Wilson and Kevin Costner.
Ghost, Koch, Paramount. Produced by Lisa Weinstein.
The Godfather Part III, Zoetrope, Paramount. Produced by Francis Ford Coppola.
GoodFellas, Warner Bros. Produced by Irwin Winkler.

Actor

Kevin Costner in *Dances with Wolves* (Tig, Orion).
Robert De Niro in *Awakenings* (Warner Bros.).
Gerard Depardieu in *Cyrano de Bergerac* (Hachette Premiere/Camera One, Orion Classics).
Richard Harris in *The Field* (Granada, Avenue).
★ Jeremy Irons in *Reversal of Fortune* (Reversal Films, Warner Bros.).

Actress

★ Kathy Bates in *Misery* (Castle Rock, Columbia).
Anjelica Huston in *The Grifters* (Scorsese, Miramax).
Julia Roberts in *Pretty Woman* (Touchstone, Buena Vista).
Meryl Streep in *Postcards from the Edge* (Columbia).
Joanne Woodward in *Mr. and Mrs. Bridge* (Merchant Ivory, Miramax).

Supporting Actor

Bruce Davison in *Longtime Companion* (American Playhouse, Goldwyn).
Andy Garcia in *The Godfather Part III* (Zoetrope, Paramount).
Graham Greene in *Dances with Wolves* (Tig, Orion).
Al Pacino in *Dick Tracy* (Touchstone, Buena Vista).
★ Joe Pesci in *GoodFellas* (Warner Bros).

Supporting Actress

Annette Bening in *The Grifters* (Scorsese, Miramax).
Lorraine Bracco in *GoodFellas* (Warner Bros.).
★ Whoopi Goldberg in *Ghost* (Koch, Paramount).
Diane Ladd in *Wild at Heart* (Polygram/Propaganda, Goldwyn).
Mary McDonnell in *Dances with Wolves* (Tig, Orion).

Director

Francis Ford Coppola for *The Godfather Part III* (Zoetrope, Paramount).
★ Kevin Costner for *Dances with Wolves* (Tig, Orion).
Stephen Frears for *The Grifters* (Scorsese, Miramax).
Barbet Schroeder for *Reversal of Fortune* (Reversal Films, Warner Bros.).
Martin Scorsese for *GoodFellas* (Warner Bros.).

Writing

(SCREENPLAY WRITTEN DIRECTLY FOR THE SCREEN)
Alice, Rollins-Joffe, Orion. Woody Allen.
Avalon, Tri-Star. Barry Levinson.
★ *Ghost*, Koch, Paramount. Bruce Joel Rubin.
Green Card, Green Card Co., Buena Vista. Peter Weir.
Metropolitan, Westerly Film-Video, New Line. Whit Stillman.

(SCREENPLAY BASED ON MATERIAL FROM ANOTHER MEDIUM)
Awakenings, Columbia. Steven Zaillian.
★ *Dances with Wolves*, Tig, Orion. Michael Blake.
GoodFellas, Warner Bros. Nicholas Pileggi and Martin Scorsese.
The Grifters, Scorsese, Miramax. Donald E. Westlake.
Reversal of Fortune, Reversal Films, Warner Bros. Nicholas Kazan.

Cinematography

Avalon, Tri-Star. Allen Daviau.
★ *Dances with Wolves*, Tig, Orion. Dean Semler.
Dick Tracy, Touchstone, Buena Vista. Vittorio Storaro.
The Godfather Part III, Zoetrope, Paramount. Gordon Willis.
Henry & June, Walrus & Associates, Universal. Philippe Rousselot.

Art Direction—Set Decoration

Cyrano de Bergerac, Hachette Premiere/Camera One, Orion Classics. Ezio Frigerio; Jacques Rouxel.
Dances with Wolves, Tig, Orion. Jeffrey Beecroft; Lisa Dean.
★ *Dick Tracy*, Touchstone, Buena Vista. Richard Sylbert; Rick Simpson.

The Godfather Part III, Zoetrope, Paramount. Dean Tavoularis; Gary Fettis.

Hamlet, Icon, Warner Bros. Dante Ferretti; Francesca Lo Schiavo.

Sound

★ *Dances with Wolves*, Tig, Orion. Russell Williams II, Jeffrey Perkins, Bill W. Benton, and Greg Watkins.

Days of Thunder, Simpson/Bruckheimer, Paramount. Charles Wilborn, Donald O. Mitchell, Rick Kline, and Kevin O'Connell.

Dick Tracy, Touchstone, Buena Vista. Chris Jenkins, David E. Campbell, D. M. Hemphill, and Thomas Causey.

The Hunt for Red October, Neufeld/Sherlock, Paramount. Richard Bryce Goodman, Richard Overton, Kevin F. Cleary, and Don Bassman.

Total Recall, Carolco, Tri-Star. Nelson Stoll, Michael J. Kohut, Carlos deLarios, and Aaron Rochin.

Music

(ORIGINAL SONG)

"Blaze of Glory" (*Young Guns II*, Morgan Creek, 20th Century-Fox); Music and lyrics by Jon Bon Jovi.

"I'm Checkin' Out" (*Postcards from the Edge*, Columbia); Music and lyrics by Shel Silverstein.

"Promise Me You'll Remember" (*The Godfather Part III*, Zoetrope, Paramount); Music by Carmine Coppola. Lyrics by John Bettis.

"Somewhere in My Memory" (*Home Alone*, 20th Century-Fox); Music by John Williams. Lyrics by Leslie Bricusse.

★ "Sooner or Later (I Always Get My Man)" (*Dick Tracy*, Touchstone, Buena Vista); Music and lyrics by Stephen Sondheim.

(ORIGINAL SCORE)

Avalon, Tri-Star. Randy Newman.

★ *Dances with Wolves*, Tig, Orion. John Barry.

Ghost, Koch, Paramount. Maurice Jarre.

Havana, Universal. David Grusin.

Home Alone, 20th Century-Fox. John Williams.

Film Editing

★ *Dances with Wolves*, Tig, Orion. Neil Travis.

Ghost, Koch, Paramount. Walter Murch.

The Godfather Part III, Zoetrope, Paramount. Barry Malkin, Lisa Fruchtman, and Walter Murch.

GoodFellas, Warner Bros. Thelma Schoonmaker.

The Hunt for Red October, Neufeld/Sherlock, Paramount. Dennis Virkler and John Wright.

Costume Design

Avalon, Tri-Star. Gloria Gresham.

★ *Cyrano de Bergerac*, Hachette Premiere/Camera One, Orion Classics. Franca Squarciapino.

Dances with Wolves, Tig, Orion. Elsa Zamparelli.

Dick Tracy, Touchstone, Buena Vista. Milena Canonero.

Hamlet, Icon, Warner Bros. Maurizio Millenotti.

Makeup

Cyrano de Bergerac, Hachette Premiere/Camera One, Orion Classics. Michele Burke and Jean-Pierre Eychenne.

★ *Dick Tracy*, Touchstone, Buena Vista. John Caglione, Jr. and Doug Drexler.

Edward Scissorhands, 20th Century-Fox. Ve Neill and Stan Winston.

Sound Effects Editing

Flatliners, Stonebridge Entertainment, Columbia. Charles L. Campbell and Richard Franklin.

★ *The Hunt for Red October*, Neufeld/Sherlock, Paramount. Cecelia Hall and George Watters II.

Total Recall, Carolco, Tri-Star. Stephen H. Flick.

Short Films

(ANIMATED)

★ *Creature Comforts*, Aardman Animations Limited. Nick Park, producer.

A Grand Night Out, National Film & Television School. Nick Park, producer.

Grasshoppers. Bruno Bozzetto, producer.

(LIVE ACTION)

Bronx Cheers, American Film Institute. Raymond De Felitta and Matthew Gross, producers.

Dear Rosie, World's End. Peter Cattaneo and Barnaby Thompson, producers.

★ *The Lunch Date*. Adam Davidson, producer.

Senzeni Na? (What Have We Done?), American Film Institute. Bernard Joffa and Anthony E. Nicholas, producers.

12:01 P.M., Chanticleer Films. Hillary Ripps and Jonathan Heap, producers.

Documentary

(SHORT SUBJECTS)

Burning Down Tomorrow, Interscope Communications, Inc. Kit Thomas, producer.

Chimps: So Like Us, Simon & Goodman Picture Co. Karen Goodman and Kirk Simon, producers.

★ *Days of Waiting*, Mouchette Films. Steven Okazaki, producer.

Journey into Life: The World of the Unborn, ABC/Kane Prods. International, Inc. Derek Bromhall, producer.

Rose Kennedy: A Life to Remember, Sanders & Mock Prods. & American Film Foundation. Freida Lee Mock and Terry Sanders, producers.

(FEATURES)

★ *American Dream*, Cabin Creek. Barbara Kopple and Arthur Cohn, producers.

Berkeley in the Sixties, Berkeley in the Sixties Production Partnership. Mark Kitchell, producer.

Building Bombs, Mori/Robinson. Mark Mori and Susan Robinson, producers.

Forever Activists: Stories from the Veterans of the Abraham Lincoln Brigade. Judith Montell, producer.

Waldo Salt: A Screenwriter's Journey, Waldo Prods., Inc. Robert Hillmann and Eugene Corr, producers.

Foreign Language Film

Cyrano de Bergerac (France).

★ *Journey of Hope* (Switzerland).

Ju Dou (People's Republic of China).

The Nasty Girl (Germany).

Open Doors (Italy).

Irving G. Thalberg Memorial Award

Richard D. Zanuck and David Brown.

Jean Hersholt Humanitarian Award

Not given this year.

Gordon E. Sawyer Award

Stefan Kudelski.

Honorary Awards

Sophia Loren, one of the genuine treasures of world cinema who, in a career rich with memorable performances, has added permanent luster to our art form (statuette).

Myrna Loy, in recognition of her extraordinary qualities both on screen and off, with appreciation for a lifetime's worth of indelible performances (statuette).

Special Achievement Award

For Visual Effects: Eric Brevig, Rob Bottin, Tim McGovern, and Alex Funke for *Total Recall*, Carolo, Tri-Star.

Scientific or Technical

ACADEMY AWARD OF MERIT (STATUETTE)

Eastman Kodak Co. for the development of T-Grain technology and the introduction of EXR color negative films which utilize this technology.

SCIENTIFIC AND ENGINEERING AWARD (PLAQUE)

Bruce Wilton and Carlos Icinkoff of Mechanical Concepts, Inc., for the development of the Mechanical Concepts Optical Printer Platform.

Engineering Dept. of Arnold & Richter for the continued design improvements of the Arriflex BL Camera System, culminating in the 35BL-4S model.

Fuji Photo Film Co. Ltd., for the development and introduction of the F-Series of color negative films covering the range of film speeds from EI64 to EI500.

Manfred G. Michelson of Technical Film Systems, Inc., for the design and development of the first sprocket-driven film transport system for color print film processors which permits transport speeds in excess of 600 feet per minute.

John W. Lang, Walter Hrastnik and Charles J. Watson of Bell & Howell Co. for the development and manufacture of a modular continuous contact motion picture film printer.

TECHNICAL ACHIEVEMENT AWARD (CERTIFICATE)

William L. Blowers of Belco Associates, Inc., and Thomas F. Denove for the development and manufacture of the Belco/Denove Cinemeter. This digital/analog exposure meter was specifically and uniquely designed for the cinematographer.

Iain Neil for optical design; Takuo Miyagishima for the mechanical design; and Panavision, Inc., for the concept and development of the Primo Series of spherical prime lenses for 35mm cinematography.

Christopher S. Gilman and Harvey Hubert Jr. of the Diligent Dwarves Effects Lab for the development of the Actor Climate System, consisting of heat-transferring undergarments.

Jim Graves of J&G Enterprises for the development of the Cool Suit System, consisting of heat-transferring undergarments.

Bengt O. Orhall, Kenneth Lund, Bjorn Selin and Kjell Hogberg of AB Film-Teknik for the development and manufacture of the Mark IV film subtitling processor, which has increased the speed, simplified the operation, and improved the quality of subtitling.

Richard Mula and Pete Romano of HydroImage, Inc., for the development of the SeaPar 1200 watt HMI Underwater Lamp.

Dedo Weigert of Dedo Weigert Film GmbH for the development of the Dedolight, a miniature low-voltage tungsten-halogen lighting fixture.

Dr. Fred Kolb, Jr. and Paul Preo for the concept and development of a 35mm projection test film.

Peter Baldwin for the design; Dr. Paul Kiankhooy and the Lightmaker Company for the development of the Lightmaker AC/DC HMI Ballast.

All-Union Cinema and Photo Research Institute (NIKFI) for continuously improving and providing 3-D presentations to Soviet motion picture audiences for the last 25 years.

MEDAL OF COMMENDATION

Roderick T. Ryan, Don Trumbull, and Geoffrey H. Williamson, in appreciation for outstanding service and dedication in upholding the high standards of the Academy of Motion Picture Arts and Sciences.

Points of Interest

1. Nothing to it: Kevin Costner wins Best Director for directorial debut.
2. Renaissance man: Kevin Costner wins as Producer of Best Picture and Director and also nominated for Actor.

Rule Changes

1. Here we go again: Visual Effects considered a Special Achievement Award.

Eligible Films That Failed to Be Nominated for Best Picture

The Grifters, Reversal of Fortune, Mr. and Mrs. Bridge, Longtime Companion, Metropolitan, Postcards from the Edge, The Russia House, The Sheltering Sky, Edward Scissorhands, Henry & June, Tie Me Up! Tie Me Down!, The Cook, The Thief, His Wife & Her Lover, Last Exit to Brooklyn, Without You I'm Nothing, Rosalie Goes Shopping, Mountains of the Moon, Akira Kurosawa's Dreams, The Witches, Pump Up the Volume, Vincent & Theo, Henry: Portrait of a Serial Killer, Sweetie.

Submitted Films Rejected by the Foreign Language Film Award Committee

Ay, Carmela (Spain), directed by Carlos Saura; *Taxi Blues* (U.S.S.R.), directed by Pavel Lounguine.

1991

Picture

Beauty and the Beast, Disney, Buena Vista. Produced by Don Hahn.

Bugsy, Tri-Star. Produced by Mark Johnson, Barry Levinson, and Warren Beatty.

JFK, Camelot, Warner Bros. Produced by A. Kitman Ho and Oliver Stone.

The Prince of Tides, Barwood/Longfellow, Columbia. Produced by Barbra Streisand and Andrew Karsch.

⋆ *The Silence of the Lambs*, Strong Heart/Demme, Orion. Produced by Edward Saxon, Kenneth Utt, and Ron Bozman.

Actor

Warren Beatty in *Bugsy* (Tri-Star).

Robert De Niro in *Cape Fear* (Amblin Entertainment/Cappa/Tribeca, Universal).

⋆ Anthony Hopkins in *The Silence of the Lambs* (Strong Heart/Demme, Orion).

Nick Nolte in *The Prince of Tides* (Barwood/Longfellow, Columbia).

Robin Williams in *The Fisher King* (Tri-Star).

Actress

Geena Davis in *Thelma & Louise* (Pathe Entertainment, MGM).

Laura Dern in *Rambling Rose* (Carolco, Seven Arts/New Line).

⋆ Jodie Foster in *The Silence of the Lambs,* (Strong Heart/Demme, Orion).

Bette Midler in *For the Boys* (20th Century-Fox).

Susan Sarandon in *Thelma & Louise* (Pathe Entertainment, MGM).

Supporting Actor

Tommy Lee Jones in *JFK* (Camelot, Warner Bros.).

Harvey Keitel in *Bugsy* (Tri-Star).

Ben Kingsley in *Bugsy* (Tri-Star).

Michael Lerner in *Barton Fink* (Barton Circle, 20th Century-Fox).

⋆ Jack Palance in *City Slickers* (Castle Rock Entertainment, Columbia).

Supporting Actress

Diane Ladd in *Rambling Rose* (Carolco, Seven Arts/New Line).

Juliette Lewis in *Cape Fear* (Amblin Entertainment/Cappa/Tribeca, Universal).

Kate Nelligan in *The Prince of Tides* (Barwood/Longfellow, Columbia).

⋆ Mercedes Ruehl in *The Fisher King* (Tri-Star).

Jessica Tandy in *Fried Green Tomatoes* (Act III Communications/Electric Shadow, Universal).

Director

⋆ Jonathan Demme for *The Silence of the Lambs* (Strong Heart/Demme, Orion).

Barry Levinson for *Bugsy* (Tri-Star).

Ridley Scott for *Thelma & Louise* (Pathe Entertainment, MGM).

John Singleton for *Boyz N the Hood* (Columbia).

Oliver Stone for *JFK* (Camelot, Warner Bros.).

Writing

(SCREENPLAY WRITTEN DIRECTLY FOR THE SCREEN)

Boyz N the Hood, Columbia. John Singleton.

Bugsy, Tri-Star. James Toback.

The Fisher King, Tri-Star. Richard LaGravenese.

Grand Canyon, 20th Century-Fox. Lawrence Kasdan and Meg Kasdan.

⋆ *Thelma & Louise*, Pathe Entertainment, MGM. Callie Khouri.

(SCREENPLAY BASED ON MATERIAL PREVIOUSLY PRODUCED OR PUBLISHED)

Europa, Europa, CCC-Filmkunst/Les Filmes du Losange, Orion Classics. Agnieszka Holland.

Fried Green Tomatoes, Act III Communications/Electric Shadow, Universal. Fannie Flagg and Carol Sobieski.

JFK, Camelot, Warner Bros. Oliver Stone and Zachary Sklar.

The Prince of Tides, Barwood/Longfellow, Columbia. Pat Conroy and Becky Johnston.

★ *The Silence of the Lambs*, Strong Heart/Demme, Orion. Ted Tally.

Cinematography

Bugsy, Tri-Star. Allen Daviau.

★ *JFK*, Camelot, Warner Bros. Robert Richardson.

The Prince of Tides, Barwood/Longfellow, Columbia. Stephen Goldblatt.

Terminator 2: Judgment Day, Carolco, Tri-Star. Adam Greenburg.

Thelma & Louise, Pathe Entertainment, MGM. Adrian Biddle.

Art Direction—Set Decoration

Barton Fink, Barton Circle, 20th Century-Fox. Dennis Gassner; Nancy Haigh.

★ *Bugsy*, Tri-Star. Dennis Gassner; Nancy Haigh.

The Fisher King, Tri-Star. Mel Bourne; Cindy Carr.

Hook, Tri-Star. Norman Garwood; Garrett Lewis.

The Prince of Tides, Barwood/Longfellow, Columbia. Paul Sylbert; Caryl Heller.

Sound

Backdraft, Trilogy Entertainment Group/Grazer, Universal. Gary Summers, Randy Thom, Gary Rydstrom, and Glenn Williams.

Beauty and the Beast, Disney, Buena Vista. Terry Porter, Mel Metcalfe, David J. Hudson, and Doc Kane.

JFK, Camelot, Warner Bros. Michael Minkler, Gregg Landaker, and Tod A. Maitland.

The Silence of the Lambs, Strong Heart/Demme, Orion. Tom Fleischman and Christopher Newman.

★ *Terminator 2: Judgment Day*, Carolco, Tri-Star. Tom Johnson, Gary Rydstrom, Gary Summers, and Lee Orloff.

Music

(ORIGINAL SONG)

★ "Beauty and the Beast" (*Beauty and the Beast*, Disney, Buena Vista); Music by Alan Menken. Lyrics by Howard Ashman.

"Belle" (*Beauty and the Beast*, Disney, Buena Vista); Music by Alan Menken. Lyrics by Howard Ashman.

"Be Our Guest" (*Beauty and the Beast*, Disney, Buena Vista); Music by Alan Menken. Lyrics by Howard Ashman.

"(Everything I Do) I Do It for You" (*Robin Hood: Prince of Thieves*, Morgan Creek, Warner Bros.); Music by Michael Kamen. Lyrics by Bryan Adams and Robert John Lange.

"When You're Alone" (*Hook*, Tri-Star); Music by John Williams. Lyrics by Leslie Bricusse.

(ORIGINAL SCORE)

★ *Beauty and the Beast*, Disney Buena Vista. Alan Menken.

Bugsy, Tri-Star. Ennio Morricone.

The Fisher King, Tri-Star. George Fenton.

JFK, Camelot, Warner Bros. John Williams.

The Prince of Tides, Barwood/Longfellow, Columbia. James Newton Howard.

Film Editing

The Commitments, Beacon Communications, 20th Century-Fox. Gerry Hambling.

★ *JFK*, Camelot, Warner Bros. Joe Hutshing and Pietro Scalia.

The Silence of the Lambs, Strong Heart/Demme, Orion. Craig McKay.

Terminator 2: Judgment Day, Carolco, Tri-Star. Conrad Buff, Mark Goldblatt, and Richard A. Harris.

Thelma & Louise, Pathe Entertainment, MGM. Thom Noble.

Costume Design

The Addams Family, Rudin, Paramount. Ruth Myers.

Barton Fink, Barton Circle, 20th Century-Fox. Richard Hornung.

★ *Bugsy*, Tri-Star. Albert Wolsky.

Hook, Tri-Star. Anthony Powell.

Madame Bovary, MK2/C.E.D./FR3, Goldwyn. Corinne Jorry.

Makeup

Hook, Tri-Star. Christina Smith, Monty Westmore, and Greg Cannom.

Star Trek VI: The Undiscovered Country, Paramount. Michael Mills, Edward French, and Richard Snell.

★ *Terminator 2: Judgment Day*, Carolco, Tri-Star. Stan Winston and Jeff Dawn.

Visual Effects

Backdraft, Trilogy Entertainment/Grazer, Universal. Mikael Salomon, Allen Hall, Clay Pinney, and Scott Farrar.

Hook, Tri-Star. Eric Brevig, Harley Jessup, Mark Sullivan, and Michael Lantieri.

★ *Terminator 2: Judgment Day*, Carolco, Tri-Star. Dennis Murren, Stan Winston, Gene Warren, Jr., and Robert Skotak.

Sound Effects Editing

Backdraft, Trilogy Entertainment/Grazer, Universal. Gary Rydstrom and Richard Hymns.

Star Trek VI: The Undiscovered Country, Paramount. George Watters II and F. Hudson Miller.

★ *Terminator 2: Judgment Day*, Carolco, Tri-Star. Gary Rydstrom and Gloria S. Borders.

Short Films

(ANIMATED)

Blackfly, National Film Board of Canada. Christopher Hinton, producer.

★ *Manipulation*, Tandem Films. Daniel Greaves, producer.

Strings, National Film Board of Canada. Wendy Tilby, producer.

(LIVE ACTION)

Birch Street Gym, Chanticleer Films. Stephen Kessler and Thomas R. Conroy, producers.

Last Breeze of Summer, American Film Institute. David M. Massey, producer.

★ *Session Man*, Chanticleer Films. Seth Winston and Rob Fried, producers.

Documentary

(SHORT SUBJECTS)

Birdnesters of Thailand (aka Shadow Hunters), Antenne 2/National Geographic Society/M.D.I./Wind Horse. Eric Valli and Alain Majani, producers.

★ *Deadly Deception: General Electric, Nuclear Weapons and Our Environment*, Women's Educational Media, Inc. Debra Chassnoff, producer.

A Little Vicious, Film and Video Workshop, Inc. Immy Humes, producer.

The Mark of the Maker, McGowan Film and Video, Inc. David McGowan, producer.

Memorial: Letters from American Soldiers, Couturie Co. Bill Couturie and Bernard Edelman, producers.

(FEATURES)

Death on the Job, Half-Court Pictures Ltd. Vince DiPersio and William Guttentag, producers.

Doing Time: Life Inside the Big House, Video Verite. Alan Raymond and Susan Raymond, producers.

★ *In the Shadow of the Stars*, Light-Saraf Films. Allie Light and Irving Saraf, producers.

The Restless Conscience: Resistance to Hitler Within Germany, 1933–1945. Hava Kohav Beller, producer.

Wild By Law, Florentine Films. Lawrence Hott and Diane Garey, producers.

Foreign Language Film

Children of Nature (Iceland).

The Elementary School (Czechoslovakia).

★ *Mediterraneo* (Italy).

The Ox (Sweden).

Raise the Red Lantern (Hong Kong).

Irving G. Thalberg Memorial Award

George Lucas.

Jean Hersholt Humanitarian Award

Not given this year.

Gordon E. Sawyer Award

Ray Harryhausen.

Honorary Award

Satyajit Ray, in recognition of his rare mastery of the art of motion pictures and for his profound humanitarian outlook, which has had an indelible influence on filmmakers and audiences throughout the world (statuette).

Scientific and Technical

SCIENTIFIC AND ENGINEERING AWARD (PLAQUE)

Iain Neil for the optical design; Albert Saiki for the mechanical design; and Panavision, Inc. for the concept and development of the Primo Zoom Lens for 35mm cinematography.

Georg Thoma for the design, and Heinz Feierlein and the engineering department of Sachtler AG for the development for a range of fluid tripod heads.

Harry J. Baker for the design and development of the first full fluid-action tripod head with adjustable degrees of viscous drag.

Guido Cartoni for his pioneering work in developing the technology to achieve selectable and repeatable viscous drag modules in fluid tripod heads.

Ray Feeney, Richard Kenney, and Richard J. Lundell for the software development and adaptation of the Solitaire Film Recorder that provides a flexible, cost-effective film recording system.

Faz Fazakas, Brian Henson, Dave Housman, Peter Miller, and John Stephenson for the development of the Henson Performance Control System.

Mario Celso for his pioneering work in the design, development, and manufacture of equipment for carbon arc and xenon power supplies and igniters used in motion picture projection.

Randy Cartwright, David B. Coons, Lem Davis, Thomas Hahn, James Houston, Mark Kimball, Peter Nye, Michael Shantzis, David F. Wolf, and the Walt Disney Feature Animation Department for the design and development of the "CAPS" production system for feature film animation.

George Worrall for the design, development, and manufacture of the Worrall geared camera head for motion picture production.

TECHNICAL ACHIEVEMENT AWARD (CERTIFICATE)

Robert W. Stoker, Jr. for the design and development of a cobweb gun for applying non-toxic cobweb effects on motion picture sets with both safety and ease of operation.

James Doyle for the design and development of the Dry Fogger, which uses liquid nitrogen to produce a safe, dense, low-hanging dry fog.

Dick Cavdek, Steve Hamerski, and Otto Nemenz Intl., Inc.

for the opto-mechanical design and development of the Canon/Nemenz Zoom Lens.

Ken Robings and Clairmont Camera for the opto-mechanical design and development of the Canon/Clairmont Camera Zoom Lens.

Century Precision Optics for the opto-mechanical design and development of the Canon/Century Precision Optics Zoom Lens.

AWARD OF COMMENDATION (SPECIAL PLAQUE)

Pete Comandini, Richard T. Dayton, Donald Hagans, and Richard T. Ryan of YCM Laboratories for the creation and development of a motion picture film restoration process using liquid gate and registration correction on a contact printer.

MEDALS OF COMMENDATION

Richard J. Stumpf and Joseph Westheimer for outstanding service and dedication in upholding the high standards of the Academy of Motion Picture Arts & Sciences.

Points of Interest

1. Nothing to it: John Singleton nominated for Director and Original Screenplay for film debut.
2. Youth must be served: John Singleton, twenty-four, becomes youngest Director nominee, breaking Orson Welles' record.
3. The family way: Laura Dern and Diane Ladd first mother and daughter nominated in same year.
4. Never too late: Jessica Tandy, eighty-two, ties with Eva LeGallienne as oldest performer ever nominated for an Oscar.
5. Triple play: For the first time, three Song nominees from one movie, *Beauty and the Beast*.
6. Boo!: *The Silence of the Lambs* becomes first horror movie to win Best Picture.
7. Home movie: *The Silence of the Lambs* becomes first Best Picture already on home video when it wins.
8. Who needs actors?: *Beauty and the Beast* first cartoon nominated for Best Picture.
9. The big wait: Jack Palance's thirty-eight-year gap between nominations ties Helen Hayes' record.
10. Know your competition: Sound engineer Gary Rydstrom first person to compete against himself in two different categories.

Rule Changes

1. The name game: "Screenplay Based on Material from Another Material" becomes "Screenplay Based on Material Previously Produced or Published"; "Scientific or Technical Awards" becomes "Scientific and Technical Awards."
2. Here we go again: Visual Effects again becomes a regular competitive category.

Eligible Films That Failed to Be Nominated for Best Picture

Thelma & Louise, Boyz N the Hood, Fried Green Tomatoes, My Own Private Idaho, Naked Lunch, Europa, Europa, Paris Is Burning, Barton Fink, La Femme Nikita, Switch, An Angel at My Table, Impromptu, Madame Bovary, Cape Fear, Straight Out of Brooklyn, City of Hope, Dead Again, The Rapture, Life Is Sweet, Strangers in Good Company, Rambling Rose, The Man in the Moon, Poison.

Submitted Films Rejected by the Foreign Language Film Award Committee

The Double Life of Veronique (Poland), directed by Krzysztof Kieslowski; *High Heels* (Spain), directed by Pedro Almodovar; *Rhapsody in August* (Japan), directed by Akira Kurosawa; *Toto le Heros* (Belgium), directed by Jaco Van Dormael.

Index

Courtesy of Pictorial Parade, Inc.

About the Authors

MASON WILEY, a coauthor of *The Official Preppy Handbook,* has not missed an Oscar telecast in two decades.

DAMIEN BONA, a graduate of New York University School of Law, has been going to the movies since 1958. *Inside Oscar,* however, is his first book.